Oxford Dictionary of National Biography

Volume 37

Oxford Dictionary of National Biography

IN ASSOCIATION WITH

The British Academy

From the earliest times to the year 2000

Edited by

H. C. G. Matthew

and

Brian Harrison

Volume 37

Martindale–Meynell

OXFORD

UNIVERSITY PRESS

OXFORD
UNIVERSITY PRESS

Great Clarendon Street, Oxford OX2 6DP

Oxford University Press is a department of the University of Oxford.
It furthers the University's objective of excellence in research, scholarship,
and education by publishing worldwide in

Oxford New York

Auckland Bangkok Buenos Aires Cape Town
Chennai Dar es Salaam Delhi Hong Kong Istanbul Karachi
Kolkata Kuala Lumpur Madrid Melbourne Mexico City Mumbai Nairobi
São Paulo Shanghai Taipei Tokyo Toronto

Oxford is a registered trade mark of Oxford University Press
in the UK and in certain other countries

Published in the United States
by Oxford University Press Inc., New York

© Oxford University Press 2004

Illustrations © individual copyright holders as listed in
'Picture credits', and reproduced with permission

Database right Oxford University Press (maker)

First published 2004

British Library Cataloguing in Publication Data
Data available

Library of Congress Cataloging in Publication Data
Data available: for details see volume 1, p. iv

ISBN 0-19-861387-3 (this volume)
ISBN 0-19-861411-X (set of sixty volumes)

Text captured by Alliance Phototypesetters, Pondicherry
Illustrations reproduced and archived by
Alliance Graphics Ltd, UK
Typeset in OUP Swift by Interactive Sciences Limited, Gloucester
Printed in Great Britain on acid-free paper by
Butler and Tanner Ltd,
Frome, Somerset

LIST OF ABBREVIATIONS

1 General abbreviations

AB	bachelor of arts		BCnL	bachelor of canon law
ABC	Australian Broadcasting Corporation		BCom	bachelor of commerce
ABC TV	ABC Television		BD	bachelor of divinity
act.	active		BEd	bachelor of education
A$	Australian dollar		BEng	bachelor of engineering
AD	*anno domini*		bk *pl.* bks	book(s)
AFC	Air Force Cross		BL	bachelor of law / letters / literature
AIDS	acquired immune deficiency syndrome		BLitt	bachelor of letters
AK	Alaska		BM	bachelor of medicine
AL	Alabama		BMus	bachelor of music
A level	advanced level [examination]		BP	before present
ALS	associate of the Linnean Society		BP	British Petroleum
AM	master of arts		Bros.	Brothers
AMICE	associate member of the Institution of Civil Engineers		BS	(1) bachelor of science; (2) bachelor of surgery; (3) British standard
ANZAC	Australian and New Zealand Army Corps		BSc	bachelor of science
appx *pl.* appxs	appendix(es)		BSc (Econ.)	bachelor of science (economics)
AR	Arkansas		BSc (Eng.)	bachelor of science (engineering)
ARA	associate of the Royal Academy		bt	baronet
ARCA	associate of the Royal College of Art		BTh	bachelor of theology
ARCM	associate of the Royal College of Music		*bur.*	buried
ARCO	associate of the Royal College of Organists		C.	command [identifier for published parliamentary papers]
ARIBA	associate of the Royal Institute of British Architects		*c.*	*circa*
ARP	air-raid precautions		c.	*capitulum pl. capitula*: chapter(s)
ARRC	associate of the Royal Red Cross		CA	California
ARSA	associate of the Royal Scottish Academy		Cantab.	Cantabrigiensis
art.	article / item		cap.	*capitulum pl. capitula*: chapter(s)
ASC	Army Service Corps		CB	companion of the Bath
Asch	Austrian Schilling		CBE	commander of the Order of the British Empire
ASDIC	Antisubmarine Detection Investigation Committee		CBS	Columbia Broadcasting System
ATS	Auxiliary Territorial Service		cc	cubic centimetres
ATV	Associated Television		C$	Canadian dollar
Aug	August		CD	compact disc
AZ	Arizona		Cd	command [identifier for published parliamentary papers]
b.	born		CE	Common (*or* Christian) Era
BA	bachelor of arts		cent.	century
BA (Admin.)	bachelor of arts (administration)		cf.	compare
BAFTA	British Academy of Film and Television Arts		CH	Companion of Honour
BAO	bachelor of arts in obstetrics		chap.	chapter
bap.	baptized		ChB	bachelor of surgery
BBC	British Broadcasting Corporation / Company		CI	Imperial Order of the Crown of India
BC	before Christ		CIA	Central Intelligence Agency
BCE	before the common (*or* Christian) era		CID	Criminal Investigation Department
BCE	bachelor of civil engineering		CIE	companion of the Order of the Indian Empire
BCG	bacillus of Calmette and Guérin [inoculation against tuberculosis]		Cie	Compagnie
BCh	bachelor of surgery		CLit	companion of literature
BChir	bachelor of surgery		CM	master of surgery
BCL	bachelor of civil law		cm	centimetre(s)

Cmd	command [identifier for published parliamentary papers]	edn	edition
CMG	companion of the Order of St Michael and St George	EEC	European Economic Community
		EFTA	European Free Trade Association
Cmnd	command [identifier for published parliamentary papers]	EICS	East India Company Service
		EMI	Electrical and Musical Industries (Ltd)
CO	Colorado	Eng.	English
Co.	company	enl.	enlarged
co.	county	ENSA	Entertainments National Service Association
col. *pl.* cols.	column(s)	ep. *pl.* epp.	*epistola(e)*
Corp.	corporation	ESP	extra-sensory perception
CSE	certificate of secondary education	esp.	especially
CSI	companion of the Order of the Star of India	esq.	esquire
CT	Connecticut	est.	estimate / estimated
CVO	commander of the Royal Victorian Order	EU	European Union
cwt	hundredweight	ex	sold by (*lit.* out of)
$	(American) dollar	excl.	excludes / excluding
d.	(1) penny (pence); (2) died	exh.	exhibited
DBE	dame commander of the Order of the British Empire	exh. cat.	exhibition catalogue
		f. *pl.* ff.	following [pages]
DCH	diploma in child health	FA	Football Association
DCh	doctor of surgery	FACP	fellow of the American College of Physicians
DCL	doctor of civil law	facs.	facsimile
DCnL	doctor of canon law	FANY	First Aid Nursing Yeomanry
DCVO	dame commander of the Royal Victorian Order	FBA	fellow of the British Academy
DD	doctor of divinity	FBI	Federation of British Industries
DE	Delaware	FCS	fellow of the Chemical Society
Dec	December	Feb	February
dem.	demolished	FEng	fellow of the Fellowship of Engineering
DEng	doctor of engineering	FFCM	fellow of the Faculty of Community Medicine
des.	destroyed	FGS	fellow of the Geological Society
DFC	Distinguished Flying Cross	fig.	figure
DipEd	diploma in education	FIMechE	fellow of the Institution of Mechanical Engineers
DipPsych	diploma in psychiatry		
diss.	dissertation	FL	Florida
DL	deputy lieutenant	*fl.*	*floruit*
DLitt	doctor of letters	FLS	fellow of the Linnean Society
DLittCelt	doctor of Celtic letters	FM	frequency modulation
DM	(1) Deutschmark; (2) doctor of medicine; (3) doctor of musical arts	fol. *pl.* fols.	folio(s)
		Fr	French francs
DMus	doctor of music	Fr.	French
DNA	dioxyribonucleic acid	FRAeS	fellow of the Royal Aeronautical Society
doc.	document	FRAI	fellow of the Royal Anthropological Institute
DOL	doctor of oriental learning	FRAM	fellow of the Royal Academy of Music
DPH	diploma in public health	FRAS	(1) fellow of the Royal Asiatic Society; (2) fellow of the Royal Astronomical Society
DPhil	doctor of philosophy		
DPM	diploma in psychological medicine	FRCM	fellow of the Royal College of Music
DSC	Distinguished Service Cross	FRCO	fellow of the Royal College of Organists
DSc	doctor of science	FRCOG	fellow of the Royal College of Obstetricians and Gynaecologists
DSc (Econ.)	doctor of science (economics)		
DSc (Eng.)	doctor of science (engineering)	FRCP(C)	fellow of the Royal College of Physicians of Canada
DSM	Distinguished Service Medal		
DSO	companion of the Distinguished Service Order	FRCP (Edin.)	fellow of the Royal College of Physicians of Edinburgh
DSocSc	doctor of social science		
DTech	doctor of technology	FRCP (Lond.)	fellow of the Royal College of Physicians of London
DTh	doctor of theology		
DTM	diploma in tropical medicine	FRCPath	fellow of the Royal College of Pathologists
DTMH	diploma in tropical medicine and hygiene	FRCPsych	fellow of the Royal College of Psychiatrists
DU	doctor of the university	FRCS	fellow of the Royal College of Surgeons
DUniv	doctor of the university	FRGS	fellow of the Royal Geographical Society
dwt	pennyweight	FRIBA	fellow of the Royal Institute of British Architects
EC	European Community	FRICS	fellow of the Royal Institute of Chartered Surveyors
ed. *pl.* eds.	edited / edited by / editor(s)		
Edin.	Edinburgh	FRS	fellow of the Royal Society
		FRSA	fellow of the Royal Society of Arts

FRSCM	fellow of the Royal School of Church Music
FRSE	fellow of the Royal Society of Edinburgh
FRSL	fellow of the Royal Society of Literature
FSA	fellow of the Society of Antiquaries
ft	foot *pl.* feet
FTCL	fellow of Trinity College of Music, London
ft-lb per min.	foot-pounds per minute [unit of horsepower]
FZS	fellow of the Zoological Society
GA	Georgia
GBE	knight or dame grand cross of the Order of the British Empire
GCB	knight grand cross of the Order of the Bath
GCE	general certificate of education
GCH	knight grand cross of the Royal Guelphic Order
GCHQ	government communications headquarters
GCIE	knight grand commander of the Order of the Indian Empire
GCMG	knight or dame grand cross of the Order of St Michael and St George
GCSE	general certificate of secondary education
GCSI	knight grand commander of the Order of the Star of India
GCStJ	bailiff or dame grand cross of the order of St John of Jerusalem
GCVO	knight or dame grand cross of the Royal Victorian Order
GEC	General Electric Company
Ger.	German
GI	government (*or* general) issue
GMT	Greenwich mean time
GP	general practitioner
GPU	[Soviet special police unit]
GSO	general staff officer
Heb.	Hebrew
HEICS	Honourable East India Company Service
HI	Hawaii
HIV	human immunodeficiency virus
HK$	Hong Kong dollar
HM	his / her majesty('s)
HMAS	his / her majesty's Australian ship
HMNZS	his / her majesty's New Zealand ship
HMS	his / her majesty's ship
HMSO	His / Her Majesty's Stationery Office
HMV	His Master's Voice
Hon.	Honourable
hp	horsepower
hr	hour(s)
HRH	his / her royal highness
HTV	Harlech Television
IA	Iowa
ibid.	*ibidem*: in the same place
ICI	Imperial Chemical Industries (Ltd)
ID	Idaho
IL	Illinois
illus.	illustration
illustr.	illustrated
IN	Indiana
in.	inch(es)
Inc.	Incorporated
incl.	includes / including
IOU	I owe you
IQ	intelligence quotient
Ir£	Irish pound
IRA	Irish Republican Army

ISO	companion of the Imperial Service Order
It.	Italian
ITA	Independent Television Authority
ITV	Independent Television
Jan	January
JP	justice of the peace
jun.	junior
KB	knight of the Order of the Bath
KBE	knight commander of the Order of the British Empire
KC	king's counsel
kcal	kilocalorie
KCB	knight commander of the Order of the Bath
KCH	knight commander of the Royal Guelphic Order
KCIE	knight commander of the Order of the Indian Empire
KCMG	knight commander of the Order of St Michael and St George
KCSI	knight commander of the Order of the Star of India
KCVO	knight commander of the Royal Victorian Order
keV	kilo-electron-volt
KG	knight of the Order of the Garter
KGB	[Soviet committee of state security]
KH	knight of the Royal Guelphic Order
KLM	Koninklijke Luchtvaart Maatschappij (Royal Dutch Air Lines)
km	kilometre(s)
KP	knight of the Order of St Patrick
KS	Kansas
KT	knight of the Order of the Thistle
kt	knight
KY	Kentucky
£	pound(s) sterling
£E	Egyptian pound
L	lira *pl.* lire
l. *pl.* ll.	line(s)
LA	Lousiana
LAA	light anti-aircraft
LAH	licentiate of the Apothecaries' Hall, Dublin
Lat.	Latin
lb	pound(s), unit of weight
LDS	licence in dental surgery
lit.	literally
LittB	bachelor of letters
LittD	doctor of letters
LKQCPI	licentiate of the King and Queen's College of Physicians, Ireland
LLA	lady literate in arts
LLB	bachelor of laws
LLD	doctor of laws
LLM	master of laws
LM	licentiate in midwifery
LP	long-playing record
LRAM	licentiate of the Royal Academy of Music
LRCP	licentiate of the Royal College of Physicians
LRCPS (Glasgow)	licentiate of the Royal College of Physicians and Surgeons of Glasgow
LRCS	licentiate of the Royal College of Surgeons
LSA	licentiate of the Society of Apothecaries
LSD	lysergic acid diethylamide
LVO	lieutenant of the Royal Victorian Order
M. *pl.* MM.	Monsieur *pl.* Messieurs
m	metre(s)

m. *pl.* mm.	membrane(s)
MA	(1) Massachusetts; (2) master of arts
MAI	master of engineering
MB	bachelor of medicine
MBA	master of business administration
MBE	member of the Order of the British Empire
MC	Military Cross
MCC	Marylebone Cricket Club
MCh	master of surgery
MChir	master of surgery
MCom	master of commerce
MD	(1) doctor of medicine; (2) Maryland
MDMA	methylenedioxymethamphetamine
ME	Maine
MEd	master of education
MEng	master of engineering
MEP	member of the European parliament
MG	Morris Garages
MGM	Metro-Goldwyn-Mayer
Mgr	Monsignor
MI	(1) Michigan; (2) military intelligence
MI1c	[secret intelligence department]
MI5	[military intelligence department]
MI6	[secret intelligence department]
MI9	[secret escape service]
MICE	member of the Institution of Civil Engineers
MIEE	member of the Institution of Electrical Engineers
min.	minute(s)
Mk	mark
ML	(1) licentiate of medicine; (2) master of laws
MLitt	master of letters
Mlle	Mademoiselle
mm	millimetre(s)
Mme	Madame
MN	Minnesota
MO	Missouri
MOH	medical officer of health
MP	member of parliament
m.p.h.	miles per hour
MPhil	master of philosophy
MRCP	member of the Royal College of Physicians
MRCS	member of the Royal College of Surgeons
MRCVS	member of the Royal College of Veterinary Surgeons
MRIA	member of the Royal Irish Academy
MS	(1) master of science; (2) Mississippi
MS *pl.* MSS	manuscript(s)
MSc	master of science
MSc (Econ.)	master of science (economics)
MT	Montana
MusB	bachelor of music
MusBac	bachelor of music
MusD	doctor of music
MV	motor vessel
MVO	member of the Royal Victorian Order
n. *pl.* nn.	note(s)
NAAFI	Navy, Army, and Air Force Institutes
NASA	National Aeronautics and Space Administration
NATO	North Atlantic Treaty Organization
NBC	National Broadcasting Corporation
NC	North Carolina
NCO	non-commissioned officer
ND	North Dakota
n.d.	no date
NE	Nebraska
nem. con.	*nemine contradicente*: unanimously
new ser.	new series
NH	New Hampshire
NHS	National Health Service
NJ	New Jersey
NKVD	[Soviet people's commissariat for internal affairs]
NM	New Mexico
nm	nanometre(s)
no. *pl.* nos.	number(s)
Nov	November
n.p.	no place [of publication]
NS	new style
NV	Nevada
NY	New York
NZBS	New Zealand Broadcasting Service
OBE	officer of the Order of the British Empire
obit.	obituary
Oct	October
OCTU	officer cadets training unit
OECD	Organization for Economic Co-operation and Development
OEEC	Organization for European Economic Co-operation
OFM	order of Friars Minor [Franciscans]
OFMCap	Ordine Frati Minori Cappucini: member of the Capuchin order
OH	Ohio
OK	Oklahoma
O level	ordinary level [examination]
OM	Order of Merit
OP	order of Preachers [Dominicans]
op. *pl.* opp.	opus *pl.* opera
OPEC	Organization of Petroleum Exporting Countries
OR	Oregon
orig.	original
OS	old style
OSB	Order of St Benedict
OTC	Officers' Training Corps
OWS	Old Watercolour Society
Oxon.	Oxoniensis
p. *pl.* pp.	page(s)
PA	Pennsylvania
p.a.	per annum
para.	paragraph
PAYE	pay as you earn
pbk *pl.* pbks	paperback(s)
per.	[during the] period
PhD	doctor of philosophy
pl.	(1) plate(s); (2) plural
priv. coll.	private collection
pt *pl.* pts	part(s)
pubd	published
PVC	polyvinyl chloride
q. *pl.* qq.	(1) question(s); (2) quire(s)
QC	queen's counsel
R	rand
R.	Rex / Regina
r	recto
r.	reigned / ruled
RA	Royal Academy / Royal Academician

RAC	Royal Automobile Club		Skr	Swedish krona
RAF	Royal Air Force		Span.	Spanish
RAFVR	Royal Air Force Volunteer Reserve		SPCK	Society for Promoting Christian Knowledge
RAM	[member of] Royal Academy of Music		SS	(1) Santissimi; (2) Schutzstaffel; (3) steam ship
RAMC	Royal Army Medical Corps		STB	bachelor of theology
RCA	Royal College of Art		STD	doctor of theology
RCNC	Royal Corps of Naval Constructors		STM	master of theology
RCOG	Royal College of Obstetricians and Gynaecologists		STP	doctor of theology
			supp.	supposedly
RDI	royal designer for industry		suppl. *pl.* suppls.	supplement(s)
RE	Royal Engineers		s.v.	*sub verbo* / *sub voce*: under the word / heading
repr. *pl.* reprs.	reprint(s) / reprinted		SY	steam yacht
repro.	reproduced		TA	Territorial Army
rev.	revised / revised by / reviser / revision		TASS	[Soviet news agency]
Revd	Reverend		TB	tuberculosis (*lit.* tubercle bacillus)
RHA	Royal Hibernian Academy		TD	(1) *teachtaí dála* (member of the Dáil);
RI	(1) Rhode Island; (2) Royal Institute of Painters in Water-Colours			(2) territorial decoration
			TN	Tennessee
RIBA	Royal Institute of British Architects		TNT	trinitrotoluene
RIN	Royal Indian Navy		trans.	translated / translated by / translation / translator
RM	Reichsmark			
RMS	Royal Mail steamer		TT	tourist trophy
RN	Royal Navy		TUC	Trades Union Congress
RNA	ribonucleic acid		TX	Texas
RNAS	Royal Naval Air Service		U-boat	*Unterseeboot*: submarine
RNR	Royal Naval Reserve		Ufa	Universum-Film AG
RNVR	Royal Naval Volunteer Reserve		UMIST	University of Manchester Institute of Science and Technology
RO	Record Office			
r.p.m.	revolutions per minute		UN	United Nations
RRS	royal research ship		UNESCO	United Nations Educational, Scientific, and Cultural Organization
Rs	rupees			
RSA	(1) Royal Scottish Academician; (2) Royal Society of Arts		UNICEF	United Nations International Children's Emergency Fund
RSPCA	Royal Society for the Prevention of Cruelty to Animals		unpubd	unpublished
			USS	United States ship
Rt Hon.	Right Honourable		UT	Utah
Rt Revd	Right Reverend		*v*	verso
RUC	Royal Ulster Constabulary		v.	versus
Russ.	Russian		VA	Virginia
RWS	Royal Watercolour Society		VAD	Voluntary Aid Detachment
S4C	Sianel Pedwar Cymru		VC	Victoria Cross
s.	shilling(s)		VE-day	victory in Europe day
s.a.	*sub anno*: under the year		Ven.	Venerable
SABC	South African Broadcasting Corporation		VJ-day	victory over Japan day
SAS	Special Air Service		vol. *pl.* vols.	volume(s)
SC	South Carolina		VT	Vermont
ScD	doctor of science		WA	Washington [state]
S$	Singapore dollar		WAAC	Women's Auxiliary Army Corps
SD	South Dakota		WAAF	Women's Auxiliary Air Force
sec.	second(s)		WEA	Workers' Educational Association
sel.	selected		WHO	World Health Organization
sen.	senior		WI	Wisconsin
Sept	September		WRAF	Women's Royal Air Force
ser.	series		WRNS	Women's Royal Naval Service
SHAPE	supreme headquarters allied powers, Europe		WV	West Virginia
SIDRO	Société Internationale d'Énergie Hydro-Électrique		WVS	Women's Voluntary Service
			WY	Wyoming
sig. *pl.* sigs.	signature(s)		¥	yen
sing.	singular		YMCA	Young Men's Christian Association
SIS	Secret Intelligence Service		YWCA	Young Women's Christian Association
SJ	Society of Jesus			

2 Institution abbreviations

All Souls Oxf.	All Souls College, Oxford
AM Oxf.	Ashmolean Museum, Oxford
Balliol Oxf.	Balliol College, Oxford
BBC WAC	BBC Written Archives Centre, Reading
Beds. & Luton ARS	Bedfordshire and Luton Archives and Record Service, Bedford
Berks. RO	Berkshire Record Office, Reading
BFI	British Film Institute, London
BFI NFTVA	British Film Institute, London, National Film and Television Archive
BGS	British Geological Survey, Keyworth, Nottingham
Birm. CA	Birmingham Central Library, Birmingham City Archives
Birm. CL	Birmingham Central Library
BL	British Library, London
BL NSA	British Library, London, National Sound Archive
BL OIOC	British Library, London, Oriental and India Office Collections
BLPES	London School of Economics and Political Science, British Library of Political and Economic Science
BM	British Museum, London
Bodl. Oxf.	Bodleian Library, Oxford
Bodl. RH	Bodleian Library of Commonwealth and African Studies at Rhodes House, Oxford
Borth. Inst.	Borthwick Institute of Historical Research, University of York
Boston PL	Boston Public Library, Massachusetts
Bristol RO	Bristol Record Office
Bucks. RLSS	Buckinghamshire Records and Local Studies Service, Aylesbury
CAC Cam.	Churchill College, Cambridge, Churchill Archives Centre
Cambs. AS	Cambridgeshire Archive Service
CCC Cam.	Corpus Christi College, Cambridge
CCC Oxf.	Corpus Christi College, Oxford
Ches. & Chester ALSS	Cheshire and Chester Archives and Local Studies Service
Christ Church Oxf.	Christ Church, Oxford
Christies	Christies, London
City Westm. AC	City of Westminster Archives Centre, London
CKS	Centre for Kentish Studies, Maidstone
CLRO	Corporation of London Records Office
Coll. Arms	College of Arms, London
Col. U.	Columbia University, New York
Cornwall RO	Cornwall Record Office, Truro
Courtauld Inst.	Courtauld Institute of Art, London
CUL	Cambridge University Library
Cumbria AS	Cumbria Archive Service
Derbys. RO	Derbyshire Record Office, Matlock
Devon RO	Devon Record Office, Exeter
Dorset RO	Dorset Record Office, Dorchester
Duke U.	Duke University, Durham, North Carolina
Duke U., Perkins L.	Duke University, Durham, North Carolina, William R. Perkins Library
Durham Cath. CL	Durham Cathedral, chapter library
Durham RO	Durham Record Office
DWL	Dr Williams's Library, London
Essex RO	Essex Record Office
E. Sussex RO	East Sussex Record Office, Lewes
Eton	Eton College, Berkshire
FM Cam.	Fitzwilliam Museum, Cambridge
Folger	Folger Shakespeare Library, Washington, DC
Garr. Club	Garrick Club, London
Girton Cam.	Girton College, Cambridge
GL	Guildhall Library, London
Glos. RO	Gloucestershire Record Office, Gloucester
Gon. & Caius Cam.	Gonville and Caius College, Cambridge
Gov. Art Coll.	Government Art Collection
GS Lond.	Geological Society of London
Hants. RO	Hampshire Record Office, Winchester
Harris Man. Oxf.	Harris Manchester College, Oxford
Harvard TC	Harvard Theatre Collection, Harvard University, Cambridge, Massachusetts, Nathan Marsh Pusey Library
Harvard U.	Harvard University, Cambridge, Massachusetts
Harvard U., Houghton L.	Harvard University, Cambridge, Massachusetts, Houghton Library
Herefs. RO	Herefordshire Record Office, Hereford
Herts. ALS	Hertfordshire Archives and Local Studies, Hertford
Hist. Soc. Penn.	Historical Society of Pennsylvania, Philadelphia
HLRO	House of Lords Record Office, London
Hult. Arch.	Hulton Archive, London and New York
Hunt. L.	Huntington Library, San Marino, California
ICL	Imperial College, London
Inst. CE	Institution of Civil Engineers, London
Inst. EE	Institution of Electrical Engineers, London
IWM	Imperial War Museum, London
IWM FVA	Imperial War Museum, London, Film and Video Archive
IWM SA	Imperial War Museum, London, Sound Archive
JRL	John Rylands University Library of Manchester
King's AC Cam.	King's College Archives Centre, Cambridge
King's Cam.	King's College, Cambridge
King's Lond.	King's College, London
King's Lond., Liddell Hart C.	King's College, London, Liddell Hart Centre for Military Archives
Lancs. RO	Lancashire Record Office, Preston
L. Cong.	Library of Congress, Washington, DC
Leics. RO	Leicestershire, Leicester, and Rutland Record Office, Leicester
Lincs. Arch.	Lincolnshire Archives, Lincoln
Linn. Soc.	Linnean Society of London
LMA	London Metropolitan Archives
LPL	Lambeth Palace, London
Lpool RO	Liverpool Record Office and Local Studies Service
LUL	London University Library
Magd. Cam.	Magdalene College, Cambridge
Magd. Oxf.	Magdalen College, Oxford
Man. City Gall.	Manchester City Galleries
Man. CL	Manchester Central Library
Mass. Hist. Soc.	Massachusetts Historical Society, Boston
Merton Oxf.	Merton College, Oxford
MHS Oxf.	Museum of the History of Science, Oxford
Mitchell L., Glas.	Mitchell Library, Glasgow
Mitchell L., NSW	State Library of New South Wales, Sydney, Mitchell Library
Morgan L.	Pierpont Morgan Library, New York
NA Canada	National Archives of Canada, Ottawa
NA Ire.	National Archives of Ireland, Dublin
NAM	National Army Museum, London
NA Scot.	National Archives of Scotland, Edinburgh
News Int. RO	News International Record Office, London
NG Ire.	National Gallery of Ireland, Dublin

NG Scot.	National Gallery of Scotland, Edinburgh
NHM	Natural History Museum, London
NL Aus.	National Library of Australia, Canberra
NL Ire.	National Library of Ireland, Dublin
NL NZ	National Library of New Zealand, Wellington
NL NZ, Turnbull L.	National Library of New Zealand, Wellington, Alexander Turnbull Library
NL Scot.	National Library of Scotland, Edinburgh
NL Wales	National Library of Wales, Aberystwyth
NMG Wales	National Museum and Gallery of Wales, Cardiff
NMM	National Maritime Museum, London
Norfolk RO	Norfolk Record Office, Norwich
Northants. RO	Northamptonshire Record Office, Northampton
Northumbd RO	Northumberland Record Office
Notts. Arch.	Nottinghamshire Archives, Nottingham
NPG	National Portrait Gallery, London
NRA	National Archives, London, Historical Manuscripts Commission, National Register of Archives
Nuffield Oxf.	Nuffield College, Oxford
N. Yorks. CRO	North Yorkshire County Record Office, Northallerton
NYPL	New York Public Library
Oxf. UA	Oxford University Archives
Oxf. U. Mus. NH	Oxford University Museum of Natural History
Oxon. RO	Oxfordshire Record Office, Oxford
Pembroke Cam.	Pembroke College, Cambridge
PRO	National Archives, London, Public Record Office
PRO NIre.	Public Record Office for Northern Ireland, Belfast
Pusey Oxf.	Pusey House, Oxford
RA	Royal Academy of Arts, London
Ransom HRC	Harry Ransom Humanities Research Center, University of Texas, Austin
RAS	Royal Astronomical Society, London
RBG Kew	Royal Botanic Gardens, Kew, London
RCP Lond.	Royal College of Physicians of London
RCS Eng.	Royal College of Surgeons of England, London
RGS	Royal Geographical Society, London
RIBA	Royal Institute of British Architects, London
RIBA BAL	Royal Institute of British Architects, London, British Architectural Library
Royal Arch.	Royal Archives, Windsor Castle, Berkshire [by gracious permission of her majesty the queen]
Royal Irish Acad.	Royal Irish Academy, Dublin
Royal Scot. Acad.	Royal Scottish Academy, Edinburgh
RS	Royal Society, London
RSA	Royal Society of Arts, London
RS Friends, Lond.	Religious Society of Friends, London
St Ant. Oxf.	St Antony's College, Oxford
St John Cam.	St John's College, Cambridge
S. Antiquaries, Lond.	Society of Antiquaries of London
Sci. Mus.	Science Museum, London
Scot. NPG	Scottish National Portrait Gallery, Edinburgh
Scott Polar RI	University of Cambridge, Scott Polar Research Institute
Sheff. Arch.	Sheffield Archives
Shrops. RRC	Shropshire Records and Research Centre, Shrewsbury
SOAS	School of Oriental and African Studies, London
Som. ARS	Somerset Archive and Record Service, Taunton
Staffs. RO	Staffordshire Record Office, Stafford

Suffolk RO	Suffolk Record Office
Surrey HC	Surrey History Centre, Woking
TCD	Trinity College, Dublin
Trinity Cam.	Trinity College, Cambridge
U. Aberdeen	University of Aberdeen
U. Birm.	University of Birmingham
U. Birm. L.	University of Birmingham Library
U. Cal.	University of California
U. Cam.	University of Cambridge
UCL	University College, London
U. Durham	University of Durham
U. Durham L.	University of Durham Library
U. Edin.	University of Edinburgh
U. Edin., New Coll.	University of Edinburgh, New College
U. Edin., New Coll. L.	University of Edinburgh, New College Library
U. Edin. L.	University of Edinburgh Library
U. Glas.	University of Glasgow
U. Glas. L.	University of Glasgow Library
U. Hull	University of Hull
U. Hull, Brynmor Jones L.	University of Hull, Brynmor Jones Library
U. Leeds	University of Leeds
U. Leeds, Brotherton L.	University of Leeds, Brotherton Library
U. Lond.	University of London
U. Lpool	University of Liverpool
U. Lpool L.	University of Liverpool Library
U. Mich.	University of Michigan, Ann Arbor
U. Mich., Clements L.	University of Michigan, Ann Arbor, William L. Clements Library
U. Newcastle	University of Newcastle upon Tyne
U. Newcastle, Robinson L.	University of Newcastle upon Tyne, Robinson Library
U. Nott.	University of Nottingham
U. Nott. L.	University of Nottingham Library
U. Oxf.	University of Oxford
U. Reading	University of Reading
U. Reading L.	University of Reading Library
U. St Andr.	University of St Andrews
U. St Andr. L.	University of St Andrews Library
U. Southampton	University of Southampton
U. Southampton L.	University of Southampton Library
U. Sussex	University of Sussex, Brighton
U. Texas	University of Texas, Austin
U. Wales	University of Wales
U. Warwick Mod. RC	University of Warwick, Coventry, Modern Records Centre
V&A	Victoria and Albert Museum, London
V&A NAL	Victoria and Albert Museum, London, National Art Library
Warks. CRO	Warwickshire County Record Office, Warwick
Wellcome L.	Wellcome Library for the History and Understanding of Medicine, London
Westm. DA	Westminster Diocesan Archives, London
Wilts. & Swindon RO	Wiltshire and Swindon Record Office, Trowbridge
Worcs. RO	Worcestershire Record Office, Worcester
W. Sussex RO	West Sussex Record Office, Chichester
W. Yorks. AS	West Yorkshire Archive Service
Yale U.	Yale University, New Haven, Connecticut
Yale U., Beinecke L.	Yale University, New Haven, Connecticut, Beinecke Rare Book and Manuscript Library
Yale U. CBA	Yale University, New Haven, Connecticut, Yale Center for British Art

3 Bibliographic abbreviations

Adams, *Drama* — W. D. Adams, *A dictionary of the drama*, 1: *A–G* (1904); 2: *H–Z* (1956) [vol. 2 microfilm only]

AFM — J O'Donovan, ed. and trans., *Annala rioghachta Eireann / Annals of the kingdom of Ireland by the four masters*, 7 vols. (1848–51); 2nd edn (1856); 3rd edn (1990)

Allibone, *Dict.* — S. A. Allibone, *A critical dictionary of English literature and British and American authors*, 3 vols. (1859–71); suppl. by J. F. Kirk, 2 vols. (1891)

ANB — J. A. Garraty and M. C. Carnes, eds., *American national biography*, 24 vols. (1999)

Anderson, *Scot. nat.* — W. Anderson, *The Scottish nation, or, The surnames, families, literature, honours, and biographical history of the people of Scotland*, 3 vols. (1859–63)

Ann. mon. — H. R. Luard, ed., *Annales monastici*, 5 vols., Rolls Series, 36 (1864–9)

Ann. Ulster — S. Mac Airt and G. Mac Niocaill, eds., *Annals of Ulster (to AD 1131)* (1983)

APC — *Acts of the privy council of England*, new ser., 46 vols. (1890–1964)

APS — *The acts of the parliaments of Scotland*, 12 vols. in 13 (1814–75)

Arber, *Regs. Stationers* — F. Arber, ed., *A transcript of the registers of the Company of Stationers of London, 1554–1640 AD*, 5 vols. (1875–94)

ArchR — *Architectural Review*

ASC — D. Whitelock, D. C. Douglas, and S. I. Tucker, ed. and trans., *The Anglo-Saxon Chronicle: a revised translation* (1961)

AS chart. — P. H. Sawyer, *Anglo-Saxon charters: an annotated list and bibliography*, Royal Historical Society Guides and Handbooks (1968)

AusDB — D. Pike and others, eds., *Australian dictionary of biography*, 16 vols. (1966–2002)

Baker, *Serjeants* — J. H. Baker, *The order of serjeants at law*, SeldS, suppl. ser., 5 (1984)

Bale, *Cat.* — J. Bale, *Scriptorum illustrium Maioris Brytannie, quam nunc Angliam et Scotiam vocant: catalogus*, 2 vols. in 1 (Basel, 1557–9); facs. edn (1971)

Bale, *Index* — J. Bale, *Index Britanniae scriptorum*, ed. R. L. Poole and M. Bateson (1902); facs. edn (1990)

BBCS — *Bulletin of the Board of Celtic Studies*

BDMBR — J. O. Baylen and N. J. Gossman, eds., *Biographical dictionary of modern British radicals*, 3 vols. in 4 (1979–88)

Bede, *Hist. eccl.* — *Bede's Ecclesiastical history of the English people*, ed. and trans. B. Colgrave and R. A. B. Mynors, OMT (1969); repr. (1991)

Bénézit, *Dict.* — E. Bénézit, *Dictionnaire critique et documentaire des peintres, sculpteurs, dessinateurs et graveurs*, 3 vols. (Paris, 1911–23); new edn, 8 vols. (1948–66), repr. (1966); 3rd edn, rev. and enl., 10 vols. (1976); 4th edn, 14 vols. (1999)

BIHR — *Bulletin of the Institute of Historical Research*

Birch, *Seals* — W. de Birch, *Catalogue of seals in the department of manuscripts in the British Museum*, 6 vols. (1887–1900)

Bishop Burnet's History — *Bishop Burnet's History of his own time*, ed. M. J. Routh, 2nd edn, 6 vols. (1833)

Blackwood — *Blackwood's [Edinburgh] Magazine*, 328 vols. (1817–1980)

Blain, Clements & Grundy, *Feminist comp.* — V. Blain, P. Clements, and I. Grundy, eds., *The feminist companion to literature in English* (1990)

BL cat. — *The British Library general catalogue of printed books* [in 360 vols. with suppls., also CD-ROM and online]

BMJ — *British Medical Journal*

Boase & Courtney, *Bibl. Corn.* — G. C. Boase and W. P. Courtney, *Bibliotheca Cornubiensis: a catalogue of the writings … of Cornishmen*, 3 vols. (1874–82)

Boase, *Mod. Eng. biog.* — F. Boase, *Modern English biography: containing many thousand concise memoirs of persons who have died since the year 1850*, 6 vols. (privately printed, Truro, 1892–1921); repr. (1965)

Boswell, *Life* — *Boswell's Life of Johnson: together with Journal of a tour to the Hebrides and Johnson's Diary of a journey into north Wales*, ed. G. B. Hill, enl. edn, rev. L. F. Powell, 6 vols. (1934–50); 2nd edn (1964); repr. (1971)

Brown & Stratton, *Brit. mus.* — J. D. Brown and S. S. Stratton, *British musical biography* (1897)

Bryan, *Painters* — M. Bryan, *A biographical and critical dictionary of painters and engravers*, 2 vols. (1816); new edn, ed. G. Stanley (1849); new edn, ed. R. E. Graves and W. Armstrong, 2 vols. (1886–9); [4th edn], ed. G. C. Williamson, 5 vols. (1903–5) [various reprs.]

Burke, *Gen. GB* — J. Burke, *A genealogical and heraldic history of the commoners of Great Britain and Ireland*, 4 vols. (1833–8); new edn as *A genealogical and heraldic dictionary of the landed gentry of Great Britain and Ireland*, 3 vols. [1843–9] [many later edns]

Burke, *Gen. Ire.* — J. B. Burke, *A genealogical and heraldic history of the landed gentry of Ireland* (1899); 2nd edn (1904); 3rd edn (1912); 4th edn (1958); 5th edn as *Burke's Irish family records* (1976)

Burke, *Peerage* — J. Burke, *A general* [later edns *A genealogical*] *and heraldic dictionary of the peerage and baronetage of the United Kingdom* [later edns *the British empire*] (1829–)

Burney, *Hist. mus.* — C. Burney, *A general history of music, from the earliest ages to the present period*, 4 vols. (1776–89)

Burtchaell & Sadleir, *Alum. Dubl.* — G. D. Burtchaell and T. U. Sadleir, *Alumni Dublinenses: a register of the students, graduates, and provosts of Trinity College* (1924); [2nd edn], with suppl., in 2 pts (1935)

Calamy rev. — A. G. Matthews, *Calamy revised* (1934); repr. (1988)

CCI — *Calendar of confirmations and inventories granted and given up in the several commissariots of Scotland* (1876–)

CClR — *Calendar of the close rolls preserved in the Public Record Office*, 47 vols. (1892–1963)

CDS — J. Bain, ed., *Calendar of documents relating to Scotland*, 4 vols., PRO (1881–8); suppl. vol. 5, ed. G. G. Simpson and J. D. Galbraith [1986]

CEPR letters — W. H. Bliss, C. Johnson, and J. Twemlow, eds., *Calendar of entries in the papal registers relating to Great Britain and Ireland: papal letters* (1893–)

CGPLA — *Calendars of the grants of probate and letters of administration* [in 4 ser.: England & Wales, Northern Ireland, Ireland, and Éire]

Chambers, *Scots.* — R. Chambers, ed., *A biographical dictionary of eminent Scotsmen*, 4 vols. (1832–5)

Chancery records — chancery records pubd by the PRO

Chancery records (RC) — chancery records pubd by the Record Commissions

CIPM	Calendar of inquisitions post mortem, [20 vols.], PRO (1904–); also Henry VII, 3 vols. (1898–1955)
Clarendon, Hist. rebellion	E. Hyde, earl of Clarendon, The history of the rebellion and civil wars in England, 6 vols. (1888); repr. (1958) and (1992)
Cobbett, Parl. hist.	W. Cobbett and J. Wright, eds., Cobbett's Parliamentary history of England, 36 vols. (1806–1820)
Colvin, Archs.	H. Colvin, A biographical dictionary of British architects, 1600–1840, 3rd edn (1995)
Cooper, Ath. Cantab.	C. H. Cooper and T. Cooper, Athenae Cantabrigienses, 3 vols. (1858–1913); repr. (1967)
CPR	Calendar of the patent rolls preserved in the Public Record Office (1891–)
Crockford	Crockford's Clerical Directory
CS	Camden Society
CSP	Calendar of state papers [in 11 ser.: domestic, Scotland, Scottish series, Ireland, colonial, Commonwealth, foreign, Spain [at Simancas], Rome, Milan, and Venice]
CYS	Canterbury and York Society
DAB	Dictionary of American biography, 21 vols. (1928–36), repr. in 11 vols. (1964); 10 suppls. (1944–96)
DBB	D. J. Jeremy, ed., Dictionary of business biography, 5 vols. (1984–6)
DCB	G. W. Brown and others, Dictionary of Canadian biography, [14 vols.] (1966–)
Debrett's Peerage	Debrett's Peerage (1803–) [sometimes Debrett's Illustrated peerage]
Desmond, Botanists	R. Desmond, Dictionary of British and Irish botanists and horticulturists (1977); rev. edn (1994)
Dir. Brit. archs.	A. Felstead, J. Franklin, and L. Pinfield, eds., Directory of British architects, 1834–1900 (1993); 2nd edn, ed. A. Brodie and others, 2 vols. (2001)
DLB	J. M. Bellamy and J. Saville, eds., Dictionary of labour biography, [10 vols.] (1972–)
DLitB	Dictionary of Literary Biography
DNB	Dictionary of national biography, 63 vols. (1885–1900), suppl., 3 vols. (1901); repr. in 22 vols. (1908–9); 10 further suppls. (1912–96); Missing persons (1993)
DNZB	W. H. Oliver and C. Orange, eds., The dictionary of New Zealand biography, 5 vols. (1990–2000)
DSAB	W. J. de Kock and others, eds., Dictionary of South African biography, 5 vols. (1968–87)
DSB	C. C. Gillispie and F. L. Holmes, eds., Dictionary of scientific biography, 16 vols. (1970–80); repr. in 8 vols. (1981); 2 vol. suppl. (1990)
DSBB	A. Slaven and S. Checkland, eds., Dictionary of Scottish business biography, 1860–1960, 2 vols. (1986–90)
DSCHT	N. M. de S. Cameron and others, eds., Dictionary of Scottish church history and theology (1993)
Dugdale, Monasticon	W. Dugdale, Monasticon Anglicanum, 3 vols. (1655–72); 2nd edn, 3 vols. (1661–82); new edn, ed. J. Caley, J. Ellis, and B. Bandinel, 6 vols. in 8 pts (1817–30); repr. (1846) and (1970)

DWB	J. E. Lloyd and others, eds., Dictionary of Welsh biography down to 1940 (1959) [Eng. trans. of Y bywgraffiadur Cymreig hyd 1940, 2nd edn (1954)]
EdinR	Edinburgh Review, or, Critical Journal
EETS	Early English Text Society
Emden, Cam.	A. B. Emden, A biographical register of the University of Cambridge to 1500 (1963)
Emden, Oxf.	A. B. Emden, A biographical register of the University of Oxford to AD 1500, 3 vols. (1957–9); also A biographical register of the University of Oxford, AD 1501 to 1540 (1974)
EngHR	English Historical Review
Engraved Brit. ports.	F. M. O'Donoghue and H. M. Hake, Catalogue of engraved British portraits preserved in the department of prints and drawings in the British Museum, 6 vols. (1908–25)
ER	The English Reports, 178 vols. (1900–32)
ESTC	English short title catalogue, 1475–1800 [CD-ROM and online]
Evelyn, Diary	The diary of John Evelyn, ed. E. S. De Beer, 6 vols. (1955); repr. (2000)
Farington, Diary	The diary of Joseph Farington, ed. K. Garlick and others, 17 vols. (1978–98)
Fasti Angl. (Hardy)	J. Le Neve, Fasti ecclesiae Anglicanae, ed. T. D. Hardy, 3 vols. (1854)
Fasti Angl., 1066–1300	[J. Le Neve], Fasti ecclesiae Anglicanae, 1066–1300, ed. D. E. Greenway and J. S. Barrow, [8 vols.] (1968–)
Fasti Angl., 1300–1541	[J. Le Neve], Fasti ecclesiae Anglicanae, 1300–1541, 12 vols. (1962–7)
Fasti Angl., 1541–1857	[J. Le Neve], Fasti ecclesiae Anglicanae, 1541–1857, ed. J. M. Horn, D. M. Smith, and D. S. Bailey, [9 vols.] (1969–)
Fasti Scot.	H. Scott, Fasti ecclesiae Scoticanae, 3 vols. in 6 (1871); new edn, [11 vols.] (1915–)
FO List	Foreign Office List
Fortescue, Brit. army	J. W. Fortescue, A history of the British army, 13 vols. (1899–1930)
Foss, Judges	E. Foss, The judges of England, 9 vols. (1848–64); repr. (1966)
Foster, Alum. Oxon.	J. Foster, ed., Alumni Oxonienses: the members of the University of Oxford, 1715–1886, 4 vols. (1887–8); later edn (1891); also Alumni Oxonienses … 1500–1714, 4 vols. (1891–2); 8 vol. repr. (1968) and (2000)
Fuller, Worthies	T. Fuller, The history of the worthies of England, 4 pts (1662); new edn, 2 vols., ed. J. Nichols (1811); new edn, 3 vols., ed. P. A. Nuttall (1840); repr. (1965)
GEC, Baronetage	G. E. Cokayne, Complete baronetage, 6 vols. (1900–09); repr. (1983) [microprint]
GEC, Peerage	G. E. C. [G. E. Cokayne], The complete peerage of England, Scotland, Ireland, Great Britain, and the United Kingdom, 8 vols. (1887–98); new edn, ed. V. Gibbs and others, 14 vols. in 15 (1910–98); microprint repr. (1982) and (1987)
Genest, Eng. stage	J. Genest, Some account of the English stage from the Restoration in 1660 to 1830, 10 vols. (1832); repr. [New York, 1965]
Gillow, Lit. biog. hist.	J. Gillow, A literary and biographical history or bibliographical dictionary of the English Catholics, from the breach with Rome, in 1534, to the present time, 5 vols. [1885–1902]; repr. (1961); repr. with preface by C. Gillow (1999)
Gir. Camb. opera	Giraldi Cambrensis opera, ed. J. S. Brewer, J. F. Dimock, and G. F. Warner, 8 vols., Rolls Series, 21 (1861–91)
GJ	Geographical Journal

Gladstone, *Diaries* — *The Gladstone diaries: with cabinet minutes and prime-ministerial correspondence*, ed. M. R. D. Foot and H. C. G. Matthew, 14 vols. (1968–94)

GM — *Gentleman's Magazine*

Graves, *Artists* — A. Graves, ed., *A dictionary of artists who have exhibited works in the principal London exhibitions of oil paintings from 1760 to 1880* (1884); new edn (1895); 3rd edn (1901); facs. edn (1969); repr. [1970], (1973), and (1984)

Graves, *Brit. Inst.* — A. Graves, *The British Institution, 1806–1867: a complete dictionary of contributors and their work from the foundation of the institution* (1875); facs. edn (1908); repr. (1969)

Graves, *RA exhibitors* — A. Graves, *The Royal Academy of Arts: a complete dictionary of contributors and their work from its foundation in 1769 to 1904*, 8 vols. (1905–6); repr. in 4 vols. (1970) and (1972)

Graves, *Soc. Artists* — A. Graves, *The Society of Artists of Great Britain, 1760–1791, the Free Society of Artists, 1761–1783: a complete dictionary* (1907); facs. edn (1969)

Greaves & Zaller, *BDBR* — R. L. Greaves and R. Zaller, eds., *Biographical dictionary of British radicals in the seventeenth century*, 3 vols. (1982–4)

Grove, *Dict. mus.* — G. Grove, ed., *A dictionary of music and musicians*, 5 vols. (1878–90); 2nd edn, ed. J. A. Fuller Maitland (1904–10); 3rd edn, ed. H. C. Colles (1927); 4th edn with suppl. (1940); 5th edn, ed. E. Blom, 9 vols. (1954); suppl. (1961) [see also *New Grove*]

Hall, *Dramatic ports.* — L. A. Hall, *Catalogue of dramatic portraits in the theatre collection of the Harvard College library*, 4 vols. (1930–34)

Hansard — *Hansard's parliamentary debates*, ser. 1–5 (1803–)

Highfill, Burnim & Langhans, *BDA* — P. H. Highfill, K. A. Burnim, and E. A. Langhans, *A biographical dictionary of actors, actresses, musicians, dancers, managers, and other stage personnel in London, 1660–1800*, 16 vols. (1973–93)

Hist. U. Oxf. — T. H. Aston, ed., *The history of the University of Oxford*, 8 vols. (1984–2000) [1: *The early Oxford schools*, ed. J. I. Catto (1984); 2: *Late medieval Oxford*, ed. J. I. Catto and R. Evans (1992); 3: *The collegiate university*, ed. J. McConica (1986); 4: *Seventeenth-century Oxford*, ed. N. Tyacke (1997); 5: *The eighteenth century*, ed. L. S. Sutherland and L. G. Mitchell (1986); 6–7: *Nineteenth-century Oxford*, ed. M. G. Brock and M. C. Curthoys (1997–2000); 8: *The twentieth century*, ed. B. Harrison (2000)]

HJ — *Historical Journal*

HMC — Historical Manuscripts Commission

Holdsworth, *Eng. law* — W. S. Holdsworth, *A history of English law*, ed. A. L. Goodhart and H. L. Hanbury, 17 vols. (1903–72)

HoP, *Commons* — *The history of parliament: the House of Commons* [1386–1421, ed. J. S. Roskell, L. Clark, and C. Rawcliffe, 4 vols. (1992); 1509–1558, ed. S. T. Bindoff, 3 vols. (1982); 1558–1603, ed. P. W. Hasler, 3 vols. (1981); 1660–1690, ed. B. D. Henning, 3 vols. (1983); 1690–1715, ed. D. W. Hayton, E. Cruickshanks, and S. Handley, 5 vols. (2002); 1715–1754, ed. R. Sedgwick, 2 vols. (1970); 1754–1790, ed. L. Namier and J. Brooke, 3 vols. (1964), repr. (1985); 1790–1820, ed. R. G. Thorne, 5 vols. (1986); in draft (used with permission): 1422–1504, 1604–1629, 1640–1660, and 1820–1832]

IGI — *International Genealogical Index*, Church of Jesus Christ of the Latterday Saints

ILN — *Illustrated London News*

IMC — Irish Manuscripts Commission

Irving, *Scots.* — J. Irving, ed., *The book of Scotsmen eminent for achievements in arms and arts, church and state, law, legislation and literature, commerce, science, travel and philanthropy* (1881)

JCS — *Journal of the Chemical Society*

JHC — *Journals of the House of Commons*

JHL — *Journals of the House of Lords*

John of Worcester, *Chron.* — *The chronicle of John of Worcester*, ed. R. R. Darlington and P. McGurk, trans. J. Bray and P. McGurk, 3 vols., OMT (1995–) [vol. 1 forthcoming]

Keeler, *Long Parliament* — M. F. Keeler, *The Long Parliament, 1640–1641: a biographical study of its members* (1954)

Kelly, *Handbk* — *The upper ten thousand: an alphabetical list of all members of noble families*, 3 vols. (1875–7); continued as *Kelly's handbook of the upper ten thousand for 1878* [1879], 2 vols. (1878–9); continued as *Kelly's handbook to the titled, landed and official classes*, 94 vols. (1880–1973)

LondG — *London Gazette*

LP Henry VIII — J. S. Brewer, J. Gairdner, and R. H. Brodie, eds., *Letters and papers, foreign and domestic, of the reign of Henry VIII*, 23 vols. in 38 (1862–1932); repr. (1965)

Mallalieu, *Watercolour artists* — H. L. Mallalieu, *The dictionary of British watercolour artists up to 1820*, 3 vols. (1976–90); vol. 1, 2nd edn (1986)

Memoirs FRS — *Biographical Memoirs of Fellows of the Royal Society*

MGH — Monumenta Germaniae Historica

MT — *Musical Times*

Munk, *Roll* — W. Munk, *The roll of the Royal College of Physicians of London*, 2 vols. (1861); 2nd edn, 3 vols. (1878)

N&Q — *Notes and Queries*

New Grove — S. Sadie, ed., *The new Grove dictionary of music and musicians*, 20 vols. (1980); 2nd edn, 29 vols. (2001) [also online edn; see also Grove, *Dict. mus.*]

Nichols, *Illustrations* — J. Nichols and J. B. Nichols, *Illustrations of the literary history of the eighteenth century*, 8 vols. (1817–58)

Nichols, *Lit. anecdotes* — J. Nichols, *Literary anecdotes of the eighteenth century*, 9 vols. (1812–16); facs. edn (1966)

Obits. FRS — *Obituary Notices of Fellows of the Royal Society*

O'Byrne, *Naval biog. dict.* — W. R. O'Byrne, *A naval biographical dictionary* (1849); repr. (1990); [2nd edn], 2 vols. (1861)

OHS — Oxford Historical Society

Old Westminsters — *The record of Old Westminsters*, 1–2, ed. G. F. R. Barker and A. H. Stenning (1928); suppl. 1, ed. J. B. Whitmore and G. R. Y. Radcliffe [1938]; 3, ed. J. B. Whitmore, G. R. Y. Radcliffe, and D. C. Simpson (1963); suppl. 2, ed. F. E. Pagan (1978); 4, ed. F. E. Pagan and H. E. Pagan (1992)

OMT — Oxford Medieval Texts

Ordericus Vitalis, *Eccl. hist.* — *The ecclesiastical history of Orderic Vitalis*, ed. and trans. M. Chibnall, 6 vols., OMT (1969–80); repr. (1990)

Paris, *Chron.* — *Matthaei Parisiensis, monachi sancti Albani, chronica majora*, ed. H. R. Luard, Rolls Series, 7 vols. (1872–83)

Parl. papers — *Parliamentary papers* (1801–)

PBA — *Proceedings of the British Academy*

Pepys, *Diary*	*The diary of Samuel Pepys*, ed. R. Latham and W. Matthews, 11 vols. (1970–83); repr. (1995) and (2000)
Pevsner	N. Pevsner and others, Buildings of England series
PICE	*Proceedings of the Institution of Civil Engineers*
Pipe rolls	*The great roll of the pipe for . . .*, PRSoc. (1884–)
PRO	Public Record Office
PRS	*Proceedings of the Royal Society of London*
PRSoc.	Pipe Roll Society
PTRS	*Philosophical Transactions of the Royal Society*
QR	*Quarterly Review*
RC	Record Commissions
Redgrave, *Artists*	S. Redgrave, *A dictionary of artists of the English school* (1874); rev. edn (1878); repr. (1970)
Reg. Oxf.	C. W. Boase and A. Clark, eds., *Register of the University of Oxford*, 5 vols., OHS, 1, 10–12, 14 (1885–9)
Reg. PCS	J. H. Burton and others, eds., *The register of the privy council of Scotland*, 1st ser., 14 vols. (1877–98); 2nd ser., 8 vols. (1899–1908); 3rd ser., [16 vols.] (1908–70)
Reg. RAN	H. W. C. Davis and others, eds., *Regesta regum Anglo-Normannorum, 1066–1154*, 4 vols. (1913–69)
RIBA Journal	*Journal of the Royal Institute of British Architects* [later *RIBA Journal*]
RotP	J. Strachey, ed., *Rotuli parliamentorum ut et petitiones, et placita in parliamento*, 6 vols. (1767–77)
RotS	D. Macpherson, J. Caley, and W. Illingworth, eds., *Rotuli Scotiae in Turri Londinensi et in domo capitulari Westmonasteriensi asservati*, 2 vols., RC, 14 (1814–19)
RS	Record(s) Society
Rymer, *Foedera*	T. Rymer and R. Sanderson, eds., *Foedera, conventiones, literae et cuiuscunque generis acta publica inter reges Angliae et alios quosvis imperatores, reges, pontifices, principes, vel communitates*, 20 vols. (1704–35); 2nd edn, 20 vols. (1726–35); 3rd edn, 10 vols. (1739–45); facs. edn (1967); new edn, ed. A. Clarke, J. Caley, and F. Holbrooke, 4 vols., RC, 50 (1816–30)
Sainty, *Judges*	J. Sainty, ed., *The judges of England, 1272–1990*, SeldS, suppl. ser., 10 (1993)
Sainty, *King's counsel*	J. Sainty, ed., *A list of English law officers and king's counsel*, SeldS, suppl. ser., 7 (1987)
SCH	Studies in Church History
Scots peerage	J. B. Paul, ed. *The Scots peerage, founded on Wood's edition of Sir Robert Douglas's Peerage of Scotland, containing an historical and genealogical account of the nobility of that kingdom*, 9 vols. (1904–14)
SeldS	Selden Society
SHR	*Scottish Historical Review*
State trials	T. B. Howell and T. J. Howell, eds., *Cobbett's Complete collection of state trials*, 34 vols. (1809–28)
STC, 1475–1640	A. W. Pollard, G. R. Redgrave, and others, eds., *A short-title catalogue of . . . English books . . . 1475–1640* (1926); 2nd edn, ed. W. A. Jackson, F. S. Ferguson, and K. F. Pantzer, 3 vols. (1976–91) [see also Wing, *STC*]
STS	Scottish Text Society
SurtS	Surtees Society
Symeon of Durham, *Opera*	*Symeonis monachi opera omnia*, ed. T. Arnold, 2 vols., Rolls Series, 75 (1882–5); repr. (1965)
Tanner, *Bibl. Brit.-Hib.*	T. Tanner, *Bibliotheca Britannico-Hibernica*, ed. D. Wilkins (1748); repr. (1963)
Thieme & Becker, *Allgemeines Lexikon*	U. Thieme, F. Becker, and H. Vollmer, eds., *Allgemeines Lexikon der bildenden Künstler von der Antike bis zur Gegenwart*, 37 vols. (Leipzig, 1907–50); repr. (1961–5), (1983), and (1992)
Thurloe, *State papers*	*A collection of the state papers of John Thurloe*, ed. T. Birch, 7 vols. (1742)
TLS	*Times Literary Supplement*
Tout, *Admin. hist.*	T. F. Tout, *Chapters in the administrative history of mediaeval England: the wardrobe, the chamber, and the small seals*, 6 vols. (1920–33); repr. (1967)
TRHS	*Transactions of the Royal Historical Society*
VCH	H. A. Doubleday and others, eds., *The Victoria history of the counties of England*, [88 vols.] (1900–)
Venn, *Alum. Cant.*	J. Venn and J. A. Venn, *Alumni Cantabrigienses: a biographical list of all known students, graduates, and holders of office at the University of Cambridge, from the earliest times to 1900*, 10 vols. (1922–54); repr. in 2 vols. (1974–8)
Vertue, *Note books*	[G. Vertue], *Note books*, ed. K. Esdaile, earl of Ilchester, and H. M. Hake, 6 vols., Walpole Society, 18, 20, 22, 24, 26, 30 (1930–55)
VF	*Vanity Fair*
Walford, *County families*	E. Walford, *The county families of the United Kingdom, or, Royal manual of the titled and untitled aristocracy of Great Britain and Ireland* (1860)
Walker rev.	A. G. Matthews, *Walker revised: being a revision of John Walker's Sufferings of the clergy during the grand rebellion, 1642–60* (1948); repr. (1988)
Walpole, *Corr.*	*The Yale edition of Horace Walpole's correspondence*, ed. W. S. Lewis, 48 vols. (1937–83)
Ward, *Men of the reign*	T. H. Ward, ed., *Men of the reign: a biographical dictionary of eminent persons of British and colonial birth who have died during the reign of Queen Victoria* (1885); repr. (Graz, 1968)
Waterhouse, *18c painters*	E. Waterhouse, *The dictionary of 18th century painters in oils and crayons* (1981); repr. as *British 18th century painters in oils and crayons* (1991), vol. 2 of *Dictionary of British art*
Watt, *Bibl. Brit.*	R. Watt, *Bibliotheca Britannica, or, A general index to British and foreign literature*, 4 vols. (1824) [many reprs.]
Wellesley index	W. E. Houghton, ed., *The Wellesley index to Victorian periodicals, 1824–1900*, 5 vols. (1966–89); new edn (1999) [CD-ROM]
Wing, *STC*	D. Wing, ed., *Short-title catalogue of . . . English books . . . 1641–1700*, 3 vols. (1945–51); 2nd edn (1972–88); rev. and enl. edn, ed. J. J. Morrison, C. W. Nelson, and M. Seccombe, 4 vols. (1994–8) [see also *STC, 1475–1640*]
Wisden	*John Wisden's Cricketer's Almanack*
Wood, *Ath. Oxon.*	A. Wood, *Athenae Oxonienses . . . to which are added the Fasti*, 2 vols. (1691–2); 2nd edn (1721); new edn, 4 vols., ed. P. Bliss (1813–20); repr. (1967) and (1969)
Wood, *Vic. painters*	C. Wood, *Dictionary of Victorian painters* (1971); 2nd edn (1978); 3rd edn as *Victorian painters*, 2 vols. (1995), vol. 4 of *Dictionary of British art*
WW	*Who's who* (1849–)
WWBMP	M. Stenton and S. Lees, eds., *Who's who of British members of parliament*, 4 vols. (1976–81)
WWW	*Who was who* (1929–)

Martindale, Adam (1623–1686), nonconformist minister, was born in September 1623 at High Heyes, Windle, in Prescot parish, Lancashire, and baptized at Prescot parish church on 21 September, the youngest child among the four sons and two daughters of Henry Martindale (*c*.1578–1658), yeoman, and his wife, Jilian or Julia Dombill (*d*. 1632).

Education and early life In January 1630 Martindale attended the free school at St Helens. His own account, found in 'The life of Adam Martindale written by himself', composed towards the end of his life, presents a picture of a somewhat haphazard education under the tutelage of incompetent teachers and the companionship of boys less able than himself. Subsequently he studied under a former schoolmaster from the school at Winwick. In retrospect, Martindale found him equally unsatisfactory—'he was a very silly and unconstant man, always making new laws, in-so-much that if a boy had beene absent a day or two, he knew not how to behave himself for feare of transgressing some new ridiculous order or other' (Martindale, 13). Martindale later attended schools at Rainford and received tuition from various other schoolmasters. By mid-1639 he had acquired sufficient education for him to consider Oxford. However, 'the university was not so readie for me; warres being coming on, that soone after turned Oxford … into a garrison, and many scholars into souldiers' (ibid., 28).

After failing to gain university entrance, Martindale entered the household of one Mr Shevington of Booths in Eccles parish, as tutor to his children. In addition, he apparently undertook the duties of secretary until his dismissal at Christmas 1641. He returned to his father's house, and subsequently, for about three months, taught at a school at Holland in Wigan parish. He recorded this as an unsuccessful experience owing to a shortage of pupils 'in those days of constant alarms', his lodgings among papists, drunkards, and quartered soldiers, and his reputation as a 'roundhead' which he could not 'cleare myself from … by swearing and debaucherie but would have been quiet and meddled on no side' (Martindale, 34–5). There followed a period of schoolteaching in Rainford. About this time Martindale heard a sermon preached at St Helens by Mr Smith, presumably Timothy Smith, minister of Rainford Chapel in Prescot parish, who was later described by the Commonwealth church survey of Lancashire in 1650 as 'an orthodox preaching minister' (Fishwick, 79). This sermon influenced Martindale greatly, and he seems to have experienced a conversion: 'I was rouzed to purpose and this proved a sharp needle, drawing after a silken thread of comfort in due season, so as if I may, without presumption, lay claim to a work of grace' (Martindale, 36).

Martindale found teaching unprofitable, and turned instead to employment as clerk to Colonel John Moore, MP for Liverpool and governor of the parliamentarian garrison in 1644. Having again failed to prosper, he became clerk to a foot regiment, where his literacy enabled him to assist the quartermaster. The army gave him the opportunity of discussion with devout puritans, who read scripture and prayed together. About this time he took the solemn league and covenant with the rest of his regiment. There he continued until Liverpool was taken by Prince Rupert in June 1644, which led to his imprisonment for about nine weeks and the loss of most of his possessions. On release he became schoolmaster at the free school at Over Whitley in Great Budworth parish, Cheshire. There he embarked on an impressive programme of self-education, and resolved to enter Oxford or Cambridge University should the opportunity present itself. Martindale's determination to defend his rights led to his steadfast refusal to provide free education to a family who had been born in another parish. This in turn led to an argument during which he and the father came to blows. Martindale stayed at Over Whitley until April 1646, when, being of the age for ordination, he accepted an invitation to Gorton Chapel in the parish of Manchester, having apparently gained preaching experience at Middleton and St Helens.

The move to Gorton gave Martindale the opportunity to observe the lively debate over church government between the presbyterians Richard Hollinworth of Manchester, John Harrison of Ashton under Lyne, and Thomas Johnson of Stockport and the Independents Samuel Eaton and Timothy Taylor, ministers of Duckinfield Chapel in Stockport parish. Martindale was reluctant to accept the Scottish model of presbyterianism advocated by such men as Hollinworth, Harrison, and John Tilsley, minister of Deane, Lancashire. He disapproved of the Independent gathered churches, considering them harmful to the common good, as was 'the preaching of gifted brethren not intending the ministrie' (Martindale, 66). He was, however, firmly of the opinion that the doctrine and liturgy of the English church would benefit from a thorough reformation. In Manchester on 31 December 1646 Martindale married Elizabeth (*b*. 1620/21, *d*. in or after 1686), second daughter of John Hall of the Clock-House, Droylsden, and his wife, Elizabeth Low, who had in 1626 married James Jollie. Elizabeth Martindale was therefore half-sister to the future nonconformist ministers Thomas *Jollie and John Jollie. The Martindales had four sons and four daughters born between 1648 and 1665.

Martindale's ministry: 1647–1662 Towards the end of 1646 or at the beginning of 1647, Martindale approached the veteran puritan minister John Angier with a view to ordination by the newly formed Manchester classis. At a meeting of the classis on 4 March, Martindale presented himself for examination for ordination. The classis signified its approval of him, but—since Angier was deputed to ask the reason for Martindale's non-attendance for ordination—it appears that he had last-minute doubts. Meanwhile his work at Gorton was apparently attracting attention. During 1647 and 1648 Martindale was invited by six parishes in Yorkshire and five in Cheshire to leave Gorton and minister to them. One such was the large Cheshire parish of Rostherne, the living there being vacant following the death of the incumbent, William Shenton, in September 1647. However, some of the parishioners, 'thinking themselves undervalued, and not liking a man of my kidney' (Martindale, 78), attempted to block Martindale's appointment by enlisting the help of the patron, Peter Venables, Baron Kinderton, who had served in the royalist armies. The Manchester classis was informed that Martindale's appointment was not universally popular, and on 21 November 1648 it agreed to delay his ordination until the parish sanctioned the appointment. Martindale and his supporters retaliated by petitioning the committee for plundered ministers, who on 26 March 1649 appointed him to the parish. Again in June and July 1649, Martindale's supporters and opponents made their various views known to the classis. Impatient of the delay, Martindale signified that he would no longer trouble the Manchester classis with his ordination. He travelled to London, where he was examined and ordained by the eighth London classis on 25 July 1649. While in London he obtained a licence to publish his tract *Divinity Knots Unloosed*, written 'for the strengthening of the younger sorts of christians of our parish' (ibid., 85–6), in which he examined the nature of scripture and exact doctrine in the light of the antinomianism and anabaptism, which, he feared, were rife in Rostherne and surrounding parishes.

In 1650 Martindale took part in a debate, conducted at a meeting of ministers at Warrington, as to the legality of taking the engagement to the Commonwealth government. Biblical precedent was searched for an answer to a question that deeply troubled Martindale. Could he, in all conscience, take the engagement? Should ministers pay allegiance to usurpers? The question continued to exercise him until *A Discourse Concerning the Engagement, or, The Northern Subscribers Plea* was published later in 1650. This treatise 'by a friend to the commonwealth' examined arguments for and against the engagement and concluded that, being far from the centre of influence and action, and lacking information, ministers should in conscience subscribe and thereby defuse a potentially dangerous situation. These arguments appear to have reassured Martindale, and when called on to subscribe, he did so, although the matter continued to trouble him.

From his appointment to Rostherne parish in 1649 until his ejection in 1662, Martindale tackled his duties as parish minister with an enthusiasm not always appreciated by his parishioners. Not only did he attend to the normal parish duties, but he preached regularly in the parish, and also in its chapels. In addition, he attended and preached on the exercise circuits in Cheshire, Staffordshire, and Lancashire.

In common with his presbyterian colleagues in Lancashire and Cheshire, Martindale showed a willingness to shoulder an impressive workload in the effort to bring godly reformation to the church. A direct challenge to this ambition was posed by alternative strands of puritan ideology. Both Martindale and his fellow presbyterian Henry Newcome, then minister of Gawsworth, east

Cheshire, left accounts of the activities of the followers of Samuel Eaton of Duckinfield Chapel. Eaton was respected as a godly minister, episcopally ordained and formerly rector of West Kirby, on the Wirrall. However, the practice of lay preaching among his followers was not welcomed, particularly when carried on in the parish regarded by Martindale as his own preserve. The latter entered into public debate with those Independents who were frequently preaching at Tabley Chapel in the parish, with little success. The lay preachers were as determined to pursue their course as Martindale was to prevent it. In an attempt to counter the Independent threat, Martindale preached at Tabley, where he 'answered all the material arguments I had met with for the preaching of gifted men, not intending the ministry, showed the irregularity of such men's thrusting their sickle into my harvest' (Martindale, 107) and asked that such intruders be discouraged.

As a result of these differing notions as to doctrine, the dissemination of radical ideas by the army, and the growing influence of the Quakers, Martindale published *An Antidote Against the Poyson of the Times* (1653), a catechism intended to provide his parishioners with a clear account of orthodox doctrine. As a defence against rising sectarian activity, a number of ministers met at the exercise day in Knutsford on 20 October 1653 when it was agreed to form the voluntary association of Cheshire. Martindale subscribed to the association, which was drawn up along the lines proposed by Richard Baxter's model of the Worcestershire association. In the Cheshire association ministers had no power over each other's parishes. The rules and conditions were advisory rather than compulsory. Interpretation of the conditions as to parish discipline and the appointment of elders seem to have been left to the discretion of the individual minister. To Martindale 'these termes were approved as rationall and moderate by many, onely the proud, the grossely ignorant, (especially if ancient) and the scandalous liked not these termes' (Martindale, 114). Although Martindale referred to this association as the classis, it had none of the organization or authority of the formally convened Lancashire classes. Cheshire men seeking ordination had to request the authority of the Manchester classis or that of Wirksworth (Derbyshire) or Bridgnorth (Shropshire) classes to give them legitimacy.

In the summer of 1655 Martindale entered into public debate on Knutsford Heath with the Quaker missionary Richard Hubberthorne, a formidable opponent from an area of growing Quaker strength. In contrast to the ill-thought-out and irrational argument that he had encountered in other public debates with radical sectarians, Hubberthorne was, Martindale found, 'the most rationall calme-spirited man of his judgment that I ever publicly engaged against' (Martindale, 115). The rising influence of the Quakers in the north-west led the Lancashire presbyterians and Independents to form the Accommodation of Ministers in 1659. Although the Cheshire ministers did not subscribe to the accommodation, Martindale bemoaned the fact that there had not been more attempt to reach agreement in preceding years, particularly in the debate between presbyterians and Independents that he had witnessed at Gorton in 1646.

The late 1650s were a period of uncertainty for presbyterians in the north-west. The ill-fated Cheshire rising on behalf of Charles II led by Sir George Booth in September 1659 implicated many of the presbyterian clergy. Apparently Martindale was aware of plans for Booth's rising, and sympathetic to its aims, but he did not join it, although he considered reasons for and against so doing. In later years, and perhaps with the benefit of hindsight, he wrote that although he had feared that supporting a restoration of the monarchy would result in his ejection from his ministry, such a risk was an improvement on the uncertain political climate and insecure government that prevailed. When the monarchy was restored in May 1660 Martindale welcomed it, 'that I might be freed from the yoke of usurpers' (Martindale, 143), and despotism thwarted.

As Martindale's appointment at Rostherne had been occasioned by the death of the previous incumbent, the Act for Settling Ministers confirmed his appointment as vicar. Following the Fifth Monarchist rising in January 1661, Martindale was ordered to read orders for the suppression of conventicles to the congregation. By dint of searching the text for loopholes, he persuaded himself that he need not comply. On 25 February he appeared before the justices, where he was 'secured as a countenancer of seditious meetings' (*CSP dom.*, 1660–61, 515). He was imprisoned at Chester, but released upon a bond of £1000 before 30 April 1661, when Henry Newcome wrote to Richard Baxter: 'Blessed be God Mr. Martindale is a freeman now, and returns you hearty thanks for your kindness to him' (Keeble and Nuttall, 2.14).

Martindale welcomed the Restoration, but deplored the return of traditional custom and ritual. When on 1 May 1660 local youths set up a maypole, he preached that 'many learned men were of the opinion that a May-pole was a relique of the shamefull worship of the Strumpet Flora in Rome' (Martindale, 157). To reinforce his message he invited Thomas Brooke, minister of Congleton, to preach. Elizabeth Martindale solved the problem in a more practical manner when one night, assisted by some women friends, she took a saw to the maypole.

The winter of 1661–2 saw Martindale once more in trouble. He was indicted for refusing to read the Book of Common Prayer, but he appears to have avoided punishment by proving that although he had not read it, he had not refused to do so because no copy of the book had been supplied to the church, the churchwarden having neglected this responsibility. It was a short reprieve, for on 29 August 1662 he was deprived of his living by the bishop of Chester under the Act of Uniformity, having conducted his last services twelve days earlier.

Dissent: 1662–1686 After ejection Martindale moved, with his family, to a house at Camp Green, not far from the vicarage. He returned to teaching and taking in scholars, which with income from other sources allowed him sufficient income to support his family. In the early days he formed the habit of hearing the sermons of Benjamin

Crosse, his successor as vicar. These he would repeat to sympathetic supporters, adding a discourse of his own. He began to fear that he would be prevented from taking in scholars, following an anti-nonconformist sermon preached by the bishop of Chester at nearby Bowden. He therefore considered a change of career. He was encouraged to learn physic, but prudently decided, 'the time would be long, practice uncertaine, and above all, the lives of men were not to be jested with' (Martindale, 175). He decided on the study of mathematics, encouraged and helped by Lord Delamere (the former Sir George Booth), who subsequently presented him to the school at Warrington.

In 1665, following the passing of the Five Mile Act, Martindale moved his family to Birkenheath, in Rostherne parish, while he went to Manchester to teach mathematics at the grammar school. In 1668 he published *The Description of a Plain Instrument*, in which he described the uses of a scientific instrument designed for geometric and navigational measurement. In August 1668 Henry Newcome learned that 'certificates from the bishop were issued' (*Calamy rev.*, 343) against Martindale and Edmund Jones, formerly minister of Eccles parish in Lancashire, for preaching at Gorton. Martindale may have been referring to this when he recorded being brought before the sessions of the peace in the late 1660s. On this occasion he had a good advocate, and the jury returned a verdict of not guilty.

About 1670 Martindale was invited to be private chaplain to Lord Delamere at Dunham Massey, an appointment that lasted until Delamere's death in August 1684. Under the declaration of indulgence of 1672 he was licensed to be a presbyterian teacher at the house of Henry Peacock at Rostherne. Following the retraction of the declaration he continued as chaplain to Delamere, in 1674 moving his family to Millington to bring them nearer to Dunham. About this time he wrote *The Country Almanack*, three editions of which were published in 1675 and 1677.

Throughout the period from ejection until his death, Martindale travelled widely to meet sympathetic and like-minded friends, on several occasions visiting Hoghton Tower, Lancashire, where dissenting clergy frequently met under the patronage of Sir Charles Hoghton. The 1670s and the 1680s were in large part overshadowed by his worries regarding his children, only four of whom had survived infancy. In 1673 his eldest daughter, Elizabeth (b. 1648), died. His eldest son, Thomas (b. 1649), whose extravagant lifestyle in London had been a severe worry to his father, died in 1680. The youngest daughter, Hannah (b. 1665), was struck down by a crippling illness. In May 1681 the surviving members of the family moved to Hough Heath in Mere, where Martindale wrote his *Country Survey Book* (1682). In Calamy's *Account of the Ministers* he 'appears to have been a judicious divine, by a little book which he published relating to the Arminian controversy intitled *Truth and Peace Promoted* (1682)' (Calamy, *Abridgement*, 2.135). In May 1684 the family moved for the final time, to Leigh in Rostherne parish, to a tenement that

Martindale had purchased in 1655 as a home for his wife and family should he predecease them, the rents from which had supplied some of his income since ejection.

Martindale was imprisoned at Chester in June and July 1685 on the groundless suspicion of involvement in Monmouth's rebellion. Later in 1685 he was involved in litigation as a witness in a civil action. He died at Leigh in September 1686 and was buried at Rostherne on 21 September. Thomas Jollie recorded that:

> the loss of soe faithfull a brother must needs bee grevious to mee and the rather becaus his day was not soe cleer in the evening thereof as might bee desired, he dyed in the close of his great climatericall year (63) which is accounted most dangerous, I dout he had too deep apprehensions thereof. (Jolly, 78–9)

He was survived by his wife and two daughters, Martha (b. 1657) and Hannah. The 'Life' was edited from a manuscript in the British Museum and published in 1845.

CATHERINE NUNN

Sources The life of Adam Martindale, ed. R. Parkinson, Chetham Society, 4 (1845) · The autobiography of Henry Newcome, ed. R. Parkinson, 2 vols., Chetham Society, 26–7 (1852) · The diary of the Rev. Henry Newcome, from September 30, 1661, to September 29, 1663, ed. T. Heywood, Chetham Society, 18 (1849) · The notebook of the Rev. Thomas Jolley, ed. H. Fishwick, Chetham Society, new ser., 33 (1895) · H. Fishwick, ed., Lancashire and Cheshire church surveys, 1649–1655, Lancashire and Cheshire RS, 1 (1879) · W. A. Shaw, ed., Minutes of the Manchester presbyterian classis, 3 vols., Chetham Society, new ser., 20, 22, 24 (1890–91) · F. V. Driffield, ed., Prescot parish register, Lancashire Parish Register Society, 76 (1938) · H. Brierley, ed., Parish register of Manchester, Lancashire Parish Register Society, 55 (1918) · E. Calamy, ed., An abridgement of Mr. Baxter's history of his life and times, with an account of the ministers, &c., who were ejected after the Restauration of King Charles II, 2nd edn, 2 vols. (1713) · Calendar of the correspondence of Richard Baxter, ed. N. H. Keeble and G. F. Nuttall, 2 vols. (1991) · VCH Lancashire, vol. 4 · CSP dom., 1660–61 · Calamy rev. · G. L. Turner, ed., Original records of early nonconformity under persecution and indulgence, 1 (1911) · R. N. Dore, The civil wars in Cheshire (1966) · J. S. Morrill, Cheshire, 1630–1660 (1974) · C. M. Nunn, 'The ministry of Henry Newcome: presbyterianism in south-east Cheshire, 1648–1662', MPhil diss., University of Manchester, 1998 **Archives** BL, 'Life', Add. MS 4239

Martindale, Cyril Charlie (1879–1963), Jesuit and scholar, was born on 25 May 1879 in Kensington, London, the only child of Sir Arthur Henry Temple Martindale (1854–1942) and his first wife, Isabel Marion (d. 1879), daughter of Captain C. F. Mackenzie. Although the family originated in Martindale in the Lake District, Martindale was born in the Kensington home of his grandfather Ben Hay Martindale, general manager of the London and St Katharine Docks Company. His mother having died within some months of his birth and his father being in the Indian Civil Service, he was brought up by his aunts in the family home. Precocious and lonely, he early developed scholarly and somewhat exotic tastes. At the age of ten he asked for and got an ancient Egyptian grammar as a Christmas present. As a schoolboy at Harrow School he seems to have been influenced by the Yellow Book culture. After leaving Harrow he became a Roman Catholic in 1897 and later in the same year entered the Jesuit noviciate. He was to become the most famous English Jesuit of the twentieth century.

In the course of his Jesuit training Martindale went to Pope's Hall (later renamed Campion Hall), Oxford, where his classical scholarship reached its full flower. In addition to firsts in honour moderations (1903) and literae humaniores (1905), he won the Hertford and Craven scholarships (1903), the chancellor's Latin verse and the Gaisford Greek verse prizes (1904), was twice placed second for the Ireland scholarship, and was later awarded the Derby scholarship (1906) and the Ellerton theological essay prize (1907). He was ordained in 1911, taught at Stonyhurst from 1913, then in 1916 returned to Oxford to lecture in classics. The First World War altered the whole nature of his apostolate. The university had been turned into a vast hospital and Martindale began to minister to the spiritual needs of the wounded soldiers. Suddenly this shy, donnish priest discovered in himself a totally unexpected ability to communicate with these tough Australians, perky cockneys, and taciturn Scots.

Although Martindale stayed on at Oxford for some years after the war his interest in pure scholarship was declining and in 1927 he joined the staff of the Farm Street Church in Mayfair, where his spiritual clientele was drawn from every level of society—from dukes to dustmen. He was, for example, involved in the declaration of the nullity of the ninth duke of Marlborough's marriage to Consuelo Vanderbilt. Equally he involved himself in such enterprises as a settlement for working-class boys in the East End of London. He became known for his sermons, which were not rhetorical exercises, but the direct, reasoned, taut productions of a man who never used three words where one would do. His reputation as a broadcaster grew rapidly, so able was he to present the abiding truths in language which could be grasped by the average man and yet appealed to the mind of the sophisticated intellectual.

Whereas Martindale's earliest written works—such collected pieces as Waters of Twilight (1914) and The Goddess of Ghosts (1915)—reflected his classical preoccupations even while these were related to his Christian convictions, he soon turned to more directly religious themes. One of his greatest achievements was to rescue the trade of hagiography from its cliché ridden conventionality. He produced, over the years, in addition to biographies of such contemporaries as R. H. Benson and C. D. Plater, a score of saints' lives which presented their subjects in the round and in the context of their age. Martindale's Letters from their Aunts (1939) was delightful and eccentric.

In all, Martindale published over eighty books, some sixty pamphlets, and hundreds of articles, all aimed at the presentation of Christian truth in a way which would show it to be intellectually respectable and genuinely humane. Like his friend Teilhard de Chardin, although in a less spectacular way, he was regarded with some suspicion by ecclesiastical authorities who found his fresh, almost pioneering approach to theological ideas too novel for their taste. They may have feared he would become, like George Tyrrell, a modernist theologian.

Meanwhile Martindale was becoming internationally known. Two concerns in particular were responsible for this development. His university background involved him in a Roman Catholic international university movement. He was also to become a member of the central committee which planned the Eucharistic Congresses which occur periodically in different parts of the world. He visited Switzerland, Yugoslavia, and Hungary in 1923, Poland, Hungary, and Germany in 1924, and in 1928 New Zealand and Australia. Later he travelled to South Africa and South America. Wherever he went he was in demand for sermons, lectures, discussions, speeches, retreats, broadcast talks. His sea voyages opened his eyes to another problem—the spiritual needs and anxieties of sailors. They too were added to his already excessively large parish, just as he concerned himself with the activities of a home for mentally defective boys.

In April 1940, having been invited to give a course of lectures in Denmark, Martindale arrived in Copenhagen on the very eve of the German invasion. This meant that he was marooned there until the end of the war. He chafed at his exile at a time when he felt he was not sharing the dangers of his fellow countrymen; his health, always precarious, was seriously affected. However, he lived and worked on for almost eighteen years after his return to England in September 1945. He retired from Farm Street in 1953 and died at Petworth, Sussex, on 18 March 1963.

THOMAS CORBISHLEY, *rev.*

Sources P. Caraman, *C. C. Martindale* (1967) · personal knowledge (1981) · *WWW* · *The Times* (19 March 1963)
Likenesses S. Elwes, portrait, Campion Hall, Oxford · R. Fletcher, bronze relief, Priest's lodgings, Farm Street, Mayfair, London

Martindale, Hilda (1875–1952), civil servant, was born on 12 March 1875 in Leytonstone, London, the third daughter of William Martindale (1833/4–*c*.1874), City merchant, and his second wife, Louisa *Martindale (1839–1914), daughter of James Spicer and his wife, Louisa. Hilda was born six months after the death of her father and of one of her sisters. Her mother, Louisa, who was widowed after only three years of marriage, brought up Hilda and her elder sister, Louisa *Martindale (1872–1966), as well as two half-brothers and two half-sisters from their father's first marriage. Hilda's mother and uncle, Albert Spicer, proved a strong influence on Hilda's adult interests.

Family and education Hilda's mother, a woman of strong initiative and independence, whose family were Liberal and nonconformist (Congregational), took her children to live in Penzance, Eisenach in Germany, and Vevey on Lake Geneva. While living in Germany and Switzerland, Hilda learned German. In 1880 the family returned to England and lived in Lewes for five years. Louisa Martindale prized her daughters' education highly and in 1885 they moved to Brighton so Hilda and her sister could attend Brighton high school, a Girls' Public Day School Company school. As well as ensuring that Hilda received an academic education and an annual holiday on the continent, Louisa Martindale brought her into contact with the women's movement's and Liberal Party's activities and thought.

Louisa Martindale had a long-standing interest in higher education, and she decided on the higher education of both her daughters. In 1893 she sent Hilda to Royal Holloway College at Egham for two years. Hilda's uncle, Albert Spicer, had served on the committee of the State Children's Association and he interested Hilda in the care of children. In the late nineteenth century and early twentieth century philanthropists took an especial interest in the upbringing of children in care.

Hilda wanted to work with children in care and, as no social work courses with children existed, she carved out a personal training programme. In the mid-1890s she attended lectures on hygiene and sanitation at the Royal Sanitary Institute, visited places which came under sanitary inspectors, passed the institute's examination, and became an associate. In 1897–8 she studied hygiene and public health at Bedford College, London, for a year under Sir Thomas Legge, and obtained a certificate in hygiene. On the advice of Graham Wallas she read social science publications and visited a range of institutions for the poor. One day a week she worked for the Charity Organization Society. She helped at an epileptic colony, at a Dr Barnardo's home which fostered out babies, and briefly as a travelling inspector for the Children's Country Holiday Fund. Overseas travel was not unusual for educated, middle-class women at this time, and in 1900 her mother took Hilda and her sister Louisa on a year's world tour; Hilda met social workers, and visited institutions for the poor as well as children's homes.

Factory inspector On her return from the world tour Hilda Martindale was asked by Henrietta Barnett to speak on work for children in the countries she had visited at a meeting of the State Children's Association. Adelaide Anderson was in the audience and after the meeting offered Martindale a temporary post as woman factory inspector. Thomas Legge, by now a medical inspector at the Home Office, urged Martindale to accept. Martindale entered the civil service, not by a formal process of rigorous examination and interview but through her connections, relevant knowledge, and luck (it was not until 1925 that the government permitted women to sit the annual administrative grade entry examinations for the civil service).

In 1900 Martindale launched herself on one of the earliest successful civil service careers for a woman. Her work as an inspector was typical of the type of work undertaken by the few educated women who joined the civil service at this time. Ability and tenacity helped her inexorable rise within the service. Her personal circumstances enabled her to devote herself to a career: she remained single so was not forced to resign by the ban on married women's employment in the civil service, and she always employed paid domestic help.

From 1901 to 1933 Martindale served in the factory department of the Home Office. In her early years as an inspector she continued her work for children's welfare: the world of work was not an exclusively adult world; many children worked long hours in harsh conditions.

Her training was brief: on her fifth day, with little knowledge of the law, she inspected alone, and before long she was prosecuting employers in court. The women inspectors dealt with firms employing women and girls producing and finishing a wide range of goods, including lace, boots and shoes, chains and nails, paper bags, and hosiery. Women also worked in laundries, which required close inspection because of their heat, steam, wet floors, gas fumes, and dangerous machinery.

Women active in a number of organizations, including the Women's Trade Union League, campaigned vigorously during these years for improvements in working-class women's conditions of work. The anti-sweating movement attacked some of the worst conditions of women in the sweated trades and, although as a civil servant Martindale did not join these organizations, her day-to-day work supported some of the greatest concerns of organized women; the reports she and her colleagues produced were grist to the mill for the campaigners. Martindale's writings, which are realistic and unsentimental, reveal her great respect and sympathy for women workers. They also document the complexity of many of the issues with which inspectors had to deal and the difficulties of inspection.

Initially Martindale was a peripatetic inspector in England, visiting a breathless range of workplaces. In 1904, for instance, she visited factories from Truro to Leeds employing women under the china and earthenware special rules; she made a special inquiry into the employment of mothers in the Potteries, which included visiting women at home; she made various additional inspections around the country, and for two weeks she was in charge of her colleague, Lucy Deane's, west London special district. In 1905 she was posted to Ireland where she worked for seven years, the first three living out of a suitcase and travelling the length and breadth of the island. In 1908 she was promoted to senior lady inspector and based in Belfast. As well as disagreeable living conditions the work proved more awkward than in England. Irish employers misled her (not uncommon in England) and the workers treated her with apprehension as they had to avoid any suspicion of being an informer to a representative of the British government.

In 1912 Martindale was delighted to return to England, close to her mother and friends, as senior lady inspector for the midlands. As a senior lady inspector she required a close knowledge (either through her own or her staff's visits) of the working conditions in her area; she worked with her colleagues in trying to enforce the Factory Acts; and visited annually works employing women and girls under special regulations. Martindale had special responsibility for investigating accidents to women and girls in laundries and clothing factories, and cases of industrial poisoning among women and girls. Martindale and her colleagues dealt with a multitude of trades, including the metal and engineering trades of Birmingham; brick, hollow-ware, and chain works of the Black Country; the lace and net industry of Nottinghamshire; the hosiery, boot, and shoe trades of Leicestershire; the saddlery and leather trades of Walsall; the glass industry of south Staffordshire and the Potteries. The main work in the midlands related to industrial poisoning and trades operating under special regulations or with special dangers.

During the First World War the work of all the women inspectors expanded. There were fewer male inspectors, and whereas before the war women were confined to inspecting women's conditions of work, the dilution of labour and substitution of women for men in industry meant that no clear distinctions could now be drawn; indeed the women inspectors worked closely with employers and workers in negotiating the terms and conditions of women's wartime work. Martindale dealt with exemption orders from the hours laid down in the Factory Acts; she advised employers taking on women for the first time, and she worked closely with the Ministry of Munitions' Health of Munition Workers Committee, and with women trade unionists. Alarmist reports of excessive drinking among workers flush with increased wages prompted the central liquor control board to set up a committee to inquire into the supply of intoxicating drink to girls under the age of eighteen on which Martindale, along with Ellen Pinsent, sat. In 1918 she acted as deputy principal lady inspector while Rose Squire was on secondment to the Ministry of Munitions. She then became senior lady inspector for the south-eastern division.

Despite the blurred scope of women's and men's work in the inspectorate, and a departmental committee which recommended the amalgamation of the women's and men's branches at the end of the war, Martindale was one of the women who opposed the merger. She feared prejudice and opposition from male colleagues, especially from those who would have to work under women, and she also suspected that women did not match their male colleagues for technical knowledge. She subsequently felt the first of these concerns justified, but not the second. The amalgamation, in 1921, led to Martindale's appointment as a superintending inspector, with men working under her. In 1925 she was appointed deputy chief inspector. Over the following eight years all factory department staffing matters gradually came within her remit. Martindale was also active in the council of women civil servants.

Director of women's establishments From 1933 to 1937 Martindale was director of women's establishments at the Treasury. She was initially loath to take on the work, for which she had not applied. Martindale was sorry to leave her work and colleagues at the factory department of the Home Office, but her lack of enthusiasm reflected deeper misgivings. Although Martindale had previously argued for separate posts for women and men inspectors, by the early 1930s she had become critical of separate posts and wary of a post dealing exclusively with women civil servants' employment for three reasons: she no longer thought women's and men's problems so different as to require separate treatment; a post which was only advisory was unsatisfactory to the holder, and gave a false sense of security to women; and the holder of such a post gained limited and one-sided experience instead of performing a range of duties appropriate to the grade which would qualify her for an interchange of work and further promotion.

As director of women's establishments Martindale fought in difficult circumstances for women's interests. Often she was the only woman present in meetings and conferences. She unsuccessfully pressed for equal pay for women and men civil servants, and for the civil service to lift the bar on married women's employment. She sat on an interdepartmental committee which considered women's entry into the foreign and diplomatic service. Martindale and Muriel Ritson, the one other female member, signed a minority report in which they argued unsuccessfully for women's entry. Martindale sat on appointments boards as the sole woman. Conscious of how few women applied for the administrative grade, she conducted a recruitment campaign. She spoke at universities and to organizations such as the British Federation of University Women. She also kept in close touch with the heads of women's colleges. The number of women applicants to the civil service gradually rose. Meanwhile, her previous expertise gained in the factory department was not forgotten. She was a technical adviser for British delegates to international labour conferences in Geneva. In 1935 Martindale's work was recognized with her appointment as CBE.

Martindale had been pressing for an end to special posts for women in various departments, and by 1937 her advice had been taken and the posts phased out. She felt this an appropriate moment to end her own special post and resigned; a woman who undertook work with both women and men replaced Martindale.

Women's organizations and women MPs campaigned throughout these years for an end to discrimination against women in the labour market. Women entered the civil service in increasing numbers, but there were very few senior women, and the terms and conditions of service were worse for women than for men. Martindale had struggled within the civil service for equality; she had publicly urged more women to apply for the administrative grade, and on her retirement she wrote *Women Servants of the State, 1870–1938* (1938), a history of women in the civil service which presented the case for women civil servants. Martindale was critical of a system which worked to women's disadvantage, and she highlighted the prejudice of second-rate men, but she was careful to give credit by name to those men in the civil service who she believed had encouraged women. Retirement afforded Martindale time for reflection and writing, and she also published *From One Generation to Another, 1839–1944* (1944), and *Some Victorian Portraits and Others* (1948). Martindale's memoirs give away little of her personal feelings, except her strong admiration for her mother.

After her retirement Martindale pursued her interests in education and welfare, especially of children. She sat on the council of Dr Barnardo's and on the governing body of Bedford College. She chaired two all-women committees which ran almshouses for elderly women in Brixton and Camberwell. She never married. She died in London on 18 April 1952; on 8 May a memorial service conducted by the dean of St Paul's was held for her at All Souls, Langham Place.   HELEN JONES

Sources H. Martindale, *From one generation to another, 1839–1944* (1944) · H. Martindale, *Women servants of the state, 1870–1938: a history of women in the civil service* (1938) · L. Martindale, *A woman surgeon* (1951) · H. Martindale, *Some Victorian portraits and others* (1948) · *The Times* (19 April 1952) · *The Times* (8 May 1952) · *The Times* (9 May 1952) · O. Banks, *The biographical dictionary of British feminists*, 2 (1990) · H. Jones, 'Women health workers: the case of the first women factory inspectors in Britain', *Social History of Medicine*, 1 (1988), 165–81 · 'Chief inspector of factories and workshops', *Parl. papers*, various years [annual reports] · *CGPLA Eng. & Wales* (1952)
Wealth at death £50,864 7s. 8d.: probate, 15 July 1952, *CGPLA Eng. & Wales*

Martindale [*née* Spicer]**, Louisa** (1839–1914), women's activist, was born on 25 June 1839 at 9 York Place, City Road, London, the eldest child of James Spicer (1807–1888), head of a wholesale stationers, and his wife, Louisa, *née* Edwards. The Spicers' was a homoeopathic, Congregationalist household (eventually Louisa was joined by five brothers and five sisters), which, while conforming to the patriarchal structure typical of Victorian families, also allowed space for self-development in which Louisa revelled. At fourteen years of age she was sent to a fashionable private school near Hyde Park, which did little to instil in her anything but a sense that the formal education she received was wanting in breadth, scope, and inspiration. Travels abroad, and there were many in her life, were more fulfilling, and at eighteen she accompanied her parents on her first venture to Europe, a religious jamboree organized by the Evangelical Exchange. Upon her return to the family's Elizabethan home on Woodford Green, she founded a small society, the Mutual Improvement Association, and threw herself into a 'lady bountiful' role by founding Sunday schools and the Ray Lodge Mission Station in 1865, a 'democratic' working-class alternative to the often alienating experience of organized religion. On 2 May 1871 she married a 37-year-old widower and father of four, William Martindale, a merchant. Their marriage ended abruptly after only a few years when he succumbed to heart trouble about 1874, and Martindale was left a widow with two small daughters, Louisa and Hilda (a third daughter, Mary, had died in infancy). From this time onward mother and daughters lived a peripatetic life that took them from Penzance to Germany, Switzerland, Lewes (which proved too conservative and intellectually stultifying for Louisa), and finally to Brighton. There Martindale held open houses for governesses and shop assistants, became a moving force in establishing the Women's Liberal Association in 1891, the Women's Co-operative Movement, and a dispensary for women staffed by women (later the New Sussex Hospital for Women and Children). She also worked on behalf of her brother Albert *Spicer, who had been elected to Monmouth Boroughs in 1892, and involved herself with the

British and Foreign Bible Society, the Women's Suffrage Society, and the German church.

Louisa Martindale had become interested in women's rights in 1867, and firmly believed that the Liberal Party would enfranchise women. In the 1890s she spoke in her brother's constituency on the topic of women's admission to county councils, wrote lectures on the 'rights' of women (personal, property, and as citizens), on women in India, and co-operative kitchens, and corresponded with Elizabeth Wolstenholme Elmy. She supported women's right to preach, and built a Congregational church in Horsted Keynes, Sussex, where she moved in 1903, to serve this end. She welcomed the arrival of the suffragettes as a breath of fresh air, but always believed that the vote would be won by non-militant means, and worked within the National Union of Women's Suffrage Societies. As a pacifist she believed that women should become public and political creatures in order to promote peace. On 15 March 1914, a few months before the First World War erupted, Louisa Martindale died from pneumonia at Cheeleys, her home in Horsted Keynes; she was buried in Horsted Keynes. She was 'saved', her daughter Hilda writes, 'from what would have been a great sorrow to her' (H. Martindale, 39)—war, and the realization that women would get the vote in 1918 arguably as a result of their war work. The careers of her two daughters, Louisa *Martindale as a gynaecologist and Hilda *Martindale in the civil service, were a personal testament to Martindale's commitment to the cause of women's rights.

LORI WILLIAMSON

Sources H. Martindale, *From one generation to another, 1839–1944* (1944) · L. Martindale, *A woman surgeon* (1951) · P. Levine, *Feminist lives in Victorian England* (1990) · O. Banks, *The biographical dictionary of British feminists*, 2 (1990) · P. Levine, *Victorian feminism, 1850–1900* (1987) · b. cert. · m. cert. · d. cert.

Likenesses photograph, repro. in Martindale, *From one generation to another*

Wealth at death £1425 7s. 6d.: probate, 20 May 1914, *CGPLA Eng. & Wales*

Martindale, Louisa (1872–1966), gynaecologist and suffragist, the elder daughter of William Martindale (1833/4–c.1874), a City of London businessman, and Louisa Spicer [see Martindale, Louisa (1839–1914)], his second wife, was born at Gainsborough Lodge, Leytonstone, London, on 30 October 1872. Her father was an evangelical Anglican, her mother a Congregationalist. Louisa Spicer came from a large family who combined evangelical Christianity with social reform, Liberal politics, charitable works, homoeopathy, and a love of travel. William Martindale died in his early forties when Louisa was three, leaving four children from his first marriage and Mrs Martindale pregnant with Hilda. Two infant children of the marriage had died in the same week as their father.

After her father's death Louisa Martindale lived first in Penzance before moving to Thuringia in Germany in 1877, where she and Hilda attended a kindergarten run by Fräulein Trabert, a pupil of Froebel. In 1879 the family moved to Switzerland, to a village near Vevey overlooking Lake Geneva, and in 1880 to Lewes in Sussex. Here Louisa Spicer

Louisa Martindale (1872–1966), by Frank O. Salisbury, exh. Ehrlich Galleries, New York, 1925

Martindale revealed her progressive ideas about the upbringing of Louisa and Hilda: she converted stables into a gymnasium, paid a gymnastics teacher, gave them bicycles, and had them taught to ride horses astride rather than side-saddle.

In 1885 Mrs Martindale moved into Brighton so that Louisa and Hilda could attend the Brighton High School for Girls, a Girls' Public Day School Company school opened in 1876. The girls were escorted to and from school by a governess to ensure that they were both chaperoned and educated on the journey. Mrs Martindale had open house on alternate Saturdays for German governesses working in Brighton, and for shop assistants. The latter group included Margaret Bondfield, later the first woman cabinet minister, then sixteen.

Louisa Martindale attended Royal Holloway College (1890–92), and then the London School of Medicine for Women. She graduated with her MB (Lond.) and BS (Lond.) in 1899. After a brief spell as locum for Dr Mary Murdoch in Hull, Louisa, Hilda, and their mother spent a year travelling around the world. Louisa visited hospitals in Vienna, India, Australia, and the USA. From 1901 to 1906 she was in partnership with Dr Murdoch in Hull, a period which included three months' further study in Vienna. Louisa Martindale left Hull to do postgraduate work in Berlin and London, took the London MD in 1906, and then set up a private practice in Brighton. Here one vital source of income was retainers as medical officer at local girls' schools, including Roedean and the Brighton High School for Girls. Once qualified Louisa Martindale was active in four ways: as a medical woman who worked to open women's hospitals and to promote the interests of women in the profession at home and overseas, as a pioneer of radium therapy, in the governance of the medical profession, and as a feminist and suffragist.

While Louisa Martindale was in private practice in Marlborough Place, Brighton, she joined the staff of the Brighton Dispensary for Women and Children founded by her mother and Dr Helen Boyle. Fund-raising to open a general hospital for women staffed by women went on in Brighton from 1893, and the Brighton Dispensary gradually expanded to become the New Sussex Hospital for Women and Children. When the New Sussex Hospital, Windlesham Road, was opened free of debt by Lady Astor in 1921 it became one of five general women's hospitals in Britain. Supporters included Elizabeth Robins and Octavia Wilberforce. Martindale became the senior surgeon in 1911; her professional colleagues were leading women pioneers in medicine including Louisa Aldrich Blake, Helen Scatliff, and Gladys Wauchope. In 1913, when the British Medical Association met for its annual conference in Brighton, she was the honorary secretary of the obstetrics and gynaecology section. During the First World War she remained in Brighton, but spent her holidays with the Scottish Women's Hospital at Abbey de Royaumont in France.

In 1923 Martindale moved to London and set up a private practice there, although she continued to operate at the New Sussex Hospital, as well as the East Grinstead Hospital. She was active in the work of the British Medical Women's Federation, serving as its president in 1931. She was also instrumental in establishing the Medical Women's International Association after its foundation meeting in 1919 in New York, serving as honorary secretary from 1924 to 1929, and then as honorary treasurer. She was president from 1937 to 1947. In 1921 she gave the inaugural address at the Royal Free School of Medicine for Women, which led to the publication of *The Woman Doctor and her Future* (1922). Working with Christine Murrell, Martindale also ensured that the British Postgraduate Medical School was open to women from its inception in 1931, and she became its first woman governor. In 1924 Martindale was a guest of honour at the American Medical Association's annual convention in Chicago. In 1933 she was made a fellow of the Royal College of Obstetricians and Gynaecologists and became the only woman on the council in 1934 when she was co-opted. In her autobiography she claimed to have performed more than 7000 operations.

Martindale was a pioneer of radium treatment for uterine and ovarian cancer in Britain. She had seen the work of Gauss and Kronig in Freiburg in 1913, and after 1921 she worked with Helen Chambers (a pathologist) and Elizabeth Hurdon (a physicist) implanting small amounts of radium surgically in cancerous organs. The trio were the Medical Women's Federation team in the Medical Research Council trials of radium therapy, their radium funded by the Medical Research Council and the King Edward's Hospital Fund. Operating at four women's hospitals the trio collaborated on 300 implants. Chambers and Martindale were on the committee that raised funds to open the Marie Curie Hospital specializing in women's cancers in 1929. As well as the innovative treatment the medical women conducted long-term follow-ups of patients, eventually producing epidemiological data on 13,800 patients.

Martindale held to the feminist position common in the nineteenth century that women were morally superior to men, and should exhort men to abstain from sex outside marriage and practise restraint within it. She opposed family planning ('conception control') and campaigned against prostitution. Martindale was involved in suffrage campaigning in Hull and Brighton, and she was briefly on the national executive of the National Union of Women's Suffrage Societies. She was not a militant, but did shelter a fellow campaigner being sought by the police under the 'Cat and Mouse'. Her social circle included the Fawcetts, and it was at Millicent Fawcett's urging that Martindale became embroiled in a public controversy. Martindale published a small volume on the evils of prostitution, *Under the Surface*, written from a feminist perspective. Anti-suffrage peers tried to get the book banned for obscenity in 1908. Martindale had focused on the links between prostitution and venereal diseases with explicit details of the medical symptoms. The book argued that enfranchising women would lead to national moral uplift, because women's greater moral sensibility would generate legislation on purity issues, and that sexual equality including equal pay would cause prostitution to wither away.

Louisa Martindale's personal life was women centred. Her autobiography reports little contact with her older half-siblings, in contrast to her close relationship with Hilda, her full sister. After the death of her mother in 1914, and of Dr Murdoch in 1916, Louisa's main adult relationship was with the Hon. Ismay Fitzgerald (1872–1946) who lived with her from 1911 until her death. Ismay Fitzgerald was the daughter of John David, Lord Fitzgerald of Kilmarnock, an Irish judge, and Jane Mary Matilda Southwell. One of the baron's thirteen children, she was a devout Roman Catholic and loved horses. The two women entertained and visited Ismay's aristocratic relatives and often travelled in Italy, on one occasion having an audience with the pope. After leaving Brighton, Louisa and Ismay lived at Colin Godman's House in Chelwood Gate, Sussex, at Weymouth Street, London, and later at Little Rystwood, Forest Row, East Grinstead, Sussex, and in Manchester Square, London. Martindale's obituaries describe her as small, always beautifully dressed and shod in the current fashion, and fond of parties and entertaining. A dog lover, her memoir devotes a chapter to her pets.

Louisa Martindale was one of the first women JPs in Brighton (from 1924) and was later a JP in East Grinstead. Created a CBE in 1931, she retired in 1947, and published her autobiography, *A Woman Surgeon*, in 1951. In her old age she became blind. She died on 5 February 1966 at her home, 14 Avenue Lodge, Avenue Road, St John's Wood, London.   SARA DELAMONT

Sources L. Martindale, *A woman surgeon* (1951) · H. Martindale, *From one generation to another, 1839–1944* (1944) · *BMJ* (26 Feb 1966), 493–556 · *Octavia Wilberforce: the autobiography of a pioneer woman doctor*, ed. P. Jalland (1989) · M. Fawcett, *What I remember* (1924), 214–15 · H. Malleson, *Life of a woman doctor: Mary Murdoch of Hull* (1919) · A. H. Bennett, *English medical women* (1915) · L. Bland, *Banishing the beast: English feminism and sexual morality, 1885–1914* (1995), 242–8 · H. M. Swanwick, 'Committee of inquiry into sexual morality', *The sexuality debates*, ed. S. Jeffreys (1987), 210–15 · b. cert. · d. cert. · d. cert. [Ismay Fitzgerald] · *CGPLA Eng. & Wales* (1966)
Archives Wellcome L., corresp. and papers; diaries and note-books
Likenesses F. O. Salisbury, oils, exh. Ehrlich Galleries, New York, 1925, New Sussex Hospital, Brighton [*see illus.*]
Wealth at death £4916: probate, 6 April 1966, *CGPLA Eng. & Wales*

Martindale, Miles (1756–1824), Methodist minister, son of Paul Martindale, who emigrated to the West Indies, was born at Moss Bank, near St Helens, Lancashire. He had only a slender education but taught himself French, Latin, and Greek, the last in order to read the New Testament in the original. When quite young he had a vivid mystical experience; he was then influenced by Voltaire and Rousseau and became an agnostic, but by 1780 was attracted to Methodism. In 1776 he moved to Liverpool and in the following year married Margaret King (*d.* 1845). From 1786 to 1789 he was a local preacher in the Wirral, where he found the people to be 'the most ignorant he ever laboured among'. In 1789 he was ordained, and until 1816 served as an itinerant Methodist preacher, being chairman of the Newcastle and York districts. In that year he was appointed governor of Woodhouse Grove School near Bradford, founded in 1811 as the Methodists' second boarding-school. In this position he was astute and effective, a matter acknowledged by the Wesleyan conference. He was a pioneer in the teaching of English language. Beside sermons, Martindale published an elegy on the death of Wesley (1791) and a *Dictionary of the Holy Bible* (1810), and translated from French works by John Fletcher and Abbé Besplas.

Martindale died of cholera on 6 August 1824, while attending the Wesleyan conference at Leeds. He was survived by his wife, who died in 1845, and their three daughters: Sophia, who married the Revd John Farrar, a noted Wesleyan theologian; Margaret, who married the Revd James Brownell; and Maria, who became matron of Wesley College, Sheffield.

C. W. Sutton, *rev.* John Munsey Turner

Sources F. C. Pritchard, *Methodist secondary education* (1949) · F. C. Pritchard, *The story of Woodhouse Grove School, Bradford* (1978) · J. T. Slugg, *Woodhouse Grove School: memorials and reminiscences* (1885) · H. W. Starkey, *A short history of Woodhouse Grove School* (1912) · *Wesleyan Methodist Magazine*, 48 (1825), 233 · *Minutes of conference of Wesleyan Methodists*, 5 (1824), 472 · G. Osborn, *Outlines of Wesleyan bibliography* (1869) · *Arminian Magazine*, 20 (Jan–Feb 1797) [autobiographical memoir]
Likenesses Ridley, stipple, NPG; repro. in *Methodist Magazine* (1820)

Martindale, William (1840–1902), pharmacist, was born on 12 June 1840 at Hesket, near Carlisle, Cumberland, the third son of the eight children of Richard Martindale (1807–1874), farmer, and his wife, Charlotte Stalker. After education in a Carlisle private school he was apprenticed in 1856 to his great-uncle, William Robinson Martindale, a chemist and druggist in the market place of that town. Martindale's uncle died two years later and his apprenticeship was completed with Andrew Thompson, of English Street, Carlisle, a loyal member of the Pharmaceutical Society of Great Britain. Aged twenty-two Martindale went to London to gain further experience; for two years he worked with James Merrell, who had established his own pharmacy in Camden after an apprenticeship in Tewkesbury and seven years at the famous Bell pharmacy in Oxford Street.

Martindale attended the Pharmaceutical Society's school of pharmacy at Bloomsbury Square, passed the 'minor' examination in 1864 and the 'major' two years later, by which time he had moved to the prestigious pharmacy and manufacturing house of T. N. R. Morson in Southampton Row. After two years as a qualified assistant, he was appointed pharmacist in 1868 to the University College Hospital, where also he taught pharmacy in the medical school and became demonstrator in materia medica; in 1872 he edited the hospital's own pharmacopoeia. While there he carried out original research, such as that on carbolic acid plaster and dressings with Joseph Lister, and he improved excipients for pills, and bases for pessaries and suppositories. He became a close friend of Sydney Ringer, famous for his work on the effects of electrolytes in body fluids, and the two of them published a paper on jaborandi in 1875.

In May 1873 Martindale took over the New Cavendish Street pharmacy of Hopkin and Williams, two other former assistants at Morsons. The business became one of the most important and scientifically advanced in London, and here Martindale developed an analytical service, besides increasing prescription numbers twentyfold. In the same year he began a ten-year spell as an examiner for the Pharmaceutical Society. Elected to the society's council in 1889, Martindale became treasurer in 1898 and then president for the year 1899–1900. From 1869 he was a frequent contributor to the British Pharmaceutical Conference; he held the position of treasurer for two years and was president in 1891 and 1896. He became a member of many other societies such as the Royal Society of Arts, the Chemical Society, the Sanitary Institute, the Linnean Society, and as a member of the Royal Botanic Society's council he encouraged improvement in the teaching of botany.

Martindale was an inventor and developer of dosage forms, being particularly well known for his work on glyceryl trinitrate in a cocoa-butter base for sublingual administration as a vasodilator in angina pectoris. He was the originator of amyl nitrite in crushable glass ampoules known as vitrellae, and was also one of the earliest pioneers of parenteral medication, writing on the subject as early as 1870, and in 1872 describing what he termed 'antiseptic pharmacy'. A regular feature of the *Pharmaceutical Journal* was its 'Dispensing memoranda', to which Martindale was a frequent contributor, answering scientific and practical questions. It was these notes which formed the basis for his famous book *The Extra Pharmacopoeia* (1883), to which Dr Wynn Westcott later added valuable medical details. The book was immediately successful, and ten editions appeared in Martindale's lifetime.

Martindale married Maria Hannah Harrison (*b. c.*1842), daughter of a Yorkshire farmer, at Kentish Town, London, on 14 August 1872. They had four children: two sons, William Harrison (1874–1933) and Leonard; and two daughters, Elizabeth ('Elsie') (1877–1949), who, against the wishes of her parents, married the novelist Ford Madox Ford (1873–1939), and Mary, who may also have had an affair with Ford. In later life Martindale bought land and a house at Winchelsea and a farm at Icklesham, Sussex. There he continued his experiments but also became interested in the archaeology and history of the area. He became a freeman, a jurat, and mayor of Winchelsea, which led to him becoming a baron of the Cinque Ports in 1893.

An almost obsessive worker when his poor health allowed, Martindale became much depressed, until finally on the morning of 2 February 1902 he took his own life by means of prussic acid. He was found dying by the maid in the study of his home at 19 Devonshire Street, London, but was dead before Sydney Ringer arrived. Martindale's father had also died by suicide. Martindale was survived by his wife and the flourishing pharmacy and manufacturing business, as well as the publication of *Martindale* (as it is still known to the pharmaceutical world), was carried to even greater heights by his eldest son, William.   JUANITA BURNBY

Sources A. Wade, 'The Martindales and their book', *Pharmaceutical Journal*, 248 (1992), 787–8 · T. D. Whittet, 'A history of pharmacy at University College Hospital', *Chemist and Druggist* (6 June–11 July 1953) · *Pharmaceutical Journal*, 14 (1902), 110–11, 123–4, 194 · W. H. Martindale, 'Links with Lister', *Pharmaceutical Journal and Pharmacist*, 64 (1927), 616 [letter] · *Chemist and Druggist* (23 April 1927) · *Chemist and Druggist* (18 June 1927) · N. W. Blacow, 'Martindale's Extra pharmacopoeia', *M&B Pharmaceutical Bulletin* (1968), 5–7 · *Chemist and Druggist* (15 April 1933), 414 · A. Morson, *Operative chymist* (1997), 251 · private information (1998) · M. Saunders, *Ford Madox Ford: a dual life*, 1 (1996) · *CGPLA Eng. & Wales* (1902)
Likenesses F. Taubman, clay model · F. Taubman, marble bust, Pharmaceutical Society, London · photographs, Pharmaceutical Society, London
Wealth at death £15,665 4s. 10d.: probate, 13 March 1902, *CGPLA Eng. & Wales*

Martindell [Martindale, Martindall], **Sir Gabriel** (1754/5–1831), army officer in the East India Company, was probably born in India, son of John Martindale (*d.* 1769), an officer in the Bengal army, and his wife, Lettice. Contemporary records suggest that he changed his name to Martindell. At a very young age he became a cadet in the East India Company's Bengal army, attached to 'the Select Picket' while awaiting the commission which was awarded him in 1776. In November 1798, having spent much of his service in Bengal European regiments, he was given command of the newly raised 2nd battalion 13th native infantry which became known as Martdeel-ki-paltan ('Martindell's battalion'). He served with distinction in the Second Anglo-Maratha War, taking command in turbulent Bundelkhand and driving out the Pindaris

(irregular bands of marauders). He defeated Raja Ram Singh on 2 July 1804, and took Jaipur by storm on 28 July. Martindell earned the 'approbation and applause' of the governor-general for his success, and more especially for capturing the fort of Ajaigarh in 1809 (BL OIOC, F/4/325).

However, Martindell's unsuccessful attack on the hill fort of Kalinjar in Bundelkhand in 1812 entailed heavy casualties, and his failure to fulfil orders when leading a force into Rewah in 1813 led to his resigning his command in March 1814 and to a posting to Cawnpore. These reverses seem to have drained him of self-confidence and drive. Lord Moira, governor-general and commander-in-chief, appointed Martindell to command the 2nd field division of the Bengal army in the Anglo-Nepal War of 1814–16. He did so mainly because of 'the difficulty of finding any other unemployed officer of rank sufficient to exercise so large a command', but also in 'the hope that the occurrences attending his command in Rewa … would stimulate him to exert himself' (*Papers Respecting the Nepaul War*, 737). Martindell assumed his command in the Sirmur hills on 19 December 1814, finding morale low following the death of his predecessor, Major-General Robert Gillespie, who had been killed while leading a reckless and unsupported charge at Kalanga, near Dehra Dun. Martindell delayed and dithered, to the frustration of his officers and his commander-in-chief. His incompetence brought disaster, causing William Fraser, the governor-general's political agent, to write to his brother Alexander 'I cannot tell you how much General [Martindell's] management is scorned and reviled by the army for indecision, want of promptness, energy and enterprise' (Fraser MSS, National Register of Archives for Scotland 2696, xxxiv, 254). Martindell's eventual offer to resign was overtaken by the victory of Major-General David Ochterlony at Malaun which brought the first campaign of the war to an end. Both officers were made KCB in April 1815.

Martindell was sent with a strong force in 1816 to quell a rising in Cuttack in Orissa, and in 1818 commanded a column in the Third Anglo-Maratha War. From 1820 he commanded the 1st division Bengal field army until 1824 when he was made divisional commander Cawnpore. In September 1824, at Chunar, Bishop Reginald Heber met Martindell, whom he described as 'a fine, mild, unaffected old officer' (Heber, 1.173). Seniority having long been the paramount consideration for promotion in the Bengal army, Martindell was made lieutenant-general in 1825. In 1827 he was given command of the fortress of Buxar where, still serving, he died on 2 January 1831, aged seventy-six. He was buried in Buxar cemetery.

Martindell may have married in 1777, though further details are obscure; however, he is known to have had at least ten children, presumably with one or more Indian mistresses. Of his six known sons, one, William Martindell, was commissioned in the Bengal cavalry; another, conceived when Martindell was seventy-two, died in infancy. A third, 'H. M.' (Henry Martindell), had inscribed on Martindell's tomb in Buxar cemetery, 'He was an affectionate father, a kind friend, and his charities knew no bounds.' Two of his four daughters, Mary and Jane, were at school when their father died. The inventory of his estate suggests that he lived in comfort in his old age, even if he was not possessed of a large fortune.   A. P. COLEMAN

Sources V. C. P. Hodson, *List of officers of the Bengal army, 1758–1834*, 4 vols. (1927–47) · 'List of old inscriptions, Bihar and Orissa', BL OIOC [Buxar cemetery, tombs 83 and 84] · inventory of Martindell's estate, BL OIOC, L/AG/34/27/98 and 106 · board collections, pt II, 1810–20, BL OIOC, F/4/325 · BL OIOC, Home misc., vols. 649, 652 · *Papers respecting the Nepaul war* (1824) · A. P. Coleman, *A special corps: the beginnings of Gorkha service with the British* (1999) · NRA Scotland, Fraser MSS, 2696 · R. Heber, *Narrative of a journey through the upper provinces of India*, [new edn], 2 vols. (1844) · F. G. Cardew, *A sketch of the services of the Bengal native army to the year 1895* (1903) · J. Pemble, *The invasion of Nepal: John Company at war* (1971) · CUL, Ludlow MSS · J. Philippart, *East India military calendar*, 3 vols. (1823–6)
Wealth at death lived in comfort, but not possessed of large fortune: inventory, BL OIOC, L/AG/34/27/98 and 106

Martine, George (1635–1712), historian, was born in Fife on 5 August 1635, the eldest son of James Martine (1614–1684), minister successively of Cults (1636), Auchtermuchty (1641), and Ballingry (1669), all in Fife, and his wife, Janet Robertson (1615/16–1644). His grandfather was Dr George Martine, principal of St Salvator's College, St Andrews. About 1663 Martine became secretary to Archbishop James Sharp of St Andrews. In this capacity he accompanied Sharp on his frequent travels between St Andrews, Edinburgh, and London, keeping a detailed memorandum book listing all the archbishop's travelling expenses, as well as household expenditure and charitable bequests. In August 1666 he became commissary clerk of St Andrews, remaining so for the next twenty-four years. He married, on 30 June 1668, Catherine, daughter of James Winchester of Kinglassie, Fife; they had several children. Martine also acquired the lands of Clermont that year, and is sometimes called Martine of Clermont.

Martine is best known for his *Reliquiae divi Andreae, or, The State of the Venerable ... See of St Andrews*, written in 1683 but not published until 1797. Robert Wodrow's contention that he was prevented from publishing it by the revolution of 1688 is very plausible considering the episcopalian bias of the work at a date when presbyterianism had been officially established. In any case, Martine was a Jacobite: his refusal to take the assurance of loyalty to King William and Queen Mary cost him his St Andrews clerkship in 1690. This may explain why, although in 1702 he was considered by some to be 'the greatest antiquary now in Scotland' (Wodrow, 1.xxxiv) he passed the last years of his life in comparative obscurity. He died on 26 August 1712.

ALEXANDER DU TOIT

Sources W. Macfarlane, *Genealogical collections concerning families in Scotland*, ed. J. T. Clark, 2, Scottish History Society, 34 (1900), 183–98 · *Fasti Scot.*, new edn, 5.58, 126, 138 · J. Stirton, 'The household book of James Sharp, lord archbishop of St Andrews, 1663–1668', *Leaves from my manuscript portfolio* (1929), 19–21 · G. Martine, *Reliquiae divi Andreae, or, The state of the venerable and primitial see of St Andrews* (1797), vii–viii · R. Wodrow, *Analecta, or, Materials for a history of remarkable providences, mostly relating to Scotch ministers and Christians*, ed. [M. Leishman], 4, Maitland Club, 60 (1843), xxxiv–

xxxv · *Miscellany of the Maitland Club*, ed. J. Dennistoun and A. MacDonald, 2 vols. (1840), 2.497–541
Archives U. Edin., Laing collection
Wealth at death Clermont estate, Fifeshire

Martine, George (1700–1741), physician, was born at Claremont, St Andrews, Fife, the son of James Martine (*d.* 1725), owner of the Claremont estate, and his wife, Margaret McGill. He matriculated at the University of St Andrews in 1713/14, and paid fees for his bachelorship in 1716. Having decided on a medical career, in 1720 he studied under Alexander Monro *primus*, who taught medicine outside the University of Edinburgh prior to the foundation of the faculty of medicine there. He then moved to the University of Leiden, in the Low Countries, and matriculated in 1721 to study under Hermann Boerhaave. On his return in 1722 he obtained his degree of MD at St Andrews on testimonials signed by six eminent British physicians. He practised as a physician in St Andrews until late 1725. In that year he and William Graeme MD opened a medical school in the basement of the Surgeons' Hall, Edinburgh, where he taught the theory and Graeme the practice of medicine. The school was not a success, and Martine returned to St Andrews before 1728.

On his father's death Martine inherited Claremont, which he sold in 1732, though he remained at St Andrews until 1739. In his early years Martine had published several articles, in the form of letters or essays, dealing with the blood and organs of the human body, and by this time had developed an interest in the temperature of the circulating blood and animal heat generally. The difficulties of measuring temperature led him to investigate the unsatisfactory business of thermometer manufacture and the impossibility of comparing observations that had been made with a variety of instruments graduated to individual scales. Some of these referred to a single point, often the freezing point of water, and calculated higher points from the expanded volume of thermometric fluid (oil, mercury, or spirits of wine). He spent some of the latter part of 1739 in Paris, doubtless investigating the work of Réaumur and Delisle on this topic, from where he wrote to Cromwell Mortimer, secretary of the Royal Society. Martine came out strongly in favour of graduating thermometers with reference to two fixed points, one being the boiling point of water—with due attention to barometric pressure—the other being the melting point of ice. He also urged the adoption of mercury, as spirits of wine came in many strengths and could not be brought to the boiling point of water, while oil tended to adhere to the inside of the tube.

In December 1739 Martine was appointed physician to Lord Cathcart, commander-in-chief on the expedition to the West Indies. He spent the early part of 1740 in London, where his essays on thermometry were read to the Royal Society. He presented to the society copies of his books published in 1740, *De similibus animalibus et animalium calore* and *Essays Medical and Philosophical*. In the latter, two medical essays, 'On the period and crises of diseases' and 'On the specific operation of cathartic medicine', were followed by a discourse on the history of thermometers and the evolution of their various scales, a comparison of the best-known reproducible scales, and an essay on the heating and cooling of matter, in which Martine challenged the conventional view that denser fluids heated more slowly by showing that a mercury thermometer responded faster than one containing spirit. The final long essay dealt with the degrees of heat and cold found in nature, ranging from the body heat of man and beast, and of fish and insects, to the heat of the sun and planets, the highest and lowest recorded temperatures of the atmosphere, the melting and boiling points of a variety of metals and minerals, and the temperatures of flame and fire. The *Essays … on Thermometers* went through several editions; that of 1792 contained additions and Joseph Black's tables, to serve the students to whom Black had recommended the book. After his death Martine's work was also translated into French.

Martine was elected an honorary fellow of the Royal College of Physicians of Edinburgh early in 1740. He had sailed to the West Indies by the time that he was proposed for membership to the Royal Society on 15 May; he was elected on 11 December. He died of a fever at Cartagena, in what is now Colombia, some time before April 1741.

ANITA MCCONNELL

Sources R. C. Mackenzie, 'George Martine MD, FRS (1700–1741), an early thermal analysist?', *Journal of Thermal Analysis*, 35 (1989), 1823–36 · W. E. K. Middleton, *A history of the thermometer and its use in meteorology* [1966], 59, 97, 115–16, 124 · E. Mendelsohn, *Heat and life* (1964), 81–4, 92, 96

Martineau, Edith (1842–1909), watercolour painter, was born on 19 June 1842 at 30 Mason Street, West Derby, Liverpool, one of eight children of Dr James *Martineau (1805–1900), Unitarian theologian and minister, and his wife, Helen (1804–1877), daughter of Edward Higginson. She was the niece of the author Harriet *Martineau. After early training at the Liverpool School of Art, Martineau moved with her family to London, where she enrolled in classes at Leigh's School of Art. In 1862, at the age of twenty, she was one of the first women to be admitted to the Royal Academy Schools. According to the *Magazine of Art* (1883, 329) she also attended classes at the Slade School of Fine Art.

Martineau began her exhibiting career while still a student, submitting her *Study of Fungi and Moss in the Highlands* to the Society (later Royal Society) of British Artists in 1862. Over the next four decades she exhibited widely, selling her works to private collectors. She contributed to numerous annual exhibitions including, most regularly, those of the Royal Society of Painters in Water Colours, the Walker Art Gallery in Liverpool, the Royal Society of Artists in Birmingham, the Manchester City Art Gallery, the Royal Academy, and the Society of Women Artists. In 1888, after twenty-six years of professional activity, Martineau was elected an associate of the Royal Society of Painters in Water Colours, one of only nine women in the Old Watercolour Society to attain that honour. She was also a member of the Dudley Watercolour Society (1883–6) and the Hampstead Art Society. Her first major exhibition was held together with her elder sister Gertrude (1837–1924),

also a watercolourist, at the Modern Gallery in 1906. A second joint exhibition was held at the New Dudley Gallery in 1910 in commemoration of Edith Martineau's death.

Martineau's paintings are highly detailed and usually small. Working primarily on paper in watercolour heightened with bodycolour, she experimented with a variety of styles, including the classicism of *Early Steps* (exh. Royal Institute of Painters in Water Colours, 1885; ex Sothebys, 30 March 1994), the aestheticism of *The Pot of Lilies* (1883; ex Sothebys, 5 July 1977), and a rustic cottage style similar to that of Helen Allingham (1848–1926) (*A Duckling in Danger*, 1891; ex Sothebys, 21 May 1981). She undertook a number of portraits, occasionally ethnographic in nature, as in *Head of an Arab* (1879; ex Sothebys, 10 November 1998). Most representative, however, are Martineau's highland landscapes, such as *Hillside Near Aviemore, in Early June* (V&A), her flower paintings, including *June Riches* (Manchester City Galleries), and her peasant genre scenes, such as *Rustic Courtship* (1888; ex Sothebys, 6 November 1991) and *Potato Harvest* (1888).

Edith Martineau never married, maintaining close ties with her immediate family throughout her life. Along with Gertrude she edited a posthumous collection of her father's unpublished sermons (*National Duties and other Sermons and Addresses*, 1902). She died at home, 5 Eldon Road, Hampstead, on 19 February 1909, from heart failure following influenza. She was sixty-six.

KRISTINA HUNEAULT

Sources *Art Journal*, new ser., 29 (1909), 110 · W. Sparrow, *Women painters of the world* (1905) · Mallalieu, *Watercolour artists*, vol. 1 · P. Gerrish Nunn, *Victorian women artists* (1987) · C. Petteys, *Dictionary of women artists* (1985) · C. Weeks, 'The Slade girls', *Magazine of Art*, 6 (1882–3), 329 · C. E. Clement, *Women in the fine arts* (1904) · J. Johnson and A. Greutzner, *The dictionary of British artists, 1880–1940* (1976), vol. 5 of *Dictionary of British art* · exhibition catalogues (1862–87) [Society of British Artists] · exhibition catalogues (1887–1909) [Royal Society of British Artists] · exhibition catalogues (1862–1909) [Royal Scot. Acad.] · exhibition catalogues (1862–8) [Society of Female Artists, London]; (1869–98) [Society of Lady Artists, London]; (1899–1909) [Society of Women Artists, London] · The exhibition of the Royal Academy (1862–1909) [exhibition catalogues] · exhibition catalogues (1862–1909) [Royal Hibernian Academy, Dublin] · exhibition catalogues (1862–1909) [Royal Glasgow Institute of the Fine Arts] · d. cert. · b. cert. · *DNB*
Archives V&A
Wealth at death £116,076 17s. 2d.: resworn probate, 22 April 1909, CGPLA Eng. & Wales

Martineau, Harriet (1802–1876), writer and journalist, was born in Norwich on 12 June 1802, the sixth of eight children of Thomas Martineau (1764–1826), a cloth manufacturer descended from an old Huguenot family, and his wife, Elizabeth (1770/71–1848), the eldest daughter of Robert Rankin, a sugar refiner in Newcastle upon Tyne.

The making of a writer Thomas Martineau was a gentle, unassertive man; Elizabeth Martineau was a highly intelligent, largely self-educated woman of considerable force of character. Harriet Martineau's childhood was, according to her own account, a difficult one, marked by digestive and other physical disorders and by more than usual fears and isolation. She admits in her autobiography to having been a difficult child: the degree of blame she

Harriet Martineau (1802–1876), by George Richmond, 1849

places on her mother for her unhappiness may have been unfair, but her younger brother, James *Martineau (1805–1900), also noted (in his autobiographical memoranda) Elizabeth Martineau's reserved and formidable aspect.

Harriet Martineau had deficient senses of taste and smell, and her progressive deafness had become virtually total by the age of twenty, adding to her sense of isolation. From about 1830 she regularly used an ear trumpet, which was an enduring, and sometimes daunting, feature in contemporaries' recollections of her. Many disliked it, among them Sydney Smith (1771–1845), though with his booming voice he scarcely needed it, while Nathaniel Hawthorne (1804–1864) recalled it 'as an organ of intelligence and sympathy … a sensitive part of her, like the feelers of some insects'.

Harriet Martineau was taught largely at home, but for two years from 1813 to 1815 she attended an excellent school headed by the Revd Isaac Perry (1777–1837), who had left the Congregationalists for the Unitarians in 1812; he was, she recalled, 'made to be a girls' schoolmaster' (*Autobiography*). For fifteen months in 1818–19 she was a boarder in a small school in Bristol run by an aunt. While living in Bristol she also received religious instruction from the Revd Lant Carpenter (1780–1840), minister at Lewin's Mead Chapel, who made a powerful impression on her, though she was very dismissive of him in her autobiography.

Surviving correspondence from the early 1820s reveals a high-spirited and happy family. The Martineaus attended the Octagon Chapel in Norwich, one of the leading Unitarian congregations in the country. Company in the town was plentiful and lively: having long since abandoned the old Calvinist traditions of the dissenters, the Martineaus played cards and danced, and there were long visits to relatives elsewhere. But the letters also record the high seriousness of discussions of political and religious questions. As a child, Harriet Martineau had found consolation in religious reading and fancies, and serious study of her Unitarian inheritance underlay the main preoccupations of her early writing. In 1822 her first published essay, comparing Anna Laetitia Barbauld and Hannah More as devotional writers, appeared in the Unitarian *Monthly Repository* (17, 1822, 593–6, 746–50). *Devotional Exercises* followed two years later, reflecting her enchantment with romantic poetry and importantly qualifying the usual perception of Unitarians as chilly rationalists. In 1831 she gained denomination-wide fame by winning all three prizes in a contest for the best essays aimed at converting Roman Catholics, Jews, and Muslims to Unitarianism.

By inheritance a political radical and dedicated dissenter, Harriet Martineau consistently criticized the Church of England, particularly for what she considered the craven submission of its clergy to creeds and hierarchical authority. No one was more insistent on the obligation to speak out, or even to suffer martyrdom, on matters of principle. Especially significant was her early and lasting commitment to necessarianism, the philosophical determinism then dominant among Unitarian ministers and many educated laymen. Derived from David Hartley (1705–1757) through Joseph Priestley (1733–1805), the most important figure in the emergence of Unitarianism from presbyterianism, necessarianism denied free will, arguing that every seemingly voluntary act was inexorably determined by prior motives formed by association from external impressions. But external impressions could be controlled and so motives could be changed, opening broad opportunities for education, reform of social arrangements, and the discipline of experience to bring behaviour into conformity with divine law. Moreover, to Unitarians, Jesus was not a god but a perfect man, whose death on the cross was an example of self-sacrifice, not a substitutionary atonement. Thus, under providence and God's foreknowledge, every human being could win salvation, alone or with the help of the truly enlightened. Harriet Martineau elaborated this world-view in a series of articles in the *Repository* at the end of the 1820s, when that journal was edited by W. J. Fox. Although she eventually withdrew from Unitarianism, she never forsook necessarianism.

Political economy and literary London: 'A national instructor'
The growing sense of mission conveyed in the above description of Martineau (it is Fox's) and her early development as philosopher and writer were set in a time of much personal and family trouble, from which her literary work offered a welcome deliverance. Her beloved elder brother Thomas (*b*. 1795) died of tuberculosis in 1824; her father's business suffered badly in the economic collapse of 1825, and he died the next year. In May 1827 came the death of her fiancé, John Hugh Worthington (*b*.

1804), a young minister at Cross Street Chapel, Manchester, who had been a college friend of James Martineau. The brief attachment had been doubtful from the first, as Worthington's ardent hopes came up against her reluctance, compounded of uncertainty about his health, worries about the prospect of marriage, and family pressures. A manifest sense of relief is conveyed in her oddly detached letters at the time of his death and in the celebration of single life recorded in her autobiography, although she delighted in children and was always happy in a domestic circle.

The failure of the family firm in 1829 threw Harriet Martineau on her own resources. Rejecting the alternative of governessing, she determined to live by her pen rather than her needle, although needlework remained an enjoyable recreation throughout her life. Up to that point her work for Fox had been unremunerated, but he now began to pay her £15 a year. She wrote for other publishers as well. *Traditions of Palestine, or, Times of the Saviour* (1829) attracted notice on both sides of the Atlantic and foreshadowed her later interest in the Near East. Of her apprentice tales, *The Rioters* (1827), which dealt with machine breaking, and *The Turn Out* (1829), on wages and strikes, were more immediately prophetic.

At about the time of these modest successes, Martineau had encountered *Conversations on Political Economy* (1816) by Jane Marcet (1769–1858), an event that soon led to a bold new project. In 1831, with Fox's strong encouragement and with his brother Charles as the not particularly generous publisher, she began work on *Illustrations of Political Economy*, a series of twenty-three tales in twenty-five parts published monthly from February 1832. Based on rapid study of economic principles, particularly in the works of James Mill and T. R. Malthus, and with a generally effective if sometimes forced and wooden narrative style, the tales made her famous almost overnight. A failure in so far as they were intended to make the working classes think rightly about economic laws, the stories reinforced middle-class convictions and were welcomed accordingly, while reviews ranged from enthusiastic to extremely hostile, according to the reviewers' political prejudices. She was quickly invited to write four additional volumes, *Poor Laws and Paupers Illustrated* (1833), and a further five tales, *Illustrations of Taxation* (1834), to improve prospects for reform in those areas under the whig government.

John Stuart Mill commented acutely that Martineau reduced political economy to an absurdity by simply carrying it out logically to all its consequences (*Monthly Repository*, 2nd ser., 8, 1834, 321), and she has remained famous as an advocate of the most doctrinaire version of the science. It is true that she remained loyal to the central tenets of free trade and non-intervention, and, ever the manufacturer's daughter, she continued to think that social problems were more likely to arise from the rapid growth of towns than from factory evils. But, though she never favoured trade unions, her later visit to America persuaded her of the virtues of the Rappite and Shaker communities, and she came to look benevolently on association, particularly consumers' co-operatives, as one

solution to economic ills. In 1855 she wrote an article that argued so severely against government-required fencing of dangerous machinery that the *Westminster Review* rejected it, and it was published as a pamphlet by the National Association of Factory Occupiers. But a few years later she supported the new round of factory legislation, and thought that if the market did not solve pressing social problems then the state must intervene.

In late 1832 Martineau moved to London to enjoy the celebrity she had earned, living first in lodgings in Conduit Street and then in a small house taken by her mother in Fludyer Street, near Downing Street, Westminster, but now vanished from the map. In an article in the *London and Westminster Review* (32, 1839, 261–81) in April 1839 she wrote critically about the phenomenon of literary lionizing, and further recollections appear, delightfully, in her autobiography. She was well connected by family ties to radical London, but W. J. Fox was her main point of entry to intellectual circles. She came to know most of the prominent political figures in the reform era, among whom Lord Durham was a hero to her, while Lord Brougham she found by turns fascinating and untrustworthy.

Of average height, with a plain face, grey-green eyes, and brown hair, Harriet Martineau had a pleasant voice and manner and could converse confidently, even boldly, on almost any subject: Sydney Smith once deplored a sleep-destroying dream in which he was chained to a rock, and was being talked to death by Harriet Martineau and Macaulay. Some years later, Hawthorne described her as 'a large, robust (one might almost say bouncing) elderly woman', with a face 'so kind, cheerful and intelligent … that she is pleasanter to look at than most beauties'. Her talking still struck him as remarkable, 'like the babbling of a brook' (*English Notebooks*, ed. R. Stewart, 1941, 77). She approved of none of the portraits of her until that by George Richmond in 1849; the drawing was so good, she reported, that people agreed there was nothing to say about it: 'It is just me' (H. Martineau to L. Hunt, 24 Jan 1851, BL, Add. MS 38 111, fols. 1–6).

American tour, 1834–1836 Harriet Martineau had been frequently prostrated by her active London life and by constant writing to deadline, so when the series were drawing to completion, the need for a change determined a new and fateful step: she would observe the creation of a new society in the United States. Accompanied by Louisa Jeffrey, a young Unitarian woman she had met in London, she sailed for America on 9 August 1834. From New York she travelled through western Massachusetts to Albany and on to Niagara, then to a personal shrine in Northumberland, Pennsylvania, where Priestley had lived his last years and was buried. After extended stays in Philadelphia, Baltimore, Washington, and Charleston, she travelled across the south to the Mississippi, sailed to Kentucky, where she saw Mammoth cave, and stayed for three weeks in Lexington before ten days in Cincinnati and a return up the Ohio and through Virginia to New York. Without her companion, she toured New England in the autumn of 1835, spent the winter in Boston, and headed west, again to Niagara and on to Detroit and Chicago, returning on the Great Lakes to Cleveland and thence to New York, where she sailed for England on 1 August 1836.

The rigours of the journey were compensated for by the intense but critical interest Harriet Martineau took in what she saw. Her way was smoothed in most cities by Unitarian connections and made rougher by the reputation that preceded her. She made no secret of her sympathy with the whig party against the Jacksonian democrats, and her already vocal opposition to slavery was strengthened by seeing the institution in practice. In Boston she aligned herself with the most radical wing of the abolitionists, led by William Lloyd Garrison, and in those circles made one of the closest friendships in her life, with Maria Weston Chapman, her literary executor and first biographer. No cause, in a life devoted to causes, so preoccupied her as opposition to slavery, not only in America but in the world at large.

Back in London, Martineau published *Society in America* (1837), a two-volume analysis that, other than Alexis, comte de Tocqueville's, contemporaneous *Democracy in America* (1835; trans. 1835–40), may be regarded as the best book among the vast outpouring of travel writing on the great transatlantic experiment. She had originally intended the title to promise an explicit discussion of theory and practice, and, partisan and personal though the book is, the acute observation and the high level of generalization transcend a mere travel account to make it a historical document in its own right and a pioneering work of sociological analysis. The next year *Retrospect of Western Travel* offered a more conventional, though delightful and revealing, record of the journey. She received £900 for the first book, £600 for the second. Also in 1838 her contribution to a series of guides on various subjects by different hands returned to the analytical level to discuss principles of social observation: this remarkable little book was called *How to Observe: Morals and Manners*.

Like most writers Martineau was expected to turn her hand to a novel. *Deerbrook* (1839) was her sole large-scale effort in the form, although the sympathetic portrayal of Toussaint l'Ouverture and the Haitian revolution in *The Hour and the Man* (1840) evoked much admiration, and the four long tales making up *The Playfellow* (1842) remained in print for over a century to enforce their stern lesson of willingness to suffer for the right. *Deerbrook* had a similar moral aim. Although the novel offers in Mrs Rowland a splendid, eventually humbled, villain, the plot turns on an unfortunate marital choice, forcing the leading male character, an apothecary, to choose between duty and emotion. At times it justifies Thomas Carlyle's description of it as 'very ligneous, very trivial-didactic' (*Collected Letters of Thomas and Jane Welsh Carlyle*, ed. C. R. Sanders and K. J. Fielding, 15 vols., 1970–87, 11.87); undoubtedly over-long and occasionally extravagant in its rhetoric, it fairly soon fell into neglect. It has recently evoked new interest, partly for the psychological insights it offers into its author, and partly as a sympathetic portrayal of a hero from the middle ranks of society, a point very important

to her, at the very height of the craze for 'silver fork' novels.

These major books of Martineau's second London period were surrounded by an array of journalism in the leading reviews and by efforts to advance a number of causes in addition to anti-slavery, notably the legal and economic advancement of women. Here, again, was a campaign that drew new force from her stay in Boston, and the famous Seneca Falls meeting in 1840, usually seen as the fountainhead of modern feminism, found her among its most enthusiastic endorsers. She was never in entire sympathy with the campaign for the political rights of women—for example, she is very severe in her autobiography about Mary Wollstonecraft—giving priority to women's claims in the labour market and to female education in schools and in the home. She approached the latter subject with genuine originality in a series of essays collected in 1849 as *Household Education*.

New turnings: mesmerism and positive philosophy In 1838 Harriet Martineau began to suffer acute physical symptoms and the next year collapsed during a visit to Venice. The problem was a prolapsed uterus almost certainly caused by an ovarian cyst. She moved to Newcastle to be near her doctor, her brother-in-law T. M. Greenhow (1791–1881), and eventually took up residence in rented rooms in Tynemouth, where after 1842 she was largely confined to her couch. Despite the debility and frequent suffering, she led an active philanthropic and literary life and entertained a stream of visitors. The experience was turned to account in *Life in the Sickroom* (1844), an inspirational and instructive volume for other sufferers that evoked much admiration and almost equal hostility.

Writing to Jeanie Walsh in January 1843, Jane Carlyle, a difficult friend, deplored what she saw as 'a dreadful state of "self-consciousness" of late' in Martineau (*Collected Letters of Thomas and Jane Welsh Carlyle*, ed. C. R. Sanders and K. J. Fielding, 16.34–5). This was soon to be evident from her book, and could be seen already in two ostensibly principled actions that annoyed or alienated many old friends. One was a much publicized refusal to accept a civil-list pension offered to help in circumstances inevitably reduced by illness (her income for 1842 was £120). She had once before refused such assistance, at the time of the political economy tales, and was to do so again when W. E. Gladstone made an offer in 1873, although she accepted the proceeds from a private campaign organized by her close friend the younger Erasmus Darwin (1804–1881). The other was to demand the return of her letters, on pain of being denied all future correspondence. Some friends reluctantly complied (her brother James first made shorthand abstracts, now transcribed in the library at Harris Manchester College, Oxford), but others refused and were (mostly) cut off. She forbade publication of her letters, arguing that, as 'written speech', they were entitled to the same protection.

None of these passages, however, matched the stir created by the cure which Martineau insisted was a result of mesmerism. For some years she had been interested in phrenological and mesmeric phenomena, which seemed to suggest the imminent discovery of new laws of thought, and as the craze mounted to its height in the early 1840s the urging of friends found her a willing subject. Even Dr Greenhow persuaded himself that, given her susceptibilities, it might have some good effect. At the hands of several practitioners, including her own personal maid, the symptoms of her illness disappeared. She published an account of the cure in six letters to *The Athenaeum* in November and December 1844 and so became one of the most celebrated medical cases of the century. She regarded Greenhow's defensive pamphlet, *Medical Report of the Case of Miss H— M—* (1845), which described his treatment of her condition and her symptoms in detail—'not even written in Latin' (*Autobiography*)—as an act of treachery that warranted her refusal to see him again.

Whatever the medical and psychological explanation, Martineau was able to resume an astonishingly strenuous life. Its high point was her extensive tour of Egypt and the Near East in 1846–7. Like *Society in America* the resulting book, *Eastern Life: Present and Past* (1848), combined a travel account with acute observation and important reflections. While sharing the emotion evoked in so many of her travelling contemporaries by the sights and historical resonance of the Holy Land, she was confirmed in her growing sense of the historicity of the Christian dispensation and of its present irrelevance. In 1851 she published an exchange of letters with a mesmeric adviser who had become a close friend, Henry George Atkinson, under the title *Letters on the Laws of Man's Nature and Development*. The bulk of the book is Atkinson's, with promptings from Harriet Martineau, but she associated herself fully with the result, not only underlining her faith in mesmerism but proclaiming a rejection of all religion. Again a publication brought notoriety and broken friendships.

The most traumatic of these breaks was no doubt inevitable, but its timing and its occasion could scarcely have been worse. Many years before, in 1824, Martineau had gone on a walking tour of the Scottish highlands with her brother James, then a ministerial student. The main subject of their long conversations was, in her recollection (which he substantially confirms), the doctrine of necessity, which he had recently suggested might offer an answer to some of her metaphysical concerns. From the early 1830s, however, he began to move away from their shared philosophy. Rediscovering free will and convinced that religion was an essential human need that carried conviction not because of external evidences but because the soul commanded it, he rose to prominence as the leader of the 'new school' of Unitarianism, as against the 'old school' descended from Priestley. Harriet had observed this growing estrangement with genuine puzzlement, tinged with the old affection. In May 1851 James Martineau published a very hostile review of the Atkinson letters in the *Prospective Review* (7, 1851, 224–62), which he edited with three friends; he later insisted disingenuously that the book had fallen to him in the ordinary editorial rota. It was a terrible blow to Harriet. Characteristically, James could not quite understand his sister's feelings and tried on a few occasions to effect a reconciliation,

but to no avail. In the mid-1860s, when he was a leading candidate for the chair of philosophy at University College, London, she was a willing conspirator in the campaign led by the psychologist Alexander Bain to deny him the professorship, on the grounds that appointing a minister to so crucial a post in an avowedly secular foundation was wrong.

Whatever the personal cost of her new direction, Martineau never looked back. In her autobiography, written in 1855, she is forthright about her unbelief and the emancipatory process by which she arrived at it; less appealingly, she voices contempt for nearly all the Unitarians who had nurtured her early intellectual development and mediated the mental structures which she never abandoned. In 1859 she welcomed Charles Darwin's *On the Origin of Species* with almost unmeasured warmth, regretting only that he occasionally mentioned a creator or a first cause, a prudential reticence that she feared would allow believers to cling to outworn prejudices.

In 1851 Martineau had acquainted herself with the *Cours de philosophie positive* by the French philosopher Auguste Comte, whose system charted the evolution of the sciences from the superstitious through the metaphysical to the positive stage, in which law, rather than supernatural influences or abstract systems, became the basis for understanding. The roots of this positive philosophy lay in the teachings of the comte de Saint-Simon. In the W. J. Fox circle in 1831 Harriet Martineau had been impressed by the Saint-Simonian missionaries then visiting London, whose diverging course from the master competed with Comte's system, which was in some ways more extravagant. At times in her writings of the 1830s she seemed almost to anticipate the law of three stages. Martineau's translation and abridgement of the *Cours* appeared in 1853 as *The Positive Philosophy of Auguste Comte*, by which vehicle the English-speaking world was first introduced to Comte's text. Martineau never accepted many aspects of Comte's philosophy: she rejected the theocratic structure of the later positive polity and powerfully dissented from his subordination of women. But to the end of her life, she continued to uphold him as a guide to the right mode of thought for the nineteenth century. Although this can be seen as a natural evolution from her Priestleyanism and her early essays on the art of thinking, she regarded it as a fundamental departure.

A consummate journalist In 1845 Harriet Martineau settled in the Lake District and in 1846 moved into a charming house, The Knoll, which was built for her in Ambleside. There she maintained a happy and industrious household, with the usual succession of well-known callers and extended, welcome visits from young nieces and nephews. She supervised a 2 acre farm—writing a book on the subject, of course—and continued to engage in extensive charitable effort. Mrs Chapman gives her income for one unspecified year in the 1850s as around £800, of which about half was from current and past work, and most of the rest from investments; in 1871, after retirement, her income was £470, mostly from investments (M. W. Chapman, 'Memorials', in *Autobiography*, and

Weston MSS, Boston Public Library). In both years she appears to have laid out about a third of her income in good works.

Martineau knew the famous local residents, including William Wordsworth; she was an intimate in the household headed by Mary Arnold, the widow of Thomas and mother of Matthew, and corresponded with many literary and political figures elsewhere. In addition to the major books, she continued to turn out periodical writing of a quality that led George Eliot to say, in admiring an article on the great German historian B. G. Niebuhr (1776–1831), that she was 'the only English woman that possesses thoroughly the art of writing' (G. Eliot to Mr and Mrs C. Bray and S. S. Hennell, 2 June 1852, *George Eliot Letters*, ed. G. S. Haight, 2, 1954, 32).

In 1852 Martineau began writing leading articles for the *Daily News* in London, a connection established when the editor, Frederick Knight Hunt, published her letters from Ireland, and thereupon suggested that she contribute two or three leaders a week, a schedule made possible by improved rail and postal services, which ensured that an article posted in the evening in Ambleside would be on the editor's desk in London the following morning. By the time she retired in 1866, she had written more than 1600, along with occasional letters and non-editorial pieces, among them a brilliant set of portraits of leading Victorians later collected as *Biographical Sketches* (1869).

It was a natural métier. The Martineau household in Norwich had been highly engaged politically, and she had herself been deeply impressed in the 1820s by George Canning's prediction that the world would soon see a great war of opinion that would set right against might—a conflict she was led to see in every war that broke out for the remainder of her life. A principled reformer and an astute observer of national and international affairs, she was also a brilliant contemporary historian. In 1848 she accepted an invitation from the publisher Charles Knight to write a history of her times, a project Knight himself had begun but had had to abandon. The *History of the Thirty Years' Peace*, covering the years 1815–45, appeared in 1849–50; later editions carried it back to 1800 and down to 1850. Annalistic in construction and opinionated in tone, the book has an acuteness and immediacy that support its claim to being, perhaps, her masterpiece. The tone of her editorial writing is confident, the style impeccable, the range astonishing. Old enthusiasms are there—anti-slavery, education, the condition of women, political economy (somewhat modified) and free trade, ecclesiastical and clerical malignity. New interests to which she returned repeatedly included Ireland and India, the reforms proposed by Florence Nightingale, and the deterioration of politics: she profoundly distrusted Palmerston, Gladstone, and Disraeli, and placed her confidence in men of secondary rank such as Sidney Herbert and George William Frederick Howard, Lord Morpeth, later seventh earl of Carlisle. Above all, she was the paper's expert on America, a subject which the outbreak of the civil war in 1861 gave her ample opportunity to exploit.

Nor did the *Daily News* exhaust Martineau's capacities. In the early 1850s she wrote for *Household Words* and the *Westminster Review*; in 1858 she transferred her allegiance to the *Edinburgh Review*, of which her cousin Henry Reeve (1813–1895) had become editor three years earlier. In 1861 she became European correspondent of a New York abolitionist paper, the *Anti-Slavery Standard*, a post she used to scold as much as to encourage the Americans into courses of which she approved. After her retirement in 1866 she could still re-enter the lists: in 1868 she used a review of a book on the Salem witchcraft episode in colonial New England to denounce the spiritualist circles much talked of in that decade, which she regarded as utterly unscientific (*Edinburgh Review*, 128, 1868, 1–47). The next year, in a succession of addresses and open letters (printed in Chapman's 'Memorials', appended to Martineau's *Autobiography*), she gave her firm support to the campaign of Josephine Butler to repeal the Contagious Diseases Acts.

Last illness and autobiography In 1855 Harriet Martineau had been once more stricken with illness, caused, she believed, by heart disease—a not inaccurate, but insufficient, diagnosis. She died on 27 June 1876 at The Knoll, Ambleside. The attending physician gave as the cause of death fatty degeneration of the heart and an ovarian tumour; the tumour, which the autopsy showed to be of enormous size, had grown, severely compressing and distending the internal organs and producing the symptoms that reduced her to invalidism in the last twenty years of her life. She remained mentally alert and an excellent correspondent almost to the moment of death. Her investments brought some ease to her old age, as did the generosity of the many admiring friends who came to share the hospitality at The Knoll. She was buried on 1 July in the family plot in the general cemetery, Key Hill, Birmingham. Her personal estate was valued for probate at under £10,000.

When, in 1855, she expected death to strike at any moment, Martineau wrote her autobiography in the space of three months, having it stereotyped so that it would be published unchanged when her death occurred; she also wrote and filed with the *Daily News* the character sketch the paper ran as an obituary on 29 June 1876. If these moves suggest (correctly) that she was concerned about how the world saw her, she was not concerned that the image be uniformly favourable. Indeed, when the autobiography was published in 1877, the frequent tone of asperity, added to candid judgements as severe on herself as on others, seriously undercut her reputation. She has never lacked admirers, but a major upsurge in interest happened in the 1960s, in part because she was rediscovered by feminist scholars. Extensive and newly available manuscript collections, no longer subject to her prohibition against publication, have revealed her as a magnificent correspondent. The autobiography, too, is now generally recognized as one of the best self-studies of the century.

One must regret that two of Martineau's greatest contemporaries, George Eliot and Matthew Arnold, who knew her well, never wrote the appreciations each had once expressed the wish to do. Both would have found much in her life and work to object to: most contemporaries did. Certainly, no one who ever met her forgot her. She could be charming, affectionate, and immensely generous, but she was also judgemental and could be difficult in personal relationships, as a trail of broken friendships shows, not in that perhaps very different from many contemporaries in an age that prized individuality and even eccentricity.

In the end it is Harriet Martineau's work that counts, in itself and as a striking example of what a single woman could accomplish in unpropitious times. She herself said, in the *Daily News* obituary, that she worked well only within a limited range and had no originality of mind. But the limits were pretty widely extended, and the combination of talents and interests argue an originality in the whole that the parts might lack. Above all, she was a person of singular faithfulness, whatever small digressions may have appeared along the way, to a philosophical position and a political commitment that projected the assumptions of the 1820s and 1830s, with no small effect, into the more complex world of the late Victorians.

R. K. WEBB

Sources *Harriet Martineau's autobiography*, ed. M. W. Chapman, 3 vols. (1877) · R. K. Webb, *Harriet Martineau: a radical Victorian* (1960) · S. Hoecker-Drysdale, *Harriet Martineau, first woman sociologist* (1992) · *Harriet Martineau in the 'London Daily News': selected contributions, 1852–1866*, ed. E. Sanders Arbuckle (1994) · *Harriet Martineau's letters to Fanny Wedgwood*, ed. E. Sanders Arbuckle (1983) · *Harriet Martineau: selected letters*, ed. V. Sanders (1990) · V. Sanders, *Reason over passion: Harriet Martineau and the Victorian novel* (1986) · *Harriet Martineau on women*, ed. G. G. Yates (1985) · J. Martineau, and W. S. Coloe, abstracts of Harriet Martineau's letters, Harris Man. Oxf. · J. Martineau, autobiographical memoranda, Harris Man. Oxf. · U. Birm., Harriet Martineau MSS · U. Cal., Berkeley, Bancroft Library, R. S. Speck collection of Harriet Martineau · R. L. Wolff, *Strange stories and other explorations in Victorian fiction* (1971) · Boston PL, Weston MSS · d. cert. · T. M. Greenhow, *Medical report of the case of Miss H— M—* (1845) · T. S. Wells, 'Remarks on the case of Miss Martineau [pt 1]', *BMJ* (14 April 1877), 550 · T. S. Wells, 'Remarks on the case of Miss Martineau [pt 2]', *BMJ* (5 May 1877), 543

Archives Bodl. Oxf., letters · Boston PL, corresp. and papers · Cumbria AS, Carlisle, letters · Dorset RO, letters · Harris Man. Oxf., letters · Hunt. L., letters · TCD, letters · U. Birm. L., special collections department, corresp., literary MSS, and papers · Women's Library, London, corresp. · Wordsworth Trust, Dove Cottage, Grasmere, letters | Armitt Library, Ambleside, letters to Mrs Ogden and others · BL, letters to George Grote and Harriet Grote, Add. MS 46691 · BL, letters to George Holyoake, Add. MS 42726 · BL, letters to Macmillans, Add. MS 55253 · BL, corresp. with Florence Nightingale, Add. MS 45788 · BL, letters to Edward Smyth Pigott, RP629 [copies] · BL, corresp. with Francis Place, Add. MS 35149 · Bodl. Oxf., letters to John Chapman · Bodl. Oxf., letters to Edward Moxon · Harris Man. Oxf., letters to Philip Pearsall Carpenter · Harris Man. Oxf., letters to Helen Martineau · Harris Man. Oxf., corresp. with James Martineau · Harvard U., Houghton L., letters to Ralph Waldo Emerson · Herts. ALS, letters to Lord Lytton · Lambton Park, Chester-le-Street, co. Durham, letters to Lord Durham and Lady Durham · Lpool RO, letters to Anne Holt · NL Scot., corresp. with Samuel Brown · NL Scot., corresp. with George Combe · U. Cal., Berkeley, Bancroft Library, R. S. Speck collection · UCL, letters to Lord Brougham · UCL, letters to Society for the Diffusion of Useful Knowledge · UCL, letters to William Tait

Likenesses Finden, stipple, pubd 1833 (after M. Gillies), BM, NPG · R. Evans, oils, 1833–4, NPG · G. Richmond, chalk drawing, 1849, NPG [*see illus.*] · M. Bowness of Ambleside, carte-de-visite, NPG · D. Maclise, lithograph, BM, NPG; repro. in *Fraser's Magazine*, 6 (1833) · D. Maclise, pencil study, V&A · attrib. C. Osgood, Essex Institute, Salem, Massachusetts · A. Whitney, statue; formerly at Wellesley College, Massachusetts; [destroyed by fire, 1914] · death mask, Armitt Library, Ambleside, Cumbria · woodcut (after M. Bowness), NPG

Wealth at death under £10,000: probate, 5 Aug 1876, *CGPLA Eng. & Wales*

Martineau, James (1805–1900), Unitarian minister, was born in Magdalen Street, Norwich, on 21 April 1805, the seventh child of a middle-class merchant family. His father, Thomas (1764–1826), a cloth manufacturer, was a descendant of the surgeon Gaston Martineau, a Huguenot, who had settled in Norwich after the revocation of the edict of Nantes; his mother, Elizabeth Rankin (1770/71–1848), was the eldest daughter of the grocer and sugar refiner Robert Rankin of Newcastle upon Tyne. James's earliest memory at the age of four was of travelling to Newcastle to visit his grandfather, a monotonous journey in a post-chaise that lasted four days which was only lighted by the inspiring view of Durham Cathedral.

Childhood and education, 1805–1821 The house in which Martineau was born and brought up still stands in Magdalen Street, Norwich: although the ground floor, at the time of writing, is used as a second-hand shop, with a little imagination one can picture how this spacious building must have been in the opening years of the nineteenth century. A steady stream of visitors called, and intense discussions took place round the fireside in the evenings, especially on a Sunday, when Thomas Madge (1786–1870), the Unitarian minister, would call. The whole family worshipped at the nearby Octagon Chapel, and it was on this fellowship that its social and cultural life was centred. Built by the English presbyterian Dr John Taylor, the chapel had been founded on non-sectarian lines; however, by the early years of the nineteenth century it had moved, like most English presbyterian congregations, towards Unitarianism.

Martineau's home had its own invigorating atmosphere. There were eight children, and the older children played their part in the formal education of the younger: Thomas, the eldest, taught Latin, while Elizabeth taught French, and Henry writing and arithmetic. All this activity took place with the enthusiastic support of their parents, who knew the importance of discerning encouragement in education: Martineau later said of his father that he was always ready to strain every nerve to advance the education of his children. From 1815 to 1819 he was a day pupil at the public grammar school in the cathedral close, then under the headmastership of Edward Valpy (1754–1836). There were some 230 pupils in the school, several of whom later rose to prominence in civil and military life, including James Brooke, the raja of Sarawak, George Borrow, the writer, and Edward Rigby and John Dalrymple, who became eminent in the field of medicine. However, his schooldays were not happy as he suffered bullying; his intellectual impulses were frustrated, too, as the ethos of the school was centred on classics and grammar, while his interest lay in the direction of mathematics and science.

James Martineau (1805–1900), by George Frederic Watts, 1873 [replica]

His unhappiness came to an end through the intervention of his sister, Harriet *Martineau, who returned to Norwich full of enthusiasm for the classes of Dr Lant Carpenter (1780–1840) that she had attended in Bristol. Thomas Martineau provided the 100 guineas a year to meet the fees and enrolled James in Carpenter's school.

Carpenter carried his wide range of interests with him into the classroom: he was a man of the world who read the daily papers to the pupils around the dinner table and kept them in touch with the parliamentary debates. He encouraged his pupils to start their own debating society and to care for the poor from their own funds. He laid great stress on moral and religious education, and introduced his pupils to contemporary biblical criticism. The school curriculum at Bristol included lessons in science, history, geography, and in the Greek Testament, as well as in classics and mathematics. This curriculum widened Martineau's horizons and gave him a foundation which enabled him to cope with the scientific revolution of the nineteenth century. Even more important than the subject matter and the patterns of thought developed at Bristol was the immediate influence of the man: Lant Carpenter was both a deeply religious man and a profound thinker, and his spirit stayed with Martineau for the rest of his life.

Training and early ministry, 1821–1828 On the completion of Martineau's schooling in the autumn of 1821 the family took a holiday in the Lake District, staying with friends near Cockermouth. The view of the distant mountains with their sunny knolls and dark hollows filled James with wonder. It awakened within him a love of mountaineering and, like many others of his time, he found a new world in the beauty of nature. At the end of the holiday he travelled to Derby to begin his training with James Fox at his engineering works. Although Fox was a kind and practical man, he was unable to give Martineau a satisfactory theoretical and mathematical grounding for his mechanical interests. This disappointment, combined with the death of his cousin Henry Turner, the young minister of High Pavement Church, Nottingham, and his courtship of Helen Higginson (1804–1877), daughter of the Unitarian minister Edward Higginson and his wife, Sarah (née Marshall), channelled Martineau's aspirations in the direction of the ministry. In 1822, against the advice of his father (who had warned him he would face poverty but nevertheless found the money to support him), he entered Manchester College, York, to train for the ministry.

The members of the Manchester College staff, Charles Wellbeloved (1769–1858), John Kenrick (1788–1877), and William Turner (1788–1853), were all competent men. It was the admirable teaching of Turner, in particular, which gave fresh impetus to Martineau's mathematical studies and enabled him to achieve his ambition of reading Newton's *Principia*. Martineau also greatly admired the principal, Charles Wellbeloved, and from him received not only the principles of sound biblical criticism but also an overriding view of the catholicity of the church. John Kenrick had just returned from studying with F. D. Schleiermacher, the father of modern German theology, in Berlin, and shared with his pupils the results of his recently gained knowledge; he and Martineau became lifelong friends. In addition to his studies Martineau joined a college missionary society, which went regularly to visit the village of Welburn, almost at the gates of Castle Howard. The small congregation to which they preached so increased that the students decided to build a chapel: Martineau was appointed the architect and on one visit to oversee the building work he met Sydney Smith, the local incumbent and a famous wit, observing the rising walls. In order to deflect Smith's good-natured grumbling Martineau pointed out that without a chapel the people for whom it was meant would go nowhere; Smith replied, 'So long as you only gather and tame my refractory parishioners, I shall look upon you as my curates, to get people ready for me' (Martineau, 'Biographical memoranda').

While Martineau was still a student his father died, leaving the family with great financial burdens; through the generosity of the college James was awarded a bursary which enabled him to complete his five years' study at York. In 1827 the illness of Lant Carpenter and his consequent absence from the school resulted in Mrs Carpenter inviting Martineau to Bristol to take charge of the fourteen pupils. He undertook this post for one year, and it provided him with two important opportunities. The first came through the good offices of Dr James C. Pritchard, who introduced Martineau to a private philosophical society. He looked back on the evening meetings of the society as one of the most precious passages of his life, when he heard able local men discuss the newest questions of the time and the greatest questions of all time. This society broadened his outlook and prepared him for the part he was later to play in the famous Metaphysical Society, and for his defence of theism against those who propounded a purely mechanical evolutionary theory. The second opportunity was that of hearing the great Baptist preacher Robert Hall (1764–1831) on Thursday evenings at Broadmead Chapel. His style of preaching, which captivated Martineau, influenced the congregation not by addressing them, but rather by thinking aloud before them. Martineau subsequently adopted a similar form of preaching himself, composing thoughtful meditations, and kept to it in spite of later persuasions by Francis Newman (1805–1897) to change and become a more popular preacher.

Dublin, 1828–1832 In the summer of 1828, after one year in Bristol, Martineau accepted the post of junior minister of Eustace Street Presbyterian meeting-house, Dublin, with the Revd Joseph Hutton (1765–1856), grandfather of Richard Holt Hutton (1826–1897), as his colleague. At the end of that year, on 18 December, he married Helen Higginson, and settled down to his teaching and ministerial work with the hope of a long and fruitful stay in Dublin. In the event his ministry lasted under four years, owing to his refusal to accept any part of the *regium donum*, the annual grant bestowed by parliament on presbyterian ministers. During his Dublin years he published *A Collection of Hymns for Christian Worship* (1831), containing 273 hymns, five of which were by his sister Harriet. Martineau drew his hymns from a wider spiritual tradition than had many previous compilers of Unitarian and non-subscribing presbyterian hymnbooks, with the hymns of Isaac Watts and Bishop Reginald Heber well represented. His residence in Dublin coincided with Daniel O'Connell's political agitation, and although Martineau was ministering to a protestant congregation he made several friends among the Catholic population, including the old Irish patriot Hamilton Rowan (1751–1834), in whose home he was often a guest. His sympathy with the Roman Catholic population caused him some difficulty: he signed a petition for Catholic emancipation, only to be told that ministers should not meddle in politics by a member of his congregation who, nevertheless, thought it was Martineau's duty to sign on the other side.

In the summer of 1832 the Martineaus left their first home, said farewell to their friends, stood in silence together in the French churchyard by the little grave of their first-born child, a daughter, Helen Elizabeth, and then crossed the sea with their surviving son and daughter to enter upon the most formative and productive period of Martineau's life.

Liverpool, 1832–1857 On his arrival in Liverpool, Martineau took up the position of minister of Paradise Street Chapel in June 1832. It was here that he formed a close association with J. H. Thom (1808–1894), Charles Wicksteed (1810–1885) of Liverpool, and John James Tayler (1797–1869) of Manchester. They were aided by Joseph Blanco White

(1775–1841), the turbulent Spanish Roman Catholic priest who became an Anglican and member of the Oriel College senior common room before being introduced by Thom into Liverpool Unitarian circles. For several years, while editing the *Prospective Review*, the four friends met once a month at Tayler's home, dining, spending the evening together, and often staying overnight. These were memorable occasions for all of them, and they interacted to stimulate and promote one another's thoughts.

In 1836 Martineau published a remarkable little book under the title *The Rationale of Religious Inquiry*, which went into four editions and was republished after his death under the title *What is Christianity?* The impact of this book was extensive. It was read and reviewed in America, and in England it was seen as an important attempt to examine Christianity philosophically. In the preface Martineau maintained that religion and philosophy had traditionally occupied different spheres with little or no contact between them, except in the field of natural religion. Martineau published this volume in the hope of providing an improved philosophical method for investigating Christianity, namely, that religious truth must not be contrary to reason. Martineau was not advocating that the Christian faith must lie within the limits of reason, but rather that, although it goes beyond what reason can prove, it does not go against reason. He expressed this in the phrase, 'A divine right, therefore, to dictate a perfectly unreasonable faith cannot exist.' In the development of Martineau's religious thought there were two movements taking place at this time: one was towards a more critical approach to the scriptures and religious tradition, while the other was towards a religion based on feeling which emphasized worship and devotion to Christ. Both these elements can be found within *The Rationale*, although the critical element dominates. The Wesleyan Conference meeting the following year was urged to make special appointments to Liverpool to refute the brilliant Martineau.

The Liverpool controversy of 1839 and the removal of Manchester College from York back to Manchester had a profound effect on Martineau's thought. The Liverpool controversy was occasioned by the Revd Fielding Ould and twelve other Anglican clergymen inviting, by poster and in the press, the Unitarians of the city to attend a series of lectures in which the errors of their beliefs would be exposed. On the Unitarian side Martineau, together with John Hamilton, Thom, and Henry Giles, accepted the invitation and issued a reciprocal invitation to the Anglicans of Liverpool to hear a reply to each lecture. Martineau gave five of these replies; his papers were well-argued and closely reasoned treatises, containing many of the ideas which came to fruition in his later works. At the end of the controversy Blanco White declared that the Unitarians were the outright winners. The controversy caused Martineau to set down systematically his developing views on a wide variety of theological issues. His lectures show that he had abandoned the idea of revelation as a body of truth, the authenticity of which was assured by miracles, and had replaced it by the view that revelation had to be received by the individual soul, and that its appeal was not to external authorities but to the conscience and the affections. Miracles were still important, but they were performed not to guarantee truth, which could be verified internally, but as a compassionate act of Christ in response to human need. By the close of the Liverpool controversy Martineau had taken his first tentative steps against philosophical necessity, which was one of Joseph Priestley's favourite doctrines.

The removal of Manchester College from York back to Manchester in 1840 provided an opportunity to enlarge the institution: Martineau was appointed professor of mental and moral philosophy and logic, while at the same time he continued his ministerial duties in Liverpool. The preparation of the lectures for his new appointment caused him finally to break away from the influences of Priestly in regard to his biblical and philosophical thought. In his new post he enjoyed close friendships with his colleagues John James Tayler and Francis Newman, the gifted brother of John Henry Newman. During his remaining seventeen years in Liverpool, Martineau wrote some forty-five major articles and contributed to several journals, as well as producing his outstanding hymnbook *Hymns for the Christian Church and Home* (1840) and his fine collection of sermons *Endeavours after the Christian Life* (1843). The former, which drew from a wide variety of Christian spirituality, exerted a powerful influence on English Unitarianism, becoming the most widely used hymnbook in the movement. The latter had a powerful influence outside English Unitarianism: avidly read by Anglicans such as John William Colenso and F. W. Robertson, its ideas and images were often reproduced in their sermons. Also during his ministry at Liverpool, Martineau started his classes for young ladies. Among those to benefit from his teaching were the Winkworth sisters, Catherine (1827–1878) and Suzanna (1820–1884), and Anna Swanwick (1813–1899), who felt grateful for the rest of her life to Martineau for his assistance and guidance in her youth; their friendship continued over the following sixty-five years.

During the 1840s Martineau began to feel that the Paradise Street church building—conducive to eighteenth-century rationalism—was inappropriate for his new theological emphasis. Like the members of the Oxford Movement, he too had been affected by romanticism. Hope Street Church was accordingly built in 1848 to rehouse the congregation: Thomas Barry and William Brown designed a beautiful Victorian-Gothic building, with statues, stained-glass windows, chair pews, and a high altar that was never used but which helped to create an atmosphere of medieval gloom, conducive to Martineau's etherial voice and aesthetic sermons.

While Hope Street Church was being built Martineau took his family for a prolonged stay in Germany, and spent several months studying in Berlin, reading the works of Plato and Hegel, as well as observing the great democratic revolutions. He also attended several lecture courses, including those of Professor Trendelenburgh, the well-known German theologian. He likened the German experience to passing through a second education. From that time onwards he read German theological journals and kept abreast of German scholarship. He later said that in Berlin he found only one professor who thoroughly understood Hegel, but sadly no one could understand that professor. He returned to Liverpool in 1849, and preached the 'hauntingly beautiful' sermon 'Watchnight Lamps' at the opening of the new church.

The year 1851 saw the end of Martineau's long and happy relationship with his sister Harriet. The two had always been close to each other; as children they had enjoyed each other's company and as young people they had undertaken walking tours together in Scotland. It was James who had originally encouraged Harriet to start writing articles. Early in 1851 Harriet and her friend Henry George Atkinson published *Letters on the Laws of Man's Nature and Development*; in May, in the *Prospective Review*, James savaged the book, the main criticism being that it propounded atheism, not in the sense of a denial of a first cause, but the denial that the first cause was God as the intending and governing mind. This hurtful review destroyed the close relationship between James and Harriet, and although they occasionally met they never again corresponded with each other. In his 'Biographical memoranda' James devoted several pages to vindicating his position, but even he admitted that the consequences of the review caused an 'epoch' in his life.

London, 1853–1885 In 1853 Manchester College faced a financial crisis, and after a long and bitter struggle it was decided to move the college to London which, it was argued, would provide better scientific and literary opportunities for students and staff. Martineau retained his post within the college, and for the next four years commuted to London to deliver his lectures. In 1857 John James Tayler was appointed principal of the college and Martineau appointed a full-time tutor. For one and a half years he devoted himself solely to his academic work, but with the death of Edward Tagart in 1858 he combined his post with that of joint minister of Little Portland Chapel. The removal of the college to London was also the occasion of the appointment of James's eldest son, Russell *Martineau (1831–1898), to Manchester College as lecturer in Hebrew on the recommendation of the German theologian H. G. A. Ewald. Russell was promoted to professor in 1866, but had to retire only a few years later owing to his epilepsy.

It was during James Martineau's London years that he entered into his major controversies. He disliked confrontation and often felt himself badly equipped for it; but he was drawn into controversy, and even seemed to attract it and create it. In 1862 he engaged in a major debate with Herbert Spencer on agnosticism, following the publication of Spencer's *First Principles*. In October of that year Martineau wrote an article for the *National Review* under the title 'Science, nescience and faith', which was chiefly a criticism of Spencer's work and one of the best apologies of the nineteenth century for the theistic position.

In the spring of 1866 the chair of philosophy of mind and logic at University College, London, became vacant;

Martineau's name was put forward and his candidature received the recommendation of the senate. However, the preference of the senate was overturned by the college council through a coalition of those who wanted no minister of religion to be appointed and those who wanted only a minister of the Church of England. The episode caused Augustus De Morgan (1806–1871) to resign his chair of mathematics at University College; he later wrote to Martineau:

> I came here on the understanding that a man in office may have any theology provided he sticks to his own subject in his class; if the stipulation is to be that a man shall have no theology, I am just as much disqualified as you; and the College instead of respecting conscience, snubs conscience. (Martineau, 'Biographical memoranda')

Croom Robertson, who was appointed to the chair, went on to exert a powerful influence on philosophy in England, while Martineau returned to Manchester College, of which institution he became principal in 1869, and from where he launched his assaults on the materialism of John Tyndall.

Societies and controversies In 1867 Martineau and J. J. Tayler hosted a meeting in the library of Manchester College to launch the Free Christian Union, a society aimed at promoting Christian unity between liberal Christian churches and individuals. The union called on those who loved God and their fellow men to a common action and a search for divine truth, based on religious sympathies rather than theological agreement. Its members included Henry Sidgwick, the Cambridge philosopher, and Kegan Paul, the vicar of Sturminster Marshall; Tayler had also persuaded Ananase Coquerel of the French Protestant church to be actively involved. At the end of the first year the movement gained considerable momentum, but with Tayler's death in 1869 was removed the one person who had the ability to hold the enterprise together.

In the year following the formation of the Free Christian Union, Martineau was involved in the foundation of the Metaphysical Society. The original plan drawn up by Dean Arthur Penrhyn Stanley, Archbishop Manning, and James Knowles was to form a society of believers to discuss questions of theology and to refute agnostics. When Martineau was approached to join, he said that he had no wish to belong to a society of 'gnostics to put down agnostics'. At his insistence the plan was enlarged to form a society comprehending all schools of thought, theological and scientific. Its membership included John Tyndall, Thomas Huxley, and Alfred Tennyson. In this influential society he formed many friendships.

The nineteenth-century debate on science and religion is often portrayed by the famous confrontation between Thomas Huxley and Samuel Wilberforce which took place in the University Museum in Oxford. Although this encounter captured the public imagination, it can be argued that the major battle of the conflict between science and religion was not centred on Huxley and Wilberforce but on the debate of 1872 between James Martineau and Professor John Tyndall. Martineau's campaign was largely defensive and concentrated on two fundamental issues: he argued against matter being self-sufficient, able to create and construct out of its own necessity, and thus removing the need for God, and he vigorously opposed religion relinquishing to science the intellectual sphere and thus being confined to the emotional realm of human nature. It was Martineau's defence of religion against the claims of some scientists that caused Owen Chadwick to remark that there came a time after Darwin when even orthodox churchmen came to look upon Martineau as a champion of faith.

Later life and assessment Martineau retired from Manchester College in 1885 and over the following eight years wrote several important books, including *The Seat of Authority in Religion* (1890), *Types of Ethical Theory* (1895), and *A Study of Religion* (1888). However, some of his work was already appearing dated by the time it came out in print; this was in part due to the fact that he was writing up and publishing his four-year cycle of lectures. His major contribution was not his many articles on science and religion, nor his ethical or theological writing, but his devotional writing. His two volumes of sermons, *Endeavours after the Christian Life* (1840) and *Hours of Thought on Sacred Things* (1876–9), still convey many splendid insights into the human condition and contain ideas and imagery that will continue to speak to other generations as vividly as they did to his own. His prayers also have a lasting quality. He both edited and wrote large sections of *Common Prayer for Christian Worship* (1862); and here for the first time, it has been suggested by Horton Davies, nonconformity produced a liturgical editor of rare genius. His *Home Prayers* (1892) contain deeply devotional and beautiful expressions of the Christian faith; these prayers have often been reprinted in other anthologies, sometimes without acknowledgement.

Martineau was too broad-minded to belong to any school. Eclectic by nature, he gathered ideas from any source that appealed to his own intellectual and emotional character. His philosophical theology was shaped more by his personality and the movements of the age than by specific adherence to one particular school of thought. He in himself was a record of nineteenth-century theology; born only three years after the death of Kant and living on into the twentieth century, he engaged or commented on almost every theological personality or movement of the age, as can be seen from his volumes of collected *Essays, Reviews and Addresses* (1890–91). Although a lifelong Unitarian, he rarely felt at home in Unitarianism and indeed disliked the name being applied to a church or a movement, believing that it should be kept to describe individual belief. Had he been an Anglican his influence would have been greater, but the Church of England was too narrow for him: Stopford Brooke once asked Dean Stanley if the Church of England would broaden sufficiently to allow James Martineau to be made archbishop of Canterbury. During the course of his long life Martineau often changed his mind. But this tall, wiry theologian, who enjoyed mountaineering and who had little small talk, was large-hearted and would give unstintingly of his time and effort to everyone who sought his help.

James Martineau died at 35 Gordon Square, London, on 11 January 1900 and was buried in Highgate cemetery. Of his eight children, four daughters, including Edith *Martineau, and one son survived him.   RALPH WALLER

Sources R. Waller, 'James Martineau', PhD diss., King's Lond., 1986 · R. Waller, 'James Martineau: the development of his religious thought', *Truth, liberty, religion: essays celebrating two hundred years of Manchester College*, ed. B. Smith (1986), 227–64 · E. Carpenter, *James Martineau* (1905) · J. Drummond and C. B. Upton, *James Martineau, life and letters* (1901) · R. Waller, 'James Martineau revisited', *Faith and Freedom*, 38 (1985) · R. K. Webb, 'James Martineau', *The encyclopaedia of religion*, ed. M. Eliade, 9 (1987), 229–30 · *DNB* · J. Martineau, 'Biographical memoranda', Harris Man. Oxf. · A. Hall, *James Martineau: the story of his life* (1906)

Archives DWL, lecture notes · Harris Man. Oxf., corresp., literary MSS, and papers · St Hilda's College, Oxford, lecture notes | BL, letters to Sir A. Wills, Add. MS 63084 · Co-operative Union, Holyoake House, Manchester, letters to G. J. Holyoake · Devon RO, letters to W. I. E. Hickson etc. · DWL, letters to Thomas Chatfeild Clarke; letters to A. Lazenby; letters to Priestly Prime; letters to W. G. Tarrant · Hunt. L., letters mainly to Frances Power · Trinity Cam., letters to Henry Sidgwick · U. Nott. L., letters to William Hugh

Likenesses silhouette, 1813, Harris Man. Oxf. · bust, *c.*1845, Harris Man. Oxf. · C. Agar, oils, 1846, Harris Man. Oxf. · E. Armitage, group portrait, pencil study, 1870, DWL · G. F. Watts, oils, 1873, Harris Man. Oxf. · G. F. Watts, oils, replica, 1873, NPG [*see illus.*] · E. R. Mullins, terracotta bust, 1877, DWL · H. R. Hope-Pinker, statue, 1878, Harris Man. Oxf. · C. Martineau, pencil drawing, 1887, NPG; related silverpoint drawing, DWL · H. Allingham, drawing, 1891, Harris Man. Oxf. · S. P. Hall, pencil drawing, 1893, NPG · H. R. Hope-Pinker, marble statue, 1897, Harris Man. Oxf. · C. Martineau, pastel drawing, 1899, DWL · E. Armitage, group portrait, fresco, DWL · Elliott & Fry, carte-de-visite, NPG · H. R. Hope-Pinker, plaster statuette, NPG; related statuettes, DWL · C. Martineau, pastels, Harris Man. Oxf. · E. Martineau, watercolour drawing, DWL · P. Pieraccini, plaster bust, DWL · chromolithograph, NPG · relief bust on memorial, Rochdale

Wealth at death £29,871 16s. 11d.: probate, 27 March 1900, *CGPLA Eng. & Wales*

Martineau, Jane (1812–1882), college administrator, was born in London, the first child of the seven children of John Martineau (1789–1831), sugar refiner and mechanical engineer, and his wife, Jane (1792–1868), daughter of Samuel Taylor. She was educated at Miss Byerley's school at Stratford upon Avon. In 1831 the family emigrated to America, but was forced to return to London following John Martineau's death on board ship. The family was very close, and the sisters who remained unmarried, Anna, Clara, and Jane, lived together long after their mother's death.

Jane Martineau continued her education as an adult, attending classes with her mother, Anna, and Clara at the ladies' college in Bedford Square, London, which was founded by her friend and fellow Unitarian Elisabeth Jesser Reid. She registered for courses at Bedford College in astronomy, drawing, English, geography, mathematics, moral philosophy, and political economy between 1849 and 1855. She also took lessons in bookkeeping to help her manage the family accounts. She organized the family's correspondence and arranged all the details of their trips abroad. She also acted as honorary secretary at a school in Harp Alley, Farringdon Street, in London.

All of this proved useful training for Jane Martineau's

Jane Martineau (1812–1882), by unknown photographer

work at Bedford College, and showed that she had a talent for administration. Her involvement in the management of the college dated from its foundation in 1849 when she became, along with her mother and Clara, one of the Lady Visitors who chaperoned students and helped run the college. She represented the Lady Visitors on the council from 1852 to 1855, and her administrative skills and commitment to the college were recognized in 1855 when she was appointed honorary secretary. She held this post, on an unpaid basis as with all her work for the college, until her retirement in 1876. Contemporaries commented on her attention to detail: her account and minute books were always accurate and impressively neat. Rachel Notcutt noted that 'a blot or an erasure was an offence to her' (Notcutt, 5). She demanded the same high standards from others, which led a friend to tell Elisabeth Reid that 'Jane is such a tyrant I dare not disobey her' (Tuke, 104).

Elisabeth Reid made Jane Martineau one of the three Reid trustees in 1860, thus increasing her power within the college. She now had control over the two trust funds which Elisabeth Reid had set up to run the college's boarding house and to provide money for women's education. She also became part owner of the leases on the college's buildings in Bedford Square and Grenville Street. The trustees, who were required to be single women, assumed responsibility for the governance of the college for a year after Elisabeth Reid's death, steering it through a series of changes designed to improve the standard of education offered. Jane Martineau collaborated with Elizabeth Bostock, one of the other trustees, in 1868 to force the closure of the school attached to the college, allowing the college to concentrate on higher education for women. The trustees realized Elisabeth Reid's aim of ensuring that the college was run by women, for women.

As well as being an able administrator, Jane Martineau showed a great interest in students' academic progress.

Two former Bedford College students recalled how on one occasion she gave up an hour a week to help students who were struggling in Richard Holt Hutton's arithmetic class (Armstrong and Jecks, 31). She devoted her life to the cause of women's education, and Rachel Notcutt commented that when she died she left behind her 'a fine example of a well-spent life' (Notcutt, 5). An acute attack of bronchitis led to her death at her home, 11 Craven Hill, Hyde Park, London, on 2 January 1882.   SOPHIE BADHAM

Sources R. Notcutt, *Bedford College Magazine* (March 1901), 4–5 · M. J. Tuke, *A history of Bedford College for Women, 1849–1937* (1939) · F. Armstrong and A. Jecks, 'Recollections of the earliest boarding house of the college', *Bedford College Magazine* (June 1900), 31 · Royal Holloway College, Egham, Surrey, Elisabeth Jesser Reid MSS · Bedford College register of students, Royal Holloway College, Egham, Surrey · D. Martineau, *Notes on the pedigree of the Martineau family* (1907) · d. cert.
Archives Royal Holloway College, Egham, Surrey, Bedford College MSS; Elisabeth Jesser Reid MSS
Likenesses photograph, repro. in Tuke, *History of Bedford College for Women* · photograph, Royal Holloway College, Egham, Surrey [*see illus.*]
Wealth at death £13,780 13s. 9d.: probate, 31 Jan 1882, *CGPLA Eng. & Wales*

Martineau, Robert Braithwaite (1826–1869), genre and portrait painter, was born on 19 January 1826 in Guilford Street, London, the fifth son of eight children of Philip Martineau (1791–1860), solicitor and taxing master to the court of chancery, and his wife, Elizabeth Frances (*d.* 1875), daughter of Dr Robert *Batty of Fairlight Lodge, Hastings. The family was descended from Gaston Martineau, a French Huguenot refugee and surgeon, who fled to England following the revocation of the edict of Nantes in 1685, settling in Norwich. Martineau's mother was an accomplished watercolour painter; several volumes describing her European travels with her brother were published, illustrated with engravings from their sketches.

Martineau was educated at University College School, London, and followed his two older brothers into the law. He was articled to a firm of solicitors from 1842 to 1846 but decided to pursue an artistic career. He studied first at Cary's drawing school, and in 1848, at the age of twenty-two, entered the Royal Academy Schools, where he was awarded a silver medal for drawing. About 1851 he asked William Holman Hunt, a member of the Pre-Raphaelite Brotherhood, if he could become his pupil. Hunt agreed, after warning him of the difficulties of making a living from art and being assured that: 'To him [Martineau] the lucrativeness of the pursuit was not at first a vital question, which removed the scruples I had against anyone native born needing to live by his profession from becoming a painter in this country' (Hunt, 1.301–2). It is clear that Martineau had a sufficient private income to support himself, and only when he married at the age of thirty-nine did he need to earn a living from his art. His wife, whom he married in 1865, was Maria (*b.* 1840), eldest daughter of Henry Wheeler of Bolingbroke House, Wandsworth, London. They had three children, the youngest of whom, Helen (1868–1950), was the author of several articles on

her father's work, and bequeathed most of the works in her possession to public collections on her death.

In 1852 Martineau exhibited for the first time at the Royal Academy, showing an illustration of a scene from Charles Dickens's *The Old Curiosity Shop* entitled *Kit's Writing Lesson* (Tate collection), painted in Holman Hunt's studio. Martineau exhibited ten further works at the Royal Academy before his early death in 1869. These works included illustrations from literature such as *Katherine and Petruchio* (exh. RA, 1855; Ashmolean Museum, Oxford) from Shakespeare's *The Taming of the Shrew*, and *Picciola* (exh. RA, 1856; Tate collection) from Saintine's novel of 1837; genre scenes such as *The Last Chapter* (exh. RA, 1863; City of Birmingham Art Gallery), showing a young woman finishing her novel by firelight, and *The Allies* (exh. RA, 1861; Johannesburg Art Gallery); and portraits such as *Bertie, Son of Hubert Martineau*, the artist's nephew (exh. RA, 1867; priv. coll.) and *Portrait of Master Toke* (exh. RA, 1862).

However, the work for which Martineau is best-known is *The Last Day in the Old Home* (Tate collection) which was shown in the British picture galleries at the International Exhibition in South Kensington in 1862. These galleries were arranged as a major retrospective of British art from the time of Hogarth and *The Last Day in the Old Home* was, according to the artist William Bell Scott, one of the two 'most popular of all the thousands of works … shown in the International Exhibition' (Minto, 2.48)—the other was Ford Madox Brown's *The Last of England*. Its subject, an old and titled family brought to financial ruin by the gambling habits of the husband, was hugely popular with Victorian audiences who loved piecing together the narrative from the ample visual clues in such 'incident pictures'.

Martineau and Holman Hunt remained close friends, sometimes sharing studios or lodgings. Martineau was part of a lively artistic circle which included Hunt, Dante Gabriel Rossetti, Arthur Hughes, George Price Boyce, Edward Burne-Jones (whose wife, Georgiana, credits him with advising them that the Grange in Fulham, the Burne-Jones' home for thirty years, was available to let), Ford Madox Brown (Martineau modelled for the gentleman on horseback in Brown's *Work*), and Val Prinsep. He regularly attended the artistic and social gatherings at the Prinseps' home, Little Holland House in Kensington, as well as at Rossetti's house in Chelsea. William Michael Rossetti described him as 'a very sensible person, not given to much talk, and with a mind rather steady going than lively, highly trusty and well principled, and worthy of the utmost regard' (Rossetti, *Reminiscences*, 2.158), and in a private letter he was described as a man 'of whom nothing but good is thought and said by all who know him' (A. J. Lewis to A. Wheeler, 13 Sept 1864, priv. coll.). He was a founder member and treasurer of the short-lived Hogarth Club (1858–61), where *The Last Day in the Old Home* was shown privately before the International Exhibition, and a member of the Cosmopolitan Club on Charles Street, where an exhibition of his paintings and drawings was held shortly after his death in 1869. In addition to his talents as a painter, he had a natural gift for music and composed several small studies. He also had a wonderful sense of humour and fun, as is evident from his private correspondence.

Martineau's pictures were purchased by some of the foremost patrons of the day, including James Leathart, Thomas Fairbairn, and Kirkman Hodgson. He was working on a large canvas, *Christians and Christians* (Walker Art Gallery, Liverpool), possibly for Fairbairn, at the time of his early death. Martineau died at Lancaster Lodge, Campden Hill, London, on 13 February 1869 from heart disease brought on by earlier bouts of rheumatic fever. He was buried in Kensal Green cemetery.

Appreciation of Martineau's work has fallen and risen with the popularity of Victorian painting. *The Last Day in the Old Home*, so universally popular in 1862 that, according to an article in 1899, it 'made a triumphant progress through the country after the close of the Great Exhibition' (*Cornhill Magazine*, 6 Jan–June 1899, 183), was by 1951 described as 'no more than a painstaking inventory of a Victorian drawing room' (C. A. Bertram, *A Century of British Painting*, 1951, 35). In the 1990s this painting is again appreciated for the insights it gives into Victorian social values, and the realistic manner in which it is painted.

PENELOPE GURLAND

Sources P. Gurland, 'Robert Braithwaite Martineau's *The last day in the old home*', MA diss., Courtauld Inst., 1986 · C. A. Crofton, *Pedigrees of the Martineau family* (1972) · H. Martineau, 'Robert Braithwaite Martineau: a follower of the Pre-Raphaelites', *The Connoisseur*, 90 (1942), 97–101 · *The Athenaeum* (20 Feb 1869), 281 · *Art Journal*, 31 (1869), 117 · *DNB* · Graves, *RA exhibitors* · H. Martineau, 'Echo of a Pre-Raphaelite painter', *The Studio*, 134 (1947), 78–9 · H. Martineau, 'A Pre-Raphaelite painter', *The Studio*, 87 (1924), 207–8 · F. T. Palgrave, *Handbook to the fine art collections in the International Exhibition of 1862* (1862) [exhibition catalogue, International Exhibition, London, 1862] · *Works by the late Robert B. Martineau* (1869) [exhibition catalogue, Cosmopolitan Club, London, 1869] · *Works by the late R. B. Martineau* (1922) [exhibition catalogue, Brook Street Art Gallery, London, 10–23 Jan 1922] · D. Cherry, 'The Hogarth Club', *Burlington Magazine*, 122 (1980), 237–44 · W. H. Hunt, *Pre-Raphaelitism and the Pre-Raphaelite Brotherhood*, 2 vols. (1905) · G. Burne-Jones, *Memorials of Edward Burne-Jones*, 2 vols. (1904) · E. Burne-Jones, *The Little Holland House album, 1859* (1981) · F. M. Hueffer [F. M. Ford], *Ford Madox Brown: a record of his life and work* (1896) · W. M. Rossetti, *Some reminiscences*, 2 vols. (1906) · W. M. Rossetti, ed., *Ruskin, Rossetti, Pre-raphaelitism: papers, 1854–1862* (1899) · *Autobiographical notes of the life of William Bell Scott: and notices of his artistic and poetic circle of friends, 1830 to 1882*, ed. W. Minto, 2 vols. (1892)

Archives FM Cam. · priv. coll., letters · V&A

Likenesses F. M. Brown, group portrait, oils, 1852–65 (*Work*), Man. City Gall. · W. H. Hunt, red and black chalk drawing on toned paper, 1860, Walker Art Gallery, Liverpool · J. M. Cameron, photograph, priv. coll. · W. H. Hunt, group portrait, oils (*London bridge at night. rejoicings in honour of the marriage of the prince and princess of Wales, 10th March 1863*), AM Oxf. · photographs, priv. colls.

Wealth at death under £3000: administration, 17 April 1869, CGPLA Eng. & Wales

Martineau, Russell (1831–1898), Hebraist and librarian, was born on 18 January 1831 in Dublin, the eldest son of James *Martineau (1805–1900), Unitarian minister, and Helen (1804–1877), eldest daughter of Edward Higginson. He was educated at home and in Germany before entering University College, London, where he gained a BA degree in 1850 and an MA in classics in 1854. However, his London affiliation was punctuated by studies at the universities of Berlin (whence his family had temporarily moved) and Göttingen, where he studied under Heinrich Ewald. He continued his studies during the years 1854–7, when he was employed as a private family tutor. By the time that he was appointed to the staff of the British Museum Library and to a lectureship in Hebrew at Manchester New College, London, in 1857, his linguistic accomplishments included Sanskrit, Arabic, and Persian, in addition to the classical languages and German.

It was typical of Martineau's all-round abilities that, though he was not employed in the British Museum in any area in which he had previously specialized, he none the less made a significant contribution to the work of the library; this was recognized by successive promotions until he reached the rank of assistant keeper in 1884. He retired from this post in 1896 in accordance with civil-service superannuation rules. At the library he specialized in early printed books: he collected first editions of Luther's works for the museum, contributed significantly to the scheme for cataloguing the library, and completed the heading 'Bible' in the catalogue.

Martineau's appointment to Manchester New College was on the recommendation of Heinrich Ewald, who was the colossus of German Old Testament scholarship at that time, and Martineau was promoted to full professor in 1866, resigning from the college in 1874. Because Manchester New College had a strong, though not exclusive, unitarian tradition, Martineau was able to teach the results of critical scholarship freely, and there was probably no other lecture room at that time in Britain where students were kept so well informed of the latest results of critical research. His lecture notes indicate a strong dependence upon Ewald's moderately critical position, though the researches of Bishop J. W. Colenso, which called into question the historical accuracy of some Old Testament narratives and which proposed radical theories of the authorship of biblical books, were carefully assessed. Martineau was a presenter of critical scholarship rather than an original contributor to it, and his importance in the development of critical scholarship in Britain lay in his translation work. He took responsibility for the English translation of the first two volumes of Ewald's *History of Israel* (1867) and advised on the translation of later volumes, as the initiator and financial supporter of the project, Charlotte Lupton, wished to remain anonymous. In 1877 he published *Mythology among the Hebrews*, a translation of a work by Ignaz Goldziher. He also worked on the textual criticism of the Song of Solomon, on which he published two books, in 1892 and 1896, reprinted from articles in the *American Journal of Philology*.

Martineau appears to have had a complex, almost contradictory character. On the one hand there is abundant evidence of his wide interests and talents, for, in addition to the accomplishments already mentioned, Martineau was an expert conchologist, an enthusiastic botanist, and a considerable musician, in which latter capacity he helped to edit and compose new tunes for his father's *Hymns of Praise and Prayer* (1876). He also contributed to James Murray's *New English Dictionary* and published notes on the pronunciation of English vowels in the seventeenth century. Yet he seems to have had few social graces and few friends. As a teacher he did not appreciate the limitations of his students and was more effective in informal situations than in the lecture hall. Increasingly bad health, which interrupted his normal work, left its mark upon his appearance, and he developed a speech impediment that hindered him from expressing his thoughts fluently. A tendency to epilepsy is mentioned. At the same time those who came to know him well appreciated his humour, warm-heartedness, and loyalty. Martineau married Frances (b. 1836/7), daughter of Edward Bailey, an ironmonger, on 26 March 1861, and they enjoyed a relationship of mutual support and deep affection. There were no children. Martineau's latter years were marked by declining health and he died at Glen View, Sidmouth, Devon on 14 December 1898. He was survived by his wife.

J. W. ROGERSON

Sources *The Inquirer* (24 Dec 1898) · *Christian Life* (24 Dec 1898) · R. Martineau, lecture notes, Harris Man. Oxf. · J. Rogerson, *Old Testament criticism in the nineteenth century: England and Germany* (1984) · *CGPLA Eng. & Wales* (1899)
Archives Harris Man. Oxf., J. Martineau MSS
Wealth at death £12,111 18s. 11d.: probate, 20 Feb 1899, *CGPLA Eng. & Wales*

Martineau, Sir Thomas (1828–1893), lawyer, was born on 4 November 1828 in Bristol Road, Edgbaston, Birmingham, the son of Robert Martineau, a manufacturer and prominent local figure, and his wife, Jane, daughter of Samuel Smith, another local industrialist. A descendant of a Huguenot family that had settled in Norwich during the late seventeenth century, Martineau was a nephew of the Revd James *Martineau and Harriet *Martineau. On the death of the latter he became sole literary executor and co-executor of her estate with his brother. Martineau grew up in and remained a prominent member of Birmingham's Liberal and Unitarian circle. He was educated at the Birmingham and Edgbaston proprietary school (1838–44), where he developed a close friendship with Alfred Wills, who later became a judge and well-known alpinist. At school they set up and ran a library, a magazine, and later a debating society.

Martineau left school in 1844 and was articled to Arthur Ryland, solicitor of Birmingham, and his mother's first cousin. From 1849 his legal education continued with Ryland's agents in London, Sharpe, Field & Co., and later in the chambers of the conveyancer, John Wilson, and the special pleader, T. H. Baylis. He was admitted in 1851 and immediately joined Ryland in partnership, the firm being known as Ryland and Martineau until the death of Ryland in 1877. Martineau succeeded his late partner to the prestigious post as law clerk of the Birmingham assay office. By this time he had achieved a high reputation in the local profession. However, it was not until this point in his career that he became fully active in the public life of Birmingham. Nevertheless, he had exhibited a keen interest in local affairs since the 1850s and had taken his first steps in the political and cultural life of the town. Soon after qualifying he became active in local Liberal politics, later

acting as an election agent. It was also at this time that Martineau was a member (and later president) of the Birmingham and Edgbaston Debating Society. It was through this society that he was to develop a friendship with Joseph Chamberlain. About the year 1860 he was elected to the council of the Birmingham and Midland Institute, which had been established by his partner, Ryland, in 1853. Martineau subsequently held office as honorary secretary and vice-president. In 1860 he married Emily, daughter of Timothy Kenrick, a hardware manufacturer of West Bromwich. Her sisters were married to Joseph Chamberlain and Charles Gabriel Beale.

In 1876, Martineau entered the town council as representative for the Edgbaston ward and began a notable municipal career, which illustrates well the important role of eminent solicitors in provincial public life. In 1883 he was elected alderman and in 1884 became mayor for the first time. He was re-elected in 1885 and again in 1886. In addition to being thrice mayor he served on a variety of committees, his legal knowledge and experience proving invaluable. Indeed, the three major improvement projects for which he became widely known saw a convergence of his professional and political interests and drew extensively on his professional skills. As chairman of the parliamentary committee in 1882 Martineau took responsibility for the Birmingham Consolidation Bill. This measure affecting the government of Birmingham engendered considerable local opposition which continued through the courts and both houses of parliament. Much of the parliamentary work fell to Martineau, which necessitated a stay in London of several weeks to monitor the progress of the bill and shepherd it through its various stages.

It was, perhaps, with the creation of Birmingham as an assize town and the erection of the Victoria Law Courts in Corporation Street that Martineau attracted most public recognition. As a member of the Birmingham Law Society he had been active in the promotion of an assize scheme and made his maiden speech in the town council on the subject. After much debate and several attempts, assize status was granted in 1884. Though assizes were commenced soon afterwards, it was not until 1887 that building work on the new courts was started. Queen Victoria laid the foundation stone during her jubilee year and was received by Martineau as mayor. Two days later, on 25 March 1887, the honour of a knighthood was conferred upon him at Windsor.

The third project with which Martineau was associated again drew heavily on his legal expertise and negotiating skills. The Birmingham water scheme required his attendance before the House of Commons select committee on the bill. He successfully piloted the bill through parliament in 1892, but was to die before the scheme was started.

Martineau was involved in many other local movements and aspects of civic life. He held positions on the governing bodies of numerous charitable, educational, and cultural organizations. He was appointed a borough justice in 1880 and acted regularly until his death. A keen gardener, he established the Gardeners' Association of which he was first president. Towards the end of his life he was president of the midland iron and steel wages board; a further recognition of his local prominence and abilities in arbitration and negotiation. In the late 1880s he served on the royal commission on market rights and tolls.

Martineau's health began to deteriorate in 1888, but he did not retire from practice until the beginning of 1893. He died on 28 July 1893 at his residence, West Hill, Augustus Road, Edgbaston; he was survived by his wife, Lady Martineau, and his children, Ernest and Clara.

ANDREW ROWLEY

Sources *Birmingham Faces and Places*, 2 (1889–90), 56–60 · *Edgbastonia*, 4 (1884), 1–4 · *Birmingham Daily Gazette* (29 July 1893) · *Law Journal* (5 Aug 1893), 550 · Boase, *Mod. Eng. biog.* · *Law Times* (5 Aug 1893), 335 · *CGPLA Eng. & Wales* (1893)
Likenesses H. von Herkomer, oils (after F. Holl), priv. coll. · F. Holl, oils, Birmingham Museums and Art gallery
Wealth at death £62,650 6s. 1d.: probate, 15 Aug 1893, *CGPLA Eng. & Wales*

Martins, Emmanuel Alhandu [Orlando] (1899–1985), actor, was born on 8 December 1899 in Lagos, Nigeria, the son of Emmanuel Akinola Martins and Madam Paula Idowu Soares. His paternal grandfather, a freed Portuguese slave, was a wood seller who was said to have lived to the age of one hundred and twenty. Orlando Martins was educated at the Eko Boys' High School in Lagos. He left in 1916 to work as a bookkeeper for a French firm. During the First World War his grandmother became a prisoner of war when the Germans held the Cameroons, and it was her suffering at German hands that caused him to give up his job in Africa and travel to London in 1917, hoping to join the British navy. He joined the merchant marine, serving until the end of the war.

Having settled in London in 1919, Martins made an early theatrical appearance in 1920 when the Diaghilev Ballet, led by Anna Pavlova, arrived in London and recruited him to appear as a Nubian slave. In 1983 he recalled: 'I hated the part, but as I was young and hungry, I had no other choice' (Folami, 21). Afterwards he survived by taking a variety of jobs. He was a porter at Billingsgate fish market; a wrestler known as Black Butcher Johnson; a snake charmer with Lord John Sanger's Circus; a night watchman; a kitchen porter; a road sweeper; and an extra in silent films.

In 1928 Martins joined the Mississippi Chorus of the musical *Show Boat* at the Theatre Royal, Drury Lane, and he later toured Britain with the production. He acted in two plays starring Paul Robeson: *Stevedore* (1935) and *Toussaint L'Ouverture* (1936), the latter written by the Trinidadian C. L. R. James and presented at the Westminster Theatre by the Stage Society. In 1939 he appeared in *Colony* for the left-wing Unity Theatre.

After playing a number of small roles in films, Martins played the role of the influential witch doctor Magole in the melodrama *Men of Two Worlds* (1946). At the time most critics considered this 'ground-breaking' film a sincere attempt at exploring the conflict between modern medicine and the power of African witch doctors. However, in spite of Thorold Dickinson's sensitive documentary-style

Emmanuel Alhandu Martins (1899–1985), by unknown photographer

direction, the film reflected a still condescending view of Africans.

Men of Two Worlds helped establish Martins as one of Britain's most sought-after character actors. One of his most popular roles was that of the Basuto warrior in *The Hasty Heart*, which he played on the London stage (1945) and on film (1949). Other London stage appearances included *Cry, the Beloved Country* at St Martin-in-the-Fields, Trafalgar Square (1954) and *The Member of the Wedding* at the Royal Court (1957). He first appeared on BBC television as early as 1937 and, among other roles, played the runaway slave Jim in the BBC's serialization of *Huckleberry Finn* (1952).

In British films of the 1950s Africa remained a colourful, exotic backdrop for white settlers or adventurers in dramas with titles such as *Where No Vultures Fly* (chosen for the 1951 royal film performance), *West of Zanzibar* (1954), *Simba* (1955), *Safari* (1956), and *Tarzan and the Lost Safari* (1957). Almost without exception these films provided Martins with employment, though he was invariably typecast as a friendly African native. Occasionally he played roles in a British setting, such as the nightclub doorman in *Good Time Girl* (1948) starring Jean Kent, and the barman in *Sapphire* (1959), but few of his film roles gave him any scope as an actor.

In 1959 Martins returned home to Lagos, Nigeria, and thereafter accepted only occasional acting assignments. Towards the end of his career he appeared in two films by Nigerian writers: Wole Soyinka's *Kongi's Harvest* (1970) and Chinua Achebe's *Things Fall Apart* (1971). In 1970 the British actors association, Equity, awarded him life honorary membership in recognition of his long career in British films. He had started as an extra in *If Youth but Knew* (1926) and continued into the mid-1960s with roles in *Sammy Going South* (chosen for the 1963 royal film performance) and *Mister Moses* (1965). In 1982 he was made a member of the order of the Niger (MON), and in 1983 the National Award in Theatre Arts was presented to him at an impressive ceremony at the University of Calabar, Nigeria, by the Society of Nigerian Theatre Artistes.

Martins died in Lagos, Nigeria, on 25 September 1985 and was buried at the Ikoyi cemetery in Lagos. 'Proudly', he had told his biographer, 'I am very very happy to say that I am one of the pioneers, if not *the* pioneer African film star, when it comes to representing Africans and Nigeria in particular in the film world' (Folami, 73).

STEPHEN BOURNE

Sources T. Folami, *Orlando Martins: the legend* (Lagos, 1983) · 'Let him blossom out … as Martins!', *The Cinema Studio* (Oct 1951) · E. M. Martins and P. Noble, interview, *Film Quarterly* (spring 1947) **Likenesses** photograph, priv. coll. [*see illus.*]

Martinus (*d.* 353/4), Roman administrator, was *vicarius* of the Britains, the head of the Roman civil administration: the 'vicar' or deputy of the praetorian prefects supervised the governors of the four provinces into which Roman Britain was now divided. Nothing is known of his origins or connections (the name is a common one), nor of his previous career. Only the manner of his death is known, in an episode recorded by the late-Roman historian Ammianus Marcellinus. After the death (on 10 August 353) of the western usurper, Magnentius, the legitimate emperor, Constantius II, sent a special emissary to Britain called Paulus (nicknamed the Chain) to arrest some officers who had supported Magnentius. When Paulus exceeded his instructions by making many other arrests, Martinus protested to him and threatened to resign. Paulus then threatened to arrest him as well (it is not recorded whether Martinus had been appointed by Magnentius or by Constantius), and Martinus drew his sword; but his 'failing hand' prevented him from striking a mortal wound, so he killed himself instead. Paulus returned to the imperial court with many prisoners who were subsequently condemned (Ammianus Marcellinus, 14.5.7–8). Since Ammianus calls them *ingenui* (gentry), it has been suggested that their fate is reflected in a decline of British towns and country houses (villas) after the mid-fourth century, but until this decline has been more closely dated and quantified, it would be unwise to attribute it to this single episode. None the less, the name of Martinus 'deserves to be remembered in Britain' (P. Salway, *Roman Britain*, 1981, 358).

R. S. O. TOMLIN

Sources Ammianus Marcellinus, *History*, ed. and trans. J. C. Rolfe, 3 vols., rev. edn (1971), 14.5.7–8 · A. H. M. Jones, J. R. Martindale, and J. Morris, *The prosopography of the later Roman empire*, 1: AD 260–395 (1971), 508, 565, 744–5 · A. R. Birley, *The fasti of Roman Britain* (1981), 321–2

Martival, Roger (*c.*1250–1330), bishop of Salisbury, was almost the last of a knightly family named from the Norman village of Martinvaast, near Cherbourg. On the death of his father, Sir Anketil de Martival, in 1274 he became lord of Noseley in Leicestershire. His father had endowed a chantry chapel in the manor house, which in the fourteenth century the son further endowed and converted into one of the earliest chantry colleges.

Roger Martival was born *c.*1250: he was a minor in December 1269 and in 1268 was presented, as an acolyte, to the rectory of Arnold, Nottinghamshire. He apparently used the rectory's income to support himself at Oxford University, where he studied under Gilbert Seagrave (*d.* 1312). At the university in 1274 he was a party to the terms of peace agreed between the northern and southern scholars. The claim that he was a fellow of Merton College rests on inadequate evidence. In 1280, as a master of arts, he was granted protection on going overseas, evidently to the University of Paris, where he was studying in 1282.

In 1286 or 1287 Oliver Sutton, bishop of Lincoln (*d.* 1299), collated Martival to the archdeaconry of Huntingdon and to the prebend of Sleaford. He apparently continued to teach and study at Oxford: in 1293, as a doctor of theology, he became chancellor of the university. He resigned the chancellorship in 1295, shortly after being collated to the archdeaconry of Leicester, which in turn he resigned in 1310 on being elected dean of Lincoln. Meanwhile he had been collated to the prebend of Netheravon in Salisbury Cathedral in 1298 by Bishop Simon Ghent (*d.* 1315), his predecessor both as chancellor of Oxford University and as bishop of Salisbury, and formerly a fellow archdeacon in Lincoln diocese. He was also prebendary of Flixton in Lichfield Cathedral from 1306 and, having resigned Arnold, was rector of Thurcaston, Leicestershire, until 1315. Lincoln chapter records show that after he had journeyed to the papal court in 1306–7, Martival was in residence at Lincoln for at least eight months in each year until 1315. As dean, he was in dispute with the chapter about the exercise of his jurisdiction; this was resolved in 1314, when Bishop John Dalderby (*d.* 1320) confirmed that the dean should act in principal matters only with the chapter's consent.

Martival was elected bishop of Salisbury on 11 June 1315. Although Thomas of Lancaster, his overlord at Noseley, was then powerful at court, the election was apparently made freely by the chapter of which he was a member, the last such election at Salisbury during the middle ages apart from that in 1417. A conscientious and effective diocesan, Martival played little part in national affairs, though he was appointed to the king's council in 1318 following the treaty of Leake between Edward II and Lancaster. In his fifteen years as bishop he appears to have been out of the diocese for a total of less than a hundred weeks, and nearly a third of that total was during 1318–19. He was active in consecrating churches, in attempting to persuade John XXII to moderate papal provisions, and in ordaining and augmenting vicarages. The novel arrangement of his registers reflects the efficiency of his diocesan administration and his pioneering activity in church court matters. His concern for the well-being of the cathedral was marked by his endowment of the choristers and the vicars-choral, and particularly by the formulation of his constitutions of 1319, fulfilling his predecessor's intention to ensure the observance of St Osmund's statutes. He died on 14 March 1330, and was buried in a tomb, which survives, on the north side of the cathedral presbytery.

C. R. ELRINGTON

Sources The registers of Roger Martival, bishop of Salisbury, 1315–1330, ed. K. Edwards, C. R. Elrington, S. Reynolds, and D. M. Owen, 4 vols. in 5 pts, CYS, 55, 57–8, 68 (1959–75) [esp. 'General introduction' by K. Edwards] · Emden, Oxf. · G. F. Farnham and A. H. Thompson, 'The manor of Noseley', Transactions of the Leicestershire Archaeological Society, 12 (1921–2), 214–71 · C. Wordsworth and D. H. Robertson, 'Salisbury choristers', Wiltshire Archaeological and Natural History Magazine, 48 (1937–9), 201–31, esp. 204–7 · C. Wordsworth and D. Macleane, eds., Statutes of Salisbury cathedral (1915) · K. Edwards, The English secular cathedrals in the middle ages: a constitutional study with special reference to the fourteenth century, 2nd edn (1967) · Fasti Angl., 1066–1300, [Lincoln] · Fasti Angl., 1066–1300, [Salisbury] · Fasti Angl., 1300–1541, [Lincoln] · Fasti Angl., 1300–1541, [Salisbury] · Fasti Angl., 1300–1541, [Coventry] · J. Nichols, The history and antiquities of the county of Leicester, 2/2 (1798), 739–40 · J. Nichols, The history and antiquities of the county of Leicester, 3/2 (1804), 1059 · W. St J. Hope, 'On the tombs of two bishops in the cathedral church of Salisbury', Proceedings of the Society of Antiquaries of London, 2nd ser., 28 (1915–16), 174–90, esp. 186–8 · R. M. T. Hill, ed., The rolls and register of Bishop Oliver Sutton, 4–5, 8, Lincoln RS, 52, 60, 76 (1958–86) · VCH Leicestershire, 2.12, 46–7; 5.266 · VCH Wiltshire, vol. 3 · H. Bradshaw and C. Wordsworth, eds., Statutes of Lincoln Cathedral, 3 vols. (1892–7), vol. 1

Archives Wilts. & Swindon RO, Salisbury diocesan records
Likenesses casement (for a lost brass on tomb), Salisbury Cathedral
Wealth at death held Noseley manor; other lands in Leicestershire; provided endowments of £500 in total for choristers and vicar choral of Salisbury Cathedral: Wordsworth and Robertson, 'Salisbury choristers', 207

Martyn, Bendal (1700–1761). See under Martyn, Henry (bap. 1665, d. 1721).

Martyn, Benjamin (1698–1763), writer and government official, born on 8 September 1698, was the eldest son of Richard Martyn (1667–1715?), commissioner of stamp duties and linen draper of London, and nephew of Edward Martyn, professor of rhetoric at Gresham College, and of Henry Martin, the economist. Their forebears were of Aldbourne, Wiltshire. Benjamin was educated at the Charterhouse School (1709–14), and bound apprentice to his father on 10 July 1714. Soon afterwards the father went to Buenos Aires as agent for the South Sea Company, and died there; his Relation of the voyage thither and expedition to Potosi was published in London in 1716. Benjamin became an examiner of the outport books in the London custom house, probably by favour of his uncle Henry, who was inspector-general of the exports and imports.

Martyn wrote a tragedy, Timoleon, which was rejected by the Drury Lane management until resubmitted 'with a Command which they durst not disobey' (Daily Journal, 29 Jan 1730). Martyn's play was disparaged in Remarks on Timoleon by Philomusas, and ridiculed in James Miller's Harlequin–Horace and John Lloyd's The Play; a Satire, but ran successfully for fourteen nights in January and February 1730, and was revived occasionally later. Such fame as it had was owing to a ghost scene which echoes Hamlet and Macbeth. The printed play was dedicated to George II.

The patron who helped Martyn in the staging and dedication of Timoleon has not been identified, but it was Alderman George Heathcote, a wealthy West India merchant and opposition whig MP, who recommended him in July 1732 for the post of secretary to the board of trustees for establishing the colony of Georgia in America, describing him as 'a very ingenious young man' who 'has some employment under the Government, and is a sober young man, who out of his little maintains his mother and sisters' (Egmont Diary, 1.286). Martyn acted gratis at first, but was receiving £50 a half-year by the end of 1733 and £75 by 1737; he also kept his examinership, worth £100 p.a., in the custom house. In 1734 he displeased some of the Georgia trustees by inviting the suspected deist Thomas Rundle (1688–1743) to preach before them: it was also said that Martyn had 'too little regard to the religious part' of the council's designs in Georgia, and that he was politicking on his own account (ibid., 2.23–4, 41, 44); but Martyn retained his position.

As well as conducting official correspondence Martyn publicized Georgia in pamphlets, the most substantial of which are A New and Accurate Account of … Georgia (1732) (sometimes wrongly attributed to James Oglethorpe, the prime mover of the Georgia project), Reasons for Establishing the Colony of Georgia (1733), An Impartial Enquiry into the State and Utility of … Georgia (1741), and An Account Showing the Progress of … Georgia (1742). This last was a vindication of the Oglethorpe administration against a hostile pamphlet by colonial malcontents, though Martyn knew far less about Georgia than his opponents did. Martyn is perhaps the seated figure with pen and paper in hand in the centre foreground of Willem Verelst's conversation piece The Common Council of Georgia Receiving the Indian Chiefs (painted in London 1734–5, now in the H. F. Dupont Museum, Winterthur, Delaware, USA). On 20 December 1752 Martyn was recommended for the profitable post of agent for Georgia.

In May 1736 Martyn was a committee member of the Society for the Encouragement of Learning, as was his friend Thomas Birch (1705–1766): their correspondence, 1737–62, is in British Library Add. MS 4313. According to his tombstone Martyn was 'the first promoter' of the Shakespeare monument in Westminster Abbey. Other contemporary references to this project (such as periodicals and George Vertue's notebooks) do not mention Martyn, but he wrote a special prologue for a performance of Shakespeare's Julius Caesar at Drury Lane on 28 April 1738 to raise money for the monument.

At some time in the 1730s the fourth earl of Shaftesbury, one of the Georgia trustees, commissioned Martyn to write a life of the first earl from family papers. The work, unfinished at Martyn's death in 1763, was revised in turn by Gregory Sharpe and Andrew Kippis and printed privately about 1790 (nearly twenty years after the fourth earl's death). The fifth earl disapproved, so most of this impression was destroyed, but a copy which escaped was edited and published in 1836 by George Wingrove Cooke.

In the last decade of his life Martyn suffered from gout; he died unmarried at Eltham, Kent, on 25 October 1763, and was buried in Lewisham churchyard on 31 October. By his will, proved on 27 October 1763, he bequeathed nearly £4000 to relatives; works of art in his New Bond Street lodgings (collected during tours on the continent) were bequeathed to friends.   JAMES SAMBROOK

Sources *Manuscripts of the earl of Egmont: diary of Viscount Percival, afterwards first earl of Egmont*, 3 vols., HMC, 63 (1920–23) · Martyn's letters to Thomas Birch, 1737–62, BL, Add. MS 4313, fols. 101–69 · E. Chamberlayne and J. Chamberlayne, *Magnae Britanniae notitia* (1745) · B. Marsh and F. A. Crisp, eds., *Alumni Carthusiani: a record of the foundation scholars of Charterhouse, 1614–1872* (1913), 70 · J. Ward, *The lives of the professors of Gresham College* (1740), 334 · D. Lysons, *The environs of London*, 4 (1796), 523 · P. Bayle and others, *A general dictionary, historical and critical*, 9 (1739), 189 · IGI · A. A. Ettinger, *James Edward Oglethorpe: imperial idealist* (1936) · J. Sambrook, *James Thomson, 1700–1748: a life* (1991) · A. H. Scouten, ed., *The London stage, 1660–1800*, pt 3: *1729–1747* (1961) · C. Atto, 'The Society for the Encouragement of Learning', *The Library*, 4th ser., 19 (1938–9), 263–88 · G. W. Cooke, *Life of the first earl of Shaftesbury* (1836), preface · W. D. Christie, *Memoirs of the earl of Shaftesbury* (1871) · DNB

Archives PRO, papers relating to Georgia, T 1/ 335–350, 353, 356, 370, 388, 394, 400, 407, 412 | BL, letters to Thomas Birch, Add. MS 4313, fols. 101–69

Likenesses W. Verelst, 1734–5 (of Martyn?, in *The common council of Georgia receiving the Indian chiefs*), H. F. Dupont Museum, Winterthur, Delaware, USA; A. E. Dyer, copy, Rhodes Memorial Hall, Atlanta, Georgia, USA

Wealth at death £3926; plus valuable art works and other property: will, PRO, PROB 11/892, sig. 479

Martyn, Caroline Eliza Derecourt (1867–1896), Christian socialist, was born on 3 May 1867 in Manson Street, Lincoln, the eldest of the nine children of James William Martyn, a police superintendent, and his wife, Kate Eleanor (*née* Hewitt) (*d.* in or after 1896). The Martyns were devout high Anglicans, and active Conservatives. After attending Beaumont House School, Lincoln, Caroline became a governess at the age of eighteen. In common with many other young girls of her class she found this unsatisfying and opted for schoolteaching, first at a church school and then in 1890 at a board school in Reading.

Caroline Martyn's first political involvement was with the Primrose League. This altered during her stay in Reading when she lodged with her mother's sister, Mrs Bailey, a lady of more leftward views. The combination of her influence and a sustained reading of the New Testament made Caroline Martyn increasingly aware of other political ideologies and she flirted briefly with radicalism before committing herself to socialism. In 1891 she moved to London. She went to take up a post as governess at the Royal Orphanage Asylum in Wandsworth, and also to be in a location where she could more fully involve herself in socialism. She joined the London Fabian Society on arrival. The following summer, when a health breakdown forced her to resign her post, she was able to devote herself completely to the socialist cause. She never married.

The religion in which she was raised always remained an important part of Caroline Martyn's political beliefs. She violently opposed the 'hard and bitter materialism' of her Marxist contemporaries (Mayo, *Recollections*, 226). She relied on Bible teachings more than revolutionary or economic rhetoric, and 'The social teachings of Jesus', 'The

brotherhood of man', and similar titles featured heavily in her lecture list. Religion and socialism constantly intertwined in her work, allowing her politics to surface in unusual places. From the spring of 1893 she wrote regularly for the *Christian Weekly* on social questions of the day. However those who knew her well noted that socialism often forced her to compromise some of her religious beliefs. Her friend Isabella Fyvie Mayo sadly commented that Caroline, who always sought to help those in trouble, was often 'less than loyal to her own best instincts … (and showed) apparent approval of some whom I know she despised and mistrusted' (ibid., 227).

A feminism which stemmed from a belief in the equality of all also underpinned Caroline's political life. As a socialist she rejected a distinct campaign for 'women's rights as something separate and apart from all other rights'. She believed instead that men and women should work together to remove the 'false social and economic conditions' that oppressed both sexes (*Labour Prophet*, July 1893). She believed women were of 'different but equal value' to men (*Christian Weekly*, 23 Sept 1893), and her writings urged women socialists to expand their superior female influence into all spheres of life.

Although she published widely in radical journals it was as a lecturer rather than a writer that Caroline Martyn was best known to her contemporaries. Ironically, despite her teaching background, she initially feared public speaking, and only the encouragement of friends persuaded her into lecturing. This brought her national recognition, and she attracted large audiences whenever she appeared. One Independent Labour Party (ILP) member who often heard her speak claimed that at her meetings:

> she reaches the mind of the dullest by her simplicity and by her pathos and religious fervour she carries the whole argument upward to the plane of unworldliness and self-sacrifice. She makes the 'smart' man of commerce feel mean, and the man whose object is to get on meaner still. The effect of her teaching is to … enlarge and ennoble the motive and aims of the socialist reformer. (*Labour Chronicle*, 1 Aug 1895)

Unfortunately the lifestyle of an itinerant speaker did not suit Caroline Martyn's health. She confided her emotional dissatisfaction to friends such as Mrs Mayo on more than one occasion: she missed the stability of a fixed home and felt she was merely a speaking machine. Long journeys by third-class rail, poor sleeping accommodation, and a sense of always having to move on also took their toll physically. Her 1896 election to the ILP's national executive added to her schedule. She died suddenly of pneumonia at 107 Murraygate, Dundee, on 23 July 1896 and was buried the next day in Dundee at Balgay cemetery.

Caroline Martyn's unexpected death at the age of twenty-nine shook the socialist movement. Keir Hardie wrote that she was the leading socialist of her day, with 'a power of intellect and moral-force' that was unmatched (*Labour Leader*, 1 Aug 1896). The *Glasgow Commonweal*, referring to her work in a recent Aberdeen by-election, remarked that all ILP branches in the area had lost their best member. A subscription in *The Clarion* raised money for a mobile propaganda van which bore her name. Added poignancy came from the fact that Caroline Martyn had just taken over the editorship of *Fraternity*, the journal of the International Society for the Brotherhood of Man, and was about to commence as trade union organizer among Dundee's women. In many senses it appeared her best work was about to begin.   KRISTA COWMAN

Sources I. F. Mayo, *Recollections of what I saw, what I lived through, and what I learned, during more than fifty years of social and literary experience* (1910), 225–8 · L. Wallis, *Life and letters of Caroline Martyn* (1898) · J. Edwards, 'Caroline Martyn', *Liverpool Labour Chronicle* (Aug 1895) · 'Tributes', *Labour Leader* (1 Aug 1896) · C. Martyn, 'Women in the world', *Labour Prophet* (July 1893) · *Glasgow Commonweal* (Aug 1896) · I. F. Mayo, 'Our new editor', *Fraternity* (July 1896) · *Fraternity* (Sept 1896) · C. Martyn, 'Women's work and wages', *Christian Weekly* (23 Sept 1893) · d. cert. · b. cert.
Archives U. Warwick Mod. RC, MSS letters and press cuttings, MSS 21/1738
Likenesses J. Hindle, photograph, repro. in *Labour Prophet* (July 1895) · line drawing, repro. in *Labour Leader*

Martyn, Edith How (1875–1954), suffragist and advocate of birth control, was born on 17 June 1875 at Bexley Road, Lessness Heath, Erith, Kent, the daughter of Edwin How, grocer, and his wife, Anne Darley. She was educated at The Hall, Cheltenham, and North London Collegiate School for Girls, and studied at University College, Aberystwyth. She was awarded a BSc (external) by the University of London in 1903 and gained an MSc in economics in 1922. The first woman associate of the Royal College of Science (mathematics and physics), she lectured in mathematics at Westfield College for a short time. On 4 August 1899 she married George Herbert Martyn, a science teacher. The couple, who were married for fifty-five years, did not have any children.

How Martyn later admitted that she had 'been a rebel ever since I can remember', adding, 'I was always in hot water at school, even in my very earliest school days, because I resented the difference made between boys and girls, and the greater amount of liberty allowed to the former' (*The Vote*, 19 March 1910, 244). Her suffrage career began in the Women's Social and Political Union (WSPU), which she joined after going to a meeting. The women present 'were like a revelation to me. For the first time I felt I had met women who were strong and self-reliant … My imagination was fired' (ibid.). She resigned her post at Westfield College to devote the whole of her time to the WSPU. She first spoke in public in the deputation to Asquith on 21 June 1906, and was one of the first women to be imprisoned that year. In 1907, however, disillusioned by the WSPU's undemocratic structure, she and others founded the Women's Freedom League (WFL), a non-violent, militant organization. How Martyn became a leading strategist at the height of the suffrage campaign and was unanimously appointed honorary secretary of the League.

From 1910, when she joined the Malthusian League, How Martyn attempted to promote public discussion of contraception, at the time a very contentious issue avoided by suffrage organizations. Her beliefs were not motivated by Malthusian doctrine, but by her feminism: by the view that women had the right to sexual fulfilment

and by her concern for women's welfare. Disliking Mrs Despard's authoritarian style of leadership, she retired on health grounds as head of the WFL's political and militant department in April 1912.

In 1918 How Martyn was one of the first women parliamentary candidates, standing as independent (liberal) in Hendon, Middlesex. She was elected as the first woman councillor in Middlesex county council in 1919 and served for three years. In 1921 she helped the Malthusian League establish one of the first birth control clinics in Britain. During the 1920s she helped to mobilize public opinion in Britain to promote birth control both as morally acceptable and as an essential aspect of sexual relations. She was the linchpin of an extensive campaign to bring birth control to poorer women through local authority provision, arguing that birth control information was a 'legitimate and natural extension of the work of Maternity and Child Welfare Centres' (How Martyn).

How Martyn continued to debate suffrage issues, and in 1927 she wrote that she agreed with both sides in the dispute between new and old feminism within the National Union of Societies for Equal Citizenship (NUSEC). She shared Mrs Abbott's definition of equality and feminism, yet, as one anxious to realize this equality, 'I soon find myself ranged as an ardent supporter of Miss Eleanor Rathbone' (*Time and Tide*, 218). In October 1932, just back from visiting Russia, she claimed that its government 'has established complete political, economic and social equality between men and women, while their organisation for the welfare of mothers and children compares very favourably with that of any other country in the world' (*Jus Suffragii*, 4). In 1928 she founded the Suffragette Fellowship with Lilian Lenton, to preserve memories of the fight for women's suffrage; its records have provided much of the primary source material for the historiography of the Edwardian suffragettes.

From 1915 Edith How Martyn had worked with the American Margaret Sanger aiming to bring contraceptive knowledge to women all over the world. They felt women's needs were being ignored in international debate where many interests—religious, scientific, medical, and eugenic and sexual reformism—jostled with politico-economic considerations. They wanted women to have access to safe, cheap, reliable methods of contraception which could be used in homes without basic sanitation, water, or privacy, and where females had little control over sexual initiative. In 1927 How Martyn set up a small office in Geneva, hoping to establish a permanent bureau close to the League of Nations for international exchange of birth control information. In 1934 she made the first of several visits to India, perceiving that, as India emerged from colonialism, it might be possible to integrate women's reproductive needs into programmes for social and health reform. She introduced Margaret Sanger to Mahatma Gandhi, but they could not convince him of the benefits of contraception. How Martyn also visited China, Ceylon, Burma, Malaya, the Philippines, Japan, Hawaii, Jamaica, and North America. Finances were always meagre and ultimately How Martyn's Birth Control International Information Centre was amalgamated with the other voluntary organizations which eventually formed the Family Planning Association and International Planned Parenthood.

Shortly after the outbreak of the Second World War, Edith How Martyn set out on another propaganda tour, accompanied by her husband. They spent a year in New Zealand, and then went on to Australia. They did not return to England (or go on to South Africa as intended) but settled in Australia. Increasing ill health and penury clouded the remaining years of How Martyn's life. She died in Sydney on 2 February 1954. Her husband died a few months later.   HILARY FRANCES

Sources private information (2004) · Eileen Palmer MSS, BLPES, Coll. misc. 0639 · New York University, Margaret Sanger papers project, MSS · BL OIOC, MS Eur. D 1182 · London Guildhall University, Calcutta House, Old Castle Street, London, MSS Fawcett Library · Wellcome L., MSS · *The Times* (4 Feb 1954) · *Daily Telegraph* (4 Feb 1954) · *Manchester Guardian* (4 Feb 1954) · *The Vote*, 1–10 (1909–15) · E. How Martyn, *An appeal for equality of knowledge* [n.d.] [Birth Control Movement Information Centre pamphlet] · b. cert. · m. cert. · *The Vote* (19 March 1910) · *Time and Tide* (4 March 1927) · *Jus Suffragii* (Oct 1932)
Archives BL OIOC, diaries and papers, MS Eur. D 1182 · Women's Library, London, MSS | BLPES, Eileen Palmer collection, MSS diaries of propaganda tours, Coll. misc. 0639 · New York University, Margaret Sanger papers project, corresp. · Wellcome L., Birth Control International Information Centre archives
Likenesses Women's Freedom League, photographs (taken during Edwardian suffrage campaign), London Metropolitan University
Wealth at death died in penury: correspondence of personal friends · £3000 legacy to the Suffragette Fellowship: *Women's Bulletin* (31 July 1859)

Martyn, Edward Joseph (1859–1923), playwright and politician, was born on 30 January 1859 in Tillyra Castle, Ardrahan, co. Galway, the son of John Martyn (*d.* 1860) and Annie May Josephine Martyn, *née* Smyth (1830–1898). His father's family traced its descent from the crusader Sir Oliver Martin, who came to Ireland with Strongbow in 1170, and the Martyns, although Catholic, were loyal enough to retain their estates in penal law times through a special act of parliament. Martyn had no recollection of his father, who died shortly after he was born, and his devout and austere mother, the daughter of an upwardly mobile Galway land speculator, continued to exert a dominant influence over him until her death. A younger brother died in early manhood, shortly after taking a commission in the British army.

After some years at Belvedere College in Dublin, Martyn's mother moved him to another Jesuit school, Beaumont College in England. The intellectual curriculum did not suit him, and an unsuccessful attempt to blow up the school nearly led to his expulsion. His feeling of isolation was intensified at Christ Church, Oxford, where he matriculated in May 1877, partly because he found few fellow Catholic undergraduates, but largely because his ignorance of Latin and Greek made his time there a humiliation. By way of compensation, he threw himself into the aesthetic movement, and travelled much in the vacations, developing a lifelong love for Wagner, Ibsen, Greece, and architecture.

Leaving Oxford after two years, and without a degree, Martyn kept rooms in London, but returned frequently to Galway where he extensively rebuilt Tillyra Castle. Agrarian agitation was at its height (there was a subsequent attempt to assassinate his agent), and he was noted for his uncompromising position as a magistrate, a stance reinforced by lifelong disdain for the people. He rebuffed his mother's attempts at matchmaking, and remained unmarried and a lifelong misogynist. His emotional energy went rather into religion, and he became an unusually devout Catholic, destroying a long poem because of its supposed pagan tendency. There was little to indicate the future president of Sinn Féin, yet he soon became vehemently pro-nationalist and anti-English. His cousin the novelist George Moore thought this a return to his genuine beliefs after the death of his mother in May 1898, while he himself ascribed his conversion to his reading Lecky's *History of Ireland in the Eighteenth Century*. His first published work, *Morgante the Lesser* (1890), a prose satire influenced by Swift and Rabelais, contrasts a hellish vision of the modern world with the utopian Agathopolis, a womanless state, classical in art, Catholic in religion, and enlightenedly despotic in politics. Perhaps in an attempt to create something of this in Ireland, he began to support a wide variety of cultural organizations. He became a prominent member of the ruling council of the Gaelic League, and was particularly eager to re-Gaelicize the upper and middle classes, a policy he urged in his pamphlet *Ireland's Battle for her Language* (1900). He also sat on the Irish committee of the Pan Celtic Association from 1898, and helped to plan its first congress in Dublin in 1900. At the same time Martyn was elected a vice-president of the Feis Ceoil, a cultural and musical organization, which he supported not only financially but also practically, by acting as a judge at its competitions. This taste for Irish music was predated by his interest in Wagner and church music. He made the pilgrimage to Bayreuth, and founded the Dublin Palestrina Choir in 1899, subsequently expending a great deal of time and money in persuading the Catholic hierarchy to merge this into the Cathedral Choir of Dublin, an ambition he achieved in 1903 at a personal cost of £10,000. These initiatives were part of a more general campaign to improve Irish ecclesiastical art. He induced the department of technical instruction to establish classes in stained glass at the Dublin Metropolitan School of Art, and helped finance Sarah Purser's stained-glass co-operative, An Túr Gloine (Tower of Glass), which opened in Dublin in 1903 and from which he commissioned windows for his local church. He also advised the bishop of Clonfert on the use of Irish artists in decorating a new cathedral at Loughrea.

Martyn had met W. B. Yeats in London in 1896 through Arthur Symons, and the two stayed with him for the first time that summer at Tillyra. By this time he had already written an Ibsenite play, *The Heather Field*, with George

Moore's help, and was completing a more symbolical piece, *Maeve*, which he paid Arthur Symons to revise. Unsuccessful in getting either play produced commercially, in June 1897 he resolved, with Yeats and Lady Gregory, to establish an Irish Literary Theatre in Dublin. Martyn agreed to underwrite any financial loss, recruited potential subscribers, helped to find a venue for the first productions, and successfully lobbied Irish MPs to change the laws governing theatrical performances in Dublin.

Although they met frequently in Galway, Dublin, and London from 1896 to 1900, Martyn was always suspicious of Yeats's unorthodox religious beliefs, and shortly before the first season of the new society threatened to abort the whole project by withdrawing his financial guarantees because he objected to several passages in Yeats's *Countess Cathleen* on theological grounds. Yeats enlisted influential Catholic churchmen to counter these suspicions; the performances went forward, and the enthusiastic reception of *The Heather Field* gave Martyn the greatest triumph he was to know in the theatre. Even international success seemed to beckon when the play was staged in New York. *Maeve* was also well received at the second Irish Literary Theatre season in February 1900, and Martyn had begun work on a third play, a satire on Anglo-Irish relations entitled *The Tale of a Town*. He had received considerable help with the writing of his previous plays, and George Moore and Yeats with singular lack of tact now began a radical revision of this one under the title *The Bending of the Bough*. Mortified, Martyn repudiated the new version and began to reconsider his position in the Irish Literary Theatre.

Meanwhile, Martyn had openly declared his nationalism. At a Christmas celebration at Tillyra in 1899 he refused to allow a band to play 'God Save the Queen', and when Lord Clonbrock suggested that he had compromised his position as deputy lord lieutenant and commissioner of the peace for co. Galway, he promptly resigned these offices, explaining that he no longer shared the views of the Unionist Party in which he had been brought up. The cool response to the publication of his plays *The Tale of a Town* and *An Enchanted Sea* disappointed him, while Yeats's alliance with the Fay brothers of the Irish National Dramatic Society indicated that the direction of the theatrical movement would be toward poetic and folk drama, rather than the psychological, Ibsenite plays he preferred. Early in 1902 he let it be known that he was withdrawing from what remained of the Irish Literary Theatre, and turned his attention to the Players' Club, a semi-professional company which produced *The Heather Field* in June 1903, and his homo-erotic four-act tragedy *An Enchanted Sea* in April 1904. Although Moore thought it was the play which most fully expressed Martyn's essential paganism, Dublin critics found it monotonous and far-fetched.

In May 1903 Martyn, Maud Gonne, and Arthur Griffith founded the National Council, the immediate purpose of which was to oppose an impending royal visit to Dublin, but which outlasted this occasion, and in September 1908

became one of the planks in the Sinn Féin movement. By that time Martyn had been elected president of Sinn Féin at its first annual convention in November 1905. His political affiliations had already led to his resignation as the president of the Catholic Association, and, as a consequence of a speech made to the National Council, he was expelled from the Kildare Street Club, a bastion of ascendancy values. To general astonishment, he took an action disputing its right to do this, won his case, and defiantly remained a member of the club until his death. His presidency of Sinn Féin was far shorter: in July 1908 he told Yeats that he had 'left the Sinn Fein organization and retired from politics altogether'. Yeats suspected that the organization had made inordinate demands on his pocket, but reported that he was 'busy writing as ever, is very amiable' (W. B. Yeats to J. B. Yeats, 17 July 1908).

Martyn's interest in the theatre continued: he was a regular patron of the Abbey Theatre, as well as serving simultaneously on the committees of several drama societies. In October 1905 the National Players' Society, of which he was a vice-president, produced *The Tale of a Town*, and when in 1906 actors seceding from the Abbey set up the Theatre of Ireland, Martyn agreed to become its president. In May 1908 it revived *Maeve* to a hostile reception, while the return of *The Heather Field* to the Abbey stage in April 1909 aroused little interest. In January 1912 Count Markiewicz's Independent Dramatic Company produced his domestic melodrama *Grangecolman* to mixed reviews, and he despaired of finding an Irish theatre group that could give him the theatre he wanted. Nevertheless, when the poets Thomas MacDonagh and Joseph Plunkett proposed a new company, the Irish Theatre, he jumped at the chance of becoming one of the three directors.

The company's first production, in 1914, was Martyn's heavy-handed comedy *The Dream Physician*, in which the absurd George Augustus Moon was his revenge for George Moore's ridicule of him in *Hail and Farewell*. The following year the company revived the play in its new Hardwicke Street venue, and in November 1915 premièred his three-act play *The Privilege of Place*. The Irish Theatre was severely afflicted by the Easter rising in 1916, but, despite the execution of Martyn's fellow directors Plunkett and MacDonagh, it reopened in November with a revival of *The Heather Field*, followed in December by the production of Martyn's 'symbolist extravaganza' *Romulus and Remus*. This clumsy satire on Moore, Yeats, and Lady Gregory, first published in the *Irish People* in 1907, transposes the quarrels in the Irish Literary Theatre to a hairdresser's salon. In 1917 *Grangecolman* was revived in Hardwicke Street, and Martyn offered a £10 prize for the best psychological play of Irish life. But his hopes of creating a new national theatre were fading, and the company limped on in its cramped theatre, playing to tiny audiences. *The Heather Field* was revived in April 1918, and in April 1919 Martyn presented his wordy new 'drama in elective moods', *Regina Eyre*. The reviewers panned it, as they did a lugubrious production of Chekhov in June 1919, and the Irish Theatre came to an end early in 1920. The resignation of the main director, the deteriorating political situation, the frequent curfews, and the refusal of Joseph Plunkett's mother to continue the lease on Hardwicke Street all contributed to its demise.

The breakdown of law and order during the Irish War of Independence revived all Martyn's old mistrust of the people, and he tried to sell Tillyra, but could not find a buyer. He began to regret his early support for Sinn Féin, although this did not save him from the attentions of the crown forces; his rooms in Dublin were raided by the military, and the fine village hall he had built at Ardrahan was burnt by the Black and Tans. In autumn 1922 Martyn suffered a stroke, and was almost entirely incapacitated. He supported Griffith and the signing of the Anglo-Irish treaty, but, although there was republican activity in his area, Tillyra escaped burning. Martyn was operated on for a brain tumour, and died a few days later at Tillyra Castle on 5 December 1923. In his will he left his body to be dissected, and his library to the Discalced Carmelites in Clarendon Street, Dublin. JOHN KELLY

Sources D. Gwynn, *Edward Martyn and the Irish revival* (1974) • J. MacDonagh, 'Edward Martyn', *Dublin Magazine*, 1 (Feb 1924), 463–7 • G. Moore, *Hail and farewell*, 3 vols. (1937) • J. Setterquist, *Ibsen and the beginnings of Anglo-Irish drama*, 2, *Edward Martyn* (1960) • d. cert. • J. Holloway, diaries, NL Ire. • letters to John Hogan, NL Ire. • correspondence with George Moore, W. B. Yeats, NL Ire. • NL Ire., Count Plunkett papers [re *Irish Review*] • photostat of agreement with Irish Theatre, 1914, NL Ire. • correspondence with George Moore, Lady Gregory, and others, NYPL, Humanities and Social Sciences Library, Berg collection • Yeats–Lady Gregory correspondence, NYPL, Humanities and Social Sciences Library, Berg collection • University of Delaware, Newark, Hugh M. Morris Library, Frank Hugh O'Donnell papers • E. S. M. Archer, *Genealogy of the family of Martin of Ballinahinch Castle* (Winnipeg, 1890) • *Lady Gregory's diaries, 1892–1902*, ed. J. Pethica (1996) • *Lady Gregory's journals*, ed. D. Murphy, 2 vols. (1978–87) • Lady Gregory, *Our Irish theatre* (1913) • W. B. Yeats, *Autobiographies* (1955) • W. B. Yeats, *Memoirs*, ed. D. Donoghue (1972) • M.-T. Courtney, *Edward Martyn and the Irish theatre* [1956] • 'The Martyns of Galway', *Tuam Herald* (12 April 1930) • 'The National Council Convention of Sinn Fein', *Freeman's Journal* [Dublin] (29 Nov 1905)

Archives NL Ire., corresp., MS 13068, etc. | NL Ire., letters to John J. O'Horgan

Likenesses N. French McLachlan, oils, NG Ire.; repro. in M. Bence-Jones, *Twilight of the Ascendancy* (1987) • S. Purser, oils, Municipal Gallery of Modern Art, Dublin • J. B. Yeats, pencil drawing, NG Ire.

Wealth at death £10,643 8s. 9d.: probate, 7 March 1924, *CGPLA Eng. & Wales*

Martyn, Francis (1782–1838), Roman Catholic priest, born in Norfolk in February 1782, was sent to Sedgley Park School, near Wolverhampton, at the age of eight, and in 1796 proceeded to St Mary's College, Oscott. Because the English seminaries on the continent had closed as a result of the French Revolution he remained at Oscott to study for the priesthood; when ordained by Bishop Milner in December 1805 he was the first Roman Catholic priest since the Reformation to have received his entire training in England. After being stationed for a short time at Brailes, Warwickshire, and Louth, Lincolnshire, he was appointed in 1807 to the mission at Bloxwich, Staffordshire, which became the base for his pioneer missionary

work in Walsall and West Bromwich. In 1831 he was transferred to Wolverhampton. Martyn's ministry in the Black Country was publicized in the *Orthodox Journal* of W. E. Andrews, and he was a frequent contributor to that journal. He died at Walsall on 18 July 1838, and was buried there at St Mary's Mount. The Revd George Spencer, the missioner at the church Martyn had founded at West Bromwich, preached the funeral sermon, which was printed at Birmingham in 1838, with a memoir by the Revd Robert Richmond.

THOMPSON COOPER, *rev.* G. MARTIN MURPHY

Sources J. Bossy, *The English Catholic community, 1570–1850* (1975), 317–18 • *Catholic Directory* (1839), 89–93 • *The Oscotian*, 2nd ser., 4 (1885), 17, 272 • G. Every, 'The Catholic community in Walsall, 1720–1824', *Recusant History*, 19 (1988–9), 313–31 • *London and Dublin Orthodox Journal*, 7 (1838), 63, 80, 173 • *Catholic Magazine*, 5 (1834), 307–13 • J. A. Mason, *The triumph of truth* (1827) • J. A. Mason, *The conversion of Edward Corser … also the address … by the Revd Francis Martyn* [1838]

Likenesses Holl, engraving, repro. in *Catholic Directory*

Martyn, Henry (*bap.* 1665, *d.* 1721), essayist, was baptized on 28 November 1665 at Aldbourne, Wiltshire, the eldest son of Edward Martyn of Upham, in that parish, and his wife, Elizabeth. His younger brother, Edward Martin (*b.* 1666), went on to become Gresham professor. He himself matriculated from Pembroke College, Oxford, on 13 March 1684, and graduated BA in 1687 and MA (from Oriel) in 1690. He went on to study at the Middle Temple, but due to ill health never practised as a lawyer. He married Sarah Bendall on 31 December 1698.

Martyn wrote for *The Spectator* and *The Guardian*. He was almost certainly the Philarithmus of *Spectator* number 180, and has been linked to articles in other issues of the paper including numbers 143 (Cottilus), 200, and 232. In issue number 555 Richard Steele praises Martyn highly, and acknowledges his indebtedness to his work, listing him alongside—indeed, ahead of—Alexander Pope, John Hughes, Henry Carey, Thomas Tickell, Thomas Parnell, and Laurence Eusden. Martyn was one of the leading lights in the movement to set up *The British Merchant, or, Commerce Preserved*, a paper designed to focus opposition to a proposed trade treaty with France being negotiated at the Utrecht peace talks in 1713–14. The paper was thus in opposition to Defoe's *Mercator*. According to another of the founders, Charles King, Martyn's work was instrumental in making a success of the paper and ensuring the rejection of the treaty. Martin became inspector-general of imports and exports, in which capacity he wrote various papers now in the British Library dealing with the financial affairs of the country. He died at Blackheath on 25 March 1721.

Henry Martyn's only son, **Bendal** [Bendall] **Martyn** (1700–1761), composer, was born in London on 8 January 1700. Bendal attended Eton College, then King's College, Cambridge, where he was admitted as a scholar on 3 February 1719. He graduated BA in 1722, and was made a fellow of the college. He was also registered at the Middle Temple on 14 April 1721. Between 1736 and his death he held the post of secretary to the excise, and in 1740 he inherited a good estate from an aunt. He died on 20 December 1761 at Highgate. He was reputedly an excellent musician, and in 1763 fourteen trio sonatas, written by him, were published.

A. E. J. LEGGE, rev. MATTHEW STEGGLE

Sources C. King, 'Preface', *The British Merchant* (1721) • Foster, *Alum. Oxon.* • 'The *Spectator* project', Rutgers University, harvest. rutgers.edu/projects/spectator/, 22 April 2002 • P. Platt, 'Martyn, Bendall', *New Grove* • Venn, *Alum. Cant.* • IGI

Martyn, Henry (1781–1812), missionary and translator, was born on 18 February 1781 in Truro, Cornwall, the third of the four children of John Martyn, a clerk in a merchant's office. His mother, his father's second wife, about whom little is known, died when he was two. The family's exact economic and social status remains uncertain, but Henry, delicate from childhood, was prepared for one of the professions through a sound classical education at Truro grammar school between 1788 and 1797, followed by university education at St John's College, Cambridge. By 1801, when he graduated as senior wrangler and winner of several prizes, he had proved his intellectual strengths, particularly in mathematics and Latin. In 1802, when he was elected a fellow at St John's, he seemed set for an academic or legal career.

The turning point in Martyn's life, which confirmed a missionary vocation already encouraged by the evangelical piety of his Cornwall home and the influence in particular of his younger sister, was occasioned by contact with Charles Simeon, the strongly evangelical vicar of Holy Trinity, Cambridge. Simeon's reports of the recent impact in Bengal of the first Baptist missionary to India, William Carey, and Martyn's own reading about new opportunities for overseas missionary work recently opened up by the evangelical revival and colonial expansion, stimulated his interest in overseas evangelism. After ordination as deacon in 1803, at Ely Cathedral, he nevertheless remained for a further two years in the Cambridge evangelical circle, working as Simeon's curate at Holy Trinity, with responsibility for a rural congregation. He took his MA degree in 1804, followed by a BD in 1806. Hopes of a full missionary posting to India had meanwhile been dashed when responsibility for an unmarried sister, following the loss of family property, obliged Martyn to accept the better-paid post of chaplain in the East India Company's rapidly expanding Bengal presidency. While awaiting departure he returned briefly to Cornwall, where his love for a local woman, Lydia Grenfell, six years his senior and also strongly evangelical, was revived. Failure to overcome his grief at her refusal to accompany him to India, though they were to maintain a close correspondence, was one of the factors responsible for his intermittent depressions.

Martyn reached Calcutta in early 1806 but found the British capital's dominance by worldly Europeans uncongenial to his evangelical temperament. He was posted for the next four years to military cantonments on the middle Ganges: first at Dinapore, near Patna, in Bihar, from 1806

Henry Martyn (1781–1812), by William Say (after Thomas Hickey, 1810)

to 1809; and second, until 1810, at Cawnpore, a busy trading city. Employed to serve the British community's ecclesiastical needs, he was prohibited by the Company's 'neutrality' pledge from engaging in evangelistic activity among Indians; however, he managed to open some schools. There were scarcely any converts in this region during his lifetime, though an influential early Indian Muslim convert to Christianity, the Revd 'Abd al-Masih, later attributed his subsequent baptism, soon after Martyn's departure, to overhearing by chance a sermon given by the chaplain. In spite of the prohibition of direct preaching in the bazaars, the presence in Calcutta and at a neighbouring cantonment of some likeminded 'pious chaplains', notably David Brown and Daniel Corrie, who were also in communication with the Simeonites in Cambridge, provided an evangelical network which proved supportive to Martyn's self-deprecating temperament. Led by Brown they planned for the future evangelization of the region. By mutual agreement Martyn abandoned the study of Sanskrit, which was in any case less congenial to him, to concentrate on learning Arabic, Persian, and also Hindustani (Urdu), the principal vernacular of north India, which, with the help of a leading orientalist scholar, John Gilchrist, he had already begun in England. Assisted by local munshis (translators), Martyn put his outstanding linguistic skills to immediate use in translating the Bible into these three languages, for distribution in the Arabic script among the Muslims of India and the Middle East. However, suffering from a recurrence of tuberculosis, which made preaching increasingly painful, and despairing of conversions in north India, he decided that Arabia and Persia would provide a more congenial environment, free of colonial restraints, to improve his translations of the Bible into the languages of the Islamic world. Having obtained leave to travel via Calcutta and Bombay, he left north India in October 1810.

Martyn was proved correct, for the revised Persian manuscript of the New Testament was rapidly completed in 1811–12 in Shiraz, where he also engaged local scholars and Sufis in discussions about the nature and proofs of religious truth. He compiled two tracts in Persian in reply to the evidences for Islam, particularly from miracles, proposed by these scholars, and a third work entitled 'On the vanity of the Sofee system and on the truth of the religion of Moses and Jesus'. Yet despite the seemingly more receptive atmosphere, resistance to conversion was just as strong as in India, leading within a few months to Martyn's departure. Apart from his anxiety to complete further revisions of the scriptures and to ensure their publication in the Arab world as well as in India and Persia, Martyn's by now frenetic journey westward was impelled by hopes of a further meeting with Lydia Grenfell. However, on 16 October 1812 he died a lonely death from tuberculosis at Tokat in Anatolia, *en route* for Constantinople. He was thirty-one. He was buried in an Armenian graveyard.

In his efforts 'to burn himself out for God', Martyn set himself goals which were unrealistic. His evangelical certainties distorted his perceptions of Islam, whose beliefs and practices he denigrated, like most missionaries of his generation. Some contemporaries thought that he was temperamentally, as well as physically, unsuited to the role of itinerant missionary. Nevertheless, Martyn's longterm influence has been very significant. His Urdu New Testament, usually regarded as his greatest contribution to evangelical objectives, was published in Bengal in 1814. The British ambassador to Persia, Sir Gore Ousley, who sympathized with Martyn's aims, presented his Persian New Testament to the shah of Persia and also sent it to St Petersburg where it was printed in 1815. The manuscript of the Arabic New Testament, which was with Martyn at his death, was forwarded to Charles Simeon in Cambridge, who ensured its publication in Calcutta in 1816. The New Testament was thus made available to missionary societies in the languages known to Muslims immediately after the easing in 1813 of the East India Company's embargo on evangelical activity. The impact was most direct in India, where re-editions of Martyn's Bible translations were published repeatedly, with various revisions, until the late nineteenth century.

In addition, Martyn's 'Persian tracts', generated in discussion with scholars in Shiraz, eventually came to missionary attention through their inclusion in Professor Samuel Lee's *Controversial Tracts on Christianity and Mohammedanism* (1824). These tracts, which emphasized a rational, evidential approach to apologetics, dictated by Martyn's Persian discussants rather than by his own preference for the 'word' of the New Testament, seemed increasingly inappropriate in the high evangelical age, whose missionaries sought exclusively biblical tests for truth. Some influential Indian missionaries of the mid-

nineteenth century, including Karl Pfander in Agra, and John Wilson in Bombay, acknowledged their debts to his apologetic writings, but other critics in India ridiculed his seriousness. Martyn's private journals, in which he recorded a deep conviction of his spiritual unworthiness, suggest a despondent personality. In contrast his evangelical friends, notably the children's novelist Mrs Sherwood, stressed his cheerfulness, and some company officials who disapproved of his evangelical objectives nevertheless valued his company for his conversational powers and good humour. In Anglican evangelical tradition he is remembered as 'saint and scholar: the first modern missionary to the Mohammedans' (the sub-title of George Smith's biography of 1892), a perception which underlies more recent biographies. Further critical evaluation is awaited of his contribution to Biblical translation and of his relations with Muslims. AVRIL A. POWELL

Sources S. Wilberforce, *Journals and letters of the Rev. Henry Martyn*, 2 vols. (1837) • J. Sargent, *Memoir of the Rev. Henry Martyn, B.D.* (1816) • G. Smith, *Henry Martyn, saint and scholar, first modern missionary to the Mohammedans, 1781–1812* (1892) • C. E. Padwick, *Henry Martyn: confessor of the faith* (1922) • A. A. Powell, *Muslims and missionaries in pre-mutiny India* (1993) • C. Bennett, 'The legacy of Henry Martyn', *International Bulletin of Missionary Research*, 16/1 (Jan 1992), 10–15

Archives St John Cam. • U. Birm. L., letters and papers • U. Birm. L., Church Missionary Society archive, letters and sermons | British and Foreign Bible Society, Swindon, letters to Col. Sandys of Helston • Canterbury Cathedral, archives, corresp. with Daniel Corrie

Likenesses T. Hickey, oils, 1810, Henry Martyn Hall, Cambridge • W. H. Hay, oils, 1865, St John Cam. • W. Say, engraving (after T. Hickey, 1810), NPG [*see illus.*]

Martyn, John (1617/18–1680), bookseller, was born in London, the son of John Martyn of the Merchant Taylors' Company. He was apprenticed to a bookseller, Humphrey Robinson, on 4 February 1635, and became a freeman of the Stationers' Company on 1 March 1643 and a liveryman in 1657. From 1651 he worked from The Bell in St Paul's Churchyard, developing a prosperous partnership with James Allestry, and becoming one of the most prominent booksellers of Restoration London. He published works by Abraham Cowley, Samuel Butler, Margaret Cavendish (duchess of Newcastle), Thomas Blount, and John Graunt, whose sister Sarah he married. At the same time he established important links with the continental book trade.

The most significant of Martyn's activities involved publications on natural philosophy, and especially the works of the newly formed Royal Society. In its charter Charles II gave the society the right to license its own publications and to appoint privileged printers. In 1663 Martyn and Allestry were sworn into the position. In their capacity as the Royal Society's 'printers' (neither was in fact a printer himself) Martyn and Allestry played an important role in the establishment of experimental philosophy, publishing such key works as the *Micrographia* (1665) of Robert Hooke and the *History of the Royal Society* (1667) by Thomas Sprat. Allestry died in 1670, but Martyn continued as the Royal Society's main link with the book trade for another decade.

Martyn and Allestry also produced the first 'scientific' journal, the *Philosophical Transactions*, edited by Henry

Oldenburg, which became by far the most important international forum for natural philosophy and eventually the official journal of the Royal Society. Readers attributed to Martyn a degree of responsibility for the content of the journal, and some sent their comments to him rather than to Oldenburg. Scholars and gentlemen were much given to complaining of the venality and corruption of stationers, but Martyn was to a large extent an exception. He was portrayed as the 'thinking' bookseller and by the 1670s his shop had become a place where London's intellectual élite could expect to meet, gossip, and scheme.

Martyn died on 3 July 1680, aged sixty-two, at the home of his brother-in-law in Brockley in the parish of Deptford, London. Hooke attended the funeral. He was buried under the still-skeletal St Paul's of Sir Christopher Wren, in the chapel of St Faith's, where his monument was placed.

ADRIAN JOHNS

Sources L. Rostenberg, *Literary, political, scientific, religious, and legal publishing, printing and bookselling in England, 1551–1700: twelve studies*, 2 vols. (1965) · L. Rostenberg, 'John Martyn, printer to the Royal Society', *Papers of the Bibliographical Society of America*, 46 (1952) · C. A. Rivington, 'Early printers to the Royal Society, 1663–1708', *Notes and Records of the Royal Society*, 39 (1984–5), 1–27 · *The correspondence of Henry Oldenburg*, ed. and trans. A. R. Hall and M. B. Hall, 13 vols. (1965–86) · Stationers' Company, Stationers' Hall, London, London Stationers' and Newspaper Makers' Company records

Martyn, John (1699–1768), botanist, was born on 12 September 1699 in Queen Street in the City of London, the son of Thomas Martyn (*d.* 1743), a merchant trading with Hamburg, and Katherine Weedon, who died the year after her son's birth. He was sent to a private school in the City of London, where he evidently received an excellent classical education, and left at sixteen to work in his father's counting-house off Cheapside. By then, however, botany had developed into a strong competing interest and he began to turn his sights to a more congenial career in medicine. He owed this change of direction to his acquaintance with John Wilmer (1697–1769), a young apothecary with a fondness for plant-hunting and entomology, whom he met in 1718, and through whom he presently gained introductions to several leading figures in botanico-medical circles.

A particularly fruitful contact proved to be Patrick Blair, then in Lincolnshire struggling to rebuild his medical fortunes after being imprisoned because of his involvement in the Jacobite rebellion. Cut off from fellow spirits there, Blair entered into a correspondence with Martyn, which was to last several years, discussing with him a possible natural system of classifying plants based on their cotyledons and stimulating him to extend his collecting to birds and their eggs. After Blair's death in 1728 Martyn saw his *Pharmaco-botanologia* through the press. *The Compleat Herbal* (1716–30), a translation of the Latin edition of Tournefort's *Elémens de botanique* attributed to Martyn, may have been started by Blair.

Martyn was a devotee of Tournefort's writings and, having acquired and translated his *History of Plants Growing about Paris* in 1720, conceived the idea of producing a London equivalent. To that end he made many excursions

John Martyn (1699–1768), by unknown artist

into the surrounding countryside, attended the 'herbarizings' of the Society of Apothecaries, and began to put together a *hortus siccus*. Within a year he had taken the further step of forming a botanical society, the earliest one known in Britain to have been formally constituted. Taking on the secretaryship himself, he recruited as president Dillenius, just then a newcomer from Germany; the other members, of whom there were scarcely ever more than twenty, were medical students in the main. For the next six years the society met each Saturday evening in the Rainbow Coffee House on Watling Street and, as one surviving minute book attests, listened to papers on a good spread of topics. Many finds of rarities reported by its members were later published in Martyn's eventual version of Tournefort's book, which by the time it appeared in 1732 had assumed the character of a national flora and was tantamount to a supplement to the standard handbook of the period, Dillenius's edition of Ray's *Synopsis*.

Early in the society's existence Martyn delivered a series of lectures to it expounding current botanical terminology. These he subsequently published and, after the society's demise, worked up into a more general botanical course which he offered on a commercial basis. This led to an invitation in 1727 to repeat the lectures for the benefit of the medical students at Cambridge. The occupant of the university's chair of botany, Richard Bradley, though skilled in the applied and experimental aspects of the subject, was ill-equipped to provide the standard fare of contemporary medical teaching and the students were apparently desperate. Martyn, who was recommended by Hans

Sloane and William Sherard, made the most of this opportunity and honour by hastily producing at his own expense an updated version of Ray's Cambridgeshire flora and distributing free copies to those attending his course. An interleaved copy of this rare octavo volume, *Methodus plantarum circa Cantabrigiam nascentium*, copiously annotated by him, survives in the university's department of plant sciences.

This taste of academia evidently heightened Martyn's ambitions. That same year he secured election to the Royal Society and set up in practice, apparently as an apothecary, in St Helen's, in the heart of the City of London, augmenting his income by lecturing on botany and materia medica. The first part of what was to be his boldest and most sumptuous venture, *Historia plantarum rariorum*, followed in 1728. Noteworthy for some of the earliest examples of colour printing from a single plate, the work of Elisha Kirkall, it drew extensively on drawings by the Dutch flower painter Jacob van Huysum for its illustrations, and on the expertise of Philip Miller for its horticultural notes. Like all too many such productions, though, it failed to attract sufficient support and, after four further parts, had to be discontinued in 1737.

A further setback to Martyn's ambitions was an unsuccessful bid to become second secretary of the Royal Society, on the death of William Rutty in 1730. That same year his ready pen found a further, if surprising, outlet in a new satirical weekly, the *Grub-Street Journal*. Its proclaimed policy was 'to restrain the enormities of our worse brethren, proceeding from their want of integrity and knowledge'. Joint editor at first for a year and then an occasional contributor, Martyn sheltered behind pseudonyms to hold up to ridicule a variety of leading learned figures. Prominent among these was the hapless Bradley, who had published his Cambridge lectures on materia medica and, because of his misuse of the word in one of those, became a thinly disguised 'Professor Hecatomb'.

This sniping at Bradley had a deeper motive: Martyn coveted his chair, which, although it had no endowment, carried prestige and could be expected to advance a medical career. On Sloane's advice Martyn resolved to arm himself with a university degree. To that end he returned to Cambridge in 1730 and, in the steps of his great-grandfather, entered Emmanuel College as a fellow-commoner. After keeping five terms, however, the calls of his London practice and, in 1732, marriage to Eulalia, daughter of John King DD, rector of Chelsea and prebendary of York, put paid to his intention of graduating. In consideration of his earlier lecturing services Martyn nevertheless felt that he was owed the professorship of botany, and on Bradley's death in 1732 canvassed energetically to succeed him. After countering a baseless rumour that he was a nonjuror, he secured election in February 1833. He began well, taking his students out on field excursions, but after three years the lengthy absences from his London practice told afresh and, on the pretext of the lack of a botanic garden to enable him to illustrate his teaching, he turned into the stereotype of an eighteenth-century absentee professor and had no more to do with Cambridge for almost thirty

years, resigning only in 1762 on the election of his son Thomas *Martyn in his place.

Martyn became disillusioned, and his botanical activity diminished after his university débâcle. However, his correspondence with Linnaeus, initiated by his receipt from the Swedish naturalist about 1737 of a copy of his recently published *Flora Lapponica*, was noteworthy. Always a keen Latinist, Martyn devoted his later years to producing an edition of Virgil, with a translation and natural history notes. Of this, he published the *Georgicks* in 1741 and the *Bucolicks* in 1749, but of the *Aeneids* he left only fragmentary material, which was seen into print after his death.

In 1730 Martyn left the City of London on account of an asthmatic condition and went to live and practise in the more salubrious environment of Chelsea, where the Physic Garden was conveniently close. His first wife, with whom he had three sons and five daughters, died in 1749. The next year he married Mary Anne, daughter of Claude Fonnereau, a London merchant; they had one son. Two years later he retired from practice and moved out to Hill House, a farm on Streatham Common. Persistent attacks of gout, however, undermined his enjoyment of that rural existence and eventually he retreated back to Chelsea, where he died on 29 January 1768. He was buried in the churchyard of what is now Chelsea Old Church.

'Mus. Martyn', as Martyn's herbarium is still known, was presented to Cambridge University along with his botanical library and collection of materia medica when his son succeeded to the chair, but much of it was subsequently lost through poor curation. The surviving portion contains some type specimens and incorporates one or two small collections of historic interest made by botanist contemporaries. A genus of tropical American plants, *Martynia*, was named by his friend William Houstoun in his honour. The later recognition of a new family, Martyniaceae (unicorn plants), has resulted in his being commemorated at that higher level as well.

D. E. ALLEN

Sources T. Martyn, 'Some account of the late John Martyn, FRS, and his writings', in G. C. Gorham and T. Martyn, *Memoirs of John Martyn … and of Thomas Martyn* (1830) · S. M. Walters, *The shaping of Cambridge botany* (1981) · D. E. Allen, 'John Martyn's Botanical Society: a biographical analysis of the membership', *Proceedings of the Botanical Society of the British Isles*, 6 (1967), 305–24 · R. Williamson, 'John Martyn and the Grub-street Journal, with particular references to his attacks on Richard Bentley, Richard Bradley', *Medical History*, 5 (1961), 361–74 · B. Henrey, *British botanical and horticultural literature before 1800*, 2 (1975), 50–51 · K. M. Albu, 'John and Thomas Martyn: a bibliography', DipLib diss., U. Lond., 1956 · R. Pulteney, *Historical and biographical sketches of the progress of botany in England*, 2 (1790), 205–18 · DNB

Archives NHM · U. Cam., department of plant sciences, annotated catalogues · U. Cam., department of plant sciences, herbarium | BL, letters to Thomas Birch, Add. MS 4313 · Bodl. Oxf., Patrick Blair MSS · NHM, letters to Patrick Blair

Likenesses oils, NPG [*see illus.*] · portrait, repro. in *House and Garden*, 34/8 (1979), 206

Martyn, Richard (d. 1483), bishop of St David's, is first recorded in 1448, when he supplicated as bachelor of canon law, at Oxford; he had incepted in canon law by

1478. He served as chaplain to John Tiptoft, earl of Worcester (d. 1470), from 1458 until at least 1464. He subsequently passed into the service of the crown, and the archdeaconry of London in 1469, and prebends in St Paul's, London, and St Stephen's Chapel, Westminster, both in 1471, may have been among his early rewards.

Among the complaints against Edward IV in 1469 was the king's inability to command the regular services of a body of lords. The deficiency was made up by the appointment of professional men retained by annuities, while the title of counsellor was extended to more than a score of doctors of law. Martyn, who had become a chancery clerk, was prominent among these. In May 1471 he arranged the funeral of Henry VI at Chertsey Abbey, and in February 1472 was appointed one of the tutors and counsellors of Edward, prince of Wales. He served as a master of chancery from 1472 to 1478, and was a member of the king's council and royal chaplain by 1478.

Martyn was also a diplomat, closely associated with Edward IV's tortuous foreign policy. He was one of the commissioners to treat for peace with Scotland in August 1471, and to treat with the ambassadors of Burgundy about the handing over of Henry Tudor, earl of Richmond, in March 1472. In 1475, during Edward IV's invasion of France, Martyn was employed in unsuccessful negotiations with Duke Charles of Burgundy, failing to persuade the duke to raise the siege of Neuss and come to Edward's aid. In March 1477 he treated with King Ferdinand of Aragon (r. 1479–1516) for the marriage of the latter's daughter, Isabella, to Edward, prince of Wales, and requested Ferdinand and his wife, Isabella of Castile (r. 1474–1516), to send an embassy to England. Thereafter he acted as an intermediary between Edward IV and Louis XI of France (r. 1461–83). In 1480 he was one of a large embassy sent to treat with Louis for the pension he had agreed to pay Edward in 1475. At a secret meeting the dispute between Louis XI and the Flemings was discussed, and also Edward's wish to arbitrate between Louis and the emperor's son, Maximilian of Austria. While this was going on Edward, presumably without Martyn's knowledge, was negotiating a marriage between the prince of Wales and Anne, daughter of the duke of Brittany, which was intended as a prelude to the invasion of France.

Martyn had more success applying Edward's domestic policies after 1471, being associated with the king's collection of revenues. The 'benevolences' by which Edward sought to raise money for his invasion of France of 1475 raised £22,000, and a letter survives commissioning Richard Martyn 'our counsellor to go to London t'exite and induce by all reason that you can or may make to us good and loving grants' (BL, Harley MS 980, art. 23). Martyn was also involved in Edward IV's efforts to enforce law and order in his second reign, and was appointed to a number of commissions of the peace in Gloucestershire, Herefordshire, Shropshire, and Worcestershire between February 1473 and May 1474, along with Richard, duke of Gloucester, Anthony Woodville, Lord Rivers, and George, duke of Clarence. He was appointed chancellor of Ireland in February 1478, but may not have taken up office.

Martyn was closely identified with the advance of the Woodvilles in Wales at the expense of the Herberts. He was appointed chancellor of the earldom of March for life in 1471, and on 26 February 1482 was nominated by the king for the bishopric of St David's. Papal provision followed on 26 April, and the temporalities were restored on 1 July. During his brief episcopate Martyn seems to have had little to do with his diocese, which he claimed to have found impoverished and heavily in debt. By 1478 he had become archdeacon of Hereford, and he was allowed to keep this and other benefices, to the value of 300 florins, nominally to allow him to repair dilapidated buildings at St David's. But there is no evidence that he actually financed any works. He died in 1483, probably on 25 March, and perhaps in London, since he was buried not in his own cathedral but in St Paul's Cathedral, by the crucifix near the north door. He endowed a yearly exhibition for the choristers to sing before this crucifix. His obit was observed in Christ Church Cathedral priory, Canterbury, to which he left his mitre and crozier.

JONATHAN HUGHES

Sources J. F. Baldwin, *The king's council in England during the middle ages* (1913) · C. Ross, *Edward IV* (1974) · C. L. Scofield, *The life and reign of Edward the Fourth*, 2 vols. (1923) · Emden, *Oxf.*, 2.1236–7 · BL, Harley MS 980, art. 23 · *Fasti Angl., 1300–1541*, [Hereford] · *Fasti Angl., 1300–1541*, [Welsh dioceses] · W. Dugdale, *The history of St Paul's Cathedral in London*, new edn, ed. H. Ellis (1818), 15, 246, 255 · G. Williams, *The Welsh church from conquest to Reformation* (1962), 257

Martyn, Thomas. See Martin, Thomas (1520/21–1592/3).

Martyn, Thomas (1735–1825), botanist, was born at Cambridge on 23 September 1735, the eldest surviving child of three sons and five daughters born to John *Martyn (1699–1768), professor of botany at the University of Cambridge, and his first wife, Eulalia (1703–1749), daughter of John King DD, rector of Chelsea. He was raised at his grandfather's house in Church Lane, Chelsea, and later recalled his visits during this time to the aged Sir Hans Sloane, bearing copies of his father's publications. From the age of five and a half until he was seventeen Martyn was educated under the Revd Rothery at Paradise Row, Chelsea, from where he entered Emmanuel College, Cambridge, as a pensioner in 1752. At Cambridge, Martyn studied classics under Richard Hurd; he gained two scholarships and an exhibition, but was held back by his dislike of mathematics and graduated fifth senior optime in 1756.

Martyn was always a keen student of botany, but although brought up by his father on the works of John Ray, he absorbed the works of Linnaeus on their first appearance, and was a convert and early proponent of Linnaean views. As fellowships at Emmanuel were temporarily suspended, Martyn was elected fellow at Sidney Sussex College, Cambridge, and ordained deacon in 1758, when he also proceeded MA, and priest in the following year. From 1760 to 1774 he acted as tutor of his college.

Following his father's resignation in 1762 Martyn was elected university professor of botany, a post he held for sixty-three years, though he only lectured until 1796, botany not being a very popular subject. When Dr Richard Walker gave the site of the Austin friary for a botanical

Thomas Martyn (1735–1825), by Giovanni Vendramini, pubd 1799 (after John Russell)

garden, Martyn became the first reader in botany under this endowment. In 1763 he gave his first course of lectures, based on the Linnaean system which was now gaining public and academic recognition. In the same year he published his first work, *Plantae Cantabrigienses*, and spent the long vacation in the Netherlands, Flanders, and Paris. In 1766 he graduated BD, and in 1770 he stood in when the garden's curator Charles Miller went to the East Indies.

In 1773 Martyn and his fellow tutor John Lettice, having bought the Italian original of *The Antiquities of Herculaneum* for £50 and laboured for five years on a translation, began publication; they issued only the first part, with fifty plates, before being stopped by objections from the Neapolitan court. Martyn resigned his fellowship to marry, on 9 December 1773, Martha Elliston (*d*. 1829), sister of Dr William Elliston, master of Sidney Sussex College. They had one child, John King Martyn. Martyn was presented by the bishop to the sequestration of Foxton and went to live at Triplow, near Cambridge, where he took pupils until 1776. At the beginning of 1774 his pupil John Borlase Warren presented him to the rectory of Ludgershall, Buckinghamshire, and in 1776 to the vicarage of Little Marlow, which became his headquarters until 1784.

In 1778 Martyn accompanied his pupil and ward, Edward Hartopp, of Little Dalby Hall, Leicestershire, for a two years' tour on the continent, taking with him his wife and infant son. After settling for some time at Vandoeuvres, near Geneva, they went as far south as Naples,

and returned to England by Venice, Tyrol, Cologne, and Brussels. Martyn kept a journal, part of which he afterwards published, and made a large collection of minerals to illustrate lectures on general natural history, with which he now found it expedient to supplement those on botany.

In 1784 Martyn went to London for his son's education, and, having purchased the Charlotte Street Chapel, Pimlico, from Dr Dodd, resigned the rectory of Ludgershall, in which he was succeeded by his half-brother, Claudius. At this time he produced his most popular work, *Letters on the Elements of Botany* (8 edns), a translation and continuation of the original work by Jean-Jacques Rousseau. He also began his most considerable undertaking, his edition of Philip Miller's *Gardener's Dictionary*, a new work on the Linnaean system, which he undertook in 1785 for White and Rivington for 1000 guineas, expecting to complete it in eleven years. It was not, however, published as a whole until 1807. He was elected FRS in 1786, and fellow of the Linnean Society in 1788, and afterwards acted as vice-president of the latter society.

Martyn contributed twenty letters to the *Gentleman's Magazine* in 1783–1800, principally on natural history, especially botany. In 1784 he entered into a polite exchange of seven letters on trees with Thomas Holt White in that periodical, in which he continued to espouse the Linnaean system of botanical nomenclature. In 1791, at the request of Sir J. B. Warren, he became secretary to the Society for the Improvement of Naval Architecture, which lasted until 1796. In 1793, after thirty years' work, his professorship at Cambridge was made a royal one, and he was given a pension of £100 per annum.

In 1798 Martyn moved to Pertenhall rectory, Bedfordshire, the home of his cousin, the Revd John King, who in 1800 resigned the living to the professor's son and only child, John King Martyn, fellow and mathematical lecturer of Sidney Sussex College, who in turn, in 1804, resigned it to his father. Martyn passed the remainder of his life in Pertenhall. He continued to preach until he was eighty-two, when his biographer, George Cornelius Gorham, became his curate. Martyn died at Pertenhall on 3 June 1825, and was buried in the chancel of his church, where a marble slab was placed to his memory.

G. S. BOULGER, *rev.* ARTHUR SHERBO

Sources G. C. Gorham and T. Martyn, *Memoirs of John Martyn … and of Thomas Martyn* (1830) · G. R. De Beer, 'Chelsea and John and Thomas Martyn', *Chelsea Society Report* (1947), 37–41 · 'The Rev. Thomas Martyn and the Surrey list of plants', *Phytologist*, new ser., 86 (1862), 163–73 · T. Faulkner, 'Interesting letter from the late professor Martyn', *GM*, 1st ser., 96/1 (1826), 291–2 · Nichols, *Lit. anecdotes*, 3.156–8 · *GM*, 1st ser., 95/2 (1825), 85–7
Archives Linn. Soc., annotated catalogue · NHM, corresp., drawings · U. Cam. Botanic Garden, annotated catalogue | Beds. & Luton ARS, letters to Miss G. Bell · BL, corresp. with John Strange, Add. MS 33349; Egerton MS 1970 · Linn. Soc., letters to Richard Pulteney · Linn. Soc., letters to Sir James Smith
Likenesses J. Farn, stipple (after S. Drummond, 1796), BM, NPG; repro. in *European Magazine* (Dec 1796), facing p. 395 · Holl, engraving (after J. Russell) · G. Vendramini, engraving (after J. Russell), priv. coll.; repro. in R. J. Thornton, *The philosophy of botany*, 2 vols. (1799) [*see illus.*]

Martyn, Thomas (*fl.* 1779–1811), natural history illustrator and pamphleteer, was said to be a native of Coventry, Warwickshire (Nichols, 8.432). Martyn developed a talent for coloured depictions of insects and shells. He purchased shells brought back from Cook's third voyage, although, as he wrote to Henry Seymer on 9 December 1780, 'I have purchased, amounting to 400 gns, more than 2 thirds of the whole brought home, Nevertheless I do not abound either in the variety of the new or many duplicates of the known ones that are valuable' (Dance, 100). He sold many of the shells, but the paucity of new species led him to modify his original plan to figure two different shells on each plate. Martyn sought to impose order on his subject: his *Universal Conchologist* bore the subtitle 'A new systematic arrangement by the author'. It had 160 hand-coloured plates, the whole being published in four folio volumes between 1784 and 1787, making it the greatest of all books on shells.

Since Martyn's illustrations were hand-coloured he needed the assistance of professional artists, but, finding that miniaturists were unwilling to interrupt their normal work to paint shells, he decided to recruit his own workforce and train boys to paint in a uniform style. His first boy joined him about 1779; others followed, and eventually he had ten young men at work in his 'academy' at 10 Great Marlborough Street, Westminster. In the first three and a half years over 6000 paintings were produced; at the end of that time Martyn saw that the standard had greatly improved, and decided to scrap the earlier plates and copies and begin again. This cost him dear, in time and money, but the splendour of the *Conchologist* brought him rewards in the form of gold medals from Pope Pius VI, the German Emperor Ferdinand, and the king of Naples, and flattering letters from lesser dignitaries.

Turning thereafter to insects, Martyn produced his *English Entomologist* (1792), followed by *Aranei, or, A Natural History of Spiders* (1793), a quarto in two parts. It included much of Eleazar Albin's well-known work on English spiders, Martyn having purchased Albin's drawings at the sale of the dowager duchess of Portland's museum. *Psyche: Figures of Non-Lepidopterous Insects* (1797) was probably produced privately and only about ten sets of its thirty-two stipple engravings are known to have been published. His only venture into botany, *Figures of Plants* (1795), consisted of forty-three coloured plates without text or captions.

Martyn reacted to the balloon flights of Lunardi and Blanchard in 1784 by issuing a pamphlet, *Hints of important uses to be derived from aerostatic globes. With a print of an aerostatic globe … originally designed in 1783* (1784). The design of his 'globe' and its undercarriage was utterly impractical, the proposed uses being to elevate military signals in wartime and to serve as bases to explore the upper atmosphere. Military matters seem to have held some fascination for Martyn. In 1804 he published *A Dive into Buonaparte's Councils on his Projected Invasion of Old England*, in which he advised the duke of York, as commander-in-chief of the king's forces, on the enemy's probable invasion tactics. He also offered advice on how to keep the British troops in good heart, by the provision of good food

and clothing, and medals for the brave. The preface states that the duke had recommended Martyn's son for a commission in the royal army or reserve. In patriotic mood, Martyn's *Great Britain's Jubilee Monitor* (1810) was merely a verbose and flattering expression of royalist sentiments. Nothing is known of his wife and family, nor of the circumstances of his death. ANITA MCCONNELL

Sources H. Buchanan, *Nature into art* (1979) · S. P. Dance, *Shell collecting: an illustrated history* (1966) · Nichols, *Lit. anecdotes*, 8.432 · T. Martyn, *A short account of the … private establishment instituted for the purposes of instructing youth in the art of illustrating and painting subjects in natural history* (1789) · T. Martyn, *Hints of important uses to be derived from aerostatic globes* (1784)

Martyn, William (*bap.* 1562, *d.* 1617), lawyer and historian, was baptized at St Petrock's, Exeter, on 19 September 1562, the eldest son of Nicholas Martyn (*d.* 1599) of Exeter and his first wife, Mary (*d.* 1576), daughter of Lennard Yeo of Hatherleigh. After having been sent to the grammar school at Exeter, Martyn matriculated at Broadgates Hall (afterwards Pembroke College), Oxford, in the autumn of 1581. He was admitted to the Middle Temple on 1 May 1582, and was called to the bar in 1589.

Martyn married at St Petrock's, on 28 November 1585, Susan, daughter of Thomas Prestwood of Exeter, with whom he had three sons, Nicholas (*d.* 1654), William, and Edward, and one daughter, Susanna. He represented Exeter in the 1597–8 parliament, and was its recorder from 1607 until his death. Susan Martyn died in January 1606, and Martyn then married Jane, daughter of Henry Huishe of Sands in Sidbury, Devon.

Martyn was the author of a work of morality (directed towards his son Nicholas) entitled *Youth's Instruction* (1612). He then turned to medieval history in *The historie, and lives, of the kings of England from William the Conqueror unto the end of the raigne of Henrie the Eight* (1615), containing preliminary verses from his three sons and his son-in-law and an appendix of 'succession of dukes and earles' and other particulars. A second edition appeared in 1628, which was illustrated with portraits of the kings by R. Elstrack, most of which were sold by 'Compton Holland over against the Exchange'. An enlarged third edition appeared in 1638 with lengthier lives of Edward VI, Mary I, and Elizabeth I. This was written by 'B. R., Master of arts' who lifted his accounts nearly verbatim from William Camden's *Annales* and Francis Godwin's *Annales* of Edward and Mary.

Martyn's history reaches no further back than the Norman conquest, like many of his contemporary historians. Unlike Francis Bacon, Camden, John Hayward, and Samuel Daniel, however, his history is suffused by moral rather than political judgements (of the same flavour as his *Youth's Instruction*) which make it appear sententious. The sermonizing character of many of his verdicts on particular kings, especially the Scottish Stuarts, may have offended James I, who only a year earlier had caused Sir Walter Ralegh's *History of the World* to be called in. On 25 February 1615, barely a month after Martyn had dated the preface to his book, he was arrested and taken before the council. It fell to Bacon, a future historian himself and then attorney-general, to charge Martyn with having written a history with offensive passages. He was soon released, after apologizing, and returned to Exeter. Fuller's remark that the king forgot the offence seems correct since subsequent issues of the book were unaltered.

But the incident proved too much for Martyn, and he died at Exeter, having never recovered his 'former cheerfulnesse' (Fuller, 1.306; Wood, 2.199), on 7 April 1617. He was buried on 12 April in St Petrock's Church. By his will, drawn up on 18 September 1610 and amended on the day of his death, he expressed assurance of salvation 'by a lively faith in Christ Jesus my Saviour and Redeemer' and made provision for his wife and children, who survived him, from various properties in Devon (PRO, PROB 11/130, sig. 81).   D. R. WOOLF

Sources Wood, *Ath. Oxon.*, new edn, 2.199 · *Report on records of the city of Exeter*, HMC, 73 (1916), 55, 132 · Fuller, *Worthies* (1811), 306 · H. A. C. Sturgess, ed., *Register of admissions to the Honourable Society of the Middle Temple, from the fifteenth century to the year 1944*, 1 (1949), 53 · *APC, 1615–6*, 62, 67, 73, 100 · D. MacLeane, *Oxford college histories: Pembroke College* (1900), 34 · D. R. Woolf, *The idea of history in early Stuart England* (1990), 72–5 · will, PRO, PROB 11/130, sig. 81 · DNB

Marvell, Andrew (*c*.1584–1641), Church of England clergyman, was born at Meldreth in south-west Cambridgeshire, one of the two sons of Andrew Marvell (*d*. 1628), yeoman, and his wife, Johanne (*d*. 1615). The family, which had long been settled in the area, farmed some 50 acres of land in the village. Marvell was admitted in 1601 to Emmanuel College, Cambridge, and elected scholar in 1604, graduating BA in 1605 and proceeding MA in 1608. After entering the diaconate at York in March 1607 he was in November licensed by the bishop of Ely to serve as curate and schoolmaster at Melbourne, adjacent to his birthplace. By January 1609 his signature as curate appears in the register of burials at Flamborough in the East Riding, and he was ordained priest in York Minster on 30 May (Trinity Sunday).

At Cherry Burton near Beverley, on 22 October 1612, Marvell married Anne Pease (*d*. 1638), whose precise parentage remains unknown though the surname was a local one. On 23 April 1614 he was formally inducted as rector of Winestead in Holderness, a parish to the east of Kingston upon Hull, where all his five children were baptized. Of his two sons only Andrew *Marvell (1621–1678), the poet, reached manhood; John (*b*. 1623) died on 20 September 1624, ten days before the corporation of Hull appointed Marvell lecturer at Holy Trinity Church. Shortly afterwards he obtained the mastership of the Charterhouse Hospital, outside the north walls, which became his home. There he was joined in 1626 by his father and his brother Edward and family, perhaps fleeing the plague or Charles I's forced loan. In due course his daughters became the wives of Hull townsmen, Anne (*b*. 1615) marrying James Blaydes in 1633, Mary (*b*. 1617) marrying Edmund Popple in 1636, and Elizabeth (*b*. 1618) marrying Robert More by 1642.

During Marvell's stewardship of the Charterhouse the number of almspeople was increased, the fabric and chapel were extensively repaired, and annual accounts

faithfully rendered. Otherwise, according to his son, he 'lived with some measure of reputation, both for Piety and Learning: and he was moreover a Conformist to the established Rites of the Church of *England*, though I confess none of the most over-running or eager in them' (Marvell, *Rehearsal*, pt 2, 128). It is true that early on he fell out with the vicar of Hull about preaching, and as late as 1639 was ordered by the diocese to read, in hood and surplice, more of the prayer book liturgy before his weekly lecture. Yet some autograph complaints against local separatists (manuscript in Hull Local History Library) and notes on the necessity of observing church ritual (BL, Harley MS 6356, fols. 197r–197v) indicate only a moderate puritanism.

Thomas Fuller's anecdotal account derives from a son-in-law of Marvell. It portrays him as 'most *facetious* in his *discourse*, yet *grave* in his *carriage*; a most excellent preacher, who, like a good husband, never *broached* what he had new *brewed*, but preached what he had pre-studied some competent time before' (Fuller, *Worthies*, 159). Several of his sermons survive in manuscript. Besides those still preserved in Hull, 'Israel and England parallel'd' (London, Inner Temple Library) was dedicated in 1627 to Anne Sadleir of Standon, Hertfordshire, sister of his traditional benefactor Bridget Skinner of Thornton Curtis, Lincolnshire. A copy of the address which, although himself recently under quarantine from the plague, he delivered at the funeral of John Ramsden, mayor of Hull, on 8 December 1637 survives in BL, Harley MS 6356, fols. 153–62. He corresponded on theological matters with brother ministers (for example BL, Lansdowne MS 891, fol. 118), sometimes acrimoniously, while Fuller mentions that his 'excellent comment upon Saint *Peter* is daily desired and expected'.

Marvell's first wife died in 1638 and was buried at Holy Trinity on 28 April. On 27 November of the same year he married, at Norton in Derbyshire, Lucy (1592–1664), widow of William Harris, by birth a member of the Alured family who were Marvell's neighbours at the Charterhouse; he was her third husband. The merchants and civic authorities of Hull continued to show their appreciation of his services by gifts and bequests until his death by drowning on 23 January 1641, in a '*Barrow-boat*' that became '*sand-warpt*' while crossing the Humber. His sole contemporary memorial is an anonymous verse-elegy jotted into the parish register of Pickering, North Riding of Yorkshire.   W. H. KELLIHER

Sources A. Marvell, *The rehearsal transpros'd*, pt 2 (1673) · Fuller, *Worthies* · P. Legouis, *André Marvell: poète, puritain, et patriote* (Paris, 1928); abridged Eng. edn as *Andrew Marvell: poet, puritan, patriot*, 2nd edn (1968) · *The complete works in verse and prose of Andrew Marvell*, ed. A. B. Grosart, 4 vols. (1872–5) · *N&Q*, 6th ser., 2 (1880), 174 · *N&Q*, 227 (1982), 33–44 · *N&Q*, 229 (1984), 379–85 · *N&Q*, 230 (1985), 172–80 · R. Marchant, *The puritans and the church courts in the diocese of York, 1560–1642* (1960) · L. M. Stanewell, ed., *City and county of Kingston upon Hull: calendar of the ancient deeds, letters, miscellaneous old documents, &c. in the archives of the corporation* (1951) · *VCH Cambridgeshire and the Isle of Ely*, vol. 8 · *VCH Yorkshire East Riding*, vols. 1–2 · *Proceedings of the Cambridge Antiquarian Society*, 70 (1980), 172 · Ely diocesan records, CUL

Archives BL, Harley MS 6356, fols. 153–62, 197r–197v · BL, Lansdowne MS 891, fol. 118 · Hull Central Library, Wilson-Barkway MS of sermons, etc.

Marvell, Andrew (1621–1678), poet and politician, was born on 31 March 1621, 'being Easter-even', in the rectory at Winestead, in the Holderness region of the East Riding of Yorkshire, and baptized in the church of St German there on 5 April. He was the fourth child and elder son of the Revd Andrew *Marvell (c.1584–1641) and his first wife, Anne Pease (d. 1638). In September 1624 the family moved to Kingston upon Hull, one of the most important trading centres in the north of England. Marvell's boyhood was passed in the master's house of the Charterhouse hospital, a small community of alms-people, which, with its chapel and gardens, stood in a rural suburb half a mile north of the walls. Of his schooldays he later recalled the Latin scansion 'that we learn'd at [the] Grammar-School' (*Mr. Smirke*, 1676, 6) at the heart of the seaport.

Cambridge and the continent On 13 December 1633, three months before his thirteenth birthday, Marvell matriculated from Trinity College, Cambridge. If entry to the university at such an early age suggests precocity it may also explain why he graduated after five years instead of the normal three. As a sub-sizar, the lowest rank of student, he carried out day-to-day tasks for seniors for an annual allowance of 6s. 8d., with a further 4d. each week for food. The scholarship to which he was elected in April 1638 more than doubled his income, and further funds would have come from the 'dry' chorister's place that he appears to have held from 1640 to 1642 (BL, Add. MS 5846, fol. 133v). Although this post, which his contemporary Abraham Cowley also enjoyed, did not carry any duty of singing, Marvell's love of music is apparent throughout his poetry. His only known compositions at this time are some Greek verses and a Latin reworking of an ode of Horace that he wrote, in anticipation of the birth in March 1637 of Princess Anne, for the university's congratulatory *Sunwdia*. After subscribing for his BA degree on 27 February 1639, the young puritan fell under the influence of Catholic proselytizers. As his earliest editor puts it, some 'Jesuits … seeing in him a Genius beyond his Years' enticed him from the university, but after 'some Months his Father found him in a *Bookseller's* shop in *London*, and prevailed with him to return' (*Works*, ed. Cooke, 1.5).

At home in Hull, the death of Marvell's mother in April 1638 had been followed in November by his father's marriage to Lucy Harris, and his drowning on the Humber in January 1641. The Revd Andrew died intestate, but, on 23 July, Jane Grey, the remarried widow of his brother Edward (d. 1631), made over to young Andrew 47½ acres of copyhold land that the Marvells had long farmed in Meldreth, Cambridgeshire (LMA, H1/ST/E79/24, m.37). These he at once mortgaged to his brothers-in-law Edmund Popple and James Blaydes for £260, repayable in two instalments by the eve of his majority; nine years later they were still unredeemed. At the same time he paid a fine of £3 to retain the house and 2½ acres which can be identified with the property traditionally known as the Marvells and

Andrew Marvell (1621–1678), by unknown artist, c.1655–60

nowadays as Meldreth Court. The sudden inheritance and his release from paternal control freed Marvell to turn his back on academic life. On 24 September 1641 an entry in the college conclusion book warned that he and four other graduates 'in regard that some of them are reported to be maryed and the other looke not after their dayes nor Acts … shalbe out of their places unles thei show just cause … for the contrary in 3 months'.

Early in 1642 Marvell was in London, taking the protestation oath on 17 February as a resident of Cowcross Street in the fashionable area of Clerkenwell, not far from the inns of court. In the same month he witnessed three deeds transferring lands in Yorkshire from Sir William Savile of Thornhill to Thomas, first Viscount Savile. At some unknown date, possibly following the outbreak of serious hostilities in August, he left England and in doing so escaped the first civil war entirely. Much later he was to pass over his failure to engage himself with the paradox that 'the Cause was too good to have been fought for' (*Rehearsal Transpros'd*, 135). All that is known of the extent of his itinerary comes from Milton's remark that he had passed four years in Holland, France, Italy, and Spain 'to very good purpose, as I beleeve & the gaining of those 4 languages' (Milton to J. Bradshaw, 21 Feb 1653, PRO, SP 18/33/75). While a later allusion to his 'Fencing-master in Spain' (*Poems*, 2.324) suggests that he had lived in some style, his own resources would hardly have sufficed for such a prolonged stay. The likeliest explanation is suggested by a later report of his having been employed as governor to a young nobleman on his travels. A fixed point is provided by his brilliant if cruel lampoon 'Fleckno, an

English priest at Rome', which belongs to Lent 1646. Richard Flecknoe was a literary protégé of the second duke of Buckingham and his brother Lord Francis Villiers, former contemporaries of Marvell at Trinity who in the previous autumn had taken a house in Rome.

Poetry and politics Marvell was back in England at the latest by 12 November 1647, when he sold the Meldreth house, apparently for £80, attending the transfer in person. Although the deed describes him as 'of Kingstone super Hull Gentleman', some poems that he wrote over the next three years imply close contact with literary circles in London. 'An elegy upon the death of my Lord Francis Villiers', who had met his death in July 1648 during a brief royalist uprising, represents Marvell's first independent, though anonymous, venture into print. Commendatory verses 'To his noble friend Mr. Richard Lovelace', published in the *Lucasta* of May 1649, were followed in June by a lament on the death of the nineteen-year-old Henry, Lord Hastings, written for Richard Brome's commemorative *Lachrymae musarum*. But his pronounced royalism had changed by June 1650, when he wrote 'An Horatian Ode upon Cromwell's Return from Ireland', one of the greatest political poems in English. While reflecting sympathetically on Charles I's conduct at execution, it hails Cromwell as the dominant figure in the new republic. Critics and historians have debated at length the precise extent of Marvell's conversion to the parliamentarian cause, especially since 'Tom May's Death', written in November, denounces a former royalist poet for turning 'Chronicler to *Spartacus*' (ll. 73–4). What probably provoked this outburst was the grant of a state funeral to May while his rival Davenant, whose poetry Marvell admired, lay under threat of death. The safest reading of his politics in the 1650s is probably that he was prepared to accept any government that would operate within a constitutional framework, and that his admiration of Cromwell was conditional on his remaining 'still in the *Republick's* hand'.

Nun Appleton Composition of the 'Horatian ode' coincided with the resignation of Thomas, third Lord Fairfax, from supreme command of the parliamentary forces, largely in opposition to the Scottish campaign, which the poem welcomes. On Fairfax's withdrawal to his native Yorkshire, Marvell was employed as tutor in languages to his twelve-year-old daughter Mary. It says much about his character and religious temper that her devoutly Presbyterian parents and formidable grandmother Lady Vere found him, in Milton's phrase, 'of an approved conversation' (PRO, SP 18/33/75). By the winter he was praising his pupil in some English verses prefaced to the translation of James Primrose's *Popular Errors* (1651) by the Hull physician Robert Witty.

Marvell's new surroundings proved both congenial and conducive to poetry. The family domain stretched eastward from Fairfax's birthplace at Denton, above the River Wharfe, to his town house on Bishophill in York, taking in the country retreats of Bilbrough and the former nunnery of Nun Appleton, his favourite seat. All are celebrated in a series of English and Latin verses dedicated to the

employer who had left the world of action for a life of rural contemplation. The longest of these, 'Upon Appleton House', stands out among contemporary estate and topographical poems by sharp perception of the natural setting, and startling images. The mower sequence of poems, which sets the 'wild and fragrant Innocence' of fields above the 'enforc'd' culture of gardens, has also been ascribed to this interlude, though 'The Garden' itself, with its Latin counterpart, may date from an altogether later period. That Marvell was still writing lyric verse after the Restoration is confirmed by the graceful epitaph 'Enough: and leave the rest to fame' (March 1672).

Cromwell's poet By the winter of 1652–3 Marvell was back in London, where in mid-February the prospect of a career at the centre of public life presented itself by the death of Rudolph Weckherlin, assistant to the blind Milton in the Latin secretaryship to the council of state. On 21 February Milton wrote to President Bradshaw recommending Marvell in strong terms both as 'a scholler & well read in the Latin and Greeke authors' and as 'a man whom both by report, & the converse I have had with him, [is] of singular desert for the State to make use of' (PRO, SP 18/33/75). Soon after, Marvell marked an English naval victory with 'The Character of Holland', in which he calls on personal experience to satirize Dutch manners, and proclaims the new regime at home as the 'Darling of Heaven'. Despite failing to obtain the government post he was taken up by Cromwell himself as governor to his protégé William Dutton, nephew and heir of Cromwell's wealthy friend John Dutton of Sherborne in Gloucestershire. As prospective husband for Cromwell's youngest daughter, Frances, it was essential that the youth be brought up in sound religious doctrines. On 28 July, Marvell wrote to his employer of their reception in the house of the puritan John Oxenbridge, vicar of Windsor and fellow of Eton College. The friendship that he developed with their hosts is confirmed by the Latin epitaph for Oxenbridge's wife, while the hymn of religious exile 'Bermudas' has been traced to recollections of the Oxenbridges' retreat there from Laudian persecution. A year later Marvell was promising to study a presentation copy of Milton's *Defensio secunda* 'even to the getting of it by Heart' (*Poems*, 2.306).

Two important poems that Marvell wrote at this time extol Cromwell and promote his political aims. In December 'The First Anniversary of the Government under O. C.' drew on musical and biblical analogies to celebrate the political harmony created by a protector who declines to be king. It was issued anonymously by a government printer in mid-January 1655. Some months later Marvell sent a long verse-letter in Latin to Nathaniel Ingelo, a fellow of the college who had gone as choirmaster to Bulstrode Whitelocke's embassy to Kristina of Sweden. Its overtly political message was reinforced by the message of the well-known Latin tetrastich that Marvell composed to accompany the gift of Cromwell's portrait to the queen.

Late in the same year Samuel Hartlib in London jotted down some information sent by John Worthington, an occasional visitor to Eton, about:

one Marvel of 40. *years* of age who hath spent all his time in travelling abroad with Noblemens so*nn*es and is skilled in several Languages, who is now again to goe with one's so*nn*e of 8. thous*and* a *year* who is fitter to be a Secretary of State &c. (Sheffield University Library, H50/29/5/50A)

By the following January, Marvell and his charge had passed through Paris and reached Saumur in the Loire valley, a leading centre of protestantism favoured by the well-to-do of several nations for the education of their sons. On 15 August a royalist visitor, James Scudamore, reported that he had seen virtually no Englishmen of note but 'Mr Dutton called by the french Le Genre [that is, *Gendre*, son-in-law] du Protecteur whose Governour is one Mervill a notable English Italo-Machavillian' (BL, Add. MS 15858, fol. 135). Marvell seems to have been promoting republican writings there; he is evidently the learned friend whom twelve months later Milton mentioned to Oldenburg as having sent back word of local interest in the *Defensio*. In all likelihood the death of Dutton's uncle early in 1657 brought to an end three and a half years of close fellowship.

Civil servant Nothing certain is known of Marvell's activities for most of this year. The verses on Blake's victory at Santa Cruz in April, separately printed in 1674 and incorporated in the posthumous *Miscellaneous Poems* (1681), do not seem to be his (see Duncan-Jones). But on 2 September he finally entered the civil service as Latin secretary in the office of John Thurloe, secretary to the council of state and head of the government's intelligence service. His salary was £200 per year and his duties included writing letters to heads of state, translating foreign documents, acting as interpreter, and occasionally even receiving foreign envoys. After the Restoration he was to deny having had 'the remotest relation to publick matters' until taking up this post, 'which I consider'd to be the most innocent and inoffensive … of any in that usurped and irregular Government' and which he claimed to have discharged 'without disobliging any one person' (*Rehearsal Transpros'd*, 203). In November he wrote two lyrics to be sung at the festivities in Whitehall for the wedding of Viscount Fauconberg and Mary, third daughter of the music-loving protector; they include a tactful glance at the marriage of Frances Cromwell to Lord Rich one week earlier. Ten months later Cromwell was dead, and Marvell and Milton were granted six yards of mourning to walk in procession with Dryden, Hartlib, and Peter Sterry at his state funeral. 'A Poem upon the Death of O. C.', besides conveying the writer's sense of awe and personal loss, dwells on the human side of a great public figure. Although it was scheduled for publication in January 1659 along with elegies by Dryden and Sprat, its place was taken by a reprint of Waller's elegy.

Member of parliament Under the new protector, Richard Cromwell, Marvell not only retained his civil service post but was returned in January 1659 as one of the two MPs for Hull. In the Commons he voted with the majority against the opposition until the fall of the protectorate in May, when the restoration of the Rump saw him unseated by his predecessor, the younger Harry Vane. The regicide Thomas Scott now replaced Thurloe as Marvell's superior

in the civil service and by July Marvell had been granted lodgings in Whitehall; when the council was dissolved in October his salary was £86 in arrear. That winter he may have spoken at the Rota, the political club founded by his 'intimate friend' the republican James Harrington. Marvell was returned at the elections of 2 April 1660 to the Convention Parliament that recalled the Stuarts, coming a distant second to his partner in defeating Hull's republicans. There he was not entirely allowed to forget his recent affiliations: in July he was ordered to help in replying to a letter of congratulation on the Restoration, and in December was rebuked when he offered a complaint on the treatment of Milton, whom he had defended while his life was at stake during the indemnity debates. Unlike his friend he was not implacably opposed to monarchy, and had moreover been encouraged by Charles's promise of 'a liberty to tender consciences' at Breda. Marvell's own religious position has never been clearly defined. While more than sympathetic to dissent, and bitterly opposed both to Catholicism and episcopacy, he seems himself to have been a conforming Anglican. But a failed attempt in November to bring in a bill for a modified episcopacy, on which he acted as teller for the ayes, was an early indication of how little headway comprehension was to make in the Restoration settlement.

Marvell's continued exertions on Hull's behalf after the December dissolution were rewarded by re-election in April 1661. In the Cavalier or Pensionary Parliament he retained his seat for all but the sixteenth and last session, receiving from the borough a salary of 6*s*. 8*d*. per day while the house sat, besides expenses and occasional barrels of ale. He proved an able and attentive constituency member, his zeal reflected in the self-mocking description of how

The portly *burgess*, through the Weather hot,
Does for his Corporation sweat and trot
(*Last Instructions*, ll. 831–2)

and in the newsletters that he addressed to 'my very worthy friends'. Almost 300 of these, written between November 1660 and his death, still survive, though there are considerable gaps in the series. In the general dearth of parliamentary reportage at this period they provide a useful firsthand account of public business. Though more impersonal than might be wished—in October 1675 he remarked that 'I am naturally and now more by my Age inclined to keep my thoughts private' (*Poems*, 2.166)—they do not lack an occasional dry wit. In the Commons he proved by the standards of the day moderately active, attending regularly when not absent abroad and acting as teller in eight divisions. He was named to 120 committees, though evidence of his work there is largely confined to examination of an informant in December 1666 as to the causes of the great fire. Records survive of his speaking on fourteen occasions only, and as late as 1677 he was apologizing for lack of practice (Grey, 4.330). His effectiveness as a politician was doubtless hampered by the fact that he 'had not a generall acquaintance' (*Brief Lives*, 2.54). Cooke alleges affiliations with two leading opposition figures, Prince Rupert, whose 'Tutor' in political matters he was said to be, and William Cavendish, later first duke of Devonshire (*Works*, ed. Cooke, 1.10–11). His natural loyalties lay with the country party, that:

> Gross of *English Gentry*, nobly born,
> Of clear *Estates*, and to no Faction sworn
> (*Last Instructions*, ll. 285–306)

but his tendency to act according to his own lights made him difficult to manage. Moreover his behaviour in the house could be unruly; in March 1662 he was forced to apologize for having provoked Thomas Clifford into striking him.

Embassy to Russia The extent of Marvell's involvement in Hull's affairs is also witnessed by sixty-nine surviving letters to the Trinity House there, two-thirds of which relate to a plan for a lighthouse at Spurn Head. On 8 May 1662 he advised the wardens that 'by the interest of some persons too potent for me to refuse … I am obliged to go beyond sea' (*Poems*, 2.250). Promoting this unstated errand was a former member of Cromwell's bodyguard, Charles Howard, newly created earl of Carlisle, whose brother-in-law Sir George Downing was playing host to Marvell at The Hague by 24 May. When an extension of his stay over the following winter led Lord Bellasis, the royalist steward of Hull, to urge his replacement in parliament, he abandoned his 'private concernments' and was back in his seat by 2 April. But on 20 July, one week before the house rose, he wrote again of an immediate departure, with leave from the house and 'his Majestyes good liking', as secretary to Carlisle's embassy to the northern powers (ibid., 2.254). The main purpose was to secure the restoration of privileges revoked from English merchants at Archangel by Tsar Alexis following the execution of Charles I. An account that was published later by Marvell's assistant Guy de Miège describes how, after landing at Archangel in August, they were delayed for three months at Vologda before taking sledge to Moscow. Exception taken to a Latin form of address used by Marvell of Alexis at an audience in February 1664 drew from him a learned but ultimately unsuccessful defence. In June the embassy, with some bitterness at Carlisle's returning the tsar's gifts, left for audiences with the kings of Sweden (14 September) and Denmark (30 October) in an equally unproductive attempt to secure backing for war with the Dutch. Near Hamburg, in December, Marvell threatened an uncooperative waggoner with his pistol and had to be rescued from a 'barbarous rout', sparking off a general skirmish (Miège, 430–31). After an almost continuous absence of two and a half years he returned to the house a month before it rose in March 1665.

On 4 March 1665 Charles declared war on the Dutch. The progress of the long campaign was followed in a series of satirical poems that took their rise from Waller's panegyric *Instructions to a Painter* on the duke of York's leadership in the battle off Lowestoft in June 1665. Recent editorial opinion inclines to Marvell as the author of the *Second* and *Third Advice* (April and October 1666), as he was of the later and more ambitious *Last Instructions to a Painter* (September 1667). From his seat in parliament he was well placed to observe political developments, while his maritime expertise was to be acknowledged by his election in May 1674 as an elder brother of the Deptford Trinity House, of which in the year of his death he rose to be younger warden. In *Last Instructions* the debates of October 1666 on a measure to impose a general excise are made the occasion for a mock-heroic catalogue of members (ll. 121–334); a section describing the progress of Dutch warships unopposed up the Thames almost to the heart of the capital (ll. 523–760) leads to an attack on administrative failures. Marvell derides attempts to shuffle the blame onto the navy commissioner Peter Pett (ll. 765–90), whom he defended in the house also, being named (17 October) to the committee to consider the conduct of the war and the sale of Dunkirk.

During Marvell's absence abroad the predominantly Anglican and loyalist parliament had repealed the Triennial Act and passed a law against conventicles, thus concluding the series of measures that became known as the Clarendon code. Whatever his views on the administration, and despite having given voice to popular suspicions of misappropriation in 'Clarindon's house-warming' (July), Marvell now argued against shaming the chancellor in a vote to the king and opposed precipitate action to impeach him on the ground of his 'not being likely to ride away post' (Grey, 1.14). In November his call for substantiation of Clarendon's alleged remark regarding Charles's unfitness to govern drew his fellow poets Denham to testify to it and Waller to call for its retention in the articles (ibid., 1.36–7).

In February 1668 Marvell attacked the new chief minister, Arlington, 'somewhat transportedly', for buying his place and title, but when asked to elaborate said that the matter 'was so plain, it needed it not' (Grey, 1.70). Arlington was instrumental in the same month in concluding with the Netherlands and Sweden a triple alliance for consolidation of protestant liberties, but any hopes that it raised in Marvell were dispelled over the next two years by the increasingly pro-French policies of king and government. Marvell's private letters testify to a growing fear of civil and religious absolutism, and his anger at the treatment of protestant dissenters. On 21 March 1670 he sent his nephew William Popple a bleak account of affairs (*Poems*, 2.315), deploring recent enlargements of royal authority, particularly in the establishment of a Scottish militia and in the renewal of the bill against nonconformist conventicles, which he had opposed in the house, and now described as 'the Quintessence of arbitrary Malice'. Altogether, he concluded, no king since the conquest was 'so absolutely powerful at Home', and the diminution of Stuart powers now became one of his main concerns. His disillusion with Charles sought expression in satirical ballads, the jocular manner of 'The King's Vows' (early 1670) eventually giving way to the darker tone of 'Upon his Majesty's being Made Free of the City' (December 1674). 'The Loyal Scott' (1669/70) redeploys the Douglas episode from *Last Instructions* as part of a bitter attack on Episcopal opposition to union with Scotland.

A year later, when the prorogation of parliament threatened his livelihood, Marvell entertained hopes of some unspecified 'honest fair Employment into *Ireland*' (*Poems*, 2.323). A report of 1671 appears to link him, in a faction formed against Ormond by Buckingham, with Thomas Blood, whose attempt on the crown jewels in May gave Marvell the cue for a sharp epigram on clerical cruelty. Despite his manifest patriotism and his complaining that summer of how we 'truckle to *France* in all Things' (ibid., 2.325), he drafted five Latin distichs in response to Colbert's prize competition for an inscription for the pediment of the Louvre. By Christmas he was at Winchendon, a seat of the prominent dissenter Philip, fourth Lord Wharton, acting as moderator in the search for a bride for his eldest son. They shared an interest in poetry, and in April 1667, 'having nothing of mine own to deserve your acceptance', he had sent Wharton Simon Ford's Latin and English verses on the great fire.

Controversial writings In the following autumn there appeared the first part of the work by which Marvell was best-known in his own time and for long after: *The Rehearsal Transpros'd*. Its target was Samuel Parker, later bishop of Oxford, whom Marvell had first met in Milton's house in 1662–3, before the zealous young dissenter had conformed, risen in the church, and turned on his former fellows. By 1670 Parker was upholding the power of the civil authority over religious externals in *A Discourse of Ecclesiastical Polity*, but it was the attack on toleration of nonconformity that he prefaced to Bramhall's *Vindication* (September 1672) that finally provoked Marvell to respond. The title of his anonymously published reply, and the name Bayes which he uses to mock his opponent, derive from Buckingham's satirical play *The Rehearsal*, where the protagonist—a caricature of Dryden to which Marvell was to return in his prefatory verses to the second edition of *Paradise Lost*—defines his practice of turning prose into verse as 'transversing'.

Marvell's tract pursues no coherent line of argument but is framed in what Wood called 'the then, but newly, refin'd art of sportive and jeering bufoonery' (Wood, *Ath. Oxon.*, 4.231). Ill-advised innuendos about the love life of 'Mr Bayes' were repaid with interest by the writers of five printed replies and a scurrilous verse-lampoon entitled 'A love letter to the author of the RT' who accused Marvell of sodomy and impotence, alleging that he had been surgically castrated. A second issue was allowed to pass by the censor, L'Estrange, with only slight changes, after the king read it and let it be known that 'Parker has done him wrong, and this man has done him Right' (Leics. RO, Finch MSS, DG7, box 4985) over the recent declaration of religious indulgence (March 1672). The forced withdrawal of this hasty measure twelve months later aided Parker in his long *Reproof*, to which Marvell replied with a second part (1673), issued under his own name. This defiantly quotes on its title-page a threat made against his life if he should publish any further 'Lie or Libel' against his opponent. The verdict of contemporaries was that the 'victory lay on Marvell's side' (Wood, *Ath. Oxon.*, 4.231), and a generation later Swift, hailing him as an innovative genius,

remarked that 'we still read *Marvel's* Answer to *Parker* with Pleasure' ('Apology' to *Tale of a Tub*, 1710).

In March 1672 Charles II joined Louis XIV in a third war against the Dutch. Marvell, who was ultimately to play a part in framing the parliamentary address for peace, seems to have been active in a Dutch fifth column headed by Peter Du Moulin and including John Ayloff. Spies of Secretary Williamson reported a brief conference early in 1674 between William of Orange and a member of parliament, 'a thicke short man … much like Mervell' who went under the name of Mr George, and, in June, giving his code name as Mr Thomas, alleged that a difference of opinion with his fellows had led to his retiring into the country (Hayley, 57–8, 62–3). If so, his place of retreat may have been the Highgate property, known much later as Marvell's Cottage, where in the next summer he resolved to 'sequester my self one whole day' (*Poems*, 2.341). In a clever and libellous mock speech (*Poems on Affairs of State*, 1704, vol. 3) composed perhaps as early as the following February, he anticipated Charles's inevitable plea for supply at the reassembly of parliament on 13 April. Its exposure of the king's wayward inclinations is matched in a series of related verse-satires comprising 'The statue in Stocks-Market' (after October 1674), 'The Statue at Charing Cross' (July 1675), and 'A Dialogue between the Two Horses' (late 1675), the attribution of which to Marvell has sometimes been disputed. During the same session he acted as teller for the yeas in a failed bill to prevent MPs accepting public offices, a device much used by Lord Treasurer Danby to buy off opposition, as satirized that year in 'The Chequer Inn'. It was no small part of the emerging Marvell legend that the alleged royal bribe offered to him in his modest lodging in Maiden Lane by Danby himself should have been firmly rejected (*Works*, ed. Cooke, 1.11–14). Before the house rose he was named to the committee on the bill to disable Catholics from sitting in parliament and appointed a commissioner for recusancy in his native Yorkshire.

During the fifteen-month prorogation that followed, Marvell took it on himself to defend the views of an Anglican dignitary while continuing his attack on episcopacy. Herbert Croft, bishop of Hereford, had argued in *The Naked Truth* (1675) for an accommodation with the nonconformists and had been taken to task by Francis Turner in *Animadversions* (1676), written in an attempt at bantering humour. Marvell's *Mr. Smirke, or, The Divine in Mode* (May 1676), published under the pseudonym Andreas Rivetus junior—the borrowed identity makes a convenient anagram of *res nuda veritas* ('naked truth')—mocks Turner in the character of Lady Bigot's 'pretty spruce' chaplain in George Etherege's *Man of Mode*. Croft had drawn on precedents from the primitive church; Marvell followed him in *A Short Historical Essay, Concerning General Councils*, which he appended to the tract, and in which he explored the origins of disputes between rival sects in the third century, concluding that 'the true and single cause then was the Bishops' (*Mr. Smirke*, 71). Government attempts at prosecution failed, though Nathaniel Ponder suffered a brief imprisonment for publishing the work without licence.

On 27 March 1677 Marvell made his longest recorded speech (Grey, 4.321–5), opposing a bill for educating royal children in the protestant faith that had been inspired by the prospect of the duke of York's succession to the throne. Faced with a difficult choice, he concluded that whether the bill would 'prevent Popery, or not' it would 'secure the promotions of the Bishops'. Two days later a friendly tussle with Sir Philip Harcourt was drawn to the attention of the house by the speaker and debated; despite an initial smart rejoinder Marvell submitted himself to censure.

In September, Marvell wrote 'an excellent epitaph', now lost, on James Harrington, but suppressed it because it 'would have given offence' (*Brief Lives*, 1.293), perhaps because of his increasing apprehension of personal danger. Early in the previous year had occurred the collapse of a banking partnership set up by a group of London merchants that included two of his distant relatives, Edward Nelthorpe and Richard Thompson. After commissions of bankruptcy were issued against them they went into hiding in July 1677 in a house in St Giles-in-the-Fields that Marvell had taken for the purpose. An appeal for their discovery was published in the *London Gazette* for 28–31 January 1678, and Marvell himself was named to a committee to consider their case. Not content with harbouring fugitives, he risked prosecution with a work written largely in the autumn and given the finishing touches in December 1677. *An Account of the Growth of Popery and Arbitrary Government* marks Marvell's final abandonment of any hopes that he had in Charles II. It opens with the bold contention that 'There has now for diverse Years, a design been carried on, to change the Lawfull Government of *England* into an Absolute Tyrrany, and to convert the established Protestant Religion into down-right Popery.' The stages of this alleged conspiracy are traced from the triple alliance to Charles's adjournment of parliament in July 1677, the declaration of indulgence is presented as a Catholic subterfuge, and the heroes are Buckingham, Wharton, and the two other lords committed in February 1677 for questioning the legality of the recent prorogation. The tract, timed to appear before the next session of parliament in April 1678, alarmed the government, which in the *Gazette* for 21 February – 5 March offered £50 for the discovery of author and publisher. Marvell himself told Popple in June that 'great Rewards have been offered in private', but affected to make light of the matter (*Poems*, 2.357). L'Estrange replied from a tory perspective in *An Account of the Growth of Knavery* (1678), and much later a hostile critique and scurrilous personal attack appeared in Parker's posthumous *History of his Own Time* (1727, 335–49).

For his last published work Marvell intervened in a theological dispute between two nonconformist ministers. *Remarks upon a Late Disingenuous Discourse*, issued anonymously under an imprimatur dated 17 April 1678, defends views on a question framed by Robert Boyle that had been expressed in John Howe's *Reconcileableness of God's Prescience* against the Calvinist interpretation offered by Thomas Danson in *De causâ dei*. Following a visit to Hull in

July 'about the Towns affaires' Marvell contracted the tertian ague which brought about his end on 16 August 1678, in the rented property on the north side of Great Russell Street, a few yards to the west of the present British Museum. A professional report alleged medical incompetence, and concluded that an ounce of quinine might have saved him. Two days later he was buried under a window in the south aisle of the old church of St Giles-in-the-Fields.

Marriage No will was found, and, though Marvell is said to have owned a house in Hull, Thompson's mention of a 'small paternal estate' remains unverified (*Works*, ed. Thompson, 3.480). But a surprising light was thrown on Marvell's last years by a series of chancery suits now initiated by the third member of the failed banking partnership. John Farrington, desperate to release hidden assets, searched the Maiden Lane lodgings soon after in the vain hope of recovering a bond for £500 formerly made out to Marvell by Nelthorpe, who himself died one month later. During his search he is said to have removed 'trunks bonds bills & other goods', leaving only 'a few Books & papers of a small value' (Tupper, 374 n. 42). Then, having secured the administration of Nelthorpe's affairs, he enlisted Marvell's eldest sister, Anne Blaydes, to forestall any similar attempt on the poet's estate. But in September 1680 Marvell's housekeeper, Mary Palmer, laid claim to be his widow and by the following March had been granted administration jointly with her lawyer, one of his creditors. In February 1682 Farrington challenged the marriage on the grounds that it was unsuspected even by Marvell's close friends, and that the widow of a poor tennis-court keeper—one Thomas Palmer—was no fit match for a learned man and an MP. In reply (7 April) she asserted that the ceremony had taken place 'on or about' 13 May 1667 at Holy Trinity, Little Minories, as 'by the Register Book … may appear'; moreover, 'the difference in their Conditions … might be (as this Defend' believes it was) One reason why the said M' Marvell was pleased to have the Marriage kept private' (Tupper, 380). Holy Trinity was one of only two London churches that were licensed to celebrate clandestine marriages, the number there rising from over 500 in 1661 to almost 1000 in 1677. Attempts were periodically made to suppress them, and early in 1678 Marvell and his colleagues had to swear that they had not stolen the engrossed bill to abolish this popular practice (*Poems*, 2.219). Although the relevant Holy Trinity register is now missing, there is no reason to doubt that it would have been available to the court authorities of the time. It may be significant that in the year of their marriage a bookseller of the same name as Mary's son, Thomas Palmer, who traded in Westminster Hall, was pilloried for selling *Directions to a Painter* (CSP dom., 1665–6, 159), and again in March 1671 for *Advice to a Painter* (*Poems*, 1.376).

Posthumous reputation After Marvell's death a collection of his *Miscellaneous Poems* was issued in 1681 by Robert Boulter, one of the original publishers of *Paradise Lost*, who that summer was to be arrested for predicting the imminent fall of the monarchy. The prefatory note, dated 15 October 1680 and signed 'Mary Marvell', describes them as being 'Printed according to the exact Copies of my late dear Husband, under his own Hand-Writing'. It served to authenticate the contents for a general readership, to whom Marvell's poetic talents were known, if at all, from his commendatory verses to the second edition (1674) of Milton's epic, and perhaps from some satires. The folio volume includes religio-philosophical dialogues; verses on the pleasures (both sensuous and spiritual) of the retired life in pastoral surroundings; poems that depict innocence on the verge of sexual maturity; love lyrics, from the classic persuasion of 'To his Coy Mistress' to the dark complaint of 'The Unfortunate Lover'; and some Latin epigrams and epitaphs. Almost the only public response to such late-appearing metaphysical poems is Wood's grudging statement that the volume was 'cried up as excellent' by those of the author's own persuasion (Wood, *Ath. Oxon.*, 4.232).

Failure of nerve during a temporary crisis in whig fortunes had led to excision of the three Cromwell pieces before sale from almost all known copies of the work. It is scarcely surprising therefore that the collection did not include any of the political satires that were to be claimed for Marvell in anthologies printed after the revolution of 1688, from *A Collection of the Newest ... Poems ... Against Popery* (1689) to successive editions of *Poems on Affairs of State* (1697–1704). Definitive authentication, hampered by lack of demonstrably authorial texts and a marked disparity in style from Marvell's other poems, is further hindered by the tendency for a topical genre or subject to attract a number of writers. But to judge from the commonly accepted pieces, Parker's sneering allusion to Marvell's 'proper trade of Lampoons and Ballads' (*Reproof*, 526) was not wholly undeserved, for though they address serious issues, they do so chiefly through burlesque and ridicule. Marvell himself told Aubrey that the earl of Rochester was 'the only man in England that had the true veine of Satyre' (*Brief Lives*, 2.54, 304).

Aubrey, who knew Marvell personally in the 1670s, praised him as 'an excellent poet in Latin or English: for Latin verses there was no man would come into competition with him', recalling that he 'kept bottles of wine at his lodgeings ... to refresh his spirits, and exalt his Muse'. Yet he was:

> in his conversation very modest and of very few words. Though he loved wine he would never drink hard in company: and was wont to say, *that he would not play the good-fellow in any mans company in whose hands he would not trust his life.*

In appearance he was 'of a middling stature, pretty strong sett, roundish faced, cherry cheek't, hazell eie, browne haire' (*Brief Lives*, 2.53), a description borne out in the oil portrait, executed about 1655–60 by an unidentified artist, that was presented by Marvell's grand-nephew Robert Nettleton in 1764 to the British Museum and is now in the National Portrait Gallery. A line engraving of a related type, but with image reversed, appears as frontispiece to *Miscellaneous Poems*, and a smaller version was executed by

John Clark for Cooke's edition of 1726. Another oil, in Hull City Art Gallery, which belonged to Ralph Thoresby and later to Thomas Hollis, bears an inscription that gives the sitter's age as forty-two; it was engraved by Cipriani for Hollis (1760) and by Basire for Thompson's edition (1776). Vertue attributed to Lely a now unlocated portrait that belonged before 1726 to the Hon. Maurice Ashley, Marvell's nephew by marriage (BL, Add. MS 23070, fol. 22*v*).

In September 1678 Hull voted £50 for Marvell's funeral expenses and 'to perpetuate his memory by a Grave-stone' (Tupper, 373–4 n. 42), but the rector is said to have objected. Mary was buried in St Giles's on 24 November 1687, under the surname of her first husband. In the next year Popple wrote an epitaph, of which a slightly altered version was placed on a tablet set up in the new church in 1764 by Nettleton. Verse elegies survive by John Ayloffe (*Poems on Affairs of State*, 1697, 160–61) and two anonymous admirers (ibid., 122–3, and Davies). Marvell's posthumous reputation as a proto-whig defender of constitutional liberties and a 'sincere and daring Patriot' encouraged Thomas Cooke in 1726 to reprint the lyrics alongside the satires in a collection grandly entitled *The Works of Andrew Marvell Esq.* A brief biography was prefixed, and some private letters were supplied by 'the Ladys his Nieces' (vol. 1, p. x), daughters of William Popple. Fifty years later the same spirit led Captain Edward Thompson, a native of Hull, to publish a luxurious folio edition to which Burke and Wilkes subscribed, and Thomas Hollis and T. J. Mathias contributed material. Here the expurgated Cromwell poems were first brought to public notice.

Over the next hundred years Marvell's poetry was increasingly praised by poets and anthologists in Britain and America, earning pride of place in Alexander Grosart's comprehensive edition of the *Complete Works* in 1872. T. S. Eliot's influential essay for the Hull tercentenary volume of 1921 pointed the way to a major critical reassessment that was facilitated by H. M. Margoliouth's 1927 Oxford edition of the *Poems and Letters* and Pierre Legouis's biographical and critical study of 1928, *André Marvell*. Since then the ambiguity of Marvell's poetry and the elusiveness of his personality have helped to make him of all seventeenth-century lyrists the subject of the most extensive exegesis.   W. H. KELLIHER

Sources A. Marvell, *Miscellaneous poems* (1681) · *The works of Andrew Marvell esq.*, ed. T. Cooke, 2 vols. (1726) · *The works of Andrew Marvell esq.*, ed. E. Thompson, 3 vols. (1776) · *The complete works of Andrew Marvell*, ed. A. B. Grosart, 4 vols. (1872) · *The poems and letters of Andrew Marvell*, ed. H. Margoliouth, rev. P. Legouis, 3rd edn, 2 vols. (1971) · A. Marvell, *The rehearsal transpros'd, and The rehearsal transpros'd: the second part*, ed. D. I. B. Smith (1971) · P. Legouis, *André Marvell: poète, puritain, patriote* (1928); repr. with additions (1965) · W. H. Kelliher, *Andrew Marvell, poet & politician, 1621–1678: an exhibition to commemorate the tercentenary of his death* (1978) · G. de Miège, *A relation of three embassies* (1669) · S. Parker, *History of his own time* (1727) · A. Grey, ed., *Debates of the House of Commons, from the year 1667 to the year 1694*, new edn, 10 vols. (1769) · HoP, *Commons, 1660–90* · *Brief lives, chiefly of contemporaries, set down by John Aubrey, between the years 1669 and 1696*, ed. A. Clark, 2 vols. (1898) · Wood, *Ath. Oxon.*, new edn · W. R. Chaplin, *The corporation of Trinity House of Deptford*

Strond from the year 1660 [1950] · E. M. Tomlinson, *A history of the Minories* (1907) · *Diary of John Milward, esq.*, ed. C. Robbins (1938) · G. de F. Lord and others, eds., *Poems on affairs of state: Augustan satirical verse, 1660–1714*, 7 vols. (1963–75) · P. Beal and others, *Index of English literary manuscripts*, ed. P. J. Croft and others, [4 vols. in 11 pts] (1980–), vol. 2, pt 2, pp. 17–67 · E. S. Donno, *Andrew Marvell: the critical heritage* (1978) · D. S. Collins, *Andrew Marvell: a reference guide* (1981) · F. S. Tupper, 'Mary Palmer, alias Mrs. Andrew Marvell', *Proceedings of the Modern Language Association*, 53 (1938), 366–92 · P. Burdon, 'Marvell after Cambridge', *British Library Journal*, 4 (1978), 42–8 · E. E. Duncan-Jones, 'Marvell, R. F., and the authorship of "Blake's victory"', *English Manuscript Studies, 1100–1700*, 5 (1995), 107–26 · L. A. Davies, 'An unpublished poem about Andrew Marvell', *Yearbook of English Studies*, 1 (1971), 100–01 · conclusion book, 1608–73, Trinity Cam., p. 169 · PRO, SP 18/33/75 · K. H. D. Hayley, *William of Orange and the English opposition, 1672–4* (1953) · BL, Add. MS 5846, fol. 133*v* · LMA, H1/ST/E79/24, M.37 · Sheffield University Library, H50/29/5/50A · Leics. RO, Finch papers, DG7, box 4985

Archives NRA, corresp. and papers · U. Hull, Brynmor Jones L., letters | Bodl. Oxf., MS Eng. poet. d. 49 · City Archives, Hull, letters to the corporation · Trinity House, Hull, letters to the wardens

Likenesses oils, *c*.1655–1660, NPG [*see illus.*] · oils, *c*.1662–1663, City Art Gallery, Hull · line engraving, BM, NPG; repro. in A. Marvell, *Miscellaneous poems* (1681) · mezzotint (after unknown artist), NPG

Wealth at death see F. S. Tupper, 'Mary Palmer', 366–92

Marvin, Charles Thomas (1854–1890), writer on Russia, was born on 10 June 1854 at Plumstead, Kent, the son of Charles Woodward Marvin, draughtsman, and his wife, Catherine Martha, *née* Law. He was employed in a warehouse in Watling Street, London, in 1868. At the age of sixteen he went to Russia to join his father, who was assistant manager of an engineering works on the Neva. He remained there until 1875, and acquired a good knowledge of the language. For eighteen months he was the correspondent of *The Globe and Traveller* at St Petersburg. Returning to London in 1875 Marvin passed the civil service examination, and in January 1876 was appointed a temporary writer in the custom house. He was also transferred for a short time to the Inland Revenue department, and to the Post Office.

On 16 July 1877 Marvin entered the Foreign Office, and here, although only a writer, he was, on 29 May 1878, entrusted to make a copy of a secret treaty with Russia, the 'Project de memorandum'. The same evening he supplied *The Globe and Traveller*, from memory, with a summary of the document. On 1 June Lord Salisbury, in the House of Lords, claimed that this summary was 'wholly unworthy of their lordships' confidence'. On 14 June *The Globe and Traveller* printed the complete text of the treaty from Marvin's extremely retentive memory. On 26 June he was arrested, but discharged on 16 July as he had not committed an illegal act. In 1878 he published *Our public offices, embodying an account of the disclosure of the Anglo-Russian agreement, and the unrevealed secret treaty of 31 May, 1878*. During the Russo-Turkish War in 1878 he contributed to twenty publications.

Marvin published prolifically during the 1880s. In 1880 his first book on the Russo-Indian question, *The Eye-Witnesses' Account of the Disastrous Campaign Against the Akhal Tekke Turcomans*, appeared; it was adopted by the Russian government for military libraries, and commended by General Skobelev. In 1881 he printed *Merv the Queen of the World and the Scourge of the Man-Stealing Turcomans*, in which he predicted that the next Russian advance would be pushed to Panjdeh. In 1882 he was sent to Russia by Joseph Cowen, the radical politician and journalist, to interview the leading generals and statesmen on the Russo-Indian question. On his return he wrote *The Russian advance towards India: conversations with Skobeleff, Ignatieff, and other Russian generals and statesmen on the central Asian question*. The following year he travelled to the Caucasus, and published in 1884 an account of his exploration of the Russian oil-producing districts, under the title *The Region of the Eternal Fire*. The most popular of his works was, however, *The Russians at the Gates of Herat* (1885), a book of 200 pages, written and published within a week, which sold 65,000 copies.

The date of Marvin's marriage is not known; his wife, Mary Ann Georgina, survived him. He died at Grosvenor House, Heavitree Road, Plumstead Common, Kent, on 4 December 1890, and was buried in Plumstead new cemetery on 10 December.

G. C. BOASE, *rev.* CHANDRIKA KAUL

Sources *The Times* (17 July 1878), 11 · *The Times* (5 Dec 1890), 8 · *London Figaro* (13 Dec 1890), 11 · *CGPLA Eng. & Wales* (1891) · b. cert.

Likenesses portrait, repro. in *London Figaro*, 11

Wealth at death £1844 2s. 7d.: probate, 26 May 1891, *CGPLA Eng. & Wales*

Marvin [*née* Deverell], **Edith Mary** (1872–1958), inspector of schools, was born at Attington, near Tetsworth, Oxfordshire, on 29 July 1872, the daughter of Alfred Deverell JP, a coal merchant and farmer, and his wife, Mary Seymour. Brought up as a Congregationalist, she was educated at home and then at a private school at Weston-super-Mare. She was an undergraduate at Somerville College, Oxford, from 1892 to 1895 and was a contemporary of several women who were to become prominent in public affairs and the academic world. A select discussion group called the Associated Prigs, whose early members included Margery Fry, Hilda Oakeley, and Eleanor Rathbone, first met in her room at Somerville in January 1894 to discuss 'social subjects' ranging from an analysis of the London school board elections to factory legislation and women. After obtaining second-class honours in modern history in 1895 (graduating MA from Trinity College, Dublin, in 1910, Oxford degrees not then being open to women), she was on the staff of Morley College, 1896–9, holding research studentships at the London School of Economics, 1896–8, and at Somerville, 1898–9. While in London she worked as an unpaid research assistant for A. L. Bowley for his classic study *Wages in the United Kingdom in the Nineteenth Century*.

In 1900 Edith Deverell was appointed as woman sub-inspector, under the Board of Education, to assist HM inspectors in inspecting girls' and infants' departments in elementary schools. The first year was spent in Liverpool and then she moved to a part of London which she knew well from her research days, West Ham. She was appalled at the neglect of children and, possessing a lively social conscience, she devoted much of her energies to improving the health and welfare of children in schools. Within five months of joining she wrote direct to Sir John Gorst, vice-president of the committee of the privy council on education, on the inadequate lighting conditions especially in infant classrooms. In April 1901, along with five women colleagues, she became a junior inspector. She urged that teachers should be able to recognize outward signs of physical and mental weakness in children, and was appointed a member of the interdepartmental committee on the model course of physical exercises, which reviewed the course of physical training laid down for children in elementary schools. Its report (1904) recommended that future teachers should receive suitable instruction in physiology and hygiene.

During her time in the West Ham district Edith Deverell met a remarkable fellow inspector, Francis Sydney Marvin (1863–1943), who belonged to the band of English positivists. They were married at Tetsworth parish church on 25 June 1904, and had a family of three sons. It was originally proposed that Frederic Harrison should conduct a positivist marriage ceremony, but Edith rejected elements of the alternative service which emphasized the subordinate role of women. They initially settled in Leeds, where Francis Marvin was inspector for training colleges. She resigned from the inspectorate following her marriage but remained active in the National Union of Women Workers, where she pressed for improved school facilities. Her speech at the union's 1904 annual conference, 'Practical hygiene for teachers and managers of schools', drew attention to the need for more practical teaching of physiology to teachers, especially in relation to younger children. She called for the appointment of more women school managers and more women school inspectors, urging their special qualification to report on questions of health and sanitation. The lack of opportunities for women inspectors was highlighted in her speeches and articles. Her own advice on medical inspection in schools was valued by Sir William Anson, parliamentary secretary to the Board of Education.

Edith Marvin advocated women's suffrage and belonged to the small committee responsible for presenting the Women Graduate Suffrage Petition to Campbell-Bannerman in May 1906. Among her close friends was Margaret Gladstone, wife of Ramsay MacDonald, who consulted her on educational matters. One of her later schemes, in 1934, was to help unemployed young teachers find posts by granting retirement pensions for the profession at the age of sixty. Edith Marvin died at her home, 66 Cross Oak Road, Berkhamsted, Hertfordshire, on 20 May 1958.   PETER GORDON

Sources P. Gordon, 'E. M. Deverell', *History of Education Society Bulletin*, 22 (1978) · *Somerville College register, 1879–1971* [1972] · Bodl. Oxf., Marvin MSS · M. D. Stocks, *Eleanor Rathbone: a biography* (1949) · b. cert. · m. cert. · d. cert.
Archives Bodl. Oxf., MS Eng. Lett. c.257
Wealth at death £12,256 13s. 10d.: probate, 8 Aug 1958, *CGPLA Eng. & Wales*

Marwick, Sir **James David** (1826–1908), legal and historical writer and local government official, was born James Marwick on 15 July 1826 at Leith, the eldest of the nine surviving children of William Marwick (1798–1856), general merchant of Kirkwall and Edinburgh, and his wife, Margaret Garrioch (1798–1871). He was, by his own account, an Orcadian of Scandinavian descent on both sides of his family. When he was three or four his father was struck by what seemed to be a fatal illness and he was adopted by his paternal grandfather, also James Marwick, a merchant in Kirkwall. His uncle David was a member of this new family circle and young James took his name in addition to his own.

Education; early professional life; Edinburgh town councillor Marwick was sent initially to a subscription school under the auspices of the Secession church and later to Kirkwall grammar school. His grandfather appears to have influenced him to take a liberal and broad view of church matters. In 1842 he was sent to Edinburgh University with the intention of studying medicine and then going to India. Instead he began an apprenticeship in the solicitor's office of James B. Watt, and attended law classes at Edinburgh University, where he was an active member of a literary group that later became the Tuscalan Society. These activities brought him into contact with John Hill Burton, Joseph Robertson, and John Stuart, founders of the Spalding Club, and Cosmo Innes—friendships which led into Marwick's subsequent interest in and contribution to antiquarian research. From Watt's office he moved to a junior position in the office of a writer to the signet who specialized in conveyancing and estate management. This provided him with invaluable, if badly paid, experience for his later career and, by his own account, was the only job he ever had to apply for.

In 1850 Marwick went to Dundee, where he later became a procurator in the sheriff courts of Forfarshire, and entered into partnership with David Barrie, the son of Dundee's then town clerk. In the former position he acted as one of the agents for the poor and as court-appointed defence counsel in the sheriff and police courts. In 1854 he returned to Edinburgh to join Hugh Watt, the son of his former employer, in what became the successful legal firm of Watt and Marwick. He married Watt's sister Jane on 9 July 1855; they had two sons and two daughters. Personal reasons were cited for his refusal of Dundee town clerkship just prior to his marriage.

Marwick witnessed many of the public events in Edinburgh of the time; his account of the rejection of T. B. Macaulay at the general election of 1847 is a good example of his acute observation and ready wit. In the mid-1850s he began to play a more prominent political role, as convenor of the whig committee of St Bernard's ward, and as a last-minute candidate he was elected to the town council for the Stockbridge ward, in 1856. As a councillor he supported the rebuilding of Trinity Church, demolished to make way for Waverley Station, putting him at odds with his fellow dissenters, and on the parochial board of the city parish he was convenor of a committee which proposed the incorporation of the whole of Edinburgh into one area for poor-law purposes. This was not carried into effect, but Marwick saw the experience as useful when he came later to be involved in Glasgow's municipal extension. On the board of the Edinburgh Water Company he represented the popular demand for increased supplies. He was a prominent supporter of Sir David Brewster, who was elected principal of Edinburgh University in 1859—the fruition of a dissenters' movement for a layman to hold the post, as was permitted by the 1858 Universities Act.

Edinburgh town clerk After retiring from the council in 1859 Marwick took up the position of Edinburgh town clerk, in December 1860, after a twelve-month waiting period dictated by a self-denying ordinance. As town clerk he regarded himself not merely as a recorder of proceedings and a legal agent and adviser, but as the upholder of continuity in policy. His contribution to legislation affecting Edinburgh and other Scottish burghs was his most significant work. With the provost of Leith and the crown agent he was responsible for revising what became the General Police Act (1862). In 1867 another act confirmed the Edinburgh provisional order which Marwick had drawn up to extend police provision in the city. With H. D. Littlejohn, the medical health officer for Edinburgh, Marwick was responsible for a report to the council on a local outbreak of smallpox which prompted the passing of the 1863 Vaccination Act for Scotland. He was consulted on the clauses affecting Scottish burghs in the parliamentary reform act of 1868, and helped to draft the subsequent Municipal Elections (Scotland) and Municipal Elections Amendment (Scotland) Acts of 1868 and 1870 respectively. He piloted a measure in 1869 to take Edinburgh's water supply into public ownership and was later elected law agent and clerk of the newly created Edinburgh and District Water Trust. He held this position until 1872 when, as a supporter of an extended supply, he was replaced by newly elected trustees who opposed it.

Publications and honorifics Marwick published widely on the conduct of municipal business. After the passage of the Ballot Act in 1872 he put out material for the guidance of returning officers; he produced suggestions for the conduct of elections to school boards (1873 and 1876) and in 1879 published *Observations on the Law and Practice with Regard to Municipal Corporations in Scotland*. These became indispensable handbooks for town clerks.

Marwick appeared to great advantage on formal civic occasions, with a gift for writing sonorous prose and having a 'stately presence and manner' which 'were always impressive' (McKendrick, 27). In 1863 he was part of a delegation to Windsor which presented an address on the marriage of the prince of Wales and Princess Alexandra; on that occasion Dublin was called before Edinburgh, and a famous controversy was sparked over precedence. Marwick drafted Edinburgh's case, published as *Precedence of Edinburgh and Dublin: Proceedings in the Privy Council on the Question* (1865). In February 1864 a privy council committee reported that neither party had established a definite claim.

In 1861 Marwick was appointed clerk of the convention of the royal burghs of Scotland. After discovering that the records of this body dealt not only with burghal history, but also with Scotland's commercial relations with other countries, he decided that they should be published, and a series of volumes appeared under his editorship from 1866. Marwick was a founder and the first secretary of the Scottish Burgh Records Society. Under its aegis, and with the initial supervision of Cosmo Innes, and latterly the assistance of Robert Renwick, he published numerous monumental compilations of Glasgow and Edinburgh charters and records dating from the earliest times. He also published a national survey entitled *The Municipal Institutions of Scotland* (1904). Among his other works were a history of the collegiate church and hospital of the Holy Trinity in Edinburgh (first published 1871), a report in 1890 on markets and fairs in Scotland, and volumes on the history of the River Clyde and the Clyde burghs, the Glasgow water supply, and the Edinburgh guilds. Marwick's published works linked factual material with a minimum of general statements and cited authorities for every paragraph, and contrasted with his 'vehement and almost passionate' participation in conversation unless in a mediating role (Neilson, 268).

In 1861 Marwick was elected a fellow of the Society of Antiquaries of Scotland; in 1864 he was made a fellow of the Royal Society of Edinburgh; and he was the first president of the Edinburgh Photographic Society—he had arranged for items in Register House, Edinburgh, to be reproduced by the newly invented photozincography process. His contacts among Edinburgh's civic élite were further augmented by his membership of St Augustine's Church, a Congregationalist centre in Scotland, and by his connection with the golf club at St Andrews.

Town clerk of Glasgow: boundary extension; last years In 1872 Marwick's health broke down from overwork, and on medical advice he accompanied delegations to exhibitions in Copenhagen and Moscow that summer. Later the same year he was approached by James Watson, lord provost of Glasgow, to become its town clerk. After initial reluctance, largely caused by the prospect of the loss of his private legal practice, Marwick accepted the post. His salary of £2500 made him the highest-paid local government official in Britain, and his move to Glasgow broadened his connections, consolidating his position among the élite of late nineteenth-century Scotland.

On taking office in 1873 Marwick set about reorganizing the town clerk's office; his proposals for the appointment of deputies and the establishment of a clear chain of command met with the approval of councillors. During his spell in office he built himself an immensely powerful position, and according to one source was involved at different stages with more than a hundred parliamentary bills affecting the city. These included measures to further the development of Glasgow's water supply, to construct works for purifying the Clyde, to introduce a municipal tramway system, and to establish an electricity department. His most significant achievement, however, was to expand Glasgow's city boundaries, to create the 'greater

Glasgow' first envisaged by the Lord Provost Andrew Orr in the 1850s and set out in Marwick's own *Statement of Municipal Expansion* (1879), which became a classic text. By the 1870s the exodus of the prosperous to the suburbs had left Glasgow to provide amenities from a shrinking rate-revenue base. The collapse of the City of Glasgow Bank in 1878, and the inability of the suburban police burghs to compete with Glasgow on rates left the town council as a beacon of financial probity. Marwick made the most of this and zealously campaigned to present Glasgow in general as a model municipality. By the 1880s and 1890s municipal extension had come to be associated with unionism, calls for a 'greater Britain', and in particular the ideas of Joseph Chamberlain: Marwick privately supported the Liberal Unionists in 1886, and as he grew more conservative in later life he expressed anxiety at the incursion of socialist principles into municipal policy. His efforts were finally crowned with success in 1891 when a large-scale extension of the city boundary was effected, and in 1893 by the passage of an act drafted by Marwick raising the city to the status of a county.

Marwick was made deputy lieutenant and JP of the new Glasgow (he also held the latter office for Lanarkshire), having earlier refused these offices in Edinburgh on the ground that his close relations with the provost would cause suspicions of favouritism. He also received an LLD degree from the University of Glasgow in 1878 and was knighted in 1888 on the occasion of a royal visit to Glasgow. In 1893 he received the freedom of Kirkwall.

Marwick's retirement in December 1903 was marked by disagreement with Glasgow corporation over his pension—ultimately, he received only the £1500 minimum agreed on his appointment. After his departure, the wide-ranging role of the town clerk that he had created was given a major reappraisal. In retirement he published privately a volume of memoirs, *A Retrospect* (1905), which covered his life up to his move to Glasgow in 1873. Since that time he had been a member, and also a deacon and manager, of Trinity Church in the city, though in later years his sympathies were said to lie with the Church of Scotland. He enjoyed relatively good health and maintained an impressive physical presence into his eighties, despite having had a severe attack of pneumonia in 1875 and having considered resigning office in 1881 from ill health. Marwick eventually succumbed again to pneumonia, dying at his home, 19 Woodside Terrace, Glasgow, on 24 March 1908; his wife survived him. He was buried on 28 March at Warriston cemetery, Edinburgh.

GORDON F. MILLAR

Sources J. G. McKendrick, *Memoir of Sir James D. Marwick* (1909) · J. D. Marwick, *A retrospect* (privately printed, Glasgow, 1905) · *The Scotsman* (25 March 1908) · *Glasgow Herald* (25 March 1908) · *WWW*, 1897–1915 · W. H. Fraser and I. Maver, eds., *Glasgow*, 2 (1996) · *The Scotsman* (26 March 1908) · *The Scotsman* (30 March 1908) · *Glasgow Herald* (26 March 1908) · *Glasgow Herald* (30 March 1908) · G. Neilson, 'Scottish burgh records', *SHR*, 8 (1910–11), 264–70 · G. E. Todd, *Who's who in Glasgow in 1909* (1909), 142–3 · *DNB* · bap. reg. Scot., 1798 · m. reg. Scot., 1855 · General Register Office for England · *IGI* · I. Maver, 'Politics and power in the Scottish city: Glasgow town council in the nineteenth century', *Scottish elites*, ed. T. M. Devine (1994), 119–20

Archives U. Edin. L., letters to David Laing, La iv 17

Likenesses G. S. Templeton, marble bust, 1905, Art Gallery and Museum, Glasgow · G. Frampton, bronze bust · G. Frampton, marble bust, Glasgow Art Galleries · R. Herdman, portrait · photograph, repro. in Fraser and Maver, eds., *Glasgow*, pl. 36; courtesy of Mitchell L., Glas. · photographs, repro. in McKendrick, *Memoir of Sir James D. Marwick*

Wealth at death £42,202 9s. 2d.: confirmation, 22 May 1908, *CCI* · £1374 15s. 6d.: additional estate, 21 Sept 1908, *CCI*

Marwood, William (1820–1883), public executioner, born at Horncastle, Lincolnshire, was by trade a cobbler throughout his life. A married man, he was a local preacher, and lived in Church Lane, Horncastle. Becoming interested in executions, he suggested that, for reasons of humanity, criminals ought not to be choked to death. By carefully ascertaining a criminal's weight, and by employing a proportionate length of rope, he showed that the descent of the body into the pit beneath the scaffold would instantaneously dislocate the vertebrae, and thus cause immediate death. He became a pupil of the executioner William Calcraft and obtained his first engagement as a hangman at Lincoln in 1871; his 'longdrop' system worked with success on that and many subsequent occasions. The sheriffs of London and Middlesex appointed him to succeed Calcraft (of whom Marwood said 'He hanged them—I executed them') in June 1874, at an annual retainer of £20 and a fee of £10 per execution; as was usual, he was also entitled to the hanging rope and the clothes of his victims. Among the more celebrated criminals whom he put to death were Charles Peace, Percy Lefroy Mapleton, Dr Lamson, Kate Webster, and Henry Wainwright; he also hanged the Phoenix Park murderers in Dublin. Gustave Doré drew Marwood while he was hanging Wainwright on 21 December 1875; it was entitled *L'execution à Londres*.

Marwood outlined his methods in a letter reprinted in the *St Stephen's Review* of 3 November 1883; a pamphlet by D. D. D. of 1883 described a visit to Marwood at Horncastle, concluding that Marwood took great pride in his work, which he regarded as a surgeon might view an operation, and aimed to give value for money to his employers. A 'respectable-looking' man with broad shoulders, short legs, dark curly hair, and side-whiskers, he was said also to have a 'cruel mouth' and one eye half closed. He died of pneumonia and jaundice on 4 September 1883 at his home in Horncastle; he was buried there in the Trinity churchyard two days later. There was brisk competition for the purchase of his effects, his travelling bag fetching £3 and one of his ropes £4 10s. A wax effigy of Marwood in the act of hanging Charles Peace (with a piece of the original rope) joined Madame Tussaud's chamber of horrors.

G. C. BOASE, rev. J. GILLILAND

Sources B. Binns, *The life of W. Marwood* (1883) · Ward, *Men of the reign* · J. Bland, *The book of executions* (1993) · B. Bailey, *Hangmen of England* (1989) · S. Fielding, *The hangman's record, 1868–1899*, 1 (1994) · H. Bleackley, *Hangmen of England* (1929) · J. Atholl, *Shadow of the gallows* (1954) · *Law Journal* (8 Sept 1883), 490 · *St Stephen's Review* (3 Nov 1883), 9, 20 · *N&Q*, 165 (1933), 231 · R. W. Postgate, *Murder, piracy and treason* (1926) · Boase, *Mod. Eng. biog.*

Likenesses G. Doré, portrait · portrait, repro. in Binns, *Life* · portrait, repro. in Bleackley, *Hangmen of England* · portrait, repro. in *Illustrated Police News* (15 Sept 1883)

Marx [*known as* Marx-Aveling], (**Jenny Julia**) **Eleanor** (1855–1898), socialist writer and activist, was born on 16 January 1855 at 28 Dean Street, Soho, London, the sixth child of Karl *Marx (1818–1883), revolutionary socialist philosopher, and his wife, Jenny (1814–1881), daughter of Baron Johann Ludwig von Westphalen, Trier city councillor, and his wife, Caroline. Eleanor, who quickly acquired among her intimates the lifelong nickname Tussy, was the youngest by eleven years of three sisters, the other three children of the Marx household having died in infancy. Although born in a cramped and insalubrious flat in Soho, Eleanor spent her early years in a terraced house in Kentish Town, to which the Marxes moved in September 1856, before settling in a spacious villa in Maitland Park in 1864. She attended the South Hampstead College for Ladies, leaving at the age of fourteen with rather a haphazard education.

The Marx household itself, however, provided Eleanor with extensive exposure to politics and literature, which were to be her lifelong intellectual and practical interests. Her mother described her as 'political from top to toe'. She visited Ireland with her father's collaborator, Friedich Engels, in 1869 and passionately supported the Fenian cause. But it was the Paris Commune of 1871 and its bloody suppression that marked her serious introduction to political activism. Both her sisters married Frenchmen who were committed to the socialist cause, and both settled in France. Eleanor was active in helping to organize aid for the French refugees in London and was herself briefly arrested while on a visit to France in August 1871.

The commune also left Eleanor Marx with a very different kind of legacy. She fell in love with, and became engaged to, Hyppolite Prosper Olivier Lissagaray, one of its more flamboyant refugees, who belonged to an old Basque family and was exactly twice her age. Both her parents strongly disapproved. She took a post in a ladies' seminary in Brighton for six months in 1873, but returned to London to look after her father, whose health had seriously and permanently deteriorated. Forbidden by parental authority to see Lissagaray, Eleanor threw herself into literary activity. She went regularly to the British Museum, where she worked for Frederick Furnivall's Philological, Chaucer, and Shakespeare societies. She became friendly with actors such as Ernest Radford and Dolly Maitland, and planned unsuccessfully for a career on the stage. Increasingly imprisoned by the ill health of her parents, to whose interests she felt she had 'sacrificed the best, precious years of my life', she was liberated only by the death of her father in 1883.

In 1884 Eleanor began to live openly with Edward Bibbens *Aveling (1849–1898), a married man and a well-qualified zoologist with oratorical talent, whose commitment to socialism was as genuine as his character was fickle. Her attachment to Aveling (whose name she used

(Jenny Julia) Eleanor Marx (1855–1898), by unknown photographer

in conjunction with her own) did, however, provide Eleanor with a firm sense of direction. She began to give public addresses on social and political matters, thus developing her talents in explaining Marxism with reference to the practical needs and interests of her audience. She had been active in the early years of the Social Democratic Federation, sitting on its executive committee, but resigned in 1885 together with (among others) Belfort Bax and William Morris to found the Socialist League. Nor did she neglect her writing: she published a pamphlet entitled *The Woman Question* (1886), translated Lissagaray's *History of the Commune* (1886), produced the first English version of Flaubert's *Madame Bovary* (1886), and even learned Norwegian to translate Ibsen. From 1887 onwards she became more directly involved in labour unrest: she made frequent visits to the East End of London, where she was particularly involved in the defence of Jewish workers, was active in support of the gas workers' and dockers' strikes of 1889, and sat for several years on the council of the Gas Workers and General Labourers Union. Further afield, she was present at the founding congress of the Second International in Paris in 1889, where she was an indefatigable translator and interpreter. Her finest hour was perhaps her speech at the Brussels Congress of the International in 1891. Published later as a penny pamphlet under the title *Report from Great Britain and Ireland*, it was a lengthy document presented in the name of the Gas Workers and

General Labourers Union, the Legal Eight Hours and International Labour League, the Bloomsbury Socialist Society, and the Battersea Labour League.

Although she attended the founding conference of the Independent Labour Party in Bradford in 1893 and again addressed the Zürich Congress of the International in the same year, Eleanor's morale began to undergo a slow but fatal descent. Always close to Engels, she felt herself increasingly excluded, particularly by his new housekeeper Louise Freyberger. There were several disagreements about how Marx's manuscripts should be dealt with, though Eleanor did edit and publish editions of her father's writings on eighteenth- and nineteenth-century history and politics. The death of Engels in September 1895 and his revelations about the paternity of Marx's illegitimate son, Frederick Demuth, whose paternity Engels had assumed and to whom Eleanor was very close, were hard blows from which she never recovered. She continued to lecture, began to collaborate again with the Social Democratic Federation, and was secretary to the committee organizing the 1896 London Congress of the International. But Eleanor Marx felt sidelined, as it was becoming clear that the influence of Marxism on the British socialist movement would be limited, and the mid-1890s saw a reversal of what had seemed an irresistible tide of working-class political progress. Her death was precipitated by Aveling's secret marriage to Eva Frye in June 1897. Eleanor learned about this in August, and although she continued to live on and off with Aveling she committed suicide by taking prussic acid on 31 March 1898 at her home, 7 Jews Walk, Sydenham, Kent. She was cremated on 5 April at Woking. DAVID MCLELLAN

Sources Y. Kapp, *Eleanor Marx*, 2 vols. (1972–6) • D. McLellan, *Karl Marx: his life and thought* (1973)

Archives BL, notes and essay by Havelock Ellis relating to subject • Internationaal Instituut voor Sociale Geschiedenis, Amsterdam, letters to Benno Karpeles

Likenesses photograph, *c*.1874, repro. in McLellan, *Karl Marx* • photograph, repro. in Collison, *The apostle of free labour* (1913) [see illus.]

Wealth at death £1909 3s. 10d.: probate, 16 April 1898, *CGPLA Eng. & Wales*

Marx, Enid Dorothy Crystal (1902–1998), designer, was born in London, at Belsize Lodge, 3 Garlinge Road, Kilburn, on 20 October 1902, the younger daughter and youngest of three children of Robert Joseph Marx, a mechanical engineer particularly involved in the paper industry (and a second cousin, twice removed, of Karl Marx), and his wife, Annie Marie Neuberger. Her elder sister, Marguerite, who lived in Paris as a young woman, was an important early influence, and Enid's artistic bent was encouraged. At an early age she delighted in collecting samples from ribbon shops. Small in stature, with bird-like speed and alertness, she always retained a child's curiosity and freshness of vision. She was educated in Hampstead and at Roedean School, Sussex, where she benefited from an excellent art teacher, and entered the Central School of Arts and Crafts, in London, in 1921. After a year's study, during which several important friendships were formed, she proceeded to the Royal College of Art in 1922

as a contemporary of Henry Moore, Edward Bawden, Eric Ravilious, and other notable artists. Her drawing was not conventionally correct and her painting was influenced by European modernism. Together with Moore she attended classes at Leon Underwood's studio. Her independence was encouraged by the college's principal, Sir William Rothenstein, but she and other rebels were failed for the diploma in 1925. She continued to practise painting and drawing none the less, and observation of nature was the basis even of her abstract design work.

On the recommendation of Paul Nash, a part-time teacher at the Royal College of Art, Marx had already been commissioned to engrave a design for a pattern paper on wood for the Curwen Press. The potter Norah Braden introduced her to the handblock textile printers Phyllis Barron and Dorothy Larcher, and she joined them as an apprentice, learning the craft that Barron had revived in the previous ten years. With her own independent textile printing workshop from 1927 to 1939 Marx cut designs on wood and lino, and printed lengths to order. The designs were often influenced by ethnic pieces in the British Museum. Cecilia, Lady Sempill, who sold Marx's textiles in her own shop, wrote in 1979:

> The linens were lovely for curtains and covers, and there was a particularly good red and brown striped one which we used for the seats of the chairs which Eric Ravilious designed for us. The organdies, mostly starry patterns on pale or spotted grounds, were much used for under-curtains and no doubt also for dresses. (*Enid Marx: a Retrospective Exhibition*, 11)

Marx knew many of the leading figures of the 1920s crafts revival but was also interested in designing for industry under appropriate conditions of artistic independence. In 1935 she was commissioned by Christian Barman of London Underground to design new seating moquettes. 'It couldn't be a dazzling design, or something too directional, in case people travelling began to feel seasick', she recalled ('Enid Marx: in celebration'). The counterchange pattern in red and green was lively and hard-wearing, responding to the different light conditions in tunnel and open air. Barman believed that Marx's craft background gave her 'the ability to seize the major points of a concrete problem and to provide a solution that will have something more than interest or charm: the fitness and simplicity of the finest craftsmanship' (Barman, 47).

The war brought an end to handblock printing, but Marx found new occupations in illustrating children's books and painting for the Recording Britain scheme. In 1943 she was commissioned by Sir Gordon Russell to design textiles for the Utility Furniture Design Panel set up by the Board of Trade, and relished the restrictions of colour and yarn, from which she still managed to produce lively patterns. In 1944 she was created a royal designer for industry by the Royal Society of Arts. After spending the war mostly in London she lived for a time in St Andrews, where her friend the historian Margaret Lambert (1905–1995) held a university teaching post, before returning to London and teaching in art colleges at Gravesend and Croydon, where she was head of three departments at once. She increased her production of book illustrations (usually wood engravings but sometimes lithographs) and in the course of a long and productive relationship with the publishers Chatto and Windus designed a standard pink and sky-blue jacket for the translations of Marcel Proust's *A la recherche du temps perdu*. For the new reign in 1952 she designed borders for the queen's head for the low-value definitive stamps, an area of design to which she returned with the Christmas stamps of 1976.

With Margaret Lambert, Marx collaborated on a book, *When Victoria Began to Reign* (1937), a scrapbook of words and images of the year 1837. This led to a collaboration on *English Popular and Traditional Art* (1946), in Collins's Britain in Pictures series, and *English Popular Art*, published by Batsford in 1951. Other artist contemporaries shared their excitement about the stimulus that the folk art of the industrial revolution offered to the modern eye. As a designer and craftsman Marx was interested in how things were made but equally in customs surrounding their naming and use. Many of the illustrations for Lambert and Marx's books were taken from their own collections, which are now in the Enid Marx Collection, Compton Verney House Trust, Warwickshire.

Like many of the anonymous producers of popular art Enid Marx liked to use animals as motifs, making up illustrated alphabets and simple tales about them or incorporating them in illustrations and large linocuts; a Noah's ark was used by London Underground to advertise the zoo under the slogan 'Carried in comfort'. At home she kept Siamese cats, whose misdeeds formed a frequent topic of conversation with the many visitors whom she entertained right up to the end of her life. Those who came to learn about the past were invariably drawn into lively discussion of current events in the world of art and design, and she campaigned ceaselessly for the continuation of the direct, unaffected, but human design values that her generation had established before the war. Enid Marx died in London, at the Royal Free Hospital, Camden, on 18 May 1998. She never married. ALAN POWERS

Sources *Enid Marx: a retrospective exhibition organised by the Arkwright Arts Trust for the Camden Arts Centre* (1979) · 'Enid Marx: in celebration of her Camden Shows', *Designer Magazine* (1979), 8–10 · F. MacCarthy, *The Guardian* (19 May 1998), 14 · F. Sweet, *The Independent* (19 May 1998), 21 · [A. Powers], *Daily Telegraph* (21 May 1998), 33 · *Designers*, 2/11 (July–Aug 1998), 9 · C. Barman, 'Enid Marx', *Signature*, 4 (Nov 1936), 47–8 · A. Powers, 'Sources of inspiration: Enid Marx', *Crafts* (March–April 1990), 34–7 · C. Weaver, 'Enid Marx: textile designer for industry', MA diss., University of Central England, 1987 · E. Marx, 'Pattern papers', *Penrose Annual*, 44 (1950), 51–3 · E. Marx, 'Student days at the RCA', *Matrix: a review for printers and bibliographers*, 16 (1996), 145–50 · E. Marx, 'Design and print in the 1930s', *Matrix: a review for printers and bibliographers*, 15 (1995), 162–4 · personal knowledge (2004) · b. cert. · d. cert. · *CGPLA Eng. & Wales* (1998)

Archives priv. coll. · U. Reading L., Chatto and Windus archive · V&A NAL, autobiographical notes

Likenesses E. D. C. Marx, self-portrait, *c*.1925, priv. coll. · E. Ravilious, drawing, *c*.1925, priv. coll.

Wealth at death £310,558: probate, 17 Sept 1998, *CGPLA Eng. & Wales*

Marx, Karl Heinrich (1818–1883), revolutionary and thinker, known from student days to his intimates as

Karl Heinrich Marx (1818–1883), by unknown photographer, 1867

Mohr (the Moor), was born on 5 May 1818 at Brückengasse 664, in Trier, a recent addition to the kingdom of Prussia, the third of nine children and only surviving son of the lawyer Heinrich Marx (1781/2–1838) and his wife, Henriette, *née* Pressburg. As was then not unusual, four of his siblings died in infancy or youth.

Family background and religion Marx's parents both came from rabbinical families, which had customarily tended to intermarry. Both his grandfather Meier Halevi Marx, the descendant of a priestly line, and his uncle Samuel became rabbis of the Jewish community in Trier, then a small but ancient country town, proud of its Roman heritage. Meier's wife, Chaje Lwow, Karl Marx's grandmother, came from an even more distinguished rabbinical lineage descended from, as the name implies, the scholar Moses Lwow of the then Polish, and subsequently Austrian, Polish, Soviet, and Ukrainian, city. Her father, grandfather, and great-grandfather had been rabbis of Trier and elsewhere in Franconia and Alsace since the later seventeenth century. Another line led from the Minz family which emigrated, presumably from Mainz, in the mid-fifteenth century to Padua, where its members were rabbis and heads of the Talmudic college. On his mother's side, as the name Pressburg implies, the family came from Hungary, whence they had migrated to the Netherlands, where Henriette's grandfather became rabbi of Nijmegen. Her sister broke the rabbinical chain by marrying the banker Lion Philips, grandfather of the founder of the well-known Dutch and international industrial concern, who after Heinrich's death acted as trustee for Karl Marx's mother.

Given this family background, it seems at first surprising that Heinrich Marx decided to be baptized at the age of thirty-five—in the evangelical rather than the locally prevalent Roman Catholic faith—in 1816 or 1817, and had Karl and all his surviving siblings baptized in 1824, followed in 1825 by Marx's mother. The immediate reasons were almost certainly practical. After Trier became Prussian in 1815 Jews were excluded from all public posts, the practice of law being classified as a public post on 4 May 1816. Even so, the decision to abandon the religion of his forefathers can be understood only if we bear in mind the extent to which the culture of the eighteenth-century Enlightenment had penetrated the world of the educated professional strata in the Rhineland and the experience of the first generation of Jewish emancipation under the French. Marx's father was a deist who found his God in Locke, Newton, and Leibniz and not in the Torah. His son already grew up in something close to an emancipated and assimilated German household, steeped in secular literary and philosophical culture of the ancient and modern European classics, although Marx's mother, brought up in the old ways, was never at ease either in writing or in speaking the High German language. Nevertheless, Heinrich Marx's conversion meant a complete break with his family. There appears to have been no further contact with any other Marxes. Karl's only known relation with his Jewish kin in later life appears to have been with his mother's relatives, the Dutch Philipses, with whom he continued to be on close terms. Lion Philips was also the only known correspondent to whom he wrote as one Jew to another—an identity he was elsewhere at pains to disclaim.

Education and marriage The young Karl Marx's five years at the Friedrich-Wilhelm Gymnasium in Trier (1830–35) were uneventful and not strikingly distinguished. Only hindsight can read more into the seventeen-year-old's essay 'Considerations of a young man on choosing his career' than the adolescent's idealist desire to serve humanity: 'If he is working only for himself, he can become a famous scholar, a sage, a distinguished writer, but never a complete, a truly great, man.' He appears to have formed no lasting friendships except with the brother of his future bride, Jenny (Johanna Bertha Julie Jenny von Westphalen; 1814–1881), to whom he became engaged at the age of eighteen, at the end of his first academic year at the University of Bonn. Intellectually, the major influences in his school years appear to have come from his father and his future father-in-law, privy councillor (*geheimer Regierungsrat*) Johann Ludwig von Westphalen, son of an official of the duke of Brunswick, who was distinguished in the Seven Years War, ennobled, and married into the Wishart family, kin to the earls and later dukes of Argyll, a connection which Mrs Marx did nothing to conceal during her years in England.

Westphalen, who served, in turn, the Guelphs, the

French kingdom of Westphalia, and Prussia, shared his enthusiasm for the Greek poets and Shakespeare with the young Marx, and, more surprisingly, introduced him to Saint-Simon; his ideas were clearly more advanced than those of his eldest son, who was to become Prussian minister of the interior in the 1850s. His daughter Jenny, four years older than Karl, was the beauty of Trier, and was still remembered in the town as such even in the early 1860s, as Marx noted with satisfaction when he revisited his birthplace in 1863. That a man of this background and standing should have consented to the marriage of his daughter to a young, even if converted, Jew without visible prospects is convincing evidence that, even as a schoolboy, he must have deeply impressed at least one good judge.

That the brilliant, sarcastic, darkly handsome youth also deeply impressed both contemporaries and seniors became clear at the universities in Bonn (1835–6) and especially Berlin (1836–41), where Marx gradually shifted from his original subject of law to philosophy, though also tempted by Romantic poetry, for which his surviving verses show no great aptitude. The student was father to the man. A number of what proved to be Marx's permanent characteristics emerged during his university years, finally completed by a doctoral dissertation, 'Die Differenz der Demokritischen und Epikurischen Naturphilosophie' ('The difference between Democritus' and Epicurus' philosophy of nature'), at the philosophical faculty of Jena (April 1841): a tendency to indulge in Herculean bouts of overwork (at the expense of his health); an inability to finish his projects, except under extreme pressure; and—not least—a cavalier attitude to the problems of earning a living and to the relation between income and expenditure. These darkened his relations with his father, a conflict which can be followed in a moving exchange of letters that ended with Heinrich Marx's premature death in 1838, after which relations with Marx's mother also deteriorated. Perhaps the father, though complaining about Karl's extravagant debts, would have been more tolerant of the nineteen-year-old's impassioned but ill-defined struggles to reunite art, science, and philosophy single-handed had he not, by his engagement to the daughter of an established Trier family, undertaken commitments, by the standards of contemporary reason and convention, which he showed no sign of recognizing. Indeed, for the rest of his life Marx was never to succeed by his own efforts in solving his economic problems, or acquiring any regular or predictable income.

Berlin and Paris In Berlin, the home of Hegelian thought, the undergraduate Marx was quickly accepted by his seniors in the so-called 'postgraduate club' (*Doktorklub*) of Young Hegelian philosophers, representing the philosophical and political avant-garde, that is to say the critique of state and religion. There was no prospect of an academic career for a brilliant but philosophically (though by no means yet socially) subversive young intellectual inclined to activism. However, he had made a sufficiently strong impression to be asked to contribute to a new journal, the *Rheinische Zeitung*, financed by a group of wealthy Cologne men in business and the professions and representing the moderate but loyal liberalism of the (non-clerical) Rhineland bourgeoisie. After six months and a number of articles, which were almost his first excursions into real politics and his first into economic questions, he became its editorial director and remained so until the paper was closed down by the censor in early 1843, though evidently without hard feelings, for shortly after he resigned from the editorship the Prussian government appears to have offered him a post as editor in the state service. Indeed his posture as editor of the *Rheinische Zeitung* had been militant but politically moderate. In any case, until then, in spite of its urgency and prominence in the early 1840s, he had as yet shown no interest in the much discussed 'social question', nor did he as yet sympathize with what he regarded as the superficial communism which was already attracting the paper's young Berlin contributors. It was not, he felt, based on serious thought. Proud, abrasive, and confident of his gifts, he had begun to make a name. Nevertheless, it was clear that no serious opposition writing would be tolerated in Germany.

Marx therefore accepted the offer (by Arnold Ruge, one of the most prominent voices of liberal opposition) of a salaried joint editorship of a proposed journal to be published abroad, the *Deutsche-Französische Jahrbücher*. This brought him to Paris in late 1843 as a literary emigrant and, after April 1844, when the Prussian government issued an arrest warrant against its editors on the grounds of high treason and *lèse-majesté*, as a permanent, and soon stateless, political refugee. He surrendered his Prussian citizenship in December 1845, a fact which was later used to disqualify his application for naturalization in Britain on the grounds that he had 'behaved disloyally to his King' (*Collected Works*, 24.564), although actually he tried unsuccessfully to reclaim his Prussian citizenship in 1862. In Paris he set up his first married household—he had married on 12 June 1843—and had his first child, Jenny Caroline (1844–1883). Here also the household was joined by its lifelong member Helene (Lenchen) Demuth, a young servant of the Westphalen family who was transferred, in a somewhat feudal manner, from Trier to Jenny Marx by her mother. Under Prussian pressure Marx was expelled from Paris by the French government in January 1845 and moved to Brussels, which remained his base of operations until the 1848 revolutions. Two further children were born in Brussels, (Jenny) Laura (1845–1911)—all his daughters were named Jenny, after his wife—and the short-lived Henry Edgar, who died in Soho (1846–1855). The rest of the Marxes' children, Henry Edward Guy (1849–1850), (Jenny Eveline) Frances (1851–1852), and (Jenny Julia) Eleanor *Marx (1855–1898), were born and died in England.

The Karl Marx we know was born in the months between his marriage and his expulsion from Paris. He thought his way through to communism by means of an intensive critique of Hegel's philosophy of law and the state, via the *Vorläufige Thesen zur Reform der Philosophie* (1843) (*Preliminary Theses on the Reform of Philosophy*) of the radical philosopher Ludwig Feuerbach and an impassioned study of the history of the French Revolution. By the end of 1843, when Marx wrote 'Zur Kritik der Hegel'schen Rechtsphilosophie' ('Introduction to the critique of Hegel's philosophy of law') for the *Jahrbücher* (published in 1844), he had concluded that the proletariat alone was the necessary agency for the emancipation of humanity. In Paris he found himself in the capital of both revolution and socialism, and in the midst of an international community of the political avant-garde, most of whom were soon to become victims of his critique—Bakunin, Proudhon, Ruge and the German emigration, Leroux, Louis Blanc, and the other French socialists, but not the sceptical poet and temporary communist sympathizer Heinrich Heine, for whom, all his life, Marx retained 'a sincere affection' (Prawer, 66). He was already known as both the ablest and least tolerant of the revolutionary intellectuals.

Marx and Engels Stimulated by his study of the French Revolution and by a 'Umrisse zu einer Kritik der Nationalökonomie' ('Outlines of a critique of national economy') submitted in 1844 to the magazine by Frederick *Engels (1820–1895) on the basis of his British experience, Marx began, with his usual titanic energy, to plunge into the literature of economics. The two young men found they had converged on the same point by different routes: the one via politics and the French Revolution, the other via the experience of Britain's industrial revolution in his family's Manchester cotton business. By the late summer of 1844, when Engels spent ten days in Paris with Marx on his way back from Manchester, the two young men found themselves 'in agreement in all theoretical areas' and about to begin their lifelong co-operation. With Engels, Marx made his first visit to Britain—London and Manchester—a few months later (July–August 1845).

The partnership with Engels, never broken on either side, was so central to the remainder of Marx's life that a brief comment on it is relevant. For Marx, Engels was to be the permanent intellectual collaborator and partner, the ever reliable source of information, notably about the actual operations of capitalist industry, the constant, unconditional (if not uncritical) backer, and the fount of intellectual, and especially material, support. Without Engels he could not have survived his years in Britain. For Engels, Marx, in his own graveside words, was 'the greatest living thinker', the Darwin of the law of human historical evolution, the pathbreaker for humanity's future, a genius to whom he, a mere man of talent and intelligence, was justified in devoting his mind and money—even at the cost of continuing in the hated family cotton business to provide him with an income.

Marx and the origins of Marxism With and without Engels, Marx now launched himself into a series of writings in which he tried to elaborate his new theory, and which form the basis of what later came to be called Marxism—a term from which he took his distance when it came into use at the end of his life. However, although he actually received in 1845 a publisher's advance for a two-volume critique of politics and national economy, his major work—or that part of it which was actually completed under the title *Das Kapital: Kritik der politischen Oekonomie*—was not published until 1867. As Ruge had observed: 'He never finishes anything; he is always breaking off, and then plunges again into an infinite ocean of books' (Blumenberg, 55). Only ideological disagreement and personal polemic seemed to spur him into publication—with Engels against various Germans (*Die heilige Familie, oder, Kritik der kritischen Kritik*, Frankfurt, 1845), alone against Proudhon (*La misère de la philosophie*, Brussels and Paris, 1847). Major texts, such as the so-called 'Paris manuscripts' of 1844, the 'Theses on Feuerbach' (1845), and the enormous *Die deutsche Ideologie* ('German ideology') of 1845–6, written in collaboration with Engels, in which his 'materialist conception of history' was first elaborated, were to be published posthumously between 1888 and 1932.

The *Communist Manifesto* and the 1848 revolutions Of more immediate significance was the conversion of the most important secret German revolutionary fraternity, the League of the Just, renamed the Communist League, with whom both had had increasingly close contacts for some years, to the views of Marx and Engels. This body, an offshoot of French secret societies of the 1830s, was primarily composed of militant expatriate German craftsmen, but also attracted some young intellectuals, among them the future leaders of Germany's major working-class parties, Ferdinand Lassalle and Wilhelm Liebknecht. Marx visited Britain for the second time (27 November to 13 December 1847) to take part in the Second Congress of the now reformed organization at the Communistischer Arbeiterbildungsverein ('Communist Workers' Educational Club'), then in Soho, just off Shaftesbury Avenue. Here he and Engels were commissioned to draw up a manifesto, which he completed—not without a deadline and ultimatum from the league—for publication at the end of February, a nose ahead of the 1848 revolutions. It presented communism as the necessary and inevitable product of the historical development of capitalism. As the *Communist Manifesto*, this irresistible combination of utopian confidence, moral passion, hard-edged analysis, and—not least—a dark literary eloquence was eventually to become perhaps the best-known and certainly the most widely translated pamphlet of the nineteenth century. Its publication went almost unnoticed. The Communist League and its network remained Marx's main political resource during the ensuing years of revolution.

The 1848 revolution gave Marx a political role adequate to his talents. Expelled from Belgium shortly after the outbreak of the February revolution in France, he returned to Paris by invitation of the new republican government and prepared for the now certain German revolutions which triumphed in March. Within weeks, and on a temporary French passport, he was back in Cologne with Engels, who raised most of the money to found the daily *Neue Rheinische Zeitung: Organ der Democratie*, of which Marx was editor-in-chief, assisted—for the paper was run, in Engels's words, 'simply as the dictatorship of Marx'—by Engels and a team of communists. It has been described as 'the best newspaper of that year of revolution' (Blumenberg, 87).

Certainly it was the most coherent voice of the democratic left, which believed that 'the domination of the bourgeoisie cannot be reached by compromise with the feudal powers', recommended a revolutionary war against Russia, and held that 'German unity, like the German Constitution, can only emerge as the result of a movement in which both the inner conflicts and the war with the East are brought to resolution' (*Neue Rheinische Zeitung*, 7 June 1848). Fortunately Marx's pen felt the discipline of the need for daily comment. He had to write rapidly, and the *Neue Rheinische Zeitung* gave him practice in the genre of instant analytical history he was to make his own and which he perfected after 1848, notably in the masterly 'Der 18te Brumaire des Louis Napoleon' ('The eighteenth Brumaire of Louis Napoleon') (*Die Revolution*, 1, 1852), written within weeks of the French *coup d'état* of December 1851.

Marx in London Though Marx and his friends did not recognize that the defeat of the revolution was irreversible until 1850, the increasingly radical paper closed down as Marx was expelled from Prussia at twenty-four hours' notice in May 1849. The family made its way to Paris by various routes. In France he was, once again, a suspect subversive, offered permission to reside only if he remained far from Paris in southern Brittany. Instead, planning a revived expatriate *Neue Rheinische Zeitung*, he chose exile in Britain, where he arrived at the end of August, to be joined by his family on 15 September. From then on to the end of his life Marx had his domicile in London at—omitting temporary lodgings—4 Anderson Street, Chelsea (October 1849 – April 1850), then at two addresses in Dean Street, Soho (December 1850 – September 1856), in Grafton Terrace, Kentish Town (October 1856 – March 1864), at 1 Modena Villas (1864–75), and finally, further up Maitland Park Road at 41 (1875–83), where both Jenny Marx and he died.

The next few years were the hardest and most frustrating in Marx's life, although the British Museum Library, to which he obtained access in June 1850, offered some escape from the miseries of politics and everyday troubles. His political hopes, both general and personal, collapsed. For a few months he kept up hopes of a revolutionary revival as he published six issues of a short-lived *Neue Rheinische Zeitung: Politisch-Ökonomische Revue* (including his analysis of the French revolution later republished as *Die Klassenkämpfe in Frankreich, 1848 bis 1850* and in English as *The Class Struggles in France, 1848–50*), while sketching a prospect of the possible passage from democratic to proletarian revolution ('permanent revolution') for the benefit of the Communist League. Yet, unlike many other of the refugees crowding into London, he soon accepted that the revolutionary era was at an end. In the overheated atmosphere of inquest, rivalry, recrimination, and mutual accusation that tends to follow lost revolutions, the German Workers' League in London broke away from Marx and Engels—never the best of committee men—as did most of the London communists, leaving them politically quite isolated, while in 1851 the police succeeded in virtually destroying the Communist League in Germany.

It was formally dissolved by Marx in November 1852. Politically he was at zero point. Intellectually few could even read him, for attempts to publish his writings in 1851 came to little, as did his hopes, excessively optimistic as usual, to complete his economic work. Ferdinand Lassalle, shortly to be founder of the first mass workers' party in Germany and an admirer of Marx (who did not return the admiration), arranged for the publication of a first instalment, *Zur Kritik der politischen Ökonomie* (Berlin, 1859), which Marx failed to follow up. The enormous preparatory manuscripts of 1857–8 became influential after their publication under the title *Grundrisse* in 1939–41. The contrast between his talent, promise, and achievement and his political isolation visibly embittered Marx, and made him even more intolerant, both in public and in private.

At the same time Marx's material situation was catastrophic. With no gift for domestic financial management and living the hand-to-mouth life of the political refugee, without a predictable source of income since 1844, he had been harried by money troubles since the mid-1840s, but with the end of the *Neue Rheinische Zeitung* these became constant and acute. The squalor in which the Marxes—six persons—lived in their two furnished rooms in Soho was vividly described by visiting Prussian police spies, and the daily Dickensian struggle with butchers, bakers, landlords, and pawnbrokers emerges in Marx's correspondence with the ever loyal Engels, on whose financial aid he now relied permanently. Three of the Marx children died during these terrible years and were buried in the churchyard of Whitefield's Tabernacle in Tottenham Court Road, Mrs Marx having to beg £2 from a neighbouring French political refugee to pay for the coffin of one of them. Not surprisingly Jenny Marx's nerves often gave way, as did Karl's hardly equable temper. 'At home a constant state of siege' he reported to Engels in 1851; 'Am annoyed and enraged by streams of tears all night long … I'm sorry for my wife. She bears the brunt of the pressure, and *au fond* she is right. In spite of this … from time to time I lose my temper' (Marx to Engels, 31 July 1851, *Collected Works*, 38.398). It should be remembered that Mrs Marx was not only in charge of the household but also acted as her husband's secretary. It may be that those times of what must have been intolerable pressure led to the birth of Helene Demuth's son, Henry Frederick, who (according to one interpretation) was Marx's child, on 28 June 1851. Jenny Marx seems to have been kept in ignorance, thanks to the faithful and notoriously unbourgeois Engels, who tacitly allowed paternity to be attributed to himself until shortly before he died. We may assume that Marx was not in a position to take responsibility for an illegitimate son. Still, the episode leaves a bad taste in the mouths of Marx's biographers. Befriended later by Marx's daughters, Frederick Demuth, the only member of the Marx family actually to be a class-conscious proletarian (a toolmaker and member of the Amalgamated Engineering Union), died in 1929. It has been suggested that the authorities of the young USSR, anxious to avoid potentially embarrassing claims from illegitimate descendants of Marx, paid him a substantial sum, probably in the mid-1920s, presumably in return for silence about his paternity. The documentation about Demuth was sufficiently important to be submitted to Stalin himself in 1934, who decided that 'the material should stay buried in the archive' (Kapp, 'Frederick Demuth', 18–19, 26–7).

Ironically, the main victim of those years was not Helene Demuth, who continued as the loved and respected friend, member, and housekeeper of the Marx family until her employer's death and is buried in the family grave, but Jenny Marx.

> In all these struggles [she was to write some twenty years later] we women have the harder part to bear, because it is the pettier one. A man draws strength from his battles with the world outside, invigorated by the very confrontation with the enemy, be their number legion. We sit at home and darn stockings. That doesn't save us from worry, and the little everyday miseries slowly but surely grind down the will to live. (J. Marx to W. Liebknecht, 26 May 1872, *Collected Works*, 44.580; slightly modified translation)

In the last decade of her life, when Marx's work made less demand on her time, Jenny's life—passionate but not entirely conventional by the standards of Haverstock Hill—turned increasingly round the domestic problems of children and grandchildren. Her daughters, from whom surprisingly few letters to her appear to have survived, talked of her with a sort of amused condescension and made fun of her conscientious reading of *Das Kapital*. Not so Karl Marx, who thought the most important thing about what he regarded as the first English publication that did his ideas justice was that he received it in time 'so that my dear wife had the last days of her life still cheered up. You know the passionate interest she took in all such affairs' (ibid., Marx to F. A. Sorge, 15 Dec 1881, 46.163).

If anything Marx's financial problems became worse in the course of the 1850s, although journalism, mainly for the *New York Daily Tribune*, whose editor, Charles Dana, he had got to know in 1848 and for which he acted as London correspondent, provided some fairly regular income. Some of these articles were written for Marx by Engels, notably those later published as *Revolution and Counter-Revolution, or, Germany in 1848*, edited by Eleanor Marx Aveling (1896). In 1862, when the American Civil War had lost Marx this source of income, he reached the nadir of his financial fortunes. His wife attempted to sell his books and (with recommendations from a Philips cousin) Marx actually felt obliged to seek employment as a clerk for the Great Western Railway. He was turned down because of his sensationally illegible handwriting, which has also been the bane of Marxian scholars. In spite of constant, desperate, and always successful appeals for money to Engels, some legacies, and various complex (and sometimes shaky) speculations and credit transactions, the Marx finances were not stabilized until 1869 when Engels, about to retire from the Manchester cotton business, offered to pay all his debts and to provide an annuity of £350, which Marx agreed he could live on—illness and other unforeseen contingencies apart—though he also admitted that he had exceeded this sum in the past. In fact the Marxes continued to rely on Engels's extraordinary generosity, as the need arose.

The problem of the Marxian finances had been particularly intractable for two reasons: the Marxes felt it essential to maintain the public expenditure of a successful professional household, especially after their move into a middle-class district, and they were spectacularly bad at budgeting. Hence the surprising combination of what was then a substantial annual expenditure with almost constant and desperate financial embarrassment. Moreover, matters were made even more difficult by the ill health which increasingly racked Marx's powerful body from 1849. He suffered annual and increasingly severe liver and gall-bladder attacks. From the early 1860s he developed disabling and Job like boils and abscesses—the famous carbuncles, for which he hoped the bourgeoisie would one day pay. He also suffered from rheumatic pains and occasional paralysis, and, fairly persistently, from headaches, inflammation of the eyes, neuralgia, and chronic insomnia, not to mention from bronchial and lung problems, which were to be the official cause of his death ('cachexy as a result of consumption'). In his last thirty years he was, for practical purposes, under constant medical attention. It is possible that some of his medical problems were psychosomatic ('of a nervous nature'), as his doctor suggested on at least one occasion. They were almost certainly aggravated by his diet, smoking, and drinking habits, and quite certainly by the enormous workload he imposed on himself by day and night.

The International and *Das Kapital* These were the conditions under which Marx entered the second, and very much more rewarding, decade of his British exile, when he became a well-known figure in British politics and an influential one in international labour politics, and also produced the only volume of *Das Kapital* published in his lifetime as well as virtually all of the manuscript of what was to be published posthumously as volumes 2 and 3 of that work and the *Theorien über den Mehrwert* ('Theories of surplus value').

Since 1846 Marx had established relations with the British Chartists—notably G. J. Harney, who appears to have been the main British contact for the Communist League, and later Ernest Jones. However, his contacts with the main body of the post-Chartist labour movement, the trade unions, were probably mediated through old Communist Leaguers among German workers in Britain, who retained their admiration for him, such as the tailor G. Eccarius, who in 1863 arranged his participation in a trade union meeting in favour of the north in the American Civil War, presided over by John Bright. This initiated his relations with leading figures of the British trade union and labour movement such as Robert Applegarth, W. R. Cremer, and George Odger. The British unions were to provide the crucial organizational backing for the new International Working Men's Association, to the inaugural meeting of which, on 28 September 1864, Marx was invited as a reprcsentative of the German workers, and to whose provisional committee he was elected.

Although Marx at this time had few supporters anywhere, sheer intellectual superiority immediately made him the leading figure in this organization. Since, unlike in the Communist League, he was in no position to exercise authority directly, he now also demonstrated a political tact not evident in his earlier career. Composed of representatives of virtually all tendencies on the European left, ranging from moderate trade unionists to anarchist insurrectionaries, the 'International' was to acquire considerable public prominence, coinciding as it did with a marked growth in labour activity and organization in Europe, which it attempted to inspire and co-ordinate. While uninterested in revolutionary projects the British unions, engaged in the struggle for electoral reform and union rights, found Marx's insistence on class-based political action congenial and welcomed the International's efforts to prevent the import of strike-breakers from abroad. Marx became the chief draftsman of its documents, beginning with its rules and inaugural address (1864), and indeed was chiefly instrumental in holding its disparate elements together until they broke apart under the strain of the battle between Marx, the champion of state power and politics, and Bakunin, the anti-political anarchist, and in the aftermath of the Paris commune of 1871. Most of the British trade unionists abandoned the International after its, or rather Marx's, 'Address on the commune', better known as *The Civil War in France* (1871)—the third of his remarkable pamphlets on the contemporary history of France. This document, which profoundly influenced subsequent revolutionaries from Lenin to Mao, abandoned the deliberate moderation of the earlier statements of the International to return to 'the old boldness of speech' (Marx to Engels, 4 Dec 1864, *Collected Works*, 42.18), thus reinforcing the impression that the International, identified with Marx, was the heart of international revolution, which had been gaining ground for some time. Although the British government did not take these attacks seriously, Marx himself was not displeased that 'I have the honour to be AT THIS MOMENT THE BEST CALUMNIATED AND MOST MENACED MAN OF LONDON. That really does one good after a tedious twenty years' idyll in the swamp' (ibid., Marx to Kugelmann, 18 June 1871, 44.158). His prominence in the International also attracted attention to his writings. Volume 1 of *Das Kapital* was published in 1867, its preface dated from London on 25 July 1867, the only one of Marx's major works which was published in his lifetime (its first English translation, edited by Engels and translated by S. Moore and Eleanor Marx Aveling, was published by Swan Sonnenschein in 1887). Between 1869 and 1872, for the only time in his lifetime, new editions of his earlier writings were published: *The Eighteenth Brumaire* (1869), the *Communist Manifesto* (1872), and the second and much rewritten edition of *Das Kapital* (1872). On the other hand the breakup of the International in 1872—its relics were dispatched to New York—virtually ended his life as a practising politician.

Although the 1870s left Marx with far more time and without serious financial worries, they also virtually brought to an end his theoretical work. While he continued to read endlessly in a variety of languages—he now learned Russian—after 1872 he wrote little, published less, and added hardly anything to the vast but uncoordinated mass of manuscript written in the 1860s, although he made an attempt to return to the second volume of *Das Kapital* in 1877-8, which he said he hoped to complete within a year. Engels's shock at the fragmentary state of the material after his friend's death is comprehensible: he had been given the impression that it was close to completion. Why Marx never concluded his *magnum opus* has been endlessly discussed since his death, but there is no doubt that with the end of the International something went out of his life.

However, he was by this time a personage of some note, or notoriety, in various countries. Indeed, his (unsuccessful) application for naturalization in 1874 was intended to safeguard himself against action by the authorities in newly united Germany and the Austrian authorities at Karlsbad where, under the watchful eye of the local *Bezirkshauptmann*, he took the cure with his daughter Eleanor, until a nervous Habsburg government intimated its intention to expel this 'outstanding leader of the democratic-social party' (Kisch, 31, 73) if he were to return. He began to attract interviewers. More to the point, in Germany the two labour and socialist parties, both founded by his disciples, merged in 1875 (on terms which he bitterly denounced in the so-called 'Critique of the Gotha programme' of that year, posthumously published by Engels in *Die Neue Zeit*, 1891) to form what was to become the largest of pre-1914 Marxist parties. More surprisingly, the translation of *Das Kapital* into Russian (1872) gained him immediate and profound influence among Russian intellectuals. The censors of St Petersburg had authorized its publication on the grounds that 'it is possible to state with certainty that very few people in Russia will read it and even fewer will understand it' (Figes, 139). While he had been in touch with Russian exiles since the 1840s, his links with Russian intellectuals, in whose country—to cite a British report of 1879—he expected 'a great and not distant crash' (*Collected Works*, 24.581), now became extremely close. His relations also remained close with France, the only other country in which a translation of *Das Kapital* appeared in Marx's lifetime (1872-5); two of his daughters, Jenny and Laura, married Frenchmen—respectively Charles Longuet (1833-1903) and Paul Lafargue (1842-1911)—while a third, Eleanor, was for some years engaged to another, the communard and historian of the Paris commune Hippolyte Prosper Olivier Lissagaray (1838-1901), and would almost certainly have married him but for a paternal veto.

In Britain, where *The Times* and some other newspapers were to receive the news of his death from the Paris papers, Marx remained little known and intellectually isolated. Not surprisingly he resented the fact that even his earliest British disciple, founder of the Democratic (from 1884 Social Democratic) Federation, H. M. *Hyndman, initially thought it advisable not to mention his name, on the grounds that the English did not like the word socialism and 'have a dread of being taught by a foreigner' (Marx to Hyndman, 2 July 1881, *Collected Works*, 46.102). Such contacts as he had earlier, mainly with the radicals of the *Fortnightly Review*, appear to have been

mediated by the small band of positivists (E. S. Beesly, Frederic Harrison), themselves supporters of the International and among the rare British sympathizers with the Paris commune. Characteristically, Sir Mountstuart Elphinstone Grant Duff's letter of 1 February 1879 to the Empress Friedrich (ibid., 24.580-82) passes naturally from a lengthy account of a meeting with Marx to some gossip about the English positivists.

A number of writers have left very similar impressions of Marx in his last decade: a 'firm neck' (Kisch, 70) on still massive shoulders supported 'the head of a man of intellect and the features of a cultivated Jew' (*Collected Works*, 24.568) framed by long grey hair and beard, 'which contrast strangely with a still dark moustache' (ibid., 24.580) and dark bushy eyebrows (Kisch, 70). Few failed to remark on the sharp, sparkling eyes. He looked old, almost certainly older than his years—the *Chicago Tribune's* reporter thought 'he must be over 70 years of age' in December 1878 (*Collected Works*, 24.568). He seemed to enjoy life. He was cultured, witty, a gifted raconteur: 'varied by many quaint turns and little bits of dry humour … it was all very *positif*, slightly cynical, interesting' (ibid., 24.580). He impressed by the sheer range of his knowledge—'a most impressively cultivated anglo-german *gentleman*' (Maxim Kovalevsky, quoted in Blumenberg, 151); 'his talk was that of a well-informed, nay, learned man' (*Collected Works*, 24.580). All were struck by the contrast between his incendiary reputation and continued belief in revolution on one hand and the dispassionate tone of the elderly scholar–observer on the other. 'It will not be he who whether he wishes it or not will turn the world upside down' observed Sir Mountstuart Elphinstone Grant Duff as he reported to the future Empress Friedrich of Germany that his impression of Marx 'was not at all unfavourable and I would gladly meet him again' (ibid., 24.582).

Final years With Engels's move to London in 1870—he lived a short walking distance away and saw Marx daily—and with the French sons-in-law as communard refugees in London, Marx now lived close to family and friends. From 1876 he acquired Longuet grandchildren, to whom he became very attached. But for his health, the natural exuberance and *joie de vivre* on which visitors to the family parties remarked would have been even more evident. However, his health continued to deteriorate, and from 1873 his doctors insisted on annual cures at a spa—Harrogate, Karlsbad, in the Black Forest, Malvern—as well as seaside rest in Jersey, Ramsgate, and finally, in 1882, in Algiers and on the Isle of Wight. So, and somewhat more rapidly, did the health of Jenny Marx deteriorate; she died, beloved, emaciated, and stoical, of liver cancer on 1 December 1881, leaving her husband bereft. On the day she died, thought Engels, the Moor also died (Mehring, 528). He outlived her for little more than a year. He suffered his last blow with the death of Jenny, his favourite daughter, on 11 January 1883, aged thirty-seven, probably of cancer of the bladder. On the afternoon of 14 March 1883, sitting in his easy chair in his house at 41 Maitland Park Road, London, he died. He was buried in Highgate cemetery on 17 March, in his wife's grave, in the presence of his daughter Eleanor, her partner Ernest Aveling, Ernest Radford (a friend of Engels), some old comrades from the Communist League, his two French sons-in-law, Wilhelm Liebknecht who spoke for the German Social Democratic Party, and two fellows of the Royal Society—the communist chemist Karl Schorlemmer from Manchester and the biologist Ray Lankester, a friend of Marx's last years. Engels's lapidary words at the graveside, quoted in every life of Marx since, remained unpublished at the time, except in the Zürich journal of German social democracy, then illegal under Bismarck's anti-socialist law. Engels said:

> As Darwin discovered the law of evolution in organic nature, so Marx discovered the law of evolution in human history … that human beings must first of all eat, drink, shelter and clothe themselves before they can turn their attention to politics, science, art and religion.   (Mehring, 531)

Marx died intestate. His youngest daughter, Eleanor, being the only relative resident in Britain, was granted letters of administration for his estate, valued at £250 (Kapp, *Eleanor Marx*, 1.282). The complex fortunes of the voluminous papers of Marx and Engels after their deaths form part of the troubled history of the twentieth century. 'What works?' Marx is reported as having said, bitterly, when asked about them. At his death there seemed little to show for a lifetime of sacrifice in the cause of changing the world. And yet scarcely any nineteenth-century figure has left a larger mark on history either as a thinker or as the inspirer of political action. As a thinker he was destined to make a greater impact—though in a very different manner—than any of his other contemporaries except Darwin. His intellectual gifts and achievement—'not only originality but also scientific ability of the highest order' (Schumpeter)—could not but impress even his critics. A century after the publication of *Das Kapital* he appeared more frequently than anyone else in the index of the *International Encyclopaedia of the Social Sciences*, with references to every single one of its sixteen volumes. As for his practical impact, within little more than fifty years of his death regimes officially devoted to Marxism ruled a third of the human race, without counting the many millions who lived under the governments of social democratic parties, many of which also claimed direct descent from him.

How far was this due to Marx, how far to the parties and movements claiming him as their inspiration? His personal contribution is not to be underestimated. 'The philosophers have only interpreted the world in various ways: the point is to change it' Marx had noted down in 1845 (*Collected Works*, 5.5). To the object of changing the world he devoted his life. Even sceptical critics noted 'the enormous vigour with which he created an arsenal of ideas for a political party and a host of slogans which could be used immediately and which were of magnificent effectiveness … the glowing passion which fascinated members of his party and his opponents and … the tone of the prophet which made his work unique' (Schumpeter, 119). He died no doubt hopeful, but also frustrated and disappointed.

And yet few unarmed prophets were destined to a century of such posthumous success.

Marx's thought   Marx's intellectual influence has been so wide-ranging that a brief summary of his thought is unusually difficult. Since his death, no field of thinking about man and nature has, at one time or another, lacked serious debates about the relevance of his ideas to it. He himself is a major figure in the history of philosophy, economics, sociology, and historiography, though he cannot be adequately contained under any of these headings. The absence of any systematic and comprehensive account of his thought by Marx himself adds to the difficulty. The various posthumous systematizations or 'Marxisms' do not necessarily represent his own views, although the version devised between 1883 and 1895, mainly by Frederick Engels, could clearly claim to be based on a lifetime's partnership with him.

Marx's starting point was a reflection on human nature. Like other humanist philosophers he assumed that it had a permanent essence, but he historicized this by defining what human beings 'really' are—not as a collection of permanent and unchanging qualities embodying some arbitrary ideal, but as a process of development inherent in their social existence. Humans produced both themselves and their world, and they did so through 'labour', the interaction of man and the non-human environment, by which they both transformed external nature and modified their own. Yet historically the inability of humans to recognize themselves in the man-made universe which surrounded them ('alienation') made impossible the realization of their full human potential—until the conditions for ending alienation came into existence in Marx's own times.

There were thus two strands in Marx's thinking—utopian or teleological, and historical or evolutionary—both relying on a coherent but non-linear ('dialectical') analysis and linked by the concept of social practice: only through praxis could man both change himself and the world and arrive at an understanding of what he was doing. In its Hegelian origins it was utopian, or rather eschatological: history was an objective process moving towards a final end—in Marx's case communism, the situation in which humanity would be able to determine its own development in freedom, no longer enslaved and blinded by the material forces it had created. Yet if this objective was achievable, it was not because it was desirable, but because it was historically inevitable. Moreover, Marx claimed to show why only the modern 'bourgeois' society could create the conditions for, and indeed the mechanism of, its realization, both by its capacity to revolutionize human society worldwide and by generating its own 'grave-digger'.

This required an understanding of how societies in general developed and changed, and, specifically, of the nature and dynamics of the new capitalist society, which was creating the conditions for human life to move into the realm of freedom. The 'materialist conception of history', elaborated between 1843 and 1846, provided the first; Marx's political economy, which developed the classical lines of thought from Quesnay and Adam Smith to Ricardo, set out to provide the second. Meanwhile recent French historical experience provided both a model of revolution and political action and the concept of history as a struggle between 'classes', one of which acted as the predestined and necessary agent of social transformation. In capitalist society this was to be the function of the propertyless and wage-dependent proletariat, created by the system, whose auto-emancipation would 'constitute … a transition to the *abolition of all classes* and to a *classless society*' (*Collected Works*, 39.62), and therefore to the end of human alienation.

In its most general form the materialist conception of history could be stated concisely and (except in one respect) remained substantially unchanged: 'It is not the consciousness of men that determines their existence, but their social existence that determines their consciousness' (*Collected Works*, 29.263–4). The motor of historical change was the secular tendency of man's 'material productive forces' to grow and to come into conflict with the rigidities of the ensemble of 'social relations of production', which humans necessarily had to establish to ensure 'the social production of their means of existence'. More precisely, the conflict was with the 'juridical and political superstructure' of the prevailing mode of production, which had become a fetter on its further development. Periodic 'epoch[s] of social revolution' would ensue until the revolutionary era (which Marx believed to be imminent) would—and here analysis gave way to millennial hope—eliminate capitalism, 'the last antagonistic form of the social process of production' and thus end 'the prehistory of human society'.

However, under the impact of Darwin the 'materialist conception' was broadened out into the concept of human historical evolution as an aspect of general (natural) evolution and essentially subject to the same 'scientific laws'. This was later to become the compendium 'dialectical and historical materialism', so influential in the Soviet period. While Engels developed this line of thought from the 1870s rather than Marx, who wrote little on these as on other matters in his last decade, Marx clearly showed a growing interest in the natural sciences at this time.

Unlike the materialist conception of history, the 'anatomy of civil society', Marx's political economy, which he began to study seriously in 1843, was constantly elaborated and never adequately presented and synthesized. *Das Kapital* attempted to combine three strands of thought: (1) an analysis of commodity production, comprising an exposition of 'alienation' in its specifically capitalist form—for example, the so-called 'fetishism of commodities', in which what are essentially social relations between humans 'masquerade as things or relations between things' (Kolakowski, 1.276); (2) a theory of class exploitation (through the appropriation by an employing class of the 'surplus value' created by those whose labour power is hired for wages); and (3) a model of the contradictory *modus operandi* of a capitalist economy, which

eventually creates the conditions for its supersession. The accumulation of profit-seeking capital, which constitutes the engine of capitalist growth, depends on the surplus value extracted from labour ('variable capital'), the ratio of which to 'constant capital' must decline with technological progress, thus leading to a tendency for the average rate of profit to decline. This leads both to increased exploitation of labour, made easier by the 'reserve army' of the unemployed, continuously reinforced by labour-saving technical progress, and to economic concentration. Thus capitalism moves through periodic crises, and a secular tendency towards economic concentration and social polarization, to the moment when, in the course of capitalist development, 'centralisation of the means of production and socialisation of labour at last reach a point where they are incompatible with their capitalist integument' (*Collected Works*, 35.750). Marx's writings contain virtually nothing about the post-capitalist economy.

How far Marx believed these tendencies of capitalism had developed in his lifetime is unclear. How they intersected with the history of men and movements, about which he was far from determinist, could not be predicted a priori. It is safe to say that at the time of his death he did not believe the end of capitalism was immediately to hand. Almost certainly he believed that it would be ended, when the time was ripe, by the socially explosive forces in the mature industrialized societies, although a revolution in the periphery of world capitalism—he confidently expected one in Russia—might act as the detonator for their explosion. However, in democratic countries he did not exclude the possibility of a non-violent transition.

E. J. E. Hobsbawm

Sources works *Karl Marx, Frederick Engels: collected works*, ed. and trans. R. Dixon and others, [49 vols.] (1975–) · K. Marx and F. Engels, *Correspondence* [Marx–Engels Gesamtausgabe] · Marx–Engels Nachlass, International Institute for Social History, Amsterdam family correspondence and iconograpy *Karl Marx album*, Institut für Marxismus-Leninismus beim ZK der SED (Berlin, 1953) · *Friedrich Engels, Paul et Laura Lafargue: correspondance*, ed. E. Bottigelli, 3 vols. (Paris, 1956–9) · O. Meier and E. Trebitsch, eds., *Les filles de Karl Marx: lettres inédites* (1979) biographies and biographical materials *Karl Marx: Chronik seines Lebens in Einzeldaten* (Zürich, 1934) · F. Mehring, *Karl Marx: the story of his life*, trans. E. Fitzgerald (1936) · W. Blumenberg, *Karl Marx: an illustrated biography*, trans. D. Scott (1972) · A. Cornu, *Karl Marx und Friedrich Engels: Leben und Werk*, 2 vols. (1953–61) · Y. Kapp, *Eleanor Marx*, 2 vols. (1972–6) · Y. Kapp, 'Frederick Demuth: new evidence from old sources', *Socialist History*, 6 (1994), 17–27 · G. Mayer, *Friedrich Engels: eine Biographie*, 2 vols. (1920–34) · *Karl Marx: eine Sammlung von Erinnerungen und Aufsätzen* (Zürich, 1934) · *Reminiscences of Marx and Engels* (Moscow, [n.d., 1956?]) · W. Liebknecht, *Karl Marx: biographical memoirs* (1901) · D. McLellan, *Karl Marx: his life and thought* (1973) · d. cert. related sources O. Figes, *A people's tragedy: the Russian Revolution, 1891–1924* (1996) · C. Grünberg, 'Marx als Abiturient', *Archiv für die Geschichte des Sozialismus und der Arbeiterbewegung*, 11 (1925), 424–44 · *Archiv für die Geschichte des Sozialismus und der Arbeiterbewegung*, 12 (1926), 239–40 · E. E. Kisch, *Karl Marx in Karlsbad* (1968) · A. E. Laurence and A. N. Insole, *Prometheus bound: Karl Marx on the Isle of Wight* [n.d., 1981?] · S. S. Prawer, *Karl Marx and world literature* (1978) · F. Regnault, 'Les maladies de Karl Marx', *Revue Anthropologique*, 43 (1933), 293–317 · J. Schumpeter, *Economic doctrine and method* (1954) · B. Wachstein, 'Die Abstammung von Karl Marx',

Festskrift i anledning af Professor David Simonsen's 70-aarige fødselsdag (1923), 277ff. · L. Kolakowski, *Main currents of Marxism: its rise, growth, and dissolution*, 3 vols. (1978) · K. Willis, 'The reception of Marx in England', *HJ*, 20 (1977), 417–59
Archives Internationaal Instituut voor Sociale Geschiedenis, Amsterdam, corresp. and papers
Likenesses photograph, 1867, Marx Memorial Library, London [*see illus.*] · photographs, Internationaal Instituut voor Sociale Geschiedenis, Amsterdam
Wealth at death £250: administration, 18 Aug 1883, *CGPLA Eng. & Wales*

Mary [Mary of Blois], **countess of Boulogne** (*d.* 1182), princess and abbess of Romsey, was the youngest daughter of *Stephen of Blois (*c.*1092–1154), king of England, and *Matilda (*c.*1103–1152), countess of Boulogne and queen of England. Born in France, at Blois, she was destined for the cloister as a child, and was accordingly placed, with some nuns of St Sulpice, Rennes, in the nunnery of Stratford, Middlesex. But discord arose and a new nunnery was founded for Mary in 1150–52 by her parents at Lillechurch (Higham) in Kent. This nunnery was linked with St Sulpice. Although she is not given the title of prioress, a charter of Henry II dating from 1155–8 confirms Lillechurch to her and her nuns, suggesting she was in a position of authority. Two of her charters, with her seal, date from this period. Some time before 1160 she went to Romsey, an older and more prestigious nunnery, and became abbess. But in 1160, after the death of her brother *William of Blois made her the sole heir of the Boulogne lands, she left the cloistered life and was married to Matthew, younger son of the count of Flanders. Most of the sources suggest this was against her will (although Matthew Paris describes her as willing and eager), and imply that the marriage was forced on her by Henry II. Such marriage of a nun was regarded by most chroniclers as an outrageous breach of canon law, and it caused dissent with Thomas Becket and other ecclesiastical authorities. A Flemish source suggests that the pope's permission was given, but no record of a dispensation has survived and Pope Alexander III wrote to the archbishop of Rheims deploring the marriage and Matthew's subsequent actions. An interdict was imposed and the pope supported Constantia, wife of Mary's elder brother, *Eustace, who had died some fourteen years before, in her claim to the Boulogne inheritance. In 1167 Matthew tried to affirm his right, through Mary, to the earldom of Mortain. Henry II eventually promised to pay Matthew the huge sum of £1000 on condition that he renounce all claims to the parts of his wife's estate still in royal hands. But this was not enough to secure Matthew's loyalty and he again rebelled against Henry. There is intriguing evidence of Mary's dislike of Henry II in a document written by her, as countess of Boulogne, to the French king telling him of her conversation at Boulogne with ambassadors of the emperor Frederick Barbarossa. She informs King Louis of Henry II's—'the fraudulent king's'—machinations against him.

Mary had two daughters, Ida and Matilda, who, after their father's death, were apparently brought up by their uncle Philippe, count of Flanders.

In 1169–70 Mary returned to the religious life, entering the Benedictine nunnery of St Austrebert near Montreuil, apparently as a simple nun. One source suggests that this retirement from the world was due to pressure from Matthew's dying father and the emperor Frederick Barbarossa. Her re-entry to a convent resulted in the lifting of the interdict. Matthew subsequently married Eleanor, sister of his elder brother's wife, and died in 1173. Mary died and was buried at the nunnery in 1182.

S. P. THOMPSON

Sources M. Bouquet and others, eds., *Recueil de historiens des Gaules et de la France / Rerum Gallicarum et Francicarum scriptores*, 24 vols. (1738–1904), vol. 13, pp. 185, 277, 314, 414, 422, 435, 517, 705; vol. 15, p. 867; vol. 16, p. 144 · M. A. E. Green, *Lives of the princesses of England*, 1 (1849), 191–212 · M. A. E. Wood, *Letters of royal and illustrious ladies of Great Britain*, 3 vols. (1846), vol. 1, pp. 11 · D. de Sainte-Marthe and others, eds., *Gallia Christiana in provincias ecclesiasticas distributa*, 16 vols. (1715–1865), vol. 10, pp. 1318–19; vol. 14, p. 787 · L. Delisle and others, eds., *Recueil des actes de Henri II, roi d'Angleterre et duc de Normandie, concernant les provinces françaises et les affaires de France*, 4 vols. (Paris, 1909–27), vol. 1, pp. 143–4 · L. d'Achery, *Spicilegium, sive, Collectio veterum aliquot scriptorum qui in Galliae bibliothecis detiluerant*, 2 (1723), 812, 818 · E. Baluze, *Histoire généalogique de la maison d'Auvergne*, 2 vols. (Paris, 1708), vol. 1, p. 89; vol. 2, pp. 97–8 · *Matthaei Parisiensis, monachi Sancti Albani, Historia Anglorum, sive ... Historia minor*, ed. F. Madden, 3 vols., Rolls Series, 44 (1886–9) · A. Saltman, *Theobald, archbishop of Canterbury* (1956), 52–4, 379–80 · P. Oudegherst, *Les chroniques et annales de Flandres* (1571), 135 · J. H. Round, 'Faramus of Boulogne', *The Genealogist*, new ser., 12 (1895–6), 145–51 · J. H. Round, *Studies in peerage and family history* (1901), 147–80 · P. Jaffé, ed., *Regesta pontificum Romanorum*, rev. G. Wattenbach, 2nd edn, 2 (Leipzig, 1888); repr. (1956), no. 10793 · P. Anger, 'Cartulaire de l'Abbaye de Saint-Sulpice-la-Forêt, Ille-et-Vilaine', *Bulletin et Mémoires de la Société Archéologique du Département d'Ille-et-Vilaine*, 34–5, 37–40 (1903–11); repr. in P. Anger, *Cartulaire de l'Abbaye de Saint-Sulpice-la-Forêt, Ille-et-Vilaine* ([Rennes], 1911) · H. G. D. Liveing, *Records of Romsey Abbey, 907–1558* (1906) · St John Cam., MSS 46.27, 46.58
Archives St John Cam., MSS 46.27, 46.58
Likenesses carving (of Mary of Blois?), Romsey Abbey, Hampshire

Mary [Mary of Woodstock] (1278–*c.*1332), princess and Benedictine nun, was born at Woodstock, Oxfordshire, on 11 or 12 March 1278, the sixth daughter of *Edward I (1239–1307) and *Eleanor of Castile (1241–1290). *Joan, countess of Hertford and Gloucester was her sister. She took the veil at Amesbury Priory, Wiltshire, in 1285 at the insistence of her grandmother, *Eleanor of Provence, who resided there, and to the annoyance of her mother. As a daughter house of Fontevrault, the burial place of the Angevin kings, Amesbury had a strong connection with the English royal house. Although a nun, Mary enjoyed a lifestyle appropriate to her rank. She was granted £100 p.a. for life in 1285, and this was doubled after the death of her grandmother in 1291. In 1292 she was granted forty oaks a year from royal forests, and twenty tuns of wine from Southampton. Plans that she should go to Fontevrault on Eleanor of Provence's death were cancelled, probably at Edward I's insistence.

Mary was not confined to a cloistered life at Amesbury. Accounts testify to her frequent presence at court. In 1293 she spent some time with her brother Edward. In 1297 she was at court for five weeks, making her farewells to her sister Elizabeth who was about to go to join her husband in Holland. In 1302 her financial provision was changed; she received a number of manors and the borough of Wilton in place of the £200 p.a., to hold as long as she remained in England. Her income, however, proved insufficient for her needs. By 1305 she was substantially in debt, and the escheator south of the Trent was ordered to pay her £200 so that she could pay off her creditors. She had an extravagant entourage; one account shows that she came to court with twenty-four horses to transport her household, while gambling at dice must have added to her costs. After her death, John de *Warenne, earl of Surrey (1286–1347), arguing for a divorce, claimed to have had an affair with Mary. While her presence at court makes this possible, there is no corroboration for the story.

*Edward II continued his father's support of his sister Mary, and she continued to visit court regularly. She also went on frequent pilgrimages. A request from Edward in 1317 that she should conduct a visitation of the English daughter houses of Fontevrault was unsuccessful; although her high birth gave her some influence within the order, she never obtained significant office. She did, however, have custody of several young aristocratic nuns at Amesbury. Her cultural interests are testified to by Nicholas Trevet's dedication of his chronicle to her. She died about 1332 and was buried at Amesbury.

MICHAEL PRESTWICH

Sources M. A. E. Green, *Lives of the princesses of England*, 2 (1849) · L. Guilloreau, 'Marie de Woodstock: une fille d'Édouard Ier, moniale à Amesbury', *Revue Mabillon*, 9 (1914), 341–59 · J. C. Parsons, *Eleanor of Castile: queen and society in thirteenth-century England* (1995)

Mary [Mary of Gueldres] (d. 1463), queen of Scots, consort of James II, was probably born in Gueldres, the eldest daughter of Arnold, duke of Gueldres, and Catherine, duchess of Cleves. From an early age she enjoyed the support of her powerful uncle, Philip the Good, duke of Burgundy, at whose court she was brought up. Scottish diplomatic success in finding prestigious European husbands for four of James II's sisters (in France, Brittany, Austria, and Veere) may have led to raised expectations on the part of the Scottish commissioners—William, Lord Crichton, the chancellor, John Ralston, bishop of Dunkeld, and Nicholas Otterburn, official of St Andrews—in their pursuit of a marriage alliance in Burgundy, Gueldres, and Cleves.

Negotiations appear to have been tough and protracted. *James II (1430–1460) enlisted the aid of his kinsman, Charles VII of France, as early as January 1448, and gave full powers to the Scottish ambassadors on 6 May. But it was not until 1 April 1449 that the marriage contract was finally drawn up at Brussels. The long delay was caused by the fact that Duke Arnold of Gueldres's original plan, drawn up on 6 September 1448, had been to marry his eldest daughter, Mary, to Duke Albrecht of Austria, brother of Friedrich, king of the Romans (Emperor Friedrich III), while Arnold's second daughter, Margaret, was to marry the Scottish king. Both marriages were to be negotiated by Philip of Burgundy. It seems likely that the final deal, whereby James II obtained the hand of Mary, was the result not so much of tough talking by the Scots commissioners as of an agreement between Philip of Burgundy,

who was to pay Mary's dowry, and the Scottish king's ally Charles VII, who stood surety for the bride's Scottish dower (10,000 crowns) in the event of James II's death. Significantly the Franco-Scottish alliance was renewed on 31 December 1448, during the course of the Burgundian negotiations which resulted in the treaty of Brussels.

Mary of Gueldres came to Scotland not only with the promise of a dowry of 60,000 gold crowns (to be paid over two years by Philip the Good), but also at the duke of Burgundy's expense, in a magnificent fleet of fourteen vessels which sailed from Sluys on 9 June 1449, reaching Leith on the 18th after a detour to visit the chapel of St Adrian on the Isle of May. The marriage treaty was duly ratified by James II a week later, and on 3 July James and Mary were married at Holyrood, with Mary's coronation taking place on the same day. The queen's dower lands included the lands of the earldoms of Strathearn and Atholl, the castle and lordship of Methven, and the palace of Linlithgow, as well as the great customs of the burgh of Linlithgow. These were supposed to yield the huge sum of 10,000 crowns, the equivalent of £5000 Scots. The fact that this ambitious total was not even approached, taken together with James II's fear that Burgundy might withhold the substantial balance of Mary's dowry if an adequate Scottish dower was not forthcoming, probably played a role in the king's assault on the Livingston family in 1449–50 and in his subsequent efforts to wrest the earldom of Wigtown from the Black Douglases. Significantly, the queen played a considerable role in the first parliament of James II's active rule, held in Edinburgh in January 1450. Not only did she back the Scottish bishops in their complaint to the crown that the estates of deceased prelates were being requisitioned by royal officers, but she also secured the widest possible support for the payment of her dower, assigned by the estates on the day after the axe fell on two of the forfeited Livingstons.

Throughout the 1450s Mary of Gueldres acted as a dutiful wife, providing her husband with four sons and two daughters. The most crucial period from the point of view of the continuing Stewart succession, however, came in the early 1450s. At Stirling on 19 May 1450 the queen gave premature birth to a child who lived only six hours; about a year later she had a daughter Mary; but no surviving male child was born to the royal couple until May 1452, by which time James II was embroiled in the greatest crisis of his reign and was forced to send his wife from the storm centre of Stirling to the comparative safety of the episcopal castle at St Andrews. There, towards the end of May 1452, the future *James III was born. Further children followed: Alexander *Stewart, duke of Albany and earl of March, most probably in 1454, David, earl of Moray, in 1456, John *Stewart, earl of Mar, in 1457 or early 1458, and a second daughter, Margaret, in 1459–60. With the exception of David, all these children survived into adulthood.

The sudden death of Mary's husband, James II, aged only twenty-nine, killed by the explosion of one of his own cannon at the siege of Roxburgh on 3 August 1460, ended the queen's lengthy preoccupation with childbirth and forced on her the new task of stateswoman, a role which she performed equally well during the last three years of her life. Within five days of James II's death the queen had brought her eldest son, the eight-year-old James III, to the siege; Roxburgh was taken, and the new king was crowned at Kelso on 10 August. A contemporary chronicler comments, albeit disapprovingly, that at the first parliament of the new reign (February 1461), the estates 'left the king in keping with his modere the queen and governing of all the kinrik' (McGladdery, 170). Mary lost no time in appointing her own men as keepers of the vital castles of Edinburgh, Stirling, Blackness, and Dunbar; and she made James Lindsay of Covington, a man mistrusted by her late husband because of his Douglas connections, keeper of the privy seal.

In foreign policy the queen dowager followed James II's line of playing off Lancaster and York in England in order to recover Scottish strong points on the borders. In this she was spectacularly successful. By offering sanctuary to the refugee Lancastrian king and queen, Henry VI and Margaret of Anjou, she was able to recover Berwick by negotiation in March 1461. When it became clear that the Lancastrian cause was lost in England, Mary of Gueldres switched to dealings with the Yorkist Edward IV; she paid large sums to be rid of Margaret of Anjou, sending her from Kirkcudbright to Brittany in April 1462 to seek French aid, while Queen Mary herself went to Dumfries to meet the Yorkist earl of Warwick. The queen's great rival, Bishop James Kennedy of St Andrews, who was pro-French and Lancastrian by conviction, tried to upset Mary's more realistic inclination towards Burgundy and the Yorkists, partly by besmirching the queen's name through accusations of causing divisions and bloodshed, and ultimately by forcing her into an abortive raid on Norham Castle (July 1463). Mary died on 1 December 1463. Her legacy was the peace process with Yorkist England, into which even Kennedy was drawn after her death; the spectacular Fife castle of Ravenscraig, on which the queen spent at least £600 Scots between 1460 and 1463; and Holy Trinity Church in Edinburgh, on which she lavished the huge sum of £1100 Scots, and in which she was buried in December 1463. Stories that circulated in later generations, alleging that Queen Mary had been the mistress successively of Edmund Beaufort, duke of Somerset (d. 1471), and Adam Hepburn, without much doubt originated in confusion with another maligned queen mother, James I's widow, Joan. NORMAN MACDOUGALL

Sources 'Auchinleck Chronicle', NL Scot., Asloan MS Acc. 4233, fols. 109r–123v · G. Burnett and others, eds., *The exchequer rolls of Scotland*, 5–7 (1882–4) · *APS*, 1424–1567 · *Chronique de Mathieu d'Escouchy*, ed. G. Du Fresne de Beaucourt, new edn, 3 vols. (Paris, 1863–4) · Archives Départmentales du Nord, Lille, B427, 308 [documents relating to marriage, 1448–9] · J. H. Baxter, 'The marriage of James II', *SHR*, 25 (1927–8), 67–72 · A. I. Dunlop, *The life and times of James Kennedy, bishop of St Andrews*, St Andrews University Publications, 46 (1950) · C. McGladdery, *James II* (1990) · N. Macdougall, *James III: a political study* (1982), chap. 3
Likenesses double portrait, Seton Armorial, 1591 (with James II), NL Scot.

Mary (1496–1533), queen of France, consort of Louis XII, was born in the first half of 1496, probably in March, the third daughter and fifth child of *Henry VII (1457–1509) and *Elizabeth of York (1466–1503).

Tudor princess Elizabeth and Henry had eight children, one of whom died in infancy, two others within the first year, and one at the age of three. *Arthur, the eldest, died at fifteen, while *Margaret, *Henry, and Mary survived their parents. Mary would have had no recollection of her younger siblings, and grew up as the youngest member of a close family. Arthur died early in her seventh year, and her mother before it was complete. Seven months later her sister Margaret, a few weeks short of her fourteenth birthday, departed for Edinburgh to marry James IV of Scotland. As a result of these changes, and of her father's declining health and close preoccupation with business, Mary grew close to her remaining brother, Henry, nearly five years her senior. The bond of affection between them was lasting, and was to be of great importance to her.

As the only princess of the royal blood remaining at court Mary enjoyed her own retinue of attendants, but they remained an integral part of the royal household. She was not given an independent endowment. Little is known of her upbringing beyond what can be learned from the household accounts. She had her own physician, apothecary, and schoolmaster, as well as attendant ladies. Frequent references to medication suggest delicate health, but they may prove no more than conscientious accountancy. It can be deduced that her schoolmaster taught her Latin and French—although probably not to the same rigorous standards as her brother—because later in life she is known to have had some intellectual interests. Thomas Linacre and John Palsgrave accompanied her to France, and the latter began to write a French grammar for her. She also had a reputation for piety in the humanist mode, and received the dedications of several devotional works. She also learned, although not from the same person, the courtly accomplishments of music and dancing, and the feminine art of embroidery. Princesses were pawns on the chessboard of royal politics, and Mary's hand was first sought in November 1498, when she was about two and a half. The hopeful suitor was Massimiliano, the son of Ludovico Sforza, duke of Milan, a child of about her own age. Sforza was in earnest, but was overreaching himself, and his bid was politely rejected.

The royal marriage market Visitors to the English court occasionally commented upon Mary as an attractive child, but her real début did not come until 1506, when at the age of ten she helped her father to entertain Philip the Handsome, formerly archduke of Austria and now king of Castile, during his unintended visit to Windsor. She danced, played the lute, and generally made a gracious and desirable impression. Philip died later that year, but Mary's efforts had not been wasted because his father, the emperor Maximilian, then sought her as a bride for his grandson, Philip's eldest son Charles of Ghent (later the Emperor Charles V), who was six. This idea had been aired earlier, and was a proposal very much to Henry's liking, so the negotiation was seriously pursued. The terms were agreed by the end of 1507, and on 21 December a marriage treaty was signed at Calais. It was not until 17 December 1508, however, that the formal betrothal *per verba de praesenti* took place at Richmond, with the sieur de Bergues standing as proxy for Charles. At this point Mary was nearly thirteen, and although attractive, well schooled, and well disciplined, was thought young for her age. Records do not reveal what she thought of her commitment to Charles, but, as he was some five years her junior, she would have plenty of time to grow up before being required for the duties of childbearing.

Both sides to the bargain were pleased. Henry had bestowed his younger daughter as royally as possible, and in a direction that should have been greatly to his kingdom's advantage. At the same time Maximilian, whose resources never matched his imperial dignity, had managed to extract a loan of 100,000 crowns from his granddaughter-in-law's father, which is in itself an eloquent testimony to Henry's enthusiasm for the match. When the king died in April 1509 Mary was officially styled archduchess of Burgundy and princess of Castile, and it was under the latter title that she was recognized in the will of her grandmother Margaret Beaufort, who died very shortly after her son. Many things changed with Henry VII's death, however. Henry VIII sought war and glory, and his ambitions were directed to re-establishing an English presence in France, which made both Spain and Maximilian necessary allies. So the young king married his widowed sister-in-law Katherine of Aragon, with momentous consequences, and was keen to see his sister's marriage consummated. In October 1513, when Henry and Maximilian were already companions-in-arms, a new treaty was made, stipulating that the union should be completed at Calais not later than 15 May 1514, which must have been the earliest date that Charles's age would have permitted. Mary had been exchanging tokens with Charles since shortly after her father's death, and at the age of fifteen seems to have been looking forward to the reality of marriage with some enthusiasm.

Queen of France However, political unions were slippery properties. First Ferdinand of Aragon made a separate peace with France. Henry was furious, and Katherine distressed, but worse was to follow. The more the English pressed for the marriage to be completed, the more Maximilian vacillated. There were divided councils in Brussels, and tempting offers from France. The treaty date passed, and the excuses became lamer. By the summer of 1514 it had become clear to Henry that Maximilian intended to make a separate peace, and marry his grandson elsewhere. To avoid the humiliation of being stranded in this way, the king moved fast, impelled by the man who was now his chief adviser, Thomas Wolsey. On 30 July Mary solemnly repudiated her marriage contract, and a week later was pledged to Louis XII of France (1462–1515) by the terms of the peace treaty that brought the war to an end. Romantic fiction has attributed to Mary a bargain with her brother, whereby she agreed to exchange her youthful bridegroom for a broken man of fifty-two on the condition that she could have her own choice next time. However, nothing is known about her feelings. Her repudiation of Charles was a formal statement, written for her, and she is not known to have raised any objection to being unexpectedly raised to the dignity of queen of France. At eighteen Mary was beautiful, poised, and charming: a desirable bride for any king. A French observer described her as 'a nymph from heaven' and 'one of the most beautiful young women in the world' (Russell, 5–6). She was also apparently a dutiful and obedient sister, prepared to serve the political purposes of a brother for whom she had a genuine affection and respect. On 18 August she was married by proxy, *per verba de praesenti*, for the second time, the duc de Longueville representing Louis. On the 22nd she appointed the earl of Worcester as her own proxy to repeat the ceremony in Paris, and that was done on 14 September. The ceremony at Greenwich had been enhanced by a symbolic gesture of consummation, presumably to make it more binding, but this time neither party had any intention of reneging, and Mary embarked with a suitable retinue at Dover on 2 October.

After a stormy crossing, during which one ship was wrecked, an extremely seasick princess was literally carried ashore near Boulogne the following day. Hasty repairs to Mary's poise and magnificence ensued before she could join the French king at Abbeville on 8 October, and their marriage was celebrated with great pomp the following day. However pleased Louis may have been with his bride, he was not pleased with her entourage, which numbered over a hundred, and was exclusively English. Whether such tactlessness was calculated is not clear, but Louis had had trouble with the Breton attendants of his first wife, and was not going to be caught again. His reaction was equally unmannerly, and the day after the wedding most of the queen's retinue was dismissed. Mary was perfectly at home in the French language, but felt suddenly isolated and vulnerable. She complained bitterly to her brother, and a diplomatic storm was narrowly averted. Louis refused to modify his orders, but he did condescend to explain the reasons for them, and both Henry and Mary professed themselves content. A handful of English ladies (including Anne Boleyn) were allowed to remain. The new queen of France was crowned at St Denis on 5 November, and entered Paris in great state the next day. Mary's reign was an almost continuous round of jousts and triumphs, and partly for that reason was extremely brief. Louis died on 1 January 1515, danced to death, it was said, by his energetic young consort.

The possibility that this might happen had occupied Wolsey's mind for some weeks, and was one of the reasons why the delegation of honour led by Charles *Brandon, duke of Suffolk (c.1484–1545), had lingered in Paris after the coronation. Ostensibly the captain of the English jousting team, Brandon had also been entrusted with the delicate task of suggesting an offensive alliance against Ferdinand of Aragon, and with the even more delicate (and secret) responsibility of safeguarding the queen if Louis's fragile health should indeed collapse. Believing that all was well, Henry had recalled him before Christmas, and then rushed him back to France as soon as the news of the king's death was received. A widowed queen not yet nineteen years old was extremely vulnerable, and Louis was scarcely buried before her name was being linked with both the duke of Savoy and the duke of Lorraine. Such a match would not have been at all in Henry's interest, and he also knew that Brandon, who was his closest friend, aspired to marry her himself. Before Suffolk returned to France it was agreed that such a marriage might take place, but only after a seemly interval and once the pair were back in England.

Marriage to Charles Brandon Mary, however, had other ideas. She may well have been fearful of being used in another political match that might have been personally distasteful. Neither Henry, nor François I, Louis's successor, could be altogether trusted when a sudden advantage beckoned. Nor was François, a notorious womanizer, altogether trustworthy in other respects. Suffolk was a desirable partner, and he was immediately available, so ignoring the conventions of 'shamfastness', and with a courage born equally of lust and desperation, the dowager queen virtually forced him to marry her secretly in mid-February. It was the one decisive action of her life, and it nearly ruined both of them. Suffolk's mission, apart from escorting the king's sister home, had been to establish good relations with the new king of France. He did that, but not quite in the way that Henry had envisaged, by seeking and securing François's support for his secret marriage. Henry was furious; mainly because he had been deceived and his honour tarnished, rather than because he had any other destination in mind for his sister. The crisis also impinged immediately upon the politics of the English court. Wolsey, humbly begged for his intercession, supported Suffolk. The Howards, and most of the rest of the council, denounced him, some out of envy of Suffolk and some out of hostility to Wolsey. It soon transpired that Wolsey was the best judge of the king's mind. For about two months Suffolk did his best to redeem himself by extracting the balance of his wife's dower, the jewels that she claimed Louis had given her, and a continuation of her French income from a reluctant François. Eventually a complex bargain was struck, which recovered a portion of what was claimed. This ruined the rest of Suffolk's intended diplomacy because he had become heavily dependent upon François's goodwill, and in mid-April with repeated messages of self-abasement he and Mary set out apprehensively to return to England.

In a sense their concern was exaggerated. When Henry met his sister at Birling on 3 May his anger had largely evaporated. He did not pretend to be pleased, but he attended their public wedding at Greenwich on the 13th, and was publicly reconciled to his old friend. Wolsey's ascendancy was firmly re-established, but Suffolk became little more than his client. This was useful as the duke recovered Henry's favour, but was based upon a sense of obligation rather than common purpose. In spite of the king's apparent indulgence, the financial settlement imposed upon the erring couple was onerous. Mary was to pay her brother £2000 a year for twelve years, drawn from the income of her dower lands in France, which can have left her with very little independent income. Suffolk lost the wardship and marriage of Lady Lisle, but kept control of her lands until she should come of age. On 12 May the duke and duchess entered into the enormous recognizance of £100,000 to abide by the terms of the settlement. Thereafter Suffolk discovered urgent (and genuine) business to attend to on his estates, particularly in East Anglia where he was trying to establish himself on the former de la Pole lands. He soon returned to regular attendance at the council, but Mary became only an occasional visitor to the court. However passionate the origin of her relationship with her husband, her children arrived only after discreet intervals. Henry was born on 11 March 1516, Frances [see Grey, Frances, duchess of Suffolk] on 16 July 1517, Eleanor at some time between 1518 and 1521, and a second Henry in 1522, after the death of the first-born of that name.

Later life Mary's occasional appearances at court over the next decade are duly chronicled. In 1517 the Suffolks escorted Queen Katherine to Walsingham; in the spring of 1518 Mary was taken ill at Woodstock and attended by the royal physicians; in October of the same year she attended the espousal of Princess Mary to the dauphin at Greenwich. In 1520, in spite of further illness, she accompanied her brother, both in his meeting with Charles V and to the competitive festivities of the Field of Cloth of Gold, where it was she, rather than Queen Katherine, who provided the 'female lead'. The treaty of the More with France in 1525 finally settled outstanding issues relating to her dower, which had fallen into arrears as a result of the war, and in May 1526 she was again at Greenwich as the king's guest. The troubles over Henry's Great Matter, which began in 1527, and the fall of Wolsey in 1529 made little difference to the fortunes of the Suffolks, although the duke's successful request to Clement VII in 1528 for a bull protecting his marriage from being impugned on grounds of precontract may have been prompted by his brother-in-law's concerns.

Mary did not, however, approve of Anne Boleyn. The two women exchanged insults of a semi-public nature, and when Anne accompanied Henry VIII to Calais for a meeting with François I in 1532, Mary refused to attend, although her health may also have been a reason for that. It is possible that Anne knew something about the origins of Mary's relationship with her husband, and had attempted to use that knowledge in a manner that led to personal as well as political estrangement. Mary died at Westhorpe in Suffolk on 25 June 1533, and was interred in Bury St Edmunds Abbey. Her quarrel with the king over his second marriage does not seem to have been reconciled, and in spite of the close relationship that they had once enjoyed, he left no recorded reaction to her death. She was survived by her second son, Henry, earl of Lincoln (who died in 1534), and by her two daughters, Frances and Eleanor. On 7 September Charles Brandon married his fourteen-year-old ward, Catherine Willoughby.

Mary was important for who she was rather than for

what she did, although for a few months in 1514–15 her actions and reactions affected the high politics of the realm. Apart from the circumstances of her marriage to the duke of Suffolk, her main impact on the history of the period came in the claim to the English throne that she transmitted via her elder daughter, Frances, to Jane and Katherine Grey, Frances's daughters from her marriage to Henry Grey, seventh marquess of Dorset. Her younger daughter, Eleanor, married Henry Clifford, later second earl of Cumberland, in 1535, and died in 1547. A number of portraits of Mary survive. The best known of these, now at Woburn Abbey, represents her with Charles Brandon and was probably painted shortly after their marriage. It bears eloquent testimony to her good looks.

DAVID LOADES

Sources *LP Henry VIII*, vols. 1–6 · *CSP Spain, 1485–1525*, 1–2 · *CSP Venice, 1527–33*, 1–4 · W. C. Richardson, *Mary Tudor: the white queen* (1970) · S. J. Gunn, *Charles Brandon, duke of Suffolk, c.1484–1545* (1988) · M. Perry, *The sisters to the king* (1998) · J. G. Russell, *The Field of Cloth of Gold: men and manners in 1520* (1969)
Archives PRO, domestic state papers, SP1
Likenesses school of the Clouets, chalk drawing, Bibliothèque Méjanes, Aix-en-Provence, France · J. Corvus, engraving, Sudeley Castle, Gloucestershire · chalk drawing, Uffizi, Florence, Album of the Medicis · chalk drawing, Château de Chantilly, France, Album Destailleur · double portrait, oils (with Charles Brandon, first duke of Suffolk), Woburn Abbey, Bedfordshire · drawing, Bibliothèque Nationale, Paris · portrait, St Mary's Church, Bury St Edmunds

Mary [Mary of Guise] (**1515–1560**), queen of Scots, consort of James V, and regent of Scotland, was the eldest of the twelve children of Claude, first duc de Guise (1496–1550), and his wife, Antoinette de Bourbon (1493–1583), daughter of François, third comte de Vendôme (1470–1495).

Childhood and first marriage Born on 20 November 1515 in the castle of Bar-le-Duc, she was baptized there twelve days later. When she was four her father's mother, Philippa of Gueldres, entered the convent of Poor Clares at Pont-à-Mousson and Mary's parents went to live in her former residence, the family's ancestral castle of Joinville. Some years later Mary was sent to her grandmother to be educated in the convent, perhaps with the intention that she should become a nun, but when she was about fourteen her uncle Antoine, duc de Lorraine, and his wife visited her and decided that it would be a waste to keep a handsome, eligible girl like Mary shut away from the world. Exceptionally tall, like the rest of her father's family, she had auburn hair, grey eyes, and a charming manner. Her uncle took her back to Nancy, and then to the French court to witness the coronation of François I's new wife, Eleanor of Austria. Mary was presented to the king and queen, rode in the royal procession when Eleanor made her formal entry into Paris, and attended the royal banquet afterwards. She was soon a great favourite, the king treating her almost as if she were his own daughter.

Among those who had played a leading part in the queen's coronation was Louis, duc de Longueville (1510–1537), grand chamberlain of France. His lands lay in Normandy, to the north of the Guise possessions, and in 1534 he and Mary were betrothed. Louis settled on her the

Mary [of Guise] (**1515–1560**), by Corneille de Lyon

castle and lands of Châteaudun, while she brought with her a dowry of 80,000 livres, augmented by 40,000 livres from François I. They were married on 4 August 1534 in the Louvre, before the entire court, the celebratory banquets and tournaments lasting for sixteen days afterwards.

Mary and her husband were happy together and their first son, born in their castle at Amiens on 30 October 1535, was christened François after the king. They travelled round their estates in the summer months, but much of their time was spent at court and on 1 January 1537 they attended the wedding of Madeleine, the elder daughter of François I, to *James V, king of Scots (1512–1542). By then Mary was pregnant again, but on 9 June 1537 her husband died of a fever in Rouen, leaving her a widow at twenty-one. Her second son was born at Châteaudun on 4 August 1537 and named Louis after his father.

Second marriage Mary's intention was to live quietly at Châteaudun, running the Longueville estates for her elder son, but two months after her husband's death she was dismayed to receive a letter from François I informing her that she was to marry the widowed king of Scots. Queen Madeleine, always delicate, had died on 7 July 1537, and James V now wanted another French bride. Soon afterwards Henry VIII of England announced that he too was a suitor for Mary. His third wife, Jane Seymour, had just died and he wanted to prevent his nephew James V from strengthening Scotland's traditional alliance with France by taking James's intended wife for himself. When the French ambassador asked Henry why he was so set on marrying the duc de Guise's daughter, the English king replied that Mary was big in person and he needed a big wife. 'I may be big in person', she commented dryly when she heard this, 'but my neck is small' (Fraser, 7).

In December 1537 Mary's infant son Louis died and in the midst of her grief she received a letter from François I ordering her to proceed with the Scottish marriage. Bowing to the inevitable she sent a representative to court, and was horrified to learn that the king had decided that although he himself would supply 30,000 livres of her dowry of 150,000 livres, the rest was to come not from her father but from the lands and revenues settled on her by her first husband. This would be very prejudicial to the interests of her surviving son, for it meant that part of his inheritance was in effect being transferred to the king of Scots. Mary urged her friend Marguerite de Navarre, sister of François I, to speak to the king, and Marguerite must have done so to some effect, for when the contract was signed in Lyons at the end of March 1538, the offending clause had been removed. François I would provide no less than 70,000 livres and Mary's father would contribute the remaining 80,000 livres. If James V died first, his heirs would return to Mary one third of the dowry if there were children of the marriage, one half if there were none. As her jointure she would receive Falkland Palace and the castles of Stirling, Dingwall, and Threave, the earldoms of Strathearn, Ross, Orkney, and Fife, and the lordships of Galloway, Ardmannach, and the Isles. Were she to be widowed, she would be free to return to France if she wished, and she would continue to draw the revenues from her jointure lands.

Mary's grandmother Philippa of Gueldres had been the niece of James's great-grandmother Mary of Gueldres, the wife of James II, and so James wrote to the pope for the necessary dispensation of consanguinity. He decided not to return to France to collect his new bride in person, but instead sent Robert, fifth Lord Maxwell, to France as his proxy. Mary's second wedding took place on 9 May 1538 in the castle of Châteaudun, Maxwell placing upon her finger a diamond spousing ring which had cost James considerably less than the ring with which he had married Madeleine. Mary could not take her small son with her to Scotland, for his inheritance lay in France, and so she left him with her mother, who was expecting her twelfth child. The little duke would be happy in the nurseries at Joinville with Mary's young brothers and sisters, some of whom were about his own age. Several weeks after the proxy wedding Mary's family escorted her to Rouen. Her father, her sister Louise, and a retinue of French servants would accompany her to Scotland, and they embarked at Le Havre on 10 June aboard the same three galleys which had carried James V and Madeleine north the previous year.

On Trinity Sunday (16 June) 1538 Mary of Guise set foot in her new country for the first time, landing at Balcomie in Fife. She spent the night in Balcomie Castle, and in the morning her new husband arrived with a procession of courtiers to escort her to St Andrews. There she was greeted with a pageant specially composed by Sir David Lindsay, the lord Lyon (the Scottish king of arms), and next morning the royal marriage was solemnly confirmed and blessed at a service in the cathedral. Even the sophisticated French were impressed by 'the magnificent novelties' with which the guests were subsequently entertained (Marshall, *Mary of Guise*, 60). The celebrations lasted for forty days and included archery contests, hunting, hawking, and a series of tournaments in which the duc de Guise played a prominent part. He and the other French courtiers remained in Scotland until August, when James took his queen on a tour of her various jointure lands. She finally made her formal entry into Edinburgh on St Margaret's day, 16 November 1538.

Queen of Scots Despite homesickness, Mary expressed tactful pleasure at all she saw, while the Scots for their part were delighted with this impressive, well-made mother of sons, so different from fragile Madeleine. James treated Mary kindly and soon she was thinking of ways of improving her surroundings, sending to her mother for French masons to work at Falkland Palace and Stirling Castle, begging a French friend for cuttings from fruit trees, and trying to obtain young wild boars for the forests of Falkland. She also urged her mother to dispatch experienced miners from Lorraine to exploit the valuable minerals of Crawfordmuir, high up in the hills of western Scotland.

As the months went by, however, there was a good deal of concern that Mary of Guise showed no sign of pregnancy, and it was noticeable that she had not yet been crowned queen of Scots. She would have to produce a son to secure her position. In August 1539 she and James V made a pilgrimage to St Adrian's shrine on the Isle of May, a well-known source of help for barren women, and not long afterwards she found that she was pregnant. She was crowned in Holyrood Abbey on 22 February 1540, and on 22 May her child was born at St Andrews, a son, who was baptized James when he was a week old. On 24 April in the following year another son, Robert, was born to her in Stirling Castle.

A week after that alarming news arrived from Fife. Prince James was seriously ill. The king rode at once for St Andrews, but by the time he got there his elder son was already dead. Even as he left the chamber where the baby lay, an anxious messenger arrived from Stirling to tell him that Prince Robert had also fallen ill. The infant was still alive when his father reached the castle, but he died a few hours later. The little princes were buried together in Holyrood Abbey, and James's mother observed that the king and queen were said to be in great distress. Clad in deepest mourning they made a progress through Perth and Aberdeen that summer, returning to Edinburgh by way of Falkland. Early the following year Mary was pregnant once more.

The death of the king Relations between Scotland and England were now deteriorating rapidly. James V had ignored Henry VIII's urgings to follow his example and break with the Roman Catholic church and Henry decided that he could no longer tolerate the threat from his northern neighbour. In spring 1542 he not only instructed his archbishop of Canterbury to search through the ancient records for any document which would prove his claim to be overlord of Scotland, but he also considered the cheaper and quicker expedient of having his agents kidnap James.

The archbishop's search failed to yield anything and Henry decided to invade Scotland. Mary of Guise walked 7 miles to Our Lady of Loretto, just outside Edinburgh, to pray for the safety of her husband and his kingdom, but on 24 November 1542 the Scots were defeated at the battle of Solway Moss. James was not present at the battle but the defeat plunged him into despair. Riding first to Tantallon Castle, where he kept a mistress, he made his way to Linlithgow to see Mary and then travelled on to Falkland, 'his mind near gone through dolour and care' (Lesley, 2.258–9). On 8 December 1542 the queen gave birth to her first daughter. James was lying ill in bed when they told him, and it was then that he made his famous remark, 'It cam' wi' a lass and it will gang wi' a lass', meaning that although his family had gained the throne through a woman, Robert I's daughter Marjorie, a male heir was now vital in such troubled times. He died on 14 December, just before midnight, leaving Mary of Guise a widow for the second time, at the age of twenty-seven. Hitherto clad in gorgeous purple, crimson, and tawny silks encrusted with gold passementerie, she now put on the mourning black which she would wear for the rest of her life.

Although her marriage contract entitled Mary to return to France, she decided to stay in Scotland to protect the interests of her baby daughter, known to posterity as *Mary, queen of Scots. Traditionally, a widowed Scottish queen could expect to act as regent for her child, but Mary of Guise was lying in childbed at Linlithgow while Cardinal David Beaton, primate of Scotland, and James, second earl of Arran, head of the house of Hamilton and heir presumptive to the throne, were locked in a determined struggle for the regency. Meanwhile, the threat from England remained. Henry VIII had immediately seen the possibilities of the changed situation. He would persuade the Scots to marry their infant queen to his young son Edward, take her into his own hands, and Scotland would be his.

The rough wooing On 3 January 1543 the Scottish lords chose the earl of Arran as regent. The lord governor, as he was styled, believed that a further invasion of Scotland could only be averted by making peace with England. Mary of Guise supported Cardinal Beaton, who was known to favour the French alliance, for now, virtually Arran's prisoner in Linlithgow, she feared that he would hand her daughter over to Henry VIII. In fact she wished to be regent herself, but in the present emergency it suited her to collaborate with the cardinal, just as he hoped to profit from her influence in France. Desperate to counteract the lord governor's influence, they together decided to invite back to Scotland the earl of Lennox, Arran's great rival, then living in France. Lured on by illusory promises that Mary of Guise would consider marrying him, Lennox returned, but his rival's very presence did much to strengthen Arran's wavering resolve to pursue an English alliance. The treaties of Greenwich were concluded on 1

July 1543. There would be peace between Scotland and England and Mary, queen of Scots, would be married to Henry VIII's son Edward. Mary of Guise's opposition to the match was well known, and when a French fleet was sighted off the east coast there were immediate rumours that the ships had come to take her and her daughter to France. Arran at once set about fortifying Linlithgow Palace, but Lennox and Beaton marched against him and he was forced to agree that Mary could move her daughter to Stirling Castle.

The treaties of Greenwich had not yet been ratified, and while Mary did her best to influence the Scottish lords against them, Beaton persuaded Arran to abandon the English alliance. On 8 September 1543 the lord governor did public penance for his recent support of the protestants, promising to take no action without the advice and consent of the cardinal. The following day Mary, queen of Scots, was crowned in the Chapel Royal at Stirling. Mary of Guise now became the principal member of a new council of regency and in December the Scottish parliament solemnly declared the treaties of Greenwich to be null and renewed their ancient alliance with France. Vowing vengeance, Henry VIII sent a fleet to the River Forth in May 1544 and the first of the series of devastating invasions later known as the 'rough wooing' began. While Mary of Guise and her daughter remained in the safety of Stirling Castle, the English burned Holyrood Abbey, where her husband and sons were buried. A general council meeting at Stirling on 29 May blamed Arran for his failure to drive back the English and ordered him to resign the regency in favour of Mary of Guise and a council of twelve advisers, but the lord governor clung to power and Mary was not powerful enough to dislodge him.

On 27 February 1545 Arran won a resounding victory over the English at Ancrum Moor and that April the Scots rejected English requests that negotiations be reopened on the basis of the treaties of Greenwich. In response to Mary of Guise's pleas for help, the French sent assistance in the form of a force led by Jacques de Montgomery, seigneur de Lorges, but that autumn Henry VIII's forces were back, burning the abbeys of Kelso, Melrose, Dryburgh, and Jedburgh. Henry himself died on 28 January 1547, but Lord Protector Somerset, commander of the previous invasions, continued his policy towards Scotland, marched north in August, and routed Arran and the Scots at the battle of Pinkie on 10 September 1547.

The French alliance Sending her daughter to the secluded island of Inchmahome, on the Lake of Menteith, Mary of Guise pleaded with the French ambassador, Henri Cleutin, seigneur d'Oysel, for further help. It was not in the interests of France to see Scotland overrun by the English, and so Henri II instructed d'Oysel to persuade Mary of Guise to agree to a new scheme. Her daughter should marry the king's son, the dauphin, François. England would then be trapped irrevocably between France and Scotland. In return for Mary of Guise's compliance, he would send her substantial assistance.

Mary was relieved, even though it meant agreeing to her daughter being brought up at the French court. At least she would be safe there. The following February the English invaded yet again, and Mary sent the little queen west to Dumbarton Castle. Not until mid-June did the promised French assistance arrive, led by André de Montalembert, sieur d'Essé. Mary of Guise urged him to recapture Haddington from the English but he was reluctant, for the French wanted the new treaty to be signed before they did anything. However, when Mary personally rallied the Scots, urging them to join with the French in driving out the enemy, the siege began, and the treaty of Haddington was signed on 7 July 1548. Mary, queen of Scots, would marry the dauphin, and Henri II promised to defend Scotland as he did his own realm, while maintaining Scottish laws and liberties.

Touring the French and Scottish camps at Haddington two days later, Mary of Guise narrowly escaped death when English guns from the town fired on her cavalcade, killing and wounding sixteen of her gentlemen as well as other members of her household. She fainted with horror, but she was unhurt. As soon as she had heard masses for the dead, she left for Dumbarton to see her daughter embark for France. The young Queen Mary set sail on 7 August 1548 and the earl of Arran was persuaded, somewhat against his will, to make the journey to the French court too. Henri II then rewarded him for agreeing to Mary's marriage by making him duc de Châtelherault.

In June 1549 yet another English fleet sailed into the River Forth, but at Mary's instigation newly arrived French reinforcements managed to seize the strategically important island of Inchkeith which the English had captured. When France and England signed a peace treaty the following April, she decided to take advantage of the opportunity to visit the French court herself. She was, of course, anxious to see her children, but there were urgent matters of public business too. She wanted to press Henri II for financial assistance and she needed his support if she was to oust Châtelherault from his position as lord governor.

Return to France In the middle of August 1550 Henri sent Leon Strozzi with six galleys to bring Mary of Guise from Scotland, and after a series of delays she finally embarked at Leith, arriving at Dieppe on 19 September. She was accompanied by a large number of Scottish noblemen whom she had not dared leave behind for fear of the trouble they could cause in her absence. The duc de Châtelherault had remained at home, however, for he was too satisfied with his new title to cause any trouble, and the French ambassador d'Oysel, now lieutenant-general of Scotland, would keep a watchful eye on him.

Mary's father had died earlier in the year, but her brothers the duc de Guise and the cardinal of Lorraine were waiting to escort her to Paris. She made a ceremonial entry into the city with her retinue of Scottish noblemen, and was reunited with her children. Mary, queen of Scots, was seven now, and her son François, duc de Longueville, was fourteen. She had not seen him for twelve years. When he was small, her mother had sent her pictures of him and even a length of cord to show his height, but in more recent times he had been able to write to her himself, telling her that he longed to come to Scotland to fight in her cause. After a delighted reunion Mary lost no time in engaging the French king and his advisers in serious discussions about the future of Scotland. Some of the French said that since Mary, queen of Scots, would so soon be the bride of the dauphin, a Frenchman should be appointed to govern Scotland in her name, but Mary insisted that she herself should rule as regent. In November she went with the court to Chartres and then on to Blois, where they spent the winter. Secret discussions continued, the Scots who had come with Mary received lavish bribes, and the English ambassador complained that the queen dowager of Scotland was exercising far too much influence.

The discovery of a plot to poison her daughter caused Mary of Guise to cancel her plans to return to Scotland in the spring of 1551, and she remained with the French court throughout the summer, visiting Tours, Angers, and Nantes and then making a progress through Brittany. When Henri II moved to his favourite residence of Fontainebleau, he agreed that she could visit Joinville. Her old home was sadly changed, with her father dead, her mother in deepest mourning, and her brothers and sisters grown up and living elsewhere, but she stayed there until early September. When she then moved to Amiens to begin the preparations for her journey back to Scotland, another family crisis intervened. Her son had gone with her to see her off, but when they reached Amiens he fell ill and although Mary nursed him tenderly, he died in her arms. 'Our Lord must wish me for one of His chosen ones, since He has visited me so often with such sorrow. Praised be He by all', Mary wrote sadly to her own mother (Pimodan, 380). After the funeral she hastened the preparations for her departure and sailed from Dieppe in mid-October.

Mary of Guise had decided to visit Edward VI on her way back to Scotland, and so she crossed the channel and made her way to Hampton Court, where she was welcomed by a large delegation of English courtiers. Next day she sailed along the Thames to the bishop of London's palace and then on 4 November went in procession to the palace of Westminster, where Edward VI entertained her to a banquet. The following day he sent her a gift of two horses and a ring set with a diamond. She left London on 6 November 1551, escorted for the first part of the journey by the duke of Northumberland, the earls of Pembroke and Wiltshire, and many other lords and ladies and their retinues. As she passed through each shire on the way north she was accompanied by the local dignitaries until she finally reached Berwick, where she was welcomed by various Scottish noblemen including the earl of Bothwell and Lord Hume.

She had come back with her status greatly enhanced by her reception in Paris and London, but even so she could not wrest the regency from Châtelherault right away. In the summer of 1553 she welcomed the accession of Mary I to the English throne but when she heard disturbing rumours that the earl of Lennox was plotting to seize the government of Scotland for himself, she decided that the time had come to act. She sent d'Oysel to France to consult Henri II, and when he returned worked with him to persuade Châtelherault to relinquish his position. He was predictably reluctant, but on 19 February he capitulated in return for promises of financial benefit, grants of property to various relatives, and the position of lieutenant-general, currently held by d'Oysel. Parliament met on 12 April 1554, Châtelherault resigned his office, d'Oysel placed the crown of Scotland on Mary of Guise's head, and handed her the sceptre and the sword of state. At last she was queen regent of Scotland.

Queen regent Mary of Guise replaced Châtelherault's men with her own supporters, rewarded her adherents with gifts of land and money, and bribed those who were liable to waver. She also aroused much hostility by appointing Frenchmen to various public positions. Monsieur de Rubay, one of the French king's counsellors, would keep the king's seal, Bartholomew de Villemore would control the customs, Monsieur Bonet, a member of her own household, became her bailie of Orkney, and in 1557 the Frenchman Jean Roytell was appointed principal master mason. At the same time she tried to restore firm central government. She attended parliament personally in 1555 and much of its legislation dealt with the administration of justice and the regulation of trade. That summer she went to Dumfries to try border thieves, and the following year she held justice eyres throughout the north of Scotland, telling clan chiefs that she intended to continue her late husband's policy of making them responsible for the behaviour of their clansmen.

The Scots viewed Mary of Guise's activities with deep suspicion, and when parliament met early in 1557 she was unpleasantly surprised by the hostility of its members. They complained bitterly that her daughter was still not married to the dauphin, and wondered openly if the wedding would ever take place. The continuing uncertainty undermined the queen regent's position, and although she wanted to fortify the borders against English raids, she doubted whether she would be able to raise the money from her unco-operative subjects. Ruling the country was no easy task, she told the cardinal of Lorraine, adding, 'God knows, brother, what a life I lead. It is no small thing to bring a young nation to a state of perfection …. Happy is he who has least to do with worldly affairs. I can safely say that for twenty years past I have not had one year of rest' (Marshall, *Mary of Guise*, 211).

No one was more anxious than Mary of Guise to see her daughter married to the dauphin, but there was little she could do about it, and her position became even more difficult when France went to war with Spain that autumn and Henri instructed her to create a diversion by sending an army to invade England, Spain's ally. She dutifully summoned all able-bodied men between the ages of sixteen and sixty, and addressed them herself, but when they reached the borders the Scots turned and marched home again. Her relatives were, however, in an increasingly influential position at the French court, not least because the duc de Guise had in January 1558 captured Calais from

the English. Henri therefore decided to go ahead with his son's marriage to the young Scottish queen.

Scottish commissioners were sent to France to negotiate the contract, the couple were formally betrothed on 19 April, and the marriage finally took place on 24 April 1558. The marriage contract ostensibly safeguarded Scotland's independence and stated that Mary of Guise was to act as regent as long as her daughter was out of the country, but the Scots' worst suspicions would have been realized had they known that Mary, queen of Scots, had also signed secret clauses. If she died childless, Henri II would inherit Scotland and he would enjoy all Scottish revenues until he had been repaid for the money he had spent in defence of his daughter-in-law's kingdom.

The Scottish Reformation Apart from Scottish hostility to the French, the situation in Scotland was complicated by the growing tide of protestantism, and on 1 September 1558, St Giles's day, a riot broke out in Edinburgh when the saint's image was carried in procession through the streets. That winter the protestants presented Mary of Guise with a series of petitions demanding the right to convene publicly or privately, hear services in the vernacular, and take communion in both kinds. They likewise demanded the repeal of all the laws against heresy. Mary regarded their religious demands as a mere cloak for sedition, but they gained a valuable ally when Mary I of England died on 17 November 1558 and her protestant half-sister Elizabeth succeeded to her throne.

On 1 January 1559 protestants pinned to the doors of the Scottish friaries copies of a document known as 'beggars' summons', demanding that the friars give up their property to the poor. The signing of the treaty of Cateau Cambrésis that spring brought peace between France and Spain. Scotland and England were comprised in the treaty, but religious disturbances continued in Scotland and Mary of Guise resolved to outlaw the protestant leaders. Shortly before they were to appear before her, John Knox the energetic protestant preacher arrived back in Scotland, and his inflammatory sermon in St John's Church in Perth roused up the townspeople to smash images, tear down furnishings, and drive friars out of their friaries.

Mary of Guise and Châtelherault rode to Perth at the head of an army, intending to disperse the protestants, but they were outnumbered and on 29 May 1559 it was agreed that both armies would disband. Mary of Guise entered Perth, gave orders for the repair of the damaged buildings, and replaced the protestant provost with one of her own supporters. She then garrisoned the town with Scottish soldiers in French pay, and withdrew to her palace at Falkland. The lords of the congregation, as the protestant leaders now called themselves, immediately declared that the queen regent had broken the truce and hostilities were renewed.

Mary herself had fallen ill and she remained at Falkland while Châtelherault and d'Oysel marched to confront the rebels at Cupar, in Fife. Realizing that they were outnumbered once more, the royal commanders entered into discussions with the rebels and reached a new agreement. The queen regent would grant the protestants freedom of worship, they would disband their army, and the French soldiers would retire to Lothian. Well aware that it was unsafe for her to remain in Fife, Mary crossed to Edinburgh and then sought shelter in Dunbar Castle, on the east coast. If all else failed she could escape from there to France. Her precautions were justified, for the congregation marched to Stirling and then entered the capital.

When she heard that Scotland's coining irons had been seized by the congregation, Mary was affronted. She ordered Châtelherault and d'Oysel to march on Edinburgh but, recognizing that they were not strong enough, they seized Leith instead and entered into negotiations once more. Agreement was reached on Leith Links on 23 July 1559. The congregation would deliver up the coining irons and leave Edinburgh the following day. In future they would obey the authority of the queen regent and molest neither churches nor churchmen. In return, Mary would grant the people of Edinburgh freedom of worship and no one would interfere with the protestant preachers. Two days later the royal army entered Edinburgh, the congregation dispersed, and Mary herself returned when order had been restored.

The final months The appearance of peace was no more than an illusion, however, for the protestants were engaged in secret negotiations with Elizabeth I and on 7 August 1559 the English queen sent Sir Ralph Sadler north. He was to stir up further opposition to the French, urge Châtelherault to abandon Mary of Guise, and persuade her nobles to force her to make a treaty of perpetual peace with England. Mary meanwhile learned that Henri II had died as the result of a jousting accident and, to add to her troubles, Châtelherault's protestant son James, third earl of Arran, arrived back from France. Within twenty-four hours the duc had changed sides and joined the congregation.

Sending urgent pleas to France for assistance, Mary persuaded d'Oysel to fortify Leith, and she took refuge there when she heard that the congregation were marching on Edinburgh once more. Her health was deteriorating rapidly—she seems to have been suffering from chronic heart disease—and her remaining supporters were diminishing daily. Her once sumptuous furnishings were worn and threadbare, and her wardrobe was reduced to a sparse collection of black garments, some of them lined with fur to keep out the cold. Personal splendour no longer mattered. She was desperately short of money, for she had inherited a deficit of £30,000 when she took over as regent from Châtelherault, and although an appeal to Rome brought grants of ecclesiastical subsidies, her attempts at introducing new forms of lay taxation aroused great opposition. On 21 October the lords of the congregation announced that her regency was suspended, and transferred her authority to a council of regency under the leadership of Châtelherault. Mary sent a defiant reply when she was told, and d'Oysel managed to drive off a protestant assault on Leith. Mary determinedly entered the capital once more but a fortnight later she was so seriously ill that her friends despaired, and reports of her grave condition continued to circulate throughout November. By the end of the month she was said to be recovering a little, although 'without hope of long life' (*CSP for., 1559–60*, 146–7).

The French were enjoying some success in Fife early in the new year when word came on 22 January 1560 that an English fleet had been sighted off the east coast. At the same time a French fleet coming to Mary's aid was driven back by storms. Worse was to follow, for on 27 February 1560 Elizabeth I signed the treaty of Berwick with the congregation, taking Scotland into her protection and promising the protestants her assistance. She then sent an army north to besiege Leith. Mary of Guise left her palace of Holyroodhouse for Edinburgh Castle, where she held lengthy discussions with English envoys in a desperate attempt to play for time. The siege of Leith dragged on, the queen's health continued to decline, and her pleas to her brothers in France for men and money seemed to be going unanswered. Even so, when the bishop of Valence arrived to try to mediate between Scotland and England, he found Mary 'in want especially of health and of everything else except greatness of spirit and good understanding, for she is quite undaunted by these troubles' (Teulet, *Papiers d'état*, 1.574).

On 27 May Mary had a relapse and her companions could see that her condition was very grave. She was suffering from dropsy and a high fever, and from 1 June she was unable to take any nourishment. By 7 June she knew that she was dying. She sent for the duc de Châtelherault, her stepson Lord James Stewart, and her other lords, urging them to maintain the alliance with France and asking their forgiveness if she had ever offended them. The following evening, at about seven o'clock, she dictated a simple will, requesting that her servants' wages and her debts be paid and nominating her executors. After that, she sank into semi-consciousness and died in Edinburgh Castle about half an hour after midnight on 11 June 1560, Lord James Stewart and Archibald Campbell, fifth earl of Argyll, at her side. Her embalmed body lay in state on a black satin bed until it was taken in a lead coffin to St Margaret's Chapel in the castle. There it remained for many months. On 6 July the French, Scots, and English signed the treaty of Edinburgh, agreeing that all foreign soldiers, French and English alike, would withdraw from Scotland, and in August the Scottish parliament passed legislation making the country officially protestant. Not until the following year was permission given for Mary of Guise's burial. On 16 March 1561 her coffin was taken from the castle at midnight and put aboard a ship for France.

Mary of Guise was buried in July at Rheims, in the convent of St Pierre, where her sister was abbess, and a public funeral service was held in the cathedral of Notre Dame, Paris, in the presence of Mary, queen of Scots. The priest who gave the eulogy compared the dead queen to Judith, the heroine in the biblical Apocrypha who had saved her city of Bethulia by cutting off the head of the besieging Assyrian general Holofernes, nor was the comparison inappropriate. Sacrificing her own comfort, interests, and ultimately her life, Mary of Guise had fought a long, desperate, and, in the end, hopeless struggle to preserve Scotland as a pro-French, Roman Catholic nation for her daughter. In so doing, the witty, vivacious, and popular young woman who had been such a favourite at the French court developed qualities of determination and endurance which impressed even her enemies. Charming, highly intelligent, and hard-working, with a diplomatic manner and an ability to fight on regardless of hostility, disappointment, and ill health, Mary was never merely a pawn of the French king. Her correspondence makes it clear that her ambitions were not necessarily those of the French monarchy, and indeed both she and her mother worried that not only François I and later Henri II but also her own brothers would ignore her interests and simply use her for their own political advantage. While it is true that Mary saw Scotland as an ally for France, she seems to have viewed her daughter's realm as an independent nation, albeit an infant one which she would have to organize and transform into a well-governed state. She intended doing this on her own terms and indeed, if it had not been for her determination, the French would probably have come to an agreement with the English in 1559, rather than having to wait until she was dead.

John Knox detested Mary of Guise because for him she stood for Roman Catholicism and the mass, but later historians have viewed her with a kindly eye. Not only have her biographers, Strickland in the nineteenth century, McKerlie and Marshall in the twentieth, been unanimous in praising her intelligence and fortitude, but other writers discussing mid-sixteenth-century Scotland have also signalled their approval. 'Her methods were diverse', wrote Gordon Donaldson in 1974, 'but in the main they were along the lines of conciliation, which was always the key to the successful government of Scotland' (Donaldson, 35). In the end Mary of Guise failed in what she was trying to do, and the Scots became the protestant allies of England, but her dignity and dedication have won her the lasting admiration of protestants and Catholics alike. Her life is indeed best summed up by the emblem she chose for herself: a crown set above a rock beaten by winds and waves, with the motto 'And yet it stands'.

ROSALIND K. MARSHALL

Sources R. K. Marshall, *Mary of Guise* (1977) • *Foreign correspondence with Marie de Lorraine, queen of Scotland: from the originals in the Balcarres papers*, ed. M. Wood, 2 vols., Scottish History Society, 3rd ser., 4, 7 (1923–5) • *The Scottish correspondence of Mary of Lorraine*, ed. A. I. Cameron, Scottish History Society, 3rd ser., 10 (1927) • *John Knox's History of the Reformation in Scotland*, ed. W. C. Dickinson, 1 (1949) • G. Dickinson, ed., *Two missions of Jacques de la Brosse*, 3rd ser., Scottish History Society, 36 (1942) • H. Forneron, *Les ducs de Guise et leur époque* (1877) • R. de Bouillé, *Histoire des ducs de Guise* (1849) • G. de Pimodan, *La mère des Guises: Antoinette de Bourbon* (1925) • E. Bapst, *Les mariages de Jacques V* (1889) • D. Mayer and R. K. Marshall, 'Iconography and literature in the service of diplomacy', *Stewart style, 1513–1542: essays on the court of James V*, ed. J. H. Williams (1996), 273–88 • R. K. Marshall, 'The queen's table', *Tools and traditions: studies in European ethnology*, ed. H. Cheape (1993), 138–41 • R. K. Marshall, '"Hir Rob Ryall": the costume of Mary of Guise', *Costume*, 12 (1978), 1–12 • E. M. H. McKerlie, *Mary of Guise-Lorraine, queen of Scotland* (1931) • J. de Beaugué, *Histoire de la guerre d'Écosse*, ed. J. Bain, Maitland Club, 2 (1830), 2 • E. M. Goldsmid, ed., *The journal of King Edward's reign*, Clarendon Historical Society Reprints, 2 (1884) •

C. Merigot, *La vie de la serenissime Philippe de Gueldres* (Paris, 1627) • C. d'Espence, *Oraison funèbre* (1561) • A. Strickland and [E. Strickland], *Lives of the queens of Scotland*, 1 (1850) • J. B. A. T. Teulet, ed., *Papiers d'état, pièces et documents inédits ou peu connus relatifs à l'histoire de l'Écosse au XVIème siècle*, 3 vols., Bannatyne Club, 107 (Paris, 1852–60), vol. 1 • A. Teulet, ed., *Inventaire chronologique des documents relatifs à l'histoire de l'Écosse conservés aux archives du Royaume à Paris*, Abbotsford Club, 14 (1839) • *The historie and cronicles of Scotland … by Robert Lindesay of Pitscottie*, ed. A. J. G. Mackay, 1, STS, 42 (1899) • *APS*, 1424–1567 • R. Holinshed, *The chronicles of England, Scotland and Ireland*, 6 vols. (1807–8); facs. edn (New York, 1965), vol. 5, pp. 601–3 • G. Donaldson, *Mary, queen of Scots* (1974) • A. Fraser, *Mary, queen of Scots* (1969) • *CSP for., 1559–61* • J. Lesley, *The history of Scotland*, ed. T. Thomson, Bannatyne Club, 38 (1830)

Archives Archives du Ministère des Affaires Étrangères, Paris, Mary's testament, Angl. reg., vol. 15, fols. 112–13 • Archives Nationales, Paris, quittances for Longueville jointure, 1537, 1540, KK 907, fol. 3, KK 908, fol. 9 • Bibliothèque Nationale, Paris, Guise family expenses during Mary's childhood, suppl. Franc. 2568, cahiers 1–6 • NL Scot., corresp. and papers • NL Scot., state papers • NRA, priv. coll., letters | NA Scot., Exchequer records, 'Depences de la maison royale', 1543–4, E33/34 • NA Scot., Exchequer records, roll and number of persons in the service of the queen, c.1543, E34/23 • NL Scot., Balcarres papers, accounts and corresp.

Likenesses double portrait, oils, 16th cent. (with James V), Hardwick Hall, Derbyshire • Janet [F. Clouet], chalks, BM • C. de Lyon, oils, Scot. NPG [*see illus.*] • H. Monro, oils (after unknown artist), Scot. NPG • double portrait, oils (with James V), Blair Castle, Blair Atholl, Perthshire • drawing, priv. coll. • oils, priv. coll. • watercolour, Scot. NPG

Mary [Mary Stewart] (1542–1587), queen of Scots, was born in Linlithgow Palace on 8 December 1542, the only surviving child of *James V, king of Scots (1512–1542), and *Mary of Guise (1515–1560).

Early life and upbringing, 1542–1560 Mary's father died at Falkland on 14 December 1542, lamenting that his Stewart dynasty 'come witht ane lase, it will pase witht ane lase' (*Historie and Cronicles*, 1.407). The prophecy proved inaccurate, but it was made during a crisis for Scotland, at war with England and recently humiliated at the battle of Solway Moss (24 November). Mary's succession was accepted without question, although before her coronation she was referred to officially as 'the princess', while 'the queen's grace' meant her mother. Her existence opened the way to a peace settlement involving her betrothal to the future Edward VI. This was agreed (treaty of Greenwich, 1 July 1543) but soon renounced by the Scots. Anglo-Scottish war, later dubbed the 'rough wooing', was renewed.

Details of Mary's early life are sparse. On 26 July 1543 her mother took her from Linlithgow to Stirling Castle, where she remained under the formal charge of lords Livingstone and Erskine. She was crowned there hurriedly on 9 September, the day after the regent, the earl of Arran, had publicly repudiated his flirtation with England. Her mother usually remained with her, using the influence that this gave her to bolster Scotland's links with France. After the disastrous Scottish defeat at Pinkie (10 September 1547) Mary was sent briefly to the island priory of Inchmahome, in the Lake of Menteith.

The Scots now sought French military aid, the price of which turned out to be the queen's delivery to France and betrothal to the dauphin, subsequently François II (1544–

Mary (1542–1587), by Nicholas Hilliard, c.1578

1560). On 29 February 1548 Livingstone and Erskine took her to Dumbarton to await transport to France. On 7 July the Scottish parliament agreed to the betrothal on condition that Scottish liberties were respected. She and her company—including the aristocratic four '*Queen's Maries' with whom she was long associated—embarked on French royal galleys on 7 August, landing at Roscoff on 13 August. Mary's arrival consolidated the political prominence of her French family: her grandfather Claud, first duc de Guise (d. 1550), and then her uncles, François, second duc (1519–1563), and Charles, cardinal of Lorraine (1524–1574). As the dauphin's prospective bride she was adopted by the French royal family, living mainly in the royal palaces with him and his brothers and sisters. Elisabeth, later queen of Spain, became a special friend. Mary remained connected to the Guises, and they carefully cultivated their dynastic prize. Her grandmother Antoinette de Bourbon monitored her closely.

Mary's education was courtly rather than academic, developing her considerable talents in music, singing, dancing, needlework, and horsewomanship. She was taught Latin and the rudiments of some other languages, but not written Scots or English. Autograph letters of hers in Scots exist, but she usually wrote to educated people like Elizabeth or Sir William Cecil in French. In spoken language she was bilingual. For her formal 'oration' at the opening of parliament in 1563, 'she wrote yt in Frenche, but pronunced it in Englishe with a verie good grace' (*CSP Scot.*, 1563–9, 10). She was an accomplished poet in French, and occasionally in Latin.

People wanted a princess to be beautiful, and it seems that Mary really was: her beauty was universally and fulsomely praised, along with her charm, wit, and grace. She was unusually tall, like her mother. Yet she herself seems hardly to have exploited her appearance. Most authentic portraits of Mary were commissioned in her teens by the French royal family—notably three or four of c.1555–1559 attributed to François Clouet. In Scotland she patronized musicians and poets but few portraitists. For twenty years her portrait was available almost solely on coins, which remained mundane objects, however well suited her classical profile was to them. During her English captivity she learned the value of the image as propaganda, and occasional miniatures were produced. The best known and most securely attested was one by Nicholas Hilliard (c.1578) which served as the model for most of the many images of the queen in later life.

Mary's thirteen years in France made her effectively a Frenchwoman by upbringing. Her four Scottish Maries were cherished but kept at a discreet distance. Even after leaving France she felt personally closer to her French Guise and royal relations than to anyone in Scotland. In her will of 1566, there was greatest warmth in the bequests to her French connections. Her last letter, written on the morning of her execution, was to her brother-in-law Henri III, and she asked to be buried in Rheims. This did not endear her to the Scots. French court culture was alien to Scottish nobles like Lord Ruthven, who masterminded the murder of Riccio. He feared Mary's wiles, 'because she was trained from her youth in the Court of France' (Keith, 3.275). Ruthven adhered to what he regarded as a straightforward code of honour and vengeance; when Mary outwitted him she was not playing fair.

Nevertheless, a point on which Mary was most thoroughly educated was her dynastic position and destiny. This was not in itself French. Queen of Scots from infancy, she was also, as the granddaughter of Margaret Tudor, poised to inherit the crown of England. While in France she used these positions to benefit France, but as personal ruler of Scotland she pursued indigenous Scottish policies. As claimant to the English succession she sought above all to make herself acceptable to the English political establishment. From the English perspective, Mary in Edinburgh represented a conservative candidate to succeed Elizabeth, with her personal Catholicism a crucial issue. Her French background was unimportant; she was not seen as Charles IX's candidate. Only in her English captivity did her French connection regain diplomatic significance.

In 1550–51 Mary saw her mother for the last time, when Mary of Guise visited the French court, accompanied by a train of Scottish nobles, whose support she hoped to win in a bid for power in Scotland. Mary of Guise was finally granted the regency by the Scottish parliament on 12 April 1554. She was aided by having her daughter declared of age a year early, in December 1553, allowing her nominally a personal choice. The young queen also obtained her own household on 1 January 1554. The new regent set out to assimilate Scotland to France, a policy that would prove deeply unpopular.

Mary and François were married splendidly in Notre Dame on 24 April 1558. The official marriage agreement (15 April, 25–26 June 1558) was that Scotland would remain a distinct kingdom, although ruled by the same monarch. A separation was envisaged should the marriage produce no male issue (a daughter would inherit Scotland but not France). Meanwhile (4 April) Mary signed secret documents making the French crown her heir if she had no issue, and assigning her kingdom to France in pledge until the French were reimbursed for their military costs in Scotland and her own upbringing. This in effect authorized a French military takeover of Scotland. The fifteen-year-old queen's acceptance of the duplicitous measures urged on her by those she trusted is unsurprising, but it is worth noting that she was now committed to two inconsistent policies. The simultaneous pursuit of incompatible policies would be a recurring phenomenon in her career.

With the death of Queen Mary of England (17 November 1558), the Tudor blood of the 'queen–dauphiness' suddenly became an immediate issue. The legitimacy and religion of the new queen, Elizabeth, were doubtful and England and France were at war, although peace negotiations were in train. Wanting peace, Henri II was cautious about proclaiming his daughter-in-law queen of England, but the English royal arms came to pervade the already-febrile French royal pageantry and iconography about Mary, to English fury. Then Henri died (10 July 1559), and Mary became queen of France. Power passed to her Guise uncles, possibly assisted by her new status. Mary's prestige had never been higher.

But Mary's native throne was being rocked by a protestant and anti-French uprising (1559–60). English military intervention on the side of the insurgents led to the treaty of Edinburgh (6 July 1560) by which the French occupying forces agreed to evacuate the country, leaving Scotland in the hands of a noble coalition that swiftly enacted protestantism in the Reformation Parliament (August). Her mother's death, of which she was told on 28 June, distressed her deeply; otherwise she was hardly involved in the revolution. In November it was apparently François alone who received the coalition's emissary to France.

The death of François on 5 December 1560 hit Mary as a personal tragedy, and transformed her political position. She could theoretically have been married to her eleven-year-old brother-in-law, now Charles IX, but the new regent was the queen mother, Catherine de' Medici, who wanted to take the Guises down a peg. The French dynasty thus had no further direct use for Mary, and she ceased using the English arms or title.

Return to Scotland Until François's death, Mary had fulfilled her glittering but symbolic role admirably. Now she had to find a new one—or rather, her Guise relatives had to find one for her. She spent her period of strict mourning with her grandmother Antoinette, and went to Lorraine in the spring. The Guises in January 1561 put in a bid for her to marry Don Carlos, eldest son of Philip II, but in April this was blocked by Catherine de' Medici. Nor did any other suitable marriage emerge.

Return to Scotland was thus an obvious move. Mary had already informed the Scottish estates in January that she hoped to return as soon as her affairs permitted, and that she would be willing to overlook the recent offences against her authority. She wanted to renew the Franco-Scottish alliance, but without French troops it would be a shadow of its former self. She might still use domestic Scottish forces to overthrow the protestant regime. The two alternatives—confrontation with the regime or acceptance of it—were put to the queen in April, with near-simultaneous visits from Catholic and protestant representatives. John Leslie, future bishop of Ross, invited her to land at Aberdeen, where the earl of Huntly would raise 20,000 men to support her in restoring Catholicism. Lord James *Stewart, Mary's illegitimate half-brother and one of the protestant leaders, promised her that she could retain a private Catholic mass if she were to work with the regime.

Mary accepted Lord James's offer, which was in line with her existing policy. Lord James probably pointed out Huntly's unreliability: although a Catholic he had co-operated with the anti-French insurgents. Leslie's plan would also have invited renewed English military intervention at a time when the Guises could offer no French support. Mary would have liked to restore Catholicism, but she was in no hurry and did not want to take risks. Lord James's colleague, the secretary William Maitland of Lethington, worked out the details of the arrangement, and in June practical preparations for the journey began. Elizabeth refused Mary a passport through England (changing her mind too late), so she went by sea. Her party, including the four Maries and three of her Guise uncles, arrived at Leith on 19 August 1561.

Although the widowed queen's return was natural, Mary's co-existence with protestantism made it an experiment, even an adventure. It has sometimes been thought that her major interest in Scotland was the English succession, but she could have pursued that from a French château. Her interest in the English succession is obvious, but she also wanted to be queen of Scotland for its own sake. Even in her later English captivity, she directed her main diplomatic efforts towards fostering a party of Scottish supporters who would restore her to her northern throne.

On Mary's first Sunday, 24 August, she heard mass in her chapel at Holyroodhouse, protected by Lord James from the threats of more militant protestants encouraged by John Knox. A proclamation, perhaps improvised in response to the incident, was issued next day, commanding that no attempt was to be made to alter the present (that is, protestant) form of religion, on pain of death, until parliament should settle the religious question. This proclamation and its reissues remained the legal basis for religion throughout her personal reign. She governed with the aid of her privy council, unlike previous Scottish monarchs who had regarded a privy council as a device for a royal minority, an *alternative* to royal government. Conciliar government may reflect the growing administrative sophistication of the Scottish state, but Mary's sex also mattered; men tended to insist that female rulers should take as much male counsel as possible. Lord James and Maitland were her leading councillors.

The religious compromise was behind several governmental initiatives of the early personal reign. In December 1561, for instance, all surviving Catholic benefice holders were ordered to give up one-third of their income, to finance both crown and protestant ministers. Meanwhile, Mary herself tried four times to argue politely with Knox; the effort usually reduced her to tears, but also exposed Knox's marginal position, since the protestant establishment represented by Lord James and Maitland was prepared to accept her. The hostility to the settlement of the earl of Arran, who had aspired to marry Mary on her return, was nullified when he became insane in 1562. Meanwhile the queen firmly suppressed radical anti-Catholic moves by the burgh council of Edinburgh (October 1561).

The stability of Mary's regime was based ultimately on the pursuit of détente with Elizabeth. Her leading nobles and ministers owed their positions not primarily to their own queen, but to the English-backed revolution of 1559–60. With Mary's return, it was not obvious how she would fit into this new establishment, but it was her ministers' task to find her a role in it. The new-found Anglo-Scottish 'amity' had to develop traditions and mechanisms, and it was soon realized that Mary's position in the English succession was crucial. Scots and English alike assumed that the unmarried Elizabeth had to name a successor, and Mary's policy was to ensure that it would be her. Her ministers, too, saw the dynastic issue as vital; it would be dangerous for Scotland if any other candidate were to succeed.

So, only days after Mary's arrival in Scotland, she sent Maitland to England to ask Elizabeth for the succession. Elizabeth told him that she knew no better right than Mary's, but that she did not want to nominate a successor because it would undermine her own position, as she had learned when heir apparent to her sister. Maitland took this at face value, as an opening position in negotiations. With hindsight it can be seen that Elizabeth's refusal to name a successor was adamantine and non-negotiable; to all but Elizabeth at the time, a negotiated settlement seemed likely and Maitland saw clearly the lines that it should take. Mary wanted Elizabeth's friendship, and an assurance of her throne after her death. Elizabeth wanted Mary's friendship, renunciation of her 1558 claim to *be* queen of England, and commitment to protestantism in Scotland and England. The treaty of Edinburgh had included a pledge by her not to bear the English arms or title, which might be interpreted as renouncing the succession. Mary had not yet ratified this treaty, much to Elizabeth's frustration. Guided by Maitland, Mary presented her demands to Elizabeth as a simple clarification of the treaty. She would renounce the English throne in return for a clear promise of the succession.

In England, however, things were not so simple. Not only was there Elizabeth's personal touchiness to contend with, but English politicians were by no means agreed that if a successor were to be named it should be Mary. Her religion was a serious objection. Whether Mary would have converted to protestantism if offered the succession in return is a fascinating if ultimately unanswerable question. She might well have been swayed by the Guises' advice, which in 1562 was that conversion might be necessary. At any rate it suited neither queen to rule out concessions, and so the negotiations proceeded on what were perhaps false premises. In spring 1562 it was agreed that the queens should meet at Nottingham in the autumn. But in July the English intervened to support the Huguenots in the deteriorating French civil war, while Mary remained neutral. The meeting was postponed—indefinitely as it turned out. At this point (24 July) Mary reluctantly received the pope's envoy, Nicholas of Gouda, and told him firmly that the time was not right for Catholic initiatives.

Progresses and policy, 1562–1564 The queen now undertook the first of her extended progresses around her kingdom, a visit to the north-east (August–November 1562). This demonstrated, perhaps deliberately, how far her wooing of the Anglo-Scottish protestant establishment had marginalized her Catholic subjects. In order to advance protestantism in the north-east, Mary had decided to establish Lord James in the earldom of Moray, currently being administered by the Catholic earl of Huntly. Mary did not intend to destroy Huntly, but he was to be cut down to size. As the royal party approached his domains, Huntly staged a half-hearted protest which spiralled into open revolt. His small army was defeated at Corrichie (28 October) and he died of natural causes in his captors' hands. Huntly's downfall demonstrated to the English that Mary was willing to maintain protestantism, and further entrenched a domestic regime that could claim to be benefiting all concerned in it.

Mary's frequent progresses became important governmental devices. She covered over 1200 miles between August 1562 and September 1563, visiting not just the north but also the south and west. In 1564 she reached Inverness again, travelling through the central highlands via Blair Atholl—a remarkable venture. In Inverness she had the court wear what passed for highland dress. Like her grandfather James IV, she was solving the problem of governing a decentralized kingdom by bringing her court physically to the localities. Her personal charm was deployed to maximum effect among local élites. Most of the lords whom she visited would espouse her cause during the civil wars that followed her deposition.

Although Mary had failed to meet Elizabeth, she continued to pursue the English succession. She made a declaration renouncing the English throne in one of her parliaments, probably that of 1563 or 1564. Although this fell short of ratifying the treaty of Edinburgh, it did indicate that Mary was seeking *only* the succession. Yet to the English establishment, represented by Cecil, the prospect of

Mary's succession was never welcome. The Scottish establishment, represented by Moray and Maitland, recognized their dependence on England and hoped to keep their queen on a conciliatory course.

One of the main ways in which Mary could demonstrate her protestant and pro-English commitment was to make an acceptable marriage. Yet her first major marriage project was spectacularly unacceptable to the English. In February 1563 she reopened negotiations for the hand of Don Carlos. Maitland hinted to Philip that she might otherwise marry Charles IX, and Philip was initially beguiled. But by early 1564 he decided against the marriage. The Don Carlos project may have been a feint to put pressure on Elizabeth. If so, Elizabeth initially responded as Mary must have hoped. She told Maitland in June 1563 that she would regard a Habsburg marriage as a hostile act, but would show all favour to Mary if she married suitably. When asked who a suitable husband would be, Elizabeth prevaricated and dropped vague hints. Eventually, in March 1564, the English ambassador Thomas Randolph told Mary that the husband Elizabeth had in mind for her was her own favourite, Lord Robert Dudley.

This remarkable proposal astonished the Scots and still puzzles historians. Was Elizabeth sincere, or was she using Dudley (a man over whom she had complete control because he still hoped that she would marry him) purely to deflect Mary from a continental marriage? There is no positive evidence for the latter theory, and in any case Dudley was definitely reluctant. He was created earl of Leicester (29 September) to enhance his eligibility, but what Mary and her advisers wanted was a firm promise of the succession. Elizabeth would make only vague promises, which never elicited more than a polite but unenthusiastic response in Scotland. Randolph remained hopeful, but by early 1565 the plan was dead in the water.

Marriage to Darnley When the Leicester match lost momentum, Elizabeth moved to stall Mary's marriage completely. She would ideally have wished to keep her permanently unmarried—a traditional Tudor policy towards potential dynastic rivals, which she had recently inflicted on Catherine Grey. With Mary she had less influence than with one of her own subjects, but she could still aim to stave off a marriage for a while. Thus she declared on 5 March 1565 that she had decided not to name a successor until she herself had either married or decided not to marry. This said to Mary, in effect, that she could retain English friendship only by marrying Leicester or one of her own subjects, or by remaining unmarried—and none of these would secure the English succession.

There remained one theoretical candidate for Mary's hand, however: her cousin Henry *Stewart, Lord Darnley (1545/6–1567), who stood next to her in the English succession. Darnley's father, the earl of Lennox, had been exiled to England for opposing the Hamiltons in the 1540s. Having been born in England, Darnley might even have a better claim to the succession than Mary, who was technically an alien at English common law—a minor point, but one that had been made against her in the English 1563

parliament. Although a Mary–Darnley match was highly undesirable to Elizabeth, because uniting the two claims would prevent her playing them off against each other, she assumed that she could always block it because Darnley was an English subject, and his parents were her dependants with lands in England. Elizabeth had originally asked Mary to restore Lennox in June 1563, as a gesture of Anglo-Scottish amity. Mary and her advisers had agreed, since the proposal mainly damaged the Hamiltons who were then in partial eclipse. Lennox returned to Scotland in September 1564, and his restoration to his estates (16 October) was confirmed by parliament on 13 December. He pressed for Darnley to join him, and this was agreed in January with the apparent blessing of both Leicester and Cecil; he arrived on 11 February. There is no evidence for the popular theory that Elizabeth sent Darnley deliberately to trap Mary into an unwise marriage; the theory is also quite irreconcilable with the desperate English shifts and manoeuvres as the marriage loomed. Darnley's release proved a major blunder.

Mary first took up the idea of a Darnley marriage as a means of putting pressure on Elizabeth to retract her declaration of 5 March. During April she also conceived a personal attraction to him, though its exact nature—romantic, sexual, even maternal—is unknown. But such feelings would have led at most to light courtly dalliance if he had not possessed solid dynastic credentials. On paper his credentials were impressive. His religion, like his father's, was also attractively ambiguous: while his mother was a committed Catholic, in mid-1565 Darnley generally posed as a protestant, absenting himself from his own wedding mass. Nevertheless, the marriage offered Mary advantages with the Catholic powers, keeping both France and Spain friendly; had she married a Habsburg she would have forfeited Valois support, and vice versa. Perhaps, though, Darnley won Mary's hand mainly by being, apart from Leicester, the sole remaining candidate in the field. Mary might have avoided disaster if she had married Leicester after all, abandoning her Catholic friends and resigning herself to a future of being bossed around by Elizabeth. But if she wanted more than that, she simply had to marry Darnley and hope to overcome English displeasure.

Randolph realized in mid-April that marriage to Darnley could be imminent. The English council debated the Darnley problem on 1 May, and sent Sir Nicholas Throckmorton as a special envoy. Formally, the nearest Mary ever came to the English succession was now, when his instructions came close to offering it if Mary were to marry Leicester. Elizabeth also offered the duke of Norfolk or earl of Arundel, though with no assurances on the succession. But this was too little, too late. On 15 May Mary created Darnley earl of Ross, effectively announcing their engagement. This was bad news to Moray and Maitland, and also to the Hamiltons, traditional foes of the Lennox Stewarts. Lennox was attracting a new, heterogeneous party from all those dissatisfied with the regime to date. Prominent among these were the earl of Huntly, now rehabilitated after his father's downfall, and James *Hepburn, fourth earl of Bothwell (d. 1578), whom Moray had forced into exile in 1562. Frantic at the way in which Darnley was precipitating a redrawing of the political map to their disadvantage, Moray and the Hamiltons broke with Mary during May and June, and made vague military gestures in the hope of securing English support.

Seeing the danger, Mary carefully refrained from making open anti-protestant moves during the summer. She reissued the proclamation of August 1561, and made it clear that her mass remained a personal one. She nevertheless needed papal approval, and asked the cardinal of Lorraine to obtain a dispensation. By July she assumed that this would be on its way; in fact it was issued only on 25 September, but backdated to 25 May to cover the possibility that the marriage might already have taken place. Her banns were called on 22 July and she was married in her own chapel at Holyroodhouse on the 29th. She also proclaimed Darnley king.

The English reacted with open hostility. Their refusal to recognize the marriage or address Darnley by his new titles left Mary's diplomatic relationship with Elizabeth in tatters. 'All ther sisterly famyliarite was cessit, and insted therof nathing bot jelousies, suspitions and hattrent' (Melville, 156). On 16 July Mary even mentioned the possibility of warfare against 'oure auld inymeis' (Keith, 2.328). The breach was a failure of English policy, but in the long run it would harm Mary more.

Encouraged by the English stance, Moray and the Hamiltons now rebelled openly. However, Mary kept the allegiance of most protestants, notably the earl of Morton, head of the Douglases. Sporadic military manoeuvres began in late August, later dubbed the Chase-about Raid. Mary's forces were greatly superior, and when the English saw that, they reluctantly abandoned the rebels to their fate. On 6 October they all fled over the border, except Argyll who retreated to the highlands.

The murder of Riccio and its aftermath The key to Mary's problems from 1565 onwards does not lie in her relationship with Darnley as such, nor in her religious policy, nor in factionalism among the Scottish nobles. All these played their part, but they were all exacerbated by the single overriding fact of the breakdown of her relations with the English establishment. This was linked to religion, since protestantism was an inextricable part of the Anglo-Scottish 'amity' that Mary's marriage had disrupted. A hostile England would inevitably succour Mary's protestant enemies and make life awkward for her protestant friends. The playing of the protestant card by rebels would also tend to drive Mary towards a pro-Catholic policy; on the whole she resisted this, but on one occasion she did not.

With Maitland's eclipse and Moray's rebellion, Mary had to choose new councillors, and did so mainly from a range of conservative protestants. Catholics were more prominent than before, and her largely Catholic household had more political prominence. Here one notorious adviser was David Riccio, a Savoyard musician who in late

1564 had become secretary for her French correspondence. Riccio became a confidant, advising her on patronage, though it seems unlikely that he made policy as Maitland had done. During the Moray–Hamilton rebellion there was a brief flurry of appeals to Spain, France, and the papacy for financial and military support; Spain sent a subsidy, but it never reached Scotland.

Darnley, for whom Mary had done so much, rapidly proved himself vain, foolish, idle, and violent, with a rare talent for offending people, including his wife. He had been proclaimed king the day before his marriage, and Mary seems to have promised to get him the crown matrimonial in parliament. This honour, which François had received, would have granted Darnley equal power with his wife in the government. On realizing Darnley's incapacity Mary declined to grant him the crown matrimonial, causing him deep offence. By late October the marriage was already on the rocks—and Mary was known to be pregnant.

After her bloodless victory over the Moray–Hamilton rebellion, the queen's instincts turned to conciliation. It accorded with Scottish tradition, especially from the nobles' point of view, that dissident nobles should eventually be reintegrated into the body politic. In December she detached the Hamiltons from their allies by conditionally restoring them. This angered Darnley and Lennox; Darnley suddenly became ostentatiously Catholic in protest at Mary's wooing of professed protestants. A parliament was proclaimed (18–19 December) for March 1566, to which the other exiles were summoned to be forfeited, but it was assumed that the threat would not be carried out. Until mid-January 1566 Mary continued to make conciliatory gestures.

In late January, however, Mary reversed her policy abruptly. She evidently felt secure in her position, and she was encouraged into an aggressive stance by the cardinal of Lorraine and others on the continent. The impending parliament took on a new character when she announced that it really would forfeit the exiles. She also pressed ahead suddenly with open promotion of Catholicism, urging the nobles who had given her political support to attend mass (with limited success) and apparently planning to legalize the mass in the parliament. This plan horrified many leading nobles and royal officials, who had acquiesced only reluctantly in the ejection of Moray from power. There was no consensus that he should suffer permanent forfeiture; and yet there was no guarantee that the parliament would cross the royal wishes. If Mary was going to be stopped, it would have to be soon and it would have to be sensational. About 9–10 February, the exiles' Scottish friends started to plan a coup.

The plot's immediate aim was to discharge the parliament before it could forfeit the exiles and legalize the mass. In the longer term it aimed to take permanent control of Mary's council, if necessary by coercing her. What has become known as 'the murder of Riccio' was not primarily about him; it was simply a seizure of political power. Such a coup had to use the legitimating ideology of the ancient nobility whose right and duty it was to counsel the monarch. Since Mary was to be accused of taking the wrong advice, an adviser had to be sacrificed. Riccio, a low-born foreigner, was a necessary but largely symbolic grievance. The plotters rapidly gathered wide support. Maitland co-ordinated the early stages, the leading noble involved was Morton, and Knox and Randolph approved. The most remarkable recruit was Darnley. Only a week earlier he had been ultra-Catholic, with the exiles his chief enemies. But the plotters fanned his jealousy of Riccio with insinuations against Mary's honour, and promised him what she had refused—the crown matrimonial. Darnley was largely a pawn, but as king he added legitimacy to the coup. He and his father also increased the threat to Mary personally: nobody else sought her death, which might lead to a disputed succession, but one of the candidates for that succession was Lennox. It was Darnley who insisted that the assassination should be in the pregnant queen's presence.

The parliament assembled on 7 March 1566. Mary heard but dismissed a warning of plots. On the 9th her supper-chamber at Holyroodhouse was entered unexpectedly, first by Darnley, then by a band of armed men led by Lord Ruthven and George Douglas (Morton's henchman and Darnley's uncle). Darnley seized the queen, Ruthven harangued her on the iniquity of her recent policies, and Douglas and others dragged Riccio into the next room and stabbed him to death. The plotters barred the palace gates (Bothwell and Huntly escaped out of a window) and showed every sign of staying. Darnley publicly assured the Edinburgh burgesses that the queen was well, and ordered the parliament to disperse. Imprisonment of the queen in Stirling Castle was discussed.

Mary met the crisis with courage and resourcefulness. She skilfully detached Darnley from the plotters, who saw that they could not now retain her in captivity; they were reduced to seeking a pardon for their offence. This was drafted and redrafted, but Mary delayed signing. She manoeuvred the plotters into giving Darnley responsibility for her guards, and then staged a daring midnight escape to Dunbar (11 March), where she and Bothwell assembled an army that soon swept her back to power. She pardoned Moray and the other exiles, and the plotters fled to England where (as Melville commented) they might find the other lords' nests still warm. The plotters' immediate aim had succeeded. The parliament did not reassemble, there were no forfeitures, and the mass was not legalized. Their long-term aim, though, had failed, and Mary was back in charge. Scottish politics now had to cope with the simultaneous presence in royal favour of two hostile and unpopular factions, Moray and his friends against Bothwell, Huntly, and theirs. Mary tried with difficulty to remain above the factions.

In April Mary took up residence in Edinburgh Castle in order to await her child's birth, and on 19 June 1566, after a difficult labour, Prince James [see James VI and I] was born. The birth of a male heir enhanced the queen's dynastic attractiveness, and Patrick Adamson, a Hamilton client, published a Latin poem in Paris describing James as prince of Scotland, England, France, and Ireland—to the fury of the English government, who demanded Adamson's punishment.

Over all this loomed the problem of Darnley, in disgrace with everyone and yet still king. Governmental documents ran in the joint names of king and queen until the very day of his murder. Occasional efforts at reconciliation did not last. In early October Mary and her courtiers went to Jedburgh to hold a justice ayre for trials of border malefactors. There she received news that Bothwell had been wounded in Liddesdale. On the 15th or 16th she, Moray, and others visited Bothwell at Hermitage Castle, a 50 mile round trip. On her return she soon became seriously ill. She vomited blood and green matter, was feverish, and repeatedly lost consciousness. On the 25th her life was despaired of, and she made a moving deathbed speech, but by early November she had made a partial recovery. The French ambassador attributed her problems to depression at her relations with Darnley, who had paid her a brief and unwelcome visit in Jedburgh.

Mary returned fully to public life on 20 November on her arrival at Craigmillar Castle near Edinburgh. There she discussed the Darnley problem with Bothwell, Huntly, Maitland, Argyll, and Moray. According to a later account (sympathetic to Mary and written by Leslie for Huntly and Argyll to sign), divorce was ruled out, and an understanding was reached that Maitland and others would pursue an unspecified solution that might offend the scrupulous Mary and Moray when they heard of it, but would receive parliamentary approval. This may refer to a murder plot, to a scheme to put Darnley on trial, or (perhaps most likely) to something in between, such as a plan to have him killed resisting arrest.

The court was now taken up with preparations for the prince's baptism at Stirling Castle. Ambassadors arrived from France and England. Three days of festivities ensued, the high point being the siege of a mock fortress. The baptism itself (17 December) was a Catholic service, so the English ambassador, Bedford, absented himself, as did most Scottish nobles including Huntly, Moray, and Bothwell. Darnley too stayed away, although he was still posing as a Catholic; he preferred a stance of open opposition to the court rather than exposing himself to its contempt. The festivities were the high point of the Renaissance culture that Mary had fostered at her court, sending a political message of reconciliation under a glorious monarchy. Alongside this splendid and public Catholic gesture, Mary was carefully making practical concessions to the protestant church; and on 24 December Morton and the remaining murderers of Riccio were pardoned and returned from England. The pardon was regarded as Bothwell's initiative. His reconciliation with Morton was ominous for Darnley, since Morton was likely to seek vengeance for his betrayal by Darnley at the time of Riccio's murder. One Catholic concession was the restoration of Archbishop Hamilton's consistorial jurisdiction (23 December). This enabled him to grant divorces, though not for the queen (that would have been reserved to the pope). Moray opposed the move, so Bothwell probably supported it; he may already have been foreseeing a need to call on the archbishop's services.

The murder of Darnley In early 1567 Mary's career suffered a series of disasters culminating in her deposition. The first disaster was Darnley's murder—an abiding historical whodunnit, generating a mass of contradictory evidence, and with a large cast of suspects since almost everyone had a motive to kill him. One of these suspects is Mary, and here three main views have been taken. The extreme anti-Mary case is that from late 1566 onwards she was conducting an illicit love affair with Bothwell, with whom she planned the murder. The extreme pro-Mary case is that she was wholly innocent, knowing nothing of the business. In between these two extremes, it has been argued that she was aware in general terms of plots against her husband, and perhaps encouraged them.

The Bothwell love affair can readily be dismissed. Once the casket letters (discussed below) are discarded as forgeries, there is no contemporary evidence for it, merely the loudly proclaimed later assertions of men whose political survival required them to make such assertions. Along with this falls the Bothwell–Mary murder plot. The extreme pro-Mary case is equally untenable, since her main apologist, Leslie, conceded in his account of the Craigmillar conference that she had discussed a variety of options for disposing of Darnley. The question thus becomes: how much encouragement, if any, did she give to a murder plot? There is no direct evidence either way, but it is necessary to explain Mary's motives in seeking a reconciliation with Darnley in late January, when her dislike and distrust of him were vivid. Darnley had fallen ill (officially with smallpox, possibly in fact with syphilis) and was staying with his father in Glasgow. Mary went there (20 January) and persuaded him to complete his convalescence in Edinburgh, whereupon she would resume marital relations with him. This move to the notorious house at Kirk o' Field looks suspicious in retrospect, but is sufficiently explained by contemporary evidence of her concern to forestall Darnley's schemes against her. One can speculate that she wanted to facilitate a murder plot, but it is equally plausible that she was taking Darnley under her personal protection to prevent his murder.

As for who did kill Darnley, a consensus soon emerged that Bothwell was the main culprit. Despite what was said later, he probably did not act alone; Morton is his likely chief associate. There are several pointers to Douglas involvement, and Morton would later be executed for the murder (1581). A murder bond was drawn up (later carefully suppressed), and probably many others signed it.

In the early hours of 10 February 1567 the house at Kirk o' Field was blown up with gunpowder and the strangled bodies of Darnley and his servant found in the garden. The murder made international headline news, and the courts of Europe and the common folk of Edinburgh both expected queen and council swiftly to identify and punish the culprits. The Scottish nobility, accustomed to vengeance killings, had no such expectation, which indeed was hardly realistic when leading councillors like Bothwell, Morton, and Maitland had been involved. For Mary

to have made a show of prosecuting some underlings would have implicated their masters. Moray himself, possibly as innocent as Mary, urged Cecil (13 March) not to expect speedy results from the enquiries that the council claimed to be making. The one man who really wanted the murderers punished, Lennox, was fobbed off with a rigged acquittal of Bothwell (12 April). Then a parliament was held (14–19 April) at which most leading nobles extracted concessions for themselves.

Mary's own involvement in this was minimal, since she suffered a nervous breakdown after the murder. She had been depressed for some time, and had probably not fully recovered from her physical collapse in October–November 1566. The breakdown may well have been prompted by guilt feelings—she had wished Darnley dead, and now he was. There were reports of her 'melancholy'. Her council, concerned for her health, urged her to mitigate the seclusion of her formal mourning. On 8 March she received the English ambassador in a darkened room: she was clearly ill, possibly so ill as to have had one of her ladies impersonate her. She did not recover fully for months—especially since Darnley's murder was not the last of her problems.

Marriage to Bothwell As the parliament closed, Bothwell was already bidding to marry the queen. He invited the leading lords to a banquet (20 April) known as 'Ainslie's supper' from the tavern in which it was reportedly held. Nine earls, seven lords, and eight bishops signed a bond pledging themselves to promote his marriage to Mary. They represented a wide cross-section of the mainly protestant political establishment. Morton's name was prominent, and there were several other former Riccio murderers and Chase-about raiders. Many of these men were soon to rise in revolt against the Bothwell marriage, but the Ainslie bond shows that they were not initially hostile to it. Mary later claimed that they had urged Bothwell forward insincerely, hoping to use him to destroy both himself and her. But the most straightforward interpretation of the Ainslie bond is that Morton and his friends, having helped Bothwell to get rid of Darnley, were still prepared to work with him. They did not trust him; although a protestant he had a record of opposition to the Anglo-Scottish 'amity'. But for that very reason it was important to sign the bond to keep him in line. A marriage to the queen that they promoted could benefit them as well as him.

What changed their minds was what happened next. Bothwell at once took the bond to the queen and proposed marriage—and she refused him. He then made the disastrous mistake of striking out on his own. Mary went to Stirling on 21 April to visit her son. On her return on the 24th, Bothwell with a large troop of horsemen intercepted her party at Bridge of Almond and carried her captive to Dunbar.

The abduction is a major impediment to the theory of a Mary–Bothwell love affair, and believers in the theory have had to claim that it was collusive. There is one piece of evidence for this: Sir William Kirkcaldy's letter of 24 April, announcing Bothwell's abduction plan and exclaiming, 'Judge ye geif it be with hyr will or no!' But

Kirkcaldy in Edinburgh had no means of knowing the intentions of the queen in Stirling, and is likely to have been led astray by Bothwell's own claims that Mary had consented. Kirkcaldy's letter is of a piece with his earlier assertion (20 April) that Mary had said she would marry Bothwell 'and sall go with him to the warldes ende in ane white peticote or sho leve him' (*CSP Scot.*, 1563–9, 322, 324). This malicious gossip is flatly contradicted by Mary's refusal to marry Bothwell on that very day. Believers in the Mary–Bothwell love affair have of course made the most of Kirkcaldy's 20 April letter too, but accepting it at face value forces the improbable conclusion that Mary was simultaneously declaring her intentions openly to Bothwell's enemies and engaging in an elaborate and demeaning deception to conceal those intentions. Sir James Melville, who was in Mary's company and was taken to Dunbar with her, wrote:

> Then the Erle Bodowell boisted to mary the quen, wha wald or wha wald not; yea whither sche wald hir self or not … the quen culd not bot mary him, seing he had ravissit hir and lyen with hir against hir will.   (Melville, 177)

Mary too came as close as she could to admitting that she had been raped: 'Albeit we fand his doingis rude, yit wer his answer and wordis bot gentill' (Labanoff-Rostovskii, 2.38).

Mary thus had to go through with the marriage: 'as it is succeedit we mon tak the best of it' (Stevenson, 177). On 6 May Bothwell brought her back to Edinburgh, accompanied by his one committed ally, Huntly, having secured a rapid divorce from his existing wife, Huntly's sister. On 12 May Mary declared formally that although she had not welcomed the abduction, she was now a free agent and willing to marry Bothwell. On 15 May the marriage was celebrated at Holyroodhouse with little festivity and by protestant rites. The whole experience deepened her depression and distress; she and Bothwell argued constantly and she more than once threatened suicide.

Whatever Morton and his friends thought about abduction and rape, they were now faced with a Mary–Bothwell match that they had not promoted and from which they had no prospects of benefiting. When they signed the Ainslie bond they had assumed that they, Bothwell, and the queen would all be part of a new post-Darnley regime. But Bothwell was now making no efforts to include them in his plans. From 1 May onwards a large confederacy assembled at Stirling, including Morton, Argyll, and the young prince's keeper the earl of Mar. Their professed intentions were to avenge Darnley's murder, with which they charged Bothwell, and to liberate the queen from his thraldom. Military manoeuvres began in early June. The confederate lords occupied Edinburgh and captured the privy council machinery, while Mary and Bothwell were increasingly driven back on Bothwell's own followers. They operated first from Borthwick Castle, then from Dunbar. Eventually two armies confronted each other at Carberry Hill in Haddingtonshire (15 June). The day passed in fruitless negotiations and challenges to single combat

until the queen's army began to dwindle. Mary surrendered to the confederates on a promise (not kept) of honourable treatment; Bothwell fled to Dunbar and eventual exile. The queen was now a captive for a second time. As she was led into Edinburgh, the lords' soldiers cried out 'Burn the whore'. She was imprisoned in a burgess's house in a state of collapse.

Downfall and flight to England, 1567–1568 What happened next flowed from the confederates' general political position: to support protestantism and the Anglo-Scottish 'amity'. Mary's recent record here was far from appealing. Some of the confederates took their original aim—her liberation from Bothwell—seriously; but many were determined to seize the opportunity provided by her public humiliation. They had to act quickly, for the Hamiltons were assembling an army for a rescue attempt. On the night of the 16th Mary was sent as a prisoner to the island fortress of Lochleven.

The period between then and 24 July, when her abdication was extorted, is crucial. Various options for Mary were initially discussed by her captors: conditional restoration; enforced abdication and exile; enforced abdication, trial for murder, and life imprisonment; enforced abdication, trial for murder, and execution. The idea of the murder trial was linked to the confederates' demand for justice for Darnley's killers. After some of Bothwell's servants were executed in late June, it was dropped. Sir Nicholas Throckmorton had been sent by Elizabeth to demand Mary's restoration, but he did not himself believe in this demand and was probably more effective in preserving her life. He probably discouraged the idea of exile for her, since it was against English interests for her to go to France; indeed he tried to get Mary's son sent to England. The options were thus narrowing, with enforced abdication and imprisonment without trial looking more likely. But restoration remained conceivable. There were intense negotiations with the queen's supporters, presumably about the conditions on which this might be possible.

One essential precondition for restoration was divorce from Bothwell. This would have meant personal shame and disgrace for Mary, especially since by the time of Carberry she probably knew that she was pregnant. She could not bastardize her child. There is also no evidence that the confederates seriously offered to restore her if she would agree to a divorce. From the outset they claimed that she was refusing to abandon Bothwell, and milked this refusal for all it was worth. It was the formal rationale for her arrest warrant (16 June). A rumour was circulated that the lords had intercepted a letter from Mary to Bothwell written on the night of her arrival, 'calling him her dear hart' and saying that she would not leave him. This letter, never produced, was suspected even at the time to have been 'invented' (Melville, 185). It was not the last time that letters would be fabricated to blacken Mary's reputation.

Gradually, then, the confederates reached a consensus that Mary should be deposed, though this cost them some defections, notably Argyll. They ascertained from Throckmorton that English objections would be pro forma. On 24 July lords Lindsay and Ruthven presented the queen with deeds of abdication, telling her that she would be killed if she did not sign. Mary was then prostrate with illness, having on top of everything else suffered a recent miscarriage. She received messages from Throckmorton and others advising her that she should sign to save her life, since a deed extorted under duress would be invalid. She signed.

The effect of Mary's deeds of abdication was to make her son king (he was crowned on 29 July), and to appoint an interim regency council until Moray could return from France and assume the regency. The regime now had no further use for her. Perhaps Moray scrupled to order her murder; perhaps Elizabeth's lobbying on her behalf was effective. At any rate, the regent seemingly intended to keep the 24-year-old queen in prison for the rest of her life.

In the later months of 1567 Mary, in her enforced seclusion, gradually recovered her physical and mental health. On 2 May 1568 she escaped from Lochleven Castle and was met by Lord Seton and some of the Hamiltons. Both they and the regent rushed to arms. Mary offered Moray a compromise settlement if he would accept her restoration, but he refused. Mary's initial support came mainly from the Hamiltons and Argyll, though many more supporters would have rallied to her in time. The queen's forces headed for the stronghold of Dumbarton, and Moray was based at Glasgow, so a battle ensued at Langside near Glasgow (13 May). It was lost by Mary's commander, Argyll, whose fainting fit prevented the reinforcement of his advance guard. Few were killed, but the queen's forces were scattered and many captured.

The queen now panicked. 'Efter the tincell [loss] of this battaill hir majeste tint curage, quhilk sche did never befoir, and tok sa gret fear that sche rested never untill sche was in England' (Melville, 202). Her party initially made for Dumbarton, but finding the way blocked they turned to the south, led by Lord Herries. Mary later recalled with a shudder the frantic night ride, without food or drink for the first twenty-four hours. Finally she reached Herries' house, Terregles, near Dumfries, where she stayed a day or two, and resolved to go to England to seek Elizabeth's support. On 16 May she embarked near Dundrennan and crossed the Solway Firth in a fishing boat, landing at Workington.

Mary's decision can easily be criticized, but her other options were hardly attractive. In retrospect it is evident that her best bet was to remain in Scotland as a focus for a regrouped queen's party. Her mistake was not to recognize that Langside was an indecisive defeat. Here she was evidently swayed by her long and desperate flight after the battle. Although the queen herself made the decision at Terregles, it was a natural extension of Herries' decision to flee southwards from Langside; the momentum of Mary's flight from Langside carried her across the Solway. Her critics have sometimes urged that she should have gone to France, where she had estates, friends, and relatives. But even if a ship could have been found, France offered merely a comfortable refuge for an exile, not military assistance to restore her to her protestant throne.

Mary still accepted Scotland's link with England and relied on regaining the support of the Anglo-Scottish protestant establishment. To that end it was natural that she should go to England. At best, English arms and diplomacy would restore her; at worst, she could always go on to France later. It was hardly likely that Elizabeth would deny her that right.

Mary in England: the shaping of English policy, 1568–1570
Elizabeth, who had initially welcomed Mary's escape from Lochleven, was in a dilemma. Her standing with continental powers, and perhaps her domestic position too, would suffer if she appeared to sanction rebellion. But Moray and his colleagues were her most reliable friends. Mary herself was not necessarily an enemy, but if her restoration would involve Moray's destruction, this would harm English interests. The English government quickly got Mary into its hands and away from the Catholic earl of Northumberland. She was well guarded, but it was not yet entirely clear that she was a prisoner—largely because she herself did not wish to leave. Still, Elizabeth stressed that she was not to go to France.

Elizabeth's attitude to Mary was driven mainly by *realpolitik*—a wish to promote her own and her regime's interests. She had not forgotten Mary's claim to the English throne in 1558, nor her failure to ratify the treaty of Edinburgh. Mary was thus a potential enemy. But Elizabeth also experienced other feelings: a wish for friendship with her closest relative, and a sense of solidarity with a fellow monarch afflicted by rebels. She was never vindictive towards her. She later told the parliament that petitioned for Mary's execution (12 November 1586) that she wished 'that we were but as two milk-maids, with pails upon our arms', so that she might forgive her offence (Neale, 2.117). Her chief adviser, Cecil, focused on *realpolitik* alone. He was clear that Mary could not be restored unconditionally, but the main line of English policy in the summer and autumn of 1568 was to work for a conditional restoration. The treaty of Edinburgh would be ratified, Moray's position guaranteed, and the queen limited by a great council and parliament. It would be a signal achievement of English diplomacy.

This required three-cornered negotiations between Elizabeth, Mary, and Moray. The idea took shape during the summer of a conference to inquire into Mary's and Moray's charges against each other and to resolve their differences. Neither proved keen, and each wanted the conference to concentrate on hearing their own charges against the other. Mary also hesitated to compromise her sovereign status. But she agreed to the conference on being given the impression that she was going to be restored whatever the outcome; at worst the English might insist on guarantees for Moray's position. Moray, however, was told that if Mary were proven guilty of murder she would not be restored.

The conference convened at York in early October, with Moray present in person but Mary confined in Bolton. Mary's commissioners, principally Leslie and Herries, treated the conference as being about how Elizabeth was going to restore their mistress. The English commissioners, led by Norfolk, also began that way, and were impressed by Mary's case. Compromise was in the air. But Moray had other ideas, sensing that if Elizabeth were forced to choose between him and Mary, she would choose him. He had brought with him the casket letters, documents which purported to prove her adultery with Bothwell and complicity in Darnley's murder. In November Elizabeth moved the conference to Westminster, whereupon it became almost wholly an inquiry into Mary's guilt. Moray, after much hesitation, made a formal murder accusation on 26 November. Mary's commissioners protested her innocence but soon withdrew (6 December), realizing that continued co-operation could not benefit her.

It was then, with no hostile witnesses present, that Moray produced the casket documents (7 December). His aim was twofold: to convince the English commissioners of Mary's guilt, and to show Elizabeth that compromise between him and Mary was now impossible, he having accused his sister of murder. The first aim seems to have failed, since Norfolk, the chief commissioner, was soon seeking to marry Mary; but the second and more important aim succeeded. In political terms her actual guilt or innocence mattered little, so long as the English accepted that Moray and his regime were committed to maintaining her guilt.

The casket letters, consisting of eight letters (written in French but surviving only in translations) and twelve French love-sonnets supposedly written by Mary to Bothwell early in 1567, and two draft contracts of marriage, are crucial to any understanding of Mary's career and reputation. If genuine, they prove Mary's adultery and complicity in the murder of Darnley. It is obvious, however, that they have been extensively tampered with, largely by blending Mary's genuine letters with existing material from other sources. The sonnets date on stylistic grounds from about 1520. A passage about 'mes subjects' spoils the metre and is an obvious interpolation, while they contain various passages that could not have been written by Mary. Of the letters, four are flowery love letters which probably come from the same source as the sonnets—most likely one of the romantic manuscript collections that circulated in Renaissance courts. The other four letters are Mary's own, straightforward and businesslike in tone, but with places, dates, and addresses manipulated, and passages interpolated. Letter two is the only really important one. It purports to have been written in late January 1567 by Mary in Glasgow to Bothwell in Edinburgh, describing her mission to fetch Darnley to his fate at Kirk o' Field. Most of the text is probably genuine, though some passages suggest that it was addressed to someone other than Bothwell. The forgers' demonstrable practice of interpolation means that the passages alluding to adultery and murder cannot be accepted as evidence of Mary's guilt.

The letters' provenance is also suspicious. Morton testified in December 1568 that George Dalgleish, Bothwell's servant, had been captured on 20 June 1567 with a casket containing them. Yet Dalgleish's deposition, dated 26 June, had mentioned neither casket nor letters. The dossier probably evolved gradually. In July 1567 a single letter was mentioned that sounds like a more explicit version of letter two than the one which eventually emerged. George Buchanan, drafting Mary's indictment during 1567, mentioned only a letter or letters from Glasgow (presumably a version of letter two) in June, but by the autumn the evidence against her was being described as numerous letters written on different occasions. Forgery of legal documents was frequent, and Mary's italic hand easy to simulate. Once the production of an incriminatory dossier had been decided, the necessary skills would easily have been procured.

The documents were not intended for publication, only for private use by the English commissioners. They did not even have to be convincing, so long as they were plausible and forced the necessary breach between Moray and Mary. The same applies to the 'book of articles', the narrative indictment of Mary by Buchanan that was presented along with the letters; it was wildly inaccurate, but the English commissioners could not know this. Even when Buchanan's lies were published (1571), they did not generate the kind of debate that modern scholars would have expected. Sixteenth-century polemicists primarily used a priori reasoning to support entrenched positions, and when Buchanan was condemned it was on the grounds that his partisanship made him untrustworthy.

The original casket documents returned to Scotland in 1569. Their last known possessor was the first earl of Gowrie; after his execution in 1584 they disappeared. They may or may not have come into James VI's hands, and much has occasionally been made of his apparent failure to publish them. All that can safely be said is that if the letters were forgeries, it was against his interest to expose the fact while Mary lived.

After inspection of these dramatic documents, the York–Westminster conference ended in anticlimax. Elizabeth declared (10 January 1569) that nothing had been sufficiently proved by either side against the other. But her actions were far from even-handed. It seems that Cecil had been resigned to the necessity for Mary's restoration before the conference, but seized upon Moray's evidence as a means of avoiding it. Moray went home to govern Scotland, with a £5000 English subsidy; Mary remained in England, although she had no further reason to stay. She was now unambiguously a prisoner, and was moved to more secure (if insalubrious) accommodation, Tutbury Castle in Staffordshire.

Mary's imprisonment was obviously illegal. She was accused of no crime in England, and Elizabeth's jurisdiction over her was questionable. But political reality was pressing. Early in 1569 Elizabeth had the theoretical option of allowing her to go to France, where she would probably have been welcomed politely but not aided, especially since her scandalous protestant marriage. By 1572, when France and England signed a formal alliance, Mary would have become a back number. However, Moray's regime in Scotland was precarious and memories of the Franco-Scottish alliance were green. It was unthinkable that the French should be given another opportunity to dabble in Scotland. In fact Elizabeth in early 1569 was still discussing another scheme for Mary's restoration to Scotland; Moray dragged his feet and rejected it in October.

Moreover, the main danger that Mary eventually posed to Elizabeth came in the form of assassination plots. There was no reason why these should cease once Mary was free. So long as she was a prisoner, any plotters seeking to place her on the English throne had to prevent her jailers killing her; Mary was effectively a hostage for Catholic good behaviour. To Elizabeth's councillors, who worried about what would happen if the English queen died (she had a serious illness early in 1572, for instance), the detention of her rival also offered the prospect of a breathing-space in which to settle the succession.

So Elizabeth, encouraged by hawkish councillors, kept Mary in captivity to retain the initiative. The rising of the northern earls in late 1569, and Elizabeth's excommunication by the pope in 1570, closed Mary's prison door more firmly by showing that her religious and dynastic position threatened her cousin's throne. In 1570 there were still fitful negotiations for her restoration, but soon Cecil was exploring the possibility of returning Mary to Scotland for imprisonment or execution there. Intermittent discussions continued until 1576, but the Scots were unwilling.

Mary in England: efforts at release, 1568–1572 Mary in England had two choices, once it was clear that Elizabeth intended neither to restore her nor to allow her to go to France. First, she could try to rehabilitate herself with the Anglo-Scottish protestant establishment, which had tolerated her for some four years, though most of it had never welcomed her. Mary had some benefits to offer Elizabeth: Scottish stability; legitimacy; links with the continental powers. If Mary had pursued this course it might have been politically advantageous for her to convert to protestantism. Second, she could become actively hostile to Elizabeth, capitalizing on her Catholicism and her direct claim to the English throne on the assumption of Elizabeth's illegitimacy. This would involve throwing in her lot with the militant Counter-Reformation movement and with Spain, in order to attempt to overthrow and replace Elizabeth.

What Mary in fact did was to adopt both options. She always publicly professed friendship and loyalty towards Elizabeth, even offering to sign the bond of association (1584); but she did also plot against her. As early as 24 September 1568 she wrote to the queen of Spain, offering to risk her life for the re-establishment of Catholicism in England if she had foreign aid. She surely recognized that the two stances were inconsistent; but whether she fully grasped what effect it would have on English attitudes to her is questionable. The point, to her, was that both options were legitimate. The plots were genuine, and when plotting she really did want to overthrow Elizabeth; but the negotiations with Elizabeth were genuine too. If a deal had been struck to restore her to her Scottish throne, she might well have performed her side of the bargain in good faith. What she did not foresee was that the English would see it differently. They regarded her plotting as sincere, and her professions of friendship towards Elizabeth as hypocritical.

Mary's main immediate aim between 1569 and 1571 was to marry the duke of Norfolk. This was originally discussed as part of a plan to restore her to Scotland under Elizabeth's auspices, but although Norfolk was a protestant the match increasingly acquired a Catholic cast. Norfolk, politically naïve, was manoeuvred into heading a faction at the English court that would oust Cecil and reverse his policy of confrontation with Spain. The bid for Mary's hand was intended to procure Cecil's disgrace. Elizabeth consequently vetoed it in mid-September 1569. Norfolk, frustrated, left the court in disgrace, and was soon arrested (October). This was followed by the rising of his Catholic supporters, the earls of Northumberland and Westmorland (November–December). Mary was hurriedly moved south to Coventry to forestall any rescue attempt.

The Norfolk match revived after his release in August 1570. It was now definitely subversive. In early 1571 Mary wrote to the banker and papal agent Roberto Ridolfi denouncing the French and soliciting Spanish aid. She also wrote to France seeking aid, and to Elizabeth assuring her that her hopes of the English succession rested on the queen. She was thus pursuing not two but three incompatible policies. But her most significant line of action concerned what came to be known as the Ridolfi plot. This called simultaneously for an uprising of English Catholics, the release of Mary, and an invasion of England by the Spanish army in the Netherlands. Elizabeth would be arrested by Norfolk, who would marry Mary and place her on the English throne. The scheme was grandiosely and incompetently co-ordinated by Ridolfi with the support of Mary's ambassador, Leslie. Mary gave her full approval in March 1571. The English government gradually unravelled the plot during the summer, and Norfolk was arrested in September.

The year 1572 was a turning point—one of the worst periods for Mary's career, through a concatenation of English, Scottish, Dutch, and French events over which she had no control. Norfolk was convicted of treason in January, though Elizabeth hesitated to put him to death. The English parliament of May–June wanted Mary executed, or at least excluded from the succession. Elizabeth was forced to have Norfolk executed to deflect the clamour. A commission was established for Mary's trial also, but nothing came of it. By the end of 1572, stability had returned to English politics. Mary's continental friends also suffered setbacks. The Spanish position in the Netherlands was shaken by an uprising in April 1572 and Mary's French hopes were simultaneously shattered by the Anglo-French treaty of Blois, in which she was not mentioned.

Mary's most solid prospects in 1570–71 lay in Scotland, where her party had recovered from the disasters of 1567 and 1568. In late 1569 Moray's regency began to crumble, and in January 1570 he was assassinated by a Hamilton.

Civil war was renewed, with the 'queen's party' looking strong. But they were not a cohesive group. To the extent that they really were Mary's friends, their war aims involved her restoration; and instead of offering this, the English sent troops to support the 'king's party'. The leading Marian nobles gradually made their peace with successive regents, and by 1572 those who remained in arms were hoping to do the same. The last nobles surrendered in February 1573. A few diehards remained holed up in Edinburgh Castle, but it fell to English artillery in May. Mary's cause was at its lowest all over Europe. Almost a decade elapsed before it showed signs of revival.

Life in captivity, 1568–1583 Although deposed and incarcerated, Mary was always treated as a queen. She maintained her own household under her keepers' supervision, corresponded freely (until 1585), and received guests. Her position could be regarded as house arrest rather than imprisonment. Her household aimed to be a royal court, with privy and presence chambers, dais, throne, and cloth of state. She usually had about forty servants, and guarding them was an administrative challenge—some were armed with swords and even pistols. Closest to her were her secretaries, gentlewomen of the chamber, and (usually) a Catholic priest under the guise of an almoner. One of the four Maries, Mary Seton, served her until 1583, when in poor health she retired to a French convent. As dowager queen of France, Mary enjoyed large revenues (though reduced in 1576). She paid her servants' wages, while her keepers (subsidized haphazardly by the English government) provided their food and accommodation. The head of her French council, James Beaton, exiled archbishop of Glasgow, skilfully maintained her diplomatic presence in France. Her household's funds were remitted via the French embassy in London. The Guises stayed in contact, and in 1574 provided her with a new secretary, Claude Nau.

For most of the period 1569–84, Mary's keeper was the sixth earl of Shrewsbury, a wealthy midland magnate. She was treated as his personal guest; he and his formidable countess, Bess of Hardwick, were her regular companions. Mary and Bess spent many hours in embroidery, producing a large output which influenced the decorative fashions of the Sheffield region for generations. Mary spent fourteen years in Sheffield (1570–84), mainly alternating between Shrewsbury's adjacent residences of Sheffield Castle and Sheffield Lodge. She was occasionally allowed to visit the spa at Buxton, a social centre where she once met Cecil, now Lord Burghley, and twice met Leicester. In Shrewsbury's household she acquired some new relations when in 1574 Darnley's brother Charles married Bess's daughter Elizabeth Cavendish. Their daughter Arabella was born in 1575, and Mary involved herself with her welfare, trying unsuccessfully to get her the earldom of Lennox. Mary was embroiled in the Shrewsburys' marital breakdown in 1583, with Bess spreading the wild rumour that she had borne a child to Shrewsbury. Her health, never good, declined markedly during this period. She suffered from recurrent vomiting

and abdominal pains that have been attributed to porphyria—a hereditary condition that may also have contributed to her mental problems in 1566–7. She fretted at being deprived of fresh air and exercise. Arthritis in her arms and legs became severe, and by the 1580s she could often hardly walk.

Mary's diplomatic prospects revived briefly in 1576 when Don John of Austria, Philip II's dashing half-brother, became governor of the Netherlands. His martial image was such that he seemed likely to subdue the rebellious Netherlands and then lead a crusade against England, culminating in his marriage to Mary, whom he would place on the English throne. Mary herself was never committed to the idea, rightly seeing it as improbable. Don John's governorship collapsed in 1577 and he died the next year.

Mary continued to take a strong interest in Scotland. As James grew up, she looked forward to a time when he would espouse her cause like a dutiful son. Despite her self-presentation on the continent as a committed Catholic, for Scottish audiences she retained her pose as a tolerant *politique*. James later recalled that 'in all her letters (whereof I received many) she never made mention of religion, nor laboured to perswade me in it' (*Workes*, 301). She attended protestant services regularly, and was never a recusant. Her servants were mainly Catholic but some, including her steward Andrew Melville, were protestants. She did not adopt the Gregorian calendar reform of 1582. As with her pluralist approach to politics, she probably saw both her religious positions—commitment to the Counter-Reformation and willingness to compromise with protestants—as legitimate.

Mary's last serious effort to rehabilitate herself with the protestant establishment came in the early 1580s, when her son showed signs of rejecting English tutelage. The association scheme, devised by Mary in October 1581 and discussed between February 1583 and October 1584, would have freed Mary and restored her to a nominal joint sovereignty with her son. She offered to live in England and resign the executive government to him. In three-cornered negotiations she skilfully persuaded both James and Elizabeth that the other favoured the scheme, but it was eventually called off when they both realized that this was not so. An Anglo-Scottish league was soon being discussed, and was concluded in June 1586 without reference to Mary.

Plots against Elizabeth, 1583–1586 Even while the association scheme was being discussed, Mary was moving into the final stage of her career as a plotter. She was probably involved (her trusted agents certainly were) in the Throckmorton plot, exposed in November 1583, by which the duc de Guise would invade England with Spanish support in order to place her on the English throne. After her son disappointed her over the association scheme, plotting became her main political activity. She was playing for high stakes; the risks were great but so were the benefits. She knew that she had nearly been executed over Ridolfi. It would be anachronistic to say that she should have refrained from plotting because it was dangerous; she thought the risks worthwhile.

The mid-1580s saw increasing international tension, with prospects of Spanish support for plots better than they had been since 1572. After the assassination of William of Orange in July 1584 the Dutch resistance against Spain began to crumble, and English armed intervention in the Netherlands became increasingly likely; it finally came in August 1585. This sharpened Anglo-Spanish conflict, increasing Mary's symbolic value if not her ability to take initiatives. Her French background was a problem to Spain, as was her son's heresy. In early 1586 Philip II was already planning to invade England and depose Elizabeth. In negotiations with the pope he agreed that Mary would be placed on the English throne, but married to a husband of Philip's choice, and succeeded not by James but by Philip's nominee (he intended to nominate his eldest daughter, Isabella). Philip's reservations about Mary were reciprocated. In the 1570s she had often placed high hopes in France, and had been hesitant about any pro-Spanish moves that might alienate France. Nevertheless, on 20 May 1586 in connection with the Babington plot, Mary informed the Spanish ambassador of her intention to bequeath her kingdoms and rights to Philip if James remained protestant. On 23 November 1586, after her conviction for treason, she announced this to the pope in a letter which, because it became public, Philip regarded as a suicide note.

English actions towards Mary were also provocative. The English council on 19 October 1584 sponsored a bond of association by which thousands of loyal Englishmen swore to defend their queen, and to 'prosecute to death' any 'pretended successor' in whose name any assassination attempt might be made. Subscriptions flooded in. With the Act for the Security of the Queen's Royal Person (27 Eliz. I c. 1, debated from 1 December 1584 to 13 March 1585) this was modified: instead of lynch law, a special commission would be established for the trial of the 'pretended successor'. The act also confined itself to Mary (who was of course not named), in contrast to the original bond which would also have excluded her son. In January 1585 she was imprisoned more strictly under Sir Amyas Paulet. She was allowed no correspondence except via the French ambassador, and that was inspected by Paulet. In December she was moved to Chartley Hall in Staffordshire.

A new plot took shape in May–June 1586 around Anthony Babington, a Catholic gentleman who had been a page to Mary's former gaoler Shrewsbury. It involved a Catholic uprising, assassination of Elizabeth, and invasion by Spain. Sir Francis Walsingham's double agents knew of the plot throughout, and fostered it carefully in the hope that Mary would commit herself to it. A channel of communication with Mary was arranged, with packets of coded letters hidden in beer barrels; unknown to the plotters, Walsingham saw all Mary's correspondence. The plot was thus a frame-up, a point of which Mary's defenders sometimes complain. It is not, however, obvious that the English government was obliged to nip the plot in the bud to prevent Mary from incriminating herself. The frame-up was directed almost as much against Elizabeth as against Mary.

Babington could never have organized an uprising; his preliminary enquiries showed that most Catholics would support the government. The assassination, however, was perfectly conceivable and some of those in the plot were committed to it. Under surveillance, Babington wrote to Mary (6 July) proposing invasion, rescue, and 'dispatch of the usurper' by 'six noble gentlemen' (Pollen, *Babington Plot*, 21–2). Mary replied (17 July), endorsing the plot in detail and making numerous recommendations. The plot as she saw it was that English Catholics would make military preparations, alleging self-defence against the 'Puritans'. Elizabeth would then be assassinated—'sett the six gentlemen to woork' (ibid., 41). Immediately thereafter, Mary herself would be rescued, and defended until a Spanish army could arrive. This 'Bloody Letter' (as Thomas Phelippes, the code-breaker, dubbed it) gave Walsingham enough evidence against Mary, but he hoped for more. He had her letter sent on to Babington, with a forged postscript asking for the names of the six gentlemen and the intended assassination method. However, the postscript was never effective; Babington had made only a general interim reply (3 August) by the time the authorities pounced. He and most of the plotters were rounded up on 14 August. Mary's secretaries, Claude Nau and Gilbert Curle, were arrested on the 11th and her papers seized. It was they who had written out and encoded the 'Bloody Letter'; their confessions (5 September) authenticated it, as did Babington's own. The evidence of Mary's complicity in the plot could not be suppressed, as it was needed to convict the other plotters.

Trial and execution, 1586–1587 Burghley and Walsingham dragged Elizabeth reluctantly into appointing (9 September) a commission for Mary's trial in terms of the act of 1585. Elizabeth was never told that the plot had been a frame-up, and to her the danger seemed immediate. Mary was moved to Fotheringhay Castle for the trial. In a two-day hearing (14–15 October) she defended herself with skill and dignity, but the evidence was clear and the verdict never in doubt. The trial was continued to the Star Chamber at Westminster (25 October), where the commissioners pronounced that:

> the aforesaid Mary pretending title to the crown of this realm of England, hath compassed and imagined within this realm of England, divers matters tending to the hurt, death and destruction of the royal person of our sovereign lady the Queen. (Steuart, 61)

Mary was thus condemned for plotting political assassination. She herself always claimed to be a martyr for her religion, and it was said after her death that she had been offered a pardon in return for conversion to protestantism. The truth was, as the English authorities made clear to her on the scaffold, that she was welcome to convert to protestantism but would still be executed. If her pose as a Catholic martyr was genuine, it was because political Catholicism encouraged the assassination of its opponents.

The verdict had brought Mary several steps nearer the

block, but there was now a pause—mainly to overcome Elizabeth's reluctance, but also to assess the international situation. One way of pressurizing Elizabeth was to summon a parliament, and this her councillors persuaded her to do in early September when the Babington plot was in the headlines. Parliament met on 29 October, explicitly to consider Mary's position. Elizabeth absented herself; she must have guessed that parliament would launch itself at Mary's throat, and it duly did, petitioning forcefully for her execution (12 and 24 November). On 4 December the sentence of death was publicly proclaimed, stressing parliament's responsibility. The likely reaction in France and Scotland had to be gauged. Henri III sent a special ambassador to intercede for Mary, but it soon emerged that France could or would do little. Scotland was more of a problem, politically volatile and deeply involved. James VI's honour required him to make a display of diplomatic activity on his mother's behalf, which he duly did. But although he huffed and puffed, his only effective move would have been to break the Anglo-Scottish league, imperilling his own succession claim. By mid-December Elizabeth saw that he would not do this. His final appeal (26 January 1587) urged clemency on the feeble grounds that it would damage his reputation among his own subjects if Mary were executed and he took no action.

On 1 February 1587 Elizabeth finally signed the long-prepared warrant authorizing Mary's execution. She gave it to William Davison, Walsingham's recently appointed colleague as principal secretary, with vague and contradictory instructions. She also told Davison to get Walsingham to write to Paulet and his colleague Sir Dru Drury (1 February) asking them to assassinate Mary—as the bond of association conceivably committed them and others to do. Paulet had been willing to kill her to forestall a rescue attempt; but (as Davison predicted to the queen) they refused outright assassination, either on principle or fearing that an assassin would become a scapegoat. The episode reveals much about Elizabeth: most relevantly, it shows that she was no longer aiming to keep Mary alive, merely to preserve her own reputation. Elizabeth was genuinely distraught by the execution; her claim that it had been against her wishes was not strictly true, but may be understandable when it is recalled how long and how hard she had resisted the pressure for it.

Meanwhile, Davison sealed the execution warrant as soon as he received it, and convened the leading councillors (3 February). At Burghley's prompting they agreed on its immediate implementation without further reference to the queen. The warrant was sent up to Fotheringhay and practical preparations made. Mary was informed on the evening of 7 February that she was to be executed. She was ready for the news and took it calmly, stressing her view that she was being condemned for her religion. On the morning of 8 February 1587 she mounted the scaffold in the great hall of Fotheringhay, attended by two of her women servants. Denied the services of a Catholic priest, she refused protestant ministrations with dignity and made her own Latin prayers. The axe severed her head with three blows.

Posthumous reputation Mary's execution prompted a howl of protest from Catholic Europe, presenting her as a martyr for her faith. This was offset by the grim English insistence that she had died for treason, not religion. There were mass demonstrations of sorrow in Paris, and of joy in London. The execution achieved its purpose, since plots against Elizabeth's life ceased. It is sometimes said that the Spanish Armada (1588) was a reprisal for Mary's death, but plans for the Armada were already well under way.

Contrasting images of the dead queen—a tragic Catholic martyr, or a murderous traitor—were sharply etched. Yet the images soon became blurred. There were occasional Catholic reports of miracles at Mary's tomb, but her dubious past ruled out canonization. As the prospect of her son's succession grew during the 1590s, Catholic writers deserted her cause while protestants discreetly glossed over her faults. When James at last succeeded Elizabeth, Mary's image was at its most anodyne. In 1606 he commissioned a tomb for his mother in Westminster Abbey; her remains were transferred there from Peterborough Cathedral (where she had been buried on 1 August 1587) on the tomb's completion in 1612. Her verse epitaph by the crypto-Catholic earl of Northampton avoided controversy. James's successful succession, by drawing a line under the succession disputes of the 1590s, nevertheless enabled Catholics to revive the notion of Mary as martyr—an image which enjoyed fitful circulation for much of the seventeenth century.

There matters rested until the revolution of 1688, when dynastic strife intensified partisan arguments about Mary. Buchanan was translated, while Jacobite sympathizers began to expose his untruths. But the polite muting of religious passion among the most prominent eighteenth-century writers soon led to the creation of an 'unfortunate' Mary. There was keen debate over the casket letters, but those on both sides could treat her as a victim of circumstances, or perhaps of her own tragically flawed nature—a precursor of the later flowering of Marian romanticism. Religion regained prominence in nineteenth-century views of the queen. Assaults on her once again tended to come from protestants—or, in the prominent case of J. A. Froude, from a disillusioned former Anglo-Catholic. Religion also anchored Mary's story to a broader historical perspective: the triumph of the Reformation, of Anglo-Scottish union, and ultimately of the Enlightenment and modern progress. In the leading British fictional representation of her, that of Sir Walter Scott in *The Abbot* (1820), her Catholicism was emphasized. While romantically alluring, she was also ultimately wrong—a historical dead end.

But a more modern Mary was already under construction, a Mary who could float free of long-term historical context. In his play *Maria Stuart* (1800), Friedrich Schiller created the first dramatically satisfying Mary, both guilty and sympathetic. When he allowed her to meet Elizabeth, as everyone wished she had, he personalized their story. The broader significance of the two queens for subsequent British history never concerned Schiller's German audience, and it declined in British significance too. Scott's novel led to one opera, but Schiller's play inspired three, including Donizetti's classic *Maria Stuarda* (1835). Schiller gave Mary a stage triumph in death over Elizabeth which showed that the latter, however charismatic in her own way, could no longer match Mary's romantic appeal. For the liberal Schiller, the passionless Elizabeth and her scheming sidekick Burghley were archetypes of repression and tyranny. This was a crucial reversal, since for Buchanan it had precisely been Mary's unbridled passions that made *her* a tyrant; his ideal would have been Elizabeth's rational triumph over desire. The 'virgin queen' now symbolized only sterility and frustration, while Mary's sexual activity was celebrated as life-affirming.

This gave Mary one of her most important modern roles: as a popular image in women's fantasy. In the twentieth century this required her to have a worthy sexual partner, and she was duly provided with an upgraded Bothwell, a masterful, wickedly attractive libertine. Neither Scott nor Schiller had put Bothwell on stage, but he now came to dominate Mary's story and his alleged romantic and sexual relationship with her was embroidered. Buchanan had asserted that Bothwell had raped Mary in September 1566; to him this was just another piece of mud to sling, but novelists fused it imaginatively with the real rape at Dunbar to perpetrate a genre of ugly romances (including one of literary merit, Margaret Irwin's *The Gay Galliard*, 1941) in which Mary responded passionately to Bothwell's violent advances.

Conclusions Twentieth-century research on Mary was marked by the decline of religious partisanship and by fresh directions in scholarship. Many traditional assumptions were overturned by M. H. Armstrong Davison's detailed textual analysis of the casket letters in 1965. By demonstrating how far they had been manipulated by Mary's accusers, he freed scholars from any obligation to believe in her guilt over Darnley's murder. Antonia Fraser seized the opportunity thus presented and produced a detailed and highly sympathetic biography in 1969 which has enjoyed both a wide general readership and a high reputation among scholars ever since. The studies of noble politics published by Gordon Donaldson between 1965 and 1983 offered factional, rather than primarily religious, interpretations of the conflicts of Mary's reign, and demonstrated the extent of Scottish support for her after her deposition and even into the 1580s. The fourth centenary of Mary's death produced two new scholarly contributions in 1988. Jenny Wormald attempted to reduce the issue to one of Mary's personal incompetence, while Michael Lynch edited a collection of essays taking a more nuanced view of her; Lynch later produced a review article comprehensively rebutting Wormald's central claims.

Meanwhile the commanding position enjoyed by Fraser's biography among general readers has permitted sympathy with Mary's tragedy to flourish unchecked. Fraser's own conclusions were generally judicious, but were so presented as to allow the emergence of a popular Mary–Elizabeth story that unequivocally favoured Mary. This was noticeable, for instance, in the film *Mary, Queen of Scots* (1971), with its Schiller-inspired meetings between the two queens. A jealous Elizabeth tricked Mary into an unsuitable marriage; she imprisoned her unjustly; she (or her scheming ministers) framed her deceitfully over the Babington plot; she executed her although lacking jurisdiction to do so.

But one can respect Mary and even regret her execution while still recognizing that this is mostly unfair to Elizabeth. She did not want the Darnley marriage. The evidence of Mary's plotting, however obtained, was genuine—and if Mary's plots had succeeded she would have become queen of England and Elizabeth would have been killed. This is also relevant to the legalities of Mary's captivity; freeing her would have harmed English political interests. Mary was well aware of the rules of the political game in which she was engaged, and in claiming that Elizabeth had no jurisdiction over her, she was playing another card in that game. She lost the game, but need not lose our respect: Elizabeth won, but by the rules of the game she won fairly. Elizabeth was the more skilled player, and also held more of the cards. However, the game itself was not of their making; both queens saw themselves as being forced by circumstances into enmity. In happier times they might have met and been friends. Mary's deep and long-standing wish for such a friendship is a striking memorial to her character.

One should thus turn the spotlight away from Elizabeth and towards her ministers, associates, and protégés: Burghley, Walsingham, Moray, Morton, and ultimately James VI. They shared a coherent Anglo-Scottish religious and political programme. Could Mary ever have found a place in it? Critics have argued that her downfall was due primarily to her own errors, notably her marriage to Darnley, flight to England, and plotting against Elizabeth. But a cannier politician than Mary could have been forgiven for misreading the tortuous English diplomacy of early 1565. Flight to England looks less foolish in the light of Elizabeth's repeated efforts to negotiate her restoration, abandoned only in 1570. Mary's plots were all undertaken after she had seen other avenues close; she knew the risks, but would not abandon hope. She was not an outstanding politician, but she scored some notable successes: integrating herself with the Scottish regime in 1561, seeing off the Moray–Hamilton challenge in 1565, and outmanoeuvring the Riccio murderers in 1566. Her personal breakdown in 1567 can hardly be called a political error, however disastrous its consequences.

From the moment that Mary returned to Scotland, she was in a minefield. The Anglo-Scottish protestant establishment found a French Catholic queen with a claim to the English throne highly inconvenient. It tolerated her at first because it had to, but it allowed her minimal room for her own initiatives, as the reaction to her second marriage showed. After she had angered the establishment twice—over Darnley and over the plan to forfeit Moray early in 1566—her enemies were determined to pounce on even the slightest mistake. Her sex, too, was obviously crucial.

Darnley was a problem only because a male consort, however useless and insufferable, was expected to play a political role. Darnley's tragedy was that he never had the chance to grow up. Mary's was quite different. Any woman ruler, even Elizabeth, had to appeal to the emotions of a patriarchal world; Mary did so forcefully. Her charisma, intelligence, and determination to maintain her status were frequently noted and impossible to ignore. The English parliament of 1572 complained that she had written to Norfolk with 'great discourses in matters of State (more than woman's wit doth commonly reach unto)' (Neale, 1.249). Her religion was just tolerant and flexible enough to make her a passable ruler of a protestant Scotland, and a plausible candidate to rule a protestant England; but it was still the wrong religion and her persistent attempts to advance her career were fraught with danger. A woman's political career also depended on marriage, and many men wanted to marry her. Yet few were politically suitable—certainly not Darnley, Bothwell, or Norfolk. In late sixteenth-century Britain an attractive, talented, and ambitious woman with Mary's background was bound to make more enemies than friends. Only by jettisoning ambitions, principles, or both would she stand a chance of success—and failure could easily be fatal. Mary remained true to herself, and paid the price. Ultimately one is left with a historical Mary remarkably close to the popular image: a romantic tragedy queen. JULIAN GOODARE

Sources CSP Scot. · Lettres, instructions et mémoires de Marie Stuart, reine d'Écosse, ed. A. Labanoff, 7 vols. (1844) · J. Anderson, ed., Collections relating to the history of Mary, queen of Scotland, 4 vols. (1727–8) · Reg. PCS, 1st ser., vol. 1 · T. Thomson, ed., A diurnal of remarkable occurrents that have passed within the country of Scotland, Bannatyne Club, 43 (1833) · Memoirs of his own life by Sir James Melville of Halhill, ed. T. Thomson, Bannatyne Club, 18 (1827) · J. H. Pollen, ed., Papal negotiations with Mary queen of Scots during her reign in Scotland, 1561–1567, Scottish History Society, 37 (1901) · C. Nau, The history of Mary Stewart from the murder of Riccio until her flight into England, ed. J. Stevenson (1883) [Mary's own memoirs as told by her secretary] · R. Keith, History of the affairs of church and state in Scotland from the beginning of the Reformation to the year 1568, ed. J. P. Lawson and C. J. Lyon, Spottiswoode Society, 1 (1844) [incl. numerous documents] · J. Stevenson, ed., Selections … illustrating the reign of Mary, queen of Scotland, MDXLIII–MDLXVIII, Maitland Club, 41 (1837) · J. B. A. T. Teulet, ed., Relations politiques de la France et de l'Espagne avec l'Écosse au XVIème siècle: papiers d'état, pièces et documents inédits, new edn, 5 vols. (Paris, 1862) · John Knox's History of the Reformation in Scotland, ed. W. C. Dickinson, 2 vols. (1949) · J. H. Pollen, ed., Mary, queen of Scots, and the Babington plot, Scottish History Society, 2nd ser., 3 (1922) · Lord Herries [John Maxwell], Historical memoirs of the reign of Mary queen of Scots, ed. R. Pitcairn, Abbotsford Club, 6 (1836) · I. B. Cowan, ed., The enigma of Mary Stuart (1971) [anthology of extracts from contemporary and later writings] · W. A. Gatherer, ed., The tyrannous reign of Mary Stewart: George Buchanan's account (1958) · The historie and cronicles of Scotland … by Robert Lindesay of Pitscottie, ed. A. J. G. Mackay, 3 vols., STS, 42–3, 60 (1899–1911) · A. F. Steuart, ed., Trial of Mary, queen of Scots, 2nd edn (1951) · James I, The workes of the most high and mighty prince, James, by the grace of God kinge of Great Brittaine, France and Ireland (1616) · A. Fraser, Mary, queen of Scots (1969) · M. Lynch, ed., Mary Stewart: queen in three kingdoms (1988) [also published as Innes Review, 38 (1987)] · G. Donaldson, All the queen's men: power and politics in Mary Stewart's Scotland (1983) · M. Loughlin, 'The career of Maitland of Lethington, c.1526–1573', PhD diss., U. Edin., 1991 · M. H. Armstrong Davison, The casket letters (1965) · G. Donaldson, The first trial of Mary, queen of Scots (1969) [the conference of 1568–9 incl. text of Moray's 'Book of articles'] · E. Furgol, 'The progresses of Mary, queen of Scots, 1542–1548 and 1561–1568', Proceedings of the Society of Antiquaries of Scotland, 117 (1987), 219–31 [with daily itinerary in attached microfiche] · J. D. Leader, Mary, queen of Scots, in captivity (1880) · J. E. Phillips, Images of a queen: Mary Stuart in sixteenth-century literature (1964) · R. H. Mahon, The tragedy of Kirk o' Field (1930) · C. Read, Mr Secretary Walsingham and the policy of Queen Elizabeth, 3 vols. (1925) · M. Levine, The early Elizabethan succession question, 1558–1568 (1966) · J. E. Neale, Elizabeth I and her parliaments, 2 vols. (1953–7) · J. E. Lewis, Mary, queen of Scots: romance and nation (1998) [literary works about her, to c.1900] · P. Collinson, The English captivity of Mary, queen of Scots, Sheffield History Pamphlets (1987) [incl. chronology and documents] · M. Lynch, 'Queen Mary's triumph: the baptismal celebrations at Stirling in December 1566', SHR, 69 (1990), 1–21 · H. Smailes and D. Thomson, The queen's image: a celebration of Mary, queen of Scots, Scottish National Portrait Gallery (1987) · J. Wormald, Mary, queen of Scots: a study in failure (1988) · M. Lynch, 'Mary, queen of Scots: a new case for the prosecution', Journal of Ecclesiastical History, 41 (1990), 69–73 [review of Wormald] · M. Lee, 'The daughter of debate: Mary, queen of Scots, after 400 years', SHR, 68 (1989), 70–79 · J. E. A. Dawson, 'Mary, queen of Scots, Lord Darnley, and Anglo-Scottish relations in 1565', International History Review, 8 (1986), 1–24 · A. S. MacNalty, Mary, queen of Scots: the daughter of debate (1960) [has appendix on her medical history]

Archives NL Scot., letters | BL, Cotton MSS, letters and MSS · BL, Sloane MSS, letters and papers [mainly copies] · Hatfield House, Hertfordshire, letters and MSS · Morgan L., letters · Scottish Catholic Archives, Edinburgh, letters to James Beaton · W. Sussex RO, letters to Elizabeth I

Likenesses coins, 1542–65 (electrotype replicas), Scot. NPG · crayon drawing, 1555, Musée Condé, Chantilly, France · double portrait, silver medal, 1558 (with François II), Scot. NPG · P. Sacquio, bronze bust, c.1559–1560, Scot. NPG · F. Clouet, two drawings, c.1560, Bibliothèque Nationale, Paris · miniature, 1560–65, Uffizi, Florence · double portrait, silver medal, 1565 (with Darnley), Scot. NPG · miniature, c.1575–1580, St Mary's College, Blairs, Aberdeen · N. Hilliard, miniature, c.1578, Royal Collection [see illus.] · double portrait, oils, 1583 (with James I), Blair Castle, Tayside region · oils, c.1604–1620, Trustees of St Mary's College, Blairs, Aberdeen · C. and W. Cure, alabaster tomb effigy, c.1606–1616, Westminster Abbey; replicas, NPG, Scot. NPG · watercolour drawing, c.1608 (The execution of Mary), Scot. NPG · oils, c.1610 (Sheffield or Oudry type; after N. Hilliard), Hatfield House, Hertfordshire; versions, Hardwick Hall, Derbyshire; NPG · oils, c.1610–1615, Scot. NPG · J. Barry, group portrait, etching, pubd 1808 (after J. Barry), NG Ire. · A. Duncan, double portrait, line engraving, 1830 (with Chastelard; after H. S. Fredelle), NG Ire. · D. Allen, pencil and chalk drawing, Scot. NPG · D. Allen, pencil, ink, and wash drawing, Scot. NPG · J. Primavera, medal, BM; electrotype, NPG, Scot. NPG · chalk drawing, Scot. NPG · double portrait, oils (with Darnley; after a miniature type, c.1660–1665), Hardwick Hall, Derbyshire · line engraving, NPG · oils, Scot. NPG · oils (after F. Clouet), Scot. NPG · oils (Anamorphosis), Scot. NPG · pen-and-ink drawing, NPG · pencil and chalk drawing, Scot. NPG

Mary, princess royal (1631–1660), princess of Orange, consort of William II, was born at St James's Palace on 4 November 1631, the eldest daughter of King *Charles I (1600–1649) and his queen, *Henrietta Maria (1609–1669). Since at first it seemed unlikely she would survive, she was baptized in a sober ceremony by William Laud, bishop of London, on the same day. Her childhood was spent under the tuition of Jean Ker, née Drummond, countess of Roxburghe, and she and her siblings lived alternately at Richmond and in London.

Mary, princess royal (1631–1660), by Adriaen Hanneman, 1656?

The marriage to William of Orange, 1641 On 2 May 1641, only nine years old, Mary was married to William II (1626–1650), son of Frederick Henry, prince of Orange. The tentative overtures between the English and Spanish in the late 1630s caused much alarm in the Dutch republic, as it was feared this would greatly jeopardize Dutch trade at sea. In 1639 an ambassador was sent from The Hague to England to discuss a possible treaty between England and the United Provinces, and in January 1640 another Dutch envoy, Johan Polyander van Kerckhoven, Lord Heenvliet, arrived in London to negotiate a match between William and Mary. Should Charles accept this marriage, it was reasoned, the Spanish king Philip IV, set on a match between his son and Mary, would certainly not be satisfied with Charles's second daughter Elizabeth as an alternative. Charles, however, proposed not Mary but Elizabeth as William's future wife, and after some deliberation this proposal was approved both by the Dutch authorities and Frederick Henry, as well as by the English parliament. Another Dutch embassy crossed the North Sea in order to discuss the conditions of the marriage treaty, but once in London it appeared Charles had changed his mind. The English–Spanish negotiations having failed, and Spain backing out because of troubles in Portugal and Catalonia, he now offered his eldest daughter to William, on the condition of a political alliance with the Dutch republic. This, however, was not accepted by the Dutch, who feared they might be implicated in the troubles between king and parliament, and in the end Charles had to succumb. His wish that Mary should stay in England until she had reached the age of twelve, when, according to English

marriage laws, she officially had to agree to the match, was granted by the Dutch. The marriage articles stipulated that Mary's dowry from England should be £40,000, while the prince of Orange agreed that Mary and members of her court were allowed to exercise religion according to the rites of the Church of England; that she would keep all her English servants while any vacant post would be filled from England; that all household expenses would be paid for by her husband; that in addition she would receive £1500 per annum and that her Dutch dower would be £10,000 a year with two residences, were her husband to die. Prince William and his entourage of 250 people arrived in Gravesend on 19 April 1641, and some days later he was received in Whitehall Palace, presenting members of the royal party with diamonds, pearls, and other jewellery, worth almost £23,000. The couple were married by the bishop of Ely in the Chapel Royal at Whitehall Palace on 2 May. The groom, wearing a suit of crimson velvet, was accompanied by the Dutch ambassadors, while Mary, dressed in a silver robe, her train borne by sixteen ladies dressed in white satin, was led in by her brothers Charles, prince of Wales (later *Charles II), and James, duke of York (the future *James II). A Roman Catholic, Henrietta Maria did not attend the Anglican ceremony, but watched the wedding from an upstairs gallery. Afterwards, the party dined, and later in the evening William was led to Mary's bedchamber, where the royal family had assembled. For an hour and a half, the young couple lay beside each other on the bed, the princess wrapped from head to toe in a sheet, and then the prince was taken back to his own quarters. A few days later he dutifully reported to his parents that 'although we were at first very solemn towards each other, now we feel more at ease; I find her to be more beautiful than the painting'—a Van Dyck portrait of the princess that had been sent to Holland before—'I love her very much and I believe she loves me too' (Groen van Prinsterer, 2nd ser., 3.460). On 29 May os (8 June ns) William returned to the Netherlands.

Princess royal in the Dutch republic, 1642–1650 Less than a year later, in March 1642, Mary followed her husband. She was brought over by Henrietta Maria, who, under the pretext of accompanying her daughter, was bringing large quantities of jewels and plate, planning to trade them in the Netherlands for money and weapons for Charles's campaigns. Mary, Henrietta Maria, and their train of almost 400 courtiers were received with great pomp. They were met by Prince William, *Elizabeth, the exiled queen of Bohemia, and some of her children, and escorted into The Hague, where cannon were fired and all the streets were richly decorated. In the following weeks they travelled to various Dutch towns and cities, and in every one of them they were entertained on a grandiose scale.

In February 1644 Mary was officially installed in her conjugal position, fulfilling from that moment onwards all functions of state, and in March 1647, after Frederick Henry had died and William had succeeded his father as stadholder of the main provinces of the republic, she became princess of Orange. With her father-in-law, the prince of Orange, Mary had stood on good terms, while her aunt Elizabeth of Bohemia quickly became one of her greatest friends and allies in The Hague, but with her mother-in-law, Amalia van Solms, relations were strained from the beginning.

Mary's royal status gave her precedence over members of the house of Orange, which on several occasions caused friction at the court. Also, Amalia bitterly complained about the sumptuous lifestyle of her son and his wife, and Mary's ladies had been overheard saying that 'it was time the princess should run the country', because Amalia had done so long enough (Visser, 431). The 'English' match was often discussed, and greatly regretted, by members of the Orange entourage, and in 1648 Amalia was reported to be 'hateful of all things English' (ibid., 540). When, in 1648, and again in 1649, the prince of Wales and the duke of York came to The Hague to seek support for the royalist cause, William not only lent them large sums of money, but also paid for all their expenses, which led Amalia and others to object that supporting four households would certainly bankrupt the house of Orange.

Meanwhile, the fact that Mary did not get pregnant was another worrisome matter. Her relationship with her husband was never cordial, and the couple did not spend much time together. After a miscarriage in October 1647, it was rumoured she could not conceive again, and in 1649 one of Mary's servants was dismissed because she had given the princess something 'to prevent her from having children' (Visser, 700). However, when on her nineteenth birthday, on 14 November 1650 NS, Mary gave birth to a son, there was not much ground for celebration. Eight days before, on 6 November, her husband had died of smallpox.

Widow and mother, 1650–1660 On 15 January 1651 NS the young prince was baptized in the Great Church of The Hague, his mother being absent from the ceremony. Only a few days after his birth discord had risen between Mary and Amalia, his mother preferring to name the baby Charles, and his grandmother intent on naming him William—which name eventually was decided upon [see William III and II (1650–1702)]. The 'royal' character of the baptism was frowned upon by some, who did not take well the fact that 'halberdiers were riding on the side of the Prince's coach, and also that the Child was dressed in fur, black on white' (Royal Archives, The Hague, account of the baptism 1651, inv. A-16-I-3).

Other disputes arose soon after the burial of Mary's husband on 8 March 1651 NS. First, it had to be decided whether William should be elected as stadholder, succeeding his father, but the states general, despite petitions from both Amalia and Mary, decided against this and resolved to take over all offices themselves. Second, the guardianship over the young prince proved to be a cause of such conflict that it took the supreme court to settle the matter in August 1651. The court decided upon the appointment of three guardians: Mary, with one vote, on one side, and Amalia and the elector of Brandenburg, sharing one vote, on the other side. Under supervision of these guardians, the administration of William's estate would be executed by the Nassau estates council. Not only

was Mary thought too young and too ignorant of national affairs to become sole guardian, but Amalia in particular suspected that 'her Daughter-in-law … will spend all his estate upon her family and party; that shee and they have undone her son' (*Mercurius Politicus*, 37, 603).

Although after 1651 the support for the English royalist exiles in Holland had diminished and it was thought that the 'great disbanding of the English [should] be attributed to the death of the Prince of Orange, whose onely study and indeavor was to win the hearts of the strangers wholly to himself' (*Mercurius Politicus*, 38, 616), Mary tried to assist them financially whenever she could. She was supported by her faithful courtiers, staunch royalists and Anglicans themselves, such as her personal chaplain Thomas Browne, who would never allow Mary to attend services in the English Reformed church in The Hague. Especially the dominating influence of Catherine Stanhope (later countess of Chesterfield), first lady of honour, and her Dutch husband, Lord Heenvliet, superintendent of Mary's household, was greatly feared, by both the Dutch and the English. Sir Edward Hyde, chancellor to Charles II, despaired in 1653 that the princess would not take counsel from anyone but 'subjects herself solely to Henfleet and his lady' (*Clarendon State Papers*, 2.169), and Mary indeed preferred staying at their country house in Teylingen over her own residence in The Hague.

Cromwell's spies reported that royalists were plotting against him at The Hague, 'which is a nest of malignant vypers. The princess royall's and queen of Bohemia's court nourishes those creatures' (Thurloe, *State papers*, 2.344). The outbreak of the First Anglo-Dutch War in 1652 temporarily roused Dutch sympathy for the royalist party, but the peace treaty of May 1654 stipulated that enemies of England would not be tolerated in Holland. Having hosted her brothers, Charles II, James, duke of York, and *Henry, duke of Gloucester, on several occasions in The Hague, Teylingen, and her own country estates during the early 1650s and in 1654 (and as she was to again in 1657), Mary was now officially forbidden to receive them on Dutch territory. From that moment onwards she travelled extensively in France, Germany, and the Spanish Netherlands to meet her brothers and the exiled English court whenever she could. During these travels rumours circulated in Europe about a possible marriage between Mary and several candidates, among whom were the king of Sweden, George Villiers, second duke of Buckingham, the dukes of Savoy and Brunswick, and Prince Radziwill of Poland. Her everyday movements were duly reported in newspapers and in intelligence sent to Cromwell, informing him that she had gone, for example, in July 1654, to take the waters at Spa, where she was to meet Charles, and that she then would travel with him to Aachen and Cologne. In the summer of 1655 she visited her brother at his Cologne residence, staying until November, and in January 1656 she was royally received in Paris by her mother and the French court: 'On the 16th [February] the grand Balet, called *Psyche* or the Power of Love, was danced at the Louvre, in presence of the Queen, the Princess of Orange … with many great Lords and Ladies' (L. Hotson,

The Commonwealth and Restoration Stage, 1928, 137). She returned to The Hague in February 1657, almost a year later.

By that time the conflict between Mary and her mother-in-law had flared up again, focusing on Mary's claims to the regency over the princedom of Orange in the south of France. William II had died without an official will, but in a sealed letter of 24 February 1649 NS to Count Dohna, governor of Orange, he had left instructions that, in case of his death, only Mary's orders should be followed. Dohna—a protégé of Amalia's—had ignored the instructions, pledging loyalty instead to young Prince William, while Mary had found a copy of the letter when she opened a chest containing her husband's papers, which had been sealed immediately after his death. Defending her rights, and firmly opposing Dohna's position, she had assented in August 1651 to submit the case to the court of Holland and the supreme court, which, in February 1652, dismissed her claims. During her visit to Paris in 1656 she asked Louis XIV to intervene; he denounced Dohna and his followers as rebels, and on 24 August 1658 NS the *parlement* of Orange declared Mary sole regent, which position she formally accepted in October. When, in 1659, and again in 1660, Louis XIV sent troops to Orange, the states general forced Mary to recall the French intervention, but she was too late, for in March 1660 Orange capitulated to Louis's troops. The conflict would continue after Mary's death, resulting ultimately in the loss of Orange to France.

Death and aftermath On 14 May 1660 NS Mary notified the Dutch government that the English parliament had invited her brother to the throne of England. Together with her young son and her brothers she took part in the celebrations in Breda and The Hague, and witnessed Charles's embarkation for England from Scheveningen. The Restoration placed both Mary and her son—now fifth in succession to the throne of England—in a completely different position in the Dutch republic. In the following weeks they were officially received and entertained in several Dutch cities, and in Amsterdam allegorical pageants were staged, representing the tragedies and triumphs of the house of Stuart. Encouraged by the change in attitude towards her, Mary once again asked the Dutch states to consider reinstating her son in his father's dignities, referring to a similar request of her brother to the state pensionary of Holland. Although some provinces looked upon her demands favourably, Holland required time for deliberation. Meanwhile, Mary made plans to travel to England, confessing to Charles that to stay in the Netherlands would be 'the greatest punishment of this world' (Thurloe, *State papers*, 1.662), but when she left in September 1660, only the education of the young prince had been officially settled. Even before arriving, she learned that her brother Henry, duke of Gloucester, had suddenly died of smallpox, and thus her visit was deeply coloured by mourning. Her only public act was the recognition of £10,000 presented to her by parliament in November, while in the same month Charles appointed a committee to investigate her claims to the yet unpaid dower of £40,000.

A Dutch embassy, sent over to congratulate Charles on his restoration and to renew the alliance between England and the Dutch republic, sought Mary's assistance when some difficulties over the treaty arose in late November. However, she was already feeling ill, and when it became clear that she was suffering from either measles or smallpox, court physicians started to bleed her frequently, causing her to take a turn for the worse. Anxious to settle her affairs, Mary dictated her will to her secretary Nicolas Oudaert on 24 December 1660 OS (3 January 1661 NS). Asked repeatedly what she wanted with regard to her son, she answered that she trusted her brother and mother completely with his well-being: 'My greatest pain is to depart from him. Oh my child, give him my blessing' (Royal Archives, The Hague, report Oudaert 1661, inv. G1-6II-H, fol. 41). The same evening, after one last bloodletting incision, according to an eyewitness, 'her eyes did look so dim that it was obvious to all she was dying. After that, she had no signs of great pain, but every instant did visibly decay, till she lost her senses' (Green, 6.328). She was buried, as she had wished, near her brother Henry, in Henry VII's chapel, Westminster Abbey, on 29 December 1660. In the same year a double biography of Mary and Henry was published by Thomas Manley, who lamented their untimely death:

> What raging Seas of dangers, and what storms,
> What foaming billows of Tempestuous harmes:
> The royal Issue has escap'd! Then ar'
> The *Fates* more cruel in their Peace, than *War*!
> (Manley, 114)

Immediately after her death Oudaert started settling Mary's estate, discovering that already many valuables had disappeared: Lady Stanhope had taken all jewellery, plate, and linen from the bedchamber, while the duchess of York was seen wearing Mary's pearls. His first concern was to separate Mary's own possessions—to be inherited by her brother and mother—from jewellery that had once belonged to her husband, because 'my Sonnes Jewels, being those I found in his Fathers Cabinet expressed in a note of them to be delivered to him' should be returned to Holland (Royal Archives, The Hague, will of princess royal, inv. A15-XIII-1). He drew up a detailed 'Representation of estates, concerns and debts', including payment due to all Mary's servants (PRO, SP 84/164, fols. 118–24), and specified all moneys borrowed by her father and brother from the prince of Orange in the 1640s, as well as the outstanding dower, to be restituted with interest. In 1667 these affairs were still not settled. Although in her will Mary had named Charles II as guardian over her son William, this was accepted neither by the other guardians nor by the states of Holland, who feared the English influence over the Dutch prince. After long, and often bitter, deliberations, it was decided in September 1661 that Amalia van Solms would have custody over the young prince.

Dutch historians, in particular those writing from a republican point of view, have, for the most part, evaluated Mary's significance in history in rather negative terms. Her marriage to William II in 1641 caused the involuntary involvement of the princes of Orange and the Dutch republic in the English troubles of the 1640s. This put a heavy strain on the finances of the house of Orange, while the interference of Mary and her English councillors in Dutch politics of the 1650s is generally considered to have had disastrous consequences, as in the case of Orange. Her Dutch contemporaries judged her for her 'royal' arrogance, her obstinacy to accept anything Dutch, and her refusal to learn the language, and after her death state pensionary John de Witt was appalled by the fact she had not named her son universal heir, leaving him 'not even a stiver' (Geyl, 133). On the other hand, her English contemporaries and biographers praised her continuous support to the royalist case of her brother, and it was said that her love and zeal in this respect 'deserved to be engraved with a diamond pen upon tablets of brass, that its memory might never pass away' (Green, 6.188). As she died before the age of thirty, her most important accomplishment came posthumously when, in 1689, her son became William III of England. MARIKA KEBLUSEK

Sources M. A. E. Green, *Lives of the princesses of England*, 6 (1855) · Thurloe, *State papers* · J. Visser, ed., *Gloria parendi: dagboeken van Willem Frederik, stadhouder van Friesland, Groningen en Drenthe, 1643–1649, 1651–1654* (The Hague, 1995) · *Calendar of the Clarendon state papers preserved in the Bodleian Library*, ed. O. Ogle and others, 5 vols. (1869–1970) · T. Manley, *A short view of the lives of those illustrious princes, Henry, Duke of Gloucester, and Mary* (1661) · P. Geyl, *Oranje en Stuart, 1641–1672*, 2nd impression (Zeist, 1963) · G. Groen van Prinsterer, ed., *Archives ou correspondance inédite de la maison d'Orange-Nassau* (Leiden, 1835–1915) · *Mercurius Politicus* (13–27 Feb 1651) · PRO, SP 84/116, 164 · Archives of Nassau Estates Council, National Archives, The Hague · Archives Frederick Henry, Royal Archives, The Hague · Archives William II, Royal Archives, The Hague [incl. Mary Stuart] · Archives William III, Royal Archives, The Hague · Bodl. Oxf., Clarendon MSS · Bodl. Oxf., MS Rawl. 155 · S. Groenveld, *Verlopend getij: de Nederlandse republiek en de Engelse burgeroorlog, 1640–1646* (Dieren, 1984)

Archives Royal Archives, The Hague, Archives William II

Likenesses A. Van Dyck, group portrait, oils, 1634? (three eldest children of Charles I), Galleria Sabauda, Turin · A. Van Dyck, group portrait, oils, 1635 (three eldest children of Charles I), Royal Collection · A. Van Dyck, group portrait, oils, 1637 (five eldest children of Charles I), Royal Collection · C. Johnson, oils, 1639, NPG · studio of Van Dyck, oils, 1641, Gov. Art Coll. · G. van Honthorst, oils, 1647, Rijksmuseum, Amsterdam · G. van Honthorst, oils, c.1647, Ashdown House, Oxfordshire · A. Hanneman, oils, c.1650–1655, Syon House, Brentford, Middlesex · G. van Honthorst, oils, 1652, Raadhuis, Breda, Netherlands · A. Hanneman, oils, c.1655, Royal Collection · B. van der Helst, oils, c.1655–1660, Rijksmuseum, Amsterdam · A. Hanneman, portrait, 1656?, priv. coll. [*see illus.*] · A. Hanneman, oils, 1659, Scot. NPG · A. Hanneman, oils, 1660, Royal Collection · A. Hanneman, oils, c.1664, Mauritshuis, The Hague · A. Hanneman, oils, Holkham Hall, Norfolk · A. Van Dyck, portrait (wedding), Rijksmuseum, Amsterdam · engravings · medals and coins

Wealth at death approx. £50,000, but debts of even larger amount: *CSP for., 1661*; PRO, SP 84/116

Mary [Mary of Modena] (**1658–1718**), queen of England, Scotland, and Ireland, consort of James II and VII, was born Maria Beatrice Anna Margherita Isabella d'Este on 25 September/5 October 1658 at the Palazzo Ducale, Modena, Italy, the first of two surviving children of Alfonso IV d'Este, duke of Modena and Reggio (1634–1662), and his

Mary [of Modena] (**1658–1718**), by Willem Wissing, c.1685

wife, Laura (1639–1687), daughter of Giralamo Martinozzi and his wife, Margherita Mazarini. Through her maternal grandmother Mary Beatrice was a great-niece of Cardinal Mazarin. On the death of her father on 6/16 July 1662 and the succession of her infant brother, Francesco II, to the dukedom, her mother became regent of the duchy and her uncle, Prince Rinaldo d'Este, her joint guardian. Her education was entrusted to the nuns of the local Carmelite convent. She later recalled with pleasure the summers she had spent at d'Este's summer palace of Sassuolo. The family was well aware that a marriageable daughter was a potential diplomatic bonus. Following the death of Henrietta, duchess of Orléans, in 1670, Mary Beatrice's great-uncle Cardinal d'Este hinted to Cardinal d'Estrées that she might make a suitable second wife for Orléans. Even so, there was an assumption that she would probably enter the local Convent of the Visitation and she herself believed that she had a vocation.

Marriage, 1673 The future of the young Mary Beatrice was transformed by the death of *James, duke of York's first duchess, Anne Hyde, in March 1671. York's wish to remarry was a matter of the utmost dynastic importance. The growing likelihood that Charles II's wife, Catherine of Braganza, would never bear any children made it ever more probable that any surviving son born to York's future wife would eventually inherit the British throne. That the newly converted York was determined to choose a Catholic bride meant that the marriage was bound to be controversial. His groom of the stole, the second earl of Peterborough, was appointed to investigate the various candidates. Klaudia Felizitas, daughter of the late Archduke Ferdinand Karl of the Tyrol (who instead married

Emperor Leopold I); Marie Anna of Württemberg, daughter of Prince Ulrich of Neuenburg; Elizabeth, widow of Louis Joseph, duc de Lorraine-Guise; and Eleonore Magdalene, daughter of the elector palatine of Pfalz Neuburg (and Leopold I's future third wife), were among the possibilities considered.

Peterborough, on the advice of the Modenese representative in Paris, Abbé Rizzini, instead favoured Mary Beatrice, a choice which was also acceptable to Louis XIV. Initial indications from Modena were, however, unfavourable, either because the intention was to honour her wish to enter a convent or, more probably, because the king of Spain, Carlos II, was preferred as a bridegroom. Her aunt Leonora, sister of Alfonso IV, was promoted as one possible alternative bride for York and Mary Beatrice bluntly told Peterborough when she first met him that she would prefer to become a nun. In the end pressure applied by the French government in the person of the marquis de Dangeau persuaded the Duchess Laura to capitulate. The decision distressed her daughter who cried for several days on being informed of her fate. Several problems remained. Another of the bride's great-uncles, Cardinal Barberini, lobbied the pope, Clement X, for a dispensation to allow her to marry someone who had not yet publicly declared himself a Catholic, but objections were raised as to whether Mary Beatrice would be able to worship in public and about whether any children would be brought up as Catholics, and the pope recalled the dispensation at the last minute. The Modenese decided to proceed anyway, although the bishop of Modena refused to officiate. The wedding took place on 20/30 September 1673 in the Palazzo Ducale with Peterborough standing in as proxy for York. The new duchess set out for England five days later, her fifteenth birthday, accompanied by her mother and Prince Rinaldo.

What diplomatic importance the dukes of Modena enjoyed was as the traditional pro-French counterweight to the papacy in central Italy and it was understood by everyone that the marriage reinforced Charles II's alliance with Louis XIV. This made the match all the more unpopular in England. The House of Commons presented a protest to Charles II on 3 November 1673 asking him to cancel the marriage and the Fifth of November commemorations in London that year were much larger than usual. These protests were ignored on the grounds that the marriage had already taken place and suggestions that Mary Beatrice should delay her arrival were rejected.

The bride landed at Dover on 21 November and was greeted on the beach by her new husband. That evening, in the presence of the bride and groom, Bishop Crewe of Oxford formally acknowledged the validity of the ceremony which had taken place in Modena. Five days later the couple sailed up the Thames to Whitehall. The reception there was marred when a number of peeresses objected to the king's offer of a chair to the new duchess of York's mother. Such disputes over the right to sit in the royal presence often occurred during the visits of foreign royalty, but on this occasion the protest seemed designed to cast aspersions on the marriage, for the implication was

that the Duchess Laura was not royalty and that York had once again married beneath himself. The incident embarrassed the duchess, who cut short her stay in England.

Mary Beatrice was never considered a great beauty. In this respect, her most striking feature, her long, narrow face, was a disadvantage. Shortly before her arrival in England, Peterborough's nephew, Henry, Lord O'Brien, joked that parliament planned to reward his uncle by granting him a pair of spectacles. Those who distrusted her for political reasons were quick to criticize her appearance. Others were more positive. The third Viscount Conway thought that she was:

> a proper hansome Lady, she hath very good eyes, very good features, and a very good complexion, but she wants the Aire which should sett off all this, and having been bred in a Monastry, knows not how to set one foot before another with any gracefulnesse. (*Conway Letters*, ed. M. H. Nicolson and S. Hutton [1930], rev. edn, 1992, 376)

When she visited Cambridge in 1680 she was considered to be 'a very handsome, gracious looking person, pretty tall, not very big, black eyed, something pale-faced and a little outlandish-like swarthy colour' (*The Diary of Samuel Newton*, ed. J. E. Foster, 1890, 80). Similar comments were made five years later by the marquis d'Auvers who described her as tall and well proportioned, with a white complexion, beautiful eyes, and a mouth which was a little too large. The person least concerned by any shortcomings in her appearance was perhaps her husband, who had a reputation for choosing his mistresses for their personalities rather than their beauty. What he really wanted from his new wife was an heir.

Duchess of York, 1673–1685 Mary Beatrice soon settled into her new life at the English court. Charles II and Queen Catherine made her feel welcome and she got on well with her two stepdaughters, the elder of whom, Princess Mary, was only four years younger than she was. The countess of Peterborough was appointed as her groom of the stole as a reward to her husband for his efforts as royal matchmaker, and a number of her Italian servants were allowed to remain in the duchess's service. The one restriction placed on her was that, unlike Queen Catherine, she was required to conduct her religious devotions in private. This contravened the marriage treaty but, as her husband had still not publicly acknowledged his conversion, this had some advantages because the two of them were therefore able to attend private services together in her closet chapel. She was permitted the handful of Catholic priests she needed for that purpose.

There was no doubt that the duchess was fertile. The rate of her pregnancies during the first eleven years of her marriage bears comparison with the more celebrated fertility of her younger stepdaughter. As with Princess Anne, the problem was that the pregnancies ended in miscarriage or that the children were short-lived. A miscarriage in May 1674 was followed by the birth of a daughter on 9 January 1675. Much to Charles II's annoyance, the child was baptized Catherina Laura in secret by the duchess's Jesuit chaplain, Antonio Galli. The king insisted on a second Anglican baptism and all three of the later children born before 1685 had to be baptized as protestants. Mary Beatrice again miscarried on 14 May 1675 but became pregnant almost immediately, only to lose that child on 4 October in her shock at the death of Catherina Laura the previous day. A second daughter, Isabella, was born on 28 August 1676 and she survived until 1681. Moreover, on 7 November 1677, just three days after Princess Mary had married the prince of Orange, Mary Beatrice was delivered of the longed-for son. He was baptized Charles and granted the dukedom of Cambridge. For the next five weeks it seemed as if Princess Mary's marriage might, after all, prove to be of only secondary importance. The infant duke, however, died on 12 December.

For the time being Mary Beatrice was largely sheltered from political controversy. Burnet believed that she avoided any involvement in public affairs while her husband remained duke of York (*Bishop Burnet's History*, 2.43). It was instead those around the duchess who caused problems. Her French Jesuit confessor, Pierre de Saint-Germain, was forced to flee to France in November 1675 when he was accused of attacking another French priest, Hippolite Chastelet, alias de Luzancy, who had taken refuge in England after deciding to become a protestant. Her secretary, Edward Colman, had to be dismissed in December 1676 after he was caught leaking military secrets.

It was, however, always going to be only a matter of time before the duchess's life was to be thrown into confusion by a more substantial anti-Catholic panic. Any political moves against Catholics had to be seen as a potential threat to York and his wife, but what was not predictable was the series of revelations, deceits, and coincidences which conjured up the Popish Plot of 1678. This time bad luck, together with the resolve of their political opponents, came close to ruining them both. The seizure of Colman's papers on 29 September 1678 replaced the unsubstantiated allegations of Titus Oates with hard facts. As it happened, Mary Beatrice had already planned a trip to the Netherlands to visit Princess Mary. She and Princess Anne set out on 1 October and did not return until 16 October. The earl of Ossory accompanied them in order to brief the prince of Orange on the true nature of Oates's evidence. In Mary Beatrice's absence the full implications of Colman's letters became apparent, but the assumption that she and her husband must have known what Colman had been doing was to be the least imaginative part of the emerging conspiracy theory. It was also unfair. Colman's position as the duchess's secretary had been entirely nominal and the job had remained unfilled after his dismissal. The only definite secrets about Mary Beatrice that came to light in his papers were that she had used the disgraced Father Saint-Germain as a contact at the French court during the first half of 1676 to seek support for the proposal that her uncle should become a cardinal and to press the case of the English Carmelites at Antwerp who wished to move to Lille. Mary Beatrice's involvement in the broader conspiracy was often implied by York's critics but was one line of speculation which remained undeveloped. The duchess's absence in the Netherlands also provided her with the perfect alibi against any direct complicity in the death of Sir Edmund Berry Godfrey and by late December the evidence of Miles Prance had shifted attention to the supposed involvement in the plot by Catholic members of the queen's household.

When the new parliament met in March 1679, Charles II decided that it would be better if the duke and duchess left the country. They reached Brussels on 17/27 March and took up residence at the Hôtel de Bassigny, the house of the prince de Ligne. Three months later Mary Beatrice expressed disappointment that the trial of the five Catholic peers accused of complicity in the plot had been postponed, as she thought that they would each have been acquitted. She correctly foresaw that the dissolution of the 1679 parliament would not remove her husband's problems. Letters of denization were granted to her by the king on 24 September 1679 so that deeds confirming her jointure could be sealed on 26 and 27 September. This was intended to clarify her legal status at a time when her husband's future was uncertain. In the following month she and her husband were recalled to London, but almost immediately they were sent to Scotland. They arrived in Edinburgh on 24 November and held court at the palace of Holyroodhouse. Their return to England in February 1680 turned out to be only temporary, as the decision to allow parliament to assemble in October 1680 made it necessary for them to return to Scotland. This second Scottish exile was to be even longer than the first. On 2 March 1681, in Mary Beatrice's absence, her daughter, Isabella, died at St James's. By November 1681 she knew that she was pregnant once more, although she came close to another miscarriage on 16 December when she had, in the words of her physician, William Waldegrave, a 'dangerous fall' while out riding (Cambs. AS, R.51.17.31). Her expectant condition was one reason why she and James were allowed to leave Scotland in May 1682. Her mother visited England in order to be present at the birth. A daughter, Charlotte Maria, was born on the morning of 15 August 1682 but she lived only until 6 October. Mary Beatrice suffered two further miscarriages in October 1683 and on 8 May 1684. She was therefore childless when she became queen on the death of Charles II on 6 February 1685.

Queen, 1685–1688 No English queen consort in living memory had conformed to the Church of England but what made Mary Beatrice's position different was that her husband also openly acknowledged that he was a Catholic. The two of them attended mass in public for the first time on 15 February 1685. Despite the fact that it was a protestant ceremony, Mary Beatrice was crowned along with her husband in Westminster Abbey on 23 April 1685, becoming the first consort since 1603 to participate in a coronation. The frame of her coronation crown survives in the collections of the Museum of London, while her diadem, state crown, sceptre, and ivory rod remain part of the crown jewels. She seems to have adjusted well to her new role. John Evelyn noted with approval in July 1686 that 'her outward affability [had] much changed to statelinesse &c. since she has ben exalted' (Evelyn, 4.519). She remained in good health, although she did receive minor injuries in another riding accident in October 1685 and she suffered a bout of shingles in April 1686.

The major reorganization which James imposed throughout his own household did not extend to that of his wife. Her household was modelled on that which had been provided for Catherine of Braganza and, before her, for Henrietta Maria. Comparable financial arrangements were also made to meet its costs. Revenues from the Post Office (almost £20,000), the excise on beer (£18,000), her lands, and other sources gave her an annual income of about £40,000. In the event this income was not quite sufficient as her actual expenditure reached almost £50,000. She was therefore granted a further £10,000 in December 1686 in the form of an official annuity to cover the difference. It was agreed that these payments would be continued as her jointure after James's death. The death of her maternal grandmother, Margherita Martinozzi, in June 1685 brought her some property in Italy. She also benefited from her husband's building projects at Whitehall. In May 1685 work began on a range of new state apartments for her and these were ready by 1687. In the following year attention shifted to her privy apartments, which were rebuilt by Sir Christopher Wren as the dominant feature on the palace's river frontage. Mary Beatrice, however, never got the chance to occupy them as they were not quite finished when she fled the country. In January 1686, in the absence of a prince of Wales, she was granted St James's Palace.

Contemporaries almost certainly overestimated Mary Beatrice's role in policy-making. The duke of Monmouth's attempts to use her influence to save himself from the block came to nothing. Her subsequent request to be granted 100 of his supporters who were due to be transported to the West Indies, in order to collect the money made from their sale as indentured labour, has often been condemned. Seen from her point of view, however, the request could hardly seem callous as the deal was a purely financial transaction which made no practical difference to the prisoners themselves. Her principal concern during the first half of the reign was to persuade Pope Innocent XI to elevate her uncle Prince Rinaldo to the cardinalate. This request was granted on 23 August/2 September 1686. In November 1687 James disregarded her advice that it would be unwise to appoint his Catholic clerk of the closet, Edward Petre, to the privy council. Her secretary, John Caryll, claimed that she was also overruled when she tried to dissuade her husband from removing Cardinal Howard as cardinal-protector of England in order to appoint the new Cardinal d'Este to that position. Even so, the general fear was that she herself or those around her might use her position to meddle in politics, particularly that she might do so to support the Catholic interest. Her stepdaughter Princess Anne made it clear to her sister, the princess of Orange, that she was unconvinced that the queen could not be manipulated:

> The Queen, you must know, is of a very proud, haughty humour, and though she pretends to hate all forms and ceremony, yet one sees that those that make their court this way, are very well thought of. She declares always that she

loves sincerity and hates flattery, but when the grossest flattery in the world is said to her face, she seems extremely well pleased with it. It really is enough to turn one's stomach to hear what things are said to her of this kind, and to see how mightily she is satisfied with it. (*Letters and Diplomatic Instructions*, 30–31)

A number of courtiers, most notably the two Catholic converts the earl of Sunderland and the earl of Melfort, exploited this weakness to charm their way into her favour, although in both cases this was only a secondary factor in the influence they were able to exercise over the king. The Catholic earl of Dumbarton gained his position as a gentleman of the bedchamber in July 1687 in part because of the queen's backing. What complicated the question of Mary Beatrice's potential influence was her disapproval of the king's continuing affair with Catherine Sedley. The banishment of the new countess of Dorchester in early 1686 was a temporary victory for the queen, but this incident was the most obvious indication that the marriage was not an entirely happy one.

News of the death of Mary Beatrice's mother at Rome on 9/19 July 1687 reached London by 26 July and six months of official court mourning commenced five days later. One of the duchess of Modena's final acts had been to visit Loreto to pray that her daughter might produce a male heir and the progresses of the king and queen that summer had been planned with the same aspiration in mind. While James made his own pilgrimage to Holywell his wife remained at Bath to take the waters in the hope that both undertakings would aid the conception of a son. These measures appeared to work: the future prince of Wales was probably conceived shortly after James had been reunited with Mary Beatrice at the end of his progress.

In late November 1687 the first rumours of the queen's pregnancy began to circulate. An official announcement confirming the fact was made on 23 December. Days of thanksgiving were held on 15 January 1688 in London and on 29 January elsewhere. Unfortunately these public celebrations were out of step with the unease felt by most of the king's protestant subjects. The implications of a surviving Catholic male heir were obvious to all. The more paranoid took refuge in claims of popish deception in high places. The rumours that the birth would be faked, which had first circulated in 1682 when she was pregnant with Charlotte Maria, were recycled. By the middle of March 1688 Princess Anne was already claiming in private that these suspicions seemed well founded. Her main misgiving was that the queen seemed too healthy. The original intention was that the birth would take place at Windsor, mainly because that was where the court usually spent the summer. The date on which the queen intended to move there, 15 June, would in any case have been too late, but the change of plan was used by those who wished to create a mystery about these events. The queen had decided that she would stay at St James's, which was still her principal residence, and it was there that she went into labour on the morning of 10 June 1688. A son, *James Francis Edward, was born shortly before 10 a.m. after a short confinement made difficult only by the crowd of witnesses crammed into her bedchamber. In accordance with contemporary post-natal practice, she remained in seclusion for one month after the birth, making her first public appearance on 9 July.

The birth clinched the prince of Orange's decision to invade. That the child was a son seemed to confirm the predictions of those who were determined to believe that the birth was suppositious. All this wild speculation played into William's hands and the need to establish the truth about the birth was cited by him in his declaration of 1/10 October as one of the reasons justifying his actions. William's use of the rumours in this way required some sort of response. An extraordinary meeting of the privy council was held at Whitehall on 22 October to hear the testimonies of all those who had been present. Five days later these were enrolled in chancery as permanent proof of the prince's authenticity but it was already too late as only the weather was delaying the departure of the Dutch invasion fleet. On 17 November, twelve days after William had landed at Torbay, James set out from London to join his army at Salisbury. Mary Beatrice and a subcommittee of the privy council which had been appointed to assist her were left behind to manage events in the capital. The will which James signed that same day named her as regent in the event of his death. There was in truth little that Mary Beatrice could do from London to help her husband once the desertions to William's side began.

By the time James returned to London on 26 November, withdrawal abroad already seemed the most prudent option. The comte de Lauzun offered to organize Mary Beatrice's escape. On 1 December it was decided by James that she would leave on the night of 3 December. The subsequent failure to get the prince of Wales out of the country, as well as highlighting just how dangerous any escape would be, made it necessary to delay the plan until the following week. The queen finally left Whitehall early on the morning of 10 December disguised as a laundry woman, taking her son with her and accompanied only by Lauzun and a few of her most trusted servants. She boarded one of the royal yachts which was lying off Gravesend later that morning. Bad weather prevented their sailing until early the next day, 11/21 December, and it then took them about six hours to reach Calais. After a short stay at Boulogne, waiting for news of James, Mary Beatrice set out for Paris. She was greeted by Louis XIV at Chatou, 6 miles to the west of the French capital, on 27 December 1688/6 January 1689, whereupon Louis presented her with the use of his palace at St Germain-en-Laye. James joined her there the following day.

Exile, 1689–1718 St Germain was to be Mary Beatrice's home for the rest of her life. In some ways her time there was to be more congenial than it had been in England. She and James were honoured guests at the greatest court in western Europe, all their domestic needs were well provided for, and most of her closest servants had been able to join her. Louis XIV, who always had a soft spot for her, made sure that she was treated as a queen. As the public status of Louis XIV's morganatic wife, the marquise de

Maintenon, remained ambiguous, Mary Beatrice outranked every other woman at Versailles. What tarnished it all was the sense of disappointment and failure which inevitably pervaded the court James and Mary created for themselves at St Germain. Efforts to reverse the setbacks they had suffered brought their own problems. The seventeen months James now spent in Ireland was the longest period of separation during their years of marriage. For his wife, the hope that he might regain his three kingdoms was offset by the fear that he might die in the attempt. After his return, late in 1691 Mary Beatrice became pregnant once again. On 23 March/1 April 1692 James issued summonses to several leading English peeresses to attend the birth, which was then expected to take place some time around the middle of May. This time the estimate was too optimistic and it was not until 18/28 June that she gave birth to a daughter, Louise-Maria. This weakened but did not dispel the beliefs of those that wanted to think that there had been something suspicious about Prince James's birth. The defeat of the French invasion fleet at La Hogue the previous month had ended any real possibility of an early Stuart restoration and James was realistic enough to nickname this daughter La Consolatrice. The earl of Ailesbury, seeing Mary Beatrice in 1693 for the first time in over four years, noticed how much she had aged. As she pointed out to him, 'Afflictions alter people fast' (T. Bruce, *Memoirs of Thomas, Earl of Ailesbury*, 2 vols., 1890, 324).

Religion became even more important to the exiled queen. Whereas James found spiritual solace in the time he spent at the Cistercian monastery of La Trappe, Mary Beatrice regularly retreated to the Convent of the Visitation at Chaillot, the founder of which had been her late mother-in-law, Queen Henrietta Maria. Her devotion to the memory of the order's founder, François de Sales, had been a constant theme in her life and while at Chaillot she could feel that she was, in part, fulfilling the vocation that she had been forced to abandon. Another key strand in her piety was her interest in the devotion to the Sacred Heart. Claude de la Colombière, the Jesuit priest who had been instrumental in the movement's development, had been one of her French chaplains in the late 1670s.

One recurring issue of the years of exile was the question of Mary Beatrice's jointure. She was able to argue that if, as the 1689 convention had assumed, her husband was legally dead, she was entitled to the payments of £50,000 per annum which she had been promised for her widowhood. The French took up the issue during the peace negotiations at Rijswijk in 1697. The English government indicated that payments would be forthcoming but this undertaking came to nothing as no payments had been made by the time hostilities with France were renewed in 1702. In 1706 Mary Beatrice indicated that, in return for this money, she would pay off the bills she still owed to tradesmen in England. Her attempts to claim the personal property of her brother following his death in 1694 were equally unsuccessful. Cardinal d'Este, who had withdrawn from holy orders on succeeding to the dukedom as Rinaldo I, aligned himself with the League of Augsburg against Louis XIV and, although they were never broken off, relations between uncle and niece were strained thereafter. Modena was occupied by French troops in 1698.

James's health was declining fast, and in the spring of 1701 Mary Beatrice accompanied him on his trip to Bourbon to take the waters. She was, however, not present when James died on 5/16 September 1701, as it was not thought appropriate for queens to attend royal deathbeds and she had retired to her own apartments after taking her final leave from him. On receiving the news and after paying her respects to her son, Mary Beatrice withdrew to Chaillot. By James's will of 28 August/8 September 1701, Mary Beatrice became his sole executor and guardian of their son. For the next five years she was, in Jacobite eyes, the *de jure* regent of England, Scotland, and Ireland. In 1702 she opposed the idea that her son should go to Scotland to oppose the accession of his half-sister Anne. It made little sense to seek his restoration while his mother remained regent. Her own health was not good. In the autumn of 1703 she was operated on for breast cancer. The tumours reappeared and she underwent a second operation in 1705.

On 10/21 July 1706 James Stuart (the Old Pretender James III) came of age. Mary Beatrice's public role then shrank to that of the matriarchal figure presiding over the court at St Germain, which, even from a Jacobite point of view, was facing a period of slow, terminal decline. Two separate developments in 1712 deprived Mary Beatrice of the company of both her children. On 7/18 April 1712 Louise-Maria died of smallpox. Four months later her son was forced to move to Chalons in order to allow the French to commence peace negotiations with the British. On the other hand, the conclusion of the treaty of Utrecht in the following year revived hopes that her jointure might finally be paid. In December 1713 Queen Anne authorized the payments of those sums which were owed from the previous Lady day onwards, with the payments to be made via the heirs of Sidney, Lord Godolphin, Mary Beatrice's former lord chamberlain, who had been the last surviving of the trustees for her jointure appointed in 1685. However, none of this money ever reached her. Anne died eight months later and George I had no reason to resolve the issue. In June 1715 Mary Beatrice visited her son at Bar-le-Duc. She saw him for the last time early the following year when he stopped off at St Germain on his return from Scotland. Before long he had moved first to Avignon and then to Italy. By this time Mary Beatrice's main preoccupation was the question of who her son should marry.

Mary Beatrice died at Château de St Germain on 26 April/7 May 1718. The cause of death was believed to be inflammation of the lungs, complicated by an abscess on her left side remaining from her most recent cancer operation. Her body was interred in the chapel at Chaillot on 16/27 June, while her viscera were buried before the monument containing her husband's brain in the Collège des Escossois in Paris. The tomb at Chaillot was destroyed, along with the other Stuart tombs and the rest of the convent, during the French Revolution.

Most of her biographers to date have shown Mary Beatrice to have been a fairly typical princess of the seventeenth century. The life of a royal bride married off to a foreign prince was always difficult, but she had the advantages of intelligence, charm, and diffidence and she quickly adapted to life at the English and French courts. On a purely personal level, James's marriage to her was one of the better decisions he made. Her virtues should not, however, be overstated. Too often, the way in which her popular biographers have presented her life, as being particularly romantic, ill-fated, and Catholic, has owed more to the manner in which those historians have also interpreted those other imprudent or ineffectual Stuart queens, Mary, queen of Scots, Henrietta Maria, and Catherine of Braganza. Stuart queens are expected to be tragic. Some of the sympathy which Mary Beatrice has thus been accorded is, however, understandable, given the undoubted unfairness of many of the misfortunes which befell her. Historians of her husband's reign have, on the other hand, been much more hard-headed, portraying her influence on James as generally misguided, although this has sometimes been exaggerated. The circle of courtiers around her, which may yet prove to be the key to understanding the true nature of that influence, has been little studied.

ANDREW BARCLAY

Sources A. Strickland, *Lives of the queens of England* (1851–2); reprinted (1972), vol. 6 • M. Haile [M. Hallé], *Queen Mary of Modena: her life and letters* (1905) • M. Hopkirk, *Queen over the water* (1953) • C. Oman, *Mary of Modena* (1962) • J. Southorn, *Mary of Modena, queen consort of James II and VII* (1992) • household papers of Mary of Modena, 1683–1716, Bodl. Oxf., MS Rawl. C. 987 • Marquise Campana de Cavelli, ed., *Les derniers Stuarts à Saint-Germain en Laye*, 2 vols. (Paris, 1871) • *CSP Venice, 1673–5* • *Calendar of the Stuart papers belonging to his majesty the king, preserved at Windsor Castle*, 7 vols., HMC, 56 (1902–23), vols. 1–4 • F. Madan, ed., *Stuart papers relating chiefly to Queen Mary of Modena*, 2 vols. (1889) • *The life of James the Second, king of England*, ed. J. S. Clarke, 2 vols. (1816) • R. Halstead [H. Mordaunt, second earl of Peterborough], *Succinct genealogies of the noble and ancient houses* (1685) • M. R. Toynbee, 'An early correspondence of Queen Mary of Modena', *N&Q*, 188 (1945), 90–94, 112–18, 135–40; 193 (1948), 292–5 • *The letters and diplomatic instructions of Queen Anne*, ed. B. C. Brown (1935) • *The manuscripts of Sir William Fitzherbert … and others*, HMC, 32 (1893) • J. Dalrymple, *Memoirs of Great Britain and Ireland*, 2 vols. (1771–3) • Evelyn, *Diary* • *Bishop Burnet's History* • J. P. Kenyon, *Robert Spencer, earl of Sunderland, 1641–1702* (1958) • M. Bini, *Gli Estensi: la corte di Modena* (1999) • J. H. McMaster and M. Wood, eds., *Supplementary report on the manuscripts of his grace the duke of Hamilton*, HMC, 21 (1932), 111 • *CSP dom., 1673–5*, 24–5 • P.-A. de Sainte-Marie, marquis d'Auvers, *Un voyageur français à Londres en 1685*, ed. G. Roth (1968), 75 • R. Warden, 'Accounts as treasurer to Mary of Modena', 25 March 1687–25 March 1688, PRO, LR 8/418, unfol. • PRO, PC 2/72, fols. 166–76 • PRO, C21 2/7, mm. 5–19 • W. A. Shaw, ed., *Calendar of treasury books*, 27, PRO (1955), 547, 549

Archives Bodl. Oxf., household papers, MS Rawl. C. 987 • Royal Arch., corresp. and related material | BL, letters to Cardinal Guamario, Add. MSS 46493–46498 • BL, Caryll papers, Add. MSS 28225–28226 • BL, Gualterio corresp., Add. MS 20293 • BL, letters to F. A. Gualterio, Add. MSS 31254, 31258 • W. Sussex RO, letters to duchess of Gordon

Likenesses P. Lely, oils, 1673–80, Ranger's House, London • S. Verelst, oils, *c.*1675, Royal Collection • B. Gennari, oils, *c.*1677, Royal Collection • attrib. P. Lely, oils, *c.*1677, Royal Collection • W. Wissing, oils, *c.*1685, NPG [*see illus.*] • W. Wissing, oils, second version, 1687, Scot. NPG • B. Gennari, double portrait, oils, 1690 (with prince of Wales); Sothebys (9 April 1997) · P. Mignard, group portrait, oils, 1694, Royal Collection · F. de Troy, oils, c.1698, Sizergh Castle and Garden, Cumbria · P. Gobert, oils, 1713–15, priv. coll. · R. de Hooghe, group portrait, etching (after his portrait), NG Ire. · P. Lely, oils, Althorp, Northamptonshire; version, c.1675–1680, Royal Collection · J. Smith, mezzotint (after G. Kneller), BM, NG Ire., NPG · J. Smith, mezzotint (after N. de Largillière), BM, NPG · T. Trumpton, pastel drawing, NG Ire. · G. Valck, mezzotint (after P. Lely), NPG · medals, BM · mezzotint (after P. Lely), BM, NPG · mezzotint (after W. Wissing), BM, NPG

Mary, Princess (1723–1772), landgravine of Hesse-Cassel, consort of Friedrich II, was born on 22 February 1723 (between eight and nine o'clock in the evening) at Leicester House, London, the fourth daughter and eighth child of *George II (1683–1760) and Queen *Caroline (1683–1737). She was carefully brought up by her mother and, after the queen's death, by her elder sister Princess Caroline. The *Memoirs of the House and Dominions of Hesse-Cassel*, published in 1740, described her as 'a lover of reading, and far more solicitous to improve the mind than to adorn the body' (Hall, 127). When she was seventeen a marriage was arranged for her with Prince Friedrich of Hesse-Cassel (1720–1785), the only surviving son and heir of Landgrave Wilhelm, then ruling in Kassel as regent for his elder brother, King Fredrik I of Sweden. Parliament voted the princess a marriage portion of £40,000 and the proxy wedding took place at the Chapel Royal, St James's Palace, in the evening of 8 May 1740, the bride's brother William Augustus, duke of Cumberland, standing in for the bridegroom. Princess Mary sailed from Greenwich on 6 June and travelled via the Netherlands to Kassel, where she was married in person on 28 June. Her husband, although tall and handsome, was profligate and brutal, and Mary's married life was very unhappy. In the October following her marriage the statesman Jacob Friedrich von Bielfeld saw her at a fancy dress ball at Herrenhausen and described her as tall, and handsome enough to be a painter's model (*faite à peindre*). Horace Walpole, who had played with her when they were both children, said she had 'the softest, mildest temper in the world' (Walpole, *Corr.*, 19.295) and referred to her husband as a boor and a brute. In late 1746 she paid an extended visit to Britain to recover from her mistreatment at Kassel. Mary gave birth to four sons, of whom the eldest died in infancy and the youngest was born in September 1747.

In 1749 Prince Friedrich was converted in secret to the Roman Catholic faith, believing that by so doing he would be reunited in the afterlife with his dying Catholic mistress. His conversion was made public in 1754, giving Mary the excuse to separate from him in February 1755. George II urged his daughter to return to England, but she felt that her place was with her young sons and she received much support from her father-in-law, since 1751 reigning landgrave as Wilhelm VIII, who provided a residence for her at Hanau, a sovereign county of the Holy Roman empire, which he had acquired in 1736 through a family arrangement. In 1757 the French invaded Hesse-Cassel and Mary with her father-in-law and children fled to Hamburg, where their circumstances were such that William Pitt

Princess Mary (1723–1772), by John Faber junior (after Arthur Pond)

the elder anticipated the meeting of parliament by remitting the sum of £20,000 to provide for their immediate expenses. In 1758 a life annuity of £5000 was settled on the princess. Landgrave Wilhelm VIII died at Rinteln on 1 February 1760 and was succeeded by Mary's estranged husband as reigning Landgrave Friedrich II. Wilhelm had made provision for Mary's eldest surviving son, also called Wilhelm, to become reigning count of Hanau with his mother as regent until he came of age on 13 October 1764. The landgravine, as she now was, possessed coinage rights, and very handsome thalers and half-thalers were struck bearing her bust, the coats of arms of Hesse-Cassel and Great Britain, and her name and titles in the fashion of a reigning sovereign.

Mary continued to reside at Hanau during her son's rule there. She continued to play an active part in the life of the British royal family from Hanau through correspondence. Her niece Caroline Matilda, queen of Denmark, was reported to have appealed for her help in 1769 against the Danish queen mother, Juliane Marie. In the same year her nephew William Henry, duke of Gloucester and Edinburgh, visited her at Hanau as part of his continental tour. After suffering some years of failing health, she died at Hanau at seven o'clock in the morning on 14 January 1772. She was buried in the Reformed church (now the Marienkirche) there on 1 February. Landgrave Friedrich II married secondly on 10 January 1773 Philippine, daughter of Friedrich Wilhelm, margrave of Brandenburg-Schwedt, but they had no children and on his death on 31 October 1785 he was succeeded by his eldest surviving son from his first marriage, Landgrave Wilhelm IX, subsequently

Elector Wilhelm I of Hesse. He and his two younger brothers, Karl and Friedrich, who both had distinguished military careers and to whom their mother bequeathed the bulk of her property, left numerous descendants, several of whom (including Edward VII's queen, Alexandra, and Mary, queen to George V) married back into the British royal family. DAVID WILLIAMSON

Sources H. M. Lane, *The royal daughters of England*, 2 vols. (1910–11) · M. Huberty and others, *L'Allemagne dynastique* (Hesse-Reuss-Saxe, 1976) · D. Williamson, *Brewer's British royalty* (1996) · N. D. Nicol, *Standard catalog of German coins: 1601 to present*, ed. C. W. Bruce (1994), 382 · W. D. Craig, *Coins of the world, 1750–1850*, 3rd edn (1976) · *LondG* (May 1740) · *GM*, 1st ser., 24 (1754), 527; 25 (1755), 330; 27 (1757), 374; 30 (1760), 102; 42 (1772), 44 · *The Grenville papers: being the correspondence of Richard Grenville … and … George Grenville*, ed. W. J. Smith, 1 (1852), 206 · *Correspondence of William Pitt, earl of Chatham*, ed. W. S. Taylor and J. H. Pringle, 4 vols. (1838–40), vol. 1, p. 244 · *Correspondence of John, fourth duke of Bedford*, ed. J. Russell, 2 (1842), 337 · J. F. Bielfeld, *Lettres familières et autres*, 2 vols. (1763), vol. 1, pp. 209–10 · Walpole, *Corr.* · *DNB* · M. Hall, *The royal princesses of England* (1857), 126–37

Likenesses W. Hogarth, group portrait, oils, c.1731–1732 (*The family of George II*), Royal Collection; version, NG Ire. · B. Lens III, miniature, 1739, Kenwood House, London · silver coin, 1764, repro. in Nicol, *Standard catalog*, 382 · J. Faber junior, mezzotint (after A. Pond), BM, NPG [*see illus.*] · attrib. P. Mercier, group portrait, oils, Chatsworth House, Derbyshire · C. Shirmer, silver medal, BM · J. Simon, mezzotint (after E. Seeman), NPG · J. Simon, print, BM, NPG · J. S. Tanner, gold, silver, and copper medal, BM · group portrait, line engraving (*The royal family of Great Britain*), BM · mezzotint, BM, NPG

Mary, Princess, duchess of Gloucester (1776–1857). *See under* George III, daughters of (*act.* 1766–1857).

Mary [Princess Mary of Teck] (1867–1953), queen of Great Britain and Ireland, and the British dominions beyond the seas, and empress of India, consort of George V, was born in Kensington Palace on 26 May 1867, in the room in which Queen Victoria was born. Baptized Victoria Mary Augusta Louise Olga Pauline Claudine Agnes, she used the names Victoria Mary officially until she became queen, but in her family she was known as May. Her father was Francis, prince (later duke) of Teck (1837–1900), the only son of Duke Alexander of Württemberg by his morganatic marriage with Claudine, Countess Rhédey, of a protestant Hungarian family. Her mother was Princess *Mary Adelaide Wilhelmina Elizabeth (1833–1897), younger daughter of *Adolphus Frederick, duke of Cambridge, and a first cousin of Queen Victoria. Princess May was their only daughter and eldest child. Three brothers followed: Prince Adolphus of Teck (1868–1927), later first marquess of Cambridge, Prince Francis of Teck (1870–1910), and Prince Alexander of Teck (1874–1957), who became earl of Athlone [*see* Cambridge, Alexander Augustus Frederick William Alfred George].

Early life The Tecks were a devoted, though tempestuous, couple, with widely differing temperaments. The liberal, cheerful duchess, though a bad manager and notoriously unpunctual, was deservedly popular because of her efforts on behalf of charity. The conservative and quick-

Mary (1867–1953), by Bertram Park, 1927

tempered duke, who lacked a private fortune, lived a life of enforced idleness in Britain, which led to disappointment, ill health, and a fixation with protocol. Both were deeply conscious of their high social status but, inept about finance, they could not live in a style in keeping with their expectations on the duchess's annual parliamentary grant of £5000. The expense of life at Kensington Palace and White Lodge in Windsor Park led to their humiliating near bankruptcy, which deeply influenced their daughter's childhood. It was notable that she rarely discussed her youth in later life. Once, when asked about a lengthy trip to Florence as a girl, she replied: 'my parents were always *in short street* so they had to go abroad to economise' (Pope-Hennessy, 112).

Princess May's parents also economized on her studies. In keeping with conventions about female royalty, she received little formal education beyond the accomplishments of the drawing-room. She led a sheltered childhood with a social life largely restricted to visiting the houses of her royal cousins and her mother's friends and German relatives. But she spent more time with her mother than was typical of royal children, and it was at her mother's side that she first engaged in social work and came to sympathize with the lives and aspirations of the working classes. With the help of her liberal-minded Alsatian governess, Hélène Bricka, she took it upon herself to extend the range of her education. During the eighteen months that she spent in Florence in 1883–5 she was put in the hands of competent French and Italian tutors and developed an interest in literature and art history. Upon her return to England she pressed ahead with her studies and became proficient in French and German, and took a greater interest in German politics. Unlike her future husband and most of her relatives, she was bookish.

An acquaintance in Florence described Princess May of Teck as 'a remarkably attractive girl, rather silent, but with a look of quiet determination mixed with kindliness which augured well for the future' (Pope-Hennessy, 127). Various commentators spoke of her shyness, gravity, and youthful good looks. Yet she was not so attractive that her looks turned men's heads or became a distraction. As a young woman, she was less concerned about winning a beauty pageant than about avoiding the obesity that had embarrassed her mother. Only in middle age did she acquire the imposing presence that courtiers called regal. She said of herself that she looked too much like Queen Charlotte, the Mecklenburg princess with the full jaw and turned-up nose who had married her great-grandfather George III. What Princess May lacked in beauty, she made up for in intelligence and alertness; and despite her outward reserve, she possessed a sense of the ridiculous, which is always an advantage for a member of the royal family.

Duchess of York and princess of Wales The first purpose of female royalty is to marry, but because of her father's morganatic birth, Princess May's marriage prospects were thought to be limited. As her biographer put it, she was 'too Royal to marry an ordinary English gentleman, and not Royal enough to marry a Royalty' (Pope-Hennessy, 186). But Queen Victoria, who had no objection to morganatic blood, thought her a suitable wife for her eldest grandson, Albert Victor, duke of Clarence, who stood in the direct line of succession. The marriage was wonderfully convenient. Princess May was the only available English princess not descended from Queen Victoria, and it was widely felt in the royal family that she might stabilize the wayward duke. Thus their engagement had an air of inevitability about it. It was announced publicly at the end of 1891, but the sudden death of the duke of Clarence in January 1892 dashed the marriage only weeks before the scheduled wedding. The princess was devastated, for just at her moment of triumph everything was taken from her. But what Queen Victoria thought a great misfortune was probably a blessing in disguise, for the unstable and dissipated duke was never likely to make much of a husband, however assiduous the wife. His sudden death was a close escape for both the princess and the crown

Royalty is nothing if not resilient, and the death of one prince turned the mind of the royal family to the next prince in the direct line of succession, the younger brother of the duke of Clarence, Prince George Frederick Ernest Albert [see George V (1865–1936)], who was created duke of York in May 1892. The duke of York was everything his brother was not: candid, dutiful, and devoted to domestic life, with more than a passing resemblance to Queen Victoria. Nor was he a playboy, though he had some experience of the opposite sex. He had also fallen in

love, chastely it seems, with Miss Julie Stonor, the daughter of one of the princess of Wales's ladies-in-waiting. But marriage to a commoner was never a possibility. Not surprisingly, the queen encouraged an alliance with Princess May, and was delighted when the engagement was announced in May 1893 and the marriage solemnized in the Chapel Royal, St James's Palace, on 6 July. At its inception the match could not have been described as a romance, but it took the princess off the shelf, offered the prince a settled life, and satisfied expectations in the country. As the faithful husband commented years later when George V:

> We suit each other admirably & I thank God every day that he should have brought us together, especially under the tragic circumstances of dear Eddy's death, & people only said I married you out of pity & sympathy. That shows how little the world really knows what it is talking about.   (Royal Archives, Geo. V, CC 4/86)

They may have suited 'each other admirably', but Princess May suffered from her husband's reticence. As a consequence, she had little sense of how successful she was in dealing with her role. Expressions of affection and appreciation from her husband were rare, and largely confined to his letters. The royal couple corresponded on a daily basis when separated, and in the year of his accession George V wrote a letter to Queen Mary that suggested the formality in their marriage that sometimes caused her grief:

> I fear darling my nature is not demonstrative, but I want you to understand, that I am indeed grateful to you, for all you have done all these busy months for me & to thank you from the bottom of my heart for all your love & and for the enormous help & comfort which you have been to me in my new position.   (Pope-Hennessy, 426)

She replied: 'What a pity it is you cannot *tell* me what you write for I should appreciate it so enormously—It is such a blessing to know that I am a help to you' (ibid.).

The duke and duchess of York settled into a domestic routine on the prince of Wales's Sandringham estate. They moved into the unpretentious York Cottage, which had been a wedding present from the prince of Wales; during extended stays in London they lived at York House and, after 1901, at Marlborough House. While the marriage of convenience developed into a romance, country life suited the duke rather more than the duchess. At Sandringham, a benign tyranny reigned from the big house, which the duchess often found suffocating. She found less scope for her charitable interests than she would have liked because her mother-in-law dominated the local charities. Moreover, her enthusiasms and intellectual interests were little valued at Sandringham by her relatives, including the prince of Wales, whose idea of a good time was shooting birds and entertaining plutocrats. It was said of George V that as duke of York he 'did nothing at all but kill animals and stick in stamps' (Nicolson, 162); this was an exaggeration, but it is suggestive of the environment in which the duchess, who preferred urban to rural pursuits, had to live.

Over the years a life of some frustration for the duchess was leavened by the birth of six children: Prince Edward (later King *Edward VIII), Prince Albert (later King *George VI), Princess *Mary (later the princess royal), Prince *Henry (later duke of Gloucester), Prince *George (later duke of Kent), and the invalid Prince John. In later years Queen Mary remarked on the curious fact that three of her five sons had died sudden deaths: Prince John in 1919, the duke of Kent in 1942, and King George VI in 1952. Sadly for her marriage, and the children, the family idyll had its tensions. The unimaginative duke of York confused fatherhood with a variation on naval drill. In matters of discipline Princess May felt obliged to support her sovereign, but she sought to provide a refuge for the children when she felt that he was treating them unfairly. In later life the duke of Windsor, who was so often the victim of his father's wrath, recalled that 'she was a different human being away from him' (Duke of Windsor, 1).

Despite her isolation at Sandringham and the demands of motherhood, the princess was not inactive on the public stage. There were frequent tours of British cities, visits to Coburg and Copenhagen for royal weddings, state visits to Ireland in 1897 and 1899, Queen Victoria's diamond jubilee, and helping her mother supervise the ladies of the Needlework Guild. Charitable duties, particularly hospital work, mounted with the Second South African War. In 1901 she supported her husband in successful tours of Australia, New Zealand, and Canada, an experience that strengthened her pride in the British empire. Upon their return the couple's status underwent a marked change, for on 9 November 1901 the new King Edward VII proclaimed the duke of York prince of Wales. As the wife of the heir to the throne, Princess May was increasingly on royal parade and in the public eye. An early indication of their new responsibilities as prince and princess of Wales took place in January 1902, when they took their seats on chairs of state at the opening of parliament. Increased travel was another feature of their elevated rank, capped by a well-publicized tour of India in 1905. India so charmed the traditionalist princess that she could never conceive of it becoming an independent state. When it did so in 1947, she compared her sense of loss to another Queen Mary's feelings over the loss of Calais.

In May 1906 the royal couple travelled to Madrid to attend the wedding of Princess Ena of Battenberg to the king of Spain. What promised to be a happy royal event ended in tragedy as an anarchist dropped a bomb on the wedding procession, killing several soldiers and many in the crowd. The experience reinforced Princess May's hostility to radical movements. A week after returning from Madrid, the Waleses sailed on the royal yacht to attend the coronation of the king and queen of Norway. The Norwegian court admired the princess for her dignity and jewellery—it was said that no other European royal could move so freely under such a weight of jewels—but found her stiff and forbidding. This view was consistent with opinion at home, for the old-fashioned prince and princess were out of the swim of the Edwardian smart set. When King Edward died on 6 May 1910, the princess of Wales became queen consort, dropped her first name, Victoria, and became known as Queen Mary.

Queen consort The new king and queen became the subject of jibes, some of which stuck: 'The King is duller than the Queen' ran the refrain. Queen Mary could be mordant and laconic, but she lacked small talk and disliked gossip. Friends called her shy; critics called her dreary. Beatrice Webb, who looked down her nose at successive generations of royalty, noted after a dinner at Buckingham Palace that the queen was 'stiff in manner, curt in words and lifeless in expression, and really looks like an exquisitely executed automaton—a royal robot … she was painfully at a loss of what to say to me' (*The Diaries of Beatrice Webb*, ed. N. Mackenzie and J. Mackenzie, 2000, 494). While cosmopolitans lamented the loss of brilliance at court, an 'exquisitely executed automaton' was arguably just the ticket in a burgeoning social democracy, especially when combined with an exceptional sense of duty.

At the accession of George V the portents for the monarchy were ominous. Industrial unrest, troubles in Ireland, and an emerging Labour Party with a vocal republican element were taken by the king and queen to be threats to the monarchy's survival. Queen Mary's politics had been formed in the ultra-tory atmosphere of her youth at White Lodge, where Gladstone was thought to be a dangerous radical. The queen had her limitations, but naïveté was not among them. She was highly attuned to politics as it applied to the crown, but had to keep her views under wraps as the consort of a constitutional monarch. Privately, however, she was horrified by industrial strife and the militant rhetoric, with its implied republicanism, which sought to capitalize on divisions between capital and labour. In a letter to the king early in the reign, she turned on the Liberal government: 'I do think the unrest is due to their extraordinary tactics in encouraging Socialism all these years & in pandering to the Labour Party' (Pope-Hennessy, 469). Highly sensitive to the suffering caused by the coal strike in 1912, she wrote with her customary forcefulness: 'If only one could act, but like this one feels so impotent, & all this time our blessed & beloved country is in a state of stagnation & misery' (ibid., 466).

In a political no man's land, the royal family felt obliged to consider a more coherent strategy of self-defence than palace precedent provided. Friends and courtiers advised the royal family to bring the throne and the people into line, to show that the monarchy was sensitive to the deteriorating social conditions and sympathetic to working-class aspirations. The strategy that emerged had more to do with the royal traditions of social service than with the monarch's 'dignified' role as head of state. For her part, the queen lamented that there was little she could do on the political front, but assisting the poor was a royal prerogative. From her perspective, charitable work not only ameliorated distress but was a way of squaring deference with democracy and enticing the labouring classes into the royal camp. Feeling besieged by strikers, sneering socialists, and tiresome suffragettes (the orderly queen abhorred disorderly women), the royal family stepped up its social work and sought greater publicity for it. Queen Mary and King George knew what was in their own interest, but thought it synonymous with the nation's.

Unlike Edward VII and Queen Alexandra, the king and queen saw themselves as a team and worked in effective partnership, a point brought home by the praise the queen received during their second visit to India for the durbar in 1911–12. As the more intelligent of the two and the better informed on social questions, Queen Mary took a leading role in developing and implementing royal social policy. Drawing on the philanthropic training imbibed from her mother, she mixed easily with cottage and factory wives. On advice, the royal couple stepped up their appearances in the mining and industrial regions with a series of goodwill visits. In June 1912, for example, they penetrated the colliery districts of Glamorgan and the Merthyr valley. Queen Mary wrote to her aunt Augusta in Strelitz: 'We are assured on all sides that our visit wld do more to bring peace and goodwill into the district than anything else & that we had done the best days work in all our lives!' Keir Hardie, she added, 'will not have liked it' (Royal Archives, Queen Mary to grand duchess of Mecklenburg-Strelitz, 29 June 1912). (The Labour leader, a trenchant anti-royalist, had described the trip as a 'ruse' to 'whitewash the mine owners' (The Times, 15 June 1912, 10).) The various tours and patronage work generally brought out and publicized the queen's good qualities, while giving shape to her role as consort. Her long experience in the charitable field would turn out to be the most fitting preparation for the cataclysm to come.

The First World War offered Queen Mary fresh opportunities for self-expression, as to women of every class and background—arguably marking her greatest contribution to national unity and well-being. With strong ideas of female responsibility and women's sphere of usefulness, she seized every opportunity to be of service. On 6 August 1914 she wrote in her diary: 'Very busy seeing people about the various Relief schemes' (Pope-Hennessy, 490). Like her mother, she was a charitable bulldozer, clearing a path for hundreds of thousands of volunteers. The Needlework Guild, now called Queen Mary's Needlework Guild, took up the cause with frenzied determination, and the state apartments of St James's Palace soon turned into a warehouse piled high with gifts for distribution to needy cases. In touch with the efforts of other charities, among them the National Relief Fund, the St John Ambulance Brigade, and the Red Cross, she became a one-woman co-ordinating body for the administration of wartime charity.

An unemployment crisis, albeit temporary, was a consequence of the war, and Queen Mary concluded that women needed work more than anything else. She thus formed the Queen's Work for Women Fund as a female branch of the National Relief Fund. An unlikely ally was Mary Macarthur, the secretary of the Women's Trade Union League, with whom she formed an effective partnership. Macarthur wrote to the queen in August 1914: 'May I venture to express to Your Majesty on behalf of the working women whom I have the honour to represent the deep gratitude which we feel we owe to your Majesty at

this time' (Royal Archives, GV CC49/28). Given the queen's view of trade unionism, it must have been a pleasing tribute and may even have softened her view of socialism. Raising money and visiting the many projects identified the queen with a sensitive working-class cause during the national emergency. Wherever she turned her attention, practical work was the priority. A lady of the bedchamber noted that the number of the queen's engagements trebled during the war, among them countless dispiriting visits to hospitals. At the palace, meanwhile, she and the king imposed a regime of legendary frugality, in keeping with the national sense of crisis. As a token of gratitude for the queen's war service, the nation presented her with a magnificent dolls' house designed by Edwin Lutyens, which became a centrepiece of the British Empire Exhibition in 1924 and is now on permanent display at Windsor.

The end of the war only increased royal fears. Given the collapse of the German, Russian, and Austrian monarchies, a degree of paranoia was understandable in palace circles. The monarchy had also to deal with post-war scarcity and high unemployment, with a new mass electorate unsettled by war, and with the distinct possibility of a Labour government, now armed with an explicitly socialist constitution. Highly sensitive to the dangers facing the monarchy, Queen Mary made no small contribution to ensuring its continued popularity. Everyone in the royal family was conscious of the need for vigilance. Eventually the king kept a chart in Buckingham Palace that chronicled his family's public work. The self-indulgent young prince of Wales needed to be encouraged to step up his royal duties. The queen wrote to the king three weeks after the armistice: 'I think David ought to return home before very long, as he must help us in these difficult days' (Ziegler, 108). She had 'some capital talks' with the prince of Wales, and noted that 'he is quite ready to do anything we want' (Pope-Hennessy, 515). It was Queen Mary, as much as anyone else, who encouraged the reluctant prince to cultivate the image of a social crusader.

There was never any doubt about the commitment of the queen to social causes, and she set a benchmark for the rest of the family. Few government ministers have ever visited as many hospitals or child welfare centres. In 1921 Sir George Newman, the chief medical officer at the Ministry of Health, said that the queen's philanthropic work was 'invaluable' and her social influence 'sound and statesmanlike'. And he noted, in passing, that her beneficent labours were 'enormously strengthening the influence of the Crown with the people' (Royal Archives, GV CC47/672). The queen made her own unique contribution to the implementation of post-war royal strategy, which the king's private secretary, Lord Stamfordham, had set out in 1918:

We must endeavour to induce the working classes, Socialists and others, to regard the Crown not as a mere figurehead … but as a living power for good, with receptive faculties welcoming information affecting the interests and social well-being of all classes, and ready not only to sympathize with those questions, but anxious to further their solutions. (Royal Archives, GV/O 1106/65)

In the post-war years the monarchy kept open its lines of communication and showed particular sensitivity to the first Labour government, with which it had ideological differences. Though palace advisers developed much of royal policy during the reign, Queen Mary was determined to take a lead on a national scale. Never content to stay in the shadows, she pressed ahead with her many patronages and social work in working-class constituencies. Meanwhile she and the king invited aspiring Labour MPs, trade unionists, and their wives to teas, dinners, and garden parties. The object was to take the republican edge off socialism by showing that the monarchy was a living institution that mattered. To the dismay of left-wing republicans, who complained of the toadying and house-training of Labour wives, royal efforts had the desired effect. Despite the war, industrial unrest, depression, and high unemployment that marked George V's reign, the monarchy was more popular at the end of it than it had been at the beginning.

Queen Mary's official biographer described her 'dominant characteristics' as 'patriotism, a love of order, an earnest desire to relieve distress and a concern about social conditions' (Pope-Hennessy, 490). Propriety might be added to the list, for the queen always carried out her social duties with an eye to her exalted station and royal prerogatives. Patronage work gave her ample opportunity to fly the royal standard and express her unique style. On countless public outings to baby camps and bazaars, to hospitals and city centres, her much noted reserve and dignified bearing—topped off by the ubiquitous toque—enhanced the sense of occasion, but could make presiding officials tremulous. On one memorable visit to a London hospital she refused to plant a tree because the red carpet that had been rolled out before her did not extend to the commemorative spade. Before the ceremony could proceed, a footman had to cut off the carpet at the other end and place the remnant at her feet.

Over the years Queen Mary devoted much of the time not spent on public duties to her 'one great hobby'—that of building up the royal art collection. Like her mother, she had a passion for objects, but, unlike her mother, she had the money to pay for them, despite her occasional reluctance to spend it. She read widely in art history, visited museums, and rummaged through antique shops. The king, who had little interest in collecting apart from stamps and snuff boxes, did not object to her enthusiasms. Her mind was absorbent and classifying rather than analytical; her taste was catholic and conventional but favoured the historical. Anything to do with the British royal family tempted her collector's eye, though she could get equally excited about gewgaws or budgerigars. In the early years of the reign she concentrated her energies on conservation, but after the war she began the process of garnering, organizing, and cataloguing the Royal Collection and rearranging the treasures in the royal residences. In later life she continued to add to her own collection of curios, the quality of which, as an earlier memoir put it, 'would have profited had she paid more for less' (DNB).

Life at Buckingham Palace was a sombre affair between the wars, not least because of the king's exhaustion. When he fell seriously ill in 1928 of an acute form of septicaemia, the queen's steely self-control astonished her family. 'Through all the anxiety', remarked the duke of York, 'she has never once revealed her feelings to any of us. She is really far too reserved' (Pope-Hennessy, 546). She had to call on all her reserves and strength of character in the years left to the king, for he was physically unfit to carry out many of his public duties without her. He lived to enjoy the hugely popular silver jubilee celebrations in 1935, but died in the presence of his family eight months later at Sandringham. 'Am brokenhearted', Queen Mary wrote in her account of his death (ibid., 559). Immediately upon the king's death, in a gesture that was entirely in character, she kissed the hand of her eldest son, Edward VIII.

To a dutiful queen with such an exalted notion of kingship, her son's abdication at the end of 1936 was abhorrent. That a king of England should give up the throne for a woman was unprecedented. 'Really! This might be Roumania!' she was heard to remark (Pope-Hennessy, 577). The abdication was the greatest humiliation of her life. In 1938 she wrote to her son:

> It seemed inconceivable to those who had made such sacrifices during the war that you, as their King, refused a lesser sacrifice … My feelings for you as your Mother remain the same, and our being parted and the cause of it, grieve me beyond words. After all, all my life I have put my Country before everything else, and I simply cannot change now. (Ziegler, 385)

In the aftermath of the abdication it was Queen Mary, along with her daughter-in-law, Queen Elizabeth, who stiffened the resolve of King George VI against Mrs Simpson's desires. Ever after she refused to receive the duchess of Windsor. It was ironic that the first occasion at which the duchess found herself amid the royal family was in 1967 when she accompanied her husband to the dedication of a plaque to the memory of Queen Mary.

Last years In widowhood Queen Mary moved to Marlborough House. She continued to work on the Royal Collection and visit museums, exhibitions, and the theatre. She also became a regular visitor to the Wimbledon tennis championships. In May 1939 she had a terrible shock when a lorry carrying a load of steel tubing overturned her Daimler. 'Nothing, perhaps, that Queen Mary has done', one commentator remarked, 'has ever become her so well as … the manner of leaving the wrecked car' (Pope-Hennessy, 595). When war broke out she retired to Badminton, where she visited evacuees, opened hospitals, and salvaged scrap. She also executed a carpet in gros point needlework which became celebrated at the end of the war when sold to a Canadian women's organization for $100,000. She gave the money not to charity, as advised by her friends, but to the national exchequer, an artful act of benevolence which elicited not only great publicity but a letter of thanks signed by the entire Labour cabinet. But she was less than enthusiastic about Labour policy, particularly the nationalization of the hospitals. Like all members of the royal family, she remained a voluntarist at heart.

George V, as his eldest son famously remarked, was engaged in a 'private war with the twentieth century'. Queen Mary was also out of tune with the political changes taking place in her day, but—blessed with robust health, without constitutional duties, and with a wider breadth of view than her husband—she was able to move with the times in a way that he could not. She was rigid in conduct, but, being practical in all things, open to change. Beneath her adamantine self-control were wide sympathies which endeared her to those she sought to assist or represent. Her life must be seen in the context of a pre-feminist view of women's role and the waning of the crown's political authority. If she has not worn well in the historiography it is in large measure due to cultural changes which have led to an increase in the expectations of women and a decline in deference. It has been said that George III was the first of the Victorians; it could be said that his great-granddaughter was the last.

In the reign of George V the monarchy was undergoing a difficult adjustment to social democracy. The consequent increase in royal attention to the demands and institutions of civil society offered the female members of the royal family an ever more prominent role. Queen Mary represented a civic-minded monarchy with unflagging industry. The fact that the monarchy came through a period of unprecedented social and political change with its reputation enhanced was in no small measure due to her serene purposefulness, which betrayed no hint of party to the public. She did more than any member of the royal family in her generation to turn the monarchy into an agency of welfare, thus making it more broadly based on the popular will. George V's admission that he felt 'lost' without her underscored the enormous service she performed for the crown. Indeed, she and her daughter-in-law, Queen Elizabeth, effectively kept the royal show on the road in the first half of the twentieth century.

In 1952 Queen Mary mourned the loss of her son George VI. In keeping with her exacting sense of royal obligation, she was the first to kiss the hand of the new monarch, just as she had kissed the hand of her son on the death of her husband. She died, after a short illness, at Marlborough House, on 24 March 1953, three months before her grand-daughter's coronation. She was buried beside George V in St George's Chapel, Windsor, on 31 March 1953. Among her monuments is the official biography, *Queen Mary*, by James Pope-Hennessy, which brings her vividly to life.

FRANK PROCHASKA

Sources J. Pope-Hennessy, *Queen Mary* (1959) · *DNB* · J. Gore, *King George V: a personal memoir* (1941) · K. Rose, *King George V* (1983) · F. Prochaska, *Royal bounty: the making of a welfare monarchy* (1995) · Royal Arch., Queen Mary papers · Royal Arch., George V papers · Royal Arch., Edward VIII papers · Duke of Windsor, *A king's story: the memoirs of HRH the duke of Windsor* (1951) · P. Ziegler, *King Edward VIII* (1990) · private information (2004) · H. Nicolson, *Diaries and letters, 1945–1960*, ed. N. Nicolson (1971)

Archives Royal Arch., papers of Queen Mary and George V | BL, corresp. with J. E. Burns, Add. MS 46281 · BL, letters to Bishop Carpenter, Add. MS 46722 · BLPES, letters to V. R. Markham · CAC Cam., corresp. with Lord Esher · CCC Cam., letters to Lady Isobel Gathorne-Hardy · CUL, corresp. with Lady Hardinge · Herts. ALS, letters to Lady Desborough · Lpool RO, corresp. with seventeenth earl of Derby · NA Scot., letters to Lady Airlie · NL Scot., letters to Lord Haldane · NL Scot., corresp. with and papers relating to Sir George Smith and Lady Lilian Smith · NRA, priv. coll., letters of her and her mother, duchess of Teck, to Jane, dowager countess of Aylesbury · priv. coll., Athlone papers, corresp., etc. · PRO NIre., letters to Lady Londonderry · Royal Arch., papers of King Edward VIII · St George's Chapel, Windsor, Berkshire, letters to A. V. Baillie, dean of Windsor · V&A NAL, letters to Sir Cecil Harcourt-Smith | FILM BFI NFTVA, actuality footage · BFI NFTVA, documentary footage · BFI NFTVA, news footage · BFI NFTVA, other footage | SOUND BL NSA, current affairs recording

Likenesses M. H. Carlisle, miniature, 1890–99, NPG · E. Hughes, oils, 1890–1900, Royal Collection · H. von Angeli, oils, before 1893, Royal Collection · L. Fildes, oils, 1893, Royal Collection · L. Tuxen, group portrait, oils, 1893, Royal Collection · L. Tuxen, group portrait, oils, 1896 (*Marriage of Princess Maud and Prince Charles of Denmark*), Royal Collection · G. Koberwein, oils, before 1900 · Tyrell, oils, before 1900 · E. A. Abbey, group portrait, oils, 1904 (*The coronation of King Edward VII, 1902*), Royal Collection · A. Hughes, photogravure, 1905, NPG · S. March, bronze bust, 1905, Royal Collection · A. Drury, marble bust, c.1906, Bradford City Art Gallery · W. Llewellyn, oils, 1911–12, Royal Collection; versions, Queen's College, Oxford; Liverpool corporation · G. Frampton, marble bust, 1912, Royal Collection · J. Lavery, group portrait, oils, 1913 (*The royal family at Buckingham Palace, 1913*), NPG; *see illus. in* George V (1865–1936) · J. Lavery, oils, 1913, Royal Collection; study, NPG · S. J. Solomon, oils, 1914, NPG · F. D. Salisbury, oils, c.1918, Harewood House, West Yorkshire · I. Snowman, oils, c.1924, Royal Collection · A. J. Munnings, group portrait, oils, 1925 (*The majesties return from Ascot*), Tate collection · R. Jack, oils, c.1926–1927, Royal Collection · B. Park, bromide print, 1927, NPG [*see illus.*] · L. C. Taylor, oils, 1928, Royal College of Music, London · D. Jagger, oils, c.1930, Bethlam Royal Hospital, Beckenham, Kent; version, Royal Collection · S. Elwes, oils, 1930–39, Royal Collection · J. Lavery, group portrait, oils, 1933, NPG · O. Birley, oils, 1934, Royal Collection · C. Beaton, pen-and-ink drawing, 1935, NPG · F. O. Salisbury, group portrait, oils, 1935 (*Thanksgiving service of the king's silver jubilee*), Guildhall, London · F. O. Salisbury, group portrait, oils, 1935 (*Jubilee service*), Royal Collection · A. T. Nowell, oils, c.1937, Royal Collection · W. R. Dick, bronze bust, 1938, NPG; version, Royal Collection · M. L. Williams, oils, 1938, St Thomas's Hospital, London · W. G. John, bronze model, 1939, NMG Wales · J. H. F. Bacon, group portrait, oils, Royal Collection · W. R. Dick, marble tomb effigy (with King George V), St George's Chapel, Windsor · photographs, NPG · photographs, Royal Collection · portraits, Royal Collection

Mary, princess royal (1897–1965), was born Victoria Alexandra Alice Mary at York Cottage, Sandringham, on 25 April 1897, the third child and only daughter of the future King *George V (1865–1936) and Queen *Mary (1867–1953). Among her godparents were Queen Victoria and the Empress Maria of Russia. Known as Princess Mary until her marriage, she was brought up quietly at Sandringham, Marlborough House, and later at Buckingham Palace. As an only daughter among five brothers, her childhood interests tended to the outdoor sports which they enjoyed, and for some time she shared their lessons. Her reading was frequently boys' adventure stories, and her favourite exercise was riding. She became an expert horsewoman and enjoyed hunting, while her lifelong interest in horse-racing was probably partly inherited from her father and, after her marriage, encouraged by her husband.

During the First World War Princess Mary assisted her

mother in many charities, such as those for helping the mothers, wives, and children of men serving with the forces. She took a great interest in voluntary aid detachment (VAD) work, passing the advanced course in nursing with honours. It was a disappointment to her that she was not allowed to serve in France. Another of her great interests was the Girl Guide movement. She helped also in canteen work, insisting on taking her share of the dull routine tasks. It was her own idea after the war to visit the various women's organizations at a number of places in France. In 1918 Princess Mary came of age, and that year went to the Hospital for Sick Children in Great Ormond Street as a VAD probationer. She had early told her mother she thought nursing was her true vocation and her intense care and interest in the children continued long after she left the hospital in 1920.

On 28 February 1922 the princess married Henry George Charles *Lascelles, Viscount Lascelles (1882–1947), elder son of the fifth earl of Harewood. It was the first royal pageant since the war and aroused great public excitement and enthusiasm. After her marriage she was known as Princess Mary, Viscountess Lascelles, and after her husband's succession to the earldom in 1929 as Princess Mary, countess of Harewood, until in 1932 she was created princess royal. The many interests she shared with her husband included a love of horse-racing and hunting, old furniture, interior decoration, and Yorkshire life. During her father-in-law's lifetime their Yorkshire home was Goldsborough Hall and after his death they moved into Harewood House. Their London home was Chesterfield House and they occasionally stayed at Portumna Castle, co. Galway, which her husband had inherited from his great-uncle, the eccentric marquess of Clanricarde.

The princess in 1918 became colonel-in-chief of the Royal Scots (the Royal regiment), in 1930 of the Canadian Scottish, and in 1935 of the Royal Signals, and later of other signal corps in Australia, Canada, India, and New Zealand, and in 1958 of the Prince of Wales Own regiment of Yorkshire, in 1961 of the Royal regiment of Canada, and in 1963 of the Royal Newfoundland regiment. In 1926 she was appointed commandant-in-chief of the British Red Cross detachments. The Second World War brought many additional duties. In 1940 she was made chief controller and in 1941 controller commandant of the Auxiliary Territorial Service (later the Women's Royal Army Corps). She was energetic in visiting and inspecting these troops; but she never overcame her dislike of inspecting ranks of men, which she regarded as a man's job. In addition, she paid visits to war canteens and similar welfare organizations.

The war brought its personal anxieties to the princess and her husband. Their elder son, George, Viscount Lascelles, who had been born in 1923, was wounded and taken prisoner in Italy when serving with the Grenadier Guards, and their younger son, Gerald, born in 1924, was on active service with the rifle brigade. However, the end of the war saw the family once more united. The loss of her husband, who died on 24 May 1947, a few months after

their silver wedding, increased rather than diminished her activities, as well as leading to a financial crisis caused by death duties, which resulted in opening Harewood to the public. She became chancellor of Leeds University in 1951, enjoying her work as such and being particularly gratified that among those upon whom she conferred honorary degrees was her elder son.

During the monarch's absences abroad the princess was a counsellor of state in 1939, 1943, 1944, 1947, 1953, 1954, 1956, and 1957, as also in 1951 during the king's illness. During the last decade of her life she conscientiously carried out many royal duties. In 1956 she visited France, and the next year Nigeria, and in 1960 she toured for four months in the West Indies, two years later representing the queen at the celebrations on granting independence to Trinidad. In 1964, as colonel-in-chief of the Royal Newfoundland regiment, she visited them on the fiftieth anniversary of the re-forming of the regiment in 1914. In October the same year she represented the queen at Lusaka for the independence celebrations when Northern Rhodesia became Zambia. Only shortly before her death she represented the queen at the funeral in Stockholm of Queen Louise of Sweden. The princess royal died suddenly at Harewood House on 28 March 1965.

The princess was appointed CI in 1919, GBE in 1927, and GCVO in 1937. She received the honorary degree of DCL from Oxford and the LLD from Cambridge, Leeds, Sheffield, St Andrews, Manchester, McGill, Laval, and Lille. She became a dame grand cross of the venerable order of St John of Jerusalem in 1926 and an honorary FRCS in 1927.

A conscientious devotion to her royal duties was perhaps the keynote of the princess's character. Although she never overcame her shyness, which made many of her official duties a trial to her, she never for that reason avoided them or found them a burden. Once she knew people she could talk with them easily and freely, as many senior Girl Guides and Red Cross members could testify, although her son observed that 'she was conditioned to communicate only on as uncontroversial a level as possible' (Memoirs of Lord Harewood, 27). She was probably happiest in her home life with her family and in the quiet rural life in Yorkshire, to which county she was particularly attached. G. K. S. HAMILTON-EDWARDS, rev.

Sources E. Graham, *Princess Mary, Viscountess Lascelles* (1930) · M. C. Carey, *Princess Mary* (1922) · J. Pope-Hennessy, *Queen Mary* (1959) · *The Times* (29 March 1965) · *The tongs and the bones: the memoirs of Lord Harewood* (1981)

Archives Bodl. Oxf., corresp. with Lord Woolton · York Minster Library, letters to Archbishop Garbett | FILM BFI NFTVA, 'The wedding of HRH Princess Mary to the Viscount Lascelles, D.S.O. at Westminster Abbey', Gaumont Graphic, 2 March 1922 · BFI NFTVA, current affairs footage · BFI NFTVA, documentary footage · BFI NFTVA, news footage

Likenesses J. Lavery, group portrait, 1913 (*The royal family at Buckingham Palace, 1913*), NPG; *see illus. in* George V (1865–1936) · S. Elwes, portrait, 1933, Royal Scots Regimental Museum · G. Hudson, portrait, 1933, Royal Scots Regimental Museum · O. Birley, portrait, Harewood House, Yorkshire · A. C. D. Houston, portrait, WRAC HQ Mess, Guildford · G. Kelly, portrait · A. Munnings, portrait, Harewood House, Yorkshire · F. O. Salisbury, portrait, Harewood

House, Yorkshire · J. S. Sargent, portrait, Harewood House, Yorkshire · E. Seago, portrait, WRAC Regimental Museum · photographs, Hult. Arch.

Mary I (1516–1558), queen of England and Ireland, was born at Greenwich Palace on Monday 18 February 1516. Although she was not the male heir desired by her parents, *Henry VIII (1491–1547) and his first wife, *Katherine of Aragon (1485–1536), her birth and early survival offered hope that a healthy son would follow. Henry's desire for a male heir dominated Mary's first twenty years. The fear of anarchy caused by a disputed succession was never far from the minds of contemporaries who could well remember the Lancastrian–Yorkist conflicts. The recent troubles over succession, the relative novelty of the Tudor dynasty, contemporary opinion about the nature of women, diplomatic considerations, and the law, directed Henry's actions in regard to his daughter. In spite of elements in her education working to a contrary effect, conventional, conservative attitudes about women affected Mary's entire life.

Childhood, 1516–1527 Henry and Katherine celebrated Mary's baptism with the pomp and solemnity befitting a royal princess on 20 February in the church of the Observant friars adjoining Greenwich Palace. The important nobility attended: the countess of Surrey carried her to the font assisted by the dukes of Norfolk and Suffolk, while Catherine Courtenay, countess of Devon and daughter of Edward IV, Margaret Pole, countess of Salisbury and daughter of George, duke of Clarence, and the duchess of Norfolk served as her godmothers; the godfather was Cardinal Thomas Wolsey.

Henry and Katherine gave Mary unusually close attention during her early years because she was the only survivor of Katherine's many pregnancies and because the pretty and precocious child obviously delighted both parents. The women in charge of the infant's household changed frequently in the early years, as Margaret Bryan replaced the first governess, Elizabeth Denton, only to be replaced by a woman of higher social status, the countess of Salisbury, in 1519. Since the countess of Salisbury was too closely connected with the third duke of Buckingham, executed in 1521, Henry wanted the dowager countess of Oxford to take over governance of the household, but when the latter's health prevented such service, he appointed Sir Philip Calthorpe as chamberlain and his wife, Jane, as governess at £40 per year. By 1525 the countess of Salisbury had returned to her post and remained a powerful influence on Mary. From the beginning Catherine, wife of Leonard Pole, served as Mary's nurse; Richard Sydnour, dean of Totnes, filled the office of treasurer, while Henry Rowle became her chaplain and clerk of the closet. One gentlewoman (Alice Baker), four rockers, and a laundress completed the first household. By her third year Mary's household had expanded to include six gentlemen, nine valets, three grooms, one yeoman of the chamber, and twelve grooms of the household, as well as Beatrice ap Rice, the laundress who served Mary for the rest of her life. In these early years no expense was spared: the cost of Mary's household, estimated at £1400, amounted

Mary I (1516–1558), by Anthonis Mor, 1554

to about 18 per cent of the outlay of the whole royal household.

The proud parents enjoyed displaying their attractive and gifted child to foreign ambassadors who commented on her pleasing appearance, good health, and precocious behaviour. In February 1518 Sebastian Giustinian, the Venetian ambassador, reported the famous occasion at court when Henry carried the two-year-old Mary in his arms and she, recognizing Friar Dionisio Memo, the organist of St Mark's, Venice, called out 'priest' until he played for her. The incident, which charmed the ambassador, was later interpreted as a harbinger of her staunch Catholicism, but was in fact no more than the action of a happy, confident child.

While Mary was not the desired male heir, she was still a valuable asset in the dynastic marriage and diplomatic power game that Henry played with the Valois and Habsburgs. Henry and Wolsey used the two-year-old child to seal the new alliance with France and general European peace embodied in the treaty of London of 1818. Mary's espousal to the infant François, dauphin of France (1518–1536), took place with great ceremony and celebration at Greenwich on 5 October 1518. Dressed in cloth of gold with a heavily jewelled cap on her head, she received a diamond ring from the dauphin's proxy. However, as the treaty of London began to unravel in the following three years, and as Charles V came into his own as Holy Roman emperor, Henry used Mary to seal a new alliance. The unpublished treaty of Bruges (1521) provided for the future marriage of Mary and Charles, a man sixteen years her senior. The emperor's six-week visit to England in 1522 afforded him some opportunity to observe his six-year-old cousin. At one court occasion Mary demonstrated her social skills by dancing for him. In spite of this successful trip, Henry and Wolsey, wishing in 1524 to neutralize Scotland, now entertained a proposed alliance which included Mary's marriage to the youthful James V. Although no betrothal resulted, this marriage prospect remained a valuable negotiating tool for a year, until Charles V changed the whole European diplomatic configuration by capturing the French king, François I, at Pavia.

When Charles subsequently announced he would marry Isabella, the daughter of the king of Portugal, the English and French responded with a proposed universal peace reinforced by Mary's marriage to either François I or his second son, Henri, duc d'Orléans. Many problems arose during subsequent negotiations in 1527, not the least of them Henry's refusal to allow Mary to leave the realm because she was only eleven. To impress the French envoys Mary again demonstrated her skills in language, music, and dancing, but her small stature made them hesitate about the viability of an immediate marriage. They found her 'admirable by reason of her great and uncommon mental endowments; but so thin, sparse, and small as to render it impossible for her to be married for the next three years' (*CSP Venice*, 1527–33, 105).

Education While all these diplomatic manoeuvres and marriage negotiations provided Henry with a chance to present Mary at elaborate court occasions and gave her high expectations for her future life as a royal consort, they barely interfered with the course of her young life, which revolved around her household. The early records do not show who first taught her to read and write English and Latin, or the other skills compatible with her station such as playing the lute and virginals, singing, dancing, and riding. However, when Henry established her household at Ludlow in 1525, the schoolmaster he appointed was a noted scholar, Richard Fetherston, who was executed in 1540 for denying the royal supremacy. In 1526 Henry ordered her council to consult on Mary's health and 'virtuous education' at least once a month (*LP Henry VIII*, 4/1, no. 2331). As she matured, music played an increasing role in her life and she developed her skill on the lute, virginals, and spinet with the aid of Philip Van Wilder and Paston. However, it was Queen Katherine, who had received a humanist education from her mother, Isabella of Castile, who really took an active interest in her daughter's training and intellectual development. At certain points Katherine herself probably instructed her daughter in Latin, and when they were separated in 1525, she asked to see Mary's Latin exercises. The queen's well-known interest in education inspired Thomas Linacre to write a Latin grammar, *Rudimenta grammatices*, for Mary's use in 1523, and the princess's French tutor Giles Duwes to produce a similar work for that language.

The celebrated Spanish humanist Juan Luis Vives came to England at Katherine's invitation in 1523, and she commissioned him to write a treatise on the general education of women, *De institutione feminae Christianae*, and an outline of studies for Mary, *De ratione studii puerilis*. Vives delivered a mixed message, for while he advocated the education of women, an advanced idea at that time, he still saw women as the inferior sex. The list of acceptable reading included scripture, the church fathers, but only a few pagan classics, and no medieval romances, because he believed women could be led astray all too easily. Nevertheless, in *De ratione studii* Vives recommended that Mary read the dialogues of Plato, works that endow women with the same virtues as men and develop a notion of women as guardians or governors. More's *Utopia* and Erasmus's *Institutio Christiani principis* rounded out her educational programme. Thus while Mary received an exceptional humanist education for a woman of her era, marriage negotiations and court appearances reinforced the conventional belief that her true destiny was to be a royal wife and mother, not a ruler in her own right.

The impact of the divorce, 1527–1536 During these early years Mary remained a loved, confident child, but the cloud of the succession gradually overshadowed her life. While it is difficult to date Henry VIII's decision to set Katherine aside, he undoubtedly turned to other women. A year after Katherine's last failed pregnancy in 1518, Henry's mistress Elizabeth Blount gave birth to a healthy boy whom Henry immediately recognized as Henry Fitzroy, but even his elevation to the dukedom of Richmond in 1525 could not solve the question of succession. Katherine's forceful objections to Henry's favourable treatment of his illegitimate son may have forced him to send Mary to govern Wales, the traditional role for the legitimate heir to the throne. Although some contemporaries referred to her as princess of Wales, there is no evidence that Henry formally invested Mary with the office. Nevertheless her father had enhanced her position as heir to the throne while she learned more about her future royal duties, even if these were largely ceremonial.

Her nineteen-month sojourn in the marches initially insulated Mary from court gossip as Anne Boleyn, who refused to be just another royal mistress, captured Henry's heart. By the time Mary returned to court in 1527, her parents' relationship had altered, and Anne threatened Mary's own status. If the situation at court had not penetrated Mary's consciousness earlier, the increasing tension at court could hardly have escaped the notice of this precocious teenager when she visited her parents on several occasions during the stressful period leading to Katherine's banishment in 1531. While Henry found himself caught between two powerful women, Mary sided with her mother from the beginning and found a rationale for maintaining her devotion to both parents by viewing Anne as a Jezebel, the creator of all her distress. Indeed, Henry saw Mary less and less, as Anne did her best to keep father and daughter apart until she could secure her own position by marrying the king and producing the all-important male heir. At this juncture the psychological toll on Mary began to manifest itself in various physical ailments. After a week's visit with Katherine in May 1531, she could not keep food down for three weeks, and after she was forbidden to see her mother in July, reports of her various illnesses increased. As the separation of mother and daughter continued, Mary's health deteriorated to the point that Henry sent his own physician to her and moved Mary closer to her mother so that Katherine's physician could attend her, but even then she was never allowed the comfort of seeing her mother.

What Mary endured psychologically and physically before Katherine's banishment from court in 1531 was trivial compared with what followed Henry's marriage to Anne and the birth of their daughter *Elizabeth on 7 September 1533. While Henry had risked his throne for yet another girl, he could still hope for a male heir; but Mary, who defied her father and fought the succession of humiliations that followed, risked all with little hope for the future. She had acquired a firm identity as a princess from her early years at court, and when denied that status she acted every inch the Tudor. From the outset she refused to relinquish the dignity of princess, of which she was deprived after Henry announced his marriage to Anne in April 1533. Her very serious illness that summer demonstrated the personal cost of defying her father. After Elizabeth's birth, the council again ordered Mary to stop calling herself princess. She continued to refuse her demotion to the status of 'lady'. Henry, enraged by what he repeatedly called her Spanish stubbornness, failed to recognize that she was as obstinate as he. In December, intent on being obeyed at any cost, Henry sent the duke of Norfolk to Newhall to break up Mary's household and transfer her to Hatfield, where the hated Boleyns had charge of Princess Elizabeth. Mary stoutly defended the validity of her title to Norfolk, but complied after drafting a written protest to her father.

At Hatfield the situation was intolerable not only because she had been deprived of all but two servants, but also because Lady Shelton, Anne's aunt who governed the household, had been given permission to treat her harshly, even beat her, if she continued to resist the king's commands. Henry tried to increase the pressure when he visited Hatfield in early 1534, making his seeing Mary conditional on her renunciation of her title. Mary again resisted, but counting correctly on her father's love, the eighteen-year-old dramatically presented herself 'on a terrace at the top of the house' on her knees with her hands joined (*LP Henry VIII*, 7, no. 83). Henry acknowledged her and his train followed suit. Nevertheless, although Mary could still exploit her father's affection, she could not alter the course of events caused by Henry's marriage to Anne. The Succession Act of March 1534 formally declared Mary illegitimate, elevated Anne's children as the king's heirs, and demanded an oath to that succession. While there is no evidence that either Katherine or Mary was asked to swear the oath at this stage, they were formally presented with the statute and their answer requested, so both courted danger by further defiance.

No matter the psychological or physical cost to herself, Mary maintained her principles as long as possible, showing remarkable courage in the face of tremendous pressure as she refused to swear the oath of supremacy and continued to defend her title and precedence over Elizabeth. Caught between her mother's advice to obey Henry while maintaining her titles, and her father's use of isolation to break her resolve, she learned the art of resistance. Although Mary occasionally glimpsed the support that she and her mother commanded when she was moved from one residence to another, Henry increasingly deprived her of friendly visitors and consolation. The danger to Mary increased as she was gradually separated from her mother, friends, and trusted servants until the emperor's ambassador, Eustache Chapuys, became her only adviser and intercessor at court. Even his access was curtailed. In the absence of decisive action from Charles V, Chapuys urged caution and painted a graphic picture of the dangers of resistance.

Such a situation required considerable political wisdom on the part of an isolated young woman and Mary did her best to play on court sympathies when she could. At one time she forced Elizabeth's servants to remove her from a litter, and another time she arrived at Greenwich before her sister. But, when rumours circulated in 1535 that Anne meant to have Mary murdered, an emotionally exhausted Mary begged Chapuys to arrange her escape to the continent. Before any viable escape plan could be developed she fell ill at Greenwich. She was seriously ill at least twice more that year, and court physicians acknowledged the emotional component of her physical problems when they attributed her state to grief and despair. The effect of these events on Mary's further development as an adult is impossible to calculate. She had learned valuable lessons of resistance, but this education did not provide her with the critical skills she would later need to be an astute political leader.

Defeat and recovery, 1536–1547 The year 1536 began with the most painful events of Mary's young life, but ended with a reversal of fortune. Her mother's death on 7 January 1536 was an incalculable loss and Mary's grief was profound. Katherine's death exposed Mary to even greater danger, but by April Anne Boleyn's life was at risk and her execution on 19 May opened the way for Mary's reconciliation with her father. Henry demanded a very high price for that reconciliation: nothing less than complete submission, the destruction of Mary's conscience and will. She held out for as long as possible, telling Henry she would submit to him 'in all things next to God', and playing on her gender and Henry's affection asked her father to consider that 'I am but a woman, and your child' (*LP Henry VIII*, 10, no. 1022). Finally Cromwell and Henry convinced Chapuys, and through him Mary, that she either had to accept the invalidity of her mother's marriage and the supremacy or she would follow others to the scaffold. Deprived of her mother's support, faced with the arrest of her friends at court (Sir Anthony Browne, Sir Francis Bryan, and Lady Hussey), and under the cruel pressure exerted by her father, Mary capitulated on 22 June. About two weeks later Henry and his new queen, Jane Seymour, visited her at Hunsdon. The subsequent re-establishment of Mary's household and new talk of her marriage prospects signalled her rehabilitation. While her household was not as large and grand as before, some of her loyal servants were restored to her side. As the year drew to a close Mary spent more time at court. Her relationship with Queen Jane was amicable, and as she became reacquainted with her father she probably acquired a better understanding of him. He did nothing, however, to alter the Succession Act and nothing could erase her memories and psychological scars.

Mary reacted with relief to the birth of Prince *Edward in autumn 1537. As the long-desired male heir naturally occupied the centre of attention, Mary happily accepted the decline in her political importance. She served as godmother at Edward's baptism, and then settled into a life as a member of the royal family. Her privy purse expenses show she now moved freely about the countryside and court. Jane the fool, music, minstrels, greyhounds, betting on card games, and purchases of jewellery became a normal part of her entertainment. While fewer illnesses were reported, her childhood health never returned. From her rehabilitation in 1536 until the end of Henry's reign marriage proposals and negotiations continued. Some proposals were serious adjuncts to Valois–Habsburg diplomacy, while some were court rumours about a woman whose unwed status was somewhat anomalous.

Henry's refusal to legitimate Mary or to determine her place in the succession until 1543 precluded any serious negotiations. No one dared advance any internal candidate for her hand, and in 1542 Mary described herself as the 'unhappiest woman in Christendom', indicating her understanding of her rightful destiny as a royal consort (LP Henry VIII, 17, no. 371).

Even though Mary now lived a life more in keeping with her status as the king's unmarried daughter, danger and sadness were never far away. Jane Seymour's death represented another blow as Mary entered her twenties. Her relations with the king's third wife had always been good and Mary's grief prevented the full performance of her duties as chief mourner at the late queen's obsequies. Then late in 1538 Mary's closeness to the Pole family proved risky. Goaded by his dislike of Cardinal Reginald *Pole, Henry attacked the whole family, including the countess of Salisbury, who had contributed so much to Mary's happy childhood years and who had staunchly supported Mary and her mother in the Boleyn era. Cromwell ominously warned Mary not to allow strangers in her household. Henry's marriage to Anne of Cleves was too brief to alter Mary's circumstances, but after Henry married Katherine Howard in 1540, Mary frequently resided on the queen's side of court, even though the two women were not particularly friendly. When Katherine was arrested and her household dissolved late in 1541, Henry dispatched Mary to Prince Edward's household. She had another serious illness in May 1542 with a strange fever and heart palpitations, but by Christmas she was back at court 'with a great number of ladies' and there she remained for a number of months (LP Henry VIII, 17, no. 1212). One of those ladies, a new addition to Mary's household, Katherine Parr, attracted Henry's attention, and in the following July of 1543 Mary with only seventeen others witnessed Henry's last marriage ceremony.

The next three years were the most tranquil and enjoyable of Mary's adult life. Her portrait, painted by Master John in 1544, shows a sombre but serene woman who is still young and attractive. She and Katherine became close and for the remainder of her father's reign Mary seems to have been based at court. Separated in age by only four years, the two women enjoyed a love of fashion, and having both received humanist educations, they shared intellectual interests as well. When Katherine commissioned a new translation of Erasmus's Paraphrases on the New Testament, Mary worked on the 'Book of St John' until illness forced her to turn it over to Francis Mallet, who had recently left Katherine's employ to become one of Mary's chaplains. Friendship and a shared interest in humanist studies also bridged the gap between their divergent religious views. Mary had accepted her father's ecclesiastical settlement in 1536, but her attachment to the Catholic faith, while strong, was a conventional one tempered by humanist criticism. She practised her faith privately and although she gave alms generously, she had never indulged in public exercises of piety such as the visitation of shrines and pilgrimage sites. Her open, even frivolous, enjoyment of court life attracted her young brother's critical comment in a letter to Katherine. He asked that Mary 'attend no longer to foreign dances and merriments' because it was not becoming a 'Christian princess' (LP Henry VIII, 21/1, no. 802). Although this comment was probably only a schoolboy's exercise, it foreshadowed the more sombre life that awaited Mary when her brother became king.

Catholic magnate, 1547–1550 When Henry VIII died, on 28 January 1547, the men at court kept Mary and Katherine in the dark as the new king's uncle, Edward Seymour, earl of Hertford but soon to be duke of Somerset, and his allies took political control. Mary's relationship with the Seymours had been cordial, and even though the Habsburgs considered Mary the only legitimate heir, Somerset had little fear on that score because Mary genuinely loved her brother, and since 1537 had expressed her relief that there was a male heir to the throne. She continued to live in the dowager queen's household until April 1547, and only gradually learned that Henry's will had reaffirmed her place in the order of succession and endowed her with substantial estates in East Anglia. She was given some of her own favourite residences such as Hunsdon and Newhall, as well as substantial properties recently forfeited by the Howards, along with that family's politically important affinity in East Anglia. Mary was now able to develop her own following for the first time, and she used the opportunity to sustain resistance to further religious change. As Edward's government shifted its focus from the Henrician concentration on papal power, purgatory, and relics to central theological ideas like the nature of the mass, Mary increasingly defended her father's settlement and made her religious observance more obvious. Throughout Edward's reign she held fast to the position that her father's religious settlement should stand until her brother reached his majority and in so doing she became the focus of hope for religious conservatives.

Mary initially protested against religious change in autumn 1547 when she wrote to Somerset about the first set of royal injunctions. Somerset boldly reminded her that she had seen the light about papal authority in 1536, and suggested that she needed further instruction now. Mary responded with silence until 1549, when the Act of Uniformity drew a line which she refused to cross and prompted her to resist Somerset's religious policy. By having mass celebrated with great ceremony at Kenninghall, Mary not only signalled her opposition to religious legislation during Edward's minority but also defied his authority as king. The council advised her to conform. Mary, however, answered 'I have offended no law unless it be a late law of your own making for altering of matters of religion, which in my conscience, is not worthy to have the name of law' (*Acts and Monuments*, 6.7). The council, naturally disturbed by this attitude toward the king and parliament, summoned three of Mary's household servants, Robert Rochester, Sir Francis Englefield, and her chaplain John Hopton, in an effort to influence her. Mary's assertion of conscience was similar to her claims in 1536, but in this case Mary was no longer a mere girl of twenty, she was a 33-year-old landed magnate with a following of her own and the support of Charles V, who promptly asked the council to provide a written statement of her exemption from the Act of Uniformity. A public dispensation such as Charles desired was out of the question during the rebellious summer of 1549, so the council offered a compromise: Mary could hear mass privately until the king came of age. This compromise on the eucharist failed to work, because Mary persisted in ignoring the difference between public and private affairs, and in any case the political situation changed in the autumn of 1549.

In September and October 1549 John Dudley, earl of Warwick, skilfully allied with conservative councillors and others to oust Somerset. Although there is evidence that Mary was approached about the possibility of a regency, she played no part in this political coup, and Warwick, having secured his position, turned on the conservatives. He then promoted further religious change, setting the stage for a showdown with Mary. By providing mass in the 'very public privacy' of her household for anyone who came, the princess was clearly abusing the council's spirit of compromise (Loades, *Mary Tudor*, 152). Consequently by spring 1550 Mary's position resembled that in her standoff with Henry VIII. As before she had three relatively distasteful alternatives: she could submit to the king and council, press Edward for a foreign marriage, or flee the realm. She decided to flee and urged Van der Delft, the imperial ambassador, to devise an escape plan. On 30 June 1550 two imperial ships appeared off Maldon ready to spirit Mary out of England. Following her reportedly hysterical last-minute indecision, given a farcical colouring in the account by Jehan Dubois, the ambassador's secretary, Robert Rochester, her comptroller, persuaded Mary to stay by citing the dangers involved and arguing that she would forfeit any right to the throne if she left. Her hesitancy not only reflected her awareness of the substantial risk involved, but also shows her responding to conflicting advice from the Spanish and her trusted household officer, foreshadowing a situation that recurred during her reign. In 1550 Mary listened to her household men and made the right decision.

Defiance, 1551–1553 In December 1550 the uneasy truce over Mary's nonconformity collapsed. As the council and the princess exchanged letters about who could attend her services, their disagreement intensified. In January 1551 Edward intervened, asserting his authority as king: 'in our state it shall malcontent us to permit you, so great a subject, not to keep our laws' (*Acts and Monuments*, 6.11–12). Even if Warwick instigated the January letter, as has been claimed, Edward was now old enough to understand his rights as king and his growing evangelicalism made him eager to bring his sister around to the true faith. The council now insisted that only a few personal servants could hear mass with her. In March 1551 Edward summoned his sister to court. Mary's entry into London accompanied by 130 supporters each holding a rosary leaves no doubt that she knew how to make a theatrical demonstration of her religious conservatism when she chose to do so. At the meeting with her brother and the council she stressed her faith and conscience while Edward emphasized her disobedience. The council added to the pressure on her by having Sir Anthony Browne arrested for hearing mass at Newhall and ordering Rochester to appear before the council, but nothing was resolved.

As the council came to view Mary as the focus of opposition to change by religious conservatives at home and Charles V abroad, it determined to eliminate mass in Mary's household no matter how private. On 14 August 1551 the council ordered Rochester, Englefield, and Edward Waldegrave to convey the decision over their strenuous objection to Mary. When Mary refused to comply, the council responded by imprisoning her servants for contempt and sending Lord Chancellor Rich, Sir Anthony Wingfield, and Sir William Petre to deliver the order to Mary again. She treated their authority with contempt, saying they should show more favour to her for her father's sake who 'for the most part made [you] of nothing'. When the councillors conveyed Edward's desire to replace Rochester, Mary replied she was 'old enough to appoint her own officers'; and, even though she was doing her own accounts, 'her mother and father had not brought her up with baking and brewing' (*CSP dom.*, 1547–53, no. 534). It was a performance worthy of her heritage and it worked, for a new truce followed, albeit a fragile one. Although Mary's servants remained in custody until May 1552, and although the ban on the mass continued, no attempt was made to enforce it. Mary made a state visit to court in June 1552 without apparent reference to her continued defiance.

In autumn 1552 parliament passed another Act of Uniformity, one even more objectionable to religious conservatives, but within months Edward's health began to fail. In February 1553 he was too ill to see Mary for several days when she came to court and he never recovered from this pulmonary infection. Warwick (created duke of Northumberland in October 1551) began to make overtures to Mary, suggesting a recognition of her position as heir to the throne. However, that attitude changed some time in April after parliament had ended. Fearing the destruction of true religion, Northumberland and Edward decided to alter the succession. Mary's well-known attachment to the old religion was probably consistent with the outlook of most of her future subjects and therefore no reason to exclude her, but her well-established habit of relying on Charles V for guidance was more alarming to the current political leaders. Consequently Edward and Northumberland produced a 'Devise for the succession' which excluded both Mary and Elizabeth in favour of the male heirs of Henry VIII's younger sister, Mary, even though no such heirs existed at the time. Then, after Henry's great-niece Lady Jane Grey had married Northumberland's youngest son, Guildford, the document was altered to vest the succession in Jane and her male heirs. As Edward continued to decline physically, Northumberland took the lead in bullying councillors and judges into approving the altered succession. While some hesitated to sign and some called for a parliamentary confirmation of the alteration, most of the judges and councillors signed the letters patent and swore to uphold Jane's succession. Meanwhile the government did its best to conceal first Edward's critical condition and then his death on 6 July 1553.

Securing the crown, 1553 Edward's death precipitated a succession crisis which called on all Mary's powers of resistance. Although she was the legal heir to the throne according to the Act of Succession of 1543, she appeared isolated at first, and with Northumberland in power in London, her cause seemed hopeless. Yet within two weeks the powerful councillors who had supported Jane were proclaiming Mary as queen amid bonfires and great rejoicing. This reversal in fortune occurred because Mary had been warned that Edward's death was imminent, the Catholic gentlemen of her household were ready and able to rally their co-religionists in East Anglia, and the provincial gentry of Norfolk and Suffolk, as well as of Oxfordshire, Buckinghamshire, and the Thames valley, supported her. Mary fled to Kenninghall in Norfolk via Sir John Huddleston's manor at Sawston and the countess of Bath's estate at Hengrave near Bury St Edmunds. Both the earl of Bath and Huddleston joined Mary while others rallied the conservative gentry of Norfolk and Suffolk. Men like Sir Henry Bedingfield arrived with troops or money as soon as they heard the news, and as she moved to the more secure fortress at Framlingham, Suffolk, local magnates like Sir Thomas Cornwallis, who had hesitated at first, also joined her forces.

Although Edward's 'Devise' had mentioned the danger that his half-sisters might marry a foreigner who would take over the government, he nevertheless named Jane to succeed him, and she, although protestant, was certain to be dominated by her father-in-law Northumberland, a relatively new member of the nobility. As the days went by and prominent men rallied to Mary's side, through

respect either for her legitimacy or for her religious conservatism, her support surprised those at the centre of politics. The Spanish ambassadors, the council, and especially Northumberland all seriously miscalculated the shrewdness and boldness of Mary's household officers, her own willingness to take a stand, and her popularity with the provincial aristocracy as well as the common people. When Northumberland left London with troops to capture Mary, the increasingly nervous councillors in the Tower began to divide, and on 19 July a substantial number led by the earls of Shrewsbury, Bedford, Pembroke, and Arundel proclaimed Mary as queen in London to general rejoicing with 'everie strett full of bon-fyres' (*Diary of Henry Machyn*, 37). The plot to alter the succession had collapsed. On 3 August, dressed in a gown of purple velvet and a kirtle of purple satin 'all thicke sett with gouldsmiths worke and great pearle' Mary triumphantly entered London with a large and magnificent retinue, which the populace greeted with joy and traditional festivities. As she entered the Tower there was 'a terrible and great shott of guns' which had never been heard before 'lyk to an earthquake' (Wriothesley, 2.93–4). The size of Mary's retinue, her dress, and the cannonade at the Tower left no doubt about her regal position.

Establishing a regime Now Mary had to rule, a burden she had not desired and a task for which she had had little training or preparation. Up to this point in her life she had been resolute in the face of serious challenges to her principles, surviving several crises which tested her political mettle. But she had learned the lessons of resistance, not the skills of leadership. From the beginning she indicated she would take an active part in governance. This she did throughout her short reign, working long hours in trying to solve problems that would have tested the most skilled of England's rulers. As she assumed the throne Mary, an unmarried woman of thirty-seven, small in stature and near-sighted, appeared older than her years and often tired, because of her generally poor health. For the past seventeen years Mary had settled for life as a royal magnate, and she held the views about marriage and the hierarchical order of society conventionally espoused by the early-sixteenth-century aristocracy. Since Mary was the first woman to rule England in her own right issues of gender dominated and complicated the early days of her reign. On the legal level, a suggestion that parliament meet before the coronation to confirm her title seemed to threaten her regal powers, but that danger was quickly recognized and the coronation preceded the opening of parliament. Her first parliament then reinforced the Act of Succession of 1543 by declaring the validity of the marriage of Henry and Katherine so that the issue of Mary's legitimacy could not be associated with the abolition of the royal supremacy and the restoration of papal authority. At a personal level her advisers assumed that her marriage was as important a consideration as her coronation and the first parliament. Rumours about her marriage circulated at the court in August and September as Mary concentrated on forming her government and looking for a political adviser she could trust implicitly.

Although she had the nucleus of her council and court from her days as princess, and although she had chosen a council at Kenninghall to direct her military effort, Mary now had to create a government out of two groups who naturally distrusted each other, at least at first: her faithful inner circle of servants and the supporters of Jane Grey, powerful men experienced in government. Critics of the size and operation of this council have neither understood how it was formed nor have they separated the tensions of its early days from the working body that soon developed. Mary retained her emergency military council and rewarded her trusted household servants. Members of the old Howard affinity remained on the council, because Mary had to rely on these local gentry to stabilize East Anglia, an area that had spawned rebellion in 1549 and now suffered from unrest and food shortages, making the region appear particularly volatile in July and August 1553. Meanwhile those councillors who had supported Northumberland's attempted coup besieged Mary with apologies.

Mary now had to weigh these men's fine words of apology against their actions in order to select as councillors either seasoned professionals or powerful, conservative nobles, who would be loyal and put their knowledge of royal administration at her service, thereby compensating for the inexperience in national affairs of her trusted household servants. She also added a few men who had suffered under the previous regime, notably the old duke of Norfolk and Stephen Gardiner, bishop of Winchester, whom she named lord chancellor. This combination of the experienced Henricians and Edwardians, her household officers, and emergency councillors produced a council larger than those of the recent past. Although their different experience and roles before August 1553 inevitably gave rise to tensions, the men Mary chose shared a loyalty to the Tudor regime. They might differ on policy at times and they might have old personal quarrels to settle, but they were above all servants of the crown. The council was neither hopelessly faction-ridden nor too large to operate efficiently and effectively, since an inner working group quickly emerged. The imperial ambassador, Simon Renard, reported in September that for many the title of councillor was honorary. Subsequent criticism of the council's size had more to do with Paget's objections to those who constituted the regular working body than numbers. The circumstance that made it most difficult for Mary to govern during her critical first year was not the number of men on the council, but the absence of one single person she could trust implicitly and whose concepts of policy matched her own. Gardiner and Mary shared a common religious ideal, and he bore the burden of restoring Catholicism until late 1554, but the chancellor vigorously opposed her marriage to Philip; Paget, an experienced councillor since the 1540s, who actively supported her choice of husband, obstructed her religious programme, causing her relationship with him to be permanently strained after the spring of 1554. Mary's distant cousin Cardinal Reginald Pole might have filled the void, but his intransigence on the politically explosive issue of returning church lands meant that Mary with the aid of Charles V had to delay his return to England until November 1554.

With the obvious exception of the privy chamber, where the queen's gender dictated a complete change of personnel, considerable continuity characterized the organization of her royal household. The household officers who had served her as princess, men like Rochester, Waldegrave, and Sir Henry Jerningham, were rewarded with equivalent responsibilities at court, while her long-standing female servants such as Susan Clarencius, Jane Dormer, Mary Finch, Frances Waldegrave, and Frances Jerningham formed the nucleus of the privy chamber and ladies at court. In the absence of trusted family members, Mary added religiously conservative women, wives and daughters of privy councillors, and the conservative aristocracy to her chamber and court. Close personal contact with the novice queen gave these women a measure of influence, especially in the first year of her reign, before the personnel of government had become settled and Mary had found an adviser on policy with views to match her own. In particular they could facilitate access to the queen: thus Anne Bacon, wife of Nicholas, helped her husband and her brother-in-law, Sir William Cecil, to gain admission to Mary, while Mary Finch interceded for her half-sister, the wife of Sir Thomas Wyatt, after the latter's rising in 1554. Renard voiced his fear of their influence until Mary announced her marital choice, and they protected her during her false pregnancies.

The subdued court Mary created at the beginning of her reign reflected the quiet life she had enjoyed since 1536. A lively, glamorous court like her father's would have been extraordinary given the queen's matronly age, the circumstances of her accession, and the insecurity of the early months. Her court was not short of talented women, as a contemporary poem noted: Anne Bacon was 'cumly' and 'in bookes sets all her care in lerninge', Catherine 'Briges prayeth with harte and voise' while Baynum was noted for her 'stedfasteness' and 'chastity', and Dorothy Mancell was 'a merye one' (Loades, *Tudor Court*, 212–13). But as Mary, the first English queen regnant, sought to project an image of sobriety and maturity, so her court reflected her public serious side, her mission to fulfil God's plan by ruling well and restoring Catholicism, rather than the private woman who enjoyed music, fine jewels, fashion, dancing, and gambling at cards.

Symbols and ceremonies Two important ceremonies, Edward's funeral and Mary's coronation, set a symbolical tone for the new regime, while two important issues requiring immediate resolution, religion and the queen's marriage, initially divided her council and court. Mary wanted a Catholic funeral for Edward, but some of the council feared that would inflame religious passions. Mary's acceptance of a compromise that provided a public protestant ceremony while she attended a private mass demonstrated the sensitivity to popular sentiment that made the Tudors generally successful rulers. The grandeur of Mary's coronation on 1 October spoke for itself, sweeping away the initial conciliar bickering and fears about her safety. Her procession from the Tower to Westminster dazzled the London crowd as she passed through the streets dressed in her magnificent gown of blue velvet trimmed with powdered ermine. A gold trellis-work cap and a gold garland, both studded with jewels and pearls, were too heavy for the head of a small woman, and she had to hold them up with her hands as she rode in a chariot covered with cloth of gold beneath the canopy of state. Knights, judges, bishops, councillors, and peers preceded her as the parade passed by elaborate pageants accompanied by the sound of trumpets and church bells.

On the morning of the coronation, wearing a mantle of crimson velvet, Mary entered Westminster Abbey where Gardiner, in the absence of the schismatic archbishops of Canterbury and York, presided over an otherwise traditional coronation ceremony. He anointed Mary with holy oil which she had secretly obtained from the continent (thereby avoiding the use of oil tainted by consecration during her brother's reign), while she had previously examined the wording of her coronation oath to ensure that in swearing to uphold the laws she was not committing herself to the religious changes instigated by her father and brother. Historians have criticized Mary for missing a golden opportunity to define the nature of her rule during the celebrations surrounding her entry into London and the coronation. But although Mary's entry into London on 3 August attested to her capacity for a dramatic gesture when necessary, no guidance for the coronation of a woman as a ruler in her own right existed. The only precedents were those for the coronation of a queen consort. Mary's ceremony, which followed the tradition as it had developed for male rulers, invested her with all the power exercised by her ancestors. She had restored the rightful order of succession, and she also saw herself as an instrument of God's will for the restoration of the religion of her childhood, giving symbolic expression to her vision by adopting the motto 'Truth the daughter of time', a motto that first appeared on her great seal in 1553. Mary now expanded the concept of herself as a potential royal consort, which she had developed in childhood, to embrace her new duties as a ruler, and she further articulated this idea in her Guildhall speech during Wyatt's rebellion in 1554 by saying she was married to the realm first.

The Spanish match No matter how well these rites and ceremonies served to establish Mary's rule in the minds of her subjects, contemporaries soon criticized the proposed Catholic restoration and her decision to marry *Philip II of Spain. The religious settlement came as no surprise, but her choice of Philip, no matter how understandable, astonished many and complicated the implementation of her religious programme. Although gender had not been an issue during the succession crisis, since both contenders were female, prevailing opinions on the issue resurfaced quickly afterwards. Mary shared the contemporary opinion that a woman could not rule alone. At the age of thirty-seven she privately preferred to remain single, but she accepted the danger of childbirth in order to fulfil her public duty to her faith and her kingdom. The

realm expected that personal sacrifice, but not the husband she chose.

Although Mary found herself in a unique position for a woman of royal birth, because she had complete freedom to choose her husband, in fact there were few candidates and Mary further restricted herself by turning to Charles V for advice. Charles, with little concern for Mary, seized the opportunity to increase his influence over England by proposing his son Philip. He entrusted the delicate but not difficult task of proposing Philip's name to his ambassador, Renard, who readily exploited Mary's habitual reliance on imperial ambassadors and who also had the benefit of Paget's expert advice and assistance. No other candidate could match Philip's appeal, for he was not only Spanish but also an intelligent, experienced ruler far superior to foreign candidates proposed for her in years past. The only plausible English candidate was Edward Courtenay, newly created earl of Devon, whose lineage as a great-grandson of Edward IV made him eminently eligible. However, Courtenay's dissolute behaviour following his release in August after years in the Tower demonstrated his inability to be the serious helpmate Mary sought.

As rumours about Mary's choice spread about the court in October, councillors, courtiers, and the women of the privy chamber all disagreed on the issue. Gardiner, Rochester, and other long-time servants favoured Courtenay. After Mary announced her choice both Rochester and Waldegrave considered leaving her service. Renard worried about the influence of her ladies, but unnecessarily, it seems. Two of Mary's longest-serving and closest confidantes, Susan Clarencius, who had ties to Courtenay, and Frideswide Strelly, supported Philip, though Mary Finch, another trusted servant, voiced her concern about the eleven-year age difference. In making her decision Mary, aware that Gardiner and her old faithful household servants supported Courtenay, did not consult the council as she pondered the pros and cons of Philip's marriage proposal, which was delivered on 10 October. She waited until the end of the month to announce her decision to twenty-eight councillors, the largest gathering of that body during the reign.

In deciding to marry Philip, Mary made her first and most serious political error. She either failed to comprehend or chose to disregard the depth of an English xenophobic sentiment which was made all the more powerful for being combined with anxiety about the potential power of a male consort. The prospect of a foreign ruler created considerable opposition in parliament and throughout the realm; on 16 November a delegation from parliament went to the queen to try to dissuade her. Although Mary accepted conventional ideas of the inferiority of women where her private affairs were concerned, she reacted forcefully to parliament's unprecedented action. When the speaker of the Commons suggested she marry an English subject, not a foreign prince, Mary angrily swept Lord Chancellor Gardiner aside to tell the delegation she would not subject herself in marriage to an individual whom her position made her inferior. She then repudiated the notion that parliament could dictate her marriage partner, declaring indignantly that they would not have behaved thus in her father's reign.

Nevertheless Gardiner, Rochester, and Paget exploited the opposition expressed by parliament to hammer out a remarkably favourable marriage treaty, designed to preserve all Mary's legal rights as queen as well as to keep Spanish influence and power to a minimum. The eldest son of the union would inherit England and Philip's lands in southern Germany and Burgundy, while his own son from his first marriage, Don Carlos, would inherit Spain and the Habsburg lands in Italy, which would come under English control only if Philip and Mary had issue but Don Carlos had none. The children and the queen herself could not be taken from England without parliamentary approval. If Mary remained childless and predeceased Philip, he would have no right of succession; in fact he was forbidden to influence it. Although Philip could style himself king of England, the treaty denied him regal power while requiring his assistance to the queen in the administration of her realm in so far as the 'rights, laws, privileges and customs' of both kingdoms permitted. Finally England was not to be involved in Habsburg wars. In spite of the favourable terms obtained by her councillors, however, the treaty failed to calm fears of foreign domination and privately Philip repudiated it.

Religious stalemate In contrast to Mary's determined action in regard to her marriage, she demonstrated her flexibility and political sensitivity when she accepted changes in her religious legislation during her first parliament. Although most English people had neither absorbed nor fully accepted the reforms of Edward's reign, Mary's view that a small political cabal had imposed religious change proved mistaken. She had at first signalled a cautious approach to religious change, issuing a proclamation on 18 August 1553 saying she would not coerce any of her subjects into Catholicism until parliament could be called. Consequently the scope of the legislation designed to turn the clock back to 1529 surprised the political nation, and threatened the titles to ecclesiastical lands of those who had acquired them since Henry's first monastic dissolution in 1536. As resistance to the legislative package emerged in October, Mary had the sense to accept Gardiner's judgement that connecting a restoration of church land with a return to Rome would be fatal to the Catholic cause, and ultimately she accepted a compromise that simply abolished the Edwardian legislation. Unfortunately the announcement of Mary's intention to marry Philip obscured her willingness to moderate this first attempt to restore Catholicism in England.

Wyatt's rebellion Wyatt's rebellion in January 1554 demonstrated that the queen's marriage and religious change had already been conflated in the public mind. Alarmed by the Spanish marriage and unaware of the favourable treaty accompanying it, some members of parliament plotted to prevent the match by co-ordinating four separate risings in Kent, Hereford, Devon, and Leicestershire in March 1554. However, when the conspiracy began to come

to light in January, the council acted promptly: the Devon conspirators fled; the Hereford revolt never materialized; and only a few men joined Jane Grey's father, the duke of Suffolk, in Leicestershire. Kent, where Sir Thomas Wyatt raised between 2500 and 3000 men, was the only area where the conspirators had any success. Wyatt himself clearly feared foreign domination; others joined him for reasons both religious and political. The rebellion became dangerous when the trained bands of London led by the aged duke of Norfolk deserted before a possible engagement with Wyatt at Rochester on 28 February. With London and Westminster exposed, Mary and her council handled the critical situation as best they could.

Mary refused to flee; she refused imperial aid, which would only have exacerbated resentment against foreigners; and while her councillors raised troops, she put her faith in the City of London. The queen's instincts proved correct. When she went to the Guildhall to rally the City she rose to the occasion, demonstrating all the courage and eloquence of a Tudor as she declared Wyatt a traitor and defended her religious programme as well as her proposed marriage. She declared herself 'already married to this Common Weal and the faithful members of the same', and she vowed she would stay to shed her royal blood to defend them (Proctor, 239–40). The combination of Mary's speech, correct tactical decisions, and Wyatt's fatal hesitation defeated the rebellion. In its aftermath the government rejected a policy of vengeance, and in spite of Charles V's advice to treat political opponents harshly, the queen and her council punished only the leaders. The two women who had the potential to be the focus for future rebellions suffered as well: Jane Grey lost her life, because of her father's treason, and Elizabeth went to the Tower. But despite the varied motives of leaders and followers, the government chose to emphasize the religious component of the revolt and ignore the opposition to Philip. Thus queen and council equated protestantism with treason, a tactic Elizabeth would later adopt in her effort to crush English Catholicism.

By the time parliament met in April 1554 Wyatt's rebellion had imparted a sense of urgency to the supporters of Catholic restoration. Gardiner's attempt to restore the heresy laws, which resulted in an unseemly political battle in the Lords with Paget, demonstrated that much more needed to be done, but also that further measures to reduce heresy and revive the old faith would have to wait for Pole's arrival and England's formal reconciliation with Rome. The implications of Mary's impending marriage also provided work for parliament, which ratified the marriage treaty with all its clauses, in an act reaffirming the queen's power in relation to a foreign consort. The reasons for another act dealing with the queen's royal power remain unclear, but whether due to Wyatt's rebellion or to the prospective Spanish marriage, its extent was manifestly felt to need clarifying.

Philip and Mary As soon as Mary dissolved parliament, her attention turned to her marriage. After lengthy delays Philip arrived in England on 19 July. Their first meeting turned out well in spite of the obvious age difference. On the feast of St James, 25 July, dressed in a golden robe, Mary arrived at Winchester Cathedral with a large company of councillors and ladies to meet Philip, who was also dressed in gold. Having no close male relatives, Mary was given away by four councillors, the marquess of Winchester, and the earls of Derby, Bedford, and Pembroke. After a nuptial mass the king and queen walked slowly under the canopy of state to the bishop's palace, which had been hung in gold and silver for the wedding banquet. Following a few more days in Winchester the couple moved at a leisurely pace to Windsor and then to London so that Mary's subjects could view her husband. For Mary the wedding should have brought relief, giving her the fellowship of a ruler who could help her manage the myriad problems England faced.

The joy of the wedding was soon enhanced by a doctor's assurance in the autumn that Mary showed all the signs of pregnancy. Unfortunately for Mary's hopes and plans both she and the doctor were deluded, but that did not become obvious until June 1555. She publicly celebrated her pregnancy with a procession and Te Deum at St Paul's just as her second parliament convened in late November 1554. But although the ambassadors reported the obvious signs of pregnancy, her physical condition was the result of a combination of long-standing menstrual problems and a great deal of wishful thinking. Her subsequent failure to produce an heir represented the ultimate failure for a sixteenth-century woman. However, until disillusionment set in the time between the wedding and Philip's departure in September 1555 has always been considered the high point of Mary's reign and presumably the happiest part of it for her.

Two portraits painted between June and December 1554 depict Mary during this period. They not only reflect the different views of the English and Habsburg courts but cast doubt on this so-called idyllic time. Hans Eworth's picture, though lacking the complicated symbolism of later portraits of Elizabeth, displays a somewhat idealized, ageless, good-looking woman. This portrait makes a simple statement of Mary's life and goals shortly before her marriage, showing her wearing a pearl given to her by Philip and a cross at her neck, while she holds the Tudor rose in her hand. The more famous and most frequently reproduced portrait, painted by Anthonis Mor, probably in November or December 1554, does not reflect the happiness Mary is usually presumed to have experienced after her marriage, her assumed pregnancy, and England's reconciliation with Rome. She looks uncomfortable as she sits stiffly on her throne holding the Tudor rose and wearing Philip's pearl, but without a cross. Moro's portrait is more realistic than most court portraits, and though it may reflect a Habsburg view of royalty (Philip commissioned it), it clearly depicts a face that was beginning to suffer the ravages of illness and age.

Although Philip took his position in England seriously, the nature and extent of his influence on English affairs has been debated from the sixteenth century onwards, thanks to conflicting sources: the Spanish ambassadors assigned him a significant role in public affairs, while the Venetian ambassador thought his political contribution negligible. Mary and her councillors certainly expected Philip to assist the queen forcefully if necessary. His arrival with a complete household, only to find an English one established for him, caused some friction, but initially at least Mary's government did all it could to help him understand English political problems. But although the council ordered the secretaries to translate the minutes into Latin so that he could read them, he could only communicate with some individuals through an interpreter, which constituted a considerable handicap. When Philip left England in 1555, he and Mary appointed a small group of councillors to correspond with him and act on his behalf. The few surviving letters from Philip to this 'council of state', as he called it, attest his famous attention to detail, but cannot be interpreted as constituting government from afar, or reform of the council. As the months passed England receded from the centre of Philip's attention, and Mary's unsuccessful attempt to secure legislation making him king, followed early in 1556 by Henry Dudley's anti-Spanish conspiracy, confirmed Philip's sense that his influence in England had decided limitations.

There is little doubt, however, that Philip's arrival broke the religious stalemate. To facilitate England's reunion with Rome and the revitalization of Catholicism, he initially employed Dominican friars: Father Pedro de Soto, who later received a chair at Oxford, helped negotiate the return of Pole to England in November; Juan de Villagarcia, who also received a chair of divinity at Oxford, was instrumental in obtaining Cranmer's recantations. These two were so effective at Oxford that John Jewel later commented, 'one could scarce believe that so much mischief could have been done in such a short time' (*CSP for.*, 1558–9, 269–70). A third Dominican, Bartolomé Carranza, became Mary's confessor. Alfonso de Castro, a Franciscan who was an authority on heresy, remained a member of Philip's household; he argued for a more determined campaign against dissent, while expressing misgivings about the use of the death penalty to punish it.

Catholic restoration Cardinal Reginald Pole, the man Mary relied upon to direct her kingdom's return to orthodoxy, did not arrive in England until November 1554. His intransigence on the issue of returning church lands caused Charles V to delay his journey to England so that the marriage to Philip could proceed with as little trouble as possible and without being unduly associated with that political quagmire. Pole had considerable experience and talent to bring to the revitalization of the faith. He had developed a solid reputation as a humanist, and was an advocate for reform at the early sessions of the Council of Trent. Mary arranged the ceremonial restoration of the Roman primacy so that it would have a maximum effect on MPs, who would then return home with news of Pole's conciliatory tone and impressions of the beauty of pre-Reformation ceremony. Pole's speech, delivered on 30

November before Mary, Philip, and the assembled parliament, offered reconciliation in exchange for the revocation of all ecclesiastical legislation after 1529 with the notable exception of laws pertaining to ecclesiastical lands. With carefully chosen words he assured the audience that he came 'to reconcyle, not to condemne, … not to destroy but to build, … not to compel but to call agayne'. He also advanced the idea of Mary's marriage to the kingdom when he emphasized how God had 'miraculously' preserved the queen, 'a virgin, helples, naked and unarmed' who had prevailed over tyranny (Nichols, *Chronicle of Queen Jane*, 157, 159).

With Mary's approval and support, Pole, at first as papal legate and later as archbishop of Canterbury, was free to pursue his humanist vision of a reformed Catholic church in England. However, his twenty-year absence had not prepared him for the extent of damage to the ecclesiastical structure and finance, and ultimately these issues absorbed most of his time and energy. The programme which he developed concentrated on the education of the clergy and through them the laity, and he rejected one more rapid, based on missionary work by the Jesuits. Most of Pole's programme was outlined in his London synod of 1555–6. He gave particular emphasis to episcopal and clerical leadership and to training: bishops had to hold regular diocesan visits to detect disorder and audit finances, and priests had to be resident, while his decrees provided a plan for clerical education that later became a model on the continent. The ranks of the clergy had been reduced over the years of religious change and recently by Mary's deprivation of married clergy before her second parliament. Although Pole generally pardoned those who abandoned their wives, his high standards guaranteed that it would take time to provide adequately trained men for all the benefices in England. Only then could those born in the last twenty years be instructed properly and participate in the ancient liturgy in all its fullness.

Pole's appointments to the episcopate reflect both his own and Mary's intellectual interests. Many of the new bishops were highly regarded scholars who began to produce solid defences of the Catholic faith. The Marian regime was well aware of the educational value of the printing press, and promoted a number of religious treatises, sermons, and catechisms. Thomas Watson, bishop of Lincoln, wrote *Holsome and Catholic Doctrine Concerning the Seven Sacraments* while Edmund Bonner, the restored bishop of London, produced a book of homilies entitled *A Profitable and Necessarye Doctryne* and a children's catechism which Pole endorsed for use throughout the realm. Mary and Pole also emphasized the beauty of the pre-Reformation church by ordering the restoration of rood screens and other forms of church decoration, while the royal chapel encouraged the recovery of liturgical music. Most of what Pole achieved was carried out without papal help after the election of Pope Paul IV in summer 1555. A hardline traditionalist, the new pope later revoked Pole's legatine authority and demanded his return to Rome to answer charges of heresy; he also delayed the confirmation of bishops, leaving Elizabeth in the happy position of having several important ecclesiastical vacancies to fill at her accession.

Pole's programme of Catholic restoration was generally positive, as he had promised, but it had one negative side, the pursuit of heresy, and attitudes towards this have coloured all subsequent evaluations of Mary's religious policy, and indeed of her entire reign. The question of responsibility for the active pursuit of heretics remains difficult to resolve, both because conclusive evidence is lacking and also because, quite naturally, the biographers of the critical players tend to deflect blame from their subject. Most sixteenth-century people agreed that heresy was a cancer that must be excised for the health of society; Pole and Mary believed that the country had been misled by a small group, whose elimination would speed the restoration of Catholic worship. That they were mistaken became clear following the reinstatement of the fourteenth-century heresy laws in 1555, which resulted in the burning of Hugh Latimer and Nicholas Ridley in 1555 and Thomas Cranmer in 1556, as well as of the popular preachers John Rogers and Rowland Taylor, but which failed to discredit protestantism. After executing the leaders, the government expanded its pursuit of heretics until about 290 individuals, largely from the lower classes in south-east England, had been executed by the end of the reign. The Venetian ambassador noted the unpopularity of the London burnings and Mary's advisers divided on the issue. Pole attempted to restrain Bonner's energetic pursuit of heretics in London, only to have the council sternly order Bonner to continue. Gardiner, who initially saw eliminating heretics as an effective policy, quickly recognized that prosecutions had become counterproductive, but others like Sir John Baker, another privy councillor, continued to encourage the prosecutions in Kent. Apart from Mary's determination to execute Cranmer, there is little explicit evidence for her continuing involvement, except for the obvious fact that as queen she could have halted the process at any moment.

The prejudice against Mary and her religion which developed in Elizabeth's reign has continued to obscure the positive aspects of the former's reign. She laboured mightily to cope with a series of highly complex problems inherited from her brother and father. Debt plagued the regime from the outset, with government finance proving particularly intractable. The marquess of Winchester, Sir John Baker, and Sir Walter Mildmay, all men skilled in the arcane workings of the exchequer, started to restore the supremacy of that office, though their policies took time to implement and even longer for their effects to be felt. The currency too was problematic, the result of years of debasement. The council took vigorous action against forgers of domestic and foreign coins, but while the queen's financial advisers discussed a major recoinage, dearth and the disruption of war in Mary's last two years prevented action. Still, these advisers had laid the foundation for the Elizabethan recoinage. Mary's commercial policy was forward-looking and earned the support of the merchant community. Shrinking markets and dependence on the Calais staple led to a search for new markets in Guinea, the Baltic, and Russia. The latter resulted in the formation of the Muscovy Company in 1555. When the government overhauled the book of rates in 1558, adding substantially to its revenue, the merchants registered only a mild protest. During her last two years Mary and her council also tried to provide relief to localities afflicted by a series of poor harvests and the epidemics that followed.

War and the loss of Calais: Mary's death From the beginning of the reign Mary and most of her council had understood that any involvement in continental hostilities would place England's fiscal resources under intolerable strain, any reforms notwithstanding. Mary saw herself as an advocate for peace and she succeeded in bringing the two antagonists, the Habsburgs and Valois, to the table in 1555 at Gravelines. But in spite of the efforts of Pole and his colleagues neither side was willing to make the necessary territorial concessions and the talks collapsed. Worse, although they signed a peace at Vaucelles in February 1556 without English participation, it lasted only long enough for the combatants to regain their fighting strength. When Philip invaded the Papal States in September 1556, Mary and her council, with the exception of Paget, watched events with considerable dismay because they realized it was probably only a matter of time before England became involved. There were many good reasons for remaining on the sidelines: in particular, plans for fiscal solvency would be compromised and popular support for the government and its religious reform would be damaged.

The advocates of peace, Mary's trusted household servants, constituted a majority on the council until Philip returned to England in March 1557 to plead his case for English support before her sceptical advisers. Even then the council repeated their concerns about crown finance, the possibility of a Scottish invasion, the predictable decline in England's trade with France, and the effect of bad harvests on the realm. While Philip and Mary were doing their best to persuade individual councillors, the English protestant exile Thomas Stafford sailed from France to invade England. Local forces easily dealt with his troops when he landed at Scarborough, but when the 'invasion' news reached the council those against the war had lost the political battle. Militarily England was better prepared to meet the challenge than she had been since Henry's reign. Mary's government had overhauled the administration and finances of the navy and her ships were in good repair. Having realized the inadequacy of the old feudal and national levies, the council had also begun to reorganize England's land forces. In 1558 parliament passed a Militia Act which gave responsibility for raising troops and to muster commissions in the counties to the lord lieutenants. Mary's council and competent military leaders together achieved a number of successes at first. In summer 1557 the navy aided Philip by clearing French shipping from the channel and successfully ferried English forces to the continent. Land forces under the earl of Pembroke participated in the capture of St Quentin in August 1557, while another army defended the northern border against a threatened Scottish attack. Nevertheless,

the war has been viewed as foolish because Calais and its associated forts fell to the French in January 1558. As the last remnant of the English claim to continental monarchy, Calais had a symbolic value which arguably outweighed its economic and military importance. Its loss was certainly felt as a humiliation.

Mary received the news of Calais stoically, perhaps encouraged by the belief that she was pregnant (the story that she declared that the word 'Calais' would be found engraved on her heart appears to be apocryphal). Her profound desire to produce an heir resulted in another disappointment, and she appeared depressed in the spring. Over the years her general health had deteriorated as severe headaches and dysmenorrhoea took their toll. As summer ended Mary had an unusual bout of fever, probably induced by the influenza that carried away so many in 1558. Although she rallied in September, by the end of October another serious fever signalled the end. Mary's gradual decline in autumn 1558 allowed Elizabeth to plan for her succession even though Mary postponed the inevitable naming of her half-sister until the last minute. Although their relations were not always overtly hostile, Mary had long disliked and distrusted Elizabeth. She had resented her at first as the child of her own mother's supplanter, more recently as her increasingly likely successor. She took exception both to Elizabeth's religion and to her personal popularity, and the fact that first Wyatt's and then Dudley's risings aimed to install the princess in her place did not make Mary love her any more. But although she was several times pressed to send Elizabeth to the block, Mary held back, perhaps dissuaded by considerations of her half-sister's popularity, compounded by her own childlessness, perhaps by instincts of mercy. On 6 November she acknowledged Elizabeth as her heir. Feria, the Spanish ambassador, devoted his last dispatches of the reign largely to an analysis of the princess and her plans for the realm.

Mary died on 17 November 1558, before many of her policies could come to fruition. She was buried in Henry VII's chapel in Westminster Abbey. Her early death at forty-two thus left an incomplete programme and a country at war, one that was also suffering from two years of poor harvests, famine, and a flu epidemic, but her successor had the decided advantage of being the second woman to rule and of having had the opportunity to learn from her sister's successes and failures.

Assessments The shift in religious policy which came in 1559 brought with it increased criticism both of Mary's Catholic restoration and of her achievements. The vehement anti-Catholicism fostered by John Foxe and by Elizabeth's advisers merged in the sixteenth century with England's sense of national identity and in the nineteenth century with notions of predestined English greatness, a potent combination that has made it difficult even for Mary's most sympathetic defenders to escape the bonds of a history written by the political and religious victors. In the mid-twentieth century, as the work of A. G. Dickens shifted the focus of discussion and research from the level of the political and ecclesiastical élite to that of the man and woman in the pew, he opened a debate about the nature of religious change, on the strengths and weaknesses of Catholicism, and on the numbers and influence of protestants, which has yet to be resolved. By then historians were also beginning to challenge the black and white picture painted by religious polemic and hagiography. J. A. Muller produced a biography of Gardiner in 1926 which started to free him from the venom of Foxe's portrayal, E. H. Harbison looked at Mary's reign from the perspective of the rival ambassadors at her court, and in 1953 H. F. M. Prescott tried to present an objective biography. A collection of essays on the mid-Tudor period edited by J. Loach and R. Tittler in 1980, and authoritative studies of Mary's reign by D. M. Loades, heralded new interpretations of such issues as parliament, the council, and the military, reinforced between 1990 and 2000 by biographies of Gardiner, Pole, and Cranmer. A growing interest in women's history has led to a fruitful discussion about female succession and the presentation of a woman as ruler, although most of this writing has centred on the evolution of Elizabeth's image, which took a long time to develop, and not on the short reign of Mary and her very different sense of herself. Thus Mary still stands condemned by ideology, no longer for her religious faith but for her failure to challenge the place of women in a patriarchal society.

There is no question that while Mary's choice of husband made sense in terms of her personal history, with its long-standing reliance on her Spanish relatives, it was a political mistake because it exacerbated English xenophobia and complicated the implementation of her main objective, the restoration of the Catholic church. This marital alliance, with the aid of expert Elizabethan propaganda, stamped Catholicism as an alien presence in England, and has consequently prevented 'a just assessment of the aims and achievements of the Marian Church' (Duffy, 524). In fact the revived Catholicism that Mary left to her sister took a considerable effort over more than five years for Elizabeth to reverse.

In the political arena, although Mary was a conscientious and hard-working ruler, she lacked the personal charisma needed to lead the realm through a difficult period. There was much more continuity than change in Mary's administration, and co-operation largely characterized her work with parliament and the council. There were moments of tension: members of parliament wanted to protect the ecclesiastical lands they had acquired before they were ready to consider sweeping religious change; and they refused to crown Philip. However, Mary was generally willing to compromise or wait for a more auspicious time to enact her religious programme because she realized the value of the support of the political nation. The personal rivalry between Gardiner and Paget as well as their differences over policy initially deprived Mary of an adviser she could trust completely, but the council was still able to carry out its many functions effectively. Indeed, it did a remarkable job in leading a reluctant nation during the war of 1557–8. Circumstances beyond her control such as bad weather and the flu epidemic

exacerbated Mary's problems, but above all she was not given the time she needed to consolidate her initiatives in religion and finance, which were predicated on a longer reign and her hopes for a child who would carry on her policies. Consequently the economic, naval, and administrative reforms enacted by parliament benefited Elizabeth more than they did Mary.

In the final analysis, it seems more profitable for historians to compare Mary's five years as queen with the first five years, not the whole forty-five, of her sister's reign. Mary demonstrated that a woman could rule the kingdom in her own right. Her marital choice, by revealing the problems that a foreign marriage could create, gave her sister good reason to resist pressure to marry. In forming her government Elizabeth retained some of Mary's experienced councillors, who continued to work toward fiscal reform. Both queens had to make compromises in their initial religious legislation, and both had to deal with a body of dissent, but Elizabeth had learned the futility of religious persecution, and was more adept in applying Mary's equation of religious dissent with treason. Given a fair chronological comparison, and the perspective provided by the secularized culture of the late twentieth century, Mary emerges as a much more sympathetic person and conscientious ruler than was previously allowed, one who belies the simplistic bloody tyrant of protestant mythology.

ANN WEIKEL

Sources *LP Henry VIII*, vols. 1–21 · *CSP Spain, 1550–58* · *CSP Venice, 1509–58* · R. A. Vertot, ed., *Ambassades des messieurs de Noailles en Angleterre* (1861–1903) · *CSP dom., 1547–58* · *CSP for., 1553–60* · *APC, 1542–58* · D. MacCulloch, 'The *Vita Mariae Angliae Reginae* of Robert Wingfield of Brantham', *Camden miscellany, XXVIII*, CS, 4th ser., 29 (1984), 181–301 · J. G. Nichols, ed., *The chronicle of Queen Jane, and of two years of Queen Mary*, CS, old ser., 48 (1850) · *The diary of Henry Machyn, citizen and merchant-taylor of London, from AD 1550 to AD 1563*, ed. J. G. Nichols, CS, 42 (1848) · *The acts and monuments of John Foxe*, ed. S. R. Cattley, 8 vols. (1837–41), vol. 6, pp. 1–23, 356–590 · F. E. Madden, ed., *Privy purse expenses of the Princess Mary* (1831) · J. Proctor, 'The history of Wyatt's rebellion', *Tudor tracts, 1532–1588*, ed. A. F. Pollard (1903), 207–57; repr. (1964) · C. V. Malfatti, ed., *The accession, coronation, and marriage of Mary Tudor* (1956) · C. Wriothesley, *A chronicle of England during the reigns of the Tudors from AD 1485 to 1559*, ed. W. D. Hamilton, 2 vols., CS, new ser., 11, 20 (1875–7) · J. G. Nichols, ed., *The chronicle of the grey friars of London*, CS, 53 (1852) · D. Loades, *Mary Tudor: a life* (1989) · J. Loach, *Parliament and the crown in the reign of Mary Tudor* (1986) · G. Redworth, *In defence of the church Catholic: the life of Stephen Gardiner* (1990) · D. Loades, *The reign of Mary Tudor: politics, government and religion in England, 1553–58*, 2nd edn (1991) · D. Loades, *The Tudor court* (1987) · D. M. Loades, *Two Tudor conspiracies* (1965) · R. Tittler, *The reign of Mary I*, 2nd edn (1991) · S. E. James, *Kateryn Parr: the making of a queen* (1999) · D. E. Hoak, 'Two revolutions in Tudor government: the formation and organization of Mary I's privy council', *Revolution reassessed: revisions in the history of Tudor government and administration*, ed. C. Coleman and D. Starkey (1986) · C. Merton, 'The women who served Queen Mary and Queen Elizabeth: ladies, gentlewomen and maids of the privy chamber, 1553–1603', PhD diss., U. Cam., 1992 · J. M. Richards, 'Mary Tudor as "Sole Quene"?: gendering Tudor monarchy', *HJ*, 40 (1997), 895–924 · J. M. Richards, '"To promote a Woman to Beare Rule": talking of queens in mid-Tudor England', *Sixteenth-Century Journal*, 28/1 (1997), 101–21 · J. M. Richards, 'Love and a female monarch: the case of Elizabeth Tudor', *Journal of British Studies*, 38/2 (1999), 133–61 · M. V. de la Torre, 'Sex, subjugation and the succession: gender and politics in early Elizabethan England', PhD diss., New York University, 1997 · E. Duffy, *The stripping of the altars: traditional religion in England, c.1400–c.1580* (1992), 524–65 · J. D. Alsop, 'The act for the queen's regal power, 1554', *Parliamentary History*, 13/3 (1994), 261–76 · E. Russell, 'Mary Tudor and Mr. Jorkins', *Historical Research*, 63 (1990), 263–76 · D. M. Loades, 'Philip II and the government of England', *Law and government under the Tudors: essays presented to Sir Geoffrey Elton*, ed. C. Cross, D. Loades, and J. J. Scarisbrick (1988), 177–95 · G. Redworth, '"Matters impertinent to women": male and female monarchy under Philip and Mary', *EngHR*, 112 (1997), 597–613 · J. Loach, 'The Marian establishment and the printing press', *EngHR*, 101 (1986), 135–48 · 'The count of Feria's dispatch to Philip II of 14th November 1558', ed. M. J. Rodríguez-Salgado and S. Adams, *Camden miscellany, XXVIII*, CS, 4th ser., 29 (1984) · J. N. King, *Tudor royal iconography* (1989) · J. Woodall, 'An exemplary consort: Antonis Mor's portrait of Mary Tudor', *Art History*, 14 (1991), 192–224 · A. Carter, 'Mary Tudor's wardrobe', *Journal of the Costume Society*, 18 (1984), 9–28 · D. M. Loades, *The Tudor navy* (1992), 159–77 · T. Glasgow, 'The navy in Philip and Mary's war, 1557–1558', *Mariner's Mirror*, 53 (1967), 321–42 · R. C. Braddock, 'The royal household, 1540–1560', PhD diss., Northwestern University, 1971 · R. K. Marshall, *Mary I* (1993) · E. H. Harbison, *Rival ambassadors at the court of Queen Mary* (1940) · J. Loach and R. Tittler, eds., *The mid-Tudor polity, c.1540–1560* (1980) · P. L. Hughes and J. F. Larkin, eds., *Tudor royal proclamations*, 3 vols. (1964–9) · H. F. M. Prescott, *Mary Tudor*, 2nd edn (1962) · D. Starkey, *Elizabeth: apprenticeship* (2000) · T. F. Mayer, *Reginald Pole, prince and prophet* (2000) · A. G. Dickens, *The English Reformation*, 2nd edn (1989)

Archives BL, Add. MS 26748; Egerton MS 3723F · PRO, Exchequer, E 101, 179, 350 · PRO, Foreign, SP 69 · PRO, Lord Chamberlain's Office, LC 2, 5 · PRO, Privy Council, PC 6–8 · PRO, state papers, domestic, SP 11 · S. Antiquaries, Lond., list of offices and fees and account of her coronation | BL, Arundel MS 151 · BL, Cotton MSS Otho C.x, E.ix; Titus A.xiv, B.ii, C.viii; Vespasian C.xiv, F.xiii; Vitellius C.i · BL, Egerton MS 2986 · BL, Harley MSS 283, 289, 416, 3504, 6234, 6807, 6949 · BL, Lansdowne MSS 3, 170 · BL, Sloane MS 1583 · BL, Stowe MSS 141, 354, 571

Likenesses attrib. L. Horenbout, miniature, *c*.1521–1525, NPG · H. Holbein the younger, chalk drawing, *c*.1536, Royal Collection · H. Eworth, oils, 1544, NPG · Master John, oils, 1544, NPG · group portrait, oils, *c*.1545, Royal Collection · H. Eworth, oils, 1554, S. Antiquaries, Lond. · A. Mor, oils, 1554, Museo del Prado, Madrid [*see illus.*] · J. da Trezzo, medal, *c*.1555, BM; electrotype, NPG · double portrait, oils, 1557 (with Philip), Woburn Abbey, Bedfordshire · H. Eworth, miniature, Buccleuch estates, Selkirk, Scotland · W. Hollar, engraving (after H. Holbein), NPG · A. Mor, oils, other versions, Isabella Stewart Gardner Museum, Boston, Massachusetts; Castle Ashby, Northamptonshire

Mary II (1662–1694), by Sir Godfrey Kneller, 1690

Mary II (1662–1694), queen of England, Scotland, and Ireland, was born on 30 April 1662 in St James's Palace. She was the eldest child of James, duke of York, the future *James II (1633–1701), and his first wife, Anne Hyde [*see* Anne (1637–1671)]. Her maternal grandfather was Edward *Hyde, first earl of Clarendon, architect of the restoration of Charles II. She was named after her aunt, *Mary, princess of Orange, who had recently died. At her baptism her godparents were Prince Rupert and the duchesses of Buckingham and Ormond. These relationships identified the princess with the Stuart dynasty and its survival from her birth.

Childhood and education Apart from a sojourn in York from 1665 to 1667, to escape the last visitation of the plague, Mary lived in the south of England until she married. The question of her education was extremely sensitive, given her father's Roman Catholicism and the fact that her mother also exhibited Catholic sympathies before her death from breast cancer in March 1671. After her mother died Mary lived at Richmond Palace, where her upbringing was entrusted to a governess, Lady Frances Villiers. To avoid any suspicions being aroused about Mary's protestantism she was educated by George Morley, bishop of Winchester, Henry Compton, bishop of London, and Edward Lake, archdeacon of Exeter, who instructed her in the principles of the Church of England, to which she became devoted. Although she learned no Latin or Greek, she did acquire French from Pierre de Laine, who in 1667 published a grammar written for the princess. According to her teacher she was 'absolute mistress of the French tongue' (Laine, 8). Her drawing-master was the dwarf Richard Gibson, who later went with her, together with his equally diminutive wife, to the Netherlands. Among Mary's other accomplishments were playing music on the lute and the harpsichord, and dancing, at which she was so proficient that on 2 December 1674 she appeared at court in the title role of John Crowne's ballet, *Calisto, or, The Chaste Nymph*. When Crowne published it in 1675 he dedicated it to her. Another work dedicated to her was one by Basu Makin on female education published in 1673, which hailed her as principal among all 'Ingenious and Vertuous ladies' (A. Fraser, *The Weaker Vessel: Women in Seventeenth Century England*, 1984, 321). 'Her Age and her Rank had denied her opportunities for much study', observed Abel Boyer in 1701, 'yet she had read the best Books in English, French and Dutch' (Maccubbin and Hamilton-Phillips, 4). She showed her own concern for education in 1693 by helping to establish the College of William and Mary in Virginia. Mary spent much of her leisure time gardening, doing needlework, and playing at cards, her addiction to card games earning her a rebuke from her tutor Dr Lake, especially when she played on Sundays.

Marriage The question of Mary's marriage partner was already being openly discussed when she was only eight years old. The deaths of her mother and her brother Edgar in 1671 made her second in the line of succession to the throne. In the absence of any legitimate children of *Charles II, her uncle, Mary became heir to the crown after her father, James. The disposal of her hand thus became a crucial issue in British politics and European diplomacy. From the start, the claims of *William of Orange were pressed by protestants. William himself visited England in the winter of 1670–71 'to pretend to the Lady Mary' (*Memoirs of Sir John Reresby*, ed. A. Browning, M. K. Geiter, and W. A. Speck, 1991, 82). Although Charles II was in favour of the match, James was not, and had to be bullied into it by his brother. For a while James held off, hoping to arrange a marriage between Mary and the French dauphin. Meanwhile William had benefited from the coup in the Dutch republic in 1672 which removed the de Witt brothers and elevated him to the position of stadhouder. He himself then cooled on the question, as he did not wish to identify himself with the English court and its pro-French foreign policy. With the ending of the Third Anglo-Dutch War in 1674, however, the negotiations for a marriage treaty were reopened. The earl of Danby, who was by then the chief minister in England, was particularly keen on this protestant match. Sir William Temple discussed it in a two-hour conversation with William in the Netherlands in which he enthused about the princess's eligibility. William visited England again in the autumn of 1677, when his marriage to Mary was arranged between himself and her father and uncle. She was then informed of the outcome on 21 October 1677, at which she 'wept all that afternoon and the following day' ('Diary of Dr Edward Lake', 5).

Mary's reaction was natural in an attractive young woman of fifteen when faced with the prospect of being married to the Dutchman who was so unappealing, with his blackened teeth and hooked nose, that her sister *Anne called him Caliban. Mary was taller than her husband, being all of 5 feet 11 inches while he was 5 feet 6½ inches in height. She was also a passionate woman, while he was cold and regarded as unfeeling. Mary's highly emotional nature was expressed in the adolescent letters she wrote to her friend Frances Apsley, in which she described herself as the wife and her correspondent as her husband. Much of the passion she displayed can be dismissed as the excess of adolescence. The correspondents were consciously play acting, for they also signed their names Mary Clovin and Aurelia, based on characters in Philip Massinger's play *The Maid of Honour*. Nevertheless, the emotion which Mary put into her letters was very strongly expressed, in that peculiar spelling of hers which was atrocious even by the lax standards of the time. Thus about 1675, when she was thirteen, she wrote:

> I love you with more zeal then any lover can, I love you with a love that ner was known by man, I have for you excese of friendship more of love than any woman can for woman and more love then ever the constanest love had for his Mrs, you are loved more then can be exprest by your ever obedient wife vere afectionate friand humbel sarvant to kis the ground where one you go to be your dog in a string, your fish in a net your bird in a cage your humbel trout.
> (Bathurst, 60)

The reference to the love of a man for his mistress is one of many in the correspondence, revealing how exposure to the dissolute courts of Charles II and her father affected her early impressions of married life. She once observed to Frances that 'in tow or three years men are alwais wery of thier wifes and look for Mrs as sone as thay can gett them' (ibid., 51). Such youthful cynicism was a good preparation for marriage to William, who took a mistress, Mary's friend Elizabeth Villiers, even before two years had elapsed.

Their wedding took place at nine o'clock at night in Mary's bedchamber on 4 November 1677, which was also William's twenty-seventh birthday. Significantly the king and not her father gave Mary away. Charles 'was very pleasant all the time'. Thus 'when the prince endowed her with all his worldly goods, hee willed to put all up in her pocket, for 'twas clear gains' ('Diary of Dr Edward Lake', 6). As part of the settlement Mary received jewels worth £40,000 and an annual allowance of £10,000 plus £2000 a year pin money. Sir Edmund Waller composed an epithalamium for the occasion, which included the lines

> Not Belga's fleet (his high command)
> Which triumphs where the sun does rise
> Nor all the force he leads by land,
> Could guard him from her conquering eyes.
> (*The Poems of Edmund Waller*, ed. G. T. Drury, 2 vols., 1893, 2.80)

The last line was especially unfortunate. Mary's eyesight was always affected by migraine-like aching, which made it at times impossible for her to read or write. At the same time William was scarcely smitten by her, at least in the early stages of their marriage which he regarded as purely diplomatic, and treated her with indifference.

The departure of the newly married couple for the Netherlands was delayed, initially because Mary was reluctant to leave London where her sister Anne was ill with smallpox at St James's Palace. They also had to stay until *Catherine of Braganza's birthday was celebrated on 15 November. The celebrations included a ball at which it was observed that William danced only once with his wife. There was court gossip about 'the prince's sullennesse, or clownishness, that he took no notice of the princess at the playe and balle' ('Diary of Dr Edward Lake', 9). The royal party left for Margate on 19 November,

Mary weeping all the morning. When the queen tried to cheer her up by relating the similar circumstances which attended her own nuptials, when she had left her native land for a strange country, Mary replied 'But madam you came into England; but I am going out of England' (ibid., 10). Contrary winds held them up, so they made a leisurely journey to the coast by way of Canterbury. They eventually set sail on 28 November, Mary in the *Katherine*, William in the *Mary*. The crossing was rough, and because Rotterdam was icebound they had to land at Terheyde. They went straight to Honselaarsdijk, which was to become Mary's favourite Dutch palace. On 14 December they ceremonially entered The Hague to a magnificent reception. Although the Dutch found her more appealing than the other Mary Stuart they had known, William's mother, her husband's insistence on strict protocol upset many of them. For William insisted that, while his wife could kiss the cheeks of noblemen's wives, she could not extend the same favour to those of the burghermasters.

Princess of Orange Mary miscarried in spring 1678 and again a year later. After the first miscarriage her father wrote 'Pray let her be more careful of herself another time' (*CSP dom.*, 1678, 126). These miscarriages were bitter disappointments to her maternal aspirations and dynastic ambitions in the Netherlands and in Britain. She apparently never conceived again. This, together with her sister's failure to leave an heir after many pregnancies, suggests that there was a hereditary problem, though whether inherited from their father, as has been suggested, or their mother is impossible to determine.

Although Mary scarcely found wedded bliss with the unfaithful William, she was able to transform some of the mock affection she had shown for Frances Apsley into real devotion to him. Thus she wrote to her friend on 3 March 1678:

> I suppose you know the prince is gone to the Army but I am sure you can guese at the troble I am in, I am sure I coud never have thought it half so much, I thought coming out of my own contry parting with my friands and relations the greatest that ever coud as long as thay lived hapen to me but I am to be mistaken that now I find till this time I never knew sorow for what can be more cruall in the world then parting with what on loves and nott ondly comon parting but parting so as may be never to meet again to be perpetually in fear for god knows when I may see him or wethere he is nott now at this instant in a batell.   (Bathurst, 88–9)

Mary's pining for her absent husband might have been inspired as much by loneliness as by love. For her life in the Netherlands appears to have been very solitary. Although she moved around her husband's palaces— Dieren, Honselaarsdijk, Hoofdyke, the House in the Wood, and, when it was eventually built in the 1680s, Het Loo—she was not invited to other people's residences. This could have been partly her fault, since she seems to have felt that as a princess her status was so far above the Dutch regents that she could not accept invitations. Consequently her existence was spent in card playing, needlework, and religious devotions. This pattern was only occasionally disturbed by visits, such as that which her stepmother and sister paid her in October 1678, followed by

her father in February 1679, and all three in September 1679. Mary got on well with *Mary of Modena while she was duchess of York. In their correspondence the duchess addressed the princess as 'the lemon', by contrast with the prince or 'the orange'. Anne's visits were also very welcome. James's second visit was to be the last time he was in the presence of his daughter. Otherwise her routine was mundane. As the author of 'The character of … Queen Mary II' observed of her regular practice when she returned to England, it repeated a pattern established in the Netherlands:

> What an enemy she was to idleness, even in Ladies, those who had the Honor to serve her, are living witnesses. It is well known how great a part of the Day they were employed at their needles … the Queen herself, when more important business would give her leave, working with them. And that their minds might be well employed at the same time it was her custom to order one to read to them while they were at work either Divinity or some profitable History.   (*The Royal Diary*, 8)

As another observer noted:

> the course of her life in her Court abroad (being indeed all little else but one unvaried scene) affords but little matter of particular memoirs worthy a peculiar relation; there happened nothing of importance or weight … till the death of … Charles the second.   (Laine, 49)

At the time of the king's death Mary and her husband were entertaining Charles's illegitimate son, the duke of Monmouth, at The Hague. Monmouth relieved the tedium of Mary's life in the Netherlands, attending magnificent balls and skating with the princess on the ice. One of the first communications from her father, now James II, which Mary received was a polite request to dismiss Monmouth from court. The duke went off to raise his fatal rebellion in England. In 1686 Gilbert Burnet took refuge from James II in the Netherlands and was kindly received by Mary and William, who invited him to their court. There he found that:

> she knew little of our affairs till I was admitted to wait on her. And I began to lay before her the state of our court, and the intrigues in it, ever since the restoration: which she received with great satisfaction, and shewed true judgment, and a good mind, in all the reflections that she made. (*Bishop Burnet's History*, 3.134)

Burnet claimed that, until he pointed it out, Mary was ignorant of the fact that, if she became queen, William would not be king. She expressed surprise and asked him to propose an alternative, which led him to suggest that she should give her husband the real authority and try to get it legally invested in him. Although Burnet insisted that it was his own idea, and that 'no person living had moved me in it', the earl of Dartmouth, when he glossed this passage, took it for granted 'that the prince ordered him to propose it to the princess before he would engage in the attempt upon England: and she must understand it so' (*Bishop Burnet's History*, 3.138–9).

Mary appears to have become more concerned about the state of affairs in England following Burnet's account of them. Thus she intervened in favour of Bishop Compton of London when her father used the commission for ecclesiastical causes to suspend him from his spiritual duties. She also gave £200 to the ejected fellows of Magdalen College, Oxford. When James issued the declaration of indulgence in July 1687 she endorsed her husband's objections to it. Their views were made public in *Pensionary Fagel's Letter to James Stewart* 'giving an account of the Prince and Princess of Orange's thoughts concerning the repeal of the Test and Penal Laws'. This open letter to Stewart, a Scottish presbyterian lawyer, dated from Amsterdam 4 November 1687, was published in Dutch and English shortly afterwards. 'Their highnesses have often declared', Fagel wrote, 'that no Christian ought to be persecuted for his conscience'. They therefore offered 'full liberty of conscience' even to Roman Catholics. But they were not prepared to agree to the repeal of the Test Acts, which were a necessary safeguard for the Church of England.

In view of these gestures in support of that church it is surprising that James sought to convert his daughter to Catholicism. Nevertheless, in November 1687 he wrote to Mary a letter explaining why he had converted from the Anglican to the Catholic church. She replied that:

> though she had come young out of England, yet she had not left behind her either the desire of being well informed, or the means for it. She had furnished her self with books, and had those about her who might clear any doubts to her.
> (*Bishop Burnet's History*, 3.200)

Among the latter were her chaplains. George Hooper had accompanied her to the Netherlands in 1677. He had incurred William's wrath by insisting that she worshipped exclusively according to the liturgy of the Church of England, and by recommending Anglican works such as Richard Hooker's *Laws of Ecclesiastical Polity*. In 1679 he had been succeeded by Thomas Ken, whom William also disliked because he complained to the prince about the effects his infidelity were having on Mary. When Ken returned to England, where he became bishop of Bath and Wells, John Covel succeeded him from 1681 until 1685. In October 1685 Covel indiscreetly wrote to Bevil Skelton, English ambassador at The Hague, to inform him that 'the Princess's heart is ready to break; and yet she, every day, counterfeits the greatest joy … The Prince hath infallibly made her his absolute slave' (Singer, 2.165). When William was told about the contents of this letter he was so incensed that he gave Covel three hours' notice to leave the country. William Stanley replaced him as Mary's chaplain. Burnet also acted as her spiritual adviser, for although James had demanded his removal from her presence he still influenced her, reading the king's letter and helping her to compose a reply:

> Thus … she gave him the trouble of a long account of the grounds upon which she was persuaded of the truth of her religion; in which she was so fully satisfied, that she trusted by the grace of God that she should spend the rest of her days in it.   (*Bishop Burnet's History*, 3.202)

James replied with a reading list of relevant books, recommending her to discuss them with an English Jesuit, Father Morgan, who was then in The Hague. Mary undertook to read the books but not to see Morgan, on the grounds that conferences with a Jesuit would not be kept secret and that news about them would do her a great deal

of harm. Mary informed her sister Anne, Bishop Compton, and (by means of her chaplain Dr Stanley) William Sancroft, archbishop of Canterbury, of her father's attempts to convert her. These included sending her the printed account of her own mother's conversion before she died. James's efforts ended when Mary protested against the recall of the English regiments from the Netherlands. She was relieved at being spared reading more devotional literature, which had taken up a good deal of her time without in any way shaking her Anglican faith.

The revolution of 1688 Mary expressed her shock at the trial of the seven bishops, getting Dr Stanley to write to Archbishop Sancroft on behalf of herself and her husband 'to express their real concern for your grace and your brethren' (Strickland, 5.484). She also expressed scepticism about the birth of the prince of Wales in June 1688. Her conviction that there was 'quelque tromperie' ('some deceit') in the queen's pregnancy partly arose from her perplexity in reconciling the conviction that God would preserve the church through her, with the fact that she herself had not been blessed by providence with an heir (Bentinck, 71, 92–3). Although she ordered prayers for the prince in her chapel, she sent her sister Anne a long list of questions concerning the circumstances of Mary of Modena's pregnancy and lying-in. The first of these was 'whether the Queen desired at any time any of the Ladies … to feel her belly, since she thought herself quick?' (Dalrymple, vol. 2, appendix, part 1, 305). Mary became convinced that the prince was a supposititious child, and stopped the prayers for him. The thoughts that her father was capable of perpetrating such a fraud, and that humanly speaking the only way to save the church and the state in England was for her husband to dethrone him by force, afflicted her severely over the summer of 1688. She spent much of it at the newly finished palace at Het Loo, in remote Gelderland, where she was rarely disturbed by visitors. She had much time on her own, and spent it in meditation. She thanked God that her eyes were better than they had been for many years, and that she was able to read and write as well as to reflect. In September she moved to Dieren, but was still sufficiently remote in the country, and felt a spiritual tranquillity there despite the preparations that were being made by William to invade England.

Then in October Mary went to The Hague to be present at the prince's departure. William told her that if it so turned out that they never met again, she should remarry, though not to a papist—'paroles qui me percèrent le coeur' ('words which pierced my heart'; Bentinck, 80). She told him that she loved him only and could never love another. Besides, having been married so long and not been blessed with a child, she believed that was enough to prevent her ever thinking of what he proposed. She went with him to the river where he boarded the boat to take him to Briel. The thought of never seeing him again if the expedition miscarried was so terrible that it deprived her of her senses, and she sat immobile in her carriage for as long as she could still see him. A storm rendered the first embarkation abortive, and the task force had to return to port. This occasioned a second farewell which might have been anticlimactic after the first, but which Mary insisted 'm'étoit plus sensible encore que la première, et lorsqu'il me quitta, c'étoit comme si l'on m'eut arraché le coeur' ('was to me even more affecting than the first, and as he left me it was as if one had torn out my heart'; Bentinck, 86). That was the last time she saw William before she herself followed him to England the following February.

Burnet saw Mary just before the expedition left, and noted that 'she seemed to have a great load on her spirits, but to have no scruple as to the lawfulness of the design'. He urged upon her the importance of her backing William up to the hilt, since any sign of discord would be ruinous to the enterprise.

> She answered me that I need fear no such thing: if any person should attempt that, she should treat them so, as to discourage all others from venturing on it for the future. She was very solemn and serious, and prayed God earnestly to bless and direct us.   (Bishop Burnet's History, 3.311)

While the expedition was under way she worshipped four times a day, and the rest of the time meditated and composed prayers. When she learned that William had successfully landed she allowed herself to relax four days a week, but refrained from playing cards. She still kept herself away from the public during the weeks of the revolution in England, coming out of her self-enforced seclusion only to entertain the Elector Frederick III of Brandenburg and his wife.

One of the prayers that Mary composed was for the proceedings in the Convention which was discussing the arrangements for the disposal of the crown. There was a strong party led by the earl of Danby which wanted her to be queen regnant. Danby wrote to urge her to insist on her hereditary right, claiming that her insistence would sway the Convention to declare her queen. Mary replied 'that she was the prince's wife, and never meant to be other than in subjection to him, and that she did not thank anyone for setting up for her an interest divided from that of her husband' (Strickland, 5.521). Until her views were known, however, her supporters argued strenuously against those who wished William to be king. Thus where the latter were in favour of the view that the throne was vacant, Mary's supporters contested it on the grounds that James had forfeited the crown through his Catholicism and that all other Catholics were similarly disbarred, so that the succession went automatically to the next protestant heir, who was Mary. Had Mary been present in England, notwithstanding her own preference, this view might have gained more adherents. It certainly appears that William did not encourage her to leave the Netherlands until he was assured of the crown. He got this assurance when he indicated that he had not gone over to England to be 'his wife's gentleman usher'. On or about 3 February 1689 he held a meeting of leading politicians and told them that if Mary were to be declared queen 'he could not think of holding any thing by apron strings'. Unless he were offered the crown 'he would go back to Holland and meddle no more in their affairs'. This announcement

'helped not a little to bring the debates at Westminster to a speedy determination'. What clinched them was Mary's own wish, conveyed by Burnet, to rule jointly with her husband (Bishop Burnet's History, 3.395–6). The declaration of rights then declared William and Mary king and queen, though giving him the sole executive power. Mary was quite happy with this solution. 'My opinion', she wrote in her memoirs, 'has ever been that women should not meddle in government' (Doebner, 23).

Queen Mary finally arrived in England on 12 February 1689. Although she expressed sadness at leaving the Netherlands where she had been so happy, her cheerful deportment when she entered Whitehall was noted and condemned by many observers as not acting with due decorum. 'She ran about it, looking into every closet and conveniency, and turning up the quilts of beds, just as people do at an inn' wrote one admittedly hostile observer (An Account of the Conduct of the Dowager Duchess of Marlborough, 1742, 26). But even Burnet confessed he 'was one of those that censured this in my thoughts' (Bishop Burnet's History, 3.406). She put it down to guidance she had received from William that she should not betray any misgivings about entering a place from which her father had so recently fled. The very next day she went with William to the Banqueting House in Whitehall to assent to the declaration of rights and to accept the crown.

Their coronation took place in Westminster Abbey on 11 April. Bishop Compton of London officiated at it since ominously the archbishop of Canterbury, William Sancroft, declined on conscientious grounds. Mary herself felt scruples about the 'pomp and vanity' of the ceremony and the stress on the Anglican communion during it, which she felt arose from 'worldly considerations' (Doebner, 13). Throughout the ceremony the unprecedented nature of the dual monarchy was stressed. Thus where Mary or William would have received the crown kneeling on the steps of the altar if they had been mere consorts, both sat in specially made coronation chairs. The two sovereigns took a new form of coronation oath. Where James had sworn to confirm the laws and customs granted to the English people by his predecessors, they undertook to govern according to the statutes agreed on in parliament. Again, where their predecessor had agreed to uphold rightful customs, they took the oath to maintain the protestant religion. A medal struck to commemorate the coronation depicted William as Jove thundering against James II as Phaeton leaping out of a chariot at Jove's anathemas. But Jacobites claimed that the chariot represented Mary as the Roman matron Tullia, who had driven out Tullius to set up Tarquin, and that she was dethroning her father.

Far more devastating to Mary's peace of mind was a letter she received from her father at this time, saying that previously he

> had wholly attributed her part in the revolution to obedience to her husband; but the act of being crowned was in her power, and if she were crowned while he and the prince of Wales were living, the curse of an outraged father

would light upon her, as well as of that God who has commanded duty to parents.   (Strickland, 6.9)

Jacobites kept up throughout her reign the charge that she had behaved unnaturally in replacing James. In June 1689 they exploited the queen's discomfiture at a production of Dryden's *The Spanish Fryar*. The plot, involving a queen of Aragon who had usurped the throne, was grist to their mill.

In one place, where the queen of Arragon is going to church in procession, tis said by a spectator, Very good, she usurps the throne, keeps the old king in prison and at the same time is praying for a blessing on her army … Twenty more things are said which may be wrested to what they were never designed.   (Dalrymple, vol. 2, appendix 2, 79)

In 1690 a Jacobite poem imagined her lying in bed 'at dead of night … in her own father's lodgings at Whitehall'. The ghost of her mother draws back the curtain and upbraids her saying:

Can quiet slumber ever close thine eyes?
Or is thy conscience sunk too low to rise?
From this same place was not thy aged Sire
Compelled by midnight-summons to retire? …
Had he been murdered, it had mercy shown
'Tis less to kill a king, than to dethrone.
(Lord, 5.298–9)

To most of her subjects, however, Mary was more acceptable than her father or for that matter her husband, who was hated as a Dutchman and despised as an alleged homosexual. William was well aware of this, and told the marquess of Halifax in June 1689 that 'if hee left us, the Queen would governe us better' (Foxcroft, 2.222). According to Burnet, in December he came close to bringing this about:

He thought he could not trust the tories, and he resolved he would not trust the whigs: so he fancied the tories would be true to the queen, and confide in her, though they would not in him. He therefore resolved to go over to Holland and leave the government in the queen's hands.   (*Bishop Burnet's History*, 4.71)

In the event wiser counsels prevailed.

Soon after the coronation in Westminster Abbey, commissioners arrived from the convention which had met in Edinburgh to offer the crown of Scotland to William and Mary. The formal ceremony was held in the Banqueting House where the king and queen accepted the claim of rights, the Scottish equivalent of the declaration of rights, and took the coronation oath. They thereby became king and queen of Scotland as well as England. Their claim to Ireland, however, was currently being disputed by James II, whose landing in Kinsale was reported to them on their coronation day in England. James was effective ruler of Ireland for over a year.

William's decision to go to Ireland in June 1690 posed for the first time the problem of what arrangements should be made for the governing of the country in his absence. It seems that initially he was reluctant to leave Mary in charge at all, preferring to appoint a council which would simply report to her but be answerable to himself. Thus he told Halifax that 'there must be a Councell to governe in his absence, and that the Queen was not to meddle' (Foxcroft, 2.246). This suggests that his earlier threat to abdicate, leaving her in charge, was a deliberate bluff. In the event, however, he was persuaded that it was most convenient to pass an act of parliament vesting the administration in Mary. The Regency Act stated that, notwithstanding the Bill of Rights:

whensoever and so often as it shall happen that his Majesty shall be absent out of this realm of England it shall and may be lawful for the Queen's Majesty to exercise and administer the regal power and government of the kingdom.   (*Statutes of the Realm*, 11 vols., 1810–28, 6.170)

Some members of parliament objected to the arrangement. As one put it 'if the king should die in this expedition and the queen be regent, what if, out of duty to her father, if he land she should not oppose him?' 'The question is', riposted another, 'whether you will trust the government in the queen's hands or not at all?' All objections were removed by pointing out that 'the king is resolved to trust the queen' (Cobbett, *Parl. hist.*, 6, 1690, 611–18).

Mary came out of virtual retirement to take on her new responsibilities. For much of 1689 after the coronation she had devoted herself to the same kind of interests she had cultivated in the Netherlands. Thus she had brought her collection of Chinese porcelain to Hampton Court where the royal pair spent the summer. In the autumn they had moved nearer to London to Holland House, and just before Christmas acquired Kensington Palace. Mary herself remarked on the difference between the tranquillity she had enjoyed in the Netherlands and the bustle which surrounded her in England: 'et ce qui m'afflige' she wrote to Mademoiselle la Baronne de Wassenaer d'Obdam on 10 August 1689, 'c'est le peu d'apparence que je voie d'estre encore si heureuse' ('what afflicts me is the small prospect I see of ever being so happy again'; Bentinck, 119).

The major disturbance to Mary's domestic peace had been a disagreement with her sister over Anne's intrigues with members of parliament to get a financial settlement for herself. This was the first round in a quarrel which was to estrange Mary from Anne completely. Mary thought that her sister should be content to depend on herself and her husband for her finances. But Anne, who had agreed to set aside her hereditary claim to the throne in William's favour, thought that an adequate parliamentary grant was a fair compensation, especially since she was in financial difficulties. The matter came to a head in the House of Commons in December, when Anne's supporters voted her an annual allowance of £50,000, much to Mary's chagrin. On 3 March 1690 she observed privately that there was a Jacobite party and a republican party in England, 'et que j'ay raison de craindre que ma soeur en forme une troisieme' ('and that I have reason to fear that my sister is forming a third'; Bentinck, 95). Apart from this foray into public affairs, however, Mary had been very much left at leisure to pursue her hobbies of gardening and needlework. As Burnet observed, 'she seemed to employ her time and thoughts in any thing rather than matters of state' (*Bishop Burnet's History*, 4.87). Now she had to take over the government of the country.

Queen regnant, 1690 Mary was not left alone to govern, for although the Regency Act made no mention of a council, William appointed one to advise her. It consisted of nine of the principal ministers of state. He apparently gave her his views of them, for in July she wrote to him 'I thought you had given me wrong characters of men, but now I see they answer my expectation of being as little of a mind as a body' (Dalrymple, 2/2, 143). Their disagreements stemmed from the fact that five were tories while four were whigs, the outcome of William's preference for mixed ministries. Experience did not endear them to Mary, her own comments on each of them being negative. Of Thomas Osborne, marquess of Carmarthen, better known by his former title of earl of Danby, although William had particularly recommended him to her, she wrote that he was 'of a temper I can never like'. The earl of Devonshire she found 'weak and obstinate', while the earl of Dorset was too lazy. The earls of Monmouth and Pembroke she described as 'mad', while the earls of Marlborough and Nottingham were untrustworthy. Sir John Lowther was 'a very honest but weak man'. Finally Edward Russell, though he 'was recommended to me for sincerity, yet he had his faults' (Doebner, 29–30). Mary was clearly not impressed by any of them.

At first the regency council were equally clearly not overimpressed by Mary's abilities. She confessed to William that 'as I do not know when I ought to speak and when not, I am as silent as can be'. 'Every one sees how little I know of business and therefore will be apt to do as much as they can' she further informed him. 'I find they meet often at the Secretary's [Nottingham's] office, and do not take much pains to give me an account' (Dalrymple, vol. 2, appendix, part 2, 119, 121). They were to find that they had underestimated her. Carmarthen, for instance, felt that as president of the council he should have the prevailing influence. One Jacobite libel asserted that 'she's governed in Council by the marquis [of] Carmarthen' (Lord, 5.193). In fact she was quite able to divide and rule the nine. Perhaps realizing that Carmarthen, a tory, was trying to monopolize her, which her trimming spouse would dislike, she made a point of cultivating the whig Edward Russell, telling him 'that I desired to see him sometime, for being a stranger to business I was afraid of being too much led or persuaded by one party'. When the whigs tried to take advantage of her by offering £200,000 if she dissolved parliament she told Monmouth, who made the offer, that even if the whole privy council advised this step she would still have to consult the king about it (Dalrymple, vol. 2, appendix, part 2, 122, 141). Mary's deference to William in fact resolved a problem which had agitated debates on the Regency Bill as to the division of the executive power between them. There had been some concern about the consequences of their not seeing eye to eye. In fact the situation never arose because Mary was anxious to prevent it. 'That which makes me in pain', she wrote to William, 'is for fear what is done may not please you. I am sure it is my chief desire ... as much as may be to act according to your mind' (Dalrymple, vol. 2, appendix, part 2, 129). She stuck by the resolution adopted

at the first meeting of the nine that 'all business that will admit delay must be sent to the king that his pleasure may be known' (Finch MSS, 2.378).

A crisis arose during Mary's first experience of government, however, which demanded decisions which could not be referred to the king. The defeat inflicted on the English fleet by the French at Beachy Head in June 1690 called for urgent action by the regents. Mary rose to the occasion. 'Heaven seems to have sent us one of the most threatening junctures that England ever saw', a newspaper claimed, 'merely to set off with the greater lustre the wisdom magnanimity and justice of a princess who has made good some people's fears and other's hopes in deserving the character of another Queen Elizabeth' (Mercurius Reformatus, or, The New Observator, 1 Aug 1690). Burnet, who saw her every week that summer, observed that she 'shewed an extraordinary firmness ... her behaviour was in all respects heroical' (Bishop Burnet's History, 4.98). She also kept a cool head, as the treatment of the earl of Ailesbury, a suspected Jacobite, reveals. In July she issued an order for the arrest of several Jacobites, including Ailesbury. He got his wife to communicate to the queen how mortified he was that, as a suspect on bail, he could not pay his duty to her. He recalled:

> The Queen's answer was in these very words: 'Tell my Lady of Ailesbury that I love to do good to all persons as far as I can, but more especially to her husband and his family, whom I knew so well in my youngest years ... and therefore, for his sake, I will break through the common forms and direct him to come at four tomorrow afternoon.'

Ailesbury accordingly waited on 'that good and incomparable Queen' and even played cards with her, to the astonishment of her companions (Memoirs of ... Ailesbury, 1.264–5).

The loss of the battle of Beachy Head was attributed to the incompetence or even treachery of the earl of Torrington, the English admiral. Mary determined to dispense with his services and to imprison him in the Tower to await the outcome of a judicial inquiry into his actions. Fortunately the immediate crisis was offset by William's victory at the battle of the Boyne. Mary was relieved to learn that her husband had won and, despite Jacobite calumnies to the contrary, that her father had managed to escape unscathed. Her relief that both had been spared was genuine enough in the letter she wrote to the electress of Hanover. 'La conservation et la victoire d'un mary d'un côté, et la préservation de la personne d'un père de l'autre ... étoit plus que je n'osois espérer' ('the conservation and the victory of a husband on one side, and the preservation of a father on the other ... was more than I dared to hope'; Bentinck, 107).

The question of replacing Torrington presented Mary with another problem which she had to cope with on the spot. She had initially referred the decision to William, but the advice he gave, that Edward Russell and Richard Haddock should replace the admiral, proved abortive, for Russell declined the appointment. Mary then proposed that Haddock should serve with Sir John Ashby, a proposal endorsed by the nine. When the commissioners of the

Admiralty were brought in to be informed of this, however, one of them, Sir Thomas Lee, objected that they should have been consulted earlier and invited to recommend a replacement. To this Mary replied 'then the king … could not make an admiral which the admiralty did not like?' Lee answered 'no, no more he can't' (Dalrymple, vol. 2, appendix, part 2, 147). Although in the end she got her own way, backed up by the nine, Mary discovered how much such matters were accomplished 'by partiality and faction'. As she confessed to the electress of Hanover in a letter of 14 August 'les animosités personelles, que les gens ont l'un contre l'autre, sont bien désagréables, et les partis différents sont trop difficiles à ménager pour moi' ('the personal animosities that men have for one another are disagreeable enough, and the different parties are too difficult for me to manage'; Bentinck, 107). She was clearly bruised by the experience, writing to William, 'when I … see what folk do here, it grieves me too much, for Holland has really spoiled me in being kind to me' (Dalrymple, vol. 2, appendix, part 2, 3). Mary's first real experience as queen had been a searing one, and she was relieved when her husband returned in September and expressed himself 'very much pleased with her behaviour' (Doebner, 34).

Queen regnant, 1691–1694 By the time William left England again in January 1691, this time for the Netherlands, the previous year's experience had established a routine for the running of the country in his absence abroad. During his stay on the continent which, apart from a brief return in mid-April, lasted until October, the regency council dealt with routine business while Mary coped with any crises. Unlike 1690, there was no emergency like Beachy Head. There was concern about the discovery of a Jacobite plot involving Lord Preston, but this was dealt with by the king when he returned briefly to England. Mary's involvement in the process was limited to an exchange with Preston's daughter, whom she found admiring a portrait of James II at Kensington and asked her why she did so. The young girl answered 'I am reflecting how hard it is that my father should be put to death for loving your father' (Dalrymple, 1.466–7). The only alarm the queen faced was a disastrous fire at Whitehall, which destroyed much of the palace, and forced her to escape in her nightdress, just before the king returned in April. Otherwise Mary was able to pass her time in public playing cards and arranging a ball for her sister's birthday, and in private meditating that God would bring success to their undertakings. These meditations were not just for the blessing of providence in general, but for particular enterprises. Thus she asked God to:

> Regarde avec un oeil de compassion ceux qui sont en Irlande, et, si c'est ta volonté, mets fin à cette malheureuse guerre. Bénis pour cette fin les efforts de notre général, Mr de Ginkle, et les autres qui sont employé à cet oeuvre.   (Regard with a compassionate eye those who are in Ireland, and, if it is Thy will, put an end to this unhappy war. Bless for this end the efforts of our general, Mr van Ginkel, and the others who are employed in this work. Bentinck, 101)

'The only thing of business' she dealt with, according to

her memoirs, 'was the filling the Bishoprics' (Doebner, 37). The bishoprics which had to be filled were those occupied by the nonjurors. It is sometimes claimed that William left all episcopal appointments to his wife. Certainly Burnet maintained that 'the king left the matters of the church wholly in the queen's hands' (*Bishop Burnet's History*, 4.211). But that was not in fact the case. 'The Queen shall give no bishoprics', he informed Lord Halifax on the eve of his first departure in 1690 (Foxcroft, 2.251). When Canterbury became vacant in 1694 on Tillotson's death, he translated Thomas Tenison to it, whereas she would have preferred Edward Stillingfleet (*Bishop Burnet's History*, 4.244). The sensitive business of depriving Archbishop Sancroft and other nonjuring bishops, however, he did leave to his wife. She handled it admirably. In close co-operation with the high-church earl of Nottingham she chose John Tillotson as Sancroft's replacement at Canterbury. Tillotson was just the man to bring the Church of England through its gravest crisis following the revolution of 1688. 'Had it been put to a poll', William Sherlock claimed, 'there had been vast odds on his side that he would have been voted into the see of Canterbury' (Sherlock, 17). Mary was even prepared to risk offending her husband by promoting George Hooper to the deanery of Canterbury, for William had expressed his dislike of the new dean. Hooper had apparently said that 'if her husband retained his throne it would be by her skill and talents for governing' (Strickland, 6.62).

Relations with Anne continued to deteriorate over the summer of 1691. This time they involved perceived slights to Anne's husband, George, prince of Denmark. George had already felt insulted by the king, whom he had accompanied to Ireland the previous year. William virtually took no notice of his brother-in-law, ignoring his part in the battle of the Boyne. To the insult offered to George's military prowess the king added another relating to his naval expertise. George told William that he wished to join the navy as a volunteer, an ambition the king did nothing to curb before his own departure in January 1691. He gave orders to Mary, however, that the prince was not to be allowed to serve, and she had the invidious task in May of sending Lord Nottingham to George with orders forbidding him to join a ship to which he had already consigned his baggage, which had to be removed. The upshot was, according to a contemporary report, that 'the two sisters quarreled terribly' (Gregg, 80).

They were to quarrel even more fiercely when William returned from the campaign in October 1691 complaining about the conduct of the earl of Marlborough, Anne's favourite. The king accused Marlborough of corresponding with the exiled James II and of conniving with his wife to alienate Anne from her sister and himself. Certainly John and Sarah Churchill, the earl and countess of Marlborough, were Anne's most intimate confidants in her dispute with William and Mary. Their intrigues, which did indeed include correspondence with James, led William to cashier the earl from all his offices and to ban him from court in January 1692. Although the ban undoubtedly extended to Marlborough's wife, Anne provocatively took

Sarah to court at Kensington Palace on 4 February. Mary restrained herself from remonstrating with her sister at the time, on the grounds of the princess's pregnancy. But she wrote to her the very next morning to complain that she had 'all the reason imaginable to look upon your bringing her as the strangest thing that ever was done' (Strickland, 5.344–6). She concluded by virtually ordering Anne to dispense with Sarah's services. When Anne refused Mary evicted her from her apartment at the Cockpit. Before quitting the Cockpit, Anne sought an interview with her sister who, according to Sarah, 'was as insensible as a Statue' (Gregg, 88). Anne and Prince George moved to Syon House. In April Mary sent the earl of Rochester to Anne to demand the immediate dismissal of Sarah, upon which the princess and her husband could be reinstated in their former residence. Anne gave the spirited reply that she was quite content with her new abode, so much so 'that should the Monsters grow good natured and endulge her in everything she could desire … she would be hardly persuaded to leave her retirement' (Gregg, 90). William had become a monster, 'Caliban', the 'Dutch abortion', to the princess before this. Now Mary was identified with him in Anne's eyes. Mary attempted a reconciliation with her sister by visiting her after she had given birth to a stillborn child on 17 April. But her insistence on the dismissal of Sarah made the attempt futile. It was the last time that the sisters met. Mary made the breach permanent by issuing an order that nobody could appear in court who had visited Anne. She even forbade the mayor of Bath who had received the princess, though when she did so, according to the earl of Nottingham, she 'could not refrain from tears, and said "Thus it becomes a Queen to act, but I cannot forget she is my sister"' (Gregg, 96).

Mary was again queen regnant under the terms of the Regency Act when William was out of the country from 5 March to 18 October 1692. She appears to have been more reluctant than before to take decisions without reference to William. Perhaps he had criticized her for some of those she had taken the previous year, possibly concerning the replacing of the nonjurors. Or it could be that she was reprimanded for her initial flippancy when she was asked to round up the usual Jacobite suspects and presented with a list headed by Ailesbury. According to him she replied that he had been arrested in 1690 for nothing, and ordered his name to be eliminated. Nottingham then replied that they had orders from the king, at which 'with warmth' Mary demanded to see his orders:

> On which the Secretary replied 'Madam we have received orders to clap up a certain number.' On which she laughed, and with life and judgement added, 'I thought persons were to be taken up for crimes and not to make up numbers as they empanel jurymen.' So other names of persons were presented to her, and finding at the top, Robert of Scarsdale, 'Stop there, my Lord. Since you will have your number, put in that Lord's name insted of my Lord Ailesbury's, and if titles please you, there is an Earl for an Earl. What is sauce for one is sauce for another.' (*Memoirs of … Ailesbury*, 1.298)

If this story reached William he might not have seen the joke and instructed his wife to take his orders more seriously. At all events the earl of Nottingham noted of one

decision that her advisers thought it 'very reasonable for the Queen to grant … but her Majesty would take no resolution without the king' (*Finch MSS*, 4.40). Mary was later criticized in parliament for referring matters to William, one member expressing the wish that 'she had dispatched more herself without sending abroad for orders' (*The Parliamentary Diary of Narcissus Luttrell*, ed. H. Horwitz, 1972, 251).

There was unease among officers of the armed forces at the disgrace of Marlborough, who spent some weeks in the Tower this year, that it was the prelude to a general purge. So serious was this alarm felt to be that Mary was moved to reassure naval officers of her faith in their loyalty. Nottingham passed on a message to them:

> that she reposes an entire confidence in them all, and will never think that any brave English seaman will betray her or his country to the insolent tyranny of the French, and as it is their duty and their glory to defend the government, it shall be her part to reward their service. (*Finch MSS*, 4.141–2)

This appeal inspired sixty-four naval officers to sign an address of loyalty, pledging to venture their lives in defence of her rights and the liberty and religion of England. They went on to win the battle of La Hogue, and with it the command of the sea. The queen was as good as her word and rewarded the seamen with a substantial sum of money, and pledged herself to establish a hospital at Greenwich for those who were disabled. Mary might have left more to William than she needed to have done in 1692, for whatever reason; but as this episode reveals she could still rise to the occasion when it was required. Both houses of parliament recognized this when they thanked her for her administration of the government during William's absence. The Lords congratulated her on her resolute conduct 'by which the danger of an invasion was prevented and a glorious victory obtained at sea' (*JHL*, 15.115). The Commons noted that while Europe was engulfed in war:

> we, your Majesty's subjects under your auspicious reign, enjoyed the blessings of peace at home, and … saw your Majesty's fleet return with so complete and glorious a victory as is not to be equalled in any former age and can never be forgotten by Posterity. (*JHC*, 10.698)

Although she might have treated the Jacobites leniently, Mary's feelings for her father hardened during the course of this year. When James issued a declaration on the eve of La Hogue offering vague concessions to English protestants, Mary allowed it to be published in England in order to discredit him. And when she discovered that he was involved in a plot to assassinate her husband it removed the last vestiges of respect for the former king.

The following year, however, produced friction between Mary and William. She noted in her memoirs that her administration during his absence from 24 March to 29 October 1693 'was all along unfortunate, and whereas other years the King had almost ever approved all was done, this year he disapproved almost every thing' (Doebner, 59). The main reason was that Mary's attachment to the tories was stronger than ever, while William began to move decisively towards the whigs. In April the queen was godmother at the baptism of the earl of Nottingham's fourteenth child. Yet the previous month, before setting out for the Netherlands, William had appointed the whigs John Trenchard and John Somers to the second secretaryship of state and the lord keepership. The whigs in the cabinet criticized Nottingham's conduct of naval affairs, particularly his alleged failure to protect a merchant fleet bound for the Mediterranean which was attacked by the French. These criticisms were distressing to Mary, who described Nottingham as 'the man I found the most constant in serving the king his own way, and who was the man who really toock the most and greatest pains to do so' (Doebner, 59). Yet when William returned he dismissed Nottingham from the senior secretaryship and offered it to the whig duke of Shrewsbury. 'When I begin to reflect on this year', Mary noted at the end of 1693, 'I am almost frighted and dare hardly go on; for t'is the year I have met with more troubles as to publick matters than any other' (ibid., 58).

What Mary made of further moves towards the whigs in 1694 can only be surmised, for her memoirs unfortunately stop abruptly at the end of 1693. She complained in April of infirmities which she attributed to advancing years, or to 'le chagrin et les inquiétudes qu'on a si régulièrement tous les estés' ('the grief and anxieties that I have so regularly every summer'; Bentinck, 146). It seems, though, that Mary played less of a role as regent than usual while William was absent from 6 May to 9 November. She continued to preside at meetings of the privy council, which met almost twice a week. But she rarely attended cabinet meetings. The major decision to have the fleet winter in the Mediterranean was taken entirely by the cabinet in consultation with the king. She was thus less involved in the government of the country in 1694 than she had been in 1690. This made it easier for William to manage in later years when he was sole monarch. Nevertheless, he had been abroad for over two and a half years in all since his first departure from England in 1690, rather more than half the time. During those years Mary had played a crucial role in the development of a system of government with the first regularly absent monarch since the fifteenth century.

Mary's legacy Mary smoothed the path for William in other ways more crucial to the survival of the revolution settlement than the exercise of executive authority. Had he been sole ruler from the start he would have been king of only half the nation. Jacobitism, by no means a negligible force, would have become even more formidable. It was no coincidence that the most serious Jacobite plots against the regime took place after the queen's death. By that time, however, the settlement was reasonably secure. Mary had reconciled many tories to the dual monarchy because they could, if they chose to ignore her half-brother as being suppositious, which many did, regard her as next in line to the throne by hereditary right. As Aphra Behn put it on Mary's arrival in England in 1689:

The murmuring world till now divided lay,
Vainly debating whom they shou'd Obey

Till you great Cesar's Off-spring blest our Isle
The differing Multitudes to Reconcile.
(*The Works of Aphra Behn*, ed. J. Todd, 7 vols., 1992–6, 1.307)

Mary reconciled herself to the revolution by attributing it to providence. God had weighed her father in the balance and found him wanting. She and her husband were therefore the instruments of divine judgment. As Burnet recorded, she was fully convinced 'that God had conducted her by an immediate hand and that she was raised up to preserve that Religion which was then everywhere in its last Agonies' (Burnet, *Essay*, 95). Mary's belief in providence was absolute. 'I cannot tell, if it should be his will to suffer you to come to harm for our sins', she wrote privately to William in Ireland, 'for though God is able, yet many times he punishes the sins of a nation as it seems good in his sight' (Dalrymple, vol. 2, appendix, part 2, 130). The victory at the battle of the Boyne was a clear sign that providence still smiled on their cause. But it could readily frown if the English mocked it by continuing in their sinful ways.

What was needed to ensure the permanence of the revolution of 1688 was a moral revolution. To inspire this Mary set an example of piety and devotion. Services in royal chapels became more frequent and more public. She surrounded herself with clergymen who had been foremost in the campaign against popery and vice under her father and her uncle. She publicized their sermons by having many which were preached before her printed. Thus where under Charles II a mere three a year had appeared by command of the king, an annual average of seventeen sermons were published by Mary's command. After her death the average commissioned by the court dropped to four a year. Preaching a sermon on the occasion of her demise Thomas Manningham noted that:

Tis to the Queen that we owe many of those Pious Treatises which have been lately Publish'd amongst us; And that multitude of plain, useful and Practical Sermons, which she approv'd of, and caused to be printed, are Her Gift to the Publick. (Claydon, 98)

Her efforts to promote piety included schemes to eliminate pluralism and non-residence in the Church of England by putting pressure on clergymen guilty of these practices 'when not enforced by real necessity' to abandon those livings where they were not resident. Just before her death she admitted that 'she had no great hope of mending matters, yet she was resolved to go on' (*The Royal Diary*, 5).

Besides setting an example at court, Mary also supported the societies for reformation of manners in their efforts to get the country to mend its ways in order to avert God's wrath. In July 1691 she issued a proclamation to the justices of the peace for Middlesex for the suppressing of profaneness and debauchery. The following year 'the queen, in the king's absence, gave orders to execute the laws against drunkeness, swearing and the profanation of the Lord's day; and sent directions over England to all magistrates to do their duty in executing them' (*Bishop Burnet's History*, 4.181–2). Some of the measures undertaken by the queen to prevent the profanation of Sunday provoked ridicule. Lord Dartmouth noted against this passage in Burnet's *History of my Own Time*:

> There came forth at this time several puritanical regulations for observing the sabbath in London, savouring so much of John Knox's doctrine and discipline, that Burnet was thought to have been the chief contriver. One was that hackney coaches should not drive upon that day; by another, constables were ordered to take away pies and puddings from anybody they met carrying of them in the streets; with a multitude of other impertinences so ridiculous in themselves, and troublesome to all sorts of people, that they were soon dropt, after they had been sufficiently laughed at. (*Bishop Burnet's History*, 4.182)

Mary even tried by fiat to suppress vice in the army and navy, though without much success. Notwithstanding that some of them were excessive, the result of all Mary's endeavours, according to the dissenters who presented William with an address of condolence on her death, was 'that the Court, that is usually the centre of vanity and voluptuousness became virtuous by the impression of her example' (Bates, 25).

Mary died on 28 December 1694. She had not been well since 24 November, when she was present at a service conducted by Archbishop Tillotson at which he had collapsed with a stroke from which he never recovered, dying a few days later. The first signs of Mary's fatal illness appeared on 19 December. She shook these off initially, so that it was hoped she only suffered from measles. But by the end of Christmas day it became clear that she was suffering from the most virulent smallpox. Archbishop Tenison felt duty bound to inform her that she was dying, for which she thanked him, since 'she had nothing then to do, but to look up to God and submit to his will' (*Bishop Burnet's History*, 5.247). Her death occurred at Kensington Palace about one o'clock on the morning of the 28th.

Jacobites of course tried to present the event as a judgment of God upon Mary. One pamphleteer even noted that she died in the same month that her father laboured under an unnatural rebellion, while she was cut off in her prime—she was only thirty-two—according to the punishment threatened to breakers of the fifth commandment. A Jacobite 'Epitaph' appeared:

> Here ends, notwithstanding her specious pretences,
> The undutiful child of the kindest of princes.
> Well here let her lie, for by this time she knows,
> What it is such a father and king to depose.
> (Strickland, 6.130)

But the Jacobite mud did not stick. Mary's admirers turned the tables on her detractors, claiming that her death was a judgment on the nation for its sins. 'We have just cause to fear our sins have hastened her death' preached the duke of Newcastle's chaplain:

> God in his goodness sent us such a princess as was both a patroness and an example of goodness: a glass by which this crooked age might have rectified itself; and seeing he has waited divers years, and found no amendment, what was it but just to take the mirror from us? What should they do with a light who will not walk by it? (Pead, 19)

'Natural causes had their share in this evil', conceded Archbishop Tenison, 'but it was the immorality, the sin of the nation which hastened it as a judgment' (Tenison, 26).

In a curious and almost macabre way Mary continued to sustain the state even after her death. Her body was embalmed the day she died, a prudent precaution in view of the putrescent effects of smallpox. It took from 28 December 1694 to 21 February 1695 to prepare for her lying-in-state, the arrangements for which cost over £50,000. She then lay in state from noon until five o'clock every day until 5 March. Four ladies of honour stood about the corpse, being relieved by four others every half hour. On 5 March she was buried with elaborate ceremony in Westminster Abbey. Sir Christopher Wren supervised the construction of a railed walk from the Banqueting House to the abbey, the rails being covered in black cloth and the walkway with gravel. Along this the funeral procession made its way in a blinding snowstorm. For the first time in English history the coffin of a monarch was accompanied by members of both houses of parliament, since normally they were dissolved by the death of a king or queen regnant. There were those who argued that parliament should have been dissolved by Mary's death, but they were overruled by those who insisted that William's surviving her as sole monarch created a unique situation. Consequently Mary's funeral procession was the largest ever held for an English monarch. It entered the abbey to the solemn strains of Purcell's specially composed funeral anthem. The casket was laid under a black velvet canopy while the archbishop of Canterbury preached a sermon, and then it was lowered into the tomb. A wax effigy of the dead queen was placed on display in the abbey, so that Mary's image would be perpetuated beyond the grave.

Her reputation was fiercely disputed between Jacobites and Williamites. A Jacobite epitaph summed up the view of James's supporters:

> Between vice and virtue she parted her life,
> She was too bad a daughter and too good a wife.
> (Strickland, 6.130)

On the other hand John Somers, the whig leader, stated in parliament 'I believe her the best woman in the world' (Cobbett, *Parl. hist.*, 5.631). Mary generated these contrary responses in her subjects. The public image she projected could foster both. Her behaviour on taking over Whitehall Palace in 1689 certainly seemed unfeeling in a daughter, while her toleration of William's infidelity did seem to be beyond the call of duty, even given the lax court morals of the age. At the same time her piety struck many observers as being sincere. 'If any person came to visit her in the morning before she pour'd forth her prayers', observed one admirer, 'she sent them back with this expression *That she was first to serve the King of Kings*' (*The Royal Diary*, 2). Her private memoirs, letters, and meditations, however, leave little doubt that the eulogists were nearer the truth than the detractors. The survival of these papers, some preserved in French, gives a rare insight into her private thoughts. They document a simple piety and devotion to the Church of England. Of course she was no saint, as she readily admitted to herself. Her treatment of her sister Anne could be called an unnecessary vendetta. Yet she clearly felt affection for her father until he forfeited it by countenancing the death of her husband. And, although their marriage got off to a rocky start, William and Mary did come to respect and even perhaps to love each other with the passage of the years. Certainly he was distraught at the onset of her fatal illness, risking infection from smallpox himself by insisting on ministering to her, and her death devastated him.

Mary was a passionate and intelligent woman, which made her sensitive to her position. She was very aware of the role which, in her view, she had been called upon by providence to play. And she played it well. Her actions at the time of the revolution of 1688 reconciled many Anglicans, who were uneasy about replacing James with William, to the new regime. She did not wish to rule as well as to reign, being more than content to let her husband exercise the executive authority. But, when called upon in his frequent absences to administer affairs, she showed that she was quite able to do so, and to stand up to the cynical and experienced politicians with whom she had to work.

Perhaps above all Mary was prepared for death. She read Charles Drelincourt's *Art of Dying Well* (its published title was *The Christian's Defence Against the Fears of Death*) seven times over. She often expressed indifference to dying, only wishing that she would die before William. She got her wish. And after the delirium in the first onset of her final illness, in which she raved alarmingly, she became perfectly composed and conscious of her fate. Mary had learned Drelincourt's lesson and died an exemplary death.   W. A. SPECK

Sources J. Dalrymple, *Memoirs of Great Britain and Ireland*, 2 vols. (1771–3) · Countess Bentinck, ed., *Lettres et mémoires de Marie, reine d'Angleterre* (1880) · B. Bathurst, ed., *Letters of two queens* (1924) · R. Doebner, *Memoirs of Mary, queen of England* (1886) · *Bishop Burnet's History* · *The life and letters of Sir George Savile … first marquis of Halifax*, ed. H. C. Foxcroft, 2 vols. (1898) · *Memoirs of Thomas, earl of Ailesbury*, ed. W. E. Buckley, 2 vols., Roxburghe Club, 122 (1890) · *Report on the manuscripts of Allan George Finch*, 5 vols., HMC, 71 (1913–2003), vols. 2, 4 · G. Burnet, *An essay on the memory of the late queen* (1695) · W. Bates, *A sermon preached upon the … death of … Queen Mary* (1695) · T. Tenison, *A sermon preached at the funeral of her late majesty Queen Mary* (1695) · D. Pead, *A practical discourse upon the death of our late gracious queen* (1695) · [P. de Laine], *The life of that incomparable princess Mary* (1695) · *The royal diary: to which is prefixt the character of his Royal Consort Queen Mary II* (1705) · 'Diary of Dr Edward Lake … in the years 1677–8', ed. G. P. Elliott, *Camden miscellany*, I, CS, 39 (1847) · G. de F. Lord and others, eds., *Poems on affairs of state: Augustan satirical verse, 1660–1714*, 7 vols. (1963–75), vol. 5 · W. Sherlock, *A sermon preached … December 30, 1694* (1694) · A. Strickland and [E. Strickland], *Lives of the queens of England*, new edn, 6 vols. (1901–4), vols. 5, 6 · E. Gregg, *Queen Anne* (1980) · R. P. Maccubbin and M. Hamilton-Phillips, eds., *The age of William III and Mary II: power, politics and patronage* (1989) · L. Schwoerer, ed., *The revolution of 1688–1689: changing perspectives* (1992) · T. Claydon, *William III and the godly revolution* (1996) · *The correspondence of Henry Hyde, earl of Clarendon, and of his brother Laurence Hyde, earl of Rochester*, ed. S. W. Singer, 2 vols. (1828)
Likenesses P. Lely and B. Gennari, group portrait, oils, 1670–80 (with James II and family), Royal Collection · P. Lely, oils, c.1672, Royal Collection · P. Lely, oils, c.1677, Royal Collection · portrait, c.1677, Het Loo Palace, Appeldoorn, The Netherlands · R. ver Hulst, bust, 1683, Mauritshuis, The Hague · G. Netscher, oils, before 1684, Althorp, Northamptonshire; version, Rijksmuseum, Amsterdam · W. Wissing, oils, c.1685, Royal Collection · W. Wissing, oils, c.1685, Royal Collection; copy, NPG · J. vander Vaart, oils, 1688, Audley End, Essex · J. vander Vaart, oils, c.1689, Petworth House, Sussex · J. vander Vaart?, oils, c.1689, NPG · G. Kneller, oils, 1690, Royal Collection [see illus.] · medal, c.1690, BM · effigy, 1694, Westminster Abbey, London · W. Faithorne, mezzotint (after J. vander Vaart, 1698), BM, NPG · P. van Gunst, line engraving (after J. H. Brandon), BM, NPG

Mary Adelaide, Princess [Princess Mary Adelaide of Cambridge], **duchess of Teck** (1833–1897), philanthropist, was born Mary Adelaide Wilhelmina Elizabeth on 27 November 1833 in Hanover, the youngest of the three children of the seventh son of George III, *Adolphus Frederick, duke of Cambridge (1774–1850), and his wife, Princess Augusta (1797–1889), the daughter of the landgrave of Hesse-Cassel. When she was four, her family moved to Kew, where she had the conventional training of a princess, strong on female accomplishments and the history of the royal family. A lively, imperious girl, she was highly conscious that she derived from the Hanoverian line—the 'old royal family'—and not the Saxe-Coburgs.

The first duty of a princess is marriage, but Princess Mary's obesity must have alarmed prospective suitors (the American minister estimated that she weighed 250 pounds). In 1856 she declined a proposal from the widowed king of Sardinia. Just as she was becoming reconciled to remaining a 'jolly old maid', the prince of Wales (later Edward VII) discovered a handsome young officer in the Austrian army, Prince Francis of Teck (1837–1900), the son of the duke of Württemberg. Queen Victoria, perhaps remembering the prince consort's wish to introduce 'strong dark blood' into the royal family, approved of the match. After a brief courtship, the couple married at Kew on 12 June 1866. They lived in Kensington Palace, but in 1870 moved to White Lodge in Richmond Park. They had three sons, among them Alexander *Cambridge, earl of Athlone, and a daughter, Princess Victoria *Mary (Princess May), who married George, duke of York, later George V. The penniless Prince Francis, who became the first duke of Teck in 1871, lacked employment but found distractions in gardening, feuding over questions of precedence, and arranging the jewels on his wife's dresses. The duchess had a passion for objects but little idea of how to pay for them, although Angela Burdett-Coutts helped out in emergencies. It was a volatile marriage.

The duchess of Teck was remarkable for her benevolence, and she increased her overdrafts by giving away at least 20 per cent of her annual allowance of £5000 granted by parliament. She came from a notable philanthropic background (her father had been the patron of about thirty institutions), but few other members of the royal family so happily transformed good works into a career. A devout Anglican, her charity, like her jewellery, was highly polished and ready to be worn at a moment's notice. Appeals and begging letters bombarded her daily at White Lodge, and though discriminating, she obliged a large number of supplicants each year. Caught up in the craze for bazaars, she had as many as six of them on the go at any one time. The public loved to see her acting as a shop-woman. She enjoyed the part, but often stipulated

Princess Mary Adelaide, duchess of Teck (1833–1897), by Camille Silvy, 1860 [standing, with her mother, Augusta Wilhelmina Louisa, duchess of Cambridge]

to the Royal Hospital, Chelsea. She died of heart failure at White Lodge on 27 October 1897, after an operation for a strangulated hernia, and was interred in the royal vault at Windsor Castle on 3 November. FRANK PROCHASKA

Sources C. K. Cooke, *A memoir of her royal highness Princess Mary Adelaide, duchess of Teck, based on her private diaries and letters*, 2 vols. (1900) · S. W. Jackman, *The people's princess: a portrait of HRH Princess Mary, duchess of Teck* (1984) · J. Pope-Hennessy, *Queen Mary, 1867–1953* (1959) · *The Times* (28 Oct 1897) · *The letters of Queen Victoria*, ed. A. C. Benson, Lord Esher [R. B. Brett], and G. E. Buckle, 9 vols. (1907–32) · F. Prochaska, *Royal bounty: the making of a welfare monarchy* (1995)
Archives Royal Arch. | BL, letters to Lady Holland, Add. MS 52114 · Hove Central Library, Sussex, letters to Lord and Lady Wolseley · Staffs. RO, letters to duchess of Sutherland · Warks. CRO, letters to Lady Aylsford · Wellington College, Crowthorne, corresp. with P. H. Kempthorne
Likenesses C. Silvy, photograph, 1860 (with Augusta Wilhelmina Louisa, duchess of Cambridge), NPG [*see illus.*] · H. Weigall junior, portrait; in possession of second marquess of Cambridge in 1959 · photographs, Royal Arch., Queen Mary's albums
Wealth at death £35,471 7s. 4d.: administration, 25 Nov 1897, CGPLA Eng. & Wales

Mary of Blois. *See* Mary, countess of Boulogne (*d.* 1182).

Mary of the Cross. *See* MacKillop, Mary Helen (1842–1909).

Mary of Woodstock. *See* Mary (1278–c.1332).

Mascall, Edward James (1757/8–1832), civil servant, may have been the Edward Mascall baptized at St Katharine Cree, London, on 3 October 1757, the son of William Mascall and Mary, *née* Kilby. He entered government service probably in 1779. He was appointed examiner of the outport quarter books on 12 January 1813, and collector of customs for the port of London, at a salary of £1500 per annum, on 9 October 1816. His books on the customs, sanctioned by the commissioners, provided merchants with information about the changes made between 1784 and 1817. The first, *The Consolidation of the Customs and other Duties*, appeared in 1787, and a revised edition of his *A Practical Book of Customs* (1799) was published in 1813. He also produced *A Digest of the Duties of Customs and Excise* (1812). He married, on 19 September 1793, at Croydon, Juliana Anne, eldest daughter of Robert Dalzell of Tidmarsh, Berkshire. She died on 24 July 1823. Mascall died, aged seventy-four, at Yateley Cottage, Yateley, Hampshire, on 6 March 1832, 'after six weeks extreme suffering from a gradual mortification of the foot' (*GM*, 379). He was buried on 12 March at Yateley.

W. A. S. HEWINS, *rev.* M. C. CURTHOYS

Sources *GM*, 1st ser., 63 (1793), 956 · *GM*, 1st ser., 93/2 (1823), 188 · *GM*, 1st ser., 102/1 (1832), 379 · *Monthly Review*, new ser., 30 (1799), 469–70 · *Monthly Review*, new ser., 36 (1801), 429 · 'A return of all persons in the civil and military establishments', *Parl. papers* (1822), 18.46, no. 328 · parish register (burial), 12 March 1832, Yateley · IGI

Mascall, Eric Lionel (1905–1993), Church of England clergyman and theologian, was born on 12 December 1905 at 2 Earlsthorpe Road, Sydenham, London, the second of the two children (his elder brother had died in infancy) of John Richard Strutt Mascall, commercial traveller, and his wife, (Susan) Lilian, daughter of William Grundy and his

that if she attended a sale, she could not be expected to purchase the goods.

With the years, the duchess was often on charitable parade opening schools, visiting orphanages, and laying foundation stones. She was highly visible in philanthropic causes associated with the queen's jubilee year, 1887. In her prime, she was arguably the hardest working member of the royal family. Her many charities included Dr Barnardo's, the National Society for the Prevention of Cruelty to Children, the Royal Cambridge Asylum, the St John Ambulance Association, the Young Women's Christian Association, and a dozen or so London hospitals. She was particularly assiduous in her work for the Needlework Guild, which recruited large numbers of middle-class women to make clothes for the poor. Although she had the common touch with the working classes, she could be sharp with ladies who obstructed her charitable administration. As a frequent visitor to the East End, where she was known as 'Fat Mary', she sought to reduce social distress while encouraging deference in the poor.

The duchess of Teck was a pillar of the monarchy's policy of cultivating civil society. Her association with good causes, like that of other members of the royal family, brought the crown and the middle classes into alliance. It raised the prestige and reaffirmed the importance of the monarchy in a time when it was retiring from national politics. Not the least of her services to the crown was the inculcation of charitable habits in her daughter, later Queen Mary, who further expanded the monarchy's welfare role. The duchess's last public appearance was a visit wife, Susan Anne. From Latymer Upper School in Hammersmith, he went in 1924 to Pembroke College, Cambridge, with an open scholarship in mathematics, eventually obtaining first-class honours in 1928. But his hope to go on to an academic career did not materialize. Nor was he at this stage contemplating ordination. His first employment was as senior mathematics master at Bablake School in Coventry. His three years there were the unhappiest of his life for, in his own words, he 'had no training in teaching, … was no good at athletics and … was a bad disciplinarian' (Mascall, 97). However, during his time in Coventry he published two articles on Christianity and science in *Theology*, and in 1931 decided to offer himself for ordination. He proceeded to Ely Theological College for one year. Mascall had already become a committed Anglo-Catholic while still at school. At Cambridge particular influence on his religious life was exercised by the dean of Pembroke, Edward Wynn, later bishop of Ely, and by Mascall's old school friend Christopher Waddams, soon to become chaplain of St Catharine's College. Mascall's lifelong involvement with the Eastern Orthodox church began towards the end of his student days, when he attended the Second Anglo-Russian Student Conference. By 1929 he was already chairman of the executive committee of the Fellowship of St Alban and St Sergius.

Mascall served two short curacies, under the same vicar, at St Andrew's, Stockwell Green, and St Matthew's, Westminster. Especially in Stockwell, he was noted for his classes and talks on the Christian faith. He also published an article in *Theology* entitled 'Three modern approaches to God', and his first book, *Death or Dogma: Christian Faith and Social Theory* (1937), arose out of talks given to a study group at Stockwell. His introduction to the so-called Christian sociology of Maurice Reckitt and the Christendom Group began towards the end of his time in Westminster.

In 1937 Mascall was invited to become sub-warden of Lincoln Theological College. He threw himself into the tasks of teaching ordinands and writing philosophical theology. His first major book, *He who is: a Study in Traditional Theism*, appeared in 1943. It was a lucid re-examination of natural theology and established Mascall's reputation as an exponent of Thomism. It was submitted for, and received, the Cambridge BD the same year.

During vacations Mascall often stayed at All Saints, Margaret Street, London, and helped in setting up the Anglo-Catholic publishing house the Dacre Press, for which he wrote a short work on St John of the Cross and two paperbacks in the Signposts series, which he jointly edited. One of these, *Man: his Origin and Destiny* (1940), reflected his continuing interest in the Christendom Group. Soon after his move to Lincoln he made his profession as a member of the Oratory of the Good Shepherd, a society of celibate priests and laymen living under a rule.

In 1945 Mascall was persuaded to apply for a short-term lectureship in theology, with some chaplaincy duties, at Christ Church, Oxford. In fact he was to remain there for seventeen years, as student (fellow), tutor, and university lecturer in the philosophy of religion. His steady stream of publications consolidated his position as one of the country's leading Anglo-Catholic theologians. Particularly noteworthy were *Christ, the Christian and the Church* (1946), a study of the incarnation and its consequences; *Existence and Analogy* (1949), recommended to all students of analogy; *Christian Theology and Natural Science*, the Bampton lectures for 1956, and for many years regarded as the standard work on the subject; *The Recovery of Unity* (1958), a substantial contribution to ecumenism, commending, first and foremost, common study of the truth of Christian doctrine; and *The Importance of being Human* (1958), the American Bampton lectures, offering a reasoned Christian anthropology. Mascall's works were hardly original. They were full of long quotations from other authors, but they constituted an unparalleled attempt to set out, rationally, the truth content of the classical Christian tradition and to relate it, without a hint of accommodation or reduction, to the discoveries of the sciences. In a broadcast review of *The Recovery of Unity* Owen Chadwick observed that 'among the living thinkers of the Christian Church, Dr Mascall is in a minority of one', but also that he, like Hooker, exhibited 'the sane, clear-headedness of a devout mind'. The stature of his work was marked by further higher degrees, the Oxford DD in 1948 and the Cambridge DD in 1958. (Later honours included an honorary DD from St Andrews in 1967 and fellowship of the British Academy in 1974.)

Mascall carried out his chaplaincy role as best he could, offering Cyprus sherry and tea, playing records, and appearing, rather implausibly, on the river bank and the touchline. His shyness made it difficult for undergraduates to get to know him, but those who persevered learned to appreciate his courtesy, his pastoral concern, and above all his quirky sense of humour, made public in two volumes of comic verse—the first, *Pi in the High*, published towards the end of his Oxford time. In the intellectual fraternity of beleaguered Christians, Mascall was a natural member of the Socratic Club (dominated by C. S. Lewis) and the Metaphysicals, an informal group of Christian philosophers.

Having already turned down the offer of the Ely chair at Cambridge, Mascall, in 1962, accepted the invitation to become professor of historical theology at King's College, London, where he remained until retirement in 1973. His writings during these years and well into his retirement consisted mostly of reasoned rebuttals of various widely publicized books by liberal theologians. *Up and Down in Adria* (1963) was a response to *Soundings* (1962), edited by Alec Vidler. *The Secularisation of Christianity* (1965) contained a response to John Robinson's *Honest to God* (1963). *Theology and the Gospel of Christ* (1977) contained a response to *The Myth of God Incarnate* (1977), edited by John Hick. And *Whatever happened to the Human Mind?* (1980) contained a response to Geoffrey Lampe's *God as Spirit* (1977). These books showed Mascall's polemical conservatism at its best. Less appealing were his extraordinary arguments against the ordination of women and his defence of literal belief in the devil and the controlled practice of exorcism.

The one major, positive work during his London time was *The Openness of Being*, the Gifford lectures for 1970–71. This was a wide-ranging exposition of contemporary natural theology, especially noteworthy for introducing a whole generation of students to the work of the so-called 'transcendental Thomists'—Karl Rahner, Emerich Coreth, and Bernard Lonergan—and for advancing the influential metaphysical position known as critical realism.

Mascall's London home was the clergy house of St Mary's, Bourne Street, in Pimlico. *Whatever happened to the Human Mind?* was dedicated to the priests and people of this parish, 'who for many years have provided this grateful author with an altar and a home'. He was also at home, surprisingly, in the National Liberal Club and, later, the Athenaeum.

Increasingly, Mascall was invited to lecture abroad—Canada, the United States (nine visits in all), and South Africa—and to visit church leaders and groups in Belgium, Romania, and Yugoslavia. But his favourite destination was Rome. His several visits 'ad limina Apostolorum' were assuredly more congenial than that of Karl Barth. Mascall remained, nevertheless, quintessentially a Catholic Anglican. Eventually illness forced Mascall to leave Bourne Street for a nursing home, St Mary's House, King's Mead, Seaford, Sussex, where he died on 14 February 1993. A memorial service was held in the chapel of King's College, London, on 4 May 1993. BRIAN HEBBLETHWAITE

Sources E. L. Mascall, *Saraband: the memoirs of E. L. Mascall* (1992) · H. P. Owen, 'Eric Lionel Mascall, 1905–1993', *PBA*, 84 (1994), 409–18 · *The Times* (17 Feb 1993) · *The Independent* (17 Feb 1993) · private information (2004) · *WWW*, 1991–5

Archives Pusey Oxf., papers

Likenesses B. Jones, drawing, repro. in *The Independent* · photograph, repro. in *The Times* · photograph, repro. in Owen, 'Eric Lionel Mascall', 408

Wealth at death £259,726: probate, 14 Oct 1993, *CGPLA Eng. & Wales*

Mascall, Leonard (*d.* 1589), translator and author, was a near kinsman of Eustace Mascall (*d.* 1567), clerk of the works at Christ Church, Oxford, Hampton Court Palace, and other buildings of Henry VIII; he may have been the son of Eustace's brother, Evan Mascall (*fl.* 1531). In 1569 his *Booke of the Art and Maner, howe to Plante and Graffe All Sortes of Trees* was published. This was partly a translation of Davy Brossard's *L'art et maniere de semer, et faire pepinieres des sauvageaux*, and was partly 'taken out of diuerse Authors' (sig. A4v); the last third was from a Dutch or German work. Thirteen further editions, one of them a piracy, appeared between 1572 and 1656.

By 1573 Mascall was clerk of the kitchen to Matthew Parker, archbishop of Canterbury. In this year he transcribed the parish register of Farnham Royal, Buckinghamshire, with Thomas Cromwell's injunctions and English verses of his own on the keeping of such records, at the request of Eustace Mascall, 'because their Friends were Christend Marryd & buryed in yt Parish' (Wright, fols. 101v–102). This transcript appears no longer to be extant. In 1581 he produced *The Husbandlye Ordring and Gouernmente of Poultrie*, which was based on French versions of Lucius Junius Moderatus Columella's work on

agriculture (*De re rustica*), and Charles Estienne's *Praedium rusticum*. It was dedicated to Katherine Woodford of Britwell, near Farnham Royal, whose husband James was chief clerk of the kitchen to the queen. (Mascall's two other dedications were both to aristocrats with Buckinghamshire marriage connections.) A book of recipes for removing stains, dyeing, dressing leather, gilding and soldering various metals, and hardening and softening iron and steel, translated from Dutch or German, followed in 1583; a translation of selected apothecarial recipes from the Latin *Dispensatorium ad aromaticos* attributed to Nicolaus Praepositi appeared in 1587; and a book on animal husbandry, claiming to draw on the practice of 'straungers as of our owne country men' (sig. A3v) was published in the same year. This work appeared in numerous editions, well into the seventeenth century, and, like others by Mascall, was a source for Gervase Markham's very successful writings.

Mascall's last book, entered in the Stationers' Company's registers in 1587 and published posthumously in 1590, was *A Booke of Fishing with Hooke and Line* (with a long appendix on traps for vermin); this was based on the *Treatyse of Fysshynge wyth an Angle* which had accompanied the *Book of St Albans* since 1496, and was a major source for Izaak Walton's *Compleat Angler*. It contains the story that one of the Mascalls of Plumstead in Sussex (a family to which the writer was not related) introduced carp and pippins into England, and this has, mistakenly, been taken as an autobiographical statement. Leonard Mascall was buried at Farnham Royal in early May 1589.

JOHN CONSIDINE

Sources N. Wright, response to questionnaire, 1712, Bodl. Oxf., MS Rawl. D. 1480, fols. 101–2 · Tanner, *Bibl. Brit.-Hib.* · I. Walton, *The compleat angler, 1653–1676*, ed. J. Bevan (1983) · B. Henrey, *British botanical and horticultural literature before 1800*, 1 (1975) · F. C. Carr-Gomm, *Records of the parish of Farnham Royal, Bucks* (1901) · F. N. L. Poynter, *Bibliography of Gervase Markham, 1568?–1637* (1962) · *LP Henry VIII*, vol. 5 · H. M. Colvin and others, eds., *The history of the king's works*, 4 (1982)

Likenesses R. Gaywood, etching, pubd 1662, BM

Mascall, Robert (*d.* 1416), bishop of Hereford, is said by the sixteenth-century bibliographer John Bale to have been born in Ludlow. He became a Carmelite, and is also said to have been prior of the friary at Ludlow, where he probably received some schooling as a boy. He refers in his will to his only known kinsman, one John Gase. His family background appears to have been undistinguished. He had received the degree of DTh from Oxford University by 3 October 1393, when he took part in the trial of the suspected Lollard Walter Bryt (also recorded as Brut and Bryte) at Hereford. He preached before Richard II at Candlemas 1396. But the fact that he became confessor to Henry IV as soon as that king seized the throne points to a gap in the known details of Mascall's career. There is no evidence that he had shared Henry Bolingbroke's exile, but, as his title of duke of Hereford indicates, Henry had considerable interests in the west midlands and Welsh march, much of it through his late wife, Mary de Bohun, and may have encountered Mascall accordingly. On 24

December 1400 Mascall was granted the temporalities of the vacant see of Meath in Ireland, being licensed on 22 and 25 January 1401 to stay in England and collect the revenues (for what they were worth) by attorney. On 13 February he was referred to as 'elect' of Meath and dispensed to hold the church of Kildalke in Ireland to augment the revenue. However, in 1402 Robert Montain was provided to the see, and Mascall's remuneration at court readjusted.

Mascall remained in constant attendance on the king until his dismissal was demanded and ceded, for no specific reason, in the parliament of January 1404, the latest in a line of unpopular royal confessors of unpopular kings. It happened that the see of Hereford fell vacant on 29 March, for which Mascall might well have been an obvious candidate anyway. Adam Usk, not the most reliable of autobiographers, would claim later that he himself was nominated by the pope, and it is true that Mascall travelled to Rome in person to secure provision on 2 July and consecration there four days later; but this journey may have been in part a dignified withdrawal from his detractors at home. In August or early September 1404, returning from Middleburg in Zeeland to England, he was captured by Flemish pirates and detained at Dunkirk with at least the tacit consent of the duchess of Burgundy, but released, if maybe for a ransom, before 25 September. On 20 March 1406 he received £10 from the crown for his losses during Owain Glyn Dŵr's rebellion. He attended parliaments regularly, but otherwise was fully resident in his diocese. Bale refers to Mascall as a noted preacher and of upright character, although, in the absence of any explicit slur on him and given his career, Bale might simply have been settling for the obvious. Mascall made a perfunctory will on 23 November 1416 in London, with a codicil on 16 December. He died on 22 December 1416, in London, and was probably buried, as he requested, in the Carmelite church at Ludlow, which he had reputedly rebuilt in large part, although a series of antiquarians have preferred to believe he was buried at the London house. Bale attributes a number of writings to him, including a collection of sermons preached before the king, but none of them is known to survive.

R. G. DAVIES

Sources Emden, Oxf., 2.1239 · R. G. Davies, 'The episcopate in England and Wales, 1375–1443', PhD diss., University of Manchester, 1974, 3.clxxxix–cxc · E. F. Jacob, ed., The register of Henry Chichele, archbishop of Canterbury, 1414–1443, 2, CYS, 42 (1937) · J. H. Parry, ed., Registrum Roberti Mascall, CYS, 21 (1917) · Bale, Cat.
Archives Hereford Diocesan RO, Hereford, episcopal register

Mascarene, (Jean-)Paul (1685–1760), army officer and colonial administrator, was born Jean-Paul Mascarene in October or November 1685 in Languedoc, France, the only child of Jean Mascarene and his wife, Margaret de Salavy. Shortly after the birth of his son, Jean Mascarene was imprisoned and then expelled from France as a Huguenot, following the revocation of the edict of Nantes. Jean-Paul was eventually smuggled out of the country and made his way in 1696 to Geneva, where he was cared for by the Rapin family, relatives of his father. He went later to Utrecht, and then to England, where he joined the army.

Commissioned as a lieutenant in 1706, he went to North America in 1709 with the expedition intended to capture the French colonies of Acadia and Canada, under the command of Samuel Vetch and Francis Nicholson. The following year Mascarene assisted at the capture of Port Royal (Annapolis Royal, Nova Scotia) and mounted the first British guard at the fort. In spite of many attempts to find other avenues of employment—especially in the more congenial environment of Massachusetts, where he married Elizabeth Perry (d. 1728) in 1714—Mascarene spent the remaining forty years of his career tied to the new British colony of Nova Scotia.

Mascarene was commissioned captain in 1717 in Philipps's regiment (later the 40th). He was also appointed one of the members of the new governing council of Nova Scotia, the colony's first civil government, in 1720. Over the next thirty years he was to serve that government in many capacities, especially in attempts to deal with and regulate the Acadians (the French inhabitants) and the native peoples of the region. In 1731 he led an unsuccessful attempt to entice New Englanders to resettle in Nova Scotia. The 1720s and 1730s brought repeated disappointments in Mascarene's efforts at self-advancement. Although nominated for the lieutenant-governorship of Massachusetts by Governor Andrew Belcher, he was passed over, probably owing to his lack of patronage in London. He increasingly spent time in Boston, especially after the death of his wife on 1 January 1728 left him with four young children. A stint as commanding officer at the fishing outport of Canso appears to have involved him briefly in the profitable smuggling business with nearby Louisbourg. When advancement did come, it was ironically not in Boston but in Annapolis Royal, from where he had tried so hard to break free. With Governor Richard Philipps a long-time absentee, the death of Lieutenant-Governor Lawrence Armstrong in 1739 brought Mascarene hastening to Nova Scotia from Boston. After a brief struggle he emerged as president of the governing council, a position he held until 1749. From 1742 he was also the senior military officer. In spite of claims by later historians, he never attained the rank of lieutenant-governor, the parsimonious Philipps repeatedly refusing to pay the necessary salary.

In spite of Mascarene's best efforts, the colony was poorly equipped to deal with the outbreak of the War of the Austrian Succession in 1744, with the Annapolis Royal fortifications in disrepair and the garrison inadequate. Only through the intervention of Massachusetts was Mascarene able to stave off repeated French and native attacks. Even the capture of the French fortress of Louisbourg by New Englanders in 1745 and the subsequent peace treaty of 1748 did not lead to military stability in Nova Scotia. Mascarene's major contribution towards peace in the colony during this difficult period lay in his efforts to conciliate the Acadians. In spite of the religious differences which separated them, Mascarene had developed a strong sympathy for the Acadians' predicament, as both France and Britain attempted to use them as pawns in the struggle for control of north-eastern North America. Among officials in Nova Scotia and Massachusetts, Mascarene was nearly alone in his view that reasonableness and time, not force, would eventually make of these people 'good British subjects', but his ability to keep them largely neutral in the conflict contributed materially to the defence of the colony.

After the conclusion of the war, London for once acted quickly and decisively in respect to Nova Scotia. The founding of the new administrative and military centre of Halifax in 1749 meant that both Annapolis Royal and Paul Mascarene were to be replaced—the latter by a new governor, Edward Cornwallis. Having handed over the reins of government, Mascarene remained in the colony for another year and then in 1750 quietly retired to his home in Boston, where he lived comfortably, surrounded by his children and grandchildren. He sold his lieutenant-colonel's commission (ironically to Charles Lawrence, who in 1755 ordered the expulsion of the Acadians) and received the rank of brevet colonel.

Mascarene's lively intellectual interests—in the classics, in debate on religious issues, and in translating the plays of Molière into English—made it natural for him to prefer cosmopolitan Boston to tiny Annapolis Royal. Yet he had remained an outsider wherever he went: a Huguenot in France, in Britain a military officer without strong patronage connections, a devout Anglican in largely Congregationalist Massachusetts. Able and dedicated officer that he was, nowhere did his talents find full expression. He died in Boston on 22 January 1760.   BARRY MOODY

Sources BL, Sloane MS 3607, Add. MSS 19069–19071 · Paul Mascarene papers, Harvard U., Houghton L., Sparks collection · Mass. Hist. Soc., Miscellaneous bound, 1706–13, 1714–18, 1723–27, 1728–33 · Mass. Hist. Soc., Belcher MSS · Mass. Hist. Soc., Belknap MSS · Mass. Hist. Soc., Mascarene family MSS · Public Archives of Nova Scotia, Halifax, Nova Scotia, Record Group 1, vols. 5–12, 14, 18 · NA Canada, Manuscript Group 11, Nova Scotia A ser., vols. 3–7, 15–17, 20, 23, 25, 33–6 · PRO, colonial office 5, vols. 893, 901; 217, vols. 3, 4, 39 · *The notebook of John Smibert* (1969) · A. M. MacMechan, ed., *Original minutes of his majesty's council at Annapolis Royal, 1720–1739*, 2 vols. (1908) · C. B. Fergusson, ed., *Minutes of his majesty's council at Annapolis Royal, 1736–1749* (Halifax, NS, 1967) · T. B. Akins, ed., *Selections from the public documents of the province of Nova Scotia*, trans. B. Curzen (1869) · J. B. Brebner, *New England's outpost: Acadia before the conquest of Canada* (1927) · J. B. Brebner, 'Paul Mascarene of Annapolis Royal', *Dalhousie Review*, 8 (1928–9), 501–16 · B. M. Moody, '"A just and disinterested man": the public career of Paul Mascarene', PhD diss., Queen's University, Kingston, Canada, 1976 · M. Sutherland, 'Mascarene, Paul', *DCB*, vol. 3 · R. Symthies and H. Raymond, *Historical records of the 40th (2nd Somersetshire) regiment, now the 1st battalion the prince of Wales's volunteers (south Lancashire regiment), from its formation, in 1717, to 1893* (1894)

Archives BL, corresp. and papers, Add. MSS 19069–19071 · Mass. Hist. Soc., papers · NA Canada, letter-book and papers [copies]

Maschiart, Michael (1544–1598), Latin poet and Church of England clergyman, born in St Thomas's parish, Salisbury, was elected scholar of Winchester College in 1557, probationary fellow of New College, Oxford, on 29 January 1560, and full fellow in 1562 (the same year as George Coryate, his fellow Latinist from the same parish). He became BCL on 9 December 1567, DCL on 13 October 1573, and advocate of Doctors' Commons in 1575. In April 1572

he was appointed by his college vicar of Writtle, Essex. He gained a reputation for Latin poetry, and was 'not only esteemed an able civilian, but also excellent in all kinds of human learning' (Wood, *Ath. Oxon.*, 1.673). His poems were probably never published, and seem almost entirely lost. A fragment is preserved in Camden's *Britannia*, two 'pretily versified' couplets on Clarendon Park, near Salisbury:

> Nobilis est lucus, cervis clausura, Saronam
> Propter …
> A famous parke for Stag and hind, neere Salisburie doth lie.
> (in Philemon Holland's translation, Camden, 1610, 250)

Holland notes in the margin, 'this name [Sarona, for Sarum, or Salisbury] poetically devised'. This quotation does not appear in Camden's original *Britannia* of 1586, although other verses on Wiltshire do, from Daniel Rogers, 'vir eruditus', and Alexander Neckam, 'non Apolline plenus' (Camden, 1586, 118–19). Apart from a talent for coining names that will fit the metre, and explaining the presence of twenty groves, each a mile in circumference, these lines reveal little of Maschiart's poetic genius. One may note merely that they are not quite so dull in Latin as in Holland's English. Maschiart died in Writtle in December 1598 and was buried there the same month.   D. K. MONEY

Sources Wood, *Ath. Oxon.*, new edn, 1.673 · Foster, *Alum. Oxon.* · R. Benson and H. Hatcher, *The history of modern Wiltshire*, ed. R. C. Hoare, 6 (1843) · G. Camdeno [W. Camden], *Britannia, sive, Florentissimorum regnorum, Angliae, Scotiae, Hiberniae* (1586) · W. Camden, *Britain, or, A chorographicall description of the most flourishing Kingdomes, England, Scotland, and Ireland*, ed. and trans. P. Holland (1610) · *DNB*

Maschwitz, (Albert) Eric (1901–1969), writer and broadcaster, was born on 10 June 1901 at 13 Carpenter Road, Edgbaston, Birmingham, the son of Albert Arthur Maschwitz, a general merchant, and his wife, Leontine Hilda Bockemann. He was educated at Arden House preparatory school, Henley in Arden, and Repton School, and went on to read modern languages at Gonville and Caius College, Cambridge. Maschwitz worked in an editorial capacity with *Hutchinson's Magazine* (1922–3), and then undertook a number of assignments as a freelance writer and editor, including a stint in 1925 with a film studio in France. In 1926 he became a publisher's reader with A. M. Heath, the firm of literary agents.

Maschwitz joined the BBC in 1926 in the outside broadcast department but his first important job was in the editorial office of the *Radio Times*. In 1927 he became editor of the magazine. Maschwitz graduated from that in 1933 to the variety department of which he became a driving force and innovator. He detached the department (which in later years would be renamed light entertainment) from the stuffy atmosphere of Broadcasting House to the nearby St George's Hall where the atmosphere was more free and easy, and the best of the pre-Second World War entertainment shows were born.

In addition to helping to create the successful magazine programme *In Town Tonight* Maschwitz was a songwriter, penning the lyrics of 'These foolish things' and 'A nightingale sang in Berkeley Square'. He wrote, together with George Posford, the operetta *Goodnight Vienna*, which opened a new chapter of entertainment in the expanding world of radio (still called, in the 1930s, the wireless). Many other operettas followed in association with various authors and proved hugely successful with the growing radio audience, as well as on stage. These included *Balalaika* and *Magyar Melody*. *Balalaika*, which ran for 570 performances at the Adelphi from 1936, was a great hit. Less successful was *Waltz without End* in 1942, in which he tried to present Chopin in a popular format.

Eric Maschwitz promoted the dance bands of the day and was responsible for ending the monopoly of the so-called BBC Dance Band. He encouraged the BBC to employ the many dance orchestras of the time whose music was popular, and especially those of Ambrose, Billy Cotton, Geraldo, and Joe Loss. From 1933 until 1937, when he briefly joined MGM in Hollywood, his flair and energy helped to promote radio as entertainment. In so doing he helped to dilute the more sombre educational/political view of what should be broadcast beloved of the corporation's director-general, Sir John Reith.

While running variety Maschwitz was constantly looking for new ideas and new talent; 'Only occasionally', he claimed, 'did talent "drop as manna out of heaven"' (Briggs, 2.103). But drop it did and Maschwitz was largely responsible for the broadcasting careers of Arthur Marshall, Beryl Orde, Vic Oliver, Claud Dampier, Sandy Powell, and many others. However, the demands on talent were enormous. When the BBC proved reluctant to install its own talent-spotting department Maschwitz employed the young Canadian Carroll Levis to provide a 'discovery' show which would put new and untried talent before the microphone. Levis was an immediate success.

On 25 January 1926 Maschwitz married the intimate revue and cabaret star Hermione Ferdinanda *Gingold (1897–1987), daughter of James Gingold, a stockbroker. Appearing on the wireless as herself, or under the pseudonym Mrs Pullpleasure, an itinerant harpist, Gingold was in constant demand. They divorced in April 1945 and on 14 November 1945 Maschwitz married Phyllis Crawford Gordon, daughter of Thomas Crawford Gordon and divorced wife of John Taylor Galey, who died in September 1969. There were no children.

When war came in 1939 Maschwitz joined the army, and from 1940 to 1945 he served in the intelligence corps. In due course he became head of a War Office broadcasting section in the department of welfare and education, where he became involved in army entertainment at home and abroad. He pressed for the creation of a forces programme run in healthy competition with the Home Service. At the end of the war Maschwitz acted as the story editor of the official D-day film, *True Glory* (1945). He left the army in 1945 with the rank of lieutenant-colonel. After the war Maschwitz became intimately associated with the Music Publishers' Association, constantly arguing for a greater proportion of British music in the BBC output and a correspondingly smaller American input which he dismissed as merely 'the latest fads'.

Maschwitz in 1948 had another great success with *Carissima*, its delightful lyrics set to the music of Hans May. Other effective productions were *Belinda Fair* (1949), *Zip Goes a Million* (1951), *Love from Judy* (1952), and *Happy Holiday* (1954).

In 1956 Eric Maschwitz rejoined the BBC as head of light entertainment television and was a stimulating force in fighting back against the energetic programme-makers of ITV, newly established in 1955. Between 1961 and 1963 he was assistant and adviser to the controller of television programmes. Under his benign leadership BBC television came up with *The Rag Trade*, *Black and White Minstrel Show*, and sitcoms for Harry Worth, Charlie Drake, and Eric Sykes. He retired from the BBC in 1963 but re-emerged as a freelance producer of the television series *Our Man at St Marks* for Associated Rediffusion. In broadcasting terms his importance to BBC light entertainment cannot be understated. He wrote a novel, *A Taste of Honey*, in 1924, and an autobiography, *No Chip on my Shoulder*, in 1957. He was appointed OBE in 1936. Eric Maschwitz died on 27 October 1969 at Ascot Nursing Home, Sunninghill, Berkshire.

BARRY TOOK

Sources B. Took, *Laughter in the air: an informal history of British radio comedy*, rev. edn (1981) · A. Briggs, *The history of broadcasting in the United Kingdom*, 4 vols. (1961–79) · CGPLA Eng. & Wales (1970) · b. cert. · m. certs. · d. cert. · *The Times* (29 Oct 1969) · WWW · personal knowledge (2004)

Archives FILM BFI NFTVA, documentary footage |SOUND BL NSA, performance recordings

Likenesses photograph, Hult. Arch.

Wealth at death £20,080: probate, 13 Jan 1970, *CGPLA Eng. & Wales*

Masefield, John Edward (1878–1967), poet and novelist, was born at The Knapp, Ledbury, Herefordshire, on 1 June 1878. He was the third of the six children of George Edward Masefield (d. 1890), solicitor, and his wife, Caroline Louisa Parker. His mother died following childbirth in 1885, after which his father became increasingly unbalanced, until his own death in hospital in 1890. The children were brought up by an uncle and an aunt (who tried to repress Masefield's addiction to reading), and by a succession of governesses. Nevertheless, his early years in the Herefordshire countryside were very happy ones (Smith). In 1888 he was sent to Warwick School and then, in 1891, to HMS *Conway* in Liverpool, to train as an officer in the merchant marine. Life there was rough and he did not escape bullying, though there were compensations too, and he took delight in the great sailing ships.

In 1894 Masefield sailed for Chile, via the Cape, on the four-master *Gilcruix*, an experience on which he later drew in one of his finest narrative poems, *Dauber* (1913). But despite his love of the sea he was an indifferent sailor and was eventually shipped home as a DBS—'distressed British seaman'. Soon after this, on another voyage, he jumped ship in New York to travel rough in the United States. This was followed by a spell as a barman in Greenwich Village and then by steadier work in a carpet factory in Yonkers. While in New York, Masefield read voraciously, and with

John Edward Masefield (1878–1967), by William Strang, 1912

the help of the local booksellers discovered such favourite authors as Chaucer, Malory, and the Romantic poets. It was at this time that he realized that poetry was his vocation. On 4 July 1897 he returned to England with, as he said, '£6 and a revolver' (Smith, 49), determined either to find work or to shoot himself.

Back in London, Masefield began to write seriously while working as a clerk. He first attracted attention with *Salt-Water Ballads* (1902), *Ballads* (1903), and, in 1910, *Ballads and Poems*. Some of these poems, such as 'Sea-fever' and 'Cargoes', have remained popular ever since, providing the first introduction to poetry for generations of school children. Coming after the verse of the *fin de siècle*, they are strikingly vigorous. Like Kipling, Masefield celebrates the common man—as his poem 'A Creed' puts it, 'Not the ruler for me, but the ranker'—though his focus is on England itself rather than the empire. A poem that was especially important to him is 'The Wanderer', which depicts the beauty and decline of the tall ships, thus initiating the theme of defeated endeavour to which he often returned in later books. A crucial event of these early years was Masefield's meeting with W. B. Yeats in 1900, and through him with J. M. Synge in 1903. With Yeats he found literary companionship and an entry into the literary world. Soon after, in 1901, he became a full-time writer.

Masefield married Constance de la Cherois Crommelin (1866/7–1960) on 23 July 1903 in London. She was Irish, of French Huguenot descent, eleven years older than he, and considerably better off. She was a graduate of Newnham

College, Cambridge: at the time of the marriage she was the proprietor of a girls' school in London, having previously been senior mistress at Roedean. She had some influence on Masefield's social views, particularly on women's suffrage. They had a daughter, Judith, a book illustrator (*b.* 1904), and a son, Lewis (*b.* 1910), a novelist, who died in action in north Africa in 1942. Masefield had many relationships—all platonic as far as is known—with other women, often with women older than himself, such as the actress Elizabeth Robins, to whom at one point he wrote as often as nine times in a day, and Florence Lamont, who supported his theatre work, and with whom he had an important correspondence.

In 1911 Masefield published *The Everlasting Mercy*, which has been described as 'a bigger literary sensation than … *Barrack-Room Ballads*' (Spark, 3). It is certainly quite unlike most of the verse of the period. Its story of a reformed wastrel was widely admired and debated for its 'low' comic dialogue and its revelation of the more squalid side of rural life. The brutally realistic boxing bout is enough to cast doubt on the notion that Masefield was ever a 'Georgian' poet. The poem was attacked by clerics, but it was also recited in public houses in the East End of London—not usually an audience for modern verse.

The second decade of the twentieth century saw the publication of most of Masefield's finest verse. *Dauber* appeared to similar acclaim in 1913. Its demotic dialogue and the vivid description of a storm off the Cape show Masefield as both a naturalist and a romantic, having learned from Conrad and Melville, as well as from Kipling. Indeed, he always saw himself as a teller of tales. In old age he told Muriel Spark that, 'My main concern has always been to tell stories … to living audiences' (Spark, 80–81). At the outbreak of the First World War Masefield, who had previously had pacifist leanings, went with the British Red Cross to the Dardanelles; on his return he published *Gallipoli* (1916), one of the finest accounts we have of modern warfare. Though an 'official' commission, it gives a graphic insight into the life of the common soldier, in both its horror and its heroism. During the war Masefield went to the United States, under government auspices, to help to explain the British war effort, and in 1917 he received honorary doctorates from both Yale and Harvard universities, the first of many such awards. At this time he declined a knighthood (and did so again several times in later years). He preferred to be a common man himself, as well as a poet of the common man.

Masefield's most popular poem, *Reynard the Fox*, appeared in 1919. It is less disturbing than *Dauber*, and was perhaps a reaction to the horrors of war. Amy Lowell called it 'a cry of hunger for the past' (Sternlicht, 70), though there is nothing dreamy or ruminative in its nostalgia for rural England. The inspiration for the meet is clearly Chaucer's 'Prologue', and the hunt itself, seen from the fox's point of view, is as full of pace and dash as of pathos. Perhaps the greatest pleasure the poem offers lies in its observant relish of the natural world. Masefield wrote other fine narrative poems in those years, such as *The Widow in the bye Street* (1912) but none was so successful.

At the same time he was also producing work of many other kinds, from naval history to his essay on Shakespeare as a poet (1911).

From 1905 until 1926 Masefield was also deeply involved with drama, partly as a result of the influence of Yeats and Synge. His most successful play was *The Tragedy of Nan* (1909); however, his theatrical work received at best a mixed response. It ranged from versions of Racine to dramas on the life of Christ and involved him in collaborations with, among others, Granville Barker and Gilbert Murray. Perhaps the most significant aspect of these activities was Masefield's championship of live poetry reading. He set up his own theatre in his house at Boars Hill, near Oxford, to which he had moved in 1917, and invited many friends (and successive generations of Oxford undergraduates, including Robert Graves, whose landlord he was) to his productions. Some of this work was continued when he became poet laureate in 1930. This honour set the seal on his popularity and he took its responsibilities more seriously than many of his predecessors had done. Apart from writing much occasional verse, he read his poetry in public widely and often. He also worked tirelessly as president of the Society of Authors (from 1937) and of the National Book League (1944–9). In 1935 he was elected to the Order of Merit.

Masefield was never simply a poet. He was also a prolific novelist for most of his writing life, particularly novels of action, which ranged, as his poems did, from eighteenth-century seaports to ancient Troy and beyond. Among his most rewarding novels are *Lost Endeavour* (1910), *The Bird of Dawning* (1933), and the uncanny *Dead Ned* (1938). Great claims cannot be made for his fiction, but it is nearly always readable and often vivid. He is better known now as an author of children's books, the best of which, such as *The Midnight Folk* (1927) and *The Box of Delights* (1935), have become classics. Beside all this, he regularly published verse—right into old age. He no doubt wrote too much, but there are good poems in all his later books, albeit less vigorous ones than those of his best period. Masefield also wrote several memoirs in his later years, although these tend to conceal as much as they reveal of his early days. By the end of his life his *Collected Poems* had sold over 200,000 copies—an unprecedented figure for a modern poet, indicating his popularity with ordinary readers. He was also a tireless letter writer; one scholar has estimated that he wrote no fewer than 250,000 letters.

Masefield was essentially a traditional poet and he always thought of himself as a Victorian. He relied on conventional forms and metres and he addressed his verse to the common reader rather than to the literati. After he became laureate his work went increasingly out of fashion; but more recently it has begun to be rediscovered. Readers have ventured beyond the more 'poetical' later verse to what Edward Thomas called the 'fidelity to crudest fact' (p. 116) of his best work. Masefield's narrative poems are particularly admired. However, his audience now seems mainly confined to devotees of pre-modernist verse, to the general reader, and to schools. His name is not one that figures largely in critical accounts of modern poetry, nor is it much cited by contemporary poets. Masefield's work has perhaps been the victim of its own popularity: many readers do not realize that at its best it is both more challenging and more modern than its conventional reputation would suggest.

In appearance Masefield was tall, thin, and blue-eyed, with what one friend called 'an expression of perpetual surprise' (Spark, 32). Everyone remarked on his courtesy and friendliness. His manner was simple and unaffected—never that of 'the laureate' or the 'great man'. He took special pleasure in helping younger writers.

Masefield's wife, Constance, died in 1960 and Masefield himself died on 12 May 1967, at Burcote House, his home near Abingdon, as a result of a gangrenous foot which he refused to have amputated. His daughter looked after him in his final years. On 20 June 1967 his ashes were interred in Westminster Abbey, London, in Poets' Corner, next to Browning's. Another memorial to him might be his own early poem 'Biography' (1912):

> When I am buried, all my thoughts and acts
> Will be reduced to lists of dates and facts.

Masefield cherished the storyteller's traditional anonymity.   DAVID GERVAIS

Sources C. B. Smith, *John Masefield: a life* (1978) · G. Handley-Taylor, *John Masefield OM: a bibliography* (1960) · C. Lamont, *Remembering John Masefield* (1971) · S. Sternlicht, *John Masefield* (1977) · M. Spark, *John Masefield* (1953) · F. Drew, *John Masefield's England* (1973) · P. Carter, correspondence, Masefield Society · J. Masefield, *In the hill* (1941) · J. Masefield, *New chum* (1944) · J. Masefield, *On the hill* (1949) · J. Masefield, *So long to learn* (1952) · J. Masefield, *In glad thanksgiving* (1967) · *A language not to be betrayed: selected prose of Edward Thomas*, ed. E. Longley (1981) · b. cert. · m. cert. · d. cert.
Archives Bodl. Oxf., corresp., papers, and literary MSS · Bodl. Oxf., letters to his family · Bodl. Oxf., papers relating to battle of the Somme · Harvard U., Houghton L., corresp., papers, and literary MSS · Hereford City Library, MSS · Hunt. L., letters · L. Cong., letters · London Library, letters · LUL, Sterling Library, MSS · LUL, watercolours and drawings, photographs and papers · New York University, Fales Library, letters · NL Scot., letters · Theatre Museum, London, letters · Theatre Museum, London, letters and papers relating to *The coming of Christ* · University of Arizona, Tucson, corresp. · Yale U., Beinecke L., letters and literary MSS | BL, corresp. with Sir Sydney Cockerell, Add. MS 52735 · BL, letters to Harley Granville-Barker, Add. MS 4789 · BL, corresp. with League of Dramatists, Add. MS 56854–56856 · BL, letters to Lillah McCarthy, Add. MS 47897 · BL, letters to George Bernard Shaw, Add. MS 50543 · BL, corresp. with Society of Authors, Add. MSS 56575–56626 · Bodl. Oxf., letters to Robert Bridges · Bodl. Oxf., letters to Celia Brown · Bodl. Oxf., letters to Nevil Coghill · Bodl. Oxf., letters to J. L. L. Hammond · Bodl. Oxf., letters to Phyllis Horne · Bodl. Oxf., letters to Grace Hunter · Bodl. Oxf., corresp. with Gilbert Murray · Bodl. Oxf., corresp. with Audrey Napier-Smith incl. two albums of watercolours and photographs · Bodl. Oxf., corresp. with H. W. Nevinson and E. S. Nevinson · Bodl. Oxf., letters to James Shelley · Bradford Art Galleries and Museums, letters to Butler Wood · CAC Cam., letters to Cecil Roberts · Col. U., letters to Cyril Clemens and literary MSS · CUL, letters to Siegfried Sassoon · Dorset County Museum, Dorchester, letters to Florence Hardy · Forbes Magazine, New York, corresp. with John Galsworthy · Harvard U., Houghton L., letters to Sir William Rothenstein · JRL, letters to *Manchester Guardian* · King's AC Cam., letters, mainly to Charles Ashbee · King's AC Cam., letters and postcards to Rupert Brooke · Litchfield Historical Society, Connecticut, letters to Dorothy Bull · London School of Hygiene and Tropical Medicine, corresp. with Sir Donald Ross · LPL, letters to G. K. A. Bell · LUL,

corresp. with Thomas Sturge Moore · LUL, letters to Ethne Thompson · News Int. RO, corresp. with *The Times* · NL Scot., letters to Lillian Adam Smith · NL Scot., letters to Alice V. Stuart · PRO NIre., letters to Margaret Dobbs, Mic 152 · Royal College of Physicians and Surgeons of Glasgow, corresp. with Sir Ronald Ross · Royal Society of Literature, London, letters to Royal Society of Literature · U. Birm. L., letters to Ada Galsworthy · U. Birm. L., letters to Francis Brett Young · U. Leeds, Brotherton L., letters to Edmund Gosse · U. Leeds, Brotherton L., letters to Thomas Moult · University of Kent, Canterbury, letters to Hewlett Johnson |SOUND BL NSA, performance recordings

Likenesses W. Strang, oils, 1912, Man. City Gall. · A. L. Coburn, photogravure, 1913, NPG · E. Kapp, drawing, 1917, Barber Institute of Fine Arts, Birmingham · W. Rothenstein, drawing, 1920, FM Cam. · J. Lavery, oils, 1937, priv. coll. · H. Coster, photographs, 1940–50, NPG · F. Man, photograph, *c*.1945, NPG · M. Gerson, photograph, 1961, NPG · H. Lamb, pencil drawing, NPG · T. Spicer-Simson, plasticine medallion, NPG · W. Strang, etching (after his oil portrait, 1912), NPG [*see illus.*] · W. Strang, oils, Wolverhampton Art Gallery · portraits, repro. in *William Strang RA* [1980] [exhibition catalogue, Sheffield, Glasgow, and London, 6 Dec 1980 – 28 June 1981]

Wealth at death £71,162: probate, 6 Nov 1967, CGPLA Eng. & Wales

Maseres, Francis (1731–1824), colonial administrator and author, was born in London on 15 December 1731, the son of Peter Abraham Maseres, a physician in Broad Street, Soho, and his wife, Magdalena, daughter of Francis du Pratt du Clareau. He spent his childhood in Soho and at Betchworth on the North Downs, which gave him a lifelong affection for Surrey. A Huguenot by descent, he was raised on stories of persecution in France which left him with an interest in seventeenth-century history and a hostility to Catholicism that was 'part of his very frame' (Cobbett, 234). Educated at Kingston upon Thames grammar school under the Revd Richard Wooddeson, Maseres, together with his brother Peter, was admitted to Clare College, Cambridge, in July 1748. Taught by John Courtail, another Huguenot by descent, Maseres graduated BA in 1752 with first-class honours in mathematics and was awarded the first chancellor's medal for classics. A fellow of Clare from 1756 until August 1759, he pursued his mathematical interest and retained his enthusiasm for Latin authors for the rest of his life. In 1758 he published a textbook to 'remove from some of the less abstruse parts of algebra, the difficulties that have arisen therein from too extensive use of the Negative Sign', which he argued should be used only as the symbol of subtraction (*Dissertation on the Use of the Negative Sign in Algebra*, 1758, preface, i); he dedicated this work to the duke of Newcastle, then chancellor of Cambridge University. Two years later he applied unsuccessfully to Newcastle for the Lucasian chair of mathematics at Cambridge, which went instead to Edward Waring. He was also a fine chess player and even held out for two hours against François-André Philidor.

Maseres combined his academic career with studying law. He had been admitted to the Inner Temple in 1750 and was called to the bar from the Middle Temple in 1758. He practised with little success on the western circuit and as a common pleader in London. Promotion, even 'a Welsh Judgeship' (*Maseres Letters*, 74), evaded him and it was probably the hope of future advancement that led him to accept the potentially demanding post of attorney-general of Quebec in 1766, a province in which French-speaking British officials were in short supply. Recommended by Charles Yorke, attorney-general in Rockingham's administration, he replaced George Suckling and set sail on 23 June 1766.

Maseres arrived in Quebec in September to join the administration, headed by the newly appointed Guy Carleton, of a lightly governed province that had been ceded to Britain only in 1763; one of the judges was a ship's surgeon. The population consisted of a small community of British merchants, 'the violent gentlemen of the army' (*Maseres Letters*, 18), and the French Catholic majority. Maseres wrote on 19 November 1767 that he believed 'the right way of settling this province would be to take away their religion (that is, discourage it without persecution, and powerfully encourage the Protestant religion)'; at the same time the French should be left with 'their … innocent, useful and compendious laws', which were so much to be preferred to 'the voluminous, intricate, unknown laws of England' (ibid., 57–8). The trouble was, as Maseres perceived, that while the treaty of 1763 had promised toleration of Catholicism 'as far as the laws of Great Britain permit', 'the laws of England do not at all permit the exercise of the Catholic religion'. He commented, 'Tis difficult [for a Catholic people] to be well-affected to a set of governours whom they look upon as enemies of God, deserving of, and destined to, eternal damnation' (ibid., 54). His preferred solution was to produce a code of the French and English laws applicable to Quebec.

During his three years in office Maseres managed to offend both the merchants and the military. He antagonized the former by claiming in 1766 that Britain had inherited the powers of the former regime to collect customs duties on rum, and by attempting to introduce English bankruptcy laws in 1767. He earned the enmity of the latter by treating as murder the death of a soldier, Donald Mackenzie, who had died after a vicious flogging, and by attempting to prosecute six army officers for assaulting a magistrate. His fiscal policies had to be dropped after his customs proposals were dramatically resisted by a jury of 'pretended patriots' who followed the lead of their American neighbours in resisting imposed taxation. His prosecution of the six officers failed because of the evidence provided by an unreliable witness. As a result, his position was seriously weakened.

Maseres was 'a good deal out of heart' at the failure of his 'schemes for the benefit of the province' (*Maseres Letters*, 86) and began to yearn for his beloved Surrey. Rigid he may have been, but Maseres was simply trying to uphold order in a turbulent community where even the basis of law was uncertain. Tensions came to a head in February 1769 when the governor, Carleton, bluntly rejected his long-awaited report on methods of reconciling French and English law. He granted his attorney-general indefinite leave, hoping that 'some Opportunity may offer this Gentleman in a Situation more agreeable to his own Inclinations, and where the Fervor of his Zeal can be of no essential disadvantage to the King's Service' (ibid., 24).

Back in Britain, Maseres kept his interests in Canada alive by lobbying on behalf of the merchants at the time of the Quebec Act of 1774 and by writing copiously about Canadian affairs in a series of pamphlets published under the title *The Canadian Freeholder* (3 vols., 1776–9). In 1773 the influence of the lord chancellor, Henry Bathurst, then Lord Apsley, secured his appointment to the virtual sinecure of cursitor baron of the exchequer, which gave him an income of between £300 and £400 a year. Contemporaries often referred to him as Baron Maseres, but this was not a peerage title. He became a bencher at the Inner Temple in 1774 and its treasurer in 1782. From 1780 until 1822 (when he was over ninety) he served as a judge of the sheriff's court in the city of London. His life was bound up with the Temple: his rooms were at 5 King's Bench Walk, and although out of term he used to dine at his home in Rathbone Place, which he inherited from his brother John, he always returned to the Temple to sleep. Just as he spoke the French of Louis XIV, so to the end of his life he wore clothes from the time of George II, including a 'three-cornered hat, tye-wig and ruffles' (*GM*, 573). He was very sociable and delighted in entertaining visitors, many of whom were eminent mathematicians, to dinner.

Maseres was a prolific author. He pursued his mathematical studies and published a number of treatises on subjects such as trigonometry, logarithms, and algebra, which Joseph Priestley declared were 'original and excellent' (J. T. Rutt, *Life and Correspondence of Joseph Priestley*, 2 vols., 1831–2, 2.490). Elected FRS on 2 May 1771, he contributed papers to the *Philosophical Transactions* for 1777, 1778, and 1779. He had acquired a lifelong fascination for history in his youth when he had set himself the task of reading the whole of Rapin's *History of England*, paying special attention to the sources used. He showed a keen interest in the civil wars of the seventeenth century, and in 1815 edited for the first time a collection of important tracts, which he attempted to contextualize in his introduction. He edited a number of reprints of historical works, including Thomas May's *History of the Parliament of England which Began 1640* and Sir John Temple's *History of the Irish Rebellion*, both of which revealed his anti-Catholic prejudices. A fellow of the Society of Antiquaries, he wrote a 'View of the ancient constitution of the English parliament' which was published in *Archaeologia* (2.301–40), eliciting a response from Charles Mellish. According to William Cobbett, Maseres 'had no asperity in his nature; he was naturally all gentleness and benevolent' (Cobbett, 233). He was generous to refugees from revolutionary France, Catholic priests included. A whig in politics, he was always stirred by injustice; he visited Cobbett during his imprisonment in Newgate in 1810, wearing his wig and gown to underline his protest. Jeremy Bentham hailed him as 'one of the most honest lawyers England ever knew' (*Maseres Letters*, 33), while Cobbett admired him for refusing to accept a salary increase. Someone, Maseres said, would have to meet the cost 'and the more I take the less that somebody must have' (Cobbett, 233). In later life he associated with advanced whigs such as the radical William Frend but,

despite writing over thirty books and pamphlets, he generally kept out of political disputes.

Maseres could afford to be lofty about money. 'He was by no means stingy' (Cobbett, 233) but his bachelor life was frugal. Legacies inherited from his father and brother grew into a massive fortune. Cobbett recalled Maseres as a loyal Anglican, who endowed a Sunday afternoon service at Reigate, where he had a country home, The Barons, to provide an additional opportunity for church attendance. He was not blind, however, to the abuses in the contemporary church and wrote two pamphlets proposing reforms, such as the division of populous parishes and an end to pluralism and non-residence, though he stopped short of advocating equalization of clerical incomes. In old age he moved towards the Unitarians, a conversion that Cobbett dated to 1812 when Maseres was over eighty. However, this may simply have represented the late flowering of radical protestant ideas common among Huguenots. Robert Fellowes, a young Anglican clergyman leaning to Unitarianism, became his unofficial chaplain, and then his principal heir. When Maseres, who was unmarried, died at his house in Church Street, Reigate, on 19 May 1824, £30,000 was bequeathed to relatives, while Fellowes scooped about £200,000. Fellowes erected a monument to his memory in Reigate churchyard.

GED MARTIN

Sources *The Maseres letters, 1766–1768*, ed. W. S. Wallace (1919) · E. Arthur, 'Maseres, Francis', *DCB*, vol. 6 · *DNB* · W. Cobbett, *Rural rides*, new edn (1967), 232–9 · *GM*, 1st ser., 94/1 (1824), 569–73 · Nichols, *Illustrations*, 9.556–7 · Venn, *Alum. Cant.* · C. Lamb, *The old benchers of the Inner Temple*, ed. F. D. Mackinnon (1927)
Archives Inner Temple, London, papers · RS, papers · U. Edin. L., mathematical notes, ref. Dc 5 7 · UCL, logarithms · Yale U., Farmington, Lewis Walpole Library, exchequer accounts | Bodl. Oxf., letters to Stephen Rigaud · NMM, letters to Andrew Mackay
Likenesses C. Hayter, oils, 1815 · P. Audinet, line engraving (aged eighty-three; after C. Hayter, 1817), BM, NPG; repro. in Lamb, *The old benchers*, facing p. 26

Masham. For this title name *see* individual entries under Masham; *see also* Lister, Samuel Cunliffe, first Baron Masham (1815–1906).

Masham [*née* Hill], **Abigail, Lady Masham** (1670?–1734), royal favourite, was the elder daughter of Francis Hill (*d. c.*1690), an Anabaptist and merchant of Smyrna and, after 1657, of London, and his wife, Elizabeth (*bap.* 1642, *d.* 1691x9), the youngest daughter of Sir John Jenyns of St Albans. Her parents were married in 1663, but the only source for 1670 as her date of birth is an inscription on an unauthenticated portrait now in the National Portrait Gallery (Piper, 226–7). It does, however, fit with the evidence that she was 'a grown woman' by 1690 (*Memoirs of Sarah, Duchess of Marlborough*, 126). On her mother's side Abigail was the first cousin of Sarah (Jenyns) Churchill, duchess of Marlborough, and on her father's the second cousin of Robert Harley, first earl of Oxford. Her paternal grandparents were William Hill of Teddington, one of the auditors of the revenue, and Abigail, the daughter of Richard Stephens of Eastington, Gloucestershire, whose niece and namesake married the father of Robert Harley. These two kinships drew her into court politics.

Early years Towards the end of the 1680s Francis Hill went bankrupt and he died shortly after, leaving his family destitute. Abigail appears to have joined the household of the newly married wife of Sir George Rivers, fourth baronet, of Chafford, Kent. The Rivers were neighbours of the Packers of Groombridge, a family connection of the Harleys, but Abigail's position was such a menial one that it cast doubt on her subsequent status as a gentlewoman. When Sarah Churchill, in high favour at the court of Princess Anne, was told of the Hill family's plight, she made herself responsible for their future support. Elizabeth Hill told her that her greatest concern was for her children, 'that they might have a subsistence in this vally of tears when I shall be no more' (BL, Add. MS 61454, fol. 194). Sarah put the younger son John *Hill into St Albans grammar school in 1690–91 and took Abigail into her own household nearby, meanwhile asking the princess to reserve a place for her as one of her bedchamber women, whenever a vacancy should occur (BL, Add. MS 61415, fol. 32). Jealous references to 'that enchantress' Mrs Hill in Anne's letters to Sarah of the 1690s have sometimes been taken as evidence that Abigail Hill was intimately involved in the royal friendship at this early stage; a novel by Doris Leslie (1950) based on her life takes its title from this epithet. In fact, in the famous correspondence between Mrs Morley and Mrs Freeman it was Sarah's friend Lady Fitzhardinge who figured as Mrs Hill. Abigail is not recorded among Anne's household until 1700, when she was 'Mother of the Maids'. When Anne succeeded to the throne Abigail's appointment as bedchamber woman was confirmed on 3 June 1702 with a salary of £500 a year.

Bedchamber woman and royal favourite As Abigail's own account makes clear, her duties were essentially those of royal chambermaid, dressing her mistress and waiting on her at table (*Letters to and from Henrietta*, 292–3). Despite a somewhat volatile temperament she proved herself a devoted servant and there was soon a degree of emotionalism in her relations with the queen. During the court's visit to Bath in 1703, when Abigail refused to sleep in the lodging assigned to her, the queen followed her about, begging her to go to bed, and 'calling her Dear Hill twenty times over' (Gregg, 235). By 1705 she was regarded as the most influential of the queen's personal servants after the duchess of Marlborough, whose growing estrangement from her mistress over politics was not yet public knowledge.

Robert Harley's political association with Abigail must have begun about 1706, when, as secretary of state, he began to part company with the Marlborough–Godolphin ministry over the appointment of the whig junto to cabinet office and realized that his cousin might be a useful ally in the royal bedchamber. A contemporary historian with inside information wrote of their night-time meetings 'under colour of concerts of music, at which the Queen herself is also said to have been present' (Cunningham, 2.76). In the spring of 1707 it first came to Sarah's

attention that her cousin had begun to speak to the queen about politics, and soon she was taxing Anne with taking all her advice from Harley and Abigail, who constantly fed 'Mrs Morley's passion for the torrys' (BL, Add. MS 61417, fol. 76). The queen insisted that Abigail's only role was that of a useful servant.

Royal favour also brought Abigail Hill the prospect of marriage. According to a whig lampoon of 1708, *The Rival Dutchess, or, Court Incendiary*, she was suspected 'of having too great a Regard' for her own sex, because she had remained so long unmarried. In fact her want of fortune and beauty were more than sufficient to account for this; Swift, who otherwise admired her, admitted that she was not handsome. All the evidence suggests that she was susceptible to the younger male courtiers. By Sarah's account she had been in love with one of the equerries, William Breton, 'but not to have an affair that ever I heard of' (BL, Add. MS 61422, fol. 156). There were also protracted negotiations with another young man, in which the indigent Lady Newport acted as go-between. Again the detail comes from *The Rival Dutchess*, but the duchess of Marlborough testified that the account was essentially true.

Finally in the spring or summer of 1707 Abigail was secretly married to **Samuel Masham** (1678/9–1758), courtier and army officer, the eighth son of Sir Francis Masham, third baronet (c.1646–1723), of Otes, in whose house John Locke had spent his later years, and his wife, Mary, *née* Scott. Masham, who had been first page and then equerry (1701) and was now groom of the bedchamber to Prince George, was several years younger than his wife, and Harley was said to have been instrumental in the match by pointing out to him the advantages of marriage to a royal favourite. Masham's family were certainly fully aware of these, but he himself assured them that it was a love match. The queen was present at the ceremony, made a privy purse payment of £2000 to Abigail as a dowry, and, to allow for her necessary absences as a married woman, appointed her younger sister Alice as a supernumerary bedchamber woman.

It was the belated discovery of the queen's collusion in this marriage which confirmed Sarah's suspicions about her cousin as a political rival. Realizing that Abigail had been in the queen's confidence for much longer than she had suspected, she decided that this underhand influence had been entirely responsible for her own loss of favour and the queen's resistance to her political advice. Her constant invective against her cousin from this time on, and particularly the insinuation that there was an unnatural element in Anne's affection for her bedchamber woman, turned the queen completely against her.

In the winter of 1707–8 Harley's attempt to form a moderate political ministry failed and he was forced to resign. But in the course of this crisis it became public knowledge that he had the support of his cousin in the queen's bedchamber, 'a great and growing favourite of much industry and insinuation' (*Correspondence of Jonathan Swift*, 1.69). Even after his resignation he boasted that he would continue to 'play [her] against any body' (*Private Correspondence of Sarah, Duchess of Marlborough*, 1.113), and before he retired into the country in May 1708 they arranged to keep up a correspondence in a code ingeniously based on the financial problems of their shared kinfolk. By this means he continued to feed her with accounts of the 'Pride, Ambition and Covetousness' of the Marlboroughs and their whig allies, and their mismanagements at home and abroad, 'which I think very necessary to be communicated to my aunt' (Longleat, Portland MSS, X, 16 Oct 1708). When Harley returned to London, Abigail arranged for him and his associates to have backstairs access to the queen at both Windsor and St James's. Probably she also encouraged press attacks on their opponents. When Delriviere Manley's *New Atalantis* was published in 1709 the duchess of Marlborough noted that 'it was said that Mrs Masham had given the author money' (*Private Correspondence*, 1.238).

Matters came to a head in January 1710 when the queen, on Harley's advice, instructed Marlborough to give a regiment vacant on the death of the whig earl of Essex to Abigail's brother John. Seeing this as a public blow to his authority in the army, and believing that Harley and Abigail were trying to force his resignation by this means, Marlborough urged his whig colleagues that 'now is the time or never for getting rid of … Mrs M[asham]' (Harris, 164). When they began canvassing support for a parliamentary address to remove her from court, Abigail was alarmed and contemplated resignation herself, but, since she had already done her work in helping Harley and his associates to re-establish relations with the queen, the attempt was too belated to be effective. The queen managed to rally tory support against it and by the end of the year the Godolphin ministry was dismissed, Harley restored to office, and the duchess of Marlborough forced to resign all her court offices.

Keeper of the privy purse and peeress   The post of keeper of the privy purse was bestowed on Abigail Masham on 24 January 1711. She kept her accounts with Hoare's Bank (in 1726 her daughter Anne was to marry Henry Hoare II), but these are uninformative, stating only the amounts and dates of withdrawals, often in the form of round sums to herself. She was also authorized by royal warrant to give full receipts in her own right, 'notwithstanding coverture' (BL, Add. MS 63093, fol. 45). But the queen was always reluctant to bestow a peerage on the Mashams, saying that she would 'lose a useful servant about her person, for it would give offence to have a peeress lie on the floor and do several other inferior offices' (Burnet, 6.36n.). She was only brought to consent in December 1711, when there was a need to create a batch of tory peers to ensure the passage through parliament of the preliminaries to the treaty of Utrecht, and then only on condition that Abigail remained as bedchamber woman, 'and did as she used to do' (ibid.).

Although Swift berated Lady Masham whenever she absented herself from court for family reasons, her political involvement remained remarkably sustained after her marriage, in spite of five pregnancies and at least one miscarriage in six years. Her first child, Anne, was born in September 1708; the second, Elizabeth, a year later;

George, who died as an infant, in September 1711; Samuel [*see below*] in November 1712; and Francis in 1714. Like several of the tory women at court she employed the man-midwife Hugh Chamberlen, and believed that she owed her life to him.

Once Harley was restored to office he had less need of his cousin as intermediary, a common pattern with such backstairs allies. But he noted that, 'following the example of the Duchess of Marlborough', she still expected that nothing should be done 'without her privity and consent' (*Portland MSS*, 5.661), and took care to maintain their confederacy, believing that she still had power to 'pull down' if she chose (Holmes, 216). In 1711 Swift could still come upon them alone together, 'settling the nation' (Swift, *Journal*, 412). But it was not long before Abigail began to grow suspicious of her cousin, now Lord Oxford, and to shift her allegiance to his rival Bolingbroke. The accusation that he had bribed her with illicit profits from the Assiento contract comes from Oxford's family and is unreliable (*Portland MSS*, 5.661), but he was the more thorough-going tory of the two and also more willing to further the career of her brother John. In return she privately conveyed his opinions and associates, including the Jacobite earl of Mar, to the queen. Whether she actually favoured the Pretender herself is uncertain. A work purporting to be an account by Nicolas Mesnager of his negotiations at the English court, which represents Lady Masham as the only one of the queen's advisers who was willing to speak to him openly about the restoration of the Pretender, is now known to be by Defoe. As the queen's health failed, Abigail maintained the partnership with Oxford for her sake. But by the last weeks of Anne's life, when he was in decline himself with drink and indecision, she became completely disillusioned with him, and rejoiced in, even if she did not bring about, his dismissal.

Conclusion   Abigail appears to have been genuinely grief-stricken at the queen's death, and gossip about her depredations afterwards was probably unfounded. When she was accused of making away with some of the queen's jewels, the duchess of Marlborough testified that none were missing: 'in this manner I justify'd Lady Masham, who I believed never rob'd any body but *me*' (Harris, 205). With her political role at an end under the Hanoverians, Abigail lived the rest of her life in obscurity, first at Langley, near Windsor, and, after the death of her husband's father in 1723, at Otes, in Essex. She died there after a long illness on 6 December 1734 and was buried in High Laver church.

Reacting against contemporary exaggerations, modern accounts of court politics under Queen Anne tend to minimize Abigail Masham's role. In the last resort the exact nature and extent of all such unofficial influence is unknowable, but what is significant in the context of women's roles in public life is the seriousness of her political aims. In minor matters of patronage, by which the influence of court women was normally measured, she was reluctant to exert herself and made no secret of her impatience with importunate courtiers. What she wished above all, as her letters to Harley make clear, was to shape policy, and like the duchess of Marlborough she was quite ready to risk alienating the queen with her hectoring in order to achieve her ends. Her frustration when Anne was unresponsive and her complaints about the limits of her influence should be read in this light, and not simply as objective evidence of her impotence.

Abigail's husband, described by the duchess of Marlborough as 'a soft, good-natured, insignificant man, always making low bows to everybody, and ready to skip to open a door' (Butler, 191), rose to be brigadier-general, was MP for Ilchester in 1710, and in 1716 succeeded by reversion to the office of remembrancer of the exchequer. He survived his wife by many years, and died on 16 October 1758, aged seventy-nine. His son **Samuel Masham** (1712–1776), courtier, who succeeded him as second Baron Masham, following an education at Westminster School and Christ Church, Oxford, was made auditor-general of the household of George, prince of Wales, and a lord of the bedchamber in 1762. He was married twice, first on 16 October 1736 to Henrietta Winnington (d. 1761) and second on 4 February 1762 to Charlotte Dyve (d. 1773), but had no heirs. When he died, heavily in debt, on 14 June 1776, his titles became extinct. The collections of John Locke, which had remained at Otes until then, were dispersed by his principal creditor.   FRANCES HARRIS

Sources Blenheim MSS, BL, Add. MSS 61415–61425, 61454 · Portland MSS, BL, Add. MSS 70116, 70290 · Lady Marlborough [S. Churchill] MS correspondence, BL, Althorp Papers, D14 · Wentworth MSS, BL, Add. MS 22225 · arrivals in London from overseas, BL, Add. MS 34015 · Longleat House, Wiltshire, Portland MSS · E. Masham's letter-book, Newberry Library, Chicago · Hoare's Bank archive, Fleet Street, London · manorial records, Herts. ALS · E. Chamberlayne, *Angliae notitia, or, The present state of England*, 19th edn (1700) · *The Rival Dutchess, or, Court incendiary* (1708) · D. Defoe, *Minutes of the negotiations of Monsieur Mesnager at the court of England* (1717) · J. Oldmixon, *The history of England, during the reigns of King William and Queen Mary, Queen Anne, King George I* (1735) · A. Cunningham, *The history of England from the revolution of 1688 to the accession of George I* (1787) · *Letters to and from Henrietta countess of Suffolk*, ed. J. W. Croker, 2 vols. (1824) · *Bishop Burnet's History* · *Private correspondence of Sarah, duchess of Marlborough*, 2 vols. (1838) · *The manuscripts of his grace the duke of Portland*, 10 vols., HMC, 29 (1891–1931), vols. 4–5 · N. Hooke, *Memoirs of Sarah, duchess of Marlborough*, ed. W. King (1930) · J. Swift, *Journal to Stella*, ed. H. Williams, 2 vols. (1948) · *The correspondence of Jonathan Swift*, ed. H. Williams, 5 vols. (1963–5) · D. Piper, *Catalogue of seventeenth-century portraits in the National Portrait Gallery, 1625–1714* (1963) · J. C. Sainty and R. Bucholz, eds., *Officials of the royal household, 1660–1837*, 1: *Department of the lord chamberlain and associated offices* (1997) · R. O. Bucholz, *The Augustan court: Queen Anne and the decline of court culture* (1993) · I. Butler, *Rule of three* (1967) · M. Gray, 'An early professional group? The auditors of the land revenue in the late 16th and early 17th centuries', *Archives*, 20 (1992), 45–59 · D. Green, *Sarah, duchess of Marlborough* (1967) · E. Gregg, *Queen Anne* (1980) · F. Harris, *A passion for government: the life of Sarah, duchess of Marlborough* (1991) · G. S. Holmes, *British politics in the age of Anne* (1967) · P. Laslett, 'Masham of Otes: the rise and fall of an English family', *History Today*, 3 (1953), 535–43 · GEC, *Peerage* · private information (2004) · *Old Westminsters*, 2.629 · Foster, *Alum. Oxon.*

Archives Hoare's Bank, Fleet Street, London, privy purse accounts | BL, Blenheim MSS, letters, etc., Add. MSS 61415–61425, 61454 · BL, letters to Lord Oxford, Add. MS 70290 · BL, Portland MSS, letters, Add. MSS 70116, 70290 · Newberry Library, Chicago, letter-book of Esther Masham
Likenesses portrait, 1700–10, NPG · engraving, BL, Add. MS 20818, fol. 65

Masham [née Cudworth], **Damaris**, **Lady Masham** (1658–1708), philosopher and theological writer, was born in Cambridge on 18 January 1658. Her father was Ralph *Cudworth (1617–1688), the philosopher and a leading member of the Cambridge Platonists. In 1645 he became regius professor of Hebrew, a post which he held until his death. Her mother, Damaris (d. 1695), possibly the daughter of Mathew Cradock, a London merchant, had been married to Thomas Andrewes of London before her marriage to Cudworth. The younger Damaris was Cudworth's only daughter, but she had a stepsister, a stepbrother, and at least three brothers.

Cudworth, whom his daughter was to defend against critics including Leibniz, was an 'unusually open-minded controversialist' and Damaris was brought up in a rare atmosphere of free enquiry and intellectual independence (Wallas, 75). From a young age she was distinguished by her learning and the keen mind she brought to all her studies. When on 25 June 1685 she married Sir Francis Masham (c.1646–1723), son of William Masham and his wife, Elizabeth Trevor, she acquired nine step-children. In 1686 her only son, Francis Cudworth Masham, was born. He was to become accountant-general to the court of chancery. Sir Francis later served as MP for Essex.

Damaris Masham first met John Locke in 1682 when she was twenty-three. They became close friends. In her Locke found 'a soul not of ordinary alloy' (*Correspondence*, ed. Rand, 14). He taught Damaris philosophy and divinity. At Otes in Essex, where she and Sir Francis lived, Damaris obviously found life frustrating, as in 1687 she wrote to Locke complaining that he 'might advise me to converse with the dead since here [at Otes] are so few living that are worth it' (HoP, *Commons, 1690–1715*). After returning from exile in Holland in 1688 Locke became increasingly ill in London and in 1691, aged fifty-nine, he was persuaded to leave the city for his health's sake. Already a frequent and welcome visitor at the home of Sir Francis and Lady Masham, Locke was invited to live with them. This he did for thirteen years until his death in 1704. His influence on Damaris, both as a writer and as a mother, was profound. Without Locke's influence she would almost certainly have been ignored, despite the fact that she was a most remarkable and learned woman. Early on in his time at Otes, Locke, in a letter to Limborch of 1690–91, acknowledged her rare qualities:

> The lady is so well versed in theological and philosophical studies, and of such an original mind, that you will not find many men to whom she is not superior in wealth of knowledge and ability to profit by it. (DNB)

Locke's *Some Thoughts Concerning Education* was to be Masham's guide in her son's upbringing. According to Locke she taught her son Latin 'without knowing it herself when she began' (Wallas, 86). Despite some natural reluctance she followed Locke's guidance on the importance of sun and fresh air for children to the extent of providing her son with thin-soled shoes. This was at a time when children were carefully shielded from the elements. After Locke's death Damaris wrote that:

> my first acquaintance with him began when he was past the middle age of man and I but young … I had for a great part of above two years conversed freely with him, and he favoured me sometimes with his correspondence in Holland.
> (*Correspondence*, ed. Rand, 13)

Life at Otes provided a stimulating and sympathetic atmosphere in which to live and write and Locke benefited greatly from it, although his health did not improve. He continued to supervise Lady Masham's studies as well as the education of her son. He made time for a close friendship with Esther Masham, the stepdaughter of Damaris, and acted as medical adviser to old Mrs Cudworth, who since her husband's death had made her home at Otes. Edward Clarke, husband of Locke's cousin, was a frequent visitor with his children, Edward, on whom Locke tried out his theories of education, and Elizabeth.

Against those who thought this life was merely a preparation for the next, Damaris Masham defended a life of reason—this was particularly bold as most people thought women had no business being reasonable. Her first published work was *A Discourse Concerning the Love of God* (1696), an essay on morality. Although published anonymously it was widely known to be hers. It was an answer to the works of John Norris. Norris, who had known Damaris Masham for some time and had been impressed by her piety and learning, dedicated his *Reflections upon the Conduct of Human Life* (1690) to his friend under the mistaken notion that she had gone blind. Her friends promptly informed him that he was wrong and that Damaris had not lost her sight, but this did not persuade Norris to withdraw his book. As she commented in *A Discourse*, Norris, 'having fitted his Epistle to that supposition, could not be hindered from publishing it' (Masham, *Discourse*, preface). It was an incident that finally severed Masham's friendship with Norris. In *A Discourse* Damaris Masham responded to volume 3 of Norris's *Practical discourses upon several divine subjects* (1693). She characterized Norris's position as being that 'God's creatures have no warrant for our love, having as they do "no Efficiency at all to operate upon us"; they are simply the "occasional Causes of those Sentiments which God produces in us"' (Pyle, 560). Her object was to refute Norris's understanding of divine love as 'morally subversive and a dangerous imposture as a principle of Christianity' (ibid.). Her most profound concern was that Norris's account:

> provides no foundation for virtuous conduct. Additionally, it may cause positive harm by encouraging people to strive for a love of God which they cannot possible attain 'and opposite to their very Constitution and Being in this world', while failing to recognize that their ideal indeed 'Destroys all the Duties and Obligations of Social Life'.   (ibid.)

Damaris Masham's second work, *Occasional thoughts in reference to a vertuous or Christian life* (1705), argues against social prejudice for the rational life, and 'that the Pursuit of virtue must be based upon a rational commitment to sound religious principles acquired through education'

(Pyle, 560–61). She saw such prejudice as responsible for the ignorance of daughters of the middle and upper classes. 'Girls', she wrote, 'betwixt silly Fathers and ignorant Mothers, are generally so brought up that traditionary Opinions are to them, all their lives long, instead of Reason' (Masham, *Occasional Thoughts*, 162). Parents, she saw, were afraid of the consequences of learning in their daughters. 'They might be in danger of not finding Husbands' (ibid., 197). She shared Locke's conviction that mothers should be able to educate their children—boys as well as girls. Men would not welcome learning in their wives but 'if Men did usually find Women the more amiable for being knowing, they would much more commonly, than now they are, be so' (ibid., 204). Unhappy marriages were common and education in women could counter discontent. It was not advice easily followed. A woman must 'order the Course and Manner of her Life somewhat differently from others of her Sex and Condition' (ibid., 198). From her own experience as a learned woman she knew the difficulties and the opposition to be met.

Damaris Masham died at Otes on 20 April 1708 and was buried in the middle aisle of Bath Abbey. Over her grave it was written of 'her Learning, Judgement, Sagacity, and Penetration together with her Candor and Love of Truth' (Ballard, 337).

BRIDGET HILL

Sources [D. Masham], *A discourse concerning the love of God* (1696) • D. Masham, *Occasional thoughts in reference to a vertuous or Christian life* (1705) • *The correspondence of John Locke and Edward Clarke*, ed. B. Rand (1927) • H. R. Fox Bourne, *The life of John Locke*, 2 vols. (1876) • A. Wallas, *Before the bluestockings* (1929) • D. Garber and M. Ayers, eds., *The Cambridge history of seventeenth-century philosophy*, 2 vols. (1998) • G. Ballard, *Memoirs of several ladies of Great Britain* (1752) • *DNB* • J. Peile, *Biographical register of Christ's College, 1505–1905, and of the earlier foundation, God's House, 1448–1505*, ed. [J. A. Venn], 2 vols. (1910–13) • HoP, *Commons, 1690–1715* • A. Pyle, ed., *The dictionary of seventeenth-century British philosophers*, 2 vols. (2000), 2.559–562 • T. Birch, 'Account of the life and writings of R. Cudworth', in R. Cudworth, *The true intellectual system of the universe* (1743), preface

Archives Bodl. Oxf., corresp. and papers relating to Masham Trust | Bodl. Oxf., Locke MSS, letters to John Locke

Masham, Samuel, first Baron Masham (1678/9–1758). *See under* Masham, Abigail, Lady Masham (1670?–1734).

Masham, Samuel, second Baron Masham (1712–1776). *See under* Masham, Abigail, Lady Masham (1670?–1734).

Masham, William (1615/16–1654/5), politician, was the son and heir of Sir William Masham, baronet (*c*.1592–1656), of Otes, or Oates, in the parish of High Laver, Essex, and his wife, Elizabeth (*d*. in or after 1663), widow of Sir James Altham and daughter of Sir Francis Barrington, baronet. He was educated at St Catharine's College, Cambridge, where he matriculated in 1633; in the following year he was said to be aged eighteen. Entering Lincoln's Inn in 1635 no less a figure than Oliver St John, future lord chief justice of the common pleas and Masham's brother-in-law, stood surety for him. Although he does not appear to have been called to the bar both he and his father held masterships in the court of common pleas, but their functions appear to have been performed by deputies. At an unknown date Masham married Elizabeth (*d.* in or after 1656), daughter of Sir John Trevor, like his father a member of the Long Parliament. So heavily connected was he with the leading parliamentarian dynasties of the day that it would have been surprising had he made no entry on the public stage, and in 1646 he was himself recruited to a vacant Commons seat at Shrewsbury. His election at this time, amid the ripening conflicts at Westminster between different political factions, might repay closer examination were there source material adequate to the task.

Masham's early career at Westminster was undistinguished to the point of indiscernability. He formally dissented from the 5 December 1648 vote of the House of Commons to continue peace talks on 8 February 1649, the same day as his father, who had avoided participating in the trial of the king. Having been more or less perpetually submerged in a parliament of several hundred members Masham began to stand out a little more in a Rump of several dozen, and in the months and years that followed he was nominated to a large number of committees of the house. In spring 1649 he joined the board of governors of Westminster School. In November 1651 he was elected to the fourth Commonwealth council of state, coming in way down the poll, with just 47 votes. He was appointed to several standing conciliar committees, including those for admiralty business, foreign affairs, examinations (a body active in the sphere of security), and the control of timber stocks (a key strategic responsibility of the council), as well as numerous *ad hoc* bodies. He attended about two-fifths of the council's meetings in the ensuing year, but was not re-elected in November 1652, possibly falling victim to the political fallout from the decidedly uncertain start to the war at sea with the Dutch. During the protectorate he was personally nominated by Cromwell as one of the treasury commissioners, on 2 August 1654, and was also appointed as an ejector in Essex. He died some time between August 1654 and 15 January 1655, when the Commons' journal refers to his being dead, predeceasing his father. His eldest son, William, inherited the baronetcy on the death of his grandfather in 1656, and Masham and his wife had at least one other child, a son, Trevor.

SEAN KELSEY

Sources GEC, *Baronetage*, 1.182 · *JHC*, 4 (1644–6); 7 (1651–9) · *CSP dom.*, 1651–2 · R. Zaller, 'Masham, William', Greaves & Zaller, *BDBR*, 2.225–6 · J. Peacey, 'Led by the hand: manucaptors and patronage at Lincoln's Inn in the seventeenth century', *Journal of Legal History*, 18 (1997), 26–44 · Venn, *Alum. Cant.*

Maskell, Daniel [Dan] (**1908–1992**), tennis player and broadcaster, was born on 11 April 1908 at 15 Everington Street, Fulham, London, the fourth and youngest son and seventh of eight children of Henry George Maskell (*b.* 1873), engineer, and his wife, Emma Pearce (1875–1922). He had an entirely happy childhood, though his upbringing was firm. His father, Harry, insisted that all the younger members of the family address him as 'sir'. The younger Dan won a place at Upper Latymer School, a grammar school in nearby Hammersmith, but the family could not afford the fees. He went instead to Everington

Daniel Maskell (1908–1992), by unknown photographer, 1977

Street School, close to the family home. There his talent for sport soon emerged. He was captain of the school soccer team, and during school holidays he became a part-time ballboy at Queen's Club, near his home. He said it was 'a better way of earning pocket-money than queueing for meat or delivering bread' (Maskell, 28). As well as tennis and other racket sports, Queen's was also the venue at that time for a range of sports, including the Oxford and Cambridge football, rugby, and athletics matches. Maskell never forgot witnessing performances from the future Olympic champions Harold Abrahams and Lord Burghley, nor acting as a ballboy for the future duke of York (later George VI), who competed at Wimbledon in 1926.

Lawn tennis became Maskell's main interest. He was a natural timer of the ball, and the game came easily to him. He seized the opportunity to impress in matches against the younger Queen's members and professionals. In 1923, aged fifteen, he became a full-time ballboy. When the maharaja of Baroda, a Queen's member, presented a trophy for the annual competition between the ballboys, Maskell won his first tennis prize. Just a year later he was appointed a junior teaching professional, and in 1926 was given a five-year contract by Queen's to teach lawn tennis, real tennis, rackets, and squash. Tournament tennis at the time was mostly for amateur players. Professionals could not compete. But in October 1927 Maskell helped create the first world professional championship, played at Queen's Club, and defeated Charles Read in three straight sets for a first prize of £50. A year later he beat the same player to become British professional champion—a title he won sixteen times between then and 1951.

In 1929 Maskell left Queen's to become the first teaching professional at the All England Club, Wimbledon, where his duties also included coaching juniors with Davis cup and Wightman cup potential. He had already been a spectator at Wimbledon many times, starting in 1924 when he saw Britain's Kitty McKane defeat Helen Wills (Moody) in the ladies' final—the only match the American woman lost at Wimbledon in a career that took her to eight Wimbledon singles titles. Maskell joined the club in pre-practice week prior to the championships fortnight in June, and his first task was to practise with legendary champions such as Helen Wills, Jean Borotra, and Dorothy Round. He also became coach to the British Davis cup team. Led by the inspirational Fred Perry, the British team regained the cup in 1933, defeating France in Paris, and retained it for the next three years on the centre court at Wimbledon, beating the United States and Australia. Perry was Wimbledon champion three years running from 1934 to 1936, and with Dorothy Round winning the ladies' singles in 1934 and 1937, Maskell was part of the golden age of British tennis. On 26 August 1936 he married Constance Eileen (Con) Cox (1916–1979), secretary. They had one daughter, Robin, and one son, Jay.

During the Second World War, Maskell served in the Royal Air Force and, from 1940, was its first rehabilitation officer, based at the Palace Hotel in Torquay, and then Loughborough. Maskell's task was to devise exercises and activity for wounded aircrew. He was devastated when bombing destroyed part of the Palace Hotel and killed over twenty patients and medical staff while he was on a weekend away. He rose to the rank of squadron leader, and was appointed OBE in 1945. After the war he resumed his career at the All England Club, became chairman of the Professional Tennis Coaches Association, and continued to play professional tournaments. He also gave private tennis coaching to members of the royal family.

Maskell's broadcasting career began in 1949 when he joined the BBC radio commentary team for Wimbledon as an expert summarizer. In 1951 he moved to television, and soon became the leading commentator—a role he continued for the next forty years until he retired in 1991, by which time he had not missed a day's play at Wimbledon since 1929. Such was his impact that the 1992 Wimbledon championships began with a presentation to him in the royal box of a silver salver engraved with the landmarks of his career. The All England Club had already honoured him nearly forty years earlier, in 1953, by making him the first professional member of the club. As a television commentator, he believed in meticulous preparation and economy of words. 'The picture tells the greatest part of the story', he said (Maskell, 218). One of his golden rules was never to talk during a rally. Nevertheless his rich, even plummy, voice became almost the traditional sound of an English summer. His reaction to winning shots, with such phrases as 'Oh, I say!' and 'a dream of a backhand!', became legendary. He was never controversial nor outspoken, but was always looking to emphasize the positive aspects of players and the game. Following his retirement from the All England Club in 1955, he worked for the Lawn Tennis Association until 1973, devoting himself to coaching and development work. In 1982 he was appointed CBE for his services to tennis. In 1988, when tennis was restored to the Olympic games after an absence of sixty-four years, he fulfilled a life's ambition by attending the games in Seoul, Korea, as a member of the BBC team. Colleagues were astonished when the eighty-year-old Maskell, after the long and tiring flight from London, insisted on going straight to the Olympic Stadium to see the opening ceremony.

Maskell's personal life was struck by two tragedies. In 1970 his only son, Jay, a licensed pilot, was killed in an air crash in the Bahamas, and in 1979 his first wife, Connie, was drowned in the West Indies. He married second, on 20 August 1980, Kathleen (Kay) Latto (d. 1993), a voluntary worker. Away from tennis he had an intense passion for skiing, which he took up in the 1930s. Asked on a radio programme what he would do if given only one further day of sport, he opted for skiing. He was also a keen golfer, and for twenty-two years served on the committee of Wimbledon Common Golf Club, where he first swung a club as a seventeen-year-old. In his last years he suffered from cancer of the prostate. He died of heart failure in his sleep, on 10 December 1992, at East Surrey Hospital, Redhill, and was cremated on 17 December at Randalls Park, Leatherhead, Surrey. He was survived by his second wife and by the daughter of his first marriage. A memorial service was held on 15 March 1993 at All Souls, Langham Place.   JONATHAN MARTIN

Sources D. Maskell, *From where I sit* (1988) • *The Times* (11 Dec 1992) • *The Times* (16 March 1993) • *The Independent* (11 Dec 1992) • *The Independent* (18 Dec 1992) • *Daily Telegraph* (11 Dec 1992) • personal knowledge (2004) • private information (2004) [Mrs R. Charlton, family] • d. cert.
Archives Loughborough University, papers | FILM BBC WAC • BFI NFTVA, current affairs footage • BFI NFTVA, documentary footage
Likenesses photograph, 1977, Hult. Arch. [*see illus.*] • photograph, repro. in *The Times* (11 Dec 1992) • photograph, repro. in *The Independent* (11 Dec 1992) • photograph, repro. in *Daily Telegraph*
Wealth at death £313,870: probate, 17 March 1993, CGPLA Eng. & Wales

Maskell, William (1814–1890), Roman Catholic convert and liturgical scholar, the only son of William Maskell (1777–1841), solicitor, and Mary Miles (1772–1854), was born on 17 May 1814 at Shepton Mallet, Somerset. In 1823 the family moved to fashionable Bath. Maskell matriculated on 9 June 1832 at University College, Oxford. He graduated BA in 1836, and proceeded MA in 1838, having taken holy orders in the previous year. From the first an extremely high-churchman, in 1840 he attacked the latitudinarian bishop of Norwich, Edward Stanley, for supporting the movement for the relaxation of subscription. In 1842 he became rector of Corscombe, Dorset, but within a year he resigned his living to devote himself to research into the history of Anglican ritual. His *Ancient liturgy of the Church of England … and the modern Roman liturgy, arranged in parallel columns* appeared in 1844 and was followed by his *Monumenta ritualia ecclesiæ Anglicanæ, or, Occasional Offices of the Church of England* (3 vols., 1846; 2nd edn, 1882). In 1970 there was a facsimile reprint of this work.

These works at once placed Maskell in the front rank of English ecclesiastical antiquaries. His diocesan, Edward Denison, bishop of Salisbury, to whom he had dedicated his *Monumenta*, recommended his appointment as domestic chaplain to the bishop of Exeter, Henry Phillpotts, and in July 1847 he was instituted vicar of St Mary Church, Torquay. His first major duty was to assist the bishop in his examination of the Revd George Cornelius Gorham, concerning his views on baptism, after his presentation to the vicarage of Brampford Speke, near Exeter. Maskell was peculiarly well qualified for this duty, in view of his extensive knowledge of the history of the doctrine and practice of baptism. The Gorham case inspired his *Holy Baptism: a Dissertation* (1848). In 1849 he published a volume of sermons in which high-church views both of baptism and of the holy eucharist were expounded; and in *An Enquiry into the Doctrine of the Church of England upon Absolution* (1849) he attempted to justify the revival of the confessional.

However, the Gorham case changed Maskell's view of the Church of England. Initially he had agreed wholeheartedly with the bishop of Exeter that Gorham's teaching on baptism was heretical and he deplored Gorham's appeal to the privy council against the bishop who had refused to institute him; but as the case unfolded, Maskell underwent a period of anguished reflection, and came to the conclusion that the privy council committee, though composed of laymen, was indeed the legitimate arbiter of the doctrinal dispute, and that Gorham's views on baptism were not repugnant to the formularies of the Church of England. He published his volte-face in three provocative pamphlets between February and June 1850: *The Royal Supremacy and the Authority of the Judicial Committee of the Privy Council*, *The Want of Dogmatic Teaching in the Church of England*, and *Correspondence of the archbishop of Canterbury and the bishop of Exeter with the Rev. W. Maskell*. These pamphlets made it clear that Maskell's faith in the Church of England was collapsing.

Soon afterwards, having sought advice from J. H. Newman, Maskell resigned his living, and was received into the Church of Rome. He publicized his secession in his *Letter to the Rev. Dr. Pusey on his Receiving Persons in Auricular Confession* (1850). As a Roman Catholic he refrained from controversy until the decree of the Vatican council defining the dogma of papal infallibility. In his pamphlet entitled *What is the Meaning of the late Definition on the Infallibility of the Pope?* (1871), he espoused the views propounded by liberal Roman Catholics such as Newman, and challenged the interpretation of the decree put forward by the archbishop of Westminster, Henry Manning, in his pastoral letter of 1870. For this Maskell was violently attacked in the ultramontane *Tablet* and had his pamphlet examined for heresy by the archbishop. However, he made his peace with Manning and in 1872 published under the title *Protestant Ritualists* some very trenchant remarks on the privy council case of *Sheppard v. Bennett* and the position of the Tractarians in the Church of England. W. J. E. Bennett had been charged with heresy for his extremely high views on the eucharist, but had been acquitted. In a final burst of controversy in 1876 Maskell castigated Sabine Baring-Gould's biography of the poet Robert Stephen Hawker, and defended his friend Hawker against the allegation that he had secretly subscribed to Roman Catholicism while officiating as vicar of Morwenstow.

Maskell never took orders in the Church of Rome. Although a widower at the time of his conversion in 1850, he told Newman emphatically that he was 'quite sure' he

'never should or would' ask for holy orders in the Church of Rome. This was probably because he had three young sons to care for. His second marriage in 1852 made priesthood impossible. He spent his later life in retirement, residing at Bude, Cornwall, and dividing his time between the activities of a country gentleman and antiquarian pursuits. He was judged to be a man of considerable literary and conversational powers. Thanks to a fortune inherited from his father, he amassed a considerable library of patristic literature, and collected medieval service books, enamels, and carvings in ivory, many of which he gave to the British and South Kensington museums. For the committee of council on education he edited in 1872 *A Description of the Ivories, Ancient and Modern, in the South Kensington Museum*. He was a JP and a deputy lieutenant for the county of Cornwall.

Maskell was married twice, first in 1837 to Mary Scott (*d.* 1847); second in 1852 to Monique Stein (*d.* 1895). With his first wife he had one daughter and three sons: Mary (1838–1845); William (1839–1898), registrar of the University of New Zealand; Stuart (1843–1912), solicitor; and Alfred (1845–1912), art historian. He died at 1 Alexandra Terrace, Penzance, on 12 April 1890 and was buried at Penzance.

A conscientious and profound liturgical scholar, Maskell was also a keen theological controversialist. Particularly adept at legalistic and historical argument, he would castigate his opponents with firm belief in his superior logic and in the complete righteousness of his cause.

J. M. RIGG, *rev.* DAVID MASKELL

Sources Gillow, *Lit. biog. hist.* · P. B. Nockles, *The Oxford Movement in context: Anglican high churchmanship, 1760–1857* (1994) · G. C. B. Davies, *Henry Phillpotts, bishop of Exeter* (1954) · H. P. Liddon, *The life of Edward Bouverie Pusey*, ed. J. O. Johnston and others, 4 vols. (1893–7), vol. 3 · *The letters and diaries of John Henry Newman*, ed. C. S. Dessain and others, [31 vols.] (1961–), vols. 13–14, 25–6, 28–9 · F. J. Cwiekowski, *The English bishops and the First Vatican Council* (1971) · C. E. Byles, *The life and letters of R. S. Hawker* (1905) · J. C. S. Nias, *Gorham and the bishop of Exeter* (1951) · E. S. Purcell, *Life of Cardinal Manning*, 2 vols. (1896) · *The Times* (15 April 1890) · *Church Times* (18 April 1890) · *The Athenaeum* (19 April 1890), 502–3

Archives BL, corresp. and papers, Add. MSS 37824–37826 · BL, notebook, Add. MS 38721 · BL, printed catalogue of books used in sixteenth-century church services with his MS notes and additions · Bodl. Oxf. · LPL, MS of 'Enquiry into the doctrine of the Church of England' · priv. coll. | Archives of the British Province of the Society of Jesus, London · BL, corresp. with W. E. Gladstone, Add. MSS 44364–44444 · Bodl. Oxf., J. C. Crosthwaite MSS · Bodl. Oxf., R. S. Hawker MSS · Bodl. Oxf., F. G. Lee MSS · Bodl. Oxf., H. E. Manning MSS · Downside Abbey, Somerset · Pusey Oxf., G. A. Denison MSS · Sion College, London, W. Scott MSS

Likenesses oils, *c.*1836, priv. coll. · Richmond, drawing, *c.*1850, repro. in Byles, *Life and letters* · Mayall, photograph, *c.*1860, priv. coll.

Wealth at death £2986 19s. 5d.: probate, 11 June 1890, *CGPLA Eng. & Wales*

Maskelyne, John Nevil (1839–1917), magician, was born on 22 December 1839 at 20 White Hart Row, Cheltenham, the son of John Nevil Maskelyne, a saddler, and his wife, Harriet Brunsdon. He was descended from the astronomer royal Nevil Maskelyne, who had a crater on the moon named after him. He was apprenticed to a watchmaker, and as a boy was a keen amateur conjuror, giving a public performance of his own tricks at the age of sixteen. In 1865 his exposure of the famous spiritualists the Davenport Brothers as impostors led Maskelyne and his friend George Alfred Cooke, a cabinet-maker, to embark on a joint career as professional magicians. Their first appearance, billed as 'the only Successful Rivals of the Davenport Brothers', was on 19 June 1865 at Jessop's Aviary Gardens, Cheltenham. Meanwhile, on 10 December 1862, Maskelyne married Elizabeth Taylor (1859–1911), the daughter of Thomas Taylor, a stagecoach driver.

After touring the provinces for eight years, Maskelyne and Cooke began a short season in 1873 at St James Hall, Piccadilly, with their 'entertainment of pure trickery'. This was so successful that in May 1873 they took a lease on the Small Hall at the Egyptian Hall in Piccadilly, but soon moved into the Large Hall, where they remained until its demolition in 1904. The Egyptian Hall became known as England's 'Home of Mystery', and was as essential for family outings as the Tower of London or London Zoo. In 1904 the show moved to St George's Hall, Langham Place, and on Cooke's death in 1905 the famous magician David Devant became Maskelyne's partner. The era of 'Maskelyne and Devant's Mysteries' lasted until 1915, when the partnership ended.

Maskelyne's repertory included many famous tricks and illusions which were repeated and improved upon over the years. One of his earliest tricks, first performed in 1865, was 'escaping from a box', in which he managed to escape from a locked, roped, wooden box inside a cabinet in seven seconds. This box escape was later incorporated into *Will, the Witch, and the Watch*, a musical dramatic sketch performed more than 10,000 times over four decades. Maskelyne developed many of these dramatic sketches, which embodied tricks and illusions: two of the most famous were *Elixir vitae*, which involved the illusion of decapitation, and *A Spirit Case, or, Mrs Daffodil Downing's Light and Dark Seance*, which conjured up a ghost to the sounds of a violin suspended in the air. One of his most famous illusions was his *Levitation*, which he first performed in 1867, when he caused his wife to rise from the stage. He created several automatons, the most celebrated being Psycho, which first performed in 1875. Psycho was a cross-legged Hindu figure, 22 inches high, which played whist with the audience and solved arithmetical problems set by them. Psycho made more than 4000 consecutive appearances before it was withdrawn in 1880. Another of Maskelyne's specialities was plate-spinning— he traced his first ambition to be a conjuror to his experience as a boy watching a famous plate-spinner, Antonio Blitz.

In addition to developing his own tricks and illusions, Maskelyne was important as an impresario, booking guest performers to appear in his show. Many successful magicians began their careers at the Egyptian Hall: one who never performed there was Houdini, who wrote asking for an engagement in 1898, before he became famous, and was refused. Maskelyne entered into several lawsuits. One of the best known followed his offer of £500 to anyone who could reproduce the box used in his box trick. He

disputed the design of the trick box produced by Stollery and Evans, and the case went to the House of Lords, who ruled against Maskelyne. Throughout his career he attacked and exposed bogus spiritualists, including Eusapia Palladino. Among his publications was *Modern Spiritualism* (1876).

Maskelyne took out patents on more than forty commercial inventions, including a cash register (patented in 1869), which won a major award at the Paris Universal Exhibition, a typewriter (1889), and his coin-operated lock for public lavatories (1892), which was used in England until the 1950s.

Maskelyne died on 18 May 1917, at St George's Hall, 4 Langham Place, London, and was buried on 22 May at Brompton cemetery. His wife had predeceased him, on 23 July 1911. He was survived by his sons Nevil and Edwin and a daughter. Nevil and his sons, Clive, Noel, and Jasper, kept the entertainments going at St George's Hall until 1933, when the Maskelyne tradition of magic finally came to an end. ANNE PIMLOTT BAKER, *rev.*

Sources J. Fisher, *Paul Daniels and the story of magic* (1987) · E. A. Dawes, *The great illusionists* (1979) · *The Times* (19 May 1917) · *Era Almanack and Annual* (1912) · B. Hunt, ed., *The green room book, or, Who's who on the stage* (1906) · J. Parker, ed., *The green room book, or, Who's who on the stage* (1907–9)
Likenesses portrait, repro. in Fisher, *Paul Daniels and the story of magic*, 103
Wealth at death £5366 19s. 7d.: probate, 21 Nov 1917, *CGPLA Eng. & Wales*

Maskelyne, Mervyn Herbert Nevil Story- (1823–1911), mineralogist, born at Basset Down House, near Wroughton, Wiltshire, on 3 September 1823, was the eldest son in the family of two sons and four daughters of Anthony Mervyn Reeve Story FRS (1791–1879), and his wife, Margaret (d. 1858), only child and ultimate heir of Nevil *Maskelyne, astronomer royal. The father acquired through his wife the Maskelyne estates in Wiltshire, and in 1845 adopted the surname of Story-Maskelyne. One of the mineralogist's sisters, Antonia, married Sir Warington Wilkinson Smyth.

After spending ten years at Bruton grammar school in Somerset, Story-Maskelyne was admitted to Wadham College, Oxford, as a commoner in 1840, where he was taught by the positivist Richard Congreve. He graduated BA with a second class in mathematics in Easter term 1845. He proceeded MA in 1849. On leaving Oxford he studied for the bar at the Inner Temple, but he had, almost from boyhood, taken a keen interest in natural science, and his early studies in photography led to a friendship with William Henry Fox Talbot. Fox Talbot introduced him to David Brewster, who encouraged his scientific interests. He was persuaded to abandon the law for science in 1847 by Benjamin Brodie the younger, and in 1850 was invited to deliver lectures on mineralogy at Oxford. He accepted this invitation on condition that a laboratory should be assigned to him, where he could teach mineralogical analysis and chemistry in general. A suite of rooms under the Ashmolean Museum was allotted Story-Maskelyne, and there he lived and worked from 1851 to 1857. Among his earliest students were William Thomson, afterwards archbishop of York, and Henry Smith, later professor of geometry and a life-long friend. He remained actively interested in the applications of photography, helping Fox Talbot in his unsuccessful legal action to protect his patent in December 1854.

Story-Maskelyne was a strong advocate of the recognition of natural science in the Oxford curriculum, and was examiner in the new school of natural science in 1855 and 1856. He was one of the small group of scholars, who included H. H. Vaughan and Mark Pattison, who advocated an extension of the professoriate and disciplinary specialization. He moved in radical circles and opposed the power of the clergy in the university. In 1856 he became professor of mineralogy at Oxford in succession to Dean William Buckland, but the chair was very poorly endowed. In 1857 he accepted the newly created post of keeper of the minerals at the British Museum and, although he retained his Oxford professorship, he moved to London. His income was now sufficient to marry, on 29 June 1858, Thereza Mary, eldest daughter of John Dillwyn Llewelyn, a coal-owner and pioneer of photography.

Since 1851 no one at the British Museum had taken any special interest in mineralogy. Story-Maskelyne undertook the rearrangement of all the minerals under his charge according to the crystallochemical system of Rose. He also maintained and developed the collections so that they became the largest and best arranged series of minerals and meteorites in existence. During his tenure of the keepership no fewer than 43,000 specimens were added to the collection. He published a catalogue of minerals at the museum in 1863 (new edn, 1881) and a *Guide to the Collection* in 1868. His friend John Ruskin brought his work in arranging the mineralogical collections to public notice in 1866.

Story-Maskelyne was always much interested in meteorites, which he was one of the first to study by means of thin sections for the microscope. He published the results of his numerous researches, of which the most important are those on the nature and constitution of the Parnallee, Nellore, Breitenbach, Manegaum, Busti, Shalka, and Rowton meteorites. Chief among his mineral researches were those upon Langite, Melaconite, Tenorite, Andrewsite, Connellite, Chalkosiderite, and Ludlamite. New minerals described by him were Andrewsite, Langite, Liskeardite, and Waringtonite. Asmanite, Oldhamite, and Osbornite, constituents of meteoric stones, were first isolated and determined by him, though the first named, described by him in 1871, was later regarded as identical with the mineral tridymite. He was also the first to recognize the presence of enstatite in meteorites.

Deeply interested in the history of the diamond, he wrote on the Koh-i-noor stone (*Chemical News*, 1, 1860, 229; *Nature*, 44, 1891, 555; *Nature*, 45, 1891–2, 5). In 1880, following a controversy, he proved that the diamonds claimed to have been manufactured by the Glasgow chemist James Mactear were in reality a crystallized silicate. He also studied the occurrence of the diamond in South Africa, and

described the enstatite rock which is associated with it in that part of the world (*Philosophical Magazine*, 7, 1879, 135).

Story-Maskelyne gave some notable courses of lectures on crystallography both in London and Oxford. In a course delivered in 1869 he announced an important proof of the number and mutual inclinations of the symmetry planes possible in a crystalloid system. His general views were stated in a series of lectures before the Chemical Society in 1874. On his lectures he largely based his textbook *The Morphology of Crystals*, which was published in 1895. In his mathematical as well as in his purely scientific treatment of his theme his writing was characterized by distinction and charm of style. It became his practice to invite the most promising of his Oxford pupils, who included Professor W. J. Lewis, Dr L. Fletcher, and Sir Henry A. Miers, to work with him at the British Museum. He thus extended the usefulness of both his London and Oxford offices, and trained many distinguished members of the next generation of British mineralogists.

Story-Maskelyne's scientific attainments were widely recognized. Elected a fellow of the Royal Society in 1870, he was vice-president from 1897 to 1899. He received in 1893 the Wollaston medal of the Geological Society, of which he became a fellow in 1854, was chosen an honorary fellow of Wadham College in 1873, and was made honorary DSc in 1903. He was corresponding or honorary member of the Imperial Mineralogical Society of St Petersburg, of the Society of Natural History of Boston, of the Royal Academy of Bavaria, and of the Academy of Natural Sciences in Philadelphia.

On the death of his father in 1879 Story-Maskelyne succeeded to the Basset Down estates, and thenceforward became an active country gentleman. He resigned his post at the British Museum the next year, but continued to hold the professorship of mineralogy at Oxford until 1895. By that time funds were obtained for securing the whole time of a resident professor, and he was succeeded by Henry A. Miers.

Story-Maskelyne entered the House of Commons in 1880, when he was elected as Liberal MP for Cricklade. He opposed Irish home rule and from 1886 until his defeat in July 1892 he sat as a Liberal Unionist. He was not prominent in debates, and was mainly interested in local questions such as protecting the upper reaches of the Thames, which resulted in safeguards for the wildlife and improved towpaths. He was a member of the Wiltshire county council from its foundation in 1889 until 1904, when he was over eighty years of age, and was for many years chairman of the agricultural committee. He was an active member of the Bath and West of England Agricultural Society, and it was at his suggestion that the first itinerant dairy school was established. He was a good scholar and was one of the few scientific men who read Homer until late in life. He formed a valuable private collection of antique engraved gems, and he privately printed (1870) a catalogue of the intaglios and cameos at Blenheim Palace known as the Marlborough gems. He retained an enthusiasm for scientific advances, exclaiming, when his life was threatened by illness in 1904, 'I must live, I want to know more about radium' (*PRS*, liv). Story-Maskelyne died at Basset Down House on 20 May 1911, after a prolonged illness, and was buried at Purton, Wiltshire. He was survived by his wife and three daughters, of whom the second, Mary Lucy, married Hugh Oakeley Arnold-Forster, sometime secretary of state for war, and the third, Thereza Charlotte *Rucker, became wife of Sir Arthur Rucker FRS, in 1892.

HENRY ALEXANDER MILLAR and
ARTHUR WILLIAM RUCKER, rev. M. C. CURTHOYS

Sources Burke, *Gen. GB* · *The Times* (21 May 1911) · A. W. R. and H. A. M., *PRS*, 86A (1911–12), xlvii-lv · *Mineralogical Magazine*, 16 (1911–13), 149–56 · V. Morton, *Oxford rebels: the life and friends of Nevil Story Maskelyne, 1823–1911* (1987)
Archives NHM, notebooks and papers | NHM, corresp. relating to NHM; papers relating to Royal Society's expedition to Rodriguez Island
Likenesses photographs, *c.*1850–1858, repro. in Morton, *Oxford rebels*, pp. 46, 140 · J. Collier, oils, 1895, Basset Down House, Swindon · Elliott & Fry, photograph, 1898, repro. in *Mineralogical Magazine*, pl. 8
Wealth at death £137,837 17s.: resworn probate, 21 July 1911, *CGPLA Eng. & Wales*

Maskelyne, Nevil (1732–1811), astronomer and mathematician, was born on 5 October 1732 in Kensington Gore, London, the third of the four children of Edmund Maskelyne (1698–1744), one of the clerks of the duke of Newcastle, secretary of state, and his wife, Elizabeth (*d.* 1748), the only child of John Booth of Chester, a distant cousin. In his own words, written about 1800, Nevil was 'the last male heir of an antient family long settled at Purton in the County of Wilts, which from the name probably came from Normandy, where there is or was 50 years ago a family of that name Masqueline' (autobiographical notes, CUL, RGO MS.4/320:8). All Nevil's siblings were born in Kensington: William in 1725, Edmund in 1728, and Margaret in 1735. The following year the family moved to Tothill Street, Westminster, saving a walk of more than 2 miles each way to Edmund senior's office in Lincoln's Inn Fields, and to Westminster School, where the two eldest boys were king's scholars. In January 1741 Nevil followed his brothers to Westminster, becoming a town boy.

In March 1744 their father died, leaving a somewhat meagre inheritance in trust for the three younger children. Then, in the winter of 1748–9, their mother died also. William and Edmund were already provided for. Nevil became a boarder in Vincent Bourne's house in Westminster, and Margaret went to live with her aunts in Wiltshire until 1752, when she sailed to India to join her brother Edmund, whose friend and colleague Robert Clive she married in Madras in 1753.

Preparations for astronomy It was while Nevil was still at Westminster School that he decided that astronomy was the career for him. For this, the study of mathematics was essential, and he decided he must follow his eldest brother to the University of Cambridge. After leaving Westminster in July 1749 he entered St Catharine's College as a sizar in November, and migrated in July 1750 to Pembroke College, where he matriculated. In 1752 he

Nevil Maskelyne (1732–1811), by Louis van der Puyl, 1785

moved again, to Trinity, the college of his brother William, where he took the mathematical tripos for the BA degree in 1754 and graduated as seventh wrangler.

Maskelyne wanted to be an astronomer—and an important one. The first hurdle was the mathematical tripos. Then, fellowship of Trinity would be an enormous advantage, not only for its academic distinction but also because it would pay a small stipend and give free board and lodging in college until marriage. While waiting for the appropriate moment to apply, he decided to anticipate one of the fellowship requirements, the taking of holy orders. At Michaelmas 1755 he was ordained to the curacy of Chipping Barnet in Hertfordshire, where he came under the rector of East Barnet. In 1756 he was elected a fellow of Trinity, and, after proceeding to the MA degree, in July 1757 was elected to his major fellowship.

It was about this time that Maskelyne was introduced to the astronomer royal, James Bradley, who, in January 1758, was one of those signing a certificate recommending Maskelyne, 'well versed in Mathematical Learning and Natural Philosophy', for fellowship of the Royal Society, to which he was duly elected on 27 April 1758, at the age of twenty-five.

Expedition to St Helena Of Maskelyne's activities in Chipping Barnet, pastoral or scientific, little is known, but he began to see his way ahead in an astronomical career on 14 July 1760, when he was appointed by the Royal Society to go to St Helena to observe the transit of Venus, a phenomenon which was to occur on 6 June 1761. This was part of an international programme of observers all over the world (in the event somewhat frustrated by the Seven Years' War) to measure the sun's parallax and thereby derive the mean distance between the earth and sun, a fundamental quantity known today as the astronomical unit.

With Robert Waddington as second observer, Maskelyne sailed for St Helena in the East Indiaman *Prince Henry* on 18 January 1761. While on passage he became involved for the first time in practical navigation at sea, in the development of which he was later to play such an important role. He had with him a 20 inch Hadley quadrant by Bird and, thanks to Bradley, a copy of Mayer's solar and lunar tables, so was able to try out the lunar-distance method of measuring longitude, effectively continuing the 1757–9 trials of Captain John Campbell.

Maskelyne's first task on arrival at St Helena on 6 April 1761 was to find a site and to set up the instruments for observing the transit of Venus on 6 June. Sadly, clouds covered the sun at the critical moment. Waddington left the island immediately, but Maskelyne remained to continue scientific observations, principally to measure the annual parallax of the star Sirius, which passes nearly overhead there. However, after many months of inconsistent results he decided there was a defect in his zenith sector, so he sailed for home in the East Indiaman *Warwick* in February 1762, taking further lunar-distance observations for longitude while on passage. He reached Plymouth on 15 May.

Maskelyne resumed his pastoral duties at Chipping Barnet. At the same time he assiduously attended Royal Society meetings and wrote *The British Mariner's Guide*, published in April 1763, containing an English edition of Mayer's tables and giving simple instructions for finding longitude at sea by lunar distance, with worked examples from his observations in the *Warwick*.

Finding longitude Meanwhile, the board of longitude was giving much attention to the rival method of finding longitude—by chronometer. The longitude watch (H4) of John Harrison had been tried out on a voyage to Jamaica in 1761–2, but the results did not satisfy the board, which decided that, if Harrison was to qualify for the full reward offered by the Longitude Act of 1714, there must be another sea trial to the West Indies. In August 1763 Maskelyne agreed to sail on the board's behalf (with Charles Green, assistant at the Royal Greenwich Observatory) to establish the longitude of Barbados by observations of the eclipses of Jupiter's satellites, so that the accuracy of H4 could be assessed. Maskelyne and Green left from St Helens Roads off the Isle of Wight in HMS *Princess Louisa* on 23 September, and on 7 November reached Bridgetown, Barbados, where they set up an observatory and began observations. John Harrison's son William arrived with H4 on 13 May 1764, when he objected to Maskelyne being involved because, he said, the latter was a candidate for a reward on behalf of the lunar-distance method. Maskelyne was greatly upset by this slur on his character. Why this objection was not raised before Harrison left England is not clear, but a compromise was reached so that Maskelyne and Green made observations on alternate days. Harrison, Green, and H4 sailed for home on 4 June; Maskelyne

remained until 30 August to complete his longitude observations and continue some lunar observations started in St Helena.

Maskelyne reached London on 12 October 1764 to be greeted with the news that Bradley's successor as astronomer royal, Nathaniel Bliss, had died on 2 September and that he, Maskelyne, was a strong candidate for the vacant post. The royal warrant appointing him director of the Greenwich observatory was dated 8 February 1765. The very next day he was at the Admiralty in London attending his first meeting as an *ex officio* member of the board of longitude. At what was probably the most important meeting of that body in the 114 years of its existence, the board recommended awards to Harrison for his watch—only half the major award—and to Mayer and Euler for the lunar tables. They also approved a proposal by Maskelyne that the board should publish annually a nautical almanac containing tables for facilitating the lunar-distance method of finding longitude at sea, to be edited by Maskelyne himself. With minor amendments, these proposals were ratified by parliament in May.

Astronomer royal Maskelyne took up residence at the Greenwich observatory on 16 March 1765. According to the king's instructions:

> forthwith to apply yourself with the most exact Care and Diligence to the rectifying the Tables of the Motions of the Heavens, and the Places of the fixed Stars, in order to find out the so much desired Longitude at Sea, for perfecting the Art of Navigation   (royal warrant, 8 Feb 1765)

Maskelyne's primary task was astronomical observation. Top priority was given to the moon: the astronomer royal and his assistant took observations on every possible occasion it crossed the meridian, the former noting the time of crossing with the transit instrument, the latter measuring the zenith distance with the mural quadrant. The sun and planets were observed likewise, though at lower priority. As for star positions, Maskelyne decided that enough such data existed on some 3000 stars for the time being, so, except in special circumstances, limited his observations to thirty-six stars, lying near the celestial equator and bright enough to be visible through a telescope in daylight, needed to ascertain the going of the clocks. With one assistant only, Maskelyne followed this policy for more than forty-five years, and some 90,000 observations were made. Through the Royal Society, the results were published every ten years or so, something his predecessors had failed to do.

Many occasional observations had to be taken at Greenwich in addition to the routine meridian observations—the timing of predictable phenomena used for finding longitude, such as the eclipses of Jupiter's satellites; the occultation of stars and planets by the moon; solar and lunar eclipses; and measuring the places of newly discovered bodies, such as Uranus in 1781, Ceres and two other minor planets in 1801–4, and fairly frequent comets. Then there was the transit of Venus of 1769, when Maskelyne was not clouded out as he had been in St Helena in 1761.

The annual *Nautical Almanac and Astronomical Ephemeris*

and its companion *Tables Requisite* were undoubtedly Maskelyne's greatest contribution to the improvement of navigation and astronomy and to science as a whole. It was almost entirely through his efforts and persistence that they came to be published in the first place—for the year 1767—and he was the first editor. As such he superintended the complex calculations, the precision of which was improved year by year as a result of work by mathematicians and astronomers throughout Europe with whom, despite the bellicose state of that period, Maskelyne kept in touch. He was entirely responsible for the first forty-nine issues of the almanac, from 1767 to that for the year 1815, published in 1811, the year of his death; and for three editions of the *Tables Requisite*, published in 1766, 1781, and 1801. He also had to oversee the production of some eighteen other works published by the board of longitude.

Other work for the board of longitude kept Maskelyne extremely busy, particularly arranging for and assessing the performance of timekeepers submitted for trial at Greenwich, which led to acrimonious disputes with Harrison (in 1765–7), Thomas Mudge (in 1774–93), and John Arnold and Thomas Earnshaw (in 1798–1807). He was also responsible for the planning of the scientific sides of voyages of exploration to which the Royal Society or board of longitude appointed observers—for the 1769 transit of Venus, for the first fleet to New South Wales, and the voyages of Cook, Phipps, Vancouver, and Flinders.

Density of the earth Maskelyne's other responsibility was to the Royal Society, to whose council he was elected in December 1766, and on which he remained, except for two short breaks, until his death. In the summer of 1774, having obtained the king's leave of absence, he went on the Royal Society's behalf to conduct an experiment which he had himself proposed, to determine the earth's density—to 'weigh the world'—by measuring the deviation of a plumb line produced by the gravitational attraction of the mountain Schiehallion in Perthshire, and by observing stars near the zenith on both the north and south sides of the mountain. From the results he postulated that the density of the whole earth was 4.5 times that of water; the current accepted value is 5.52. For this work he was given the society's highest award, the Copley medal, in November 1774. In the society's dissensions in 1784 he strongly supported Dr Charles Hutton (who had carried out the analysis of the Schiehallion results) against the president, Sir Joseph Banks.

In 1768 Maskelyne took the degree of bachelor of divinity at Cambridge, followed in 1777 with that of doctor of divinity. In 1775 he was presented by his nephew Lord Clive with the living of Shrawardine in Shropshire, and in 1782 by Trinity College to the rectory of North Runcton, Norfolk. On 21 August 1784, in St Andrew's, Holborn, he married Sophia Rose (1752–1821), the second daughter and coheir of John Pate Rose of Cotterstock, Northampton, and Jamaica; she was twenty years his junior. Their only child, Margaret, was born in Greenwich on 27 June 1785. Nevil's eldest brother, William, had died in 1772, leaving him Pond's Farm, Purton Stoke, Wiltshire, which became

his 'country cottage' after he married, and where the family used to go for five weeks or so each autumn.

Maskelyne was elected fellow of the American Academy of Arts and Sciences at Cambridge, Massachusetts, in 1788, and received honours from Hanover, Russia, and Poland, but the honour he appreciated most was his election in 1802 as one of only eight foreign members of the Institut de France, established in 1795.

Final years Maskelyne's final years were as busy as ever, and he had a large amount of paperwork to deal with, particularly on *Nautical Almanac* business and during the Earnshaw affair of 1806. He took what proved to be his last recorded astronomical observation on 1 September 1810. The same year he attended all three meetings of the board of longitude, and on 6 December took the chair—his 150th attendance (he missed only one, when on Schiehallion); he was also at the Royal Society council meeting on 13 December. Then, in mid-January, he fell ill, and he died at the Greenwich observatory on 9 February 1811 in his seventy-ninth year, having completed forty-six years as astronomer royal. He was buried on 20 February at the church of St Mary, Purton, Wiltshire. He was survived by his widow, Sophia, and his daughter, Margaret, who in 1819 married Anthony Mervyn Story (who subsequently took the additional name of Maskelyne); their eldest son, Nevil Story Maskelyne, became a distinguished mineralogist.

The evidence from the large body of correspondence that has survived proves that, pompous and a bit of a bore as he might have seemed to some, Maskelyne was almost universally liked and admired by his contemporaries—except perhaps by some chronometer makers and their families. The reputation that survives in some popular twentieth-century books of Maskelyne as the evil genius who tried to deprive the poor illiterate carpenter of his just rewards—out of personal spite and because of his own involvement in the rival lunar-distance method of finding longitude—was certainly not one that was held generally in his own day, nor is it in any way justified by modern research: he was a member of the board of longitude, appointed by parliament to advise on the award of large sums of public money; there is no evidence whatsoever that he at any time abused his position as a public servant, still less that he lined his own pocket.

Although he promoted the cause of astronomical science through his routine work at Greenwich—and, most important, made it available to mathematicians and astronomers the world over by ensuring the prompt publication of results—Maskelyne never lost sight of the principal object of the observatory's existence, the improvement of navigation. But undoubtedly his greatest achievement was to set in motion the annual publication of Britain's *Nautical Almanac*, the model for similar ephemerides now published worldwide, and the reason why the international system of time and longitude measurement are today based upon the Greenwich meridian.

DEREK HOWSE

Sources D. Howse, *Nevil Maskelyne: the seaman's astronomer* (1989) · parish register, St Andrew's, Holborn [marriages]

Archives CUL, Board of Longitude MSS, RGO MS 14 · CUL, corresp. and papers · NMM, account books (microfilm) · priv. coll., letters and three account books · RS, MS vols. 371, 372 (class Gh) · RS, corresp.; observations · St John Cam., papers · Wilts. & Swindon RO, corresp. and papers, 1390 | Armagh Observatory, corresp. with J. A. Hamilton · MHS Oxf., corresp. with Lewis Evans · NL Wales, letters to John Walsh · NRA, corresp. with Sir Joseph Banks · RAS, corresp. with Sir William Herschel; letters to Nathaniel Pigott · W. Yorks. AS, Leeds, Yorkshire Archaeological Society, remarks by him on memoranda of John Edwards relating to telescopes
Likenesses attrib. J. Russell, black and red chalk, c.1776, repro. in Howse, *Nevil Maskelyne*; priv. coll. · J. Downman, oils, 1779, NMM · L. F. G. van der Puyl, oils, 1785, RS [*see illus.*] · M. Byrne, miniature, 1801, priv. coll. · Threed junior, miniature, 1801, priv. coll. · J. Russell, pastel, 1804, priv. coll. · stipple, pubd 1804, BM · J. F. Skill, J. Gilbert, W. and E. Walker, group portrait, pencil and wash (*Men of science living in 1807–8*), NPG · portraits, repro. in Howse, *Nevil Maskelyne*

Mason, (Frances) Agnes (1849–1941), founder of the Community of the Holy Family, was born at the parsonage, Laugharne township, Carmarthenshire, on 10 August 1849, the second daughter in the family of three daughters and four sons of George William Mason (1819–1891), justice of the peace and deputy lieutenant, of Morton Hall, Nottinghamshire, and his wife, Marianne Atherton, daughter of Joseph George Mitford of Laugharne. Her family was active in Church of England causes. Her eldest brother, William Henry Mason (1846–1936), was a member of the Woodard Corporation; another brother, Arthur James *Mason, was a divinity professor at Cambridge; her elder sister, (Marianne) Harriet *Mason, had a career in social work. Between 1876 and 1883 Agnes gained experience of social and educational work while assisting her brother (George) Edward Mason (1847–1928) in his parish at Whitwell, Derbyshire, where he was rector. In 1883 she entered Newnham College, Cambridge, taking the moral sciences tripos with second-class honours in 1886. For two years (1886–8) she was lecturer in mental and moral science at Bedford College, London, and then taught privately in London until 1892. She was secretary to the Guild of the Epiphany, founded by Canon Francis Holland for religious teaching, from 1887 until 1895 when she resigned in order to found the Anglican Community of the Holy Family.

Agnes Mason was first called to found the community while visiting Florence. It was to be dedicated to the religious teaching of women of all ages, worldwide, and to be expressly for scholars and artists. In this calling she was helped by Frederick Temple, archbishop of Canterbury, Charles Gore, bishop of Oxford, William Collins, bishop of Gibraltar, Walter Frere, bishop of Truro, George Congreve of the Society of St John the Evangelist, Charles Lindley Wood, second Viscount Halifax, president of the English Church Union, and the Roman Catholic theologian Baron von Hügel. With the help of von Hügel she was able to study the methods of the Sisters of the Assumption in Paris and a congregation of teaching Dominicanesses at Nancy. The four novices of the Community of the Holy Family were professed on 19 October 1898, Temple being celebrant, Gore as gospeller, and Arthur Mason, her

brother, as epistoler. Following her immediate election by the sisters, Agnes Mason was installed by the archbishop as their mother superior.

Mother Agnes Mason was drawn to biblical studies in Greek and Hebrew, and also the mystics, such as St Teresa of Avila, whose *Foundations* she translated from the Spanish in 1909, St John of the Cross, Gertrude More, and Julian of Norwich. She published essays in *Theology* (1922–36), various devotional works, including *The Way of Beauty* (1920), and school books for the Society for Promoting Christian Knowledge. Herself a fine watercolourist, Mother Agnes collected the works of Myra Luxmoore, and purchased sepia photographs of Italian art in Florence for use in teaching. Later she arranged for artist sisters to teach in the community's school in India, Naini Tal, and on their journey spend time in Florence to study its religious art.

The community's rule drawn up by Mother Agnes is probably the best among the Anglican communities. Learned, yet joyous, it quotes Shakespeare, 'Who chooses me must give and hazard all he hath'. The rule states that 'Every Sister ought to be so systematically studying at least one subject that she makes real progress from month to month', and elsewhere affirms that 'A sin against beauty is a sin against God'. In 1911 she gained the Lambeth diploma in theology by thesis, the sisters of her community shaping, and tutoring in, that programme from its beginning. Though the community never became large, the excellent scholarship of its sisters ensured that it prospered. There were schools at London and then, from 1913, at St Leonards, and at All Saints' College, Naini Tal, India (1915–45), and houses of study at Leeds (1906–11), and then Cambridge (1911–39). The house of prayer at St Pega's Hermitage, Peakirk, Northamptonshire, was given to the community by Miss Bertha James in 1937. In 1913 the community acquired its mother house, Holmhurst St Mary, St Leonards, Sussex, where Agnes Mason, who was mother superior until 1933, died on 19 December 1941. She was buried in the community's graveyard under a cross of Sussex oak. JULIA BOLTON HOLLOWAY

Sources Community of the Holy Family, *In memoriam, Mother Agnes, C.H.F.* (1941) · J. B. Holloway, *Mother Agnes Mason* (1995) · M. Dunn, *The Community of the Holy Family, 1898–1958: the first 60 years* (1958) · V. Markham, *Newnham College Roll Letter* (1942), 32–3 · Burke, *Gen. GB* (1914) [Mason of Morton Hall] · b. cert.
Likenesses photographs
Wealth at death £56 18s. 10d.: administration, 22 June 1942, *CGPLA Eng. & Wales*

Mason, Alfred Edward Woodley (1865–1948), novelist, was born on 7 May 1865 at Enfield Villa, Upper Grove Lane, Camberwell, London, the youngest son of William Woodley Mason, chartered accountant, and his wife, Elizabeth Hobill, daughter of Joseph Gaines, a plumber and glazier of Leicestershire. He was first educated at a dame-school and then tutored at Hove with several other boys, but his parents settled in Dulwich, London, in 1878, and at the age of thirteen Mason entered Dulwich College. In 1884 he proceeded to Trinity College, Oxford, where he won an exhibition in classics in 1887, being placed in the second class of the honours list in classical moderations (1886) and in the third class in *literae humaniores* (1888). He was a notable speaker in the Oxford Union, but after playing Heracles in the Oxford University Dramatic Society's *Alcestis* in May 1887 he turned his attention to acting, and for some years toured the provinces, usually with Edward Compton or Isabel Bateman. In 1894, although appearing in the first production of Shaw's *Arms and the Man*, he failed to find further West End work and, encouraged by Oscar Wilde and Arthur Quiller-Couch, he produced his first novel, *A Romance of Wastdale* (1895). In the following year *The Courtship of Morrice Buckler* placed him in the front rank of the 'cloak and dagger' story-tellers, although *Miranda of the Balcony* (1899) won him fame as a contemporary novelist. *Parson Kelly* (1900), written in collaboration with Andrew Lang, and *Clementina* (1901) both showed an advance in historical fiction, but the success of *The Four Feathers* (1902) turned Mason to the novel of contemporary adventure for the next thirty years. This, his most famous book, combining excitement with careful character analysis, represents a new development in his and indeed most other popular fiction, which had hitherto so often been content with simple characterization, the whole interest being focused on the action. Mason followed up his success by applying the same method to the detective story with the first of the Inspector Hanaud series, *At the Villa Rose* (1910).

Not content with writing adventurously, Mason sought adventure exploring in Morocco, sailing, and alpine climbing. Of these experiences he made good use in fiction, as he also did of his five years (1906–10) as Liberal member of parliament for Coventry. He also wrote about his adventures in the First World War, in which he took up a commission in the Manchester regiment and then became a major in the Royal Marine light infantry. He finished his military service as a naval intelligence officer in Spain, Morocco, and Mexico.

Returning to literature, Mason achieved increased success with the next three Hanaud stories, *The House of the Arrow* (1924), *The Prisoner in the Opal* (1928), and *They wouldn't be Chessmen* (1935), his thriller *No other Tiger* (1927), and the last historical novels, which show deeper insight and more subtle understanding of character in action. Of these, *Fire over England* (1936) and *Königsmark* (1938) represent both popular and artistic success, but with *Musk and Amber* (1942) he touched the fringes of greater literature: as a novelist he will be remembered for this book, as a story-teller for *The Four Feathers*, and for his detective series. Mason was less successful as a dramatist, his best play being *The Witness for the Defence* (St James's Theatre, 1911), but he wrote a notable volume of stage history, *Sir George Alexander and the St. James's Theatre* (1935).

Mason was tall, broad, with pronounced features, wore an eye-glass, was a member of many famous clubs, a guest much sought in society and at country houses, a brilliant raconteur, a generous listener whose laugh, said E. V. Lucas, was 'famous in both hemispheres', a good friend, and a man who enjoyed every moment to the full. His books were best-sellers for fifty years, and the films made from them, notably *The Drum* (1938), for which he wrote his own scenario, and *The Four Feathers* (1939), were among the most popular in their time. He was elected a fellow of Trinity College in 1943. He never married, refused a knighthood since 'such honours mean nothing to a childless man', and died in his sleep at his home, 51 South Street, Mayfair, London, on 22 November 1948.

R. L. GREEN, *rev.* REBECCA MILLS

Sources R. L. Green, *A. E. W. Mason* (1952) · WWW · J. Foster, *Oxford men, 1880–1892: with a record of their schools, honours, and degrees* (1893), 406 · Foster, *Alum. Oxon.* · *The Times* (23 Nov 1948) · WWBMP, 2.244 · *CGPLA Eng. & Wales* (1949)

Archives NRA, corresp. and literary papers · Ransom HRC, papers | BL, letters to Lady Aberconway, Add. MSS 52554–52555 · BL, corresp. with Macmillans, Add. MS 54971 · BL, corresp. with Society of Authors, Add. MS 56745 · LPL, corresp. with Archbishop Benson

Likenesses O. Birley, oils, 1946, Trinity College, Oxford · Max [M. Beerbohm], caricature, Hentschel-colourtype, NPG; repro. in *VF* (10 June 1908) · K. Pollak, photographs, NPG · photograph, repro. in *The Times*

Wealth at death £70,646 9s. 7d.: probate, 23 Feb 1949, *CGPLA Eng. & Wales*

Mason, Arthur James (1851–1928), Church of England clergyman and theologian, was born on 4 May 1851 at Laugharne, Carmarthenshire, the third son and fifth child of George William Mason (1819–1891) of Morton Hall, Retford, Nottinghamshire, a former high sheriff of Nottinghamshire, and his wife, Marianne Atherton, daughter of Captain Joseph George Mitford of the East India Company. His sisters were (Frances) Agnes *Mason and (Marianne) Harriet *Mason. Educated at Repton School, he went to Trinity College, Cambridge (matriculated 1868, scholar 1869), where he graduated as eighth classic in the 1872 tripos (MA 1875, BD 1887), and was a fellow from 1873 to 1884. Following a short time as an assistant master at Wellington College, where he formed a lifelong, devoted, almost romantic friendship with the headmaster, Edward White Benson, who was to greatly influence his future career, he returned to Cambridge in 1874 as assistant tutor of Trinity. In 1874 he was ordained deacon and in 1875 priest, in which year Trinity appointed him perpetual curate of St Michael's Church, Cambridge. In 1877 Benson, then bishop of Truro, appointed him diocesan missioner and honorary canon of Truro Cathedral, posts he held until 1884. His post as missioner was tailored to suit his gifts and was a pioneering development in the church. Benson in particular urged him to counter what he regarded as the bad effects of popular revivalism upon the people of his diocese. James Adderley commented in 1916 that Mason was 'one of the most picturesque figures in the English Church …. He would have liked to be a preaching friar; but the Church authorities persuaded him out of it—and perhaps they were right' (Voll, 78). In 1884 Benson, then archbishop of Canterbury, appointed Mason vicar of All Hallows Barking by the Tower, a benefice with few parishioners and a large endowment, where he was able to establish a college of mission preachers for work among the educated classes of London, and where Mason established himself as a popular lecturer and preacher. In 1893 he was appointed an honorary canon of Canterbury Cathedral and examining chaplain to the archbishop. In 1895 he was elected Lady Margaret professor of divinity at Cambridge, with a professorial fellowship at Jesus College, while he was also made a residentiary canon at Canterbury. In 1903 he resigned his professorship to become master of Pembroke College (1903–12). During 1908–10 he acted as vice-chancellor of the university. In 1912 he resigned as master of Pembroke in order to concentrate on his Canterbury duties. Mason remained celibate for many years to devote himself to mission work, but in 1899 he married Mary Margaret, daughter of the Revd George John Blore, headmaster of King's School and honorary canon of Canterbury. They had two sons and two daughters and she survived her husband.

Mason was a traditionalist, hostile to 'modernity', and favoured ancient custom and picturesque ceremonial. As a moderate high-churchman Mason believed that the reformed Church of England and the Book of Common Prayer had retained the essentials of Catholic faith and order, and concluded *Thomas Cranmer* (1898) with the affirmation that Cranmer 'was able to preserve by means of the Prayerbook, the Ordinal, and the Articles, a truly catholic footing for the Church of England' (*Cranmer*, 202). In his most substantial and well-known theological work, *The Relation of Confirmation to Baptism* (1893), he advanced F. W. Puller's recent thesis (later championed by L. S. Thornton and G. Dix) that although real gifts of the Holy Spirit are conveyed in baptism, the full gift of his indwelling presence is reserved to confirmation. Mason's solution of the pastoral problem of the division of the two acts of Christian initiation was to reunite them in one rite to be administered at the age of discretion. While the book's central thesis has been frequently criticized and much of it has dated, it remains valuable as a comprehensive collection of patristic texts on confirmation. In an earlier work intended as a manual of doctrine for the educated laity, *The Faith of the Gospel* (1888), Mason presented an early version of the kenotic theory of the incarnation (p. 170), developed a few years later by Charles Gore. Many of his later writings were defences of the high-church position. In *John Wesley: a Lecture* (1908) he blamed Wesley, 'who lacked the virtue of patience' (*Wesley*, 46), for the Methodist schism; and contrasted him unfavourably with Bishop Butler, 'the greatest thinker' and holiest man of the age (ibid., 40). In 1894 Mason joined with Bishop Mandell Creighton and other like-minded colleagues to form the Church Historical Society. Its object was to promote the study of the 'history and position of the Church of England, to spread information, and to repel attacks' (*Life and Letters*, 95). The majority of Mason's publications reflect a similar apologetic purpose—to promote a moderate high-church view of Anglicanism.

Mason published lectures entitled *Principles of Ecclesiastical Unity* (1896) and *Purgatory, the State of the Faithful Departed, Invocation of the Saints* (1901). *The Church of England and Episcopacy* (1914) was a defence of episcopacy written in response to a crisis in 1913, when Bishop Frank Weston petitioned Archbishop Davidson to discipline a fellow bishop in east Africa for communicating non-Anglican missionaries. He summed up his criticisms of popular revivalism and described an authentically Anglican approach to parochial mission in his pastoral handbook *The Ministry of Conversion* (1902), originally delivered as pastoral theology lectures at Cambridge in 1892. Mason also published two memoirs of his episcopal friends G. H. Wilkinson (1909) and W. E. Collins (1912). His final publications, *What became of the Bones of St Thomas?* (1920) and *A Guide to the Ancient Glass in Canterbury Cathedral* (1925), reflected his love of the cathedral. The dean and chapter's 'fabric' documents acknowledge the encouragement given to 'antiquarian enquiry' by Mason and a fellow canon (fabric collection, 5), and include Mason's correspondence about the possible discovery of Becket's bones, the restoration of the high altar to its original position, and the placing of the archbishop's throne in the vacated space. Mason wrote a number of hymns, some of which were published in *Hymns Ancient and Modern*, and a collection of privately published *Canterbury Sonnets* (1919). After a short illness he died at his home, 13 The Precincts, Canterbury, on 24 April 1928. PETER DAVIE

Sources DNB · *Clergy List* (1899) · A. C. Benson, *The life of Edward White Benson*, 2 vols. (1899) · D. Voll, *Catholic Evangelicalism* (1963) · *The Times* (25 April 1928) · *Kentish Gazette and Canterbury Press* (28 April 1928) · A. J. Mason, *The faith of the gospel* (1888) · A. J. Mason, *The relation of confirmation to baptism as taught by the western fathers: a study in the history of doctrine* (1893) · A. J. Mason, *Thomas Cranmer* (1898) · A. J. Mason, *John Wesley: a lecture* (1908) · A. J. Mason, *The ministry of conversion* (1902) · A. J. Mason, *The Church of England and episcopacy* (1914) · L. von Glehn Creighton, *Life and letters of Mandell Creighton*, 8th edn, 2 (1913) · J. D. C. Fisher, *Confirmation then and now* (1978) · B. M. G. Reardon, *Religious thought in the Victorian age: a survey from Coleridge to Gore*, 2nd edn (1995) · Venn, *Alum. Cant.* · *CGPLA Eng. & Wales* (1928) · dean and chapter of Canterbury, fabric collection, Canterbury Cathedral Library

Archives Canterbury Cathedral, dean and chapter · LPL, diaries mainly as Truro diocesan missioner · LPL, corresp. and papers relating to reunion with Moravian church, MS 2785 · NRA, priv. coll., corresp. and diaries | King's AC Cam., letters to Oscar Browning, ref. OB · LPL, the Revd Canon Lancelot Mason

Likenesses G. Henry, oils, c.1914, Pembroke Cam. · A. Hayward, oils, Pembroke Cam.

Wealth at death £17,778 16s. 6d.: probate, 16 June 1928, *CGPLA Eng. & Wales*

Mason, Charles (1616/17–1677/8), Church of England clergyman, was born at Bury St Edmunds, Suffolk, the son of Pomfit Mason. He was reputedly born at Christmas time 1616; if so there was an unusually long gap between his birth and his baptism in St Mary's Church, Bury, on 9 September 1617. He was educated at Eton College from about 1628. On 10 March 1632 he was admitted a scholar of King's College, Cambridge, graduating BA in early 1636 and proceeding MA in 1639. Chosen as a fellow on 10 March 1635 he was a lecturer in the college from Christmas 1636 to Michaelmas 1639 and proceeded BD in 1642. On 1 November of that year he was created DD of Oxford University. Mason was one of the five fellows of King's College ejected by the parliament in 1644, but was chosen by the college as rector of Stour Provost in Dorset in 1646. His institution was ordered by the Lords on 1 March 1647, and he seems to have retained the living until his death.

On the Restoration Mason was created DD of Cambridge University (1660). On 15 June 1661 he was presented by the king to the rectory of St Mary Woolchurch, London, but the church was destroyed in the great fire of 1666 and the parish annexed to that of St Mary Woolnoth. In 1662—with the support of Gilbert Sheldon, bishop of London—Mason petitioned the king for the rectory of Chipping Barnet in Hertfordshire; on 3 September a warrant for his grant was drawn up, but he does not appear to have been instituted. Although, on 31 December 1663, Mason was collated to the prebend of Portpool in St Paul's Cathedral, he wrote in January 1665 to William Sancroft, then dean of St Paul's, complaining of poverty and ill health, and begging for preferment. On 14 May 1669 he was presented to the rectory of St Peter-le-Poer, Broad Street; there, on 27 August 1675, James Fleetwood (*d.* 1683) was consecrated bishop of Worcester, and Mason arranged the use of a neighbouring hall for the consecration feast. On 15 July 1671 he was installed in the prebend of Beaminster Prima, in Salisbury Cathedral, and in 1675 he was appointed president of Sion College. Mason published several sermons, including *Miles Christianus: a sermon preached to the artillery company, October 16 1673 at St Michael's in Cornhill*, in which a preface to Sir John Robinson, lieutenant of the Tower of London, explains that it appeared in print partly because 'I am told that my trumpet was not shrill enough to be heard by those at a distance'. Mason held his two prebends and the rectory until his death, which occurred between 22 December 1677, when he made his will, and the grant of probate on 25 January 1678. He left all his property to his wife, Barbara, his two daughters having earlier married.   STEPHEN WRIGHT

Sources W. Sterry, ed., *The Eton College register, 1441–1698* (1943) • Venn, *Alum. Cant.* • *CSP dom.*, 1660–62 • will, PRO, PROB 11/356, sig. 6 • *Fasti Angl.*, 1541–1857, [St Paul's, London] • *Fasti Angl.*, 1541–1857, [Salisbury] • G. Hennessy, *Novum repertorium ecclesiasticum parochiale Londinense, or, London diocesan clergy succession from the earliest time to the year 1898* (1898)

Mason, Charles (1728–1786), astronomer and mathematician, was born early in 1728 at Wherr in the parish of Bisley, near Stroud, Gloucestershire, the third child of Charles Mason, a baker, and his first wife, Ann, *née* Damsel, and was baptized in Sapperton church on 1 May 1728. Details of his early life and education are lacking, but it seems likely that between 1730 and 1750 he had the help of Robert Stratford, a schoolmaster and mathematician of Sapperton, to give him the necessary mathematical skills to be appointed—in 1756 at the age of twenty-eight—to the Royal Greenwich Observatory as assistant to the astronomer royal, James Bradley, who had been born in Gloucestershire and whose wife, Susannah Peach, came from Chalford, near Sapperton. At a meagre £26 a year Mason was able to acquire the skills of observational astronomy; his recorded observations at Greenwich span the period between October 1756 and November 1760. But his mathematical ability was also much appreciated by Bradley, particularly in helping to assess the accuracy of Tobias Mayer's solar and lunar tables submitted to the board of longitude in 1757—with which Mason was to be

much concerned later in his career. His first wife, Rebekah, died at Greenwich on 13 February 1759, leaving two sons, William and Isaac.

In 1760, on Bradley's recommendation, the Royal Society chose Mason to go to Sumatra to observe the 1761 transit of Venus, assisted by Jeremiah Dixon. An encounter with a French frigate delayed their final sailing, and as they could not reach Sumatra in time they landed at the Cape of Good Hope, from where they successfully observed the transit on 6 June 1761. On the passage home they landed at St Helena and, after discussion with Nevil Maskelyne (whose observation of the transit had been thwarted by clouds), Dixon returned temporarily to the Cape with Maskelyne's clock to carry out gravity experiments, while Mason assisted Maskelyne with astronomical and tidal observations at St Helena. Mason and Dixon eventually reached England early in 1762.

In August 1763 Mason and Dixon signed an agreement with Thomas Penn and Frederick Calvert, Lord Baltimore, hereditary proprietors of the provinces of Pennsylvania and Maryland, to help local surveyors define the disputed boundary between the two provinces. After arriving in Philadelphia with their instruments in November, they began operations the following month at the north-east corner of Maryland. Proceeding along the parallel of 39° 43′ 17″.6 N, they surveyed and marked the boundary for 244 miles; hostile Indians prevented the survey of the last 36 miles. When late in 1766 work for the proprietors was completed on what was to become the famous Mason–Dixon line—popularly regarded as the boundary between the northern and southern states—they began, on the Royal Society's behalf, to measure a degree of latitude on the Delmarva peninsula in Maryland and to make gravity measurements with the clock sent out by the society, the same that Maskelyne had had in St Helena and Dixon had taken to the Cape in 1761. Having completed their task on 21 June 1768, they sailed for England on 11 September. Before leaving, both were admitted as corresponding members of the American Society for Promoting Useful Knowledge, in Philadelphia.

In December 1768 Mason was appointed to be one of the Royal Society's observers of the second transit of Venus, which he successfully observed on 3 June 1769 at Cavan, near Strabane, in northern Ireland; in July 1773 he was appointed by the Royal Society to make a tour of Scotland to find a mountain suitable for experiments to 'weigh the earth' by measuring the deflection of a plumb line by the gravitational attraction of the mountain. He recommended Schiehallion in Perthshire as a suitable site for the experiment and was immediately offered the task of leading the expedition for doing this. However, he declined, nominally on financial grounds, though perhaps, after South Africa, America, and Ireland, fieldwork no longer appealed to him. He retired to Gloucestershire to look after his growing family, having married his second wife, Mary, about 1770.

Meanwhile Mason had been commissioned by the board of longitude to complete the computation of Bradley's

Greenwich observations, which resulted in the publication in 1771 of a catalogue of the places of 387 stars in the *Nautical Almanac* for 1773. Secondly, he was commissioned to improve Mason's solar and lunar tables, which had been used by the computers of the annual *Nautical Almanac* since its first publication in 1767. He presented his first results in November 1772, then improved tables in November 1777, and again in March 1781. They were used immediately for computing the *Nautical Almanac* and were published in 1787. For the first set of tables Mason received £417 10s.; for the last he asked originally for £5000 but had to be content with £800. In 1786 he emigrated to America with his wife, seven sons, and a daughter. Having been taken ill while on passage, he died at the George tavern, on the corner of Arch and Second, Philadelphia, on 25 October 1786. He was buried at Christ Church burial-ground, Philadelphia. In 1793 his widow presented to the board of longitude various papers concerning the lunar tables, for which she received an additional £200 reward.

Mason should not be confused with the Revd Charles Mason FRS (1699?–1771), Woodwardian lecturer in the University of Cambridge.   DEREK HOWSE

Sources H. W. Robinson, 'A note on Charles Mason's ancestry and his family', *Proceedings of the American Philosophical Society*, 93 (1949), 134–6 · T. D. Cope and H. W. Robinson, 'Charles Mason, Jeremiah Dixon and the Royal Society', *Notes and Records of the Royal Society*, 9 (1951–2), 55–78 · T. D. Cope and H. W. Robinson, 'The astronomical manuscripts which Charles Mason gave to provost the Reverend John Ewing during October 1786', *Proceedings of the American Philosophical Society*, 96 (1952), 417–23 [incl. account of Mason's lunar tables] · *The journal of Charles Mason and Jeremiah Dixon … 1763–1768*, ed. A. H. Mason (1969) · C. Mason and J. Dixon, 'Observations made at the Cape of Good Hope', *PTRS*, 52 (1761–2), 378–94 · W. Hirst, 'An account of an observation of the transit of Venus over the sun', *PTRS*, 52 (1761–2), 396–8 · N. Maskelyne, 'Introduction to the following observations', *PTRS*, 58 (1768), 260–63 · C. Mason and J. Dixon, 'Astronomical observations, made in the forks of the River Brandiwine', *PTRS*, 58 (1768), 329–35 · C. Mason and J. Dixon, 'Observations for determining the length of a degree of latitude in the provinces of Maryland and Pennsylvania', *PTRS*, 58 (1768), 274–328 · C. Mason, 'Astronomical observations made at Cavan, near Strabane', *PTRS*, 60 (1770), 454–96 · minutes, CUL, Board of Longitude MSS, RGO 14, vols. 5 and 6 · petitions and memorials, CUL, Board of Longitude MSS, RGO 14, vol. 12
Archives CUL, Maskelyne MSS

Mason, Charlotte Maria Shaw (1842–1923), teacher and writer on education, was born on 1 January 1842 in Bangor, the only child of Joshua Mason, a Liverpool merchant, and his wife, Charlotte. Her mother's poor health made sea air desirable, and she spent her early years on the Isle of Man. She had a lonely childhood. Her education was undertaken by both her parents, using prescribed texts. In 1858 her parents died.

Charlotte Mason regarded teaching as her vocation from her early adolescence. In 1860 she began her training as an infant teacher at the Home and Colonial Training College, London. As she had been left penniless, the Home and Colonial Society made an unusual arrangement for her, organizing a teaching position at a school in Worthing before she had completed her training. In 1861 she became headmistress of the Davison infant school, where

Charlotte Maria Shaw Mason (1842–1923), by Fred Yates, 1901

she remained until 1873. In 1863 she was awarded a first-class certificate.

In 1874 Mason became a lecturer in education, hygiene, and physiology, and vice-principal at the Bishop Otter College in Chichester. While there, she indulged her passion for long walks and put together her first book, *The Forty Shires: their History, Scenery, Arts and Legends* (1880). In 1878 she gave up teaching for two years, following a breakdown in her health. She moved to Bradford in 1880, and developed the principles first delivered in a series of lectures in 1885–6 and expounded in *Home Education* (1886). Her later works included *A Liberal Education for All: the Scope of Continuation Schools* (1919) and *An Essay towards a Philosophy of Education* (1923).

Mason's principles were in accordance with the child-centred views of Heinrich Pestalozzi, Friedrich Froebel, and Herbert Spencer. It was imperative, in her view, that education meet the physical, intellectual, and moral needs of the child, and that children be respected and seen as the active agents in their own education. The task of parents and teachers was to supply books and information, to provide sympathy and encouragement, and sometimes to sum up and enlarge on particular questions. But the actual work of learning was always that of the child. She always insisted on the active and determining role of the child, rejecting absolutely any analogy between the growth of a child and the growth of plants because of the power of the gardener to prune a plant.

Although she trained teachers for infant schools, Mason was not in favour of nursery schools, believing that a home education was the best kind. As a result, much of her effort went to training mothers in the best ways to care for small children. These ideas became the basis for the Parents' Educational Union, which was established in 1887 in Bradford. It became the Parents' National Education Union in 1892 as branches developed in several cities. In 1891 Mason moved to Ambleside and started the House of Education to prepare for the teaching and care of children. She started the Parents' Review School in 1891 (from 1907 the Parents' Union School), a correspondence school which sent out work to all children enrolled. She devoted herself to the 'liberal education for all' movement. In her view, a liberal education was the birthright of every child and she tried hard to persuade the Board of Education that any form of continuing education should be based on the humanities rather than on technical training. In July 1889 she was reported to have been among the signatories of a pro-suffrage manifesto.

Despite her love of exercise, Mason's health had been poor since her early adulthood and she was bedridden for many years. She was unmarried. She died on 16 January 1923 at Seale Row, Ambleside, Westmorland.

BARBARA CAINE, rev.

Sources *In memoriam Charlotte Mason* (1923) · E. Cholmondeley, *The story of Charlotte Mason* (1960) · 'Women's suffrage: a reply', *Fortnightly Review*, 52 (1889), 123–39 · *CGPLA Eng. & Wales* (1923) **Archives** Armitt Library, Ambleside, papers · LUL, papers | King's AC Cam., letters to Oscar Browning **Likenesses** F. Yates, oils, 1901, National Educational Association, Esher, Surrey [*see illus.*] **Wealth at death** £10,057 0s. 5d.: probate, 5 June 1923, *CGPLA Eng. & Wales*

Mason, Edmund (d. 1635), dean of Salisbury, was the son of William Mason of Egmanton, Nottinghamshire. He went up to Clare College, Cambridge, about 1590, graduating BA about 1594 or 1595 and proceeding MA in 1598, when he became a fellow of Pembroke College under its master, Lancelot Andrewes. Later Mason gained a number of preferments in the midlands, becoming rector of Walton by Louth, Lincolnshire, in 1613, of Warsley, Huntingdonshire, and Ordsall, Nottinghamshire, in 1614, and of Newark, Nottinghamshire, in 1618, although he resigned from both Walton and Ordsall in 1619.

Mason was a tutor to the future Charles I, and subsequently, from May 1633, to his eldest son, and he served James I as a chaplain-in-ordinary from at least 1621. A noted Calvinist conformist, his 1622 court sermon *A Sermon Preached at Oatlands* is one of only twenty-three James commanded to be printed in his reign, alongside ten homilies by Andrewes.

In 1628 Mason resigned from Newark, being presented on 16 July to the rectory of Cottenham, near Cambridge, vacant by the appointment of Leonard Mawe as bishop of Bath and Wells. In the same year he proceeded DD, and was incorporated at Oxford in 1633. In November 1626 he had petitioned his former royal pupil in vain for the archdeaconry of Nottingham in succession to Dr Joseph Hall, but just over three years later, on 11 February 1630, he was granted the deanery of Salisbury when John Bowle was made bishop of Rochester.

Although he was dean for little more than five years, his ministry at Salisbury showed Mason to be rather more of a conformist than his bishop, John Davenant; in March 1633, for instance, he complained to Secretary Windebank that Davenant had watered down the charges brought against the Salisbury dissident Henry Sherfield, while asserting that he himself favoured reviving the medieval reconciliation of schismatics. In his final years Mason lost a good deal of credibility with his chapter during altercations over the competing rights of his chancellor, Humphrey Henchman, and of Matthew Nicholas, a member of the chapter and brother of the secretary of state, Edward Nicholas. Henchman was a kinsman of Bishop John Williams of Lincoln, whom his elder brother served as a chaplain, and it was thought that Davenant owed his see to the disgraced bishop. Nicholas hoped that Mason would support his claims in order to counterbalance those of the Williams party but lost Mason's support. Nicholas half suspected that Mason's growing friendship with Bishop Davenant might suggest that he too was in cahoots with Williams, 'as both these bishops drive in one yoke', as Nicholas wrote to his brother on 23 July 1633 (M. Nicholas to his brother, 23 July 1633, PRO, SP 16/243/24). Mason for his part alleged scandalous behaviour against members of the close and made unwarranted attacks on Richard Steward, one of the canons. On this somewhat unhappy note Mason seemingly left the close. He died on 24 March 1635 at Petty France in Westminster and was buried on 27 March in Westminster Abbey.

NICHOLAS W. S. CRANFIELD

Sources Venn, *Alum. Cant.* · Foster, *Alum. Oxon.* · PRO, SP 16 16/233/88, SP 16/243/24, SP 16/246/59, SP 16/247/87 · E. Mason, *A sermon preached at Oatlands* (1622) · Bodl. Oxf., MS Rawl. 83, fol. 140 [May 1633] · Bodl. Oxf., MS Carte 77, fol. 409r [March 1635] · K. Fincham, ed., *Visitation articles and injunctions of the early Stuart church*, 2 (1998), 128, 274 · N. W. S. Cranfield, 'Chaplains in ordinary at the early Stuart court: the purple road', *Patronage and recruitment in the Tudor and early Stuart church*, ed. C. Cross (1996), 120–47, esp. 132, 142

Mason, Eudo Colecestra (1901–1969), German scholar, was born in Colchester, Essex, on 26 September 1901, the third son of Ernest Nathan Mason (1867–1935), engineer's draughtsman, and his wife, Bertha Betsy, *née* Kitton (1872–1940), a governess. His father, who had published a study entitled *Ancient Tokens of Colchester* (1902), named him after Eudo Dapifer, an eleventh-century governor of Colchester (see the book by his brother Bernard Mason, *Clock and Watchmaking in Colchester*, 1969). After attending Colchester Royal Grammar School, and the Perse School in Cambridge, he matriculated at Oxford in 1922 as a noncollegiate student to read English language and literature. After graduating with second-class honours in 1926 he held posts as English lektor in the universities of Münster, Leipzig, and Basel, returning to England briefly to take the second part of the modern languages tripos at Cambridge, where he was a member of Jesus College, in 1932.

At Leipzig, where he was lektor from 1932 to 1939, Mason was awarded a doctorate *summa cum laude* in 1938 for his thesis, 'Lebenshaltung und Symbolik bei Rainer

Maria Rilke', published in book form the following year. He became a world authority on the poet, producing over thirty articles, reviews, and translations, and seven books, including *Rilke und Goethe* (1958), *Rilke, Europe and the English-Speaking World* (1961), and *Rainer Maria Rilke: sein Leben und sein Werk* (1964). In Basel from 1939 to 1946, Mason wrote for the Swiss press on German and English literature and began research on the painter–poet J. H. Füssli, his book, *The Mind of Henry Fuseli*, appearing in 1951.

Appointed lecturer in German at Edinburgh University in 1946, Mason succeeded to the chair in 1951 when W. H. Bruford returned to Cambridge. Besides Rilke and Füssli, his eclectic interests inspired writings on Goethe, Hölderlin, Novalis, Rudolf Kassner, James Joyce, T. S. Eliot, and Shakespeare, and his comparative study, *Deutsche und Englische Romantik*, was published in 1959 with subsequent editions in 1966 and 1970. In his later years he was collecting material on the devil in European literature. His last book, *Goethe's 'Faust': its Genesis and Purport*, appeared in 1967. His literary achievements were recognized in the award of a DLitt from Oxford in 1963, the degree of doctor of philosophy *honoris causa* from the University of Bern in 1965, and in 1967 both the gold medal of the Goethe Institut in Munich and the prize of the Deutsche Akademie für Sprache und Dichtung for his services to the study of German language and literature abroad.

Mason's tall stature, domed head, and dark bushy eyebrows presented an imposing appearance which concealed a deep-seated insecurity. Sensitive and highly strung, he found solace in constant research and writing. His few leisure activities were pursued with the same energy and attention to detail bestowed on his literary and academic endeavours. His collection of eighteenth- and nineteenth-century children's books and periodicals, including also games and toy theatres with paper actors, is preserved in the National Library of Scotland. The Royal Botanic Garden in Edinburgh has inherited some of his fine herbarium of alpine plants. Scottish country dancing and strenuous hill walks were ways of relaxing in the company of others. He was most at ease with young people and delighted in taking his final honours class on long rambles in the Pentland hills near Edinburgh, and in the glens of Angus during study weekends, outpacing all his walking companions despite being forty years their senior.

Mason's last completed paper was on a man with whose attitude to literature and life he felt a strong affinity—*C. S. Lewis: ein Unzeitgemässer* ('a man behind the times'); this description he also applied to himself, but as his friend Professor A. A. Parker emphasized at the memorial service held on 1 July 1969, 'not with proud defiance but with the inner anguish that was always near the surface of his life.' Deeply religious and with the Christian tradition at the forefront of his thought and writings, Mason nevertheless found difficulty in committing himself to any form of dogmatic Christian belief. Eventually in 1964 he became a Roman Catholic, although he viewed with dismay the changes taking place in many of the ancient traditions of the church, particularly the introduction of the vernacular into the liturgy.

Mason was given unstinting devotion by his wife, Esther Giesecke (1912–1966), whom he met in Leipzig. They married on 16 August 1939 and during their happy years at 20 Warriston Gardens she shielded him from the pressures of life, affording him peace to work without interruption. Her death in August 1966 while they were climbing in the south Tyrol was a devastating blow from which Mason never recovered. In 1969 he decided to retire two years early. Instead of coming to the farewell party arranged for him on the evening of 10 June he went walking in the border hills near Peebles, where he was found dead the following day, overcome by the unusually extreme heat of that Scottish summer. A requiem mass was held at the Roman Catholic chaplaincy, University of Edinburgh, 24 George Square, and he was buried beside his wife in Warriston cemetery on 17 June, beneath a quotation from Goethe's *Urfaust*: 'Wir sehn uns wieder!' ('We shall see each other again').   SHEILA M. WAGG

Sources personal knowledge (2004) · N. A. Furness, 'Eudo C. Mason, 26.9.1901–10.6.1969', *Jahrbuch für Internationale Germanistik*, 1/2 (1970), 83–9 · A. A. Parker, address at the memorial service held for Eudo C. Mason in the University Chaplaincy Centre, 1 July 1969 · report of the committee appointed to advise the University Court on the future of the chair of German at Edinburgh, 12 March 1951 · 'Mason, E. C.', *Who's Who in Europe* (1964) · Oxf. UA · b. cert. [Bertha Betsy Kitton] · b. cert. [Ernest Nathan Mason] · m. cert. [Ernest Nathan Mason and Bertha Betsy Kitton]

Archives David Hume Tower, George Square, Edinburgh, department of German, handwritten lecture notes from student years in Oxford and Cambridge · NL Scot., collection, 18th- and 19th-century books, periodicals, games, and toy theatres · NL Scot., corresp. and bibliographical notes · Royal Botanic Garden, Edinburgh, herbarium of wild plants, mainly alpine, from Europe and California · U. Edin. L., special collections division, corresp. and poems

Likenesses photograph, 1914, U. Edin. L., special collections department · photograph, c.1964, U. Edin., department of German · two colour slides, c.1968, priv. coll.

Wealth at death £41,209 12s. 0d.: confirmation, 1 Sept 1969, NA Scot., SC 70/1/1851/133–9

Mason, Francis (1565/6–1621), Church of England clergyman and religious controversialist, was born in co. Durham; his parents are unknown. He matriculated from Oriel College, Oxford, on 10 May 1583, aged seventeen, and was elected a probationer fellow of Merton College in 1586. Although he graduated BA from Brasenose College, on 27 January 1587, it was Merton that presented him for both his MA (4 July 1590) and BD (7 July 1597) and for his licence to preach (30 June 1597). The only hint of his later controversialist temperament came in 1591 when he was censured for objecting vehemently to the divinity defence of Thomas Aubrey. On that occasion he successfully defended himself against the decision to suspend him from full membership of the university. During the royal visit to Oxford the following year he was one of the defendants before Queen Elizabeth in the after-dinner Latin debate 'whether civil disorders are useful to a state' at which the French ambassador was also present (Merton College, Oxford, Registrum Annalium, 1567–1603, 158).

On 23 November 1599 he was presented to the rectory of Sudbourn, with the chapelry of Orford in Suffolk, an appointment that he held for the rest of his life. Within a few years he married Elizabeth Price. They had three children, two of whom, Elizabeth and Samuel, were baptized at Orford respectively on 9 September 1604 and 4 May 1606.

Mason's first work, *The Authority of the Church in Making Canons and Constitutions*, appeared in London in 1607. It derived from a sermon that Mason preached in the summer of 1605 at the Green Yard at Norwich and was dedicated to Archbishop Richard Bancroft. Against the puritans Mason reiterated the validity of a church over which James VI and I was supreme governor, and in which only the king could authorize the making of canon law, and urged the superiority of bishops. 'The ministers of England are not in popular paritie, but our Bishops are advanced above the rest, being indued with power by giving orders and the exercise of ecclesiasticall jurisdiction' (p. 16). In support of this opinion Mason adduced the biblical witness of the letters of Timothy and Titus before appealing for a learned ministry to be established in each parish in accord with canon 34. While he admitted that where there was no apostolical injunction for ceremonies such as the use of the surplice, the ring in marriage and the sign of the cross at baptism, and kneeling at communion, he claimed that to 'transgress the law of his Prince' was to 'leave his pastorall charge, and make a rent in the Church of Christ' (p. 38). Discipline, especially the ceremonies, 'is for the most part variable, according to circumstance of time and place' (p. 34). Such a moderate defence of the present state of the church was principally intended to remind all parties in the church that division was a much greater scandal than that alleged in the enforcement of ceremonies. Mason hoped that 'this olive branch', 'an exhortation to holy obedience', would serve to correct those carried away 'rather from weaknesse then of wilfulnesse' (sig. A2). A revised edition was entered at the Stationers' Company on 26 August 1632, to be printed in London, but it was stayed at the printers. Not until 1634, when, according to Thomas Crosfield, Dr Brian Duppa, then vice-chancellor of Oxford, ordered it to be reprinted 'in opposition to what Dr Prideaux read his lecture upon' at the Act of 12 July (Oxford, Queen's College, MS 390, fol. 68r), was it published, by John Lichfield at Oxford.

A more vigorous defence of the Church of England, this time against Romish attacks on the validity of Anglican episcopacy in the context of the controversy over Anglican orders begun by George Downham's rigorist consecration sermon of 1608, appeared with Mason's name on the title-page in 1613. *Of the Consecration of the Bishops in the Church of England* was dedicated to Archbishop George Abbot and is framed as a discourse between one Philodox, a seminary priest, and Orthodox, a minister of the Church of England. Using archival evidence from Lambeth Palace, the book traced the episcopal succession in England from the reign of Edward VI to refute the claims of Bellarmine, Nicholas Sanders, Richard Bristow, Thomas Harding, William Allen, Thomas Stapleton, Robert Parsons, and other leading Romanists. In particular it sought to end the controversy of the 'Nag's Head' story and to show that the consecrations of Matthew Parker and the first Elizabethan bishops had been canonically valid and that the full apostolic succession had been maintained in England since before the Reformation:

> I have set downe the successive Ordination, and Golden Chaine of the most reverend Father George, now [Lord] Archbishop of Canterbury, extending linke by linke unto the Bishops in the time of King Henry the 8, which our adversaries acknowledge to be canonicall. (p. 142)

On 12 May 1614, according to Mason in a note on the flyleaf of the copy of his book surviving at Merton College, Oxford, Archbishop Abbot showed the archival evidence to 'some of their discreet catholics'—John Cottington, Thomas Leake, and Thomas Laithwaite SJ—that 'they might view and consider whether they be true, or counterfeit'.

Whether or not Mason wrote the defence in its entirety has been disputed, despite his autograph note in the copy that he presented to his Oxford college. George Davenport, a friend of John Cosin in Paris, later claimed that according to Cosin, who had been Bishop John Overall's secretary and chaplain from 1616, it was written by the bishop of Norwich himself. 'Mr Mason indeed added something to it, with the approbation of the Bishop, and printed it in his own name at the desire of the Bishop whose Chaplain (I think) he was' (Bodl. Oxf., MS Tanner 52, fol. 103). According to Cosin, Mason had lodged with Overall in London at the time and may have held the same posts in the household in which Cosin succeeded him. Both Overall and Mason are credited with writing *The Validity of the Ordination of the Ministers of the Reformed Churches beyond the Seas* that finally appeared in 1641 as part of the debate over moderate episcopacy.

The 1613 vindication was roundly answered by Anthony Chamney in *A Treatise of the Vocation of Bishops and other Ecclesiasticall Ministers* (1616), published at Douai and dedicated to the archbishop of Canterbury. Later reprinted in Latin at Paris, it was the first of several antagonistic responses to the calm assertiveness of the original work, and Thomas Fitzherbert, Henry Fitzsimon, and Matthew Kellison joined in the attack. Mason's work was reissued in 1618 and at Abbot's prompting he began to translate it into Latin.

On 13 December 1619 Mason was chosen archdeacon of Norfolk by Abbot, who had the right of presentation following Bishop Samuel Harsnett's promotion; he was instituted on 18 December. However, the following year illness curtailed his activities, although he still attended the king as a royal chaplain and preached before him in January 1621. 'Upon David's Adultery' and 'Upon David's Politick Practice', published as *Two Sermons Preached at the Kings Court* (1621), censured James for going after foreign women, and in the prelude to the Spanish match are part of the literature drawing admonitory models of James from King David, attacking the rhetoric of 'carnall Concupiscence' so often found in the court of princes. Mason died at Orford in December 1621 and was buried in the chapel there on 21 December. The funerary monument put up by his widow depicts him in academic dress kneeling in prayer. His *De ministero Anglicano* was completed and published by Nathaniel Brent. An amplified version, *Vindiciae ecclesiae Anglicanae* (1625), was dedicated to Bishop Henry de Gondy of Paris. The Latin editions extend the scope of the original, not only by taking the allegations of Champney and others into account but also defending the ordinal of Edward VI and the impropriety of speaking of sacrifice in the eucharist.

Mason's younger brother, **John Mason** (*b.* 1576/7), Church of England clergyman, matriculated at Merton College, Oxford, on 15 October 1591, aged fourteen, and graduated BA from Corpus Christi College, Oxford, on 23 July 1599. He proceeded MA on 9 July 1603, when he became a fellow. He obtained his BD in June 1610 only after recanting opinions that were regarded as unorthodox. He was granted a licence to preach on 12 May 1612 and may have become in 1620 vicar of Yazor, Herefordshire. Nothing further is known of him.

NICHOLAS W. S. CRANFIELD

Sources Registrum Annalium, 1567–1603, Merton Oxf. • Bodl. Oxf., MS Tanner 52 • LPL, Abbott 2, registers • Foster, *Alum. Oxon.* • Queen's College, Oxford, MS 390 • PRO, E 331 Norwich/1 • admonitions, 1621, Norfolk RO, Norwich consistory court, fol. 267
Likenesses funerary monument, 1622, Orford Chapel, Suffolk
Wealth at death see admonitions, Norfolk RO, Norwich, Norwich consistory court, 1621, fol. 267

Mason, Francis (1837–1886), surgeon, youngest son of Nicholas Mason, a lace merchant, of Wood Street, Cheapside, London, and his wife, Ann, was born at Islington on 21 July 1837. He received his early education at the Islington proprietary school, of which John Jackson, afterwards bishop of London, was then the headmaster. Mason subsequently attended the King's School, Canterbury, and, matriculating at the London University, he pursued his medical studies at King's College, London, of which he was made an honorary fellow. While in the medical school attached to King's College, Mason became a friend of Sir William Fergusson, who formed such a high opinion of Mason's surgical skill that he made him his private assistant. Mason was admitted a member of the Royal College of Surgeons on 25 July 1858. He served as house surgeon at King's College Hospital in 1859–60, and he was granted the diploma of fellow of the Royal College of Surgeons on 11 December 1862.

In 1863 Mason was appointed an assistant surgeon to King's College Hospital, and surgeon to the St Pancras and Northern Dispensary. In 1867 he became assistant surgeon to, and lecturer on anatomy at, the Westminster Hospital, and he became full surgeon there in 1871. Later the same year Mason accepted an invitation to join the medical staff of St Thomas's Hospital as assistant surgeon and lecturer on anatomy. He became full surgeon there in 1876, when he resigned the lectureship of anatomy for that of practical surgery. From 1879 to 1886, Mason was editor of the hospital's *Reports*.

Mason filled many important offices at the Medical Society of London, being orator in 1870, Lettsomian lecturer in 1878, president in 1882, and subsequently treasurer. Throughout his professional career he published a number of works, including *On Harelip and Cleft Palate* (1877) and *On the Surgery of the Face* (1878), which were well received.

Mason was a man of genial character and had great musical talents. He died of acute erysipelatous inflammation of the throat, at his home at 5 Brook Street, Grosvenor Square, London, on 5 June 1886, leaving a widow; there were no children. He was buried at Highgate.

D'A. POWER, *rev.* JEFFREY S. REZNICK

Sources *BMJ* (12 June 1886) • *The Lancet* (12 June 1886) • *St Thomas's Hospital Reports*, new ser., 15 (1886), 249–52 • *Medico-Chirurgical Transactions*, 70 (1887), 17–18 • private information (1893) • CGPLA Eng. & Wales (1886) • V. G. Plarr, *Plarr's Lives of the fellows of the Royal College of Surgeons of England*, rev. D'A. Power, 2 vols. (1930) • *IGI*
Likenesses portrait, 1893, St Thomas's Hospital • Lock & Whitfield, photograph, Wellcome L.
Wealth at death £5298 14s. 9d.: probate, 23 July 1886, CGPLA Eng. & Wales

Mason, Sir Frank Trowbridge (1900–1988), naval officer and engineer, was born in Ipswich on 25 April 1900, the elder son and elder child of Frank John Mason MBE, draper and later JP and mayor of Ipswich, and his wife, Marian Elizabeth Trowbridge. He was educated at Ipswich School, passing into the Royal Navy (executive branch) as a special entry (public school) cadet in 1918. After two years as a cadet and midshipman in HMS *Collingwood* and HMS *Queen Elizabeth*, he volunteered to specialize in engineering (E). He underwent specialist engineering training at the Royal Naval colleges at Greenwich and Keyham. In 1923 he qualified for his engineering watch-keeping certificate in HMS *Malaya* and was promoted to lieutenant (E), continuing his service in that ship as a fully qualified mechanical and marine engineer until appointed in 1925 to HM Dockyard, Malta.

In 1928 Mason was appointed to HMS *Rodney*, a new battleship then undergoing severe problems with her novel 16-inch guns. His engineering skill in securing improved reliability led him to specialize in ordnance engineering and to his reappointment after a short period with Messrs Vickers at Elswick. After promotion to lieutenant-commander (E) he served for three years in the naval ordnance department and in 1933–4 he again served in HMS *Rodney*, but this time as senior (second) engineer, responsible to the commander (E) for all propulsion, electricity generating, and 'hotel services' machinery and equipment. Following his next promotion to commander (E) in December 1934, he served again for three years in the naval ordnance department. From there he was appointed as engineer officer (chief engineer) to a new cruiser, HMS *Galatea*, then flagship of the rear-admiral, destroyers. In 1939 he became the first commander (E) to serve in HMS *Excellent*, then the naval gunnery school. He was appointed in 1943 as fleet gunnery engineer officer to the Home Fleet in Scapa Flow, and at the same time received promotion to captain (E).

From 1944 Mason served again in the naval ordnance department in the Admiralty (Bath) and in 1947 became chief gunnery engineer officer and deputy director of naval ordnance. In 1949 he was the first engineering specialist to become a student at the Imperial Defence College (later the Royal College of Defence Studies) and, on promotion to rear-admiral, from 1950 to 1952 he held the post of deputy engineer-in-chief of the fleet. After a year on the staff of the commander-in-chief, the Nore, he was promoted to vice-admiral (E) in 1953 and assumed the post of engineer-in-chief of the fleet. He was appointed CB in 1953 and KCB in 1955. He was placed on the inactive list of the Royal Navy in 1957.

By the 1950s Mason was among the last of those naval officers still serving who had entered under the Selborne–Fisher scheme of 1903, whose aim was to put engineers in the main stream of naval life. The scheme was cancelled in 1923 and the navy entered the Second World War technologically bereft. In the immediate post-war era Mason and others determined to resurrect it, in the face of great resistance. But Mason's influence and the battle experience of many senior officers of all specializations carried the day. In 1956 the new arrangements came into being. It was Mason's great service to the navy that he was at the centre of bringing about a general list of officers.

For thirty years after leaving the active list Mason devoted himself to the national, but greatly neglected, engineering aspects of manufacturing industry and to education in general. He was president of the Institution of Mechanical Engineers (1964) and of the Institute of Marine Engineers (1967), as well as being a member of the Institute of Plant Engineers and chairman or vice-chairman of many other professional bodies. He was a member of the Council for Scientific and Industrial Research (1958–63), and its vice-chairman in 1962–3, a member of the National Council for Technological Awards (1960–64), a founder fellow of the Fellowship of Engineering (1976), a member of the Smeatonian Society of Civil Engineers, and assistant to the court of the Worshipful Company of Shipwrights. He served on the councils or governing bodies of the Further Education Staff College (1964–74), Brighton Polytechnic (1969–73), the Royal Naval School in Haslemere (1953–83), Hurstpierpoint College (1966–80), and Ipswich School (1961–72), and was chairman of the steering committee of the National Engineering Laboratory (1958–69) and of the Standing Conference on Schools Science and Technology (1971–5). He was an active member of the council of the Navy League (1967–73) and from 1967 held the life appointment of high steward of Ipswich. He was FEng, honorary FI MechE, honorary MI PlantE, and FIMarE.

Mason was good-looking and his expression was that of a man at peace with himself. Of medium build, he was always impeccably turned out, and, as he grew older, his white hair added to his aura of long and deep experience and benign but firm authority. He was a committed and practising Christian. On 23 April 1924 he married Dora Margaret (Margot) (d. 1993), daughter of Sydney Brand JP, who, like Mason's father, was a draper. They were a devoted couple who had one son, who became archdeacon of Tonbridge, and two daughters, one of whom was appointed OBE. While suffering from cancer of the lung, Mason died from heart failure at his home, Townfield House, 114 High Street, Hurstpierpoint, Sussex, on 29 August 1988. His body was cremated at the Sussex and Surrey crematorium at Worth, Sussex.

LOUIS LE BAILLY, rev.

Sources *The Times* (31 Aug 1988) · personal knowledge (1996) · private information (1996, 2004) [Ann and Diana Mason, daughters] · *CGPLA Eng. & Wales* (1988)
Likenesses G. Wheatley, portrait, oils, priv. coll. · portrait photograph, Ipswich Town Hall
Wealth at death £96,265: probate, 22 Nov 1988, *CGPLA Eng. & Wales*

Mason, George (1725–1792), revolutionary politician in America, was born in Fairfax county, Virginia, the eldest son of George Mason (1690–1735), a prominent tobacco planter, and Ann, *née* Thomson (1700–1762). Mason was nine years old when his father drowned in the Potomac in December 1735. Circumstances forced him into an early maturity, so that by the time contemporaries were going to college Mason was running a large plantation on Virginia's Northern Neck. His education was left to several Scottish tutors, who grounded their pupil in Latin and classical literature.

Mason's business acumen and spirited service on the Truro parish vestry led him into a circle that included the Washingtons, Lees, and others who would be prominent in the resistance movement from 1765 onward. His fortune was supplemented by marriage in 1750 to a Maryland heiress, Ann Eilbeck (1734–1773), and five years later he built an elegant home which he named Gunston Hall.

Early on Mason exhibited strong opinions and an impatience with government interference. When the Stamp Act crisis erupted in 1765, he and his neighbour George Washington were prominent in the resistance movement, and favoured a boycott of British goods until the obnoxious act was repealed. When parliament finally withdrew the legislation, Mason issued a warning that 'Such another Experiment as the Stamp-Act wou'd produce a general Revolt in America' (*Papers*, 1.70). Parliament, however, failed to heed this advice, and passage of the 1773 Boston Port Bill placed the colonies and the crown on a collision course. In Virginia money and supplies were raised to help the beleaguered Bostonians, and Mason took the lead among northern Virginians ready to consider armed resistance. Perhaps at Washington's urging, he wrote the Fairfax Resolves (1774) which called for a ban on the importation of British goods, beseeched parliament to stop the slave trade, and denounced lukewarm colonists for their cowardice. Washington carried the Resolves to the Virginia house of burgesses at Williamsburg. On his departure to serve in the continental army he was replaced by Mason, who, suffering from gout, frequently begged off public duties. None the less the opportunity to help shape the future brought Mason to the forefront at the Virginia convention in the spring of 1776.

Placed on committees preparing a constitution and bill of rights, Mason took his assignment as a mandate for radical change. A key witness reported that Mason's plans 'swallow'd up all the rest', as his draft of the Virginia declaration of rights, the first such document to deal with a citizen's rights, called for a free press, free speech, and 'the free exercise of religion' (*Papers*, 1.274, 289). Mason's draft also expressed the idea that all men were due their right 'to life, liberty, and the pursuing and obtaining happiness and safety' (ibid., 1.283). Mason's work was hurried into print in the Williamsburg newspaper, and was broadcast up and down the Atlantic seaboard in a matter of weeks. Soon constitutional framers in other new states enacted their own versions of his handiwork, not least Thomas Jefferson, who borrowed some felicitous phrasing for his own draft of the Declaration of Independence.

Mason refused to serve in the continental congress, but was a key figure on the Virginia committee of safety, which maintained civil government during most of the war. After the return of peace, Mason stayed at home to care for his family (his first wife had died in 1773) and for business matters. In April 1780 he married Sarah (1730–1806), widow of George Brent of Stafford county. During this period Mason received numerous entreaties to re-enter public service. He kept his ties with Patrick Henry, and probably at Henry's request accepted a post on the Virginia delegation to the federal convention in 1787.

'The Expectations & Hopes of all the Union center in this Convention' Mason wrote to his son from Philadelphia. Mason feared that a fragmented confederation would fail to address 'the Evils which threaten us' (*Papers*, 3.880). Frequently on his feet, Mason spoke 134 times and was responsible for the tax ban on interstate commerce, and for the impeachment clause 'for high crimes and misdemeanors'. Mason harboured fears that northern shipping interests might inflict monopolistic laws on southern planters, but his efforts to thwart such legislation (commonly called 'navigation laws') failed. His late effort to add a bill of rights was also rejected. A disappointed Mason refused to sign the finished draft. He then opposed ratification of the constitution, chiefly citing the fact that it lacked a bill of rights. Mason's 'Objections' were printed in a pamphlet that began 'There is no Declaration of Rights': that first sentence became the rallying cry of antifederalists everywhere.

Energized by the federalists' efforts to speed the ratification process by a quick resolution, Mason sought allies in Virginia. He joined Patrick Henry in opposing Virginia's ratification, and at the Richmond convention in June 1788 he delivered a powerful attack on the constitution, because, among other flaws, 'it authorises the importation of slaves for twenty years, and thus continues upon us that nefarious trade' (*Papers*, 3.1066). Mason had spoken out against slavery before, calling it an evil that invited the judgment of divine providence, but he remained a slaveholder himself, enmeshed in the dilemma that plagued most southern public men.

By a narrow margin Virginia ratified the constitution, and Mason accepted defeat without bitterness. Once the federal government was in operation, however, he criticized treasury secretary Alexander Hamilton's financial system. As he told James Monroe early in 1792, 'Our new

Government is a Government of Stock-jobbers and Favourtism' (*Papers*, 3.1256). Mason worried about the American Indians on the frontier, and agreed with Jefferson that the government should seek to make Native Americans farmers instead of warriors. If 'we cou'd bring the Indians to live, by cultivating the Ground', he wrote to Monroe, 'we shou'd probably hardly ever hear of another Indian War' (ibid., 3.1260).

James Madison, who spoke of Mason as 'a powerful reasoner, a profound statesman, and a devoted Republican', introduced a bill of rights in the first congress, a move which Mason applauded (29 Dec 1827, Madison MSS, Library of Congress). Mason turned down a seat in the United States senate and devoted himself to his children and his thriving plantation. Jefferson—who once characterized Mason as a citizen 'of the first order of greatness' (Miller, 144)—last visited Mason shortly before the master of Gunston Hall died, at his home, on 7 October 1792. He was buried the following day at the family cemetery at Gunston Hall.   ROBERT ALLEN RUTLAND

Sources *The papers of George Mason*, ed. R. A. Rutland, 3 vols. (1970) · H. H. Miller, *George Mason: gentleman revolutionary* (1975) · R. A. Rutland, *George Mason: reluctant statesman* (1997) · L. Cong., manuscript division, George Mason MSS · B. Tarter, 'Mason, George', *ANB* · family bible, Gunston Hall, Fairfax county, Virginia · vestry books, Truro parish, L. Cong.

Mason, George (1735–1806), writer and book collector, was baptized on 17 September 1735 at St Alban, Wood Street, London, the second son and fourth child of John Mason (1686–1753/4), a wealthy malt distiller in Deptford, who on 23 February 1728 had married Amelia (c.1698–1782), the illegitimate daughter of General George *Wade (1673–1748). Two other children of this marriage, John (b. 1729) and Sarah (b. c.1733), survived into adulthood; three died young.

Mason was admitted to the Middle Temple on 5 June 1752 and matriculated at Oxford from Corpus Christi College on 7 February 1753. By his father's will, proved on 19 January 1754, the distillery business, valued at £15,000, and property in Deptford and Greenwich went to his brother John, who was charged to pay an annuity of £500 p.a. to their mother. She was given a life interest in more valuable property in Hertfordshire, Essex, and Ormonde Street, London, all of which was to descend to George on her death; George also received £8000 and Sarah £5000. Their mother married on 20 November 1755 George Jubb (1718–1787), later the regius professor of Hebrew at Oxford; she died on 4 February 1782, but long before her death (perhaps from the date of her remarriage or his majority a year later) George Mason had part ownership and use of the landed property bequeathed to her. He left Oxford without graduating, was called to the bar from the Inner Temple in 1761, became a manager of the Sun Fire Office in 1770, and lived comfortably at Porter's, Shenley, near St Albans, Hertfordshire, as a country gentleman, landscape gardener, and bibliophile. His anonymously published *Essay on Design in Gardening* (1768), intended to supplement the 'Unconnected thoughts on gardening' in Shenstone's *Works* (vol. 2, 1764), shows familiarity with gardens in many parts of England, but refers to his own practice only in general terms. Its main theoretical concern is to draw a line between desirable contrast and undesirable incongruity.

In 1772 Mason and his mother, as joint owners, sold Porter's to Admiral Richard Howe, then Viscount Howe, and Mason went to live at nearby Aldenham, another of his estates. He became friendly with Howe, of whom he wrote a eulogistic *Life* (1803). His knowledge and his library contributed a little to Thomas Warton's *History of English Poetry* (1774–81). In 1780 John Mason became insolvent. Funds inherited by their mother for the future benefit of both brothers went to pay his debts, and George, complaining of John's 'knavery' (Nichols, 4.554), was forced to retrench. He relinquished his coach, but continued to live at Aldenham Lodge and remained a keen collector of incunabula. His select and extremely valuable library boasted some of the rarest works of Greek, Latin, and English literature, including Pynson's original edition of Chaucer's *Canterbury Tales*, two early editions of *La Morte d'Arthur*, and Caxton's *Blanchardyn and Eglantine*. In 1793 'a stroke on the forehead' resulted in visual impairment and a 'perpetual debility' in his 'tottering knees', from which he suffered for the rest of his life (Mason, *Earl Howe*, 89–90). He sought relief in electrical treatment, seemingly in vain. He also belatedly returned to authorship, evidently in quarrelsome mood. In 1795 he published a revised and greatly enlarged edition of *An Essay on Design in Gardening*, in which he now disparaged the gardening theories of Thomas Whately and Uvedale Price. Whately was dead but Price hit back in the second edition of his *Essay on the Picturesque* (1796–8), to which Mason responded testily in 1798 with two appendices to his own *Essay*.

Mason assisted the antiquary William Herbert (1718–1795) in revising Joseph Ames's *Typographical Antiquities* (1785–90), and in 1796 he published a creditable edition of Thomas Hoccleve's poems, selected from a manuscript in his possession, now in the Huntington Library. His finical correspondence with Samuel Pegge the younger (1733–1800) about the notes and glossary for this edition is published in Nichols's *Illustrations* (4.561–70). He sold a considerable part of his library in four sales between January 1798 and April 1799, raising about £2500, including £73 10s. for a perfect copy of Dame Juliana Berners's *Boke of Haukyng and Huntyng* (1486). Dibdin comments that 'it must have been a little heart-breaking for the collector to have seen his beautiful library, the harvest of many a year's hard reaping, melting away piece-meal, like a snowball' (Dibdin, 419n.).

Mason's belligerent *Supplement to Johnson's English Dictionary* (1801), intended to rectify Johnson's 'palpable errors' and supply his 'material omissions', received a hostile notice in the *British Critic*, to which Mason made a blistering reply in a supplement to his *Review of the Proposals of the Albion Fire Insurance* (1806), an attack on a commercial rival, disclaimed by Mason's fellow Sun Fire managers. This incongruous mixture of financier's and lexicographer's controversy was Mason's last publication. In it he implied that he was the author of letters signed 'Superior of the Jesuits' which in 1771 'put Junius to silence'. These letters have not been traced; neither has *A British Freeholder's Answer to T. Paine*, attributed to Mason in Nichols's *Illustrations* (4.551).

Mason never married. He died of apoplexy at Aldenham Lodge on 4 November 1806. He had settled Aldenham Lodge and other landed property on his brother John's son, Bryant. After other small bequests the residue of his estate went to Mrs Anna Maria Dalby, *née* Carteret (*bap.* 28 Dec 1764), who, according to Nichols, was Mason's natural daughter. Bryant Mason and his son Frank were drowned on the way back from India in 1809.

JAMES SAMBROOK

Sources Nichols, *Illustrations*, 4.550–70, 8.287 · G. Mason, *The life of Richard Earl Howe* (1803), 2, 34, 68, 89–90 · will, PRO, PROB 11/806, fols. 154v–157v [John Mason, father] · will, PRO, PROB 11/1456, fols. 222v–224r · *GM*, 1st ser., 52 (1782), 94 · *GM*, 1st ser., 57 (1787), 1031–2 · *GM*, 1st ser., 76 (1806), 1169 · *IGI* · *VCH Hertfordshire*, 2.155, 270–71; 3.314–15 · Foster, *Alum. Oxon.* · will, PRO, PROB 11/1087, fols. 285v–286r [Amelia Jubb, mother] · G. Mason, *An appendix to an essay on gardening* (1798), 4 · H. A. C. Sturgess, ed., *Register of admissions to the Honourable Society of the Middle Temple, from the fifteenth century to the year 1944*, 3 vols. (1949) · J. E. Cussans, *History of Hertfordshire*, 3/1 (1881), 311–12, 315, 319–20 · P. G. M. Dickson, *The Sun Insurance office, 1710–1860* (1960), 96, 274–5, 280 · *The correspondence of Thomas Warton*, ed. D. Fairer (1995), 405 · *DNB* · T. F. Dibdin, *Bibliomania, or, Book madness: a bibliographical romance*, new edn (1876) · parish register, Shenley, 6 Jan 1754 [burial, John Mason]

Archives BL, letter to Thomas Warton, Add. MS 42561, fols. 29–32

Wealth at death unknown but probably very considerable: will, PRO, PROB 11/1456, fols. 222v–224r

Mason, George Heming (1818–1872), landscape painter, the son of George Miles Mason and his wife, Eliza Heming, was born on 11 March 1818 at Fenton Park, near Stoke-on-Trent. The Mason family, whose fortune derived from the invention and manufacture of Mason's ironware china, later lived at Wetley Abbey, a large Gothic house between Stoke and Leek, built in the 1820s. Mason was educated at Anderton's school in Newcastle under Lyme. Mason seems to have inherited an interest in literature and the arts from his father, but, despite this, when he left school he was articled to William Royden Watts, a surgeon in Birmingham. In 1843, however, he gave up his medical training to travel in Europe and to study art. Travelling with his brother Frederick Miles, George Mason visited France and Switzerland and eventually arrived in Rome in 1845. In due course, the two brothers joined in the patriotic campaign to free Rome from foreign control; in 1848 Frederick Miles Mason joined the Roman legion, and served in the military campaign against the Austrians, while George tended the wounded during the siege of Rome by the French in 1849.

When George Mason first lived in Italy he found time to explore Rome and the surrounding countryside. However, a financial crisis at home meant that remittances were stopped and for a period Mason suffered dire poverty. He seems to have turned to painting in earnest as a means of supporting himself. Gradually he gained the support of a circle of English visitors to Rome, including fellow Staffordshire man David Watts Russell, and of William Cornwallis Cartwright (later a Liberal MP) with whom, in 1851, Mason explored the Sabine hills. Mason met the Italian painter Giovanni Costa at Ariccia in 1852, when Costa was lying low from the papal authorities following the suppression of the patriotic uprising, in which he had played a part. Costa and Mason made painting expeditions into the Roman campagna, and it was Costa who encouraged Mason to sketch directly from nature. Mason entered upon a close friendship with Frederic Leighton from the time of their first meeting in Rome in 1853. In 1855, Mason travelled to Paris with George Aitchison to visit the Universal Exhibition, where he studied the works of contemporary French landscape painters, notably Antoine Hébert and Gabriel-Alexandre Decamps. In Paris Mason sold a Roman landscape to the English artist J. B. Pyne. He and Aitchison then travelled on to England for a short visit.

Mason's early paintings seem to have been conventional rustic subjects but, as he became increasingly entranced by the landscape scenery of the campagna, an intense and poetic quality entered his works. Like Costa, Mason sought to represent the landscape of the Lazio region in a specific and authentic way, with reference to the hardships and endurance of the working people. He returned to Italy for a further period after 1855, working on increasingly ambitious paintings such as the scene showing horses being watered at a campagna farmstead known as *An Italian Landscape* (Tate collection), or *Ploughing in the Campagna* (Walker Art Gallery, Liverpool), which was the first painting he exhibited at the Royal Academy, in 1857.

Finally, in 1858 Mason moved back to England, to marry, on 5 August that year, his cousin Mary Emma Wood; they had seven children, five of whom survived their parents. Following the death of Mason's father in 1859, the couple set up home at Wetley Abbey. In these years Mason struggled to earn enough to support his family; in addition he suffered from bouts of depression and poor physical health. Frederic Leighton encouraged him to allow the Staffordshire landscape to become the inspiration of his painting: *Wind in the Wolds* (Tate collection, on loan to Leighton House, London) of 1863, which Mason painted in response to a commission from Leighton, marks his new interest in subjects set in the English countryside. From this time on Wetley, and its immediate vicinity (which includes hills and moorland and the impressive Wetley Rocks), became the dominant motif of his art. In 1863 Costa visited Mason at Wetley Abbey, finding 'in the structure and outlines of that upland landscape a resemblance in the distribution of particular hillsides in the remote Maremma region, while the distinguished appearance of the Staffordshire people was reminiscent of the Etruscan physical type' (Costa, *Quel che vidi e quel che intesi*, 1927, 159). After a stay of three months, the two artists travelled together to London, and then on to Paris to see the Salon exhibition, where that year Costa was showing two works.

From 1864, the Masons lived principally in Hammersmith, London, first at Westbourne House, Shaftesbury Road, and later at 7 Theresa Terrace.

In the late 1860s and early 1870s Mason's reputation as one of the most aesthetically advanced painters of the day was confirmed by works shown at the Royal Academy and Dudley Gallery, as well as by the exhibition of seventy-one paintings by him shown at the Burlington Fine Arts Club after his death. In 1868 *The Evening Hymn* (previously Wyndham collection; probably destroyed) was, according to Algernon Charles Swinburne, 'the finest … of his works, admirable beyond all where all are admirable'. Swinburne went on to describe the subject:

> A row of girls, broken in rank here and there, stand and sing on a rough green rise of broken ground; behind them is a wild spare copse, beyond it a sunset of steady and sombre fire stains red with its sunken rays the long low space of the sky; above this broad band of heavy colour the light is fitful and pale.   (repr. Swinburne, 366)

The success of *The Evening Hymn* led to Mason's election as an associate member of the Royal Academy. Mason's later paintings are of the same panoramic landscape type that he had devised in Italy, but with a subtlety of mood and soft tonality adapted to the English countryside. Figures occur, often engaged in some rural occupation—harvesting or plodding home from the fields at the end of a day's labour—and by these motifs Mason suggested in symbolical terms the very cycle of existence.

Girls Dancing (priv. coll.), later known as *A Pastoral Symphony*, was shown at the 1869 Royal Academy exhibition, where its intense and wistful mood and an atmosphere of romantic enticement was admired. The French critic Philippe Burty mentioned Mason in his review of the exhibition as:

> the landscapist who touched me most deeply. He introduces to his vistas something that is vibrant and impassioned … He has a feeling for romantic colour, and a quality of light which fills the open spaces and loses itself beneath the leaves like the waves of sound of a shepherd's song.
> (P. Burty, 56)

This beautiful painting was one of a group in the exhibition in which the *Art Journal* found:

> manifest the idealism and the realism, the romance and the naturalism, which are so strangely blended in certain new phases of the English school; to these characteristics may be added signs of the growing sway of Continental styles, together with tendency to intensity of sentiment, and to a sustained rhapsody of colour.   (*Art Journal*, 1869, 199)

Mason died on 22 October 1872 at 7 Theresa Terrace. He was buried in Brompton cemetery on 28 October. His wife survived him. *The Harvest Moon* (Tate collection), his last painting, became his most famous work, appearing at a succession of exhibitions in the years after Mason's death and through to the turn of the twentieth century. It was reproduced in an etching by Robert Walker Macbeth, published in 1891, and it was the work that moved critics to compare Mason with Jules Breton, Jean-François Millet, and Charles Daubigny among French painters.

CHRISTOPHER NEWALL

Sources S. Colvin, 'English artists of the present day: George Mason, ARA', *The Portfolio*, 2 (1871), 113–17 · *Art Journal*, 34 (1872), 300 · *Collected works of the late George Mason* (1873) [exhibition catalogue, Burlington Fine Arts Club, London] · A. Meynell, 'George Mason: a biographical sketch', *Art Journal*, new ser., 3 (1883), 43–5, 108–11, 185–8 · *DNB* · J. F. White, 'The pictures of the late George Mason', *Contemporary Review*, 21 (1872–3), 724–36 · G. Aitchison, 'George Hemmings Mason', *The Architect* (1879), 379 · S. Reynolds, 'George Heming Mason and the idealised landscape', *Apollo*, 113 (1981), 106–9 · R. Billingham, ed., *George Heming Mason* (1982) [exhibition catalogue, Stoke-on-Trent City Museum and Art Gallery, 1982] · C. Newall, *The Etruscans: painters of the Italian landscape, 1850–1900* (1989) [exhibition catalogue, Stoke-on-Trent City Museum and Art Gallery, 1989] · N. Costa, *Quel che vidi e quel che intesi*, ed. G. G. Costa (Milan, 1927) · G. A. Simcox, 'Mr Mason's collected works', *The Portfolio*, 4 (1873), 40–43 · P. Burty, 'Exposition de la Royal Academy', *Gazette des Beaux-Arts*, 2nd ser., 1 (1869), 44–61 · *Art Journal*, 31 (1869), 199 · A. C. Swinburne, *Essays and studies* (1897), 366 · *CGPLA Eng. & Wales* (1873)
Archives Kensington Central Library, London, family corresp. | Leighton House Museum, London, letters to his wife Mary
Likenesses V. C. Prinsep, oils, c.1870, NPG · J. Watkins, carte-de-visite, NPG · wood-engraving, NPG; repro. in *ILN* (8 May 1869)
Wealth at death under £5000: probate, 10 June 1873, *CGPLA Eng. & Wales*

Mason, George Henry Monck (1824–1857), administrator in India, was born at Southampton on 23 October 1824, the only son of Captain Thomas Monck Mason RN (d. 1838), of co. Wicklow, Ireland, and his second wife, Mary (d. 1863), eldest daughter of Sir George Grey, first baronet. His father was a brother of Henry Joseph Monck Mason, writer, and William Monck Mason, historian of Ireland, and a nephew of John Monck Mason, writer on Shakespeare.

Mason was educated at King William's College, Isle of Man. In 1842 he entered the Bengal army as an ensign and in June 1843 was attached to the 74th regiment of native infantry, first at Nowgong and afterwards at Hoshangabad and Mhow. He was promoted lieutenant in October 1845, and in March 1847 was made assistant to the governor-general's agent in Rajputana. In this post he acquired a reputation for energy and resourcefulness, undertaking several arduous expeditions to hunt down Sindhi robber chiefs who raided the border areas of Rajputana.

In October 1854 Mason was appointed political agent at Karauli. Dalhousie admired his political skills and in March 1857, at the relatively young age of thirty-two, Mason was promoted to resident at Jodhpur. He was popular with the maharaja, Takht Singh, who, grateful for British backing in his struggles against his unruly nobles, stuck to the British throughout the uprising of 1857. Jodhpur remained quiet during the early months of the rising, but towards the end of August the Jodhpur legion mutinied at Erinpura and sought protection at Awah, a stronghold which was controlled by one of Takht Singh's most recalcitrant chiefs, Thakur Kushal Singh. Kushal Singh had no quarrel with the British and approached Mason with assurances that the rebels would surrender if they were guaranteed safety and a resumption of their old employment. Mason rejected this offer out of hand; he had just received orders forbidding any deals with rebels who were still in arms and he was wary of alienating

Takht Singh by treating with one of his enemies. Rebuffed, Kushal Singh threw his lot in with the rebels.

In September, Brigadier-General George Lawrence approached Awah with a small force, intending to reduce it quickly. Ignoring Takht Singh's warnings of danger, Mason insisted on leading a few of the maharaja's troops to Lawrence's assistance. However, by the time he arrived at Awah, on 18 September, the battle was already raging. He dismounted and set off alone through the jungle in search of Lawrence's camp, but was almost immediately shot and cut down by rebel sowars. Lawrence, meanwhile, was forced to retreat.

Mason was survived by his wife, Sarah Louisa, daughter of Dr John Cheyne, queen's physician in Ireland, whom he had married at Calcutta on 10 February 1850, and by three surviving small children—a son, Gordon George Monck (b. 1850), who went on to join the Indian Civil Service, and two daughters, Secelia Mary Monck (b. 1850) and Alice Frances Monck (b. 1853). A second son, Leslie Arthur Cheyne Monck, had died in infancy.

KATHERINE PRIOR

Sources M. Irving, *A list of inscriptions on Christian tombs or monuments in the Punjab, North-West Frontier Province, Kashmir, and Afghanistan*, ed. G. W. de Rhé-Philipe, 2 (1912) · R. M. Mathur, *Rajput states and East India Company* (1979) · I. T. Prichard, *The mutinies in Rajpootana: being a personal narrative* (1860) · ecclesiastical records, BL OIOC · BL OIOC, Cadet MSS · K. S. S. Henderson, ed., *King William's College register, 1833–1927* (1928)

Mason, (Marianne) Harriet (1845–1932), poor-law inspector, was born at 61 York Terrace, Marylebone, Middlesex, on 19 February 1845, the daughter of George William Mason (1819–1891) and his wife, Marianne Atherton, *née* Mitford. (Frances) Agnes *Mason was a younger sister and Arthur James *Mason was one of her brothers. By 1869 the family was resident at Morton Hall, East Retford, Nottinghamshire, where George Mason was a JP. Harriet Mason was educated at home and did not marry. Until the age of forty she was the voluntary supervisor of all poor-law boarding-out committees in Nottinghamshire; she was also vice-president of the Nottinghamshire poor-law department of the Girls' Friendly Society and central head of the Young Men's Friendly Society. Her official career began in 1885 when she was appointed by the Local Government Board to conduct a preliminary inspection of poor-law children boarded-out 'beyond the union'. Her first report (which appeared as part of the fifteenth 'Annual report of the Local Government Board', *Parl. papers*, 1886, 31.51–61) praised the work being done on behalf of boarded-out children but emphasized the pressing need for systematic government inspection. She became the board's only inspector and travelled widely in England and parts of Wales (Scotland had a separate system) to visit boarded-out children. In 1898, after thirteen years of working alone, she suffered a breakdown in health, and the board appointed another inspector (Florence Chapman). Harriet Mason was made senior inspector in 1899 and worked in this capacity until her retirement in 1910.

The boarding-out of poor-law children to selected foster

families for money (generally 4s. a week per child) was part of government policy to remove children from the workhouses and to 'graft' them to new families. Initially only orphaned or deserted children were boarded-out, but gradually other categories of children (such as those whose parents were in prison) were included in the scheme. Most children were kept within the union and were the responsibility of local poor-law guardians, but those who were sent beyond their poor-law unions were the responsibility of the Local Government Board. Harriet Mason's work consisted of visiting children and their foster families (she saw about 300 children a year) and advising local voluntary boarding-out committees. Although she was not required to do so, she maintained contact with many children after they had grown up and helped them to find work and accommodation. Over the years she gained a unique knowledge of the poor law as it related to children and was often asked to speak about her work to a wider audience (for example, she gave a speech to the Congress for the Protection of Children in 1902). In all twenty-five of her annual reports ('Annual report of the Local Government Board', nos. 15–29) she provided forthright accounts of the children and families she had met and described in detail how she had conducted her inspections. She castigated local poor-law guardians for failing to carry out regular inspections and demanded that all boarded-out children should be thoroughly physically examined for signs of abuse and deliberate neglect. She appealed for the appointment of more women inspectors because she felt that they could more appropriately conduct physical examinations of children, and she was specific that children's underclothing and bedding should be checked at each visit. In her final report she reviewed the improvements that had taken place in boarding-out practice since 1885 and claimed that boarding-out had helped raise standards of childcare in the wider community. She wrote articles and pamphlets about the care of poor-law children, including *Classification of Girls and Boys in Workhouses* (1884), as well as a book of traditional nursery rhymes and country songs. She was called to give evidence to the 1909 royal commission on poverty shortly before her retirement and forcefully defended her outspoken views on the poor law and her working practices.

Harriet Mason also had a lifelong interest in botany, and after her retirement she travelled widely in southern Africa with her brother Canon Edward Mason (principal of a theological college in the Transkei), where she studied and painted African plants. In 1913 she published 'Some flowers of eastern and central Africa' in the *Journal of the Royal Horticultural Society*, and was made a fellow of the Royal Geographical Society in the same year. In 1916 an exhibition of her watercolours was held in London. She bequeathed all her botanical manuscripts to the Royal Botanic Gardens at Kew. She is commemorated in the names of three species of plant: *Indigofera masoniae*, *Watsoniae masoniae*, and *Crocosmia masoniae*. Harriet Mason had homes in London and Cape Town, and after her retirement retained connections with several philanthropic organizations, including the Charity Organization Society and the National Association for the Care of the Feeble Minded. She was a practising Anglican and a member of the Psychical Research Society: she also wrote about thought-reading and conducted amateur experiments on the subject. She died at her home in South Africa, Morton, Eureka Road, Rondebosch, on 7 April 1932.

KATHERINE FIELD

Sources *The Times* (9 April 1932), 14 • H. Martindale, *Women servants of the state, 1870–1938: a history of women in the civil service* (1938) • *WWW*, 1929–40 • G. E. Mitton, ed., *The Englishwoman's year book and directory* (1909), 220–21 • G. D. R. Bridson, V. C. Phillips, and A. P. Harvey, *Natural history manuscript resources in the British Isles* (1980) • Desmond, *Botanists*, rev. edn • M. Gunn and L. E. Codd, *Botanical exploration of southern Africa* (1981) • b. cert. • *CGPLA Eng. & Wales* (1932)

Archives RBG Kew, archives, botanical corresp. from South Africa; drawings; papers

Likenesses photograph, 1921, RBG Kew • M. Tayer, drawing, RBG Kew

Wealth at death £4395 10s. 6d.: probate, 19 Aug 1932, *CGPLA Eng. & Wales*

Mason, Henry (1575/6–1647), Church of England clergyman, was born at Wigan, Lancashire, a younger son of John Mason, a minor tradesman. He entered Brasenose College, Oxford, as a servitor in 1592, was elected an exhibitioner in 1593 and matriculated on 23 November aged seventeen. He graduated BA on 22 January 1596 and proceeded MA from Corpus Christi College, where he became chaplain in 1602, on 11 May 1603. Showing early signs of his later anti-puritan commitment, in 1603 he was a party to the attempt at Corpus Christi to learn the contents of the university's response to the millenary petition in advance of its publication.

Mason proceeded BD in June 1610, and on 15 January 1611 was collated to the vicarage of Hillingdon, Middlesex, which he resigned in December 1612 when he became rector of St Matthew's, Friday Street, London. He was appointed chaplain to John King, bishop of London, and subsequently, on 14 February 1613, collated to St Andrew Undershaft with St Mary Axe, London. In October 1616 he was installed prebendary of Willesden in St Paul's Cathedral.

Mason became an important figure within English Arminianism. In a series of seven devotional tracts published between 1624 and 1634 he distanced himself from both Roman Catholic and Calvinist doctrines. Already a controversial cleric by 1625 when, in *Christian Humiliation, or, A Treatise of Fasting*, he criticized the position of the reformed church on Lenten fasting, in 1633 he co-authored with Samuel Hoard the unlicensed Arminian tract, *God's Love to Mankind*; in 1635 he attacked the clergy who 'do nible at the orders of our Church, and the Government of the present State' and the

> ambitious professors, who talk still in a popular language, and speak for the good of their country, and finde fault with the errors in our government, and like zealous *Patriots* indeed, take part with the Commoners, against their Aldermen, and with the subjects against their Soveraigne; and all that they may steale the hearts of the multitude.
> (*Hearing and Doing the Ready Way to Blessedness*, pp. 31, 429)

Instead, Mason identified himself with the doctrinal positions of bishops John King and William Juxon, and said of the Church of England, 'I am also perswaded in my soule, that she is the purest, best reformed Church in Europe' (*Christian Humiliation*, sig. A4).

Mason resigned his prebend on 29 March 1637, and Anthony Wood reports that when the 'puritan or presbyterian began to be dominant' in London in 1641, Mason also resigned his rectory and retired to Wigan (Wood, *Ath., Oxon.*, 3.220–21). In receipt of an annuity of £20 from the Lancashire gentry family of Ince, Mason disappeared into humble, but not uncontroversial, obscurity. Wigan was a hotly contested county town during the civil war and Mason suffered at the hands of parliamentarians; in his will of June 1647 he requested that the mayor and recorder, 'help me & the poor against their oppressors who are well known so that I need not to name them' (Lancs. RO, WCW). Several of Mason's close associates, including his cousin the pewterer Geoffrey Scott to whom Mason bequeathed his personal Bible, supported the royalists at Wigan. Mason died at Scoles, Wigan, and was buried in the churchyard of All Saints, Wigan, on 7 August 1647. He had in his lifetime (in 1632 and 1639) bestowed £240 in trust for the relief of the poor of the town, and gave most of his library to the grammar school. Mason's publications were frequently reprinted during his lifetime, and in some instances up to 1656. They influenced an individual as markedly different as Sir Simonds D'Ewes, who in 1627 adopted Mason's rules on fasting as his lifelong guide.   J. D. Alsop

Sources wills of Robert Mason, 1640, Henry Mason, 1646, Henry Mason, BD, 1647, Lancs. RO · 7 Aug 1647, Wigan Archives Service, Leigh, D/DZ, A13/1; P/WI, 7 Aug 1647 · J. Arrowsmith and F. Wrigley, eds., *Register of the parish church of Wigan* (1899) · J. D. Alsop, 'A high road to radicalism? Gerrard Winstanley's youth', *Seventeenth Century*, 9 (1994), 11–24 · D. Sinclair, *The history of Wigan*, 2 vols. (1882), 1.198–9, 202–3, 219–21; 2.5–6, 23 · G. T. O. Bridgeman, *The history of the church and manor of Wigan, in the county of Lancaster*, 3, Chetham Society, new ser., 17 (1889), 716 · *The autobiography and correspondence of Sir Simonds D'Ewes*, ed. J. O. Halliwell, 1 (1845), 353 · *Walker rev.*, 54 · Wood, *Ath. Oxon.*, new edn, 3.220–21 · Foster, *Alum. Oxon.* · BL, Add. MS 28571, fols. 181–6 · N. Tyacke, *Anti-Calvinists: the rise of English Arminianism, c.1590–1640* (1987) · *Hist. U. Oxf.* 4: 17th-cent. Oxf.

Wealth at death died solvent: will, Lancs. RO, WCW

Mason, Henry Joseph Monck (1778–1858), legal writer and antiquary, was born at Powerscourt, co. Wicklow, on 15 July 1778, the son of Lieutenant-Colonel Henry Monck Mason of Kildare Street, Dublin, and his second wife, Jane, the only daughter of Bartholomew *Mosse MD. His uncle was John Monck and his brother William Charles Monck *Mason, the antiquarian scholar. After attending schools at Portarlington and Dublin, Mason entered Trinity College, Dublin, on 7 October 1793. He was elected a scholar in 1796, and was awarded the gold medal, along with his BA, in 1798. During his time at college he befriended the poet Thomas Moore; their friendship continued into later life.

In Trinity term 1800 Mason was called to the Irish bar, but he did not practise. Under judges Radcliffe and Keatinge he held the post of examiner to the prerogative court. About 1810 he was asked by the record commissioners for Ireland to prepare a draft catalogue of the manuscripts of Trinity College, Dublin. Although he never finished the project, his work in progress was eventually acquired by the college and deposited in the manuscript room, and he was elected a member of the Royal Irish Academy on 22 June 1812. In Easter term 1814 he was appointed assistant librarian of the King's Inns, Dublin, and in 1815 he became chief librarian; he was awarded the honorary degrees of LLB and LLD by the University of Dublin in 1817. During a tour in Cumberland in 1814 Mason came to know Robert Southey, and they corresponded for twenty years. In 1816 he married the Hon. Anne Langrishe; they had two sons and four daughters.

In 1818, with the help of Bishop Daly, Mason founded the Irish Society for 'promoting the scriptural education and religious instruction of the Irish-speaking population chiefly through the medium of their own language', and he also acted as its secretary for many years, writing many papers to further its causes. At his suggestion two scholarships (the Bedell scholarships) and a bursary, to be held at Dublin University, were founded in 1844 to encourage the study of the Irish language, and it was largely due to his influence that a chair of Irish was established at the university. In 1818 he also helped to found an association for the improvement of prisons and of prison discipline in Ireland, and in 1819 he published a pamphlet on the objects of the association. He also visited prisons in the hope of rehabilitating first offenders.

Mason's most enduring work of scholarship was his *Essay on the Antiquity and Constitution of Parliaments in Ireland* (1820), which offered a concise account of his history of Irish common and statute law from the period of the Anglo-Norman invasion to the reign of Charles I. Originally intended as an introduction to a projected work on the annals of the early Irish which would describe developments to the year 1782, the sequel was never finished or published. Yet his essay was still being reprinted as late as 1891, when a short biography of its author was appended by the Revd John Canon O'Hanlon. In 1830 Mason also published a *Grammar of the Irish Language* (2nd edn, 1839), in which he admitted that he was acquainted with Irish only as a written language. Following a letter to the *Christian Examiner* in September 1833 (pages 618–32), ostensibly criticizing Owen Connellan's edition of the Irish prayer book, but accusing both Mason and Connellan of serious errors in their knowledge of Irish grammar, it was also suggested that the Irish Society's pocket edition of Bedell's *Irish Bible* was a mass of errors. Connellan published a defence entitled *A Dissertation on Irish Grammar* (1834).

However well or badly the work was translated, Mason is also thought to have been the editor of an Irish-language edition of the Book of Common Prayer which was published in Dublin in 1825. He also wrote many pamphlets in support of the Irish Society and the Association for the Improvement of Prisons, and a series of papers for the *Christian Examiner*. In 1836 he published a letter addressed to Thomas Moore, entitled *Primitive Christianity in Ireland*, in refutation of some statements made by Moore in the first volume of his *History of Ireland*.

In 1851 Mason resigned as librarian of King's Inns and

left his house in Henrietta Street, Dublin, and moved to Dargle Cottage, near Bray, co. Wicklow, where he died on 14 April 1858. He was buried in the old cemetery of Powerscourt Demesne.

GORDON GOODWIN, rev. SINÉAD AGNEW

Sources Boase, *Mod. Eng. biog.* • J. S. Crone, *A concise dictionary of Irish biography*, rev. edn (1937), 152 • D. J. O'Donoghue, *The poets of Ireland: a biographical and bibliographical dictionary* (1912), 304 • Burtchaell & Sadleir, *Alum. Dubl.* • private information (1893) • J. O'Hanlon, 'Life', in H. J. M. Mason, *Essay on the … parliaments in Ireland*, ed. J. O'Hanlon, rev. edn (1891) • *GM*, 3rd ser., 4 (1858), 570
Wealth at death under £3000: probate, 22 May 1858, *CGPLA Ire.*

Mason, Hugh (*fl.* 1707–1734). *See under* Fortnum, Charles (1738–1815).

Mason, Hugh (1817–1886), mill owner and philanthropist, was born at Stalybridge on 30 January 1817, the third and youngest son of Thomas Mason (1782–1868) and his wife, Mary Woolley (*née* Holden). His father was a joiner, his mother kept a smallware shop, where she sold tapes and gingerbread. During the boom of 1822–5, Thomas Mason moved to nearby Ashton under Lyne, where he became a cotton spinner with three jennies; his son went to school at Stamford Academy in the town. Thomas had first entered the mill at the age of eight, his son Hugh did so at the age of ten, working a 72-hour week for seven years. He then spent the years 1834–8 in a local bank. At the age of twenty-one he entered the mill for a second time but as a partner, and the same year was elected a member of the Manchester exchange. He rapidly became the driving force within the business, and took over its reins from his brothers and his father, who retired in 1862. He extended his horizons beyond the confines of the counting-house, and followed the example set by his father, an ardent advocate of education and social reform. He became an active supporter of the Ashton Mechanics' Institute established in 1839, funding lectures out of his own pocket, and a founder member in 1847, with other radical dissenters and ex-Leaguers, of the Lancashire Public Schools Association.

The 'Oxford Colony' Mason's greatest achievement was to transform the two Oxford mills, built in 1845 and 1851, into the nucleus of the 'Oxford Colony' of his workfolk. Not merely did Mason treble employment from 200 in 1840 to 620 in 1861, but he also became a convinced and thoroughgoing paternalist, dedicated to improving the welfare of his employees. He came to view himself as simply the steward of his own wealth and his employees as his own brothers and sisters. He built 150 houses with four or six rooms apiece, in the interests of morality and decency. He actively discouraged the employment in the mill of mothers of families. The colonists established their own clutch of associations: a burial club, a friendly society, a band, a choir, and a gardeners' society. Mason sought to provide alternative attractions to the 'man traps' of public houses. He provided in 1861 a library, lecture hall, reading-room, and smoking-room. In 1868 he inaugurated the Oxford Institute with an enlarged lecture hall, picture gallery, and baths, supplemented in 1870 by a recreation ground. During the winter season a course of lectures was organized, concluding with a tea party. Mason 'gathered round him a band of the élite of the working classes' (*Ashton Reporter*, 28 April 1866, 4, vi), for whom he acquired a profound respect. He received their tributes in the form of a series of addresses and testimonials. He also earned the praise of two factory inspectors for the 'noble example' he set to his fellow employers (*Factory Inspectors' Reports*, 31 Oct 1862, 26; *Ashton Reporter*, 18 April 1868, 7, vi). He resigned from the local employers' association and denounced trade unions, whether of masters or men, as pernicious to commerce. The contrast between the success of the Oxford Colony and the failure of the Owenite 'villages of co-operation' remains noteworthy.

Mason became a town councillor in 1856, a magistrate in 1857, a deputy lieutenant of Lancashire by 1864 and, finally, an alderman in 1866. He served as the mayor of Ashton for three terms of office (1858–60), and proved to be more effective than any of his predecessors. He rooted out bribery, set officials to rights, and infused a new public spirit into the life of the town. He built a new market place, helped to establish the Ashton Penny Bank, and enforced the proper administration of the burial laws. As chairman of the governors of Ashton Infirmary he introduced a more economical system of bookkeeping. He also forced down the price of the gas supplied by the Ashton Gas Company, to the benefit of all consumers.

The cotton famine In 1861 Mason warned, with remarkable prescience, that 'a time of trial for both masters and workpeople seems to be approaching us' (*Ashton Reporter*, 29 June 1861, 4, iii). During the subsequent cotton famine he achieved national eminence by his untiring philanthropy. First, he remained a strenuous supporter of the cause of the North in the American Civil War, a leading spirit of the Union and Emancipation League, and a fearless critic of those hotheads who favoured armed intervention to end the blockade of the cotton ports. Second, he continued to run his own mills full time throughout; only ten other millowners out of two thousand did so. Thereby he maintained both employment and wages, enabling his own operatives to contribute in their turn to the relief of the unemployed. Immediately trade recovered he raised wages by 10 per cent without any solicitation and so confirmed his position 'in the front rank of those who have acknowledged the rights and claims of the working classes' (*Ashton Reporter*, 28 April 1866, 7, i). Third, he became the prime mover in relieving distress throughout Ashton. That borough was more afflicted by the shortage of cotton than any other in the whole region, and it had almost no middle class to fund the relief of distress. Political and religious feelings ran so high that two separate relief committees were established, representing respectively the Anglican–Conservative interest and the Liberal dissenting interest. It was Mason's achievement to reconstitute his own committee, the Borough Committee, upon a broader basis, and to secure its recognition as the sole responsible agency. At first Mason had thought that relief should be given in the form of food and fuel rather than in money or clothing, because money might be used for gambling and clothes might be pawned. He quickly changed his opinion and favoured the payment of relief in money rather than in kind as being more acceptable to working people. He admired the independence of character of those workmen who disdained to seek relief. He strove to secure increases in the scale of relief, and set an example to other employers by conceding a moratorium upon the payment of cottage rents. He disapproved of both the workhouse test and the labour test. He presided over the rapid construction of the Albion Sunday school in 1861–2, and used the new building to house sewing and reading classes for the unemployed. Fourth, Mason prevented the riots in Stalybridge from spreading to Ashton by his courage and his promptness on 23 March 1863 in reading the Riot Act, a service he repeated during the Murphy riots of 1868. Fifth, he served on the central executive committee in Manchester (1862–9), first deploring any appeal for aid to London, and then in 1864 urging the government to invest £500,000 in a programme of public works. Finally, he sought to extend the sources of cotton supply so as to avert any recurrence of similar distress in the future.

Mason had been a far-sighted founder in 1857 of the Cotton Supply Association, becoming a member of its executive committee. He also became chairman of the executive committee of the Manchester Cotton Association established in 1860. On 23 September 1862 he boldly called in public for the impeachment of Sir Charles Wood, secretary of state for India, for his consistent obstruction of the efforts made by Lancashire to develop the supply of cotton from India. To the same end he rebuked the government in 1871 for failing to admit the 'commercial element' to membership of the Council of India. He also became disturbed by the incidence of speculation in the Liverpool cotton market. He was elected president of the Cotton Spinners' Association, established in 1861 in self-defence against the merchants of Liverpool. He supported the passage of the Cotton Statistics Act of 1868, and sought in 1871 to improve its administration, so as to reduce the violent fluctuations in the price of cotton.

Other interests Hugh Mason devoted his great abilities, and his leisure hours, to the service of his fellows, identifying himself fully with the great movements of the age. His natural capacities were those of a leader of men. He was 'an exceedingly strong man', 'a man of inflexible will and unswerving integrity' (I. Petrie, *From Tinder-Box to the 'Larger' Light: Threads from the Life of John Mills, Banker*, 1899, 88), 'a man of great intensity, fixed in his convictions, indomitable in spirit, untiring in energy' (*The Congregationalist*, 227). As a Sunday school teacher he early mastered the art of public speaking and he honed it to perfection as a temperance advocate. He developed an early preference for the public meeting to the private canvass in order 'to get at the working man'. Lacking in suavity of manner, he preserved an abiding love of plain speech and secured an appreciative response from his audiences. He was elected to the Society of Arts in 1861; he established his own newspaper, the *Ashton News* (1868–74) and proposed in 1870 the local adoption of the Public Libraries Act, donating 1000

volumes to the library when it opened in 1882. He nevertheless remained an apostle of the spoken word and always had a long speech ready for any occasion. Sometimes he spent every evening of the week in chairing a local meeting. In Manchester in the 1870s he would be greeted by audiences of working men with tempestuous cheers and deafening applause.

In the sphere of religion he embodied the best elements of the puritan tradition of the seventeenth century and incarnated 'the dissidence of Dissent' from the Anglican church. 'In many points he was a nineteenth-century edition of the finest type of the old Puritanism' (*The Congregationalist*, 229). He remained a devout worshipper, attending church upon week nights as well as twice on Sundays. Born and bred within the Methodist New Connexion, he transferred his loyalty to the leading Congregational church of the region. He became a member of Albion Congregational Church in 1846, its treasurer in 1858, and a deacon in 1860. He presided at the bi-centenary conference held in Manchester on 13 January 1862, which decided to commemorate the expulsions of 1662 by the erection, in association with the English Congregational Chapel Building Society, of thirty memorial chapels and schools in Lancashire, as well as the restoration of the Independent chapel in Dukinfield, the oldest in the region. As a true nonconformist he became an ardent member of the Liberation Society, and a keen supporter of the British and Foreign Bible Society and the London Missionary Society. In 1863 he chaired a public meeting of the Liberation Society, and in 1873 he opened the restored chapel at Dukinfield.

As a Liberal and a Cobdenite, Mason became in 1866 a founder both of the Cobden Club and of the Manchester Reform Club. In 1871 he reduced the working week at the Oxford mills by two hours, generalizing the Saturday half-holiday throughout Tameside and anticipating the Factory Act of 1874. He became a director of the Manchester chamber of commerce in 1864, a vice-president in 1871, and its president for three terms in 1871–4. Thereby he became the spokesman for the country's staple trade, with its 2 million dependants, as Thomas Bazley had been in the 1850s, and Charles Macara was to be in the 1890s. Mason, however, became the chief executive of the Manchester trade at the period of its greatest importance in the supply of the world market. He infused new spirit into the chamber, extending its remit over the whole sphere of British commerce, reporting to regular quarterly meetings and drafting detailed annual reports. He travelled to Paris as well as to London as the representative of the chamber, sponsored a drive to extend membership, and was honoured by a double vote of thanks on his retirement from office. Three speeches proved highly effective. First, he reproved the banks in 1873 for their reckless competition for business. Second, he boosted in 1873 the campaign against the Indian import duties on Lancashire goods. Third, he criticized in 1875 the mania in Oldham for floating limited companies. Those speeches led to the suspension of mill building in Bombay in 1874 and of company flotation in Oldham in 1875. Mason was appointed by the government in 1872 as a member of the Mersey Docks and Harbour Board, the first member recruited from outside Liverpool. His interests in the Liverpool–Manchester traffic secured his election to the boards of the Bridgewater Navigation and the Midland Railway. When the Manchester Ship Canal was projected, he foretold in 1883 that it would prove to be a ruinous failure.

Later life Mason was removed from the bench of aldermen in 1874 by his political opponents and withdrew thereafter from local politics. A typical Manchester man and a representative Lancashire radical, his interests extended to embrace the dialect literature of Waugh, Brierley, and Laycock. His zeal, courage, and sagacity enabled him to become a leader of the region's Liberals and nonconformists, and to reach the heights of his fame as a speaker. He served the Liberal Party well as vice-chairman from 1861 of the South Lancashire Registration Association. He secured the holding in Ashton in 1882 of the annual conference of the National Liberal Federation, founded in 1877 by the Birmingham radicals. He had served the Steam Users' Association as a vice-president since 1864, and he became its president in 1875. He also became president of the Society for the Promotion of Scientific Industry in 1875. He was appointed a life governor of Owens College in 1875 and endowed it with a scholarship. Above all, he devoted himself to the temperance agitation, having become a teetotaller in 1870 and a vice-president of the United Kingdom Alliance in 1875. He became president of the Manchester and Salford Temperance Union and of the Band of Hope Union. His crusade against smoking generated his first printed speech, *On the Use of Tobacco* (Manchester Anti-Narcotic League, 1885). As the Liberal MP for Ashton (1880–85) he secured the passage of the Local Option Bill in 1880 and of a Boiler Explosions Bill in 1882, but failed in an 1883 bid to enfranchise women; he was narrowly defeated in the general election of 1885.

Mason died at his home, Groby Lodge, Jowetts Walk, off Manchester Road, Ashton under Lyne, at the age of sixty-nine on 2 February 1886; he was buried in Dukinfield cemetery on the 6th. His estate of nearly £290,000 may be compared with that of his father, who left less than £20,000. He was married three times: in 1846 to Sarah Buckley; probably in 1853 to Betsey Buckley; and in 1864 to Anne Ashworth. His third wife, two sons, and two daughters survived him. He was commemorated by the erection in 1887 of the first public statue in Ashton. The Oxford Colony survived the demise in 1955 of the firm of Thomas Mason & Son; the Oxford Mills Institute and Social Club bought in 1956 the premises which it had previously leased.   D. A. FARNIE

Sources minutes of the Manchester Chamber of Commerce, 1871–4 • *The Builder*, 15 (1857), 685–7 • *The City Jackdaw*, 1/3 (3 Dec 1875), 25–6 • *Momus* (11 April 1878), 1 • *Ashton under Lyne Reporter* (6 Feb 1886), 5–7 • *Ashton under Lyne Reporter* (13 Feb 1886), 6 • *Alliance News*, 32 (6 Feb 1886), 88–9 • *The Congregationalist*, 15 (1886), 224–30 [J. G. Rogers] • W. H. Mills, 'The passing of Henry Stonor', *Manchester Guardian* (13 April 1914), 12; repr. in W. H. Mills, *Grey pastures* (1924), 35–40 • W. M. Bowman, *England in Ashton under Lyne* (1960), 459–64 • J. Holland, 'Hugh Mason: a cotton master and puritan', *Ashton Reporter* (28 Dec 1973), 5 • O. Ashmore and T. Bolton, 'Hugh Mason and the Oxford mills', *Transactions of the Lancashire and Cheshire Antiquarian Society*, 78 (1975), 38–50 • A. Howe, *The cotton masters, 1830–1860* (1984) • E. A. Rose, 'Mason, Hugh', DBB • N. Kirk, *The growth of working class reformism* (1985), 286, 294–7 • m. cert. • d. cert. • *Ashton under Lyne Reporter* (5 March 1864), 3ii • J. G. Rogers, *An autobiography* (1903), 105–11

Archives Man. CL, Manchester Archives and Local Studies, Lancashire Public Schools Association Archives • Man. CL, Manchester Archives and Local Studies, Wilson MSS

Likenesses C. A. Duval, photograph, 1863, Man. CL, Manchester Archives and Local Studies • statue, 1884, Chester Square, Ashton under Lyne, Lancashire • W. G. Baxter, cartoon, repro. in *Momus* • McLachlan and Shields, group portrait (Cotton Famine Relief Committee)

Wealth at death £289,342 9s. 3d.: resworn probate, May 1887, CGPLA Eng. & Wales (1886)

Mason, James (c.1723–1805), landscape engraver, was listed in 1744 by George Vertue as one of a group of new engravers being employed by the publisher Arthur Pond. Nothing is known of his early life, but he was probably born about twenty years earlier. For Pond he engraved ten landscapes by Gaspard Poussin and three by Claude, the earliest dated 1743, and he also engraved illustrations for Anson's voyages. In April 1746 Mason himself co-published with Peter Canot six landscapes after Jean-Baptiste Chatelain. He rapidly established a reputation as a talented landscape engraver, working after Thomas Smith (1749–51), William Bellers (1754–63), George Lambert (1745–61), Paul Sandby (1754), Jean Pillement (1759–62), Thomas Gainsborough (1763), Francesco Zuccarelli (1765), William Woollett (1766), and Richard Wilson (1767), and he was one of a group of talented landscape engravers whose work attracted favourable notice throughout Europe during the 1760s.

In 1763 Mason was living in Phoenix Alley, Hart Street, Covent Garden, but in the late 1760s he moved to Windmill Street and finally, in 1771, to Winchester Row, Paddington, where he remained for the rest of his life. He was a fellow of the Society of Artists but exhibited with them only before trouble broke out between the court faction and the rank and file and after the mass resignation of the court faction. In the mid-1760s he exhibited with the Free Society of Artists. He produced several prints of sea fights and some important colonial views, notably four views of Halifax, Nova Scotia, after Dominic Serres, but his most highly regarded prints were three large landscapes after Claude for John Boydell's *Collection of Prints Engraved after the most Capital Paintings in England*. While he engraved several more landscapes after old masters for Boydell, he seems to have engraved less and less after 1780. He died at his home in Winchester Row in April 1805, and was buried at St Mary, Paddington, on 27 April. In his will, proved on 20 May 1805, he called himself engraver and shopkeeper. The sale after his death held by King and Lochée on 3 April 1806 consisted chiefly of his own proof prints and others by fellow landscape engravers, and the catalogue reveals nothing of the nature of his shop. He left a widow, Mary Magdalen, two unmarried children, Benjamin James and Mary Elizabeth, another son, Michael, a widowed daughter, Elizabeth Wareup, and a grandson, William Mark

Wareup, and was able to leave modest annuities to all of them. The apparent difference in age suggests that Michael and Elizabeth might have been children of an earlier marriage.

F. M. O'DONOGHUE, rev. TIMOTHY CLAYTON

Sources will, PRO, PROB 11/1425, fols. 423v–425r · *A catalogue of the prints and etchings of Mr. James Mason, engraver, lately deceased* (1806) [sale catalogue, King & Lochée, 3 April 1806] · T. Clayton, *The English print, 1688–1802* (1997), 198–9 · Graves, *Soc. Artists* · L. Lippincott, *Selling art in Georgian London: the rise of Arthur Pond* (1983) · L. Lippincott, 'Arthur Pond's journal … 1734–1750', *Walpole Society*, 54 (1988), 220–333 · 'Catalogue of prints and drawings', www.nmm.ac.uk, 28 Nov 2000

Wealth at death modest annuities to widow, four children, grandchild: will, PRO, PROB 11/1425, fols. 423v–425r

Mason, James (1778/9–1827), writer, was the son of James Mason, draper, of St John's Hill, Shrewsbury, and his wife, Sarah, daughter of Arthur Heywood, banker in Liverpool. Mason lived in Shrewsbury all his life. He was captain of the Shrewsbury Volunteers, and was involved in politics and literature. He was a supporter of Charles James Fox, advocating the abolition of slavery and Roman Catholic emancipation. In 1804 his *Considerations on the Necessity of Discussing the State of the Irish Catholics* appeared. This was followed by *A Brief Statement of the Present System of Tythes in Ireland, with a Plan for its Improvement*. He took part in the Shrewsbury election of 17 October 1806, and next year issued *A Letter to the Electors of Shrewsbury*. His other political pamphlets were *Observations on Parliamentary Reform* (1811) and *A Review of the Principal Arguments in Favour of Restricting Importation, and Allowing the Exportation of Corn* (1814).

Mason's published literary work included a tragedy, *The Natural Son* (1805), which should be distinguished from Richard Cumberland's earlier comedy with the same title, and in 1809 he issued two volumes of *Literary Miscellanies*. The first contained 'Mortimer', a novel in a series of letters, and translations from the classics; the second contained two tragedies, 'The Renown' and 'Ninus', and two comedies, 'The School for Husbands' (an original play, unlike John Ozell's translation from Molière) and 'The School for Friends'. A comedy, under the same name as the last, by Marianne Chambers, was produced at Drury Lane in December 1805, and published the same year. In 1810 Mason published a verse translation, *The Georgicks of Publius Virgilius Maro*. Robert Watt, in his *Bibliotheca Britannica*, also attributes to him, probably wrongly, *A Plea for Catholic Communion in the Church of God* (1816).

Mason died at Shrewsbury on 27 April 1827, aged forty-eight. G. LE G. NORGATE, rev. H. C. G. MATTHEW

Sources GM, 1st ser., 97/2 (1827), 189 · Watt, *Bibl. Brit.* · H. Pidgeon, Salopian Annals, 1827, Local Studies Library, Shrewsbury, vol. 5 · *Shrewsbury Chronicle* (4 May 1827)

Mason, James Neville (1909–1984), actor, was born on 15 May 1909 at Huddersfield, the youngest of three sons (there were no daughters) of John Mason, a textile merchant of that town, and his wife, Mabel Hattersley, only daughter of J. Shaw Gaunt, also of the West Riding of Yorkshire. He was educated at Marlborough College and at

James Neville Mason (1909–1984), by Dennis Reed, 1947 [in the film *Odd Man Out*]

Peterhouse, Cambridge, where he took a first in architecture in 1931. At Cambridge he discovered a taste for acting and the theatre. His performance as Flamineo in a Marlowe Society production of *The White Devil* by John Webster was well reviewed by the theatre critic of the London *Daily Telegraph*. Thus encouraged, he began to reconsider his decision to become an architect (he was skilful at drawing for the rest of his life). He was stage-struck, of course, but also shrewd about himself. He knew that he had a good voice, a true ear, and other graces of body and mind. He also knew that in acting, as in the other performing arts, a broad gulf divides the talented amateur from the employable professional. He believed, though, that he could bridge it. His interest in films was that of a young intellectual. The thought of working in them (except, possibly, as an avant-garde director) had not yet occurred to him.

Mason had no formal training as an actor, but served an older, informal kind of apprenticeship: that of answering advertisements in *The Stage*, of presenting himself for auditions, of living cheaply, of taking ill-paid jobs in provincial touring and repertory companies, of making friends in the theatre, of doing the best he could with unsuitable parts, and of making the suitable ones seem better. He made his professional début at the Theatre Royal, Aldershot, in 1931 playing the Grand Duke Maritzi in a play called *The Rascal*. Two years later he made his first London appearance in *Gallows Glorious* at the Arts Theatre. Between 1934 and 1937 he continued his stage education with the Old Vic Company and at the Gate Theatre, Dublin. He played his first film part in 1935. This was in *Late*

Extra, a low-budget 'quickie' of the kind then being made by the dozen in England to enable film exhibitors to comply with the Quota Act.

Mason played in more quota films, and in doing so began to identify and acquire the special skills needed to act effectively for the camera. He also made new friends, among them Roy Kellino, a cameraman turned director, and his wife, Pamela. She was the daughter of Isidore Ostrer, who, with his brothers, then controlled half of the British film industry, including the Gaumont-British cinemas and the Shepherd's Bush and Islington studios. He was not, however, an indulgent father. When, in 1937, Mason and the Kellinos decided to make a film of their own, using their own pooled savings and a script written by the three of them, they were unable to get it properly distributed. *I Met a Murderer* (1939) was an intelligent little crime thriller and well received by the better critics, but the Ostrers were reluctant to exhibit in their cinemas a British film that had not been made in their studios. Mason returned to the stage to repair his fortunes and was in rehearsal for the BBC at Alexandra Palace when television production was halted there in August 1939.

Mason had an eventful but confusing war. He was estranged from his family, who disapproved of his living with Mrs Kellino, not yet divorced. His attempt to register as a conscientious objector was frustrated by a tribunal which directed him to non-combatant military service. His appeals against this ruling, however, became in the end irrelevant. After he and Pamela were married in 1941, he found that work in the film industry had been declared of national importance. As long as he worked in films his call-up would be deferred and he would remain a civilian. He had worked his way through some very bad films when, at the Islington studios of Gainsborough Pictures, he played the wicked Lord Rohan of *The Man in Grey* (1943). It was the first of a series of costume melodramas which had a phenomenal popular success. *Fanny by Gaslight* (1944), *They were Sisters* (1944), and *The Wicked Lady* (1945, with Margaret Lockwood) followed. In 1944 he was polled by the New York *Motion Picture Herald* as Britain's top box-office star. In the following year he appeared, with Ann Todd, in *The Seventh Veil*, the film that introduced him to American audiences. *Odd Man Out* (1946, directed by Carol Reed), an exceptionally good film made shortly after the war ended, established Mason as a fine actor as well as a star. In less than four years he had become what Hollywood then called 'a hot property'.

In post-war England the problems of managing a success of that sort were unfamiliar; and, perhaps inevitably, the solutions were decided upon by the property himself, assisted by his wife. Determined at that time to produce films as well as act in them, Mason proceeded to dissipate much of his potential influence as a star by writing newspaper articles and open letters denigrating the British film industry in general (lacking in glamour, third-rate) and J. Arthur Rank, by then its major proprietor, in particular. He made other mistakes. In deciding which of his Hollywood suitors to accept, he used his own judgement rather than his agent's. As a result he spent most of his first year in America preoccupied with an expensive lawsuit. He won the suit, but not all the costs of it. He needed work and was glad to play in two minor Hollywood films directed by Max Ophüls. It was his successful portrayal of a German field marshal in *Rommel, Desert Fox* (1951) that re-established him as a box-office attraction, and his Brutus in the 1953 film version of *Julius Caesar* reminded the public of his qualities as an actor.

In his fifty years as a screen actor Mason appeared in over 100 films. Those of his middle years were perhaps the best. His fine performance in George Cukor's version of *A Star is Born* (1954) brought him an Oscar nomination; his portrait of a middle-aged man infatuated with a teenage girl in the film of Vladimir Nabokov's *Lolita* (1962) was a triumph. He was remarkably versatile and could always make even a small part memorable. *Georgy Girl* (1966) and James Ivory's *Autobiography of a Princess* (1975) are examples.

Mason's marriage to Pamela was dissolved in 1965, when he left Hollywood. They had a daughter, Portland, and a son, Morgan. In 1971 he married the Australian actress Clarissa Grace Kaye, daughter of Austin Knipe, racehorse training manager, of Sydney, Australia. There were no children of this marriage. The Masons settled in Corseaux sur Vevey in Switzerland, where they were near neighbours of Sir Charles Chaplin and his wife, Oona. Corseaux was their base from which they travelled and went to work in other places. They took up bird-watching. Their favourite subjects were a family of crows which occupied the large pine on the lake side of their house. Mason died in hospital in Lausanne on 27 July 1984.

ERIC AMBLER, *rev.*

Sources *The Times* (28 July 1984) · F. Gaye, ed., *Who's who in the theatre*, 14th edn (1967) · J. Mason, *Before I forget* (1981) · S. Morley, *Odd man out: James Mason* (1989) · D. de Rosso, *James Mason* (1989) · personal knowledge (1990)
Archives BFI, corresp.
Likenesses D. Reed, photograph, 1947, BFI NFTVA [*see illus.*]

Mason, Sir John (*c.*1503–1566), diplomat and member of parliament, was born of humble parents in Abingdon, Berkshire. While the identity of his father is unknown, his mother was the sister of a monk at Abingdon Abbey (possibly the last abbot, Thomas Rowland); she was still living in Abingdon, as a widow, in 1533. After attending Abingdon grammar school Mason was sent to Oxford University, with support from the abbey. As a young man he was apparently destined for a clerical career, as he was ordained an acolyte in 1521. That year he was elected a fellow of All Souls and admitted to the BA degree, and in 1525 he incepted MA. His career path changed at Oxford, after he attracted the attention of Sir Thomas More, perhaps by delivering the welcome oration for Henry VIII's visit to the university in 1529. With More's support he secured a royal exhibition to study in Paris. In 1531 his old patron (and perhaps uncle) the abbot of Abingdon presented him to the first of his many ecclesiastical benefices: the rectory of Kingston Bagpuize, Berkshire; but he remained in France. In 1532 he attended the meeting between François I and Henry VIII at Calais.

On leaving Paris in 1533, Mason embarked upon a diplomatic career, and was soon employed carrying letters between London and Paris. To further his knowledge of foreign lands, he went from France to Spain, and by July 1534 he was at Valladolid. That year he seemed to exhibit conservative religious views, lamenting the imprisonment of Sir Thomas More and Bishop John Fisher. In 1535 he was with Emperor Charles V's court in Sicily, from where he wrote to his colleague Thomas Starkey at Padua. Both men belonged to the cadre of young scholars and diplomats recruited and directed by Thomas Cromwell. By late 1536 Mason was back in England, his basic diplomatic training complete. At this time he was rewarded by Cromwell with the canonry of Crediton (Exeter), and was named a chaplain to the bishop of Lincoln.

In 1537 Mason received his first major assignment, as secretary to the new English ambassador to the emperor, Sir Thomas Wyatt. The embassy included Edmund Bonner, at that time an anti-papalist and loyal servant of Cromwell, and almost immediately relations between Bonner and Mason were tense. Bonner complained that Wyatt listened only to Mason, relying upon him 'as a God almighty'. Denouncing the secretary as 'as glorious and as malicious a harlot as any that I know', Bonner also accused Mason of treasonous contact with Cardinal Pole and described him as a papist. Aware that these complaints derived from malice, Cromwell protected Mason, and throughout 1539 and 1540 the secretary remained at work in the Netherlands. As a token of Cromwell's continued favour, in February 1540 Mason added the canonry of Timsbury (Hampshire) to his growing sheaf of benefices. During a brief visit to England, in late December that year he married Elizabeth (d. 1594), widow of Richard Hill (d. 1539) of Hartley Wintney, Hampshire, and daughter of Thomas Isley of Kent. Although he acquired Hill's estate through his marriage, and was licensed to continue holding his benefices despite it, Mason soon set off to rejoin Wyatt. His journey was cut short, however, for in the turmoil following the fall of Cromwell Bonner's earlier charges of treason were revived, and on 25 January 1541 Mason was urgently recalled to London, to join Wyatt in the Tower. With Wyatt's support, however, he was soon cleared, and on 21 March Mason and his master were pardoned.

Following his release Mason did not immediately return abroad, but instead remained in England, where his acknowledged administrative acumen led to his appointment in late September 1541 as a clerk of the privy council, as a deputy for William Paget. In October 1542 Mason replaced Sir Brian Tuke as French secretary. He also regularly acted for Paget as clerk of parliaments and, upon Paget's appointment as principal secretary, in May 1543 Mason was named clerk of the council for life. The summer of 1544 found him once more across the channel, serving as a royal secretary at the siege of Boulogne. In November 1545 Mason and Paget were appointed joint masters of the posts, while at the same time a second French secretary was appointed to alleviate Mason's heavy workload. Mason finally resumed diplomatic work in April 1546, when he visited a number of German princes to promote a league with England (designed to frustrate French diplomacy) and to propose a council to resolve religious differences within the empire. Neither suggestion found much favour, forcing Mason to admit failure and to seek speedy recall. While waiting to return, he attended the emperor's court at Speyer; he arrived home some time between July and November.

Mason's labours were rewarded with a knighthood at the coronation of Edward VI in February 1547. Although not a member of Protector Somerset's inner circle, he remained active in royal service, and there were rumours in April 1547 that he was to become English ambassador to the emperor. On 11 May his stepdaughter Mary Hill married the king's tutor John Cheke. Mason prepared a manuscript treatise on the superiority of the English crown over Scotland, apparently for the protector. With the overthrow of Somerset in the council coup of October 1549, Secretary Paget's power was further enhanced, which in turn had important consequences for his friend and protégé Mason, whose wife was also a relative of the Dudleys. Despite being a married layman, on 2 November Mason was presented by the crown to the deanery of Winchester. He had no chance for leisure, however, for in January 1550 it was reported that he was soon to be sent to France to negotiate peace. To enhance his diplomatic stature, on 19 April he was sworn of the privy council, and four days later he departed for France. By mid-June he was in Paris, and then joined the peripatetic French court. Negotiations dragged on (from Poissy to Blois to Amboise), while Mason complained repeatedly about the twin curses of early modern diplomatic life: ill health and poverty. His appeals to return to England were not ignored: by February 1551 he had been joined in France by his replacement, but the council ordered Mason to remain until a peace treaty was settled. At last, on 20 July 1551, a marriage treaty was concluded at Angers (between Edward VI and a daughter of Henri II), and a relieved Mason departed for England. By mid-September he was back at the council board, but one lasting legacy of his stay in Paris was the publication, which he had arranged while there, of Edward Wotton's treatise on botany, *De differentiis animalium* (1552).

Mason was an active member of the Edwardian privy council: hearing the case against Bishop Cuthbert Tunstall (1551); investigating tampering with the coinage (1552); and reporting on Irish mines (1553). His standing is illuminated by the fact that, after a by-election in Reading in which the borough had unsuccessfully tried to return a kinsman of Somerset, on 18 January 1552 Mason was certified as its new MP; he had no previous connection with the town. He also served as a clerk of parliament. In early 1553 he was to be sent as ambassador to the emperor, but excused himself as too old. As a councillor Mason witnessed the will of Edward VI which altered the succession, and was directly involved in the crisis which followed the king's death on 6 July. On 12 July Mason was chosen to meet the anxious imperial ambassadors to discuss the fate of Princess Mary, and the council's intentions. Despite his role as a spokesman, Mason was an astute political survivor and, realizing that Jane Grey's cause was doomed, quickly made his peace with Mary. Indeed, by 30 July he had joined Mary's privy council. Suspicions undoubtedly remained, for in early September reports circulated that Mason (and Paget) would retire from court. Before the month was over, however, Mason had been named to replace Thomas Thirlby as English ambassador to the emperor. In late 1553 Thirlby briefly returned to Brussels and Mason to England. Misfortune befell his family in early 1554 when two of his brothers-in-law were executed for their parts in Wyatt's rebellion, despite Mason's anxious appeals for clemency. None the less, he was elected MP for Hampshire to the parliament which opened on 2 April. He was in London on 15 April, but soon after returned to the Netherlands. Still mistrusted in some quarters, he was reported by the imperial ambassador that year to be hostile to Catholicism, yet in 1555 he was rumoured as a possible candidate for the post of chief secretary. Although opposed to Mary's proposed Habsburg marriage, Mason remained as ambassador to Charles V but he was in Windsor in March 1556 and finally recalled to England that summer. As a layman, and married, Mason was stripped of his ecclesiastical benefices that year and in October was compelled to resign his chancellorship at Oxford in favour of Cardinal Pole. However, he was compensated with a substantial pension. In October 1557 there were rumours that Mason, an active Marian councillor, would shortly replace William Petre as principal secretary, and on 31 October 1558 (not long before her death) the queen appointed him treasurer of the chamber. He served again as knight of the shire for Hampshire in that year's parliament.

Upon the accession of Elizabeth in November 1558 Mason was the sole senior household officer (treasurer of the chamber) to retain his post (and also the richest): testimony to his strong administrative ability and sound political judgement. Despite the distrust of some protestants, Mason also remained at the council board, where during the early weeks of the reign he pressed for peace with France, even at the price of abandoning claims to Calais. Elizabeth soon drew upon his considerable diplomatic experience, unhappy with the lack of progress by English negotiators at the peace talks at Cateau-Cambrésis. Dispatched to the conference in mid-March 1559 to deliver a royal rebuke to the English commissioners, Mason found that a treaty had been concluded a few days earlier. He was soon back in England as a councillor; rumours that he was to be sent as ambassador to Madrid came to nothing. While he was personally closer to his old friends Paget and Petre than to William Cecil, Mason's opposition to the secretary's intervention in Scotland and the Newhaven (Le Havre) expedition owed more to his pragmatism than to factional politics. Despite recurring bouts of ill health, Mason continued freely to offer counsel, warning of the perils of foreign military adventures and urging the queen to pursue peace. He last attended the council in June 1565. Meanwhile he was again MP for Hampshire in

the parliaments of 1559 and 1563, and was re-elected chancellor of Oxford in June 1559, serving until his resignation in December 1564.

Throughout his career Mason worked to protect and promote the interests of his native Abingdon. As a Berkshire chantry commissioner he was involved in the suppression of the Hospital of St Helen, which he later restored as Christ's Hospital (May 1553), serving as its first master. In 1549 Mason became steward of the lands of the dissolved abbey, and was a patron of the local grammar school. Although in 1551 he wrote to William Cecil opposing Abingdon's bid for a borough charter, it seems likely that he assisted in securing that charter in 1556, earning him the effusive praise of Francis Little in *A Monument of Christian Munificence* (1627), as one 'whose memory deserves and ought to be honoured with a statue advanced in the most conspicuous place of this town' (p. 47). During his final years he divided his time between his principal estate at Hartley Wintney and the house of his son-in-law Francis Spelman at Gunnersbury, Middlesex. The ambiguity surrounding Mason's religious views was shared by many of his colleagues, and continued to the end of his life: in 1564 the bishop of Winchester reported that he was favourable to true religion, while at his death the Spanish ambassador claimed he was a Catholic. There is no evidence of Catholicism in his will, in which he asked forgiveness for his sins from God 'who hathe saved us not according unto workes of Justice that we have doon but acording unto his Mercie' (PRO, PROB 11/49, fol. 10r). Among its many beneficiaries were his half-brother Thomas Wikes, or Wykes, of Drayton, near Abingdon, Thomas's children, and the children of another half-brother, John Wikes. His overseers were named as Secretary of State Sir William Cecil, the master of the rolls, Sir William Cordell, the archdeacon of Surrey, John Watson, and Robert Creswell. He died on 20 or 21 April 1566 and was buried in the north choir aisle of St Paul's Cathedral in London, where his widow and his heir, his nephew Anthony Wyckes (later Mason), erected a monument; his son Thomas had predeceased him, although he was survived by several stepdaughters.

The monument proclaimed that Mason had faithfully served four Tudor monarchs as ambassador and councillor, successfully weathering a succession of religious and political storms. His political longevity testified to his discretion in keeping his own counsel, and his adroitness in rendering himself indispensable to the crown. His diplomatic skill and personal affability were noticed by his contemporaries. On one occasion, during a dinner-table debate the scholar Roger Ascham observed how Mason, 'after his maner, was verie merie with both parties, pleasantlie playing both' (Ascham, sig. B1v). Mason himself claimed that his motto was 'do and say nothing' (BL, Sloane MS 1523, fol. 39). Yet he had consistently promoted scholarship, and his scholarly interests were praised by John Leland in his *Encomia*. He bequeathed at least a dozen volumes to the library of All Souls. P. R. N. CARTER

Sources D. G. E. Hurd, *Sir John Mason, 1503–1566* (1975) • *CSP for.*, 1547–53; 1558–9 • Emden, *Oxf.* • T. F. T. Baker, 'Mason, Sir John', HoP,

Commons, 1509–58 • A. Harding, 'Mason, Sir John', HoP, *Commons, 1558–1603* • *CSP Spain, 1538–58* • *LP Henry VIII*, vols. 6–21 • *APC, 1547–58* • will, PRO, PROB 11/49, sig. 2 • N. R. Ker, *Records of All Souls library, 1437–1600* (1971) • S. Alford, *The early Elizabethan polity: William Cecil and the British succession crisis* (1998) • W. T. MacCaffrey, *The shaping of the Elizabethan regime: Elizabethan politics, 1558–1572* (1968) • BL, Lansdowne MS 7 • BL, Sloane MS 1523 • R. Ascham, *The scholemaster* (1870) • BL, Add. MS 6128 • D. S. Chambers, ed., *Faculty office registers, 1534–1539* (1966)
Archives BL, Add. MS 6128
Likenesses H. Cheere, bronze bust, 1756, All Souls Oxf. • portrait, Christ's Hospital, Abingdon, Oxfordshire
Wealth at death £631 p.a. fees: PRO, SP 12/39/59

Mason, John (*b.* **1576/7**). *See under* Mason, Francis (1565/6–1621).

Mason, John (1586–1635), founder of New Hampshire, was born in King's Lynn, Norfolk, the son of John Mason and Isabel Mason (*née* Steed), and baptized there on 11 December 1586. His father was apparently the John Mason who in 1575 had bought his freedom of the borough. The records of Magdalen College, Oxford, suggest that some time before the younger John's matriculation there on 25 June 1602 the family had moved to Southampton. In 1606 he married Anne Greene (*d.* 1655), daughter of a London goldsmith. In 1610 he commanded a small fleet sent by James VI and I to help put down resistance to Scottish rule in the Hebrides. He fitted out the expedition at his own expense on the promise of reimbursement from the Scottish treasury, which never happened because of the death of the treasurer. His failure to gain immediate reimbursement may have been a factor in his appointment in 1615 as governor of Newfoundland, where a company of adventurers of London and Bristol had established a colony in 1610 in order to exploit the north Atlantic fishery. The title captain by which he is invariably known dates at least from this period if not earlier.

During his six-year governorship Mason oversaw the expansion of settlement, explored thoroughly, wrote an important promotional tract, and drew the first accurate map of the island. *A Briefe Discourse of the New-Found-Land*, his tract published in Edinburgh in 1620, helped persuade Sir William Alexander to sponsor a colony in Nova Scotia. After his return to England in 1621 Mason became closely associated with Sir Ferdinando Gorges, governor of Plymouth Fort and treasurer of the council for New England, and on 9 March 1622 became the second beneficiary of a grant of land from the council. This was a sizeable strip of land between the Naumkeag and Merrimac rivers, including Cape Anne, which Mason named Mariana. The entire grant is within the present bounds of Massachusetts; neither Mason nor his heirs ever successfully defended it against the conflicting claims of the Massachusetts Bay Company.

Later in 1622, however, Mason and Gorges became joint proprietors of the council's third grant in New England, a much larger piece between the Merrimac and the Kennebec called the province of Maine. The Spanish and French wars, 1624–30, during which he served as commissary-general in the expedition against Cadiz and then as treasurer and paymaster of the English armies, kept both

Mason and Gorges from moving ahead with their New England project at once. At the end of the war with France in 1629 the partners turned their attention once again to the province of Maine, and agreed to divide it between them. Mason took the part between the Merrimac and Piscataqua (or Pascataqua) rivers. Since he was living in Portsmouth, Hampshire, the place from which he had conducted his military and naval affairs during the wars and with which he and his family may have been associated before that, he named his province New Hampshire. The Council for New England confirmed the arrangement the same year by granting separate new patents for Maine and New Hampshire to Gorges and Mason respectively. Gorges and Mason, together with other associates, received two more joint grants, the Laconia patent in 1629, intended to forward the interior fur trade, and the Pascataqua patent of 1631. The first of these latter grants reflected a vague understanding of American geography. Both overlapped the adjoining provinces of Mason and Gorges and were of extremely short duration; both helped to stimulate settlement of the Piscataqua region under Mason's sponsorship.

Besides investing in his own province and sending over agents, settlers, equipment, and livestock, Mason became increasingly involved in colonial affairs in general. In April 1632 he warned the secretary of state, Sir John Coke, about trading encroachments by Dutch 'interlopers' on the coast between Cape Cod and Delaware Bay, and in June of the same year joined the Council for New England. The council thereafter met frequently at his London house in Fenchurch Street, which he maintained in addition to his house in Portsmouth. By the time of its dissolution in April 1635, three days after it issued a new grant to Mason for New Hampshire along with a 10,000 acre tract to the east to be called Masonia, he was the council's vice-president. At the same time as he was active in the council, he led the way in developing the fishery in the Hebrides and became treasurer of a company chartered for the purpose by the king.

In 1634 Mason was appointed captain of Southsea Castle, commanding Portsmouth harbour, and inspector of forts and castles on the south coast. In 1635 he was named a judge of the court of oyer and terminer for Hampshire, and appointed vice-admiral of New England, a position in what was intended as an elaborate viceregal government for all of New England to be headed by Gorges. Mason's death and a shipwreck prevented either man from sailing to put the plan into effect.

Mason died in London between 26 November and 22 December 1635 after providing in his will, dated 26 November, that the sons of his only daughter, Anne Tufton, should become the heirs to his New England lands provided they adopt the surname Mason. Only one of the grandsons, Robert Tufton Mason, lived to come of age. The subsequent history of New Hampshire until 1746 is in large measure the story of his ultimately unsuccessful efforts, and those of his representatives and heirs, to gain permanent and secure possession of the lands granted to his grandfather against the contending claims of politically powerful settlers. Mason's will was admitted to probate on 22 December. He is probably buried somewhere in Westminster Abbey in accordance with his wishes, but neither his grave nor a record of his burial has been located.   CHARLES E. CLARK

Sources J. W. Dean, *Capt. John Mason, the founder of New Hampshire* (1887) · DNB · CSP col., 1.28, 32, 102, 135, 138, 143–4, 153–4, 156, 204, 212, 214, 292–3 · J. R. Daniell, *Colonial New Hampshire: a history* (1981) · O. G. Hammond, 'The Mason title and its relation to New Hampshire and Massachusetts', *Proceedings of the American Antiquarian Society*, new ser., 26 (1916), 245–63 · Foster, *Alum. Oxon.*
Archives Berks. RO, warrant reciting that prize ship has been given to him in part satisfaction of debt owed by crown

Mason, John (*c.*1601–1672), army officer and colonial official, was born in England. His parentage and place of birth are unknown. He served in the Low Countries under Sir Thomas Fairfax, who reportedly wrote to him at the outbreak of the civil war to urge his return; in *A Brief History of the Pequot War* Mason mentions Grubbendunk, who commanded Bois-le-Duc ('s-Hertogenbosch) during the siege of 1629 (Mason, v, 3).

By 1632 Mason had migrated to Massachusetts, where he was appointed to chase away pirates harassing the coast. In 1633 he was promoted captain. Mason represented Dorchester at the first general court that included deputies (1635). Later that year he moved to Connecticut, where he helped to found Windsor. The influx of settlers into New England in the 1630s heightened tensions with Native Americans. After a series of skirmishes Connecticut voted to attack the Pequots. Mason led the expedition and persuaded Mohegans and Narragansetts to join him. The combined force attacked a Pequot fort at Mystic on 26 May 1637, slaughtering as many as 700 people, most of them non-combatants, in less than an hour. Fighting continued into the summer before ending in a resounding success for the English; most Pequots were either killed or captured to be sold into slavery within New England or elsewhere.

His role in the Pequot War ensured Mason's place as the premier military commander in Connecticut. Although a number of older sources state that Mason was elevated to the rank of major shortly after the war, contemporary references to him invariably style him as captain until 1654, major thereafter. The war apparently created in Mason an abiding loyalty to Uncas, a Mohegan leader who fought with him at Mystic. Mason repeatedly defended Uncas against other Indian leaders and even against his fellow colonists. Considered an expert on Indian affairs, Mason was called upon repeatedly to amass information about, give advice on, collect tribute from, or otherwise intimidate the Native Americans. Decades later, at the behest of the colony, Mason composed a history of the Pequot War, which was not published under his name until Thomas Prince saw it into print in 1736. Mason's account, as might be expected of a history commissioned by a 'puritan' Commonwealth, casts the war in a providential framework, glorying in the gruesome victory as a sign of God's approval. Along with other contemporary accounts it has fuelled a vociferous debate about the brutality of the English conquest.

Mason served on the Connecticut general court from 1637, rising from deputy in the 1630s to magistrate in 1642. Nothing is known of his first marriage except that it produced one daughter and ended in his wife's death in 1639. Later that year he married Anne Peck (1619–1671), daughter of Robert Peck, minister of Hingham, and Peck's first wife, Anne. After New Haven, Connecticut, Plymouth, and Massachusetts formed the United Colonies in 1642, Mason served repeatedly as a commissioner (1647, 1654–7, 1661). The Connecticut government requested that he move to Saybrook Fort in 1647. Mason and his family resided at Saybrook until 1659, when they helped found Norwich. This town stands in the heart of Pequot country, and settling it was part of an effort to keep that region under Connecticut's control. Mason had earlier laboured to prevent Indians from using the old Pequot hunting grounds, clashing with John Winthrop junior over the issue. He also defended Connecticut's interests against other colonies that laid claim to the region. The significance of the town and of Mason's role in it was not lost on the Indians, who reportedly attempted to assassinate him at the new town site in 1660. For his work on this and other colonial business Mason was frequently granted large tracts of land. He became deputy governor in 1660, a position which Charles II confirmed in the charter granted in 1662.

Mason's views contrasted with those of Roger Williams, who none the less called him his 'Honrd deare and ancient friend' (*Correspondence of Roger Williams*, 609). Unlike Williams, who traded with the Indians and learned their language, Mason may never have mastered Algonquian, and he invariably recommended military solutions to tensions, where Williams might work for peace. The two men also differed on religious toleration, a topic Mason thought unworthy of discussion. Late in life Mason advised his colony to drop its boundary dispute with Rhode Island. He wanted to avoid royal intervention, but he also worried that the settlers whom Connecticut would absorb by seizing the land from Rhode Island were unsuited to 'any Tollrable Christianlike society' (Ellis, 325–6).

Mason retired from public office in 1671, 'in Extream misery with the Stone or Strangury or some such desease' ('Bradstreet's journal', 9.46). He died on 30 January 1672. In 1889 Norwich residents erected a statue of a colonial-era soldier in Mason's honour. In 1996, after an extended controversy over celebrating a man guilty of genocide, it was removed and relocated elsewhere.

CARLA GARDINA PESTANA

Sources J. Mason, *A brief history of the Pequot War*, ed. T. Prince (1736) · *The correspondence of Roger Williams*, ed. G. W. LaFantasie and others, 2 vols. (1988) · 'Bradstreet's journal, 1664–83', *New England Historical and Genealogical Register*, 9 (1855), 43–51 · G. E. Ellis, 'Life of John Mason, of Connecticut', *The library of American biography*, ed. J. Sparks, 25 vols. (1834–48), vol. 13, pp. 309–438 · J. H. Trumbull and C. J. Hoadly, eds., *The public records of the colony of Connecticut*, 15 vols. (1850–90), vols. 1–2 · D. Pulsifer, ed., *Acts of the commissioners of the united colonies of New England* (1859), vol. 9 of *Records of the colony of*

New Plymouth in New England, ed. N. B. Shurtleff and D. Pulsifer (1855–61) · A. A. Cave, *The Pequot War* (1996) · *The journal of John Winthrop, 1630–1649*, ed. R. S. Dunn, J. Savage, and L. Yeandle (1996) · *DAB* · J. Savage, *A genealogical dictionary of the first settlers of New England*, 4 vols. (1860–62) · R. D. Karr, '"Why should you be so furious ?": the violence of of the Pequot War', *Journal of American History*, 85 (Dec 1998), 892

Mason, John (1646?–1694), Church of England clergyman and millenarian, was probably the son of Thomas and Margaret Mason, who were mentioned in the parish registers at Irchester, Northamptonshire, as the parents of Thomas (*b.* 3 April 1643) and Nicholas (*b.* 2 Feb 1644); an unnamed child of theirs referred to in March 1646 was probably John. Contemporary biographical sources suggest that Mason's early life was spent in Northamptonshire. Certainly Mason's contemporary biographer Henry Maurice mentioned a school in Strixton, where one teacher said of Mason 'that if he liv'd, he was like to be a violent Zealot' (Maurice, 25). On 16 May 1661 Mason was admitted as a sizar at Clare College, Cambridge, from where he graduated BA in 1665 and proceeded MA in 1668. It was at university that he began to fulfil the prediction of his former teacher, and was known to be 'but careless in some part of his Life there, that he would be sometimes starting of Questions, in reference to the usages of the Church of *England* (which seem'd to discover some dissatisfaction)' (ibid., 26).

From 1668 until 1674 Mason was the vicar of Stantonbury, Buckinghamshire. In this he seems to have been the beneficiary of the patronage of John Wittewronge, who had been a parliamentary officer in the civil wars. At the funeral of Wittewronge's daughter, Clare, on 22 October 1669 Mason preached a sermon (later published as *The Waters of Marah Sweetned* (1671), based on Hebrews 9: 27–8; this seems to be the first indication of his increasing interest in the second coming. It is unclear exactly when Mason married, but it was while he was at Stantonbury. He had a family of six children including John (1677–1722/3), who became a dissenting minister and whose son John (1706–1763) edited the *Select Remains of John Mason* in the 1740s; and William (1681–1744), who became a Church of England clergyman. In 1674 Mason became the rector of Water Stratford, Buckinghamshire, where he lived until his death.

In 1683 Mason published *Spiritual Songs, or, Songs of Praise*. This was extremely popular, going into its sixteenth edition in 1761. It is usually cited as among the first compositions in English hymnology. One can find elements borrowed from it in the works of Isaac Watts, and it allegedly influenced John and Samuel Wesley. However, the importance of song in Mason's beliefs suggests that the compositions have more significance than is usually thought. Mason 'was a rigid *Calvinist*, and not a little inclining to *Antinomianism*', and he also believed strongly in predestination (Maurice, 27). His interest in the millennium is hard to pinpoint. Maurice's account divides Mason's life into two separate stages: before 1690 he was a moral, hard-working, moderate cleric, 'a Man of severe Morals' (ibid., 26); Richard Baxter allegedly wrote that he was 'the

glory of the Church of England' (*Select Remains*, xii). Christopher Hill seems to concur with Maurice that between 1690 and his death in 1694 Mason became 'increasingly odd' (Hill, 332). However, some letters written by Mason, included in *Some Remarkable Passages in the Life and Death of Mr John Mason*, published in 1694, pre-date 1690 and suggest some continuity in his beliefs. Indeed, it was possibly in the 1680s that Mason first became interested in the millennium. Maurice wrote that it was the minister of the nearby town of Haversham, James Wrexham, who was 'the very Man that put him first upon *Revelation Thoughts*'; Wrexham owned a copy of one of John Henry Alsted's works of millenarian chronology (Maurice, 31). The catalyst for Mason's change has been seen as Wrexham's death and that of Mason's wife shortly afterwards in February 1687, both of which affected Mason greatly.

It is certainly around this date that Mason's fame seems to have been made by his preaching of a sermon based on the parable of the ten virgins, published in 1691 under the title *The Midnight Cry*. This is millenarian in tone and interprets apocalyptic passages of scripture in the light of events such as the Thirty Years' War. At the same time Mason started to preach exclusively on the subject of Christ's personal reign on earth, believing that this was to begin shortly in Water Stratford. He began to attract followers, and a community of about 100 gathered south of the village of Water Stratford in an area they named the Holy Ground. Here all possessions were shared, no work was done except that connected to basic survival, and singing and dancing were carried out continuously day and night. Song seems to have been an important part of Mason's eschatology. He believed that Christ 'would have all sorts of Musick to attend Him' (Maurice, 13), and so thought it fitting to have constant singing and dancing in preparation for his arrival. Music also heightened the spiritual process. His followers 'found great raisings of their *affections* by it' (*Some Remarkable Passages*, 5).

It was in this fervent atmosphere that at 1 a.m. on 16 April 1694 Mason had a vision of Christ. He appeared in 'a Crimson Garment, his Countenance exceeding Beautiful' with 'a deep *Scarlet Robe* down to his Feet' (Maurice, 6; *Some Remarkable Passages*, 1). This image is reminiscent of Revelation 19: 13, which described Christ as 'clothed with a vesture dipped in blood'. Mason believed that this appearance of the Son of God heralded the start of Christ's personal reign on earth—and as a result Mason stopped giving the sacrament, preaching, and praying. Mason saw himself in relation to the appearance of Christ and, indeed, his followers 'witnessed, That their Prophet was the very Person spoken of, *Rev.* 1.1. *He sent and signified it by his Angel to his servant John. ... Mr. Mason was that Elijah*' (Maurice, 10). Another spiritual predecessor cited by Mason was Noah, and Water Stratford was for Mason the ark where the elect would be safe until the Lord removed them to the New Jerusalem. Also, just as John the Baptist was the Elias who heralded the first appearance of Christ on earth, Mason was the Elias heralding his second coming. However, although Mason styled himself as the messenger and minister of Christ, there is a suggestion that his followers saw him quite differently, believing him to be Christ. Maurice's account of 1695, while sceptical of Mason's claims, does excuse him as a well-meaning but misled clergyman; however, towards Mason's followers Maurice is not so lenient: 'I can't forbear expressing my resentment and indignation against all such, as would rob, as would dethrone God, that they may Deifie a Man' (ibid., 59–60).

Mason published a number of minor works: *Dives and Lazarus*, which was appended to the 1685 second edition of *Spiritual Songs*; *A Little Catechism, with Little Verses and Little Sayings, for Little Children* (1692); and *Penitential Cries* (1692). He died from quinsy (possibly linked to the smoking that Maurice claimed he was fond of) in May 1694 at Water Stratford, where he was buried on 22 May. His community did not believe in his death, and Mason's successor, Isaac Rushworth, was forced to exhume his body to prove that he was not about to be resurrected. None the less, the community survived, still believing that Christ would return to earth. Although they were evicted from the land, remnants of the group existed until 1710 and even survived until about 1740.   K. HARVEY

Sources H. Maurice, *An impartial account of Mr John Mason of Water-Stratford* (1695) · *Some remarkable passages in the life and death of Mr John Mason* (1694) · Venn, *Alum. Cant.* · J. L. Myers, 'John Mason: poet and enthusiast', *Records of Buckinghamshire*, 7 (1892–7), 9–42 · B. Willis, *The history and antiquities of the town, hundred, and deanry of Buckingham* (1755), 344–5 · C. Hill, 'John Mason and the end of the world', *Puritanism and revolution* (1958), 311–23 · J. Bransby, *A brief account of the remarkable fanaticism prevailing at Water Stratford* (1835) · *The trial and condemnation of the two false witnesses* (1694) · M. Holms, 'On a mystical vision of Christ seen by John Mason', 1694, BL, Add. MS 34274, fols. 142–4 · *DNB* · *Select remains of John Mason*, ed. J. Mason (1745)

Mason, John (1706–1763), Independent minister and author, was born at Dunmow, Essex, the son of John Mason (1677–1723), an Independent minister. His grandfather was John *Mason (1646?–1694), vicar of Water Stratford, Buckinghamshire, the millenarian and hymn writer. He began his training for the ministry under John Jennings at Hinckley about 1722, but this was probably completed in London following Jennings's death in 1723. In the mid-1720s he became private tutor and chaplain to the family of John Feake, for several years governor of Bengal, at his seat near Hatfield, Hertfordshire. Mason commenced his first ministry in 1729 at West Street Independent Chapel in Dorking, Surrey, where on 10 April 1732 he married Mary Walters, daughter of the Revd James Walters of Uxbridge, Middlesex. He was pressed to move to a ministry at Uxbridge in 1744, but declined the offer.

In September 1746, however, Mason accepted the call to follow John Oakes as minister of the large congregation meeting at Crossbrook, Cheshunt, Hertfordshire, which had been formed in 1733 by a union of Presbyterians and Independents. He had come into prominence the previous year with the publication of his *Treatise on Self-Knowledge*, which quickly became one of the most popular works of moral advice and self-help of its time, with a popular appeal that lasted into the following century. By 1836 it had gone through more than twenty editions, both in

Britain and America, and had been translated into Welsh and several European languages. Many of the later editions varied greatly from the original version. It was 'esteemed by able and impartial judges, as one of the most useful treatises on practical piety that was ever written in English, or perhaps in any language' (Good, 9). In consideration of this book and his *Plea for Christianity* (1733) Mason was awarded an MA degree by Edinburgh University. This was probably conferred between 1746 and 1749 when the names were not recorded, as his name does not appear in the list of Edinburgh graduates.

Mason was considered a sound but not outstanding preacher. 'In the pulpit he pleased by a grave simplicity, but never rose to the higher excellencies of a preacher' (Bogue and Bennett, 2.590). His theological views, presented with a quiet determination, were conservative rather than radical, though he studiously avoided controversy. However, in private he was a lively conversationalist and expressed himself differently: 'his early works show that he was a believer in the trinity, which however he gave up some years before his death' (Good, 23).

While at Cheshunt, Mason prepared young men for the ministry, who had the benefit of his wide culture and learning. His attitude to study was encapsulated in *The student and pastor, or, Directions how to attain to eminence and usefulness in those respective characters* (1755), his second most popular work. The sound advice he offers is as valid today as it was in the mid-eighteenth century: 'Consult your own genius and inclination in the study you intend to pursue. You will else row against the tide, and make no progress that is either comfortable, or creditable to yourself' (*The Student and Pastor*, 22). His success as an author lay in an ability to explain his views in a popular way to an intelligent, if non-expert, eighteenth-century readership. His books on elocution (1748), the power of numbers (1749), and on becoming a minister of religion (1753) all went to several editions, and his sermons for both young and old also appeared in numerous volumes and editions. He published a book of the sayings of his grandfather, together with a memoir, in 1742, the content of which was praised in a foreword by Isaac Watts.

Mason continued in the ministry at Cheshunt until his death there of a chill on 10 February 1763. He was buried in the parish churchyard on 20 February, survived by his wife. His name was inextricably linked with his *Treatise on Self-Knowledge*, and his claim to fame rests on the sensible moral advice which he gave, linked with broadly accepted Christian principles. His chief tenet is summed up in the preface to early editions: 'The great end of all philosophy, both natural and moral, is to know ourselves and to know God. The highest learning is to be wise, and the greatest wisdom is to be good'.   ALAN RUSTON

Sources J. M. Good, 'Memoir', in J. Mason, *Self-knowledge, a treatise*, 14th edn (1802), 5–28 · *DNB* · E. E. Cleal, *The story of congregationalism in Surrey* (1908), 356 · *IGI* · J. Hodge, *Funeral sermon for John Mason, 20 Feb 1763* (1763) · D. Bogue and J. Bennett, *History of dissenters, from the revolution in 1688, to … 1808*, 2nd edn, 2 (1833), 590 · *Calendar of the correspondence of Philip Doddridge*, ed. G. F. Nuttall, HMC, JP 26 (1979), 197, 233, 242 · *BL cat.* [John Mason] · J. Julian, ed., *A dictionary*

of hymnology, rev. edn (1907); repr. in 2 vols. (1915), 717 • W. Musgrave, *Obituary prior to 1800*, ed. G. J. Armytage, 2, Harleian Society, 45 (1900), 306
Archives DWL, MSS

Mason, John Charles (1798–1881), East India Company servant, was born in London in March 1798, the only son of Alexander Way Mason, chief clerk in the secretary's office of the East India Company's home establishment, and one of the founders and editors of the *East India Register* in 1803. His grandfather Charles Mason served with distinction in the expedition to Guadeloupe in 1758–9 and with the allied army in Germany in 1762 and 1793–6. Mason was educated at Monsieur de la Pierre's Commercial School, Hackney, and at Lord Weymouth's Grammar School, Warminster. For three years he worked in the office of Dunn, Wordsworth, and Dunn, solicitors, at 32 Threadneedle Street, until, in April 1817, he received an appointment as a clerk in the secretary's office at East India House on the ground of his father's services to the company.

From 1817 to 1837 Mason was almost wholly employed upon confidential duties under the committee of secrecy: in 1823 in negotiating a treaty with the government of the Netherlands for the exchange of settlements in India and the Malay peninsula and archipelago, in 1829 in arranging the secret signals for the East India Company's ships, in 1833 in negotiating for the renewal of the company's charter, and in 1834 in advising the parliamentary inquiry on matters connected with China. The company granted him several gratuities for his confidential work, which included transcribing the secrecy committee's papers from 1829 to 1834. In 1822 he compiled an *Index to the Debates at the East India House, 1815–1822*; this was followed in 1825–6 by *An analysis of the constitution of the East India Company, and of the laws passed by parliament for the government of their affairs at home and abroad*.

In 1837, on a salary of £1000, Mason was appointed assistant in the newly formed marine branch of the secretary's office; under his management the Indian navy was improved and the coasts of India were surveyed. At the outbreak of the uprising of 1857 he expedited the transportation of 50,000 troops to India. In September 1858, upon the transfer of the government of India from the company to the crown, Mason retired from the service, but in January 1859 he was recalled to duty as secretary of the marine and transport department. The evidence he furnished to the select committees in 1860, 1861, and 1865 on the transport of troops to India led to his appointment in 1865 as the government of India's representative on the committee on the Indian overland troop transport service.

Mason retired in April 1867 with fifty years' service to his credit. With his wife, Jane Augusta (*d.* 1878), daughter of James Ensor, he had five daughters and an only son, Charles Alexander James (*b.* 1832), who in 1848 followed his father into the Indian home establishment. He became assistant secretary in the military department and retired in 1882. Mason died at his home, 12 Pembridge Gardens, Bayswater, London, on 21 December 1881.

G. C. Boase, *rev.* Katherine Prior

Sources *The Times* (24 Dec 1881), 1 • *The Times* (31 Dec 1881), 6 • home establishment records (accountant-general's department), BL OIOC, L/AG/30/12, L/AG/30/17/2 • *Allen's Indian Mail* (27 Dec 1881) • *Allen's Indian Mail* (2 Jan 1882) • *Allen's Indian Mail* (9 Jan 1882) • *Allen's Indian Mail* (18 Jan 1882) • *Homeward Mail* (27 Dec 1881) • *Homeward Mail* (9 Jan 1882) • private information (1893)
Archives JRL, corresp. and papers
Wealth at death £18,452 5s.: probate, 18 Jan 1882, *CGPLA Eng. & Wales*

Mason, John Monck (1726?–1809), literary scholar and politician, eldest son of Robert Mason of Mason-Brook, co. Galway, and Sarah, eldest daughter of George Monck of St Stephen's Green, Dublin, was born in Dublin. After attending Mr Young's school in Dublin, he entered Trinity College, Dublin, on 12 August 1741, graduated BA in 1746 and proceeded MA in 1761. He was called to the Irish bar from the Middle Temple in 1752 and in 1761 was elected to the Irish House of Commons. There he represented Blessington, co. Wicklow, from 1761 to 1768 and 1769 to 1776, and St Canice, co. Kilkenny, from 1776 to 1800. On 11 July 1766 he married Catherine, the second daughter of Henry Mitchell of Glasnevin, co. Dublin. They had no children.

In 1765 Mason was appointed a commissioner of barracks for Dublin, and in 1772 a commissioner of revenue, a position he held until 1795, whereupon he became a commissioner of the Treasury. In 1761 he had introduced a bill allowing Catholics to invest money in mortgages on land, which was rejected by the English privy council. The same bill failed when introduced again in 1772 and 1773. A staunch supporter of the administration, Mason became so unpopular that in 1779, during the free trade agitation, he feared for his life and would not attend the house. He was, however, gratified to be made a privy councillor on 23 December 1783. He retired in 1799 on a pension of £1200 p.a. and voted for the Union in the last Irish parliament.

Mason combined his parliamentary activities with a deep interest in Elizabethan drama. He first came to notice with a four-volume edition of the plays of Philip Massinger, an inauspicious beginning, as his edition was fraught with errors and was severely criticized. The reviewer for the *Gentleman's Magazine* (1st ser., 49, February 1779, 887–8) praised Tom Davies's account of Massinger, prefixed to the edition, but wasted no word on the edition itself. Not so the reviewer for the *Critical Review*, who was merciless from the first paragraph on. Acknowledging that he had never heard of Mason before but had learned that he was one of the commissioners of revenue in Ireland, he sincerely hoped that

> he has more knowledge of his *Majesty's customs* than those of the *drama*. To be plain, and to use the mildest terms we can think of, we do not remember, since the commencement of our literary labours, to have had any work pass through our hands, in which we have found such absolute insufficiency in an editor, joined with such perfect confidence and self-complacency. (*Critical Review*, 47, April 1779, 293–300)

Mason next planned a complete edition of Shakespeare's plays but was beaten to it by the publication of Isaac Reed's edition in 1785. Mason confined himself to *Comments on the Last Edition of Shakespeare's Plays* (1785), that consisted of remarks, notes, and corrections to Reed's text. In

John Monck Mason (1726?–1809), by Charles Knight, pubd 1791 (after Sylvester Harding)

the preface he blamed the errors in his edition of Massinger on 'the negligence of the person entrusted with the conduct of it' (J. M. Mason, *Comments*, x).

Mason's scholarly reputation and abilities were viewed ambivalently by his contemporaries. His fellow Shakespearian scholar, George Steevens, in the advertisement prefixed to his own edition of Shakespeare's plays of 1793, noted that he included 'a large proportion of Mr. Monck Mason's strictures on a former edition of Shakespeare', namely Reed's, although 'a small number of his proposed emendations are suppressed through honest commiseration' (*The Plays of William Shakespeare*, ed. S. Johnson and G. Steevens, 15 vols., 1793, 1.x). None the less, Steevens incorporated a number of Mason's notes in the edition. In a letter to Bishop Thomas Percy, dated 11 January 1788, Steevens blew hot and cold. Mason, he wrote,

is often ingenious and sometimes right; but occasionally outdoes even Dr. Warburton in absurdity of conjecture. There is also somewhat of ferocity in his manner which had better been avoided. Still, with all his extravagances, I must allow that he is a man of thinking and erudition. (Nichols, *Illustrations*, 7.1)

Percy, in a letter to Edmond Malone, dated 3 July 1785, told him:

We have a Volume of Criticism by M[r] Monck Mason, who never saw one ancient Edition. I have promised to lend him the 1 st and 3[d] folios, and some of the *Quartos*, &&. You will then see what he makes of them. (*Percy Letters*, 1.28)

If Mason made use of the folios, he did not think it incumbent upon him to acknowledge Percy's kindness when he re-edited his *Comments on … Shakespeare* in 1807. Francis Douce praised Mason's Shakespearian efforts, aligning him with Steevens, Malone, and Thomas Tyrwhitt, the

great editors of the eighteenth century, in his *Illustrations of Shakespeare and Ancient Manners* (1807). Mason's *Comments* of 1785 and 1807 have not been entirely forgotten by the editors of the twentieth-century variorum editions of Shakespeare's plays.

Mason also published *Comments on the Plays of Beaumont and Fletcher* (1798), which he dedicated to Steevens, despite their differences over the Shakespeare editions. This work won praise from the *Critical Review*, but Mason was criticized as 'rather deficient in his acquaintance with old English books—the only source from which our authors of the 17th century can be illustrated' (*Critical Review*, new ser., 32, June 1800, 155). He was a member of the Dublin Society from 1768 and of the Royal Irish Academy from 1792. He died in Dublin on 2 April 1809.

ARTHUR SHERBO

Sources DNB · Nichols, *Illustrations* · The Percy letters, ed. A. Tillotson, vol. 1: *The correspondence of Thomas Percy and Edmond Malone* (1944) · E. M. Johnston-Liik, *History of the Irish parliament, 1692–1800*, 6 vols. (2002), 5.201–3 · A. Sherbo, *The birth of Shakespeare studies* (1986)
Likenesses F. Wheatley, group portrait, oils, 1780 (The Irish House of Commons), Leeds City Art Gallery · C. Knight, engraving, pubd 1791 (after S. Harding), NPG [see illus.] · C. Knight, stipple (after S. Harding), BM, NPG; repro. in S. Harding, *Shakespeare illustrated* (1793)

Mason, Joseph (b. 1799?), farm labourer and radical, lived in the Hampshire village of Bullington, approximately 7 miles north of Winchester. Little is known about Joseph Mason or his brother **Robert Mason** (b. 1806?) but briefly in 1830–31 they came to public notice as participants in the Captain Swing rising.

Doubtless educated by their mother (b. c.1764)—a former schoolteacher who had taken pupils into her home—the Mason brothers were more adept at reading and writing than were most nineteenth-century farm workers. Joseph and Robert spent their days at work for neighbouring farmers and devoted their evenings to their rented small-holding of 3½ acres, where they kept bees, a cow, and some pigs. Living and working in what the radical journalist and farmer William Cobbett called the 'hard parishes' of northern Hampshire (Micheldever, Stoke Charity, Wonston, Sutton Scotney, Barton Stacey, and Bullington), where fuel was scarce and the soil flinty, the Masons were not prosperous but of above average means for farm workers: they maintained a comfortable subsistence without drawing upon the poor rates.

During their spare hours the Mason brothers took part in a local political club that convened in cottages and alehouses throughout their district. Club members, after partaking in beer and song, turned their attention to local and national politics, discussing in particular the radical reform programme that was set out in William Cobbett's writings, most notably the *Political Register*. At a meeting at Michaelmas 1830, held at The Swan inn at Sutton Scotney, the Masons and their colleagues adopted Cobbett's advice to petition the king for parliamentary reform. Joseph Mason was appointed to draft the petition, and in it he followed Cobbett's example of attacking sinecures in government, indirect taxation, tithes, and the national debt, and adding to these issues a variety of local grievances, particularly complaints about extreme hunger and poverty among Hampshire village workers.

The 1500-word petition, upon being signed by 176 workers from the hard parishes (at least eighteen of which would reappear on the indictment rolls of the Winchester special commission) was walked some 60 miles by Joseph Mason to the Brighton Pavilion, where William IV was in residence. Arriving on 21 October, Joseph was informed by the king's private secretary that the king would not receive the petition, and that it should be directed instead to the secretary of state for the Home department. Vexed at the fruitlessness of his journey, Joseph returned home, again by foot. On 13 November another meeting, attended by ten people, was convened at Sutton Scotney, this one angrier in tone because of the rejection of the petition at Brighton. Those present spoke of the 'sovereign people' and of the need for parliamentary reform; they also addressed the lowness of agricultural wages and the farmers' use of the labour-saving threshing machine.

Within a week of the 13 November meeting the hard parishes were in open revolt: crowds of village workers moved about breaking threshing machines, demanding increased wages, and aggressively requesting levies from farmers and passers-by. The principal role of Joseph Mason in the rising was to serve as spokesman for the crowd at the East Stratton estate of Sir Thomas Baring, where a £10 levy was peaceably obtained from the steward. Robert Mason—younger and rather more impetuous than Joseph—was more heavily involved in the protests; it was said at his trial that he led some of the wage negotiations with farmers and assisted in the selection of threshing machines for destruction.

For their involvements in the Captain Swing rising the Mason brothers were charged by the Winchester special commission with 'demanding money'. Sentences of death, commuted to transportation for life to New South Wales, were recorded. Joseph Mason, declared the judge Sir John Vaughan 'is a person moving in a better class, and ought to have set a different example. He, therefore, must not expect any further mitigation of his punishment than that of sparing his life' (A Report of the Proceedings at the Special Commission, 90).

It is clear from the correspondence of the Masons, as well as from the information gleaned about their lives and politics by William Cobbett, that landowners and the government were misguided about the character and motivations of some of the Swing rioters. In their correspondence from prison and later from Australia the Mason brothers expressed deep concern about the well-being of their widowed mother and of Joseph's daughter and wife, all of whom had lived with and depended upon the two brothers. Following their transportation, Joseph's wife was forced to go into farm service. Joseph and Robert also expressed anger and bitterness towards their accusers, particularly the landowner Sir Thomas Baring who they knew to have been active in seeking their conviction. The brothers were also disturbed by the extensive role of the local clergy in obtaining convictions against the rioters.

Subsequently Robert abandoned the church altogether and Joseph, upon arriving in New South Wales, turned from the established church to the Methodist chapel.

In New South Wales the Mason brothers were assigned a master who supplied them with employment, clothing, and housing. Robert was sent to Port Macquarie and Joseph to Parramatta, from where he wrote home about the fair wages and good food that he received. It was Joseph's view that his material life in Australia was much superior to that of his friends and fellow workers in Hampshire. Although pardoned in the mid-1830s along with most others who were transported for their involvement in the riots, the Masons appear to have remained in Australia for the rest of their days; nothing is known of their deaths.   IAN DYCK

Sources A. M. Colson, 'The revolt of the Hampshire agricultural labourers and its causes, 1812–1831', MA diss., U. Lond., 1937 · I. Dyck, William Cobbett and rural popular culture (1992), chap. 7, appx 2 · A report of the proceedings at the special commission, holden at Winchester (1831) · Calendar of prisoners, in the county gaol at Winchester, for trial at the special comission…December 18 1830 (1830) · Journals and correspondence of Francis Thornhill Baring, ed. Thomas George, earl of Northbrook [T. G. Baring] and F. H. Baring, 2 vols. (privately printed, Winchester, 1902–5) · W. Cobbett, 'To the Hampshire parsons', Cobbett's Weekly Political Register (15 Jan 1831), 144–65 · W. Cobbett, 'To the labourers of England', Cobbett's Weekly Political Register (2 April 1831), 1–23 · W. Cobbett, 'To the electors of England', Cobbett's Weekly Political Register (16 June 1832), 641–70 · W. Cobbett, 'To the working people', Two-Penny Trash, 11, 12 (July 1832), 265–88 · The Times (25 Dec 1830) · The Times (3 Jan 1831) · Hampshire Telegraph (3 Jan 1831) · A. Somerville, The whistler at the plough, 3 vols. (1852–3), 261–4

Mason, Sir Josiah (1795–1881), pen-nib manufacturer and philanthropist, was born on 23 February 1795 at Mill Street, Kidderminster, the second son of Josiah Mason, carpet weaver, and his wife Elizabeth Griffiths. At the age of eight he commenced selling cakes in the streets, and afterwards fruit and vegetables, which he carried from door to door on a donkey. He taught himself shoemaking in 1810, and was afterwards a carpenter, a blacksmith, and a house-painter. In 1814 he became a carpet weaver, and from 1817 to 1822 he acted as manager of the imitation-gold jewellery works of his uncle, Richard Griffiths of Birmingham. On 18 August 1817 Mason married the latter's daughter, his cousin Anne Griffiths (d. 24 Feb 1870). They had no children. Mason subsequently became manager of Samuel Harrison's business producing split rings in 1824, and a year later he purchased the business for £500. He then invented a device for making split keyrings by machinery, which proved to be profitable.

Other manufacturers, including John and William Mitchell and Joseph Gillott, had already commenced making steel pens, and in 1829 Mason also began to produce them. He made the acquaintance of James Perry, a stationer, of Red Lion Square, London, and acted as his pen maker for many years. These pens, however, bore the name of the seller, Perry, and not of the manufacturer, Mason. The first order of 100 gross of pens was sent to London on 20 November 1830. About twelve workpeople were employed, and up to 1 hundredweight of steel was rolled in a week. In 1874 one thousand persons were employed, the quantity of steel rolled every week exceeded 3 tons, and on an average one and a half million pens were produced from each ton of steel. By this time Mason had become the owner of the largest pen-nib manufactory in the world.

In 1844 George *Elkington (1801–1865) took out a patent for the use of cyanides of gold and silver in electroplating, and, requiring capital to develop the business, he and his cousin Henry Elkington were joined by Mason. The electroplated spoons, forks, and other articles soon came into use, and their popularity was much increased after the Great Exhibition of 1851. Having made a large sum of money in this connection, Mason retired from the firm in 1856. But, with Elkington, he also established copper-smelting works at Pembrey, Carmarthenshire, and became a nickel smelter. In December 1875 he sold his pen manufactory to a limited liability company. Mason died at Norwood House, Erdington, Warwickshire, on 16 June 1881. His estate was valued at £51,729 5s. 7d.

Much of Mason's wealth (estimated to be in the order of half a million pounds) had been spent on charitable causes during his own lifetime. In 1858 he founded almshouses in Erdington village for thirty aged women and an orphanage for fifty girls. Between 1860 and 1868 he spent £60,000 on the erection of a new orphanage at Erdington, and then, by a deed executed in August 1868, he transferred the edifice, together with an endowment in land and buildings valued at £200,000, to a body of seven trustees. This orphanage was capable of receiving three hundred girls, one hundred and fifty boys, and fifty infants, and remained in existence until 1960. On 30 November 1872 he was knighted. His most important work, the establishment of a scientific college at Birmingham, which cost him over £200,000, was opened on 1 October 1880, and in 1893 had 556 students. The purpose of the college was originally to provide instruction in science, but by 1881 the trustees were permitted to extend this to all branches of science, art, languages, and literature. Mason College was subsequently absorbed into the University of Birmingham, which was founded and incorporated in 1900. Mason's heraldic crest, representing a mermaid, forms part of the coat of arms of the university.

G. C. BOASE, rev. ERIC HOPKINS

Sources J. T. Bunce, *Josiah Mason: a biography* (1882) · [J. Hogg], ed., *Fortunes made in business: a series of original sketches*, 1 (1884), 129–83 · R. K. Dent, *Old and new Birmingham: a history of the town and its people*, 3 (1880), 524, 570, 591–3, 604 · *Edgbastonia*, 1 (1881), 48–9 · *Stationery Trades Journal* (28 Nov 1890), 604–5 · *ILN* (11 Sept 1869), 247–8 · *Illustrated Midland News*, 1 (1869), 8 · *Calendar of Mason College* (1892), 3–8 · E. W. Vincent and P. Hinton, *The University of Birmingham: its history and significance* (1947) · M. Cheesewright, *Mirror to a mermaid* (1975) · C. L. Penney, ed., *Sir Josiah Mason's Scientific College centenary* (1975) [exhibition catalogue, U. Birm., June–Oct 1975] · Boase, *Mod. Eng. biog.*

Archives Mason College, Birmingham | Birm. CA, records of orphanage management

Likenesses albumen print, pubd 1882, NPG · H. J. Munns, oils, U. Birm., Great Hall · F. J. Williamson, bronze statue, U. Birm. · portrait, repro. in *Illustrated Midland News*

Wealth at death £51,729 5s. 7d.: resworn probate, July 1882, CGPLA Eng. & Wales (1881)

Mason, Kenneth (1887–1976), geographer and mountaineer, was born on 10 September 1887, at Glenmore, Brighton Road, Sutton, Surrey, son of Stanley Engledue Mason, merchant, and Ellen Martin Turner. He was educated at Cheltenham and at the Royal Military Academy, Woolwich. At Cheltenham, he set his heart on the survey of India after reading Francis Younghusband's *Heart of a Continent*. He was commissioned second lieutenant in the Royal Engineers in 1906, and spent two years at the School of Military Engineering, Chatham, where he worked on the development of stereoplotting machines.

Mason was posted to Karachi to join the survey of India in 1909, and spent several years surveying in Kashmir. There he taught himself to ski, and he once considered himself the first person to bring skis to India. He also climbed many of the peaks between the Sind, Liddar, and Warwan valleys. In 1911–12, he climbed the highest peaks of the Kolahoi group (17,799 ft) with his shikari, Abdulla Bhat, and Ernest Neve, a medical missionary. After a colleague's death in 1912, he took over an extended survey of the Taghdumbash Pamir intended to link previous Indian and Russian surveys. With Captain R. W. G. Hingston, a doctor, and several Gurkha soldiers and Hunza porters, he spent 1913 in arduous work plotting peaks in the western Karakoram using stereoscopic photography.

During the First World War, Mason, by this time a captain, served in France (1914–15), where he was wounded at Loos, and in Mesopotamia (1916–18), where he was awarded the Military Cross during the relief of Kut. In the Tigris corps, he was promoted brevet major, thrice mentioned in dispatches, and became chief intelligence officer. On 25 June 1917 he married Dorothy Helen (1893/4–1974), daughter of Captain Arthur Robinson, Royal Engineers, at the garrison church of St George, Aldershot, Hampshire. They had two sons and one daughter.

After the war, Mason returned to India, and was disappointed not to be chosen for the early Everest expeditions. He began research in the records of the survey of India and published many papers on the history of surveying. In 1926 he led an expedition to survey the remote Shaksgam valley and the Aghil ranges in the Karakoram, areas that Younghusband visited in 1887. For this work, the Royal Geographical Society (RGS) awarded him the Cuthbert Peek grant in 1926, and the founder's gold medal in 1927. In 1928 he was appointed assistant surveyor-general of India, and, in 1929, deputy director of surveys. In 1928 he co-founded the Himalayan Club in Delhi, and its publication, the *Himalayan Journal*, became under his editorship from 1929 to 1945 an authoritative record of mountaineering in the Himalayas. He was superintendent of the survey of India in Burma during 1931–2.

Oxford had had a reader in geography (jointly funded by the university and the RGS) since 1887, a school of geography since 1899, and a graduate diploma in geography since 1900, but by the end of the Second World War the subject languished. It had few supporters within the university from either natural scientists or those in favour of 'modern humanities', and outside it its diploma holders faced stiff competition from geography graduates from other universities. By 1930 there were just seven candidates for the diploma, and numbers for the biennial summer school were also shrinking. In 1928 the committee for geography renewed its call for an honours degree in geography at Oxford and the university responded in 1930 by establishing a new honours school and a new chair, the first holder of which was Mason (1932–53). Mason retired as lieutenant-colonel to take up the chair and a fellowship of Hertford College. Although he had strong backing from the RGS, Mason was by no means an obvious choice for a department seeking to re-establish its academic credentials. In some ways he proved surprisingly successful. During his term of office the school was a success in numerical terms: it was first examined in 1933, by 1939 it had thirty-nine, or 4 per cent, of both men and women honours finalists, and it continued to grow rapidly after the end of the Second World War.

Mason also revitalized the links between geography at Oxford and practical service. These had begun with the RGS's involvement in the establishment of the discipline at Oxford and were fostered by Halford Mackinder and particularly his successor, A. J. Herbertson. Under Mason, with his extensive contacts in the military services, government, the city, and the RGS, the school consolidated its practical focus, linked to regional planning, surveying, exploration, teaching, and colonial service. A notable product was the Admiralty handbooks produced during the war when the school became an intelligence unit. Mason also had ambitious plans for establishing a geographical research institute partially funded by the Rockefeller Foundation: but although during his term of office the school's library grew, a large lecture hall was built, and the staff expanded, plans for a research institute, a second chair in geography, and a chair of planning attached to the geography school failed. Mason's own publications, such as they were, were wholly devoted to surveying and mountaineering and, except for Marjorie Sweeting, the staff he appointed were products of the Oxford school with little commitment to research and publication. The school was thus ill-equipped to conduct research of the type which was beginning in both other Oxford schools and other British geography departments.

Mason served the RGS as a council member (1932–45 and 1952–4), vice-president (1937–42), and briefly as acting president. He also served on the committee organizing the Everest expeditions from 1933 to 1940 and during this period the India Office frequently consulted him when deciding who should be given permission to scale peaks in the Himalayas. During the Second World War Mason was active in the inter-services topographical intelligence department located at Oxford, organized a series of *Admiralty Handbooks* on overseas countries, and co-authored a volume for naval intelligence on western Arabia and the Red Sea. After his retirement from Oxford in 1953, he published his *magnum opus*, *Abode of Snow* (1955), a valuable and encyclopaedic history of surveying and climbing in the Himalayas that epitomizes the early twentieth-century

view of mountaineering as exploration and conveys the allure of 'blanks on the map'.

Mason was also freeman of the Drapers' Company, City of London, and elected master in 1949. He was made an honorary fellow of the RGS (1965), honorary member of the Alpine Club (1973) and the French Alpine Club (1930), and an honorary fellow of Hertford College (1953). In the 1970s he was one of the interviewees for the BBC's oral history *Plain Tales from the Raj*. Contemporaries admired him as an attractive and accurate writer, an efficient administrator with a gruff military bearing, and as energetic, kindly, and generous. He died of renal failure and coronary thrombosis on 2 June 1976 at his home, Sylvanway, West End Road, Mortimer West End, Hampshire.

PETER H. HANSEN

Sources *The Times* (3 June 1976) · J. Morris, 'In memoriam: Lieut-Colonel Kenneth Mason', *Alpine Journal*, 82 (1977), 271–2 · *Himalayan Journal*, 34 (1974–5) · *GJ*, 142 (1976), 566–7 · *Mountain*, 54 (1977), 17 · *Mountain*, 53 (1977), 20 · A. F. Martin, *Geographical Magazine*, 48 (1975–6), 627 · A. Salkeld, 'Mapping the Himalaya: Kenneth Mason and the Indian survey', *Mountain*, 118 (1987), 38–43 · D. Scott, 'Foreword', in K. Mason, *Abode of snow* (1987), ix–xiii · C. Allen, ed., *Plain tales from the raj* (1975) · *Plain tales from the raj: a catalogue of the BBC recordings*, India Office Library and records (1981) · *Hist. U. Oxf.* 8: *20th cent.* · D. I. Scargill, 'The RGS and the foundations of geography at Oxford', *GJ*, 142 (1976), 438–61 · C. Firth, *The Oxford school of geography* (1918) · R. Symonds, *Oxford and empire: the last lost cause?* (1986) · P. Coones, 'The centenary of the Mackinder readership at Oxford', *GJ*, 155 (1989), 13–22 · *WWW* · b. cert. · m. cert. · d. cert.
Archives BL OIOC, L/PS/12/4236 · RGS | Bodl. Oxf., corresp. with J. L. Myres · Bodl. Oxf., corresp. with Sir Aurel Stein | SOUND BL NSA · BL OIOC, MSS Eur. R.42/1–7 · IWM, London, 004941/07 · SOAS, OAI/42/1–7
Wealth at death £44,428: probate, 30 July 1976, *CGPLA Eng. & Wales*

Mason, Martin (*fl.* 1655–1676), religious writer, was probably the son of John Mason (*d. c.*1675), 'gentleman', of St Swithin's, Lincoln. Mason's knowledge of Latin suggests a grammar school education. By 1655 he had become a Quaker, possibly 'convinced' during the visits of George Fox and William Dewsbury to Lincoln the previous year. Mason's first books were published in 1655. *A Check to the Loftie Linguist* refuted the assertions made by George Scortreth, a preacher at Lincoln Cathedral, in a debate with the town's sheriff, Robert Craven, whom Fox had convinced in 1654. Mason's other 1655 publication, *The Proud Pharisee Reproved*, attacked the Independent Edward Reyner's *Precepts for Christian Practice* (8th edn, 1655); Reyner, too, was a preacher at Lincoln Cathedral. Mason challenged the Baptist Jonathan Johnson in a letter (apparently lost), and then replied to his response in *The Boasting Baptist Dismounted* (1656). When Johnson renewed the debate in *The Quaker Quasht* (1659), Mason answered in *Sion's Enemy Discovered* (n.d. [1659]), arguing in part for the Friends' conception of the Christ who suffers within believers, enabling them to experience an unquenchable fire.

At the Restoration, Mason contributed to the chorus of Quaker advice to King Charles and parliament in two broadsides, *Charles, the King of England, the Infinite Being* (1660) and *To both Houses of Parliament* (2 November 1660), calling for religious toleration. In *A Faithful Warning, with Good Advice* (7 January [1661]), he protested against incarcerating the innocent, the conspiracy of priests and people against God's annointed, and charges that Quakers were plotters. England's rulers, he argued, should be nursing fathers to Zion, and should bury revenge in 'the grave of Eternal forgetfulness' (*Faithful Warning*, 6). By 2 February he was in the Lincoln town prison, where he composed *A Loving Invitation, and a Faithful Warning to All People*, complaining that innocency was now a crime and warning of imminent divine vengeance. Reflecting the Quakers' belief in the pre-eminence of spirit over word, he averred that recourse to the Bible could not save England; 10,000 bibles were nothing without Christ's presence. Dutch and German translations of the tract appeared the same year. From his prison cell he issued another work on 18 February, *Innocence Cleared*, defending the Friends' right to meet for worship, denouncing oaths, and espousing a view of government limited to preserving peace and curtailing wickedness. When the validity of a Quaker marriage was challenged in Nottinghamshire (*Ashwell* v. *Theaker*) Mason wrote to two judges of assize on 2 August 1661, arguing that refusal to recognize Quaker matrimony would undermine religion, make Quakers fornicators, and bastardize their children; the verdict upheld Quaker marriage. Mason joined John Whitehead in September 1662 in an appeal to bishops to reform themselves, their clergy and ecclesiastical courts, their parishioners, and their worship; restrained in tone, *An Expostulation with the Bishops* politely explained why Friends could not in good conscience belong to the Church of England. Two months later, writing against the background of Charles's proposed indulgence, Mason addressed *A Friendly Admonition* to Catholics, urging them to repudiate compulsion as an instrument of religion.

Imprisoned again by 20 March 1665, Mason published meditations entitled *One Mite More Cast into God's Treasury* (1665), condemning professional clergy and persecutors, and depicting Quakers as a handful of harmless people. Increasingly attracted to poetry, Mason completed a broadside in verse on 1 May 1665, *Love and Good-Will to All*, cautioning his adversaries that they strove against God, not the Friends. Physically ill, he consulted with the German physician Albertus Otto Faber in 1666–8, obtaining relief. By April 1669 he was again in the Lincoln prison; he was released by the royal pardon of September 1672. Among his fellow Quaker correspondents were Rebecca Travers (February 1671) and John Pennyman (April 1669). Mason's last published work was a tribute in verse to John Perrot, written on 17 October 1676 and printed on the back of the title-page of *The Vision of John Perrot* (1682). Perrot had challenged Fox's authority by claiming to have had a divine revelation against men removing their hats during prayer; for this, Fox accused him of destroying Quaker unity. Mason admired Perrot, and, like George Whitehead, espoused a moderate position on wearing hats during prayer, deeming the issue inconsequential. Mason saluted the spiritual power in Perrot's works:

In Shilohs Holy Ink thy Learned Pen
Was dipt, which Ravished the Sons of Men.
(*Vision of John Perrot*)

The date of Mason's death is unknown. He was apparently survived by his son, Martin, who was married in Lincoln on 29 July 1679. His daughter, Abigail, was interred in the Quakers' burial-ground in Lincoln on 4 April 1658.

RICHARD L. GREAVES

Sources J. Smith, ed., *A descriptive catalogue of Friends' books*, 2 (1867), 153–6 · *DNB* · *The Christian progress of that ancient servant and minister of Jesus Christ, George Whitehead*, ed. [J. Besse?] (1725), 358 · C. W. Horle, *The Quakers and the English legal system, 1660–1688* (1988), 234–5 · 'Dictionary of Quaker biography', RS Friends, Lond. [card index] · *The journal of George Fox*, ed. N. Penney, 1 (1911), 149, 423 [Robert Craven]
Archives RS Friends, Lond., MSS

Mason, Philip [*pseud.* Philip Woodruff] (**1906–1999**), administrator in India and writer, was born on 19 March 1906 in Finchley, London, the eldest son of Herbert Alfred Mason (1876–1968), general practitioner at Duffield, Derbyshire, and his wife, Ethel Addison Woodruff (1880–1956). He was educated at Stancliffe Hall, Derbyshire, Sedbergh School, and Balliol College, Oxford, where he graduated with a first-class degree in philosophy, politics, and economics and passed first into the Indian Civil Service in 1927. After remaining at Oxford for an additional year of study in oriental languages, he sailed to India in 1928 and served first in the Bareilly district of the United Provinces, followed by a brief spell as city magistrate of Lucknow. In 1933 he was transferred to the defence department of the government of India in New Delhi. There he met and on 6 June 1935 married (Eileen) Mary (1912–2000), daughter of Courtenay Hayes, of Charmouth, Dorset. They had two sons and two daughters. It was a perfect marriage which lasted for sixty-three years.

The Masons began their married life in Garhwal, a steeply mountainous district between Kashmir and Nepal, comprising 50,000 square miles with only 20 miles of motor road, where Mason was the deputy commissioner and mainly engaged in supervising the updating of the survey of land use on which government taxation was based. Six to nine months of every year were spent on tour, travelling on horseback and sleeping under canvas. His itinerary was well publicized, and those with grievances or petitions could intercept him as he passed. The more serious issues were referred to his campsite meetings in the evening. Garhwal became for him the epitome of imperial rule in rural India, of which the essential functions were to provide stability under the law and to protect the poor from the exactions of their landlords. This was an aspect of British India which neither E. M. Forster nor even Rudyard Kipling ever seriously addressed.

The Masons' four-year idyll ended with the outbreak of the Second World War, when Mason was recalled to Delhi; there he soon combined the duties of deputy secretary of the defence department and secretary of the chiefs of staff committee. This brought him into daily contact with Auchinleck and Wavell, and when, in 1944, Mountbatten was appointed as supreme allied commander for south and south-east Asia, Mason was seconded by the Indian

Civil Service to serve him in the same capacity. The 'Supremo's' daily meetings were apt to last half the day and when emerging from one of them, a senior general was heard to say, 'I have no idea what we decided, but Philip will tell us' (Mason, *A Shaft of Sunlight*, 194–5). He was appointed OBE in 1942 and CIE in 1946.

The British decision to leave India at the earliest possible moment after the end of the war caused Mason no personal dismay. He approved of the policy, and he had in any case long decided to retire from the Indian Civil Service after the twenty years needed to earn a pension. He was not prepared to face separation from his four children and he hoped to live by farming a smallholding in England and developing it as the home base for a mainly literary second career. During his later years in India he wrote stories and novels for recreation, using as a pseudonym his mother's maiden name of Woodruff. One early novel, entitled *Call the Next Witness* (1945), owed much to his experiences as a young magistrate. Another, *The Wild Sweet Witch* (1947), was set in a mountain district reminiscent of Garhwal. The writer Peter Fleming, a frequent visitor to Delhi during the war, introduced Mason to the publisher Jonathan Cape, who accepted his manuscripts with enthusiasm.

The Masons finally returned to England in 1947, and found the smallholding of their Indian dreams on the hills overlooking Charmouth, Dorset. As an economic enterprise it soon proved a failure but, remarkably, Mason's four years as a farmer were also his most prolific as a writer. During them he wrote five novels, a film script, and the first draft of what became his best-known book: a collection of attractively written biographical studies of leading figures in the establishment of the British empire in India. It appeared first in two volumes as *The Founders* (1953) and *The Guardians* (1954) under the pseudonym Philip Woodruff, but from 1985 and in later editions as *The Men who Ruled India*, signed, like all his later works, with his own name. By this time the Masons had moved from the Dorset farm to the Lyon House at Sherfield English near Romsey; accessible enough for mid-week work in London, it remained their home until 1970.

In 1952 Mason found the part-time employment he needed at the Royal Institute of International Affairs (Chatham House) as director of studies in the experimental and still poorly defined area of race relations. It was the period when the scale of the post-war immigration of people from the Caribbean colonies was becoming politically sensitive; at the same time people were continuing to emigrate in some numbers from Britain to eastern, central, and southern Africa, under the illusion that they and their descendants would remain permanently privileged within the 'multiracial' societies emerging there. It was Mason's business both to undertake research himself, and to seek out and help steer to publication scholarly work in a variety of disciplines which might assist public discussion of these problems. For his own first study he chose Southern Rhodesia, then seeking to extend its influence into Northern Rhodesia and Nyasaland to form a central

African federation. In *The Birth of a Dilemma* (1958), he presented brilliantly the predicaments involved in creating a colony of settlement within territory already well occupied by indigenous peoples. The successor volume, *The Two Nations* (1959), which dealt with the period of colonial rule, he left to a younger colleague, but he contributed the third and most topical study, *The Year of Decision* (1960), published just as the federation was about to break up. Meanwhile in London the scope of Mason's work was outgrowing the capacity of Chatham House to support it, and its sponsors there encouraged the emergence of an independent institute of race relations, able to seek its own funding from the great international foundations. This came into being in 1958, and its first large project was the report *Colour and Citizenship in Britain* (1969), by E. J. B. (Jim) Rose and Nicholas Deakin. Thereafter Mason's own interests moved increasingly to Latin America, where he set in motion several studies and summed up their main conclusions in *Patterns of Dominance* (1970), the last of his books written for the institute before he retired as director in 1969.

Their children having by this time grown up, the Masons moved in 1970 to Hither Daggons, a charming, isolated farmhouse in the wooded hills of the Hampshire and Dorset border, west of Fordingbridge. There Mason wrote all but one of his nine later books, which included *A Matter of Honour* (1974), a short history of the Indian army; *The Glass, the Shadow and the Fire* (1975), a life of Rudyard Kipling; *The Dove in Harness* (1976), based on his Bampton lectures given at Oxford in 1975; and two delightful volumes of autobiography, *A Shaft of Sunlight* (1978) and *A Thread of Silk* (1984). It was there also that the Masons came to feel the need to change their religious allegiance. Hitherto they had been devout, high-church Anglicans, always finding enough people round them who shared their outlook. But as they moved deeper into the English countryside, among Anglicans of every degree of belief or none, they began to feel themselves to be 'schismatics within a schismatic church'. The conviction crystallized in 1978, when they were on holiday in Venice, where they sat together in rapt contemplation of Titian's great altarpiece of the Assumption in the church of the Frari. He said to her, 'I believe in that picture.' Soon after their return home he said to her at breakfast, 'Why not now?', and she replied 'Why not, indeed? I was thinking just the same' (Mason, *A Shaft of Sunlight*, 196–7). They joined the Roman Catholic church in the following year. It was a characteristic decision, swiftly taken, even after half a century of searching, and it was adhered to with confidence to the end. In 1996 Mason published *Since I Last Wrote*, a collection of his essays contributed to *The Tablet*.

In 1987 the Masons were constrained by failing health and oncoming blindness to leave Hither Daggons, first for a flat in Fordingbridge, and then for the home of their daughter Sarah Irons and her doctor husband at 97 Glebe Road, Cambridge, where Mason died on 25 January 1999. He was buried at the city cemetery, Newmarket Road, Cambridge, on 2 February. His wife died on 26 April 2000. They were survived by their four children.

In his public life Mason was very much an 'establishment' figure, working from an office in Jermyn Street and dispensing genial hospitality at the Athenaeum or the Travellers' Club to those able to help the Institute of Race Relations with intellectual or financial contributions. In contrast his private life was private indeed, concentrated on family and garden and books, and on the daily struggle with the written word. In his later years he usually described himself as a writer, and certainly what flowed from his pen was always beautifully written and effortless to read. In all his writings he addressed himself to people of experience in every walk of life.   ROLAND OLIVER

Sources P. Mason, *A shaft of sunlight* (1978) · P. Mason, *A thread of silk* (1984) · R. Oliver, *In the realms of gold* (1997) · *The Times* (1 Feb 1999) · *The Independent* (2 Feb 1999) · *The Guardian* (3 Feb 1999) · *WWW* [forthcoming] · personal knowledge (2004) · private information (2004) [Sarah Irons, daughter; and others]
Archives Borth Inst., typescript history of Institute of Race Relations and related papers | Bodl. RH, corresp. with M. Perham and related papers
Likenesses double portrait, photograph, 1937 (with his wife, Mary), repro. in *The Independent* (2 Feb 1999) · photograph, 1965, repro. in *The Guardian* · photograph, repro. in *The Times*

Mason, Richard [*name in religion* Angelus à Sancto Francisco] (**1599/1600–1678**), Franciscan friar, was reputedly born in Wiltshire. Of his parents it is known only that his mother, who died in Limerick before 1656, was a resolute Roman Catholic. In the preface to his later *Apologia pro Scoto Anglo* (1656) he recalled his ordination by an Irish Catholic bishop (about 1624) and appointment as dean of Emly. However, about 1630 he left the secular priesthood to become a Recollect friar, a Franciscan of strict observance. Having gone to the friary–seminary of St Bonaventure at Douai, he was approved for missionary work in England in 1632 but was recalled two years later to become vicar and novice-master at St Bonaventure's, dedicated to serving the needs of the English mission. 'A man of great energy and resourcefulness' (Allison, 20), he inspired a burgeoning of literary activity there to which he contributed four titles during the 1630s: his translation into English, *The Rule and Testament of the Seraphical Father S. Francis* (1635), the first edition of his handbook *A Manuell of the Arch-Confraternitie of the Cord of the Passion* (1636), and two Latin works, *Sacrarium privilegiorum quorundam seraphico patri S. Francisco … indultorum* (1636) and *Questionum theologicarum resolutio* (1637).

In 1637 Mason became superior or guardian of St Bonaventure's and professor of theology there. He helped the third order nuns of Brussels to escape the plague and high prices of that city by moving to Nieuwpoort in Flanders. He continued to assist them there as commissary concerned with the English Franciscan province's subjects in the Southern Netherlands from 1640 to 1646. He dedicated to their abbess the second part of *The Rule of Penance of the Seraphicall Father S. Francis* (1644), the first part having been dedicated to the Franciscan provincial, John Gennings. His translation of *A Manuall of the Third Order of … St Francis* (1643) was dedicated to the dowager Countess Rivers. He also acted as visitor of the Franciscan province of Brabant and presided at the meeting of its chapter.

Mason may have been briefly in England in 1647 acting as a definitor assisting the provincial but by that October he was again guardian of St Bonaventure's as he still was two years later according to the title page of his celebrated account of the English Franciscan province, *Certamen seraphicum provinciae Angliae pro sancta Dei ecclesia* (1649). Here he treated of three aspects of the English Franciscan experience: mission, martyrdom (including the recent execution of four confrères), and the apostolate of the printed word. He published a second edition of his *Manuell of the Arch-Confraternitie* in 1654, relating to a sodality for lay people associated with the Franciscans and flourishing in the English midlands by 1657 with 'cordbearers' listed in surviving records. His *Apologia pro Scoto Anglo* (1656) was an entry into the debate on the origins of the Franciscan theologian John Duns Scotus.

The 1650s found Mason in England again—he writes from London in 1653—and was again a definitor involved in running the province. Latterly lauded for his fruitful exertions in the English vineyard he became provincial in 1659 for a *triennium* during which his brethren created him a doctor of divinity. *En route* for the 1661 general chapter of the order in Spain he visited a colony of nuns from Nieuwpoort in Paris beset by jurisdictional difficulties from which he extricated them by smoothing their path to a different order.

Mason was at Douai in 1663 but for much of the next decade he was at Wardour, Wiltshire, the only Franciscan in the Arundell family's long roll of Catholic chaplains. He served as chaplain to Henry, third Lord Arundell, who had links with the order both as a financial intermediary and through having a daughter and a niece in the Poor Clare convent in Rouen. In dedicating to his patron *A Liturgical Discourse of the Holy Sacrifice of the Mass* (first part published 1670, second part 1669) Mason extolled his piety and his royalist role in the civil wars. An abridgement has a dedication to Lady Arundell acknowledging her many kindnesses and her religious zeal. This, the final item of Mason's forty-year output of printed words, appeared in 1675, his last year in England whence, 'that he might live for God in his old age' as he put it (Thaddeus, 272) he retired to St Bonaventure's, where he died on 30 December 1678 aged seventy-eight. He was buried at the English Recollects' church at Douai.   J. ANTHONY WILLIAMS

Sources Angelus à Sancto Francisco [R. Mason], preface, *Apologia pro Scoto Anglo* (Douai, 1656) · Father Thaddeus [F. Hermans], *The Franciscans in England, 1600–1850* (1898) · W. F. Skehan, *Priests of Cashel and Emly* (1991) · R. Trappes-Lomax, ed., *The English Franciscan nuns, 1619–1821, and the Friars Minor of the same province, 1618–1761*, Catholic RS, 24 (1922) · J. Gillow and R. Trappes-Lomax, eds., *The diary of the 'blue nuns' or order of the Immaculate Conception of Our Lady, at Paris, 1658–1810*, Catholic RS, 8 (1910) · A. F. Allison, 'Franciscan books in English, 1559–1640', *Biographical Studies*, 3 (1955–6), 16–65 · D. Rogers, 'The English recusants: some mediaeval literary hints', *Recusant History*, 23 (1996–7), 483–507 · A. F. Allison and D. M. Rogers, eds., *The contemporary printed literature of the English Counter-Reformation between 1558 and 1640*, 2 vols. (1989–94) · Gillow, *Lit. biog. hist.* · W. P. W. Phillimore, J. L. Whitfield, and J. H. Bloom, eds., *Franciscan registers of St Peter's, Birmingham* (1904–6), vol. 3 of *Warwickshire parish registers* · J. Berchmans Dockery, *Christopher Davenport: friar and diplomat* [1960] · A. M. C. Forster, 'The chronicles of the

English Poor Clares of Rouen [pts 1–2]', *Recusant History*, 18 (1986–7), 59–102, 149–91 • T. H. Clancy, *English Catholic books, 1641–1700: a bibliography*, rev. edn (1996) • P. Guilday, *The English Catholic refugees on the continent, 1558–1795* (1914) • J. A. Williams, *Catholic recusancy in Wiltshire, 1660–1791* (1968)

Likenesses M. Baes, portrait, repro. in Angelus à Sancto Francisco [R. Mason], *Sacrarium privilegiorum quorundam seraphico patri S. Francisco* (Douai, 1636)

Mason, Robert (1579–1635), lawyer and politician, was the son of Stephen Mason of Kingsclere, Hampshire. He was admitted to Lincoln's Inn on 26 February 1592, was called to the bar in 1617 and made a bencher of Lincoln's Inn in 1633. Mason married twice: his first wife was Edith, daughter of John Foyle of Dorset, and his second Hester, daughter of Edward Richards of Yaverland on the Isle of Wight.

Mason was the author of *Reasons Monarchie* (1602), a work on the nature of reason, dedicated to Sir John Popham, chief justice of king's bench, which ends with some verses entitled 'The Minds Priviledge'. In 1605 he published *Reasons Academie*, at the end of which are some verses entitled 'Reasons Moan', attributed to Sir John Davies. The book was reprinted in 1609 under the title *A Mirrour for Merchants with an Exact Table to Discover the Excessive Taking of Usurie*. In 1616 Mason was secondary of the Poultry Compter prison in London, but for most of his career his main offices lay in his home county, where he served as steward and recorder of Basingstoke from 1624, recorder of Winchester from 1628, and recorder of Southampton from 1633. He acted as legal counsel to Winchester Cathedral and to the earl of Southampton (to the latter he also lent money). In 1627 he received a commission of oyer and terminer for Southampton, renewed in 1635.

Mason's parliamentary career began in 1626 with his return for Ludgershall, Wiltshire, contested and upheld in a by-election. He supported the Commons in their proceedings against George Villiers, duke of Buckingham, together with Sir Benjamin Rudyerd assisting Mr Herbert in the delivery of the impeachment charges to the Lords on 3 May, and later motioning for the commitment of the duke. On 17 May, following the imprisonment of Sir John Eliot and Sir Dudley Digges for their speeches at a joint conference, Mason spoke eloquently of the privileges of parliament men, noting that 'We sit not here as private men but as public vessel[s] for the commonwealth's service' (Bidwell and Jansson, 3.271). In 1628 he was returned for Winchester. His parliamentary maturity is apparent by 1628. He spoke frequently and assisted at several conferences related to the drafting of the petition of right. Arguing passionately against the use of martial law in peacetime, against unparliamentary taxation, and for cause to be shown on warrants he said 'We sit here not only to take men out of jail but to keep them free' (Johnson and others, 3.188). His speeches are masterpieces of legalese honed and shaped for fellow lawyers. While serving in the Commons he was counsel for Sir Simeon Steward and in 1629 defended Sir John Eliot in his case against the crown. Throughout the early 1630s there is little evidence of the pattern of his career. He was greatly respected by Attorney-General Noy and in 1634, in the heat of the ship-money controversy, the king appointed him recorder of London. In that capacity he was ordered by the council to appear before them regularly with an account of London moneys raised for ships. His term as recorder was short but the judge Sir Richard Hutton wrote that Mason was a good recorder, and a man of great intelligence whose death would be lamented (*Diary*, 106). Mason died in London on 20 December 1635 and was buried in Winchester Cathedral on 6 January 1636. His contribution to the *Perfect Conveyancer, or, Several Select and Choice Presidents Collected by Four Sages of the Law, Ed. Hendon, Robert Mason, Will. Noy, and Henry Fleetwood*, was published posthumously in London in 1650.

Mason is not to be confused with two namesakes. Confusingly, Robert Mason (*b.* 1570/71) of Shropshire also entered Lincoln's Inn in the 1590s; following his matriculation at Balliol College, Oxford, in 1591, he was admitted to Lincoln's Inn on 8 October 1597. **Robert Mason** (1588x90–1662), civil lawyer, was the son of George Mason of New Windsor, Berkshire, and his wife, Barbara, daughter of John Parkins of Flintshire. He was admitted a scholar of St John's College, Cambridge, in 1606, graduating BA in 1610 and proceeding MA in 1613; his MA degree was incorporated at Oxford in 1617. He was a fellow of his college from 1610 to 1632 and senior proctor of the university in 1619–20. In 1626 he was actively involved in the election of the duke of Buckingham as chancellor of the University of Cambridge and sat in parliament as MP for Christchurch, Hampshire. He served as Buckingham's secretary on the expedition to the Île de Ré the following year. His fidelity to the duke was rewarded by a legacy of £500 in the latter's will and his creation as LLD by royal mandate in 1628. In 1629 he was granted full admission to Doctors' Commons. He subsequently held positions in the ecclesiastical and admiralty courts. He served as chancellor of the diocese of Winchester from 1628 until the civil war and as commissary of the archdeaconries of Surrey and Winchester. At the Restoration he was restored to Winchester and also became chancellor of the diocese of Rochester. He served on the admiralty courts in London and Hampshire and was a commissioner for piracy in both places. He was appointed a master of requests about 1635. On 11 July 1633 he married Judith, daughter of Sir Charles Buckle. He died and was buried at Bath in 1662, leaving his library to St John's College, Cambridge.

MAIJA JANSSON

Sources W. R. Prest, *The rise of the barristers: a social history of the English bar, 1590–1640* (1986) • W. P. Baildon, ed., *The records of the Honorable Society of Lincoln's Inn: admissions*, 1 (1896), 125 • W. B. Bidwell and M. Jansson, eds., *Proceedings in parliament, 1626*, 4 vols. (1991–6), vol. 2, p. 246; vol. 3, pp. 204, 271 • *APC, 1627*, 318 • *CSP dom., 1634–5*, 221, 241, 466; *1635*, 319 • R. C. Johnson and others, eds., *Proceedings in parliament, 1628*, 6 vols. (1977–83), vol. 2, pp. 364, 461; vol. 3, pp. 123, 188 • R. R. Sharpe, *London and the kingdom*, 3 vols. (1895), vol. 3, pp. 113–14 • *The diary of Sir Richard Hutton, 1614–1639*, ed. W. R. Prest, SeldS, suppl. ser., 9 (1991), 106 • B. P. Levack, *The civil lawyers in England, 1603–1641* (1973), 253–4 • J. G. Nichols and J. Bruce, eds., *Wills from Doctors' Commons*, CS, old ser., 83 (1863), 91 • will, PRO, PROB 11/170, fols. 103–104v • *The obituary of Richard Smyth … being a catalogue of all such persons as he knew in their life*, ed. H. Ellis, CS, 44 (1849) • J. Baigent and J. E. Millard, *A history of the ancient town and manor of Basingstoke* (1889)

Wealth at death see will, PRO, PROB 11/170, fols. 103–104v

Mason, Robert (1588x90–1662). *See under* Mason, Robert (1579–1635).

Mason, Robert (*b.* 1806?). *See under* Mason, Joseph (*b.* 1799?).

Mason, Stewart Carlton (1906–1983), educational administrator, was born on 28 February 1906 in St John's Wood, London, the only child of Carlton Willicomb Mason, musician, and his wife, Alys Kastor. Educated at Uppingham School, but denied family support because of his desire to teach, he was able to take up an exhibition at Worcester College, Oxford, where he read Spanish and French, only through the generosity of a wealthy patron. Accordingly, after graduating in 1928 he taught first at Berkhamsted (1930–31) and was then a modern languages master at Harrow School under Cyril Norwood, whom he greatly admired. In 1937, momentously as it turned out, he joined the inspectorate and as an inspector in Cambridgeshire was deeply impressed by the work of the chief education officer, Henry Morris.

In 1941 during wartime secondment to the Admiralty, a first marriage having been dissolved, Mason married Ruth Elizabeth Wise; they had four sons. In 1944 he went as inspector to Leicestershire, from where his family originated and where the chief education officer, Sir William Brockington, was in his seventies. Seizing his opportunity, there being no deputy director, he virtually compiled single-handedly the authority's development plan for implementing the 1944 Education Act and duly succeeded Brockington in 1947.

Something of a mystic, Mason was convinced that 'all the fates' had determined this almost unprecedented career reorientation and he eagerly set about guiding this nominally conservative but largely non-political shire authority through the immediate post-war years. During his first decade, supported by the paternal Sir Robert Martin, chairman of both the county council and the education committee, he laid the foundations of what became a vast collection of fine art for the embellishment of schools, while, at the same time, designating strategically placed 'community colleges' on the Cambridgeshire model. Simultaneously, he supported his music adviser, Eric Pinkett, in the creation of the internationally renowned Leicestershire Schools Symphony Orchestra. He encouraged the primary schools, meanwhile, to adopt the progressive practices which had enchanted him at the village school at Quy in Morris's Cambridgeshire—practices which attracted many American observers to Leicestershire in the 1960s.

Hitherto Mason had unquestioningly supported the tripartite structure of post-1944 universal secondary education but, gradually, he became disturbed by the injustices that eleven-plus grammar-school selection could impose on families, including his own. Accordingly, in March 1957, after much pondering, he persuaded the authority to accept a 'limited experiment' in a two-tier system of secondary education which, consisting of high schools for those aged eleven to fourteen and upper (grammar) schools for those aged fourteen to eighteen, not only eliminated the dreaded selection examination but also effectively guaranteed access to grammar schools to all children whose parents promised to keep them there until the age of sixteen. By 1969 the 'Mason plan', described in his booklet *The Leicestershire Experiment and Plan* (1960; rev. edn, 1964), covered the whole county—the first shire authority to turn comprehensive; it was Mason's finest achievement.

In 1959, with Leicestershire's reputation as a patron of fine art fully established, Mason was invited to serve on the National Advisory Council on Art Education and virtually began a second career. First as vice-chairman (1961–70) and later chairman (1970–74) of the National Council for Diplomas in Art and Design he not only presided over the reorganization of art education but, believing, as an employer of artists in a qualification-conscious world, that artists needed degrees, led it against virulent opposition into the mainstream of higher education via the Council for National Academic Awards. He also served on both the advisory council of the Victoria and Albert Museum (1961–73) and the Standing Commission on Museums and Galleries. Similarly, at regional level he chaired the visual arts panels of both the East Midlands Arts Association (1971–5) and, having retired to Suffolk, the Eastern Arts Association (1972–80), where he converted the local Tolly Cobbold art exhibition into a national competition for contemporary artists.

Significant though these activities were, however, Mason's greatest and most lasting achievement outside the education field was made as a trustee of the Tate Gallery (1966–73), when in the summer of 1972, salvaging a previously abandoned scheme, he engineered the establishment of the Institute of Contemporary Prints at the Tate under the Sir Robert McAlpine Trust. Through the generosity of donors and Mason's assiduity as curator (1972–6) in approaching artists, some 3000 prints were acquired which the gallery could never have afforded to buy. Whereas print acquisition hitherto had been the province of the Victoria and Albert and British museums, the Tate now had its own core collection; a fitting memorial to Mason's work on behalf of both artists and the art-loving public.

Mason died of spinal cancer at St Mary's Hospital, Paddington, London, on 23 November 1983, survived by his wife. He was fortunate to have been ideally placed to exploit the massive post-war educational expansion at a time when local education authorities provided scope for people with vision. Not everything he touched turned to gold, however, and in the harsher climate of subsequent decades some of the innovations in both primary and secondary schools that he encouraged may have appeared controversial and even ill-advised. There was also a protracted dispute between himself and Robin Pedley, a lecturer in education at Leicester University, over the origins of the idea of the two-tier system of secondary school reorganization. His adversarial style, moreover, did not always endear him to those in high places, which possibly explains why he was made CBE in 1968 but he never received the coveted knighthood. Nevertheless, there is no denying the contemporary national impact of the developments that he fostered across a remarkably broad front. Many had been pioneered elsewhere, but his bringing them together in a single authority designates him as one of the great directors of education of the post-war era.   DONALD K. JONES

Sources D. K. Jones, *Stewart Mason: the art of education* (1988) · S. C. Mason, ed., *In our experience* (1970) · D. Crook, 'The disputed origins of the Leicestershire two-tier comprehensive schools plan', *History of Education Society Bulletin*, 50 (1992), 55–8 · *WW* · personal knowledge (2004)
Likenesses photographs, repro. in Jones, *Stewart Mason*, 95–6
Wealth at death £227,484: probate, 20 March 1984, *CGPLA Eng. & Wales*

Mason, Thomas (1579/80–1649), Church of England clergyman and author, was born in Hampshire. He claimed to be the grandson of Sir John *Mason (c.1503–1566), sometime member of Queen Elizabeth's privy council. He matriculated from Magdalen College, Oxford, on 29 October 1594, aged fourteen, graduated BA on 13 December 1602, and proceeded MA on 12 June 1605. A fellow of the college between 1603 and 1614, Mason took his BD on 1 December 1613 and was awarded his doctorate the following 18 May.

Mason acquired two Hampshire vicarages, Newton Valence in 1606, and Odiham. From Odiham he signed the preface to *Christ's Victorie over Sathans Tyrannie* (1615), addressed to Sir Edmund Coke and Archbishop Abbot, in which he described himself as 'your daily and faithful orator, being a professed soldier under Christ's banner'. In his epistle to the reader, it was estimated on the basis of biblical prophecies that there remained 'about 46 years to come until God shall call together the kings of the earth to destroy Rome'. In the meantime, however, Mason acquired the rectories of Littleton, Middlesex, on 26 October 1616, North Waltham, Hampshire, in 1623, and Weyhill, Hampshire, in 1624. He was resident at Odiham when signing *A Revelation of the Revelation … whereby the Pope is most Plainely Declared and Proved to be Antichrist*, in 1619.

On 25 August 1624, Mason was collated to the Salisbury prebend of Alton Australis (South Alton), and on 7 October 1626 he was elected as the next canon residentiary of Salisbury when a vacancy should arise. However, when the time came another prebend, Humphrey Henchman, was on 28 May 1633 admitted to residence at the request of the dean, Edmund Mason. Thomas Mason and another pre-elected canon, Matthew Nicholas, decided to contest the admission. After a long and complex wrangle, which takes up much space in the state papers of 1633–4, and in which King Charles himself was involved, Henchman's appointment was confirmed, but Mason and Nicholas were to have the next two vacant places. Mason was still in occupation of South Alton on 6 May 1634 but was in residence at the chapter house by 20 November.

In 1646 Mason was ejected by the Wiltshire county committee from his residence; he was charged with having used the rents of the dean and chapter to support the royalist cause. It was alleged that when parliamentarian forces were in Salisbury he refused to preach. Refusing the solemn league and covenant, Mason responded that he would stand for the Book of Common Prayer until the day of his death, comparing the parliamentarian cause with the rebellion of Absalom. Thomas Mason died on 7 November 1649 and was buried at Weyhill. His will was proved on 5 May 1655 by his widow, Elizabeth.

STEPHEN WRIGHT

Sources *Walker rev.*, 377 · *Fasti Angl., 1541–1857,* [Salisbury] · *CSP dom., 1633–4* · Foster, *Alum. Oxon.* · Wood, *Ath. Oxon.*, new edn

Mason, Sir Thomas (1844–1924), civil engineering contractor, was born in Airdrie, Lanarkshire, Scotland, the son of John Mason, builder, and his wife, Marion Hamilton. He was educated at Anderson's University, Glasgow, before starting an apprenticeship as a mason. In 1861 he moved to Edinburgh, where he was mainly involved with railway works, both as a mason and as a subcontractor. After six years in Edinburgh, Mason was taken on as foreman mason by the contractor James Brand, and put in charge of the building of the Ayr Viaduct for the Glasgow and South Western Railway. He worked for Brand until 1875, in charge of his tramway contracts, including one for the Govan and Greenock Tramway Company.

In 1875 Mason won a contract for the building of the Stobcross docks (later the Queen's docks) in Glasgow, and shortly after this he joined the building firm John Morrison & Co., with the job of tendering for and managing future contracts at Queen's Dock. The name of the company was changed to Morrison and Mason in 1879. During the 1880s the firm began to win railway contracts, including the building of the first section of the Cathcart Circle, a local railway on the south side of Glasgow, in 1884–6, and the Paisley Canal branch line of the Glasgow and South Western Railway. They also built the Citadel Station at Carlisle. Morrison and Mason branched out into waterworks with the construction of the Thirlmere Reservoir for Manchester corporation, and a joint contract with the structural engineer William Arrol for 26 miles of aqueducts in connection with the Thirlmere waterworks. The company also tendered for public building contracts, building offices for the Clyde Navigation Trust in Glasgow in 1883–6, and the municipal buildings for Glasgow corporation in 1883–8.

The firm became a limited company, Morrison and Mason Ltd, in 1889, with capital of £100,000: Morrison was chairman. While continuing to build reservoirs, such as those at Criagmaddie for the Glasgow waterworks, in 1893–4, the company began to build bridges, including the Great Western Bridge in 1890, the Glasgow Bridge in 1895, and the Rutherglen Bridge in 1896. They also continued to build offices, with new offices for the *Glasgow Herald* completed in 1910, and won contracts for hospitals, including the Ruchill Fever Hospital, finished in 1900. Morrison and Mason Ltd undertook major dock-building projects on the Clyde, notably a new dock at Clydebank, and work for Arrol on the new dockyard for Yarrows at

Scotstoun in 1907. As the European powers built up their navies in preparation for war, the company won lucrative Admiralty contracts, including in 1907 one of £1 million to build lock gates at the entrance to Portsmouth naval dockyard, and a £0.5 million contract for a dock for battleships, also at Portsmouth. During the First World War the company was mainly engaged in building harbour defences.

Mason, a Liberal, was elected to Glasgow town council in 1891, and represented the city on the board of the Clyde Navigation Trust. After he left office he remained on the board as a representative of the Merchant's House. As chairman from 1908 to 1919 he was involved in the deepening and widening of the river, and also the construction of the Rothesay Dock at Clydebank and the installation of hydraulic power at Princes Dock. While he was on the board the tonnage of shipping using the Clyde doubled, from 7 million to 14 million tons. Mason was knighted in 1909. Following the death of John Morrison in 1919, Mason sold the company to Sir William Arrol & Co. He was a director and chairman of Arrols, and the two companies had collaborated on many projects from 1876 onwards, when Morrison and Mason worked for Arrol on a bridge over the Clyde for the Caledonian Railway.

Mason was married twice; first to Jeanie Paton, and second to Charlotte Wyllie. He had two sons and three daughters. At one point he owned a small stable of racehorses, and he continued to own racehorses at Newmarket. He died on 26 April 1924 at his home on the south side of Glasgow, Craigie Hall, 6/8 Rowan Road, Bellahouston, survived by his second wife. ANNE PIMLOTT BAKER

Sources N. J. Morgan, 'Mason, Sir Thomas', *DSBB* · *CCI* (1924) · *Engineering* (2 May 1924)
Likenesses photograph, repro. in Morgan, 'Mason, Sir Thomas'
Wealth at death £138,129 10s. 3d.: confirmation, 15 Aug 1924, *CCI*

Mason, Timothy Wright (1940–1990), historian and university teacher, was born at Birkenhead on 2 February 1940, the eldest child of Walter Wright Mason, a teacher of physics and then lecturer at a teacher training college, and his wife, Isabel Anna Smith (d. 1990), a French teacher. He was educated at Birkenhead School (1951–8) and then at Corpus Christi College, Oxford, where he graduated with first-class honours in modern history in 1962. In the same year he went to St Antony's College, Oxford, as a scholar and began his doctoral research on the German working class and Nazism. In the following year he went to Germany as Theodor Heuss research fellow and in 1964 he was appointed assistant lecturer and then lecturer in history at the recently founded University of York. In 1965 he returned to Germany for a year, having been offered a research post at the Free University of Berlin, and in 1966 was elected to a research fellowship at St Antony's College, where he remained until he was elected to a tutorial fellowship in modern history at St Peter's College, Oxford, in 1971. In 1972 he was awarded his doctorate. Between 1967 and 1970 he was assistant editor of the historical journal *Past and Present*. He was married twice: first, to Ursula Vogel, a historian of political theory, in 1970; second, to

Simonetta Piccone Stella, a sociologist, in 1987. He retired from St Peter's College on grounds of ill health in 1984 and thereafter lived in Rome, where he died in a hotel, by suicide, on the night of 4–5 March 1990.

Mason was one of the outstanding British historians of his time and his work on German Nazism, although its argument was by no means universally accepted, transformed the way historians studied the National Socialist Party. He approached Nazism as a Marxist, but his own Marxism was pluralistic; to the point, indeed, where he was, in the eyes of some German historians, a 'liberal'. He was much influenced by two texts, E. P. Thompson's *The Making of the English Working Class* (1963) and Franz Neumann's *Behemoth: the Structure and Practice of National Socialism* (1942), both of which represent different kinds of Marxism: the one defines class as a product of the daily experience of individual men and women; the other defines it as system and structure. As influences, they were not, however, always easy intellectual bedfellows. Mason himself drew more heavily on the Marx of *The Eighteenth Brumaire of Louis Bonaparte*, Marx the historian, than on the rather crude political teleology of *Capital*. Mason's famous essay 'The primacy of politics' (1966), a critique of East German interpretations of Nazism, clearly drew upon *The Eighteenth Brumaire*. Here he saw Nazism as a neo-Bonapartist movement which saved the capitalist élites despite themselves, rather than as a simple manifestation of capitalist power politics.

Mason's most significant contribution to the study of Nazism—one grounded in Marxism—was to place the industrial working class squarely in the centre of his analysis. Since Nazism was not its party, he argued, but since it was essential for the achievement of the Nazi 'programme', the need to contain the working class, via bribery, persuasion, or coercion, largely determined the form of German domestic and external policy. It even, indirectly, drove Hitler into a war in 1939 which was not the war he wanted. This was an exceptionally bold argument brilliantly developed in two major works—*Arbeiterklasse und Volksgemeinschaft: Dokumente und Materialien zur deutschen Arbeiterpolitik, 1936–1939* (1975) and *Sozialpolitik im Dritten Reich* (1977; English translation, *Social Policy in the Third Reich*, 1993), a version of the introduction to the first work—and a number of essays. Much of what he wrote became canonical, not least the work on women under Nazism (published in the first two numbers of the *History Workshop Journal*), even though two elements of the argument—his account of the forces that drove Hitler to war and his interpretation of some forms of working-class resistance to the regime—were, though powerful, never wholly convincing. After he went to live in Italy his preoccupation continued to be with working-class resistance to fascism, and this produced, among other things, an impressive essay on the Turin strikes of 1943. His chief articles were posthumously collected and edited by Jane Caplan as *Nazism, Fascism and the Working Class* (1995).

Mason was a devoted teacher: patient, kind, and exceptionally tolerant of all sorts of students and opinions. He also had a profound influence on the development of history both in Oxford and in Britain generally: with Raphael Samuel, Joaquin Romero Maura, and Gareth Stedman Jones he established in Oxford the social history seminar which shaped a generation of graduates, and he was a founder editor of the journal *History Workshop*, for which he wrote several of his most important essays. To be taught by him was both a challenge and a privilege. In Oxford, his tutorials rarely stopped after the statutory hour but few undergraduates regretted the long haul. It was impossible for anyone attending his classes and seminars, even if they were unsettled by the silences which often preceded his comments, to be unaware that they were listening to a remarkable historical intelligence. Those who heard his moving and penetrating paper on Rosa Luxemburg and Leo Jögiches would be unlikely ever to forget it. Increasingly, however, these silences became longer; and they came to represent not the familiar manner of the tutorial or seminar but the silence born of a despair which eventually overwhelmed him. For much of his adult life he suffered from a manic-depressive condition and in the late 1970s had a serious breakdown, from which recovery was slow and never complete. Throughout the next decade depression and a sense of failure—a sense astonishing to anyone else—took a tighter hold. Praise surprised him and increasingly he discounted it. By the end of his life depression and withdrawal were almost total.

It is impossible for anyone to know exactly the origin of Mason's despair, but there were in his life tensions which were perhaps never resolved. He was, for instance, a familiar figure to many in his Hamburg docker's cap which was, in a way, the badge of a carefully nurtured loyalty. Less familiar, particularly as he grew older, was the cricketer or tennis player (he was very good at both) in his carefully pressed whites—unique among the sportsmen of St Antony's College. The docker's cap and the pressed whites suggest two sides of his personality which were never really reconciled. Equally ambivalent was his view of Oxford. It often dismayed and frustrated him; yet he remained deeply attached to it, and attachment grew the longer he was away from it. Ambivalence marked him as a historian: he combined a rigorous adherence to scholarly conventions and rules of evidence with a readiness to make almost apocalyptic political judgements which could startle even his friends. How far his own historical writing tormented him cannot be known. He certainly carried the burden of early achievement. His essay 'Some origins of the Second World War' (*Past and Present*, 1964), written when he was a graduate student, was a piece of astonishing precocity: a review of A. J. P. Taylor's *The Origins of the Second World War* (fifth impression, 1963) which effectively destroyed that book's thesis; and a review the more effective because of its restraint. And, of course, he carried the burden of his subject. He was asked once whether he might write a general history of Nazism even if it were, in his own eyes, only an interim one. He declined on the grounds that the story 'has to end in Auschwitz', and he had not got that far yet. It is hard to believe that a story which ended in Auschwitz was not one of the demons which preyed upon him.

ROSS MCKIBBIN

Sources personal knowledge (2004) · private information (2004) [L. Mason] · *History Workshop Journal*, 30 (1990) · J. Caplan, 'Introduction', in T. Mason, *Nazism, fascism and the working class*, ed. J. Caplan (1995) · B. Harrison, 'Tim Mason: a memory', *Pelican Record*, 38/1 (1991–3), 68–72 · H. Mayr-Harting, 'Tim Mason: a personal memoir', *St Peter's College Record* (1990), 66–9 · archival material, St Peter's College, Oxford · C. Matthew, 'In memoriam', *Oxford Magazine*, noughth week, Trinity term (1990), 6
Likenesses photograph, repro. in *History Workshop Journal*

Mason, William (*fl.* 1672–1716), stenographer and writing-master, is of unknown origins. He wrote that from his youth he 'delighted in the Art of Short-Hand' (W. Mason, *La plume volante*, 1707, 'To the reader'). In 1736 it was noted, 'As for Mr. Mason he has obtained a very great Reputation in the world (and that deservedly) as a short-hand writer' (Gibbs, 51). Mason's shorthand system may be described as a perpetual work-in-progress. For a half century he taught and made radical modifications to his system, which was originally based, as Mason acknowledged, on that of Jeremiah Rich (more accurately called the William Cartwright–Jeremiah Rich system).

In 1672, 'to delight the Ingenious, and to encourage the Industrious', Mason published his first shorthand treatise, *A Pen Pluck'd from an Eagles Wing*. The alphabet contained nineteen of Rich's characters; by contrast, the alphabet of his second treatise, *Arts Advancement* (1682), contained only six. Elaborately engraved, *Arts Advancement*, which sold for only a shilling, had ornamental borders with a bird's feather and quill pen motif and a handsome oval portrait of Mason by Benjamin Rhodes. Both works were among the shorthand books in the library of Samuel Pepys. Even fewer echoes of Rich's system were found in Mason's last and most influential treatise, *La plume volante* (1707), which he had taught in manuscript from around 1692. All three versions of Mason's system had subsequent editions, and Mason also published broadsheet learning aids to accompany his texts.

A self-described teacher of 'Fair-Writing, Arithmetick, Merchants Accompts, and Short-Hand' (*Aurea clavis*, 1695, 'Advertisement'), Mason was also 'very famous, in writing many things in a little Compass' (Turner, pt 3, chap. 13, p. 26), a reference to his skill in miniature writing. Indeed, John Bagford claimed that he 'graved in the Compass of an Heart the number of Letters, words, Chapters and verses in the Bible' (Heal, 73). In *Arts Advancement* Mason announced his intention to engrave and print the entire Bible in 'Character' (i.e. shorthand—a task evidently never completed) and also wrote a collection of aphorisms. His name appeared among the recommenders of the 1678 and 1700 editions of Edward Cocker's *Cocker's Arithmetick*.

In the tradition of the great seventeenth-century writing-masters, Mason was a keen advertiser and promoter of both his personal qualifications and his very moderately priced books. A successful teacher who emphasized his many years' experience, Mason boarded pupils and advertised that he would instruct students at convenient hours in their own houses. On 27 August 1700 the *Post Man* announced the removal of Mr Mason's academy the Hand and Pen (previously in Prince's Court, Lothbury, and in Talbot Court and Bell Yard off Gracechurch Street) to Scalding Alley 'over against Stocks Market' near the Royal Exchange. As late as 1716, Mason advertised his services:

> William Mason, designs to teach [shorthand] twice a Week at his very next Door, being Leaden-Hall Coffee House in Leaden-Hall Street, where is a Room for that Purpose, called the Stenographical Club Room, to teach in [sic] Monday and Thursday Evenings, for two Hours together, at such Times as all may agree to, for One Shilling a Week … where all will receive ample Satisfaction. (*Monthly Catalogue*, November 1716)

By 1719 his pupil Joseph Smith was instructor at the Hand and Pen, suggesting that Mason had either died or retired.

Mason's *La plume volante* 'shaped the destiny of shorthand reporting' (Butler, 40), for it was adapted and published by Thomas Gurney, official shorthand writer to the Old Bailey (T. Gurney, *Brachygraphy*, 1750; eighteen editions by 1884), who maintained what amounted to a rigid copyright. Through the medium of Gurney and his stenographic family, Mason's system profoundly influenced the use and status of shorthand in the eighteenth-century law courts and continued in use well into the nineteenth century. The 'secret diaries' of William Byrd of Westover, Virginia, who may have studied with Mason while Byrd was a student in London, are written in Mason's system. Mason is now generally regarded as one of the greatest stenographers of the seventeenth century. PAGE LIFE

Sources W. J. Carlton, *Shorthand books* (1940), pt 4 of *Bibliotheca Pepysiana: a descriptive catalogue of the library of Samuel Pepys*, 77–87 · J. J. Gold, 'The battle of the shorthand books, 1635–1800', *Publishing History*, 15 (1984), 5–29 · A. Heal, *The English writing-masters and their copy-books, 1570–1800* (1931); repr. (Hildesheim, 1962) · P. Gibbs, *An historical account of compendious and swift writing* (1736) · J. H. Lewis, *An historical account of the rise and progress of shorthand* (privately printed, London, 1825?) · I. Pitman, *A history of shorthand*, 3rd edn (1891) · A. Paterson, 'William Mason's "arts advancement"', *Phonetic Journal*, 58 (1899), 742 · A. Paterson, 'Some early shorthand systems, no. 3: William Mason's *La plume volante*', *Phonetic Journal*, 45 (1886), 201–2 · L. B. Wright, 'A shorthand diary of William Byrd of Westover', *Huntington Library Quarterly*, 2 (1938–9), 489–96 · E. Arber, ed., *The term catalogues, 1668–1709*, 3 vols. (privately printed, London, 1903–6) · *A Catalogue of All Books, Sermons and Pamphlets Published in May 1714 and in Every Month to This Time* (1714–17); repr. as *The monthly catalogue, 1714–1717*, 3 vols. in 1 (1964), vol. 3, p. 33 · *Post Man and the Historical Account*, 795 (24–7 Aug 1700) · *Post Man and the Historical Account*, 836 (10–13 May 1701) · *N&Q*, 2nd ser., 3 (1857), 254–5 · *N&Q*, 5th ser., 3 (1875), 24–5 · E. H. Butler, *The story of British shorthand* (1951) · W. Turner, *A compleat history of the most remarkable providences* (1697) · N. A. Smith, ed., *Printed books* (1978), vol. 1 of *Catalogue of the Pepys Library at Magdalene College, Cambridge*, ed. R. Latham, 119

Likenesses B. Rhodes, line engraving on copper, 1682?, BM; repro. in W. Mason, *Arts advancement* (1682), frontispiece · B. Rhodes, woodcut, 1682?, BM; repro. in W. Mason, *La plume volante*, 5th edn [1719]

Mason, William (1725–1797), poet and garden designer, was born on 12 February 1725 at Holy Trinity Church vicarage, Vicar Lane, Kingston upon Hull, the only son of the Revd William Mason (1694–1753), incumbent of Holy Trinity from 1722 to 1753, and his first wife, Mary Wild (*d.* 1725). He was baptized at his father's church on 11 March 1725. His mother died before he was a year old, and was buried at Holy Trinity on 26 December 1725; his father remarried twice. Mason's ancestors had included locally important merchants, civic and ecclesiastical officials. His great-grandfather Robert (*d.* 1718) had been successively sheriff (1675) and mayor (1681 and 1696) of Hull, and his grandfather Hugh was controller of the customs at the port of Hull from 1696 and patron of the church livings at Sutton-on-Hull as well as Thorp Brantingham.

Mason's family was staunchly whig, with some antiquarian interests, well connected, and considerably influenced his life's direction. Mason was distantly related to his first patron, Robert D'Arcy, fourth earl of Holdernesse (1718–1778), secretary of state for the north from 1751 to 1761. Matthew Hutton, archbishop of York from 1747 to 1757, and later of Canterbury, gave Mason his first church preferment, the prebend of Holme, at York Minster in 1757. His brother John Hutton left Mason a considerable landed estate at Marske, North Riding of Yorkshire, in 1768, said to be worth £1500 in rents (Nichols, *Lit. anecdotes*, 2.241), which gave him the financial independence to abandon church ambitions, and to pursue his artistic and political projects.

Education and entry into the church Mason's father exercised influence over his early development in religion, politics, poetry, and painting, as acknowledged in a 1746 poem 'To the Author's Father' (Mason, *Works*, 1.172–5). Mason began his formal education at the nearby Hull grammar school, thus literally following in the footsteps of Andrew Marvell, whom he greatly admired. His teachers there included John Clarke (1687–1734), an advocate of Locke's educational ideas, and John Blyth (1708–1762). Mason lived with his father and stepmothers until he went to St John's College, Cambridge, being admitted on 1 July 1742. He graduated BA in 1746, MA in 1749 at Pembroke College, and was a fellow of the latter college from 1749 to 1759. He grew to prefer the social life of Cambridge and London, and then Aston's rural retreat, to Hull's bustle and pollution. His native town, and the Humber shoreline are, however, glimpsed in works throughout his career, such as the 'Ode to Independency' (ibid., 1.38–41), his tribute to Marvell, and 'On Expecting to Return to Cambridge' (1747):

> Commerce, riding on thy refluent tide,
> Impetuous HUMBER! Wafts her stores
> From Belgian or Norwegian shores
> And spreads her countless sails from side to side.

The death of his childhood friend Marmaduke Prickett MD (1724–1753) on 18 September 1753 (F. F. Prickett, *The Pricketts of Allerthorpe*, 1929, 72), only weeks after losing his father, was a turning point; from then on he was only an occasional visitor to Hull, usually on family business.

William Mason (1725–1797), by Sir Joshua Reynolds, 1774

His father's death, on 26 August 1753, deprived Mason of a paternal allowance, leaving him with only a fellowship of £100 per year, and the will excluded Mason completely, leaving the estate to his father's third wife and their daughter. Mason's career as a Cambridge fellow and promising young writer was thus interrupted; these financial implications virtually obliged him to enter the church—which was perhaps his father's intention. After a period of indecision lasting more than a year, during which he served as private secretary to Lord Holdernesse, Mason was ordained deacon on 17 November 1754 in St Margaret's, Westminster, made a priest a week later, and was then presented by Holdernesse on 27 November 1754 to the living of Aston, West Riding of Yorkshire, where he remained rector for forty-three years. For some years until his 1768 inheritance Mason actively pursued preferment, holding five church offices by 1777. Through the duke of Devonshire, he was made a royal chaplain in 1757, relinquishing the post in 1772. His most significant post was as precentor of York Minster, held for thirty-five years from 1762, in which his activities, compositions, and writings affected the development of provincial church music (see N. Temperley, 'Jonathan Gray and church music in York, 1770–1840', Borthwick Papers, 51, University of York, 1977, 7–8).

Entry into the church vitally affected the kind of writer Mason was to become, giving much of his work a tone, varying from piousness to bombast, Miltonic romance to sentiment, which rendered it highly fashionable to a contemporary audience, and increasingly unacceptable to subsequent Romantic and modern tastes. The church provided him with a framework for his life and polymathic activities in poetry, music, antiquities, gardening, art, politics, and a rich social life. He became a man of letters, but 'never was an author for bread. The aim of all his writings was to dignify the poetic art' (Coleridge, 454). He was 'as a man, as a poet, as a politician, and as a divine … highly respectable' (ibid., 397), and adopted anonymity, and later a pseudonym, Malcolm MacGreggor, when publishing his satires, most famously An Heroic Epistle to Sir William Chambers (1773).

Mason's friends and his poetry At Cambridge, Mason sought out a series of older men who became his mentors and friends: firstly, his tutors William Powell and Thomas Balguy, then his lifelong friends Thomas Gray, William Whitehead, Richard Stonhewer, and Richard Hurd. Another important influence was William Warburton (1698–1779), bishop of Gloucester, who, as the friend and literary executor of Alexander Pope, offered Mason an example of combining the ecclesiastical and literary life. Much of his early verse was written to impress or memorialize these and other friends, notably in Odes (1756) and Elegies (1763). At Pembroke College, Gray and Mason were regarded as being at the head of the university's 'polite scholars', who 'confined all merit to their own circle' and 'looked down with fastidious contempt on the rest of the world' (Nichols, Lit. anecdotes, 5.613). Perhaps too much emphasis has been placed on Gray's very early view of Mason as having 'much Fancy, little Judgement, and a good deal of Modesty … he reads little or nothing, writes abundance, & that with a Design to make his Fortune by it' (Mitford, 195).

Mason's first works were imitations of Milton, written as an undergraduate in 1744 (Mason, Works, 1.158–65, 166–71) and his first widely praised poem was 'Musaeus: a Monody to the Memory of Mr Pope, in Imitation of Milton's Lycidas' (ibid., 3–15), which brought him to the attention of Gray. Mason's 'Ode for Music' was performed in the Senate House at Cambridge on 1 July 1749 at the installation of the duke of Newcastle as chancellor of the university, set to music by William Boyce, master of the king's music. Hurd and Gray were at this time close advisers, though Mason by no means always accepted their views: for instance, Mason's use of a chorus in his dramatic poem Elfrida (1752), written 'on the model of the ancient Greek tragedy', was much against Gray's advice. This experiment was continued by Caractacus (1759), described by Warburton as 'a prodigiously fine thing, vastly above Elfrida' (E. H. Pearce and L. Whibley, eds., The Correspondence of Richard Hurd and William Mason, 30 Nov 1757). Both were successfully adapted for the London stage during the 1770s. Mason's most historically significant work, The Poems of Mr Gray, to which are Prefixed Memoirs of his Life and Writings (1775) was in essence to establish the rank of Gray's reputation, and, using Gray's entertainingly waspish letters to his friends in censored, sometimes bowdlerized forms, it succeeded. The format—five sections of letters interspersed with biographical commentary, leading to an edition of Gray's poems—was innovative, and is credited with introducing the 'life and letters' mode to biography. Its plan was taken up by Boswell's *Life of Johnson* (1791) and by a host of nineteenth-century imitators.

Mason's work also had consequences for copyright law: his successful lawsuit in 1777 against the Scottish bookseller John Murray for having reprinted fifty lines by Gray from the memoirs without his permission, greatly extended the rights of authors. Murray had wanted to settle out of court, and then issued a virulent 'Letter to W. Mason' (May 1777), impugning his motives, but it was pursued by Mason as an important test case. Mason's own poetry was often criticized by contemporary critics for its rhetorical flourishes, and over-fondness for alliteration, but he was a fashionable author, satirized by Churchill in 'The Rosciad' (1762), by Charles Lloyd and George Colman in their 'Odes to Obscurity and Oblivion' (1760), and especially condemned by Dr Johnson who became his favourite enemy.

On 25 September 1765 Mason was married at St Mary's, Lowgate, Hull, to Mary Sherman (*c*.1738–1767), daughter of William Sherman, the local garrison storekeeper. On 27 March 1767 she died of consumption (tuberculosis) at Bristol Hot Wells (now Clifton) where she had been taken for the waters, and was buried at Bristol Cathedral, with a pious but moving epitaph by her husband, which is still to be seen there: 'Take, Holy Earth, all that my soul holds dear'. It was singled out by Wordsworth in his 'Essay on epitaphs' (3, 1810, 82–3; *Prose Works of William Wordsworth*, ed. W. Owen and J. Smyser, 2, 1974).

Mason did not have a unified identity. The highly respected author of odes, elegies, epitaphs, dramatic poems, and epic blank verse was at the same time the subversive satirist Malcolm MacGreggor. One side of his work is 'correct', informed by history, romance, religion, and sentiment; the other is informed by virulent political and personal attacks. He has been often stigmatized as a dilettante: conventional, pious, monotonously high-flown, a dull imitator of Gray and Milton. But he was an undeniably restless literary experimenter. He can be seen as a vital transitional figure between the late Augustan and Romantic modes, by way of the picturesque. This is most obvious in his *magnum opus*, *The English Garden* (4 books, 1772–81), over 2400 lines of blank verse based on Virgil's *Georgics*, a didactic poem concerning landscape, art, and gardening—with an occasional vein of romanticized autobiography. Mason started out as a very ornamental, 'Parnassian' poet and evolved towards the much more natural language of his satires and the birthday sonnets of his last years. His student imitations of Milton, Chaucer, and Spenser in 'Musaeus' (written 1744, published 1747) were already moving away from the dominant Augustan modes. With Gray and Hurd, Mason shared an antiquarian interest in the British Muse, in its Anglo-Saxon, Scandinavian, and especially Celtic sources (see his commonplace book, York Minster Archives, Add. MS 25). Mason concluded his writing with a series of birthday sonnets during the 1790s, a lengthy exposition of his faith, 'Religio clerici', and a versification of a chapter in the book of Job, sent to Hurd a few days before his fatal accident.

Mason and gardens Gardening, like politics, formed both a subject for Mason's writing and a sphere of practical activity. His two major poems, *An Heroic Epistle to Sir William Chambers* (1773), which ridicules the royal taste for chinoiserie, especially at Kew Gardens, and *The English Garden*, both deal with garden history and aesthetics, albeit in radically different manners. Mason frequented the houses and estates of his friends and patrons throughout his life, and designed several flower gardens for them, notably for Hurd at Thurcaston in Leicestershire; for Lord Jersey at Middleton Park; and most spectacularly for Lord Harcourt at Nuneham Courtenay, Oxfordshire. Mason believed in hybrid arts,

> Those magic seeds of fancy, which produce
> A Poet's feeling, and a Painter's eye.
> (*English Garden*, 1.20–21)

He absorbed some of his garden tastes from an early love of poetry, but had more practically seen the work of William Kent, and Launcelot 'Capability' Brown (1715–1783) whose epitaph at Fenstanton church, Suffolk, Mason later wrote (Mason, *Works*, 1.143). Mason's gardens were themselves very literary, with classical and modern busts, memorials, and verse inscriptions taken from Milton, Marvell, Gray, and Rousseau, to give a melancholy, sentimental atmosphere; his gardens were to be places of spiritual refreshment and aesthetic contemplation.

Mason's horticultural masterpiece was for George Simon (1736–1809), Lord Nuneham until 1778, thereafter second Earl Harcourt. The walled garden was created in 1772–3, improved in 1784, and was regarded by visitors for generations as one of the most beautiful in Britain. It is the only one of Mason's gardens which still survives, having been restored in the 1970s. Mason created a series of points of interest in the picturesque manner (later more associated with his friend William Gilpin), and irregularly shaped flower beds containing wild, native, and imported flowers. The gently sloping ground was covered with patches of flowers including roses, lupins, tulips, hollyhocks, and sweet-scented mignonette; and trailing garlands of clematis, bryony, and creepers draped the surrounding trees, in imitation of Julie's garden in Rousseau's *La nouvelle Héloïse* (1760). Mason describes it in the fourth book of *The English Garden*, with Lord Harcourt as 'Alcander'. Mason's gardening style became fashionable, inspiring numerous imitators, and Queen Charlotte wanted a Mason garden for Frogmore, Windsor. Mason's gardening has been seen as his most original cultural contribution: the informal flower garden was without precedent (see Batey, 11–25).

Politics and social concerns Mason spent much of his adult life in opposition to the government of the day—to the policies of Lord Bute, and Lord North during the American war in particular. Mason's major political involvements were with the Yorkshire Association, and he was particularly active during the 1780 and 1784 general elections, being Christopher Wyvill's deputy from 1779 to 1785, and with the anti-slavery campaign. His whig politics affected both his personal and literary relations: the mutual antipathy between him and the tory Dr Johnson had a political as well as a personal element. In his satires tory ministers, pensioners, and placemen were ruthlessly pursued; but Charles James Fox also suffered: the *Heroic Epistle* ends with the inveterate gambler being seized by Jewish moneylenders and circumcised in public (P. J. Toynbee, *Satirical Poems Published … by William Mason*, 1926, 52). Eventually disillusioned by the infighting of whig politicians, and their failure to deliver even moderate reforms, Mason switched his allegiance in 1784 to the young William Pitt, as the best hope for parliamentary reform and for the abolition of slavery, a decision which cost him friends, notably Horace Walpole (Walpole, *Corr.*, 29.xxviii). Mason was a friend of William Wilberforce, and of Bielby Porteous, bishop of London, and was himself one of the earliest abolitionists. His sermon 'God the universal and equal father of all mankind', delivered in York Minster on 27 January 1788, was widely circulated. Perhaps to annoy his tory archbishop William Markham, he baptized a young American black man, Benjamin Moor, in the minster on 11 May 1777 (*Yorkshire Archaeological and Topographical Journal*, 6, 1881, 393). Mason's social and charitable concerns stretched widely, to include the treatment of prisoners and lunatics in York (see A. Digby, 'From York Lunatic Asylum to Bootham Park Hospital', *Borthwick Papers*, 69, University of York, 1986, 8–10).

Mason's music Mason knew, observed, and sometimes collaborated with, leading composers and performers—Boyce, Giardini, and Avison—and was a friend of Charles Burney. Thomas Arne composed the incidental music for Mason's dramatic poems *Elfrida* and *Caractacus* when they were adapted for the stage in 1772 and 1776 respectively. Mason was an accomplished amateur musician, playing several keyboard instruments, and had strong progressive views about both cathedral and parochial music (Mason, *Essays on English Church Music*, 1795; and see *MT*, 114, 1973, 894). He concerned himself with the state of church music in practical ways and in his essay 'On parochial psalmody' he criticized the habit of leaving the choice and conduct of metrical psalms to the parish clerk, and the music in the hands of a self-appointed choir and band. He also criticized many of the verse translations in use, and proposed using a 'judicious selection' of passages from the metrical psalms; Mason advocated unison singing in which all could easily join, with the accompaniment of an organ or barrel organ and tunes to be sung faster and more rhythmically. Congregational devotion through music had been his aim. Mason's best-known anthem was 'Lord of all pow'r and might', which was sung in the Chapel Royal, Windsor, and in York Minster. In 1782 he published *A Copious Collection of those Portions of the Psalms of David … which have been Set to Music and Sung as Anthems … and Published for the Use of the Church of York*. He introduced a new form of the piano to Britain, actually a combination harpsichord-pianoforte, which he brought back from Hamburg, Germany, in 1755 and is said to have popularized at court. He invented the celestinette, which according to his friend Mrs Delany had 'a delicate, exquisite sound, something between a fiddle and the musical glasses' (Barr and Ingamells, 18).

Mason had a squint in his right eye, giving him a roguish leer somewhat at odds with his cultivated manners and priestly duties. In maturity he was a stout, short man; his voice was said to incline towards a nasal whine. He could be disputatious, but on a visit to Aston in 1788, the poet Richard Polwhele found 'a kind of sedate benignity in his countenance' (R. Polwhele, *Traditions and Recollections*, 1826, 2.217). Sarah Siddons recorded that Mason 'spoke broad Yorkshire, and good-naturedly allowed us to accuse him of affectation in so doing', adding that 'he was a great humorist, but with all his oddities, a benevolent man' (P. Fitzgerald, *The Kembles*, 2 vols., 1871, 1.252–3).

Death and subsequent reputation On Friday 31 March 1797 Mason fell and injured his leg while entering his carriage. The wound became inflamed over the weekend and his curate reported:

Mr Mason was suddenly seized with a violent shivering fit & never spoke afterwards … It seemed as if his whole frame had given way at once; for the malady was so rapid that he died the day following [Wednesday 5 April 1797] at two in the afternoon.   (Brunskill to William Gilpin, Bodl. Oxf., MS Eng. Misc. d.571)

He had died at his rectory in Aston, and was buried at All Saints Church, Aston, on 11 April. Among the obituaries of Mason which appeared, that in the *Gentleman's Magazine* (April 1797) praised him, but in ways which presaged subsequent attitudes through the nineteenth and early twentieth centuries:

Mr Mason was an acknowledged scholar, and possessed high claims to a considerable degree of poetical reputation. All that could be gathered from the Greek and Roman stores certainly contributed to embellish his mind, but it may be reasonably questioned whether it was enriched by great share of original genius.   (*GM*, 359)

Accounts of Mason's life and works appeared in books such as Hartley Coleridge's *Worthies of Yorkshire and Lancashire* (1836, 397–462), and R. W. Corlass's *Sketches of Hull Authors* (1879, 54–63) viewed him as a respected if old fashioned figure. Coleridge called Mason 'the most considerable Yorkshire poet since Marvell', adding that, 'With the great poets in any department of poetry, Mason cannot be numbered. Yet he was, for many years of his life, England's greatest living poet' (Coleridge, 462). Later critics, Edmund Gosse and Leslie Stephen in particular, severely deprecated Mason's silent mutilation of Gray's letters—and this proved an essential element in the radical downgrading of his reputation. Stephen reached the damning verdict that Mason 'mistook himself for a poet … his serious attempts at poetry are rather vapid performances' (*DNB*). George Saintsbury dismissed him as 'one of the paltriest and most pretentious poetasters who ever trespassed on the English Parnassus' (Saintsbury, *A History of English Prosody*, 2, 1910, 518).

Most twentieth-century critical attention has found Mason 'typical' of his class and era, an imitator of Milton and Gray, notably J. W. Draper in his *William Mason: a Study in Eighteenth-Century Culture* (1924). The only significant publication of Mason's works in the twentieth century was an edition of his satirical poems (Oxford, 1926), edited by Paget Toynbee, with notes by Horace Walpole written in 1779. There is evidence that interest in Mason has revived in recent decades, certainly in his gardening, and also in his combative role in the political and aesthetic debates of his time. A wide-ranging exhibition of Masoniana, including portraits, manuscripts, and first editions, was held in York Art Gallery and York Minster Library from 16 June to 15 July 1973, organized by Bernard Barr and John Ingamells. A one-day conference to mark the bicentenary of Mason's death was held at the King's Manor, York, under the auspices of the Yorkshire Gardens Trust, on 24 July 1997.

Mason was one of the most famous, fashionable—and most often satirized—poets of his era. He wrote one of the best-selling poems of the eighteenth century, the *Heroic Epistle*, and critically influenced another, Gray's 'Elegy in a Country Church-Yard'. His debates with Walpole, Gray, Hurd, and later William Gilpin, were instrumental in forming the ideas of the picturesque and the Gothick, and were an important influence on the Romantic movement. Mason's polymathic activities make him one of the most comprehensive cultural figures of his age. He survives as a name in the indexes of books about his contemporaries, from Dr Johnson to Sarah Siddons, Sir Joshua Reynolds to David Garrick. His influence has been felt in the most diverse spheres. But as a poet of at least historical importance, he still awaits resurrection.   JULES SMITH

Sources W. Mason, *The works of William Mason, M.A.*, 4 vols. (1811) · W. Mason, commonplace book, York Minster Archives, Add. MS 25 · B. Barr and J. Ingamells, eds., *A candidate for praise: William Mason, 1727–97, precentor of York* (1973) [exhibition catalogue, York Art Gallery and York Minster Library, York, 16 June – 15 July 1973] · J. W. Draper, *William Mason: a study in eighteenth-century culture* (1924) · P. Gaskell, *The first editions of William Mason* (1951) · E. W. Harcourt, ed., *The Harcourt papers*, 14 vols. (privately printed, London, [1880–1905]) · Walpole, *Corr.*, vol. 29 · *The correspondence of Thomas Gray and William Mason*, ed. J. Mitford (1853) · H. Coleridge, 'The Rev. William Mason', *Lives of the illustrious worthies of Yorkshire* (1835), 397–462 · J. Foster, *Pedigrees of the county families of Yorkshire*, 3 (1874) · L. Whibley, 'William Mason, poet and biographer', *Blackwood*, 222 (1927), 514–27 · M. Batey, 'William Mason, English gardener', *Garden History* (Feb 1973), 11–25 · *GM*, 1st ser., 67 (1797) · *DNB*
Archives BL, letters to Christopher Alderson, RP 1458B [copies] · BL, corresp. with Horace Walpole (extracts), Add. MSS 32563, 32569 · Bodl. Oxf., treatise, MS Johnson c.8 · Hunt. L., papers · Hunt. L., letters · Pembroke Cam., letters and literary MSS · Yale U., Lewis Walpole Library, letters · York Minster Library, MSS and some letters, commonplace book, books | BL, letters to Thomas Wharton, Egerton MS 2400, fols. 236–71 · Bodl. Oxf., William Gilpin letters, MSS Eng. misc d.570–571 & d.582 · N. Yorks. CRO, corresp. with Christopher Wyvill · Notts. Arch., letters to F. F. Foljambe · NRA, letters to Christopher Alderson · Yale U., Lewis Walpole Library, letters to Horace Walpole
Likenesses F. Mapletoft, silhouette, *c.*1765, Pembroke Cam. · J. Reynolds, oils, 1774, Pembroke Cam. [*see illus.*] · W. Doughty, oils, 1778, NPG; version, York City Art Gallery · W. Doughty, mezzotint, 1779, York City Art Gallery · R. Page, stipple, pubd 1815 (after L. Vaslet, 1771), NPG · S. W. Reynolds, mezzotint, pubd 1837 (after J. Reynolds), BM, NPG · J. Bacon, relief medallion on monument, Westminster Abbey · attrib. J. Plott, miniature on ivory, NPG
Wealth at death considerable landed estate (at Marske, North Yorkshire), said to be worth £1500 p.a. in rents: *DNB*; Foster, *Pedigrees* · £1750 in money and stocks left to individuals: will, proved 1 May 1797

Mason, William Charles Monck (1775–1859), historian, was born in Dublin on 7 September 1775, the eldest son of Henry Monck Mason, colonel of engineers. His mother, Jane, Henry Mason's second wife, was a daughter of Dr Bartholomew *Mosse (1712–1759), founder of the Dublin Lying-in Hospital. Henry Joseph Monck *Mason, writer, was William's brother. He was an uncle of George Henry Monck Mason (1825–1857). Mason's father held an office in the household of the lord lieutenant as well as the post of 'land waiter for exports' in the revenue department at Dublin. When Mason was twenty-one, in 1796, he succeeded to the land-waitership. Throughout his life Mason worked on the history and topography of Ireland; he collected rare books and manuscripts, and transcribed many documents. His ambition was to produce a topographical account of Ireland similar to Samuel and Daniel Lysons's *Magna Britannia* (1806–22) and George Chalmers's *Caledonia* (1807–24). The intended title was 'Hibernia antiqua et hodierna: being a topographical account of Ireland, and a history of all the establishments in that kingdom, ecclesiastical, civil, and monastick, drawn chiefly from sources of original record'. The first part, published in 1819, was devoted to the history of St Patrick's Cathedral. More than one third of the book was taken up by a biography of Jonathan Swift. It remains an important source for the history of Dublin. Mason hoped to publish a companion volume on Christ Church, Dublin, but although engravings were prepared under his direction, the work was not printed.

In 1823 Mason issued a prospectus for a history of the city and county of Dublin, hoping to revise the work of historians such as Walter Harris, but subscriptions were not forthcoming. The plan was abandoned, and Mason's manuscript collections for it remained unrevised and unsorted. His excerpts from Dublin municipal archives were superseded by J. T. Gilbert's publication of the calendars of the ancient records of Dublin.

About 1826 Mason left Ireland for the continent, having been granted a government pension on the abolition of his office in the revenue department at Dublin. During his travels and residence abroad he collected many valuable works on continental literature and the fine arts; these were auctioned in London in 1834–7. Mason moved to England in 1848, and devoted himself mainly to the study of philology. Once again he formed a very large library, which he sold at auction at Sothebys in 1852. Also at Sothebys in 1858 he sold by auction his literary collections and compositions relating to Irish history and philology.

Mason was married, but the name of his wife is not known. He died at Surbiton Hall in Kingston upon Thames, where he had been living, on 6 March 1859.

J. T. GILBERT, *rev.* MARIE-LOUISE LEGG

Sources *GM*, 3rd ser., 6 (1859), 441 · personal knowledge (1893)
Archives BL, notes, collections, and MS additions to printed works on Ireland · NL Ire. · TCD, extracts from Dublin parish records · TCD, historical notes · Yale U., Beinecke L., corresp. | BL, Egerton MSS, corresp. with Sir Robert Peel, Add. MSS 40226–40515 · Dublin City Library, Gilbert MSS · Hunt. L., letters to Charles O'Conor

Mason, William Shaw (1774–1853), statistician and bibliographer, was born in Dublin, the son of Henry Mason, described as *publicanus* (Burtchaell & Sadleir, *Alum. Dubl.*). He was educated, first, under a Mr Carpendale, and then at Trinity College, Dublin, to which he was admitted in 1791, graduating BA in 1796. In conjunction with two others he was appointed by patent in 1805 to the office of remembrancer or receiver of the first-fruits and twentieth parts in Ireland; to this was added in September 1810 the post of secretary to the commissioners for public records in Ireland. Sir Robert Peel, while chief secretary to the lord lieutenant of Ireland, conceived a high opinion of Mason, and encouraged him to undertake an Irish statistical work similar to that executed by Sir John Sinclair for Scotland. The first volume of Mason's publication was issued at Dublin in octavo, with maps and plates, in 1814, as *A Statistical Account or Parochial Survey of Ireland, drawn up from the Communications of the Clergy*. The second volume appeared in 1816, and a third followed in 1819. Mason devoted much attention to the subject of the census of Ireland, and compiled a *Survey, Valuation, and Census of the Barony of Portnahinch* in Queen's county. This was printed in 1821 in a folio volume, and submitted to George IV during his visit to Ireland as a model for a statistical survey of the whole country. Mason's annotated catalogue of the books relating to Ireland that he had collected for Peel was published as *Bibliotheca Hibernicana* (1823). During an investigation into the integrity of the Irish records, their keeper alleged that Mason had refused him the keys on the grounds of being 'servant to the Record Commissioners, and not of the Lord Lieutenant' ('Observations', 19), and said that Mason had been threatened with dismissal by the lord chancellor. Mason died in Camden Street, Dublin, on 11 March 1853.   J. T. GILBERT, *rev.* ALAN YOSHIOKA

Sources N. D. Palmer, 'Sir Robert Peel's "select Irish library"', *Irish Historical Studies*, 6/22 (1948–9); repr. in W. S. Mason, *Bibliotheca Hibernicana*, facs. edn (1970) • 'Observations on the report from the select committee … on the record commission', *Parl. papers* (1837), 39.369, no. 177 • J. S. Crone, *A concise dictionary of Irish biography* (1928) • Burtchaell & Sadleir, *Alum. Dubl.*
Archives TCD, corresp.; corresp. relating to his *Statistical … survey of Ireland* | BL, corresp. with Sir Robert Peel, Add. MSS 40226–40515

Masquerier, John James (1778–1855), painter, was born in Chelsea, London, on 5 October 1778, of French Huguenot parents. He had two elder brothers, both of whom emigrated to America; Louis (or Lewis) married in Bourbon, Kentucky, in 1798 and named his first daughter Mary Barbot (later Barbett), preserving the maiden name of his mother, who was born in 1742 or 1743. His father, Lewis Masquerier (1735/6–1803), returned with his family in 1789 to Paris, where his wife and daughter opened a school. Masquerier entered the Académie Royale as a painting student in the studio of François Vincent. In 1792 he made a drawing of his father (BM), who remained in Paris until his death in 1803. From the vantage point of Vincent's second-floor studio in the Palais du Louvre, Masquerier witnessed many of the unfolding events of the French Revolution. He knew Danton especially well, as he used to come and practise speaking English to the boy. After the massacres of the first reign of terror in September 1792, rumours circulated that all foreigners would be arrested. Masquerier fled to England, while his mother and sister remained in Paris. Though imprisoned, they were eventually released and continued to run the school in Paris until 1814. Masquerier enrolled at the Royal Academy Schools on 31 December 1792. He received the silver medal in 1794 and in the following year exhibited his first work in the annual exhibition, a self-portrait. In 1796 he exhibited *The Incredulity of St Thomas*, his only attempt at grand-manner history painting; thereafter he concentrated primarily on portraiture. He is said to have worked as an assistant to John Hoppner, but soon gained a clientele of his own, thanks to support from one Alexander (an MP whose portrait was exhibited at the Royal Academy in 1803) and Major John Scott Waring (whose portrait he painted in 1801).

In 1800 Masquerier returned to Paris, and was granted access through Mme Tallien to Napoleon to make drawings of him from life. On his return to London he created a composition, *Napoleon Reviewing the Consular Guard in the Court of the Tuileries*. The work was exhibited in a house in Piccadilly in 1801 and excited intense interest as the first true likeness of the first consul seen in England. The sale of tickets reputedly brought the artist £1000, along with an accusation from 'Peter Porcupine' (William Cobbett) of acting as an enemy agent, which he refuted by the production of the register of his birth in England.

Masquerier was again in Paris in 1802, assisting Joseph Farington and others among the many English artists who flocked to the city during the peace of Amiens. On this occasion he probably painted the portrait of Mme Tallien which he showed at the Royal Academy in 1803. The mezzotint after this portrait by William Bond published the same year reveals, aptly, a debt to David. Masquerier continued to maintain contacts with some of the leading French artists: his surviving papers include an undated invitation to visit the studio of Gérard and a letter from Girodet in 1823 expressing gratitude for numerous visits from Masquerier over the years.

Masquerier had by now gained a particular reputation among patrons from Ireland and Scotland, but failed to establish any individual style. He fluctuated between the manner of Romney, of Hoppner, and of Lawrence; his Scottish sitters are often painted in conscious emulation of Raeburn. In 1810 he spent five months as guest of George Augustus, second marquess of Donegal, completing eleven canvases. It was, however, through his Scottish connections that he met his future wife, Rachel Scott (*née* Forbes-Mitchell), whom he married in 1812. She was the widow of Robert Eden Scott (1770–1811), professor of moral philosophy at Aberdeen University, and descended on both her father's and her mother's side from aristocratic Scottish families. She died in 1850. Thus he came to paint the portrait of the poet James Hogg, the Ettrick Shepherd, and John McDairmid, through whom he became acquainted with many of the circle of Sir Walter

Scott. His small-scale portrait of the playwright and poet Joanna Baillie seated in an interior (1831; University of Glasgow), reminiscent of the style of Francis Wheatley or perhaps of Louis Boilly, is one of his more unusual and original works.

While his annual submissions to the Royal Academy were almost exclusively portraits, Masquerier produced occasional fancy and historical pictures for the British Institution. It was there that he showed in 1816 *Sketch of a Meeting between the Duke of Wellington and Marshal Blucher at the Belle Alliance after the Victory of Waterloo*, based on a visit to the battlefield. The appearance of paintings of Italian monuments in 1819 presumably derives from a further continental visit in 1818. Masquerier painted a royal sitter only once. This was the duke of Sussex; the portrait was exhibited in 1812 and engraved by Hodgetts in 1813. Other notable sitters included Lady Hamilton in 1804 and Michael Faraday, who retained a lifelong affection for the painter.

In 1823 Masquerier effectively retired from his practice as portrait painter, accepting commissions only from family and close friends. He moved to Brighton in 1824, but made frequent trips abroad over the next twenty-five years, often in the company of Henry Crabb Robinson. During these final years he formed a special relationship with Baroness Burdett-Coutts; it seems to have dated from 1828, when she sat for him as the duchess in *The Lay of the Last Minstrel to the Duchess of Buccleugh* (exh. British Institution, 1828). Baroness Burdett-Coutts subsequently owned many paintings from all periods of Masquerier's career (most were sold at Christies on 4 May 1922). Masquerier died at his home, 10 Western Cottages, Brighton, on 13 March 1855, and was buried on 20 March in St Andrew's Church, Hove.   TIMOTHY WILCOX

Sources R. R. M. See, *Masquerier and his circle* (1922) · Farington, *Diary* · R. Walker, *National Portrait Gallery: Regency portraits*, 2 vols. (1985) · Thieme & Becker, *Allgemeines Lexikon* · Engraved Brit. ports. · *GM*, 2nd ser., 43 (1855), 540–42 · W. T. Whitley, *Art in England, 1800–1820* (1928); repr. (1973) · parish register, Hove, St Andrew's, 20 March 1855 [burial] · *The Post Office directory of Brighton* · *The exhibition of the Royal Academy* (1796–1823) [exhibition catalogues] · J. Guiffrey, 'Logements d'artistes au Louvre', *Nouvelles archives de l'art français* (1873), 148 · *Diary, reminiscences, and correspondence of Henry Crabb Robinson*, ed. T. Sadler, 3 vols. (1869)
Archives DWL, corresp. and MSS
Likenesses L. Parez, oils, exh. Royal Society of British Artists 1830 · J. J. Masquerier, self-portrait (aged sixteen), repro. in *Connoisseur* (Sept 1918), 11 · J. Opie, oils; photograph, NPG

Massasoit (*c*.1600–1661), leader of the Algonquian Indians, was born near Bristol, Rhode Island. The exact date of his birth and the names of his parents are unknown. He rose to become sachem (chief) of a band of southern New England Algonquian Indians later known to the English as the Wampanoag Pokanoket. In March 1621 he entered into an alliance with a group of English separatist puritans who had established a small and vulnerable village at Plymouth. That alliance and the aid he extended to the English made possible the survival of a colony that had lost nearly half its population during the previous winter. It also secured for Massasoit and his people a position as a major power in the region. His motives have been the object of much speculation. The pilgrims themselves believed that he had been forced into an unwanted friendship by the hand of God, who had intervened to restrain the naturally murderous proclivities of the savages in order to save his new chosen people. Suspecting that Indians might well be the agents of Satan, the puritans were never truly at ease with their new allies. Later historians, romanticizing events such as the work of Squanto, who taught the pilgrims to plant Indian corn, and the interracial celebration at Plymouth of the first Thanksgiving, portrayed the chief as a 'noble savage' who acted out of his natural sense of goodness and charity. A more dispassionate, modern assessment of Massasoit's policy stresses self-interest. Massasoit, it is said, sought English aid to counter the power of his enemies, the Narragansetts, a powerful tribe residing in what is now Rhode Island that had been unaffected by the epidemic disease (of European origin) that had recently killed about 90 per cent of the population adjacent to the eastern Atlantic coast. Taking full advantage of that circumstance the Narragansetts soon subjected the more vulnerable tribes in the region to tributary status. Alliance with the pilgrims gave Massasoit the means to resist Narragansett demands.

Of Massasoit's background almost nothing is known. It is estimated that he was about twenty-one at the time of his encounter with the English. Trading land for European goods such as cloth, horses, knives, kettles, and guns, his English connection brought his people not only security but power, and some wealth. Plymouth in the early years of the alliance interceded with the Narragansetts to protect Wampanoag independence. Massasoit returned the favour many times over by serving as a pro-English advocate with other Algonquian peoples. He also offered some assistance to the missionary efforts of John Eliot, who established 'praying villages' within Wampanoag territory, but Massasoit personally refused to accept the Christian religion. In other respects he was by English lights an ideal Indian, loyal to Plymouth until his death in 1661.

Massasoit was succeeded by his son Wamsutta. Named Alexander by the English, Wamsutta never enjoyed their trust. He died in 1662, following his interrogation by Plymouth officials concerned with rumours about anti-English Indian conspiracies. His brother and successor *Metacom (*c*.1630–1676), known to the English as Philip, was unable to preserve the peace. After a series of provocations, including the trial and execution by Plymouth of three of his people for killing a Christian Indian allegedly privy to a Wampanoag war plan, Metacom yielded to pressure to attack English settlements, thereby triggering one of the costliest wars in American history. Massasoit's policy of peace and alliance, so effective in its day, was undermined by the growth of English population, by the economic marginalization of the Indian population, and by the puritan colonists' deep-seated lack of respect for

Native American cultural and political autonomy, a disdain intensified by their fear and suspicion of Indians as the Devil's agents.   ALFRED A. CAVE

Sources A. T. Vaughan, *New England frontier* (1965) • N. Salisbury, *Manitou and Providence—Indians, Europeans and the making of New England* (1982) • W. Bradford, *Of Plymouth Plantation, 1620–1647*, ed. S. E. Morison (1952) • E. Arber, ed., *The story of the pilgrim fathers, 1606–1623* (1897) • *The complete writings of Roger Williams*, ed. P. Miller, 7 (1963) • *John Winthrop's journal: 'History of New England', 1630–1649*, ed. J. K. Hosmer, 2 vols. (1908) • A. A. Cave, *The Pequot War* (1996) • E. S. Johnson, *'Some by flatteries and others by threatening': political strategies among native Americans of seventeenth century New England* (1993) • F. Dockstader, *Great North American Indians* (1977)

Massereene. For this title name *see* Clotworthy, John, first Viscount Massereene (*d.* 1665); Skeffington, John, second Viscount Massereene (*bap.* 1632, *d.* 1695); Skeffington, Clotworthy, second earl of Massereene (1742–1805); Skeffington, John Skeffington Foster, tenth Viscount Massereene and third Viscount Ferrard (1812–1863) [*see under* Skeffington, Clotworthy, second earl of Massereene (1742–1805)].

Massey family (*per. c.*1760–1891), makers of clocks, watches, and nautical instruments, had as its most important member **Edward Massey junior** (*bap.* 1768, *d.* 1852), who was baptized on 18 August 1768 in Newcastle under Lyme, Staffordshire, the first of eight children of **Edward Massey senior** (1740–1813), clock- and watchmaker, and his wife, Ann (*d.* 1805). He had two sisters and five brothers, three of whom died before reaching maturity. The family were Roman Catholics, and Edward senior moved to Newcastle in 1763, having served his apprenticeship elsewhere. Although declared bankrupt in 1778, he was clearly a competent and versatile mechanic who supplied tools such as cutters and Lancashire files to the pottery manufacturer Josiah Wedgwood, and maintained the machines in his factory. Edward junior was made a freeman of Newcastle on 17 March 1790, having served an apprenticeship with his father, and married Jane Roulstone (*d.* 1841) on 2 November that year. He had seven sons, all of whom became watchmakers or nautical instrument makers, and one daughter, who married William Poynter, a watch pallet jeweller and nephew of the recusant Bishop Poynter, at Prescot, Lancashire, in 1828.

Soon after he became a freeman of Newcastle, trade directories list Edward junior as a clock- and watchmaker in the nearby pottery towns of Burslem and Hanley, but by 1806 he had returned to Newcastle to manufacture mechanical logs and sounders, to designs patented by him in 1802 and 1806. Accounts of Massey's patent sea log and sounding machine were published in Liverpool (1805) and London (1806), and a German version was published in Danzig (1818). An important forty-one page statement 'of the Case of Mr Edward Massey of the City of Coventry and of Scholes near Prescot Lancashire, Most respectfully offered to the notice of every Member of Parliament' was published in 1820. This contained details of the development and trials of his sounding machines and the number of machines purchased by the Navy Board, testimonies of sailors who had used the machines, and his objections to the lords commissioners of the Admiralty's discontinuing the purchase of his machines in favour of less satisfactory devices. Massey claimed that £700 paid by the board of longitude and the treasurer of the navy was 'not equivalent to half the travelling expenses he has incurred in bringing this machine to maturity'. Letters from Earl St Vincent, admiral of the British fleet, and Vice-Admiral Sir Charles Cotton, dated 1807, commend the machine, and Cotton adds that:

> Mr. Massey, having now been embarked more than two months (in consequence of the long detention of the squadron in Torbay by the westerly gales) and being very anxious to return to his wife and numerous family, I intend, in compliance with his earnest request, to send him into port by the first opportunity.

Additional patents for nautical instruments were taken out by members of the Massey family in 1834, 1836, 1844, 1848, 1854, 1857, 1858, 1860, 1865, 1868, 1876, and 1884. These include designs for taffrail logs, electric logs, and deep-sea sounders. As well as being used by merchant and national navies throughout the world, Massey nautical instruments were used on the great early nineteenth-century voyages of discovery, by the US coast and geodetic survey, and for deep-sea sounding for the transatlantic telegraph cables, beginning in 1857.

The Massey family continued to develop and manufacture mechanical logs and sounders on the same basic principle until the firm was taken over by Thomas Walker & Son Ltd, Birmingham, early in the twentieth century, after the death of the unmarried grandson of Edward junior, **(John) Edward Massey** (1831–1891). Thomas Walker was reputed to be a nephew of Edward Massey.

Entries in London trade directories record that John Edward Massey, trading as 'Edward Massey, successors of the original inventor and sole manufacturer by special appointment of patent logs and sounding machines to Her Majesty's Royal Navy', received the only gold medal awarded at the International Fisheries Exhibition, London (1883), and another medal at the International Inventions Exhibition, London (1885). In 1876, following a patent taken out in 1875, he also advertised as: 'Stamp makers, die sinkers and engravers; sole inventors and patentees of the new post office lock stamps used for dating, defacing and impressing or any purpose requiring the secure use of movable type'.

The younger Edward Massey was by no means the first person to have the idea of measuring the distance travelled through water by mechanically recording the revolutions of a dragged or falling vaned rotor, designed to turn at a constant rate. However, his designs were the first to produce instruments which worked well in practice and which ordinary mariners could afford to buy.

An interesting reference to the development of his log at Newcastle is found in the papers of the Liverpool antiquary, jeweller, and goldsmith Joseph Mayer (1803–1886), who was also born and raised in Newcastle under Lyme:

> On dismissal from school almost every Saturday afternoon several of my school fellows went to the canal where opposite the Cotton Factory … Massey tried his log machine

and we thought it a privilege to be allowed to trail the machines by running them along the canal.

During this period, Edward Massey junior also developed various horological devices, and in 1808 he patented a design for an improved cock or tap. In 1803 the Society of Arts awarded him 20 guineas for the design of a clock striking train which did not use a fly, for accurate indication of time during astronomical observations, and another 50 guineas for two clock escapements. After the death of his father in 1813 he moved to Ironmonger Row, Cross Cheaping, Coventry, where he continued to manufacture logs and sounders, and to exploit the horological inventions which he patented in 1812 and 1814, especially his new design for a detached lever escapement for watches. The inventions also include a robust keyless winding mechanism and an adjustable temperature compensation curb for watches, a remontoir chronometer escapement, and a gravity escapement for a pendulum regulator clock. Entries in trade directories and an advertisement in *The Times* for 21 April 1815 suggest that the Masseys soon concentrated on manufacturing, supplying, and fitting parts for their patented devices, rather than on manufacturing complete watches or chronometers. Coventry was an obvious place to set up such a business as it already had a reputation for exploiting apprentice labour in workshops to finish the rough movements produced in the Prescot area of Lancashire, rather than using the skilled watch finishers working in areas like Liverpool and Clerkenwell. Many watches with Massey's escapement from this early period were signed by Edward Massey, or marked 'Massey's Patent', but many more were signed by other manufacturers or retailers, and marked 'Patent Detached Lever', with escapements fitted or supplied by the Masseys.

Massey's version of the detached lever escapement was by far his most important contribution to horology, and exists in a number of variant forms. These, unlike the earlier versions produced by such eminent London watchmakers as Thomas Mudge and Josiah Emery, could be inexpensively produced in large numbers, and it appears that Massey was the first maker to use 'draw' as a matter of course in his lever escapements, from around 1820. This is an escapement design feature which limits intermittent friction when a watch is carried on the person, and is essential for the satisfactory performance of lever watches. It may have been the subject of a patent applied for in 1820 for which no specification was ever filed.

From 1812 until the late 1840s Massey's was the dominant form of detached lever escapement used in English watches, produced in great numbers, especially by the Liverpool watchmakers. It can be seen as the precursor of both the English single table roller lever escapement and the Swiss double roller escapement, which were produced in ever greater numbers from the second half of the nineteenth century. Through the many watches exported to the USA, Massey also influenced the development of the great American watch factories. The first American machine-made watches (manufactured by H. and J. Pitkin of Hartford, Connecticut, from 1838) had a version of his

escapement. The Massey design and the layout of the early Massey escapement watches can themselves be seen as a development of the rack lever watches produced in the Liverpool area following Peter Litherland's patents of 1791 and 1792.

By 1819 the Masseys had opened a manufactory at the Scholes, a sixteenth-century recusant house near Prescot (apparently because the skilled workmen required to develop Edward's chronometer escapements were not available in Coventry), and by 1825 another manufactory at Clerkenwell, to exploit the London market. By the early 1830s Edward and all his children were working at various addresses in the cities of London and Westminster, manufacturing patented nautical instruments, horological devices, and other items such as early fountain pens (according to designs patented in 1833 and 1834). Special items supplied by the Masseys include fast beating stopwatches (originally designed to ascertain accurately distance by sound in gunnery), and seconds beating 'journeyman' watches (to carry the time from a fixed regulator or chronometer about an observatory or ship). Further patents for various horological devices were taken out by Edward junior in 1838 and 1841, and by his son Francis Joseph (1801–1845) in 1841.

After trials at the Greenwich Royal Observatory in 1842, Massey's chronometer no. 1 was purchased for the Royal Navy for 50 guineas, 'their Lordships having been pleased in order to mark the superior performance of it to assign to it a proportionately increased price to that usually given'. However, the only member of the Massey family who seems to have produced a significant number of chronometers was Edward John (1810–1872), probably a nephew of Edward junior, who worked in Liverpool from the early 1830s. Edward Massey junior died at his home, 17 Chadwell Street, Clerkenwell, London, on 10 May 1852 of 'age and debility', and was buried at St John's Church, Duncan Terrace, Islington.

The Massey family enjoyed for many years a virtual monopoly of supply of logs and sounders for Royal Navy and merchant ships. Taken as a whole, their products did much to advance the arts of navigation and hydrography and thereby to improve maritime safety.

A. ALAN TREHERNE

Sources A. Treherne, *The Massey family* (1977) · CUL, Board of Longitude MSS, RGO 14/19, 14/25 · *A statement of the case of Mr Edward Massey* (1820) [Edward Massey jun.] · J. E. Willmot, *A short history of the firm of Thomas Walker and Son Ltd* (1951) · Keele University, Staffordshire, Wedgwood archives · Newcastle Borough Museum, Brampton Park, Newcastle under Lyme, Staffordshire, Newcastle under Lyme borough records · Gillow, *Lit. biog. hist.* · E. Smith, *On the use of the new patent sea log and sounding machine invented by Edward Massey of Hanley, Staffordshire* (1805) · R. Bill, *A short account of Massey's log and sounding machine* (1806) · A. McConnell, *No sea too deep* (1982), 25–32 · parish register, Newcastle under Lyme, St Giles, 18 Aug 1768, Staffs. RO [baptism, Edward Massey jun.] · parish register, Stoke on Trent, 2 Nov 1790, Staffs. RO [marriage, Edward Massey jun.] · d. cert. [Edward Massey jun.] · UK patents, 1802–44

Massey, Daniel Raymond (1933–1998), actor, was born on 10 October 1933 at 21 Wilton Crescent, Westminster, the only son and elder child of the Canadian actor Raymond

Daniel Raymond Massey (1933–1998), by Dorothy Wilding, c.1957

Hart *Massey (1896–1983) and his actress wife, Gladys Allen (b. 1907), who acted under the name Adrianne Allen. Given that his godfather was Noël Coward, everything conspired to lead Massey towards a life in the theatre, and after Eton College and two years in the Scots Guards, he went up to King's College, Cambridge, and made his stage début in the 1956 Footlights revue, *Anything May*, whose writers included Michael Frayn and Bamber Gascoigne.

Tall, lean, aristocratic, and blessed with a resonant musical voice, Massey was untypical of the new school of regional working-class actors emerging in the late 1950s. But his debonair charm and transatlantic inheritance—his father became a naturalized American in 1944—quickly enabled him to find work in both London and New York. He made his début in both theatrical capitals in 1957, scoring a particular success as a gauche young American in a frothy West End comedy, *The Happiest Millionaire*. But it was his performance as a Portobello Road Wedgwood dealer in a musical by Monty Norman and David Henneker, *Make me an Offer*, at the Theatre Royal, Stratford East, in 1959 that marked him out as an actor of exceptional grace and style.

For much of the next decade Massey moved easily between classics, musicals, and comedies. He took up semi-permanent residence at the Theatre Royal, Haymarket, appearing as Charles Surface in *The School for Scandal* (1962), Jack Absolute in *The Rivals* (1966), and John Worthing in *The Importance of being Earnest* (1968). But he also commuted to Broadway to play opposite Barbara Cook in a delightful American musical, *She Loves Me*, in 1963, and starred as the adoring husband in the West End

version of Neil Simon's *Barefoot in the Park* in 1965. He gave his most distinctive screen performance playing his own godfather in the ill-fated 1968 film about Gertrude Lawrence, *Star!* Coward confided to his diaries: 'Daniel Massey was excellent as me … he was tactless enough to sing better than I do, but of *course* without my special matchless charm!' (*Coward Diaries*, 667).

As if to prove that he was more than a graceful stylist, Massey deliberately widened his range over the next decade. In 1974 he memorably played Lytton Strachey, with gently fluting voice and lily-white hands suspended from his arms as if on wires, in Peter Luke's *Bloomsbury* at the Phoenix Theatre. He went on to appear, less convincingly, as Othello at Nottingham Playhouse, but was a fine guilt-racked John Rosmer in a 1977 West End revival of Ibsen's *Rosmersholm*. But it was through his work with the national companies that Massey both stretched his talent and showed himself to be a first-rate classical actor. He had a particular affinity with Shaw and appeared, to great effect, at the National Theatre in *The Philanderer* (1979), as John Tanner in *Man and Superman* (1981), and, in 1994, as General Burgoyne in *The Devil's Disciple*: this last was a perfect study of a man who adopts a pose of ironic languor to disguise his moral outrage at the loss of the American colonies.

Massey also enjoyed a rich spell with the Royal Shakespeare Company in the 1980s. Both as the Duke in *Measure for Measure* and as the politician–hero of Harley Granville-Barker's *Waste* he suggested the pathos of the public idealist slowly awakening to the emptiness of his private life. But he was also at home in new plays. In 1979 he created the role of Robert, the deceived and deceiving husband, in Harold Pinter's *Betrayal* at the National Theatre. In 1984 he played Nikolai, a wealthy Russian aristocrat and thwarted pioneer of talking pictures, in Stephen Poliakoff's *Breaking the Silence* for the Royal Shakespeare Company. He also played the tortured hero, Ben, in the 1987 London première of Stephen Sondheim's musical *Follies*.

Massey's own life had its share of anguish. His parents divorced when he was six, and he later became bitterly estranged from his mother, whom he at one point compared to the Moors murderer Myra Hindley. He also married three times. His first marriage, on 30 September 1961, was to the actress Adrienne Corri, daughter of Louis Reccoboni, hotelier; the marriage ended in divorce in 1968. Massey had a son, Paul, by another relationship before marrying, on 12 December 1975, his co-star in *Betrayal*, Penelope Alice Wilton, daughter of Clifford William Wilton, company director. They had a daughter, Alice. The marriage ended in divorce in 1984. Massey's third marriage, on 21 June 1997, was to Penelope's younger sister, Linda Mary (Lindy) Wilton. In 1992 he was diagnosed with Hodgkin's disease, which for a time he successfully fought off with chemotherapy. Although the illness affected his career and gave his aquiline features a ravaged look, he gave one last magnificent stage performance in 1995, in both London and New York, as Wilhelm Furtwängler in Ronald Harwood's *Taking Sides*. Classical music was one of Massey's private passions, and he made his audience understand both the conductor's belief in the transformative power of music and his residual guilt over his complicity with Nazi tyranny. It was both a magisterial performance and a reminder that Massey, having started out as an aristocratic charmer, later revealed a positive genius for playing damaged idealists. He died on 25 March 1998 at the Brompton Hospital, Chelsea, London, and was survived by his third wife, Lindy, his son Paul, and his daughter Alice. A memorial service was held on 16 June 1998 at St Paul's, Covent Garden.   MICHAEL BILLINGTON

Sources I. Herbert, ed., *Who's who in the theatre*, 17th edn, 2 vols. (1981) · *The Times* (27 March 1998) · *The Guardian* (27 March 1998) · *The Independent* (27 March 1998) · *The Noël Coward diaries*, ed. G. Payn and S. Morley (1982) · *WWW* · b. cert. · m. cert. [Adrienne Corri] · m. cert. [Penelope Alice Wilton] · m. cert. [Linda Mary Wilton] · d. cert.

Archives King's Cam., letter to G. Rylands

Likenesses D. Wilding, photograph, c.1957, NPG [*see illus.*] · photograph, 1985, repro. in *The Independent* (28 March 1998) · N. Clark, photograph, repro. in *The Guardian* · photograph, repro. in *The Times* · photographs, Hult. Arch.

Wealth at death £399,830—gross; £387,216—net: probate, 4 Feb 1999, *CGPLA Eng. & Wales*

Massey, Sir Edward (d. 1674), parliamentarian and royalist army officer, was the fifth of eleven sons of John Massey of Coddington, Cheshire, and Anne (b. 1582), daughter of Richard Grosvenor of Eaton, Cheshire. He was probably born between 1610 and 1615. The family were long-established minor gentry with various estates in Coddington and Bechin. Two younger brothers, George and Robert, served under Edward's command in Gloucester and he also had seven sisters. He never married. Much of the early evidence about Massey is uncertain because it derives from Clarendon, who detested him, but other sources concur that he saw military service in the Low Countries. In the bishops' wars of 1639–40 he served as a captain of pioneers under Colonel William Legge. According to a later diatribe 'hee had not 12d. some time in his pockett to pay for his dinner' (Firth, 2.159). Clarendon says that he was with the king's forces in York in June 1642 but, despairing of preferment, went to London and was appointed lieutenant-colonel to the earl of Stamford's regiment. Massey himself later wrote that he had initially been uncertain when both king and parliament seemed to profess the same beliefs, but was convinced by parliament's declarations that it never intended to alter government by king, Lords, and Commons and had taken up arms to defend the king's authority and its own privileges, punish evil counsellors and restore pure worship to the church by removing superstitious practices. He remained a rigid presbyterian throughout his career, adhering equally firmly to the oaths of allegiance and supremacy, the protestation, and the covenant.

Governor of Gloucester, 1642–1645 In the autumn of 1642 Massey marched with Stamford to Gloucester, and was left behind with one regiment when Stamford continued into Devon. Although not officially appointed governor until June 1643 he worked closely from the outset with the strongly parliamentarian aldermen of the city and the local deputy lieutenants in the military government of Gloucester. When Prince Rupert sacked Cirencester on 2 February 1643 this also shattered the self-defence forces which had been raised locally before Massey's arrival and made Gloucester the sole focus of the local parliamentarian cause. From now until May 1645 Massey defended the city against a wide array of royalist commanders from within and outside the county. Although Gloucester was vital to parliament's cause Massey rarely had much practical help and the garrison became notorious for hard service and bad pay. His dashing leadership and the general belief that the defence of Gloucester was the turning point of the war brought him hagiographic treatment from the press—notably in the account by his personal chaplain, John Corbet, which was first published in 1647. In March 1643 Massey's troops joined Waller's army and overwhelmed Lord Herbert's Welsh forces at Highnam Court, taking 1500 prisoners. They then cleared the Forest of Dean and recaptured Tewkesbury.

Despite being worsted by Prince Maurice at Ripple Field on 12 April, Massey took Hereford in May. However, after the royalists stormed Bristol in July, Gloucester became totally isolated. Massey's conduct before the siege is the most controversial aspect of his career. Clarendon says that his former commander William Legge sent him a cordial message and that, while publicly roaring defiance, Massey intimated that he would not fight against the king in person. This swayed the debate and on 10 August the king's army appeared before the walls. Massey wrote to the Commons of his lack of men and the treacherous inclinations of the citizens. It appears that he was seeking to save his skin whatever the outcome, but in the event, he signed Gloucester's defiant answer to Charles's summons and led a sturdy defence. The royalists besieged the town until forced to retreat when the earl of Essex's army arrived on 5 September. By then the garrison was down to three barrels of powder and its numbers were shrinking rapidly. Massey was voted £1000 plus all his arrears in thanks. He probably never received either. Throughout the winter he was desperately short of men and money, and subject to constant alarums from royalists forces on all sides. He fought at least fourteen minor battles between November and April as he sought to enlarge the garrison's quarters. Finally, after a relief convoy slipped through with £8000 and large amounts of material, Massey took the offensive. In April he drove Sir John Winter's forces from the Forest of Dean and marched into Herefordshire. He then doubled back to take Beverstone Castle through the governor's treachery on 21 May, then Malmesbury and, on 4 June, Tewkesbury. With Waller's help, Sudeley Castle was reduced on 9 June.

Just as the military situation was improving, however, Massey became embroiled in a vicious feud with most of the Gloucestershire county committee, which both sides pursued locally and through parliament over the next year. The initial focus was control of the two new regiments that were raised in the associated counties of Gloucestershire, Herefordshire, and south Wales. Massey believed that some committeemen were trying to raise

Sheriff Thomas Stephens's horse under their own authority while systematically starving the regiments he controlled of pay and men. While there was an overlap in authority between Massey and the deputy lieutenants—which he hoped to have resolved by an ordinance confirming him as governor—this was mainly a clash of personalities. Massey's enemies included both conservatives like Isaac Bromwich and radicals like Alderman Thomas Pury and William Sheppard, later Cromwell's law reformer. He had also squabbled with his future political ally Waller over the allocation of money when both forces were in Gloucestershire. Massey's letters to the committee of both kingdoms, the Harleys and Sir Samuel Luke, which chronicled the feud throughout, are shrill, petulant, and self-pitying in tone.

None the less, despite this and his being barely in control of the mutinous troops, Massey continued to fend off the royalists. Colonel Mynne was defeated and killed at Redmarley on 2 August, after which Massey went briefly to London to pursue his case against the committee. On his return he marched first towards Bath, then drove Langdale's Northern horse from around Corse Lawn, destroyed Winter's naval station at Beachley and took Monmouth on 24 September. Beachley had to be retaken, after being abandoned for lack of men to garrison it, on 14 October; Massey's headpiece was knocked off by a musket-butt during the assault. In November, when Massey was ordered away to Oxfordshire, Monmouth was lost again, which sparked off more bitter recriminations on both sides. Only in February 1645, when royalists trapped Stephens's forces at Rawden House, Wiltshire, and forced him to surrender, was the feud somewhat defused. In March, Massey defeated Winter at Lancaut and moved into Herefordshire. Although beaten by Rupert at Ledbury on 22 April (he later wrote that he and Rupert had shot each other's horses from under them, though neither knew it at the time), he withdrew in good order and flushed Winter out of the Forest of Dean, then stormed Evesham on 26 May.

Presbyterian leader, 1645–1649 In the same month, after repeatedly requesting to leave Gloucester, Massey was appointed general of the western association forces. He helped in the relief of Taunton on 29 June and routed Porter's horse at Ilminster on 8 July when the royalists tried to surprise Taunton again. He took part in the battle of Langport two days later and the storming of Bridgwater on 23 July, then returned to Taunton to blockade Goring. He spent the winter reducing the few remaining royalist garrisons in the west as Fairfax swept away the field armies. His men committed major disorders in Dorset, Wiltshire, and Somerset. Massey was already a known enemy of the Independent party in parliament and the army, and some hoped to use his brigade as a counterweight to the New Model. For this reason the disbandment of his troops became a major issue after May 1646, but obstacles were continually put in the way until Fairfax finally disbanded them at Devizes in October. On 18 June 1646 Massey took his seat in the Commons as member for Wootton Bassett, Wiltshire.

Thanks to his popularity in London and his enduring military reputation Massey rapidly became an influential figure in parliament. He was appointed lieutenant-general to command the army in Ireland on 2 April 1647, but the troops strongly opposed this. With Waller and others he vainly tried to persuade them to enlist at Saffron Walden. On 6 June he rode the streets of London urging the citizens to defend themselves against the madmen in the army who sought to put the best men in parliament and the city to death. When the army arrived on 16 June the officers laid articles of impeachment for high treason against eleven MPs, including Massey, for trying to start a new civil war. To let matters cool down, these 'eleven members' withdrew temporarily. In late July, with the presbyterians briefly in control again, he was named to the reconstituted committee of safety and as commander of the 40,000 men the city proposed to raise. However, on 3 August, London capitulated. Massey and Poyntz fled to the Netherlands from where they published a vindication, reciting their past services, justifying their withdrawal and vowing to return to settle the peace and restore the covenant to religion. Massey and his past were the subject of heated argument in the London mercuries at this time. From some of these we have the only extant descriptions of him. One says that he was 'of a sanguine complexion, of a middle age, brown trizld hair' (*A Speedy Hue and Crie after Generall Massie*), while a satirical skit attributed to Lilburne describes 'A strange fat unlickt, [s]mall-faced fellow' (*Generall Massey's Bartholomew Fairings for Collonell Poynts and the London Reformadoes*). Now, and again later, Massey was accused of amassing vast riches by extorting money from Gloucestershire royalists and embezzling moneys raised from taxation and other sources. These allegations are unproved; for his part, Massey complained that he never received the £1000 per year plus lands and iron mills voted to him from Winter's estates at various times. He was back in England by August 1648, when certain presbyterians planned to put him at the head of a body of infantry to be raised to restore Charles I. He was secluded from the Commons and imprisoned in St James's after Pride's Purge on 6 December, but on 18 January 1649 he slipped out by an open door and escaped to the Netherlands.

Royalist exile, 1649–1660 Here, Clarendon was later to grouse, Massey presented himself to Charles II 'with as much confidence, and as a sufferer for the King his father, as if he had defended Colchester' (Clarendon, *Hist. rebellion*, 4.467). Shortly before going abroad he penned another personal vindication, professing his fidelity to the original principles of the parliamentarian cause and calling the regicides the vilest of traitors. With the other presbyterian exiles in the Netherlands, Massey established contact with Charles II soon after Charles's return from Scotland in October 1649. His estates were consequently sequestered. In December he encountered the council of state's agent, Sir Walter Strickland, who wrote of Massey's vain attempts to dissuade locally resident members of the West India Company from taking the engagement: 'truly I have not seen a man thrust himself into a business with less advantage than he did. It seems that he had rather play at a small game than stand out' (Scrope and Monkhouse, 3.144). Massey later joined Charles II in Scotland, served as lieutenant-general of the duke of Buckingham's horse regiment and as governor of Kirkcaldy, and took part in the battle of Inverkeithing on 20 July 1651. As Charles's army marched towards Lancashire he sent Massey to rally the local presbyterian gentry. With the earl of Derby, Massey addressed a meeting at Warrington on 18 August, urging them to put past differences aside, but they found little practical support. He rejoined Charles at Stoke next day and volunteered to raise support in Worcestershire and Gloucestershire. Fighting with his customary tenacity to defend a house he had fortified near Upton Bridge, he was badly wounded in the thigh, arm and hand by 'rag-shot' on 28 August and was too ill to take any part in the battle of Worcester. Afterwards, he fled as far as Droitwich but, unable to keep up, parted from Charles and threw himself on the mercy of the countess of Stamford at Broadgate Manor, Leicestershire. Here his wounds were treated—they were so severe that a deathbed declaration was published in his name—but he was kept a prisoner. On 24 November Lord Grey sent him to London. He tried to escape by spurring his horse away, but was recaptured and confined in the Tower. The Rump had earlier listed him among eleven who should face trial for treason, but clemency prevailed after Derby's execution. Massey survived to escape to the Netherlands again on 30 August 1652, this time out of a chimney.

Charles II trusted Massey implicitly. He apparently called Massey 'my dear and faithful friend' at a tearful farewell during the retreat from Worcester (Ormerod, 2.739), and regarded him as a useful link to the presbyterians. Massey was twice in England on such business, in 1654 and 1656, as well as in Denmark in 1655. To many other royalists, his past and his character counted against him; Clarendon thought him 'a wonderfully vain, weak man', though he acknowledged Massey's courage and devotion (Clarendon, *Hist. rebellion*, 3.144). From late 1658 Massey became more actively involved in royalist plotting. He returned to London on 5 March 1659 and in May went west to revive faltering plans for an uprising in Gloucestershire. He spent most of the next three months in hiding with the Veel family in Symondshall, distributing commissions and drumming up support among local gentlemen and presbyterian clergymen for a rising on Gloucester. From the outset, this was hampered by internal divisions. Lord Mordaunt, who was co-ordinating the plot, relied mainly on the ultra-cautious John Howe, and Massey frequently complained that Mordaunt and Howe were ruining his best efforts. Some support was raised in the Stroudwater clothing district and the Forest of Dean and the rising was planned for 1 August. However, the rebel activity was all too obvious and Sir Richard Willis had betrayed much detail to the government. The Gloucester militia seized Massey and others on 31 July, and the risings here and around Bath fizzled out. While being brought over Nympsfield Hill to Gloucester at dusk, Massey contrived yet another improbable escape by making his horse stumble, rolling downhill and fleeing in the dark. He spent the next few months in the Southern Netherlands and Holland, preparing to return. On 14 January 1660 Charles commissioned Massey to return to England, authorizing him to use his own judgement as to where to act but urging him to revive the Bristol and Gloucester business if possible. He arrived by 27 January. Again friction arose because Mordaunt appointed Howe commander-in-chief above him and again Clarendon had to smooth things over. Massey was in the Bristol area in early February seeking to promote the rising, then returned to London to agitate for the readmittance of the MPs secluded at Pride's Purge. Events rapidly overtook him, though, and he did little more than report on national events and complain.

The later years, 1660–1674 On Monck's advice Massey went to Gloucester to seek election to the Convention Parliament in March. Despite opposition from some citizens and garrison troops, which led to scuffling as Massey went to dine with the mayor on 30 March, he was made a freeman and elected. He was arrested, but the Convention subsequently acquitted him of causing the riot. He worked intensively for the king's restoration in the Convention, putting forward motions to take down republican insignia and to increase the king's supply to £50,000 per annum. He was voted £1,944 6s. 2d. plus interest for his past arrears and expenses and took command of Twiselton's regiment until its disbandment in October. Charles knighted him at Canterbury on 27 May. In December he was granted a further £3000 from the excise. He was again elected for Gloucester in the Cavalier Parliament in April 1661. Presumably for this reason he did not take up the governorship of Jamaica which the king had earmarked for him in September 1660 at the request of the merchant adventurers. Massey was a moderately active MP, serving on 110 committees over the next fourteen years. He spent much time in Ireland between 1661 and 1664, after receiving a command in the Irish army and a grant of an estate on very favourable terms at Abbey Leix, now in Queen's county. He may have lost favour for trying to defend the Gloucester corporation when it was purged in 1662–3 under the Act for the Well Governing and Regulation of Corporations, for he never again held any significant posts. During the Second Dutch War he served in the Dover prize office and as the commander of auxiliary troops. Just as in Gloucester twenty years before, he was popular with the townsfolk but appears to have alienated many of the town council. In 1673 he spoke in support of bills to ease restrictions on protestant dissenters and backed Lord Arran's complaints of Catholic worship going unchecked in Ireland after the declaration of indulgence. He died in Ireland between 6 February 1674, when he last spoke in parliament, and 30 May, when his will was proved, and was buried at Abbey Leix.

Massey rose from obscurity through a mixture of outstanding qualities of military leadership, courage, sheer luck, and a talent for publicizing himself. The successful defence of Gloucester made him a nationally important figure. However, he was ill at ease in the world into which his success thrust him. Rigid, self-righteous, humourless, and paranoid to the point where his very sanity might be questioned, he was unable to work with others and invariably annoyed allies and enemies alike. It was largely because of his character defects that he never really scaled the military and political heights. Conversely, his courage, doggedness, and consistent devotion to his version of the cause of 1642 made him too useful to ignore, and he was never far from the public spotlight.

ANDREW WARMINGTON

Sources J. Corbet, 'An historicall relation of the military government of Gloucester', *Bibliotheca Gloucestrensis*, ed. [J. Washbourne], 1 (privately printed, Gloucester, 1823), 1–152 • Clarendon, *Hist. rebellion* • A. R. Warmington, *Civil war, interregnum and Restoration in Gloucestershire, 1640–1672* (1997) • G. Ormerod, *The history of the county palatine and city of Chester*, 2nd edn, ed. T. Helsby, 2 (1882) • HoP, *Commons, 1660–90*, vol. 3 • D. S. Evans, 'The civil war career of Major-General Edward Massey, 1642–1647', PhD diss., U. Lond., 1993 • *Calendar of the Clarendon state papers preserved in the Bodleian Library*, 4–5, ed. F. J. Routledge (1932–70) • *CSP dom., 1644–5* • *JHC*, 3–5 (1642–8) • S. R. Gardiner, *History of the great civil war, 1642–1649*, new edn, 1–3 (1893); repr. (1965) • *The Clarke Papers*, ed. C. H. Firth, 2, CS, new ser., 54 (1894) • 'The vindication of Major-Generall Edward Massey', 1649, BL, MS E 541 (7) • PRO, SP 25 [calendared in *CSP dom., 1644, 1644–5*] • R. Scrope and T. Monkhouse, eds., *State papers collected by Edward, earl of Clarendon*, 3 vols. (1767–86), vol. 3 • D. Underdown, *Royalist conspiracy in England, 1649–1660* (1960) • H. Cary, ed., *Memorials of the great civil war in England from 1646 to 1652*, 2 (1842) • *The letter books of Sir Samuel Luke, 1644–45*, ed. H. G. Tibbutt, Bedfordshire Historical RS, 42 (1963) • *The Nicholas papers*, ed. G. F. Warner, 4, CS, 3rd ser., 31 (1920), vol. 4 • Bodl. Oxf., MSS Tanner 60–62 • *The declaration of Generall Massey and Colonell Generall Poyntz* (1647) [Thomason tract E 401(12)] • *A short declaration by Colonel Edward Massie* (1649) [Thomason tract E 541(7)] • R. Howes, 'Sources for the life of Colonel Massey', *Transactions of the Bristol and Gloucestershire Archaeological Society*, 112 (1994), 127–41

Archives Bodl. Oxf., Tanner MSS • Bodl. Oxf., Clarendon MSS

Likenesses attrib. A. Van Dyck, oils, *c.*1639–1640, repro. in 'Notes on portraits of Sir Edward Massey', *Transactions of the Bristol and Gloucestershire Archaeological Society*, 43 (1921); priv. coll. in 1923 • R. Walker, oils, 1642–9, repro. in F. Hyett, 'Notes on portraits of Sir Edward Massey', *Transactions of the Bristol and Gloucestershire Archaeological Society*, 143 (1921); priv. coll. in 1923 • oils and half-tone print, *c.*1643–1645; priv. coll. in 1923 • half-tone print, *c.*1645, Gloucester City Museum and Art Gallery • P. Lely, oils, *c.*1650, National Gallery of Canada, Ottawa • R. Cooper, engraving, repro. in J. Ricraft, *England's champions* (1847) • crude wood caricature, BL • engraving (after W. Strewin, in or after 1670), repro. in Edward, earl of Clarendon, *The history of the rebellion* [A. H. Sutherland's grangerized edn, AM Oxf., Print Room, Sutherland Collection] • woodcut, BL

Massey, Edward, senior (1740–1813). *See under* Massey family (*per. c.*1760–1891).

Massey, Edward, junior (*bap.* 1768, *d.* 1852). *See under* Massey family (*per. c.*1760–1891).

Massey, (John) Edward (1831–1891). *See under* Massey family (*per. c.*1760–1891).

Massey, Eyre, first Baron Clarina (1719–1804), army officer, born on 24 May 1719, was the sixth son of Colonel Hugh Massey of Duntrileague, co. Limerick, and his wife, Elizabeth, the fourth daughter of George Evans, father of George, first Baron Carbery. His eldest brother, an MP and office-holder in Ireland, was Hugh, first Baron Massy. In a

'Memorial' of his services he stated that he 'purchased a pair of colours' in the 27th foot in 1739, and went with them to the West Indies as lieutenant of the grenadiers. The 27th foot, of which General William Blakeney (later Baron Blakeney; 1672–1761) was colonel, was at Admiral Edward Vernon's capture of the port and treasure of Porto Bello (on the north side of the isthmus of Darien) in 1739, and the few survivors returned home in December 1740. The dates of Massey's commissions in the 27th foot as ensign were 25 January 1741 and 3 November 1741. He served with his regiment against the Jacobites in Scotland in 1745–6, and was wounded at the battle of Culloden (16 April 1746). He was made captain-lieutenant and captain in the regiment by William Augustus, duke of Cumberland, apparently in 1747, captain on 24 May 1751, and major on 10 December 1755. In 1757 he went to North America as a major in the 46th foot, of which he became lieutenant-colonel in 1758, and in summer 1759 he commanded the regiment in the expedition against the French Fort Niagara, succeeding to the command of the king's troops after Brigadier-General John Prideaux was accidentally killed by a British mortar shell on 19 July. Massey stated in his 'Memorial' that, as Sir William Johnson (1715–1774) was in command of a large force of American Indians, who were lukewarm in the British cause, he waived the chief command in favour of Johnson. Massey commanded in the action at La Belle Famille (24 July 1759), where, with 500 of the 46th and some Indians and New York provincials, he ambushed and routed the relief force of 1800 French regulars and French Canadians together with 500 of the Five Nations Indians; almost all the French officers were killed or captured. This action took place in view of Fort Niagara, which surrendered that day, leaving the whole Upper Ohio region in British hands. According to Massey's 'Memorial', this was the first time American Indians had been defeated in the war. At his request Massey was transferred to his old regiment, the 27th (Inniskilling) regiment, and in 1760 he commanded the grenadiers of the army in James Wolfe's advance on Montreal. He commanded a battalion of grenadiers at the capture of Martinique in 1761 and at the conquest of Havana in 1762, though he was wounded several times. Massey commanded the 27th at New York, Quebec, and Montreal from 1763 to 1769, and afterwards in Ireland, and was its colonel from 19 February 1773 until his death. On 27 December 1767 Massey married Catherine (*d.* 1815), the daughter of Nathaniel Clements and the sister of Robert Clements, first earl of Leitrim; they had two sons and two daughters. Massey went to Nova Scotia in 1776 and commanded the troops at Halifax for four years. He was promoted major-general in 1777, and later he commanded at Cork. In 1782 he was promoted lieutenant-general, and he was reportedly marshal of the army in Ireland.

For many years Massey appears to have remained unemployed. In letters to General Sir John Vaughan about 1793–4 he wrote about his disappointments in not obtaining a command (as lieutenant-general), and he regarded as heartbreaking the appointment by George Nugent-

Temple-Grenville, first marquess of Buckingham, the lord lieutenant, of 'Popish children' (Master Talbot, aged eight, Master Skerritt, aged nine, and others), to ensigncies in his regiment. The carrying of the standards taken at Martinique in 1794 in state to St Paul's angered him: 'We had no such honours paid to our noble and brave commander, General Monckton!' (BL, Egerton MS 2137). From 1794 until promoted full general in 1796 he held the Cork command. It was a critical one, with, among other problems, the difficulties with new regiments, which the government persisted in 'drafting' against their recruiting engagements. He quelled a potentially serious mutiny of 2000 of these young troops at Spike Island, Cork Harbour, in 1795. Massey was MP for Swords, co. Dublin (1790–97), and governor of Limerick (1797–1804) and of the Royal Hospital, Kilmainham. In a letter to William Cavendish Cavendish-Bentinck, third duke of Portland, dated 9 November 1800, Charles, first Marquess Cornwallis stated that Massey had 'most strongly urged upon him' that his wife should be made a peeress in her own right, as a reward for his own 'long and faithful services as a soldier and his zealous loyalty as a subject' (*Correspondence of …Cornwallis*, 3.301). Massey was raised to the Irish peerage on 27 December 1800 as Baron Clarina, of Elm Park, co. Limerick; his was one of nine peerages conferred on commoners on the last day of such creations before the union with Great Britain. He died at his residence in Bath, Somerset, on 17 May 1804, and was buried at Bath Abbey on 24 May. He was succeeded by his second and only surviving son, Nathaniel William Massey (1773–1810), army officer. His widow, Catherine, died on 27 January 1815, aged seventy-one. H. M. CHICHESTER, rev. ROGER T. STEARN

Sources GEC, *Peerage* · 'Memorial of services', PRO, Home Office papers, Ireland, vol. 440 · F. Parkman, *Montcalm and Wolfe*, 2 vols. (1884) · *British military library*, 8 (1799) · *GM*, 1st ser., 74 (1804), 487 · Burke, *Peerage* (1924) · Fortescue, *Brit. army*, vol. 2 · W. C. Trimble, *The historical record of the 27th Inniskilling regiment* (1876) · R. F. K. Goldsmith, *The duke of Cornwall's light infantry (the 32nd and 46th regiments of foot)* (1970) · T. Pocock, *Battle for empire: the very first world war, 1756–63* (1998) · J. Black, *Britain as a military power, 1688–1815* (1999) · J. Holland Rose and others, eds., *Canada and Newfoundland* (1930), vol. 6 of *The Cambridge history of the British empire* (1929–59) · J. C. Beckett, *The Anglo-Irish tradition* (1976) · *Correspondence of Charles, first Marquis Cornwallis*, ed. C. Ross, 3 vols. (1859)
Archives PRO, corresp., 30/55 | BL, letters to C. Jenkinson and others · U. Mich., Clements L., corresp. with T. Gage
Likenesses J. J. Van den Berghe, stipple, pubd 1800 (after R. Bull), BM · plaster medallion (after J. Tassie), Scot. NPG

Massey, (Thomas) Gerald (1828–1907), poet and writer, born in a hut at Gamble wharf on the canal near Tring, Hertfordshire, on 29 May 1828, was the son of William Massey, a canal boatman, and his wife, Mary. His father brought up a large family on a weekly wage of some 10s. in circumstances of extreme poverty and hardship. Massey said of himself that he 'had no childhood'. After occasional attendance at the national school at Tring at the age of eight, he was put to work in a silk mill there. His hours were from 5 a.m. to 6 p.m., and he earned from 9d. to 1s. 3d. a week. He then tried straw-plaiting, but the marshy districts of Buckinghamshire induced ague. He later recalled

that it was his mother who supplemented his meagre education by acquiring for him the Bible, *The Pilgrim's Progress*, and Wesleyan tracts.

At fifteen Massey went to London and worked as a clerk and later as an errand-boy. He read voraciously, devoting his leisure to a study of Cobbett's *French without a Master*, and of books by Tom Paine, the comte de Volney, and William Howitt. His first verses, on the sufferings of the poor and the power of knowledge to redeem these people, were published in provincial papers. In 1848 they were collected in his first volume, *Poems and Chansons*, at Tring, and he sold some 250 copies at 1s. each to his fellow townsfolk. He became involved in the radical working-class politics of the day and joined the Chartists in February 1848. With John Bedford Leno, a Chartist printer from Uxbridge, he edited in 1849, at twenty-one, a paper written by working men called 'The spirit of freedom'. The following year he contributed some forcible verse to *Cooper's Journal*, a venture of the Chartist Thomas Cooper. But Massey's sympathies veered to the religious side of the reforming movement, and in the same year he associated himself with the Christian socialists under the leadership of Frederick Denison Maurice, who wrote of him at the time to Charles Kingsley as 'not quite an Alton Locke' but with 'some real stuff in him' (*Life of … Maurice*, 2.36). Massey acted as secretary of the Christian Socialist Board and contributed verse to its periodical, the *Christian Socialist*. Also in 1850 he brought out a second volume of verse, *Voices of Freedom and Lyrics of Love*, which showed genuine poetic feeling, though the style was rough and undisciplined. On 8 July 1850 he married Rosina Jane Knowles (*d.* March 1866); they had three daughters and a son.

Massey fully established his position as a poet of liberty, labour, and the people with his third volume, *The Ballad of Babe Christabel and other Poems*, which appeared in February 1854 and which was welcomed by a storm of critical acclaim. The book, which dealt with conjugal and parental affection as well as with democratic aspirations, passed through five editions within a year and was reprinted in New York, where Massey's position was soon better assured than in London. Despite obvious signs of defective education and taste, his poetry deserved its welcome. Hepworth Dixon in *The Athenaeum* (4 February 1854) called him 'a genuine songster'. Alexander Smith likened him to Robert Burns, and Walter Savage Landor in the *Morning Advertiser* compared him with John Keats, Hafiz, and Shakespeare as a sonneteer. Tennyson was hardly less impressed, though he thought that the new poet made 'our good old English crack and sweat for it occasionally' (A. Tennyson, *Life*, 1.405). Ruskin regarded Massey's work 'as a helpful and precious gift to the working classes'. Sydney Dobell, a warm admirer, became a close personal friend, and Massey named his first born son after him.

Babe Christabel was succeeded by five further volumes of verse: *War Waits* (1855, two edns), poems on the Crimean War; *Craigcrook Castle* (1856); *Robert Burns, a Song, and other Lyrics* (1859); *Havelock's March* (1860), poems on the Indian mutiny; and *A Tale of Eternity and other Poems* (1869). Many of Massey's ballads have intense martial and patriotic ardour, such as 'Sir Richard Grenville's Last Fight' and his tribute to England's command of the sea in 'Sea Kings'. His narrative verse embodies mystical speculation and was less successful; his range and copiousness suffered from laxity of technique; but his reputation endured both in England and in the United States. In 1857 Ticknor and Field of Boston published his *Complete Poetical Works*, with a biographical sketch, and in 1861 a similar collection appeared in London with illustrations and a memoir by Samuel Smiles. In *Self-Help* (1859) Smiles set Massey high among his working-class heroes. After 1860 Massey gradually abandoned poetry for other interests which he came to deem more important, and his vogue as a poet declined. In 1899 his eldest daughter, Christabel, collected his chief poems in two volumes under the title of *My Lyrical Life*.

Massey had long sought a livelihood from journalism. For a time he worked with the publisher John Chapman, and Mary Ann Evans (George Eliot) who was also in Chapman's employ (1851–3) afterwards based some features of her novel *Felix Holt—the Radical* (1866) on Massey's career. From 1854, on the invitation of the editor, Hepworth Dixon, Massey wrote poetry reviews for *The Athenaeum*. He was also a contributor to *The Leader*, edited by Thornton Leigh Hunt. Charles Dickens accepted verse from him for *All the Year Round*, and he sent a poem on Giuseppe Garibaldi to the first number of *Good Words* in 1860. He also wrote for *Chambers's Journal of Popular Literature, Science and Arts* and Hugh Miller's *The Witness* in Edinburgh.

Despite his popularity and his industry, Massey found it no easy task to bring up a family on the proceeds of his pen. With a view to improving his position, he had in 1854 left London for Edinburgh, where he lectured at literary institutes on poetry, Pre-Raphaelite art, and Christian socialism. His earnestness drew large audiences. In 1857 he moved from Edinburgh to Monk's Green, Hertfordshire, and then to Brantwood, near Coniston in the Lake District, which was at the time the property of a friend, William James Linton; it was acquired by Ruskin in 1871. During four years' subsequent residence at Rickmansworth, Hertfordshire, Massey found a helpful admirer in Lady Marian Alford, who resided with her son, the second Earl Brownlow, at Ashridge Park, Berkhamsted. In 1862 Lord Brownlow provided him with a house on his estate, called Ward's Hurst, near Little Gaddesden. In 1863, on Lord Palmerston's recommendation, Massey received a civil-list pension of £70, which was augmented by Lord Salisbury in 1887. Lord Brownlow died in 1867, and his brother and successor married the following year; both episodes were commemorated by Massey in privately printed volumes of verse. In January 1868, two years after the death of his first wife, Massey married Eva Byron; they had four daughters and a son. While at Ward's Hurst he closely studied Shakespeare's sonnets. In his article to the *Quarterly Review* (April 1864) he argued that Shakespeare wrote most of his sonnets for his patron, the third earl of Southampton. He amplified his view in 1866 in a somewhat idiosyncratic volume called *Shakespeare's Sonnets Never before Interpreted*, later rewritten as *The Secret Drama of Shakespeare's Sonnets* (1888).

At Ward's Hurst, Massey also developed an absorbing interest in psychic phenomena, especially after the death of his first wife who had been a professional clairvoyant. In 1871 he issued a somewhat credulous book on spiritualism which he afterwards withdrew. Subsequently he made three lecturing tours through North America. The first tour (September 1873 to May 1874) included California and Canada, where he gained unenviable notoriety by the delivery of a lecture, 'Why does not God kill the Devil?'. The second (October 1883 to November 1885) encompassed Australia and New Zealand as well. The third American tour began in September 1888, but the fatal illness of one of his daughters, brought it to an early close. His lectures dealt with many branches of poetry and art, but they were chiefly concerned with mesmerism, spiritualism, and mystical interpretation of the Bible. He printed privately many of his discourses. His faith in spiritualistic phenomena was lasting and monopolized most of his later years.

On leaving Ward's Hurst in 1877, Massey lived successively at New Southgate, London (1877–90), Dulwich (1890–93), and from 1893 at South Norwood. His last years were devoted to a study of the ancient Egyptian civilization, in which he thought to trace psychic and spiritualistic problems to their source and to find their true solution. *A Book of the Beginnings*, in two massive quarto volumes, appeared in 1881, and a sequel of the same dimensions, *The Natural Genesis*, appeared in 1883. His final publication was *Ancient Egypt the Light of the World, in Twelve Books* (1907), which he saw as 'a work of reclamation and restitution'. In the preface he described this as the 'exceptional labour which has made my life worth living'.

Massey died on 29 October 1907 at his home Redcot, South Norwood Hill, South Norwood, London, and was buried in Southgate cemetery, Middlesex. Two daughters of each marriage survived their father.

SIDNEY LEE, rev. SAYONI BASU

Sources S. Smiles, 'Memoir', in *Massey's poetical works* (1861) · biographical sketch of G. Massey, *The ballad of babe Christabel: with other lyrical poems*, 5th edn (1855) · *The Times* (30 Oct 1907) · C. Knight, ed., *The English cyclopaedia: biography*, 6 vols. (1856–8) [suppl. (1872)] · *Men of the time* (1856) · *Men of the time* (1875) · J. C. Collins, *Studies in poetry and criticism* (1905), 42–67 · *The Athenaeum* (2 Nov 1907), 553 · A. H. Miles, ed., *The poets and poetry of the century*, 10 vols. (1891–7) · Allibone, *Dict.* · A. T. C. Pratt, ed., *People of the period: being a collection of the biographies of upwards of six thousand living celebrities*, 2 vols. (1897) · *The life of Frederick Denison Maurice*, ed. F. Maurice, 2 vols. (1884) · private information (1912) · *Review of Reviews*, 36 (1907), 576–7 · *Book Monthly* (July 1905) · *Book Monthly* (Sept 1907)
Archives Hunt. L., letters mainly to James Thomas Fields · Royal Literary Fund, London, letters to the Royal Literary Fund
Likenesses R. & E. Taylor, woodcut, NPG; repro. in *Illustrated Review* (4 Sept 1873) · J. & C. Watkins, cartes-de-visite, NPG · portrait, repro. in *Review of Reviews* · portrait, repro. in *Book Monthly* (Sept 1907)
Wealth at death £106 os. 1d.: probate, 11 Nov 1907, *CGPLA Eng. & Wales*

Massey, Sir Harrie Stewart Wilson (1908–1983), physicist, was born on 16 May 1908 in St Kilda, a suburb of Melbourne, Australia, the only child of Harrie Stewart

Massey, hunter and prospector, and his wife, Eleanor Wilson. His father discovered gold in Hoddles Creek, and turned himself into a proficient practical engineer, operating his mine with machines of his own design, but he did not attain great wealth from this, and after 1914 he changed to sawmilling. Until Harrie was twelve the family lived in Hoddles Creek, a small country town, with a school of only twenty to thirty pupils. He was a precocious student, possessing an extremely good memory and the ability to work fast. This gave him time to pursue many interests in and out of school, such as natural history, astronomy, debating, and cricket (at which he was later reputed to be of professional standard). As a scholarship student in the University of Melbourne from 1925 he took the unusual and demanding course of undertaking full honours courses in both chemistry and natural philosophy in three years. In the first year of his studies he married Jessica Elizabeth, a teacher and daughter of Alexander Barton-Bruce, manager of timber mills near Perth, Australia. They had one daughter, Pamela Lois. Massey received the degree of BSc in 1927 and BA in mathematics in 1929 (both with first-class honours), and, prompted in the direction of physics by the lectures of E. O. Hercus, he accepted the suggestion of Professor Laby to take wave mechanics as the topic of his MSc dissertation. The resulting 460 page dissertation was a magisterial survey of the most current work on the new quantum mechanics, much of it originally published in German.

Massey's next step was to Trinity College and the Cavendish Laboratory in Cambridge, where he worked from 1929 to 1933, obtaining the degree of PhD in 1932 and being involved in one of the laboratory's most fruitful periods of experimental research under the direction of Sir Ernest Rutherford. Against Rutherford's advice Massey pursued both theoretical and experimental studies; throughout his career he was to retain an unusually wide grasp of current work in physics. Experiments on the deflection, or scattering, of very fast particles when passing through matter were responsible for the discoveries of the neutron and positron then opening up particle physics in Cambridge and elsewhere. Massey chose to concentrate in particular on collision theory—an understanding of which was crucial to experiments of this kind—and the theoretician Nevill Mott asked him to collaborate in a book on the subject. Published in 1933 *The Theory of Atomic Collisions* was quickly recognized as the standard text in the field, and Massey alone was responsible for the revisions incorporated in two subsequent, much enlarged editions in 1949 and 1965.

Massey's interest in collision theory was to underlie his entire research career, leading him from electron and atom scattering to studies of negative ions and the upper atmosphere (following a suggestion from Laby) and thence into rocket research and the utilization of the space programme for basic scientific research from the 1950s. His particular gifts lay in the direction of synthesis rather than analysis: as he put it, 'I look for relations between things and have a pattern of linkages that helps me keep in touch with a very wide area of things' (Robertson, 137). In addition to publishing over 200 papers, this unusual talent is manifested in the important research monographs he wrote, including his books on *Negative Ions* (1938, with editions in 1950 and 1976), and, with E. H. S. Burhop, *Electronic and Ionic Impact Phenomena*, five volumes (1952 with a second edition 1969–74).

From 1933 to 1938 Massey was independent lecturer in mathematical physics at the Queen's University in Belfast, managing both to stretch the brighter students and support the weaker students in his undergraduate classes. In 1938 he became Goldsmid professor of mathematics at University College, London (and in 1940 he was elected fellow of the Royal Society) but he was soon taken up with war work, at first with the Admiralty on magnetic mines before being appointed in 1943 to lead a large group of theorists working at Berkeley on the separation of fissionable from natural uranium. This research was closely related to the Manhattan project to build an atomic weapon. However, the extent to which the work of the group affected the outcome of the project is unclear. Five years after his return to a war-damaged University College, Massey moved departments to become Quain professor of physics, a post he retained until retirement in 1975, serving as vice-provost at the college from 1969 to 1973.

Under Massey's direction the physics department at University College quickly changed its focus from metal physics and liquids to research on atomic and ionic collisions, particularly in relation to studies of the upper atmosphere and particle physics. The books *Ancillary Mathematics* (with H. Kestelman, 1959), *Basic Laws of Matter* (with A. R. Quinton, 1961), and *Atomic and Molecular Collisions* (1979) demonstrate his commitment to undergraduate teaching and the clarity of his expositions of physics. He also popularized particle physics and astrophysics through such books as *Atoms and Energy* (1953), *The New Age in Physics* (1960), and *Space Physics* (1964). He oversaw the amalgamation of physics and astronomy into the one department at University College, and its passage into the era of 'big science'. In space research and high energy physics a pattern was established of planning, instrument development, and data analysis being undertaken at University College while experiments were carried out with facilities outside the college such as the Conseil Européen de Recherches Nucléaires laboratory in Geneva, NASA in the United States, and the rocket testing site at Woomera in Australia.

Massey's leading role in science policy in Britain, Europe, and the Commonwealth began in this period, initially in areas of physics in which he was closely involved—and while he continued an active programme in research. He served as a member of the nuclear physics subcommittee of the Department of Scientific and Industrial Research from 1956, as chairman of the Royal Society British national committee on space research from 1959, and as the first chairman of the council of the European Space Research Organisation in 1964–5. Sir Robert Boyd comments that it was thanks to Massey's energy and initiative that Britain had a well-established domestic space research programme unparalleled elsewhere outside the superpowers (Bates, Boyd, and Davis, 488). Massey's prediction to the press in 1957 that rockets should soon be capable of reaching the moon made him a subject of the satirical efforts of *Punch* magazine. From 1965 to 1969 Massey was chair of the newly created Council of Science Policy, the key advisory body to the Ministry of Education and Science (later the Department of Education and Science). On giving up this position he served as physical secretary and vice-president of the Royal Society from 1969 to 1978.

Massey was a short, wiry man, with time for others, remarkable powers of concentration, and an unaffected enjoyment of a broad range of activities. Students and colleagues such as D. G. Davis and Francis Crick remembered his leadership for its light touch and sure supportiveness (Bates, Boyd, and Davis, 461, 463, 499–500). He enjoyed many fruitful collaborations, including one with Courtney Mohr, a fellow student in both Melbourne and Cambridge, which outlasted their spatial separation of thousands of miles for many years. A constant traveller, Massey returned to Australia over twenty times, and the family garden in Surrey incorporated several eucalyptus trees. He received many honours, including the Royal Society's Hughes and royal medals (1955 and 1958), a knighthood in 1960, and honorary doctorates of twelve universities. He died after a long illness in his home, Kalamunda, 29 Pelham's Walk, Esher, Surrey, on 27 November 1983. He was survived by his wife.   RICHARD STALEY

Sources D. Bates, R. Boyd, and D. G. Davis, *Memoirs FRS*, 30 (1984), 445–511 • P. Robertson, 'Sir Harrie Massey: a profile', *Australian Physicist*, 18 (1981), 135–8 • H. S. W. Massey, 'T. H. Laby, FRS', *Australian Physicist*, 17 (1980), 181–7
Archives UCL, corresp. and papers | SOUND NL Aus., oral history recording with Hazel de Berg, 13/4/1970 • University of Adelaide, Physics department, pyrox magnetic wire recording of two lectures, 8/1949
Likenesses W. Stoneman, photograph, c.1940, RS • D. H. Rooks, photograph, 1980, repro. in Bates, Boyd, and Davis, *Memoirs FRS*, facing p. 445 • photographs, RS
Wealth at death £17,607: probate, 23 Jan 1984, *CGPLA Eng. & Wales*

Massey, John (1650/51–1715), dean of Christ Church, Oxford, and Roman Catholic convert, was born at Wedhampton, Wiltshire, the son of John Massey, a puritan minister. He matriculated at University College, Oxford, on 16 March 1666, aged fifteen (as John Macie), and was listed among the college's servitors in 1669/70, Anthony Wood recording that he was servitor of Obadiah Walker, fellow of University College. (Foster, *Alum. Oxon.*, confuses this John Massey with a John Massey who matriculated at Magdalen College in 1669.) He graduated BA from University in 1670, and on 10 April 1672 was admitted probationer fellow of Merton College, from where, on 29 January 1676, he proceeded MA. His academic career was undistinguished, with no known published works. He drank, and quarrelled, with Anthony Wood; assisted the Maurists by collating St Augustine; and was one of the six who took 'a course on chimistrie' in September 1683, joining the Philosophical Society on 26 March 1684 (Günther,

1.47). He served as proctor in 1684–5, after which he was a delegate to raise a regiment of scholars and a troop of horse to combat Monmouth's rebellion.

This support for James II must have drawn Massey to the king's attention, and he was rewarded in October 1686 with the deanery of Christ Church. The king's patent, dated 16 December, specifically exempted Massey from the oaths of allegiance and supremacy, subscribing the Articles, and (unusually for the dean of an Anglican cathedral) celebrating or receiving the sacrament of the Church of England. The king promised him exemption from all prosecution, 'notwithstanding that the said John Massey is not consecrated priest, or is or at any rate hereafter shall be a convict Recusant' (Bodl. Oxf., MS Tanner 30, fol. 163v). Clearly he was, or at any rate was about to be, a Catholic, influenced probably by the vicar apostolic of all England, John Leyburn, more than Walker.

Massey's tenure of the deanery was short but energetic. In March 1687 he declared himself a Catholic, furnished an oratory, and appointed a Jesuit chaplain named Ward. As a justice of the peace from July 1687 he dealt with scoffers who disrupted services at his own and Walker's chapels. He helped Walker to print Catholic works, including those of Abraham Woodhead, provoking considerable anti-Catholic response. When the king visited Oxford later that year he attended Massey's chapel on Sunday 4 September and, speaking the following day, the king alluded to the attacks on Catholic chapels, urging all to practise charity. Despite this the subdean and canons of Christ Church consistently opposed Massey. Ignoring the king's dispensation they denounced him for not receiving the sacrament and forged a note purporting to be from Sunderland ordering Massey to expel all non-Catholic students. Massey saw through this and reported it to the king, who commended him for his integrity. Although Hearne believed that Massey 'lived amongst them with great respect' (*Remarks*, 8.343), in reality the senior members of Christ Church 'did everything they could to give him a rough ride', while undergraduates were 'insolent and unruly' (Beddard, 935). The university pointedly ignored the king's request to make him a DD.

The Dutch invasion in autumn 1688 extinguished Massey's career, and he had to flee Oxford before daybreak on 30 November. From London he escaped to the exiled court in St Germain disguised as a trooper. He entered the English College at Douai on 14 December 1692, moving soon afterwards to the oratorian seminary at St Magloire, where he was supported by Mary of Modena, wife of the exiled James II. He was ordained by August 1695, when he became confessor to the famous blue nuns in Paris, moving into the convent at rue de Charenton, faubourg St Antoine, Paris, as chaplain on 23 December 1699. He presided at professions and jubilees of the community, who referred to him as 'our worthy Confessor' (Gillow and Trappes-Lomax, 65). A friend of Hearne visited him there and found him 'in a very chearfull condition' (*Remarks*, 8.343). There he died, on 11 August 1715, and was buried in the church, leaving his rented property and library to the convent charities.   JEROME BERTRAM

Sources R. A. Beddard, 'James II and the Catholic challenge', *Hist. U. Oxf. 4: 17th-cent. Oxf.*, 907–54 · Bodl. Oxf., MSS Tanner 30, 460 · *The life and times of Anthony Wood*, ed. A. Clark, 3, OHS, 26 (1894) · Wood, *Ath. Oxon.: Fasti* (1820) · J. Gillow and R. Trappes-Lomax, eds., *The diary of the 'blue nuns' or order of the Immaculate Conception of Our Lady, at Paris, 1658–1810*, Catholic RS, 8 (1910) · G. C. Brodrick, *Memorials of Merton College*, OHS, 4 (1885) · T. F. Knox and others, eds., *The first and second diaries of the English College, Douay* (1878) · Foster, *Alum. Oxon.* · L. du Four de Longuerue, *Longueruana, ou, Recueil de pensées, de discours et de conversations*, ed. J. de Guijon and N. Desmarest (Berlin [i.e. Paris], 1754) · R. T. Gunther, *Early science in Oxford*, 15 vols. (1920–68) · *VCH Wiltshire*, vol. 11 · *Remarks and collections of Thomas Hearne*, ed. C. E. Doble and others, 8, OHS, 50 (1907), 343 · Merton Oxf., archives, MCR 1.3, 481 · University College, Oxford, archives, UC:BU4/F/9

Wealth at death 88 livres p.a. rent; library sold for 582 livres; 249 livres, 13 sous remained after debts paid: Gillow and Trappes-Lomax, eds., *Diary*, 68–9

Massey, Raymond (1896–1983), actor and director, was born on 30 August 1896 in Toronto, Canada, the son of Chester Massey (*d.* 1926) and his wife, Anna Vincent Dobbins (1859–1903). His paternal ancestors had emigrated to America in 1630 and had become one of the most prominent families in Canada: for three years his father was president of Massey-Ferguson, the manufacturers of agricultural implements. His mother, who died during a family visit to Europe in 1903, was American and a graduate of Smith College, and in 1952 his elder brother (Charles) Vincent *Massey became the first governor-general of Canada to have been born in that country. The family had been deeply religious and suspicious of, if not actively hostile to, the theatre, but Massey began to develop an interest in theatre-going while still at school in Ontario.

The outbreak of the First World War found Massey touring France with his brother Vincent. He returned to Canada, enrolled at the University of Toronto, and worked briefly in the family firm before enlisting for military service. Wounded in France, he eventually joined a Canadian expeditionary force to Siberia, where the intention was to support the White Russians against the Bolsheviks. During a period of enforced idleness in Vladivostok he helped to organize a 'minstrel show', which stimulated his interest in stage performance.

In 1919 Massey was admitted to Balliol College, Oxford, where he was distinguished more for his rowing than for his academic prowess. He belonged to a play-reading circle rather than the University Dramatic Society, but after two years he left Oxford without a degree, subsequently admitting that he had frittered away his time. During a holiday in Cornwall he met Margery Fremantle, an art student who in 1920 became his first wife. They were divorced in 1929: he later wrote that 'we both displayed an astonishing lack of judgement, and we were soon aware of it' (Massey, *A Hundred Different Lives*, 14).

By now convinced that his future career lay in the theatre, Massey found employment at the newly established Everyman Theatre in Hampstead where he remained for several productions before experiencing his first West End success with a small part in the comedy *At Mrs Beam's* (1923) by C. K. Munro. He was cast in two small roles in George Bernard Shaw's *Saint Joan* in 1925, and began to

Raymond Massey (1896–1983), by Dorothy Wilding, *c.*1930

appear in, stage manage, and, eventually, direct numerous Sunday night performances, at that time the principal means of trying out new plays.

In collaboration with Allen Wade and George Carr, Massey entered into the management of the Everyman, directing and appearing in new plays and classic revivals, until financial difficulties following the general strike in 1926 put a stop to the enterprise. By 1926 his position as an actor in the West End was well established, and he used his wider managerial experience in helping to organize the actors' union Equity. He was equally at home playing English and American parts, and scored a success playing the Khan Aghaba in *The Transit of Venus* (1927). 1929, the year of his divorce, saw his second marriage, to the actress Gladys Allen, whose stage name was Adrianne Allen. His first appearance in New York followed in 1931, as Hamlet, in a spectacular production by Norman Bel Geddes: from then onwards he was to appear regularly in the United States and Canada.

In 1930 Raymond Massey began his film career, with a brief stint in Hollywood: during his lifetime he appeared in more than seventy films, under directors including James Whale, John Wayne, Alexander Korda, and William Powell, with whom he formed a close friendship. His career in the theatre continued with the title role in the stage adaptation of Edith Wharton's *Ethan Frome* at the National Theatre, New York, which he regarded as 'just about the best dramatization of a novel ever to be seen in the theatre' (Massey, *A Hundred Different Lives*, 197). He was best remembered by the American public, however, for his performance as Lincoln in Robert Sherwood's *Abe Lincoln in Illinois*, which began its lengthy run in October 1938 and was subsequently made into a film; the author had asked him to play Lincoln after seeing his performance as Hamlet, impressed both by his abilities as an actor and by the tall, gaunt appearance which fitted him physically for the role.

Massey was divorced (amicably) from his second wife in 1939, and in that year married Dorothy Ludington Whitney, a lawyer whom he described as 'a Connecticut woman of the same Puritan ancestry as myself' (Massey, *A Hundred Different Lives*, 248). His career was now based in the United States, where his appearances ranged from 'acting one heavy after another' (ibid., 272) in films under contract to the Warner brothers to playing Sir Colenso Ridgeon in the New York production in 1942 of *The Doctor's Dilemma* by George Bernard Shaw. In the same year he enlisted in the Canadian army, but, finding himself unable to do anything worthwhile as a 'desk warrior' (ibid., 290), he soon returned to the stage. In 1944 he played the stage manager in Thornton Wilder's *Our Town* to United States troops on service in Europe, and in the same year he became a naturalized citizen of the United States.

In the post-war theatre, Massey's reputation as a serious and intelligent actor ensured that he was rarely out of work. Although Conservative politically and traditional in his approach to the craft of acting (he distrusted the Stanislavsky-based 'method') he was associated with many of the attempts to enlarge the horizons of the American stage. In 1952 the only play of which he was the author, *The Hanging Judge*, based on a novel by Bruce Hamilton, had a successful run at the New Theatre, London; in America in the same year, Charles Laughton directed him in a dramatized reading of Stephen Benét's poem *John Brown's Body*, whose simple but powerful format proved highly popular. Massey's last Broadway appearance took place in 1958, when he played Mr Zuss in Archibald McLeish's poetic drama *JB*.

In 1959 Massey moved from his Connecticut home to Beverly Hills in Los Angeles in order to be closer to the opportunities offered by the expanding television industry, and in 1960 he was invited to play Dr Gillespie in *Dr Kildare*. Over the next five years he was to become familiar to a vast public in this popular series. Although arthritis was now making it more difficult for him to appear on the stage, in 1970, at the age of seventy-five, he returned to London's West End in Robert Anderson's *I Never Sang for my Father*. In his final stage appearance, in 1975, he played the 93-year-old Jonathan Coffin in Tennessee Williams's *The Night of the Iguana*.

Massey wrote two volumes of autobiography, *When I was Young* (1977) and *A Hundred Different Lives* (1979), and was awarded seven honorary degrees from universities in Canada and the United States. Two of his children, Anna and Daniel *Massey, followed him into the theatre. Raymond Massey died in Los Angeles in July 1983.

MICHAEL ANDERSON

Sources R. Massey, *A hundred different lives* (1979) · R. Massey, *When I was young* (1977) · I. Herbert, ed., *Who's who in the theatre*, 16th edn (1977) · *The Times* (1 Aug 1983)
Archives FILM BFI NFTVA, performance footage | SOUND BL NSA, oral history interviews · BL NSA, performance recordings
Likenesses D. Wilding, photograph, c.1930, NPG [see illus.] · photographs, Hult. Arch.

Massey, (Charles) Vincent (1887–1967), diplomatist and patron of the arts, was born in Toronto, Ontario, on 20 February 1887, the eldest son of Chester Daniel Massey (1850–1926) and his wife, Anna Dobbins Vincent (1859–1903). Raymond *Massey, the film actor and director, was his younger brother. The family house, 519 Jarvis Street, in Toronto, where Vincent grew up, had been the home of his paternal grandfather, Hart Almerrin Massey (1823–1896), a manufacturer of farm implements. The successful family farm implement business, originally a sole proprietorship, became the Massey-Harris Company, Massey-Ferguson Ltd, and eventually, in 1987, the Variety Corporation. Vincent Massey was president of the Massey-Harris Company from 1921 to 1925. Chester Daniel Massey was both a manufacturer and philanthropist and endowed the University of Toronto with a substantial neo-Gothic building, Hart House (completed in 1919). Vincent's mother, an American by birth and a Methodist of Huguenot descent, died in 1903, and his father married Margaret Phelps in 1907.

Vincent Massey was educated at five different schools (the last was St Andrew's College, a private school in Toronto). At the age of nineteen he enrolled at the University of Toronto, where he graduated BA in 1910, then in 1911 he entered Balliol College, Oxford, where he graduated with a second in modern history in 1913. Between 1913 and 1915 he was a lecturer in modern history and dean of residence at Victoria College, University of Toronto. In 1915 he married Alice Stuart Parkin (1879–1950). Her father, Sir George Robert *Parkin, had been the first administrator of the Rhodes scholarships, and she met Vincent while he was an undergraduate at Oxford. Alice and Vincent had two sons, Lionel (b. 1916) and Hart (b. 1918).

During the First World War Massey served on the staff of military district no. 2, Canada, achieving the rank of lieutenant-colonel. The war committee of the federal cabinet provided him with administrative experience of government as an associate secretary. After the war he worked on resettling ex-servicemen in domestic employment in Canada. This provided him with further administrative experience that he found valuable in his later diplomatic posts. From 1921 to 1925 he was president of the family business, the Massey-Harris Company.

In 1925 the Canadian prime minister, Mackenzie King, invited Massey into the cabinet. However, he failed to secure a parliamentary seat in the House of Commons and was subsequently made a delegate representing Canada at the Imperial Conference of 1926 in London and then first Canadian minister to the United States, a post he held from 1926 to 1930. It was as president of the National Liberal Federation (1932–5) that he first experienced a strain in his relationship with King. This strain continued, and King later accused Massey of 'self-aggrandizement' (Massey). Massey, nevertheless, found a fitting role for his talents and personality when in 1935 he was appointed Canadian high commissioner to Britain, an appointment interrupted and delayed from 1930 when King's Liberal government was defeated in the general election. It was with distinction, particularly because of his social skills, that he served in this role at Canada House in London until 1946. The post suited him admirably because he brought to it the complex view of what it was to be Canadian, yet he was also an inveterate Anglophile. He savoured the considerable ceremony that went with the post in London, moved in aristocratic and political circles, and enjoyed both London and the English countryside.

King kept Massey in office in London for a considerable time despite their clear differences of political opinion. Their personal and political relationships were always rather formal and tense. The political differences developed over divergent attitudes towards empire and Massey being seen by King at times as rather too pro-British or friendly towards Whitehall. During the Second World War Winston Churchill marginalized Massey's importance by using the British high commissioner in Ottawa, Malcolm MacDonald, for communications with King. With General Andrew McNaughton, commander of the Canadian troops in Britain, having separate wartime military headquarters in London, Massey's influence with London and Ottawa was overshadowed. However, his longevity in office at the high commission would suggest that King was happy with most of his work, and particularly his tireless wartime activities. The Masseys helped to organize two centres for Canadians in Britain during the war, and Alice showed compassion and understanding of the losses being experienced by Canadians at home and abroad, personally corresponding with thousands of Canadian families with regard to Canadian personnel serving in Europe. Through the Massey Foundation, Vincent secured a convalescent home for Canadians, Garnons, in Hereford, and, through his contacts with Waldorf and Nancy Astor, the Cliveden estate in Buckinghamshire was made available as a convalescent hospital. The Masseys promoted a positive relationship between the Astors and Canada and procured some useful confidences on visits to Cliveden. Early in the war the Masseys created a Canadian officers' club in London, and in 1940, with less élitism and with a financial cost to themselves, they set up and helped to run the Beaver Club for all enlisted Canadian servicemen in the city. Among Massey's staff at the high commission was the future Canadian prime minister Lester Bowles Pearson.

Massey was a great patron of the arts (trustee of the National Gallery in London, 1941–6; the Tate Gallery, 1942–6; and the National Gallery of Canada in Ottawa, 1948–52), and he presented a substantial collection of his paintings to the National Gallery of Canada. In 1949 he was appropriately appointed as chairman of the royal commission on national development in the arts, letters, and sciences, providing him with the opportunity to diagnose the cultural problems of Canada. This royal commission, set up by the then prime minister, Louis St Laurent, commonly became known as the Massey commission, although it has also been referred to as the Massey-Lévesque commission. Father Georges-Henri Lévesque was a member of the religious order of Dominicans and a crucial French-Canadian representative for the commission.

The mandate of the royal commission included consideration of television, radio, cultural institutions, and federal scholarships. Massey clearly saw its work as concerning broad human activities relating to Canadian life, and that it should not be associated exclusively with the more esoteric notion of 'culture'. The commissioners attempted to address both urban and rural concerns about the nature of Canadian life and commissioned some forty specialized studies. While the commission tried to be democratic in approach, it was inevitably accused of being élitist. Massey was very proud of the contribution he made in advancing the debates about Canadian life in many forms. Early criticism of the royal commission, notably from the province of Quebec, was that its work and mandate infringed upon the autonomy of provinces. The subsequent report of the commission, which was much debated, recommended the creation of the Canada Council, a body established in 1957.

In 1952 St Laurent appointed Massey the first native-born governor-general of Canada. This was another official responsibility which he held with distinction, and his first five-year term was extended until 1959, when he formally retired. It appeared an entirely appropriate appointment, given his love of all the traditions of the crown and the ceremony that accompanied the position. He also did not stint on trying to reach all Canadians, undertaking trips throughout the country totalling over 180,000 miles by the end of his tenure. These trips included visits to the Inuit and First Nations of Canada in 1956, the photographs of which make him appear much less aloof and less formal than his official position normally warranted.

A number of honours were bestowed on Massey, but the one that gave him exceptional pleasure was the Companion of Honour (1946), though King withheld his own approval of this honour until close to the time of its bestowal by George VI. Massey delivered the Romanes lecture at Oxford in 1961 on 'Canadians and their Commonwealth', a subject of both personal and political significance to him. In his honour, the Canadian Broadcasting Company created the Massey lectures in 1961. A further legacy was provided when he oversaw the creation and construction of Massey College, a college for graduates at the University of Toronto funded from the Massey Foundation.

Although Massey died on 30 December 1967, at the King Edward VII Hospital in London, he was buried neither in England nor in the rather grand family tomb at Mount Pleasant cemetery in Toronto. Instead, after a state funeral in Ottawa on 4 January 1968, his remains were interred on 5 January in the unostentatious cemetery of the Anglican church of St Mark's at Port Hope, Ontario. He had broken from strict Methodism earlier in his life and found a modest resting place beside his wife and elder son, Lionel (*d.* July 1965). 　　　　MARTIN THORNTON

Sources V. Massey, *What's past is prologue: memoirs* (1963) · C. Bissell, *The young Vincent Massey* (1981) · C. Bissell, *The imperial Canadian: Vincent Massey in office* (1986) · *The Times* (1 Jan 1968) · P. Litt, *The muses, the masses, and the Massey commission* (1992) · *DNB*
Archives Massey College, Toronto, papers | BL, corresp. with Albert Mansbridge, Add. MS 65253 · Bodl. Oxf., corresp. with L. G. Curtis · HLRO, corresp. with Lord Beaverbrook · Tate collection, corresp. with Lord Clark | FILM BFI NFTVA, documentary footage · BFI NFTVA, news footage
Likenesses two group portraits, photographs, 1923–45, Hult. Arch. · G. Lunney, photograph, NA Canada · L. T. Newton, oils, Government House, Ottawa · L. T. Newton, oils, University of Toronto, Hart House · L. T. Newton, oils, priv. coll. · photograph collection, NA Canada

Massey, William (1691–1764?), writer and translator, born in January 1691 of Quaker parents, learned Latin, Greek, and French at a private grammar school kept by William Thompson at Nottingham, and afterwards took lessons in Hebrew from a clerk of the parish of St Gregory, Norwich. In 1712 he became Latin usher in a boarding-school at Half-Farthing House, Wandsworth, Surrey, kept by Richard Scoryer, after whose death in 1714 he continued in the same employment for about a year under Scoryer's successor, Edward Powell, a noted writing-master and accountant. Afterwards he ran a boarding-school of his own for many years at Wandsworth which proved popular with Massey's fellow Quakers.

Massey's first published work was *Musa paraenetica, or, A Tractate of Christian Epistles, on Sundry Occasions, in Verse* (1717, repr. 1746), and he went on to compose further works of a religious or scholarly nature. These include a translation of Ovid's *Fasti*, and *Synopsis sacerrima, or, An Epitomy of the Holy Scriptures, in English Verse* (1719, repr. 1801). The latter is a whistle stop tour of the Bible, 'chiefly designed for children, to be got by heart when they have learn'd to read'. Also of interest are his *Remarks upon Milton's Paradise Lost, Historical, Geographical, Critical, and Explanatory* (1761) and *Corruptae Latinitatis index* (1755). The latter is an attack on post-classical Latin neologisms; of *flatuosus*, for example, he remarks: 'This word is not, that I can find, in the Classics. Whatever Occasion some Modern Physicians may have for it, other Writers ought to reject it.' Massey's most substantial work is *The Origin and Progress of Letters, an Essay* (1763). The first part deals with the origin of writing and includes discussions of writing materials, printing, and alphabets. The second part, treating of calligraphy, is 'a compendious account of the most celebrated English penmen'.

Dr Birch notes that on 24 March 1764 Massey was seized with the dead palsy on his right side, and on 28 August he adds: 'I visited him at his house on Cambridge Heath, near Hackney, and found him very ill of the stone, added to the palsy.' Probably he died shortly afterwards.
　　　　THOMPSON COOPER, rev. SARAH ANNES BROWN

Sources BL cat. · W. Massey, *The origin and progress of letters: an essay in two parts* (1763) · W. Massey, *Synopsis sacerrima, or, An epitomy of the holy scriptures in English verse* (1719) · W. Massey, *Corruptae Latinitatis index* (1755) · Watt, *Bibl. Brit.* · J. Smith, ed., *A descriptive catalogue of Friends' books*, 2 (1867) · E. F. Rimbault, 'Notes concerning Edward Cocker and his works', *N&Q*, 2nd ser., 2 (1856), 310–11 · BL, Add. MS 6211, fols. 123, 127 · A. Heal, *The English writing-masters and their copybooks, 1570–1800* (1931)
Archives Yale U., Beinecke L., treatises

Massey, William Ferguson (1856–1925), prime minister of New Zealand, was born at Limavady, co. Londonderry, on 26 March 1856, the eldest child of John Massey, a small farmer, and his wife, Mary Anne Ferguson. The family background was Ulster-Scots. In 1869 John Massey emigrated to New Zealand and settled in Auckland, William being left behind to continue his schooling. He arrived in Auckland on 10 December 1870.

In 1876 William Massey began farming on his own account at Mangere, near Auckland, where on 5 April 1882 he married Christina Allen Paul (1863–1932), from a neighbouring farming family. They had seven children, of whom two daughters and three sons survived infancy; two of the latter became MPs in New Zealand. He took a prominent part in local organizations, especially in farming, and was nicknamed Farmer Bill by some. In 1891 he was elected president of the Auckland Agricultural (and Pastoral) Association, and soon became leading spokesman for Auckland farmers.

In 1891 a strongly conservative political body, the National Association, was formed. Massey became its Auckland vice-president, thus aligning himself with the opposition in politics. He stood unsuccessfully in the 1893 general election, but was returned at a by-election in 1894. The opposition was in low water during the 1890s, unable to adjust to the new party politics as practised by the masterful Liberal premier R. J. Seddon. Massey, a vigilant, hard-working member among less industrious colleagues, became party whip in 1896. In 1903 he was elected leader over some senior members.

Massey was chosen as reorganizer, and made ground as party chief slowly. He was basically a freehold farmers' champion, and accepted state leasehold settlement only if tenants had ready access to the freehold. Massey proclaimed himself the foe of socialism and land nationalization. His rise to power was generally in proportion to divisions within the Liberal Party under Seddon's successor, J. G. Ward. He asserted that Ward could not stand up to his left wing and militant labour.

Massey's arrival in power as leader of the Reform Party (the name was adopted in 1909) was delayed until July 1912, when Liberal disintegration in the house tipped the balance. The changes which he made were not great: he had long accepted Liberal legislation and undertook to administer it more 'soundly' (Gardner, 'The rise of W. F. Massey', 22).

Massey chose an able cabinet and headed New Zealand's first disciplined party organization. In 1912–13 he faced unprecedented industrial upheaval, which led to a general strike. He regarded militant labour, 'the Red Feds' (Olssen), as challenging law and order with force. In this spirit, he crushed the strikes with superior force. A bitter

William Ferguson Massey (1856–1925), by Sir William Orpen, 1919

election in December 1914 did not yield the reward he expected, and he retained office only in political deadlock.

The formation of a national wartime cabinet in the United Kingdom in May 1915 led to demands for similar steps in New Zealand. In August, Massey reluctantly agreed to share power with Ward and the Liberal Party, while remaining as prime minister. Ward, who insisted on otherwise equal political status, became minister of finance. As war leader, Massey, the Ulster Presbyterian, was yoked with Ward, of Cork Catholic descent—a sore trial for both men.

With almost universal approval, Massey pledged and delivered full support to the United Kingdom in August 1914. Yet the country had no experience of a total war effort, and the task of swiftly mounting one was achieved with difficulty. For a small, remote society the human cost was heavy: out of a total of 103,000 serving overseas, about 17,000 lost their lives. At home, farming prospered in response to the British commandeer of produce, and land values rose sharply. Yet the burdens placed on civilians by continuing war generated complaint and dissension from which the new Labour Party benefited, to Massey's intense annoyance. Massey's wife was extremely active in war work, and for this and later service was made CBE in 1918 and GBE in 1926.

In September 1916 Massey and Ward arrived in Britain to attend an Imperial Conference and to take part in the imperial war cabinet. The two leaders had two further visits to Britain in 1918–19. Massey attended the Paris peace conference and signed the treaty of Versailles on behalf of New Zealand. Though he had no faith in the League of Nations,

he gained the mandate over Western Samoa, a German colony which had been occupied by New Zealand at the outbreak of the war. A share in Nauru Island phosphate was his welcome legacy to New Zealand farming. Massey attended imperial conferences in 1921 and again in 1923, when he was the senior prime minister present.

Massey was the strongest imperialist among the dominion prime ministers of his time. He was privately attracted to British Israelism. While insisting on New Zealand's autonomy, he regarded the British empire and navy as the guarantors of its members' security and prosperity. However, his hope that a closer union would develop from wartime co-operation proved vain. Post-war turmoil alarmed him, and he was quick to denounce opponents of his views as 'Bolsheviks' (Gardner, 'W. F. Massey in power', 28).

Massey faced the 1919 election with some disgruntled followers and a party organization in decay: wartime prosperity still held, however, and against expectations he won his only clear, if narrow, victory. Its benefits were short-lived. In 1920–22 export prices fell and the frenzied wartime speculation in farm land collapsed. In response to demands that New Zealand should reward its defenders, Massey put more than 7000 returned soldiers on overpriced farms. In depression, many were ruined, and Massey was widely, if unfairly, held to blame. Established farmers survived on increased production, and put pressure on Massey to establish state-sponsored meat and dairy boards to control marketing. Massey put aside his free-enterprise views when farmers made their needs plain.

The 1922 election reflected current economic problems and the growing urban electorate. Massey held office only with the votes of independents. To the strains and uncertainties of party manoeuvring was added the onset of cancer. Massey became increasingly overbearing and irascible, though the 'Old Man' (Lee, 47) continued to dominate the house by stature and experience. The apparent return of prosperity in 1924–5 convinced him that full victory was within his reach: yet his hand was not strong enough to grasp it. Following an unsuccessful operation, Massey died at his residence in Tinakori Road, Wellington, on 10 May 1925. He was buried on 14 May at Point Halswell, Wellington harbour.

Massey has not achieved his rightful place in New Zealand history. He lacks a full biography—and a local statue: yet he held office for more than twelve years, standing second only to Seddon by three months. He faced far more difficult, crisis-ridden times than Seddon, and with weaker political resources. Massey's career lay in the shadow of traumatic events which changed New Zealand irrevocably. Their effects remained; the confused politics of his tenure of power have left no lasting mark.

A man of large frame and commanding presence, Massey inspired widespread respect while falling short of Seddon in popularity. Labour denounced him as the defender of class interests. As head of state he met crisis with courage and fixity of purpose. He owed much to F. H. D. Bell, whose legal talents complemented his own political prowess, and to James Allen, acting prime minister in his absence. Massey rejected the 'conservative' label and proclaimed himself a 'True Liberal' (Gardner, 'The rise of W. F. Massey', 25–6). His pragmatic continuance of Liberal policies and extension of state power place him well within the mainstream of New Zealand politics.

W. J. GARDNER

Sources B. Gustafson, 'Massey, William Ferguson', *DNZB*, vol. 2 · W. J. Gardner, *William Massey* (1969) · W. J. Gardner, 'The rise of W. F. Massey, 1891–1912', *Political Science*, 13/1 (1961), 3–30 · W. J. Gardner, 'W. F. Massey in power, 1912–1925', *Political Science*, 13/2 (1961), 3–30 · G. H. Scholefield, *The Right Honourable William Ferguson Massey, MP, PC, prime minister of New Zealand, 1912–25: a personal biography* (1925) · A. H. McLintock, ed., *An encyclopaedia of New Zealand*, 3 vols. (1966) · W. J. Gardner, 'William Ferguson Massey', *New Zealand's Heritage*, pt 71 (1972), 1965–70 · M. Bassett, *Three-party politics in New Zealand, 1911–1931* (1982) · B. Macdonald, *Massey's imperialism and the politics of phosphate* (1982) · W. J. Gardner, *The farmer politician in New Zealand history* (1970) · W. D. Stewart, *Sir Francis Bell: his life and times* (1937) · R. D. Batt, ed., *The Massey collection* (1977) · E. Olssen, *The red feds: revolutionary industrial unionism and the New Zealand federation of labour, 1908–1913* (1988) · J. A. Lee, *Rhetoric at the red dawn* (1965)

Archives Massey University of Manawatu, Palmerston North · NL NZ, Turnbull L. · University of Canterbury, New Zealand, Macmillan Brown Library | HLRO, political coresp. with Lloyd George | FILM Film Archive, Wellington, Massey farewells NZ troops, September 1914 · Film Archive, Wellington, George V reviews NZ troops, Salisbury Plain, May 1917 · Film Archive, Wellington, Massey and Sir Joseph Ward visit NZ troops, Western Front, July 1918 | SOUND Radio NZ, Christchurch, archives, address on the British Empire, 1917, HMV D841 [only known reproduction of voice, 78 record] · Radio NZ, Christchurch, archives, contemporary reminiscence by W. D. Stewart

Likenesses W. Stoneman, photograph, before 1917, NPG · W. Orpen, oils, 1919, NPG [*see illus.*] · F. D. Shurrock, stone medallion, *c.*1929, Massey Memorial, Point Halswell, Wellington Harbour, New Zealand · P. Flannagan, bronze statue, Limavady Borough Council Offices grounds, Northern Ireland · J. Guthrie, group portrait, oils (*Statesmen of World War I*), NPG · J. Guthrie, oils, NPG, Scot. NPG · photograph, NL NZ, Turnbull L.

Wealth at death £48,597 16*s.* 2*d.*: probate, New Zealand

Massey, William Nathaniel (1809–1881), politician and historian, son of William Massey, was a distant member of the Clarina family. He was called to the bar in 1844, and became recorder of Portsmouth in 1852 and of Plymouth in 1855. In the same year he was returned to parliament in the Liberal interest as member for Newport in the Isle of Wight, which he represented until 1857, when the moderate Liberal Party in Manchester invited Robert Lowe to oppose T. Milner-Gibson and John Bright in that city and extended a similar invitation to Massey to contest Salford against Sir Elkanah Armitage. Massey, wiser than Lowe, responded to the summons, and won the seat with an ease astonishing to all who were not acquainted with the personal unpopularity of his opponent.

Massey was under-secretary in the Home Office from August 1855 to March 1858, and, though opposing Russell's Reform Bill in 1860, was chairman of ways and means and deputy speaker from 1859 to 1865. He continued to sit for Salford until 1863, when he succeeded Samuel Laing as financial member of the government of India, a position which he held until 1868, when he unsuccessfully contested Liverpool. Massey possessed high qualifications for this important post, but his efficiency in it, as well as in the chair of the house in committee, was thought to be impaired by his indolence. He was sworn a privy councillor on his return to England, was elected for Tiverton in 1872, and sat until his death, but took no prominent part in politics, and did not again hold office. He married first, in 1833, Frances Carleton (*d.* 1872), daughter of the Revd John Orde, and second, in 1880, Helen Henrietta, the youngest daughter of Patrick Grant, sheriff-clerk of Inverness-shire. Massey had at least one child, Charles Carleton, probably from his first marriage.

Massey was a devoted follower of Palmerston, and both by conviction and temperament averse to political innovation. He was personally popular both in the house and among his constituents; his abilities were considerable, his legal and financial knowledge extensive, but he lacked energy and ambition. He published an essay on legal reform, *Common Sense versus Common Law* (1850), but his only important literary performance is an unfinished history of the reign of George III until the Peace of Amiens (4 vols., 1855–63). In writing this book he had the assistance of the extensive materials collected by E. H. Locker for his intended biography of George II; Massey's style is lucid, and his general treatment of the subject sensible and impartial, but his work is devoid of all distinctive characteristics, and exhibits the qualities neither of a picturesque nor of a philosophic historian.

Massey died at his home, 71 Chester Square, London, on 25 October 1881 and was buried at Kensal Green cemetery.   RICHARD GARNETT, *rev.* H. C. G. MATTHEW

Sources *The Times* (27 Oct 1881) · *Annual Register* (1881) · Boase, *Mod. Eng. biog.* · *Dod's Parliamentary Companion*

Likenesses wood-engraving, NPG; repro. in *ILN* (11 March 1865)

Wealth at death £17,913 14*s.* 7*d.*: resworn probate, June 1882, CGPLA Eng. & Wales

Massie, James William (1799–1869), missionary and abolitionist, born in Ireland, was taught by Dr David Bogue, presumably at the missionary college at Gosport, Hampshire, and began his independent ministry as a missionary to India, where he lived and worked from 1822 until 1839. His *Continental India* was published in two volumes in 1840. At some point, Massie married; he and his wife had three children: a son, Milton, and two daughters, Elizabeth and Isabella. Massie then worked as a pastor in Perth, Dublin, and Salford, and travelled through Belgium, Switzerland, and Germany, before moving to London where he was secretary to the Home Missionary Society from 1848 to 1859.

Massie was an advocate of free trade and for the anti-slavery movement, and he was an ardent member of the union and emancipation societies that were formed during the American Civil War. He published *The American Crisis, in Relation to the Anti-Slavery Cause* (1862) and *America: the Origin of her Present Conflict: her Prospect for the Slave, and her Claim for Anti-Slavery Sympathy* (1864). Massie was a frequent visitor to America; his last trip was as a member of a deputation appointed to deliver the address adopted at the ministerial anti-slavery conference held in the Free Trade

Hall, Manchester, on 3 June 1863. He was also often in Ireland for 'revival work', and he published *The Evangelical Alliance: its Origin and Development* (1847).

Before his death, Massie was granted the degrees of DD and LLD and was elected a member of the Royal Irish Academy. He died at 28 Adelaide Street, Kingstown, near Dublin, on 8 May 1869.

GORDON GOODWIN, rev. LYNN MILNE

Sources T. Cooper, ed., *The register, and magazine of biography, a record of births, marriages, deaths and other genealogical and personal occurrences*, 1 (1869), 472 · E. Walford, ed., *The register, and magazine of biography, a record of marriages, deaths and other genealogical and personal occurrences*, 2 (1869), 54 · J. G. Wilson and J. Fiske, eds., *Appleton's cyclopaedia of American biography*, 7 vols. (1887–1900) · *CGPLA Eng. & Wales* (1869)

Likenesses S. Bellin, group portrait, engraving, pubd 1850 (*The meeting of the council of the anti Corn Law League*; after J. R. Herbert), BM, NPG · Holl, engraving (after Wageman), repro. in E. Evans, *Catalogue of a collection of engraved portraits*, 2 vols. (1853) · stipple and line engraving, NPG

Wealth at death under £1500: administration with will, 9 June 1869, *CGPLA Eng. & Wales*

Massie, John (1842–1925), biblical scholar and politician, was born on 3 December 1842 at Newton-le-Willows, Lancashire, the son of Robert Massie, a Congregational minister, and his wife, May Soutter. In 1848 the father moved to Atherstone, Warwickshire. Massie was educated at Atherstone grammar school and subsequently at St John's College, Cambridge, where he was admitted as a sizar in 1862 and became a scholar in 1864. He obtained a second class in the classical tripos in 1866. During his first few years as a graduate he lived at Highgate, Middlesex, and prepared pupils for university entrance. In 1869 he became classical tutor at the Congregational theological college at Spring Hill, Birmingham. Two years later he was appointed professor of New Testament exegesis at that college, and was known as an accurate and congenial teacher. He held this post at Birmingham, together with his classical tutorship, until 1886, when the college moved to Oxford. On 19 July 1876 he married Edith Mary (*b.* 1848/9), daughter of Alexander Ogilvie, civil engineer, of Sizewell House, Suffolk, and the couple settled at Leamington Spa. Massie became involved in local politics, and in 1878 he was elected to the town council at Leamington Spa, later becoming an alderman. He remained a member of the council until 1887.

In 1886 Spring Hill College was closed, its endowments being transferred to Mansfield College, the new Congregational theological institution at Oxford which replaced it. Mansfield began its work at 90 High Street, Oxford, in October 1886. Three years later its new premises, built in spacious gothic style, were opened.

Massie moved to Oxford, took up residence at Headington, and from 1886 to 1903 continued his scholarly occupation as Yates professor of New Testament exegesis at Mansfield. He became associated with the university as an incorporated MA at Corpus Christi College. At Mansfield he was initially the only member of staff apart from the principal, the Revd Andrew Martin Fairbairn. In the college Massie commanded respect for his teaching ability, his friendliness towards the students, and his performances on the cricket field. His scholarly writing was equally sound, though small in quantity—appearing as commentaries on the first and second epistles to the Corinthians (published in the Century Bible, 1901) and as articles in biblical dictionaries and religious magazines. In 1901, when he attended the tercentenary celebrations at Yale University as Mansfield College representative, he was awarded an honorary DD of that university.

Massie was devoted to educational work outside Mansfield as well as within it, and to political work for the Liberal Party. From 1890 he was vice-chairman of the council of Leamington High School for Girls. In 1894 he became an assistant commissioner to the royal commission on secondary education, in which capacity he wrote an official report on secondary schools in Warwickshire. On the political side, he was on the executive of the National Liberal Federation from 1894 to 1906, and again from 1910, and was treasurer of the federation from 1903 to 1906. He published political pamphlets in the 1890s against dogmatic teaching in schools and on university education for Catholics in Ireland. His political nonconformity was indicated by his spells as president of the Liberation Society (or Society for the Liberation of Religion from State Patronage and Control), and as president of the Oxford and District Free Church Council for twenty-five years (1896–1921). He also had a period as president of the Body of Protestant Dissenting Deputies. He served the Congregational Union of England and Wales as chairman of its council and of its committees for education and general purposes, as well as being a benefactor of, and loyal attender at, its churches. Massie's many roles were liable to draw him into conflict with others, but he was genial by nature and upheld his opinions without bitterness, so managing to maintain friendships with persons whose views were far removed from his own.

Massie took part in the nonconformist opposition to the Education Bill of 1902, and after the bill had gone through he passively resisted paying the local education rate. In 1903 he relinquished his professorship in order to give more time to public and political work. He was given a fairly promising parliamentary seat to fight (the Cricklade division of Wiltshire), and entered parliament in the Liberal landslide of January 1906, holding the seat for the Liberals by a substantial majority of 1578 (7294 votes to 5716) over a Liberal Unionist. He lost the seat to a Unionist by 635 votes in January 1910. In the Commons he spoke frequently, if usually briefly, in support of the Liberal government's unsuccessful education bills, and on ritualism, disestablishment, and the Irish University Bill of 1908. He also spoke against women's suffrage—a subject on which he joined Asquith and others in a minority of the Liberal MPs—and he became treasurer of the Women's National Anti-Suffrage League. 'Massie is tiresome and loses himself in petty detail', Cromer told Curzon in September 1910, 'but one must bear with him'; by listening 'to all the paltry tittle-tattle' Massie causes 'a great deal more friction than he allays' (Cromer to Curzon, 14 and 29 Sept 1910, Curzon MSS, BL OIOC, MS Eur. F/112/33).

Massie did not sit again in parliament after January 1910, but he remained active in public life for many years. As well as the denominational and wider free church activities already mentioned, and work for the National Liberal Federation, he was a diligent JP for Oxfordshire. From 1916 to 1921 he chaired the Oxfordshire committee established under the War Pensions Act. He died at 84 Harley Street, London, on 11 November 1925, as the result of double pneumonia accelerated by the shock of being knocked down by a taxi-cab. He was survived by his wife.

IAN MACHIN

Sources *The Times* (12 Nov 1925) · E. Kaye, *Mansfield College, Oxford: its origin, history and significance* (1996) · *Hansard 4* (1906–8), vols. 152–99 · *Hansard 5C* (1909), vols. 1–13 · R. Tudur Jones, *Congregationalism in England, 1662–1962* (1962) · G. I. T. Machin, *Politics and the churches in Great Britain, 1869 to 1921* (1987) · *WWW, 1929–40* · *McCalmont's parliamentary poll book: British election results 1832–1918*, ed. J. Vincent and M. Stenton, 8th edn (1971) · B. Harrison, *Separate spheres: the opposition to women's suffrage in Britain* (1978) · Venn, *Alum. Cant.* · b. cert. · m. cert. · d. cert. · *CGPLA Eng. & Wales* (1926)
Archives Mansfield College, Oxford, minute books of the Mansfield College board of education · Mansfield College, Oxford, minute books of the Mansfield College council
Wealth at death £110,296 17s.: resworn probate, 22 Jan 1926, *CGPLA Eng. & Wales*

Massie, Joseph (*d.* **1784**), writer on trade and economics, was of unknown origins. Likewise it is not known if he married or had children. Several of his early writings exhibit an in-depth familiarity and interested concern with the West Indian sugar trade which suggests that he was a merchant or factor in this branch of business for some years. In the 1750s he began to establish a reputation as a writer, statistician, and economic theorist. During the Seven Years' War and its aftermath he was particularly active as a pamphleteer in support of, and probably in the pay of, William Pitt. Possibly he entertained hopes of a post as a Treasury civil servant or as an official historian of commerce. One of Massie's chief claims to fame is as a bibliographer of economics. Between 1748 and 1764 he formed an unprecedented collection and a catalogue of books and pamphlets on trade and commerce dating back to 1557. He hoped that this collection would provide a resource for the development of economic theory as a science, and for the training of students in the theory and practice of trade. He attempted unsuccessfully to persuade either the City of London or the government to buy this collection and make it the centrepiece of a projected academy of commerce. The indexed catalogue of this collection and other works on economics, last updated in 1764 and then listing more than 2400 titles, is to be found among the Lansdowne manuscripts in the British Library. Later in life Massie became bitter at the repeated rejection of his schemes and advances for patronage; his publications and memorandums then became cranky and paranoid.

Massie's name has been linked with a pioneering work of economic theory published anonymously as *An Essay on the Governing Causes of the Natural Rate of Interest* (1750), but the evidence of authorship is unclear (most of Massie's later writings were signed). This work argued that the natural rate of interest was regulated by the profits of trade rather than by the amount of circulating money as John Locke and other writers had previously assumed. Massie's approach to economics was profoundly shaped by his reading of economic literature as it had developed since the sixteenth century as well as his own experience of trade. He bemoaned the fact that 'some writers have considered commerce as a science, and endeavoured to deduce the knowledge of it from axioms and maxims &c. while many others have treated it as a branch of history, and given narratives' (*Representation*, preface) and that there was little consensus on first principles, and his ambition was to unite the historical and the scientific deductive approaches to the subject of economics. In pursuance of this goal he planned but did not complete a detailed history of British trade divided into its separate branches which he hoped would facilitate the formulation of general maxims. This project was influenced by the Baconian intellectual tradition and the methods of the Royal Society. Although the next generation of political economists preferred to use more abstract and systematic models of the economy, Massie's essay may still be considered one of the more interesting attempts at generating a unified body of economics prior to the work of Adam Smith.

Commerce for Massie was an essential art and he hoped that the subject would soon become an accepted component of a liberal education. These views were stated most clearly in his *Representation Concerning the Knowledge of Commerce as a National Concern* (1760). Massie also continued to pursue the statistical work begun by the political arithmeticians and produced several interesting calculations on population, social structure, consumption, and taxation. The most significant of these productions first arose from a polemical broadside against the sugar planters whose title is a précis of its argument: *A computation of the money that hath been exorbitantly raised upon the people of Great Britain by the sugar planters … shewing how much money a family of each rank, degree or class hath lost by that rapacious monopoly* (1760). One of the work's most interesting elements is a tabular representation of English and Welsh social structure and income distribution based on the returns of the hearth-tax and his own estimates. Similar material is also contained in his *Calculations of Taxes for a Family of each Rank, Degree or Class* (1756). These have proved useful resources for modern social and economic historians.

For most of his career as a writer Massie lived in Covent Garden, London. He died on 1 November 1784 and was buried on 7 November at St Andrew's, Holborn.

R. D. SHELDON

Sources *DNB* · J. Massie, *A state of the British sugar colony trade* (1759) · J. Massie, *A representation concerning the knowledge of commerce as a national concern* (1760) · P. Mathias, 'The social structure in the eighteenth century: a calculation by Joseph Massie', *Economic History Review*, 2nd ser., 10 (1957–8), 30–45 · W. A. Shaw, *Bibliography of the collection of books and tracts on commerce, currency and poor law* (1557–1763) (1937) · W. Cunningham, 'The progress of economic

doctrine in England in the eighteenth century', *Economic Journal*, 1 (1891), 73–94 · BL, Add. MS 33056, fol. 285
Archives BL, Lansdowne MSS, catalogue of subject's collection of books and pamphlets on trade and commerce, 1049 · BL, 'Memorandum relating to the defence of Great Britain', 1759, Egerton MS 3444, fols. 231–40 · BL, draft memorandum to the principal landowners of Britain, 9 Jan 1768, Add. MS 33065, fol. 285

Massie, Thomas Leeke (1802–1898), naval officer, was born at Coddington Hall, Cheshire, on 20 October 1802, the second son (of twenty-two children, eighteen of whom survived to maturity) of the Revd Richard Massie (1771–1854). He entered the navy in October 1818 on the *Rochefort*, flagship in the Mediterranean of Sir Thomas Francis Fremantle and later of Sir Graham Moore, and continued in different ships in the Mediterranean. He was wrecked in the brig *Columbine* on the coast of the Morea (25 January 1824), was in the *Martin* at the demonstration against Algiers, was frequently in boat actions against Greek pirates, and was in the *Asia* at Navarino (20 October 1827). For this he was rewarded with promotion to lieutenant on a death vacancy on 11 November 1827. Thereafter he served mostly on the channel, North Sea, and Lisbon stations, but was three years on the South American station with Captain Robert Smart in the *Satellite* and two years in the Mediterranean as first lieutenant of the *Carysfort* with Henry Byam Martin. On 28 June 1838 Massie was made commander, and in 1839 was, with others, sent to Constantinople to assist in organizing the Turkish navy. They were, however, recalled after about six months, and in March 1840 Massie was appointed (as second captain) to the *Thunderer* with Maurice Frederick Fitzhardinge Berkeley, afterwards Lord Fitzhardinge. In the *Thunderer* he took part in the operations on the coast of Syria in the summer and autumn of 1840, culminating in the capture of Acre, for which he was promoted captain on 17 March 1841. On 8 February 1844 he married Charlotte Hester, the only daughter of E. V. Townsend of Wincham Hall, Cheshire.

In April 1849 Massie was appointed to the *Cleopatra*, which he commanded in the East Indies and China and during the Second Anglo-Burmese War. In September 1854 he commissioned the *Powerful*, which during the latter part of 1855 and 1856 was on the North American station. He had no further service, but became rear-admiral on 7 November 1860, vice-admiral on 2 April 1866, and admiral on 20 October 1872, having been placed on the retired list in 1866. He died at his home, 3 Stanley Place, Chester, on 20 July 1898.

J. K. LAUGHTON, rev. ROGER MORRISS

Sources O'Byrne, *Naval biog. dict.* · *The Times* (2 July 1898) · *Navy List* · G. S. Graham, *The China station: war and diplomacy, 1830–1860* (1978) · A. D. Lambert, *The last sailing battlefleet: maintaining naval mastery, 1815–1850* (1991) · *WWW, 1897–1915* · Boase, *Mod. Eng. biog.* · Venn, *Alum. Cant.* · *CGPLA Eng. & Wales* (1898)
Archives Meteorological Office, Bracknell, Berkshire, National Meteorological Library, meteorological journal kept during voyage to China · NMM, letter-books, log books, and diaries
Wealth at death £4779 9s. 8d.: probate, 10 Sept 1898, *CGPLA Eng. & Wales*

Massingberd, Sir Archibald Armar Montgomery- (1871–1947), army officer, was born Archibald Armar

Sir Archibald Armar Montgomery-Massingberd (1871–1947), by Lafayette, 1927

Montgomery on 6 December 1871 in London, the second son of Hugh de Fellenberg Montgomery (1844–1924), landowner and politician, of Blessingbourne, Fivemiletown, co. Tyrone, and his wife, Mary Sophia Juliana (May) (d. 1928), daughter of the Revd John Charles Maude, rector of Inniskillen and son of the first Viscount Hawarden. Hugh Maude de Fellenberg *Montgomery was his brother. He added the name Massingberd to his own in 1926 when his wife, Diana Massingberd (1872–1963), daughter of Edmund Langton, whom he married on 2 April 1896, inherited through her mother the Massingberd estates in Lincolnshire.

During his education at Charterhouse School and at the Royal Military Academy, Woolwich, Montgomery did not prove outstanding in any activity except horsemanship, to which he had a lifelong devotion. Yet he was from a 'good' family background: tall, good-looking, charming, articulate, and persuasive. These characteristics stood him in good stead during his military career. He was commissioned into the Royal Field Artillery in November 1891 and served with it for most of the Second South African War of 1899–1902, though he had a staff job in Cape Town for the last few months. He was present both at the British defeat at Magersfontein and at the Boer surrender at Paardeburg. During his war service Montgomery developed a strong reputation for being resilient in the face of adversity and a good improviser. His natural charm and careful diplomacy made him especially skilled in the handling of his superiors.

Montgomery's early war service seems to have inspired him to take a more serious, studious attitude to his profession. According to his own account it was reading, at this period in his life, the celebrated study of Stonewall Jackson by the military historian G. F. R. Henderson which inspired him to seek entry to the Staff College at Camberley. He joined that institution in January 1905. While there he formed a firm friendship with the commandant, Sir Henry Rawlinson. Rawlinson reported very favourably on Montgomery and the latter gained a series of staff appointments most beneficial to the advancement of his career. Their future careers were to be intimately connected.

In August 1914 Rawlinson was an instructor at the Staff College. Shortly after the outbreak of war he was appointed a staff officer with the 4th division. Rawlinson took over this division on 23 September 1914, the previous commander having been injured during the battle of the Marne, and by then Montgomery was acting as its principal staff officer. A partnership between commander and his chief of staff was forged which, most unusually, was carried through several levels of command and lasted from this early stage in the war virtually to its end. When Rawlinson was promoted to command the 4th corps in October 1914, he managed to have Montgomery appointed his chief of staff, and Montgomery remained Rawlinson's principal staff officer when the latter was appointed to command the newly formed Fourth Army in February 1916. The chief of staff of an army was a job which carried the rank of major-general. After being an acting major-general for nearly a year, Montgomery was made substantive in that rank in January 1917, having risen from major to major-general in two-and-a-half years. It was a rate of promotion made all the more remarkable by the fact that Montgomery never held a field command in the First World War.

The Rawlinson–Montgomery partnership was certainly close. Montgomery, however, was generally very discreet, content to remain a grey eminence. It is rarely possible to delineate with any clarity his particular role in planning and executing Rawlinson's military operations. Fourth Army's record in the Somme campaign of 1916 considered as a whole was very mixed and no senior officer serving in that headquarters can escape a share of responsibility for the catastrophe of 1 July 1916 with which it opened. But there is evidence that Montgomery had favoured a much more limited and cautious sort of attack than that which, under pressure from Haig and general headquarters, was finally adopted. Fourth Army did not play a major role in the operations of 1917. Its heyday was the final campaign of 8 August to 11 November 1918 in which, commencing with the battle of Amiens, it won a series of stunning victories, playing a greater role than any other allied army in forcing the Germans to sign the humiliating armistice of 11 November. Montgomery wrote a detailed account of these last battles, *The Story of the Fourth Army in the Battles of the Hundred Days* (1919), which some astute observers considered to be one of the finest works of military history to be produced in the immediate aftermath of the war.

After the armistice Montgomery served as chief of staff with the British army of occupation on the Rhine and subsequently became deputy chief of staff to Rawlinson while the latter was commander-in-chief in India. On his return from India he successively commanded the Welsh territorial division and the 1st division at Aldershot. As a lieutenant-general, in the late 1920s, he was in charge of southern command which included the Salisbury Plain area where pioneering exercises with mechanized forces were being held. Montgomery's temperament was conservative and he was somewhat sceptical about the ambition of radical officers in the Royal Tank Corps (RTC) to effect a revolution in the army's structure. In 1928 his influence helped terminate one series of experiments, though it was a series which had in any case largely run its course. He incurred during this period the deep and lasting hostility of the influential military journalist Basil Liddell Hart. Montgomery's historical reputation has suffered massively from Liddell Hart's distinctly prejudiced, exaggerated, and unfair portrayal of him, in influential books, as an archetypal military reactionary. Montgomery, however, continued to impress his superiors. He was promoted full general in 1930 and appointed adjutant-general in March 1931, becoming an army council member. In February 1933 he became chief of the Imperial General Staff (CIGS) and in 1935 he was promoted field marshal. He never held a field command in war, and his role as Rawlinson's chief of staff in the Fourth Army (1916–18) was, for the most part, exercised too discreetly to enable his role in decision making to be discerned. It is, therefore, on his performance as CIGS in the critical period 1933–6 that his reputation must depend.

Although not an early advocate of independent armoured forces, Montgomery-Massingberd seems to have become a convert by the time he became CIGS, or very shortly afterwards. At this period he enjoyed good relations with the two most important advocates of armoured formations in the RTC: George Lindsay and Percy Hobart. He took the decision, in November 1933, to establish the 1st tank brigade as a permanent formation and gave great encouragement to its work, gaining glowing praise from Hobart, its commander. He followed this up in late 1934 with a decision to form the British army's 1st armoured division (initially called the mobile division) though this decision could not be implemented until after his retirement. He played a major part in the early planning of rearmament and was a strong proponent of making the British army ready to fight alongside the French against the Germans. Montgomery-Massingberd seems to have been a Francophile and strongly advocated maintaining close relations with the French general staff. Regarded by at least one reputable observer as the best CIGS of the inter-war period at putting the general staff's case in committee, he gained the agreement of the chiefs of staff and of Stanley Baldwin's government to prepare the regular army for a continental campaign, though the Territorial Army was not so lucky.

In a memorandum on the future organization of the

British army completed on 9 September 1935, he advocated the preparation of a regular field force to be sent to the continent on the outbreak of war which would include four infantry divisions plus the mobile division, to be reinforced at intervals by rearmed divisions of the Territorial Army. The field force was to be very highly mechanized by the standards of the time, having enough lorries to lift an entire infantry division if required, as well as a large amount of armour. In addition to the mobile division, it was to have a light tank battalion attached to each infantry division for reconnaissance and screening. There were also to be army tank battalions (one per infantry division) consisting of heavily armoured tanks to assist the infantry in the assault. In the same document Montgomery-Massingberd demonstrated a good grasp of German operational methods, especially the use of airpower to facilitate deep penetration by a highly mobile land force.

Having, in his own view, laid a foundation for the army's rearmament, Montgomery-Massingberd decided to retire early in the spring of 1936 in order to make room for a younger man to execute the programme. He had been appointed CB (1918), KCMG (1919), KCB (1925), and GCB (1934). In retirement he resided at his country house at Gunby Hall, Spilsby, Lincolnshire. During the Second World War the lord lieutenant of Lincolnshire, who was attached to the Air Ministry, asked Montgomery-Massingberd to take charge of organizing and recruiting the Home Guard in Lincolnshire, work he undertook for nine months, at the end of which the lord lieutenant returned to the county and personally took command. Montgomery-Massingberd died on 13 October 1947, at Gunby Hall, leaving no children.   J. P. HARRIS

Sources J. P. Harris, *Men, ideas and tanks: British military thought and amoured forces, 1903–1939* (1995) · B. Bond, *British military policy between the two world wars* (1980) · R. H. Larson, *The British army and the theory of armored warfare, 1918–1940* (1984) · B. H. Liddell Hart, *The memoirs of Captain Liddell Hart*, 1 (1965) · *DNB* · m. cert. · *CGPLA Eng. & Wales* (1948)
Archives King's Lond., Liddell Hart C., papers | CAC Cam., corresp. with Sir E. L. Spears · King's Lond., Liddell Hart C., corresp. with Sir B. H. Liddell Hart
Likenesses W. Stoneman, two photographs, 1922–33, NPG · Lafayette, photograph, 1927, NPG [*see illus.*] · O. Birley, oils, Gunby Hall, Lincolnshire · F. E. Hodge, oils, Gunby Hall, Lincolnshire
Wealth at death £5354 13s. 1d.: probate, 29 June 1948, *CGPLA Eng. & Wales*

Massingberd, Emily Caroline Langton (1847–1897), women's club founder and temperance campaigner, was born on 19 December 1847 at Gunby Hall, Lincolnshire, the first of the three children of Charles Langton Massingberd (1815–1887), a landowner, and his first wife, Harriett Anne (d. 1855), daughter of Richard Langford. On 2 March 1867 Emily married her cousin, Edmund Langton, the only son of the Revd Charles Langton. The couple had two girls and one boy. They lived principally at Bournemouth; Emily Langton built the Red House in Knyveton Road, and gave entertainment to the workmen employed on the villa. After her husband's premature death on 28 November 1875 she devoted herself to temperance work and later enthusiastically supported the suffrage cause, to which she was partially drawn by the recollection of her late husband's keen interest in the advancement of women.

On the death of her father on 9 February 1887 Emily Langton succeeded to the family estate in Lincolnshire, and on 20 May 1887 she resumed her maiden name of Massingberd by royal licence. After managing the estate personally for four years, she let the property and moved to London, where she was active in the capital's temperance, anti-vivisectionist, and women's movements.

Much of Massingberd's temperance work was in association with the British Women's Temperance Association, a loose federation of county associations and local units founded in 1876. She was also a vice-president of the (prohibitionist) United Kingdom Alliance and honorary treasurer to Lady Henry Somerset's Cottage Homes for Inebriates, at Dunsworth. At Westminster town hall in 1882 she made her first speech in favour of women's suffrage.

In 1892 Massingberd founded the Pioneer Club, which was to become one of the most popular of the many women's clubs established in London in the late nineteenth century to provide middle-class women (especially the single) with an alternative social environment to their homes. Within three years the membership increased from about fifty to more than 300, which necessitated two changes of premises. The club found a permanent home at 22 Bruton Street, Berkeley Square, the former residence of Lord Hastings. There were three drawing rooms, a library, and four bedrooms. Meals and (non-alcoholic) refreshments were available to members and their guests, and lectures, debates, and discussions were held every Thursday evening, covering a variety of themes—social, political, and literary.

Emily Massingberd was the sole proprietor and president of the Pioneer Club until her death. She determined its rules and personally undertook all financial and management responsibilities. In organizing the club's activities she was assisted by several committees. The essential requirement for membership was an interest in any movement for the advancement of women. An annual subscription of 3 guineas was charged. Professional and other working women joined the Pioneers, including typists, dressmakers, and milliners. To stress the unimportance of social position, each member was called by a number rather than by her name. The Pioneer Club acquired a reputation for being strongly feminist, although visitors were surprised that most members did not wear the cropped hair and masculine dress of the stereotypical 'new woman'.

Late in 1896 Emily Massingberd fell ill and underwent a serious surgical operation at Llandudno, where she died on 28 January 1897. Her obituarist described her as a generous, sympathetic, and warm-hearted woman with a keen sense of humour and possessed of musical, artistic, and dramatic talents. In her will she provided for the maintenance of the Pioneer Club for as long as it remained teetotal. Its feminist character was diluted after her death.   MARK CLEMENT

Sources *Englishwoman's Review*, 28 (1897), 128–31 • Burke, *Gen. GB* (1972) • B. S. Knollys, 'The Pioneer Club in Bruton Street', *The Englishwoman* (April 1895), 120–25 • H. Friederichs, 'A peep at the Pioneer Club', *Young Woman*, 4 (1895–6), 302–6 • M. Vicinus, *Independent women: work and community for single women, 1850–1920* (1985) • P. T. Winskill, *Temperance standard bearers of the nineteenth century: a biographical and statistical temperance dictionary*, 2 (1898) • P. Levine, *Feminist lives in Victorian England: private roles and public commitment* (1990) • L. L. Shiman, *Crusade against drink in Victorian England* (1988)

Wealth at death £23,380 9*s.* 4*d.*: probate, 30 April 1897, *CGPLA Eng. & Wales*

Massingberd, Francis Charles (1800–1872), Church of England clergyman, the son of Francis Massingberd, rector of Washingborough, near Lincoln, and Elizabeth, his wife, youngest daughter of William Burrell Massingberd of Ormsby Hall, was born at his father's rectory, on 3 December 1800, and baptized on 30 December. After preparatory education at a school at Eltham, Kent, he entered Rugby School in 1814. He matriculated at Magdalen College, Oxford, and was elected a demy on 23 July 1818. He gained a second class in *literae humaniores*, and graduated BA on 5 December 1822 and MA on 26 June 1825. He was ordained deacon by Edward Legge, bishop of Oxford, on 13 June 1824 and priest by Bishop Tomline of Lincoln on 5 September 1825, and was instituted to the family living of South Ormsby, Lincolnshire, on 9 December of that year.

The previous summer, together with his friend William Ralph Churton, Massingberd had accompanied Thomas Arnold, headmaster of Rugby School, on a visit to Italy, undertaken by Arnold to identify the line of Hannibal's passage over the Alps, and to explore the battlefields of his campaign, for the purposes of his history of Rome. He returned to Rome for health reasons in the early 1840s. On 15 January 1839 he married at Putney church Fanny (*d.* 2 April 1891), eldest daughter of William Baring MP and his wife, Frances, *née* Paulett Thompson. They had two sons: Francis Burrell, a captain in the 5th lancers, and William Oswald, an Anglican clergyman.

Massingberd was an exemplary rural clergyman. He rebuilt Driby church and thoroughly restored that at Ormsby; he erected a new rectory on a better site, and built premises for schools that developed from classes he had started in a kitchen. In 1840, at the request of his lifelong friend, Edward Churton, he wrote on the leaders of the Reformation, volume 21 of the Englishman's Library, of which Churton was editor. Published in 1842, it reached a fourth edition in 1866. It reflects a distinct but unembittered high-churchmanship in the tradition of John Keble, as do his other main publications, *The Educational and Missionary Work of the Church in the Nineteenth Century* (1857) and *Lectures on the Prayer Book* (1864). In 1846 he declined an offer from Bishop Phillpotts of Exeter to move into that diocese with the prospect of appointment to the first vacant archdeaconry. He was appointed to the prebendal stall of Thorngate in Lincoln Cathedral by Bishop Kaye on 15 May 1847, and was made chancellor and canon residentiary by Bishop Jackson on 11 December 1862.

From an early period Massingberd was a strenuous advocate for the revival of the deliberative functions of convocation. In 1833 he published *Reasons for a Session of Convocation*, and when that object was attained he was one of its most active members, first as proctor for the parochial clergy in 1857, and subsequently, in 1868, for the chapter. He frequently sat on committees and drew up their reports, and took a large share in the debates, proving himself a persuasive, if prolix, speaker. As chancellor of Lincoln he directed his efforts to the increase of the practical efficiency of the cathedral. Together with other minor reforms, he was the first to institute an afternoon nave sermon, and during successive Lents he delivered courses of lectures on the prayer book and on church history. He died at 2 Cambridge Place, London, of congestion of the lungs on 5 December 1872, and was buried at South Ormsby. EDMUND VENABLES, *rev.* H. C. G. MATTHEW

Sources Boase, *Mod. Eng. biog.* • private information (1894)

Archives Lincs. Arch., corresp., papers, and literary remains

Wealth at death under £12,000: probate, 22 April 1873, *CGPLA Eng. & Wales*

Massinger, Philip (1583–1640), playwright, was born in November 1583, probably in Salisbury, and baptized at St Thomas's, Salisbury, on 24 November 1583. He was the son of Arthur Massinger (*c.*1550–1603), fellow of Merton College, Oxford, MP, general agent for the earls of Pembroke, and examiner to the council of the Welsh marches, and of Anne Crompton (*d.* in or after 1614), whose father was a merchant of Stafford and London. According to John Aubrey, Philip Massinger was married and his widow, who lived and died in Cardiff, continued to receive from the earl of Pembroke and Montgomery a pension formerly paid to her husband. Nothing further is known of the marriage.

Massinger went up to St Alban Hall, Oxford, in 1601 or 1602. Gerard Langbaine and Anthony Wood credit him with three or four years at Oxford—studying hard, says Langbaine; sidetracked by poetry and romances, says Wood—but he left without a degree so his departure probably occurred sooner than that, perhaps at about the time of his father's death in 1603. Conceivably he became an actor; in his poem 'The Copy of a Letter' (*c.*1615–1620) he speaks of not being 'knowne beyond A Player or A Man' (*Plays and Poems*, 4.390). But nothing certain is known about Massinger's activities from his arrival in Oxford until (probably) 1613, when, with his fellow playwrights Nathan Field and Robert Daborne, he wrote from the Clink prison to ask Philip Henslowe for £5 that was owed to them for an unidentified play. (By 1629, when Massinger apparently owed Field's brother Nathaniel £60, his credit must in some respects have improved.)

Another area of some uncertainty is Massinger's religious affiliation; a tradition grew up in the nineteenth century that he was a Roman Catholic. There is no strong evidence for this; the tradition was based mainly on the presence of Catholic characters and contexts in two of his plays with Mediterranean settings—*The Maid of Honour* and *The Renegado*—and a third, *The Virgin Martyr*, which was set at the time of the early church. Perhaps more significantly it is known that Massinger's uncle Anthony Crompton was a recusant in the 1580s and that another

Vera ac Viva Effigies
PHILIPPI MASSINGER, Gen̅
J. Cross fecit

Philip Massinger (1583–1640), by Thomas Cross, pubd 1655

uncle, Thomas Crompton, was suspected of being a Catholic although he later became chancellor of the diocese of London and vicar-general for the archbishop of Canterbury. Massinger also had a number of Catholic friends or associates, including Sir Aston Cokayne and the playwright James Shirley, but this in itself proves little.

Collaborations Writing collaborative drama was Massinger's principal occupation between 1613 (or before) and the early 1620s. There has been a strong measure of agreement among scholars as to his share in these works. About 1613 he is believed to have contributed part of act III of *The Honest Man's Fortune*, which was written mainly by Nathan Field and John Fletcher. He is given a more substantial role in his other collaborations with Field and Fletcher of about 1616–18 (*The Knight of Malta*, *The Queen of Corinth*, and the lost *Jeweller of Amsterdam*); with Field alone (*The Fatal Dowry*, 1616–18?); with Thomas Dekker (*The Virgin Martyr*, probably 1620); and in the series of plays written with Fletcher mostly between about 1618 and 1623. Often Massinger writes the opening and closing scene (or sometimes the whole of act I and act V); partly as a result his share contains a somewhat higher percentage than his partners' of expository, rhetorical, and forensic material and a lower percentage of comic material. (One of his best

early opportunities for forensic oratory occurs in the judicial and quasi-judicial scenes of *The Fatal Dowry*.)

The collaboration between Fletcher and Massinger was at its height about 1619–22 and included such plays as *The Custom of the Country* (c.1619–1620), *The Double Marriage* (c.1621), *The False one* (1620?), *The Prophetess* (licensed 14 May 1622), and *The Spanish Curate* (licensed 24 October 1622). Almost all the Fletcher/Massinger pieces are either comedies or tragicomedies in the tradition established earlier by Fletcher and Francis Beaumont. In the summer of 1619, however, they produced the controversially topical *Tragedy of Sir John Van Olden Barnavelt*, concerning the fall of the Dutch statesman and opponent of Prince Maurice. Barnavelt was executed on 3 May and the play was ready for performance by the King's Men by mid-August when, as Thomas Locke wrote to Sir Dudley Carleton, they 'at th' instant were prohibited by' the bishop of London (Bentley, 3.415). (This is the first of several known instances when a Massinger play encountered censorship problems.) Somehow, Locke reports on 27 August, 'Our players have fownd the meanes to goe through with the play of Barnavelt, and it hath had many spectators and receaved applause' (ibid.).

How Massinger and others regarded his collaborative work is largely uncertain. The 'toyes I would not father' in 'The Copy of a Letter' (*Plays and Poems*, 4.390) probably refers to such work but could, of course, be disingenuous or could, since the poem may date from as early as 1615, pre-date prestigious co-operation with Field and Fletcher, the leading actor and leading playwright of the day. (According to Sir Aston Cokayne in *A Chain of Golden Poems* (1658), Massinger and Fletcher were 'great friends' as well as collaborators (p. 186).) It seems likely that at the time Massinger's role in the plays was known and even celebrated; in 1620, before any recorded non-collaborative work, John Taylor, the 'water poet', lists him among the best-known playwrights in *The Praise of Hemp-Seed*. And clearly even after Fletcher's death in 1625 Massinger continued to engage with their joint work; it is evident that in a number of plays datable in their original form to 1622 and after his role is that of reviser. This is almost certainly the case, for instance, in two plays performed in 1634: *Cleander*, a revision of Fletcher's *The Lovers' Progress*, and *A Very Woman*. Several of the plays, moreover, continued to flourish on stage during Massinger's later career. As Fletcher's original joint-author, reviser, or both Massinger worked, in addition to plays already mentioned, on *The Little French Lawyer* (1619–23), *The Sea Voyage* (1622), *The Elder Brother* (1625?), and *Love's Cure* (1625?). He may also, less certainly, have had some role in *Beggars' Bush* (1615–22) and a revised version of *Thierry and Theodoret* (before 1621).

The work with Fletcher and others may, then, have contributed much to Massinger's earnings and renown. This fact—to the detriment of his reputation during the later seventeenth and eighteenth century in particular—was subsequently obscured by the complete omission of his name from the Beaumont and Fletcher folios of 1647 and 1679. Only Massinger's friend Cokayne is known to have protested about this state of affairs, and then chiefly out of concern for Fletcher's honour:

> In the large book of Playes you late did print
> (In *Beaumonts* and in *Fletchers* name) why in't
> Did you not justice? give to each his due?
> For *Beaumont* (of those many) writ in few:
> And *Massinger* in other few; the Main
> Being sole Issues of sweet *Fletchers* brain.
> (A. Cokayne, *A Chain of Golden Poems*, 1658, 217)

Plays, 1621–1625 About 1620 Massinger started to work with companies other than the King's Men, for whom he had so far co-scripted almost all his surviving plays. *The Virgin Martyr* was performed at the Red Bull, probably in 1620 and probably by His Majesty's Revels. And between about 1621 and 1625, while not breaking his connection with the King's Company, he wrote in all five unaided plays—four tragicomedies and a comedy—for the companies based at the Phoenix or Cockpit theatre. Another tragicomedy, *The Great Duke of Florence*, was licensed for performance by the queen's company at the Phoenix in July 1627. Since it is Massinger's only non-King's play after 1625—unless, as seems unlikely, Donald S. Lawless is right that *The Maid of Honour* was first performed in 1630 and not merely revived—this has caused some puzzlement. It seems probable either that *The Great Duke* was written a year or two earlier and remained the property of the Phoenix company or that it was written in 1627 in fulfilment of an earlier obligation.

In the Phoenix tragicomedies—*The Maid of Honour* (1621/2?), *The Bondman* (1623), *The Renegado* (1624), *The Parliament of Love* (1624), and *The Great Duke of Florence* (1627)—romantic plots are so shaped, as in many other Massinger plays, as to emphasize ethical themes and dilemmas. Seeming uprightness is often undermined or forced to rethink itself. For instance Leosthenes, in *The Bondman*, falls victim to the belief that military success gives him right of conquest over Cleora and, particularly where the disguised Pisander is concerned, that physical slavery is an index of moral slavery. More immediate political concerns are also explored. *The Bondman* fairly evidently, in its opening scenes, suggests support for the new anti-Spanish views embraced by Prince Charles and by the duke of Buckingham since their return from Spain in October 1623; the play was performed before the prince on 27 December 1623 at Whitehall. But it also, more subtly—potentially less palatably—sounds a warning note through the slaves' rebellion and through Pisander's lecture on the wider issue of a perceived 'descent from a benevolent patriarchy to governmental tyranny' (Patterson, 85) Similarly *The Maid of Honour* (1621/2?) explores, without risking censorship or imaginative limitation, a situation at least analogous to the affairs of Frederick, elector palatine, and James I's policy of non-intervention on his behalf.

The comedy *A New Way to Pay Old Debts* (1625) scores more direct hits at the universally vilified monopolist Sir Giles Mompesson, from whom the rapacious Sir Giles Overreach is at least in part developed. Set in the country (although drawing on many of the conventions of 'city comedy') the play pits aristocratic virtue against *nouveau riche* greed, which it defeats by encouraging it to overreach itself. That *A New Way* became overwhelmingly Massinger's most popular play in later generations, however, is mainly the result of Sir Giles's energy of language and activity. Forever concocting new schemes, berating his underlings, walking 'to get me an appetite' (II.iii), triumphing over his enemies, and in defeat violent, insane, hallucinating, he is more like the protagonist of a revenge tragedy than the central figures in most contemporary comedy.

Patronage Massinger says in his 1624 dedication of *The Bondman* to Philip Herbert, earl of Montgomery, that 'When it was first Acted, your Lordships liberall suffrage taught others to allow it for currant' (*Plays and Poems*, 1.313). Many of the issues explored in Massinger's plays at this time—attitudes to engagement in foreign wars, for instance—were dear to the heart of Montgomery, Montgomery's brother the third earl of Pembroke, and their associates. It was at this point very probably, therefore, that the playwright succeeded in gaining Montgomery's patronage, perhaps in the form of the pension referred to by Aubrey. His first known attempt to attract the notice of the 'Honourable House' in whose service his father 'Many years … happily spent' (*Plays and Poems*, 1.313) was 'The Copy of a Letter' (c.1615–1620), addressed to Pembroke. Later evidence of patronage by Montgomery (from 1630 also fourth earl of Pembroke) is the poem 'Sero, sed serio' (1636), addressed to him as 'my most singular good Lord and Patron'. The poem, on the death of the earl's son Charles, starts apologetically from Massinger's failure to write in honour of his marriage in 1634:

> I cursd my absence then
> That hindred itt, and bitt my Star-crost pen
> Too busie in Stage-blanks, and trifeling Rime.
> (*Plays and Poems*, 4.419)

Massinger also sought the patronage of Robert Dormer, Philip Herbert's son-in-law, to whom *A New Way to Pay Old Debts* was dedicated on its publication in 1633.

Lady Katherine Stanhope (later countess of Chesterfield), Massinger's first known patron, was the sister of Fletcher's patron the earl of Huntingdon and was of fairly similar political persuasion to the Herberts. *The Duke of Milan* was dedicated to her in 1623; she is acknowledged as Massinger's 'Lady and Mistress' in his poem 'A Newyeares Guift' (c.1622). In 1630 he dedicated *The Renegado* to George Harding, Lord Berkeley, Stanhope's relative by marriage, and in 1632 he dedicated *The Emperor of the East* to Lord John Mohun, her son-in-law, noting that:

> My worthy friend Mr *Aston Cokaine* your Nephew [also Stanhope's nephew], to my extraordinarie content, deliver'd to mee, that your Lordship at your vacant hours sometimes vouchsaf'd to peruse such trifles of mine, as have passed the Presse, and not alone warranted them in your gentle suffrage, but disdain'd not to bestow a remembrance of your love, and intended favour to mee. (*Plays and Poems*, 3.403)

As well as these aristocratic patrons Massinger attracted the attention and the money of, among others, Sir Francis Foljambe, recipient of an autograph poem to accompany a copy of *The Duke of Milan* in 1623 and co-dedicatee of *The*

Maid of Honour in 1632; the Norfolk landowner Sir Philip Knyvett, co-dedicatee of *The Roman Actor* in 1629, to whose daughter Massinger addressed 'The Virgin's Character' (*c.*1625–1630); Sir Thomas Jay, a close associate of Massinger, also from Wiltshire, co-dedicatee of *The Roman Actor*; Sir Robert Wiseman—'for many yeares', the playwright tells him in the 1636 dedication to *The Great Duke of Florence*, 'I had but faintly subsisted, if I had not often tasted of your Bounty'; and Sir Warham St Leger and his son Sir Anthony, the former commemorated in 'A Funerall Poem Sacred to the Memorie of the Trewly Noble … Sir Warham Sentliger' (1631?), the latter dedicatee of *The Unnatural Combat* in 1639.

The King's Men By 1625 Massinger was well established as a playwright. Payment for plays and pensions or gifts from well-connected patrons mean that he may also have become fairly prosperous. (No doubt he was not rich, but the later perception of his knowing extreme poverty results mainly from the early 'tripartite letter' and over-literal reading of references such as that, in the 1639 dedication of *The Unnatural Combat*, to his 'necessitous fortunes'.) He became all the more well known when he succeeded Fletcher as company dramatist of the King's Men in 1625 or soon afterwards. (Fletcher had died in the major plague outbreak of that year, which was the subject of Massinger's poem 'London's Lamentable Estate, in any Great Visitation'.) Although no contract survives it is clear that there must have been one; all Massinger's remaining plays were for this company with the exception of *The Great Duke of Florence*.

Contact with the king's company appears to have been maintained during Massinger's Phoenix years since he wrote for it the tragedies *The Duke of Milan* (*c.*1621) and *The Unnatural Combat* (*c.*1624). These explore, respectively, obsessional jealousy and a father's incestuous passion for his daughter; here seemingly brave and admirable public figures—exposed or redeemed in the tragicomedies and comedies—are destroyed by private flaws. *The Roman Actor*, as performed in 1626 and published in 1629, is somewhat more complex in effect. This inaugural fanfare for and by the company's new staple dramatist draws on many classical sources in a way that is likely to excite comparison with Ben Jonson's Roman tragedy *Sejanus*, itself another of Massinger's sources. And with its three inset plays and impassioned defence by Paris of the moral, reformative function of the stage, *The Roman Actor* encourages debate on the very premises of drama. The 'most perfit birth of my *Minerva*' (*Plays and Poems*, 3.15) is presented confidently in print, complete with six commendatory poems: one in Latin; several, including one by the esteemed classicist and playwright Thomas May, stressing the appropriate Roman dignity of the work; and one by Joseph Taylor, the leading King's Men 'sharer', who first played Paris, professing 'our loves Antiquitie' (*Plays and Poems*, 3.20).

The Roman Actor was followed by several lost plays, which include *The Judge* (1627), *The Honour of Women* (1628), and *Minerva's Sacrifice* (1629). (Eight plays written by Massinger after 1625 are known to be lost and a number of other titles have been more conjecturally attached to his name.) *The Picture* (1629), a tragicomedy, subtly and often humorously examines jealousy, vanity, and double sexual standards before arriving at the deceptively simple conclusion:

> And to all married men be this a caution
> Which they should duly tender as their life:
> Neither to dote to[o] much nor doubt a wife.
> (V.iii)

In the process audiences were provided with some scenes that help to explain the dramatist's presence in the library of love studied by 'our courtly dames' in John Johnson's *Academy of Love* (1641). For instance Queen Honoria enters masked, with '*Musicke above, a song of pleasure*', to offer or seemingly offer Mathias:

> This moist palme, this soft lippe, and those delights
> Which Darkenesse should onely judge of.
> (P. Massinger, *The Picture*, 1629, III.v)

According to the author, *The Picture* 'in the presentment found … a generall approbation' (*Plays and Poems*, 3.195).

Massinger's last surviving tragedy, *Believe as you List* (1631), returns to the ancient world but only as a result of censorship. On 11 January 1631 Sir Henry Herbert, master of the revels:

> did refuse to allow of a play of Massinger's, because itt did contain dangerous matter, as the deposing of Sebastian king of Portugal, by Philip the [Second], and ther being a peace sworen twixte the kings of England and Spayne. (*Plays and Poems*, 3.293)

Probably there was also too evident a parallel between the hero's plight and that of Frederick of Bohemia, but changing the story of Sebastian (or the pretender claiming to be him) to the conveniently similar story of King Antiochus was apparently sufficient for Herbert to grant the revised play its licence on 6 May. Hearers may have rejoiced in the disingenuousness of the prologue to *Believe as you List*, which blames the apparent similarity of ancient things to 'a late, and sad example' on the author's ignorance of '*Cosmographie*' (*Plays and Poems*, 3.305). As with *Barnavelt* and, in 1638, *The King and the Subject*, the non-publication of the play (until 1849) may suggest that it was too dangerous or too immediately topical to print, but this did not preclude its stage success.

It seems likely, although performances are not recorded, that *The City Madam* (1632) was successful in the theatre. This city comedy features a tester tested: Luke Frugal secretly observed by his brother Sir John as he uses the intended reformation of the wilful Frugal wife and daughters as an excuse for unreasonable harshness, revenge, and personal financial gain. Luke provides a central role popular with actors, especially in the nineteenth century. (Nineteenth-century adaptations of the play, however, give a somewhat exaggerated impression of Luke's importance; *The City Madam* is less a one-man play than *A New Way to Pay Old Debts*.) Luke's rapt soliloquy ''Twas no phantastick object, but a truth' (III.iii), on the gold, silver, and jewels he thinks his own, is one of the more psychologically convincing speeches in Massinger.

The 'untun'd kennell' quarrel Massinger's commenders' confident proclamation of the excellence of *The Roman*

Actor in 1629 may have been directed at sections of the literary community who were more doubtful about his worth. This at least is suggested by the fact that in the same year the playwright became embroiled in a quarrel over the place and function of professional playwrights and their work. The dispute began, or perhaps only simmered over, when William Davenant's *The Just Italian* was badly received at the Blackfriars theatre in October. Davenant's supporters, led by the poet Thomas Carew, attacked James Shirley's contrastingly well received *The Grateful Servant*, given at the Phoenix in November, as work for a stage:

> where not a tong
> Of th' untun'd Kennell, can a line repeat
> Of serious sence.
> (*The Poems of Thomas Carew*, ed. R. Dunlap, 1949, 96)

Shirley's supporters replied in kind in the verses attached to the 1630 quarto of his play. They included Massinger, who used terms similar to those in which his own commenders often praised his own work to contrast Shirley's 'well/Exprest and ordred' composition with Davenant's 'forc'd expressions', 'rack'd phraze', and

> Babell compositions to amaze
> The tortur'd reader.
> (*Plays and Poems*, 4.416)

The documents of the second, more vitriolic phase of the struggle remained unpublished until 1980; Massinger contributed a prologue for a 1630 revival of his Phoenix play *The Maid of Honour*, which attacked those resolved to dislike any play performed at that theatre and also censured Carew's Italianate 'Chamber Madrigalls or loose raptures' (Garrett, 60); a reply, almost certainly by Davenant, defends Carew, his 'ditties fit onely for the eares of Kings' and all 'Ingenious Gentlemen' and attacks Massinger and the actors—as a professional playwright he is merely their 'hireling' (Garrett, 62–3). Finally, in a furious counter-defence, 'A charme for a libeller', Massinger attacks the libeller for hiding behind the so-called 'poets tribune' Carew as well as for slander and immorality, upholds writing plays for money on classical precedent, and maintains that 'witlesse malice' cannot overthrow:

> The buildinge of that Meritt whiche I owe
> To knoweinge mens opinions.
> (Garrett, 65)

It is clear that this is less an argument between rival companies than one between professional dramatists and newer courtly rivals. (Massinger remains staple dramatist at the Globe and Blackfriars while rallying to the defence of Phoenix actors and playwright.) How long the quarrel went on, whether it ended in any sort of reconciliation, and how consistently seriously the participants took it—it was no doubt good for trade at both the Blackfriars and the Phoenix—are unknown. But it may explain a number of references to discontent with Massinger's plays—by, for example, the 'gallants' of Henry Parker's manuscript poem 'To his honoured frend Mr Phillip Massinger, having not had that just applause for one of his playes which was due to him' (T. A. Dunn, *Philip Massinger: the Man and the Playwright*, 1957, 33) or by:

> [the] *tribe*, who in their *Wisedomes* dare accuse,
> this ofspring of thy *Muse*.
> (Shirley's poem printed with *The Renegado*; *Plays and Poems*, 2.14)

In 1631 or 1632 the dramatist himself says that *The Emperor of the East* has:

> suffer'd by the rage,
> And envie of some Catos of the stage.
> (*Plays and Poems*, 3.408)

It is clear from several remarks in its front matter, and probably from its early publication in 1632, that *The Emperor*, a tragicomedy with sources in Byzantine history, was one of Massinger's least popular plays.

Later career Either the 'untun'd kennell' affair rumbled on for some time or there were similar 'wars of the theatres' soon afterwards. The prologue of *The Guardian* (1633) speaks of two plays failing, of two years' silence (mystifying commentators since this was clearly not the case), and of the need to confute rumours that the author has 'quite forgot to make a Play' (*Plays and Poems*, 4.114). *The Guardian*, performed at the Blackfriars in 1633 and 'well likte' at court in January 1634, seems an appropriate play with which to 'regain his credit lost'. For while there are elements of serious testing and moral interrogation here, and a shadowing of some contemporary issues in the Robin Hood-like code observed by Severino and his bandit followers, on the whole the play is less morally absolute and more light-hearted and festive than most of Massinger's earlier work. (Its title-page in *Three New Playes*, 1655, bills it as 'A Comical-History'.) That this is the case is due, above all, to the presence of the energetic, generous, red-blooded, sometimes outrageous Durazzo, the eponymous guardian whose love of hunting, good living, and no-nonsense lust is set against the more swooning amours of his nephew and ward Caldoro and his beloved Caliste.

However much sniping may have continued from supporters of Davenant or some other rival, Massinger's career in the 1630s continued to thrive, perhaps buoyed up, indeed, by the publicity attendant on the 'untun'd kennell' affair and the brush with censorship over *Believe as you List*. It can be argued that the publication of six of Massinger's plays between 1630 and 1633 suggests decreasing popularity since companies often (if by no means invariably) protected work from publication while it was likely to be reusable. But confidence in achievements so far is suggested by Massinger's action, about 1632–3, in having copies of his then published seven unaided plays, together with *The Fatal Dowry*, bound into what is now called the Harbord volume (Folger Shakespeare Library, Washington). The volume contains corrections in Massinger's hand up to about half way through. Perhaps he intended to present the collection to a patron but he may also have been at least thinking ahead to putting together his works, following the example of the Jonson and Shakespeare collections of 1616 and 1623. And if non-publication is indeed a sign of continuing theatrical viability it may be significant that only two of Massinger's hitherto unpublished plays were printed between 1633 and his death in 1640: *The Great Duke of Florence* in 1636 and *The Unnatural Combat* in 1639.

Massinger's last decade was one of undiminished business—of making good 'in some labor'd Song' that 'Though he grow old, *Apollo* still is yong' (epilogue to *The Guardian*, *Plays and Poems*, 4.197). He produced at least a play a year, besides working on poems for patrons and friends (usually left in manuscript; a number of similar works may have perished) and revision of Fletcher or Fletcher/Massinger plays, including *A Very Woman* (1634) and *Cleander* (a version of Fletcher's *The Lovers' Progress*), which was presented before Queen Henrietta Maria at Blackfriars in May 1634. There were also court productions, untouched or more lightly revised, of the Massinger/Fletcher collaborations—*The Spanish Curate* in 1638 and 1639, and *The Custom of the Country* in 1630 and 1638—and *The Fatal Dowry*, which was given at the Cockpit-in-Court, Whitehall, on 3 February 1631. A second edition of *The Bondman* was brought out in 1638.

In 1636 *The Bashful Lover*, Massinger's last surviving play, exploited the fashion for romance and Neoplatonism particularly associated with Henrietta Maria. Galeazzo, the suitor of the title, exemplifies noble, selfless, sometimes self-abnegating love and ultimately wins Matilda through it. But that this was by no means the only sort of drama Massinger was writing in the late 1630s is shown by the one speech that survives from the tragedy *The King and the Subject* and begins:

Monys? Wee'le rayse supplies what ways we please,
And force you to subscribe to blanks.

Sir Henry Herbert recorded it because some time before June 1638 Charles I himself, 'readinge over the play at Newmarket, set his marke upon the place with his owne hande, and in thes words: "This is too insolent, and to bee changed"'. 'Note', Herbert continues, that 'the poett makes it the speech of a king, Don Pedro, king of Spayne, and spoken to his subjects' (*Plays and Poems*, 1.xxxix); he might have added that Charles probably understood, and the playwright and company perhaps intended, an allusion to his raising of forced loans. Following a change of title (possibly to *The Tyrant*, which appears in Humphrey Moseley's 1660 list of Massinger plays) and 'reformations' which were to be 'most strictly observed' in performance, *The King and the Subject* was licensed on 5 June, a day after Herbert was 'given … power from the king to allowe of the play'.

When dedicating *The Unnatural Combat* to Anthony St Leger in 1639 Massinger looked back with pride and a degree of nostalgia on 'this old Tragedie, without Prologue, or Epilogue, it being composed in a time (and that too, peradventure, as knowing as this) when such by ornaments, were not advanced above the fabricque of the whole worke' (*Plays and Poems*, 2.197). But his plays do not generally seem to have been perceived as old-fashioned. The last of them, the lost *The Fair Anchoress of Pausilippo* (1640) may, to judge from the title, have been in the fashionable vein of *The Bashful Lover*. And where older plays were concerned, in August 1639 the lord chamberlain protected the five Phoenix plays of the 1620s for the King and Queen's Young Company, and in August 1641 he protected from publication, for the King's Men, seven plays wholly by Massinger (*The City Madam*, *The Guardian*, *The Bashful Lover*, and four late lost works), and eleven of the collaborations.

Death and reputation Massinger died in March 1640 in a house on Bankside, 'neer the then playhouse'; 'he went to bed well, and dyed suddenly—but not of the plague' (*Plays and Poems*, 1.xliv, xliii). He was buried on 18 March in Southwark Cathedral, either, as Aston Cokayne says, in the church and in the same grave as John Fletcher or, according to the probably less reliable testimony of Aubrey and Wood, in the Bull-Head churchyard. Since he was a 'stranger'—resident outside the parish—the burial fee was doubled to £2.

Almost nothing is known of Massinger's personal life and character as opposed to his literary associations. His friends or acquaintances included John Selden, the jurist; among his fellow dramatists were John Ford and James Shirley. In a younger generation, Philip Edwards and Colin Gibson point out, a group of men who were at Oxford in the early 1620s seem to have shared 'an enthusiasm for the theatre and an admiration for the dramatist who was twenty years their senior' (*Plays and Poems*, 1.xxxviii); one of these was the minor poet James Smith, whom Massinger hailed (in a largely humorous context) as his 'son' ('To his sonne, upon his *Minerva*', c.1635?; *Plays and Poems*, 4.423). He also had contacts at the Inner Temple, to his 'Honored, and selected friends' at which he dedicated *The Picture* in 1630, mentioning no names mainly because 'I had rather injoy (as I have donne) the reall proofes of their friendship, than mountebancke like boast their numbers in a Catalogue' (*Plays and Poems*, 3.195). Particularly in the nineteenth century Massinger was supposed, on flimsy evidence, to be of a gentle, grave, melancholy nature. The subsequently discovered irate 'Charm for a libeller', where he does not rule out the possibility of confuting his critic with a cudgel, is one useful corrective to this image.

The only known likeness of Massinger is the engraving by Thomas Cross in *Three New Playes* (1655); all other representations of him derive from it but adapt it to accord with different generations' perceptions of the author. Eighteenth-century editions use Grignion's engraving based fairly closely on Cross; Massinger is more vigorous and earnest in the 1820 engraving by John Thurston, and more melancholy and uncertain in the R. Bocourt version used as the frontispiece of Arthur Symons's selection of 1887.

Massinger's reputation has undergone a series of fluctuations; it reached its zenith in the late eighteenth and early nineteenth century and its nadir in the early to mid-twentieth century. Commenders of his work in his own lifetime emphasize its constructive skill and strength, and the purity, dignity, and theatrical appropriateness of its language; for example Sir Thomas Jay praises *A New Way to Pay Old Debts* for:

The craftie *Mazes* of the cunning plot;
The polish'd phrase, the sweet expressions; got

Neither by theft, nor violence; the conceipt
Fresh, and unsullied.
(*Plays and Poems*, 2.296)

Those who disagreed, then as often later, perceived crude moralizing and dull dialogue—Davenant's 'rude/Modells of vice and virtue unpursued' (Garrett, 62) or what Abraham Wright, about 1640, saw as 'onely plaine downright relating the matter; without any new dress either of language or fancy' in *A New Way* (*Plays and Poems*, 2.379).

During the 1640s and 1650s Massinger was quite well represented in such miscellanies as Cotgrave's *English Treasury* (1655). Then and for the rest of the century he features in lists of notable poets much more frequently than such subsequently more popular contemporaries as Webster, Marston, Ford, or Middleton. While the theatres were closed *The Guardian*, *A Very Woman*, and *The Bashful Lover* first became available to readers in 1655, and *The City Madam* in 1658. With other pre-interregnum successes a number of Massinger's plays remained popular on the early Restoration stage. *The Bondman* seems to have appealed most; between 1661 and 1666 Samuel Pepys saw and read the play several times with enthusiasm, and praised especially Thomas Betterton's Pisander and the Cleora of Mrs Saunderson (later Mrs Betterton). On the whole, however, Massinger's fame declined markedly during the remainder of the century. Unmentioned in the Beaumont and Fletcher folios he did not share those authors' high renown. Nicholas Rowe's *The Fair Penitent* (1703), founded on *The Fatal Dowry*, was popular throughout the eighteenth century; Rowe's failure to acknowledge his original suggests to what extent Massinger's star had waned.

From the mid-eighteenth century, however, this trend began to be reversed. Massinger fared well in such selections as *The British Muse* (1738) and Dodsley's *Select Collection* (1744), and full editions followed in 1759 (reissued in 1761) and 1779. The plays were studied for their historical interest and admired for their 'flowing, various, elegant, and manly' diction, clear morality, strength of characterization, and, concomitantly, their theatrical viability (Garrett, 93). From about 1780 performance of some of the plays, above all *A New Way to Pay Old Debts* (somewhat adapted) became more frequent. After John Henderson first played Sir Giles in 1781 the part was soon established as one which all leading male actors would wish to attempt. It was one of Edmund Kean's most successful roles from 1816; audiences, among them Byron, Mary Shelley, and William Hazlitt, were deeply affected by Sir Giles's outrageous boldness and sudden and total overthrow, and by Kean's suitably spasmodic and passionate style. The play remained immensely popular in Britain until at least the 1860s and in America until the 1880s, with some productions in the early twentieth century. *The City Madam* enjoyed not inconsiderable but briefer success in such adaptations as Sir James Bland Burges's *Riches, or, The Wife and Brother*, first performed in 1810.

Massinger was at his most well known, partly because of such productions, in the early nineteenth century. He was established, in repeated references to his 'sentimental biography', as a noble, 'melancholy' figure. William Gifford's editions of 1805 and 1813 were the most thorough that had so far been accorded a contemporary of Shakespeare. In some quarters, however, critical disenchantment soon began to make itself felt; in particular, clarity of language and morality began to seem to some, as in the playwright's own time, insipid. Hazlitt found him harsh, crabbed, unpoetic; Charles Lamb, in his influential *Specimens of English Dramatic Poets* (1808), judged him inferior in 'the higher requisites of his art' to 'Ford, Webster, Tourneur, Heywood, and others'—'He never shakes or disturbs the mind with grief. He is read with composure and placid delight' (Garrett, 116). While Massinger still had his partisans, notably Coleridge, such perspectives became, increasingly—with the addition, later in the century, of complaints about his 'indecency'—the critical orthodoxy. Lamb's and Hazlitt's views are essentially repeated in the mostly unfavourable Victorian verdicts of Leslie Stephen and Edmund Gosse and, most famously, in T. S. Eliot's essay of 1920, where the dramatist is easy, bland, an initiator of the 'dissociation of sensibility' (T. S. Eliot, 'Philip Massinger', *The Sacred Wood*, 1920, 123–43).

Eliot long seemed to have delivered the *coup de grâce* to Massinger's reputation. By the 1970s, however, some interest in him was reviving in scholarly circles, much helped by a major edition in 1976. Study has concentrated especially on social and political aspects of the plays. *A New Way to Pay Old Debts* continued periodically to be revived in the theatre.   MARTIN GARRETT

Sources *The plays and poems of Philip Massinger*, ed. P. Edwards and C. Gibson, 5 vols. (1976) • D. S. Lawless, *Philip Massinger and his associates* (1967) • M. Garrett, ed., *Massinger: the critical heritage* (1991) • G. E. Bentley, *The Jacobean and Caroline stage*, 7 vols. (1941–68) • P. Beal, 'Massinger at bay: unpublished verses in a war of the theatres', *Yearbook of English Studies*, 10 (1980), 190–203 • A. Patterson, *Censorship and interpretation: the conditions of writing and reading in early modern England* (1984) • C. Hoy, 'The shares of Fletcher and his collaborators in the Beaumont and Fletcher canon', *Studies in Bibliography*, 8 (1956), 129–46; 9 (1957), 143–62; 11 (1958), 85–106; 12 (1959), 91–116; 13 (1960), 77–108; 14 (1961), 45–67; 15 (1962), 71–90 • D. S. Lawless, 'On the date of Massinger's *The maid of honour*', *N&Q*, 231 (1986), 391–2 • J. H. P. Pafford, 'A new poem by Philip Massinger', *N&Q*, 223 (1978), 503–5 • *Aubrey's Brief lives*, ed. O. L. Dick (1949)
Archives Folger, autograph corrections in texts of six of the printed plays gathered as the Harbord volume
Likenesses T. Cross, etching, 1655, BM, NPG; repro. in P. Massinger, *Three new plays* (1655) [*see illus.*]

Massingham, Henry William (1860–1924), journalist, was born on 25 May 1860 at Old Catton, Norwich. He was the second of the three sons of Joseph Massingham (*d.* 1866) and his wife, Marianne Riches. Methodist lay preacher, active in local politics, and secretary to Joseph Gurney, a Norwich banker, Joseph Massingham died when his son was only six. Two men subsequently profoundly shaped Massingham's personal and intellectual development: Jacob Henry Tillett, his guardian, and his headmaster, Dr Augustus Jessopp. The former inspired Massingham's passion for Liberalism and nonconformity; the latter, a lifelong love and critical judgement of literature.

Henry William Massingham (1860–1924), by Sir Benjamin Stone, 1891

From 1870 to April 1877 Massingham attended King Edward VI's School, Norwich. He did not choose to go to university. Instead, he was articled as a reporter to the *Eastern Daily Press*, part of a newspaper group in which Massingham's family was a substantial shareholder. Massingham was closely associated with the editor, James Spilling. He met William Hale White (Mark Rutherford), whose work he greatly admired. In 1883 he succeeded Rutherford as author of the London letter for the *Norfolk News*. He married on 9 June 1883 Emma Jane (d. 1905), daughter of Henry Snowdon, a Norwich draper. He was also a contributor to the National Press Agency, and was present with Dawson Rogers at the meeting with Herbert Gladstone on 16 December 1885, which produced the agency's sensational scoop that W. E. Gladstone had been converted to home rule. In 1888 he joined the staff of T. P. O'Connor's halfpenny evening newspaper, *The Star*. In July 1890 he was made editor but within six months had resigned after a quarrel with the proprietor. For a short interval he edited Michael Davitt's weekly, *Labour World*, before joining the *Daily Chronicle*. He was in turn appointed leader writer, literary editor, special parliamentary representative, and, within the year, assistant editor.

When A. E. Fletcher resigned in 1895, Massingham was the inevitable choice as editor. He enhanced the *Chronicle*'s political influence and maintained its literary distinction. Yet, in November 1899, he was obliged to resign. The ostensible reason was his strong opposition to the war in South Africa. Up to the outbreak of war, he had given unstinted support to the government. His sudden volte-face was reflected in a sharp drop in the *Chronicle*'s circulation and advertisement revenue. His credentials and reputation as a radical were, however, considerably enhanced. In March 1900 he became the *Manchester Guardian*'s London correspondent, providing parliamentary sketches. It was never a happy relationship and he left at the first possible opportunity, in January 1901. He joined the *Daily News*, succeeding Sir Henry William Lucy as the parliamentary correspondent. He was rarely seen at Bouverie Street, haunting instead the corridors of Westminster, where few secrets escaped his notice. His first wife died in March 1905, after the birth of their sixth child, and in 1907 he married her sister, Ellen; as marriage to a deceased wife's sister was still not permitted under United Kingdom law, the ceremony took place in Guernsey.

In March 1907 Massingham was appointed editor of *The Nation*, a Liberal weekly which replaced *The Speaker*. *The Nation* was livelier, more comprehensive, and much more controversial than its predecessor or most of its contemporaries. He collected about him a small but brilliant editorial team who were complemented by writers some of whom were already celebrated and successful, while others aspired to literary fame. He 'encouraged, criticised … gave them all a place' (Havighurst, 174). Nevertheless, except for one year, 1922, *The Nation* made a loss and depended upon an annual subsidy from its owners, the Rowntree Social Service Trust.

The Nation, upon its first appearance, had been widely and enthusiastically greeted as 'the authoritative organ of the Liberal party' (*British Weekly*, 21 Feb 1907). The declared aspiration of its mercurial editor, however, was not so much to support the Liberal government as to interrogate it. Before the First World War he constantly challenged the Liberal Imperialist-inspired foreign policy pursued by Edward Grey, while in domestic politics he advertised and popularized the new Liberals' programme of radical social and financial reforms. During the war he made certain that his paper was a primary forum for the discussion and promotion of radical ideas and particularly designs to prevent future wars. He supported Lord Lansdowne's plea for a peace settlement in November 1917. President Woodrow Wilson's fourteen points and League of Nations were, Massingham believed, 'the best means of achieving peace for ever' (*The Nation*, 16 Nov 1918). But peace brought him only disillusionment. Despairing of Liberalism, he now promoted Labour as 'the only political party with a scrap of principle' (*The Nation*, 9 Dec 1922). He was bitterly disappointed in Lloyd George as prime minister. He wrote to J. L. Garvin, 'All I have cared about in politics has lapsed hopelessly into the hands … [of] a totally irresponsible, non-moral personality' (Massingham to J. L. Garvin, 10 Dec 1922, Garvin MSS, Humanities Center, University of Austin, Texas).

In April 1923 Massingham resigned as editor of *The Nation*. It was generally supposed that the cause of the breach was a protracted quarrel between the editor and the proprietors over Lloyd George's policies. It was not policy, but finance that finally sundered a partnership that had long been uncertain and troubled. Massingham showed a total indifference to the need for economies, declaring that his only responsibility was editorial and it was the board's concern to look after finance. He had been in the habit of regularly offering his resignation. This time his impulsive gesture was accepted. Thereafter he deeply, if silently, lamented the loss of his editorship.

The possibility of Massingham's editing a new weekly or a Sunday was discussed. Whether or not such a venture could have been financed, it rapidly became apparent that his health would no longer support the strain of editing. From the autumn of 1923 he settled to work as a freelance. He had already transferred his popular 'Wayfarer's diary' to the *New Statesman*. He wrote London letters for the *Haagshe Post* and the *Christian Science Monitor*. He also made occasional contributions to H. W. Brailsford's *New Leader*, *The Spectator*, and the *Daily Herald*, and he reviewed for *The Observer*.

In journalism Massingham found the expression of his ardent and impatient spirit. His interests were varied and he wrote with eager appreciation of everything in which he discerned excellence. Among his best work must be counted his literary and dramatic criticism. He wrote with intense vigour and breadth. For epigrams or delicate subtleties he cared nothing. Every sentence had to seize the reader immediately. An outstanding and versatile reporter and commentator, he possessed brilliant descriptive powers.

Massingham's highest distinction was a passionate energy for human welfare. Irrespective of party loyalties, he appreciated the outstanding personality, recklessly choosing one hero after another, only to be disappointed. It was never enough that those who had earned his disapproval should be abandoned; they had to be trampled in the dust. And this was as true of an idea—like Fabianism— as it was of individuals, like the Webbs, or Rosebery, or Lloyd George. 'I am not an idealist', he insisted, 'but an opportunist' (*Daily News*, 11 March 1907). As a witness and commentator upon Liberal contradictions and the quarrels among its leaders, he allowed circumstances to shape the expression of his political philosophy. As his disillusion for Liberalism increased, so his sympathies for socialism grew. He was close to Ramsay MacDonald, and in 1923 finally joined the Labour Party. Not that it ended his political odyssey for, attracted to guild socialism and the ideas of Henry George, he sought what he termed 'practicable socialism', but was disappointed by the narrow materialism pursued by trade unionists.

Friends and admirers surrounded Massingham all his working life. Yet few, if any, felt themselves really intimate with him. Particularly following the death of his first wife, he became excessively secretive, never revealing his essential self to anyone. His personality is not easily understood. He himself spoke of his struggle with his two opposed natures: a Rabelais and a St Francis. As an editor he was demanding, impatient of slipshod workmanship; he was prodigal with blame and grudging with praise. But without exception, the distinguished company of brilliant writers who had contributed to *The Nation* shared G. B. Shaw's judgement that Massingham was in the very

first flight of editors (Scott, 164). In a real sense, as one of his own sons acknowledged, '*The Nation* rather than his family were his offspring' (ibid., 162).

Massingham was the author of *The Gweedore Hunt: a Story of English Justice in Ireland* (1889) and *Humphrey's Orchard* (1894). A collection of articles, originally written for *Leisure Hour*, were collected and published as *The London Daily Press* (1892). He edited and introduced *Labour and Protection* (1903) and *Why we Came to Help Belgium* (1914). He wrote an introduction for Winston Churchill's *Liberalism and the Social Problem* (1909), and also for the memorial edition of the *Works of Mark Rutherford* (1923).

Massingham died suddenly, on 27 August 1924, while on a family holiday, at the Castle Hotel, Tintagel, Cornwall, and was buried on 2 September in Old Brompton cemetery, London. His eldest son, Harold John *Massingham, the author and journalist, edited a posthumously published selection of his writings (1925).

H. W. NEVINSON, *rev.* A. J. A. MORRIS

Sources A. F. Havighurst, *Radical journalist: H. W. Massingham* (1974) • *The Times* (3 Sept 1924) • H. J. Massingham, *Remembrance: an autobiography* (1942) • H. W. Nevinson, *Changes and chances* (1923) • H. W. Nevinson, *More changes, more chances* (1925) • F. W. Hirst, *In the golden days* (1947) • WW • J. W. R. Scott, *We and me* (1956)
Archives Norfolk RO, corresp. | BL, letters to John Burns • BL, corresp. with Lord Gladstone, Add. MS 46042 • BL, corresp. with W. E. Gladstone, Add. MS 44521–44526 *passim* • BL, corresp. with Lord Northcliffe, Add. MS 62176 • BL, letters to George Bernard Shaw, Add. MS 50543 • Bodl. Oxf., corresp. with Sir William and Lewis Harcourt • Bodl. Oxf., letters to H. W. Nevinson • Bodl. Oxf., letters to Lord Ponsonby • CAC Cam., Stead MSS, letters to W. T. Stead • HLRO, corresp. with J. St L. Strachey • Ransom HRC, letters to J. L. Garvin • U. Newcastle, Robinson L., corresp. with Walter Runciman
Likenesses B. Stone, photograph, 1891, NPG [*see illus.*] • photograph, repro. in Scott, *We and me*, facing p. 144
Wealth at death £9664 13s. 5d.: administration, 18 Nov 1924, CGPLA Eng. & Wales

Massingham, (Harold) John (1888–1952), rural writer, was born in London on 25 March 1888, the eldest of the six children of the radical Liberal journalist Henry William *Massingham (1860–1924) and his first wife, Emma Jane Snowdon (d. 1905). John Massingham won an exhibition from Westminster School to Queen's College, Oxford, which he attended from 1906 to 1910, but appendicitis prevented him from graduating. After convalescing he worked in London as a journalist, notably for his father on *The Nation* and for the guild socialist *New Age*. Through the latter he met the poet Ralph Hodgson, whose minor verse included a poetic invective against the fashion for women to wear exotic bird feathers. It inspired Massingham to form in 1919 the Plumage Bill Group, which successfully secured a parliamentary ban on the trade in 1921. It marshalled some notable supporters, including John Galsworthy, Thomas Hardy, and the ornithologist and nature writer William Henry Hudson. Hudson became a crucial influence on Massingham, who self-consciously adopted his mantle as a nature writer in a lineage he saw extending back to Gilbert White of Selborne.

Massingham's first nature books, appearing shortly before Hudson's death in 1921, were largely descriptive and undistinguished. The emergence of his own voice as a writer, and the foundations of a highly individual personal philosophy, came later in the 1920s through a brief but intense period of interest in archaeology. He joined the staff of the department of anthropology at University College, London, working closely with its professor, Grafton Elliot Smith. He became an enthusiastic proponent of Smith's argument that archaic civilizations shared a common Egyptian origin. Massingham's *Downland Man* (1926) remains a substantial and highly readable testimony to now-discredited diffusionist theory. Yet it was clear he was not temperamentally suited to an academic career. In his introduction (p. 24) Elliot Smith archly referred to Massingham's 'honest attempt to interpret human nature' and his preference for 'common sense and common honesty' over 'the vagaries of pseudo-technical phraseology'. These qualities were much in evidence in Massingham's writing and he quickly rejected any trappings of conventional academic thinking. By the early 1930s he had arrived at a forcible and opinionated style. This alone would invite comparison with William Cobbett, without taking into account Massingham's increasingly mordant view of progress and concern for the condition of rural England.

This style and outlook distinguished all Massingham's work from the publication of *Wold without End* (1932) until his death. This output included twenty-six books, six edited or co-authored volumes, and a weekly column in *The Field* from 1938 until 1951. It was framed by a personal contentment that sharply contrasted with his earlier life in London: an unhappy first marriage in 1914, to Gertrude Speedwell Black, the daughter of Arthur Black of Brighton, was dissolved and in 1933 Massingham married Anne Penelope Webbe, the daughter of A. J. Webbe. They made their home in the Chilterns at Long Crendon, Buckinghamshire, and thenceforth Massingham was an infrequent and reluctant visitor to London. He wrote swiftly and was able to spend much of his time studying the English countryside and, especially, its craftsmen. He accumulated an important collection of hand tools (now held by the Rural History Centre at the University of Reading), which formed the basis of his pioneering study *Country Relics* (1939). A close study of this material had been forced on him when he was confined to his home following a freak accident in 1937, when he tripped over a rusting trough obscured by long grass. The injury eventually led to the amputation of his leg and, in 1940, to near-fatal complications.

Massingham's output as a writer continued unabated, but the crisis shaped his philosophy. First, after a lifetime of agnosticism, he converted to Christianity, choosing to be baptized by a Roman Catholic priest in order to underline his respect for the eternal verities—as he saw them—of the medieval church. He did not, however, become a practising Roman Catholic, choosing instead a loose affiliation to the Church of England out of respect for the eternal verity—as he saw it—represented by the parish church's central role in the life of each rural community. The cumulative effect was to make his writing at times wearisome. His friend the historian Arthur Bryant, in an otherwise handsome obituary, compared Massingham's treatment of 'the indispensable link between God, man and Nature' to that of 'Charles I's head for Mr Dick; it crept into everything he wrote—on topography, horticulture, archaeology, history, literature, agriculture, music, painting, craftsmanship' (contribution to 'In memoriam Harold John Massingham', 80).

A second change in Massingham's outlook after 1937 stemmed from enforced rest and the opportunity to read more widely. Two books influenced him profoundly. The first was *Bio-Dynamic Farming and Gardening* (1938) by Ehrenfried Pfeiffer, a Swiss scientist and follower of Rudolf Steiner. Pfeiffer's attack on mechanized agriculture, chemical fertilizers, and over-production found a receptive reader in one who had long sought the restoration of traditional husbandry and craftsmanship. Yet more important, though, was Gerald Vernon Wallop, Viscount Lymington's, *Famine in England* (1938), a bleak prognosis of a debased industrial agriculture bringing the ruin of civilization in its wake. Massingham wrote to Lymington: 'in the sacred cause of restoring the English land … it is a pivotal book'; and he called for 'a fatherly general organization' to which various elements opposed to the modernization of agriculture might affiliate (letter, 24 Nov 1939, Hants. RO). From this casual suggestion there emerged in 1941 the Kinship in Husbandry, a select group of writers and landowners gathered to influence rural reconstruction. Its members included Lymington, Bryant, the poet Edmund Blunden, and the novelist Adrian Bell. Massingham was its main literary force, editing *England and the Farmer* (1941), a collection of essays by the group. 'I am prouder of it than of any of the something under forty books I have written or edited', he wrote in his autobiography (Massingham, *Remembrance*, 102–3). A further collection, *The Natural Order: Essays in the Return to Husbandry*, followed in 1945.

The Kinship's capacity to influence post-war rural reconstruction was severely limited, not least by its members' profound distaste for contemporary political developments. For Massingham the general election of 1945 marked 'a bound forward to despotism unknown since the dictatorships of Henry VIII and Cromwell' (*The Small Farmer*, 1947, 63). Its call for ecologically sensitive farming was also out of step with political and economic imperatives to maximize agricultural production, though it did contribute directly to the formation in 1945 of the Soil Association, on whose council Massingham served. Although he made no secret of his anti-democratic sentiments, he did not let these stand in the way of collaborating with the socialist Edward Hyams in his most forceful prediction of ecological crisis, *Prophecy of Famine*, published posthumously in 1953 with a preface by Penelope Massingham. Her husband had died at their home, Reddings, Long Crendon, on 22 August 1952; he was buried in Long Crendon.   MALCOLM CHASE

Sources H. J. Massingham, *Remembrance: an autobiography* (1941) · 'In memoriam Harold John Massingham', *Wessex letters from Springhead*, 4 (winter 1952) · *DNB* · Hants. RO, Wallop papers, 15

M84/F148 · M. Chase, 'This is no claptrap, this is our heritage', *The imagined past*, ed. C. Shaw and M. Chase (1988) · W. J. Keith, *The rural tradition* (1975) · D. Matless, *Landscape and Englishness* (1998) · R. J. Moore-Colyer, 'Feathered women and persecuted birds', *Rural History*, 11/1 (2000) · *A mirror of England: an anthology of the writings of H. J. Massingham*, ed. E. Ableson (1988) · P. Conford, *The origins of the organic movement* (2001)

Archives U. Reading, Rural History Centre, corresp. · U. Reading L., literary papers, diary, corresp. | BL, corresp. with Society of Authors, Add. MSS 63298–63301 · Hants. RO, Wallop papers, corresp. · JRL, letters to *Manchester Guardian* · U. Reading L., corresp. with Jonathan Cape Ltd · U. Reading L., letters to Macmillans · U. Sussex, letters to Maurice Reckitt · University of Auckland, New Zealand, Fairburn papers, corresp. · University of Delaware, Newark, Cobden Sanderson papers, corresp.

Likenesses P. Evans, crayon drawing, *c.*1941, NPG; repro. in Massingham, *Remembrance* · photograph, repro. in Massingham, *Remembrance*

Wealth at death £10,607 12*s.* 0*d.*: probate, 31 Oct 1952, *CGPLA Eng. & Wales*

Masson, Charles [*formerly* James Lewis] (1800–1853), traveller in Afghanistan and archaeologist, was born James Lewis in Aldermanbury, London, on 16 February 1800, the eldest child of George Lewis, oil dealer, of 58 Aldermanbury, and his wife, Mary, daughter of Thomas and Elizabeth Hopcraft, of Croughton, Northamptonshire. Nothing is known of his education and early years. He served briefly in the King's 24th regiment of foot and then enlisted on 12 October 1821 as a private soldier in the East India Company's infantry, later transferring to the Bengal European artillery. He was present at the siege of Bharatpur in 1826 but deserted in early July 1827 in Agra and changed his name.

Masson travelled to Afghanistan and embarked on a decade of pioneering travel and antiquarian investigation. During this period he collected well over 80,000 ancient coins and other objects which first provided a chronology of the dynasties of central Asia in the unknown centuries after the death of Alexander the Great. From 1834 Masson published news of his discoveries in the *Journal of the Asiatic Society of Bengal*. The following year he was recruited by the East India Company as news writer in Afghanistan, in return for a free pardon for his desertion and a small allowance.

Masson became bitterly critical of Britain's Afghan policy in the years before the First Anglo-Afghan War. He left Afghanistan in 1838 and during the ensuing British invasion remained in Sind, writing up his researches and travels for publication in London (*Ariana antiqua*, 1841, and *Narrative of Various Journeys*, 3 vols., 1842). In attempting to return to Afghanistan in 1840, he became accidentally embroiled in the Baluchistan revolt and was imprisoned by the British authorities without either charge or good reason (described in *Narrative of a Journey to Kalat*, 1842).

Masson returned to England in 1842, embittered and short of money, although from 1845 he received a small pension from the East India Company. On 19 February 1844 he married eighteen-year-old Mary Anne (*d.* 1855/6), daughter of John Kilby, farmer. He published a book of verse and some contributions to learned journals, but his efforts to obtain financial compensation, to publish an

illustrated *magnum opus* about his Afghan years, to return to Afghanistan, and even to complete a half-finished novel all came to nothing. Masson was the pioneer of Afghan archaeology and numismatics, although he lacked the knowledge fully to interpret his discoveries. As an accurate observer of, and extensive traveller in, a virtually unknown land he was unrivalled. He died in Church Street, Edmonton, Middlesex, on 5 November 1853; his wife died two years later, leaving two children.

GARRY ALDER, *rev.*

Sources G. R. Kaye and E. H. Johnston, eds., *Catalogue of manuscripts in European languages belonging to the library of the India Office*, 2/2: *Minor collections and miscellaneous manuscripts* (1937) · C. Masson, *Narrative of various journeys*, new edn, 1 (1975) · G. Whitteridge, *Charles Masson of Afghanistan* (1986) · BL OIOC · d. cert. · m. cert.

Archives BL OIOC, corresp., journals, notes, and papers, MSS Eur. A 31, B 98–101, C 90, D441–442, E 161–170, F 61–65 · BL OIOC, papers, MS Eur. B 218 | PRO, corresp. with Henry Pottinger, FO 705

Masson, David Mather (1822–1907), biographer, university teacher, and editor, was born on 7 December 1822 in Aberdeen, the son of William Masson, a stonecutter, and his wife, Sarah Mather. Educated at Aberdeen grammar school (1831–5) under the tutelage of James Melvin, Masson received a bursary to study at Marischal College, Aberdeen, and matriculated there in October 1835; he finished first among the masters of arts recipients in April 1839. Intending to enter the ministry, he studied at the Divinity Hall of Edinburgh University from 1839 to 1842, where one of his admired teachers was Thomas Chalmers. Having decided against the ministry as a vocation (perhaps because of the turmoil preceding the disruption of the Church of Scotland in 1843), Masson returned to Aberdeen to edit *The Banner* (1842–4), a weekly newspaper associated with the Free Church cause. During summer 1843, on his first visit to London to meet Alexander Bain, his friend and fellow Aberdonian, he was introduced to Jane Carlyle and John Stuart Mill. While on a more extended London stay, in 1844, he met Thomas Carlyle, who with his wife and Mill became Masson's lifelong friends. In that year, encouraged by Carlyle, who introduced him to George Nickisson of *Fraser's Magazine*, Masson began writing for periodicals with several contributions to *Fraser's* and also to *The Athenaeum*. In August 1844 George Lillie Craik introduced him to the publishing firm W. and R. Chambers, of Edinburgh. For several years he wrote articles for *Chambers's Edinburgh Journal* and books for the firm's various series: *History of Greece* (1845), *History of Rome* (1848), and *Medieval History* (1855) for Information for the People; *The British Museum, Historical and Descriptive* (1848) for the Instructive and Entertaining Library; *Medieval History* (1855) and *Modern History* (1856) for the Educational Course; and 'The myths', 'Dante', and 'Critique of Mill's logic' for Papers for the People.

Once Masson took up London residence in 1847 he got to know many of the mid-nineteenth century's leading literary and artistic figures. George Henry Lewes introduced him to the Museum Club, whose members included Douglas Jerrold, Charles Knight, Shirley Brooks, and T. K.

David Mather Masson (1822–1907), by Sir George Reid, 1896

Hervey, editor of *The Athenaeum*. When Our Club succeeded the Museum Club, Masson came to know Mark Lemon, William and Henry Mayhew, William Makepeace Thackeray, Hepworth Dixon, Charles Dickens, Robert Chambers, and William Hazlitt junior, among others. Coventry Patmore, then librarian at the British Museum, introduced Masson to Charles and Eliza Orme, whose home at Avenue Road, Regent's Park, was a noted gathering place for those associated with the Pre-Raphaelite movement: Holman Hunt, the Rossettis, and Thomas Woolner, besides Patmore. Masson joined the London Scottish Volunteers, and inspired by European revolutionary events of the 1840s became a member of the London Society of the Friends of Italy, serving as its secretary in 1851–2. His concern for the Italian situation was intensified through his introduction to, and subsequent friendship with, Giuseppe Mazzini. During the late 1840s and early 1850s he continued writing for periodicals, notably *The Athenaeum*, the *North British Review*, and the *British Quarterly Review*.

In 1852 Masson succeeded Arthur Hugh Clough as professor of English language and literature at University College, London. In the following year, on 27 August, he married the Ormes' eldest daughter, Emily Rosaline. They had four children: Sir David Orme *Masson (1858–1937), Flora, Helen, and Rosaline. After marrying the Massons lived in the Ormes' home and continued to share in their circle of friends; besides the Pre-Raphaelite figures these included Ralph Waldo Emerson, Herbert Spencer, and Horatio and Matilda, children of Alfred, Lord Tennyson. While teaching Masson persisted with writing. In addition to his work

for Chambers he published *Essays, Biographical and Critical: Chiefly on English Poets* (1856) and *British Novelists and their Styles* (1859). He had also begun working on a biography of Milton, the first volume of which appeared in 1859. His plan was that the work should be not only a biography of the poet but also 'in some sort, a continuous History of his Time' (D. Masson, *The Life of John Milton*, [1859–94], 1.xi). Consequently it alternated chapters describing Milton's life with chapters of history, an arrangement not generally approved by critics at the time. Already associated with Macmillan, which published the biography as well as Masson's books on the British poets and novelists, with Alexander Macmillan he had started planning a new monthly magazine as early as the end of 1858. The first number of *Macmillan's Magazine*, edited by Masson, appeared on 1 November 1859, two months before its rival, *Cornhill*, which Thackeray edited. Under Masson's supervision *Macmillan's* published serial fiction (as well as the usual review articles) by Thomas Hughes, Charles and Henry Kingsley, Margaret Oliphant, and R. D. Blackmore—all Macmillan authors. Masson continued editing the magazine until 1868. He also initiated *The Reader* (1863–7), a weekly paper of literature, science, and the arts. His edition of the poetical works of Milton was published in 1864.

Masson returned to Scotland in 1865, when he was invited to succeed William Edmonstoune Aytoun as professor of rhetoric and English literature at Edinburgh University. When he began his thirty-year tenure there (1865–95) the university's chancellor was still Lord Brougham (soon replaced by Thomas Carlyle), its principal Sir David Brewster. Among his colleagues were John Stuart Blackie, James Lorimer, Peter Gutherie Tait, and Lyon Playfair. All told, Masson taught 5000 students during his career. Besides his official university duties he was active from the first in the Edinburgh Association for the University Education of Women. He lectured on English literature in every session after its opening, served as vice-president, and was considered one of its guiding lights. He supported medical education for women as well as women's rights. On more than one occasion he spoke at the annual meetings of the Edinburgh branch of the National Society for Women's Suffrage. Masson completed the final six volumes of *The Life of John Milton* and revised the first volume (1859–81). He edited Oliver Goldsmith's works, adding a biographical introduction (1869). In 1873 he published another major biography, *Drummond of Hawthornden*. It was followed by *The Three Devils* (1874), *Chatterton* (1874), *Wordsworth, Shelley, Keats and other Essays* (1875), and *De Quincey* (1878). From 1879 to 1899 he was editor of the privy council register of Scotland, in succession to John Hill Burton. Of the fourteen volumes of records that he supervised he wrote introductions for twelve. In tribute to his friend Carlyle he gave a series of lectures that were published as *Carlyle, Personally and in his Writings* (1885). His fourteen-volume *Collected Writings of Thomas DeQuincey* was published in 1889–90. He revised some of his periodical essays to form *Edinburgh Sketches and Memories* (1892).

Having retired from the university Masson continued to

edit the privy council records; for his service to the council he was named historiographer-royal for Scotland in 1893. In recognition of his support for women's education the Edinburgh Association for the University Education of Women named Edinburgh University's new residence for undergraduate women Masson Hall. He was elected an honorary member of the Royal Scottish Academy and designated professor of ancient literature (1896). He received honorary degrees from Aberdeen (LLD), Dublin (LittD), and Moscow. In his retirement he continued writing. From this period came *James Melvin: Rector of the Grammar School of Aberdeen* (1895), a tribute to his legendary teacher. He collected memories of his early friends and experiences into two volumes: *Memories of London in the 'Forties* (1908) and *Memories of Two Cities: Edinburgh and Aberdeen* (1911). Both were published after his death by his daughter Flora. Having lived in Edinburgh at 10 Regent Terrace (1869–78) and at 58 Great King Street in the 1880s, he spent his last years at 2 Lockharton Gardens. He died on 6 October 1907 at 41 Drummond Place. Following funeral services at the Grange United Free Church, he was buried in the Grange cemetery, Edinburgh, on 10 October. His wife survived him.

J. M. Barrie recalled in *An Edinburgh Eleven* (1889, p. 29) that Masson's Edinburgh students thought he bore a physical and intellectual likeness to Carlyle. It was a similarity more imagined than real. George Saintsbury, Masson's successor at Edinburgh, wrote in a memorial tribute that a 'granite-like solidity, a keenness of intellect, a never-failing energy, a rugged genuineness, a love of letters and learning, and, not least, a knowledge of men and women were the predominant features of his character' (Saintsbury). Forming an accurate estimate of Masson's life and work is complicated because after his death his widow and daughters announced his request that no one should write his biography or publish his letters (*The Scotsman*, 17 Oct 1907). Moreover so much of his writing was published anonymously, or lies scattered in prefaces and introductions to various books, that the extent and quality of his *œuvre* has not been accurately estimated. He wrote for the leading nineteenth-century periodicals: the *North British Review*, *Dublin University Magazine*, the *British Quarterly Review*, the *Westminster Review*, *Fraser's*, *The Athenaeum*, and the *National Review*. Although he re-edited and published some of these articles in books most were never collected or even identified as his. He also contributed to the *English Cyclopedia of Biography* and the eighth and ninth editions of the *Encyclopaedia Britannica*. His reputation during the twentieth century was based primarily on the biography of Milton. Because of its thoroughness and detail all students of Milton, whatever their bias, have depended upon the facts that it contains. William Riley Parker, the major biographer of Milton after Masson, said that in writing his work he 'perched like a pygmy on Masson's noble shoulders' (W. R. Parker, *Milton: a Biography*, 1968, 1.vi). Finally Masson's work as periodical writer and editor, literary biographer, and critic has overshadowed his importance as a teacher. From his earliest tutoring while a student at

Aberdeen and Edinburgh, through his official appointments at London and Edinburgh universities, he left an indelible mark on generations of students. At the time of Masson's death Saintsbury described him as a notable representative of the older type of Scots professor. But he did not belong just to the past. Whatever his enthusiasm for the lives and work of writers from earlier days, his warm acquaintance with so many writers of his own day enabled him to bring vitality and intensity to the emerging discipline of English literature studies. Because, as his first *DNB* biographer observed, 'his broad-minded patriotism [was] untainted by the parochialism which he heartily condemned, [he] was accepted by his contemporaries as the representative of what counts for best in Scottish character'.

Though there is a tendency to associate Masson with England because of his work on Milton and other English writers he was thoroughly a Scot. However, a tension between things English and Scottish existed throughout his career. Scottish education, which introduced aesthetics and criticism into Latin classroom instruction, developed the frame of mind and provided Masson with the critical tools that he used in studying English writers. Concern for the cultural symbiosis between the Scots and English—a concern that he shared with other 'young patriots', as George Elder Davie describes them (G. E. Davie, *The Democratic Intellect*, 1964, 207)—drove him to the study and criticism of English literature. While teaching in London he worked for publishers and publications associated with Scotland. At the University of Edinburgh he introduced Scottish students to English as well as Scottish writers. The results that Masson derived from this tension he himself best described in his essay on Scott in *British Novelists and their Styles*:

> [Scotticism] may exist internally as a mode of thought; … it may be the internal Scotticism, working on British, or on still more general objects, and not the Scotticism that works only on Scottish objects of thought, that may be in demand in literature as well as in other walks.   (pp. 211–12)

G. G. SMITH, *rev.* SONDRA MILEY COONEY

Sources H. Wilson, 'David Masson', *Nineteenth-century British literary biographers*, ed. S. Serafin, DLitB, 144 (1994), 188–203 · D. Masson, *Memories of London in the 'forties* (1908) · F. Masson, *Victorians all* (1931) · D. Masson, *Memories of two cities: Edinburgh and Aberdeen*, ed. F. Masson (1911) · *The Scotsman* (8 Oct 1907) · *The Scotsman* (11 Oct 1907) · G. Saintsbury, 'Tribute', *The Scotsman* (8 Oct 1907) · J. M. Barrie, *An Edinburgh eleven* (1889) · *Quasi cursores* (1884) · bap. reg. Scot. · d. cert.

Archives U. Edin. L., lecture notes | BL, corresp. with Macmillans, Add. MS 54792 · Edinburgh Central Reference Library, letters to Hew Morrison · NL Scot., corresp. with Thomas Carlyle · NL Scot., W. and R. Chambers archive, Dep. 341 · NL Scot., letters to Alexander Campbell Fraser · NL Scot., corresp. mainly with Lord Rosebery · U. Birm. L., letters to Edward Arber · UCL, letters to G. C. Robertson

Likenesses G. Reid, oils, 1896, Scot. NPG [*see illus.*] · W. Hole, etching, repro. in *Quasi cursores* · photograph, repro. in Masson, *Memories*

Wealth at death £802 7s. 7d.: confirmation, 8 Nov 1907, *CCI*

Masson, Sir David Orme (1858–1937), chemist, was born on 13 January 1858, probably in Avenue Road, Hampstead,

London, the second child of four and only son of David *Masson (1822–1907), the historiographer royal for Scotland, who was then professor of English literature at University College, London, and his wife, Emily Rosaline, eldest daughter of Charles Orme, of Hampstead. In London and then in Edinburgh, Masson's childhood and youth were strongly coloured by the literary influences of his father's and mother's circles, which included the Tennyson brothers, the Pre-Raphaelite Brotherhood, Coventry Patmore, Giuseppe Mazzini, Thomas Carlyle, Robert Browning, and T. H. Huxley.

In 1865 the family moved to Edinburgh, where Masson attended first Oliphant's School and then Edinburgh Academy. In 1873 he entered Edinburgh University, later graduating in both arts and science. After a period at Göttingen, he joined the staff of University College, Bristol, in 1880, engaging in work with William Ramsay on atomic volumes. He returned in 1881 to Edinburgh and was awarded a research fellowship in chemistry; he published several papers on glyceryl trinitrite and trinitrate, and on salts of organic bases such as sulphines. On 5 August 1886 he married Mary (1862–1945), second daughter of Sir John *Struthers (1823–1899), professor of anatomy in Aberdeen University. They had three children: their son, Sir (James) Irvine Orme Masson [see below], a chemist, became vice-chancellor of the University of Sheffield, and their two daughters were noted writers, particularly the elder, Marnie Bassett. The younger, Elsie Rosaline (d. 1935), was married to the anthropologist Bronislaw Malinowski (1884–1942). After his marriage Masson emigrated to Australia, having been appointed to the chair of chemistry in the University of Melbourne. During the next fifty years he was to be one of the most prominent figures in Australian science, doing much to advance its cause in both Melbourne and the nation, both of which were growing rapidly. His wife became much involved in voluntary community work, for which she was created CBE in 1918.

Despite the handicaps of isolation and heavy teaching responsibilities, Masson's original scientific work was extensive and of a high quality. Apart from studies associated with the periodic classification of the elements, his chief interests lay in the development of the theory of solution as originally put forward by Svante A. Arrhenius, Jacobus Hendricus van't Hoff, Wilhelm Ostwald, and their school, and in interpreting the chemical dynamics of such reactions as that of hydrogen peroxide on potassium cyanide, the decomposition of cyanates, and the decomposition of persulphuric acid and its salts in aqueous solution. His paper on the velocity of the migration of ions was a particularly valuable contribution in its time (PTRS, 192, 1899). He was attracted by problems of theoretical interpretation rather than by those of design or manipulation of apparatus, and in his later years he contributed much to the development of ideas on the constitution of atoms, and to the theory of dissociation of electrolytes in water.

From 1910 Masson became absorbed more and more in university administration and in outside public work. In 1911–13, as president of the Australasian Association for the Advancement of Science, he took the leading part in organizing the visit of the British Association to Australia in 1914. He actively assisted the first expedition under Douglas Mawson to the Antarctic in 1911–14, and in 1929–31 he was chairman of the committee responsible for the British, Australian, and New Zealand Antarctic research expedition. During the First World War he served on many special committees dealing with munitions and naval matters and did notable work from 1915 onwards in drafting the scheme leading to the establishment in 1920 of a Commonwealth Institute of Science and Industry, which in 1926 was reorganized as the Council for Scientific and Industrial Research, on which he served until his death. Retirement from active teaching in 1923, when he was made emeritus professor, gave him increased opportunity for outside interests which included service on several business directorates.

The Melbourne University Chemical Society, the Society of Chemical Industry of Victoria, and the Australian Chemical Institute were all founded by Masson, as was (with Sir T. W. Edgeworth David) the Australian National Research Council. He presided over the second Pan-Pacific Scientific Congress held in Melbourne and Sydney in 1923.

Masson was elected FRS in 1903, and appointed CBE in 1918, and KBE in 1923; he received the honorary degree of LLD from Edinburgh University in 1924. A Masson lectureship was established in his honour by the National Research Council, and a Masson memorial scholarship by the Australian Chemical Institute.

His personal charm, originality, and independence of mind, and his perfect integrity made Masson a powerful influence in his adopted university and country. Together with his colleagues Sir Walter Baldwin Spencer, biologist, and Sir Thomas Lyle, physicist, he shaped the science schools of Melbourne University, particularly with respect to the teaching of advanced laboratory subjects; many of his students became successful in academia and industry. He died of cancer at his home at South Yarra, Melbourne, on 10 August 1937, and was cremated after a private funeral.

Sir (James) Irvine Orme Masson (1887–1962), chemist, was born in Melbourne on 3 September 1887. He was educated at Melbourne grammar school and at Ormond College (University of Melbourne). He was awarded an 1851 Exhibition scholarship, which he held at University College, London, under William Ramsay. In 1912 he was appointed to the staff of University College's chemistry department and in the following year he married Flora Lovell, daughter of G. Lovell Gulland, later professor of medicine at Edinburgh University.

Masson's tenure at University College was interrupted by the First World War, during which he worked at the research department of the Royal Arsenal in Woolwich. In 1924 he was appointed professor of chemistry and head of the department of pure science at the University of Durham. In 1938 he went to the University of Sheffield as vice-chancellor, remaining there until his retirement in 1952. During these years he moulded the university into an expanded and modern institution.

Masson's interests spanned physical chemistry, the history of chemistry, and science education. He was author of *Three Centuries of Chemistry* (1925) and *Problems in the National Teaching of Science* (1931). During the Second World War, in addition to his duties as vice-chancellor, he supervised a large group involved in explosives research. Outside the sciences he had a keen interest in typography and contributed several articles to *Transactions of the Bibliographical Society*. He was elected FRS in 1939 and was awarded honorary LLDs from Edinburgh and Sheffield. He was knighted in 1950.

Masson retired to Edinburgh, where he spent many hours in bibliographical pursuits. His years there were saddened by the long illness of his wife, who died in 1960. Masson himself died in Edinburgh on 22 October 1962. He left one son.   DAVID RIVETT, *rev.* K. D. WATSON

Sources A. C. D. Rivett, *Obits. FRS*, 2 (1936–8), 455–64 • N. T. M. Wilsmore, 'The life and work of Sir David Orme Masson', *Australian Journal of Science*, 3 (1941), 139–44 • I. W. Wark, 'David Orme Masson, 1858–1937', *Proceedings of the Royal Australian Chemical Institute*, 25 (1958), 533–41 • J. Read, *Nature*, 140 (1937), 534–6 • A. C. D. Rivett, *JCS* (1938), 598–603 • L. W. Weickhardt, 'Masson, Sir David Orme', *AusDB*, vol. 10 • *Testimonials in favour of Mr Orme Masson, candidate for the chair of chemistry in the University of St Andrews* (1884) • *WWW*, 1961–70 [Sir J. I. O. Masson] • *The Times* (23 Oct 1962) • private information (1949) • personal knowledge (1949)
Archives Australian Academy of Science, Canberra, Basser Library, corresp. and papers • State Library of Victoria, Melbourne • University of Melbourne, corresp. • Wellcome L., paper relating to nitroglycerine | NL Aus., letters to Alfred Deakin • UCL, Ramsay MSS
Likenesses photographs, 1893–1933, Basser Library, Canberra • W. B. McInnes, oils, University of Melbourne, chemistry department • photograph, repro. in Rivett, *Obits. FRS* • photograph, repro. in Wark, 'David Orme Masson', 531

Masson, Francis (1741–1805), botanist, was born in August 1741 at Aberdeen. He made his way to London, where he obtained a gardening appointment at the Royal Botanic Gardens, Kew. In 1771 or 1772 he was selected by Aiton, the superintendent, on the advice of Sir John Pringle, as the fittest person to undertake a journey to the Cape for the purpose of collecting plants and bulbs—the first collector thus sent out by the authorities at Kew.

Masson made Cape Town his headquarters and undertook at least three separate journeys into the interior, the first of which was from 10 December 1772 to 18 January 1773, with F. P. Oldenburg; the second, in company with C. P. Thunberg, the Swedish naturalist, lasted from 11 September 1773 to 29 January 1774; and the third, also in 1774, was begun on 26 September and brought to an end on 29 December. Having for the time thoroughly supplied the wants of Kew from that locality, Masson was sent on a like errand in 1776 to the Canaries, Azores, Madeira, and the West Indies, more especially to St Kitts. He returned to England in 1781, and remained at home until 1783, when he was dispatched to Portugal and Madeira. In 1786, when once more sent out to the Cape, he confined his botanical excursions, by the advice of Sir Joseph Banks, to a circuit of 40 miles round Cape Town. He remained there until 1795.

Masson spent some two years in England with his friends, and prepared and published in 1796–7 his well-known book, *Stapeliae novae, or, … new species of that genus discovered in the interior parts of Africa*. The work was issued in four instalments and contains forty-one charming coloured plates by Masson, only one of which was copied from another drawing. In 1798 he set out for North America, where he died at Montreal, on 23 December 1805.

Many plants common in conservatories were first sent to Britain by Masson. *Massonia*, a genus of eight southern African bulbous species, was named after him, as were the southern African shrubs *Thamnea massoniana* and *Protea massonii*.   B. B. WOODWARD, *rev.* F. NIGEL HEPPER

Sources F. R. Bradlow, *Francis Masson's account of three journeys at the Cape of Good Hope, 1772–1775* (1994) • M. Gunn and L. E. Codd, *Botanical exploration of southern Africa* (1981) • Desmond, *Botanists*, rev. edn • M. C. Karsten, 'Francis Masson: a gardener–botanist who collected at the Cape', *Journal of South African Botany*, 24 (1858), 203–18; 25 (1859), 167–88, 283–310; 26 (1860), 9–15; 27 (1861), 15–45 • H. C. Andrews, *Botanical repository*, 1 (1799), pl. 46 • A. Rees and others, *The cyclopaedia, or, Universal dictionary of arts, sciences, and literature*, 45 vols. (1819–20), vol. 22 • J. Britten, 'Francis Masson', *Journal of Botany, British and Foreign*, 22 (1884), 114–23; 42 (1904), 2–3; 55 (1917), 70–71 • *The Banks letters*, ed. W. R. Dawson (1958) • K. Lemmon, *The golden age of plant hunters* (1968) • A. M. Coates, *The quest for plants* (1969) • L. C. Rookmaker, *The zoological exploration of southern Africa* (1989)
Archives BM, department of prints and drawings, drawings • Mitchell L., NSW • NHM, drawings • RBG Kew, archives, drawings | Boissier Herbarium, Geneva • NHM, corresp. with Sir Joseph Banks • NRA, corresp. with Sir Joseph Banks • U. Cam.
Likenesses G. Garrard, oils, Linn. Soc.
Wealth at death £35 0s. 3½d.: Rees and others, *The cyclopaedia*; Bradlow, *Francis Masson's account*

Masson, (George Joseph) Gustave (1819–1888), French scholar and teacher, was born in London on 9 March 1819, the son of Emile Masson, who served under Napoleon and having survived the retreat from Moscow lived in exile in London where he met and married Masson's English mother. Gustave Masson received his primary and secondary education in Tours. As the eldest son of a highly decorated officer's widow Masson was, ironically enough, exempted from military service, but he quickly developed into a precocious scholar and earned the diploma of *bachelier-ès-lettres* at the Université de France in August 1837 when he was still only eighteen years old. On completion of his studies Masson embarked on a decade of intense but ultimately futile literary struggle in Paris. On 26 September 1844 he married Janet, daughter of George Clarke. They had two sons and two daughters. In 1847, with his resources at an end, Masson accepted an invitation to cross the channel and serve as private tutor to a wealthy family in Harrow, Middlesex. The decision to settle in Harrow was a fortuitous one and it was followed, in 1855, by Masson's appointment as French master at the renowned Harrow School. Over the next thirty-three years Masson proved an able administrator, a beloved teacher, and an innovative librarian (of the Vaughan Library), who balanced his official duties with an ambitious scholarly agenda that ranged from the middle ages to the nineteenth century, but placed emphasis on articulating the development and main contours of modern French literature.

Indeed, Masson was a critic, editor, translator, lexicographer, linguist, textbook compiler, and journalist on a prodigious scale, whose chief works on French literature, language, and history include *Introduction to the History of French Literature* (1860), *La lyre Française* (an anthology in the Golden Treasury series, 1867), *A Compendious Dictionary of the French Language* (1874), *Outlines of French Literature* (1877), *Early Chronicles of Europe: France* (1879), *The Huguenots: a Sketch of their History* (1881), *French Literature* (1888), and *Medieval France from Hugues Capet to the Sixteenth Century* (1888). In addition, Masson published original monographs of Richelieu (1884) and Mazarin (1886), and numerous successful school and university editions of French classics, including Molière, Racine, Corneille, Madame de Sévigné, Voltaire, Regnard, Musset, Victor Hugo, George Sand, and Germaine de Staël (Clarendon Press, Oxford, 1867–80). In terms of scope, lucidity, and contemporary importance, Masson's contributions to French studies in Victorian England may be compared to Thomas Carlyle's and George Saintsbury's construction, respectively, of German and English literary history during the same period.

While engaged in producing a vast and, for its time, innovative body of scholarship for specialists and valuable study aids for students and pupils, Masson was also a frequent contributor to *The Athenaeum* and the regular reviewer of French literature for the *Saturday Review* from 1872 to 1880. He gave up his Harrow mastership in 1888 and died a few weeks later on 29 August at Woodlands, Tooting Common, Streatham, Surrey, while on a visit to his good friend Sir Henry Doulton. Masson was buried in Harrow churchyard. He was survived by his wife and four children. THOMAS SECCOMBE, *rev.* GREGORY MAERTZ

Sources 'French literature', *Saturday Review* (8 Sept 1888) · Allibone, *Dict.* · *The Times* (31 Aug 1888) · *The Times* (1 Sept 1888) · *Annual Register* (1888), 169 · *The Athenaeum* (1 Sept 1888) · Boase, *Mod. Eng. biog.*, 2.788

Archives CUL, corresp.

Wealth at death £8831 18s. 6d.: probate, 19 Sept 1888, *CGPLA Eng. & Wales*

Masson, Sir (James) Irvine Orme (1887–1962). *See under* Masson, Sir David Orme (1858–1937).

Massue de Ruvigny, Henri de, earl of Galway, and marquess of Ruvigny in the French nobility (1648–1720), Huguenot leader, army officer, and diplomat, was born in Paris, probably in the Faubourg St Germain, on 9 April 1648, the eldest son of five surviving children of Henri de Massue, first marquess of Ruvigny (1599/1610–1689), general, diplomat, and deputy general of the Huguenots to Louis XIV, and his wife, Marie (*d.* 1698), daughter of Pierre Tallemand and Marie de Rambouillet.

From France to England: soldier and diplomat As a young man Ruvigny served in the French army, first under Schomberg in Portugal, where he was present at the siege of Fort de la Garda, and then under Turenne on the Rhine. In 1674 he was granted a pension for his distinguished service, and by 1677 had achieved the rank of colonel and

Henri de Massue de Ruvigny, earl of Galway, and marquess of Ruvigny in the French nobility (1648–1720), by John Simon, pubd *c.*1704 (after Philip de Graves)

command of a regiment. In 1678 Louis XIV sent him to England on a successful diplomatic mission aimed at reaching an accommodation with the earl of Shaftesbury and the parliamentary opposition to preserve English neutrality in the final phase of the third Dutch war. In 1679 he left the army and succeeded his father as deputy general of the Huguenots. Thereafter he worked diligently on behalf of the Huguenots at the French court, although there was some criticism that he was the too compliant protégé of the marquess of Seignelay, whose interests he sought to gratify. The revocation of the edict of Nantes in 1685 and subsequent severe persecution of protestants in France undermined his position, and at the end of the year he emigrated to England with his father and younger brother Pierre, seigneur de la Caillemotte. The family did not, however, at that stage forfeit their property in France, and received the special privilege of being allowed to take with them whatever personal goods they chose.

Ruvigny's father, a former French ambassador to England and related through his sister to the whig family of Russell, dukes of Bedford, had prudently obtained letters of naturalization as an English subject in 1680. He settled at Greenwich and became one of the most important of the refugees' leaders in England. Before his death in July 1689 he was influential in the formation of four Huguenot regiments to serve William of Orange. Command of one of the infantry regiments went to la Caillemotte, who was killed in Ireland at the battle of the Boyne. Ruvigny himself had initially avoided military service against France in order to preserve his title to the extensive family estates in

Picardy and Champagne. In January 1691, however, he accepted a major-general's appointment with the Williamite army in Ireland and was given the vacant command of Schomberg's cavalry regiment. In June he was present at the siege of Athlone, where he was one of those to advocate the hazardous assault across the river which ultimately won the town for William. At the closely fought battle of Aughrim in co. Galway on 12 July he turned the tide in favour of the Williamites by achieving a vital breakthrough on the right wing, where he led a force of cavalry, including some of his own regiment, along a narrow causeway near Aughrim Castle into the heart of the enemy position. The Jacobite resistance crumbled as a consequence, and in the ensuing collapse James's army suffered as many as 7000 casualties. On the battlefield Ginckel, the Williamite commander, publicly embraced Ruvigny in gratitude for his conduct and courage in helping to win the decisive victory of the war. Subsequently he took part in the second siege of Limerick, where he commanded the cavalry force which crossed the Shannon to cover the Jacobite cavalry in Clare. He played a role in the preliminary contacts which led to the negotiation of the Jacobite surrender, and later took part in the victory celebrations in Dublin before crossing to England in November.

On 3 March 1692 Ruvigny was created Baron Portarlington and Viscount Galway in reward for his military services, made an Irish privy councillor, and sent back to Ireland as commander-in-chief of the forces there in succession to Ginckel. However, in response to the French invasion threat he was called back to England, where he was appointed second-in-command of a proposed expedition against St Malo and spent much of the year at Portsmouth until the project was abandoned. He returned to Ireland in January 1693, departing again the following April to join William's army in Flanders. In July he played an important role at the battle of Landen, covering William's retreat by defending the bridge at Neerhespen against the entire French cavalry. He was slightly wounded in the engagement and made prisoner, but soon afterwards freed by his magnanimous French captors, who thereby preserved him from a traitor's fate.

In December 1693 Galway was promoted lieutenant-general and appointed to command the British forces in Savoy. On 14 February 1694 he was given the additional appointment of envoy-extraordinary to Victor Amadeus, duke of Savoy. He brought with him a considerable sum of money for the relief of the Vaudois and the French protestant refugees, and persuaded Victor Amadeus to allow the Vaudois limited toleration. War had ruined the Savoyard economy, and he sought to promote commercial links, especially in textiles, with England. Despite the high hopes of the allies, very little was achieved on the military front in 1694 except the capture of Fort San Giorgio. The duplicitous Victor Amadeus completely deceived Galway as to his trustworthiness. He was secretly in touch with the French, who in 1695 surrendered Casale to him after a token siege. He would not agree to Galway's proposals for combining with the English navy to attack

Toulon and Nice, and in 1696 he made a separate peace with France and withdrew from the war. Having declined to accept a gift from Victor Amadeus, Galway retired into the Milanese with the English contingent before rejoining William in Flanders in October.

Lord justice of Ireland and Huguenot champion In 1697 Galway was appointed one of the lords justices of Ireland, an office he retained until 1701. His French nationality prevented him from being made lord lieutenant, but the absence or indolence of his colleagues made him effective head of the Irish administration. On 12 May 1697 he was advanced to the earldom of Galway and given a grant of £3000 per year out of the forfeited estates of Ireland. His achievements in Ireland included the establishment of a system of discipline and regulations for the army together with an extensive programme of barrack building. He was trusted and liked by William for his frankness and spirit, and repaid the confidence with total loyalty. Although labelled a whig, he had neither the tone nor the temper of a partisan in British politics. The forfeiture of his French estates led him to write to William in 1692, reminding him of a promise that he should get something of the order of £25,000 in compensation for his loss. As a result he was given possession of the 36,000 acre Portarlington estate of the outlawed Jacobite Sir Patrick Trant. This was made an absolute title in 1696. Thus Ireland was effectively his home in the 1690s. He liked Dublin and praised the plentiful crops and fine fish.

Galway, throughout his life, used his wealth and influence on behalf of the exiled Huguenots. Described as 'their head, their friend, their refuge, their advocate, their support [and] their protector' (Agnew, *Protestant Exiles from France*, 1.162), effectively he continued to act as their deputy general, working tirelessly to improve their general position and to lobby on behalf of individuals. In England he maintained his father's practice of dispensing hospitality and bounty to Huguenot supplicants who crowded his house from early in the morning. In 1689 he paid for the release of Huguenot slaves from Algiers, and in 1696 was known to be maintaining eighty refugees in Switzerland. As early as 1692 he was planning a French colony in Ireland. He spent much of his brief visit that year viewing suitable locations and settling refugees, including half-pay officers and their families. In 1693 he was involved in an abortive scheme to establish a French university at Kilkenny, and in 1694 he discussed the possibility of settlement in Ireland with the leaders of the exiled Waldenses in Switzerland.

Following Galway's return to Ireland in 1697 the settlement of the French proceeded in earnest, especially when the Huguenot regiments, including his own, were brought there for disbandment in 1698 after the treaty of Ryswick. He helped secure pensions for 120 officers and settled 500 French people on his Portarlington estate, financing the construction there of two churches, two schools, and more than a hundred houses. His vision did much in the 1690s to establish Ireland as a fit haven for Huguenot refugees. Almost a score of settlements, large and small, were established, and the number of Huguenots in the kingdom was greatly increased. He is said to have paid for the grandsons of Viscount Clanmaliere, a previous owner of Portarlington, to be educated at Eton College and to have promised to restore them to their family lands if they converted to the protestant religion. He complained that his expenditure and a reduction in his emoluments had left him virtually penniless, and in 1700 he lost his Portarlington estates when William's land grants in Ireland were cancelled by the Act of Resumption. It was even mooted that as a foreigner he might be precluded from serving in the army. William wrote to Galway of his grief over the matter, and compensated him with a general's appointment in the Dutch forces and command of his prized regiment of Dutch footguards, which he held until 1711.

Galway's term of office as a lord justice coincided with the enactment by the Irish parliament of the first of the notorious anti-Catholic laws and its ratification of only a severely mutilated version of the 1691 treaty of Limerick. Then, and since, the suggestion has been made that these measures were Galway's revenge. He seems, however, to have been motivated throughout by the government's need to placate the Irish parliament rather than by any personal spleen. In part the contemporary criticism was undoubtedly founded on the genuine, if perhaps mistaken, suspicions of the exiled Irish Catholics and their supporters. An element of 'black propaganda', emanating from the French court, may also have been involved, motivated by Louis's vindictive determination to thwart any attempt by Galway to recover his estates in France under the private clauses of the treaty of Ryswick. In May 1698 William's close adviser the earl of Portland made representations to Louis at Versailles about a possible restoration, but to no avail, and Galway's French estates were eventually granted to Cardinal Polignac. Louis also persuaded President d'Harlay to betray a private trust covering moneys which he held for the Ruvigny family. An even more sinister explanation was Louis's need to discredit Galway in Catholic circles before the disclosure of damaging information Galway had acquired in Savoy relating to Louis's complicity in Jacobite plans to have William assassinated.

Galway left Ireland in 1701, and in July accompanied the earl of Marlborough to Holland, where he met William at Het Loo and was sent on an unsuccessful diplomatic mission to detach the elector of Cologne from alliance with France. Next he returned to England to negotiate on William's behalf with lords Somers and Sunderland to gain their support for the coming war. William's death found him without public or military employment in Britain, but with an annual pension of £1000. He retired to the manor house of Rookley in Hampshire, which he evidently leased because of its proximity to Stratton House, the residence of Rachel, Lady Russell, his kinswoman and friend.

The Peninsular War In July 1704 Galway was called out of retirement by Queen Anne, given £10,000, promoted general, and sent with 4000 reinforcements to take command of the English forces in Portugal. He arrived at Lisbon on 10 August, where he found the Portuguese army to be of poor quality and ill paid, the clergy hostile to protestants, and the politicians corrupted by French bribes. An early offensive against Ciudad Rodrigo was undertaken, although he counselled against it because of the deficiency in supplies. His view was vindicated when lack of provisions forced the army to retreat. During the winter he reinforced Gibraltar and busied himself in preparing his forces for the 1705 campaign. There were a number of councils of war with the quarrelsome and incompetent earl of Peterborough, who had arrived with a fleet to take command of the allied forces in Spain. Eventually it was decided that Peterborough, accompanied by Archduke Charles, the Habsburg claimant to the Spanish throne, would attack Barcelona, while Galway and the Portuguese under Las Minas invaded Estramadura. His plan for an immediate attack on Badajoz was postponed until Valencia d'Alcántara and Albuquerque had been reduced, and only on 2 October was the siege of Badajoz opened. While he was supervising the erection of a battery, a cannon shot from the fortress carried off his right arm a little below the elbow. His injury forced him to withdraw, and the siege was raised. Marshal de Tessé, the French commander, allowed him a pass to go to Olivenza for his recovery and sent his own physicians to attend him there. During his convalescence he received sympathetic letters of gratitude for his service from both the king of Portugal and Queen Anne. He later learned to write with his left hand.

Encouraged by Peterborough's capture of Barcelona, Galway resumed his command in the spring of 1706, mounting a fresh offensive with the 25,000 men at his disposal to take advantage of the French preoccupation with Catalonia. Although physically so weak that he had to be lifted into the saddle, he conducted a vigorous and successful campaign. The numerically weaker Hispano-French forces under the duke of Berwick were driven back, and were powerless to prevent the capture of Alcántara and Ciudad Rodrigo. After some delay the reluctant Portuguese were persuaded to continue the offensive towards Madrid, which was occupied without resistance in the name of King Charles on 27 June. The event occasioned much public rejoicing when news of it reached England. It had less impact in Spain, because most of the Spanish grandees had already left the city, and Peterborough and Charles, despite repeated requests from Galway, failed to put in an appearance in the capital. While the allies delayed, Berwick was reinforced and given time to mobilize Spanish support. On 6 August French troops reoccupied Madrid, which Galway had vacated finally to join Peterborough and Charles at Guadalajara. The meeting of the allied leaders was marked by recriminations. Galway's generous proposal that Peterborough should assume overall command of their united forces was rejected by the other generals. After spending a month at Chinchón, the allies withdrew to winter quarters in Valencia.

Galway sought to be recalled to England, but instead in

February 1707 orders came appointing him commander of all the British forces in Spain while Peterborough was summoned home. Reinforced from England, but without the Catalan and German troops which were brought north by Charles to garrison Catalonia and Aragon, he planned a fresh attack on Madrid. However, to consolidate the security of Valencia, he delayed the offensive to reduce first the potential French bases in Murcia. Meanwhile Berwick, having received substantial reinforcements from France under the duc d'Orléans, opened his own offensive in Murcia. Galway, mistakenly believing that the French reinforcements had yet to arrive, advanced on 25 April against Berwick's position outside Almanza, only to find that his army was heavily outnumbered. The left wing gave way before the French and the Portuguese cavalry on the right fled from the field leaving the infantry to be massacred or made prisoner. Galway himself behaved courageously, but he lost direction of the battle when severely wounded by a sabre cut to the face, which cost him the sight of his right eye. He managed to leave the field, but his army was virtually destroyed. Although the war was to drag on for several years, Almanza was probably the decisive engagement which ensured that the throne of Spain would go to the French claimant.

In the immediate aftermath of the battle Aragon, Murcia, and Valencia fell to the French, while Galway concentrated on the defence of Catalonia, where he displayed considerable energy in reorganizing the remnants of his broken infantry into five battalions and raising four more of Catalans. However, he was powerless to prevent the fall of Lérida in November. He became the focus of growing criticism in England over the set-backs in the peninsula, and in December he was replaced by James Stanhope as commander of the British in Spain. Debilitated by his war wounds, deafness, and gout, he had long sought to be recalled. Instead, as a mark of the government's approbation, he was sent as envoy to Lisbon and resumed command of the English forces in Portugal. He had little influence with King Pedro, the new Portuguese monarch, who was pro-French and was only kept in the allied alliance by his fear of the English fleet. Apart from diplomatic duties he was largely inactive in 1708. In 1709 he participated in a fresh offensive in Estramadura, which was ended on 17 May by a sharp reverse on the banks of the Caya, during which his horse was killed beneath him and he narrowly escaped capture. The defeat was largely caused by the rashness of the Portuguese commander, but the set-back renewed criticism of Galway in England, and in 1710, much to his relief, he was finally recalled, arriving at Falmouth on 21 October.

Ireland again, retirement, and death A month later, despite the fall of the Godolphin and Marlborough faction with whom Galway was associated, he was kindly received at St James's Palace by Queen Anne on 18 November. In January 1711, however, the management of the disastrous Peninsular War was the subject of several acrimonious debates in the House of Lords. He and Peterborough gave conflicting accounts, and although Marlborough defended

Galway's conduct, for entirely political reasons the house, by sixty-eight votes to forty-eight, chose to believe Peterborough and voted to censure him. He then retired to Rookley, where he remained until 1715, when he was summoned from retirement to serve once more as a lord justice of Ireland with the young duke of Grafton. His appointment was probably intended to preserve the military security of Ireland at the time of the Jacobite rising in Scotland. He landed with Grafton at Dublin on 1 November, and found the Irish parliament and establishment totally loyal. His plan to improve the legal position of the presbyterians was thwarted by the bishops in the House of Lords, but it was some compensation that parliament granted him a military pension of £500 per year. He was recalled in January 1716, when he retired for the final time to Rookley. In 1718 he was named as first governor in the charter establishing the French Hospital in London. His mind remained clear to the end of his life. On 3 September 1720 he died at the age of seventy-two, while visiting Lady Russell at Stratton House, and was buried three days later in nearby Micheldever churchyard. Ruvigny was unmarried and left no immediate family, so that at his death all his honours both French and English became extinct. Under his will, after legacies of £12,670 mainly to Huguenot charities, the residue of his estate went to Lady Russell.

Although the many failures and vicissitudes of Galway's career suggest that his abilities were limited, contemporaries generally held him in high esteem. In France, as a young man, the writer Benoit judged him 'handsome in person, and mentally he was affable, sagacious and intelligent, brave without temerity, prudent without meanness, agreeable to the king, beloved by all the court, and on excellent terms with His Majesty's ministers … his merits procured him neither enemies nor detractors' (Agnew, *Henri de Ruvigny, Earl of Galway*, 33). In later life the whig bishop Burnet thought him 'one of the finest gentlemen in the army, with a head fitted for the cabinet as well as the camp; is very modest, vigilant and sincere, without pride or affectation; wears his own hair [and] is plain in his dress and manners' (GEC, *Peerage*). This assessment provoked the partisan and probably unfair response of the tory dean Swift that he was 'a deceitful, hypocritical, factious knave, [and] a damnable hypocrite of no religion' (GEC, *Peerage*).

HARMAN MURTAGH

Sources D. C. A. Agnew, *Henri de Ruvigny, earl of Galway: a filial memoir, with a prefatory life of his father, le marquis de Ruvigny* (1864) • D. C. A. Agnew, *Protestant exiles from France in the reign of Louis XIV, or, The Huguenot refugees and their descendants in Great Britain and Ireland*, 2nd edn, 1 (1871), 144–219 • C. E. J. Caldicott, H. Gough, and J.-P. Pittion, eds., *The Huguenots and Ireland: anatomy of an emigration* (1987), 205–54, 297–320 • GEC, *Peerage* • C. Petrie, *The marshal duke of Berwick* (1953), 162–219 • G. Story, *A continuation of the impartial history of the wars of Ireland* (1693) • J. G. Simms, *The Williamite confiscation in Ireland, 1690–1703* (1956), 61–2, 68, 86–9, 139, 112–13 • *CSP dom.*, 1685; 1697–1702 • C. Dalton, ed., *English army lists and commission registers, 1661–1714*, 6 vols. (1892–1904), vols. 3, 5–6 • C. Reid and F. Waddington, eds., *Mémoires inédits de Dumont de Bostaquet, gentilhomme, Normand* (1864) • K. Danaher and J. G. Simms, eds., *The Danish force in Ireland 1690–1691* (1962), 112, 122–3, 128, 134 • G. Symcox, *Victor Amadeus II: absolutism in the Savoyard state 1675–*

1730 (1983), 106–17 • T. Murdoch, *The quiet conquest: the Huguenots 1685 to 1985* (1985), 81–2 • A. D. Francis, *The first Peninsular War, 1702–1703* (1975)

Archives BL, corresp., Egerton MS 891 • Chatsworth House, Derbyshire, letters | BL, letters to William Blathwayt, Add. MS 19771 • BL, letters to John Ellis, Add. MSS 28056–28057 • BL, letters to Lord Godolphin, Add. MSS 28879–28885 • BL, corresp. with Lord Lexington, Add. MS 46583 • CAC Cam., letters to Thomas Erle • CKS, corresp. with James Stanhope • CUL, letters to Sir Robert Walpole • Longleat House, Wiltshire, corresp. with Matthew Prior • Northants. RO, corresp. with duke of Shrewsbury • PRO, state papers, Savoy and Sardinia, no. 31 • TCD, corresp. with William King • U. Nott. L., corresp. with first Earl Portland • U. Nott. L., letters to Lady Russell and corresp. with the monarch • UCL, letters to Jacques Muysson • Yale U., Beinecke L., letters to William Blathwayt, etc.

Likenesses J. Simon, mezzotint, pubd *c.*1704 (after P. de Graves), BM, NPG [*see illus.*] • oils (in middle age), Corsham Court, Wiltshire; repro. in E. Black, *Kings in conflict: Ireland in the 1690s* (1990) • oils, Corsham Court, Wiltshire

Wealth at death legacies of £12,670 and undisclosed residue: Agnew, *Henri de Ruvigny*, 33

Massy, William Godfrey Dunham (1838–1906), army officer, was born on 24 November 1838 at Grantstown, co. Tipperary, Ireland, the eldest of four sons of Major Henry William Massy (1816–1895) of Grantstown and Clomaine, co. Tipperary, and his wife, Maria, daughter of Patrick Cahill. Educated at Trinity College, Dublin, he graduated BA in 1859, and was made LLD in 1873.

Massy joined the army as an ensign on 27 October 1854, and was promoted lieutenant on 9 February 1855. He went out to the Crimea in 1855, and in the assault on the Redan, on 8 September 1855, he led the grenadiers of the 19th foot (Green Howards). Returning to the trenches for reinforcements, he was dangerously wounded by a ball which passed through his left thigh, shattering the bone. When the assaulting troops were compelled to retire, Massy was left on the field. The enemy, believing him to be dying, did not take him prisoner, and he was subsequently rescued. Although his chance of recovery was considered hopeless, Massy survived six months on a camp stretcher, and eventually recovered. His gallantry and fortitude were brought to the notice of the commander-in-chief, and he became known throughout the army as Redan Massy. He was promoted captain on 26 February 1858, and was awarded the fifth class of the Légion d'honneur and the Turkish order of the Mejidiye. In 1858 he joined the newly formed 5th Royal Irish Lancers.

On 23 January 1863 Massy became major while serving as assistant adjutant-general in India. In 1869 he married Elizabeth Jane, eldest daughter of Major-General Sir Thomas *Seaton of Ackworth, Suffolk, and widow of George Arnold. They had one daughter, Gertrude Annette, who married in 1893 Colonel James George Cockburn (*d.* 1900). On promotion to lieutenant-colonel on 31 October 1871 Massey commanded the 5th Royal Irish Lancers in India until 1879.

On 4 September 1879 Massy, who was temporarily commanding the Kurram field force in the absence of Major-General Sir Frederick Roberts on leave in Simla, was on his way with a small escort to Kabul when the news of the massacre of Sir Louis Cavagnari and his companions

reached him at Shutar Gardan. He at once telegraphed the news to Roberts who returned forthwith. During the renewed Anglo-Afghan War Massy commanded a cavalry brigade and took a prominent part in the battle of Charasia on 6 October 1879, capturing seventy-five Afghan guns. He was sent in pursuit of the enemy on 7 October during the subsequent operations in the Chardeh valley, but he failed to cut off the Afghan line of retreat. Next, taking part in the operations round Kabul, he was ordered (11 December 1879) to start from Sherpur with the cavalry to join up with General Macpherson's brigade, but he advanced too far and was cut off by 10,000 Afghans at Killa Kazi. After an unsuccessful charge and the loss of his guns, Massy was extricated from a very difficult situation by the timely arrival of Roberts with the main body. Roberts in his report laid at least part of the blame for the disaster on Massy, whom he had already judged as lacking in the qualities necessary in a good cavalry leader. Massy was recalled to India by the commander-in-chief, India, Sir Frederick Haines, but Massy had influential friends and a good record as a regimental commander. He was reappointed to a brigade by the duke of Cambridge, commander-in-chief at the Horse Guards. The formal grounds for Massy's removal were given in a letter from the adjutant-general, India, to Roberts dated 9 February 1880 (NAM, Roberts MSS, RP 101-23-147-3). Massy received the Afghan medal with two clasps.

Massy became major-general on 28 August 1886 and was made CB on 21 June 1887. He commanded the troops in Ceylon from 1888 to 1893, when, on 21 January, he was promoted lieutenant-general. On 4 October 1896 he became colonel of the 5th Royal Irish Lancers and was placed on the retired list. He was a JP and deputy lieutenant for co. Tipperary, and high sheriff in 1899. Massy died on 20 September 1906 at the family residence, Grantstown Hall, co. Tipperary.   H. M. VIBART, *rev.* JAMES LUNT

Sources *The Times* (21 Sept 1906) • *The Times* (22 Sept 1906) • Lord Roberts [F. S. Roberts], *Forty-one years in India*, 30th edn (1898) • H. B. Hanna, *The Second Afghan War*, 3 (1910) • J. Duke, *Recollections of the Kabul campaign* (1883) • P. Macrory, *Signal catastrophe: the story of a disastrous retreat from Kabul, 1842* (1966) • [S. P. Oliver], *The Second Afghan War, 1878–80; abridged official account*, rev. F. G. Cardew (1908) • A. W. Kinglake, *The invasion of the Crimea*, 8 vols. (1863–87) • Burke, *Gen. GB* • J. R. Harvey, *History of the fifth royal Irish lancers* (1923) • W. T. Willcox, *A history of the fifth (royal Irish) lancers* (1908) • G. Powell, *The history of the Green Howards: three hundred years of service* (1992) • *CGPLA Ire.* (1906) • NAM, Roberts MSS

Likenesses S. Marks, mezzotint, BM • black and white illustration, repro. in Willcox, *History*, p. 200 • wood-engraving (after a photograph by Sawyer and Bird), NPG; repro. in *ILN* (11 Oct 1879)

Wealth at death £11,786 4*s.* 11*d.*: Irish probate sealed in London, 8 Dec 1906, *CGPLA Eng. & Wales*

Master, John (*bap.* 1637, *d.* in or after 1684). *See under* Master, William (*bap.* 1627, *d.* 1684).

Master, Richard (*d.* 1587/8), physician, was a younger son of Robert Master (*d.* before 1551) of Street End, near Canterbury, Kent. A fellow of All Souls College, Oxford, from 1533 to 1541, Richard Master graduated BA in 1533 and MA in 1537. Later he would claim that he became a protestant at about this date through reading the works of Heinrich Bullinger, and that he gave up a lucrative benefice c.1538–9 because he considered himself unsuitable for the post, and 'Popery, though officially abolished flourished in reality' (Robinson, *Original Letters*, 1.177). Master certainly met Bullinger's associate, Rudolph Gwalther, on 11 March 1537 during his visit to England and subsequently corresponded with him. Master's enthusiasm for the protestant cause was tempered by a native shrewdness: he suspended the correspondence with Gwalther during the reign of Mary.

Master began studying medicine about 1541. In 1545 he was admitted BM at Oxford University with licence to practice. From 1547 he studied at Christ Church and graduated DM on 29 July 1555, despite suffering severe illness through much of 1549 and 1550. Master's medical standing rose steadily throughout the 1550s. In March 1553 he became a fellow of the College of Physicians. He was censor of the college in 1556–8 and 1560, and elect in 1558. He was also incorporated MD at Cambridge in 1571.

Master's appointment for life as royal physician on 26 June 1559 represented the zenith of his career. Other preferment soon followed. In 1561 he was elected president of the College of Physicians. In 1563 he was granted the lucrative prebend of Fridaythorpe in the East Riding of Yorkshire and lands in Sheriff Hutton near York. He was appointed master of the hospital of St Mary the Virgin, Newcastle upon Tyne, and consiliarius of the College of Physicians in 1564. In September 1566 he was moderator of the physic act kept there before the queen at Oxford. In 1568 Elizabeth I granted him a coat of arms. In the same year he was granted the reversion of the site of the former abbey of Cirencester in return for £590, where, after buying out the sitting tenants, he built a substantial house. Further grants of property in Huntingdonshire, Sussex, Lincolnshire, Oxfordshire, Middlesex, Hertfordshire, and Essex occurred in 1577 and 1581. His standing is also indicated by his being chosen as dedicatee of a translation of a French tract on gout by Christopher Arbaleste in 1577. Master's good relationship with the queen is suggested by his exchange of gifts with her on new year's day of 1562, 1578, and 1588, one of which was almost certainly a fine silver covered cup bearing the badge of Anne Boleyn, the queen's mother ('Reports of the itinerary', 32). Master had married Elizabeth, daughter of John Fulnetby of Fulnetby near Wragby, Lincolnshire, by 1560; they had seven sons.

Richard Master made his will on 10 January 1587; he was buried on 15 January 1588 at St Olave, Silver Street, London. He was survived by his wife, who received the lease estate, income from Bisley Wood in Gloucestershire, and two thirds of the marriage settlement of their eldest son George. George inherited the Cirencester house and estates in Gloucestershire and Wiltshire. Master set aside £310 for the purchase of Sinckley Manor, Gloucestershire, for his son John. Henry received his father's house in Silver Street, St Olave, London, and his father's 'books of phisick and books of philosophie' (PRO, PROB 11/72, sig. 34). His other sons received annuities. Four of Master's

sons had distinguished careers. George, of St John's College, Oxford, and Lincoln's Inn, was MP for Cirencester in 1586 and 1588. Thomas (1560–1628), BTh, master of the Temple in 1601, became canon of Lichfield in 1613 and archdeacon of Shropshire in 1614. Robert (1565–1625), DCL, was principal of St Alban Hall, Oxford, 1599–1603, chancellor of Rochester and Lichfield, and MP for Cricklade in 1601. Henry, MA, was principal of St Alban Hall 1603–14.

In addition to some of his correspondence with Rudolph Gwalther, a number of other letters by Richard Master survive. These include his undated reply to Elizabeth I concerning her question about the general causes of disease (Strype, 4.271) and several letters to William Cecil, Lord Burghley, which give advice concerning loose teeth, gout, and pains in the head and neck (PRO, SP 12/141/33; BL, Lansdowne MS 46.38, 121.19).

MAX SATCHELL

Sources H. Robinson, ed. and trans., *The Zurich letters, comprising the correspondence of several English bishops and others with some of the Helvetian reformers, during the early part of the reign of Queen Elizabeth*, 2, Parker Society, 8 (1845), 5, 25, 28, 48 • H. Robinson, ed. and trans., *Original letters relative to the English Reformation*, 1 vol. in 2, Parker Society, [26] (1846–7), 177, 198 • J. Strype, *Annals of the Reformation and establishment of religion … during Queen Elizabeth's happy reign*, new edn, 4 (1824), appx, 271 • BL, Lansdowne MS 19.83; Lansdowne MS 46.38; Lansdowne MS 121.19 • PRO, SP 12/141/33 • PRO, PROB 11/72, sig. 34 • *CPR, 1558–60*, 94; *1560–63*, 507; *1563–6*, 402, 1042; *1575–8*, 2346; *1578–80*, 1808; *1580–82*, 157 • R. E. G. Kirk and E. F. Kirk, eds., *Returns of aliens dwelling in the city and suburbs of London, from the reign of Henry VIII to that of James I*, Huguenot Society of London, 10/1 (1900), 307 • C. Arbaleste, *The overthrow of gout and a dialogue betwixt gout and Christopher Ballista*, ed. S. McKeown (1990) • P. Boesch, 'Rudolph Gwalthers Reise nach England im Jahre 1537', *Zwingliana*, 8 (1947), 433–71 • Cooper, *Ath. Cantab.*, vol. 2 • *Fasti Angl.*, *1541–1857*, [York], 36 • J. Philipott, 'The visitation of the county of Kent taken in the year 1619 [pt 1]', *Archaeologia Cantiana*, 4 (1861), 241–72, esp. 259 • Munk, *Roll* • *DNB* • private information (2004) [A. H. Nelson] • R. Reece, 'The abbey of St Mary, Cirencester', *Transactions of the Bristol and Gloucestershire Archaeological Society*, 81 (1962), 198–202, esp. 200 • [G. McN. Rushforth and W. H. Knowles], 'Reports of the itinerary: Tuesday, 7 July 1931', *Transactions of the Bristol and Gloucestershire Archaeological Society*, 53 (1931), 27–35, esp. 32
Archives PRO, MSS, SP 12/141/33 | BL, Lansdowne MSS 19.83, 46.38, 121.19
Wealth at death very wealthy: will, PRO, PROB 11/72, sig. 34

Master, Sir Streynsham (1640–1724), administrator in India, was born on 28 October 1640, probably at the family home of East Langdon, near Deal, Kent, the thirteenth child and eighth son of the twenty children of Richard Master (1604–1669), landed gentleman, and his wife, Anne (1606–1705), daughter of Sir James Oxenden. Master was relatively well educated. At the age of eight he attended Mr Latham's school at Sutton, and in 1654 he was taught by a Mr Cullen and a Mr Brett. He went to Canterbury in 1655 to study under a Mr Powndall, and in the same year proceeded to London, where he was taught by Mr Thomas Fox.

On 4 April 1656, at age fifteen, Master proceeded to India with his uncle and godfather George Oxenden, arriving at the East India Company's Surat factory (trading station) in November. In January 1659 Oxenden returned to England, leaving Streynsham under the charge of his brother Christopher Oxenden. That year Master was employed as cape-merchant on a voyage to the Persian Gulf and the Red Sea, returning to Surat in December. There, in January 1660, he was appointed a company factor, and was employed subsequently both at Surat and, from May to December 1662, at Ahmadabad.

In 1668 Master was appointed warehouse keeper and a member of the Surat council, and in September 1668 he was one of the company's commissioners who received the charge of the island of Bombay from the king's officers. At Surat, where the company's accounts were in a state of confusion, Master devised a new, efficient system of bookkeeping that was subsequently adopted at other factories and 'had a commanding influence on the public accounts of the English in India for a long time afterwards' (*Diaries*, 1.2).

Later in 1668 Master sailed south to resettle the company's factors at Karwar and Calicut, where he narrowly escaped with his life during a Moplah riot. In 1664, and again in October 1670, he was involved in the defence of Surat from the attacks of the Maratha leader Shivaji. On Master's return to England in June 1672 he was awarded a gold medal by the company in recognition of his gallant defence of the factory during the 1670 attack. Soon after his arrival in England he purchased the estate of Wallett's Court, near Dover, and on 17 May 1674 he married Diana, daughter of Sir Thomas Bendyshe, bt, of Bumsted, Essex. However, she died later that same year.

On 10 September 1675 Master was appointed to succeed Sir William Langhorne as agent and governor of Fort St George (Madras) when the latter's term of office expired in January 1677, until which time Master was to serve as second in council. Master sailed for India on 8 January 1676, and arrived at Fort St George on 7 July. His own proposals for the better administration and regulation of the company's factories were incorporated into his commission, and shortly after his arrival he set off again on a tour of inspection of the factories at Masulipatam and Bengal, not arriving back at Madras until 17 January 1677. When Langhorne returned to England at the end of that year Master formally succeeded him and made significant improvements in the administration at Madras. Perhaps his two most enduring accomplishments at Madras were the founding, in 1678, of the Anglican church of St Mary in the Fort, the first English church in India, and, secondly, the establishment in August 1683 of a court of judicature.

In common with many other company employees at this time, Master engaged in considerable private trading. In particular, he dealt in diamonds, and built up a considerable fortune thereby. In 1679 he again visited Masulipatam, and on 1 August of that year embarked for a tour to Bengal. The extravagant nature of these tours was one reason, or perhaps excuse, for the court's subsequent condemnation of him. Indeed, there is evidence of a largely unwarranted conspiratorial opposition to Master within East India House, an opposition which even gained the support of the king at one time. As a consequence, Master was formally dismissed his post on 3 July 1681 and the agency transferred to William Gyfford. Master was permitted to remain at Madras one year longer in order to settle his affairs before returning to England a wealthy man. However, he was never able to recover the substantial sums of money which were left owing to him at Madras. In September 1682 the company filed a suit in chancery against him, and it was not until October 1691 that the case was settled out of court to Master's advantage.

On 25 September 1690 he married, secondly, Elizabeth (d. 1714), daughter of Richard Legh of Lyme, Cheshire. They had three children: Anne (1691–1788) [*see* Coventry, Anne], Legh (1694–1750), and Streynsham (1697–1759). Although Master and his family resided mainly at their house in Red Lion Square, Holborn, London, in 1692 he also purchased the estate of Codnor Park, Derbyshire, and in 1698 he sold Wallett's Court and acquired Stanley Grange, near Morley, Derbyshire. Also in 1698 he was appointed one of the directors of the 'new' or 'English' East India Company, and on 14 December of that year—at which time Master happened to be chairman of the court of directors—he was knighted by King William at Kensington Palace. Master is also recorded as one of the trustees in the building of the church of St George the Martyr, Bloomsbury, London.

Sir Streynsham Master died on 28 April 1724 at New Hall in Lancashire, and was buried in a chapel of Macclesfield church. As Henry Yule concluded, he 'was a worthy, religious, methodical, and liberal man, and one of strong family affection' (*Diary of William Hedges*, 2.cclv). However, he was also clearly 'a strong man, who went his own way' (*Diaries*, 1.129) and made enemies thereby.

ANDREW GROUT

Sources *The diary of William Hedges … during his agency in Bengal; as well as on his voyage out and return overland (1681–1687)*, ed. R. Barlow and H. Yule, 2, Hakluyt Society, 75 (1888), ccxxii–cclv · *Diaries of Streynsham Master*, ed. R. C. Temple, 2 vols. (1911) · H. D. Love, *Vestiges of old Madras, 1640–1800*, 4 vols. (1913) · F. E. Penny, *Fort St George* (1900) · E. L. Saxe, 'Fortune's tangled web: trading networks of English entrepreneurs in Eastern India, 1657–1717', PhD diss., Yale U., 1979 · S. Mentz, 'English private trade on the Coromandel coast, 1660–1690: diamonds and country trade', *Indian Economic and Social History Review*, 33 (1996), 155–73 · *LondG* (8 Aug 1698) · *LondG* (15 Dec 1698)
Archives BL, MSS, Add. MSS · BL OIOC, papers, MS Eur. E 219 · NRA, priv. coll., MSS | Tamil Nadu State archives, Madras, India, 'A memoriall of Streynsham Master', MS bound with consultation books
Likenesses attrib. C. D'Agar, oils, 1714, NPG; repro. in Temple, ed., *Diaries of Streynsham Master*, vol. 1, frontispiece
Wealth at death substantial: will; *Diary*, ed. Barlow and Yule, vol. 2, p. cclii

Master, Streynsham (1681–1724), naval officer, was born on 7 March 1681, at Great Bartholomew Close, Smithfield, London, and baptized on the following day at St Bartholomew-the-Great, West Smithfield, the fourth but only surviving son of James Master (1626/7–1702), of East Langdon, Kent, and his wife, Joyce (1645/6–1719), daughter of Sir Christopher *Turnor, baron of the exchequer. Master was originally intended for the law, being admitted on 22 May 1699 to Gray's Inn (where his father had entered in 1648). However, the influence of his brother-in-law Sir

George *Byng (who had married his elder sister, Margaret) led him instead to embark upon a naval career.

With Byng as a patron, Master served on board the *Ranelagh* as a midshipman, becoming a lieutenant in 1704, and being 'much hurt in the leg' (Laughton, 143) during the capture of Gibraltar in July of that year. When Byng was in command in the Mediterranean, he appointed Master to command the *Fame* prize on 15 July 1709. On 22 March 1710 Sir John Norris made him captain of the *Ludlow Castle*, and on 7 December 1712 he was appointed to command the *Ormonde*. He commanded the *Ormonde* in July 1715 when it was one of the extra ships commissioned to deal with the Jacobite threat. In 1716–17 he was captain of the *Dragon* serving under Byng and Norris in the Baltic. On 14 March 1718 he was in command of the *Superb* again in the Mediterranean, and on 31 July 1718 was in action at the battle of Cape Passaro. In this action he took part in the capture of the Spanish flagship and her admiral, being much lauded as the first captain to achieve that honour.

Master returned to England, and saw no further service. On 10 February 1724 he married Elizabeth (1691–1759), only daughter of Richard Oxenden and Mary, daughter of Henry Oxenden. She was the heir of Brook, Kent. Master died on 22 June 1724 of a fever; he is not to be confused with his kinsman the Indian administrator Sir Streynsham Master, who also died in 1724 (28 April). His will, made the previous day, left Brook to his wife, but ordered other property to be sold in order to pay his seven surviving sisters £1000 apiece. Interestingly, he still possessed a chamber at Gray's Inn, which was also to be sold. He was buried in the parish church of Wingham, Kent.

J. K. LAUGHTON, rev. STUART HANDLEY

Sources DNB · J. Charnock, ed., *Biographia navalis*, 6 vols. (1794–8) · J. Philipott, 'The visitation of the county of Kent taken in the year 1619 [pts 2–3]', *Archaeologia Cantiana*, 5 (1863), 223–56, esp. 239–41; 6 (1866), 251–301, esp. 278 · D. Syrett and R. L. DiNardo, *The commissioned sea officers of the Royal Navy, 1660–1815*, rev. edn, Occasional Publications of the Navy RS, 1 (1994), 303 · J. Foster, *The register of admissions to Gray's Inn, 1521–1889, together with the register of marriages in Gray's Inn chapel, 1695–1754* (privately printed, London, 1889), 350 · will, PRO, PROB 11/599, fols. 193v–194r · *Memoirs relating to the Lord Torrington*, ed. J. K. Laughton, CS, new ser., 46 (1889), 52, 143 · IGI · E. A. Webb, *The records of St Bartholomew's Priory and of the church and parish of St Bartholomew the Great, West Smithfield*, 2 (1921), 470 · *The Byng papers: selected from the letters and papers of Admiral Sir George Byng, first Viscount Torrington, and of his son, Admiral the Hon. John Byng*, ed. B. Tunstall, 3, Navy RS, 70 (1932), 87
Archives BL OIOC, papers, MS Eur. E 219
Likenesses portrait, Panton House, Lincolnshire

Master, Thomas (1602/3–1643), poet and amanuensis, was born in Coates, Gloucestershire, where his father, William Master (d. in or after 1637), was rector. He studied under Henry Topp at Cirencester grammar school and in 1617 advanced to Winchester College on a scholarship. He was nineteen on 15 November 1622 when he matriculated from New College, Oxford; he was named perpetual fellow before graduating BA on 22 November 1625. He proceeded MA on 6 June 1629. According to Anthony Wood, he 'was esteemed a vast scholar, a general artist and linguist, a noted poet, and a most florid preacher' (Wood, *Ath. Oxon.*, 3.84).

Master contributed Latin and English poems to no fewer than ten Oxford University collections, including *Carolus redux* (1623), *Musarum Oxoniensium* (1633), and *Horti Carolini rosa altera* (1640). Some of this poetry is substantial, such as 'Oceani convivium' in *Britanniae natalis* (1630). Wood mentions three poems not included in any of these collections: 'On Bishop Lake' (1626), 'On Ben Jonson' (1637), and 'On Vaulx'. Master is the author of a Greek ode, dated 19 April 1633, on the crucifixion. It was first published as an appendix to Sir Henry Saville's *Oratio* (1658), along with a Latin translation by Henry Jacobs, and an English translation, entitled 'Christs passion', by Abraham Cowley.

In the 1630s Master served as an amanuensis to Edward Herbert, Lord Herbert of Cherbury, and according to John Aubrey he lived with Herbert until 1642. The Bodleian Library holds four manuscript volumes related to Herbert's *The Life and Raigne of King Henry the Eighth*. The first three volumes (Jesus College MSS 71–73) are original drafts, party in Master's handwriting, of the three-volume printed work. A fourth volume (Jesus College MS 74) comprises research notes in Master's hand and 'is dated internally to 1635–1638' (Hoyle, 54). Wood suggests that Master translated several of Herbert's books into Latin, but this has not been confirmed. At Herbert's request in 1636 Master composed a Latin poem, *Mensa lubrica*, on the game of shuffleboard. It was published in 1651 and republished, with an English version entitled 'The shovel-board table turn'd', as an appendix to Saville's *Oratio*.

In August 1637 Master travelled from Montgomeryshire to Lincolnshire to be inducted into the sinecure living of East Wickham, near Louth. He recounts his journey in a Latin letter to his father, dated 25 September 1637. He apparently became ill near Lincoln and had to stay briefly with his uncle at Stockwith before attending the ceremony and returning to Montgomeryshire. Written in prose and verse, the letter was later edited by his travelling companion George Ent and published as *Iter boreale* (1675).

Shortly after receiving his BD, on 25 March 1641 Master preached an English sermon on Luke 1: 26–7 at New College. It was later published as *The Virgin Mary* (1665) and achieved some measure of popularity, with reprints in sermon collections throughout the eighteenth century. On 19 March 1642 Viscount Newark wrote to the bishop of London to recommend Master for an ecclesiastical preferment. There is no evidence, however, that his petition was successful. About a week later, in the chapel of New College, Master delivered a Latin oration on the British monarchy, surveying the reigns of Elizabeth I and James I and concluding with praise of Charles I. The oration was later edited by the history professor John Lamphire of New College and published as *Monarchia Britannica* (1661).

According to Wood, Master died 'either in Dec. or Jan. in sixteen hundred forty three' (Wood, *Ath. Oxon.*, 3. 86), having succumbed to the so-called Oxford camp disease, but the date of Master's death is probably closer to 31 August 1643: his replacement at New College, Thomas Brickenden, was admitted as a scholar on 9 September. Master may have died in Oxford or at Louth, but is said to have been buried in 1643 in the north part of the outer chapel of New College. Edward Herbert's *Occasional Verses* (1648) concludes with a poem dedicated to Master and a Latin epitaph on 'Amate Master'.   EDWARD A. MALONE

Sources Wood, *Ath. Oxon.*, new edn · R. W. Hoyle, 'Thomas Master's narrative of the Pilgrimage of Grace', *Northern History*, 21 (1985), 53–79 · F. Madan, *Oxford books: a bibliography of printed works*, 3 vols. (1895–1931); repr. (1964) · *Reg. Oxf.*, 2/1–4 · Foster, *Alum. Oxon.* · PRO, SP 46/128, fol. 1; SP 46/127, fol. 312 · New College, Oxford, MS 9751, p. 388 · *DNB* · *Brief lives, chiefly of contemporaries, set down by John Aubrey, between the years 1669 and 1696*, ed. A. Clark, 2 vols. (1898) · E. Herbert, *Lord Herbert of Cherbury's 'De religione laici'*, ed. H. Hutcheson (1944) · private information (2004) [C. Brown, Bodl. Oxf.; P. R. Evans, Glos. RO; C. Dalton, New College, Oxf.]
Archives Jesus College, Oxford, collections to illustrate life of Henry VIII for Lord Herbert of Cherbury

Master, Sir William (1600/01–1662). *See under* Master, William (*bap.* 1627, *d.* 1684).

Master, William (*bap.* 1627, *d.* 1684), Church of England clergyman, was baptized on 7 September 1627 at Cirencester, the second son, in a family of six sons and six daughters, of **Sir William Master** (1600/01–1662), local politician, and his wife, Alice Estcourt (*d.* 1660). Sir William was the son of George Master (*b.* 1556?) and Bridget Cornwall, and the grandson of Elizabeth I's physician, Richard *Master—the family was one of the most important in the Cirencester area. He was admitted to the Inner Temple in November 1612 and knighted on 3 December 1622. He was MP for Cirencester in 1624 and high sheriff of Gloucestershire in 1627, when he was also among twelve county commissioners who refused either to pay the forced loan or to enforce it on others. He was present when Lord Chandos tried unsuccessfully to execute the commission of array at Cirencester on 15 August 1642 and afterwards smuggled Chandos away through his house to escape the wrath of the mob. Prince Rupert and Prince Maurice quartered at his house and batteries were sited in his garden prior to the sack of Cirencester on 2 February 1643. During the civil war he was a moderately active royalist, though not in arms. He was nominated to the royalist commission of the peace in March 1643 and to several other administrative commissions. Sir William surrendered to the county committee in August 1644 but then entertained the king at his house on the night of 31 October 1644. The estates, already severely reduced in value, were consequently sequestered. He took the covenant and the negative oath on 18 February 1647 and petitioned to compound for his estates, claiming that he had only acted as he had to prevent worse damage. In 1650 he compounded for £1200, plus a further £282 for undervaluations in 1652. He died on 3 March 1662 at the age of sixty-one, a year and a half after the death of his wife, Alice Estcourt, on 5 September 1660, and was buried at Cirencester.

The younger William Master matriculated at Christ Church, Oxford, on 2 April 1647 and was admitted as a fellow of Merton College while still an undergraduate by order of the parliamentary visitors on 25 March 1650. He graduated BA on 7 November 1650 and MA on 19 November 1652. He also took a BD, according to Anthony Wood. In 1653 he published *Essayes and Observations Theologicall and Morall*, a series of twenty-five short, well-written essays on the humours of the age, under the pseudonym 'A student in theologie'. These actually skirted around theological matters and did not openly express Master's firmly Anglican views. Instead, he contrasted the wise government under bishop or presbyter in the primitive church with the false certainties of contemporary saints who 'take upon themselves to be Daniels, persons greatly beloved of God and yet have no better authoritie for their assurance, than that of a presumptuous fancy'. Master also took a wry dig at Cromwell, noting that 'Alexander's way with Gordian knots is too well knowne in this age, and too much practised' (Master, 52–3, 86). In 1654 he published, again anonymously, *Drops of Myrrhe*, seven prayers and meditations on such matters as 'a distracted Church and state' and the spirit of moderation and discernment. Wing's *Short-Title Catalogue* also attributes to Master an anonymous tract of 1653 entitled *Master John Goodwins Quere Questioned*, which rebutted Goodwin's denial of the magistrate's right to enforce observation of the sabbath and generally upheld his powers in religious matters. The beliefs this expresses are similar to Master's, but the writing style is different.

At some stage before 20 May 1658 Master was presented to the vicarage of Preston, near Cirencester, the advowson of which was in the family. On that date he officiated at the wedding of George Bull, the future bishop of St David's and a close friend of the family, using the proscribed Anglican form. Master became rector of Woodford, Essex, on 13 February 1661 and prebendary of Chamberlainwood at St Paul's on 17 July 1663. On 18 May 1665, at Woodford, he married Susanna Yate, daughter of the Revd Job Yate, rector of Rodmarton, Gloucestershire. They had two sons and a daughter: Richard, Thomas, and Elizabeth. He resigned the prebend of Chamberlainwood in 1666 and was collated to the rectory of Southchurch, Essex, on 3 July 1666 by Archbishop Sheldon. He resigned this living after he was appointed by royal prerogative to the prebend of Caddington Major in St Paul's on 14 February 1667. On 29 April 1671 Sheldon conferred on him the rectory of St Vedast-alias-Foster, London, with the united parish of St Michael-le-Querne, which he retained until his death. His wife was living when he made his will on 27 April 1684; he was buried at Woodford on 6 September 1684.

John Master (*bap.* 1637, *d.* in or after 1684), physician, was William Master's younger brother and their parents' fifth son. He was baptized at Cirencester on 25 September 1637, although he was said to be forty-eight years old in 1682. He matriculated at Christ Church, Oxford, on 20 July 1654, graduated BA on 3 February 1657, proceeded MA from St Mary Hall on 25 June 1659, and was created MD from Christ Church on 4 July 1672. He was unmarried. He assisted the noted medical author Thomas Willis in some of his publications and was admitted an honorary fellow of the Royal College of Physicians on 30 September 1680. He is last recorded on 27 April 1684, when William Master named him an executor of his will.

ANDREW WARMINGTON

Sources Wood, *Ath. Oxon.: Fasti*, 2nd edn, vol. 2 · S. Rudder, *A new history of Gloucestershire* (1779) · R. Newcourt, *Repertorium ecclesiasticum parochiale Londinense*, 2 vols. (1708–10) · [W. Master], *Essayes and observations theological and morall* (1653) · *CSP dom.*, 1627–9; addenda, 1625–49; 1645–7 · M. A. E. Green, ed., *Calendar of the proceedings of the committee for compounding … 1643–1660*, 5 vols., PRO (1889–92) · *DNB* · R. Atkyns, *The ancient and present state of Glostershire*, 2 pts in 1 (1712) · D. Lysons, *The environs of London*, 2nd edn, 2 vols. in 4 (1811) · *A letter sent to a worthy member …* (1642) [BL, E 113 (6)] · 'A particular relation of the action before Cyrencester', *Bibliotheca Gloucestrensis*, ed. J. Washbourne (1823) · Bodl. Oxf., MS Drydale 19 · R. Nelson, *The life of Dr George Bull*, 2nd edn (1714) · will, 1684, PRO, PROB 11/377, sig. 116 · M. T. Chester, *The visitation of the county of Gloucester: begun … in 1682, and finished … in … 1683* (1884) · W. H. Cooke, ed., *Students admitted to the Inner Temple, 1547–1660* [1878] · Wing, *STC*

Wealth at death considerable; bequeathed £2150 in cash and goods; £98 p.a. endowments; plus main estate to first son; lands in Essex, Gloucestershire, and Wiltshire: will, 1684, PRO, PROB 11/377, sig. 116

Masterman, Charles Frederick Gurney (1874–1927), politician and author, the son of Thomas William Masterman (d. c.1893), of Rotherfield Hall, Sussex, and his wife, Margaret Hanson, daughter of Thomas Gurney, of New Park Lodge, Brixton Hill, was born at Spencer Hill, Wimbledon, Surrey, on 25 October 1874. He was the fourth of six brothers, and also had one sister. The family was evangelical in tone. His father had been a farmer but a nervous breakdown rendered him a permanent invalid. His mother came from the Quaker banking family.

Education and early career Charlie Masterman—as he was known throughout his life—was educated at St Aubyn House in Brighton, Weymouth College, and at Christ's College, Cambridge, matriculating in 1892. His father died intestate and Masterman quickly lost his £2000 inheritance by investing in fraudulently run companies. His career at Cambridge was academically brilliant, with first classes both in the natural science tripos (1895) and in the moral science tripos, part two (1896). While at Cambridge he 'began the habit of reckless work at late hours and started the insomnia that stayed with him all his life' (Masterman, 21). He was one of the best speakers at the Cambridge Union, and became president of the society in 1896. In 1897 he and his brothers ran a boarding-school at Horsemonden which soon went bankrupt. In 1897 he was awarded the Arnold Gerstenberg scholarship and returned to Cambridge. He was interested in psychical research and worked on it with Frederic Myers. In 1900 he was elected a fellow of his college. At Cambridge, Masterman associated chiefly with members of the liberal and progressive school of thought which found expression in *The Heart of the Empire* (1901), a collection of essays by Masterman, G. M. Trevelyan, Noel Buxton, G. P. Gooch, and others. The volume deplored imperialism, which the authors saw as a force for national decadence, not greatness.

Masterman's liberalism was strongly tinged with Christian socialism, then under the leadership of men such as Bishop Westcott, Canon Scott Holland, and Charles Gore. He was a member of the Christian Social Union. On moving to London he lived in 1900–01 in a tenement in south London, having already spent some time in the university settlement at Camberwell. The contrast between the squalor of the slums and the luxury of Mayfair stirred his emotional nature, and an indignant pessimism inspired his next two books, *From the Abyss* (1902) and *In Peril of Change* (1905). These writings and his success as a platform speaker made Masterman a welcome recruit to the political Liberalism which regained ground after the Second South African War. He soon gained a footing in Fleet Street, and contributed to the *Independent Review*, *The Pilot*, *The Commonwealth*, the *Daily News*, of which he became literary editor, *The Speaker*, then under the editorship of J. L. Hammond, and afterwards to *The Nation* under the editorship of H. W. Massingham. At the lunches held for the staff of *The Nation* his witty and often cynical sayings found an appreciative audience.

Politics and marriage In 1903 Masterman stood for parliament, contesting Dulwich unsuccessfully. With the assistance, however, of John Burns, then a power in London, he was returned for West Ham (North) in 1906. He was on the back benches during Campbell-Bannerman's 1905–8 government, and played an important role in maintaining contacts with the Webbs and urging the cause of social reform on a government which many back-benchers found too 'old-Liberal' (see his 'Politics in transition', *Nineteenth Century*, 73, January 1908, cited in Gilbert, 249). He established something of a rapport with Winston Churchill. When Asquith became prime minister in 1908 he appointed Masterman under-secretary of the Local Government Board under Burns (Churchill having declined the post). Fearing that office would hamper his ability to call for reform, Masterman reluctantly accepted, with the condition that the board was reorganized. He assisted Burns in passing the Housing and Town Planning Act of 1909, but he found working with the increasingly cautious Burns a trial, and tried to get Asquith to replace Burns. Lucy Lyttelton's diary for 10 February 1910 records: 'C[harles] went to see Asquith on his own job. He said Asquith talks to him as if he and C. were a pair of nurses running the child J. B[urns]' (Masterman, 125).

On 2 June 1908, having become engaged in Westminster Abbey during a break in the Commons' debates, Masterman married Lucy Blanche Lyttelton [**Lucy Blanche Masterman** (1884–1977)], the eldest of the three daughters of Sir Neville Gerald *Lyttelton (1845–1931) and his wife, Katherine Sarah. They had one son, Neville, and two daughters. Marriage connected Masterman with one of the great Liberal dynasties (W. E. Gladstone was Lucy's great-uncle by marriage). Lucy Masterman had a sharp, bright mind, and soon became one of the noted hostesses of the day. Her unconventional beauty is still evident from her photograph (Masterman, 96). She was an energetic diarist and had a toughness that her husband, fatally for a politician, lacked. Cabinet ministers treated her as something of a political equal, but perhaps even more as an effective conduit. Lloyd George, for example, who knew of her diary, gave her details in 1910 of his plans for a coalition government. The Mastermans shared an intense religious commitment laced with a strong sense of social justice, and their terminology, common enough a generation earlier, began to seem out of place in the new Liberal era. They worked closely together, with Lucy at times almost a surrogate minister.

A month after his marriage Masterman was appointed under-secretary to the Home Office where, in 1910, Churchill, to his relief, became his superior; when appointing him, Asquith asked him to continue his assistance to Lloyd George on financial details. The Mastermans had been suffragists, and remained so in principle, taking care, for example, that their daughters were as well educated as their son (Masterman, 383); but Charles's experiences at the Home Office made his sympathy go 'rather on the wane' (Masterman, 166). In the general elections of January and December 1910 Masterman retained his seat, but the latter victory occasioned a petition of objection. He and Lucy accompanied Lloyd George on his famous visit to Nice in January 1911, during which the details of the National Insurance Bill were thrashed out. On their return Masterman lost his seat in June 1911 when the petition against his return for North West Ham in December 1910 was granted; his agent had muddled the finances. Another London constituency (the very marginal South-West Bethnal Green) was found for him, and he was back in the house in July 1911.

During 1911 Masterman was in charge of the land clauses of the Finance Bill and of the Development Bill, the Shop Hours Bill, the Coal Mines Bill, and other measures, as well as helping with the preparations for the National Insurance Bill and the Finance Bill, for both of which his wife believed him to have been 'very nearly all-powerful' with respect to many of the details, a view not fully supported by subsequent commentators (Masterman, 202). He was thus active at the heart of the government's domestic programme. An investigation in conditions at Heswall reformatory school found that Bottomley's *John Bull* had been exaggerated in its accusations; this earned Masterman the dangerous hostility of Bottomley. Masterman's work on the details of the insurance bill led to his appointment as first chairman of the National Insurance Commission, with the task of giving the bill practical effect; he brought in Sir Robert *Morant to assist with the health aspects of the bill. He soon found himself in conflict with Morant on a variety of issues, some substantial, some personal (for Morant would brook little opposition, even though Masterman was the chairman). In February 1912 Masterman was appointed financial secretary to the Treasury as well as chairman of the Insurance Commission, a stepping stone to the cabinet. He continued to work effectively with Lloyd George in what has been called 'a teasing friendship of equals' (David, 'New Liberalism', 28). He supported Lloyd George's

land campaign and sustained him during the Marconi affair.

In February 1914 Masterman was appointed chancellor of the duchy of Lancaster with a seat in the cabinet. He lost the by-election consequent on this appointment by twenty-four votes. 'So our cycle of ill-luck began' remarked his wife (Masterman, 263). Masterman stood unsuccessfully for Ipswich at a by-election in May 1914, and was thus in the cabinet but not in parliament. The chief whip gave him a year to find a seat, but the electoral pact between the government and the opposition meant that vacancies were hard to arrange, and no suitable constituency was found, and the whips do not seem to have been energetic on Masterman's behalf. In August 1914 there was a vacancy in Swansea—normally an unopposed Liberal seat—by the death of the sitting MP. The Welsh Nationalists threatened to oppose Masterman (as a carpetbagger); he failed to get Lloyd George to encourage the nationalist not to stand and on Asquith's advice did not contest the seat. He resigned from the cabinet in February 1915.

Wellington House and wartime propaganda Masterman was a strong supporter of British intervention in August 1914 and was placed in charge of Wellington House, as the propaganda department was called. Wellington House was the converted premises of the Insurance Commission, and Masterman brought many of the commission's staff with him. At meetings on 2 and 7 September he brought together a strong team of writers, including A. J. Toynbee, L. B. Namier, and John Headlam (Morley), to which John Buchan was soon added as an external contributor. The initial focus was on seeing that public opinion in the USA was favourable to the allies. By June 1915 more than 2 million books and other publications in seventeen languages had been published, almost entirely without the readers' knowledge that these were sponsored by the British government. The first propaganda film, *Britain Prepared*, was issued in December 1915 and released all over the world, and a wide variety of other forms of propaganda was employed. Masterman set a high standard for British propaganda. The insistence that any materials released were to be accurate and rather factual—with the reader as far as possible reaching his or her own conclusions—led to accusations that the allied case should be as vociferously and as duplicitously made as the German. In February 1917, following a report prepared by Robert Donald, editor of the Liberal *Daily Chronicle* and a man critical of Masterman, Lloyd George (now prime minister) appointed John *Buchan director of information, with a department of four sections, including Masterman's at Wellington House. This was a demotion for Masterman: his salary was reduced and Wellington House now dealt only with printed materials, photographs, and the works of war artists, which Masterman had been instrumental in commissioning (he was insistent that artists be given a free and roving commission; thus their direct propaganda value was not great or primary, but the long-term interest of their output was very considerable).

Buchan soon found himself being accused of the same

failings as Masterman, and both their positions were rather curtly terminated at the end of the war, neither receiving any public honour at a time when such things were generously distributed by Lloyd George. Buchan later commented on Masterman's propaganda work: 'The idea, held by many, that his chief talent lay in a kind of emotional appeal was the reverse of the truth. I always felt that his real *métier* was practical administration' (Masterman, 375).

Post-war politics Masterman continued his attempts to re-enter parliament, and was heavily defeated at West Ham (Stratford) in December 1918, standing as a Liberal against a coupon Conservative (despite his Lloyd Georgian connections, he did not become a Lloyd George Liberal and was a prominent critic of Lloyd George's post-war government). He was eventually successful in the Rusholme division of Manchester in the general election of 1923, standing as a Liberal. However, he was heavily defeated there in 1924—he 'broke down' the day before the poll— and did not stand again. Initially he was a leading opponent of Liberal reunion, attacking Lloyd George's 'adulterous alliance with the hereditary enemies of liberalism' (speech in Glasgow, cited in David, 'New Liberalism', 34). But he became disillusioned with Asquith's leadership, considered joining the Labour Party, but instead became Lloyd George's 'chief lieutenant' (Bentley, 95). He hoped at times for a 'coalition of convenience' between advanced Liberals and the Labour Party (Freeden, *Liberalism Divided*, 211). He chaired the industrial policy committee of the National Liberal Federation in 1920–21, his recommendations anticipating the spirit of the *Yellow Book*. He assisted with the Liberal summer schools, and helped to prepare *Britain's Industrial Future*, published after his death.

Publications Masterman always made time to write. Two of his books remain central texts. His *The Condition of England* (1909) was one of the best contributions to the new liberalism, and its large sales helped establish the respectability of its reforming message. The post-war years, his wife recalled, 'were the hardest we had' (Masterman, 318). The Mastermans had to retrench substantially, and his writings articulated the concerns of the middle classes whose savings had been taken to pay for the war and who felt themselves very hard done by. *England after War; a Study* (1922) 'is perhaps the most revealing description of the English middle classes as they saw themselves at this fraught moment' (McKibbin, 50), and the shift in his position as reflected in the two books encapsulates the shift in liberalism. *England after War* was written at Bembridge on the Isle of Wight, where Ruskin had lived—Masterman was always a keen exponent of some of Ruskin's views. The book sold poorly, with half the print run of 5000 unsold. He also published *From the Abyss; or its Inhabitants, by one of them* (1902), *In Peril of Change* (1905), *To Colonise England* (1907), and studies of Tennyson as a religious teacher (1900) and of F. D. Maurice (1907). He published *The New Liberalism* and *How England is Governed* in 1920. In 1927 he produced a one-volume digest of Morley's life of Gladstone.

He wrote capaciously as a journalist, notably a weekly letter for the high-church newspaper *The Guardian*, and a column, 'At St. Stephen's', for *The Nation*. Beaverbrook gave him a regular slot in the *Sunday Express*.

Final years In his later years Masterman's health declined. He always suffered acutely in the summer from hay fever, but other, undisclosed, troubles afflicted him, including excessive drinking. He died in a nursing home, Bowden House, Harrow, on 17 November 1927. In Masterman, and in his wife's biography, which she published in 1939, there is a clear sense of promise unfulfilled. Indeed, Lucy ended her well researched biography, much of it based on her own diaries, with a comment on 'the vivid, tormented man I loved' (Masterman, 368). In this Masterman epitomized many Liberals of his time. He was unlucky in the absence of a safe seat, and the war sidetracked him, but, even so, there was some further uncertainty. Despite holding important offices he did not fully inspire confidence. He had, Frank Swinnerton recalled, 'a lazy, slightly oily voice' (Masterman, 378) and was careless about his dress. He spoke well in the Commons and as a lecturer, but was less effective on the hustings. A. G. Gardiner believed that:

> If he had been made of harder metal he would have ridden the wave … But he was a man of moods, and he carried too much sail of emotion for his mental and physical capacity … feeling always had the whip-hand of calculation.
> (Masterman, 374)

Lucy Masterman lived until 1977, an active Liberal to the end, and, as one of the relics of the epoch of Asquithian government, became in her later years something of an icon.

H. C. G. MATTHEW

Sources M. Freeden, *The new liberalism* (1978) · M. Freeden, *Liberalism divided* (1986) · *DNB* · *The Times* (18 Nov 1927) · L. Masterman, *C. F. G. Masterman* (1939) · E. David, 'The new liberalism of C. F. G. Masterman', *Essays in anti-labour history*, ed. K. D. Brown (1974), 17–41 · F. M. Mason, 'Charles Masterman and national health insurance', *Albion*, 10 (1978), 54–75 · M. L. Sanders, 'Wellington House and British propaganda during the First World War', *HJ*, 18 (1975), 119–46 · M. L. Sanders and P. M. Taylor, *British propaganda during the First World War, 1914–1918* (1982) · M. Bentley, *The liberal mind, 1914–1929* (1977) · B. B. Gilbert, *The evolution of national insurance in Great Britain: the origins of the welfare state* (1966) · P. Jalland, *Women, marriage and politics, 1860–1914* (1986) · R. McKibbin, *Classes and cultures: England 1918–1951* (1998) · E. David, 'Charles Masterman and the Swansea district by-election', *Welsh History Review / Cylchgrawn Hanes Cymru*, 5 (1970–71), 31–44 · *CGPLA Eng. & Wales* (1928) · private information (2004)

Archives U. Birm. L., corresp. and papers | BL, corresp. with G. K. Chesterton and F. A. Chesterton, Add. MSS 73238, fols. 173–8; 73454, fols 25, 34, 38, 53, 59v · BL, corresp. with Lord Gladstone, Add. MSS 46061–46068 · BL OIOC, letters to Lord Reading, MSS Eur. E 238, F 118 · Bodl. Oxf., letters to Margot Asquith · Bodl. Oxf., letters to Gilbert Murray · Bodl. Oxf., letters to Arthur Ponsonby · HLRO, corresp. with David Lloyd George · HLRO, corresp. with Herbert Samuel · HLRO, corresp. with John St Loe Strachey · U. Newcastle, Robinson L., corresp. with Walter Runciman | FILM BFI NFTVA, news footage

Likenesses Stearn & Sons, group portrait, photograph, 1899, NPG · M. Beerbohm, caricature, drawing, 1911, AM Oxf. · E. Kapp, drawing, 1914, Barber Institute of Fine Arts, Birmingham

Wealth at death £452 9s. 4d.: probate, 15 March 1928, *CGPLA Eng. & Wales*

Masterman, Sir John Cecil (1891–1977), college head and intelligence officer, was born on 12 January 1891 at Crescent Lodge, Kingston upon Thames, the younger of the two children, both sons, of Commander (later Captain) John Masterman RN (1847–1916) and his wife, Edith Margaret Hughes (1859/60–1946). Originally destined to follow in his father's footsteps, after attending Evelyns, a preparatory school, Masterman spent five years as a naval cadet at the Royal Naval College at Osborne and Dartmouth. But he became increasingly aware of his unsuitability for a career in the mechanized navy and in a noteworthy feat of self-awareness and determination dropped out in 1908, much to the dismay of his parents. In 1909 he was elected to a scholarship in modern history at Worcester College, Oxford. Academic life immediately fulfilled his expectations and thereafter commanded his lifelong devotion.

Masterman often confessed to following habitually the conventional course. Nevertheless, between gaining his first-class degree in 1913 and election as a student of Christ Church in 1919, fate intervened with decidedly unconventional results. The outbreak of war caught him towards the end of a post-graduate year in Germany, leading to his internment for the duration at Ruhleben camp outside Berlin. Masterman always regretted this misfortune as a shameful episode, a reaction perhaps accentuated by a belated attempt at escape followed by a humbling agreement not to break out again in exchange for a safe return to Ruhleben.

As history tutor and censor (1921–6) at Christ Church, Masterman developed an ever-widening range of acquaintances. His attractive personality and dedication to teaching left a lasting impression on undergraduates, many of whom attained distinction in later life. He blamed the war and administrative duties for his failure to develop into a publishing scholar, protesting rather unconvincingly that at thirty-five he was already too old for research. Still, his reputation was such that by 1933 he could well have been appointed headmaster of Eton College had he not preferred to remain at 'the House' instead. His standing as 'that quintessential Establishment figure' (Annan, 5) was assured decades before the term caught on in the sixties. With little interest in money or politics, he was admired and consulted as an expert judge of character. The modest young don himself excelled at games, then widely believed to be a form of character-building, and was well known far beyond Oxford as an outstanding all-rounder. Cricket was his first love but he played hockey well enough to represent England, and lawn tennis well enough to compete at Wimbledon in the 1920s.

His self-confessed 'political blindness' led to Masterman's being surprised a second time by the outbreak of war against Germany. He was called up in June 1940 and soon found himself employed as secretary of a War Office committee. Concerned about his lack of military background, he replied when asked by a general 'Can you write the King's English?' that this was almost his only qualification (Masterman, 201, 206). Fortunately he was seconded from the intelligence corps to MI5 and appointed by the director-general to chair the new Twenty (XX) Committee

Sir John Cecil Masterman (1891–1977), by Walter Stoneman, 1950

set up in January 1941 to funnel the flow of information through double agents to the enemy. Thus he found himself in a position for which the qualifications were indeterminate but where success would more than make up for Ruhleben.

Masterman wrote his celebrated *The Double-Cross System* (1972) as a highly classified MI5 report in 1945, beginning with a description of the origins of the system early in the war, when the overriding concern was security against German espionage, and building up to the implementation of cover and deception for the cross-channel invasion in 1944. Thanks to the Official Secrets Act, however, the book's only character sketches were of the double agents themselves. Identification of the roles played by Masterman and his anonymous colleagues had to wait until the publication of the official history of strategic deception in 1990 and the subsequent release of MI5 files at the Public Record Office.

The XX Committee had no directive but operated pragmatically, acting as a forum for information about the agents and their traffic, making suggestions as to how to answer the questionnaires they received from their *Abwehr* controllers, devising schemes to elicit intelligence, including signals intelligence, and so forth. It belonged to section B1a, which was effectively run by its chief, Major T. A. Robertson, with the help of Masterman and John Marriott, secretary of the XX Committee. Masterman, accordingly, had a significant say in policy decisions. Robertson, an MI5 professional, formed an excellent working relationship with the recruit from Oxford, whose wealth of contacts he particularly appreciated. Wartime Whitehall was heavily populated by former students and acquaintances whom Masterman had only to ring up for guidance or a ruling on some item of business. The chairman's self-deprecatory aside about merely providing the weekly tea and a bun cannot disguise the fact that the XX Committee could easily have become fractious and unco-operative under different management. Masterman kept the membership as small as possible at just over a dozen and conducted business 'with supreme tact, equanimity and common sense', according to Lieutenant Commander Ewen Montagu (Montagu, 48), an original member not known for bestowing accolades lightly. The chairman also shrewdly ensured that no MI5 proposal was ever voted down.

Among the relevant documents first released at the Public Record Office in the 1990s were batches of decrypts of *Abwehr* wireless communications. Masterman permitted himself only the most oblique and guarded references to Most Secret Source (MSS or Ultra), so that revelation of the enormous advantages it provided was delayed until well after the Ultra secret became public in 1974. MSS, for example, was decisive in penetrating the inner workings of the *Abwehr* and in confirming by mid-1942 that there was no undetected network of German agents at large in the country; only then did Robertson propose making the double agents available as a channel for strategic deception. Yet it would be a mistake to accept that MSS, combined with the *Abwehr*'s frequent inefficiency and corruption, drained risk from the XX game. Quite rightly, Masterman assumed he was playing with dynamite, and half-expected the system to explode before D-day. Uncontrolled agents, for instance, posed a threat either if they guessed right and were believed by the German high command or if they devalued all agents' reports by making outrageous guesses; then again, a well-meaning German defector might blow double agents by 'betraying' them to the allies. Simply keeping the network together took unremitting attention to detail, not to mention nerve and perhaps some old-fashioned gamesmanship. Everything more than paid off, though, when a mere handful of agents played an unexpectedly decisive role in putting across the brilliant cover plan (*Fortitude South*) of Supreme Headquarters Allied Expeditionary Force, which tied down German reserves in the Pas-de-Calais not only before but well after D-day.

Appointed OBE in 1944, Masterman returned to Oxford the following year, taking an illicit copy of his XX report with him. He was elected provost of his beloved Worcester College in 1946 and knighted in 1959, having served as vice-chancellor in 1957–8. In 1952 he published a popular, slightly arch guide to Oxford, *To Teach the Senators Wisdom*, which reflected his dedication to the system of residential colleges and tutorial instruction. He belonged to the club of Oxford's élite. 'Humane, humorous and loyal he was wonderful company and a very good friend' (*DNB*). He also made enemies—not surprisingly, given the strength of his convictions and well-founded suspicions of influence

exerted behind the scenes. A. J. P. Taylor, for one, always blamed him for sabotaging his appointment as regius professor in 1957. This was all the more galling, according to Taylor, because Masterman had made a career of nominating 'bishops and headmasters' and little else (A. J. P. Taylor, *A Personal Life*, 1983, 189). Soon after the provost's retirement in 1961 the public schools and ancient universities came under fire as privileged and out-dated. Masterman particularly disliked demonstrations. Ironically enough, however, he was planning an act of defiance of his own: to publish his XX report even if it meant going to an American publisher to evade the Official Secrets Act.

Once again Sir John displayed a ferocious fixity of purpose. His stated motive was to rehabilitate the reputation of MI5—and with it, it must be strongly suspected, the establishment as a whole. If so, he failed: where he succeeded was in setting the record straight before garbled versions of his story inevitably leaked out. To charge that he was vainglorious or bent on slighting the successful deception practised by A force in the Middle East is to overlook the constraints under which the 1945 report was written. Masterman enjoyed an unexpected success, especially in the United States, possibly because his themes of penetration and deception reflected the ethos of the cold war. Sparely but stylishly written, *The Double-Cross System* gave a boost to the nascent discipline of intelligence studies, though claims for an avalanche effect on the publication of official histories and release of documents at the Public Record Office have been overstated. Masterman never married. He died of old age at eighty-six in the Acland Hospital, Oxford, on 6 June 1977; he was cremated and his ashes were scattered in the lake at Worcester College.   JOHN P. CAMPBELL

Sources J. C. Masterman, *On the chariot wheel: an autobiography* (1975) · PRO, ADM/223/792–4, NID 17m (Montagu) files on deception · minutes of the Twenty Committee, PRO, KV 4/63–9 · M. Howard, *British intelligence in the Second World War*, 5: *Strategic deception* (1990) · F. H. Hinsley and C. A. G. Simkins, *British intelligence in the Second World War*, 4: *Security and counter-intelligence* (1990) · J. Curry, *The security service, 1908–1945: the official history* (1999) · R. Winks, *Cloak and gown: scholars in the secret war, 1939–1961* (1987) · E. Montagu, *Beyond top secret U* (1977) · N. Annan, *Our age: portrait of a generation* (1990) · *DNB* · *The Times* (7 June 1977) · *CGPLA Eng. & Wales* (1977) · private information (2004)

Archives Bodl. Oxf., corresp. and literary papers · PRO, records, e.g. KV 4, CAB 154, PREM 3 | Bodl. Oxf., corresp. with Lord Monckton · IWM, Mure MSS · Nuffield Oxf., corresp. with Lord Cherwell · U. Reading L., letters to Bodley Head Ltd

Likenesses W. Stoneman, photograph, 1950, NPG [*see illus.*] · A. Gwynne-Jones, oils (aged eighty), Christ Church Oxf. · E. Halliday, oils (aged sixty-one), Worcester College, Oxford

Wealth at death £17,214: probate, 31 Aug 1977, *CGPLA Eng. & Wales*

Masterman, Lucy Blanche (1884–1977). *See under* Masterman, Charles Frederick Gurney (1874–1927).

Masters, John (1914–1983), army officer and novelist, was born on 26 October 1914 at Fort William, Calcutta, India, the elder son (there were no daughters) of Captain John Masters (1883–1963) of the 16th Rajput regiment and his wife, Ada Coulthard (1882–1971) of Scarborough, Yorkshire. The Masters family connection with India went

John Masters (1914–1983), by unknown photographer, 1946

back five generations to 1804 when William Masters (1774–1819) of the King's Royal Irish light dragoons arrived in Calcutta. His sons and their descendants all served in the Indian army and young Masters followed in the family's footsteps.

In 1928 Masters was sent to Wellington College, where he won a prize cadetship to the Royal Military College, Sandhurst. Commissioned into the Indian army in 1934, he spent his first year back in India with the 1st Duke of Cornwall's light infantry before transferring to the 4th Prince of Wales's Own Gurkha rifles. With them he served on the north-west frontier and in Baluchistan. In 1941 his regiment was part of the expeditionary force which was sent to Iraq to oust the pro-Hitler government of General Rashid Ali. At its conclusion he was sent to the Indian Army Staff College in Quetta. After passing out first in his course Masters was appointed brigade major in the 114th Indian infantry brigade, then training in north India as part of 7th Indian division.

This was a key posting as the brigade's senior operations officer, but Masters had placed his career in jeopardy by embarking on an affair with Barbara Rose, née Allcard (b. 1910), the wife of Captain Hugh Rose, 3rd Gurkha rifles. Masters was determined to marry her even though there would be difficulties over the divorce and the custody of her two children, Elizabeth and Michael (later Lieutenant-General Sir Michael Rose). Normally, being involved in a divorce case meant that an officer had to resign his commission but the war had altered many peacetime shibboleths; however, under the divorce settlement Rose won custody of the children. Masters and Barbara Rose married on 18 March 1945; they were to have two children, a son and a daughter.

In April 1943 Masters had transferred to the 111th Indian infantry brigade which was part of a special long range penetration force (known as the Chindits), founded by Major-General Orde Wingate. Their task was to fight behind Japanese lines in Burma using fortified bases supplied by air. They were given special training and equipment but when the force went into action in March 1944

its impact was reduced by Wingate's death in an air crash. As a result, its commanding officer, Brigadier W. D. A. (Joe) Lentaigne, replaced Wingate and Masters himself took over command of 111th brigade. During the fighting retreat out of Burma, Masters distinguished himself as a competent and determined commander and he was made DSO. Following his promotion to lieutenant-colonel, he was appointed chief of staff to the 19th Indian infantry division during the liberation of Burma. At the end of the war he was given a senior staff appointment at the Military Operations Directorate in Delhi and made an OBE. As India was due to become independent in 1947, Masters had to reconsider his future. Although he would have preferred to remain in India, he was posted to the Staff College, Camberley, as the Indian army instructor in mountain warfare.

However, life in peacetime Britain was not to Masters's liking; he resigned his commission in 1948 and decided to emigrate to the United States. His birth in India almost prevented his entry to the country, but he was allowed to stay on a visitor's visa. His idea was to create and sell Himalayan adventure holidays; although the project failed, it led to a writing career. An article on Hollywood and India was published in *Atlantic Monthly* and as a result he determined to write books based on British rule in India. A preliminary list suggested that he could produce thirty-five adventure novels beginning with the arrival of the East India Company in 1600 and ending with independence in 1947.

Although Masters proved to be a prolific writer, acceptance was slow in coming and his first novel, *The Nightrunners of Bengal*, was not published until 1951. Set in the Indian mutiny of 1857, it was an immediate success, selling 300,000 copies in six months, and it made Masters's name. His second novel, *The Deceivers* (1952), was also well received: the reviewer in the *New York Herald Tribune* hailed him as the best writer on India since Rudyard Kipling. In fact Masters had few literary pretensions as a writer, preferring to produce simply told adventure stories which are strong on characterization and background description. Among his many novels set in India are: *The Lotus and the Wind* (1953), *Coromandel* (1955), *Far, Far the Mountain Peak* (1957), and *Venus of Konpara* (1960).

In 1954 Masters became a United States citizen. In the same year he produced *Bhowani Junction*, a thinly disguised autobiographical novel based on the events surrounding the end of British rule in India. It is one of the few books about India which deals compassionately with the fate of people of British and Indian parentage who were accepted by neither community. Here Masters was also writing from experience: it was a family secret that they had Indian blood through his great-grandfather's marriage. The novel was made into an equally successful film in 1955 starring Stewart Grainger as the officer in the Indian army who falls in love with a Eurasian girl played by Ava Gardner.

Masters wrote two autobiographical works about his life and career in the Indian army. *Bugles and a Tiger* (1956) is an affectionate account of military life in India before the war, while *The Road Past Mandalay* (1961) deals with his wartime career. A third volume, *Pilgrim Son* (1971), recounts his experiences as a writer in the United States. His early years in the country were spent in a number of homes near New York before he settled in Santa Fe, New Mexico.

Later books by Masters included his *Loss of Eden* trilogy, a panoramic family saga set in the First World War which brings together fictional and historical characters caught up in the conflict. Although the novels were praised for the accuracy of the background detail, much of which came from contemporary newspaper accounts, they had a less certain touch than his earlier Indian fiction and received mixed reviews. There were also difficulties over his use of excessively graphic sexual descriptions, and his publishers forced him to tone down the details of a homosexual relationship and a rape scene in the first volume, *Now God be Thanked* (1979). The other volumes are *Heart of War* (1980) and *By the Green of the Spring* (1981). Towards the end of his life Masters suffered from heart disease and he died on 7 May 1983 in the Presbyterian Hospital, Albuquerque, New Mexico, following the failure of a bypass operation. He was buried in the Pecos Wilderness, outside Santa Fe. TREVOR ROYLE

Sources J. Clay, *John Masters: a regimented life* (1992) · J. Masters, *Bugles and a tiger* (1956) · J. Masters, *The road past Mandalay* (1961) · J. Masters, *Pilgrim son* (1971) · *Daily Telegraph* (7 May 1983) · *New York Times* (8 May 1983) · *The Guardian* (9 May 1983) · *The Times* (9 May 1983)

Likenesses photograph, 1946, repro. in Masters, *The road* [*see illus.*]

Masters, John White (1791–1873), botanist and poet, was born on 16 January 1791 and baptized on 23 January at St Mary's, Ashford, Kent, the last of eight children of William Masters (*c.*1749–1837), weaver and workhouse master, and his wife, Martha (*c.*1750–1817), workhouse mistress, both of Wiltshire. Comparatively little is known of Masters's early years. His parents became master and mistress of Chartham workhouse, near Canterbury, in 1801. Perhaps as a result of this environment, Masters was sympathetic towards the poor throughout his life. He was probably educated and trained in horticulture in Canterbury.

Until 1830 Masters worked as a gardener in Sheldwich, near Faversham, and then in Faversham itself, but travelled widely. Later he wrote that in Kent 'there is scarce a field that I have not been into' and that he had visited Essex, Sussex, Lincolnshire, and Yorkshire (*Transactions of the Agricultural and Horticultural Society of India*, 5, 1838, 8). About 1820, while in Faversham, Masters wrote a poem of 100 four-line stanzas, mostly in Kentish dialect, entitled *Dick and Sal, or, Jack and Joanses Fair*; although he disparaged it as 'doggerel', it was, in fact, well written. Possibly influenced by the botanist John Ray's *Collection of English Proverbs* (1670) and *Collection of English Words* (1673) and by Robert Bloomfield's *Richard and Kate, or, Fair-Day: a Suffolk Ballad* (1802), Masters was innovative in handing over the narration almost entirely to a Kentish voice, which tells an

amusing and fast-moving tale of a visit to Canterbury Michaelmas fair, with comments on several contemporary local residents. Perhaps as a result of his horticultural training, Masters showed a praiseworthy ability to observe and classify dialect objectively. By 1910 at least seventeen editions of *Dick and Sal* had been printed, each with a slightly different text, thus recording changes in Kentish dialect and in ideas about dialect during the century. The text of the first edition was reprinted in 1999, in Arthur Percival's *A First Anthology of Faversham Verse*. Even the title was changed to the one by which the poem came to be better known: *Dick and Sal at Canterbury Fair*. The poem was imitated in Sussex by Richard Lower (alias Uncle Tim) in his *Tom Cladpole's Jurney to Lunnon* (1831), and seems to have started a dialect genre on the theme of 'country lad and country lass venture by some means outside their area and find adventure'. Examples were soon to be found in, among other counties, Essex, Lincolnshire, and Lancashire, where the theme merged with the flowering of dialect writing in northern England.

On 29 August 1819 Masters married Sarah (1787–1826), the daughter of John and Sarah Drewry of Eastling, Kent. Their only child, Leah, was baptized on 2 September 1821. There is a family story that, about a year after Sarah died, Masters was walking with Leah when 'a savage bull charged them; whereupon the father, in his anxiety to save his child, threw her over a fence with the result that one of her legs was damaged and she was lamed for life' (private information).

In June 1830, leaving his daughter with relatives, Masters sailed to Calcutta, where initially he taught in his nephew's school and was appointed the equivalent of a parish overseer, distributing 'pensions to aged and infirm Paupers of all denominations including several hundred Hindoos and Moosulmans' (*Calcutta Annual Directory*, 1835, 131). He also became a very active member of the Agricultural and Horticultural Society of India, publishing several papers on horticulture and botany in the *Transactions/Journal of the Agricultural and Horticultural Society of India*, 1836–50. In 1836 he was appointed head gardener of the East India Company's botanic gardens in Calcutta, a post which he resigned in 1838 after a misunderstanding. He then started compiling 'Calcutta flora', which was published in the *Transactions* (7, 1840, 39–85).

In June 1839 the newly formed Assam Company appointed Masters head superintendent of the first commercial tea estates in India. Situated in Upper Assam, these were intended to overcome the Chinese monopoly of tea. Despite an unhealthy climate, illness, and living conditions like those of paupers in Kent, he established the well-known tea estates in the Brahmaputra valley surrounding Nazira, the headquarters of the plantation. He provided his Assamese labourers with a staffed clinic and school, learned their language, and protested to the Calcutta board of directors about their low wages. Following company policy, he cleared of jungle as much suitable land as possible. In 1842 he produced over 31,000 lb of tea from 1645 acres. But, since this was about 25 per cent less tea than he had predicted, the income did not cover the company's ambitious expenditure. The board suspended him and he resigned in July 1843.

While working for the Assam Company, Masters continued to pursue his interests in botany. By 1843 he had completed two collections of more than one thousand plants each, which he sent to Calcutta. They eventually reached Sir William Hooker at Kew Gardens, where their meticulous labelling was noted. In total he made at least six large collections of Assamese plants for 'the promotion of Science'. In honour of Masters's achievements William Griffith, botanist, named after him at least two species Masters himself had collected: a small palm, *Calamus mastersianus*, and a beautiful flower, *Camellia mastersia*. After Masters returned to England, George Bentham named a genus of twiners *Mastersia assamica*.

After leaving the Assam Company, Masters became sub-assistant commissioner and magistrate for the Golaghat district of Assam, where he continued to study plants and geological specimens. In 1863 he retired as an uncovenanted civil servant and returned to Faversham, where he donated Assamese specimens to the Faversham Institute. Inspired, no doubt, by the continuing popularity of *Dick and Sal*, he wrote an inferior sequel in standard English: 'Richard and Sarah', Waiting for the Train (1868), which was not published until 1897, in the *Faversham Institute Journal* (August, 445–7). Masters died at his home, 19 Court Street, Faversham, on 15 February 1873, and was buried at St Mary's Church, Faversham, on 20 February.

TONY FAIRMAN

Sources GL, Assam Company-under Inchcape, 9925–30, 27047, 27052 · P. Griffiths, *The history of the Indian tea industry* (1967) · Masters family biographies, private information · T. Fairman, 'Dick and Sal, or, Jack and Joanses fair', *Antiquarian Book Monthly*, 23 (1996), 10–15 · *Transactions/Journal of the Agricultural and Horticultural Society of India* (1836–50) · *Calcutta Annual Directory and Kalendar* (1835) · *Calcutta Annual Directory and Kalendar* (1830–63) · East India letters, Kew Gardens, vol. 55, 213 · *Faversham Institute Journal* (Aug 1897), 445–7 · H. A. Antrobus, *The history of the Assam Company, 1839–1953* (1957) · CKS, 2360/8/18 [microfiche] · Canterbury Cathedral, U3/146/1/33 · d. cert. · J. McClelland, ed., *Palms of British East India* (1850), pl. 206 · L. Berlèse, *Iconographie du genre camellia* (1841), pl. 66 · *Transactions of the Linnean Society of London*, 25 (1866), pl. 34 · *The posthumous papers of William Griffith*, ed. J. McLelland (1854) · militia records, CKS, PS/US/39, 45

Archives RBG Kew, corresp.

Likenesses photograph, 1863?, priv. coll.

Wealth at death under £200: Masters family biographies, private information

Masters, Mary (*fl.* 1733–1755), poet and letter-writer, was born of humble parents who, by her admission, 'always brow-beat and discountenanc'd … her Genius to Poetry' (Masters, *Poems*, preface, A2), her father endeavouring 'to prevent [her] from acquiring the use of the Pen or a proper Pronunciation in Reading', since he maintained that 'Writing would only qualify [women] for intrigue' (Masters, *Familiar Letters*, 52–3). Though 'ill-provided with the gifts of Fortune' (ibid., preface) she published two original volumes, *Poems on Several Occasions* (1733) and *Familiar Letters and Poems on Several Occasions* (1755), whose lengthy subscribers' lists, which included Elizabeth Carter, Hester

Chapone, Samuel Johnson, Charlotte Lennox, John Newbery, Samuel Richardson, and Christopher Smart, show that Masters was well promoted within élite literary networks. In fact such 'genteel' (Landry, 8) social connections mean that Masters, unlike Mary Collier, Mary Leapor, and Ann Yearsley, was not a typical plebeian poet. Despite Boswell's unsubstantiated claim that Johnson 'revised' her volumes, 'illuminated here and there with a ray of his own genius' (Boswell, 8.241), Masters's work not only discloses whatever scant biographical information can be pieced together but conveys the mind of a determined, self-possessed woman. The biographical facts are oblique at best, glimpsed through hints of extended sojourns in various London households, Edward Cave's among them, and a period of residence in Derbyshire. The volumes, in effect, establish and confirm Masters's literary presence, their fleeting attention to geography notwithstanding. Her response to 'ingenious letters' from the then elderly poet Jane Barker was praise of 'such Indications of the clearest Mind' and 'such steady Sense' (Masters, *Poems*, 86–7). Whether imitating Dryden or Horace, recommending to female correspondents books such as Francesco Algarotti's explications of Newton, or annotating her copy of poet and prose writer Elizabeth Rowe's work, Masters, as she justified herself to an intemperate *London Magazine* critic in the *Gentleman's Magazine* (April 1739), let her 'Themes themselves … for their Author plead' (Masters, *Familiar Letters*, 285).

These themes include the vagaries of courtship and marriage, women's intellectual equality, and the transformations and raptures of Christian charity. 'Never distrest [with] am'rous Cares', Masters did not marry, preferring 'a safe Part … out of the Snare' of Cupid (Masters, *Familiar Letters*, 219). However, in poems and prose letters she held forth on love, marriage, and childbirth, pointedly opposing the union of a foolish man and a witty woman, since 'those who are not Fools, will Fools despise', but approving the marriage of two minds where 'wit to Wit gives, mutually, Delight' (ibid., 193–4). Convinced that 'Souls have no Sex' Masters devoted several letters and poems to proto-feminist issues: the desire 'to rescue [her] Sex from so base a Slavery as some of them undergo who are Married to such as Delight to keep them in a mean Subjection' (ibid., 77), the asseveration that 'as I'm born, I will be, free' (ibid., 80), and the opinion that the intellectual 'difference between Men and Women … proceeds only from the difference in Education' (ibid., 313). Answering a female correspondent who argued for women's inferiority and for 'female poets fall[ing] short of Milton' Masters contended that 'Female Authors have thoughts as sublime as his can possibly be', citing such exemplars of acumen and artistry as the biblical Deborah, the Socratic Diotima, Pope Joan, and Catherine the Great, along with Mary Astell, Alison Cockburn, and Elizabeth Rowe (ibid., 313–15). Both volumes, especially the first, show her expertise in blending humility and self-aggrandizement; an 'unletter'd Maid … wholly unpractis'd in the learned Rules', she insists that she writes 'simple Nature unimprov'd by Art', yet clings to 'distinguishing Defects to prove them Mine' (Masters, *Poems*, 45). From early child-hood, during which she was particularly affected by the narrative of the friendship of David and Jonathan, the Bible provided a storehouse of allusion and metaphor. Masters's paraphrastic verse translations of several psalms garnered rhymed epistles from Thomas Scott, attesting that:

> the soft melodious Hebrew's Voice
> In your sweet, echoing Notes rejoice.
> (ibid., 231)

Masters was also an adept imitator whose skill verged on parody. Her two-part extension of Thomas Gray's 'Ode on the Death of a Favourite Cat', aiming to comfort Selima's grieving young mistress, installs the favourite 'on Clio's Lap Divine' with 'two snow-white cows' attending to dispense 'Nectareous Milk of Taste and Hue', of which Selima 'has all the Cream' (Masters, *Familiar Letters*, 253–6). Her response to Dryden's version of Catullus's berating of Lesbia for 'the Lechery of Deceit' adroitly turns the tables—in the manner of Christopher Marlowe's articulate nymph—in its observation on the philandering of men, charmed by 'dear Variety' and loving 'to range' (ibid., 89–90). Like so many enigmas of her life, the place of Masters's death is unknown.

PATRICIA DEMERS

Sources M. Masters, *Poems on several occasions* (1733) · M. Masters, *Familiar letters and poems on several occasions* (1755) · D. Landry, *The muses of resistance: laboring-class women's poetry in Britain, 1739–1796* (1990) · J. Boswell, *The life of Samuel Johnson*, ed. J. W. Croker, rev. J. Wright, [another edn], 10 vols. (1835) · *GM*, 1st ser., 9 (1739) · Blain, Clements & Grundy, *Feminist comp.*

Masters, Maxwell Tylden (1833–1907), botanist and journal editor, was born at Canterbury, Kent, on 15 April 1833. He was the youngest son of William Masters (1796–1874), a nurseryman and hybridizer of plants. William Masters was also the compiler of a valuable catalogue, *Hortus Duroverni* (1831), and a correspondent of Sir William Hooker. He later became alderman and mayor of Canterbury, and was founder of the Canterbury Museum in 1823.

After education at King's College, London, Maxwell Masters qualified licentiate of the Society of Apothecaries in 1854 and MRCS in 1856. He graduated MD *in absentia* at St Andrews in 1862. While at King's College he attended the lectures of Edward Forbes and those of John Lindley at the Chelsea Physic Garden; he always described the latter as the most interesting he ever heard. When the Fielding herbarium was acquired by the University of Oxford in the early 1850s Masters was appointed subcurator under Charles Daubeny (1795–1867), the professor of botany; his first paper, one on air-cells in aquatic plants, was communicated to the Ashmolean Society in 1853. He also delivered courses of lectures on botany at the London and Royal institutions, and from 1855 to 1868 lectured on botany at St George's Hospital medical school. In 1856 he began to practise as a general practitioner at Peckham. In 1858 he married Ellen Anne Ruck, daughter of William Tress, with whom he had four children.

In the mid-1850s Masters's attention was first drawn to the study of malformations in plants, especially those of the flower, and their connection with the theory of the foliar nature of its parts. His first teratological paper, one on *Saponaria*, was published in 1857 in the *Journal of the Linnean Society*. After other preliminary papers, he published *Vegetable Teratology* (1869), a pioneer work issued by the Ray Society. Although he never had leisure to prepare a second edition, he furnished many additions to the German translation, *Pflanzen-Teratologie* (1886), and in 1893 he prepared a descriptive catalogue of the specimens of vegetable teratology in the museum of the Royal College of Surgeons. In November 1865 Masters was appointed principal editor of the *Gardeners' Chronicle*, and horticulture became his dominant interest. Under his direction the journal maintained a high standard, with eminent botanists contributing articles across a wide variety of topics. A gentle and kindly man, Masters encouraged beginners and the first publications of many notable botanists and horticulturists appeared in the *Gardeners' Chronicle*.

Masters acted as secretary to the International Horticultural Congress of 1866, and edited its *Proceedings*. Part of the large financial surplus from this event was used to purchase Lindley's library for the nation: it was vested in trustees, of whom Masters was chairman, and put in the care of the Royal Horticultural Society. Masters assiduously supported the society, and succeeded Sir Joseph Dalton Hooker as chairman of its scientific committee. He also kept in close touch with the progress of horticulture on the continent.

Masters still continued to work at pure botany, studying in the herbarium of the Royal Botanic Gardens, Kew, from 1865. He was a large contributor to Lindley's and Moore's *Treasury of Botany* (1866; rev. edn, 1873), and elaborated the Malvaceae and allied families and the passion flowers (Passifloraceae) for Oliver's *Flora of Tropical Africa* (2 vols., 1868–71), and the Passifloraceae and Aristolochiaceae for the *Flora Brasiliensis* (1872–6). He also prepared a monograph on the family Restionaceae for Alphonse and Casimir de Candolle's *Monographiae Phanerogamarum* (1878). On the conifers (Coniferae), he published papers in the journals of the Linnean Society and of the Royal Horticultural Society, the *Journal of Botany, British and Foreign*, and the *Gardeners' Chronicle*; in 1892 he presided over the conifer conference of the Royal Horticultural Society. He also contributed to Hooker's *Flora of British India* and to his edition of Harvey's *South African Plants*, and to the *Flora Capensis*.

As lecturer and examiner Masters knew the requirements of students, and met them successfully in thorough revisions of Henfrey's *Elementary Course of Botany*, which he brought abreast of the times. He also published two primers, *Botany for Beginners* (1872) and *Plant Life* (1883), both of which were translated into French, German, and Russian, and he contributed articles on horticulture and botany to the *Encyclopaedia Britannica* (9th edn.).

Masters was elected a fellow of the Linnean Society in 1860 and of the Royal Society in 1870, and a correspondent of the Institut de France in 1888; he was also a chevalier of the order of Leopold. He died at his home, 9 Mount

Avenue, Ealing, London, on 30 May 1907 and was cremated in Woking on 4 June. His wife and two daughters survived him. The Royal Horticultural Society commemorates his services by an annual Masters memorial lecture relating to science and horticulture. In 1865 Bentham named *Mastersia*, a genus of flowering plant, in his honour, and in 1930 Gilg-Benedict gave the name *Mastersiella* to a genus within the Restionaceae.

G. S. BOULGER, rev. WILLIAM T. STEARN

Sources W. B. Hemsley, 'Botanical works of the late Dr Masters', *Gardeners' Chronicle*, 3rd ser., 41 (1907), 377–8, 398, 418–19 · *Bulletin of Miscellaneous Information* [RBG Kew] (1907), 325–34 · *Proceedings of the Linnean Society of London*, 120th session (1907–8), 54–6 · K. F. P. von Martius and others, *Flora Brasiliensis*, 1 (1906), 185 · CGPLA Eng. & Wales (1907)
Archives RBG Kew, papers
Likenesses photographs, 1873–97, repro. in *Gardeners' Chronicle*, 368 · photograph, 1877, RBG Kew · photograph, priv. coll.; repro. in E. Nelmes and W. Cuthbertson, eds., *Curtis's botanical magazine dedications, 1827–1927* (1932), 190 · photograph, RBG Kew
Wealth at death £6787 18s. 9d.: probate, 5 July 1907, CGPLA Eng. & Wales

Masters, Robert (1713–1798), historian, was born on Christmas day 1713 at Hetherset, Norfolk, son of William Masters (1681–1759) and his wife, Anne Fish (d. 1758) of Hetherset, and was descended from the royalist Sir William Masters. His parents had two other sons, who died in infancy, and a daughter. Nothing is known of his schooling; he entered Corpus Christi College, Cambridge, as a sizar in 1731, and proceeded BA in 1735, MA in 1738, and BD in 1746. He was ordained priest at Ely in September 1738, the same year that he was elected into a fellowship of his college. There he remained for twenty years, filling at times the offices of dean, bursar, and tutor; his pupils remembered his plain-speaking. In 1752 he was presented to the vicarage of St Benet, Cambridge, and he eventually became a rural parish priest in Corpus livings at Landbeach from 1756 to 1797 and Waterbeach from 1759 to 1784. Masters married at Landbeach on 12 August 1757 Constance Cory (c.1730–1764), daughter of John Cory, vicar of Impington and Waterbeach in Cambridgeshire. She died on 29 August 1764 leaving a son, William, and three daughters: Anne, who married the Revd Andrew Sprole, Mary, who married the Revd Thomas Cooke Burroughes, and Constance, who died young.

Although Masters published a timely sermon entitled *The Mischiefs of Faction and Rebellion Considered*, delivered in October 1745 when a Jacobite invasion from Scotland was expected daily, his real passion was the past. He belonged to a small and intimate group of antiquaries whom William Cole dubbed the Benedictines because of their association with Benet (Corpus Christi) College. Cole, who acted very uncomfortably as Masters's curate at Waterbeach for two years, admitted that much of what he recorded about him was 'wrote with too much acrimony', and as a witness he is not always to be relied on. Both were strong-minded and liked their own way. That Masters had a rough edge and did not court popularity is, however, evident; his attempt to have his son elected a fellow of Corpus failed,

he was embroiled in a controversy with the young architect James Essex in 1748 and appears to have been in the wrong, and he later engaged successfully in litigation about his parochial rights to tithes. Masters contributed a few papers to *Archaeologia*, the journal of the Society of Antiquaries, to which he was elected in May 1752. The first of them, a scholar's remarks on Horace Walpole's *Historic Doubts* on Richard III (*Archaeologia*, 2, 1771, 198), only confirmed the dislike that Walpole had been taught by Cole and alienated him from the society. Masters also wrote on stone coffins and skeletons discovered at Cambridge Castle (ibid., 8, 1785, 63), and on a stained-glass pedigree of the Stewart family (ibid., 8, 1786, 321). He compiled *Memoirs of the Life and Writings of the Late Rev. Thomas Baker*, the nonjuror of St John's College, using materials of Zachary Grey to which he appended a catalogue of manuscripts (1784) and a *Catalogue of the several pictures in the public library and respective colleges in the University of Cambridge* (1790).

Of greater value than such works was Masters's first major book, which attracted favourable attention and proved durable. In 1749 he printed a biographical list of the alumni of Corpus, and was led to compile a large *History of the College of Corpus Christi* (in two parts, 1753–5) which is the first published account of its kind of any college at Oxford or Cambridge. He had permission to inspect the archives and printed what by the standards of the time are well-edited documents together with a narrative history in which biographical material predominated. His interleaved and extra-illustrated copy at Corpus shows a painstaking concern. John Lamb, master of the college, continued and revised the history, bringing it down to 1831. The second pioneering historical work that Masters undertook came at the end of his life when he issued in an edition of only twenty-five copies *A Short Account of the Parish of Waterbeach* (1795) 'by a late vicar', which is the first separate Cambridgeshire parish history. It allowed him to settle an old score with Bishop Yorke of Ely and remains of interest for its evidence about the agriculture of a fenland parish on the eve of enclosure.

In typical eighteenth-century fashion, Masters resigned the living of Waterbeach in favour of his son William who, however, predeceased him, dying in 1794, and the Landbeach parish to his son-in-law, Thomas Burroughes, with whom he lived until his death at Landbeach on 5 July 1798. He was buried in Landbeach church. His considerable library had been sold by auction at London some months before he died.

JOHN D. PICKLES

Sources Nichols, *Lit. anecdotes*, 3.479–84; 7.256, 626 · Walpole, *Corr.*, vols. 1–2 · *Masters' History of the college of Corpus Christi and the Blessed Virgin Mary in the University of Cambridge*, ed. J. Lamb (1831), 395–6 · R. Willis, *The architectural history of the University of Cambridge, and of the colleges of Cambridge and Eton*, ed. J. W. Clark, 1 (1886), 242, 298–30; 3 (1886), 64 · R. Barber, *Letter of the Corpus Association* (1997), 14–20 · C. Smyth, 'Robert Masters and his college history', *Church Quarterly Review*, 155 (1954), 270–80 · F. G. Stokes, *The Blecheley diary of the Rev. William Cole* (1931) · W. M. Palmer, *William Cole of Milton* (1935) · 'A peasant's voice to landowners', by John Denson of Waterbeach ... reprinted with 'Masters' history of Waterbeach', ed. J. R. Ravensdale (1991), xiii–xv, 77–125 · DNB · Venn, *Alum. Cant.* · *Miscellanea Genealogica et Heraldica*, 2nd ser., 4 (1890–91), 101 · GM, 1st ser., 68 (1798), 634–5

Archives CCC Cam., notes and extracts relating to Waterbeach · CUL, Ely Diocesan archives · CUL, Cambridgeshire collections · St John Cam., notes and papers
Likenesses Facius, stipple, pubd 1795 (after T. Kerrich), BM, NPG; repro. in Ravensdale, ed., *A peasant's voice to landowners*, 78

Mastertown, Charles (1679–1750), minister of the Presbyterian General Synod of Ulster and religious controversialist, was born in Scotland, probably near Linlithgow, on 23 March 1679, and was educated at Edinburgh University, whence he graduated MA on 28 June 1697. He was licensed to preach by the presbytery of Linlithgow probably in 1703 and, having moved to Ireland, his credentials were accepted by the synod of Ulster at Antrim on 1 June 1703. He accepted a call from the congregation of Connor and was ordained there by Antrim presbytery on 17 May 1704. His ministry in this charge earned him a growing reputation as a preacher and a scholar. In view of their future disagreements it is worth noting that in 1718 he headed a protest against synod's decision to force John Abernethy, a leading non-subscriber, to move to Dublin, a decision which Abernethy at this time refused to obey.

The installation of Samuel Haliday in the First Belfast congregation in 1720, in spite of his refusal to subscribe to the Westminster confession of faith, alienated several members of both Presbyterian congregations in Belfast. On 4 July 1721 a subscription list was opened for the building of a third meeting-house. Generous help was forthcoming, including gifts from Scotland, and the new church was opened in 1722; the congregation called Mastertown to be their minister, and he was installed on 20 February 1723. It is a remarkable tribute to his ability that so soon afterwards, on 18 June 1723, he was elected moderator of the general synod, meeting at Dungannon. The controversy over subscription was now at its height. Mastertown's own contribution to the debate was substantial. In 1723 he published *An Apology for the Northern Presbyterians in Ireland*, defending the practice of subscription in reply to Abernethy's *Seasonable Advice to the Protestant Dissenters in the North of Ireland* (1722). Abernethy replied with his *Defence of the Seasonable Advice* (*c*.1725) and Mastertown answered with his *Short Reply*, published in 1726; this was a pamphlet of considerable importance that dealt with the doctrinal issues that lay behind the subscription controversy.

Meanwhile Mastertown had published in 1725 a sermon entitled *Christian Liberty Founded on Gospel Truth*. Against Abernethy's argument that sincerity is enough and that truth is founded on 'personal persuasion' Mastertown maintained that a Christian's knowledge of the truth must be based on the persuasion of the Holy Spirit speaking through scripture. It was not a liberty to embrace error, but to accept the revelation given by God. His most significant work was undoubtedly *The Doctrine of the Holy Trinity*, originally published in Belfast in 1725. This went through several editions—in Belfast, London, and Edinburgh—during the author's lifetime. Mastertown himself contributed a supplement to the 1745 edition, entitled *The Great Importance of the Scripture Doctrine of the Ever-Blessed Trinity*. After his death it was reprinted a number of times.

The final edition (1880) contained a biographical memoir by his great-grandson the Revd Hope Masterton Waddell.

Mastertown suffered considerable opposition from Samuel Haliday and James Kirkpatrick, the ministers of the First and Second Belfast congregations, both before and after the separation of the non-subscribing congregations into the separate Presbytery of Antrim in 1725 and the exclusion of that presbytery from the jurisdiction of synod in 1726. Mastertown pursued his ministry calmly but firmly and built up a large congregation. He attended the general synod in 1745 but by the next year was no longer capable of preaching; William Laird was appointed his assistant and successor on 16 September 1747. Mastertown died in Belfast on 15 July 1750. His only child, Susan, married John Poaug in 1725 and had numerous descendants. After his death Mastertown's friends arranged for the publication of two of his sermons in one pamphlet, which was printed in Belfast in 1753. The first was the farewell sermon that he had preached at Connor in 1722 and the second was a reprint of his 1725 sermon *Christian Liberty*.

Charles Mastertown was probably the most capable and influential proponent of orthodoxy in the synod of Ulster as it tried to deal with the contentious issue of subscription in the 1720s. His attitude appears rigid but his writings reveal that he might have proved less inflexible had the non-subscribers been more forthcoming about their doctrinal views. He was above all else an able and gifted minister who built up a strong congregation while at the same time contributing significantly by his writings to the support of orthodox doctrine not only in Ireland but beyond.　　　　　　　　　　A. W. GODFREY BROWN

Sources H. M. Waddell, 'Memoir', in C. Mastertown, *The doctrine of the Holy Trinity* (1880) · T. Witherow, *Historical and literary memorials of presbyterianism in Ireland, 1623–1731* (1879) · J. S. Reid and W. D. Killen, *History of the Presbyterian church in Ireland*, new edn, 3 (1867) · A. W. G. Brown, 'Irish Presbyterian theology in the early 18th century', PhD diss., University of Belfast, 1977 · *Orthodox Presbyterian*, 1 (1829), 131 · T. Hamilton, *Biographical sketches of Irish worthies* (1875), 43 · *Records of the General Synod of Ulster, from 1691 to 1820*, 1 (1890) · D. Laing, ed., *A catalogue of the graduates … of the University of Edinburgh*, Bannatyne Club, 106 (1858), 58 · *DNB*

Mastin, John (1747–1829), topographer, was born on 30 September 1747 in Epperstone, Nottinghamshire, to William Mastin (*d*. 1779), a freeholder husbandman, and his wife, Ann (*c*.1721–1792), daughter of John Baguley, of Stoke Bardolph, Nottinghamshire. After education at a dame-school and at establishments at Woodborough and Nottingham, Mastin returned home to Epperstone when about twelve and entered the service of a succession of gentlemen and clergymen. Over the next ten years his self-education continued with his employers' encouragement. He was both competent and energetic, and in his later teenage years was well known locally as a wrestler. About 1771 he obtained his first senior post, as a steward at Rickmansworth, Hertfordshire. In 1772, however, he resigned after eloping to marry the seventeen-year-old Mary Gurney (1754/5–1811), a modestly wealthy minor whose prospects he checked by journeying to London to inspect the will of her deceased father, William Gurney, a freeholder and wheelwright of Rickmansworth.

In 1773 a kinsman offered Mastin a curacy if he could qualify himself, which he did in 1777 after instruction by a clergyman. By the end of the same year he had been appointed to the curacies of Husbands Bosworth, Leicestershire, and of Naseby, Northamptonshire. Ordained priest in 1779, he was appointed sequestrator at Naseby in 1781, the year his seventh and last child was born. He became vicar of Naseby in 1783 and moved there, to the newly refurbished parsonage, in 1787. In 1791, a year after he surrendered his curacy of Husbands Bosworth, he began to write a history of Naseby. At the instigation of George Ashby, the patron of the living, this was published for some 600 subscribers in 1792. Although *The History and Antiquities of Naseby* was conventionally cumulative, perhaps not least because of the guidance Mastin received from the Leicestershire historian John Nichols, it nevertheless owed much to Mastin's own curiosity, observations, and fieldwork, including archaeological excavation. As well as sections on church and manorial history, soils, fossils, agriculture, and plants it included a lengthy discourse on the battle of 1645, reprinting various primary sources and recording a few local traditions. It was enlivened with biographical sketches of the parish's 'ingenious mechanics' such as John Tresler, blacksmith and whitesmith, caster of metals, locksmith, and maker of steel crossbows for shooting rooks with balls. The book was well received, and an offer was made (but declined) to propose Mastin as a fellow of the Society of Antiquaries. A second edition, with additions and engravings, was published in 1818.

Mastin remained vicar of Naseby until his death. During that time he served in addition numerous terms as curate or stipendiary priest in nearby parishes. In 1802 he became vicar of Dunton Bassett, Leicestershire, and in 1822 vicar of Cold Ashby, which adjoins Naseby. He was reportedly a formidable figure, 'largely formed, but not corpulently covered. His dress was of the old school, black coat and waistcoat and knee breeches with black stockings' (Foard, 353). Throughout his adult life he also maintained an active interest in farming and land management, and acted both on his own behalf and as agent for others. He submitted several communications to the board of agriculture, from which he received a silver plate in 1801 for an essay, probably on the conversion of grass levels to tillage. In his old age he wrote a manuscript autobiography.

Mastin died aged eighty-one in his daughter's arms at Naseby vicarage on 15 January 1829 after a long decline, and was buried in his own church.   PAUL STAMPER

Sources 'Memoirs of Revd. John Mastin', Northants. RO, accession no. 1991/129 · P. Stamper, 'Northamptonshire', *English county histories: a guide*, ed. C. R. J. Currie and C. P. Lewis (1994), 291–301 · Board of Agriculture minute book BV1, 10 Nov 1801, U. Reading, Rural History Centre · Board of Agriculture letter book BXV, U. Reading, Rural History Centre, 172 · Board of Agriculture, Register of Letters BXII, May 1813 · G. Foard, *Naseby: the decisive campaign* (1995), 353 · *IGI* · memorial tablet, Naseby church, Northamptonshire

Archives Northants. RO, memoirs

Matcham, Francis [Frank] (1854–1920), architect, was born on 22 November 1854 in Newton Abbot, Devon, the eldest son and second of nine children of Charles Matcham, subsequently manager of Mary Bridgeman's Torquay brewery, and his wife, Elizabeth. He was educated at Babbacombe School, Torquay, which he left at fourteen to join the office of George Bridgeman, an architect in Torquay, to whom he returned after being apprenticed to a quantity surveyor in London.

In the 1870s Matcham's career as a theatre architect grew rapidly. He joined the practice of Jethro Thomas Robinson, who was not only theatre architectural adviser to the lord chamberlain but was also responsible for the surviving interiors of the Old Vic in London (1872) and the Theatre Royal in Margate (1874). On 9 July 1877 Matcham married Robinson's younger daughter Maria, with whom he had two daughters. In 1878 Robinson died and Matcham took over his late father-in-law's architectural practice which, in the preceding seven years, had created seven successful theatres and was currently rebuilding the Elephant and Castle Theatre, London, which Matcham completed.

Between 1879 and 1912 Matcham built or rebuilt over 150 theatres, an achievement approached in Great Britain only by C. J. Phipps, who designed seventy-two. Matcham's work covers the entire span of late Victorian and Edwardian theatre architecture, from the grand London Coliseum to smaller suburban and variety theatres, most of which were later destroyed either by enemy bombers during the Second World War or by later developers. Innovative only in using cantilevers for the galleries and hence abolishing intrusive columns, he was uniquely pragmatic in his architectural and technical responses to the commercial manager's brief, which was to seat ever larger audiences on ever tighter city-centre sites. Few Matcham exteriors excite but his interiors are always exuberant and eclectic. The interiors encompassed Tudor strap-work, Louis XIV detail, Anglo-Indian motifs, naval and military insignia, delicate rococo panels, classical statuary, and robust baroque columns supporting heavy entablatures, often with more than one style competing in a single auditorium. Whatever the style, Matcham was always prepared to bend the architecture to satisfy both the sight-lines and the all-important connection of performer to audience: tier fronts slope down towards boxes which frame the proscenium arch and, as an architectural ensemble, draw out rather than distance the performer.

In 1896 Edwin O. Sachs criticized Matcham for the impurity of his sloping tiers and juxtaposition of styles. However, this was before the opening of his masterpiece, the London Coliseum, in 1905. For half a century after Matcham's retirement his theatres were widely disparaged by architects and others who preferred unbuilt European projects to what the public and theatre profession still prized as 'real theatres'. It was only after 1970 that

Matcham's genius was widely recognized. In 1995 the Theatre Museum, Covent Garden, acquired well over 7000 of his drawings. Of these *c.*500 are highly finished drawings and represent over seventy-five theatres or cinemas and about one-sixth of his total life's output.

Other major Matcham theatres which survive include: the Everyman Theatre, Cheltenham (1891); Grand Opera House in Belfast, Grand Theatre in Blackpool, and Opera House in Wakefield (all 1894); Lyric Theatre, Hammersmith (1895; dismantled, 1972; auditorium only re-erected on a new site in 1979); Empire, Langton (1895); Tivoli, Aberdeen (1896 and 1909); Richmond Theatre, Surrey (1899); Gaiety, Douglas, Isle of Man (1900); Hackney Empire, London, and Hippodrome in Brighton (both 1901); Opera House in Buxton, Derbyshire, Devonshire Park Theatre in Eastbourne, Shepherd's Bush Empire, London, and Royal Hall in Harrogate (all 1903); King's, Glasgow (1904); King's, Southsea (1907); His Majesty's in Aberdeen, and Olympia in Liverpool (both 1909); London Palladium (1910); and the Victoria Palace, London (1911).

Matcham died at his home, 28 Westcliff Parade, Westcliff-on-Sea, Essex, on 17 May 1920 and is buried in Highgate cemetery.   IAIN MACKINTOSH, *rev.*

Sources B. Walker and others, *Frank Matcham: theatre architect* (1980) · C. Brereton and others, *Curtains!!!, or, A new life for old theatres* (1982) · V. Glasstone, *Victorian and Edwardian theatres* (1975) · E. O. Sachs and E. A. Woodrow, *Modern opera houses and theatres*, 3 vols. (1896–8) · *CGPLA Eng. & Wales* (1920)
Archives Theatre Museum, London, papers, incl. architectural plans and blueprints
Wealth at death £86,389 18s. 8d.: probate, 22 July 1920, *CGPLA Eng. & Wales*

Matcham, George (1753–1833), traveller, was born at or near Bombay, India, the only surviving son of Simon Matcham (*d.* 1776), superintendent of the Bombay marine of the East India Company, and his wife, Elizabeth, formerly Bidwell. Matcham's travels began when he was sent from Bombay to Charterhouse School, and put under the guardianship of Henry Savage, a director of the East India Company. On leaving Charterhouse in 1769 he returned overland to India and entered the Bombay civil service in 1771, subsequently becoming the East India Company's resident at Broach until its cession to the Marathas in 1783.

His father's death left Matcham with a good inheritance. In 1777 his mother sailed to England, to live near Canterbury, while he travelled overland to join her, spending his home leave exploring England and Ireland, where he had cousins. In 1780 he again crossed the desert on his way back to India. Matcham followed various routes: sometimes taking a ship through the Mediterranean to explore the Greek islands and view their antiquities; on another journey, he sailed through the Red Sea; at other times his route carried him through Kurdistan, Turkey, and the Balkan lands, into western Europe. He normally crossed the desert on horseback, either alone or in the company of other Europeans, and accompanied by Arab guides and servants. From the frequency of these expeditions, he was well known to such British diplomats

as Sir Robert Murray Keith at Vienna and Sir Joseph Yorke at The Hague, and on one occasion he was presented at the court of the emperor Joseph II, to whom he recounted his travels. Accounts of these journeys were said to appear in James Capper's *Observations on the Passage to India* (1783) and Eyles Irwin's *Voyage up the Red Sea* (1780; 3rd edn, 1787, 2 vols.) but Matcham's precise route is difficult to establish from these sources.

Matcham retired from the service in 1785, and the following year settled with his mother at Enfield, near Bath. There he met Catherine (Kitty; 1767–1842), daughter of the Revd Edmund and Catherine Nelson, and sister of Horatio, later Viscount Nelson (1758–1805). Two months later, on 26 February 1787, they were married at Burnham Thorpe, Norfolk, by her father, and they stayed at Barton Hall, near Norwich, for the birth in 1789 of George Matcham [*see below*]. The Matchams then moved to Ringwood, Hampshire, where their subsequent seven children were born. In 1797 they decided to move to Bath for the sake of the children's education, and subsequently to Ashfold Lodge, Sussex. Throughout these moves, they kept in close contact with the Nelson family, and followed with interest the progress of their famous naval relative.

On his Hampshire and Sussex estates, Matcham was concerned with the planting and improvement of his property; he took pleasure in guiding the education of his children, and in his own liberal studies. He sent many letters to the higher authorities of the state, proposing various improvements. These were mostly ignored, one exception being the conversion of some marshy ground into a public pleasure garden in St James's Park. His patent (no. 2676 of 1803) for a method of raising sunken vessels or other heavy objects was likewise ignored, as it was completely impractical. His specification described a leathern bag filled with water, and attached to a rope led over a pulley and counterweighted. When air was pumped into the bag, the counterweight would, he supposed, raise the air-filled bag and the wreck to the surface. Matcham died at Kensington on 3 February 1833; Catherine spent her widowed years at Holland Park, Kensington, where she died on 2 April 1842.

Their son **George Matcham** (1789–1877) was born on 7 November 1789, and entered St John's College, Cambridge, in 1808, where he graduated LLB in 1814 and LLD in 1820. He was an advocate of Doctors' Commons, 1820–30. On 20 February 1817 he married Harriet, eldest daughter and heir of William Eyre, of Newhouse, Whiteparish, Wiltshire. They are known to have had at least one son, William Eyre Matcham, his father's sole executor, since his mother died before his father. George Matcham maintained his association with Wiltshire, serving as justice of the peace and deputy lieutenant of the county, and in due course residing at Newhouse. He became chairman of Wiltshire quarter sessions in 1836, an office he continued to hold until 1867. He drew on his lifelong antiquarian pursuits to contribute accounts of the hundreds of Downton and Frustfield to R. C. Hoare, *Modern History of Wiltshire* (1825), and published a collection entitled *Notes on* *the Character of Lord Nelson* (1861). He died at Newhouse in 1877, in the words of an obituarist:

> Ripe in years, and honoured and revered by all his relatives and friends, with a vigorous mind unimpaired to the last, he passed away on 18 January last, leaving a character almost peculiar to our nation, of an accomplished, an able, and useful country gentleman. *(Law Magazine and Review, 416)*

ANITA McCONNELL

Sources *GM*, 1st ser., 103/1 (1833), 276–8 · R. L. Arrowsmith, ed., *Charterhouse register, 1769–1872* (1974), 253 · M. E. Matcham, *The Nelsons of Burnham Thorpe* (1911) · E. Irwin, *A series of adventures in the course of a voyage up the Red sea*, 2 vols. (1787), 2.290–330 · BL OIOC, MSS Eur. A 209 · Venn, *Alum. Cant.* · Boase, *Mod. Eng. biog.* · Bombay baptisms, BL OIOC, N/3/1, fol. 383 · parish register, Norwich, St Stephen · 'The late Dr George Matcham', *Law Magazine*, 4th ser., 2 (1876–7), 416–18 · d. cert. [George Matcham the younger] · *CGPLA Eng. & Wales* (1877)

Wealth at death under £8000—George Matcham the younger: probate, 14 March 1877, *CGPLA Eng. & Wales*

Matcham, George (1789–1877). *See under* Matcham, George (1753–1833).

Mather, Alexander (1733–1800), Wesleyan Methodist preacher, was born in February 1733 at Brechin in Forfarshire. His parents, of whom little is known, instructed him 'early in the principles of religion' and consequently he was 'an utter stranger to the vices common among men'. When he was 'about ten years old', on hearing his schoolteacher pray, he 'was struck with strong convictions' and gained 'a desire to be a Christian' (Mather, 91). In 1745 'out of a childish frolic' he fought at the battle of Culloden for the Pretender, and in an attempt to evade the English authorities he spent a brief period living with an uncle near Perth. Although caught and arrested, he was soon released, and commenced work with his father as a baker.

In May 1752 Mather 'determined to go abroad' and stayed at Perth for several months, during which time he began to attend the Scottish Episcopal church. In June 1752 he travelled to London, where, after a short time working in different households, he gained employment with Thomas Marriott, a baker in Norton Folgate. He was married on 14 February 1753, although his wife's name is unknown. Due to his strict sabbatarian views he persuaded his employer and other local bakers to cease working on Sunday. At the request of Marriott he began to attend meetings at the Foundery, John Wesley's headquarters in London. He heard Wesley preach for the first time on 14 April 1754, at West Street Chapel, and consequently experienced an evangelical conversion, all his 'sorrow, and fear, and anguish of spirit, being changed into a solid peace' (Mather, 99). He soon became a band leader, the leader of a class, and a preacher. Having 'not eight hours sleep in a week' (Mather, 148), he would preach in the evening, work most of the night, and preach again at five in the morning. In 1757, due to the 'searching preaching of Thomas Walsh', Mather professed the experience of Christian perfection, claiming 'uninterrupted communion with God, whether sleeping or waking' (ibid., 203). Later in August of that year he was appointed as an itinerant preacher.

Alexander Mather (1733–1800), by William Ridley, pubd 1796

As a preacher Mather faced fierce opposition and violence at various places, including Darlaston, Birmingham, and Monmouth. At Wolverhampton the chapel in which he preached was pulled down and his effigy burnt, while at Boston he was so severely molested by the mob that, as he stated, 'it was a full year, before I quite recovered the hurts which I then received' (Mather, 151). In 1761, assisted by his wife, his preaching brought about a significant holiness revival at Wednesbury. Three years later, at the request of Wesley, he visited Wales to 'regulate the Societies there' (ibid., 157). A successful and tireless preacher, Mather became a close friend of Wesley. In 1788 he, with Thomas Rankin and Henry Moore, was ordained superintendent by Wesley for the English work. In 1792 he was elected president of the Methodist conference. His high-church principles were revealed in his criticisms of Alexander Kilham in *An Affectionate Address to the Members of the Methodist Society, in Leeds, and Elsewhere*, published jointly with John Pawson in 1794. Mather sat on all conference committees until 1797 and served as district chairman on five occasions from 1791 to 1796.

Mather died at York on 22 August 1800. In character many saw him as 'a man of strict integrity, of exemplary conduct, and of great zeal' (Benson, 552). Abel Stevens, in recognition of his contribution to the establishment of the Methodist connection, described him as 'a main pillar of the Wesleyan edifice' (Stevens, 2.354).

SIMON ROSS VALENTINE

Sources A. Mather, 'An account of Mr Alexander Mather', *Methodist Magazine*, 3 (1780), 91–9, 146–60, 199–207 · T. Jackson, ed., *The lives of early Methodist preachers, chiefly written by themselves*, 3 vols. (1837–8) · J. Pawson, 'A further account of the late Mr Alexander Mather', *Methodist Magazine*, 24 (1801), 112–19, 158–67 · 'Epistolary remains of the Rev. Alexander Mather', *Wesleyan Methodist Magazine*, 61 (1838), 26–9 · J. Benson, 'A sermon preached on the death of Mr Mather', *Methodist Magazine*, 23 (1800), 531–57 · *The journal of the Rev. John Wesley*, ed. N. Curnock and others, 8 vols. (1909–16) · T. Marriott, *Methodist Magazine*, 38 (1815), 802 · A. Stevens, *The illustrated history of Methodism*, 2 vols. (1873–4)

Archives JRL, Methodist Archives and Research Centre, letters, mainly to William Marriott

Likenesses portrait, 1780, repro. in *Methodist Magazine* (1780), 80 · W. Ridley, stipple engraving, pubd 1796, NPG [*see illus.*] · portrait, repro. in Curnock, ed., *Journal of John Wesley*, vol. 5, p. 51

Mather, Cotton (1663–1728), minister in America and author, was born on 12 February 1663 in North End, Boston, Massachusetts, the first of ten children born to Increase *Mather (1639–1723), minister and president of Harvard College, and his wife, Maria (1641–1714), daughter of John Cotton. Both grandfathers, Richard *Mather and John Cotton, were founding ministers of Massachusetts.

Mather entered Harvard College at the unprecedentedly early age of eleven. He was by then fluent in Latin, familiar with Greek and Latin literature, and had started Greek and Hebrew grammar. Young as he was, he already exhibited several lifelong characteristics. He habitually directed others how to improve their spiritual lives. He was a voracious reader and became easily the widest-read man in Anglo-America. He acquired a personal library inferior to none. Passionate, voluble, and extroverted, he was also vain and sensitive to slights real or imagined. He expounded on all subjects at the drop of a hat. He wrote and published as much as he talked, kept a large journal, and carried on an equally large correspondence with men in England, Scotland, and throughout Europe. His writing was always self-referential, and despite incessant protestations of modesty, he was immodestly aware of his extraordinary mental powers: 'Proud thoughts flyblow my best performances' (Levin, 'Trying to make', 170). His writing was larded with quotations from and allusions to classical Greek and Roman literature, as well as patristic and Reformation scholarship. He freely invented new words.

Of his approximately 380 separate published titles, these are thought to be the most important: *Memorable Providences Relating to Witchcraft and Possessions* (1689); *The Wonders of the Invisible World* (1692); *Magnalia Christi Americana* (1702); *Bonifacius, Essays to do Good* (1710); *The Christian Philosopher* (1721); *Parentator* (1724); *Manuductio ad ministerium* (1726); *Ratio disciplinae* (1726). Book-length manuscripts unpublished at Mather's death included 'Biblia Americana', 'Angel of Bethesda', and 'Triparadisus'. The last two were published in the twentieth century.

Mather suffered at Harvard College, where he was roughly handled by the older students and developed a stammer that he largely overcame later. His brilliance was quickly recognized, and he received important preaching requests before he was twenty. He was ordained teacher in his father's North Church in Boston in 1685, and preached there the rest of his life. Shortly after ordination he married, on 4 May 1686, his first wife, Abigail Phillips (1670–1702). The couple had nine children, but miscarriage, infant mortality, accident, and disease took a heavy toll. Four children survived their mother in 1702: Katharine

Cotton Mather (1663–1728), by Peter Pelham, in or before 1727

(1690–1716), Abigail (1694–1721), Hannah (b. 1697), and Increase (1699–1724).

Witchcraft Shortly after Mather's marriage he brought home Martha Goodwin, an emotionally disturbed girl who was believed to have been a victim of witchcraft. He laboured to exorcise the evil spirits. During this exhausting face-to-face encounter with a disturbed but physically active teenage woman, Mather believed he was engaging in the great contest over materialism and atheism. His traditional view was that a myriad of invisible, malicious spirits filled the air. They 'swarm like the frogs of Egypt in every chamber of our houses' (Silverman, *Life*, 91). He believed that failure to come to grips with this reality would open the door to materialism, disbelief in Satan, and ultimately atheism itself. After six months Martha Goodwin left, completely restored, thus confirming Mather in his world-view and his belief in the power of prayer. He wrote his first important book about that experience, *Memorable Providences Relating to Witchcraft and Possessions* (Boston, 1689). It was immediately successful and published in both London (1691) and Edinburgh (1697).

When eighteen people were executed in Salem for witchcraft three years later, in 1692, other ministers questioned the trial procedures, but Mather, intent on the reality of evil spirits, wrote another book, *The Wonders of the Invisible World*, in which he defended the judges. The Salem witchcraft trials became a fixture in American historical memory, and those two widely read books ruined Cotton Mather's reputation there for ever.

Public life When William of Orange landed in England in 1688 Increase Mather was already in London to negotiate a new colonial charter. Cotton Mather found himself in charge of the large, influential North Church. Before his father returned he admitted the first new members under the half-way covenant, an important step toward wider access to the church, as it extended baptism to the children of baptized adults. He found himself drawn increasingly into public life. When Boston learned of the success of William in England, the city arrested the governor, Sir Edmund Andros, and disarmed his two regiments and a frigate in the harbour.

That afternoon a 'Declaration of the Gentlemen, Merchants and Inhabitants of Boston, and the Country Adjacent', which declared Boston loyal to William and Mary, was read to the crowd in the streets. The declaration spoke largely in the terms of English civil liberties rather than the providential language of puritanism. Although there is no direct evidence, many scholars believe Cotton Mather composed it. One month afterwards he was chosen by the magistrates to deliver the election day sermon, a much sought-after privilege never before given to one a mere twenty-six years old. It was the high point of Mather's political reputation.

Political developments after 1690 centred on the new colonial charter and the royal governor provided for in it. The Mathers, father and son, supported the new governor, Sir William Phips (1651–1695), who was a member of their church but a poor choice for governor. Afterwards they were unable to gain the good graces of his successor, Joseph Dudley (1647–1720). Their nemesis in the world of New England politics was the Cook family. Elisha Cook (1637–1715), a physician and contemporary of Increase Mather, and his son, a merchant, also Elisha Cook (1678–1737), thought to be the wealthiest man in New England, actively opposed both Mathers. They finally managed to remove Increase from the presidency of Harvard College, and later prevented Cotton from attaining that cherished post.

Mather's puritan New England In 1693 Cotton Mather began work on his *magnum opus*, a history of puritan New England. By 1700 he was able to send to London a large manuscript, about 850 folio pages, *Magnalia Christi Americana, or, The Ecclesiastical History of New England*. It was published in London in 1702 in a large folio volume closely printed in double columns. *Magnalia* is an ambitious project that envisages the movement of Christian civilization from Europe to America. Mather fancied himself as Boston's Virgil. The opening lines of his general introduction, 'I write the wonders of the CHRISTIAN RELIGION, flying from the Depravations of Europe, to the American Strand', echo George Herbert's

> Religion stands on tiptoe in our land,
> Readie to pass to the American strand.
> (Murdock, 89)

The whole comprises seven 'books' very disparate in character. These include important biographies of governors and ministers, some already published separately, histories of Harvard College, the conflicts with the American Indians, and selected churches, and an engraved 'Ecclesiastical map of the country'.

Magnalia was at once controversial. The British historian John Oldmixon used its information, but ridiculed its pedantry and errors. The University of Glasgow, on the other hand, awarded Mather an honorary degree of doctor of divinity in 1710. In 1818 the editor of the *North American Review* described *Magnalia* in a way characteristic of detractors for three centuries:

> a chaotick mass of history, biography, obsolete creeds, witchcraft, and Indian wars, interspersed with bad puns, and numerous quotations in Latin, Greek and Hebrew which rise up like so many decayed, hideous stumps to arrest the eye and deform the surface.

He called Mather a 'credulous, pedantick, and garrulous writer' (Murdock, 33). But two years later, in 1820, Thomas Robbins, a bibliophile in Connecticut, published the first American edition (2 vols., 1820; 2nd edn, 1853, 1855). It was the American editions that were important in the American literary renaissance of the mid-nineteenth century. For Herman Melville in 1856, 'His style had all the plainness and unpoetic boldness of truth' (Silverman, *Life*, 54). Ralph Waldo Emerson (1803–1882), Nathaniel Hawthorne (1804–1864), Harriet Beecher Stowe (1811–1896), and Elizabeth Stoddard (1823–1902) are among the American writers who were inspired by *Magnalia*. Twentieth-century scholars continued these opposing patterns: for some, scathing ridicule of Mather's pedantic, overblown prose, and for others, admiration for the coherence, power, and influence of his vision.

In 1702, the year that *Magnalia* was published in London, Abigail, Mather's wife of sixteen years, died in Boston after a miscarriage and a long illness, on 28 November. Eight months later, on 18 August 1703, Mather married Elizabeth (1684?–1713), daughter of John Clark, a Boston physician, and widow of four years of Richard Hubbard. She and Cotton had six children, of whom one died in infancy and three more succumbed with their mother in a single month in 1713 to measles and smallpox. Two children from this marriage survived her: Elizabeth (1704–1726), who in 1724 married Edward Cooper, a shipmaster, and Samuel (1706–1785).

Through the ten years of this second marriage Mather continued to work furiously. Once his concerned father wrote from London, 'do not Let him kill Himself. He will do it if you do not hinder him' (Silverman, *Life*, 77). Cotton published no fewer than 135 separate titles in the first decade of the new century. By far the most important of these was *Bonifacius, Essays to do Good* (1710, title varies).

Bonifacius is a small book by Mather's standards, and perhaps for that reason his most widely read. He published it anonymously in Boston in 1710. There was a second Boston edition in 1845, and many London editions appeared throughout the nineteenth century under the title *Essays to do Good*. Writing to 'all Christians' Mather put the question 'What service is there that I may now do for my Saviour, and for His People in the world!' (Levin, introduction, 31). He answers with practical suggestions, first for 'the Duty to Oneself', and then in separate chapters suggestions for doing good in family, neighbourhood, and among several different occupations and social classes.

The book is 'warm, friendly, helpful, encouraging' (Holmes, 1.92). It was the perfect book to introduce the new century of pietism and experiential religion. Although Benjamin Franklin started out ridiculing it, in his mature years he gave credit to *Bonifacius* for being an important influence on him. *Bonifacius* put Mather squarely in the mainstream of the German pietism emanating from the university at Halle and reaching America's middle colonies. In 1711 he opened a correspondence with August Herman Francke at Halle that lasted many years, and brought Mather into contact with like-minded men around the world.

Natural science Many of Mather's letters to England were about the natural sciences. In 1712 he sent the first of several accounts of unusual natural phenomena to John Woodward, a prominent English geologist. He followed up with letters addressed to John Waller, secretary of the Royal Society, with the hope that they be published in the society's *Philosophical Transactions*. From 1712 to 1724 Mather sent a total of eighty-two such letters, known collectively as 'Curiosa Americana'. Many were printed in the *Transactions*. Mather made no secret of his wish to be included among the circle that made up the Royal Society, and was elated when news came of his election to the fellowship in 1713. Thereafter with great pride he put FRS after his name. In 1714 he sent to London a large manuscript epitomizing the science of the day that was published in 1721 as *The Christian Philosopher*. The chapter on astronomy, according to a modern historian, is 'The finest example of how Newtonian Science came to America and was disseminated' (Theodore Hornberger in Holmes, 1.137). Already the indefatigable Mather had started another large survey, this time of medical practice. He called it 'Angel of Bethesda'. Like the other, it reviewed the work of scores of European scientists. Mather sent the manuscript to England in 1724, but it remained unpublished until the twentieth century. He was

> the first native-born American colonial to advance beyond the status of a mere field agent for European scientists in the New World and to demonstrate a genuine *philosophical* approach to science, with scientific *ideas* and *hypotheses* of his own. (Stearns, 426)

Mather's contributions to the *Transactions* often seem rather credulous by recent standards. Twice, however, he made experiments that have stood the test of time. In 1712 he experimented in his own garden with strains of Indian corn that produced red and black kernels. Reasoning correctly from the evidence, he described the process of plant hybridization.

His most famous scientific experiment was the use of inoculation against smallpox. Accounts from Turkey had already appeared in the *Transactions*, and Mather had word-of-mouth accounts from Africa. He and his friend Dr Zabdiel Boylston, in the face of vicious public protests, inoculated over 200 people during an epidemic in Boston in 1721. They kept statistical records that raised the whole procedure from the realm of anecdote. The following year

he sent a full description to the Royal Society, which considered it at three consecutive meetings. Mather and Boylston provided Britain with first-hand evidence that inoculation against smallpox worked, in Mather's words, 'upon both *Male* and *Female*, both *Old* and *Young*, both *strong* and *weak*; *Whites*, and *Blacks*; on *Tawnies*, Women in *childbed* … on Women *with child*, at all Seasons' (Silverman, *Life*, 362). As usual, Mather's every action spurred extremes of hostility. In Boston someone tried to assassinate him. At this time of heated pamphleteering over inoculation, Benjamin Franklin, a youthful sixteen, lampooned *Bonifacius* with an enduring literary character, Silence Dogood.

Later years Eighteenth-century Boston was no longer a city upon a hill. Merchant wealth fostered English fashions in dress, homes, and thought; big houses and new churches sprang up everywhere. Disgruntled members broke from Mather's North Church to form the New North Church three blocks away. Church of England chapels multiplied, Quakers built a meeting-house, and, a sure sign of religious pluralism, in 1718 Cotton Mather himself helped install the pastor at the new Baptist church, observing 'Liberty of Conscience is the Native Right of Mankind' (Silverman, *Life*, 302).

Mather's second wife, Elizabeth, died on 8 November 1713 in a measles epidemic. A year and a half later he found a third wife in Lydia (*d.* 1734), daughter of the well-known puritan Samuel *Lee (1625?–1691), and widow of John George, a wealthy Boston merchant. George died in November 1714 and left Lydia a large fortune. Mather and Lydia married on 5 July 1715, after signing a pre-nuptial agreement that gave her the entire control of her fortune and left Mather unprotected. It turned out to be an unfortunate marriage. Lydia was emotionally unstable. Her wide swings of mood tormented Mather. He was sued for debts arising from her first husband's business affairs, and as a consequence was repeatedly thrown on the mercy of wealthy members of his church. He and Lydia had no offspring; she outlived him and died on 17 January 1734.

Mather's father died in 1723. Cotton wrote a large, fulsome biography, *Parentator*, in imitation of Increase's famous biography of his own father, Richard Mather. The two books are in sharp contrast. Increase's is slim, anonymous, written in the third person. Cotton's biography fits the new, post-puritan century. It is personal, immodest, ornate, and rich in its praise. It was followed five years later by yet a third of these father–son biographies, when Mather's son Samuel published a biography of Cotton himself, *The Life of the Very Reverend and Learned Cotton Mather* (1729).

In 1724 Cotton's first-born son, named Increase after his grandfather, died at sea. Two years later, in 1726, his daughter Elizabeth, now Elizabeth Cooper, died, and only two of Mather's many children remained alive—Hannah, who had been badly scarred in childhood and remained unmarried, and Samuel (1706–1785). Despite these disappointments and being besieged by creditors, Mather remained as energetic as ever. He continued adding to a huge compendium of scriptural comments, 'Biblia Americana', but failed to get it published. He maintained his very large correspondence. In 1726 he brought out two more noteworthy books: *Manuductio ad ministerium* and *Ratio disciplinae fratrum Nov-Anglorum*.

Manuductio ad ministerium: Directions for a Candidate to the Ministry (1726, 1781, 1789) is an urbane summary of a life spent in the ministry. In it Mather advised young men to do good, and also to study languages, sciences, poetry and style, natural philosophy, mathematics, and history, in short to imitate himself. He urged young candidates to an evangelical ministry. Perry Miller thought it the culmination of one century and 'the beginning of a new era', the age of reason (Holmes, 2.631). *Manuductio* is said to have been in use in Britain into the nineteenth century.

Ratio disciplinae fratrum Nov-Anglorum (1726) is a description of Congregational practice in Massachusetts. Mather began it in 1701, but as happened so often with his projects, he kept working on the text for many years. By 1726 his ecumenical description of the church contrasted sharply with his grandfather Richard Mather's famous description of the early puritan church, *Cambridge Platform* (1648). In 1726 Mather no longer wrote of New England as 'Immanuel's land', as his father had. That signature of seventeenth-century puritanism had faded with the passage of time. Silverman (*Life*, 404) describes *Ratio disciplinae* as a statement to the world of a uniquely American church, comparable to Hector St John de Crèvecoeur's description of the distinctively American citizen in *Letters from an American Farmer* (1782).

Mather had always been an eager millenarian. Between 1720 and 1726 he broke away from his father's literalist interpretations to a preterite position similar to the new philological interpretations in Europe. This decisive break with his father's generation and his own earlier thinking provides a link to Jonathan Edwards's postmillenarianism of the 1740s.

In or before 1727 Peter Pelham painted Mather's portrait in oil on canvas, a shoulder-length frontal view that shows a cheerful, rubicund face under a large, fashionable wig. Contemporaries said that it was not a good likeness, but did resemble Mather's loyal son Sammy. Pelham also engraved an often-reproduced mezzotint, said to have been 'the first mezzotint known to have been made in the New World' (Silverman, *Life*, 410); it shows a more serious expression.

Early in 1728 Mather became ill, and by 10 February he was confined to bed with a cough, asthma, and a fever. On 13 February 1728 he died at home (probably Ship Street, North End), peacefully, surrounded by friends and family, aged sixty-five, in a Boston that he had left only to attend college across the river. He died intestate. The mandatory inventory of his estate does not mention the great library. Without it the estate amounted to £235 10s. 10d., and '500 Acres of wast land' in Scituate valued at £36. Two children survived: Hannah and Samuel. After a state funeral, Mather was buried on 19 February in the family crypt on Copp's Hill in Boston's North End.

Cotton Mather was the most influential writer of his generation in America. He brought the puritan period of New England history to an end and started towards the evangelical pietism of the eighteenth and nineteenth centuries. His vision of Christian religion flying to America inspired nineteenth-century writers on America's manifest destiny. In the twentieth century his writings were an inexhaustible source for a revivified intellectual history: 'He was the one man of his time in America not dwarfed beside the virtuosi of the continent' (Silverman, introduction, xvii). MICHAEL G. HALL

Sources K. Silverman, *The life and times of Cotton Mather* (1984) · T. J. Holmes, *Cotton Mather: a bibliography of his works*, 3 vols. (1940) · D. Levin, *Cotton Mather: the life of the Lord's remembrancer, 1663–1703* (1978) · D. Levin, introduction, in *Bonifacius: an essay upon the good by Cotton Mather*, ed. D. Levin (1966), vii–xxxi · R. Smolinski, introduction, in *The threefold paradise of Cotton Mather: an edition of 'Triparadisus'* (1995), 1–86 · D. Levin, 'Trying to make a monster human', *Forms of uncertainty: essays in historical criticism* (1992), 157–76 · K. Murdock, 'Cotton Mather', 'The *Magnalia*', in C. Mather, *Magnalia Christi Americana*, ed. K. B. Murdock and E. W. Miller, new edn (1977), 1–48 · K. Silverman, introduction, in *Selected letters of Cotton Mather* (1971), ix–xxxvi · R. P. Stearns, *Science in the British colonies of America* (1970) · S. Bercovitch, 'Cotton Mather', *Major writers of early American literature*, ed. E. Emerson (1972), 93–149 · P. Miller, *From colony to province* (1953) · S. Mather, *The life of … Cotton Mather* (1729) · R. Lovelace, *The American pietism of Cotton Mather: origins of American evangelicalism* (1979) · C. Robbins, *A history of the second church, or Old North in Boston* (Boston, 1852), 216–17 · 'The autobiography of Increase Mather', *Proceedings of the American Antiquarian Society* [ed. M. G. Hall] (1962), 271–360
Archives American Antiquarian Society, Worcester, Massachusetts, family papers · Mass. Hist. Soc., papers · RS, corresp. · University of Virginia, Charlottesville, MSS | BL, Sloane MSS, letters to J. Woodward · Boston PL, Prince collection · Hunt. L. · Massachusetts Archives, Boston · NL Scot., Robert Wodrow collection, letters to John Stirling and Robert Wodrow
Likenesses P. Pelham, mezzotint, 1727, American Antiquarian Society, Worcester, Massachusetts · P. Pelham, oils, in or before 1727, American Antiquarian Society, Worcester, Massachusetts [*see illus.*] · P. Pelham, mezzotint (after his earlier work), BM
Wealth at death £235 10s. 10d.: inventory taken by law, 23 July 1728; Suffolk county probate records, 5 Aug 1728, Suffolk county, Boston

Mather, Ebenezer Joseph (1849–1927), founder of the Royal National Mission to Deep Sea Fishermen, was born on 12 June 1849 at Foregate Street, Stafford, the son of Henry Penkett Mather (*c*.1805–1886), a shoe manufacturer, and his wife, Elizabeth, *née* Douthwaite. Although raised a member of the Plymouth Brethren, Mather later joined the Church of England (about 1883) and remained an Anglican for the rest of his life. Following his education at Mr Charles Hammer's private academy, Rhyll, in 1861, Mather worked as a junior clerk in a Worcester bank and later as a market gardener. He became an auditor about 1869 and was licensed as a broker of the City of London. On 4 September 1872 he married his first wife, Caroline Eliza (1849–1925), *née* Lough, at Islington register office; they had eight children, two boys and six girls. In 1880 he was appointed as secretary to the Thames Church Mission (TCM), which had been founded in 1844 following the demise of the Episcopal Floating Church Society, to continue the Church of England's work among seafarers on the Thames.

In 1881 Samuel Hewett, owner of the Short Blue [fishing] Fleet, invited Mather to visit his employees in the North

Sea. Following this visit, and in the light of growing public concern with conditions in the fleets, Mather gave a paper on Christian work at sea to the Newcastle church congress in October 1881. He also urged the TCM committee to employ a 'sailing Bethel' for evangelistic work among the fishing fleets, and the *Ensign* was launched on 14 June 1882, the new venture becoming known as the Mission to Deep Sea Fishermen (MDSF). The TCM committee, however, found the development increasingly burdensome, and in 1884 sought to separate the two aspects of its work. This led, in 1886, to the MDSF being reconstituted as an independent organization under the direct control of Mather and a new council (which included Sir Frederick Treves, R. M. Ballantyne, Dr A. T. Schofield, and G. A. Hutchison). The MDSF quickly moved off in new directions involving the establishment of 'sailing hospitals' and a highly publicized campaign against the North Sea liquor trade engaged in by vessels known as copers ('coopers'). These developments, however, led to severe financial worries, and in 1887 Mather published his history of the MDSF, *Nor'Ard of the Dogger*, in an attempt to increase public support. With the growing financial burdens, Mather found himself the butt of increasing criticism. He became the subject of inquiry by his council regarding financial irregularities, and was forced to resign in August 1889. When the magazine *Truth* picked up the story, Mather, encouraged by R. M. Ballantyne, sailed in January 1890 for Australia, where he spent two years researching details for a popular travel book which he published as *The Squatter's Bairn*.

Details about the remaining thirty-seven years of Mather's life are very sparse. He spent some time as an editor with the *Church Family Newspaper*, and in 1918 was awarded a civil-list pension of £50 p.a. 'in consideration of his valuable work in connection with the Fishermen's Mission and of his inadequate means of support' (*Fish Trades Gazette*, 6 July 1918). In retirement he lived on Canvey Island, Essex, where he published (anonymously) his biography, *Memories of Christian Service*. Following the death of his wife he married his nurse, May Ethel Timewell (1873–1957?), on 16 June 1925, but was to survive only two further years before dying, at their home in Cotswold Gardens, Canvey Island, of heart failure on 23 December 1927. He was buried in the grounds of the nearby church of St Nicholas.

STEPHEN FRIEND

Sources [E. J. Mather], *Memories of Christian service* (c.1922) · *Toilers of the deep* [Royal National Mission to Deep Sea Fishermen] [minutes, correspondence] · b. cert. · m. certs. · d. cert. · archives, Royal National Mission to Deep Sea Fishermen, London
Archives British and International Sailors Society, Southampton · International Association for the Study of Maritime Mission, York · Mission to Seamen, London · Royal National Mission to Deep Sea Fishermen, London
Likenesses photograph, repro. in *The Christian* (3 Feb 1888) · photograph, Royal National Mission to Deep Sea Fishermen · photograph, International Association for the Study of Maritime Mission, York

Mather, Increase (1639–1723), Congregational minister, was born in Dorchester, Massachusetts, on 21 June 1639,

Increase Mather (1639–1723), by Robert White (after Jan van der Spriet, 1688)

the youngest son of Richard *Mather (1596–1669), minister, and Katherine (d. 1655), daughter of Edmund Holt, who had migrated to New England from Lancashire, England, in 1635. At the age of twelve he went to live and study with the Revd John Norton in Boston, and then attended Harvard College, graduating BA in 1656. In 1657 he followed his brothers Samuel *Mather and Nathaniel *Mather to England, and then settled briefly in Ireland, graduating MA from Trinity College, Dublin, in 1658 and preaching in Magherafelt and Ballyscullion, co. Derry.

Mather moved to England in 1659 where he substituted for his brother Nathaniel's friend John Howe as minister at Great Torrington, Devon. When Howe returned from London in 1659 Mather moved on, serving briefly as a minister in Guernsey and Gloucester. With no settled congregation, he was not one of the ministers ejected from their posts after the Restoration of 1660 but clearly his religious views were incompatible with the new regime and he returned to Massachusetts in 1661.

On 6 March 1662 Mather married Maria (1642–1714), daughter of the New England minister John Cotton. Cotton *Mather was their first child. Nine others survived childhood. At the same time Mather was engaged in the controversy over the half-way covenant, opposing the proposed expansion of membership by relaxing the rules concerning religious conversion. In 1664 he was ordained teacher of the North Church in Boston, Massachusetts, and over the next twenty-five years he emerged as the foremost figure in American puritanism. During the next two decades he published nearly fifty books, including sermons and works of theology, natural science, and history. He criticized what he saw as a decline from the standards of the founders and was the key figure in the reforming synod of 1679 which called for a moral cleansing of the society and covenant renewals. He was involved in the affairs of Harvard College and accepted the presidency in 1685 but continued in his post at North Church and to live in Boston.

Part of Mather's stature derived from his key role in maintaining the link between English and American puritanism through his continuing connection with English dissenters such as Thomas Jollie. He both gave and received advice and assistance and aided others in their correspondence with transatlantic friends. When New Englanders were criticized by English dissenters for their treatment of Baptists, Mather defended the colonists. He argued that the colonial Baptists were not Calvinists and did not value a learned ministry and were therefore different from the Particular Baptists with whom English congregationalists (and he himself when he had been in England) found it possible to co-operate.

In 1684, when the government of Charles II demanded that Massachusetts surrender its charter, Mather urged the citizens of Boston to resist, but without success. The Bay colony was incorporated, along with the other New England colonies and then New York, into the dominion of New England. In 1688, distressed with Sir Edmund Andros's policies as governor-general of the dominion, Mather slipped away from Boston and sailed to England to seek redress for the colonists. Initially he had three audiences with James II in which he pleaded for restoration of the old charter. Following the revolution of 1688 he was granted access to King William through the intercession of English friends and attempted to gain royal acceptance of the colonial revolt that had overthrown the dominion in reaction to news of England's revolution, and to gain a return of the old Massachusetts charter. At the same time he immersed himself in the affairs of the English dissenters, preaching to their congregations, associating with their leaders such as Richard Baxter, and playing an active role in the short-lived 'heads of agreement' that united congregational and presbyterian clergymen.

Mather failed to gain restoration of the old charter but was instrumental in obtaining a new charter for the colony in 1691. He was also allowed to nominate the first royal governor and member of the governor's council. On his return to Boston he found the colony embroiled in the Salem witchcraft hysteria. Mather certainly had done his share to warn people of the dangers of the devil, but he was disturbed by the nature of the court proceedings. Though he was slow to make public his concerns, his publication, *Cases of Conscience Concerning Evil Spirits* (1692), criticizing the use of spectral evidence, played a key role in bringing the trials to a close.

Over the remaining decades of his life Mather's star was in the decline. He was criticized, though not as much as his son Cotton, for his role in the witchcraft episodes. His efforts to curtail the spread of liberal and latitudinarian influences in New England led to his losing the Harvard presidency in 1701. Though a believer in ministerial associations he was critical of a movement to create regional clerical boards that he felt impinged too much on congregational autonomy. Those dissatisfied with aspects of the new charter government criticized him unrealistically for not having achieved a restoration of the old. His support of his son Cotton's promotion of inoculation during a smallpox epidemic in 1721 was also unpopular. Yet he continued to publish—forty new volumes in the first two decades of the new century—and was recognized as the region's greatest link to the founding generation. His wife, Maria, died on 4 April 1714 and the following year he married Anne (1663–1739), widow of Maria's nephew John Cotton of Hampton and daughter of Thomas Lake, a merchant of Boston. Following his death on 23 August 1723 an immense procession followed Mather's coffin to its burial place on Copps Hill, not far from the North Church that he had served for over half a century. His wife, Anne, survived him; she died on 29 March 1739.

FRANCIS J. BREMER

Sources J. L. Sibley, *Biographical sketches of graduates of Harvard University*, 1 (1873) • F. J. Bremer, *Congregational communion: clerical friendship in the Anglo-American puritan community, 1610–1692* (1994) • *Calamy rev.* • R. L. Greaves, *God's other children: protestant nonconformists and the emergence of denominational churches in Ireland, 1660–1700* (Stanford, 1997) • *Mather papers, Collections of the Massachusetts Historical Society*, 4th ser., 8 (1866) • M. G. Hall, *The last American puritan: the life of Increase Mather, 1639–1723* (1988) • K. B. Murdock, *Increase Mather: the foremost American puritan* (1925) • R. Middlekauff, *The Mathers: three generations of puritan intellectuals* (1971) • M. Lowance, *Increase Mather* (1974) • M. G. Hall, 'Mather, Increase', *ANB*
Archives American Antiquarian Society, Worcester, Massachusetts, library, diaries, sermon books and corresp. • Boston PL, papers • Harvard U., papers • Mass. Hist. Soc., corresp. and papers • Mass. Hist. Soc., records of the North Church | Bodl. Oxf., letters to Anthony Wood
Likenesses J. van der Spriet, oils, 1688, Mass. Hist. Soc. • R. White, line engraving (after J. van der Spriet, 1688), NPG [*see illus.*]
Wealth at death less than 20 li in silver and bills; most of considerable library and personal possessions to son, Cotton: will

Mather, Joseph (1737–1804), file cutter and songwriter, was born either at Chelmorton, Derbyshire, or in Cack Alley, Sheffield. Nothing is known of his parentage or early life but after serving an eight-year apprenticeship (1751–9) Mather became a journeyman file cutter (otherwise known as file hewer) in the Sheffield workshop of Nicholas Jackson. At one stage he seems to have become a 'small mester' himself before reverting to journeyman status. He struggled to maintain himself, his wife, Nell, and their five (or more) children, and he served terms of imprisonment for debt in the town gaol at Pudding Lane.

Starting in the 1770s, Mather began to supplement his income by making up and setting to well-known tunes ballads which he sang at fairs and races, in streets and taverns. He could read, but his inability to write meant that the process was entirely oral, although later some items were taken down from his dictation and printed on broadsides:

> our author used to 'raise the wind' by vending his songs in the streets, seated on a grinder's donkey, or on the back of Ben Sharp's bull. Should it chance to begin raining, he would ride the animal into the nearest alehouse. (*Songs*, vii)

Mather's high spirits were reflected in his lively celebrations of the pleasures of artisan life, from horse-racing, bull-baiting, and cock-fighting to singing, dancing, and drinking, but he turned more and more to virulent invective, drawing on vocabulary and imagery which derived from his assiduous reading of the Old Testament. For several years he was a Methodist, though by 1787 he had left the sect after succumbing to the temptation of the alehouse and falling into sin. So said a contemporary, James Montgomery (Hobday, 78); a more recent commentator suggests that Mather rejected 'Methodism's egocentric obsession with individual salvation for a morality based on solidarity with his fellows' (ibid.).

An orientation of this kind is undoubtedly reflected in many of Mather's songs, of which the best-known was 'Watkinson and his Thirteens', written in 1787 in response to the campaign thought to be led by the master cutler of the day to lower piece rates by demanding that workers supply thirteen items for the price of a dozen. Its subject, Jonathan Watkinson, was forced on a memorable occasion to leave the theatre when the audience in the gods struck up the song with its vitriolic chorus:

> And may the odd knife his great carcase dissect,
> Lay open his vitals for men to inspect
> A heart full as black as the infernal gulph,
> In that greedy blood-sucking bone-scraping wolf.
> (*Songs*, 63)

In the same song Mather wished 'Success to our Sovereign who peaceably reigns' (*Songs*, 65), yet only six years later he was identified with the Jacobin movement in Sheffield and parodying the national anthem as 'God Save Great Thomas Paine' (1793). In 1795, after what has been called Sheffield's rehearsal for Peterloo (Palmer, *The Sound of History*, 26), when the local volunteer corps fired on an unarmed crowd in Norfolk Street, Mather wrote ballads attacking the 'Raddle-neck'd Tups', as he called them, and their commander, 'beef-headed Bob' (Colonel Robert Althorpe).

Mather's being bound over to keep the peace for a year, and thus prevented from singing in public, may date from this time. He wrote again when the ban had expired—one of his songs has the refrain 'I was muzzled a year'—but gradually reverted from radicalism to religion in the shape of Wesleyan Methodism. One of his last pieces, 'Repentance', stayed in the Methodist repertory for many years, while in a different context—that of 'loosings' and 'foot ales', theatre galleries and public houses—his radical songs remained in oral tradition.

Embittered by illness and poverty, Mather declined into his last years and died at his home in Pond Hill in Sheffield on 12 June 1804. The affection felt in the town for this stocky, pugnacious man was demonstrated at his funeral in St Paul's Church when 'his remains were followed to the grave by many of the working classes of the town, who regarded him as their champion' (*Songs*, x).

In 1811 fifty-four items by Mather were gathered together and printed under the title *A Collection of Songs, Poems, Satires, &c. Written by the Late Joseph Mather*. The publisher was John Crome (1757–1832), a Scot who settled in Sheffield and became a lifelong radical. A further edition of Mather's songs appeared in 1862 with a memoir by John Wilson which included a great deal of information culled from veteran cutlers. After a long period of eclipse during which the songs might be briefly quoted in histories of the cutlery trades, Mather's work was rediscovered in the 1960s through the influence of the folk music revival of the time, with its interest in industrial material. Some of Mather's songs were sung again, in Sheffield and elsewhere. Anthologists sought them out. The 'filesmith' (Armitage, 320) or 'sansculotte' (Hobday, 61) poet found fresh audiences. ROY PALMER

Sources *The songs of Joseph Mather*, ed. J. Wilson (1862) · R. Palmer, *The sound of history* (1988) · C. Hobday, 'Two sansculotte poets: John Freeth and Joseph Mather', *Writing and radicalism*, ed. J. Lucas (1996), 61–83 · J. L. Baxter and D. E. Martin, 'Mather, Joseph', *DLB*, vol. 8 · W. H. G. Armitage, 'Joseph Mather: poet of the filesmiths', *N&Q*, 195 (1950), 320–22 · R. Palmer, ed., *A touch on the times* (1974) · G. I. H. Lloyd, *The cutlery trades* (1913) · R. Lonsdale, ed., *The new Oxford book of eighteenth-century verse* (1984)

Mather, Sir Kenneth (1911–1990), geneticist, was born on 22 June 1911 in Nantwich, Cheshire, the elder child and only son of Richard Wilson Mather, furniture-maker, of Nantwich, and his wife, Annie, daughter of John Mottram, agriculturist, of Nantwich. His formal education started in 1915 at the Church of England boys' elementary school, Nantwich. He won a Cheshire county scholarship in 1922 to Nantwich and Acton grammar school, where the headmaster developed Mather's interest in mathematics but suggested a future in biological research. In 1928 he won a Cheshire county university scholarship to read botany at Manchester University, where he obtained first-class honours in 1931. He was then awarded a research scholarship by the Ministry of Agriculture and Fisheries, to work at the John Innes Horticultural Institution, Merton, London, on chromosome behaviour (cytology) with C. D. Darlington. Here Mather developed his skills and enthusiasm, within four months was writing his first paper (published in 1932), and within two years was awarded a London University PhD (1933).

In 1933 Mather went to Svalöf, Sweden, where he decided that traditional genetics would not take the plant breeder very far with the problems that he encountered and that a different genetical methodology was needed. He returned in 1934 to work under R. A. Fisher in the Galton Laboratory, University College, London:

> My greatest gain was … working closely with Fisher and learning from him the principles and practice of statistical analysis, estimation and hypothesis testing; how to design experiments; how to wring information efficiently from data; and how to measure the amount of information available for the analytic purpose in mind. For this I owe him a debt which has lasted all my working life.

In 1937 Mather married a fellow botanist, Mona (*d.* 1987),

daughter of Harold Rhodes, managing director of a colour printer's firm in Saddleworth. They had one son.

A Rockefeller fellowship allowed Mather to visit the USA for the year 1937–8 and he spent time at the California Institute of Technology and Harvard. In 1938 he returned to the John Innes Horticultural Institution as the head of the genetics department. While continuing his cytology work (for which he obtained a DSc in 1940) and collaborating with Fisher, he paid increasing attention to the analysis of characters showing quantitative variation (biometrical genetics). In 1948 he became the first professor of genetics at Birmingham University. He built up his department, with support from the Agricultural Research Council, which established a unit of biometrical genetics. Mather expanded his work on biometrical genetics and published widely. In 1965 he was appointed vice-chancellor of the University of Southampton, where he experienced mixed fortunes. The student unrest of the 1960s and Mather's more traditional approach did not mix easily; he found this period trying and frustrating. Nevertheless, he was successful in persuading the University Grants Committee to authorize a new medical school, which he developed. In 1971 he returned to Birmingham as an honorary professor and senior research fellow, to concentrate his efforts on his passion—biometrical genetics. He worked there until the day before his death.

Mather wrote 283 scientific papers, gave twenty-four broadcasts, and published the following books: *The Measurement of Linkage in Heredity* (1938), *Statistical Analysis in Biology* (1943), *Elements of Genetics* (1949), *Biometrical Genetics* (1st edn, 1949; 2nd and 3rd edn, with J. L. Jinks, 1971 and 1982), *Human Diversity* (1964), *The Elements of Biometry* (1967), *Genetical Structure of Populations* (1973), *Introduction to Biometrical Genetics* (1977), and (with C. D. Darlington) *The Elements of Genetics* (1949) and *Genes, Plants and People* (1950).

Mather was appointed CBE in 1956 and knighted in 1979. He was presented with honorary degrees by Southampton (LLD, 1972), Bath (DSc, 1975), Manchester (DSc, 1980), and Wales (DSc, 1980). He was elected a fellow of the Royal Society in 1949 and was awarded the Weldon medal (Oxford, 1962) and the Darwin medal (Royal Society, 1964). He was president of the Genetical Society of Great Britain (1949–52) and an honorary member in 1981. He served on many research councils, advisory bodies, and committees.

Mather was short and stockily built, had swept-back hair and glasses, and invariably had a pipe in his mouth or hand. He did not suffer fools gladly and tended to make this clear, but he would spend whatever time was needed to explain an idea to a genuine enquirer. His determination and self-commitment were without question; he would sit with his pipe firmly gripped and would pursue an idea until he resolved it. Interruptions on trivial matters often resulted in large quantities of smoke and short sentences. The opportunity to try out an idea or the prospect of a new approach was welcomed warmly. Despite his commitment to genetics he showed a fascination and knowledge of British military (especially naval) history.

Mather died of a heart attack on 20 March 1990, at his home, the White House, 296 Bristol Road, Edgbaston, Birmingham. PETER D. S. CALIGARI, *rev.*

Sources autobiographical notes, RS · D. Lewis, *Memoirs FRS*, 38 (1992), 249–66 · *The Times* (30 March 1990) · *The Independent* (27 March 1990) · CGPLA Eng. & Wales (1990) · personal knowledge (1996)
Archives John Innes Centre, Norwich, corresp., research notes and papers
Likenesses photographs, repro. in Lewis, *Memoirs FRS*
Wealth at death £435,316: probate, 29 June 1990, CGPLA Eng. & Wales

Mather, Leonard Charles [Len] (1909–1991), banker, was born on 10 October 1909 at Port Sunlight in Cheshire, the son of Richard and Elizabeth Mather. He was educated at Oldershaw School, Wallasey. After leaving school at the age of fifteen, he spent a year in a Liverpool shipping office before joining the staff of the Midland Bank branch at Dale Street, Liverpool, in 1926. In 1937 he married Muriel Armor Morris (*d.* 1991). They had no children.

Midland's Dale Street branch was part of a distinctive Liverpool tradition in banking, and Mather thrived on learning the special banking techniques which were needed in the city's cotton and shipping markets. There was even a time in the 1930s when he was tempted to move across to an appointment in the Booth Steamship Company. In 1937, however, he was promoted to a succession of appointments at the bank's headquarters at Poultry in London. Initially he was a branch superintendent's assistant—an appointment at the centre of the branch network—but during the war years he was the right-hand man of G. P. A. Lederer, chief general manager of the bank between 1943 and 1946. His duties included liaison with head office departments which had been evacuated from London, and he was also responsible for contacts with Whitehall departments.

Between 1945 and 1948 he was manager of Midland's branch in Bolton—an appointment which he later described as 'the most satisfying period of my career'. Decades later the Bolton office was still being described by customers as 'Mr Mather's branch' (Holmes and Green, 246). He returned to Poultry in 1948 as principal of the legal department and became an assistant general manager in 1950. Between 1954 and 1955, and again between 1956 and 1958, he was *de facto* in charge of the Midland Bank Executor and Trustee Company. These duties in the trust company, although essential to the fortunes of the bank at that time, probably delayed Mather's journey to the most senior management posts.

In 1958 Mather was promoted to become a joint general manager. He then joined the 'magic circle' of Midland's management committee, where his contemporaries included Howard Thackstone, Bernard Clarke, and Tony Hellmuth. He was promoted to become assistant chief general manager in 1964, and deputy chief general manager in 1966. In 1968, on Thackstone's retirement, he was appointed a director of the bank, the first occasion on which a new chief executive was given a seat on Midland's board. Mather's appointment to the most senior management position in the bank was not the clear run which it seemed, as Midland's chairman, Sir Archibald Forbes, regarded his chairmanship as a fully executive task. Consequently, for the next four years Mather, although he was perhaps the most experienced and best-qualified banker in the country, did not have the full command of strategy and management which he may have wished for. Nevertheless, in his new role he oversaw a revolution in Midland's management structure; the highly centralized systems of the previous seven or eight decades now made way for a new network of regional head offices. He was an inspirational chief, especially in his commitment to the branch network and the importance of local banking knowledge. Mather believed, 'based on long tradition, that a bank's success could be earned only by the services provided in its branches and the standing and influence of its men on the spot' (Holmes and Green, 246).

Mather was also realistic about the bank's prospects and the need to simplify the branch structure. In 1969, along with the other clearing banks, the Midland fully disclosed its profits for the first time; and the figures revealed, to surprise inside and outside the bank, that Midland's profitability was below that of its main competitors. Shortly afterwards the introduction of the 'competition and credit control' regime in 1971 put the earnings of all the main clearing banks under severe pressure. It was a reflection of Mather's traditional banking skills that Midland was able to treble its profits between 1969 and 1973, without suffering from the property and overseas losses then being incurred by some of its competitors.

Mather also made an important contribution to the development of the banking profession. He was well suited to a teaching role, as early in his career he had obtained not only the qualifications of the Institute of Bankers and the Chartered Institute of Secretaries but also an external BComm degree from the University of London. In the 1930s he taught banking law at the Liverpool College of Commerce; in the mid-1940s his views were an important factor in the Institute of Bankers' decision to upgrade the associateship examinations; and in the 1950s he produced a series of publications which became standard textbooks of modern banking practice. His books included *Banker and Customer Relationship and the Accounts of Personal Customers* (1956), which was given the premier award of the Institute of Bankers. He was also in regular demand as a lecturer and speaker, and he delivered the Gilbart lectures at the University of London in 1957 and 1961, and the Ernest Sykes memorial lectures in 1966.

These contributions led to his election to the council of the institute in 1961 and to the deputy chairmanship in 1967. He was a popular choice as president of the institute in 1969–70. In 1974 he was made an honorary fellow of the institute, at that time one of only fourteen honorary fellowships to have been awarded. His input to the literature of banking was also recognized by Loughborough University, which awarded him an honorary doctorate in 1978.

Since the late 1960s he had been instrumental in setting up Loughborough's degree in banking and finance.

Mather retired as Midland's chief general manager in 1972, but he remained on the board as vice-chairman until 1974 and as a director until 1984. In 1974, however, at the invitation of the Bank of England, he accepted the chairmanship of United Dominions Trust. This company, then the largest of the British finance houses, was being supported by the 'lifeboat' arrangements for companies affected by the secondary banking crisis of 1973–4. Mather's astute management of the business over the next few years was widely applauded in the City as a return to the basics of banking and finance. Under his chairmanship United Dominions' lifeboat borrowings were reduced from £500 million to under £100 million, and in 1981 the company, profitable once more, was sold to the Trustee Savings Bank. His contribution to this major rescue was recognized by a CBE in 1978—although there were many in the banking world who placed him even higher in their own estimates of achievement.

Len Mather's ebullience, sense of fun, and frankness brought him affection and influence not only at Midland but throughout the banking community. A large and avuncular figure, he was a committed supporter of Midland's sports and social societies and he enjoyed golf and bridge with the same enthusiasm. Outside the bank, he served as captain and chairman (for two terms) of Wildernesse Golf Club, and he was a vice-president of the Society of Lancastrians in London. Len Mather died in hospital at Tunbridge Wells on 8 May 1991, and was survived by his wife (who died on 18 September 1991).

EDWIN GREEN

Sources A. R. Holmes and E. Green, *Midland: 150 years of banking business* (1986) • E. Green, *Debtors to their profession: a history of the Institute of Bankers, 1879–1979* (1979) • B. Goldthorpe, 'Leonard Mather', *The Independent* (14 May 1991) • J. A. Brooks, memorial address, 24 July 1991, HSBC Group Archives, London, Midland bank archives [unpublished] • M. Reid, *The secondary banking crisis, 1973–1975* (1982) • HSBC Group Archives, London, Midland Bank archives

Archives Chartered Institute of Bankers, London • HSBC Group Archives, London

Likenesses photograph, c.1970, HSBC Group Archives, London, Midland Bank archives • photograph, c.1970 (with Queen Elizabeth II), HSBC Group Archives, London, Midland Bank archives • photograph, c.1972 (with C. E. Trott), HSBC Group Archives, London, Midland Bank archives • photographs, HSBC Group Archives, London, Midland Bank archives

Wealth at death £801,799: probate, 28 May 1991, *CGPLA Eng. & Wales*

Mather, Nathaniel (1630–1697), Independent minister, was the second son of Richard *Mather (1596–1669), minister, and Katherine (d. 1655), daughter of Edmund Holt. He was born in Much Woolton, Lancashire, on 20 March 1630 and in 1635 travelled with his family to Massachusetts, where his father became minister for the town of Dorchester. He attended Harvard College, and graduated MA in 1647. He soon returned to England, probably at the same time as his brother Samuel *Mather in 1650 and perhaps inspired by Oliver Cromwell's call for ministers in Ireland. On his arrival he wrote to his Harvard friend John

Rogers that "Tis a notion of mighty great and high respect to have been a New-English man, 'tis enough to gayne a man very much respect, yea almost any preferment' (*Mather Papers*, 4). And indeed Mather was soon placed in the ministry, serving first as an assistant to George Mortimer at Harberton, Devon, and then succeeding Mortimer in 1655. The next year he was presented by Oliver Cromwell to the living of Barnstaple in Devon. He befriended John Howe and became a member of the Devonshire Association. He also served as an assistant to the Devon commission of triers. During this period he married Mary (*d.* 1699x1706), daughter of the Revd William *Benn of Dorchester, England. Their only child died in infancy in 1660. Nathaniel was possibly one of the delegates at the congregationalists' Savoy conference in 1658.

Mather was disappointed by the Restoration and he was ejected in 1660. Like most nonconformists he was horrified by the 1661 uprising led by the radical Thomas Venner and signed the declaration against it. He then left England with the aid of Matthew Mead and became pastor of an English congregation in Rotterdam. Calamy says that he briefly ministered to a congregation in Sudbury, Suffolk, in 1671. When his brother Samuel died in 1671 he accepted the call to replace him as pastor of the New Row congregational church in Dublin. He laboured to bring some of Samuel's works to print and led a drive to raise funds in Dublin for the relief of New Englanders suffering from King Philip's War. In the early 1680s his congregation experienced difficulties due to declining membership and a division over the selection of the young Nathaniel Weld as Mather's assistant. In the aftermath of the Rye House plot of 1683 persecution of dissenters in Dublin was stepped up and Mather's congregation was forced to meet privately. In 1688 Mather left Ireland to accept the pastorate of the Lime Street Church in London, succeeding another former New Englander, John Collins, who had died in November 1687.

Nathaniel provided his brother Increase *Mather and other colonists with information on English and Irish religious and political developments and followed events in New England closely. In the 1660s he wrote a foreword to his father's treatise in favour of the half-way covenant, a move aimed at expanding numbers in New England churches by allowing the children of congregation members to join as partial or 'half-way' members before they had experienced religious conversion. He worked with Increase when the latter went to England in 1688–92 to seek a reversal of the policies that had led to the formation of the dominion of New England. Nathaniel is also believed to have worked with John Howe, George Griffith, and other dissenting clergymen in support of the revolution of 1688–9 which placed William of Orange on the English throne.

Nathaniel was initially a supporter of the 'heads of agreement', the union of congregational and presbyterian clergy that his brother Increase had helped to organize, and he was one of the original managers of the common fund for the support of such clergy in the early 1690s.

But while his brother Samuel had been a leading proponent of interdenominational co-operation, and Increase a supporter of the movement, Nathaniel was much less eirenic and more suspicious of presbyterians. He was one of the clergy who attacked Daniel Williams in 1693 for preaching Arminian views, a dispute which led to the break-up of the union and the withdrawal of the Presbyterian clergy from the jointly sponsored Pinners Hall lectureship. Mather was one of those then named to the vacant positions at Pinners Hall.

Mather died in London on 26 July 1697 and was buried in Bunhill Fields. He was survived by his wife, whose will of 29 April 1699 was proved in 1706. Mather was said to have been of a 'most amiable spirit and … an unaffected modesty' in his personal relationships, and as a preacher 'his aspect was venerable, his gesture pleasing, and his pronunciation agreeable', although 'in addressing sinners, he possessed an awfulness in his manner' and he had 'a certain heaviness in the pulpit, which rendered him unpopular' (Sibley, 159).   FRANCIS J. BREMER

Sources J. L. Sibley, *Biographical sketches of graduates of Harvard University*, 1 (1873) · F. J. Bremer, *Congregational communion: clerical friendship in the Anglo-American puritan community, 1610–1692* (1994) · *Calamy rev.* · R. L. Greaves, *God's other children: protestant nonconformists and the emergence of denominational churches in Ireland, 1660-1700* (Stanford, 1997) · *Mather papers, Collections of the Massachusetts Historical Society*, 4th ser., 8 (1868) · *DNB*
Archives American Antiquarian Society, Worcester, Massachusetts, corresp. and papers · Mass. Hist. Soc., corresp. and papers
Likenesses portrait (of Mather?), American Antiquarian Society, Worcester, Massachusetts

Mather, Richard (1596–1669), minister in America, was born in Lowton, within present-day Liverpool, son of Thomas Mather and his wife, Margarite Abrams, of whom little is known except that they were modest landowners. Mather attended the nearby grammar school at Winwick until, in 1611, the master there, William Horrock, recommended his pupil to be teacher at a newly organized school at neighbouring Toxteth Park. Here Mather was profoundly influenced by the pious puritan Edward Aspinwall and his family, with whom he boarded, and experienced his own spiritual conviction in 1614.

In 1618 Mather matriculated at Brasenose College, Oxford, but his experience there was unhappy, and he left within a few months to return to Toxteth Park, now as the minister in a newly built chapel. He was ordained in March 1619 by Thomas Morton, bishop of Chester. On 29 September 1624 Mather married Katharine (*d.* 1655), daughter of Edmund Holt of Bury, Lancashire. The couple purchased a house at Much Woolton and while there had three sons—Samuel *Mather (*b.* 13 May 1626), Timothy (*b.* 1628), and Nathaniel *Mather (*b.* 20 March 1630). In 1633 Mather was suspended after a frank exchange of views with Archbishop Richard Neile's visitor, who is said to have remarked: 'What … preach fifteen years and never wear a Surpless? It had been better for him that he had gotten Seven Bastards' (Mather, 27).

Having read of the recent experiments of puritans in Massachusetts with a congregational form of church polity, the Mathers decided to emigrate to New England; they reached Boston, Massachusetts, in 1635. They settled at Dorchester, where they had two more sons, Eleazar (*b.* 13 May 1637) and Increase *Mather (1639–1723). The local church was in its infancy. From his arrival Mather played a leading role in shaping Congregationalism, a role all the more remarkable because he alone of the leading ministers was without a university degree. The early years were contentious. Recent scholarship has emphasized the different views represented by John Cotton's emotional 'spiritism' and Thomas Shepard's logical intellectualism. Mather's particular genius was a knack for expressing arcane matters plainly and the ability to find a middle ground between the positions of brilliant and opinionated fellow clergymen. Not only did Mather reconcile their disputes, but he navigated between what his learned colleagues wanted and the often very different expectations of the lay members of churches.

The proof of Mather's growing stature among both the ministers and the governing magistrates was their use of him in the 1630s and 1640s to respond to inquiries from England about the new polity. Criticisms by Charles Herle, a former neighbour of Mather's, Samuel Rutherford, the Scottish apologist, and others who favoured a presbyterian polity, were countered in three responses published in London which served to define and justify the New England church and its congregationalist autonomy—*Church-Government and Church Covenant Discussed* (1643), *A Modest and Brotherly Answer to Mr. Charles Herle* (1644), and *A Reply to Mr. Rutherfurd* (1646). However, another, non-political side of Mather is evidenced by his contributions to *The Whole Book of Psalms* (1640), soon known as *The Bay Psalm Book*, the first book printed in English America, at the press in Cambridge, Massachusetts. It comprised translations of psalms from the Hebrew into metred English verse, so that they could be sung, after a fashion, in the puritan church services.

None the less Mather's most important achievement by far was to provide the working draft for the results of a synod in 1646, printed in 1649 on the Cambridge press as *A Platform of Church-Discipline*, and known since as the Cambridge *Platform*. Although a full third of the house of deputies voted against its adoption, possibly because in it the lay brothers and sisters lost authority to the elders, the Massachusetts general court adopted the *Platform* as an advisory model, and it became the standard description of the New England way. Mather's text reveals his own characteristic gentleness and leniency: 'The weakest measure of faith is to be accepted in those that desire to be admitted into the church. … Severity of examination is to be avoyded' (Walker, *Creeds*, 222).

Mather's first wife, Katharine, having died in Dorchester in March 1655, he married on 26 August 1656 John Cotton's widow, Sarah (*née* Hawkridge and widow, first, of John Story), thus uniting two of the most influential families in New England. Richard Mather's fifth son, Increase, later married Sarah Cotton's daughter Maria, and their eldest son was Cotton *Mather (1663–1728).

Richard Mather had always argued for leniency in regard to baptism, and he pleaded for open baptism to the children of non-members, of whom his son Timothy was one, if at least one of their grandparents was a church member. At a synod in 1662 this issue was fiercely debated. John Davenport, the last surviving great figure of Mather's own generation, and Mather's son Increase both opposed him, but the change won out among the ministers present, and the proposal, known ever since as the half-way covenant, passed, although it brought a storm of disapproval from lay members and was not generally adopted for another generation. In this as in parts of the Cambridge *Platform* Richard Mather was less puritanical than the general population.

In the 1660s Mather's health deteriorated. He lost the sight of one eye, his hearing failed, and he suffered from kidney stones. In 1669, while moderating one of the most contentious church disputes in New England history, one that resulted from the call of John Davenport from New Haven to the First Church of Boston, Mather collapsed. Within the week, on 22 April 1669, he died from the stoppage of urine, while in bed at home. He was buried in Dorchester. He was survived by his wife.

MICHAEL G. HALL

Sources I. Mather, 'The life and death of that reverend man of God, Mr. Richard Mather, teacher of the church in Dorchester in New England', *Two Mather biographies*, ed. W. J. Scheick (1989) · W. Walker, 'Richard Mather', *Ten New England leaders* (1969), 95–134 · B. R. Burg, *Richard Mather of Dorchester* (1976) · M. G. Hall, *The last American puritan: the life of Increase Mather, 1639–1723* (1988) · T. J. Holmes, *The minor Mathers: a list of their works* (1940) · W. Walker, *The creeds and platforms of Congregationalism* (1960) · S. Foster, *The long argument: English puritanism and the shaping of New England culture, 1570–1700* (1991) · J. Knight, *Orthodoxies in Massachusetts: rereading American puritanism* (1994)
Archives American Antiquarian Society, Worcester, Massachusetts, family MSS · Mass. Hist. Soc., bound MSS · Massachusetts State Archives, Boston | Boston PL, Prince collection · Harvard U., Harvard College archives
Likenesses J. Foster, woodcut, *c.*1670, Mass. Hist. Soc. · oils, American Antiquarian Society, Worcester, Massachusetts

Mather, Robert Cotton (1808–1877), missionary and translator, was born at New Windsor, Manchester, on 8 November 1808, the second son of James Mather, Congregational minister of Sheffield and formerly of Clapton. He was educated at Edinburgh and Glasgow universities (MA Glasgow 1831) and at Homerton College. On 1 June 1833 he was ordained at Lendal Chapel, York, and soon afterwards he sailed for India as a missionary with the London Missionary Society. He had recently married, and his wife, Elizabeth, *née* Sewell (d. 1879), a worshipper at Hew Court Chapel, Carey Street, London, accompanied him.

In September 1834, after ten months at Calcutta, Mather moved to Benares and then, in May 1838, to Mirzapur, where he founded a small but viable mission with churches, schools, and an orphan school press. Schools, he discovered, were almost the only way of establishing contacts with Hindus. He became an excellent Hindustani scholar and was well placed to witness and foster the emergence of Khari Boli Hindi as a major written language; a tiny magazine which he issued from his press, *Balko ke liye Phulo ka har*, was one of the first publications in

Robert Cotton Mather (1808–1877), by John Cochran (after Henry Room)

Khari Boli Hindi for children. He also revised the Bible in Urdu, in 1860, and compiled an English–Urdu New Testament, a Hindi Bible in roman script, an Urdu commentary on the New Testament, and the beginnings of another on the Old Testament. He saw his new Urdu Bible through the press while back in England on furlough in 1857–61 and was thus ideally positioned to issue speedily *The Indian Church during the Great Rebellion* (1859), compiled by his son-in-law, the Revd M. A. Sherring, who covered for Mather at Mirzapur during his absence. While the rebellion was still raging Mather also published *Christian Missions in India* (1858). In common with other evangelicals he viewed the rebellion as proof that God would let no political administration survive, no matter how sound, if it were not underpinned by true religion.

Mather returned to India in February 1861. In 1862 Glasgow University honoured him with the degree of LLD for his new Urdu Bible. He returned to England permanently in 1873 to work on his Bible commentaries and died at his home, 5 Torrington Park Villas, North Finchley, Middlesex, on 21 April 1877. After his death his widow, Elizabeth, who had published an Urdu dictionary of the Bible and many improving booklets in Hindustani for Indian women and children, joined the female mission at Mirzapur. She died on 29 March 1879. The Mathers' youngest son, Dr C. B. Mather, became a medical missionary in German East Africa.

C. W. SUTTON, rev. KATHERINE PRIOR

Sources B. H. Hadley, *Indian missionary directory*, 3rd edn (1886) · W. I. Addison, ed., *The matriculation albums of the University of Glasgow from 1728 to 1858* (1913) · S. Vedalankar, *The development of Hindi prose literature in the early nineteenth century, 1800–1856* (1969) · *Congregational Year Book* (1878) · *Bengal Directory and General Register* (1834)

Archives SOAS, Council for World Mission archives, official corresp.

Likenesses J. Cochran, engraving (after H. Room), NPG [*see illus.*]

Wealth at death under £1000: probate, 9 June 1877, *CGPLA Eng. & Wales*

Mather, Samuel (1626–1671), Independent minister, was the eldest son of Richard *Mather (1596–1669) and his wife, Katherine Holt (d. 1655). He was born at Much Woolton, Lancashire, on 13 May 1626, and emigrated with his parents and three brothers to New England in 1635. He was educated at Harvard College, graduating MA in 1643. He was the first graduate named a fellow. Mather preached to what became the Second Church of Boston (North Church), but refused an offer to become that congregation's pastor, choosing to return to England instead. His New England connections with leading English Independents secured for him a position as chaplain to Thomas Andrewes, the lord mayor of London, who had earlier been a member of Thomas Goodwin's Arnhem congregation. Mather preached at Gravesend and Exeter and in 1650 became a chaplain at Magdalen College, Oxford, where Thomas Goodwin was president. He became a close friend of Sidrach Simpson and accompanied Simpson to Scotland with the English commissioners. During the next two years he preached occasionally at Leith.

In 1654 Philip Nye recommended Mather as a preacher to the council of state in Ireland. Two years later he was called to the ministry of the church of St Nicholas in Dublin, where most Dublin aldermen worshipped; he was ordained in a congregationalist ceremony. His colleague at St Nicholas was Samuel Winter. Mather was also a lecturer at Christ Church, a fellow of Trinity College, Dublin, and one of the leading puritan clergy in the country, with a close relationship to Henry Cromwell during the latter's administration of Irish affairs. He served as a commissioner for approbation of ministers in co. Cork. For part of this time he had the companionship of his brother Increase *Mather, who received an MA from Trinity in 1658. In that same year Samuel married a sister of Sir John Stevens. They had four or five children but only one, named Catherine, lived to maturity.

Mather accepted the accession of Charles II but preached a sequence of two controversial sermons in September 1660, urging Charles to assume the role of a reforming Hezekiah and identifying as needing reform the use of the clerical surplice, signing with the cross in baptism, kneeling at communion, bowing to the altar, use of cathedral music, and other targets common to the puritan agenda. He warned that if such reforms were not initiated and, worse, 'If you super-adde the sin of Persecution to the sin of Superstition, you will be quickly ripe for final Ruine', as 'the Lord himself will fight against you' (Greaves, 56). He was prohibited from further preaching and ordered to deliver his sermon notes, but instead sent them to New England where they were published in 1670 through the efforts of his brother Increase.

Deprived of his living, Mather returned to his Lancashire homeland and ministered at Burtonwood until ejected in 1662. He was advised that the repression of dissent was less thorough in Ireland and returned to Dublin, where he preached regularly to a congregation on New Row. Though briefly incarcerated in 1664 for holding a conventicle, he was able to continue his ministry. In 1666 or the following year Mather preached a sermon justifying withdrawal from the Church of Ireland, 'the wicked party'. He urged co-operation between congregationalist, Baptist, and presbyterian dissenters, particularly in *Irenicum, or, An Essay for Union*, which was published posthumously in 1680. In that work he pointed with approval to the fact that the dissenters attended each others' services in Dublin. But Mather's eirenic interests were limited to orthodox Calvinists. He was critical of the Fifth Monarchist Jeremiah Marsden and preached *A Defence of the Protestant Christian Religion Against Popery* (1672). Another of his interests was typology, and his sermons on *The Figures or Types of the Old Testament* were published by his brother Nathaniel *Mather in 1683.

Mather's first wife died in 1668 and by the time he wrote his will on 18 August 1671 he was married to Hannah, whom he named one of his executors. They seem to have had no children and Mather's daughter, Catherine, was his heir. He died on 29 October 1671 and his widow proved his will on 7 March 1672. He was soon succeeded by his brother Nathaniel as pastor of the New Row congregation.   FRANCIS J. BREMER

Sources J. L. Sibley, *Biographical sketches of graduates of Harvard University*, 1 (1873) • F. J. Bremer, *Congregational communion: clerical friendship in the Anglo-American puritan community, 1610–1692* (1994) • *Calamy rev.* • R. L. Greaves, *God's other children: protestant nonconformists and the emergence of denominational churches in Ireland, 1660–1700* (Stanford, 1997) • *Mather papers*, Collections of the Massachusetts Historical Society, 4th ser., 8 (1866) • *DNB* • L. Withington, 'Will of Samuel Mather', *New England Historical and Genealogical Register*, 52 (1898), 366–8
Archives American Antiquarian Society, Worcester, Massachusetts, corresp. and papers • Mass. Hist. Soc., corresp. and papers
Likenesses portrait, American Antiquarian Society, Worcester, Massachusetts
Wealth at death £900—personalty: probate, 7 March 1672, will as of Oxmonton (present-day Oxmanstown), Dublin, 18 August 1671

Mather, William (*fl.* 1657–1708), pamphleteer and schoolmaster, was born in Bedford. Nothing is known about his family, other than that his grandfather was a mayor of Hull. Appointed a surveyor of highways, Mather trained as a schoolmaster, and kept a private school in Bedfordshire. The latter post inspired his chief literary work, an enhanced primer entitled, *A Very Useful Manual, or, The Young Man's Companion*, which was printed in London in 1681. Eclectic in range, the text contained advice on a diverse array of subjects from the traditional curriculum, and incorporated additional exercises in husbandry, housekeeping, and legal matters. Mather intended that his manual should be read in tandem with the Bible, and emphasized, in his address to the reader, the importance of self-awareness in achieving purity in religion (sig. A2v).

Popular and respected, the text ran to twenty-four editions, and Mather's son Samuel, who died at the age of twenty-two, added verses and fourteen further chapters to the fourth edition in 1695.

Initially a conformist within the Church of England, about 1661 Mather with his wife became a Quaker, a shift of commitment and loyalty which dominated Mather's later works. In November 1657 he was imprisoned for thirty-two weeks for non-payment of tithes and, later, in 1683, after a prosecution in the ecclesiastical court, he was subjected to a second period of imprisonment on a writ *de excommunicato capiendo* (Besse, 1.3, 11). By this time the Quaker population of Bedford was estimated at thirty (ibid., 1.xxxviii), and Mather resorted to writing pamphlets as a means of vindicating his own position and attracting support. In 1694 his two texts, *An Instrument from that Little Stone Cut out of the Mountain without Hands* and *A Novelty, or, A Government of Women Distinct from Men*, were distributed in order to promote Mather's own mistrust of segregated meetings (which could ultimately result in 'Unscriptural Government'), and to justify his personal patronage of Margaret Everard, who had preached of God's grace to a crowd gathered in his own house in June 1694.

In the following year Mather offered chronological discussions of Quakerism from its semantic origins to the core of its creed (*A Brief Character of the Antient Christian Quakers*), but a simultaneous sense of disillusionment can also be detected from this date. This culminated in published attacks advertising the flawed nature of scripture (*Of the Quakers Despising the Holy Scriptures*, 1700), and denouncing the efforts of 'Lifeless Preachers … who are Taught to preach neither by Grace nor Holy Scriptures' (W. Mather, *An Answer to the Switch for the Snake*, 1700, 9). In 1701 this breach became permanent, and Mather, careful throughout to reassure that he entertained no quarrels with individual Quakers, articulated his public dissatisfaction with their spirit:

> That the Substance and Summ of the Religion of the Quakers, turns upon one Single Hinge, viz That the Spirit by which they are moved, and inspired, is really the Holy Ghost, or the Universal Spirit of God … we have clear evidence, and can make it appear to all, who are not wilfully blind, that their Spirit is not the Holy Ghost, but a Spirit of Error. (Mather)

Consonant again with the teachings of the English church, Mather sought to stress that his absence had been in part due to his desire for martyrdom and his love of habit and harmony (pp. 1–5). His final work, *A letter from a Quaker-preacher to a church-man* [Mather] (*who had been a Quaker forty years.*) *With the church-man's answer* was printed in 1708. It is not known when Mather died.

ELIZABETH HARESNAPE

Sources W. Mather, *A vindication of William Mather and his wife; who having lived about forty years professed Quakers, have now renounced that perswasion, and returned to the communion of the Church of England* (1701) • *A letter from a Quaker-preacher to a church-man (who had been a Quaker forty years.) With the church-man's answer* (1708) • J. Whiting, *A catalogue of Friends books; written by many of the people called Quakers from the beginning or first appearance of the said people* (1708) • J. Besse,

A collection of the sufferings of the people called Quakers, 1 (1753), 3, 11 · *DNB* · *BL cat.* · Wing, *STC*

Mather, Sir William (1838–1920), mechanical engineer and textile equipment manufacturer, was born in John Street, Manchester, on 15 July 1838, the son of William Mather senior (*d.* 1858) and his wife, Amelia, daughter of James Tidswell of Manchester. The family operated a small machine works and iron foundry in Salford which had been established about 1824 by William Mather senior and his father, Colin Mather, who had come to Manchester from Montrose.

After attending a private day school in Salford, William Mather became an apprentice in the family business between 1850 and 1852. Meanwhile he continued his schooling at Accrington under a Swedenborgian teacher, the Revd Dr Bagley. His studies under Bagley included a spell in Dresden (1854–5), before he returned to the Salford factory. By 1852 Colin Mather had formed a partnership with William Platt (owner of the Salford Iron Works) for the manufacture of boilers, pumps, and textile machinery. In 1858, on the death of his father, William Mather became assistant manager in the works and then, in 1863, partner. On 2 September 1863 he married Emma Jane (*b.* 1842/3), the daughter of Thomas Watson of Highbury, London, at the Swedenborgian chapel in Argyle Square, London. Soon afterwards, Mather and his growing family (the couple eventually had nine children) settled at a residence in Lower Broughton, which was close to the works.

In the following decades Mather assumed control of the business. He became sole manager in 1871 and senior partner in 1877 (when the older members of the Mather and Platt families retired). He was appointed chairman in 1892, when Mather and Platt became a private limited company, with paid-up capital of £135,000 (Mather holding two-thirds of the shares). Under his direction the business expanded steadily, the number of employees swelling from about 300 when he became partner to about 4000 before the First World War. Mather and Platt was also consistently profitable, especially in the decade before 1914, when dividends never fell below 10 per cent. In 1900 Mather and Platt acquired land at Newton Heath and by 1912 most of the chief departments had been removed there. The company's prosperity stemmed partly from the enormous growth of the Lancashire cotton industry (with Mather and Platt's reputation resting upon its ability to supply most of the equipment for a modern mill). However, it also drew on Mather's commitment to scientific methods and technical education, his interest in overseas markets, and his promotion of good labour relations.

A competent engineer (he became a member of the Institution of Mechanical Engineers in 1867), Mather designed many pieces of equipment for textile finishing (such as the steam-ager in the 1870s and the chain-mercerizer in 1898). The firm diversified into electrical machinery, food manufacturing equipment, and fire-fighting equipment. In 1885 Mather and Platt undertook under licence the manufacture of Grinnell sprinklers for extinguishing fires in cotton mills and warehouses. It

built and marketed Edison dynamos, and in 1889 it began supplying electrical equipment for the London underground railway. In 1894 Dr Edward Hopkinson joined the firm from Siemens to supervise electrical machine manufacture. Outside the company Mather founded the Chloride Electrical Storage Company in 1891 and in 1895 the Castner-Kellner Company Ltd, manufacturing batteries, chlorine, and caustic soda.

The company's reputation was international, reflecting Mather's indefatigable overseas journeys in Europe and America. He was a particularly frequent visitor to Russia, having first visited the country in 1860. Over the next fifty years he made up to fifty trips to Russia, leading him to say that 'I must have spent nearly half my life there' (Mather, 32). The company also had offices in Berlin, Bombay, and Calcutta, and Mather took a personal interest in trade with China through his vice-presidency of the British Engineers' Association.

Mather was profoundly interested in education. His son attributed this to his father's apprenticeship in the works, where he came 'into contact with [ordinary skilled workmen] and learned to respect them' (Mather, 89). In 1873 William Mather started the Salford Iron Works evening science school for his staff. When a royal commission on technical education was set up in 1881, Mather became one of its special commissioners and reported on education in the USA and Canada. He published several pamphlets on technical education and labour relations. He was one of the advocates of the 8-hour day in the 1890s and experimented in 1893 with a scheme for a 48-hour working week. Holiday, welfare, and sports facilities were also launched at Mather and Platt.

William Mather supported the development of Owens College (later Manchester University) by various benefactions and the establishment of a department of Russian language and literature (the university awarding him an honorary LLD in 1908). He was the first president of the Association of Technical Institutions, formed in 1894. In the Sudan, which he visited in 1902, he donated workshops and equipment to Gordon College, Khartoum.

Mather sat as Liberal MP for the southern division of Salford (1885–6), for the Gorton division of Lancashire (1889–95), and for the Rossendale division of Lancashire (1900–04). Though not a noted parliamentarian or debater, he helped to push through the Technical Instruction Act (1890) and the Local Taxation (Customs and Excise) Act (1890), which raised funds (notably the so-called 'whisky money') made available to local authorities for subsidizing technical education. He was knighted in 1902 for helping to reorganize the War Office during the Second South African War, and was sworn of the privy council in 1910.

After 1896 the purchase of country and London residences signalled an end to his active business career. About 1908 he moved to Bramble Hill Lodge, at Bramshaw in the New Forest. He relinquished the chairmanship of Mather and Platt in 1916 at the age of seventy-eight, and made his last visit to his native city in the following year. He died at Bramble Hill Lodge on 18 September 1920, leaving an estate of £405,841; his son, Loris Emerson Mather

(1886–1976), became manager of Mather and Platt. William Mather was buried at Prestwich parish church on 22 September 1920. GEOFFREY TWEEDALE

Sources L. E. Mather, *Sir William Mather, 1838–1920* (1926) • H. Coles, 'Mather, Sir William', *DBB* • *Manchester Guardian* (20 Sept 1920) • *Manchester Guardian* (23 Sept 1920) • *Lancashire leaders: social and political* (1897) • m. cert. • d. cert. • *CGPLA Eng. & Wales* (1920)
Archives U. Durham L., diaries of journeys to Sudan and India | Bodl. Oxf., letters to Sir William Harcourt and Lewis Harcourt • Museum of Science and Industry, Manchester, Mather and Platt records • U. Durham L., corresp. with Sir Reginald Wingate
Likenesses photographs, repro. in Mather, *Sir William Mather*
Wealth at death £405,840 16s. 9d.: probate, 27 Nov 1920, *CGPLA Eng. & Wales*

Mathers, Samuel Liddell (1854–1918), occultist, was born on 8 January 1854 at 11 De Beauvoir Place, Hackney, Middlesex, the son of William Mathers, a merchant's clerk, and his wife, Mary Ann, formerly Collins (d. 1885). From 1866 to 1870 he received a classical education at Bedford School, before going to live with his widowed mother at Bournemouth, where he worked as a clerk and developed his twin passions of 'magic and the theory of war' (Yeats, 183). His occult studies were first guided by his neighbour and fellow freemason, Frederick Holland, and they were admitted together, in 1882, into the Societas Rosicruciana in Anglia, where Mathers was befriended by William Wynn Westcott, with whom he later created the Hermetic Order of the Golden Dawn.

Mathers's military zeal was expressed by joining a local volunteer regiment and by translating and adapting a French military manual, published in 1884 as *Practical Instruction in Infantry Campaigning Exercise*. He also took up both fencing and boxing and delighted in aiding the authorities—as a civilian—in quelling public disturbances. It was in the context of his militarism that his less desirable personality traits first appeared. Fantasies about his social status are apparent in an early photograph in which he is wearing the uniform of a volunteer lieutenant (he was never commissioned), and his inability to accept defeat with a good grace was recorded by A. E. Waite, who noted that Mathers debarred a potential candidate for the Golden Dawn who had beaten him in a fencing match. Nor could Mathers accept that others matched his knowledge of occultism: he rejected Holland in the early 1880s because he was the better scholar, and Westcott ten years later for the same reason. In this respect Mathers was transparent; Waite described his learning as 'undigested' (*Occult Review*, 199) and to W. B. Yeats he 'had much learning but little scholarship, much imagination and imperfect taste' (Yeats, 87). His imagination was nowhere more apparent than in his Celtic pretensions—already in 1878 he was adding MacGregor to his name and styling himself comte de Glenstrae—which were to become an increasingly important part of his self-perception.

After the death of his mother in January 1885 Mathers moved to London and became active in occult circles. By 1887 he had published his first esoteric work, *The Kabbalah Unveiled*, and was helping Westcott to develop the rituals that formed the basis of the Hermetic Order of the Golden Dawn. In March 1888 they brought the order into being and, in company with William Woodman, became its first chiefs. One of the first initiates was the artist Mina Bergson (1865–1928), the sister of the philosopher Henri Bergson, who became Mathers's wife in June 1890 and lent her artistic talents to the creation of a second order, the Rosae Rubeae et Aureae Crucis. The rituals of this wholly magical inner order were entirely the work of Mathers who was, without question, a ritualist of genius.

However, magicians must eat, and Mathers was desperately poor despite his writing; he had published a small book on tarot cards in 1888 and a masterly edition of *The Key of Solomon the King* in 1889. Escape from poverty came by way of Annie Horniman, who was both a friend of Mina Mathers and a prominent member of the Golden Dawn. She obtained a post for him at her father's private museum and made the couple a regular allowance even when they settled in Paris in May 1892. Mathers fitted well in *fin de siècle* Paris, moving in its occult circles and establishing, in 1894, the Ahathoor Temple of the Golden Dawn. He was also becoming arrogant and quarrelsome towards London members of the order, engineering Westcott's removal from office, demanding ever more money from Annie Horniman, and expelling her in 1896 when she cut off his allowance.

By this time Mathers was showing signs of paranoia, but he continued to work on magical texts—his most significant work, *The Book of the Sacred Magic of Abra-Melin the Mage*, appeared in 1898—and he set up a new occult activity in Paris, the Rites of Isis. He also continued to direct the activities of the Golden Dawn, albeit in an increasingly erratic manner. Matters came to a head in 1900 when Mathers wrote to Florence Farr telling her that Westcott had forged the documents on which the order's authority was founded. In the furore that followed Mathers refused to justify his allegation, expelled the 'rebels' and sent Aleister Crowley to take possession of the London headquarters. On their part the members expelled Mathers and had Crowley bodily ejected. Mathers fired off a barrage of manic, abusive letters but for all practical purposes he had lost his influence. Only the rump of the Golden Dawn remained loyal to him and he was taken in by two adventurers, a couple named Horos, whose criminal activities opened the order to public ridicule at their trial in 1901.

Nor was this the end of Mathers's woes. Two of his unpublished works, an edition of a magical text, the *Lesser Key of Solomon*, and a *Book of Correspondences*, were 'borrowed' by Crowley and published under his name in 1904 and 1909. Even worse, in 1910 Crowley went on to publish the rituals of the Golden Dawn in his journal, *The Equinox*, Mathers having failed to stop the publication by legal means. Mathers lapsed into complete obscurity. When he died at his home, rue Ribera, Paris, on 20 November 1918 of influenza, no one outside occult circles noticed his death. This was in keeping with his own expectations. In 1898 he had declared: 'for the opinion of the ordinary literary critic who neither understands nor believes in Occultism, I care nothing' (Mathers, *Abra-Melin*, xxxviii).

R. A. GILBERT

Sources E. Howe, *The magicians of the Golden Dawn* (1972) · I. Colquhoun, *Sword of wisdom: MacGregor Mathers and the Golden Dawn* (1975) · R. A. Gilbert, *Revelations of the Golden Dawn* (1997) · M. K. Greer, *Women of the Golden Dawn: rebels and priestesses* (1995) · W. B. Yeats, *Autobiographies* (1955) · A. E. Waite, *Shadows of life and thought* (1938) · A. E. Waite, *Occult Review*, 29/4 (April 1919) · S. L. Mathers, *The kabbalah unveiled* (1926), introduction · S. L. Mathers, *The book of the sacred magic of Abra-Melin the mage* (1898) · b. cert. · m. cert.
Archives NRA, priv. coll., Golden Dawn archives · Societas Rosicruciana in Anglia, London, High Council Library, Westcott MSS · Warburg Institute, London, Yorke collections
Likenesses Nesbitt, photograph, 1882, priv. coll. (NRA), Golden Dawn archives; repro. in Colquhoun, *Sword of wisdom* · Russell & Sons, photograph, 1889, Societas Rosicruciana in Anglia, High Council Library, Westcott MSS · M. Mathers, oils, *c*.1896, priv. coll.

Matheson, Sir Alexander, first baronet (1805–1886), merchant and banker, was born on 16 January 1805 at Attadale, Ross-shire, the eldest of the seven children of John Matheson and Catherine, daughter of Captain Donald Matheson of Shinness, and sister of Sir James Matheson, first baronet (1796–1878).

Following his education at the University of Edinburgh, Matheson pursued a career in commerce in Asia, first at Calcutta, and subsequently at Canton (Guangzhou), where he joined his uncle James's firm of Jardine, Matheson & Co. Founded in 1832, that partnership was an agency house of major importance, undertaking marketing for correspondent merchants in Britain, India, and parts of south-east Asia. As the firm developed, it was also active in finance, insurance, and shipping. Its most profitable commodity was opium, which was sold, illegally, both at Canton, and along the coast of China; but the firm avoided drawing on its own account for large-scale speculation in opium.

A partner in the firm from 1835, Matheson found himself in the midst of the incidents which led to the First Opium War (1839–42). In the late 1830s the Chinese imperial government was determined to crush the opium trade, and for that purpose it appointed Lin Zexu imperial commissioner at Canton. Arriving in March 1839, Lin demanded the surrender of all the opium stocks of foreign merchants, and he held as hostages James Matheson and fifteen other merchants. James sent Alexander down to the Gulf of Canton to manage the firm's opium fleet during the crisis. Thus, when the British superintendent of trade, under severe pressure from Lin, directed the merchants to surrender their opium supplies, Alexander Matheson was responsible for gathering Jardine Matheson's quantity (7000 chests) for destruction by Chinese officials.

Not long after the release of the hostages in May 1839, Matheson returned to London to pursue the company's claim for compensation from the British government. He and his partner, William Jardine (1784–1843), lobbied for a forceful response by the government, and both men testified before the parliamentary committee on China. During this stay in Britain, Matheson married, in 1840, Mary, the daughter of James Macleod, a neighbour of the Mathesons in Ross-shire. However, his young wife died early in 1841.

By the spring of 1841, Matheson was *en route* for China,

accompanying the new British plenipotentiary, Sir Henry Pottinger. He returned to the Far East a lonely man. Often experiencing poor health, he was also characteristically dyspeptic in temperament. Arriving at Macao in August 1841, Matheson resumed his role in the firm's business. In the course of the First Opium War, British forces had taken possession of Hong Kong, and as early as the spring of 1842, Matheson was writing to a London correspondent that Hong Kong 'has already thrown Macao into the Shade' (Matheson to T. C. Smith, 10 May 1842, CUL, letter-book C6/2). The island was formally acquired by the treaty of Nanking (Nanjing; 1842). Two years later, Jardine Matheson moved its headquarters to Hong Kong, and the staff celebrated their first night there with a dinner at Alexander's bungalow in Happy Valley.

In the aftermath of the war, Britain's trade opportunities in China expanded dramatically, but opium itself remained an illegal commodity. Alexander Matheson hoped that Pottinger would not succeed in getting the opium trade legalized. He wrote to a major supplier in India: 'You may rest assured that if ever the trade is legalized, it will cease to be profitable from that time. The more difficulties attend it, the better for you and us' (Matheson to Jamsetjee Jeejeebhoy, 10 Sept 1843, CUL, letter-book C6/3). With the trade in opium increasing after the war, he was contemptuous of those at home who objected to it on moral grounds. 'The cry against the drug trade in England is certainly very absurd, & I sincerely hope the saints will fail in their attempt to interfere with it' (ibid., 28 March 1843).

Following James Matheson's departure from China early in 1842 Alexander Matheson became the *taipan* of Jardine Matheson, dividing his time between Hong Kong and Macao. He remained the senior partner until 1852, but he left China in 1847, arriving in London as a banking crisis was about to jeopardize many of the major financial institutions in the City. Upon discovering that the firm of Magniac Jardine was vulnerable, Matheson engineered the rescue of that firm, with financial assistance from his uncle and from the portion of William Jardine's estate inherited by Andrew Jardine. In the following year the firm was reorganized as a new partnership, Matheson & Co., which was to function as the agency house in London for Jardine Matheson. Alexander Matheson served as senior partner of Matheson & Co. into the 1870s. Under his leadership that firm was vital to the growth of Jardine, Matheson & Co. as a commercial giant in the Far East. As Jardine's London representatives, Matheson & Co. imported into Britain a broad range of commodities, including teas and silks, and exported to the Far East coal, machinery, metals, wines, and liquors. Moreover, they recruited personnel to staff the expanding Jardine enterprises.

Just after his return from China in 1847, Matheson was elected MP for the Inverness burghs, and held that seat until 1868, when his uncle retired from the Commons. He thereupon succeeded his uncle as MP for the county of Ross and Cromarty, which he represented as a Liberal until 1884. He served as a deputy lieutenant for Ross and Cromarty, for Inverness, and for the City of London.

Matheson's purchases of Scottish estates had begun during his brief return home in 1840–41, with the acquisition of 6000 acres south of Lochalsh. The ancestral lands of his family at Lochalsh, Ross-shire, were added in 1851, and ten years later he purchased the ancestral properties at Attadale. He spent nearly £0.75 million buying estates in Ross-shire, where he held over 220,000 acres; the total purchase and improvement costs of his Scottish estates exceeded £1.46 million.

Matheson served as a director of the Bank of England, 1847–84; he was also for many years chairman of the Highland Railway, and was credited with a central role in the construction of the railways throughout northern Scotland. In 1882, in reward for his public service, he was awarded a baronetcy. His second marriage, in 1853, was to Lavinia Mary (d. 1855), the youngest daughter of Thomas Stapleton of Carlton, Yorkshire. They had a son and a daughter. In 1860 Matheson married his third wife, Eleanor Irving (d. 1879), the daughter of Spencer Perceval and Anna Macleod. This marriage produced three sons and four daughters.

Although he left China in 1847, Alexander Matheson was head of the firm from 1842 to 1852. When his cousin, Donald Matheson, resigned on conscience grounds in 1848, Matheson participation in the senior management on site in China effectively ended. None of Alexander's sons pursued a business career in the Far East. The Mathesons focused their attention on Matheson & Co. in London for another thirty years until the Jardine family became predominant in that firm. Matheson apparently experienced financial problems in his last four years, but it is not known whether these were caused by ill-judged investments or the effect of the agricultural depression on his vast land holdings. He nevertheless left estate in the UK worth over £600,000 at his death on 26 July 1886, at 38 Hill Street, off Berkeley Square, London. Sir Kenneth Matheson, his son and heir, was required to part with the greater portion of the lands, but the family was able to retain possession of the ancestral estates in Ross-shire including Attadale.   RICHARD J. GRACE

Sources A. Matheson, personal letter-book, CUL, Jardine, Matheson & Co. MSS · J. Matheson, personal letter-book, CUL, Jardine, Matheson & Co. MSS · A. Mackenzie, *History of the Mathesons*, 2nd edn (1900) · M. Keswick, ed., *The thistle and the jade: a celebration of 150 years of Jardine, Matheson & Co.* (1982) · J. Steuart, ed., *Jardine, Matheson & Co., afterwards Jardine, Matheson & Co. Limited: an outline of the history of a China house … 1832–1932* (privately printed, Hong Kong, 1934) · *CGPLA Eng. & Wales* (1887)
Archives CUL
Likenesses G. Chinnery, portrait; formerly at Number One House, East Point, Hong Kong · marble bust, Matheson & Co., 3 Lombard Street, London
Wealth at death £643 11s. 4d.—effects in England: probate, 6 Sept 1887, *CGPLA Eng. & Wales*

Matheson, George (1842–1906), theologian and hymn writer, known as 'the Blind Preacher', born at 39 Abbotsford Place, Glasgow, on 27 March 1842, was the eldest son in the family of five sons and three daughters of George Matheson, a prosperous Glasgow merchant. His mother, Jane Matheson, his father's second cousin, was the eldest daughter of John Matheson of the Fereneze print works at Barrhead. As a child he suffered much from defective eyesight, and while still young he became blind. This calamity did not deter him from an early determination to enter the ministry.

After attending two private schools, Matheson went in 1853 to Glasgow Academy, where, notwithstanding his disability, he gained a competent knowledge of the classics, French, and German, and carried off many prizes. At Glasgow University, which he entered in 1857, he had a distinguished career, graduating BA in 1861 (the last occasion on which the degree was granted) with 'honourable distinction in philosophy', and proceeding MA in 1862. In the latter year he passed to the Divinity Hall, where he was much influenced by John Caird, the Hegelian philosopher.

In January 1867, after being licensed by the presbytery of Glasgow, he was appointed assistant to the Revd Dr MacDuff of Sandyford church, Glasgow, and on 8 April 1868 became minister of Innellan church on the shores of the Firth of Clyde, then a chapel of ease in the parish of Dunoon, but through Matheson's efforts soon erected into a parish church. There Matheson was minister for eighteen years, and his preaching gifts rapidly matured. For a time he grew dissatisfied with the Calvinist theology in which he was brought up, and according to his own account was inclined to reject all religion (Macmillan, 121–2). But a study of Hegelian philosophy saved him from agnosticism. Innellan afforded Matheson leisure and tranquillity for study and writing. In 1874 he published anonymously *Aids to the Study of German Theology*, in which he sought to show that German theology was positive and constructive. The work passed into a third edition within three years. In 1877 appeared *The Growth of the Spirit of Christianity* in two volumes, a philosophical presentation of the history of the church to the Reformation. In *Natural Elements of Revealed Theology* (Baird lecture, 1881) he used arguments from comparative religion to defend Christianity. In his *Can the Old Faith Live with the New? or, The Problem of Evolution and Revelation* (1885), he argued that the acceptance of evolution was calculated to strengthen belief in the Christian faith. While at Innellan, Matheson also began a long series of devotional books which had a wide appeal, and wrote much sacred poetry. A selection of his verses appeared as *Sacred Songs* in 1890. The third edition (1904) included the hymn 'O love that wilt not let me go', which long enjoyed great popularity.

In October 1885 Matheson preached at Balmoral to Queen Victoria, by whose direction the sermon was printed for private circulation. Meanwhile in 1879 he declined an invitation to succeed Dr John Cumming of Crown Court Church, London, but in 1886 he became minister of St Bernard's parish church, Edinburgh. His ministry in that charge was successful, his influence being especially strong among the professional classes. Despite his blindness, he was a dramatic preacher. In 1897 poor health led him to seek assistance in the parish, and the joint pastorate lasted until July 1899, when he finally retired. The later years of his life were devoted almost entirely to study and authorship. He was made DD of Edinburgh in 1879, and LLD of Aberdeen in 1902, but declined the Gifford lectureship at Aberdeen. In 1890 he was elected a fellow of the Royal Society of Edinburgh.

Matheson's many devotional works included *My Aspirations* (Cassell's Heart Chords series, 1883) and *Words by the Wayside* (1896), both of which were translated into German. His contributions to theology other than those cited included, among many, *The Psalmist and the Scientist, or, The Modern Value of the Religious Sentiment* (1887), which popularized the views set forth in *Can the Old Faith Live with the New?*; *The Distinctive Messages of the Old Religions* (1892); *The Lady Ecclesia* (1896), an allegorical treatment of the development of the spirit of Christ in the church and in the individual; and *Studies of the Portrait of Christ* (vol. 1, 1899; vol. 2, 1900), a popular book, characteristic of Matheson's thought. Matheson, whose learning was varied rather than profound, was a conspicuous and effective representative of liberal theology. He was regarded as invariably radiant and cheerful. He died at Avenell House, North Berwick, East Lothian, after a brief illness, on 28 August 1906, and was buried in the family vault in Glasgow necropolis on 1 September. He was unmarried. He shared his home with his eldest sister, Jane Gray Matheson, to whom he attributed much of his happiness and success.

W. F. GRAY, rev. H. C. G. MATTHEW

Sources D. Macmillan, *The life of George Matheson* (1907) · G. Matheson, *Times of retirement … with a biographical sketch by D. Macmillan* (1901) · *CGPLA Eng. & Wales* (1907)
Likenesses O. Leyde, oils; at St Bernard's parish church, Edinburgh, 1912
Wealth at death £37,845 3s. 1d.: Scottish confirmation sealed in London, 11 Jan 1907, *CGPLA Eng. & Wales*

Matheson, Hilda (1888–1940), intelligence officer and director of radio talks, was born on 7 June 1888 at 13 Dealtry Road, Putney, the elder of two children of Donald Matheson, Presbyterian minister, and his wife, Margaret Orr. Since both parents were Scottish the family spent most of their summer holidays in the Scottish highlands where Hilda became a skilled mountaineer. For four years she boarded at St Felix School in Southwold and her history teacher persuaded her to study history at Cambridge. But she had to leave school, aged eighteen, when her father suffered a breakdown and the family moved to the continent. Within three years Hilda became proficient in French, German, and Italian, having lived in France, Stuttgart, and Florence. The family returned to England in 1908 when her father was appointed chaplain to Oxford University's Presbyterian undergraduates, and she enrolled in the Society of Oxford Home Students, now known as St Anne's College, to read history. As a day student she experienced little of the social side of college life, although she participated in the dramatic society, playing a young king in *Eagerheart* and then Andromache in Gilbert Murray's version of *The Trojan Women*; she was also active in the Student Christian Movement.

Matheson's first employment, in 1911, was as part-time secretary to H. A. L. Fisher at New College, the husband of her economic history tutor, who had just been appointed editor of the Home University Library. She later worked in a similar capacity for David George Haworth, keeper of the Ashmolean Museum. On the outbreak of war in 1914 she joined the Voluntary Aid Detachment in Wandsworth, but in 1916 was assigned to military intelligence (MI5), and ended her war service working for the British military control office in Rome. Then she worked for Lord Lothian, who recommended her as political secretary to the first female member of parliament, Nancy, Lady Astor. Astor introduced her to the realms of politics, literature, and society. It was while representing Lady Astor that Matheson first met John Reith, who offered her a senior position in the fledgeling British Broadcasting Company. She accepted the appointment, at a salary of £900 a year, with Lady Astor's blessing, as well as a large farewell cheque, in 1926.

Nominally employed to assist J. C. Stobart administer the BBC's education department, Matheson soon became the first director of talks and established the first news section when the company became the British Broadcasting Corporation in 1927. 'Always ready to try something different' (Woodruff, 81), she sought the advice of Lord Lothian and Nancy's husband, Viscount Astor, in helping to determine how the BBC could become a major provider of the news. They recommended that she employ Philip Macer-Wright, the assistant editor of the *Westminster Gazette*, and his eleven-page report, 'Suggestions for the improvement of the BBC news service', which he submitted in September 1928, was referred to constantly during the ensuing decades as the BBC refined and expanded its news presentation.

At a time when all broadcast talks had to be scripted, Matheson devoted much time to helping prospective broadcasters express themselves clearly by teaching them how to 'write for the ear'. Genuinely interested in ideas as well as people, Matheson saw that BBC talks offered a unique opportunity to bring to the microphone the leading figures of the day, such as H. G. Wells, G. B. Shaw, Winston Churchill, and Harold Nicholson, who later portrayed her in his 1932 novel *Public Faces* as a 'woman of tact, gaiety and determination … [whose] office table was unencumbered [who] liked being a female [and] displayed this liking in every curve of her tiny body' (Nicholson, 1946, 24).

Matheson's colleague Lionel Fielden described her two great qualities as leadership and encouragement, and offers the following account of what it must have been like working during the early days of the BBC at Savoy Hill:

> The microphone was a gateway to great things; but in what form and to what audience? As the first Director of Talks you held in your hands (at one guinea per talk, then, and the rest persuasion) the most powerful instrument devised by man to mould public opinion for good or ill … [W]ork was the innumerable letters and interviews which you packed into six years, the reputations you built and fostered, the ceaseless struggle for wider horizons of toleration, the hours

of rehearsal and experiment, the frequent 'crises', the everlasting search for ideas, and the whole queer business of discovering, by trial and error, the 'technique' of the spoken word over the air.   (Matheson)

Harold Nicholson was one of those whom Matheson introduced to the new medium of broadcast talks, in 1928, as was his wife, Vita Sackville-*West (1892–1962), with whom she immediately became involved in an intense lesbian relationship. This did not end until 1931, which coincided with Matheson's resignation from the BBC. Hilda's love letters to Vita, of over 800 pages, remain in Nigel Nicholson's hands.

The primary reason for Matheson's resignation was a change in policy imposed by Reith. The regime of talks she had instituted, by 'left-wing liberals', evoked criticism in the 'right-wing' daily press. To deal with these objections Reith imposed a regime of censorship, which even embargoed reviews of new novels, declaring that he wanted to instil a sense of 'responsibility to the older generation' (explaining Fielden's remark about her departure as ('the Blimps were on the warpath and you and your kind were doomed'; Matheson, 36). For her part, Matheson believed it was 'equally part of our responsibility to provide for the intellectual needs of the intervening generations' and stated that she 'could not loyally administer a policy which seemed to be turning into a reversal of what I had been instrumental in helping to build up' (Astor MS 1416/1/1/962).

Matheson's resignation was announced in December 1931 and caused a stir in the columns of Liberal and left-wing newspapers, and Lady Astor even tried to persuade the MP Walter Elliott to use his influence to have Matheson appointed to the BBC board of governors (Astor MS 1416/1/1/962, 9 Dec 1931). But Matheson was already involved in new ventures, rejecting an offer from Leonard Woolf to administer the Hogarth Press (Leonard Woolf archives, Sx MS 13) so that she could become the radio critic on the Astor-owned *Observer* and write a column in the *Week-End Review*. Matheson's revenge on Reith was sweet when her old friend H. A. L. Fisher commissioned her to write a book for the Home University Library, *Broadcasting*, which was published in 1933 and is still quoted. As soon as this was published Lord Lothian, at the Royal Institute of International Affairs, persuaded the Carnegie Trust to finance an important research study on British colonial policy, and Matheson was paid £400 a year for working two days a week. Its director was Sir Malcolm (later Lord) Hailey, whose work on the Government of India Act prevented him from taking up his duties until 1935, and ill health during 1937–8 meant that the burden of producing the *African Survey*, of over 2000 pages, published in 1938, devolved on Matheson, for which she was made OBE in 1939.

After leaving the BBC in January 1932 Matheson developed a stable relationship with the poet Dorothy Violet *Wellesley, duchess of Wellington (1889–1956), and made her home on Wellesley's estate in Sussex. It was Dorothy who suggested a recuperative visit to the Riviera in December 1938, and there they met W. B. Yeats and his wife, George. In 1937 Dorothy had co-edited a series of the *Broadsheet* with W. B. Yeats, who regularly stayed at her country estate, Penn on the Rocks. In what was to be the last week of his life Yeats asked Hilda to compose a setting for one of Dorothy's poems, which she sang for him. A longtime member of the Bach Choir, Hilda counted Dame Ethel Smyth among her close friends, and also the Australian composer and writer W. J. Turner, who was a fellow guest at the soirée with Yeats and later figured prominently in Matheson's last venture.

By the summer of 1939 Matheson was again involved in military intelligence, having turned down an offer of the principalship of her alma mater. She became founder director of the joint broadcasting committee on a salary of £1000 per annum, responsible for arranging the broadcasting by foreign radio stations of British information and opinions, recording programmes in German and Italian, and scripting programmes for dispatch to neutral countries. Among others, her staff included Guy Burgess, W. J. Turner, Elspeth Huxley, and the former foreign director at the BBC, Isa Benzie. By February 1940 there were over thirty on her staff, out of a projected forty-five, and the committee's programmes were broadcast regularly in eight neutral European countries and three in Latin America. As well as setting this up, in competition to the BBC, Matheson was also responsible for initiating a publishing venture entitled Britain in Pictures, designed to counteract the publication in Germany of illustrated books glorifying the German empire and its soldiers, musicians, poets, cities, and mountains, distributed in neutral countries. Almost 140 volumes of Britain in Pictures were eventually published. Dorothy Wellesley was a director, alongside Hilda and W. J. Turner, and the first books were published from Rocks Farm, Withyham, in Sussex, which was Matheson's home on Dorothy's estate.

On 14 October 1940 Matheson wrote to Lady Astor soliciting her recommendation of an American publisher for this venture. But on 30 October she died of Graves' disease (a toxic goitre), following surgery for partial thyroidectomy, at Kettlewell Hill Nursing Home, Horsell, Surrey. Dorothy Wellesley erected a memorial to 'that wonderful friend [who] understood poetic genius' at Penn on the Rocks, inscribed 'Amica amicorum'. Michael Carney, Matheson's biographer, believed the *African Survey* was her most enduring work, which British colonial policy makers regularly consulted until the 1960s, and extensive comments on radio drama from her book *Broadcasting* figure in Tim Crook's *Radio Drama: Theory and Practice* (1999).

FRED HUNTER

Sources [M. Matheson], ed., *Hilda Matheson* (1941) • W. J. West, *Truth betrayed* (1987), 116–18 • overseas and emergency publicity expenditure committee paper no. 82, joint broadcasting committee, 1939, PRO, T162/858/E39140/4 and 6 • M. Carney, *Britain in pictures: a history and bibliography* (1995) • M. Carney, 'Stoker': the life of *Hilda Matheson OBE, 1888–1940* (privately published, Pencaedu, Llangynog, Wales, 1999) • D. Wellesley, *Far have I travelled* (1952) • F. Hunter, 'Hilda Matheson and the BBC, 1926–40', *This working-day world: women's lives and culture(s)*, ed. S. Oldfield (1994), 169–74 • P. Macer-Wright, 'Suggestions for the improvement of the BBC news service', 24 Sept 1928, BBC WAC, R/28/177/1 • U. Reading, Lady

Astor archive, MS 1416/1/1/962 · U. Sussex, Leonard Woolf MSS, Sx MS 13 · H. Nicholson, *Public faces* (1932); repr. (1946) · private information (2004) · V. Glendinning, *Vita: the life of Vita Sackville-West* (1983) · *The Times* (1 Nov 1940) · *The Star* (1 Nov 1940) · *New Statesman and Nation* (6 Nov 1940) · *The Spectator* (22 Nov 1940) · D. Woodruff, 'Debates and discussions: a criticism', *BBC Quarterly*, 1/3 (Oct 1946), 81 · d. cert. · b. cert. · T. Crook, *Radio drama: theory and practice* (1999)
Archives BBC WAC | U. Reading, Lady Astor archive
Wealth at death motor car to brother · £9374 10s. 7d.: probate, 6 March 1941, *CGPLA Eng. & Wales*

Matheson, Hugh Mackay (1821–1898), overseas trader and Presbyterian lay supporter, was born on 23 April 1821 in Edinburgh, son of Duncan Matheson (1784–1838), advocate and afterwards presiding magistrate of Edinburgh, and his wife, Annabella (1796x9–1829), daughter of Thomas Farquharson of Howden. He had an elder brother and two sisters. He was educated in Leith, in Edinburgh at the high school, and at Cunningham's academy, and later in part-time classes in logic and moral philosophy at Glasgow University. He had a devout upbringing and was convinced from an early age of his need to seek God's guidance in all matters by Christian prayer and scriptural readings.

Matheson became a clerk in the Glasgow merchant house of James Ewing in 1836, and in 1843 he was invited to join the Hong Kong trading firm of Jardine Matheson, in which his uncle, afterwards Sir James Matheson, was a partner. He declined, apparently out of scruples at the firm's involvement in the Chinese opium trade, but accepted a post with their London correspondents, Magniac, Jardine & Co. In an attempt to improve his health he took leave of absence in 1845, and spent eighteen months touring the Orient and studying British trade there. His meetings with both merchants and missionaries convinced him that Christianity must be the salvation of the East: Europeans were superior in civilization to oriental people (so he concluded) because of their Christian faith. He returned to Britain fired with an ardour to spread biblical teachings; for the rest of his life he was committed to the Presbyterian church's China mission, of which he was successively treasurer and convenor.

Magniac Jardine was reconstituted as Matheson & Co. in 1848 with Hugh Matheson as managing partner. Based in Lombard Street, its chief business initially was importing China tea and silks on Jardine Matheson's behalf, but in the 1850s the firm began exporting Lancashire cotton piece-goods and other commodities to China as well as importing Indian commodities to Britain. During the 1860s the firm managed Indian tea estates, and was involved with Jardine Matheson in promoting railways and cotton mills in China. It indirectly profited from the opium trade which Matheson had publicly indicated that he found 'objectionable' (*The Times*, 3 Feb 1870).

After the shah of Persia in 1872 granted an exclusive concession to Baron Julius de Reuter to build and operate all Persian railways, tramways, and canals, and to exploit natural resources, Matheson attempted to raise the finance to exploit this concession. He was more successful in 1873 when he formed an international consortium to buy from the Spanish republican government the state-owned pyrites mines at Rio Tinto. Having paid £3.68 million, the Rio Tinto Company began working the concession in 1874 with Matheson as its first chairman. Under Matheson's leadership the company surmounted various financial, marketing, and political obstacles to become the world's largest supplier of sulphur and copper. The Rio Tinto mines were technologically advanced and well-managed (mainly by Scots; these expatriate managers were also responsible for introducing soccer to Spain).

As a businessman Matheson was shrewd at appraising risks and bold at hazardous moments. He was a hard negotiator who could be ruthless in pressing his advantages and was adept at winning the confidence of others. As a Christian, Matheson was protective of his Spanish employees, and provided houses, churches, stores, medical services, and schools (he was personally involved in the curriculum). However, his concern for the spiritual and economic welfare of his workers did not prevent him from justifying the use of Spanish troops to repress their political aspirations.

In the 1840s Matheson was shocked by the decline of Presbyterianism in England and as soon as he had the means dedicated himself to its revival. At the time of his death he was acknowledged as Presbyterianism's leading lay advocate south of the Tweed. He financed Presbyterian newspapers, educational initiatives, church building, and doctrinal work. Holy Trinity Church, near his home in Hampstead, was erected with his money. For many years, when in London, he went from his City office to Whitechapel or Spitalfields at the end of his working day to rescue prostitutes and drunkards. He was a strict sabbatarian. His religion was bigoted: he was an entrenched opponent of Roman Catholicism, and had an even more violent antagonism against ritualism and Anglo-Catholicism. Although given to many private charities he was thought harsh and offensively righteous even by some fellow Presbyterians. He was exceedingly conservative in his domestic arrangements and social attitudes but was president of the Hampstead Liberal and Radical Association and was much besought as a radical parliamentary candidate. He supported Irish home rule and the widening of electoral suffrage. Notwithstanding his commercial interests he hated the jingo policies of the Conservatives and was never a business imperialist. He enjoyed high standing in the City of London but pointedly did not join its hierarchy. Though a deputy lieutenant and magistrate in the City, and chairman of the committee of London merchants during the Anglo-Chinese negotiations of 1870, he desired neither the lord mayorship nor the accompanying baronetcy. He was, unusually for a Liberal, a bimetallist.

In 1855 Matheson married Agnes Ann (1830–1900), daughter of David McFarlen of the Indian Civil Service. They had a son and two daughters. In 1858 he bought an estate in the Scottish highlands, Elswick House, near Strathpeffer, in Ross-shire, along with nearby property at Lower Scatwell. King Alfonso XII of Spain invested him as a knight grand cross of the order of Isabella the Catholic in 1882. He died of heart disease on 8 February 1898, at Heathlands, Hampstead. His widow published the *Memorials of Hugh M. Matheson* in 1899.

RICHARD DAVENPORT-HINES

Sources A. A. Matheson and Rev. J. O. Dykes, *Memorials of Hugh Mackay Matheson* (1899) · D. Avery, *Not on Queen Victoria's birthday: the story of the Rio Tinto mines* (1974) · C. E. Harvey, *The Rio Tinto Company: an economic history of a leading international mining concern, 1873–1954* (1981) · E. Bond, *Working his purpose out* (1948) · *The Times* (10 Feb 1898) · *The Times* (3 Feb 1870) · *The Times* (19 March 1870) · *CGPLA Eng. & Wales* (1898) · C. Harvey, 'Matheson, Hugh Mackay', *DBB* · Burke, *Gen. GB*
Archives CUL, Jardine, Matheson & Co. MSS · PRO, Foreign Office MSS · London, Rio Tinto Zinc Corporation, MSS
Likenesses portrait, repro. in Avery, *Not on Queen Victoria's birthday*, 138
Wealth at death £96,169 18s. 7d.: probate, 23 April 1898, *CGPLA Eng. & Wales*

Matheson, Sir (Nicholas) James Sutherland, first baronet (1796–1878), merchant and politician, was born on 17 November 1796 at Shinness, near Lairg, Sutherland, the second son in the family of three sons and five daughters of Captain Donald Matheson of Shinness, and his wife, Katherine, daughter of the Revd Thomas MacKay, minister of Lairg. He was educated at Inverness Royal Academy, the Royal High School, Edinburgh, and the University of Edinburgh, after which he spent two years learning commerce with a London agency house.

India attracted Matheson about 1815, and, with free merchants' indentures from the East India Company, he joined the agency house of Mackintosh & Co. at Calcutta. But his first business experience there was unsuccessful and inauspicious; he therefore left that firm and formed a partnership in 1818 with an elderly merchant named Robert Taylor. Their ventures had only limited success, and within two years Taylor died. While sailing as supercargo on ships carrying their country trade goods between India and China, Matheson first visited Canton (Guangzhou) during the tea season of 1818, and he was settled in the area of Macao and Canton from 1820. By 1821 he held an appointment as Danish consul at Canton, which put him beyond the jurisdiction of the East India Company and allowed him to fly the Danish flag on ships he engaged.

As a partner in the firm of Yrissari & Co., which he helped to form at Macao in 1821, Matheson served as agent for merchants in Singapore and India; and, dealing in export and import commerce, he speculated in the opium trade which, although illegal in China, offered the greatest profits.

After the death of Xavier Yrissari in 1826, Matheson continued the firm briefly, but wound up its affairs in 1828. In that year, a fellow Scot, William Jardine, brought Matheson into the firm of Magniac & Co., reconstituted in 1832 as Jardine, Matheson & Co. Of the two, Jardine was the dour, disciplined business planner, while Matheson was the more mercurial and intellectually curious entrepreneur. Their combined experience built the most influential agency house in Canton. Jardine Matheson engaged in banking, shipping, insurance, and marketing, principally on commission for businesses remote from China. Their

Sir (Nicholas) James Sutherland Matheson, first baronet (1796–1878), by Henry Cousins, pubd 1837 (after James Lonsdale)

legitimate trade may have exceeded their opium trade, but it was their hard-currency resources from opium sales which gave them primacy among the foreign merchants in Canton.

Official Chinese policy confined the commerce of British merchants (and nearly all other foreign merchants) to Canton, and channelled their transactions through a loose organization of Chinese merchants known as the 'Cohong', who functioned as middlemen to control the foreign trade. When Matheson returned to Britain for an extended visit in 1835–6, he articulated his ideas on free trade in a booklet entitled *The Present Position and Prospects of British Trade with China* (1836). Resentful of the haughty contempt shown towards foreign merchants by the Chinese imperial government, he argued that providence had blessed the Chinese with a vast portion of the most desirable parts of the earth, from which they were trying to exclude foreigners, in defiance of the laws of nature. To correct that situation he urged the British government to make a resolute approach to the Chinese emperor in order to establish a proper commercial relationship.

No such arrangement had been achieved by 1839, when Jardine retired from China, leaving Matheson as the managing partner. In March 1839, two months after Jardine's departure, imperial commissioner Lin Zexu confiscated foreign inventories of opium, and forcibly detained sixteen merchants, including Matheson. Upon their release in May, Lin expelled Matheson from China for ever, but the Scot retreated first to Macao and then to Hong Kong, to resume opium sales in secret, with 200 per cent profits on fresh supplies from India. During the First Opium War (1839–42), after Hong Kong was occupied by a British expedition, Matheson purchased for his firm the first plots of land offered for sale on the island.

For medical reasons (asthma) Matheson retired to London in 1842, and there found his partner terminally ill. When Jardine died in 1843, Matheson succeeded him as Liberal MP for Ashburton, Devon, 1843–7. He then sat for Ross and Cromarty, 1847–68. He also pursued finance, and in 1848 helped to reorganize the banking firm of Magniac Jardine, which as Matheson & Co. became a financial giant in the City, and within which he became known as 'Uncle James'. On 9 November 1843 he married Mary Jane, daughter of Michael Henry Perceval, of Spencer Wood, Canada, a member of the Quebec legislative council. They had no children. His nephews succeeded him in directing Jardine Matheson and Matheson & Co.

In his China days Matheson had joined with Jardine and others to organize the Medical Missionary Society in Canton and a hospital in Macao. He repeatedly showed kindness toward old British merchants, newly down on their luck. Also, with a small hand press, in 1827 he started the *Canton Register*, China's first English-language newspaper. He had begun acquiring extensive estates in Sutherland before he left China, and in 1844 he purchased the Isle of Lewis, largest of the Outer Hebrides, from the Seaforth Mackenzies. At Stornoway he and Lady Matheson built the Lews Castle and developed elaborate gardens on the castle grounds. As proprietor of Lewis, Sir James was considered to be a kind laird in his efforts to improve conditions of life in many ways. For his generous relief to the people of Lewis during the great famine of the late 1840s he was made a baronet in 1850. However, in later years the estate management of his tyrannical factor, Donald Munro, led to much discontent among the population of the island and caused the so-called 'Bernera riot' in 1874. That incident led to Munro's disgrace, but residual hard feeling diminished somewhat the people's memory of Sir James's generosity.

Matheson was appointed lord lieutenant and sheriff principal of the county of Ross in 1866. Elected FRS in 1846, he led an active public life into his eighth decade, and for many years served as chairman of the Peninsular and Oriental Steam Navigation Company.

Sir James died at the spa town of Menton in the south of France on 31 December 1878. He was buried, not far from his birthplace, in the cemetery at Lairg under a funeral monument strikingly reminiscent of imperial India where his career as a merchant began. He was survived by his wife.   RICHARD J. GRACE

Sources CUL, Jardine, Matheson & Co. MSS · J. Matheson, 'Brief narrative', CUL, Jardine, Matheson & Co. MSS [concerning events at Canton, March–April 1839 during hostage crisis] · J. Matheson, *The present position and prospects of British trade with China* (1836) · monument, 1880 [at Lews castle, Stornoway, erected by Lady Matheson] · Valuation rolls of the county of Ross and Cromarty, 1868–9 · Valuation rolls of the county of Ross and Cromarty, 1872–3 · Valuation rolls of the county of Ross and Cromarty, 1877–8 · M. Keswick, ed., *The thistle and the jade: a celebration of 150 years of Jardine, Matheson & Co.* (1982) · J. K. Fairbank, *Trade and diplomacy on the China coast: the opening of the treaty ports, 1842–1854*, 2 vols. (1953); repr. in 1 vol. (Cambridge, MA, 1964) · P. W. Fay, *The opium war* (1975) · M. Greenberg, *British trade and the opening of China, 1800–42* (1951) · J. S. Grant, *A shilling for your scowl* (1992) · A. Mackenzie, *The history and genealogy of the Mathesons*, 2nd edn (1900) · private information (1995) · D. MacDonald, *Lewis: a history of the island* (1978) · *CGPLA Eng. & Wales* (1879)

Archives CUL, Jardine, Matheson & Co., private letter-books | CUL, Jardine, Matheson & Co., private letter-books, William Jardine · CUL, Jardine, Matheson & Co., letter-books, Yrissari & Co. · CUL, Jardine, Matheson & Co., letter-books, Taylor & Matheson · NMM, Peninsular and Oriental Steam Navigation Co.

Likenesses H. Cousins, engraving, pubd 1837 (after J. Lonsdale), NPG [*see illus.*] · group portrait, Lodge Fortrose, Stornoway, Lewis · photographs, Stornoway, Lewis · portraits, repro. in Keswick, *The thistle and the jade*

Wealth at death £169,685 6s. 11d.: confirmation, 28 May 1879, *CCI* · under £25,000—effects in England: probate, 9 May 1879, *CGPLA Eng. & Wales*

Mathew, Anthony (1905–1976). *See under* Mathew, David James (1902–1975).

Mathew, David James (1902–1975), Roman Catholic bishop, was born at Lyme Regis, Dorset, on 15 January 1902, the elder son of Francis James Mathew, barrister and novelist, and his wife, Agnes Elizabeth Anna, daughter of James Tisdall Woodroffe, advocate-general of Bengal from 1899 to 1904, who was a son of the rector of Glanmire, co. Cork. His father was a nephew of Sir James Mathew and a great-nephew of the Roman Catholic priest Theobald Mathew (1790–1856), and thus belonged to a prominent family in co. Tipperary.

Mathew was educated at Osborne and Dartmouth, serving as a midshipman in the last year of the First World War. In 1920 he went to Balliol College, Oxford. Awarded a second class in modern history (1923), he received a war memorial scholarship and then the Amy Mary Preston Read scholarship, which enabled him to spend two more years in Oxford. His research, which was to bear fruit partly in *The Reformation and the Contemplative Life* (1934), written with his younger brother Anthony (known as Gervase) [*see below*], attracted him to the Carthusian life. He put aside the intention of entering for a fellowship at All Souls and went to the Beda College in Rome to prepare to go as a priest to the Charterhouse in Sussex. He was ordained under his own patrimony in 1929, but ten months as a novice at Parkminster proved that he was not to be a monk—the chief obstacle apparently being his inability to master plainchant. He used to say that for the Carthusian life one needed to have no imagination: it was suitable for the products of provincial grammar schools who were good at games—but how much he wished that he was one of them!

Mathew now offered himself to the diocese of Cardiff. He spent four happy years as a curate at St David's Cathedral, enjoying the pastoral work in the dock district. In 1933 he was awarded the degree of LittD by Trinity College, Dublin, for *The Celtic Peoples and Renaissance Europe*, his first book; it was, at 500 pages, his most substantial, and dealt, in a series of impressionistic studies, with the effects on Roman Catholics on the Celtic fringe of the Elizabethan settlement and the Counter-Reformation. In

1934, since he had a small private income, he was able to become chaplain to Roman Catholics in the University of London, a post which he held until 1944. He divided his days between the British Museum and his widely spread flock, some of whom found his elliptical humour baffling but many became lifelong friends.

In 1936 Mathew published *Catholicism in England, 1535–1935*, subtitled 'Portrait of a minority: its culture and tradition'. Crisp, intuitive, and witty, this represents David Mathew at his best. It provided English Roman Catholics with a fresh sense of their identity and helped thereby to articulate the confidence of a whole generation, many of whom also had Oxford connections. Mathew's characteristically toneless and deadpan epigrams extended even to judgements on the recently deceased Cardinal F. A. Bourne: 'In such a character, with its strength and mastering sense of duty, it is almost inevitable that a desire for centralization should have been found and a tendency to concentrate authority. Monarchical institutions appealed to him' (Mathew, 243).

In 1938, at the age of thirty-six, Mathew became bishop auxiliary of Westminster. Bourne's successor, Arthur Hinsley, evidently taking advice from Mathew's circle of friends, may well have been surprised by his own decision. As the war came, he clearly placed more and more trust in his young auxiliary. An intrepid pastor in the blitz, Mathew was also at the centre of the Catholic laity in London who sought greater participation in national life, particularly through the Sword of the Spirit movement.

Hinsley was thought by some to have wanted Mathew to succeed him, but at his death in 1943 Bernard Griffin was appointed. Though loyally accepted, it is impossible to exaggerate the blow that Griffin's preferment was to Mathew. At that time, auxiliary bishops had to be reappointed by the new ordinary: Griffin reappointed Mathew, after some delay, but made no difficulties when the Vatican chose him as apostolic visitor to Ethiopia in 1945 (his cousin had been judicial adviser to the emperor throughout the war). This was obviously a trial run for the Vatican diplomatic service. Mathew's report to the Holy See was hailed as brilliant: it included an unprecedented account of Ethiopian flora and fauna. In 1945–6 he delivered the Ford lectures in Oxford, published as *The Social Structure in Caroline England* (1948). But Griffin, on his visit to Rome late in 1945, had persuaded the authorities to choose Mathew as apostolic delegate to the British colonies in Africa, east and west, and so, with the dignity of archbishop of Apamea, he moved to Mombasa in 1946.

His seven years as a diplomat in Africa were undoubtedly successful, although to him they felt like exile. He carried out the Vatican's policy of preparing the way for native bishops. His greatest triumph was the appointment in 1953 of Rugambwa as bishop (vicar apostolic of Lower Kenya); he was later the first African cardinal. In 1953 Mathew also published the last volume of his trilogy of novels—*In Vallombrosa* (1950–53)—and signified that he had served in Africa long enough. The Vatican offered him the important nunciature at Bern. His refusal displeased Pius XII and seemed incomprehensible to Monsignor

Montini. But Mathew, having apparently demonstrated his qualities as a pastor and an administrator, dearly wanted a diocese in England; the prospect of a career which would no doubt lead to high office in some Vatican dicastery did not attract. He returned home in 1953 at the age of fifty-one and at the height of his powers, apparently not knowing, or anyway unwilling to believe, that 'lack of the common touch' and 'impaired health' had already become the accepted reasons that excluded him from consideration. His cryptic manner in conversation and increasingly eccentric appearance no doubt worked against him, but in 1954 he was appointed Roman Catholic bishop-in-ordinary to the forces: his early connection with the Royal Navy served as a pretext. The bishops were thus able to accommodate him, while many senior officers learned to dread entertaining him in the mess. His curial office was in Stanhope Lines, Aldershot, but his quarters were, for most of this period, in the ladies' annexe of the Athenaeum.

In 1960 the Vatican called upon Mathew to become secretary to the preparatory commission on missions for the forthcoming general council of the church, a demanding task which excited him, although he found living in Rome wearisome. A great deal had happened in the few years since he left Africa: forces which he had himself helped to release made him something of an anachronism. When the council opened in 1962 he was not even elected a member of the commission, let alone reinstated as secretary. He attended the first session of the council and was horrified, when he cast his vote against substantial changes in the Roman liturgy, to find what sort of bigoted theological company he was keeping. In March 1963 he resigned as bishop to the forces and went into retirement.

Mathew spent the next ten years with Lord and Lady Camoys at Stonor, near Henley-on-Thames, publishing several books in that genre of light biography which he had perfected—*James I* (1967), *Lord Acton and his Times* (1968), *The Courtiers of Henry VIII* (1970), and *Lady Jane Grey* (1972). He could now make frequent visits to Oxford to stay with his brother at Blackfriars or take him travelling in England or the Mediterranean. The two brothers, always in correct clerical dress, though otherwise distressingly dishevelled and unkempt, were often to be seen in the streets of Oxford, sometimes arm in arm, as they made their way somewhat ponderously to a small French restaurant for a special celebration, or pottering over to Blackwell's to leaf through the latest book by one of their many friends. The enigmatic silences, the sudden hilarity which ended with the disconcerting abruptness with which it began, and the oracular manner, which the brothers shared, alarmed many people; but many others found in their love for one another, and in the absolute simplicity of their religion, a touchstone of fidelity.

To save it from demolition in 1938 David Mathew bought the ruins of Thomastown Castle, co. Tipperary, the mansion where Theobald Mathew was born. He was proud to have inherited his chalice, but pictures also show a strong family likeness between David Mathew and the apostle of temperance—'a broad, solid-looking man, with grey hair, mild, intelligent eyes, massive rather aquiline nose and countenance', as Thomas Carlyle described him when he saw him in Liverpool in 1843 (*Collected Letters*, 16.315).

As his strength failed Mathew moved to the Hospital of St John and St Elizabeth in London, where he was able to receive his friends to the last. He died there on 12 December 1975, a few weeks after the death of Cardinal Heenan, whose catafalque he visited on his last outing. There was thus no archbishop of Westminster to preside at Mathew's funeral in Westminster Cathedral. He was buried at Downside Abbey in Somerset.

His younger brother, **Anthony Mathew** (1905–1976), Dominican friar and scholar, who received the name in religion of Gervase when he entered the Dominican order, was born in Chelsea, London, on 14 March 1905. He was educated privately, partly by his father, with whom he also travelled a good deal in the Mediterranean immediately after the First World War. He went to Balliol College, Oxford, in Hilary term 1925 and read modern history, in which he received a third class in 1927. In 1928 he joined the Dominican friars and was ordained priest in 1934 at Blackfriars, Oxford, where he spent the rest of his life. He began to lecture on the Greek fathers in 1937. His published work ranged over many fields—classical antiquity, Byzantine art, historical theology and patristics, fourteenth-century English literature and society. He deserves to be remembered as a main creator of Byzantine studies at Oxford. In 1947 he was appointed university lecturer in Byzantine studies, a post which he held until 1971 and for which he never drew a salary. During this period he took part in archaeological investigations in east Africa and southern Arabia and offered advice on medieval art in Cyprus and Malta. In 1963, with Roland Oliver, he edited the first volume of a *History of East Africa* sponsored by the Colonial Office. In the same year he published *Byzantine Aesthetics*, no doubt his most important book. In nearly forty years of teaching in Oxford he drew on his polymathy to illuminate hundreds of students in various disciplines. He conducted many retreats, particularly for nuns, and had great gifts of insight as a confessor. His collaboration in most of his brother's writing was always generously acknowledged. He suffered from emphysema for many years and survived his brother by four months, almost to the day, dying in Oxford on 4 April 1976.

FERGUS KERR, rev.

Sources *The Times* (13 Dec 1975) · *The Times* (18 Dec 1975) · *The Times* (6 April 1976) [Anthony Mathew] · *The Times* (20 April 1976) [Anthony Mathew] · *The Times* (11 May 1976) [Anthony Mathew] · private information (1986) · *The collected letters of Thomas and Jane Carlyle*, ed. K. J. Fielding, 16–18 (1990) · D. Mathew, *Catholicism in England*, 2nd edn (1948) · *CGPLA Eng. & Wales* (1976)
Archives Downside Abbey, near Bath, archives, corresp., and papers | St Ant. Oxf., Middle East Centre, corresp. with W. R. Hay
Wealth at death £43,524: probate, 5 Aug 1976, *CGPLA Eng. & Wales*

Mathew, Sir George Benvenuto [*formerly* George Byam] **Buckley-** (1807–1879), politician and diplomatist, was the son of George Mathew (1760–1846), of the Coldstream Guards, and his wife, Euphemia, the daughter of J. Hamilton. In 1835 he substituted the name of Benvenuto for that of Byam and in 1865 he added that of Buckley (on inheriting West Indian estates). Mathew entered the army in 1825, joining the light infantry; by 1833 he was a captain in his father's regiment. He retired from the army in 1841 as captain in the Grenadier Guards. In 1835 he married Anne Hoare (1808–1872), the only child and heir of the banker Henry Hoare of Stourhead and his wife, Charlotte, *née* Dering. This marriage, which enabled him to enter politics, was soon in difficulties, ending in what Mathew called a 'Scotch divorce' in 1849 (Disraeli, 253n.). His second wife, whom he married in 1850, was another heiress, Rosina Adelaide Handley, the daughter of J. C. Handley, and his third was the daughter of J. W. Gerard of New York (she was also the niece and coheir of General Sumner of Boston). In 1835 Mathew was elected MP for Athlone, as a tory. In 1838 he became MP for Shaftesbury when J. S. Poulter's election was declared void on petition, but he failed by seventeen votes to hold the seat in 1841.

Mathew, frustrated in his political career, was appointed governor of the Bahamas in 1844, beginning a long career in the Americas. He was consul at Charleston from 1850 to 1853 and at Philadelphia from 1853 to 1856, when his exequatur was removed by the president of the USA. After serving in the Black Sea (1856–8), he was secretary and then chargé d'affaires of the legation first in Mexico and afterwards for the Central American republics, for whom he was minister from 1861 to 1863. He moved to be minister to Colombia (1865–6), Argentina (1866–7), and Brazil (1867 – April 1879). He was made CB in 1863 and KCMG in May 1879, and lived latterly at Leamington Spa. He died at 16 Suffolk Street, London, on 22 October 1879. His various marriages produced at least five sons and two daughters. His was a rather miserable career, with the loss of his seat not compensated by his minor diplomatic appointments, despite the wealth supplied by his marriages.

H. C. G. MATTHEW

Sources *Colonial Office List* · *FO List* · *Benjamin Disraeli letters*, ed. J. A. W. Gunn and others (1982–), vol. 4
Archives Glamorgan RO, Cardiff, copies of dispatches · Lpool RO, corresp. | BL, letters to Sir Austen Layard, Add. MSS 39994–39120 · Bodl. Oxf., corresp. with Sir John Crampton · Bodl. Oxf., letters to Lord Kimberley · Lpool RO, corresp. with fifteenth earl of Derby
Wealth at death under £3000: probate, 29 Nov 1879, *CGPLA Eng. & Wales*

Mathew, Sir James Charles (1830–1908), judge, was born on 10 July 1830 at his father's residence, Lehenagh House, co. Cork, Ireland, the eldest son of Charles Mathew and his wife, Mary, daughter of James Hackett of Cork. Father Theobald *Mathew, the temperance campaigner, was his uncle, and it was largely because of his influence that Mathew, after being taught at a private school at Cork, was allowed in 1845 to enter Trinity College, Dublin, an exceptional occurrence at that time for the child of a Roman Catholic family. Here, without changing his religion, he graduated as senior moderator and gold medallist in 1850. Having obtained an open studentship in 1850, on 6 June

1851 Mathew entered as a student at Lincoln's Inn. He read in the chamber of Thomas Chitty, the special pleader, and was called to the bar on 26 January 1854. He did not take silk before being made a bencher in Easter term 1881.

Mathew's first ten years of practice were slow in progress, but he found scope for his debating and argumentative skills at the Hardwicke Society, which he helped to found, and he became renowned on the home circuit for his sarcastic humour. When business at last came his way, his thorough knowledge of the intricacies of pleading and practice put him in a good position to take advantage of his new opportunities. He had a strong aptitude for grasping the essentials of a case and, impatient with mere technicalities, applied his common sense to good effect in the courts. His services were in particular demand at the Guildhall sittings, where the heavy City special jury cases were then tried. After Mr (later the Right Hon.) Arthur Cohen took silk in 1874, Mathew and Charles (later Lord) Bowen were invariably in demand for these cases. In 1873 Mathew was among the Treasury counsel for the prosecution of Arthur Orton in the celebrated Tichborne case.

In March 1881, though still a junior counsel, Mathew was appointed a judge in the Queen's Bench Division and was knighted on 1 April of the same year. After an uncertain start as a judge when he showed himself prone to impatience on the bench, he eventually emerged as one of the most respected *nisi prius* judges of his time. Despite little previous experience in criminal law matters, he developed acuteness and common sense, although he was occasionally thought by his colleagues to lean too far to the side of the defendant. His most notable contributions, however, were in the commercial court.

Having already served on a royal commission appointed to inquire into the question of costs and legal procedures before his elevation to the bench, Mathew persuaded the other judges of the Queen's Bench to assent in 1895 to the formation of a special list for commercial cases to be heard in a particular court, presided over by the same judge sitting continuously and with a free hand as to his own procedure. Mathew, who was the first and the most successful occupant of this position, swept away written pleadings, narrowed the issues, and allowed for no dilatoriness on the part of counsel. His own judgments were widely approved for their concision and terseness by both lawyers and businessmen, and earned him a good deal of esteem among his colleagues. His hopes to reform the chancery courts along the same lines, in order to make what he considered to be a cumbersome medieval survival efficient and modern, were less successful, however, and many resented him for criticizing the *status quo*.

Shortly after the return of the Liberal Party to office in August 1892, Mathew was made chairman of a royal commission on evicted tenants in Ireland, with particular reference to their reinstatement and resettlement. The selection was controversial. On 26 December 1861 Mathew had married Elizabeth Biron; they had two sons and three daughters, the eldest of whom, Elizabeth [see Dillon, Elizabeth (1865–1907)], in 1895 married John Dillon, the Nationalist MP. The elder son was the lawyer and wit Theobald

*Mathew. This family connection, combined with Mathew's personal home-rule tendencies, meant that he was regarded with distrust by the landlords and the unionists generally. The opening day of the commission, 7 November 1892, was marked by an altercation between the chairman and Edward Carson. The landlords as a body refused to take any further part in the proceedings. The commission, however, continued to take evidence, and reported in due course; some of its recommendations eventually bore fruit in the clauses of Wyndham's Land Purchase Act of 1903. Furthermore, the lines of procedure as laid down by Mathew were afterwards consistently followed in many royal commissions.

It is probably because of this episode that Mathew was not raised to the Court of Appeal until 1901. As an appeal judge, he showed common sense in his judgments and gave short shrift to counsel who attempted to cite too many authorities before him; which he dismissed as the 'old umbrellas of the law'. On 6 December 1905, while at the Athenaeum, he suffered a stroke; his resignation was announced shortly afterwards. He died in London on 9 November 1908, and was buried in St Joseph's cemetery at Cork. He was survived by his wife.

Mathew, although convinced of his own Catholic faith and political sympathy for home rule, was known to all as an articulate and humorous man. His private religious and political beliefs did not interfere with his ability to make friends with those of diametrically opposed views; he had happy relations with many unionists and was a welcome visitor in the homes of many dignitaries of the Church of England. A cultured and likeable man, he was valued as sincere, humorous, and loyal.

J. B. ATLAY, rev. SINÉAD AGNEW

Sources J. Foster, *Men-at-the-bar: a biographical hand-list of the members of the various inns of court*, 2nd edn (1885), 308–9 · *WWW*, 1897–1915 · *Men and women of the time* (1899), 732–3 · A. T. C. Pratt, ed., *People of the period: being a collection of the biographies of upwards of six thousand living celebrities*, 2 (1897), 150 · *Annual Register* (1892), 62 · W. P. Baildon, ed., *The records of the Honorable Society of Lincoln's Inn: admissions*, 2 (1896), 252 · *The Times* (10 Nov 1908) · H. S. Cunningham, *Lord Bowen: a biographical sketch* (1896) · J. D. Woodruff, *The Tichborne claimant: a Victorian mystery* (1957), 221, 252, 255, 323, 388
Likenesses Lock & Whitfield, woodburytype photograph, 1883, NPG · Barraud, photograph, NPG · Spy [L. Ward], chromolithograph caricature, NPG; repro. in *VF* (12 March 1896)
Wealth at death £60,580 5s. 9d.: resworn probate, 12 Dec 1908, *CGPLA Eng. & Wales*

Mathew, Mary (1724–1777), diarist, was the eldest daughter of the six children of Theobald Mathew (*d.* 1745) and his wife, Catherine Shelley. The family were wealthy landowners with estates in co. Galway, co. Limerick, and co. Tipperary. Nothing is known of the early life of Mary Mathew. In adult life she lived in co. Dublin, and began to keep a diary from August 1772. It is for this diary, written during 1772 and 1773 and providing glimpses of her day-to-day life, that she is known.

Mary Mathew was wealthy in her own right, inheriting money from relatives and the rental of some property from her father. Her finances appear, however, to have been controlled by her brother Thomas, who succeeded to the family property on the death of his father in 1745. Mary refers to the difficulty of getting the money owed to her from Thomas, and her frustration at his delay in forwarding her moneys is evident from her diary.

Mary Mathew also kept a record of her expenditure between 1747 and 1777. There are references to payments made to servants, and her expenditure on clothing and household goods is also noted. The accounts, which appear in the back of the same manuscript as the diary, are most detailed after 1760. Mathew was on friendly terms with many of the titled families of the time who were regular visitors to her home in Portmarnock, co. Dublin. Her diary provides an insight into the work and wages of servants of the period, as well as an account of the life of a lady of leisure. She enjoyed an active social life, visiting the theatre and attending balls and assemblies. Like many diarists of the period she hoped that the discipline of keeping the diary would allow her to lead a more useful life or at least be conducive in making her use her time and energy in a more worthwhile manner. However, her diary shows her to have been unreflective, and she felt she gained little from the diary, concluding in August 1773: 'This day ends the year of this journal. I think my time past in so trifling a manner tis not worth recording so here I end' (*Diary*, 46). She died, unmarried, in Dublin in 1777.   MARIA LUDDY

Sources *The diary of Mary Mathew*, ed. M. Luddy (1991) · Burke, *Gen. Ire.* (1976)
Archives NL Ire., cookery recipes, household accounts, and diary, MS 5102

Mathew, Theobald (1790–1856), Capuchin friar and temperance campaigner, was the fourth son of Ann Mathew, *née* Whyte, and James Mathew, a cousin of Francis Mathew of Thomastown Castle near Cashel in co. Tipperary. James, who was descended from a Catholic line of the family, had been adopted by Francis, who had conformed to the established church to secure his property and later became the earl of Llandaff, and was employed by Francis as an agent at Thomastown Castle, where Theobald was born on 10 October 1790. While the title derives from the family's Welsh origins, the Mathews's association with Tipperary went back to the seventeenth century, when George Mathew of Llandaff in Glamorgan married the widow of Viscount Thurles.

Education and early life Mathew spent much of his childhood at Thomastown Castle, even after his father took a farm at nearby Rathcloheen, and Lady Elizabeth Mathew, who was later to inherit the castle and estate, took an interest in his education. He attended a school in Thurles and, in 1800–07, a school in Kilkenny (which later became St Kieran's College). In 1807 he went to St Patrick's College, Maynooth, to train for the priesthood, but left about 1809 when he was caught entertaining some friends in his room, which was considered a serious breach of college regulations. He continued his studies for the priesthood, this time in the Capuchin order of Franciscans in Dublin, and at Easter 1814 was ordained by Dr Daniel Murray who later, as archbishop of Dublin, was to become a firm supporter of Mathew's temperance work. While an assistant

Theobald Mathew (1790–1856), by Edward Daniel Leahy, 1846

priest in a poor parish in Kilkenny, Mathew was wrongly accused of a breach of regulations concerning the administration of paschal communion, and was transferred in late 1814 to Cork by the provincial of his order.

In Cork, Mathew was assigned as assistant to a Father Donovan at a chapel known as the Little Friary in Blackamoor Lane, a poor part of the city. He gained a reputation for his non-sectarian outlook in religion and politics, and as an effective preacher of charity sermons. Above all, he became known for his concern for the poor of Cork city. He set up schools for both boys and girls, organized charities for the poor and visits to the sick, and founded a cemetery in the south of the city where the Catholic poor could be interred free or for a nominal charge. He noticed that, in a city where brewing and distilling were major industries, many of the problems of the poor were related to excessive drinking.

The temperance movement There had been temperance societies in Cork city from 1831, but as they were promoted mainly by Anglicans, Quakers, and other protestant nonconformists few Catholics had joined them. By the time Mathew was persuaded publicly to promote temperance by agreeing to become leader of the Cork Teetotal Society in 1838, the earlier pledge to drink in moderation had given way to a teetotal pledge which demanded total abstinence from all alcoholic drink except when prescribed for medicinal purposes. The public attachment of such a well-loved and charismatic figure as Mathew to the temperance cause enabled the movement to grow rapidly, especially among the Catholic poor in the city, and by the end of 1838, 6000 people had taken the pledge. Teetotal 'missionaries' were sent to towns around co. Cork, and by the autumn of 1839 crowds were arriving daily from all over Ireland to take the pledge in person from Mathew.

At the end of 1839 Mathew conducted the first of many crusades outside Cork when he spent several days administering the pledge to large numbers in Limerick, where the native population had been swelled by thousands who had come into the city from the surrounding countryside. This was followed by equally successful missions in Waterford, Clonmel, Galway, and Dublin, and by 1842 almost every district in Ireland had been reached by one of his missions. In 1842 he made the exaggerated claim that 5 million people had taken the pledge, but even half that figure would have justified J. G. Kohl's reference to the enormous numbers flocking to take the pledge as 'extraordinary occurrences, for which the historian can hardly find a parallel' (*Travels in Ireland*, 1844, 100).

Temperance societies were established in towns throughout the country, providing mutual support for members who had pledged themselves to avoid drinking in a society where drinking had previously played such an important part. They organized confessional meetings and social gatherings, provided coffee houses and reading rooms, founded provident and savings schemes for members, and arranged processions with temperance bands and banners that offered an alternative to the drink-related entertainments of the fair day, the pattern, and the racecourse. Mathew reinforced these new attitudes by visiting and revisiting towns, encouraging teetotallers to persist with the pledge, and, while he was careful to explain that the pledge entailed no vow in the religious sense, many of his supporters at a local level were less scrupulous, and stories were current about the misfortunes that had befallen those who abandoned the pledge. But whether maintained by Mathew's charismatic influence, by the work of temperance societies, by superstitious rumours, or by individual commitment to a better way of life, there can be no doubt that for a number of years the Irish temperance movement succeeded in changing habits to the extent that social pressure to drink gave way to social pressure to abstain.

In the years before the famine of 1845–9 alcohol consumption decreased dramatically in Ireland and there was a substantial reduction in crimes, especially those relating to intoxication. Although other factors besides Mathew's work contributed to those improvements, and the improvements did not endure into the second half of the century, many people who knew Ireland well saw his crusade as having a lasting effect on Irish life. One of them, Samuel Hall, writing fifteen years after Mathew's death, noted that while heavy drinking had once been acceptable in Ireland it was no longer so, but had become 'a shame and a reproach' (*A Book of Memories of Great Men and Women of the Age*, 1871, 409).

From 1842 the number of Mathew's crusades around Ireland began to decrease, partly because of his chaotic financial situation. This had come about by his poor financial organization, by parishes failing to reimburse him for medals he had bought and distributed, by his generous contribution to charities, and by his hopes of a legacy from Lady Elizabeth Mathew, the heir to the Thomastown estates, who, when she died in 1842, left him nothing. Attempts to raise money by public subscription to enable his work to continue met with only limited success because he was resentful of the interference that was thought necessary to put his financial affairs in order.

In England Mathew made a successful visit to Scotland in 1842, and although he had been invited to England as early as 1840 did not take up the offer of a major crusade there until the summer of 1843. The timing was partly determined by his wish to be away from Ireland while Daniel O'Connell's campaign for the repeal of the union with Britain was reaching its height. While he was not opposed to repeal, he was reluctant to have his temperance movement associated with it; but, as great numbers of people belonged to both movements, it was proving impossible to keep the two apart. Despite Mathew's opposition, many temperance bands were taking part in repeal meetings, and repeal speakers were referring to his work as Ireland's preparation for self-government.

Mathew was unable to escape from political and religious issues in England, however, where some newspapers, such as the *Morning Herald*, insisted on associating his movement with repeal and with 'popery'. His refusal to allow political issues to be raised on his platforms and his consistent respect for the representatives of all creeds that he encountered in England, as in Ireland, were sufficient to deflect the most prejudiced criticisms, and there was general approval of his work in the Irish quarters of English cities. There was opposition from brewers, who were suspected of offering free beer to men to disrupt some of his meetings in London. A few Catholic clergymen also had reservations about his mission, fearing it would interfere with the prospects of employment for Irish immigrants in England. Having pledged 200,000 people, most of them Irish, Mathew returned to Ireland in September 1843 in time to witness the decline in repeal agitation that followed the government's banning of the 'monster' meeting planned for Clontarf.

In Ireland and the United States From as early as 1840 there had been suspicions that some of Mathew's supporters were breaking their pledges. Cordials containing alcohol and dispensations from doctors were among the stratagems employed by waverers to adhere to the letter, if not the spirit, of the pledge. With the onset of the famine there were increased accusations that many were abandoning the pledge, accusations which Mathew vigorously denied. In time he had to accept, however, that in the great social disruption that accompanied the potato failure of the late 1840s many of his followers would die of starvation, many would emigrate, and many of those who remained in Ireland would abandon the pledge for ever.

From 1846 Mathew's own energies became increasingly

absorbed in famine relief work, although he continued to make regular, if less frequent, visits to promote temperance. He was on the Cork Relief Committee and worked tirelessly soliciting aid from abroad, advising and assisting government relief officers, publicizing the virtues of the controversial 'yellow meal', and even turning his own home in Cove Street into a soup kitchen for the starving.

Mathew was disappointed not to have been appointed bishop of Cork by the Vatican, having been the preferred candidate of the clergy of the diocese. Some of the Irish bishops, while supporting his crusade against drink, were suspicious of what they saw as his accommodating attitude towards British power in Ireland. He suffered an attack of paralysis, probably brought on from overwork, in 1848, from which he made a rapid but incomplete recovery.

In 1849 Mathew went to America, where he immediately became embroiled in a series of controversies. Catholics and protestants in New York vied with one other to welcome him, Irish nationalist immigrants condemned him for having received a pension from the British government in 1848 as a solution to his financial problems, abolitionists vilified him for not condemning slavery in public in America as he had done in Ireland seven years earlier, and politicians from southern states denounced him for having condemned slavery in the first place. He successfully steered his way through the various minefields, and large numbers, mostly Irish Americans, took the pledge in hundreds of towns and cities in twenty-five states over a period of two and a half years. His exertions in America weakened him further, and after his return to Ireland in December 1851 he was unable to take part in any further temperance crusades, although people continued to visit Mathew at his brother's home, where he was living, at Lehenagh near Cork to take the pledge.

Death and influence Father Mathew had a stroke early in 1856 and died on 8 December of the same year at Queenstown, near Cork. His friend and biographer, John Francis Maguire, recorded that he left no property except his watch and the altar plate and sacred vestments which belonged to him as a priest, so it was perhaps appropriate that he was buried in the cemetery which he founded many years earlier for the poor of Cork.

Considered attractive as a child, Mathew retained his good looks into middle age. Kohl described him in 1842 as having the same height and figure as Napoleon, 'really a handsome man', with a fresh complexion, large eyes, and a nose that was 'a little too arched in the middle' (J. G. Kohl, *Travels in Ireland*, 1844, 97). W. M. Thackeray, who met him the same year, recalled 'a stout, handsome, honest-looking man' (*The Irish Sketch Book*, 1843, 113). Towards the end of his life, Mathew acknowledged that his cherished aim of banishing drunkenness from Ireland had not been achieved and he became more sympathetic towards legislative changes to prevent the abuse of alcohol. His personal influence on the Irish temperance movement was enormous, however, and several successful campaigns

against drink in the late nineteenth century, both in Ireland and among the Irish in Britain, owed their inspiration to him and to those of his followers who had kept the pledge. The wider influence of his work, especially the activities of the temperance societies he encouraged, has been controversially viewed by H. F. Kearney as contributing to the modernization of Irish life. While there will continue to be discussion among historians on the influence of his work, his enigmatic personality—with his single-minded commitment to opposing drunkenness and his reputation for personal sanctity—will ensure that he remains a revered figure among the heroes of nineteenth-century Ireland.   COLM KERRIGAN

Sources J. F. Maguire, *Father Mathew: a biography* (1863) • H. F. Kearney, 'Fr. Mathew, apostle of modernisation', *Studies in Irish history presented to R. Dudley Edwards*, ed. A. Cosgrove and D. McCartney (1979), 164–75 • E. Malcolm, 'Temperance and Irish nationalism', *Ireland under the Union: varieties of tension*, ed. F. S. L. Lyons and R. A. J. Hawkins (1980), 69–114 • C. Kerrigan, *Father Mathew and the Irish temperance movement, 1838–1849* (1992) • J. Quinn, 'Father Mathew's crusade: temperance in Ireland, 1838–1856', Ph.D diss., Notre Dame University, 1993 • Fr. Augustine, *Footprints of Father Theobald Mathew OFM Cap., apostle of temperance* (1947) • P. Rogers, *Father Theobald Mathew: apostle of temperance* (1943) • F. Mathew, *Father Mathew: his life and times* (1890) • D. Mathew, 'Father Mathew's family: the Mathews of Tipperary', *Capuchin Annual* (1956–7), 143–52 • *The Constitution* [Cork] (9 Dec 1856) • *Cork Examiner* (10 Dec 1856)

Archives Capuchin Archives, Dublin | CKS, corresp. with duke and duchess of Cleveland • CKS, letters to Lord Stanhope

Likenesses J. P. Haverty, oils, c.1840, NG Ire. • J. Hogan, bust, 1840, Capuchin friary, Dublin • J. Doyle, caricature, 1843, BM • E. D. Leahy, oils, 1846, NPG [*see illus.*] • J. Foley, statue, 1864, Patrick Street, Cork • M. Redmond, statue, 1893, O'Connell Street, Dublin

Wealth at death 'his watch, and altar plate and sacred vestments, which belonged to him as a priest, he had nothing to give or bequeath': Maguire, *Father Mathew*, 554–5

Mathew, Theobald (1866–1939), lawyer and wit, was born in London on 5 December 1866, the elder son of the judge Sir James Charles *Mathew (1830–1908) and his wife, Elizabeth, daughter of Edwin Biron, vicar of Lympne, Kent. The family hailed from Tipperary and Theobald was a great-nephew of his namesake, Father Theobald Mathew, the temperance advocate, and, through his elder sister Elizabeth *Dillon, a brother-in-law of John Dillon. His parents, devout Roman Catholics and admirers of Cardinal Newman, sent him to the Oratory School, Edgbaston. From there he went to the cardinal's old college, Trinity College, Oxford, where he matriculated in 1885 and graduated with a second class in modern history in 1888. Throughout his life he remained greatly attached to his old college and cherished the friendships which he formed there.

Mathew was called to the bar by Lincoln's Inn (his father's inn) in 1890 and was in chambers with Joseph Walton, afterwards judge of the High Court. Here he acquired a profound knowledge of English law and an unswerving respect for its traditions. He practised as a junior on the common law side until he was over seventy years of age. Like his father, he never took silk, preferring to keep his forensic work within reasonable dimensions. He became a bencher of Lincoln's Inn in 1916.

Mathew first came to public notice in 1896 as the editor of *Commercial Cases*, a series of reports on the proceedings before the commercial court, which began its existence in 1895 under the inspiration of Mathew's father, its first judge. Mathew's introduction to the opening volume of the series was regarded as the most authoritative statement of the reasons that led to the formation of this tribunal, and in 1902 he published a small volume entitled *Practice of the Commercial Court*, which was revised and reissued in 1967. He was recorder of Margate from 1913 to 1927 and of Maidstone from 1927 to 1936. In 1898 he married Ruth, daughter of the Revd George Henry Rigby and niece of Sir John Rigby, and they had five sons and two daughters.

Mathew's fame among his contemporaries was based less on his professional career than on his reputation as one of the great wits of his generation. With Irish intuition he saw the funny side of everything and he had the rare gift of expressing himself at the luncheon table, in chambers, at the Garrick Club, and elsewhere, in swift and impromptu sayings which gained a wide currency among his peers. He was also an accomplished after-dinner speaker, the purveyor of a hundred or more 'grouse in the gunroom' stories which he seemed never to forget.

Mathew's humour was helped by his personal appearance. He was small in stature and wore pince-nez, but had a deep and resonant voice which was apt to break into a chuckle with the delivery of a joke, 'his solemn face wreathing into a triumphant smile as the shaft of wit found the mark' (*The Times*, 22 June 1939). Some of these witticisms now seem period pieces, notably his greeting to a white friend in the library of an inn that was home to many African lawyers, 'Dr Livingstone, I presume', a remark that acquired legendary status during his lifetime. Some of his caricatures also played on racial stereotypes, such as the avaricious Jewish moneylender, in a way that would nowadays be deemed offensive. But Theo, as he was universally called, was held in genuine affection by contemporaries as a generous and tolerant man as well as a funny one.

The origin of much of Mathew's humour lay in the legal profession, and it was there that his most appreciative audience was to be found. In 1925 he began to contribute to the *Law Journal* a weekly series of 'Forensic fables', illustrated by his own skilful pen-and-ink caricatures. These were subsequently published in four volumes (1926–32) and threw humorous and often penetrating light on the *cursus curiae* as it presented itself to the practising lawyer of the day. Mathew did not hesitate to portray in his gallery, in the thinnest disguise, famous personalities of the time. Contemporaries had no difficulty identifying the 'tearful performer'; the 'old hand', with his somewhat unprofessional methods; the fashionable leaders, who settled the case when neither of them could understand the question addressed to them by the erudite judge; and the sagacious solicitor, who had the popular primer *Law for the Million* bound in a cover displaying the name of an old law report. Complete editions of *Forensic Fables* were published in 1961 and 1999. With *For Lawyers and Others* (1937), a volume of articles that he contributed from time to time to periodicals, Mathew's wit reached a wider audience. He died at his home, 5 Queen's Gate Place, London, on 20 June 1939.　　　P. A. LANDON, *rev.* MARK POTTLE

Sources *The Times* (21–4 June 1939) · O. [T. Mathew], *Forensic fables* (1961); repr. (1999) · T. Mathew, ed., *Reports of Commercial Cases* (March–Aug 1895) · T. Mathew, *For lawyers and others* (1937) · A. D. Colman, *Mathew's Practice of the commercial court* (1967)
Likenesses W. Orpen, sketch on dinner menu, repro. in Mathew, *Forensic fables*; in family possession in 1949
Wealth at death £12,700 3s. 3d.: probate, 24 July 1939, CGPLA Eng. & Wales

Mathew, Sir Theobald (1898–1964), lawyer and public servant, was born in London on 4 November 1898, the elder son of Charles James Mathew (1872–1923), barrister and briefly (1922–3) Labour MP for Whitechapel, and his wife, Anna, daughter of James Archbold Cassidy, of Monasterevan, co. Kildare. Educated at the Oratory School and later at Sandhurst, he served with the Irish Guards in the First World War, from 1917 to 1920; he was awarded the MC in 1918 when a lieutenant. In the following year he was appointed aide-de-camp to Sir Alexander Godley.

In 1921 Mathew was called to the bar by Lincoln's Inn, but practised for only four years in that branch of the profession before getting himself disbarred and becoming articled to the well-known firm of London solicitors, Charles Russell & Co., whose senior partner, Sir Charles Russell, bt, was an uncle of his wife. In 1923 Mathew had married Phyllis Helen, daughter of Cyril Russell, stockbroker, and granddaughter of Lord Russell of Killowen, a nineteenth-century lord chief justice. They had one son, John Charles, who became a senior treasury counsel at the central criminal court, and two daughters. In 1928 Mathew was admitted a solicitor and became a partner in Charles Russell & Co. In April 1941 he left private practice and joined the Home Office as a wartime civil servant. A year later he became head of that department's criminal division, where he remained until appointed director of public prosecutions in 1944.

His work as head of criminal division caused Herbert Morrison, then home secretary, quickly to form a high opinion of his talents. It was Morrison who recommended his appointment as director of public prosecutions to the prime minister on the retirement of Sir Edward Tindal Atkinson. The appointment caused a certain amount of surprise and comment in legal circles as Mathew was the first solicitor to hold that office, hitherto regarded as one reserved for the bar. It proved, however, a completely successful appointment, and one which amply justified Morrison's confidence.

In 1946 Mathew was appointed KBE, and this year found him presiding over a rapidly expanding department. The problems of the immediate post-war years were manifold and, on the part of the director of public prosecutions, called for administrative as much as legal skills. Mathew's talents in both spheres were quickly apparent, and his ability to win the loyalty and affection of a greatly increased staff (most of them straight from the forces) was a mark of his success. He fought successfully with the treasury to secure more resources for his department,

Sir Theobald Mathew (1898–1964), by Walter Stoneman, 1946

including the creation of a new post of assistant solicitor; and he managed to find the right balance between delegating and retaining responsibility. Unlike his predecessor, Sir Archibald Bodkin, he was content to let his staff prepare cases for trial.

Mathew was a good lawyer, but perhaps what is more important in someone concerned with the administration of the criminal law, he had an abundance of common sense and great humanity. Allied to these qualities was a keen sense of humour. He was one of the most approachable holders of high office, which was symbolized by his insistence that the door of his room be kept open, save when he was in conference. He was incisive and could reach decisions quickly and he was also a master of the written word, managing to stamp all his letters and minutes with his own brand of urbane literacy.

Mathew sat on numerous official committees concerned with aspects of the administration of criminal justice and his advice was frequently sought and generously given. He had a strong feeling for his office and its constitutional role, and was always ready to lecture on the subject. He was fond of opening his lectures with the words, 'I direct no one and there's no such thing as a public prosecution', to underline the principle that criminal justice in this country rests basically on the rights and duties of the private individual. He recognized a distinction between public and private morality and, as he informed the select committee on the Obscene Publications Bill in 1957, strongly disapproved of his department being placed in the position 'of being a censor of novels or other literary publications' (Rozenberg, 28). Yet he felt obliged to accept, and to act upon, what he perceived to be the current state of public opinion. This immensely difficult position led him, with much hesitation, to proceed with the prosecution of Penguin, the publishers of *Lady Chatterley's Lover*, at the Old Bailey in 1960 under the Obscene Publications Act of 1959. In this he was supported by the attorney-general, Sir Reginald Manningham-Buller. The act had redefined obscenity and this test case, in which Penguin were acquitted, thereafter 'enabled the full force of the reformed law to be exploited on behalf of recognized literature' (Robertson and Nicol, 109).

Of medium height and lithe figure, Mathew had a memorably bushy pair of eyebrows. Away from the calls of office he was very much a family man with a keen interest in horse-racing. He died suddenly in the Middlesex Hospital, London, on 29 February 1964, a few months short of retirement. He was survived by his wife. During the twenty years that he held office, he served under eight attorneys-general, and became something of a father figure to the many on his staff who had grown up under his benign and efficient reign. Although brought up in the law—his father was a silk, his grandfather Lord Justice Mathew, and an uncle the inimitable Theo Mathew of 'forensic fables' fame—he was refreshingly free of those foibles often associated with lawyers in the lay mind.

MICHAEL EVELYN, *rev.* MARK POTTLE

Sources *The Times* (2 March 1964) · J. Rozenberg, *The case for the crown: the inside story of the director of public prosecutions* (1987) · N. Skelhorn, *Public prosecutor: director of public prosecutions, 1964–1977* (1981) · *Law Journal*, 114 (13 March 1964), 178 · G. Robertson and A. Nicol, *Media law* (1984) · T. Mathew, 'The office and duties of the director of public prosecutions' [lecture, U. Lond., 9 March 1950] · A. Travis, *Bound and gagged: a secret history of obscenity in Britain* (2000) · personal knowledge (1981) · private information (1981) · *CGPLA Eng. & Wales* (1964)

Likenesses W. Stoneman, photograph, 1946, NPG [*see illus.*] · photograph, repro. in *The Times*, p. 17

Wealth at death £14,161: administration with will, 29 May 1964, *CGPLA Eng. & Wales*

Mathews, Basil Joseph (1879–1951), writer on the missionary and ecumenical movement, was born at Oxford on 28 August 1879, the eldest son of Angelo Alfred Hankins Mathews, insurance broker, and his wife, Emma Colegrove. The Mathews line has been traced to Sir David Mathew, who was standard-bearer to Edward IV at the battle of Towton and whose tomb is in Llandaff Cathedral. The name acquired its final 's' in the lifetime of William Mathew of Bristol (1746–1830), author, and publisher to John Wesley and Hannah More.

Mathews's formal schooling, which was begun at the Oxford high school, ended through family misfortunes at the age of fourteen. After working in the Bodleian and in Oxford public libraries Mathews became private secretary to A. M. Fairbairn, principal of Mansfield College, Oxford. Contact with Fairbairn strengthened a natural aptitude for study and hard work and while still in his employ Mathews entered the university through what was then the non-collegiate delegacy. In 1904 he took second-class honours in modern history. With journalism in view he joined the staff of the *Christian World* and in 1910 attended as a reporter the World Missionary Conference at Edinburgh, a turning point in the modern history of the ecumenical movement. This experience kindled in Mathews a lifelong enthusiasm for Christian missions and in the same year he became editor of the London Missionary Society's publications. It was quickly apparent that missionary propaganda under Mathews's pen was entering a new phase. To the skill of a professional journalist he joined natural teaching gifts, a fine understanding of a great field of Christian thought and action, and the persuasiveness of a man who believed what he wrote and wrote what he believed. One of his earliest books, *Livingstone the Pathfinder* (1912), won speedy and widespread popularity and set the pattern for a successful series of missionary biographies.

The First World War brought Mathews into a fresh field of activity. He joined the staff of the Ministry of Information and became chairman and secretary of its literature committee. After the war his widening range of interests included work with the opium commission of the League of Nations in 1923. In the meantime he had in 1919 left the London Missionary Society to become editor of the Far and Near Publications Company, a task which included the editorship of a short-lived but valiant monthly journal, *Outward Bound*. From 1920 to 1924, as head of the press bureau of the Conference of British Missionary Societies, he served all the British missions and was active in the affairs of the United Council for Missionary Education and its counterpart in the United States, the Missionary Education Movement. From 1924 until 1929 he was literary secretary to the World's Committee of Young Men's Christian Associations in Geneva. In addition to his editorial work he was in growing demand as a public speaker, especially to student audiences. In these years he travelled widely in the Near East, west Africa, and India, and in 1931 paid his first visit to the United States. From 1932 to 1944 he was first visiting lecturer and then resident professor of Christian world relations in the school of theology of Boston University and at the Andover-Newton Theological Seminary, Massachusetts. From 1944 to 1949 he held a similar professorship at Union College, University of British Columbia, from which he received the honorary degree of LLD in 1949.

Mathews married first, in 1905, Harriett Anne, daughter of William Henry Passmore, farmer; she died in 1939; second, in 1940, Winifred Grace, daughter of John Wilson, chemist. There were no children from either marriage.

Mathews was a prolific writer. In addition to editorial work and a constant stream of articles, he published more than forty books, many of which appeared in translations. Among the best known, apart from his biography of Livingstone, were those on John R. Mott (1934) and Booker T. Washington (1949) and his presentation of racial and ethnic problems in *The Clash of Colour* (1924) and *The Jew and the World Ferment* (1934). Much of his writing was topical, but behind a vivid popular style there lay great industry and a power of discernment which made his work more than transient. Students remembered him as an inspiring teacher, and men and women of many nationalities took delight in his friendship. He endured a long illness, in which he knew that he was under sentence of death, with fortitude and grace. To the end his pen was busy and he still conversed with zest on the great causes to which he had dedicated uncommon gifts. In the history of the ecumenical movement during the twentieth century Mathews represented, in his writing and standpoint, a significant period; it was one in which, primarily through practical co-operation in the missionary enterprise, the course was being set towards the churches' deeper understanding of their unity and mission. He died on 29 March 1951 at the Warneford Hospital in Oxford.

NORMAN GOODALL, *rev.*

Sources *The Times* (31 March 1951) · *The Times* (3 April 1951) · private information (1971) · *CGPLA Eng. & Wales* (1951)
Archives IWM, corresp. with Sir C. K. Webster
Wealth at death £3706 16s. 5d.: probate, 14 Aug 1951, *CGPLA Eng. & Wales*

Mathews, Charles (1776–1835), actor, the seventh son of James Mathews, a bookseller and Wesleyan local preacher, and his wife, Elizabeth, was born on 28 June 1776 at 18 Strand, London. His youth was spent in his father's bookshop in Richmond, Surrey, where he acquired an early interest in the literature of the theatre. By the time he was twelve years old, he could usually be found in a large room above the nearby stable which he and a friend had converted into a theatre for the purpose of entertaining their youthful companions. After two years in that stable theatre, in 1790, at the age of fourteen, Charles Mathews applied to Henry Harris, the manager of the Covent Garden Theatre, for the position of leading comedian: Harris did not consider Mathews ready for leading comic business.

For three years Mathews studied the contemporary plays which the leading comedians of the day were performing and the classic comedies of Shakespeare and Jonson, building a repertory of roles. In September 1793 he paid the manager of the Richmond Theatre in Surrey 10 guineas for the privilege of playing Richmond in *Richard III* (he had selected the role for his début because it gave him a chance to display his fencing abilities against Richard in the last act). Two years later he accepted a position with a company of players in Dublin, and in September 1794 made his first appearance before an audience in comic imitations of famous actors. His imitations of Joseph Munden, John Kemble, and Mr Wathen were received with roars of laughter, marking his early beginnings in the area of impersonation.

One year later, in September 1795, disillusioned by lack of promotion, lack of salary, and lack of support, Mathews decided to give up the prospect of the stage and set sail for London. The ship, which also carried Montague Talbot, another actor, met rough weather and came to rest at Swansea. In an effort to profit from their enforced loss of time, Talbot and Mathews agreed to appear with the Swansea company for two nights. The venture led to a three-year stay with this provincial company, during

Charles Mathews (1776–1835), by Rembrandt Peale, *c.*1822

which, on 19 September 1797, Mathews married Eliza Kirkham Strong (1772–1802) [*see* Mathews, Eliza].

In January 1798 Mathews heard that John Emery, the principal comedian with the York company, was about to move to London, and he applied to Tate Wilkinson, the manager of the York company, for the vacated position. The York circuit was considered a nursery and preparatory school for metropolitan performers. In August 1798 he arrived in York, and by the end of 1799 he enjoyed all the roles he requested, and played leading comic business for the following three years. During that period his first wife died, and on 28 March 1803 he married Anne Jackson (*d.* 1869), an actress with the York company. Also during that three years he continued to perfect his imitations of the leading actors of the day, and he acquired a knack for ventriloquism.

On Monday 16 May 1803 Mathews made his London début, as Jabel in Richard Cumberland's *The Jew* and as Lingo in *The Agreeable Surprise*, under George Colman at the Theatre Royal, Haymarket. The following night he repeated the performance by command for King George III and his family. At the close of the 1803 season, after signing a contract with Colman for three further seasons, he joined the company at Liverpool for the winter. Charles James *Mathews, the couple's only child, was born on 26 December 1803. Mathews's second season at the Haymarket was as successful as the first, and reviewers ranked him with the best London comedians, finding him less flippant than John Fawcett, as natural as John Bannister, and less laboured than Joseph Munden.

In the summer of 1804 Mathews and his wife signed a joint contract with the Theatre Royal, Drury Lane, for five years. The following autumn (18 September 1804), as Don Manuel in Colley Cibber's comedy *She Would and She Would Not*, Mathews established himself as one of the leading comedians of London.

The summer of 1805 again found Mathews before the audiences of the Haymarket Theatre, and another new piece was written for him. More and more, he began to appear as a character who disguised himself as someone else. It was later said that he had the faculty of putting on another man's thoughts with his clothes, and many plays written for him were skeletons left for his elaboration. One year after Bannister's solo performance at Covent Garden in *Bannister's Budget* (1807), Mathews conceived the idea of performing an entertainment that would eliminate his dependence on provincial companies for work outside the London season. He constructed a 'solo' entertainment and displayed it for the first time in Hull on 12 April 1808 (in fact his wife also took part in it).

This entertainment, called *The Mail Coach Adventure, or, Rambles in Yorkshire*, was intended solely for the consumption of the provincial audiences, and, when he created it, Mathews probably had no idea that ten years later it would launch him on a totally new career. The structure of this early entertainment—provided by James Smith—was crude and disjointed, with the last act, the monopologue that came to be Mathews's trademark, absent. Mrs Mathews played a minor role in *The Mail Coach Adventure*, and the couple performed this entertainment with some regularity nearly every season between 1808 and 1811, when Mrs Mathews retired from the company of two. In that latter year Mathews created his second entertainment, based on the first, *The Travellers, or, Hit or Miss*, this time joining forces with Charles Incledon.

The difference between the entertainment of 1808 and that of 1811 was that, instead of using the novelty as an intermittent rest from the regular drama, Mathews now began to produce it in a regularly scheduled tour of the provinces. This two-man show lasted only one season. There are some indications that the provinces saw Mathews periodically between 1812 and 1817 in a one-man version of *The Mail Coach Adventure*. In 1817 he wrote to his wife: 'During my performance at Brighton, Mrs George Farron's mother and sister went to see me "At Home".' This reference marks 1817 as the date Mathews first associated the title 'At Home' with his entertainment. In that same year Mathews joined Frederick Yates to tour England with *The Actor of All Work*, and with him played the two-man show in Paris.

In 1809 Drury Lane burnt down and Mathews moved with the company to the Lyceum. He left in 1811 because of a disagreement with the management. After touring the provinces for a year, he returned to the city in 1812, this time to Covent Garden. From then until 1814 his career progressed smoothly. In the summer of that year he fell from his carriage and suffered a broken hip: the accident left him lame for the rest of his life.

After a brief retirement for rest and recovery, Mathews returned to Covent Garden to fulfil his contract, but he now walked with an obvious limp and was cast in the roles of gout-stricken old men, as he could no longer handle the demanding physical activity required for the leading comic roles. Finally, in 1816 Mathews asked Henry Harris, the manager, to release him from his contract. Harris agreed, but made Mathews promise not to play anywhere in London for its duration.

Mathews returned to the provinces. He appeared in Scotland and Ireland before returning to London for the summer season of 1817 at the Haymarket. The following autumn he appeared before London audiences for the first time in the one-man version of *The Mail Coach Adventure*. S. J. Arnold saw him perform and gave him a contract to appear at the English Opera House every spring for the next seven years. The title 'At Home' was first used publicly by Mathews in London during the 1817 season. It was structured as a table entertainment in which a monologue provided the avenue for anecdote, jest, and song that carried his audience through a series of amusing adventures and provided the opportunity for imitations of all the human oddities encountered along the way. It was followed by a farce, in which he played multiple characters using his skills in quick changes and ventriloquy. The 'At Home' was to be given annually in April and May, leaving Mathews free to tour the provinces for the remainder of the year. The 'At Homes' succeeded, and the people of London and the provinces flocked to see them each year. Each new entertainment was the talk of the town for months before it began, and everyone speculated on the topic of the next one-man show. Annually, with the assistance of two or three highly gifted writers, Mathews devised new and varied delights. Richard Peake, James Smith, Charles James Mathews, and others contributed to the scripts.

In search of variety and material, and in hopes of large profits, Mathews devised a tour of America. He set sail in August 1822 and after thirty-five days at sea arrived at New York, then plagued by yellow fever. He opened in Baltimore, and he was triumphant. The critics universally praised his performances, and he was the hit of the season. The popular and critical success did not however, produce the financial bonanza he had anticipated. Mathews returned to England as *the* comedian of the age. After a summer of rest, he again entered the fray at the English Opera House for the month of August in the regular drama. Following another month in Dublin, he took up residence in London and retired for the winter to prepare his new entertainment. *A Trip to America*, perhaps his finest venture, opened at the English Opera House on 25 March 1824. From then until 1834, in the spring of each year apart from 1828, Mathews was 'At Home' for forty nights. In addition, he played short-term engagements at the patent houses in the regular drama and undertook brief tours through the provinces. In 1828 there was no 'At Home', as Price, the manager of Drury Lane, offered him an extravagant salary to perform there for the 1827–8 season. His nightly salary was then the highest ever paid to a comic performer.

In the spring of 1828 Mathews paid £17,000 for a half-share of the Adelphi Theatre, and commenced as manager. The Adelphi held the 'At Homes' until the death of the host. The last London 'At Home' was in 1834, when Mathews advertised a succession of selections from his old entertainments. He was fifty-eight years old. He had spent forty of those years as a professional actor, but he could not retire, as, although he had earned large sums of money, bad investments had rendered him nearly impoverished. So, when an American agent came to him in the spring of 1834 and offered financial independence in exchange for another crossing of the Atlantic, Mathews accepted. The offer, the details of which have been obscured by time, would supposedly have made Mathews wealthy after only one year in the United States.

Mathews designed the tour himself. He intended to remain absent from England for at least eighteen months and possibly for as long as two years, because he wanted to extend his tour to the Canadian provinces. He had also decided to appear only in his monodramatic performances and to maintain his independence of the American managers. He was destined never to see Canada, and his dependence on the American managers was ordained before landing by the illness he contracted while on board ship. Before leaving England, however, he gave a farewell performance at Richmond on 25 July: his last performance in England was thus on the very stage where he first appeared in public in 1793.

With each day of the crossing Mathews became weaker, and by the time New York was in view he held in his lungs the infection that would kill him in less than a year. In addition to his illness, the tour had an awkward beginning: the public was somewhat opposed to his appearances because of the reports that had preceded him concerning his *A Trip to America* show. When he arrived at the theatre, he found bills posted calling him a scoundrel and an ungrateful slanderer, suggesting he be pelted from the stage for his insult to the American people in his London productions on their national character. In spite of this polemic, he appeared in his *A Trip to America*: his audience made no effort to hinder the production, and the entertainment was acclaimed throughout the American theatrical capitals.

The Philadelphia papers were universal in their praise, often comparing this visit with the first, marvelling at Mathews's ability 'to look through the windows of the heart'. But behind the footlights Mathews was changed, even though he tried to hide his pain and discomfort as he brought himself before his auditors. By December 1834 his condition was worse, but still he clung to the American venture out of desperation. Notices regularly appeared indicating that he could not appear as the result of a severe cold. All the plans fell through. By January he had given up the 'At Homes' entirely. He was forced to keep to the drama, being too weak to do his table acts because the necessary energy was too severe an exertion on his lungs. In six months he performed on only thirty-two nights. He had lost a year's income.

Mathews and his wife returned to England and arrived in Liverpool on 10 March 1835, after nineteen days at sea.

Mathews died in Plymouth on 28 June 1835, his fifty-ninth birthday, and was buried there two days later at St Andrew's Church.   RICHARD L. KLEPAC

Sources A. J. Mathews, *Memoirs of Charles Mathews, comedian* (1839) · P—, 'Personal recollections of the late Charles Mathews', *The Court Magazine and Belle Assemblée* (Aug 1835) · B. Mathews and L. Hutton, eds., *Actors and actresses of Great Britain and the United States* (1886) · R. L. Klepac, *Mr Mathews at home* (1979) · T. A. Brown, *History of the American stage* (1870) · 'Mathews the comedian', *Blackwood*, 45 (1839) · H. B. Baker, *History of the London stage and its famous players, 1576–1903*, 2nd edn (1904) · *The London theatre, 1811–66: selections from the diary of Henry Crabb Robinson*, ed. E. Brown (1966) · A. J. Mathews, ed., Published criticisms etc. upon the performances of Charles Mathews, comedian, scrapbook, Harvard TC · W. B. Wood, *Personal recollections of the stage embracing notices of actors, authors and auditors, during a period of forty years* (1855) · G. C. D. Odell, *Annals of the New York stage*, 15 vols. (1927–49) · H. S. Wyndham, *The annals of the Covent Garden Theatre: from 1732 to 1897*, 2 vols. (1906) · *Boston Evening Transcript* (16 Dec 1834) · *Oxberry's Dramatic Biography*, 5/65 (1826)

Archives BL · NYPL · Princeton University Library, New Jersey, papers · Yale U. | BL, lord chamberlain's collection of plays · Harvard TC · NYPL, Stead and Players collections

Likenesses S. De Wilde, oils, 1810–12, Garr. Club · S. De Wilde, oils, exh. 1813, Garr. Club · G. H. Harlow, oils, exh. RA 1814, Garr. Club · S. Joseph, plaster bust, 1822, NPG · R. Peale, oils, c.1822, NPG [*see illus.*] · J. Lonsdale, oils, exh. RA 1827, Garr. Club · G. Clint, group portrait, oils, exh. RA 1830, Garr. Club · G. Clint, oils, exh. RA 1832, Garr. Club · G. Clint, oils, NPG · S. De Wilde, drawings, Garr. Club · G. H. Harlow, pencil drawing, NPG · E. Landseer, pen-and-ink drawing, NPG · prints, BM, NPG

Charles Edward Mathews (1834–1905), by Sarony

Mathews, Charles Edward (1834–1905), mountaineer, born at Kidderminster on 4 January 1834, was the third of six sons of Jeremiah Mathews, a Worcestershire land agent, and his wife, Mary Guest. Of his five brothers, the eldest, William (1828–1901), educated at St John's College, Cambridge (twentieth wrangler, 1852), was one of the leading pioneers of alpine exploration and the largest contributor to *Peaks, Passes, and Glaciers* (1859 and 1862); he was also president of the Alpine Club (1869–71). The fourth brother, George Spencer Mathews (1836–1904), fellow of Gonville and Caius College, Cambridge (seventh wrangler in 1859) and a land agent, was also a noted mountaineer. Both brothers were prominent figures in municipal and social life in Birmingham.

Charles Edward Mathews was educated at King Charles I's School, Kidderminster, served his articles in Birmingham and London from 1851, and was admitted solicitor in 1856. He practised with great success in Birmingham, and acted as solicitor to the Birmingham school board and as clerk of the peace from 1891 until his death. In 1860, he married Elizabeth Agnes Blyth; they had two sons and two daughters.

Mathews was a member of the town council from 1875 to 1881 and for nearly fifty years exerted much influence on the public and social affairs of Birmingham. He was one of the founders, and subsequently chairman, of the parliamentary committee of the National Education League. In 1864, with Dr Thomas Pretious Heslop, he founded the children's hospital and took part for many years in its management; he agitated for the reorganization of King Edward's School, and served as a governor of the school from its reconstitution in 1878 until his death. A lifelong friend of Joseph Chamberlain, he was from 1886 one of the local leaders of the Liberal Unionist Party, but declined proposals to stand for parliament.

Beside professional and civic concerns, Mathews's main interest was mountaineering. He was introduced to the Alps in 1856 by his brother William. In November 1857 the two brothers, a cousin, Benjamin Attwood Mathews, and Edward Shirley Kennedy decided to form the Alpine Club. Kennedy, aided by Thomas Woodbine Hinchliff, took the leading share in its actual formation (between December 1857 and January 1858). Charles Edward Mathews played his part in the conquest of the Alps during the succeeding decade, and he continued to climb vigorously for more than forty years, long after all the other original members of the Alpine Club had retired from serious mountaineering. He was president of the club from 1878 to 1880, and was active in its affairs until the last year of his life. He was a voice for prudence in alpinism—except perhaps on the occasion when a sudden thirst caused him, descending from the Aiguille Verte, to drain the emergency half-bottle of champagne, to the outrage of his guide Melchior Anderegg. He was also one of the founders (1898) and the first president of the Climbers' Club, an association formed with the object of encouraging mountaineering in Great Britain and Ireland.

Besides numerous papers in the *Alpine Journal*, Mathews contributed articles on the guides Melchior and Jakob Anderegg to *Pioneers of the Alps* (1887) and a retrospective chapter to C. T. Dent's *Mountaineering* (1892) in the Badminton Library series, but his most important work in alpine literature is *The Annals of Mont Blanc* (1898), which contains a critical analysis of the original narratives of the early ascents of the mountain and a history and description of all the later routes by which its summit had been reached.

Mathews died at his home, 14 Farquhar Road, Edgbaston, Birmingham, on 20 October 1905, and was buried at Sutton Coldfield, his home for the previous twelve years. A monument to his memory was built in the garden of Couttet's Hotel at Chamonix. Another was proposed for Snowdonia, in honour of his British mountaineering interests: he climbed Mont Blanc twelve or thirteen times, but Snowdon and Cadair Idris about a hundred times each. 　　　　　A. L. MUMM, *rev.* JULIAN LOCK

Sources H. B. George, 'In memoriam: Charles Edward Matthews', *Alpine Journal*, 22 (1905), 592–600 · *The Times* (21 Oct 1905) · *Birmingham Daily Post* (21 Oct 1905) · *Birmingham Daily Post* (23 Oct 1905) · *Birmingham Daily Post* (24 Oct 1905) · *Birmingham Daily Post* (25 Oct 1905) · R. L. G. Irving, *A history of British mountaineering* (1955) · A. Lunn, *A century of mountaineering* (1957) · private information (1912) · Venn, *Alum. Cant.* · CGPLA Eng. & Wales (1906)
Likenesses Sarony, photograph, Alpine Club, London [*see illus.*]
Wealth at death £11,360 15s. 4d.: probate, 22 Jan 1906, *CGPLA Eng. & Wales*

Mathews, Charles James (1803–1878), actor and playwright, the only child of Charles *Mathews (1776–1835) and his second wife, Anne Jackson (*d.* 1869), was born in Basnett Street, Liverpool, on 26 December 1803, and baptized at St Helen's Church, York.

Education and early career After attending preliminary schools at Hackney and Fulham, Mathews went to Merchant Taylors', where he boarded with Thomas Cherry, the headmaster, who is said to have taken a strong dislike to him. He was then moved to a private school on Clapham Common kept by the lexicographer Charles Richardson, where he formed friendships with John Mitchell Kemble and Julian Young, and was one of Richardson's assistants in copying extracts for his *New English Dictionary*. On 4 May 1819 he was articled to Augustus Pugin as an architect, and designed the picture gallery for his father's cottage in Kentish Town, where he later met Byron, Scott, Moore, Coleridge, Lamb, Leigh Hunt, and other men of eminence. In company with his master he visited York, Oxford, and various provincial towns, executing sketches, some of which were inserted in architectural works.

A visit with Pugin to Paris, in which Mathews saw the principal French comedians, fostered a lurking disposition towards the stage. After his return he made his first appearance as an amateur, under the name of M. Perlet, at the Lyceum Theatre on 26 April 1822, playing Dorival, a comedian in *Le comédien d'étampes* (a French piece subsequently adapted by him under the title *He would be an Actor*), singing a song as M. Émile of the Théâtre Porte St Martin. He also acted under his own name as Werther in *The Sorrows of Werther*, by John Poole, in which his mother took the part of Charlotte. His imitations of French actors were received with much favour. His father urged him to adopt the stage, but he liked his profession. When his articles expired he refused a renewed invitation to join the architect John Nash, and went instead in 1823 to Ireland to build a house for Lord Blessington at Mountjoy Forest, co. Tyrone. Very little progress, or none at all, was made with the scheme. Mathews remained hunting, shooting, and fishing, and discussing details of the house, never to be built, and then accepted an invitation from his patron to accompany him to Italy. In Naples he stayed a year at the Palazzo Belvedere, where the party included his host and hostess, Miss Power, the sister of Lady Blessington, and Count D'Orsay, with whom he had a misunderstanding almost leading to a duel. His imitations of Italian life and manners were the delight of a fashionable world, English and foreign.

Becoming a professional actor After a couple of years spent in Wales as architect to a Welsh iron and coal company at Coed-talon, Flintshire, where he built Hartsheath Hall, an inn, a bridge, and some cottages, Mathews was employed by Nash, but kept on an office in Parliament Street as a practising architect. He occupied his leisure time in writing songs for his father's 'At Homes' and trifling pieces for the theatre, including *Pongwong* and *The Court Jesters*. On 30 April 1827, in company with D'Egville, he started once more, on an allowance from his father, for Italy. They visited Milan, Venice, and Florence, where Mathews caught smallpox. At the Palazzo San Clementi, Mathews played comic characters, such as Peter in *Romeo and Juliet*, Launcelot Gobbo, and Falstaff in *1 Henry IV*, at Lord Normanby's private theatre. From Rome, where Mathews suffered much from malaria, they returned to Venice, and at the close of 1830 Mathews arrived back in England on crutches. The next five years of desultory life, financed by his father, were spent in visiting the houses of noblemen and the like. His father's financial collapse forced him to accept the post of district surveyor at Bow, but this did not last long.

The death in 1835 of Mathews's father put an end to this idle career, and on 28 September 1835 he turned his attention seriously to the theatre: in conjunction with Frederick Yates, his father's partner, he opened the Adelphi Theatre. The first piece was *Mandrin*, an adaptation by Mathews of a well-known French melodrama. But the speculation failed, and Mathews retired from management. On 6 November 1835 he appeared at the Olympic in his own piece *The Humpbacked Lover*, in which he played George Rattleton, and in a farce by Leman Rede, *The Old and Young Stagers*—John Liston, who recited a prologue, being the old stager, and Mathews the young. His performance was fashionable, though his success was not triumphant.

Marriage and the stage On 11 January 1836 Mathews joined Madame Vestris [*see* Vestris, Lucia Elizabeth (1797–1856)] at the Olympic in *One Hour*; this was the beginning of a celebrated partnership. In their production of *The Old and Young Stagers*, their desire for authenticity led them to place carpets in the rooms on stage for the first time in any theatre. On 18 July 1838, at Kensington church, the couple were married, primarily to placate American sentiment before their forthcoming tour of the USA. None the less, the visit was unsuccessful. Mathews then reappeared at the Olympic in his own *Patter versus Clatter*, which remained a favourite piece. On 30 September 1839 Mathews and his wife opened at Covent Garden with an elaborate, but unsuccessful, revival of *Love's Labour's Lost*; the company included Robert Keeley, George Bartley, Louisa Nisbett, and Anne Humby. *Love* by Sheridan Knowles followed, introducing Ellen Tree (later Mrs Charles Kean), with little better result, and Mathews found himself involved in debts from which he was unable to free himself. *The Beggar's Opera*, with William Harrison as Macheath and Madame Vestris as Lucy Lockett, was more successful, and *The Merry Wives of Windsor*, with Mathews as Slender and Mrs Nisbett and Madame Vestris as the wives, proved a draw. During the period in which he held possession of Covent Garden, Mathews produced more than a hundred plays, operas, interludes, farces, melodramas, and pantomimes, including *A Midsummer Night's Dream*, given seventy times. Among the novelties were Leigh Hunt's *A Legend of Florence* (7 February 1840), performed thirteen times; *The Baronet*, a comedy by Haynes Bayly, hissed from the stage; *The Bride of Messina* (subsequently known as *John of Procida*), by Sheridan Knowles (19 September 1840); *The Greek Boy*, a musical afterpiece by Samuel Lover; Boucicault's *London Assurance*, in which Mathews played Dazzle; Knowles's *Old Maids*, a failure; and several farces, some of them (including *You Can't Marry your Grandmother*) his own works. Charles Kemble accepted an engagement and performed at the theatre. On 2 November 1841 Adelaide Kemble appeared as Bellini's Norma, with a success that drew the attention of the proprietors, who pressed Mathews for arrears of rent, and so sealed his ruin. He had incurred many debts and was paying 60 per cent interest, often borrowing from one to make a payment to another. His management finished on 30 April 1842. Arrested for debt and declared bankrupt, he was released under conditions with regard to his creditors that deprived him of all chance of shaking off the burden. A flight to Paris was followed by a fresh bankruptcy.

In October 1842 Mathews and his wife were engaged for Drury Lane by W. C. Macready, but they soon quarrelled with him, and transferred their services to the Haymarket. There they appeared on 14 November 1842, respectively as Charles Surface and Lady Teazle. On 29 August 1843 Mathews made a great hit as Giles in Planché's *Who's your Friend?*, and on 6 February 1844 a still greater success as Sir Charles Coldstream in Boucicault's *Used up*. On 22 February 1843 Mathews, with his wife, made his first appearance in Edinburgh, playing Mr Charles Swiftly in *One Hour* and in *Patter versus Clatter*. Because of a failed tour of Ireland as a result of the potato losses there, on 8 May 1845 he again found himself in the bankruptcy court, for £28,000. After performing at the Surrey and at the Princess's, and in various provincial towns, Mathews opened at the Lyceum on 18 October 1847 with *The Light Dragoons*, *The Two Queens*, and *The Pride of the Market*. For seven years the theatre was remuneratively conducted, but without enabling Mathews to get free from debt, and he gave it up on 24 March 1855. The next season saw him in his usual roles at Drury Lane. While playing in the provinces, he was arrested for bad debt on 4 July 1856 and imprisoned in Lancaster Castle.

Second marriage and further stage career On 8 August 1856 Mathews's wife died. A year later, after playing at Drury Lane, where he was acting-manager, he revisited America. There he met and married in 1857 his second wife, Mrs Elizabeth (Lizzie) Davenport, *née* Jackson (d. 1899), who, formerly married to William West, was also known as Lizzie Weston; she was an actress at Burton's Theatre, New York. He played for sixty nights at Burton's Theatre, the longest star performance ever known in New York at that time. In October 1858, with his wife as Lady Gay Spanker, he reappeared at the Haymarket as Dazzle in *London Assurance*. He performed a round of his favourite characters, including, for the first time, Paul Pry, and Goldfinch in Thomas Holcroft's *The Road to Ruin*. In 1860–61 he was again at Drury Lane, where he played Will Wander in a wild melodrama adapted by himself and called *The Savannah*, and on 25 November 1861 he appeared with his wife at the concert room (then called the Bijou Theatre) in Her Majesty's Theatre in an entertainment called *Mr and Mrs Mathews at Home*, illustrated by pictures by John O'Connor, from sketches by Mathews. *My Wife and I* and a burlesque by H. J. Byron, *The Sensation Fork, or, The Maiden, the Maniac, and the Midnight Murderers* were also given. In 1863 Mathews was again at the Haymarket, and the same year he played in Paris, at the Théâtre des Variétés, in *Un Anglais timide*, his own French version of W. B. Jerrold's *Cool as a Cucumber*. This experiment was repeated in the autumn of 1865, when, at the Vaudeville, he played in *L'homme blasé* (*Used up*). Both engagements were successful but were not renewed, though Mathews in July 1867 played *Un Anglais timide* at the St James's, for the benefit of Ravel, and gave *Cool as a Cucumber* the same night at the Olympic. Between these performances, Mathews had acted at the St James's in *Woodcock's Little Game* and in *Adventures of a Love-Letter*, his own adaptation of Sardou's *Pattes de mouche*. A scheme for a journey round the world led to a benefit at Covent Garden on 4 January 1870, in which, in scenes from various plays, the principal actors of the day took part. Mathews himself played his favourite character of Puff in the second act of *The Critic*, with Mrs Mathews appearing as Tilburina.

Final years, death, and reputation On 9 April 1870 Mathews made his first appearance at the Theatre Royal, Melbourne, in *Patter versus Clatter* and *Married for Money*. Various parts were played, and Ballarat, Sydney, and Adelaide were visited. The Australian trip ended on 31 January 1871, when Mathews set sail for Auckland. He performed *Used up* and *Cool as a Cucumber* at 11 a.m. on 7 February and sailed three hours later for Honolulu, where he acted for one night. On the 12th he arrived at San Francisco, where he performed for one week, then proceeded to New York and fulfilled a six-week engagement. A tour in the United States and Canada followed, and on 1 June 1872 he took his farewell of America at Wallack's Theatre, New York, as Sir Simon Simple in H. J. Byron's *Not such a Fool as he Looks*.

On 7 October 1872 Mathews appeared at the Gaiety Theatre, London, in *A Curious Case* and *The Critic*. A second engagement at the same house began on 26 May 1873, and a third on 29 September of the same year. In 1874 he was again at the Gaiety, and on 13 September 1875 produced there his own adaptation *My Awful Dad* (*Un père prodigue*). This was his last new part. The periods between these performances were spent in the provinces. In November 1875 he went to India, and played at Calcutta before the prince of Wales. In 1876 he was again at the Gaiety, and in 1877 at the Opéra Comique, where, in Samuel Foote's *The Liar* and G. H. Lewes's *The Cosy Couple*, he reappeared on 2 June 1877. The following year he started on a provincial tour with a company under the management of Sarah Thorne. On 8 June he made his last appearance, playing at Stalybridge in *My Awful Dad*. He died on 24 June 1878 at the Queen's Hotel in Manchester. His body was moved to 59 Belgrave Road, his last London residence, and was buried in Kensal Green cemetery on 29 June.

Mathews played some 240 characters, very many of them in his own pieces. His most conspicuous successes were obtained in light comedy and farce; passion and pathos seemed wholly alien to his nature. He was, within limits, an admirable comedian. In his early days he was a model of grace, brightness, and elegance. George H. Lewes tells how the youth of the day were wont to worship him, and says of his Affable Hawk in *The Game of Speculation* that its artistic merit was so great 'that it almost became an offence against morality, by investing a swindler with irresistible charms, and making the very audacity of deceit a source of pleasurable sympathy'. Lewes owns, however, that Mathews was 'utterly powerless in the manifestation of all the powerful emotions: rage, scorn, pathos, dignity, vindictiveness, tenderness, and wild mirth are all beyond his means. He cannot even laugh with animal heartiness. He sparkles; he never explodes.' Mathews had, however, airiness, finesse, aplomb, and, in spite of an occasional tendency to jauntiness, repose and good breeding, and he possessed powers of observation and gifts of mimicry. His popularity was indescribable, and at times embarrassing. His frequent imprisonment and the class of parts he played gained him a character he did not wholly deserve of 'a gay dog'. He was not at all the reckless character popularly supposed, and was a little shy in the presence of strangers.

Of Mathews's plays, mostly adaptations, no full catalogue seems to be in existence. A list of his own pieces and of those in which he had appeared constitutes an appendix to Charles Dickens's *Life of Charles James Mathews* (1879). Such of the plays as are printed are included in T. H. Lacy's Acting Edition and Benjamin Webster's *Acting National Drama*. The British Museum collection is meagre. In *The Chain of Events*, a drama in eight acts, Mathews collaborated with Slingsby Lawrence (Lewes). With the exception of this piece and *The Savannah*, a four-act melodrama, his plays were generally in three acts or fewer. His three-act pieces included *Black Domino*, *Dead for a Ducat*, and *Soft Sex*.

In two acts are *Aggravating Sam*, *Impudent Puppy*, *Kill Him Again*, and *Who Killed Cock Robin?* He wrote many one-act pieces, including *Cherry and Blue*, *His Excellency*, *Little Toddlekins*, *Mathews & Co.*, *Methinks I see my Father*, *My Mother's Maid*, and *Paul Pry Married and Settled*. Many of these are trifles, intended to serve a temporary purpose, and most have been long forgotten. Mathews also collaborated on a large number of works, and translated plays both from and into French.

JOSEPH KNIGHT, rev. RICHARD L. KLEPAC

Sources *The life of Charles James Mathews*, ed. C. Dickens, 2 vols. (1879) • H. S. Wyndham, *The annals of the Covent Garden Theatre: from 1732 to 1897*, 2 vols. (1906) • *The Times*, various • G. H. Lewes, *On actors and the nature of acting* (1875) • A. Mathews, *Memoirs of Charles Mathews* (1838) • private information (1894)
Archives BL, letters to Royal Literary Fund • Garr. Club, letters • Harvard TC • Hunt. L., letters; commonplace book • Princeton University Library, papers • Shakespeare Birthplace Trust RO, Stratford upon Avon, corresp. • Theatre Museum, London, letters • University of Pennsylvania Library, Philadelphia
Likenesses J. F. Lewis, pencil and chalk drawing, 1827, NPG • J. W. Childe, watercolours, 1835–45, Garr. Club • Queen Victoria, drawings, 1837, Royal Collection • Ape [C. Pellegrini], chromolithograph, NPG; repro. in *VF* (2 Oct 1875) • R. W. Buss, oils (as George Rattleton), Garr. Club • Hennah & Kent, cartes-de-visite, NPG • Mayall, cartes-de-visite, NPG • H. Watkins, cartes-de-visite, NPG • oils (after drawing by S. De Wilde), Garr. Club • photographs, NPG • prints, BM, Harvard TC, NPG
Wealth at death under £20,000: probate, 6 July 1878, *CGPLA Eng. & Wales*

Mathews [*formerly* West]**, Sir Charles Willie**, baronet (1850–1920), lawyer, was born on 16 October 1850 in New York, the son of William West and Elizabeth (Lizzie), *née* Jackson (*d.* 1899). His mother was an actress at Burton's Theatre, New York, under the stage name of Lizzie Weston. She remarried twice. Her third marriage in 1857 was to Charles James *Mathews (1803–1878), the actor and dramatist, whose second marriage it was. This theatrical background strongly influenced her son. Charles Willie Mathews, who assumed his second stepfather's surname by deed poll, was educated at Eton College. On leaving school at the age of eighteen, he spent three years in Europe before becoming a pupil in the chambers of Montagu Williams, a celebrated criminal barrister and a family friend. Williams recorded that Mathews was 'the very best pupil I ever had' (Williams, 294). He was called to the bar of the Middle Temple in 1872, and started practice, initially 'devilling' for Williams, at 5 Crown Office Row, moving from there in 1880 to 1 Essex Court. In 1886, on Williams's retirement as junior counsel to the Treasury at the Old Bailey, the position was divided, and Mathews was appointed as one of two joint holders. In 1888 he became one of the two senior counsel. On 11 August of the same year he married Lucy, daughter of Edward Hugh Lindsay *Sloper, a well-known musician. He stood unsuccessfully for parliament as Liberal candidate for Winchester in the general election of 1892. He was made recorder of Salisbury in 1893, and in 1901 a bencher of the Middle Temple. In 1907, on the occasion of the opening of the new central criminal court by Edward VII, he was knighted. In 1908 he succeeded Lord Desart as director of public prosecutions, an office which he discharged until his death. He was made a KCB in 1911, and a baronet in 1917.

Mathews was much in the public eye as an advocate in the more sensational criminal trials at the Old Bailey and on the western circuit and also, unusually for a criminal advocate, in many notorious civil cases. He was skilled in criminal law, an adroit advocate and cross-examiner, especially of expert witnesses. A small man, agile and quick, with a dapper figure and a face 'somewhat feminine in appearance' (Marjoribanks, 90), he was a fluent speaker of real eloquence despite a weak, high-pitched voice which some found unpleasant. His manner, exquisitely polished and precise, was somewhat foppish and artificial; his forensic style, like that of his pupil master, was dramatic and 'carefully rehearsed' (ibid., 90). 'If you saw and heard him in action on the Circuit or at Hampshire Sessions', Lord Simon recalled, 'you did not need to be told that he was the son of an actor' (Simon, 289). In timing, emphasis, and gesture, in choice of language and beauty of diction, in rhetorical appeals, surprise effects, stage whispers, and 'the singular inflexions of his voice' (The Times), he was of the school of Henry Irving (a friend of Montagu Williams). He could move a jury to tears or rouse it to its feet by the pathos he injected into a single sentence. Even on counsel and judges his impact could be mesmeric. Out of court too he was often histrionic. Christmas Humphreys remembered him in chambers outlining a projected prosecution 'as if it were a passionate speech to the jury or an appeal for mercy from the scaffold' (Humphreys, 71).

Murder trials in which Mathews appeared for the defence included the Penge mystery, involving homicide by starvation, and the trial of the poisoner Dr Lampson. He prosecuted in R. v. Dudley and Stephens (1884), the classic case of cannibalism by shipwrecked mariners. After 1888 he prosecuted in many important criminal cases: the Hansard Union fraud case (1892–3), the trial of the Jameson raiders (1896), the trial of Louise Masset, who murdered her illegitimate child, and of Arthur Deveureux, who poisoned his wife and sons, the trial for high treason of 'Colonel' Arthur Alfred Lynch (1903), and of Robert Wood in the Camden Town murder (1907). He exercised great skill in turning a court's sympathy from the defendant to the crown. His description of the abortionist Dr Laerman playing the piano to drown the screams of his dying victim, was harrowingly effective. His melodramatic techniques, however, went out of fashion. Even at the time some judges found them too contrived. Mr Justice Cave once discountenanced him in a murder trial by deliberately interrupting his opening speech for the crown at the dramatic moment.

Mathews's appearances in the civil courts included the Oscar Wilde libel suit, the Colin Campbell divorce, and the Jockey Club arbitration proceedings, in which Sir George Chetwynd was awarded a farthing's damages for defamation. As director of public prosecutions, he showed himself a persistent, aggressive, some thought unfair, even vindictive advocate for the crown: to hear him cross-examine a defence witness 'was at times painful' (Bowen-Rowlands, 97), and defence counsel bridled.

Yet afterwards Mathews, laughing it off as 'pure advocacy' (Abinger, 239), would win over his ruffled opponent with the irresistible charm and genuine good nature that gained him many lifelong friends. Indeed his human sympathies provoked charges of complacency. When the Charing Cross Bank failed through the gross and protracted fraud of a director, he long refused to prosecute out of compassion for the delinquent's family. He was a modest man, who declined the opportunity of judicial office. He was once offered a brief to appear before the privy council. Creeping in to observe the procedure, immediately afterwards he asked the solicitors to let him refuse the brief, as he did not feel up to the task. On the day of his knighthood, when his name was mistakenly announced as 'Mr Charles Williams', he modestly kept silent and did not step forward for the royal accolade: only after others had resolved the error did the investiture duly take place. Conscientious and painstaking, he postponed his retirement as director of public prosecutions because of the First World War, and maintained a punishing workload into his late sixties, to the detriment of his health.

Willie Mathews, as he was familiarly known, was a cultivated and highly sociable man of varied interests, a practised horseman and assiduous attender at race meetings, a discriminating lover of literature and a regular 'firstnighter', a member of the Turf, the Garrick, and the Beefsteak clubs. 'A delightful combination of Etonian, Bohemian, courtier and lawyer' (The Times), he was a lively companion and after-dinner speaker, with a ready supply of vivid anecdotes and a fastidious wit, which quelled, with a gentle flick, any undue familiarity. A gifted linguist, fond of travel, he was an amiable and popular man, engaging, courteous, and kindly, who was counted a friend by both Edward VII and George V. Having suffered for some time from nephritis, he died in a nursing home at 4 Dorset Square, London, on 6 June 1920. His wife survived him. There were no children of the marriage.   A. LENTIN

Sources The Times (7 June 1920) · DNB · Law Journal (12 June 1920) · E. Marjoribanks, The life of Sir Edward Marshall Hall (1972) · S. Jackson, Mr Justice Avory (1935) · F. W. Ashley, My sixty years in the law (1936) · E. Bowen-Rowlands, In court and out of court: some personal recollections (1925) · [J. Allsebrook, first Viscount Simon], Retrospect: the memoirs of the Rt. Hon. Viscount Simon (1952) · E. Abinger, Forty years at the bar (1930) · C. Humphreys, Both sides of the circle (1978) · D. G. Browne, Sir Travers Humphreys: a biography (1960) · R. Jackson, Case for the prosecution: a biography of Sir Archibald Bodkin (1962) · T. Humphreys, Criminal days (1946) · M. Williams, Leaves of a life, 2 vols. (1890), vol. 1 · m. cert. · d. cert.

Archives BL, corresp. with Lord Gladstone, Add. MSS 46065–46084

Likenesses R. Wood, sketch, 1907, repro. in Marjoribanks, Life of Sir Edward Marshall Hall · W. Stoneman, photograph, 1917, NPG · H. Furniss, pen-and-ink sketches, NPG · Spy [L. Ward], chromolithograph caricature, repro. in VF (6 Feb 1892) · photograph (with Sir Richard Muir), repro. in R. Muir, A memoir of a public prosecutor (1927)

Wealth at death £23,848 17s. 10d.: probate, 21 July 1920, CGPLA Eng. & Wales

Mathews [née Strong], **Eliza Kirkham** (1772–1802), novelist and poet, was born in Exeter, one of at least four children born to George S. Strong (d. 1796), a physician, and his wife, Mary, about whom nothing is known. The sole survivor of her family and penniless by 1796, she first published, by subscription, *Poems*, a collection of sonnets, odes, ballads, love songs, and eulogies memorializing her recent dead—both parents, a brother, two sisters, and two women friends. Contributing to the *Monthly Mirror*, teaching in a girls' school, and existing hand to mouth, on 19 September 1797 she hastily married the impecunious comedian Charles *Mathews (1776–1835), who 'inadvertently' had proposed to her out of 'pity' at their first introduction (Mathews, 199–200).

According to Charles Mathews's second wife, 'whom he *really* loved' (Mathews, 200), the first Mrs Mathews wrote incessantly, secretly, and badly for the remainder of her short life, hoping to alleviate the couple's poverty. The later writing was supposedly an outgrowth of the early talent she evinced in her home town, where she was 'a triton among the minnows' (ibid., 241). However, other than the *Poems*, most of her pre-1797 canon cannot be firmly ascribed to her. It probably included the four volumes of *Constance: a Novel*, 'The First Literary Attempt of A Young Lady' (1785); *The Pharos: a Collection of Periodical Essays* 'by the Author of *Constance*' (1787); and the epistolary work *Argus: the House-Dog at Eadlip* 'by the Author of *Constance* and the *Pharos*' (1789). At least two early publications generally ascribed to her, *Simple Facts, or, The History of an Orphan* (1793) and *Perplexities, or, The Fortunate Elopement* (1794), by a 'Mrs. Mathews', cannot be the works of Eliza Kirkham Mathews, as they pre-date her marriage (Grundy, 289).

Containing at least one (unpublished?) play revision for her husband's 'benefit' (Mathews, 245), Mathews's later canon appeared under her married name. From 1801 to 1803 were published *Mornings' Amusement* and *Afternoon Amusements*, both educational nature texts for children, and *Lessons of Truth* (1802). Her most important work during this period is the novel *What has been* (1801), a realistic treatment of the vicissitudes of a woman writer, the sole support of a husband and baby, as she peddles to publishers her 'found' manuscript about a doomed female forebear. In a reversal of the male *Bildungsroman* this novel features the motif of women wanderers coming of age as they starve and narrate their lives to other women; her theme finds unusual reflection in sonnet 17, 'The Indian', from the 1802 edition of *Poems*. Several novels, thematically similar, appeared posthumously: *Ellinor, or, The Young Governess* (1809); *Griffith Abbey, or, Memoirs of Eugenia* (1808); and *Adelaide, or, Trials of Fortitude* (1813).

Mathews died on 25 May 1802 in London, after a lingering haemorrhagic lung disease afflicted her 'small' frame (Mathews, 201)—the result of 'a withering sickness' from the womb that 'form'd thy cradle but to form thy tomb', according to her husband's elegy that accompanied the posthumous edition of her poems. The volume was edited and introduced by Charles Mathews in 1802.

Polly Stevens Fields

Sources A. J. Mathews, *Memoirs of Charles Mathews, comedian*, 2 vols. (1838) • Blain, Clements & Grundy, *Feminist comp.*, 726–7 • private information (2004) [I. Grundy] • I. Grundy, '"A novel in a series of letters by a lady": Richardson and some Richardsonian novels', *Samuel Richardson: tercentenary essays* (1989), 223–6, 288–90 • V. Woolf, *The common reader: the first series* (New York, 1925)

Mathews, (Charles) Elkin (1851–1921), publisher and antiquarian bookseller, was born on 31 August 1851 at Gravesend, Kent, one of the nine children of Thomas George Mathews, timber and slate merchant, and his wife, Frances Elkin. Although born in Gravesend, downstream from London on the Thames where his family for generations had been engaged in shipbuilding, shipping, and other related enterprises, Mathews spent most of his childhood and youth in the village of Codford St Mary in the Vale of Wylye on the edge of Salisbury Plain in Wiltshire. His father had retired early from business, and he and his family of three sons and six daughters were largely supported by his wife's well-to-do father. Here, in a house known as The Poplars, Elkin, like his siblings, was allowed to follow his own inclinations, which were antiquarian and literary. In reply to a reporter's question in 1906 as to how he came to select his profession, Mathews replied: 'I have been a collector of old poets and *belles lettres* all my life and, therefore, when the time came for me to choose a vocation, it seemed natural that I should turn my hobby to a practical use' ('A chat with Mr. Elkin Mathews', 417).

Having learned accounting from his older brother, Thomas George, Mathews followed him to London, and was employed by Charles John Stewart of King William Street, Strand, who was known as the last of the learned old booksellers. Following his apprenticeship, Mathews managed Peach's popular library at Bath for several years before returning to London, where he found employment in the firm of Messrs Sotheran in Piccadilly. Ambitious to go into business for himself, in 1884 Mathews used the £125 he had acquired from an uncle to open an antiquarian and general bookshop at 16 Cathedral Close, Exeter.

In 1887 Mathews became acquainted with a young bibliophile from Devon, John Lane, who was working for Mathews's brother as a clerk in the railway clearing house at Euston Station, London. Aspiring to the role of bookseller and publisher, Lane persuaded Mathews that setting up shop in London with himself as silent partner would be advantageous. Mathews with some reluctance at length agreed and, through Lane's agency, leased premises at 6B Vigo Street near Burlington House. Since Robert Dunthorne, the shop's previous occupant, had decorated his small 'cabinet of fine arts' with a sign designating it 'the Rembrandt Head', Mathews and Lane replaced it with one bearing the physiognomy of Sir Thomas Bodley, an association Mathews had brought with him from Exeter, the birthplace of the famous book collector. Thus the new firm which opened for business in September 1887 became known as the Bodley Head.

Although Mathews had dabbled in publishing at Exeter, he and Lane soon developed plans to publish on a larger scale, commencing what would become one of the most illustrious and successful publishing firms of the late nineteenth and early twentieth centuries. Some of its early authors were the leading young avant-garde writers and artists of the 1890s, including Oscar Wilde, Ernest

Dowson, W. B. Yeats, Arthur Symons, Aubrey Beardsley, and Max Beerbohm.

As the Bodley Head prospered, Mathews established himself and his sisters in a home at 1 Blenheim Road, in the fashionable and arty suburb of Bedford Park. His next-door neighbour was John Butler Yeats and his family, which included his son, the poet W. B. Yeats, and his younger son, the artist Jack Yeats. Mathews married the artist Edith Calvert on 16 July 1896. They had one child, a daughter, Nest Elkin Mathews. After their marriage the couple lived for a time at 13 Addison Road, London, but in 1903 moved to a house called Russettings, Shire Lane, in the Hertfordshire village of Chorleywood, which became Mathews's residence until his death.

In January 1892 Lane ceased to be a silent partner and joined the Bodley Head full-time. The partners soon found, however, that their quite different temperaments and business styles were incompatible. Mathews, a quiet, mild-mannered man (later described in *Punch* as the 'monkish, medieval Mathews'), did not suit well with the aggressive and manipulative Lane. In April 1894 Mathews viewed his deliberate exclusion from the dinner celebrating the first number of the *Yellow Book* as the last in a series of provocations and affronts engineered by Lane. After a struggle between the two proprietors over the firm's authors, the partnership was dissolved on 30 September 1894. Mathews remained in the premises at 6B Vigo Street, while Lane, taking the Bodley Head sign with him, moved to new quarters across the street in Albany.

After Mathews resumed business on his own, he continued the practice of the early Bodley Head, bringing out books and periodicals central to the decadent and symbolist movements of the 1890s—Dowson's *Dilemmas* (1895), Lionel Johnson's *Poems* (1895), and Yeats's *The Wind among the Reeds* (1899). As the firm of Elkin Mathews entered the new century, its publisher brought out a whole host of books crucial to the rise of modern literature. Among his major authors was Ezra Pound who as a young, unknown American poet arrived on the firm's doorstep in the autumn of 1908 'sans sous' (as he later recalled). At this crucial stage of Pound's career, Mathews played an indispensable role as his publisher and as his entrée to London literary society. As a result of bringing out Pound's first regularly published book *Personae* (1909), Mathews found his announcement parodied in *Punch*: 'Mr. Welkin Mark [Elkin Mathews] … begs to announce that he has secured for the English market the palpitating works of the new Montana (U.S.A.) poet, Mr. Ezekiel Ton [Ezra Pound].' In addition to Pound's *Cathay* (1915), and the infamous *Lustra* (1916), Mathews published Wilfrid Gibson's *Urlyn the Harper* (1902), John Millington Synge's *The Shadow of the Glen* and *Riders to the Sea* (1905), James Joyce's *Chamber Music* (1907), several of Jack Yeats's illustrated books, R. D. Aldington's *Images of Desire* (1919), and Nancy Cunard's first book of poems, *Outlaws* (1921).

Dedicated to making poetry more widely accessible, Mathews inaugurated two series of books of poetry in paperback which sold for 1s. each. The first of these series was edited by Laurence Binyon and was entitled Elkin

Mathews' Shilling Garland. It included editions of such popular successes as Stephen Phillips's *Christ in Hades, and other Poems* and Henry Newbolt's *Admirals All, and other Verses*. The Vigo Cabinet series of paperback books comprised 145 titles published between 1900 and 1918, leading Mathews to claim that it was 'the longest series of original contemporary verse in existence'. Among its most notable titles were John Masefield's *Ballads* (1910), Yeats's *The Tables of the Law* and *The Adoration of the Magi* (1904), James Elroy Flecker's *The Bridge of Fire* (1907), and Max Weber's *Cubist Poems* (1914).

Having lost his lease on the Vigo Street premises, Mathews moved to 4A Cork Street in January 1913, where he continued his rare book and publishing business until his death in 1921. Looking back over Mathews's publishing career of some thirty years, one must concede that his support for young, often unknown poets earned him many successes and, indisputably, the place of honour Robert Scholes gives him among that handful of 'small publishers who were so influential in British literary developments around the turn of the century', those courageous 'men who had a direct hand in the shaping of new literature' ('Grant Richards to James Joyce', *Studies in Bibliography*, 16, 1963, 139). After a brief bout of pneumonia, Mathews died on 10 November 1921 at his home in Chorleywood, where he was buried in the parish churchyard.

JAMES G. NELSON

Sources J. G. Nelson, *Elkin Mathews: publisher to Yeats, Joyce, Pound* (1989) · J. G. Nelson, *The early nineties: a view from the Bodley Head* (1971) · 'A chat with Mr. Elkin Mathews', *Publisher and Bookseller*, 2 (24 Feb 1906), 417–18 · 'Books and the man: Mr. Elkin Mathews', *Bookman's Journal and Print Collector*, 1 (1920), 245 · 'About Mr. Elkin Mathews', *St James's Budget*, 29 (1894), literary suppl., 26 · J. L. May, *John Lane and the nineties* (1936)
Archives U. Reading L., business corresp. and papers · U. Reading L., working diaries | Bodl. Oxf., letters from Michael Field
Likenesses J. B. Yeats, drawing, Dec 1893, repro. in Nelson, *Elkin Mathews*; priv. coll. · photograph, c.1912, U. Reading, Elkin Mathews archive; repro. in Nelson, *Elkin Mathews* · J. B. Yeats, drawing, U. Reading, Elkin Mathews archive; repro. in Nelson, *Elkin Mathews* · portraits, repro. in Nelson, *Elkin Mathews*
Wealth at death £4011 5s. 7d.: probate, 5 Jan 1922, CGPLA Eng. & Wales

Mathews, Dame **Elvira Sibyl Maria** [Vera] **Laughton** (1888–1959), director of the Women's Royal Naval Service, was born at 130 Sinclair Road, Hammersmith, Middlesex, on 25 September 1888, the daughter of Sir John Knox *Laughton (1830–1915), naval instructor, and his second wife, Maria Josepha di Alberti (d. 1950). She was educated at the convents of the Religious of St Andrew, Streatham, then (like her mother) at Tournai, and then at King's College, London.

As a girl, Vera Laughton joined the militant Women's Social and Political Union, and women's rights remained an important thread of her life thereafter. She joined the Catholic Women's Suffrage Society (later the St Joan's Social and Political Alliance) at or soon after its foundation in 1911 and nearly fifty years later presided over the St Joan international meeting at Geneva in summer 1959. She employed her journalistic skills, first as sub-editor of *The*

Dame Elvira Sibyl Maria Laughton Mathews (1888–1959), by
unknown photographer

Suffragette, working in London and Glasgow, and in 1914 as
acting editor.

In the early part of the war Laughton applied to work at
the Admiralty, only to be told that no women were
allowed; she then moved to sub-edit a journal, the *Ladies
Field*. When the Women's Royal Naval Service (WRNS) was
formed in 1917 she hastened to join it, and after an officer's course, went as WRNS unit officer to HMS *Victory VI*, a
naval training depot at Crystal Palace. There she kept a
happy ship, inspiring her crew with confidence to tackle
the daunting tasks now for the first time imposed on service women. She was also public-spirited, active in legislative reforms and arranging lectures on matters of public
interest. A keen sportswoman herself, she encouraged
and promoted all kinds of inter-service sports during and
after the war.

Laughton was appointed MBE when the WRNS unit was
disbanded in 1919. After demobilization she published a
booklet entitled *The Wrens: a Story of their Beginnings and
Doings in Different Parts*. She was active in the Association of
Wrens, and as its first vice-president founded and edited
its magazine, *The Wren*, from February 1921. She also
launched *Time and Tide*, bringing out its first number in
May 1920. In 1921 she sat on the committee of the International Women's Franchise Club, which supported
women's emancipation. She was the first captain of the

Sea Ranger ship *Wren*, being enrolled with her company
by Lady Baden-Powell in July 1922.

These activities were inevitably curtailed when Laughton sailed to Japan to marry in the Roman Catholic church
in Kobe on 10 June 1924 (and then in a civil ceremony at the
British consulate). Her husband was Ernest Gordon Dewar
Mathews (1880/81–1943), an engineer. Their first child,
Elvira, was born in Japan; two sons followed after their
return to London. In Japan, Mrs Laughton Mathews, as she
became known, acquired some knowledge of Japanese
language and culture; she was also appointed commissioner for British guides in Japan, running her own company and travelling extensively to attend rallies.

The family returned to Britain in 1927, settling at 57
Carlton Hill, Maida Vale, London. Laughton Mathews
resumed her concern with women's rights, compiling
with Phyllis Challoner *Towards Citizenship: a Handbook of
Women's Emancipation* (1928). Her work with the guides and
rangers expanded as she became a division commissioner,
then, in 1930, district commissioner for Camberwell. In
1928 she became captain of the Sea Ranger ship *Golden
Hind*, a responsibility she held until 1939. Every year she
took the Sea Rangers of the *Golden Hind*, together with her
husband and children, to camp, often abroad. While
chairman from 1932 to 1939 of the St Joan's Social and Political Alliance she gave evidence on their behalf before the
select committee of the House of Lords on the age of marriage, urging that it should be raised to sixteen for boys
and girls. She was active in many other organizations
working for the benefit of society in general and for
women and young people in particular.

With the re-formation of the WRNS in 1939 Laughton
Mathews was appointed director, with Ethel Goodenough
as her deputy. During her service she travelled to virtually
every establishment where Wrens were posted. The CBE
was conferred on her in 1942, the DBE in 1945. Dame Vera,
as she became, won great acclaim within the Admiralty, in
parliament, and among her own Wrens for the humanity
and common sense with which she led her force. After the
war she worked to forge the Wrens into a permanent service, retiring in 1947.

Dame Vera's capabilities were immediately called on by
the post-war government; she was appointed chairman of
the Domestic Coal Consumers' Council set up when the
coal industry was nationalized; and when the gas industry
was nationalized she sat on the South Eastern Gas Board,
the first woman in gas management in Britain, a post she
held until shortly before her death. These positions led to
her service on various subsidiary bodies dealing with the
consumption of domestic fuels. Dame Vera's last public
act was to preside at the lord chancellor's unveiling of the
memorial to Christabel Pankhurst in July 1959. She died at
her home, 14A Ashley Gardens, London, on 25 September
1959.   LESLEY THOMAS

Sources *The Times* (28 Sept 1959) · J. Woollacombe, *The Times* (6 Oct
1959), 13c · C. Fry, 'Farewell', *The Wren* (Oct 1959), 5 · *WWW* ·
E. Crawford, *The women's suffrage movement* (1999), 391 · M. Lloyd,
Tablet (3 Oct 1959), 846 · P. C. Challoner, *Tablet* (10 Oct 1959), 865 · b.
cert. · m. cert. · d. cert. · *CGPLA Eng. & Wales* (1959)

Likenesses W. Stoneman, photograph, 1958, NPG · A. Devas, oils, IWM · photograph, NPG [*see illus.*]

Wealth at death £13,660 19s. 2d.: probate, 3 Nov 1959, *CGPLA Eng. & Wales*

Mathews [Matthews], **Lemuel** (*b.* 1643/4, *d.* in or before 1725), Church of Ireland clergyman, was one of at least three sons of Marmaduke *Matthews (*c.*1606–*c.*1683), clergyman and ejected minister, and his wife, whose name is unknown. On 25 May 1661, aged seventeen, he matriculated from Lincoln College, Oxford. That same year, at the visitation of the diocese of Connor, he was recorded as being a schoolmaster at Carrickfergus, co. Antrim. Some time before 1667 Mathews received the degree of MA and later became DD. It is unknown which universities granted either of these degrees. After leaving Oxford he became chaplain to Jeremy Taylor, bishop of Down, Connor, and Dromore. In 1666 Taylor presented him to the vicarage of Glenavy and the prebendary of Cairncastle in the diocese of Connor. However it appears from the diocesan succession lists that Mathews did not gain possession of the vicarage of Glenavy until 1680. In 1667 he published in honour of his recently deceased patron *A Pandarique Elegie*.

Mathews was installed as vicar of Aghagallon, Magherameske, and Aghalee on 7 October 1668. On 2 November 1674 he was appointed archdeacon of Down. In 1689 he was one of the many Anglican clergymen in Ireland attainted by James II's Irish parliament. However, in 1690 he was made vicar-general of the united diocese of Down and Connor. In December 1693 a royal commission was established to inquire into and correct various abuses alleged to have been committed by the bishop and clergy of the diocese of Down and Connor. In February 1694 this commission held an extraordinary visitation at Lisburn, and subsequently Mathews was deprived of all his livings. The articles against Mathews claimed that he had not resided on his livings for the past twenty years but instead had lived at Lisburn. Furthermore he was accused of neglecting his cures by not endowing vicars on any of his livings. Instead it was said that he had appointed unqualified and unfit curates to his parishes and only paid them an insufficient allowance. Other charges brought against him included the maladministration of diocesan business, such as altering the visitation books, issuing blank licences for marriage, and presenting unfit candidates for ordination. Mathews was also charged with simony. It was alleged that he paid £200 for the archdeaconry of Connor to be granted to his nephew, Philip Mathews.

The day following his deprivation Mathews left for London to appeal against the judgment. For the next ten years he attempted to lodge an appeal against the verdict in the courts. He addressed a series of appeals to lord chancellors Cox, Freeman, and Phipps, the House of Commons, and the House of Lords, both in Ireland and England, King William, and Queen Anne, as well as to one of the commissioners, the bishop of Derry, William King. He set out his arguments in a series of pamphlets which appear to have been issued privately. In 1703 he printed *The Proceedings Against Lemuel Mathews, at the Regal Visitation Held at Lisburn*

1693 and *A Letter to the Right Reverend William Lord Bishop of Derry. Demonstrations that the lord chancellor of Ireland is bound by the statute and common law and also by his commission and oath as chancellor to grant a commission of delegates to Archdeacon Mathews upon his appeal* was published in 1704, as was *The Argument for a Commission of Delegates upon his Appeal and Querel of Nullities*. That same year he published his petition, *To the Honourable the Commons of England in Parliament Assembled*, and *Notes on the case and petition of Archdeacon Mathews to the honourable the Commons of England in parliament assembled*. In his defence Mathews claimed that he was not obliged to reside on his cures but as archdeacon was required to reside at Lisburn, where the cathedral of the diocese was located. Moreover he claimed that as chancellor he was excused from parochial residence by law. He also claimed that the charges against him were general and non-specific, and that the proceedings against him were hasty, speedy, and arbitrary in manner. He argued that the commission had overreached its terms of reference and likened it to the high commission, as there appeared to be no form of redress. He also implied that the real reason for his deprivation was that he prosecuted the rights of the church too vigorously. Furthermore he believed that there was a conspiracy against him formulated by members of the laity who felt threatened by his activities.

Nevertheless Mathews's repeated attempts to bring his appeal to court were unsuccessful for over a decade. However, in 1705 the Irish House of Lords was receptive to his petition and addressed the lord lieutenant, the duke of Ormond, to intercede with Queen Anne on Mathews's behalf. The lord lieutenant replied that he would take care of it in the most effectual manner he could. Subsequently it seems that Mathews was restored to the prebendary of Cairncastle but not to his other livings. It is not clear exactly when Mathews died. It would appear that he survived into the second decade of the eighteenth century as he continued to petition for the archdeaconry in the 1710s. Moreover, Mathews's successor to the prebend of Cairncastle was collated as late as 1720. Furthermore Walter Harris claimed in 1745 that his death occurred some twenty years previously. On this basis it seems that Mathews, who is not known to have married, died in or before 1725. CHARLOTTE FELL-SMITH, *rev.* CIARAN DIAMOND

Sources J. B. Leslie, *Clergy of Connor* (1993) · J. B. Leslie, *Biographical succession list of the diocese of Down* (1936) · *Whole works of James Ware*, ed. W. Harris, 2 (1745) · H. Cotton, *Fasti ecclesiae Hibernicae*, 3 (1849) · Foster, *Alum. Oxon.* · *Journal of the House of Lords [of Ireland]* (1780) · BL, Add. MS 21132 · BL, Lansdowne MS 446 · L. Mathews, *The proceedings against Lemuel Mathews, at the regal visitation held at Lisburn 1693* (1703) · L. Mathews, *A letter to the Right Reverend William Lord bishop of Derry* (1703) · L. Mathews, *Demonstrations that the lord chancellor of Ireland is bound by the statute and common law and also by his commission and oath as chancellor to grant a commission of delegates to Archdeacon Mathews upon his appeal* (1704) · L. Mathews, *The argument for a commission of delegates upon his appeal and querel of nullities* (1704) · *CSP dom.*, 1694–5 · T. Sweeney, *Ireland and the printed word: a short descriptive catalogue of early books … relating to Ireland, printed, 1475–1700* (Dublin, 1997) · F. T. G. Robinson Gaverley, D. R. Esslemont, and P. J. Wallis, *Eighteenth-century British books: an author*

union catalogue, 4 (1981) · DNB · R. Mant, History of the Church of Ireland, 2 (1840)
Archives BL, petitions, Add. MS 21132 · Representative Church Body Library, Dublin, ecclesiastical form book

Mathews, Sir Lloyd William (1850–1901), slavery abolitionist and politician in Zanzibar, was born on 7 March 1850 at Funchal, Madeira, the son of Captain William Mathews, a pioneer of the volunteer movement, and his wife, Jane Penfold of Sussex. He entered the Royal Navy in 1863 as a naval cadet, became a midshipman on 23 September 1866, and in 1868 was stationed in the Mediterranean.

Mathews first saw active service in the Second Anglo-Asante War of 1873–4. He received the war medal and was promoted lieutenant. On 27 August 1875 he was appointed lieutenant on board HMS *London*, which was engaged in suppressing the slave trade on the east coast of Africa. A capable and enterprising officer, he drilled his own recruits, captured many Arab dhows, and was commended by the Admiralty. He retired from the navy with the rank of lieutenant in 1881.

In 1877 Mathews had been selected to command the army of Bargash, the sultan of Zanzibar, and to drill his troops on the European model. He trained and equipped a military force of 1000 regulars and 5000 irregulars, and worked entirely for the Zanzibar government. He was given the rank of brigadier-general in the Zanzibar army, and in 1881 he captured the Arab slave dealers who had murdered Captain Brownrigg of the Royal Navy. Mathews retained the confidence of Bargash's successors, and was successful in urging the suppression of slavery. In 1889 a decree was issued purchasing the freedom of all slaves who had taken refuge in the sultan's dominions and from 1890 the traffic of slaves was prohibited in Zanzibar. In November 1890, in accordance with the Anglo-German convention, Zanzibar was formally declared a British protectorate. In 1891 Mathews was appointed British consul-general for east Africa, but he never took up the post, preferring to remain in the sultan's service. In October 1891 British influence got Mathews appointed first minister and treasurer of Zanzibar, despite the sultan's initial hostility. Mathews proved a reforming administrator. His strong personality influenced successive sultans: in 1896, on the death of Sultan Hamed bin Thwain, he opposed Khalid's attempt to seize the throne; after the bombardment of the palace by British warships Khalid was compelled to submit. Mathews then secured the installation of Sultan Hamed bin Mahommed, who favoured British interests (27 August 1896). Mathews's reforming energies brought about the abolition of legal slavery in 1897 and compensated the slave owners. Farms were established for the cultivation of new products, and Western methods of agriculture were introduced.

The British government officially recognized Mathews's valuable work, and created him CMG in 1880, and KCMG in 1894. He also held the first class of the Zanzibar order of the Hammudie, and the order of the crown of Prussia. His prestige remained high during the whole of his career and his name became a household word throughout the European colonies in east Africa for strict justice and honest administration. He died of malaria at Zanzibar on 11 October 1901, and was buried in the British cemetery outside the town. [ANON.], rev. LYNN MILNE

Sources The Times (12 Oct 1901) · R. N. Lyne, Zanzibar in contemporary times (1905) · R. N. Lyne, An apostle of empire (1936) · H. S. Newman, Banani: the transition from slavery to freedom in Zanzibar (1898) · E. Younghusband, Glimpses of east Africa and Zanzibar (1910) · Oxford history of east Africa, 3 vols. (1963–76)
Likenesses portrait, repro. in Lyne, Zanzibar, 100

Mathews, Lucia Elizabeth. *See* Vestris, Lucia Elizabeth (1797–1856).

Mathews, Thomas (1676–1751), naval officer, eldest son of Colonel Edward Mathews (d. 1700), and Jane, daughter of Sir Thomas *Armstrong, was born in October 1676 at Llandaff Court, Glamorgan, the seat of the family for many generations, later the palace of the bishops of Llandaff. His father was a fervent whig convert; his wife's father was a whig martyr, executed for his thoroughgoing complicity in the Rye House plot. Mathews entered the navy about 1690, on the *Albemarle* with Sir Francis Wheeler. On 31 October 1699 Admiral Matthew Aylmer promoted him lieutenant of his flagship, the *Boyne*. The promotion was confirmed on 16 March 1700 when the Admiralty appointed him to the *Deal Castle*.

Early career, 1703–1717 Mathews took post on 24 May 1703 in the *Yarmouth* in the West Indies under John Graydon; he remained with Graydon's squadron as it suffered near ruin from Caribbean summer, chilling September fog off Newfoundland, and a stormy passage home. He commanded the frigate *Kinsale* in the channel in 1704, and after that the *Dover* (50 guns), in which he crossed to North America, convoying home the New England trade in late 1706. March 1708 saw the *Dover* with the squadron under Sir George Byng that was hurrying to Scotland to prevent Forbin's Dunkirk fleet from landing a Franco-Jacobite invasion force. On sighting Byng's ships off the Firth of Forth, Forbin fled northwards. The heavier British ships were unable to close, but the *Dover* and another clean ship did so. The cannonading, which was plainly audible ashore, began off Montrose at about 4 p.m. on 13 March. Mathews tried to advance to engage *Le Mars*, in which he presumed (correctly) the Pretender was embarked, but French warships blocked his path. The chase continued during the night past Aberdeen, but in the end only the *Salisbury* was forced to surrender. Byng ordered Mathews to scout further north, a foul-weather mission that found nothing because the invasion force had headed home. After a brief command of the *Gloucester*, Mathews moved to a new ship, the *Chester* (54 guns), in 1709. In late March he was with Lord Dursley in the Soundings when Du Guay Trouin was sighted. Most of Trouin's ships outsailed Dursley's and escaped, but Mathews caught up with the *Gloire* (44 guns) and after staying close through the night engaged and captured her.

In 1710 the *Chester*, under Commodore George Martin, participated in the conquest of Nova Scotia, playing a

Thomas Mathews (1676–1751), by Claude Arnulphi, 1743

prominent role in the capture of Port Royal, which was renamed Annapolis Royal. When Martin went home Mathews remained as senior officer on the New England station; he joined the fleet that came to Boston in the following summer under Sir Hovenden Walker for the purpose of attacking Quebec. Cruising at the entrance of the Gulf of St Lawrence in July 1711, Mathews captured a small French warship whose master was subsequently induced by Walker to serve as chief pilot for guiding the fleet up the river. The expedition was terminated after seven of its troop transports smashed upon the north-west shore. A few weeks later the *Chester* was assigned to convoy home the New England mast ships. When the ship was paid off Mathews settled down to life as a squire at Llandaff Court. Although he had found time for marriage in 1705 to Henrietta Burgess (d. 1737), daughter of a physician of Antigua and Shoreditch, he had been much at sea and compiled an enviable record in seamanship, combat, and command.

Mediterranean command, 1718–1743 Mathews returned to duty in early 1718 and as captain of the *Kent* (70 guns) went out to the Mediterranean with the fleet commanded by Byng. In the action off Cape Passaro the *Kent*—again Mathews commanded a fast ship—was one of four ordered ahead during the night to catch the Spanish main body. On the next morning (1 August) Mathews engaged and took possession of the *San Carlos*, and then assisted the *Superb* in engaging and capturing the Spanish admiral. Thus Mathews had a distinguished share in the great victory, and afterwards Byng appointed him commander of the small squadron responsible for blockading Messina. Although he was unable to capture George Camocke, rear-admiral in the Spanish service, who escaped in a small

boat, his squadron performed diligently and effectively for over a year. In August 1719 he was ordered to cruise off Palermo to intercept incoming Spanish supplies. The *Kent* returned to England in 1720.

Mathews was next appointed commodore of a squadron ordered to assist the East India Company in suppressing piracy in the Indian Ocean. Immediately upon arriving in the *Lion* (64 guns) at Bombay on 27 August 1721, he quarrelled with the governor over whether the fort or the ship should salute first. Continuing hostility marked subsequent relations between him and the company; such conflicts were not unusual, but Mathews's contentiousness seems excessive. The joint operation of 1721 involving Portuguese troops from Goa against the troublesome Angria on the Malabar coast would probably have failed anyhow. It was the complete failure of Mathews's subsequent cruise against the pirates round Madagascar in 1722 that did greatest injury to his reputation, especially because some of the *Lion's* movements were evidently designed to generate personal trading profits rather than hunt down pirates. Back in England in 1724 he was court martialled and mulcted four months' pay for misdemeanours, one of the charges being that he had received disallowed merchandise on board a navy ship. The directors of the company sued him in civil court for £13,677 as recompense for his illegal trading, but intercession by the Admiralty in 1728 led to the matter's being dropped. It is very likely that Mathews accepted the East Indies command in order to amass a fortune, and that having made some money—one need not imagine that he netted the figure calculated by the company—he sought no further employment at sea. In 1727 and again in 1734 he contested the tory-controlled Cardiff Borough seat on behalf of the whig interest but was unsuccessful on both occasions.

After refusing an offer to serve in the Russian navy because the empress would not make him an admiral, Mathews, in 1736, became dockyard commissioner at Chatham. His wife died in 1737, and on 9 November 1738 he married Millicent (d. after 1751), daughter and coheir of John Fuller, formerly sheriff of London. Mathews was an effective commissioner, popular with the yard workers yet capable of satisfying his Navy Board colleagues and his superiors at the Admiralty.

With Britain at war with Spain and war with France likely, Mathews, who had been passed over for promotion to flag-rank in the 1730s, was promoted at one step on 13 March 1742 vice-admiral of the red (full restoration of rank), and was also made commander-in-chief in the Mediterranean, and plenipotentiary to the king of Sardinia and the states of Italy. Only an acute shortage of capable senior flag officers excused the elevation of someone who had not seen sea service for eighteen years. In favour of Mathews, however, were his performance as a commander at sea before 1720, his experience as a dockyard commissioner, and his knowledge of the Mediterranean theatre. He was well thought of by Sir Charles Wager and was politically connected with William Pulteney (later earl of Bath), who was then in ascendancy.

Although Mathews comes down to posterity, as Admiral

Sir Herbert Richmond remarked, 'with a cheap tag attached to his name that he was stupid' (Richmond, 3.254), his performance both as theatre commander and plenipotentiary displayed sense, foresight, diligence, and a high degree of success. The dual assignment was complex and strewn with pitfalls. Chiefly he was charged with frustrating Spanish military designs on Italy; the inshore waters between Marseilles and Genoa were therefore the primary focus. Yet British warships were needed far and wide, from the coast of Spain to the Adriatic. Mathews's crusty disposition did not please the diplomatic corps but may have materially benefited the cause: when he ordered Captain William Martin to Naples to 'use his utmost to lay the said city in ashes, unless the King of the two Sicilies' agreed immediately to stop assisting the enemy, the threat was believed and the purpose achieved (ibid., 1.212). A similar threat at Genoa was also effective. Above all, for twenty months Mathews managed to maintain a correct balance of concentration and dispersal, not allowing the large Franco-Spanish fleet at Toulon to deter him from deploying most of his ships on the mundane tasks of sea power. Only when he was sure the combined fleet was being readied for sea in December 1743 did he order a concentration.

Toulon, 1744 Effective intelligence arrangements sped the news of the Toulon fleet's weighing, but it took two days for the British fleet to clear Hyères Roads and even then, on 10 February 1744, the light, variable winds prevented formation of a line. Fortunately an easterly breeze prevented Admiral de Court (commanding sixteen French and twelve Spanish ships of the line) from taking advantage; instead, he steered away southward in line ahead. Yet he did not flee, which his ships could have done thanks to cleaner hulls. At 3 p.m. Mathews ordered a line abreast and headed downwind towards the combined fleet. The situation, foreseen in his orders, permitted him to treat the French as enemies even though no war between Britain and France was yet declared. When darkness fell, both fleets brought to. Mathews's signal for the line abreast was still flying when he ordered the halt. Vice-Admiral Richard Lestock, whose rear squadron (eight of the line) was separated far to windward, brought to immediately instead of using the favouring wind to achieve the line abreast. Irregular drifting during the night put the rear squadron even further away.

At 8.30 a.m. on 11 February Mathews signalled for a line ahead. A battle plainly loomed. Rear-Admiral William Rowley attained his station in the van, but despite Mathews's signals to make more sail (reinforced twice by a lieutenant sent in a boat) Lestock's squadron remained far behind. By noon Mathews concluded that the aim of the Franco-Spanish fleet was to lure him away from the coast so that Spanish troops could be embarked for an invasion of Italy. The fleet might also have been trying to join with a Brest squadron known to have sailed, in which case he would be overmatched. In any case, as a British admiral with a superior force he simply had to try to bring on an engagement.

After a shouted conversation with Captain James Cornewall of the *Marlborough* next astern, Mathews hoisted the signal to engage and led his centre division towards the Spanish flagship. By isolating the Spanish ships he might induce the French to slow down to assist them and thus bring on a general engagement. Rowley steered for the French admiral. Through all this Mathews kept the signal for the line ahead flying, a proceeding much criticized later, though it may have encouraged three captains of the van to stretch forward to inhibit the half-dozen leading French ships from doubling back. Because gaps developed in the Spanish portion of line and the British van fell upon the rear of the French portion, some British ships lacked opponents. Far in the rear were four Spanish ships—so far behind that Lestock's squadron could have cut them off. But he chose not to engage and they slowly rejoined their admiral unopposed.

Only a few ships bore the brunt of the battle. Mathews's flagship, the *Namur*, was substantially disabled aloft and her captain lost an arm. The *Marlborough* was heavily engaged with the Spanish flagship and suffered severe damage and casualties, including Captain Cornewall, who was killed. All in all Mathews and Rowley and six or seven captains of the van and centre, including Edward Hawke, were in the thick of it. Astern of Mathews four captains of his division kept too great a distance. Lestock's squadron missed the battle.

In the final phase de Court tacked, realizing that he must shield the Spaniards, and the move was successful. Both sides made repairs during the night. The enemy's course change had placed Lestock in the lead and the next day his undamaged squadron moved out ahead. The chase forced the Spanish to cease towing a disabled warship, which Mathews ordered be burnt. The following morning, 13 February, Lestock was sure, though 12 miles distant, that he would overtake the fleeing Spanish because they were trying to protect some crippled ships. Just before noon, however, Mathews called off the chase. He believed that the Riviera blockade held priority and was also worried that the Brest fleet might be near. It was a bad decision. The Brest squadron was not in the Mediterranean and a strong adverse wind frustrated the attempted return to the Riviera. Although most of the enemy would have undoubtedly escaped, four or five crippled Spanish men-of-war must have been captured had the chase continued.

Mathews wrote to Lestock straight away, asking why he had brought to on the evening before the battle without achieving a line abreast, the result being that his squadron had fallen astern 'full five Miles …, which is notorious to the whole Fleet'. He further asked why Lestock did not respond to the signal to engage by bearing down on the four Spanish stragglers. In response Lestock pointedly criticized Mathews's inadequate and contradictory signals, and added that there were four unengaged ships of his centre division which could have been ordered to deal with the lagging Spaniards. This provoked an angry reply: 'You would not yourself do it, or order any of your Division to do, what you are pleased to tell me I ought to have done', yet 'it was absolutely in your Power' to oppose those four ships (*Original Letters*, 22).

Parliamentary inquiry and court martial, 1745–1746 On 16 March 1744 Mathews suspended Lestock and ordered him home. Next day he sent copies of their correspondence to the duke of Newcastle, then secretary of state for the southern department, and asked to be ordered home to defend himself against Lestock's accusations. Lestock arrived in London three months before Mathews and quickly published his version of the battle in a long pamphlet. Nevertheless public opinion ran strongly in Mathews's favour. It appears that most people accepted the view that the signal to engage plus the example set by the centre and van required Lestock to fall upon the Spanish ships that were within his reach. Lestock defended himself chiefly by conveying the impression that Mathews as fleet commander had been sloppy, reckless, and impatient; the battle, he contended, could have been fought with a complete, well ordered line if only Mathews had waited for him to join.

An unstable political situation enabled Lestock and his friends to push successfully for a parliamentary inquiry. It was a major political event; hearings occupied the House of Commons on two full days every week from 12 March to 4 April 1745 and these were followed by passionate debates. This inquiry was an extraordinary innovation, never repeated, in which naval operations were examined in the political forum prior to courts martial. During the proceedings Mathews sat as MP for Glamorgan, having wrested the seat from its traditional tory control in a by-election victory in January. This gave him no advantage, however, because it set all tories against him while failing to bring solid allegiance from the faction-ridden whigs. Henry Fox, a rising star in debate, emerged as an outspoken advocate of Lestock. Although Mathews fared well in the pamphlet war, the parliamentary inquiry damaged him severely. Lestock's cool manner of reasoning impressed the MPs. Mathews was perceived as 'a hot, brave, imperious, dull, confused fellow' (Walpole, 19.33), and he harmed his credibility by unwillingness to criticize the four captains of his own division who had failed to engage more closely.

Hundreds of witnesses were brought home from the Mediterranean for the courts martial. Seven captains and four lieutenants were tried in 1745 at Chatham, where the trials of the admirals were feverishly anticipated. For two days in October the yard was at a standstill as the workers 'assembled at the dock gate, to the number of about eight hundred, and examined everyone that went in or out whether for Mathews or Lestock, and were all strong for Mr Mathews'. The Board of Admiralty, pondering whether there might be riots 'if upon the courts martial it should appear that Mr Lestock has not been so much to blame as thought and Mr Mathews should be found guilty', ordered the venue changed to Deptford (Hattendorf, 522). Key members of the board apparently contrived to ensure that the composition of the court for the admirals' trials would not favour Mathews (Sandwich to Bedford, 22 Oct 1745, Woburn MSS, 10, fols. 110–11). In the event Lestock was

acquitted of all charges on 20 June 1746 and, despite his poor health, immediately appointed to an important command. That did not bode well for Mathews.

During his trial, which lasted four months, Mathews is reported to have 'calmed all his passions', becoming 'sensible of the advantages of an even temper and decent behaviour' (*Du Cane MSS*, 135). Nevertheless the court, in spite of overwhelming evidence to the contrary, presumed that a classic line-of-battle action could have been fought. They excused Mathews's decision to attack with only part of his force on the technical ground of superior strength, but rejected his claim that he 'had no chance of bringing the French to action, unless by making the signal for engaging and bearing down' on the Spaniards. More reasonably, the court also faulted him for failing to coerce the four lagging captains of his division into closer engagement and neglecting to stay in close touch with the fleeing enemy during the moonlight night of 12 February. On 22 October 1746 he was deemed to be a principal cause of the miscarriage and was cashiered. Mathews had clearly made many mistakes during and after the battle. The astonishing thing is that Lestock was found completely faultless.

Aftermath and final years, 1747–1751 It is undeniable that Mathews lacked some of the qualities wanted in a commander-in-chief. His imperious temper showed too readily, and not only when talking: his official letters from the Mediterranean were too often disfigured by expressions of wrath. Worse, he allowed a long-developed dislike of Lestock to prevent a discussion of possible tactics before the battle. The Admiralty and the leaders of government must share some responsibility in this regard. The mutual animosity of the two men was well known. Mathews, upon accepting command, had asked for Lestock to be removed, and Lestock himself had asked for a new assignment. The complacent assumption that they would co-operate for the good of the service proved disastrous.

It is said that Mathews accepted the outcome of his trial with equanimity, at least on the surface. He could take comfort in knowing that his method of attack was the only way to bring on an engagement and that he had risked life and limb while his critic and accuser remained aloof. His bluntness was evidently matched with natural honesty. He readily admitted to the court that under pressure of combat he had made mistakes. All in all there seems to have been a genuine basis for his popular support, and George II remained grateful to him for his services to the allied cause. Though parliamentary opinion still flowed strongly against him he found friends among those who were inclined to perceive his disgrace and Lestock's exoneration as high-handed acts of an increasingly powerful political combination at the Admiralty.

By arrangement Mathews agreed to give up his Glamorgan seat and accept Carmarthen Boroughs for the election of 1747, and was thus returned to parliament. In 1749, feeling himself in failing health, he settled in Bloomsbury Square, London, and there he died on 2 October 1751. He was buried in St George's, Bloomsbury. His only child,

Thomas William, by his first wife, resigned his commission as major in the army upon his father's disgrace in 1746 but sat three years for Glamorgan (1756–9).

DANIEL A. BAUGH

Sources H. W. Richmond, *The navy in the war of 1739–48*, 3 vols. (1920) • B. Tunstall, *Naval warfare in the age of sail: the evolution of fighting tactics, 1650–1815*, ed. N. Tracy (1990) • P. G. G. Thomas, 'Glamorgan politics, 1688–1790', *Glamorgan county history*, ed. G. Williams, 4: *Early modern Glamorgan* (1974), 394–429 • Cobbett, *Parl. hist.*, vol. 13 • P. A. Luff, '*Mathews v. Lestock*: parliament, politics and the navy in mid-eighteenth-century England', *Parliamentary History*, 10 (1991), 45–62 • *Original letters and papers between Adm—l M—ws, and V. Adm—l L—k* (1744) • C. Downing, *A history of the Indian wars*, ed. W. Foster (1924); repr. (Lahore, 1978), xix–xxv • J. Burchett, *A complete history of the most remarkable transactions at sea* (1720) • *Report on the manuscripts of Lady Du Cane*, HMC, 61 (1905) • J. H. Owen, *War at sea under Queen Anne, 1702–1708* (1938) • G. S. Graham, ed., *The Walker expedition to Quebec, 1711*, Navy Records Society (1953) • P. D. G. Thomas, *Politics in eighteenth-century Wales* (1998) • *The Royal Navy and North America: the Warren papers, 1736–1752*, ed. J. Gwyn, Navy RS, 118 (1975) • J. B. Hattendorf and others, eds., *British naval documents, 1204–1960*, Navy RS, 131 (1993) • P. D. G. Thomas and R. S. Lea, 'Mathews, Thomas', *HoP, Commons, 1715–54* • *The manuscripts of the House of Lords*, new ser., 12 vols. (1900–77), vol. 8 • Woburn Abbey, Woburn MSS, vol. 10, fols. 110–11 • M. E. Matcham, *A forgotten John Russell* (1905) • *The Byng papers: selected from the letters and papers of Admiral Sir George Byng, first Viscount Torrington, and of his son, Admiral the Hon. John Byng*, ed. B. Tunstall, 2, Navy RS, 68 (1931) • T. Lediard, *The naval history of England*, 2 vols. (1735) • Walpole, *Corr.*

Archives BL, papers relating to his conduct off Toulon, Add. MS 29512 • PRO

Likenesses C. Arnulphi, portrait, 1743, NMM [*see illus.*] • print (after portrait), repro. in Tunstall, *Naval warfare in the age of sail*, 83

Mathias, Benjamin Williams

Mathias, Benjamin Williams (1772–1841), Church of Ireland clergyman, was born on 12 November 1772 in Dublin, the only surviving child of Benjamin Mathias, originally of Haverfordwest, Pembrokeshire, who settled in Dublin about 1760 as a woollen cloth manufacturer; both parents died about 1782. He was educated at Trinity College, Dublin, from 1791, where he was elected a scholar in 1794, and graduated BA in 1796 and MA in 1799. In 1797 he was ordained to the curacy of Rathfriland, co. Down, and in January 1804 he married a daughter of Mr Stewart of Wilmont, co. Down. They had at least two sons; the second, John Alexander Mathias, became archdeacon of Colombo, Ceylon.

In 1805 Mathias became chaplain of Bethesda Chapel, Dorset Street, Dublin, and he was soon one of the most popular evangelical ministers in the city, his preaching being considered so powerful that the provost of Trinity College, Dublin, forbade students from attending his services. In 1828 he helped to found the Established Church Home Mission with the aim of reviving the church by evangelizing Roman Catholics; and with Joseph Singer he was a founder of the Hibernian Bible Society. Mathias wrote a number of controversial works, including, *An Inquiry into the Doctrines of the Reformation and of the United Church of England and Ireland, respecting the Ruin and Recovery of Mankind* (1814), *A Compendious History of the Council of Trent* (1832), and a volume of *Twenty-one Sermons* (1838).

In May 1835 Mathias resigned his chaplaincy because of illness. He died in Merrion Avenue, Dublin, on 30 May 1841, and was buried in Mount Jerome cemetery. His congregation erected a tablet to his memory in Bethesda Chapel and a monument in the cemetery. The memorial tablet was later moved to the porch of St George's, Dublin.   GORDON GOODWIN, *rev.* DAVID HUDDLESTON

Sources *Brief memorials of the Rev B. W. Mathias* (1842) • D. Bowen, *The protestant crusade in Ireland, 1800–70* (1978) • H. B. Swanzy, *Succession lists of the diocese of Dromore*, ed. J. B. Leslie (1933), 145 • J. B. Leslie, biographical succession list of clergy for the diocese of Dublin, PRO NIre., T 1075/1, 21 • W. B. S. Taylor, *History of the University of Dublin* (1845), 493 • [J. H. Todd], ed., *A catalogue of graduates who have proceeded to degrees in the University of Dublin, from the earliest recorded commencements to … December 16, 1868* (1869), 378 • Burtchaell & Sadleir, *Alum. Dubl.* • private information (1894)

Likenesses C. Turner, mezzotint, pubd 1821 (after Mrs Taylor), BM • stipple, 1825, NPG • J. Horsburgh, engraving (after M. Gregan), repro. in B. W. Mathias, *Twenty-one sermons* (1838)

Mathias, Thomas James

Mathias, Thomas James (1753/4–1835), satirist and Italian scholar, was the eldest son of Vincent Mathias (*c.*1711–1782), sub-treasurer in the queen's household, and his wife, Marianne (1724–1799), daughter of Alured Popple, secretary to the Board of Trade and governor of Bermuda. Mathias's uncle Gabriel was an artist, and held a post in the office of the keeper of the privy purse. Another uncle, James, was a Hamburg merchant, well-known amateur singer, and minor enemy of Mrs Thrale. Mathias's brother George, queen's messenger from 1792, was a long-standing friend of Charlotte Burney, who found him 'excessive comical' (*Early Diary*, 2.302–12). Andrew, the other brother, became surgeon-extraordinary to the queen. His sister Albinia was (as Mrs Skerrett) the addressee of a poem written in 1805 by Anna Seward. The family lived in Middle Scotland Yard. Mathias once owned a picture of the family by Hogarth.

Education and early work Mathias is said to have been educated at Eton College, and he had a strong personal interest in the college; but on his admission as a pensioner at Trinity College, Cambridge, on 2 July 1770, aged sixteen, he was recorded as having come from the Revd Richard Woodeson's school at Kingston upon Thames. He was admitted as a scholar of the college on 26 April 1771 and took an *aegrotat* degree in 1774. In August 1775, as a middle bachelor, he gained one of the members' prizes (15 guineas) for the best dissertation in Latin prose; in 1776, as a senior bachelor, he took a similar prize. These dissertations were printed and survive in signed copies. In 1776 he was elected as a minor fellow of the college (his Latin letter to Dr Lort about the election is in Nichols, *Anecdotes*, 2.676–8); he subsequently became a major fellow. In 1777 he graduated MA and served as third, second, and first sublector over the period 1777–80. He became intimate with Spencer Perceval, apparently acting as a kind of private tutor to him. In 1780 he published, anonymously, *An Heroic Epistle to the Rev. R. Watson*, ridiculing Watson's hopes of surveying the deserts of Arabia and Tartary; *An Answer to the Heroic Epistle* provoked from Mathias a further *Heroic Address in Prose* of the same year. In 1781 Mathias published *Runic Odes Imitated from the Norse Tongue*, which addressed Icelandic, Ossianic, and Welsh themes 'in the manner of Mr. Gray'.

Mathias's father died on 15 June 1782 aged seventy-one, and Mathias left Cambridge to become successively sub-treasurer to the queen, vice-treasurer, and treasurer of the accounts of the queen's household. In 1783, aided by Dr Glynn, who had access to some of Chatterton's manuscripts, Mathias produced a somewhat indeterminate *Essay on the Evidence Relating to the Poems Attributed to Thomas Rowley*. The anonymous *Rowley and Chatterton in the Shades* (1782), sometimes attributed to Mathias, is probably by George Hardinge. The wide range of Mathias's interests and connections is indicated by his election as fellow of the Society of Antiquaries in January 1795, and fellow of the Royal Society in March 1795. He was 'particularly agreeable & pleasant as well as cultivated and sensible' in social circles, according to Fanny Burney, who mentioned that he 'can't determine upon matrimony' (*Journals and Letters of Fanny Burney*, 3.101, 4.31). (He never did marry.)

Pursuits of Literature and other satires Mathias's *Pursuits of Literature, or, What you will*, a wide-ranging satire with extensive notes on the conceit and licence of contemporary authors, appeared anonymously in four dialogues, the first on 7 June 1794, the second and third on 14 July 1796, and the fourth on 19 July 1797. The poem was issued as a whole in a 'fifth edition revised' in 1798, alongside several editions of a translation of the classical passages quoted in the poem. The attacks on Payne Knight's *Worship of Priapus* and Lewis's *The Monk* are concerned with obscenity, and Mathias ridicules the 'Black-Letter Kennell' of antiquarians (especially George Steevens), W. H. Ireland, Parr, Darwin, and Gilpin, on literary grounds. There is praise for Gray, Mason, Beattie, Burns, Cowper, Ann Radcliffe, Capell, Johnson, Isaac Reed, and Jacob Bryant, as well as for several of Mathias's own works. But the poem is confessedly of its political moment, declaring openly that literature is an important tool of government. Held up for censure are Sheridan, Fox, Priestley, Paine, Horne Tooke, and Godwin. The vehement distrust of Catholics in the poem was also expressed separately in *A Letter to the Lord Marquis of Buckingham* (1796).

The *British Critic* approved of the poem as a 'strenuous enemy and assailant of democratical principles, and of that monster, French, or Frenchified philosophy' (8.353–6). When the fourth part came out, the *Monthly Review* accused Mathias of scaremongering: 'our literary Mesmer very successfully magnetizes his readers into a perpetual hysteric, and convulses them with the titillatory spasms of ever-varying fears' (new ser., 24.219). William Cobbett wrote to the anonymous author that 'Your matchless poem … is become very fashionable in the libraries of the Americans' (Smith, 1.244–5). Mathias's comments on the French Revolution and on women radicals were enthusiastically endorsed by Richard Polwhele in *The Unsex'd Females*, addressed to Mathias in 1798, though this did not prevent Mathias from disparaging Polwhele in a later edition. Steevens's perceptive point that the poem was 'merely a peg to hang the notes on' brought a rebuttal in the poem itself (iv.15). Southey commented 'they tell me I am civilly wiped in that stupid poem' (*New Letters*, 1.139). The most successful public response was that by William

Boscawen, whose translation of Horace had been censured by Mathias in *Pursuits*. His *Progress of Satire: an Essay in Verse* (1798) argued that local and topical satire was inferior to general satire and attacked Mathias's arrogance and spite. It was reissued with a supplement in 1799. Reviewers tended to agree with Boscawen. Other responses of 1798 included the anonymous *Impartial Strictures on the Poem called The Pursuits of Literature*, which contained a vindication of *The Monk*; *The Egotist*, which depicted the overweening author quarrelling with his interlocutor; John Mainwaring, *Remarks on 'The Pursuits of Literature'*, to which Mathias replied in *A Letter to the Author of a Pamphlet, Entitled, Remarks*; and Thomas Dutton, *The Literary Census. A Letter to the Executor of the Deceased Author of 'The Pursuits of Literature'* appeared the following year, and William Burdon's *An Examination of the Merits and Tendency of 'The Pursuits of Literature'* came out in two parts between 1799 and 1800.

The *Monthly Magazine*, reviewing Dutton, said that there seemed to be 'a train in preparation' for discovering the authorship of the *Pursuits* (7.505–6). Fanny Burney thought it was by Mason, but Farington recorded in November 1797 that the poem was ascribed to Mathias, with help from Dr Rennell and Mansell, the master of Trinity (Farington, *Diary*, 1.219). Mathias's anonymity was partly removed by 'Andrew Oedipus, an injured author', in *The Sphinx's Head Broken, or, A Poetical Epistle … to Thomas James M*th**s, Cl*rk to the Q***n's Tr**s*r*r* (1798), though the *Monthly Review* was not convinced by the 'very angry and scurrilous' pamphlet (new ser., 25.473) and the *British Critic* asked for more proofs against the 'ingenious and amiable' Mathias (11.677). Samuel Denne, happy with his mention in the poem, guessed Mathias to be the author (Nichols, *Illustrations*, 6.770). Peter Pindar, another victim, referred to Mathias as 'one of the smaller rats of the Queen's Closet' and claimed that he 'giveth the little Animal a good Drubbing' (Pindar, 'Argument'). He abused Mathias as 'human *toad*' and descanted on the poem's 'enormity of falsehood and impudence' (note to line 108). Mrs Thrale forgave Mathias her mention in the poem because of his 'being a Scholar, and a Christian, and … a firm Aristocrate' (*Piozzi Letters*, 2.399–401).

Alongside the *Pursuits*, Mathias produced a series of conservative topical satires in Popean couplets. *The Political Dramatist*, an attack on Sheridan, complete with adulation for Pitt, appeared in 1795 and was reissued with a postscript attacking the declaration of the Whig Club in 1796. *The Imperial Epistle from Kien Long, Emperor of China, to George the Third* (1795), using an idea of Peter Pindar, offered a mock invitation to Pitt in a general satire on the state of Europe. In 1796 Mathias also published *An Epistle in Verse to the Rev. Dr Randolph* and *An Equestrian Epistle in Verse, to the Right Honourable the Earl of Jersey*, both concerned with the embarrassing loss of some private letters of the princess of Wales. *The Grove*, a Popean vision of literature and society, was published in 1798, containing 'abundant abuse of about some ten dozen of his cotemporary wits' and others (*Monthly Review*, new ser., 25.472); the *Monthly Magazine* said it displayed 'the pedantry of a schoolmaster, the vulgarity of a poissard, and the malevolence of a—' (5.507). *The Shade of Alexander Pope. On the Banks of the Thames*, an attack on Henry Grattan, followed in 1799, occasioning a further attack by William Burdon (*A vindication of Pope*, 1799), and an anonymous riposte, *An Interview between the Spirit of Pope and the Shade that assumed his Name* (1799); Grattan's own lines on the matter appear in Wrangham's *English Library* (409–10). *Pandolfo attonito!*, a light stanzaic poem about the removal of armchairs from the Opera House, completed Mathias's satiric efforts in 1800.

Italian scholarship and later life　Mathias's mother died on 6 January 1799, occasioning a warm tribute, probably by Mathias (*GM*, 1st ser., 69, 1799, 82). She left him £3000. Mathias brought out a quarto edition of his *Works*, and in 1801 published a selection of items from newspapers, *Prose on Various Occasions, Literary and Political*. Thereafter Mathias, who had apparently studied Italian at Cambridge under Agostino Isola, embarked on a series of editions of Italian texts, and translations into Italian. These included *Sonetti de piu illustri poeti d'Italia* (1802), critical works by Tiraboschi, Crescimbeni, Menzini, Redi, Monti, and Gravina, an Italian version of Mason's *Saffo* (1809), and one of Milton's 'Lycidas' (1812). Byron, responding to a letter of praise from Mathias, chided him for being 'too much devoted to a foreign Muse' and hoped that 'some national *Pursuit* will enable us once again to claim your muse entirely our own' (*Byron's Letters and Journals*, 2.176).

Mathias became librarian at the queen's house about 1813. He continued to revise *Pursuits*, and made many textual changes between the fourteenth edition (1808) and the sixteenth (1812), but the poem still received a mixed reception. Byron called the poetry 'the worst written of it's kind' and thought 'it's sole merit lies in the Notes, which are indisputably excellent' (*Byron's Letters and Journals*, 2.86–7). De Quincey saw it as marked by 'much licence of tongue, much mean and impotent spite, and by a systematic pedantry without parallel in literature' (*De Quincey's Works*, 142). Ireland contrasted its 'sea of gall' with the 'rivulet narrow of poor praise' in *Scribbleomania* (p. 96). Mathias made peace with Samuel Parr by sending him several of his later works, and Parr kept seventeen of his letters in a bundle marked 'MOST PRECIOUS'. Among his numerous other correspondents of this period were Sir Walter Scott, Spencer Perceval, and William Roscoe. Mathias derived considerable knowledge of Thomas Gray from the Revd Norton Nicholls, on whose death in 1807 Mathias composed a letter of eulogy. Mathias was a beneficiary of Nicholls's will. In 1814 he published an edition of *The Works of Thomas Gray* in two quarto volumes, with substantial prose extracts from Gray's manuscripts, under the sponsorship of Pembroke College. At 7 guineas it could not compete with the cheap editions by John Mitford and others and it 'sank with the weight of lead upon the market' (Dibdin, 732), causing Mathias some personal loss.

In his official capacity Mathias was responsible for the quarterly payments of Fanny Burney's pension from 1794 until 1816. Burney reported that Mathias suffered an 'alarming stroke & attack' in spring 1817 and decamped to Italy for his health (*Journals and Letters of Fanny Burney*, 10.773). Southey met him on the way in Paris in May 1817. He fitted effortlessly into expatriate circles in Rome and Florence before settling in an old palace on the Pizzofalcone in Naples. He received a pension from the Royal Society of Literature, of which he was a royal associate. Some of his books and manuscripts were sold by R. H. Evans in 1820. He produced an edition of *Lyrica sacra, excerpta ex hymnis ecclesiae antiquis* (1818), and translated into Italian poems by Akenside (1821), Mason (1823), Armstrong (1824), Beattie (1824), Spenser (1826), and Thomson (1826). He also produced several editions of *Poesie liriche toscane* between 1818 and 1825, and revised versions of his lyric poetry. Mathias visited Scott at Naples during his last illness, contributing to his 'comfort and amusement' by helping him collect local ballads (Lockhart, 10.147–8).

Mathias's death in August 1835 was noted in *The Athenaeum* (22 August 1835, 650), which printed some recollections, almost certainly by Lady Blessington. According to her, the litterati of Naples bestowed 'the warmest eulogiums on the purity and precision' of Mathias's written Italian. He 'maintained an independent and respectable station, and was a welcome guest in all the houses occupied by the English residents'. He was 'below the middle size, being scarcely taller than Mr. Godwin. In face he bore a striking resemblance to Sir Francis Burdett. He was particularly neat in his attire, and scrupulously clean in his person.' Among other 'nervous peculiarities' he had a bizarre dread of getting run over in the street; his attempts to cross the highway were a source of amusement to his acquaintances. He was 'a gastronome in the full extent of the word, took a lively interest in the first appearance of green peas, and was a connoisseur of wild boar'. He enjoyed the 'cheapness of the luxuries he liked', and shuddered if anyone mentioned returning to England. 'Any allusion to the *Pursuits of Literature* was extremely offensive to him', and he persisted in denying his authorship to the end. Dawson Turner, a friend to whom Mathias wrote over ninety letters and who once owned a volume of letters written to the anonymous author, with some replies by Mathias (now BL, Add. MS 22976), wrote that the authorship 'was scarcely made a secret by his family after he went to Italy' (*N&Q*, 1st ser., 3.276); but even in 1824 Dibdin was not sure that Mathias was the author. Further anecdotes, from Lady Blessington's *Idler in Italy*, were reprinted in *The Times* (23 March 1839).

PAUL BAINES

Sources　J. S. Mabbett, *Thomas James Mathias and 'The pursuits of literature'* (1964) • O. M. Brack, jun., 'A critical review and analysis of Thomas James Mathias's *The pursuits of literature* (1794–1812)', PhD diss., U. Texas • *The Athenaeum* (22 Aug 1835), 650 • *The journals and letters of Fanny Burney (Madame D'Arblay)*, ed. J. Hemlow and others, 12 vols. (1972–84) • *GM*, 1st ser., 52 (1782), 311, 360; 1st ser., 69 (1799), 82; 1st ser., 80 (1810), 346–51; 2nd ser., 4 (1835), 550–52 • Nichols, *Lit. anecdotes*, 2.676–8 • Nichols, *Illustrations*, 5.65–83; 6.770; 7.33; 8.212–14, 577 • N. P. Willis, *Pencillings by the way*, 3 vols. (1835), 1.100–02 • *N&Q*, 1st ser., 3, 276; 2nd ser., 10, 41–2, 282–4; 2nd ser., 12, 221; 2nd ser., 184–7, 219–20 • *The Piozzi letters*, ed. E. A. Bloom, 4 vols. (1989–96), 2.399–401; 4.106–9 • *The early diary of Frances Burney*, ed. A. R. Ellis, 2 vols. (1913), 2.302–12 • [J. Watkins and F. Shoberl], *A biographical dictionary of the living authors of Great Britain and Ireland*

(1816) · P. Pindar [J. Wolcot], *Nil admirari* (1799) · *Byron's letters and journals*, ed. L. A. Marchand, 12 vols. (1973–82), 2.86–7, 171, 176 · *Admissions to Trinity College, Cambridge*, ed. W. W. Rouse Ball and J. A. Venn, 5 vols. (1911–16) · J. Lockhart, *Memoirs of the life of Sir Walter Scott, bart.*, 10 vols. (1851), 10.147–8 · *British Critic*, 8 (1796), 353–6; 11 (1798), 677 · *Monthly Review*, new ser., 24 (1797), 219; new ser., 25 (1798), 472–3 · *Monthly Magazine*, 5 (1798), 507; 7 (1799), 505–6 · E. Smith, *William Cobbett: a biography*, 2 vols. (1878), 1.244–5 · *New letters of Robert Southey*, ed. K. Curry, 1 (1965), 139 · Farington, *Diary*, 1.100, 105, 219 · *De Quincey's works*, 16 vols. (1862–71), 5.88–9, 142 · W. H. Ireland, *Scribbleomania* (1815) · *The works of Samuel Parr, LL.D.*, ed. J. Johnstone, 8 vols. (1828), 8.59–82 · T. F. Dibdin, *The library companion* (1824) · *The Times* (23 March 1839)

Archives BL, corresp., Add. MS 22976 · Eton | BL, letters to Charlotte Broome, Egerton MS 3700a · BL, Hardwicke papers · CUL, corresp. with Spencer Perceval · Harvard U., Houghton L., letters to George Hardinge · Lpool RO, corresp. with William Roscoe · NL Scot. · Trinity Cam., letters to Dawson Turner · U. Edin., letters

Mathias, William James (1934–1992), composer, was born on 1 November 1934 at Cilhawl, North Road, Whitland, Carmarthenshire, the only child of James Hughes Mathias (1893–1969) and his wife, Marian, *née* Evans (1896–1980). His father, who had a keen interest in music, was a history teacher at Whitland grammar school and his mother was a respected amateur organist and piano accompanist. Mathias showed an early interest in the piano and at the age of six he began formal lessons. Composing seemed to be a natural extension of his piano studies, and he wrote a large number of works, without any official tuition, while at school. A school song, written when he was twelve, is still in use today.

In 1952 Mathias went to University College of Wales, Aberystwyth, to read English, French, and philosophy, but soon transferred to music. He was tutored by Professor Ian Parrott and graduated with first-class honours in 1956. He then gained an open scholarship to the Royal Academy of Music in London to study composition with Lennox Berkeley and piano with Peter Katin. While there he met his future wife, (Margaret) Yvonne Collins, another scholarship student, also from south Wales, who was studying voice. They married in 1959 and had one daughter, Rhiannon (*b.* 1968). Among their peers at the academy were Cornelius Cardew and Harrison Birtwistle, yet out of this furnace of avant-garde ideas Mathias emerged with his own lyrical, compositional style. His music soon came to the attention of Alan Frank, the entrepreneurial music editor at Oxford University Press, who wooed the young composer into the ranks of the press's house composers—who at that time included Ralph Vaughan Williams and William Walton.

In 1959 Mathias took up a lectureship at the University College of North Wales, Bangor. This, coupled with his marriage the same year, gave him the professional, emotional, and financial security to build on his increasing reputation as a composer. In 1968 he took the position of senior lecturer at the University of Edinburgh. However, Wales remained his natural home, and in 1970 he was appointed professor of music back in Bangor, and the family moved into Y Graigwen, a beautiful house on the island of Anglesey overlooking the Menai Strait. He took early retirement to devote more time to composition in 1988.

William James Mathias (1934–1992), by Hugh Knott

Mathias wrote with great fluency in a style that was largely consolidated by the time he left the academy. His stylistic hallmarks were a modal tonality, frequent harmonizations at the interval of a 4th or 7th, ostinati motifs, a penchant for syncopated rhythms, and the construction of forms through contrasting and often quite discrete musical episodes. His character was present in his music's energy and jauntiness and in a seam of Celtic romance. His prolific output—nearly 250 catalogued works—covered most genres, and the quality was variable. He made a significant contribution to the canon of twentieth-century organ music both with the organ concerto, op. 81 (1984), and with shorter works such as the dazzling *Carillon* (1990). He also wrote well for choir, moving easily between sacred and secular texts. He regarded *Lux aeterna*, op. 88 (1982), dedicated to the memory of his mother, as his 'choral best'; it was a glorious work in the great tradition of other British works written for the Three Choirs festival. During the 1980s Mathias made frequent visits to the United States and Canada, where there was a constant demand for new anthems. This popularity was in part precipitated by the enormous interest in 'Let the people praise thee, o God', op. 87 (1981), commissioned for the wedding of the prince and princess of Wales and consequently heard at its première by over 750 million people worldwide.

Mathias's chamber and orchestral music conveyed a sort of nationalism born not out of the politics of confrontation but out of a deep empathy with the history, spirit, and natural beauty of Wales. The concertos for flute and oboe were distinctly pastoral in places, and the harp concerto, op. 50 (1970), showed a marvellous understanding of the possibilities of the Celtic emblem. He wrote three symphonies, a single opera (*The Servants*, to a libretto by

Iris Murdoch), a number of successful works for youth orchestras, ten concertos, three string quartets, a piano trio, and other works for assorted forces. His final three large-scale works, the third symphony (1991), the violin concerto, and *In Arcadia* (1992), were all affirmatory and pointed to a man who was determined to live life to the full. In the last few months of his life Mathias revised a number of early works but continued to compose afresh, even commencing a fourth symphony.

Mathias received many honours, including being made a fellow of the Royal Academy of Music (1965) and a doctor of music of the University of Wales (1966); he was awarded the Bax Society prize (1968) and the Guild for the Promotion of Welsh Music's John Edwards memorial award (1981), and was appointed CBE (1985). He was diligent in his public roles as president of the Incorporated Society of Musicians (1979–80), member of the music advisory committee of the British Council (1974–83), member of the Welsh Arts Council (1974–81), and vice-president of the Royal College of Organists (1985–6). He also founded the St Asaph festival in 1972 and remained its artistic director until his death. He died, from cancer, at his home in Anglesey on 29 July 1992, survived by his wife and daughter.

HELEN C. THOMAS

Sources S. R. Craggs, *William Mathias: a bio-bibliography* (1995) · *New Grove* · *Oxford composers: William Mathias catalogue* (1992) · *The Times* (31 July 1992) · *The Independent* (31 July 1992) · WWW [forthcoming] · personal knowledge (2004)

Archives NL Wales, corresp. and papers, music MSS | SOUND BL NSA, interview, 6 Sept 1988, B3202/13 · BL NSA, *Talking about music*, 224, 1LP0202853

Likenesses C. Williams, oils, 1973, priv. coll. · H. Knott, oils, unknown collection; copyprint, NPG [*see illus.*] · photograph, repro. in *The Times* · photograph, repro. in *The Independent*

Wealth at death £345,789: probate, 2 Sept 1992, CGPLA Eng. & Wales

Mathieson, (James) Muir (1911–1975), director and conductor of film music, was born on 24 January 1911 in Stirling, the son of John George Mathieson, an artist. Nothing further is known of his early life but after studying at the Royal College of Music he joined Alexander Korda's recently formed production company, London Films, in 1931 as assistant to the then musical director Kurt Schroeder. This was in the years following the introduction of synchronized sound on film and when the whole process of providing recorded music to accompany the images was being developed. Schroeder contributed a reasonable though hardly memorable background score to Korda's first major success, *The Private Life of Henry VIII* (1933). However, as the political situation changed, Schroeder felt that his place should be in a German studio and he returned to Germany in 1934, leaving the post of music director to be filled by the now experienced Mathieson. It was often reported—erroneously—in the popular film and music press that film music had been composed by Mathieson; this was because Mathieson's name appeared on so many British films during the years following his appointment. But Mathieson's abilities lay not only in his masterly knowledge of how to assemble and conduct scores but in an early talent for selecting the right composer for the job,

(James) Muir Mathieson (1911–1975), by Baron, 1942

and many, now well-known composers wrote some of their finest work for the British cinema under his patronage. Indeed composers who had never shown any interest in writing for films often found a hidden aspect of their art revealed in the meticulous and exact processes required to score a film effectively.

Mathieson's first work as musical director was to conduct Mischa Spoliansky's score for *The Private Life of Don Juan* (1934), a rather flat attempt to revive the flagging career of the silent matinée idol Douglas Fairbanks. This score was by no means exceptional but Spoliansky was commissioned the following year to work on *Sanders of the River* (1935), a dramatization of Edgar Wallace's tale of colonialism in Africa. The songs written for Paul Robeson in the latter film were magnificent and did much to popularize the film in its day. During the same period Mathieson was instrumental in acquiring the services of composers such as Arthur Benjamin (whom he had met while studying at the Royal College of Music), who contributed scores for *The Scarlet Pimpernel* (1934), *Wings of the Morning* (1937), *The Return of the Scarlet Pimpernel* (1937), and *Under the Red Robe* (1937). Richard Addinsell wrote for *Dark Journey* (1937), *Farewell Again* (1937), *South Riding* (1937), and *Fire over England* (1936). Georges Auric was specially imported from French studios for *The Man who could Work Miracles* (1936); Miklos Rozsa wrote for *The Four Feathers* (1939) and *The Thief of Baghdad* (1940). Most famously Arthur Bliss's score for *Things to Come* (1935) has earned its place in British film music history as supposedly the first contribution by a major British composer to cinema, which of course it was not. There is no escaping the quality of the film, its music, and the grandeur of the overall concept in adapting this unwieldly science fiction story by H. G. Wells. It was Mathieson who insisted that Bliss was brought in to the film's production early on and indeed much of the film was edited to Bliss's score rather than the other way round. Various movements of the final score were arranged into a concert suite, now familiar on modern orchestral recordings. The score was thought to be a breakthrough in first-class symphonic film music and parts were released on a set of Decca 78s, which were best-sellers in their day and which helped to elevate the status of film music in the public eye.

With the outbreak of the Second World War, in September 1939, Mathieson became musical director to the Ministry of Information, Royal Air Force, and army film units. In this capacity he used his considerable experience to involve composers of the quality of Richard Addinsell, for *Men of the Lightship* (1940), William Alwyn for *Fires were Started* (1942), and by no means least, Ralph Vaughan Williams for *Coastal Command* (1942). Indeed it was Mathieson who had enticed the ageing Vaughan Williams to the screen, in the previous year, with an offer to write the score for the propaganda feature film *49th Parallel* (1941), which was being produced by Michael Powell and Emeric Pressburger and photographed on location in Canada. Mathieson visited Vaughan Williams at his home in Dorking, where the composer, then aged sixty-nine, was puzzled as to how he might effectively contribute to the war effort; so far he had managed to collect salvage and was often seen pushing his little cart around the town. In the magnificent prelude to Michael Powell's superb film Vaughan Williams was able to show that he was master of the idiom; the opening ten minutes of this film serve as an example of first-class, effective, and superbly controlled film writing. During his work with the various documentary units during the war Mathieson also managed to commission scores from composers of the quality of John Greenwood, Clifton Parker, and Alan Rawsthorne, all of whom continued their film work after the war.

Perhaps the most celebrated film composer whom Mathieson encouraged during the war years was William Walton. This was after J. Arthur Rank had appointed Mathieson as music director for the Rank Organisation's film productions; he persuaded Walton to supervise the score for *Henry V* (1944), one of the greatest and most imaginative productions of the war period. Walton produced a score of almost unparalleled beauty in its melody, orchestration, and construction. Olivier recognized the quality of the music and the way in which it enhanced the effect of every scene of the film.

In the post-war period Mathieson supervised the music of nearly all the major productions emanating from the various independent units under Rank's control. These included Two Cities, The Archers, and Cineguild. Among the more notable films of the day for which Mathieson conducted the score were *Great Expectations* (1946; composer Walter Goehr), *Oliver Twist* (1948; composer Arnold Bax), *Brief Encounter*, which famously employed the second piano concerto of Rakhmaninov (1945), *Blithe Spirit* (1945; composer Richard Addinsell), *Odd Man Out* (1946; composer William Alwyn), *The Brothers* (1947; composer Cedric Thorpe Davie), and *Men of Two Worlds* (1946; composer Arthur Bliss). This period also produced a further Walton score of note, that for Olivier's 1948 film of *Hamlet*.

Around this time Mathieson himself made several appearances on screen as a conductor, including the films *The Seventh Veil* (1945) and *Girl in a Million* (1946). During the war he also conducted regular public concerts, occasionally including suites from the more celebrated film music that he had introduced on the screen.

One of Mathieson's most valuable and enduring works was his own production in 1946 of *Instruments of the Orchestra*, which he personally directed. This twenty-minute film was produced under the auspices of the Crown Film Unit and was intended for non-theatrical exhibition to schools as a music education film describing the various orchestral instruments. Mathieson commissioned a new work from Benjamin Britten, who had composed for documentaries in the 1930s, but not even Mathieson could have foreseen the quality of the work which resulted, which was originally entitled *The Young Person's Guide to the Orchestra* and later became known (minus the specially written narration by Eric Crozier) as *Variations and Fugue on a Theme by Purcell*. Under Mathieson's direction Malcolm Sargent conducted the London Symphony Orchestra and also addressed the camera, which represented a non-existent studio audience. Playing through the music Sargent was able to present each instrument both singly and as part of its orchestral group, while the culmination, a fugue, presented the entire orchestra playing together. The music was recorded at Wembley town hall and the film was later shot to 'playback' at Pinewood Studios. For the final shot, where the camera tracks right back to show the full orchestra, the sound stage had to be enlarged. This was, for its day, a very effective film, which has occupied an honoured place in the development of educational films as well as being a milestone in the history of the London Symphony Orchestra. Britten's work quickly established itself as a staple work in the concert repertoire.

In 1948 a second educational film of the same type was produced, entitled *Steps of the Ballet*, for which Mathieson's old professor at the Royal College of Music, Arthur Benjamin, produced the score, and Robert Helpmann and other leading dancers of the day described the principal steps of ballet and how a complete stage production is put together. Although it was an effective film at the time it has not been frequently revived and has consequently not enjoyed the fame of the earlier production. The Festival of Britain year found Mathieson appearing in the official industry feature, *The Magic Box* (1951), which portrayed the life of cinema pioneer William Friese-Greene. Mathieson played the part of Sir Arthur Sullivan, guest conductor of the Bath Choral Society.

During the early 1950s Mathieson continued to be a principal force in the musical design of British feature films, encouraging new film composers such as Malcolm Arnold, who wrote the score to David Lean's *The Sound Barrier* in 1952; the following year Mathieson suggested to Larry Adler that he contribute his solo harmonica theme to *Genevieve* (1953). Other notable features of the period included a further Walton score, this time for Olivier's *Richard III* (1955), and William Alwyn's tracks for films such as *Carve her Name with Pride* and *A Night to Remember* (both 1958). In the same year Mathieson achieved another major success, under unusual circumstances, when he had the opportunity to conduct Bernard Herrmann's celebrated score for Hitchcock's *Vertigo*.

During this period Mathieson continued his extensive work with documentary units such as British Transport Films, and he actively encouraged composers of the quality of Clifton Parker, Leighton Lucas, Elizabeth Lutyens, Doreen Carwithen, John Greenwood, and Edward Williams, many of whom had already enjoyed long associations with British cinema. What is often forgotten about Mathieson is that he was active in non-film work as well, and during the 1960s he became more active in the world of youth orchestras. His final studio work, of which he was very proud, repeated his old Crown Film Unit success of 1946; in 1966 he wrote and directed an ambitious series of twenty-four short films, entitled *We Make Music*, this time shot in colour.

On 21 December 1935 Mathieson married Hermione Marie Louise Darnborough (*b.* 1914/15), principal ballerina of Sadler's Wells, with whom he had one son and three daughters. He was appointed OBE for his services to music. He was a governor of the British Film Institute and a vice-president of the Greater London Arts Association. He died at the Radcliffe Infirmary, Oxford, on 2 August 1975 and was survived by his wife.

ANDREW YOUDELL

Sources J. Huntley, *British film music* (1947) · D. Quinlan, *British sound films* (1984) · *Journal of the Guild of British Film Editors*, 46 (Dec 1975), 24–5 · *International Film Collector*, 12 (Dec 1975), 20 · *Film Music Notebook* (summer 1975), 31 · *CGPLA Eng. & Wales* (1975) · m. cert. · d. cert. · database, British Film Institute, London, BFI
Archives FILM BFI NFTVA, documentary footage | SOUND BL NSA, performance recordings
Likenesses Baron, photograph, 1942, Hult. Arch. [*see illus.*] · group portrait, photograph, 1970, Hult. Arch.
Wealth at death £17,215: administration with will, 5 Nov 1975, *CGPLA Eng. & Wales*

Mathieson, William Law (1868–1938), historian, was born at Wardie, Leith, Edinburgh, on 25 February 1868, the third surviving son of George Mathieson, shipowner, and his wife, Isabella Melrose. He was educated at Edinburgh Academy and Edinburgh University; at the latter he distinguished himself in the history classes and won the lord rector's prize in 1893. Possessed of modest means which he supplemented by tutoring, he settled down to a scholar's uneventful life in Edinburgh. In 1910 he married Christian Mary (*d.* 1941), third daughter of James Shaw JP, sheriff of London and Middlesex in 1874–5; they had no children.

In his early years Mathieson contributed to W. E. Henley's *National Observer* and reviewed for *The Athenaeum*. By his first historical work, *Politics and Religion: a Study in Scottish History from the Reformation to the Revolution* (2 vols., 1902), he stepped into the front rank of contemporary historians. *Scotland and the Union … 1695–1747* (1905), *The Awakening of Scotland … 1747–1797* (1910), and *Church and Reform in Scotland … 1797–1843* (1916) completed his interpretation of Scottish history. Primarily interested in movements, especially in the connection between church

and state, Mathieson was the historian of the growth of the moderate tradition in Scotland. Based on a thorough study of the printed sources, his interpretation was distinguished by 'a philosophic charm and impartiality which humanized controversies and periods which are still too often the prey of partisan bitterness'. Qualities of apt illustration, historical portraiture, and wit characterize all his work, although his later style tended to be too concentrated.

Mathieson next turned to cognate aspects of English history in *England in Transition, 1789–1832* (1920) and the more original *English Church Reform, 1815–1840* (1923), a sketch of a hitherto neglected subject. Finally, his studies of the slave trade, a virtually unworked field, won him a place among the historians of the British empire. He published four volumes between 1926 and 1936, the first being *British Slavery and its Abolition, 1823–1838*, and the last *The Sugar Colonies and Governor Eyre, 1849–1866*. He also wrote the chapter 'The emancipation of the slaves, 1807–1838', for the *Cambridge History of the British Empire*, 2 (1940).

A scholar of genial personality, Mathieson died at his home, 9 Wardie Avenue, Edinburgh, on 26 January 1938. He had received the honorary degree of LLD from Aberdeen University in 1912.

H. W. MEIKLE, *rev.* H. C. G. MATTHEW

Sources *The Scotsman* (27 Jan 1938) · *The Times* (3 Feb 1938) · [T. Henderson and P. F. Hamilton-Grierson], eds., *The Edinburgh Academy register* (1914) · B. Dickens, 'Thumbnail sketch of an Edinburgh scholar', *Edinburgh Bibliographical Society Transactions*, 2 (1938–45), 450–51 · personal knowledge (1949) · *CCI* (1938)
Archives NL Scot., draft account of 1865 Jamaica rebellion
Likenesses D. G. Shiels, oils, 1934, Scot. NPG
Wealth at death £8975 10s. 6d.: confirmation, 1 April 1938, *CCI* · £129 11s. 9d.: eik additional estate, 5 Nov 1938, *CCI*

Mathison, Thomas (*bap.* 1721, *d.* 1760), writer on golf, was baptized in Edinburgh on 13 August 1721, the youngest of the eight children of William Mathieson, wright, of Edinburgh, and Elspet Mark. Thomas, whose name was usually spelt Mathison, as distinct from his father's Mathieson, began his career in the legal profession as a writer in Edinburgh. The work for which he is known, *The Goff, an Heroi-Comical Poem*, was published anonymously in Edinburgh in 1743. Its significance, and that of its author, lies in its claim to be the first printed book devoted entirely to golf.

The Goff, a poem of more than 300 lines, recounts with irony and satire a game of golf on Leith links, then Edinburgh's playground on the shores of the Firth of Forth. This was a match between Castalio, identified by C. B. Clapcott in his 1946 commentary on the poem as Alexander Dunning, an Edinburgh bookseller and a proficient golfer, and the much younger Pygmalion, Mathison himself. The latter, according to the poem, was 'skilled in Goffing art'. The poem continues:

small is his size, but dauntless his heart,
Fast by a desk in Edin's domes he sits
… length'ning out the writs

—a clear reference to Mathison's profession as a legal writer.

The poem gives much important information as to how

golf was played at the time, the equipment used, and the course at Leith links, and there is little doubt that the contest actually took place. In his work, Mathison refers to the leading golfers of the day, the 'Caledonian Chiefs' who frequented the links at Leith. These were men of Edinburgh's social and professional élite: eminent lawyers, surgeons, academics, and aristocrats. There was Robert Biggar, an Edinburgh merchant, 'Gigantic Biggar … [whose] bulk enormous scarce can scape the eyes', Duncan Forbes of Culloden, lord president of the court of session, and John Rattray, Bonnie Prince Charlie's surgeon at the 1745 uprising, renowned for his golfing skill. These men were among the founder members of the world's earliest known golf club, the Company of Gentlemen Golfers, formed in 1744. This was a socially exclusive society to which Mathison, the young writer, could not aspire.

Soon after he wrote *The Goff*, Mathison's career changed and he studied divinity at Edinburgh from 1744 to 1748; he was licensed as a probationer by the presbytery of Dalkeith on 1 November 1748. Mathison held an appointment in the north of England before being ordained as assistant minister of Inverkeilor in Arbroath presbytery on 27 September 1750. He married Margaret Whyte on 22 April 1752; they had three daughters—Anne, born in 1753, Margaret, born in 1756, and Mary, born in 1758. Mathison was appointed minister of Brechin on 11 July 1754.

Only one other work by Mathison is known, *A Sacred Ode Occasioned by the Late Successes Attending to the British Arms*. This was published in Edinburgh in 1760. Thomas Mathison died at Brechin on 19 June 1760.

OLIVE M. GEDDES

Sources T. Mathison, 'The goff', ed. C. B. Clapcott, NL Scot., MS 3999 • A. J. Johnston and J. J. Johnston, *The chronicles of golf, 1457–1857* (1993) • O. M. Geddes, *A swing through time: golf in Scotland, 1457–1743* (1992) • J. Kerr, *The golf book of East Lothian* (1896) • Brechin commissariat register of testaments, 1760 • Edinburgh baptismal registers, 1700–22 • Presbytery of Dalkeith minutes, 1742–57
Wealth at death £58 13s. 5d.: Brechin commissariat register of testaments, 1760

Matilda [Matilda of Flanders] (d. **1083**), queen of England, consort of William I, was the daughter of Baudouin (V), count of Flanders (d. 1067), and Adela (d. 1076), daughter of Robert the Pious, king of France, and his wife, Constance of Aquitaine. She had two brothers, Baudouin (VI) of Mons, count of Flanders (d. 1070), and Robert the Frisian, count of Flanders (d. 1093).

Marriage and monastic patronage In 1050, or at the latest 1051, Matilda married William (II), duke of Normandy [see William I]. Accompanied by her father she travelled from Flanders to Eu on the Norman border where she met her fiancé, his mother, Herleva, and his stepfather, Herluin of Conteville, and many others. From there they went to the capital, Rouen, where the wedding ceremony took place. The marriage negotiations had probably started in 1048 and were definitely under way in October 1049 when, at the Council of Rheims, Pope Leo IX forbade the union on unknown grounds. Twelfth-century historians like Orderic Vitalis and the anonymous author of the life of Lanfranc suggest that consanguinity was the problem, but

they add that in 1059 Pope Nicholas II retrospectively approved the marriage on condition that the couple founded one monastery each. Subsequently Duke William founded St Étienne, dedicated in 1077, and his wife Ste Trinité at Caen, which was dedicated in June 1066. Matilda is also credited with founding the church of Notre Dame du Pré at Emendreville, a suburb of Rouen. The foundation was expanded by her son Henry and turned into a priory of Le Bec.

Children and family Over a period of seventeen years Matilda gave birth to eight or nine children. She had four sons, of whom *Robert Curthose, born in 1051 or 1052, was the eldest. He was duke of Normandy from 1087 to 1106 and died in captivity in England in 1134. The second son was Richard, who died as a youth during a hunting accident between 1069 and 1074. William Rufus, king of England, as *William II, from 1087 to 1100, was the third son. *Henry I, the youngest child, born in 1068, was the son who ultimately reunited his father's realm of Normandy, Maine, and England; he died in 1135. There were four or five daughters: *Adelida (d. before 1113) was the eldest, who after a series of collapsed marriage alliances retired as a nun to St Léger at Préaux; Cecilia was given as an oblate to Ste Trinité in 1066, professed in 1075, became abbess in 1113, and died in 1126; Constance married Alain Fergant, duke of Brittany, in 1086 and died in 1090; *Adela was born after her father became king of England—she married c.1080 Stephen, count of Blois, and died as a nun at Marcigny in 1137. A daughter Matilda is known from a reference in Domesday Book, whereas Agatha, who is only mentioned once as a daughter by Orderic Vitalis, may never have existed. Matilda of Flanders was also godmother of St Simon, count of Amiens, Valois, and Vexin from 1074 to 1077, who died at Rome in 1082 and for whose tomb she paid, and of Edith (more often known as *Matilda), later the wife of her son Henry I.

Matilda was on excellent terms with her children of whom her eldest, Robert Curthose, was particularly dear to her. Despite Robert's quarrels with his father and his time in exile, Matilda supported him and remained upset by their disagreement. Once, when St Simon's intervention between William and Robert had failed, Matilda was so upset that she was, according to the biographer of St Simon, 'choked by tears and could not speak' ('Vita B. Simonis', col. 1219). Without William's knowledge, Matilda used to send her son vast amounts of silver and gold. When the king discovered his wife's generosity, he threatened to blind the Breton messenger Samson used for these missions. Through the queen's counsel Samson escaped and became a monk at St Evroult, where Orderic Vitalis heard his story. Samson, too, may have told the story of how Matilda sent messengers to a certain hermit in Germany to ask for his prophecy on the future. The German foretold the dire circumstances of the Norman duchy during the next generation but added that the queen would not suffer because she would be dead before the troubles started. As for her other sons, Richard, while he was still alive, William, and Henry, they appear relatively often in the presence of the king and queen, suggesting a cordial relationship. That none of her sons married during her lifetime, despite Robert's shortlived engagement to Margaret of Maine, is an interesting coincidence, which is perhaps not entirely unconnected with William Rufus's homosexual inclinations. Of her daughters, it seems that Constance and Adela did not leave home until their marriages in respectively 1086 and 1080, while Adelida and Cecilia, despite their life as nuns, stayed relatively close at home in Préaux and Caen.

Matilda remained in touch with her own country and family. According to Orderic Vitalis she was grieved by her father's death, her mother's bereavement, and her brother Robert's usurpation of Flanders after the battle of Kassel, where her nephew Arnulf died. Before her father's death, Matilda and her husband arranged for Abbess Elisabeth of Montivilliers to pay her mother, Adela, an annual pension of £100 in return for her gift of land in the Pays-de-Caux. Her cousin Beatrix, daughter of Christian de Valenciennes, married Gilbert d'Auffay, a distant cousin of Duke William. Among Matilda's servants was a chamberlain called William the Fleming who became a benefactor of Ste Trinité. She probably introduced Arnulf de Chocques to the ducal court, where he taught Cecilia before she became a nun. Through her he became a chaplain of Robert Curthose and later travelled with Bishop Odo of Bayeux to the Holy Land, where he was promoted to the archbishopric of Jerusalem.

Political activities Matilda acted as regent in Normandy for her husband after 1066, probably in collaboration with her son Robert Curthose and sometimes under the guidance of Roger de Montgomery and Roger de Beaumont. Her first visit to England took place in 1068, when at Whitsun she was crowned queen. Among her followers on that occasion was Gui, bishop of Amiens, who had by then already written the *Carmen de Hastingae proelio* ('Song of the Battle of Hastings'). She had a share in about one quarter of her husband's gifts: thirty-nine pre-conquest and sixty-one post-conquest charters bear her name. This charter evidence supports the chroniclers who say that she was sometimes left with overall responsibility in Normandy. Her prominence in the government of Normandy was maintained in the 1070s and 1080s. In 1075, for example, she is named at the head of a group who were present when St Simon restored Gisors to Rouen Cathedral, while in late 1080 she was acting on her husband's behalf in Normandy in a land plea when William and Robert Curthose were in England. Alongside her important role in Normandy, she was very often present at the great crown-wearings which were a prominent feature of William's kingship in England. She heard land pleas as well. 'Royal preoccupations', according to Gilbert Crispin, prevented her from attending the dedication of the abbey church of Le Bec in 1077, instead of which she sent a benefaction. There is no evidence of contacts with foreign officials other than the French abbots to whom she sent gifts and the German hermit mentioned above, with the exception of Pope Gregory VII (*r.* 1073–85) who corresponded with her mainly, it seems, to encourage her to use her influence over her husband by quoting the Bible, which says that an unfaithful man can only become faithful through his wife. A large quantity of evidence shows Matilda as playing the central political and familial role typical of the most active medieval queens.

Wealth and gifts Matilda was the sole donor of two gifts to Ste Trinité at Caen and one each to Malmesbury Abbey and Wells Cathedral. Her pre-conquest income derived from her relatively meagre dowry consisting of estates in the Pays-de-Caux at Bures-en-Bray, Maintru, and Osmoy-St Valéry. She gave the monks of Marmoutier a new refectory and a cope. In support of her husband's invasion of England she gave him the ship *Mora*, on the prow of which stood the figure of a small gilded boy who with his right hand pointed to England and with his left hand held a horn to his lips. This description given by the anonymous author of the *Brevis relatio* comes close to, but is not identical with, the picture of the *Mora*'s stern on the Bayeux tapestry. After the conquest of England, Matilda became a wealthy landowner in England, where she held lands in the counties of Surrey, Hampshire, Wiltshire, Dorset, Devon, Cornwall, Buckinghamshire, and Gloucestershire. The manor of Sandford, Devon, was presented by her to Muriel (perhaps a confidante or servant) upon her marriage to Roger of Bully. She gave the monks of St Evroult £100 to pay for a refectory, a mark of gold, a chasuble decorated with gold and pearls, and a cope for the chanter. Among her other gifts were a vase decorated with gold and precious stones for St Corneille at Compiègne, a golden chalice for St Florent at Saumur, and a chasuble 'that was so rigid because of the metal that it could not be folded' (Musset, 'La reine Mathilde', 193) for the great Burgundian abbey of Cluny. Matilda is also the most likely identification for the anonymous English queen who in the late 1070s approached Abbot Adalelme of La Chaise-Dieu in the Auvergne for a cure for lethargy in return for which she sent a liturgical vestment and £100 towards the cost of the monks' dormitory. The nuns of Ste Trinité at Caen received as her bequest, apart from her regalia mentioned below, a chalice, a chasuble made in Winchester by the wife of Aldred, a mantle of brocade kept in the queen's chamber to be used as a cope, two golden chains with a cross, a chain decorated with 'emblems' for hanging a lamp in front of the altar, several large candelabras made at St Lô, the draperies for her horse, and all the vases 'which she had not yet handed out during her life' (Musset, *Les Actes*, no. 16). In contrast to her generosity there is only one note suggesting greed. Not surprisingly, this comes from England, where in the 1130s the monks of Abingdon remembered her as one of their foreign despoilers who shortly after the conquest demanded a great number of the abbey's treasures. Both Orderic Vitalis and William of Malmesbury state that her English lands and money went after her death to her youngest son, Henry.

Relationship with the Conqueror and death Matilda's relationship with her husband was happy. When, during a stay at Cherbourg between 1063 and 1066, William fell seriously ill, Matilda prayed for his recovery and made a gift at the main altar while wearing her hair loose. Her informal appearance, as a sign of distress, was significant enough for the monks to write it down, presumably as a means to jog people's memory of the gift. William the Conqueror is the first Norman duke for whom no evidence of concubines or illegitimate children survives, an absence on the whole interpreted as a sign that his marriage was a happy one. The only story contradicting such a conclusion comes from William of Malmesbury, who professed himself sceptical about its reliability. He relates the rumour that Matilda had William's mistress, a daughter of a priest, hamstrung by her servant; the perpetrator was disinherited and Matilda, in revenge, was beaten to death with a horse's bridle. In fact the chronicles and charters confirm Matilda's natural death: in the late summer of 1083 she fell ill and died on 2 November. She was buried at her own request at Ste Trinité at Caen, where the original tombstone with inscription carved round the edge has survived. All her epitaphs remember her for her royal descent on her maternal side. That her royal origin and state were important for her is also clear from the protocol to her bequest of land and movables to Ste Trinité, dated to the year before she died. Among the treasures she left to the nuns were her crown and sceptre, a gesture which was imitated by her husband when he left his regalia to St Étienne at Caen.   ELISABETH VAN HOUTS

Sources L. Musset, 'La reine Mathilde et la fondation de la Trinité de Caen (Abbaye aux Dames)', *Mémoire de l'Académie Nationale des Sciences, Arts et Belles Lettres de Caen*, 21 (1984), 191–210 · *Les actes de Guillaume le Conquérant et de la reine Mathilde pour les abbayes caennaises*, ed. L. Musset (Caen, 1967) · M. Fauroux, ed., *Recueil des actes des ducs de Normandie de 911 à 1066* (Caen, 1961) · Ordericus Vitalis, *Eccl. hist.* · 'Vita B. Simonis', *Patrologia Latina*, 156 (1853), 1211–24 · G. Crispin, 'Vita Herluini', in *The works of Gilbert Crispin, abbot of Westminster*, ed. A. S. Abulafia and G. R. Evans (1986), 183–212 · Milo Crispin, 'Vita B. Lanfranci', *Patrologia Latina*, 150 (1854), 29–58 · William of Poitiers, *The history of William the Conqueror*, ed. and trans. R. H. C. Davis and M. Chibnall, OMT (1997) · *The Gesta Normannorum ducum of William of Jumièges, Orderic Vitalis, and Robert of Torigni*, ed. and trans. E. M. C. van Houts, 2 vols., OMT (1992–5) · *Willelmi Malmesbiriensis monachi de gestis regum Anglorum*, ed. W. Stubbs, 2 vols., Rolls Series (1887–9) · J. Stevenson, ed., *Chronicon monasterii de Abingdon*, 2 vols., Rolls Series, 2 (1858) · *Das Register Gregors VII*, ed. E. Caspar, 2 vols., MGH Epistolae Selectae, 2 (Berlin, 1920–23) · *Letters and charters of Gilbert Foliot*, ed. A. Morey and others (1967), 66 (no. 26) · D. M. Wilson, ed., *The Bayeux tapestry* (1985) · *Reg. RAN*, vol. 1 · E. M. C. van Houts, 'The ship list of William the Conqueror', *Anglo-Norman Studies*, 10 (1987), 159–83 · G. Beech, 'Queen Matilda of England (1066–83) and the abbey of La Chaise-Dieu in the Auvergne', *Frühmittelalterliche Studien*, 27 (1993), 350–74

Matilda. *See* Maud (*d.* 1131) *under* David I (*c*.1085–1153).

Matilda [Edith, Mold, Matilda of Scotland] (**1080–1118**), queen of England, first consort of Henry I, was a daughter of *Malcolm III, king of Scots, and his wife, *Margaret, granddaughter of Edmund Ironside (*d.* 1016). She was born probably in the late summer or autumn of 1080, as her godfather, Robert Curthose (*d.* 1134), the eldest son of William I, was in Scotland then, but so far as is known at no other time. She was baptized Edith, but contemporaries

knew her only as Matilda (or one of its variants). Her education was entrusted to her maternal aunt Christina, a nun who appears to have spent time at both Romsey and Wilton. The girl was compelled by her superiors to dress as a nun, and since visitors saw her wearing the habit, some assumed that she was a nun. During the summer of 1093 William II, Alan Rufus, count of Richmond, and her father all observed her wearing the veil. Malcolm was so angered that he snatched it from her head, declaring that he would rather see her married to Count Alan than a nun. His enigmatic outburst has created confusion over whether Malcolm had betrothed his daughter to the count, or whether the comment was intended sarcastically. Malcolm evidently took his daughter with him back to Scotland. Before the end of the year, however, Alan, Malcolm, and Margaret were all dead, and Donald (*d. c*.1099), the new king of the Scots, drove most of Margaret's children out of his realm. Matilda found shelter in England with the help of King William and of her uncle, her mother's brother Edgar Ætheling. Anselm, archbishop of Canterbury (*d.* 1109), ordered the bishop of Salisbury to compel the 'lost daughter' of the Scottish king to return to the monastery, but whether action was taken on this order is not known, nor are Matilda's whereabouts from 1093 to late 1100 ascertainable. During these years Earl William de Warenne (*d.* 1138) asked for her hand, but according to a contemporary chronicler, 'it was reserved for a loftier bridegroom' (Ordericus Vitalis, *Eccl. hist.*, 4.272).

*Henry I was no sooner king, in August 1100, than he proposed to marry Matilda. There was, however, the question of Matilda's freedom for marriage, since Anselm considered her a runaway nun. Matilda approached the archbishop and told him her story; he and an assembly of bishops, nobles, and clergy decided, after careful inquiry, that she had never taken vows nor been pledged to the cloister, and was therefore free to marry. She received their verdict 'with a happy expression', and on 11 November 1100 Anselm performed the wedding and crowned her queen at Westminster Abbey. This marriage proved popular with Henry's English subjects, particularly within the city of London, and had the additional benefit of securing England's northern border through an alliance with the Scots. Matilda received a generous dower settlement. No accurate assessment of the wealth she controlled can be gleaned from the existing evidence, but records which include some twenty-five charters issued by the queen, do show that she controlled the abbeys of Waltham, Barking, and Malmesbury, lands in Rutland, and property in London, including the wharf that later became known as Queenhithe, and that she received the tolls of the city of Exeter. Her staff included two clerks who were promoted to bishoprics. One chronicler reports that Matilda was 'in childbed' in Winchester in July 1101, when Curthose invaded England to press his rights to the throne. If so, she must have been in the early stages of the difficult pregnancy that resulted in the birth of a daughter, *Matilda, near Abingdon in February 1102. A son, *William, was born late in 1103. Unreliable traditions posit the births and early deaths of other children; none of these is likely to be correct.

As queen, Matilda attended meetings of the king's council; she often chaired these meetings in Henry's absence. By 1103 Matilda had persuaded Robert Curthose to give up the pension from England secured to him by his treaty with Henry in 1101. She corresponded with many leading ecclesiastical figures during the investiture controversy, including Archbishop Anselm, Pope Paschal II (r. 1099–1118) and bishops Ivo of Chartres, Marbod of Rennes, and Hildebert de Lavardin. A letter from the German emperor, Henry V, thanking her for efforts on his behalf, presumably refers to negotiations concerning the emperor's marriage to her daughter. Matilda evidently sympathized with the clergy who were taxed harshly in 1105, but declined to intercede on their behalf. On 15 August 1105 she was travelling through the kingdom and stopped for services at Abingdon. When Anselm returned from his three-year exile in 1106, she provided a personal welcome, and then rode ahead along his itinerary to secure comfortable lodgings and lead welcoming ceremonies. She visited Normandy in 1106 or 1107; while there she may have heard a guitar performance by Adelard of Bath. In 1111 she was present at the translation of St Æthelwold's relics at Winchester. In 1112 Matilda travelled to Gloucester to witness the presentation of gifts to the monks there. In 1116, while in London, she ordered the release of an unjustly condemned prisoner. Later that year she chaired a council to deal with the issue of admitting papal legates in England, and on 28 December she attended the consecration of St Albans Abbey church.

Like her mother, Matilda was pious and practised bodily mortifications, especially during Lent. She was particularly interested in the care of lepers, and on one occasion washed and kissed the feet of a group of sufferers who had been invited into her chamber. She built a leper's hospital outside London and patronized several other institutions dedicated to their care. Matilda's interest in works of practical charity probably led to her patronage of the Augustinian canons. Working with Anselm, she established one of England's first Augustinian priories, Holy Trinity, Aldgate, in London. She was also an early patron of Merton Priory. Her good works included the construction of several bridges in Surrey and Essex and a public bathhouse at London's Queenhithe. Matilda is also known for her literary and musical interests. Several continental bishops addressed poetic elegies to her. She commissioned a biography of her mother, a genealogical account of the royal house of Wessex, and was most likely the patron of the Anglo-Norman version of the life of St Brendan. She may also have inspired and helped to pay for the writing of William of Malmesbury's *Deeds of the Kings of England*.

When Matilda died at Westminster on 1 May 1118, the canons of Holy Trinity and the monks of Westminster both claimed burial rights. She was interred in Westminster Abbey near the tombs of her relative Edward the Confessor and his queen. The occurrence of several 'signs and miracles' at Matilda's tomb led to an early interest in the possibility of her sainthood, but the cult waned after the wreck of the *White Ship* and the accession of King Stephen. Despite William of Malmesbury's complaint that she allowed her bailiffs to fleece her tenants to provide funds for her patronage, she is, in English tradition, emphatically 'Mold the Good Queen'. Not only was the Confessor's prophecy of the regrafting of the 'green tree' fulfilled through her descendants, but chroniclers over and over again ascribe to her a direct, personal, and beneficial influence on the condition of England under Henry I.

LOIS L. HUNEYCUTT

Sources *Reg. RAN*, vol. 2 [incl. most of Matilda's charters] · *S. Anselmi Cantuariensis archiepiscopi opera omnia*, ed. F. S. Schmitt, 6 vols. (1938–61); repr. with *Prolegomena, seu, Ratio editionis* (1968) · *Eadmeri Historia novorum in Anglia*, ed. M. Rule, Rolls Series, 81 (1884) · Hermann of Tournai, *Liber de restauratione S. Martini Tornacensis*, MGH Scriptores [folio], 14 (1956) · Hildebertus Cenomanensis, *Patrologia Latina*, 171 (1854) · Ordericus Vitalis, *Eccl. hist.* · J. Stevenson, ed., *Chronicon monasterii de Abingdon*, 2 vols., Rolls Series, 2 (1858) · William of Malmesbury, *Gesta regum Anglorum / The history of the English kings*, ed. and trans. R. A. B. Mynors, R. M. Thomson, and M. Winterbottom, 2 vols., OMT (1998–9) · L. L. Huneycutt, 'Another Esther in our own times: Matilda II and the creation of a queenly ideal in Anglo-Norman England', PhD diss., U. Cal., Santa Barbara, 1992 · G. A. J. Hodgett, ed. and trans., *The cartulary of Holy Trinity Aldgate*, London RS, 7 (1971) · Ivo Carnotensis, *Patrologia Latina*, 162 (1854), 11–290 · C. N. L. Brooke and G. Keir, *London, 800–1216: the shaping of a city* (1975) · A. Strickland and [E. Strickland], *Lives of the queens of England*, new edn, 1 (1902)

Likenesses wax seal, Durham Cath. CL, charters 1.3 Ebor 13 and Durham 1.2.Spec 23

Matilda [Matilda of England] (1102–1167), empress, consort of Heinrich V, was the elder of two children and only legitimate daughter of *Henry I (1068/9–1135), king of England, and his first wife *Matilda (1080–1118), the daughter of *Malcolm III, king of Scots. She was born probably at Sutton Courtenay on about 7 February 1102. A granddaughter of *Margaret of Scotland, marked out from birth for an illustrious marriage, she probably received some early instruction in letters and morals in her mother's circle, which was cultured and religious. When King Henry went to Normandy in the autumn of 1108 he entrusted her and her younger brother William to the spiritual care of Anselm, archbishop of Canterbury and former abbot of Bec: the special devotion to the monks of Bec that she showed to the end of her life may have originated in her childhood memories of Anselm. In 1109 King Henry arranged for her marriage to the German king, Heinrich V (1086–1125); a dowry estimated at 10,000 marks in silver was arranged, and she was betrothed to him by proxy in the Whitsun court held at Westminster on 13 June 1109. She made her first formal appearance in her father's court on 17 October 1109, when she added her cross to a royal charter establishing the see of Ely as 'Matilda, betrothed wife of the king of the Romans' (*sponsa regis Romanorum*; *Reg. RAN*, 2, no. 919).

Marriage and years in Germany In February 1110 imperial envoys, including Burchard, later bishop of Cambrai, arrived to escort Matilda to her future husband. She left with a retinue of nobles and clergy, including Roger, son

Matilda [of England] (1102–1167), manuscript drawing [seated second from right]

of Richard de Clare, and Henry, archdeacon of Winchester. Although Orderic Vitalis claimed that her husband sent them all home, it is possible that Archdeacon Henry, later bishop of Verdun, and some Norman knights remained with her. Her education, however, was to be completed in Germany, and it was in her husband's dominions of Germany and northern Italy that she was to spend the next sixteen years of her life.

Matilda landed at Boulogne and travelled to Liège, where she met her husband, a man about twenty-four years old, and performed the first of her new duties by agreeing to intercede for the disgraced Godfrey, count of Lower Lorraine (whose daughter Adeliza was later to become her stepmother). The royal cortège then moved to Utrecht, and the formal betrothal took place there at Easter (10 April). The dower she received in return for her princely dowry probably included lands in the region of Utrecht. Her coronation took place at Mainz on 25 July, the feast day of St James; she was anointed by Friedrich, archbishop of Cologne, while Bruno, archbishop of Trier, held her reverently in his arms. Bruno, one of Heinrich V's most loyal counsellors, was appointed her guardian when Heinrich himself led an expedition, partly financed by her dowry, to Italy to secure his position there, and to extort coronation as emperor from Pope Paschal II. In his absence she remained at Trier to learn the German language and German customs, so as to be ready to undertake the duties of queen when she reached the canonical age for marriage.

On 6 or 7 January 1114, shortly before her twelfth birthday, Matilda was married to the newly crowned emperor at Worms and then crowned again at Mainz. The magnificent nuptials were attended, according to one anonymous German chronicler, by five dukes, five archbishops, thirty bishops, and innumerable counts and abbots. The hopes that she would become the mother of an heir to the empire were disappointed; no children survived from this marriage, though one chronicler stated not implausibly that she gave birth to one child who did not live. She proved to be a loyal and able queen consort, who carried out the onerous duties of her office with dignity. From the first she frequently sponsored royal grants and acted as intercessor in presenting petitions to her husband. During a reign in which his realm was torn by civil war, and he himself was excommunicated as a result of quarrels with the pope over investiture, she gave him loyal support, and frequently acted as regent during his absence on campaigns. She accompanied him on his second Italian expedition in 1116, when he went to seek reconciliation with Paschal II and to establish his position in Tuscany by taking up his contested rights under the will of Matilda, countess of Tuscany. The expedition crossed the Alps by the St Bernard Pass in March 1116, and proceeded through Lombardy to the Tuscan castle of Canossa. There feudal vassals of the old Matilda welcomed the royal pair in the hope that the new young Matilda might, with her husband, take the place of the old. Unfortunately it proved impossible to make peace with Paschal II, who withdrew in panic to Monte Cassino when the German army approached Rome in March 1117. Since a formal crown-wearing was customary when an emperor visited Rome at Easter, and neither the pope nor any of the cardinals was willing to participate, the papal envoy Maurice Bourdin, archbishop of Braga (later the antipope Gregory VIII), consented to act; he probably crowned Heinrich and Matilda in the basilica of St Peter at Easter, and certainly did so at Pentecost (13 May), by which time he had been excommunicated. Matilda later claimed to have been twice crowned in Rome with papal approval; a hundred years later her right to the imperial title would certainly have been questioned. But the title was then used more loosely by many chroniclers and in many chanceries: Heinrich V, who had unquestionably been crowned emperor in 1111, sometimes continued to call himself simply king of the Romans. Matilda, his betrothed and crowned wife at that date, assumed the title queen of the Romans and used it on her seal. Whatever the legality of the events in Rome in 1117 she consistently called herself empress in her charters to the end of her life, and the title seems never to have been questioned.

When her husband returned to Germany in 1117, to deal with rebellion there, Matilda remained with the army in Italy, presided at courts held at Roca Carpineta and Castrocaro, and pronounced judgments. By November 1119 she had rejoined him at Liège. His reconciliation with the church took place, after years of turmoil, at Worms in November 1122; during the negotiations Matilda could have made the acquaintance of the papal legates and made her first contacts with the papal curia. When the emperor died at Utrecht on 23 May 1125 he entrusted the imperial insignia to her, and placed her in the care of his nephew Friedrich, duke of Swabia, who inherited the family lands. She was persuaded to hand over the insignia to Adalbert, archbishop of Mainz, who presided over an imperial election at which not Friedrich, but his rival Lothar, duke of Saxony, was chosen. As a childless widow she had no further duties in Germany, though Friedrich could have arranged a second marriage for her with one of the German princes who, according to William of Malmesbury, sought her hand. However, her father, King Henry, whose only legitimate son, William, had been drowned in the *White Ship* in 1120, wished to make her his heir and persuaded her to return to Normandy. She appears to have surrendered her lands in Germany; but she was allowed to bring away her magnificent jewels and personal regalia, and one precious relic from the imperial chapel, the hand of St James. Her years as empress had given her valuable experience of European diplomacy; she had also seen the political dangers involved in a quarrel with the church, and had witnessed the change in her husband's formerly devoted chancellor, Adalbert, who after he was rewarded with the archbishopric of Mainz became a leader in the ecclesiastical opposition to his former master. She had been trained in a hard school, where enemies were ruthlessly punished; but she had learned that it was unwise to bear resentment, and that former opponents could become useful allies.

Heir to England and Normandy Matilda's mother had died in 1118, and although her father quickly married Adeliza of Louvain there were no children of the marriage. Henry I wished to secure the succession to England and Normandy in his own line by recognizing her as his heir. She crossed the channel to England in 1126, and in January 1127 he obtained oaths of allegiance to her from all the bishops and magnates present at his Christmas court. Among the latter was his nephew, Stephen of Blois, count of Mortain, who had been brought up at the English court and given the hand of Matilda, the heir of Boulogne. Although Stephen had a hereditary claim to the throne through his mother, Adela, daughter of William I, and his wife was Matilda's first cousin, the claim of the empress was stronger, and he appears to have taken the oath willingly. Shortly afterwards Matilda was betrothed to Geoffrey Plantagenet (1113–1151), son of Foulques, count of Anjou, a youth more than eleven years her junior. Some of the Norman magnates later complained that they had not been consulted about the betrothal. King Henry was anxious to secure the southern frontier of Normandy by an alliance with Anjou; and with that object he had arranged a marriage between his son William and Count Foulques's daughter Matilda in 1119, only a few weeks before William's death put an end to the union. When young Geoffrey of Anjou married Matilda at Le Mans on 17 June 1128, Count Foulques surrendered the county of Anjou to him and left for Jerusalem to marry Queen Melisende.

Matilda's second marriage, like the first, was purely political; its purpose was to provide a male heir to her father's throne. Unfortunately Geoffrey's position was never made clear, and no oaths were ever taken to him. Matilda herself, as an empress, may have felt disparaged by marriage to a mere count. There was an open rift between her and her husband within a year, and she returned to her father at Rouen. In 1131 he took her to England, though Geoffrey had demanded her return and promised to receive her with the honour due to her station. But at a council held at Northampton on 8 September 1131, after the magnates had renewed their homage to her and recognized her as Henry's heir, she agreed to return to her husband. Her eldest son, who was to become *Henry II, was born at Le Mans on 5 March 1133; thereafter the marriage survived as a partnership for the benefit of the couple's joint inheritance. A second son, Geoffrey, was born at Rouen at Pentecost 1134; his birth nearly cost Matilda her life, but she recovered and the inheritance seemed secure. However, Geoffrey of Anjou quarrelled with King Henry over the castles in southern Normandy which were Matilda's dowry, but which Henry continued to occupy. When the king died on 1 December 1135, Matilda was in Anjou and Henry's nephew Stephen of Blois was in his wife's county of Boulogne. He immediately crossed to England, hurried to London, and laid claim to the English throne. He was crowned at Winchester on 22 December by the archbishop of Canterbury, with the encouragement of his brother, Henry de Blois, bishop of Winchester. Shortly afterwards the Norman barons decided not to divide the inheritance, and accepted him as duke of Normandy also. Stephen further secured his position by a successful appeal to Pope Innocent II, whose support was essential if he were not to be charged with violating his oath to Matilda, and by Easter he had won the support of almost all the Anglo-Norman bishops and magnates.

Beginnings of civil war Meanwhile Matilda, caught at a disadvantage, was asserting her rights. She made straight for the castles of her dowry, and the castellan, Wigan the Marshal, handed over to her as his liege lady the castles of Argentan, Exmes, and Domfront. She established herself in the impregnable fortress at Argentan, where her third son, *William FitzEmpress, was born on 22 July 1136. Geoffrey led annual raids into Normandy for the next three years; in October 1136 Matilda brought a troop of men to support him during an unsuccessful siege of Le Sap. There was some support for her in the Cotentin. But not until her half-brother, *Robert, earl of Gloucester, renounced his allegiance to Stephen in 1138 were Matilda's forces strong enough to make further inroads into Normandy. She then began a new initiative and directly challenged Stephen's position.

Early in 1139 Matilda appealed to the papal court. Her case, based on her claim as her father's heir and the oaths sworn to her, was heard at the Second Lateran Council, which opened on 4 April 1139. Stephen's delegation was led by Arnulf, archdeacon of Sées and later bishop of Lisieux, who countered her claim with technicalities, arguing that she could not be Henry's heir because her mother had been a nun and she was therefore illegitimate. This was never proved; and indeed her mother, though educated in a nunnery, was not known to have taken any vows, and Anselm of Canterbury himself had celebrated her marriage. Innocent refused either to pronounce sentence or to adjourn the case, and it was never finally settled by his successors, who preferred to await the outcome of events and hope for a compromise. For the time being, however, Stephen's coronation was not invalidated, and this led to his continued acceptance by most of the English bishops, until his authoritarian treatment of church rights led some to desert his cause.

Matilda's next step was to carry her challenge to England. Sporadic rebellions in support of her claim had already broken out in the west country, and her uncle, David, king of Scots, had invaded the north; but both initiatives had been halted. On 30 September 1139 she and her half-brother, Earl Robert, landed in Sussex; he immediately slipped away to Bristol with a small bodyguard, and she took refuge in Arundel Castle. Here she was under the protection of her stepmother, the dowager queen Adeliza, who had become the wife of William d'Aubigny, earl of Arundel. Although William was a staunch supporter of Stephen, Adeliza's protection could not be disregarded, and Stephen agreed to grant Matilda a safe conduct to proceed to Bristol, under the escort of Henry, bishop of Winchester, and Waleran, count of Meulan. Miles, castellan of Gloucester, immediately hurried to Bristol to recognize her as his liege lady. As even the hostile *Gesta Stephani* recorded:

> he was so unquestioning in his loyalty to King Henry's children as not only to have helped them, but likewise to have received the countess of Anjou herself with her men and always behaved to her like a father in deed and counsel. (*Gesta Stephani*, 96–7)

Another of King Henry's circle to be equally loyal and fatherly in his conduct towards her was *Brian fitz Count lord of Wallingford, one of her most steadfast and eloquent supporters. Matilda joined Miles at Gloucester, a royal castle held by him under Earl Robert, where she probably felt more at home than as a poor relation with Robert in Bristol. When her power increased she rewarded Miles with the earldom of Hereford, and he was one of her chief military commanders until he was killed in a hunting accident at Christmas 1143.

Lady of England Although Matilda's position was now strong enough for attempts at mediation to be made, they came to nothing. The situation changed only when King Stephen's army met the combined forces of Robert of Gloucester and Robert's son-in-law Ranulf (II), earl of Chester, in the battle of Lincoln on 2 February 1141, when the king was defeated and captured. With Stephen held a prisoner at Bristol, and with even Stephen's brother, Henry of Winchester, now papal legate, ready to abandon his cause, many of Stephen's vassals began to turn to her. Since her husband, Geoffrey of Anjou, took advantage of her victory to press further into Normandy, those with extensive estates across the channel began to look for reconciliation. On 2 March Bishop Henry met the empress at Wherwell; and after she had given security to consult him on all major business, particularly on the gift of bishoprics and abbeys as long as he preserved his fealty to her, he agreed to receive her as 'lady of England'. On the following day he received her ceremoniously in his cathedral at Winchester, where she walked in procession with six other bishops and a number of abbots. At a legatine council, celebrated on 7 April, she was formally accepted as 'lady of England and Normandy', and arrangements were put in hand for her coronation at Westminster. At this stage she seems to have hoped to rule in her own right until her son came of age.

In spite of her apparent victory, Matilda's position was more precarious than her adherents were willing to admit. Archbishop Theobald of Canterbury, though a former abbot of Bec who knew her personally and respected her, was a man of principle, who refused to renounce the allegiance he had sworn to Stephen unless Stephen surrendered the crown, which he refused to do. The writs and charters issued by the empress in the summer of 1141 show that her support was mostly in the west of England, the Welsh marches, parts of the Thames valley, and Wiltshire. In the north King David remained loyal and gave her such help as his own Scottish interests allowed, but he had no influence in Yorkshire, and his attempt to force his chancellor, William Cumin, into the bishopric of Durham poisoned Matilda's relations with the church. In East Anglia, Hugh Bigod (d. 1176/7) gave nominal support and was rewarded with the earldom of Norfolk. Although Geoffrey de Mandeville, the powerful earl of Essex, came over to her side for a few weeks, he turned back to Stephen in the hour of Matilda's greatest need. William de Mohun, another waverer, supported her just long enough to be made earl of Somerset. Ranulf, earl of Chester, was clearly hesitant; and Ranulf's half-brother, William de Roumare, earl of Lincoln, was still unwilling to offer substantial help to her cause. She alienated the Londoners by refusing to grant the concessions they demanded. Although she succeeded in securing the election of Robert de Sigillo, the former head of her father's writing office and now a monk of Reading, as bishop of London, her support for William Cumin at Durham angered the legate. Hostile chroniclers, in particular the author of the *Gesta Stephani*, attacked her as haughty and intractable; it is likely that she wished to keep up the state she had experienced in Germany, but when she met opposition peremptorily, with all the firmness that had been accepted, however reluctantly, from her father, it was regarded as unwomanly, arrogant, and obstinate in her. The legate, Henry of Winchester, in spite of having accepted her, remained sufficiently hesitant to seek papal approval for his change of allegiance; and Innocent II's reply, when it came, reiterated support for Stephen and ordered Henry to recognize him. Moreover the empress had to contend with a woman as resolute as herself. Stephen's queen, Matilda, never gave up the fight. With all the wealth of her own county of Boulogne and the honour of Boulogne in England behind her, and the support of William of Ypres at the head of a formidable band of Flemish mercenaries, she was in a position to win waverers back to Stephen's side. When the empress reached Westminster at midsummer, hoping to be crowned queen, the rival Matilda was encamped with her army on the south bank of the Thames, threatening the city of London. At the last minute the Londoners poured out of their city to attack the empress, and she was forced to beat a hasty and somewhat ignominious retreat. She reached Oxford, where she rewarded those magnates still loyal to her and reconsidered her position.

Matilda rallied her supporters, who included King David, Robert, earl of Gloucester, and another half-brother Reginald, earl of Cornwall, Baldwin de Revières, earl of Devon, William de Mohun, Hugh Bigod, and Geoffrey de Mandeville, to whom she promised concessions similar to those previously made by Stephen. However, since the lands and castles offered to Geoffrey were in Essex, London, Middlesex, and Hertfordshire, which she did not control, Geoffrey decided within a few weeks that his interests would be better served by returning to the side of the queen. Since Henry of Winchester did not come to Oxford, and was already in communication with the queen, Matilda decided at the end of July 1141 to march on Winchester. While her army besieged the bishop's palace, the queen's forces under William of Ypres, supported by the Londoners and Mandeville, advanced to encircle the besiegers and cut off their supplies. In the rout that followed Matilda escaped with Brian fitz Count and Reginald of Cornwall, while Robert of Gloucester, who was protecting her rear, was himself captured on 14 September. Matilda reached first Ludgershall, then Devizes; for part of the way she rode astride like a man for greater speed. Finally exhaustion compelled her to be carried on a litter between two horses, so giving rise to a legend that she escaped hidden in a coffin. Earl Robert was able to negotiate his release in exchange for the release of King Stephen by 3 November; the only lasting advantage he could secure was that the castles and lands seized by the empress after the king's capture should not be restored. These included the castles of Oxford and Devizes, and for the next twelve months she kept her court at Oxford, meeting her adherents on at least two occasions at the more convenient centre of Devizes.

Last years in England Matilda's next step was to appeal to her husband, Geoffrey, for military aid. Geoffrey, however, was fully occupied in attempting to establish his authority firmly in Normandy; he replied that he would negotiate only with Earl Robert, whom he knew personally. Leaving his sister in Oxford, where she seemed relatively safe, Robert crossed to Normandy at the end of June 1142, and spent some weeks helping to complete the conquest of the region between Falaise, Caen, and Avranches. He returned bringing some 300 men and Matilda's son Henry, now a boy of nine. But during his absence Stephen's army laid siege to Oxford; and before Robert could arrive with a relieving force the garrison was on the brink of surrender. Matilda was obliged to make the most dramatic escape of her perilous career. Early in December 1142, with only three or four knights, she slipped out of the castle, probably by a postern gate, and crossed the frozen Thames. She and her escort, wearing white cloaks as camouflage, walked through the snow to Abingdon. From there she rode to Wallingford, to reach the protection of Brian fitz Count, and was taken by him to Devizes. There she established her base in the almost impregnable castle which King Stephen had taken from Roger, bishop of Salisbury. She remained there for the next six years, during which time neither side could gain a decisive advantage in England. In Normandy, however, Geoffrey

completed his conquest by 1144, and was recognized as duke of Normandy. Young Henry's time was divided between his uncle and mother in England, and his father in Normandy. From 1142 Matilda definitely recognized that her struggle was rather to secure Henry's inheritance than to win the crown for herself.

Matilda's charters and the coins issued in her name show that she and her party were able to control a limited area, with its solid core in the great lordship of Gloucester, including also parts of Somerset, Wiltshire, and Dorset. Her channel port was at Wareham; she controlled mints at Bristol, Cardiff, and Wareham after Oxford was lost. In Wiltshire her principal military commander, John FitzGilbert, the marshal, held firmly to his castle of Marlborough, though he could never succeed in capturing Malmesbury. Matilda rewarded her knights with gifts of lands from the royal demesne, and provided for adequate castle guard. She made use of royal demesne and forest lands for gifts to churches, so consolidating her power in disputed border lands. Some gifts were purely tokens of thanks, not politically motivated; she gave her laundress, probably when she left England, a substantial hereditary estate in Somerset. During these years there were changes in allegiance among the magnates. Those like Waleran of Meulan and William de Roumare, whose principal estates lay in Normandy, finally abandoned Stephen and became her vassals to preserve their patrimonies. Ranulf, earl of Chester, had, like Geoffrey de Mandeville, supported Stephen for a time; but Stephen did not trust them and both returned to her party when they found themselves threatened by him. A war of sieges followed, in which neither side could achieve a decisive victory.

Matilda and Geoffrey fared better by diplomacy. Matilda had contacts in Rome, and Stephen's relations with the church deteriorated. Innocent II's successors withheld final judgment on the rights of the claimants, and refused to recognize Stephen's son Eustace as heir to the throne. In Normandy, on the other hand, after Geoffrey's victories in 1144, all the bishops including Arnulf of Lisieux, once a bitter enemy, recognized Geoffrey as duke and Henry as his heir.

Retirement to Normandy In March 1148 the empress decided to leave England and return to Normandy. Her brother Robert had died the previous year; Brian fitz Count was no longer active and had possibly taken religious vows before his death. Moreover her position in Devizes was becoming difficult. Legally Devizes belonged to the bishop of Salisbury, and Pope Eugenius III was demanding its restoration to the church. Threatened with excommunication if she did not surrender it, she prevaricated as long as possible; after leaving England she instructed her son in somewhat general terms to comply with the pope's mandate. Young Henry adroitly succeeded in evading it. By June 1148 she was at Falaise; within a few months she had moved to Rouen. There on 11 October, together with her husband and her three sons, she made a grant to the abbey of Mortemer. Probably at this time plans were agreed for her future. In March 1149 Geoffrey of Anjou made a grant possibly intended for her support;

he gave three prebends in the church of St Étienne at Bures-en-Bray to the priory of Notre Dame du Pré, a cell of Bec at Quevilly, just across the river from Rouen, and it was here that Matilda spent the last nineteen years of her life, either in the royal residence that Henry I had built in his park at Quevilly, near to the priory, or in quarters attached to the priory itself. Her charters were dated either at Rouen or at Le Pré. Her way of life recalls that of her mother at Westminster, where the royal palace stood beside the abbey church. Like her mother she was equally active in the work of government, helping her son in much the same way as her mother had helped Henry I.

After Matilda's return to Normandy she never used the title 'lady of England' or 'of the English' in her charters, but she retained the title of empress and never called herself countess of Anjou. In April 1149 her son went to England to take control of the struggle for the throne. He was knighted by his great-uncle King David at Carlisle. In the autumn he returned and his father Geoffrey invested him with the duchy of Normandy. In September 1151 Geoffrey took him to Paris and persuaded Louis VII to recognize his claim to the duchy in preference to that of Stephen's son Eustace. There is no indication that Matilda accompanied them; she may have been busy maintaining order in Normandy. Henry did homage to King Louis. On the way home Geoffrey unexpectedly fell ill and died, leaving Henry as count of Anjou and duke of Normandy. England, however, was less than half conquered; and the situation was further complicated in May 1152 when Henry married the former wife of King Louis, Eleanor of Aquitaine, and added her vast inheritance to his own, while at the same time reawakening the hostility of Louis himself. Matilda was to have an important role in Normandy while Henry was forced to campaign elsewhere.

Although Matilda must have met Eleanor, there is no record of her views on the marriage, or of her relations with her new daughter-in-law. Eleanor came to Normandy only very rarely, whereas Matilda was actively involved there, sometimes acting as Henry's regent and trying to ensure the loyalty of the Norman magnates, in particular the volatile Waleran of Meulan, who had considerable property in France. Her worst moments came during Henry's absence in England in 1153. She had to admit that she was unable to protect the monks of Mortemer who were attempting to settle in her new foundation at Le Valasse, and her second son, Geoffrey, who may have had some responsibility in Anjou, was captured and imprisoned by the lord of Amboise. On Henry's return after a successful campaign in England, during which Eustace of Blois had died and Henry was recognized as Stephen's heir, she persuaded him to secure Geoffrey's release from a harsh imprisonment by dismantling the fortifications of the castle of Chaumont. The years of greatest peril ended when Stephen died on 25 October 1154, and Henry came into the inheritance his mother had helped to preserve for him.

The king's mother Thereafter Matilda remained at Quevilly. Rouen was a thriving commercial, judicial, and administrative centre, and Matilda was able to combine active involvement in the business of the duchy with a semi-religious retreat. The monks of Bec in the priory of Le Pré were her friends and spiritual counsellors, and she was warmly praised both by Robert de Torigni, who left Bec to become abbot of Mont-St Michel in 1148, and by the monk Étienne of Rouen, author of the long historical poem *Draco normannicus*. She helped to finance the building of a new stone bridge over the Seine, linking Rouen with the royal park at Quevilly and the priory of Le Pré. From time to time when Henry II was in Rouen she heard cases with him in her court, particularly if a religious house in her patronage was involved. He always treated her with great respect, putting her name before his in any joint charters. In his absence she sometimes acted on his behalf, confirming the election of a prelate, or issuing a writ to protect monastic property. He was prepared to listen to her advice on matters of policy; when in 1155 he was considering the possibility of attempting to conquer Ireland and give it to his brother William, she made her opposition to the project known. Her motives are conjectural, but she must have realized that Henry's resources were already overstretched. William, who received very extensive estates in England instead of in Ireland, was able to give practical support to his brother in the early years of the reign, up to his premature death in 1164. Her intimate knowledge of Germany may have been useful during the negotiations with the emperor, Frederick Barbarossa (r. 1152–90), who wrote to Henry II asking for the return of the hand of St James that she had brought with her from Germany. The precious relic was retained for the abbey of Reading, and Frederick was pacified with magnificent gifts. They included a tent said to have been large enough for a coronation ceremony, which he took on his campaigns in Italy—a gift probably suggested by Matilda's practical experience of the Roman expedition she had undertaken with her first husband. Only after the death of Archbishop Theobald in 1162, when she advised against the election of Henry's chancellor and close friend, Thomas Becket, as his successor and was overruled, did her influence over her son visibly weaken.

Matilda may have feared that Becket would act like the emperor Heinrich V's chancellor Adalbert after his election as archbishop of Mainz almost fifty years previously. But she did not raise any objection when in 1163 Becket banned the marriage of her youngest son, William, to Isabel de Warenne, the widow of William de Blois, on the grounds of consanguinity. William's death shortly afterwards was attributed by his friends to his disappointment. But if Matilda resented Becket's action she did not harbour a grudge against him, and when disagreement with King Henry over the constitutions of Clarendon forced Becket into exile in 1164 she was cautiously prepared to attempt mediation. Her views were written down by Nicholas, prior of the hospital of Mont-St Jacques at Rouen, in a remarkable letter describing a private interview, which she had reluctantly agreed to give him when he interceded with her on Becket's behalf. At her request he read the constitutions to her in Latin and explained them in French. Her views were practical and pragmatic. She thought it had been a great mistake on her son's part to write down the constitutions and require the bishops to swear to uphold them; she preferred the more flexible customs that had guided conduct in her father's and grandfather's time. She was less concerned with the legal principles determining the procedure for judging criminous clerks than with the measures needed to prevent the crimes; she blamed the bishops for ordaining too many clerks without benefices, so that poverty drove them to robbery and violence, while on the other hand some wealthy clerks held as many as four or even seven churches or prebends, contrary to the canon law that forbade more than two. Although she claimed that her son did not consult her about his relations with the church because he knew that she rated the freedom of the church more highly than the royal will, she refused to allow any diminution of the royal dignity, and censured Thomas Becket for his rigid opposition and lack of humility. Many thought that she might have been able to bring about a reconciliation, but the task was beyond her. Her genuine respect for ecclesiastical authority appears at this time in her refusal to receive the envoys of Frederick Barbarossa after his excommunication by Alexander III, though the business that brought them to Rouen included negotiating the marriage of her granddaughter Matilda to Henry the Lion, duke of Saxony. Her son had no scruples about receiving them. But if she failed to find a solution for the Becket controversy, she had more success in negotiations with the king of France, when a minor quarrel that nearly led to war broke out about the transmission of money collected at Tours for the Holy Land. And in 1164 King Louis wrote to her, as the person exercising authority in Rouen, on behalf of one of his merchants who had become involved in a lawsuit there. She was known to have some authority in government, and was respected as a peacemaker.

Death and benefactions   In 1160 Matilda suffered a serious illness, but after her recovery she remained active in government until she died on 10 September 1167. The statement of Geoffroi de Vigeois that she took the veil as a nun of Fontevrault is unsupported and unreliable; he probably confused her with her sister-in-law, Matilda, who had retired to Fontevrault in her widowhood. The monk Étienne of Rouen describes in detail in the *Draco normannicus* her solemn funeral rites, conducted by Rotrou, archbishop of Rouen, in the presence of Arnulf of Lisieux and many monks and clergy. She was buried in accordance with her own wishes before the high altar in the abbey of Bec. Two lines of her epitaph became particularly famous:

Ortu magna, viro major, sed maxima partu,
Hic jacet Henrici filia, sponsa, parens.
('Great by birth, greater by marriage, greatest in her offspring,
here lies the daughter, wife, and mother of Henry.')

She gave her treasures and regalia to various religious houses; Bec received the richest vestments and church ornaments as well as two crowns, one of which was so heavy that it had to be supported on two silver rods when worn for a royal coronation. Some treasures had already gone to St Denis; and a dalmatic given to the austere hermit monks of Grandmont is still preserved at Ambazac. A beautiful reliquary given to the monks of Le Valasse is preserved at Rouen. Her tomb was damaged by fire in 1263; during the restoration in 1282 her body was found sewn into an ox-skin. When the church was pillaged by the English in 1421 the tomb was again seriously damaged; in 1684 it was restored by the Maurists, who then wrapped her bones in an embroidered silk cloth and enclosed them in a coffin of wood and lead. The abbey church was destroyed by Napoleon, and Matilda's remains were not discovered until 1846, when they were taken to Rouen and reinterred in the cathedral. Ironically the final resting place of the empress was not the one she herself desired, but that chosen by her father.

Matilda's church benefactions were numerous, and often directed towards the newer religious orders, though she made some gifts to Cluny and was commemorated throughout the Cluniac order. In Germany she granted land at Oostbroek near Utrecht for the foundation of a very strict Benedictine house by a group of knights who wished to retire to the monastic life. During her years in England her gifts were partly politically motivated; she refused to acknowledge Stephen's right to give away royal demesne lands, and took over any lands he had given to religious houses as her own donations. After Waleran of Meulan founded the abbey of Bordesley out of royal demesne received from Stephen, she appropriated the foundation and brought Bordesley into the royal patronage. Her gifts to the Shropshire abbeys of Shrewsbury and Haughmond were partly intended to assert her rights and neutralize Stephen's gifts; but she also regarded Shropshire as territory that could be recovered after 1142. When she took the newly founded house of Arrouaisian canons at Lilleshall under her protection, territorial interest may have been to the fore. The same is true of her work, with her son Henry, in replacing the hermitage of Radmore in Staffordshire with a Cistercian house, which was moved shortly afterwards to Stoneleigh. Wiltshire too was contended territory, and there she and her son established another Cistercian abbey (Drownfront, later Stanley) as a daughter house of Quarr.

In Normandy, Matilda used part of her wealth and the dower lands she held to favour the Cistercians. At Le Valasse she took over the foundation of a house begun by Waleran of Meulan, whose motives she did not trust, and after a stormy beginning during the disorders of 1152–3 she secured the establishment there of Cistercian monks from the royal abbey of Mortemer, with the assistance of one of her illegitimate half-sisters, Matilda, abbess of Montivilliers. At the end of her life, in 1166, she began the foundation of another Cistercian house at La Noë. She refounded the house of secular canons, Notre Dame du Voeu, which her grandfather *William I had established at Cherbourg, and placed there a community of regular canons from the reformed house of St Victor in Paris. She also completed the foundation of a house of Premonstratensian canons at Silly-en-Gouffern, which, according to the chronicle of the abbey, she had begun after the birth of her son William in 1136, partly out of a regard for St Norbert, whom she had known at the court of the emperor, her first husband. Drogo, one of her knights who had returned to Normandy with her, became in time the first abbot. The establishment of full religious life there seems to have been interrupted by wars and disorders; the foundation proper was apparently delayed until some years after her return to Normandy in 1148, for her charters date from 1157-8. She made gifts to Mortemer for the building of two guest houses large enough to accommodate four different categories of pilgrims: rich and poor, monks and knights. Lannoy Abbey also received gifts from her. After recovering from a serious illness in 1161 she gave her silk mattress to be sold for the benefit of the leper hospital of Mont-St Jacques at Rouen. She was a generous benefactor of Bec and its priory of Notre Dame du Pré. Apparently she had a special devotion to the Virgin Mary; although the foundation of the chapel of St Julien at Petit-Quevilly about 1160 was attributed to her son Henry, she may have had a voice in the decoration of the building: the beautiful paintings on the vaults of the choir and apse show scenes from the life of the Virgin.

Character, historical significance, and posthumous reputation
Matilda's royal status ensured that writers would seek her patronage. When she was still a young bride in Germany, Hugh of Fleury dedicated his chronicle of the recent Frankish kings (*Liber qui modernorum regum Francorum continet actus*) to her, praising her high birth and lofty status. Shortly after her return to England in 1126 the monks of Malmesbury sought her patronage. William of Malmesbury had undertaken to write his *Gesta regum Anglorum* at the request of Queen Matilda, but her death in 1118 deprived him of a patron. A dedicatory letter was addressed to the empress through her uncle King David; the monks stressed the distinction of her birth, and the value history had always had for kings and queens in the past. When, later, she seemed to have the crown within her grasp, Philip de Thaon dedicated his *Livre de sybille* to her. If the subject chosen was not merely conventional, it may imply that she shared the fashionable interest of court circles in the prophecies of Merlin and the sibyls. These works all spoke respectfully of her lineage; there is a more personal touch in a poem addressed to her by Hildebert de Lavardin, archbishop of Tours, who implied that learning was one of her virtues.

A life of the empress said to have been written by Arnulf of Lisieux, a former adversary who became a devoted supporter, has not survived. Arnulf wrote two laudatory epitaphs, praising Matilda's royal lineage and imperial marriage, but claiming that her virtues were even greater than her noble blood, and that though a woman she was without feminine weakness. She was said, whether conventionally or truly is not known, to have been extremely beautiful, and she was remembered in Germany as 'the good Matilda'. Her greatest successes came during three periods: the first during the time when she was consort in Germany before 1125; the second when, from 1142, she helped to secure the claim of her son Henry as heir to the throne of England; and the last when she supported him

in the governance of Normandy. She then showed that she had inherited many of her father's talents for government. As herself a claimant to the throne of England in 1139-41 she was less successful; partly, perhaps, through lack of experience in leadership and the inherent weakness of any opposition to a crowned king, or through the handicap of her sex, and the impression she sometimes gave of pride and harshness. Years later Prior Nicholas of Mont-St Jacques, even after the interview in which she said much that pleased him, noted that she was 'of the stock of tyrants', determined to uphold her son's rights. But there were at all times elements of grandeur in her character that attracted and held the loyalty of such men as Miles, earl of Hereford, and Brian fitz Count. The loyalty and affection of the monks of Bec, with whom she spent the last years of her life, never wavered. Her piety was more than conventional; the chronicler of Le Valasse wrote that her devotion to the Lord God came from the heart. Ralph de Diceto considered that her nobility of character and her masculine courage set an example of fortitude and patience to sustain her three granddaughters—Matilda, duchess of Saxony, Joanna, queen of Sicily, and Eleanor, queen of Castile—through all the trials and hardships of their lives.

Although Matilda failed to overcome the difficulties in the way of female succession in early twelfth-century England and Normandy, and never became a reigning queen, she was able to learn from some mistakes made during the early years of her struggle with Stephen. Her lasting achievement in the long run was to secure—by courage, determination, and shrewd political judgement—the succession of her son Henry II, and so the establishment of the Angevins in preference to the house of Blois–Flanders as rulers of England. This achievement was recognized by most Angevin historians in the century after her death, and by many others later. Her reputation in later centuries, however, fluctuated according to the sources studied by writers and the conditions governing succession to the throne. The succession question during the Tudor period made writers alive to the problems she had faced, not least the question of the rights of a queen's husband. As long as historians consulted mainly narrative sources their assessments depended on their selection of authorities; the vivid and hostile picture of her failures in 1141-2 given by the author of the *Gesta Stephani* was responsible for many unfavourable interpretations of her character, including that of Sir James Ramsay. She fared better with those familiar with continental chronicles, notably Kate Norgate, whose balanced narrative has stood the test of time. The publication of charters and financial documents made possible an appreciation of her political skills in government; Léopold Delisle was the first to recognize her positive and important work in the government of Normandy. Her turbulent career shows how much could, and could not, be achieved by a female heir to the English throne in the twelfth century.

The epitaph on Matilda's first tomb is lost, but possibly the description of her preserved in the chronicle of Bec was taken from it:

the most noble lady Matilda, empress of the Romans, daughter of the first Henry king of the English, wife first of Henry emperor of the Romans, and then countess of Anjou, queen of England and mother of Henry II king of the English.   (Chibnall, *Empress Matilda*, 191)

In 1684 a new inscription for her tomb, composed by Jean Mabillon and printed in A. A. Porée's *Histoire de l'abbaye du Bec* (2.615), more correctly avoided describing her as queen of England.

There are two formal representations of Matilda. One on coins struck in her mints shows her in profile. The other is on the only seal she is known to have used all her life; she is depicted sitting majestically with her feet resting on a footstool, wearing a crown of three points and a long garment with full sleeves, and holding in her right hand a long sceptre terminating in a fleur-de-lis. The legend is 'St Mathildis Dei gratia Romanorum regina'.

MARJORIE CHIBNALL

Sources *Reg. RAN* · L. Delisle and others, eds., *Recueil des actes de Henri II, roi d'Angleterre et duc de Normandie, concernant les provinces françaises et les affaires de France*, 4 vols. (Paris, 1909–27) · William of Malmesbury, *The Historia novella*, ed. and trans. K. R. Potter (1955) · K. R. Potter and R. H. C. Davis, eds., *Gesta Stephani*, OMT (1976) · M. Chibnall, *The Empress Matilda* (1991) · R. H. C. Davis, *King Stephen*, 3rd edn (1990) · Ordericus Vitalis, *Eccl. hist.* · R. Howlett, ed., *Chronicles of the reigns of Stephen, Henry II, and Richard I*, 4, Rolls Series, 82 (1889) · J. C. Robertson and J. B. Sheppard, eds., *Materials for the history of Thomas Becket, archbishop of Canterbury*, 7 vols., Rolls Series, 67 (1875–85) · A. A. Porée, *Histoire de l'abbaye du Bec*, 2 vols. (1901) · G. Meyer von Knonau, *Jahrbücher des deutschen Reiches unter Heinrich IV und Heinrich V*, 6, 7 (1890–1909) · M. Chibnall, 'The charters of the Empress Matilda', *Law and Government in Medieval England and Normandy*, ed. G. Garnett and J. Hudson (1994), 276–96

Likenesses impression of her great seal, *c.*1142 (affixed to charter granting lands to Cluniac priory of St James), King's Cam. · coin, NMW · manuscript drawing, CCC Cam., MS 373, fol. 95*v* [*see illus.*] · seal, BL, Add. Ch. 75724

Matilda [Matilda of Boulogne] (*c.*1103–1152), queen of England, consort of King Stephen, was the only legitimate child and heir of Eustace (III), count of Boulogne and one of the wealthiest landholders in England. Her mother, Mary, was the younger daughter of Queen *Margaret and *Malcolm III, king of Scots, whose elder daughter, *Matilda, had married *Henry I of England. Boulogne, with the port of Wissant, controlled one of the most important channel crossings to England, and the extensive properties of the honour of Boulogne in England, particularly in Essex and the south-east, made the marriage of its heir of paramount importance to King Henry. He approved her union with his favourite nephew, *Stephen, already count of Mortain. In 1125, after the marriage, Count Eustace abdicated to retire to a Cluniac monastery, and Matilda became countess of Boulogne in her own right.

The granddaughter on one side of Margaret of Scotland and on the other of Ida, countess of Bouillon, Matilda was a woman of strong and pious character, and her upbringing prepared her for the tasks of government. When in 1135 Henry I died, and Matilda's husband Stephen seized the English throne in defiance of the claims of Henry's daughter, the Empress *Matilda, the new queen (as she was always styled, though there is no evidence of a formal

coronation) proved an invaluable help and support to her husband. She used her knowledge of continental politics, and her control of an effective fleet and an important stretch of the channel coast round Boulogne, to the best advantage. She was also instrumental in securing the support of a strong and ruthless troop of Flemish mercenaries, led by her kinsman William of Ypres. Her kinship network was valuable in her work as a negotiator and peacemaker, though, since her cousin and rival the empress shared some close family contacts with her, the advantage was not always on the queen's side in the long run.

Hostilities between Stephen and the empress (aided by her second husband, Geoffrey, count of Anjou) began immediately; but it was when widespread resistance broke out in England in 1138 that Matilda's practical help was needed. She brought up a land force to besiege Dover, held for the empress by Walchelin Maminot, and sent word to her friends and kinsmen and vassals in Boulogne to blockade the port by sea, so reducing the garrison to surrender. Her next direct interventions in the struggle were through diplomacy. According to Richard of Hexham, she played a leading part in securing peace with her uncle, David, king of Scots, who, though defeated in the battle of the Standard in August 1138, remained a threat to the north of England. The outcome of the negotiations was the peace of Carlisle (9 April 1139), which (as Richard of Hexham notes) was opposed by some English magnates, and (according to Orderic Vitalis) seen by some of King David's counsellors to be to the advantage of the Scots. David was heavily bribed with territory in the north of England, and his son Henry was betrothed to Ada de Warenne, daughter of the earl of Surrey.

After completing the negotiations Matilda accompanied Henry south to Nottingham, to join Stephen's court for the confirmation of the treaty. Next, relying on her continental connections, she set about brokering the marriage of her son *Eustace with Constance, sister of Louis VII of France. After the empress came to England in 1139 and established a centre of resistance with her half-brother, Robert, earl of Gloucester, the importance of France as a bulwark against Geoffrey of Anjou's attacks on Normandy became clearer than ever. Stephen had already taken Eustace on his one visit to Normandy in 1137, and had persuaded Louis to receive Eustace's homage for the duchy. In February 1140 Matilda took her son overseas for betrothal to Constance, and brought his bride back to England. At Whitsuntide she assisted the papal legate, Henry, bishop of Winchester, in an unsuccessful attempt to negotiate a peace between the two contending parties. But it was during the ensuing period of open war, and near disaster for Stephen, that she played her most important role in government.

After Stephen's defeat and capture at the battle of Lincoln (2 February 1141) and the temporary defection of Henry of Winchester to the side of the empress, the queen acted as regent and kept up the struggle on behalf of her husband. Appeals for his release fell on deaf ears, and she turned her attention to raising troops and working tirelessly by persuasion and purchase to win back Geoffrey de

Mandeville and other magnates who had gone over to the empress. By bringing William of Ypres and his Flemish mercenaries to threaten London, she induced the Londoners, already disillusioned by the intransigence of the empress, to rise against her and prevent her coronation. At Guildford the queen met Henry of Winchester, already wavering in his support of the Angevins, and secured his return to the king's cause. When he was besieged by the empress in his cathedral city of Winchester, she brought up her Flemish troops and a strong band of Londoners, as well as the magnates loyal to her, and besieged the besiegers. In the ensuing rout Robert of Gloucester was captured and brought to her castle of Rochester, to be kept in honourable captivity until he could be exchanged for the king. At Christmas 1141 Matilda wore her crown beside Stephen in Canterbury Cathedral.

In the later stages of the civil war Matilda played an important, if less dramatic part, watching the continental alliances and trying to smooth relations between Stephen and the church, so as to secure the coronation of their son Eustace. When a quarrel between Stephen and Archbishop Theobald in 1148 led to the expulsion of the latter from England, she provided a refuge for him in St Omer until peace could be re-established. Her influence was not strong enough to persuade the pope to permit the coronation of Eustace. But her courage and determination was decisive in enabling Stephen to retain the throne as long as he lived.

Much of Matilda's energy in her last years went into pious works. Her great wealth had made donations to religious foundations possible from an early age. She had a close friendship with Gervase, abbot of Arrouaise, whom she had known at her father's court, and it was probably she who encouraged the settlement of the first Arrouaisian canons in England. She gave generously to the templars to found the preceptories of Temple Cowley (Oxfordshire) and Cressing (Essex), both in 1136. Perhaps her most important new foundation, made jointly with her husband, was at Faversham, an abbey first colonized by Cluniac monks from Bermondsey, but (like Henry I's abbey at Reading) thereafter freed from dependence on any other Cluniac house; in 1148–9 she spent some time in Canterbury, at St Augustine's, to supervise its foundation. She also established a nunnery at Lillechurch (later known as Higham), to provide for her daughter *Mary of Blois, who had been placed as a child in Stratford Priory, but was now made prioress of the new house at Lillechurch. Matilda also founded the hospital of St Katharine by the Tower in London, dependent on Holy Trinity, Aldgate. Support for the Cistercians was shown in her foundation, with her husband, of Coggeshall Abbey in 1140, and in her donations to Mortemer before Normandy was captured by the Angevins. In April 1152 she fell ill at Castle Hedingham, Essex, where she died on 3 May, three days after sending for her confessor, Ralph, prior of Holy Trinity, Aldgate. She was buried at Faversham Abbey.

Two of her children, Baldwin and Matilda, predeceased her. Eustace, who had assumed the title of count of Boulogne in 1146, died in 1153, and *William, who was count

of Boulogne from 1153, died during the Toulouse campaign of 1159. Her daughter Mary was then made to return to the world and marry, in order to preserve the Boulogne inheritance.

MARJORIE CHIBNALL

Sources Reg. RAN, vol. 3 · K. R. Potter and R. H. C. Davis, eds., Gesta Stephani, OMT (1976) · William of Malmesbury, The Historia novella, ed. and trans. K. R. Potter (1955) · The chronicle of John of Worcester, 1118–1140, ed. J. R. H. Weaver (1908) · R. Hexham, 'De gestis regis Stephani et de bello standardi', Chronicles of the reigns of Stephen, Henry II, and Richard I, ed. R. Howlett, 3, Rolls Series, 82 (1886) · Ordericus Vitalis, Eccl. hist. · The historical works of Gervase of Canterbury, ed. W. Stubbs, 2 vols., Rolls Series, 73 (1879–80) · R. H. C. Davis, King Stephen, 3rd edn (1990) · A. Saltman, Theobald, archbishop of Canterbury (1956) · S. Thompson, Women religious (1991) · H. J. Tanner, 'The expansion of the power and influence of the counts of Boulogne under Eustace II', Anglo-Norman Studies, 14 (1991), 251–86 · C. N. L. Brooke and G. Keir, London, 800–1216: the shaping of a city (1975) · cartulary of Holy Trinity, Aldgate

Matilda, countess of Chester (d. 1189), magnate, was the granddaughter of *Henry I by his illegitimate son *Robert, earl of Gloucester (d. 1147), and Sibyl, the daughter of Roger de Montgomery, earl of Shrewsbury (d. 1157). Before 1135 she married *Ranulf (II), fourth earl of Chester (d. 1153), with whom she had a son, *Hugh (d. 1181), who subsequently succeeded his father to the earldom. Matilda's marriage thus created a strong kinship alliance between two of the most powerful earldoms in twelfth-century England which was to prove especially significant during the disturbances of King Stephen's reign.

Matilda may have played a central role in the capture of Lincoln Castle in December 1140, a key turning point in the conflict that set in train the series of events that led eventually to the capture of Stephen. While their husbands were besieging Lincoln Castle, Matilda and her sister-in-law Hawise, countess of Lincoln, made a friendly social visit to the wife of the castellan. Under the pretext of providing an escort for his wife's safe return to his armed camp, Earl Ranulf penetrated and captured the castle. On the subsequent approach of the king's army towards Lincoln, it is unclear whether Matilda held the castle while Ranulf attempted to rally support or whether she was captured. None the less Ranulf escaped from the castle leaving his wife and sons to face the besieging royalists. Robert, earl of Gloucester, went to the aid of Ranulf since he was worried about the safety of his daughter and grandchildren. In the subsequent battle of Lincoln on 2 February 1141 King Stephen was captured.

Matilda survived her husband by forty-four years and remained unmarried throughout that period. She had dower of lands of the earldom of Chester valued at over £22 in 1185. She was occasionally involved in the public affairs of her husband's administration: for example she witnessed his charter in 1147–8 of a grant to the monks of Lenton, Nottinghamshire, which was witnessed also by, among others, the Welsh prince Cadwalader ap Gruffudd (d. 1172). Between 1141 and 1145 she received maritagium at Campden, Gloucestershire, lands that were strategically important to her husband, strengthening his position in the more southerly areas of his lordship. She also held maritagium at Great Gransden, Huntingdonshire. She was an active patron of religious houses. When married to Earl Ranulf she granted lands to Belvoir Priory, Leicestershire, between 1141 and 1147, to Bordesley Abbey, Worcestershire, in 1153, and refounded Repton Priory, Derbyshire, c.1150–1154. She witnessed her husband's charters to Garendon Abbey, Leicestershire, and to the nuns of St Mary's, Chester. In 1154–7, jointly with her son, she gave a charter to Walter, bishop of Chester, in reparation for the injuries inflicted by Earl Ranulf which had resulted in his dying excommunicate. As a widow she continued to patronize religious houses, making benefactions to her favourite priory at Repton. In 1185 she held dower in Waddington, Lincolnshire, worth £400. Matilda died on 29 July 1189.

SUSAN M. JOHNS

Sources Ordericus Vitalis, *Eccl. hist.* · William of Malmesbury, *The Historia novella*, ed. and trans. K. R. Potter (1955) · K. R. Potter and R. H. C. Davis, eds., *Gesta Stephani*, OMT (1976) · GEC, *Peerage* · G. Barraclough, ed., *The charters of the Anglo-Norman earls of Chester, c.1071–1237*, Lancashire and Cheshire RS, 126 (1988) · J. H. Round, ed., *Rotuli de dominabus et pueris et puellis de XII comitatibus* (1185), PRSoc., 35 (1913) · W. Farrer, *Honors and knights' fees … from the eleventh to the fourteenth century*, 2 (1924)

Matilda, duchess of Saxony (1156–1189), princess, the third child and eldest daughter of *Henry II, king of England, and his wife, *Eleanor of Aquitaine, was baptized in the church of the Holy Trinity, Aldgate, by Archbishop Theobald of Canterbury (d. 1161). She had four surviving brothers: *Henry (1155–1183), *Richard I (1157–1199), *Geoffrey, duke of Brittany (1158–1186), and *John (1167–1216); and two sisters: Eleanor (b. 1161) and *Joanna (1165–1199). In 1160 the queen took Matilda to join the king in Normandy; they seem to have brought her back with them in January 1163. Early in 1165 an embassy came from the emperor, Frederick Barbarossa, to ask in marriage two of Henry's daughters, one for Frederick's son, the other for his cousin, Henry the Lion, duke of Saxony. Both couples were betrothed, but while Henry II appears to have dropped the project of a marriage between his daughter and Frederick's son, the marriage between Matilda and Henry went ahead. After visiting Normandy again, Matilda returned in the autumn of 1166. The earliest extant register of English tenants-in-chief and their holdings, still preserved in the Red and Black Books of the Exchequer, was probably compiled with a view to the assessment of the aid levied by the king for his daughter's marriage. In 1167 the duke sent envoys to fetch his bride. She sailed about Michaelmas from Dover to Normandy, and thence proceeded, probably after Christmas, to Germany. The duke met her at Minden, and they were married there by Bishop Werner in the cathedral church on 1 February 1168.

Henry the Lion was twenty-seven years older than Matilda; he had been married long before she was born, and divorced from his first wife in 1162. First cousin to the emperor, he was duke of Bavaria and Saxony. Brunswick was his main residence in Saxony; there the newly married couple held their wedding feast; and there their first child, Richenza, was born during her father's absence on pilgrimage in 1172. Two sons were born in the next eight years, probably in 1173 or 1174 and 1174 or 1175. Henry occupied a quasi-regal position in Saxony, and he laid much stress on the status conferred by his marriage to Matilda, who was referred to on a number of occasions as the daughter of a king and granddaughter of an empress. His power and its ruthless exercise had long aroused opposition among other lay and ecclesiastical magnates. In the late 1160s Frederick had been able and willing to mediate between the two groups, but after the ending of the papal schism in 1177 the opposition to Henry found renewed intensity, and this time Frederick, who had come to have his own quarrels with Henry, was not prepared to intervene. After Henry had refused to obey a series of summonses to assemblies at which charges against him were to be heard, he was outlawed for contumacy at an assembly at Würzburg in January 1180 and his lands declared confiscated.

From the spring of 1180 there followed eighteen months of campaigning in Saxony, at the end of which Henry submitted to Frederick at Erfurt in November 1181. He regained his allodial possessions, but had to go into exile, not to return without Frederick's consent; the sources differ on whether a term was set for the exile and if so how long, and on whether Matilda was also exiled or joined Henry in exile voluntarily. The couple left the Reich in July 1182, accompanied by two of their sons; Lothar remained in Saxony, perhaps as a hostage. They reached Argentan in the summer of 1182, and soon afterwards their fourth son was born there. It was probably at this point that the troubadour Bertrand de Born met Matilda; he apostrophized her under the name Elena in two poems and praised her beauty and wit. On 12 June 1184 Matilda travelled to England, and in that year her fifth son, William, was born at Winchester. In November she was in London with her husband; at Christmas both were at Windsor with the king. In 1185 Henry and Matilda were allowed to return to Saxony, in part through the mediation of Henry II. In the spring of 1189 the emperor demanded that Henry the Lion should either accompany him on crusade, or go into exile again until his return. Henry again sought refuge in England, but Matilda remained at Brunswick and died there on 28 June. She was buried at the church of St Blaise and St Giles, Brunswick. Her husband returned to Brunswick after Frederick's death; he died there in 1195 and was buried at her right hand, 'choosing to sleep beside her in death as in life' (Pertz, 231). In the early thirteenth century their tombs were provided with stone effigies, probably as part of a larger project for a family memorial put in hand by their son Otto IV (d. 1218). Arnold of Lübeck called Matilda 'a most religious woman, whose memory is of note before God and man, whose good works and sweet disposition enhanced the lustre of the long royal line whence she sprang; a woman of profound piety, of wondrous sympathy for the afflicted, a great distributor of alms, and, being given to prayers, a most devoted frequenter of masses, of which she had many sung' (*Arnoldi chronica Slavorum*, 11–12).

Little is known of the part Matilda played in the government of her husband's territories, although she acted in effect as regent in his absence, for example during his crusade in 1172 and in the last few months of her life. She acted not only as a transmitter of Anglo-French cultural impulses to the court at Brunswick, which, certainly in the reign of her son, Otto IV, was more advanced than most princely courts in the Reich, but was also closely associated with Henry in his efforts to build up Brunswick as a princely residence, with a palace, cathedral-like church, and art treasures. Most prominent of these is the 'Evangeliary of Henry the Lion', now in Wolfenbüttel, in which Matilda appears both in the dedicatory miniature and in a further miniature depicting Christ crowning (in what sense is disputed) herself and Henry the Lion, surrounded by their ancestors.

Matilda's eldest child, Richenza, is almost certainly identical with the daughter whom the English chroniclers call Matilda, who was left in Normandy with her grandparents in 1185, returned to England with them in 1186, was married, first, in 1189, to Geoffroy, count of Perche, and second, between 1200 and 1205, to Enguerrand (III) de Coucy, and died before 1210. The eldest son, Henry, assumed the title of duke of Saxony on his father's death, became count palatine of the Rhine in 1196, and died in 1227 survived by two daughters, Irmgard and Agnes, his only son, Henry, having predeceased him. His brother Otto, nominated by his uncle Richard I as earl of York in 1190 and count of Poitou in 1196, was elected emperor in 1198 in opposition to the Staufer candidate, crowned at Rome in 1209, excommunicated and declared deposed the following year, and died childless in 1218, having lost all royal power after the defeat of the Welf and Angevin forces at Bouvines in 1214. Lothar died in 1190. The boy born at Argentan in 1182 is never heard of again, and presumably died very young. Matilda's youngest child, the English-born William of Winchester, died in 1213. He and his wife, Helen, daughter of Waldemar I of Denmark, had a son named Otto, who became sole heir male of the family on the death of his uncle Henry in 1227. From him are descended the ducal house of Brunswick-Lüneburg, and the British royal house of Windsor.

KATE NORGATE, *rev.* TIMOTHY REUTER

Sources *Arnoldi chronica Slavorum*, ed. J. M. Lappenberg, MGH Scriptores Rerum Germanicarum, [14] (Hanover, 1868) · Gerhard of Stederburg, 'Annales Stederburgenses', [*Annales aevi Suevici*], ed. G. H. Pertz, MGH Scriptores [folio], 16 (Stuttgart, 1859), 179–232 · J. Ahlers, *Die Welfen und die englischen Könige, 1165–1235*, Quellen und Darstellungen zur Geschichte Niedersachsens, 102 (1987) · K. Jordan, 'Heinrich der Löwe und seine Familie', *Archiv für Diplomatik*, 27 (1981), 111–44 · K. Jordan, *Henry the Lion: a biography*, trans. P. S. Falla (1986) [Ger. orig., *Heinrich der Löwe: eine Biographie* (1979)] · D. Kötzsche, ed., *Das Evangeliar Heinrichs des Löwen: Kommentar zum Faksimile* (Frankfurt am Main, 1989) · L. Clédat, *Du rôle historique de Bertrand de Born* (1879) · M. W. Garzmann, *Eine kunstsinnige Prinzessin aus England in der Braunschweiger Welfenresidenz* (1989) · A. Saltman, *Theobald, archbishop of Canterbury* (1956) · Herzog-August-Bibliothek, Wolfenbüttel, evangeliary of Henry the Lion, fols. 19, 171v · psalter of Henry the Lion, BL, Lansdowne MS 381/1, fol. 10v **Likenesses** manuscript illustration, 1170–90, BL, psalter of Henry the Lion, Lansdowne MS 381/1, fol. 10v · manuscript illustrations, 1175–88, Herzog-August-Bibliothek, Wolfenbüttel, evangeliary of Henry the Lion, fols. 19, 171v · stone effigy, 1200–40, St Blaise and St Giles Cathedral, Brunswick · group portrait, painting on wood, 15th cent. (probably a copy of a thirteenth-century work), Herzog-Anton-Ulrich Museum, Brunswick

Matilda (*fl. c.*1200). *See under* Women medical practitioners in England (*act. c.*1200–*c.*1475).

Matilda of England. *See* Matilda (1102–1167).

Matilda [Maud] **of Lancaster, countess of Ulster** (*d.* 1377), noblewoman, was a daughter of *Henry, third earl of Lancaster (*d.* 1345), and his first wife, Maud, daughter of Patrick Chaworth of Kidwelly. She was thus a sister of *Henry of Grosmont, first duke of Lancaster (*d.* 1361), who often forwarded her interests. Matilda's marriages drew her into a connection with Ireland that proved doubly tragic. In 1327 she married William de *Burgh (*d.* 1333), grandson and heir of Richard de Burgh, earl of Ulster and lord of Connacht (*d.* 1326), whose wardship had been granted to her father. The earl was murdered near Carrickfergus in June 1333; his widow at once fled to England with their only child, Elizabeth, who in 1341 was to be betrothed to the king's son, *Lionel. During the 1330s Matilda exploited her relationship with *Edward III. Unable in practice to obtain her Irish dower, through her absence and the disturbed state of the de Burgh lordships (some of the more valuable parts of which were already held in jointure by her mother-in-law, Elizabeth de *Clare), she was compensated with the custody of the lands of alien priories. By petitioning Edward she continued to exert influence in Ireland. In 1337 she ensured that the justiciar was forbidden to pardon her husband's murderers. In 1339 she had Hugh de Burgh, once her wardrobe clerk, appointed to the treasurership of the Dublin exchequer, and in 1342 inquisitions taken by him confirmed the problematical nature of her dower, which consisted partly of the rents and services of Gaelic leaders, including Énrí Ó Néill, the most powerful chief in Ulster.

By June 1343 Matilda was married to Ralph *Ufford (*d.* 1346), a younger brother of the earl of Suffolk. She was in Avignon during August of that year, when Clement VI granted her and her husband various privileges and excused her from a vow to visit Santiago de Compostela. Ufford was soon appointed justiciar of Ireland, and the couple arrived in Dublin in July 1344 with 40 men-at-arms and 200 archers. The Dublin annalist thought Ufford was under the influence of his wife. Certainly his retinue included a significant Lancastrian element, and in 1345 he led an expedition to Ulster, which had seen little government action for a decade, deposing Énrí Ó Néill. By November 1345 Matilda was said to be pregnant at Kilmainham. Shortly afterwards Ufford fell ill. His death in April 1346 was followed by her second hasty departure from Ireland with an infant daughter. The Dublin annalist views her plight unsympathetically, remarking gleefully:

> that one who had gloriously entered the gates of the city of Dublin, with regal pomp and a great company of paid soldiers, should, after only a brief spell of playing the queen in the island of Ireland, slip away furtively with her retainers through the postern gate of the castle of that city in order to avoid the jeers of the crowd, who were angry at her inability to repay the debts she had contracted. (Gilbert, 2.388)

After Matilda's return to England, Edward III again made financial provision for her. However in 1347 she decided to take the veil. Leaving her affairs in the hands of executors headed by her brother she became an Augustinian canoness at Campsey Ash in Suffolk, where Ralph Ufford was buried, and where she endowed a secular college to staff a chantry offering prayers for the souls of both her husbands. In 1354 the college was transferred to nearby Bruisyard, where her son-in-law, Lionel, duke of Clarence, later founded a Franciscan nunnery. In 1364 Matilda had papal permission to become a Minoress, an intention she claimed to have harboured since childhood; in 1369 she was living at Bruisyard, and it was probably there that she died on 5 May 1377; she was buried at Campsey Ash. Her elder daughter, the countess of Ulster and duchess of Clarence, had died in Dublin in 1363. Matilda, her daughter with Ralph Ufford, married Thomas de Vere, earl of Oxford (d. 1371), and lived until 1413.

ROBIN FRAME

Sources *Chancery records* · PRO · J. T. Gilbert, ed., *Chartularies of St Mary's Abbey, Dublin: with the register of its house at Dunbrody and annals of Ireland*, 2, Rolls Series, 80 (1884) · R. Frame, *English lordship in Ireland, 1318–1361* (1982) · R. Frame, 'The justiciarship of Ralph Ufford: warfare and politics in fourteenth-century Ireland', *Studia Hibernica*, 13 (1973) · *CEPR letters* · D. Knowles, *The religious houses of medieval England* (1940) · GEC, *Peerage* · A. J. Otway-Ruthven, *A history of medieval Ireland* (1968) · G. O. Sayles, ed., *Documents on the affairs of Ireland before the king's council*, IMC (1979) · *The annals of Ireland by Friar John Clyn and Thady Dowling: together with the annals of Ross*, ed. R. Butler, Irish Archaeological Society (1849)

Matlack, Timothy (1736?–1829), revolutionary politician and army officer in America, was born in Haddonfield, New Jersey, most likely on 28 May 1736, though three other dates appear in biographical sources. He was the seventh child and eldest son of his father's eleven children. His parents were Timothy Matlack (1695–1752) and his second wife, Martha Burr Haines, who were married in March 1730. The elder Timothy was of an English Quaker farming family that settled in West Jersey. In 1726 he moved to Haddonfield and opened a shop. The younger Timothy attended Haddonfield Friends' School, probably from 1742. In 1746 the family moved to Philadelphia, where his father kept a shop and also owned a brewery. Here the younger Timothy continued his education, most likely at Penn Charter School. His father died ruined by creditors, but a stepson preserved enough of the estate so that Timothy could open a hardware shop, about 1762, and perhaps continue the brewery.

In 1758 Matlack married Ellen Yarnall (d. 1791) at a Friends' meeting-house. They had five children. Matlack went bankrupt in 1765. The Quakers disowned him for failure to tend to his enterprises and to attend meetings, but some Friends helped him revive his business. Although only marginally successful economically, before the revolution he socialized with very prominent colonial leaders—lapsed Quaker Joseph Galloway of the Pennsylvania assembly and fellow fighting-cock owner James DeLancey of the New York legislature. In 1780 he was elected a member of the American Philosophical Society.

In 1781 he helped organize the Society of Free Quakers, composed of Friends who had been disowned for abandoning pacifism.

Matlack first joined in the struggle against Britain after the battles of Lexington and Concord. He may have immediately enlisted in a volunteer company. His activism led Charles Thomson to get the second continental congress to appoint him as Thomson's clerk. In October 1775 he was also appointed storekeeper of army supplies. Matlack throughout his career evidently lived on the salaries from such bureaucratic posts. In August 1775 he appeared in politics for the first time, as a radical-mechanic candidate for the Philadelphia committee of observation. He was re-elected in February 1776, became a designated leader of this committee, and advocated Pennsylvania's endorsement of independence from Britain. As a delegate to the Pennsylvania constitutional convention of July 1776, Matlack was a drafter of this radical, democratic instrument, and incorporated in it his ideas about freedom and equality, protection of individual rights, and opposition to aristocracy. The voters of Philadelphia rejected him as too radical for the state legislature. His allies, the constitutionalist majority, in March 1777 appointed him as secretary of the Pennsylvania supreme executive council. He maintained this post, and other minor salaried state offices, including prosecutor of Benedict Arnold, until 1783. His chief legislative service was as delegate to congress for three months in 1780. Here he advocated that the states dedicate funds to restore congress's credit. The opponents of the Pennsylvania constitution took power in the 1780 legislative election, and retired Matlack as delegate.

In late 1775 Matlack became colonel of a rifle battalion of Pennsylvania militia. He performed only minor duties until December 1776, when he led his battalion into New Jersey to assist General George Washington's continentals. After the battle of Trenton, Matlack's troops and the other militia battalions chased the British out of nearby Bordentown and Burlington, New Jersey. Matlack saw no further battlefield action.

Matlack harshly attacked the policies of his political enemies such as James Wilson, although in 1779 he helped disperse the mob that attacked Wilson's home. In 1783 his opponents got their revenge by charging him with misappropriating public funds. The supreme executive council dismissed him and the assembly barred him from holding office again. The council of censors in 1784 declared this action unconstitutional, whereupon the assembly rescinded its ban. However, the state in 1787 obtained a judgment against him for an account shortage of less than £40. Matlack could not pay and was sent to debtors' prison.

Thereafter, Matlack's foes ceased political persecution. He gained his freedom and by 1789 was again making his living serving the state in official posts. In 1790 he became clerk of the state senate for the next ten years, and after that state master of the rolls until 1809. He served as Philadelphia alderman (1813–18) and as a court officer (1817–22). In 1797 he married his second wife, Elizabeth Claypoole

Copper (b. 1751). Matlack died on 14 April 1829, in Holmesburg, Pennsylvania, where he and his wife, who survived him, lived with his daughter and son-in-law. He was buried at the Free Quaker Meeting-House, Philadelphia.

BENJAMIN H. NEWCOMB

Sources G. J. Saldino, 'Matlack, Timothy', *ANB* · A. M. Stackhouse, *Col. Timothy Matlack: patriot and soldier* (1910) · C. Johnson, 'Matlack, Timothy', *DAB* · S. Rosswurm, *Arms, country, and class: the Philadelphia militia and the 'lower sort' during the American revolution, 1775–1783* (1987) · R. A. Ryerson, *The revolution is now begun: the radical committees of Philadelphia* (1978) · R. L. Brunhouse, *The counter-revolution in Pennsylvania, 1776–1790* (1942) · P. H. Smith and others, eds., *Letters of delegates to congress, 1774–1789*, 26 vols. (1976–2000) [continuing] **Likenesses** C. W. Peale, oils, 1826, Independence National Historical Park, Philadelphia, Pennsylvania

Maton, Robert (b. 1606/7, d. in or after **1646**), religious writer, was the second son of William Maton of North Tidworth, Wiltshire, and his wife, Thomazin Hayter of Langford. He entered Wadham College, Oxford, as a commoner at Michaelmas 1623 and matriculated, aged nineteen, on 3 November 1626, graduating BA on 25 October 1627 and MA on 10 June 1630. Very little else is known of his life, although he is reported to have taken holy orders.

In 1642 Maton published a notable work, *Israel's Redemption*, which predicted the coming millennium. It was clearly much influenced by Joseph Mede, the Cambridge biblical scholar who had sought to systematize and render mutually consistent the apocalyptic prophecies of the books of Daniel and Revelation. Maton was supremely confident that the days of Satan's 'pompous clergy, of his princely and magistracy mastering pontiffs' were numbered, and that those of the millennium approached: for

> it is not to be doubted but that God will have the victory in the end, and the longer, and more eagerly any truth of his hath been opposed and supprest, the more suddenly and more powerfully shall she break forth again, to the amazement and confusion of her adversaries.

Christ would soon return to establish his reign on earth, and the Jews would share in its spiritual riches: 'both Jew and gentile are sick in the same disease … never will the happiness of either receive perfection … till both are folded together' (Maton, *Israel's Redemption*, preface).

Maton's book was published in London, but his ideas had their greatest initial impact among the independent congregations of the Netherlands: such was their influence that Alexander Petrie, minister of the Scottish church at Rotterdam, felt impelled to launch an attack, signed in August 1644 within a year of his arrival, upon Maton's literalist interpretation of the prophecies. Maton countered in December 1646 with a lengthy response, *Israel's Redemption Redeemed*, later republished as *Christ's Personall Reign on Earth One Thousand Years* (1652). Maton's ideas were influential during the English Commonwealth. His response to Petrie was republished again in 1655 as *A Treatise of the Fifth Monarchy*, though he is not known to have been associated with the Fifth Monarchists. It may be that he died shortly afterwards, for nothing more is heard of him. STEPHEN WRIGHT

Sources R. B. Gardiner, ed., *The registers of Wadham College, Oxford*, 1 (1889) · R. Maton, *Israel's redemption, or, The propheticall history of our* Saviour's kingdom on earth (1642) · A. Petrie, *Chiliasto mastix* (1644) · R. Maton, *Israel's redemption redeemed, or, The Jewes generall and miraculous conversion … and our Saviour's personall reigne on earth cleerly proved* (1646) · R. Maton, *A treatise of the Fifth Monarchy* (1655) · T. Phillipps, ed., *Visitatio heraldica comitatus Wiltoniae*, A.D.1623 (1828) **Likenesses** T. Cross, line engraving, BM; repro. in Maton, *Treatise of the Fifth Monarchy*

Maton, William George (1774–1835), physician, was born in Salisbury on 31 January 1774, the eldest son of George Maton (d. 1816), a wine merchant in that city. He was educated at Salisbury's Free Grammar School (where he showed an early interest in natural history) and entered Queen's College, Oxford, in July 1790. At Oxford he gave much time to botany, and acquired the friendship of the subject's then professor, John Sibthorp (1758–1796). Maton graduated BA in 1794 and was elected a fellow of the Linnean Society in the same year. Although originally intended by his father for the church, Maton continued his academic studies. He graduated MA in January 1797, and began medical studies at Westminster Hospital in the spring of that year. He gained his MB (Oxford) in 1798 and his MD in 1801, and was elected FRS in 1800. Elected a fellow of the College of Surgeons in 1802, he was Goulstonian lecturer in 1803, censor (1804, 1813, and 1824), treasurer (1814–20), and Harveian orator (1815). He was physician to the Westminster Hospital in 1800–08.

While at university Maton published several antiquarian works. He wrote parts of the *Salisbury Guide*, and Hutchins's *History of Dorset*, as well as a paper on Stonehenge in the *Archaeologia* for 1794. Travels in Dorset, Devon, Cornwall, and Somerset led to his *Observations relative chiefly to the natural history, picturesque scenery, and antiquities of the western counties of England, made chiefly in the years 1794 and 1796* (2 vols., 1797). In it he concluded that the Cornish language was extinct—a conclusion based on his inability to find a single person who could speak it.

After several years of practising medicine in London, Maton took to residing at Weymouth during 'the season'. There he found time to pursue his botanical interests and was often seen rambling in the neighbourhood. Indeed, he was identified to the royal family (spending the season at Gloucester Lodge) as the person to name a specimen of *Arundo* (later *Calamagrostis*) *epigejos*, which one of the botanically minded princesses had obtained. As a result, he acquired the confidence of the royal family, and in 1816 was appointed physician-extraordinary to Queen Charlotte. In 1820 he attended the duke of Kent in his last illness, and afterwards became physician-in-ordinary to the duchess and to the infant Princess Victoria. His practice increased and between 1823 and 1835 'shared with Sir Henry Halford the best business of the town' (Munk, *Roll*).

In 1816 Maton's father had died, deeply in debt. By 1827 Maton had paid off in excess of £20,000. The mayor and corporation of Salisbury, in testimony of his honourable conduct, gave him the freedom of the city in a gold box. He bought a country seat near Downton, Wiltshire, but six months later became very ill and died on 30 March 1835 at his house in Spring Gardens, London. In addition to his antiquarian works, Maton published several papers in the *Transactions of the Linnean Society* (of which he served as vice-president) and of the College of Physicians. A woodpecker, a shellfish, and a genus of plants were all named after him. NORMAN MOORE, rev. PETER OSBORNE

Sources Desmond, *Botanists*, rev. edn · J. A. Paris, *Biographical sketch of William George Maton* (1838) · Munk, *Roll*
Archives BL, collections relating to Wiltshire and Salisbury, Add. MSS 22835–22838, 22840 · BL, travel journals, Add. MSS 32442–32443 · Devon RO, travel journals · NHM | Bodl. Oxf., letters to Richard Gough · Dorset RO, letters to Thomas Rackett · Linn. Soc., letters to Sir James Smith · RCP Lond., collection of papers by and about Richard Pulteney, incl. diplomas, etc.
Likenesses M. Carpenter, oils, c.1820, RCP Lond. · W. Belnes, bust, Linn. Soc. · R. W. P., chalk drawing, BM · T. Rackett, pencil drawing, Wellcome L. · engraving, RS; repro. in Paris, *Biographical sketch*, frontispiece · oils, RCP Lond. · pencil drawing, Botanical Garden Library, Oxford

Matonabbee (1736/7–1782/3), fur trader and explorer, was born near Churchill Fort, in what is now Churchill, Manitoba, the son of Chipewyan parents; his father was a hunter for the Hudson's Bay Company (HBC). His mother and father had met on the west coast of Hudson Bay when his mother was freed from the captivity of Cree fur traders by Richard Norton, chief factor of the HBC's post at Churchill. Matonabbee's background gave him the rare ability to move smoothly between British and Chipewyan cultures. Orphaned at an early age, he was adopted by Richard Norton, who introduced him to the fur trade. On Norton's retirement in 1741 Matonabbee's father's relatives took him to their homeland north-west of Hudson Bay. There he learned the survival skills he would use later in life. In 1752 he returned to Churchill, where he worked as a hunter to supply HBC company employees with fresh meat. Later he began forays into the Cree territory around Lake Athabasca. The Cree and the Chipewyans were longstanding enemies; however, Matonabbee was able to broker a peace with the encouragement of the HBC, which believed that warfare interfered with trading opportunities. Although the peace was temporary, its impact on Matonabbee's reputation was permanent. At Churchill he received the titles ambassador and mediator (Hearne, *Journey*, 225).

In 1762 Matonabbee was asked by Moses Norton, Richard's son, to find the northern copper mines, rumours of which had been heard at Churchill since 1716. Matonabbee and a companion, Idotyazee, returned to Churchill five years later with a copper sample. Together, Matonabbee, Idotyazee, and Norton created a map to guide an HBC expedition to the mine. However, by the time Norton had finished the preparations, Matonabbee, his choice for expedition leader, had disappeared.

Beginning in 1769, the explorer, fur trader, and HBC employee Samuel Hearne twice tried and failed to reach the copper source. Matonabbee met Hearne as he returned from the second attempt, and quickly attributed previous failures to the lack of Chipewyan women. Matonabbee told Hearne: 'there is no such thing as travelling any considerable distance, or for any length of time, in this country, without their assistance' (Hearne, *Journey*,

35). Matonabbee agreed to lead a third expedition, which included his seven wives. The eighteen-month trek became one of the most celebrated Arctic adventures, unique because Hearne acquiesced to Matonabbee's seasoned knowledge of geography, diplomacy, and survival. In one of its best-known episodes a group of Chipewyan joined the expedition to attack a group of Inuit, camped by the mouth of the Coppermine River, in revenge for recent unexplained illnesses; twenty-one Inuit were killed. The expedition reached the mythic source of copper soon after but, as Matonabbee and others had intimated before to the HBC, the mines were of little commercial value. Hearne and Matonabbee searched for more than four hours to find one sizeable piece. When the expedition returned to Churchill on 30 June 1772 Norton immediately proclaimed Matonabbee chief of all the Chipewyans.

Matonabbee's prominence as a trader ended prematurely in the autumn of 1782 or winter of 1782–3 when he arrived with furs at Churchill to discover the settlement in ruins and abandoned following an attack by two French frigates returning from the American War of Independence. One year later Hearne and a small crew returned to reopen Churchill. It was, however, too late for Matonabbee. On seeing the basis of his livelihood and reputation reduced to rubble, he had hanged himself. As testimony to Matonabbee's indelible influence, Hearne devoted much of his published narrative about the journey to the Coppermine River to expressions of admiration for the abilities and character of the Chipewyan chief.

HEATHER ROLLASON DRISCOLL

Sources S. Hearne, *A journey from Prince of Wales's Fort in Hudson's Bay to the northern ocean*, ed. R. Glover (1958) · S. Hearne, 'Mr. Hearne's narrative', 1791, BL, Stowe MSS, vol. 307, fols. 67–89 · S. Hearne, 'Hearne's journal, 1770–72, from the original in the possession of the Hudson's Bay Company', BL, Dropmore MSS, Grenville MS, Add. MS 59237, fol. 47 · J. Helm, 'Matonabbee's map', *Arctic Anthropology*, 26/2 (1989), 28–47 · G. Williams, ed., 'Remarks on the French raids on Churchill, York, 1782', *Hudson's Bay Miscellany, 1670–1870* (1975), 94 · B. Gillespie, 'Matonabbee', *DCB*, vol. 4 · G. Warkentin, 'Andrew Graham becomes a scholar of Bayside life', *Canadian exploration literature: an anthology* (1993), 103 · London correspondence inwards from Churchill, 1764–73, Provincial Archives of Manitoba, Winnipeg, Hudson's Bay Company Archives, A.11/14, fols. 78d, 132, 144 · Churchill post journal, 1771–2 and 1776–7, Provincial Archives of Manitoba, Winnipeg, Hudson's Bay Company Archives, B.42/a/83, fol. 73d; B.42/a/94, fols. 8d–9 · Churchill correspondence book, 1768–9, 1770–71, 1777–8, 1779, 1779–80, and 1783–4, Provincial Archives of Manitoba, Winnipeg, Hudson's Bay Company Archives, B.42/b/15, fols. 3, 4d; B.42/b/9, fol. 6; B.42/b/18, fols. 14d, 10–11; B.42/b/23, fol. 3; B.42/b/24, fol. 7; B.42/b/25, fol. 4; B.42/b/26, fols. 3d, 16, 16d
Archives Provincial Archives of Manitoba, Winnipeg, Hudson's Bay Company Archives, Matonabbee's map of how to get to the northern copper mines from Churchill Fort, G.2/27

Matteis, Nicola (*fl. c.*1670–*c.*1698), violinist and composer, came from Naples; nothing else is known about his origins. His contemporary Roger North related that 'his circumstances were low, and it was say'd that he travelled thro' Germany on foot with his violin under a full coat at his back' (BL, Add. MS 32536). Matteis arrived in England *c.*1670. The earliest account of his playing comes from

John Evelyn, who first heard him at a private music meeting in November 1674. Evelyn's reaction (recorded in his diary) was to be echoed by many others:

> I heard that stupendious Violin Signor *Nicholao* (with other rare Musitians) whom certainly never mortal man Exceeded on that Instrument: he had a stroak so sweete, & made it speake like the Voice of a man; & when he pleased, like a Consort of severall Instruments: he did wonders upon a Note: was an excellent Composer also … nothing approch'd the *Violin* in *Nicholas* hand: he seem'd to be *spiritato'd* & plaied such ravishing things on a ground as astonish'd us all.

Matteis was supported (and persuaded out of what were considered arrogant Italian manners) by Roger L'Estrange, William Waldegrave, and William Bridgeman, all of whom had strong interests in music and were sympathetic to Roman Catholics.

In 1676 Matteis published his *Arie diverse per il violino*, a collection of 120 pieces for solo violin and continuo bass. A second edition with an English title-page together with a second part containing a further seventy pieces (*Other Ayrs*) appeared about two years later. These publications were important for various reasons, not least the fact that they helped establish in Britain the technology of engraving music (which had been little utilized since one landmark publication in 1613). Like all Matteis's subsequent publications, they seem to have been produced with pupils in mind. An advertisement in the *London Gazette* announcing the 1676 publication indicated his willingness to teach 'such as desire to learn Composition, or to Play upon the Violin' and mentioned the availability in manuscript of second treble and tenor (viola) parts.

In November 1678 Matteis applied to go to France (perhaps because London seemed unsafe for Catholics while hysteria about the Popish Plot was at its height). He was, however, back in England within a year (Evelyn heard him play again in November 1679). About this time he published an important treatise on thoroughbass realization for the five-course guitar, an instrument on which he was also (according to North) a 'consummate master'. This treatise (*Le false consonanse della musica*) appeared in an expanded English-language edition (*The False Consonances of Music*) in 1682. Three years later he published the third and fourth parts of the *Ayres for the Violin*, and as before this was followed by an expanded second edition (1687). Three features stand out in the edition of 1687. First, it includes a concerto for three trumpets with strings and/or recorders partly based on a violin piece in the *Ayres* of 1685. Second, Matteis's pedagogical interests are again to the fore: the table of contents is categorized according to difficulty, and pieces requiring the violinist to use multiple stops (that is, to play on more than one string at a time) have lower parts indicated with a dotted-outline notation enabling less skilled violinists to omit them. Third, Matteis published a companion volume, *The Second Treble of the Third and Fourth Parts*, thus turning what were essentially solo violin pieces into trio sonatas.

Matteis appears to have married in or before about 1678, and had a son, Nicola, whom, according to North, he had 'taught upon the violin from his cradle'. By the early 1690s the younger Nicola was coming to prominence as a performer. His age is uncertain: his will of 1737 (in Vienna) suggests that he was born *c.*1677, while a marriage licence issued in 1692 describes him as 'ab᷑ 25' at that time. This, as Simon Jones has pointed out, makes it difficult to know whether references to Nicola Matteis after *c.*1695 denote father or son.

A Matteis was listed in 1695 (together with Henry Purcell) as a teacher for a planned royal academy. Two volumes of *A Collection of New Songs* appeared under the same name, the first (1696) 'made purposely for the use of his Scholers' and the second (1699) 'being all teaching Songs, made for his Scholars'. Nicola Matteis is named in advertisements in the *London Gazette* (and on a broadsheet copy of the poem) as the composer of the now lost St Cecilia's day ode 'Assist, assist! You mighty sons of art' of 1696. This ode was first performed on 23 November 'being the sequel of St. Cecilia's day' and was repeated a few days later at a St Cecilia's day celebration in Oxford (for which Matteis was named as a steward) and again at a public concert in the York Buildings in January 1697. In May 1698 the *London Gazette* reported another concert in the York Buildings featuring 'Mr Nicholas's Consort of Vocal and Instrumental Musick'. It is possible that all of these refer to the younger Nicola Matteis.

Roger North claimed that Matteis lived with a woman 'as one that was married' and that they had a child and moved to a great house where the violinist dissipated his by-now considerable wealth and undermined his health in extravagant living. It has been assumed that North was alluding to a marriage in 1700 to Susanna Timperley (*fl.* 1685–1715). But the younger Matteis's will proves that it was he who had married this widow. The confusion may have arisen very early, since the *London Post* reported in January 1700 that 'Signor Nicolao, the famous Italian Musician, is married to one Madam Timperley …'. (Despite the younger Matteis's growing reputation, it seems unlikely that he would be described then as a famous Italian musician.) The elder Matteis may well have been dead by this time. He features as one of the imagined writers in the third edition of Thomas Brown's *Letters from the Dead to the Living* (1707).

Matteis's works were still very much in demand. Roger published five books of *Les solos de Nicolas Mathys* in 1702, and in the following year Walsh brought out a new edition of the first two parts of the *Arie* together with second treble parts (presumably those mentioned in the advertisement for the original publication of 1676) to complement those published earlier for volumes 3 and 4.

Matteis made an extraordinary contribution to violin playing in England. He was technically innovative and set new standards of virtuosity and expressiveness performing his own music, which in North's words in *The Musicall Grammarian* 'shewed him a very exquisite harmonist, and of a boundless fancy, and invention'. 　PETER WALLS

Sources BL, R. North, Add. MSS 32506, 32533, 32536 · *Roger North on music*, ed. J. Wilson (1959) · *LondG* (15 Feb 1677) · *LondG* (29 Oct 1688) · *LondG* (4 Jan 1697) · *LondG* (30 May 1698) · Evelyn, *Diary* · *London Post* (29 Jan 1700) · *The Observator* (30 Nov 1682) · *Daily Courant*

(26 April 1707) • M. Tilmouth, 'Nicola Matteis', *Musical Quarterly*, 46 (1960), 22–40 • P. Walls, 'The influence of the Italian violin school in 17th-century England', *Early Music*, 18 (1990), 575–87 • A. Pinnock and B. Wood, 'A counterblast on English trumpets', *Early Music*, 19 (1991), 436–43 • P. Holman, 'English trumpets: a response', *Early Music*, 19 (1991), 443–4 • P. Downey, 'What Samuel Pepys heard on 3rd February 1681: English trumpet style under later Stuart monarchs', *Early Music*, 18 (1990), 417–28 • G. Proctor, 'The works of Nicola Matteis, sr.', PhD diss., University of Rochester, 1960 • G. Ryan and L. J. Redsome, *Timperley of Hintlesham* (1931) • W. Rye, *Norfolk families*, 2 vols. in 5 pts (1911–13) • M. Tilmouth, 'A calendar of references to music in newspapers published in London and the provinces (1660–1719)', *Royal Musical Association Research Chronicle*, 1 (1961), esp. 3, 5, 7, 18, 24, 31, 69 • M. Tilmouth, 'The royal academies of 1695', *Music and Letters*, 38 (1957), 327–34 • S. Plank, 'A song in imitation of Mr Nicola's manner', *Bach Quarterly*, 17 (1986), 16–23 • J. Congleton, '"The false consonances of music": Nicola Matteis's *Instructions for the playing of a true bass upon the guitar*', *Early Music*, 9 (1981), 463–9 • S. Garnsey, 'The use of hand-plucked instruments in the continuo body: Nicola Matteis', *Music and Letters*, 47 (1966), 135–40 • M. Mabbett, 'Italian musicians in Restoration England', *Music and Letters*, 67 (1986), 237–47 • J. Westrup, 'Foreign musicians in Stuart England', *Musical Quarterly*, 27 (1941), 70–98 • Hereford Cathedral Library, MS R II, xlii • *Roger North's The musicall grammarian, 1728*, ed. M. Chan and J. C. Kassler (1990) • private information (2004) [Simon Jones] • S. Jones, 'The legacy of the "stupendious" Nicola Matteis', *Early Music*, 29 (2001), 553–68

Likenesses G. Kneller, oils, 1684, Llandudno, William Barrow collection

Matthew. *See also* Mathew.

Matthew, (Henry) Colin Gray (1941–1999), historian and founding editor of the *Oxford Dictionary of National Biography*, was born at 31 Island Bank Road, Inverness, on 15 January 1941, the eldest child of Henry Johnston Scott Matthew (1914–1997), consultant physician, and his wife, Joyce Mary (Maisie) McKendrick (*b.* 1915). John Gray *McKendrick (1841–1926), professor of physiology in Edinburgh and Glasgow, was his great-grandfather.

Background and early life While Matthew was still a young child his family moved to Edinburgh, where his father became a distinguished physician. He was very conscious of being a member of the Edinburgh upper-middle class, though his attitude to that class and its mores was, to say the least, ambivalent. In part, this was due to his difficult relationship with his father. There was little intimacy between the two, except perhaps towards the end of his father's life. There was also a wider ambivalence towards Scotland generally. He was in many ways very Scottish, and was intellectually involved in Scottish culture and politics—he was even an excellent piper—but reacted against what he took to be the introversion of Scottish life and the petty snobberies of Edinburgh. This was not helped by his time at the Edinburgh Academy, a school he strongly disliked, and from which he was removed. He crossed the border and went to Sedbergh School, where he was very happy. In particular, he liked the history teaching at Sedbergh and acknowledged that as part of his intellectual development. He was head boy at the school.

In 1960 Matthew went to Christ Church, Oxford, to read modern history. The college was an institution he always much respected, as he did his tutors, particularly C. H. Stuart, a man whose own views were in many ways antithetical to Matthew's. What united them was a deep affection for Christ Church as a great nineteenth-century institution, not as the one founded by Henry VIII, and for the traditions of nineteenth-century scholarship. (Their mutual respect was marked by Matthew's address at Stuart's memorial service, given at Stuart's request.) Matthew graduated in 1963 with second-class honours and was not even very close to first-class honours. Given his later distinction as a historian this may seem surprising but the Oxford examination system did not suit him. His ruminative intellectual processes, the careful thought, were unsuited to the snappy demands of the three-hour examination. Furthermore, especially as a younger man, his first drafts—which is what exam answers are—were awkward, in many ways sketches. The mandarin style of the

(Henry) Colin Gray Matthew (1941–1999), by Judith Aronson, 1993

older man was the product of hard work, practice, and considerable rewriting.

After graduation Matthew went to east Africa, first to Makerere University College, Kampala, Uganda, where he completed a diploma in education, and then to newly independent Tanzania, where he was a teacher. The three years he spent in east Africa were doubly important. First, he met his future wife, Sue Ann Curry (b. 1941), also a teacher, who was to play an absolutely central role in his own life and in those of his family and friends. She was an American, born in Ohio, the daughter of Clarence William Curry and his wife, Ruth Richardson. Second, he gained an understanding of a decaying imperial system which still, none the less, had considerable authority. Matthew found himself teaching largely English constitutional history of a whiggish kind to classes for whom it was increasingly alien, though not necessarily unpopular. This experience was in a way formative: when he returned to Oxford in 1966, a return assisted by Charles Stuart, he worked briefly with Robert Blake and Roy Harrod for an uncompleted diploma in politics and economics but soon transferred to do a doctorate, under the supervision of A. F. Thompson, on the imperial wing of the late Victorian and Edwardian Liberal Party. The doctorate was completed in 1970 and published in 1973 as *The Liberal Imperialists: the Ideas and Politics of a Post-Gladstonian Élite*. This was Matthew's first attempt to grapple with Gladstone and his legacy to British politics, but also with the empire and its legacy to British politics. He married Sue Curry on 17 December 1966. They had three children: David, Lucy, and Oliver.

Gladstone In 1970 Matthew was appointed lecturer in Gladstone studies at Christ Church—though he might well have gone to the University of Malaysia had the offer of a post there not been sent by sea mail—with a brief to assist M. R. D. Foot in the publication of the Gladstone diaries. The first two volumes had been published in 1968, with Foot as sole editor; the second two were published in 1974 under the joint editorship of Foot and Matthew. In 1972 Matthew became sole editor, and the remaining ten volumes (including the index) were his alone. The publication of the diaries was an immense undertaking, and it established his reputation not just as an editor, but as a scholar and, indirectly, as a teacher.

Matthew was an impeccable scholarly editor: he left nothing unexamined or to chance. He also drew upon an extraordinarily wide range of expertise, and thus, often willy-nilly, acquired an extraordinarily wide intellectual acquaintance. He was very persuasive in drawing upon not only the gratuitous help of friends and colleagues, but also that of his family—especially his indispensable aunt Jean Gilliland. He was a hard man to refuse. His abilities as editor were not merely academic or persuasive. Having been characteristically slow in computerizing himself, he then characteristically learned to use the sophisticated software which produced the remarkable index to the diaries, a scholarly resource in its own right, for which he was awarded the Wheatley medal by the Society of Indexers.

Under Matthew's editorship the principles by which the diaries were published underwent two important changes. The first involved the content of the published diaries themselves. The initial six volumes consisted of the diary entries alone. This was possible because the entries were full enough and of sufficient intrinsic interest; indeed, their revelations of the younger Gladstone's religious and sexual anxieties—which Matthew handled frankly and sensitively—had a dramatic quality which earned the diaries wide publicity. As Gladstone's political significance increased, however, the diary entries became more austere and bitty; sometimes merely lists. Matthew therefore decided to accompany the entries with the appropriate cabinet 'minutes' and associated personal political correspondence. This permitted, as he noted, 'by far the fullest documentary account of a British administration in peacetime' (H. C. G. Matthew, ed., *The Gladstone Diaries*, 7, 1982, v), and enormously widened both the scope and scholarly utility of the published diaries. It also imposed new burdens on the editor.

The second change lay in the character of the introductions to each volume: they became steadily longer and more argumentative. Matthew increasingly used them to make a powerful statement about the nature of nineteenth-century British politics, with Gladstone's career as its pivot. He had reacted strongly against what was then perhaps the predominant view: that the 'faddism' which later ravaged the Liberal Party was a result of Gladstone's personal obsessions—with Ireland, for instance—and that Gladstone was somehow out of tune with the development of mass politics. Matthew increasingly came to the view that Gladstone was the first 'modern' politician. In doing so he was much influenced by Max Weber's argument that Gladstone and Lincoln were the prototypes of the demagogic politicians of the twentieth century. The Gladstone who emerges from Matthew's introductions is, among much else, a pioneer in manipulating the modern media, the man who shaped not so much the political rhetoric of the twentieth century as the notion that there should be a political rhetoric appropriate to an age when the 'masses' rather than the 'classes' dominated the electorate. Matthew also strongly defended, if not in all their details, Gladstone's Irish policies. Ireland, he argued, was not Gladstone's obsession but the obsession of others. His attempt to unblock British politics by a final settlement of the Irish question was frustrated by those—particularly in the Conservative Party—who had a selfish and cynical interest in ensuring that the question was never settled.

Matthew's interpretation of Gladstone was an evolving one. In part that was due to his development as a historian. As he increasingly thought of history in structural and comparative terms, the context in which he placed Gladstone became wider in scope and explanation. He moved from a simple biography of Gladstone to a 'biography' of nineteenth-century political culture via Gladstone. It was also a result of his reflections on the history of British political institutions after Gladstone's death: in a sense on Gladstone's 'lesson' for his successors. Matthew was all his adult life a member of the Labour Party, and though he was maddened by the behaviour of much of the party in the early 1980s he never left it or lost his loyalties to its social democratic traditions. The extent and character of his political engagement can be measured in his 'In vacuo' essays, which appeared regularly in the house journal of Oxford University, the *Oxford Magazine*. These were the politics of a man who was obviously hostile to the predominant spirit of his age but who felt that many of the country's historic institutions—not least Oxford University—had left themselves open to attack because they had been unwilling to reform themselves. There was an implied contrast here with the nineteenth century, and especially with Gladstone, but arguably his analysis of the politics of his own time—particularly, perhaps, the travails of the Labour Party—encouraged him to think of Gladstone, for all his flaws, as the model of a reforming political leader. He came to believe, for example, that Gladstone's view that 'progressive' electoral majorities could most effectively be mobilized around great legislative acts ('big bills') was almost certainly correct.

The size and importance of Matthew's introductions to the diaries allowed him to publish them, somewhat reassembled, as a two-volume biography, *Gladstone* (1986, 1995), which remains his master work and for which he was awarded the Wolfson prize for history. Matthew's Gladstone is a towering figure—central to the political, religious, and intellectual history of the nineteenth century, such that someone like Disraeli seems a mere dilettante. Matthew as historian benefited from this. To master Gladstone he had to master much of the history of the nineteenth and early twentieth centuries; and not just of Britain. Gladstone's own preoccupations drew Matthew into the history of Germany and Italy and allowed him to place Gladstone within a European framework to a degree that few previous students of Gladstone had done.

This range had its consequences for the Oxford history syllabus. Matthew was an originator of two of its special subjects: the first on late Victorian and Edwardian social policy, the second on church and state in Victorian Britain. Both demanded a detailed knowledge of subject and period which few other than Matthew possessed. Another proposal, which he and a colleague drafted, for a comparative course on the financial and constitutional crises in the major European states on the eve of the First World War, never got off the ground, largely because it was too demanding for any history syllabus. Since the mastering of Gladstone required him to think in the largest terms it also encouraged him to write essays on British history of great sweep designed for a wider public, as in the *Oxford Illustrated History of Britain* (ed. K. O. Morgan, 1984) and the *Short Oxford History of the British Isles: the Nineteenth Century* (2000), which he himself edited and which was published posthumously. It also set him upon the work which he thought would be his *summa* but which he never finished: a study of the evolution of the political rhetoric and culture of the nineteenth century. In practice, much of this work, one way or another, was already written, though Matthew had still to sort out the apparent antithesis between the 'demagogic' nature of Gladstone's political

rhetoric and what Matthew thought to be the highly rational rhetoric of the Edwardian Liberal Party—which, he had argued, eventually brought it to ruin.

Matthew's success as editor inevitably brought him success in academic life. In 1976 he was elected a research student (in effect a senior research fellow) of Christ Church, which, however, was coterminous with his position as editor of the diaries. Security was guaranteed when he was elected to a tutorial fellowship at St Hugh's College, Oxford, in 1978. That was primarily a teaching post and as a teacher he was outstandingly good, both academically and pastorally. The grief and shock his death caused generations of graduates and undergraduates were a poignant testimony to this. He was attached to St Hugh's in every way and served the college in several capacities, among them as senior tutor and librarian. As the editor of a great scholarly enterprise he was in demand for posts which drew upon this experience. He was for four years (1985–9) literary director of the Royal Historical Society, was a curator of the Bodleian Library, Oxford, and was on the committee of the Oxford Historical Monographs Series. None of these posts he regarded as a sinecure. He was elected a fellow of the British Academy in 1991 and as a member of its council and vice-president was influential in its affairs. He was very 'chuffed' (as he would have said) to have been appointed a trustee of the National Portrait Gallery, a relationship established when he wrote a marvellous essay on Millais's portraits of Gladstone.

The new *Dictionary of National Biography* Matthew had given some thought to what he might do when the publication of the diaries was complete, but he was initially undecided. Although he would have continued as a college tutor happily enough, he probably would have been restless. The issue arose unexpectedly when Oxford University, the British Academy, and Oxford University Press decided to embark upon a new edition of the *Dictionary of National Biography*, a dictionary which would incorporate and revise the old one but which would be an entirely new project. Matthew was asked whether he would agree to become editor. Although he sought the advice of friends and colleagues—a number of whom advised against his taking it—it is unlikely that he ever thought seriously of refusing. He had been a brilliant success as an academic entrepreneur, as well as scholar, and was excited by the prospect of overseeing such an undertaking: what would become the largest research project in the humanities in Britain. He was also attracted by the possibility of reconstructing a great nineteenth-century creation   to do for an institution what he had done for the Gladstone diaries. He had, furthermore, as a younger man been involved in another project, which never came to fruition, to examine the ways in which Oliver Cromwell's career had been put to ideological and political use in British history—he had worked, *inter alia*, on the controversy over the erection of the Cromwell statue which now stands outside Westminster Hall—and he saw this as in some sense a model for the project to create a new *Dictionary of National Biography*. In 1992 he was formally appointed editor and the university recognized his distinction by electing him to a personal chair.

Such hesitation as Matthew had before accepting the post was probably 'political'. That some of the funding for the new *Dictionary* came indirectly from the government at a time when, in the eyes of many, including Matthew, it was becoming increasingly unwilling to fund research into the humanities at adequate levels, made the new dictionary politically problematic. He was also aware that the writing of national history via individual biographies went against historiographical developments, both in Britain and abroad. Matthew, however, argued that these objections could be overcome. He believed that the popularity of historical biography as a genre in Britain was something which had to be recognized and exploited, rather than deplored. One way to do this was to make the new edition of the dictionary as wide-ranging as possible. Here Matthew was much more sympathetic to the dictionary's first editor, Leslie Stephen, who believed that all human life should be represented, than to Stephen's successor, Sidney Lee, who had a much more 'national-celebratory' view of the dictionary. Above all Matthew was determined that the category of women, the most conspicuous absence in the *Dictionary of National Biography*, should achieve a different status in the new edition of the dictionary. He was himself exceptionally open to suggestions and he and the staff of the dictionary canvassed very widely before drawing up a definitive list of names—and the list remained undefinitive for a long time. The list was also opened to foreigners whose visits to Britain 'may have been short but whose observations have been influential', as it was to iconic figures (like Britannia and John Bull), and to people who might never have existed (like King Arthur) or who have never been identified (like Jack the Ripper), but whose resonance in historical memory is sufficiently strong to justify inclusion. There was, as well, to be a more generous interpretation of individuals whose lives were lived under British imperial rule, and this embraced the pre-1776 American colonists. The result was a biographical dictionary of more than 50,000 names, with no significant area of British historical experience absent.

A second way of ensuring that the revised *Dictionary of National Biography* did not become over-individualized was to combine certain individuals into group entries—landed families or family firms, for example—as well as to give collective representation to movements. With the old technology, even had it been thought desirable, this would have been very difficult. With electronic technology, however, the possibilities of which had excited Matthew since he began to compile the index to the Gladstone diaries, sophisticated cross-referencing and highly sensitive indexing made collective representation easier. The only problem with this, as he himself remarked, 'is that it will be at once complained that it is not extensive enough' (Matthew, *Leslie Stephen*, 27).

The third principle, an important one, was to include within the new edition of the dictionary all the entries from the old—though all revised or rewritten. This not only avoided all the problems of starting over again, it gave the new dictionary itself a historical character. Matthew argued that while many of the entries in Stephen's dictionary—the legions of clergy are an example—would not have been included in a dictionary begun *de novo*, that they were important to the Victorians is itself historically significant. The new edition of the dictionary is, therefore, a collective account of the attitudes of two centuries: the nineteenth as well as the twentieth, the one developing organically from the other. There was, it must be said, some tension within this principle, as Matthew knew. He was trying to endow the new edition of the dictionary with a certain timelessness, a proof against changing fashion, by emphasizing the historicity of individual lives—he was anxious that the changing historical reputations of individuals should be emphasized in their entries—but he was also conscious of how far great enterprises, such as the new edition of the *Dictionary of National Biography*, are products of the particular concerns of their time (and he believed that the last quarter of the twentieth century was a particularly climacteric moment in British history) which become not so much timeless as historical artefacts themselves. None the less he had devised a structure which made the new edition of the dictionary as proof against changing fashion as any structure could.

The old *Dictionary of National Biography* was published alphabetically by name, *seriatim*, over a period of fifteen and a half years. This was a procedure that Matthew rightly did not repeat. Instead he decided that the new edition of the dictionary should be published as a whole in 2004, twelve years after its inception. This made possible the organization of the project first into general areas, some defined by period and some by subject (such as art or business), supervised by consultant editors, and then into specialist blocks (such as eighteenth-century naval officers, or twentieth-century physicists), supervised by associate editors. (Matthew was himself consultant editor for the nineteenth and twentieth centuries.) He had in addition one more resource unavailable to Stephen or Lee: a large professional scholarly community—mostly, though not altogether, university-based. Whereas the old dictionary was substantially written, often in house, by generalists who frequently wrote very many entries, the new edition was essentially written by specialists, whose work was co-ordinated and polished by an expert in-house research team. Oxford University Press, moreover, provided him with invaluable editorial, technical, and administrative support.

While as general editor of the dictionary Matthew was answerable to a supervisory committee, all the major strategic decisions as to its organization and production were his. He was not, however, an intrusive general editor. Once the rules had been established he was inclined to let people get on with the job, as indeed it was all the easier for them to do thanks to the clear lines of command he had established. The atmosphere at the dictionary's offices was, therefore, exceptionally congenial yet also purposeful. Matthew's personal qualities, his equability, his capacity to encourage and to guide, the qualities we normally associate with leadership, made him an inspiring editor, and his death caused as much dismay to the staff of the dictionary as it did to his students. He did not, of course, live to see its publication, but it is none the less very largely his creation.

Matthew was not merely an editor: he wrote numerous entries himself, including several on Britain's recent monarchs. That is not as surprising as it seems: although politically on the left, Matthew had a strong interest in those great British institutions—the Union, crown, church, parliament, Oxford—which had undergone major reforms in the nineteenth century but which were often ill adapted, as he thought, to the twentieth. How they might adapt was one of his intellectual preoccupations and had emerged from his study of Gladstone. Indeed, the last of his writing to be published during his life was an essay in the *London Review of Books* on Scotland and the future of the Union.

Matthew's editorship of both the Gladstone diaries and the new edition of the *Dictionary of National Biography* brought him international as well as national recognition. He went quite regularly to Italy and also to Canada, Australia, and New Zealand. He was an adviser to the committee which supervised the publication of Bertrand Russell's correspondence, and was awarded an honorary doctorate at McMaster University in Canada. He was a willing speaker at universities, schools, and branches of the Historical Association.

Character and assessment There was another side to Matthew: that of the wife-supporting husband. When their children had reached a safe age Sue Matthew returned to teaching, a career in which she was as successful as he was in his. As his friend and colleague Peter Ghosh wrote:

> Although, for many, the abiding image of Colin Matthew will be of the scholar and the public man, pondering what might become of Britain in the future, for the parents of south Oxford it will be that of the devotedly loyal husband who would always turn out on weekday evenings for events at St Ebbe's First School [of which Sue Matthew was head teacher], and who, as a special treat, would play the bagpipes at the summer fete. (*The Guardian*, 2 Nov 1999)

The extent of Matthew's writing and editing was prodigious, and was the result of self-discipline and remarkable powers of concentration. Whatever else he did, he wrote every morning from seven until eight, and was very efficient in his use of time. His rooms, particularly his Christ Church room, which was once Gladstone's, looked utterly chaotic to the outsider, but had a clear internal order for Matthew. He was careful, however, not to let his work dominate him. He and his family, who gave him intense happiness and satisfaction, always went to Scotland in August, and he and his wife nearly always took a little break abroad after Christmas. He was a good fisherman (though he eventually gave it up in deference to his daughter's anti-fishing views) and became an enthusiastic photographer. There was nothing to make anyone suspect ill health. He complained of shortness of breath only a few

days before his death: he was, in fact, on his way to the doctor when, on 29 October 1999, outside St Hugh's College, he had the heart attack from which he died later that day at the John Radcliffe Hospital, Oxford. After a funeral service at Christ Church Cathedral on 4 November 1999 he was cremated at Oxford crematorium, and his ashes were buried in the churchyard of St Thomas's Church, Elsfield. He was survived by his wife, Sue, and their three children. A memorial service was held at the university church of St Mary the Virgin on 12 February 2000.

Matthew's was a remarkably successful career. But it did not come easily. As a younger man, particularly, he felt that he had to work harder than others to achieve what he deserved, and this led to a certain prickliness. He himself conceded that he did not always have a good bedside manner. In part, this gruffness was a natural way of speech. In reporting his election to the fellowship at St Hugh's he told a friend: 'St Hugh's. News. Good' (private information). But there is no doubt that in the early days people could be puzzled and sometimes alienated by his manner, even those who later became friends and admirers. Given how much he had once thought himself an outsider, he would have been less than human had he not felt a certain satisfaction at 'showing them' they had been wrong—a satisfaction he did not always conceal. But success mellowed him. By the time of his death he was enormously respected and liked, indeed 'loved' would be the better word. As Sir Keith Thomas said of his death: 'A sense of shock and desolation ran through Oxford and was rapidly disseminated outwards to all the learned world. Colin Matthew was one of the few wholly irreplaceable people in this university' (Thomas, funeral address, 4 Nov 1999). In any case, even at his spikiest, those who knew him well found him utterly staunch—a word he himself often used—and he was always distressed if he felt that he had offended a friend. He was a striking figure: his hair prematurely white, nearly always informally dressed—a collar and tie were almost contrary to his nature. There is a fine photograph of him, in characteristic mode, in the St Hugh's College Library, and another, in a group portrait of the trustees, in the National Portrait Gallery. After his death the Colin Matthew Fund, for the encouragement of historical research within the University of Oxford, and the Colin Matthew lecture for the public understanding of history were established in his memory.

Ross McKibbin

Sources H. C. G. Matthew, *Leslie Stephen and the 'New Dictionary of National Biography'* (1997) · *The Times* (1 Nov 1999) · *Daily Telegraph* (1 Nov 1999) · *The Guardian* (2 Nov 1999) · *The Independent* (1 Nov 1999) · K. Thomas, funeral address (privately printed, 2000) · *WWW* · personal knowledge (2004) · private information (2004) · b. cert. · d. cert.

Archives priv. coll. | Oxford University Press, *Oxford DNB* archive

Likenesses J. Aronson, photograph, 1993, priv. coll. [see illus.] · photograph, St Hugh's College, Oxford · photograph, repro. in *The Times* · photograph, repro. in *The Guardian* · photograph, repro. in *The Independent* · photograph, repro. in *Daily Telegraph* · photographs, *Oxford DNB* archive · portrait (with NPG trustees), NPG

Wealth at death £324,288—gross: probate, 7 March 2000, *CGPLA Eng. & Wales*

Matthew [*née* Barlow; *other married name* Parker], **Frances** (1550/51–1629), benefactor, was the fourth daughter of William *Barlow (d. 1568), at that time bishop of Bath and Wells, and Agatha Wellesbourne, a former nun; William *Barlow (1544–1625) was her brother, and her four sisters all married future bishops. One of the first generation of clergy children born after the Reformation, Frances was given a strict protestant upbringing by her parents; her son subsequently recalled how his mother 'was ever upon all occasions wont to be as busy with Scripture as if it had been some glove upon her fingers' ends' (Mathew, 131). She was also a skilled embroiderer, wrote a neat italic hand, and may possibly have understood Latin. On 29 December 1569, at the age of eighteen, she married Matthew Parker (1551–1574), the second son of Archbishop Matthew *Parker. He died prematurely in December 1574 and his young widow moved to live with her sister Elizabeth and her husband, William Day, at that time provost of Eton, where Frances's first son, Matthew, was born in July 1575; he lived for less than a year. Early in 1577 Frances married again, her second husband being the Oxford scholar Tobie *Matthew (1544?–1628), at this stage of his career dean of Christ Church, prebendary of Salisbury, and chaplain to the queen; their first child, Toby (or Tobie) *Matthew (1577–1655), was born at Salisbury the following October. During the next six years Frances gave birth to four more children, of whom only two, John and Samuel, survived beyond infancy.

In 1583 Tobie Matthew was appointed dean of Durham and, especially in their early years there, Frances Matthew intensely disliked the unfamiliar north of England, imploring her husband to seek fresh promotion in the south. She never realized this ambition but was at least able to visit London fairly regularly when Tobie Matthew preached at court and, later, took his place in the House of Lords. On Matthew Hutton's elevation to the archbishopric of York in 1595 Tobie Matthew succeeded him, first as bishop of Durham and then, when Hutton died in January 1606, as archbishop of York.

Even as Frances's husband was scaling the heights of his profession disaster struck. The Matthews' precocious eldest son, Toby, had matriculated at his father's college, Christ Church, in Oxford in March 1590, when only twelve years old, and graduated BA in 1594 and MA in 1597. Oblivious of the need for economy the young man time and again applied to his mother to pay his debts, provoking his father's wrath yet further at his wife's exploitation. Soon after James I's accession, and upon his promise not to venture beyond France, Toby Matthew gained his parents' consent to travel on the continent, but once across the channel he proceeded directly to Italy where, after taking instruction from Robert Persons, he was received into the Church of Rome. After his return to England, Archbishop Bancroft attempted in vain to procure his reconversion, and all the rest of her life his mother, devastated by grief, prayed for his restoration to the fold. Neither of the two younger children could compensate for their elder brother's delinquency. John, the second son, not blessed with Toby's academic prowess, proved another spendthrift; the third son, Samuel, of whom his mother cherished great hopes, died in 1601 while a student at Peterhouse in Cambridge.

Disappointed in their children Frances and her husband turned to the Barlow kin. In 1614 the archbishop granted a prebend in York Minster to his wife's nephew, Henry Wickham, son of the late bishop of Winchester, who subsequently became archdeacon of York and chancellor of the minster. He was also almost certainly behind the appointment to the deanery of York of John Scott, the husband of Dorothy, Frances's godly niece. To these relatives and their families Frances Matthew in her last years introduced her two granddaughters, Frances and Dorcas, whom she had removed from their father (John Matthew) to be educated under her own supervision.

At his death on 29 March 1628 Archbishop Matthew, virtually disinheriting his two sons, bestowed his whole estate upon his wife of fifty years, 'relying with all confidence upon her care and providence' (Tobie Matthew, will). Among his effects were his 3000 books, valued at £600 and reputed to be the largest private library in England. Frances Matthew conferred the entire collection upon the dean and chapter of York, a deed which her beneficiaries believed deserved 'to live as long as the church itself', and so laid the foundations of the present York Minster Library (Drake, 512).

On 9 August 1628 Frances Matthew drew up her will, asserting her 'firm resolution to pour out my last breath' within 'this church of England wherein I have learned the profession of Christian and saving doctrine' (will, fol. 397r). Like her husband she almost completely ignored her sons, leaving Toby a diamond ring and John merely the interest on £500 intended for his daughters, and instead lavished her generosity upon her four grandchildren and host of nephews, nieces, great-nephews, great-nieces, and godchildren. Her cash bequests alone, which included £200 for a scholarship at Peterhouse, exceeded £2500; she left the residue of the estate to her granddaughters.

Frances Matthew died, aged seventy-eight, on 8 May 1629 and was buried in the lady chapel of York Minster, where her monument paid tribute to her 'exemplary wisdom, gravity, piety, bounty and … other virtues not only above her sex, but the times'; it also recorded the fact, in which she had evidently taken great pride during her lifetime, that 'a bishop was her father, an archbishop her father-in-law; she had four bishops her brethren and an archbishop her husband' (Drake, 512).

CLAIRE CROSS

Sources F. Matthew, 'The birth of all my children', York Minster Library, Add. MS 322 · F. Matthew, will, Borth. Inst., PROB Reg. 40, fols. 397r–398v · T. Matthew, will, Borth. Inst., PROB Reg. 40, fol. 195r · chancery wills inventory; inventory of the goods of Archbishop Tobie Matthew, 10 April 1628, Borth. Inst. · A. H. Mathew, ed., *A true historical relation of the conversion of Sir Tobie Matthew* (1904) · C. Clusius, *Aulae Caesareae quondam familiaris exoticorum libri decem*, Leiden, 1605, York Minster Library [Frances Matthew's copy] · F. Drake, *Eboracum, or, The history and antiquities of the city of*

York (1736), 482, 512 · CSP dom., 1595–7, 168 · Correspondence of Matthew Parker, ed. J. Bruce and T. T. Perowne, Parker Society, 42 (1853) · R. Thoresby, Vicaria Leodiensis, or, The history of the church of Leedes in Yorkshire (1724) · B. Willis, A survey of the cathedrals of York, Durham, Carlisle … Bristol, 2 vols. (1727), vol. 1 · J. B. Gavin, 'Elizabethan bishop of Durham: Tobias Matthew, 1595–1605', PhD diss., McGill University, 1972 · A. H. Mathew and A. Calthrop, Life of Sir Tobie Matthew (1907) · G. E. Aylmer, 'Funeral monuments and post-medieval sculpture', A history of York Minster, ed. G. E. Aylmer and R. Cant (1977), 430–86 · C. B. L. Barr, 'The Minster Library', in G. Aylmer and R. Cant, A history of York Minster (1977), 487–539 · J. Berlatsky, 'Marriage and family in a Tudor élite: familial patterns of Elizabethan bishops', Journal of Family History, 3 (1978), 11–12 · P. Collinson, The religion of protestants (1982) · R. Marchant, The puritans and the church courts in the diocese of York, 1560–1642 (1960) · C. H. Garrett, The Marian exiles: a study in the origins of Elizabethan puritanism (1938)

Archives York Minster Library, 'The birth of all my children', Add. MS 322

Likenesses monument, York Minster; repro. in Aylmer and Cant, eds., History of York Minster, pl. 142

Wealth at death exact sum unknown but wealthy; bequests of £2650; plus rent charge of £160; plus plate and jewels: will, Borth. Inst., probate register 40, fols. 397r–398v

Matthew, Sir Robert Hogg (1906–1975), architect, was born on 12 December 1906 at 8 West Mayfield, Edinburgh, second son in the family of four sons (the first of whom died in infancy) and one daughter of John Fraser Matthew, architect, and his wife, Annie Broadfoot Hogg. His father was the partner of Sir Robert Lorimer, the most celebrated Scottish architect of his day. From Melville College, Edinburgh, Robert Matthew passed into Edinburgh University, but after a year moved to the college of art to study architecture. It was while they were both students that he met, and on 25 December 1931 married, Lorna Louise (b. 1909/10), daughter of Robert Stuart Pilcher, general manager of the Manchester corporation transport department; they had a son and two daughters.

Matthew's professional career falls into three parts, the first and last centred in Edinburgh. With Lorimer's death in 1929, followed by the world slump, his father's practice could not support him, and for two years he lived on a college studentship which enabled him to study slum housing and to confirm his interest in the social role of architecture. On the advice of a family friend, Professor L. B. Budden of Liverpool, in 1936 he took employment in the Department of Health for Scotland, which gave him an insight into the present limitations and future potential of a public office. It was also through Budden that he came to the notice of Patrick Abercrombie, with whom he worked on the wartime Clyde valley regional plan from 1940 to 1945. He made the first sketches for the new towns of East Kilbride and Glenrothes, and on a visit to Sweden to buy timber cottages he was much taken by the attractive co-operative housing, in particular the modestly scaled 'point blocks' of flats going up in the wooded fringes of Stockholm. In 1945 he became chief architect and planning officer to the health department for Scotland and a member of the RIBA's reconstruction committee. At its first meeting in London, Sir Charles Reilly, Budden's successor, urged him to apply for the vacant post of chief architect to the London county council (LCC).

This second period of Matthew's career lasted only

Sir Robert Hogg Matthew (1906–1975), by Elliott & Fry, 1950

seven years (1946–53) but it was of permanent significance for London and for architecture. Convinced that city planning, housing, and architecture were inseparable, and that only in this unison could quality be combined with quantity, he was able to persuade the council to remove housing from the valuer's department, where it had been recently and unhappily placed in the interest of productivity, and reunite it with planning and architecture under his charge. But he rejected the traditional hierarchical structure in favour of group working with fully delegated responsibility; this made his office, despite its size, especially attractive to the young and in due course the most highly regarded urban housing authority in the world. He and his chief housing architect, Whitfield Lewis, proceeded to scrap all existing designs and to substitute, under Scandinavian influence, the 'mixed development' of little towers and terraces whose prototype was the delightful Ackroyden estate on Putney Heath (c.1950–56). Simultaneously, with his chosen deputy (and successor), Leslie Martin, he initiated the LCC's permanent contributions to the 1951 Festival of Britain—the charming Lansbury neighbourhood in the East End and the Royal Festival Hall.

For a time the design philosophy of the LCC was the subject of passionate internal debate between the empiricists and the modernist intellectuals, and the final victory of the latter may have been a factor in Matthew's return to Scotland. In 1953 he accepted the Forbes chair of architecture at Edinburgh University. His enlargement of the role of his school now went hand in hand with the creation of a private practice which became internationally known as RMJM when he invited Stirrat Johnson-Marshall, whose work at the Ministry of Education he admired, to take charge of its London end. His own first significant job was Turnhouse airport (1956), whose human scale and unaffected use of timber again showed Scandinavian influence. The dramatic silhouette of Cockenzie power station, the romantically sited Stirling University, and the Commonwealth Pool at the foot of Arthur's Seat were the work of his office, and he was influential in Scotland as a member of its Historic Buildings Council and Royal Fine Art Commission. Despite living in Edinburgh New Town and in Nash's London, Matthew was never a classicist, and it was he who proposed that New Zealand House at the foot of Haymarket (1962) should have a high tower, though the romantic silhouette he intended did not survive the development of the design in the London office of RMJM.

In 1962 Matthew succeeded Sir William Holford as president of the RIBA, and he subsequently had much to do with the expansion of the institute's work and influence. His shrewd judgement and quiet authority had by now made him a father figure at international conferences, as president of the International Union of Architects (1961–5) and creator of the Commonwealth Association of Architects (of which he was president, 1965–8). He was an honorary fellow of the American Institute of Architects (1951) and of the Canadian (1964) and New Zealand (1959) institutes, and an honorary LLD of the University of Sheffield (1963). In 1970 he received architecture's highest award—the royal gold medal. He was appointed CBE in 1952 and knighted in 1962.

Although a private man, not given to self-exposure, Matthew was sociable and able to endure international bonhomie without a sign of strain. Partly this stemmed from a profound sense of obligation to, and affection for, the developing world. But behind his distinguished looks, his charm of manner, and his soft lowland voice lay an iron determination to get his way—the way he thought right for a liberal and caring society. He was the most conspicuous of the new kind of architect that emerged in Britain after 1945, who believed that if the country could get the system right, the rest would follow. He died at his country house, Keith Marischal, at Humble near Edinburgh, on 21 June 1975. His wife survived him.   LIONEL ESHER

Sources *The Times* (23 June 1975) · *Building* (27 June 1975), 39 · *WWW, 1971–80* · personal knowledge (2004) · private information (1986) · private information (2004) · b. cert. · m. cert. · d. cert.
Archives RIBA · U. Edin. L., papers
Likenesses Elliott & Fry, photograph, 1950, NPG [*see illus.*] · bust?, RIBA?
Wealth at death £254,456.02: probate, 1976, *CGPLA Eng. & Wales*

Matthew, Tobie (1544?–1628), archbishop of York, was born in Bristol, the son of John Matthew of Ross-on-Wye in Herefordshire and his second wife, Eleanor Crofton of Ludlow in Shropshire. The Matthew family had a long connection with the city and Tobie was said to have been born

Tobie Matthew (1544?–1628), by unknown artist, 1610

at Bristol Bridge, the heart of the mercantile community. The uncertainty about his birth date stems in part from the conflicting evidence of his own statements in later life—though his funeral monument before its near destruction recorded 1546, he himself claimed in 1588 that he was just short of his third birthday when Henry VIII died and that his mother, who was still alive at the time, could verify the fact. It seems therefore that a birth date in early 1544 is most likely.

Career at Oxford Matthew's parents are reported by John Strype to have been disaffected in religion, presumably meaning that they were Catholics. During Mary's reign Matthew attended school at Wells before proceeding to Oxford, where he is said to have matriculated as a probationer of University College in 1559. By 1561 he was at Christ Church, where the Scottish protestant James Calfhill, a cousin by marriage and a formative influence on the young Matthew, was a canon. He graduated BA in 1564 and MA in July 1566, by which time he was a student—a fellow—of Christ Church, and he was ordained deacon in the same year, apparently at the suggestion of Calfhill and to the dismay of his parents. Christ Church under the former exile Thomas Sampson was a strongly Calvinist college, and in 1565 Sampson was removed from the deanery for his objections to the imposition of the surplice and other vestments. Matthew wrote a lengthy letter to that great patron of godly Calvinists, Robert Dudley, earl of Leicester, complaining about the government's action, and he remained a correspondent and friend of Sampson throughout the latter's life.

At this time Matthew was identified as one of the rising Oxford stars and 'he was much respected for his great learning, eloquence, sweet conversation, friendly disposition and the sharpness of his wit' (Wood, *Ath. Oxon.*, 2.870), qualities which were to play an important part in his subsequent career. More immediately they gained him a part, along with another rising star, Edmund Campion, in the disputation held before the queen in St Mary's Church on 3 September 1566, and he was chosen to make the oration on her departure from Christ Church at the end of her visit. His eloquence and presence attracted Elizabeth's attention, and she continued to show an active interest in his career thereafter, making him a royal chaplain-in-ordinary in 1572, soon after his ordination to the priesthood by John Jewel, bishop of Salisbury, on 10 June 1571. By this time Matthew's Oxford career was becoming well established; he had been chosen as public orator by the university in 1569 and made a canon of Christ Church in 1570, succeeding to the stall held by his cousin James Calfhill. In 1571 he was presented to the rectory of Algarkirk in Lincoln diocese by Bishop Thomas Cooper, a former dean of Christ Church, and on 15 May 1572 he was appointed to the prebendal stall of Teynton Regis in Salisbury Cathedral. On 28 November in that same year he renewed his earlier connection with Wells on his appointment as archdeacon of Bath.

These promotions were chiefly intended to support Matthew's Oxford commitments, for on 17 July 1572 he was elected president of the recent foundation of St John's College, with which Christ Church was closely connected. He was the fifth president to have been elected in the college's short history and he had to grapple with its poor finances and a divided fellowship, among whom were many sympathizers with the old religion, including his long-time acquaintance the future Jesuit martyr Edmund Campion. Matthew was elected reader in Greek in 1573, in which year he also proceeded BTh. His attempts to improve the fortunes of St John's met with little success: he raised money in an attempt to found a library there but the plans came to nought, and the penury of the college undermined other developments. Matthew continued as a canon of Christ Church, and his work there led the college visitors in 1574 to complain that his cathedral duties prevented him from giving proper attention to St John's. He became DTh in 1574, and was given the stall of Combe IX in Wells Cathedral that same year. His reputation as a theologian committed to the Calvinist position and his links with Leicester's circle led to his admission to the godly legal community of Gray's Inn in London under special dispensation in 1575.

In 1576 Matthew was appointed dean of Christ Church and subsequently resigned the presidency of St John's on 8 May 1577. His new position at the head of both a chapter and a wealthy college made Matthew a formidable figure in Oxford, and his marriage early in 1577 to Frances Parker (*d.* 1629) [*see* Matthew, Frances], the widow of the late archbishop's son and the daughter of William Barlow, bishop of Bath and Wells, further strengthened his growing authority. Matthew was a vigorous dean who devoted considerable energy to building up the college library, making several gifts of his own, including a copy of the 1576 edition of Foxe's *Actes and Monumentes*, and encouraging others to follow his example. He was also active in university affairs, being a member of the commission to root out papists from Exeter College in 1578, and was appointed vice-chancellor in 1579, on the recommendation of the earl of Leicester.

It was through Leicester that Matthew also came into contact with two distinguished foreign scholars at Oxford. He was a patron of the Italian protestant jurist Albericus Gentilis, who had fled from Italy in 1579, welcoming him to Christ Church and subsequently defending his views on the legitimacy of the theatre against the more puritan scholars associated with John Rainolds, president of Corpus Christi College. In recognition of the support he had received from Matthew, Gentilis dedicated to him his *Commentarius de maleficis et math.* (1593); a copy survives heavily annotated by Matthew. The other visitor, Jean Hotman, arrived in Oxford in 1581 as an alumnus of Calvin's academy and the Genevan church, and was also provided with rooms in Christ Church by the dean. Hotman had a wide circle of Oxford contacts, and, although less closely identified with Matthew in person, was highly influential in introducing the works of Beza to Oxford protestants. It was in 1581 also that the greatest public confrontation at Oxford during Matthew's time took place, when Edmund Campion published his *Decem rationes* in defence of the Roman church, placing copies on the seats in St Mary's Church at commencements on 27 June. Campion identified Matthew, among others, as one not learned enough in scripture and the fathers to fulfil his office, a barb that Matthew underlined in his own copy of Campion's work. Although William Whitaker was chosen to respond officially to Campion, Matthew's was the first public response, in a Latin sermon based on Deuteronomy 32: 7 preached in St Mary's on 9 October that year. The sermon gained some celebrity and circulated in manuscript until it was finally published as *Concio apologetica adversus Campianum* in 1638.

Dean and bishop of Durham By the time of the sermon against Campion, Matthew was beginning to play an active if minor role in ecclesiastical affairs outside the university. As dean of the cathedral he had ordered the seeking out of papists in the diocese of Oxford (left vacant between 1568 and 1589), and in 1581, as prolocutor of the lower house of convocation, he was among those who unsuccessfully petitioned Elizabeth I to lift Archbishop Grindal's suspension, an act that secured the queen's displeasure. He was a natural candidate for further advancement (a view that he held himself), and when the deanery of Durham fell vacant late in 1581 he let his interest be known. The other candidate for Durham was Robert Bellamy, a member of the chapter and chaplain to Bishop Richard Barnes. Bellamy had the support of the queen's cousin Lord Hunsdon, but Matthew commanded the support of several godly preachers in the chapter, including the Pilkington brothers and Thomas Lever, as well as that of the earls of Leicester and Huntingdon and, most crucially, William Cecil, Lord Burghley. Despite such powerful backing negotiations took over a year and Matthew was not installed until 3 September 1583, resigning from Christ Church early in 1584. Matthew's departure from Oxford was the occasion of a celebrated sermon, and he was accompanied north by his friend Richard Eales who composed a lengthy elegiac poem, 'Iter Boreale', recording the event (Bodl. Oxf., MS Rawl. B.223, fols. 1–16). This was neither the first nor the last time that Matthew was to inspire verse: William Gager, a student at Christ Church, had already dedicated several verses to him (BL, Add. MS 10943, fols. 51, 68–71, 74–76v); he was later to be the dedicatee of Barnabe Barnes's *A Divine Centurie of Spirituall Sonnets* (1595) and of John Ashmore's translations of Horace's odes, published in 1621, while John Earle, the future bishop of Salisbury, composed a private elegy on Matthew's death in 1628 (Bodl. Oxf., MS Eng. poet. e.97, pp. 50–53).

Matthew did not always view his promotion with pleasure, especially in the early years when his defeated rival proved a focus for opposition within the chapter and Lord Hunsdon's powerful influence still counted against him. He regarded the deanery as merely a stepping-stone to higher things, and his determined pursuit of promotion has left him, somewhat unfairly, with a reputation for ecclesiastical jobbery. Despite the presence of committed protestants in the chapter from the beginning of Elizabeth's reign, large areas of the diocese were still missionary territory, with the added complication of a shared border with a foreign power. Matthew was energetic in sustaining the preaching and pastoral effort required, mostly through personal example by preaching weekly at several churches in the diocese. In addition he exploited the opportunities to embellish the library that he had brought with him from Oxford by astute purchases from the estates of deceased members of the chapter. He made this resource available to local clergy engaged in combating recusancy, and was also assiduous in enforcing the laws against Catholics. As a crown appointee, Matthew was a trusted negotiator on its behalf with the Scottish authorities, and in particular Francis Stewart, fifth earl of Bothwell, in the years following the execution of Mary, queen of Scots. Trusted by the more advanced protestants on the privy council Matthew was hopeful of promotion to the see of Durham when Barnes died in 1587, but in the end Matthew Hutton, dean of York, was preferred, though the dean, still thwarted by his old opponent Hunsdon, was able to resist removal to the diocese of Salisbury and remained in the deanery. His income was subsequently increased when he was presented to the wealthy rectory at Monkwearmouth in 1590, which he held in plurality, but he continued to sue for promotion and was disappointed not to be made bishop of London in 1594.

The death of John Piers, archbishop of York, on 28 September 1594 occasioned another series of moves on the episcopal bench and Matthew was determined to succeed Hutton, the new archbishop of York, at Durham and not to be fobbed off with a less well endowed see. After some delay he achieved his ambition, being consecrated bishop of Durham on 13 April 1595, whereupon he settled his debts to his old patron Burghley, giving him £100 in gold,

with other presents to Burghley's secretary Michael Hickes and to his son Robert Cecil, a transaction that has been described as 'one of the more patently documented cases of simony in the Elizabethan Church' (Collinson, 47). At Durham, Matthew also looked after the interests of his family, most infamously in 1604 when he secured a lease of the extensive episcopal manor of Tunstall for his son Toby. Yet whatever may have been his dealings with his temporal estate, Matthew proved an assiduous bishop to a poorly staffed diocese in which traditional attitudes predominated and where less than half the parishes had preaching ministers and there was a high incidence of non-residence. He himself continued his preaching activity but 'neglected not his proper Episcopal Acts of Visitation, Confirmation, Ordination &c. he confirmed sometimes 500, sometimes 1000 at a Time, yea, so many that he hath been forced to betake himself to his Bed for Refreshment …' (Thoresby, 165).

In addition to the demands of his spiritual duties, as prince-bishop Matthew played a prominent part in local administration in co. Durham and, following the death of the third earl of Huntingdon in 1595, was the *de facto* lord lieutenant of the county. As such he was soon engaged on the government's behalf in border affairs where the warden of the middle march, the 95-year-old Sir John Forster, had proved ineffectual in dealing alike with border raids and with recusancy among the local landowners. Forster was removed from office in 1595 with some difficulty, and on 25 September 1596 a border commission was set up with Matthew as its head. He played a key role in the Anglo-Scottish settlement of 5 May 1597, and preached regularly at Berwick while negotiations proceeded. Border affairs continued to occupy the bishop; he did not enjoy good relations with Forster's successor as warden, Ralph, third Baron Eure, who proved equally ineffective in controlling faction among the marcher gentry. Religion lay behind many of these disputes and the diocese contained many gentry with traditional values against whom the magistrates were unwilling to act and whose status rendered them immune from effective discipline by the bishop. Nevertheless it was during Matthew's years at Durham that concerted action was taken both against recusancy and to bolster protestantism.

Unable to overcome the gentry Matthew was assiduous in pursuit of missionary priests, and a number of them, including an old Oxford associate, John Boste, were executed during the 1590s. Matthew employed a network of spies to hunt down priests, led by the energetic Henry Sanderson, a customs official responsible for the disruption of a system of recusant safe houses, for which he was rewarded with the leases of episcopal coalmines. Matthew also secured the services of former priests to inform on their colleagues, the most famous of them being the prolific polemicist Thomas Bell, who was given access to the bishop's library in pursuit of his work. In order to promote protestantism Matthew successfully used his patronage within the chapter to secure preachers, and rather less successfully tried to make local patrons restore the fabric of churches and install resident preaching ministers in key border parishes after the Anglo-Scottish treaty of 1597. By 1601 this had only produced four licensed preachers in the whole of Northumberland, though almost half the Durham parishes had preaching ministers by that date. His efforts on behalf of the church were widely recognized and Archbishop Hutton thought that, on the death of Whitgift in 1604, Matthew might be promoted to Canterbury.

The see of York As a key political figure Matthew occasionally antagonized local opinion by an over-assiduous attention to his own rights, as when he confiscated the goods of Scottish merchants at Durham in 1597 or when he contested the charter of the city in 1601, but he was a trusted servant of the state, and especially of the Cecils, and played a key role during the arrival of James I in England. Although his earlier negotiations do not appear to have given Matthew a high opinion of his new king, he quickly set out to make amends. He met James at Berwick, where he preached before him, and was in constant attendance as a preacher in the first four months of the reign, then returning north to welcome the new queen. He played a prominent part in the Hampton Court conference, preaching the closing sermon. He also preached before the king on the Sunday following the Gunpowder Plot, and before the English and Scottish commissioners upon the designed union of the two kingdoms. His advice was often sought by James in these crucial months. On 16 April 1606 he was appointed archbishop of York, a promotion that recognized his overall contribution to the national church and his effective administration at Durham where, by the time he moved on, protestantism had made significant inroads beyond the cathedral city, and the bishop had become the effective temporal ruler of the palatinate and the chief source of royal authority in the border regions.

Matthew's involvement in political affairs increased further through his work as archbishop with the council of the north, many of whose members were already good friends and shared his antipathy for Catholicism. He formed good relationships with the magnates Gilbert Talbot, seventh earl of Shrewsbury, whose funeral sermon he preached in 1616, and Francis Clifford, fourth earl of Cumberland, whom Matthew appointed as keeper of his estate at Scalme Park in Nottinghamshire and who, with his household, was a regular visitor to Bishopthorpe, the archbishop's principal residence. The secretary of the council, Sir John Ferne, was appointed steward of the archiepiscopal manors of Cawood, Wistow, and Sherburn, and his successor, Sir Arthur Ingram, was granted a long lease of the archbishop's house in the cathedral close, building there a substantial 'palace'. Matthew remained on close terms with Sir Thomas Fairfax of Denton, whose lands adjoined the archiepiscopal manor of Otley and whose son Henry was briefly Matthew's household chaplain. Perhaps his closest colleague on the council, however, was Sir Thomas Posthumous Hoby, the strongest defender of protestant interests in that Catholic stronghold, the North Riding. Matthew trusted Hoby's

local judgement, asking him to nominate curates to unprovided-for chapelries and supporting his actions in the secular courts with a vigorous campaign against recusants at the visitation of 1615. Hoby's actions did not always endear him to his fellow protestants in the region but Matthew continued to support him and in 1617 appointed him high steward of Ripon. This was an important post as Ripon was a parliamentary borough, which gave Hoby considerable political influence in what was a well-known recusant stronghold where the crown, with Matthew's encouragement, had recently attempted to strengthen the position of the established church through the re-endowment of the minster there.

During these years, largely through Matthew's efforts, a vigorous and active group of Calvinist gentry took over the effective running of the council, but their ambitions were threatened by the appointment of the pro-Catholic Emanuel, eleventh Baron Scrope, as president in 1619. Matthew, among others, let his disapproval of Scrope be known, with the result that in 1620 he was warned by James I to give the president due precedence at official ceremonies in York Minster. Though now in his seventies Matthew continued to be an active force in the north, but his influence on politics at the national level had waned by this date. He had preached the sermon at the opening of parliament in 1614, during which he indicated his opposition to royal policy over taxation, but his influence had probably already declined with that of his patron Robert Cecil, and dwindled still further with the latter's death in 1612. He entertained James I at Bishopthorpe on the king's journey north in 1617, and in 1622 he exchanged his London residence, York Place, which later became Whitehall, with the crown for the manors of Acomb, Beckhay, and Sancton in Yorkshire, further testimony to his close association with James but also, perhaps, a pointer both to his withdrawal from national affairs and to his tendency, previously noted at Durham, to accommodate lay patrons at the expense of the church's interests. His reputation for wit, too, may well have affected his reputation in temporal matters—he has often had his own words to Matthew Hutton quoted against him by historians: 'God loveth, as do princes, a cheerful giver' (*Correspondence*, 95).

Recusants and separatists Matthew's influence in ecclesiastical affairs remained crucial to the religious history of the north until his death in 1628. On arriving in his new diocese Matthew was faced with both the anticipated problem of recusancy and the less expected problem of separatism, each of which he addressed immediately. Matthew revived prosecutions against Catholics, using the high commission which in Hutton's later years had been less active, and he was deeply suspicious of the oath of allegiance, tendered to Catholics after 1607. In a sustained drive between 1612 and 1615 the high commission imposed heavy fines on the Catholic gentry, and a number of Calvinist clergy were appointed to confer with obstinate recusants. At his visitation in 1615 Matthew paid particular regard to recusancy, asking especially detailed questions, and his determined thoroughness in uncovering Catholics remained a feature of every visitation up to and including that of 1627. Ambition was not always matched by achievement, however, and despite his efforts many lay Catholics still found it relatively easy to evade the full force of the law, not surprising in a region where many court officers had recusant relations. Indeed, on the eve of his promotion to York, Matthew acquired one of his own: his antipathy to Catholicism was of long standing, but was given an added piquancy by the conversion of his eldest son, Toby (or Tobie) *Matthew, in 1606, an event that was a continual source of unhappiness to the archbishop and his wife until their deaths. Matthew also encouraged polemicists like Alexander Cooke and scholars like John Favour to take up in print the intellectual defence of the Reformation, making available to them his extensive library, and he encouraged godly preachers such as Edmund Bunny, who was based during these years at the episcopal residence at Cawood, to preach in towns throughout the province.

Separatism was a less expected issue. A number of clergy based in parishes on the Nottinghamshire, Yorkshire, and Lincolnshire borders had failed to subscribe to the canons of 1604, and were cited before the ecclesiastical courts. It was against this background that the separatist preachers John Robinson and John Smyth had gained support from some clergy and from members of their congregations by the time of Matthew's arrival in the diocese. The new bishop sought to act against the separatists as swiftly as possible, trying to drive a wedge between them and the puritan clergy who had scruples over the canons. This he did in his primary visitation, adding one of the centres of separatism, Bawtry, to his preaching venues with a sermon specifically against the Brownists. He then placed the clergy of the area directly under his own supervision rather than that of the archdeacon, secured the subscription of the more moderate puritan ministers such as Richard Bernard, vicar of Worksop, whom he subsequently made a canon of Southwell, and picked off the leading lay separatists for prosecution in the courts. So successful was this strategy that in 1608 the congregations removed themselves to exile in Amsterdam.

Preacher and theologian Using his authority to deal with the opponents of the church was only one aspect of Matthew's work; he was also active in sustaining the continued vigour of the early Calvinist reformers. By this date he was one of the few men left with direct experience of the struggles of the early Elizabethan church, and this no doubt informed his churchmanship. In addition to his support of godly writers and preachers he was a particular champion of that quintessential element of the reformed ministry, the exercise, in which clergy of a neighbourhood met to hear each other preach and to discuss matters of theology. He himself preached in that held at Mansfield, Nottinghamshire, in 1609 and 1613, while his chaplain John Favour was the leader of the famous exercise at Halifax, which exerted considerable influence upon the religious life of the West Riding in this and succeeding generations. It was during his archiepiscopate that the foundations laid by his predecessors began to bear fruit; a graduate preaching ministry became established in many parts of the diocese, and Matthew played his part in this through careful use of patronage within the minster as well as in the diocese. Only three clergy ordained by him at York were non-graduates, and even these had attended university.

The touchstone of the ministry as perceived by Matthew was preaching, an activity in which he was both preeminent and indefatigable. Matthew's preaching diary has become a standard source for the pastoral objectives of his generation of Jacobean bishops. In it he recorded those sermons preached by him following his appointment to Durham, 721 as dean and 550 as bishop, and then a further 721 as archbishop until 1622 when the diary ceased, though not the preaching. This was a weekly routine, and Matthew recorded his distress if illness prevented him from maintaining a programme of at least forty sermons a year. These included great occasions before court and parliament, and visits to small country churches 'through high waters and foul ways' where congregations were sparse, though the situation he found on his arrival at Acomb on the outskirts of York in 1622 when there were 'neither priest nor people, although they had warning over night' (York Minster Library, Add. MS 18) appears to have been unique. The Pauline epistles often provided him with his text, and his industry was matched by his style, plain but elegant 'In that still voice, that voice that God was in', according to the poem by John Earle, himself a future bishop (Bodl. Oxf., MS Eng. poet. e.97, pp. 50–53). Both in his audiences and by his example Matthew's preaching extended his influence well beyond his diocese, and this was strengthened further through contacts with other bishops, men like Arthur Lake and James Montague, and with university divines like Samuel Ward. To evangelical divines such as these preaching had to be based on scriptural learning, in the pursuit of which Matthew had acquired an extensive library of almost 3000 volumes by his death. It was acquired by gift, by assiduous purchases from deceased friends and colleagues, and from the Frankfurt book fair whose catalogues were marked up annually by Matthew with his requirements. Many of his books can be identified by his monogram, his motto *Vita Christus, mors lucrum*, and by his copious annotations, suggesting that he used his library regularly in preparing his sermons.

The collection reveals Matthew as a man of wide theological interests of an evangelical nature who, in addition to scriptural works and studies of the fathers, had a special interest in Italian works and in the troubles of French protestants during the wars of religion. He was clearly one of those who saw the English church as part of the wider protestant communion and as having a responsibility towards co-religionists elsewhere. His library was put at the disposal of other godly ministers, and the public purposes of print were formally acknowledged by him in 1602, when he gave £50 to the Bodleian Library, and in 1615, when he established a library in his home town of Bristol, to which he continued to add from duplicates in his own collection until his death. These volumes can still be identified at Bristol, as can those of his personal library which he had intended to leave to his son Toby; however, having disinherited the latter, he bequeathed them to his wife, Frances, who subsequently gave them to the minster, where they formed the basis of the present library. The library was equipped and the books catalogued following a gift of £40 for that purpose from Matthew's former colleagues on the council of the north.

Impact and legacies Matthew's career had been forged in the reign of Elizabeth, and his ecclesiastical contacts and pastoral priorities reflect that fact. However by the 1620s his brand of evangelical Calvinism was being challenged by the Arminians, whose style of churchmanship was very different. They already had some support in the chapter at York by the time of Matthew's death, when his generation of godly conforming protestants no longer commanded the heights of the established church, and he was followed as archbishop by a succession of Arminian churchmen in George Mountaine, Samuel Harsnett, and Richard Neile. By the time of his death the theological and pastoral priorities that had shaped Matthew's career, and indeed that of the church he served, were being replaced among the hierarchy by those of a younger generation of clerics whose attachment to Calvinism was much less strong, but Matthew's own care in the exercise of his office and of the patronage that it bestowed played no small part in ensuring that the churchmanship he represented continued to be attractive to a significant portion of both the parochial clergy and the substantial laity of the northern province in the decades following his death. That could not have been said of the archdiocese at the time of his arrival in those parts in 1583.

Matthew and his wife, Frances, had five children, three of whom survived infancy—Toby and John, who also became a Catholic, and Samuel, who died in 1601 while still a student at Peterhouse, Cambridge. Both Toby and John were great disappointments to their father, who in his will recalled the large sums he had spent on them— £14,000 in the case of Toby. He bequeathed to each simple tokens of plate worth 20 marks. Perhaps surprisingly, Matthew left no money for public charitable purposes, giving the rest of his estate to the care of his widow, who died on 8 May 1629, 'relying with all confidence upon her care and prudence' (Borth. Inst., probate register 40, fol. 195). Most notable among his effects was the library of 3000 volumes, valued at £600 and said to be the largest private library in England. In addition to his books, Matthew was reputed to have several manuscript pieces at his death and these seem to have passed to Henry Wickham, a canon of the minster and his wife's nephew, eventually coming into the possession of Archbishop John Sharp, but all that survives is an eighteenth-century copy of his preaching diary. The inventory of his Yorkshire residences, whose contents were valued at over £3000, reveal a lifestyle in which hospitality played no small part, and Matthew was as much famed for this as for his preaching by contemporaries. Indeed his eloquence was central to both activities and he was celebrated for his puns, fine

examples of which were known as 'Tobys' among his circle in Yorkshire.

Both preaching and hospitality were prominent features of the epitaph on Matthew's fine classical monument placed in York Minster. The monument was largely destroyed by fire in 1829, but an engraving was published in Francis Drake's *Eboracum* (1736) where the inscription is also recorded. All that survives is the much restored effigy, now placed on the north side of the lady chapel. Matthew's portraits reveal him as a small man with a thin face, and not the commanding presence described by contemporaries, thus perhaps providing further evidence for the power of his oratory. He died at his residence at Cawood on 29 March 1628 and was buried in York Minster.   WILLIAM JOSEPH SHEILS

Sources J. Newley, 'A life of Tobias Matthew, archbishop of York, 1546–1628', MA diss., Bristol University, 1998 · J. P. Gavin, 'An Elizabethan bishop of Durham: Tobie Matthew, 1595–1606', PhD diss., McGill University, 1972 · K. Fincham, *Prelate as pastor: the episcopate of James I* (1990) · W. J. Sheils, 'An archbishop in the pulpit: Tobie Matthew's preaching diary, 1606–1622', *Life and thought in the northern church, c1100 – c1700*, ed. D. M. Wood, SCH, Subsidia, 12 (1999), 381–405 · J. Raine, *A catalogue of the printed books in the library of the dean and chapter of York* (1896) · *Hist. U. Oxf.* 3: *Colleg. univ.* · C. B. L. Barr, 'The Minster Library', in G. Aylmer and R. Cant, *A history of York Minster* (1977), 487–539 · Tobie Matthew's preaching diary, York Minster Library, Add. MS 18 · will, Borth. Inst., probate register 40, fol. 195 · inventory of goods of Tobie Matthew, Borth. Inst., chancery wills, 1628 · R. Thoresby, *Vicaria Leodiensis, or, The history of the church of Leedes in Yorkshire* (1724) · P. Collinson, *The religion of protestants* (1982) · *The correspondence of Dr Matthew Hutton, archbishop of York*, ed. [J. Raine], SurtS, 17 (1843) · F. Drake, *Eboracum, or, The history and antiquities of the city of York* (1736) · M. E. James, *Family, lineage and civil society: a study of society, politics and mentality in the Durham region, 1500–1640* (1974) · S. J. Watts and S. J. Watts, *From border to middle shire: Northumberland, 1586–1625* (1975) · R. Marchant, *The puritans and the church courts in the diocese of York, 1560–1642* (1960) · F. Heal, *Of prelates and princes: a study of the economic and social position of the Tudor episcopate* (1980) · R. R. Reid, *The king's council in the north* (1921) · C. M. Dent, *Protestant reformers in Elizabethan Oxford* (1983) · J. Strype, *Annals of the Reformation and establishment of religion … during Queen Elizabeth's happy reign*, new edn, 4 vols. (1824) · Wood, *Ath. Oxon.*, new edn, 2.869–77

Archives BL, corresp., Add. MSS 4274, fols. 16, 178, 231, 233, 237–8, 240, 242ff.; 4275, fols. 219, 234; 4277, fol. 66; 39829, fols. 81, 83 · Bodl. Oxf., notes of sermons at Oxford, MS Rawl. B. 323 · Borth. Inst., corresp. · PRO, state papers, domestic; official corresp. · York Minster, preaching diary, notes on sermons, Add. MS 18 | N. Yorks. CRO, Hutton MSS, letters

Likenesses oils, 1610, Christ Church Oxf. [*see illus.*] · oils, second version, 1616, NPG · R. Elstrack, line engraving (after Powell?), BM, NPG; repro. in A. M. Hind, *Engraving in England, 17th centuries*, 2 (1966), pl. 102 · funeral tomb effigy, York Minster · line engraving, BM, NPG; repro. in Boissard, *Bibliotecha chalcongraphica* (1650) · portrait, Auckland Castle, Durham · portrait, York Minster · portrait, NPG · portrait, Red Lodge, Bristol

Wealth at death over £3000—excl. lands: inventory, Borth. Inst., chancery wills, 1628

Matthew, Sir Toby [Tobie] (**1577–1655**), writer and courtier, was born at Salisbury on 3 October 1577, the first son of Tobie *Matthew (1544?–1628), later archbishop of York, and Frances, *née* Barlow (*d.* 1629) [*see* Matthew, Frances], widow of Matthew Parker, son of the former archbishop of Canterbury. On 13 March 1590 he matriculated at Christ Church, Oxford, where his father was dean; he graduated

Sir Toby Matthew (1577–1655), by James Gammon, pubd 1660

BA on 5 June 1594 and proceeded MA on 5 July 1597. He was selected to act in 1595 in a 'device' presented in the queen's presence for which Francis Bacon wrote the dialogue, which was the beginning of their lifelong friendship (Sutherland, 36). In 1598 he went to France to visit one of the Throckmortons of Coughton, but after returning was seriously ill. He showed an interest in politics after being admitted to Gray's Inn on 15 May 1599, and was returned as MP for the Cornish borough of Newport iuxta Launceston in the last Elizabethan parliament in 1601. He fell ill again 'with a long shrewd fit of his old infirmitie' (*Letters of John Chamberlain*, 1.144) in May 1602 but later, with Bacon's help, he was returned as MP for St Albans for the first session of parliament in 1604. Before it adjourned his political interest waned for, on 3 July 1604, he secured a licence to travel for three years.

Conversion In April 1605 Matthew went to The Hague to visit his friend Dudley Carleton and then to Italy, contrary to the wishes of his parents. In Florence he associated with resident English Catholics and then proceeded to Rome, where he often met the superior of the English Jesuits, Robert Persons, as well as Cardinal Pinelli. After he returned to Paris in January 1607 a spy informed William Trumbull: 'Mr. Mathew is neither fish nor flesh. He discourseth with priests and hath been at the mass, but of

late also at my lord ambassador's sermons' (*Downshire MSS*, 2.223). Matthew returned to Florence to attend the Lenten services and, as he wrote later: 'purposed fully to become a Roman Catholic' (Matthew, 'True historicall relation', 156). In late March at the church of the Annunciata a Jesuit preacher, Lelio Ptolemei, performed the traditional rites.

Upon his arrival in England, by September 1607, Matthew's conversion created a stir in the established church. There were planned serious polemical debates with Launcelot Andrews, bishop of Chichester, Alberico Gentili, professor of civil law at Oxford, Sir Christopher Perkins, and Thomas Morton, bishop of Chester. A tenacious adversary was George Bancroft, archbishop of Canterbury, who after many conferences sent him to the Fleet prison when he refused the oath of allegiance. In February 1608 Matthew was brought before the privy council, where the earl of Salisbury informed him that he was granted six weeks 'to set his affaires in order and depart the realme' (*Letters of John Chamberlain*, 1.255).

An odyssey of nine years In May 1608 Matthew settled down in Florence, where he regaled Dudley Carleton with news that he was in 'an excellent coole terrene' and able to 'eate good melons, drinke wholesome wines, looke upon excellent devout pictures [and] heer choyse musique' (Stoye, 79). However, a hostile visitor, Henry Wotton, ambassador to Venice, disdained him as a leader of 'a certain knot of bastard Catholiques … who with pleasantness of conversation and force of example do much harm' in their hospitality to English visitors (ibid., 76–7). In 1609 Matthew arrived in Madrid, where he joined the entourage of Sir Robert Shirley, who was commissioned by the shah of Persia to negotiate with Philip III a military alliance against the Turkish empire. Since the Spanish court was not ready to do this Shirley left for England but Matthew remained to visit famous sites and read the works of Spanish theologians. Meanwhile, between 1608 and 1614 he was engaged in a major poetical endeavour in which he composed a series of twenty-nine sonnets of high quality, of which eighteen reflected his private devotion to the saints and eleven others some very personal experiences. Apparently he dedicated these poems to George Gage (c.1582–1638), his close companion of these years.

Early in 1611 Matthew returned to Paris, where an informant wrote to Trumbull that he 'appeared stronger in his perversion and professing popery than ever', but in such poor health that 'at first we could scarce know him' (*Downshire MSS*, 3.12). In 1612 Gage and Matthew began a two-year tour of Italy, after arriving in Venice by way of Basel and Milan, so that they did not reach Rome until a long itinerary was completed. Here on 20 May 1614 Cardinal Bellarmine ordained Matthew to the priesthood. Later they visited Leipzig, where in March 1615 Matthew confided to the second earl of Arundel that he was there 'to satisfy my curiosity about these northern parts' and had concluded 'they are to be held little less than barbarous' (*Downshire MSS*, 5.154). Afterwards they purchased paintings in Flanders on behalf of Dudley Carleton. By this time the burden of travel and poor health forced Matthew to seek help from friends so as to return to England, although there were unfriendly voices at court such as Archbishop Abbot's, who advised Trumbull: 'I have little to say in favour of … Toby Matthew' and gave a long list of grievances (*Downshire MSS*, 5.532). Finally, after his parents appealed to Buckingham to influence King James, he was allowed to return to England in May 1617.

First translations Once again Matthew made an extended visit to Bacon at Gorhambury and as a token of gratitude he translated into Italian a collection of thirty-eight essays by the lord chancellor. In London his first book was printed in 1618 entitled *Saggi morali … con un altro trato della sapienza*, with a dedication to Cosimo (II) de' Medici, grand duke of Tuscany, wherein Matthew praised the high quality of Bacon's learning. More startling to the court was the news that Matthew had guided the conversion of Frances Brydges, second wife of the earl of Exeter, as Chamberlain lamented: 'I heard yt now two several wayes that he hath perverted her to become a Romane Catholique' (*Letters of John Chamberlain*, 2.128). Possibly this incident led King James to insist that Matthew take the oath of allegiance which, after his refusal, once again meant exile.

This, however, proved to be a productive period of writing, since between early 1619 and late 1621 Matthew published six books at St Omer: four translations of well-known Italian and Spanish writers; a fifth was his well-received version of Augustine's *Confessions*; and a sixth was his original essay in English on the value of private devotions entitled *The Widdowes Mite*. Published in 1619 this last work included his new poem of 32 pages named 'A Prayer for the Love of God'. The *Confessions*, which appeared in 1620, was the first English translation of Augustine's thirteen books in a text of 800 pages with a long preface and annotations added to help the reader. However, while his prose was elegant Matthew's accuracy was questioned at times, since he had to rely on a flawed Latin text. For his translations from the Italian he chose two unusual biographies: in 1619 he published the text, first translated by 'a dying Freind' of Vicenzo Puccini's *Suor Maria Magdalena de Patsi*, to which he added marginal notes and a preface (*The Life of the Holy and Venerable Mother*, sig. *3r*); and then in 1620 he brought out a version of Giuseppe Biondi's narrative of the repentance of a former bandit called *A Relation of the Death of … Troilo Savelli*. He commented in the preface that this latter story had already been translated into other languages, 'though not at all into ours, nor yet as carefully into others … as I could have wished' (sig. A1r–v). He also chose two leading Spanish writers. In 1620 appeared the *Audi filia: a Rich Cabinet of Spiritual Jewels* by Juan de Ávila, a famous preacher of the Counter-Reformation in Andalusia, who completed this popular tract in 1557. In 1621 Matthew published twenty chapters from the *Imitación de Cristo* by Francisco Arias, a Jesuit professor of theology in Córdoba, entitled *The Judge … how Christ … is to Judge the World*. Meanwhile, when Matthew learned that Bacon had suffered his political downfall Matthew wrote such an eloquent letter to him that Bacon commented that it seemed 'as if it had been in old gold'

and it may have been a source for his essay *De amicitia* (*Letters and Life of Francis Bacon*, 7.344–5).

The courts at Vienna and Madrid Although Matthew never received a diplomatic post officially he was asked twice to assist in major negotiations. In 1621 Lord John Digby asked him to be his principal agent and assistant in Vienna when he was ambassador-extraordinary to the court of Ferdinand II to discuss the palatinate crisis. Pleased with Matthew's skill in languages and political advice Digby later pleaded successfully on his behalf with King James and he was allowed to return to England by December. Back in London, Matthew completed *Of the Love of our Only Lord*, a new treatise, which was printed at St Omer in 1622 and contained ninety-six short chapters of his reflections. Of far greater satisfaction to him was the king's reception of him, which Chamberlain duly reported in September 1622. Apparently when Matthew went to visit his father he carried a message that the archbishop should 'now receve him to favour upon his reconciling to his Majestie' (*Letters of John Chamberlain*, 2.452). Soon after this Matthew, sensing a danger to the Catholic community, revealed to the duke of Buckingham in a letter of 29 September 1622 that there was a plan by certain 'indiscreet English Catholiques' to ask the pope to appoint five titular bishops for England that 'will much offend the kinge and many poore Catholiques … will yet smart for it in the end' (BL, Harley MS 1581, fol. 82). After his disclosure the plan did not proceed further.

Matthew's second unofficial diplomatic mission began in spring 1623 when the king asked him to assist Prince Charles and Buckingham in Madrid in the treaty to be negotiated for the marriage to the infanta. As a skilled linguist and friend of Gondomar and Digby, Matthew performed many services but an unusual one was his appeal in a letter to young Philip IV that protested the rigorous terms imposed on the prince by the 'theologi'. He warned that they would break up the treaty and leave the English Catholics 'in a lamentable state' unless their terms were reduced. He advised Philip 'to give the Prince some foot of ground … as whereupon he may with honour stay and perfect the treaty' (*Cabala*, 303). Upon Matthew's return to England, King James conferred a knighthood upon him at Royston on 20 October 1623, which was an extraordinary gesture to a Catholic priest. Matthew later wrote, in 1640, that 'a visible marke of particular honour' had been given to him by James, 'at the instance of his Majestie that now is' which implied that this was a reward for unusual services in Madrid (Matthew, 'Truc historicall relation', 158).

Matthew's father, having been dismayed at his conversion, now arranged a meeting of Sir Toby with several clergymen who sought to alter his views. Matthew, however, remained unmoved and wrote later: 'It was strange to see how they wrung their hands and their whites of eyes were turned up and their devout sighes were sent abroad' (Matthew, 'True historicall relation', 158). In November 1623 he had the role of chief mourner, 'clad in black cotton or bayes down to the heeles' in the obsequies at the Spanish embassy for the Catholics killed accidentally while attending mass at Blackfriars (*Letters of John Chamberlain*, 2.525).

Early in the reign of Charles I, Matthew produced a new series of translations. He began with thirty-four chapters from *The Practice of Perfection and Christian Virtues* (1609) by the well-known Castilian Jesuit, Alfonso Rodríguez (d. 1616), which appeared as *A Treatise of Mentall Prayer* in 1627. Later at St Omer he published in 1630 his second English tract anonymously entitled: *Charity Mistaken, with the Want Thereof Catholikes are Unjustly Charged*, which has been mistakenly attributed to Matthew Wilson. There followed in the same year translations of two different sections of the *Imitación de Cristo* of Francisco Arias: *A Treatise of Patience* and *A Treatise of Benignity*. Finally, in 1632 he published two other translations from Alfonso Rodríguez: *The Two First Treatises of … Christian Perfection* and *A Treatise of Humilitie*, that had forty chapters.

The courtier After 1630 Matthew appeared more frequently at the court, as can be seen in his letters to Henry Vane the elder, ambassador to The Hague, where details abound of royal favourites and of his own visits to the residences of notables. He especially admired the countess of Carlisle: 'the highest creature Sir Tobie has known in all kinds of excellency' (*CSP dom.*, 1631–3, 437). In June 1634 the marquis de Fontenay-Mareuil, an ambassador who had observed Matthew for three years, considered him 'the cleverest of the Catholic seminarists [secular clergy], a man of parts, active, influential, an excellent linguist', who was able to 'penetrate cabinets' and 'insinuate himself into all kinds of affairs and knows the temper and purpose of those who govern the kingdom, especially of the lord treasurer [Richard Weston]'. However, his sole ambition was 'the relief and benefit of the Catholics' (von Ranke, 5.448).

The marquis was correct in noting that Matthew had won the confidence of several influential courtiers. He accompanied Wentworth to Ireland for a brief period in 1633 and was a welcome visitor to Lord Cottington, Sir Francis Windebank, and Sir John Winter, secretary to Henrietta Maria. He was also regularly seen in the company of Endymion Porter, Kenelm Digby, and Walter Montague, who were prominent in Henrietta's court at Somerset House. However, many others resented Matthew's presence as the Newport affair in November 1637 proved. The conversion of Anne Boteler, wife of Mountjoy Blount, earl of Newport, enraged her husband, who publicly denounced Matthew and Walter Montague to King Charles for covertly influencing her. The anger of the king against the two men was so intense, although neither had been in fact involved, that Secretary Conway remarked: 'don Tobiah was in such perplexitie that I find he will make a very ill man to be a martyr' (Albion, 213 n. 2). It was later established that Anne Boteler had been influenced by her Catholic sister, her aunt, the duchess of Buckingham, and George Con, the papal representative to Henrietta.

During the first bishops' war in 1639 a political squib circulated that identified Matthew as an 'abettor' of a popish plot at the court, who encouraged Winter and Queen Marie de' Medici to make a 'laughing stock' of England (*CSP dom.*, 1639–40, 246). Later, another squib claimed that Winter and Matthew were 'court papists' who were informants of Rome (Hibbard, 126). In September 1640 a spy named Habernfeld disclosed to William Boswell, ambassador at The Hague, fanciful details of a 'Jesuitical' plot to murder King Charles and Archbishop Laud, wherein Toby Matthew had a leading role, since he was 'a most vigilant man of the chief heads … never quiet, always in action and perpetual motion' (ibid., 158–9). This sensational fiction led some radicals in the Long Parliament to denounce Matthew and others as treasonous 'court papists' who endangered the kingdom (ibid., 190–92). By 17 March 1641 both houses had voted that Matthew and two others must be banned from the precincts of the court at once. With imprisonment also likely Matthew sought protection at Raglan Castle with the earl of Worcester, but left England for the last time in April 1641.

Last years in Ghent Escaping the turmoil of the civil war Matthew found safety in the English Jesuit college at Ghent, where he started to write again. In 1642 there appeared *The Flaming Hart: the Life of the Glorious S. Teresa*, a translation of Teresa of Avila's autobiography. His preface noted that although it was translated earlier, that author 'seemed to have lost a little of the puritie of his owne Englishe tongue' but 'not to have acquired enough of the Spanish', and so a new text was called for (Allison and Rogers, 2.154). In 1647 his last book appeared in Louvain entitled *A Missive of Consolation … to the Catholics of England*. In eleven chapters he offered personal reflections from the Bible and philosophy on the virtue of patience which Catholics needed during their current trials. In the same year he made his last will in which he gave a major part of his personal estate to the English Jesuits and entrusted his manuscripts to Walter Montague. After a grave illness he died unmarried on 13 October 1655 at the English Jesuit college in Ghent and was buried in its chapel's crypt with his coffin inscribed: 'Hic jacet D. Tobias Matthaei'.

Matthew left unpublished two completed books. On 8 September 1640 he had finished a 234-page manuscript entitled: 'A true historicall relation of the conversion of Sir Tobie Matthew', which remained in private hands until lost in the nineteenth century. Before its disappearance W. C. Neligan selected excerpts at random for a limited private edition that has been used in later printings. In 1651 Matthew had made ready for publication 'The life of Lady Lucy Knatchbull', who died in 1629 after an exemplary career as abbess of the Benedictine convent in Ghent. This text survived unpublished until 1931 when it was edited by David Knowles.

Toby Matthew's career at the early Stuart court was notable for its striking reverses. Under James I he was exiled twice (1608–17 and 1619–22) but in 1623 was reconciled and knighted. Under Charles I he gained many influential friends but in 1641 suffered demonization as a court papist in parliament and fled to Flanders. His achievement as a writer, despite exile and illness, was significant indeed. His superior linguistic skills enabled him to prepare polished English versions of not only classic autobiographies by Augustine and Teresa, but also translations of two unusual biographies by Italian authors and nine recent treatises on spirituality by leading Spanish contemporaries. He also produced four personal essays of pastoral advice for his beleaguered fellow Catholics in Britain.

A. J. LOOMIE

Sources [T. Matthew], 'A true historicall relation of the conversion of Sir Tobie Matthew', in W. H. Smith, *Bacon and Shakespeare* (1857), 155–62 • A. G. Petti, 'Unknown sonnets by Sir Toby Matthew', *Recusant History*, 9 (1967–8), 123–58 • A. F. Allison and D. M. Rogers, eds., *The contemporary printed literature of the English Counter-Reformation between 1558 and 1640*, 2 (1994) • C. M. Hibbard, *Charles I and the Popish Plot* (1983) • *The letters of John Chamberlain*, ed. N. E. McClure, 2 vols. (1939) • *Report on the manuscripts of the marquis of Downshire*, 6 vols. in 7, HMC, 75 (1924–95), vols. 2–3, 5 • *The letters and life of Francis Bacon*, ed. J. Spedding, 7 vols. (1861–74), vol. 7 • J. W. Stoye, *English travellers abroad, 1604–1667*, rev. edn (1989) • N. M. Sutherland, 'Matthew, Tobias (1577–1655) of London', HoP, *Commons, 1558–1603* • L. von Ranke, *A history of England, principally in the seventeenth century*, 5 (1875) • *Cabala, sive, Scrinia sacra: mysteries of state and government in letters of illustrious persons*, 3rd edn (1691) • *CSP dom.*, 1603–49 • *The journal of Sir Simon D'Ewes*, ed. W. Notestein (1923) • *Memorials of affairs of state in the reigns of Q. Elizabeth and K. James I, collected (chiefly) from the original papers of … Sir Ralph Winwood*, ed. E. Sawyer, 3 vols. (1725), vol. 3 • G. Albion, *Charles I and the court of Rome* (1935) • *STC, 1475–1640* • Wing, *STC* • *A true historical relation of the conversion of Sir Tobie Matthew*, ed. A. H. Matthew (1904) • BL, Harley MS 1581, fol. 82 • *DNB*
Archives BL, letters to Lord Doncaster, Egerton MSS 2592–2595
Likenesses J. Gammon, line engraving, BM, NPG; repro. in T. Matthew, ed., *A collection of letters* (1660) [*see illus.*]

Matthews. *See also* Mathews.

Matthews, Alfred Edward [Matty] (1869–1960), actor, was born at Bridlington, Yorkshire, on 22 November 1869, the son of William Matthews (1829/30–1906) and his wife, Alice Mary Long. His father was one of the Matthews brothers of the original Christy Minstrels and his great-uncle was the famous clown Thomas Matthews, who had been a pupil of Grimaldi. He was educated at Stamford, Lincolnshire. Thereafter, according to his own story (Matthews had plenty of stories), he proceeded to an office-boy's desk in London on which were carved the initials 'J. H. B.', which he was told were those of Henry Irving, whose original name was Brodribb. Inspired by this coincidence he got himself a job as a theatre call-boy. He soon rose, via stage management and understudying to touring actor and in, 1889, he toured South Africa with Lionel Brough. In 1893–6 he toured Australia and then returned to the West End of London in a long list of plays. In 1909 he married Caroline May (1875–1953), divorced wife of Richard Cave Chinn and daughter of James Blackwell. Under the name May Blayney she enjoyed a relatively successful stage career. They had twin sons and a daughter; the marriage ended in divorce. In 1910 he made his first trip to New York, where he played Algernon Moncrieffe in Oscar Wilde's *The Importance of being Earnest*, his wife playing Cecily Cardew. By then Matty (as he was often known) was in great demand at home and overseas, and he had appeared in plays by Pinero, Galsworthy, and Barrie.

After the First World War, Matthews replaced such actors as Gerald Du Maurier (in Sapper's *Bulldog Drummond*, 1921, New York and London), Owen Nares, or Ronald Squire. Yet, at all times, like other actors in his constellation, his star, though minor, was truefixed and constant, only waiting for the opportunity to show it had no fellow in its chosen firmament. It had to wait another twenty years. Meanwhile, however, in the twenty-five years after 1918, he was in a further thirty different plays. In 1940 he married the actress Patricia Lilian, divorced wife of William Robson Davies and daughter of Jeremiah O'Herlihy, solicitor. Her stage name was Pat Desmond.

Matthews began his connection with the film industry early, being in 1916–18 managing director of the British Actors' Film Company. He regularly appeared in films, including *The Lackey and the Lady* (1919), *Quiet Wedding* (1940), *Three Men in a Boat* (1956), and (made shortly before his death) *Inn for Trouble* (1960).

In 1947, in his seventy-eighth year, A. E. Matthews at last became a great star in his own right in the line of Sir Charles Hawtrey and Du Maurier—the part was the Earl of Lister, the play William Douglas-Home's *The Chiltern Hundreds*, the theatre the Vaudeville, where he had once been call-boy. In 1949 he went to New York in the same play (renamed *Yes, M'Lord*) and he then returned to make the film at Pinewood in his eightieth year. He was appointed OBE in 1951; he published *Matty*, his autobiography, in 1952; he repeated his success as Lord Lister in a sequel to *The Chiltern Hundreds* in 1954; and he went on acting in both films and plays. Aged ninety, he was indomitable to the last and working still: 'How do I do it?' he echoed an enquiring reporter, 'Easy! I look in the obituary column of *The Times* at breakfast and, if my name's not in it, I go off to the studio.'

Matty was a playwright's dream: the grand old man of the theatre without being remotely grand; the oldest actor acting with the youngest mind; the best-dressed member of the Garrick Club, even though he would travel by underground on a wet day in a deerstalker hat and a pyjama coat over his tweed suit and gumboots. He knew more about the technique of light-comedy acting than many of his colleagues, yet, such was his spontaneity, he succeeded in giving the impression that he knew nothing at all. On stage he was as selfish as any actor ever was but in private he was kindness personified. He was crotchety but he had a heart of gold. He was unpredictable, easily bored, perhaps a shade close with the drinks, but he had as much charm as any man in any other walk of life and he loved beauty in women and animals and he encouraged youth. Matthews died at Bushey Heath on 25 July 1960.

WILLIAM DOUGLAS-HOME, rev. K. D. REYNOLDS

Sources *The Times* (26 July 1960) • A. E. Matthews, *Matty* (1951) • J. Parker, ed., *Who's who in the theatre*, 6th edn (1930) • *Halliwell's filmgoer's companion*, 5th edn (1976) • R. Low, *The history of the British film, 1918–1929* (1971) • *WWW* • personal knowledge (1971) • private information (1971)

Matthews, Sir Bryan Harold Cabot (1906–1986), physiologist, was born on 14 June 1906 in Clifton, Bristol, the younger son and youngest of the three children of Harold Evan Matthews, manufacturing pharmacist, who had a factory and shop in Clifton, and his wife, Sarah Susannah

(Ruby) Harrison, pharmacist. His elder brother was Leonard Harrison *Matthews, zoologist. Educated at Clifton College, Bristol, and at King's College, Cambridge, he graduated second class in part one (1926) and first class in part two (1927) of the natural sciences tripos.

Matthews worked in Cambridge all his life except during the Second World War. In 1928 he became Beit memorial fellow for medical research, and in 1932 assistant director of research, a post he held until 1948. Before the war he made a major contribution to the development of neurophysiology. Previously single nerve impulses had been recorded, but only with difficulty and distortion; now Matthews developed an instrument, the moving iron oscillograph, with its associated amplifiers, which had the necessary sensitivity and frequency response to record single nerve impulses. Moreover, it was easily photographed, unlike the cathode ray oscilloscopes. With this system he worked out the basic physiology of muscle spindles, including mammalian spindles, work which formed the basis of much subsequent receptor and control system physiology. With E. D. Adrian, and using his newly developed differential amplifier, he investigated potentials from the surface of the brain and from the human brain through the skull, laying the foundation for later electroencephalography. He also worked with D. H. Barron on the potentials which could be recorded from spinal roots. This work advanced knowledge of the way nerve impulses converge on cells in the spinal cord and set up graded potential changes, which in turn initiate further impulses in other nerve cells.

During this time in Cambridge Matthews also developed his interest in high altitudes. He started with a theoretical study showing that heat lost through breathing becomes greater than that gained from the utilization of oxygen at altitudes above 30,000 feet. He participated as a subject in work on the effects of prolonged exposure to low oxygen tensions, and in this and many experiments during the war he was prepared to act as a subject in situations which were potentially dangerous. In 1935 he was a member of an expedition to the Andes to study physiology at high altitudes. He spent longer at the highest camp than anyone else and made significant scientific as well as physical contributions to the expedition.

In August 1939 Matthews moved to Farnborough to head the Royal Air Force physiological laboratory, which in 1944 became the RAF Institute of Aviation Medicine, with Matthews as its first director. He had great success both in his own work and as director of the laboratory in finding quick and easy solutions to immediate and important problems facing aircrew: lack of oxygen, decompression sickness, and acceleration. At the same time he laid the foundations for the more sophisticated solutions needed for the jet age.

After the war Matthews returned to Cambridge in 1946 and in 1948 became a reader in physiology. He was professor of physiology from 1952 to 1973. He continued his research on the nervous system, but his main task, as head of the department, was to build it up again once staff could be recruited. His overriding priority was to recruit only those of outstanding scientific ability. He made changes in the administration of the department, with a view to improving the distribution of resources, and left his staff to develop their own ideas. He was a fellow of King's College from 1929, director of studies there from 1948 to 1952, and a life fellow from 1973. He became a fellow of the Royal Society in 1940 and was a vice-president in 1957 and 1958. Appointed CBE in 1944, he was knighted in 1952.

An imposing bearded figure, Matthews had a vigorous personality and was a friendly, likeable, and at times commanding person. He had a love of activities with an element of challenge to the natural elements, such as skiing, canoeing, and, above all, long-distance sailing. He cruised widely and spent much time at sea. He was an expert navigator and developed instruments and techniques for use in cruising short-handed, some of which became commonplace. In 1926 he married Rachel Katherine (d. 1994), daughter of Gustav Eckhard, Manchester shipping agent, and sister of the wife of the economist F. W. Paish. They had a son, Professor P. B. C. Matthews FRS, neurophysiologist, as well as two daughters. Their marriage broke up at the beginning of the war and he was then supported for nearly thirty years by the close friendship of his sailing companion, Constance Biron, who changed her name to Matthews by deed poll. In 1970, after his relationship with Constance had come to an end, he divorced Rachel and in the same year married Audrey Wentworth, widow of Air Vice-Marshal William Kilpatrick Stewart and daughter of Francis Tyndale, a lieutenant-colonel in the Royal Army Medical Corps. Matthews died in Cambridge on 23 July 1986.   JOHN GRAY, rev.

Sources *Annual Report of the Council* [King's College, Cambridge] (1987) · J. Gray, *Memoirs FRS*, 35 (1990), 265–79 · personal knowledge (1996) · private information (1996) · *CGPLA Eng. & Wales* (1986)
Likenesses photograph, repro. in Gray, *Memoirs FRS*, 265
Wealth at death £116,243: probate, 29 Oct 1986, *CGPLA Eng. & Wales*

Matthews [*née* Marlar], **Charlotte** (*bap.* **1759**, *d.* **1802**), businesswoman, was baptized Charlotta Marlar on 23 March 1759 at the church of All Hallows-the-Great, London, the second of the six children of John Marlar (1712–1791), merchant and banker, and his wife, Ann (d. 1800). She married William Matthews (d. 1792), merchant, on 1 August 1776 at Monken Hadley, Middlesex. During their marriage, which was childless, they lived at 6 Green Lettice Lane in the City of London, and at Croydon Lodge, near Croydon, Surrey. Although it is not known how or where Charlotte was educated she was literate at the time of her marriage, during which she appears to have received the training that enabled her to run her husband's business successfully after his death.

Depending on the custom of the trade or borough many widows carried on their late husbands' businesses on their own account. It appears that in the years of her marriage Charlotte Matthews had discovered a latent talent for, and love of, commercial life that she had no intention of surrendering. In the ten years of her widowhood she brought her experience of business, learned under the tutelage of her husband, to the enterprise that she now controlled. She worked long hours, attending business meetings, which necessitated her walking between venues in the City, as well as spending much time in her counting house, supervising her two male clerks, who had also worked for her husband, and making up the books. She rationalized William Matthews's many commercial interests, retaining only those that she considered essential. She disposed of his London house and, in 1795, moved to 13 London Street, Fenchurch Street, which remained her town home and office until her death. In these premises, chosen to suit her new business profile, she concentrated on insurance, banking, and bill discounting. She was elected a member of Lloyds of London, by virtue of being William Matthews's widow. She transacted business with many major London banking and merchant houses, moved her funds between several bank accounts, and was the part owner of a ship, the *Sally*, which traded to the Levant.

There was one business connection of William Matthews's that Charlotte Matthews was most anxious to continue: his provision of credit to the Birmingham partnership of Boulton and Watt. They were not the only customers for her banking services but they were probably the most well known, and it is arguable that Matthew Boulton and James Watt would have found it difficult to fulfil their contracts without her assistance. She provided them with regular and reliable credit to facilitate the production and sale of the numerous and very different items made on their Birmingham premises, from buttons to steam engines, from coins to silver tableware. The moneys she advanced were unsecured, and were dependent on a relationship of mutual trust. They were enormous for their time and fluctuated between a few thousand and many tens of thousands of pounds, repayable from remittances which Charlotte Matthews received on their behalf. She also used her contacts in the City of London to answer Boulton and Watts's enquiries about the financial soundness of potential customers, and to report how the money markets were moving and popular reaction to contemporary events. She was well known as their agent, active in the pursuit of their interests in London, and solicited for introductions by people who wanted to do business with them. She negotiated on their behalf with officials of the government and of the East India Company to ensure that contracts were executed and payments made to the partners. Copper coins minted by Boulton on behalf of the British government in 1797–9 were distributed to the public from her London premises as well as from the Soho Mint in Birmingham.

Despite her extensive business interests Charlotte Matthews enjoyed a full social life. She dined with friends and attended the theatre; she was an accomplished and knowledgeable horsewoman. She was a woman with a gift for friendship, who helped to hold together a network of business and sociability for, without the protection of limited liability or formal credit vetting agencies, it was important to know as much as possible of the personal lives and reputations of those with whom one did business. She continued the exchange of visits, initiated during her husband's lifetime, with Boulton and Watt, and enjoyed, during her widowhood, annual holidays at Boulton's Birmingham home, Soho House. She provided a sympathetic audience for Boulton, flattering him and fussing over his health. It was a friendship he valued highly.

Charlotte Matthews died at Croydon Lodge on 9 January 1802, aged forty-three, after an illness of a few weeks' duration. She was buried on 16 January 1802 at the church of St John the Baptist, Croydon, but her body was subsequently removed to an unknown resting place. For the purposes of legacy duty her personal estate was valued at £5000; she left most of her property to her sisters and nieces and nephews. Her business was taken over by the sons of Boulton and Watt, who continued to employ her two clerks, as their London banking operation. They closed the business in 1833. CHRISTINE WISKIN

Sources Birm. CL, Matthew Boulton MSS, boxes 281, 325/327 · W. R. Dawson, *The roll of Lloyds* (1931) · H. W. Dickinson and R. Jenkins, *James Watt and the steam engine* (1927) · IGI · parish register, 16 Jan 1802, St John the Baptist, Croydon, Surrey [burial]
Archives Birm. CA, corresp. with Matthew Boulton, boxes 325–7
Wealth at death £5000: PRO, death duty registers, IR 26/59/99; will, PRO, PROB 11/368/49

Matthews, Denis James (1919–1988), pianist and composer, was born on 27 February 1919 in Coventry, the only child of Arthur Matthews, director of the Norman Engineering Company at Leamington Spa, and his wife, Elsie Culver, schoolteacher. His father committed suicide when Denis was twelve. He was educated at Warwick grammar school, where his musical gifts brought him to the attention of visiting adjudicators including Herbert Howells, who encouraged him to consider a career in music. Another was the pianist Harold Craxton, who offered to teach him. He won the Thalberg scholarship to the Royal Academy of Music in 1935, and studied composition with William Alwyn and the piano with Craxton, who welcomed him into a large and musical family circle, giving him a home as well as tuition and encouragement. His interests were initially in composition, and early works included songs and chamber music, which he later described as 'cosily derivative and romantic'. However, a piano trio, performed at a student concert, excited favourable press attention; and in 1937 he added a composition scholarship to that for piano. His performing and composing abilities were sometimes combined, as when Sir Henry Wood conducted his symphonic movement for piano and orchestra. The list of his compositions eventually included a violin sonata, five sketches for violin and piano, a string quartet, and a partita for wind quintet for a fellow student, the horn player Dennis Brain.

Though some of his works were taken up by performers, and even published, Matthews found that his deepening interest in the classics—Bach, Mozart, and Beethoven, in particular—was directing him towards playing. His professional début came with a Promenade Concert in 1939, when he played Beethoven's third piano concerto under

Sir Henry Wood. Beethoven was to remain central to his interests, and was the subject of many lecture recitals, some records expounding the sketch-books, and two BBC music guide booklets, *Beethoven Piano Sonatas* (1967) and *Brahms Piano Music* (1978). Matthews's writings also included a chapter on Beethoven, Schubert, and Brahms in a symposium he edited, *Keyboard Music* (1972), *Arturo Toscanini* (1982), and an autobiography, *In Pursuit of Music* (1966).

Having graduated from the Royal Academy of Music in 1940 with the LRAM (to which he added the Royal College of Music's ARCM, as well as the Worshipful Company of Musicians medal, 1938, for the most distinguished student), Matthews earned a living accompanying for opera and ballet classes, playing for social occasions such as City dinners, and occasionally giving concerts either alone or with student friends. He remained all his life an excellent sonata pianist, though latterly he seldom accompanied singers in lieder.

In 1940 Matthews was called up, entered the Royal Air Force, and, together with a number of other musicians who were to go on to make distinguished careers, joined the RAF central band at Uxbridge. He toured Germany at the end of the war with the central band, playing piano solos at the Potsdam conference to Josef Stalin, Winston Churchill, and Harry S. Truman. He also shared the keyboard with Truman.

Demobilized in 1946, Matthews was taken up by musicians including Dame Myra Hess, and solo engagements began to come in. He played concertos with John Barbirolli, Malcolm Sargent, Sir Thomas Beecham, Sir Adrian Boult, and other leading conductors, and toured widely; he had also begun making records in 1941, in a repertory centring on Mozart and Beethoven (and including a classic version of Beethoven's horn sonata with Dennis Brain), but also embracing modern British composers. He was closely associated with the London Mozart Players, founded in 1949 by another friend from the central band, Harry Blech. Concerts and recordings brought him wide popularity, and he embarked upon a career that took him all round the world. In 1955 he settled in Henley, where he and his friends took part in festival music-making. However, divorce in 1960 brought him back to London.

With the emergence of a post-war generation of virtuosi, Matthews found his career prospering less well in the 1960s. To his friends, he was candid about his powers, believing that he had been fortunate to make a career at a time when competition was less fierce. He was never a great technician, but the musicality of his playing gave his performances at their best an illuminating quality, and a sense of the music's essential structure and meaning. His interest in conveying this found a new outlet when in 1971 he was invited to be the first professor of music at the University of Newcastle. He ran an enterprising and successful department, while continuing to maintain a performing career. He retired in 1984. He was appointed CBE in 1975, and had honorary degrees from St Andrews (1973), Hull (1978), and Warwick (1982).

Though prey to private melancholy, Matthews was an amusing and warm-hearted companion. He was slightly built, with sandy hair and an expressive face that remained impassive during performance but could take on a lively, animated expression in the discussions about music which were his greatest joy. He retained a somewhat boyish appearance and manner. He married three times. In 1941 he married Mira Howe, a cellist, and they had one son and three daughters. The marriage was dissolved in 1960 and in 1963 he married Brenda, who had been brought up by Dr Samuel McDermott, a general practitioner in Swindon, and taken his surname. They had one son and one daughter. The marriage was dissolved in 1985 and in 1986 he married Beryl, a piano teacher, daughter of Arthur Harold Jordan Perry, owner of a textile firm. Matthews died by his own hand in Birmingham, on 24 December 1988, having suffered from bouts of severe depression, particularly after his marriage to Brenda McDermott broke up.   JOHN WARRACK, *rev.*

Sources D. Matthews, *In pursuit of music* (1966) [autobiography] · *The Independent* (28 Dec 1988) · private information (1996) · personal knowledge (1996) · *CGPLA Eng. & Wales* (1990) **Archives** U. St Andr. L., letters to Cedric Thorpe Davie **Likenesses** photograph, Hult. Arch. **Wealth at death** £110,848: probate, 9 March 1990, *CGPLA Eng. & Wales*

Matthews, Drummond Hoyle (1931–1997), geologist and marine geophysicist, was born on 5 February 1931 at 29 Devonshire Street, St Marylebone, London, the only child of Charles Bertram Matthews (1897–1942), solicitor, and his wife, Enid Mary Hoyle (1899–1966). Throughout his life he was universally known as Drum. His father, who was a captain in the Royal Flying Corps in the First World War, had been badly wounded and traumatized during heavy aerial combat in March 1918. As a result, after the war, he moved to Porlock, Somerset, to help run a family horse-riding school. Matthews's love of the outdoors, and of the sea, sailing, and ships in particular, undoubtedly derived from his childhood experiences at Porlock. For much of the Second World War he attended The Downs preparatory school in Malvern, transferring in 1944 to Bryanston School in Dorset. At both schools he attained the position of head boy, admired by staff and peers alike for his reliability and integrity, and his thoughtfulness for others. At Bryanston he was instrumental in reviving interest in the sea cadets, and on leaving in 1949 undertook his national service within the Royal Navy. This provided him with additional training in seamanship and leadership which was to prove valuable in his subsequent career. At the end of his national service he was a sub-lieutenant on HMS *Gravelines*, and he remained a member of the Royal Naval Volunteer Reserve until 1967, when he was awarded the Royal Naval Volunteer Reserve officers' decoration.

From 1951 to 1955 Matthews studied natural sciences at King's College, Cambridge. In 1954 he obtained a first in part one and was awarded an exhibition by the college. In part two he specialized in geology and petrology and he and others hoped that he would go on to study for a PhD. However, following a disappointing result in his final examinations, he took a job as a geologist with the

Drummond Hoyle Matthews (1931–1997), by Godfrey Argent Studios

Falkland Islands Dependencies Survey (later to become the British Antarctic Survey). During the next two years he spent three arduous field seasons in the South Orkney Islands, producing a geological map of Coronation Island and helping to map part of Signy Island. In late 1957, following his return to the UK, he was diagnosed as having diabetes, which meant that he was unable to carry out further field work in the Antarctic. He returned to Cambridge in January 1958 to embark on a PhD under Maurice Hill, his mentor as an undergraduate in King's College and head of the marine geophysics group of the department of geodesy and geophysics. As the first geologist to be recruited by this group, he was assigned the task of studying rocks dredged from the north-east Atlantic Ocean. In 1960 he was awarded a fellowship at King's College and became a senior assistant in research at the department of geodesy and geophysics, positions he held until 1966. He gained his PhD in 1961 and was then appointed to organize the initial British contribution to the International Indian Ocean Expedition.

In late 1962, aboard HMS *Owen*, Matthews set himself the unusual and then difficult task of surveying in detail a relatively small area (50 x 40 nautical miles) on the crest of the Carlsberg Ridge in the north-west Indian Ocean. It was the data from this survey that led to his best-known work. Together with his first graduate student, Fred Vine, he suggested that the linear anomalies in the earth's magnetic field over oceanic areas might be due to a combination of sea-floor spreading from the crests of the mid-

ocean ridges, such as the Carlsberg Ridge, and reversals of the earth's magnetic field. Although initially regarded as too speculative a hypothesis, within a few years it was convincingly confirmed following the acquisition of additional data. This led to widespread acceptance of the validity of sea-floor spreading and continental drift, and paved the way for the formulation of the plate tectonic paradigm. This provides a unified explanation for the major topographic features at the solid earth's surface such as major faults, mountain ranges, mid-ocean ridges, and oceanic trenches.

On 1 May 1963 Matthews married (Elizabeth) Rachel McMullen (b. 1939), social worker, daughter of Launcelot McMullen, brewer. They had one son and one daughter. Following the untimely death of Maurice Hill in 1966, Matthews was promoted to be assistant director of research and appointed head of the marine geophysics group. Under his leadership during the following sixteen years the group, typically fifteen to twenty strong at any one time, took part in seventy-two cruises and expeditions and published nearly 200 papers. These included studies of plate boundaries such as the Azores–Gibraltar 'ridge', the Gulf of Oman, and the Hellenic arc, and the development of new seismic refraction techniques that revealed thinning of the continental crust beneath the North Sea basin. The latter provided compelling evidence for a radical model for the development of such sedimentary basins proposed at that time (1978) by Dan McKenzie.

By the late 1970s the period of remarkable discoveries relating to the evolution and structure of the deep-sea floor was coming to an end and Matthews sensed the need to change tack. In 1979 he spent a sabbatical at Cornell University, with Jack Oliver, to learn about the US land-based deep-crustal seismics programme, for by then knowledge of the structure of the deep continental crust was lagging way behind that for oceanic areas. On returning to the UK, and together with Derek Blundell, he was successful in obtaining funds to set up the British Institutions Reflection Profiling Syndicate (BIRPS), and in 1982 he became its first scientific director. In 1971 he had been appointed to the permanent position of reader in marine geology in the department of geodesy and geophysics. However he chose to resign from this post, and to be reappointed to a three-year contract, so that the marine geophysics group could continue separately under new leadership.

In using marine seismic techniques to study continental crust covered by shallow seas, notably around the British Isles, BIRPS obtained much better data than comparable programmes that were, unavoidably, restricted to land areas. It revealed previously unknown structures in the lower crust and upper mantle to a depth of 50 km. Appropriately one of the most significant profiles was the DRUM (Deep Reflections from the Upper Mantle) profile north of Scotland. In the light of its outstanding success, funding for the BIRPS project was repeatedly renewed; but in 1990, in failing health, Matthews took early retirement. His long struggle with diabetes had led to a deteriorating heart condition and in 1989 he suffered a heart attack.

From 1980 to 1990 he was a fellow of Wolfson College, Cambridge. He enjoyed a very happy retirement, initially in Porlock and then in Wells, Somerset, with his second wife, Sandra (Sandie) Adam (b. 1949/50), author, daughter of Frank Trevor Howard Whiting, builder. They had married on 17 June 1987, Matthews's first marriage having ended in divorce in 1980.

Matthews was an unassuming, often self-deprecating person with an unusual, often whimsical, sense of humour. His legacy was a greatly improved understanding of the evolution of the earth's surface and numerous students who themselves became established and respected scientists. His outstanding contributions to geology and geophysics were recognized by election to fellowship of the Royal Society in 1974 and by numerous honours and prizes, including the Balzan prize in 1982. He died of a heart attack, at Taunton Hospital, Somerset, on 20 July 1997, and was buried in Porlock church on 29 July. He was survived by both wives, and by the two children of his first marriage.

F. J. VINE

Sources R. S. White, *Memoirs FRS*, 45 (1999), 275–94 · curriculum vitae, U. Cam., department of earth sciences, Matthews MSS · R. White and others, *Old Bryanston Yearbook*, 62 (1998), 77–86 · *WWW* [forthcoming] · R. S. White, 'Drummond Hoyle Matthews', *Nature*, 388 (1997), 524 · *The Independent* (1 Aug 1997) · *The Independent* (14 Aug 1997) · *The Times* (12 Aug 1997) · *The Guardian* (14 Aug 1997) · b. cert. · m. certs. · personal knowledge (2004) · private information (2004)
Archives U. Cam., department of earth sciences
Likenesses Godfrey Argent Studios, photograph, c.1974, RS; repro. in *The Independent* (1 Aug 1997) · Godfrey Argent Studios, photograph, Godfrey Argent Studios [*see illus.*] · photograph (after his retirement), U. Cam., department of earth sciences · two photographs, repro. in White, *Memoirs FRS*
Wealth at death £271,875: probate, 19 Dec 1997, *CGPLA Eng. & Wales*

Matthews, Henry (1789–1828), judge and traveller, fifth son of John *Matthews (d. 1826), physician and poet, of Belmont, Herefordshire, and Elizabeth (1756/7–1823), daughter of Arthur Ellis of Marcle, Herefordshire, was born in Hereford on 21 June 1789. He was educated at Eton College and at King's College, Cambridge, graduating BA in 1812 and MA in 1815. He was a fellow of King's from 1811 until 1821. In 1817 ill health forced him to the continent, where he travelled widely, and on returning he published *The Diary of an Invalid* (1820), which enjoyed considerable success. In 1821 he was called to the bar at Lincoln's Inn, and married Emma (d. 1861), daughter of William Blount, of Orleton Manor, Herefordshire, in August; they had a son and two daughters. In November 1821 he was appointed advocate fiscal of Ceylon, an office he held until his promotion in October 1827 to the judicial bench. His contemporaries thought him a fine advocate: quick-thinking and accurate but not unfeeling or unduly harsh. He died in Ceylon on 20 May 1828 and was buried in St Peter's Church, Colombo. His only son, Henry *Matthews, was made Viscount Llandaff in 1895.

THOMPSON COOPER, rev. KATHERINE PRIOR

Sources J. P. Lewis, *List of inscriptions on tombstones and monuments in Ceylon of historical or local interest, with an obituary of persons*

uncommemorated (1913), 13–14 · Venn, *Alum. Cant.* · H. E. C. Stapylton, *The Eton school lists, from 1791 to 1850*, 2nd edn (1864) · HoP, *Commons* · Burke, *Peerage* (1939)
Likenesses lithograph, BM, NPG

Matthews, Henry, Viscount Llandaff (1826–1913), lawyer and politician, was born on 13 January 1826 in Ceylon, the second of three children and only son of Henry *Matthews (1789–1828), a puisne judge in Ceylon, and his wife, Emma (d. 1861). His father, the son of John *Matthews of Belmont, Herefordshire, was of Welsh descent. His mother, the daughter of William Blount, of Orleton, Herefordshire, came of an old Catholic family. His father dying young, his mother took him with her at the age of six to live in Paris. His education was varied and cosmopolitan. He attended a school run by a German protestant, but was brought up in the Roman Catholic faith, to which he remained conspicuously loyal. In his youth he met such celebrities as Lamartine, Guizot, and Macaulay. Debarred by his religion from Oxford and Cambridge, he graduated at the Sorbonne as *bachelier-ès-lettres* at the precocious age of sixteen, before proceeding in 1845 to University College, London, where he took his BA with first-class honours in classics and mathematics in 1847 and an LLB in 1849. He was called to the bar at Lincoln's Inn in 1850.

After a slow start, Matthews gradually acquired a large legal practice in London and the leading practice on the Oxford circuit. To 'a mind of lightning acumen' he added meticulous preparation and an extraordinary proficiency in foreign languages which enabled him to examine witnesses in Italian, German, and even Yiddish. He was an authority on canon law and in such recondite areas as Austrian, Roman-Dutch, and old French law. He took silk in 1868. Trials in which he distinguished himself as counsel included *Borghese* v. *Borghese* (1860–63), which concerned the will of the last Catholic earl of Shrewsbury; *Lyon* v. *Home* (1868), an action for the return of moneys advanced to a so-called 'spiritualist'; and the Tichborne case (1869). His cross-examination of Sir Charles Dilke in the divorce proceedings in *Crawford* v. *Crawford* (1886) was considered masterly: it helped to destroy Dilke's political career and to launch his own. 'This man must have office,' Queen Victoria declared (Leslie, 7).

Yet Matthews's mannered style of advocacy, much admired on the circuit, was also frowned on as theatrical; and despite his success at the bar, which reached its height between 1874 and 1886, he was never seriously considered for the bench. On his mother's death in 1861, followed by that of three aunts, he inherited considerable private means which freed him from dependence on his practice. Tall, upstanding, with jet black hair, a fine physique, and commanding presence, he was an engaging public speaker and conversationalist, with a well-stocked, cultivated, and literary mind, and a fashionable bon vivant, who joined in the festivities of the bar mess and rode enthusiastically to hounds. He travelled abroad, frequented the main European capitals, and regularly wintered in Vienna. He became widely known for his charm, intelligence, and wit, and as an eligible bachelor, though

Henry Matthews, Viscount Llandaff (1826–1913), by Sir Benjamin Stone, 1895

he never married. Behind his elaborate punctilio lay a certain reserve.

In 1868, standing as an independent Liberal-Conservative, Matthews won the Irish borough of Dungarvon. As a Catholic, he then voted with Gladstone for the disestablishment of the Church of Ireland in 1869. Disraeli held out to him the prospect of office as solicitor-general; but he lost Dungarvon in the general election of 1874 and failed to regain a seat until the general election of 1886, when he was returned for East Birmingham, the first Conservative to represent that city. His ability in a celebrated case persuaded Lord Randolph Churchill to secure his unexpected appointment as home secretary in Lord Salisbury's first administration. He was the first Roman Catholic since the reign of Elizabeth I to become a minister of the crown.

Matthews proved a conscientious official, but not the successful politician which his talents seemed to promise; and his career as home secretary from 1886 to 1892 was dogged with controversy. As a parliamentarian, he failed to win the confidence of the House of Commons. He lacked the common touch. The wit which delighted the bar he considered unbecoming in the house, and declined to indulge. His forensic fluency at the dispatch box passed for legerdemain, and his elegance of address, polished, courtly, deliberate, and aloof, was caricatured by 'Spy' as a flippant and languid complacency. He was likened to a Jesuit and even to 'a French dancing master'. Indeed Alphonse Daudet was astonished to learn that he was not a Frenchman. In a number of murder cases, when it was his duty to determine whether to recommend reprieve from execution, his decisions gave rise to criticism, sometimes

rancorous, especially in the radical press. In the case of Israel Lipski (1887), his decision to let the law take its course was vindicated by Lipski's eleventh-hour confession. Through his failure to satisfy the Commons over the questionable arrest of Elizabeth Cass (1887), however, the government actually lost a division; and in the case of the Davies brothers (1890), who killed their father for maltreating their mother, his decision to reprieve the younger, a boy of sixteen, while allowing sentence to stand in the case of his twenty-year-old brother, was widely condemned. Privately he opposed capital punishment and agonized over his decisions; but his mind once made up, he disdained to bend to popular agitation or conciliate his critics. His fair-mindedness was commended by Lord Chief Justice Coleridge; but his parliamentary 'indiscretions' suggested to Lord Salisbury 'an innocence of the ways of the world which no one could have expected in a criminal lawyer of sixty' (Southgate, 134). He concealed his genuine humanity behind an impassive public mask, his fastidious integrity was taken for airy indifference, and he was denounced for being 'as hard as the marble chimney-pieces of Whitehall' (Leslie, 9). Also damaging to his career were the violent public disorders in Trafalgar Square on 'Bloody Sunday', 13 November 1887. As home secretary, he bore much of the odium for the heavy-handedness of the Metropolitan Police commissioner, Sir Charles Warren; and discontent with the government generally was visited on his head.

On the Conservatives' return to power in 1895, Matthews's reappointment was as stoutly opposed as it had earlier been canvassed by Queen Victoria, to whose wishes Lord Salisbury deferred. Considered too accident-prone for judicial office, he was raised to the peerage as Viscount Llandaff. As a Conservative MP in opposition, he had scrupulously refrained from participating in the debate on Gladstone's bill to remove remaining Catholic disabilities (which his Conservative colleagues opposed), while opposing on principle the disestablishment of the Church in Wales. As a peer, however, taking little part in party politics, he vigorously championed the rights of his co-religionists. He was active in securing the passing of the Accession Declaration Act (1910), which abolished the monarch's obligation to condemn transubstantiation and other Catholic beliefs. He was among the founders of Westminster Cathedral.

Llandaff was a bencher of Lincoln's Inn, a fellow of University College, London, and a member of the Senate of London University. From 1897 to 1899, he served as chairman of the royal commission on the London water supply, which led to the formation of the Metropolitan Water Board in 1902. He published learned articles in the legal journals, light-hearted reminiscences of the hustings at Dungarvon in the *Dublin Review*, and a critique, polite but pointed, in the *National Review* on the separation of church and state in France. In later years he was crippled with rheumatism and constantly in pain. He died at 6 Carlton Gardens, London, on 3 April 1913, and was buried with Catholic rites in the Anglican family vault at Clehonger, Herefordshire.   A. LENTIN

Sources S. Leslie, C. Darling, and J. Rose, 'Henry Matthews, Lord Llandaff', *Dublin Review*, 168 (1921), 1–22 · *The Times* (4 April 1913) · *VF* (10 Sept 1887) · *The Tablet* (12 April 1913), 561–2 · *Hansard 3* · *Hansard 4* (1892) · A. B. Keith, *The British cabinet system, 1830–1938* (1939), 61, 104, 430 · J. Pellew, *The home office, 1848–1914* (1982) · S. Petrow, *Policing morals: the Metropolitan Police and the home office, 1870–1914* (1994) · R. C. K. Ensor, *England, 1870–1914*, reprint of 1936 edn (1992), 173, 180–81, 204 · D. Southgate, 'The Salisbury era, 1881–1902', *The conservative leadership, 1832–1932*, ed. D. Southgate (1974), 101–50, esp. 133–5 · *WWW* · *DNB* · Burke, *Peerage* · *CGPLA Eng. & Wales* (1913)

Archives Bodl. Oxf., corresp. and papers | BL, corresp. with Lord Ripon, Bishop Carpenter, Lord Gladstone, Lady Knightly · Ches. & Chester ALSS, letters to Rhoda Broughton · CKS, letters to Edward Stanhope · UCL, corresp. with E. Chadwick

Likenesses B. Stone, photograph, 1895, NPG [*see illus.*] · London Stereoscopic Co., photograph, NPG · Spy [L. Ward], chromolithograph caricature, repro. in *VF* · etching (after photograph by London Stereoscopic Co.), NPG · wood-engraving (after photograph by J. Collier), NPG; repro. in *ILN* (14 Aug 1886)

Wealth at death £259,749 2s. 7d.: resworn probate, 27 May 1913, *CGPLA Eng. & Wales*

Matthews, Jessie Margaret (1907–1981), actress, was born in Soho, London, on 11 March 1907, the seventh of eleven surviving children of George Ernest Matthews, owner of a greengrocery stall in Berwick Street market, and his wife, Jane, daughter of Charles Henry Townshend, a timber porter. She went to Pulteney Street School for Girls, Soho, and showed such promise as a dancer that her oldest sister, Rosie, arranged for her to be trained in classical ballet by Mme Elise Clerc. When Mme Clerc died suddenly, Rosie determinedly arranged for Jessie to train as a chorus girl with Miss Terry Freedman of Terry's Juveniles.

Jessie Matthews made her first London appearance in 1919 in *Bluebell in Fairyland*, produced by E. Seymour G. Hicks. Four years later she played in Irving Berlin's *Music Box Revue*, presented by Charles Cochran. In his book *I had Almost Forgotten* (1932) Cochran described her as 'an interesting looking child with big eyes, a funny little nose, clothes which seemed a bit too large for her, and a huge umbrella' (Cochran, 163).

At sixteen Jessie Matthews made her New York début in the chorus of *André Charlot's Revue of 1924*. Gertrude Lawrence was the leading lady in that show, and when she fell seriously ill with pneumonia in Toronto, Jessie Matthews took over her part. She reached full star status in *The Charlot Show of 1926* when she danced in ballet numbers with Anton Dolin and in musical comedy items with Henry Lytton junior (Lord Alva Lytton; d. 1965), son of Henry Alfred Lytton, actor. She married Henry Lytton in 1926 but from the outset the marriage was a failure, and in 1929 it was dissolved. At this time she also obtained a £25,000 contract from Cochran, and in 1927 she starred in *One Dam Thing After Another* by Ronald Jeans, with music by Lorenz Hart and Richard Rodgers. A co-star was John Robert Hale Monro (Sonnie Hale), and she found in him the perfect dancing partner. The next year they appeared together in *This Year of Grace* by Noël Coward, in which they sang Coward's romantic duet, 'A Room with a View'. The critics acclaimed her performance, which was followed by similar triumphs in Cole Porter's *Wake up and*

Jessie Margaret Matthews (1907–1981), by Dorothy Wilding, c.1928

Dream (1929) and *Ever Green* (1930). She had now reached the peak of her theatrical career.

Sonnie Hale (d. 1959), son of the actor Robert Hale, was married to Evelyn Laye, another highly successful actress. In 1930 they divorced and Jessie Matthews received much unwelcome publicity as the woman responsible for the break-up of the marriage. Her own divorce had been finalized and in 1931 she and Hale married. In that year she made her first sound film, *Out of the Blue*, which was a failure, but her second, *There Goes the Bride* (1933), was a triumph, and led to her becoming Britain's first international film star. During the 1930s she starred in fourteen films, including *The Good Companions* (1933) opposite John Gielgud, *Friday the Thirteenth* (1933) opposite Ralph Richardson, and *Evergreen* (1934), all directed by Victor Saville.

During the filming of *Evergreen* Jessie Matthews had her first nervous breakdown; many, more serious, were to follow. In 1934 her first baby, a son, lived only four hours; the doctors advised the desolate mother to adopt a child, and early in 1935 she and her husband adopted a baby girl, Catherine. In 1936 there was another serious nervous breakdown. In spite of Jessie Matthews's spectacular successes she was always beset by feelings of insecurity; at the beginning of her autobiography, *Over my Shoulder* (1974), she wrote: 'All my life I had been frightened' (Matthews and Burgess, 1). She was now directed by her husband in *Head over Heels* (1937) and feared it would be a failure; but it made money. *Gangway* (1937) and *Sailing Along* (1938), however, were disappointments, and relations with Sonnie Hale were becoming more and more strained. Her only Hollywood film was *Forever and a Day* (1943).

The Hales returned to the stage in 1939 in their own musical production *I Can Take It*. Its provincial tour was a great success and it was due to open at the London Coliseum on 12 September 1939; war broke out on 3 September, and cancellation of the show meant financial disaster. In 1941 Jessie Matthews had an offer to appear on Broadway in *The Lady Comes Across*, and her husband urged her to accept. She reluctantly left him and Catherine, and set off alone for New York but before the show could open she was ill again and the play flopped. At the age of thirty-four her doctors predicted that her theatrical career was over. During her absence in America her husband was having an affair with Catherine's nurse, Mary Kelsey, and in 1942 he and his wife parted company; two years later they divorced.

Jessie Matthews resumed her stage career in the West End in Jerome Kern's *Wild Rose* (1942). While appearing in concerts with the Entertainments National Service Association she met Lieutenant (Richard) Brian Lewis, of the Queen's Royal regiment, who was twelve years her junior; in 1945 they married. Lewis was the son of Norman Percy Lewis, a schoolmaster, from West Hartlepool. Four months later Jessie Matthews had a stillborn son and her doctors warned her that another pregnancy would threaten her life. In 1948, after six years' absence, she reappeared on the London stage in *Maid to Measure*, followed in 1949 by the revue *Sauce Tartare*. She also appeared in *Pygmalion* (1950) and *Private Lives* (1954). She and Brian Lewis divorced in 1958.

Jessie Matthews returned to films in *Tom Thumb* (1958), and demonstrated that she could still command an audience when she sang one of her well-known songs, 'Dancing on the Ceiling', in the 1960 *Night of One Hundred Stars*. By this time she had lost her sylphlike figure but not her charm. In 1963 the BBC invited her to take over the matronly role of Mrs Mary Dale in the radio serial *The Dales*; she played this part for the next six years. She also appeared frequently in television drama and returned to the stage in such plays as *The Killing of Sister George* (1971) and *Lady Windermere's Fan* (1978). In 1979 her one-woman show *Miss Jessie Matthews in Concert*, produced in Los Angeles, won the US Drama Critics award. She was appointed OBE in 1970. Jessie Matthews's last appearance was at the National Theatre, London, in *Night of One Hundred Stars* on 14 December 1980. She died at Eastcote, London, on 19 August 1981. H. F. OXBURY, *rev.*

Sources *The Times* (21 Aug 1981) · J. Matthews and M. Burgess, *Over my shoulder* (1974) · M. Thornton, *Jessie Matthews* (1974) · D. Shipman, *The great movie stars: the golden years*, rev. edn (1979) · J. Richards, *The age of the dream palace: cinema and society in Britain, 1930–1939* (1984) · C. B. Cochran, *I had almost forgotten* (1932) · *CGPLA Eng. & Wales* (1981)

Archives FILM BFI NFTVA, current affairs footage · BFI NFTVA, performance footage | SOUND BL NSA, oral history interview · BL NSA, performance recordings

Likenesses D. Wilding, bromide print, *c*.1928, NPG [*see illus.*] · photographs, Hult. Arch.

Wealth at death £56,503: probate, 26 Oct 1981, *CGPLA Eng. & Wales*

Matthews, John (1701?–1719), printer, was probably born in August 1701, the second son and probably the youngest of three children of John Matthews (*d.* 1716?), printer, and his wife, Mary. In 1719 Matthews became the first and last printer to be executed in England for printing a seditious and treasonable libel. His dramatic death at such a young age attracted much public attention; it was the occasion of riotous behaviour by apprentice and journeymen printers and resulted in the publication of at least five supposed dying declarations espousing the Jacobite cause.

According to broadsheets printed to mark his execution, John Matthews went to grammar school 'as soon as possible' (PRO, SP 35/19/133), and received 'a liberal Education'. The biographical account printed by the Jacobite Francis Clifton claimed that 'his sprightly Genius enabled him soon to out-ship many of his Seniors' (PRO, SP 35/19/128). Matthews was apprenticed in September 1715 to his father, described by Thomas Gent as 'an eminent printer' (*Life*, 91). When John Matthews senior died the business was transferred to his wife, Mary, but seems to have been principally carried on by their elder son, George. John Matthews, the younger son, although technically still an apprentice, involved himself in printing treasonable pieces: 'For about three Years past, he has been frequently taken up for Printing Thing's against the Government; but in Consideration of his Youth, was always dismiss'd by the Government, with Caution not to offend again' (*Weekly Journal, or, British Gazetteer*, 7 Nov 1719). At John Matthews's trial his older brother admitted these previous 'misfortunes', and explained that he had given orders to the household to report to him if John, 'did, or talked any thing against the government' (*State trials*, 15.1369).

On 19 February 1718 a warrant was issued against John Matthews, 'for printing and publishing treasonable Libels' (PRO, SP 44/79A/131) and he was duly arrested with a well-known Jacobite, Captain Leonard. In May 1718 he escaped custody, but was soon rearrested. The notorious Jacobite newspaper printer, Nathaniel Mist, visited him in gaol in October 1718. He was released from custody later that year.

As a youth Matthews seems to have been heavily influenced by the infamous Jacobite and nonjuring clergyman Robert Orme, who ran a meeting-house in Trinity Court, Aldersgate Street, and by whom he 'was several years instructed' (*St James Post*, 9 Nov 1719). James Alexander, Orme's clerk or churchwarden, deeply involved in the production of Jacobite propaganda, used Matthews for printing subversive works on some occasions and may well have been the agent who commissioned the fatal pamphlet in 1719. He had certainly commissioned a version of it to be printed by Claudius Bonner in May of that year, a month earlier than Matthews's edition.

At some point in the first week of June 1719 Matthews printed the eight-page pamphlet *Vox populi, vox Dei* in his mother's printing shop, aided by Laurence Vezey, an older journeyman, and William Harper, a young apprentice.

According to Harper, about 1000 copies were printed. Vezey claimed that Matthews paid his two assistants 14s. for their help. One of the prosecuting counsel at the subsequent trial lamented: 'it is to be feared that they were dispersed, and God knows what mischief they may have done' (*State trials*, 15.1340).

Vox populi, vox Dei claimed to prove that, whether from the standpoint of hereditary right or from the 'Whiggish Principle' of 'the Sense of the Majority of the People', 'the Chevalier' (James Edward Stuart, the Jacobite pretender) was the rightful monarch. It concluded with the rousing call to arms: 'I hope some Patriot will rouze up the People to shake off this Arbitrary Government … Sure you ought to fight with more Resolution for Liberty than your Oppressors do for Domination. COUNT YOUR NUMBERS' (PRO, SP 35/19/135). Such a pamphlet had to be taken seriously by the authorities at a time when the latest Jacobite rising, with Spanish troops, had only just been defeated in Scotland, and when the much more serious conflict of 1715 was still fresh in people's minds.

Matthews was arrested at his mother's house between 8 and 9 a.m. on 7 July. Apparently he 'behaved in a passion' (*State trials*, 15.1343) while two king's messengers searched his clothes and the room he kept at his mother's house. One of the arresting officers claimed that the printer admitted, 'I deserve to be hanged' (ibid., 15.1347). On being questioned, Matthews claimed that he had printed the pamphlet for money as 'his brother did not give him his allowance' (ibid., 15.1357), but he steadfastly refused to divulge the name of its author.

His refusal to provide evidence of the authorship of *Vox populi, vox Dei* ultimately proved fatal to Matthews. It was clear to all that Matthews himself had neither the maturity nor the education to have written the pamphlet, but the government was determined to discover the author. A reprieve from the death penalty was evidently on offer if Matthews was prepared to talk. Harper and Vezey were rewarded with £200 as an encouragement for 'Printers' Servants, who alone can do it, to inform against those who employ them' (PRO, SP 43/63, Charles Delafaye to Lord Stanhope, 3 Nov 1719).

After being held by messengers for two months, Matthews was moved to Newgate on 9 September. On the 16th he wrote requesting an audience as he had 'Something of Importance to declare to the Right Honourable the Lords of the Regency' (PRO, SP 43/63). Clearly the government expected information about the author of the pamphlet, but was disappointed as Matthews in fact had little to say. George Matthews also pleaded his brother's case and warned of the bad effects 'three or four nonjuring ministers', who had gained access to the prisoner, were having on him (PRO, SP 43/63, Charles Delafaye to Lord Stanhope, 3 Nov 1719). Orders were given to prevent nonjurors from visiting Matthews, and instead to provide him with reliable Anglican clergy. However, the only other concession obtained by these negotiations was to reprieve the dead body from being quartered.

Matthews's main defence counsel, the tory MP John Hungerford, found various arguments to delay the trial and challenged as many jurors as he was allowed. Eventually the trial began in front of ten judges at the Old Bailey on 30 October 1719. The prosecution, led by the attorney-general, proved that Matthews had printed and published *Vox populi, vox Dei*, and explained its treasonable content. In addition to the evidence of Vezey and Harper and the two arresting messengers, George Matthews was pushed into identifying his brother's handwriting, an action for which he was much criticized after the trial.

Hungerford put forward a wide-ranging defence: that the act of parliament passed in the reign of Queen Anne was not appropriate to this offence; that Matthews was too young to have any malice of intent; that Matthews was not acting advisedly as 'he doth not appear so much as to have read it'; that he was not 'directly' responsible as he was not the 'author, contriver, or publisher'; that the witnesses contradicted each other; and that the pamphlet was not treasonable (*State trials*, 15.1360–63). All of this was to no avail, however. As one newspaper reported: 'The Tryal lasted from the Morning 'till Eleven at Night, when the Jury thought fit to bring him in Guilty, and Sentence of Death was accordingly pass'd upon him' (*Weekly Packet*, 31 Oct 1719). Matthews was described at the trial as 'behaving himself both before and after with a surprising Hardiness, not at all like an heroick Boldness peculiar to Innocence and a good Cause, but with an obdurate Heart, the Effect of Rage and Prepossession, Enmity and Rebellion' (*Thursday's Journal*, 5 Nov 1719). The jury was out for only 'a short stay' (*State trials*, 15.1394).

The execution took place at Tyburn, in the rain, on 6 November 1719, alongside two other felons, and attended by Church of England clergymen. Matthews was drawn through the streets to the scaffold on a sledge. The eyewitness Thomas Gent observed: 'his clothes were exceeding neat, the lining of his coat a rich Persian silk, and every other thing as befitted a gentleman. I was told he talked like a philosopher of death … and suffered with a perfect resignation' (*Life*, 91). Mist's newspaper reported that Matthews 'seemed mighty composed, and died without showing any Terror or Dread at the Punishment' (*Weekly Journal, or, Saturday's Post*, 7 Nov 1719). His body was taken to an undertaker in Fleet Street and he was buried at St Botolph's Church in Aldersgate Street in the early hours of the morning of Sunday 8 November.

The significance of the Matthews case, attested by the high-profile nature and wide reporting of his trial, was further demonstrated by extensive wrangling over his state of mind, and his political and religious allegiance at his death. The authorities were determined to prevent Matthews from making a Jacobite dying speech from the scaffold, which might establish him as a popular martyr. Having excluded nonjuring ministers from the prisoner's company, the under-secretary of state, Charles Delafaye, recorded with satisfaction that 'he dyed penitent & made no Speech having before given under his hand a declaration of his abhorence of the Nonjurors principle that brought him to this shamefull End' (PRO, SP 43/63, Charles Delafaye to Lord Stanhope, 6 Nov 1719).

Despite all government efforts, no less than five dying

speeches or declarations were published which attested to Matthews's continued Jacobite principles and nonjuring beliefs. In the aftermath of the trial Jacobite newspapers published pieces in defence of George Matthews and Robert Orme, whereas Vezey and Harper experienced considerable hostility and even violence in retaliation for their role in John Matthews's conviction.

At least two other versions of *Vox populi, vox Dei* are known to have been printed, one before and one after the Matthews edition. These cases also led to arrests and prosecutions, but no other execution. It is difficult to escape the conclusion that John Matthews died because he was young and vulnerable, a convenient scapegoat for the administration's problems in controlling the London press and public opinion. It is a reasonable supposition that he was set up as an expendable pawn by Jacobite publicists, and executed as a warning to others by the Hanoverian government. Both sides then disputed their claim to his memory with bitterness, acrimony, and scant regard for the truth.   PAUL CHAPMAN

Sources *State trials* · PRO, State Papers Domestic 35 · PRO, State Papers Domestic 43 · Bodl. Oxf., Nichols newspapers · BL, Burney collection of newspapers · R. J. Goulden, 'Vox populi, vox Dei: Charles Delafaye's paperchase', *Book Collector*, 28 (1979) · *The last dying words, character, portraiture, prison prayers, meditations, and ejaculations of Mr. John Matthews* (1719) · *The declaration of John Matthews, deliver'd to a friend two days before his death* (1719) · *The copy of a paper deliver'd by Mr. John Matthews to a friend of his before his execution* (1719) · P. M. Chapman, 'Jacobite political argument in England, 1714–66', PhD diss., U. Cam., 1983 · *Mr. John Matthews, the printer, his last farewell to the world* (1719) · *The life of Mr Thomas Gent … written by himself*, ed. J. Hunter (1832) · R. J. Goulden, 'Jacobite pamphlets in the Public Record Office', *Antiquarian Book Monthly Review*, 3 (1976)
Likenesses woodcut, 1719, PRO, SP 35/19/128; repro. in *Last dying words* · woodcut, 1719, PRO, SP 35/19/134; repro. in *Mr. John Matthews*

Matthews, John (*bap.* 1755, *d.* 1826), physician and poet, baptized on 30 October 1755 at Linton, Herefordshire, was the only surviving child of William Matthews (*d.* 1799), of Burton in Linton, and his wife, Jane (*d.* 1768), daughter of Philip Hoskyns of Bernithen Court, Herefordshire. He matriculated from Merton College, Oxford, on 14 February 1772, and graduated BA in 1778, MA in 1779, MB in 1781, and MD in 1782. On 30 September 1782 he was a candidate for the Royal College of Physicians, and a year later he became a fellow. On 9 November 1778, Matthews married at Marcle, Herefordshire, Elizabeth (1756/7–1823), daughter and heir of Arthur Ellis. They had eight sons and six daughters. Among their sons were Charles Skynner Matthews, the friend of Byron, and Henry *Matthews (1789–1828), author of *The Diary of an Invalid* (1820).

From 20 April 1781 to his resignation in 1783 Matthews was the physician to St George's Hospital, London, and in 1784 he delivered the Goulstonian lectures. He then retired from medicine and returned to Herefordshire. He acquired the estate of Clehonger, near Hereford, and by 1790 had built there the mansion of Belmont. A sapling planted by him in 1788 became famous as Colonel Matthews's oak, and was marked by a cast-iron tablet. For the rest of his life Matthews took a leading part in county affairs. He acted as mayor of Hereford in 1793, and was

senior alderman and magistrate for twenty years. He was also colonel of the first regiment of Hereford militia, chairman of quarter sessions, and member of parliament for the county from 31 March 1803 to 1806.

John Matthews was a man of versatile disposition and generous tastes, which frequently left him at a financial loss. His works were published anonymously. The best-known of them is *Eloisa en dishabille: being a new version of that lady's celebrated epistle to Abelard, done into familiar English metre by a lounger* (1780), which is a parody of Pope's 'Eloisa to Abelard'. It was reprinted in 1801, and again in 1822, when the bookseller put on the title-page that it was 'ascribed to [Richard] Porson'. Matthews wrote other verse, some of it described as 'contemptible' by contemporaries, and much of it badly received. He died after a long illness at Belmont on 15 January 1826. A monument to his memory was placed in the south aisle of Clehonger church.   W. P. COURTNEY, *rev.* CLAIRE L. NUTT

Sources Munk, *Roll* · Foster, *Alum. Oxon.* · *GM*, 1st ser., 96/1 (1826), 368 · J. Duncumb and others, *Collections towards the history and antiquities of the county of Hereford*, 2 (1812), 387–8, 402 · J. Duncumb and others, *Collections towards the history and antiquities of the county of Hereford*, 3 (1882), 174, 215 · *The life of Lord Byron, with his letters and journals*, ed. T. Moore, new edn (1847), 129 · C. J. Robinson, *A history of the mansions and manors of Herefordshire* (1873), 66, 181 · S. C. Lawrence, *Charitable knowledge: hospital pupils and practitioners in eighteenth-century London* (1996)
Likenesses Wedgwood medallion, *c.*1790, Wedgwood Museum, Stoke-on-Trent

Matthews, Lemuel. *See* Mathews, Lemuel (*b.* 1643/4, *d.* in or before 1725).

Matthews, Leonard Harrison (1901–1986), zoologist and naturalist, was born on 12 June 1901 in Clifton, Bristol, the elder son and eldest of three children of Harold Evan Matthews, manufacturing pharmacist, and his wife, Sarah Susannah (Ruby) Harrison, pharmacist. His sister, Marjorie Violet (later Mrs Marshall Sisson), was an exhibitioner at Newnham College, Cambridge, and became an educational psychologist. His younger brother, Bryan Harold Cabot *Matthews, became professor of physiology at Cambridge. Leo Matthews was brought up at Clifton, where his father had a pharmaceutical factory and chemist's shop, and went to Bristol grammar school. In 1919 he went up to King's College, Cambridge, where he obtained a first class in part one of the natural sciences tripos (1922) and a second class in part two (1923). He was also awarded the Frank Smart prize in zoology. He spent much time during his vacations studying the fauna of the Bristol Channel and on trawlers, visiting the Faeroes, Iceland, the White Sea, and Brazil, confirming a liking for hands-on zoology that was to last his lifetime.

In 1924 Matthews married a dancer, Dorothy Hélène, daughter of Henry Charles Harris, of independent means; they had a son and a daughter. The same year he applied for, and obtained, a post with the *Discovery* committee to work on whale biology in South Georgia. This committee (known by the name of its research vessel) had been set up by the British government to conduct an intensive scientific research programme in the Southern Ocean to provide data for the rational management of the whaling industry, the expansion of which was causing concern. Matthews was attracted by the prospect of working in this remote spot on the largest and most impressive of all living things, and mixing with the hard men engaged in whaling. He travelled to South Georgia in the autumn of 1924 to establish a marine laboratory at King Edward Cove, next to the whaling station where he was to do most of his work. This resulted in major monographs on humpback, sei, right, and sperm whales, published in *Discovery* reports. There were other papers on seals, birds, and invertebrates and his first book, *South Georgia: the British Empire's Subantarctic Outpost* (1931), which remained the definitive text for fifty years. Besides these, there were three books, *Wandering Albatross* (1951), *Sea Elephant* (1952), and *Penguin* (1977), aimed at the general public, which vividly captured the life of the sealers and whalers whose company Matthews had so relished.

Matthews relinquished his post with the *Discovery* committee in 1928, and returned to Bristol to work part-time in the family firm and help his brother develop scientific instruments. They established Clifton Instruments Ltd. He also took his Cambridge MA, which was followed by an ScD in 1937. In 1935 he was appointed a special lecturer at Bristol University. Here he continued to work on his South Georgia material and widened his field to include African mammals. Reproductive physiology held a fascination for him and he was intrigued by the uncertainty surrounding the sex of the spotted hyena, regarded by Pliny as a facultative hermaphrodite. In 1935 he organized an expedition to the Balbal plains, west of the Ngorongoro crater in Tanganyika, and there collected and dissected 103 hyenas. He was the first to describe the extraordinary penile clitoris and apparent absence of a vulva in the female that had given rise to Pliny's misapprehension.

During the Second World War, Matthews became a radio officer in anti-aircraft command (1941), and senior scientific officer in the telecommunications research establishment (1942). He worked at the Petersham radio-location school, undertaking confidential work on radar gun-laying and, later, radar position-indicating systems for the Pathfinder bombers.

Matthews returned to Bristol in 1945 as research fellow. He continued to produce a wide variety of papers on the biology of animals, from bats to basking sharks. In 1952 he was appointed scientific director of the Zoological Society of London (the London Zoo), a post he held until retirement in 1966. He was highly successful in developing the scientific activities of the society and his own research, particularly on reproduction in seals. In 1954 he was elected FRS. Unfortunately, his later years at the zoo were clouded by disagreement with the secretary, Sir Solly Zuckerman.

Matthews's retirement, at the Old Rectory, Stansfield, Suffolk, was an active period. He continued to produce important texts, including *The Life of Mammals* (2 vols., 1969–71) and *The Natural History of the Whale* (1978). His last book was *Mammals in the British Isles* (1982). He was, perhaps, the last of the great naturalists, a man with a wide interest in animals, less concerned with laboratory experimentation than with animals' life in the field.

In appearance Matthews was tall and well built and always well groomed, not to say dapper, which was surprising in one who had spent so much time in rigorous field conditions. In later life he sported a goatee beard and had a liking for bow-ties. He was excellent company, something of a bon viveur, and a most entertaining companion, always able to produce an appropriate yarn from his travels. He sketched and painted in a delightful free style and his illustrations appeared in several of his published works. He amassed a notable library and a remarkable collection of curios from his travels. Matthews died at home at the Old Rectory, Stansfield, Suffolk, on 27 November 1986.   NIGEL BONNER, *rev.*

Sources R. Harrison, *Memoirs FRS*, 33 (1987), 411–42 · N. Bonner, *Journal of the Zoological Society of London*, 213 (1987), 1–5 · *Daily Telegraph* (3 Dec 1986) · *The Times* (31 Nov 1986)
Archives priv. coll. | Rice University, Texas, Woodson Research Center, Huxley MSS | FILM priv. coll.
Likenesses photograph, NPG, RS

Matthews, Marmaduke (*c*.1606–*c*.1683), clergyman and ejected minister, was born at Swansea, the son either of Matthew Matthews of Swansea, or of Matthew Jones of Nydfywch, Llangyfelach, and his wife, Mary. On 20 February 1624 he matriculated from All Souls College, Oxford, graduating BA on 25 February 1625 and proceeding MA on 5 July 1627; a possible brother, Edward Matthews, son of Matthew Jones of Swansea, matriculated at Oxford on 11 July 1634, aged nineteen. Nothing is known of Matthews's life in the decade after his graduation, but in 1636 he was recorded as vicar of Penmain in the Gower by William Laud, then bishop of St David's, in his annual account, which noted further that Matthews expressed puritan sentiments against Laud's wishes and that he was 'preaching against the keeping of all holy-days, with divers other, as fond or profane opinions' (LPL, MS 943). As a consequence, he was 'inhibited' by the bishop, and proceedings were initiated against him in the court of high commission.

Some time between 1636 and 1638 Matthews emigrated to New England to avoid censure by the state and church authorities. He was perhaps among the 'severall Welsh Gentlemen of Good note … procured' by Edward Winslow of the Pilgrim Church at Plymouth, Massachusetts, to assist Robert Blinman of Gloucester after his acceptance of the pastorate of the branch church at Mansfield in 1639 (Dodd, 30). After a visit to the West Indies, Matthews returned to New England and became a 'teaching-elder' of the church at Maldon. Here he became involved in a dispute about a fast, and as a result his election as a full freeman of the colony was deferred. In 1640 he was appointed as the pastor of Yarmouth, Massachusetts, and in 1649 was a minister at Hull, south of Boston, but again he became embroiled in a dispute with local magistrates. Although Matthews received the support of his congregation, he was denied the privilege of preaching 'untill he hath given satisfaction to the Elders that heard the errors chardged and proved against him' (ibid., 31). He subsequently moved on to two other pastorates within the Boston area.

During his time in New England, 'whilst I yet lived in the midst of wild men, and wild Beasts, amongst the Lords Exiles', Matthews and his family were sustained financially, as he later acknowledged, by Colonel Philip Jones (Dodd, 35). In 1654 they returned to Wales at Jones's behest, and through his patronage Matthews was appointed in 1655 minister of St John's, Swansea, 'a good living' (Calamy, 2.732). He became a member of the committee for the approbation of public preachers (the 'triers') in Wales, and in 1656 signed the *Humble Representation and Address from South Wales* to Oliver Cromwell. During the late 1650s there is evidence that he was opposed by radical Quaker preachers, of whom he was described as 'an envious persecutor', for instance pinching Alice Birkett so hard that 'her blood came forth' and threatening to 'box' Robert Coldbeach of Swansea (Gawler, 27). For many years, as Matthews explained in *The Messiah Magnified by the Mouthes of Babes in America* (1659), he had been trying to convert the ungodly, 'to see their teares trickle, their lips quiver, their hue to change, their joynts to tremble; and to observe … their weeping for the piercing of Christ' (Matthews, 8). That year he also published *The Rending Church Member Regularly Call'd Back*.

In 1662 Matthews was ejected, but in spite of financial constraints, 'preached, by the connivance of the magistrates, in a little chapel at the end of the town' (Palmer, 3.504). His *The Reconciling Remonstrance* appeared in 1670, and on 12 April 1672 he obtained a licence, under the declaration of indulgence, to preach as an Independent. He conducted services at his house in Swansea and was described as 'a very pious and zealous man, who went about to instruct the people from house to house', receiving a mixed reception (Calamy, 2.732). In his later years he 'lived above the world', and was supported by the 'children of God, his own children, and the children of the world' (ibid.). His sons (whose mother's name is unknown)—Manasseh, Mordecai, and Lemuel [*see* Mathews, Lemuel]—also became nonconformist ministers, but later conformed to the established church. Matthews died in Swansea about 1683.   RICHARD C. ALLEN

Sources M. Matthews, *The Messiah magnified by the mouthes of babes in America* (1659) • LPL, MSS 943, 972, fol. 379 • 'Great book of sufferings', RS Friends, Lond., vol. 2, fols. 3, 4 • F. Gawler, *A record of some persecutions … in south Wales* (1659), 5–7, 27–8 • *DNB* • *DWB* • T. Rees, *History of protestant nonconformity in Wales* (1861), 59–60 • T. Rees, *History of protestant nonconformity in Wales*, 2nd edn (1883), 35–6, 53–4, 177 • E. Calamy, ed., *An abridgement of Mr. Baxter's history of his life and times, with an account of the ministers, &c., who were ejected after the Restoration of King Charles II*, 2nd edn, 2 vols. (1713), vol. 2, pp. 732–3 • Foster, *Alum. Oxon.* • T. Richards, *Religious developments in Wales, 1654–1662* (1923), 22, 93, 134, 180, 484, 488, 512 • T. Richards, *Wales under the indulgence, 1672–1675* (1928), 98, 101–2, 115, 158, 192, 235 • *The nonconformist's memorial … originally written by … Edmund Calamy*, ed. S. Palmer, [3rd edn], 2 (1802), 627–8; 3 (1803), 504 • A. H. Dodd, 'New England influences in early Welsh puritanism', *BBCS*, 16 (1954–6), 30–37 • E. S. John, 'Bywyd, gwaith a chyfnod dau Biwritan Cymreig, Marmaduke Williams a Richard Blinman', PhD diss., U. Wales, Bangor, 1987 • E. S. John, 'Marmaduke Williams a Richard Blinman: en teuluoedd a'u cyfraniad', *Y Cofiadur*, 60 (1996), 3–25

Matthews [*née* Gee], **Sarah Magdalene** (1846–1929), temperance leader, was born at Denbigh in January 1846, the second daughter of the prominent Calvinistic Methodist minister, publisher, and politician Thomas *Gee (1815–1898), and his wife, Sarah, daughter of John Hughes of Plas Coch, Llangynhafal. All nine children of the Gees received a full education, and Sarah attended schools in Denbigh and Birmingham. In marrying John Matthews (1838–1916), son of a prominent shopkeeper and surveyor from Aberystwyth, she found a partner who came from a middle-class, Welsh-speaking, Calvinistic Methodist, Liberal background similar to her own, and shared her interest in temperance. In the early years of their marriage the Matthewses lived in Aberystwyth, but later moved to Anglesey, where John Matthews became manager of the National Provincial Bank at Amlwch. They had three surviving children.

By the beginning of the 1890s Sarah Matthews, who had long been involved with local temperance associations, felt that the time had come for more co-ordinated action. Although not an ardent feminist, she saw that many women had insufficient outlets for their talents and felt that a women's temperance association could develop these untapped resources while bringing together scattered groups working towards similar ends. With the help of her elder sister, Mary Gee, and a friend from Bala, Miss Parry, she organized a women's conference at Blaenau Ffestiniog in 1892, delegates being invited from existing temperance groups. The conference decided to set up Undeb Dirwestol Merched Gogledd Cymru (UDMGC, the north Wales women's temperance union), to unite and focus the women's efforts. Sarah Matthews was elected president, a post which she held for four years, during which time membership rose to 11,821 women in over 100 branches throughout the six north Wales counties and in the large Welsh communities of Liverpool and Manchester.

Recognizing the importance of Welsh as the language of home and religious life for the vast majority of women in the temperance movement, and being very conscious of the distinct culture and traditions of Wales, from the outset Sarah Matthews politely but firmly rejected the possibility of working within the England-based British Women's Temperance Association (BWTA) which was already recruiting in north Wales. By formally establishing UDMGC as a bilingual association from the start, she ensured the support of those who spoke little English, while also creating for such women new opportunities outside home—giving them a chance to learn new skills in administration, public speaking, and even creative writing. Despite pressure from the BWTA, UDMGC remained independent, agreeing only, from 1895 onwards, to affiliate as a body. The constitution of UDMGC required that both the president and secretary be bilingual, and one of the organization's main aims was the publication of suitable literature in Welsh on temperance and the related question of sexual morality.

Sarah Matthews possessed great determination and a firm conviction of the rightness of her cause, which helped her to persevere when faced with enormous prejudice against women as public speakers and accusations that women's activities in the public sphere, such as temperance work, were leading them away from their duties as wives and mothers at home. Her ability to keep calm and polite even when faced with the most virulent masculine opposition is said to have been one of her greatest assets.

Although Sarah Matthews was particularly active in Anglesey, where she was often assisted by her husband, she also travelled widely throughout north Wales and beyond, taking part, for instance, in mass meetings held for Welsh women in London in 1895 and 1896. Her deeply felt religious, social, and political convictions permeated every aspect of her life and are reflected in the most mundane family letters. Her unmarried daughter, Emily, who lived with her mother, also became an active member of UDMGC and was one of the first women JPs in north Wales. Sarah Matthews died at her home, Trehinon, in Amlwch on 29 December 1929. In her will she left £50 to the temperance union she had founded.

CERIDWEN LLOYD-MORGAN

Sources C. Peris [A. G. Jones], *Er cof a gwerthfawrogiad o lafur Mrs Mathews* (1930) · H. Williams, 'Y Diweddar Mrs Matthews, Amlwch', *Y Gymraes* (Feb 1930), 17–20 · C. Peris [A. G. Jones], 'Mrs Matthews', *Y Gymraes* (Feb 1930), 22–6 · C. Lloyd-Morgan, 'From temperance to suffrage?', *Our mother's land: chapters in Welsh women's history, 1830–1939*, ed. A. V. John (1991), 135–58 · T. G. Jones, *Cofiant Thomas Gee* (1913) · Adroddiad Blynyddol (Annual Report), 1893–1929, Undeb Dirwestol Merched Gogledd Cymru · A. C. Prichard, *Boreu oes* (1910)
Archives NL Wales
Likenesses photograph, repro. in Peris, *Er cof a gwerthfawrogiad o lafur Mrs Matthews* · photographs, repro. in Williams, 'Y Diweddar Mrs Matthews, Amlwch', *Y Gymraes*, 17–22
Wealth at death £3275 1s. 3d.: probate, 20 March 1930, *CGPLA Eng. & Wales*

Matthews, Sir Stanley (1915–2000), footballer, was born at 89 Seymour Street, Hanley, Stoke-on-Trent, on 1 February 1915, the third of four sons of John Matthews and his wife, Ada Hewitt. Jack Matthews had a barber's shop in Market Street but he was also a boxer, with 300 fights as a featherweight. He was addicted to physical fitness, and transmitted both his enthusiasm for training and his passion for sport to his sons, and to Stanley in particular. Stanley was presented with a pair of spiked running shoes for his fourth birthday and his father took him outside for daily breathing exercises, even on freezing mornings. At six he was entered for a handicap race for boys at local elementary schools. He won off 45 yards, bringing Dad a substantial betting profit. Stanley's father hoped he would follow him into the boxing ring, but it soon became clear that it was football which fascinated the boy. He played or practised whenever he could, and quickly developed into an outstanding schoolboy player for Wellington Road and

Sir Stanley Matthews (1915–2000), by unknown photographer, 1956

Hanley schools. In 1929 he was chosen to play in the international trial England v. the Rest and then for England schoolboys against Wales.

On leaving school Matthews was an apprentice bricklayer for a time but at fifteen he became an apprentice at Stoke City at a wage of £1 a week. As soon as he was eligible, on his seventeenth birthday, he signed professional forms which produced a £10 signing-on fee and wages of £5 a week in the season, with a £1 winning bonus, and £3 a week in the summer. Half his wages went into a savings account and half was given to his mother. Matthews played his first league game away to Bury in 1932 and his 700th and last at home to Fulham in February 1965, at the age of fifty. He is the oldest outfield player to appear in a Football League match. Between 1934 and 1957 he played fifty-four times for England, having become an international celebrity before the days of worldwide television and the revolution in electronic communications. His name was synonymous with what was best in British sport.

In fact, Matthews had two careers. From 1932 to 1947 he was a right-winger for Stoke. His balance, control, and above all his speed, made him a handful for most fullbacks. Even when he was in his forties he showed a surprising turn of pace over the first crucial yards. Matthews was nevertheless not only quicker in his youth but more direct: he scored forty-seven goals in six pre-war seasons as against twenty-four in sixteen post-war ones. In 1934 he scored four against Leeds, and his hat-trick for England against Czechoslovakia in 1937 effectively turned a defeat into a narrow victory. After the war he became more of a provider of scoring opportunities for others, either by means of accurate crosses deep into the penalty area or by infiltrating defences by reaching the opposition goal line and pulling the ball back for an incoming forward: the classic example was the goal which he laid on for Perry to win the 1953 cup final.

The press christened Matthews the 'wizard of dribble', the Germans, more poetically, *Der Zauberer*, the magician. His method did not involve a slalom-like wriggle through a packed defence. His aim rather was to defeat his immediate marker, the left back. Spectators would be charmed and amazed by the way he did it as he brought the ball, often quite slowly, almost to the feet of the defender, showing him the ball in order to tempt him into a tackle. As the full-back shifted his balance to move forward, so Matthews would suddenly accelerate away in another direction. He liked to deceive opponents by feinting to his left before actually setting off at speed down the right touchline. Some likened the manoeuvre to that of a dragonfly, arms outstretched, almost hovering close to his opponent before darting off unpredictably. Others likened it to a man teasing children. Matthews was still doing it at the age of forty-one when he tormented the famous Brazilian defender Nilton Santos in England's 1956 victory over Brazil. Matthews's ability was more instinctive than analytical. He claimed not to know how he performed his body swerve and could produce it only under the pressure of actual match conditions. Matthews often established a psychological domination over his marker and was known to torment his opponents by repeatedly taking the ball past them during the course of a single attack.

Matthews's second career began when he was transferred to Blackpool in 1947. He had been posted there as an RAF physical training instructor during the war and had played for the club as a wartime guest. He liked the seaside and he and his wife, Betty, took over the Romford Hotel in the town. Matthews had not had an easy relationship with the Stoke manager, Bob McGrory; in 1938, when the club refused to pay the full amount of a bonus due to him, he had asked for a transfer. This provoked a remarkable display of local feeling as leading manufacturers in Stoke organized a public protest meeting claiming that their workers had asked them to do it. Three thousand people packed the Kings Hall with at least a further thousand locked outside. The press joined the 'Matthews must stay campaign' and in 1938 he did. But by 1947 he was thirty-two, an age at which most footballers began to think of becoming publicans or small shopkeepers, and still at odds with McGrory. This time Matthews did leave Stoke, to join Blackpool for £11,500.

But far from being finished Matthews was to play an important role in the golden age of another previously unfashionable club. Blackpool reached three cup finals in five years between 1948 and 1953. The first two were both lost and the press began to make much of the fact that

Matthews had no cup winner's medal. By 1953 television had made certain that the cup final was an event which many more than Wembley's 90,000 could watch. Ten million viewers ensured that the so-called 'Matthews final' was engraved on to the collective memory of the English. In truth it was not much of a game, punctuated by poor passing and goalkeeping errors. Bolton played with virtually ten men for the whole of the second half after an injury to Bell, yet led 3–1. Only in the last twenty minutes did Blackpool seize control and Matthews become influential: the game was won 4–3, with the 38-year-old making the pass for the winning goal.

The 1950s were the high point of Matthews's fame. These were the years when people would travel long distances in order to say that they had seen a middle-aged maestro play football. The marks of public recognition began to accumulate. He had already been voted by British football writers footballer of the year in 1948; in 1956 he became the first European footballer of the year, defeating such international stars as Alfredo di Stefano and Ferenc Puskas. Matthews played in all seven England matches in 1957, when he was forty-two. His skill and long playing career were recognized by the award of the CBE in 1957, the first national honour to be offered to a professional footballer.

Although a knee injury prompted thoughts of retirement, Matthews was transferred for a fee of £3500 back to Stoke as a 46-year-old in 1961. Stoke were then close to the bottom of the second division with average gates of 10,000 when he arrived. Attendances then rose to 30,000, relegation was avoided, and established stars such as Jimmy McIlroy and Denis Viollet were attracted by the scent of glory. In two years the championship of the second division was won. Matthews had been a member of the Stoke team that had won the same title thirty years earlier. Footballer of the year again in 1963, Matthews was knighted in the 1965 new year's honours list, the first and only such honour for a professional still playing the game. By now he was playing mostly in Stoke City reserves and retirement soon followed. In 1965 Matthews became the manager of the other Potteries club, Port Vale. It was not a success. The club was expelled from the Football League for financial irregularities and, although they were immediately re-elected, Matthews resigned. He continued to enjoy passing on his knowledge and experience to the young, and over the next twenty years he was in demand all over the world, particularly in Australia, Canada, Ghana, Malta, South Africa, and the United States.

Matthews had all the qualities most of the English prefer in their heroes, including modesty and a reluctance to seek the limelight. He was even-tempered and never cautioned or sent off. In fact he eschewed physical contact, and part of his endearing attraction was that he did not look much like an athlete. Thin, slightly stooping, with bony knees and a receding hairline, he was not bigger, stronger, or more physically gifted than many of those who turned up to watch. He fulfilled the fantasies of many middle-aged fans as he ignored those critics who proclaimed that footballers were past it by thirty. In many ways he was the master craftsman of football, dedicated to fitness and practice, who worked at the game. His tools were his body and his boots, and he made sure those were maintained in good order. He neither smoked nor drank. He liked new boots, and once told a journalist, 'I liked the shine on them. You could look at the shine, as you do with ordinary shoes and it does something to you; it makes you proud; it makes you more alive.'

Football was Matthews's life. In 1934 he married Elizabeth (Betty) Hall Vallance, the daughter of the Stoke City trainer. He was, perhaps, not always the easiest man to live with, with his diet of carrot juice at lunchtime and steak and salad for dinner. He fasted every Monday. If there was increasingly something ascetic about all this, it was the explanation for his exceptional longevity as a player. A son, Stanley, and a daughter, Jean, were children of the marriage. In 1967 Matthews met Mila Winterova, a cultural assistant at the American embassy in Prague. She was thirteen years younger than he and introduced him to a new kind of lifestyle. They were married after his divorce from Betty in 1975 and lived in Malta, South Africa, and Canada before returning to Stoke in 1989. By that time Sir Stanley had been presented with an honorary degree by the University of Keele and in the same year, 1987, a statue by Colin Melbourne was erected in the new pedestrian precinct in Hanley. Some Conservative councillors objected to ratepayers' money being spent in such a way, but then Matthews had always had his critics. He had been too unpredictable, too individualistic, too slow to release the ball, and, it was increasingly said, too old. Yet this modest loner not only became emblematic of his birthplace but also came to exemplify the good name of English football wherever the sport was played.

Matthews died in the North Staffordshire Nuffield Hospital, Clayton Road, Newcastle under Lyme, on 23 February 2000. His wife had died the previous year. He was survived by his son Stanley, and his daughter Jean Gough. Another statue, depicting the three ages of his playing career, was unveiled outside Stoke City's new Britannia Stadium in October 2001.   TONY MASON

Sources S. Matthews, *Feet first* · D. Miller, *Stanley Matthews: the authorized biography* (1989) · S. Matthews, *My autobiography: the way it was* (2000) · T. Mason, 'Stanley Matthews', *Sport and the working class in modern Britain*, ed. R. Holt (1990), 159–78 · *The Independent* (31 Jan 1995) · *World Sports* (April 1953) · *World Sports* (Nov 1953) · *The Guardian* (24 Feb 2000) · *The Times* (24 Feb 2000) · *The Independent* (25 Feb 2000) · b. cert. · d. cert.
Archives FILM BFI NFTVA, 'Match of their day', BBC 2, 3 Nov 1998
Likenesses photograph, 1956, Hult. Arch. [*see illus.*] · photographs, Hult. Arch.

Matthews, (John) Thomas [Tom] (1805–1889), clown, was born on 17 October 1805. As a boy he entered the office of the *Independent Whig* (later known, after other changes, as the *Sunday Times*). The stage was popular with those associated with the paper, and after working on it for four years Matthews sought a career in the theatre. He established a reputation at various London theatres during the late 1820s, including the Olympic and Sadler's Wells, and became known as the last of the old-fashioned singing clowns. He had the proper instruction for this pursuit, having learned the trade from Joseph Grimaldi. He went on to appear at Covent Garden for a series of seasons in such pantomimes as *Puss in Boots*, *Old Mother Hubbard*, *Whittington and his Cat*, and *Grammar Gurton*. At Drury Lane, where he filled the post of principal clown for nearly forty years, he created a sensation by imitating Duvernay in *La cachuca*. Having been engaged by W. C. Macready in July 1837 at £3 per week, he reappeared at Covent Garden, where he brought out *Fair Rosamond* and danced a mock bayadère dance. He visited Scotland and played in Edinburgh and other provincial cities, then returned to the Olympic in Nelson Lee's pantomime *Riddle me, Riddle me Ree*. He crossed the channel in August 1843 to oversee and appear in *Arlequin* at the Théâtre des Variétés in Paris. Théophile Gautier spoke of his costume in this production as a 'rare fantasy' and praised his parody of the 'Cachuca' (*L'histoire de l'Art Dramatique en France*, 1859, 2.260).

Matthews alternated between pantomime and dance when he appeared in a ballet at Vauxhall Gardens alongside the Payne family and Rosina Wright and carried on playing the clown at Drury Lane, the Adelphi, and Covent Garden. On the provincial circuit he was familiarly known for singing such songs as 'Hot Codlings', 'Tippitywitchet', and 'The Life of a Clown', the last of which was composed for him by Michael Balfe. His last appearance was at Drury Lane in 1865 in *Hop o' my Thumb*. In that year, after forty years in the theatre, Matthews retired and soon afterwards moved to Brighton, where he spent the last two decades of his life. In the months leading up to his death he was bedridden, but was assisted by his daughter, Clara Matilda Lawrence. He died at his home, 28 Walpole Terrace, on 4 March 1889, and was buried in Brighton cemetery.   JOSEPH KNIGHT, *rev.* BRENDA ASSAEL

Sources *The Era* (9 March 1889), 10 · D. Pickering, ed., *Encyclopaedia of pantomime* (1993) · R. Toole-Stott, *Circus and allied arts: a world bibliography, 1500–1970*, 3 (1962), 284 · CGPLA Eng. & Wales (1889)
Wealth at death £259 5s.: probate, 9 April 1889, CGPLA Eng. & Wales

Matthews, Victor Collin, Baron Matthews (1919–1995), businessman, was born on 5 December 1919 at 14 Cloudesley Square, Islington, London, the son of Abraham Cohen Matthews, a master tailor, and his wife, Jenny, *née* Edwards. His father disappeared soon after his birth, and he was brought up by his mother. Educated at Highbury School, he never lost his cockney accent, or his love of Arsenal football team. He left school at fourteen, and his first job was as an office boy for a tobacco company. During the Second World War he served in the Royal Naval Volunteer Reserve and took part in the evacuation from Dunkirk and in the Dieppe raid; he ended the war with the rank of able seaman. On 7 March 1942 he married Joyce Geraldine (1922/3–1995), a typist, daughter of Alfred Ernest Pilbeam, a builder's foreman; they had one son, Ian.

After demobilization Matthews joined the building firm of Trollope and Colls as a trainee surveyor; he rose to be contracts manager before moving to a small building products firm, Clark and Fenn, as a director. In 1960 he

Victor Collin Matthews, Baron Matthews (1919–1995), by Sue Adler, 1985

struck out on his own, acquiring the Brixton-based building firm Bridge Walker; within four years he had increased its turnover eightfold, to about £2 million. Among his major clients was Nigel *Broackes. When a take-over bid was launched for Bridge Walker in 1964, Broackes, who was keen to diversify, agreed to take a 49 per cent stake in the company, with an option on the remainder. The partnership worked well, and in 1967 Matthews merged the rest of his company with Trafalgar House and joined the board. In 1968 he became group managing director, and in 1973 deputy chairman.

Under the leadership of Broackes and Matthews, Trafalgar House expanded rapidly into a conglomerate covering construction, leisure, and shipping, with a value at one point estimated to be in excess of £2 billion. Among its major acquisitions were Trollope and Colls in 1966, the Cunard shipping line in 1971, and the Ritz Hotel in 1976. Broackes, shrewd and audacious, provided the brains, while Matthews combined managerial skills with on-site experience. As group managing director (1968–77), deputy chairman (1973–85), and group chief executive (1977–83), Matthews was Broackes's right-hand man, though they were never close socially: in all their years together neither visited the other's home. Matthews, short, dark, and decisive, was a blunt cockney of humble origin. By contrast, the patrician Broackes, educated at Stowe School before national service in the 3rd hussars, was a smooth entrepreneur with a touch of arrogance.

Matthews became a press lord almost by accident when he and Broackes acquired Beaverbrook Newspapers in 1977, at the knock-down price of £15 million. The controlling family interests sold out to forestall the marauding Rupert Murdoch. The group was heavily in debt after years of decline following the death in 1964 of its founder, Lord Beaverbrook, though the fixed assets were worth over £50 million and the three main titles—the *Daily Express*, the *Sunday Express*, and the London *Evening Standard*—still

managed to sell 20 million copies a week. Broackes made no secret of the fact that his main consideration in acquiring Beaverbrook Newspapers was to give Matthews a new role away from Trafalgar House. The two were still partners, but there was mounting tension between them. By 1977 the builder was becoming disenchanted with the demands of big business. At one time he was managing nearly 200 companies. Now he was talking of retiring to pursue his hobby, training racehorses with his son Ian. In his autobiography, *A Growing Concern* (1979), Broackes described Matthews at this point as 'morbid and morose' (Broackes, 245). Matthews replied with a stinging rebuttal in the *Evening Standard*.

In fact, taking on Beaverbrook's mantle perfectly suited Matthews, who felt he still had much to offer at fifty-eight. He was fiercely patriotic and greatly admired the Canadian tycoon's empire crusades. As a young boy delivering newspapers, he had dreamed of becoming a *Daily Express* reporter. Shy and quiet, with piercing brown eyes, he swept into Fleet Street in his Rolls-Royce determined to succeed in his new role as chairman and chief executive. The *Daily Express* had been transformed from broadsheet to tabloid—he pronounced it 'tab-o-loid'—shortly before his arrival without any discernible improvement in its fortunes. He immediately poached as editor of the *Express* the managing editor of the *Daily Mirror*, Derek Jameson, another fatherless cockney from north London. The satirical magazine *Private Eye* immediately dubbed the pair Lord Whelks and Sid Yobbo.

Matthews renamed the group Express Newspapers and got down to tackling the excessive demands of the notoriously difficult print unions. The engineers were first to knock at his door, demanding a 75 per cent pay increase. For once management stood firm and the confrontation turned nasty. There was a publishing room fire and editorial cars were vandalized. The police were called in and barbed wire was erected around the *Express*'s black glass headquarters, known as the Black Lubyanka. Faced with Matthews's refusal to yield—he had been outraged by the engineers' demanding twice as much money for half the work they did in the building trade—the union backed off. Matthews subsequently won court injunctions to prevent the unions usurping what he called the right of management to manage. It was the beginning of a new era in Fleet Street. Ultimately Matthews won the reluctant support of the unions, telling the *Sunday Times*: 'Fleet Street is not overmanned but under-employed.' In 1978 he decided to use some of the group's excess printing capacity, and in the process secured hundreds of jobs, with the launch of the *Daily Star*, Britain's first new national newspaper for 75 years. In 1980 he negotiated a merger between the two loss-making London evening papers, the Express group's *Evening Standard* and Associated Newspapers' *Evening News*, to form a single, profitable *Evening Standard*; Associated Newspapers subsequently bought full control of the paper.

A natural Thatcherite and reputedly the biggest individual donor to the Conservative Party, Matthews was rewarded with a life peerage, as Baron Matthews, in 1980.

(Broackes was knighted in 1984.) Apart from taming the print unions, his other great achievement as chairman of Express Newspapers was to unfreeze the treasure trove locked into Reuters, then a co-operative jointly owned by newspapers. Ironically the revenue raised by the news agency's flotation made Trafalgar's publishing interests, from 1982 demerged into Fleet Holdings, with Matthews as chairman, ripe for take-over. In 1985 the group succumbed to a hostile bid by the rival United Newspapers, headed by David Stevens. Under Matthews's skilful management, the group's value had multiplied more than twentyfold, to £317 million. Matthews's personal stake was worth around £8 million. He severed his remaining links with Trafalgar and retired to Jersey. Lonely and all but forgotten in his last decade, he died at his home, Waverley Farm, Mont Arthur, St Brelades, Jersey, on his seventy-sixth birthday, 5 December 1995, two months after Joyce, his wife of fifty-three years. He was survived by his son Ian.   DEREK JAMESON

Sources C. Wintour, *The rise and fall of Fleet Street* (1989) · N. Broackes, *A growing concern* (1979) · S. Jenkins, *The power and the money* (1979) · D. Jameson, *Touched by angels* (1988) · *The Times* (7 Dec 1995) · *The Guardian* (7 Dec 1995) · *The Independent* (7 Dec 1995) · *Daily Telegraph* (7 Dec 1995) · *The Observer* (1 Feb 1989) · W. D. Rubinstein, *The Harvester biographical dictionary of life peers* (1991) · personal knowledge (2004) · m. cert.

Archives FILM BBC · BFI NFTVA · ITN

Likenesses photograph, *c.*1977, repro. in *The Guardian* · photograph, 1978, repro. in *The Independent* · B. Griffin, photograph, 1979, NPG · S. Adler, photograph, 1985, NPG [*see illus.*] · photograph, repro. in *The Times* · photograph, repro. in *Daily Telegraph*

Walter Robert Matthews (1881–1973), by Karl Pollak, *c.*1948

Matthews, Walter Robert (1881–1973), dean of St Paul's and theologian, was born on 22 September 1881 in Camberwell, London, the eldest of four children (three boys and a girl) of Philip Walter Matthews, a banker, and his wife, Sophia Alice Self. After being educated at Wilson's Grammar School, Camberwell, he spent five years as a clerk in the Westminster Bank. He then became a student at King's College, London, where he graduated in 1907. He was ordained in the same year. From 1908 to 1918 he was a lecturer in philosophy at King's College, London. From 1918 to 1932 he was dean of the college and professor of the philosophy of religion. He was appointed chaplain to Gray's Inn in 1920 and preacher in 1929. He later became an honorary bencher. He was chaplain to the king in 1923–31. In 1931 he became dean of Exeter, and in 1934 he succeeded W. R. Inge as dean of St Paul's, where he remained until his retirement in 1967. Among the public questions on which he spoke during his time in St Paul's he became known chiefly (and was sometimes unfairly criticized) for his opposition to unilateral disarmament.

Matthews was a prolific writer. He poured out a constant stream of books, articles, reviews, and published sermons. Among the more important of his books are *Studies in Christian Philosophy* (1921), *God in Christian Thought and Experience* (1930), and *The Problem of Christ in the Twentieth Century* (1950), which consisted of the Maurice lectures of 1949 delivered at King's College, London. The second of these books was widely read and was, in its day, one of the most significant contributions to the study of theism.

Matthews's main interest was in philosophical theology. His work in this area bears comparison with similar work produced by such distinguished philosophical theologians of his period as William Temple and John Baillie. But he also wrote perceptively on both the theoretical and the practical aspects of ethics. His thought was governed by a determination to give due weight to all the elements in Christian faith and so to establish the right relation between them. This led him to avoid extremes and to achieve a new synthesis at many major points. Thus while he held that Christian revelation is a supernatural reality that can be discerned only by spiritual experience, he also insisted that all claims to religious truth must satisfy the appropriate rational criteria. A theological 'label' cannot be applied to him. His belief in natural theology distinguished him from the disciples of Karl Barth. Also, although he spoke of medieval theology with respect, he did not belong to the movement known as neo-Thomism or, indeed, use scholastic modes of thought. He was sometimes called, with his consent, a modernist. Certainly he shared the modernists' conviction that the theologian must take full account of modern knowledge; but he never attenuated traditional Christianity for the sake of accommodating it to non-Christian presuppositions; and he remained unwavering in his adherence to the Christian doctrines of creation, the incarnation, and the Trinity in their traditional forms. Thus although he used psychological categories in order to interpret the person of Christ, he admitted that the metaphysical terminology adopted by the fathers was ultimately required in order to affirm belief in the incarnation.

Matthews was capable of writing with equal effectiveness at different levels for different audiences. In the books cited, as well as in other books and in many articles, he wrote in a manner suited to meet the technical requirements of professional philosophers and theologians. Yet (as his Saturday sermons contributed to the *Daily Telegraph* over a period of twenty-four years show) he could also put profound truths simply and with a lucidity that characterized everything he wrote. The approach he adopted in his published work was nearly always objective. He rarely referred to his own religious experience even in his autobiography. Yet such references as there are confirm the impression, indirectly given by all his writings, of a sincerely and deeply held personal faith which, though instilled in childhood, developed through a continuing process of rational re-examination. Among his personal qualities those that especially impressed people who knew him well were his modesty and his combination of firmness with gentleness. He also possessed a distinctive sense of humour.

In 1912 Matthews married Margaret Bryan (*d.* 1963), the daughter of a schools inspector. They had two sons and one daughter. One of the sons was killed in action in 1940. The other son, (Walter) Bryan, became professor of clinical neurology in the University of Oxford. Matthews was appointed KCVO in 1935 and CH in 1962. He was honoured with the degree of DD by the universities of Cambridge, St Andrews, Glasgow, Trinity College, Dublin, and Trinity College, Toronto. He died in London on 4 December 1973.

H. P. OWEN, *rev.*

Sources *The Times* (5 Dec 1973) · W. R. Matthews, *Memories and meanings* (1969) · H. P. Owen, *W. R. Matthews: philosopher and theologian* (1976) · private information (1986) · *CGPLA Eng. & Wales* (1974) **Archives** King's Lond., lecture drafts and sermons | LPL, corresp. with H. R. L. Sheppard | FILM BFI NFTVA, documentary footage · BFI NFTVA, news footage **Likenesses** W. Stoneman, photograph, 1945, NPG · K. Pollak, photograph, *c.*1948, NPG [*see illus.*] · W. Bird, photograph, 1962, NPG · L. J. Fuller, oils, St Paul's, London, The Deanery · photograph, repro. in Matthews, *Memories and meanings*, frontispiece **Wealth at death** £33,939: probate, 18 Feb 1974, *CGPLA Eng. & Wales*

Matthews, Sir William (1844–1922), civil engineer, was born at Penzance on 8 March 1844, the eldest son of John Matthews, borough surveyor of Penzance, and his wife, Alice, daughter of Thomas Richards of Penzance. He was educated locally at a school kept by a Mr Teague, and on leaving served a short part of his apprenticeship in the engineering works of Sandys, Vivian & Co., near Hayle, Cornwall. Later he entered his father's office, where he worked for some years.

When he was about twenty Matthews prepared a survey of Penzance harbour for John Coode, the harbour engineer, and as a result was invited to become a pupil in Coode's London office, and later joined his staff. Matthews speedily rose to be chief assistant, and he was entrusted in time with home business when Coode was abroad. In 1892, the year of Coode's death, Matthews was made a partner of Sir John and his son, J. C. Coode, the firm taking the style of Coode, Son, and Matthews.

The firm, of which Matthews was senior consulting engineer for nearly forty years, acted as consulting engineers to the crown agents for the colonies. It was frequently employed by the Admiralty in connection with works at naval bases, including acting as chief engineers for the naval harbour at Dover, a work which occupied thirteen years (1896–1909). It was also consulted by the Board of Trade, the India Office, the Mersey conservancy, the Humber conservancy, the Tyne commissioners, and other public bodies. Matthews was engaged in the construction of a wet dock and a graving-dock at Singapore, and in the reconstruction of the main wharf. He visited and inspected these works in 1901 and 1905. At the same time he advised the Straits Settlements administration as to the advisability of taking over the works of the Tanjong Pagar Dock Company. For the Admiralty, Matthews reported upon the naval harbour in Malta in 1900, and in 1901 he served on a committee to inquire into the naval works at Gibraltar. He also visited and inspected harbour works in progress in Ceylon, Hong Kong, Cyprus, and at the Cape. For his services in connection with colonial harbours he was appointed CMG in 1901 and created KCMG in 1906. He was also made an officer of the order of Leopold for services in connection with the harbour of Zeebrugge in 1894.

Matthews was a member of the royal commission on coast erosion (1906), of the international technical commission on the Suez Canal (1908), and of the royal commission on oil fuel and engines (1912), and he acted as chairman of the British Standards cement committee (1912). Matthews became an associate of the Institution of Civil Engineers in 1870 and a member in 1876, and was elected president in 1907. He retired from active work at the end of 1917 but continued in an advisory capacity until 1920. He died, unmarried, at his home 14 Strathray Gardens, Eton Avenue, Hampstead, on 8 January 1922.

E. I. CARLYLE, *rev.*

Sources *The Times* (10 Jan 1922) · *PICE*, 213 (1921–2), 418–21 · Boase & Courtney, *Bibl. Corn.*, vol. 3 · *CGPLA Eng. & Wales* (1922) · *DNB* **Likenesses** M. S. A. Forbes, oils, 1908; in Inst. CE, 1937 **Wealth at death** £101,115 18s. 10d.: probate, 21 Feb 1922, *CGPLA Eng. & Wales*

Matthews, Zachariah Keodirelang (1901–1968), university teacher and political leader in South Africa, was born on 20 October 1901 in his grandmother's home at Winter's Rush, near Kimberley, in the Barkly West district of Cape Colony, the second son of Motsielwa Peter (Rre-Dinku) Matthews, who had been a mine worker at Kimberley, and Martha Mooketsi (*d.* 1959), a domestic worker. Always known as Z. K. or Zac, he grew up in the house which his father built in the Kimberley African location and first attended the United Mission School in Kimberley, then the Lyndhurst Road School, from where he won a scholarship to Lovedale in the eastern Cape. He entered South African Native College, Fort Hare in 1918, and in January 1924 became the first African to obtain a BA degree from the University of South Africa (UNISA).

Matthews then taught at Adams College in Natal, where in 1925 he became the first African principal of the high school. He studied part-time for a law degree at UNISA and was the first African to obtain such a law degree, in 1930. He was pondering a law career when offered a scholarship to go to Yale. There in 1934 he presented a thesis entitled 'Bantu law and Western civilization in South Africa', for which he obtained an MA degree. Before returning to South Africa he attended B. Malinowski's famous anthropology seminar at the London School of Economics, and met Jomo Kenyatta and other future African leaders. In January 1936 he became a lecturer in social anthropology and native law at Fort Hare. Had the legislation of that year permitted black people to be members of parliament, he would probably have been elected. Instead, he stayed at Fort Hare, becoming professor and head of African studies in 1945. His varied activities included being a member of the royal commission which reported on higher education in east Africa in 1937.

Matthews was not only an outstanding teacher; he also did much to build up Fort Hare and served as its acting principal from 1954. But he was increasingly drawn into political activity, both as a member of the natives representative council from 1942 and in the African National Congress (ANC), after brief initial involvement in the all-African convention. He chaired the committee which drew up the key document 'Africans' claims' which the ANC adopted in 1943, and in 1949 was elected its Cape leader. After resigning from the natives representative council in protest at government policy in 1950, he was involved in preparations for the defiance campaign, but then left to become a visiting professor at the Union Theological Seminary in New York.

It was as Cape leader of the ANC that in August 1953 Matthews suggested a congress of the people be called, at which a charter of rights should be drawn up. After the congress was held in 1955, he was, though acting principal of Fort Hare, arrested with others and charged with high treason. He was a dominant figure at the trial in Pretoria until the charges against him were dropped. In 1959 he boldly resigned from Fort Hare, forfeiting his pension though he was close to retirement, in protest against legislation which downgraded the institution to the status of an ethnic college and brought it under state control. Rhodes University then gave him an honorary doctorate, but in 1961, after being detained in the 1960 state of emergency, he left the country of his birth, where his enormous talent had not been used. A staunch Anglican, he spent five years in Geneva, Switzerland, working for the World Council of Churches, before in 1966 becoming Botswana's first ambassador to the United States and representative at the United Nations.

An urbane, affable man of great integrity and liberal views, who commanded widespread respect and exercised a moderating influence on more radical elements in the ANC in the early 1950s, Matthews remained committed to reconciliation despite all the adversities he suffered because of his colour. In 1928 he had married Frieda Bokwe (1905–1997), daughter of a leading Xhosa-speaking

missionary, and they had five children. One became a nurse, another a teacher, two doctors, and one a lawyer, Joe, who in 1994 became a deputy minister in South Africa's first democratic government.

Matthews died in Washington, DC, on 11 May 1968 and was buried in Gaborone, Botswana. His autobiography, *Freedom for my People*, completed by Monica Wilson, a fellow anthropologist, was published in 1981, and in 1996 his widow published her autobiography, *Remembrances*.

CHRISTOPHER SAUNDERS

Sources *Freedom for my people: the autobiography of Z. K. Matthews*, ed. I. M. Wilson (1981) · F. Matthews, *Remembrances* (1996) · S. du Rand, *Z. K. Matthews* (1993) · T. J. Juckes, *Opposition in South Africa* (1995) · W. Saayman, *A man with a shadow: the life and times of Professor Z. K. Matthews* (1997) · P. Rich, *State power and black politics in South Africa* (1996) · C. Kros and Z. K. Matthews, *Perspectives in education*, 12 (1990) · T. Karis, G. M. Carter, and G. M. Gerhardt, eds., *From protest to challenge: a documentary history of African politics in South Africa, 1882–1990*, 5 vols. (1972–97) · J. Hendricks, 'From moderation to militancy: a study of African leadership and political reactions in South Africa, 1936–1960', PhD diss., U. Mich., 1983 · J. Grobler, 'Matthews, Zachariah Keodirelang', *New dictionary of South African biography*, ed. E. J. Verwey, 1 (1995)

Archives NRA, corresp. and papers · University of South Africa, Pretoria [microfilm at University of Cape Town] | University of the Witwatersrand, South Africa, Cullen Library, Karis and Carter collection of South African political materials

Likenesses photograph, repro. in Wilson, ed., *Freedom for my people* · photograph, repro. in Matthews, *Remembrances* · photograph, repro. in du Rand, *Z. K. Matthews*

Matthey, George (1825–1913), refiner and metallurgist, was born on 8 May 1825, the fourth son of John Matthey, a stockbroker and foreign-exchange dealer, and his wife, Elizabeth, *née* Green. George was educated at Arragon House in Twickenham, but his career was determined by an agreement between his father and Percival Norton Johnson, a family friend and business client. This allowed for two sons of the former to enter Johnson's business in Hatton Garden, London, in return for the injection of new capital, believed to be about £10,000. Thus in 1838 Johnson, who at this time was refining gold, silver, and platinum on a modest scale, took on George Matthey as an apprentice.

Initially working in the assay laboratory, Matthey benefited from the knowledge and experience of Johnson and had William John Cock (1813–1892) as his mentor. In 1845 Matthey was put in charge of platinum refining, and it was due mainly to his persistent scientific endeavour over many years that the refining and fabrication of platinum was developed from a laboratory activity into a successful industrial enterprise. He persuaded Johnson to participate in the Great Exhibition in 1851; his display of platinum received a prize, but was outshone by a French competitor, who exhibited a large platinum still, used for the concentration of sulphuric acid. This spurred Matthey into deciding to become pre-eminent in the platinum business.

The first source of natural platinum was the Chocó region of South America. Then, in the 1820s, significant platinum was found in the Ural Mountains in Russia; to begin with, this was subjected to an imperial monopoly, but in 1850 some mine owners there appointed George Matthey as their refiner and selling agent. Almost immediately, in 1851, he was taken into partnership by Johnson, and the firm became Johnson and Matthey. From then on Johnson began to relinquish control of the company's affairs, and on his retirement in 1860 Matthey became senior partner, the other two partners being Matthey's younger brother, Edward, and John Scudamore Sellon, a nephew of Mrs Percival Norton Johnson. The former concentrated on the gold- and silver-refining side of the business, while Sellon was largely responsible for commercial affairs. In 1891 George Matthey became the first chairman of Johnson Matthey & Co., a position he held until his retirement in 1909.

Until the early 1900s an important use of platinum was for the manufacture of boilers in which the relatively dilute sulphuric acid produced by the chamber process could be concentrated up to about 95 per cent, or even higher. Originally this was done in small glass retorts, but their fragile nature resulted in many accidents and significant losses. Early platinum vessels were operated on a batch principle, the weak acid being boiled down to the required specific gravity before being poured or siphoned out and the operation repeated. However, at the Paris Universal Exhibition of 1855 Johnson and Matthey exhibited a platinum boiler designed for continuous operation. This had been developed in collaboration with William Petrie (1821–1908), one of the earliest chemical engineers, and was more economical to operate. Later, Matthey's invention of platinum fusion welding, using a blowpipe flame, was to reduce the cost and greatly improve the quality of such boilers. The 1855 exhibition was particularly significant, for there Matthey became friendly with Paul François Morin, an associate of Professor Henri Sainte-Claire Deville and Jules Henri Debray. In 1857 Deville and Debray devised a lime-block furnace in which platinum could be melted and refined on a large scale for the first time; the British patent rights to the process were taken up by Matthey.

At the Universal Exhibition in Paris in 1867, Johnson Matthey displayed some 15,000–20,000 ounces of manufactured platinum. A gold medal was awarded for the exhibit, and George Matthey became a chevalier of the Légion d'honneur. Discussions held at this exhibition led to the formation of the international metric commission. Platinum with 10 per cent iridium was selected for the fabrication of standard metres and kilograms, and over many years Matthey played an important part in the production of such standards. Crucially, he refined the constituents by a new method which he described in a paper to the Royal Society in 1879. In the same year he was elected FRS. Over the years, his acute business sense enabled him to see opportunities for the expansion of the platinum business and these he developed until both technical and commercial success were achieved. With the platinum business firmly established, Matthey maintained mutually beneficial contacts with the scientific community. An eminent member of several scientific and technical bodies, he was active in the establishment of the City and Guilds colleges at South Kensington and Finsbury. At times he held directorships in a variety of companies. Elected to the Goldsmiths' Company in 1853, he became a member of its court in 1853, and served as prime warden in 1872 and 1894.

In 1853 Matthey married Charlotte Ann Davies (d. 1919), daughter of Richard Davies of South Hackney. They had eleven children, of whom Richard Davies Matthey (1858–1929) and Percy St Clair Matthey (1863–1928) subsequently entered the family business. George Matthey died at Rosemount, his Eastbourne residence, on 14 February 1913.

Almost 150 years later Johnson Matthey was still successfully engaged in the refining, fabrication, and marketing of gold and silver, and the platinum metals; in 1994–5 the company was the largest gold refiner in the world, and the sole marketing agent and joint refiner for Rustenburg Platinum Mines, the world's largest source of the platinum metals.

IAN E. COTTINGTON

Sources D. McDonald and L. B. Hunt, *A history of platinum and its allied metals* (1982), 270–315 · D. McDonald, 'A history of Johnson Matthey & Co. Limited', vol. 1, 1860–1914, Johnson Matthey plc, Cockspur Street, London · E. Matthey, private memoirs, Johnson Matthey plc, Cockspur Street, London · L. B. Hunt, 'George Matthey and the building of the platinum industry', *Platinum Metals Review*, 23 (1979), 68–77
Archives NRA, priv. coll., corresp. | Johnson Matthey plc, Cockspur Street, London, corresp.
Likenesses portrait, c.1845, Johnson Matthey plc, London · portrait, 1880–89, Johnson Matthey plc, London
Wealth at death £305,252 6s. 5d.: probate, 3 May 1913, CGPLA Eng. & Wales

Matthiessen, Augustus (1831–1870), chemist and physicist, was born in London on 2 January 1831, the son of William Matthiessen and his wife, Jane. His father, who died while Matthiessen was quite young, was a merchant. A paralytic seizure during infancy produced a permanent and severe twitching of Matthiessen's right hand. Notwithstanding the taste for chemistry which he displayed as a boy, on leaving school he was sent by his guardians to learn farming with a Dorset farmer, as being the only occupation suited to his condition. He then considered a business career, but became interested in the new subject of agricultural chemistry and, on coming of age, went to the University of Giessen in Germany, where he studied under Will and H. L. Buff, and graduated PhD. From 1853 he spent nearly four years under Professor Robert Wilhelm Bunsen at Heidelberg, and by means of his electrolytic method isolated the metals calcium and strontium in the pure state for the first time. In Professor Kirchhoff's physics laboratory he studied the electrical conductivity of these new metals and of many others, publishing his results in Germany and England. He returned to London in 1857 with a thorough knowledge of the methods of physics and of inorganic chemistry, and studied organic chemistry with Professor August Wilhelm von Hofmann at the Royal College of Chemistry. Work done under Hofmann's direction led the way to Matthiessen's considerable researches on the opium alkaloids of later years. Matthiessen soon fitted up his own laboratory at 1 Torrington Place, where he began a series of investigations on the physical properties of pure metals and alloys which has become a classic.

The preparation of copper of the greatest conductivity had great practical importance in connection with telegraphy; Matthiessen showed that the discrepancies of previous observations and the low conductivity of certain supposedly pure samples were due to the presence of minute quantities of other elements. He embodied his results in a report presented in 1860 to the government committee appointed to inquire into the subject, and in a paper with M. Holzmann, published in the *Philosophical Transactions*. In 1861 he became a fellow, and afterwards a member, of the council of the Royal Society. In 1862 he was elected to the lectureship on chemistry at St Mary's Hospital, a post which he held until 1868. During 1862–5 he undertook important voluntary work for the British Association committee on electrical standards, and in the latter year constructed for them ten standards of resistance and several copies of these, made from various metals and alloys.

In 1867 Matthiessen summarized his work on the constitution of alloys in a lecture given before the Chemical Society. Besides demonstrating that tin, lead, zinc, and cadmium behaved differently in alloys from other metals, he made two general suggestions of great importance: first, that small amounts of impurity in a metal do not produce the remarkable changes in physical properties by their direct action, but by causing the metal with which they are alloyed to assume an allotropic, or different, form; and second, that in most cases alloys must be considered as 'solidified solutions'. In 1868 Matthiessen was appointed lecturer on chemistry at St Bartholomew's Hospital in conjunction with Professor William Odling; on the latter's resignation in 1870 he became sole lecturer. In 1869 he was awarded a royal medal by the Royal Society 'for his researches on the electric and other physical and chemical properties of metals and their alloys'. Besides his other work he had a large private practice as a consulting chemist, and from January 1869 to June 1870 was one of the editors of the *Philosophical Magazine*. In 1870 he was appointed examiner to the University of London. On 6 October of the same year he committed suicide in his laboratory at St Bartholomew's. He left a note saying that he had been charged with indecent assault on a boy, and that he was innocent, but could not bear to face the proceedings. At the time of his death he was a member of a committee inquiring into the chemical nature of pure cast iron, and he was also experimenting with the construction of a standard pyrometer.

Matthiessen was a prolific author of scientific papers. His researches showed remarkable acuteness, experimental skill, and conscientiousness, together with a distinct power of generalization. That with his physical defect he should have accomplished so much delicate and exact work is a proof of rare perseverance and his contemporaries thought highly of him.

P. J. Hartog, rev. Anita McConnell

Sources *The Times* (8 Oct 1870), 5e · *Nature*, 2 (1870), 475, 517–18 · *Pharmaceutical Journal and Transactions*, 3rd ser., 1 (1870–71), 317 · *Chemical News* (14 Oct 1870), 189 · *JCS*, 24 (1871), 615 17 · *American Journal of Science*, 2nd ser., 1 (1870), 437 · *PRS*, 18 (1869–70), 111–12 · *CGPLA Eng. & Wales* (1871) · *IGI*

Wealth at death under £7000: double probate, Jan 1871, *CGPLA Eng. & Wales* (1870)

Mattingly, Harold (1884–1964), numismatist and ancient historian, was born at Market Hill, Sudbury, Suffolk, on 24 December 1884, the son of Robert Mattingly, a clothier who became a JP and mayor of Sudbury, and his wife, Gertrude Emma Boggis. In January 1896 he went to the Leys School in Cambridge, where he concentrated on classics. In 1903 he went up to Gonville and Caius College, Cambridge, gaining firsts in both parts of the classical tripos (1906, 1907). Between 1907 and 1909 he studied under Eduard Meyer in Berlin and Ernst Fabricius in Freiburg, the research undertaken in Germany on the Roman administration being published as *The Imperial Civil Service* (1909). After returning to a fellowship at Gonville and Caius College for 1909–10, he was then appointed to a post in the department of printed books in the British Museum and transferred to the department of coins and medals in 1912.

Mattingly's arrival in the department of coins and medals coincided with the heyday of the printed descriptive catalogue of the museum's collections; in 1873 the publication of the catalogues of the Greek coins, of notable austerity, had begun; H. A. Grueber, whose interest lay in English coinage, had been set to work on the coins of the Roman republic, publishing the catalogue in three volumes in 1910; and Mattingly was set to work on the coins of the Roman empire.

The traditional way of arranging the coins of the Roman republic was in alphabetical order of the names of the *gens* of the monetary magistrate responsible for an issue, with a rough attempt at chronological order of the issues of, say, the Aemillii. The coins of the Roman empire had traditionally been grouped by emperor, then arranged in alphabetical order of the reverse legends. In the case of the coins in the trays of the British Museum, the republican series had been assigned to what he believed to be the correct mints and dates by Count John de Salis between 1859 and 1869; and it is the view of those who worked in the department after Mattingly that de Salis had done the same for the bulk of the imperial series, but that Mattingly had restored much of it to the traditional arrangement. Unfortunately de Salis had left no written explanation of his criteria. In the case of the republican series, Grueber broke new ground by including in his catalogue a long introduction and very extensive annotation; much of both consists of plaintive attempts to make sense of de Salis's arrangement, which he evidently regarded as sacred. Mattingly, on the other hand, did much work on organizing the imperial series for himself. When the first volume of the catalogue, *Coins of the Roman Empire in the British Museum*, appeared in 1923 its introduction and notes represented his justification of his own arrangement; but the preface by G. F. Hill and occasional notes in other publications make it clear that to a large but unknowable extent Mattingly followed de Salis. On any showing, however, the volume made extraordinary progress in ordering the imperial series, and above all made the critical breakthrough of rendering the imperial series intelligible to non-specialists. The model was not replaced until the 1970s and 1980s. The briefer presentation of the coinage in the first volume of *Roman Imperial Coinage*, written in collaboration with E. A. Sydenham and also published in 1923, naturally depended on the research undertaken for the British Museum catalogue.

In the First World War, Mattingly served initially with the London regiment, then in the postal censorship bureau. His horror of war brought on a nervous breakdown, which was repeated in the Second World War; shortly before the end of the First World War he joined the Society of Friends. On 23 January 1915 he married Marion Grahame (1890/91–1958), the daughter of John Young Meikleham, a merchant; they had a daughter and three sons.

The volumes of *Roman Imperial Coinage* and *Catalogues of the Coins of the Roman Empire in the British Museum* continued to appear throughout Mattingly's career; but an interest in the chronology of the republican series, adumbrated in an article of 1922, occupied more and more of his attention. An article of 1933, written with E. S. G. Robinson (published in the *Proceedings of the British Academy* for 1932), set the cat among the pigeons by dating the inception of the denarius nearly a century later than had always been believed. The article's clarity of exposition, however, was not rivalled in his later production, which also tended increasingly to resort to *ex cathedra* statements. At the same time, the later volumes of the British Museum catalogues were marked by less reading than had been apparent hitherto; his general historical work was conventional; and his attempts at economic history did not involve any significant use of comparative material.

Mattingly was remembered by all who knew him as a model of kindness and helpfulness; he edited the *Numismatic Chronicle* from 1936 to 1952, and served as president of the Royal Numismatic Society from 1942 to 1948. He was elected a fellow of the British Academy in 1946, and was made CBE in 1960. After retirement as an assistant keeper at the British Museum in 1948, he moved initially to Cambridge, but found little welcome, and later moved to Chesham, Buckinghamshire, where he died at his home, 9 Missenden Road, on 26 January 1964.

MICHAEL H. CRAWFORD

Sources R. A. G. Carson, 'Harold Mattingly', *PBA*, 50 (1964), 331–40 · R. A. G. Carson, 'Harold Mattingly', *Numismatic Chronicle*, 7th ser., 5 (1965), 239–54 · R. A. G. Carson and C. H. V. Sutherland, eds., *Essays in Roman coinage presented to Harold Mattingly* (1956) · private information (2004) [R. A. G. Carson; Harold B. Mattingly, son] · b. cert. · m. cert. · d. cert.
Archives Bodl. Oxf., letters to O. G. S. Crawford
Likenesses W. Stoneman, photograph, 1946, repro. in Carson, 'Harold Mattingly', *PBA*, facing p. 331 · P. Vincze, medal
Wealth at death £9163: probate, 14 April 1964, *CGPLA Eng. & Wales*

Mattison, Francis Charles (1860–1944), businessman, was born on 6 May 1860 in Alnwick, Northumberland, the son of a house painter, John Mattison, and his wife, Mary Ann, *née* Alder. The community into which he was born was part of the estates of the duke of Northumberland, a member of the Percys, one of the great landowning families of England, who had owned Alnwick Castle since 1309. Although his family was of modest means, young Francis was born at a time when the resident duke was taking a particular interest in the welfare of the county and making great efforts to improve the conditions of the poor, and it is likely that the boy received decent basic schooling. Little is known of his upbringing, but a sound education and a good brain he must have had for he went into banking and eventually became manager of a Liverpool and Martins branch bank in Bexleyheath, Kent, an impressive achievement for the son of a house painter. In 1892 he married Annie Maude, daughter of Julius Hewett, civil engineer; they lived for several years at Blackheath, and raised at least two children.

In his capacity as bank manager Mattison met Andrew Pringle, a customer who was also a director of the newly formed photographic manufacturing company, Kodak Limited. The recent death of Kodak's joint managing director, George Dickman, had left a vacancy for a managerial assistant with a financial background, and Pringle asked the bank manager if he could advise; to his surprise, Mattison suggested himself. After further discussions to establish whether Mattison was serious, he was offered the post and joined Kodak in March 1899. His bank was astonished that he should desert banking for trade and promised Mattison that should he reconsider before the end of the year they would find a job for him. In his early years with Kodak there were times when Mattison regretted not taking advantage of this offer but he persevered and promotion to company secretary in 1903 extinguished any lingering doubts. Thereafter he steadily progressed. In 1909 he became deputy managing director and in May 1911 was appointed to the board as a director in place of the recently deceased Sir G. W. des Voux GCMG. In January 1920 he was appointed managing director and became chairman of the board in 1927.

Mattison joined Kodak during an eventful period in the company's history. Although built on products marketed by the American entrepreneur George Eastman, Kodak Limited was registered in November 1898 as a British company. In 1901, however, soon after Mattison joined, a proposal by the Treasury to tax company profits to help pay for the Second South African War prompted Eastman to set up the Eastman Kodak Company of New Jersey. Eastman's new company immediately acquired the stock of Kodak Limited and associated companies in Europe and America, and overall control reverted to the United States.

Mattison's first post at Kodak was as assistant to the deputy managing director, George Davison, a distinguished landscape photographer who had been associated with the company from its earliest days. Davison was an active left-wing socialist with a reputation for being impulsive in business and cold and impersonal with his staff. He had little in common with the conservative Mattison, a precise, dignified man whose hobby was church-bell ringing. Eastman gradually lost confidence in the controversial Davison and in 1908 replaced him with an American, Charles Gifford, a man much more to Mattison's liking. Mattison was being groomed for the future and began to carry an increasing burden of the company's business, particularly during the First World War when Gifford was often away. Gifford retired in 1919 and a year later Mattison was appointed managing director. He began to assume wider responsibilities but his health failed when he developed pernicious anaemia. Although warned by colleagues that Mattison might not recover, Eastman had great respect for his abilities and to give the invalid the opportunity to regain his health, temporarily appointed the British scientist, C. E. K. Mees, in his place. The arrangement was successful; to the surprise of many, Mattison made a complete recovery and Mees was able to return to his laboratory within a year. Working closely with Eastman, Mattison played a prominent part in promoting Kodak's fortunes in Europe. Particularly important was the takeover of Charles Pathé's film company in 1927. By the end of the 1930s Kodak dominated the European motion picture market and was winning an ever increasing share of the amateur materials and equipment market.

Mattison was unusual in showing little interest in the manufacturing or scientific side of Kodak's business and he is said rarely to have visited the Harrow factory unless accompanied by Eastman. Yet he played a critical role in helping to develop Kodak into a multinational concern and the foremost photographic manufacturing company in the world. By 1943, although still in post as chairman, he was a sick man and confined to a wheelchair. He resigned at the end of the year and died at his home, Bridge House, West Overcliffe Drive, Westbourne, Bournemouth, on 14 December 1944. He was survived by his wife.   JOHN WARD

Sources M. D. Gauntlet, 'A history of Kodak Limited to 1977', 1978 · E. E. Blake, 'Reminiscences', 1959 · private information (2004) · *British Journal of Photography* (12 May 1911), 370 · *British Journal of Photography* (16 Jan 1920), 42 · *British Journal of Photography* (29 Dec 1944), 461 · C. W. Ackerman, *George Eastman* (1930) · C. E. K. Mees, *From dry plate to ektachrome* (1961) · F. M. L. Thompson, *English landed society in the nineteenth century* (1963) · b. cert. · m. cert. · d. cert. · *CGPLA Eng. & Wales* (1945) · *Kelly's directory*
Archives Kodak Ltd, Harrow, European archives
Likenesses photograph, Kodak Ltd Archives, Harrow
Wealth at death £227,657 14s. 7d.: probate, 29 March 1945, *CGPLA Eng. & Wales*

Mattli, Giuseppe Gustavo (1907–1982), fashion designer, was born in Locarno, Switzerland, and grew up in Lugano with one brother and twelve younger sisters. At an early age he showed an interest in clothing when he began making clothes for his sisters. In 1925 he was apprenticed to an oil company in Geneva; however, after showing no interest in pursuing such a career, he soon left. Keen to develop a career in the growing fashion industry of the mid-1920s, Mattli moved to England in 1926 in order to learn tailoring skills and English. Following initial training in London he moved to Paris in order to continue learning couture skills at the House of Premet, founded in 1911. Having learned

the skills necessary to produce his own collections Mattli returned to London and opened his own couture house in 1934. His premises, shared with a fellow couturier, Charles Creed, were located behind Harrods in an increasingly fashionable area, noted for its top fashion designers. Later described in *Vogue* in 1953 as 'charming and a perfectionist whose favourite phrase is "it's not quite …"', Mattli created stylish couture outfits as well as ready-to-wear garments, which were initially modelled by his wife, Olga, whom he had married before 1934. Early success meant that by 1938 he was showing collections in Paris, but further growth in Paris was curtailed by the outbreak of the Second World War. In 1941–2 he joined the recently established Incorporated Society of London Fashion Designers, whose work included promoting their designs abroad, especially in North and South America. However, postwar fashions were dominated by Parisian designers such as Christian Dior, although Mattli continued to produce quality designs that frequently featured in articles on the London collections in *Vogue* during the 1950s and early 1960s. 'Mattli's clothes have charming wearable qualities. Always one can rely on him for the perfect "little black dress". One feels he cares more about dressing women than putting over fashion themes, good though his are' (*Vogue*, March 1953, 125). As well as the quintessential black dress, Mattli was noted for his feminine evening and cocktail dresses, theatre coats, and understated tailored suits. His style was characterized by softly draped fabrics and easily wearable designs. Some of his outfits had matching hats designed by Olga. Mattli contributed regularly to *Reynolds News* during the 1950s. In 1955, however, the company with whom Mattli worked went into liquidation, bringing to an end his couture line. But he continued to produce ready-to-wear collections throughout the 1960s. The House of Mattli closed in the early 1970s, a couple of seasons after Mattli himself retired. He died at his home, Grange Farm Cottage, Curridge Common in Curridge, near Newbury, Berkshire, on 9 February 1982. Examples of clothing designed by Mattli are in the Victoria and Albert Museum, London, the Museum of London, the London College of Fashion, and the Museum of Costume in Bath.   REBECCA QUINTON

Sources C. McDowell, *McDowell's dictionary of twentieth century fashion* (1984) · G. O'Hara, *The encyclopaedia of fashion* (1986) · T. Glenville, F. Anderson, and E. Damon, 'Selected glossary of British designers, 1947–1997', *The Cutting* (1995) · N. Cawthorne, *The new look: the Dior revolution* (1996) · C. McDowell, *Forties fashion and the new look* (1997) · V. Mendes and A. de la Haye, *20th century fashion* (1999) · 'Are they worth it?', *Vogue* (Sept 1960) · G. Perint, 'Leading looks from London', *Vogue* (March 1963) · 'If you dressed at …', *Vogue* (Sept 1956) · 'London's fashion centres … London', *Vogue* (March 1953) · 'The London collections', *Vogue* (March 1959) · 'The London collections', *Vogue* (Aug 1950) · 'The London way', *Vogue* (March 1950) · 'The London collections', *Vogue* (March 1951) · 'The London collections', *Vogue* (March 1956) · d. cert. · *CGPLA Eng. & Wales* (1982)
Likenesses photograph, Sept 1960, repro. in 'Are they worth it?', *Vogue* · N. Parkinson, photograph, repro. in 'London's fashion centres', *Vogue*
Wealth at death £114,857: probate, 11 March 1982, *CGPLA Eng. & Wales*

Mattocks, George (1734/5–1804). *See under* Mattocks, Isabella (1746–1826).

Mattocks [*née* Hallam]**, Isabella** (1746–1826), actress and singer, was born at 3 Lambeth Street, Whitechapel, London, in 1746, and baptized at St Mary, Whitechapel, on 25 May, the daughter of Lewis *Hallam (1714?–1756?) and his wife, Sarah *Hallam (*d.* 1774) [*see under* Hallam, Lewis]. Both her parents were actors, as were her father's sister Ann and his brothers, Adam, George, and William. Her paternal grandfather, the actor Thomas Hallam, had been accidentally killed by Charles Macklin during a greenroom quarrel in 1735, and she was also related to the family of John Rich, the Covent Garden patentee. Her father was in financial difficulties by the early 1750s and in 1752 went to North America as manager of a group of English actors, taking his wife and three older children but leaving Isabella in the care of his sister Ann and her second husband, the actor John Barrington.

Isabella believed that she took her first acting role at the age of four and a half, when she appeared as the Parish Girl in John Gay's *The What D'Ye Call It* for her uncle's benefit at Covent Garden. This must have been on 1 April 1752, when she was nearly six and was so small that a gentleman commented 'he could hear her very well, but he could not see her without a glass' ('Biographical sketch of Mrs Mattocks', 323). The Barringtons were members of the Covent Garden company, and during the next six years the young Isabella made a few appearances there each season, acting the Parish Girl, the Duke of York in *Richard III*, and various pages, including Robin in *The Merry Wives of Windsor*. She later wrote that her aunt and uncle became parents to her in the tenderest sense of the word, and gave her 'an expensive and a finished education' (ibid.). It seems likely that she was at school from 1758 to 1762, when she made very few stage appearances. During the summer season at Jacob's Wells Theatre, Bristol, in 1760 she sang and played the guitar at her aunt's benefit. In April 1761, at Ann Barrington's Covent Garden benefit, she played her first adult role, Juliet, with her aunt as Lady Capulet, and for the Barringtons' joint benefit the following year she again acted Juliet and also sang Laura in William Boyce's musical afterpiece *The Chaplet*.

In autumn 1762 the sixteen-year-old Isabella joined the Covent Garden company, where she remained, apart from the two seasons 1784–5 and 1785–6, for the next forty-six years. She took eighteen roles during her first season alone, in both comedies and tragedies, including Dorinda in George Farquhar's *The Stratagem*, Miss Hoyden in John Vanbrugh's *The Relapse*, and Serina in Thomas Otway's *The Orphan*. 'Having an exceeding good natural voice, improved by a knowledge of music' (*Theatrical Biography*, 2.13), she created many roles in English operas and musical afterpieces, beginning with Lucinda, the lively second heroine of Isaac Bickerstaff's *Love in a Village* (8 December 1762). During the next two seasons Miss Hallam sang Nysa in Kane O'Hara's burletta *Midas*, Sylvia in the nineteen-year-old Charles Dibdin's *The Shepherd's Artifice*, and Theodosia in Bickerstaff's *The Maid of the Mill*. The

Isabella Mattocks (1746–1826), by Gainsborough Dupont, *c.*1793–4 [as Catherine in *Catherine and Petruchio* by David Garrick]

handsome tenor George Mattocks [*see below*] was the young male lead in these pieces, and he and Isabella were married in the first few days of April 1765, during the Easter break. They reputedly eloped to France because the Barringtons opposed the match, possibly for economic reasons or because of George Mattocks's earlier love affairs. However, friendly relations with her aunt and uncle were soon re-established. Mr and Mrs Mattocks sang together in Bickerstaff's *Lionel and Clarissa* (25 February 1768), O'Hara's *The Golden Pippin* (6 February 1773), Sheridan's *The Duenna* (21 November 1775), and other less long-lasting works. Isabella Mattocks also sang in Gloucester at the 1769 Three Choirs meeting and in some of the Covent Garden oratorio seasons. Although successful as Ophelia, she was considered too short and not beautiful enough for leading parts in tragedy. Younger sopranos took over her musical roles in the early 1780s, but by then she was firmly established as a favourite comic actress, specializing in pert servant girls, vulgar citizens' wives, old maids, and gossips.

Both George and Isabella Mattocks were rumoured to have indulged in short-lived infidelities, she with the actor Robert *Bensley (1741/2?–1817) and he with Elizabeth (*d.* 1780), the wife of the theatre musician John Abraham Fisher, but their marriage endured. She accompanied her husband to the various summer theatres of which he was the manager and, after the death of John Barrington in January 1773, her aunt acted with them in the Liverpool summer seasons for the next few years. Isabella Mattocks left Covent Garden in June 1784 to work full-time with her husband in his Liverpool and Manchester theatres, but after two years of an over-ambitious programme he was ruined financially. In autumn 1786 she returned to Covent Garden, where, until her retirement twenty-two years later, she played numerous parts every season in revivals and new plays. John O'Keeffe, who called her 'sweet Mrs Mattocks' (O'Keeffe, 2.411), wrote Betty Blackberry for her in *The Farmer* (1787) and Mrs Cockletop in *Modern Antiques* (1791). She created Widow Warren in Thomas Holcroft's *The Road to Ruin* (1792), Mrs Placid in Elizabeth Inchbald's *Every One has his Fault* (1793), Lady Sarah Savage in Frederick Reynolds's *The Rage!* (1794), and Miss Lucretia Mac Tab in George Colman the younger's *The Poor Gentleman* (1801), where she was said to have worn the dress that was made for her when she first played Lucinda in *Love in a Village*. She was much admired as a speaker of epilogues, particularly those written for her by Miles Peter Andrews. Some critics found her manner and facial expressions too vulgar, and James Boaden commented:

> in her private manners she was rather refined, and had some of the graceful ease of the old school. On the stage she had a taste for the greatest *breadth* of effect, and excited probably as much laughter as [William] Lewis himself. (Boaden, *Kemble*, 1.84)

In the summer she generally joined her husband in Liverpool, where he was treasurer of the theatre, and she acted in his last benefit there in 1802, two years before his death. Mrs Mattocks gave her final performance at Covent Garden on 7 June 1808, playing Flora in Susannah Centlivre's *The Wonder*, 'with all the freshness and spirit of a woman in her prime' and speaking a simple, affecting farewell, 'having changed her stage dress for the lady-like attire of black silk' ('Mrs Mattocks', 430).

George and Isabella Mattocks had one daughter, Isabella Anne (*b.* 31 October 1773), 'a very accomplished young lady' (*GM*, 1st ser., 74, 1804, 884), who married a barrister, Nathaniel Huson, in 1801. Huson died ten years later, leaving his wife and young daughter unprovided for. John Genest records that Mrs Mattocks, who had given her son-in-law power of attorney, discovered after his death that he had sold her £6000 of stocks and spent the money. On 24 May 1813 a benefit performance was organized for her at the King's Theatre, which raised the impressive sum of £1092. Isabella Mattocks died at her home in High Street, Kensington, on 25 June 1826 and was buried on 1 July at St Mary Abbots, Kensington.

George Mattocks (1734/5–1804), singer and theatre manager, sang as a boy at Southwark fair in September 1746, and in August 1748 was advertised as singing and dancing at Bartholomew fair. A Miss Mattocks, perhaps his elder sister, acted minor roles at Southwark fair and at the Goodman's Fields Theatre in autumn 1746 and appeared at Covent Garden in early 1748. The young George Mattocks sang at Drury Lane in February and March 1749 in *The Triumph of Peace*, Thomas Arne's masque celebrating the treaty of Aix-la-Chapelle. He remained at Drury Lane until summer 1752, singing between the acts and in musical pieces and acting Donalbain in *Macbeth*. After appearing in the provinces during the next few

years, he returned to London to play Macheath in *The Beggar's Opera* at Covent Garden on 1 November 1757, advertised as having 'never appeared on that stage or any other these 6 years' (Stone, 623). In fact, he had sung the role for his benefit at Norwich earlier in 1757. Mattocks has been claimed as the father of two of the children of the actress Harriet *Pitt (1748?–1814) [*see under* Pitt, Ann], Harriet Pitt and George Cecil Pitt (*d.* 1820), but although there was gossip before his marriage implying that he had many love affairs, there seems to be no contemporary source connecting him to Harriet Pitt or her children.

Mattocks remained at Covent Garden for another twenty-seven years, performing incidental music, taking a few speaking parts, and creating the tenor young-lead roles in many English operas and afterpieces. He was the first Young Meadows in *Love in a Village* (1762), Apollo in *Midas* (1764), Lord Aimworth in *The Maid of the Mill* (1765), Lionel in *Lionel and Clarissa* (1768), Tom in Joseph Reed's *Tom Jones* (1769), Ferdinand in *The Duenna* (1775), and Don Fernando in O'Keeffe's *The Castle of Andalusia* (1782). *The Smithfield Rosciad* found 'Miss Molly Mattocks' (p. 18) soft and affected and *Theatrical Biography* complained of his stiffness and want of feeling, but *Thespis* praised his 'tender strain, so delicately clear' (Kelly, 2.24) and John Bernard found him, 'with the exception of [Joseph] Vernon, the best acting vocalist I ever saw' (Bernard, 1.3).

Bernard, a stage-struck boy in Portsmouth in the late 1760s, admired Mattocks walking to morning rehearsal in a gold-laced suit of green and white: 'such a swan-like dignity about him, such a fascinating glitter, and "stand-out-of-the-way" consequence; his feather floating, his skirts flying, his sword dangling, and his stick thumping, as he proceeded' (Bernard, 1.3). Mattocks acted in the provinces every summer, and in 1771 he became a lessee of the Portsmouth theatre. The following year, in partnership with the Covent Garden prompter Joseph Younger, he leased the newly built Theatre Royal at Liverpool. Then, in 1775, he and Younger also took a twenty-one-year lease on the Manchester theatre, and in 1779 Mattocks was involved with a theatre in Birmingham. Isabella Mattocks made summer appearances at these theatres, returning to Liverpool many times, while George Mattocks concentrated on management. In London he gradually lost his roles to younger singers, and he left Covent Garden at the end of the 1783–4 season, moving with his wife to the north of England. Younger died in September 1784, leaving Mattocks in sole charge of the Liverpool and Manchester theatres. He established a strong company, with an impressive array of visiting stars in the summer, but after two years had sustained heavy losses, so that his wife was forced to return to Covent Garden. The bankruptcy of George Mattocks of Liverpool was announced in May 1788. After his financial ruin he apparently worked for Major John Halliday, a gentleman 'well known through the kingdom for theatrical talent, which he frequently displayed for charitable purposes' (*GM*, 1st ser., 64, 1794, 672). Following Halliday's death in 1794, Mattocks was employed by the theatre manager Francis Aickin in a position variously described as treasurer and stage manager, working at Liverpool, at both Edinburgh and Liverpool in 1801–2, and, after Aickin lost the Liverpool lease in early 1803, solely in Edinburgh. George Mattocks died at his lodgings in 5 Shakespeare Square, Edinburgh, on 14 August 1804. His funeral at the Calton burying-ground on 18 August was attended by 'a number of respectable friends and all the theatrical persons in Edinburgh' (*GM*, 1st ser., 74, 1804, 884). OLIVE BALDWIN and THELMA WILSON

Sources G. W. Stone, ed., *The London stage, 1660–1800*, pt 4: *1747–1776* (1962) · C. B. Hogan, ed., *The London stage, 1660–1800*, pt 5: *1776–1800* (1968) · Genest, *Eng. stage*, vols. 5–8 · I. Mattocks, letter, Harvard TC, TS 990.1, v.III, p. 30 · 'Biographical sketch of Mrs Mattocks', *Monthly Mirror*, 9 (1800), 323–4 · 'Memoir of Mrs Mattocks', *European Magazine*, 52 (Oct 1807), 247–56 · 'Mrs Mattocks', *New Monthly Magazine* (1826), pt 3, 430–31 · J. Bernard, *Retrospections of the stage*, 2 vols. (1830), vol. 1 · *Theatrical biography*, 2 (1772) · [J. Haslewood], *The secret history of the green rooms: containing authentic and entertaining memoirs of the actors and actresses in the three theatres royal*, 2 vols. (1790) · *Smithfield Rosciad* (1763) · H. Kelly, *Thespis*, 2 (1767) · J. O'Keeffe, *Recollections of the life of John O'Keeffe, written by himself*, 2 (1826) · J. Boaden, *Memoirs of the life of John Philip Kemble, esq.*, 2 vols. (1825), vol. 1 · *Memoirs of Mrs Inchbald*, ed. J. Boaden, 2 vols. (1833) · parish register, St Mary Whitechapel, Middlesex, 25 May 1746 [baptism] · parish register, St Pancras, Middlesex, 28 Nov 1773 [daughter's baptism] · D. Lysons and others, *Origin and progress of the Meeting of the Three Choirs*, new edn (1865) · R. Jenkins, *Memoirs of the Bristol stage* (1826) · H. Ackroyd, *The Liverpool stage* (1996) · 'Provincial drama', *Monthly Mirror*, 14 (1802), 418 · J. L. Hodgkinson and R. Pogson, *The early Manchester theatre* (1960) · T. Wilkinson, *The wandering patentee, or, A history of the Yorkshire theatres from 1770 to the present time*, 4 vols. (1795) · J. Winston, *The theatric tourist* (1805) · S. Rosenfeld, *Strolling players and drama in the provinces, 1660–1765* (1939) · J. C. Dibdin, *The annals of the Edinburgh stage* (1888) · G. O. Seilhamer, *History of the American theatre*, 3 vols. (1888–91); repr. (1968), vol. 1 · R. Wright, *Revels in Jamaica, 1682–1838* (1986) · *Crosby's pocket companion to the playhouses* (1796) · *GM*, 1st ser., 74 (1804), 884 · *GM*, 1st ser., 64 (1794), 672 · *GM*, 1st ser., 58 (1788), 470 · *Theatrical portraits* [n.d., c.1780] · W. Hawkins, *Miscellanies in prose and verse, containing candid and impartial observations on the principal performers belonging to the two Theatres-Royal, from January 1773 to May 1775* (1775) · R. Ryan, *Dramatic table talk*, 2 (1825) · A. Pasquin [J. Williams], 'The children of Thespis', *Poems*, 2 [1789] · *Monthly Mirror*, new ser., 3 (1808), 464 · *The Times* (24 May 1813) [benefit performance]

Archives Harvard TC, letter

Likenesses double portrait, line engraving, watch-paper, pubd 1773 (George Mattocks as Apollo in O'Hara's *Midas*, with Elizabeth Baker as Daphne), BM · C. Grignion, double portrait, line engraving, pubd 1777 (George Mattocks as Ferdinand in Shakespeare's *The Tempest*, with Ann Brown as Miranda; after R. Dighton), BM, Harvard TC · double portrait, mezzotint, pubd 1777 (George Mattocks as Ferdinand in Sheridan's *The duenna*, with John Quick as Mendoza), BM, Harvard TC · R. Laurie, mezzotint, pubd 1779 (George Mattocks; after R. Dighton), BM, Harvard TC · Terry, line engraving, pubd 1779 (as Hermione in Shakespeare's *The winter's tale*), BM, Harvard TC · Terry, line engraving, pubd 1779 (George Mattocks as Achilles in Gay's *Achilles*), BM, Harvard TC · Cook, line engraving, pubd 1780 (speaking epilogue to Murphy's *Know your own mind*; after Dodd), Harvard TC · R. Laurie, mezzotint, pubd 1780 (after R. Dighton), BM, Harvard TC · line engraving, pubd 1781 (as Isabella in Centlivre's *The wonder*), BM, Harvard TC · Barlow, line engraving, pubd 1792 (as Mrs Warren in Holcroft's *The road to ruin*; after Cruikshanks), BM · G. Dupont, oils, c.1793–1794 (as Catherine in Garrick's *Catherine and Petruchio*), Garr. Club [see illus.] · Alais, stipple, pubd 1806 (as Jacinta in King's *Lover's quarrels*), Harvard TC · Chapman, stipple and line engraving, 1807 (as Lady Wishfort in Congreve's *The way of the world*; after Moses), repro. in *British drama* (1817) · P. Audinet, line engraving (as Lady Restless in Murphy's *All in the wrong*; after S. De Wilde), repro. in J. Bell, *Bell's British theatre* (1792) · J. Collyer, double portrait, line engraving (George Mattocks as Lord Aimworth in Bickerstaff's *The maid of the mill*, with Elizabeth Bannister as Patty; after D. Dodd), repro. in Lowndes, *New English theatre* (1782) · J. Corner, line engraving (as Elvira in Dryden's *The Spanish friar*; after S. De Wilde), repro. in J. Bell, *Bell's British theatre* (1791) · S. De Wilde, oils (as Lady Restless in Murphy's *All in the wrong*), Garr. Club · S. De Wilde, pencil and chalk drawing (as Lettice in Fielding's *The intriguing chambermaid*), BM · C. Grignion, line engraving (as Princess Catherine in Shakespeare's *Henry V*; after J. Roberts), repro. in Bell, ed., *Bell's edition of Shakespeare's plays*, 9 vols. (1773–4) [facs. edn (1969)] · B. Reading, double portrait, line engraving (as Miss Prue in Congreve's *Love for love*, with Wilson as Ben; after E. Edwards), repro. in Lowndes, *New English theatre* (1776) · W. Ridley, stipple (after Miller), repro. in *Monthly Mirror* (June 1800) · Ridley & Co., stipple (after S. Drummond), repro. in *European Magazine* (Oct 1807) · J. Roberts, drawing (as Princess Catherine in Shakespeare's *Henry V*), BM · Thornthwaite, line engraving (as Elvira in Dryden's *The Spanish friar*; after J. Roberts), repro. in J. Bell, *Bell's British theatre* (1777) · Thornthwaite, line engraving (George Mattocks as Achilles in Gay's *Achilles*; after J. Roberts), repro. in J. Bell, *Bell's British theatre* (1777) · Walker, double portrait, line engraving (George Mattocks as Macheath in Gay's *The beggar's opera*, with Ann Cargill as Polly; after R. Dighton), repro. in Lowndes, *New English theatre* (1782) · Williamson, line engraving (as Lettice in Fielding's *The intriguing chambermaid*; after S. De Wilde), repro. in Cawthorn, *Minor British theatre* (1806) · double portrait, line engraving (as Louisa in Sheridan's *The duenna*, with Leoni as Carlos), BM, Harvard TC · double portrait, line engraving (George Mattocks as Ferdinand in Sheridan's *The duenna*, with Ann Brown as Clara), BM · line engraving (as Nysa in O'Hara's *Midas*), repro. in *The Vocal Magazine* (Jan 1779) · line engraving (as Mrs Warren in Holcroft's *The road to ruin*), repro. in *Attic Miscellany*, 30 (Feb 1792) · line engraving (George Mattocks as Apollo in O'Hara's *Midas*), repro. in *The Vocal Magazine* (Aug 1778) · line engraving, watch-paper (George Mattocks, as Squire in Bickerstaff's *Thomas and Sally*), BM · watercolour drawing (as Louisa in *The duenna*), Harvard U., Widener Library

Wealth at death over £700 in stocks in 1822, and some money in the hands of her bankers, Ellis & Co. of Ludgate Hill: will, proved 11 July 1826, LMA, X19/32 · George Mattocks: will, made 1 Jan 1768, PRO

Mattos, Katharine Elizabeth Alan de [*née* Katharine Elizabeth Alan Stevenson; *pseud.* Theodor Hertz-Garten] (**1851–1939**), author, was born in Scotland, the youngest of four children of Alan *Stevenson (1807–1865), lighthouse engineer, and his wife, Margaret Scott Jones (1812–1895). Like her brother Robert Alan Mowbray *Stevenson, Katharine Stevenson was one of Robert Louis *Stevenson's favourite cousins: together, the three children enjoyed spending their holidays roaming the Scottish hills on their ponies. This friendship was to last until well into adulthood and the early years of R. L. Stevenson's marriage to Fanny van de Grift Osbourne. According to Robert Louis Stevenson's biographer, Frank McLynn, Katharine became a charismatic and very intelligent woman: Stevenson's appreciation is evident in his affectionate dedication to her of *The Strange Case of Dr Jekyll and Mr Hyde* (1886).

Katharine Stevenson shocked her friends and family when she decided to wed the Cambridge atheist and notorious philanderer William Sydney de Mattos (*b.* 1850/51). The union proved to be an incompatible one almost immediately after their marriage on 25 June 1874: Katharine had to beg for financial assistance and, finally, opted for a judicial separation in 1881. The couple had two children who were left in the care of their mother; William de Mattos later emigrated to Canada.

After the break-up of her marriage Katharine de Mattos settled in London and tried to support herself and her children by writing. Stevenson assisted her by introducing her to some of his friends, including the poet William Ernest Henley. Henley not only adopted her as a member of his circle but, according to Charles Baxter and Stevenson, also nourished a passion for her. She started to write for the *Magazine of Art*, which was edited by Henley, and for other periodicals including the *Saturday Review*, *Sylvia's Journal*, the *Windsor Magazine*, the *Yellow Book*, and *The Athenaeum*. She became widely known, however, for her part in the breach between W. E. Henley and R. L. Stevenson in 1888. In a now-famous letter to Robert Louis Stevenson, Henley accused Fanny Stevenson of having plagiarized one of Katharine de Mattos's stories. The row was fierce and protracted, leaving many people deeply hurt: Stevenson came to blame Katharine for all that had happened—'I regard her as the wicked mainspring of all this distress' (*Letters*, 6.200)—and he considerably reduced her share in his final will in spite of his father's wishes.

By that time, however, Katharine de Mattos had succeeded in establishing her career as a professional writer, although Stevenson had, at one time, articulated his reservations about her writing talents and had thought of acting as a ghost writer for her. Some of her (admittedly small) living derived from translations and a few short stories published under the pseudonym Theodor Hertz-Garten. One translation, that of Vicomte Henri Delaborde's *La gravure*, was published under her brother's name in 1885. Her main source of income from 1886 up to 1908, however, must have stemmed from her anonymous pieces in *The Athenaeum*, to which she contributed, at the peak of her involvement (mainly in the 1890s), an average of seventy reviews a year. Considering that she was paid £10 a book in 1906, those top years yielded an income of about £350 a year. She usually reviewed a great number of new novels, also the 'novels of the week', some of the short stories, and exceptionally a book in the 'Our library table' column. It is unclear what happened to Katharine de Mattos after 1908, when she ceased to contribute to *The Athenaeum*. She died of 'senile decay' on 13 April 1939, at Beaufort Mansions, Chelsea.   MARYSA DEMOOR

Sources *The letters of Robert Louis Stevenson*, ed. B. A. Booth and E. Mehew, 8 vols. (1994–5) • M. Demoor, 'An American in Britain: anonymous comments on Henry James in *The Athenaeum*, 1890–1910', *Bell* (1993), 7–14 • F. McLynn, *Robert Louis Stevenson: a biography* (1993) • J. Connell, *W. E. Henley* (1949) • M. Demoor, *Their fair share: women, power and criticism in the Athenaeum, from Millicent Garrett Fawcett to Katherine Mansfield, 1870–1920* (2000) • *The Athenaeum* (1886–1906) • m. cert. • d. cert.

Mattos, Moses Lumbrozo de (*d.* **1759**). *See under* Mocatta family (*per.* 1671–1957).

Mattuck, Israel Isidor (1883–1954), rabbi, was born on 28 December 1883 in Shirvint, Lithuania, the third child of the seven children of Benjamin and Bessie (their original surname is unknown), who took the name Mattuck on arrival in the USA, *c.*1890. Israel Mattuck was enrolled at the Classical High School in Worcester, Massachusetts, and in 1901 gained entry to Harvard University, where he specialized in Semitics. His teachers included C. H. Toy, the eminent biblical scholar, and George Foot Moore, the outstanding authority on rabbinic Judaism. In his leaving testimonial of 1905 Toy described Mattuck as 'an exceptionally promising man, both in scholarship and character' (*Liberal Jewish Monthly*, June 1954). Moore was equally impressed.

From an early age Mattuck had studied the Talmud with his father. His interpretation and practice of Judaism would diverge radically from that of his traditional background, not least when he enrolled at the Hebrew Union College, Cincinnati, the foremost seminary for the training of Reform rabbis. Part of his studentship was spent in leading a congregation in Lincoln, Nebraska, where he met his wife-to-be, Edna Minna Mayer (1888–1957). They married on 3 November 1910, had their first child, Robert, in 1911, and subsequently also had two daughters, Dorothy and Naomi. Theirs was a happy and compatible marriage.

After ordination in 1910 Mattuck became rabbi of a fledgeling congregation in Far Rockaway, New York. He was to stay only a few months. By 1911 the Jewish Religious Union, established in London in 1902, had grown to the stage where it required a rabbi to expound its distinctive message. The movement acquired a building in Hill Street, near Regent's Park, and founded the Liberal Jewish Synagogue (LJS). Mattuck accepted the invitation to become its first minister. His inaugural sermon on 20 January 1912 was entitled 'The aim of Liberal Judaism'. Those who heard it, and those who heard him from the pulpit during the subsequent four decades, recall an exceptionally powerful, compelling preacher. Small of stature, slim, ascetic-looking, decisive in his judgments, thoroughly grounded in Jewish sources and well read in general culture, his eloquence laced with humour, Mattuck had the rare gift of being able to communicate with all manner of people at the appropriate level, from children to university dons. Under his leadership, the LJS developed rapidly. He was fortunate in having gifted co-workers in Claude Montefiore, a distinguished scholar, and the Hon. Lily Montagu, daughter of Edwin Montagu, the first Lord Swaything (the triumvirate was called 'the three Ms'); but it was the force of Mattuck's personality, the sway of his preaching, and the quality of his religious instruction that turned curious newcomers into ardent disciples.

The congregation outgrew its Hill Street premises. Mattuck, although personally diffident about fund-raising, spearheaded the building appeal which resulted in the imposing sanctuary behind stone pillars that stands opposite the Grace gate of Lord's cricket ground. His consecration sermon of 13 September 1925 contained a summation of his own credo: 'In the simple, the almost austere beauty of this synagogue, I feel a token of our faith. It has for us the beauty of simplicity, and it is austere in the demands it makes' (Mattuck MSS, London). Implementation of those demands elevated Mattuck to a leading role among clergy of whatever denomination in the UK. He was controversially sympathetic to the workers' cause during the general strike of 1926, in 1927 co-founded with W. R. Matthews, dean of St Paul's, the (London) Society of Jews and Christians, the first inter-faith group in the country, and for several years conducted Sunday morning services in addition to the regular sabbath ones, which many non-Jews would attend in order to hear his views on topical issues. He considered it his task to spread Liberal Judaism beyond the LJS. Conferences were organized in London and the provinces. These provoked lively reactions from Orthodox Jewish opponents, but usually his eloquence, personal charm, and formidable Jewish knowledge carried the day and led to the establishment of several new Liberal congregations.

Mattuck wrote numerous pamphlets, monographs, and essays, and broadcast regularly. Substantial and lasting works of his include *What are the Jews?* (1937), a religious interpretation of Jewish history and mission, *The Essentials of Liberal Judaism* (1947), a concise summation of its principles and beliefs, and the three volumes of the *Liberal Jewish Prayer Book* (1926; rev. edn, 1937), radical compilations that combined a drastically pruned traditional liturgy with material from the Bible, the Apocrypha, later Jewish literature, English poetry, and many of Mattuck's own compositions. On 1 November 1940 an enemy bomb partially destroyed the synagogue, but services continued throughout the war, at Lord's, then in a neighbouring church hall, and finally in the homes of local congregants. Those years took a heavy toll on his health. In 1948 he retired as senior minister of the LJS, and became minister emeritus. Three years later he was taken critically ill with coronary thrombosis, but he recovered sufficiently to give a stirring address at the reconsecration service of the rebuilt synagogue in September 1951.

The respite was brief. Although he managed to write two books, *The Thought of the Prophets* (1953) and *Jewish Ethics* (1953), and was planning another, Mattuck's health was deteriorating. He was too ill to celebrate publicly his seventieth birthday in December 1953, and died four months later, on 3 April 1954 at home at Wildwood, North End, London. He was buried three days later in the Liberal Jewish cemetery at Willesden. His death was reported on the BBC national news, received obituary notices in the major newspapers, and occasioned widespread tributes in Anglo-Jewry and beyond. DAVID J. GOLDBERG

Sources *Liberal Jewish Monthly* (June 1954) ['In memoriam' issue] • lecture by Rabbi John D. Rayner, 'Israel I. Mattuck', 28 June 1957, London, Mattuck MSS • J. D. Rayner, 'Rabbi Israel Mattuck: a man of the past—and the future?', *Manna Journal* (winter 1993) • letter of Rabbi John Rayner to Dr Ellen Umansky, 9 Dec 1982, London, Mattuck MSS • private information (2004) [D. Edgar] • d. cert.

Archives Liberal Jewish Synagogue, London, MSS • LMA, corresp. and papers incl. sermons and MS essays • Union of Liberal and Progressive Synagogues, London, JRU-ULPS Archives • World Union for Progressive Judaism, New York, archives, MSS | c/o The Liberal Jewish Synagogue, minutes of the London Society of Jews and Christians

Likenesses A. Pan, oils, 1949, Liberal Jewish Synagogue, London
Wealth at death £11,625 3s. 11d.: probate, 7 July 1954, *CGPLA Eng. & Wales*

Maturin, Basil William (1847–1915), Roman Catholic priest and religious writer, son of the Revd William *Maturin (1806–1887) and his wife, Jane Cooke Beatty, was born at All Saints' vicarage, Grangegorman, Dublin, on 15 February 1847, the third of ten children. The Maturins were a religiously earnest family of Tractarian persuasion, three of the sons becoming clergymen and two of the daughters nuns. Educated at home, at a day school, and at Trinity College, Dublin, where he took his BA in 1870, Basil (or Willie as he was called at home) intended to join the Royal Engineers until a serious illness about 1868 and the death of his brother Arthur made him decide instead to take holy orders.

Maturin was ordained deacon in 1870 and became curate at Peterstow, Herefordshire, where Dr John Jebb, an old friend of his father, was rector. In 1873 he joined the Anglo-Catholic Society of St John the Evangelist, founded in 1866 at Cowley St John, Oxford, by R. M. Benson. In 1876 he was sent to the United States in order to begin a mission in Philadelphia. He worked first as an assistant priest and in 1881 became rector of St Clement's, Philadelphia, where he remained until he was recalled to the society's mother house in Oxford in 1888 because of his doubts about Anglicanism. After a six-month visit (1889–90) to the society's house at Cape Town, Cape Colony, he spent seven further years preaching, conducting retreats, and holding missions, mainly in England but with occasional trips to the continent.

At length, on 5 March 1897, after much agonizing, Maturin was received into the Roman Catholic church at the Jesuit Beaumont College, near Windsor. He then went to the Canadian College, Rome, to study theology and was ordained a Roman Catholic priest in 1898. Upon his return to England he wished to join the Society of Jesus but was told that it would be better to wait; Archbishop Herbert Vaughan then suggested that Maturin live with him and undertake missionary work in the diocese of Westminster. He moved to London, where he stayed at Archbishop's House, Westminster, and served as a priest at St Mary's, Cadogan Street, before joining the new society of Westminster diocesan missionaries in 1905 and becoming parish priest of Pimlico in the same diocese.

Maturin continued to be drawn to the idea of the monastic life, and in 1910 tried his vocation with the Benedictines at Downside, near Bath; but he never joined the order and returned to London as an itinerant preacher who worked some of the time at St James's, Spanish Place. In 1914 Maturin was offered simultaneously the parish of the Holy Redeemer in Chelsea, and the Catholic chaplaincy at the University of Oxford. He accepted the second position but had hardly taken it up when the First World War broke out and the university was left empty of undergraduates.

In 1915 he returned to the United States, where he preached some Lenten sermons before setting sail for England on the *Lusitania* in May. The ship was torpedoed and sunk on 7 May and Father Maturin eventually drowned. Before the ship went down he gave absolution to fellow passengers, and lowered a child into a lifeboat, saying 'Find its mother.' His body was found washed ashore without a lifebelt, and it was generally supposed that he had refused one because there were not enough to go round. His funeral service was held at Westminster Cathedral.

Maturin wrote several devotional and pastoral works, including *Some Principles and Practices of the Spiritual Life* (1896), *Practical Studies on the Parables of Our Lord* (1897), *Self-Knowledge and Self-Discipline* (1905), *Laws of the Spiritual Life* (1907), and *The Price of Unity* (1912), the last describing his conversion to Roman Catholicism. After his death a volume of *Sermons and Sermon Notes* was edited and arranged (1916) by his friend, Wilfrid Philip Ward, and a *Memoir* of his life was published by Maisie Ward (1920). Maturin's career was not crowned with achievement: he failed to enter a monastery, his jobs as a Catholic missionary priest lacked continuity, and he never had the chance to make a success of the chaplaincy at Oxford. But he was a kindly confessor (who was thought psychologically shrewd by his penitents) and was notable for having no bitterness towards either the Roman Catholic or the Anglican church. His sermons, though thought too long by some, were generally acknowledged to be earnest and vivid.

C. C. MARTINDALE, *rev.* DAVID HUDDLESTON

Sources M. Ward, *Father Maturin: a memoir* (1920) · B. W. Maturin, *The price of unity* (1912) · *New Catholic encyclopedia*, 18 vols. (1967–89), vol. 9, pp. 504–5 · *WW* · *Letters of the late Father B. W. Maturin to Lady Euan-Smith*, ed. J. M. Bampton [1928] · *CGPLA Eng. & Wales* (1915)
Likenesses Sarony of New York, photograph, 1915, repro. in Ward, *Father Maturin*
Wealth at death £835 19s. 10d.: probate, 6 Aug 1915, *CGPLA Eng. & Wales*

Maturin, Charles Robert (1780–1824), writer and Church of England clergyman, was born in Dublin on 25 September 1780 (not 1782 as asserted by many previous sources), the last of the six children of William Maturin and his wife, Fidelia, *née* Watson. On his father's side Maturin came from a long line of protestant clergymen, beginning with Gabriel Maturin, a Huguenot pastor who emigrated to Ireland in the seventeenth century. Pierre Maturin, Gabriel's son, had been dean of Killala, while Gabriel James Maturin, Charles Robert's grandfather, succeeded Swift in the deanery of St Patrick's. William Maturin departed from family tradition by entering government service where he enjoyed a lucrative career in the Post Office until November 1809 when he was dismissed on a false charge of malversation. Charles Robert Maturin entered Trinity College, Dublin, in 1795. An active member of the Historical Society, he was awarded a scholarship before graduating with a BA in 1800. On 7 October 1803 Maturin married Henrietta Kingsbury, a society beauty famous for her musical accomplishments, who was also from a clerical family. According to one memoir, Maturin was 'the most uxorious man living' (*New Monthly Magazine*, 11, 1819, 167). The Maturins had four children. The eldest, William *Maturin (1806–1887), was also a clergyman, while the second son, Edward (1812–1881), emigrated to

Charles Robert Maturin (1780–1824), by Henry Hoppner Meyer, pubd 1819 (after William Brocas)

the USA where he was a professor of Greek and an author.

Maturin was ordained and appointed to the curacy of Loughrea, co. Galway, in 1803, returning to Dublin in 1804 as the curate of St Peter's. Although it was a highly fashionable church, the curacy carried a meagre stipend of £80 to £90 per annum. At his own expense Maturin published a Gothic romance, *The Fatal Revenge* (1807), under the 'vulgar and *merely* Irish sounding' pseudonym of Dennis Jasper Murphy (*Dublin and London Magazine*, 2, 1826, 248), followed by *The Wild Irish Boy* (1808). His father's dismissal from the Post Office in 1809 increased the financial pressure on Maturin. In that year he rented a house in York Street where he remained until his death, supplementing his income by tutoring students for entrance to Trinity. Maturin sold the copyright of his next romance, *The Milesian Chief* (1812), to Colburn for £80. In 1810 Sir Walter Scott momentously reviewed *The Fatal Revenge* in the May issue of the *Quarterly*. Scott singled out Maturin's work from the 'flat imitations' of Radcliffe, remarking that the evidently youthful author was talented, though wayward. He advised him to seek professional advice, which Maturin did by writing to Scott himself in 1812. Thereafter Scott guided Maturin, doing him innumerable favours, frequently interceding on his behalf, and, on at least one occasion, sending him money (£50 in 1813). The resulting correspondence is the single best source of information about Maturin, with the bulk of it about *Bertram*. Maturin wrote his play in 1814, inspired by Richard Lalor Sheil's *Adelaide*, which had enjoyed a great success at the Crow

Street Theatre, Dublin. Worried that a Dublin production would injure his clerical reputation, Maturin turned to Scott for advice. Scott judiciously excised a scene in which the devil appears bodily on stage, and, after first trying John Kemble, sent the play to Byron, then on the newly formed management committee for Drury Lane. Byron was entranced by the text, and gave it to George Lamb, who also could not put it down. The play opened on 9 May 1816, and was a sensation, running to over forty performances. Murray published the amended version of the play, and even at the exorbitant price of 4s. 6d. it went through at least seven editions within the year. Maturin received £350 from Murray, and £500 for his share of the box office. He visited London for a week in late May 1816 after the committee invited him to the capital to be lionized, but was intensely disappointed by his reception. It was Maturin's only trip outside Ireland.

Bertram's brilliant success brought out the flamboyant side of Maturin's character: 'tradesmen of all hues and callings were ordered to York-Street, to paint, furnish, and decorate, with suitable taste and splendour, the mansion of the great new-born tragic poet of Ireland' (*Irish Quarterly Review*, 2, 1852, 161). According to the memoirs he was extremely fond of dancing, especially the quadrille, which he prided himself in doing 'certainly better than any other divine of the Established Church' (ibid., 162). He would even darken 'his drawing-room window', and indulge his passion 'in the day-time' (*Dublin University Magazine*, 46, 1855, 448). He was a notorious dandy:

> tall, slender, but well proportioned, and on the whole, a good figure, which he took care to display in a well made slack coat, tight buttoned, and some odd light-coloured stocking-web pantaloons, surmounted in winter by a coat of prodigious dimensions, gracefully thrown on, so as not to obscure the symmetry it affected to protect.   (*Irish Quarterly Review*, 2, 1852, 160)

Among other eccentricities, he was renowned for pasting 'a wafer on his forehead, whenever he felt the *estro* of composition coming on him' as a sign to his family that he was not to be interrupted (*Dublin University Magazine*, 46, 1855, 448).

Maturin's next two plays flopped. *Manuel* (1817) was written for Kean, who wanted the opportunity to act the part of 'aged distress', given that *King Lear* was off-limits owing to sensitivities regarding George III's mental condition. Unfortunately, Kean lost interest after the first night, and sabotaged the play by walking through his part. *Fredolfo* (1819) also failed, while Maturin's final play, *Osmyn,* was mislaid by Kean. Maturin could not sustain these failures as after 1810 he was in terrible debt having stood security for a 'friend' whose affairs collapsed. Meanwhile his clerical career had also stalled, owing, Maturin thought, to his novel-writing. After he had broken cover with *Bertram*, an article appeared in the *Morning Chronicle* alleging his job was at risk, but enough fuss was caused to force Maturin's superiors into denying the rumours. Subsequent evidence suggests that the true reason for Maturin's lack of preferment was the eccentricity of his character and religious

views. Maturin styled himself a 'high Calvinist', in opposition to the low Calvinism of nonconformist Methodism that was then popular in Dublin, but it was a stance which irritated the church hierarchy who largely held Arminian views.

One memoir claims that as a writer Maturin was apt unconsciously to adopt 'something of the last book he read' (*New Monthly Magazine and Literary Journal*, 19, 1827, 404); the reviews commented on his undisciplined originality. Both views have substance. *The Fatal Revenge* reveals Maturin's early love of Ann Radcliffe and Matthew Lewis while adding a new complexity to the genre through its exuberant proliferation of plot. *The Wild Irish Boy* and *The Milesian Chief*, though inspired by the examples of Maria Edgeworth and Lady Morgan, make significant contributions to the emerging genre of the Irish national tale. The early works up to and including *Bertram* reflect their Irish obsessions in often coded references to usurpation and dispossession. *Women, or, Pour and contre* (1818) marks a departure: the plot is once again based upon the story of a dispossessed and scattered family, but its main theme is salvation through faith. A satire on Methodism and depictions of Dublin undergraduate life are among its novelties.

In 1820 Maturin published his masterpiece, *Melmoth the Wanderer*, the book for which he is chiefly remembered. On the surface it is a return to the Gothic mode of his first romance, where he initially displayed his talent for 'darkening the gloomy, and of deepening the sad; of painting life in the extremes, and representing those struggles of passion when the soul trembles on the verge of the unlawful and the unhallowed' (preface, *The Milesian Chief*, 1812, iv–v). However, it too carries on the religious preoccupations of his last phase. With its Chinese box structure of tales within tales, and its obsessive elaboration of its Faustian theme, it constitutes a high-water mark in the Gothic genre. On the surface its most salient quality is its anti-Catholic paranoia, but its real achievement is to invest the form with a new, poetic intensity. On the whole *Melmoth* was given a hostile reception on the grounds that Maturin impersonated his wicked characters with immoral eloquence. Maturin's last novel, *The Albigenses* (1824), was modelled on *Ivanhoe*, and is a historical romance based on the Cathar rebellion, a pre-Reformation setting apparently chosen for its uncontroversial nature. Maturin received £510 for the copyright, £10 more than for *Melmoth*. In 1819 Constable published Maturin's sermons which were a reasonable success, going into a second edition in 1821. His final work was *Five Sermons on the Errours of the Roman Catholic Church* (1824). Despite its title, it was equally aimed at the errors of nonconformity. Preached at St Peter's, the sermons were a sensation.

Maturin died on 30 October 1824 at his home, 37 York Street, Dublin, and was buried in the churchyard of St Peter's. The *Morning Register* reported that the 'immediate cause of Mr. Maturin's death was … his having taken a lotion, containing a large quantity of laudanum, in mistake for medicine intended for the stomach' (Henderson,

215). Although it has been much repeated, there is no evidence to substantiate the claim. This is typical of Maturin's biographical record; the numerous memoirs that appeared after his death had a tendency to recycle anecdotes and rumours, a situation worsened by the destruction of the Irish Public Record Office in 1922, and by Maturin's own mythopoeic tendencies. He had been particularly fond of relating different versions of the family history, and was notoriously evasive and inconsistent about his own financial difficulties in the early years of the nineteenth century. However, according to his widow, at his death he left his family 'totally unprovided for' (*Correspondence of … Scott and … Maturin*, 103). Scott agreed to publish Maturin's collected works, with a biography, but was prevented by his own financial difficulties. There was a rumour that William Maturin was so humiliated by his father's authorial reputation that he burnt all his papers, although this is contradicted by William's assiduity in promoting *Osmyn* after its discovery in 1825. The play was produced in Dublin for the benefit of the Maturin family by R. L. Sheil and W. C. Macready in 1830. Maturin was widely known throughout Europe, but especially in France, where all the major works were quickly translated. Balzac thought *Melmoth* 'the greatest creation of one of the greatest geniuses of Europe'. Maturin's descendant Oscar Wilde honoured Maturin by adopting the sobriquet Sebastian Melmoth on his release from Reading gaol.

ROBERT MILES

Sources The correspondence of Sir Walter Scott and Charles Robert Maturin, ed. F. E. Ratchford and W. H. McCarthy (1937) · S. Smiles, *A publisher and his friends: memoir and correspondence of the late John Murray*, 2 vols. (1891) · N. Idman, *Charles Robert Maturin: his life and works* (1923) · D. Kramer, *Charles Robert Maturin* (1973) · P. M. Henderson, *A nut between two blades: the novels of Charles Robert Maturin* (1980) · 'Memoir of the Rev. C. R. Maturin', *New Monthly Magazine*, 11 (1819), 165–7 · 'Maturin', *Dublin and London Magazine*, 2 (1826), 248 · 'Conversations of Maturin—no. I', *New Monthly Magazine and Literary Journal*, 19 (1827), 401–11 · 'Conversations of Maturin—no. II', *New Monthly Magazine and Literary Journal*, 19 (1827), 570–77 · 'Recollections of Maturin—no. III', *New Monthly Magazine and Literary Journal*, 20 (1827), 146–52 · 'Recollections of Maturin—no. IV', *New Monthly Magazine and Literary Journal*, 20 (1827), 370–76 · Melmoth, a new edition, with a memoir and bibliography of Maturin's works, 3 vols. (1892) · 'Rev. R. C. Maturin', *GM*, 1st ser., 95/1 (1825), 84–5 · 'Rev. Charles Robert Maturin', *Irish Quarterly Review*, 2 (1852–3), 140–70 · 'The dramatic writers of Ireland—no. VIII: the Rev. C. R. Maturin', *Dublin University Magazine*, 46 (1855), 444–9 · N. Cox, *Seven Gothic dramas, 1789–1825* (1992)
Archives NL Scot., letter-books | BL, letters to Hurst & Robinson, Add. MS 41996, fols. 27–46 · BL, letters to Royal Literary Fund, loan 96 · NL Scot., Archibald Constable · NL Scot., Constable and Constable papers, letters to Archibald Constable · NL Scot., letters to Sir Walter Scott
Likenesses W. Brocas, oils, NL Ire. · H. H. Meyer, stipple (after W. Brocas), BM, NPG; repro. in 'Memoir of the Rev. C. R. Maturin', 165 [see illus.]
Wealth at death negligible: *Correspondence of … Scott and … Maturin*

Maturin, William (1806–1887), Church of Ireland clergyman, was born in Dublin, the son of Charles Robert *Maturin (1780–1824), novelist and dramatist, and Henrietta, daughter of Thomas Kingsbury of Dublin. He was educated at Dublin University, where he graduated BA in

1831 and accumulated the degrees of MA, BD, and DD in 1866. He took holy orders in 1831 and after serving for some years a curacy in Dublin, Maturin was presented in 1844 by William Le Fanu to the perpetual curacy of Grangegorman, co. Dublin. On 17 August of the preceding year he had married Jane Cooke, eldest daughter of Captain Arthur Beatty; they had two sons, including Basil William *Maturin.

A high-churchman formed by the movement of Pusey and Newman, Maturin was unreserved in the expression of his views. This led Archbishop Richard Whately and others to neglect him, so that, in spite of his great talents as a preacher and his devotion to parochial details, Maturin remained all his life merely incumbent of All Saints, Grangegorman, with an income never exceeding £100 a year, though about 1860 his friends obtained for him the additional post of librarian in Archbishop Marsh's Library, Dublin. In England he would have been considered a moderate churchman, but to the Irish evangelicals he always appeared as little removed from a Roman Catholic and to a large section in Dublin his name was a term of theological reproach. After speaking of the great qualities of his sermons, Sir John Pentland Mahaffy, the provost of Trinity College, Dublin, wrote of Maturin:

> He was a grim Dantesque sort of man, with deep affection for his family and friends hidden under a severe exterior. He was perfectly certain and clear in his views—a quality rare in modern preachers and fatal to modern preaching; his simple and burning words reflected the zeal of his spirit … I saw him crush by his fiery words a mob of young men, who came to disturb his service on Protestant principles, and drive them cowed and slinking from his church. (*Athenaeum*, 54)

Besides several pamphlets, single sermons, and addresses to the Irish Church Society, Maturin wrote *Six Lectures on the Events of Holy Week* (1860) and *The Blessedness of the Dead in Christ*, a collection of twenty-four of his sermons (1888). He died at 11 Alma Road, Seapoint, co. Dublin, on 30 June 1887, and after lying in state for four days before the altar was buried in All Saints' Church, Grangegorman, on 4 July.

THOMAS SECCOMBE, rev. DAVID HUDDLESTON

Sources The Athenaeum (9 July 1887), 54 · Irish Times (4 July 1887), 6; (5 July 1887) · J. B. Leslie, biographical succession list of clergy for the diocese of Dublin, PRO NIre., T 1075/1 [typescript] · BL cat., 215.292 · [J. H. Todd], ed., *A catalogue of graduates who have proceeded to degrees in the University of Dublin, from the earliest recorded commencements to … December 16, 1868* (1869), 378 · Burtchaell & Sadleir, *Alum. Dubl.*, 2nd edn · R. B. McDowell, *The Church of Ireland, 1869–1969* (1975) · H. E. Patton, *Fifty years of disestablishment* (1922)
Wealth at death £8135 14s. 3d.: letters of administration, 1887 · £1889 14s.—effects in England: administration, 16 Aug 1887, CGPLA Ire.

Maty, Matthew (1718–1776), physician and librarian, was born on 17 May 1718 at Montfoort, 6 miles south-west of Utrecht, the eldest child of Paul Maty (1681–1773), French protestant minister, and his wife, Jeanne Crottier Desmarets. Both parents were Huguenots. Before moving to the Netherlands the Maty family, which originated in the Île de Ré, had lived in Dauphiné, and the Crottier Desmarets family of Amsterdam were refugees from Lyons. After being educated at Utrecht University, Paul Maty was ordained in 1709 and became minister to the Huguenots of Montfoort. As the congregation there was small he moved to The Hague, where he became a teacher. A book on the Trinity which he published in 1729 led to his excommunication by synods at Kampen and The Hague in 1730. Having failed to establish himself in England he moved to Leiden in 1731 and joined the remonstrant church. After Matthew moved to London, Paul lived for much of the rest of his life with him, and died in Matthew's apartments in the British Museum on 21 March 1773.

Matthew Maty entered Leiden University on 31 March 1732 and studied philosophy and medicine; he submitted dissertations in both fields which gained him doctorates in 1740. He was taught medicine by the noted physician Herman Boerhaave (1668–1738), of whom he published a life in 1747. A French version of Maty's philosophical dissertation (entitled *Essai sur l'usage*) was published at Utrecht in 1741.

At the end of 1740 Maty and his parents moved to London, where he practised medicine and became a contributor to the *Bibliothèque Britannique* (The Hague, 1732–47) and the *Bibliothèque raisonnée des ouvrages des savans de l'Europe* (Amsterdam, 1728–53). He became known in London literary circles as a result of frequenting various coffee houses, and made the acquaintance of notable figures in the medical world, such as Dr Richard Mead (whose life Maty wrote in 1755, expanded from an article in the *Journal Britannique* of 1754) and Sir John Pringle. Both of these supported his election as a fellow of the Royal Society in 1751. As a foreigner he had only a 'bishop's licence' to practise medicine, and in 1765 he was summonsed by the Royal College of Physicians for illegal practice, but in the same year he became a licentiate of the college. He was an enthusiast for inoculation against smallpox (the precursor of Jenner's method of vaccination) and campaigned vigorously against those who opposed it.

Despite his father's excommunication by the Huguenot church, Maty remained in touch with the Huguenot community in England, and chose his wife from among them. She was Elizabeth de Boisragon (d. 1750), the daughter of Louis Chevalleau, seigneur de Boisragon. They were married on 13 December 1743 in Spring Gardens Chapel, one of several small chapels belonging to the Huguenot church of the Savoy. Their first child, Henri Paul (later Paul Henry *Maty (1744–1787), was born on 18 December 1744, followed by two daughters, Louise (b. September 1746) and Anne Gillette (b. March 1748). Elizabeth died in August 1750, soon after the birth in July of their third daughter, Susanne, who also died in August. On 25 July 1752 Maty married again; his second wife was Mary Dolon de Ners (d. 1802) of Marylebone, also of Huguenot descent, the daughter of Peter Anthony Dolon, seigneur de Ners. In July 1753 a daughter, Jeanne, and in June 1756 a son, James, were born; both probably died young. In March 1758 Maty's last child, Marthe, was born.

As the *Bibliothèque Britannique*, which reviewed British publications for the benefit of readers on the continent, came to an end in 1747, Maty decided to found a successor. This was entitled *Journal Britannique*, and the first number

appeared in 1750. For the first two years it appeared each month, but from 1752 issues were published every two months. Written in French and published at The Hague, it was successful in publicizing British books and periodicals abroad, and soon gained an authoritative reputation. Many of the contributions were written by Maty himself, but he also enlisted other writers, such as Thomas Birch, John Jortin, Jean Des Champs, and César de Missy.

An article by Maty in the July–August 1755 issue on Samuel Johnson's *Dictionary* was probably the cause of Johnson's dislike of Maty. When it was suggested in 1756 that Maty should assist Johnson with a new review which he planned (but which never appeared), the latter's comment was: 'the little black dog! I'd throw him into the Thames' (Boswell, *Life*, 1.284). The review had implied that after dedicating the 'plan' (1747) of the *Dictionary* to Lord Chesterfield, Johnson had failed to make acknowledgement to Chesterfield when the *Dictionary* was published in 1755. This ignored the fact that Johnson had, in a letter dated 7 February 1755, criticized Chesterfield's failure to assist him while the work was in preparation. Maty had been on friendly terms with Chesterfield at least since 1745, when he had dedicated to him (as M.L.C.D.C., that is Monsieur le comte de Chesterfield) his *Ode sur la rebellion de MDCCXLV en Écosse*, in which Maty expressed his hatred of Catholicism. He and Chesterfield were both friends of the mathematician Abraham de Moivre (1667–1754), whose life Maty wrote in the *Journal Britannique* of September–October 1755, and subsequently published separately.

At the end of 1755 Maty gave up the *Journal Britannique*, which was rather unsuccessfully continued for two more years by De Mauve, of whom little is known. In 1756 he applied for a post in the British Museum (founded in 1753) to the earl of Hardwicke, who as lord chancellor was one of the three principal trustees responsible for appointments to the new institution. Maty's successful application was supported by Hardwicke's eldest son, Lord Royston, and by John Jortin, later archdeacon of London (whose son in 1776 married Maty's daughter Louise). Jortin said that if Maty were appointed he would be naturalized (apparently he never was), and that he had been elected a foreign member of the Academy of Sciences of Berlin in January 1755. He was elected in 1759 to the Royal Society of Haarlem and in 1765 to the Royal Academy of Sciences of Sweden.

In June 1756 Maty was appointed one of the three original under-librarians (keepers) of the British Museum and put in charge of the department containing Sir Hans Sloane's books and manuscripts. After the gift of the Royal Library by George II in 1757, Maty took charge of its printed books, as well as the Sloane printed books and those of Major Arthur Edwards, while his colleague Charles Morton dealt with the Sloane, Cotton, Harley, and Royal manuscripts. From 1758 these two departments were called the departments of printed books and manuscripts respectively. The third department, named the department of natural and artificial productions, contained Sloane's collections of natural history and antiquities.

Maty drew up a scheme in 1757 for arranging the books of the Royal Library, and in 1759 for improving the (very restricted) way in which the public were admitted to view the museum. Both these proposals were approved by the trustees. In 1759 he also put forward a scheme for cataloguing the printed books, but this work did not reach fruition until the 1780s. In 1765, when James Empson, the first under-librarian of the department of natural and artificial productions, died, Maty took charge of that department, relinquishing the control of the department of printed books to Samuel Harper. Maty was particularly interested in the collections of birds and made considerable additions to them.

In 1760 Maty withdrew his application for the post of secretary of the Society for the Encouragement of Arts, Manufactures, and Commerce because of the disapproval of his patron, Lord Royston, but in 1762 he became assistant secretary for foreign correspondence to the Royal Society. In 1765 he succeeded his friend Thomas Birch (whose executor he became when Birch died in 1766), one of the original trustees of the British Museum, as joint secretary of the Royal Society. In 1750, when visiting the continent, he called on Voltaire, in 1763 he showed Casanova round the British Museum, and in 1766 he met Rousseau. In 1758 he helped Edward Gibbon with his first publication (*Essai sur l'étude de la littérature*), which appeared in 1761.

Despite his poor health Maty was promoted in July 1772 to succeed Gowin Knight, the first principal librarian (director) of the British Museum. He did not achieve a great deal during his four-year tenure of this post, but he was more energetic than his notoriously idle successor, Charles Morton. Some important acquisitions of books were made during Maty's principal keepership at the sales of the libraries of James West, Anthony Askew, and César de Missy, and of duplicates from the library at Dresden.

After the death of the earl of Chesterfield in 1773, Maty wrote a biography of him which was published as the preface to Chesterfield's *Miscellaneous Works* (1777). This work was seen through the press by John Obadiah Justamond, a surgeon who was the assistant librarian of the department of natural and artificial productions, and who married Maty's daughter Anne Gillette in 1767. In 1774 Maty became physician to the hospital for French protestants.

Maty died at the British Museum on 2 August 1776. In accordance with his instructions a post-mortem examination was carried out by two fellows of the Royal Society, whose report, published in the *Philosophical Transactions*, indicates that he died of cancer of the intestine. He was buried on 8 August at St Anne's, Soho, and a sermon in memory of him was preached on 11 August at Oxendon Street Chapel by the minister there, his nephew Charles Peter Layard, later dean of Bristol. In his will Maty instructed his sole executor, his wife, Mary, who died in 1802, to burn all his papers. He left to the British Museum his portrait, painted when he was aged about thirty-six by the Swiss painter Barthelémy Dupan, and busts of Petrarch, Boccaccio, Machiavelli, and Dante. In 1762 he had presented to the museum seventeen busts which he had bought at Roubiliac's sale after the sculptor's death that year; Maty and Roubiliac had both worshipped at the Huguenot chapel in Spring Gardens. Maty's son Paul Henry Maty, who was on the staff of the British Museum from 1776 until his death in 1787, sold his father's library in 1777.   P. R. HARRIS

Sources U. Janssens-Knorsch, *Matthieu Maty and the Journal Britannique, 1750–1755* (1975) • W. Minet and S. Minet, eds., *Registres des églises de la Savoye, de Spring Gardens et des Grecs*, Publications of the Huguenot Society of London, 26 (1922) • H. Wagner, 'The Maty family', *The Genealogist*, new ser., 22, 188–9 • Munk, *Roll* • minutes of the general meeting, BM, CE1 • minutes of the standing committee, BM, CE3 • original papers, BM, CE4 • register of donations, BM, CE30 • IGI • *The record of the Royal Society of London*, 4th edn (1940) • BL, Birch papers, Add. MSS 4441 and 4449 • BL, Hardwicke papers, 35606 and 36269 • will, PRO, PROB 11/1023/368 • records of St George, Bloomsbury, LMA, P82/GE0 1/63 [searchers' reports] • parish register, St Anne, Soho, City Westm. AC [burial; baptisms] • 'A short account of Dr Maty's illness and of the appearance of his dead body', *PTRS*, 67 (1777), 608–13 • Boswell, *Life*, 1.284 • C. P. Layard, *A sermon preached at Oxendon Chapel on … August 11th, 1776, occasioned by the decease of the late Matthew Maty* (1776) • *DNB*
Archives Bibliothèque Publique et Universitaire, Geneva, corresp. with Charles Bonnet • BL, letters to Lord Hardwicke, Add. MSS 35606–35613 • BL, Add. MS 36269 • BL, Add. MS 4313 • BL, Add. MS 4441 • BL, Add. MS 4449
Likenesses B. Dupan, oils, c.1754, BM • F. Bartolozzi, stipple, BM; repro. in Janssens-Knorsch, *Matthieu Maty* • L. C. de Carmontelle, engraving, repro. in Janssens-Knorsch, *Matthieu Maty*
Wealth at death in 'narrow circumstances': will, PRO, PROB 11/1023/368

Maty, Paul Henry (1744–1787), librarian, was born in London on 18 December 1744 and baptized on 18 January 1745 at St Anne's, Soho, the son of Matthew *Maty (1718–1776), librarian, and his wife, Elizabeth (*d.* 1750), daughter of Louis Chevalleau of Sieur de Boisragon. He was admitted a king's scholar at St Peter's College, Westminster, in 1758 before being elected in 1763 to Trinity College, Cambridge, where he became a scholar in 1764 and graduated BA in 1767 and MA in 1770. In 1768 he was nominated to one of the travelling fellowships of his college and spent three years abroad. In 1774 he was appointed chaplain to David Murray, Lord Stormont (afterwards second earl of Mansfield), British ambassador at the court of France. He vacated his fellowship in 1775 on his marriage to Harriet, daughter of Joseph Clerke of Wethersfield, Essex, and sister of Captain Charles Clerke, the successor to Captain Cook.

In 1776 doubts conceived as to the consistency of the Thirty-Nine Articles, especially on such points as predestination and original sin, compelled Maty to refrain from seeking any further ecclesiastical appointment; his scruples, which approached Arianism, were printed in full in the *Gentleman's Magazine* for October 1777. Fortunately for him, however, on his father's death in July 1776 he obtained the situation of an assistant librarian in the British Museum, and in 1782 was promoted to under-librarian in the department of natural history and antiquities. He also succeeded in 1776 to the foreign secretaryship of the Royal Society, of which he had been elected a member on 13 February 1772, and on 30 November 1778, on the withdrawal of Dr Horsley, he became

Paul Henry Maty
(1744–1787), after
James Tassie, 1778

principal secretary. In this capacity he became involved in the controversy which raged about the virtual dismissal of Dr Charles Hutton from the post of foreign secretary by the president, Sir Joseph Banks. In a heated pamphlet entitled *An history of the instances of exclusion from the Royal Society … with strictures on the formation of the council and other instances of the despotism of Sir Joseph Banks, the present president* (1784), he proposed that, as a means of protest against the president, the dissatisfied minority should form themselves into a solid phalanx, and resolutely oppose any admission whatsoever into the society, a proposal from which all moderate supporters of Maty's views dissented. Having tried in vain to organize a regular opposition under Horsley, Maty resigned his office on 25 March 1784, and his resignation helped to restore peace to the society. As secretary and an officer of the society he had not been expected to take any active part in the debate but here, as elsewhere, 'his vivacity outran his judgment'. The loss of his office involved a reduction of income which he could not afford, and he was only moderately successful in making up the difference by giving instruction in classical and modern languages.

In January 1782 Maty had started the *New Review*, which aimed at giving a bird's-eye view of foreign publications, and he continued this considerable work, almost unassisted, until September 1786. Edward Gibbon referred to him as the 'angry son' who wielded the rod of criticism with but little of 'the tenderness and reluctance' of his father. Horace Walpole spoke of some of his comments as 'pert and foolish' (cf. *Canons of Criticism Extracted from the Beauties of Maty's Review*).

Three works by Maty appeared in 1787: *A General Index to the Philosophical Transactions, vols. i–lxx*, which he had prepared some time previously; a translation of the work by Riesbeck as *Travels through Germany, in a Series of Letters* (3 vols.); and a French translation of the text to the first volume of *Gemmae Marlburienses*, to accompany the Latin of James Bryant. A volume of sermons delivered in the Ambassador's Chapel at Paris during the years 1774, 1775,

and 1776, in which some of Secker's sermons were inadvertently included, was published in 1788. Bishop Horsley, Dean Layard, and Dr Southgate were responsible for the editing.

Maty died of asthma on 16 January 1787 and was buried in Bunhill Fields, London. His wife and only son were left in poor circumstances. Charles Burney undertook the expense of educating Maty's son, but he died while at school.   THOMAS SECCOMBE, *rev.* REBECCA MILLS

Sources IGI · will, PRO, PROB 11/1150, sig. 80 · Venn, *Alum. Cant.*, 2/4.365 · H. R. Luard, ed., *Graduati Cantabrigienses*, 6th edn (1873), 316 · *Old Westminsters*, 2.632 · E. Gibbon, *Memoirs of the life and writings of Edward Gibbon*, 2 vols. (1827) · *An authentic narrative of the dissensions and debates in the Royal Society* (1784) · A. Kippis, *Observations on the late contests in the Royal Society* (1784) · T. Lindsey, *An historical view of the state of Unitarian doctrine and worship from the Reformation to our own times* (1783), 515–25 · *Life and correspondence of Joseph Priestley*, ed. J. T. Rutt, 1 (1831), 406–7 · J. Welch, *The list of the queen's scholars of St Peter's College, Westminster*, ed. [C. B. Phillimore], new edn (1852), 369, 379–80, 536 · T. Green, *Extracts from a diary of a lover of literature* (1810), 162, 169, 173–4 · C. R. Weld, *A history of the Royal Society*, 2 vols. (1848), vol. 2, pp. 561–2 · Watt, *Bibl. Brit.*, 2. 656 · *GM*, 1st ser., 47 (1777), 466–8 · *GM*, 1st ser., 57 (1787), 92–3 · Nichols, *Lit. anecdotes*, 3.259–61, 623 · Nichols, *Illustrations*, 4.833

Likenesses plaster medallion (after J. Tassie, 1778), Scot. NPG [*see illus.*]

Wealth at death poor: will, PRO, PROB 11/1150, sig. 80

Maubray, John (*d.* 1732), man-midwife, was born probably in Scotland. Nothing is known of his early life. About 1724 or 1725 he set himself up in London as a teacher of midwifery. An unlicensed practitioner, he sought the patronage of Sir Hans Sloane, and such an eminent contact may have persuaded the Royal College of Physicians to ignore his lack of a licence. Maubray's first book was *The female physician, containing all the diseases incident to that sex, in virgins, wives and widows* (1724). His second book was *Midwifery Brought to Perfection by Manual Operation* (1725), in which he appealed for the founding of a lying-in hospital, becoming one of the first to do so. He wrote that there were many excellent hospitals but 'on this point of provision for poor miserable women in the time of their affliction, when they are in no case in a condition to help themselves we have been hitherto and are still deficient' (Spencer, 11). He cited the Hôtel Dieu in Paris as a suitable model. Maubray published his course on midwifery from his house in New Bond Street. He gave about twenty lectures between the hours of five and six twice a week; students engaged in practical work with patients, which allowed them to perform vaginal examinations (the touch) and conduct deliveries.

One object of Maubray's teaching was 'to confute and reject the barbarous and truly inhumane use of all *chirurgical tools*' (Spencer, 12). Practitioners were at that time acquiring knowledge of obstetric forceps, which Maubray probably was condemning, as he did all the other, much more barbarous instruments then being used in obstetric practice for difficult labours. According to Adrian Wilson, Maubray was among those whig men-midwives who opposed the use of forceps. He was the first to describe different shapes of bony pelvis, categorizing them as deep, large, broad, flat, oval, and round. He also coined the term 'andro-boethogynist' to describe a male practitioner of midwifery.

Despite being a pioneer in the teaching of midwifery, writing about it, and proposing a lying-in hospital, there is evidence that Maubray did not have much practical experience for he says he was only called 'occasionally' to births in London (Spencer, 8). He travelled to Venice, Germany, and the Netherlands to learn more, and it was in the Netherlands, on a Zuyder Zee ferry, that he attended a woman, who, he said, produced a Moodiwarp, 'having a hooked snout, fiery sparkling eyes, a long round neck, an acuminated tail and an extraordinary agility of feet' (Spencer, 9); it yelled and shrieked like a demon and scooted round the deck finding a place to hide. Other evidence of his gullibility is that he accepted astrologers' views on the magic number seven, believing that babies born in the seventh month of pregnancy were stronger than those born in the eighth. Eight-month babies were ruled by Saturn, an enemy to all creatures that breathe life; Maubray said that they were always weakly, with tender constitutions, and often half-witted. It was because of his holding these views that his injunction 'to watch the patient during pregnancy so as to prevent all preternatural disasters' (Spencer, 8) was misinterpreted as his trying to prevent the birth of jumping rabbits and similar strange creatures. Maubray, who was also duped during the Mary Toft affair, was a mixture of the far-sighted and the credulous in midwifery.

Maubray was chairman of the Charitable Corporation in 1730, and in 1732 he drew the attention of the House of Commons to one of the members of his committee who was misappropriating funds on behalf of the Pretender. At his death, which occurred in London on 27 October 1732, Maubray was described in the *Gentleman's Magazine* as 'justly esteemed as an honest publick-spirited man' (Spencer, 14). PHILIP RHODES

Sources A. Wilson, *The making of man-midwifery: childbirth in England, 1660–1770* (1995) • H. R. Spencer, *The history of British midwifery from 1650 to 1800* (1927) • H. Graham, *Eternal Eve* (1950) • GM, 1st ser., 2 (1732), 1031

Likenesses N. Hogarth, etching, 1726, Wellcome L.

Mauclerk, Walter (d. 1248), bishop of Carlisle, is of unknown origins. It seems unlikely that he is to be identified with a namesake, one of the sons of Girard Mauclerk, active in property transactions at Rouen as early as 1176. He may, however, have been related to another royal clerk, Robert Mauclerk, resident in Nottinghamshire, who in the 1190s had joined the rebellion of John, count of Mortain, the future king. Walter Mauclerk is recorded in 1218 holding the prebend of Woodborough in Southwell Minster, and at a later date as witness to various private charters in Nottinghamshire—facts which go some way towards substantiating a family link to the north midlands. One of his brothers, named 'R', was prior of Reading Abbey, and in 1214 was proposed unsuccessfully as the king's candidate for the vacant abbey of St Albans. A kinsman or nephew, named Ralph Barri, possibly related to the Barry family of Nottinghamshire, was appointed prior of Carlisle during Mauclerk's years as bishop, and another

(unnamed) nephew was seeking promotion to the church of Arnold near Nottingham about the year 1220. Mauclerk's father, named 'W', was later commemorated in gifts to the bishopric of Carlisle.

First recorded in 1202, as a clerk of King John's chamber involved in financial operations in Normandy, Mauclerk was promoted in the same year to the Norman church of Falaise, but following the collapse of Plantagenet power in France, joined the king in England, where John presented him to the churches of Croxton in Lincolnshire, Kings Nympton in Devon, and Mylor in Cornwall, and to a vicarage at Catfield in Norfolk, a pension in the diocese of Exeter, and the custody of various royal wards. As the king's confidential clerk, he was appointed joint sheriff of Lincolnshire in 1204, and travelled to Ireland in 1210 and 1212, perhaps in the following of John de Gray (d. 1214), royal justiciar in Ireland and bishop of Norwich, two of whose charters were witnessed by Mauclerk. In 1214 he accompanied the English military expeditions to Poitou and Flanders, and in the following year he appeared at the papal court, reporting to the king on the progress made by the rival baronial and royal proctors in Rome. In 1218 he served as royal justice in eyre in the east midlands, and in 1221 he was promoted to joint custody of the king's forests throughout England. From 1222 he served as sheriff of Cumberland, and it may be that it was the local power acquired with this office that enabled him, in the following year, to stake a claim to the vacant see of Carlisle. He was elected bishop by the canons of Carlisle before 22 August 1223, when his election received royal assent. Shortly afterwards the king appointed a proctor to oppose Mauclerk before the papal court, suggesting a temporary breach in relations; but on 26 October royal assent was renewed and Mauclerk's temporalities were restored.

As bishop of Carlisle, Mauclerk remained active in royal service. In 1225 he spent several months in Cologne, attempting to arrange a marriage between Henry III and a daughter of the duke of Austria, a mission in which he claimed to have endured shipwreck and great hardship. While abroad he consecrated a shrine in the collegiate church of the Holy Apostles at Cologne. Two years later he was sent to Poitou, and in the same year he is said to have been engaged in fruitless attempts to persuade the knights of Normandy and Brittany to abandon their allegiance to the king of France. He served as constable of Newcastle in 1228, and in the same year was promoted to be treasurer of the king's exchequer, assuming office on about 13 November. In the summer of 1232, amid the upheaval brought about at court through the influence of Peter des Roches, bishop of Winchester (d. 1238), Mauclerk received royal letters guaranteeing him life custody of the treasury, and of the castle and county of Carlisle, but despite this, he was deposed from office in January 1233, deprived of the manor of Melbourne, Derbyshire, which had also been guaranteed to him for life, and forced to fine £1000 to retain his other lands and liberties. Disgraced at court, he sought to go into exile overseas, but was detained by the king's bailiffs at Dover and roughly handled. The English bishops pronounced a sentence of excommunication against his assailants, and Mauclerk was allowed to retire to Flanders, from where he appears to have issued a sentence of his own, placing the cathedral and city of Carlisle under interdict.

Mauclerk was reconciled to court in the following year and, with the fall of Peter des Roches, assumed a leading role in the king's council. In 1235 he headed an embassy to Flanders, charged with arranging a marriage between Henry III and a daughter of the count of Ponthieu. In 1236 he was restored to custody of Carlisle Castle, and two years later fined 600 marks a year to have the county of Westmorland and the heir of John de Vieuxpont in wardship. During the king's continental expedition of 1242–3 he served as one of the principal members of the regency council set to govern England, and over the next few years he was engaged in peace negotiations with Scotland, and in a lucrative trade in royal wardships. With papal licence, he resigned the see of Carlisle on 29 June 1246, in order to enter the Dominican order at Oxford, a move inspired by piety and by advancing age and decrepitude. None the less, as a former bishop he continued to exercise episcopal functions, being appointed by Robert Grosseteste, bishop of Lincoln (d. 1253), to provide the blessing of newly elected heads of houses at Leicester and Godstow, and in May 1248 issuing an episcopal indulgence on behalf of the relics of Westminster Abbey. He died at Oxford on about 28 October 1248, leaving substantial benefactions to the Oxford Blackfriars. As bishop of Carlisle, he did much to improve the finances of his see, purchasing the soke of Horncastle in Lincolnshire together with numerous subsidiary liberties obtained through royal favour. In addition he obtained a life interest in the royal manor of Melbourne and the manor of Dalston in Cumberland as a gift from the crown. Most of this property, together with his houses in London and an estate at Salkeld, near Penrith, he bequeathed in perpetuity to the bishopric of Carlisle. Given his later contacts with the Dominican order, it is possible that it was Mauclerk who in 1233 helped to establish houses of Dominican and Franciscan friars in Carlisle. However, his chief talent appears to have lain in finance, rather than in scholarship or works of piety.

NICHOLAS VINCENT

Sources *Chancery records* · *Pipe rolls* · Emden, *Oxf.* · Paris, *Chron.* · *Ann. mon.* · H. Summerson, *Medieval Carlisle: the city and the borders from the late eleventh to the mid-sixteenth century*, 2 vols., Cumberland and Westmorland Antiquarian and Archaeological Society, extra ser., 25 (1993) · F. N. Davis, ed., *Rotuli Roberti Grosseteste, episcopi Lincolniensis*, CYS, 10 (1913) · J. Raine, ed., *The register or rolls of Walter Gray, lord archbishop of York*, SurtS, 56 (1872) · C. Harper-Bill, ed., *Norwich, 1070–1214*, English Episcopal Acta, 6 (1990) · W. W. Shirley, ed., *Royal and other historical letters illustrative of the reign of Henry III*, 2 vols., Rolls Series, 27 (1862–6) · *Quellen zur Geschichte der Stadt Köln*, ed. L. Ennen and G. Eckertz (1860–63) · MS Westminster Domesday, Westminster Abbey, fol. 395v · Rouen Chapter cartulary, Bibliothèque Municipale, Rouen, MS Y44, fols. 112–13
Likenesses wax seal

Maud (d. 1131). *See under* David I (c.1085–1153).

Maud, Princess (1869–1938), queen of Norway, consort of Haakon VII, was born prematurely on 26 November 1869

Princess Maud (1869–1938), by W. & D. Downey, 1905 [with her husband, King Haakon VII of Norway]

at Marlborough House, London. The fifth child and youngest of the three daughters of the future king *Edward VII (1841–1910) and Queen *Alexandra (1844–1925), she was baptized on 24 December Maud Charlotte Mary Victoria. She grew up in a loving, cheerful environment and was noted for mischief and high spirits. She was a tomboy, enjoying riding, cycling, fishing, and yachting: her nickname in the family was Harry. Later she found it hard to cope outside the familiar circle of family and friends, and shyness became her most striking characteristic.

The three Wales princesses were educated at home. Maud was musical and had a gift for languages; she was an avid reader and liked chess. The princess of Wales was a possessive mother who was not keen to see her daughters marry. In 1888 Prince Friedrich of Prussia made enquiries about Maud but was rejected because the princess of Wales, who never wavered in her antagonism to Prussia, did not want her daughter to marry a German. There was talk of other engagements which came to nothing; Queen Victoria began to consider possible husbands for Maud, recognizing that she was becoming impatient with her mother's attitude. But Maud was already in love with Prince Francis of Teck, a childhood friend who did not return her feelings. Finally, in 1895, she accepted a proposal from Prince Carl (Christian Frederick Carl Georg Valdemar Axel; 1872–1957), the second son of the king of Denmark, and a cousin she knew from her family's Danish holidays. They were married at Buckingham Palace on 22 July 1896.

Unable to face leaving home, Maud postponed her departure for Denmark for five months, clinging to Appleton House at Sandringham, a wedding present from her father. This made her unpopular in Denmark and she never really settled there, displaying so strong a preference for England that her mother felt obliged to remind her of her duty to her husband's country. In the early years of her marriage Maud suffered persistent minor illness, complaining of neuralgia, infections of the ear and nose, rheumatic pain, and perpetual colds. Her only child, Prince Alexander Edward Christian Frederick, was born at Appleton on 12 July 1903.

On 18 November 1905 Prince Carl was elected king of a newly independent Norway: he took the name Haakon VII, recalling the country's viking rulers, while his son became Olav. Maud left for Norway with her husband and threw herself determinedly into her new role, surprised and amused by the sudden change in her fortunes. She was delighted by the welcome given to her son and quickly took to calling him Olav, even in private. The coronation took place on 22 June 1906 in the cathedral at Trondheim. The new queen's shyness never left her, but her old mischief and sense of fun were increasingly in evidence, even on formal occasions. In 1907, preparing for an official visit to Paris, she remarked that it would be hard to stay on her best behaviour for so long. Her health improved. She learned Norwegian and in her own quiet way demonstrated a progressive and independent attitude. In 1907 she amazed many by openly espousing the cause of unmarried mothers. She was never entirely at her ease with formal ceremonial, and life in the royal palace in Oslo was markedly informal. The queen is said to have remarked 'I am so glad that I am Queen of a country in which everybody loves simplicity' (Aronson, 305).

Norway declared its neutrality in the First World War and King Haakon was unable to let his wife continue her visits to England. She felt painfully isolated, but extended her charity work by raising money to provide fuel, food, clothing, and medicine for those hardest hit by wartime austerity within Norway, and by limiting her already modest expenditure. Once peace came she resumed her visits to England and devoted more time to her own family. Her eldest sister died in 1931, her second in 1935. January 1936 saw the death of her only surviving sibling, George V, but, depressed as she was by these losses, Maud offered support by letter, and in person wherever possible, to her widowed sister-in-law Queen Mary, a lifelong friend. At home she found consolation in her husband, son, and grandchildren, and in the country pastimes she had always enjoyed, particularly in the English garden she had arranged at Bygdö Kongsgaard. But her health steadily weakened; her hearing had been poor for some time and she became increasingly prone to attacks of neuralgia and bronchitis, and to a general sense of weakness. Her last public appearance in England was made at the 1937 coronation.

In October 1938 Queen Maud was taken ill on a shopping trip to London and admitted to a nursing home. King Haakon hurried to her, but after an operation and much suffering the queen died of heart failure shortly after midnight on 19–20 November 1938, with only a nurse present. Her funeral took place in Oslo on 8 December and she was buried in the mausoleum at Akershus Castle.

CHARLOTTE ZEEPVAT

Sources general correspondence, Royal Arch. · J. van der Kiste, *Edward VII's children* (1989) · *The Times* (21 Nov 1938) · M. Michael, *Haakon, king of Norway* (1958) · J. Pope-Hennessy, *Queen Mary* (1959) · [H. Montgomery-Massingberd], ed., *Burke's royal families of the world*, 1 (1977) · T. Aronson, *Grandmama of Europe: the crowned descendants of Queen Victoria* (1973)

Archives Royal Arch., papers relating to childhood and youth, later letters to Queen Mary, George V, and others | FILM BFI NFTVA, The coronation of their majesties King George VI and Queen Elizabeth, 1937 · BFI NFTVA, news footage

Likenesses H. von Angeli, oils, 1875, Royal Collection · H. von Angeli, group portrait, oils, 1876 (*Prince and princess of Wales with Albert Victor and Maud*), Royal Collection · M. Thornycroft, double portrait, marble statue, 1877 (with her sister Princess Victoria), Royal Collection · S. P. Hall, group portrait, oils, 1883 (with her sisters), NPG · L. Tuxen, group portrait, oils, 1887 (*The royal family at the time of the jubilee*), Royal Collection · L. Tuxen, group portrait, oils, 1893 (*Marriage of King George V and Queen Mary*), Royal Collection · L. Tuxen, group portrait, oils, 1896 (*Marriage of Princess Maud and Prince Charles of Denmark*), Royal Collection · W. & D. Downey, double portrait, photograph, 1905, NPG [*see illus.*] · Byrne & Co., photographs, NPG · W. & D. Downey, photographs, NPG · R. Milne, photographs, NPG · J. Russell & Sons, photographs, NPG

Maud, (Margaret) Jean Hay, Lady Radcliffe-Maud (1904–1993). *See under* Maud, John Primatt Redcliffe, Baron Redcliffe-Maud (1906–1982).

Maud, John Primatt Redcliffe, Baron Redcliffe-Maud (1906–1982), public servant, was born on 3 February 1906 at Bristol, the younger son and last of the six children of the Revd John Primatt Maud (1860–1932), then vicar of St Mary Redcliffe, Bristol, and later bishop of Kensington, and his wife, Elizabeth Diana, eldest daughter of Canon Charles Wellington Furse, archdeacon of Westminster and rector of St John's, Smith Square, London.

Maud was educated at Summer Fields School, Oxford; as a king's scholar at Eton College (of which he was a fellow, 1964–76); and as a scholar at New College, Oxford, where he won a second in classical honour moderations (1926) and a first in *literae humaniores* (1928). In 1929, after a year studying economics at Harvard, he was appointed a junior research fellow in politics at University College, Oxford—the first full-time politics don to be appointed in Oxford—and made his speciality the subject of local government. Johannesburg invited him to write a history of its local government, and a visit in 1932 was to establish a lifelong link with South Africa. He became a tutorial fellow at University College in 1932, and dean in 1933.

In 1939 Maud was appointed master of Birkbeck College, London. The war broke out just as he took up his appointment, but he managed until 1943 to combine the mastership with work as a temporary civil servant, for a few months in the office of the regional commissioner for the southern region of England, and then in the Ministry of Food. When Lord Woolton became minister of food in

John Primatt
Redcliffe Maud,
Baron Redcliffe-
Maud (1906–1982),
by Ruskin Spear,
exh. RA 1973

April 1940 he chose Maud to be his principal private secretary. Maud's rise thereafter was rapid: to deputy secretary in 1941 and second secretary in 1944, when he moved with Woolton to the newly formed office of the Ministry of Reconstruction, at first as its deputy head and soon, when Norman Brook became secretary of the cabinet, its head.

Maud was so evidently fitted for the public service that he was invited to continue in it after the war ended. Still only thirty-eight, he was appointed permanent secretary to the Ministry of Education in 1945. This appointment engaged his concern for education as well as his knowledge of local government, and called for all his qualities of administrative skill, persuasiveness, and enthusiasm. In this period he was one of the founding fathers of UNESCO.

In 1952 Maud became permanent secretary at the Ministry of Fuel and Power. The main thrust of policy during his time was to reduce dependence on coal by increasing the substitution of oil for coal and developing alternative energy sources: for Maud the prospects of nuclear power were particularly exciting. In 1956 his attention was diverted for a time to the response to the immediate energy problems created by the closure of the Suez Canal and the need to re-establish the administrative machinery for petrol rationing.

At the beginning of 1959 Harold Macmillan asked Maud to go to South Africa as British high commissioner. After South Africa became a republic and left the Commonwealth in 1961 he became the first British ambassador to the new republic. It was the time of Macmillan's 'wind of change' speech. Wholly out of sympathy with the South African government's apartheid policies, Maud remained scrupulously correct in his behaviour and pronouncements, without compromising his integrity or betraying his convictions, and came to be widely respected in that country. He combined with his diplomatic appointment that of high commissioner for Swaziland, Basutoland, and Bechuanaland, and worked hard to promote the constitutional, economic, and educational advancement of those territories.

In 1963 the wheel came full circle: Maud returned to University College, to serve as its master until his retirement in 1976. During this time he undertook the chairmanship of a succession of public inquiries on the organization, structure, and management of local government, above all the royal commission on English local government (1966–9); its recommendations for changing the structure of local government proved to be too radical for the 1970–74 government, whose own 'reorganization' Maud regarded as a child of no great beauty. But the college came first, and he devoted himself wholeheartedly to its interests and to the welfare of its members. It was not by mere coincidence that under his mastership University College became pre-eminent among Oxford colleges in reputation and success.

Maud's publications included *Local Government in Modern England* (1932), *City Government: the Johannesburg Experiment* (1938), *English Local Government Reformed* (with Bruce Wood, 1974), *Support for the Arts in England and Wales* (1976), *Training Musicians* (1978), and *Experiences of an Optimist* (1981).

Maud was (as he said the ideal permanent secretary should be) discreet, wise, entertaining, and incorruptible; and he had in high degree the traditional attributes of the distinguished public servant: intelligence, high-mindedness, dedication, and a capacity for sustained hard work. He believed in the power of enlightenment to hold back the tide of barbarism, and in the capacity and duty of individual men and women to bring about progress. In these virtues and beliefs he was true to his Christian faith and to the value which he derived from his education. There were some who found all this—combined with his enjoyment of the rewards of his achievements, with his effortless charm and ease of manner, and with his seemingly inexhaustible zest—old-fashioned and even a little too good to be true. There were many others, more responsive to his qualities and in tune with his values, who looked to him for friendship, help, and inspiration, and were never disappointed.

Maud was a fine-looking man: tall, elegant, and distinguished. In his youth he loved and practised the art of acting, and his skill as a performer showed in his later facility as a public speaker and as a broadcaster: he had a gift for combining wisdom and wit in his matter with grace and felicity in his manner.

Music also meant much to Maud—as performer in his younger days as well as listener—though in this part of his life he played a supporting role to his wife, Jean [see below], who was, and continued to be, a professional pianist. They married on 20 June 1932; and from then on his success and his serenity were sustained by fifty years of close and happy family life. There were four children of the marriage: three daughters (one of whom died in 1941 on the day before her fifth birthday) and a son, Humphrey, who had a distinguished career in the diplomatic service.

Maud was appointed CBE (1942), KCB (1946), and GCB (1955). He was given honorary degrees by the universities of Witwatersrand (1960), Natal (1963), Leeds (1967), Nottingham (1968), and Birmingham (1968). He was FRCM (1964) and an honorary fellow of New College (1964) and University College, Oxford (1976). He was created a life peer in 1967, taking the title of Redcliffe-Maud. He took an active part in the work of the House of Lords, particularly relishing the committee work, until very shortly before his death in Oxford, where he lived, on 20 November 1982.

Maud's wife, **(Margaret) Jean Hay Maud**, Lady Redcliffe-Maud (1904–1993), pianist and hostess, was born on 6 March 1904 in Melrose, Roxburghshire, the younger daughter of John Brown Hamilton, headmaster of St Mary's School, Melrose. Educated at St Mary's School, Melrose, St Leonard's School, the Royal College of Music, and Somerville College, Oxford, she also studied with the harpsichordist Wanda Landowska in Paris and with the pianist and composer Artur Schnabel in Berlin. She became a successful concert pianist. She met Maud in Oxford, and after their marriage she supported his career and continued to perform, entertaining troops and others during the Second World War, playing in London in the 1950s, and performing in South Africa and Oxford for charity. She was also a keen amateur painter and gardener. Between 1989 and 1991 she published four volumes of autobiography, based in part on her letters and diaries. She died in Oxford on 6 November 1993, survived by her son and two daughters.   ROBERT ARMSTRONG, rev.

Sources Lord Redcliffe-Maud [J. P. R. Maud], *Experiences of an optimist* (1981) [memoirs] · *The Times* (22 Nov 1982) · personal knowledge (1990) · private information (1990) · *CGPLA Eng. & Wales* (1983) · *The Times* (4 Dec 1993) · *WWW* · Burke, *Peerage* · *CGPLA Eng. & Wales* (1994)

Archives BLPES, papers | Rice University, Houston, Texas, Fondren Library, corresp. with Sir Julian Huxley, Huxley MSS

Likenesses R. Spear, oils, exh. RA 1973, NPG [see illus.] · photograph, repro. in *The Times* · photograph, Hult. Arch.

Wealth at death £164,934: probate, 4 Feb 1983, *CGPLA Eng. & Wales* · £377,620—[Margaret Jean Hay Maud, Lady Redcliffe-Maud]: probate, 1 March 1994, *CGPLA Eng. & Wales* (1994)

Maude, Angus Edmund Upton, Baron Maude of Stratford upon Avon (1912–1993), journalist and politician, was born on 8 September 1912 at 44 Temple Fortune Lane, Hendon, Middlesex, the only child of Alan Hamer Maude (1885–1979), journalist and army officer, and his wife, Dorothy Maude Upton, only daughter of Frederic Upton,

civil servant. The Maudes were an old-established family of Yorkshire gentry and included several notable bankers and naval officers; one of Maude's forebears was an officer in Cromwell's army at Marston Moor, and another was a godson of William IV. Maude's father was a sub-editor on *The Times* and later a colonel in the Royal Army Service Corps, serving with great distinction in the First World War.

Like his father, Maude was educated at Rugby School (where he was a classical scholar) and at Oriel College, Oxford, where he served on the committees of both the Union Society and the Conservative Association and from where he graduated with a second-class degree in philosophy, politics, and economics in 1933. He then joined his father's profession, working on *The Times* (1933–4) and then the *Daily Mail* (1934–9) as a financial journalist. Commissioned as a Territorial Army officer four months before the outbreak of the Second World War in 1939, he saw action in north Africa but was captured in January 1942 and spent the rest of the conflict as a prisoner of war. Although shy, he helped to organize theatrical activities. On 2 January 1946 he married Barbara Elizabeth Earnshaw (b. 1915/16), daughter of John Earnshaw Sutcliffe, artist, of Bushey, Hertfordshire. They had two sons and two daughters.

After the war Maude found an outlet for his restless intelligence at an independent think-tank, Political and Economic Planning, where he served as a deputy director. It was an unusual posting for a man who was later associated with the anti-statist wing of the Conservative Party; the group's work suggested an active (if not directive) role for government. But the job seemed to fit Maude for a post-war Conservative Party which had accepted a more interventionist state than had existed previously. In 1949 he was chosen as the Conservative candidate for South Ealing, and in the same year his researches bore fruit in his most popular book, *The English Middle Classes*, a perceptive account of social change which he wrote with Roy Lewis. This collaboration also produced *Professional People* (1952).

Maude was returned at the general election of 1950 with a comfortable majority. As a prospective candidate he had met another young Conservative intellectual, Cuthbert ('Cub') Alport, and they had discussed forming a ginger group if they both won their seats. This was the first suggestion of what became the 'One Nation' group—formed with seven other MPs including Edward Heath, Iain Macleod, Enoch Powell, and Robert Carr. Maude played a key role in co-ordinating the work on the group's first (eponymous) pamphlet, which was widely touted as a distinctive Conservative approach to the social services at a time of economic stringency. Maude was also heavily involved in the group's next production, *Change is our Ally* (1954), which indicated a more sceptical view of the state. By the time the Conservatives returned to power in 1951, membership of One Nation was already seen as a likely passport to ministerial office. But Maude and Powell were repeatedly overlooked, suggesting that the Conservative whips had already noted them as mercurial characters.

Neither was prepared to suffer fools. In Maude's case the failure to secure a footing was particularly significant, since in addition to his One Nation work he served as director of his party's educational wing, the Conservative Political Centre, for four years after 1951. He was also an effective Commons speaker, if not quite up to the standard set by his friends Macleod and Powell. His main handicap seems to have been an inability to court influential allies; his son later described him as 'the world's worst networker' (private information).

By 1956 Maude was a disappointed man. A member of the Suez group, he resigned the Conservative whip in May 1957 and sat for a year as an independent Conservative, in protest against British policy towards Cyprus. The fact that Maude, who had always concentrated on domestic policy, should choose to associate with his party's imperialist wing revealed how disillusioned he had become. In 1958 he took this emotion to its logical conclusion, resigning his seat (much to the embarrassment of Harold Macmillan's government) and accepting the post of editor at the *Sydney Morning Herald*. Nevertheless the Australian exile lasted only three years. Before his departure friends warned him that he would be disappointed if he expected to enjoy full editorial independence, and so it proved. But he enjoyed Australia, where he also hosted an important televised discussion programme. In 1961 he was back in England, actively searching for a seat. Fortunately for him, in October 1961 Iain Macleod became chairman of the party, and by November 1962 Maude had been chosen to fight a by-election in a safe Conservative seat, South Dorset. Ironically, another old acquaintance thwarted his comeback. Viscount Hinchingbroke, whose elevation to the Lords had created the vacancy, was a fellow Suez rebel, but unlike Maude he could no longer support a Conservative leadership which was anxious to join the Common Market. Hinchingbroke threw his weight behind an independent Conservative, Sir Piers Debenham, who won 5000 votes; Maude was defeated by a narrow margin. During the by-election campaign Maude's abrasive personality attracted unfavourable press attention, and even he thought that his career was at an end. But in August 1963 he was allowed another attempt, at Stratford upon Avon, which had been represented by the disgraced minister John Profumo. Maude won the seat with a greatly reduced majority, but this was a creditable performance, since the Macmillan government was more than 10 per cent behind Labour in the national opinion polls.

After the Conservatives fell from power in 1964 there were signs that Maude was willing to play a more orthodox role within his party. When Enoch Powell stood for the leadership in July 1965 Maude voted for Reginald Maudling. Earlier Alec Home had appointed Maude opposition spokesman on aviation. It was some surprise when the new leader, Edward Heath, kept him on in this role; after all, Heath had been chief whip during the Suez crisis. A falling-out could be predicted, and it came remarkably quickly. In January 1966 *The Spectator* published an article by Maude, entitled 'Winter of tory discontent'. The author, now spokesman on colonial affairs, warned that

his party risked being regarded as an 'irrelevance', and attacked the timidity of its policy proposals. Since Maude lacked a parliamentary following, Heath could dismiss him without fearing the consequences; if the decision made the party look disunited, the errant minister had created this impression already. To underline his political innocence, he was genuinely puzzled by the furious reaction of the leadership.

Since Maude's oft-frustrated hopes of preferment were unlikely to be satisfied while Heath was leader, his decision to fight the general election in 1970 testified to his addiction to parliamentary life. He also continued to write intelligent articles, and in 1969 produced *The Common Problem*, a substantial volume which proved him a rigorous and original thinker. Combined with more tact—and, perhaps, a less forbidding aspect—these qualities should have secured high office. Instead, he seemed to be competing with Powell for the role of chief prophet without honour; *The Common Problem* has remained an unjustly neglected work of political thinking. By contrast, Maude's contribution to the *Black Papers*, which challenged current educational theory, was well publicized; but it did nothing to endear him to a party leadership unwilling to oppose the introduction of comprehensive schools. He also joined Powell in voting against the Race Relations Bill (1968). During the Heath government he was an occasional rebel, particularly over EEC membership (although he avoided a serious clash with his constituency party by abstaining, rather than voting against the British application). His main influence was exerted through a critical and widely read *Sunday Express* column. Although he had passed his sixtieth birthday by the time of the general election of February 1974, he stood again. But only the prospect of a radical change in the party's direction can have induced him to seek election in the second 1974 contest, held in October.

When Thatcher contested Heath's leadership in January 1975, Maude was an enthusiastic supporter, and he drafted the impressive statement of principles published under her name in the *Daily Telegraph* just before the election. When Thatcher won the leadership on the second ballot Maude was appointed chairman of the Conservative Research Department. In theory it was an apposite choice; Maude could be relied upon to uphold the 'Thatcherite' line in an institution which the new leadership deeply distrusted. As usual with Maude, there was an element of irony in the appointment because Powell, whose brilliance had helped to make the reputation of the research department in the late 1940s, had by this time joined the Ulster Unionists—an act of self-immolation which surpassed even the gestures of his old friend. Maude did make a significant contribution, but morale in the research department was low throughout his chairmanship, and his precise role was difficult to define since Sir Keith Joseph had been given overall charge of policy research. Maude's main achievement was to help with the drafting of *The Right Approach* (1976), which cleverly steered a middle course to paper over the divisions between Conservative 'wets' and 'dries'.

When the Conservatives won the general election in 1979 Maude was made paymaster-general, with a seat in the cabinet and membership of the privy council. It had been a tortuous career path, but at last it seemed that Maude had reached a destination suited to his talents. But he would have preferred a departmental post, preferably in education, and it was his ill fortune to be given responsibility for government policy at a time when there was no cheering news to impart. At the end of Thatcher's first year in power ministers had to admit that they had failed to meet expectations, but in the search for scapegoats Maude was always likely to be vulnerable. In January 1981 he stood down from the cabinet. Thatcher later claimed that this was at his own request, but he was most reluctant to leave. He remained on good terms with the prime minister, who awarded him a knighthood. Before the next election he was appointed chairman of a government committee on questions of policy, but this was his last official appointment. He left the Commons at the 1983 election, and was made a life peer, as Baron Maude of Stratford upon Avon, shortly thereafter.

Maude remained an active member of the Lords for many years, able at last to lend consistent support to the policies of his own party. He also had the satisfaction of seeing his son Francis rise within the ranks, becoming financial secretary to the Treasury in 1990, although his final years were touched by tragedy when his other son, Charles, died from an AIDS-related illness. Maude himself was already unwell. He died peacefully of old age and haemochromatosis at the Foscote Hospital, Banbury, on 9 November 1993 and was buried at South Newington, Oxfordshire. He was survived by his wife, Barbara, his son Francis, and his two daughters.

The leading theme of Maude's life was that of talent unfulfilled. Too self-willed to reach the top in politics, he could have achieved lasting fame as a writer but seemingly lacked sufficient application. There was some satisfaction in the success of his party, which at the time of his death seemed destined for many more years in power. But he was ill suited to the role of unthinking loyalist, and had he written a follow-up to *The Common Problem* his idiosyncratic ideas might have helped to inject much needed intellectual excitement into his party.

MARK GARNETT

Sources *The Guardian* (10 Nov 1993) · *The Times* (11 Nov 1993) · *The Times* (3 March 1994) · *The Independent* (11 Nov 1993) · *WWW, 1991–5* · M. Garnett, *Alport: a study in loyalty* (1999) · b. cert. · m. cert. · d. cert. · private information (2004) [Francis Maude, son]
Archives SOUND BL NSA, performance recordings
Likenesses photographs, 1976–9, Hult. Arch. · photograph, repro. in *The Guardian* · photograph, repro. in *The Times* (11 Nov 1993) · photograph, repro. in *The Independent*

Maude, Aylmer (1858–1938), writer and translator, was born on 28 March 1858 in Ipswich, the youngest son of Francis Henry Maude (1822–1886/7), perpetual curate of Holy Trinity Church, Ipswich, and his wife, Lucy, *née* Thorp. Educated at Christ's Hospital from 1868 to March 1874, in 1874 he went for two years to the Lyceum in Moscow where from 1877 to 1880 he worked as an English

Aylmer Maude (1858–1938), by Lafayette, 1932

tutor. On 7 August 1884 at the British vice-consulate in Moscow in an Anglican ceremony he married by special licence Louise Shanks (1855–1939), the daughter of James Stewart Shanks, a Moscow-based British businessman. Maude worked first in Moscow as a carpet salesman for the Scottish company Muir and Mirrielees. He was subsequently employed by the Anglo-Russian Carpet Company in Moscow as business manager and then as director.

In 1897, after having spent more than twenty years in Moscow, Maude considered that he had sufficient funds on which to retire. With his wife and their four sons, Arnold (b. 1885), Herbert (1886–1962), Aylmer Henry (b. 1890), and Lionel (1892–1971) (he had a twin brother who was stillborn), Maude left Moscow to settle in England. The family initially went to the Brotherhood Church in Croydon, Surrey and then later in 1897 to Wickham's Farm in Danbury, near Purleigh, Essex. In September 1898 Maude left for three months for Canada to negotiate on behalf of a cause championed by Tolstoy: that of the Dukhobors, a Christian pacifist fundamentalist sect, whose members had been brutally treated by the Russian authorities as a consequence of their refusal to do military service. Maude's good offices led to their successful resettlement in the Canadian North-West Territories, and to his publication of *A Peculiar People, the Dukhobors* in New York in 1904.

In 1901 the Maudes settled in Great Baddow, near Purleigh, Essex. Living on income generated by their investments, he and his wife devoted themselves to translating and publishing Tolstoy's writings. Maude visited Tolstoy in August 1902, October 1906, and in the autumn of 1909. First introduced to the Russian novelist in 1888 by his brother-in-law Dr P. S. Alekseyev (1849–1913), Maude recorded in his 'Recollections of Tolstoy' that 'During the winters of 1895–96 and 1896–97 I went to see him almost every week. He sometimes visited my wife and myself, and taught our boys to make paper cockerels' (Maude, 476). Correspondence between Maude and Tolstoy continued until the latter's death; indeed, Tolstoy wrote more letters to Maude than to any other Englishman. Following his visit to Tolstoy in 1902 at Yasnaya Polyana, Maude was authorized to write Tolstoy's biography. Constable published the first volume, *The First Fifty Years*, in 1908 followed by the second volume, *The Life of Tolstoy: Later Years*, in 1910.

Maude also worked on what was the first full English translation of *What is Art?* This appeared in the supplement to the June to December 1899 issue of the *New Order*, the journal of the Croydon Brotherhood Church. In 1900 Louise translated *Resurrection*. In 1901 Grant Richards' published Maude's translation of *Sevastopol and Other Military Tales*. Two years later saw Maude's compilation of Tolstoy's essays and letters in English translation published in Grant Richards' World's Classic series, a second edition of *Resurrection*, and Maude's translation of Tolstoy's *Plays* (*The Power of Darkness*, *The First Distiller*, and *Fruits of Culture*). These were the first among the Maudes' many translations, including *Anna Karenina* (1918) and *War and Peace* (1922); Aylmer usually took on Tolstoy's theoretical and political writings and Louise worked on the fiction. Maude's 'greatest achievement was undoubtedly the splendid Centenary Edition of Tolstoy's works in twenty-one volumes, published—after many hesitations—by the Oxford University Press between 1928 and 1937' (Holman, 'Half a life's work', 40).

In addition to working on his monumental edition of Tolstoy's works in translation, Maude expounded Tolstoy's ideas and enacted a lengthy public campaign, with the support of Shaw, Rebecca West, H. G. Wells, Arnold Bennett, and others, for a collected Tolstoy in English. Michael J. De K. Holman observes that the Maudes:

in the early 1930s … found themselves in greatly straitened circumstances. So much so, in fact, that had not Aylmer been granted a Civil List Pension in 1932 for his services to literature, it is questionable whether they would have been able to continue their work on the Centenary Edition. (Holman, 'Half a life's work', 51)

In 1918–19 Maude went to Russia with the north Russian expeditionary force (the British interventionist forces); he also served as a liaison officer with the Russians. His other activities and causes included defending the ideas of Dr Marie Stopes, writing *The Authorized Life of Marie C. Stopes* (1924) and *Marie Stopes: her Work and Play* (1933). He was also very active in the Fabian Society and between 1907 and 1912 was on the Fabian executive.

Maude was independently minded. He disagreed at times with some of Tolstoy's ideas but was a dedicated advocate of Tolstoy's greatness. Although he was slightly

dictatorial as an editor, 'his Oxford University Press Centenary Edition, the "Maude Tolstoy" … is an achievement unique in the history of Anglo-Russian literary relations' (Holman, 'Half a life's work', 52). Garth M. Terry thought that 'Maude's edition, is in fact, probably the best and most complete translation of Tolstoy ever made' (Terry, 223). In June 1937 Maude wrote his final 'Editor's note' which appeared in the second volume of *Anna Karenina*. He recalled:

I had no idea when I started, that the presentation of [Tolstoy's] works to the English-speaking world would be so arduous and lengthy a task, but it is one I do not regret devoting my life to, and which, I think, was worth doing. (ibid.)

Maude died, following the completion of his edition, at Great Baddow aged eighty on 25 August 1938. His close collaborator, his wife, Louise, died in 1939.

WILLIAM BAKER

Sources M. J. De K. Holman, 'Half a life's work: Aylmer Maude brings Tolstoy to Britain', *Scottish Slavonic Review*, 4 (spring 1988), 39–53 · M. J. De K. Holman, 'L. N. Tolstoy to Aylmer Maude: an unpublished letter', *Journal of Russian Studies*, 36 (1978), 3–9 · M. J. De K. Holman, 'The Purleigh colony: Tolstoyan togetherness in the late 1890s', *New essays on Tolstoy*, ed. M. Jones (1978), 194–222 · DNB · A. Maude, 'Recollections of Tolstoy', *Slavonic Review*, 7/20 (1929), 475–81 · H. Gifford, 'On translating Tolstoy', *New essays on Tolstoy*, ed. M. Jones (1978), 17–38 · G. M. Terry, 'Tolstoy studies in Great Britain: a bibliographical survey', *New essays on Tolstoy*, ed. M. Jones (1978), 223–46 · G. B. Shaw, '[Aylmer Maude's *Life of Tolstoy*]', *Fabian News* (March 1911) [repr. in *Tolstoi and Britain*, ed. W. G. Jones (1995), 217–21] · M. J. De K. Holman and D. Collins, 'Aylmer Maude's letters from Archangel, 1918–1919', *Sbornik* [(Leeds)] (1981), 6–7 · CGPLA Eng. & Wales (1938)

Archives U. Leeds, Brotherton L., corresp. | BL, corresp. with Society of Authors, Add. MSS 56746–56749 · BL, corresp. with Marie Stopes, Add. MSS 58487–58490 · Bodl. Oxf., letters to Gilbert Murray · Bodl. Oxf., corresp. with J. L. Myres · Dorset County Museum, Dorchester, letters to Thomas Hardy · JRL, letters to W. E. A. Axon · U. Edin., corresp. with C. Sarolea · University of Toronto, corresp. with James Mavor · West Yorks. AS, Wakefield, letters relating to Russian Carpet Company

Likenesses Lafayette, photograph, 1932, NPG [see illus.] · E. Shanks, double portrait (with Stella Meldrum), priv. coll. · photograph, priv. coll.; repro. in Holman, 'Purleigh colony', facing p. 195

Wealth at death £2391 16s. 1d.: probate, 24 Nov 1938, CGPLA Eng. & Wales · English probate resealed in New Westminster, 25 Feb 1939, CGPLA Eng. & Wales

Maude [née Elphinstone Fleeming], **Clementina**, **Viscountess Hawarden** (1822–1865), photographer, was born on 1 June 1822 at Cumbernauld House, Dunbartonshire, the third of the five children of Admiral Charles Elphinstone Fleeming (1774–1840) of Cumbernauld (pronounced 'Fleming'), and his wife, Catalina Paulina Alessandro (1800–1880), of Cadiz, Spain. Her father was the second son of the eleventh Lord Elphinstone and brother of Mountstuart Elphinstone (1779–1859), governor of Bombay; her mother was the daughter of Luis Alessandro, of Ancona, Italy, and Antonia Felipes, of Gibraltar. Her parents were married in May 1816 while her father was commander-in-chief at Gibraltar. A whig member of the reform parliament, he died while serving as

Clementina Maude, Viscountess Hawarden (1822–1865), by
Eden Upton Eddis, 1851

governor of the Royal Naval Hospital, Greenwich, leaving
his family with little money.

In 1841 their mother and uncle, Mountstuart Elphinstone, took Clementina and her sisters Mary Keith (c.1825–
1859) and Anne Elizabeth (1828–1925)—the latter the
mother of the traveller and scholar Robert Bontine Cunninghame Graham—to Rome, where education was less
costly. Their uncle introduced them to the city's sights and
its society, including his old friend Mary Somerville, the
mathematician and astronomer. In 1842 they returned to
London, where it was feared Clementina would risk 'getting into bad society' and her exotic beauty would prove a
'snare' (D. Erskine to M. Elphinstone, 6 Oct 1842, BL OIOC,
Mountstuart Elphinstone MS F88 4C #13). Instead she
made a love match with a future peer: on 24 March 1845
she married Cornwallis Maude (1817–1905) of the 2nd Life
Guards. When his father died on 12 October 1856 he
became fourth Viscount Hawarden and inherited Dundrum, co. Tipperary, Ireland, which made him one of Britain's 10,000 wealthiest landowners. In 1857 the family (of
ten children born between 1846 and 1864 eight survived
infancy) moved from London to Dundrum.

Lady Hawarden began photographing at the estate, in
late 1857 or early 1858. She worked with various formats,
from stereoscopic to view cameras; she made wet collodion on glass negatives and albumen prints. These were
technically demanding processes, but favoured by professionals and amateurs alike for tonal range and degree of

detail. Most of the prints were pasted into albums, from
which they were removed by cutting or tearing (hence the
missing corners) many years later.

Lady Hawarden's work centred on her family, and her
photographs reveal a deep rapport between photographer and models, mother and children. Her first photographs were stereoscopic images of the Dundrum estate,
emphasizing the Romantic qualities of the landscape and
giving no hint of the tensions between the Roman Catholic tenant farmers and their protestant landlords; often
her husband and children appear, occasionally in peasant
costume. In 1859 the family moved to a new house at 5
Prince's Gardens, South Kensington, London, though they
returned to Dundrum regularly. In this house, where her
best-known work was done, she used the entire first floor
as a studio, which was flooded with light and furnished
with a few props. From about 1862 she concentrated on
photographing her three eldest daughters—Isabella
Grace, Clementina, and Florence Elizabeth—in costume
tableaux, perhaps as an extension of their participation in
amateur theatricals and tableaux vivants. These images,
in which the girls are often twinned with each other or
with a mirror reflection, reverberate with romantic, even
sexual, feeling. The themes of identity and expression are
clear, but precise meanings remain ambiguous. There are
no titles to provide clarification: Lady Hawarden exhibited her photographs as 'Photographic Studies' and 'Studies from Life'. These terms indicate that she worked in an
established genre of art photography and followed an artistic tradition which valued form over content, and observation over narrative. Her rather enigmatic œuvre invites
comparison with the work of her better-known contemporary, Julia Margaret Cameron.

Although her work focused on her domestic life, Lady
Hawarden was not a recluse. Among her associates was
the surgeon and etcher Sir Francis Seymour Haden; some
of Haden's most renowned prints are of Dundrum scenes,
and he based at least two prints on photographs by Lady
Hawarden. Haden was a friend of Sir Henry Cole, director
of the South Kensington Museum, with whom the
Hawardens also became acquainted.

Lady Hawarden first showed her photographs at the
1863 exhibition of the Photographic Society of London
(later the Royal Photographic Society, Bath), winning a silver medal for the best contribution by an amateur and
afterwards being elected to the society. She exhibited for a
second and final time at the society's 1864 show, where
she won a silver medal for composition. Her place among
the finest photographers of the day, amateur or professional, male or female, was assured. Among her admirers
were O. G. Rejlander, and Lewis Carroll, who purchased
five of her photographs now in the Gernsheim collection
at the Humanities Research Center, University of Texas at
Austin.

When Lady Hawarden died suddenly of pneumonia on
19 January 1865, at the age of forty-two, at her home, at 5
Prince's Gardens, her photographic colleagues mourned a
'member as useful as a clasp and bright as a diamond'
(British Journal of Photography, 27 Jan 1865). She was survived

by her husband. Within a few years after her death her work and reputation had disappeared from view. However, rediscovery began in 1939 when her granddaughter Lady Clementina Tottenham donated the family collection of 775 photographs to the Victoria and Albert Museum. This collection is Lady Hawarden's testament, as it appears she left no diary or journal, and few letters.

VIRGINIA DODIER

Sources V. Dodier, *Clementina, Viscountess Hawarden: 'Studies from life'* (1998) · V. Dodier, 'Clementina, Viscountess Hawarden: " Studies from life"', *British photography in the nineteenth century: the fine art tradition*, ed. M. Weaver (1989), 141–50 · V. Dodier, 'Haden, photography and salmon fishing', *Print Quarterly*, 3 (1986), 34–50 · O. G. R. [O. G. Rejlander], *British Journal of Photography* (27 Jan 1865), 38 · Burke, *Peerage* (1867) · Burke, *Peerage* (1970) · *Journal of the Photographic Society*, 9 (1864–5), 69 · *British Journal of Photography* (16 Feb 1863), 69 · *Exhibition of photographs and daguerrotypes … ninth year* (1863) [exhibition catalogue, Photographic Society of London] · *Exhibition of photographs and daguerrotypes … tenth year* (1864) [exhibition catalogue, Photographic Society of London] · H. Gernsheim, *Lewis Carroll, photographer*, rev. edn (1969), 52 · GEC, *Peerage*, new edn, vol. 5 · HoP, *Commons* · J. Bateman, *The great landowners of Great Britain and Ireland*, 4th edn (1883); repr. with introduction by D. Spring (1971), 213 · BL OIOC, Elphinstone MSS, MS Eur. F 87 · d. cert.
Archives BL OIOC, Mountstuart Elphinstone collection · NA Scot., Elphinstone collection · NA Scot., Cunninghame Graham collection · NA Scot., Loch collection · NL Scot., Elphinstone collection · priv. coll., Polwarth collection
Likenesses oils, *c*.1838, priv. coll. · E. U. Eddis, chalk, 1851, priv. coll. [*see illus.*]
Wealth at death under £2000: administration, 17 May 1865, *CGPLA Eng. & Wales*

Maude, Cyril Francis (1862–1951), actor and theatre manager, was born on 24 April 1862 at 19 St George's Square, Westminster, London, the eldest of the seven children of Charles Henry Maude (1830–1908), a captain in the 14th Madras infantry and the grandson of the first Viscount Hawarden, and his wife, Georgiana Henrietta Emma Hanbury-Tracy (*c*.1833–1921), the daughter of the second Baron Sudeley. He was educated at preparatory schools in London, Surrey, and Hampshire and, from 1876 to 1879, at Charterhouse School, where, already intent on a theatrical career (at a time when the stage was gaining in respectability), he took part in plays. He then studied with private tutors and took lessons in dancing, elocution, and fencing. Ill health threatened his ambitions and led to his being sent with his brother Ernest to Canada in 1882 to learn farming.

With renewed health, Maude obtained an engagement in New York with Daniel Bandmann's company in 1884, and his first professional appearance was at Denver, Colorado, that April as the Servant in John Oxenford's *East Lynne*. After returning to London he was first seen in the modest part of Mr Pilkie in *The Great Divorce Case*, by John Roe and Richard Doe, at the Criterion Theatre on 18 February 1886. Greater distinction came, following work in the provinces, as the Duke of Courtland in G. H. Macdermott's *Racing*, which opened at the Grand Theatre, Islington, on 5 September 1887. Maude's career was now assured, and he became best known for his characterizations of a long line

of older—often very old—men in both classic and contemporary comedies. The next decade saw engagements at the Gaiety, the Vaudeville, the Criterion, the Avenue, the Strand, the Haymarket, the Comedy, the Lyceum, and the St James's theatres; at the last he created the part of Cayley Drummle in Pinero's *The Second Mrs Tanqueray* (27 May 1893). In 1888 he twice married the actress Winifred *Emery (1861–1924) (on 28 April, and again on 2 June), with whom he co-starred in many productions and with whom he had a son and two daughters. The second wedding (reasons for which remain obscure) took place in the Savoy Chapel, and was said to mark the 'vast alteration which has taken place in the last few years in the estimation of the stage as a profession by the British aristocracy' (*The Era*, 9 June 1888).

On 17 October 1896 Maude began a highly successful partnership with Frederick Harrison (1854–1926) at the Haymarket Theatre, when he opened in the part of Captain Larolle in Edward Rose's *Under the Red Robe*. The following nine years saw him direct and star in many important productions, including J. M. Barrie's *The Little Minister* (as Reverend Gavin Dishart), *Cousin Kate* by H. H. Davies (Heath Desmond), and Robert Marshall's *The Second in Command* (Major Christopher Bingham), as well as in such classics as *The Rivals*, *The School for Scandal*, and *She Stoops to Conquer*.

In 1905 Maude leased and rebuilt the Avenue Theatre, Northumberland Avenue, which had opened in 1882. As the work neared completion the theatre, now named the Playhouse, was largely destroyed and eight people killed when, on 5 December 1905, the roof of the adjoining Charing Cross Station collapsed. In the year before it could be restored and opened (it cost the London and South-Eastern Railway Company £20,000 to make it good) Maude took over the Waldorf Theatre for some months. He played Lord Meadows in *Toddles*, by Clyde Fitch, at the Duke of York's, at Wyndham's, and, from its opening on 28 January 1907, at his Playhouse, where the next six years saw a further string of successes. At the same time he appeared at a number of gala and royal command performances.

Maude averred that his greatest enjoyment lay in 'powder plays', and he took great pains in studying old men, even following likely models in the street; Sir Peter Teazle in *The School for Scandal* was his favourite role. His meticulous make-up included 'blueing the veins of his hands and chalking the knuckles' (*The Sketch*, 25 Oct 1893, 658–9). His greatest success, in box-office terms, was as Andrew Bullivant in *Grumpy*, by Horace Hodges and T. W. Percyval, first performed at Glasgow on 19 September 1913, given more than 1300 performances in Britain and abroad, and filmed in 1930.

Maude relinquished his lease of the Playhouse in 1915. He spent much of the period between 1913 and 1925 on tours in the United States and in 1917–18 was in Australia. Winifred Emery died on 15 July 1924. After marrying Beatrice Mary Trew, the daughter of the Revd John Ellis and the widow of P. H. Trew, on 12 October 1927, Maude lived chiefly in retirement. His last performance was as Sir

Peter Teazle, opposite Vivien Leigh, at a benefit on behalf of the RAF Benevolent Fund and the Actors' Orphanage at the Haymarket Theatre on 24 April 1942.

Maude was a 'sprightly, neat little man' (*Torquay Times*, 23 Feb 1951, 2) of 'bright spirits and high principles' (Brereton, 42) whose acting was distinguished by 'gentle pathos' (ibid., 41). He wrote two reminiscences, *The Haymarket Theatre* (1903) and *Behind the Scenes with Cyril Maude* (1927), and co-wrote a novel, *The Actor in Room 931* (1925), and a play, *Strange Cousins* (1934). He appeared in nine films, the first in 1913. He was one of the founders of the (later Royal) Academy of Dramatic Art in 1905 and was elected its president in 1936. In his last years Maude lived in Torquay, where he took up painting and became president of the Devon Art Society, as well as president of the South Devon Literary and Debating Society. He died of influenza at his home, Dundrum, Lower Woodfield Road, on 20 February 1951, and was buried at St John's Church on 23 February.

C. M. P. TAYLOR

Sources C. Maude, *Behind the scenes with Cyril Maude* (1927) · A. Brereton, *Cyril Maude: an illustrated memoir* (1913) · C. Maude, *The Haymarket Theatre* (1903) · C. Maude, 'Cyril Maude's story told by himself', *The Gentlewoman* (Dec 1905), 22–30 · C. Maude and R. De Cordova, *Parts I have played, 1883–1909* (1909) [souvenir brochure] · *The Times* (21 Feb 1951) · *Evening Standard* (24 April 1951) · *Torquay Times* (23 Feb 1951) · *The Stage* (22 Feb 1951) · M. Morley, 'Cyril Maude', Theatre Museum, London, Maude MSS · 'Mr Cyril Maude "De Senectute"', *The Sketch* (25 Oct 1893), 658–9 · *Today* (2 Oct 1895) · *The Era* (9 Dec 1905) · J. Parker, ed., *Who's who in the theatre*, 10th edn (1947) · Burke, *Peerage* (1939) · R. Low, *The history of the British film*, 4: *1918–1929* (1971) · *Debrett's Peerage* · *The Sketch* (23 Sept 1927) · *Torquay Times* (2 March 1951)
Archives Theatre Museum, London
Likenesses A. Ellis, photograph, 1894, NPG · H. Furniss, pen-and-ink caricature, 1905, NPG; repro. in *The Garrick Gallery* · Rotary photo, c.1905, NPG · Lenare, photograph, 1942, NPG · Spy [L. Ward], caricature, lithograph, NPG; repro. in *VF* (11 March 1897) · portraits, Theatre Museum, London
Wealth at death £62,516 13s. 4d.: probate, 14 April 1951, CGPLA Eng. & Wales

Maude, Sir (Frederick) Stanley

Maude, Sir (Frederick) Stanley (1864–1917), army officer, was born on 24 June 1864 at Gibraltar, the youngest son of General Sir Frederick Francis Maude VC (1821–1897) and his wife, Catherine Mary (d. 1892), daughter of the Very Revd Sir George Bisshopp, eighth baronet, dean of Lismore.

Education and early career The family claimed descent from Eustacius de Monte Alto, an Italian freebooter who came over at the conquest. Maude was educated at St Michael's School, Aldis House, Slough (1875–8) and Eton College (1878–82), where his fagmaster later described him as 'one of the nicest small boys I ever had to deal with' (Callwell, 6). Athletic, he rowed and won the steeplechase and the mile, and in 1882 was elected to Pop. He acquired a nickname, Joe. After 'cramming' at Mr Northcote's establishment, Rochester House, Ealing, he attended the Royal Military College, Sandhurst, where he was a 'show cadet' (ibid., 10) and under-officer. Over 6 feet tall, good at games, and keen on personal fitness, he never smoked.

On 6 February 1884 Maude was commissioned a second lieutenant in the 1st battalion Coldstream Guards, and stationed in Chelsea. During the 1885 Sudan campaign he accompanied the battalion to Suakin, where he fought in the battles at Hashin and Tamai and participated in the occupation of Handub. For his services he received the campaign medal with clasp and the khedive's star. Between 1888 and 1892 the battalion served in London and Windsor and he served as adjutant, despite only four years' service. On 1 November 1893 he married at St Paul's, Knightsbridge, Cecil Cornelia Marianne St Leger, daughter of Colonel Thomas Edward *Taylor (1811–1883), of Ardgillan Castle, co. Dublin, Conservative politician and chancellor of the duchy of Lancaster in Disraeli's second ministry. They had two sons, one dying in infancy, and three daughters. On 28 August 1895 he was promoted captain, then, with a special nomination from the duke of Cambridge, he attended the Staff College, Camberley (1895–6). He was appointed on 1 January 1897 brigade major of the brigade of guards. Later that year he was responsible for organizing much of the military ceremonial during Queen Victoria's diamond jubilee. Never wealthy, he suffered financial loss in 1898 which hampered his career for several years. In February 1899 he was promoted major.

Second South African War and staff appointments Following the outbreak of the Second South African War (1899–1902) Maude resigned his appointment and rejoined the 2nd battalion Coldstream Guards in January 1900, serving in the 1st division on the Modder River. He arrived too late to participate in the hard fighting in which the guards brigade had been engaged. For one month he served as second in command before being appointed brigade major. Following the battle of Paardeburg (27 February 1900) the guards moved to Klip Drift as part of Lord Roberts's offensive towards Pretoria. The guards took part in the engagements at Poplar Grove and Driefontein, and Maude was seriously injured during the latter when his horse fell. Since he did not then receive proper medical treatment he suffered a painful shoulder for the rest of his life. Despite this injury he accompanied the brigade to Johannesburg and Pretoria and fought at Diamond Hill (11–12 June 1900). The guards brigade was then redeployed southwards to oppose an attack by the Boers on Cape Colony. Since it appeared that the war was nearly over, Maude accepted an offer from the earl of Minto, the governor-general of Canada, to serve as his military secretary, and in February 1901 Maude left South Africa for England. He was appointed to the DSO and received a mention in dispatches and the campaign medal with six clasps.

Maude briefly went into hospital for treatment on his shoulder and then in May 1901 proceeded with his family to Canada. He spent the following four years serving Lord Minto at Ottawa, during which time he visited nearly all the country. He was appointed CMG (1901). Maude rejoined the 1st battalion in London in 1905, but financial pressure made him anxious to find more lucrative employment. His long absence from regimental service and his 'virtually non-military appointment' (Callwell, 85) in Canada stood in the way of his obtaining a staff appointment. Later that year he acted as private secretary to H. O. Arnold-Forster (1855–1909), secretary of state for war, but following the resignation of Balfour's government (December 1905) he became deputy assistant adjutant and quartermaster-general of coast defences at Plymouth (1906–8), beginning a long succession of staff appointments. On 26 June 1907 he was promoted lieutenant-colonel. He served on the staff of the second London territorial division (1908–9), was assistant director of the territorial forces at the War Office (1909–12), and was involved in the inauguration of the territorial force. He was promoted substantive colonel on 19 July 1911. In 1912 he served as general staff officer in the 5th division at the Curragh, and in February 1914 he joined the directorate of military training at the War Office as a GSO1.

First World War Following the outbreak of war in 1914 Maude joined the staff of 3rd corps under the command of General Sir William Pulteney, reaching France during the retreat from Mons. He took part in the battles of the Marne, Aisne, and Armentières and the ensuing fighting on the River Lys. In October 1914 he was promoted brigadier-general and placed in command of the 14th infantry brigade, part of the 5th division, engaged in the battle of La Bassée. He took part in the counter-attack at Neuve Chapelle in support of the Indian corps, and afterwards led his brigade during a period of static trench warfare at Wulverghem and then near Neuve Église, Kemmel, and St Eloi. He was wounded near St Eloi in April 1915 by a stray bullet and returned to England to recuperate. In May 1915 he received a CB and later that month rejoined his brigade in France. Six weeks later he was promoted major-general and appointed GOC 33rd division then forming in Nottinghamshire. On 15 August he was given command of the 13th division, serving at the Dardanelles, and two days later he left England.

Maude took command of the 13th division at Anzac Cove a week after receiving his new orders. It had been shattered in earlier heavy fighting for possession of the heights at Sari Bair; its total strength amounted to only that of a single brigade and it lacked artillery. Soon afterwards it was sent to Suvla Bay, and after three weeks in reserve occupied the front line trenches near Salajik. When the 10th division left for Salonika, in October, Maude assumed responsibility for the important Chocolate Hills position. When Suvla and Anzac Cove were stealthily evacuated Maude's division was sent to Helles, where it served until it was also successfully abandoned in January 1916 without arousing Turkish suspicion. Maude was twice mentioned in dispatches and made a commander of the Légion d'honneur. His division went to Egypt and then was ordered to Mesopotamia.

The war in Mesopotamia had begun in 1914 as an operation directed by the Indian government and limited to the Indian army. It led to the successful capture of Basrah, to defend crucial British oil supplies from Persia. In 1915 the campaign escalated into disaster with an understrength advance commanded by Major-General Charles Vere Ferrers Townshend up the Tigris towards Baghdad. Repulsed with heavy losses at Ctesiphon (22 November

1915), Townshend's force withdrew into Kut al Amara where he chose rather than retreating further to be besieged. In 1916 the British were desperately trying to relieve his force.

In February of that year Maude's division sailed for Basrah, and in March it trained intensively at Sheikh Saad before being sent to the front. It joined the Tigris corps, under Major-General Gorringe, with which Sir Percy Lake, the commander-in-chief, planned to relieve Townshend's force. The 13th division captured the Turkish trenches at Hannah and Felahieh on 5 April, but the 7th Indian division was repulsed at Sanna-i-yat. An attack by Maude on Sanna-i-yat three days later also failed. When the 3rd Indian division was heavily counter-attacked, after seizing the Turkish trenches at Beit Aiessa on the other side of the Tigris, Maude's troops hurriedly reinforced it, but to no avail. A final attempt to seize Sanna-i-yat was made by 7th division, supported by Maude's artillery and machine guns, but failed. After an attempt to run a steamer through to Kut also proved abortive the offensive was called off. On 29 April 1916 Kut surrendered in a disastrous and humiliating defeat.

Taves offensive Maude was appointed commander of the Tigris corps in July, despite being its most junior major-general during the three months of relative quiet following the fall of Kut. The Indian army failure in Mesopotamia, and the scandal of its mismanagement and logistic and medical breakdown, led to the War Office in July 1916 assuming control of Mesopotamian operations and the war committee on 28 July appointing Maude, selected by the chief of the imperial general staff, Sir William Robertson, to replace Lake as commander. He was made a KCB, antedated to 8 June 1916. His army was debilitated by malaria and other diseases—including scurvy among Indian and beriberi among British troops—and discouraged by defeat. He reorganized his command and improved its logistics—including port facilities at Basrah—and its medical services and welfare provision. Robertson and the War Office disliked the Mesopotamian campaign, ordered Maude to remain on the defensive, and even considered withdrawing some troops, but they adequately supplied Maude's army. It received more and better weapons, including artillery, and equipment, motor transport, armoured cars, modern aeroplanes—enabling air superiority and photo-reconnaissance—and refrigerated barges and Marmite to counter deficiency diseases. Maude was determined to resume the offensive and defeat the enemy. He persuaded Sir Charles Monro, the new commander-in-chief India, to influence the War Office to authorize an offensive. Maude's army, about 150,000 strong, outnumbered the Turks and had superiority in artillery and aircraft, and crucial intelligence from intercepted Turkish wireless messages.

Maude injected a sense of urgency into his army and improved its morale. On 13 December the 1st corps, commanded by Major-General Alexander Cobbe, bombarded Sanna-i-yat, while the 3rd corps, commanded by Major-General Sir William Marshall, that night obtained a footing on the Hai River that was quickly consolidated and expanded into a practicable bridgehead. Several days later the 1st corps also cleared the Dahra Bend of Turkish troops. On 22 February a final attack was made on Sanna-i-yat and the passage of the Tigris was forced at Shumran, and on 24 February the 1st corps occupied the whole Turkish position. Outflanked, the Turks abandoned Kut and retreated, inadequately pursued by Maude's cavalry, who entered ʿAziziyyah on 27 February, half-way between Kut and Baghdad. Following a brief pause to build up supplies, Maude advanced and captured Ctesiphon following a stiff fight at Lajj between his cavalry and the Turkish 51st division. The 1st corps crossed the Tigris and advanced on Baghdad, while the 3rd corps forced a crossing over the Diala, though again inadequate pursuit enabled the Turks to escape. On 1 March Maude was promoted lieutenant-general. On 11 March Baghdad, abandoned by the Turks, was occupied, but fighting continued elsewhere. In spite of Turkish resistance Mushaidieh was occupied three days later, Bakuba on the Dialia on 18 March, and Feluza on the Euphrates on 19 March. The British offensive continued throughout the summer to the north and east, despite the intense summer heat and continued Turkish opposition. Early in November Cobbe occupied Tikrit. While these operations progressed Maude was also occupied in consolidating and administering the conquered territory. A railway was quickly constructed between Kut and Baghdad, agriculture encouraged, and sanitation improved, especially in Baghdad, a particularly unhealthy city where cholera was endemic. Maude insisted his staff were inoculated against it but himself refused to be: 'his excuse was that a man of his age was immune' (Callwell, 310). He worked hard throughout the summer preparing for further offensive operations.

Death and assessment On 14 November Maude, showing a visiting American journalist, Mrs Egan, aspects of Baghdad, attended a theatrical entertainment, *Hamlet* in Arabic, at a Jewish school. Offered coffee, he added 'a large quantity of cold raw milk' (Barker, 431). The milk was contaminated and he contracted cholera. He died in Baghdad on 18 November 1917 of 'cardiac failure consequent on the toxaemia of a very severe cholera injection' (Callwell, 310). He was buried next day in the military cemetery beyond the north gate of Baghdad. There were bizarre rumours that he had been poisoned, but his doctor denied this and a police investigation found nothing. The army in Mesopotamia felt his loss keenly. The official historian wrote that 'his name had so come to be regarded as synonymous with success that his death was looked upon as indeed a national misfortune' (Moberly, 4.85).

Maude was a brave, chivalric, intelligent, hard-working, austere, abstemious, and tenacious soldier, staff officer, and field commander who was popular with his troops. His early career was, however, blighted by his absence from the last stages of the Second South African War and his failure to secure a command appointment. Throughout his later career Maude demonstrated repeatedly that he was a capable, hardworking, and thorough staff officer. He always tended to over-centralize, however, and to concentrate direction in his own hands. Despite this he was willing to listen to advice and generous in giving recognition to his subordinates. His successful command in Mesopotamia was the pinnacle of his career and his defeat of the Turks was a tribute to his leadership and characteristic prior preparation and planning. Although his army had advantages over the Turks and although his command was not faultless, nevertheless he crucially 'contributed to the change from failure to victory' (Moberly, 4.85).

T. R. MOREMAN

Sources C. E. Callwell, *The life of Sir Stanley Maude* (1920) · *Army List* · *DNB* · *The Eton register*, 4 (privately printed, Eton, 1907) · A. J. Barker, *The neglected war: Mesopotamia, 1914–1918* (1967) · *Despatch by Lt.-Gen. Sir Frederick Maude, commanding I. E. F. Force D on operations from end August 1916 to March 1917* (1917) · *Despatch by Lt.-Gen. Sir Frederick Maude, on the operations of the Mesopotamia expeditionary force from 1st April–30th September 1917* (1917) · F. J. Moberly, ed., *The campaign in Mesopotamia, 1914–18*, 3–4, History of the Great War (1925–7) · Kelly, *Handbk* (1917) · T. Wilson, *The myriad faces of war: Britain and the Great War, 1914–1918* (1986) · I. F. W. Beckett, *The Great War, 1914–1918* (2001) · H. Cecil and P. H. Liddle, *Facing Armageddon: the First World War experienced* (1996) · T. A. Heathcote, *The military in British India: the development of British land forces in south Asia, 1600–1947* (1995) · E. W. Shepperd, *A short history of the British army* (1950) · *CGPLA Eng. & Wales* (1918)
Archives U. Warwick Mod. RC, corresp. with W. G. Granet | SOUND IWM SA, oral history interview
Likenesses E. J. Sullivan, pen-and-ink drawing, 1917, NPG · J. S. Sargent, group portrait, oils, 1922 (*General officers of World War I, 1914–18*), NPG · photograph, repro. in Callwell, *The life of Sir Stanley Maude*
Wealth at death £1441 11s. 2d.: resworn probate, 1918, *CGPLA Eng. & Wales*

Maude, Thomas (1718–1798), poet and essayist, was born in Downing Street, London, in May 1718; he retained this family property and lived in it during visits to the capital throughout his life. A member of an established Yorkshire family, he may be the Thomas Maude, son of Edmund Maude, who was baptized at Otley, Yorkshire, on 8 May 1718. Maude entered the medical profession and in 1755 was appointed naval surgeon on board the *Barfleur*. During this time he made the acquaintance of another surgeon-writer, Edward Ives. Maude performed duties in the squadron of Admiral John Byng, executed for neglect of duty in 1757. In 1765 Maude took up the position of steward of the Yorkshire estates of Harry Powlett, sixth duke of Bolton; Maude had given evidence for the duke when, as a young naval officer in 1755, he had been court-martialled.

Maude combined his responsibilities with a career as a poet, achieving local and some metropolitan fame. His best-known poem was *Wensleydale* (1772), a celebration of the picturesqueness of that particular Yorkshire dale; by 1816 the poem had reached a fourth edition. Maude's other long poems were in a similar vein: in conscious repetition, the subject matter of *Verbeia* (1782) was Wharfedale and *Viator* (1782) offered a description of a journey from London to Scarborough by way of York. Maude's poetry enabled him to demonstrate his fondness for the Yorkshire dales and his historical and topographical knowledge, but it was conventional and unmemorable. His last collection of verse was *The Invitation* (1791), although he later published a volume of essays, *The Reaper* (1797).

An amiable man, Maude formed friendships with other

scholarly figures of the day, including the mathematician George Gargrave, and William Paley who often visited Maude at the duke's seat, Bolton Hall, in Wensley. After the death of the duke (whom inevitably Maude had eulogized in private verses), Maude moved to his own property, Burley Hall, near Otley. Maude married Cordelia Charlton at St Mary Magdalen, Old Fish Street, London, on 6 August 1746; they had a son and two daughters. He died at his home in December 1798 and was buried in Wensley churchyard in January 1799. Lines from Goldsmith's *Deserted Village* were inscribed on his tomb.

STEPHEN ROBERTS

Sources *GM*, 2nd ser., 15 (1841), 597 · *GM*, 2nd ser., 16 (1841), 35–6 · *N&Q*, 4th ser., 8 (1871), 230 · *N&Q*, 2nd ser., 8 (1859), 291 · D. C. Sutton, ed., *Location register of English literary manuscripts and letters: eighteenth and nineteenth centuries* (1995), 2.637 · *IGI* · will, PRO, PROB 11/1321, sig. 210 · *York Courant* (14 Jan 1799)
Archives BL, corresp., Add. MS 28536, fols. 21, 211
Wealth at death left land, other property, and money: will, PRO, PROB 11/1321, sig. 210

Maudeleyn, Richard (1371/2–1400), royal counsellor, was born in London, the son of John Maudeleyn, serjeant-yeoman of the king's robes, and his wife, Alice, and the brother of Agnes, wife of Robert Sewall. Between 1386 and 1391 he was a royal scholar at King's Hall, Cambridge; when granted a dispensation to be ordained a priest in 1392, he was aged twenty. He enjoyed the favour of Richard II during the later years of the reign, receiving numerous benefices, including canonries at Lincoln in 1393, at St Stephen's Chapel, Westminster, in 1396, and at York in 1397. In April 1398 he became archdeacon of Lincoln. The king demonstrated great trust in his 'Master Richard': in October 1397 he brought the duke of Gloucester's corpse from Calais to London, and in 1398 was sent to Ireland to prepare the royal chambers in Dublin Castle for the king's arrival. Maudeleyn was also made an executor of the king's will. He accompanied Richard to Ireland in 1394, and again in 1399, returning with him to Wales upon news of Henry Bolingbroke's arrival. At Conwy, where the royal party was cornered by the earl of Northumberland, Walsingham states that the king offered to abdicate on condition that his life and the lives of eight of his counsellors, including Maudeleyn, were spared; the more reliable Creton says that Maudeleyn was one of five royal counsellors whom Bolingbroke intended to try for Gloucester's death.

Together with the captive king Maudeleyn was taken to London, where in October 1399 Bolingbroke, now Henry IV, presented to the knights of parliament a 'certain scroll … containing magic arts' found in Maudeleyn's possession; summoned before convocation the next day to explain it, he confessed that it had been given to him by Richard II, but denied any knowledge of its meaning, and was released (*Johannis de Trokelowe*, 301). With Richard II imprisoned in Pontefract Castle, Maudeleyn now joined a plot to kill Henry and restore Richard to the throne. He was said to resemble the deposed king greatly, and was employed to impersonate him during the early stages of the revolt, but things went badly wrong, and Maudeleyn's

chief accomplices were killed at Cirencester or Oxford in early January 1400. Maudeleyn and William Ferriby, another royal clerk, were captured in Yorkshire—apparently they were fleeing to Scotland—and brought to London at the end of January. They were drawn, hanged, and beheaded; Maudeleyn allegedly thanked God that he died in the service of his 'sovereign lord, the noble King Richard' (Creton, 134–5). Two months later, when Richard II's corpse was brought to London for burial, Creton (who was not there, but believed that the former king was still alive) thought it must have been the body of 'Maudeleyn, his chaplain, whose face, size, height and build were so exactly similar to the king's that everyone firmly believed that it was good King Richard' (Creton, 221). Creton was almost certainly wrong. Later suggestions that Maudeleyn might have been an illegitimate child of Richard II are equally implausible, given his likely date of birth.

C. GIVEN-WILSON

Sources *Chancery records* · Emden, *Cam.* · *Johannis de Trokelowe et Henrici de Blaneforde … chronica et annales*, ed. H. T. Riley, pt 3 of *Chronica monasterii S. Albani*, Rolls Series, 28 (1866), 249–50, 301, 330 · [J. Creton], 'Translation of a French metrical history of the deposition of King Richard the Second … with a copy of the original', ed. and trans. J. Webb, *Archaeologia*, 20 (1824), 1–423, esp. 134–5, 244 · B. Williams, ed., *Chronique de la traïson et mort de Richart Deux, roy Dengleterre*, EHS, 9 (1846), 229–51 · R. R. Sharpe, ed., *Calendar of letter-books preserved in the archives of the corporation of the City of London*, [12 vols.] (1899–1912), vol. I · F. Devon, ed. and trans., *Issues of the exchequer: being payments made out of his majesty's revenue, from King Henry III to King Henry VI inclusive*, RC (1837), 266

Maudith [Mauduith], **John** (d. in or after 1343), ecclesiastic and astronomer, went to Oxford from the Worcester diocese and by 1309 had become a fellow of Merton College, where he remained until 1319. In that year he was admitted rector of Aston Cantlow, Warwickshire, and in 1320 was ordained subdeacon. He remained there until 1330, when he moved north to hold at least two livings: he was rector of Sandal Magna, Yorkshire, in 1330 and still in 1331; and rector of Hatfield, Yorkshire, 1341–3. In 1341 Maudith was granted leave of absence for a year, to take up service with John de Warenne, earl of Surrey and Sussex (d. 1347), and at about this time he became a member of the group of scholars gathered around Richard Bury, bishop of Durham (d. 1345). In 1342 he completed a theological treatise, *Tractatus de doctrina theologica*, now in Salisbury Cathedral Library. He was admitted as dean of Auckland, co. Durham, in 1343, and this is the last known record of his life.

The *Catalogus vetus* of Merton College describes Maudith as 'a good astronomer who composed astronomical tables and a physician' (Emden, *Oxf.*, 2.1243). He might have regarded astronomy as an ancillary to his medical teaching, although no medical writings by him survive. His astronomical reputation has long rested chiefly on the tables to which the Merton catalogue refers, and here there is much room for misunderstanding. That he assembled a collection of trigonometrical tables in 1310 is not in doubt, but those of sine, semidiurnal arc, tangent, solar declinations and ascensions are substantially taken from, or inspired by, the more famous collections of Toledan tables and of al-Khwarizmi (d. 846). Tables of the ascensions of signs for Oxford are an exception to his heavy borrowing.

Maudith's reputation rests not only on the tables but also on the explanatory canons to them, works by which, according to some over-enthusiastic accounts, trigonometry was introduced to Europe. If anything was responsible for this important step it was the astronomical tables from which Maudith borrowed. The two sets of canons, one lengthy, the other abbreviated, did comprise an important trigonometrical text, written perhaps not long after 1316; and yet they were almost certainly not by Maudith, but rather the work of Richard Wallingford. The writer of one of the texts indeed refers to Maudith in the third person, explaining that he composed his tables to overcome the difficulties inherent in graduating instruments such as the astrolabe and quadrant.

Richard Wallingford derived one of his own catalogues of stars from an earlier list by Maudith, dated 1316, in which a certain constant is mentioned as being 'according to Profatius in his almanac' (North, *Richard of Wallingford*, 3.157–8). The reference is to a treatise on the so-called 'new quadrant' by Jacob ibn Tibbon (Profatius; d. 1305), a Jewish astronomer of Montpellier. Why Maudith's reference is of interest is that there are independent reasons for believing that he was himself the editor of a version of the Profatius text in its Latin form, namely that surviving in Cambridge University Library, MS Gg.6.3. While it contains no significant revisions, a new star list (of eighty-six stars) with which it is associated was evidently due to Maudith, some of it on the basis of new observations by him. There is also a shorter list of eleven bright stars, which it is said 'John Maudith put on the quadrant' (North, *Richard of Wallingford*, 2.243). There is some ambiguity here as between an actual instrument and a textual recommendation, but none about Maudith's concern with problems of instrumentation, fitting perfectly with the statement by the author of the canons.

Despite Maudith's concern with astronomy during the first half of his life, during the second he appears to have written nothing whatsoever on the subject. The date of his death is unknown, but in view of his relatively high profile it was probably not long after the last known reference to him, in 1343. J. D. NORTH

Sources Emden, *Oxf.*, 2.1243–4 · *Richard of Wallingford: an edition of his writings*, ed. and trans. J. D. North, 3 vols. (1976), vol. 1, pp. 3–19, 192–7; vol. 2, pp. 155–8, 243; vol. 3, pp. 157–8 [Lat. orig., with parallel Eng. trans.] · J. D. North, 'Medieval star catalogues', *Archives Internationales d'Histoire des Sciences*, 20 (1967), 71–83 · J. D. North, *Horoscopes and history* (1986), 116, 126, 133–4
Archives CUL, MS Gg.6.3 · Salisbury Cathedral, 'Tractatus de doctrina theologica'
Wealth at death £2 bequeathed to University of Oxford: *Munimenta academica*, RS, 1, 10

Maudling, Reginald (1917–1979), politician, was born at 53 Westbury Road, North Finchley, London, on 7 March 1917, the only child of Reginald George Maudling, consulting actuary, and his wife, Elizabeth Emilie Pearson. Reggie, as he was known, enjoyed a comfortable childhood, spending his early years at Bexhill, Sussex, where

Reginald Maudling (1917–1979), by Walter Bird, 1964

his parents had moved because of the German air raids on the capital. After the family's return to London, Maudling won scholarships to Merchant Taylors' School in Hertfordshire and Merton College, Oxford. He had no interest in undergraduate politics, and team games held no appeal, but he enjoyed golf and, improbably for someone of his bulk, excelled at ice skating. He began travelling widely before university with a visit to Canada and continued during vacations with tours of the Mediterranean and Latin America.

Maudling's easy, relaxed manner disguised a quick and formidable intellect. He obtained first-class honours in Greats in 1938 and was runner-up for the John Locke scholarship in mental philosophy. Influenced by G. R. G. Mure, his tutor and a lifelong friend, he developed the pragmatic outlook that shaped his politics. Problems were better tackled by clarifying the right questions than by adopting partisan positions and winning easy cheers at party conferences. By temperament a Conservative, Maudling drew philosophical inspiration from an unlikely source: 'The Hegelian process of thesis and antithesis leading to synthesis is the essential principle of human progress. In politics it may be called the Middle Way, Butskellism or consensus. By any name it makes sense to me' (Maudling, 28).

Maudling was reading for the bar when, six days after the outbreak of war, on 9 September 1939, he married at Worthing register office Beryl, the twenty-year-old daughter of Eli Laverick, naval architect. They had a daughter and three sons. Although Beryl, who had trained as a ballet dancer and became an actress, gave up her career on marriage, Maudling's mother regarded a woman who had appeared on the stage as unsuitable for her son. In 1940 Maudling was called to the bar (Middle Temple). However, he had already volunteered for active service, and after being rejected because of poor eyesight was commissioned in RAF intelligence. He subsequently became private secretary to Sir Archibald Sinclair, secretary of state for air, and served in the air staff secretariat. This experience strengthened his interest in a political career, and he became convinced that after the war a new closer co-operation between government and industry was essential. In his first contribution to public debate, in *The Spectator* in November 1943, Maudling urged Conservatives to adopt a new, positive concept of freedom, in which the state's power would not necessarily conflict with individual freedom, but instead would underpin it (Maudling, 257–60).

Into politics After unsuccessfully contesting Heston and Isleworth for the Conservatives at the general election of 1945, Maudling joined the Conservative parliamentary secretariat (merged with the Conservative Research Department in 1948). He serviced the parliamentary party's finance committee and was economic adviser and speech-writer for Winston Churchill and Anthony Eden. Under the guidance of R. A. Butler, Maudling and his colleagues enabled the Conservatives to recapture the political middle ground by committing the party to build on, and not reverse, the post-war settlement, namely, managing the economy on Keynesian principles, guaranteeing full employment, and providing universal, state secondary education, health care, and social security. Maudling was assistant secretary to the industrial committee that produced the *Industrial Charter*, on which Conservative post-war economic policy was largely based, and as parliamentary candidate for Barnet moved the amendment at the party conference of 1947 accepting the charter as Conservative policy.

Elected to parliament in February 1950 for Barnet, a seat he represented until his death (from 1974 he sat for the Chipping Barnet division), Maudling immediately established his reputation as an economics expert in his maiden speech. Welcoming the bipartisan support for Keynesian policies, he argued that increasing savings and encouraging production offered an alternative to a budget surplus as a way of curbing inflation. 'We cannot, in this country, tax ourselves into prosperity', he declared, encapsulating his thinking throughout his career (Maudling, 51). He joined the 'one nation' group of Conservative back-benchers after the Conservatives' victory at the general election of 1951, but left in April 1952, when Churchill appointed him parliamentary secretary to the Ministry of Civil Aviation. Exceptionally, Maudling spoke on behalf of the treasury on the Finance Bill (1952), and in November, aged thirty-five, became economic secretary to the treasury.

Rising Conservative star: the treasury and supply Maudling regarded his two and a half years as economic secretary as the most exciting and satisfying period in his political career. Working closely with his mentor, Butler, he was involved in framing budget policy and in 1953 deputized for the chancellor at the World Bank and International Monetary Fund meeting. He shared the chancellor's expansionist bias, which facilitated the transition from austerity to affluence as taxes were reduced and economic controls removed. The vision that Butler held out at the Conservative Party conference in 1953 of a doubling of incomes in twenty-five years reflected Maudling's optimistic outlook. However, problems that were later to haunt Maudling were neglected in this period. Churchill's appeasement of the unions fostered pay increases that outstripped productivity improvements and pushed up costs. Much to Maudling's regret, Butler was denied the opportunity to abandon sterling's fixed exchange rate, since allowing the pound to float would have freed Britain from balance of payments crises whenever expansion was attempted.

Maudling's reputation was enhanced by his seemingly effortless command of his brief and his ability to speak simply, without notes, on complex subjects. He first captured public attention when he offered to answer any questions that viewers wished to ask on Conservative policy on a televised party political broadcast; 20,000 calls came in, jamming the switchboard. After Eden promoted him in April 1955 to become minister of supply and a privy councillor, he was tipped as a future leader. He came to agree with critics of his new ministry and recommended its abolition, as it intervened unnecessarily between customer (the armed forces) and supplier (manufacturers). His conclusion that the aircraft production industry, for which he was also responsible, could not compete with the Americans across the whole range of aircraft types provoked controversy, but Maudling had no truck with the illusion that Britain was still a first-rank world power. None the less, he supported the Suez invasion.

Sceptical of European integration; Board of Trade In January 1957, after declining to continue at supply or to become minister of health, Maudling accepted the post of paymaster-general, deputizing in the Commons for Lord Mills, the minister of fuel and power. Macmillan finally promoted him to his cabinet in September after asking him to negotiate a European free-trade area (Macmillan's so-called 'plan G') linking Britain and the six founding member states of the EEC. But the Maudling committee (he chaired the talks) was unable to dispel French suspicion that Britain was a Trojan horse for American interests, and the obduracy of General de Gaulle, the new French president, in November 1958 finally killed the project. Maudling salvaged something with the creation (November 1959) of the European Free Trade Association (EFTA) of seven non-EEC countries.

Maudling remained sceptical about European integration. Appointed president of the Board of Trade in October 1959, he warned MPs that EEC membership would conflict with British agricultural and trading interests and weaken relations with the Commonwealth. He could think of 'no more retrograde step economically or politically' than to impose EEC duties on raw-material imports from less developed countries (*Hansard 5C*, 615, 14 Dec 1959, col. 1167). When the cabinet decided in 1961 that Britain should apply for EEC membership, the advantages of belonging to a large single market persuaded Maudling to support entry. However, he never lost hope that Europe would develop as a free-trade area, and fewer than three months before his death he opposed British membership of the European monetary system (*Hansard 5C*, 959, 29 Nov 1978, cols. 493–9).

Committed to higher economic growth and decolonization By the 1960s British politicians were increasingly preoccupied by a growing sense that the economy was lagging behind others. Maudling sought to reverse Britain's declining share of world trade by launching a campaign to promote exports. He also tried to counter regional inequalities, principally by using powers in his Local Employment Act (1960) to direct car-makers to Merseyside, Scotland, and Wales. But in July 1961 a further sterling crisis prompted another 'stop' in the 'stop–go' cycle as the chancellor, Selwyn Lloyd, imposed a pay pause. Maudling began considering his prospects of returning to the treasury, but in October the continual rows between ministers over British decolonization led Macmillan to appoint Maudling as colonial secretary in place of Iain Macleod.

However, Macmillan found that 'Maudling was quite as "progressive" as Macleod. Indeed, in some respects he seemed, *"plus royaliste que le roi"*' (Macmillan, 318). Maudling chaired constitutional conferences that hastened independence for Jamaica, Northern Rhodesia (Zambia), Kenya, and Trinidad. Faced with opposition in the cabinet to his plans for Northern Rhodesia (Zambia), he threatened to resign before eventually pushing through his independence constitution. He broke the deadlock that risked disrupting Kenyan independence by tripling the land settlement scheme, giving Africans access to land, while compensating white farmers.

In the spring of 1962 Macmillan addressed the difficulties of sustaining the post-war economic objectives—steady expansion, full employment, stable prices, and a strong pound—and concluded that a voluntary incomes policy was required, together with active state intervention. Maudling was more ambitious than his relaxed appearance suggested and he seized his moment. On 20 June, the day on which Macmillan was due to present his detailed plan to cabinet, the press prominently reported Maudling's support for an incomes policy, quoting extensive extracts from a message that he was about to send his constituents. Three weeks later Macmillan sacked Lloyd and appointed the 45-year-old Maudling chancellor of the exchequer (13 July 1962).

A controversial chancellor The myth about Maudling's chancellorship is that he immediately began a frantic dash for growth and launched massive reflation. However, his initial caution irritated supporters and opponents alike, and it was not until November 1962 that he cut purchase tax and gave special help to areas of high unemployment. In January 1963 he cut the bank rate. He saw no reason why Britain should not be able to sustain the higher rate of economic growth being achieved by other countries, and favoured the 4 per cent annual growth target suggested by the recently created National Economic Development Office and endorsed in February by employers, unions, and government. His April budget was designed to meet this target and reduce unemployment, which had soared to a post-war peak of 873,000, but he believed that a voluntary incomes policy was essential for his strategy to succeed. He therefore sought union support by aiming his £270 million of tax cuts (equivalent for many workers to a wage increase of 2 per cent) at the less well-off. Overall his budget was less reflationary than many wanted at the time, but his reliefs were worth £460 million in a full financial year, and by 1964–5 the economy was recovering faster than expected.

Although Maudling's budget of 1963 was later criticized, it was a tonic for a government shell-shocked by de Gaulle's veto of Britain's EEC application (January 1963), recession, and the Profumo scandal. With Macmillan's leadership in question, most Conservative MPs preferred Maudling to Butler as they wanted someone younger, a sentiment encouraged by Maudling in a speech highlighting the Conservatives' failure among younger voters. But when Macmillan resigned through ill health in October, Maudling's hopes of becoming leader were dashed by his inability to deliver a rousing party conference speech. Whereas Macleod and Enoch Powell refused to serve the new prime minister, Sir Alec Douglas-Home, Maudling continued at the treasury. By 1964 the economic recovery was fast becoming a boom and needed restraining, but his budget increased duties by only £100 million. He pressed for an early election, but Douglas-Home's delay until October destroyed hopes of agreeing an incomes policy with the unions, while the trade deficit grew bigger than forecast. With the Conservative government's defeat at the polls he relinquished the chancellorship.

After 1964 the Labour government's repeated claim that it had inherited an '£800 million deficit' on the balance of payments tarnished Maudling's reputation. Although this figure is open to debate and Labour's mishandling of the situation made matters worse, the persistent trade deficit during the mid-1960s would have presented Maudling, had he remained chancellor, with the dilemma that Labour faced. It is impossible to say whether his expansionist bias would have led him to continue his 'growth experiment' and devalue the pound, or whether his more cautious side would have led him to abandon his strategy and deflate demand.

A shock defeat; home secretary In February 1965, when Maudling became shadow foreign secretary and deputy leader, he was succeeded as shadow chancellor by Edward Heath. When Douglas-Home resigned in July, Maudling confidently expected to win the first leadership election in the party's history, but Heath received 150 votes, Maudling 133, and Enoch Powell 15. Conservative MPs were attracted to Heath's combative style of opposition, while

Maudling's accumulation of thirteen directorships since leaving office raised doubts about his commitment. Maudling was devastated and never recovered from his defeat. He played little part in Heath's policy review, and his support for an incomes policy conflicted with party policy.

Although Maudling wanted to return to the exchequer in 1970, he accepted the Home Office. His rationality and reasonableness were ideal qualities for a humane, reforming home secretary, and enabled him to play a key role behind the scenes in the Heath administration as a masterly chairman of cabinet committees. However, his responsibilities included Northern Ireland, and he was ill suited to deal with the worsening crisis. His reputed comment to an aide after his first visit, 'What a bloody awful country' (Campbell, 425), illustrated his failure to carry forward his predecessor James Callaghan's momentum in addressing the Ulster conflict. Initially, he trusted the devolved, Unionist-dominated Stormont government and in 1971 allowed internment without trial, which proved disastrous. Following 'bloody Sunday' in Londonderry in January 1972, which resulted in the immediate deaths of thirteen people after British paratroopers fired on anti-internment demonstrators, he was physically attacked in the House of Commons by Bernadette Devlin (later McAliskey), the 24-year-old MP for Mid-Ulster. Maudling concluded that civil war in Northern Ireland could be averted only by suspending devolution and transferring responsibility to a secretary of state, and in March 1972 Whitelaw became Northern Ireland secretary.

In Britain, Maudling resisted right-wing demands to turn back the clock, but at a time of violent protest his expulsion of Rudi Dutschke, a German radical, provoked a furore. The Immigration Act (1971) further restricted entry to Britain, but Maudling skilfully removed 'repatriation' from the Conservative agenda. He introduced community service as an alternative to prison, and despite supporting capital punishment did not pursue the matter. But in July 1972 he resigned when the Metropolitan Police, for whom he was responsible, began investigating John Poulson, a former business associate who was subsequently gaoled for corruption.

Ironically, within months of Maudling's resignation Heath's government made its 'U-turn' and adopted Maudling's approach: a 'dash for growth', an incomes policy, and state intervention. Before his resignation Maudling had submitted a memorandum for cabinet discussion calling for an incomes policy. Although he withdrew it at Heath's request, it was later published. In it Maudling argued that 'the problems we are facing are not economic but political. Economic factors operate within a political framework and the old orthodoxies of economics, however coherent and self-consistent, may not apply in a changed political situation'. He went on to say that 'What determines the course of a country's society and its economy is fundamentally political power and how it is used', so 'the old traditional economics cannot begin to cope with it' (*The Times*, 12 Sept 1972). For him, this pursuit of the middle ground meant a Conservative incomes policy

and the conciliation of the trade unions, rather than tackling their power head-on.

Maudling did not return to the front bench under Heath, and it was a surprise when Margaret Thatcher appointed him shadow foreign secretary in 1975. Predictably, their personalities and politics jarred, and he was sacked in November 1976. In his last Commons speech he attacked monetarist economics and suggested that independent arbitration would make an incomes policy effective (*Hansard 5C*, 960, 13 Dec 1978, cols. 716–21).

Business dealings and reputation Maudling's final years were overshadowed by controversy over his business relationships. In 1969 he had briefly been president of the Real Estate Fund of America, a Bermuda-based investment company run by Jerome Hoffman, who was eventually imprisoned for fraud. Maudling also advised the Peachey Property Corporation, whose chairman, Sir Eric Miller, misused corporation money and in 1977 committed suicide. Although Department of Trade inspectors exonerated Maudling of any wrongdoing, he had again seemed remarkably imprudent. His association with Poulson, who recruited him in 1966, dogged him to the end. One of Poulson's companies had won a contract for a hospital on the Maltese island of Gozo that entailed a heavy loss for the taxpayer. Ten years later, in July 1977, a Commons select committee reported that Maudling should have declared his interest when arguing in the house for maintaining aid to Malta, because although Maudling received no salary, Poulson had contributed generously to a charity to which Maudling's wife was committed. However, MPs merely took note of the report and Maudling was not punished. Two remaining libel suits brought by Maudling against the media over the Poulson affair were due to come to court in 1979, but his health began to suffer during the last year of his life as he turned increasingly to alcohol. He died of cirrhosis of the liver and kidney failure at the Royal Free Hospital, Camden, London, on 14 February 1979. He was buried in St Andrew's churchyard, Little Berkhamsted, Hertfordshire, on 23 February 1979. He was survived by his wife.

The shadow cast over Maudling's career by his ill-judged business associations and his loss of political drive after losing the Conservative leadership contest in 1965 has obscured his achievement in public life. Recognition of his role in post-war politics was not helped by his self-effacing and disappointing autobiography (1978). It has been further diminished by his having left no significant archives and because, over thirty years after his death, there has been no biography. A cabinet minister at the age of forty and one of the most intellectually gifted politicians of his generation, Maudling, with better luck, might have become prime minister. The tragedy of his career is that his affability, equable nature, reasonableness, and tolerance made him an attractive personality but denied him the top prize. He was temperamentally incapable of indulging in the partisanship that rallies party conferences, or of practising the black arts that win leadership elections.

Although Maudling's role at the treasury and other economic departments has been criticized, the economy performed well by historical standards during his period in office. However, his laudable priority of raising living standards made him susceptible to 'growthmanship', which encouraged over-ambitious growth targets and led, in turn, to more state intervention. Right-wing critics later accused Maudling of having embraced the 'progressive consensus which ultimately led Conservative Governments to disaster' (*Daily Telegraph*). But his approach reflected a different analysis of inflation and the purpose of public policy. He regarded inflation as a political problem instead of a purely economic one, and believed that it was better controlled by consensus than by conflict. Whether he could have prevented the collapse of consensus had he been in office after 1972 is debatable. Opposed to the use of unemployment as a tool of economic policy and an intellectually formidable champion of Keynesian policies, he was sorely missed on the Conservative benches during the 1980s. ROBERT SHEPHERD

Sources R. Maudling, *Memoirs* (1978) · personal knowledge (2004) · *DNB* · *Financial Times* (15 Feb 1979) · *Daily Telegraph* (15 Feb 1979) · *The Times* (20 June 1962) · *The Times* (12 Sept 1972) · *Hansard 5C* (1959), 615.1075, 1093, 1162–73; (1978), 959.493–9, 540; 960.716–21 · H. Macmillan, *At the end of the day, 1961–1963* (1973) [vol. 6 of autobiography] · S. Brittan, *Steering the economy* (1971) · R. Fitzwalter and D. Taylor, *Web of corruption* (1981) · R. Shepherd, *The power brokers: the tory party and its leaders* (1991) · I. Gilmour, *Whatever happened to the tories* (1997) · J. Ramsden, *The age of Churchill and Eden, 1940–1957* (1995) · J. Ramsden, *The winds of change: Macmillan to Heath, 1957–1975* (1996) · R. Shepherd, *Iain Macleod* (1994) · R. Shepherd, *Enoch Powell* (1996) · J. Campbell, *Edward Heath* (1993) · A. Horne, *Macmillan*, 2 vols. (1988–9) · official documents, PRO · b. cert. · m. cert. · d. cert. · *CGPLA Eng. & Wales* (1979)

Archives Bodl. RH, interview on colonial problems · CAC Cam., constituency corresp. · priv. coll. | Bodl. Oxf., conservative party archive · Bodl. RH, corresp. with Sir R. R. Welensky

Likenesses W. Bird, photograph, 1964, NPG [*see illus.*] · Emwood [J. Musgrave-Wood], pen-and-ink cartoon, 1967, NPG · Cummings [M. Cummings], pen-and-ink cartoon, NPG · Papas [W. Papas], pen-and-ink cartoon, NPG · Vicky [V. Weisz], three pen-and-ink cartoons, NPG · photographs, Hult. Arch.

Wealth at death £140,690: probate, 21 May 1979, *CGPLA Eng. & Wales*

Maudslay, Alfred Percival (1850–1931), archaeologist, was born at Lower Norwood Lodge in Surrey on 18 March 1850, the eighth of nine children born to Joseph *Maudslay (1801–1861) [*see under* Maudslay, Henry] and his wife, Anna Maria, *née* Johnson (1810–1878). Joseph was the third son of the eminent engineer Henry *Maudslay, and the latter's successor as head of the family engineering firm. After Harrow School (1863–7), Maudslay went to Trinity Hall, Cambridge, and obtained a BA in natural sciences in 1872. He then enrolled in medical school, but a recurrence of bronchitis forced him to abandon medicine and leave England for a warmer climate. While investigating possible occupations in the Caribbean he was offered the position of private secretary to the governor of Trinidad. When his chief was appointed to Queensland, Maudslay went with him, but in 1875 he was assigned to the staff of Sir Arthur Gordon, the first governor of Fiji. He was to hold various posts in Fiji, Samoa, Tonga, including that of acting consul-general for the Western Pacific, all this during a turbulent period in those islands. Early in 1880, after nearly five years' service, he resigned and returned to England, evidently feeling ready to undertake ventures of his own.

In Fiji, Maudslay's private interests had turned from ornithology to the collection of ethnographic material, and eventually it was the gift of his, Sir Arthur Gordon's, and Anatole von Hügel's Fijian collections to Cambridge that led to the creation of the University Museum of Archaeology and Ethnology. But having developed a serious interest in archaeology before leaving the Pacific, Maudslay began to think of working either in Ceylon or the Maya area. He was acquainted with both areas, having visited Guatemala, immediately after graduation from Cambridge, to study tropical birds. He had been helped then with advice from a friend who knew that country well, the ornithologist Osbert Salvin. He must have seen the photographs which Salvin had taken in 1861 of the ruins of Quirigua and Copan, Honduras, for when Maudslay embarked for Guatemala in December 1880 his goal was to see those two ruined cities at first hand. Exploration of them confirmed his hopes of doing useful work in this field, and led him to visit the distant ruins of Tikal before returning home.

A revelation occurred for Maudslay at Quirigua when, on pulling moss from apparently shapeless stones, hieroglyphs and figurative designs carved in relief came to light. To record these inscriptions was clearly an urgent and important task, and one to which he, already an experienced photographer, could devote his time and money. Later he came to see that photographs alone would not yield an adequate record; plaster casts were needed. So a year later, in London, he engaged a skilled plaster-moulder for his first serious expedition, and in January 1883 embarked with him for Guatemala, with 4 tons of plaster of Paris in the ship's hold. This expedition and five others produced a comprehensive record of sculpture and inscriptions at the important ruins of Quirigua, Copan, Tikal, Yaxchilan, Palenque, and Chichen Itza, together with plans of those sites. Casts were made from the moulds and artists were engaged to draw them for publication; the casts were then displayed in the South Kensington museum. The problem of publishing these materials in appropriate format was solved when his friends Frederick Godman and Osbert Salvin offered to include them as a separate section entitled *Archaeology* (1899–1902) in the massive series they were publishing, the *Biologia Centrali-Americana*.

These five large volumes stand as a monument marking the beginning of careful research in the Maya area, and at the end of the twentieth century they still serve as an essential work of reference for epigraphers, archaeologists, and art historians. Seventy years would pass before any other systematical programme of recording Maya sculpture and inscriptions to an equivalent standard was undertaken. With due permission, Maudslay brought back superb pieces of sculpture from Copan, and these he presented, together with others from Yaxchilan, to the South Kensington museum. In 1922 they were transferred to the British Museum and exhibited on a stairway landing that was given his name—the only exhibition area in the museum ever named for a living person.

On 31 May 1892 Maudslay had married Anne (or Ann, but known as Annie) Cary Morris (1848–1926), the daughter of Gouverneur Morris (II) and his wife Patsey (or Martha) Jefferson Cary, at the American Protestant Episcopal Church in Rome. She was the granddaughter of the American statesman Gouverneur Morris. The couple began by spending a year managing a ranch in Colorado belonging to Annie's family, then Maudslay bought a small goldmine near Oaxaca, Mexico, and built a house nearby. Before settling in, however, he and Annie spent much of 1894 travelling in the highlands of Guatemala and doing another season of work at Copan. Their experiences formed the basis of a beautifully produced book written jointly by them, *A Glimpse at Guatemala* (1899). About 1905 the Maudslays settled in England, first in Montpelier Square, Knightsbridge, London, then at Morney Cross, Fownhope, Herefordshire. Here Alfred produced *The True History of the Conquest of New Spain*, a five-volume translation of the work by Bernal Diaz. Maudslay received honorary degrees from both Oxford and Cambridge, and in 1912 was elected president of the Royal Anthropological Institute. In 1926 Annie died, childless, and two years later Maudslay married his neighbour, Alice (Mrs J. M.) Purdon (*d.* 1939), the daughter of Edward Mortimer Clissold of Ravensworth, Cheltenham. For a few years before his first marriage Maudslay was involved with a woman of whom nothing is known, beyond the fact that she bore him a son. Evidently Maudslay supported them financially until his death, and beyond it—by discreetly settling on the son a considerable sum of money that bypassed his will.

Alfred Maudslay was tall, with a broad forehead and fair wavy hair parted near the middle. He was a quiet, modest man, of equable disposition, who moved at an unhurried pace; he had a notable gift for establishing trust and friendship with ordinary people, whether in Oceania or Latin America. In 1930 he published a book of reminiscences, *Life in the Pacific Fifty Years Ago*. He died at his home at Morney Cross on 22 January 1931 of heart failure, and his cremated remains were interred in the crypt of Hereford Cathedral on 27 January.   Ian Graham

Sources A. P. Maudslay, *Life in the Pacific fifty years ago* (1930) · A. C. Maudslay and A. P. Maudslay, *A glimpse at Guatemala* (1899) · priv. coll. · private information (2004) · V. Ebin and D. A. Swallow, *The proper study of mankind: great anthropological collections in Cambridge* (1984) · *The Times* (24 Jan 1931) · I. Graham, *Alfred Maudslay and the Maya: a biography* (2002)
Archives BM, department of ethnography, sculpture collections and MSS · Brooklyn Museum, New York · RGS · U. Cam., Museum of Archaeology and Anthropology, sculpture and other collections
Likenesses H. Sweet, photograph, 1889, BM · fifteen photographs (aged between eight and eighty), priv. coll.
Wealth at death £27,557 3s. 0d.: probate, 21 March 1931, *CGPLA Eng. & Wales*

Maudslay, Henry (1771–1831), mechanical engineer, was born on 22 August 1771 at Woolwich, the son of Henry Maudslay (sometimes Maudsley; *d. c.*1780) who was a native of Clapham in Yorkshire who had served in the Royal Artillery and had become a workman at the Woolwich arsenal. Maudslay's father died while he was a boy and this was probably why he himself began work in the arsenal at an early age. He demonstrated considerable skill at the forge and with machinery, and attracted the attention of the engineer and inventor Joseph Bramah (1748–1814). Bramah had already established a successful business as a manufacturer of water closets and locks, and he went on to make important innovations with hydraulic power for the operation of presses and other equipment. When Maudslay joined him in 1789 at the age of eighteen, Bramah was struggling to develop a new type of lock, and it was Maudslay who devised and constructed the machines capable of producing the precisely designed parts for this apparatus. He was probably also responsible for the self-tightening leather collar which made Bramah's hydraulic press work efficiently. In 1790 Maudslay married Sarah Tindale (1761/2–1828), who had been Bramah's housekeeper; and they had four sons and three daughters (see below).

After nine years with Bramah, Maudslay had a dispute with his employer about his wages and left to set up business on his own in 1798, acquiring premises first in Wells Road, off Oxford Street, and then in Margaret Street, Marylebone. He was brought to the attention of Marc Isambard Brunel (1769–1849), who employed him to build the series of forty-four machines which Brunel had been commissioned to construct at Portsmouth Dockyard for the production in bulk of ships' blocks, indispensable items for the rigging of sails in the naval vessels of the time. A high degree of precision was necessary in manufacture in order to ensure complete interchangeability of parts, and his outstanding success in achieving this makes it possible to represent Maudslay, together with Brunel, as a very early exponent of what was, in effect, a system of mass production.

The success of this enterprise brought Maudslay a wider reputation and brought increasing prosperity to his workshop. He took out patents (no. 2872 in 1805 and no. 3117 in 1808) for machinery to print patterns on cotton fabrics, and (no. 2948 in 1806, in conjunction with Bryan Donkin) for a differential motion for raising weights, which could be used for driving lathes. In 1807 he patented an arrangement of a steam engine, which became known as a 'table engine' (no. 3050) on account of the compact shape of the framework supporting the cylinder, and which became very popular in applications where only a small amount of power was required. With the expansion of his business, Maudslay sought larger premises and in 1810 he moved to Westminster Bridge Road, where the firm remained until the end of his life. He traded under the title of Henry Maudslay & Co. until he took into partnership Joshua Field and the firm became known as Maudslay, Field & Co. With the inclusion of Maudslay's sons it subsequently became Maudslay, Sons, and Field.

Henry Maudslay (1771–1831), by Charles Étienne Pierre Motte
(after Henri Grevedon, 1827)

The firm developed a strong interest in the expansion of steam navigation, producing a number of important improvements in the marine steam engine in the shape of the distinctive 'side-lever' engine, with the heavy overhead beam being replaced by levers alongside the engine, which lowered its centre of gravity and thus made it more suitable for ship propulsion. Maudslay also patented (no. 3538 in 1812, in conjunction with Robert Dickinson) a method of purifying sea water by blowing air through it, for use in marine engines.

Maudslay's outstanding contribution to mechanical engineering, however, derives less from the goods that he produced than from the machine tools that he devised and the workmen he trained. His machine tools—that is, the key machines such as lathes, planing machines, slotting and drilling machines, and suchlike, used for making other machines—were of superlative quality, and provided models for all subsequent mechanical engineers. He realized at the outset of his career that only the very highest standards of precision and accuracy were adequate for the mass replication of the many new machines, such as textile machines and steam engines, which were revolutionizing methods of industrial production in Britain at the turn of the eighteenth and nineteenth centuries. By insisting on the use of high quality metal for all parts of his machines, by incorporating features such as the slide-rest as a matter of routine into his workshop lathes, and by standardizing the screws and other widely used parts in his workshops, Maudslay effected a transformation in the standards of engineering workshop practice. Above all, by determining exact standards of workmanship through constant application of his micrometer, capable of measuring to within a ten thousandth of an inch (so authoritative was the regime of this instrument that it is

reputed to have been nicknamed 'the lord chancellor' in Maudslay's workshop), and by issuing his workmen with standard plane surfaces to test their own workmanship, Maudslay brought what had previously been the standards of scientific instrument makers into commonplace engineering routine.

Regarding the workmen whom he trained, Maudslay is remarkable for the number of young men who served in his workshop before going on to secure great fame and distinction as engineers in their own right. Joseph Clements, Richard Roberts, James Nasmyth, Samuel Seaward, William Muir, and Joseph Whitworth all served some years with Maudslay and absorbed his passion for accuracy and high quality. They all, moreover, were accustomed to speak of him subsequently with affection and gratitude. The testimony of Nasmyth was typical in this respect:

> The indefatigable care which he took in inculcating and diffusing among his workmen, and mechanical men generally, sound ideas of practical knowledge, and refined views of construction, has rendered, and ever will continue to render, his name identified with all that is noble in the ambition of a lover of mechanical perfection. (Buchanan, 401)

Maudslay was a large man, standing 6 feet 2 inches tall, with, in Smiles's words, a jolly and good-natured temperament. Sarah Maudslay died on 29 March 1828, aged sixty-six, and Maudslay himself died, of complications following a chill, on 15 February 1831 at Lambeth and was buried in Woolwich churchyard. His sons continued the business and two of them made their mark on its development. The eldest son, **Thomas Henry Maudslay** (1792–1864), demonstrated considerable commercial ability, which contributed to the progress of the firm both during and after his father's life. He gave evidence before a select committee of the House of Commons on steam navigation in 1831. Maudslay purchased an estate at Banstead Park, Surrey, was twice married and had at least one son. He died of heart disease at Knight's Hill, Norwood, London, on 23 April 1864 and was buried at Woolwich.

Henry Maudslay's third son, who also had gifts as an engineer, was **Joseph Maudslay** (1801–1861). Apprenticed as a shipbuilder to William Pitcher of Northfleet, he subsequently joined his father's engineering business at Lambeth and took a prominent position in it. An improved oscillating steam engine, which he patented in 1827, dispensed with a beam or slide-guides by allowing the cylinder to rock on trunnions with each stroke. He was elected a member of the Institution of Civil Engineers in 1833; and with Joshua Field he took out a patent in 1839 for a double-cylinder marine engine, which was widely adopted. He took a great interest in marine propulsion, and in 1841–2 the firm made the engine for *Rattler*, the first screw-propelled steamship built for the Admiralty, which was used for trials of various forms of screw propellers. He also invented the direct-acting annular cylinder screw engine, which formed the subject of a paper read by him to the Institution of Naval Architects in 1860. He died on

25 September 1861 at 21 Hyde Park Square, London. He was survived by his wife, Anna Maria Stamp Maudslay, and they had at least one son. R. ANGUS BUCHANAN

Sources S. Smiles, *Industrial biography: iron-workers and tool-makers*, another edn (1879), 198–235 · *James Nasmyth, engineer: an autobiography*, ed. S. Smiles, new edn (1885) · J. F. Petree, 'Henry Maudslay, pioneer of precision', *Engineering heritage: highlights from the history of mechanical engineering*, 1 (1963), 100–05 · L. T. C. Rolt, *Tools for the job: a short history of machine tools* (1965), 83–91 · *Mechanics Magazine* (26 April 1864) · *PICE*, 21 (1861–2), 560–63 [obit. of Joseph Maudslay] · R. Buchanan, *Practical essays on millwork* (1841) · *DNB* · d. cert. [Thomas Henry Maudslay] · *CGPLA Eng. & Wales* (1864) [Thomas Henry Maudslay] · [J. F. Petree], ed., *Henry Maudslay, 1771–1831, and Maudslay, Sons and Field, Ltd* (1949)
Archives Sci. Mus., letters and papers
Likenesses H. Grevedon, lithograph, 1827, NPG · C. E. P. Motte, lithograph, 1827 (after H. Grevedon, 1827), NPG [*see illus.*] · F. Chantrey, bust, Institute of Mechanical Engineers, London · J. F. Skill, J. Gilbert, W. Walker and E. Walker, group portrait, pencil and wash (*Men of science living in 1807–08*), NPG · H. Weeks, marble bust (after F. Chantrey), Institute of Mechanical Engineers, London; related plaster bust, Sci. Mus. · cast-iron tomb, St Mary's churchyard, Woolwich
Wealth at death under £200,000—Thomas Henry Maudslay: will, 1866 · under £300,000—Joseph Maudslay: will, 1861

Maudslay, Joseph (1801–1861). *See under* Maudslay, Henry (1771–1831).

Maudslay, Reginald Walter (1871–1934), motor vehicle manufacturer, was born on 1 September 1871 at 14 Oxford Square, Paddington, the son of Athol Edward Maudslay, gentleman, and his wife, Kate, daughter of Sir Thomas Lucas, founder of a large firm of building contractors. His great-grandfather was Henry *Maudslay, pioneer of marine engine building. Reginald Maudslay was educated at St David's School in Moffat, Scotland, and Marlborough College. He then secured an apprenticeship, and later an assistantship, with Sir John Wolfe Barry's London firm of civil engineers. During this period Maudslay became involved in a number of major engineering projects, from the planning and construction of Barry Dock to a survey of the West Highland Railway.

In 1902 Maudslay abandoned his civil engineering career and, with financial support from Wolfe Barry and others, moved to Coventry where he leased a small workshop for experimental purposes. In the following year he established the Standard Motor Company in larger premises in Much Park Street from where he was able to indulge his long-time passion of motor cars. Reginald's cousin, Cyril Maudslay, was at this time managing director of the nearby Maudslay Motor Company and it may have been this family link which precipitated the move from London. The title of his cousin's firm prevented Maudslay from using the family name to identify his own vehicles. The adoption of the Standard marque appears to have been influenced by the Roman standard which adorned the lounge of Maudslay's house. Standard became a public limited company in 1914, but for most of the period from its establishment to Maudslay's death in 1934 the company was under the control of its founder.

By 1913 Standard was one of Coventry's largest motor manufacturers with an output of some 750 vehicles per annum. During the First World War the company responded to government overtures by diversifying into airframes and aero-engines, producing in particular the Bristol Sopwith Pup fighter. This expansion of activities necessitated the purchase of 30 acres of land at nearby Canley in 1915, with a further 110 acres being acquired in 1918. Standard experienced a number of problems in the 1920s with some serious financial setbacks and a six-year period without dividends. The situation was reversed in the 1930s, partly as a result of the reorganization of production initiated by Maudslay's successor as managing director, John Paul Black, so that by 1939 Standard was responsible for almost 13 per cent of the total output of the 'Big Six' motor manufacturers, compared with 5.1 per cent at the start of the decade.

Maudslay married on 30 January 1908 Susan Gwendolen (*b.* 1881/2), *née* Herbert; they had two sons and a daughter. Little is known about his private life, but he acquired the reputation of a country gentleman and was fond of inspecting the shop floor wearing a deerstalker hat and matching overcoat. Maudslay's particular contribution to motor vehicle engineering and design is also little known, though he is credited with inventing the side-entry car body in place of the tonneau, as well as the all-weather body and the Starlite sliding roof. Standard's recurring financial problems suggest that Maudslay's business judgement was sometimes at fault. In 1927, for example, he allowed the company to become over-committed in the Australian market which led eventually to the firm sustaining heavy losses. However, he also had the foresight to purchase the Canley properties, begin the move into volume production and, crucially, to recognize the talent of John Black. His other important legacy to the firm was a paternalistic and welfarist style of management which included the creation of a hardship fund for Standard workers and the provision of numerous recreational facilities at the Canley works.

After a short illness, Maudslay died at Beaumont House, Beaumont Street, Marylebone, London, on 14 December 1934, survived by his wife. He was buried at Sherbourne. DAVID THOMS

Sources S. Morewood, *Pioneers and inheritors: top management in the Coventry motor industry, 1896–1972* (1990), 97–104 · J. R. Davy, *The Standard car, 1903–1963* (1967) · D. W. Thomas, 'Maudslay, Reginald Walter', *DBB* · *The Times* (19 Dec 1934) · m. cert. · d. cert.
Archives U. Warwick Mod. RC, records of the Standard Motor Company
Wealth at death £216,283 18s. 3d.: probate, 14 Feb 1935, *CGPLA Eng. & Wales*

Maudslay, Thomas Henry (1792–1864). *See under* Maudslay, Henry (1771–1831).

Maudsley, Henry (1835–1918), medical psychologist, was born on 5 February 1835 at a farmhouse called Rome, near Giggleswick, Yorkshire, the third of the four sons and fourth of seven children of Thomas Maudsley (1798–1880), yeoman farmer, and his wife, Mary Bateson (*d.* 1865), daughter of a Lancaster farmer. He was educated at Giggleswick School. At the age of fourteen he was sent as a private pupil to the Revd Alfred North, who ran a small

Henry Maudsley (1835-1918), by George Jerrard, 1881

school for dissenters in Oundle, and he spent two years pursuing classical studies there. When he was seventeen he went to study medicine for five years at University College Hospital, London, apprenticed to J. T. Clover. Awarded ten gold medals during his studentship, despite neglecting practical work, in 1856 he obtained his MB as university medical scholar, with prizes in surgery, physiology, and comparative anatomy, and MRCS, and in 1857 his LSA and MD. After working as house surgeon to Jones Quain at University College Hospital, he became assistant medical officer at Wakefield Asylum (1857–8), before a brief period at Brentwood Asylum as assistant medical officer; he was elected a member of the Association of Medical Officers of Asylums and Hospitals for the Insane (later the Medico-Psychological Association) in July 1858.

Appointed in 1859 as medical superintendent to the Manchester Royal Lunatic Asylum in Cheadle, Maudsley now committed himself to a career in 'lunacy' (that is, psychiatry), gaining his MRCP in 1861. After three successful years during which he published his first, well-received articles, in 1862, in his own words, he 'became restless and desirous of change ... and threw [himself] on London'. In private practice, and by virtue of his influential writings, Maudsley soon became the leading alienist of his generation. Joint editor of the *Journal of Mental Science* from 1863 to 1878, he was appointed physician to the West London Hospital in 1864. On 30 January 1866 he married Anne Caroline (1830–1911), the third and youngest daughter of John *Conolly, the eminent alienist, medical author, and leader of the non-restraint movement. There were no children. Maudsley was lecturer on insanity at St Mary's Hospital from 1868 to 1881, professor of medical jurisprudence at University College, London, from 1869 to 1879, and was elected FRCP in 1869. Joining B. A. Morel and W. Griesinger in 1867 in a consultation of eminent European alienists to assess the mental state of the (Habsburg) Archduchess Charlotte, empress of Mexico, he became an honorary member of the Imperial Society of Physicians of Vienna and the Medico-Psychological Society of Paris. In

1870 he was elected president of the Medico-Psychological Association and was Goulstonian lecturer to the Royal College of Physicians.

After Maudsley resigned the editorship of the *Journal of Mental Science* in 1878, he concentrated on writing (eleven books in all), medico-legal work, and a successful office practice in London. In 1884 he was made honorary LLD at Edinburgh University and an honorary member of the Medico-Legal Society of New York. In 1905 he delivered the address in medicine at the BMA annual meeting, and in 1912 became an honorary fellow of the Medico-Psychological Association (from which he had resigned for reasons unknown in 1890). In 1907 he contributed £30,000 to the establishment of a hospital for early treatment of mental illness, and for research and teaching in psychiatry, resulting in the 1914 foundation of the Maudsley Hospital, and an annual lecture in his name.

Maudsley's contemporary fame derived from an extraordinary memory, wide reading in philosophy (for example Bacon, Locke, and Comte) and literature, an extensive series of about eighty articles and pamphlets, and an admired lecturing style. Described by contemporaries as a positivist and a materialist, he was convinced of the importance of an inductive approach to science, and believed in the physical basis of mental illness; he developed the evolutionary ideas of Herbert Spencer and Charles Darwin and the neurophysiology of W. B. Carpenter and Thomas Laycock. Themes of heredity and degeneration underscored his written and clinical work, as demonstrated in *The Physiology and Pathology of Mind*, published in 1867, which was widely admired, and extensively translated, revised, and enlarged in later editions. *Body and Mind* in 1870 (his Goulstonian lectures), *Responsibility in Mental Disease* in 1874 (a much reprinted work on forensic psychiatry), *Natural Causes and Supernatural Seemings* (1886), and *Organic to Human: Psychological and Sociological* (1916), among other writings, developed these ideas, but in a style increasingly obscure and dense, and pessimistic in tone.

Maudsley's acknowledged agnosticism, his contradictory and somewhat unscientific analyses, his dismissive attitude towards women, and his convinced hereditarianism created notoriety and left him isolated. Arguments and comments at Medico-Psychological Association meetings, criticism of his editional and writing style, and the tone adopted by his contemporaries ('he was not a clubbable man') indicate considerable unpopularity among fellow alienists. A proud, often sarcastic, hypercritical man, he was of a handsome and impressive bearing, scrupulous in appearance, but he had few close friends. He had a considerable fortune, probably accrued from a private (and discreet) practice among the wealthy. Little is known of his personal life and he opposed formal biography. He enjoyed cricket, and visited Australia in 1902–3 to watch it; he was fluent in French and German, and quoted Shakespeare, Goethe, and other poets at length by heart. Maudsley died at Heathbourne House, Bushey Heath, Hertfordshire, on 23 January 1918; his body was later cremated.

T. H. TURNER

Sources *BMJ* (2 Feb 1918), 161–2 · *The Lancet* (2 Feb 1918) · T. H. Turner, 'Henry Maudsley: psychiatrist, philosopher and entrepreneur', *Psychological Medicine*, 18 (1988), 551–74 · H. Maudsley, 'Autobiography', *British Journal of Psychiatry*, 153 (1988), 736–40 · G. H. Savage, 'Henry Maudsley', *Journal of Mental Science*, 64 (1918), 117–23 · M. Collie, *Henry Maudsley, Victorian psychiatrist: a bibliographical study* (1988) · m. cert. · will, proved, London, 5 April 1918 · *CGPLA Eng. & Wales* (1918) · d. cert.
Archives Bethlem Royal Hospital, Beckenham, Kent, Archives and Museum · National Library of Medicine, Bethesda, Maryland · priv. coll. | CUL, Hunter–MacAlpine collection · Wellcome L., autograph letter series
Likenesses photograph, *c.*1860, National Library of Medicine, Bethesda, Maryland · G. Jerrard, photograph, 1881, Wellcome L. [*see illus.*] · photograph, *c.*1917, National Library of Medicine, Bethesda, Maryland
Wealth at death £65,676 18*s.* 7*d.*: probate, 5 April 1918, *CGPLA Eng. & Wales*

Mauduit, Israel (1708–1787), colonial official and political writer, was probably born at Bermondsey, London. He was descended from a French protestant family who settled at Exeter early in the seventeenth century. His father, Isaac Mauduit (1662/3–1718), the first dissenting minister at the chapel of St John's or King John's Court, Bermondsey, died on 8 April 1718, aged fifty-five; his mother, Elizabeth (1671/2–1713), died on 10 March 1713, aged forty-one. Mauduit was educated for the dissenting ministry at the Taunton Academy and he afterwards travelled abroad with several other young men of the same opinions. He preached for a time both at The Hague and in England. His career as a minister was brief, however, for soon he became a partner in a woollen draper's business in Lime Street, London, with his brother Jaspar, and with James Wright, Jaspar's son-in-law. They did an active business in Virginia, North America, and enjoyed substantial commercial success. On 13 June 1751 Mauduit was elected a fellow of the Royal Society.

In 1763, with the influence of Lord Bute, Mauduit was appointed customer of Southampton. In this period he was also helping his brother, who had been appointed agent for Massachusetts Bay in the previous year but who now suffered from ill health. In this latter capacity Israel acted mainly as a contact man and lobbyist: he obtained for the province partial compensation for military expenditures during the Seven Year's War; he organized resistance to George Grenville's Sugar and Stamp Acts; and he oversaw a bill through parliament for the promotion of whale fishing in Massachusetts. This bill reduced the duty on whale fins to a nominal figure, thereby putting colonial fishermen on a more equal footing with their British rivals. Once the Stamp Act riots erupted in America, Mauduit gradually became an outspoken critic of colonial actions and a firm supporter of George III and the North ministry. In 1765 he was chosen to succeed his brother by Governor Thomas Hutchinson, with whom Mauduit developed a friendship. Mauduit successfully pleaded Hutchinson's case for a fixed salary out of customs revenues, and in 1774, together with the British solicitor-general, Alexander Wedderburn, he defended Hutchinson against Benjamin Franklin's ill-judged attempt to remove him as governor.

Israel Mauduit (1708–1787), attrib. Mason Chamberlin, in or before 1751

Mauduit first rose to literary prominence as the author of a pamphlet entitled *Considerations on the Present German War* (1760), a work that at once established his reputation as a leading polemicist. Selling over 5000 copies in five editions within a few months, *Considerations* was a compelling attack on the policy of continental intervention promoted by William Pitt, and on the large army and expenditures that this required. The pamphlet stimulated and shaped a fervent press debate on British strategy that continued throughout the remainder of the war and turned many former supporters against the European conflict. Other pamphlets published by Mauduit included *A letter to the Right Hon. Lord B—y, being an enquiry into the merits of his defence of Minorca* (1757); *Occasional Thoughts on the Present German War* (1761); and *Some thoughts on the method of improving the advantage accruing to Great Britain from the northern colonies* (1765). He also published two histories, one of the New England colonies and one of Massachusetts Bay (both 1769), and he proposed *The Case of the Dissenting Ministers* with a bill for their relief in 1772 . During the American War of Independence he offered *Remarks upon General Howe's account of his proceedings on Long Island in the 'Extraordinary Gazette' of Oct 10, 1776* (1776) and *Observations upon the conduct of S—r W—m H—e at the White Plains, as related in the 'Gazette' of December 30, 1776* (1779). By this date Mauduit had provided Governor Hutchinson with a statement supporting American independence. On 6 May 1787 he was chosen to succeed Richard Jackson as governor of the Society for the Propagation of the Gospel in Foreign Parts. Mauduit died, unmarried, at Clement's Lane, Lombard Street, London, on 14 June 1787.

KARL WOLFGANG SCHWEIZER

Sources R. J. Taylor, 'Israel Mauduit', *New England Quarterly*, 24 (1951), 208–30 · K. W. Schweizer, 'Foreign policy and the eighteenth-century English press: the case of Israel Mauduit's *Considerations on the present German war*', *Publishing History*, 39 (1996), 45–53 · K. W. Schweizer, 'A note on Israel Mauduit's *Considerations on the present German war*', *N&Q*, 225 (1980), 45–6 · M. Peters, *Pitt and popularity: the patriot minister and London opinion during the Seven Years' War* (1980) · *GM*, 1st ser., 57 (1787), 549 · *European Magazine and London Review*, 11 (1787), 383–4 · *Acts and laws of his majesty's province of the Massachusetts Bay in New England* (1759–68)
Archives BL, Hardwicke MSS, Add. MS 35910 · BL, letters to earl of Liverpool, Add. MSS 38204–38221, 38470 · Mass. Hist. Soc., Hutchinson / Oliver family MSS · Mass. Hist. Soc., James Otis MSS · Mount Stuart, Island of Bute, Bute MSS
Likenesses attrib. M. Chamberlin, portrait, in or before 1751, priv. coll. [*see illus.*] · T. Holloway, line engraving (after M. Chamberlin), BM, NPG; repro. in *European Magazine and London Review*

Mauduit, William (*c*.1090–*c*.1158), baron, was the son of William Mauduit, royal chamberlain and a Hampshire tenant-in-chief in 1086, and his wife, Hawise, probably daughter of Benedict, a tenant of Abingdon Abbey at Weston, Berkshire. Born about 1090, Mauduit had a brother, Robert, and two sisters. On his father's death, *c*.1100, Robert Mauduit, who seems to have been the elder son, succeeded to the family chamberlainship. He was drowned in the wreck of the *White Ship* in November 1120, and his chamberlainship and his daughter Constance were purchased by William de Pont de l'Arche, a senior financial officer. However William Mauduit acquired his father's Norman estates and some of his English lands; this inheritance included the reversion of Hawise's dower. A new chamberlainship was created for him, *c*.1131, and he was among the officials listed in the *Constitutio domus regis*, composed *c*.1136.

In the early 1130s Matilda, the daughter of a former royal official, Michael of Hanslope, was granted to William Mauduit in marriage, together with her father's barony of Hanslope (Buckinghamshire). Mauduit supported the Angevin cause in 1141 and 1153, which resulted in his acquiring Michael's soke of Barrowden (Rutland), and other lands. He also followed Michael in obtaining freedom from tolls on his goods in transit, in winning pasturage rights in the royal forests, and in becoming castellan of Rockingham Castle, from which he harried the lands of Peterborough Abbey during the Angevin campaign of 1153. From Henry II he obtained some legal privileges and a confirmation of his father's chamberlainship, cutting out Robert de Pont de l'Arche, the son of Constance Mauduit and her husband. He also obtained a confirmation of his own, newer, chamberlainship. The Mauduit family's hereditary tenure of the chamberlainship perhaps inspired the appearance of the character Malduit the Chamberlain in *The Song of Roland*, and Malduit the Wise in *Erec et Enide*. William Mauduit had six children: William, who succeeded to his lands and principal chamberlainship; John, a minor royal official; Robert, who acquired the lesser chamberlainship and, by royal grant, Warminster; and three daughters: Matilda, Sibil, and Alice, who all married members of the local gentry. He died *c*.1158.

EMMA MASON

Sources E. Mason, ed., *The Beauchamp cartulary: charters, 1100–1268*, PRSoc., new ser., 43 (1980) · *Pipe rolls*, 31 Henry I · 'Constitutio domus regis' / The establishment of the royal household', R. Fitz Nigel [R. Fitzneale], *Dialogus de scaccario / The course of the exchequer*, ed. and trans. C. Johnson, rev. edn, rev. F. E. L. Carter and D. E. Greenaway, OMT (1983) · *Reg. RAN*, vols. 2–3 · *ASC*, s.a. 1137 [text E] · E. Mason, 'The Mauduits and their chamberlainship of the exchequer', *BIHR*, 49 (1976), 1–23

Mauduit, William, eighth earl of Warwick (1221x3–1268), magnate, was the son and heir of William Mauduit (*c*.1195–1257), lord of Hanslope, Buckinghamshire, and hereditary chamberlain of the exchequer, and his wife, Alice de Newburgh, the daughter of Waleran, earl of Warwick. Between August 1233 and July 1234, William was held as a royal hostage, in the custody of Herbert fitz Matthew, to ensure the loyalty of his father. In 1242 he was ordered to deputize for his father if necessary and accompany a treasure ship on its way to the royal army campaigning in Gascony, and in 1243 Henry III met the expenses he incurred in crossing to Gascony. In July 1253 William, together with John de Plessis, earl of Warwick, and the royal administrator Gilbert of Segrave, was seized by a mob at Pons, in Poitou, and imprisoned; Segrave, whose daughter Alice was William's wife, died during their captivity.

The heirs to the earldom of Warwick, William's parents, Alice de Newburgh and William Mauduit, were constrained to acquiesce in the life tenure of the earldom and its lands by John de Plessis, who held it by royal grant for life only, since Margery de Newburgh, the widowed granddaughter of Earl Waleran and the countess of Warwick in her own right, claimed that she had already remarried before Henry III designated John as her husband. In 1257 William succeeded to his father's claims and his barony of Hanslope, to the estate of Barrowden in Rutland, Hartley Mauditt, Hampshire (held by sergeanty of his chamberlainship) and to estates in Warwickshire which had formed the marriage portion of Alice de Newburgh. He also inherited the chamberlainship of the exchequer; the routine work was performed by official deputies, but the chamberlain received robes which were perquisites of office and enjoyed legal privileges.

William's political activities contrasted with those of his father, who sided with the baronial opposition in 1215–17, as well as in 1233. He was perhaps influenced by John de Plessis, a staunch supporter of the king; certainly Henry III believed him to be a potential supporter when, in February 1261, he summoned a group of the lesser barons, in an effort to shake off the restraints imposed upon him by Simon de Montfort and his supporters. William, like others who supported the king militarily, was granted an annual fee, in his case of 40 marks, payable in half-yearly instalments, which he received until May 1263. Between March 1258 and March 1264 he received regular royal summonses to render military service—a campaign against Llywelyn, the Welsh prince, was the usual reason given, but these levies helped to strengthen the king's hand against the baronial opposition.

John de Plessis eventually died in February 1263. Alice de Newburgh predeceased him, and William Mauduit, as her son, succeeded to the earldom of Warwick. In April 1263 he rendered to Henry III his homage as earl, but the comital inheritance had been mismanaged by twelfth-century earls, while the dower entitlement of the long-lived thirteenth-century countesses had further depleted its resources. William probably controlled little more than a third of the total resources of the earldom, and during the unrest in 1264 his activities were largely confined to within a 10 mile radius of Warwick Castle. A Montfortian commander, John Giffard, captured the castle, together with William and Alice. Its fortifications were destroyed, and the earl and countess were imprisoned in Kenilworth, pending payment of his ransom of 1900 marks. On 22 November 1265 William was granted forfeited estates to the value of £100, but at his death on 8 January 1268 he was in debt to the crown. He left no direct heir, and was succeeded by William (IV) de Beauchamp, the son of his deceased sister, Isabel Mauduit. William Mauduit was buried in Westminster Abbey, but his heart was interred at the Cistercian nunnery at Catesby, Northamptonshire, perhaps reflecting a devotion to the cult of Edmund Rich, some of whose relics were there.

EMMA MASON

Sources E. Mason, ed., *The Beauchamp cartulary: charters, 1100–1268,* PRSoc., new ser., 43 (1980) • *CIPM,* 1, no. 679 • E. Mason, 'The Mauduits and their chamberlainship of the exchequer', *BIHR,* 49 (1976), 1–23 • E. Mason, 'The resources of the earldom of Warwick in the thirteenth century', *Midland History,* 3 (1975–6), 67–75 • *Thys rol was laburd and finished by Master John Rows of Warrewyk,* ed. W. Courthope (1859); repr. as *The Rous roll* (1980) • W. Dugdale, *The baronage of England,* 2 vols. (1675–6)

Mauduith, John. *See* Maudith, John (*d.* in or after 1343).

Maufe [*formerly* Muff], **Sir Edward Brantwood** (1882–1974), architect, was born at Sunny Bank, Ilkley, Yorkshire, on 12 December 1882, the second of three children and younger son of Henry Muff, linen draper, a member of Lloyds and of the firm Brown, Muff & Co. Ltd, and his wife, Maude Alice Smithies, who was the niece of Sir Titus Salt, the founder of Saltaire. Muff was educated at Wharfedale School, Ilkley, but was sent in 1899 to serve a five-year pupillage with the London architect William A. Pite. His family had moved south to live in the former home of William Morris, Red House, Bexleyheath, designed by Philip Webb, which Muff acknowledged as an early architectural influence. In 1904 Muff took an unusual step, for a student in the middle of his training, and went up to St John's College, Oxford, where he obtained a BA (pass degree) in 1908. In August 1909 he changed his surname by deed poll from Muff to Maufe. When he went down, Maufe worked hard for his final examination, and attended the design class at the Architectural Association school. He became an associate member of the Royal Institute of British Architects (RIBA) in 1910. That same year on 1 October he married Gladys Evelyn Prudence (1882/3–1976), daughter of Edward Stutchbury of the geological survey of India. She was a designer and interior decorator, and later a director of Heal's. They had one son, who died in 1968. Maufe was tall and handsome while his wife was

beautiful and always romantically dressed; together they were much admired.

Maufe immediately set up in practice on his own and in 1912 received his first large commission—Kelling Hall in Norfolk for Henri Deterding. This building shows Maufe's early links with the arts and crafts movement; it has a butterfly plan, knapped flint walls, and a grey tiled and gabled roof. His other chief pre-war work was the decoration of St Martin-in-the-Fields and chapels and alterations at All Saints, Southampton, and St John, Hackney, which first brought him into notice in church circles.

During the First World War, Maufe served as staff lieutenant in the Royal Artillery in Salonika. He became a fellow of the RIBA in 1920, and first became prominent in 1924 with his design for the palace of industry at the Wembley Exhibition. He was a silver medallist at the Paris Exhibition of 1925 and began to secure a wide variety of commissions. Two buildings, particularly, made his name among architects: the church of St Bede at Clapham (1922–3) and St Saviour's, Acton (1924–6), both for the Royal Association in Aid of the Deaf and Dumb. The latter church was particularly admired for its simplification of form and for its affinities with contemporary Swedish architecture—for example, Ivar Tengbom's Hogalids church in Stockholm, which for Maufe was 'the most completely satisfying modern Swedish building' he had seen. At this period Maufe was a constant champion of modern Swedish architecture, and often wrote on this theme in the architectural press; his own buildings, with their reticent and simplified elevations, painted ceilings, and applied sculpture, show this influence. Maufe felt that Swedish architecture 'combined freshness *without* obviously breaking with tradition'.

Maufe's domestic work had a stylish modernity, in direct contrast with the new functionalism. In the architectural language of the time it was called 'modernity with manners' and very much reflected the established taste of the inter-war period. Maufe wrote and lectured a good deal: on 'furnishing and decorating the home', on furniture, and on present-day architecture. His interiors were very stylish, with built-in fitments and pastel colour-schemes, particularly pink, mauve, and cream, contrasted with silver-lacquered furniture and mirrors. One of his best houses was Yaffle Hill, Broadstone, Dorset, built in 1929 for Cyril Carter of Poole Potteries; other schemes included an extension to Baylins, Beaconsfield (1927), for Ambrose Heal, Hanah Gluck's studio in Bolton Hill, Hampstead (1932), and the studio for religious services at Broadcasting House (1931). He also designed several branch banks for Lloyds, one of the best being 50 Notting Hill Gate (1930). His own residence was a farmhouse he restored in the late 1920s at Shepherd's Hill, Buxted, Sussex.

In 1932 Maufe won the competition for the new Guildford Cathedral. When the building was dedicated in 1961, taste had moved away from its neo-Gothic exterior but the splendid proportions of the nave and aisles and, in particular, Maufe's masterly use of space won general admiration. His design carried the simplification of Gothic still further than the Liverpool Cathedral of Sir Giles Gilbert Scott and his own earlier work. Maufe has been called 'a designer of churches by conviction': he attempted to produce buildings of austere simplicity aiming directly at the creation of a religious atmosphere. At Guildford he also wanted 'to produce a design definitely of our time, yet in the line of the great English cathedrals, to build anew on tradition'.

Later works by Maufe include buildings for Trinity and St John's colleges, Cambridge, and Balliol and St John's colleges, Oxford (of which he was made an honorary fellow in 1943), the Festival Theatre at Cambridge, the Playhouse at Oxford, and the rebuilding, in the late 1940s and 1950s, in a scholarly neo-Georgian style, of the war-damaged Middle Temple and of Gray's Inn, which made him an honorary master of the bench in 1951.

From 1943 until 1969 Maufe was first principal architect UK and then chief architect and artistic adviser to the Imperial (later Commonwealth) War Graves Commission. Among his many designs for memorials are those at Tower Hill (an extension to the mercantile marine memorial by Sir Edwin Lutyens), the RAF record cloister and Canadian record building, and the RAF memorial at Cooper's Hill at Runnymede (1950–53). He was much honoured. He was elected ARA in 1938, RA in 1947, and served as treasurer from 1954 to 1959. From 1946 to 1953 he was a member of the Royal Fine Arts Commission. In 1944 he received the royal gold medal for architecture and he was knighted in 1954 for his services to the War Graves Commission.

Although Maufe was a traditionalist and admired Lutyens above all his contemporaries, he was always open-minded. His own work, particularly before the Second World War, took a middle course of well-mannered modernity without the grammar of classicism.

Maufe died on 12 December 1974, his ninety-second birthday, in Uckfield Hospital. His architectural drawings and correspondence were deposited at the RIBA.

MARGARET RICHARDSON, rev.

Sources The Times (14 Dec 1974) · The Times (28 Dec 1974) · Building, 227 (1974) · Architect's Journal (8 Jan 1975) · J. Cornforth, 'Shepherd's Hill', Country Life, 158 (1975), 906–9 · Maufe, correspondence, writings, and press cuttings, RIBA BAL · private information (1986) · b. cert. · m. cert. · d. cert.

Archives RIBA, corresp., writings, and press cuttings · University of Pennsylvania, Philadelphia, Van Pett Library, corresp. and papers | Commonwealth War Graves Commission, Maidenhead, papers relating to work for Imperial War Graves Commission

Likenesses W. Stoneman, photograph, 1950, NPG · J. L. Wheatley, oils, c.1956, NPG · H. Coster, photograph, NPG · photographs, RIBA

Wealth at death £91,585: probate, 10 June 1975, CGPLA Eng. & Wales

Mauger (d. 1212), bishop of Worcester, was of illegitimate birth, the son of a knight and a free woman, both unmarried. The date of his birth is unknown. From 1190 he was in royal service, witnessing charters of Richard I, at first as archdeacon of Évreux, and then, from June 1195, as treasurer of Normandy. He always appears as 'Master Mauger', indicating higher education, perhaps at Paris. He was the king's doctor, and Roger of Hoveden says that Richard gave him the bishopric of Worcester. His election may have taken place after Richard's death (on 6 April 1199); it was certainly before 8 August 1199. On Mauger's admission of illegitimacy, the election was referred to the pope, and he himself went to Rome. Pope Innocent III quashed the election, but allowed the electors to postulate Mauger, and consecrated him on 4 June 1200. Cardinals who had known him in the schools testified to his learning, reputation, and virtuous life; the Worcester chronicler asserts that the pope was influenced by his distinguished appearance. Mauger was enthroned at Worcester on 12 November. Thereafter he devoted himself to ecclesiastical business, and is seldom recorded at court. His predecessor had been interested in the sanctity of Bishop Wulfstan of Worcester; Mauger took the matter up, collected evidence, and travelled to Rome for the purpose, 'not considering his age' (Darlington, 184). Wulfstan's canonization was announced on 21 April 1203. A second purpose of this, or yet another, visit to Rome, was to prosecute a claim to jurisdiction over Evesham Abbey. Mauger did not attend the later stages of the case. The pope gave sentence for Evesham on Christmas eve 1205, largely on the basis of forged papal documents. Mauger's chief opponent, Thomas of Marlborough, subsequently abbot of Evesham, writing his story later, recognized that the bishop was a 'just and Godfearing man' and 'a son of truth' (Macray, 109, 119).

Mauger's last years were dominated by the dispute between King John and the pope over the election of an archbishop of Canterbury. After lengthy negotiations, Innocent consecrated Cardinal Stephen Langton on 17 June 1207. On 27 August he ordered the bishops of London, Ely, and Worcester to try to persuade the king to accept Langton, and if he refused, to declare an interdict throughout England. The bishops met the king several times in October, but without success. Mauger had already suffered temporary confiscation of property, probably for refusing to support opposition to Langton. Negotiations continued until 12 March 1208. The three bishops then ordered the interdict to take effect on 24 March. Their property was confiscated, and they were soon forced to take refuge abroad, 'enduring harsh exile' (Ann. mon., 4.396). The bishops returned briefly in August for more discussions, but without result. Early in 1209, they received new papal orders: if the king did not submit, they were to announce his excommunication. The threat led to more negotiations. The bishops came to Dover in August, met royal envoys, and drafted peace terms. But problems remained, and the terms were never ratified. The bishops, who evidently feared for their own safety, returned to France, where the king's excommunication was published in November, at Arras. Matters had reached a deadlock. In the spring of 1211, the pope sent new envoys to England.

It was perhaps at about that time that Mauger retired to the abbey of Pontigny, where he died, in the Cistercian habit, on 1 July 1212. He may earlier have stayed at the Parisian abbey of St Victor, where he, Eustace, bishop of

Ely (*d.* 1215), and other English clergy were commemorated. During his exile Mauger was sometimes in touch with his diocese, and was able to appoint his nephew to the archdeaconry of Worcester. The writings of Gerald of Wales preserve the only example of a personal letter from Mauger, written in connection with Gerald's attempt to raise the bishopric of St David's to an archbishopric.

M. G. CHENEY

Sources C. R. Cheney, *Pope Innocent III and England* (1976) · *The letters of Pope Innocent III (1198–1216) concerning England and Wales*, ed. C. R. Cheney and M. G. Cheney (1967) · *Chronica magistri Rogeri de Hovedene*, ed. W. Stubbs, 4 vols., Rolls Series, 51 (1868–71) · *Ann. mon.* · *The Vita Wulfstani of William of Malmesbury*, ed. R. R. Darlington, CS, 3rd ser., 40 (1928) · W. D. Macray, ed., *Chronicon abbatiae de Evesham, ad annum 1418*, Rolls Series, 29 (1863) · *Gir. Camb. opera*, vols. 1–4 · *The historical works of Gervase of Canterbury*, ed. W. Stubbs, 2: *The minor works comprising the Gesta regum with its continuation, the Actus pontificum and the Mappa mundi*, Rolls Series, 73 (1880), 54–115 · *Rogeri de Wendover liber qui dicitur flores historiarum*, ed. H. G. Hewlett, 3 vols., Rolls Series, [84] (1886–9) · J. C. Dickinson, 'English regular canons and the continent in the twelfth century', *TRHS*, 5th ser., 1 (1951), 71–89, esp. 88 · L. Landon, *The itinerary of King Richard I*, PRSoc., new ser., 13 (1935) · M. G. Cheney, ed., *Worcester, 1066–1212*, English Episcopal Acta [forthcoming] · C. R. Cheney, *From Becket to Langton: English church government, 1170–1213* (1956)

Maugham, Frederic Herbert, first Viscount Maugham (1866–1958), lord chancellor, was born on 20 October 1866 in Paris, the second of the four sons of Robert Ormond Maugham (1823–1884) and his wife, Edith Mary (1840–1882), elder daughter of Major Charles Snell, of the Indian army. The novelist (William) Somerset *Maugham was his youngest brother. His grandfather Robert *Maugham (1788–1862), a solicitor, was one of the founders of the Law Society in 1825 and for thirty-five years its secretary. His father, also a solicitor, had a large practice in Paris and was legal adviser to the British embassy.

Upbringing and education The family lived in the fashionable rue d'Antin, where Mrs Maugham was something of a society hostess. Among Frederic's first memories was one of temporary flight to England in 1870 during the Franco-Prussian war. After the family's return to Paris in the following year, he was educated mainly by English governesses and a tutor, but also briefly at a *lycée*, where he learned to speak fluent French. Indeed, when sent to England in 1877 with his elder brother Charles and younger brother Harry to attend boarding-school at the recently founded Dover College, he spoke English for a time 'with a slight French accent', and all his life had to make a conscious effort before pronouncing a word such as 'liqueur' (F. Maugham, 15). At school he was a good all-rounder, head prefect, and prize-winner, combining proficiency in mathematics with a love of football, cricket, and swimming.

In 1882 Maugham's mother died, and two years later his father also died—having, it emerged, lived far beyond his means and leaving only an exiguous capital sum that yielded each son barely £150 a year. Only by winning a school-leaving scholarship and an entrance scholarship in mathematics at Trinity Hall, totalling a further yearly £130, could Frederic afford to go up to Cambridge in 1885. These reduced circumstances came as a great shock to

Frederic Herbert Maugham, first Viscount Maugham (1866–1958), by Sir Gerald Kelly, 1938

him after the affluent family lifestyle in which he had grown up in Paris. For this impecunious and somewhat shy and solitary youth, Cambridge was a happy and companionable home, where his devotion to rugby and rowing made him popular. He won several cups at Henley and rowed on the winning side in the Oxford and Cambridge boat races of 1888 and 1889. He was also active in the Cambridge Union, becoming president in 1888. In the mathematical tripos of 1888 he was a senior optime. He would have done better, he believed, but for his sporting predilections, which later included fencing, shooting, and golf. He retained throughout his life a slim, upright, athletic figure.

Practice at the bar and promotion to the bench Even before leaving school, Maugham had determined on a career at the bar, and on 17 November 1890 he was called to the bar of Lincoln's Inn. He eventually entered the chambers of Charles Macnaghten, but for several years his progress as a barrister was painfully slow. On 17 December 1896 he married Helen Mary Romer (1868×72?–1950), only daughter of Sir Robert (later Lord Justice) *Romer and sister of his oldest Cambridge friend and fellow lawyer, Mark (later Lord) Romer. With a wife and soon a young family to support and few briefs coming in, Maugham's anxiety was constant and almost overwhelming. His wife's cheerful and 'rumbustious' character (R. Maugham, *All the Maughams*, 170) offset but sometimes also grated on the increasing sombreness and reserve with which he masked his yearning for success and recognition. 'The waiting for work is a terrible drawback to a young barrister', he wrote fifty years later, 'and tends to sour his whole existence. I shall never forget those unhappy days' (F. Maugham, 59).

After 1900 Maugham began to attract an increasing clientele, and by 1911 he was earning between £4000 and £5000 a year, 'a very good income for a junior at the Chancery Bar' (F. Maugham, 60). In 1913 he took silk, which was granted by Lord Chancellor Haldane, and found that he 'thoroughly enjoyed being in charge of a case, with a duty to examine and cross-examine witnesses myself and to address the judge in my own way' (ibid., 67). He appeared in some of the weightiest Chancery litigation of the time, notably the complex proceedings arising between 1909 and 1916 from the winding up of the Law Guarantee Trust and Accident Society, the dispute between the Duff Development Company and the government of Kelantan in Malaya from 1921 to 1925, and the lengthy negotiations leading to Lord Astor's purchase of *The Times* in 1922, involving, unusually, the redrawing by agreement of Lord Northcliffe's faulty will in order to carry out his intentions. 'As an advocate', wrote Lord Chancellor Simonds, 'he was forceful and lucid, courteous, and scrupulously fair, and his wide knowledge of the law and careful study of the facts of the particular case made him as formidable an opponent as any member of the bar' (*DNB*).

Maugham had accumulated one of the largest practices of his day when, on 17 April 1928, on the promotion of Mr Justice Russell to the Court of Appeal, Lord Chancellor Hailsham appointed him, at sixty-one, a puisne judge in the Chancery Division of the High Court; he was knighted on 8 May. Maugham accepted only after long hesitation—his concerns included an 80 per cent drop in income; but he proved 'the strongest judge in the Chancery courts', and 'contributed a large number of decisions of first-rate importance' (*The Times*), mostly unreserved but seldom successfully appealed. A vacancy arising on the resignation of Lord Justice P. Ogden Lawrence, the prime minister, Ramsay MacDonald, promoted Maugham to the Court of Appeal on 10 January 1934, and he was sworn of the privy council. Eighteen months later, in October 1935, on the death of Lord Tomlin, he was appointed a lord of appeal in ordinary, with a life peerage as Baron Maugham.

Lord chancellor On 9 March 1938, Lord Hailsham being in failing health, Maugham was invited by the prime minister, Neville Chamberlain, to succeed Hailsham on the woolsack. The appointment caused considerable surprise. Maugham had no political experience (Bonar Law had invited him to become solicitor-general in 1922, but Maugham had been unable to find a parliamentary seat). He had never even met Chamberlain before his appointment. Outside the law he was unknown to the public. Nor in terms of seniority was he foremost among the law lords, though at seventy-one he was the oldest member of the cabinet. Warned by Chamberlain that in the then volatile state of politics his appointment might be short-lived, he won the prime minister's agreement to his resuming his former office in that event, if there were a vacancy.

Maugham took up his parliamentary duties with energy and resolution, steering the Coal Bill through its second reading despite much opposition. Also in 1938 he secured the passing of the Inheritance (Family Provision) Act, the Limitation Act, and the Evidence Act, which abolished the prohibition on hearsay evidence in civil proceedings. Hitherto the unsworn evidence of an absentee, for example an expert witness overseas, was inadmissible in court: he or she must be present in person to testify on oath and be cross-examined. This had led, as Maugham pointed out, to much injustice. The act was thus a most important piece of reforming legislation for which he fairly claimed the credit, both as its instigator—he had himself urged the measure as a judge since 1931—and in drafting and introducing the bill in the upper house shortly before becoming lord chancellor. His appointments to the bench were uniformly good. He drew up sensible contingency plans, unnecessary as it turned out, for the removal of the law courts from London in the event of war.

On 4 September 1939, the day after war was declared, Chamberlain replaced Maugham as lord chancellor with Sir Thomas Inskip (Lord Caldecote). Maugham was created a viscount, and was almost immediately reappointed a lord of appeal in ordinary in succession to Lord Macmillan. He finally resigned from office in July 1941, but was occasionally called on subsequently to assist in appeals to the House of Lords.

Maugham relished judicial office and earned a high reputation for fairness, patience, and acuity—'an ideal judge', wrote Lord Simonds (*DNB*). His rulings reveal 'a mind of formidable analytical power' allied to 'a crisp and lucid style' (Heuston, 550). He sliced confidently through thickets of obscure drafting, bringing learning and sense to bear in such areas as patents and trade marks, and elucidating the copyright in 'Popeye the Sailor' and 'The Man who Broke the Bank at Monte Carlo'. In *Errington v. Minister of Health* (1935) he held in the Court of Appeal that a slum clearance order must be set aside when the ministry issuing the order had conferred with the local authority about local objections in the objectors' absence. In the House of Lords ruling in *Wolstanton Ltd v. Newcastle-under-Lyme Corporation* (1940) he held an alleged custom to be invalid, for failing the crucial test of reasonableness, where the lord of a manor had extracted minerals from his land without compensating the owners of buildings on the surface for damage caused by subsidence. In *Knightsbridge Estates Trust v. Byrne* (1940) he distinguished loans made to individuals from loans to limited companies, holding that the latter may lawfully be subject to a condition making them redeemable only after a long period of time. In *Crofter Hand Woven Harris Tweed Co. v. Veitch* (1942), an important authority on the civil law of conspiracy, he confirmed that, provided that the means employed are not criminal or tortious, a combination to damage someone in his trade is not unlawful if the participants' main object is to forward their legitimate interests, 'even though each of them "has his own axe to grind"'. In *Searle* v. *Wallbank* (1947), 'a most interesting judgment' (Heuston, 566), he confirmed the ancient common-law rule that no liability rests with the owner for damage done by animals not known to be dangerous which stray onto the highway.

Liversidge v. Anderson In his public life, Maugham was at his worst in the aftermath of the celebrated case of *Liversidge* v. *Anderson* in 1941. The appeal concerned the meaning of a wartime regulation 18B made under the Emergency Powers (Defence) Act of 1939. The House of Lords (lords Maugham, Romer, Macmillan, and Wright) held that no court could question the statement of the home secretary (Sir John Anderson) that in authorizing the detention of Liversidge without charge, he had 'reasonable cause to believe' him to be a danger to national security. This was, Maugham declared in his reserved judgment, 'clearly a matter for executive discretion and nothing else'. The case became a sensation when Lord Atkin, in a powerful dissenting judgment, lambasted 'the attitude of judges who … show themselves more executive-minded than the executive', said that he had heard arguments which might have been acceptable in the reign of Charles I, and quoted to telling and amusing effect from *Alice through the Looking Glass*. Maugham responded with a letter in *The Times* reproving Atkin for what he professed to be a slight on the law officers. For one judge to attack another in the press, as Atkin privately observed, was 'quite unprecedented and quite unpardonable' (Lewis, 144). Maugham made matters worse with a long and sanctimonious statement in the House of Lords. The likelihood is that the real object of his intervention was to defend not so much the law officers as the law lords—himself included—nettled as they undoubtedly were by Atkin's passion and ridicule. Atkin's judgment won the applause of the liberal bar, and was formally approved by the House of Lords in 1980; but as Professor Heuston maintained in 1964 (pp. 564–6), Maugham's own careful judgment provided a perfectly tenable alternative in holding the question to be one of statutory construction on which more than one interpretation was possible. Maugham's construction almost certainly reflected the will of parliament at a time of national peril, when it was unlikely that parliament intended the home secretary's discretion 'to be hampered by the toils of judicial review' (Bingham, 220).

An able controversialist: Munich and Nuremberg Maugham was well read, knowledgeable, and cultivated. 'I never met a man so generally well informed', wrote Kate, the eldest of his three daughters (R. Maugham, *All the Maughams*, 191). His understanding of mathematics placed him among the rare laymen able to appreciate Einstein's theory of relativity, and he had enough technical knowledge to grasp the problems of the 'Churchill' tank in 1942. He travelled widely in Europe and overseas, 'an indefatigable sightseer', who, Kate recalled, 'walked me off my feet in most of the capitals of Europe' (ibid.). A

proud collector of paintings, he was also a clear and elegant writer. While at the bar he wrote *The Case of Jean Calas* (1928), a scholarly account of that amalgam of injustice and religious bigotry exposed by Voltaire. In *The Tichborne Case* (1936) he narrated the course of the longest civil trial in the history of English law, involving a tale of protracted and improbable imposture. The story was retold, with some infidelity to truth, in the film *The Tichborne Claimant* (1998). He also published short stories under a pen-name.

During the war Maugham produced 'vigorous war pamphlets, including the famous *Lies as Allies*' (R. Maugham, *All the Maughams*, 183), which appeared in several languages. *The Truth about the Munich Crisis* (1944) was a notable polemic in which he succinctly and ably defended Neville Chamberlain's posthumous reputation in relation to the controversial events of 1938, contending that for Britain to have gone to war at that time would have been to court disaster. The booklet, assiduously circulated by Chamberlain's former adviser Sir Horace Wilson, was among the first and most cogent attempts at a revisionist view of Chamberlain's 'appeasement' policy, and Maugham declared himself 'appalled' at its hostile reception (Dutton, 129). Though Maugham himself applauded Chamberlain's conduct, had been among the ministers who welcomed him at Heston aerodrome on his return from Munich, and considered Chamberlain's critics 'blinded by prejudice' (F. Maugham, 381), he himself bore little personal responsibility for appeasement, his views being seldom canvassed. He admitted later, however, that the cabinet had underestimated Hitler's ambitions and his perfidy: 'We can only say that we did not then recognize a new kind of political reptile in human shape' (ibid., 379). (In contrast to the Munich agreement, Maugham deplored Chamberlain's gratuitous cession, earlier in 1938, of Britain's rights in the Irish treaty ports.) In *U.N.O. and War Crimes* (1951), he questioned the claim that the Nuremberg trials in 1946 were based on accepted principles of international law. In so far as crimes against peace and crimes against humanity were an innovation at the time of the trials, his strictures were valid. However, they were somewhat academic, in that only one of the twenty-one accused was convicted of crimes against peace alone, and only two were convicted of crimes against humanity alone (Heuston, 568), while the Nuremberg charter had been incorporated into international law by the United Nations shortly after the trials (Brierly, 411).

A conscientious but 'difficult man' Maugham possessed great virtues: assiduity—'never-ending hard work' (F. Maugham, 582) loyalty, integrity, and the courage of his convictions on matters of controversy. When the judges' salaries were cut by the National Government in the financial crisis of 1931, it was Maugham who drafted and presented a collective protest to Lord Chancellor Sankey on behalf of the judiciary. As his efforts to promote the Evidence Act show, he was no hidebound legal traditionalist. His amendment to the Matrimonial Causes Act (1937) reduced from five years to three the period after marriage within which a petition for divorce could be presented. He believed that a caution before statement affords unnecessary protection to malefactors, and that a judge should have a discretion to determine the admissibility of confessions. He welcomed the advent of the Legal Aid and Advice Act, of 1949, which extended access to justice.

Maugham's patriotism was active and exemplary. During the First World War, at nearly fifty he became a special constable. He assisted at least one junior barrister (a future law lord) who returned briefless from the war. He pressed for the declaration of war in 1939, and his former hostility to Winston Churchill turned to warm admiration. He made it his business personally to investigate reports from his son, then on active service in north Africa, of defects in the 'Churchill' tanks. 'On one occasion he even drove a tank around the test area' of the Vauxhall factory at Luton—'to the general alarm of all about him' (R. Maugham, *All the Maughams*, 183). He was invited to join an unofficial watching committee of parliamentarians under Lord Salisbury formed to promote the well-being of servicemen. So highly did he rate his voluntary war work that he declined the honour of becoming treasurer of Lincoln's Inn in 1940 and again in 1946, a refusal which puzzled and even vexed his fellow benchers.

Maugham's normally reserved and undemonstrative exterior left the misleading impression of a cold uncaring nature. His features were handsome and distinguished, but a proud and sometimes censorious demeanour gave the appearance of haughtiness, an image not unassisted by the monocle which he would raise disconcertingly to his eye. His manner at the bar was 'slightly supercilious and never very genial', though he showed 'courtesy and consideration' on the bench (*The Times*). He could certainly be opinionated, humourless, and high-handed. Ever on his dignity as lord chancellor, he once sat stiff and silent through a large luncheon party. When coffee was served, he turned to his wife with an air of commanding solemnity. Everyone fell silent, awaiting some ripe pronouncement, but his only utterance was to ask for the sugar (R. Maugham, *All the Maughams*, 172). On another occasion he donned 'full evening dress' for a visit to the dentist (R. Maugham, *Conversations*, 123). 'As a judge', his son recalled, 'he believed that his opinions were inviolate—within the family as well as in court' (R. Maugham, *All the Maughams*, 92). To his four children he was an ogre, distant, disapproving, and overbearing, for while craving affection from them he was constitutionally incapable of imparting it himself. It was many years, his eldest daughter records, 'before I discovered that he was human' (ibid., 173). Increasingly frustrated, 'he withdrew into his cloak of loneliness' (ibid., 175). Relations with his only son, Robert Cecil Romer *Maugham (1916–1981) (the novelist Robin Maugham), were invariably strained, and were regularly punctuated by distressing outbursts. Invalided out of the army in 1943, Robin was serving drinks at a homecoming party hosted by his parents when, in a typical incident, Lord Maugham suddenly rounded on him, 'white and quivering'. 'How dare *you* pour out *my* sherry in my house to *my* guests?' he hissed. 'How dare you?'

(R. Maugham, *Escape from the Shadows*, 137). He disparaged Robin's ambition to become a writer and even tried to suppress publication of his first book, *The Servant*. Relations with his youngest brother, Somerset (his other two brothers died young), were likewise cold, captious, and remote, though his advice saved Somerset from a libel action at the suit of the writer Hugh Walpole, who appears as Alroy Kear in *Cakes and Ale* (1930). Somerset, who regarded his brother as a 'brilliant' (R. Maugham, *Conversations*, 157) but as a 'difficult' (Heuston, 571) and even 'odious man' (R. Maugham, *All the Maughams*, 168), used him as the model for Dr Bernard Garstin in *The Painted Veil* (1925) and the judge Sir Edward Landon in his short story *The Happy Couple*.

While Neville Chamberlain averred that Maugham had 'done very well' (Heuston, 596) as lord chancellor, not everyone agreed. When he addressed the House of Lords on the Coal Bill, some mineowning peers objected that they were being lectured or even preached at on their duty not to vote 'according to private pecuniary interests' (ibid., 555). Another peer denied the efficiency on which Maugham prided himself, observing not only that he needed constant prompting on the woolsack but even that he 'will be looked upon, and rightly, as the most inefficient Speaker of the House of Lords within living memory'. 'Seldom', this critic continued, 'have I heard anybody so hopeless in putting an amendment or conveying a decision—he even blunders over the effort of adjourning a debate and adjourning the House, which he seems to think are interchangeable processes' (*Crawford Papers*, 603). He showed 'no patience with fools', according to Somerset Maugham (R. Maugham, *Conversations*, 157) and was 'not always easy to work with' (*The Times*). The lord chief justice, Lord Hewart, was infuriated by Maugham's 'interference in matters that were in Hewart's province' and by his failure to consult him before making a judicial appointment in 1939 (Jackson, 330). *The Times* agreed that Maugham's 'tenure of the woolsack will hardly be remembered as the most successful phase of his career'.

Maugham could be strangely partisan for a lord chancellor, albeit a lifelong Conservative, 'passionately loyal' to Neville Chamberlain (R. Maugham, *All the Maughams*, 179). In a speech at the Constitutional Club in December 1938 he declared that Winston Churchill, whose calls to prepare for war he considered dangerous and irresponsible, should be 'either shot or hanged', or at any rate 'impeached' (ibid.). (Churchill's riposte was characteristically vigorous.) Maugham's angularity was rooted in, and his nature to some degree warped by, the hardship of his early years at the bar, while the years of success were purchased at the price of constant overwork, aggravated by resentment at his long failure to attain judicial office. He was haunted by morbid worries about money 'even when he was making £40,000 a year' (ibid., 5). His peremptory exclusion from the government in September 1939, although an agreed condition of his appointment to the woolsack, was a blow to his pride. 'Never' he complained, 'had there been a more hardworked lord chancellor than himself' (*Crawford Papers*, 693). His domestic happiness was continually blighted by disappointment with his son, and during his career as a silk it seems that he was distracted by a passion for a woman many years younger than himself (R. Maugham, *Escape from the Shadows*, 215–16). His sad, withdrawn, and essentially vulnerable inner self, reflected in a certain hunted expression in his melancholy eyes, emerges from his portrait by Sir Gerald Kelly, at Trinity Hall, Cambridge. His carefree years at Cambridge, which he never revisited 'without emotion' (F. Maugham, 23), he looked back on as 'the happiest chapter of my life' (ibid., 50). In select male company, especially in the House of Lords, Lincoln's Inn, or the Savile Club, Freddie Maugham could unbend and disclose a more congenial side and a dry sense of humour which he seldom vouchsafed to his family.

Maugham was made a bencher of Lincoln's Inn in 1915 and an honorary fellow of Trinity Hall in 1928. His eldest daughter looked after him after Lady Maugham's death in 1950. In 1954 Maugham published his autobiography, *At the End of the Day*. The 600-page book was a *tour de force* for a man of eighty-eight; but less than one seventh of it, the most interesting part, was devoted to his own experiences, and more than half, somewhat unaccountably, to a close engagement with the campaigns and controversies of the two world wars. His family and his marriage of over fifty years he relegated to a few lines, mostly drafted by his son. Maugham died at his London home, 73 Cadogan Square, on 23 March 1958, and was buried on 26 March at Hartfield parish church, in Sussex.   A. LENTIN

Sources *DNB* · F. Maugham, *At the end of the day* (1954) · *Law reports* · R. Maugham, *Somerset and all the Maughams* (1966) · R. F. V. Heuston, *Lives of the lord chancellors, 1885–1940* (1964); 2nd edn (1987) · *The Times* (24 March 1958) · R. Maugham, *Escape from the shadows: his autobiography* (1972) · *The Crawford papers: the journals of David Lindsay, twenty-seventh earl of Crawford … 1892–1940*, ed. J. Vincent (1984) · R. Maugham, *Conversations with Willie: recollections of W. Somerset Maugham* (1978) · R. Jackson, *The chief: the biography of Gordon Hewart, lord chief justice of England, 1922–1940* (1959) · D. Dutton, *Neville Chamberlain* (2001) · G. Lewis, *Lord Atkin* (1983) · T. Bingham, 'Mr Perlzweig, Mr Liversidge, and Lord Atkin', *The business of judging: selected essays and speeches* (2000), 211–21 · *WWW, 1951–60* · J. L. Brierly, *The law of nations* (1963) · Sainty, *Judges*

Archives NRA, corresp. and papers | Bodl. Oxf., letters to A. L. Goodhart · U. Birm., Neville Chamberlain MSS

Likenesses J. Duff, double portrait, photograph, 1936 (with W. Somerset Maugham), repro. in Maugham, *Somerset and all the Maughams*, facing p. 178 · W. Stoneman, two photographs, 1936, NPG · G. Kelly, oils, 1938, Trinity Hall, Cambridge [*see illus.*] · R. G. Eves, oils, *c.*1939, Lincoln's Inn, London · R. G. Eves, oils, 1939, NPG · J. Gunn, oils, *c.*1954–1958, Althorp, Northamptonshire · J. Gunn, group portrait, oils, *c.*1954–1959, Brooks's Club, London, Society of Dilettanti · G. Kelly, oils, Lincoln's Inn, London · caricature, repro. in *The Granta* (1 March 1889) · photographs, repro. in Maugham, *At the end of the day*

Wealth at death £40,203 15s. 10d.: probate, 6 June 1958, *CGPLA Eng. & Wales*

Maugham, Robert (1788–1862), lawyer and first secretary of the Law Society, was born on 9 March 1788 in Chancery Lane, London, one of four children of William Maugham (*bap.* 1759). About 1805 he entered the office of George Barrow, attorney of Threadneedle Street, but he did not formally become an articled clerk until March 1812. He was admitted in 1817 and by the early 1820s he was working and living at 17 Great James Street. He married in 1822, and his eldest son, Robert Ormond Maugham (1823–1884), also a solicitor, was the father of Frederic Herbert *Maugham, first Viscount Maugham (1866–1958), and William Somerset *Maugham (1874–1965).

It is not clear what role Maugham played, if any, in the formation of the Law Institution in 1825 (subsequently the Law Society), but he acted as secretary to the provisional committee in March, and was subsequently appointed secretary to the committee of management on 7 June 1825. In the same year he achieved prominence with the publication of *A Treatise on the Law of Attornies*, an important work of synthesis relating to statutory and case law affecting the profession. In 1832 his position as secretary was confirmed and he was awarded a salary of £400 a year and a set of apartments in the Law Society's hall, Chancery Lane.

Although he combined his role as secretary with private practice, Maugham's major achievement was the supervision of the institution's successful development after its foundation. As the only permanent official of any significance he played a central part in ensuring the institution, later the Incorporated Law Society, had a sound constitutional and financial basis. He guided the society through its transition from a joint-stock concern to a professional association and helped secure the second royal charter in 1845, which remained the principal constitutional document.

Maugham successfully oversaw the expansion of the hall and the establishment of lectures and examinations conducted by the society. He orchestrated the passing of the Attorneys and Solicitors Act of 1843, which recognized the place of the society in the profession. The act appointed the society as registrar of attorneys and solicitors, thereby making it responsible for the administration of the roll. Maugham remained secretary until his death, during a period of great importance for the society, in which it was guided through the critical early years and established as the pre-eminent national body for the solicitors' profession.

Maugham occupied a significant place in the development of the profession and took a keen interest in many professional issues. He continued to publish works on legal subjects and in 1830 he founded and edited the *Legal Observer*, the first legal journal dealing with professional matters, other than the reporting of cases and legislation, to become successfully established. The journal was used to promote the interests of the Incorporated Law Society and the profession, and acted as a voice for the opinions of its editor. Maugham was also a campaigner for improved legal education and higher standards of qualification, believing this would raise the status of the profession. In 1846 he gave evidence before the select committee on legal education. His proposals were far-reaching and those relating to examinations were largely adopted in the Attorneys and Solicitors Act of 1860.

Very little is known of Maugham's personal life or interests outside the profession. He retired from practice in

1856, when members of the society subscribed £600 as a testimonial, which included a gift of plate. Also in 1856 he relinquished control of the *Legal Observer*, when it merged with the *Solicitors' Journal and Reporter*. Maugham died on 16 July 1862 at Chancery Lane and was buried on 22 July at Nunhead cemetery. He was survived by his wife, Mary.

ANDREW ROWLEY

Sources R. Maugham, *Somerset and all the Maughams* (1966) · *Solicitors' Journal*, 6 (1861–2), 727 · Law Society archive, 113 Chancery Lane, London · 'Select committee on legal education in Ireland', *Parl. papers* (1846), vol. 10, no. 686 · M. Birks, 'Robert Maugham, secretary of the Law Society, 1825–1862', *Law Society's Gazette*, 56 (1959), 815–17 · Boase, *Mod. Eng. biog.* · *CGPLA Eng. & Wales* (1862)
Archives University of Calgary Library, journal of tour of Lake District
Likenesses portrait, Law Society, London
Wealth at death under £7000: probate, 20 Aug 1862, *CGPLA Eng. & Wales*

Maugham, Robert Cecil Romer [Robin], **second Viscount Maugham** (1916–1981), novelist and playwright, who wrote under the name Robin Maugham, was born at 4 Collingham Gardens, Kensington, London on 17 May 1916. He was the fourth and youngest child, and the only son, of Frederic Herbert *Maugham, first Viscount Maugham (1866–1958), lord chancellor in 1938–9, and Helen Mary (1868x72?–1950), daughter of a lord justice of appeal, Sir Robert *Romer (1840–1918). Maugham was educated, not very happily, at Eton College, but enjoyed his time at Trinity Hall, Cambridge, where he wrote a thriller for the Amateur Dramatic Company and was converted to a kind of sentimental socialism. He graduated with a second in law in 1938, with the intention, at his father's insistence, of becoming a barrister.

The outbreak of war provided a temporary excuse to dodge an unwelcome future, and Maugham enlisted in the Inns of Court regiment, being commissioned in 1940 in the 4th County of London yeomanry. While fighting in the western desert, Maugham was mentioned in dispatches and suffered a head wound which may have been the cause of his erratic conduct in later life. He reached the rank of captain, and in 1944 was invalided out of the army. He put his army experiences to literary use in his first novel, *Come to Dust* (1945), warmly praised by Graham Greene, and in his play *Enemy!* (1969).

In 1945 Maugham was called to the bar but never practised. It had always been apparent that he had more in common with his cosmopolitan uncle, the novelist and playwright W. Somerset *Maugham, than with his legal relatives. Although he produced some thirty works altogether, he had unfortunately inherited an emotional sterility similar to his uncle's without the equivalent compensating literary talent. It was early in his career, in 1948, that Maugham conceived the idea for his slim novella *The Servant*, so successfully adapted for the cinema in 1965 by Harold Pinter that it is the work, inconsequential in its origins, by which he is best remembered. It was, however, almost a collaboration between uncle and nephew, Somerset Maugham going over every line in minutest detail.

Although much of Robin Maugham's autobiographical writing was embroidered, his non-fiction was superior to his fiction. In 1961 *The Slaves of Timbuktu* was given a dramatic edge with the purchase by Maugham of an African slave to prove the truth of his researches. *Somerset and All the Maughams* (1966), enthusiastically welcomed by such distinguished critics as Cyril Connolly and Norman Shrapnel, provided an essentially affectionate portrait of his sardonic uncle, whose stutter he loved to mimic. But there was a strange ambiguity about his fiction. Many of Maugham's books, *The Second Window* (1968), for example, *The Sign* (1974), or *Lovers in Exile* (1977), were compulsively readable and yet instantly forgettable. Maugham was a financially successful but basically facile writer, whose neurotic personality prevented him from working alone and whose insecurity when he failed to inherit anything from his uncle drove him to pursue quick financial returns rather than literary integrity. Some of his novels were actually ghosted.

Maugham was a brave man who survived being buried in a terrifying earthquake in Morocco, at Agadir. He could be violent, snobbish, and cruel, but he endeared himself to close friends as a kind and extravagant host and a brilliant raconteur. Unashamedly homosexual, he had a taste for the louche life, much of it enjoyed at his villa on Ibiza, and some of it reflected in the sexual adventures in exotic locations experienced by the inhabitants of his novels.

Maugham made his final home in Clifton Road, Brighton, and at sixty-four he was still a comparatively young man, although prematurely aged through increasingly heavy drinking bouts allied to diabetes, when he died at the Royal Sussex County Hospital, Brighton, on 13 March 1981. He was buried with his parents at Hartfield in Sussex. He was unmarried, and the title became extinct. After his death it was thought that his private journals might be published, but, unable to find a suitable publisher, his executors stored the diaries. Towards the end of 1991 all but six volumes were mysteriously stolen, with suggested motives ranging from curiosity about the activities of those described to a suggestion that the thieves had believed them to contain coded references to Maugham's supposed work for British intelligence. The case remains unsolved.

MICHAEL DE-LA-NOY

Sources R. Maugham, *Escape from the shadows* (1972) · R. Maugham, *Search for nirvana* (1975) · *The Times* (14 March 1981) · personal knowledge (2004) · B. Connon, *Somerset Maugham and the Maugham dynasty* (1997) · b. cert. · d. cert.
Archives U. Texas, MSS and letters | BFI, corresp. with Joseph Losey · CAC Cam., corresp. with Sir E. L. Spears
Likenesses W. Lawrence, bust, Cornell University, New York
Wealth at death £71,036: administration, 5 Nov 1981, *CGPLA Eng. & Wales*

Maugham, (William) Somerset (1874–1965), writer and playwright, was born at the British embassy, Paris, on 25 January 1874, youngest of the four sons of Robert Ormond Maugham (1823–1884), partner in Maugham et Fils, solicitors, and Edith Mary (1840–1882), daughter of Major Charles Snell and Anne Snell, who became a successful French novelist following the death of her husband. His grandfather Robert *Maugham (1788–1862) and brother

(William) Somerset Maugham (1874–1965), by Graham Sutherland, 1949

Frederic Herbert *Maugham, first Viscount Maugham (1866–1958), were distinguished lawyers and authors of legal works, while his brother Harry was a poet, essayist, and travel writer. The Maughams were a north of England family of Norman descent, not Irish as often erroneously stated.

Youth Maugham's mother died of tuberculosis when he was seven and his father of cancer three years later. He had been brought up by servants in Paris and, with his brothers at school in England, his childhood was lonely and continued to be so when he left France to live with a childless couple, his uncle, Henry Maugham, vicar of Whitstable, Kent, and Barbara, his German-born wife.

French was Maugham's first language and when he attended King's School, Canterbury, he was taunted for his inadequate English and as a result developed a defensive speech hesitancy which never entirely left him and intensified in times of stress. He moved to Heidelberg when he was sixteen to learn German and came under the influence of John Ellingham Brooks, who seduced him. Ten years his senior and an ostentatious homosexual, Brooks encouraged his ambitions to be a writer and introduced him to the works of Schopenhauer and Spinoza. Maugham returned to England when he was eighteen and, instead of becoming an accountant or a parson as his uncle proposed, enrolled as a student at St Thomas's Hospital, London, where he believed he would have personal freedom and the time to write.

Early writing Maugham managed to qualify as a doctor in 1897 but never practised medicine because he was encouraged to continue writing by the modest success of a novel, *Liza of Lambeth*, published in the same year. Set in the slums of Lambeth, it reflected the author's knowledge of local people from his experiences in the out-patients' department and on the wards of St Thomas's Hospital, and from visiting them in the grim hovels where they lived in poverty and squalor. Commenting on the slums in his preface to the 1934 edition of the novel, he said it was somewhere 'the police hesitated to penetrate but where your [doctor's] black bag protected you from harm' (p. vii). The story of Liza, a fun-loving factory worker, and her affair with Jim, a married man, was leavened by comedy to relieve stark scenes of brutality such as the street fight between the pregnant Liza and Jim's wife which leads to Liza's miscarriage and death. The story and its setting outraged the Victorian sensibilities of critics: 'it reeks of the pot-house', said the *Daily Mail* on 7 September, but added that it was cleverly written. The stir caused by the novel did Maugham no harm but the publicity took an ugly turn when he was accused in *The Academy* of 11 September of plagiarism. It asserted that he had 'imitated' Arthur Morrison: 'The mimicry, indeed, is deliberate and unashamed'. Morrison's *Tales of Mean Streets* (1894), a collection of short stories, banned in some quarters, included one about Liza Hunt of Bow to which *Liza of Lambeth* bore similarities which went beyond mere coincidence. Unwisely, Maugham denied the charge in a long and disingenuous reply. Forty years later in his volume of autobiographical reflections *The Summing up* (1938) he finally admitted to Morrison's influence. The incident had no effect on his ultimate financial success but it left a shadow of doubt over his integrity and alerted his detractors to his propensity for lying. Other novels which followed, such as *Mrs Craddock* (1902), and *The Merry-Go-Round* (1904), made little impression on the book-buying public. They did, however, gain him some prestige and he was welcomed into 'society' partly through his brother Frederic's in-laws, the wealthy Romer family. He was also introduced into bohemian literary and theatrical circles by his aesthete brother Harry, Ellingham Brooks, and Walter Adney Payne, whom he had met in Germany. He now lived with Payne, who supported him financially.

Maugham's persistent attempts to interest theatrical managements in his plays were not helped by the failure of a West End production of *A Man of Honour* in 1904. But in 1907 the Court Theatre in Sloane Square, London, put on *Lady Frederick* to replace a flop and it became a surprise success. Within a year four of Maugham's plays were running in the West End, and a sketch by Bernard Partridge in *Punch* (24 June 1908) showed a worried Shakespeare in front of the playbills. Maugham's success was repeated in New York, and he celebrated his good fortune by moving into a lavishly appointed house in Mayfair, London, with Walter Payne. As well-to-do bachelors, both men were socially popular. Contemporary photographs show Maugham, a small man, to be good looking, sexy, and fashion-conscious. His dandyism was captured by Sir Gerald Kelly in a full-length portrait of 1911 (Tate Collection).

Maugham's drama was in the tradition of Wilde and Pinero, as his major successes, including *Home and Beauty* (1919), *The Circle* (1921), and *The Letter* (1927), illustrate. In 1933, with the failure of an experimental comedy, *Sheppey*, he retired from the theatre having written over thirty plays. He continued to be represented, however, by frequent revivals and by adaptations of his stories by other writers, such as *Rain* (by John Colton and Clemence Randolph, 1922), and *Before the Party* (by Rodney Ackland, 1949).

Critical success Maugham's novel *Of Human Bondage* (1915) was a heavily revised and amplified version of an unpublished novel, a fictionalized work of autobiography, 'The artistic temperament of Stephen Carey', which he described in an address to the Library of Congress on 20 April 1946 as 'very crude and very immature'. (On this occasion he presented the manuscript of *Of Human Bondage* to the library and followed it with the manuscript of 'The artistic temperament of Stephen Carey' in 1950.) As the title indicates, his first draft examined the development of an artistic disposition, but in the new version the emphasis was on the shedding of the clutter of a conventional religious upbringing to free the individual's spirit. Through its pages, as Maugham put it in his address, he rid himself of those memories of an unhappy past which hindered him. He renamed his hero Philip and gave him a club-foot to induce sympathy and to explain his inhibitions. Most of the novel mirrors Maugham's life and contains vivid scenes set in childhood and as a young man in Heidelberg and Paris. The emotional centre of the book is Philip's sexual obsession with Mildred, a waitress in an ABC café, who is indifferent to him but ready to exploit his love as long as it suits her. She soon leaves him and he believes he is free of her until he sees her soliciting in Piccadilly; overwhelmed with pity but not lust, he gives a home to her and her newly born child. After a terrible row in which she abuses him, calling him 'Cripple!', and after smashing up his possessions, she storms off. The novel ends somewhat unconvincingly when Philip settles down to a conventional marriage and life as a country doctor but not before Mildred makes a final appearance. She is working as a prostitute again but is in the throes of venereal disease. He begs her to give up the life because she is a danger to others. Her response is true to character: 'What do I care? Let them take their chance' (*Of Human Bondage*, 1915, 611).

There is no evidence that Mildred was based on a specific individual, but in homosexual circles it was claimed by the likes of Beverley Nichols, one of Maugham's many lovers, that the original of Mildred was a youth, probably a rent boy, with whom he became infatuated. This was endorsed by another lover, Harry Philips, in a letter to Joseph Drobinsky of 16 September 1966.

The novel was coolly received in Britain and America and became a best-seller only after an effusive review by the influential American critic and distinguished novelist Theodore Dreiser in the *New Republic* (25 December 1915),

in which he described the book as of 'the utmost importance' and its author as a 'great artist'. After this it seemed that Maugham could not fail, and the public eagerly bought his novels such as *The Moon and Sixpence* (1919), and *The Painted Veil* (1925), together with volumes of his carefully crafted short stories. These included many that had appeared in magazines such as *The Cosmopolitan*. His novel most likely to survive is *Cakes and Ale* (1930), a satire on the literary world and a cynical dissection of the nature of lust. In his favourable review for *The Graphic* on 15 October 1930 Evelyn Waugh referred to Maugham's 'supreme adroitness and ease' as well as his 'brilliant technical dexterity'. The merits of the novel were overshadowed by a controversy over the identity of the central figure Edward Driffield, a grand old man of letters who was presented in an unflattering light. It was seen as a direct attack on Thomas Hardy, who had died in 1928. Maugham deflected press indignation easily enough but it was more difficult to deny that a malicious portrait of a best-selling novelist, Alroy Kear, was based on Hugh Walpole, but deny it he did. Walpole was devastated and only slightly mollified by an evasive letter from Maugham dismissing the idea that he could do such a thing to an old friend. In his preface to the Modern Library edition (1950) he admitted the truth but added that Walpole was easy to like but difficult to respect. It is now accepted that Maugham hated Walpole for reasons that have never been clear.

The most memorable character in the book was Rosie, a vulgar, cheerful country girl, who exuded sex appeal and who happily slept with any man attracted to her. Unlike Mildred in *Of Human Bondage*, to whom she bears some resemblance, she demanded nothing of her men in return for her favours. Because much of Maugham's work was fictionalized biography there was speculation as to the identity of the 'real' Rosie. It was not until his memoir *Looking Back* (1962) that Maugham revealed his eight-year affair with a woman, not named, but identifiable from numerous clues as Ethelwyn Sue Jones (1883–1948) the actress daughter of the popular playwright Henry Arthur Jones. Commentators putting two and two together became convinced that Rosie was based on Sue. However, despite Maugham's claim to have had an affair with an unnamed woman, there has never been any evidence that an affair took place or that it was with Sue Jones. The artist Gerald Kelly, who painted her portrait, believed that Maugham was in love with her.

Maugham's stories with their vivid characters proved eminently suitable for innumerable cinema and later television adaptations. These brought him even greater fame and added substantially to his wealth. It is curious that, although there have been some forty films of Maugham's work ranging from *The Magician* (1926) to *Up at the Villa* (2000), a film of *Cakes and Ale* has not been attempted. Hollywood had no problem in simplifying the more complicated *Of Human Bondage* by concentrating on the relationship between Philip and Mildred, played by Leslie Howard and Bette Davis in the first of three versions. Nor was it daunted by *The Razor's Edge* (1948), another saga of a young man's search for spiritual freedom in which the action ranged from Chicago to India via Europe. Clearly the film industry relished the exotic settings of many of Maugham's stories, such as the south seas in *Rain* (1932) and *The Beachcomber* (1938), Tahiti in the Gauguin-inspired *The Moon and Sixpence* (1942), Hong Kong in *The Painted Veil* (1934), Malaya in *The Letter* (1940), and the East Indies in *The Narrow Corner* (1933). The homosexuality implicit in the novel (1932) was carefully expunged from this and a second film adaptation in 1936. In *The Razor's Edge*, however, Elliot Templeton, an obvious closet queen, played with relish by Clifton Webb went unremarked in 1948.

British cinema did well with Maugham's short stories as source material: Hitchcock's underrated *The Secret Agent* (1936) from *Ashenden*, and *Quartet* (1948), *Trio* (1950), and *Encore* (1951). These last three films were introduced by Maugham himself. In America CBS produced nearly forty versions of the short stories for television and British television followed with its own adaptation of some of them.

Relationships Though primarily homosexual Maugham reluctantly married a divorcee, Syrie Wellcome, *née* Bernardo (1879–1955) [*see* Maugham, (Gwendoline Maud) Syrie], interior designer, in America in 1917, ostensibly to give his name to her daughter Liza, born in Rome in 1915. The marriage was unhappy and after they divorced in France in 1929 he denied that Liza was his natural daughter.

The mainstay of Maugham's life was Gerald Haxton (1892–1944), an Anglo-American whom he had first met in London before the First World War. They served together in the American Volunteer Motor-Ambulance Corps (1914–15) but parted when Haxton joined the American army and Maugham went to Switzerland, and later Russia, for British intelligence. His wartime experiences formed the basis of *Ashenden* (1928), tales of a secret agent. In 1919 Haxton was refused re-entry to the UK for reasons successive British governments have refused to disclose. This was no problem for Maugham, who had spent most of his time abroad to avoid the criminal law that had imprisoned Oscar Wilde. The two men travelled round the world together and eventually set up home at the Villa Mauresque, Cap Ferrat, on the French riviera, in 1927. It was Haxton's athleticism, charm, exuberance, and often coarse sense of humour which pleased and sometimes startled Maugham, but his role of uncredited collaborator added substance to the relationship. He was much maligned by rivals for Maugham's affections, who underestimated the bond between them.

Following the outbreak of war in 1939 they went to America where they both worked for the newly established office of strategic services (later the Central Intelligence Agency (CIA). Haxton died of tuberculosis in New York in 1944, aged fifty-two. *The Razor's Edge*, published in the same year, was the last book he influenced, and it was also Maugham's final major success.

Last years Waiting to replace Haxton was Alan Searle (1905–1985), Maugham's 'London' secretary, and, sporadically, his lover. He was seen by some as a near saint and by others, particularly the Maugham family, as a villain, but

for better or worse he was to dominate the author's life and his control was strengthened by Maugham's decline into dementia. The final years were marked by misguided legal disputes and the memoir *Looking Back* (1962), allegedly written by Maugham but owned by Searle, in which he denigrated his late former wife, was dismissive of Haxton, and made a clumsy attempt to deny his homosexuality by claiming he was a red-blooded heterosexual. These stratagems distressed his friends and made him a laughing-stock, but his status as a grand old man of letters appeared to be unaffected. He was appointed CH in 1954 and CLitt in 1961. He was a fellow of the Royal Society of Literature, a commander of the Légion d'honneur, and an honorary DLitt of the universities of Oxford and Toulouse. On his eightieth birthday the Garrick Club, largely prompted by Beverley Nichols, gave a dinner in his honour; only Dickens, Thackeray, and Trollope had received similar recognition.

It was typical of Maugham's sense of irony that he was generous to King's School, Canterbury, where he had been so unhappy. His gifts included a new library building, many of his valuable books, and a substantial legacy. As proof of his belief that he owed his success to the educational benefits of travel, he founded the Somerset Maugham award in 1947 to give young writers a similar opportunity. He also left royalties in all his work to the Royal Literary Fund. In addition to public acts of financial generosity there were many kindnesses done in private which went beyond mere monetary gifts.

Maugham died in the Anglo-American Hospital in Nice on 15 December 1965 and after cremation in Marseilles five days later, his ashes were interred in the grounds of King's School, Canterbury, on 22 December.

Posthumous reputation Released from legal restraint there were those, including his nephew Robin Maugham, Beverley Nichols, and Noël Coward, ready to reveal Maugham's homosexuality, which he had kept from the public. This was partly a reaction to the hypocrisy of *Looking Back* and to settle old scores. Opinions as to his status as a writer continue to be divided. His detractors agreed with Lytton Strachey, who categorized him as 'class II, division I' (Curtis, 169) in 1925, and with the critic Edmund Wilson, who wrote in the *New Yorker* on 8 June 1946: 'I have never been able to convince myself he was anything but second rate'. Maugham in *The Summing up* (1938) complained: 'When clever young men write essays about contemporary fiction they never think of considering me' (p. 221). Yet his list of admirers was impressive, including W. H. Auden, Cyril Connolly, Paul Dottin, Christopher Isherwood, and Desmond MacCarthy. It was typical of the man that even in old age, with honours heaped upon him, he still believed he had not received his full due. The fact remains that he was one of the most commercially successful and gifted writers of the twentieth century, whose work remains in print in the twenty-first.   BRYAN CONNON

Sources B. Connon, *Somerset Maugham and the Maugham dynasty* (1997) · R. Maugham, *Somerset Maugham and all the Maughams* (1966) · T. Morgan, *Somerset Maugham* (1980) · R. Calder, *Willie*

(1989) · A. Curtis, *The pattern of Maugham* (1974) · F. Raphael, *Somerset Maugham* (1989) · B. Nichols, *A case of human bondage* (1966) · *DNB* · private information (2004) [Honor Earl; Mrs Diana Marr-Johnson; Lord Glendevon]

Archives King's AC Cam., letters · L. Cong., papers | BL, letters to Sir Gerald Kelly and Lady Kelly, RP 2505 [photocopies] · BL, corresp. with League of Dramatists, Add. MS 63414 · BL, corresp. with Society of Authors, Add. MS 63302 · Bodl. Oxf., corresp. with Sibyl Colefax · CAC Cam., letters to Cecil Roberts · CKS, letters to Ghita Stanhope · HLRO, corresp. with Lord Beaverbrook · King's AC Cam., letters to G. H. W. Rylands · Royal Society of Literature, London, letters to Royal Society of Literature · Stanford University Library, corresp. with Bertram Alanson · Tate collection, letters to Graham Sutherland [microfiche copies] · Theatre Museum, London, letters to the Lord Chamberlain's licensee | SOUND BL NSA, performance recordings

Likenesses G. Kelly, oils, 1907, U. Texas · G. Kelly, oils, 1911 (*The jester*), Tate collection · H. Coster, photographs, 1930, NPG · P. Steegman, oils, 1931, NPG · D. Low, caricature, pencil sketches, c.1934, NPG · G. Kelly, oils, 1934–60, U. Texas · H. A. Freeth, etching, 1946, NPG · Y. Karsh, bromide print, 1947, NPG · C. Beaton, bromide print, 1949, NPG · G. Sutherland, oils, 1949, Tate collection [*see illus.*] · G. Sutherland, pencil and crayon, 1949, NPG · H. Cartier-Bresson, bromide print, 1951, NPG · J. Epstein, bronze cast of head, 1951, Tate collection · G. Sutherland, black chalk, pencil, and gouache, 1953, NPG · G. Sutherland, chalk on tracing paper, 1953, NPG · G. Sutherland, lithograph, 1953, NPG · G. Sutherland, oils, c.1954–1955, Beaverbrook Art Gallery, Fredericton, Canada · M. Gerson, photograph, 1955, NPG · W. Stoneman, photograph, 1955, NPG · B. E. Wendkos, pastel drawing, 1956, U. Texas · D. Wilding, photographs, 1958, NPG · I. Penn, platinum palladium print, 1962, NPG · I. R. Jones, plaster bust, 1963, Beaverbrook Art Gallery, Fredericton, Canada · F. Behn, terracotta head, Musée de la Ville, Nice, France · P. Evans, pencil drawing, NPG · S. Ryan, plaster head, Walsall Museum and Art Gallery · G. Sutherland, drawings, studies for oil portraits, FM Cam. · G. Sutherland, lithograph, Maidstone Museum and Art Gallery · Madame Yevonde, photographs, NPG

Wealth at death £98,307 effects in England: probate, 15 Feb 1966, *CGPLA Eng. & Wales*

Maugham [*née* Barnardo; *other married name* Wellcome], (**Gwendoline Maud**) **Syrie** (1879–1955), interior decorator, was born on 10 July 1879 at The Cedars, Banbury Road, Hackney, London, the eldest daughter and third of seven children of Thomas John *Barnardo (1845–1905), medical doctor and philanthropist, and Sarah Louise (Syrie) Elmslie (1850?–1945?), daughter of William Elmslie, Lloyds underwriter and charity worker, and his wife. Her father was Irish, and her mother English; both their families were members of an American religious sect, the Open Plymouth Brethren, and their eldest daughter, Syrie (a compression of Sarah Louise), grew up in a paradoxical background of philanthropy and affluence, reading the Bible with her family and forbidden from attending the theatre.

At sixteen Syrie Barnardo was engaged to the son of a wealthy family from Richmond, only to discover that the man had a mistress. In 1901 she escaped from this unhappy situation—and her religious family life—on a trip to Egypt, and met Sir Henry *Wellcome (1853–1936), the wealthy American pharmaceutical manufacturer, twenty-six years her senior. Their marriage, which took place on 25 June 1901, lasted nine years, during which she 'acquired poise and sophistication but grew weary of an

(Gwendoline Maud) Syrie Maugham (1879–1955), by Nitscher

elderly companion who was said by her to be sexually inadequate' (Connon, *Somerset Maugham*, 57). A son, Henry Mounteney, born in 1903, was diagnosed as mentally handicapped, and was later fostered by a farming family. Irritable and distrustful, Wellcome accused his wife of infidelity with an American financier, Archer Harman. In 1910 the couple separated.

Living independently on an allowance of £2400 a year, in 1913 Syrie Wellcome was introduced to (William) Somerset *Maugham (1874–1965), already one of London's best-known playwrights, and a relationship developed. Their daughter, Elizabeth Mary (Liza), was born in Rome on 5 May 1915, at which point Syrie was still married to Henry Wellcome (who named Maugham as co-respondent and uncovered 'proof' of his wife's infidelity with several men, among them Gordon Selfridge).

During the war Somerset Maugham became an ambulance driver, and met Gerald Haxton, with whom he began a disastrous relationship. He was now working for the secret service, and Somerset Maugham and Syrie married in Jersey City, New Jersey, on 26 May 1917. With her husband often away—usually with Haxton—Syrie pursued her interest in interior design, having acquired experience when working for the antiques department of Fortnum and Mason. The American decorator Elsie de Wolfe, Lady Mendl, is said to have told her in 1920 that 'the decorating field is already overcrowded' (Fisher, 16). None the less she launched her decorating business in London's Baker Street in 1922, financed by the sale of her own house.

Combining French art deco (with its eighteenth-century references) and European modernism, Maugham produced her distinctive look: sleek, sophisticated interiors, a de luxe hedonism of lambskin carpets and elongated sofas. She patronized designers such as Marion Dorn and Oliver Messel; her motifs were the plaster palm frond and the sea shell in a 1920s version of rococo. 'With the strength of a typhoon she blew all colour before her,' wrote Cecil Beaton. 'For the next decade Syrie Maugham bleached, pickled or scraped every piece of furniture in sight' (Beaton, 208). Above all, white became her signature. Her house in the King's Road, Chelsea, and the Villa Eliza in Le Touquet became society showrooms for her wares (Somerset Maugham complained that bits of furniture would vanish from their house overnight). Like her Chelsea neighbour and rival, Sibyl Colefax, Syrie Maugham was an adept hostess, claiming to have thrown the first-night party for Noël Coward's *The Vortex*, a sensational success much compared to Maugham's play *Our Betters* (1923, written after hearing Syrie's stories of her affairs and Gordon Selfridge's offer to settle £5000 per annum on her). Her interiors of 1927 and 1930 respectively for Coward's country and town houses resembled sets from his plays: the Syrie sofas, zebra-print cushions, and limed Louis Quinze chairs as upholstered, seductive symbols of an elegant if amoral age.

The Maughams were now leading separate lives; they divorced in May 1929, leaving Syrie to bring up their daughter, Liza. Pursuing the lucrative American market, she opened shops in New York, Chicago, Palm Beach, and Los Angeles; in England her commission in 1936 to decorate Fort Belvedere, on the edge of Windsor Great Park, for the then prince of Wales was 'perhaps her best job', claimed *House and Garden*, 'a series of romantic rooms … enhanced by the reflection, in huge mirrors, of swans on the lake outside' (Fisher, 34).

But reality was encroaching on this inter-war fantasy. Maugham spent part of the Second World War in New York, and in 1944 returned to London, her finances 'much reduced' (Fisher, 68). She continued to work—mostly abroad—until illness prevented her. She died at her Park Lane flat on 25 July 1955, aged seventy-six, and was buried in the Oxfordshire village where her daughter (later Lady Glendevon) lived. In 1964 Beaton, Coward, Rebecca West, Beverley Nichols, and others presented a bust by the Russian sculptor Fyodor Shubin of Catherine the Great to the Victoria and Albert Museum in her memory.

It was a memory already vilified by Maugham's memoirs, *Looking Back*, published in 1962, claiming that he was not the father of their daughter, Liza. Enraged by Maugham's treatment of his wife, Nichols published his own gossipy diatribe, *A Case of Human Bondage* (1966); to Coward this was just 'another essay in bitchiness' (*Coward Diaries*, 633). The playwright's own response to *Looking Back* was *A Song at Twilight* (also 1966) in which an embittered writer is confronted with his homosexuality by his ex-wife.

Richard Fisher described Syrie Maugham as 'strikingly beautiful … of average height, with jet black hair, an ivory skin of Rossettian perfection, and an exquisite figure' (Fisher, 8). Her voice was high pitched, and her manner autocratic; yet she attracted loyal friends and remained supportive of Maugham, refusing to return his vindictiveness. Coward noted, 'One could test the intelligence of one's friends by seeing if they had noted that Syrie was much more intelligent than Willie' (Morgan). Although forever associated with her 'no-colour' phase—Beaton noted that she later adopted 'the vivid colours of lobster salad' (Beaton, 209), as her designs for Stephen Tennant at Wilsford Manor, Wiltshire, in 1938 indicated—she was the first English woman to pursue interior decoration as a career, and was a lasting influence on such decorators as David Hicks.   PHILIP HOARE

Sources R. B. Fisher, *Syrie Maugham* (1978) · E. Morgan, *Somerset Maugham* (1980) · B. Connon, *Somerset Maugham and the Maugham dynasty* (1997) · B. Connon, *Beverley Nichols* (1991) · P. Hoare, *Noël Coward: a biography* (1995) · P. Hoare, *Serious pleasures: the life of Stephen Tennant* (1990) · H. Vickers, *Cecil Beaton* (1985) · C. Beaton, *The glass of fashion* (1954); repr. (1989) · *The Noël Coward diaries*, ed. G. Payn and S. Morley (1982) · CGPLA Eng. & Wales (1955)
Archives Wellcome L. | priv. coll., Cecil Beaton archives
Likenesses photographs, 1920–49, Cecil Beaton archives · Nitscher, photograph, Wellcome L. [*see illus.*] · double portrait, photograph, Wellcome L. · line drawing, repro. in Beaton, *Glass of fashion* · photograph, repro. in Morgan, *Somerset Maugham*, pl. 34
Wealth at death £3643: administration with will, 1 Oct 1955, CGPLA Eng. & Wales

Maulay [Malo Lacu], **Peter** (**I**) **de** (*d.* 1241), knight and royal counsellor, took his name from Maulay in France, in the border region separating the provinces of Poitou and the Touraine. The identity of his father and mother remains unknown. By contemporaries it was said that he had risen from relatively humble origins, and that he abandoned his estates in France to his younger brother, Aimery de Maulay. Peter de Maulay is first recorded in 1202, granted land in the region of Loudun by King John. According to the chronicler Walter of Guisborough (likely to be a good source, though late, thanks to Guisborough's proximity to Maulay's castle at Mulgrave), it was Maulay, acting on royal orders, who carried out the murder of the king's nephew, Arthur, duke of Brittany, last heard of in 1203. Certainly Maulay enjoyed the close confidence of the king and came to be numbered among John's evil counsellors by the chronicler Roger of Wendover. Following the loss of Normandy in 1204 he joined the king in England. There he received a series of royal escheats, including the manor of Upavon in Wiltshire. In 1213 he travelled as royal ambassador to Rome, and in the following year played a leading role in the king's expedition to Poitou, where he took command of the garrison of La Rochelle. In the same year, in return for a proffer of 7000 marks, he was granted the marriage and lands of Isabella, sole daughter and heir of Robert of *Thornham (*d.* 1211), a former royal seneschal of Poitou. The fine was later pardoned in return for Maulay's services to the crown. By his marriage Maulay rose to a leading position among the Yorkshire baronage, with control over the Fossard barony, with its 30 knights' fees and its honour divided between Doncaster in the West Riding of Yorkshire and Mulgrave in Cleveland.

With the outbreak of civil war in 1215 Maulay was appointed constable of Corfe Castle in Dorset, with custody of the king's treasure and of King John's youngest son, Richard, the future earl of Cornwall. At Corfe, Maulay acted as gaoler to many state prisoners, including Eleanor (*d.* 1241), the sister of Arthur of Brittany, and several barons captured during the civil war, from whom he extracted heavy ransoms and whom he retained in prison long after the end of hostilities, an action that earned him widespread dislike. Appointed sheriff of Dorset and Somerset in 1216, he failed to respond to the orders of the royal exchequer and instituted a regime of profiteering at the expense of the local gentry. In 1220 he was forced to relinquish custody of Richard of Cornwall, and in the following year, in a coup orchestrated by the justiciar, Hubert de Burgh (d. 1243), Maulay was accused of treasonably plotting with the French, and was stripped of his offices. He retired to his estates in Yorkshire, where from around 1220 he was engaged in building a new castle at Mulgrave. In 1230 he served on the king's expedition to Brittany, and returned to court in 1232 as a protégé of his fellow alien, Peter des Roches, bishop of Winchester (d. 1238).

In the following year Henry III restored him to possession of the manor of Upavon, seized back by the crown following Maulay's disgrace, and since conferred upon Gilbert Basset by royal charter. Maulay's restoration to Upavon was widely considered an illegal exercise of royal power, and precipitated a revolt by Basset and his overlord, Richard Marshal, earl of Pembroke (d. 1234). Despite temporary disgrace Maulay survived the ensuing storm, and in 1236 was briefly appointed sheriff of Northamptonshire. Having taken the cross as long ago as 1220, in 1241 he set out on crusade together with his former ward, Richard of Cornwall. He died, probably in the Holy Land, later that same year. Although mistrusted as an alien by the native English baronage, his marriage to Isabella of Thornham, who predeceased him, established Peter de Maulay and his descendants as major Yorkshire landowners. Maulay himself bestowed land upon several local monasteries, including Meaux, where he founded a chantry in memory of his wife. He was succeeded by his eldest son, Peter (II) Mauley (d. 1279), the ancestor of a succession of Mauley lords of Mulgrave [see Mauley family]. The Mauley coat of arms, recorded by Matthew Paris, combined a maunch, probably Peter's original coat, with the Fossard arms: or, a bend sable.   NICHOLAS VINCENT

Sources Chancery records · Pipe rolls · N. Vincent, Peter des Roches: an alien in English politics, 1205–38, Cambridge Studies in Medieval Life and Thought, 4th ser., 31 (1996) · GEC, Peerage · Paris, Chron. · J. Raine, ed., The register or rolls of Walter Gray, lord archbishop of York, SurtS, 56 (1872) · Chronica monasterii de Melsa, a fundatione usque ad annum 1396, auctore Thoma de Burton, ed. E. A. Bond, 3 vols., Rolls Series, 43 (1866–8) · The chronicle of Walter of Guisborough, ed. H. Rothwell, CS, 3rd ser., 89 (1957) · Cartulary of St Thomas Acon, BL, Cotton MS Tiberius C.v, fol. 255r · T. D. Tremlett, H. Stanford London, and A. Wagner, eds., Rolls of arms, Henry III, Harleian Society, 113–14 (1967)

Maule, Fox [later Fox Maule-Ramsay], **second Baron Panmure and eleventh earl of Dalhousie** (1801–1874), army officer and politician, was born on 22 April 1801 at Brechin Castle, Forfarshire, the eldest son of William Ramsay *Maule (1771–1852), first Baron Panmure of Brechin and Navar, Forfarshire, and second son of the eighth earl of Dalhousie, and his wife, Patricia Heron (d. 1821), daughter of Gilbert Gordon from Halleaths in Dumfriesshire. The Maule family claimed eleventh-century Norman origins and were prominent in the Jacobite uprisings. Named after Charles James Fox, a political and personal friend of his father, he had two brothers, Lauderdale (1807–1854), a

Fox Maule, second Baron Panmure and eleventh earl of Dalhousie (1801–1874), by Maull & Polyblank, c.1856

lieutenant-colonel in the Cameron Highlanders, and William (1809–1859), and seven sisters: Patricia (d. 1859), Elizabeth (d. 1852), Mary (d. 1864), Georgiana (d. 1833), Ramsay (d. 1884), Christiane, and one unidentified. His father married second Elizabeth Barton in 1822, but had no further children. Two of Fox Maule's uncles, James (1772–1837) and John (1775–1842), became lieutenant-generals, the ninth earl, George (1770–1838), a general. Maule was educated first at a private school in Clapham, then at Charterhouse School in central London between 30 June 1809 and May 1818. While he was at Charterhouse his father and mother separated. Fox Maule supported his mother and never saw his father again, being settled with a £100 annual allowance and an army commission. After briefly attending Edinburgh University, he therefore joined the 79th regiment of foot (or Cameron Highlanders) as an ensign on 3 June 1819, advancing to lieutenant on 29 July 1824, brevet captain on 8 April 1826, and regimental captain on 31 October 1826. During these years Fox Maule served as aide-de-camp to his uncle Lieutenant-General the earl of Dalhousie, then commander of the forces in North America, leaving Canada with him in August 1828. A year later Maule was at the regimental depot in Dublin, and formally retired on 5 April 1831.

Maule had married Montagu (d. 1853), eldest daughter of George, second Lord Abercromby (d. 1853), the day before, on 4 April 1831; they had no children. After leaving the army Maule settled at Dalguise in Perthshire but soon entered politics as Liberal MP for Perthshire (1835–7), then Elgin burghs (1838–41), and Perth until he succeeded to his father's peerage on the latter's death, on 13 April 1852.

Under Lord Melbourne, except for a short period in 1837–8 when he was not in parliament, he served as under-secretary of state in the Home department (1835–41). In 1841 he became a privy councillor and was briefly vice-president of the Board of Trade. Maule was appointed to the War Office as secretary at war in Lord John Russell's government in July 1846, entering the cabinet in that post in October 1851 and succeeding Lord Brougham as president of the Board of Trade in January 1852. A month later the government fell. Before taking charge of the War Office in 1846, he had shown a close interest in military administration on matters such as the reopening of Kilmainham Hospital to Irish pensioners and ration allowances for troops in the colonies. He wrote, too, several papers about measures to combat Chartist disturbances. Once in office, he dealt with a vast range of issues involving pensions, accounts, contracts, and patronage.

A mutiny in New Zealand, unrest at the Cape of Good Hope, feared insurrection in Ireland, desertions from regiments in Canada all claimed his attention, too, besides more general governmental concerns about India, the Spanish occupation of Cuba, and the Don Pacifico affair. Prolonged inquiries by a parliamentary select committee on army and ordnance expenditure took up a considerable amount of his time between 1849 and 1851. When Palmerston succeeded Lord Aberdeen as prime minister in February 1855, Panmure became secretary of state for war and as such had ministerial responsibility for the Crimean campaign. He quickly insisted that a chief of staff (Sir James Simpson) be appointed to ensure that the orders of the British commander, Lord Raglan, were 'quickly and implicitly obeyed' and also 'to enquire into the manner in which the Staff Officers perform their duties and to report fully thereon' (Hibbert, 253). Referring to dissatisfaction at home arising from 'the grievances in the camp', Panmure harshly (and wrongly) assailed Raglan for not visiting his soldiers, adding: 'Your staff must be changed, at least that will satisfy the public and that radically' (ibid., 254). Before the end of February 1855 he revealed his transparent preoccupation with personal survival: 'I must do something to satisfy the House of Commons' (ibid., 257).

The deficiencies in support services, highlighted by use of pensioners to care for the sick and wounded, and of exhausted soldiers to undertake non-military maintenance and construction duties, and the reliance on civilian contractors for land transport led to a number of *ad hoc* bodies being sent to the theatre of war. Panmure's predecessor (the duke of Newcastle) had dispatched a mounted staff corps to assist with camp policing and a civil engineering corps to build a railway between the port of Balaklava and the trenches. Panmure additionally established a military Land Transport Corps, which evolved into a permanent post-war organization, and the civilian Army Works Corps for manual non-operational work, which foreshadowed the Royal Pioneer Corps. More immediately, he sponsored fundamental, lasting military reform at home. Hitherto, the master-general of the ordnance had commanded the artillery and engineers as a separate corps quite independent from the rest of the army. He had also controlled the civilian Board of Ordnance, which provided military supplies generally and a wide range of financial, supply, and administrative services for overseas garrisons. Within a week of becoming secretary of state, Panmure drew up proposals for 'placing the purely military branch of the Ordnance forces under the C-in-C, and the civil branches under the Minister (Secretary of State) of War' (Sweetman, *War and Administration*, 70). On 6 June 1855 an order in council achieved the desired changes, which were truly fundamental. Panmure had achieved something of a palace coup: the master-general (Raglan), being otherwise engaged in the Crimea, could only belatedly and vainly protest. Brusquely the secretary of state replied: 'The change at the O [*sic*] is effective and I am sorry to hear you anticipate so much confusion from it' (Sweetman, *Raglan*, 316). Seeking to show initiative as complaints mounted of unsatisfactory conditions at the front, Panmure sent Sir John McNeill and Colonel Alexander Tulloch to the Crimea to investigate criticisms of the supply system. Their two reports caused such high dudgeon among those blamed that Panmure appointed a board of general officers under Sir Alexander Woodward to examine their complaints and interview the aggrieved. The board vindicated senior officers such as lords Lucan and Cardigan and was widely dismissed as a whitewash. That was hardly Panmure's fault. He was more culpable over Lord Lucan, recalled from the Crimea following heated objection to Raglan's view that, as the divisional commander who ordered the light brigade up the valley to destruction, he (Lucan) bore responsibility for its fate. Lucan clashed with Panmure once in London, and according to Lord Granville 'Mars [Panmure] had invited the latter [Sir Henry Hardinge, the army commander-in-chief] to break Lucan' (Fitzmaurice, 219). The commander-in-chief refused, believing Lucan had been provoked, whereupon 'Mars had sworn at Hardinge, and threatened to turn the whole press loose upon him' (ibid.). Granville recorded that the prince consort suspected these exchanges had hastened Hardinge's death from a stroke. Frustrated by the failure of the allied forces to advance aggressively against the Russians once the main part of Sevastopol had fallen, Panmure hectored Sir James Simpson into resignation, vigorously defending himself to the queen (11 October): 'In that message [the dispatch containing news of Simpson's resignation] there is not a word which Lord Panmure was not fully justified in using' (Douglas and Ramsay, 1.436).

Patently, Panmure did not lack self-confidence. In cabinet meetings on 11 and 21 December 1855 Granville whimsically noted that 'Mars then gave us his strategical views of the operations in the Crimea', and after 'an interesting letter was read from Miss Nightingale … Mars said it only showed that she knew nothing of the British soldier' (Fitzmaurice, 130, 133). Visiting Panmure, who was suffering from gout 'in both arms and both legs' on 13 January 1856, Granville found him 'reading a book of Scotch divinity; very pompous and oracular on literature and politics'. The bedridden secretary of state declared that 'Macaulay's History is not a history; it is merely pot-house gossip' and went on to discuss the current diplomatic moves to end hostilities. 'I am neither warlike nor peaceable', he exclaimed, 'but I say that if we cannot have an honourable peace, we must have a bloody war' (ibid., 141).

Even as peace hopes rose in January and February 1856 a convalescent Panmure composed lengthy memoranda for the duke of Cambridge in Paris and Sir William Codrington, Simpson's successor as British commander in the Crimea, on the future conduct of operations. After the armistice on 29 February, he immersed himself in details of the army's peacetime establishment, celebratory firework displays in the London parks, the strength of coastal defences, and the building of Netley Military Hospital. On 21 February 1856, in the Lords, 'Mars spoke like Apollo' (Fitzmaurice, 167) in arguing that ambiguity in the responsibilities of the secretary of state and the commander-in-chief of the army must be clarified. Five months later, he unequivocally established the authority of his office over that of the commander-in-chief.

Panmure's energy remained seemingly boundless, but his hot temper (reputedly inherited from his father) caused offence. His nickname the Bison was not wholly due to his unruly mop of hair. He did not serve in any government after Palmerston's first ministry fell in February 1858, and according to Granville was so angry that he threatened to sit on the cross-benches when Palmerston excluded him from his new ministry in 1859. Difficulty in working with colleagues and even the prime minister may explain his exile. Granville thought 'Mars more pompous than ever' over the Indian mutiny (Anderson, 256); Clarendon, though, considered him 'a much more wily creature than he used to be ... there is no other single member of the Cabinet who can defy the Prime Minister' (Fitzmaurice, 114). Not unnaturally, perhaps, Newcastle was 'sore and hates Mars' for taking credit for many reforms that his predecessor had set in train (ibid., 161). Panmure's petulant and stubborn refusal in the Lords on 24 July 1857 to countenance a public memorial to Raglan scarcely extended his range of political supporters. Influential military figures also deplored his treatment of Raglan, who had written to a nephew, 'sometimes I think Lord Panmure believes I am either criminally negligent or a lunatic' (Hibbert, 264). Panmure had an unhappy knack of offending too many people.

Panmure supported the Free Church of Scotland from its formation in 1843, and engaged in years of fractious correspondence about crown patronage in the Church of Scotland. He commented unfavourably on 'the Puseyite principles of Gladstone and Sidney Herbert' (Fitzmaurice, 345). Granville dubbed him 'a Scotch divinity ... more fitted to conduct a campaign in the General Assembly of the Church of Scotland than on the shores of the Black Sea' (ibid., 102). He became deeply involved in the efficiency of Scottish universities, and was made lord rector of Glasgow University in 1842. Between 1850 and 1871 he served as the first non-Catholic governor of Charterhouse since Cromwellian times, being 'particularly industrious in the

work he found fixed upon him ... and always took a pleasure in promoting the true interests of the School' (The Carthusian, 135). On 19 December 1860 he succeeded as eleventh earl of Dalhousie to the Scottish estates of his cousin James Andrew Ramsay, governor-general of India (1847–56). By royal licence in 1861 Maule added Ramsay to his own name. He was a knight of the Scottish Order of the Thistle, knight grand cross of the Bath, keeper of the privy seal of Scotland, lord lieutenant of Forfarshire, and a commissioner of the royal military asylum. The barony of Panmure became extinct when he died without issue on 6 July 1874 at Brechin Castle, his birth place. He was buried at Panbride, Forfarshire, on 14 July. His cousin Admiral George Ramsay succeeded him as earl of Dalhousie.

JOHN SWEETMAN

Sources Army List · The Panmure papers, being a selection from the correspondence of Fox Maule, ed. G. Douglas and G. D. Ramsay, 2 vols. (1908) · Burke, Peerage (1887) · E. G. Petty-Fitzmaurice, The life of Granville George Leveson Gower, second Earl Granville, 2nd edn, 1 (1905) · C. Hibbert, The destruction of Lord Raglan [1961] · O. Anderson, A liberal state at war (1967) · The Carthusian (Aug 1874) · J. Sweetman, Raglan: from the Peninsula to the Crimea (1993) · J. Sweetman, War and administration (1984) · T. A. Mackenzie, J. S. Ewart, and C. Findlay, eds., Historical records of the 79th queen's own Cameron highlanders (1887) · Historical records of the queen's own Cameron highlanders, 1 (1909) · DNB

Archives NA Scot., corresp. and papers | BL, corresp. with Florence Nightingale, Add. MS 43397 · BL, corresp. with G. D. Ramsay, Add. MSS 46446–46447 · Borth. Inst., corresp. with Lord Halifax · Chatsworth House, Derbyshire, corresp. with Joseph Paxton · NA Scot., corresp. with Sir Andrew Leith Hay · NAM, corresp. with Sir William Codrington · NAM, corresp. with Lord Raglan · NL Scot., corresp. with Sir George Brown · NL Scot., corresp. with John Lee · NL Scot., letters to Andrew Rutherford · PRO, corresp. with Lord John Russell, PRO 30/22 · U. Durham L., letters to third Earl Grey · U. Southampton L., corresp. with Lord Palmerston · University of York, corresp. with Lord Halifax · W. Sussex RO, letters to duke of Richmond

Likenesses T. Duncan, wash drawing, c.1838, NPG · J. Porter, mezzotint, pubd 1838 (after T. Duncan), BM, NPG · Maull & Polyblank, photograph, c.1856, NPG [see illus.] · C. Smith, oils, 1861, Church of Scotland Assembly Hall, Edinburgh · J. W. Gordan, oils, Scot. NPG · Posselwhite, stipple (after a photograph by Mayall), BM, NPG · D. J. Pound, stipple (after a photograph by Mayall), BM, NPG; repro. in Drawing room portrait gallery (1859) · F. Schenck, lithograph (after a drawing by W. Crawford, 1845), BM, NPG · Southwell Bros., photograph, NPG

Maule, Harry, styled fifth earl of Panmure (1659–1734), Jacobite army officer and scholar, was born on 18 October 1659, the sixth son of George Maule, second earl of Panmure (1619–1671), and his wife, Lady Jean Campbell (1624/5–1703), eldest daughter of John, earl of Loudoun, lord high chancellor of Scotland. His brothers included John, who was born in January 1650 and died young; George, third earl of Panmure (c.1650–1686); and James *Maule, fourth earl of Panmure (1658/9–1723). Although he does not appear to have had any formal education, his early and extensive travels in England and on the continent developed the keen interest in politics, religion, and scholarship for which he later became famous. In his home county of Forfarshire he acquired the lands of Kelly from his father and his brother James. He also bought additional lands of Arbirlot and Cuthlie from the archbishop

Harry Maule, styled fifth earl of Panmure (1659–1734), attrib. John Scougall

of St Andrews so that he was able to obtain a charter for the whole estate of Kelly in 1687. In the tradition of the Maules he was a firm supporter of the Stuart dynasty and, as a consequence, he and his brother James were both fined considerable sums of money when they walked out of the Scottish parliament for refusing to recognize the convention of estates' decision to declare that James VII of Scotland had forfeited his crown (1689). In addition he was fined for refusing to recognize the authority of William and Mary by taking the oath of allegiance. His seat was declared vacant and eventually filled by Francis Mollison in 1694. He was also at this time a commissioner of supply for Forfarshire. On 7 March 1695 he married Mary Fleming (d. 1702), daughter of William, fifth earl of Wigtown; they had five children, three sons (including William *Maule) and two daughters. Following Mary's death he married Anne Lindsay (d. 1729) in 1704. The couple had six children, all of whom died young except John *Maule (1706–1781), who was later to become one of the barons of the court of exchequer in Scotland. At the time of the union Harry Maule was a writer to the signet in Edinburgh and closely allied both personally and politically to his nephew the earl of Mar.

In 1715 Maule came out for the Jacobites at the battle of Sheriffmuir but, perhaps significantly, preferred to ride out with several other gentlemen volunteers rather than join the Forfarshire regiment raised by his brother James. John Sinclair, in his *Memoirs of the Insurrection in Scotland in 1715*, quotes Harry Maule as saying 'never were men so idly brought in for their lives and fortunes as we were' (Sinclair, 52). Whatever his private feelings, his involvement in the battle became both personal and heroic when he

rescued his wounded brother from the bothy prison close to the battlefield in which he was being held by government troops. This stirring incident is commemorated in the Jacobite ballad on the battle: 'With brisk men about / Brave Harry retook / His brother, and laughed at them a' man'. The Maules' involvement in this uprising led to the forfeiture of their titles and lands in Forfarshire and, in the case of the earl, continuous exile on the continent until his death in 1723. Harry was less persecuted by the government and enjoyed more freedom in Scotland during his lifetime, although he was not allowed to purchase the forfeited estates of his family when they were offered for sale by the government (he offered £60,300 but the York Buildings Company £60,400). While living in the Netherlands in 1718 he wrote to Mar expressing his view about his prospects of returning to Scotland: 'expecting but little satisfaction in Scotland … [I] cannot think of the insolent usage I might meet with from the man who has management there, who threatens extirpation and, I am told, regrets that Harry Maule was not forfaulted' (*Stuart Papers*, 7.507).

Only Jacobite sympathizers referred to Maule as the fifth earl of Panmure after the death of his brother. Denied political office he devoted his time to the study of feudal and canon law, and was seen in his old age as a kind of umpire between the different schisms of the Scottish Episcopal church that were developing during this period. His correspondence with James Greenshields, an Episcopalian clergyman of Edinburgh who had been thrown into prison for using the English prayer book, illustrates the depth of his religious knowledge. His scholarship and judgement, as revealed in the many personal, political, and religious letters that have survived, were fully recognized by his contemporaries. While living on the continent Harry and his eldest son, James, carried out extensive research into the history of the Maules, tracing back the family pedigree over 700 years, and in the process accumulated valuable manuscripts relating to the early history of Scotland. In 1874 John Stuart was commissioned by the earl of Dalhousie to edit this collection into two volumes entitled *Registrum de Panmure*. This magnificent work, of which only 150 copies were privately printed, is a lasting tribute to Maule's scholarship. A portrait of the author in armour, copied from the original, is reproduced in this work. His principal residence in Scotland was Kelly Castle in Forfarshire, although he also owned property in Edinburgh from 1711 near the Nether Bow. Maule's second wife died on 12 August 1729 and Maule himself died in Edinburgh on 23 June 1734. He was buried in the abbey church, Holyrood, on 25 June, an honour that reflects the high esteem he was eventually accorded.

HEW BLAIR-IMRIE

Sources H. Maule, *Registrum de Panmure*, ed. J. Stuart, 2 vols. (1874) • NA Scot., Dalhousie MSS, GD 45 • J. Sinclair, *Memoirs of the insurrection in Scotland in 1715*, ed. W. Scott (1858) • *Scots peerage*, 7.22 • J. Foster, *Members of parliament, Scotland … 1357–1882*, 2nd edn (privately printed, London, 1882) • A. J. Warden, *Angus or Forfarshire: the land and people*, 5 vols. (1880–85), vol. 1, p. 403 • G. Lockhart, *The Lockhart papers: containing memoirs and commentaries upon the affairs of Scotland from 1702 to 1715*, 2 vols. (1817) • *The Panmure papers, being a* *selection from the correspondence of Fox Maule*, ed. G. Douglas and G. D. Ramsay, 2 vols. (1908), vol. 1, p. 4 · *Report on the manuscripts of the earl of Mar and Kellie*, HMC, 60 (1904) · *Calendar of the Stuart papers belonging to his majesty the king, preserved at Windsor Castle*, 7 vols., HMC, 56 (1902–23) · GEC, *Peerage*

Archives NA Scot., corresp. and antiquarian collections | NA Scot., letters to earl of Mar

Likenesses attrib. J. Scougall, Scot. NPG [*see illus.*] · portrait (in armour), priv. coll.; repro. in Stuart, ed., *Registrum de Panmure*

Maule, Henry (1676–1758), Church of Ireland bishop of Meath and educational reformer, was the son of William Maule, comptroller of the customs at Dublin, and Jane, daughter of Roger West. Born perhaps at Arklow, Ireland, and educated at Mr Young's school in Dublin, he entered Trinity College, Dublin, in 1691, aged fifteen. He graduated BA in 1696 and later received the degrees of LLB and LLD (in 1719) from the same institution. He was ordained in 1699, and in 1702 he was beneficed in the diocese of Cloyne. His preferment led to a protracted dispute between the bishop, eager to uphold his rights of presentation, and a too independent vicar-general. The wrangle seems to have stimulated Maule's own legal skills and brought him to the attention of clerical superiors, notably Archbishop King of Dublin. In 1706 he was appointed rector of St Mary's, Shandon, in the north of Cork city, a populous parish reckoned to yield an annual £300. There he presided over the establishment of almshouses and a charity school, complete with library. He put into effect what he had seen as he travelled in the Low Countries and England, and what he had read about in Halle. He became a corresponding member of the SPCK, whose London meetings he attended in 1716 and 1718. When in Dublin to forward business he helped to organize an association modelled on the SPCK. Maule used some of his own ample means to finance the Shandon initiatives. His pamphlet of 1721, *Pietas Corcagiensis*, shrewdly publicized what had been achieved through gifts of money and books and the record of pupils already apprenticed to tradespeople in the locality. As a member of a family enriched by office-holding, and married to Lady Anne Barry, daughter of Richard, second earl of Barrymore, he moved confidently among those whose support was vital to his charitable endeavours. Some contemporaries disliked the political and diplomatic dexterity which he displayed. He was suspected, too, of a residual toryism. These traits, when coupled with his birth and upbringing in Ireland and a supposed attachment to Irish as against English interests, delayed further preferment. In 1720 he was appointed dean of Cloyne. Despite the low yield of the deanery (£60 or £70 p.a.), he carried out physical improvements there. He missed the lucrative deaneries of Derry and Down, but in 1726 he was consecrated bishop of Cloyne. In 1732 he was translated to Dromore and then in 1744 to Meath. Following the death of his first wife Maule married twice again, first Catherine Rooth, formerly Stawell, and second, in 1725, Dorothy Roffen (*d.* 1755), a widow of Rossmore.

Much of the credit for drawing the hitherto haphazard ventures to provide protestant education into a coherent system through the Incorporated Society of 1733 went to

Henry Maule (1676–1758), by Andrew Miller, pubd 1747 (after Anthony Lee, 1747)

Archbishop Boulter. However, in 1746 the then lord lieutenant, Chesterfield, gave Maule his due when he acknowledged that without the latter's 'care and perseverance', the charity schools 'would hardly have existed' (J. Ainsworth, ed., *The Inchiquin Manuscripts*, 1961, 160). As bishop of Dromore he continued to set an example, subsidizing a charter school at Ballynahinch. Ardbraccan, his seat as bishop of Meath, saw a similar venture. He also backed the projects of the Royal Dublin Society and the Physico-Historical Society to survey and publicize the natural resources of Ireland as a prelude to their more effective exploitation. In 1733 he made the work of protestant instruction the theme of his sermon before the lord lieutenant and House of Lords on the anniversary of the 1641 uprising. Through a network of schools he aimed to entrench the British and protestant interests in Ireland and bit by bit overcome what he—in common with many contemporaries—saw as the linked evils of ignorance, idleness, and Catholicism. He argued that only by concentrating on the training of the young could the future prosperity and stability of Ireland within the Hanoverian empire be secured. These views differed from those of his fellow Church of Ireland clergyman John Richardson, who wished to use the Irish language to win converts, and it was Maule's approach which was adopted in eighteenth-century Ireland. Maule died on 13 April 1758.

TOBY BARNARD

Sources minutes of Green Coat School, Shandon, Cork · minutes, CUL, SPCK MSS · W. King, correspondence, TCD, Lyons collection, MSS 1995–2008 · W. Wake, correspondence, Christ Church Oxf., Wake MSS 12–14 · W. M. Brady, *Clerical and parochial records of Cork, Cloyne, and Ross*, 3 vols. (1863–4) · H. Cotton, *Fasti ecclesiae Hibernicae*, 6 vols. (1845–78) · Burtchaell & Sadleir, *Alum. Dubl.* ·

Armagh Public Library, Physico-Historical Society MSS · K. Milne, *The Irish charter schools, 1730–1830* (1997) · T. C. Barnard, 'Protestants and the Irish language, c.1675–1725', *Journal of Ecclesiastical History*, 44 (1993), 243–72 · GEC, *Peerage* · *GM*, 1st ser., 23 (1753), 197
Likenesses A. Miller, mezzotint, pubd 1747 (after A. Lee, 1747), NG Ire. [*see illus.*] · engraving, exh. NL Ire. 1999, probably NL Ire. · J. Latham, oils, NG Ire.
Wealth at death see will, abstract by J. B. Leslie, NL Ire., MS 2678, p. 12

Maule, James, fourth earl of Panmure (1658/9–1723), Jacobite sympathizer, was the fifth son of George Maule, second earl of Panmure (1619–1671), and his wife, Lady Jean Campbell (1624/5–1703), eldest daughter of John *Campbell, first earl of Loudoun; Patrick *Maule, first earl of Panmure, was his other grandfather. His first significant public appointment was as an excise commissioner in Forfarshire in October 1680. On 27 July 1681 he had a charter of the lands and mains of Ballumbie, Forfarshire. Maule of Ballumbie, as he was known, travelled abroad and in 1684 served as a volunteer at the siege of Luxembourg. On 1 February 1686 he succeeded the third earl, his brother George (c.1650–1686), as fourth earl of Panmure (the third earl's only son having died before May 1685). He took the oaths in the Scottish parliament on 29 April 1686 and on 13 May he was sworn a member of the Scottish privy council. On 5 February 1687 Panmure was contracted to marry Lady Margaret Hamilton (d. 1731), youngest daughter of William Douglas, third duke of Hamilton [*see* Hamilton, William] (all the children of this marriage took their mother's name). They had no children. In March 1687 he was 'laid aside' (Maule, 2.344) from the privy council for refusing to support James II's declaration of indulgence.

In January 1689 Panmure left Scotland to travel to London, presumably in an attempt to influence the revolutionary settlement in Scotland, in which his father-in-law played a crucial role. On 1 March he was given a pass to return to Edinburgh. By 14 March he was attending the Scottish convention, and on 16 March he signed the declaration that it was a free and lawful meeting. However, he opposed the recognition of William and Mary and retired to his estates. He refused the oaths to the new king and never sat in parliament again, although he held local office as a commissioner of supply in Forfarshire and Aberdeenshire in 1689–94 and again in 1704. During Queen Anne's reign Panmure crops up in Jacobite correspondence as a man to be relied upon: in 1705 his name appeared on a list of those 'who have distinguished themselves for their loyalty since the Revolution' (Hooke, 1.229). He opposed the union with England in 1707, and it was probably his nephew John Erskine, earl of Mar, who protected him from arrest in 1708. In 1709 Panmure's extensive reconstruction of Brechin Castle was completed, a project begun in the 1690s. His name was included on a list of non-juring Scottish peers in July 1713.

In August 1715 Panmure was still adding to his extensive estates, purchasing property from the Lindsays of Edzell for over £16,000. After some initial hesitation, and much to the surprise of those such as the lord justice clerk, he left Edinburgh in 1715 and sailed to his northern estates.

James Maule, fourth earl of Panmure (1658/9–1723), by Sir Godfrey Kneller, 1690

He proclaimed the Pretender (James Stuart) as James III at Brechin and raised a regiment of foot which numbered 415 men and fought at the battle of Sheriffmuir on 13 November. Panmure was wounded in the battle, captured 'so very ill cut in the head that he was left for dead in a house by the enemy' (Sinclair, 227), and then rescued by his brother Harry *Maule (1659–1734). In January 1716 he entertained James III at Brechin Castle, and following the collapse of the rebellion in February he escaped to France. In consideration of his services James III made him a knight of the Thistle on 8 April 1716 (the same day as the duke of Ormond). He was duly attainted by act of parliament for not surrendering himself to justice by 30 June 1716. Panmure joined the Jacobite court at Avignon and travelled with it into Italy. By May 1717 he was 'in a dismal way, and full of his old splenetic notions' (*Stuart Papers*, 4.253), feeling neglected and kept out of secrets. By February 1718 he was *en route* for France via Venice, in the hope that judicious bribery would enable him to return to Britain. The earl of Mar put his disillusionment down to his doctor, who had cured his wounds but not his mind, and 'to his natural temper and want of knowing the world, having never been much in business nor conversed much with those that were' (ibid., 6.90).

Once in Paris, Panmure made contact with the British ambassador, the earl of Stair, but found the way to a pardon blocked 'unless I would make engagements never to act according to the principles I have all my life been of' (*Stuart Papers*, 7.669–70). He settled in Paris and made a trip to Maule in France, where he established a family connection to the Maules and Valoniis of Normandy. Panmure died of pleurisy in Paris on 11 April 1723, aged sixty-four. He was survived by his wife, who died on 6 December 1731. In 1717 she had been the beneficiary of an act of parliament which provided maintenance for her as if her husband was already dead. After a determined rearguard action by Lady Panmure, in which she enlisted the aid of two lords of session, the family estates, valued at £3456 per annum, were sold to the York Building Company for £60,400 in October 1719. The company leased them back to Lady Panmure and Harry Maule in 1724. The family regained the estates when William *Maule (1699/1700–1782), son of Harry, purchased them in 1764.

STUART HANDLEY

Sources GEC, *Peerage* · *First report*, HMC, 1/1 (1870); repr. (1874), 117–19 · *Calendar of the Stuart papers belonging to his majesty the king, preserved at Windsor Castle*, 7 vols., HMC, 56 (1902–23), vols. 2, 4–7 · H. Maule, *Registrum de Panmure*, ed. J. Stuart, 2 vols. (1874) · A. Boyer, *The political state of Great Britain*, 25 (1723), 467 · P. Gouldesbrough, 'The Dalhousie muniments in the Scottish Record Office', *Archives*, 5 (1961), 65–74 · *Scots peerage*, 7.24–6 · J. Sinclair, *Memoirs of the insurrection in Scotland in 1715*, ed. W. Scott (1858) · A. H. Millar, ed., *A selection of Scottish forfeited estate papers, 1715, 1745*, Scottish History Society, 57 (1909), xviii · *Correspondence of Colonel N. Hooke*, ed. W. D. Macray, 2 vols., Roxburghe Club, 92, 95 (1870–71) · B. Lenman, *The Jacobite risings in Britain, 1689–1746* (1995) · A. J. Warden, *Angus or Forfarshire: the land and people*, 5 vols. (1800–05), vol. 1, pp. 400–2 · R. Patten, *The history of the late rebellion* (1717)
Archives NA Scot., corresp. · NL Scot., collection of music books | NA Scot., Dalhousie MSS, papers
Likenesses G. Kneller, portrait, 1690, Brechin Castle, Scotland [*see illus.*] · H. Maule, engraving (after a portrait), repro. in Maule, *Registrum de Panmure* · D. Patton, miniature, Lennoxlove House, East Lothian · attrib. J. Scougall, Scot. NPG

Maule, John, of Inverkeilor (1706–1781), politician, was the second surviving son of Harry *Maule, styled fifth earl of Panmure (1659–1734), and his second wife, Anne (d. 1729), daughter of Patrick Lindsay, who from 1669 assumed the surname and arms of Crawford of Kilbirnie, Ayrshire. Whereas Maule's father was a Jacobite, active in the 1715 rising and afterwards in exile, Maule had a successful career because of his being a staunch whig. He was admitted to the Faculty of Advocates in Scotland in 1725, though it was said of him in 1744 that, in the law, 'bussiness or practice' had he not (Shaw, 70). Instead he became, in the late 1730s, confidential political secretary to Archibald, earl of Ilay, and, in 1737, keeper of the register of sasines. He was 'an irrepressible, hard-drinking bachelor' whose correspondence with Ilay's political associates, notably Andrew Fletcher, Lord Milton of the court of session in Scotland, abounds with 'earthy asides' (Lindsay and Cosh, 65). Maule was a well-oiled cog in a well-oiled machine for the control of Scottish politics.

Maule's elder half-brother William *Maule, in 1743 created earl of Panmure of Forth in the Irish peerage, was another staunch whig, and it was he who engineered Maule's return as MP for the Aberdeen burghs at a by-election in 1739. The whig Maules, none the less, found it hard to escape suspicions of Jacobitism. During the 1745 rising the magistrates of Edinburgh searched John Maule's house. The maid refused them entrance to a locked room, which she said was full of arms. These proved to be coats of arms, collected by Maule's father, who had been an antiquary as well as Jacobite. Maule and his brother Lord Panmure sent a memorandum to Henry Pelham, denying the charges of Jacobitism against them made by the duke of Cumberland and others in 1746, and John Maule was unanimously re-elected MP in 1747. In August 1748 he stepped down, having been appointed—through the influence of Ilay, from 1743 third duke of Argyll—a baron of the court of exchequer in Edinburgh. A court of session judge wrote at the time that 'mr Maule is to be our Baron, of which I wish him joy. It is an honourable and genteel retreat from more publick business' (Shaw, 70). John Maule died, unmarried, on 2 July 1781.

JOHN M. SIMPSON

Sources M. Bricke, 'The Pelhams vs. Argyll: a struggle for the mastery of Scotland, 1747–1748', *SHR*, 61 (1982), 157–65 · GEC, *Peerage* · R. R. Sedgwick, 'Maule, John', HoP, *Commons, 1715–54*, 2.248 · I. G. Lindsay and M. Cosh, *Inveraray and the dukes of Argyll* (1973) · J. Maule, correspondence, NL Scot., Fletcher of Saltoun MSS · A. Murdoch, 'The people above': politics and administration in mid-eighteenth-century Scotland (1980) · letter-book of J. Maule, 1748–61, NL Scot., MS 10781 · *Scots peerage* · J. S. Shaw, *The management of Scottish society, 1707–1764: power, nobles, lawyers, Edinburgh agents and English influences* (1983)
Archives NA Scot., corresp. · NL Scot., catalogue of his library · NL Scot., letter-book | NA Scot., letters to John Clerk · NL Scot., corresp. with General Campbell

Maule, Patrick, first earl of Panmure (1585–1661), courtier, was born on 29 May 1585, probably at Bolshan, Forfarshire, the son of Patrick Maule (1548–1605), fiar of Panmure, and Margaret (d. 1599), daughter of Sir John Erskine of Dun. In March 1600 his father succeeded Thomas Maule as laird of Panmure. By 1603 the seventeen-year-old Maule was serving as page to James VI, who had been impressed by his 'cariage' in royal hunting expeditions (MacFarlane, 2.153). In April he accompanied the king to England and served as groom of the bedchamber under Sir George Home, who arranged for his livery and annual payment of £20. On 1 May 1605 Maule succeeded his father as thirteenth laird of Panmure, but remained at Whitehall, where he was then earning £65 per annum as one of the king's servants. On 7 March 1610 the king granted him the lands and barony of Panmure. In 1616 Maule married Frances, daughter of the late Sir Edward Stanhope of Grimston, Yorkshire. Before her death in January 1624, the couple had four children: George Maule, Lord Brechin (1619–1671); Henry Maule (bap. 1621, d. 1667) of Balmakellie; Jean (d. 1685); and Elizabeth (d. 1647). Maule was appointed to supervise repairs at Eltham Park on 28 March 1621, and by early 1625 was made its keeper.

Retaining his personal popularity with King Charles, on 4 May 1625 Maule was given the manor of Collyweston in Northamptonshire (which he sold to Attorney-General Sir Robert Heath in 1631). His inoffensive personality gained him the support of the duke of Buckingham, who wrote to the king while on campaign in France (August 1627), recommending that Maule be appointed gentleman usher. It was during this period that he married his second wife, Mary Waldrum (d. 1637), a maid of honour to the queen. Maule maintained his Scottish connections with his receipt of Downie barony in March 1629 and through his personal appearance at Holyroodhouse on 5 September 1632 to accept the principal sheriffship of Forfar. This was soon followed by his honorary appointment as burgess of Dundee 'for the innumerable benefits which he has conferred on the said Burgh' (Millar, 144). He expanded his business interests in the 1630s, obtaining a special grant of British exports to Africa (13 October 1634) and a thirty-one-year monopoly on soap manufacture (6 November). After his grant of the baronies of Brechin, Navar, and Balmakellie on 15 October 1634, he began to take a keener interest in Scottish affairs, serving as JP for Forfar and depute of the admiralty between Southwater and Bruchtie, in addition to asserting his rights over appointments to the magistracy of Brechin, over those claimed with equal vehemence by the bishop. Maule also happened to be present in Scotland during the prayer book riots of 1637.

On 15 July 1639 Maule married his third wife, Lady Mary Erskine (d. 1672), widow of William *Keith, fifth Earl Marischal, and daughter of John *Erskine, eighteenth earl of Mar. Throughout this period he expressed sympathies with the supplicants and later with the covenanters, as shown in his correspondence with his nephew Alexander Erskine of Dun and the earl (later marquess) of Montrose, though he never wavered in his personal loyalty to the king. From 1642 to 1643 he attended Charles at York and Oxford, and was eventually elevated to the peerage on 2 August 1646 as the earl of Panmure, Lord Maule of Brechin and Navar. He was one of the few bedchamber servants to remain with the king, and reputedly the last to leave him at Carisbrooke Castle, though there is no evidence to suggest that he followed the king from Hampton Court to the Isle of Wight in 1647. His reputation for loyalty led to a place on the commission of war for Kincardine and Forfar on 15 February 1648, and by 2 March he was in attendance at parliament in Edinburgh, listed thirtieth among thirty-two earls.

Oliver Cromwell seems to have distrusted Panmure, perhaps resenting his implication in Charles's escape from Hampton Court on 11 November 1647 and his subsequent gift of £2000 to the exiled Charles II in 1651. In April 1654 the protector fined him £10,000 under the Act of Grace and Pardon, a massive sum which was reduced to £4000 in March 1655. After issuing payment on 26 June, Panmure spent his last years trying to secure revenues, such as that of the Irish customs, and serving as commissioner to collect assessments in Forfar. Throughout his bedchamber career he had been able to revitalize his family's estates which had reached a low ebb in the late sixteenth century under his grandfather Thomas. Panmure himself died on 22 December 1661, probably at Panbride, and was soon afterward buried in the family vaults at Panbride. His widow died in December 1672.

J. R. M. SIZER

Sources GEC, *Peerage*, new edn, vol. 10 · *First report*, HMC, 1/1 (1870); repr. (1874) · *CSP dom.*, 1603–49 · *Reg. PCS*, 2nd ser. · testament, NA Scot., CC 3/3/6 · H. Maule, *Registrum de Panmure*, ed. J. Stuart, 2 vols. (1874) · NA Scot., GD 406/1/971; 973; 1000; 8348 · P. Donald, *An uncounselled king: Charles I and the Scottish troubles, 1637–41* (1990) · K. M. Brown, *Noble society in Scotland: wealth, family and culture, from Reformation to Revolution* (2000) · W. Macfarlane, *Genealogical collections concerning families in Scotland*, ed. J. T. Clark, 2, Scottish History Society, 34 (1900) · letters, NL Scot., Morton MS 84 · A. H. Millar, *Roll of eminent burgesses of Dundee, 1513–1886* (1887)
Archives NA Scot., corresp. and papers | NA Scot., Dalhousie muniments, GD 45: especially sections 16 and 17 · NA Scot., Hamilton muniments, GD 406 · NL Scot., Morton papers, letters, MS 84, II
Wealth at death testament valued at £17,333; additional debts owing to him approx. £19,400: NA Scot., CC 3/3/6, fols. 274v–275r, 25 Feb 1664

Maule, William, earl of Panmure of Forth (1699/1700–1782), politician and landowner, was the third but eldest surviving son of the five children of Harry *Maule (1659–1734) and his first wife, Lady Mary Fleming (d. 1702), daughter of William, fifth earl of Wigtown. William Maule was the last male of the house of Maule, a family that could trace an unbroken descent in the male line for 760 years. His father was the younger brother of James *Maule, fourth earl of Panmure (1658/9–1723). Both his father and uncle were ardent Jacobites who fought at Sheriffmuir and, as a consequence, forfeited their estates in Forfarshire and spent many years abroad in exile. Maule was educated at Leiden (1718) and the Scots College in Paris (1719) and despite his unfortunate family affiliations was presented at court on the succession of George II in 1727. He appears to have been a committed Hanoverian and was able to obtain a commission at that time in the 25th infantry regiment, although his progress in the army was not as rapid as he might have wished. However, after service at Dettingen in the War of the Austrian Succession (1743) he was raised to an Irish peerage as Viscount Maule of Whitechurch and earl of Panmure of Forth. Two years later he served at the battle of Fontenoy; further commissions in the Royal Scots Fusiliers and the Scots Greys and a posting to Gibraltar in 1753 led to his eventual promotion to the rank of colonel in 1770.

Under the patronage of the earl of Ilay, Panmure became MP for Forfarshire in 1735, an office he held until his death, despite a vigorous challenge by Thomas Lyon (son of the earl of Strathmore) in 1768. Lyon's bid led supporters of both candidates to create votes through artificial divisions of their estates. This resulted in a multitude of appeals and counter appeals to the court of session and the House of Lords, and a temporary dislocation of the Forfarshire commission of supply as it split on the question of the division of the cess. The resulting conflict cost Panmure in the region of £20,000, and prompted him to strike a deal with Lyon to prevent future contests. In the whole of his forty-seven years as a member of parliament there are no recorded instances of his speaking in the House of Commons.

As the eldest son at his father's death (23 June 1734), Panmure took on the responsibility of regaining the family's

William Maule, earl of Panmure of Forth (1699/1700–1782), by Allan Ramsay, 1749

forfeited land. During the 1730s he negotiated with the York Buildings Company to buy back the estates, currently leased to Sir Archibald Grant and Garden of Troup on a 29-year tack. Panmure attempted to purchase the lease or to have a superior lease inserted between the York Buildings Company and the existing tenant to strengthen his position should the land come up for sale. The company's disorganized financial situation was such that lengthy and costly legal discussions yielded few tangible results, and it was not until 1763 that his friend Alexander Forrester finally piloted a bill through the House of Commons authorizing the auction of the Panmure estate. In Edinburgh on 20 February 1764 Panmure, the sole bidder, bought back his family estates for £49,157 18s. 4d., somewhat less than the £72,000 that he had estimated. A popular, benevolent, and charitable man, as a landlord Panmure showed considerable interest in his tenants' well-being and in the improvement of his estates. His efforts provide a good example of the rehabilitation of former Jacobite families back into the Scottish landed establishment during the second half of the eighteenth century. Panmure died, unmarried, on 4 January 1782, at which point his estate was entailed to George, eighth earl of Dalhousie, the husband of his sister Jean.

HEW BLAIR-IMRIE

Sources H. Maule, *Registrum de Panmure*, ed. J. Stuart, 2 vols. (1874) • HoP, *Commons, 1715–54* • GEC, *Peerage* • Dalhousie MS, NA Scot., GD 45.16 • A. J. Warden, *Angus or Forfarshire: the land and people*, 5 vols. (1880–85) • *Scots peerage* • *The Panmure papers, being a selection from the correspondence of Fox Maule*, ed. G. Douglas and G. D. Ramsay, 2 vols. (1908), vol. 1

Archives NA Scot., corresp. and military papers | NA Scot., letters to Sir John Ogilvy • NRA, priv. coll., letters to earl of Southesk
Likenesses A. Ramsay, portrait, 1749, priv. coll. [*see illus.*]

Maule, Sir William Henry (1788–1858), judge, was born on 25 April 1788 at Edmonton, Middlesex, the son of Henry Maule, a medical practitioner, and his wife, Hannah, *née* Rawson, a Quaker from Leeds. Maule was educated at a private school run by his uncle, John Maule, rector of Greenford, Middlesex, who was described by Charles Greville, a fellow pupil at the school, as 'an excellent scholar and a great brute' (C. Greville, *Memoirs*, 1885, 2.101). Greville described Maule himself as 'a very clever boy'. In October 1806 Maule matriculated from Trinity College, Cambridge, where he was senior wrangler in the mathematical tripos of 1810 and also won the first Smith's prize. In October 1811 he was elected a fellow of Trinity. After taking his MA degree he stayed in Cambridge for some time, working as a mathematical coach. Among his pupils was Edward Ryan, afterwards chief justice of Calcutta, who remained a lifelong close friend. Another of his Cambridge friends was Charles Babbage, the mathematician.

In the autumn of 1810 Maule became a student at Lincoln's Inn. While still a student there he was offered, but declined, the professorship of mathematics at East India College, Haileybury. In 1814 he was called to the bar, took chambers at 3 Essex Court, Temple, and joined the Oxford circuit. His progress at the bar was slow at first, but he gradually obtained a reputation and business as a commercial lawyer, becoming an authority on marine insurance. He became king's counsel in Easter term 1833 and in 1835 was appointed counsel to the Bank of England in succession to Sir James Scarlett, who had been appointed chief baron. Not only did this position earn him a good deal of money but it also enabled him to act as leading counsel for the sitting member in the county Carlow election petition. His success in the case led to his being returned for Carlow borough as a Liberal MP at the general election in August 1837.

In March 1839 Maule was appointed a baron of the exchequer in succession to Baron Bolland and was knighted. In Michaelmas term 1839 he was transferred to the common pleas on the death of Mr Justice Vaughan. He continued a member of that court until June 1855, when he resigned because of ill health. Shortly after his resignation, Maule was sworn of the privy council, and acted as a member of the judicial committee until his death.

Maule was considered by his colleagues to be an excellent judge who combined common sense with legal knowledge, and was affectionately remembered for his humorous irony. At the Warwick assizes, for instance, while sentencing to one day's imprisonment a poor man convicted of bigamy, whose first wife had deserted him and lived with another man, Maule outlined at length to the bemused prisoner the various legal steps which he must take in order to obtain a divorce at the cost of about £1000.

Maule died unmarried on 16 January 1858 at the home

he shared with his widowed sister, Emma Maria Leathley, and his unmarried niece, Emma Leathley, at 22 Hyde Park Gardens, London.

J. D. FitzGerald, rev. Hugh Mooney

Sources E. Foss, *Biographia juridica: a biographical dictionary of the judges of England … 1066–1870* (1870) • *Law Magazine*, new ser., 5 (1858), 1–34 • *Solicitors' Journal*, 2 (1857–8), 236 • *Law Times* (23 Jan 1858), 247–8 • *CGPLA Eng. & Wales* (1858)
Likenesses J. Bailey, bust, 1858, Lincoln's Inn, London • G. Richmond, drawing, 1862 (after drawing, 1852), Lincoln's Inn, London
Wealth at death under £35,000: probate, 1858, *CGPLA Eng. & Wales*

Maule, William Ramsay, first Baron Panmure (1771–1852), aristocrat, second son of George Ramsay, eighth earl of Dalhousie (*d.* 1787), and his wife, Elizabeth, daughter of Andrew Glen, and niece and heir of James Glen of Longcroft, Stirlingshire, was born on 27 October 1771. His father's maternal uncle, William Maule, earl of Panmure of Forth, died unmarried in 1782, and left his property to the eighth earl of Dalhousie, with remainder to Dalhousie's second son, William. Dalhousie died in 1787, when William succeeded to the valuable Panmure estates and adopted the name of Maule. He was twice married: first, on 1 December 1794, to Patricia Heron (*d.* 1821), daughter of Gilbert Gordon of Halleaths; they had three sons and seven daughters. On learning of his dissolute activities in London, his wife left him and returned to her family in Ireland. When his eldest son, Fox *Maule (later eleventh earl of Dalhousie), took his mother's part, Maule cut him off with only £100 a year and never saw him again. Maule's second wife, whom he married on 4 June 1822, was Elizabeth Barton (*d.* 1867), daughter of John William Barton of Hospitalfield, Forfarshire; they had no children.

In 1788 Maule purchased a cornetcy in the 11th dragoons, and afterwards raised an independent company of foot, which was disbanded in 1791. He was MP for Forfar, in April–May 1796, and in 1803–31. He joined the Whig Club in 1798 and was a steady adherent of Fox, after whom his eldest son was named. He virtually never spoke in the Commons, but supported the whigs on most major divisions until 1813. He was a founder member of the Hampden Club and helped secure Joseph Hulme's election for Aberdeen burghs.

On 9 September 1831 Maule was raised to the peerage as Baron Panmure. As a young man he was one of the most dissipated and extravagant, even of the Scottish gentry of his younger days, and survived them, thanks to a constitution of extraordinary strength and a fortune of vast resources. He did not alter his manner or morals as he grew older, and scandalized Victorian observers. He was devoted to his friends so long as they remained complaisant, and violent and implacable to all who thwarted him. His uncontrollable temper eventually alienated him from nearly all his family in his latter years, yet he performed many unostentatious acts of charity. In politics he was a liberal, and his views were invariably humane; in private life he was an immovable despot. He died at Brechin Castle, Forfarshire, on 13 April 1852.

J. A. Hamilton, rev. K. D. Reynolds

Sources HoP, *Commons* • GEC, *Peerage* • *The Panmure papers, being a selection from the correspondence of Fox Maule*, ed. G. Douglas and G. D. Ramsay, 2 vols. (1908) • J. Paterson, *Kay's Edinburgh portraits: a series of anecdotal biographies chiefly of Scotchmen*, ed. J. Maidment, 2 vols. (1885) • Boase, *Mod. Eng. biog.*
Archives NA Scot., corresp. | NA Scot., Dalhousie MSS, corresp., GD45 • NA Scot., corresp. with Colonel Andrew Leith Hay • NRA, priv. coll., letters to Sinclair • W. Sussex RO, letters to duke of Richmond
Likenesses I. C. Smith, oils, Scot. NPG

Mauleverer, John (*c.*1610–1650). *See under* Mauleverer, Sir Thomas, first baronet (*bap.* 1599, *d.* 1655).

Mauleverer, Sir Richard, second baronet (*bap.* 1623, *d.* 1675). *See under* Mauleverer, Sir Thomas, first baronet (*bap.* 1599, *d.* 1655).

Mauleverer, Sir Thomas, first baronet (*bap.* 1599, *d.* 1655), politician and regicide, was born at Allerton Mauleverer, Yorkshire, and baptized there on 9 April 1599, the eldest son of Sir Richard Mauleverer of Allerton Mauleverer (*c.*1528–1603), high sheriff of Yorkshire in 1588, and his second wife, Katherine, daughter of Sir Ralph Bourchier of Beningbrough and his first wife, Elizabeth. He matriculated from St John's College, Cambridge, in 1616 and was admitted to Gray's Inn on 22 October 1617. His first wife was Mary, daughter of Sir Richard Hutton, justice of the common pleas. In 1622 he married his second wife, Elizabeth (*d.* 1653), daughter of Thomas Wilbraham of Woodhey, Cheshire. In 1630 he was prosecuted for failure to compound in distraint of knighthood and during the 1630s he served regularly as a West Riding JP alongside Ferdinando Fairfax. In July 1640 he signed the Yorkshire gentry's petition against the king's billeting of soldiers, and he was elected MP for Boroughbridge that November. The king created him baronet of Allerton Mauleverer on 4 August 1641, but his association with the Fairfaxes led him to sign their anti-royalist declaration at Otley on 29 August 1642. Ferdinando, now Baron Fairfax and parliament's general in Yorkshire, appointed him to negotiate the neutrality treaty concluded at Rothwell on 29 September, but the truce soon collapsed and Mauleverer was besieged by royalists in his home at Allerton Mauleverer. On 23 October, Fairfax sent a troop of horse to rescue him, and Mauleverer was subsequently appointed a colonel, raising a troop of horse and regiment of foot.

In January 1643 Mauleverer appeared sixth on the royalists' list of Yorkshire traitors and he has been described as 'one of the most zealous parliamentarians in Yorkshire' (Cliffe, 338). Thomas Gent defamed him as 'one of those Black-Guards of Usurpation', alleging that his unruly soldiers 'in a sacrilegious Manner, broke the windows and defac'd the Monuments' in the collegiate church of Ripon (T. Gent, *Ancient and Modern History of the Loyal Town of Ripon*, 1733, 118). By May 1643 he was a sequestrator and a member of parliament's county committee. He was among Fairfax's army routed at Adwalton Moor on 30 June, but escaped with Fairfax on a boat from Selby to Hull. With the royalists about to besiege Hull, on 27 August Fairfax appointed him to seek out traitors and spies in the town. In January 1644 Mauleverer accompanied Sir Thomas Fairfax into Cheshire to relieve Nantwich. During his absences Allerton Mauleverer was plundered, and he later accused Sir William Ingram of seizing corn valued at £500 in his tithe barn.

On 7 November 1645 Mauleverer informed Speaker Lenthall that the parliamentarian forces refused to reduce Skipton Castle, urging their immediate payment, the removal of the Scots from Yorkshire, and that excise money be used locally. On 3 May 1647 he submitted his pay accounts, and his son-in-law, Thomas Scot, brought his petition before the Commons for reimbursement of his £15,000 war expenses. Both houses voted £1000 from the excise and ordered the committee for northern affairs to organize further repayments. Mauleverer attended the king's trial and signed the death warrant [see also Regicides]. He remained as a West Riding JP, but his public career ended when the Rump Parliament was dismissed in 1653. He had died by 9 June 1655, but was exempted from the Restoration Act of Pardon.

His eldest son, **Sir Richard Mauleverer**, second baronet (*bap.* 1623, *d.* 1675), politician, was born at Allerton Mauleverer and baptized there on 28 September 1623. He was admitted to Gray's Inn on 12 July 1641, and on 10 August the next year married Anne (*b. c.*1622), daughter of Sir Robert Clarke of Pleshey, Essex. His father granted him an annuity of £500, which was subsequently removed for his disobedient royalism. He was knighted for his royalist service at Christ Church, Oxford, on 27 March 1645. After the war he petitioned that he declared himself to the committee for compounding, and owing to his debts of £1500 he was fined only £4 6s. 6d. until his annuity could be recovered. Declared an outlaw in 1654, he was captured during a royalist rising in Yorkshire the following year. He made a daring escape from Chester Castle on 26 March, reaching The Hague in June. Imprisoned on his return to London in 1659, he was released on bail in September. He joined the king at Breda and was appointed a gentleman of the privy chamber in June 1660. He was commissioned as colonel of militia, and his baronetcy and estates, valued at £1200 per year, were restored. He was elected MP for Boroughbridge on 8 April 1661 and was commissioned as captain in Lord Gerard's regiment in 1666. He remained an inactive court MP, and was granted £200 royal bounty on 30 April 1675. He was buried in Westminster Abbey on 25 July 1675.

John Mauleverer (*c.*1610–1650), army officer, was the eldest son of John Mauleverer of Letwell, Yorkshire, and his second wife, Margaret, daughter of John Lewis of Marr, Yorkshire. He married Dorcas, daughter of John Matthew and granddaughter of Toby Matthew, archbishop of York. In the civil wars he sided with the Fairfaxes, who commissioned him as colonel. He headed the list of prisoners taken by the royalists in Bradford in July 1643 but escaped or was exchanged, because by 1644 he commanded Hull's garrison regiment. The Fairfaxes nominated him as Hull's

lieutenant-governor, and the town's MP, Peregrine Pelham, informed the corporation on 15 April 1645:

> I p'ceive by your Northerne Burgesses that they have noe desire that Mr Malleveror should command at Hull. They say he is strange to them, and soe he is to most of the House. He would not have been nominated in the House without much difficulty. (T. Tindall Wildridge, ed., *The Hull Letters: Documents from the Hull Records, 1625–46*, 1886, 63)

On 14 April 1646 Mauleverer was admitted as an elder brother to Hull Trinity House, and on 13 June Fairfax thanked him for refusing Mrs Hotham's demands to search Sir John Hotham's townhouse for property Fairfax had confiscated. In 1648 Mauleverer's regiment helped besiege Pontefract and in 1650 they were allotted to Cromwell's army invading Scotland. He died from fatigue at Edinburgh in December 1650, and Cromwell recalled: 'he had a spirit very much beyond his natural strength of body, having undergone many fits of sickness during his hard service in the field' (T. Carlyle, *Letters and Speeches of Oliver Cromwell*, ed. S. C. Lomas, 3 vols., 1904, 3.272).

ANDREW J. HOPPER

Sources GEC, *Baronetage*, vol. 2 · J. T. Battick, 'Mauleverer, Sir Thomas', Greaves & Zaller, *BDBR*, 2.228–9 · Keeler, *Long Parliament* · P. A. Bolton, P. Watson, and J. P. Ferris, 'Mauleverer, Sir Richard', HoP, *Commons, 1660–90* · J. T. Cliffe, *The Yorkshire gentry from the Reformation to the civil war* (1969) · *DNB* · *Fourteen articles of peace propounded to the king and parliament by the county of York* (1642) · *A perfect narrative of the late proceedings of the parliament of Scotland in relation to the affaires of England; also the manner of the funeral of the Right Honourable Ferdinando Lord Fairfax* (1648) [Thomason tract E 433(13)] · York Minster Library, civil war tracts, 42-09-08; 42-10-04; 42-11-03; 42-12-16; 43-02-04 · F. W. Slingsby, ed., *Registers of the parish church of Allerton-Mauleverer*, Yorkshire Parish Record Society, 31 (1908) · J. Lister, ed., *West Riding sessions records*, 2, Yorkshire Archaeological Society, 54 (1915) · *The parliamentary or constitutional history of England*, 2nd edn, 24 vols. (1751–62), vol. 12 · Margaret, duchess of Newcastle [M. Cavendish], *The life of William Cavendish, duke of Newcastle*, ed. C. H. Firth, 2nd rev. edn (1906) · J. W. Clay, ed., *Yorkshire royalist composition papers*, 3, Yorkshire Archaeological Society, 20 (1896), 5 · Hull City RO, BRS/7/19 · PRO, SP 19/116/25–27, 28/252/363, 23/215/263, 28/138/5 · Venn, *Alum. Cant.* · T. Malbon and E. Burghall, *Memorials of the civil war in Cheshire and the adjacent counties*, ed. J. Hall, Lancashire and Cheshire RS, 19 (1889) · *The manuscripts of his grace the duke of Portland*, 10 vols., HMC, 29 (1891–1931), vol. 1 · will, PRO, PROB 6/31, fol. 126r · J. Foster, ed., *The visitation of Yorkshire made in the years 1584/5 ... to which is added the subsequent visitation made in 1612* (privately printed, London, 1875) · F. W. Brooks, ed., *The first order book of Hull Trinity House, 1632–1665*, Yorkshire Archaeological Society, record ser., 105 (1941) · J. Foster, ed., *Pedigrees of the county families of Yorkshire*, 3 vols. (1874)

Archives Hull Central Library, MSS relating to the Hothams and the civil wars · U. Nott., Galway of Serlby MSS

Wealth at death three manors, incl. 3000 acres at £1500 p.a.: Clay, ed., *Yorkshire royalist composition papers*

Mauleverer, Sir Thomas, third baronet (*c.*1643–1687), politician and army officer, was the eldest son of Sir Richard *Mauleverer (*bap.* 1623, *d.* 1675) [see under Mauleverer, Sir Thomas (*bap.* 1599, *d.* 1655)], the second baronet, and his wife, Anne (*b. c.*1622), daughter of Sir Robert Clarke of Pleshey, Essex. He succeeded his father to the title on the latter's death in July 1675. He first attempted to enter parliament for the seat of Aldborough at a by-election in July 1678, in the court interest, but was unsuccessful. He then represented Boroughbridge, Yorkshire, near his family seat at Allerton, in the parliaments of March and October 1678, 1681, and 1685. He remained in the court interest throughout the exclusion crisis: Shaftesbury marked him as 'base' in 1679, and he was listed as one who 'abhorred' the campaign of petitioning the king to meet his prorogued parliament in 1680. His support was not particularly active, however, since he may not even have attended the second Exclusion Parliament or the third Exclusion Parliament of 1681.

Mauleverer held a commission as major in a regiment of foot from 1678, probably until his death. As the second to the colonel of his regiment, he ran his opponent through in a duel in November 1678, and three years later he received a cut to the face when he tried to separate two fellow officers in a quarrel. He was a commissioner for the (taxation) assessment for the West Riding from 1673 to 1680, and in the latter year was appointed deputy lieutenant and JP for Yorkshire, positions he held until his death.

In January 1684 Mauleverer and some other Yorkshire gentry tried to show their diligence for the king's service, and at the same time discredit the local potentate Sir John Reresby, by claiming that the latter was protecting the town of York from *quo warranto* proceedings which would have led to the forfeiture of the town's charter, but the more politically adept Reresby frustrated them by showing that the town was being run very much in the court's interest. On news of the death of Charles II in February 1685 Mauleverer took action to stifle rumours that the king had been poisoned, and during the duke of Monmouth's rebellion four months later he raised an independent troop of horse to help secure the north. James II's Catholicizing policy, however, strained his loyalty. Danby marked him among the parliamentary opposition in 1685, and he resolutely resisted inducements by the king during the latter's 'closeting' campaign in 1687; but he died suddenly in that year before the king could punish him by removing him from his offices.

Mauleverer had married Katherine, the daughter and heir of Sir Miles Stapleton of Wighill, Yorkshire, but the marriage was not a success and they had no children, though Mauleverer fathered at least one illegitimate child. He was buried in Westminster Abbey on 13 August 1687, and the baronetcy passed to his younger brother Richard. His widow then married her cousin John Hopton of Ingerskill, Yorkshire, and died, still without children, in 1704.   ROBIN CLIFTON

Sources HoP, *Commons, 1660–90* · A. Browning, *Thomas Osborne, earl of Danby and duke of Leeds, 1632–1712,* 3 vols. (1944–51) · *DNB* · GEC, *Baronetage,* 2.117 · *Memoirs of Sir John Reresby,* ed. A. Browning, 2nd edn, ed. M. K. Geiter and W. A. Speck (1991) · *CSP dom.,* 1675–87

Mauley family (*per. c.*1226–1415), barons, of Mulgrave, Cleveland, emerged from obscurity in the early thirteenth century as a result of royal patronage, and are in many ways representative of the middling peerage of later medieval England. Despite the problems of untangling individual careers, seven successive lords of Mulgrave can be shown to have reached their majority and tended to their local interests in Yorkshire, and to the related burdens of military service and shire administration; yet they also made occasional forays into national politics. Indeed, the Mauleys were one of a small group of families summoned to parliament consistently throughout the fourteenth century, from 1295 until the failure of the male line in 1415.

The continued importance of the Mauley family was based on their extensive Yorkshire estates. The Fossard portion of the barony of Doncaster, held by Peter (I) de Maulay in right of his wife, provided the nucleus, and this impressive patrimony was augmented steadily by later generations through marriage to members of the local baronage and gentry. Connections were thus forged with the families of Brus, Clifford, Furnival, Sutton, and Neville. In 1279 the family estates were worth £321. Though precise valuations are elusive, by the early fifteenth century the family estates were worth in the region of £250, with concentrations of Mauley influence at Mulgrave Castle near Whitby, in the barony of Doncaster, and in the East Riding around Beverley. Whitby Abbey, Grosmont in Eskdale, and the Franciscan establishment at Doncaster were among those local religious houses to feel the benefits of the Mauleys' prosperity in the form of endowments and bequests.

The foundations of the family were laid by Peter (I) de *Maulay (*d.* 1241), a Poitevin nobleman who found advancement in the service of King John. None of Peter (I)'s descendants were quite as well connected, or conspicuous in national affairs, but what they lacked in national prominence they more than made up for in regional importance. By this token the career of his son **Peter (II) Mauley** (*c.*1226–1279) was undistinguished: his personal life—apart from two apparently uneventful marriages—is obscure, while his military exploits were characterized by debt and disgrace. In 1253–4 Mauley earned Henry III's displeasure by returning home from Gascony without leave, and in 1268 he owed his Jewish creditors 2000 marks, one of several barons so indebted. His son and heir, **Peter (III) Mauley**, first Lord Mauley (1249–1308), was of more typical stock, making his mark both in military and civil affairs. His marriage to Nichola (*d.* 1284), daughter and coheir of Sir Gilbert de Gaunt of Healaugh, proved lucrative, and having obtained livery of his lands in 1279 he embarked on a long and distinguished military career, serving in Edward I's Welsh wars during the 1280s, in Gascony in 1294–5, and frequently in Scotland until 1304. Mauley's opinion on military matters was obviously valued for he attended a royal assembly at Shrewsbury in June 1283, and a military council at Gloucester three years later. From 1295 onwards he was summoned to parliament. This activity brought both risks and rewards: the king's grant, in 1297, of the marriage of Thomas Multon of Gilsland must be balanced against Mauley's debts of over £600 incurred in Gascony, for which he was initially held hostage in 1299, though later pardoned. Towards the end of his life Mauley found more sedate employment as a justice of trailbaston in 1305 and 1307, and as a justice of oyer and terminer.

The example set by the first Lord Mauley was followed by the next three generations. **Peter (IV) Mauley**, second Lord Mauley (1281–1336?), was knighted with the prince of Wales in 1306, and was evidently a rather volatile man. Having married Eleanor, daughter of Thomas, Lord Furnival, Mauley was implicated in numerous transgressions, including, in 1316, the robbery of Watton Priory in Yorkshire. Moreover, the second Lord Mauley seems to have cultivated a dangerous association with the Lancastrian coalition against Piers Gaveston (d. 1313), but was shrewd enough to distance himself from the increasingly belligerent Thomas, earl of Lancaster, before the battle of Boroughbridge in 1322. Notwithstanding these peccadilloes Mauley made an important contribution to Edward II's Scottish campaigns and to the military administration of the marches, where he served as a warden in 1315. His son and heir, **Peter (V) Mauley**, third Lord Mauley (d. 1355), was from a similar mould. In 1332 the future Lord Mauley was granted a huge portion of his father's estate comprising no less than sixty knights' fees spread throughout Yorkshire. Typically, military service formed a small but important dimension of Mauley's life. Peter (V)'s early experience in Scotland with his father doubtless proved useful at the battle of Nevilles Cross in 1346, and perhaps in Edward III's French campaign of the same year where he may also have served. However, a significant portion of Mauley's time was spent tending to domestic affairs, and in this respect he found a formidable wife in Margaret (d. 1382), daughter of Robert *Clifford, first Lord Clifford (d. 1314). After her husband's death Margaret was energetic in defending those prerogatives attached to her dower, and even her decision to retire to a convent in 1381 was accompanied by a substantial yearly settlement of 800 marks to be paid by her son and heir, **Peter (VI) Mauley**, fourth Baron Mauley (d. 1383). This Peter was next to take on the dual mantle of soldier and administrator, first in France where he fought at Poitiers in 1356, and subsequently in northern England where his presence was constantly required. A successful public career was matched by marriages to two well-connected brides, first Elizabeth (d. 1368), the widow of John, Lord Darcy of Knaith, and daughter and heir of Nicholas, Lord Meynill; and second Constance (d. 1401), daughter and coheir of Sir Thomas Sutton of Bransholme and Sutton in Holderness.

The eclipse of the Mauleys began with the premature death of **Peter (VII) Mauley** (d. 1378×83), which left the five-year-old **Peter (VIII) Mauley**, fifth Baron Mauley (c.1378–1415), as heir to the family estates on the death of his grandfather in 1383. During his long minority wardship and custody of a large portion of his inheritance were granted by the king to Sir Thomas Percy. Mauley finally obtained livery of his lands in May 1399 and immediately re-established the family's profile by supporting Henry Bolingbroke against Richard II, for which he was knighted on the eve of Henry's coronation in October 1399, and by marrying Maud (d. 1438), daughter of Ralph *Neville, first earl of Westmorland, in 1400. Ultimately, however, the Mauleys' fortunes were undermined by an all too common problem—a lack of male heirs. On the death of the

last Lord Mauley in 1415 his estates were partitioned between his widow, Maud, and his daughters, Constance, wife of Sir John Bygod, and Elizabeth, wife of George Salvayn. The family arms displayed variations on or a bend sable.

RICHARD GORSKI

Sources Chancery records · C. L. Kingsford, 'The barons de Mauley', EngHR, 11 (1896), 515–20 · F. Palgrave, ed., The parliamentary writs and writs of military summons, 2 vols. in 4 (1827–34) · VCH Yorkshire East Riding · [J. Raine], ed., Testamenta Eboracensia, 2, SurtS, 30 (1855) · J. C. Atkinson, ed., Cartularium abbathiae de Whitby, 2, SurtS, 72 (1881) · Chronica monasterii de Melsa, a fundatione usque ad annum 1396, auctore Thoma de Burton, ed. E. A. Bond, 3 vols., Rolls Series, 43 (1866–8) · W. P. Baildon and W. Clay, eds., Inquisitions post mortem relating to Yorkshire, Yorkshire Archaeological Society, 59 (1918) · Ypodigma Neustriae, a Thoma Walsingham, ed. H. T. Riley, pt 7 of Chronica monasterii S. Albani, Rolls Series, 28 (1876) · accounts various, PRO, E 101 · C. Given-Wilson, The English nobility in the late middle ages (1987) · CIPM, 20, no. 468
Wealth at death approx. £250: CIPM

Mauley, Peter de. See Maulay, Peter (I) de (d. 1241).

Mauley, Peter (II) (c.1226–1279). See under Mauley family (per. c.1226–1415).

Mauley, Peter (III), first Lord Mauley (1249–1308). See under Mauley family (per. c.1226–1415).

Mauley, Peter (IV), second Lord Mauley (1281–1336?). See under Mauley family (per. c.1226–1415).

Mauley, Peter (V), third Lord Mauley (d. 1355). See under Mauley family (per. c.1226–1415).

Mauley, Peter (VI), fourth Baron Mauley (d. 1383). See under Mauley family (per. c.1226–1415).

Mauley, Peter (VII) (d. 1378×83). See under Mauley family (per. c.1226–1415).

Mauley, Peter (VIII), fifth Baron Mauley (c.1378–1415). See under Mauley family (per. c.1226–1415).

Maunche, John (d. 1465), merchant, was Venetian by birth, but had settled in London by 1439, when he imported a cargo of madder, currants, and linen cloth worth just over £35 on the Jacob captained by William Johnson. However, trading on his own account does not seem to have been the main purpose of his presence in the capital. From April 1440, together with his fellow Venetians, James Trott and Lorenzo Marconovo, he was regularly assigned to the supervision of the English mercer and royal wardrobe supplier Thomas Chalton. Chalton's summaries of their trade show that the trio worked as factors for Lorenzo's relative Giovanni Marconovo, who had been resident in London during the 1420s and 1430s, and—along with Trott—had been named among the grocers' livery in the 1430s.

In this capacity Maunche and his associates offloaded goods from the Venetian galleys which stopped at London, as well as handling goods coming into the capital from Sandwich and Southampton. Their business consisted partly of grocery—luxury spices such as currants, cloves, nutmeg, pepper, mace, green ginger, and cinnamon, which would yield very high profits—and partly of useful chemicals for the English cloth industry—dyestuffs such as brasil, saffron, madder, and woad, and the mordant alum. They also sold raw silk and small quantities of gold and silver thread to London silkwomen, including the royal wardrobe supplier Isabel Norman. They dabbled in luxury fabrics, such as the gold baldachins worth nearly £110 which they sold to the earl of Gloucester in March 1442. Although they bought piece tin from Londoners like Philip Malpas and Nicholas Yeo, their particular export interest was cloth, and in this respect Maunche's freedom of the Drapers' Company proved useful to their enterprise. Indeed, he and his associates were valuable clients for the London drapers. In October and November 1440, they spent just over £770 on purchases of 'Western' cloths from Simon Eyre alone, and in June 1442 they bought 'Ludlow' cloths worth £560 from John Gedeney. Their occasional forays outside London to buy wool were also lucrative for provincial English merchants, with whom they spent over £2000 in February 1443; again, this could work in favour of an individual such as Margery Page, who had sold Cotswolds wool worth almost £430 to Maunche and his colleagues in March 1442.

On 26 November 1443 Maunche was granted letters of denization, which cost him 10 marks, and he was admitted to the freedom of the city a few months later, on 8 February 1444. His freedom came at exactly double the price of naturalization. At first he continued at his usual residence in Langbourn ward, where he had lived since at least 1441, but he moved to the more prestigious Broad Street and Bishopsgate area by September 1449, where he was still recorded as a Venetian by the English authorities despite his changed nationality. He stayed there until at least 1451. His name featured in four suits in the mayor's court during 1444–6, two of them involving the debts of Francesco de San Cassiano, for whom Maunche may also have worked as a factor. He traded in his own name on the Venetian galleys in 1445, importing ginger and silk worth almost £130; and in 1450 he imported in his own name again, this time a small cargo including sweet wine, madder, miniver, and linen thread, with a total value of £32, but the record for his independent business activities indicates a much more limited range and capital than that to which he was accustomed as an employee.

Together with Lorenzo Marconovo, Maunche was among the witnesses to the Venetian Antonio Zane's will in 1440, and in 1450 he acted as administrator on the death of his long-standing colleague James Trott. Maunche died at some time between February and November 1465, describing himself in his will as a citizen and draper. He was to be buried under a marble slab at the Austin Friars— the most popular place of interment for fifteenth-century Italians in London—and left a £2 fee to the friars. His parish church was St Margaret, Lothbury, nearby, to which he left £1 for maintenance of the building and 2s. for the high altar. The entire residue of his estate was bequeathed to his widow and principal executor, Margaret, 'therwith to do and dispose her owne free wille' (PRO, PROB 11/5/11). Margaret afterwards married the draper Thomas Asby,

and both were pardoned any debts due to the crown from her late husband within a year of his death, in respect of accounts for his office as aulnager (inspector of cloths) in Wiltshire.   H. L. BRADLEY

Sources Exchequer, King's Remembrancer, Accounts Various, PRO, E101/128/33, 128/31 · will, PRO, PROB 11/5/11 · Exchequer, King's Remembrancer, Lay Subsidy Rolls, PRO, E179/144/52, 144/50, 144/42, 144/45 · Exchequer, King's Remembrancer, Customs Accounts, PRO, E122/73/10, 73/25, 203/3 · PRO, E179/235/23 · City of London RO, MC 1/3/181, 257, 266, 283 · GL, manuscripts section, 9171/4 f.52, 9171/4 f.287 · R. R. Sharpe, ed., *Calendar of letter-books preserved in the archives of the corporation of the City of London*, [12 vols.] (1899–1912), vol. K · *CPR, 1441–6; 1461–7* · journal, CLRO, 4, 4, f. 15
Wealth at death see will, PRO, PROB 11/5/11

Maund, Benjamin (*bap.* 1790, *d.* 1864), botanist and horticulturist, was born at Terrills in Tenbury, Worcestershire, and baptized on 7 November 1790, the middle son of Owen Maund (*c.*1753–1813), a farmer, and his wife, Mary (*c.*1761–1848). His published works testify to his having had some formal education before he was apprenticed, on 5 December 1806, to Thomas Griffiths, stationer, printer, and bookseller in Ludlow, then at its fashionable height. Griffiths's work was sometimes careless, an ironic start for Maund whose taste and standards were later so widely praised. On Christmas day 1813—the day his father was buried—Maund bought the Market Place printing and bookselling business of Sarah Thompson in Bromsgrove, moving by 1818 to the High Street where he prospered as a bookseller, stationer, printer, bookbinder, publisher, and chemist in a combination normal for the time. He specialized in veterinary medicines, preparing some—like 'Drench for Staggers'—to his own formulae. In his large garden to the rear he experimented with seeds and plants obtained from around the world and with varieties of wheat which he exhibited in London. On 30 January 1817 he married Sarah Green (1792–1857). A deeply religious man, 'of gentlemanly appearance, quiet, modest and unassuming' (Humphreys), Maund was active in the town's affairs as churchwarden, member of several parish committees, director of a bank, and prime mover in the building of a new town hall and cattle market. He was also a keen freemason, appointed provincial grand steward in 1852.

'Man, by nature, inherits the love of flowers', Maund wrote in the preface to volume one of the *Botanic Garden* (13 vols., 1825–51). He sought to share his lifelong passion by producing an interesting and useful publication affordable to everyone. Each monthly issue contained a plate with four engraved and hand-coloured figures of hardy ornamental flowering plants and eight pages of text. The principal artist was Edward Dalton Smith, of Chelsea, and the engraver, S. Watts. Maund, it is claimed, started the fashion for inserting additional material at the end of monthly numbers of botanical periodicals. With the *Botanic Garden* he issued *The Auctarium* (1833), a miscellany of practical advice and information; the *Floral Register* (1834), a source for newly introduced plants; and *The Fruitist* (inserted into the last three volumes), a forum for disseminating knowledge through notes and readers' questions. In 1827 he became a fellow of the Linnean Society and by the 1830s widespread favourable reviews—and a gold snuffbox from an admiring king of Prussia—had earned him a reputation sufficient to enlist several distinguished contributors, including the professors of botany at Cambridge and Edinburgh, and leading artists, such as Mrs Withers, 'Flower painter in ordinary to Queen Adelaide', for his second periodical, *The Botanist* (5 vols., 1836–42), a more ambitious work issued monthly with four plates and descriptive letterpress. Again, Maund published additional material, a short yearly supplement, a basic introduction to botany with volume two, and a *Dictionary of English and Latin Terms*, meant to accompany the large quarto edition but instead published separately in 1850. In 1837 Maund and William Holl, proprietor and editor of the *Worcester Herald*, edited volume one of *The Naturalist* (5 vols., 1837–9), a Worcestershire-based enterprise.

Two of Maund's daughters, Elizabeth and Sarah, began helping their father in their teens, together contributing over 200 illustrations. John *Maund (1823–1858), his middle son, had a short but illustrious medical career in Australia. In 1851 Maund took Alfred Palmer into partnership and in 1859 he retired with his three daughters, to Leamington Spa, then Folkestone, and in 1862 to Sandown in the Isle of Wight where he died, at Clapton Villa, Sandown, on 21 April 1864. He was buried in Brading. In 1928 a memorial tablet was unveiled in St John's parish church, Bromsgrove. It is of Maund's head surrounded by a wreath of *ribes acanthiordes*—a plant he introduced to Britain.

MARGARET COOPER

Sources J. Britten, 'Maund's *The Botanist* (1836–1842?)', *Journal of Botany, British and Foreign*, 56 (1918), 235–43 • Bentham MSS, RBG Kew, 1 (2720–27) • 'The botanical periodicals', *Gardener's Magazine*, 15 (1839), 90–91 • 'The botanical periodicals and their illustrations', *Gardener's Magazine*, 14 (1838), 171–7 • *Moore's Almanack* (1842) [Maund's edn: priv. coll.] • Henslow MSS, CUL, Add. MS 8176, nos. 29 and 211 • G. K. Stanton, 'The late Mr Maund: interesting reminiscences', *Bromsgrove, Droitwich and Redditch Weekly Messenger* (20 Nov 1897) • J. Humphreys, 'A great Bromsgrovian', *Bromsgrove, Droitwich and Redditch Weekly Messenger* (12 June 1926) • R. C. Gaut, *A history of Worcestershire agricultural and rural evolution* (1939) • parish registers, Bromsgrove, St John the Baptist, Worcs. RO, b 850, B.A. 9135 • churchwarden's account book, 1833–59, and order book, 1820–78, Bromsgrove, St John the Baptist, Worcs. RO, b 850, B.A. 9135 • 'The late Dr Maund', *Australian Medical Journal*, 3 (1858), 194–200 • parish register, Tenbury, St Mary, 7 Nov 1790 [baptism] • parish register, Bromsgrove, St John, 2 Dec 1848 [burial; Mary Maund] • PRO, IR/1 70–72 • d. cert. • parish register, Brading, 1864 [burial]
Archives CUL, Henslow corresp. • RBG Kew, Bentham corresp.
Likenesses H. Harvey, marble memorial plaque, 1928, St John's Church, Bromsgrove
Wealth at death under £8000: probate, 5 July 1864, *CGPLA Eng. & Wales*

Maund, John (1823–1858), physician and analytical chemist, was born in High Street, Bromsgrove, Worcestershire, on 12 March 1823, the fourth of the six surviving children of Benjamin *Maund (*bap.* 1790, *d.* 1864), bookseller, botanist, and horticulturalist, and his wife, Sarah Green (1792–1857). Dogged by a delicate constitution, he was tutored

privately in Kidderminster by William F. Matthews from 1834 to 1838 before being apprenticed to Mr Welsby, a surgeon of Prescott, Lancashire. In 1843 he went to the University of Glasgow where he gained several prizes, including first prize in pharmacology. In 1844 he moved to London, where he was assistant surgeon at St Pancras Infirmary. In 1845 to 1846 he visited Paris to further his medical training. He gained membership of the Royal College of Surgeons (1844–5), the licence of the Society of Apothecaries (1846–7), a doctorate of medicine from St Andrews University (1849), and certificates from the Royal College of Chemistry and the Royal Polytechnic Institution in London. In 1853, having sold his practice in Harlow, Essex, he emigrated to Australia with his eldest sister, Eliza, intending to take up less fatiguing work as an analytical chemist. However, Maund, a man of exceptional personal qualities, could not ignore the tremendous medical problems facing Melbourne in the early gold rush years and immediately set up again in general practice. In 1855 he helped unite two professional bodies into the Medical Society of Victoria, and in 1856 was founding editor of the *Australian Medical Journal*.

Maund's greatest achievement arose from his concern for the many mothers whose babies were being born in tents, at the roadside, even on the wharf, and in 1856, together with Dr Richard Tracy, he founded the first lying-in hospital (later the Royal Women's Hospital). He was awarded a doctorate of medicine *ad eundem* from the University of Melbourne. As Victoria's first analytical chemist he undertook important research into Melbourne's water supply, especially on the Yan Yean Reservoir scheme. Maund died unmarried on 3 April 1858 at his home, 53 La Trobe Street East, Melbourne, from a sudden attack of what was probably typhoid and was buried in Melbourne general cemetery two days later. He was deeply mourned for his professional skills, his personal qualities, and his devotion to the poor. The hospital commissioned his portrait, his father unveiled a memorial window to him in St John's, Bromsgrove, and Ferdinand Mueller named a new genus of the rush family after him, *Juncanigineae Maundia*. In 1964 the annual Tracy–Maund memorial lectures were instituted by the Australian Medical Association.

MARGARET COOPER

Sources 'The late Dr Maund', *Australian Medical Journal*, 3 (1858), 194–200 • *London and Provincial Medical Directory* (1852) • *The Argus* [Melbourne] (18 Jan 1853) • *The Argus* [Melbourne] (15 Feb 1853) • *The Argus* [Melbourne] (28 Feb 1853) • *The Age* [Melbourne] (5 April 1858) • J. Maund, 'Report on analysis of water from Yan Yean', *Australian Medical Journal*, 3 (1858), 163–4 • *Catalogue of valuable household furniture, books, surgical instruments, horses, carriages, harness, etc. … of the late Dr. Maund* (1858) • J. Maund, 'Gangleon treated by the lanceolate director', *Medical Times*, new ser., 2 (1851), 35–6 • J. Maund, 'On the deterioration of grain and flour', *Transactions and Proceedings of the Victorian Institute*, 1 (1855), 48–53 • J. Maund, 'On the mineral waters of Victoria', *Transactions and Proceedings of the Victorian Institute*, 1 (1855), 70–74 • J. Maund, 'The water of the Plenty River', *Transactions and Proceedings of the Victorian Institute*, 1 (1855), 136–43 • E. A. Mackay, 'Medical practice during the goldfields era in Victoria', *Medical Journal of Australia* (26 Sept 1936), 421–8 • 'Happenings of the now long past: the centenary of the Medical Society of

Victoria', *Medical Journal of Australia* (16 Aug 1952), 213 • C. Macdonald, ed., *John Maund: a book of remembrance* (1956), 1.33–6 • C. E. Sayers, *The Women's … a social history* (Melbourne, 1956) • private information (2004) • *AusDB* • parish registers, Bromsgrove, Worcestershire • baptismal certificate
Likenesses N. Chevalier, oils (posthumous), Royal Women's Hospital, Melbourne

Maunder [*née* Russell]**, Annie Scott Dill** (1868–1947), astronomer, was born on 14 April 1868 in Strabane, co. Tyrone, the second of three children and the younger daughter of William Andrew Russell (1824–1899), minister of the Presbyterian church in that town, and his wife, Hester (Hessy) Nesbitt Russell, *née* Dill, who belonged to a prominent Ulster family. She was educated at home and at the Ladies' Collegiate School (later Victoria College), Belfast. She entered Girton College, Cambridge, at the age of eighteen on an open scholarship and took part one of the mathematical tripos in 1889 with second-class honours. After a year as a mathematics mistress at the ladies' high school in Jersey she obtained a post at the Royal Greenwich Observatory in September 1891 as a 'lady computer', and was assigned to the solar department under Edward Walter *Maunder (1851–1928). She also had to take her place with other computers on the observing rota for the transit circle, which meant regular night duty. Annie spent four years on the Greenwich staff, and resigned on 31 October 1895 before her marriage to Maunder on 28 December.

Annie Maunder continued with determination to pursue practical astronomy within the limitations of her new circumstances. She accompanied her husband on eclipse expeditions, three of which were favoured by good weather. With a modest grant from Girton in 1897 she acquired a short-focus camera, which she used with great success to photograph the outer solar corona in India in 1898, capturing a coronal streamer extending to fourteen solar radii, the longest ever recorded up to that time. This, and her other photographs of the corona and of the Milky Way, were included in *The Heavens and their Story* (1910), published under the Maunders' joint names but in fact principally her work.

Annie Maunder collaborated with her husband in his well-known work on the periodicity of sunspots. She also produced independently a catalogue of some 600 recurrent sunspot groups recorded at Greenwich (1907). Another, less fortunate, analysis (1907), showing an apparent east–west imbalance in the visibility of spots on the sun's surface during the previous sunspot cycle, caused some discussion among solar observers, but this was undoubtedly a spurious effect.

Mrs Maunder returned to her former duties at the Greenwich observatory as a wartime volunteer from 1915 to 1920. In 1916 she became a fellow of the Royal Astronomical Society, following the admission of women to membership. She had joined the British Astronomical Association as early as 1892 and served it assiduously in various capacities, including fifteen years as editor of its journal. In her later years she acquired an interest in ancient astronomies and came to be regarded as an authority in this field. Her very last paper (1936) was a revised estimate of the date for the origin of the constellations, which she placed at 2900 BC.

Annie Maunder survived her husband by almost twenty years, and died at her home, 52 Elms Crescent, Wandsworth, London, on 15 September 1947, in her eightieth year. She had no children.   M. T. BRÜCK

Sources M. A. Evershed, 'Mrs Walter Maunder', *Journal of the British Astronomical Association*, 57 (1946–7), 238 • M. T. Brück, 'Alice Everett and Annie Russell Maunder, torch-bearing women astronomers', *Irish Astronomical Journal*, 21 (1993–4), 281–91 • M. T. Brück and S. Grew, 'The family background of Annie S. D. Maunder (*née* Russell)', *Irish Astronomical Journal*, 23 (1996), 55–6 • M. T. Brück, 'Lady computers at Greenwich in the early 1890s', *Quarterly Journal of the Royal Astronomical Society*, 36 (1995), 83–95 • K. T. Butler and H. I. McMorran, eds., *Girton College register, 1869–1946* (1948) • *The Witness* (Oct 1899) • d. cert.
Archives British Astronomical Association, album of photographs, 1909, by E. W. Maunder and A. S. D. Maunder • NMM, Royal Observatory, Greenwich, archives, letters
Likenesses photograph, repro. in Brück and Grew, 'Family background of Annie S. D. Maunder'
Wealth at death £8912: probate, 9 Feb 1948, *CGPLA Eng. & Wales*

Maunder, Edward Walter (1851–1928), astronomer, was born at 5 Chesterfield Street, St Pancras, London, on 12 April 1851, the fourth of seven children and the youngest of the three sons of George Peter Maunder (1813–1878), a Wesleyan minister, and his wife, Mary Ann, *née* Frid. He was educated at University College School in Gower Street and afterwards attended classes in science at King's College, London. Having been employed for a while with a bank in London, he was appointed in 1873 by civil service examination to a newly instituted post at the Royal Greenwich Observatory, that of photographic and spectroscopic assistant, with principal responsibility for the solar department.

In the field of solar physics Maunder extended observations beyond the required daily photography of the sun to include the positions, sizes, and movements of sunspots. His statistical analyses of these unique records after several decades led to some important results: the famous 'butterfly diagram' demonstrating the latitude drift of sunspots during the sunspot cycle (1904) and the correlation of geomagnetic disturbances with the occurrence of individual large sunspots on the solar disc (also 1904). His later study (1922) using data from various sources of the dearth of sunspots in the sixteenth century, the so-called Maunder minimum, assumed significance later in theoretical research on the sun's variability. Maunder's work in spectroscopy, including visual measurements of radial velocities of stars made in association with W. M. Christie, was less spectacular, though useful at the time.

Maunder was an active fellow of the Royal Astronomical Society, to which he was elected in 1875; he served as a member of council, as secretary, and as vice-president successively between 1885 and 1897. At the same time he was an enthusiastic supporter of amateur astronomy. He was the founder in 1890 of the British Astronomical Association, the first editor of its publications, and its president from 1894 to 1896. He led a group of members on a total solar eclipse expedition to the Scandinavian Arctic in 1896 which, though frustrated by bad weather, provided valuable experience for later successful expeditions to India in 1898 and to Algeria in 1900. In his professional capacity Maunder also observed eclipses in the West Indies in 1886 and in Mauritius in 1901, obtaining photographs and spectra of the corona.

Maunder was the author of numerous popular articles and books and completed editing stints on the magazines *The Observatory* (1881–7) and *Knowledge* (1895–1904). Among his books were a history of the Greenwich observatory (1900) and *The Astronomy of the Bible* (1908, reprinted 1922), in which he brought together his extensive biblical and astronomical knowledge.

Maunder's first wife, Edith Hannah, *née* Bustin, whom he married on 11 September 1875, died in 1888 leaving him with a family of three sons and two daughters. On 28 December 1895 he married the astronomer Annie Scott Dill Russell (1868–1947) [*see* Maunder, Annie Scott Dill]. There were no children of this marriage. His obituarist H. P. Hollis recalled his popularity as a lecturer, with 'his silver tongue' and 'his amiability of manner' (Hollis, 229), while the children of a colleague remembered him 'with his long beard, very much the picture-book astronomer' (M. Wilson, *Ninth Astronomer Royal: the Life of Frank Watson Dyson*, 1951). He retired in 1913 after forty years of service, but, with his wife, resumed his duties during the First World War, when many of the Greenwich staff were absent on military service. He died at his home, 8 Maze Hill, Greenwich Park, London, on 21 March 1928, one month short of his seventy-seventh birthday.

M. T. BRÜCK

Sources H. P. Hollis, *Journal of the British Astronomical Association*, 38 (1927–8), 229–33 · *Monthly Notices of the Royal Astronomical Society*, 89 (1928–9), 313–18 · *The Observatory*, 51 (1928), 157–9 · H. Macpherson, *Astronomers of to-day and their work* (1905), 192–200 · W. H. Newton, *The face of the sun* (1958), 128 · M. Stix, *The sun* (1989) · d. cert. · b. cert. · m. certs.
Archives CUL, papers | British Astronomical Association, photo album, 1909, by E. W. Maunder and A. S. D. Maunder · RAS, corresp. · RAS, letters to Percy Molesworth · RAS, letters to RAS
Likenesses Elliott & Fry, photograph, before 1905, repro. in Macpherson, *Astronomers of today* · Elliott & Fry, photograph, repro. in *The Observatory*, 51 (1928) · Elliott & Fry, photograph, repro. in Hollis, *Journal of the British Astronomical Association*
Wealth at death £873 17s. 1d.: resworn probate, 28 April 1928, CGPLA Eng. & Wales

Maunder, Samuel (1785–1849), compiler of reference works, belonged to a Devon family settled near Barnstaple. His sister Ann married William *Pinnock, well known in his time as the promoter of the educational *Catechisms*, published in eighty-three parts between 1837 and 1849. Maunder took part in their preparation, although Pinnock's name alone appears on their title-page. The two were also partners in a publishing business in London, and published for two or three years the *Literary Gazette*. Pinnock's rash business speculations led to his financial ruin, and Maunder, under his own name, then compiled and issued numerous dictionaries and compact encyclopaedias, chiefly for educational purposes. They were very popular, had large sales, and were frequently revised and reprinted. William Jerdan, who knew Maunder, wrote of 'his indefatigable, painstaking and diligent research, his absence of ambition and contentment with accuracy and solidity of information ... an honourable and worthy man' (Jerdan, 343).

Maunder's first book was *The Little Lexicon, or, Multum in parvo of the English Language* (1825). His next book, *The Treasury of Knowledge and Library of Reference* (1830), sold over 200,000 copies. *The Biographical Treasury* (1838) was frequently revised and reprinted and was brought up to date by W. L. R. Cates (1873, 1882). An interesting feature, used elsewhere, is the snippets of information and moral maxims printed in the four margins of each page. Other Treasuries were devoted to belles lettres (1841), history (1844), natural history (1848), and geography (1856 and 1860).

Maunder also prepared a school edition of R. Montgomery's *Omnipresence of the Deity*, a revised edition of Shakespeare's plays (1851), and one of *Geography and History* by E. R. (22nd edn, 1859).

Maunder died at his home, 67 Gibson Square, Islington, on 30 April 1849.

G. LE G. NORGATE, rev. JOHN D. HAIGH

Sources GM, 2nd ser., 31 (1849), 652 · W. Jerdan, *Men I have known* (1866), 336–45 · 'Men I have known: Pinnock and Maunder', *Leisure Hour*, 12 (1863), 261–3 · d. cert.
Likenesses J. Waugh, portrait, 1848 · E. Finden, stipple (after J. Waugh), BM

Maundrell, Henry (*bap.* 1665, *d.* 1701), Church of England clergyman and traveller in the Middle East, was the son of Robert Maundrell of Compton Bassett, near Calne, Wiltshire, where he was baptized on 23 December 1665. In the register of Exeter College, Oxford, his father is described as 'pleb', but the family had previously been important locally. He matriculated on 4 April 1682, at the age of sixteen, and entered Exeter College, Oxford, as commoner on 27 September. He graduated BA on 15 October 1685 and MA on 19 June 1688. He was elected Sarum fellow at Exeter College on 30 June 1686 and became a full fellow of the college on 28 June 1697, the day on which he also graduated BD by decree.

Maundrell was appointed curate of Bromley, Kent, in 1689, where he remained until 1695. A tombstone in Richmond churchyard suggests that he had also been a curate there. On 15 December 1695 he preached a sermon to a body of the Levant Company's merchants at the church of St Peter-le-Poer in London (published in 1696), and on 20 December he was elected by their general court as chaplain to the Levant Company's factory at Aleppo in Turkey. The chaplains to the Levant Company's factories were often distinguished scholars, interested in holy places and in classical sites and civilizations. Their pay was normally 400 dollars (about £100) per annum, plus travel to the Levant and additional payment towards equipment, including books. Maundrell was granted £20 on 15 January 1696 for books for its library. His reasons for taking up this new appointment are not entirely clear, and there is indication that he did so with some reluctance. He seems to have had a romantic involvement in England from which he was reluctant to allow his mentors, notably his uncle Sir Charles Hedges, to extricate him by encouragement to the Aleppo post.

Maundrell arrived in Aleppo in 1696, having travelled via Frankfurt am Main to discuss aspects of the history and topography of the Holy Land with the German scholar and orientalist Job Ludolphus (Hiob Leiutholf). His daily work included the saying of the Anglican office for the factors in Aleppo. He stated in a letter to the bishop of Rochester, published as a preface to his *Journey*, that 'it is our first employment every morning to solemnize the daily Service of the Church; at which I am sure to have always a devout, a regular and full Congregation'. While in Aleppo he suffered from ill health, and he died there of fever early in 1701. The vacancy caused by his death is recorded in the Levant Company's minutes on 15 May 1701.

Maundrell is best-known for his account *A Journey from Aleppo to Jerusalem at Easter A.D. 1697*, published in Oxford in 1703, two years after his death. This scholarly narrative describes in detail the journey from Aleppo to Jerusalem and back, made by Maundrell and fourteen others in 1697. His motive was to undertake an Easter pilgrimage to Jerusalem, and the company departed at 3 p.m. on Friday, 26 February 1697. Their route took them across northern Syria to Latakia, down the coast to Acre, then to Jerusalem for the Latin Easter, then inland to the valley of the Jordan and Bethlehem, returning to Jerusalem for the Eastern churches' Easter. They returned to Aleppo via Damascus, Tripoli, and the earlier part of their outward route, returning to Aleppo on 18 May.

The *Journey* was partially intended to bring up to date George Sandys's account of 1610, *Relation of a journey begun an. dom. 1610. Foure bookes. Containing a description of the Turkish empire, of Aegypt, of the Holy Land, of the remote parts of Italy and llands adioyning*. In fact, Maundrell's account is quite different from that of Sandys, and is a major work in its own right, giving detailed descriptions of the life and landscapes of Syria, Lebanon, and Palestine, including the agricultural practices of the regions and places encountered, in addition to descriptions of places of religious significance. The factual accounts of the relict features of the ancient worlds are of interest and value, and they are accompanied by careful measurements and plans of major sites such as Baalbek. Maundrell is critical of much of what he and his companions saw and experienced, but his accounts are well informed from contemporary and much earlier, classical and biblical sources, and written in an economic but witty and informative style. Later writers valued this work. Curzon, in his *Visits to Monasteries in the Levant* (1849), says that he 'was struck with the superiority of old Maundrell's narrative over all the others, for he tells us plainly and clearly what he saw' (Curzon, 168), and Howell, in a preface to a 1963 reprint of the *Journey*, says that 'it is taut, disciplined writing from which every wrinkle of ambiguity has been ironed away' (Howell, xi). Most of the nineteenth-century writers on the Holy Land, including Henry Robinson, Dean Stanley, Carl Ritter, and

George Adam Smith, comment positively on Maundrell's account.

A Journey from Aleppo to Jerusalem went through twelve editions by 1810 and it appeared in full and condensed form in later compendia of travels in the Levant and the Holy Land, including Thomas Wright's edited *Early Travels in Palestine* (1848). It was translated into French in 1705 and 1706, into Dutch in 1717, and into German in 1737, and remains an important account of the places and peoples of the region.   ROBIN A. BUTLIN

Sources H. Maundrell, *A journey from Aleppo to Jerusalem at Easter A.D. 1697* (1703) · D. Howell, 'Introduction', in H. Maundrell, *A journey from Aleppo to Jerusalem in 1697*, reprint (1963), i–xxviii · R. Curzon, *Visit to monasteries in the Levant* (1849) · A. C. Wood, *A history of the Levant Company* (1935); repr. (1964) · T. Wright, ed., *Early travels in Palestine* (1848) · C. W. Boase, ed., *Registrum Collegii Exoniensis*, new edn, OHS, 27 (1894), 123 · Foster, *Alum. Oxon.* · *DNB* · J. Dunkin, *Outlines of the history and antiquities of Bromley, in Kent* (1815) · J. B. Pearson, *A biographical sketch of the chaplains to the Levant Company, maintained at Constantinople, Aleppo and Smyrna, 1611–1706* (1883)
Archives TCD, commonplace book | BM, Add. MSS 10623–10624 · BM, Add. MS 24107

Maunsell, Andrew (b. c.1560, d. in or after 1604?), bookseller and bibliographer, was made free of the Drapers' Company by John Wight, himself active in the book trade, on 6 December 1574. The dates and circumstances of his birth, marriage, and death are unknown. Although never a member of the Stationers' Company, Maunsell was active as a bookseller and publisher from 1576, when there were printed for him, by Thomas East, *Jehovah. A Free Pardon. First Written in Spanish*, translated by J. Danyel, and, by John Charlewood, Thomas Rogers's *A Philosophicall Discourse, Entituled, The Anatomie of the Minde*. At least five other works by Rogers, chaplain to Archbishop Bancroft, were later published by Maunsell, whose investments were chiefly in theological works and in elementary textbooks.

Between 1576 and 1596 Maunsell financed the printing of some fifty-five imprints and was listed as selling seven others, and he bound his apprentices to freemen of the Stationers' Company. Among his more ambitious enterprises was the publication in folio in 1583, with Henry Denham, Thomas Chard, and William Broome, of a translation by Anthony Martin of Peter Martyr's *Common Places*. He occupied premises in St Paul's Churchyard from 1576 to 1589, first at the north-east quarter, at The Parrot, from 1576 to 1581; then at the West End from 1582 to 1583. In 1583 he returned to the north-east quarter, trading at the Brazen Serpent from 1584 to 1589. He then removed to a shop at the south entrance of the Royal Exchange, where he is found in 1592, and from there to Lothbury in 1594 to 1595. His device, formerly that of Richard Jugge, was a pelican with its young, rising phoenix-like, out of the flames, surrounded by the motto: *Pro lege, rege, grege*, expanded below in English as 'Love kepyth the lawe, obeyeth the kynge, and is good to the commen welthe'.

In 1590 many of Maunsell's copies were transferred to Robert Dexter. There are no copies entered to him in this and the following year, and from 1592 to 1596 he appears on the title pages of only eight works, and chiefly as a bookseller rather than a publisher. It is reasonable to infer that it was at this time that he embarked on the compilation of the *Catalogue of English Printed Bookes*, which was to be his chief claim to fame. This catalogue, of which Maunsell himself completed only the first two parts, bore a triple dedication: to the Queen; to divines, 'for some soare so hie that they looke not so low, as on theire owne countrie writers'; and to the Stationers' Company. This was something like the first attempt since John Bale's *Scriptores* to construct an English national bibliography. The plan was for the first volume to contain divinity; the second, science in all its branches, and music; and the third, literature, logic, law, and history.

The first two parts appeared in 1595, printed by John Windet and James Roberts respectively. The first part, devoted to divinity, expressly excludes 'Popish' books printed overseas and books against the 'present government'. It is arranged, like the second part, chiefly in alphabetical order of authors' surnames, where earlier models such as Gesner, Simler, and Bale had listed authors under their forenames, and it also contains thematic sections, devoted, for example, to sermons, catechisms, primers, and commentaries on books of the Bible. The second part, dedicated to Robert Devereux, second earl of Essex, is also prefaced by letters to the 'professors' of mathematics and physic, to the Stationers' Company, and to booksellers in general. Both parts profess to contain only books that Maunsell has seen, and ample spaces are provided for additions.

Maunsell's catalogues provide confirmation of the existence at that time of a number of books of which no known copy survives and which are otherwise recorded only occasionally, if at all, in documentary sources. At the same time it falls short of completeness and several copies survive in which books unknown to Maunsell have been entered, among them one acquired, already sparsely annotated, by Thomas Baker, into which Baker has entered additions copied from Archbishop Harsnett's copy (Colchester, H.f.35) and added a few of his own up to 1602 (CUL, Adv.b.52.1); and another, now in the library of Trinity College, Cambridge (VI.3.60), which supplies many of the papist books omitted by Maunsell and also Latin books, arranged indiscriminately together, and copious other additions to 1595. There are several others substantially annotated (including Hunt., 54169, Harvard UL, B. 2076.1*, CUL, Syn 4.59.16, and University of Michigan, SPEC\Z\2002\451), but unfortunately no comprehensive census of annotated copies exists.

The promised third part of the catalogue (*Humanity*) did not appear under Maunsell's hand, and the want was not supplied until the appearance of the *Catalogue* of William London in 1658. It was at one time supposed that it was Maunsell's death that prevented the appearance of the third part of his *Catalogue*, but he was certainly still alive on 19 April 1596 when, in response to his petition to them, and on account of his 'paines in collecting and printinge the Catalogue of bookes', the Stationers' Company granted him a 'benevolence' in money and books 'the particulars of whiche money & bookes appere in a Booke [no longer to be found] conteyning the names of the particular persons that contributed the same' (Greg and Boswell, 54), and almost certainly on 15 October 1604 when 'Andrewe Manssell, son of Andrew Mansell, citizen and stationer of London' was apprenticed to Edmund Weaver, stationer, to serve with Thomas Wight (Arber, *Regs. Stationers*, 2.285), without any indication that his father was deceased.   ELISABETH LEEDHAM-GREEN

Sources Arber, *Regs. Stationers* · G. Goodwin, *Catalogue of the Harsnett Library at Colchester* (1888) · W. W. Greg and E. Boswell, eds., *Records of the court of the Stationers' Company, 1576 to 1602, from register B* (1930) · *STC, 1475–1640*

Maunsell, Guy Anson (1884–1961), civil engineer, was born on 1 September 1884 in Srinagar, India, the second child and only son of Lieutenant-Colonel Edward Henry Maunsell (1837–1913) and Rosalie Harriet (d. 1929) of Guernsey. He was educated at Eastbourne College and then studied engineering at the Central Institution, South Kensington, graduating with honours in 1906.

A man of great vision and energy, Maunsell became an engineering designer of flair and genius. His practical training was gained in Paris and Lausanne during 1907–8. His engineering career began in 1909 when he joined the staff of Easton Gibb & Son, contractors, building the naval base at Rosyth. During 1915–16 he was chief engineer responsible for erecting cordite factories in Ayrshire and west London. In 1917 he served in France as an officer in the Royal Engineers. A year later he was seconded to design and construct a shipyard at Shoreham to build concrete sea-going vessels. After the war he worked with Sir Alexander Gibb, chief engineer at the Ministry of Transport, preparing a tidal power scheme on the River Severn comprising a barrage and combined road and rail bridge. In 1922 he married Millicent Geraldine Mockler, with whom he had two daughters.

In 1923, as special assistant to Sir Alexander Gibb & Partners, Maunsell was engaged on the design and layout of Ipswich Dock extensions, Poole harbour, and other works. From 1924 to 1927 he was engineer and agent to Sir William Arrol & Co., working on the Falls of Clyde hydroelectric power scheme. The next three years were spent in private practice and in association with Sir Alexander Gibb & Partners. In 1931 he joined Dorman Long & Co. as agent for the widening of Sir Joseph Bazalgette's Putney Bridge. When this was completed, in 1934, he became managing director of the Anglo-Danish Construction Company, expressly formed to build the Storstrom Bridge in Denmark. Maunsell solved the difficult site erection problem by designing an ingenious floating crane capable of lifting a complete viaduct span in one piece. At the time this was the longest bridge in Europe, some 10,535 feet. The linking of the erection procedure with the design concept was a Maunsell trademark. In 1936 he formed the consulting engineering firm G. Maunsell & Partners, which he headed until his retirement in 1959. In 1940 he was invited to join Sir Alexander Gibb in the restoration of Telford's Menai suspension bridge.

During the Second World War, Maunsell's ingenuity was fully utilized in many unusual projects, which later became the inspiration for other civil engineering developments. One was the design and installation of the 'Maunsell sea forts', a series of fortified off-shore tower structures. The Admiralty naval fort in the Thames estuary comprised four towers, each weighing about 4500 tons. They were built of reinforced concrete at Northfleet and then towed out and sunk on site in 1942. This was so successful that an army fort was also installed in the Thames estuary and another in Liverpool Bay. Another wartime project was his design and production of a series of reinforced concrete floating docks for the Admiralty, capable of lifting tugs and minesweepers, but the great civil engineering achievement of the war was the Mulberry harbour, built for the allied landing in Normandy in 1944. Many engineers and Admiralty staff were involved in this project, including Guy Maunsell, who had first proposed a floating breakwater scheme to Admiral Hughes Hallet in 1940.

Maunsell travelled widely throughout his life and used his talent for painting in watercolours to record many of his engineering works. His last major work was the design of a 1000 ft span arch bridge which was being constructed at Gladesville, Sydney, Australia, at the time of his death. Maunsell died on 20 June 1961 at The Orchard, London Road, Southborough, Kent, and was buried at Southborough cemetery. He was survived by his wife.

DENIS SMITH

Sources *PICE*, new ser., 22 (1961–2), 347–8 · private information (2004) · *The Times* (23 June 1961) · G. Maunsell & Partners, 160 Croydon Road, Beckenham, Kent · d. cert. · *CGPLA Eng. & Wales* (1961)
Archives G. Maunsell & Partners, 160 Croydon Road, Beckenham, Kent
Likenesses oils (after photograph), priv. coll.
Wealth at death £92,554 2s. 8d.: probate, 31 July 1961, *CGPLA Eng. & Wales*

Maunsfield, Henry de. *See* Mamesfeld, Henry (*c*.1270–1328).

Mauny [Manny]**, Sir Walter** (*c*.1310–1372), soldier and founder of the London Charterhouse, was the fourth of five sons of Jean le Borgne, lord of Masny in the imperial county of Hainault, and Jeanne de Jenlain. The brothers probably passed their youth in the household of Jean de Beaumont, brother of William I, count of Hainault. In December 1327 Mauny came to England as a page in the household of the count's daughter, Philippa of Hainault, the new queen of England, and settled there for the rest of his life.

Career at court Mauny enjoyed a rapid rise at court. Starting as the queen's trencherman, he became the keeper of her greyhounds. In 1331 he was knighted on the king's command, and retained at a large annual fee as a member of the king's household. Mauny's chance to prove himself as a soldier came in August 1332, when he joined the small private army which invaded Scotland with Edward Balliol and Henry Beaumont, and took part in the remarkable victory over the much larger army of the Scots at the battle of Dupplin Moor. Shortly afterwards, in a skirmish at Roxburgh Bridge, he captured John Crab, the celebrated Flemish seaman and military engineer in Scottish service, whom he later sold to Edward III for 1000 marks. Mauny returned to Scotland in the following year with the English army, and took part in the siege of Berwick. He followed Edward III on the winter campaign of 1334–5 and the equally fruitless march to Perth in July and August 1335. Between June and September 1336 Mauny accompanied the king on his spectacular raid into north-eastern Scotland, which resulted in the destruction of Aberdeen. For part of this campaign he served as Edward's standard-bearer. Almost nothing is known about Mauny's personal contribution to these campaigns, but Jean le Bel says (1.110) that he distinguished himself by his extravagant gestures and reckless disregard of his own safety, both qualities which were much admired by Edward III.

The king's admiration for Mauny is borne out by the evidence of his growing wealth and influence. Edward appointed him keeper of Harlech Castle and sheriff of Merioneth for life in December 1332, and over the following years he acquired almost viceregal powers in this part of north Wales. Among other favours he received a large part of the Buckinghamshire and Norfolk estates of David Strathbogie, earl of Atholl, in 1335, after the latter's defection to the Scots. He also received valuable patronage from the king's uncle, Thomas of Brotherton, earl of Norfolk, who gave him a pension and appointed him marshal of the king's Marshalsea court.

Admiral of the north On the outbreak of the war with France, in August 1337, Mauny became admiral of the north. The office, which he held for a year, gave him jurisdiction over all the east-coast ports of England from the Thames to Berwick. Edward III appointed him to command the advance guard of the great army that he intended to dispatch to the Low Countries, and to escort to Holland the cargoes of wool that it was proposed to sell there in order to finance the invasion of France. Mauny sailed from Sandwich at the beginning of November 1337 with a fleet of 85 ships carrying some 1450 troops, 2200 seamen, some prominent wool merchants, and a small group of royal councillors. The operation was conducted with the utmost recklessness. On the way to Holland, Mauny launched a surprise attack on the Flemish port of Sluys, which was repulsed. Then, on 9 November 1337, he landed his men on the nearby island of Cadzand at the entrance to the Hondt, and spent several days in killing and plundering the inhabitants. When the Flemings from the mainland tried to intervene, they were defeated with great slaughter and their commander, Guy, half-brother of the count of Flanders, was captured. Mauny personally made £8000 in ransoms out of this enterprise, but lost many of his men and achieved nothing of any military value. He landed his army and his cargoes at Dordrecht at the end of November 1337, and returned shortly afterwards to England.

As admiral of the north Mauny had the main responsibility for assembling the fleet that carried Edward III to Brabant in July 1338. He himself joined the expedition with a company of 10 knights, 33 squires, and 50 archers, one of the larger personal retinues in the army. In addition he was joined by two of his brothers with their own retinues from Hainault. When, after long delays, the invasion of France eventually began in September 1338, Mauny was determined to be the first in action. As Edward III marched from Valenciennes to Cambrai, he separated himself from the main army and led fifty men on a raid against the undefended town of Mortagne which he plundered and partly burned before withdrawing. On 20 September 1339, as Edward III laid siege to Cambrai, Mauny captured the nearby fortress of Thun-l'Évêque on the Scheldt by bribing the commander. During the next two months he accompanied the king's army in its destructive raid through the Cambrésis and the Thiérache. Characteristically, on the night of 22 October 1339, the last of the campaign, it was Mauny who led small companies of scouts and men-at-arms past the French lines at Buironfosse, killing sentries and attacking isolated groups of soldiers a few hours before Edward's army retreated northward and dispersed.

Mauny accompanied Edward III's second invasion of the Low Countries in 1340, and fought at the naval battle of Sluys on 24 June. The patriotic poet Laurence Minot sang of him:

> Sir Walter the Mawnay, God gif him mede!
> Was bold of body in batayl to bede …
> (*Poems*, 38)

The main operation of the campaign was the long, costly, and unsuccessful siege of Tournai, which lasted from 26 July to 25 September 1340. Mauny's contribution to the siege was to lead a succession of lucrative and destructive raids against the towns of the Tournaisis and neighbouring areas of France. When the siege was abandoned, for want of money, he was one of the intimates who shared Edward III's humiliating captivity at the hands of his creditors in Ghent. Mauny lent the king some £4000 in his extremity. He was with Edward when he escaped from the Low Countries in a small boat, and was present at the famous scene in the Tower of London on 30 November 1340, when the king arrived unannounced by the Watergate to confront his ministers in the middle of the night.

Soldiering, 1341–1347 In October 1341 Mauny was appointed, jointly with Robert d'Artois, to command the expeditionary force that Edward III intended to send to Brittany to intervene in the war of succession there on the side of John de Montfort against the forces of his French-backed rival, Charles de Blois. This plan was replaced in February 1342 by a more ambitious one, involving the dispatch of no less than three successive English armies to Brittany in the next four months. Mauny was given the sole command of the first of these armies, whose objects were to secure a landing place for the others and to keep the Montfortist cause alive until they could arrive. His mission was not a success. As a result of the delay in requisitioning ships, he arrived at Brest in about early May, six weeks later than he had intended, and with only 34 men-at-arms and 200 mounted archers, less than half the force that had been planned. By this time Charles de Blois had already overrun much of Montfortist Brittany. The chronicler Jean le Bel (1.301–5, 315–22) gives a dramatic account, borrowed and embellished by Froissart, of Mauny's deeds. But it is largely fictional. Mauny's only notable exploit was a raid into Finistère to capture Hervé de Léon, the principal Breton lieutenant of Charles de Blois, and other valuable prisoners. At about the end of June he made a truce with Charles's representatives and sailed back to England. Edward promptly repudiated the truce and, although Mauny remained in high favour at court, he was never again given an independent military command.

In October 1342 Mauny returned to Brittany with Edward III and the main body of the English army. He was given the dangerous task of reconnoitring the defences of Vannes. He took part in the siege of the city which ended in failure in January 1343. In August 1345 Henry, duke of Lancaster, landed with an English army in Gascony and attacked French positions in the valleys of the Dordogne and the Garonne. Mauny served in this campaign as one of Lancaster's principal subordinate commanders. He took part in the victories at Bergerac and Auberoche and in the capture of La Réole, events that turned the tide in favour of the English in the south-west for the next three decades. While he was at La Réole, Mauny discovered the grave of his father, who had been murdered there twenty years before on his return from a pilgrimage to Santiago de Compostela, and had his body disinterred for reburial in the Franciscan convent of Valenciennes. In 1346 he served as one of the captains of Aiguillon during the four-month siege of the place by the army of Jean, duke of Normandy. Mauny led the most dangerous sorties of the siege, and when the duke eventually withdrew, on 20 August 1346, he was the first to invade the abandoned encampment of the French army and plunder what they had left there.

Mauny left the south-west with twenty companions at the end of August 1346 and travelled overland to join the army of Edward III in northern France. This rash enterprise was made possible by a safe conduct from the duke of Normandy which he had bought by remitting the ransom of one of Jean's friends. Even so, Mauny was captured near St Jean-d'Angély. He escaped from his prison but was arrested again at Orléans and taken under guard to Paris, where he was briefly imprisoned in the Louvre. Several months after his departure he found his way to Edward III's siege works outside Calais.

Mauny played a prominent part in the long siege of Calais. In July 1347, when the English strength reached its peak, he had 326 men serving under him, including 19 knights and 91 squires. Only the king, the prince of Wales, and the earls of Lancaster and Warwick had larger retinues. Mauny was one of the commissioners who represented the king of England in the brief negotiations with the leaders of the French army at the end of July 1347. And, when the negotiations failed and the French left Calais to its fate, it was with Mauny that the garrison asked to speak to negotiate the surrender of the town. He understood the shared values and bonds of mutual self-interest that united men of rank on either side and articulated it as clearly as any of his contemporaries. 'By Our Lady,' he is said to have told the king, who was contemplating putting them to death:

> I tell you that we shall not go so willingly on your service if you kill these men, for they will surely do the same to us on some other occasion when we are doing no more than our duty. (*Chronique de Jean le Bel*, 2.162)

Diplomacy, administration, and marriage After 1347 Mauny was increasingly drawn into the administrative and diplomatic business of Edward III's government. He served on judicial commissions of oyer and terminer. He sat regularly in the royal council. He was summoned to every parliament between January 1348 and his death, and was regularly appointed to the committees which heard petitions. He was an influential adviser on relations with the Low Countries, where he retained many connections. He was one of Edward III's ambassadors at the diplomatic conferences with the representatives of France and Flanders at Calais and Dunkirk in November and December 1348 and returned to represent the king at the next conference with the French ministers, at Guînes in March 1349. In 1351 Edward sent him to his native Hainault to try to reconcile the dowager empress, Margaret of Hainault, with her son.

Mauny was by now a rich man. In Hainault he had inherited the lordship of Jenlain, south of Valenciennes, from his mother. In 1340 he had obtained a grant of Wasnes from the count of Hainault while both men were engaged in the siege of Tournai. At some time after the death of his elder brothers at the battle of Stavoren in 1345, he succeeded to his family's principal domains at Masny and acquired several castles in the southern part of the county. He continued to receive largesse from the king, including property at Calais and in Gascony. In late 1353 or early 1354 he married Edward III's cousin Margaret Marshal [see Brotherton, Margaret], the daughter of his old patron *Thomas of Brotherton and widow of John Seagrave, thereby temporarily incurring the displeasure of the king, whose licence had not been sought. Margaret, one of the two coheiresses of the earldom of Norfolk, was among the richest women in England. Mauny devoted much effort to the litigious business of getting her considerable domains into his possession.

Soldiering, 1347–1360 Mauny's military career was less busy and less well recorded after 1347. Froissart (4.74, 77, 89) says that he fought with Edward III in the battle beneath the walls of Calais on 2 January 1350 and in the naval battle off Winchelsea on 29 August 1350, but there is no reliable evidence on either point. He certainly took part in the raids across Picardy and the Boulonnais mounted from Calais in the summer of 1351 by the English. But for the remainder of the 1350s he took the field only when the king was in command and his status at court demanded it. In 1355 he fought with Edward in Artois and Picardy. On his return, in November, he acted as the king's spokesman at the opening of parliament, reporting on the diplomatic and military affairs of the past eighteen months. At the beginning of the following year Mauny commanded the advance guard of the army

which went north to recapture Berwick from the Scots. He organized a brief and vigorous siege of the town and succeeded in forcing the Scots to surrender within a few days of his arrival. But he took no part in the great campaigns in France in 1356. He was in council with the king when the news arrived of the capture of the king of France by the prince of Wales at the battle of Poitiers.

In the spring of 1359, after the failure of Edward III's attempts to negotiate a treaty with the captive king of France, Mauny was sent to the Low Countries to recruit troops in preparation for the great campaign by which Edward III hoped to force the issue. He recruited a force reckoned at 1500 men in Hainault and the neighbouring principalities of the empire, and led them to Calais in the autumn, where they rioted and did a great deal of damage to the town while waiting for the rest of the army to arrive from England. On the eve of the campaign Mauny became a knight of the Garter. He then accompanied Edward III during the unsuccessful siege of Rheims in December and January, and in the *chevauchée* east and south of Paris that followed. In April 1360 he led the attack on the suburbs of the French capital in person.

Mauny's facility for maintaining amicable relations with the enemy no doubt accounted for his inclusion among the delegation chosen to negotiate the treaty of Brétigny, which brought this campaign to a close in May 1360. Five months later he was present when the treaty was confirmed at Calais, and when, on 1 November 1360, the king of France was finally released from captivity, he was one of the four knights of Edward III's household on whom Jean II bestowed lavish grants as he left.

For most of the 1360s England and France were at peace, and there is little trace of Mauny's activity. In 1361 he made a pilgrimage to Santiago de Compostela, and he spent some time in Hainault in 1364. But he remained an active member of the council, close to the king and, increasingly, to the king's ambitious younger son, John of Gaunt, duke of Lancaster. When the war with France broke out again in 1369 Mauny, now some sixty years of age, served as one of the military advisers who accompanied Gaunt's destructive raid through Picardy.

Philanthropy and final years Mauny's principal enterprise in the last two years of his life was the foundation of the London Charterhouse. This was an old project renewed. The site, beyond the city wall north of Smithfield, had been leased by Mauny from St Bartholomew's Hospital in 1349. He set it aside as a burial-ground for victims of the black death and built a small chapel on it. More ambitious plans were made for a college of priests but never executed. It was Michael Northburgh, bishop of London and former keeper of Edward III's privy seal, who suggested to Mauny the foundation of a charterhouse and asked to be associated with it. When Northburgh died in 1361 he left a contribution of £2000 towards the endowment. After prolonged negotiations with Northburgh's executors and with the general chapter of the Carthusian order in England, Mauny finally bought the site from St Bartholomew's in November 1370. His charter of foundation is dated 28 March 1371. The existing chapel became the church of the new house. The foundations of the conventual buildings were begun almost at once.

Mauny died at his wife's manor at Great Chesterford in Essex on 14 or 15 January 1372, before the new buildings had risen from the ground. By his will, which was made on 30 November 1371, he left a large bequest to the Charterhouse and directed that he should be buried in its chapel in a tomb of alabaster carved with his arms and bearing his effigy dressed as a knight. Although Mauny wished his funeral to be without pomp, it was a great occasion, attended by the king, all his sons who were in England, and a great concourse of prelates and noblemen, as well as by poor men who were entitled under his will to receive a penny each from his executor. John of Gaunt had 500 masses said for the repose of his soul.

Mauny was in some ways the model soldier of his age. He was gallant and courageous. He observed the chivalrous conventions of his class. He was one of the few prominent figures in the early part of the Hundred Years' War to receive unqualified admiration from both sides. But the truth was that he was a poor commander with little strategic grasp, whose military achievements were more spectacular than useful. He was among the first to make a large personal fortune out of loot and ransoms, but he perfectly illustrated Geoffrey de Charney's observation that an excessive interest in ransoms made a poor soldier. He owed his fame in large measure to Jean Froissart who, like Mauny, came from Hainault and to whom Mauny supplied generous gifts and tall stories during the chronicler's visit to England in the early 1360s. 'My book is decorated with his deeds', said Froissart (8.287).

Mauny was survived by his wife and by a daughter, Anne, aged sixteen at the time of his death, who had married John Hastings, earl of Pembroke.

JONATHAN SUMPTION

Sources Rymer, *Foedera*, new edn • *Chancery records* (RC) • Treaty Rolls, PRO, C 76 • Wardrobe Accounts, 1342–4, PRO, E36/204 • Various Accounts, PRO, E101 • Issue Rolls, PRO, E403 • Wardrobe Accounts, 1334–5, BL, Cotton Nero C VIII, fols. 179–325 • *Chronique de Jean le Bel*, ed. J. Viard and E. Déprez, 2 vols. (Paris, 1904–5) • *Adae Murimuth continuatio chronicarum. Robertus de Avesbury de gestis mirabilibus regis Edwardi tertii*, ed. E. M. Thompson, Rolls Series, 93 (1889) • *Chroniques de J. Froissart*, ed. S. Luce and others, 15 vols. (Paris, 1869–1975) • J. Froissart, 'Ci après s'ensieut un trettié amoureus, qui s'appelle *Le joli buisson de jonesse*', in *Œuvres de Froissart: poésies*, ed. A. Scheler, 2 (Brussels, 1871), 1–164 • J. Froissart, *Chroniques*, ed. K. de Lettenhove, 18 (1874); 22 (1875), 174–84 • *The wardrobe book of William de Norwell*, ed. M. Lyon and others (1983) • G. Wrottesley, *Crécy and Calais* (1897); repr. (1898) • *Chronicon Galfridi le Baker de Swynebroke*, ed. E. M. Thompson (1889) • *Chronicon Henrici Knighton, vel Cnitthon, monachi Leycestrensis*, ed. J. R. Lumby, 2 vols., Rolls Series, 92 (1889–95) • F. Devon, ed. and trans., *Issue roll of Thomas de Brantingham*, RC (1835) • W. St J. Hope, *The history of London Charterhouse* (1925) • *Registrum Simonis de Sudbiria, diocesis Londoniensis*, AD 1362–1375, ed. R. C. Fowler, 1, CYS, 34 (1927), 1–4 [will] • *Report from the Lords' Committees ... on all matters touching the dignity of a peer of the realm*, 5 vols. (1820–29) • *RotP* • L. Devillers, ed., *Cartulaire des comtes de Hainaut, de l'avènement de Guillaume II à la mort de Jacqueline de Bavière*, 6 vols. (1881–96) • *The poems of Laurence Minot, 1333–1352*, ed. T. B. James and J. Simons (1989) • *CIPM*, 13, no. 148 • *Calendar of the fine rolls*, PRO, 8 (1924), 153–4, 200 • *RotS*, 1.954

Wealth at death owed approx. £7500 by debtors; plus land in eighteen counties; also land in Calais, Scotland, the Welsh march, and Hainault; also two ships, silver plate, armour, horses, other personal chattels

Maurice (*d.* 1107), bishop of London, rose in the service of William the Conqueror as royal chaplain and chancellor. He was appointed bishop of London at the royal court in Gloucester, at Christmas 1085. Once, in 1082, he appears as archdeacon of Le Mans, an office he surely also owed to the king. Although there is no positive evidence, there is no reason to doubt his Norman or continental origin. As chancellor from 1078 to 1085, Maurice would have been in regular attendance on the king. Supervising the production of royal writs and charters, he had a central position in royal government. Ranulf Flambard, the leading minister of William Rufus and later bishop of Durham, is said to have served under Chancellor Maurice as keeper of the king's seal.

The event in Maurice's career which is most widely recorded by the chroniclers is his anointing and crowning of Henry I at Westminster on 5 August 1100, three days after the sudden death of William Rufus. His lasting achievements, however, were the beginning of a new cathedral and the reorganization of his cathedral chapter. Anglo-Saxon St Paul's completely burned down in June 1087, and even though no visible trace of Maurice's building remains, enough is known to show that he successfully entered the competition of Anglo-Norman cathedral builders to rival the grandeur of Winchester Cathedral. A need to restructure the temporalities of his church to sustain his ambitious building programme and the wish to provide the new cathedral with a representative body of clerics may well have been factors in the reorganization of the chapter, but there was also a general concern among the Anglo-Norman bishops with the organization of cathedral chapters. Maurice established a chapter of thirty secular canons, including a dean at their head and four archdeacons. To each of them Maurice assigned a prebend as an individual source of income. With his reforms he combined a respect for Anglo-Saxon traditions. At Chich (later called St Osyth) on the Essex coast he instituted four priests to serve the church of the Anglo-Saxon saint Osgyth.

Maurice's reputation was that of an efficient administrator and conscientious bishop. William of Malmesbury rebuked him for being too fond of women, reporting maliciously that he claimed to have to have intercourse on his doctors' prescription. But St Paul's remained a home for married clergy long after Maurice's death in late September 1107.

FALKO NEININGER

Sources C. N. L. Brooke, 'The earliest times to 1485', *A history of St Paul's Cathedral and the men associated with it*, ed. W. R. Matthews and W. M. Atkins (1957), 1–99, 361–5, esp. 18–23, 66 • M. Gibbs, ed., *Early charters of the cathedral church of St Paul, London*, CS, 3rd ser., 58 (1939) • F. Neininger, ed., *London, 1076–1187*, English Episcopal Acta, 15 (1999) • *Reg. RAN*, vol. 1 • C. N. L. Brooke, *The medieval idea of marriage* (1989), 78–89 • E. G. Whatley, *The saint of London: the life and miracles of St Erkenwald. Text and translation* (1989) • *Willelmi Malmesbiriensis monachi de gestis pontificum Anglorum libri quinque*, ed. N. E. S. A. Hamilton, Rolls Series, 52 (1870), 145 • Ordericus Vitalis, *Eccl. hist.*, 5.294, 6.144 • *Fasti Angl., 1066–1300*, [St Paul's, London], 97–8 • R. Gem, 'The romanesque architecture of old St Paul's Cathedral and its late eleventh-century context', *Medieval art, architecture and archaeology in London*, ed. L. Grant, British Archaeological Association Conference Transactions, 10 (1990), 47–63 · D. Bethell, 'The lives of St Osyth of Essex and St Osyth of Aylesbury', *Analecta Bollandiana*, 88 (1970), 75–127, esp. 90–91 · *Hugh the Chanter: the history of the church of York, 1066–1127*, ed. and trans. C. Johnson, rev. edn, rev. M. Brett, C. N. L. Brooke, and M. Winterbottom, OMT (1990), 10, 16 · *ASC*, s.a. 1083, 1084, 1085, 1099, 1100 [text E] · D. Dumville and S. Keynes, eds., *The Anglo-Saxon Chronicle: a collaborative edition* (1983–96), 3, ed. J. M. Bately (1986), 87 [MS A] · F. Barlow, *The English church, 1066–1154: a history of the Anglo-Norman church* (1979) · M. L. Colker, 'Texts of Jocelyn of Canterbury which relate to the history of Barking Abbey', *Studia Monastica*, 7 (1965), 383–460, esp. 388, 398, 418, 438 · E. U. Crosby, *Bishop and chapter in twelfth-century England* (1994), esp. 318–21 · *Florentii Wigorniensis monachi chronicon ex chronicis*, ed. B. Thorpe, 2, EHS, 10 (1849), 18, 51, 57 · H. R. Luard, ed., *Flores historiarum*, 3 vols., Rolls Series, 95 (1890), vol. 2, pp. 12, 17, 19, 40 · Henry, archdeacon of Huntingdon, *Historia Anglorum*, ed. D. E. Greenway, OMT (1996), 207–8, 211, 233, 236 · H. R. Loyn, 'William's bishops: some further thoughts', *Anglo-Norman Studies*, 10 (1987), 223–35 · Symeon of Durham, *Opera*, 1.91, 135; 2.213, 235, 239

Maurice. *See* Meurig (*fl.* 1210).

Maurice, prince palatine of the Rhine (1621–1652), royalist army officer and naval officer, was the fourth son of Frederick V (1596–1632), elector palatine of the Rhine, and his wife, *Elizabeth (1596–1662), daughter of *James VI and I of Great Britain and sister of *Charles I. Maurice was born in the castle of Küstrin, on the Oder, on 16 January 1621 NS. There George William, the elector of Brandenburg, the husband of Frederick's sister, had offered temporary refuge to Elizabeth on the flight of her family after the battle of the White Mountain, which two months earlier had ended their short-lived occupation of the Bohemian throne and residence in Prague. The new baby, baptized four days after his birth, was named after Maurice of Nassau (*d.* 1625), the hero of the Dutch resistance to Spain. He was sent to Berlin for safe keeping, while the family found protection in the Netherlands at the hands of the stadholder Frederick Henry, prince of Orange, Nassau's younger brother. Maurice stayed in the care of his Brandenburg kin in Berlin for seven years, and only joined his parents in Holland in 1628.

Exile and the beginning of the English civil war In the years that followed the White Mountain the exiled palatines at their court at The Hague were the object of international protestant conspiracy and intermittent military activity, designed to recover their patrimony. After the death of Frederick V, Elizabeth (still styled queen of Bohemia) brought up a large family, which included her eldest surviving sons, *Charles Lewis (elector after 1632), *Rupert, and Maurice, and her youngest daughter, *Sophia. While Rupert attracted attention by his angelic appearance and devilish ways, Maurice was distinguished, at least in his mother's eyes, only by his great height. With her family in exile, and their homeland under military occupation, Elizabeth had few illusions about their future prospects. She wrote to Archbishop William Laud in May 1637 that Maurice (then sixteen) would be joining the prince of Orange in the forthcoming campaign in Germany 'to learn that profession I believe he must live by' (*CSP dom.*,

Maurice, prince palatine of the Rhine (1621–1652), by William Dobson, 1645?

1637, 138). Laud approved. She may also have wished him away from The Hague, where he had got into scrapes and had even fought a duel. With Rupert at the siege of Breda in 1637, he was commended for his courage. Military service was mixed with study at a French university (perhaps at Paris, as he was in the city in 1638–9) and, possibly, Leiden. In 1640 he entered the Swedish general Banier's army. In spite of a pension provided by the English government, money was desperately short at The Hague, and Charles I, concerned for his sister's welfare, had lavishly entertained her two eldest sons at Whitehall. He now promised assistance to Maurice, to 'go to what army he pleaseth' (Bromley, 124).

But before Maurice could do so, the political crisis in the British Isles, and the uprising in Ulster, turned into civil war in all three kingdoms. When Charles I sent his queen to The Hague—ostensibly to bring their daughter Mary to join her newly married husband, the son of the stadholder, but also to seek recruits, arms, and money from the Dutch—Rupert and Maurice sprang to her side. They sailed to the north of England in August 1642 in time to appear at the raising of the royal standard, the signal for war, at Nottingham. No doubt arrangements had already been made for Rupert to be given command of his uncle's cavalry. For his part Maurice became colonel of a regiment of horse. As might be expected from his closeness to the king and his brother, the general, Maurice's regiment was a favoured unit. It was officered by professional soldiers and supported by wealthy gentlemen; many of its junior officers went on to high command in the war. It was an early and effective presence in the first skirmish, at Powick Bridge, near Worcester, on 23 September 1642. Maurice was wounded at this engagement. His regiment of four troops fought in Rupert's right wing of horse at Edgehill.

When the king's cavalry quartered around the royalist capital, Oxford, Maurice was called on to attend the council of war on six of the sixteen recorded meetings which took place between November 1642 and May 1643. The youngest of the royal counsellors (he was twenty-two), he did not impress the chancellor of the exchequer, twelve years older. Sir Edward Hyde later wrote that 'he was not qualified with parts of nature, and less with any acquired … He understood very little more of the war than to fight very stoutly when there was occasion' (Clarendon, *Hist. rebellion*, 3.67). Maurice rode with his brother in the successful assault on Cirencester in February 1643. On 2 March that year he was given his first independent command, as general of horse and foot in Gloucestershire and south Wales, with the objective of shadowing Sir William Waller, whose rapid progress in the west was causing alarm at Oxford. His little army skirmished with Waller's larger force in the Forest of Dean (Little Dean, 11 April), and the following day, at Ripple Field, near Tewkesbury, inflicted some damage.

Maurice showed flair and skill in taking his forces across the Severn and outmanoeuvring his much more experienced opponent on this narrow site. His growing reputation further recruited his cavalry unit, as it was 'accounted the most active regiment in the army'. One of his new officers reckoned that six months' service with it in summer 1643 'gave me more proficiency as a soldier … than generally in the Low Countries in 4 or 5 years' (*Military Memoirs*, 8). It was heavily involved in the unsuccessful attempt by the king and Oxford forces to relieve Reading at the end of April.

The war in the west country William Seymour, marquess of Hertford, had been given supreme command of the western counties by the king at the beginning of the war, but had been forced to retire and go to Oxford. A fragment of his forces under Sir Ralph Hopton, however, had prospered in Cornwall, and had been encouraged by the king to march east. Maurice was to return to the west to assist him and supplement his largely infantry force with a strong body of horse, as well as foot and munitions, under Hertford's nominal command. Rupert had wanted his brother to command in chief, and intrigued with the king to this effect. But Hertford, although no soldier, was of great political importance in the west country; and Maurice consented to serve under him, as lieutenant-general. Unfortunately, as Hyde commented, there were in the king's camp 'no two men of more contrary natures and dispositions', and the basis was laid for further quarrels in the high command (Clarendon, *Hist. rebellion*, 3.67).

At the first skirmish with Waller's men at Chewton Mendip, near Wells, Somerset, in June 1643 the prince was wounded with 'two shrewd hurts in his head' (Clarendon, *Hist. rebellion*, 3.87) and briefly taken prisoner. Although the Cornish stormed Waller's strong position at Lansdown on 5 July, the parliamentarian general was able to withdraw in good order, interrupt vital supplies, and pen Hopton's forces into Devizes. It was left to Maurice's cavalry to summon further help from Oxford, covering 44 miles in a desperate night ride. Wilmot, with fresh horse, brought Waller to battle at Roundway Down (13 July), shattered his wings of cavalry, and, joined with the Cornish issuing out of Devizes, put his foot to flight.

Bristol was left in a vulnerable position by Waller's defeat, in which some of the city garrison had been involved, and his army's withdrawal. The Oxford and western forces combined to storm the city on 26 July 1643. While Rupert's attack on the north-west sector of the defensive line was successful, Maurice's men and the Cornish suffered heavy casualties on the other side, which was strongly held. In the appointment of a governor of the conquered city the rivalry between the princes and Hertford erupted again. Hertford, as regional commander, nominated Hopton. Rupert claimed it for himself. The king confirmed this but made Hopton his deputy, and recalled Hertford to Oxford. Maurice was made sole general of the western forces.

With a largely infantry army Maurice followed the earl of Carnarvon's cavalry sweep through the Dorset countryside, which had been successful in persuading several formerly parliamentarian towns to make terms. But as Hopton had already noted, the Oxford horse and the Cornish foot did not mix well, and often came to blows. The prince's men were unpaid and disorderly; they now breached agreements made, and resorted to plunder. There was another quarrel, this time with Carnarvon, over a new appointment, and the earl resigned his commission. Maurice turned west to quicken the siege of Exeter. It surrendered on 4 September. Dartmouth fell to his troops in October, by which time most of the ports vital to hopes of supply from the continent were in the king's hands.

Only Plymouth remained of any significance, and Maurice was about to assist the siege there when he fell seriously ill. William Harvey and other royal physicians were sent to treat him and diagnosed 'the ordinary raging disease of the army, a slow fever with great dejection of strength' (Warburton, 2.307). As others in his entourage fell sick at the same time, the common contagion of that summer, a form of typhus, can be identified. 'The disease of the camp' (*morbus campestris*) had decimated the armies of both sides in the Thames valley earlier. Maurice survived after a month's convalescence, but the siege of Plymouth was impeded. The town could be supplied from the sea, the defences were strong, and the garrison and townsmen resolute. Initial attacks were beaten off, and it also became clear that with the loss of so many of their old leaders the Cornish foot were less effective in this and the campaigns which followed.

The king's concern for his nephew was shown not only in the dispatch of royal doctors to his side, but in his plans for Maurice to marry a rich French heiress. 'Though Mars be now most in voag', he wrote in July 1643, 'yet Hymen may sometimes be remembyred' (Scott, 32). Rupert had spurned the favoured bride, and Charles I did not want to lose a lady whose wealth might be tapped for the royalist cause. But in spite of his uncle's pleas, Maurice remained unmarried.

The southern and marcher commands, 1644–1645 In the new year Maurice was commissioned to command all the southern counties except Hampshire, where Hopton's new army was active. His first task was to besiege Lyme Regis, which threatened the royalist supply lines from the western ports to Oxford and Bristol. With a considerable force of Cornish, Devon, and Irish foot, and twelve well-equipped siege guns, he opened the assault in April 1644. He built new batteries and poured shot, including 'hot iron', 'fire-arrows', and other forms of wildfire, into the little town, burning wooden houses, and barges in the harbour. But as with Plymouth, the besieged could be reinforced from the sea, sailors fought alongside the defenders, and Robert Blake conducted a skilful resistance. Several attacks were bloodily repulsed. In a wet season, and suffering heavy casualties, Maurice's troops wasted away. When forced to raise the siege, on the approach of Essex's army in mid-June, only half his force remained.

Nevertheless, when his army was reviewed by the king, marching west on the tail of Essex's army, at Crediton on 26 July 1644, it was 2500 horse and 5000 foot strong, with a full complement of general staff. Its commander now possessed a troop of mounted lifeguards. Maurice provided the advance guard of the royal forces that pursued the parliamentarians into Cornwall and eventually compelled their surrender. For the prince, however, the Lostwithiel victory was a turning point. He found that his Cornish troops would not leave the county to follow him east with the main Oxford army, and his attempts to surprise Taunton and Bridgwater, and drive in Waller's outposts, were all repulsed. He did have some success at the second battle of Newbury, where his much reduced force held Speen Hill against the odds, and by means of a complicated manoeuvre managed to draw off the guns, placed in Donnington Castle, after the battle.

The situation was altered with the appointment of Rupert as supreme commander in November 1644. Maurice replaced him as lieutenant-general in Wales and the marcher counties, without, however, the title of president. He set up his headquarters at Worcester in mid-January 1645, and energetically reorganized the royalist war effort in the region. He agreed articles of co-operation with the local commissioners, imposed a loyalty oath, and gathered recruits, munitions, and draught horses, in short supply at Oxford. But the local parliamentarians were increasingly confident and active; in meeting the threat to Chester the garrison of Shrewsbury was weakened, and it fell to a surprise assault. With it Maurice lost his base magazine. Other set-backs followed. Several of his leading supporters were killed or captured and their houses destroyed. His men deserted, and their conduct deteriorated to the extent that public opinion, formerly favourable, turned against them. The clubman movement in Worcestershire and Herefordshire began to take shape.

Maurice played a crucial role in spring 1645, however, in the preparations for the coming campaign. Most of the royalist-controlled munitions industry lay in the region he commanded, and Rupert joined his brother to make full use of it in March and April. Early in May they brought these essential supplies to Oxford, and provided a cavalry screen, to allow the king's army to take the field. Maurice was present at the sack of Leicester, and at the battle of Naseby on 14 June. With his regiment of horse and his own troop of lifeguards, he fought alongside his brother in the right wing of horse.

In the dispersal of the royal forces after this disaster Maurice returned to Worcester. A source hostile to him admitted that he was 'in himselfe cyvyll to all and wel beeloved of the cytyzens', though too tolerant of the undisciplined and disbanded soldiery who crowded into the city at this stage of the war (P. Styles, *Studies in Seventeenth Century West Midlands History*, 229). The presence of the Scots army, its siege of Hereford, and its threat to Worcester put Maurice on the defensive. But with the aid of the king's remaining forces he raised the siege in mid-September, and brought 600–700 horse to the king in north Wales after his defeat at Rowton Heath, outside Chester.

Rupert had surrendered Bristol on 10 September, however, much to the king's indignation. In dismissing his nephew instantly he compromised the position of Maurice and many other of Rupert's appointees. While Maurice had not been named in the wild rumours of plots that reached the ears of the king, and he received a friendly letter from Charles, he left his post and joined his brother. Together with about 200 followers they challenged their uncle at Newark, on 26 October 1645. Although a council of war cleared Rupert of any treachery in his surrender of the city, both brothers applied to parliament for passes to go abroad. In the interim they stayed at Oxford, and before the fall of the royal headquarters (June 1646) the king and Rupert were reconciled.

War at sea The brothers separated on leaving England, Rupert travelling to France, Maurice returning to Holland. He took service with the prince of Orange's army in 1648, as he had before. The revolt of the English fleet altered prospects again for the exiled royalists in summer 1648, providing an opportunity for direct action against the parliamentarian authorities and the chance to win prizes for the impoverished court of Prince Charles at The Hague. Rupert and Maurice took the revolted ships (January 1649) to assist the royalists in Ireland; they raided commerce from their base at Kinsale, until Robert Blake's arrival with the main fleet and Oliver Cromwell's conquests on the mainland. They then accepted the protection of the king of Portugal, and sailed to Lisbon. But Blake followed and the brothers were forced to seek refuge in the Mediterranean, until—in the hope of further booty—they sailed to the coast of west Africa, where on 2 March 1652 Maurice raised his flag as vice-admiral on a captured English ship, renamed the *Defiance*. From there the brothers took their little privateering fleet, reduced to four ships, to the West Indies.

Disaster struck in mid-September. A hurricane caught the flotilla as it sailed close to the Virgin Islands, and continued for four days (13–16 September). Only Rupert's flagship survived. Maurice and the rest disappeared on the second day of the storm, no doubt wrecked on one of the extensive reefs of Anegada or Sombrero Islands. Rumours persisted for years that he was still alive, possibly a prisoner of the Spanish on Puerto Rico. This myth was disposed of when Sir Robert Holmes, Rupert's follower and former subordinate of Maurice, questioned captured Spanish seamen with local knowledge before the Second Anglo-Dutch War in 1664. They had heard of no survivors, and had seen among the wreckage on Puerto Rico's shores 'a great quantitie of pipestaves markt MP as all prince Maurice his cask[s] were' (Ollard, 125).

As a general and admiral Maurice was overshadowed by his elder brother, to whom he was very close, sharing his good and bad fortune unhesitatingly during the civil war and after. Like Rupert he was personally brave, and was loved and respected by his immediate followers as both a dashing cavalry leader and a good organizer. He was equally ignorant of English politics and lacking in diplomatic and debating skills, with the result that, despite his high connections, he contributed little to the overall direction of the war. Hyde accused him of being too familiar with his subordinates, which the frequent indiscipline of his troops might confirm, and not giving due respect to the leading figures of the court (Hyde no doubt included). He lacked his brother's intellectual and artistic interests. His failures before Plymouth and, particularly, Lyme lessened the reputation he had acquired earlier. His competent and popular government in the Welsh marches in 1645, however, indicated that he might have pursued a successful career had he lived to enjoy the restoration of the royalists' fortunes later.   IAN ROY

Sources letter of Maurice to Rupert, BL, Add. MS 18982, fol. 27 · administrative orders from Maurice to Sir John Owen, 1645, NL Wales, Clenennau papers [some printed in E. Warburton, *Memoirs of Prince Rupert and the cavaliers* (1849)] · notes on Maurice's regiment and general staff, BL, Harley MSS 986, fol. 83, and 6802, fol. 284 · E. Warburton, *Memoirs of Prince Rupert and the cavaliers*, 3 vols. (1849), vols. 2 and 3 · Clarendon, *Hist. rebellion*, vol. 3 · *CSP dom.*, 1637; 1644–7; 1652–3 · L. M. Baker, *The letters of Elizabeth queen of Bohemia* (1958) · G. Bromley, ed., *A collection of original royal letters* (1787) · *Military memoirs: the civil war. Richard Atkyns*, ed. P. Young (1967) · *Bellum civile: Hopton's narrative of his campaign in the West, 1642–1644*, ed. C. E. H. Chadwyck Healey, Somerset RS, 18 (1902) · *Diary of the marches of the royal army during the great civil war, kept by Richard Symonds*, ed. C. E. Long, CS, old ser., 74 (1859); repr. with new introduction by I. Roy as *Richard Symonds' diary of the marches of the royal army* (1997) · *DNB* · A. R. Bayley, *The great civil war in Dorset, 1642–1660* (1910) · J. Webb, *Memorials of the civil war … as it affected Herefordshire*, ed. T. W. Webb, 2 vols. (1879) · *Bibliotheca Gloucestrensis: a collection of … tracts relating to … Gloucester*, ed. J. Washbourne (1825) · *Diary of Henry Townshend of Elmley Lovett*, ed. J. W. Willis Bund, 4 pts in 2 vols., Worcestershire Historical Society (1915–20) · E. Scott, *Rupert Prince Palatine* (1899) · R. Ollard, *Man of war: Sir Robert Holmes and the Restoration navy* (1969) · M. A. E. Green, *Elizabeth electress palatine and queen of Bohemia*, ed. S. C. Lomas, rev. edn (1909) [based on M. A. E. Green,

'Elizabeth, eldest daughter of James I', *Lives of the princesses of England*, 5 (1854), 145–573]
Archives Devon RO, corresp. with Edward Seymour
Likenesses W. Dobson, portrait, 1645?, priv. coll. [*see illus.*] · T. Athow, drawing, wash (after W. Dobson), AM Oxf. · Honthorst, group portrait (including Maurice?)

Maurice, Sir Frederick Barton (1871–1951), army officer, was born in Dublin on 19 January 1871. He was the eldest son of Major-General Sir John Frederick *Maurice (1841–1912) and his wife, Anne Frances (Annie) Fitzgerald. At various times his father was an active soldier and professor of military art and history at the Staff College, Camberley; Maurice served with him in the Tirah campaign of 1897–8.

Although Maurice followed his father's path into military service and as a military historian, his influences and associations were more wide-ranging. His paternal grandfather, F. D. *Maurice, was an eminent Christian socialist and theologian. His own wife, Helen Margaret Marsh (with whom he shared a long wedded life, from 1899 until her death in 1942), was the daughter of F. H. Marsh (sometime professor of surgery at Cambridge University and master of Downing College) and sister of Sir Edward *Marsh, art connoisseur, literary critic, and private secretary to a succession of notable politicians, including Winston Churchill. And of Maurice's five children (one son and four daughters), one became the eminent Cambridge economist Joan Violet *Robinson and another, Nancy, wrote devotedly in support of her father. (In later life she married Sir Edward Spears, liaison officer and military historian.)

Maurice was educated at St Paul's School and the Royal Military College, Sandhurst. He was commissioned in 1892 in the Derbyshire regiment (which became the Sherwood Foresters) and saw service in the Second South African War, being mentioned in dispatches and raised at the age of twenty-nine to the rank of brevet major. Back in England after the war, he graduated from the Staff College and, among other positions, served under Sir Douglas Haig in the directorate of staff duties at the War Office.

In 1913 Maurice was appointed an instructor at the Staff College, where for most of his first year the commandant was Sir William ('Wully') Robertson, a man of lowly origins whose abilities and devotion to a military career marked him out for advancement even in so hierarchical a profession. The strong friendship which developed between Maurice and Robertson became a feature of their joint careers up to 1918.

On the outbreak of the First World War in August 1914 Maurice went to France as a staff officer with the 3rd division; he was soon promoted to head its general staff, and his level-headedness and efficiency during the thirteen-day retreat from Mons to the Marne were a subject of comment. Early in 1915 Robertson became chief of staff to Sir John French, commander of the British expeditionary force, and he soon selected Maurice to take charge of the operations section at general headquarters. They worked well together and Maurice was further promoted. Then in December Robertson was transferred to London to

Sir Frederick Barton Maurice (1871–1951), by Walter Stoneman, 1917

become chief of the Imperial General Staff and principal military adviser to the government. Maurice went with him, to become director of military operations at the War Office with the rank of major-general.

At the War Office, Robertson and Maurice worked in agreement. They endorsed a strategy of concentrating Britain's military resources and operations on the western front against the armed might of Germany, and they resisted policies which would have directed Britain's endeavours towards lesser adversaries in more extraneous theatres. During 1916 this western strategy went largely unchallenged. In 1917 it certainly came under challenge, if in no way effectually, from the new prime minister, David Lloyd *George, who at various stages advocated a campaign on the Italian front, placed Britain's forces in France under French command, and sought to divert military resources to the Turkish theatre. On 31 January 1918, according to Maurice's diary, Lloyd George, despite the imminence of a great German offensive on the western front, told Robertson that 'we were and always had been "over-insured" in the West'. This brought relations between Lloyd George and Robertson—the latter devotedly supported by Maurice—to breaking point. Robertson was elbowed out of office in mid-February 1918, and Maurice followed on 21 April.

The anticipation in April was that Haig would offer Maurice command of a division, or some even more responsible position, in France. This did not come about because of action taken by Maurice himself. On 21 March

the Germans had launched a mighty offensive against the British army in France, as Robertson (more consistently than Haig) had warned, and had made an alarming advance. Lloyd George came under criticism for having contributed to this setback by reducing Haig's forces and obliging him to extend his line. The prime minister, along with other members of the government, strongly denied these charges, citing facts and figures which appeared to show that Haig's army in France had been increased, not diminished, that the decision to extend the British sector of the western front had been taken by the military command not the politicians, and that no excessive number of divisions had been diverted to the Turkish theatre. On 6 May 1918 Maurice, now between appointments but still a serving soldier, wrote a letter to the press stating that ministerial statements were false. The letter appeared on the following morning in the Conservative *Morning Post* and *The Times*, and in the Liberal *Daily Chronicle* and *Daily News*.

Despite containing some errors of detail, the charges contained in Maurice's letter were well founded. Haig had certainly been obliged against his wishes to take over from the French the area of front where his army suffered setback on 21 March. The numbers of infantrymen available to Haig were fewer, not greater, than a year before. And there were several more 'white' divisions stationed in Egypt and Palestine at the time of the German offensive than the government had claimed. And although Lloyd George subsequently claimed that the government had been supplied with its figures concerning troop strengths on the western front by Maurice's own department (figures which happened to be inaccurate), these had only been provided after the statements by Lloyd George to which Maurice took exception, and had been corrected by the time Lloyd George made his rebuttal to Maurice in the parliamentary debate of 9 May. Whether, even so, a serving officer should have taken issue with his political masters in the public way Maurice did must remain a matter of opinion. Haig, for one, certainly thought not, as he recorded in his diary. Maurice himself took the view that, as a concerned citizen, he was obliged to rebut misleading statements by ministers which served to divert responsibility for setbacks on the battlefield from the political authorities, where it belonged, to the military. To this end he was prepared to sacrifice his career in the army.

What Maurice expected to follow from his action is unclear, and perhaps he was uncertain himself. He was hardly engaged in a conspiracy to bring down the government, as Lloyd George proclaimed ever thereafter. (Lloyd George's vituperation against Maurice was even carried into the index of volume 5 of his *War Memoirs*, published in 1936. Index entries under 'Maurice' include: 'the instrument by which the Government was to be thrown out'; 'intrigues against the Government, his mind being apparently unhinged'; 'false allegations against Lloyd George and Bonar Law published by'; and 'the tool of astuter men'.) Maurice certainly expected a full inquiry to be made into his charges, with results sufficiently damaging to the government that it would be inhibited in trying to apply its deviant views on strategy or threaten Haig's retention of command. To achieve that much, he was prepared to suffer the dismissal which he recognized would follow.

In the outcome Maurice accomplished little. The government at first offered a judicial inquiry into his charges but then withdrew, and settled for an open debate in the House of Commons. H. H. *Asquith, the former prime minister, moved for an inquiry by a select committee of the house, but did not attempt to endorse any of Maurice's charges. Lloyd George in response proved far more combative. He denounced Asquith's motion as a vote of no confidence in the government, and demolished Maurice's charges in a speech of great power, if questionable veracity. Thereby he won a commanding majority in a parliament which had absolutely no wish to displace his government. So Maurice was thwarted in his purpose.

The whole event was of less moment to military and political affairs than has sometimes been claimed. The German offensive had already riveted British strategy to the western front, whatever Lloyd George's inclinations, and had revealed that the government, whatever its carping against Haig, lacked the will to replace him. As to its political aspect, the Maurice debate certainly revealed the resentment nursed by Asquith and his section of Liberals at their exclusion from office. And when late in 1918 Lloyd George decided to call an election at which he waged unrelenting war upon Asquith's section of Liberals (if not upon Asquith himself), he cited the Maurice division as his basis for distinguishing Liberal sheep from Liberal goats. But it was not the case that every Liberal who had voted against him in the Maurice debate fell under his ban, and it was certainly the case that many Liberal candidates who had not participated in that debate suffered rejection by him. In short Lloyd George, irrespective of the Maurice incident, was making a conscious decision to locate his political future in the company, not of his pre-war associates, but of the predominantly Conservative grouping which had brought him to power in December 1916.

Maurice, having been promptly retired by the army council in May 1918, was not long unemployed. He became military correspondent first of the *Daily Chronicle* and then (when that journal fell under Lloyd George's control) of the *Daily News*, and later wrote articles for another Liberal journal hostile to Lloyd George, the *Westminster Gazette*. He had already, in 1905, written a book on the Russo-Turkish War of 1877, and after 1918 he wrote a succession of works usually, but not exclusively, centred around the 1914–18 conflict: a life of his father, another (with Sir George Arthur) of his father's associate Lord Wolseley, biographies of Lord Haldane and Lord Rawlinson, chapters in the *Cambridge Modern History*, entries in the *Dictionary of National Biography*, works on the western front battles of 1914 and of 1918 as well as of particular units, and more general studies bearing the titles *Governments and War* (1926) and *British Strategy* (1929). These works were not always as rigorous in employing quotations from original sources as one might wish, but the more important among them continue to be of value to historians.

Maurice, who had been appointed KCMG in 1918, also pursued a successful career as an educational administrator. From 1922 to 1933 he was principal of the Working Men's College, which his grandfather, F. D. Maurice, had helped to found back in 1854. In 1927 he became professor of military studies at London University, and the following year he was appointed chairman of the adult education committee of the Board of Education. From 1933 to 1944 he held the position of principal of what was to become Queen Mary College of the University of London, and oversaw successfully the removal of the college to Cambridge during the Second World War. He delivered the Lees Knowles lectures on military history at Cambridge in 1925–6, received an honorary LLD from that university in 1926, became DLitt, London, in 1930, and was elected an honorary fellow of King's College, Cambridge, in 1944. His failure in 1925 to secure appointment to the Chichele professorship of the history of war at Oxford, which went to the seemingly less well-qualified Sir Ernest Swinton, may have been influenced by the antipathy which one of the electors, Sir Maurice Hankey, felt towards him on account of his action in May 1918.

Maurice worked devotedly in the cause of British former servicemen, and was throughout the 1930s and up to 1947 a major figure in the British Legion. In September 1938, on the legion's behalf, he even endeavoured to head off the outbreak of a second world war. He flew to Berlin and offered Adolf Hitler the services of the legion in carrying out the plebiscite being proposed for the disputed regions of Czechoslovakia. For this purpose he had assembled a contingent of 1200 British former servicemen. As the plebiscite did not eventuate nothing came of this initiative. A year later, three days before Britain again became involved in war with Germany, he appealed to German former servicemen not to participate in an attack on Poland. These actions, if well intended, revealed the widespread incomprehension among British veterans of the First World War concerning the attitude towards renewed conflict of German former servicemen in general and one serviceman (now Germany's führer) in particular.

Maurice died at his home, 62 Grange Road, Cambridge, on 19 May 1951. Judgement upon him (always excepting that of Lloyd George) has largely been favourable. Tom Jones of the cabinet secretariat, at the height of the military crisis of April 1918, and a month before the famous letter, noted that Maurice 'has always impressed me as very balanced in his appreciations' (T. C. H. Jones, *Whitehall Diary*, ed. K. Middlemas, vol. 1, 1969, 54). Hankey came in time to describe him as 'a highly cultured and scientific soldier' (Hankey, 2.446). And Sir Edward Spears, not yet his son-in-law, in the 1930s remembered him as being: 'As imperturbable as a fish, always unruffled, the sort of man who would eat porridge by gaslight on a foggy morning in winter … just as if he were eating a peach in a sunny garden in August. A very tall, very fair man, a little bent, with a boxer's flattened-out nose, and a rather abrupt manner. A little *distrait* owing to great inner concentration, he simply demolished work, never forgot anything, was quite impervious to the moods of his chief [Robertson] … and

[was] his most efficient if not outwardly brilliant second'. Spears attributes the letter which destroyed Maurice's army career to 'a deep sense of civic duty inherited from a family which placed service to the country and to the people of the country above all else' (Spears, 35–6).

TREVOR WILSON and ROBIN PRIOR

Sources N. Maurice, ed., *The Maurice case* (1972) · J. Gooch, 'The Maurice debate, 1918', *Journal of Contemporary History*, 3 (1968), 211–28 · E. Spears, *Prelude to victory* (1939) · D. Lloyd George, *War memoirs*, 5 (1936) · Lord Hankey [M. Hankey], *The supreme command, 1914–1918*, 2 vols. (1961) · S. W. Roskill, *Hankey, man of secrets*, 1 (1970) · D. R. Woodward, *Lloyd George and the generals* (1983) · *The Times* (21 May 1951) · d. cert. · *CGPLA Eng. & Wales* (1951)
Archives King's Lond., Liddell Hart C., corresp. · King's Lond., Liddell Hart C., personal and family corresp. and papers · NRA, priv. coll., diary | Bodl. Oxf., letters to Herbert Asquith · CAC Cam., corresp. with Sir E. L. Spears · NL Scot., corresp. with Lord Haldane | FILM BFI NFTVA, home footage
Likenesses W. Stoneman, photograph, 1917, NPG [*see illus.*] · W. Rothenstein, sanguine drawing, 1922, NPG · W. Stoneman, photograph, 1936, NPG · H. Lamb, oils, Queen Mary College, London
Wealth at death £42,128 1s. 5d.: probate, 24 July 1951, *CGPLA Eng. & Wales*

Maurice, (John) Frederick Denison (1805–1872), Church of England clergyman and theologian, was born at Normanton, near Lowestoft, on 29 August 1805, the fifth child and only son of Michael Maurice and his wife, Priscilla, *née* Hurry, daughter of a Yarmouth merchant. Michael Maurice was preparing for the dissenting ministry at an academy at Hackney, Middlesex, when a shift in his opinions led him to Unitarianism, a decision which cost him the inheritance of an estate. In 1792 he was elected evening preacher at the Unitarian chapel in Hackney where Joseph Priestley preached in the mornings. Two years later he married, residing at Normanton until 1812, when he moved first to Clifton, and then, in the following year, to Frenchay, near Bristol. Besides Frederick, the family now consisted of seven sisters, three older and four younger than he, as well as a nephew and a niece of Mrs Maurice. The deaths of the two latter, on 18 October 1814 and 3 January 1815 respectively, greatly affected the elder sisters, to the extent indeed of bringing about a change in their religious convictions from Unitarianism to Calvinism. The eldest, Elizabeth (*b.* 1795), joined the Church of England, whereas the third, Anne (*b.* 1799), became a Baptist. Eventually their mother also embraced the Calvinistic doctrine. Unfortunately the religious persuasions which thus divided the family gave rise to vehement disagreement. That the young Frederick was confused and distressed by these disputes is of little wonder, and as he came to understand how matters stood he began to sense that need for religious unity which was to be a guiding principle of all his subsequent thinking. It likewise left him with the impression that, as he afterwards put it, 'a society merely united in opinion has no real cohesion' (*Life*, 2.276).

Education Maurice's education and upbringing by his father were on puritanical lines: reading novels was not, in the main, allowed; Bible study was insisted upon. He appears to have been an exemplary child, responsive to

(John) Frederick Denison Maurice (1805–1872), by Samuel Laurence, exh. RA 1871

teaching and always dutiful. He read a good deal on his own account, but had little inclination for games. Serious and precocious, he even at this time harboured ambitions for a life of public service.

In 1821 Maurice's mother finally left the Unitarian body, her son also having found its tenets and its narrowly sectarian outlook on life unappealing (*Life*, 1.175). No longer the dissenting ministry but the legal profession was his preferred option now. But in order to enhance his general education he judged a course at a university to be necessary, and chose Cambridge, where no religious test was imposed on entrance. Accordingly, in the October term of 1823, he took up residence at Trinity College, attending Julius Hare's lectures on the Greek drama and on Plato. Hare had little personal contact with Maurice, but sufficient to recognize in him an aptitude for philosophy. Maurice's official tutor was Frederick Field. He joined eagerly in university activities, spoke at the union, and was among the founders of the Apostles, another original member being Alfred Tennyson, whose lifelong friend he became. He also formed a close companionship with John Sterling (1806–1844), a favourite pupil of Hare's and a great admirer of Coleridge, whose talk at Hampstead had fascinated him. With Sterling he transferred in October 1825 to Trinity Hall, where fellowships were tenable by barristers and awarded for a good degree in law. Here he read for the LLB course. He moved to London to study for the bar in the long vacation of 1826, returning to Cambridge the following term for his final examination, gaining a first class in civil law. On the strength of this he stood an excellent chance of a college fellowship, but felt himself unable to subscribe to the Church of England's Thirty-Nine Articles, then still requisite for proceeding to a degree. He would not, he said, 'hang a bribe round his neck to lead his conscience', and removed his name from the college books.

While still at Cambridge, Maurice revealed a capacity for intellectual leadership, although by nature he was far from self-assertive. With the help of a friend he started the *Metropolitan Quarterly Magazine*, which ran for four issues, he himself contributing a fair proportion of the articles, including appreciative pieces on contemporary authors. Highly critical of Jeremy Bentham's views, his readiest praise was reserved for Coleridge, whose influence upon his thinking was already marked. In 1827 and 1828, and now living in London, he contributed to the *Westminster Review* and made the acquaintance of J. S. Mill. With Sterling he also edited the lately founded *Athenaeum*, to which he gave a clearly reformist tone. Unfortunately it did not pay, and he was disturbed by troubles at home. His father had lost money through unsound investments and was no longer able to take in pupils. The family moved to Southampton and to a smaller house, where Frederick joined them. In the meantime his religious beliefs had undergone change; the Unitarianism of his upbringing was rejected and he resolved on ordination in the Church of England. Preparation for this meant a return to university life, and he now chose Oxford, entering Exeter College in 1830, where a friend of Sterling's, as college tutor, was able to arrange for his Cambridge terms to count as residence. But his funds were severely limited, and although he hoped to meet his expenses by means of a novel he was trying to get published, his position proved difficult. In the end he was saved by a small legacy that happened to come his way.

At Oxford, Maurice joined an essay society in which he came to know William Ewart Gladstone and James Bruce, afterwards eighth earl of Elgin. It was the latter who introduced him to the writings of the theologically minded Scottish laird Thomas Erskine (1788–1870) of Linlathen, whose ideas, like those of Coleridge, were to prove a guiding influence on his thought, and who became a firm friend. He admitted that one of Erskine's books—*The Brazen Serpent*—was of 'unspeakable comfort' to him (*Life*, 1.108, 121). Many years later he dedicated one of his own volumes, *The Prophets and Kings of the Old Testament* (1853), to Erskine. He was also interested, as Erskine was, in the activities of Edward Irving and his congregation at the Regent Square Chapel in London. On 29 March 1831 he was baptized, thus becoming formally a member of the Church of England. In November of the same year he graduated, with a second class. The death in July 1832 of his favourite sister, Emma, at whose bedside he had attended for months, caused him much sadness.

Ordination and ministry Maurice's ordination by the bishop of Lichfield took place on 26 January 1834, to an assistant curacy at Bubbenhall, near Leamington. Shortly afterwards his novel, *Eustace Conway, or, The Brother and Sister*, at last saw print, but although it won Coleridge's esteem it was not a commercial success. His first theological publication was his pamphlet *Subscription No Bondage* (1835), appearing under the pseudonym Rusticus, in which, somewhat paradoxically in view of his own experience, he undertook to defend the obligation of subscribing to the Thirty-Nine Articles on matriculating at the University of Oxford. His contention was that such subscription was no more than a declaration of the terms on which the institution professed to teach its students and they in turn agreed to learn. It was, he considered, fairer to state those terms openly than to conceal them. Later (1853) he changed his mind and advocated the abolition of tests. It was while a curate at Bubbenhall that he set to work on composing an article, 'Moral and metaphysical philosophy', for the *Encyclopaedia metropolitana*, a task which, with its successive revisions for later editions, was to occupy him on and off for the rest of his life.

In January 1836 Maurice accepted the chaplaincy of Guy's Hospital in London, where in addition to his ordinary pastoral duties he lectured the students twice weekly on moral philosophy. His sister Priscilla kept house for him, and he also received a pupil, Edward Strachey (1812–1901), whose friendship he retained over the years. He saw much of Sterling and came to know Thomas Carlyle, with whom, however, he found a good deal to disagree on, especially his alleged pantheism (*Life*, 1.276–82). If the Scottish sage judged, even then, that Maurice's ideas were 'mainly moonshine and *Spitzfindigkeit*', Maurice could be equally caustic on Carlyle's own 'silly rant about the great bosom of nature' (ibid., 282). In 1836 the master of Downing College, Cambridge, offered him a lectureship there, but he declined the post. Soon afterwards he allowed himself to be named as a candidate for the chair of political economy at Oxford, a move supported by Newman and Pusey, who approved of his opinions on subscription. Maurice, on the other hand, was not drawn to the Tractarian theology—at least as represented by Pusey's doctrine of baptism as an instantaneously transforming act, instead of, as he himself saw it, a witness to the truth of the continuing presence of Christ in the life of humanity. On perceiving how Maurice really stood on this matter the two decided to vote against him, and his name was withdrawn.

In June 1837, when staying with Julius Hare at his Herstmonceaux rectory, Maurice met not only Sterling, who for a short time was Hare's curate, but Sterling's sister-in-law Anna Barton, whose acquaintance he had already made. He became engaged to her, and the couple were married at Clifton on 7 October 1837, Sterling himself officiating at the ceremony.

It was in this year that Maurice published certain letters addressed to his friend Samuel Clark, at that time a member of the Society of Friends but afterwards an Anglican clergyman. They subsequently appeared as *The Kingdom of Christ* (1838), one of his most significant works. A second edition, considerably revised, with a dedication to the Revd Derwent Coleridge, was published in 1842. The subtitle of *The Kingdom of Christ* was *Hints on the principles, ordinances, and constitution of the Catholic church*, and like the contemporary Oxford Tracts it expounds a firmly ecclesiastical theology grounded in scripture and tradition, while seeking to avoid what its author regarded as the dogmatic rigidity and party spirit of the Tractarians. It examines in turn the beliefs of a Quaker, an orthodox protestant, a Unitarian, and a rationalist philosopher, revealing notable insight and understanding in each case. Maurice's aim is to affirm the positive principle in the position criticized, but to show also how its overemphasis and systematic development generate error. He then looks for those signs of 'a spiritual and universal Kingdom' by which one-sidedness could be transcended. Indeed Christ's kingdom, he claims, already exists, since it is constituted by the whole body of those who witness to Christ. The signs of this spiritual society are the sacraments of baptism and the eucharist, to which must be added the creeds, the liturgy, the episcopate, and the scriptures—in fact, all the marks of catholicity as exemplified in the Church of England. However, the book was not well received by the religious press, and was to prove the ground of a sustained criticism that lasted throughout Maurice's career; to his great regret, he felt misunderstood and misrepresented, both personally and as a writer. Unfortunately his views were not easily grasped by the average reader, who was apt to find him obscure and confusing.

In September 1839 Maurice assumed part editorship of a new periodical, the *Educational Magazine*, his concern for national education having been heightened by the growing social unrest of the time, spearheaded, in the next decade, by Chartism. The following year he became sole editor, continuing to press the argument that the responsibility for schools should remain the church's, through agreement by the government with the National Society for Promoting the Education of the Poor. But the magazine was short-lived, ceasing publication in 1841. In June 1840 Maurice was elected to a professorship in English literature and history at King's College, London. The work appealed to him strongly, and his manner of lecturing was undoubtedly impressive from all accounts, but the effect of his discourses, it seems, was to elevate more than inform. Some of his students perhaps were able to understand him, though for the most part his lofty generalizations were inaccessible. That he was a man of distinction none would have questioned.

Maurice was fully alive to the ecclesiastical issues of the day. The joint Anglican–Lutheran bishopric in Jerusalem, a proposal which greatly offended Newman and his associates, he found good reason to support, as he explained in his *Three Letters to the Rev. William Palmer* (1842). He saw it as a token of the true catholicity of the church, a wider conception than that of strict institutional unity. On the other hand, when E. B. Pusey was suspended by the vice-chancellor's court from preaching in Oxford because of his sermon at Christ Church extolling a high eucharistic doctrine, which his critics deemed heterodox, he protested vigorously in a letter to the evangelical leader Lord Ashley (afterwards earl of Shaftesbury), who had presided over a meeting to denounce the Tractarian teachings. And again, in 1844, after W. G. Ward's *Ideal of a Christian Church* had caused such a stir in Oxford, he likewise protested, in *Two Letters to a Non-Resident Member of Convocation*, against a statute which permitted the author to be deprived of his degree.

John Sterling's wife died on 18 April 1843, and Sterling himself, whose health had been failing, on 18 September 1844. Anna Maurice's own death was to follow on 25 March 1845, leaving two sons, one of whom, John Frederick *Maurice, was to compose, many years later, his father's biography. This succession of bereavements affected Maurice deeply. He also blamed himself for having been, as he thought, unsympathetic to Sterling in the loss of his religious faith.

At the end of 1843, when both the principalship of King's College, London, and the preachership of Lincoln's Inn were rendered vacant by the appointment of their existing holder, Dr John Lonsdale, to the see of Lichfield, Julius Hare was hopeful that Maurice would succeed him. Maurice himself was less sanguine. Ecclesiastically he was no party man, and he was regarded with suspicion by both evangelicals and Tractarians; he feared too that the other professors would by no means welcome him as their head and might even resign. He did not, in fact, desire any sort of prominence in the church, nor was he academically ambitious. The post therefore went to R. W. Jelf. In July 1845 he was nominated Boyle lecturer by the archbishop of York, and in August Warburton lecturer by the archbishop of Canterbury. The lectures he delivered at Lincoln's Inn on the latter foundation contained the substance of his book on the epistle to the Hebrews; when this was published in 1846 it carried a preface in which Newman's theory of doctrinal development came under very critical review. The Boyle addresses appeared in 1847 as *The Religions of the World in their Relation to Christianity*, and in his lifetime were to be the most popular of his works. The choice of Maurice for these lectureships by the two archbishops seemed, in spite of what he himself might have apprehended, to indicate ecclesiastical favour, and when, in 1846, a theological department was established at King's, Jelf made him one of its professors.

In June of the same year Maurice was elected chaplain of Lincoln's Inn with a stipend of £300 a year, thus affording him an opportunity to resign from his Guy's Hospital duties, which some felt to be putting a strain on his health (*Life*, 1.361). His new responsibilities comprised the reading of morning prayers at the Inn, with a full service on Sunday afternoons. His sermons at once proved a draw and were consistently well attended, especially by the younger barristers. Among his hearers were Thomas Hughes and J. M. Ludlow, soon to be associated with him in the Christian socialist movement. He had already in 1844 made Charles Kingsley's acquaintance, and the two men were by now on very friendly terms. In 1846 he and other members of the staff at King's founded Queen's College for the higher education of women, particularly of intending governesses, in whose needs his sister Mary, herself a teacher, was interested.

On 12 November 1844 Julius Hare had married Maurice's younger sister Esther. Some five years later, on 4 July 1849, Maurice himself remarried, taking as his wife Georgina Hare-Naylor, Julius Hare's half-sister.

Christian socialism The year 1848 brought repeated news of revolutionary movements on the European continent and of Chartist agitation in England, the latter reaching its climax on 10 April with the much feared, but in the event abortive, march on parliament. Maurice's thoughts turned more and more to what he beheld as the 'spiritual destitution' of the times, and to the need, as he perceived it, of moral and social regeneration. Indeed, until the twentieth-century revival of interest in Maurice as a theologian he was chiefly remembered as the protagonist of Christian socialism, supported by his friends Charles Kingsley, parson, novelist, and publicist, and John Malcolm Ludlow (1821–1911), a barrister he had come to know at Lincoln's Inn and who, through his upbringing in France, had acquired first-hand knowledge of socialist and revolutionary groups in Paris. Moreover Ludlow possessed what Maurice lacked, an understanding of the requirements of effective political action. Others who joined them with a view to some kind of reformatory effort were Edward Vansittart Neale (1810–1892), who devoted a considerable part of his personal fortune to the cause, and Thomas Hughes, the future author of *Tom Brown's Schooldays*. Maurice was from the first recognized as the spiritual leader of this group of Christian socialists, as they came to be called, and was looked to even for its necessary practical direction. With Ludlow, he edited a newspaper, *Politics for the People*, which managed to survive for some months despite financial loss. It began publication on 6 May 1848 and rose to a circulation of about 2000 copies. The contributors included Kingsley who, choosing the pen-name of Parson Lot, assumed the role of fire-eating journalist, happy to proclaim himself a Chartist too (*Life*, 2.101). But the articles were most effective when Ludlow, radical and clear-headed, was their author. He cared nothing for the susceptibilities of the established political parties, believed in a large extension of the franchise—although he was opposed to universal suffrage—and favoured big increases in direct taxation.

In 1850 Maurice publicly accepted the designation Christian socialist for his movement. It committed him, he declared, 'to the conflict we must engage in sooner or later with the unsocial Christians and the unchristian Socialists' (*Life*, 2.35). The same year (12 November) saw the publication of another periodical, carrying the name *Christian Socialist*, Ludlow being both founder and editor. Maurice was somewhat dubious about it, however, and left Ludlow with a free hand. Its aim was to present a view of society at once Christian and socialist, since Christianity, it was claimed, had by its very nature a social mission, and as things were, the alternative to a Christian socialism was a godless one. But whereas by socialism Ludlow meant socialism as he understood it—collective control of the economy—Maurice's ideal was vaguer and more utopian. He himself was no democrat in the populist sense, and certainly no egalitarian: hierarchy he thought essential to society—a token, it could be said, of his instinctive Platonism. He disliked competition as fundamentally unchristian, and wished to see it, at the social level, replaced by co-operation, as expressive of Christian brotherhood. But politically he was a long way from radicalism, and his attitude more nearly approximated to a mild tory paternalism. He was, by disposition, impractical, and he disliked organizational activity. Basic principles were his terrain. As he once wrote to Ludlow: 'Let people call me merely a philosopher, or merely anything else … my business, because I am a theologian, and have no vocation except for theology, is not to build, but to dig, to show that economics and politics … must have a ground beneath themselves, and that society was not to be made by any arrangements of ours, but is to be regenerated by finding the law and ground of its order and harmony, the only secret of its existence, in God' (*Life*, 2.137). Ludlow shared Maurice's high moral aspirations, but doubted whether the existing churches were capable of promoting them.

Maurice held Bible classes and addressed meetings attended by working men who, although his words carried less of social and political guidance than moral edification, were invariably impressed by the speaker. But the actual means by which the competitiveness of the prevailing economic system was to be mitigated was judged to be the creation of co-operative societies, a conviction reinforced by what Ludlow had learned of French *associations ouvrières* from a recent visit to Paris. Maurice saw in them a modern application of primitive Christian communism. Twelve workshops were to be set up in London for builders, tailors, shoemakers, and other artisan trades, liberally subsidized by Vansittart Neale and helped by the subscriptions of middle-class sympathizers. The workers' own efforts were also salted by teaching on the duties of citizenship and the responsibility of the franchise. For a time the societies thrived and gained the widespread approval of working-class sentiment. Regrettably, market profitability did not match social idealism, with the inevitable result, and personal friction brought discord to the fraternal harmony. In any case, Maurice's own interest really lay in education rather than economics. Kingsley's ebullient Chartist rhetoric, moreover, did not strengthen confidence in Christian socialist objectives among his fellow churchmen, as witness the public denunciation of his views on 22 June 1851 by the incumbent of St John's, Charlotte Street, G. S. Drew (1819–1880), immediately following the sermon delivered there by Kingsley as guest preacher. This event caused a sensation and compromised Maurice's own reputation. The principal of King's College wrote to him hoping that he would disown Kingsley's utterances, which he deplored as 'reckless and dangerous'. Indeed Maurice's leadership of the movement was no insignificant factor in his eventual dismissal from King's. But by then the movement itself was in decline, those who had created it feeling an increasing divergence in their personal concerns and goals. Maurice, for all his high-mindedness and attractiveness of character, was hardly fitted to head a venture dependent above all on practicability of aim. By 1854 its course was run.

Theological controversy: eternal punishment Christian socialism did not, however, deflect Maurice from his vocation and tasks as a 'pure' theologian. In 1853 he published his *Theological Essays*, a work which, it has to be said, even his admirers have found less than satisfactory. Not well written—R. W. Church complained of its 'tormenting indistinctness'—it none the less is of first importance as a statement of Maurice's views, and in particular of his convictions on the doctrine of the eternal punishment of impenitent sinners, one which theological orthodoxy, protestant as well as Catholic, held to be indispensable for belief. Maurice denied it; at least he denied that 'eternal' and 'everlasting' are synonymous terms. His own conception, he explained, was founded on John 17: 3, 'This is life eternal, that they should know thee, the one true God, and him who thou hast sent, even Jesus Christ.' Eternal life is therefore a quality of life attainable in this world. Not to know God is to forfeit that quality, to suffer the alienation from him which is spiritual death. The notion of duration in time is irrelevant. 'I cannot', he said, 'apply the idea of time to the word eternal. I must see eternity as something altogether out of time.' Not that Maurice was a universalist, holding that in the end all would be saved: 'I dare not pronounce what are the possibilities of resistance in a human will to the loving will of God.' 'But', he added, 'I know that there is something which must be infinite in the abyss of love beyond the abyss of death' (F. D. Maurice, *Theological Essays*, 1853, 406; cf. *Life*, 2.15). He could not bring himself to believe that impenitence at death necessarily meant the soul's damnation and consignment to everlasting torments.

These scruples and hesitations failed to satisfy the many, especially among evangelicals, who, further offended by Maurice's ideas on the atonement, feared that tampering with the former doctrine would have grave practical implications in weakening the sanctions of personal morality. Jelf was perturbed. A lengthy correspondence ensued between himself and Maurice, from which he could only conclude that if his professor of theology did not believe in eternal punishment then it was unsuitable that the future training of clergymen should remain in his hands. He confronted him therefore with the choice of either resignation or dismissal. At a meeting of the college council on 27 October 1853 the bishop of London, C. J. Blomfield, had to consider a motion duly thanking Maurice for his past services but requiring his departure. Gladstone moved an amendment that 'competent theologians' should be asked to examine the *Essays*, but he lost it, and on 11 November the council, poorly attended, declared Maurice's offices vacant. It grieved him that he was not even allowed to finish his lecture courses. But he received many and warm expressions of sympathy, and Alfred Tennyson marked the occasion with a poem addressed to him in January 1854. Even if to the majority of the public who had at all considered the matter his teachings remained unclear, it was widely felt that he had not been well used. The benchers of Lincoln's Inn declined to accept his offer to resign his chaplaincy, and although he did resign his chairmanship of the committee of Queen's College, he resumed it in 1856 at the unanimous request of its members.

Disappointed as he was at this abrupt termination of his own academic career, Maurice's concern for the education of the artisan class was nevertheless undiminished.

In February 1854 he drew up a scheme for a working men's college, to some extent on the model of a 'people's college' established in Sheffield back in 1842. It opened on 31 October 1854 in Red Lion Square, London, with some 120 students and with Maurice as its principal. Later it moved, first to Great Ormond Street and then to Crowndale Road. Besides Maurice's friends Vansittart Neale and Tom Hughes, the Tudor historian J. S. Brewer helped with the teaching, as too did John Ruskin and the Pre-Raphaelite painter and poet Dante Gabriel Rossetti. It was a product of Christian socialism and an expression of its ideals.

Theological controversy: divine revelation Maurice himself deemed the most important controversy of his life to be his clash with Henry Longueville Mansel (1820–1871), Waynflete professor of moral and metaphysical philosophy at Oxford and later dean of St Paul's. At issue was the fundamental theological question of the nature of man's knowledge of God. In 1858 Mansel delivered the Bampton lectures on 'The limits of religious thought examined', in which, with incisive clarity, he sought to defend the idea of divine revelation by means of a philosophical agnosticism. The finite mind, he contended, cannot comprehend the infinite. The revelation embodied in the dogmas of orthodox Christianity affords no knowledge of God as he is in himself, such being inaccessible to the speculative reason, but a knowledge which is 'regulative' only, as adapted to the limitations and needs of the human condition. Revelation must therefore be accepted by believers simply as it is, on the substantiating evidence of miracle and prophecy, and attempts to rationalize its content on philosophical grounds are as vain as the claim to know God directly. To not a few of Mansel's hearers his arguments sounded like a final answer to all rationalist assaults on Christianity. But it stung Maurice into a quite violent rejoinder, published as *What is Revelation?* (1859). To him revelation was not oblique talk about God but a disclosure of God himself, in his love and mercy. He believed Mansel's procedure was a total misrepresentation of the real nature of both revelation and faith. To describe God's personal action merely as an imparting of propositions that can be used but never properly understood was, he objected, a travesty of the divine purpose. Unfortunately Maurice weakened his case by his blustering indignation. Even his friends were disconcerted. Mansel countered Maurice's strictures in a characteristically skilful *Examination* of them, which Maurice in turn answered with his *Sequel to the Inquiry, What is Revelation?* This restates his position in more moderate language but without showing any clear conception of what Mansel was about. The truth is that he failed to grasp the metaphysical problems inevitably raised by the claim to know God by immediate apprehension. Maurice may have had a deeper mystical sense, but Mansel was the better philosopher.

In July 1860 Maurice was presented to the living of St Peter's, Vere Street, which he was to occupy over the ensuing decade. But the appointment displeased the evangelical organ *The Record*, and an address signed by twenty-two clergymen was sent to the bishop of London, A. C. Tait, protesting against his institution. This move, however, was countered by another address, promoted by J. M. Ludlow, W. F. Hook, dean of Chichester, and others, bearing 332 clerical and 487 lay signatures, congratulating him on this 'tardy recognition' of his services to the church. Among the signatories were Gladstone, Tennyson, and Connop Thirlwall, the learned and liberal-minded bishop of St David's.

Nevertheless a new difficulty soon beset Maurice. William Colenso, bishop of Natal, and a friend of Maurice's, consulted him when working on his book on the Pentateuch. Maurice was much disturbed by the bishop's radical conclusions and suggested that people could even deem it right, in view of them, that he should resign his bishopric—to which Colenso retorted that they might well think a like course to be appropriate for Maurice himself. The latter, alarmed by the outcome of the *Essays and Reviews* (1860) furore, sensed that his own position could indeed become untenable, and judged that resignation, despite the protests of his sympathizers, would be preferable to deprivation. Although Tait would have been reluctant to accept the resignation, Maurice himself came to feel that his own insistence on it might be unfair to Colenso, whose personal confidence he had received. He therefore decided to hold on to his benefice, even though some members of his congregation were critical of what seemed to them a fussy scrupulosity (*Life*, 2.553) and took themselves elsewhere. In 1863 he replied to Colenso's newly published work, in which the bishop, in his own rather idiosyncratic way, not only denied the Mosaic authorship of the first five books of the Bible but also their compositional unity and, in some respects, their historical authenticity in a series of open letters published as *The Claims of the Bible and of Science*, an act which led to some estrangement between the two men (*Life*, 2.485).

Last years On 25 October 1866 Maurice was elected to the Knightbridge professorship of casuistry, moral theology, and moral philosophy at Cambridge, on the vacancy caused by the death of John Grote. The electors, who were all but unanimous in their decision, had evidently as much assurance of Maurice's theological orthodoxy as of his competence as a philosopher. He remained principal of the Working Men's College, though he attended there less often, as he likewise retained the Vere Street cure. But the journey to London each week for the conduct of the services proved too taxing and in October 1869 he resigned his charge on medical advice. All the same, he accepted the offer of St Edward's, Cambridge, in the gift of Trinity Hall. No stipend was attached to it and pastoral work was minimal, but it provided an opportunity for preaching to an intelligent audience. He was assiduous in his academic duties, and notwithstanding his natural shyness did his best to get to know the undergraduates personally. Besides completing his *Metaphysical and Moral Philosophy* (2 vols., 1871–2), he published his university lectures as *The Conscience: Lectures on Casuistry* (1868) and *Social Morality* (1869). His health, however, was visibly declining. Even so, he did not refuse the bishop of London's offer of

the Cambridge preachership at Whitehall, delivering sermons there in the winter months of 1871–2, as well as two university sermons in Cambridge. On 30 March he resigned from St Edward's, being very weak and mentally depressed. Two days later he lost consciousness, regaining it sufficiently to murmur a blessing before he died, on 1 April 1872 at 6 Bolton Row, Piccadilly.

A proposal was made that Maurice should be buried in Westminster Abbey, but it was the unanimous view of his family that he would not have wished it. He was, accordingly, interred at Highgate cemetery, in the vault where the remains of his parents and sisters lay.

Maurice and his intellectual legacy Maurice was a man whose presence impressed all who met him. Of slightly less than medium height and somewhat reserved in manner—if always markedly courteous—his bearing was not only dignified but, by all accounts, expressive of the spiritual and moral integrity which was felt by his friends and acquaintances to be the defining quality of his character. Kingsley thought him 'the most beautiful human soul' he had known. Others did not hesitate to describe him as 'saintlike'. Yet he was certainly a controversial figure. He would not retreat before an issue that stirred his convictions, as in his famous but mainly unfortunate dispute with Mansel. In the last decade of his life, however, his public esteem was high, especially among laymen. Thus Sir Thomas Acland wrote to him: 'For more than a quarter of a century you have been helping Englishmen to see through the theories and systems which have been invented to prop up, restore, develop or narrow the ancient edifice of their national Church' (*Life*, 2.541). He was also prescient, with little of the complacent Victorian optimist about him: 'Are we to live', he asked, 'in an age in which every mechanical facility for communication between man and man is multiplied ten-thousandfold, only that the inward isolation, the separation of those who meet continually, may be increased in a far greater measure?' (F. D. Maurice, *The Lord's Prayer: Nine Sermons*, 5.24).

As a theological thinker Maurice had depth and unquestionable originality. By his own admission his aim was 'to dig', to penetrate to the spiritual roots of human life. He had no time for mere eclecticism, but he distrusted and disliked system building. As he described it, 'dexterity is shown, not in detecting facts, but in cutting them square' (*Lectures on the Ecclesiastical History of the First and Second Centuries*, 1854, 222). His cast of mind was naturally Platonist. In addition to the influence of Plato's dialogues, that of the seventeenth-century Cambridge Platonists, and of Coleridge, is obvious. His Platonizing view that 'Christ is in every man' as the head of redeemed humanity, and that salvation is essentially the recognition of this, together with its corollary that a theology whose starting point is the fall and sin, rather than grace and redemption, is misdirected, offended evangelical belief—one of his sharpest critics was the Wesleyan Methodist divine Dr J. H. Rigg—just as it distanced him also from the Tractarians, whose exclusivist doctrine of episcopacy likewise he would have wished to qualify. Yet he firmly declined to regard himself as broad church, a position which, in its attempt to commend religious faith to contemporary thought, he considered to involve a dilution of the church's formularies, on adherence to which he, as a committed Anglican, would not compromise. He believed firmly in the role of the Church of England as a national church, at once Catholic and protestant, which he did not see as incompatible principles but as complementary aspects of the faith, with their respective truths as constitutive elements in a vital unity. What he might have learned from the broad-churchmen was a keener appreciation of the significance of historical criticism for biblical exegesis, while the possible implications of Darwinism for religious belief, which much concerned them, seemed scarcely to interest him.

Although the eminent Unitarian thinker James Martineau held that Maurice had no superior among contemporary theologians in consistency of thought and precision of language, many of his readers found his ideas somewhat mystifying, with distinctions urged where they themselves could discern no differences, or unity 'revealed' where they saw only contrariety. Lucidity, it has to be conceded, was not the prime virtue of his literary style. It may well be judged that he published too much, and with insufficient discrimination. Again, despite the fact that he was the author of a copious work entitled *Metaphysical and Moral Philosophy* (1871–2), he was not a philosopher in the sense that connotes rigorous intellectual analysis. Even as a theological thinker it was less the elucidation of principles that interested him than their application to the needs and opportunities of life. Yet his influence on later nineteenth-century Anglican thought, as the instances of F. J. A. Hort and his Cambridge associates testify, was pervasive. Even the post-Tractarians did not escape it, as the publication in 1889 of *Lux mundi*, or the foundation in the same year of the Christian Social Union, also demonstrate. He was indeed a seminal figure in this respect. After some decline in his reputation in the first half of the twentieth century, revival of interest accelerated, thanks to the studies of A. R. Vidler, Bishop Michael Ramsey, and others, as the centenary of his death approached. He is now recalled as one of the outstanding contributors to the English, and especially the Anglican, theological tradition. BERNARD M. G. REARDON

Sources The life of Frederick Denison Maurice, ed. F. Maurice, 3rd edn, 2 vols. (1884) · A. M. Ramsey, F. D. Maurice and the conflicts of modern theology (1951) · A. R. Vidler, F. D. Maurice and company: nineteenth-century studies (1966) · O. Brose, F. D. Maurice: rebellious conformist (1971) · F. M. McClain, F. D. Maurice: man and moralist (1972) · T. Christensen, The divine order: a study in F. D. Maurice's theology (1973) · J. Tulloch, Movements of religious thought in Britain during the nineteenth century (1885) · B. M. G. Reardon, Religious thought in the Victorian age: a survey from Coleridge to Gore, rev. edn (1980) · E. R. Norman, The Victorian Christian socialists (1987)
Archives CUL, family and other corresp. · Hunt. L., letters · King's Lond., corresp. and papers · Queen's College, London, corresp. | BL, corresp. with C. Kingsley, Add. MSS 41297–41298 · BL, corresp. with Macmillans, Add. MSS 55090–55091 · Bodl. Oxf., Wilberforce MSS, letters to Samuel Wilberforce · CUL, Ludlow MSS, corresp. with J. M. F. Ludlow · LPL, letters to A. C. Tait · Working Men's College, 44 Crowndale Road, London, Christian Socialist MSS
Likenesses S. Laurence, chalk drawing, c.1846, NPG · F. M. Brown, group portrait, oils, 1852–65 (Work), Man. City Gall. · J. M. Hayward, oils, 1854, NPG · drawing, 1859, Queen's College, London · S. Laurence, oils, exh. RA 1871, NPG [see illus.] · T. Woolner, bust, 1872, Westminster Abbey; replica, 1873, Squire Law Library, Cambridge · L. Dickinson, oils, 1873, Queen's College, London · L. Dickinson, chalk, 1886, Working Men's College, London · F. M. Brown, group portrait, pencil, Man. City Gall. · E. Edwards, photograph, NPG; repro. in E. Edwards, Portraits of men of eminence in literature, science and art, with biographic memoirs, ed. L. Reeve and E. Walford, 6 vols. (1863–7), vol. 1 · Elliott & Fry, cartes-de-visite, NPG · E. & M. Gillick, bronze memorial plaque, Cambridge · W. Jeffrey, cartes-de-visite, NPG · Kilburn, cartes-de-visite, NPG · Mason & Co., cartes-de-visite, NPG · Poulton, cartes-de-visite, NPG · T. Woolner, plaster death mask, NPG · photograph, NPG
Wealth at death under £3000: probate, 20 April 1872, CGPLA Eng. & Wales

Maurice, Henry (1647?–1691), Church of England clergyman, was the son of Thomas Maurice, perpetual curate of Llangristiolus, Anglesey, and grandson of Henry *Perry (or Parry), the linguistic scholar. After attending Beaumaris grammar school he matriculated on 20 May 1664 from Jesus College, Oxford, aged sixteen; he graduated BA on 28 January 1668 and proceeded MA in 1671; he was created BD in 1679 and DD in 1683. His ability as a student attracted the attention of Sir Leoline Jenkins, then principal of the college, and he was elected to a fellowship. After 1669 he became, at the request of the college, the curate of Cheltenham, Gloucestershire, where, according to Anthony Wood, he answered some 'malapert Socinians' so successfully 'that he gained himself a great reputation' (Wood, Ath. Oxon., new edn, 1813–20, 4.326). In 1671 he returned to the college, but in 1673 he left again to accompany Jenkins as his chaplain to the congress of Cologne, where the latter was an English representative in the attempts to settle a peace between the belligerents in the Third Dutch War. Jenkins returned to England in May 1674 but Maurice again accompanied him as chaplain on his mission at the treaty negotiations at Nijmegen between 1676 and 1679. During his years abroad Maurice developed his skills in modern languages and established lasting contacts with French protestant divines. In England he lived for a while with Jenkins's family at Doctors' Commons, London, and in college until 1680. Jenkins's contacts were essentially in the law, and it needed an ecclesiastical patron in the person of William Lloyd (made bishop of St Asaph in 1680) to get Maurice appointed as domestic chaplain to William Sancroft in that year.

Maurice continued in this post until 1691, and published frequently during the 1680s. He was involved in a controversy with the nonconformists Richard Baxter and David Clarkson over the existence of diocesan episcopacy in the primitive church. Maurice's A Vindication of the Primitive Church and Diocesan Episcopacy (1682) proved the necessity of episcopacy from primitive practice, defending John Tillotson's historical view of its creation as not being defined by Christ but emerging from the diocesan model used by the apostles. He believed that it was essentially episcopal government that had saved the Church of England from the internecine conflicts that plagued other European reformed churches. According to his biographer, Robert Wynne, the controversy with Baxter and Clarkson considerably raised Maurice's profile among the London clergy. He also attacked the duke of Buckingham's proposals for religious toleration, arguing like many Anglican divines that it was a neglect of their duty to look after the cure of souls to permit the 'errors' of dissent, stating that 'Penalties in matters of Religion' were designed 'to remove such evil obstructions as lie in the Passage to a man's right Reason' (H. Maurice, *The Antithelemite, or, An Answer to Certain Quaeres by the D. of B.*, 1685, 41). Wood alleged that Maurice was the author of *Animadversions on Dr Burnet's 'History of the Rights of Princes'* (1682), but this seems to have been by Thomas Comber. Maurice was also acknowledged as an eloquent extempore preacher. However, his verbal brilliance seems to have masked an apparent aversion to the act of writing itself, notwithstanding his polemical interventions in the 1680s. He only ever published one sermon (given before the king at Whitehall in 1681 on the anniversary of Charles I's death) and Wynne claims that he had to act as an amanuensis for him to produce his anti-Catholic work *Doubts Concerning the Roman Infallibility* (1688).

Under the patronage of Sancroft, Maurice received the treasurership of Chichester on 7 January 1681, the rectory of Chevening, Kent, which he held from 1681 to 1685, and, in 1685, the sinecure rectory of Llandrillo-yn-Rhos, Denbighshire. In the same year he was presented to the richly endowed rectory of Newington, Oxfordshire. Despite his closeness to Sancroft, Maurice did not support his patron's decision to refuse the oaths of allegiance to William and Mary. He wrote in favour of recognizing the new monarchs, arguing that Princess Mary was, in any case, a blood heir, and that having William as joint monarch represented only a 'small deviation' from the right line (Maurice, *The Lawfulness of Taking the New Oaths Asserted*, 3). However, like many tory jurors, he used something of a hotch-potch of arguments to press taking the oaths, insisting that as he was the nation's *de facto* protector William was owed the natural duty of obedience, and hinting at contract theory by suggesting that James's actions might have violated his coronation oath. Maurice is often cited as the author of *A Letter to a Member of the House of Commons Concerning the Bishops* (1689), which argued for leniency towards Sancroft and the other nonjuring bishops. In fact, he was the author of a reply to this pamphlet which insisted that the bishops should take the oaths or lose their places. At the very least, he contended, they should make some public declaration of loyalty. George Hickes, who seems to have guessed the pamphlet's authorship, wondered whether Maurice's apparent vindictiveness was born out of a desire to see his metropolitan 'cap and cringe' before him (Hickes, 2). It seems more likely, though, that Maurice's loyalty to the Williamite regime stemmed from his virulent hatred of popery (for which he was attacked in print in 1688 by an anonymous Catholic writer) and that he saw

the Church of England as best defended by the new government. None the less, he continued to write in opposition to further alterations to the Anglican liturgy to appease protestant dissenters after the revolution.

Maurice's opposition to such compromises helps to explain his influential position within resolutely anticomprehensionist Oxford, both diocese and university. He was chosen by the clergy of the diocese of Oxford in October 1689 to be their representative in the convocation held at Westminster. He was elected Lady Margaret professor of divinity at Oxford on 18 July 1691 (Wynne states by only six votes) and was installed in the prebend of Worcester which went with the post. He died suddenly on 30 October 1691 at the age of forty-four (according to the funeral monument to him in Jesus College chapel), probably of a heart attack at his house in Newington, and was buried in the chancel of the church there on 6 November. He was unmarried and his estate was administered by his sister, Elizabeth Clancey, a widow. He donated his library to his college. He was renowned for his generosity and saved little, keeping only a sum of £200 with his college. Wynne testified to his convivial character, saying that there 'was no man alive more capable of conveying instruction over a moderate Bottle than Dr Maurice' (Wynne, 23). EDWARD VALLANCE

Sources administration, 1691, PRO, PROB 6/67, fol. 224 · *DNB* · R. Wynne, 'Dr Henry Maurice: a manuscript life', ed. O. A. Rees, *Jesus College Record* (1963), 16–24 · J. Spurr, *The Restoration Church of England, 1646–1689* (1991), 158, 328 · R. A. Beddard, 'Tory Oxford', *Hist. U. Oxf. 4: 17th-cent. Oxf.*, 863–906, esp. 870, 904 · [H. Maurice], *The lawfulness of taking the new oaths asserted* (1689) · M. Goldie, 'The revolution of 1689 and the structure of political argument', *Bulletin of Research in the Humanities*, 83 (1980), 551 · [G. Hickes], *Reflections upon a letter out of the country* (1689) · *Calendar of the correspondence of Richard Baxter*, ed. N. H. Keeble and G. F. Nuttall, 2 (1991), 251–2 · *DWB* · G. V. Bennett, 'Loyalist Oxford and the revolution', *Hist. U. Oxf. 5: 18th-cent. Oxf.*, 9–30

Archives BL, Lansdowne MSS · Bodl. Oxf., Rawl. MSS · Bodl. Oxf., Tanner MSS

Wealth at death £200 savings: Wynne, 'Dr Henry Maurice', 21 · administration, 1691, PRO, PROB 6/67, fol. 224

Maurice, James Wilkes (1775–1857), naval officer, was born at Devonport on 10 February 1775. He entered the navy in August 1789 as able seaman on the sloop *Inspector*, and in 1793 was midshipman on the *Powerful*, which convoyed a fleet of Indiamen to the Cape of Good Hope. He afterwards served in the *Cambridge*, *Concorde*, and *Royal George*, all in the channel and off Brest, and on 3 April 1797 was promoted lieutenant of the *Glory*. In 1799 he was moved to the *Canada*. Having been appointed in September 1802 to the *Centaur*, he went out to the West Indies with Commodore Samuel Hood (1762–1814) and was present at the capture of St Lucia, Tobago, Demerara, and Essequibo. He was landed at the destruction of a battery at Petite Anse d'Arlet on Martinique on 26 November 1803, when he was severely wounded by the explosion of the magazine. He was awarded a sword valued at £50 by the Patriotic Society.

When the Diamond Rock, near the south-west end of the island, was occupied, armed (with three 24-pounders and two long 18-pounders), and commissioned as a 'sloop of war' on 3 February 1804, Maurice was appointed to the command, and his promotion to commander was confirmed by the Admiralty to 7 May 1804. For more than a year Maurice held this rock, a thorn in the sides of the French at Martinique, and yielded to an attack in force by a detachment of Villeneuve's fleet (31 May–2 June 1805) only when his ammunition and water were exhausted. In the three days the British lost two men killed and one wounded; the loss of the French, on the other hand, was severe, but has never been exactly stated. Maurice estimated it at seventy killed and wounded of the landing party alone, exclusive of those on board the ships and gunboats. Maurice was tried by court martial for the loss of his post, but was honourably acquitted and highly complimented on his conduct.

Maurice returned to England in August 1805 and was immediately appointed to the brig *Savage*, which after two years in the channel was sent to the West Indies. There, in the autumn of 1808, he was appointed by Sir Alexander Cochrane governor of Marie Galante, which had been seized in the previous March. On 18 January 1809 he was advanced to post rank.

In October 1809 Maurice was compelled by ill health to return to England, and in July 1810 he was appointed governor of the island of Anholt, in the Baltic, which had been captured, without difficulty, in May 1809 by a small squadron under the command of Captain Aiskew Paffard Hollis. The island had been found most useful as a trade depot and as a base for communicating with the continent, and when Maurice was appointed it was understood that neither Napoleon nor the Danes would lose any opportunity of recapturing it. It was garrisoned by about four hundred marines, commanded by Captain Torrens. As long as the weather remained open the British cruisers secured it from attack, as, afterwards, did the severity of the winter. As soon as the water was open an attempt was made by the Danes to retake it. Twelve gunboats convoyed the Danish transports, and in the early morning of 27 March 1811, in darkness and fog, a force of a thousand men was landed about 4 miles from the fort. The enemy were ignorant that the frigate *Tartar* and brig *Sheldrake* had arrived from England the day before; the Danish troops advanced to the assault, driving in the British advanced parties, while the gunboats fired on the coast defences. The *Tartar*'s approach made the gunboats withdraw. A small schooner attached to the island took up a position on the enemy's flank and drove them from behind the sandhills, while the direct fire from the fort was well sustained and deadly. Finding no retreat open, the Danes on the north side, to the number of 543, surrendered; the rest fled to the west end of the island, where, temporarily guarded by the reefs, they managed to board the gunboats and transports. These, however, were pursued and scattered by the British ships; four were captured and one was sunk. The loss to the Danes was heavy, but Maurice's conduct was much exaggerated in popular estimation. The decisive support of the *Tartar* and *Sheldrake* was ignored or unknown and the Danes' strength was much magnified. Maurice retained his governorship until September 1812.

He had no further employment, and was retired with the rank of rear-admiral on 1 October 1846.

Maurice married, in October 1814, Sarah Lyne of Plymouth; she died in June 1815. Maurice died at his residence, East Emma Place, Stonehouse, Plymouth, on 4 September 1857, aged eighty-two. His career was unusual in that his two principal commands were islands.

J. K. LAUGHTON, *rev.* ANDREW LAMBERT

Sources E. Fraser and L. G. Carr-Laughton, *The royal marine artillery, 1804–1923*, 2 vols. (1930) • O'Byrne, *Naval biog. dict.* • J. Marshall, *Royal naval biography*, suppl. 1 (1827) • *GM*, 3rd ser., 3 (1857), 569 • W. James, *The naval history of Great Britain, from the declaration of war by France in 1793, to the accession of George IV*, [5th edn], 6 vols. (1859–60), vol. 3

Maurice, Joan Violet. *See* Robinson, Joan Violet (1903–1983).

Maurice, Sir John Frederick (1841–1912), army officer and military writer, the eldest son of (John) Frederick Denison *Maurice (1805–1872) and his first wife, Anna, *née* Barton (*d.* 1845), was born in London on 24 May 1841. His father's ideals and principles greatly influenced him, and he wrote his biography (1884). He was educated at Forest School, Walthamstow, from 1851 to 1855, and then privately. Imbued with religious and literary culture, Maurice, whose mother was from a military family, chose a military career rather than Cambridge. He passed second into Addiscombe College, then with its closure was transferred to the Royal Military Academy, Woolwich, and was commissioned in the Royal Artillery in 1861. He served at Woolwich, Shorncliffe, Leith, and in Ireland. In December 1869 he married Anne Frances, daughter of R. A. Fitzgerald, taxing officer to the courts in Dublin. They had eleven children and she survived him. Their eldest son was Frederick Barton *Maurice.

Although Maurice showed promise by passing through the Staff College (1870) and becoming an instructor in tactics at Sandhurst in 1872, it was as the winner of the second duke of Wellington's prize essay in 1872 that Maurice came to public notice. The topic was how the British army could best be prepared to meet a continental enemy, and it was a remarkable achievement for a subaltern to triumph over forty senior officers—including Colonel Sir Garnet Wolseley, who came second—with a precocious essay that anticipated most of the reforms implemented, or at least debated, over the next thirty years.

This success brought Maurice to the notice of Wolseley, whose protégé and loyal supporter he became, initially serving as his private secretary in the Second Anglo-Asante War in 1873–4. He was posted to the Royal Horse Artillery at Woolwich until promoted captain in 1875, then served two years in Canada. He saw further active service—interspersed with War Office service—with Wolseley, mainly as a staff officer, in South Africa (1879–80), where he was seriously wounded leading an attack on Chief Sekukuni's stronghold, in Egypt (1882), and in the Sudan (1884–5). Although, to his great regret, he never commanded a large unit in action and was distinguished

Sir John Frederick Maurice (1841–1912), by W. & D. Downey, pubd 1890

rather as a military historian, theorist, and teacher, Wolseley described him as 'the bravest man I have ever seen under fire' (Luvaas, 191). The most gifted writer in the *Wolseley ring, Maurice expounded Wolseley's reforming ideas and defended his reputation, notably in the official history (1887) of the 1882 Egyptian campaign.

Maurice was professor of military art and history (a title he detested) at the Staff College, Camberley, at a critical period, 1885–92, when it was moving from rote learning and cramming to produce broadly educated and professionally skilled staff officers comparable to the Prussians. Conscientious and hard-working, Maurice played a crucial role in this by encouraging the objective study of military campaigns in depth, to train the individual officer's judgement rather than to inculcate fixed principles. He believed the Staff College should teach officers how to think for themselves. In books and articles Maurice advocated the formation of an expeditionary force and, for war with Russia, a largely Eurocentric and maritime strategy with continental allies and naval and amphibious attacks on the Russian empire, rather than the Indocentric strategy of Roberts and other 'Indians'.

Maurice's outstanding abilities as an instructor and writer were offset by defects which probably barred him from high command. He was suspicious, apparently almost paranoid, and violently argumentative, as in the controversy over his official history of the Egyptian campaign. He was notoriously absent-minded and unpractical: he frequently confused the Archduke Charles with Prince Frederick Charles, and told his class that Lord Wolseley had won the battle of Waterloo. In the 1890s he owned, edited, and contributed to the *United Service Magazine*, but he lacked business sense and had to sell out at a heavy loss.

Though frustrated in his fervent desire to wield the sword as a senior commander, Maurice's literary and historical publications had established his reputation by 1900, when he was made KCB. In 1883 he published *Hostilities without Declaration of War*, a scholarly polemic against the projected channel tunnel, showing that from 1700 to 1871 there had been fewer than ten formal declarations prior to hostilities, implying a tunnel would make Britain vulnerable to surprise invasion. His *Balance of Military Power in Europe* (1888) was a masterly survey which anticipated modern strategic studies, while his essay 'War' for the *Encyclopaedia Britannica* (1891) remains valuable. His edition of the rediscovered *Diary of Sir John Moore* (1904) was, however, criticized—notably by Sir John Fortescue—as partisan and unscholarly.

By influential articles in the *Contemporary Review* (January 1902 and January 1903) Maurice publicized the high rejection rate, on medical grounds, of would-be recruits during the Second South African War, and so contributed to the growth of the movement for 'national efficiency', the establishment of the interdepartmental committee on physical deterioration (1903), and the introduction of the 1906 school meals legislation. In 1903, following the death of Colonel G. F. R. Henderson, Maurice unwisely agreed to continue his multi-volume official history, *The War in South Africa, 1899–1902*, under restrictions which rendered a truthful and illuminating account practically impossible. Maurice, who had retired from the army at the end of 1902, had produced two volumes and begun a third before his health broke down in the autumn of 1907. He had been appointed colonel-commandant of the Royal Artillery in 1906, and in 1907 was the first British recipient of the Chesney gold medal of the Royal United Service Institution for his contribution to military literature. After a long illness he died at his home, Highland View, Camberley, Surrey, on 11 January 1912.

Professor Jay Luvaas has aptly characterized Maurice as 'the second pen of Sir Garnet Wolseley' (Luvaas, 173), but he was not a mere hack or echo of his friend and chief. They differed on details and personalities, but they thought similarly on broad defence issues. Both opposed the prevalent military tendency after 1870 to imitate everything German, supported and defended the Cardwell reforms, and appreciated sea power. Maurice was important in educating the army, and to some extent the nation, in defence issues in the later nineteenth century.   BRIAN BOND

Sources F. B. Maurice, *Sir Frederick Maurice: a record of his work and opinions* (1913) · J. Luvaas, *The education of an army: British military thought, 1815–1940*, new edn (1965) · B. Bond, *The Victorian army and the Staff College, 1854–1914* (1972) · *DNB* · *The Times* (13 Jan 1912) · J. F.

Maurice, *The balance of military power in Europe* (1888) • A. Preston and P. Dennis, eds., *Swords and covenants* (1976) • B. B. Gilbert, *The evolution of national insurance in Great Britain: the origins of the welfare state* (1966) • G. R. Searle, *The quest for national efficiency: a study in British politics and political thought, 1899–1914* (1971)

Archives King's Lond., Liddell Hart C., corresp. | BL, notes, etc., relating to his edition of Sir John Moore's diaries, Add. MS 57545 • BL, corresp. with Macmillans, Add. MS 55075 • Hove Central Library, Wolseley collections • NL Scot., corresp. with Blackwoods, MSS 4201–4634, *passim*

Likenesses W. & D. Downey, woodburytype photograph, NPG; repro. in W. Downey and D. Downey, *The cabinet portrait gallery*, 1 (1890) [*see illus.*] • portrait, Staff College, Camberley

Wealth at death £8,116 5s. 10d.: probate, 16 Feb 1912, *CGPLA Eng. & Wales*

Maurice, Mary Atkinson (1797–1858), educationist, was born at Kirby Cane, Norfolk, the second daughter of the Revd Michael Maurice, a Unitarian minister and schoolmaster, and his wife, Priscilla Maurice (*née* Hurry). She was educated by her father along with some of her sisters and neighbours, showing a particular gift for languages and literature, and as she grew older, she helped to teach her numerous younger sisters. She was the most practical and businesslike member of the family.

In 1825 Mary Maurice moved with the family to Southampton, and when they ran into financial difficulties, she opened her own school, assisted by her younger sister Priscilla. She had become interested in the ideas of Pestalozzi, and spent some time with the Revd Charles Mayo and his sister Elizabeth Mayo at their school in Cheam, studying the Pestalozzian methods adopted there. She and some of her sisters and her brother had abandoned the Unitarian views of their father, causing great hurt in the family; under the influence of Mayo and others, she now became an Anglican, and opened her school as a church school. In 1829 she published anonymously *Aids to Development*, suggesting methods of instruction by which mothers might educate their own children. Her school prospered, and the need for larger premises led her to move to Reading, where she ran a school for nearly ten years with the help of another sister, Esther. When Esther married Julius Hare in 1844, Mary gave up the school and moved to London.

Mary Maurice was already a subscriber to the Governesses' Benevolent Institution (GBI), which was attempting to alleviate and improve the lives and work of governesses. It was the experiences and persuasion of Mary and her younger sisters which led their brother, (John) Frederick Denison *Maurice, to join the institution's committee. When Mary Maurice moved to Hanover Terrace, London, she took a more active role in the institution's work, in the belief that governesses needed more than financial aid, necessary as that was; they needed education, and recognized qualifications, which would in turn lead to their being given greater respect. In *Mothers and Governesses* (1847) she wrote of the task of education as 'an honourable and dignified calling, next only to the sacred ministry of the Gospel' (p. 148). And in *Governess Life: its Trials, Duties and Encouragements* (1849) she encouraged governesses to set and maintain certain standards (which she described in some detail), both for their own sakes and for those of

their employers. Drawing on her own experience, she urged them to make use of educational opportunities, which in her view were best found under instruction from men. Thus she was one of the promoters of Queen's College, Harley Street, opened in 1848 under the auspices of the GBI, with her brother F. D. Maurice as principal. Mary Maurice was a very generous subscriber to the new college, and served as one of the early 'lady visitors'. In addition, she served on the committee of, and raised a large amount of money for, the Asylum for Aged Governesses, which the GBI also opened in Harley Street.

Mary Maurice spent the last two years of her life with her sister and brother-in-law, Lucilla and William Powell, in Kensington, finally returning to the county of her birth, where she died of peritonitis, in Apsley Terrace, Great Yarmouth, on 4 October 1858. She was buried there, in St Nicholas's Church, among her Hurry ancestors. In her memory an additional aisle was added to St John's Church in Great Yarmouth, for the building of which she had raised and personally contributed much money.

Elaine Kaye

Sources L. Powell, Record of the Maurice family, 1884, Queen's College, Harley Street, London • *The life of Frederick Denison Maurice*, ed. F. Maurice, 2 vols. (1884) • Governesses' Benevolent Institution annual reports, LMA • E. Kaye, *A history of Queen's College, London, 1848–1972* (1972) • T. Hurry-Houghton, *Memorials of the family of Hurry* (1926) • d. cert. • *CGPLA Eng. & Wales* (1858)

Archives LMA, records of the Governesses' Benevolent Institution

Wealth at death under £7000: probate, 8 Nov 1858, *CGPLA Eng. & Wales*

Maurice, Thomas (1754–1824), oriental scholar and librarian, was born at Hertford on 25 September 1754, and claimed descent from an ancient Welsh family. His father, Thomas, on retiring from West Indian commerce, opened an academy at Clapham, and married an elderly lady with some property. In 1753, shortly after the death of his first wife, Thomas married her eighteen-year-old maid; Thomas was the eldest of six children of this second marriage, although only he and one brother, William, survived to maturity. After his father's death in 1762, Thomas's mother converted to Methodism and was 'trepanned into a clandestine marriage' (Maurice, 1.4) with Joseph Wright, an Irish Methodist preacher, who mistreated her and from whom she was legally separated in 1771. Thomas was sent to Christ's Hospital, thence to Ealing, and subsequently, through his mother's influence, to the Methodist school at Kingswood, near Bath. He took chambers in the Inner Temple, but found the study of classical and English literature more attractive than that of law, and, under the tuition of Dr Samuel Parr at Stanmore, he devoted himself to the classics.

On 6 May 1774 Thomas Maurice matriculated from St John's College, Oxford, migrating after a year to University College, where he graduated BA in 1778 and MA in 1808. While at Oxford he published some poetry and a translation of Sophocles' *Oedipus tyrannus*, for which Samuel Johnson wrote a preface (Boswell, *Life*, 3.370 n.2); this was the last extended preface he wrote for anyone else, and one of his best. Maurice also studied 'practical astronomy' there. He was ordained by Bishop Lowth on leaving Oxford and became curate of Woodford, Essex; in 1779, through Johnson's influence, he was also offered the curacy of Bosworth. In 1783 he began work on his *History of Hindostan*, which was nearly completed by 1789. In 1784 he relinquished his curacy for the chapel of Epping, but about the same time a legacy from a wealthy relative enabled him to buy a chaplaincy in the 97th regiment, which was disbanded later in the same year. Maurice received half-pay for the rest of his life. On 10 August 1786 he married Hannah, the daughter of Thomas Pearce, a captain in the service of the East India Company; she died childless in 1790.

In 1789 Maurice interrupted work on the *History of Hindostan* for the more polemical *Indian Antiquities*, with a view to defending the Pentateuch from the attacks of sceptical French mythographers such as Baillie, Volney, and Dupuis, who sought to interpret religious myths, whether Hindu or Christian, as astronomical and natural allegories. Maurice was encouraged in this apologetic project by Sir William Jones, whom he had known at Oxford, and whose mythographical syncretism profoundly influenced his work. In 1795 Maurice published an elegiac poem on Jones's unexpected death. The first two volumes of *Indian Antiquities* were published in 1792; volume 3 appeared in 1793, 4 in 1794, 5 in 1795–6, and 6 in 1796. *A Dissertation on the Oriental Trinities*, extracted from the fourth and fifth volumes of *Indian Antiquities*, was published in 1800, arguing that the Hindu triads, like the Christian Trinity, were vestiges of a universally revealed monotheism. Meanwhile, Maurice set about publishing his *History of Hindostan*: volume 1 appeared in 1795, volume 2 in 1798, and volume 3 in 1799. He went on to supplement his massive study of ancient Indian history with the *Modern History of Hindostan* (2 vols., 1802–10) which brought his account up to the late eighteenth century. A staunch anti-Jacobin, he also reviewed works on oriental mythology for the tory high-church *British Critic*. In 1798 he was presented by Earl Spencer to the vicarage of Wormleighton, Warwickshire, and in the following year he was appointed assistant keeper of manuscripts in the British Museum. In 1804, on the presentation of the lord chancellor, he became vicar of Cudham, Kent. All these offices he retained until his death. In 1800 he obtained, through Bishop Tomline, the pension which had been enjoyed by William Cowper. In 1812, abandoning his earlier syncretist project of defending the historicity of the Bible from Hindu mythographical sources, he published *Brahminical Fraud Detected*. A second edition, entitled *The Indian Sceptic Refuted*, was published in 1813. Another work of apologetics, *Observations Connected with Astronomy and Ancient History*, appeared in 1816. Maurice's final publication was the uncompleted *Memoirs of the Author of 'Indian Antiquities'* (1819–22), which contains recollections of contemporary men of letters and casts new light on the composition of Johnson's *Lives of the Poets*. Maurice died on 30 March 1824 in his apartments at the British Museum.

Maurice was on intimate terms with many leading contemporary scholars and men of letters; his poetry and drama were widely read, although Lord Byron, in *English Bards and Scotch Reviewers*, described him as 'dull' and his poem 'Richmond Hill' as 'the petrifaction of a plodding brain'. He was a voluminous author, but his researches in Asiatic history and myth were hampered by ignorance of Asiatic languages, and by his overriding polemical concern to refute French scepticism. His syncretist approach to mythology was of the school of Jacob Bryant, confident in comparing and contrasting different cultures on the basis of superficial etymological resemblance, without any understanding of grammar, syntax, or sound change. This etymological approach was rejected and discredited by Franz Bopp and other German comparative grammarians in the 1810s, rendering Maurice's scholarship largely obsolete. Today his work is largely of interest to students of Romantic literature and antiquarianism on account of its influence on Coleridge, Shelley, and other contemporary writers.

NIGEL LEASK

Sources T. Maurice, *Memoirs of the author of 'Indian antiquities'* (1819–22) • *GM*, 1st ser., 94/1 (1824), 467–73 • Watt, *Bibl. Brit.*, 2.657s • [Clarke], *The Georgian era: memoirs of the most eminent persons*, 4 vols. (1832–4) • Foster, *Alum. Oxon.* • *Boswell's Life of Johnson*, ed. G. B. Hill, 3 (1887), 370, n.2 • G. Gordon, Lord Byron, *English bards and Scotch reviewers* [n.d.] • Nichols, *Illustrations*, 2.661, 663, 848; vol. 8 • Nichols, *Lit. anecdotes*, 3.242, 511 • W. R. Keast, 'Samuel Johnson and Thomas Maurice', *Eighteenth century studies in honour of Donald F. Hyde*, ed. W. H. Bond (1970), 63–79 • *IGI*

Archives BL, corresp., Add. MS 56080 | BL, letters to Lord Spencer

Likenesses W. Ridley, stipple, 1799 (after Plimer), BM, NPG; repro. in *Monthly Mirror* (Nov 1799), facing p. 259 • W. Ridley, stipple, 1801 (after S. Drummond), BM, NPG; repro. in *European Magazine* (1801) • T. Uwins, chalk and pencil drawing, BM

Maurice, William (1619/20–1680), antiquary, was the son of Lewis Maurice of Cefn-y-braich, Llansilin, Denbighshire, a man of literary interests, descended from the house of Moelyrch, and Jane, daughter of John Holland, vicar of Cegidfa. His education is unrecorded. He married first Lettice, daughter of Roger Kynaston of Cefn-y-carneddau, Ruabon; they had three sons who died young and two daughters: Ann, who married David Williams of Glan Alaw, brother of Sir William Williams (1634–1700), speaker of the House of Commons, and Lettice. From his second marriage, to Elizabeth, daughter of George Ludlow of Morehouse and widow of Thomas Gethin, he had a daughter, Elizabeth. He resided at Cefn-y-braich and Tŷ Newydd, Llansilin.

By 1638 Maurice was making copies of Welsh poetry. He became the best-read Welsh antiquary of his generation, with interest in literature, history, and law. Helped by amanuenses, he was an assiduous transcriber. His collection of manuscripts, known from copies of his own catalogue, amounted to over a hundred. His transcripts are notable for his care in recording exemplars and sources. A young associate of Robert Vaughan, he catalogued the Hengwrt manuscripts in 1658; his coarse hand appears in scores of manuscripts which survive in the Hengwrt and other collections. He is said to have built himself a three-storey library.

Maurice's scholarly virtues can best be appreciated in his *Deddfgrawn* or *Corpus Hoelianum* (Wynnstay MSS 37–38), his compilation of Welsh law: his analysis laid the basis of the modern classification of the texts. His detailed, matter-of-fact chronicle of events in north Wales from 1638 to 1647, which betrays no obvious sympathy with either side, was printed from his manuscript in 1846 before its destruction. However, in religion Maurice was radical and in 1653 he wrote a forceful tract against 'altar-worship'. His style, when polemical, as in this and his anti-quarian tracts (none was printed), whether writing in Latin, English, or Welsh, is florid and bombastic. The scholarly Humphrey Humphreys, referring to a tract on British coins, described Maurice as 'a very injudicious man' (NL Wales, MS 2029, no. 2, p. 34); other contemporaries regarded him as eccentric.

Maurice made his will on 11 March 1680, 'somewhat crasie and infirme in body', leaving his books, both printed and manuscript, to his daughter Lettice. He died on 27 March 1680 and was buried at Llansilin on 31 March. His manuscript collection was bought after his death by Sir William Williams and descended to the Williams-Wynns of Wynnstay. The greater part was lost in the fire which destroyed the Wynnstay library in 1858. Fewer than ten of Maurice's manuscripts survived the fire; a few more, and a number of his annotated printed books, survive in other collections.   DANIEL HUWS

Sources DWB · E. D. Jones, 'The Wynnstay manuscripts and documents', *National Library of Wales Journal*, 2 (1941–2), 26–32 · D. Jenkins, 'Deddfgrawn William Maurice', *National Library of Wales Journal*, 2 (1941–2), 33–6 · W. Maurice, 'An account of the civil war in north Wales, 1638–47', *Archaeologia Cambrensis*, 1 (1846), 33–42 · *Handlist of manuscripts in the National Library of Wales*, 1 [1940], xvi–xx · A. Llwyd, 'Catalogue of Welsh manuscripts, etc, in north Wales', *Transactions of the Cymmrodorion*, 2 (1828), 36–58 · *Report on manuscripts in the Welsh language*, 2 vols. in 7, HMC, 48 (1898–1910), vol. 2, pp. 868–9 · E. D. Jones, 'The Brogyntyn Welsh manuscripts, IX', *National Library of Wales Journal*, 7 (1951–2), 1–11 · NL Wales, MS 732 · Llansilin bishop's transcripts, St Asaph diocesan records, NL Wales · probate records, NL Wales, SA/1680/132 · NL Wales, MS 2029 · NL Wales, Wynnstay papers
Archives NL Wales, papers and collections mainly relating to Laws Hywel Dda
Wealth at death bequests of £600: will, NL Wales, SA/1680/132

Maverick, Samuel (*c.*1602–1670×76), colonist in America, was born in Devon, the son of the Revd John Maverick (*c.*1576–1637), a Church of England clergyman, and his wife, Mary Gye. Samuel Maverick was one of the first colonists in New England, having arrived as early as 1624, possibly with the company of Robert Gorges. He was joined by his father when John Maverick sailed from Plymouth with his congregation in March 1630 and settled in Dorchester, Massachusetts. He was residing on Noddle's Island, Massachusetts Bay, where he had built a fortified homestead, when John Winthrop arrived on his way from Salem in June 1630. In 1631 he acquired land in Maine under the patent of Sir Fernando Gorges, and in 1633 the colonial government granted him title to Noddle's Island. He owned additional lands in Massachusetts at Boston, Chelsea, and Braintree. About the year 1628 he married Amias (*fl.* 1613–1672), daughter of William Cole and widow of David Thompson. They had three children: Nathaniel, Samuel, and Mary. He was made a freeman of the colony in October 1632. A loyal member of the Church of England, he was highly critical of the New England Congregationalists, who denied him church membership and participation in the sacraments.

None the less, Maverick had important social and business connections in the Atlantic world. In 1632, and again in 1635, he sailed to Virginia, returning from the second voyage with livestock and 40 tons of cedar. He corresponded with Captain William Jackson and the chevalier de la Tour on business matters. In 1638 he purchased African slaves who had been traded for captive Pequot Indians in the West Indies (Sumner, 80–82, 90).

Maverick was noted for his hospitality to travellers, which raised suspicion in the mid-1630s when the colonial authorities feared the imminent imposition of an episcopal establishment. In March 1635 he refused to comply with a court order to abandon Noddle's Island and move to Boston. Ralph Josselyn, who stayed with Maverick twice in 1638 and 1639, pronounced him 'the only hospitable man in all the country, giving entertainment to all comers *gratis*' (*Collections of the Massachusetts Historical Society*, 3rd ser., 3, 231). In 1646 he was one of seven petitioners who signed the *Remonstrance and Humble Petition*, which demanded civil and religious liberties for non-church members. When the petitioners took their case to parliament, Maverick was imprisoned and fined £150. The fine was reduced by half in 1650, following three appeals by Maverick to the Massachusetts court.

With the restoration of the monarchy in 1660 Maverick left for England to present his long-standing grievances against the Massachusetts government. In 1664 Charles II appointed him, together with Colonel Richard Nichols, Sir Robert Cane, and George Cartwright, as commissioners to oversee the administration of the New England colonies and to reduce the Dutch in New Netherland. Massachusetts refused to obey the commissioners, who were recalled to England in 1665, with the exception of Maverick. Maverick remained in the service of the king, but had moved to New York in 1660. He continued to criticize the Massachusetts government in letters to the duke of Clarendon and to Colonel Richard Nichols. 'The loyal party which groans under the burthen of the Massachusetts government now despair of relief' (*CSP col.*, 7.31). The last record of Maverick is a letter written by him to Nichols on 15 October 1669, in which he thanks Nichols 'for his favour in procuring from H.R.H. the gift of the house in the Broadway [New York]', and reports that 'the flux, agues, and fevers have much reigned in city and country' (ibid., 7.43). Whether Maverick succumbed to one of these epidemics is unknown but likely. Nathaniel Maverick of Barbados referred to his father in his 1670 will: 'father is to have complete maintenance if he comes to Barbados' (Sanders, 1.237). By 1676, however, a deed indicates that his daughter Mary owned his New York house, indicating his death before that date.

BARBARA RITTER DAILEY

Sources C. F. Adams, *Three episodes of Massachusetts history*, [2nd edn], 2 vols. (1892) · T. Hutchinson, *The history of the colony and province of Massachusetts-Bay*, ed. L. S. Mayo, 3 vols. (1936) · 'Maverick's description of New England', *New England Historical and Genealogical Register*, 39 (1885), 33–48 · J. Greenwood, 'The Maverick family', *New England Historical and Genealogical Register*, 48 (1894), 207–9 · 'Samuel Maverick', *New England Historical and Genealogical Register*, 69 (1915), 157–8 · *Collections of the Massachusetts Historical Society* (1929), 85–7, 162, 167, 324 [*The Winthrop papers*, vol. 4] · 'Letters of Samuel Maverick', *Collections of the Massachusetts Historical Society*, 4th ser., 7 (1865), 307–20 · 'The Clarendon papers', *Collections of the New York Historical Society* (1869) [whole issue], 19–159 · CSP col., 5.15–16, 147ff.; 7.20–21, 31–2, 168–9, 329–30; 10.19–20, 276–80; 11.494–5 · W. H. Sumner, *A history of East Boston* (1858), 45–160, 719–21 · J. Winthrop, *The history of New England from 1630 to 1649*, ed. J. Savage, 2 vols. (1825–6); repr. (1972) · J. M. Sanders, *Barbados records: wills and administrations*, 1 (Houston, TX, 1979), 237
Archives Mass. Hist. Soc., Winthrop papers · New York Historical Society, Clarendon papers

Mavor, James (1854–1925), political economist, was born on 8 December 1854 in Stranraer, Wigtownshire, the eldest of nine children of the Revd James Mavor (1828–1879), a teacher from New Aberdour, Aberdeenshire, and his wife, Mary Ann Taylor, née Bridie (1828–1896), of Dundee. The family moved to Glasgow in 1862 and James, as the eldest son, left school to go to work. Evening classes at Anderson's College and some lectures at the University of Glasgow finished his formal education. His international academic stature was thus attained without benefit of an earned degree.

Early friendship with the physicist and inventor William Thomson (Lord Kelvin) led to a thirst for science rare among men of arts and letters. At one time Mavor was both editor of the *Scottish Art Review* and Scottish editor of the technology magazine *Industries*. Entering business in Glasgow he saw the social effects of pell-mell industrialization, and with the town planner Patrick Geddes pioneered housing for the poor. With his lifelong friend William Morris he co-signed the founding manifesto of the Socialist League, but wary of socialism's authoritarian bent he soon broke with it.

On 16 January 1882 Mavor married Christina Jane Gordon Balfour Watt (1850–1933), a Glasgow music teacher. They had three children, all of whom achieved distinction: James Watt Mavor, a leading biologist in the USA; Dora Mavor Moore, Canadian theatre pioneer; and Brigadier Wilfrid Mavor.

When appointed professor of political economy and statistics at St Mungo's College in 1889, Mavor already had close contacts with co-operative, union, suffragist, and Ruskinite groups in Britain; with economists in France, Germany, and America; and, through the Glasgow Fabian Society, with Pease, the Webbs, and G. B. Shaw—who sparred with him by naming Candida's social activist husband 'The Rev. James Mavor Morell'. London friends included the editor W. T. Stead, the critic Arthur Symons, the poet W. B. Yeats, and the émigré Russian biologist and anarchist Prince Peter Kropotkin. Mavor's reports on British railways solidified his academic reputation, and by 1892, when he left for Canada, he was counted among the leading British economists.

As head of the department of political economy at the University of Toronto, Mavor quickly became a catalyst in Canadian cultural and economic affairs. He championed art galleries, museums, theatre, and workers' education. His report of 1904 for the British government, *North West of Canada*, dampening prospects for wheat export, became notorious in both nations. Kropotkin enlisted his aid in Tolstoy's plan to resettle Russia's oppressed Dukhobors in the Canadian west, a massive project that claimed his attention for decades. Before the First World War, Mavor had travelled through much of Canada, Europe, China, Mongolia, and Japan as an adviser to various governments, and had written (after teaching himself Russian and visiting Tolstoy) his seminal *Economic History of Russia* (2 vols., 1914).

In Toronto, Mavor's department spawned others: political science, economy, statistics, sociology, commerce and finance. The communications prophet Harold Innis was among his professorial appointments, and his students became notable in many fields. In 1912 the university made him an honorary PhD. His autobiography, *My Windows on the Street of the World*, appeared in two volumes in 1923, and *The Russian Revolution* posthumously in 1926. He died on 31 October 1925 while visiting Glasgow, and was buried there. The playwright James Bridie (Osborne Henry *Mavor, 1888–1951) was a nephew. J. MAVOR MOORE

Sources J. Mavor, *My windows on the street of the world*, 2 vols. (1923) [autobiography] · R. Grover and F. W. M. Moore, *James Mavor and his world* (1975) · J. M. Moore, *Reinventing myself* (1994) · J. M. Moore, 'Why "James Mavor" Morell?', *Shaw Review* (May 1980) · [N. Story], *The Oxford companion to Canadian history and literature*, ed. W. Toye (1967)
Archives Harvard U. · NRA, papers · Pomona College, Claremont, California · University of Toronto | NA Canada · NL Scot., corresp. with Sir Patrick Geddes
Likenesses F. H. Newbery, oils, 1893, Art Gallery of Ontario, Toronto · N. Tregor, copper bust, 1916, Art Gallery of Ontario, Toronto · H. Walker, oils, 1920, University of Toronto · photographs, University of Toronto, James Mavor Archives

Mavor, Osborne Henry [*pseud.* James Bridie] (1888–1951), playwright, was born in Glasgow on 3 January 1888, the eldest son of Henry Alexander Mavor (1858–1915) and his wife, Janet Osborne (1860–1926). Henry Mavor was a man of many gifts who, having been compelled for financial reasons to abandon the study of medicine, subsequently made a moderately comfortable living as an engineer. 'The houses in which the Mavors lived had an atmosphere of dignity and good manners and a smell of old books and ink'. So wrote O. H. Mavor in *One Way of Living*, an autobiography which refuses, with charm and gaiety, to endow its subject with the importance he deserved. Educated at Glasgow Academy, O. H. Mavor took advantage of the solid comfort in which he had grown up to spend nine or ten years at Glasgow University, ostensibly as a medical student, but more remarkably as a source of high spirits,

Osborne Henry Mavor [James Bridie] (**1888–1951**), by Lida Moser, 1949

light verse, ingenious ragging, and talkative and persistent friendships: one of his fellow students, and a friend until death, was Walter Elliot, who was later to become secretary of state for Scotland.

Having qualified in 1913 Mavor, like Elliot, joined the Royal Army Medical Corps (RAMC) and the First World War with an enthusiasm typical of his generation. This enthusiasm somehow survived service in Flanders, was depressed in Mesopotamia, but revived in the romantic circumstances of the expedition which Major-General Dunsterville led from northern Persia to the Caspian shore of Russia. Some twenty years later, at the age of fifty-one, Mavor returned to the RAMC and a second war, and saw brief service in Norway. Although by then he had found his true vocation, it was not so exclusive as to despise a latent romanticism or reject an old-fashioned call to duty.

Mavor's medical career was respectable: he was a general practitioner, then a consulting physician to the Victoria Infirmary, and for some time professor of medicine in the Anderson College of Glasgow. The work for which he is known had its public beginnings in 1928, when *The Sunlight Sonata* was presented in Glasgow by the Scottish National Players, an amateur company which employed professional producers. Mavor had been drawn to the theatre by the work of the Glasgow Repertory Company (1909–14), an enterprise funded by the citizens who subscribed to it, and one which offered its audiences a wide range of contemporary drama. He wrote in all some forty plays, under the pseudonym James Bridie, and entered the world of the professional theatre under the

auspices of Sir Barry Jackson, who presented *The Switchback* in Birmingham in 1929 and at the Malvern Festival in 1931. *The Anatomist*, with Henry Ainley in the leading part, had a London production in the latter year, after its première in Edinburgh in 1930, and Mavor found himself the recipient of a criticism which was to dog him for the rest of his life. It was said, initially by James Agate, and endlessly repeated, that he could not construct a last act. The accusation does not hold, for his last acts are usually logical, but what may readily be admitted is that they did not always meet the expectation of critics or of an audience anticipating a conventional gesture of conclusion. Sometimes too Mavor seems reluctant to allow his darker visions to be fully realized.

The central character of *The Anatomist* is Dr Knox, the teacher of anatomy whose cadavers were supplied by Burke and Hare. In 1933 Mavor again drew a subject for drama from his professional milieu and wrote one of his best plays, *A Sleeping Clergyman*, in which he explores the interaction of genius and amorality in three generations of a medical family. However it is his biblical and apocryphal plays—*Tobias and the Angel* (1930), *Jonah and the Whale* (1932), *Susannah and the Elders* (1937)—which are the most delightful of his writings. They offer instinct with wit, insight into character, and essential common sense—or, perhaps, uncommon understanding. They are, moreover, written with a gracious and fluent command of language, and his dialogue demonstrates to perfection how phrases may be carpentered to reveal the precise meaning of their words. As popular successes, *Mr Bolfry* (1943), a sustained comic sermon with Alastair Sim in the pulpit, and *Daphne Laureola* (1949), in which Dame Edith Evans played with entrancing virtuosity, were impressive. A good play, *The Queen's Comedy*, which argues for stoicism in the face of cruelty and suffering, was insufficiently rewarded at the Edinburgh Festival in 1950; *The Baikie Charivari* (1952), Mavor's last work, is admittedly difficult, darkened as it is by undisguised pessimism and anger.

Of O. H. Mavor's importance to Scotland, as well as to the Scottish theatre, there is no doubt whatever. He was an innovator, and a creator of more than words and dramatic scenes: he created an ambience of confidence, gaiety, and affection, and while he might describe his fellow man as 'a droll wee slug wi' the shifty e'e', he loved all life and welcomed all sorts and kinds of his fellow men for their comical and unexpected contributions to it. It was Mavor who took the lead in the establishment of the Glasgow Citizens' Theatre in 1943 and the founding of a College of Drama in the city in 1950. He was chairman of the Scottish committee of the Council for the Encouragement of Music and the Arts, the precursor of the Arts Council.

Mavor himself was a man of no great physical attraction, but his appearance in maturity acquired a ponderous and craggy benignity. On 14 June 1923 he married Rona Locke Bremner (1897–1985), a woman of notable beauty, ten years his junior. She was a talented and capable person but one excessively anxious about the maladies, real and imagined, from which she believed she was suffering. They had two sons, one of whom, serving with the

Lothians and Border horse, was killed in France in 1944; the other, Ronald, having qualified in and practised medicine, chose to follow further in his father's footsteps by taking to play writing and dramatic criticism.

Mavor was appointed CBE in 1946. He died in Edinburgh Royal Infirmary on 29 January 1951 of a brain haemorrhage; he was buried in the western necropolis in his native city on 1 February. For almost twenty years he had lived by his pen and had been the first Scottish dramatist, apart from Barrie—and Barrie's base was in the south—who had been able to do so in any comfort. To a large degree this was due to his ability to please audiences furth of Scotland, with his skill, wit, and philosophical musings. It is therefore something of an irony that in the years since his death revivals of his plays have been much more common in the Scottish theatre than elsewhere, despite the fact that most of his work was premièred south of the border.   ERIC LINKLATER, rev. DAVID HUTCHISON

Sources R. Mavor, *Dr Mavor and Mr Bridie* (1988) · J. Bridie [O. H. Mavor], *Some talk of Alexander* (1926) · J. Bridie [O. H. Mavor], *One way of living* (1939) · W. Bannister, *James Bridie and his theatre* (1955) · D. Hutchison, *The modern Scottish theatre* (1977) · personal knowledge (1971) · m. cert.
Archives NL Scot., corresp. and papers, and papers relating to him · U. Glas. L., special collections department, Scottish Theatre Archive, MSS · U. Glas. L., playscripts, press cuttings, speeches, article, and corresp. relating to Citizens' Theatre | BL, corresp. with League of Dramatists, Add. MS 63415 · JRL, corresp. with Basil Dean · JRL, corresp. with Robert Donat · NL Scot., letters to Eric Capon · NL Scot., letters to Neil Gunn · NL Scot., letters to Winifred Isaac · NL Scot., corresp. with R. D. Macleod and papers · NL Scot., letters to Duncan Macrae · NL Scot., letters to his wife, R. B. Mavor · NL Scot., letters to Alexander Reid · NL Scot., letters to Alfred Wareing · Theatre Museum, London, letters to John Casson
Likenesses M. Peake, black crayon painting, 1939, Scot. NPG · K. Hutton, photograph, 1949, Hult. Arch. · L. Moser, photograph, 1949, priv. coll. [*see illus.*] · B. Schotz, terracotta head, 1953, Scot. NPG · G. Cursiter, group portrait, oils (*Authors in session, 1950*), Glasgow Art Gallery and Museum · W. O. Hutchison, pencil drawing, Scot. NPG · L. Rey, bronze bust, U. Glas. · photographs, repro. in Bannister, *James Bridie and his theatre* · photographs, repro. in Mavor, *Dr Mavor and Mr Bridie* · photographs, U. Glas. L., Scottish Theatre Archive
Wealth at death £44,356 19s. 2d.: confirmation, 27 April 1951, CCI

Mavor, William Fordyce [*pseuds.* W. F. Martyn, Numa] (**1758–1837**), author and educationist, was born on 1 August 1758 at New Deer, Aberdeenshire, the elder son of John Mavor (1726–1786), farmer, and his wife, Elizabeth Low (1735–1791). His family, which had numbered judges and exchequer officials in the sixteenth and seventeenth centuries, had, by Mavor's time, 'dwindled' to being small farmers, who further risked their fortunes by coming out for the Stuarts in the rising of 1745. He was educated at New Deer and Turriff, and at the age of seventeen set out, with only a competency in Latin, to make his fortune in England. After staying for a time in London with a Jacobite cousin, who had become a prosperous city merchant on his release from the Tower, he obtained a post as assistant master at Thomas Hunter's private school at Burford in Oxfordshire. Here, while apparently giving satisfaction

since he remained in Burford for seven years (1775–82), he commenced his writing career.

At nineteen Mavor brought out *Parnassian Springs* (1777), a youthful collection of poetry. Two years later he published *Universal Stenography* (1779), a system of shorthand which ran to ten editions. Meanwhile he was ghost-writing guides and histories for Harrison, a London publisher. Considered 'remarkably handsome' (Blagdon, 23), he was already making contacts at Oxford—with the Balliol Scots, and the Jacobites and high tories at the King's Arms. He was also preparing to take holy orders, and in October 1781 was made deacon by the bishop of Oxford at Christ Church Cathedral. Plans were already afoot to start a school of his own, and in the following year Mavor opened the Woodstock Academy, where 'Youth' were to be 'genteely boarded and carefully educated' (*Jackson's Oxford Journal*, January 1782). The school was a success, and on 17 October 1782 Mavor married, at Shipton under Wychwood, Ann Harris (*d.* 1822), daughter of the host at the Royal Oak, Loughborough corner; they had seven children by 1789.

At the outset Mavor's Woodstock career was largely dependent on patronage from members of the Marlborough family and their friends. He was ordained priest in 1784, and in time curacies became available, notably at Kiddington, where Thomas Warton, the poet laureate, was rector. Presentations followed: the vicarage of Hurley (1789), Tysoe in Warwickshire (1790), and later Bladon-with-Woodstock (1810), along with private chaplaincies to the earl of Dumfries and the earl of Moira. In 1787 Mavor was made an honorary freeman of Woodstock, and two years later he became a member of the city council and master of Woodstock grammar school; he was awarded an honorary LLD by Aberdeen University in the same year.

Mavor was an extraordinarily industrious author and published a spate of guides, grammars, miscellanies, a sequence of admirably abridged tours, travels, and histories, a women's magazine, and a newspaper, the *Oxford University and City Herald* (1806), as well as numerous essays on education. A few of his works were published under his pseudonyms, W. F. Martyn and Numa. His ideas on education were liberal; 'Dry lectures seldom leave any lasting impression,' he wrote, 'but convey the moral you wish to inculcate through an interesting story … and the effect is seldom lost' (W. F. Mavor, *A Father's Gift to his Children*, 1807, x). In 1787 he brought out *The British Nepos*, which consisted of short, lively biographies of famous Englishmen from Alfred to John Howard; it ran to fifteen editions. The following year his eldest son, who was at Charterhouse, fell ill, and to entertain him Mavor wrote *The Lady's and Gentleman's Botanical Pocket Book* and *Elements of Natural History*, both published in 1799; they were written in a suitably genteel style so as to bring no blush to the youthful cheek. The *Elements* went through several editions and was translated into French as *Le buffon des enfants*.

In 1801 Mavor published his most famous work, *The English Spelling Book*. To appeal to children it had fine woodcuts by Thomas Bewick, and simple and amusing moral stories for them to read. It ran to 500 editions, was translated into

French and Hindi, and by 1823, at its 284th edition, had sold over 2 million copies. In 1806 the board of agriculture asked Mavor to write a survey of Berkshire. Undertaken at a time of great agrarian unrest as a result of low wages and high corn prices due to Napoleon's blockade of the English ports, his *General View of the Agriculture of Berkshire* (1809) is remarkable as much for its sympathetic attitude to the agricultural poor as for its interest in modern farming methods. As a farmer's son, Mavor was well acquainted with the sufferings of agricultural workers.

Meanwhile civic honours accumulated. In 1808 Mavor was elected mayor of Woodstock, and in 1811 the duke of Marlborough appointed him rector of Woodstock, a position he had long desired. He celebrated his success by having his portrait taken by James Saxon, who had recently painted Sir Walter Scott. His appearance was 'intelligent, strongly impressed with lines of thought', though he had a florid complexion and a figure 'somewhat inclined to corpulency' (Blagdon, 23). This was perhaps unsurprising, for though a 'sworn foe to licentiousness', detesting 'every species of slavery', he also 'gloried in liberty' and was 'extremely social in his habits' (ibid.).

In 1822 Ann Mavor died. The marriage had not been happy, and the following year Mavor married Harriet Segrave (1788–1875), and started a second family. In the years that followed he continued as rector, founded the Woodstock Floral and Horticultural Society and a lending library, introduced free vaccination for the poor, planted trees, and in 1834 became mayor of Woodstock for the tenth time. He died at Woodstock rectory on 19 December 1837, active to the last. His library, which was a fine one, was sold in Oxford, and he left £9000 to his wife and daughters. He was buried at Woodstock church where he is celebrated by a commemorative plaque.

ELIZABETH MAVOR

Sources A. H. T. Robb-Smith, 'Address on the bi-centenary of the birth of the Revd William Fordyce Mavor', 1958, Westgate Library, Oxford, Centre for Oxfordshire Studies • *Public characters of 1800–1801* (1801), 167–76 • F. W. Blagdon, *The flowers of literature* (1810), 23 • E. Mavor, 'The Mavors', 1991, Elgin Public Library • *DNB* • *GM*, 2nd ser., 9 (1838), 434–5 • *GM*, 2nd ser., 16 (1841), 252 • parish records, New Deer, Aberdeenshire, Scotland
Likenesses sketch, engraving, c.1790 • line engraving, 1796, NPG; repro. in W. F. Mavor, *Historical account of the most celebrated voyages, travels and discoveries* (1801), vol. 1, frontispiece • J. Saxon, oils, c.1811 • miniature, c.1823 • C. Turner, mezzotint (after J. Saxon), BM, NPG; repro. in W. F. Mavor, *Miscellanies* (1829)
Wealth at death £9000: Robb-Smith, 'Address'

Maw, John Hornby (1800–1885), entrepreneur and artist, was born on 12 April 1800 at Ferry, in Lincolnshire, the eldest of four children of George Maw (1770–1834), a local farmer, and his wife, Ann, *née* Hornby (1769–1828). His parents married in 1799. In 1807 they and their (then) three children moved from Lincolnshire to London, and George Maw established a wholesale druggist business with his wife's cousin named Hornby. In 1814 he parted from Hornby and set up a pharmaceutical manufacturing business by purchasing a surgical plaster factory. Other sundries were soon added, including surgeons' instruments.

John Maw received schooling at Aspley Guise, Bedfordshire, and at Merchant Taylors' School, London. His father placed him, at fifteen, with a chemist at Croydon for two years and afterwards entered him at St Bartholomew's Hospital, London, in order to gain first-hand knowledge that might benefit the family business. In 1826 he was taken into partnership with the family firm. In the same year he married Mary Anne Johnson (1795–1853). He and his younger brother Solomon married sisters, the only daughters of John Johnson of Maiden Lane, assayer to the Royal Mint and to the Bank of England. His brother-in-law Percival N. Johnson founded the famous firm of Johnson Matthey, in Hatton Garden, London.

The family business prospered and in the early 1830s provided a secure financial basis for Maw to begin to indulge in the collection of paintings. His three children were born at this time: Anne Mary (1830), George (1832), and Arthur (1835). In 1835 he retired from the business for health reasons but its considerable commercial success continued throughout the nineteenth century under his brother Solomon and nephew Charles.

In 1839 Maw and his family moved to Hastings, Sussex, where they lived at West Hill House. There his friends included many well-known artists, such as William Hunt, David Cox, and J. M. W. Turner. He took lessons from Peter DeWint and fitted up a studio at his home. He was a member of the Society of Painters in Water Colours and exhibited at the Royal Academy between 1840 and 1848. His *Interior of West Hill House* (c.1842) is in the collection of Hastings Museum and Art Gallery. While at Hastings he served as mayor of the town and was involved with good works, including the provision of a water fountain for fishermen to wash their nets.

In 1849 the family left Hastings for the west country, living at Tavistock, west Devon, for a few months and then at Bideford, north Devon. It was there that Maw's interest in decorative tile-making was aroused. His daughter's journal (written c.1890) records visits with her father to a local potter who still used inlaid clays in the medieval fashion. 'It struck my father that it would not be difficult to imitate ancient encaustic tiles' (Wood). Designs were traced in local churches and the prototypes were fired by a local potter. Maw saw 'the germ of the business for his boys for which he had been searching and praying' (ibid., 53).

In 1850 Maw purchased a disused tile works at Worcester, and for two years floor tiles were made there. In 1852 the family, their workforce, and equipment moved (by special train) to Benthall, in Ironbridge Gorge, Shropshire, to be closer to sources of coal and suitable clay. The family firm grew rapidly over the next decade, the demand for decorative floor tiles being fuelled by the building and restoration of churches and grand civic buildings. Wall-tiling and glazed architectural faience were added to the product range, and designs were commissioned from leading architects. Meanwhile, the Maw family was locally involved with establishing the Coalbrookdale School of Art, lending pictures from their private collection for an exhibition at the opening of the new building in 1859. The firm achieved considerable success at the 1862 International Exhibition in London in connection with its majolica fireplace tiles in the Moorish style. Maw's sons, George and Arthur, became more prominent in running the tile works, but all members of the family travelled widely in Europe and north Africa, using the opportunity to draw and trace tile designs from other cultures. A great many tiles were exported to the British empire and the United States. By the 1880s the Maws manufacturing site at Benthall had become too restricted, and land was purchased at Jackfield, a mile downstream on the River Severn, where a new Benthall works was erected and opened on 1 May 1883. Maw's wife died on 20 August 1853, after a long illness. During the latter part of his life Maw was a devout member of the Plymouth Brethren. This led to friction within the family when his daughter fell in love with Richard Wilton, curate of Broseley. Somewhat unusually, both sides of this tragic relationship are recorded by its participants (see Wood, 59; Young, 111–27).

Maw's achievements fall into three distinct phases. His entrepreneurial flair was first demonstrated during his early years in London in the family manufacturing chemists' business. His time in Hastings was one of personal artistic development and achievement. The last thirty-three years of his life, in Shropshire, saw his business flair linked to successful artistic manufacture—the epitome of a Victorian art industry. He saw decorative tile-making develop from a few crude, handmade prototypes in 1849 to the opening of the largest decorative tile works in the world in 1883.

Maw died at his home, Barratt's Hill House, Broseley, on 28 June 1885 and was buried, with his wife, in the graveyard of the Baptist Chapel at Broseley. The largest and most representative collection of Maws tiles is held in the Jackfield Tile Museum, part of the Ironbridge Gorge Museum, Shropshire; tile designs (on paper) are held at the museum's library in Coalbrookdale. Important examples of Maws tiles *in situ* are at Shrub Hill railway station, Worcester, where majolica tiles fill panels (*c.*1865) in the cast-iron waiting room; a geometric tiled floor (1857–60) at Osgoode Hall, Toronto, Canada; and extensive and varied floor tiles (1861–2) in Battlefield church, Shrewsbury. TONY HERBERT

Sources A. M. Wood, 'Diary of Anne Mary Wood', [n.d., *c.*1890], Ironbridge Gorge Museum Trust, Telford, Shropshire [typed manuscript] · *S. Maw, Son, & Sons: history of the firm* [n.d., *c.*1900] · D. S. Macleod, *Art and the Victorian middle class: money and the making of cultural identity* (1996) · M. B. Young, *Richard Wilton: a forgotten Victorian* (1967) · M. Stratton, *Broseley: a guide through an early industrial town*, Broseley Society, Ironbridge Gorge Museum Trust (1981) · CGPLA Eng. & Wales (1885)

Archives Ironbridge Gorge Museum Trust, Telford, Shropshire, papers

Likenesses photograph, 1870–80, Ironbridge Gorge Museum, Telford, Shropshire · J. W. Fall, photograph, 1880–85, Ironbridge Gorge Museum, Telford, Shropshire · A. Chapman, photograph, Ironbridge Gorge Museum, Telford, Shropshire · photograph, repro. in *S. Maw, Son, & Sons*, 2

Wealth at death £6875: probate, 1885, *CGPLA Eng. & Wales*

Maw, William Henry (1838–1924), engineer and technical journalist, was born on 6 December 1838 in Scarborough,

the only child of William Mintoft Maw, a merchant clipper captain, and his wife, Minna Josephine Teresa, *née* Maxey. Maw's childhood was dogged by poor health, but he attended Sykes's School in Scarborough for several years. He was particularly interested in scientific facts, experiments, model making, and astronomy. His father died in 1853 and William and his mother moved to London where she died the following year.

In March 1855 Maw was apprenticed to John Gooch, engineer to the Eastern Counties Railway, at Stratford in east London. Starting in the smith's shop of the carriage and wagon department he then transferred to the locomotive and engineering department. He also took drawing classes at the London Mechanics' Institution and assisted in the department's drawing office, where his impressive talent earned him, in December 1859, the post of chief draughtsman. In effect, though, he was personal assistant to the company's engineer-in-chief, Robert Sinclair, and responsible for designing rolling stock and for much standardizing work. He continued his studies through the Department of Science and Art in South Kensington, and made contact with such important figures as Henry Bessemer and Zerah Colburn.

In 1859 Maw and other young engineers founded the Civil and Mechanical Engineers' Society; he was president from 1863 to 1866. Colburn sought Maw as co-editor of his new journal, *Engineering*. He took the job in January 1866 but with Colburn's suicide in April 1870, he and James Dredge were left as co-editors and, with Alexander Hollingsworth, as co-directors. Maw's capacity for work was enormous: he set up a practice as consulting engineer with his co-directors as partners; he often acted as an expert witness and as an arbitrator, thanks to his diverse knowledge and experience. *Engineering* owed its literary excellence and technical accuracy to Maw's untiring efforts as editor and author; its range and depth of coverage quickly cemented its reputation. He soon became one of the most significant figures in nineteenth-century technical journalism and maintained personal friendships with many engineering contemporaries.

Maw married Emily Chappell (*d.* 11 Sept 1924) in August 1867. Of eleven children, two died in infancy, and eight survived him. The family home from 1881 was at 18 Addison Road, Kensington, where he was a fine host, often indulging in dances, billiard parties, and lantern shows. Devoted to his gardens, he was especially keen on glasshouse cultivation. His country residence at Outwood in Surrey was bought in 1894 and he spent long weekends there. Maw designed observatories for his astronomical work at his houses in Kensington in 1887 and in Outwood in 1896. His lengthy study of double stars was important; his observations were published in five volumes of the Royal Astronomical Society's *Memoirs*. With astronomy, as with engineering, he built up a large, worldwide correspondence. He helped found the British Astronomical Association in 1890 and was president from 1899 to 1901 and treasurer for twenty-three years. He was elected a fellow of the Royal Astronomical Society in 1888 and was president from 1905 to 1907, serving on its council for thirty-one years.

Maw was president of the Institution of Mechanical Engineers from 1901 to 1902 and a council member for thirty-four years; he was president of the Institution of Civil Engineers from 1922–3 and a council member for thirteen years. The awards he received were numerous and he was connected with many other learned institutions and societies. During the First World War he served on many technical committees appointed by the government, particularly those connected with the Ministry of Munitions. He died at his home, 18 Addison Road, Kensington, on 19 March 1924, and was buried at Kensington Hanwell cemetery, Ealing, three days later.

ROBERT SHARP

Sources W. E. Simnett, 'William Henry Maw: a life', 1926, Sci. Mus., MS 521/1 · *Engineering* (21 March 1924), 371–4 · *The Engineer* (21 March 1924), 313 · *Institution of Mechanical Engineers: Proceedings* (1924), 533–5 · *PICE*, 218 (1923–4), 505–7 · A. S. D. M. and E. W. M., 'William Henry Maw: an appreciation', *Journal of the British Astronomical Association*, 34 (1923–4), 199–202 · E. B. K. [E. B. Knobel], *Monthly Notices of the Royal Astronomical Society*, 85 (1924–5), 311–14 · *The Times* (24 May 1924), 20

Likenesses G. H. Neale, portrait, *c*.1915, Institution of Mechanical Engineers, London · G. H. Neale, portrait, *c*.1922, Inst. CE

Wealth at death unsettled property of the gross value of £149,880, with net personalty £141,058: *The Times*

Mawbey, Sir Joseph (1730–1798), politician, was born at Ravenstone House, Leicestershire, on 2 December 1730, the fourth son and youngest child of John Mawbey (*d*. 1754) and his second wife, Martha (*d*. 1737), the daughter of Thomas Pratt. When he was about ten years old he was taken to Surrey by an uncle, Joseph Pratt, the chief owner of a vinegar distillery at Vauxhall, to be trained for the ministry of the English church. At the age of seventeen, however, he joined the family business on account of the serious illness of a cousin who was a partner in the distillery. Together with his brother John, Mawbey carried on the business, and became joint owner on his uncle's death in 1754. The firm made him a wealthy man, and it was estimated that its profits were 'sufficient to yield more than £600,000 per annum to government in subsidies' (Burke, 347). Mawbey also inherited considerable property in Surrey from his uncle and established himself as a landed proprietor; he served as sheriff of the county in 1757. On 21 August 1760 he married Elizabeth Pratt (*d*. 1790), the only surviving daughter of his cousin Richard Pratt of Vauxhall. He bought the estate of Botleys in Chertsey in 1763, and commissioned Kenton Couse to build a large Palladian house. He retired from business in 1775, having inherited another large estate upon the death of his brother-in-law Joseph Pratt in 1766. In 1770 he became chairman of the Surrey quarter sessions, a position he held for twenty-seven years. He acted in this role on the whole successfully, although he was unpopular with the gentry of the county, who considered him something of an upstart.

On 1 April 1761 Mawbey was elected MP for Southwark, a seat which he held until the general election of 1774,

when he contested the county of Surrey. Through the coalition of the interests of four other candidates he was defeated, even though 1390 votes were given for him, but he went on to win the seat at the by-election in June 1775. He topped the poll again in 1780, when he incurred the odium of some of his whig supporters through his refusal to coalesce with the opposition candidate, Admiral Keppel. In April 1784 he was returned without a contest.

Mawbey was associated with the Rockingham whigs in the early part of his political career, and he was rewarded by the Rockingham ministry with a baronetcy on 30 July 1765. But he increasingly gave his support to Wilkes and the radical cause. He presented Wilkes's petition on 14 November 1768, protesting about the treatment he had received in the *North Briton* no. 45 case. He was a founder member of the Society of Supporters of the Bill of Rights and a leading light in the petitioning movement of 1769–70, which sought to press the injustice with which Wilkes was treated in being expelled by the Commons as a member of parliament. He was an instigator of the petitions from his own county of Surrey and from his seat in Southwark, and was also heavily involved in organizing the petitions from Essex, Berwick, and York.

Mawbey played a role in the *Printers' case* which exercised parliament the following year. Wilkes, now an alderman of the City of London, wanted a confrontation with parliament, and Mawbey moved to have him summoned before the House of Commons to answer charges of falsely imprisoning a messenger of the house. The Commons wisely resisted this trap, despite Mawbey's later assertion that Wilkes had a right to attend the Commons 'in his place' (Almon, 9.251–6).

Later in his career Mawbey continued on the radical side of politics and was a leading figure in the Association movement, which sought to press major reform measures on the government. He did not follow the Foxite strand of whiggism after 1783, and instead became a supporter first of Shelburne's ministry and then of Pitt's. He left politics in 1790, feeling betrayed by Pitt's administration, which had failed to support his unsuccessful election campaign of that year.

Mawbey was a frequent speaker in the Commons, and so attracted the attention of the wits. Because he professed to be above party, he was ridiculed by speakers and writers on both sides. Walpole called him 'vain, noisy, and foolish'. Among the best-known lines in the 'Rolliad', a popular prose piece of the time, are those referring to Speaker Cornwall's 'unhappy fate' who hears Fox, North, and Burke, but hears Sir Joseph too. Wraxall was more charitable in his assessment, remarking that Mawbey 'could never obtain a patient … hearing in Parliament', yet 'spoke, nevertheless with great good sense though not with brilliancy'.

For many years Mawbey was a contributor in verse and prose to the *Gentleman's Magazine*. He wrote on both political and personal subjects; he published a poem mourning the death of his wife, who died after a long illness on 19 August 1790. Mawbey died at Botleys on 16 June 1798 and was buried beside his wife and several of his children in the family vault in the chancel of Chertsey church, Surrey.　　　W. P. COURTNEY, rev. IAN K. R. ARCHER

Sources J. Brooke, 'Mawbey, Joseph', HoP, Commons · N&Q, 4th ser., 1 (1868), 581 · P. D. G. Thomas, *John Wilkes: a friend to liberty* (1996) · G. Rudé, *Wilkes and liberty: a social study of 1763 to 1774* (1962) · J. Burke and J. B. Burke, *A genealogical and heraldic history of the extinct and dormant baronetcies of England, Ireland, and Scotland*, 2nd edn (1841) · GEC, *Baronetage* · J. Almon, ed., *The debates and proceedings of the British House of Commons*, 11 vols. (1766–75) · N. W. Wraxall, *Historical memoirs of his own time*, new edn, 4 vols. (1836) · N. W. Wraxall, *Posthumous memoirs of his own time*, 2nd edn, 3 vols. (1836) · H. Walpole, *Memoirs of the reign of King George the Third*, ed. G. F. R. Barker, 4 vols. (1894) · T. R. Keppel, *The life of Augustus, Viscount Keppel*, 2 (1842), 286–8 · Colvin, *Archs.* · GM, 1st ser., 60 (1790), 748–9 · GM, 1st ser., 68 (1798), 543
Archives BL, Lansdowne MSS
Likenesses J. Gillray, caricature, etching, pubd 1787, BM · J. Dixon, line engraving (after R. E. Pine), BM, NPG · T. Holloway, line engraving (after R. E. Pine), BM, NPG; repro. in *European Magazine* (1787) · J. Newton, line engraving (after J. de Fleury), NPG

Mawby, Raymond Llewellyn (1922–1990), trade unionist and politician, was born at 74 South Street, Rugby, Warwickshire, on 6 February 1922, the son of John Henry Mawby, armature winder, and a fervent trade unionist and Liberal supporter of David Lloyd George, and his wife, Lily, *née* Griffiths. He was educated at Long Lawford council school and then trained in Rugby as an electrician. He joined the local branch of the Electrical Trades Union and, having evinced a talent for organization, rose to be president of its Rugby branch. He also, however, had a serious interest in politics outside the trade union movement and, being a man with a very persistent nature, sought election to Rugby county council five times. He failed on four occasions, but succeeded on the fifth, when he stood as an independent. Meanwhile, he had married, on 7 October 1944, Carrie Selina Aldwinckle (*b.* 1920/21), daughter of Ernest Aldwinckle, of Leicester, herself a trade union employee. They had two children, a son who died at an early age, and a daughter. He now faced a major difficulty in his life. He was ambitious to become an MP, an ambition common to many of his coevals. However, while his trade union contemporaries sought political advancement in the Labour Party, Mawby never sought to conceal his Conservative sympathies, which puzzled his wife and, as she grew up, increasingly alienated his daughter.

The interests of two powerful men came to Mawby's rescue. In 1946, after the momentous Conservative defeat in the 1945 general election, Lord Woolton, a prominent industrialist who was appalled by the deteriorating state of the party organization, offered his services as its chairman. Winston Churchill immediately accepted the offer, and gave Woolton a free hand. One of the objectives shared by both men was the emancipation of the Conservative Party from its middle- and upper-class bias and thus the extension of its electoral appeal. Obviously, the quickest way to achieving this end was through the trade union movement—if such a way could be found. The notion was romantic, but not impossible, although the Conservatives had to wait until 1979, and the advent of Margaret Thatcher, until it was realized in any substantial way. In any event it was made known to Woolton that there was, in Rugby, a trade unionist with serious working-class credentials who was desirous of becoming a member of parliament. Woolton set about finding Mawby a seat. There was, in 1955, one available: that of Totnes, in the west country. However, though Woolton's authority within the party machine was considerable, it was not sufficient to procure the assent of a squirearchical rural party association to the nomination of a horny-handed northern electrician with few social graces as Conservative candidate for such a seat. Woolton invoked Churchill, who readily, and decisively, intervened with the Totnes association on Mawby's behalf. Mawby was duly chosen, and in May 1955 was elected as MP for Totnes. He was, none the less, never to enjoy a happy relationship with the local tory hierarchs during nearly thirty years of service.

If Mawby entertained hopes of high office—and most of those who knew him well were convinced that he did—then his hopes were dashed. He held only one minor ministerial post, that of assistant postmaster-general from March 1963 to October 1964, when the Conservatives were defeated in a general election. However, he was an assiduous party and parliamentary worker. He was, at various times, a member of the executive of the 1922 committee, of the party's west country group of MPs, of his party's backbench labour committee, and of the (somewhat moribund) National Conservative trades unions advisory committee. However, he was always a somewhat totemic figure, there to symbolize the Woolton commitment to reaching out to the working classes, rather than to enjoy real power. Yet although he never really fitted in to Conservative circles, he had his friends and admirers among them. In 1979 the fourth Baron O'Hagan was chosen as Conservative member of the European parliament for Devon. A political neophyte then, O'Hagan later testified to the warmth of Mawby's character, and to the unremitting advice and support he gave to a newcomer. If Mawby gave someone his support, he gave it without stint.

Even if he failed in whatever ministerial ambitions he harboured, Mawby made one important contribution to British legislation. Until 1957 children born to British servicemen overseas were not automatically registered as British citizens. In that year the Conservative MP for Exeter, Dudley Smith, tabled a private member's bill to correct this anomaly. Mawby gave Smith's bill powerful, unequivocal, and even eloquent support. Thus, the Registration of Births, Deaths and Marriages (Special Provisions) Bill became law in the same year. Mawby found allies for his espousal of Dudley Smith's cause even from the Labour benches, from which he was normally derided.

This episode illustrated the essence of Mawby's character as a Conservative politician. He was, above all, a fierce patriot, and, rightly or wrongly, found in the tory party the only outlet for his views. His regard was not requited, once Woolton and Churchill had departed. In 1983 the boundary commissioners decreed a redrawing of west country constituencies. Mawby, socially unpopular as he was, failed to secure another Conservative nomination.

He withdrew from political life, invested his small savings in various unsuccessful business enterprises, and was then required to seek the dole until, by virtue of an act of retrospective legislation, he became the recipient of a parliamentary pension. He died on 22 July 1990 at his home, 29 Applegarth Avenue, Newton Abbot, Devon, following a heart attack. He was survived by his wife and daughter. His life stands as a monument to the failure of grand and generous aspirations to change the social and electoral nature of the party to which he gave his unswerving allegiance. PATRICK COSGRAVE

Sources *The Times* (24 July 1990) · *Daily Telegraph* (24 July 1990) · *The Independent* (25 July 1990) · *WWW*, 1991–5 · private information (2004) [Baron O'Hagan] · *Dod's Peerage* (1981) · b. cert. · m. cert. · d. cert.
Likenesses photograph, repro. in *Daily Telegraph*
Wealth at death under £115,000: administration, 19 Oct 1990, *CGPLA Eng. & Wales*

Mawdsley, James (1848–1902), trade unionist, was born at Preston, Lancashire, on 9 January 1848, the son of Thomas Mawdsley, an operative cotton spinner, and his wife, Jane (*née* Fawcett). He entered the factory as a half-timer at the age of nine, and at sixteen began to work full-time alongside his father. He involved himself in the affairs of his local spinners' association, and became its assistant secretary in 1875. Three years later, after a rigorous competitive examination, he was appointed full-time general secretary of the Manchester-based Amalgamated Association of Operative Cotton Spinners, a post which he held until his death.

Cotton spinners, an élite group of male factory workers who enjoyed considerable independence and responsibility in the workplace and who effectively controlled recruitment to their own ranks, had a long history of militancy and organization in Lancashire. Mawdsley quickly deployed his remarkable talents as a shrewd negotiator, an efficient administrator, and a resourceful propagandist to rebuild the union after the damaging lock-out of 1878. Under his leadership, the union achieved a virtual closed shop and amassed a reserve fund sufficient to sustain its members during protracted strikes provoked by proposed wage reductions at Oldham in 1885, and more generally in the south Lancashire spinning districts in 1892–3. Alerted to the union's strength by these serious but orderly disputes, the employers' organizations in 1893 accepted the famous 'Brooklands agreement', which established a mechanism for settling future wages questions. It was hailed as a model of good industrial relations practice, and helped to secure harmony in cotton spinning for the rest of Mawdsley's life.

As leader of one of Britain's most successful and wealthy craft unions, Mawdsley dominated the Trades Union Congress in the 1880s and 1890s in a manner wholly disproportionate to the spinners' small numbers and narrow regional base. He sat on the parliamentary committee from 1882 to 1897, and served as its chairman in 1885. A forceful public speaker as well as a ruthless backstage fixer, he was a leading architect of the alliance between coal and cotton, which confined the TUC to a limited and non-partisan programme until the end of the 1890s. In particular, he masterminded the procedural coup at the 1895 congress which introduced the block vote and undermined the credibility and influence of the so-called 'new' unions and their socialist leaders.

But if Mawdsley had no time for woolly-minded socialists, he was a firm advocate of *ad hoc* state intervention in economic affairs, and signed the collectivist-inspired minority report of the royal commission on labour in 1894. In public speeches and in the pages of the *Cotton Factory Times*, as well as through the lobbying of the United Textile Factory Workers' Association, he pressed vigorously for piecemeal improvements to the Factory Acts, although he opposed a statutory eight-hour working day as liable to damage cotton's international competitiveness. Taking a broad view of the industry's problems in the 1890s, he supported bimetallism as strongly as he opposed the Liberal government's introduction of import duties in India. An unashamed pragmatist, Mawdsley saw 'labour' questions as lying outside the scope of conventional party politics, and believed that the Conservatives were at least as likely as the Liberals to help the working man. Since the 1870s a handful of trade union leaders had sat in the Commons as Liberal MPs, and he saw no reason why some should not sit as Conservatives. It was not therefore surprising that in 1899 he accepted a last-minute plea from the local Conservative leadership to fight a double by-election at Oldham as running mate of the young Winston Churchill. Despite this imaginative demonstration of tory democracy in action, Mawdsley came last in a close poll, and later regarded his decision to stand as an error of judgement: but the incident served to establish his posthumous reputation as the prototype of the rational, articulate, Conservative working man, who first flourished in Lancashire in the aftermath of the second and third Reform Acts.

Although parliamentary honours eluded him, Mawdsley was prominent in the public life of the Manchester area. He was appointed a JP in 1888, and also served on his local board of poor law guardians and district council. Brought up as a Primitive Methodist, in later years he adopted an easy-going Anglicanism, became a freemason, and was proud to be a member of the Manchester chamber of commerce. How he might have reacted to the development of the Labour Party in the aftermath of the Taff Vale judgment is a matter for speculation; for Mawdsley died at his home, Taunton Bank, Taunton, Ashton under Lyne, on 4 February 1902 as a result of complications following an accident. He left a widow, Ann (*née* Wright), whom he had married in 1871, and seven children; he was buried at Christ Church, Ashton, on 7 February. His impressive public funeral, attended by numerous representatives of employers' organizations and other political bodies, as well as by trade unionists, was a tribute to the unique position which Mawdsley had built for himself in Lancashire, while an obituary in *The Times* and an entry in the *Dictionary of National Biography*—both of which were unusual for a trade unionist at the time—were convincing evidence of his national reputation as perhaps the ablest, and certainly the most independent-minded, labour leader of his generation.   DUNCAN BYTHELL

Sources The Times (5 Feb 1902) • Manchester Guardian (5 Feb 1902) • Cotton Factory Times (7 Feb 1902) • Oldham Standard (8 Feb 1902) • Cotton Factory Times (1885) • Cotton Factory Times (1892) • Cotton Factory Times (1895) • Annual Report [Trades Union Congress] (1881–97) • A. Fowler and T. Wyke, eds., The barefoot aristocrats: a history of the Amalgamated Association of Operative Cotton Spinners (1987) • H. A. Clegg, A. Fox, and A. F. Thompson, A history of British trade unions since 1889, 1 (1964) • 'Royal commission on labour', Parl. papers (1892), vol. 34, C. 6708 [first report]; (1894), 35.9, C. 7421 [final report] • Oldham Standard (June–July 1899) • B. C. Roberts, The TUC, 1868–1921 (1958) • H. A. Turner, Trade union growth, structure, and policy: a comparative study of the cotton unions (1962) • S. Webb and B. Webb, Industrial democracy (1897)

Likenesses line drawing (after block, in possession of Oldham Standard), repro. in Cotton Factory Times, 5

Wealth at death £4189 15s. 3d.: probate, 12 April 1902, CGPLA Eng. & Wales

Mawe, John (1766–1829), mineralogist and dealer in minerals, was born in Queen Street, Derby, the younger surviving son of Samuel Maw (1735–1783), baker, and his first wife, Elisabeth Massey (d. 1777), originally from Leeds. He became a mariner in the late 1770s, and in 1790 he was appointed commander of the merchant vessel Trent, trading to St Petersburg. By 1821 he had visited Morocco, Jamaica, Bombay, and Tellicherry and once 'sounded on a coral reef in … Mozambique' (Mawe, Companion, 23). However, with the coming of the Napoleonic wars, he began 'finding a sea-faring life hazardous' and 'after a favourable voyage … left off going to sea, and with other business, commenced collecting minerals and shells' (ibid., v).

In 1793 Mawe was briefly apprenticed to the Derby marble mason Richard Brown (1736–1816), whose daughter, Sarah, he married in London on 1 November 1794. They settled at 5 Tavistock Street, Covent Garden, trading as Brown, Son, and Mawe, mineral dealers, in a new 'petrifaction warehouse' partnership.

The business's first surviving catalogue was issued about 1798. By 1799 Mawe was reported by a rival dealer as having 'been very successful … [and] a very busy man' (Elizabeth Forster to Philip Rashleigh, 9 Aug 1799, Rashleigh MSS). Certainly his activity in this period appears to have been frenetic. In 1800 he collected stratigraphically arranged specimens from Derbyshire for the cabinet of Charles IV (1748–1819) of Spain, advised on the mineral exploration of New South Wales, and undertook a long mineral-hunting tour of the Scottish highlands. In 1802 the business moved to St Helens, Derby, where technologically advanced machinery for grinding and polishing stone and marble was installed. In the same year Mawe published his Mineralogy of Derbyshire, and visited Paris during the brief peace of Amiens. There he attended lectures at the École des Mines and visited many of the leading French mineralogists, but struggled with the language, recording that he 'would rather go an East India voyage as a sailor … than … learn French' (Turner, 2.209). By 1804 Mawe claimed that collectors would 'find the largest Variety of Minerals and Shells in Europe' (Mawe, Catalogue, 1804) at his Covent Garden shop. In that year he also issued A short treatise addressed to gentlemen visiting the south seas … with a view to encouraging the collecting of natural history, which in later editions appeared as the entertaining Voyager's Companion (1821).

On 1 August 1804 Mawe set off on an ambitious voyage of commercial experiment to South America. In 1809 he was allowed by the prince regent of Portugal, later John VI (1769–1826), to travel inland to the gold and diamond mining districts of Brazil, which were at the time closed to other Europeans by the Portuguese government. Mawe's many crises and adventures there were recorded in his best-selling Travels in the Interior of Brazil (1812), which went through several English editions, was translated into eight other European languages, and was on board the Beagle with Charles Darwin. However, the book caused later problems for other European visitors: members of the Portuguese government thought that many of the facts revealed should have remained unrecorded and so once again restricted access to the mining districts.

Mawe returned to London in 1810. In 1812 he opened a new shop at 149 Strand, close to Leigh and Sothebys auction rooms—an important source of specimens. From this shop Mawe issued a series of publications, some in many editions, including A Treatise on Diamonds (1813), Descriptive Catalogues of Minerals (1815), Familiar Lessons on Mineralogy and Geology (1819), and An Introduction to the Study of Conchology (1822). He also opened a 'museum' as a retail outlet in Matlock in 1815 and, following the death of his partner, another at Cheltenham in 1816, this time in partnership with his new son-in-law, Anthony Tissington Tatlow (1789–1828). Nevertheless, Mawe still found time to travel in search of new specimens, as to Devon and Cornwall in 1817, and exchanged mineral specimens with Goethe in 1817–18. He was elected a member of the Royal Geological Society of Cornwall in 1814 and was awarded the diploma of the Jena Mineralogischen Gesellschaft in 1817. He was involved both in mining lead and in abortive attempts to set up the Derbyshire Mining and Peak Mining associations in 1825. Mawe died on 26 October 1829 at his shop in London, having helped establish commercial mineralogy in Britain. The identity of the executor of his will, Walter MacDowall (1796–1865), London printer of his books, suggests that Mawe's publications were as important to him as his commercial success. Mawe was buried at St Mary-le-Strand on 2 November 1829.

Sarah Mawe [née Brown] (bap. 1767, d. 1846), mineralogist and dealer in minerals, was baptized at All Saints, Derby, on 9 June 1767, the daughter of Richard Brown and his wife, Ann Hind. Sarah Mawe often took charge of the London shop while her husband was away for long intervals. She became a highly competent mineral appraiser, purchaser, and identifier in her own right, and supplier of shells and fossils to naturalists in Europe and North America. While John Mawe was in South America, Henry Heuland, a rival dealer in London, wrote to the mineral collector Philip Rashleigh, 'dealers of Mineralogy in a few years will be very thin in this capital, and Mrs and Mr Maw will be the moon that shines on the Collectors. Indeed that

Lady is quite grand now' (letter, 20 Dec 1808, Rashleigh MSS).

Sarah Mawe continued the business long after her husband's death. She was appointed mineralogist to Queen Victoria on the queen's accession in 1837 and continued to run the shop until 1840, when her old assistant James Tennant became sole proprietor. She died on 10 September 1846 in her Strand house, leaving a considerable estate, and was buried at St Giles's Church, Northampton. The Mawes had two children but their only son, John Saint Mawe (1797–1820), died aged only twenty-two; Sarah requested in her will that she should be buried alongside him.   H. S. TORRENS

Sources H. S. Torrens, 'Under royal patronage, the early work of John Mawe, 1766–1829, in geology and the background of his travel in Brazil, 1807–1810', *O conhecimento geologico na America Latina: trabalhos do I coloquio Brasileiro de histoira e teoria do conhecimento geologico* [Campinas 1988], ed. M. M. Lopes and S. F. de M. Figueira (1990), 103–13 • *GM*, 1st ser., 99/2 (1829), 641–2 • H. S. Torrens and M. A. Taylor, 'Geological collectors and museums in Cheltenham', *Geological Curator*, 5/5 (1990), 176 • J. Hennig, 'Goethe's interest in British mineralogy', *Mineralogical Magazine*, 28 (1949), 534–46 • *The literary correspondence of John Pinkerton*, ed. D. Turner, 2 (1830) • N. Kirkham, 'A Derbyshire umbrella in Brazil', *Notes and Queries, Derbyshire Advertiser*, 1422–4 (23 Aug–6 Sept 1946) • G. Schmid, ed., *Goethe, die Schriften zur Naturwissenschaft, zweiter Band, Schriften zur Geologie und Mineralogie, 1812–1832* (1949) • J. Mawe, *Viagens ao interior do Brasil* (1978) • *Derby Mercury* (15 April 1790), 4, col. 3 • J. Mawe, *Voyager's Companion* (1821) • parish register, St Mary-le-Strand, London, 2 Nov 1829 [burial] • M. Craven, *John Whitehurst of Derby: clockmaker and scientist, 1713–88* (1996) [Sarah Mawe] • S. P. Dance, *Shell collecting: an illustrated history* (1966) [Sarah Mawe] • Cornwall RO, Rashleigh papers • I. Lea, 'Observations on the Naiades', *Transactions of the American Philosophical Society*, new ser., 4 (1830), 63–121 [Sarah Mawe] • will, PRO, PROB 10/6413 [Sarah Mawe] • *Derby Mercury* (16 Sept 1846), 3 [Sarah Mawe] • *ILN* (19 Sept 1846), 179 [Sarah Mawe]
Archives BL • GS Lond. | NHM, letters, corresp. with members of the Sowerby family • Sutro Library, San Francisco, Banks MSS • UCL, Greenough MSS
Wealth at death PRO, PROB 11/1763 • Sarah Mawe: PRO, PROB 10/6413

Mawe, Leonard (*d.* 1629), bishop of Bath and Wells, was born in Rendlesham, Suffolk, the fourth son of Simon Mawe, gentleman, and his wife, Margery, daughter of Thomas and Alice Wyld. He went up to Cambridge at Easter 1588, a pensioner at Peterhouse. He quickly attracted attention from influential friends and, in May 1594, secured a royal mandate for election to the next vacant fellowship. He was admitted a fellow of Peterhouse in 1595 and proceeded MA the following year. He was bursar for a year in 1599 and incorporated at Oxford in the same year. Further privilege followed. In 1604 he was granted royal dispensation to hold his fellowship in plurality with the benefice of Mildenhall, Suffolk, and in 1611 the king instructed the vice-chancellor and heads of house at Cambridge to admit Mawe as DD, dispensing with the statutes for the degree and the requirement that he should first have proceeded BD. Not all the attention he received was, however, welcome. Proctor from 1609, his speech at the commencement in 1610 was an attack on the further reformation of the church which enraged the House of Commons. None the less, he became master of Peterhouse in November 1617. In 1621 he served as vice-chancellor and added the rectory of Cottenham, Cambridgeshire, to his preferments.

Mawe also held a prebend at Wells, and was chaplain to Charles, prince of Wales. When Charles was in Spain in 1623 King James sent Mawe and Matthew Wren, afterwards bishop of Ely, along with other officers and attendants, to join him, charging the chaplains to set up a chapel and to hold prayers twice a day, in an attempt to commend the Anglican faith to the Spanish. Mawe and his companions set sail on 3 April. During his journey through Spain he had a fall from his mule, 'lighting on his head and shoulders' (Wynn). The prince was obliged to send orders that the greater part of the company was to return to England without going on to Madrid, and Mawe returned through France.

As a reward for his services Mawe was appointed master of Trinity College, Cambridge, by patent in 1625. Although as master he did much towards freeing that foundation from a heavy debt, his primary loyalty remained with Peterhouse, 'my ancient nurse from which I received so many blessings and favours', to which he left in his will £300 towards the leading of the chapel roof (PRO, PROB 11/156, fol. 152). He used all his influence to secure the election of the duke of Buckingham as chancellor of Cambridge in 1626, summoning the fellows of Trinity one by one to browbeat them into voting for the duke.

In 1628 Mawe received the see of Bath and Wells in succession to William Laud, being elected on 24 June and consecrated at Croydon on 7 September. 'A good scholar, a grave preacher, a mild man, and one of gentle deportment' (Fuller, 2.333), with an extensive library (he left 'books of all sorts', including Spanish works and history), he seems to have been reluctant to leave Cambridge for Wells, 'unworthy of that high honor and calling' (PRO, PROB 11/156, fol. 152). Although in 1629 he issued a conventional set of episcopal visitation articles, he was absent from the visitation itself in July and August. By 11 August he had received letters from the king desiring him to quit Cambridge, but dispensing him from residence in episcopal houses owing to ill health. Mawe may never have reached Wells for he died in Chiswick, home of his sister's family, on 2 September 1629. Apparently unmarried, he bequeathed to his cousin, nephews, and nieces his 'worldly goods which are not many (for I never hadd, nor cared to have much)' (ibid.), but amounting none the less to over £1400 and including property in Lincolnshire and Suffolk, inherited from his father and his brother Charles. He was buried in Chiswick parish church.

WILLIAM HUNT, rev. DAVID HOYLE

Sources T. A. Walker, *A biographical register of Peterhouse men*, 2 (1930) • T. A. Walker, ed., *Admissions to Peterhouse or St Peter's College in the University of Cambridge* (1912) • Wood, *Ath. Oxon.: Fasti* (1815) • Fuller, *Worthies* (1840) • R. Wynn, 'A history of Prince Charles journey into Spain', *Historia vitae et regna Ricardi II Angliae regis*, ed. T. Hearne (1729), 297–341 • R. Willis, *The architectural history of the University of Cambridge, and of the colleges of Cambridge and Eton*, ed. J. W. Clark, 1 (1886) • C. H. Cooper, *Annals of Cambridge*, 3 (1845) • *CSP dom.* • PRO, PROB 11/156, fol. 152 • P. M. Hembry, *The bishops of Bath and Wells, 1540–1640: social and economic problems* (1967), 212, 221–2 · K. Fincham, ed., *Visitation articles and injunctions of the early Stuart church*, 1 (1994), 26, 186 · Som. ARS, D/D/Ca 277A

Likenesses oils (of Mawe?), bishop's palace, Wells · watercolour drawing, NPG

Wealth at death over £1400 in legacies and property: PRO, PROB 11/156, fol. 152

Mawe, Sarah (*bap.* 1767, *d.* 1846). *See under* Mawe, John (1766–1829).

Mawer, Sir Allen (1879–1942), scholar of place names and university administrator, was born at Bow, London, on 8 May 1879, the second child and elder son of George Henry Mawer (*b.* 1851/2), commercial traveller in fancy trimmings and secretary of the Country Towns' Mission, and his wife, Clara Isabella Allen (*b.* 1850). He was educated by his parents and at the Coopers' Company Grammar School, Bow. In 1897 he obtained first-class honours as an external candidate for the London University degree in English. He entered University College, London, as a graduate, in 1898, and was a Morley medallist there. In 1901 he went to Cambridge, as a foundation scholar of Gonville and Caius College, and in 1904 took a first-class, with double distinction, in the English sections of the medieval and modern languages tripos. After a year as a research student he was elected in 1905 to a fellowship of Gonville and Caius, which he held until 1911. On 8 July 1909 he married Lettice Mona Kathleen, daughter of the Revd Christopher Heath, vicar of Hucclecote, Gloucestershire. They had four daughters, and a son who died in infancy.

Mawer was lecturer in English at Sheffield University (1905–8), Joseph Cowen professor of English language and literature at Armstrong College, Newcastle upon Tyne (1908–21), and Baines professor of English language at Liverpool University (1921–9). In 1930 he returned to University College, London, as its provost, thus devoting his remaining years to the university where he had begun his brilliant academic career.

Mawer's scholarly interests at first centred on the Scandinavian settlements in England, and were historical rather than philological, as seen especially in *The Vikings* (1913). They were soon transferred to place names, a field in which he thereafter specialized; *The Place-Names of Northumberland and Durham* (1920) established him as one of the leading scholars in the field of name study. He took the initiative of beginning a systematic survey of English place names, and it was largely thanks to his efforts that the English Place-Name Society was founded in 1923 to finance the survey. He became its honorary director, drew up the plan of the work, and had chief responsibility for its publications. The first two volumes appeared in 1924: *Introduction to the Survey of English Place-Names*, which Mawer wrote with his long-term collaborator, F. M. Stenton, and *Chief Elements used in English Place-Names*, which was his own work. From 1925 to 1943 one volume came out regularly each year (with the exception of 1941). The series deals with sixteen counties, and testifies to Mawer's scholarship and method, his skill as an organizer, and his co-operation with fellow workers. The project, begun

with such gusto, continued and expanded throughout the twentieth century.

Mawer regarded place-name study as 'a handmaiden of historical study, and specifically English historical study' (Coates), designed to illuminate the gaps in the written historical record, especially of the pre-literate Anglo-Saxon period. As scholarship moved on and developed, the scale of Mawer's original survey expanded, to the extent that the survey of Lincolnshire was projected to take twenty-nine volumes, compared to the one-volume-per-county of Mawer's time. Mawer published widely outside the survey, his *Problems of Place-Name Study* (1929) deserving special mention. In 1929 he was awarded the British Academy's biennial prize for English studies, and he was elected FBA in the following year. He was elected an honorary fellow of Gonville and Caius College in 1935, and held the honorary degrees of LittD, Cambridge (1930), and DCL, Durham (1937). He was knighted in 1937.

Mawer's provostship fell in a critical period in the history of University College. His responsibilities and duties were especially heavy after the outbreak of war in 1939: the buildings were extensively damaged by bombing and the college was evacuated. The strain was probably a contributory cause of his premature death; he died suddenly, on a train at Broxbourne Station, Hertfordshire, on 22 July 1942, on his way to London for a university meeting. His colleagues bore witness to his professional and personal qualities, one saying

> He was one of the best and most lovable of men, gifted with a wide humanity, a sympathy as ready as it was understanding, a constant cheerfulness, and a delight in the company of his fellow-men, which made the College a better and a happier place. (*DNB*)

His wife survived him.

E. EKWALL, *rev.* K. D. REYNOLDS

Sources *The Times* (23 July 1942) · F. M. Stenton, 'Sir Allen Mawer, 1879–1942', *PBA*, 29 (1943), 433–9 · E. Ekwall, 'Sir Allen Mawer: in memoriam', *English Studies*, 24 (1942), 169–71 · *Annual report*, University College, London (1943) · private information (1959, 2004) · personal knowledge (1959, 2004) · Burke, *Peerage* (1939), (1959) · *WWW* · R. Coates, 'The survey of English place-names', *British Academy Review* (July–Dec 1999) · census returns, 1881

Likenesses P. A. de Laszlo, crayon drawing, 1935, UCL · W. Stoneman, photograph, 1938, NPG

Wealth at death £1960 2s. 7d.: probate, 20 Oct 1942, CGPLA Eng. & Wales

Mawer, John (1702/3–1763), poet and biblical translator, was the younger son of John Mawer (*b.* 1668, *d.* in or after 1729) of Upleatham, Cleveland, and his wife, Elizabeth Hart (*d.* in or after 1729). After schooling nearby at Kirkleatham he proceeded in 1721 to Trinity College, Cambridge, being elected a scholar in the following year. In 1725 he was placed eleventh in the tripos, but did not take a fellowship. Later he wrote that this was because a change in Trinity's system of choosing fellows had left him and his contemporaries stranded; others of his year, however, did obtain fellowships. He was ordained priest in 1727 and from 1731 until his death was vicar of Middleton Tyas in Richmondshire; he also held the perpetual curacy of Crathorne in Cleveland from 1732.

On 7 August 1729 Mawer married Hannah Cotesworth, *née* Watson (1693/4–1766), niece of Thomas Ryles, a prominent Hull stationer, and formerly the housekeeper and then wife of the powerful Gateshead businessman and coal owner William *Cotesworth (*c.*1668–1726). Cotesworth died leaving her an infant daughter, Henrietta (*c.*1723–1781), who later became a governess in the royal household, £100 per annum, and a bequest of £1500. Mawer and his wife had two sons, who both became clergymen and army chaplains, and a daughter.

Mawer's earliest literary efforts were in verse. Of some originality was a composition entitled *The Progress of Language* (1726), celebrating the foundation of the regius chairs of modern history and languages at Oxford and Cambridge; this was reprinted in 1743 with an introductory dissertation on philological and grammatological questions reflecting an interest and ability in oriental languages which he had cultivated from youth. Less novel were three other poems in 1727, trumpeting the capture of Gibraltar (*Liberty Asserted*) and the accession of the new king and queen—all displaying the strong whig and anti-Catholic sentiments that were a feature of Mawer's writings. In 1731, however, in the preface to a verse address to Edward Chandler, bishop of Durham, he announced what was to be his life's project: a supplement to Bishop Brian Walton's polyglot Bible of 1657, based on the Ethiopic text, with the aim of reconciling the Hebrew and Septuagint. A fuller account of the project emerges from his *Epistle to the Earl of Oxford*, published by Thomas Gent in York the following year, while another, naming the work of the German scholar Job Ludolf as a model, appeared in 1736 together with Mawer's translation of the first book of Oppian's *Cynegetics* (itself not without merit), also printed by Gent.

By 1736 Mawer, who graduated DD at Edinburgh in January that year, had prepared the section dealing with the Song of Songs; a manuscript sample of his editorial notes survives in the British Library (Add. MS 6489, fols. 139–145). He also proposed an interim edition of the Psalms for use in the East, hoping for support from the Levant Company (which he canvassed in 1738) and the Society for Promoting Christian Knowledge. But despite claiming to have won the interest of Robert Walpole and John Potter, archbishop of Canterbury, and an offer of the use of Oxford University Press's oriental types, Mawer failed to find a sponsor for either scheme. Gent states in his memoirs that he actually printed the supplement in the same year as the Oppian, but this most probably refers to a specimen sheet.

Gent was one of several publishers to print individual sermons by Mawer, and he also included some more or less irrelevant verse contributions by him in his history of Ripon (1733) and his *Compendiosa historia* (1741). Mawer's prose writings, apart from standard anti-Catholic pieces, discussions of the eucharist, and attempted reconciliations of Christian revelation with Jewish and classical thought, include an interesting dissertation on the Hebrew priest of war, with topical comments on military affairs (1740). In 1745 almost all his separately published writings reappeared as *Miscellaneous Essays in Verse and Prose*, with the addition of many short, previously unpublished translations from ancient and modern languages.

In 1736 Mawer petitioned the duke of Newcastle for relief against a troublesome Catholic lawyer, John Mayer of Yarm, and his prefaces complain about the time-consuming nature of parochial duties in an area where popery was strong. He also suffered illness in the later 1740s and the 1750s. His living did bring considerable financial benefit, however; not long after his arrival copper was found in the parish, and by leasing mining rights in the glebe Mawer raised £4000. He spent much of this on restoring the vicarage.

Mawer's last publication was a contribution to a debate on the Greek text of 1 Timothy, brought out in 1758 (though the main contents dated from the 1730s). It contains a weary account of the failure of his polyglot project, and a revised conspectus for an edition of the Ethiopic text. Mawer died on 18 November 1763 and was buried at Middleton Tyas. A verbose and gushing memorial tablet was set up in the chancel ascribing to Mawer, quite wrongly, a royal Welsh lineage and, somewhat dubiously, the mastery of twenty-two languages. This hyperbole, and the reduction of his life plan to the aim of Christianizing the already Christian kingdom of Abyssinia, attracted a fair degree of adverse comment, notably from T. D. Whitaker in his *History of Richmondshire* (1823, 1.234), who unfairly directs his remarks at the deceased rather than at the next of kin. Mawer's widow died on 22 December 1766 and was buried with him.

C. E. A. Cheesman

Sources J. Mawer, letter to the duke of Newcastle, 1736, PRO, SP 36/39, item 135 · J. Mawer, letter to the Levant Company, 1738, PRO, SP 105/109 · *The life of Mr Thomas Gent … written by himself*, ed. J. Hunter (1832), 182, 191 · papers relating to Hannah Cotesworth and John Mawer, 1726–33, Gateshead central library, Cotesworth MSS CO/1/8, CO/1/18, CO/1/29, CO/1/30, CO/1/33, CP/5/30 · chancery bill and replication in the case of *Mawer and others v. Hart*, 1729, PRO, C 11/1832/15 · T. R. Hornshaw, *Copper mining in Middleton Tyas* (1975) · T. J. Pettigrew, *Chronicles of the tombs* (1878), 398 · York Minster marriage register, 7 Aug 1729, *Yorkshire Archaeological and Topographical Journal*, 2 (1871–2), 358 · J. L. Saywell, 'Middleton Tyas vicars', *Yorkshire County Magazine*, 3 (1893), 88–91 · *Trinity College admissions book*, 71 · Venn, *Alum. Cant.*, 165 · D. Laing, ed., *A catalogue of the graduates … of the University of Edinburgh*, Bannatyne Club, 106 (1858), 240–41 · R. Davies, *A memoir of the York press: with notices of authors, printers, and stationers, in the sixteenth, seventeenth, and eighteenth centuries* (1868), 172–89, 238–9 · D. F. Foxon, ed., *English verse, 1701–1750: a catalogue of separately printed poems with notes on contemporary collected editions*, 2 vols. (1975), 1.452–3 · J. C. Hodgson, *A history of Northumberland*, 4 (1897), 145–6 · J. H., 'Enigmatical epitaph', *N&Q*, 3 (1851), 184–5

Archives BL, Add. MS 6489 · PRO, state papers, SP 36/39, 105/109

Likenesses oils, priv. coll.

Mawgan [St Mawgan, Meugan, Meigant] (*fl.* **5th–6th cent.**), holy man, belongs to the large group of saints who have been described as 'the relatively insignificant and humbler men whose fame during their lifetime was local' (Bowen, 69). Although their identities are interwoven, it is possible that Mawgan and Meugan were two different saints, the former predominantly represented in church dedications and place names in Cornwall and Brittany, the latter in Wales. But if St Mawgan and St Meugan are one and the same saint, he would belong to a group witnessed in dedications and place names across Wales, Cornwall, and Brittany which includes St Cadog, St Petroc, and St Brioc. It has been suggested that the St Machan witnessed in the early place name Ecclesmachan (in Lothian) may be the same person as St Mawgan, though this must remain uncertain. There is no biography of Mawgan or Meugan. A holy man, either Mawgan ('Maucan') or Meugan ('Moucan'), is mentioned incidentally in the life of St Cadog (late eleventh century) as intervening in a dispute between Cadog and King Maelgwn of Gwynedd; and a 'monastery of Mawgan' is mentioned in the late eleventh-century life of St David. Meugan appears in *Bonedd y Saint*, the collection concerned with graves of the saints, in a section dated to *c*.1510. It has also been stated that he was president of the 'college' at Llanilltud Fawr (Llantwit Major). None of these references can be said to add to the sum of genuine information on Mawgan or Meugan, which is so uncertain as to raise doubts about whether the two names indeed refer to one person.

DAUVIT BROUN

Sources A. W. Wade-Evans, *Life of St David* (1923), 58–62 · E. G. Bowen, *Saints, seaways, and settlements in the Celtic lands*, 2nd edn (1977), 69, 70, 95, 99 · G. H. Doble, *St Cadoc in Cornwall and Brittany* (1937), 7–8, 14 · G. H. Doble, *St Carantoc* (1937), 25 · M. Miller, *The saints of Gwynedd* (1979), 59

Mawhood, William (1724–1797), woollen draper and diarist, was born on 8 December 1724 in Duck Lane, in the parish of St Bartholomew-the-Great, West Smithfield, London. He was the youngest of the three surviving children of the thirteen born to William Mawhood (1682–1757), also a woollen draper, and his wife, Mary (1686–1760), daughter of Thomas Payce, a woollen draper of Cloth Fair and liveryman of the Merchant Taylors' Company, and widow of a woollen draper named Living. Little is known of Mawhood's early life save that he was educated at the English College, St Omer, France. On 15 May 1751 in Richmond, Surrey, he married Dorothy Kroger (1727–1798), a daughter of William Kroger, a brewer of Clerkenwell. The couple had eight children; three were baptized at St Bartholomew's, three elsewhere by Bishop Richard Challoner, and two did not survive infancy.

William Mawhood was a successful woollen draper in the tradition of his father, great-uncle, and maternal grandfather. He inherited the shop and house that had been left to his mother upon the death of her first husband. Much of his cloth came from the west country and in 1772 he noted in his account book that he had stock worth £5000 and book debts to the value of £10,000 owed by 191 customers. Some of his business was concerned with supplying army clothing to the regiment of his cousin, but although he was pleased to win the order the army was notoriously slow to pay, and it took four years to obtain the total payment of £4000.

Mawhood's father had purchased 5 acres of land in Finchley in 1741. Father and son added to these until they owned 35 acres, and by 1772 Mawhood also owned three houses in Duck Lane and two in Bartholomew Close. The family spent time both in the town and on the Finchley estate where there was a house and a home farm. Mawhood was appointed surveyor of the highways for Finchley for the years 1772 and 1773, supervising the road repairs carried out by local men as required by act of parliament.

The Mawhoods were not an old Catholic family; William Mawhood senior was a convert to Roman Catholicism, and his children and grandchildren were brought up in the faith. In their turn the Mawhood men were active members of the select vestry of St Bartholomew's, rented part of a pew in the church, and, with their wives, were eventually buried in the aisle there. Neither vestry records nor the Mawhood diaries suggest that the family were ostracized or penalized as Catholics, other than having to pay fines for release from such parish offices as churchwarden. Mawhood recorded frequent attendance at church, confession, and family prayers, together with regular visits to musical events and membership of a music society. During the Gordon riots in 1780 he narrowly escaped having his West Smithfield home and possessions damaged by the mob, while providing a safe house in Finchley for Bishop Challoner.

Mawhood's final years were not without their problems. His much loved daughter Maria had been professed as a choir nun at the English convent in Bruges in 1779. When the order was forced to seek refuge in London in 1790 William, stricken with palsy and bedridden since 1790, gave all the help he could. In 1796 his son Charles threatened to take out a commission of lunacy against him, while his elder son William John continued to request financial assistance. The Finchley estate was sold in 1793 for £2635 and Mawhood moved into a house in Portman Place, Paddington. He died there on 23 December 1797 and was buried in St Bartholomew's on 2 January 1798. His wife survived him by only three months. The diary of William Mawhood is of particular value for its evidence of the daily life of a Catholic family of the 'middling sort', and of the extent to which Catholics of the period were able to take part in civic and cultural life. A selection from the diary, covering the years 1764–70, was published in a volume of the Catholic Record Society in 1956.

POLLY HAMILTON

Sources *The Mawhood diary: selections from the diary note-books of William Mawhood, woollen-draper of London, for the years 1764–1770*, ed. E. E. Reynolds, Catholic RS, 50 (1956) · will, PRO, PROB 11/1299 · will, PRO, PROB 11/1304 [Dorothy Mawhood] **Archives** GL, diaries, family papers, etc.

Mawson, Sir Douglas (1882–1958), scientist and explorer in Antarctica, was born at Shipley, near Bradford in Yorkshire, on 5 May 1882, the son of Robert Ellis Mawson, who came from sturdy yeoman stock, and his wife, Margaret Ann Moore, of the Isle of Man. His colouring and striking physique seemed to indicate viking blood. During Mawson's childhood the family moved to Australia; he was educated at the famous Fort Street School in Sydney, and at the University of Sydney, where in 1902 he obtained his BEng in mining and a demonstratorship in chemistry, and in 1905 his BSc. During this period he came under the influence of Professor A. Liversidge, who interested him in chemical geology, and of his lifelong friend Edgeworth David.

In the New Hebrides in 1903 Mawson carried out geological investigations in dangerous jungles upon which he subsequently reported. In 1905 he went as a lecturer in mineralogy and petrology to Adelaide, where he took his DSc in 1909 and served as first professor of geology and mineralogy from 1920 until 1952.

On David's recommendation Mawson was invited to join the 1907 expedition of Ernest Shackleton as a physicist. He sailed to the Ross Sea in *Nimrod*, and was chiefly concerned with geomagnetic and auroral studies, but opened his outstanding contribution to Antarctic exploration by two notable achievements with David: the ascent and geological examination of the active volcanic cone of Mount Erebus (1908) and the attainment of the south magnetic pole (1909), a success which demanded a pioneer ascent of the high and bitter Antarctic plateaux and the man-hauling of sledges for some 1300 miles. Captain R. F. Scott asked Mawson to join his last and fatal expedition to the pole, but the scientific and mechanical age of Antarctic exploration was succeeding the 'heroic period' and Mawson preferred to concentrate on the scientific appraisal of the coastlands of what was to become the Australian sector.

Mawson organized and led the noted Australasian Antarctic Expedition of 1911–14, sailing in the *Aurora* (under Captain J. K. Davis). He left a wireless station at Macquarie Island under G. F. Ainsworth, and in the continent established his own main base at Cape Denison, in what was later to become George V Land; that of J. R. F. Wild was established on the Shackleton ice shelf in Queen Mary Land farther west. Davis and the land parties explored nearly 2000 miles of coastline, while sledge parties traversed some 4000 miles in the coastlands and hinterlands, gaining scientific information of great value. In George V Land the explorers encountered one of the most stormy and crevasse-imperilled regions of the world; on one inland sledging expedition Mawson lost both his companions, Xavier Mertz and B. E. S. Ninnis, and only survived himself by the exercise of iron determination, superb physique, and the unfailing courage evident in all his expeditions. His return to base in early February 1913 was so delayed that the party were obliged to stay another winter before they could be relieved.

On his return to Australia, Mawson found that he was famous, his name bracketed with those of Scott and Shackleton, and in 1914 he was knighted in London. He had little opportunity to rest and enjoy his celebrity, however, as he had to pay off the debts from the expedition: this he succeeded in doing by personal appeals and lecturing; he enjoyed only modest financial success from his autobiographical account of the expedition, *The Home of the Blizzard* (1915).

The outbreak of the First World War in 1914 naturally submerged the achievements of the expedition and delayed the publication of the valuable scientific information it had secured. Later, however, the reports on geography, oceanography, glaciology, biology, terrestrial magnetism, and other scientific subjects proved of major importance. In the meantime Mawson enlisted for war service; he was promoted major and carried out important work with explosives, supervising the supply of munitions to various countries, including Russia, which he visited.

After the war international rivalry developed in the Antarctic, owing mainly to the growth of the whaling industry, which was based on improved methods of locating and killing the mammals and the emergence of huge diesel-engined factory ships. In 1923 Britain established the Ross Dependency under New Zealand to preserve her whaling rights and licence fees; the Australian government secretly, and Mawson openly, urged the annexation of Antarctica from the Ross Dependency to Enderby Land, mainly on account of the eastward advance of the Norwegian whaling fleets. Britain reached a secret agreement with Norway under which that country would respect the lands discovered by Britons in this sector in return for British recognition of the Norwegian annexation of Peter I and Bouvet islands, which had been discovered by the Russians and the French. This arrangement, however, did not protect the unknown coast between Wild's area of operations in Queen Mary Land and Enderby and Kemp lands. Britain refused to annex the region without the dispatch of a further exploring expedition, which was organized by Mawson with the help of private supporters and the governments of Britain, Australia, and New Zealand, and was known as Banzare (1929–31).

Lars Christensen, the great Norwegian scientific whaler, and Mawson, in Scott's old steam vessel *Discovery*, now both had expeditions at sea, nominally with scientific but also with territorial objectives. In an almost romantic climax Mawson, after conducting scientific work on Kerguelen, possibly sighted Princess Elizabeth Land in December 1929; certainly discovered MacRobertson Land, which he named after his principal financial supporter MacPherson Robertson; and landing at Proclamation Island in Enderby Land annexed what became the western end of the Australian sector. The Norwegian explorer Riiser Larsen, in *Norvegia*, now arrived from the west, where he had been coaling after reaching and proclaiming the annexation of Enderby Land, an action which the Norwegians repudiated. The rival explorers agreed to work westwards and eastwards respectively; the Norwegian turned and steamed westwards to conduct explorations which helped to give his country the vast territory of Queen Maud Land.

In the following year Mawson landed at the scene of his earlier explorations in George V Land, which he annexed. *Discovery* and her aircraft then made a sporadic examination of the coastline right around to Princess Elizabeth Land, and to the Mackenzie Sea coast of MacRobertson Land, which the party discovered only two days before the Norwegians. Landing at Scullin Monolith in the east of

MacRobertson Land, and at Cape Bruce in the west, Mawson proclaimed further annexations.

The expedition had now fulfilled the requirements of the British government, which in 1933 annexed, with the exception of Adélie Land, the vast territory of nearly 2.5 million square miles between the Ross Dependency and Enderby Land, and handed it to Australia. Although the United States and Russia refused to recognize any annexation of Antarctic territory unless accompanied by occupation, it may be fairly said that Mawson staked for the commonwealth a legal and widely admitted claim to the Australian Antarctic.

The Banzare expedition also gained notable scientific results although publication was again delayed, on this occasion by the worldwide economic depression and the outbreak of war in 1939. Later, however, the federal government provided the means to issue the reports, which Mawson himself edited until he died.

As well as his lifelong interest in Antarctic affairs Mawson gave notable services to South Australian geology, reports on which comprise the larger part of the 123 books and articles which he published. He travelled over much of the difficult and arid regions of this state of 380,000 square miles, usually taking parties of students with him. Very early in his career he was attracted by the arc of Precambrian and highly mineralized rocks which runs eastwards from the Mount Lofty and Flinders ranges to New South Wales and contains the noted Broken Hill silver–lead deposits. Mawson postulated that these rocks should be grouped into an older 'Willyama' and a younger 'Torrowangee' series, a supposition which isotopic age determination has proved correct, as also his belief that the older series is Archaean and the younger Proterozoic. In 1906 Mawson identified some specimens as uranium minerals which were in consequence developed at Radium Hill near Olary. There, too, he discovered a new radioactive mineral which he named Davidite. Subsequent discoveries of uranium and other minerals at Mount Painter were also of importance.

Mawson's work in the Antarctic gave him an intense interest in glaciology. Proterozoic sediments and glacial beds had been found in the gorge of the Sturt River near Adelaide, and Mawson showed the existence of similar beds of extraordinary extent, thickness, and importance. Indeed, he made the remarkable discovery that these glacial formations, in some places tillite but generally glaciomarine, extend for 1000 miles in the interior of South Australia and indicate that glacial conditions existed intermittently in the Proterozoic over an immense period of time.

In addition to his knighthood, Mawson was appointed OBE in 1920; he received the king's polar medal with three bars and awards from many British and foreign learned societies, including the Antarctic (1909) and Founder's (1915) medals of the Royal Geographical Society. The University of Adelaide established in 1961 the Mawson Institute for Antarctic Research, where most of Mawson's papers are deposited. Nevertheless, although Mawson's

Antarctic nomenclature was very generous, not only to his supporters and colleagues but also to his foreign rivals, his own name was not adequately recognized in Antarctica until his death. At that time the Russians in particular proclaimed him as the outstanding scientific explorer of the Antarctic, and the Australian government named, in his honour, a Mawson coast. The region selected in MacRobertson Land was most appropriate as it was discovered by Mawson, is the site of the Mawson scientific station, and adjoins the coast named after his great Norwegian rival, Lars Christensen.

Mawson helped to make Australia more aware of the strategic potential of Antarctica and his reputation as an explorer there stands high not least because of the scope of his scientific achievements: 'He was, first and foremost, a geologist and mineralogist who regarded Antarctic exploration from a frankly utilitarian point of view' (*The Times*, 15 Oct 1958). He left a vivid and detailed record of his three Antarctic expeditions in his diaries, which in 1988 were published as *Mawson's Antarctic Diaries*. For his services to geology Mawson received medals from a number of geological societies including the Bigsby medal of the Geological Society of London. He was elected FRS in 1923; the Australian and New Zealand Association for the Advancement of Science awarded him the Mueller memorial medal in 1930 and elected him to its presidency from 1935 to 1937. The new laboratories in the school of geology at Adelaide were named after him.

Mawson married on 31 March 1914 Francisca Adriana (Paquita; 1891–1974), daughter of Guillaume Daniel Delprat CBE, the leading founder of the Broken Hill Proprietary. They had two daughters, the elder of whom, Patricia Marietje Thomas, of the University of Adelaide, continued her father's work as general editor of the Banzare publications. Humble-minded and almost retiring as Mawson was, unless he was fighting with characteristic tenacity in a worthwhile cause, he and Lady Mawson, who became an OBE for her services to infant welfare, made an important contribution to the life and development of South Australia. When Mawson died in Adelaide, on 14 October 1958, he was accorded the honour of a state funeral; he was buried on 16 October at St Jude's Anglican Church, Brighton, near Adelaide.

A. G. PRICE, *rev.* MARK POTTLE

Sources D. Mawson, *The home of the blizzard: being the story of the Australasian Antarctic expedition, 1911–1914*, abridged edn (1930) · *The Times* (15 Oct 1958) · P. Ayres, *Mawson: a life* (1999) · *Mawson's Antarctic diaries*, ed. F. Jacka and E. Jacka (1988) · *AusDB* · D. Mawson, 'Geographical narrative and cartography', *Australasian Antarctic Expedition Scientific Reports* [Sydney], ser. A, 1 (1942) · D. Mawson, 'The BANZ Antarctic research expedition, 1923–31', *GJ*, 80 (1932), 101–31 · A. Grenfell Price, *BANZARE Scientific Reports*, 1st ser., 1 (1962) · A. R. Alderman and C. E. Tilley, *Memoirs FRS*, 5 (1959), 119–27 · E. M. Suzyumov, *A life given to the Antarctic: the Antarctic explorer Sir Douglas Mawson* (Moscow, 1960) · R. A. Swan, *Australia in the Antarctic* (1961) · *Sir Douglas Mawson anniversary volume*, University of Adelaide (Adelaide, 1952) · private information (1971) · personal knowledge (1971)

Archives Scott Polar RI, log · University of Adelaide, Mawson Institute for Antarctic Research, diaries and papers | NL Scot., corresp. incl. to J. M. Wordie and relating to the discovery committee · RGS, letters to Royal Geographical Society · Scott Polar RI, corresp. with James Marr · Scott Polar RI, letters to H. R. Mill **Likenesses** photograph, *c.*1929–1931, repro. in Jacka and Jacka, eds., *Mawson's Antarctic diaries*, frontispiece · H. Haley, portrait, 1933, Mawson Institute for Antarctic Research, University of Adelaide · I. Hele, oils, 1957, Bonython Hall, University of Adelaide · I. Hele, oils, 1959, RGS

Mawson, Matthias

Mawson, Matthias (1683–1770), bishop of Ely, was born in Chiswick, Middlesex, one of at least two sons of Thomas Mawson, a prosperous brewer, and his wife, Elizabeth, of Fleet Street. He was baptized on 19 July 1683 at St Dunstan-in-the-West, London. Mawson attended St Paul's School, then Corpus Christi College, Cambridge, from 1701, where he proceeded BA in 1704, MA in 1708, BD in 1716, and DD in 1725. He was made a fellow in 1707, moderator in 1708, and taxor in 1709, and became master of the college in 1724 and vice-chancellor in 1730. Mawson was known as a reformer while he was in the latter post. He tightened up academic requirements, reduced unnecessary transference from college to college, and stopped the practice of exhuming bodies from nearby graveyards for use as cadavers. Between 1727 and 1730 he was a royal chaplain. He took his first parish, Conington in Cambridgeshire, soon after completing his DD, and became rector of Hadstoke in Essex in 1733. Barely a year after he accepted the latter living, Mawson was offered the bishopric of Gloucester, a post he turned down. However, in 1738 he accepted an appointment to the see of Llandaff at the urging of his friends, and went on to become bishop of Chichester in 1740 and bishop of Ely in 1754. He died on 23 November 1770, aged eighty-seven, at his home in Kensington Square, London. He was buried in Ely Cathedral. He never married.

Mawson seems to have been a latitudinarian. Politically he was a whig, arguing for limitations on the power of the crown. He aligned himself with the duke of Newcastle and, while at Chichester, worked assiduously for the duke's interest in Sussex. Religiously Mawson was a low-churchman. He urged toleration and unity over doctrinal precision, and preached reconciliation rather than prosecution. He believed that many of the divisions in religion came from 'enthusiasm', which caused men zealously to guard doctrines and worship practices arising out of narrow formulations of Christianity, and to coerce others to accept them. He was tolerant of most protestant sects, but could not feel the same about Catholicism. Particularly in the wake of the Jacobite rising of 1745, Mawson urged greater controls over Catholics since they continued to pose a significant political threat.

Mawson gained great wealth both from his official income and from his inheritance (the latter of which he received when his brother, who ran the family business, died), but was an extremely generous benefactor. During his lifetime he lent some £6000 or £7000 for new buildings at King's College, Cambridge, and donated thousands of pounds of his own money for improvements at Chichester and Ely cathedrals. In 1754 he presented Corpus Christi College with lands sufficient to endow twelve scholarships. Further, he gave significant sums to governments for improving lands and renovating civic buildings. At his death, he bequeathed £9000 to his old college for scholarships and building projects. The balance of his fortune went to a nephew, a niece, and two grand-nephews.

As bishop and churchman, Mawson garnered respect and appreciation. In 1749 William Clarke, rector of Buxted in Sussex and prominent antiquary, observed that he was 'a better sort of man than most of the mitred order. He is indeed awkward, absent, &c., but then he has no ambition, no desire to please, and is privately munificent, when the world thinks him parsimonious' (Nichols, *Lit. anecdotes*, 4.459). A number of his sermons, preached to the House of Commons, the House of Lords, and to other institutions on anniversary occasions, were published separately.

J. S. CHAMBERLAIN

Sources Nichols, *Lit. anecdotes*, 4.459–61 · L. P. Curtis, *Chichester towers* (1966), 12, 54, 70–72, 81, 83, 85–8, 98–9, 104 · J. S. Chamberlain, *Accommodating high churchmen: the clergy of Sussex, 1700–1745* (1997), 153 · correspondence with the duke of Newcastle and others, BL, Add. MSS 4313, 5831, 5848, 6400, 32694ff., 35598ff.; Cole MS 47, fol. 86 · Venn, *Alum. Cant.*
Archives BL, corresp. with duke of Newcastle, Add. MSS 4313, 5831, 5848, 6400, 32694, 33598
Likenesses D. Heins, oils, 1729, CCC Cam. · oils, *c.*1740–1745, bishop's palace, Ely · J. Freeman, oils, 1775, bishop's palace, Ely · oils, CCC Cam.
Wealth at death bequeathed £9000 to Corpus Christi College, Cambridge: Nichols, *Lit. anecdotes*

Mawson, Thomas Hayton

Mawson, Thomas Hayton (1861–1933), landscape architect, was born on 5 May 1861 in Nether Wyersdale, Lancashire, the second of the four children (one daughter and three sons) of John William Mawson, cotton warper, and his wife, Jane Hayton. He was educated at the local church school, and then at the age of twelve joined a builders' business in Lancaster. Two years later he returned home to help his father set up a nursery, but the venture failed. Following John Mawson's death, the family moved to London, where Thomas secured work with John Wills, a well-known floral decorator. In 1881 he took a job at Hale Farm Nurseries; not long afterwards, in order to start experimenting with his ideas on design, he accepted a partnership with a firm of contractors. When this fell through he decided to set up a family business and, with his two brothers, established a nursery and contracting firm in Windermere. From designing local private gardens the firm progressed to contracts from all parts of the country, which included the design of public parks and town planning schemes.

On 1 August 1884 Mawson married Anna (*b.* 1862/3), a nurse, daughter of Edward Prentice, surgeon, of North Walsham. They had four sons and four daughters. The eldest son, Edward Prentice Mawson, became a successful landscape architect and eventually took over the running of his father's firm.

By 1900 Thomas Mawson had left Mawson Brothers to pursue a separate career in landscape design. He achieved great success and became the leading landscape architect of the day. His clients included Queen Alexandra, the maharaja of Baroda, Andrew Carnegie, and the first Viscount Leverhulme. His public works included Haslam Park, Preston, Hanley Park, Stoke-on-Trent, and Broomfield Park, Southgate.

Mawson made several trips to America and Canada, where he was involved in major town planning schemes in Ottawa, Vancouver, Calgary, and Regina. His other significant work abroad included the gardens of the Palace of Peace in The Hague, and the royal gardens and a park system in Athens. In 1917 he was commissioned to replan Salonika, following extensive fire damage.

Mawson published two main works: *The Art and Craft of Garden Making* (1900), which ran into five editions, and *Civic Art* (1911), in which he discussed the principles of town planning. From 1910 to 1924 he lectured regularly at the school of civic design, Liverpool University. Conscious that he lacked formal education, the need for education was among his lifelong concerns. Brought up in a nonconformist household, he remained deeply religious. Politically, he was an ardent Liberal. Although by nature inclined to thought rather than action, through circumstance he became fond of hard work. A family man, he was kind and gentle, genial, and without professional airs.

Mawson was elected an honorary member of the Royal Institute of British Architects in 1903 and became a member of the Art Workers' Guild in 1905. He was made a freeman of the City of London in 1917 and an honorary liveryman of the Worshipful Company of Gardeners. In 1921 he became a fellow of the Linnean Society. In 1923 he was elected president of the Town Planning Institute and the following year he was appointed to the Royal Fine Arts Commission. In 1925 he became the first president of the Institute of Landscape Architects. From 1923 he suffered from Parkinson's disease, which caused his death at his home, Applegarth, Hest Bank, Lancashire, on 14 November 1933. His wife survived him.

HARRIET JORDAN, rev.

Sources T. H. Mawson, *The life and work of an English landscape architect* (1927) · personal knowledge (1993) · private information (1993) · b. cert. · m. cert. · d. cert. · *CGPLA Eng. & Wales* (1934)
Wealth at death £3552 15s. 8d.: probate, 7 Feb 1934, *CGPLA Eng. & Wales*

Maxey, Anthony (d. 1618), dean of Windsor, was probably a member of the Maxey family of Bradwell juxta Coggeshall, Essex. Educated as a queen's scholar at Westminster School, on 18 April 1578 he was elected to Trinity College, Cambridge. He graduated BA in 1582, proceeding MA in 1585, BTh in 1594, and DD in 1608, but failed to win a fellowship. Ordained deacon and priest in the diocese of Lincoln on 7 May 1589, Maxey was rector of Hackford, Norfolk, from that year until 1602. In 1591 he acquired the rectory of Horham, Suffolk, and held it until 1595, by when he had been installed rector of Reepham, Norfolk. He is also credited with the rectory of Winterton in the same county. He resigned from Reepham in 1612, at about the same time that he acquired yet another rectory, that of Horton in Buckinghamshire.

By the beginning of 1605 Maxey had become a chaplain-in-ordinary to James I, and frequently preached before the king. On Ascension day 1605, for instance, he eulogized James's court as 'the most religious court ... that is in Christendome' (McCullough, 130). Another court sermon of that year suggests he may have sympathized with the nonconformists recently deprived of their livings, but he was none the less careful to praise the ceremonies which had been their undoing. Maxey's incomes spiralled and honours multiplied, and on 21 June 1612 James appointed him registrar of the Order of the Garter and dean of Windsor; he was instituted on the 25th. He usually attended meetings of the Windsor chapter, which on 30 March 1614 resolved to present him to the rectory of West Isley, Berkshire. Several sermons preached before the king were published soon afterwards, all of them appearing in the posthumous editions of *Certaine Sermons Preached before the King's Majesty* (1619, 1634). These also include his address given at the marriage of Ralph Sadler to Anne, daughter of Sir Edward Coke, at the Savoy on 14 September 1601, and another given before the lords of the council in Lent 1618.

Aptly described as 'an unblushing simonist' (*Old Westminsters*, 2.634), Maxey offered money to Sir Henry Hobart, attorney-general between 1606 and 1613, in the hope of gaining preferment, while in April 1618 John Chamberlain reported that he had made the highest bid for the vacant see of Norwich, topping the offer of Valentine Carey, dean of St Paul's. But the prize eluded him. Maxey died on 3 May 1618, the day on which he made his will; probate was granted on the 18th, his executor being his kinsman Amyas Maxey. He mentions several other relations but no children, referring to his wife only as having died at least ten years earlier. He left eighty books to the library of the chapter at Windsor, and sums of money to relatives and servants; two faithful servants each received £10 and a horse, 'but unto Roger my cooke, beinge verye lewde in his tongue, and besides corruptinge my clarke Roberte Berrye with tobacco and drinkinge, nothinge' (PRO, PROB 11/131, fol. 369r). Maxey held the lease of a house in the parish of St Martin-in-the-Fields, London, and it was in St Martin's Church that he was buried.   STEPHEN WRIGHT

Sources Venn, *Alum. Cant.*, 1/3.165 · S. Bond, *Chapter acts of the dean and canons of Windsor* (1966) · S. L. Ollard, *Fasti Wyndesorienses: the deans and canons of Windsor* (privately printed, Windsor, 1950) · *Old Westminsters*, vols. 1–2 · A. Maxey, *Certaine sermons preached before the king's majesty* (1619) · J. C. Challenor-Smith, 'Some additions to Newcourt's *Repertorium* — volume 2 [pt 2]', *Transactions of the Essex Archaeological Society*, new ser., 7 (1898–9), 153–78 · P. E. McCullough, *Sermons at court: politics and religion in Elizabethan and Jacobean preaching* (1998) [incl. CD-ROM] · will, PRO, PROB 11/131, fols. 368v–369r · *Fasti Angl., 1541–1857*, [Canterbury], 375
Wealth at death see will, PRO, PROB 11/131, fols. 368v–369r

Maxfield, Thomas. *See* Macclesfield, Thomas (1585–1616).

Maxfield, Thomas (d. 1784), Methodist preacher, hailed from Bristol, but nothing is known of his parents or his early life. He was converted by John Wesley's preaching at Bristol on 21 May 1739, and, despite his youth, was soon appointed leader of a Methodist band—a small group for fellowship and mutual confession. In 1740 Charles Wesley took Maxfield to London, where he was given further

Thomas Maxfield (*d.* 1784), by Richard Houston, pubd 1772 (after Thomas Beach, 1772)

responsibility as an assistant leader in the Methodist society. In the winter of 1740–41 John Wesley put him in charge of the society at the Foundery Chapel, London, while he himself returned to his Bristol ministry. Maxfield's brief was to pray with the members and give them informal exhortation. Encouraged, however, by Selina, countess of Huntingdon, and others he began to preach, which, as a layman, he was not authorized to do. John Wesley, informed of this new development, rode post-haste from Bristol to London, and at the Foundery was met by his mother, Susanna. To his curt 'Thomas Maxfield has turned preacher, I find', she replied:

> John, you know what my sentiments have been. You cannot suspect me of favouring readily any thing of this kind. But take care what you do with respect to that young man, for he is as surely called of God to preach, as you are. Examine what have been the fruits of his preaching, and hear him also yourself.

Having done so, Wesley acknowledged, 'It is the Lord. Let him do what seemeth him good' (Moore, 1.506).

Maxfield's preaching gifts made such a profound impression on Lady Huntingdon that, in a letter to John Wesley of 31 January 1742, she described Maxfield, bearing in mind his humble origins, as 'One of the greatest instances of God's peculiar favour that I know. He has raised from the stones one to set among the princes of his people' (*Works of John Wesley*, 26.73). In early 1741 Wesley appointed Maxfield as a full-time lay itinerant preacher, the first of his many 'sons in the Gospel'. In 1745 Wesley made him an assistant—a preacher with responsibility for

overseeing a circuit, a collection of Methodist societies scattered over a wide area. In June 1745, while Maxfield was preaching in Cornwall, he was press-ganged for the navy, but, having been rejected by the captain of the ship to which he was taken, was put in prison at Penzance. He was about to be freed when, by the intervention of William Borlase of Ludgvan, a clerical magistrate and avowed opponent of the Methodists, he was conscripted for military service instead. John Wesley, on a preaching tour of Cornwall, heard of these events. He rode at once to Marazion with George Thomson, in whose church Wesley had been invited to preach, to confront the justices and contend for Maxfield's release. They were not allowed into the court room until late at night, by which time Maxfield had been sentenced to military service and the justices had dispersed.

Maxfield did eventually obtain his release, however, as he was present at the Bristol annual conference of Methodist preachers in 1746. He became one of Wesley's most trusted lieutenants, and in the minutes of conference for 1758 he is listed immediately beneath the Wesleys themselves. This placing both underlines his seniority and also may well indicate that by this date he had, at Wesley's request, been ordained an Anglican clergyman. Maxfield was ordained priest by William Barnard, bishop of Derry, on John Wesley's recommendation. Barnard, who for reasons of health was then living in Bath, received Maxfield with the words, 'I ordain you, to assist that good man, that he may not work himself to death' (*Works of John Wesley*, 21.409). Maxfield combined his Methodist itinerancy with the office of chaplain to Lady Huntingdon, and also had a pronounced influence on Thomas Coke, who was to become one of John Wesley's most loyal Anglican colleagues.

The 1760s saw the development of a painful rift between Maxfield and John and Charles Wesley. John felt it particularly strongly, since he admired Maxfield's gifts and had sought to give him the fullest scope for their exercise. Moreover, the dispute touched Wesley at a sensitive point, in that it involved the understanding of Christian perfection, a doctrine on which he placed prime emphasis. In 1760 Wesley appointed Maxfield to meet weekly with a select group of Methodists who professed to have reached a state of 'entire sanctification'. They began to claim direct divine inspiration through dreams and visions. Maxfield, according to Wesley, far from exercising a sobering influence, encouraged their 'enthusiasm'. In October 1762 Wesley recorded 'I found the society in an uproar and several of Mr. M[axfield]'s most intimate friends formed into a detached body. Enthusiasm, pride, and great uncharitableness appeared in many who once had much grace' (*Works of John Wesley*, 21.410). The dispute involved claims by Maxfield's followers that Christians should expect absolute sinless perfection in this life, as against Wesley's insistence on continuing weaknesses and infirmities, 'sin in believers'. Some of the Maxfield group claimed they would never die, and one, George Bell, prophesied that the world would end on 28 February 1763—a prophecy which Maxfield endorsed. Wesley reacted strongly against these extravagances, and in his journal for 7 January 1763, recorded:

> At this time I did not want information that Mr. M.[axfield] was at the bottom of all this; that he was the life of the cause; that he was continually spiriting up all with whom he was intimate against me; that he told them I was not capable of teaching them and insinuated that none was but himself; and that the inevitable consequence must be a division in the society. (*Works of John Wesley*, 21.403)

Eventually, some 200 Methodists left Wesley's London society and Maxfield severed connection with his erstwhile leader on 28 April 1763. Contemporary evidence suggests that Maxfield's growing consciousness of his considerable gifts, his enhanced status as Wesley's lieutenant and an ordained clergyman, together with the large fortune brought him by his wife Elizabeth Branford (*d.* 1777) may have enhanced his sense of independence of the Wesleys. He had certainly outgrown the status of a 'son in the gospel', and appears to have been reluctant to accept the role of 'fellow-labourer'. Wesley, deeply hurt by Maxfield's conduct, recorded in his journal for 23 April 1763: 'From this time, he has spoke all manner of evil of *me*, his father, his friend, his greatest earthly benefactor' (*Works of John Wesley*, 21.411). In his *Vindication of the Rev. Mr Maxfield's conduct* (1767) Maxfield rebutted Wesley's charges, though the evidence against him does not derive solely from Wesley. Among others John Fletcher, the saintly vicar of Madeley, corroborates the charges of spiritual pride against Maxfield and Bell. Fletcher wrote of Maxfield, in a letter to Wesley dated 9 September 1763: 'I believe him [Maxfield] sincere; and, though obstinate and suspicious, I am persuaded he has a true desire to know the will, and live the life of God' (Tyerman, 2.464).

Maxfield became minister to a society in Snow's Fields, London, and then moved to a meeting-house in Ropemakers' Alley, Moorfields, where he had a large congregation. His final preaching place was at Princes Street, Moorfields, where he ministered until about 1767. In the following decade he published a *Collection of Psalms and Hymns Extracted from Various Authors* (1778) and several accounts of pious deaths, including that of his wife, who died on 23 November 1777. In February 1770, at Lady Huntingdon's house in Portland Row, Wesley met Maxfield, who preached against Christian perfection, the doctrine he had previously so earnestly advocated. There were attempts at reconciliation from both sides, but the breach was never healed. There was, however, in time some softening of attitude on both sides. Charles Atmore records of Maxfield that, 'For some years before his death, he became very friendly with the Methodists; the preachers frequently supplied his chapel and preached to his congregation' (Atmore, 269). Wesley recorded a later visit in his journal for 21 December 1782 after Maxfield had been struck with a violent stroke of palsy: 'He was senseless and seemed near death. But we besought God for him, and his spirit revived, I cannot but think, in answer to prayer.' On 2 February 1783 he noted, 'Mr. Maxfield continuing ill, I preached this afternoon at his chapel. Prejudice seems

now dying away. God grant it may never revive' (*Works of John Wesley*, 23.261–2). Maxfield died at his home in Moorfields on 18 March 1784.   JOHN A. NEWTON

Sources The works of John Wesley, [another edn], 18–23, ed. F. Baker and others (1988–95) · *The works of John Wesley*, [another edn], 26, ed. F. Baker and others (1982) · H. Moore, *The life of the Rev. John Wesley*, 2 vols. (1824–5) · L. Tyerman, *The life and times of the Rev. John Wesley*, 3 vols. (1870–71) · C. Atmore, *The Methodist memorial* (1801) · H. D. Rack, *Reasonable enthusiast: John Wesley and the rise of Methodism* (1989) · J. W. Etheridge, *The life of the Rev. Thomas Coke* (1860)
Archives Westminster College, Cambridge, Cheshunt Foundation, corresp. with Selina, countess of Huntingdon
Likenesses R. Houston, mezzotint, pubd 1772 (after T. Beach, 1772), NPG [*see illus.*] · group portrait, 1772 (with his family) · T. Beach, portrait · P. Dawe, engraving (after T. Beach)

Maxim, Sir Hiram Stevens (1840–1916), engineer and inventor, was born on 5 February 1840 at Brockway's Mills, near Sangerville, Maine, USA, the elder son of Isaac Weston Maxim (1814–1883) and his wife, Harriet Boston (1815–1901), daughter of Levi Stevens of Maine. His father's family were of Huguenot and his mother's of English descent. Isaac Maxim was a farmer and wood-turner with a leaning for philosophy and a talent for invention. It is interesting, in view of Hiram Maxim's subsequent career, that his father also tinkered with the ideas of an automatic gun and a flying machine.

The Maxim farmstead was a pioneering venture, located in a clearing in dense forest with a higher population of bears than people, and Hiram's boyhood was one of adventure and self-reliance. When Hiram was nine his father abandoned farming and took up wood-turning, at which Hiram acquired considerable proficiency. He was studiously inclined and eagerly read any books which came within his reach. In particular he was attracted to geography and astronomy, and at one time he cherished the idea of becoming a sea captain. At the age of fourteen he was put to work with a carriage maker named Daniel Sweat, in the village of East Corinth; there he was obliged to work for sixteen hours a day, receiving each month goods worth $4 from a local store. He soon found employment with another master in the same trade, Daniel Flynt, where although the hours were equally long, the wages and conditions were better. From there he travelled to Montreal and various towns along the northern border of New York state, working casually as a bartender, cabinetmaker, and mechanic. He evaded service in the civil war. In 1864 Maxim joined his uncle, Levi Stevens, the proprietor of an engineering works at Fitchburg, Massachusetts, where he acquired a knowledge of draughtsmanship and continued his technical and scientific studies. Then he entered the service of Oliver Drake, gas machine builder and philosophical instrument maker, of whom he thought and spoke highly, and to whom he attributed much of his later success. At this stage his inventive genius became fairly active, and, among other contrivances, he devised a 'density regulator' for equalizing the illuminating value of coal gas. This was not his first invention, but it was more ambitious than his previous efforts.

In 1867 Maxim married an English immigrant, Louisa

Jane Budden (1841–1911); they had a son and two daughters. In 1878, unknown to his wife, he went through an apparent form of marriage with Helen Leighton, aged fifteen: they had one daughter. In early 1881 Helen learned of his marriage and contacted his wife. He agreed to leave Helen but financially support her and her child. By 1873 he was senior partner in Maxim and Welch, gas and steam engineers of New York. It was not, however, until 1878, when he became chief engineer to the United States Electric Lighting Company—the first such company to be formed in the United States—that Maxim produced anything of notable importance. His involvement in the development and construction of electricity generating machines and arc and incandescent lamps led to his successful method of building up an even coating of carbon on lamp filaments by 'flashing' them in hydrocarbon gas. This invention was of fundamental importance to the electric lighting industry but through a combination of machination and accident it became public property in England and the United States. Numerous inventions and patents followed, including an electrical pressure regulator which he displayed at the 1881 Paris Exhibition, and for which he was made a member of the Légion d'honneur. Paid off by the rival Edison group, in 1881 he went to Europe. There he was joined by Sarah (1854–1941), the attractive blonde daughter of Charles Haynes of Boston, Massachusetts. She was his secretary and mistress and, after his wife divorced him in early 1888, they married in May 1888. He allegedly continued to patronize brothels and seek the company of very young girls.

Shortly afterwards Maxim transferred his operations to London, where in 1884 he opened a workshop in Hatton Garden and directed his attention to gunnery. He formed the Maxim Gun Company in the same year and prepared a design for a fully automatic gun; in order to block any competition he assiduously patented every conceivable device concerning the firing mechanism. As soon as this weapon was constructed, it attracted high official notice and was inspected by the British commander-in-chief, the duke of Cambridge, and the prince of Wales. Lord Wolseley was greatly struck by it, and suggested certain developments in range and power, which led Maxim to make a number of variations of his original design in order to meet different conditions. The Maxim gun was adopted in the British army in 1889 and in the Royal Navy in 1892, though initial orders were disappointing. Unlike earlier machine guns it had a single barrel and completely automatic action, firing at the rate of ten rounds a second. Maxim also patented a smokeless powder, maximite, which led him into dispute with the War Office explosives committee who were developing cordite, a similar product, at the same time. His firm merged with the Nordenfeldt Company in 1888 and the joint concern established various manufactories near Crayford, in Kent, before being itself absorbed in 1896 into the company of Vickers Sons and Maxim, of which Maxim became a director; he retired from the board in 1911. Meanwhile he was a tireless arms salesman, travelling throughout Europe—sometimes with Basil Zaharoff—visiting St Petersburg

twice and Constantinople once; in addition, many heads of state came to England where he laid on impressive demonstrations of the power and speed of his guns.

From gunnery Maxim turned his attention to flying, and during the period 1889–94 produced a steam-driven test rig; this may be said, in a technical sense, to have flown, since, during a trial carried out at Baldwyn's Park, Bexley, Kent, in July 1894, the runner wheels were lifted off the rail track, but otherwise the machine failed to achieve its purpose, mainly on account of its excessive weight. It consisted of a large central plane with two curved side frames. Its engines and boilers weighed respectively 600 lb and 1200 lb, including casing, feed-water heater, dome, and uptake. For a horsepower of 300, the total weight of the motive agency, 6 lb per hp, was not unreasonable, but, unfortunately, feed-water for an hour's trip added 6000 lb to the load. £20,000 was expended on this absurd contraption. A later version, intended for demonstration at the Aero and Motorboat Exhibition held at Olympia in 1910, was not ready on time and at that point the project ended. It inspired H. G. Wells's story 'The Argonauts of the air'.

Maxim and his younger brother, Isaac (who called himself Hudson) Maxim (1853–1927), explosives engineer, had co-operated but their relationship deteriorated, culminating in a final quarrel and bitter feud. Each used the press to vilify the other. Hiram hired a New York detective agency to gain evidence against Isaac. Isaac instigated Hiram's arrest in New York and prosecution in October 1898 on a bigamy charge brought by Helen Leighton (also known as Nell Malcolm and Tug Wilson): Hiram was acquitted. The brothers were never reconciled.

A wealthy man, Maxim had by this time settled permanently in England. He became a naturalized citizen, and was knighted in February 1901. In 1900 he suffered an attack of bronchitis and was advised to pass the winter of 1901–2 at a sanatorium in Nice. This experience led him to design and have manufactured in London inhalers to ease his fellow sufferers. In 1915 he published his boastful and unreliable autobiography, *My Life*. Active and inventive to the last, he died of broncho-pneumonia and heart failure at his home, Sandhurst Lodge, High Road, Streatham, London, on 24 November 1916 and was buried at Norwood cemetery.

Maxim loved to describe himself as 'a chronic inventor'. His versatility, skill, and ingenuity encompassed many fields of science and technology and his patents were legion. He could never use a machine without seeking to improve it, and between the hours spent in his conventional work, he also made improvements (as he saw it) to the mousetrap, the merry-go-round, an automatic sprinkler, a feed-water heater, and a process for obtaining cheap phosphoric anhydride. Unlike many inventors, Maxim was fastidious about his appearance. He was about 6 feet tall and well built with fluffy hair and beard, jet black in early life and snow white in his later years. He was exceedingly vain and despite his success was consumed by jealousy of other inventors, especially Thomas Edison, his rival in electric lighting, and his own brother, Isaac. The image of the self-made man, with a hearty dislike for lawyers and labour leaders, he had no use for any religion and declared himself a citizen of the world. His machine guns, which were manufactured in several variants, not only in Britain but also under licence in Germany, Russia, and elsewhere, killed untold numbers in over fifty years of war. The British variant, the Vickers machine gun, continued in service until 1963.

BRYSSON CUNNINGHAM, *rev.* ANITA MCCONNELL

Sources H. Maxim, *My life* (1915) · I. McCallum, *Blood brothers, Hiram and Hudson Maxim: pioneers of modern warfare* (1999) · J. E. Hamilton, *The chronic inventor* (1991) · *DAB* · Walford, *County families* · P. F. Mottelay, *Life and work of Sir Hiram Maxim* (1920) · d. cert.
Archives CUL, Vickers archive · Staffs. RO, letters to duke of Sutherland relating to aircraft experiments
Likenesses F. S. Baden-Powell, silhouette drawing, 1894, NPG · J. Russell & Sons, photograph, NPG · Spy [L. Ward], chromolithograph caricature, repro. in *VF* (15 Dec 1904) · photograph, repro. in Maxim, *My life*
Wealth at death £33,090 12s. 8d.: probate, 22 Dec 1916, *CGPLA Eng. & Wales*

Max Müller, Friedrich. *See* Müller, Friedrich Max (1823–1900).

Maxse, Frederick Augustus (1833–1900), naval officer and radical, was the second son of James Maxse (1792–1864), a wealthy landowner, hunting man, and yachtsman, and his wife, Lady Caroline Fitzhardinge (1803–1886), the eldest daughter of Frederick Augustus, fifth earl of Berkeley. Sir Henry Berkeley Fitzhardinge *Maxse was his elder brother. After schooling at Brighton, Hampton, and Paris he entered the navy, and obtained his lieutenancy in May 1852. As naval aide-de-camp to Lord Raglan after the battle of the Alma (20 September 1854) he showed conspicuous gallantry in carrying dispatches, which caused his promotion to commander in December 1855. At the end of the war he was the youngest captain in the navy. From 1859 he was the friend of George Meredith, who based the hero of *Beauchamp's Career* (1875) on him. He retired from the service in 1867 and became rear-admiral in 1875.

The Crimean War was apparently for Maxse a formative experience. He returned contemptuous of what he perceived as the conservative, aristocratic establishment's bungling, and also a strong Francophile. Emotional, impulsive, and idealistic, he became an 'aristocratic democrat' (Garvin, 156), an idiosyncratic political radical who was a freethinker, anti-Christianity, vegetarian, and teetotal. He condemned aristocracy and *laissez-faire* capitalism and advocated co-operation, free secular education, land redistribution, and electoral reform, but—like his fellow wealthy radical Henry Labouchere—opposed women's suffrage. His friends included John Morley and Joseph Chamberlain, whom he introduced to each other in 1873. He was an unsuccessful radical parliamentary candidate at Southampton in 1868 (when Meredith helped him) and at Tower Hamlets, London, in 1874. Patriotic and imperialist, he broke with the Gladstonians over home rule and continued his friendship with Chamberlain. He

represented Dorking on the new Surrey county council from 1889 to March 1895.

Restless, Maxse travelled much, kept a *pied-à-terre* in Paris, and spent much time buying and building houses. He finally resided at a house he had built, Dunley Hill, near Dorking. From 1868 he published articles and pamphlets on topical political issues, including *Objections to Woman Suffrage* (1874) and his defence of Chamberlain, *Judas! A Political Tract* (1894). In 1899 he published in the *National Review* articles on the Crimean War which are of historical value.

In 1861 Maxse married Cecilia (d. 1918), the daughter of Colonel Steel of the Indian army. They were incompatible, the marriage failed, and in 1877 they separated. They had two sons and two daughters. (Frederick) Ivor *Maxse (1862–1958) had a military career, Leopold James *Maxse (1864–1932) became the owner–editor of the *National Review*, which his father paid for in 1893, and the younger daughter, Violet Georgina (1872–1958) [*see* Milner, Violet Georgina], married first Lord Edward Cecil and second Alfred, Viscount Milner.

Maxse died at 2 South Place, Knightsbridge, London, on 25 June 1900.   ROGER T. STEARN

Sources *The Times* (27 June 1900) · J. A. Hutcheson, *Leopold Maxse and the National Review, 1893–1914: right-wing politics and journalism in the Edwardian era* (1989) · *GM*, 2nd ser., 42 (1854), 497 · *GM*, 5th ser., 2 (1869), 671 · *Annual Register* (1855) · J. L. Garvin, *The life of Joseph Chamberlain*, 1: *Chamberlain and democracy* (1932) · S. M. Ellis, *George Meredith* (1920) · G. Meredith, *Beauchamp's career* (1875) · A. W. Kinglake, *The invasion of the Crimea*, [new edn], 6 (1877) · Walford, *County families* (1898) · Boase, *Mod. Eng. biog.*
Archives Bodl. Oxf., corresp. and papers · W. Sussex RO, corresp. and papers | CKS, Milner MSS · U. Birm. L., corresp. with Joseph Chamberlain
Likenesses photograph, repro. in Ellis, *George Meredith*, facing p. 238
Wealth at death £75,542 7s. 7d.: probate, 8 Aug 1900, *CGPLA Eng. & Wales*

Maxse, Sir Henry Berkeley Fitzhardinge (1832–1883), colonial governor, was the son of James Maxse (1792–1864), a wealthy landowner, and his wife, Lady Caroline Fitzhardinge (1803–1886), the daughter of the fifth earl of Berkeley. Frederick Augustus *Maxse was his brother. Henry Maxse entered the army on 1 June 1849 as a lieutenant in the Grenadier Guards, but changed on 11 June 1852 to the 13th light dragoons and on 6 July to the 21st foot. He became captain in the Coldstream Guards on 29 December 1854, and in the same year was ordered to the Crimea. He served throughout the Crimean War as aide-de-campe to Lord Cardigan, was present at the battles of Alma and Balaklava (where he was wounded) and at the siege of Sevastopol, and won the Crimean medal and clasps, besides Turkish medals and the decoration of the fifth class of the Mejidiye. In 1855 he became a major. In 1863 he was promoted to be lieutenant-colonel, but he bought himself out of the army on 22 December 1873.

In 1863 Maxse went to Heligoland as lieutenant-governor, and was appointed governor there on 6 February 1864. His long tenure as governor coincided with an eventful period in the island's history. The reformed constitution was established in 1868, the gaming tables were abolished in 1870, and Maxse had to face the consequent financial difficulties and complaints of the islanders. During his administration Heligoland was also linked by telegraph cable to the mainland. He was made CMG in 1874, and KCMG in 1877.

In 1881 Maxse became governor of Newfoundland, but he never really settled there. He was interested in Germany: he married the daughter of a Herr von Rudloff, spent a part of every year in Germany, and translated into English Bismarck's letters to his wife and sisters from the period 1844 to 1870. He was also fond of acting, and took part in amateur dramatics. He died at St John's, Newfoundland, on 10 September 1883. Leopold James *Maxse was his nephew.   C. A. HARRIS, *rev.* LYNN MILNE

Sources *Colonial Office List* (1882–7) • *The Times* (11 Sept 1883) • Burke, *Peerage*
Archives W. Sussex RO, corresp. and papers | NA Canada, letters, mainly to William Fladgate • PRO, letters to Lord Odo Russell, FO918
Likenesses wood-engraving (after photograph by G. Friederichs), NPG; repro. in *ILN* (6 Oct 1883)

Maxse, Sir (Frederick) Ivor (1862–1958), army officer, was born in London on 22 December 1862, the elder son of Admiral Frederick Augustus *Maxse (1833–1900) and his wife, Cecilia (d. 1918), daughter of Colonel James Steel of the Indian army. Leopold James *Maxse (1864–1932), his younger brother, became owner–editor of the *National Review*. His sister Violet Georgina (1872–1958) [*see* Milner, Violet Georgina] married Lord Edward Cecil, and, second, Alfred, Viscount Milner.

Maxse was educated at Mr Lake's Preparatory School, Caterham, Surrey (1875–7); Rugby School (1877–80); and, after coaching by a private tutor, the Royal Military College, Sandhurst (1881–2). He was commissioned lieutenant, Royal Fusiliers, in September 1882 (captain, October 1889). From 1883 to 1889 he served with the 2nd battalion in India, enjoying hunting, polo, racing, and big-game shooting. With family encouragement, using an army exchange agent—Admiral Maxse paid the withdrawing Coldstream captain £2200—he transferred to the Coldstream Guards in May 1891 with the rank of captain. From February 1893 to January 1894 he was aide-de-camp to Sir Arthur Lyon Fremantle, an old family friend, in command first of Scottish district, then of Malta, but finding Malta too far from London social and cultural life Maxse resigned. Active soldiering interested him more than Staff College and in 1897 he went instead to Cairo where he was seconded to the Egyptian army (major, December 1897) and saw service as a staff officer; he was a brigade-major in the battles of Atbara and Omdurman in 1898, being appointed DSO, and was a battalion commander in the final defeat of the Khalifa in 1899. On Kitchener's recommendation he was sent straight on to South Africa as a brevet lieutenant-colonel. He was a transport officer on the staff of Lord Roberts as a deputy assistant adjutant-general, and helped implement Kitchener's controversial, much-criticized centralization of army transport.

Sir (Frederick) Ivor Maxse (1862–1958), by George Charles Beresford, *c.*1921

After the capture of Pretoria he became commander of its police. He returned to England in bad health in November 1900. On 18 December 1899 Maxse married Mary Caroline Wyndham (1870–1944), known to her family and friends by her nursery pet name, Tiny, eldest daughter of Henry Wyndham, second Baron Leconfield; they had two sons and one daughter. Mary Maxse was born at Petworth, Sussex, on 17 November 1870 and educated by governesses. From 1904 to 1914 she was active in politics. From 1905 she was chairman of the Women's Unionist and Tariff Reform Association, assisted Unionist candidates at elections, supported the National Service League, and opposed women's suffrage. During the First World War her activities included speaking at recruiting meetings. A keen fox-hunter and churchwoman and a JP, domineering and uncompromising, she 'had a finger in every local pie' (Gore, 121). After illness from blood-poisoning, she died on 21 January 1944 at Little Bognor.

From 1900 Maxse's life followed the pattern of the fashionable officer once more: command of 2nd battalion, Coldstream Guards (1903–7), and brevet colonel in 1905. Yet Maxse had a quick and enquiring mind and his war experience had awakened him to the dangers threatening Britain. He published *Seymour Vandeleur* (1905), a eulogistic biography of his friend and best man, Lieutenant-Colonel C. F. S. Vandeleur (1869–1901), Etonian guards officer who served in Uganda, Nigeria, and the Sudan, and was killed in the Second South African War. In the biography Maxse criticized British public schools, amateurishness, and unpreparedness for war, during increased international competition. In 1912 Maxse bought the house and estate of Little Bognor, Fittleworth, Sussex, and in 1914 he moved there; it remained his family home for the rest of his life.

From August 1910 Maxse was brigadier-general commanding the 1st (guards) brigade. He viewed the pre-war cult of the offensive as the answer to increased firepower, and claimed that 'masses of men in sufficient lines one behind the other will go through anything' (Travers, 46). He also accepted Staff College orthodoxy on the structured battle, lecturing his troops on the three-act battle: firefight, decision, annihilation of the enemy. Maxse took the 1st brigade to France in August 1914 then led it through the campaigns of Mons, the Marne, and the Aisne, but he only saw serious action at the Aisne (14 September). At the end of September he was sent home to command and train the 18th (eastern) division of Kitchener's second New Army, in which he was known by the nickname 'the Black Man' (Baynes, 125). Unlike some regular officers he was favourably impressed by the New Army junior officers and other ranks. He proved an outstanding trainer of troops: one officer wrote that his conferences were 'like a university course on how to make a fine fighting division' (Simkins, 306). Flexible, he showed first the textbook solution then a new and better way. Sir Hubert Gough considered Maxse's 18th division one of the best in the army. It went to France in July 1915. In April 1916 Maxse was optimistic about capturing the enemy front trenches. His division took part in the tragic first day of the Somme (1 July 1916), and was on the right of the British line, in 13th corps which profited from the heavier artillery bombardment of the neighbouring French army and the rapid advance of the experienced French infantry. Maxse's division captured its objectives. On 14 July it took part in the successful surprise dawn attack on the Bazentins and Longueval which marked an abandonment of the earlier rigid linear tactics. In September 1916 the 18th division took part in the successful attack on the strongly fortified Thiepval Ridge and captured the Schwaben redoubt, and in October Maxse's troops were involved in the battle of the Ancre. In November he considered Haig's Somme attritional strategy correct.

At the beginning of 1917 Maxse was promoted temporary lieutenant-general and given 18th corps. He took part in the Passchendaele campaign of July–November 1917 and in 1918 formed part of Gough's Fifth Army during Ludendorff's March offensive. Haig and general headquarters expected a German attack would be in the north. Fifth Army to the south had to defend the longest sector with the fewest divisions, its defences were dangerously incomplete, and it was heavily outnumbered by the attacking Germans. On 21 March Gough ordered that all corps could withdraw to the Somme if necessary. Apparently Maxse understood this as an order to withdraw, and on 22 March ordered 18th corps to withdraw. Its withdrawal left its neighbour 'in the air', resulting in a broken line and a German breakthrough; 18th corps' order, dated 22 March, was subsequently missing from the files. Maxse, after the war blamed by the official historian Sir James Edmonds, claimed the retreat was planned and step by step.

The operations of Maxse's corps had been marked by the thoroughness and excellence of his preliminary training; henceforth training, thorough, professional, and based on open-minded evaluation of the lessons of battle, was the keynote of his career. He was a member of the board of inquiry—called by Lloyd George 'an utter sham' (Lloyd George, 1339)—into the collapse of the British defence against the German counter-attack at Cambrai in November–December 1917. Maxse blamed the lower ranks and especially the wounded for spreading 'false notions' of defeat (for which he was later condemned in Lloyd George's *War Memoirs*). He also alleged the troops were inadequately trained, and he contributed a note on the needs and methods of training troops. He was among the first British commanders to accept the new German concepts of attack by infiltration and defence in greater depth. In April 1918, apparently because general headquarters wanted to remove him from his command, he was given the new appointment of inspector-general of training in France. Largely because of him the British quickly learned from the German success, and he did much to amend the rigidity of British tactics and command methods: the results were seen in the offensive battles of August–October 1918, when the British decisively defeated the Germans. Maxse had been elected FRGS (1899) for exploration on the River Sobat, upper Nile, and appointed CB (1900), CVO (1907), and KCB (1917).

From June 1919 to 1923 Maxse was general officer commanding, northern command, United Kingdom. There he had a marked but regrettably short-lived influence on post-war training, organization, and tactics. He was the first and perhaps most important patron of Captain Basil Liddell Hart, and helped launch his career as a military thinker and journalist. At Maxse's request Liddell Hart was transferred to northern command headquarters to collaborate in rewriting the *War* volume of *Infantry Training*. Despite Maxse's encouragement his innovations were much diluted by the War Office before publication. Maxse also superseded the Cardwell system by drafting direct from the depots. Shortly after the war he warned against German revanche and criticized the League of Nations, telling a York club dinner in November 1919, 'I prefer a League of Tanks to a League of Nations' (Baynes, 222).

In June 1923 Maxse was promoted full general and in 1926 he retired. He became a successful commercial fruit grower at Little Bognor, trading as the Maxey Fruit Company. He was colonel of the Middlesex regiment from 1921 to 1932.

One of the ablest officers of his generation, a man of originality and drive, and a formidable personality, Maxse was described by Liddell Hart as

> short and dark, with a sallow complexion, small deep-set eyes, and a long drooping moustache, which gave him the look of a Tartar chief—all the more because the descriptive term 'a Tartar' so aptly fitted his manner in dealing with lazy or inefficient seniors and subordinates. … Maxse seized the salient points of any idea with lightning quickness, although occasionally misjudging some point because of too hasty

examination. His fierce manner concealed a very warm heart, and he particularly liked people who showed that they were not afraid of him. He was always ready to encourage and make use of new ideas. (Liddell Hart, 43)

In 1956 Maxse suffered a stroke which ended his active life, and was moved to a nursing home—Pendean, West Lavington, Sussex—where he remained until he died there on 28 January 1958; he was buried at Fittleworth, Sussex, on 3 February.

CORELLI BARNETT, rev. ROGER T. STEARN

Sources J. A. Hutcheson, *Leopold Maxse and the National Review, 1893–1914: right-wing politics and journalism in the Edwardian era* (1989) · J. Baynes, *Far from a donkey: the life of General Sir Ivor Maxse, KCB, CVO, DSO* (1995) · IWM, Maxse papers · J. Gore, *Mary Maxse (1870–1944)* (1946) · B. H. Liddell Hart, *The memoirs of Captain Liddell Hart*, 1 (1965) · H. Gough, *The Fifth Army* (1931) · *The Times* (29 Jan 1958) · *The Times* (5 Feb 1958) · *The Times* (14 Feb 1958) · *WWW* · Burke, *Peerage* (1931) · *Debrett's Peerage* (1924) · T. Travers, *The killing ground* (1990) · P. Simkins, *Kitchener's army: the raising of the new armies, 1914–16* (1988) · B. Bond, *Liddell Hart: a study of his military thought* (1977) · I. F. W. Beckett and K. Simpson, eds., *A nation in arms: a social study of the British army in the First World War* (1985); repr. (1990) · T. Wilson, *The myriad faces of war: Britain and the Great War, 1914–1918* (1986); repr. (1988) · A. T. Mitchell, ed., *Rugby School register*, 3: *From May 1874 to May 1904* (1904) · *Hart's Army List* (1913) · D. Lloyd George, *War memoirs*, 2 (1938) · F. I. Maxse, *Seymour Vandeleur: the story of a British officer* (1905) · CGPLA Eng. & Wales (1958)

Archives Bodl. Oxf., family corresp. · CKS, family corresp. · IWM, official and private papers · W. Sussex RO, corresp., diaries, and papers | U. Leeds, Brotherton L., letters to Lilias, Countess Bathurst

Likenesses F. Dodd, charcoal and watercolour drawing, 1917, IWM · W. Stoneman, photograph, 1919, NPG · G. C. Beresford, photograph, c.1921, NPG [*see illus.*] · O. Birley, portrait, repro. in Hart, *Memoirs of Captain Liddell Hart*, facing p. 82

Wealth at death £12,238 19s.: probate, 28 Feb 1958, CGPLA Eng. & Wales

Maxse, Leopold James (1864–1932), journalist and political activist, was born on 11 November 1864 in London, the second child and younger son of Admiral Frederick Augustus *Maxse (1833–1900) and his wife, Cecilia (d. 1918), daughter of Colonel James Steel, who came from a family of Cumberland squires. He was a nephew of Sir H. B. F. Maxse. Baptized Leopold, Maxse was always known as Leo. He had an elder brother, (Frederick) Ivor *Maxse, and two sisters, Olive and Violet [*see* Milner, Violet Georgina]. Violet married Lord Edward Cecil in 1894; he died in 1918, and in 1921 she married Lord Milner. Her autobiography, *My Picture Gallery, 1886–1901* (1951), describes the traumatic effect of her parents' separation in 1877 upon the young Maxses. The children were to spend more time with their father than their mother, and were actively encouraged to read and debate world politics from an early age. Leo Maxse was educated at Harrow School and Cambridge. He studied history at King's College from 1883 to 1886, not long after J. R. Seeley delivered his famous 'Expansion of England' lectures. He was a president of the Cambridge Union.

Following university, Maxse embarked on an extended tour of India, Australia, New Zealand, Canada, and the USA. In India he stayed with his brother, Ivor, an army officer whose battalion was stationed in the Nilgiri Hills near Ootacamund, and who was later to write a series of articles on the army for Leo's *National Review*. This world tour proved to be a key period in Maxse's life. Not only did he gather a large fund of knowledge about colonial society and politics, but many important contacts were made with local journalists and politicians.

On returning to England, Maxse married, in 1890, Katharine (d. 1922), the eldest daughter of Vernon *Lushington KC; there were no children. Meanwhile serious illness stood in the way of his following a legal or parliamentary career. But in 1893 Maxse's father purchased a periodical on his son's behalf: the *National Review*. The last major journal to appear in the nineteenth century, it became Maxse's labour of love. After dispensing with the services of its previous and somewhat lacklustre editor, the soon-to-be poet laureate, Alfred Austin, Maxse set about stamping his own colourful personality on the publication.

Maxse was an incredibly energetic and committed editor, who attracted articles from many well-known personalities. Although invariably dogmatic and repetitive, at its best his own writing was lively and entertaining, and widely read by the Conservative back-benchers and the party's rank and file. Many felt the rasp of Maxse's pen. Balfour and Asquith were styled A. J. Foozle and H. H. Boozle, Lloyd George was the Welsh Walpole, and Cadbury a 'cosmopolitan crank'. Ownership of the *Review* also gave Maxse the freedom to castigate and condemn all sorts of political corruption. A 'radical plutocrats enquiry' of 1912 pilloried rich businessmen in the Liberal Party for leading lives of self-indulgence while professing to be concerned for the poor; while in 1913–14, under the slogan 'White slave traffic', Maxse berated an unscrupulous 'radical' ministry for muzzling the press by bestowing honours and titles on newspaper editors and press lords. The influence of the so-called muckraking American journalists, central to the American progressive movement, is readily apparent here. Strictly speaking, Maxse was not part of the 'new journalism' in Britain, but none the less had a shrewd appreciation of the value of scandal and sensation in recruiting and retaining readers. Indeed, Maxse's main achievement in life was probably to transform what had previously been a rather lifeless publication into a vibrant and influential organ of Conservative opinion.

Yet while Maxse liked to think of himself as the spokesman of the party faithful, many have since fastened upon his more eccentric and wayward views: most famously, on Maxse's Germanophobia. He became convinced of the menace of German aggression from an early age; the Kruger telegram of 1896, in which the Kaiser congratulated the Boers for defeating the Jameson raid, was a particularly important event. Fear of Germany's economic and military strength developed into an unhealthy obsession with conspiracy theories. A keen spy-hunter, on one occasion he is even said to have advised a close friend to dispense with the services of his German nanny, whose lengthy bicycle rides in the English countryside were enough to convince Maxse that she was a secret agent. Maxse's hot-headedness also manifested itself in a deeply rooted suspicion of authority, particularly figures of authority within his own party. He repeatedly railed against the organizational inefficiencies and lack of imagination of the Conservative central office, and was a prominent member of that thorn in its side, the Tariff Reform League. Yet even in moments of great extremity, Maxse's prose was usually tempered by a healthy dose of irreverence and humour. Moreover, his core political beliefs were far from being as idiosyncratic as his critics would have us believe.

Maxse's imperialism put him in the political mainstream. Coached for Cambridge by an Australian tutor, Bernhard Wise, from an early age in life he was deeply impressed by the rapid development of the English-speaking parts of the empire, and convinced that in them lay the key to the preservation of Britain's great-power status. This desire to draw the self-governing dominions into a closer working partnership with the 'mother country' led him into an uncompromising advocacy of Joseph Chamberlain's tariff reform programme, and a full frontal assault on Jacky Fisher, who was accused of playing the game of the 'Cobdenite cheeseparers' with his naval reforms. For Maxse, tariff reform was the major political issue of the Edwardian era. In providing unequivocal support for Chamberlain, he drew not only upon his own journalistic talents, but on those of other British (J. L. Garvin) and dominion (A. R. Carman) journalists too. As a critic of Fisher and a supporter of Charles Beresford in the pre-1914 debates on naval reform, Maxse joined the Imperial Maritime League, which broke away from the Navy League in 1908. He became part of that 'Syndicate of [press] Discontent' which claimed that the Royal Navy, far from being supreme at sea, was actually fast becoming a 'fraud and danger' to the empire.

The other consistent theme of Maxse's political career was his Francophilia. As a young child he had visited France frequently, and he spent a spell between school and university in Paris to perfect his French. Maxse's admiration for France and suspicion of Germany conditioned his thinking on international affairs. After 1918 he was plagued by the possibility of war with Germany, just as he had been prior to 1914. Thus in the pages of the *National Review* the League of Nations was dismissed as a waste of time and energy, and increased armaments spending was defended as a way of deterring Germany from fighting another world war. Maxse also became a fierce opponent of abandoning Britain's imperial responsibilities; he publicized persistently the cause of the so-called tory die-hards who felt that Britain must stand up to nationalist movements in Ireland, Egypt, and India rather than buy them off with constitutional concessions.

In 1917 Maxse entered daily journalism for the first time, editing anonymously an evening paper—*The Globe*—on a trial basis. As with the *National Review*, he scored a great success, nearly doubling sales within nine months, only to resign his editorship in 1921 when *The Globe* was absorbed by the *Pall Mall Gazette*. When Leo was suddenly admitted to hospital for a major operation in 1929, it was his sister Violet (now the widowed Viscountess Milner) who

stepped into the editor's chair at the *National Review*, remaining there until 1948.

Though he was identified closely with the 'radical right' of the tory party, Maxse's temperament was neither élitist nor anti-democratic. He saw the lower classes as friends rather than enemies of Britain's imperial mission. Hence he strongly supported the efforts of fellow journalist H. A. Gwynne to fund working men who could stand as Conservative candidates for parliament in the general elections of 1910. His involvement in the Tariff Reform League and kindred extra-parliamentary organizations testifies to his belief that press campaigning and grass-roots activism could shape the agendas of political leaders. Maxse died at his home, 27 Pembroke Gardens, Kensington, London, on 22 January 1932. ANDREW S. THOMPSON

Sources A. S. Thompson, *Imperial Britain: the empire and British politics, c.1880–1932* (2000) · *DNB* · J. A. Hutcheson, *Leopold Maxse and the National Review, 1893–1914: right-wing politics and journalism in the Edwardian era* (1989) · J. D. Startt, *Journalists for empire: the imperial debate in the Edwardian stately press, 1903–1913* (1991) · D. Griffiths, ed., *The encyclopedia of the British press, 1422–1992* (1992) · J. Baynes, *Far from a donkey: the life of General Sir Ivor Maxse* (1995) · G. R. Searle, *Corruption in British politics, 1895–1930* (1987) · A. J. A. Morris, *The scaremongers: the advocacy of war and rearmament, 1896–1914* (1984)

Archives Bodl. Oxf., corresp. and papers · CKS, corresp. and MSS · W. Sussex RO, corresp. and papers | BL, corresp. with Lord Northcliffe, Add. MS 62175 · CAC Cam., letters to Henry Page Croft · CUL, letters to E. H. Blakeney · CUL, letters to Lord Harding · HLRO, letters to Blumenfeld · HLRO, corresp. with Andrew Bonar Law · HLRO, corresp. with John St Loe Strachey · IWM, corresp. with H. A. Gwynne · NL Aus., corresp. with Alfred Deakin · U. Leeds, Brotherton L., letters to Lilias, Countess Bathurst

Wealth at death £16,473 4s. 9d.—probate: 24 May 1932, *CGPLA Eng. & Wales*

Maxse, Dame (Sarah Algeria) Marjorie (1891–1975), political organizer, was born on 26 October 1891 at Villa du Palmier, Birmandreis, Algiers, one of the two children, and the only daughter, of Ernest George Berkeley Maxse (1863–1943), British vice-consul at Algiers, and his wife, Sarah Alice, *née* Miller (d. 1908). Marjorie Maxse was a cousin of Leo Maxse, for many years editor of the *National Review*, and of Sir (Frederick) Ivor Maxse, a distinguished First World War general. Her father's work for the consular service meant that she spent the first twenty-five years of her life abroad, and she acquired an understanding of foreign countries and the aspirations of other peoples that proved of value in later life. During the First World War she served for a time as an auxiliary nurse in a French military hospital. She was appointed MBE in 1918.

Maxse was a natural leader who combined powers of self-control and reserve with clear vision and a single-minded determination to achieve her goals. Her freedom from personal animus was an especially valuable attribute in the world of politics, where she made her career. In 1921 she was chosen as one of the first women area agents appointed by Conservative central office. The 1918 Representation of the People Act meant that urgent attention had to be given to organizing women voters, and the Conservative Party was in many respects in the forefront of this development. In 1923 Maxse was promoted to be the first administrator of the Women's Unionist Organization

(WUO) based at the party headquarters in London. The WUO was a highly successful political organization, whose purpose was, she told party agents in 1924, 'to teach women to be voters and Conservative voters, not to create a feminist movement within the Conservative party' (McCrillis, 62). Along with Caroline Bridgeman and Gwendolen Guinness she was one of the WUO's chief promoters. Under John Colin Campbell Davidson, Conservative Party chairman 1926–30, she became in 1928 deputy principal agent of the party. As a member of the governing body of the Junior Imperial League she helped to organize the canvassing of recently enfranchised young women voters, and dismissed the suggestion that the 'flapper vote' had played a part in the Conservatives' defeat at the general election of 1929 (ibid., 190, 216). In 1931 she was appointed chief organization officer, the first woman to occupy such a role in any political party. She held this post until 1939. Maxse was thus one of the 'principal architects' in the development of women's organization in the Conservative Party (The Times, 6 May 1975).

Women Conservatives were important for fund-raising and canvassing, and Maxse aimed as far as possible to maximize their influence in the party. She believed that men mostly did not wish to give them organizational responsibility, or indeed any 'legitimate sphere for their aspiration', and so she favoured developing separate women's branches at the constituency level (Maguire, 75). By retaining a separate organization women stood a greater chance to gain recognition of their role, as well as retain a degree of autonomy. She appreciated that this could also lead to their being marginalized, but on balance she felt that the policy brought about real advances.

Maxse also understood that a united party organization would ultimately develop, and to this end did her best to harmonize relations between the sexes. There were inevitably tensions. When Davidson took office as party chairman he perceived 'a distinct antagonism running right through the organization in the country between the men and the women', which he feared would seriously undermine party unity (Maguire, 79). An obvious area of disagreement lay between party agents and women organizers at the constituency level. The latter, who were paid officials employed by the local associations, convened committee meetings, formed branches, and taught basic political organization to interested women activists. In some places they virtually did the work of party agents, but for less money. The national society of Conservative agents, though, would not countenance admitting them to membership. While advising the women workers not to seek to usurp the position of men, Maxse sought for them greater parity with the party agents. Davidson supported her in mediating the ongoing disputes, and with powerful backing at central office she overcame much of the resentment. Davidson regarded her appointment as deputy principal agent as 'a bold undertaking', but one that he considered to have been vindicated by the growing co-operation between men and women in the party (Rhodes James, 338–9).

In 1940 Maxse was appointed director of the Children's Overseas Reception Board. In the same year she became, with Lady Iris Capell and Mary Agnes Hamilton, one of the three vice-chairs of the Women's Voluntary Services for Civil Defence (WVS), in succession to Priscilla Norman (Mrs Montagu Norman). In principle a non-political organization, the WVS had a Conservative bias, and both Maxse and her successor, Lady Hillingdon, 'played a major role' in its daily running, in contrast to their Labour colleagues, Mary Agnes Hamilton and Dorothy Archibald (Hinton, 291).

Maxse relinquished her offices at the Children's Overseas Reception Board and the WVS in 1944, when she accepted an invitation to become vice-chair of the Conservative Party Organization. The general election defeat in 1945 forced the Conservative Party to look hard at its constituency organization, and under Lord Woolton, chairman of central office, the old structure of separate men's and women's branches was abolished. There were still women's sections in the constituencies, co-ordinated by women's advisory committees, whose task it was to advance the interests of women in the party. But Woolton was determined to unify the party structure, and he valued very highly Maxse's experience of the party machine. She served as his adviser on all women's work.

The decline of Conservative Party organization in the constituencies by 1945 was seen by Maxse as a possible opportunity for the advancement of women, and yet the introduction of joint branches seemed to frustrate this hope. By being grouped with the men, women party workers lost the autonomy they had previously enjoyed without any real compensatory increase in their power or influence. As a party vice-chair Maxse was determined that the joint organization should not become the cause 'of a falling-off on the women's side, for a falling-off had undoubtedly taken place' (Maguire, 141). She feared that the party might lag behind Labour and the Liberals 'in the formulation of policy of special interest to women' (ibid., 154). At the party conference in 1945 a resolution affirming equal opportunities, 'in order to ensure that the best mind or hand shall have the same chance to excel', was rejected (Smith, 74). Conservative women badly needed encouragement, and Maxse supported the formation of a parliamentary subcommittee in November 1946 designed to forge closer links between the parliamentary party and the Conservative women's national advisory council. She would not be deflected from her belief that the best way of advancing the cause of women generally was through Conservative electoral success; thus she adamantly opposed any Conservative involvement in the Housewives' League, which she feared would detract from the party's efforts. Her policy of detachment proved sensible, for the league soon degenerated into reactionary politics before self-destructing.

In 1948 Maxse was a member of the party committee set up by Rab Butler to frame a 'women's charter': Lady Tweedsmuir and Evelyn Emmet were also members. The committee's brief was to examine all aspects of women in society, and it attacked the discrimination experienced at many levels. It also called for equal pay in at least some sectors of the economy. The committee's endeavours were warmly supported at the annual conference in 1948, though its charter was rejected: delegates preferred that the issues dealt with should be included in statements of general policy, rather than be treated as issues specific to women. But the charter did see light of day as a party document, *A True Balance*, published in March 1949 and enthusiastically endorsed at that year's women's conference.

In 1952, shortly after her retirement in 1951, Maxse was appointed DBE. She remained active in the work of the United Nations Association and also on behalf of the Anglican church in the diocese of Chichester. She died, unmarried, on 3 May 1975 at St George's Retreat, Ditchling, Sussex.   MARK POTTLE

Sources *The Times* (12 Feb 1941) · *The Times* (14 Nov 1944) · *The Times* (6 May 1975) · G. E. Maguire, *Conservative women: a history of women and the conservative party, 1874–1997* (1998) · N. McCrillis, *The British conservative party in the age of universal suffrage: popular conservatism, 1918–1929* (1998) · *Memoirs of a Conservative: J. C. C. Davidson's memoirs and papers, 1910–37*, ed. R. R. James (1969) · *WWW* · b. cert. · d. cert. · Lord Woolton, *The memoirs of the Rt. Hon. the earl of Woolton* (1959) · J. Hinton, 'Voluntarism and the welfare warfare state: Women's Voluntary Services in the 1940s', *Twentieth-Century British History*, 9/2 (1998) · H. L. Smith, *Britain in the Second World War* (1996) · J. Ramsden, *The age of Churchill and Eden, 1940–1957* (1995) · *CGPLA Eng. & Wales* (1975)

Likenesses group photograph, 1938, Hult. Arch. · photograph, repro. in *The Times* (6 May 1975), 16

Wealth at death £94,075: probate, 4 Aug 1975, *CGPLA Eng. & Wales*

Maxse, Violet Georgina. *See* Milner, Violet Georgina, Viscountess Milner (1872–1958).

Maxton, James [Jimmy] (1885–1946), politician, was born on 22 June 1885 at Pollokshaws, near Glasgow, the second of the five children of James Maxton (1843–1902) and his wife, Melvina Purdon, who were both schoolteachers. The family was middle class and respectable, presbyterian in religion and Liberal Unionist in politics. When Jimmy, as he came to be universally known, was five years old his father became headmaster of a school in nearby Barrhead. The family duly moved there and the young Maxton received his elementary education under his father (1890–97). He completed his schooling at the prestigious Hutcheson's Grammar School in Glasgow (1897–1900), to which he won a scholarship, and then trained to be a schoolteacher. Before graduating from Glasgow University in 1909, Maxton had already acquired teaching experience in Glasgow schools which was to prove formative.

Appalled by the poverty of many of his pupils, Maxton sloughed off the Conservative political leanings he had absorbed at home and adopted an outlook of social radicalism. He became a member of the Independent Labour Party (ILP) in 1904, immersed himself in the evangelical socialist culture of the time, and cultivated the powers of oratory which were largely to determine his political reputation in the years to come. His striking physical appearance, with his long mane of black hair and his tall spindly frame, and his humorous and passionate rapport with audiences distinguished him among the platform

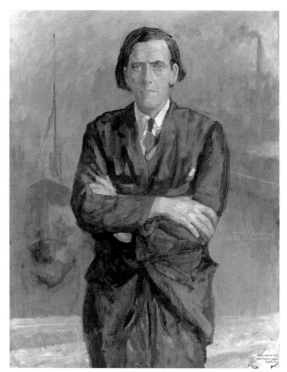

James Maxton (1885–1946), by Sir John Lavery, c.1933

troupers of his day. Although an admirer, and in educational matters a colleague, of the revolutionary socialist John Maclean, also from Pollokshaws, Maxton's socialism was at this stage decidedly reformist in character and little influenced by Marxist theory. He was elected to the national administrative council of the ILP in 1912, and from 1913 to 1919 served as chairman of the Scottish ILP.

The First World War made Maxton a public figure well beyond his native land. He opposed the war from the start, setting his face against jingoism and sacrificing his teaching post. In 1916 a speech on Glasgow Green in protest against the deportation of leading Clydeside shop stewards brought a conviction for sedition and a prison sentence. On his release in February 1917 he still refused to do war work. Perhaps more than any other labour leader or socialist agitator, Maxton seemed to personify the spirit of 'Red Clydeside' during the war, when industrial struggles and rent strikes proliferated.

Maxton stood unsuccessfully as ILP candidate for the Glasgow constituency of Bridgeton at the 1918 general election, but found paid employment soon after as an organizer with the ILP. He was also elected a member of the Glasgow Educational Authority, which allowed him to continue to pursue his social reform agenda. On 24 July 1919 he married Sarah (Sissie) McCallum, a teacher, daughter of John McCallum, a master wright; a son, James, was born in 1921. However, the boy suffered an illness requiring such attention from his mother that her own health deteriorated. Sissie died in 1922, a shock from which Maxton probably never truly recovered. In the immediate aftermath he flung himself into political work and was rewarded with decisive victory in Bridgeton at the 1922 general election. This election was Scottish Labour's coming of age; ten out of fifteen Glasgow seats were won, along with others in surrounding areas, and the send-off given to Maxton and the other Westminster-bound MPs at St Enoch's Station in Glasgow entered Scottish socialist folklore.

These Scottish MPs resolved to shake up parliament, and Maxton was certainly as good as his word. In 1923 he labelled as 'murderers' Conservative members who supported a government motion to cut health grants to local authorities. This resulted in suspension from the House of Commons, although it was not long before Maxton's warmth of personality won the affection of political foes as well as friends. Among them, Winston Churchill became a particular admirer and John Buchan something of a crony. It may even be conjectured that Maxton's emergence as a House of Commons 'character' was to limit the impact of his socialist message.

Maxton's relationship with the Parliamentary Labour Party, led by Ramsay MacDonald, was an uneasy one from the beginning. Maxton's political mentor was fellow Scot John Wheatley, with whom in the 1920s he pursued the goal of taking the Labour Party in a more left-wing and less gradualist direction. The vehicle of his campaign was the ILP, which had always claimed his first loyalty, and he became its national (British) chairman in 1926. The ILP programme of that year, 'Socialism in our time', much influenced by the underconsumptionist economics of J. A. Hobson, provided the ideological basis for Maxton's eloquent assaults on unemployment and poverty.

In 1928 the gulf between Maxton and the moderate labour leadership widened with the publication of the 'Cook–Maxton manifesto', a declaration of class war on the part of Maxton and the miners' leader A. J. Cook, and a repudiation of the idea of class collaboration as exemplified in the Mond–Turner talks of the previous year. This episode, however, also created divisions within the ILP, with Maxton being accused of undemocratic behaviour in not consulting the party executive.

During the minority Labour government's tenure of office in 1929–31 Maxton was one of its fiercest critics, and his behaviour raised questions about the relationship between the Labour Party and the ILP. These came to a head after the fall of the government. In 1932 the ILP and Maxton opted for disaffiliation, following Labour Party demands that its standing orders be adhered to. Most historians, in the light of the ILP's subsequent decline, have viewed this as a major error of judgement. On the other hand, some left-wing commentators, including Maxton's most recent biographer, have regarded it as principled opposition to gradualism, and there seems little doubt that the idea of the ILP as a propagandist 'ginger' group, useful for keeping the Labour Party alert to its values and aims, had lost validity by the time of disaffiliation.

Maxton was left to inherit the margins of political life in Britain, although his command of his Bridgeton constituency never weakened. On 14 March 1935 he married again, his second wife being Madeline Grace Glasier, his

researcher, and the daughter of George Henry Brougham Glasier, estate agent. He turned his sights increasingly to international questions in the 1930s and expounded a clear pacifist line which only deviated over his proclaimed willingness to fight for the republicans in the Spanish Civil War. When world war finally came in 1939 he opposed it. Failing health reduced steadily the impact of his interventions, and he died of cancer at Largs, Ayrshire, on 23 July 1946. He was buried at Glasgow crematorium three days later. Maxton was one of the most charismatic figures in twentieth-century British public life. He was essentially a Scottish radical whose propagandist skills for the wider British labour movement have earned him folk hero status in socialist circles.   GRAHAM WALKER

Sources G. Brown, *Maxton* (1986) • W. Knox, *James Maxton* (1987) • W. Knox, 'Maxton, James', *Scottish labour leaders, 1918–39: a biographical dictionary*, ed. W. Knox (1984) • *The Scottish socialists* (1931) • G. McAllister, *James Maxton: the portrait of a rebel* (1935) • A. McKinlay and R. J. Morris, eds., *The ILP on Clydeside, 1893–1932* (1991) • I. McLean, *The legend of red Clydeside* (1983) • J. McNair, *James Maxton, the beloved rebel* (1955) • *DNB*
Archives Mitchell L., Glas., Glasgow City Archives, personal and family corresp. and papers | BLPES, corresp. relating to the independent labour party • King's Lond., Liddell Hart C., corresp. with Sir B. H. Liddell Hart | FILM BFI NFTVA, documentary footage • BFI NFTVA, news footage | SOUND IWM SA, oral history interview
Likenesses E. Kapp, drawing, 1930, Barber Institute of Fine Arts, Birmingham • K. Kennet, bronze bust, c.1930, Art Gallery and Museum, Glasgow • H. Lavery, oils, c.1933, NPG • J. Lavery, portrait, c.1933, Scot. NPG [*see illus.*] • D. Low, pencil sketches, c.1933, NPG • E. Levy, charcoal drawing, 1936, NPG • Associated Scottish Newspapers, photograph, c.1938, NPG • B. Schotz, bronze bust, 1938, Art Gallery and Museum, Glasgow
Wealth at death £1062 2s. 7d.: confirmation, 13 Nov 1946, *CCI*

Maxwell, Sir Alexander (1880–1963), civil servant, was born at Sharston Mount, Northern Etchells, Cheshire, on 9 March 1880, the eldest son of the Revd Joseph Matthew Townsend Maxwell, a Congregational minister, and his wife, Louisa Maria Brely Snell. Educated at Plymouth College, he went up to Christ Church, Oxford, where he obtained first classes in honour moderations (1901) and *literae humaniores* (1903) and gained the Matthew Arnold (1904) and the chancellor's English essay (1905) prizes. In 1904 he entered the Home Office, where he was private secretary to successive secretaries of state. He was made an assistant secretary in 1924. In 1917 Maxwell had been acting chief inspector of reformatory and industrial schools. Brief though his tenure was, it was probably then that he became interested in delinquency, an introduction which served him in good stead in 1928 when he became chairman of the Prison Commission. There he and Alexander Paterson worked in close partnership. The first open borstal was started in 1930 at Lowdham Grange in Nottinghamshire: the idea was Paterson's but the administrative form and substance were Maxwell's.

In 1932 Maxwell became deputy under-secretary of state at the Home Office and in 1938, when Samuel Hoare was home secretary, Maxwell was promoted permanent under-secretary, a post he held for the next ten years, during which he became, by common consent, the doyen of his fellows. In this significant office, in war and in peace, Maxwell's qualities were seen at their best. Upon the Home Office rests the duty not only of maintaining law and order but also of safeguarding the liberty of the subject. That the man and the duty were in Maxwell fitly joined his political chiefs have testified. Templewood recorded that

Alexander Maxwell in particular helped me with wise and stimulating advice. How lucky I was to have him! … Unruffled amidst all the alarms and excursions that periodically shake a Ministry of public order, he possessed the imperturbable assurance essential to a department of historic traditions. (Templewood, 229)

After Maxwell had retired, J. Chuter-Ede, taking the chair for Maxwell's Clarke Hall lecture in 1949, said that

Whether he was dealing at the Home Office with broad questions of policy or with particular cases he never forgot that the decisions reached would affect, not some undifferentiated mass of humanity, but individual lives, every one of which had its peculiar problems and potentialities.

The imprisonment of enemy aliens, the treatment of those detained under the 18B regulations, and the particular case of the Mosleys illustrate both the explosive questions of policy and particular cases with which Maxwell was called upon to deal. Many aliens had been deported to Canada. It was clearly on his advice that the government in 1940 sent out Paterson to sift from the rest those whose sympathies were genuinely with this country. In offering advice, Maxwell always knew when to press his point and when not. He had the appearance and in some ways the temperament of a don, but he was at the same time a great administrator, firm and just in disciplinary matters and generous in praise. His supreme administrative gift was founded on his sheer intellectual power and capacity for work—he was usually first in the office and last out. He was able to illuminate problems, and propound solutions which were seen to be the obvious course, but which had not been apparent to his subordinates, though they were far from stupid, until he showed them the way. He was able, moreover, to set forth the principles of a subject in felicitous prose, perhaps best demonstrated in a note on the home secretary's duty to advise the sovereign on the exercise of the prerogative of mercy, after a judge had expressed a contrary view: the judge subsequently acknowledged his error.

Withal, Maxwell had a nice sense of humour and was among the most humble and gentle of men. When speaking once of deterrence he said, 'most of us, when we travel by train, intend to buy a ticket; it is just the presence of the ticket collector at the barrier which clinches the matter'. If one rang him at home, where his doctor wife practised, he would always answer, 'Dr Maxwell's telephone', perhaps a typical blend of modesty and wisdom.

On 19 August 1919 Maxwell had married, at the Friends' meeting-house at Jordans, Buckinghamshire, Dr Jessie McNaughten Campbell, daughter of the Revd John Campbell, of Kirkcaldy; they had two sons. It was so like Maxwell that he and his wife, with their two sons as waiters, should give annual parties at Toynbee Hall for the Home Office charladies, all of whom, it was said, he knew by their first names. Maxwell was appointed CB in 1924, KBE in 1936, KCB in 1939, and GCB in 1945. A valuable committee man, he presided in 1936 over the inquiry into the work of Metropolitan Police courts and in 1949 he was a member of the royal commission on capital punishment. From 1948 to 1950 he was a governor of Bedford College. He died on 1 July 1963 at his home, Chasemores, Coldharbour, near Dorking, Surrey. His wife survived him.

DUNCAN FAIRN, *rev.*

Sources *The Times* (2 July 1963) · Viscount Templewood, *Nine troubled years* (1954) · personal knowledge (1981) · private information (1981) · b. cert. · *CGPLA Eng. & Wales* (1963)
Wealth at death £5208 12s. 1d.: probate, 8 Aug 1963, *CGPLA Eng. & Wales*

Maxwell, Sir Arthur (1875–1935), banker and army officer, was born in Belfast, the son of William Maxwell. He was educated in Dublin and entered the civil service in 1893, and then transferred to the Post Office. In 1901 he married Eva, younger daughter of R. W. Jones of Belfast. In 1905 he took the unusual step of becoming joint secretary of the private bankers Glyn Mills & Co., who rarely recruited to senior positions from outside. This move may well have been prompted by the bank's use of numerical calculating machinery for cheque clearing (and in its expanding corporate registrar's business), equipment with which Maxwell would have been familiar at the Post Office.

Like many of his colleagues in the bank, Maxwell was a territorial soldier, and when war was declared in 1914 he went to France with the 8th London regiment. He was soon promoted lieutenant-colonel commanding the 8th and 23rd regiments. He was awarded the DSO in 1916 for his part in an action in which he was severely wounded. On his return to the front he was later promoted to be general officer commanding the 174th infantry brigade with the rank of brigadier-general. He served throughout the war in the trenches on the western front, being mentioned in dispatches five times, and winning a bar to his DSO in 1918; he was created CMG in 1919. He commanded the 2nd London infantry brigade, TA, from 1920 to 1924 and was honorary colonel of the 7th London regiment, the Post Office Rifles, from 1923 until his death.

When Maxwell returned to Glyn Mills, the most able of the new generation of partners had been killed, notably Charles Mills MP in 1915. General Sir Herbert Lawrence became a managing partner in 1919 and looked to Maxwell, who was appointed general manager, to help him pilot the bank through the turbulent financial world of the early 1920s. Lawrence, who was related by marriage to the bank's owning families, provided the reassurance that was vital to the success of mergers with other long-established private banks. In 1923 Glyn Mills amalgamated with Holts, a West End bank, which acted principally as army agent. Maxwell became a managing partner in the enlarged business. Within a year he was negotiating with the executors of the earl of Jersey for the acquisition of Child's, one of the oldest private banks in the City. The two banks amalgamated in March 1924 and for the rest of his career Maxwell had to manage a large unwieldy partnership.

As well as private clients Glyn Mills also had commercial customers, including the armaments manufacturer Vickers and the Oceanic Steam Navigation Co., owners of the White Star Line. When Vickers's capital was reduced in 1926 and the management reorganized, Lawrence was appointed chairman of the company. He immediately became deeply involved in all the problems of the armaments industry of the inter-war years, leaving Glyn Mills very much in Maxwell's hands. During 1926 Maxwell was himself plunged into the complex negotiations that eventually resulted in the sale of Oceanic Steam Navigation Co. to Lord Kylsant's Royal Mail group. When it became clear in the early summer of 1930 that the group was in serious financial difficulties, Maxwell was a natural choice to join Frederick Hyde and Sir William McLintock as a member of the committee of inquiry and a voting trustee with complete authority over the enormous enterprise. Maxwell's formidable task was to maintain close communications with leading figures in the City, including Montagu Norman, the governor of the Bank of England, informing them at every stage of the delicate negotiations to resolve the country's largest single corporate exposure. As Maxwell well knew, success was vital, as failure would have placed in jeopardy not just thousands of jobs but several financial institutions. For the next five years most of his time was taken up with Royal Mail and he was knighted in 1931 for his services.

After the first phase of the rescue was completed in 1933, Maxwell and McLintock joined the boards of nearly all the leading companies in the group—Royal Mail itself, Elder Dempster, Oceanic Steam Navigation Co., Coast Lines, Shaw Savill, and many others. Helped and encouraged by Norman they were charged with realizing the group's assets on behalf of the creditors. This was a hugely complicated undertaking, which at any moment could have been jeopardized by the hasty action of any one of the very large number of small creditors, many of whom were unsecured. Between 1933 and 1935 a succession of schemes were drafted and tested on City opinion by Maxwell, McLintock, and Norman; this involved hundreds of meetings and the skilful handling of the press and the courts. There is no doubt that this frantic activity, coupled with the day-to-day management of what was still the largest shipping combine in the world, contributed to Maxwell's sudden death on 20 January 1935 at 16 Cumberland Terrace, Regent's Park, London. He was survived by his wife. He was buried at St Mary's, Finchley.

As someone who had come to the City from an unusual background, Maxwell was convinced of the importance of evening classes and of professional training. He was appointed a governor of the City of London College in 1911, and he chaired the general purposes committee from 1922 and became chairman of the governors in 1934. He also served as a member of the advisory committee on commercial education of the Regent Street Polytechnic and as a member of the Board of Education's committee on examinations for part-time students, and on the London county council's advisory committee on banking education. He was president of the Institute of Bankers from 1931 to 1932. Maxwell and his wife had a daughter and a son, Arthur Terence *Maxwell (1905–1991), who became a partner in Glyn Mills and helped with the Royal Mail reconstruction; he himself had a distinguished career as a banker and industrialist.

Along with many of his contemporaries in the City, Maxwell of necessity worked discreetly behind the scenes, shunning the limelight; yet without such commitment the experience of the inter-war years would have been even more catastrophic. The financial problems they sought to resolve were so great that the simple panacea of devaluing sterling advocated by Keynes would have made little impact. MICHAEL S. MOSS

Sources E. Green and M. Moss, *A business of national importance: the Royal Mail shipping group, 1902–1937* (1982) · *Accountant's Journal*, 52 (1934–5), 877 · E. Gore Brown, *Glyn Mills and Co.* (1933), 191 · R. Fulford, *Glyn's, 1753–1953: six generations in Lombard Street* (1953) · *The Times* (22 Jan 1935) · *The Times* (23 Jan 1935) · *Shipbuilding and Shipping Record* (24 Jan 1935), 102 · *CGPLA Eng. & Wales* (1935) · private information (2004) · *WWW, 1929–40*
Archives NMM, Royal Mail Voting Trustees MSS · Royal Bank of Scotland, London, group archives
Likenesses photographs, priv. coll.
Wealth at death £58,294 18s. 7d.: probate, 28 Feb 1935, *CGPLA Eng. & Wales*

Maxwell, Arthur Terence (1905–1991), banker and company director, was born at Rosslyn, Hammers Lane, Mill Hill, near Hendon, Middlesex, on 19 January 1905, the only son, in a family of one son and one daughter, of Brigadier-General Sir Arthur *Maxwell (1875–1935), banker and company director, of Mill Hill, and his wife, Eva Jones. Educated at Rugby School and Trinity College, Oxford, where he took an MA, Maxwell travelled in Africa on a James Whitehead scholarship, and in South America, before being admitted to the bar in 1929.

Maxwell chose a career in the City, joining the long-established firm of private bankers, Glyn, Mills & Co., where his father was a managing partner. Glyn Mills's many connections, together with those that sprang from his marriage in 1935 to Beatrice Diane, daughter of Sir J. Austen *Chamberlain, MP, and his wife, Ivy, provided the tall and powerfully built young Maxwell with stepping stones for new interests. He and his wife had two daughters and a son. On his father's death in 1935, Maxwell became a director of Glyn, Mills & Co., and also succeeded him as a director of the Union Bank of Australia, one of the oldest British overseas banks, with whom the Glyn and Mills families had been associated since the 1850s.

Maxwell embarked upon a career that made a decisive contribution to British banking interests in Australia and New Zealand. He was a director of the Union Bank, and its deputy chairman and chairman in 1949 and 1950, respectively. The merger of the Union Bank and the Bank of Australasia in 1951 to form the Australia and New Zealand Bank (ANZ) signalled a revitalized British presence in Australasia after decades of declining influence. Maxwell played a key role in the creation of the new bank. It was he who was instrumental in renegotiating the terms of the merger to promote the interests of the Union Bank. He was largely responsible for the resolution of the many complex legal and operational issues still outstanding before the merger could be consummated. However, the vigour with which Maxwell pressed his own claims and those of his bank rankled the directors of the Bank of Australasia who felt that the surrender of their royal charter was more than sufficient sacrifice. In these circumstances it was not surprising that Maxwell was denied the ultimate prize of chairmanship that went to Sir Geoffrey Cokayne Gibbs (1901–1975).

As deputy chairman of ANZ Bank, now the second largest private bank in Australia, and as chairman of its standing committee, a position of *de facto* executive director, Maxwell exerted a dominant role in the new institution, overshadowing the urbane and more diplomatic Gibbs. As a frequent visitor to the Antipodes, Maxwell displayed a 'hands on' style of management. His ambitious vision of ANZ as an international bank with a significant presence in the City of London was effectively thwarted by the restrictive policies of the Australian monetary authorities in the early 1950s. Nevertheless, ANZ improved its position in its domestic markets, and spread its business into new areas such as savings banking and hire purchase. Maxwell stood down as deputy chairman in 1965. His other business interests and advancing years demanded a lessening of his commitment to the organization he had done so much to build. Maxwell sat on the board of the Australia and New Zealand Banking Group, which resulted from the merger of ANZ and the other British bank, the English, Scottish and Australian Bank, in 1969. He remained as a director until the ANZ's transfer of domicile to Australia in 1976. By that stage leadership had passed to others.

While his involvement with the Union Bank and ANZ took up much of his time, Maxwell had diverse interests. He sat on many other boards, including Vickers, and was chairman of the Powers-Samas Accounting Machines, which merged with International Computers and Tabulators to become International Computers Limited. Maxwell served in the Territorial Army of Britain from 1923 to 1935 in the 7th City of London regiment (Post Office Rifles) and in 1935 was promoted to captain in the reserve of officers. He held a number of staff posts during the war, notably that of deputy chief of military government section attached to Supreme Headquarters Allied Expeditionary Force, on the staff of General Eisenhower. His rank was that of colonel. Maxwell was also active in civic affairs, being a governor of Rugby School and the British representative on the investment committee of the International Labour Organization; he also sat on a government inquiry into rural bus services, as well as serving a number of charitable causes, including the Royal Hospital for the Incurables.

Maxwell's achievements, although considerable, never matched those of his illustrious father and father-in-law. The creation of ANZ, which remains, together with the Hongkong and Shanghai Banking Corporation, and the Standard Chartered, one of the survivors of the earlier wave of British overseas banks, is his most enduring legacy. Maxwell died at his home, Roveries Hall, Bishop's Castle, Shropshire, on 27 June 1991, after a long illness, and was buried on 2 July at Lydham parish church, Bishop's Castle. He was survived by his wife and three children.   D. T. MERRETT

Sources D. T. Merrett, *ANZ bank* (1985) · *WW* · Union Bank of Australia records · ANZ Bank records, ANZ Banking Group, Melbourne, Australia · ANZ Banking Group records, ANZ Banking Group, Melbourne, Australia · b. cert. · d. cert. · *CGPLA Eng. & Wales* (1991)
Archives ANZ Banking Group, Melbourne, Australia, archive
Likenesses photographs, ANZ Banking Group, Melbourne, Australia, archive, A. T. Maxwell file
Wealth at death £654,391 0s. 0d.: probate, 7 Aug 1991, *CGPLA Eng. & Wales*

Maxwell [*née* Brisbane], **Darcy, Lady Maxwell of Pollok** (1742/3–1810), follower of Methodism and philanthropist, was born at Brisbane in Largs, Ayrshire, the youngest daughter of Thomas Brisbane. She was educated at home and in Edinburgh. On 19 February 1760, aged seventeen, she married Sir Walter Maxwell (1732–1762) of Pollok in Nithsdale. Sir Walter died on 29 April 1762 when Lady Maxwell was nineteen, and six weeks later their only child, a son, also died. This double bereavement had a profound effect on Lady Maxwell, resulting in a religious conversion: 'I see that God requires my whole heart, and He shall have it' (Lancaster, 7). Although she took no vow, she effectively consecrated herself to a celibate life, steadfastly refusing to remarry, despite many offers. She lived in or near Edinburgh after her husband's death.

In 1764 Lady Maxwell became acquainted with John Wesley and a close lifelong friendship ensued. They corresponded regularly. When Wesley died in 1791 Lady Maxwell was delivered from grief by a quasi-visionary experience in which she 'saw' Wesley in heaven, worshipping before the throne of God. Although she had been brought up religiously in the Church of Scotland, from 1764 she worshipped in a Wesleyan chapel and joined a Methodist society. However, she still went to the Church of Scotland for holy communion—that ordinance not being generally available in Methodist chapels. In the great Calvinist–Arminian controversy among evangelicals, she sided decisively with Wesley's Arminianism. She also espoused Wesley's doctrine of 'Christian perfection', claiming in 1787 that she had herself been perfected in love. Lady Maxwell's Arminianism and perfectionism strained her working relationship with the other leading female Scottish evangelical, the Calvinist Lady Glenorchy, although their personal friendship endured unscathed.

Despite her gentry status Lady Maxwell dressed plainly and simply, and ran a fairly spartan household, in order to devote her wealth to philanthropic enterprises. In July 1770 she established a school for poor children in Edinburgh, managing its finances and superintending its activities personally. She also gave strong backing to the nascent Sunday school movement of Robert Raikes, founding two such schools in Edinburgh and one in London. Further, she financially supported a steady stream of evangelical students training for the ministry in Edinburgh University.

A contemporary pen-portrait by William Atherton, reproduced in Lancaster's biography, described Lady Maxwell as tall, slender, well-proportioned, and slightly dark in complexion, her face bold and intelligent, and her eyes piercing but sweet. Her central significance for her own day was the profound impression she made on her society—a prominent female member of the Scottish social élite whose life and personality were wholly surrendered to evangelical religion. Others found her an awe-inspiring, angelic figure. Lady Maxwell's religious experience was intense, and distinctive in its focus on the Trinity; she lived in an almost unbroken consciousness of all three persons of the godhead, Father, Son, and Holy Spirit, whom she referred to habitually as 'the Sacred Three'. Her diary and letters are a rich mine of spiritual reflections and recorded experiences. Lady Maxwell died in Edinburgh on 2 July 1810 after a long illness and was buried in the city's Greyfriars churchyard.   N. R. NEEDHAM

Sources J. Lancaster, *The life of Darcy, Lady Maxwell*, 2nd edn (1826) · R. Bourne, *A Christian sketch of Lady Maxwell*, 2nd edn (1820) · N. R. Needham, 'Maxwell, Lady Darcy', *DSCHT*

Maxwell, Gavin (1914–1969), writer and naturalist, was born on 15 July 1914 at House of Elrig, Mochrum, Wigtownshire, the youngest child of three sons and one daughter of Aymer Edward Maxwell, who died when Gavin was three months old, and his wife, Lady Mary Percy (c.1878–1965), fifth daughter of the seventh duke of Northumberland. A fragile youth of uncertain constitution, Maxwell was educated at Stowe School, and graduated in estate management at Hertford College, Oxford, in 1937, a degree he later described as 'a useless achievement'. Passionate about zoology, he collected wild geese, later given to the Wildfowl Trust, and in 1938 explored East Finnmark alone. Physically unfit for active duty, he served as an instructor with Special Operations Executive in the west highlands during the Second World War. He might have been a diplomat; he strove to be an explorer, a shark-fisherman, and, in London, a painter and a poet.

Harpoon at a Venture (1952) began Maxwell's career as a writer, describing an undercapitalized and unsuccessful Hebridean shark-fishing enterprise (1945–8) based at Soay, an island off Skye that he had bought in 1944, after his medical discharge from the army. In 1953 he went to Sicily, and wrote *God Protect Me from my Friends* (1956), the story of Salvatore Giuliano, a Sicilian separatist killed in 1950, a work which led to two successful libel actions against him by Italian politicians. He also produced *The Ten Pains of Death* (1959), and his description of the Marsh Arabs of Iraq in *A Reed Shaken by the Wind* (1957), for which he received the Heinemann award, was hailed by the *New York Times* as 'near perfect'.

Nowhere in Scotland is more evocative of a specific book than Sandaig, near Glenelg, Inverness-shire, which Maxwell disguised as Camusfeàrna in his *Ring of Bright Water* (1960). He had returned from Iraq with an otter, later acquiring another, and the personalities and habits of these two animals prompted him to write this evocative

sketch of the beauty of the sea coast, coupled with an account of a man's relationship with animals. It proved enormously popular, and was made into a film in 1968 by Jack Conffer, Maxwell being played by Bill Travers. The unforgettable title is from a poem by Kathleen Raine, with whom Maxwell had a continuing, if tempestuous, relationship. His grandfather, Sir Herbert Eustace *Maxwell, was a fine topographical writer, but Maxwell's books were more universal: he conveyed an eye for nature and a determination to live life in his own way, in elegant, readable prose, close to poetry. *The Otter's Tale* followed in 1962, but Camusfeàrna was defiled by inconsiderate visitors, and *The Rocks Remain* (1963) is a darker book. *The House of Elrig* (1965), a candid autobiography describing his calf-country, was followed by *Lords of the Atlas* (1966), about the Morocco he knew well, and two final books, *Seals of the World* (1967) and *Raven Seek thy Brother* (1968).

On 1 February 1962 Maxwell had married Lavinia Jean, elder daughter of Sir Alan Frederick Lascelles (1887–1981), but a difficult marriage was dissolved in 1964. A spare, handsome figure, above medium height, Maxwell was intellectual, had wit, charm, and a gift for self-expression, but had the mercurial temperament of a manic depressive. A bisexual, he could be gently affectionate, and several young men derived much benefit from relationships with him. Over-sanguine and extravagant in business, in other respects he was 'a reasoning pessimist, anticipating misfortune and looking upon good luck as a bonus earned against the odds' (*DNB*).

Maxwell supported the Dolci Trust, was a member of the Wildfowl Trust and the Fauna Preservation Society, and was president of the British Junior Exploration Society. He was elected a fellow of the Royal Society of Literature in 1958, and was also a fellow of the Royal Geographical Society and of the Royal Zoological Society (Scotland). In 1968 he initiated a wildlife park at Eilean Ban, Kyle of Lochalsh, but he became ill and died of cancer at the Royal Northern Infirmary, Inverness, on 7 September 1969. His ashes were buried on 18 September at Sandaig, near a memorial to Edal, his otter.

Gavin Maxwell: a Life (1993), by Douglas Botting, a long-standing member of Maxwell's entourage, deals perceptively with his relationships with Kathleen Raine and many others, including Peter Scott and another biographer, Richard Frere.   LOUIS STOTT

Sources D. Botting, *Gavin Maxwell: a life* (1993) · *DNB* · G. Maxwell, *The House of Elrig* (1965) · R. Frere, *Maxwell's ghost* (1976) · *New York Times* (9 Sept 1969) · J. Lister-Kaye, *The white island* (1972) · [J. Wakeman], ed., *World authors, 1950–70* (1975) · L. Stott, in B. D. Osborne and A. Reid, *Discovering Scottish writers* (1997) · b. cert.

Archives NL Scot., MSS, ACC10555 · U. Reading L., corresp. and literary MSS | CUL, corresp. with Sir Peter Markham Scott · NL Scot., letters to R. J. G. Payne

Likenesses P. Scott, pencil drawing, 1946

Wealth at death £8448 16s. 0d.: confirmation, 17 April 1970, NA Scot., SC 29/44/174/708–23

Maxwell, Sir George Clerk- [*formerly* George Clerk], **fourth baronet** (1715–1784), agriculturist, was born at Edinburgh in October 1715, the second son of Sir John *Clerk of Penicuik, second baronet (1676–1755), and Janet, daughter of Sir John Inglis of Cramond. He was educated at the universities of Edinburgh and Leiden. From his father he received the lands of Drumcrieff in Annandale, and through his marriage to Dorothea Clerk-Maxwell, daughter of his uncle William and his wife, Agnes Maxwell, heiress of Middlebie, Dumfriesshire, he obtained the lands of Middlebie; he also adopted his wife's surname. They had five sons and four daughters.

Clerk-Maxwell was king's remembrancer in the exchequer from 1761, a commissioner of the customs in Scotland from 1763, and a trustee for improving fisheries and manufactures in Scotland. He worked hard to promote the agricultural and commercial interests of the country. At Dumfries he set up a linen factory and he initiated a variety of projects for the mining of lead and copper in the county. In 1755 he sent two letters concerning the usual method used to treat wool to the trustees for the improvement of the fisheries and manufactures of Scotland, and these were published by the board in 1756. He was also author of a paper on shallow ploughing, published by the Philosophical Society in Edinburgh (*Essays and Observations*, 3, 1774). A clever draughtsman, he etched a variety of views of Scotland. On the death of his elder brother in 1782, he succeeded to the baronetcy and estates of Penicuik. He died on 29 January 1784, and was succeeded in the baronetcy by his eldest son, John Clerk.

T. F. HENDERSON, rev. ANNE PIMLOTT BAKER

Sources GM, 1st ser., 54 (1784), 314 • Anderson, *Scot. nat.* • *Memoirs of the life of Sir John Clerk of Penicuik*, ed. J. M. Gray, Scottish History Society, 13 (1892)
Archives NA Scot., corresp. and papers

Maxwell, Henry (1668/9–1730), politician and pamphleteer, was born in Finnebrogue, co. Down, Ireland, the son of the Revd Robert Maxwell (d. 1686?), Church of Ireland clergyman, and Jane Chichester, daughter of the Revd Robert Chichester of Belfast. His family appears to have been of Scottish descent. Educated in his early years by a Mr Harvey, he entered Trinity College, Dublin, in 1683, aged fourteen; he received the degree of BA in 1688 and that of LLD (*speciali gratia*) in 1718. He was a member of the Church of Ireland, and was married twice, first to his second cousin, Jane Maxwell, daughter of the Revd Henry Maxwell, of Armagh, and sister to John Maxwell, first Lord Farnham, and second in 1713, with a dowry of £1500, to Dorothy Brice (*bap.* 1690, d. 1725), daughter of Edward Brice, a Belfast merchant and Presbyterian of Scottish descent.

After having been successful in a by-election in 1698 Maxwell sat in every Irish parliament until his death, representing the boroughs of Bangor in co. Down (1698–1713) and Killybegs (1713–15) and Donegal (1715–30) in co. Donegal, the latter two on the interest of William Conolly, of whom he was a close adherent. Identified as a whig, Maxwell was an active participant in Anglo-Irish politics and has been associated with the reforming group of 'real Whigs' (Robbins, 6) centred around Robert Molesworth. However, Maxwell disagreed with this group in certain areas, most notably in his strong opposition to the repeal of the test imposed on protestant dissenters in Ireland. He was also associated with William Molyneux, a connection that was reflected in his writings. The first pamphlet attributed to Maxwell, *Anguis in herba, or, The Fatal Consequences of a Treaty with France* (1702), was originally published 'a little before the death of the late King William, and about the time the second Grand Alliance was formed' (*Anguis in herba*, 2). It was published for a third time in 1711, probably as part of the whig opposition to the peace negotiations in the last years of the War of the Spanish Succession. In 1703 he produced his most famous work, published the following year, *An essay upon an union of Ireland with England: most humbly offered to the consideration of the queen's most excellent majesty, and both houses of parliament* (1704), in which, motivated by discontent over the subordination of the Irish parliament to that of England, he argued that a union was the only practical solution to ongoing constitutional conflicts, as it would create greater political harmony between the two kingdoms and would be of mutual commercial and economic benefit. He also argued for a more comprehensive union than the type of union espoused by Molyneux or the Molesworth group. However, despite Irish public and parliamentary opinion becoming increasingly in favour of a union, his pamphlet made no impact in England. His continuing concern with English interference in Irish affairs under the existing constitutional relationship led to his expression of dissatisfaction with the appointment of an Englishman to the bishopric of Meath in 1715 and his association with the opposition to the Declaratory Act of 1720.

Maxwell's next excursion into political pamphleteering occurred in 1721 as part of the disputes over the establishment of a Bank of Ireland, which saw the outbreak of a pamphlet war in the autumn and winter of that year. Although many of the contributions were 'hastily written trifles' (Burns, 1.128), Maxwell's two tracts of November and December stood out as the best arguments put forward for a national bank. His first pamphlet, *Reasons Offered for Erecting a Bank in Ireland, in a Letter to H[ercules] Rowley, Esq.* (1721), which quickly went through two editions, argued for a bank on economic grounds, emphasizing how a bank would stabilize interest rates and increase the amount of currency available for trade. He also tried to assuage the fears of the landed interest that a bank would lead to a land tax and ultimately undermine the accepted land-based structure of society. His arguments prompted a response from Rowley, who appears to have been Maxwell's uncle, in opposition to a bank. Maxwell replied in *Mr Maxwell's Second Letter to Mr Rowley, wherein the Objections Against the Bank are Answered* (1721), although his arguments failed to convince his fellow MPs, and the proposals were dropped. Maxwell avoided public office for most of his political career until 1727, when he was sworn of the Irish privy council.

Maxwell died in Dublin on 12 February 1730. His father-in-law, Edward Brice, as next of kin to Maxwell's three children, Robert, Edward, and Margaret, became their guardian and the administrator of the family estate, since Maxwell had died intestate and all three children were still in their minority. Maxwell was buried in St Mary's Church in Dublin.   C. I. McGRATH

Sources Crosslé genealogical abstracts, NA Ire., 2/434/40, Maxwell envelope · *The Hamilton manuscripts, containing some account of the settlement of the territories of the upper Clandeboye, Great Ardes, and Dufferin, in the co. of Down*, ed. T. K. Lowry (1867) · C. Robbins, *The eighteenth-century commonwealthman* (1968) · J. Agnew, *Belfast merchant families in the seventeenth century* (1996) · R. E. Burns, *Irish parliamentary politics in the eighteenth century*, 2 vols. (1989–90) · J. Kelly, 'The origins of the Act of Union: an examination of unionist opinion in Britain and Ireland, 1680–1800', *Irish Historical Studies*, 25 (1986–7), 236–63 · J. B. Leslie, ed., *Clergy of Connor: from Patrician times to the present day* (1993) · M. Rider, 'The Bank of Ireland, 1721: land, credit and dependency', *HJ*, 25 (1982), 557–82 · *The journals of the House of Commons of the kingdom of Ireland*, 2–4 (1753) · S. Smyth, 'Anglo-Irish unionist discourse, c.1656–1707: from Harington to Fletcher', *Bullán: An Irish Studies Journal*, 2 (1995), 17–34 · J. C. Beckett, *Protestant dissent in Ireland, 1687–1780* (1946) · Burtchaell & Sadleir, *Alum. Dubl.* · D. W. Hayton, 'A debate in the Irish House of Commons in 1703: a whiff of tory grapeshot', *Parliamentary History*, 10 (1991), 151–63 · D. W. Hayton, 'Exclusion, conformity, and parliamentary representation: the impact of the sacramental test on Irish dissenting politics', *The politics of Irish dissent, 1650–1800*, ed. K. Herlihy (1997), 52–73 · *IGI*

Maxwell, Herbert, **first Lord Maxwell** (c.1390–1453), courtier and landowner, was the eldest son of Sir Herbert Maxwell of Caerlaverock and his wife, Katherine, daughter of John Stewart of Dalswinton. The younger Herbert succeeded his father in 1420 and was knighted at the coronation of James I in 1424. His main estate was Caerlaverock in Dumfriesshire, and he may have carried on significant building work on the castle there; he also owned lands in Roxburghshire, Haddingtonshire, Perthshire, Lanarkshire, and Renfrewshire (where in 1450 he had royal licence to build a castle at Mearns). The extent of his possessions made him one of the leading Scottish barons in the 1420s and 1430s, and about July 1445, along with several other similarly prominent nobles, he assumed a peerage title, as first Lord Maxwell. At this time he was an adherent of the Black Douglases, as indeed he had probably been throughout his formative years—his father was steward of Annandale to the fourth earl of Douglas—but when the tide turned against the Douglases after the killing of the eighth earl by James II in 1452, Maxwell appears to have been loyal to his monarch rather than to his patron. He died in late 1453, however, before the final manoeuvres by the crown against the Douglases. He is said to have married first a daughter of Sir Herbert Herries of Terregles; they had (probably) three sons and a daughter. He and his second wife, Katherine (c.1410–1468x78), daughter of Sir William Seton and widow of Sir Alan Stewart of Darnley, had five sons and two daughters.

The eldest son of Maxwell's first marriage, **Robert Maxwell** (c.1410–1485), succeeded his father as second Lord Maxwell in 1454. He made a bond of friendship to the Boyds which may have led him to support their removal of the young James III from Linlithgow to Edinburgh in July 1466. While they were pardoned, the action led to their fall in 1469; Maxwell may have escaped direct censure, although (like his father) he was seldom at court but occasionally attended parliament. He yielded the office of steward of Annandale, for which an annual fee was paid by the crown, in his eldest son's favour in 1455. About 1425, probably when a minor, he married Janet (fl. 1425–1486), daughter of Sir John Forrester of Corstorphine (d. 1450), the chamberlain of James I. They had at least five sons and two daughters; two further sons are recorded. Maxwell died about April 1485. In 1478 he had resigned the barony of Maxwell in favour of his eldest son, John, whereafter John was sometimes styled Lord Maxwell, but he was killed in 1484. His marriage c.1454 to Janet, daughter of George Crichton, earl of Caithness (d. 1454), was of great potential importance because of the standing the Crichtons then enjoyed at court. The couple had seven sons and two daughters.

The eldest son, **John Maxwell** (c.1455–1513), succeeded his father and grandfather, and is normally styled fourth Lord Maxwell. His family was engaged in some of the feuds which troubled public order during the later years of James III's reign. In 1479 a dispute in Nithsdale between 'the lord carlaverok' and William Douglas of Drumlanrig was one of those singled out in parliament as needing to be settled. And the Maxwells had a bitter feud with another Dumfriesshire family, the Murrays of Cockpool. It was probably in 1486, a year after both sides had recorded assurances that they would not bring the other to harm, that the Murrays waylaid the fourth Lord Maxwell and his followers, killing his uncle and others. A concord was sealed on 4 September 1486, whereby the Murrays undertook to attend at Dumfries or Edinburgh market cross in linen clothes and seek Maxwell's forgiveness, and also to have masses sung for the souls of the slain. Nevertheless, the fourth lord's decision to join the rebels against James III in 1488 (apparently taken only shortly before the battle of Sauchieburn) may have been heavily influenced by the support the king was giving to Cuthbert Murray of Cockpool. Maxwell established himself at James IV's court thereafter, and performed occasional service as one of the king's council in judicial affairs throughout the reign. He was active in the property market and persuaded some lairds of south-west Scotland to give him bonds of manrent. Research has suggested that these bonds, which first appear in the 1440s, show lairds who had been recently raised to the peerage seeking to enhance their status over minor lairds by securing written personal promises of loyalty, often for life, in return for maintenance of the subscribers' interests. Maxwell and his sons also persuaded some local religious houses to appoint them as bailies of their property. He was killed at the battle of Flodden on 9 September 1513, along with three of his brothers. About 1491 he married Agnes (fl. 1491–1530), daughter of Sir Alexander Stewart of Garlies. They had four sons, the eldest of whom, Robert, succeeded as fifth Lord Maxwell, and four daughters; Maxwell may have fathered two illegitimate sons.

ALAN R. BORTHWICK

Sources J. M. Thomson and others, eds., *Registrum magni sigilli regum Scotorum / The register of the great seal of Scotland*, 11 vols. (1882–1914), vol. 2 · *APS*, esp. 1424–1567 · W. Fraser, ed., *The book of Carlaverock: memoirs of the Maxwells, earls of Nithsdale*, 2 vols. (1873) · W. Fraser, ed., *Memoirs of the Maxwells of Pollok*, 2 vols. (privately printed, Edinburgh, 1863) · U. Hull, Brynmor Jones L., Maxwell-Constable of Everingham papers · various collections of manuscript estate and other papers in archive offices and in private hands in Scotland and England · G. Burnett and others, eds., *The exchequer rolls of Scotland*, 23 vols. (1878–1908) · [T. Thomson] and others, eds., *The acts of the lords of council in civil causes, 1478–1503*, 3 vols. (1839–1993) · [T. Thomson], ed., *The acts of the lords auditors of causes and complaints, AD 1466–AD 1494*, RC, 40 (1839) · *RotS*, vol. 2 · *Scots peerage*, vol. 6 · M. Brown, *The Black Douglases: war and lordship in late medieval Scotland, 1300–1455* (1998) · A. Grant, 'Acts of lordship: the records of Archibald, fourth earl of Douglas', *Freedom and authority: Scotland, c.1050–c.1650*, ed. T. Brotherstone and D. Ditchburn (2000)

Archives Mitchell L., Glas., Glasgow City Archives, Stirling Maxwell of Pollock muniments · priv. coll. · U. Hull, Maxwell-Constable of Everingham MSS

Maxwell, Sir Herbert Eustace, seventh baronet (1845–1937), politician and author, was born in Edinburgh on 8 January 1845. He was the fourth (but only survivor) of the five sons of Sir William Maxwell of Monreith, sixth baronet, and his wife, Helenora, third and youngest daughter of Sir Michael Shaw-Stewart, fifth baronet, of Greenock and Blackhall, and his wife, Catherine. His early education at home and at private schools aroused his interest in natural history and allied subjects, and it was developed and extended by the tutor who prepared him for Oxford, after what he himself described as three years of 'insensate indolence' at Eton College.

During his year at Christ Church (1864–5) Maxwell failed to pass responsions, the first step towards a commission in the Scots Fusilier Guards. Nevertheless, he had acquired much miscellaneous information outside the normal subjects of school and university, on which he was to base the self-education of later years. The lack of purpose in his early life was mainly due to the religious tenets of his parents. Belonging as they did to the Catholic Apostolic church, and believing that the second advent was imminent, neither they nor their children felt the necessity for planning for the future. Maxwell settled at Monreith, helping his father to manage the estate, acquiring a unique knowledge of the people and countryside of Wigtownshire, of which he was lord lieutenant from 1903 to 1935, and establishing his reputation as a sportsman in angling, shooting, and horsemanship. Maxwell married in 1869 Mary (d. 1910), eldest daughter of Henry Fletcher-Campbell, of Boquhan, Stirlingshire; they had two sons and three daughters.

After his father's death in 1877 Maxwell entered parliament as Conservative member for Wigtownshire (1880). His political crony was Sir Almeric Fitzroy, clerk to the privy council. He was an assiduous lord of the Treasury from 1886 to 1892, besides serving on various commissions. As chairman of the tariff reform party in the House of Commons in 1903, he was closely associated with Joseph Chamberlain's tariff reform campaign. In 1906 he

Sir Herbert Eustace Maxwell, seventh baronet (1845–1937), by William Strang, 1917

did not seek re-election owing to financial circumstances, which were also the stimulus of his literary work.

Between 1887 and 1932, beginning with novels, Maxwell wrote, in addition to several biographies, books on topography, natural, local, and national history, archaeology, horticulture, and sport, as well as making numerous contributions to scientific and other periodicals. He had a charming, if too facile, pen, but such remarkable versatility precluded deep research. His *Memories of the Months* ran to seven series (1897–1922), of which the first three reached revised editions (1931–2). *Robert the Bruce and the Struggle for Scottish Independence* (1897) and a *Life of Wellington* (1899) are typical of his historical work. His editing of the *Creevey Papers* (2 vols., 1903) provided a valuable supplement to the *Greville Memoirs*. His Rhind lecturerships in archaeology at Edinburgh (1893 and 1911), presidency of the Society of Antiquaries of Scotland (1900–13), and chairmanship of the National Library of Scotland (1925–32), testified to his services to learning. Other distinctions included that of privy councillor (1897), FRS (1898), and KT (1933). He also received honorary degrees from the universities of Glasgow and Durham.

A personality of much charm, and the most prominent of scholarly country gentlemen in Scotland, Maxwell died at Monreith House on 30 October 1937 at the age of ninety-two. Both his sons predeceased him (the younger died of wounds received at Antwerp in 1914) and he was succeeded, as eighth baronet, by his grandson, Aymer (*b.* 1911). Gavin Maxwell (1914–1969), author and conservationist, was another grandson.

H. W. MEIKLE, *rev.* H. C. G. MATTHEW

Sources H. Maxwell, *Evening memories* (1932) • W. W. Smith, *Obits. FRS*, 2 (1936–8), 387–93 • R. A. Rempel, *Unionists divided: Arthur Balfour, Joseph Chamberlain, and the unionist free traders* (1972) • A. Fitzroy, *Memoirs*, 2 vols. [1925]
Archives NL Scot., corresp. and papers | NL Scot., corresp. with Blackwoods • PRO NIre., letters to Lady Londonderry
Likenesses W. Strang, pastel drawing, 1917, Scot. NPG [*see illus.*] • W. Stoneman, photograph, 1933, NPG • W. G. Boss, pencil drawing, Scot. NPG • J. Russell & Sons, photograph, NPG • Spy [L. Ward], chromolithograph caricature, NPG; repro. in *VF* (28 Sept 1893)
Wealth at death £79,047 6s. 8d.: confirmation, 21 Feb 1938, *CCI*

Maxwell, James (*b.* 1581?, *d.* in or after 1635), scholar and theological controversialist, is said to have been the sole son of William Maxwell of Little Airds. He frequently expressed pride in being the grandson of William Maxwell of Kirkconnel (*fl.* 1540–1567), who had served James V, Mary of Guise, and Mary Stewart.

A student at the University of Edinburgh, Maxwell early distinguished himself as a scholar, at the age of nineteen compiling commentaries on Daniel and the Revelation in what subsequently became an enormous collection of prophecies, understood as detailing the rise, rule, and eventual overthrow of the papal monarchy—the great prophesied Antichrist that would be destroyed at the end of days. Maxwell immediately impressed contemporaries and, he relates, was invited to preach in various Edinburgh pulpits. Immersed in Edinburgh's rich Calvinist intellectual culture, dominated by mathematicians, astrologers, and apocalyptic exegetes such as Robert Pont and John Napier of Merchiston, Maxwell initially intended to travel to Denmark and study mathematics and astrology with Tycho Brahe. But the university's sometime principal, Robert Rollock, persuaded him to stay on at Edinburgh, and Maxwell completed his master of arts degree in 1600.

In 1601, the year of Brahe's death, Maxwell travelled to France; for several years he pursued his prophetic researches in libraries at Limoges and Cluny, then at Florence and Venice, and probably elsewhere as well, possibly even as far south as Naples. Through these researches he assembled an extraordinary and perhaps unique collection of prophetic material: Joachite, pseudo-Joachite, Galfridian, Paracelsian, Merlinic, prophecies identified with Hildegard of Bingen, Thomas the Rhymer, Wilhelm Aytinger, Paul Grebner, Nostradamus, materials collected out of John Bale, John Foxe, Flacius Illyricus, the Magdeburg centuriators, and much else. While abroad he completed his book on the papacy, the *Tyrannidi-graphia ecclesiæ militantis*, as well as several allied works. The *Tyrannidi-graphia*, dedicated to his university, was sent back to Edinburgh, where it was apparently widely read and eventually came into the hands of the prominent minister at Ayr, John Welsh. Unfortunately Welsh took the manuscript volume with him when he was banished

to France in November 1606, and it is now lost—a fate, tragically, that would await the bulk of Maxwell's writings.

By 1607 Maxwell had settled in London, where he renounced his former 'puritanisme and Geneuisme' and dedicated the rest of his life to promoting James VI and I's British project and the episcopal church that was integral to it (Maxwell, *A New Eight-Fold Probation*, 1617, 35). In London he associated with conservative protestant scholars like the royal librarian Patrick Young, the well-known antiquary Sir Henry Spelman, and the Exeter dean Matthew Sutcliffe, and for nearly fifteen years he pleaded and petitioned, continuously and unsuccessfully, for an appointment to the fledgeling Chelsea College, the projected intellectual seat of the new Britain. Constantly writing, Maxwell rushed to the crown's defence with massive replies to the fanatical counter-reformers Jacques Davy du Perron (1556–1618), Martin Becanus (van der Beeck; 1561–1624), Jacob Gretser (Gretscher; 1562–1625), and Caspar Schoppe (Scioppio; 1576–1649). But, drawing from his researches while on the continent, his central concern remained focused upon the apocalyptic promise of the new British era that James's rule appeared to be initiating.

Although most of this writing has now disappeared and can only be known through Maxwell's quaint verse summaries and relatively brief occasional pieces, his beliefs and extraordinary expectations are still abundantly clear. The new Britain was nothing less than the prophesied last world empire that would reunite Europe, the Middle East, and presumably the globe within the true Christian faith in the age immediately preceding the return of Christ. James 'the Concorder' would reconcile divided Europe into this final order—seemingly through both his diplomatic efforts and his writings, and still more through the spirit and the writings emerging from the new British church. As his religious conservatism deepened Maxwell became increasingly convinced that Rome's conversion might be accomplished without violence: 'The reforming king … shall not intend the destruction and devastation, but only the purgation and purification of the Temple' (Maxwell, *Admirable and Notable Prophecies*, 1615, 88). If the faith initially had reached Rome from Britain by means of the sword it might do so in the latter days simply by means of the Word. As he urged James:

Play David's part, our curer and our king,
In Saul's behalf, e'en the musician,
With your sweet Harp, cease not to play and sing!
Till you prove Pope Paul's physician.
(Maxwell, *The Laudable Life and Deplorable Death … of Prince Henry*, 1612, sig. D4r)

From this perspective Maxwell easily saw the Austrian Habsburgs, despite their Catholicism, as a rampart against the Ottoman empire, the 'common enemies of the Christian name' (Maxwell, *Admirable and Notable Prophecies*, 1615, 120).

The overthrow of the Ottomans, however, was an imperative, and Maxwell expected Prince Henry and, on his death, the suitably named Charles to retake Constantinople, thus restoring the eastern Roman empire under

British aegis. The huge wealth of prophecy associated with Charles V in the previous century and with Charles VIII in the century before that, Maxwell maintained, actually applied to Britain's Charles Stuart, whose role was in fact prefigured by a line of famous individuals with that name reaching back, perhaps inevitably, to Charlemagne. The destruction of Islam (anticipated to occur about the year 1630, a millennium after its advent) would be accompanied by still other eschatological events, notably the conversion of the Jews. There in the British Middle East would emerge a community of Christian Jews, possibly, Maxwell hoped, under the guidance of James himself.

> Oh happy sight to see great Britain's king
> One day descending from Mount Olivet!
> O happy song, to hear the Hebrews sing!
> For joy of heart James to congratulate.
> (*Laudable Life*, sig. E2r)

Maxwell is Scotland's closest counterpart to such contemporary or near contemporary figures as Italy's Tommaso Campanella, France's Guillaume de Postel, England's John Dee, Sweden's Johannes Bureus, and Germany's authors of the Rosicrucian manifestos. Like them he was deeply concerned to reconnect a world now religiously, politically, and intellectually fragmented, he anticipated eschatological spiritual and social renewal, and he looked to prophetic world empire. Like them he rejected Aristotelian scholasticism for a putatively more profound wisdom in Neoplatonism, astrology, and a range of magical traditions. Like Campanella—and also Francis Bacon—he sought to elevate the status of the mechanical arts in relation to the liberal arts. At once archaic and forward-looking, medieval and yet also anticipating the British imperial experience, Maxwell, like so much in Europe at the turn of the seventeenth century, is profoundly Janus-faced, exotic but curiously familiar.

By 1617 it seemed that at last a fellowship as one of the two historians at the Chelsea College, the only positions open to laymen, was within Maxwell's grasp—or so he announced in his *A New Eight-Fold Probation of the Church of England's Divine Constitution*, itself a controversial piece, hastily written in response to the Scottish Presbyterian ministers' petition to James in July of that year (sigs. B2v–B3r). But it was not to be. Worse still, three years later his religious conservatism led to disaster when he produced a tract rejecting Frederick V's claim to the Bohemian crown. The argument in the now untraceable work, probably entitled *Turba-Austriaca*, is discernible from a summary appearing in yet another pamphlet published several months earlier: the Turkish threat and eschatological moment required 'that the imperial dignity be continued yet a while in the most glorious and augustious house of Austria, and not transferred unto another, especially of smaller power than it' (Maxwell, *Carolanna*, 1619, sig. F3r). Maxwell had always claimed that the house of Stuart was genealogically close to the house of Habsburg, and this circumstance, too, necessarily figured in his thinking. Not surprisingly a protest was lodged, and the 'scribbler' found himself gaoled in the Tower on 27 June 1620. During the autumn and winter he made a series of increasingly abject recantations to the privy council, and was eventually released on 9 February 1621 (PRO, SP 14/115/176; SP 14/117/155; SP 14/118/65; SP 14/119/69; *Acts of the Privy Council of England, 1619–1621*, 230, 344).

This event cut off any chance of a Chelsea College appointment and effectively marks the end of Maxwell's career in Britain. Thereafter he is rarely heard of, his remaining published works being limited to translations. Following his humiliation he travelled to the continent, first to France, and then settled in the Spanish Netherlands. Political disaster continued to dog him. He was briefly detained in Calvinist France for his *Eight-Fold Probation* and then imprisoned at Brussels for over a year as a heretic and a British spy; he obtained his release from 'perpetuall prison', he claimed, only after falsely promising to 'turne Catholicke in the highest straine and go live in Rome'. His scholarship nevertheless impressed the Habsburgs and the counter-reformers well enough for Emperor Ferdinand II (*d.* 1637) to offer him 'spiritual preferment and the office of Imperial Antiquary and Genealogist', as well as a pension of 1000 crowns upon the death of the long-time court librarian, Sebastian Tengnagel (1573–1635). Or so he wrote to Archbishop Laud in 1631, making what was probably his last and again unsuccessful appeal for a place within the Church of England—hoping also to return home and finally publish his many works. As he told Laud, any imperial appointment of course would require his conversion to Roman Catholicism, adding that as a protestant his life itself was constantly under threat from several English Catholic exiles (PRO, SP 16/189/124–127).

Maxwell probably ended his days in France, seeking the patronage of Cardinal Richelieu—not unlike Campanella himself. His final publication, a translation of 'morall discourses' attributed to Richelieu, appeared in 1635. In the preface he noted that there existed in the world three kinds of men: natural, moral, and divine. In what was surely a reference to himself he described the last flying:

> a higher pitch than all, his soul is mounted on the wings of contemplation ... he soars with the eagle to attain those heavenly mysteries that God Himself hath revealed, and never leaves till he hath seated himself ... in the high tribunal of that Holy of Holies   (Maxwell, *Emblema animæ*, 1635, sig. A3v)

Maxwell never found a place within the British order that he so wished to serve. Appeals to James, 'an academic man to an academic king', went neglected; Laud dismissed him as 'Mountebank Maxwell' (PRO, SP 14/84/59; SP 16/189/127v). Prophecy had come to play poorly within the late Jacobean and Caroline church. In that environment Maxwell's extraordinary claims (which extended even to determining the season of the year and the day of the week when the world would likely end, which found eschatological significance in the putatively Scottish place names he located in the Middle East, and which saw Merlin's prophecies indicating James's Irish policies) found themselves drastically out of place. Yet, for all its extravagance, much within Maxwell's thinking—his apocalyptic expectations, his sense of imperial mission, his philosemitism, even his concern to reclaim 'British' Constantinople—developed and articulated attitudes which were surprisingly widespread in both England and Scotland, and which extended to powerful members of the court, like Sir William Alexander, if not to the Laudian élite. Many of these perceptions would fire the mid-century revolution and thereafter more generally under-write British achievement.   ARTHUR H. WILLIAMSON

Sources A. H. Williamson, 'Scotland, Antichrist, and the invention of Great Britain', *New perspectives on the politics and culture of early modern Scotland*, ed. J. Dwyer, R. A. Mason, and A. Murdoch (1982), 44–58 • A. H. Williamson, 'The Jewish dimension of the Scottish apocalypse', *Menasseh ben Israel and his world*, ed. Y. Kaplan and others (1989), 17–20 • A. H. Williamson, 'Number and national consciousness: the Edinburgh mathematicians and Scottish public culture at the Union of Crowns', *Scots and Britons*, ed. R. A. Mason (1994), 200–03 • *CSP dom.*, 1619–23; 1631–3 • W. Fraser, ed., *The book of Carlaverock: memoirs of the Maxwells, earls of Nithsdale*, 2 vols. (1873) • T. Fuller, *The church history of Britain*, ed. J. S. Brewer, new edn, 6 vols. (1845), vol. 5, pp. 386–97 • PRO, SP 14/84/59; SP 14/115/176; SP 14/117/155; SP 14/118/65; SP 14/119/69; SP 16/189/124–127; SP 14/18 • *APC*, 1619–21, 230, 344
Archives BL, Add. MS 24489 • BL, 'Britaines union in loue', Royal MS 18A.51

Maxwell, James, of Kirkconnel (1708–1762), Jacobite army officer and writer, was the son of William Maxwell of Kirkconnel (c.1675–1746) and Janet (c.1675–1755), eldest daughter and heir of George Maxwell of Carnsalloch, and widow of Colonel John Douglas of Stenhouse. His family is one of the oldest in Scotland, the site of Kirkconnel House having been occupied since the days of Malcolm III Cean Mór (r. 1057–93), and the Maxwells there figuring prominently in the history of Scotland since the thirteenth century. At the Reformation the Maxwells remained Catholic, and James, like many of his family, was educated at Douai (1721–8). In 1758 he married Mary, daughter of Thomas Riddell of Swinburne Castle, and they had three sons, James (later of Kirkconnel), William—a republican who commanded 'the guard escorting Louis XVI to the guillotine' (Lenman, 89), and Thomas.

Maxwell, acting with the support of his father, joined Prince Charles (Charles Edward Stuart) at Edinburgh on 18 October 1745, and was commissioned in Lord Elcho's Life-guard squadron, then newly formed. His exact rank and position in the Jacobite forces remains in doubt: various sources describe him as lieutenant, captain, major, and even lieutenant-colonel. Whatever his military position (captain subsequently promoted major is most likely, probably combined with some unrecorded aide-de-camp role on the general staff), he appears to have had privileged access to the innermost councils of the Jacobite leadership, being 'in the council, though not a member of it' (*DNB*). As a result, he was able to leave, in his *Narrative of Charles Prince of Wales' Expedition to Scotland*, one of the most useful primary sources on the Jacobite rising of 1745. In hiding after the battle of Culloden, he subsequently escaped to France, where he resided at St Germain: it was here that he composed his *Narrative* between 1746 and 1750. Its literary style and quality are noteworthy. He succeeded his father as laird of Kirkconnel in 1746, and was able to return to Scotland in 1750; subsequently he built the modern portion of Kirkconnel House in brick. After his mother's death in 1755, he sold the estate of Carnsalloch, which he had inherited from her, to Alexander Johnstone, a London merchant. He died on 23 July 1762, survived by his wife.   MURRAY G. H. PITTOCK

Sources J. Maxwell of Kirkconnel, *Narrative of Charles prince of Wales' expedition to Scotland* (1841) • *DNB* • Anderson, *Scot. nat.* • A. Lang, *Prince Charles Edward Stuart*, new edn (1903) • M. Hook and W. Ross, *The 'forty-five': the late Jacobite rebellion* (1995) • W. B. Blaikie, ed., *Itinerary of Prince Charles Edward Stuart*, Scottish History Society, 23 (1897); facs. edn (1975) • B. Lenman, 'Physicians and politics in the Jacobite era', *The Jacobite challenge*, ed. E. Cruickshanks and J. Black (1988), 74–91 • N. Bushnell, *William Hamilton of Bangour* (1957) • A. Livingstone, C. W. H. Aikman, and B. S. Hart, eds., *Muster roll of Prince Charles Edward Stuart's army, 1745–46* (1984)

Maxwell, James [*pseud.* Poet in Paisley] (1720–1800), poet and essayist, was born at Auchenback, parish of Mearns, Renfrewshire, on 9 May 1720. At the age of twenty he went to England as a packman, became a weaver, and was at various times clerk, usher, schoolmaster, and stonebreaker. In 1787 he became the recipient of a charity in the gift of the town council of Paisley, which he enjoyed until his death (Motherwell, 1828, citing council records of 11 Oct 1787). Maxwell was one of the most prolific rhymers of his day, usually designating himself Poet in Paisley, and on some of his title-pages adding to his name the letters 'SDP', meant to signify 'student of divine poetry'. He represents the terminus of the virile strain of poetry of Calvinist pietism in eighteenth-century Scotland. His work, however, rarely rises above doggerel. A bibliography of Maxwell's works, comprising fifty-two separate publications, is given in Brown's *Paisley Poets* (1.17–22). The main interest in Maxwell today follows from his vocal antagonism to Robert Burns and Thomas Paine. His essay 'On the Ayrshire ploughman poet, or poetaster, R. B.' was published in his *Animadversions on some Poets and Poetasters of the Present Age* (1788). Of some interest also, for its observation of economic history, is his poem 'The great canal, or, The Forth and Clyde Navigation' (1788). His chief works are: *Divine Miscellanies* (1756), *Hymns and Spiritual Songs* (1759), and *A New Version of the Whole Book of Psalms in Metre* (1773), in which he exemplifies his objection to the employment of the organ in church by paraphrasing all of the references to instrumental music in worship so as to suit his own views. In 1795, on his seventy-fifth birthday, Maxwell published an autobiographical poem entitled *A Brief Narrative, or, Some Remarks on the Life of James Maxwell, Poet, in Paisley*. From this the reader learns that Maxwell had married, and had had at least one son, though no more is known of his family. He died nearly five years later, in March or April 1800.

J. C. HADDEN, rev. GERARD CARRUTHERS

Sources W. Motherwell, 'James Maxwell', *Paisley Magazine* (1828), 680 • R. Brown, *Paisley poets: with brief memoirs of them and selections from their poetry*, 2 vols. (1889–90) • *Paisley Advertiser* (2 Dec 1848) [thanks from Maxwell to fellow-poets for financial help] • G. R. Roy, '"The mair they talk, I'm kend the better": poems about Robert Burns', *Love and liberty*, ed. K. Simpson (1997) • T. Leonard, ed., *Radical Renfrew* (1990) • W. Motherwell, ed., *The harp of Renfrew*, 2 vols. (1872) • J. Holland, *Psalmists of Great Britain* (1843)

Maxwell, James Clerk (1831–1879), physicist, was born on 13 June 1831 at 14 India Street, Edinburgh, the second of the two children (a daughter died in infancy) of John Clerk Maxwell (1790–1856), landowner, and his wife, Frances (1792–1839), daughter of Robert Hodshon Cay of North Charlton, Northumberland, and his wife, Elizabeth. His father, the younger brother of Sir George *Clerk, sixth baronet (1787–1867), took the name Maxwell as heir to the estate he inherited from two marriages between the Clerks of Penicuik and heiresses of the Maxwells of Middlebie. This estate consisted of farmland near Dalbeattie in Kirkcudbrightshire, and it was in the house Glenlair, built there by his father, that Maxwell spent his early years and where he later did much of his writing.

Education and early career, 1841–1865 At first educated privately at Glenlair Maxwell entered Edinburgh Academy in 1841, where some eccentricity of behaviour earned him the nickname Dafty from his contemporaries. There he established lifelong friendships with Lewis Campbell (who became his biographer) and Peter Guthrie Tait (his closest scientific correspondent). According to his own account his early interest in science was aroused by his delight in the forms of regular geometrical figures, his view of mathematics as the search for harmonious and beautiful shapes. Accompanying his father to meetings of the Royal Society of Edinburgh and the Royal Scottish Society of Arts during the winter of 1845–6, he became aware of the work of David Ramsay Hay, the Edinburgh decorative artist. Hay was engaged in studies which aimed to explain the harmony of the form of geometrical figures and the aesthetics of colour combinations by mathematical principles. At this time Hay was studying the forms of oval curves, stimulating Maxwell to develop an ingenious method of drawing ovals using string round pins placed at the foci, by analogy with the string property of the ellipse. Promoting his son's work, John Clerk Maxwell approached James David Forbes, professor of natural philosophy at Edinburgh University, who presented a paper by Maxwell to the Royal Society of Edinburgh in April 1846. Forbes remarked on the relation of these curves to the Cartesian ovals, prompting Maxwell to make a more formal study of ovals.

Maxwell's interest in the study of colour was aroused when, in April 1847, he accompanied his uncle John Cay to the laboratory of William Nicol, inventor of the polarizing prism; this led him to investigate the chromatic effects of polarized light in crystals and strained glass, 'gorgeous entanglements of colour' as he described them in 1870 (*Scientific Letters and Papers*, 2.563).

In the autumn of 1847 Maxwell entered Edinburgh University, attending Sir William Hamilton's class in logic and metaphysics, Philip Kelland's in mathematics, and Forbes's class in natural philosophy. He was impressed with Hamilton's lectures, which encouraged his abiding concern to establish the conceptual rationale of his physics by appeal to philosophical argument. Formal study helped to shape the direction of his own original investigations, largely pursued during the summer months spent at Glenlair. At the end of his first year he wrote a

James Clerk Maxwell (1831–1879), by Fergus, 1872

paper on analytical geometry, a comprehensive memoir on rolling curves, presented by Kelland to the Royal Society of Edinburgh. During the following two years he pursued his interest in the chromatic effects of polarized light, and Forbes's interest in the physics of materials helped to shape the scope of his systematic paper 'On the equilibrium of elastic solids' of 1850 (Niven, 1.30–73), written during his third session. This memoir, remarkable in its breadth of coverage and depth of analysis, is grounded on the mathematics of elastic bodies, with Maxwell mastering contemporary theory including major recent work by the Cambridge mathematician George Gabriel Stokes; it embraces the study of special cases of torsion and compression, and discussion of Sir David Brewster's work on induced double refraction in strained glass.

During his third session at Edinburgh in 1849–50 Maxwell continued to follow the traditional broad Scottish course of study, attending classes in chemistry and moral philosophy, but soon began preparations to go up to Cambridge, settling on Peterhouse (where Tait was an undergraduate), though migrating to Trinity College after his first term. He arrived at Cambridge in October 1850 as an accomplished mathematician and physicist, recommended by Forbes to William Whewell, master of Trinity. In October 1851 he became one of the pupils of William Hopkins, the pre-eminent mathematical coach of the period. According to Tait, Hopkins was appalled at the disorder of Maxwell's mathematical reading but impressed with the breadth of his knowledge, and soon realized his extraordinary promise as a physicist. The Cambridge mathematical tripos emphasized mixed mathematics, including mechanics and the theory of gravitation, as well as geometrical and physical optics, including study of the wave theory of light, the subject of Stokes's lectures on hydrodynamics and optics which Maxwell attended in May 1853. In the summer of 1853 the strain of preparing for the examination occasioned 'a sort of brain fever', as Campbell described it (Campbell and Garnett, 170), an emotional and religious crisis which reinforced a contemplative dimension to his thought, a view of science inspired by religious values. In the tripos examination in January 1854 Maxwell graduated second wrangler to Edward John Routh, but was bracketed equal Smith's prizeman with Routh in the examination for Smith's prizes which followed. He was unsuccessful at his first attempt to be elected a fellow of Trinity in 1854 (being weak in classics), but was elected in October 1855. It was at this time that he read Whewell's writings on the history and philosophy of the sciences. He later often made allusion to Whewell's notion of fundamental ideas, concepts whose negation could not be intelligibly conceived, in his emphasis on the non-empirical status of basic scientific principles.

Trinity offered a wide range of friendships, and in the winter of 1852–3 Maxwell was elected a member of the Apostles club: the papers he presented on philosophical topics, including the philosophy of science, established him as a leading intellectual (as well as a recognized mathematician) among this select group. Along with some other members of his circle, including Richard Buckley Litchfield, he became active in Frederick Denison Maurice's Christian socialist movement, and taught classes for artisans in Cambridge, and later in Aberdeen and London.

In February 1856, responding to his father's desire that he spend more time at Glenlair, Maxwell applied for the professorship of natural philosophy at Marischal College, Aberdeen, mustering an impressive clutch of testimonials. Even though his father died in April 1856 before the appointment was made, Maxwell decided to accept the post when it was offered, commencing his duties in Aberdeen with an inaugural lecture on 3 November 1856, emphasizing, in Cambridge style, the basis of physical explanation in the application of the laws of motion, but also stressing the religious value of natural philosophy and its role within the Scottish curriculum. He devoted considerable effort to his teaching in Aberdeen, introducing elements of mathematical physics to his more advanced students.

On 2 June 1858 Maxwell married Katherine Mary Dewar (1824–1886), daughter of the Revd Daniel Dewar, principal of Marischal College. The marriage, which was childless, was not popular among his family. He and his wife were united by shared Christian commitment (he served as an elder of the Church of Scotland). In 1860, following the recommendation of the parliamentary commissioners that King's and Marischal colleges be joined to form the University of Aberdeen, with a single class and professor in each subject, he was made redundant. By this time he was a candidate for Forbes's post at Edinburgh, but Tait was appointed. However, in July 1860 he was appointed professor of natural philosophy at King's College, London, a post he held, living at 8 Palace Gardens Terrace, Kensington, until his resignation in March 1865. His study of engineering structures developed from his teaching at King's College; his work on graphical analysis and reciprocal diagrams in statics led to the award of the Keith prize of the Royal Society of Edinburgh for 1869–71.

Colour vision and optics, 1849–1874 In the summer of 1849, while Maxwell was still a student at Edinburgh, Forbes introduced him to experiments on colour mixing. These consisted in observing the hues generated by adjustable coloured sectors fitted to a rapidly spinning disc, using tinted papers supplied by D. R. Hay, whose *Nomenclature of Colours* (1845) exhibited an elaborate system of colour plates which distinguished variations in colour. Maxwell's approach to colour vision was shaped by the attempts by Hay and Forbes to provide a nomenclature for the classification of colours; by Forbes's method of experimentation and his use of a triangle of colours to represent colour combinations; and by the work of another Edinburgh acquaintance, George Wilson, on the problem of colour blindness. In the early 1850s the study of colour vision was significantly advanced in major papers by Hermann Helmholtz and Hermann Grassmann, work which Maxwell absorbed into his own theory in 1854–5.

Maxwell adopted Thomas Young's three-receptor theory of colour vision; his claim that red, green, and violet should be considered the primary constituents of white light; the suggestion by Young and John Herschel that John Dalton's insensibility to red light was caused by the absence of one of the three receptors; and Young's colour diagram, with red, green, and violet placed at the vertices of a triangle, points within the triangle representing colour combinations. Maxwell showed that this depiction of colour combinations was equivalent to their representation by loaded points on Isaac Newton's circle of seven principal colours with white at the centre, and that colour combinations could also be expressed in terms of variables of spectral colour, degree of saturation, and intensity of illumination.

In his 1855 paper 'Experiments on colour, as perceived by the eye' (Niven, 1.126–54) Maxwell extended Forbes's experiments, devising a spinning top in which a second set of coloured sectors of smaller diameter was added, enabling accurate colour comparisons to be made, and obtaining quantitative colour equations which could be manipulated algebraically. He confirmed Forbes's observation that green did not result from spinning yellow and blue coloured papers, in accordance with Helmholtz's finding that green was not obtained by the mixture of spectral yellow and blue. This challenged the identity of the mixing rule for lights and pigments, supposed by Newton. The paper concluded with observations made by colour deficient observers.

In colorimetry Maxwell had established quantitative techniques and a unified theory, but he sought to make more accurate measurements, devising a series of colour boxes in which spectral red, green, and blue were mixed in varying proportions and directly compared with white light. These researches included a study of the variations of colour sensitivity across the retina, the investigation of the yellow spot on the retina, and the projection of the first trichromatic colour photograph in a lecture at the Royal Institution, London, in May 1861. This work led to the award of the Royal Society's Rumford medal in 1860, following the submission of his paper 'On the theory of compound colours' to the *Philosophical Transactions* (Niven, 1.410–44) and his appointment to read the paper as the society's Bakerian lecturer. As he was not—until May 1861—a fellow of the Royal Society, he was found to be ineligible for this appointment.

Maxwell made important contributions to geometrical optics in the 1850s. Developing a theorem due to Roger Cotes, he developed a new approach to the theory of optical instruments in which theorems expressing geometrical relations between an object and image were separated from discussion of the dioptrics of lenses. This approach was subsequently developed independently by Ernst Abbe; these methods became standard. In 1873–4 he generalized his mathematical method, appealing to concepts of projective geometry, and developed William Rowan Hamilton's idea of the characteristic function as a method of investigating lens systems.

The stability of Saturn's rings, 1856–1864 In March 1855 the subject of the University of Cambridge's Adams prize for 1857 was advertised as a study of 'The motions of Saturn's rings'. This was a problem in dynamics within the Cambridge tradition of mixed mathematics; indeed, Whewell had set a Smith's prize question in 1854 requiring candidates to show that Saturn's rings were not rigid bodies, but possibly fluid. In his classic study on the rings of Saturn Pierre Simon Laplace had established that the motion of a uniform solid ring would be dynamically unstable, while Joseph Plateau had recently suggested that Saturn's rings could be formed from the rotation of a fluid. The problem of Saturn's rings was of current interest to astronomers: in 1850 George Bond had noticed a dark ring interior to the two familiar bright rings, and Otto Struve had claimed that this ring was a new formation.

Maxwell's prizewinning essay (*Scientific Letters and Papers*, 1.438–79), completed in December 1856, was divided into two parts: on the motion of a rigid ring, and on the motion of a fluid ring or a ring consisting of loose materials. The argument rested on potential theory, Taylor's theorem, and Fourier analysis; to establish the conditions of stability of the rings he devised a mathematical method that was acclaimed by George Biddell Airy, the astronomer royal, in his review of the published memoir. He was to employ the same method in establishing stability conditions in his paper 'On governors' in 1868 (Niven, 2.105–20).

With regard to Saturn's rings, Maxwell began with the work of Laplace, concluding that a solid ring would only be stable if it was so irregular as to be inconsistent with the observed appearance of the rings. In the essay submitted for the prize he argued that if the rings were in motion they could be fluid, with waves in the fluid in the plane of the rings, and he considered the effect of disturbing causes such as the friction of the rings and gravitational irregularities, concluding that the ring system could have changed in form over time.

After the award of the prize (worth about £130) in May 1857 Maxwell began to revise the argument of his essay, corresponding with two of the examiners, William Thomson and James Challis. He soon corrected errors which had compromised his treatment of the case of a solid ring, and turned to the task of reconstructing his discussion of the condition of stability of a fluid ring. By November 1857 he had discarded his theory of waves in a fluid ring, and established that a liquid continuous ring was not dynamically feasible. He now concluded that the ring system of Saturn consisted of concentric rings of satellites; this formed the argument of his memoir *On the Stability of the Motion of Saturn's Rings* of 1859 (Niven, 1.288–376). To facilitate understanding of systems of waves in a ring of satellites he devised a model, a wheel on a cranked axle to which particles were attached; on rotation of the wheel the particles moved in wave patterns.

The memoir on Saturn's rings consolidated Maxwell's reputation as a mathematical physicist. The problems generated by this investigation also played a role in initiating his work on the kinetic theory of gases in 1859. In considering the rings as a system of particles he noted that he was unable to compute the trajectories of these particles 'with any distinctness' (Niven, 1.354). This problem alerted him to discuss the complex motions of gas particles, where he introduced a probabilistic argument, and in 1864 he attempted to apply the statistical method of his theory of gases to compute the motions of the particles of Saturn's rings. This endeavour proved abortive and remained unpublished. The problem of calculating the motions of particles was considered further in his 1873 essay (written for his Cambridge colleagues) on science and free will (*Scientific Letters and Papers*, 2.814–23), where he discussed the motion of a mechanical system subject to instabilities at points of singularity. Such instabilities were incalculable; he concluded that the physics of particles did not imply determinism.

The kinetic theory of gases and thermodynamics, 1859–1879 In completing his work on Saturn's rings Maxwell had drawn on data on gas viscosity to establish the effect of friction in disturbing the stability of the rings. In the spring of 1859 he became interested in a paper by Rudolf Clausius on the theory of gases considered as particles in motion; his work on Saturn's rings had alerted him to the problem of computing such motions. To explain the slow diffusion of gas molecules Clausius had calculated the probability of a molecule travelling a given distance (the mean free path) without collision. Maxwell had been interested in probability theory as early as 1850; his interest may have been aroused by an essay by John Herschel on Adolphe Quetelet's theory of probabilities, and there are similarities between Maxwell's derivation of the distribution law in his paper 'Illustrations of the dynamical theory of gases' of 1860 (Niven, 1.377–409) and Herschel's proof of the law of least squares.

Maxwell advanced on Clausius's procedure by introducing a statistical formula for the distribution of velocities among gas molecules, a function identical in form with the distribution formula in the theory of errors. Writing to Stokes in May 1859 he explained that he had undertaken the study of the motions of particles as an 'exercise in mechanics', but he looked for confirmation of his argument in work on gaseous diffusion; he hoped to be 'snubbed a little by experiments' (*Scientific Letters and Papers*, 1.610–11). He was able to calculate the mean free path of molecules, and established the unexpected result that the viscosity of gases was independent of their density.

Maxwell then turned to investigate the viscosity of gases at different temperatures and pressures by observing the decay in the oscillation of discs torsionally suspended in a container, experiments presented as the Royal Society's Bakerian lecture in 1866. He found that gas viscosity was a linear function of the absolute temperature, and he suggested, in his major paper 'On the dynamical theory of gases' of 1867 (Niven, 2.26–78), that gas molecules should be considered as centres of force subject to an inverse fifth power law of repulsion, a result in agreement with this experimental finding. He presented a new derivation of the distribution law, demonstrating that the velocity distribution would maintain a state of equilibrium unchanged by collisions. His theory of gases was 'dynamical' or 'kinetic', as he later termed it (*Scientific Letters and Papers*, 2.654), in that he supposed particles in motion. In the 1870s he came to contrast the certain predictive power of dynamical laws (Newton's laws of motion) with the inherently uncertain knowledge generated by the statistical method of his theory of gases, which, he argued, 'involves an abandonment of strict dynamical principles' (Niven, 2.253).

In drafting his paper 'On the dynamical theory of gases' Maxwell found that his theory seemed to have the consequence that energy could be abstracted from a cooling gas, a result in conflict with the second law of thermodynamics, stated in the early 1850s by Clausius and Thomson as denoting the tendency of heat to pass from warmer to colder bodies; this implied 'a collision between Dynamics & thermodynamics' (*Scientific Letters and Papers*, 2.269). While he corrected his argument and resolved the difficulty (reconstructing his analysis in 1873), it is likely that reflection on the problem led him to consider the bearing of his theory of gases on the interpretation of the second law of thermodynamics.

Maxwell first formulated the famous 'demon paradox' in a letter to Tait in December 1867. The term 'demon', which Maxwell did not use, was coined by William Thomson to describe the theoretical being invented by Maxwell for his thought experiment. It was incapable of doing work but was able to manipulate valves which move without friction. The purpose of Maxwell's 'finite being' was to suggest how a hot body could take heat from a colder body so as to 'pick a hole' in the second law of thermodynamics (*Scientific Letters and Papers*, 2.331–2). As he later explained to Tait, his intention was 'to show that the 2nd law of

Thermodynamics has only a statistical certainty' (ibid., 3.186).

In other words, because of the statistical distribution of molecular velocities in a gas at equilibrium there will be spontaneous fluctuations of molecules taking heat from a cold body to a hotter one. However, it would require the action of the 'finite being' to manipulate molecules so as to produce an observable flow of heat from a cold body to a hotter one, and violate the second law of thermodynamics; hence the law is statistical and applies only to systems of molecules. Moreover the law is also time directional, expressing the irreversibility of physical processes, while the laws of dynamics are time reversible. Thus the second law of thermodynamics is a statistical expression, not a dynamical theorem, as supposed by Clausius and Ludwig Boltzmann. Their opinion, Maxwell joked to Tait in December 1873, was in the realm of cloud-cuckoo-land where the 'German Icari flap their waxen wings' (*Scientific Letters and Papers*, 2.947).

Maxwell expounded his ideas on thermodynamics in various essays in the 1870s and in his *Theory of Heat* (1871), where he first made public his demon paradox. Intended as a popular exposition of the subject, this text contained an important new result, the 'Maxwell relations' between thermodynamical variables. During the 1870s he made further contributions to molecular physics: on the estimate of molecular diameters, and on intermolecular forces and the continuity of the liquid and gaseous states of matter. He also discussed the structure of molecules, which bore on one of the major problems in his theory of gases: the discrepancy between the measured values of the specific heat ratios of gases and those calculated (by the equipartition theorem) from the kinetic theory. His 1873 lecture 'Molecules' reviewed the subject; his conclusion that the identity of spectra showed an atom to be like a manufactured article, which 'precludes the idea of its being eternal and self-existent' (Niven, 2.376), used molecular physics to combat materialism.

In a paper of 1878 Maxwell developed work by Boltzmann, formulating the ergodic theorem that a system in equilibrium will, if undisturbed, pass through every state compatible with its total energy, and he introduced the concept of ensemble averaging, foreshadowing work by J. Willard Gibbs and Albert Einstein. In a paper on rarefied gases, of 1878–9, Maxwell explained William Crookes's radiometer, much discussed in the 1870s. He demonstrated that the effect of radiant heat in spinning the radiometer vanes was due to the slip of gas over their surface, generating tangential stresses. His quantitative treatment of the effect was stimulated by reading a paper by Osborne Reynolds as a referee for the Royal Society. Maxwell made public both his acknowledgement and criticism of Reynolds's paper; but Reynolds took offence, difficulties abetted by Maxwell's terminal illness.

Field theory and the electromagnetic theory of light, 1854–1873 Writing to Thomson in February 1854, after graduating at Cambridge, Maxwell declared his intention to attack the science of electricity. In the preface to his *Treatise on Electricity and Magnetism* (1873) he recalled that he had commenced his work by study of Michael Faraday's *Experimental Researches in Electricity* (1839–55). At the time he considered Faraday's experimental discoveries, of electromagnetic induction, the laws of electrochemistry, and magneto-optical rotation (the Faraday effect), to form 'the nucleus of everything electric since 1830' (*Scientific Letters and Papers*, 1.582). Faraday had explained magnetism in terms of lines of force traversing space, and electrostatics by the mediation of forces by the dielectric. Guided by Thomson, Maxwell advanced beyond the work of his mentor in grappling comprehensively with Faraday's concept of the magnetic field. He supposed that electric and magnetic forces were mediated by the agency of the field, contiguous elements of the space in the neighbourhood of the electric or magnetic bodies. He expressed the essence of his field theory in a draft in 1855: 'Faraday treats the distribution of forces in space as the primary phenomenon' (*Scientific Letters and Papers*, 1.353). In his paper 'On Faraday's lines of force' of 1856 (Niven, 1.155–229) he presented a geometrical model of lines of force in space, a representation resting on potential theory and the geometry of orthogonal surfaces, given embodiment by the physical analogy of the flow of an incompressible fluid (Niven, 1.156–8). He formulated theorems of electromagnetism, expressing the relation between magnetic forces and electric currents.

The analogy of streamlines in a fluid was proposed as illustrative of the geometry of the field, but Maxwell sought a theory of the field grounded on the mechanics of a mediating ether. He found its basis in Thomson's 1856 proposal that the Faraday magneto-optical rotation could be explained by the rotation of vortices in an ether. As early as 1857 Maxwell began to develop the idea of orienting molecular vortices along magnetic field lines, culminating in the publication of his paper 'On physical lines of force', published in four parts in the *Philosophical Magazine* in March, April, and May 1861, and in January and February 1862. He posited a honeycomb of vortices in which each vortex cell was separated from its neighbour by a layer of spherical particles, revolving in the opposite direction to the vortices. These 'idle wheel' particles communicated the rotatory velocity of the vortices from one part of the field to another. In this ether model, the most famous image in nineteenth-century physics, the analogy provides mechanical correlates for electromagnetic quantities. The angular velocity of the vortices corresponds to the magnetic field intensity, and the translational flow of the idle wheel particles to the flow of an electric current; the field equations are based on the rotation of molecular vortices in the ether. He emphasized that while the theory was mechanically conceivable, the model itself was provisional and temporary, even awkward, hardly 'a mode of connexion existing in nature' (Niven, 1.486), an argument that has generated much philosophical discussion about the role of models in physics.

It is likely that Maxwell originally envisaged the paper as being limited to discussion of magnetism and electric currents. But during the summer of 1861, while modifying the ether model to encompass electrostatics, he obtained an unexpected consequence, the electromagnetic theory of light, as he termed his theory in 1864 (*Scientific Letters and Papers*, 2.194). He introduced a displacement of electricity as an electromagnetic correlate of the elastic deformation of the vortices, an elastic property which allowed for the propagation of transverse shear waves. He established the close agreement between the velocity of propagation of waves in an electromagnetic medium (which he demonstrated to be given by the ratio of electrostatic and electromagnetic units, established experimentally), and the measured velocity of light. This led him to assert that he could 'scarcely avoid the inference that *light consists in the transverse undulations of the same medium which is the cause of electric and magnetic phenomena*' (Niven, 1.500).

Maxwell's introduction of the displacement current and his derivation of the electromagnetic theory of light have aroused claims that his argument lacks internal consistency and was subject to *ad hoc* adjustment. Analysis of his conceptualization in terms of his mechanical ether has shown that the argument is internally consistent, and that the electromagnetic theory of light rests on parameters established by experiment. He completed the theory by a quantitative treatment of the magneto-optical effect in terms of the rotation of molecular vortices, but was dissatisfied with the appeal to a mechanical model. He sought to base his theory on firmer theoretical ground, and to confirm its experimental basis.

The demands of the new technology of cable telegraphy prompted the determination of a standard of electrical resistance to aid engineers in establishing quality control, and in 1862 Maxwell joined the British Association committee on electrical standards. In May and June 1863, with Fleeming Jenkin and Balfour Stewart, he made an accurate measurement of electrical resistance in absolute units (of time, mass, and space), employing a method devised by Thomson, in which the resistance of a rotating coil was calculated from the measurement of the deflection of a magnet placed at its centre. His paper 'On governors' (1868) was the product of study of the governor designed by Jenkin for these experiments. The standard unit of resistance was issued in the spring of 1865 (though its accuracy was soon held up to question). As part of the committee's report in 1863, Maxwell and Jenkin wrote a paper introducing dimensional notation, expressing physical quantities as products of powers of mass, length, and time. For every electrical quantity there are two absolute units, the electrostatic and the electromagnetic, the ratio of these units being a power of a constant with the dimensions of a velocity. As Maxwell had established, this ratio was the velocity of waves in an electromagnetic medium, and he determined to establish its value with greater precision. Assisted by Charles Hockin, in 1868 he obtained a value for the ratio of units by an experiment balancing the (electrostatic) force between two oppositely charged discs against the (electromagnetic) repulsion between two current carrying coils (Niven, 2.125–43). The measured value still diverged from the latest value for the velocity of light, and in the *Treatise* (1873) he merely claimed that the electromagnetic theory of light was 'not contradicted by the comparison of these results' (vol. 2, p. 388), a near equivalence which was seen to provide evidence in favour of the theory.

In 'A dynamical theory of the electromagnetic field' of 1865 (Niven, 1.526–97) Maxwell achieved a more general and systematic presentation of his theory. The mechanical ether model was abandoned, yet he retained the mechanical foundations of his theory by grounding the eight sets of general equations of the electromagnetic field (the forerunners of the four Maxwell equations, as reformulated in the 1880s by Oliver Heaviside and Heinrich Hertz) on the Lagrangian formalism of abstract dynamics. But in detaching his theory from the model he altered the interpretation of the displacement current, leading to a loss of consistency, a problem resolved in the *Treatise* where he interprets the displacement current as manifested as electric charge. In Maxwell's field theory, electric charge is emergent from the field.

Maxwell began writing the *Treatise* in late 1867 and had completed a draft two years later. Interrupting the work to write the *Theory of Heat*, he resumed in November 1870, his major concern being the amplification of the mathematical argument of the book. In the *Treatise* Maxwell emphasized the expression of physical quantities freed from direct representation by a mechanical model, a style of mathematical physics that became influential. He enlarged the physical geometry and mechanical foundations of his earlier papers, deploying four fundamental mathematical ideas: quaternions (vector concepts, invented by W. R. Hamilton and developed by Tait), integral theorems (Stokes's theorem, transforming line into surface integrals), topological ideas (J. B. Listing's topology of lines and surfaces), and the Lagrange–Hamilton method of analytical dynamics (as developed by Thomson and Tait in their *Treatise on Natural Philosophy* of 1867). Maxwell's use of vector functions—he introduced the term 'curl'—was especially influential, vectors becoming pervasive in later physics, and the work abounds with innovative examples of mathematical physics, such as the polar representation of spherical harmonic functions, and the treatment of Green's function and reciprocity theorem.

The *Treatise* is divided into four parts—on electrostatics, electricity in motion, magnetism, and electromagnetism—and offers a systematic presentation, including discussion of electrical instruments and measurements. Maxwell's distinctive theory becomes most explicit in the final part: here he presents the general equations of the electromagnetic field, the electromagnetic theory of light, and the dynamical basis of his field theory. The work concludes with a rebuttal of contemporary theories (by Wilhelm Weber, Bernhard Riemann, and Enrico Betti) deriving from the tradition of considering forces acting at a distance without the mediation of a field. Maxwell argues that these theories cannot satisfactorily explain the transmission of energy, for 'there must be a medium or substance in which the energy exists'. Mediation by an ether, the seat of the electromagnetic field, is the keystone of his theory, and he stresses that it was his 'endeavour to construct a mental representation of all the details

of its action' (J. C. Maxwell, *Treatise on Electricity and Magnetism*, 1873, 2.438).

Cavendish professor, 1871–1879 In 1865 Maxwell had resigned his post at King's College, London, and subsequently retired to private life at Glenlair, where he continued with his scientific work. As an examiner for the mathematical tripos at Cambridge in the late 1860s he had set a few questions on the theories of heat, electricity, and magnetism, fostering calls within the university for the introduction of these subjects into the tripos. The university sought the establishment of a new professorship to teach these physical subjects. The chancellor of the university, the seventh duke of Devonshire, offered funds for a laboratory (which came to be named after his family), and Maxwell was appointed to the professorship of experimental physics in March 1871. In his inaugural lecture in October 1871 Maxwell presented experimental physics as liberal culture rather than workbench practice, but emphasized the value of precision measurements, experiments which became the norm of research at the Cavendish Laboratory when it opened in April 1874. He designed the laboratory and acquired the instruments, paid for largely by the duke of Devonshire and by Maxwell himself.

Maxwell's lectures on heat, electrostatics, and electromagnetism were designed to meet the expanded syllabus for the mathematical tripos, still overwhelmingly dominant as the educational path for prospective physicists at Cambridge. He gathered a small group of Cambridge graduates, including William Garnett (who became demonstrator and gave introductory lectures on physics and on laboratory methods) and George Chrystal; they were joined by Arthur Schuster, who had described experiments which suggested a deviation from Ohm's law. Under Maxwell's direction Chrystal undertook exhaustive tests, which Maxwell and Schuster reported to the British Association in 1876, confirming the accuracy of the law. Maxwell began to devise experiments to re-determine the standard unit of resistance, thwarted by Chrystal's departure for St Andrews in 1877.

Following his election as a fellow of the Royal Society in May 1861 Maxwell had refereed a wide range of papers for the *Philosophical Transactions*, a task which continued unabated in the 1870s; he often wrote substantive essays offering significant commentary. Literary work, including richly informative reviews for *Nature*, formed an important part of Maxwell's activity during this final period of his life. He also published jocular scientific poems under his thermodynamic *nom de plume dp/dt*, derived from an expression for the second law of thermodynamics in Tait's *Sketch of Thermodynamics* (1868), $dp/dt = JCM$. His edition of *The Electrical Researches of the Honourable Henry Cavendish* (1879) is a classic of scientific editing, locating Cavendish within his own period and—by undertaking experimental tests of his results and recasting his ideas into a modern idiom—relating Cavendish's work of the 1770s to the physics of the 1870s. Some of these investigations were incorporated into the second edition of the *Treatise*, published posthumously in 1881. The text *Matter and*

Motion (1876) contains subtle discussions of absolute space and the status of the laws of motion. As one of the scientific editors of the ninth edition of the *Encyclopaedia Britannica* Maxwell contributed several articles. The classic article on 'Atom' reviewed the subject from antiquity to contemporary developments, displaying his knowledge of the history of science. In 'Ether' he discussed the problem of detecting the earth's motion through the ether. His suggestion that light be propagated in opposite directions and that ether drag be detected by measuring any variation in its velocity, shortly led Albert Abraham Michelson to undertake his ether drift experiments, yielding a null result.

Maxwell died of cancer at his home, 11 Scroope Terrace, Cambridge, on 5 November 1879. He was buried at Parton churchyard, Kirkcudbrightshire, Scotland.

Historical reputation and interpretation In the 1870s Maxwell's scientific reputation was burgeoning, leading to the award of honorary doctorates from the universities of Edinburgh, Oxford, and Pavia, and the membership of academies in Amsterdam, Göttingen, Vienna, Boston, Philadelphia, and New York. His reputation initially rested largely on his kinetic theory of gases and statistical methods, further developed in the 1870s by Boltzmann. The impact of the *Treatise on Electricity and Magnetism* was at first muted, but within a few years of his death his field theory shaped the work of Maxwellian physicists: George Francis FitzGerald, Oliver Heaviside, Joseph John Thomson, and others. Following Hertz's production and detection of electromagnetic waves in 1888, Maxwell's field theory and electromagnetic theory of light came to be accepted and regarded as one of the most fundamental of all physical theories. Maxwell's equations gained the status of Newton's laws of motion, and the theory was basic to the new technology of electric power, telephony, and radio. His reputation and the status of Maxwellian physics was enhanced by the advent of 'modern' physics in the twentieth century, understood as resting on his conception of the physical field and appeal to statistical descriptions.

Although Maxwell's career traversed a period which saw the rapid professionalization of scientific endeavour, and he contributed to this development through his management of the Cavendish Laboratory, he should not be regarded as a professional scientist himself. His way of life was that of a Scottish laird, who often relied on inherited property in pursuing his own scientific interests. Indeed, in his more popular writings he expressed his traditional stance on the cultural values of science, lacking sympathy with the secularism which was becoming common in the 1870s. In his biography Lewis Campbell portrayed Maxwell as a natural philosopher pursuing science as an avocation; this has been an abiding image.

P. M. HARMAN

Sources *The scientific letters and papers of James Clerk Maxwell*, ed. P. M. Harman, 3 vols. (1990–2002) • W. D. Niven, ed., *The scientific papers of James Clerk Maxwell* (1890) • C. W. F. Everitt, 'Maxwell, James Clerk', *DSB*, 9.198–230 • L. Campbell and W. Garnett, *The life of James Clerk Maxwell* (1882) • P. M. Harman, *The natural philosophy of James Clerk Maxwell* (1998) • D. M. Siegel, *Innovation in Maxwell's electromagnetic theory: molecular vortices, displacement current, and light* (1991) • M. J. Klein, 'Maxwell, his demon, and the second law of thermodynamics', *American Scientist*, 58 (1970), 84–97 • P. M. Harman, 'Mathematics and reality in Maxwell's dynamical physics', *Kelvin's Baltimore lectures and modern theoretical physics*, ed. R. Kargon and P. Achinstein (1987), 267–97 • P. M. Harman, 'Maxwell and Saturn's rings: problems of stability and calculability', *The investigation of difficult things: essays on Newton and the history of the exact sciences*, ed. P. M. Harman and A. E. Shapiro (1992), 477–502 • P. M. Harman, *Energy, force, and matter: the conceptual development of nineteenth-century physics* (1982) • P. M. Harman, ed., *Wranglers and physicists: studies on Cambridge physics in the nineteenth century* (1985) • S. Schaffer, 'Accurate measurement is an English science', *The values of precision*, ed. M. N. Wise (1995), 135–72 • C. W. F. Everitt, 'Maxwell's scientific creativity', *Springs of scientific creativity*, ed. R. Aris, H. T. Davis, and R. H. Stuewer (1983), 71–141 • T. M. Porter, *The rise of statistical thinking, 1820–1900* (1986) • B. J. Hunt, *The Maxwellians* (1991) • J. Z. Buchwald, *From Maxwell to microphysics: aspects of electromagnetic theory in the last quarter of the nineteenth century* (1985) • E. Garber, S. G. Brush, and C. W. F. Everitt, eds., *Maxwell on molecules and gases* (1986) • E. Garber, S. G. Brush, and C. W. F. Everitt, eds., *Maxwell on heat and statistical mechanics* (1995) • C. G. Knott, *Life and scientific work of Peter Guthrie Tait* (1911) • O. Knudsen, 'The Faraday effect and physical theory, 1845–1873', *Archive for History of Exact Sciences*, 15 (1975–6), 235–81 • M. N. Wise, 'The mutual embrace of electricity and magnetism', *Science*, 203 (1979), 1310–18 • S. G. Brush, *The kind of motion we call heat: a history of the kinetic theory of gases in the 19th century*, 2 vols. (1976) • R. G. Olson, *Scottish philosophy and British physics, 1750–1880: a study in the foundations of the Victorian scientific style* (1975) • private information (2004) • d. cert.

Archives CUL, corresp. and papers • King's Lond., notebooks • NL Scot., paper presented to the Royal Society of Edinburgh • Peterhouse, Cambridge, family corresp. and papers • RS | CUL, letters to Lord Kelvin • CUL, letters to Sir George Stokes • CUL, corresp. with P. G. Tait • LMA, corresp. with C. J. Monro • U. Glas. L., letters to Lord Kelvin • U. St Andr., corresp. with James David Forbes, etc.

Likenesses W. Dyce, double portrait, oils, *c*.1837 (with his mother), Birmingham Museums and Art Gallery • photograph, 1855, Trinity Cam. • photograph, *c*.1870, Peterhouse, Cambridge • Fergus, photograph, 1872, NPG [*see illus.*] • J. E. Boehm, bust, 1879 (after engraving by G. J. Stodart), U. Cam., Cavendish Laboratory • J. Blackburn, oils, U. Cam., Cavendish Laboratory • L. Dickinson, oils, Trinity Cam. • C. H. Jeens, stipple (after unknown artist), NPG • G. J. Stodart, engraving (after photograph by Fergus of Greenock), repro. in Campbell and Garnett, *Life of James Clerk Maxwell* • double portrait, oils (with his wife), U. Cam., Cavendish Laboratory • mezzotint, watercolour on china (after photograph), NPG • photographs, RS

Wealth at death £9269 5s. 4d.: confirmation, 1 Jan 1880, CCI

Maxwell, John, fourth Lord Maxwell (*c*.1455–1513). *See under* Maxwell, Herbert, first Lord Maxwell (*c*.1390–1453).

Maxwell, John, fourth Lord Herries of Terregles (*c*.1512–1583), nobleman, was born in Dumfriesshire, the second son of Robert *Maxwell, fifth Lord Maxwell (*c*.1494–1546), and his wife, Janet, daughter of Sir William Douglas of Drumlanrig. The Maxwells were one of the most powerful border families, and normally provided the wardens of the Scottish west march. Through ties of kinship and marriage, and also through bonds of manrent, they had created a sphere of influence which included the baronies of Caerlaverock and Granane, the hereditary stewardships of Annandale and Kirkcudbright, and the ecclesiastical lordships of Dundrennan, Tongland, Sweetheart, and Holywood abbeys. Their jurisdiction as wardens extended not only over the sheriffdom of Dumfries and the two stewardships but also over some parts of the sheriffdom of Wigtown.

When his father died in 1546 John Maxwell succeeded him as warden. He immediately came under conflicting pressures from the government of the earl of Arran, the Scottish regent, and from English officials, led by Thomas, Lord Wharton, who were endeavouring to bring the Scottish borders under their own control. Wharton was anxious to secure the Maxwell strongholds of Lochmaben and Caerlaverock, and he also looked for Maxwell's support against the powerful Douglas family, led by the earl of Angus. But he found that though Maxwell was prepared to accept an English pension, he could not be trusted to carry out the undertakings which justified its payment. In February 1548 an English expedition up Nithsdale was severely mauled near Drumlanrig, leading to suspicions that Maxwell had changed sides and warned Angus of Wharton's plans. The English warden responded by hanging a number of Scottish hostages.

Maxwell may well have been influenced in his manoeuvrings at this point by the offer made to him by Arran of the hand in marriage of his ward Agnes (c.1534–1594), eldest daughter of William, third Lord Herries. The marriage took place in March 1548 and produced twelve children: William *Maxwell of Terregles, who succeeded as fifth Lord Herries, Robert, Edward, James, and John; and Elizabeth, Margaret, Agnes, Mary, Sarah, Grizel, and Nicola. Maxwell's courtesy right under Scottish custom to represent his wife's peerage was recognized only in December 1566, when he finally came into complete possession of the territorial barony of Herries, having purchased the lands and eliminated the claims which the Hamiltons had acquired from his wife's sisters.

Maxwell's casting in his lot with Arran led to his remaining march warden until March 1550. He held that office again several times, with short terms in 1552–3 and 1554–5; after his reappointment in 1557, at a time of great confusion (for much of 1559 the wardenship was unoccupied), he finally secured in 1560 an appointment which lasted until at least October 1567. The warden's office was a difficult and sometimes dangerous one, and came to be rewarded accordingly. In 1552 Maxwell became the first official to receive a supplement of £500 to his basic annual salary of £100. His being appointed several times as a border commissioner for negotiations with his English counterparts, together with a short spell as keeper of Liddesdale in 1554, indicates that his services were appreciated by both his own and the English governments. Indeed, when he returned briefly to office in 1579, Queen Elizabeth, informed by Lord Scrope of his endeavours, personally congratulated him on 'the administrations of justice and repairing and punishing on his side the disorders of those that seek to disturb the peace between England and Scotland' (*CSP Scot.*, 1574–81, 335). Earlier that year Maxwell, now Lord Herries, had presented a programme for administrative reform of the borders to Morton and his council. Its proposals included the suggestion that an armed force should be permanently based in the region, and the recommendation that the wardens should be assisted in their duties by representatives of the principal families within each march. This inevitably implied that the Maxwells would have to co-operate with the Johnstones, their great rivals in the west, and in January 1579, in acknowledgement that Herries was at least prepared to contemplate such a situation, Morton dismissed the existing warden, Lord Maxwell, and replaced him with his uncle. But the appointment was short-lived, for Herries was superseded by John Johnstone of that ilk in August, having presumably found that his advancing years made him unsuitable for such a demanding job.

Maxwell's loyalty to the Marian cause was an important aspect of his later career. This allegiance, like that of many other noblemen, flourished despite his own preference for the reformed religion, which in 1559 had resulted in his being incarcerated in Edinburgh Castle. Following his release he was a signatory of the treaty of Berwick, whereby English aid was forthcoming for the beleaguered lords of the congregation. Later in 1560 he subscribed to the first Book of Discipline. Maxwell was highly regarded by John Knox at this time; even when Maxwell began to display his Marian sympathies, Knox could still refer to him as 'a man stout and wittie' (*Knox's History*, 1.459) and of 'great judgment and experience' (ibid., 2.351).

At the time of the chaseabout raid in 1565, Maxwell attempted to mediate between the earl of Moray and the queen, and when his efforts failed he encouraged Moray to retreat to England. Following Mary's enforced abdication his position was at first ambivalent. Initially he was prominent as the outstanding representative of the queen's party, and the English ambassador Sir Nicholas Throckmorton referred to him as 'the cunning horseleech and the wisest of the whole faction; but, as the Queen of Scots says of him, there is nobody can be sure of him' (*CSP for.*, 1566–8, 324). This equivocal judgement must have seemed justified when in December 1567 Herries spoke out in favour of those who, following Mary's refusal to separate from Bothwell, had imprisoned her at Lochleven, and let it be known that he had allied himself to the party of the infant James VI. But soon afterwards he emerged as one of the queen's staunchest supporters. On 13 May 1568, following the queen's escape from Lochleven, Herries commanded Mary's cavalry at the battle of Langside where, despite being numerically superior, the Marian forces were decisively defeated. Subsequently Herries emerged as the key figure in the events surrounding Mary's flight into exile. While the queen rested at Terregles he contacted the English commander in Carlisle for permission for the refugees to enter England, while Mary's last night in Scotland was spent at Dundrennan Abbey, where one of Herries's sons was commendator. On 16 May Herries and a few other loyal followers accompanied Mary across the Solway Firth to Workington, where she placed herself at the mercy of Queen Elizabeth. The latter, concerned about Mary's presence in England but reluctant to appear to be sanctioning her overthrow in Scotland, conceived the idea of an Anglo-Scottish conference to discuss the possibility of restoring the Scottish queen. Not surprisingly, when Mary's supporters assembled shortly afterwards at Dumbarton, Herries was nominated to be one of her representatives at the forthcoming conference.

When the enquiry got under way at York in October 1568, the two main spokesmen for the Marian cause were Herries and John Lesley, bishop of Ross. Similarly when the proceedings were moved to Hampton Court in December it was principally Herries and Lesley who acted in defence of the queen against the allegations presented by the earl of Moray, leader of the king's party. But despite their efforts Elizabeth delivered a judgment in January 1569 which, though ambiguously phrased, meant in effect that Mary remained a prisoner in England. In the civil war between the king's and queen's factions which broke out in 1570 and lasted until May 1573, Herries, like so many of Mary's allies, was initially very active on her behalf, so much so that he was arrested by Moray's government in April 1569 and confined within Edinburgh Castle, where he remained until after the regent's assassination on 23 January 1570. In April of that year he joined such other leading Marians as the earls of Huntly, Argyll, and Atholl, when they gathered in Edinburgh, and he attended the parliament which they held in the capital two months later. One repercussion of their activities, and also of their sheltering English refugees from the northern risings of 1569–70, was that the king's party gave its approval to a retaliatory raid in the summer of 1570 by the earl of Sussex on the properties of Herries and other border families.

By 1571, however, Herries was becoming less involved in the Marian cause, though he continued to contact Elizabeth's government regarding the possibility of Mary's restoration, and warned the English queen that if she failed to adopt a more positive line he and his associates might look overseas for assistance. A year later he had recognized the inevitable; and while he was not himself present when Morton was elected regent, in November 1572, his son William, master of Herries, was. Shortly afterwards Morton's government repealed a number of statutes directed against Herries and his fellow Marians. Throughout Morton's regency Herries generally kept a low profile, and it was only when Morton lost office in 1578 that he reappeared on the scene. He was a member of the Argyll–Atholl faction which forced the regent's resignation, being one of those who demanded the surrender of Edinburgh Castle. Herries became a privy councillor in the short-lived administration which replaced Morton, and was also a commissioner representing the new government in talks with the church over proposed reforms. The latter appointment was made despite his having been cited for non-payment of his thirds of benefices and his also being in receipt of a comfortable pension from the bishopric of Galloway. Following Morton's return to power in the summer of 1578, Herries was one of eight nobles nominated on 8 September to assist the king in working towards 'the repose and quietness of the troubled commonwealth' (*Reg. PCS*, 26).

In 1581, unlike his nephew Lord Maxwell, who was a member of the jury which sentenced Morton to death, Herries took little part in the events which led to the ex-regent's execution. But he was a leading supporter of the duke of Lennox's faction, which briefly controlled Scottish affairs in the early 1580s, and, following the Ruthven raid of August 1582 which effectively ended the Lennox regime, he was a member of the delegation to James VI which sought (unsuccessfully) a meeting between the king and the fallen duke. It was one of his last recorded actions. Herries died in Edinburgh on Sunday, 20 January 1583, in 'an upper chamber of William Fowler's lodging', where, feeling too unwell to attend the afternoon's sermon, he had gone 'to see the boys bicker' (Calderwood, 3.232). He was buried in Terregles church. The house in which he died had once belonged to a prominent Edinburgh councillor who had also been a supporter of Queen Mary. His widow died at Terregles on 14 March 1594, and in her will asked to be buried beside her late husband.

Herries was the author of a text published in 1836, from a seventeenth-century abridgement, as *Historical Memoirs of the Reign of Mary Queen of Scots, and a Portion of the Reign of King James the Sixth*. Covering the years 1542 to 1571, it is a work of considerable value, despite its Marian perspective, as one of the comparatively few contemporary accounts of this period. But although his writings assure Herries of a niche in Scottish historiography, there is no doubt that his greatest importance lay in his activities as an administrator of the borders, where he faithfully served both Mary of Guise and Mary, queen of Scots, for more than twenty years. Even his opponent the earl of Morton recognized his talents in that capacity, for not only did Morton in 1579 adopt many of the proposals put forward by Herries for the reform of border government, but he also gave him a final stint as march warden, when he was in his late sixties.

G. R. HEWITT

Sources *Reg. PCS*, 1st ser., vol. 2 · *CSP Scot.*, 1571–81 · *CSP for.*, 1558–89 · D. Calderwood, *The history of the Kirk of Scotland*, ed. T. Thomson and D. Laing, 8 vols., Wodrow Society, 7 (1842–9), vol. 3 · *Scots peerage*, 4.407–13; 6.479–81 · W. Fraser, ed., *The book of Carlaverock: memoirs of the Maxwells, earls of Nithsdale*, 2 vols. (1873), vol. 1 · *John Knox's History of the Reformation in Scotland*, ed. W. C. Dickinson, 2 vols. (1949) · Lord Herries [John Maxwell], *Historical memoirs of the reign of Mary queen of Scots*, ed. R. Pitcairn, Abbotsford Club, 6 (1836) · D. Moysie, *Memoirs of the affairs of Scotland, 1577–1603*, ed. J. Dennistoun, Bannatyne Club, 39 (1830) · J. Spottiswood, *The history of the Church of Scotland*, ed. M. Napier and M. Russell, 2, Bannatyne Club, 93 (1850) · *DNB* · T. I. Rae, *The administration of the Scottish frontier, 1513–1603* (1966) · G. Donaldson, *The first trial of Mary, queen of Scots* (1969) · G. Hewitt, *Scotland under Morton* (1982) · G. M. Fraser, *The steel bonnets* (1971) · M. Merriman, *The rough wooings: Mary queen of Scots, 1542–1551* (2000)

Maxwell, John, earl of Morton (1553–1593), magnate, was born on 24 April 1553, the posthumous second son of Robert, sixth Lord Maxwell (*d.* 1552), and Beatrix (*d.* in or after 1583), second daughter of James Douglas, third earl of Morton. His father having died on the previous 13 September John Maxwell was raised by his uncle, Sir John *Maxwell of Terregles, the future fourth Lord Herries.

Supporter of Queen Mary On the death of his elder brother, Robert, on 16 January 1555, Maxwell inherited the family properties of Maxwell and Caerlaverock, and the bailieries of Sweetheart, Dundrennan, Holywood, and Lincluden. His early devotion to Mary, queen of Scots, alarmed the English ambassador Thomas Randolph, who in a statement of May 1565 (which may in fact refer to Herries) observed that Maxwell 'weighs more his mistress's will than her danger', being 'loth to attempt against her mind' (*CSP Scot.*, 1563–9, 169). After Mary's demission of the crown on 24 July 1568 in favour of her son, James, Maxwell joined twenty-four other disaffected nobles on the 30th in writing to the duke of Alva, the governor of the Netherlands, asking for money, thereby establishing his first contacts with Spain. In July 1569 he attended the Perth convention, voting in favour of Mary's divorce from Bothwell. Following Regent Moray's assassination on 21 January 1570, Elizabeth instructed her west march warden, Henry, Baron Scrope, to ravage Maxwell's lands in Dumfriesshire, on the grounds of his association with the English rebel Leonard Dacre. The real purpose of the sustained attacks was to prevent Maxwell and Herries from taking Edinburgh on Mary's behalf. After a pause Scrope renewed his raids and between 22 and 28 August 1570 he demolished Lord Maxwell's principal strongholds, including his castles at Dumfries.

Maxwell and Herries could not prevent Regent Lennox from occupying Paisley in early 1571, but they allied themselves with Sir John Gordon of Lochinvar and marched on Edinburgh on 14 April. After taking the capital for the queen, Maxwell attended the queen's parliament of 12 June 1571. By 20 November his kinsmen had signed an unusual bond of manrent, pledging both their support for, and confidence in, their young leader. On 17 February 1572, however, Maxwell married Elizabeth Douglas (*d.* 1637), youngest sister of the eighth earl of Angus, and in so doing was thought 'to acknowledge the kingis auctoritie', indicating an apparent swing in loyalties (Thomson, *Diurnal*, 259). They had seven children: John *Maxwell, later ninth Lord Maxwell; Robert *Maxwell, created first earl of Nithsdale in 1620; James of Kirkconnel; Elizabeth, wife of John, sixth Lord Herries; Margaret, wife of John Wallace of Craigie; Jean; and Agnes, who married her brother John's supporter William Douglas of Greenlaw.

Warden of the west march Maxwell proved outwardly amenable to the triumphant king's party under Morton, whom he personally helped to select in a special convention of earls and lords in November 1572. Having attended the king's parliament (of 30 April 1573), only weeks before the fall of Edinburgh Castle, Maxwell was confirmed in possession of Lochmaben Castle on 26 October and appointed warden of the west march. In that office he proved remarkably conscientious. He complained to the general assembly about the poor condition of the kirks of Annandale and Nithsdale in March 1574 and amazed Scrope with his judicious administration. In November 1576 Maxwell delivered forty-two bills at a single border truce day, leading the English warden to enthuse that 'the like example of justice done in one day has not been seen or heard of in these borders' (Fraser, 1.231). Even so, Maxwell found it difficult to secure the support of the

lieges of Dumfries, and on 12 December that year Morton arranged to enforce an act of 1564 requiring all nobles and property holders to attend the warden at truce days. Relations between Maxwell and the regent had up to this time been cordial (Morton hosted Maxwell's wedding celebrations at Dalkeith Palace), even though Morton suspected that Maxwell would attempt to press a claim to the earldom of Morton derived from his mother. On 25 May 1577, however, a disagreement between them led to Maxwell's resignation as warden and his replacement by his brother-in-law, the eighth earl of Angus. Warded at Edinburgh in July, and removed to St Andrews in September, Maxwell finally obtained his release on the regent's resignation in early March 1578, and on the 25th he was reappointed warden. In June he attempted to block Morton's recovery of power by voting against his membership of the king's council, and, when that failed, questioned the legitimacy of the parliament held at Stirling in July. Raising a force of 7000 men with the earls of Argyll and Erroll, Maxwell engaged to free the king from Morton's 'captivity', but was prevented by the army of 5000 raised by Angus and the last-minute arbitration of the English ambassador Robert Bowes. On 23 January 1579 Herries replaced Maxwell as warden, leading to tension between the kinsmen and Maxwell's refusal to surrender Lochmaben Castle. With Morton now back in power, Maxwell found caution to ward himself in Dundee (on 13 July 1579) and Blackness (on 27 October); he was finally released in December. By this time he was regarded as a political firebrand, widely trusted neither by the Morton regime nor by the English.

Maxwell inherited a conflict with John Johnstone, laird of Johnstone, which was worsened by the latter's appointment as march warden on 24 August 1579. Their rivalry protracted a bloody struggle for regional dominance that had lasted since at least the 1520s and which had reduced Dumfriesshire to a well-nigh permanent state of war; latterly the feud between the two families had been intensified by the participation of client surnames such as the Irvines and Armstrongs. On 4 May 1580 Maxwell was forced to appear before the privy council for withholding vital bills and scrolls which Johnstone required in order to conduct truce days with Scrope. On 2 September each signed an assurance of responsibility for the continuing good behaviour of his family members and retainers. However, his developing friendship with the king's new favourite, Esmé Stewart, earl (later duke) of Lennox, led to Maxwell's nomination as an extraordinary gentleman of the king's chamber on 24 October. As early as December he and Herries undertook to pacify the west marches, an assertion of their family's power and also a direct insult to Morton's nominee Johnstone, who relinquished his wardenship to Maxwell in April 1581.

Catholic earl On 5 June 1581, only four days after sitting on the assize that condemned Morton for his alleged involvement in Darnley's assassination, Maxwell was granted the regent's forfeited estates as a free earldom and regality, though the lands of Aberdour, Dalkeith, and Caldercleir were reserved to his ally Lennox. On 29 October Maxwell was officially created earl of Morton and Lord Carlyle and

Eskdaill. He secured his new properties by parliamentary ratification on 28–9 November 1581. Controversy followed when he criticized Scrope's refusal to punish Englishmen who took part in burning Langholm Castle and abducting its captain Herbert Maxwell in September, and threatened 'to revenge yt with burninge in like maner in England' (Bain, 1.77). Following the Ruthven raid of August 1582, Lennox was removed from power and his friend Maxwell was again ousted as warden on 19 November, ostensibly for his inability to control his Armstrong and Graham adherents in Ettrick Forest; Maxwell was succeeded once more by Johnstone. His political influence suffered serious setbacks when he failed to capture Edinburgh and Holyrood castles with Lennox on 30 November, and when Herries, his mentor and chief adviser, died on 20 January 1583. Hopeful of gaining support from the continental Catholic powers, Maxwell left for France in late May. He was back in Scotland by 4 September, having landed at Pittenweem with a store of gold and correspondence, carefully observed by English authorities, who now considered him one of the 'chief countenancers' of Border malefactors (ibid., 111).

By 1585 Maxwell's Roman Catholic sympathies had become obvious. His formal conversion in that year probably owed something to the influence of his cousin William Maxwell, fifth Lord Herries, who had converted by 1584, as well as to his own travels in Europe. He may also have been moved by political considerations, since in January 1585 he broke with James Stewart, earl of Arran, who had been in control of government since the previous summer, in dispute over the Maxwell territories of Pollok and Maxwellhaugh. Arran subsequently (on 29 January 1586) revoked the attainder on the earldom of Morton with a view to bestowing it upon Angus, a move that seriously threatened the claim by Maxwell. The latter was himself outlawed for a series of minor offences against Warden Johnstone on 26 February, and was ordered to surrender the keys of his houses to the king on 10 March. In response to an earlier Johnstone raid, Maxwell's retainers Robert Maxwell of Castlemilk and David Maxwell led a troop of 120 men to destroy Johnstone's chief residence at Lochwood on 6 April 1585. These hostile measures against the absent warden precipitated Maxwell's enforced surrender of the earldom of Morton on 10 April. Undeterred, he continued his attack on Johnstone's interests in Dumfriesshire, invading Lockerbie on 27 April, seizing two fortified stone houses within the town on 7 May, and finally capturing Johnstone himself on 21 August. Although superficially reconciled with Arran, on 1 November Maxwell joined Angus and the banished earl of Mar and master of Glamis in expelling Arran from Stirling Castle, having assembled 1300 foot soldiers and 700 horse for the expedition. Maxwell's supporters were particularly exuberant in pillaging the burgh's public buildings, with a 'great reaf of horsse and guidis' being seized by Kinmont Willie Armstrong and his sons (Moysie, 54). The subsequent political revolution caused by Arran's defeat was a personal triumph for Maxwell on all fronts: on 18 November he was reappointed warden, and he sat in parliament at Linlithgow as earl of Morton in December, when he was also granted a retroactive indemnity excusing all acts committed since April 1569. But the fact that he was discovered celebrating Christmas mass at both Lincluden College and in his own lodgings at Dumfries suggests that Maxwell misjudged his new ascendancy. After freely accepting trial he was questioned by the king and warded in Edinburgh Castle; his imminent release was announced on 14 February 1586.

Exile and return On 13 April 1586 Maxwell provided caution of £1000 to appear before the general assembly and submit to an investigation of his religious life, promising on 14 May to remain within a 4 mile radius of Edinburgh. By 21 August he was once again serving as warden, though his relations with Scrope deteriorated when he demanded the return of a Captain Case who was then an English prisoner; Scrope in turn continued to gather intelligence on Maxwell's suspected papist activities. Yet neither Scrope nor even Sir Francis Walsingham's spy network managed to detect Maxwell's plot with the sixth earl of Huntly and Lord Claud Hamilton to oust James's protestant advisers with the help of troops subsidized by Spain. Maxwell refused to sign the reformed articles presented to him at Dumfries on 16 January 1587 and, owing also to his unequivocally hostile reaction to the execution of Queen Mary on 18 February, was banished by the king on 14 April with instructions not to return without royal warrant. In his absence the Morton earldom was transferred to the earl of Angus by act of parliament on 29 July 1587. On 9 June the west march was entrusted to his cousin, the politically reliable Lord Herries.

Maxwell spent the bulk of his exile in Portugal and Spain, negotiating personally with Philip II over the possibilities of Scotland's deep-water ports being used by the Armada. However, Philip refused to commit himself to overthrowing the Scottish government, wishing instead to destabilize Anglo-Scottish relations and thus distract England from interfering with his policy of reconquest in the United Provinces. In April 1588 a disillusioned Maxwell returned to Scotland without licence, in a bid to launch an insurrection in conjunction with his fellow Catholic nobles. In response the king personally led an expedition against Maxwell, who after a dramatic boat chase was apprehended by Sir William Stewart (the brother of Arran) on 5 May and warded in Blackness in August, before being returned to Stewart's care in September. Maxwell was still lodging 'in a burghers house' at Edinburgh on 15 September 1589 (CSP Scot., 1589–93, 155). He was released in advance of the king's wedding voyage in October, and assigned to replace Sir John Carmichael as warden of the west march, but the appointment did not take effect. Maxwell's subsequent behaviour impressed Bowes, who nevertheless reported in August 1590 that the lord had 'retorned to his old papistrie far contrary to his former protestation', though not in such a way as threatened the king politically (ibid., 841). Indeed, Maxwell had moderated his conduct, in that although he remained Catholic in faith he became in practice a *politique*, who never again betrayed the king's interest. He was rewarded by an alliance with Chancellor Maitland and by readmission to the privy council in January 1591. On 9 March Maxwell appeared with the ninth earl of Erroll to subscribe articles on faith before the kirk commissioners of Edinburgh, and he attended parliament at Edinburgh on 6 August. Despite English fears of his dominance on the frontier, he was again made warden of the west march on 28 July, though the king withdrew his 'unusually ample justiciary powers' on 19 September 1592 in response to the concerns of the noblemen of Nithsdale and Galloway (Fraser, 1.287).

Defeat and death Maxwell signed the confession of faith at Edinburgh on 26 January 1593, though this was followed on 2 February by a farcical skirmish with William Douglas over seating arrangements in an Edinburgh kirk: Douglas had succeeded his father as ninth earl of Angus, and also claimed to be earl of Morton. Maxwell had continued to style himself earl, and disputes over the title between rival earls of Morton continued until 1620, when Robert Maxwell was made earl of Nithsdale instead. However, John Maxwell's attention was soon turned elsewhere by his conflict with the Johnstones after the escape from Edinburgh Castle on 10 June 1593 of James Johnstone, who had succeeded his father in June 1587. Maxwell needed little persuading to join with the barons and lairds of the west march against Johnstone as 'he loved above all things to be followed' (Spottiswoode, 2.445–6). He was granted a royal commission to apprehend Johnstone—who had been charged with assisting the first earl of Bothwell in his recent raid on the king—and in early December Maxwell marched on Annandale with 1500 men to engage Johnstone's force of 800. On the 6 December Maxwell himself crossed the River Annan with a detachment of troops, only to find Johnstone on the other side, placed atop a slope with an obvious strategic advantage. The Johnstones charged downhill into Maxwell's army, killing those who could not escape and forcing the remainder to retreat back across the river. Maxwell himself was killed in the rout on Dryfe Sands the following day, though traditions differ as to how and by whom: William Johnstone of Kirkhill, the wife of James Johnstone of Kirkton (who was said to have stabbed him with a set of tower keys), Gideon Murray of Elibank, and the laird of Johnstone himself are all reported as striking him down. One account stresses the savage nature of his death at the hand of the Johnstones, who apparently 'did cut af baith his hands, and careit the same with thayme on speir points, as a memorial of his perfidie, and for ostentatioun of ther awin glore' (Thomson, *James the Sext*, 299). Maxwell's body lay unburied until 16 February 1598, when the privy council ordered its interment within twenty days. He was then buried in Lincluden College church, as was his widow, who died in February 1637 after two further marriages.

J. R. M. SIZER

Sources W. Fraser, ed., *The book of Carlaverock: memoirs of the Maxwells, earls of Nithsdale*, 2 vols. (1873), vol. 1 · *CSP Scot., 1571–93* · *Scots peerage*, vol. 6 · K. Brown, *Bloodfeud in Scotland: violence, justice and politics in early modern society* (1986) · T. I. Rae, *Administration of the Scottish frontier, 1513–1603* (1966) · J. Bain, ed., *The border papers: calendar of letters and papers relating to the affairs of the borders of England and Scotland*, 2 vols. (1894–6), vol. 1 · D. Moysie, *Memoirs of the affairs of Scotland, 1577–1603*, ed. J. Dennistoun, Bannatyne Club, 39 (1830) · [T. Thomson], ed., *The historie and life of King James the Sext*, Bannatyne Club, 13 (1825) · *APS, 1567–92* · *Reg. PCS*, 1st ser. · J. Spottiswoode, *History of the Church of Scotland*, ed. M. Napier and M. Russell, 3 vols., Spottiswoode Society, 6 (1847–51) · T. Thomson, ed., *A diurnal of remarkable occurrents that have passed within the country of Scotland*, Bannatyne Club, 43 (1833) · GEC, *Peerage*, 8, 9 · K. Brown, 'The making of a *politique*: the Counter-Reformation and the regional politics of John, eighth Lord Maxwell', *SHR*, 66 (1987), 152–75
Archives U. Hull, Brynmor Jones L., Maxwell muniments, Scottish papers of Maxwell-Constable family of Everingham, DDEV/80

Maxwell, John, ninth Lord Maxwell (*b.* in or before **1586**, *d.* **1613**), nobleman, was the eldest son of John *Maxwell, earl of Morton and eighth Lord Maxwell (1553–1593), and Lady Elizabeth (*c.*1568–1637), daughter of David Douglas, seventh earl of Angus. He was placed under the guardianship of his father's cousin William Maxwell, fifth Lord Herries, and appears to have been brought up in Edinburgh. He was served heir to his father on 10 March 1597 and on 9 August that year he married Lady Margaret (*c.*1580–*c.*1608), daughter of John *Hamilton, first marquess of Hamilton (1539/40–1604). The couple had one son (who died young) but by 1601 were estranged. Several years later Margaret Hamilton died during divorce proceedings (instigated by Maxwell).

One of the most prominent landholders in the southwest of Scotland, Maxwell inherited a long-running feud with the Johnstone family, particularly significant as a result of the killing of his father by James Johnstone at the battle of Dryfesdale Sands. On 22 March 1599 Maxwell's father-in-law undertook a £5000 bond to ensure that Maxwell did not enter Nithsdale to confront Johnstone. In spite of this, on 15 September the privy council decided that Maxwell would be controlled better under ward in Edinburgh Castle. Maxwell was not warded as he failed to attend the council in November (and again the next June). Consequently, he was denounced as a rebel. In July 1600 a further caution for £10,000 was lodged for Maxwell not to enter Annandale, Nithsdale, or Galloway but to reside at the house of Hamilton. On 16 July 1601 he again endured warding in Edinburgh Castle but on 12 January 1602 he escaped. In February 1602 the Johnstone–Maxwell feud was heightened when Maxwell attacked and killed William Johnstone of Eschieshiels. Then, as James Johnstone of Briggs took shelter in the house of James Bratten at Dalfibble, Maxwell burnt him alive. The feud continued intermittently but was seemingly reconciled before the privy council in June 1605, when Maxwell issued a 'letter of slains' forgiving his father's killer (now styled Sir James Johnstone of Dunskellie) for his part in the murder.

Maxwell also feuded with the Douglas earls of Morton, who he felt had deprived him of his right to be earl of Morton in succession to his father. Within Dumfriesshire, Maxwell did hold local courts using the style 'earl of Morton' but he was never formally recognized as such by the government. As Lord Maxwell he attended the parliaments of March and May 1606 but in the intervening period the privy council had to intervene to prevent him duelling with William Douglas, heir to the laird of Drumlanrig. On 23 May 1607 Maxwell and Morton subscribed a band that there was no feud existing between them but on 8 August Maxwell was again denounced rebel for challenging Morton over his title. On 24 September he was placed back under ward in Edinburgh Castle and on 4 December, with the assistance of fellow inmate James McConnell, he escaped from the castle for a second time. Two weeks later he was again denounced rebel.

Maxwell was regularly out of favour with the central government because of both his volatility and his Catholicism. While in ward for the first time in Edinburgh Castle he was attended by a minister in an (unsuccessful) attempt to convert him to protestantism. In December 1606 a convention of the clergy again suggested that Maxwell undertake instruction in the reformed faith and he was warded in Leith for his beliefs. On 12 January 1608 a summons of forfeiture was issued against him. Despite strenuous efforts to capture him, he remained at large in Dumfriesshire but in April 1608 arranged to meet the laird of Johnstone finally to settle their differences. During the conference a quarrel erupted between the servants of the men and, when Johnstone attempted to find out the cause, Maxwell shot him in the back. On 28 April a proclamation was issued to capture him dead or alive. Thereafter he fled to France. In his absence, he was found guilty in parliament of three counts of treason, the murder of two Johnstones (in 1602), the breaking of ward from Edinburgh Castle in 1607, and the murder under trust of Johnstone in 1608. He was condemned to death and forfeiture of his estates and honours.

In March 1612 Maxwell returned to Scotland under the protection of George, fifth earl of Caithness. The government reissued warrants for his capture and in September he was arrested in Caithness. He was transferred to prison in Edinburgh Castle and on 10 May 1613 an order was passed in council to carry out the previously agreed sentence. On 21 May, at the Market Cross of Edinburgh, he was beheaded. Thereafter his body was removed by Mark Ker and buried at Newbattle Abbey. Five years later his brother Robert *Maxwell (b. after 1586, d. 1646) was restored to the Maxwell peerage.   ROB MACPHERSON

Sources W. Fraser, ed., *The book of Carlaverock: memoirs of the Maxwells, earls of Nithsdale*, 2 vols. (1873) · *CSP Scot., 1547–1603* · *APS, 1593–1625* · R. Pitcairn, ed., *Ancient criminal trials in Scotland*, 3 vols., Bannatyne and Maitland Clubs (1833) · *Scots peerage* · *Reg. PCS*, 1st ser. · [T. Thomson], ed., *The historie and life of King James the Sext*, Bannatyne Club, 13 (1825) · T. Thomson, ed., *Acts and proceedings of the general assemblies of the Kirk of Scotland*, 3 pts, Bannatyne Club, 81 (1839–45) · G. Ridpath, *Border history of England and Scotland*, facs. edn (1979)
Archives U. Hull, Constable-Maxwell family (Baron Herries) collection

Maxwell, John (d. 1647), Church of Ireland archbishop of Tuam, was the son of John Maxwell of Cavens in Nithsdale, Kirkcudbrightshire. He entered the University of St Andrews, where he graduated MA on 29 July 1611. In 1615 he was called and ordained minister of Mortlach parish church in Banffshire, which lay in the patronage of the crown. From 1622 he held four successive pastoral charges in Edinburgh. On 18 July 1622 he was chosen by the town council to be minister of St Giles but was translated to Trinity College Church on 25 November 1625. Three weeks later, on 14 December, however, he was nominated by the burgh magistracy to the second charge in St Giles and officially admitted on 27 January 1626. Later that year he was finally promoted to the first charge in the same incumbency. At an unknown date he married Elizabeth Innes; they had four sons, John, David, James, and Robert, and five daughters, Anne, Janet, Elizabeth, Rachel, and Bethia.

Maxwell was initially brought to the king's notice through the recommendation of his cousin James Maxwell of Innerwick (afterwards earl of Dirleton), who as a gentleman of the king's bedchamber was ideally placed to promote the interests of his kinsman. In July 1629 John Maxwell was sent to court in London, ostensibly to discuss how best the Scottish church should combat Roman Catholicism. In reality, however, his trip south had been arranged with a view to discussing the introduction of a new Scottish liturgy which conformed to, and imitated, the English prayer book. Fearful of an adverse and possibly violent reaction from Scottish public opinion Maxwell conveyed to Bishop William Laud of London the Scottish hierarchy's view that it was inexpedient simply to transpose wholesale the English liturgy to Scotland. Nevertheless Maxwell made a favourable impression on the future archbishop, and became his chief acolyte in Scotland. He returned from court in November 1629 reputedly bearing the king's instructions that the Church of Scotland was to prepare for conformity with its southern counterpart. As an enthusiast for the ceremonial and liturgical changes, he preached to his congregation in Edinburgh on Christmas day 1629 with 'not only bitter invectives, but curses also, aganis all such as would not keep such holie days' (Row, 350). In 1632 he was involved in the suspension and deposition of the Scottish presbyterians Robert Blair, John Livingstone, George Dunbar, and Josiah Welsh from office in the Church of Ireland. He also played a conspicuous part in the trial of John Elphinstone, second earl of Balmerino, in 1634 for his opposition to the crown's religious programme.

Maxwell's endeavour to suppress religious dissent was not merely predicated on loyalty to the king, however, but sprang from deeply held doctrinal convictions. Unlike the previous generation of Scottish churchmen Maxwell was a *jure divino* episcopalian. Preaching in Edinburgh on 22 and 31 July 1631 he sought scriptural justification for this belief, but it earned him a swift rebuttal from the Scottish hierarchy who wanted to distance themselves from an inflammatory and widely discredited doctrine that appeared to repudiate the biblical ideals of the protestant Reformation. Nevertheless his strident attitude and forthright courage gained him the plaudits of the growing constituency of Anglican sacramentalists who found favour with the king.

For his service to crown and church, on 23 April 1633 Maxwell was elevated to the bishopric of Ross and was consecrated in the presence of the king at some date between 15 June and 18 July that same year. He also took part in Charles's Scottish coronation. On 23 June he caused a stir at a service in St Giles attended by the king when he peremptorily dismissed the ordinary reader and replaced him with two English chaplains dressed in full ecclesiastical vestments, who, with the aid of others present, including the bishops, conducted divine worship in accordance with English practice. From as early as October 1634 he is known to have used and promoted the English liturgy in his cathedral at Fortrose in Easter Ross.

Maxwell continued to be rewarded for his stalwart service. On 19 March 1634 he gained an annual pension of £166 while his patrimony was enlarged on 22 October that year by a crown grant of the priory at Beauly in Inverness-shire and on 26 March 1636 by the addition of a number of charges and chaplaincies. His political and social ascendancy was enhanced when he was made a privy councillor and an extraordinary lord of session in December 1633 and a justice of the peace in 1634. Henry Guthry in his *Memoirs* pertinently noted that Maxwell was 'a man of great parts; but the mischief was, they were accompanied with unbounded ambition' (*Memoirs of Henry Guthry*, 16–17). His failure to secure the office of Scottish treasurer that went to John Stewart, the first earl of Traquair, in 1636 was the cause of resentment and future animosity between the pair.

Maxwell's ascendancy in Scotland was, however, cut short by the covenanting revolution of 1637–8. The Glasgow assembly excommunicated him in his absence on 13 December 1638. He signed a declinature against the assembly and in August 1639 was signatory to a protestation that declared the assembly's proceedings unlawful. He had already departed for the safety of the king's court in March 1639 after being interrupted in the course of conducting worship by a party of covenanters who swiftly requisitioned all the offending prayer books before hurling them into the Moray Firth. His wife initially took refuge with the children in the home of her brother Alexander Innes, the minister of Rothiemay, but they left Scotland in August to join Maxwell in England.

From his enforced exile Maxwell emerged as a highly effective polemicist for the royalist and episcopal cause. In 1640, his *Epistle congratulatorie of Lysimachus Nicanor of the Societie of Jesu, to the covenanters of Scotland, wherin is paralleled our sweet harmony and correspondency in divers materiall points of doctrine and practice* made his name anathema to the new regime in Scotland. He began by congratulating the covenanters as 'most worthy Brethren of the holy League', rejoicing 'in behalfe of our Mother Church of Rome at your begun returne from your former errors and heresies' and taunting them with an ironic expectation that, having 'forsaken the former erroneous Doctrine of the Protestants concerning the "Civil Magistrate", and … happily joyned with us, you will also betimes abjure all that yet remaineth' (J. Maxwell, *The Epistle Congratulatorie*,

1641, 1). He made no secret of his contempt for and opposition to the political philosophies of John Knox and George Buchanan, readily accepted and promulgated by the covenanters, that had challenged the notion that kings ruled by divine right and were therefore unaccountable to the law of the land and her people. The Scottish parliament declared him an incendiary in July 1641 and proclaimed him guilty of treason in November that same year. However, Maxwell continued to publish on the same themes as before in *Episcopacy not Abjured in his Majesties Realm of Scotland* (1641), *An answer to a gentleman who desired of a divine some reasons by which it might appear how inconsistent presbyteriall government is with monarchie*, and most notably, *Sacro-sancta regum majestas, or, The Sacred and Royall Prerogative of Christian Kings* (1644), a trenchant call for the restoration of royal authority indebted to Jean Bodin. Samuel Rutherford responded to the latter in *Lex rex*. Finally in *Burden of Issachar, or, The tyrannical power and practices of the presbyteriall government in Scotland* (1646), Maxwell defended Erastian episcopacy.

Meanwhile, Maxwell had continued high in the king's favour. On 12 October 1640 he was appointed bishop of the Irish see of Killala and Achonry by royal patent after the deposition of his fellow Scot, Patrick Adair, for his commitment to the national covenant. Trinity College, Dublin, conferred on Maxwell the title of DD the same year. On the outbreak of the Irish rising in 1641 he was forced to flee for his life from his episcopal residence at Killala. Intercepted at the bridge of Shrule, co. Mayo, he was stripped naked, beaten, and left for dead. Only the intervention of Barnabas O'Brien, sixth earl of Thomond, saved his life. After a short spell in Dublin, Maxwell made his way to the royal court at Oxford where he served as a chaplain to Charles I. On 30 August 1645 he was elevated to the archbishopric of Tuam by letter patent and returned to Ireland to take up his prestigious post. On receiving news that the king had surrendered to the Scottish army on 30 January 1647 he retired to his private chambers, where he was found dead upon his knees at prayer on 14 February. He was interred in Christ Church, Dublin.

A. S. WAYNE PEARCE

Sources *Fasti Scot.*, new edn, vol. 7 · R. Keith and J. Spottiswoode, *An historical catalogue of the Scottish bishops, down to the year 1688*, new edn, ed. M. Russel [M. Russell] (1824) · *DNB* · *APS*, 1625–41 · *The memoirs of Henry Guthry, late bishop*, 2nd edn (1747) · J. Row, *The history of the Kirk of Scotland, from the year 1558 to August 1637*, ed. D. Laing, Wodrow Society, 4 (1842) · *The letters and journals of Robert Baillie*, ed. D. Laing, 3 vols. (1841–2), vols. 1–2 · D. G. Mullan, *Episcopacy in Scotland: the history of an idea, 1560–1608* (1986) · G. Donaldson, *The making of the Scottish prayer book of 1637* (1954) · G. W. Sprott, *Scottish liturgies of the reign of James VI* (1871) · J. Spalding, *The history of the troubles and memorable transactions in Scotland and England, from 1624 to 1645*, ed. J. Skene, 2 vols., Bannatyne Club, 25 (1828–9), vol. 1, pp. 17, 53; vol. 2, pp. 40, 284
Archives NL Scot.

Maxwell, Sir John, of Pollok, eighth baronet (1791–1865), landowner and politician, was born on 12 May 1791 at Pollok House, Renfrewshire. The mansion and surrounding lands were eventually absorbed into Glasgow, and in

1966 the family gifted the estate to the city for use as public parkland. He was the second of four children and the only son of Sir John Maxwell of Pollok, seventh baronet (1768–1844), and his wife, Hannah Ann Gardiner (1764–1841), daughter of Captain Richard Gardiner, of Mount Amelia, Norfolk. Maxwell senior was a flamboyant figure who had served briefly as an army officer before devoting his energies to farming, hunting, and politics. A whig of radical inclinations, he served as MP for the textile community of Paisley between 1832 and 1834. Hannah, Lady Maxwell, enthusiastically supported her husband's politics, to the extent that their eldest daughter, Harriet, described her (in verse) as 'an ultra Reformer, the best in the nation' (Fraser, 1.428). The Maxwell family was close-knit, outgoing, and campaigning; it was also one of the oldest, wealthiest, and socially most prominent in Renfrewshire.

From the age of seven Maxwell—who was known as 'the younger', even after his father's death—received a thorough education at boarding-schools in Renfrewshire and Lincolnshire. Between 1805 and 1809 he attended Westminster School before proceeding as a gentleman commoner to Christ Church, Oxford, which he left in 1812, without taking a degree, subsequently attending classes at Edinburgh University. He had keen scholarly interests, especially a lifelong devotion to history and genealogy, and during 1813–15 undertook extensive travels across eastern Europe, Palestine, and Egypt, the antiquities of Egypt leaving a profound impression on him. However, his early career ambitions were political. In 1818 he was returned as whig MP for Renfrewshire and he represented the seat continuously until 1830, when he stood down. After unsuccessfully contesting the Lanarkshire constituency in 1831, he topped the poll the following year, in the first general election after the Reform Bill. He represented Lanarkshire until he retired from parliament in 1837.

There was consistency in Maxwell's politics throughout his years at Westminster. In 1819 he articulated his outlook in a pamphlet dedicated to 'the honest reformers of Scotland', where he stressed the need for constitutional change, while at the same time strongly criticizing the confrontational attitudes of extreme radicals; the voice of 'blasting society', as he put it (Maxwell, *A Letter Addressed to the Honest Reformers*, 18). He was writing at a time of economic depression in Scotland's textile districts, with unemployment having a dislocating impact on Renfrewshire communities, notably Eastwood, the parish where the Pollok estate and the populous weaving village of Pollokshaws were located. The threat of civil unrest was preoccupying both urban and rural élites, and Maxwell believed that tensions had been exacerbated by free-market competition in the wake of the Napoleonic wars. He consequently called for greater protection and regulation to safeguard manufacturing industry and ensure minimum standards of living for operatives, above all in the volatile hand-loom weaving sector. He also castigated those who had recently acquired wealth through speculation, adding that his own personal fortune derived from his family's careful husbandry of its resources over seven

hundred years. Evidently uneasy about his social position, there was nevertheless a conservative and paternalistic rationale underlying his defence of the upper classes. As he wrote in 1819: 'The rank, the wealth, the distinctions, they enjoy are for the interest of all classes; and of political necessity' (ibid., 19).

Parts of Lanarkshire, like Renfrewshire, were becoming heavily industrialized during the early nineteenth century, and Maxwell's priorities as MP reflected the county's rapidly changing economic profile. Hand-loom weaving had experienced a sharp fall in profit margins, causing wages to contract, while employers were beginning to invest in power-looms, primarily for cotton fabrics. The weavers' appeals for parliamentary assistance predated 1815, but from 1832 renewed efforts were made to seek improvements, notably through wage regulation. He was to the fore in furthering the weavers' cause at Westminster, supported by a small and politically diverse group of MPs, including John Fielden, the radical member for Oldham. The campaign took off in 1834, when Maxwell secured the appointment of a select committee to investigate the grievances contained in the weavers' petitions to parliament. The committee, chaired by Maxwell, was receptive to calls for empowering local boards of trade to fix wage levels, and in July 1835 he introduced a bill (drafted by Fielden) to the House of Commons. However, there was concerted opposition to the principles of interventionism and the minimum wage, and the bill was defeated under pressure from economic liberals, led by the president of the Board of Trade, Charles Poulett Thomson, one of Manchester's MPs. Despite attempts by Maxwell to revive the bill during the next parliamentary session, no further legislative progress was made.

Maxwell stood down as MP in the 1837 general election. The family's outspoken radicalism was disturbing fellow whigs in Scotland, concerned that the Lanarkshire seat would be lost. Yet even after 1837 he continued to take an interest in politics, and in a pamphlet of 1852 he expressed his antipathy to free trade, excessive taxation, overseas investment, and emigration. All, he suggested, drained the resources of the nation, while cultivation of the land, 'the surest possession we have', represented a patriotic force for regeneration (Maxwell, *Suggestions Arising out of the Present Want of Employment*, 16). He and his father were characterized by their single-mindedness and individualism, hence their reputation as nonconformists outside the whig mainstream. There were also contradictions in Maxwell's radicalism, reflected in his fascination with the family's lengthy pedigree, which he saw as testimony to the resilience of the landed interest. In 1863 he fulfilled a long-standing ambition by commissioning two elaborate, privately printed volumes which gave a detailed history of the Maxwells, and reproduced documents and charters from their extensive archives. This labour of love reputedly cost him £1500.

In later years Maxwell claimed that he had retired from parliament because he favoured the establishment in the debate over the church–state connection in Scotland and wanted to avoid dividing the Lanarkshire electorate. His own religious convictions were strong and also ecumenical. He supported the Church of Scotland by making generous financial provision for building a new parish church at Eastwood, which opened for worship in 1863. On his lands he provided low-cost sites for churches from a range of denominations. Yet, as shown by the evidence of the bequests made in his will, he was personally drawn to the Scottish Episcopal church. So, too, was his wife, Lady Matilda Harriet Bruce (1802–1857), the second daughter of Thomas *Bruce, seventh earl of Elgin and eleventh earl of Kincardine; Maxwell married relatively late in life, on 14 October 1839, and the couple had no children. After the death of Maxwell's father in 1844, they took up residence at Pollok House and thereafter devoted themselves to running their substantial lands and properties to the south of Glasgow. They were also preoccupied with charitable and philanthropic interests, such as the Industrial School of Pollokshaws, inaugurated in 1857 to give working-class children an elementary education. Perhaps reflecting the influence of his talented mother and sisters, Maxwell championed female education.

Increasingly frail in old age and suffering from neuralgia, Maxwell died at Pollok House on 6 June 1865. He was buried in the family vault at Eastwood parish church, Renfrewshire, on 10 June. His *Glasgow Herald* obituary (7 June 1865) paid tribute to his charitable and public works, and referred to him as 'a fine specimen of the polished Scottish gentleman', noted for his intellect, refined manners, and stimulating conversation. Contemporary portraits depict him as lean and angular, with dark hair and a prominent classical nose. After his death the Pollok estate and baronetcy passed to his nephew, William Stirling of Keir [see Maxwell, William Stirling], and thereafter parts of the Maxwell lands were developed for residential purposes, creating middle-class suburbs such as Pollokshields. From the 1980s the estate, which housed the celebrated Burrell art collection, became one of the most visited urban tourist attractions in Scotland.

IRENE MAVER

Sources W. Fraser, *Memoirs of the Maxwells of Pollok*, 2 vols. (privately printed, Edinburgh, 1863) • *Glasgow Herald* (7 June 1865) • *North British Daily Mail* (7 June 1865) • *The Scotsman* (7 June 1865) • *The Times* (8 June 1865) • *Glasgow Herald* (12 June 1865) • *North British Daily Mail* (5 Sept 1857) • J. Foster, *Members of parliament, Scotland … 1357–1882*, 2nd edn (privately printed, London, 1882), 245–6 • *WWBMP*, vol. 1 • P. Richards, 'The state and early industrial capitalism: the case of the handloom weavers', *Past and Present*, 83 (1979), 91–115 • J. Maxwell, ed., 'A book of newspaper cuttings, election notices, etc., chiefly relating to the elections and Paisley', 1832–57, U. Glas. L., special collections department, SM 2011 • 'A book of newspaper cuttings relating to Sir John Maxwell', 1834–41, U. Glas. L., special collections department, SM 1153 • *A letter addressed to the honest reformers of Scotland: with remarks on the poor rates, corn law, religious establishment, right of property, equality of ranks, and revolution* (1819) • J. Maxwell, *Suggestions arising out of the present want of employment for labour and capital* (1852) • J. Maxwell, *True reform, or, Character a qualification for the franchise* (1860) • *Hansard 3* (1834), 21.715–8, 1144–53; 23.1097; (1835), 29.1151–83 • M. Berg, *The machinery question and the making of political economy, 1815–1848* (1980) • A. McCallum, *Pollokshaws, village and burgh, 1600–1912: with some account of the Maxwells of Pollok* (1925) • G. Logan, 'Parish of Eastwood or Pollok', *The new statistical account of Scotland, by ministers of the respective parishes, under the superintendence of a committee for the Society for the Benefit of the Sons and Daughters of the Clergy*, volume VII, Renfrew – Argyle [sic] (1845), pp. 33–46 • H. Macdonald, *Rambles round Glasgow: descriptive, historical and traditional* (1854) • 'Select committee on … hand-loom weavers', *Parl. papers* (1835), vol. 13, no. 341 • N. Murray, *The Scottish handloom weavers, 1790–1850: a social history* (1978) • archives, Christ Church Oxf. • Burke, *Peerage* (1879) [Stirling-Maxwell] • HoP, *Commons, 1790–1820*, 4.573

Archives Mitchell L., Glas., Glasgow City Archives, corresp. and papers • U. Glas. L., newspaper cuttings, SM 1153 and 2011

Likenesses portrait, 1813–15, Pollok House, Glasgow • engraving, *c.*1826–1834, U. Glas. L., scrapbook, SM 1153 • portrait, 1835, U. Glas. L., scrapbook, Lanarkshire election poster, SM 1153 • J. R. Swinton, oils, *c.*1844–1857, Pollok House, Glasgow • J. Fillans, marble bust, Pollok House, Glasgow • portraits, repro. in Fraser, *Memoirs of the Maxwells of Pollok*

Wealth at death £39,526 14*s.* 3*d.*: NA Scot., SC 58/42/32; record of settlements and inventories, Paisley sheriff court, vol. 32, 1865, pp. 577–619

Maxwell, John (1877–1940), film financier and cinema owner, was born in Scotland. He trained as a solicitor and practised in Glasgow. In 1912 he acquired an interest in a Glasgow cinema and over the next ten years built up a circuit of twenty cinemas and set up Waverley Films as the regional distributor for a London-based company, Wardour Films. In 1923 Maxwell took over Wardour and in 1925 he moved to London. Wishing to take advantage of the Cinematograph Films Act of 1927, he expanded into the production side of the industry, buying out the troubled consortium responsible for building Elstree Studios, and establishing British International Pictures (BIP) in April 1927. True to its name, BIP recruited prestigious figures such as the German director E. A. Dupont, the American director Harry Lachman, and a promising young English director, Alfred Hitchcock, and attempted to make films for the international market. Maxwell was married, and he and his wife, Catherine (*d.* 1951), had one son and six daughters.

Unfortunately Maxwell's bold attempt to make ambitious British silent films coincided with the arrival of the 'talkies'. Maxwell responded rapidly to the change, installing American RCA sound equipment at Elstree and announcing plans for multilingual production. But when Hitchcock's modestly budgeted *Blackmail* (1929), Britain's first talkie, proved more popular with audiences than ambitious epics such as Dupont's *Atlantic* (1929)—a slow-moving account of the *Titanic* disaster made separately in English, French, and German—Maxwell reversed his policy and began making low-budget films for the domestic market. To ensure that his films had an outlet, he began to buy up cinemas. In November 1928 he registered Associated British Cinemas (ABC) as a public company with capital of £1 million. In July 1929 it had a circuit of 80 cinemas, and by the end of 1931 this had grown to 160. In September 1933 ABC, BIP, and Wardour Films were consolidated into a single company, the Associated British Picture Corporation (ABPC).

A year later in 1934 Maxwell made a bid for his only serious rival in the British film industry, the Ostrer brothers'

Gaumont-British Picture Corporation. The bid was unsuccessful, but in October 1936 Maxwell announced that he was to acquire a majority interest in Metropolis and Bradford, the holding company which controlled Gaumont-British. However, his option on the voting shares was blocked by Twentieth Century Fox, which also had shares in and aspired to control Gaumont-British. Deadlock resulted in a court case and a Board of Trade inquiry, but Maxwell had to admit defeat and abandon his dream of dominating the British film industry. Although the Gaumont-British deal failed (it was J. Arthur Rank who finally, in 1941, gained control over the Gaumont-British empire), ABPC continued to expand. In October 1937 Maxwell acquired the 168 cinemas of the Union circuit, merging them into his ABC circuit, which with a total of 493 cinemas was now the biggest in the country.

Some significant films emerged from Elstree but the studio never acquired the prestige of Alexander Korda's Denham, nor the popular identity of Michael Balcon's Ealing. John Maxwell was always more of a businessman than an impresario. But in the British film industry of the 1930s, plagued by alarming booms and slumps, Maxwell's achievement in building up a major cinema circuit, supplying it with a steady output of British films, and providing his shareholders with regular, if unspectacular, dividends, was a rare and considerable one.

Maxwell was a diabetic and had been in poor health since 1937. He died on 2 October 1940 at his home, Rockwood, Brook, Witley, Surrey, aged sixty-three. The Second World War had led to the requisitioning of Elstree Studios and at the time of Maxwell's death the blitz was threatening the prospect of cinema-going in Britain. Two years later, however, cinema attendance had risen above its prewar peak and the ABC cinema chain was making record-breaking profits.

An appreciative, if somewhat over-laudatory, obituarist in *The Times* noted Maxwell's 'deservedly high reputation for sound financial insight', adding that he had given the public the best pictures available, together with comfort and luxury (4 Oct 1940).   ROBERT MURPHY

Sources A. Eyles, *ABC, the first name in entertainment* (1993) • R. Low, *The history of the British film*, 4: *1918–1929* (1971) • R. Low, *The history of the British film*, 7: *1929–1939: film making in 1930s Britain* (1985) • A. Wood, *Mr Rank: a study of J. Arthur Rank and British films* (1952) • private information (2004) • *The Times* (4 Oct 1940)

Maxwell, Sir John Grenfell (1859–1929), army officer, was born at Aigburth, Liverpool, on 11 July 1859, the second son of Robert Maxwell (*d.* 22 Nov 1874), senior partner in the firm of A. F. and R. Maxwell, corn merchants, of 28 Brunswick Street, Liverpool, and his wife, Maria Emma, daughter of Vice-Admiral John Pascoe *Grenfell and cousin of Field Marshal Francis Wallace Grenfell, first Baron Grenfell. The marriage of Mrs Maxwell's sister Sophia to Pascoe Grenfell, Lord Grenfell's eldest brother, greatly strengthened the intimacy that arose between young Maxwell and the field marshal. John spent his boyhood with his father's parents in Scotland and was educated at Cheltenham College from January 1875 to July

1877; he was in the shooting eleven, and long continued an exceptional shot. He entered the Royal Military College, Sandhurst, in 1878, and was commissioned into the 42nd foot (Royal Highlanders) in 1879.

In 1882 the 42nd was part of Wolseley's expeditionary force to Egypt, and Maxwell was chosen by Major-General Sir Archibald Alison as his aide-de-camp for the battle of Tell al-Kebir (13 September), remaining such until Alison left for England in 1883. Maxwell stayed in Egypt with Sir Evelyn Wood as assistant provost-marshal. He lost heavily gambling in Cairo. As assistant provost-marshal and as camp commandant he spent the winter of 1884–5 up the Nile with Wolseley on the Gordon relief expedition. When, in April 1885, Sir Francis Grenfell succeeded Wood as sirdar of the Egyptian army, he summoned Maxwell to his staff, first as aide-de-camp and then as assistant military secretary, although the appointment was not made permanent until September 1886. In that capacity Maxwell took part in the Sudan frontier operations, being present at Giniss (30 December 1885), for which he received the DSO, at Gamaiza, outside Suakin (20 December 1888), which brought him the Osmanieh, and lastly (3 August 1889) at the more decisive battle of Toski, after which he was awarded a brevet majority.

Maxwell married in 1892 Louise Selina, daughter of Charles William Bonynge of New York and Dublin, a wealthy Irish American, and had one daughter, Philae (*b.* 1893), who married Clifford Carver of New York. Mrs Maxwell enjoyed a considerable fortune, and before her husband's retirement lived largely apart from him. She survived Maxwell and died in 1929.

When Sir Herbert Kitchener succeeded Grenfell as sirdar in 1892 he retained Maxwell on his staff, and there grew a lasting friendship between them. The next few years were spent planning the reconquest of the Sudan, until the crushing defeat of the Italians by the Abyssinians at Adowa (1 March 1896) facilitated a hastening of the advance. This led to the battle of Firket (7 June) in which Maxwell commanded the 3rd Egyptian infantry brigade, retaining this position until the recapture of Dongola on 23 September. During 1897 he acted as 'governor of Nubia', administering the area in which the railway was being pushed forward. During the 1898 operations he commanded the 1st Sudanese brigade at the battle of Atbara (8 April), and was transferred to the 2nd brigade for the battle of Omdurman (2 September). He was mentioned in dispatches and received the thanks of parliament. After the Dervish collapse he was governor of Omdurman, and promoted brevet lieutenant-colonel. Disappointed at not being made sirdar in succession to Kitchener, he resigned from the Egyptian army.

On the outbreak of war in South Africa in October 1899 Maxwell was still in the Sudan, but in February 1900 he went to the Cape. He commanded the 14th infantry brigade, which he led to Pretoria, distinguishing himself on the Zand River. After the capture of Pretoria (5 June) he was, on Kitchener's recommendation, appointed its military governor, and thus administered a large area of the

Transvaal. He was made KCB and appointed temporary major-general in 1900; in 1902 he received a brevet colonelcy and was appointed CMG. In 1902, before the end of hostilities, he commanded a column based on Vryburg, where he remained after the conclusion of peace on 31 May.

In the autumn of 1902 Maxwell was chosen by the duke of Connaught, then acting commander-in-chief in Ireland, as his chief staff officer at Dublin. There he remained until May 1904, when Connaught became inspector-general of the forces, and Maxwell followed him to London. At the end of 1907 Connaught was transferred to Malta as commander-in-chief and chief commissioner in the Mediterranean; Maxwell, promoted major-general at the end of 1906, once more accompanied him, and served with him until September 1908.

Maxwell left Malta to command the British troops in Egypt, a reward for his service with the duke, though he still wanted to be sirdar. His tenure of office in Egypt lasted until November 1912, shortly after his promotion to lieutenant-general, and was perhaps the most enjoyable period of his life. It was uneventful, although the Italo-Turkish War of 1912 caused him some concern. After leaving this appointment he went on half pay.

On the outbreak of the First World War Maxwell was sent to French headquarters as head of the British military mission. There he served until the opening of the battle of the Marne, when, finding little scope for his activities, he was glad to resume command in September 1914 of all the troops in Egypt. The position was important and exacting. He opposed British annexation, and proclaimed and tactfully applied martial law. He constructed defences along the Suez Canal. In February 1915 the Turks attacked the canal and were easily driven back. Events, however, rapidly increased Maxwell's responsibilities. Egypt became the base for the Gallipoli campaign (1915–16), which Maxwell himself did not favour, though he disliked withdrawal as harmful to British prestige. After the Gallipoli evacuation the troops were withdrawn to Egypt to be refitted before being sent to the Salonika front. The Palestine expedition of 1916 was also based on Egypt. Maxwell's personal position was further complicated by the system of command which grew up around him. Some 400,000 men—including British, Indian, Australian, New Zealand, and Egyptian troops—were quartered in or based on Egypt, while three different groups of higher authorities were concerned in their command and administration. After repelling an attack by the German armed and financed Senussi in the western desert in January 1916, Maxwell was recalled home in March. He had been made KCMG in 1915.

Shortly after Maxwell's return to England, on Easter Monday, 24 April 1916, the Easter rising broke out in Dublin, and was followed by a week of bitter fighting: by the next Monday the fighting was at an end. Martial law was proclaimed in Dublin on Easter Monday, and extended to the rest of Ireland the following day, so giving dictatorial power to the commanding officer. Initially this was Brigadier-General W. H. M. Lowe, but on Friday 28 April he was superseded by Maxwell—sent specially by the Asquith government—to whom devolved responsibility for the fate of the captured rebels. He was ignorant of the Irish situation, and ordered a general round-up of suspects and the trial by secret court martial of those involved in the rising. He thought his task distasteful, and was effectively in sole charge for a fortnight. He had to make difficult decisions. Those he made were understandable, if with hindsight wrong. However, the crucial decision on the prisoners' fate should not have been left to the local commander. A clear political decision should have been made by government: the fault was Asquith's, who could have prevented the executions. Maxwell commuted most of the court's death sentences but—despite the pleading of John Dillon—ordered fifteen executions, by shooting. According to his daughter 'it cost him hours of agony to sign the death-warrants of the Rebel Irish leaders' (Arthur, 313), but he believed it his duty. Initially the rising had been unpopular, but Maxwell's policy squandered this advantage and alienated many southern Irish. Asquith crossed to Ireland (11 May) and halted the executions, though Maxwell was convinced several more were required. Lloyd George wrote privately in June criticizing Maxwell's 'stupid and fatuous' administration, and alleging his lack of 'tact and restraint' was making agreement impossible (Townsend, 311). Asquith defended Maxwell against Irish and Liberal politicians' attacks. In November 1916 Maxwell was awarded the GCB and was appointed general officer commanding northern command, at York.

Maxwell remained at northern command until after the end of the war, when he was sent to Egypt as a member of Lord Milner's mission (December 1919 to March 1920) on the future relations of the UK with Egypt. He had been promoted general in June 1919, but was not re-employed, and went on retired pay in 1922. He had long excessively smoked cigarettes, which harmed his health and presumably shortened his life. His health broke down in late 1920. In his last years he travelled abroad, and in 1928, on medical advice, went to the Cape, South Africa. There he caught a chill, which turned to pneumonia. He died at Newlands, Cape Province, on 21 February 1929 and was buried at York Minster.

Maxwell was strongly built, with a prominent nose: hence his nickname, Conky. Although not a scholar nor deeply read, he was practical, a competent administrator, and ready to take action on his own responsibility. In private life he was a staunch and generous friend. He was a keen amateur Egyptologist and a friend of Lord Carnarvon and Howard Carter. Though brought up a strict Presbyterian, Maxwell was, according to his biographer, neither a religious man nor a practising church member, and 'his ignorance of Scripture history would provoke a smile' (Arthur, 94). A limited, self-important, rather lazy man, Maxwell's limitations proved disastrous in Ireland in 1916, when he was the wrong man for a very difficult task. Maxwell's daughter invited his friend Sir George Arthur to write his biography. This Arthur did to his usual low standard: among his omissions were the names of Maxwell's parents and the place and date of Maxwell's birth.

H. DE WATTEVILLE, rev. ROGER T. STEARN

Sources *The Times* (22 Feb 1929) · G. Arthur, *General Sir John Maxwell* (1932) · *Army List* · personal knowledge (1937) · E. S. Skirving, ed., *Cheltenham College register, 1841–1927* (1928) · P. Mansfield, *The British in Egypt* (1971) · T. W. Moody and others, eds., *A new history of Ireland*, 6: *Ireland under the Union, 1870–1921* (1996) · C. Townsend, *Political violence in Ireland* (1983) · F. X. Martin, ed., *Leaders and men of the Easter rising: Dublin 1916* (1964) · R. F. Foster, *Modern Ireland, 1600–1972* (1989) · *CGPLA Eng. & Wales* (1929)
Archives Princeton University Library, New Jersey, corresp. and papers incl. those of his wife · U. Durham L., letter-book | Bodl. Oxf., corresp. with H. H. Asquith · NL Aus., corresp. with Viscount Novar | FILM BFI NFTVA, news footage
Likenesses photograph, 1926, repro. in Arthur, *General Sir John Maxwell*, frontispiece · photograph, repro. in Arthur, *General Sir John Maxwell*, 308
Wealth at death £25,417 6s. 3d.: probate, 23 April 1929, *CGPLA Eng. & Wales*

Maxwell, John Hall (1812–1866), agriculturist, eldest son of William Maxwell of Dargavel, Renfrewshire (d. 1847), and Mary, eldest daughter of John Campbell of Possil, near Glasgow, was born in Queen Street, Glasgow, in February 1812, and called to the Scottish bar in 1835. He practised law until 1845, when he succeeded Sir Charles Gordon of Grimkin (also a lawyer) as secretary to the Highland and Agricultural Society of Scotland. He remained in this position until his retirement after the Inverness show of 1865 and during this period the society's influence and status greatly increased; membership rose from 2620 to 4200 and the reserve funds grew from £34,000 to £50,000. The shows under Maxwell's meticulous management expanded considerably and became annual events; he also edited the society's *Transactions* between 1853 and 1860. In the early 1850s Maxwell was involved in a pioneering attempt to collect agricultural statistics on a systematic basis, and for this and his other works he was created CB on 5 February 1856.

Maxwell married Eliza Anne Margaret, eldest daughter of Thomas Williams of Southwick Crescent, Hyde Park, London, in 1843. He invested in a range of improvements on his own estate at Dargavel, including the reclamation of wasteland. His services to the agricultural community were recognized by a presentation of 1000 guineas and a service of plate on 17 January 1866. Although suffering from heart disease, he again acted as secretary to the Highland Society until May 1866 because of the sudden illness and death of his appointed successor, Alexander Macduff. Maxwell died at his residence, Torr Hall, near Paisley, on 25 August 1866. G. C. BOASE, rev. NICHOLAS GODDARD

Sources Irving, *Scots.*, 342 · A. Ramsay, *History of the Highland and Agricultural Society of Scotland* (1879), 522–4 · The Druid [H. H. Dixon], *Saddle and sirloin, or, English farm and sporting worthies* (1870), 3–6 · *Law Times* (1 Sept 1866), 763–4
Archives Mitchell L., Glas., Strathclyde regional archives, family MSS
Likenesses Hähnisch, lithograph, 1856, priv. coll. · Hähnisch, lithograph, 1856, BM, Scot. NPG · J. B. Hunt, stipple and line engraving, pubd 1858 (after photograph), NPG · G. Steel, portrait,

priv. coll. · G. Steell, group portrait, Royal Highland and Agricultural Society of Scotland, Edinburgh
Wealth at death £8923 13s. 9d.: 22 Nov 1866, NA Scot., SC 58/42/33/805–28 · £75: additional inventory, 4 Sept 1867, NA Scot., SC 58/42/34/828–9

Maxwell, Lilly [Lily] (c.1800–1876), suffragist, was born in Scotland at the beginning of the nineteenth century. She spent many years in domestic service in the Manchester area: she apparently had a long connection with the family of Sir Bosdin Thomas Leech, later lord mayor of Manchester and pioneer of the Manchester Ship Canal. When she left domestic service, at some time between 1861 and 1865, she took a house at 25 Ludlow Street, Chorlton upon Medlock, Manchester, where she kept a small shop selling crockery, which had an annual rateable value of £11 5s. Mrs Maxwell, who was apparently a widow, came briefly to public attention on 26 November 1867, when she was the first woman known to have voted in a parliamentary election.

A by-election had been called in Manchester for November 1867, following the death of a sitting MP, one of the first elections to be called since the passing, in August 1867, of the second Reform Act, which extended the parliamentary franchise in boroughs to all adult male ratepayers. Through clerical error Lilly Maxwell's name (spelled Lily) had been entered on the new register of electors, an error discovered by a canvasser working for the return of the Liberal candidate, Jacob Bright, brother of the celebrated John Bright. The radical Bright was involved with the newly formed Manchester women's suffrage committee, and contacted Lydia Becker, the prominent suffragist, who called on Maxwell and encouraged her to use the vote she had inadvertently been given. Mrs Maxwell was 'rather timid at first', according to Becker (Rendall, 67), but because of her 'very determined political principles' (*The Times*, 3 Dec 1867), agreed to accompany Becker to the poll and give her vote for Bright. Voting was by public declaration, and Lilly Maxwell's surprise presence at Chorlton town hall was met with a round of applause; her name appearing on the electoral register, the returning officer was obliged to record it. Bright's majority was such that there was no legal scrutiny of the poll, and the legality of her vote went unchallenged.

The Times responded to the news of Mrs Maxwell's vote in a leader column heavy with sarcasm. 'If they [women] had wished for political power, they could have had it long ago', it opined: 'what mortal power could possibly resist a "Ladies' Demonstration" in Hyde Park?' (3 Dec 1867). *Punch* published a satirical poem, 'Lily Maxwell Triumphant, or, The First Person Singular' (7 December 1867), while the Manchester paper *The Free-Lance* versified on 'Lilia Jacobensis' ('Jacob's Lily'). But for the women's suffragists, she provided a test case. The Reform Act of 1867 seemed to confirm that the suffrage was a household one, that is, it was based on the payment of rates and taxes rather than on personal qualities such as age or gender. Suffragists led by Lydia Becker argued that independent single and widowed women—Mrs Maxwell among them—had no male head of household to exercise the franchise on their behalf, and that as they were ratepayers and taxpayers they should be entitled to vote. (Another group of suffragists campaigned for an adult franchise, rather than a household one, which would be open to married women as well.) Accepting his election Jacob Bright spoke about Mrs Maxwell:

> This woman is a hardworking, honest person, who pays her rates as you do, who contributes to the burdens of the State as you do, and therefore if any person should possess a vote, it is precisely such as she. (*The Times*, 3 Dec 1867)

The Manchester National Society for Women's Suffrage began a campaign to register women householders for the vote, and in 1868 took their claims to the revising barristers' courts, where they were refused. Jacob Bright, for whom Lilly Maxwell's vote had been cast, became the leader of the women's suffrage campaign in parliament after John Stuart Mill's defeat in 1868, and made the successful amendment to the Municipal Corporations Act of 1869 which enfranchised women householders in municipal elections.

Lilly Maxwell herself returned to obscurity. Lydia Becker kept in touch with her for some time, noting her removal from Ludlow Street to 17 Cowgill Street, where 'pecuniary and entirely unmerited misfortune has overtaken her' (Rendall, 74). Like many elderly working-class women, Lilly Maxwell had no resources to protect her against old age and infirmity. She became a charwoman, and on 5 April 1876 she was admitted to the Union Workhouse, Withington, Manchester, where she died from a combination of chronic bronchitis and a malignant stomach disease on 24 October 1876. Her age was given as seventy-five. A Presbyterian, she was buried in Bradford cemetery, Manchester.   K. D. REYNOLDS

Sources J. Rendall, 'Who was Lily Maxwell', *Votes for women*, ed. J. Purvis and S. S. Holton (2000), 57–83 · C. Hall, K. McClelland, and J. Rendall, *Defining the Victorian nation: class, race, gender and the British Reform Act of 1867* (2000) · *Englishwoman's Review*, 6 (Jan 1868), 395–69 · d. cert. · Withington Union Workhouse records, Man. CL, Manchester Archives and Local Studies · *The Times* (3 Dec 1867) · *Punch* (7 Dec 1867) · *First annual report of the Manchester National Society for Women's Suffrage* (1868)
Likenesses photograph, Man. CL

Maxwell, Mary Elizabeth. *See* Braddon, Mary Elizabeth (1835–1915).

Maxwell, Sir Murray (1775–1831), naval officer, the third son of James Maxwell (*b*. 1724), a captain in the 42nd regiment (himself the third son of Sir Alexander Maxwell of Monreith, Wigtownshire, second baronet) and his wife, Elizabeth, the daughter of William Maxwell of Ardwell, was born in the parish of Penninghame, near Newton Stewart, Wigtownshire, Scotland, on 10 September 1775. On 10 September 1790 he entered the navy on the *Juno*, with Captain Samuel Hood, where he served until March 1794, when he followed Hood to the *Aigle*. In November 1794 he was moved to the *Nemesis*, and was still with her when she was captured at Smyrna on 9 December 1795. He afterwards joined the *Blenheim*, and a few months later the

Princess Royal, on which he returned to England. On 10 October 1796 he was promoted lieutenant. He married on 9 September 1798 Grace Callander (*d*. 23 June 1857), the daughter of Colonel Waugh of the 57th regiment; they had one daughter and one son, John Balfour (1799–1874), who died an admiral on the retired list.

On 15 December 1802 Maxwell was promoted commander of the sloop *Cyane* in the West Indies, with which he was present at the reduction of St Lucia. He was then appointed by Hood acting captain of the *Centaur* (74 guns), bearing his broad pennant. He had thus an important part in the capture of Tobago, Demerara, and Essequibo in July and September 1803, and of Berbice and Surinam in April 1804. His commission as captain was confirmed to 4 August 1803. In 1805 he commanded the *Galatea* in the West Indies, and in 1807 was appointed to the *Alceste*, a 38-gun frigate, with which from 1807 to 1810 he served with distinction in the Mediterranean, attacking coastal forts and convoys and, in April 1808, with two brigs, a flotilla of gunboats.

In the spring of 1811 Maxwell was in the Adriatic under the orders of Captain James Brisbane, and in the autumn had for some months a semi-independent command there. On 29 November, off Lissa, his force—*Alceste*, *Unité*, and *Active* [*see* Gordon, Sir James Alexander]—fought three French frigates, capturing two (one was the *Pomone*).

In 1812 Maxwell was appointed to the *Daedalus* (38 guns), with which he sailed for India in charge of a fleet of Indiamen. On 2 July 1813 the *Daedalus* was wrecked off the coast of Ceylon. Maxwell returned to England, and, being acquitted of blame, was made a CB in 1815.

In October 1813 Maxwell was again appointed to the *Alceste*, at the desire of Lord Amherst, going out as ambassador to the emperor of China. The *Alceste* sailed from Spithead on 9 February 1816 and anchored off the Peiho (Beihe) on 28 July. Lord Amherst landed on 9 August and directed the ship to meet him at Canton (Guangzhou), whither he proposed to travel overland from Peking (Beijing). Maxwell took the opportunity of exploring the Gulf of Pecheli (Beizhili), the west coast of Korea—until then unknown except by hearsay, and drawn on the chart by imagination— and the Loo-Choo Islands. The results were afterwards ably described by Captain Basil Hall of the brig *Lyra*, then in company with the *Alceste*, in his *Account of a Voyage of Discovery to the Western Coast of Corea and the Great Loo-Choo Island* (1818). The *Alceste* arrived off the mouth of the Canton River on 2 November, and Maxwell, unable to get any satisfactory answer to his application for a pass, determined to go up the river without one. As he approached the Bocca Tigris, a mandarin came on board and ordered him to anchor at once; if he attempted to go on, the batteries would sink the ship. Maxwell sent back an angry answer, and the *Alceste* passed on, scattering the war junks which attempted to stop her, and silencing the batteries for the time by a single well-directed broadside. Without further molestation she arrived at Whampoa (Huangpu), where Lord Amherst re-embarked on 21 January 1817. The *Lyra* was sent to Calcutta with dispatches for the governor-general, and the *Alceste*, continuing her voyage by herself, entered the Strait of Gaspar on the morning of 18 February.

These straits were then little more than explored, and the charts were very imperfect. About eight o'clock the ship struck on a rock about 3 miles from Pulo Leat and sustained fatal injuries. Everyone was landed on the island, together with such stores as time permitted, but on the third day the wreck was taken possession of by Malay pirates, who threatened the encampment on shore. On the morning of 19 February Lord Amherst and his staff had been sent on to Batavia in two boats under the command of Lieutenant Henry Parkyns Hoppner, a son of John Hoppner the artist. Some 200 men remained on this inhospitable island, without clothes, with little food, and beset by ferocious enemies. They were relieved on 3 March by the arrival of the East India Company's ship *Ternate*, sent by Amherst from Batavia. On his arrival in England in August 1817 Maxwell was tried by court martial, fully acquitted, and specially complimented for his conduct before and after the wreck. Lord Amherst appeared as a witness on his behalf. On 27 May 1818 Maxwell was knighted. He was elected FRS on 18 February 1819, and on 20 May 1819 was presented by the East India Company with £1500 for his services to the embassy and in compensation for his losses in the wreck. In the July 1818 general election Maxwell was the last Admiralty (ministerial) candidate for the mass-electorate City of Westminster. He 'sustained severe personal injury from the vile rabble with which the hustings in Covent Garden is on such occasions surrounded' (*GM*, 274) and was unsuccessful, defeated by Sir Samuel Romilly and Sir Francis Burdett. Also defeated was Henry Hunt.

In 1821–2 Maxwell was captain of the *Bulwark* (74 guns), flagship of Sir Benjamin Hallowell (afterwards Carew) at Chatham, and in 1823 of the *Briton* on the South American station. In May 1831 he was appointed lieutenant-governor of Prince Edward Island, and was preparing for his departure when he died suddenly on 26 June 1831.

Of Maxwell's six brothers, three were in the army, two in the navy. Of these last, John, a captain of 1810, died in command of the frigate *Aurora* in 1826. Keith (*b. c.*1774), a lieutenant of 1794, was specially promoted commander in 1801 for cutting out the French 20-gun corvette *Chevrette* from under the batteries of Camaret Bay on the night of 21–2 July. He was promoted captain in 1804 and died in 1823. J. K. LAUGHTON, *rev.* ANDREW LAMBERT

Sources D. Syrett and R. L. DiNardo, *The commissioned sea officers of the Royal Navy, 1660–1815*, rev. edn, Occasional Publications of the Navy RS, 1 (1994) • O'Byrne, *Naval biog. dict.* • HoP, *Commons* • Burke, *Peerage* (1959) • *GM*, 1st ser., 101/2 (1831), 274 • J. Marshall, *Royal naval biography*, 2/2 (1825) • J. Marshall, *Royal naval biography*, suppl. 2 (1828) • W. James, *The naval history of Great Britain, from the declaration of war by France, in 1793, to the accession of George VI*, [6th edn], 6 vols. (1878) • P. Mackesy, *The war in the Mediterranean, 1803–1810* (1957) • H. Ellis, *Journal of the proceedings of the late embassy to China* (1817)
Likenesses T. Wageman, stipple, 1817, NPG • R. Dighton, caricature, etching, BM, V&A

Maxwell, Sir Peter Benson (1817–1893). *See under* Maxwell, Sir William Edward (1846–1897).

Maxwell, Robert, second Lord Maxwell (*c.*1410–1485). *See under* Maxwell, Herbert, first Lord Maxwell (*c.*1390–1453).

Maxwell, Robert, fifth Lord Maxwell (*c.*1494–1546), magnate, was the eldest son of John *Maxwell, fourth Lord Maxwell (*d.* 1513) [*see under* Maxwell, Herbert, first Lord Maxwell], and Agnes, daughter of Sir Alexander Stewart of Garlies. He was married after 4 July 1509 to Janet Douglas (*d. c.*1520), daughter of Sir William Douglas of Drumlanrig, and knighted before 29 November 1510. He became hereditary steward of Annandale on 10 June 1513 on his father's resignation, and held the office of admiral of the fleet when the royal army suffered its crushing defeat at Flodden on 9 September 1513, his father being among those killed. Robert was served heir on 4 November following and received the wardenship of the west march in 1515 in return for helping the duke of Albany to deprive Alexander, third Lord Home, of the latter's march wardenships. He also benefited from the distribution of Home estates following their forfeiture.

Maxwell remained loyal to Albany, and he was on the council which in 1517 established procedures for the government of the realm during Albany's absence in France. Albany returned in November 1521, and in the following autumn led a large army to attack the English west march. Maxwell served as a hostage in Carlisle during the meeting on 11 September 1522 between Albany and Thomas, Lord Dacre, warden of the English march, which led to a truce being agreed. Maxwell and Dacre subsequently stood surety for the maintenance of the truce, which was extended until March 1523, when open war was resumed. In the meantime Maxwell turned his attentions to expanding his influence in south-west Scotland, not least by securing a large measure of control over the lands of monasteries there. In 1523 his brother John became abbot of Dundrennan. Maxwell was quick to exploit his increased importance during periods of cross-border tension, especially as the government distrusted Andrew Kerr of Cessford, warden of the middle march. When hostilities resumed, Maxwell prepared resistance to an expected English invasion of south-west Scotland.

Queen Margaret had worked hard to have Albany's pro-French policies rejected, and her ascendancy brought Maxwell further rewards as he pledged his political allegiance to her, becoming one of her closest supporters. She helped him to extend his influence into Galloway, and on 9 September 1524 granted him the castles of Threave and Lochmaben as hereditary patrimony; she also appointed him steward of Kirkcudbright for nineteen years and made him principal captain of the royal guard. In addition to this she intervened directly in the burghal privileges of Edinburgh in order to secure the election of Maxwell as provost of Edinburgh. The instability of administration in the years which followed, as the queen competed for power with her estranged second husband, the sixth earl of Angus, had little effect on Maxwell's position, thanks to his indispensability on the west march, where his wardenship was repeatedly renewed. In July 1525 parliament devised an arrangement for the custody of the young king whereby four groups of prominent men would take turns to hold James for three months each; Maxwell was a member of the fourth group, along with the earls of Lennox, Montrose, and Glencairn.

The scheme foundered because the first group, led by Angus himself, refused to relinquish control of the king's person at the end of its term. Angus subsequently alienated Maxwell by the support he gave to John Johnstone of that ilk, a potential rival in the west march whose family had recently initiated what would prove to be an exceptionally long-lasting and bloody feud with the Maxwells by killing one of the Armstrongs, a powerful family on the Scottish west march who were clients of Maxwell's. The two men fell out further over the latter's attempts to stabilize the borders, where the Armstrongs had embarrassed the Scottish government by providing shelter for English rebels and by raiding across the border. Repeated complaints by Lord Dacre that no efforts were being made either to prevent such attacks or to give redress conveyed the humiliating impression that Angus was able to control neither Maxwell nor his followers. Hence, perhaps, Lady Dacre's report in May 1528 that Maxwell was in trouble with the king and dared not go to Edinburgh, but had sent his wife instead.

James V, chafing under the tutelage of Angus, viewed the inability of Angus to deal with border lawlessness as a perfect excuse to challenge his authority and condemn his actions. It is possible that Lady Maxwell was able to inform her husband of a rift between the king and Angus, as Maxwell was with the king at Stirling later in May 1528, and on 4 July he was appointed chief carver to the king in the royal household. Maxwell accompanied the king from Stirling to Edinburgh, where on 6 July he took part in a session of the lords of council and was confirmed as warden of the west march, with Lord Home replacing Angus in the east march. As James V began his personal rule, Maxwell was appointed once again to the office of provost of Edinburgh, replacing Archibald Douglas of Kilspindie. He arrived in Edinburgh in August with an armed force and surrounded the provost's house while Kilspindie and his nephews were at dinner. They were forced to flee to Tantallon and Maxwell proceeded to apply himself assiduously to royal service.

The problem of lawlessness on the borders preoccupied James V at the end of 1529, and a series of justice ayres was held in the south-west at which the king and Maxwell presided. However, the problems were far from resolved and in May 1530 it was ordained that the king should ride to the borders and execute justice, while the chief border magnates, including Maxwell, remained in ward. Maxwell appears to have accepted his warding in Edinburgh Castle, as direct royal initiative on the border was preferable to the threat of the earl of Moray assuming the lieutenancy of all three marches. Maxwell also appreciated that he had to demonstrate his loyalty to the king in order to retain his favour, and he even countenanced the execution of his tenant John Armstrong of Staplegordon or Gilnockie—the famous gang-leader Johnnie Armstrong—with whom he had a bond of manrent. A clear

message of strong royal authority having thus been delivered, Maxwell's bond for good rule was accepted by the king, and he received royal sanction for the marriage of his son Robert with Beatrice Douglas, daughter of the earl of Morton. Robert was taken to be brought up in the king's household, and Maxwell was even the recipient of some of Armstrong's escheated goods.

Maxwell's position was strengthened further when in 1536–7 he was appointed one of six vice-regents of the realm when the king was in France. In 1537 he intercepted his erstwhile patron Queen Margaret as she was fleeing to England and returned her to Stirling. He served as juror on the three major treason trials of the period 1537–40, including that of Janet Douglas, Lady Glamis. In 1538 he was entrusted with the task of travelling to France and acting as the king's proxy in his marriage to Mary of Guise; the ceremony took place on 9 May at the castle of Châteaudun, when Maxwell placed the ring on the new queen's finger and then distributed 40 crowns among the officials and minstrels in attendance. After a few weeks he escorted Mary to Rouen and then to Le Havre, where on 10 June they embarked on a ship bound for Fife. In 1540 Maxwell accompanied the king on his expedition to the isles, and on 6 June he received royal confirmation of his charters, uniting his possessions into the free barony of Maxwell, with Caerlaverock Castle as its centre.

Late in October 1542 Maxwell was ordered to bring the men of the west march to Selkirk, to join there with those of Liddesdale to meet or cut off the advance of the duke of Norfolk. The latter withdrew, however, and Maxwell and his men went back to the west march for a raid into England. The issue of who commanded the Scottish forces that came to grief at Solway Moss on 24 November has given rise to controversy. Some sources name Maxwell himself as the defeated commander, but it seems more likely that it was Oliver Sinclair of Pitcairn, of whom Sir George Douglas of Pittendriech reported on 16 December that he 'was chief captain of the army and lost the King's banner there' (*LP Henry VIII*, 17, no. 1209). There is at any rate no doubt that the Scots, caught between a river and a bog, fought valiantly before surrendering. Maxwell was the richest magnate to be taken prisoner, with landed revenues valued at 4000 marks and 3000 marks in goods.

To secure his release Maxwell became one of the 'assured lords' who at the end of December signed a bond pledging themselves to assist Henry VIII in his Scottish policies. It may have been in compliance with this undertaking that he introduced into parliament the bill enacted in March 1543 which permitted the possession and reading of the scriptures in the vernacular, though he was also alleged to have Lutheran sympathies. But although he appears to have been on bad terms with the francophile Cardinal Beaton, he made no further efforts to promote the English cause. Indeed, so lukewarm was Maxwell on King Henry's behalf that when he was arrested by the Scottish government in Edinburgh on 1 November 1544 there were rumours that he had been taken with his own connivance, and when he was released on 15 May 1545 he was swiftly taken into custody by the English forces in and around Edinburgh and carried back to London. He secured his release by placing his castles of Lochmaben and Caerlaverock in English hands, but late in November they were recaptured by the earl of Arran, and Maxwell himself was taken prisoner. Mary of Guise accepted his plea that he had acted under duress; she pardoned him and on 12 January 1546 appointed him justiciar of Annandale, Kirkcudbright, Wigtown, and Dumfries. Maxwell attended meetings of the privy council and on 3 June resumed his former office of warden of the west march. He did not hold it for long, however, for he died at Logan on 9 July 1546.

Maxwell's heir Robert was the eldest son of his marriage to Janet Douglas. They also had another son, John *Maxwell (later Lord Herries), and a daughter. Janet died about 1520 and by 1525 Maxwell had married Agnes, illegitimate daughter of James Stewart, thirteenth earl of Buchan; they had no children. Maxwell also had an illegitimate son, said to have been ancestor of the Maxwells of Logan. C. A. McGLADDERY

Sources J. Cameron, *James V: the personal rule, 1528–1542*, ed. N. Macdougall (1998) · W. K. Emond, 'The minority of James V, 1513–1528', PhD diss., U. St Andr., 1988 · W. Fraser, ed., *The book of Carlaverock: memoirs of the Maxwells, earls of Nithsdale*, 2 vols. (1873) · *LP Henry VIII · Scots peerage*, 6.479–81 · GEC, *Peerage*, 8.592–4 · M. Merriman, *The rough wooings: Mary queen of Scots, 1542–1551* (2000)

Wealth at death lands worth 4000 marks and goods worth 3000 marks, 1542

Maxwell, Robert, first earl of Nithsdale (*b.* after 1586, *d.* 1646), politician and diplomat, was the second son of John *Maxwell, eighth Lord Maxwell (1553–1593), and Lady Elizabeth (*d.* 1637), daughter of David Douglas, earl of Angus. Nothing is known of his early life or education. In May 1612 the fugitive status of his elder brother John *Maxwell, ninth Lord Maxwell (*b.* in or before 1586, *d.* 1613), led to his own warding in Edinburgh, where the Scottish privy council allowed him 100 merks per month until his release on 26 May 1613, following John's execution; having been known from 1607 as the master of Maxwell, he was now referred to as the Hon. Robert Maxwell of Caerlaverock. By 1612, the Maxwell territories encompassed the 6 merk land of Capenoch, Keri barony, Hollywood parish in Dumfries, and Keri mill, to which was added Castlegour in Kirkcudbright (16 July). As his father's heir, Maxwell received the barony of Caerlaverock in August 1615, and was able to secure his ancestral lands by a parliamentary act of rehabilitation (28 June 1617), and the reassignment of Langholm barony and the living of Maxwell by royal charter of 19 September 1621.

Maxwell's status as a border magnate was confirmed on 18 December 1617 when he accepted responsibility for his tenants in accordance with the general band of 1602. His profile was extended by his appointment as border commissioner on 4 April 1618, and his instatement as tenth Lord Maxwell on 5 October. As a mark of the royal favour he now enjoyed, the king granted him a special disbursement of £24,000 Scots (£2000 sterling). His new ascendancy was confirmed by his inclusion on the Scottish privy council on 27 March 1619, and enhanced by his marriage

on 28 October 1619, at St Mary-le-Strand, London, to Elizabeth (*d.* 1671), daughter of Sir Francis Beaumont and cousin of George Villiers, marquess of Buckingham. On 29 August 1620 he was created earl of Nithsdale, a title that caused controversy among the Scottish nobles, its precedence being based on his father's creation as earl of Morton in 1581.

On 25 January 1621 Nithsdale sat in the House of Lords as a member for the committee to raise funds for British defence and for the dowry of Princess Elizabeth. He later served as one of the lords of the articles on 25 July, and on 4 August voted in favour of ratifying the five articles of Perth. On 1 April the earl was appointed a commissioner to monitor the waters of Dumfries, Kirkcudbright, and Annandale and prevent the fishing of 'red fish, smolts, and fry' out of season (*Reg. PCS*, 1st ser., 12.640). This assignment coincided with his activities as a border triumvir, which allowed him special justiciary powers, yet his authority was challenged when the Johnstones—traditional enemies of the Maxwells—secured temporary exemption from his jurisdiction. On 17 June 1623, however, he and James Johnstone of Westray were publicly reconciled, with the latter agreeing in principle to Nithsdale's authority. It was during this period that the earl initiated construction on Caerlaverock, the Solway stronghold that had belonged to the Maxwell family since the early thirteenth century. He introduced a number of intricate architectural innovations, creating new classically styled ranges for the eastern and southern portions of the castle courtyard and embedding the Maxwell and Beaumont crests in Ionic columns along the eastern range. This ambitious building, thought to have been inspired by the prospect of a royal visit to Dumfriesshire, helped create Nithsdale's crushing debt difficulties.

On 20 May 1624 the king granted Nithsdale a special licence to travel in France, ordering his creditors not to take advantage of his absence. By 7 September he was in Italy on a mission to secure papal dispensation for the marriage of Prince Charles and Henrietta Maria of France. A severe illness confined him to Florence until the end of October, when he recovered sufficient strength to travel to Rome, returning to Britain early in January 1625. After the death of King James, helped by his friendship with his wife's cousin the duke of Buckingham, Nithsdale continued to receive favourable treatment from Charles I, on whose behalf he returned to Scotland as a collector-general of taxes for the convention of estates in October 1625. On 22 October that year the king granted him a special six-month protection 'contra creditores', indicating that his financial difficulties had not yet been resolved (*Registrum magni sigilli regum Scotorum, 1620–33*, 318, no. 883).

In 1627 Nithsdale resumed his European profile when, on 28 February, the king ordered him to raise 3000 Scottish soldiers in Lower Saxony for Christian IV of Denmark. However, his personal unpopularity within the Scottish privy council, combined with his personal arrogance and steadfast Catholicism, made recruitment difficult. Nithsdale wrote to Charles in May requesting renewed protection for his sureties during his proposed expedition to Germany, from which he would return by 23 February 1628. On this date he was in Scotland, demonstrating his loyalty to Charles by surrendering his lordship of erection. By December he had entered into diplomatic correspondence with Cardinal Richelieu, with whom he exchanged professions of amity between the British and French crowns.

On 12 January 1633 Nithsdale resumed his role as border commissioner, and on 18 June appeared in parliament at Edinburgh. By 1638 he had fortified Caerlaverock Castle to prepare for the ensuing struggle between the king and the covenanters, though he himself was forced to shelter in Carlisle until a peace was concluded in June 1639. This agreement soon deteriorated, and on 27 March 1640 Charles secretly urged Nithsdale to garrison his castles. Caerlaverock was itself besieged from 29 June, until the earl's surrender of 26 September to Lieutenant-Colonel Home, whose subsequent misuse of both it and Castle Threave led Nithsdale to complain to the king in November 1641. On 22 June 1643 the convention of estates accused him of treason and seized his estates, then valued at £3000 per annum. After launching an attack on Dumfries with Montrose on 15 April 1644, Nithsdale was excommunicated by the general assembly (23 June). His final major act was to accompany General Digby with 1500 horse in a march on Doncaster (1646), a venture that was successfully blocked by parliamentary forces. After regrouping at Skipton, Nithsdale escaped to the Isle of Man, where he died in May 1646. His wife, who survived him, died in 1671. They had two daughters, Jean (*d.* 1649) and Elizabeth, and one son, Robert (1620–1677), who succeeded as second earl of Nithsdale.   J. R. M. SIZER

Sources W. Fraser, ed., *The book of Carlaverock: memoirs of the Maxwells, earls of Nithsdale*, 2 vols. (1873), vol. 1, pp. 325–71 *passim*; vol. 2, pp. 111–12, 118, 121–7 · GEC, *Peerage* · J. M. Thomson and others, eds., *Registrum magni sigilli regum Scotorum / The register of the great seal of Scotland*, 11 vols. (1882–1914), vol. 8, p. 73, no. 228 · *APS*, 1593–1625, 561 · *Reg. PCS*, 1st ser., 9.362, 378; 10.17–18, 63; 12.640, 673–5; 13.261–2 · *Reg. PCS*, 2nd ser., 7.182 · *CSP dom.*, 1623–5, 250; *addenda*, 1625–49, 624 · NL Scot., MS 20775(43) · *CSP Venice*, 1623–5, 433, 439, 476, 558 · NL Scot., Adv. MS 34.2.12, fol. 30*r* · M. Lee, *The road to revolution: Scotland under Charles I, 1625–1637* (1985), 46, 80 · *Dumfries and Galloway*, Pevsner (1996), 141, 145–50
Archives NL Scot., Adv. MS 33.1.1, vols. 4, 9–11; 34.2.12 · U. Hull, Scottish papers of Maxwell–Constable family of Everingham, DDEV/80 Maxwell muniments
Wealth at death in 1643 Nithsdale's estates were sequestered by the Scottish estates, which collected a total of £9000 sterling from his annual rents of £3000 p. a. until 1647: Fraser, *Book of Carlaverock*, vol. 1, p. 368

Maxwell, Robert (1695–1765), agricultural improver and writer, was born at Arkland, Kirkpatrick-Durham, Kirkcudbrightshire, the eldest child of James Maxwell and his wife, Margaret, daughter of Robert Neilson of Barncaillie. The Maxwells had been landowners at Arkland since the beginning of the seventeenth century, and the Neilsons, descended from the house of Craigcaffie, Wigtown, had owned Barncaillie since 1537. After receiving an education 'becoming his rank', Maxwell engaged in agriculture, and

about 1723 he leased a farm of 130 acres, all arable, at Cliftonhall, near Edinburgh, for a rent of £50. In 1728 he married Margaret, daughter of Bailie Montgomery of Edinburgh; she predeceased him, leaving six daughters.

Maxwell devoted himself to the improvement of agriculture, and during the first half of the eighteenth century he probably did more than any other person in Scotland to encourage the practice of new methods. He was one of the earliest and most active members of the Society of Improvers in the Knowledge of Agriculture in Scotland, which was established at Edinburgh on 8 June 1723. In 1739 he proposed to the Scottish Society for the Propagation of Christian Knowledge a scheme for the application of funds in their possession to the education of boys in the new principles of agriculture. The society invited him to give a full account of the uses of the root crops which he proposed to grow, and the Society of Improvers encouraged him, but the scheme fell through. Meanwhile Maxwell had taken the main share of the work of the Society of Improvers and dealt with inquiries which were sent in from all parts of the country.

On his own farm, Maxwell paid more attention to experiments than to making a profit, and he supervised improvements on the estates of the great land proprietors. Among those who availed themselves of his advice and assistance was John, second earl of Stair. In 1743 he published at Edinburgh a book, *Select Transactions of the Society of Improvers*. A large portion of this work stemmed from Maxwell himself, and it contained many suggestions which were then new to Scotland, such as the efficacy and the mode of burning clay or subsoil, the method of cutting seed potatoes and of planting them, and the rotation of crops and root crops, in addition to information on the agriculture and manufactures of Scotland. On the dissolution of the Society of Improvers (because of the death of nearly all its founders) Maxwell transferred his energies to the Edinburgh Society for the Encouragement of Arts, Sciences, Manufactures, and Agriculture, which took its place.

In 1745 Maxwell succeeded his father in the estate of Arkland, but by this time he had exhausted his resources. Like many other improvers he was better at theory than practice. He had to surrender the lease of his farm at Cliftonhall, and in 1749 he became insolvent. At the instance of his creditors Arkland was sold on 9 January 1750, for £10,304, to John Coltart of Areeming.

After this Maxwell earned his living by acting as land valuer and supervisor of improvements, while his wife probably became a shopkeeper 'betwixt James's and Wardrop's Courts in the north side of the Lawn Market at Edinburgh' (advertisement in the *Practical Beemaster*, 2nd edn, 1750). Maxwell continued his efforts for the improvement of agriculture. He had tried to obtain the establishment of a lectureship in agriculture at Edinburgh University, and Lord Stair and the Society of Improvers had supported the scheme. Failing in this design, Maxwell, without the patronage of any public body, gave public lectures on agriculture in Edinburgh in 1756. His lectures, probably the first of the kind delivered in Great Britain, were attended by many of the farmers and landowners in the district, and he was strongly urged to publish them. Two of them were printed in *The Practical Husbandman, being a Collection of Miscellaneous Papers on Husbandry* (1757), much of which was copied from his *Select Transactions*. He also published a number of other works on husbandry, including one on bee keeping, entitled *The Practical Beemaster* (1747), which went through a number of editions. Maxwell died at Renfrew, in the house of his son-in-law, James King, on 17 May 1765.   W. A. S. HEWINS, *rev.* ROSALIND MITCHISON

Sources J. E. Handley, *Scottish farming in the eighteenth century* (1953) · T. Murray, *The literary history of Galloway*, 2nd edn (1832) · R. Maxwell, *The practical husbandman* (1757) · H. Paton, ed., *The register of marriages for the parish of Edinburgh, 1701–1750*, Scottish RS, old ser., 35 (1908) · R. Maxwell, *The practical beemaster*, 2nd edn (1750) · *Scots Magazine*

Archives Bridsen Natural History MS Resources, 1980, treatise on agriculture

Maxwell, (Ian) Robert (1923–1991), publisher and swindler, was born on 10 June 1923 in Synagogue Street, Slatinske Doly (Szlatina), a Czech village on a disputed frontier with Romania. He was one of seven children of Mehel Hoch (1887–1942?), agricultural labourer, and Chanca (*d*. 1942?), daughter of Yankel Shlomowitz and also an agricultural labourer. His mother, father, grandfather, and three youngest siblings died at Auschwitz. Originally he was named Abraham Lajbi (in Yiddish Leiby) Hoch and later Jan Ludvik Hoch. After attending a Jewish village school he had a strict religious education in the *yeshiva* (Jewish school) at Sighet and at the Pressburger Yeshiva, Bratislava. His mother wanted him to become a rabbi, but he had his sidelocks shorn, and set out to assert himself.

Hoch joined the Czech army in France in 1940 before escaping to England, where in 1941 he volunteered for the Pioneer Corps. After two years he became a private in the North Staffordshire regiment, where his linguistic fluency resulted in his recruitment to the intelligence section. Using the name Leslie Ivan du Maurier (the surname derived from his favourite brand of cigarette), he participated in the Normandy landings of 1944 as a sniper sergeant and was commissioned as a second lieutenant. During 1945 he received the Military Cross and was promoted to captain. After the collapse of the Third Reich he was a member of the branch of the Allied Control Commission in Berlin responsible for licensing films, plays, books, and newspapers (1945–7). Under military instructions he changed his surname from du Maurier to Jones in 1944, and then (apparently for military reasons) Leslie Jones in 1945 was renamed Ian Robert Maxwell. This was the name under which he was naturalized as a British subject in June 1946. Some of his enemies suspected that he began a working relationship with the KGB shortly afterwards.

On 14 March 1945 in Paris Maxwell married Elisabeth (*b*. 1921), daughter of Paul Louis Meynard, a silk mill owner who had lost his fortune. This tempestuous marriage produced four sons, five daughters, and two miscarriages. The eldest son was injured in a motoring accident at the age of fifteen in 1961 and remained in a coma in an Oxford

(Ian) Robert Maxwell (1923–1991), by Ida Kar, *c*.1960

hospital for seven years. After Maxwell agreed with a neurologist that there should be no active attempts to prolong the boy's life, Michael Maxwell died in 1968. This tragedy aside, Maxwell was a domineering, intensively possessive, and demanding parent who humiliated his children and made their home life almost unbearable. Requiring unconditional surrender from all his dependants, he relished shows of magnanimity after blistering rows. During a marital crisis of 1980–81 his wife described him as 'harsh, cruel, uncompromising, dictatorial, exceedingly selfish and inconsiderate, totally unaware of the feelings of others, least of all those who are loyal and devoted to you, those you take a sadistic pleasure in crushing and humiliating' (Maxwell, 450). Intermittently, for over thirty years, he had affairs, and he and his wife separated in 1990.

Early business life Maxwell in 1947 formed the grandiosely titled European Periodicals, Publicity and Advertising Corporation. Initially this imported German newspapers for sale to prisoners of war in Britain, but he foresaw the international demand for German scientific, medical, and technical works and obtained world distribution rights from Germany's leading scientific publisher, Ferdinand Springer. He wrote in 1949 that he had entered the 'business world without money, friends or knowledge. In this jungle the law since eternity has been "catch as catch can", no holds are barred and only the fittest can survive' (Maxwell, 201). His sharp practice resulted in a crisis with Springer in 1951. Shortly afterwards he founded Pergamon Press, to which however he gave little attention for four years because in 1951, with characteristic financial legerdemain, he acquired control of the leading British book wholesale warehouse, Simpkin Marshall. He threw his energies and overbearing character into the business. From the outset his accounting procedures were irregular, and the company made large interest-free loans to other Maxwell companies. It entered liquidation in 1955 owing £656,000.

It has been alleged that in 1948 MI6 agreed to finance Maxwell's business as a cover for spying on Soviet bloc countries; certainly he travelled extensively in eastern Europe and later in the Far East, and mastered nine languages. His incessant travels during the 1950s often had serendipitous consequences. Indeed throughout his life he had chance meetings with interesting people, who introduced him to other valuable contacts:

> Bob built up an amazing circle of acquaintances, purely on this kind of chain reaction … he had a prodigious memory, which served him well until the latter years of his life. He would remember names, faces, the most minute details of a conversation, and he possessed [an] amazing store of data gleaned from his constant reading or talks with people. (Maxwell, 245)

After the Simpkin Marshall débâcle Maxwell concentrated on Pergamon. His survival of an operation for lung cancer in 1955 increased his craving for conquest. Pergamon launched a succession of high-priced specialist scientific periodicals, to which academics were eager to contribute without remuneration, and published expensive scientific books whose authors were underpaid. He cultivated scientific contacts in the Soviet Union and in Warsaw pact countries, where his status was enhanced by Pergamon's willingness to publish sycophantic biographies of the more obnoxious dictators. Maxwell's initiatives proved a catalyst for international scientific communication and earned the grateful admiration of Sir Robert Robinson, Patrick Blackett, and other scientists. He read or scanned all Pergamon journals and books and always tried to learn from his scientific editors. The intricacies of much scientific research were beyond him, but he strove to understand the purposes and potential benefits of the work described in his publications. Although Maxwell latterly was an overbearing conversationalist, in the twenty years after 1945 his intense curiosity could seem charming. 'Bob still had everything to learn—and he knew it', according to his wife. 'If he met someone working in a field he was unfamiliar with, he would not make ordinary conversation, but would literally interrogate that person, who was generally flattered.' She considered that the 1950s were formative:

> his thirst for knowledge and his ability to use and apply it were exciting to watch. In those days, he could be enormous fun to be with; his enthusiasm for life seemed to know no bounds. You never knew what to expect next from his inventive mind. (Maxwell, 246–7)

Parliamentary career Maxwell was Labour's unsuccessful parliamentary candidate for Buckingham in 1959. He chaired the Labour Party's national fund-raising foundation (1960–69) and its working party on science, government, and industry. Richard Crossman described him in 1963: 'a very strange fellow—a Czech Jew with a perfect knowledge of Russian, who has an infamous reputation in the publishing world as the creator of the Pergamon

Press'. His scientific advice and liaison with important scientists had unexpectedly proved 'helpful, constructive and sensible' (*Backbench Diaries*, 1017). In 1964 Maxwell was elected for Buckingham. He made his maiden speech in the Commons within a few hours of taking his seat and thereafter was a frequent and strenuous speaker, especially on scientific topics. Other parliamentarians felt that he tried too hard to impress; his booming voice could seem painfully brash. 'A thrusting man who regards the House of Commons as a place where he can push himself', Tony Benn noted in 1965. 'The big struggle with Maxwell is whether you allow him to use you' (Benn, 294, 332).

Crossman in 1967 induced Maxwell to chair the Commons kitchen committee on the basis that if he succeeded, Wilson would be convinced that he could run a government department. Despite a scandal over the sale of wine, Maxwell was reckoned a success and sought his reward of ministerial office, but no cabinet minister wanted him as a junior minister. His ambition spurred him towards becoming a newspaper proprietor. He was foiled in his attempt in 1964 to buy two Labour-supporting newspapers, the *Daily Herald* and *Sunday Citizen*, and in 1968 his offer to buy 25 per cent of the shares in the *News of the World* was rebuffed. Both in 1968 and when he tried to buy *The Sun* in 1969 he was outmanoeuvred by Rupert Murdoch. When in 1968 five secretaries from Surbiton vowed to work unpaid for an extra half-hour daily to help Britain, Maxwell bustled into fronting a patriotic, populist 'I'm backing Britain' campaign. 'What a miraculous man', Crossman reflected at this time. 'However much people hate him, laugh at him, boo him and call him a vulgarian, he gets things done' (*Diaries of a Cabinet Minister*, 2.661).

Business controversy and recovery By 1964, when Pergamon was floated on the stock exchange for over £4 million, it was publishing 600 books annually and 70 journals. During the 1950s Maxwell began forming tax-free trusts, *Stiftungen*, and anonymous foundations, *Anstalten*, in the principality of Liechtenstein. These had such names as Allandra, Baccano, Corry, Hesto, Jungo, and Kiaro; he used them to buy Pergamon's books and periodicals, to increase its apparent profits. In 1969 he agreed to a £25 million take-over of Pergamon by an American company, Leasco, which withdrew its bid on discovering that he had inflated Pergamon's profit figures by transactions with his private companies and by exaggerating its encyclopaedia sales. Maxwell had also secretly supported Pergamon's share price. In the ensuing uproar he was ousted from Pergamon's board by institutional investors and Leasco.

Two inspectors from the Department of Trade and Industry who investigated Maxwell's business affairs concluded in a report published in 1971 that he was 'not … a person who can be relied on to exercise proper stewardship of a publicly-quoted company' (Bower, *Maxwell the Outsider*, 222). This famous phrase was coined by the accountant Sir Ronald Leach, who privately called Maxwell 'a wall of fat always suing us' (Bower, *Tiny Rowland*, 203). Leach understood Maxwell perfectly: 'It was his capacity to regard the world as his own, which we thought extremely dangerous' (Greenslade, 325). Two further damning reports on the encyclopaedia business and Maxwell's private companies appeared in 1972–3. The trade and industry inspectors hesitated to accuse Maxwell of criminality, and the police failed to prosecute him for fraud. He was, however, defeated in the three general elections of 1970 and 1974, and abandoned his parliamentary ambitions.

In 1974 Maxwell bought back Pergamon for about £1.5 million and kept it as a private company. It prospered, but he hankered for a return to national prominence. In 1975 he enjoyed assuming the role of saviour of the *Scottish Daily News*, a Glasgow newspaper being run by an employees' co-operative; but the experiment ended bitterly with insolvency after six months. A dawn raid in July 1980 gave Maxwell a 29 per cent stake in the British Printing Corporation at a cost of £2.9 million, and he forced his way to the post of chief executive in February 1981. Soon he was chairman too, armed with exceptional powers. Maxwell's ostracism by City institutions diminished after his brutal but successful reorganization of the company, including new union agreements and investment in new machinery. The British Printing Corporation was renamed the Maxwell Communications Corporation (MCC) in 1987.

Pergamon in 1984 bought Mirror Group Newspapers (MGN) for £90 million, and Maxwell installed himself as chairman. He thus controlled Britain's only remaining Labour-supporting newspapers, the *Daily Mirror*, *Sunday Mirror*, and *The People*. He cut the printing staff by one-third and began breaking the unions' grip on newspaper publishing. However, Maxwell swiftly compromised the editorial integrity of the *Daily Mirror*, which was the second highest selling newspaper in Britain. One million readers were lost, partly because the newspaper was used for his self-publicity. His name, photograph, and pontificating were too prominent in its pages, and he meddled constantly in its production and contents. His newspapers had diminishing political influence, partly because his political outlook was so egocentric, haphazard, and crude.

This longing for celebrity was also evident in Maxwell's sporting ventures. In 1981 he invested £128,000 in Oxford United Football Club and became chairman. His plan to merge Oxford with Reading Football Club, and thus form a new club—Thames Valley Royals—was defeated. Having failed to buy a controlling interest in Manchester United Football Club in 1984, he paid £300,000 for the debt-ridden Derby County Football Club, of which he became chairman in 1987. He had several clashes with the Football League, and he sold his interest in Derby in 1991. During 1986 Maxwell intervened to save the finances of the Commonwealth athletic games being staged in Edinburgh. His meddling brought publicity for MGN and for its publisher, but the millions he promised were never paid. Similarly his donations for AIDS research, the alleviation of Ethiopian starvation, the Gorbachov–Maxwell Institute in Minneapolis, and Balkan industrial renewal were announced with portentous publicity but were never delivered.

Deteriorating behaviour Maxwell was increasingly aggressive and uncontrollable from 1986. During that year he launched a glossy illustrated magazine, *Sportsweek* (which closed after five months with losses of £2 million), and bought the Philip Hill Investment Trust, from which he reaped £76 million by selling its components. In 1987 he launched the *London Daily News*, which was planned as the city's second evening newspaper but was abruptly relaunched by Maxwell (without consulting its editor) as Britain's first twenty-four-hour newspaper. His interventions in the printing, distribution, and strategy of the newspaper resulted in losses of about £50 million in its brief career (February–July 1987). He also tried to buy the newspaper *Today* from Tiny Rowland in 1987, but as a result of his indiscretions Rupert Murdoch again outmanoeuvred him. Maxwell's obsession with excelling Murdoch as a media tycoon became more obtrusive than ever. Also in 1987 he bought a French news agency, Agence Centrale de Presse, borrowed 750 million francs to buy a 12.5 per cent share in France's leading television channel, and was defeated in a hostile bid worth almost $2 billion for the American educational publisher and theme-park proprietor Harcourt Brace Jovanovich. During 1988, on a handshake deal with an Italian whom he met at a funeral, he paid £60 million to buy 84 per cent of the football-stickers and football-album group Panini, which further depleted his finances. He bought a 30 per cent stake in Scitex, an Israeli electronic scanning equipment manufacturer, and invested in another Israeli company, Teva Pharmaceuticals.

Maxwell wasted millions on failed projects, litigation, and sumptuous living expenses, but his downfall began with MCC's purchase of the American publishing house Macmillan (which controlled 56 per cent of the shares in the Berlitz language schools) for the exorbitant price of $2.6 billion in 1988. MCC also paid $750 million in 1988 for Official Airline Guides. Maxwell negotiated huge loans from forty-four banks eager for his business, but was soon hit by high interest rates. From 1986, when his private companies pledged 115 million MCC shares as collateral for loans, he was servicing or paying off his debts by mortgaging MCC shares (a financial device called 'pig on pork'). The banks required that if the MCC share price fell below a stipulated level, more shares had to be transferred as additional guarantees safeguarding the value of the loan. Maxwell's Liechtenstein *Stiftungen* owned the majority of MCC shares. Some 400 of his private companies of varying sizes traded with one another and with MCC in publishing, communications, printing, technology, property, currencies, gilts, and shares. He used these companies to move assets, shares, cash, and debts regardless of regulations or laws so that MCC could claim huge profits in its sumptuous brochures. To maintain the MCC share price, and thus avoid transferring more MCC shares under 'pig on pork' arrangements, he paid excessive dividends to shareholders. The profits from trading were £97.3 million in 1989, but the dividend cost £112.3 million. The cost of maintaining this charade included £17.6 million in advance corporation tax. On adjusted trading profits of £71.1 million in 1990 the extraneous tax cost was £98.8 million.

Additionally, from 1988 Maxwell set up twelve companies with London and Bishopsgate in their titles, operating from the same premises but with different activities, and thus well calculated to confuse outsiders. In 1989 London and Bishopsgate Investments began elaborate, systematic misuse of funds and fraudulent share transactions, particularly involving First Tokyo Trust. Maxwell's private company Bishopsgate Investment Trust managed nine pension funds for his 23,400 employees. These funds were siphoned to support the Maxwell businesses. He took £1.5 million from MCC's pension fund in 1986 and £9 million in 1987.

Woodrow Wyatt recorded the mistrust felt by other newspaper proprietors of Maxwell. Murdoch in 1987 predicted, 'one day Maxwell will go bust in a spectacular manner' (Wyatt, 1.375). Conrad Black told Wyatt that Maxwell was an impossible business partner because 'he was so dishonest and devious and wriggled out of things and gave you false information' (ibid., 2.475–6). Despite such perceptions, bankers continued to lend Maxwell large amounts of money. By the summer of 1990 the scale of his debts and the impossibility of servicing them made ruin inevitable. He engaged during the last fifteen months of his life in dedicated criminality. He fraudulently supported MCC's share price through the Liechtenstein *Stiftungen* and with money stolen from his employees' pension funds. In November 1990 he transferred Berlitz shares worth over $200 million from the legal ownership to his Bishopsgate Investment Trust. He began drinking heavily; his infallible memory for financial detail began to falter. Constant jet travel, meetings, and deceit were physically breaking him. Pergamon's sale for £440 million in 1991 did not solve the debt-crisis. Then, after some adroit financial manipulation, the flotation of MGN was prepared in six hectic weeks, and in May 1991 he sold 49 per cent of MGN. However, with only a 51 per cent stake, his earnings from MGN were reduced, and he could no longer use its assets as collateral. During 1991 he forged documents to inflate the profits of MCC by £37 million while his private companies' debts to MCC and MGN rose to over £600 million. As the impending doom of his empire became evident, he became more destructive.

Having purloined from *Die Zeit* of Hamburg the project of a pan-European newspaper, Maxwell had in 1990 launched *The European* with himself as editor-in-chief. His arrangements for its printing and distribution were unnecessarily expensive and inefficient. Its launch cost perhaps £50 million, and it lost £1 million a week in its first year. Despite the strains on him, in March 1991 Maxwell, in return for payment of $65 million from its owners, took over the *New York Daily News*, which was suffering from a five-month strike, corrupt employment practices, rampant expenditure, and antiquated plant. American public adulation and proximity to President George Bush at a White House dinner aggravated his delusion that (in his own words) he was 'not just a hero, [but] a cult figure' (Greenslade, 224).

Meanwhile Swiss Bank had compiled a dossier on an unpaid debt of £55.7 million that it warned would be given to the fraud squad on 5 November. The *Financial Times* simultaneously prepared a story estimating the Maxwell family's debts at £2.2 billion. Maxwell died on 5 November 1991, disappearing from his yacht, *Lady Ghislaine*, while it was cruising off Gran Canaria. It is uncertain whether he accidentally fell overboard, deliberately killed himself (knowing that his crimes would imminently be discovered), or was murdered at the instigation of an associate hoping to stop the wrecking of his assets. The hypothesis that he was murdered by secret agents seems less tenable. Roy Greenslade, who had worked for him as editor of the *Daily Mirror*, judged that 'Mr Maxwell took his own life while the balance of his mind was briefly undisturbed' (Greenslade, 351). Maxwell's corpse was retrieved from the Atlantic and was buried on 10 November on the Mount of Olives, Jerusalem.

Conclusion The sycophantic tributes paid at Maxwell's death and the eulogies pronounced at the grave were soon discredited. His empire swiftly collapsed owing about £2.7 billion; £429 million had been stolen from employee pension funds. Banks that had taken security for loans in the form of shares lost over £655 million. Maxwell's sons Ian and Kevin were subsequently arrested on criminal charges but acquitted after a gruelling trial.

Maxwell's resilience, which earned him the half-affectionate nickname the Bouncing Czech, was admirable. Yet despite his energy and bouts of ebullient charm, he aroused rancour for much of his career. This hostility partly derived from his litigious nature. Millions of pounds were spent on legal fees over the years. He threatened to issue writs and launched innumerable court actions; although these were often abandoned, they succeeded in their aim of intimidating his critics. He used the law to bludgeon his enemies into silence or stun creditors into pained compliance. During 1987–8, when he sought to suppress Tom Bower's unauthorized biography, he commissioned a hagiography from Joe Haines trumpeting his benefactions to humankind and ordered its serialization in the *Sunday Mirror* and *Daily Mirror*.

Maxwell was as ruthless and keen as any self-made businessman of his stature; but there was a flamboyant excess which was already disruptive by the 1960s, and he reacted to the stresses that accumulated from the 1980s with dictatorial behaviour that accelerated his destructive effects. In this latter period his lavatory hygiene, foul language, and table manners became increasingly primitive. Throughout, his egotism was unashamed: the bowl-sized cup from which he drank at his office was marked 'I'M A VERY IMPORTANT PERSON'. As an employer, particularly in the final decade of his life, he allowed his verbal brutality and physical presence to terrorize many of his staff. He required servility from them, and became obsessed with loyalty, secrecy, and security. He reverted to sentimental and self-serving declarations of Judaism after visiting Israel in 1985. He increasingly enjoyed his trips to Israel, where everyone who mattered to him treated him uncritically and even unctuously.

When young, Maxwell was dashingly handsome, but his features coarsened in middle age, and he became obese (ultimately weighing 22 stone). From the 1960s he was instantly recognizable, with dyed black hair, bushy eyebrows, paunch, and aggressively negligent clothes. His stentorian voice and almost pugilistic joviality attracted some and alienated others. His domestic arrangements were ostentatious and histrionic. He travelled between his homes, like a war-lord, by helicopter and assumed a monarchical pose during his incessant international journeys by private jet: his last Gulfstream cost $24 million and was code-named VR-Bob ('Very Rich Bob').

RICHARD DAVENPORT-HINES

Sources T. Bower, *Maxwell the outsider* (1988) · E. Maxwell, *A mind of my own* (1994) · R. Greenslade, *Maxwell's fall* (1992) · T. Bower, *Maxwell: the final verdict* (1995) · P. Thompson and A. Delano, *Maxwell* (1988) · J. Haines, *Maxwell* (1988) · *The backbench diaries of Richard Crossman*, ed. J. Morgan (1981) · R. H. S. Crossman, *The diaries of a cabinet minister*, 2 (1976) · T. Benn, *Out of the wilderness: diaries, 1963–67* (1987) · *The journals of Woodrow Wyatt*, ed. S. Curtis, 3 vols. (1998–2000), vols. 1–2 · T. Bower, *Tiny Rowland* (1993) · *Dod's Parliamentary Companion* · *London directory* (Post Office) · *The Times* (11 Nov 1991)
Archives CAC Cam., corresp. with Sir Edward Bullard · Fraytet, Montagnac-sur-Lède, Lot-et-Garonne, France, Elisabeth Maxwell MSS |FILM BFI NFTVA, *Dispatches*, special, Channel 4, 24 Jan 1995 · BFI NFTVA, *Inside story*, special, BBC1, 29 Oct 1996 · BFI NFTVA, current affairs footage · BFI NFTVA, documentary footage |SOUND BL NSA, performance recording
Likenesses photographs, 1950–84, Hult. Arch. · I. Kar, vintage print, c.1960, NPG [*see illus.*] · M. Frith, watercolour drawing, 1987, NPG · photographs, repro. in Thompson and Delano, *Maxwell* · photographs, repro. in Bower, *Maxwell: the final verdict* · photographs, repro. in Bower, *Maxwell the outsider* · photographs, repro. in Maxwell, *Mind of my own* · photographs, repro. in Greenslade, *Maxwell's fall*

Maxwell, William, of Terregles, fifth Lord Herries of Terregles (c.1555–1603), politician and landowner, was probably born at Hoddom, the eldest son of Sir John *Maxwell of Terregles, later fourth Lord Herries of Terregles (c.1512–1583), and his wife, Agnes Herries (c.1534–1594). He was the first cousin of John, eighth Lord Maxwell, head of the senior line of the family and the Maxwell surname. His father reunited and added to the established Herries estates during the 1560s, so that William eventually inherited extensive estates centred on Hoddom in Dumfriesshire. Like his father he may have received some education at Sweetheart Abbey.

In May 1568 William Maxwell accompanied his father to the battle of Langside which he watched with Queen Mary. He was present during Moray's suppression of the queen's followers in Dumfriesshire later that year and during the English raids of 1570. He submitted to ward to secure his father's release by the king's party on at least one occasion, but did not himself finally submit until late 1572. The attacks on Dumfriesshire, and the kirk's support for these, may have contributed to William's subsequent hostility to England, and his disaffection from the kirk. He had been raised as a protestant, but may have been influenced by Dumfriesshire Catholics in the 1570s and had converted by 1584. He married Katherine Ker (d. 1600), the daughter of Mark Ker, commendator of Newbattle, whose heir, the first earl of Lothian, married William's second sister, Margaret. Ker of Newbattle had a record of support

for religious reform but Katherine's religious views, and the date of her marriage, are unknown. Maxwell and his wife had five sons and four daughters.

William Maxwell became a gentleman of the chamber on 15 October 1580. On 20 January 1583 he succeeded to his father's peerage, being appointed to the privy council six days later. That summer Lord Scrope, the warden of the English west march, listed Herries as hostile towards England and accused him of countenancing cross-border reiving. In April 1584 Scrope thwarted Herries's efforts to support James VI against the Ruthven rebels. Herries attended the parliament which forfeited the latter, but he and Lord Maxwell were infuriated when the crown intervened to have John Johnstone elected provost of Dumfries. This re-initiated the long-running feud between the Maxwell and Johnstone families over pre-eminence in the Scottish west march, and in May 1585 Herries took part in a raid on Johnstone lands at Moffat. However, his conduct was usually less extreme. By July he was attempting to persuade Maxwell to submit, and in September he was commissioned to investigate the death of Lord Russell, killed at a day of truce on the Northumbrian border. On 9 June 1587 Herries was appointed warden of the Scottish west march. In Maxwell's absence he brought a temporary end to the feud with the Johnstones, marrying his sister to Sir James Johnstone. However, he failed to act impartially and in January 1588 was outlawed for failing to hand over offenders from his surname. He submitted in February, but was charged by the general assembly with attending mass in Dumfries. Released from outlawry in March, he was ordered by the council to suppress Catholicism. Herries had resigned his wardenry by 9 July 1588, but in August he became a commissioner for resisting the Spanish Armada.

Herries assisted Maxwell's political rehabilitation in 1589 but the Maxwell / Johnstone feud soon re-erupted. Maxwell was killed in battle with the Johnstones at Dryfe Sands on 6 December 1593, and on 22 December, Herries, who had not been present at the battle, was appointed head of a commission of local lairds to whom the wardenship was entrusted for two months. Herries subsequently acted as warden in his own right but was replaced by 21 July 1594. He was reappointed in December that year or January 1595, but by 8 November had been dismissed for attacking Johnstone settlements around Lockerbie. He came to an assurance with Johnstone, but this was broken. Brought before the council in March 1596 Herries successfully defended his conduct, but in July he was outlawed for failing to appear when summoned. He submitted and was briefly warded in Edinburgh Castle. He then co-operated with royal justice ayres to Dumfries in April and November 1597.

In March 1599 Herries again failed to appear before the council when summoned and was subsequently imprisoned in Tantallon Castle until September. He agreed to submit the Maxwell / Johnstone feud to arbitration in November, and was re-appointed warden on 17 June 1600. On 13 August, however, he was replaced by Sir James Johnstone. This re-ignited the feud and in May 1601

Herries was charged with plotting to undermine Johnstone. He had also returned to Catholicism and in November 1601 was summoned to appear before the council for attending mass and sheltering Jesuits. He appeared in December and was warded in Edinburgh Castle. He was released in January 1602 on condition that he remain in Edinburgh where ministers of the kirk could attempt to reform him. In February Herries agreed to support the kirk but once home he swiftly returned to Catholicism. In May 1602 the general assembly again sought to have him placed in the charge of a minister in Edinburgh. He returned to the capital but did not stay there for long. Herries died on 10 October 1603; his place of death and burial are not known.   JOHN STEWART RULE

Sources J. Bain, ed., *The border papers: calendar of letters and papers relating to the affairs of the borders of England and Scotland*, 2 vols. (1894–6) · *CSP Scot.*, *1563–1603* · W. Fraser, ed., *The book of Carlaverock*, 2 vols. (1894) · T. I. Rae, *The administration of the Scottish frontier, 1513–1603* (1966) · J. H. Burton and D. Masson, eds., *The register of the privy council of Scotland*, 1st ser., 14 vols. (1877–98), vols. 3–8 · D. Calderwood, *The history of the Kirk of Scotland*, ed. T. Thomson and D. Laing, 8 vols., Wodrow Society, 7 (1842–9) · D. Moysie, *Memoirs of the affairs of Scotland, 1577–1603*, ed. J. Dennistoun, Bannatyne Club, 39 (1830) · GEC, *Peerage*, new edn, 6.495 · *APS, 1424–1625* · T. Thomson, ed., *Acts and proceedings of the general assemblies of the Kirk of Scotland*, 3 pts, Bannatyne Club, 81 (1839–45) · K. Brown, 'The making of a *politique*: the Counter-Reformation and the regional politics of John, eighth Lord Maxwell', *SHR*, 66 (1987), 152–75

Maxwell, William, fifth earl of Nithsdale (1676–1744), Jacobite army officer and courtier, eldest son of Robert, fourth earl of Nithsdale (1627/8–1683), and Lady Lucie Douglas (*d.* 1713), daughter of William, first marquess of Douglas, was probably born at Terregles Castle, near Dumfries. The early death of his father ensured that he was raised by his mother, the dowager countess, who educated him to be a faithful and conventionally devout Roman Catholic and a partisan of the Stuart cause. A series of private tutors endowed him with those social accomplishments thought necessary, by his class, for a great nobleman and courtier. He was confirmed in his titles on 26 May 1696, and shortly after reaching his majority he was dispatched to the exiled court at St Germain to pay his respects to James II. While there, he met and courted Lady Winifred Herbert [*see* Maxwell, Winifred (1672–1749)], the youngest daughter of William, first marquess of Powis, and Lady Elizabeth Somerset. The couple married in Paris on 2 March 1699. On returning to his seat at Terregles, Nithsdale was careful not to present any outward show of his religion that might enrage any of his staunchly Presbyterian lowland neighbours. However, this was to no avail, and on the night of 24 December 1703 a crowd of more than 100 armed men, led by four local ministers, broke open the castle's gates and ransacked his property in search of Jesuit agents and Roman Catholic priests. Summoned to appear before the magistrates in Edinburgh on 21 February 1704, he was acquitted of harbouring foreign priests but was still stripped of his office as hereditary steward of Kirkcudbright, a title which was conferred instead upon James, duke of Queensberry.

Long suspected by the authorities of Jacobitism Nithsdale was placed under surveillance and a bond as a security for his future good conduct was demanded of him by the government, to be paid no later than 8 November 1708. Fear of the total confiscation of his lands may well have prompted him to bequeath all of his estate to his eldest son on 28 November 1712, while retaining only a liferent for his own maintenance. However, it appears that this was only a secondary consideration, and that his utter inability to manage his own affairs, and to handle money, was the real reason behind the transference of his properties.

The Jacobite rising of 1715 placed Nithsdale in a very difficult dilemma, and he initially temporized before, refusing a government summons, he joined the insurgents. Though his faith had effectively barred him from high command, he was entrusted with the unenviable task of raising the old covenanting districts of Dumfries and Galloway for the Jacobite cause. Having proclaimed James III (James Francis Edward Stuart) king at Moffat and Jedburgh, he rendezvoused with the main Jacobite forces of General Forster at Rothbury, near Hexham, on 19 October 1715. At Penrith on 2 November he brought up the main body of the troops, who pushed aside the small and dispirited militia companies which had barred the road south. He accompanied the army on its march through Kendal and Lancaster, and was placed in joint command of the gentlemen volunteers at the battle of Preston, on 12–13 November 1715. He was stationed in the parish churchyard throughout the fighting and saw his forces drawn upon as a reserve at times of crisis. However, he appears to have been one of the Scottish lords who advocated surrender once it became clear that the town was thoroughly enveloped by government troops, and his sword was delivered to generals Wills and Carpenter on Monday 14 November without the promise of any sort of favourable terms from his captors.

On 5 December Nithsdale was led into London along with the other Jacobite prisoners. Confined to the Tower, he was impeached on 9 January 1716 and was among the six Jacobite lords tried for treason at Westminster Hall over the following month. Pleading guilty to the charge, he begged George I for mercy, and argued that he had been forced into joining the rising by his compatriots who now stood accused beside him at the bar. However, his appeal was unsuccessful and he was sentenced on 9 February to be hanged, drawn, and quartered on Tower Hill. In contrast to his earlier behaviour, once this sentence was delivered Nithsdale acted with great composure and set down his 'last' testament which stressed both his commitment to Roman Catholicism and the claims of the Pretender.

Nithsdale was fortunate indeed that Winifred, Lady Nithsdale, was a woman of fortitude, intelligence, and bravery. On hearing of his capture she immediately rushed to London to be close by him and to lobby hard for his release. Combining a skilful propaganda campaign with frequent visits to the gallery of the House of Lords, she made such a favourable impression upon those she met that rumours began to circulate that her husband was about to be granted a reprieve and a full pardon. However, given the continuing opposition of George I to all such moves, it is most likely that Nithsdale would almost certainly have gone to the gallows had not his wife planned and accomplished a daring rescue. The guards at the Tower were bribed to allow Nithsdale to receive gifts and visitors, and they became confused by the frequent visits of the countess, her maid, and her friends. Under the cover of one of these visits, on the evening of 22 February—the day before his scheduled execution—Nithsdale was able to disguise himself as a woman and slip out of the Tower dressed as his wife's maid. He sought refuge in the Venetian embassy in the City of London and travelled to Dover disguised in the ambassador's livery coat. From there the Venetians helped him to charter a small boat which took him safely to Calais. The full details of his escape, which delighted partisans of the Jacobite movement and became something of a *cause célèbre*, are to be found in a letter sent by the countess to her sister, Lucy *Herbert, the prioress of the English convent at Bruges, which has been extensively reprinted (*Letter*, ed. Grace; Tayler, 46–58; Maxwell Stuart, 163–70).

Shortly after arriving in Paris, in the spring of 1716, Nithsdale fell dangerously ill but recovered. Having secured a loan from Mary of Modena, he attended the Pretender at his court in Avignon and was reunited with his wife at Lille in September 1716. On his departure for Italy in late March 1717, he chose the cheapest form of transport and consequently was almost drowned when the boat he was sailing in foundered in heavy seas. On 26 May 1717, together with the viscount of Kilsyth, he welcomed the Pretender to Rome and officiated at his court as a lord-in-waiting. The following year his wife was appointed lady-in-waiting to Clementina Sobieska, and during 1727–9 she served as governess to Henry Benedict, the titular duke of York.

Although these appointments brought with them considerable financial relief, and despite receiving (from 1717) a pension of approximately 200 livres a month from the exiled Jacobite court, until his death Nithsdale was continuously in debt. His correspondence with his brother-in-law, Charles, fourth marquess of Traquair, makes constant requests for money to be drawn from the estates of his son, while his wife lamented the raggedness of her dress and the poverty of their existence. Unable or unwilling to control his spending, Nithsdale continued to add to their difficulties and wrote of his dislike of, and boredom with, life at Rome. After 1724 the records appertaining to him tail off, and it would seem that apart from arranging the marriage of his daughter, Anne, to John, fourth Baron Bellew, in 1729, he became no more than a half-forgotten cipher at the exiled court. Nithsdale's death in Rome in 1744 obliged his son to settle £200 per annum upon the dowager countess in an attempt to fend off their creditors: Nithsdale was buried in an unknown grave in Rome.

Of his five children, only two reached adulthood; Anne, Lady Bellew, and William, commonly called Lord Maxwell. Maxwell was able to hold his family estates together as the Lords, on 21 January 1723, finally ruled that his father had forfeited only his life-rent through his part in the rebellion and not the Nithsdale lands which were held in trust for his son. The riding cloak in which Nithsdale fled the Tower still survives in the possession of the duke of Norfolk and is on display at Arundel Castle.

JOHN CALLOW

Sources DNB · W. Fraser, ed., *The book of Carlaverock: memoirs of the Maxwells, earls of Nithsdale*, 2 vols. (1873) · *A letter from the countess of Nithsdale*, ed. S. Grace (1827) · H. A. H. Tayler, *Lady Nithsdale and her family* (1939) · F. Maxwell Stuart, *Lady Nithsdale and the Jacobites* (1995) · *Diary of Mary, Countess Cowper*, ed. [S. Cowper] (1864) · Lady Dacre [A. J. Sullivan], ed., *Tales of the peerage and the peasantry*, 3 vols. (1835), vol. 1 · R. H. Cromek, *Remains of Nithsdale and Galloway song* (1810) · V. Brooke-Hunt, *Prisoners of the Tower of London: being an account of some who at divers times lay captive within its walls* (1899) · *State trials*, 15.762–806
Archives NRA, priv. coll., title deeds; legal papers; estate papers; family, personal, and household papers · U. Hull, Brynmor Jones L., family and personal papers
Likenesses J. B. Medina, oils, c.1699, Traquair House, Scottish Borders · F. Fraenkel, engraving, c.1716 (after E. M. Osborn), U. Aberdeen, Macbean Collection · engraving (after J. B. Medina), repro. in Fraser, *Book of Carlaverock*
Wealth at death debts of perhaps £300: Tayler, *Lady Nithsdale*, 244, 249

Maxwell, William (1732–1818), Church of Ireland clergyman, born on 24 August 1732, was the eldest son of John Maxwell, of Falkland, in Donagh parish, co. Monaghan, archdeacon of Clogher (1762–83), and his first wife, Isabella, daughter of the Revd John Leavens of Ardee, co. Louth. He was admitted a pensioner at Trinity College, Dublin, where he was elected scholar in 1750 and graduated BA (1752), MA (1755), and BD and DD (1777) (Todd, 381). His health suffered through study, and he travelled abroad with his relative Lord Farnham, until it improved. About 1754 he was introduced to Samuel Johnson by George Grierson, the government printer at Dublin. For several years he was assistant preacher at the Temple Church, London, when the Revd Gregory Sharpe was master; in 1775, through the influence of his relative Henry Maxwell, bishop of Meath, he obtained the rectory of Mount Temple, co. Westmeath. On his return to Ireland, Johnson, who had been for many years his 'social friend', and always 'spoke of him with a very kind regard', took an affecting leave of him. Maxwell's house at Falkland was of considerable size, with a good library, the relics of which were preserved at Trough Lodge, the seat of the Ancketills. When Maxwell was required to reside more regularly on his benefice, he resigned the rectory, and about 1780 moved to Bath, allowing the house at Falkland to fall into ruins.

Maxwell's first wife was Anne, eldest daughter of William Burrell Massingberd, of Ormsby, Lincolnshire, whom he married on 6 December 1777, and with whom he had four children. Three of them died childless; the youngest, Anne, married Henry Francis *Lyte at Queen Square Chapel, Bath, on 21 January 1818, and died at Berry Head, Brixham, Devon, on 7 January 1856. Maxwell's first wife died at Bath, and some time later he married in Ireland Miss Jane Ellis; they had no children. Maxwell died at his home in Bennett Street, Bath, on 3 September 1818, and was buried in Walcot church, where his widow erected to his memory an enormous monument, with the family escutcheon and the motto, 'Je suis prêt'. She died, aged eighty-two, on 21 May 1847, and was buried by her husband's side. Maxwell left by his will bequests for the better education of the poor at Donagh; on the old schoolhouse at Glaslough in that parish was placed an inscription to the effect that it was built in 1821 from his last designs.

Maxwell was very proud of his friendship with Johnson, copying him 'in wig, general appearance, and in manner'. He furnished Boswell with considerable collectanea (in which some of the doctor's best sayings are embodied) on Johnson's life before 1770. The greater part of them were inserted in Boswell (1st edn, 1.336–45), but some further anecdotes were given by him in the additions to the second edition. He is said to have written some political pamphlets, one on the Falkland Islands, and another addressed to Pitt on taxation as it affected Ireland.

W. P. COURTNEY, rev. MICHAEL BEVAN

Sources GM, 1st ser., 89/1 (1819), 92 · G. Monkland, *The literature and literati of Bath: an essay* (1854), and *Supplement to The literature and literati of Bath* (1855) · E. P. Shirley, *The history of the county of Monaghan* (1879) · J. Silvester, *The parish church of Walcot, Bath: its history and associations* (1888) · I. Taylor, ed., *The family pen: memorials biographical and literary, of the Taylor family of Ongar*, 2 vols. (1867) · J. Boswell, *Life of Johnson*, ed. R. W. Chapman, rev. J. D. Fleeman, new edn (1970); repr. with introduction by P. Rogers (1980) · *The diary and letters of His Excellency Thomas Hutchinson*, ed. P. O. Hutchinson, 2 vols. (1883–6) · private information (1894) [H. M. Lyte] · [J. H. Todd], ed., *A catalogue of graduates who have proceeded to degrees in the University of Dublin, from the earliest recorded commencements to … December 16, 1868* (1869)

Maxwell, Sir William Edward (1846–1897), colonial governor, was born on 5 August 1846, the younger son of **Sir Peter Benson Maxwell** (1817–1893), colonial official, who became chief justice of the Straits Settlements, and his wife, Frances Dorothea, the only daughter of Francis Synge of Glanmore Castle, co. Wicklow. His father, who was the fourth son of Peter Benson Maxwell of Birdstown, co. Donegal, was born in January 1817 and educated at Paris and at Trinity College, Dublin (BA 1839). He entered the Inner Temple in 1838, moved to the Middle Temple two years later, and was called to the bar on 19 November 1841. In 1855 Peter Maxwell published *Whom Shall We Hang? The Sebastopol Enquiry*, and the following year he was knighted. He was recorder of Penang (1856–66) and of Singapore (1866–71), and chief justice of the Straits Settlements from 1867 to 1871. In 1883–4 he reorganized the judicial tribunals of Egypt. He published two legal works of some importance, *An introduction to the duties of police in the settlement of Prince of Wales Island, Singapore and Malacca* (1866) and *On the Interpretation of Statutes* (1875). He died in France, at Grasse, Alpes-Maritimes, on 14 January 1893.

William Edward Maxwell was educated at Repton School (1860–64) and was employed from 1865 to 1869 in the supreme court at Penang and Singapore. In 1867 he qualified as an advocate at the local bar, and in September 1869 he was appointed a police magistrate and commissioner of the court of requests at Penang. In 1870 he married Lilias, the daughter of James Aberigh-Mackay, a chaplain in the Indian service. In February of that year he was placed in the same offices in Malacca, in August 1871 at Singapore, and in 1872 in Province Wellesley. In May 1874 he was nominated a temporary judge of the supreme court of Penang, and in September he was appointed assistant government agent for Province Wellesley. In November 1875 he accompanied, as deputy commissioner, the Larut field force in their retributive expedition against the murderers of James Wheeler Woodford Birch, the British resident at Perak. He was mentioned in dispatches and received a medal. Maxwell became assistant resident in Perak and a member of the state council in February 1878. In 1881 he was called to the bar by the Inner Temple, and in the following year he was commissioned to visit the Australian colonies and report on the Torrens land registration system, which resulted in *The Torrens System of Conveyancing by Registration of Title in the Straits Settlement* (1883).

On returning to the Straits Settlements Maxwell became commissioner of land titles, and in 1883 was gazetted a member of the executive and legislative councils. The following year he was employed by the Foreign Office on a successful mission to the west coast of Atchin to obtain the release of the survivors of the British ship *Nisero*, who had been in captivity for ten months; for this he was created CMG. From 1884 to 1889 he was acting resident counsellor at Penang, and in 1889 became British resident at Selangor. In 1892 he was nominated colonial secretary of the Straits Settlements, and from September 1893 to January 1895 he was acting governor.

In March 1895 Maxwell was nominated governor of the Gold Coast. He found the colony on the brink of a war with the Asante, who made frequent slave raids, and refused to pay the balance of the war indemnity due to the British government. On 17 January 1896 an expedition under Sir Francis Scott entered Kumasi without resistance, and made prisoner the Asante king, Prempeh. Maxwell, who was nominated KCMG in 1896, visited England in the summer, and addressed large meetings at Liverpool and Manchester on the future of the Gold Coast and the Asante kingdom. He returned to the Gold Coast in October, and died at sea off Gran Canaria on 14 December 1897. He was survived by his wife.

E. I. CARLYLE, rev. LYNN MILNE

Sources *The Times* (18 Jan 1893) · *The Times* (16 Dec 1896) · *Pall Mall Gazette* (8 Jan 1901) · WWW · R. S. Baden-Powell, *The downfall of Prempeh* (1896) · *ILN* (25 Dec 1897), 917 · Boase, *Mod. Eng. biog.* · Burke, *Peerage* · *CGPLA Eng. & Wales* (1895) [Peter Benson Maxwell] · *CGPLA Eng. & Wales* (1898)
Archives SOAS, notes on Perak folklore, genealogies, etc.
Likenesses portrait, repro. in *ILN*
Wealth at death £3189 15s.: probate, 1 April 1898, *CGPLA Eng. & Wales* · £8136 19s. 2d.—Peter Maxwell: resworn probate, 1895, *CGPLA Eng. & Wales*

Maxwell, William Hamilton (1792–1850), writer, was born at Newry, co. Down, on 30 June 1792, the son of James Maxwell, a merchant, and his wife, a daughter of William Hamilton, of a good, respected family. He went to school at Dr Henderson's academy in Hill Street, Newry. On 7 December 1807, when he was only fifteen years old, he entered Trinity College, Dublin. Although he wasted a good deal of time there, he graduated with some distinction as a BA in 1812.

It is difficult to establish the events of Maxwell's life in his early manhood. He was keen to follow a military career but this ambition was strongly opposed by his family, who wanted him to enter the church or the legal profession. For two or three years, it seems, the arguments between him and his family persisted. Meanwhile he spent his time in his favourite pursuits of hunting, shooting, and fishing, though he also read military history, poetry, and romances. All these activities provided him with material for his writing in subsequent years. It is sometimes said that he joined the army during this period of his life. The writer of his obituary in the *Illustrated London News* (25 January 1851, 51) claimed that he attained the rank of captain in the 88th regiment, that he participated in the last stages of the Peninsular War, and that he was present at the battle of Waterloo. But this claim is untrue, and it is possible that he gained his knowledge of recent military campaigns from talking and drinking with officers of regiments successively stationed in co. Mayo. As a young man he spent lavishly, anticipating his future income by confirming for ready money certain leases which his father had granted to tenants and by expecting to inherit money from an aunt. When the latter funds failed to materialize because of legal difficulties, he thought of taking a military commission in South America, but this plan came to nothing.

Finally, in accordance with his family's wishes, Maxwell took holy orders. He was ordained deacon at Carlow on 25 July 1813 and became a curate at Clonallan in the same year. At about this time he married Mary Dobbin, the second daughter of Thomas Dobbin, MP for co. Armagh. In 1820 the archbishop of Armagh, who was friendly with his wife's family, appointed him to two benefices in the area of Ballagh, Connemara, a place destitute of a congregation but abounding in game, and therefore a situation congenial to Maxwell. While living in a shooting lodge at Ballycroy he wrote his first novel, *O'Hara, or, 1798*, which was published anonymously in 1825 but which was unsuccessful. He seems once again to have become unsettled, but the marquess of Sligo, with whom he was on friendly terms, gave him a house rent-free to retain him at Ballagh.

In 1829 Maxwell achieved recognition as a writer when Henry Colburn published his *Stories of Waterloo*, for which he paid him £300. Three years later one of his most popular books appeared: *Wild Sports of the West* (1832). This contained lively tales and legends together with colourful descriptions of Irish people, sporting activities (such as salmon fishing and deer hunting), and the Connaught countryside. An edition of this book appeared in 1916 with an appreciative introduction by the earl of Dunraven. Maxwell had thus become a progenitor of two kinds of fiction which became popular in the 1830s and 1840s: the military novel and the rollicking story of Irish life.

Maxwell was over 6 feet tall, distinguished in appearance, and elegantly dressed. In the words of one of his friends, William Maginn, he was 'a fine, dashing-looking, long, well-knit fellow' (Maginn, vii–xii). He was vivacious and an entertaining conversationalist. Sir William Wilde thought that as a raconteur he was second only to Sheridan. Maxwell became friendly with Charles Lever in 1835, encouraging him to write novels of adventure and exchanging with him experiences and stories of Irish life and characters. As a result, it was not always possible to say who was the original author of certain incidents in their books. His easy-going temperament and fluency are reflected in his fiction, which was enthusiastically described by Maginn: 'he flings off his tales as they were so many tumblers of punch, hot and strong, pleasant and heart-cheering, hastily mixed, and hastily disposed of' (ibid.).

Maxwell contributed to periodicals, including *Bentley's Miscellany* and the *New Monthly Magazine*. Although Dickens had a poor opinion of some of his contributions to *Bentley's Miscellany*, he put a story of Maxwell's ('The Expedition') in *The Pic-Nic Papers* (1841), the compilation he edited to raise money for the widow of John Macrone, the publisher. Maxwell was a prolific writer, producing some twenty books in about twenty years. Most of them were popular, and a staple of the circulating libraries. Typical novels are *The Fortunes of Hector O'Halloran and his Man, Mark Antony O'Toole* (1842–3), illustrated by John Leech, and *Captain O'Sullivan, or, Adventures, Civil, Military and Matrimonial of a Gentleman on Half-Pay* (1846), which are picaresque narratives, as their titles indicate. In 1844 he wrote *Wanderings in the Highlands and Islands*, a sequel to *Wild Sports of the West*. He also wrote non-fiction, including the *Life of Field-Marshal His Grace the Duke of Wellington* (1839–41), which reappeared in many later editions, and a *History of the Irish Rebellion in 1798* (1845), illustrated by George Cruikshank. *The Irish Movements* (1848) was an outspoken attack on Chartism and on Irish campaigns for independence: 'Away with agitation: conciliate your best friend, England, if you can.'

In 1844 Maxwell was apparently deprived of his living for non-residence, but he had made no financial provision for the future. After spending several years in ill health and distress, he retired to Musselburgh, near Edinburgh, where he died on 28 December 1850.

DONALD HAWES

Sources *DNB* · C. McKelvie, 'Notes towards a bibliography of William Hamilton Maxwell', *Irish Booklore*, 3 (1976), 32–42 · [C. Lever], 'Our portrait gallery, no. XXI', *Dublin University Magazine*, 18 (1841), 220–25 · *GM*, 2nd ser., 35 (1851), 674–5 · W. Maginn, 'Biographical sketch of William Hamilton Maxwell', in W. H. Maxwell, *Erin-go-bragh* (1859), vii–xii · *ILN* (25 Jan 1851), 51 · J. S. Crone, *A concise dictionary of Irish biography* (1928) · W. J. Fitzpatrick, *The life of Charles Lever*, new edn [1884] · *The letters of Charles Dickens*, ed. M. House, G. Storey, and others, 1 (1965), 236, 307 · E. Downey, *Charles Lever: his life in his letters*, 2 vols. (1906) · J. Wilson, *Noctes ambrosianae*, 4 vols., new edn (1864) · *BL cat.* · *The Athenaeum* (18 Jan 1851), 83

Archives HLRO, commonplace book | BL, letters to Richard Bentley, Add. MSS 46611–46615, 46649–46652

Likenesses C. Gray, pen drawing, NG Ire. · W. Greatbach, line engraving (after S. Lover), BM, NPG; repro. in W. H. Maxwell, *Erin-*

go-bragh (1859), frontispiece · C. Grey, engraving, repro. in Lever, 'Our portrait gallery, no. xxi' · J. Kirkwood, etching (after C. Grey), NPG

Maxwell, Sir William Stirling, ninth baronet (1818–1878), art historian, historian, and book collector, was born William Stirling on 8 March 1818 at Kenmure House, Kirkintilloch, near Glasgow, the only son of Archibald Stirling of Keir and Cawder (1769–1847) and Elizabeth Maxwell (1793–1822), daughter of Sir John Maxwell, seventh baronet, of Pollok. He had two sisters, Hannah-Ann (1816–1843) and Elizabeth (1822–1845).

Family background and early life Stirling was proud to belong to one of Scotland's ancient families, who traced their descent from Walter de Striueling (*fl.* 1150), grandfather of Thomas de Striueling (*d.* 1227), chancellor of Scotland, and he encouraged William Fraser's *The Stirlings of Keir and their Family Papers* (1858). His family's loyalty to the Stuart kings was reflected in its Episcopalianism and fuelled Stirling's romantic interest in the Jacobites. His mother's equally ancient family, the Maxwells of Pollok, however, brought different traditions: they had a covenanting past and were reforming whigs, in contrast to the Stirlings' conservatism. These opposing standpoints, which sometimes caused family tensions, helped form Sir William's liberal character. His toryism was regarded by many 'as a matter of family tradition rather than of personal predilection' (*The Scotsman*, 17 Jan 1878), while his religious tolerance was demonstrated on many occasions, such as in 1853, when he supported the right of Jews to enter parliament.

Stirling was educated at private schools run by the Revd D. B. Langley at Pilton rectory, Northamptonshire, and by the Revd John Babington at Cossington rectory, Leicestershire, and then at Trinity College, Cambridge. His tutor at Trinity, where he was a fellow-commoner from 1835 to 1839, was William Whewell, and contemporaries such as Ralph W. Grey, Lord John Manners, Francis, Baron Napier, and Trinity fellow John Donaldson became his friends. He graduated BA in 1839 and proceeded MA in 1843. In 1839 he went on a grand tour of Germany, Switzerland, France, and Italy in the company of George Holland and enjoyed the opportunity to sow wild oats as well to see great art and architecture. He failed to become tory candidate for Perthshire before the 1841 election, mainly because, in the crisis over patronage in the Church of Scotland, his family had given support to the non-intrusionists who opposed the right of lairds to veto a congregation's choice of minister. Bitterly disappointed, he set out on an extended tour in 1841, this time including the Middle East, where his experience as 'a dweller in tents, by the Red Sea' resulted in his *Songs of the Holy Land* (1846), which made rich associative use of biblical language and place names.

Historian of Spain and Spanish art Stirling also paid a first brief visit to Spain, where he was enchanted by Seville. By early 1843 he had decided to write a history of Spanish art to answer a growing demand for publications on Spain. He began collecting the important source books on Spanish

Sir William Stirling Maxwell, ninth baronet (1818–1878), by George Richmond, *c.*1856

art and toured Spain again, as well as visiting British private collections containing Spanish art. The resulting three-volume *Annals of the Artists of Spain* (1848) was by far the most comprehensive and scholarly work in its field in English by that date. It was a remarkable achievement for an author of thirty and it was innovative in a number of important ways, such as its arrangement of material chronologically according to monarchs' reigns and geographical areas, its placing of art in Spain within a broad social, cultural, and historical context, and its publication of the first catalogues of the works of Velázquez and Murillo.

The *Annals* was well received at the time, notably by the art critic Richard Ford, who became a close friend. Ford compared it favourably with the shorter, less ambitious work by Sir Edmund Head which appeared the same year, describing Stirling's work in the *Quarterly Review* as 'an olla podrida … stuffed with savouries, the national garlic not omitted' (*Quarterly Review*, 83, June–September 1848, 11). The scant discussion of artistic technique, however, prompted the German writer Karl Justi to label Stirling as 'far more of a historian … and man of letters than a connoisseur' (Justi, 10). More recently, opinion has swung back in favour of Stirling's broad perspective, with Jonathan Brown's praise of the *Annals*' 'extraordinary … scope and seriousness' (Brown, 6). A project in 1857–9 to translate the *Annals* into Spanish unfortunately failed. Stirling's care over the design and illustrations of the *Annals* was typical: a bibliophile, he was fascinated by printing and reproduction. A fourth volume of twenty-five copies consisted of extra illustrations using the Talbotype photographic process developed by William Fox Talbot and became the first use of photography in an art history book.

Stirling wrote a number of other books on Spain and Spanish art. In 1855 *Velazquez and his Works* reworked the *Annals* material on the artist, with a new catalogue of prints after his works. It was soon superseded by Justi's comprehensive study but it heralded the new monographic approach in art history. A Spanish translation was serialized in the *Gaceta de Madrid* and there were also German and French translations, the latter with notes and a catalogue by the French art critic William Burger (Théodore Thoré).

Stirling's most successful book in terms of sales and editions was *The Cloister Life of the Emperor Charles the Fifth* (1852), following his two articles on the subject in *Fraser's Magazine*. It also appeared in German, Dutch, and Spanish translations. The great Renaissance figure was one of Stirling's heroes and, like many historians, Stirling was fascinated by the emperor's decision to abdicate power and retreat to a Spanish monastery. His study was inspired by an evocative drawing of the monastery at Yuste by Ford, to whom he dedicated the book, and he also composed a romantic ballad on the abdication. His book was nevertheless an important and rigorous piece of scholarship as well as a popular and accessible history, but as a standard reference work it was soon eclipsed by studies by Mignet and Gachard.

Stirling also had a fascination for Charles's illegitimate son Don John of Austria. As early as 1842 he noted that 'a good history of him in English would be popular' ('Hints on things in general', 1842, Stirlings of Keir MSS, T-SK 28/9). His two-volume *Don John of Austria, or, Passages from the History of the Sixteenth Century* (1883) was finally published posthumously and was a scholarly yet very readable history. Most of the work for the book had been completed by 1859, and in 1864 a single-volume edition of ten copies was printed. The delays reflected Stirling's perfectionism as both historian and book designer.

Bibliophile and art collector Stirling succeeded to his father's estates of Keir and Cawder in 1847, and in 1852 sold the loss-making Jamaica plantations which he had also inherited. Between 1849 and 1852 he commissioned a young London architect, Alfred Jenoure, to carry out alterations to Keir House. The ambitious scheme transformed the neo-classical pile into an idiosyncratic expression of Stirling's tastes and interests. At the centre was his magnificent two-storey library, lined in cedar, with specially designed furniture and fittings. Dr Waagen found it 'too remarkable a room not to be mentioned' and noted that every surface was carved with mottoes, 'the study of which would occupy an ordinary length of life very profitably' (Waagen, 453). The books were beautifully bound and embossed with Stirling's armorial devices, and he himself designed the *ex libris* slips which incorporated his mottoes, such as *Gang Forward* and *Poco a Poco*.

Stirling's book collecting covered several related areas, as documented by his catalogues: *An essay towards a collection of books relating to the arts of design, being a catalogue of those at Keir* (1850; updated, 1860) and *An essay towards a collection of books [of] proverbs, emblems, apophthegms, epitaphs and ana* (1860). The obsessive nature of his collecting was exemplified by his large accumulation of emblem books, now in Glasgow University Library, which numbered around 1200. It was probably the largest collection ever amassed and its owner was one of the most important figures in the nineteenth-century revival of interest in emblems.

Stirling also became an active art collector, particularly during the 1850s, when there were several important auctions of Spanish art in London, most notably of Louis-Philippe's Galerie Espagnole in 1853, and of Frank Hall Standish's collection, which had been left to the French king. Stirling's Spanish art collection became the most extensive in Britain, with works by (or then attributed to) artists 'whose names have hardly crossed the seas and mountains that bound the Peninsula' (*Annals of the Artists of Spain*, 1891, 1.61–2). Its contents reflected many of the themes of the *Annals*, such as the exploration of art patronage by Spanish rulers, which was echoed by the inclusion of many royal portraits. Similarly, as one of the first art historians of Spain to discuss the role and status of the artist, he was attracted to portraits of artists, especially self-portraits.

Perhaps surprisingly, the collection did not contain major works by Velázquez and Murillo, the best-known Spanish artists in Britain by that date, but Stirling did become the first important British collector of both El Greco and Goya, neither of whom was hitherto much known or appreciated in Britain. The majority of his Goyas, not surprisingly, were prints, most of them rare proofs acquired from his friend Valentín Carderera (1796–1880), one of the most important figures in establishing Goya's reputation in Spain. Another of Stirling's advanced tastes was for the paintings and illustrated books which accompanied the poems of William Blake. The relationship between word and image in Blake's work must have been of special interest to a collector of emblem books. He also collected paintings and prints of the Stuart kings and the Jacobite pretenders.

Stirling's collecting of copies, both painted copies and prints after paintings, was also unusual. These were the source of many illustrations for his books and often provided valuable visual references before photographs were readily available. His *Essay towards a catalogue of prints, engraved from the works of … Velazquez and … Murillo* (1873) was based on his own extensive collection and that of his friend Charles Morse. Stirling's interest in copies, and his tendency to focus more on content than on style and technique in art, certainly laid his collecting open to the criticism that it lacked connoisseurship; but equally his approach can be seen as challenging modern assumptions that 'connoisseurship' is the only important quality of a collector. He was also a better connoisseur in the traditional sense than he has generally been given credit for. Further evidence of his commitment to the multiple image was provided by his pioneering books of facsimile prints using the new photolithographic methods, including *Examples of the Engraved Portraiture of the Sixteenth Century* (1872), *Solyman the Magnificent Going to Mosque* (1563; facsimile edn, 1877), and the anatomical tables of Vesalius (1538; facsimile edn, 1874).

Public life and connections In 1852 Stirling became Conservative MP for Perthshire and gained a reputation as an independent who voted according to conscience. He lost his seat in 1868 but regained it in 1874 and held it until his death. Education, particularly higher education, became one of his principal concerns and he served on the Scottish education board and the University of London senate. In the 1860s he campaigned for separate parliamentary representation for graduates of Scottish universities, as was enjoyed by Oxford and Cambridge. He was elected rector of St Andrews University in 1863 and of Edinburgh University in 1871, and in 1875 was elected chancellor of Glasgow University. On the issue of whether women medical students should be awarded degrees, which was fiercely debated at Edinburgh at the time, he supported the women's cause, and was instrumental in getting the law changed on this matter.

From 1853 Stirling served on the government select committee on the fine arts and he later became a trustee of the National Gallery, the National Portrait Gallery, and the British Museum. He spent much of his time in the reading-room of the latter, where his private writing-case was kept for him in the inner library and was opened with a tiny key from a ring on his finger. He was also one of the founding members of the Philobiblon Society in 1854, along with his friends the duc d'Aumale and Richard Monckton Milnes, and a number of his essays and special editions were published by the society. He was a great admirer of Sir Walter Scott, and many of his ideas on history as well as politics can be traced to Scott's influence. In 1871 he was involved in organizing an exhibition in Edinburgh to celebrate the centenary of Scott's birth. He was also on the committee formed in 1856 to commission stained glass for Glasgow Cathedral, which controversially chose Munich glass. Stirling later asked the committee secretary, the architect Charles Heath Wilson, to design his family monument for Lecropt church, near Keir.

As an agriculturist, Stirling was an important breeder of traditional strains of livestock, notably shorthorn cattle and Clydesdale horses, and a pedigree which included Keir blood added considerably to an animal's value. He was honorary secretary of the Highland and Agricultural Society from 1868 and also served as president of the Glasgow Agricultural Society.

In 1865 Stirling succeeded his uncle Sir John Maxwell to the Pollok estate near Glasgow, though he continued to live at Keir. He was also permitted to succeed to the Maxwell baronetcy and became Sir William Stirling Maxwell, while in 1876 he was made knight of the Thistle, a rare honour for a commoner. On 26 April 1865 he married Lady Anna Maria Leslie Melville, daughter of the earl

of Leven and Melville; they had two sons, John and Archibald. In 1874 Lady Anna died tragically after a burning accident at Keir. On 1 March 1877, despite the opposition of some of his family, Sir William married his long-time friend Caroline Elizabeth Sarah Norton, née Sheridan (1808–1877), just months before her death on 15 June that year. His own death from a fever occurred soon afterwards in Venice on 15 January 1878. He was buried on 31 January in the Keir vault at Lecropt church.

Stirling Maxwell was remembered as a rigorous scholar and a man of enlightened views whose hospitality was enjoyed by many at Keir and his London house at 128 Park Street. His friends included Thackeray and Disraeli, while he corresponded with bibliophiles in many countries and with specialists on Spanish topics in Spain and America. He was made honorary member of Spain's Real Academia de la Historia and corresponding member of its Real Academia de Bellas Artes. He has sometimes been dismissed as a dilettante, an assessment that misses the remarkable originality and modernity of many of his ideas and his seriousness as a scholar. Photographs and descriptions highlight the fierce eyebrows which belied his kind nature. John Gray, curator of the Scottish National Portrait Gallery, lamented the lack of a good portrait which would have recorded:

> the powerful individuality of the furrowed face which one remembers so well. It is greatly to be regretted that we have no more … adequate memorial of this eminent Scotsman, than whom few indeed of our own times have been worthier of perfect portrayal and continued memory. (Gray, 41)

According to his will, Stirling Maxwell's collections were divided equally between his sons, and the elder, John (1866–1956), was required to choose between the Keir and Pollok estates. He chose the latter and succeeded to the baronetcy and represented the College division of Glasgow as a Conservative from 1895 to 1906. Keir House was sold by Sir William's grandson Lieutenant-Colonel William Stirling, and its collection dispersed. Much of his collection can, however, still be seen at Pollok House, Glasgow.   HILARY MACARTNEY

Sources W. Fraser, *The Stirlings of Keir* (privately printed, Edinburgh, 1858) · W. Fraser, ed., *Memoirs of the Maxwells of Pollok*, 2 vols. (privately printed, Edinburgh, 1863) · *DNB* · *The Scotsman* (17 Jan 1878) · R. Monckton Milnes, *The Academy* (26 Jan 1878), 75 · *The Athenaeum* (19 Jan 1878), 89 · *Glasgow Herald* (17 Jan 1878) · *The Times* (17 Jan 1878) · R. Guy, ed., 'Biographical note', in *Miscellaneous essays and addresses: the works of Sir William Stirling Maxwell*, large paper edn, 6 (1891), xxix–xxxii, 461–84 · *BL cat.* · G. F. Waagen, *Galleries and cabinets of art in Great Britain* (1857), 448–53 · J. M. Gray, *Notes on the art treasures at Keir, Perthshire* (privately printed, Edinburgh, 1887) [repr. from *The Scottish Leader*] · J. L. Caw, *Catalogue of pictures at Pollok House* (privately printed, Glasgow, 1936) · R. L. Douglas, 'Catalogue of paintings at Keir House' · H. Black and D. Weston, eds., *A short title catalogue of the emblem books and related works in the Stirling Maxwell collection of Glasgow University Library* (1988) · [R. Ford], review of E. Head, *A handbook of the Spanish and French schools of painting*, and W. Stirling, *Annals of the Spanish artists*, QR, 83 (1848), 1–37 · K. Justi, *Velazquez and his times*, trans. A. H. Keane (1889) · J. Brown, 'Observations on the historiography of seventeenth-century Spanish painting', *Images and ideas in seventeenth-century Spanish painting* (1978), 3–18 · A. Rowan, 'Keir House, Perthshire, III', *Country Life*,

158 (1975), 506–10 · 'Funeral of Sir William Stirling Maxwell', *Glasgow Herald* (1 Feb 1878) · W. W. Rouse Ball and J. A. Venn, eds., *Admissions to Trinity College, Cambridge*, 4 (1911), 414 · E. Harris, 'Sir William Stirling-Maxwell and the history of Spanish art', *Apollo*, 79 (1964), 73–7 · I. G. C. Hutchison, *A political history of Scotland, 1832–1924* (1986), p. 21 and n. 131

Archives Mitchell L., Glas., Glasgow City Archives, account by Rawdon Brown of Sir William's fatal illness, death certificate, permissions to transport body, T-SK 34 · Mitchell L., Glas., Glasgow City Archives, corresp., T-PM 119 · Mitchell L., Glas., Glasgow City Archives, corresp. and papers, incl. diaries, T-SK 28–33 · Mitchell L., Glas., Glasgow City Archives, Maxwell family MSS · Mitchell L., Glas., Glasgow City Archives, Genealogical history of the Stirlings of Keir and Cadder, 1854, T-SK 38/3 · NRA, priv. coll., letters to the Stirling family · Pollok House, Glasgow, collection · U. Glas., collection and emblem books | Bodl. Oxf., letters to Benjamin Disraeli · Bodl. Oxf., letters to J. and J. Leighton, booksellers · National Monuments Record of Scotland, inventory of Keir plans, drawings, and photographs · NL Scot., MSS · Trinity Cam., letters to Richard Monckton Milnes, Houghton MS 16 · U. Edin. L., letters to David Laing

Likenesses G. Richmond, chalk drawing, c.1856, priv. coll. [*see illus.*] · F. J. Williamson, bronze bust, 1873, Scot. NPG; related plaster bust, NPG · F. J. Williamson, marble bust, 1878, Pollok House, Glasgow · W. Douglas, oils (as a child), Pollok House, Glasgow · J. Graham-Gilbert, oils (as a young man); Christies, 22–24 May 1995, lot 477 · W. Holl, stipple (*Grillion's Club* series; after drawing by G. Richmond, c.1856), BM · R. B. Parkes, mezzotint (after photograph by T. Rodger), repro. in Guy, ed., 'Biographical note', frontispiece · T. Rodger, carte-de-visite, NPG · F. J. Williamson, terracotta bust, NPG · engraving (after G. Richmond), repro. in *Annals*, 1 (1891), frontispiece · photograph, priv. coll. · portrait, miniature, watercolour (when a child), probably priv. coll.; repro. in J. L Caw, *Catalogue of pictures at Pollok House*, 189 · wood-engraving, NPG; repro. in *ILN* (25 Nov 1871)

Wealth at death £202,817 6s. 6d.: confirmation, 26 April 1878, *CCI* · £1225 3s. 7d.: additional estate, 8 July 1886, *CCI* · £1190 11s. 3d.: additional estate, 3 April 1889, *CCI* · under £25,000 effects in England: resworn double probate, June 1878, *CGPLA Eng. & Wales*

Maxwell, Willielma. *See* Campbell, Willielma, Viscountess Glenorchy (1741–1786).

Maxwell [*née* Herbert]**, Winifred, countess of Nithsdale** (1672–1749), Jacobite courtier, was the last of the six children of William *Herbert, marquess and Jacobite duke of Powis (c.1626–1696), and Lady Elizabeth Somerset (c.1634–1691), daughter of Edward, second marquess of Worcester. She was the sister of Lady Lucy *Herbert, devotional writer and superior of the English Augustinian convent at Bruges, Flanders, and Lady Carrington, who was active in Jacobite plots. Her parents, prominent in the court of James II, moved to St Germain-en-Laye after the revolution of 1688. There she met William *Maxwell, fifth earl of Nithsdale (1676–1744), the son of Robert and Lucie Maxwell, fourth earl and countess of Nithsdale. Lady Winifred married the fifth earl in 1699. Two children survived to adulthood, William, Lord Maxwell, and Anne, Lady Bellew. Lady Nithsdale raised her granddaughter, Frances Maria Bellew, after Anne died giving birth to her second child.

When Lord Nithsdale was imprisoned and sentenced to death for his part in the 1715 Jacobite rising, Lady Nithsdale travelled to London to attempt to secure a pardon for him. She completed her journey on horseback when deep snow stopped the stagecoaches. In London she asked

Winifred Maxwell, countess of Nithsdale (1672–1749), by Sir John Baptiste de Medina, before 1710

those with power for assistance and attempted to present a petition in person to George I. He refused to accept it, and when she clutched at his robes, he dragged her to the end of the room where a guard stopped her. This incident sparked criticism of the king's rudeness and encouraged popular sympathy for Lady Nithsdale. Though Lord Dorset eventually had the petition read to the king, Lady Nithsdale believed that her husband's Catholicism would prevent any leniency. When this and other petitions failed, Lady Nithsdale organized her husband's escape from the Tower of London on 22 February 1716. With the assistance of her maid Cecilia Evans and two friends, Mrs Morgan and Mrs Mills, Lady Nithsdale confused the guards and smuggled in an extra cloak and paint to disguise Lord Nithsdale. Lady Nithsdale conducted her husband outside and then returned to his cell and pretended to converse with him for a while. When she departed, she told the guards he was at prayers and should not be disturbed. Once Lord Nithsdale was safely out of the Tower, Mrs Evans placed him with one of her friends. When the escape became known, Lady Nithsdale remained quietly in London, but once Lord Nithsdale was safe on the continent, she undertook a risky journey to Scotland to secure the family papers and arrange for the care of their property. She suffered a miscarriage during her journey to join her husband, but she recovered and became active in the exiled Jacobite court, residing first at La Flèche, in France (March 1717–July 1718), and then from 1718 to 1726 at Rome.

Lady Nithsdale's only official position at court was governess to Henry Benedict Stuart, but she also served as unofficial lady-in-waiting to Clementina Sobieska and cared for Charles Edward Stuart when Clementina moved to a convent. Many of Lady Nithsdale's letters from this period plead for money and assistance in curtailing her husband's expenditures. Despite the hardships of her later years, her devotion to James Edward Stuart and his children never wavered. She died in Rome in May 1749.

The romantic story of the earl's escape made Lady Nithsdale a popular heroine in early Jacobite writing. In a letter to her sister Lucy describing the escape, she writes that George I, whom she calls 'the Electour', said 'that I had done him more mischeif than any woman in Christendom' (Tayler, 56). Her story provided the basis for numerous popular historical accounts, plays, most notably Clifford Bax's *The Immortal Lady* (1931), and a highly romanticized historical novel, *Winifred, Countess of Nithsdale: a Tale of the Jacobite Wars* (1869), by Barbarina Olga Brand, Lady Dacre. Lady Nithsdale also became a recurring figure in books of distinguished women, where she is praised for her intrepid actions and her devotion to her husband.

LEIGH EICKE

Sources H. Tayler, *Lady Nithsdale and her family* (1939) · W. Fraser, ed., *The book of Carlaverock: memoirs of the Maxwells, earls of Nithsdale*, 2 vols. (1873)
Archives Everingham Park, Yorkshire · NRA, priv. coll., corresp. and papers | Windsor Castle, Stuart MSS
Likenesses J. B. de Medina, oils, before 1710, Traquair House, Scottish Borders [*see illus.*] · portrait, *c.*1715–1749, English Augustinian Convent, Bruges · Cook, line engraving, NPG · portrait (as a child), Powis Castle, Montgomeryshire
Wealth at death very little or none: Tayler, *Lady Nithsdale*

May, Baptist [Bab] (*bap.* **1628**, *d.* **1697**), courtier, was baptized on 4 November 1628, and was the sixth and youngest son of Sir Humphrey *May (1572/3–1630), privy councillor, and his second wife, Judith (*bap.* 1598, *d.* 1661), daughter of Sir William Poley (1562–1629). He took his first name from his uncle, Baptist Hicks, first Viscount Campden. May later told Gilbert Burnet that he had been 'bred about the king [Charles II] since he was a child' (Burnet, 2.465), and by 1648 he was one of the duke of York's pages. It is likely to have been through the influence of his mother's cousin, Henry Jermyn, Lord Jermyn, later earl of St Albans, that he had entered royal service. He was probably back in England in February 1652 when he submitted a petition to the council of state. At the Restoration he and St Albans together obtained the sinecure post of registrar of chancery, and from 1665 he and the poet Abraham Cowley were partners with St Albans in the scheme to develop St James's Square, London. An adjacent street was named Babmaes Mews after him—the use of his nickname in this context having the appearance of a private joke. Between 1662 and 1665 he served as a groom in York's bedchamber.

May is remembered as one of Charles II's most trusted servants. The office of keeper of his privy purse, to which he was appointed on 28 July 1665 on the death of Charles Berkeley, earl of Falmouth, required him to manage the king's private hoard of cash. The key influence behind his appointment seems to have been the royal mistress Barbara Villiers, countess of Castlemaine, who realized that

an ally in this office would make the payments due to her his priority. In October 1666 York nominated him as a candidate for Winchelsea, only for the electors to reject him because 'they would have no court pimp to be their burgess' (Pepys, 7.337). A courtier with a talent to amuse rather than to conspire, May had an unfortunate habit of making tactless remarks. A comment by him welcoming the great fire, because it would make the City easier to control, shocked even the king (*Life of … Clarendon*, 3.101). His alliance with Castlemaine in 1667 against Edward Hyde, earl of Clarendon, was the most public of secret court intrigues. There was in truth little that someone in May's position could do to undermine the lord chancellor except mock him. When Clarendon was brought down in November 1667, Pepys reported that May 'fell upon his knees and ketched the king about the legs and joyed him, and said that this was the first time that ever he could call him King of England' (Pepys, 8.525). Two years later he was one of those who amused the king by ridiculing Henry Bennet, Lord Arlington. The trick failed to work a second time. It was only Castlemaine's support which discouraged Arlington from seeking reprisals against him. For all his privileged access to the king, May showed little skill whenever he attempted to meddle directly in high politics. On being elected MP for Midhurst in 1670, he had plans to promote a bill to allow the king to divorce the queen, but Charles made clear his disapproval as soon as he discovered what May was up to. In 1681 when the king suspended those gentlemen of the bedchamber who persisted in supporting exclusion May came close to being suspended as well. In early 1685 he was involved with Louise Renée de Kéroualle, duchess of Portsmouth, and York's other enemies at court in plotting to have the duke sent back to Scotland. They could not have foreseen just how big a miscalculation this would prove to be.

May never enjoyed a monopoly on the king's secret finances. The French pension was paid instead through William Chiffinch, the secret service fund was controlled by the secretary to the Treasury, and Sir Stephen Fox also acted as a conduit for secret payments. The sole surviving set of late seventeenth-century privy purse accounts, which cover the years from 1666 to 1669 and which are known only from a copy transcribed by Edmund Malone (1741–1812), confirm that most of the payments made by May were very mundane (Bodl. Oxf., MS Malone 44, fols. 100–111). The privy purse may have been most important during the final years of the reign, when Charles used it to channel the surpluses from the Irish revenue to the building of his new palace at Winchester, and when, paradoxically, May was least secure in his favour. That favour was always ambiguous. Burnet thought that May:

> had the greatest and longest share in the king's secret confidence of any man in that time; for it was never broke off, though often shaken, he being in his notions against every thing that the king was for, both France, popery, and arbitrary government: but a particular sympathy of temper, and his serving the king in his vices, created a confidence much envied, and often attempted to be broke, but never with any success beyond a short coldness. (Burnet, 1.481–2)

His real secret was understanding that Charles least wanted to see those who came to him on official business. His favour, like all the other confidential servants, depended on his resisting the temptation to become too obviously involved in the political affairs his master found so tiresome.

In 1685 James II removed May as keeper to make way for James Graham. May was allowed to retain his office as ranger of Windsor Great Park, having held it since May 1671, and he continued to use the Great Lodge (later Cumberland Lodge) as his principal country seat. An attempt to become MP for New Windsor in 1690 (in partnership with Sir Christopher Wren) resulted in a double return, and he had instead to sit for Thetford. He was considered a supporter of the court throughout that parliament. He died on 2 March 1697 and was buried in St George's Chapel, Windsor. He had never married, but his will confirmed that he had had an illegitimate son, Charles, probably with Dorothy Broke of Bury St Edmunds, Suffolk (will, PRO, PROB 11/444, fols. 128v–132). ANDREW BARCLAY

Sources Pepys, *Diary* · *Bishop Burnet's History* · B. M. Crook, 'May, Baptist', HoP, *Commons, 1660–90* · W. A. Shaw, ed., *Calendar of treasury books*, 1–7, PRO (1904–16) · *The life of Edward, earl of Clarendon … written by himself*, new edn, 3 vols. (1827) · *Memoirs of Thomas, earl of Ailesbury*, ed. W. E. Buckley, 2 vols., Roxburghe Club, 122 (1890) · *Calendar of the Clarendon state papers preserved in the Bodleian Library*, ed. O. Ogle and others, 5 vols. (1869–1970) · *Report on the manuscripts of his grace the duke of Buccleuch and Queensberry … preserved at Montagu House*, 3 vols. in 4, HMC, 45 (1899–1926) · *Lorenzo Magalotti at the court of Charles II: his Relazione d'Inghilterra of 1668*, ed. and trans. W. E. K. Middleton (1980) · *Le Neve's Pedigrees of the knights*, ed. G. W. Marshall, Harleian Society, 8 (1873) · E. Ashmole, *The antiquities of Berkshire*, 3 vols. (1719) · CSP, 1651–2 · will, PRO, PROB 11/444, fols. 128v–132 · Bodl. Oxf., MS Malone 44, fols. 100–11

Likenesses oils, *c*.1650, Ickworth House, Suffolk · P. Lely, oils, 1662, Ickworth House, Suffolk · P. Lely, oils, *c*.1672, Cirencester Park, Gloucestershire · studio of P. Lely, oils, *c*.1672, Royal Collection

May, Francis (1803–1885), grocer and match manufacturer, was born at Alton, Hampshire, on 17 July 1803, the third son and fourth child of Samuel May, a prosperous merchant belonging to an old Quaker family, and his wife, Ann Curtis of Basingstoke. His older brother Charles (1801–1860), an engineer, was partner in the Quaker agricultural machinery firm Ransome and May and later became an inventor of distinction and a fellow of the Royal Society.

After leaving school Francis May was apprenticed for three years to a grocer in Epping. He then set himself up in Bishopsgate, London, as a tea dealer and grocer. In 1825 he married Jane Holmes (*d*. 1872), of Ampthill, Bedfordshire. They had two sons and five daughters. His nature was so gentle that he once wrote to his son's headmaster to protest against a caning.

About 1840 May became the retail agent of William Bryant of Plymouth, a tallow and lubricating oil producer and sugar refiner. Their agency links developed and in 1844 they went into partnership as Bryant and May, provision merchants, in Fenchurch Street and Tooley Street,

London. In 1850 they began importing matches from Carl Lundström of Sweden, and five years later bought from him the patent rights for a type of safety match. This they produced in a factory at Fairfield Road, Bow, from 1861 onwards. Bryant's eldest son, Wilberforce Bryant, then twenty-four, was appointed manager. May's stake in the partnership is not known, but he and William Bryant combined their mercantile activities with an overall supervision of the match factory.

May was not included in Wilberforce Bryant's ambitious plans to become the leader of Britain's match-making industry. In the early 1850s he moved to Reigate, Surrey; once a year the girls from the Bow factory came on the firm's outing to his house, West View, at the foot of Reigate Hill. From his garden he sent acorns to relatives in Australia.

From 1864 onwards William Bryant and his four sons, who were all partners in 1868, strove to ease May out. When he objected two Quaker arbitrators were appointed, but the Bryants disagreed with their findings and blackmailed them by threatening to take the matter to court, something abhorrent to Quakers. The quarterly meeting then pleaded with May to give in, it being far more blessed to suffer a wrong than to do a wrong. May left the firm about 1875.

May was already much involved in Quaker affairs in Reigate, where he had campaigned to make the town into a municipal borough (achieved in 1863). He helped finance the rebuilding of the meeting-house, and set up a British School there. His wife died in 1872. May was a tall, bewhiskered man of imposing appearance, even in his old age a commanding figure in the ministers' gallery of the meeting-house. Once when he rose to give testimony he began with the words, 'We of the opulent classes …' Thereafter the youngsters in the meeting nicknamed him Old Opulence. He died at his home, West View, Reigate, on 1 December 1885. T. A. B. CORLEY

Sources P. Beaver, *The match makers: the story of Bryant and May* (1985) · B. Williams, *Quakers in Reigate, 1655–1955* (1980) · Bryant and May, *Making matches, 1861–1961* (1961) · Friends' House, Quaker records · d. cert.

Archives Hackney Archives, London, records of Bryant and May Ltd

Likenesses photograph, *c*.1870, repro. in Bryant and May, *Making matches*, 3

Wealth at death £20,406 12s. 6d.: probate, 10 March 1886, CGPLA Eng. & Wales

May, George Augustus Chichester (1815–1892), judge, was born in Belfast, the son of Edward May, rector of Belfast, and Elizabeth, the eldest daughter of William Sinclair of Fort William, co. Antrim. He was educated at Shrewsbury School and then at Magdalene College, Cambridge, where he graduated BA in classics in 1838, was granted an MA in 1841, and was afterwards elected a fellow. Called to the Irish bar in January 1844, he built up a considerable chancery practice. He became QC in 1865. In 1853 May married Olivia Barrington (*d*. 1876); they had one son.

In 1867 May edited the first volumes of the Irish *Law Reports*. He was elected a bencher of the King's Inns, Dublin, in 1873, and in the following year he was appointed legal adviser at Dublin Castle. On 27 November 1875 he was appointed attorney-general by Disraeli, and on 8 February 1877 he was created lord chief justice of Ireland and sworn of the privy council. On 1 January 1878 he was transferred to the High Court of Justice as president of the Queen's Bench Division and made an *ex officio* lord justice of appeal, retaining the title of lord chief justice of Ireland. As lord chief justice May would normally have presided over the trial of Charles Stewart Parnell and his allies in the Land League conspiracy of 1880–81, but, having dismissed a motion for the postponement of the trial on 6 December 1880, he was accused of political bias and removed from the court proceedings. May resigned his post in 1887, and died on 15 August 1892 at Lisnavagh, Rathvilly, co. Carlow.   J. M. RIGG, *rev.* SINÉAD AGNEW

Sources Boase, *Mod. Eng. biog.* · J. S. Crone, *A concise dictionary of Irish biography*, rev. edn (1937), 154 · F. E. Ball, *The judges in Ireland, 1221–1921*, 2 (1926), 311–12, 316, 328, 371 · Venn, *Alum. Cant.* · *Thom's directory* (1871), 1095 · J. Haydn, *The book of dignities: containing lists of the official personages of the British empire*, ed. H. Ockerby, 3rd edn (1894), 559, 578 · *Dublin Gazette* (3 Dec 1875) · *Dublin Gazette* (9 Feb 1877) · *The Times* (12 Nov 1880), 6 · *The Times* (30 Nov 1880), 10 · *The Times* (6 Dec 1880), 10 · *The Times* (11 Dec 1880), 10 · *The Times* (17 Aug 1892), 4 · *Law Times* (20 Aug 1892), 364 · *Irish Law Times and Solicitors' Journal* (15 Jan 1887)

Archives TCD, court notebook

Likenesses M. & N. Hanhart, mezzotint, in or after 1877, NG Ire. · portrait, repro. in *The Graphic* (3 Sept 1892), 274

Wealth at death £54,813 12s. 10d.: probate, 22 Sept 1892, *CGPLA Ire.* · £25,140 10s.: Irish probate sealed in England, 24 Oct 1892, *CGPLA Eng. & Wales*

May, George Ernest, **first Baron May** (1871–1946), insurance official and government adviser, was born on 20 June 1871 at Cheshunt, the younger son of William C. May, grocer and wine merchant, and his wife, Julia Ann Mole. He was educated at Cranleigh School and joined the Prudential Assurance Company when sixteen, remaining in its employment until he retired as company secretary, in 1931, at fifty-nine. The Prudential had pioneered the development of industrial life assurance in the late nineteenth century based on the collection of small premiums from those of modest means. The company built an army of agents, accumulated vast invested funds, and its scale stimulated innovative management methods. May was a senior official when it was among the largest and most influential British businesses, with close connections in the City, in industry and commerce, and with a large working-class constituency of policyholders. This created an opportunity for him to enter public affairs, playing—as an actuary—an unexpectedly dramatic role in several important episodes in British political history.

Company secretary of the Prudential Assurance May entered the cashier's department of the Prudential as a junior clerk, was admitted a fellow of the Institute of Actuaries in 1897, transferring from the actuarial to the investment department in 1902. He married, on 15 October 1903, Lily

George Ernest May, first Baron May (1871–1946), by Walter Stoneman, 1918

Julia (*d.* 1955), younger daughter of G. Strauss of Earls Court, London. They had two sons and a daughter. At the Prudential, May rose to become controller in 1910 and company secretary in 1915. He thus came to hold formidable responsibilities. In 1915 the Prudential's assets amounted to some £95 million, its life funds substantially exceeding those of the next four largest British life companies combined. They continued to grow to reach £256 million in the year he retired. This heavy flow of funds raised problems when convention required that they were largely placed in the London market. In addition, in the Edwardian years insurance funds depreciated as interest rates rose.

In 1912 May described the strategy he had developed with his distinguished actuarial colleague Joseph Burn (May, 'The investment of life assurance funds', *Journal of the Institute of Actuaries*, 46/2, 1912, pp. 134–68). He reasoned that the conventions of insurance investment laid down by Arthur Hutcheson Bailey in 1862, which emphasized the security of capital, were not inconsistent with a wider range of securities. Indeed insurance principles suggested that greater safety lay in spreading risk across different classes of security and geographical locations. This wider conception of investment was implemented by a more professional approach to the appraisal of individual securities and a more systematic departmental management of the structure of the portfolio. This contrasted with the sometimes rather amateur or conventional investment discussion in insurance board-rooms, but was made possible by a scale of activity that could support higher management costs. Following these principles, the Prudential invested across the world, especially in the United States, and it was widely believed that the yield on its portfolio was raised.

The American interest took May into public life. His expertise (and no doubt the Prudential's large holdings) led to wartime secondment in 1915 to the Treasury American dollar securities committee. Heavy purchases in America were placing inexorable pressure on British government credit, threatening strategic supplies. May proposed informally to his directors that the Prudential should offer to sell its American securities (subsequently valued at £8,407,650) to the government to provide dollars. According to Beaverbrook, this offer enabled McKenna, chancellor of the exchequer, to trump Cunliffe, the governor of the Bank of England, who had previously kept questions of exchange under bank control. When Cunliffe could not meet the demand for dollars, McKenna responded, 'Leave it to me', and asserted Treasury control by taking up May's earlier proposal (Beaverbrook, 153–5). It was characteristic of the Prudential's efficiency that 44,000 bonds were checked in forty-eight hours, coupons attached, and dispatched to the Bank of England in six omnibuses. Only a few shillings were mislaid. May was appointed manager of the American dollar securities committee in 1916 and made similar arrangements with other British investment institutions. Alongside this, his administrative talents were deployed as deputy quartermaster-general of the Navy and Army canteens board. He was responsible for the entire forces' catering arrangements, no doubt utilizing the Prudential's experience in running a head office with some 4750 staff in 1915. His success in these activities built good relations across the City and in government. He was awarded a KBE for war service in 1918. But the strain exacerbated eye problems, requiring several operations in 1919. Eventually he lost the use of one eye and suffered periods of blindness. He trained his memory to accommodate the disability, remembering exact figures with ease in board-room discussion.

In the mid-1920s May extended the diversification of the Prudential's investments into equities at a time when few insurance companies, except those influenced by heterodox figures like Keynes, included them in portfolios. He invested the Prudential in Rootes Motors, Beecham's, and ICI. May helped to arrange the original flotation of Marks and Spencer in which the Prudential took 15 per cent and later invested heavily in retail sites for the firm. These developments extended May's connections from the City and government to industry and commerce, providing him with a detailed knowledge of British business and placing him at the centre of an impressive network. He introduced Sir George Barstow, sometime Treasury controller of supply, to the Prudential's board in 1928 (later chairman), and formed a friendship with Simon Marks the retailer.

National expenditure and import duties This position at the centre of affairs cleared the way for May to become a public figure on a grander scale. Having been created a baronet in January 1931, he retired from the Prudential in March 1931. Early in that year Philip Snowden, chancellor of the exchequer in Ramsay MacDonald's second Labour government, sought cross-party support for retrenchment in government expenditure to raise confidence in financial markets. A committee on national expenditure, comprising six extra-parliamentary nominees, mainly accountants and businessmen, was appointed to investigate government accounts and propose economies. May seemed an ideal figure to chair such a committee, and 'with all the energy and persuasive urbanity of his forceful character' (*DNB*) was able to produce a report signed by the majority of his colleagues—Patrick Ashley Cooper, Sir Mark Webster Jenkinson, Lord Plender, and Sir Thomas Royden—on 31 July. 'Treating their task as analogous to a company rescue, they [the majority] relentlessly expressed views now widely held in the financial and business communities' (Williamson, 267). The general tenor of the report is caught in its own words. 'So heavily loaded are the dice in favour of expenditure that no representation we can make is more important than to emphasise the need for caution in undertaking any commitments of a continuing character' ('Committee on national expenditure report', *Parl. papers*, 1930–31, 16.12, Cmd 3920). Within a framework that assumed that budgets must be balanced in the short run, government expenditure was interpreted in an unnecessarily austere way. Borrowing for the unemployment insurance fund, the road fund, and the sinking fund was added to conventional budget charges to produce a projected deficit for 1932–3 of £120 million on a conventional turnround of about £750 million. Proposed cuts of £96 million were focused on unemployment insurance and social services and justified in terms that rejected the advances in social security achieved in the previous twenty-five years. Furthermore, the pay of teachers and the armed services was to be reduced.

An accompanying minority report of the May committee written by the two Labour representatives, Charles Latham and Arthur Pugh, made the case for a broader view that recognized the impact such cuts would have on the economy in the short and long run. These were reinforced by Keynes, though he first wrote to Ramsay MacDonald that his views on the report were 'not fit to be published' (Skidelsky, *Keynes*, 393). These and other critics argued that the proposed cuts would reduce income and investment and therefore both employment and tax yield. The majority report took an accountant's myopic view of issues that should properly be considered in a macroeconomic and international perspective. However, nearly all contemporary non-Labour newspapers, including the *Manchester Guardian* and *The Economist*, believed that the pressure on sterling would only be relieved by the full implementation of the majority report.

The government published the May committee report immediately, on 1 August 1931, without comment or proposals. The chancellor was advised by the Treasury that 'the [deficit] figure of £120 m. will be flashed around the world' and would thus become the price of restoring international confidence (Williamson, 271). Paradoxically, a committee established to build confidence destroyed it, not least because its severe criticisms of the government's handling of national expenditure alarmed foreign investors. The government's procrastination in implementing the report led to severe pressure on gold reserves. The cabinet split, the government collapsed on 24 August and was replaced by a national government the next day. The difficulties in satisfying international financial opinion forced Britain off the gold standard on 21 September. In October the National Government won an overwhelming general election victory. The May committee thus precipitated what was probably an inevitable—even in some circles desired—political adjustment, but became a target for the bitterness this engendered in the labour movement, and an object of severe criticism in later historical writing during the high tide of Keynesianism. There is no doubt that May and his colleagues operated within a narrow financial framework that did not allow for the wider repercussions of their proposals. But the committee's terms of reference, to which the professional men involved would have paid close attention, explicitly encouraged them to exclude such considerations. The episode reflects the widespread view between the wars that most economic and many political problems could be sorted out by a consensus of hard-headed, plain-speaking businessmen. It demonstrates how ill-founded that view was then, and British governments have continued to fail to learn the lesson.

Given his role as midwife at its birth, May's reputation remained high with the new National Government. It rewarded him with a position central to industrial policy—and therefore economic recovery—for the remainder of the decade. Leaving the gold standard and overwhelming Conservative influence in the National Government opened the way for the introduction of a general tariff. May had supported this in a manifesto issued by senior City figures early in July 1931 (*The Times*, 10 July 1931). The Import Duties Act (1932) provided for an import duties advisory committee to advise the Treasury on additional duties for particular goods when in the national interest. This was intended to be removed from political pressure, so May's experience in the previous year made him an obvious and attractive chairman, a position to which he was appointed by the chancellor of the exchequer, Neville Chamberlain. His colleagues were Sir Sydney Chapman, the economist and civil servant, Sir George Powell, an administrator, with Percy Ashley as secretary and Sir Alfred Hurst, the Treasury official who had supported the work of the economy committee, as May's adviser.

May interpreted his task positively as that of using tariff policy to secure industrial change. He took the leading case of the iron and steel industry as his special concern. In a substantial official memorandum he offered higher duties if the industry was willing to reorganize along specified lines. After laying out the main direction of policy, May characteristically left the detailed work to Hurst. The higher tariff allowed the industry to negotiate from greater strength with international cartels and plan its domestic development within a new national cartel organization led by Sir Andrew Duncan, in ways that proved important for its contribution in the Second World War. But it is not clear that consumers saw much immediate benefit. Indeed, more generally the import duties advisory committee made little attempt to review the impact of its decisions before war intervened and made such work impossible. Many contemporaries saw protection as central to the industrial recovery of the 1930s, but recent scholars have questioned this view. They argue that higher costs for the imported raw materials of many important industries offset the stimulus to other sectors. When war broke out the work of the committee was suspended. May resigned on completing his last term of office in 1941. He had been elevated to the peerage in June 1935 as Baron May.

Sir George Barstow, a close associate, described May as:

> tall, slim, and erect, with an air of aloof distinction, emphasised in later life by his poor eyesight and the wearing of a monocle. He was a great believer in personal contact rather than the written word, and his charm, his remarkable memory, his ability to concentrate on essentials and to pursue his objectives with single minded purpose—these qualities, coupled with his swift and shrewd judgement of men and situations, admirably fitted him for this method of conducting affairs. (*DNB*)

Another remembered him in the 1930s as

> a dapper, white haired man of cool and easy approach … He did not involve himself unduly in detail, but he had a great shrewdness, sound judgement, and readiness to take a risk. His ability to express himself at logical length either in speech or writing was limited, but his mind was one of those that leap to a sound conclusion more quickly than logic carries others. (Hutchinson, 27)

A Prudential colleague emphasized his 'quickness of mind and commanding personality' (Crump, 537) but described how, after intense concentration to master a problem, he would lose interest and delegate responsibility to others. Most valued in the hierarchical Prudential, he would always support his juniors absolutely and never look for scapegoats.

May's splendid physique made him a fine sportsman into late middle age, playing lacrosse and tennis, and then golf later in life. Despite poor eyesight he was a demon driver, receiving several convictions for speeding, including one in his late sixties for racing a police car through Twickenham (Dennett, 411). In his years of prosperity he lived at Eyot House, Weybridge. He died in London on 10 April 1946.   OLIVER M. WESTALL

Sources S. Silcox, 'May, George Ernest, 1st Lord May of Weybridge', *DBB* · *DNB* · P. C. C. [P. C. Crump], *Journal of the Institute of Actuaries*, 77 (1946), 537–8 · *The Times* (11 April 1946) · L. Dennett, *A sense of security: 150 years of Prudential* (1998) · H. Hutchinson, *Tariff-making and industrial reconstruction: an account of the work of the import duties advisory committee, 1932–39* (1965) · P. Scott, 'Towards the "cult of the equity"? Insurance companies and interwar capital market', *Economic History Review*, 2nd ser., 55 (2002), 78–104 · P. Williamson, *National crisis and national government: British politics, the economy and empire, 1926–1932* (1992) · Lord Beaverbrook, *Politicians and the*

war, 1914–1916 (1928) • R. Skidelsky, *John Maynard Keynes, II: the economist as saviour, 1920–1937* (1992) • R. Skidelsky, *Politicians and the slump: the labour government of 1929–1931* (1967) • D. Winch, *Economics and policy: a historical study* (1969) • F. Capie, *Depression and protectionism: Britain between the wars* (1983) • M. Kitson and S. Solomou, *Protectionism and economic revival: the British inter-war economy* (1990) • *An autobiography*, 2 vols. (1934) • *CGPLA Eng. & Wales* (1946)
Likenesses W. Stoneman, two photographs, 1918–32, NPG [*see illus.*] • A. K. Lawrence, portrait, priv. coll.
Wealth at death £195,902 12s. 2d.: probate, 5 May 1946, *CGPLA Eng. & Wales*

May, Henry John (1867–1939), co-operative movement activist and internationalist, was born on 16 July 1867 at 98 Villas Road, Plumstead, Kent, the son of Henry May, painter, and his wife, Mary Jane (*née* Kimber). After an elementary education he joined the Royal Arsenal Co-operative Society (RACS) as a shop boy in 1880. Aged seventeen May followed his father into the Woolwich arsenal as an engineering apprentice. Parental influence also prompted his involvement with the management of the RACS. May subsequently chaired the education committee and edited the society's magazine, *Comradeship*. By the age of thirty he had joined the RACS management committee.

May became an active co-operative propagandist and secretary of the south metropolitan district board of the Co-operative Union. He sat on the southern sectional board, joining the union's central board in 1898. From 1905 to 1913 he held the paid appointment of secretary to the southern sectional board. An advocate of co-operative participation in politics, May was secretary of the joint parliamentary committee of the Co-operative Congress from 1909 to 1918. During the First World War, May was a member of the War Emergency Workers' National Committee established by labour and co-operative leaders to defend workers' interests. He also led co-operative representations to government on matters including food control and taxation. There followed service on governmental bodies, including the food rationing committee. May represented co-operation on the royal commission on income tax of 1919–20 and the national railway wages board from 1921. This service was recognized when May was appointed OBE.

Wartime experience confirmed May's belief in the direct political representation of co-operation. In 1917 he became secretary of the new co-operative parliamentary representation committee. May stood, unsuccessfully, as its first candidate in the 1918 Prestwich by-election and in Clackmannan at the subsequent general election. However, he withdrew from parliamentary campaigning to devote himself to co-operative internationalism.

May's work with the International Co-operative Alliance (ICA) had begun fortuitously when he deputized for its then secretary, Dr Hans Müller, at the ICA Congress at Glasgow in 1913. May assumed the post permanently, along with the editorship of the ICA *Bulletin*. During the First World War, he upheld co-operative neutrality amid what he saw as an imperialist and capitalist conflict. Contact was maintained with co-operators in belligerent

countries and included publication of English, French, and German editions of the *Bulletin*.

After the war, May re-established good relations between French, German, and Belgian co-operators, restoring the ICA's triennial congresses. He travelled throughout Europe, cementing links with national co-operative movements, and he visited North America in 1928. He wrote extensively for the *Bulletin*, from 1928 enlarged as the *Review of International Co-Operation*. May secured recognition for the ICA, and it was involved with the World Economic Congress of 1927 and of 1933, and with the League of Nations.

In 1913 the ICA represented 20 million co-operators in twenty countries; by 1930 this had increased to 56 million members in forty countries. Yet co-operative autonomy was threatened by the rise of totalitarianism, first in Italy and the Soviet Union. May's pacifism and his work with the National Peace Council and the International Peace Campaign did not preclude vigorous resistance to fascism during the 1930s. However, his personal diplomacy on behalf of German, Austrian, Bulgarian, Spanish, and Czech co-operators enjoyed little success. May co-ordinated relief for victims of the Spanish Civil War and for refugees from continental Europe. In 1937 he attempted unsuccessfully to initiate an ICA boycott of Japanese goods following aggression against China. By 1939 only twenty-eight national co-operative movements were ICA members. Thus, for May, co-operative neutrality could not be maintained in the war against fascism.

May died suddenly of cancer on 19 November 1939 at Eltham, London, survived by his wife, Ada Martha. He was cremated on 25 November and interred at Plumstead cemetery on 26 November. Despite wartime travel restrictions, several European representatives attended and co-operative journals carried overseas tributes. The 'movement's No. 1 internationalist', as he was described by *Co-operative News* on 2 December 1939, was celebrated for his idealism and his brave defence of co-operation against totalitarianism. MARTIN PURVIS

Sources *Co-operative News* (25 Nov 1939) • *Co-operative News* (2 Dec 1939) • R. Rhodes, *The International Co-operative Alliance during war and peace, 1910–1950* (1995) • R. Rhodes, 'Henry J. May, 16 July 1867 – 19 November 1939. General Secretary of the ICA, 1913–1939', *International Co-operative Alliance Review of International Co-operation*, 82/4 (1989), 99–103 • ICA press release (obituary), 25 Nov 1939, National Co-operative Archive, Rochdale, Henry May biographical file • *Review of International Co-operation* (Dec 1939) • *Review of International Co-operation* (July 1940) • S. Pollard, 'The foundation of the Co-operative Party', *Essays in labour history, 1886–1923*, ed. A. Briggs and J. Saville (1971), 185–210 • b. cert. • R. A. Palmer, 'A tribute to Henry J. May', *Co-operative Review*, 13/12 (1939), 424–5 • *DLB*
Archives International Co-operative Alliance, Geneva, Switzerland, archives
Likenesses photograph, c.1929, Co-operative College, Manchester, National Co-operative Archive, Henry May biographical file
Wealth at death £7873 17s. 9d.: resworn probate, 18 Jan 1940, *CGPLA Eng. & Wales*

May, Hugh (*bap.* 1621, *d.* 1684), architect, was baptized at Mid Lavant, near Chichester, on 2 October 1621, the seventh son of John May (*d.* 1630) of Mid Lavant, and the cousin of Baptist May (*d.* 1697), keeper of the privy purse to

Charles II; his mother was Elizabeth Hill of London. Little is known of his career before the Restoration, but it is likely that his appointment on 29 June 1660 as paymaster of the works indicates services rendered to the court in exile, rather than architectural activity. About 1653–4 May supervised the construction of a watercourse for the irrigation of meadows at Babraham, Cambridgeshire, for his cousin Thomas Bennet. He is known to have been in the service of George Villiers, second duke of Buckingham, during the 1650s, when he assisted in the transfer of works of art from York House to the Netherlands, where they were to be sold, and in 1656 he accompanied his friend the painter Peter Lely on a further visit to the Netherlands to join the exiled court, travelling with him as his 'servant'. Dutch influence is apparent in his architecture.

Although May's connection with the royal works, like that of the surveyor Sir John Denham (1615–1669), appears to have stemmed from his political activities, he proved himself, unlike Denham, to be an inspired choice. May became one of the outstanding English architects of the seventeenth century. As paymaster he was responsible for the financial arrangements for the restoration of the neglected royal palaces. In 1665–6 he joined with Sir Roger Pratt and Christopher Wren in advising on the repair of old St Paul's Cathedral, and after the great fire was appointed as one of the supervisors of the rebuilding of the City. After acting as surveyor of the works in 1666, during Denham's illness, he was promoted to the comptrollership in June 1668. He entertained hopes of succeeding Denham upon the latter's death in 1669, but was passed over in favour of Wren; he was compensated by the grant of a pension of £300 per year in recognition of 'loyal and faithful service' (Colvin, 646).

May's major architectural work for the court was the remodelling in 1674–84 of the upper ward of Windsor Castle, following his appointment as comptroller of the works there in 1673. This work, now destroyed or altered, was remarkably innovative, externally through his invention of what Vanbrugh was later to term 'the Castle Air', and internally through his creation of the first great baroque ensemble in England, combining architecture, carving (by Grinling Gibbons), and painting (by Antonio Verrio) in a grand and sumptuous suite of staterooms. The spatial complexity and dramatic lighting of the staircase at Windsor had been achieved by May on a smaller scale at the earlier Eltham Lodge, Kent, one of the quintessential Restoration houses, designed in 1664 for Sir John Shaw, and one of the few buildings by the architect to survive.

Eltham was built to the infrequently employed triple-pile plan (three ranges deep), which offered more space than the double-pile but presented the disadvantage of how to light the centre and how to organize circulation through it. At Eltham the subsequent alterations have obscured the success of Hugh May's solution to the former problem: light from the side to the staircase has been reduced by a later partition and the lantern which provided light to the first floor has been removed. Notwithstanding these changes, the drama of May's staircase is evident in its offering of alternative routes from its midway point. The exterior, an elegant essay in a classicism learned from the Netherlands, is characteristic of May's refinement as an architect.

May's other fully authenticated works, all built for men in court circles, display a comparable restraint: Cornbury House, Oxfordshire, for which he built the east front, the stables, and the chapel (1663–8); Holme Lacy, Herefordshire (1674); Cassiobury Park, Hertfordshire (c.1677–80); Berkeley House, Piccadilly (1665); and the completion of Burlington House, Piccadilly (1667–8), for the first earl of Burlington. Of these, only Cornbury and Holme Lacy survive, the latter being distinguished by particularly vigorous and up-to-date carving, a counterpoint to the quiet exterior and the traditional H-plan. Moor Park, Hertfordshire, a house now associated with Sir James Thornhill, who completely remodelled it in 1725–8, was built by May in 1679–84 for James, duke of Monmouth. Here the architect once again demonstrated his inventiveness in planning, placing his entrance hall on the short side of the house, giving onto a grand staircase in the centre, lit by a light well, with bedchambers and dressing-rooms beyond.

Until recent years May's considerable significance as one of the principal creators of the Restoration house and as the designer of the grand sequence of state apartments at Windsor has been, because of the accidents of survival, less recognized than its importance would justify. May also played an important role in the literature of architecture by prompting his friend John Evelyn to publish the influential *Parallel of the Antient Architecture with the Modern* (1664), a translation of Roland Fréart's *Parallèle de l'architecture* of 1650. Evelyn acknowledged, in the 'Epistle Dedicatory' of the work, 'the passion of my worthy Friend Mr. Hugh May to oblige the Publick ... by procuring a most accurate Edition of the Plates, [he] encourag'd me to finish what I had begun'.

May died on 21 February 1684 and was buried in Mid Lavant church, Sussex. By his will, dated 19 January 1684, he left the major part of his estate to his nephew Thomas, son of his late elder brother John. JOHN BOLD

Sources Colvin, *Archs.* · K. Downes, *English baroque architecture* (1966) · H. M. Colvin and others, eds., *The history of the king's works*, 5 (1976) · O. Hill and J. Cornforth, *English country houses: Caroline, 1625–1685* (1966) · J. Newman, 'Hugh May, Clarendon and Cornbury', *English architecture public and private*, ed. J. Bold and E. Chaney (1993), 81–7 · C. Hussey, 'Cornbury Park, Oxfordshire', *Country Life*, 108 (1950), 922–6 · A. Maguire and H. M. Colvin, 'A collection of seventeenth-century architectural plans', *Architectural History*, 35 (1992), 164–5 · J. Evelyn, 'Epistle dedicatory', in R. Fréart, *A parallel of the antient architecture with the modern*, ed. and trans. J. Evelyn (1664) · O. Millar, *Sir Peter Lely, 1618–80* (1978), 67 [exhibition catalogue, 15 Carlton House Terrace, London, 17 Nov 1978–18 March 1979] · *An inventory of the historical monuments in London*, Royal Commission on Historical Monuments (England), 5 (1930), 109–11 · Royal Commission on Historical Monuments (England), 'Eltham Lodge, London', Royal Commission on Historical Monuments (England), London [investigation report] · J. Nichols, *The history and antiquities of the county of Leicester*, 4/2 (1811), 548 · J. Dallaway, *A history of the western division of the county of Sussex*, 1 (1815), 114 · *VCH Cambridgeshire and the Isle of Ely*, vol. 6

Archives PRO, John Cary MSS, C 104/109 · Rousham Park, Oxfordshire, Cottrell MSS
Likenesses S. Cooper, miniature, 1653, Royal Collection · P. Lely, group portrait, oils, *c.*1675, Audley End House, Essex

May, Sir Humphrey (1572/3–1630), politician and administrator, was the fourth son of Richard May (*d.* in or before 1592), citizen and merchant tailor of London and of Mayfield, Sussex, and his wife, Mary Hillersden, possibly daughter of Andrew Hillersdon of Memland, Devon. Humphrey's father was probably the Richard May in receipt of foreign intelligence as secretary to the merchants in September 1586. Humphrey May matriculated at St John's College, Oxford, on 25 October 1588 aged fifteen. After graduating BA on 3 March 1592 he studied at the Middle Temple later that year. By February 1604 he was at court and had been appointed groom of the privy chamber.

May was MP for Bere Alston, Devon, from 1605 to 1610, and on 26 November 1607 he was granted the clerkship of the council for the court of Star Chamber, in reversion after William Mill and Sir Francis Bacon. Before 23 May 1611 he married Jane (*d.* 1615), sister of Sir William Uvedale of Wickham Market, Suffolk: on that date May and his wife were granted a pension of 16*s.* a day. A pension of 200 marks a year followed on 5 August, and on 10 December a grant of the clerkship of the signet, in reversion after Robert Kirkham. May was knighted in January 1613 at Newmarket and represented Westminster in the 1614 parliament. John Cusack complained of May's influence on 11 November 1615: 'Sir Hum. May can make any suit or suitor, be they ever so honest, disliked by the king' (*CSP dom., 1611–18*, 327).

In May 1615 Jane May died in giving birth to a son, Richard, and on 3 February 1616 Sir Humphrey married again at St Mary's, Bury St Edmunds, Suffolk. His second wife was Judith (*bap.* 1598, *d.* 1661), daughter of Sir William Poley (1562–1629), of Boxted, Suffolk, and his wife, Ann (*d.* 1658), daughter of Sir Robert Jermyn of Rushbrooke, Suffolk. Their youngest son was the renowned courtier Baptist *May.

In January 1618 May was appointed surveyor of the court of wards. His next objective, the chancellorship of the duchy of Lancaster, was said to have forty-three suitors. By 6 March May had provoked the duke of Buckingham's displeasure by promising the reversion of his surveyorship to both Benjamin Rudyerd and Mr Packer to secure their support. May applied for the duke's favour, but offended him by also approaching William Herbert, earl of Pembroke. Through the mediation of Pembroke and Lucy Russell, countess of Bedford, May eventually received the appointment, securing Buckingham's agreement only after he offered the lease of the duchy house in London to the duke's mother and his post in Star Chamber to the duke's brother. May himself was also made to grovel that losing Buckingham's favour was a 'matter of extreme grief and discontentment' (Lockyer, 39). He was MP for Lancaster in the parliament of 1621–2. He represented Leicester in 1624 and 1625, praising the former parliament

on 11 March 1624 for their 'clear and plain dealing' (Cogswell, 194). On 10 May 1624 May's testimony was used in the impeachment of Lionel Cranfield, earl of Middlesex. May was among his debtors, and his participation signified that the court had deserted Cranfield.

By 1624 May owned the manor and abbey of Carrow, Norfolk, in which county he accumulated church patronage. He also reportedly bought the manor of Froyle, Hampshire. He was admitted to Gray's Inn on 6 March 1625 and became a privy councillor on 28 March. Later that year he was returned for Lancaster again, and in early July endeavoured to prevent the royal decision to demand tonnage and poundage in the absence of a parliamentary grant: 'Sir Humphry May, then Chancelor of the Dutchie, who, having travaild with much industrie in that service, but in vaine, ... importund to a new attempt & triall for staie or diversion of that worke' (Thompson, 177). Having failed to persuade Buckingham himself, May sent Sir John Eliot to remonstrate with him. Nevertheless, in the House of Commons he strenuously defended Buckingham's foreign policy and urged parliament to vote the king money so they could not be blamed for future failures. He also argued against the committal of Richard Mountague for his controversial book *Appello Caesarem*. He represented Leicester again in the parliaments of 1626 and 1628–9. By May 1626 he probably maintained hopes of a barony. On 15 September 1626 he was appointed a commissioner for the sale of the king's lands and by January 1627 he was a commissioner for the forced loan. On 20 March that year Lady Hericke claimed he was 'a great favourite with the king' (*CSP dom., 1627–8*, 120).

On 7 October 1627, with Buckingham's forces on the Île de Ré in a rapidly deteriorating position, May reassured the duke of the continued favour of the king and privy council, but emphasized difficulties in supplying him, entreating him not to attempt too much:

> It is easy for us to set down on paper ships, and money, and arms, and victual, and men, but to congest these materials together, especially in such a penury of money, requires more time than the necessity of your affairs will permit. (Gardiner, 6.191)

Buckingham's campaign ended in disaster but in the parliament of 1628 May asked the House of Commons to forgive and forget, urging MPs:

> you cannot resolve too soone for the kinge, neyther can you indeede give enough. But lett our harts joyne. Let forrane states knowe wee are united. Wee have here in towne six embassadors and they every day aske after us. (C. Russell, *Unrevolutionary England, 1603–1642*, 1990, 47)

On 3 June Sir John Eliot argued that the French war had led to the sacrifice of the Palatinate and that the whole policy of the government looked pro-Spanish. When May interjected, 'If he goes on I hope that I may myself go out', the members cried, 'Begone! begone!' (Gardiner, 6.299). On 11 July 1628 May was named a commissioner for compounding with recusants in the northern counties, whose forfeitures were to maintain six warships to guard the east coast.

May defended the government on the tonnage and poundage issue on 19 February 1629, orating that he had never heard until now that an MP 'should have his goods privileged against the king' and that 'God forbid that the king's commands should be put for delinquency. When that is done his crown is at stake' (Gardiner, 7.61–3). During the ensuing debates over whether the House of Commons had the right to adjourn itself, on 2 March 1629 the speaker, Sir John Finch, was held down in his chair. May was among the privy councillors who rushed to assist him, but was overpowered. After the dissolution in April 1629 May resigned his chancellorship and was appointed vice-chamberlain. On 27 January 1630 he was also appointed commissioner for fining gentlemen that had not presented themselves for knighthood at Charles I's coronation.

Often placed in the awkward position of having to defend the government's unimpressive record, May was 'a man of some ability and of a very conciliatory disposition' (Gardiner, 5.319). He was a significant royal agent in nearly all the schemes that later came to characterize 'Thorough'. May held the reversion of the mastership of the rolls, but did not live to enjoy it. He died at his house in St Martin-in-the-Fields, Middlesex, on 9 June 1630. Rowland Woodward wrote: 'Sir Humphrey May died last night. The common speech has been that he was mad; none of his friends for a great while were suffered to speak with him' (*CSP dom.*, *1629–31*, 287). He was buried on 11 June 1630 on the north side of the chapel of kings in Westminster Abbey.   ANDREW J. HOPPER

Sources Foster, *Alum. Oxon.* · S. R. Gardiner, *History of England from the accession of James I to the outbreak of the civil war, 1603–1642*, 10 vols. (1883–4) · J. L. Chester, ed., *The marriage, baptismal, and burial registers of the collegiate church or abbey of St Peter, Westminster*, Harleian Society, 10 (1876) · *DNB* · R. Lockyer, *Buckingham: the life and political career of George Villiers, first duke of Buckingham, 1592–1628* (1981) · M. Prestwich, *Cranfield: politics and profits under the early Stuarts: the career of Lionel Cranfield, earl of Middlesex* (1966) · C. Thompson, 'Court politics and parliamentary conflict in 1625', *Conflict in early Stuart England: studies in religion and politics, 1603–1642*, ed. R. Cust and A. Hughes (1989), 168–193 · T. Cogswell, *The blessed revolution: English politics and the coming of war, 1621–4* (1989) · F. Blomefield and C. Parkin, *An essay towards a topographical history of the county of Norfolk*, [2nd edn], 11 vols. (1805–10), vol. 4 · *N&Q*, 2nd ser., 8 (1859) · J. J. Howard, ed., *The visitation of Suffolk, made by William Hervey, Clarenceux king of arms, 1561, with additions*, 2 vols. (1866), vol. 1 · *CSP dom., 1603–31*, with *addenda, 1580–1625* · W. Hervey, *The visitation of Suffolk, 1561*, ed. J. Corder, 1, Harleian Society, new ser., 2 (1981) · W. B. Bannerman, ed., *The visitations of the county of Sussex … 1530 … and 1633–4*, Harleian Society, 53 (1905) · *Fourth report*, HMC, 3 (1874) [Earl De La Warr] · F. T. Colby, ed., *The visitation of the county of Devon in the year 1620*, Harleian Society, 6 (1872) · administration, PRO, PROB 6/13, fol. 174r.
Archives BL, Add. MSS 5873, p. 59; 35832, p. 199; 36767, pp. 333, 335; 41661, p. 76 | BL, Harley MSS 1581, p. 105; 2305, p. 22; 1583, p. 91; 6799, p. 78 · BL, Sloane MSS 826, p. 49, 118b, 147; 1775, p. 41b; 3827, p. 89 · BL, Stowe MS 418, p. 2 · Norfolk RO, Fellowes MSS, account book of Robert Bransby of the Carrow estate, FEL 888, 556x6
Likenesses oils, Magd. Cam.; version, Ickworth House, Suffolk
Wealth at death see administration, 24 June 1630, PRO, PROB 6/13, fol. 174r

May, John (d. 1598), bishop of Carlisle, was allegedly a native of Suffolk. William *May, who died in 1560 as archbishop-elect of York, is commonly described as John's elder brother, but in the light of his bequest of divinity books 'to Mr John Meye my nephew' (Searle, 293) seems more likely to have been his uncle. John May was educated at Cambridge, matriculating in 1544 at Queens' College, where he was a scholar from 1545 until 1550, when he graduated BA. He subsequently proceeded MA in 1553, BTh in 1560, and DTh in 1564. Elected a fellow of Queens' in 1550, he was college bursar in 1554–5. He is also recorded as staging plays in the college, where in the late 1550s he was accused of being overfond of cards and dice. That he remained in Cambridge during Mary's reign does not seem to have been held against him afterwards, for in 1559 he was appointed master of St Catharine's College. He was remembered there a century later as a model of prudence and integrity, probably thanks to his efforts to improve the management of the college finances. He was vice-chancellor of the university in 1569–70, a time of great theological controversy in Cambridge. His firm stand against Thomas Cartwright earned him the wrath of the godly, but doubtless stood him in good stead with their opponents, led by John Whitgift.

May was ordained deacon and priest in the diocese of Norwich in 1557. Shortly afterwards he became rector of Aston Sandford, Buckinghamshire, adding the rectories of Long Stanton St Michael, Cambridgeshire, in 1560, North Creake, Norfolk, in 1562, and St Dunstan-in-the-East, London, in 1565. At an unknown date he became a prebendary in Ely Cathedral. In 1565 he preached at court on 22 March and at Paul's Cross on 26 August; notes taken from the latter address suggest a lucid and effective preacher, proclaiming a straightforward scriptural divinity—'the gospel oure certen salvation' (Bodl. Oxf., MS Tanner 50, 33). In 1569 he became archdeacon of the East Riding in the diocese of York on the queen's presentation, and in 1570 rector of Darfield in the West Riding. There is no evidence for his being active in Yorkshire, however; rather he appears to have continued to reside in Cambridge.

Elevation to the episcopate came in 1577. Following the death of James Pilkington of Durham on 23 January 1576, Richard Barnes of Carlisle was moved east across the Pennines, and May was promoted to replace him. His patron in this was George Talbot, sixth earl of Shrewsbury, who lobbied the earls of Leicester and Sussex on May's behalf. The queen's *congé d'élire* was granted on 17 May 1577, he was formally elected by the Carlisle chapter on 12 June 1577, the royal assent was given on 9 August, and he was consecrated at Fulham by the bishop of London on 29 September. Enthroned by proxy in his cathedral on 2 January 1578, he resigned his Cambridge mastership.

May was not personally rich. He was allowed five years to pay his first fruits, estimated at £478 2s. 5¾d., but his hopes of having them remitted altogether were disappointed, and they helped to create a burden of debt and financial anxiety which dogged his entire episcopate. The diocese was poor, and, when he arrived in it, afflicted by famine, so that he faced great demands on his charity—in May 1578 he told Walsingham of 'the extraordinary charge he has been at by the miserable and lamentable scarcity in this country' (*Salisbury MSS*, 2.179). He seems to have made some effort to exploit his episcopal estates, for instance by raising entry fines. He also held his Ely prebend until 1582, his Yorkshire archdeaconry until 1588, and Darfield rectory until he died; these helped to keep him afloat financially, but always in low water.

May involved himself in local government as convention required, as JP and member of the council of the north, and sometimes worked with the warden of the west march to keep the peace on the borders. Occasionally he received news of Scottish affairs which he passed on to Shrewsbury. He seems to have been a conscientious bishop who resided at his episcopal residence of Rose Castle almost without interruption; occasionally recorded at York or Durham, he never attended parliament. His primary visitation of his chapter was conducted with notable thoroughness, and he dealt effectively with routine matters like dilapidated buildings and disputes over stalls in parish churches. His greatest problem, the low quality of the resident ministry, arose from the poverty of his see, its distance from centres of learning, and the great size of many of the parishes, which were often subdivided into poorly endowed chapelries. In 1580 May himself granted parochial rights to the chapel of Matterdale in Greystoke parish. His successor, Henry Robinson, criticized 'the great facility of my predecessor in committing the charge of souls to such as were presented by those who care not how silly the clerk be, so themselves may enjoy the fat of the living' (*CSP dom.*, 1598–1601, 362–3). The charge of carelessness seems to have been less than fair. Although graduate ministers remained a minority, and would long do so, the number of university-trained incumbents (including some from the bishop's own former college of St Catharine's) certainly increased during May's episcopate, and their distribution was not limited to the wealthier livings.

May waged a continuous campaign against recusancy. He was examining die-hard Catholics early in 1584, while in 1590 he revived the constableship of Rose Castle and employed its holder to pursue seminaries. A year later he is recorded as examining the Douai-trained priest James Clayton, who subsequently died in prison under sentence of death. Early in 1597 it was May himself who feared death. About to set out to arrest another seminary, Christopher Robinson, he completed his will on 5 March in terms giving vivid expression to his fears—

> purposing tomorrow … to take a journey to Johnbie with god's favour there to apprehend a notorious Jesuite or seminarie lodged there as I am crediblie advertised and fearing that thorough the malicious dealing of such traitors I maie be wounded to death or slaine by a gunne unles by god's mightie providence I shalbe defended. (Borth. Inst., reg. 31, fol. 136*v*)

Robinson was captured and executed, after rejecting May's efforts to convert him to protestantism. The number of reported recusants in his diocese was always low, suggesting that the danger from Catholicism was less than May feared.

May's episcopate was not ended suddenly by gunshot but petered out in misery amid famine and pestilence. For four consecutive years (1594–7) the harvest failed, and in 1597–8 Carlisle diocese was also visited by plague. On 21 November 1597 Bishop Tobie Matthew of Durham wrote on May's behalf to Archbishop Whitgift telling of the distress caused by extreme dearth, exacerbated in the bishop's case by Scottish raids which robbed him of all his oxen and most of his sheep and horses; under such pressure 'the good olde fathers merrie hearte is quite kilde & starke dead' unless Whitgift helped him (LPL, MS 3470, fol. 198*v*). No effective relief was forthcoming. None the less May toiled on despite failing health—he was doing business in his bedchamber on 5 December 1597 and again on 4 February 1598. He died at Rose Castle at 8 a.m. on 15 February following, and was buried at 8 p.m. the same day in Carlisle Cathedral.

No monument to May survives, and it seems unlikely that one was commissioned. The inventory of his goods taken at Rose Castle immediately after his death suggests that he may not have been quite as impoverished as his will implies, but its record of mostly old and shabby clothes and furnishings hardly points to riches either. Probably about 1560 he married Amy, widow of John Cowel of Lancashire and daughter of William Vowel of North Creake, Norfolk; they had a son, John, and three daughters. His daughters were left 'an ould Edward' apiece 'for a remembraunce', his wife his last new year's gift from the queen. His residuary legatee was his son, who seems to have inherited little but debts. His successor at Carlisle, Henry Robinson, found both Rose Castle and the diocese generally in a poor condition, but the extent of May's responsibility should not be exaggerated, some shortcomings notwithstanding. A stranger to his diocese, he was inclined to make up for his lack of local allies by advancing the interests of his son and sons-in-law. His epistolary style suggests a man overapt to stand on his dignity, a trait commented on (along with the bishop's small stature) by the litigant who referred to him as 'Litle divine providence' (PRO, E 134/10 JAS I/MICH 17 m6). But he was diligent and hospitable—*vere hospitalis* according to Matthew—and in a letter to Burghley of 1594 denied that he was ambitious for a wealthier diocese, describing himself as 'well content to end my dayes here, where (I thanke God) I have served with credyt these xvii yeres' (BL, Lansdowne MS 76, fol. 197*v*). His record suggests that the claim was not without substance.

HENRY SUMMERSON

Sources Cumbria AS, DRC 1/3, 91–206; D & C 1/2 · inventory, 1598, Cumbria AS · PRO, exchequer, king's remembrancer, depositions, E 134/10 JAS I/MICH 17 · PRO, office of the governors of Queen's Anne's bounty and predecessors, certificates of livings, E 331/Carlisle 2–6 · PRO, office of first fruits and tenths, composition books, E334/9 · PRO, records of the court of requests, proceedings, REQ 2/178/52 · LPL, MSS 697–698, 709, 3197–3200, 3206, 3470 · Bodl. Oxf., MS Tanner 50 · Bodl. Oxf., MS St Edmund Hall 7/2 · BL, Add. MS 33207 · BL, Lansdowne MSS 68, 76, 982 · journale, 1535–59, CUL, Queens' College MSS, Book 76 (Misc. A) · Borth. Inst., reg. 30, 31; trans. CP 1580/3 · *CSP dom.*, 1598–1601; addenda, 1580–1625 · *Calendar of the manuscripts of the most hon. the marquis of Salisbury*, 2, HMC, 9 (1888) · *JHL*, 2 (1578–1614) · J. Bain, ed., *The border papers: calendar of letters and papers relating to the affairs of the borders of England and Scotland*, 2 vols. (1894–6) · J. Wilson, ed., *The parish registers of*

Dalston, Cumberland (1893) • J. Strype, *Annals of the Reformation and establishment of religion ... during Queen Elizabeth's happy reign*, new edn, 2/2 (1824) • Venn, *Alum. Cant.*, 1/3.166 • J. Nicolson and R. Burn, *The history and antiquities of the counties of Westmorland and Cumberland*, 2 vols. (1777); repr. (1976) • J. Wilson, *Rose Castle* (1912) • J. Wilson, 'The first historian of Cumberland', *SHR*, 8 (1910–11), 5–21 • W. H. S. Jones [W. H. Samuel], *A history of St Catharine's College, once Catharine Hall, Cambridge* (1936) • W. G. Searle, *The history of the Queens' College of St Margaret and St Bernard in the University of Cambridge*, 2 vols., Cambridge Antiquarian RS, 9, 13 (1867–71) • H. C. Porter, *Reformation and reaction in Tudor Cambridge* (1958) • J. B. Gavin, *The bishop of Durham, the west march border negotiations, and the treaty of Carlisle, 1597*, Transactions of the Cumberland and Westmorland Antiquarian and Archaeological Society, 2nd ser., 73 (1973), 120–42 • J. A. Hilton, 'The Cumbrian Catholics', *Northern History*, 16 (1980), 40–58

Wealth at death seriously impoverished: will, Borth. Inst., reg. 31, fols. 136v–137

May, John (*fl. c.*1606–1613), writer on aulnage, whose origins are obscure, was appointed deputy aulneger about 1606. He published *A Declaration of the Estate of Clothing now Used within this Realme of England* with an 'Apologie shewing the necessarie use of his office' (London, 1613). This treatise was written to reveal to the duke of Lennox, recently appointed aulneger-general, the 'deceits and abuses of the law' used by the manufacturers to evade statutes relating to the wool trade. The deceits occurred at every stage of manufacture, and although the law had provided for 'searchers' to look for faulty workmanship in the clothmaker's place of work, this too was abused; the searchers were frequently the clothiers themselves or else their servants. May thus presents a very grim picture where 'because of falsehood—everyone in England striveth to wear anything but cloth and the Infidel brusheth bare his garment to count the threads' (May, 28), but he claims the principal cause 'to brede these deceits' is the scattering into the countryside of these very clothiers 'where the eye of the officer is not upon their doings' (ibid., 42). To resolve the situation he urges the duke that the industry should be restricted to towns where suitable places for inspection should be provided, for searching and sealing the cloth. Nothing is known of May's life beyond this publication.

NANCY IVES

Sources J. May, *A declaration of the estate of clothing now used within this realme of England* (1613) • J. Smith, *Memoirs of wool* (1757), 1.91–8 • H. Heaton, *The Yorkshire woollen and worsted industries*, 2nd edn (1965) • E. Kerridge, *Textile manufactures in early modern England* (1985) • E. Lipson, *History of the woollen and worsted industries* (1965)

May, John (1809–1893), manufacturing chemist, was born in Harwich on 3 February 1809. His father was a ship's captain, working on the Harwich to Göteborg route, but he retired soon after John was born and the family moved to Ipswich. There John May was educated at a private school and apprenticed to F. J. Hooker, a local chemist and druggist. The 1815 Apothecaries Act had recognized the role of the chemist and druggist as a wholesale and retail supplier of medicines.

In 1830 May moved to London, finding employment in Battersea with Charles Price, a manufacturing chemist whose business lay chiefly in the preparation of health salts (sulphate of magnesia) and mercurial remedies. At that time the distinguished pharmacologist, Jonathan Pereira (1804–1853), was lecturing in chemistry at the General Dispensary, Aldersgate Street, attached to St Bartholomew's Hospital; May attended his lectures. Medical knowledge of the causes of disease was small and pharmaceutical remedies to alleviate symptoms relied on galenical and, increasingly, chemical ingredients.

In 1834 May left Price and established his own business as a manufacturing chemist, in partnership with Thomas Grimwade and Joseph Pickett, who are believed to have been fellow apprentices with him in Ipswich. The partnership rented premises in Battersea, then an industrial centre although in surroundings still largely rural in character. Pickett died in 1835 and four years later Grimwade decided to retire from manufacturing to take up farming. In 1839, therefore, May took a new partner, William Garrad Baker, like himself an East Anglian by birth, who had recently completed his apprenticeship as a chemist and druggist.

May, aged thirty-one, and Baker, aged twenty-five, signed a new partnership agreement in 1840 which lasted for thirty-six years. In the following year they bought, for £200, a plot of land in Battersea known as Garden Wharf, where the firm's factory was built; it was rebuilt several times—it remained the manufacturing premises until 1934. In the early days of the business May dealt with the sales and marketing side and Baker took charge of the manufacturing. Most of the firm's customers—wholesale drug houses—were in the London area and May visited them all, on foot, once a week. It was an extremely competitive business but May and Baker soon secured itself a place among the leading firms in the London chemical trade, which included Howards and Whiffens.

In 1851 the firm's acids, metallic salts, and pharmaceutical supplies were awarded the prize medal for quality at the Great Exhibition and, four years later, similar accolades were won at the Paris Exhibition. By then the development of the railway network was enabling May and Baker to supply customers further afield than London and, although the wholesale druggists remained its major customers, it also supplied the chemicals which were increasingly used in other industries such as brewing.

May never married and by the early 1860s was living with his unmarried sister Sarah, who was eight years his elder, at Hyde House, 41 Hyde Lane, Battersea, his home for more than thirty years. In 1862 the firm took on an apprentice, Thomas Tyrer, who recalled that May, then aged fifty-three and with completely white hair, interviewed him most searchingly. Tyrer became a great admirer of May, writing, in an obituary in the *Chemist and Druggist* in 1893:

> Mr May was always very severe upon unveracity and anything indefinite and slipshod was to him a cause of great irritation. ... His immediate relatives were the recipients of his warmest solicitude, yet he preferred a loneliness which seemed painful to me. He was as unobtrusive in his religious and political views as in his life; and loved the 'old order' of things and disliked much of the new. He was eminently a man of wise caution, a hater of deceit and a lover of truth.

At the end of 1876 May retired, selling his share of the

partnership to Richard Heath, a Warwick solicitor who bought it for his stepson, William Blenkinsop. Largely at May's insistence, Tyrer also became a junior partner in the business at the same time. With May's agreement, the firm continued to use the name May and Baker under which it was by then known as a respectable and steady business. Living in Battersea, May kept in touch with Tyrer and Baker and, in 1890 when the partnership was dissolved and the business incorporated, he agreed that his name should continue to be used. In January 1891, when he was nearly eighty-two, he became a director of the new company. He was already suffering from heart disease and, on 5 November 1893, at the age of eighty-four, he died of pneumonia at Hyde House.

The business May had founded continued to grow and in the twentieth century became well known for its discovery of the drug known as M & B 693, introduced in 1938 as a cure for bacterial pneumonia. Although the company was owned, from 1927, by the French chemical company Rhône-Poulenc, it was not until the early 1990s that use of the name May and Baker ended.　　　　JUDY SLINN

Sources J. Slinn, *A history of May & Baker, 1834–1984* (1984) · Rhône-Poulenc Rorer, Dagenham, May and Baker archives · T. Tyrer, *Chemist and Druggist* (11 Nov 1893), 698–9 · d. cert.
Archives Rhône-Poulenc Rorer, Dagenham, Essex, May and Baker archives
Likenesses portrait, Rhône-Poulenc Rorer, Dagenham
Wealth at death £25,624 2s. 7d.: resworn probate, Feb 1895, *CGPLA Eng. & Wales* (1893)

May, Peter Barker Howard (1929–1994), cricketer and insurance broker, was born on 31 December 1929 at 95 Northcourt Avenue, Reading, Berkshire, the elder son and elder child of Thomas Howard May, director of the family electrical engineering business, Callas Sons and May, and his wife and cousin, Emily Eileen Howard-May, daughter of the Revd Howard-May and his wife, Edith, *née* Whiteley. Although she died when he was only sixteen, it was through his mother, a good and very keen lawn tennis player, that May came by his interest in games and the intensity with which he played them. His father provided the wherewithal, as well as encouragement, but had been no cricketer himself.

From Marlborough House preparatory school and Leighton Park junior school, May went to Charterhouse School in September 1942, still three months short of his thirteenth birthday. In his first summer there he was already making enough runs for the advisability of his appearing in the first eleven at so tender an age to be referred to the headmaster, Robert Birley. In the event it was thought better that he should wait a year, but it was a true indication of what lay ahead. May was fortunate at Charterhouse to come into the care of George Geary, the school's cricket professional, who had played as an all-rounder for England and was as much counsellor as coach to his young protégé. In the four years he did have in the Charterhouse eleven May scored eight 100s for the school, the first of them against Harrow when he was fourteen. He finished his last year at school by making 183 not out against Eton and successive hundreds at Lord's, the first

Peter Barker Howard May (1929–1994), by Brian Griffin, 1982

for the southern schools against the Rest, the second for the public schools against the combined services, an innings of 146 when the next highest score was 18.

May did his two years of national service as a writer in the Royal Navy, combining clerical work with a limited amount of cricket. He had a place waiting for him at Pembroke College, Cambridge (he had sat and failed a scholarship for Oxford), which he took up in October 1949, reading history and economics. He took his work seriously. He was, in fact, a serious-minded person, not at all without a sense of humour but wary as to the friends he chose and possessed of a quiet yet fierce determination. May's years at Cambridge covered the last golden period in university cricket. The pitch at Fenner's was all that a batsman could ask for; Cyril Coote, Cambridge's coach-cum-groundsman, was the best of batting tutors, and among May's contemporaries were seven others who also became test cricketers. No fewer than four of the Cambridge side (May, J. G. Dewes, G. H. G. Doggart, and D. S. Sheppard) played in the test trial of 1950, the season in which Cambridge scored 594 for four declared against the first West Indian side ever to win a test series in England. The first of the nine 100s May made for Cambridge during his three years in residence was an innings of 227 against Hampshire. In 1951, a month into his second long vacation, he scored 138 against South Africa at Headingley in his first test innings. 'His equanimity from first to last stamped him as a player well above the ordinary', said *Wisden's Cricketers' Almanack*, the canonical work in such matters.

So emerged England's finest batsman of the second half of the twentieth century. May was a good 6 feet tall, upstanding, and strong in a rangy way. Although he won Cambridge blues for soccer and Eton fives as well as for cricket, he was not a noticeably free mover. As a batsman his special glory was the on-drive, and he was as ruthlessly and powerfully acquisitive as he was courteously so. He never captained Cambridge, and his highest score in the five innings he played against Oxford at Lord's was a modest 39. Yet two years after going down from Cambridge in 1952 he was Len Hutton's vice-captain in Australia, and on Hutton's retirement, shortly afterwards, May himself was given the England captaincy—at the age of twenty-five and with very little experience in the job. It was a pity, perhaps, that it came to him so soon, not because he was unsuccessful—he had too many world-class bowlers at his command for that—but that by taking so much out of him it almost certainly shortened his career. He took over the captaincy of Surrey in 1957, and led them to the last two of their record seven successive county championships.

May was of too retiring a disposition to find communication easy, and he harboured a stubborn, somewhat unsparing streak. His players, though, held him in awe for his batting, and liked and respected him as a captain for his loyalty to them and his absolute straightness. The Hutton influence was evident in his tactical approach, not only in the way he kept his own counsel but in his suspicion of flamboyance and his thriftiness in the field. On the health of both men the burden of leadership, combined with the responsibility of so often having to carry the batting, eventually took its toll.

Between 1955 and 1961 May captained England forty-one times, more than anyone before him. Of his tests in charge, twenty were won, ten lost, and eleven drawn. As captain, he knew both the joy of waving from the Oval balcony, in 1956, after the Ashes had been won, and the mortification of losing them in Australia, in 1958–9, with a well-fancied side. He also took England to South Africa in 1956–7 and to the West Indies in 1959–60. Overall they were years of plenty for English cricket, and for that May could take his full share of credit. In his first three home test series he averaged 72.75 against South Africa, 90.60 against Australia, and 97.50 against the West Indies. Of his thirteen test hundreds nine were made in England, the highest of them his 285 not out against the West Indies at Edgbaston in 1957. For a variety of reasons, on his three overseas tours as captain he was markedly less successful with the bat. In the five tests of the drawn series in South Africa in 1956–7 Neil Adcock and Peter Heine, South Africa's two fast bowlers, reduced his average to a mere 15.30; in Australia in 1958–9 he came up against three Australian bowlers with highly questionable actions; and in the West Indies in 1959–60, with a reshaped England team, he had to return home early for an operation on an ischiorectal abscess, a form of haemorrhoid, caused partly by stress, which kept him out of the whole of the English season of 1960.

In Australia in 1958–9 May took against the large press contingent following the tour when two or three of the tabloids attributed England's poor showing partly to the presence of May's fiancée, Virginia Gilligan (b. 1935/6), daughter of Alfred Herbert Harold Gilligan, company director, claiming that she was a distraction. She was there with her uncle, Arthur Gilligan, himself a former England captain to Australia. It was even rumoured that May and

Miss Gilligan had been secretly married. They married, in fact, at Cranleigh on 24 April 1959, and, as May's wife, Virginia would have been unlikely to try to dissuade him from retiring from test cricket in 1961 and from all first-class cricket two years later. She knew that he had had enough of it, and that he felt the time had come to be doing something else. In sixty-six tests he had scored 4537 runs at an average of 46.77, and in all first-class cricket 25,592 runs at 51.00.

On going down from Cambridge May had joined the insurance broking firm of E. R. Wood, as a result of personal contact. They were glad to be associated with so promising and highly regarded a sportsman. In 1970 he moved to Willis, Faber, and Dumas, who allowed him the time he needed to serve as an England selector, which he had done first from 1965 until 1968 and did again, this time as chairman, from 1982 until 1988, with a specific brief to look to the declining standard of players' behaviour. He was as conscientious in commuting to the City as in the pursuit of his selectorial duties, beset though these were with problems.

In May's first term as a selector there was the D'Oliveira affair to contend with, to which the selectors were thought to have contributed by their apparent equivocation. A 'Cape coloured' and, as such, a red rag to the South African government of the day, Basil D'Oliveira was first omitted from the Marylebone Cricket Club (MCC) touring party to South Africa and then brought in as a replacement for a different type of player who had withdrawn from the team. The upshot was the cancellation of the tour. Characteristically, May said that 'it would be grossly wrong and utterly against the principles on which our selectors work if we allowed ourselves to be influenced by considerations outside cricket' (May and Melford, 191). When May's second term as a selector began, fourteen prominent England players had just been banned for three years from test selection, for having played a series of matches in South Africa against the urgings of the Test and County Cricket Board, who had by then replaced the MCC as the ruling authority of the first-class game in England. For his services to cricket May was appointed CBE in 1981. He served on the committees of MCC and Surrey, becoming president of MCC in 1980–81 and of Surrey, *honoris causa*, in 1995. His work with Willis Faber was concerned largely with their retail operation, other than when he was acting as the most modest and charming of hosts in their company box at Lord's.

Besides being the niece of one former England captain, Virginia May was the daughter of another, so it was ironic that with such strong cricketing ties the Mays' four children should all have been daughters who excelled in the world of equestrianism. Nevertheless, their mother had once finished sixth in the Badminton horse trials championships, and three of the daughters were to achieve international honours at one level or another. Although he supported them to the hilt, May refused resolutely to take to the saddle himself. 'No brakes', he used to say, with his gentle, unaffected smile, when asked the reason why. May died of a brain tumour at his home, Hatch House, Wheatsheaf Enclosure, Liphook, Hampshire, four days before his sixty-fifth birthday, on 27 December 1994. He was survived by his wife and four daughters.

JOHN WOODCOCK

Sources P. May and M. Melford, *A game enjoyed* (1985) · *Wisden* · personal knowledge (2004) · private information (2004) · *The Times* (28 Dec 1994) · *The Independent* (28 Dec 1994) · b. cert. · m. cert. · d. cert. · *WWW, 1991–5*

Likenesses photographs, 1953–62, Hult. Arch. · R. Burton, photograph, 1957, Hult. Arch. · B. Griffin, bromide print photograph, 1982, NPG [*see illus.*] · photograph, repro. in *The Times* · photograph, repro. in *The Independent*

Wealth at death £245,491: probate, 1 April 1996, *CGPLA Eng. & Wales*

May, Philip William [Phil] (1864–1903), illustrator, was born at 66 Wallace Street, New Wortley, Leeds, on 22 April 1864, the second son and seventh child of Philip William May (1823–1873), an engineer, and his wife, Sarah Jane Macarthy (1828–1912). His grandfather, Charles May, was a squire, sportsman, and amateur caricaturist of Whittington, Chesterfield. From his mother's family Phil May had strong theatrical contacts: his grandfather, Eugene Macarthy (1788–1866), was an Irish actor and sometime manager of Drury Lane Theatre; his aunt, Maria Honnor, was a well-known actress married to the manager of Sadler's Wells and Surrey theatres. May's father had been apprenticed at George Stephenson's locomotive works at Newcastle upon Tyne, but being a poor businessman with a large family, fell on hard times.

May was sent to St George's School, Leeds, from 1872 to 1875, to two further Leeds schools from 1876 to 1877, and then sent out to work at thirteen. The young boy was gregarious, witty, and popular, and interested only in horses, the theatre, and drawing. May worked in a solicitor's office, as a timekeeper in a foundry, and in a piano saleroom before finding his niche in painting scenery for the Leeds Theatre. He joined a travelling troupe of actors and appeared at the Spa Theatre, Scarborough. Through his actress aunt's second husband, Fred Morton, he attempted to find work in London, but made no headway, being reduced to sleeping on the streets and begging for money. He eventually obtained work, publishing a cartoon of the actors Henry Irving, John Toole, and Squire Bancroft in the *portrait chargé* style of Pellegrini and in cartooning for *Society* and the newly founded *St Stephen's Review* in 1884. Again through the intervention of theatrical friends, Lionel Brough and Charles Alias of the Avenue Theatre, he received commissions to design costumes for *Nell Gwynn*. His work on the Christmas number of the *St Stephen's Review* brought recognition and when the *Review* became an illustrated paper in 1885 he joined the staff, working with established cartoonists such as Matt Morgan and Tom Merry.

May felt confident enough in the spring of 1885 to marry an old Leeds friend, Lilian Emerson (d. 1909), the widow of Charles Farrer, and to bring her to London. That autumn he was fortunate to meet the Australian publisher W. H. Traill, managing director of the *Sydney Bulletin*. Traill at

Philip William May (1864–1903), self-portrait, c.1894

once recognized May's worth and offered him a job as cartoonist on the *Bulletin* at £20 a week for three years. May had been in poor health and the change of climate was considered a good move; the Mays left in December.

The three years that May spent in Australia were formative. He had a good income, a secure job, and the pressure of work of the *Bulletin* ensured a discipline the artist needed. He was to produce nine hundred drawings for the paper and established a style of shorthand line that was to be his trademark. The rather roistering lifestyle of Sydney was very much to May's taste and he developed a liking for gambling, high living, and extravagance. When in the autumn of 1888 he was offered the money to study in Paris and Rome he gladly accepted.

Although May could not adapt to academic study, the Parisian streets and artists' studios brought him into direct contact with avant-garde continental illustration. He assimilated the work of French masters of black and white and learned much from poster art. While there, he completed the drawings for his picaresque book *The Parson and the Painter* which appeared in *St Stephen's Review* and was issued as a book in 1891. It was a best-seller and made May's name overnight. He was recruited to Harvey Thomas's *Daily Graphic* in 1892 with the possibility of a world tour in 1893 of which the climax was the Chicago World Fair, which May and his literary companion attended. But the artist did not feel at home in America and was too undisciplined to work to deadlines; the trip was aborted and May returned to a disconsolate editor, who nevertheless forgave him.

The middle 1890s were May's golden years. Editors clamoured for his work which epitomized the bohemian world of the *fin de siècle* and which was easy to reproduce in ordinary newsprint. May (like his contemporary Aubrey Beardsley) had arrived at the moment when the process block and the half-tone could interpret the subtleties of line or the absence of it to perfection. He was able to see his drawings in pure holograph in a way unknown to John Leech or Charles Keene. According to Spielmann 'the bitter experience of Melbourne [*sic*] newspaper printing presses, simplified his style to the point we now see it—in which elimination of all unnecessary lines seems carried to its furthermost limit' (Spielmann, 569). May drew in the structure of his sketches in pencil, following this with the minimum of ink lines and eliminating even some of these as he also erased the pencil. The reader was left with an image that was stark and dynamic and looked effortless, but was in reality the outcome of rigorous thought and organization. In his early days he had emulated the parallel hatching of Linley Sambourne's drawings, but by 1890 he had developed his own freedom; this control and balance was to influence a new generation of artists after 1900, among them G. L. Stampa, Bert Thomas, and George Belcher.

May had been an occasional *Punch* contributor from 1893 but was not elected to the staff until February 1895. The magazine had become very middle-class under Francis Burnand's editorship and May's raffish humour and concentration on low life was frowned on. It was his brilliant line and warm personality that won them over. After February 1895 May contributed to most numbers and almanacs. His inspiration came from the street, the music-hall, the boxing ring, and the gin palace; he was at home at racecourses, fairgrounds, or among bank holiday crowds, though seldom in the drawing-room. May was not a caricaturist, but descended from that distinguished group of illustrators including John Leech and Charles Keene who were illustrators of types. Humour lay was in the generic physiognomy of his drunks, landladies, publicans, and cabbies, not in their caricature.

The hallmark of the successful illustrator was the publication of his own annual. May achieved this very quickly: *Phil May's Winter Annual* appeared in 1892 and continued yearly until 1905; there were thirteen winter editions and three extra summer numbers, the first issue selling 53,000 copies. He supplemented this regular output with some larger albums, *Phil May's Sketch Book: Fifty Cartoons* (1895), *Guttersnipes: Fifty Original Sketches* (1896), and *Phil May's 'Graphic' Pictures* (1897). He collaborated with *Punch* colleagues in books such as F. C. Burnand's *Zig-Zag Guide* (1897) and Henry Lucy's *Essence of Parliament* (1902). He was elected a member of the Royal Institute of Painters in Water Colours in 1896, a singular honour for an illustrator whose work was only occasionally in this medium.

May's reputation was based on his drawings of the 'Arrys and 'Arriets that he saw on the streets of London, observed with tenderness and compassion. But he was a child of his time and some of his *Punch* contributions are

of a racist or antisemitic strain which has grated with subsequent generations. This contrasts with the very generous nature to which all that knew him testified. He was a popular member of the Savage and London Sketch clubs. On one occasion after a night on the town he took a hansom cab to Covent Garden at dawn and filled it with roses to lay on his wife's bed.

> He had a touchingly simple and affectionate character, but unfortunately he wasted himself and his means on a crowd of worthless strangers, who settled round his table like flies; while his terrible weakness for drink sapped his will and his physical strength.   (W. Rothenstein, *Men and Memories*, 1931, 58)

He hated pomposity and pretension, was direct in all his dealings, and very supportive of fellow artists.

In appearance May was about 5 feet 8 inches tall, slight in build, and with the look of a jockey. This was emphasized by his sporting dress: breeches and loud check jackets, garments which featured frequently in his self-portrait drawings. Contemporaries referred to his fine features and delicate hands, but most memorable was the straight fringe of his black hair which cut across his forehead.

By 1897 May's alcoholism was becoming chronic, although he was always careful not to indulge until the ladies had left the table. He could keep no regular hours or habits and his work was sustained by a continuous round of whisky and cigars. For most of his London period, May lived at Rowsley, Holland Park Road, Kensington, but latterly moved to St John's Wood. As he was confined more to his room and his bed, he lost weight and was only 5 stone when he died of phthisis and cirrhosis of the liver on 5 August 1903 at his home, 5 Melina Place, St John's Wood, London. He was buried at Kensal Green Roman Catholic cemetery. He left £803 9s. 6d. His widow received a civil-list pension of £100 per annum. Examples of May's drawings are in the British Museum and the Victoria and Albert Museum, London, and Leeds City Art Gallery.

SIMON HOUFE

Sources J. Thorpe, *Phil May: master-draughtsman and humorist, 1864–1903* (1932) · J. Thorpe, *Phil May*, 2nd edn (1948) · M. H. Spielmann, *The history of 'Punch'* (1895) · E. J. Sullivan, *The art of illustration* (1921) · D. Cuppleditch, *Phil May: the artist and his wit* (1981) · E. A. Ward, *Recollections of a savage* (1923) · M. Bryant and S. Heneage, eds., *Dictionary of British cartoonists and caricaturists, 1730–1980* (1994) · S. Houfe, *Fin de siècle: the illustrators of the nineties* (1992) · K. J. Thomas, 'Phil May: artist and actor', *Cassells Magazine* (May 1902), 662–8 · 'Life and genius of the late Phil May', *The Studio*, 29 (1903), 280–86 · *The Campfire*, 68 (19 Dec 1903), 840–41 · A. Lawrence, 'Mr Phil May at home', *The Idler*, 10 (Dec 1896), 633–48 · A. Morrison, 'Phil May', *Strand Magazine*, 32 (1906), 674–80

Archives Punch Library, London, MSS and drawings

Likenesses P. W. May, self-portrait, pen-and-ink sketch, *c*.1894, NPG [*see illus.*] · P. W. May, self-portrait, silhouette, 1894, NPG · P. F. Spence, pencil drawing, 1895, NPG · P. W. May, self-portrait, pencil caricature, 1896, V&A · Bassano, photographs, 1898, NPG · R. P. Staples, chalk drawing, 1898, NPG · P. W. May, self-portrait, charcoal caricature, *c*.1900, Leeds City Art Gallery · P. W. May, self-portrait, pencil caricature, 1901, NPG · J. Shannon, oils, *c*.1902, Tate collection · A. Collins, pen-and-ink caricature, NPG · P. W. May, self-portrait, pencil caricature, NPG · Spy [L. Ward], caricature, lithograph, NPG; repro. in *VF* (21 Feb 1895) · bronze plaque, New Wortley, Leeds · plaque, Leeds City Art Gallery

Wealth at death £803 9s. 6d.: probate, 7 Oct 1903, *CGPLA Eng. & Wales*

May, Robert (*b.* 1588?, *d.* in or after **1664**), cook and author, was born in the parish of Wing, Buckinghamshire, the second son of Edward and Joan Mayes or May. Although the narrative of Robert May's life by 'W. W.' that prefaced his cookery book *The Accomplisht Cook* (1660) states his date of birth as 1588, an entry for his baptism in the parish register of Wing was not made until 2 April 1592. Edward May was cook to the Dormers of Ascott Park, Wing, a family that had held to the Catholic cause since the reign of Mary I, to whom Jane Dormer (*d.* 1612) was maid of honour.

The only known details of May's life and professional career come from W. W.'s account. After entering the service of the Dormers through his father's influence, he was sent to France by the family to learn further secrets of the cook's profession, apparently in the household of Achille de Harlay (1536–1616), first president of the *parlement* of Paris. His son Christophe, comte de Beaumont, was a soldier and diplomatist who had been sent on various missions to England during the years 1594 to 1607. During a five-year sojourn, May, by his own account, learned the French language, studied manuscripts of French cookery, and read printed cookery books. (In later years, he stated in his own book, he read Italian and Spanish authorities on cooking.) On his return to England, at an undisclosed date, he was apprenticed to Arthur Hollinsworth of Newgate Market in London, cook to the Grocers' Company and to the Star Chamber. Thus it was a thoroughly grounded young cook who returned to the kitchens of Ascott Park some time in the early 1620s to work again alongside his father, who died in 1628. The career paths of Robert May's contemporaries are shrouded in mystery, but there can be few who, at this date, could have claimed so extensive a study of both English and French methods. May worked there until the death of his employer, Elizabeth, widow of Robert, first Baron Dormer, in 1631.

May's subsequent employers are listed in the narrative of his life, and may also be inferred from the dedicatees of *The Accomplisht Cook*. His first on leaving the Dormers was the earl of Castlehaven—either the second earl, who was beheaded for unnatural offences in 1631, or the third, who was a Catholic soldier, ultimately in Spanish pay, who died in 1684. May's next employer was Richard, Lord Lumley, a Catholic connoisseur. The third was Anthony Browne, Viscount Montague, a nephew of Lady Dormer, and also a Catholic recusant. By the outbreak of the civil war in 1642, May had entered service with Elizabeth, countess of Kent, of Wrest Park in Bedfordshire. There again there were family links with the Dormers, and the countess, by birth a Talbot, came from a proudly Catholic line. She compiled two books from the practices of her household, a collection of medical receipts, and one of cookery, *A True Gentleman's Delight* (1653), both published posthumously. Robert May draws on the latter in his own work.

Robert May's circle of employers had so far been entirely noble and Catholic, and family ties with the Dormers had often existed. During the interregnum, if

Robert May (*b.* 1588?, *d.* in or after 1664), by unknown engraver, 1660

the narrative is to be believed, he worked with people who could not be so categorized, for example a Dr Steed of Kent and Sir Thomas Stiles of Drury Lane, but in general the qualifications are repeated through Lord Rivers, Sir Marmaduke Constable, Mr Nevill of Cressing Temple, Sir Frederick Cornwallis of Brome in Suffolk, and Sir Charles Lucas of Essex, until he reached his final place in the household of Winifred, Lady Englefield of Saxelby in Leicestershire, herself a devout Catholic (her confessor was the Jesuit Thomas Harcourt), and whose father-in-law had married the sister of Lady Elizabeth Dormer.

Robert May was certainly alive to write the foreword dated September 1664 to the improved, second edition of his book which was published in 1665. *The Accomplisht Cook* was the first substantial English recipe book to appear after the Restoration and was to go into five editions by 1685. It was a book that looked back to a golden age of generous hospitality and magnificence, but also recognized more recent developments, such as the publication in France of François Pierre de la Varenne's *Le Cuisinier François* (1653). May's work was a longer and more complete collection of recipes than had appeared before in English, and made use of illustration in a way that had not yet been seen. Cookery was still a closely guarded trade mystery, which May desired to make accessible to all, though admitting that not every reader could afford his most extravagant dishes.

So far as is known, May did not marry. A portrait, possibly by Richard Gaywood, is printed as frontispiece to the first and second editions, and there are verses in his honour written by James Parry and John Town, one of which ended, 'The Book's so good, it cannot chuse but sell' (May, 1665 edn, sig. B). TOM JAINE

Sources R. May, *The accomplisht cook, or, The art and mystery of cookery* (1660); 2nd edn (1665) · A. Davidson, M. Bell, and T. Jaine, introduction, in R. May, *The accomplisht cook, or, The art and mystery of cookery*, facs. edn (1994) · parish register (baptism) for Wing, Buckinghamshire, 2 April 1592

Likenesses line engraving, 1660, AM Oxf., BM, NPG; repro. in May, *The accomplisht cook* [*see illus.*]

May, Thomas (*b.* in or after **1596**, *d.* **1650**), writer and historian, was the eldest son of Sir Thomas May (*d.* 1616) of Mayfield, Sussex, and Barbara (*d.* 1601/02), the daughter of Edward Rich of Horndon on the Hill, Essex. His grandfather, George May, had set up business as an iron-founder in Burwash, Surrey. George's son Thomas made a socially advantageous marriage into the Rich family; three years after his son's birth he purchased the manor of Mayfield; he was knighted in 1603 and seems to have had court connections, though there is no record of a formal office. His son was admitted to Sidney Sussex College, Cambridge, on 7 September 1609 as fellow-commoner, and took the degree of BA in 1613. On 6 August 1615 May was admitted to Gray's Inn. Despite this pattern of advancing family prosperity, however, his father seems to have encountered financial difficulties, perhaps heightened by a new marriage which brought four young daughters, and he steadily sold off his estates. He died in July 1616, the inquisition post mortem giving the younger Thomas's age as 20 years 6 months at most. After his death the remaining properties were sold.

Left with a small annuity, and handicapped by a stammer which equipped him badly for a legal career, May turned to literary activities. He began with the drama. The first of two comedies, *The Heir*, which may have initially received a college performance, was acted at the Red Bull and published in 1622; *The Old Couple* was not published until 1658 but there is a record of a court performance in 1636 and it may have been written earlier. Both comedies dealt with the difficulties of young heirs in gaining their inheritance, though the theme was so conventional that the plays do not necessarily reflect his own experience. Their synthesis of Jonsonian satirical comedy with the more romantic conventions of Fletcher's comedy and tragicomedy was characteristic of the drama of the time, though May refrains from the bawdy language and risqué situations which were also in fashion.

May's chief literary interest soon showed itself as the culture and politics of ancient Rome. The first among a series of distinguished translations from Latin was a rendering of the verse in John Barclay's neo-Latin *roman-à-clef*,

Thomas May (*b.* in or after 1596, *d.* 1650), by unknown engraver, pubd 1655

the *Argenis*, in Kingsmill Long's version of 1625. In the following year there appeared the first three books of his translation of Lucan's *Pharsalia*, a work which also strongly influenced his tragedy *Cleopatra*, acted in an unknown venue in the same year. The turn to Roman history may have been influenced by the rising political temperature in the last years of James I and the opening of his son's reign. The *Pharsalia* had remained untranslated until May's attempt, in part because of the poem's intense hostility to the tyranny of the Roman empire and its warm tribute to republican virtues. When May published the full ten books in 1627, he dedicated individual books to figures like the earls of Warwick and Essex who were associated with patriotic independence, at a time of great anxiety about the king's apparent subservience to the unpredictable Buckingham. May's stance was politically sensitive: the dedications were excised from most copies. His tragedy of 'Julia Agrippina', acted in 1628, drew on Lucan in a stark portrayal of imperial corruption. His Latin tragedy of 'Julius Caesar', now lost, is likely to have shared these political concerns. His *Antigone* (published in

1631) is unusual among the dramas of the period in turning directly to Greek themes and tragic models, but this play too draws on Lucan as it pits universal justice against tyrannical wilfulness. Like May's earlier comedies, the plays followed a Jonsonian precedent, in this case his rigorously scholarly Roman tragedies, but again introduced more romantic elements of love-intrigue and pathos.

John Aubrey traced May's later republicanism to his early enthusiasm for Lucan (*Brief Lives*, 2.56). He was certainly not regarded as a republican during the 'king's peace', however; on the contrary, Sir John Suckling's 'A Sessions of the Poets' implies that he became a credible candidate for succeeding Jonson as *de facto* poet laureate. In the aftermath of the Lucan translation the anti-imperial tone of his writings became somewhat muted. His verse translations were reused in Sir Robert Le Grys's new translation of the *Argenis* (1629), whose dedication emphasized that it had been commissioned by the king. Translations of Virgil's *Georgics* (1628) and some of Martial's epigrams (1629) introduced a more regal vein to his translated texts, and in 1630 he published a *Continuation* of Lucan which offered a more sympathetic view of imperial power. This he dedicated to the king, and it was at the king's command, noted on the title-pages, that he now turned to English history in verse narratives of the reigns of *Henry II* (1633) and *Edward III* (1635). These poems, while they do not follow an obvious Caroline propaganda purpose, are sympathetic to the dilemmas of royal power. His version of Barclay's *Icon animorum* (1631) was dedicated in fulsome terms to Lord Chancellor Weston, and courtly connections are also shown in verses addressed to Queen Henrietta Maria. His plays were dedicated to figures with courtly and Catholic associations: *Antigone* to the leading courtier Endymion Porter, *Cleopatra* and *Julia Agrippina* to Sir Kenelm Digby, for whose wife he composed an elegy. He wrote commendatory verses to a pastoral by Digby's friend Joseph Rutter, *The Shepherd's Holiday* (1635), and was praised by the court wit Thomas Carew. When May attended a court masque in 1634 he accidentally jostled the lord chamberlain, the earl of Pembroke, who angrily broke his staff across his shoulders, but Charles himself came to his rescue, calling him 'his poet'. (The fact that he was unknown to Pembroke, however, suggests that he was not a great frequenter of the court—where he never held any formal office.) Clarendon looked back to the May of the 1630s with some affection, praising his continuation of Lucan as 'for the learning, the wit, and the language … one of the best dramatic poems in the English language'. He found in his friend no trace of the future parliamentarian:

> since his fortune could not raise his mind, he brought his mind down to his fortune, by a great modesty and humility in his nature, which was not affected, but very well became an imperfection in his speech, which was a great mortification to him, and kept him from entering upon any discourse but in the company of his very friends. (Hyde, 924)

May kept company with the wits and scholars of Great Tew, and, persistent rumour had it, drank as convivially as any of the 'sons' of Ben Jonson. Clarendon's strong moralism might have been expected to express open disapproval if later rumours of May as a promiscuous womanizer were true; all that is known of his personal life is that he died unmarried.

It was Sir William Davenant, not May, who succeeded Jonson as laureate in 1637. This event was said by Clarendon and other royalists to have poisoned May with resentment and led to his change of political allegiance. It is true that a poem possibly dating from this time, lamenting the effect of his stammer on his fortunes, indicates a sense of grievance at princes who favour the showy at the expense of reticent virtue; but there was no major withdrawal of royal favour, for in the same year the post of chronologer to London fell vacant and the king, Pembroke, and the earl of Dorset wrote in his support. Though he failed to obtain this post too, the failure could not be blamed on the king. His next major publication, a Latin version of his continuation of Lucan (1640), may show signs of a heightening of anti-courtly sentiment, but it was also dedicated to Charles.

In the political crisis of 1640–42, however, May sided with parliament. Like many of the former Great Tew circle, he was divided in his loyalties. According to Aubrey, he had a long political discussion with his friend Sir Richard Fanshawe in the summer of 1642 before the two men parted to take up their respective parliamentarian and royalist allegiances. Rather than venting personal bitterness against the king, the treatise in which he justified his decision, *A Discourse Concerning the Success of Former Parliaments*, offers a dark view of the general tendency of monarchical institutions to threaten liberty whatever the character of the individual ruler. May's firm yet temperate style won him favour as a propagandist for parliament in pamphlets and newsbooks. *A True Relation from Hull* (1643) is the only work from this period to have been signed by May, but contemporaries assumed that he was involved in many other writings, and there is evidence for his association with *The Character of a Right Malignant* (1645), *The King's Cabinet Opened* (1645), and *The Lord George Digby's Cabinet and Dr. Goff's Negotiations* (1646). By 1645 he had gained enough notoriety both to be the object of satire in royalist newsbooks and to receive a defence in the moderate *The Great Assizes Holden in Parnassus*. In January 1646 May, along with John Sadler, was appointed secretary to parliament at a salary of £200 per annum and awarded £100 for work already undertaken. The charge to vindicate parliament's honour was fulfilled with the publication in May 1647 of *The History of the Parliament of England which Began November the Third, 1640*. May traced the origins of the civil war back to Elizabeth's reign and carried his story through to the siege of Gloucester, thus being able to end on a note of triumph. His brief as an official historian, at a time when growing divisions were emerging on parliament's side, necessitated a tone of careful impartiality despite the work's evident tendentiousness. He seems to have retained pre-war contacts with royalist poets: in 1646 he contributed commendatory verse to James Shirley's *Poems*. As political divisions widened in the post-war settlement, May sided with the emergent independent party. Charged to continue his *History*, in 1650 he produced as first instalment a Latin *Breviarium*, quickly translated into English, which condensed the 1647 volume and took the story up to the king's execution, offering a much more critical view than the *History* of the presbyterians and the Scots. He continued to work as a propagandist for parliament (*The Changeable Covenant*, 1650, may be his work), and his death on 13 November 1650 was marked by a state funeral and a memorial in Westminster Abbey.

It was also the occasion for the most vivid statement of the case against May's ingratitude, Andrew Marvell's satire 'Tom May's Death', which alleged that he choked to death in a drunken revelry. This poem's concluding vision of his expulsion from the abbey was prophetic: in September 1661 May's body was one of those exhumed by the triumphant royalists and reburied in St Margaret's, Westminster; six years later his former rival Sir William Davenant was buried in his place in the abbey. Marvell's poem perhaps spoke to suspicions of May that were found among some of the godly as well as among royalists: shortly after his death the puritan William Rowe linked him with a 'gang' of atheists including Thomas Chaloner and Henry Neville. Aubrey much later claimed that he would 'speak slightly of the Trinity' when in his cups, and that the obese poet had died when drunk by choking, because the string of his cap was too tight. Whatever substance this image of the unfaithful debauchee may have had, its later currency—as considerably amplified by Anthony Wood—can be explained by its offering a common denominator of familiar royalist and conservative parliamentarian stereotypes of the republican and the atheist. Though his translation of Lucan may have aroused suspicion, his original writings do not overtly challenge a mainstream protestantism.

Despite, or perhaps in part because of, his controversial reputation, May's writings continued to wield influence for some time after his death. Even Wood conceded the merits of his continuation of the *Pharsalia*, which continued to be regularly reprinted in continental editions of Lucan, though his English translation was superseded by Thomas Rowe's more vigorous if less faithful version. *The Heir* was reworked in Susanna Centlivre's adaptation as *The Stolen Heiress* (1703). His *Breviary*, and the Lucan translation, were reprinted at the time of the exclusion crisis. When Clarendon's *History of the Rebellion*, which originated as a response to May, first appeared, whig writers championed May's superior truth and his less ornate style, and May's *History* held its own with such readers as William Warburton and the earl of Chatham, and down to a reissue in 1854. Thereafter, however, he fell from favour until a late twentieth-century revival of interest in classicizing historiography, in which his undoubted partisanship is recognized but more attention is paid to his qualities as a writer. His adaptation of Roman republican discourse to the circumstances of an early modern

ideological civil war, his attempts to reconcile historical truth with the claims of the imagination, and his subdued sobriety of tone have earned him a new respect.

DAVID NORBROOK

Sources *DNB* · T. May, *The reigne of King Henry the Second*, ed. G. Schmidt (1999) · *Brief lives, chiefly of contemporaries, set down by John Aubrey, between the years 1669 and 1696*, ed. A. Clark, 2 vols. (1898) · E. Hyde, earl of Clarendon, *The history of the rebellion and civil wars in England*, new edn (1843) · A. Griffith Chester, *Thomas May: man of letters, 1595–1650* (1932) [includes bibliography of May's writings] · G. E. Bentley, *The Jacobean and Caroline stage*, 7 vols. (1941–68) · D. Norbrook, *Writing the English republic: poetry, rhetoric and politics, 1627–1660* (1999)

Archives BL, Add. MSS 25303, fols. 186–187; 30259, fol. 11; 33998, fol. 88 · Folger, MSS V.a.160, fols. 13–14; V.a.170, fols. 206–10 · PRO, SPD 16/68/74 | U. Nott. L., Portland collection, PW.V.305

Likenesses line engraving, BM, NPG; repro. in *A breviary of the history of the parliament*, 2nd edn (1655), frontispiece [*see illus.*]

May, Thomas Erskine, Baron Farnborough (1815–1886), clerk of the House of Commons, was born in Kentish Town, London, on 8 February 1815, the son (according to the baptismal record) of Thomas May, attorney, and his wife, Sarah. A connection with the former lord chancellor Thomas *Erskine, however, was accepted by part of Erskine's family, claimed by one of May's relatives, and hinted at by May himself, and rumours long persisted in the clerk's department. Its precise nature has not been established. May had three sisters (or half-sisters). After a private education as a pupil of Dr Brereton, headmaster of Bedford School, May was offered an Oxford exhibition, which his diary, without explanation, records his inability to accept. He was called to the bar, from the Middle Temple, in 1838.

Instead, in 1831, May became assistant to Thomas Vardon, librarian of the House of Commons. In that post May laid the foundations of his wide procedural knowledge by re-indexing the Commons *Journals*. He married (on 27 August 1839) Louisa Johanna, daughter of George Laughton of Fareham: there were no children. For most of his life May lived in an official residence in the Palace of Westminster or in Chester Square, Belgravia. In 1847, at the height of parliamentary activity on railway bills, he was appointed one of the first examiners of petitions for private bills in an effort to devolve to officials the troublesome proof of compliance with standing orders, previously the concern of committees of members. Speaker Shaw Lefevre described the office as 'by far the most laborious duty about the House'. The speaker pressed May's claim to the clerkship in 1850, but pressure from the prime minister (Russell) secured the appointment for Sir Denis Le Marchant. May had to wait until 1856 before becoming clerk assistant, and it was not until May 1871, having supported the ill-suited Le Marchant for fifteen years, that May became clerk.

May received contemporary, including prime ministerial, acclaim for his published works on constitutional history, notably *The Constitutional History of England since the Accession of George III* (2 vols., 1861–3) and *Democracy in Europe: a History* (2 vols., 1877). But it is his contribution to the modernizing of the Victorian House of Commons which

Thomas Erskine May, Baron Farnborough (1815–1886), by R. Taylor, pubd 1886 (after James Russell & Sons)

has better stood the test of time. Even before 1832 successive governments had laid increasing claim to the time of the house for their legislative and financial business. The procedural forms devised to accommodate this had to avoid damaging the ability of private members to criticize and control the executive. The most prolific source of solutions was May. His approach was one of whiggish caution. Obsolete forms were rarely without mischief, but what replaced leisurely and elaborate procedures had to respect the dignity and merit of old custom. In advice to successive speakers, in evidence to select committees (not all of which were anxious to take up the challenge), and in published articles May's fertile procedural imagination shaped the house's new practice: rules for questions to ministers were elaborated; relevance in debate was insisted on; the number of potential divisions, particularly on legislation, was drastically pruned. In order to make best use of limited time available on the floor of the house, it was essential to devise procedures for handling business which could sensibly be remitted to smaller bodies. During his career May put forward a number of solutions to this particular problem, though the preferred option, standing committees, was not originally his idea. His later years were devoted to devising schemes to enhance the powers of the chair in the face of growing unruliness, and to permit the majority to bring the house to a decision, despite the objections of the minority. Early in 1882 May twice attended the cabinet, to advise it on procedure.

These developments were recorded in May's *Parliamentary Practice*, first published in 1844 when May was aged twenty-nine and not yet a clerk. He admitted to intending a straightforward account of parliament, though he was aware of the commercial possibilities of meeting the more detailed needs of those interested in railways bills. The work was an instant success, hailed by *The Times* as 'a popular work … compact and compendious'. May edited a further eight editions, as the work deepened into an authoritative guide to procedure which, in succeeding generations, has helped to shape the development of Westminster practice, perpetuating its editor's name. At a very early stage in its career, *Parliamentary Practice* was used overseas. In 1851 the speaker of the New South Wales legislative council told May that it was 'quite impossible … to overrate the advantages which have resulted from the employment of your work in the colonial legislatures'. The text was translated for the perhaps more problematical benefit of two German diets and the Hungarian parliament. There were also French, Spanish, Italian, and Japanese versions.

With the increasing complexity of Commons procedures went the need for professional development in May's department. For all his personal ability May was ambivalent about such a change. The principle that men were promoted to the table of the house, in effect as May's successors, on merit and experience alone was enunciated by Speaker Denison and not by May. Entrance to the department depended on the clerk's nomination, and May used his powers in the interests of the sons of men already in the service of the house, of predominantly Liberal politicians, and of court officials. He resisted even limited competition for nominations. As a result, while socially, and to some extent educationally, the background of clerks changed, May's attitude delayed the development of the service of the house. Even the clerkship itself, on May's retirement, was first offered to men without departmental experience. None of these limited perspectives, however, impairs May's position as the man whose tireless professionalism at a time of political and procedural change shaped the modern clerk's department.

May's diaries bear witness to the relatively humourless ambition and hard work of their author. The impression is relieved only by a story told by Speaker Gully that as a good-looking flirtatious young man May compromised himself with a married lady and had to fight a duel with her husband at Boulogne. His preferment owed much to energy and ability, but these were assisted by the ease with which May moved in Liberal political society. Usually when promotion offered, the Liberals were conveniently in power. When in 1875 and 1885 May considered the possibility of becoming clerk of the parliaments in the Lords, they were not in power, and his ambition went unrealized. At the same time, neither May nor his department was drawn into any spoils system. In 1883 the retiring speaker, Brand, wrote to May of his legacy to the man who was to succeed him in the chair: 'the sum and substance of my advice to Peel will be to trust you and the house'.

May was created CB in 1860 and KCB in 1866 (after some discreet agitation), and became a privy councillor in August 1885. The last was an unusual, though not unique, honour for a serving official. He retired in April 1886 and on 11 May 1886 was created Baron Farnborough. He died at Speaker's Court in the Palace of Westminster on 17 May 1886 and was buried at Chippenham, Cambridgeshire.

WILLIAM MCKAY

Sources W. R. McKay, ed., *Erskine May's private journal, 1883–1886* (1984) · D. Holland and D. Menhennet, eds., *Erskine May's private journal, 1857–1882* (1972) · *The Times* (18 May 1886) · *The Times* (25 May 1886) · *The Times* (27 May 1886) · W. R. McKay and J. C. Sainty, eds., *Clerks in the House of Commons, 1363–1989* (1989) · W. R. McKay, 'The family background of Sir T. E. May', *The Table*, 52 (1984), 92–7 · *Biograph and Review*, 2 (1879), 245–51 · *Biograph and Review* (1882) · Sir C. P. Ilbert's diary, HLRO, MS. 73 [10/7/1909] · Gladstone, *Diaries* · d. cert. · baptismal register, St Martin-in-the-Fields, London [1815]
Archives HLRO, commonplace book and journal · NRA, priv. coll., official and personal papers | BL, corresp. with W. E. Gladstone, Add. MS 44154 · CUL, letters to Lord Acton · Herefs. RO, letters to George Moffat · HLRO, corresp. with H. B. W. Brand, Hampden MSS · U. Nott., letters to J. E. Denison
Likenesses R. Taylor, engraving, pubd 1886 (after photograph by J. Russell & Sons) [*see illus.*] · A. B. Joy, marble bust, 1890, Palace of Westminster, London · Ape [C. Pellegrini], caricature watercolour study, NPG; repro. in *VF* (6 May 1871) · photographs, HLRO, Erskine May MSS · photographs, Palace of Westminster, London
Wealth at death £15,441 16s. 10d.: probate, 19 July 1886, *CGPLA Eng. & Wales*

May, William (c.1505–1560), college head and archbishop-elect of York, is said to have been a native of Suffolk. Nothing is known of his parentage, and his date of birth is unrecorded, but the course of his early career suggests a date about 1505. The John May who was bishop of Carlisle between 1577 and 1598 is often stated to have been his younger brother, but seems more likely to have been the nephew of that name mentioned in his will. William May entered Trinity Hall, Cambridge, in the early 1520s, advancing to the degree of BCL in 1526. In 1531 he was awarded his DCL and elected a fellow of Trinity Hall. In the following year he began his career as an ecclesiastical lawyer, becoming chancellor to Bishop Nicholas West of Ely. Following West's death that year he served as Archbishop Cranmer's vicar-general during the vacancy of the see, though securing his position was not easy, since the privy council had to intervene to wrest the register from the hands of the previous chancellor. Following the election of Thomas Goodrich as bishop in the spring of 1534 May became chancellor once more, and entered upon a career as a professional ecclesiastical bureaucrat. In 1534 he was Cranmer's commissary for the visitation of the diocese of Norwich, and in 1536 he was one of the king's commissioners for the visitation of Ely.

In 1535 May began to reap the rewards of his services. On 27 March 1535 he was instituted rector of Bishop's Hatfield, Hertfordshire, on condition that he take holy orders within fifteen months of his institution. On 2 April he was dispensed to take two holy orders in one day, which he presumably did, and on 20 May 1538 was dispensed to hold a benefice with the rectory at Hatfield, or two without it, to the value of £9, so that he could hold the sinecure rectory of Littlebury, near Saffron Walden, to which he had already been admitted. Meanwhile his skills as an administrator had not been lost on his Cambridge community,

and in 1537 he was elected president of Queens' College, beginning a long career as an academic leader.

There is no information about May's early religious opinions, but it is clear that Cranmer and Thomas Cromwell found him useful for reforming purposes. In 1537 he was one of the twenty-five hand-picked men called to meet with the bishops of the realm to prepare the *Institution of a Christian Man*, or Bishops' Book. His own contribution to this corporate effort is unidentifiable, but his evangelical sympathies and his effectiveness on a committee continued to advance him. In 1539 he served in the lower house of convocation, where he voted for clerical marriage and for the repudiation of transubstantiation, auricular confession, private masses, and communion in only one kind.

Although there is no evidence that May served as a commissioner for the dissolution of the monasteries, he benefited from it. When the Benedictine priory of St Peter and St Etheldreda was reconstituted as the secular chapter of Ely Cathedral on 10 September 1541 May was appointed to the third prebendal stall, joining Richard Cox and Matthew Parker. He had become rector of Balsham, a few miles east of Cambridge, in the previous year.

The early 1540s was a quiet time for the president of Queens', but in 1545 May was nominated by Henry VIII to be dean of St Paul's, London. Although the cathedral chapter was sent the order for his election on 29 October 1545, he was not formally elected until 15 February following. There seems to have been some legal quibbling by the chapter about May's appointment, but an order from the privy council forced the election. Meanwhile May, who also held the prebend of Chamberlainwood in St Paul's from 1 November 1545, became very busy in government service.

On 16 January 1546, along with Matthew Parker and another head of a college, May was appointed to a commission to report on the possessions of the Cambridge colleges. A statute of 1544 had given Henry VIII the power to dissolve chantries attached to colleges. Not only was he contemplating doing so, but land-hungry courtiers were hoping that he would also dissolve the colleges themselves. Parker and May delivered the resulting survey to the king, having carefully crafted it so as to prove that every college was underfunded. It so impressed the king that he was persuaded to let the colleges keep their property.

In August 1546 May was sent on a diplomatic mission to France as the junior to Sir William Petre. They were to claim the arrears on 512,000 crowns in pensions owed by France to England under an agreement of 1529. The French arrived after the treaty had expired and the negotiations failed, but Petre's report includes a description of May: 'who … is of honest sort, wise, discreet, and well learned … Meet to serve his majesty in many ways' (*State Papers, Henry VIII*, 11.293, n. 1). The mission of 1546 did indeed begin a period of intense government service for May, in which his legal expertise was to the fore. In 1547 he served as a commissioner examining debtors imprisoned in Ludgate who wished to compound with their creditors, and he was appointed to two commissions to hear divorce appeals. In one, William Parr, first marquess of Northampton, wanted to remarry after his divorce, even though his former wife was still living. In the other Dr Robert Huick was appealing against a decision that held that he could not divorce his wife.

The accession of Edward VI brought May many new responsibilities. He was clearly thought trustworthy to carry out the protestant agenda of the new establishment, and by late 1547 he was heavily involved in reforming St Paul's, overseeing the destruction of the high altar and the abolition of obits and chantries. In November he was appointed a royal visitor to the dioceses of Salisbury, Exeter, Bristol, Bath and Wells, and Gloucester, where he and his fellow commissioners forbade the use of black copes and scapulars because they were monkish. They also tried to end ringing for the dead, and instructed that prime and the hours need not be said in Wells Cathedral in order to make time for a divinity lecture immediately after high mass. Present at the convocation at the end of 1547, May subscribed the ordinance for taking communion in both kinds and voted in favour of clerical marriage. Late in 1552 or 1553 he himself married Joan Heynes, *née* Walron, the widow of Dr Simon Heynes, the previous president of Queens' and also May's close colleague.

In November 1548, still president of Queens', May was placed on the commission to visit Cambridge University and Eton College, enforcing the dissolution of obits and chantries. As he went up to the university in March 1549 he assured Matthew Parker, now vice-chancellor, that the visitation would be orderly and moderate. It is not clear whether he favoured the proposed union of Trinity Hall and Clare College to create a college of civil law, but he was willing to vote for expelling the master and fellows of Clare for their resistance to the plan.

Over the next few years May was fully engaged in enforcing Edwardian reforms. A commissioner to search for heretics, Anabaptists, and libertines every year from 1549 to 1552, he sat on the panel that found the martyr Joan Bocher guilty of Arianism. When Bishop Bonner of London was accused of contempt of the king's order for reformation, May was appointed to the commission to try him. And after Bonner was deprived, May, as dean of St Paul's, officiated at the installation of Nicholas Ridley as the new bishop of London.

By the 1550s May had become a noted ecclesiastical lawyer, performing major tasks for the crown. Most notably he was named to the committee of thirty-two for drafting (abortively) a new canon law for the church in England. He was one of the subcommittee that drafted the *Reformatio legum ecclesiasticarum* in 1551 and 1552. He was also involved in creating the 1552 Book of Common Prayer, though in what capacity is not clear. He served on other government commissions, too, while being actively involved in St Paul's and Queens'.

All of this ended with the accession of Queen Mary in 1553. Deprived on the grounds of his marriage of the presidency of Queens', the deanship of St Paul's, and his prebend at Ely, May none the less conformed enough to

keep his rooms at Queens' from 1554 until 1558. In 1557 moreover he became rector of Pulham Norfolk, and of Stanton St Michael, Cambridgeshire.

The accession of Elizabeth brought May back into the public arena. He was named in the 'Device for alteration of religion', prepared late in 1558, as one to be consulted about revising the Book of Common Prayer in preparation for the restoration of protestantism, though the committee probably never met, and in June 1559 he resumed the presidency of Queens' College, and was readmitted as dean of St Paul's, now with the prebend of Wenlocksbarn. Later that year he was appointed a commissioner to impose the Elizabethan settlement on Cambridge, and also proctor for archbishop-elect Matthew Parker.

On 25 July 1560 May was nominated to become archbishop of York, but on 7 August, feeble and sick, he made his will. He died in London on 8 August, the same day that he was elected archbishop. Buried in St Paul's on 12 August, May left a considerable estate to his wife, Joan, to his children, William and Elizabeth, and to his stepchildren. In his will he mentions lands and bequests worth more than £732, as well as plate, horses, and uncollected debts of unspecified value. The executors of his estate were Richard Coxe, bishop of Ely, and Richard Goodrich. He named Edmund Grindal, bishop of London, John Mullens, archdeacon of London, and Thomas Yale, supervisors of his will.   NORMAN L. JONES

Sources *LP Henry VIII*, vols. 6–21 · *Correspondence of Matthew Parker*, ed. J. Bruce and T. T. Perowne, Parker Society, 42 (1853) · *CPR, 1547–53* · *Calendar of the manuscripts of the dean and chapter of Wells*, 2, HMC, 12 (1914) · *CSP dom., 1547–53* · D. S. Chambers, ed., *Faculty office registers, 1534–1549* (1966) · F. G. Emmison, *Tudor secretary: Sir William Petre at court and home* (1961), 62 · *Registrum Matthei Parker, diocesis Cantuariensis, AD 1559–1575*, ed. W. H. Frere and E. M. Thompson, 1, CYS, 35 (1928), 6 · A. Gibbons, ed., *Ely episcopal records: a calendar and concise view of the episcopal records preserved in the muniment room of the palace of Ely* (privately printed, Lincoln, 1891) · *CSP Spain, 1547–9* · M. R. James, *A descriptive catalogue of the manuscripts in the library of Corpus Christi College, Cambridge*, 2 vols. (1912) · *The chronicle and political papers of King Edward VI*, ed. W. K. Jordan (1966), 110 · 'Quene Mary's visitation: by J. Mere, present', *A collection of letters, statutes and other documents ... illustrative of the history of the University of Cambridge during the Reformation*, ed. J. Lamb (1838), 184–236 · *Fasti Angl., 1541–1857*, [St Paul's, London] · *Fasti Angl., 1541–1857*, [Ely] · *The letters of Stephen Gardiner*, ed. J. A. Muller (1933) · *The diary of Henry Machyn, citizen and merchant-taylor of London, from AD 1550 to AD 1563*, ed. J. G. Nichols, CS, 42 (1848) · 'Rex Edouard. 6. epistola', *Reformatio legum ecclesiasticarum, ex authoritate primum Regis Henrici. 8. inchoata: deinde per Regem Edouardem. 6. provecta, adauctaque in hunc modum, atque nunc ad pleniorem ipsarum reformationem in ludem aedita*, ed. T. Norton (1571) · W. G. Searle, *The history of the Queens' College of St Margaret and St Bernard in the University of Cambridge*, 2 vols., Cambridge Antiquarian RS, 9, 13 (1867–71) · J. C. Spalding, *The reformation of the ecclesiastical laws of England, 1552*, Sixteenth Century Essays and Studies, 19 (1992), 38–9 · J. Strype, *Ecclesiastical memorials*, 3 vols. (1822) · J. Strype, *The history of the life and acts of the most reverend father in God Edmund Grindal*, new edn (1821) · J. Strype, *The life and acts of Matthew Parker*, new edn, 3 vols. (1821) · J. Strype, *Memorials of the most reverend father in God, Thomas Cranmer*, ed. P. E. Barnes, new edn, 2 vols. (1853) · Venn, *Alum. Cant.* · BL, Add. MS 5813, fol. 88 · BL, Add. MS 5884, fol. 74 · BL, Sloane MS 3562, fols. 2–3 · BL, Add. MS 5842, fol. 184v · miscellaneous books, PRO, exchequer, augmentations office, E 315/440 [commissioners' report on Cambridge University, 37 Hen. VIII] · GL, MS 25184 · 'Sampson, 1536–1560', act

book of the dean and chapter of St Paul's, GL, MS 25630/1 • LPL, MS 959/28/#27 • will, PRO, PROB 11/44, sig. 16 • *State papers published under … Henry VIII*, 11 vols. (1830–52)
Wealth at death over £732: will, PRO, PROB 11/44, sig. 16

May, William (1863–1932), lawyer, was born on 4 May 1863 at 121 Castle Street, Reading, the eldest of four children of George May (1826–1909), surgeon to the Royal Berkshire Hospital, and his wife, Mary Sophia Georgiana Robinson. The Mays were an old-established Berkshire family who not only were landowners but also produced many successful professional men. Shortly after William's birth his parents moved to The Warren, Caversham, where he spent his childhood and youth.

From 1876 to 1881 May attended Charterhouse School, where he was editor of the literary magazine. He then continued his education at New College, Oxford, where he took a second in classical moderations (1883) and a fourth in modern history (1884), staying on for a further term to undertake a course in theological studies.

Early in 1885 May was articled to the firm of Ashurst Morris Crisp. The choice of firm may have been decided by his having been at school with the son of the senior partner, John Morris. He sat his qualifying examinations in January 1888 and was admitted as a solicitor in the following July. During his time with Ashurst Morris Crisp, May made the acquaintance of William Slaughter, who was an assistant solicitor with the firm. Unlike May, Slaughter came from a business and commercial background, and had qualified as a solicitor without attending university. Although the firm had a high regard for Slaughter, it seems that it was not able to offer him a partnership, and it was probably for this reason that from late in 1887 he began to practise independently at 18 Austin Friars in London. May joined him early in the following year, and in January 1889 the partners opened a joint bank account. It is believed that this was the sole formality establishing the partnership, Slaughter and May's trust in one another making a partnership deed unnecessary.

The last decade of the nineteenth century was an exceptionally favourable moment to establish a legal practice. Improvements in legal education had raised the status of solicitors, and financial stability ensured a steady flow of work in the field of commercial law. The new firm was also helped by support from Ashurst Morris Crisp, who allowed Slaughter and May to undertake work for some of their established clients, acting as their agent. During the period from 1890 to 1892 Slaughter and May acquired the freehold of their premises and had them extensively rebuilt and refurbished, creating an attractive working environment, as well as enabling them to make profitable lettings of office space which they did not require. During the building work, the firm was temporarily housed at 21 Great Winchester Street.

In 1895 May purchased Ashburton House, Send, Surrey, which became his family home. His wife, Emma Mary Blount, whom he married on 10 September 1902, was the daughter of Gilbert Blount, an architect, of Mapledurham House, near Pangbourne. The Blounts were Roman Catholics, and May incurred the disapproval of his family in converting from the Church of England to his wife's religion at the time of the marriage. Two sons were born: Michael in 1906 and George in 1910.

In contrast to Slaughter, who lived chiefly for his work, May engaged in a wide variety of leisure interests. He had considerable musical abilities, playing the piano and cello, and as a young man wrote several pieces which were commercially published. He enjoyed sports such as shooting, tennis, and cricket, and climbed both Mont Blanc and the Matterhorn. He was also a keen sailor, and frequently arranged parties on his yacht, the *Calisaya*.

Slaughter died on 10 March 1917. His death was a personal loss to May, and led to an increase in his responsibilities. He replaced Slaughter on the board of the Home and Colonial Stores, which Slaughter had done much to build up, and became chairman in 1925. May was also concerned in a number of electricity supply firms in the south of England, becoming chairman of the Reading Electric Supply Company in 1915 and chairman of the Greater London and Counties Trust in 1925. In addition he was on the boards of London Express Newspapers and several other companies.

Towards the end of the 1920s May became less active in the affairs of Slaughter and May, and by 1930 he had almost entirely withdrawn from the firm. He died, survived by his wife, on 6 May 1932 at Pitt Hall Farm, Baughurst, near Kingsclere, Hampshire, from heart failure associated with kidney problems. He was buried on 12 May at St Edward's Church, Sutton Park, Surrey, and requiem masses were also said at St Mary Moorfields, London, and at Caversham. A gifted commercial lawyer, he was also valued for his personal qualities of kindness and good fellowship, as well as scrupulous fairness. 100 years after its foundation, the firm he helped to establish had seventy-seven partners and over 1000 employees.

SHEILA DOYLE

Sources L. Dennett, *Slaughter and May: a century in the City* (1989) • *WWW* • b. cert. • d. cert.
Archives Charterhouse School, Godalming, Surrey, diaries • priv. coll., diary | Slaughter and May, London, Slaughter and May papers
Likenesses photographs, repro. in Dennett, *Slaughter and May*
Wealth at death £197,083 1s. 3d.—excl. settled land: probate, 5 Aug 1932, *CGPLA Eng. & Wales* • £19,010 2s. 1d.—settled land only: probate, 16 Sept 1932, *CGPLA Eng. & Wales*

May, Sir William Henry (1849–1930), naval officer, was born at Liscard, Cheshire, on 31 July 1849, the third son in the family of ten children of Job William Seaburne May and his wife, Anne Jane Freckleton. Since the seventeenth century the family had lived in the Netherlands, where an ancestor, John May, had been a naval architect. William Henry May's grandfather, an admiral in the Dutch navy and reportedly at the same time captain in the British navy, had assisted in restoring Prince William of Orange to the throne of the Netherlands in 1813. His father left the Netherlands in 1840 and established himself on the stock exchange in Liverpool, where he was Netherlands consul.

In 1860 May entered the Royal Institution School, Liverpool, and in 1862, when he had decided to join the Royal

Navy, he entered Eastman's naval academy, Southsea. He passed into the training ship *Britannia* twenty-second out of fifty in 1863, and a year later he passed out fourth, and embarked at once, aged fifteen, on the *Victoria*, flagship of the Mediterranean Fleet. After three years he was transferred to the frigate *Liffey*, in which he served the remaining eighteen months of his midshipman's time. Having become a sub-lieutenant in 1869, May passed his examinations in that rank so well that, as a reward, he was appointed, after a few months in the *Hercules*, to the royal yacht *Victoria and Albert*. He was advanced to lieutenant after two and a half years, gaining promotion before many of his seniors. After returning to the *Hercules* he served on her for two years (1872–4) and was then appointed to the gunnery-school ship *Excellent* to qualify as a specialist in gunnery. So far his career had been on the usual lines, but then an opportunity was presented of taking part in the Arctic expedition fitting out (1875) under Captain George Strong Nares. May at once volunteered, and was accepted as navigating officer of the *Alert*. He served on the expedition until its return in 1876, having taken part in the sledging expeditions to Lincoln Bay and in relief of the party led by Commander Albert Hastings Markham and in the search for a practicable overland route to Cape Prevost. He did much surveying, for which he was officially commended by Sir George Nares.

On his return from the Arctic expedition May joined the torpedo-school ship *Vernon*. There he played a prominent and important part in developing the Whitehead torpedo and an underwater discharging apparatus. After three and a half years (1877–80) in the *Vernon* and a few months in the frigate *Inconstant* he was promoted commander; he achieved this rank after only nine and a half years' service as lieutenant. In 1878, while in the *Vernon*, May had married Kinbarra Swene, daughter of William John Marrow, merchant; they had two sons. In 1880 he was given command of the exceptional new torpedo-ram ship *Polyphemus*. He held this command for two and a half years (1881–4) and for the next three years was second in command of the royal yacht. Aged thirty-eight, he was promoted captain.

In March 1888 May went to China as flag captain to Admiral Sir Nowell Salmon in the *Impérieuse*. On the voyage to the East he took possession, acting on secret orders, of Christmas Island. This earned him the nickname Christmas May to go with Handsome Willie May. He returned to England at the end of the commission in December 1890, and was appointed naval attaché to the European states. He served in this capacity for two and a half years, principally in France, Russia, and Germany, and then, without intermission, was appointed to the Admiralty as assistant director of torpedoes. In January 1895 he went as flag captain and chief of staff to Admiral Sir Michael Culme Seymour on the Mediterranean station, where he gave evidence of outstanding organizing ability. After two years' service in the Mediterranean he returned to England and was at once appointed flag captain to Admiral Sir Nowell Salmon, commander-in-chief at Portsmouth, acting as chief of staff during the 1897

jubilee celebrations. After this he went to the gunnery school *Excellent*, which he commanded until January 1901. He was then appointed director of naval ordnance and torpedoes.

In April 1901, aged fifty-one, May reached flag rank, having a month earlier been made third sea lord and controller of the navy. During the four years of his controllership many far-reaching changes in naval construction and dockyard administration took place. The *dreadnought* policy was initiated, though May was not a member of the 'committee of design' appointed in October 1904 to consider the characteristics of the new type; a greater sea-going capacity was given to the torpedo-boat destroyer class; the use of oil sprayed upon coal was introduced, and ships' machinery underwent great alterations. In February 1905 May, who had been created KCVO in 1904, was appointed to command the recently formed Atlantic Fleet with his flag in the *King Edward VII*. In July he took the fleet to Brest, to make a naval demonstration of the *entente cordiale*. May's presence and personality, his knowledge of French, and his able handling of the fleet in entering and leaving Brest harbour created a very good impression on French naval officers.

After two years in command of the Atlantic Fleet, May returned to the Admiralty as second sea lord. At this time (1907) great efforts were being made to cut down naval expenditure, and the Liberal government ordered a reduction of £1 million. When a further reduction of £750,000 was proposed, May, with the third and fourth sea lords, sent a memorandum to the first sea lord, Sir John (afterwards Lord) Fisher, intimating that if this was done they must resign; it was not.

In 1909 May was appointed to command the Home Fleet with his flag in the *Dreadnought*. This command included all the ships in home waters, and was, in May's opinion, too large. He concentrated on investigating the many tactical problems which the recent growth of the fleet in numbers and size, and the addition to the sea-going fleet of a fighting flotilla, had brought into existence. Gunnery, under the impulse of Percy Moreton Scott, had made great advances, though it was still far short of what came to be demanded of it in 1914. The torpedo had increased in both range and speed, and presented a new element in tactics. Many officers serving under May's command were dissatisfied with the existing tactical doctrines, and advocated new systems of handling the large and heterogeneous body of ships which formed a modern fleet command. May was open to receiving, discussing, and trying new ideas. He initiated an extensive series of tactical exercises of an enhanced scale and comprehensiveness; the cruising formations from which deployment into battle formation could most rapidly be made; the use of flotillas in a tactical offensive; the employment of fast squadrons in action; the alternative of squadronal command in place of the single line under one command—these were prominent among the tactical matters to which May devoted attention. A man of an essentially practical turn of mind, he submitted to trial new theories and suggestions 'on the scale of twelve inches to the foot'. On hauling down his flag in March 1911 May was appointed commander-in-chief at Devonport. He held this command until promoted admiral of the fleet in March 1913, when his flag came down for the last time.

During the First World War May served on the Dardanelles commission (1916–17) chaired by the earl of Cromer; as chairman of the reconstruction committee which dealt, in anticipation, with the problems of post-war reductions; and on a subcommittee on fisheries. After his retirement he lived at Coldstream, Berwickshire, where he took an active part in local affairs. He died at his residence, Bughtrigg, Coldstream, on 7 October 1930.

Few flag officers of his time had more continuous employment than Sir William May. In forty-four years' service he had only twenty months on half pay, and at no time was he unemployed for longer than seven months. He was tall, strikingly handsome, and physically active and powerful. He rowed in a race in a fleet regatta in his sixty-first year; he hunted until his horses were taken for the war; he shot, and played golf until within ten days of his death. He had the gift of eliciting the opinions and theories of his officers, encouraging their suggestions, and giving them his unbiased consideration. He was created MVO (1897), received the Légion d'honneur (1905) and the KCB (1906), and was GCVO (1909) and GCB (1911).

H. W. RICHMOND, rev. ANDREW LAMBERT

Sources A. J. Marder, *From the Dreadnought to Scapa Flow: the Royal Navy in the Fisher era, 1904–1919*, 5 vols. (1961–70) • A. Gordon, *The rules of the game: Jutland and British naval command* (1996) • A. J. Marder, *Portrait of an admiral: the life and papers of Sir Herbert Richmond* (1952) • R. F. MacKay, *Fisher of Kilverstone* (1973) • E. N. Poland, *The torpedomen: HMS Vernon's story, 1872–1986* (1993) • J. G. Wells, *Whaley: the story of HMS Excellent, 1830 to 1980* (1980) • W. H. May, *The life of a sailor* (privately printed, 1934) • *WWW, 1929–40* • *CGPLA Eng. & Wales* (1931)
Archives NMM, journals, log books, corresp. and papers | Bodl. Oxf., corresp. with Lord Selborne • NMM, corresp. with Sir Julian S. Corbett
Likenesses photograph, 1907, priv. coll. • W. Stoneman, photograph, 1917, NPG • Spy [L. Ward], chromolithograph caricature, NPG; repro. in *VF* (26 March 1903)
Wealth at death £78,710 14s. 0d.: probate, 7 Jan 1931, *CGPLA Eng. & Wales*

Mayall, John (1803–1876), cotton spinner, was born on 31 December 1803 in Lydgate, near Ashton under Lyne, the second son in the family of four sons and two daughters of Samson Mayall (1779–1860), clothier, and his wife, Betty Andrew (1785–1841), of Lees, near Oldham. At the age of seven Mayall began work in a series of textile factories. Later he bore the responsibility for maintaining his mother and siblings, after his father, given to drink and radicalism, had migrated to America in the wake of the Peterloo massacre (1819).

About 1824 he entered into partnership with three fellow cotton spinners before, in 1828, joining his brother George (1807–1883) in a rented cotton mill in Mossley, near Oldham. By 1831 they controlled 7000 spindles and, adding new mills and steam power, were to employ 510 hands by 1845. This partnership was dissolved amicably in June 1846, with each brother taking 40,000 spindles. Improved

railway communications and the burgeoning Indian market for coarse yarn stimulated the rapid growth of his firm with a series of new mills built after 1849. Mayall's mastery of technical detail and innovation optimized productivity, while the variety of mills under his control gave him the advantages of flexible specialization. He also imported raw cotton from America in his own ships. Here his success was questionable and he later imported only for his own firm. For the sale of his products he relied on two Manchester yarn agents, particularly Dilworth & Co.

But it was as a cotton spinner, not a merchant, that Mayall excelled, and by 1870 he controlled approximately 319,000 spindles, with about 1350 hands. In 1872 David Chadwick, the company promoter, reputedly offered £1.5 million to float his firm. Mayall had undoubtedly become the largest specialized cotton spinner in England (and the world), but in this period the bell-wethers of cotton industrialization had been the combined spinning and weaving firms. For this reason, Mayall's dominance was confined to the spinning sector of south-east Lancashire, and his firm never became a conspicuous leader of the cotton industry in the manner of Horrockses of Preston or Rylands of Manchester. Even in south-east Lancashire his firm was soon eclipsed by the other limited companies in Oldham.

The growth of the Pennine town of Mossley was also in large part the by-product of the rise of Mayall's business. He built a hotel, shops, and numerous houses for his workpeople, paying one-fifth of Mossley's rates. He also helped to shape the community as chairman of the board of surveyors, lighting inspector, poor-law guardian, and justice of the peace. As a politically Liberal employer, he supported the Anti-Corn Law League in the 1840s, and as a friend of the working classes provided partial employment throughout the cotton famine of the 1860s. Although baptized and buried in Anglican churches, his strongest links were with the Abney Congregational Church, which he had largely financed.

In 1824 Mayall married Elizabeth Winterbottom (d. 1860) of Lees, a piecer he employed. Both were illiterate at the time. They had five sons and two daughters. Mayall's recreations were few: he became literate, read the Bible, and subscribed to *Punch*. Prosperity eventually drove him to expenditure, acquiring servants and carriages, and building Highfield House, Mossley, with its billiard room, library, ornamental gardens, and lodge. His change in lifestyle perhaps owed something to his second marriage on 2 April 1863 to a widow, Mrs Job Lees, née Sarah Mayall (b. 1812/13), the daughter of Miles Mayall (unrelated), from the ranks of the local élite. There were no children of the second marriage. The sons of Mayall's first marriage were all initiated into the firm at an early age; a son-in-law (a doctor) acquired a mill as a dowry; and a remaining daughter married a nonconformist minister. By his retirement in the early 1870s Mayall had transferred both the firm and his wealth to his sons. He died on 7 March 1876 at Highfield House, Mossley, an example of mobility from operative to captain of industry, spurred on by poverty, aided by good luck, and displaying the full range of Smilesian virtues. He was interred in the family vault in St George's Church, Mossley.   A. C. HOWE, *rev.*

Sources Mayall MSS, Manchester City Libraries · *Ashton Reporter* (11 March 1876) · *Ashton Reporter* (18 March 1876) · censuses, 1841–71, PRO · D. A. Farnie and S. Yonekawa, 'The emergence of the largest firms in the cotton-spinning industries of the world, 1883–1938', *Textile History*, 19 (1988), 171–210 · m. cert. [Sarah Lees] · d. cert.
Likenesses photograph, Ashton under Lyne library
Wealth at death acquired a fortune and in 1872, handed over the management of 300,000 spindles to five sons from first marriage; the firm suffered losses, probably from 1877 (by his retirement in early 1870s had transferred both firm and wealth to sons): Farnie and Yonekawa, 'Emergence'; *DNB*

Mayall, John Jabez Edwin [*formerly* Jabez Meal] (1813–1901), photographer and local politician, was born on 17 September 1813 at Oldham, Lancashire, as Jabez Meal, the son of John Meal, a west Yorkshire manufacturing chemist, and his wife, Elizabeth. Virtually nothing is known of his early life. Although local tradition in his home town of Lingard, near Huddersfield, held that he followed his father into chemistry, the 1841 census listed him and his wife as flax spinners. Some time shortly after this he travelled to the United States, apparently then altering his name, which was probably of French origin. After a period in New York, he settled in Philadelphia, and it was there with the new art of daguerreotypy that Mayall made his reputation.

Late in life Mayall recalled that his first handling of a daguerreotype was on 6 January 1840; the circumstances and the precision of the date cannot be confirmed. Whether or not he had some experience in the new art before moving to America is unknown, but he must have been well informed, for he promptly established a close working relationship with two University of Pennsylvania chemists active in perfecting the daguerreotype process, Professor Hans Martin Boyé and Dr Paul Beck Goddard. In 1843–4 Mayall made a series of ten daguerreotypes illustrating the Lord's prayer, an allegorical excursion of a type previously almost unknown to the rough new art: these brought him wide acclaim for some years, but are now thought to be lost. Mayall joined another Englishman, Samuel Van Loan, in partnership in a Philadelphia daguerreotype studio, and by 1844 the Franklin Institute had awarded them a silver medal for their daguerreotype productions. In 1845 Mayall became the sole proprietor, using the name Professor Highschool, and on 20 June 1846 he sold the studio to Marcus A. Root (who was to become one of the most successful American daguerreotypists) and returned to England. There is some evidence that Mayall was facing legal difficulties over his method of hand colouring daguerreotypes and perhaps this prompted his departure.

When Mayall moved to London he worked briefly for Antoine Claudet, another pioneering daguerreotypist, but by 1847 he had set up his own studio, the American Daguerreotype Institution, at 433 Strand. It was at the Great Exhibition in 1851 that Mayall's reputation was firmly established; he was popularly believed to be an American. His seventy-two daguerreotypes, many of them from his days in America, received an honourable mention from the jurors and attracted the attention of Prince Albert, an enthusiastic patron of photography. He invited Mayall to photograph the queen and other members of the royal family and the resulting cartes-de-visite were widely popular. The queen, too, mistook his nationality: on being photographed by him in 1855, she recorded in her journal that 'Mr. Mayall … is the oddest man I ever saw but an excellent photographer. He is an American and a tremendous enthusiast in his work' (H. Gernsheim and A. Gernsheim, *Queen Victoria*, 1959, 261). On being commanded to photograph the wedding of the prince and princess of Wales in 1863, Mayall erected a special glasshouse at Windsor for the purpose (he later moved it to Brighton and turned it into a conservatory). When the fledgeling Photographic Society started up in 1853, John Edwin Mayall (as he had come to be known) was already a portrait photographer of the highest reputation and he immediately became an active participant. He was beginning to demonstrate his leadership in other ways. In common with most photographers, Mayall had by then abandoned daguerreotypy for the wet collodion negative process freely introduced by Frederick Scott Archer. He recognized the professional photographic community's debt to Archer and led the efforts to secure Archer, and then his widow, financial independence; Mayall was the largest single contributor to the Archer Testimonial Fund.

Although he continued his London studio, Mayall had become increasingly interested in Brighton, and in 1863 set up on its busy seafront another studio, which he operated personally. His sense of innovation remained active, and he was one of the first to specialize in enlarging, making spectacular life-size prints (a fine portrait of George Peabody is still preserved in the Peabody Institute in Baltimore). In 1869 Mayall became the first person to travel from London to Brighton on a velocipede. In 1881 his London studio began using electric light to illuminate its portraits.

On 23 June 1834, while still in Yorkshire, Mayall had married Eliza Parkin (1816–1870); they had three sons and a daughter. The oldest son, Edwin, took over the London studio when his parents moved to Brighton. Another son, John, became increasingly important in the Brighton studio after 1865. The 1870s marked many changes for Mayall, in addition to gradually ceding control of his studios to his children. On 14 December 1871—a year after the death of his first wife—he married a widow, Celia Victoria Hooper (*bap.* 1839), daughter of William Gardener, a surgeon, and with her had two more daughters and another son. In 1871 Mayall was made a fellow of the Chemical Society and in 1872 gave a paper before the annual meeting of the British Association for the Advancement of Science. 1871 also marked the start of his political career, when he was elected a councillor for Brighton. In 1875 he became an alderman and in 1877–8 he was mayor.

In total, Mayall and his sons operated ten studios in London (the last closed in 1941), four in Brighton (until 1908), one in Kingston upon Thames, and three in Melbourne, Australia. To the confusion over his nationality was added that over the use of his name: it is often difficult, if not impossible, to determine in particular cases if John Edwin Mayall was actually the photographer or just the famous figure behind the studio name. The name of Mayall did not die with him at The Bures, Southwick, near Brighton, on 6 March 1901. LARRY J. SCHAAF

Sources L. L. Richards and A. T. Gill, 'The Mayall story', *History of Photography*, 9 (1985), 89–107 · L. J. Schaaf, 'Mayall's life-size portrait of George Peabody', *History of Photography*, 9 (1985), 279–88 · m. cert. · d. cert. · census returns, 1841
Archives George Eastman House, Rochester, New York, MSS and photographs

Mayart, Sir Samuel (*b.* **1587**, *d.* in or after **1646**), judge, was the son of Gilbert Mayart of Ipswich (*d.* in or before 1607) and was of Flemish extraction. He matriculated from Merton College, Oxford, on 18 May 1604 and entered the Middle Temple on 16 February 1607, being called to the bar on 8 July 1614. He was admitted to King's Inns, Dublin, in 1616. In 1624 he was reported to have offered £300 to secure the place of second justice of the common pleas in Ireland. Chief Baron Sir Richard Bolton, and his son Sir Edward, solicitor-general, 'strongly' recommended the appointment of this 'man of learning and honesty', despite the fact that 'aspersions are being cast upon him' (*CSP Ire., 1625–33*, 18). Mayart received a patent for the office on 19 January 1626. He was knighted on 5 November 1631 and lived at Oxmantown, Dublin. He was named treasurer of King's Inns in 1633.

In April 1644 the Irish parliament took notice of an anonymous treatise 'A declaration how and by what means the laws and statutes of England … came to be of force in Ireland', sometimes attributed to Sir Richard Bolton. Mayart was involved in the discussion of the document and appears to have drawn up a manuscript response, approximately five times the length of the original text. Drawing heavily upon legal records stretching back over several centuries he sought to reject the notion that English made law was only valid in Ireland upon re-enactment by the Irish parliament. He was confident that 'in divers respects *Ireland* is a separate and distinct kingdom, … yet the Dominion and Government thereof is not separate from *England*' (Harris, 2.127) but rather that Ireland was under the jurisdiction of the English parliament. Though his case was based firmly upon precedent he admitted that he believed the recent rising had shown the 'inconveniency, mischief and prejudice' (Harris, 1.73) that would result if curbs were not placed upon Irish autonomy. It is unclear what response the document generated, though its arguments were addressed by Sir William Domville in 1660. The manuscript was published in *Hibernica*, a collection of sources on Irish history edited by Walter Harris under the title 'Serjeant Mayart's Answer to a Book Intitled, A Declaration'. The manuscript was presented to Trinity College, Dublin.

Despite the fact that Mayart's stance on the powers of the Irish parliament was out of step with the Dublin royalist political establishment he was among the legal figures consulted by Ormond during the lord lieutenant's negotiations with the confederate Catholics in 1645. He continued to fulfil his functions in the Irish parliament, being recorded there as late as February 1646. Little is known of his family—he is sometimes reported as having married thrice, although the name of his first wife is unknown; his second wife, Mary Smith (*d.* in or before 1631?), was twice a widow already. In 1631, and again in 1638, his wife's name is given as Dorcas (*d.* 1644?), on the latter occasion the name also given to their daughter, baptized on 9 January 1638. He had at least one other daughter, Letice (*d.* 1641), and a son, Roger (*d.* 1668). He is last heard of in 1646 and his date of death is unknown. R. M. ARMSTRONG

Sources F. E. Ball, *The judges in Ireland, 1221–1921*, 2 vols. (1926) · W. Harris, ed., *Hibernica*, 2 vols. (1747–50) · *History of the Irish confederation and the war in Ireland … by Richard Bellings*, ed. J. T. Gilbert, 7 vols. (1882–91) · *CSP Ire., 1615–47* · *Journal of the House of Lords … Ireland*, 8 vols. (1779–1800) · *Report on the manuscripts of the earl of Egmont*, 2 vols. in 3, HMC, 63 (1905–9) · H. F. Berry, ed., *Registers of the church of St Michan, Dublin, 1636 to 1685* (1907) · J. Mills, ed., *The registers of St John the Evangelist, Dublin, 1619 to 1699* (1906) · C. Kenny, *King's Inns and the kingdom of Ireland* (1992) · Foster, *Alum. Oxon.* · H. A. C. Sturgess, ed., *Register of admissions to the Honourable Society of the Middle Temple, from the fifteenth century to the year 1944*, 1 (1949) · R. Lascelles, ed., *Liber munerum publicorum Hiberniae …* or, *The establishments of Ireland*, later edn, 2 vols. in 7 pts (1852) · W. A. Shaw, *The knights of England*, 2 vols. (1906) · A. Clarke, 'Patrick Darcy and the constitutional relationship between Ireland and Britain', *Political thought in seventeenth-century Ireland*, ed. J. H. Ohlmeyer (2000), 35–55

Maybee, Robert (**1810–1891**), poet, was born on 1 April 1810 in his parents' cottage, Windmill Cottage, near the windmill on Peninnis Head, St Mary's, in the Isles of Scilly, the fifth of ten children of William Maybee, who moved to Scilly from the Isle of Wight to take up employment as a mill worker, probably in 1798, and his wife, Florence, *née* Mumford, a local girl whom he had married on 26 December 1798. The windmill closed in 1826 and William Maybee died in 1834, but Florence continued to live in the cottage together with some of her children, including Robert. During this time she compiled a list of their dates of birth and of the dates of death for four of her children who had predeceased her, and from this it appears that she may have had some ability in reading and writing; if so, she failed to pass on this accomplishment to her son Robert, who remained illiterate. Florence Maybee died in 1852, and after forty-two years' residence Robert was obliged to move out of the cottage into lodgings in Hugh Town. It was about this period that he began to compose his verses.

For all his life Maybee was poor and scraped a living from various jobs. For much of the time he was a hawker, making trips on the packet boat to Penzance to take back fruit to sell in Scilly. A verse from one of his early compositions reads:

It was many a long summer day
I hawked them round the town

And had to work till ten at night
To earn one half a crown.
(Baxter, 37)

The income he received from such trading he supplemented by reciting or singing his verses to customers. He relied on memory, but later sold his verses in printed form or at least exchanged them for a meal. He depended upon finding people to write down his words for him, one of whom was the kindly Dr Moyle, and this opens the possibility that his amanuenses may have assisted in matters such as syntax and punctuation.

In the winter months between about 1855 and 1860 Maybee worked on a farm on St Agnes; in the summer months he helped in the construction of the Bishop Rock lighthouse. In 1883, while working on Tresco, he composed an account of his life, which gave a picture of many happenings in Scilly in his lifetime and is also the main source of biographical information about him. His account was always graphic, as for instance when he described kelp-making, an important early nineteenth-century industry in Scilly, and he was always interesting, even if some of his historical detail is now discounted. He entitled the account *Sixty-Eight Years Experience on the Scilly Islands*, and in it he claimed to have composed about sixty poems, but only about nineteen were written down and are still available, the earliest being from 1871. He certainly composed some before this, because he appeared before the local magistrates in 1857 charged with selling his ballads about the streets without a licence.

Maybee's writings reveal his native charm but his verses seem childlike, and in this there may be a parallel with Alfred Wallis, the St Ives painter 'discovered' by Ben Nicholson in 1928. Both started their work late in life, untutored and lacking learning and sophistication. Wallis is termed a 'primitive' painter, and Maybee could be called a 'primitive' poet. Not for him flights of fancy or erudite allusions; instead, his verses were simple and unmannered, telling a tale (often of shipwreck) in words short, familiar, and commonplace. Some Scillonian children learned them by heart and could recite them at will. Even at the end of the twentieth century, when in the company of older Scillonians one had only to utter the first line:

Dark on the Gilstone's rocky shore

for others to complete the verse thus:

The mist came lowering down
And night with all her deepening gloom
Put on her sable crown.
(Baxter, 24)

A description of Maybee at the age of about seventy-five referred to him as 'a pathetic little man with a kind face, yellowish curls, and red-rimmed eyes' (Baxter, introduction). He spent his last five years in the local poorhouse, dying there, unmarried, in 1891. Today Maybee is remembered not only in the Scillies but also in the USA, where the Maybee Society is devoted to researching the whole Maybee family.   R. L. BOWLEY

Sources R. Maybee, *Sixty-eight years experience on the Scilly Islands* (1883) • R. M. Baxter, *Robert Maybee: the Scillonian poet*, Isles of Scilly Museum, 9 (1973) • S. Ottery, 'Robert Maybee – Scillonian poet', *Cornwall Today*, 10 (May 1995)

Maybray-King. For this title name *see* King, Horace Maybray, Baron Maybray-King (1901–1986).

Maybrick [*née* Chandler]**, Florence Elizabeth** (1862–1941), convicted poisoner, was born on 2 September 1862 at Mobile, Alabama, USA, the only daughter of William G. Chandler, banker, and his wife, Caroline, daughter of Darius Blake Holbrook. At the age of eighteen in 1881 she married an English cotton broker, James Maybrick, then aged forty-two, who maintained a mistress and offspring throughout their marriage. They lived in Virginia until 1884, when they moved to England and settled at Liverpool, from 1888 living at Battlecrease House, Aigburth. A son and daughter were born of the marriage.

James Maybrick had for many years procured arsenic without medical prescription for self-administration in greatly increasing measures. Supposedly he believed that arsenic acted as an aphrodisiac; conceivably he used it to suppress symptoms of an earlier venereal infection. Certainly he became addicted. He also habitually dosed himself with other poisons. Florence Maybrick found his sexual demands increasingly repellent, and the marriage became unhappy. She was deterred from seeking a divorce by the threat of losing her children. On 22–4 March 1889 she stayed in a London hotel with Alfred Brierley, a Liverpool cotton merchant. After quarrelling over Brierley (29 March) Maybrick gave her a black eye, but achieved a reconciliation by undertaking to pay her debts.

In April, Florence Maybrick bought fly-papers containing arsenic and steeped them in water for the purpose (she stated) of extracting the poison for cosmetic use. Maybrick was taken ill on 27 April after self-administering a double dose of strychnine. His physicians treated him for acute dyspepsia, but his condition deteriorated. On 8 May Florence Maybrick wrote a compromising letter to Brierley, which was intercepted by James Maybrick's brother, Michael, who was staying at Battlecrease. By his orders she was forthwith deposed as mistress of her house and watched vigilantly. On 9 May a nurse reported that Mrs Maybrick had surreptitiously tampered with a meat-juice bottle which was afterwards found to contain a half-grain of arsenic. Mrs Maybrick later testified that her husband had begged her to administer it as a pick-me-up; he never drank its contents. On 11 May James Maybrick died. A post-mortem revealed some arsenic in his liver, intestines, and kidney, though none in his heart or blood, as would be expected if arsenic had been administered in lethal quantities.

Once publicly branded as guilty of adultery, Florence Maybrick was treated as a murderer. She was arrested on suspicion (14 May), the inquest jury returned a verdict of wilful murder against her (27 May), and her trial opened at Liverpool crown court on 31 July. Her counsel, Sir Charles Russell, emphasized the contradictory medical evidence and the prosecution's failure to fix a certain cause of death; he contended that Maybrick did not die of arsenic

Florence Elizabeth Maybrick (1862–1941), by unknown photographer, c.1889

administered with murderous intent but of gastroenteritis caused by chemical irritation. This seems highly plausible, given that Maybrick had undermined his digestion by arsenic taking, and during his final illness was administered strychnine, arsenic, jaborandi, cascara, henbane, morphia, prussic acid, papaine, iridin, and other medicines by his physicians. There were many unsatisfactory features in both the evidence and conduct of the trial; the prejudicial, muddled remarks of the judge, Sir James Fitz-James Stephen, were justly censured. On 7 August Florence Maybrick was convicted and sentenced to death. After public outcry Henry Matthews, the home secretary, and Lord Chancellor Halsbury concluded 'that the evidence clearly establishes that Mrs Maybrick administered poison to her husband with intent to murder; but that there is ground for reasonable doubt whether the arsenic so administered was in fact the cause of his death' (*Letters of Queen Victoria*, ed. A. C. Benson and Lord Esher, and G. E. Buckle, 3rd ser., 1930–32, 1.527). The death sentence was therefore commuted to life imprisonment as punishment for a crime with which she was never charged. During the 1890s new evidence was publicized by her supporters, but there was no possibility of judicial appeal, and the Home Office was not clement.

After detention in Woking and Aylesbury prisons Florence Maybrick was released in 1904 and went to the United States, where she compiled her memoirs. About 1915 she settled as Mrs Chandler at South Kent, Connecticut, initially in comfortable circumstances but latterly dependent on her neighbours' generosity. She seemed a cultivated, self-contained woman who was devoted to local schoolboys. She was found dead at her home in South Kent on 23 October 1941 and was buried in the grounds of South Kent School. Thomas Hardy was influenced by Florence Maybrick's predicament when writing *Tess of the D'Urbervilles*.　　　RICHARD DAVENPORT-HINES

Sources *Mrs Maybrick's own story: my fifteen lost years* (1909) · J. H. Levy, ed., *The necessity for criminal appeal as illustrated by the Maybrick case* (1899) · H. B. Irving, *Trial of Mrs Maybrick* (1912) · M. Hartman, *Victorian murderesses* (1977) · V. Morris, *Double jeopardy: women who kill in Victorian fiction* (1990) · A. W. MacDougall, *The Maybrick case* (1891) · H. Densmore, *The Maybrick case: English criminal law* [1892] · C. Boswell and L. Thompson, *The girl with the scarlet brand* (1955) · L. E. X., *The Maybrick and Madeline Smith cases contrasted* (1889) · *The Times* (25 Oct 1941) · *The letters of Queen Victoria*, ed. G. E. Buckle, 3 vols., 3rd ser. (1930–32), vol. 1, p. 527 · Fifteenth earl of Derby, diary, Lpool RO, 8 Aug 1889, 10 Aug 1889, 21 Aug 1889, 23 Aug 1889, fols. 20, 223, 234–4, 244
Likenesses engraving, 1889 (after ink sketch, in possession of Culver Pictures), repro. in Morris, *Double jeopardy*, 49 · photograph, c.1889, Hult. Arch. [*see illus.*] · portraits, probably Mary Evans Picture Library, London
Wealth at death poverty: *The Times*

Maybrick, Michael [*pseud.* Stephen Adams] (1841–1913), singer and composer, was born on 31 January 1841 (not 1844, as is often stated) at 8 Church Alley, Liverpool, the fourth of the seven sons of William Maybrick (1815–1853?), an engraver, and his wife, Susannah (1815?–1883?). His grandfather and father served as parish clerk at St Peter's, Liverpool, and were minor composers; his uncle Michael (1799–1846) was organist at St Peter's, wrote sacred music, and conducted the Liverpool Choral Society. Proficient on the piano by the age of eight, the young Michael studied the organ with W. T. Best and at the age of fifteen became organist of St Peter's; he also wrote anthems and had a work performed in London. In 1865 he went to Leipzig to study keyboard and harmony with Carl Reinecke, Ignaz Moscheles, and Louis Plaidy, but later decided to perfect his fine baritone voice under Gaetano Nava in Milan. After gaining experience in Italian theatres, he was acclaimed in London on 25 February 1869 in Mendelssohn's *Elijah*. Success as Telramund in Wagner's *Lohengrin* led to appearances with Charlotte Sainton-Dolby, including her farewell concert on 6 June 1870, and to regular engagements at the English festivals and with Carl Rosa's opera company.

By the early 1870s Maybrick was already presenting his own songs, beginning with 'A Warrior Bold'. Published under the pseudonym Stephen Adams and mostly with lyrics by Fred Weatherly, these achieved extraordinary popularity: the early sea song 'Nancy Lee' sold more than 100,000 copies in two years. The composer's versatile output included other sea songs like 'The Tar's Farewell', 'They All Love Jack', and 'The Midshipmite', sentimental pieces like 'Your Dear Brown Eyes', romances like 'The Children of the City', and sacred songs like 'The Blue Alsatian Mountains', 'The Star of Bethlehem', and the well-loved 'Holy City'. He also celebrated national occasions, as in 'The Veteran's Song' for the coronation of Edward VII. He performed his ballads at St James's Hall matinée concerts, and in 1884 toured North America with them. Though later disparaged, they are direct and sincere and audiences found them ennobling. With his resonant voice and winning smile, the tall, distinguished-looking Maybrick had great presence on the stage. His character was more complex: friends spoke of his charming personality, but detractors thought him arrogant and vain.

Although Maybrick never ceased to compose, and became vice-president of Trinity College, London, he abandoned public singing after the conviction of Florence *Maybrick for the murder of her husband, James, his brother, in 1889; he wished her life to be spared (as it was), but had largely helped to instigate this controversial case. On 9 March 1893 he married his forty-year-old housekeeper, Laura Withers, and settled with her at Ryde, where he had purchased Lynthorpe; they were joined there by James's orphaned children. In a new civic career, Maybrick became chairman of the Isle of Wight Hospital, justice of the peace, and five times mayor of Ryde. He also played cricket, yachted, cycled, and was an active freemason. While convalescing at St Ann's Hotel, Buxton, from periodic gout, he died of heart failure on 26 August 1913, and was buried four days afterwards at All Saints', Ryde, survived by his wife.   PATRICK WADDINGTON

Sources A. T. C. Pratt, ed., *People of the period: being a collection of the biographies of upwards of six thousand living celebrities*, 2 vols. (1897) · Brown & Stratton, *Brit. mus.* · *The Times* (27 Aug 1913) · *Isle of Wight County Press* (30 Aug 1913) · F. H. Cowen, *My art and my friends* (1913) · H. Simpson, *A century of ballads, 1810–1910* (1910) · T. L. Christie, *Etched in arsenic: a new study of the Maybrick case* (1969) · S. Harrison, *The diary of Jack the Ripper* (1993) · D. Baptie, *A handbook of musical biography*, 2nd edn (1887) · L. Baillie and R. Balchin, eds., *The catalogue of printed music in the British Library to 1980*, 62 vols. (1981–7) · concert announcements, *The Times* (1869) · concert announcements, *The Times* (1870) · concert announcements, *The Times* (1884) · W. Ganz, *Memories of a musician* (1913) · M. S. Mackinlay, *Antoinette Sterling and other celebrities* (1906) · W. H. Jacobs, *Hampshire at the opening of the twentieth century* (1905) · *Who's who in the Isle of Wight* (1913) · *WWW* · M. R. Turner and A. Miall, eds., *The parlour song book: a casquet of vocal gems* (1972) · H. S. Wyndham and G. l'Epine, eds., *Who's who in music* (1913) · B. Ryan and M. Havers, *The poisoned life of Mrs Maybrick* (1977) · m. cert.

Likenesses photograph, repro. in Simpson, *Century of ballads* · photograph, repro. in Jacobs, *Hampshire at the opening of the twentieth century* · sketch, repro. in Harrison, *Diary of Jack the Ripper*, following p. 174

Wealth at death £23,012 2s. 7d.: probate, 13 Oct 1913, *CGPLA Eng. & Wales*

Maybury, Sir Henry Percy (1864–1943), civil engineer, the fourth son of Charles Maybury, agriculturist, and his wife, Jane Matthews, was born on 17 November 1864 at Uffington, near Shrewsbury. He passed from Upton Magna School, in Shropshire, into the office of Robert E. Johnston, chief engineer of the Great Western and London and North Western joint railways at Shrewsbury Station. In 1884 he was employed by the firm of Johnson Bros. and Slay, contractors, of Wrexham, where he later became manager. After having been successively engineer and surveyor to the Ffestiniog local board (1892) and the Malvern urban district council (1895), he was appointed county engineer and surveyor of Kent in 1904, where he gained his reputation as a pioneer in the application of tar mixtures to reduce dust on macadamized roads.

In 1910 Maybury joined the road board. He became chief engineer in 1913 and eventually manager and secretary. From the outbreak of war in 1914 he was responsible for the road work undertaken for the war department and in 1917 he was sent to France as director of roads, with the rank of brigadier-general. In 1919 he was appointed director-general of roads under the Ministry of Transport. He retired in 1928 but held the position of consulting engineer and adviser to the minister on road traffic problems until 1932. Concurrently with these posts, he also

acted as chairman of the London and home counties traffic advisory committee from 1924 to 1933, the year in which he was appointed a member of the newly formed London Passenger Transport Board. He was also chairman of several departmental committees dealing with the economics and regulation of road vehicles and the development of civil aviation in the United Kingdom.

Maybury's influence on the development of the bus and coach industry in Great Britain was substantial. Although he came to the Ministry of Transport as a road engineer, a conviction that road transport should be subsidiary to rail (whether railway or tramway) lay at the heart of his policy recommendations. Under his chairmanship, a departmental committee on the licensing and regulation of public service vehicles produced in 1925 a draft bill which became the ministry's principal exhibit before the royal commission on transport (sitting from 1928 to 1930) and which was adopted in large part in the licensing provisions of the Road Traffic Act of 1930. The three reports of the London and home counties traffic advisory committee bear the imprint of his thought. When he appeared before the joint select committee of both houses, which considered the London Transport Bill in 1931, he strongly supported the proposed London Passenger Transport Board, and regarded any private bus operator who wished to continue to trade as 'irresponsible'—a position which was founded in his defence of cross-subsidization. Maybury's contribution to the work of the royal commission and the joint select committee set the industry in a protectionist regulatory framework, with consequences which were still to be discerned a quarter of a century later.

Honours came freely to a man of such constant activity. Maybury's services in the war were rewarded by five mentions in dispatches; he was made a CB in 1917, a CMG and a KCMG in 1919, and member of the Légion d'honneur in 1917. On his retirement he was appointed a GBE (1928). In the professional world he was no less honoured. He was president of the Institution of Civil Engineers (1933–4), of the Institute of Transport (1921–2), and of the Institute of Quarrying (1919). At the time of his death he was president of the Society of Engineers and of the Smeatonian Society; the borough of Shrewsbury in 1928 elected as honorary freeman one who might almost be called one of its sons. At the University of London, the Paviors' Company (to which he had been elected in 1918) founded in 1928 a chair of highway engineering which was named after him.

Maybury was twice married: first, in 1885, to Elizabeth (d. 1929), daughter of Thomas Sheldon of Ludlow, with whom he had two sons and two daughters; second, in 1942, to Katharine Mary, daughter of Samuel William Pring, company director, of Winchester and Newport, Isle of Wight. After his retirement from public service he entered the commercial world and held a number of directorships until he died, of cerebral haemorrhage and asthma, at his home, Four Winds, Mousecroft Lane, Shrewsbury, on 7 January 1943.

Maybury is remembered for his work in remodelling the roads and the traffic system of Great Britain, and for his road work in France during the First World War. Apart from his professional skill, he possessed qualities which secured for him the confidence of successive ministers of transport, and the wholehearted support, loyalty, and devotion, not only of his staff, but of highway engineers throughout the country. His skill in negotiation enabled him to perform invaluable service for the government between the two wars in promoting vast road schemes for the relief of unemployment. His vitality was remarkable and he was indefatigable.

J. S. KILLICK, *rev.* JOHN HIBBS

Sources 'Second report: the licensing and regulation of public service vehicles', *Parl. papers* (1929–30), 17.895, Cmd 3416 [royal commission on transport] · *Annual Report of the London and Home Counties Traffic Advisory Committee*, 1 (1925); 2 (1926); 3 (1927) · 'Report from the joint select committee', *Parl. papers* (1930–31), 8.171, no. 142 [London Passenger Transport Bill] · *The Times* (9 Jan 1943) · *Journal of the Institution of Civil Engineers*, 20 (1942–3), 66–7 · *Engineering* (15 Jan 1943) · *Highways and Bridges* (13 Jan 1943) · *Highways and Bridges* (27 Jan 1943) · R. Jeffreys, *The king's highway: an historical and autobiographical record of the development of the past sixty years* (1949) · personal knowledge (1959) · *CGPLA Eng. & Wales* (1943) · d. cert.
Archives NRA, papers and press cuttings | NA Scot., Kerr MSS
Likenesses W. Stoneman, photograph, 1919, NPG · O. Birley, oils, Inst. CE
Wealth at death £72,372 10s. 7d.: probate, 6 May 1943, *CGPLA Eng. & Wales*

Mayer, John (*bap.* 1583, *d.* 1664), biblical commentator, was baptized on 16 June 1583 at Long Melford, Suffolk, the son of John and Elizabeth Mayer. He had two brothers and five sisters, all younger than himself. He matriculated from St John's College, Cambridge, about 1597, but migrated to Emmanuel College, where he matriculated on 2 March 1598. He graduated BA in 1602, and proceeded MA in 1605, BD in 1612, and DD in 1627. He was rector of Little Wratting in Suffolk from 1609 until 1631, when he became rector of Raydon, near Hadleigh. About 1613 he married Anne, with whom he was to enjoy a partnership lasting fifty years. They had one surviving son, John.

Mayer produced over the course of a number of years an entire commentary on the Bible, drawing extensively on the work of other commentators and adding notes of his own. The publication of the work was delayed by what Mayer described as 'the Hierarchicall Government that then was' (J. Mayer, 'Dedicatorie', *A Commentary upon the Whole Old Testament*, 1653). It was published in seven volumes: 1, on the Pentateuch, 1653; 2, on the historical books, 1647; 3, on Job, the Psalms, Proverbs, Ecclesiastes, and the Song of Solomon, 1653 and again in 1659; 4, on the prophets, 1652; 5, on the gospels and Acts, 1631; 6, on the epistles of St Paul, 1631; 7, on the so-called catholic epistles and Revelation, in 1627 and 1631. Mayer believed in the saying *Bonus textuarius, bonus theologus* and produced the commentaries so that 'Students in Divinity may sooner become good Textmen, to give light into any place of Scripture' (ibid.).

Mayer's works are scholarly in tone and content, but aimed at an intelligent rather than necessarily educated audience. He wrote for those who 'not being professed Divines, yet, are studious of the Scriptures' (J. Mayer, 'To the reader', *A Commentarie upon the Foure Evangelists and the Acts of the Apostles*, 1631). Mayer flouted the convention of publishing works of this nature in Latin to restrict their audience to those with the education considered a prerequisite to comprehend such matters. He declared it desirable that the people become as well versed in the fathers and learned doctors of the church as the clergy.

Mayer was a determined opponent of both popery and forms of protestant extremism. His most popular publication was *An Antidote Against Popery*, which appeared in 1625 and was republished in 1627 and 1630. In 1647 he published *Christian Liberty Vindicated from Grave Mistakes, Occasioning so Great Divisions in England*. He denounced licentious behaviour conducted under the cloak of religion, declaring that Christian liberty was 'not a liberty to any evill or sinne, because this is no liberty, but servitude to corruption' (J. Mayer, *Christian Liberty*, 1647, 4). He also rejected the suggestion that the believer's best guide to the truth was his own conscience, affirming that a lawful assembly was the surest means of resolving contentious issues.

At the Restoration, Mayer published a work dedicated to Charles II: *Unity Restored to the Church of England*. There he was bold enough to suggest to the new king the manner in which he should settle religious division in the country. He also took the opportunity to advertise another work, 'The history of the world from the creation to the year 1648', never published. His memorial stone in Raydon records that he also left in manuscript 'The topography of the three parts of the world, and the countries and most famous cities therein'.

Mayer died at Raydon on 5 March 1664 and was buried there three days later. He left most of his estate to his wife and son, but also made provision for the extended members of his family and for the poorest families of Raydon. He left detailed instructions for a black marble memorial stone, with an inscription celebrating his ministry and his writings.

NICHOLAS KEENE

Sources C. H. Spurgeon, *Commenting and commentaries: two lectures addressed to the students of the Pastors' College, Metropolitan Tabernacle, together with a catalogue of Biblical commentaries and expositions* (1876) · J. Darling, *Cyclopaedia bibliographica: a library manual of theological and general literature*, 2 vols. (1854–9) · BL, Add. MS 19165, fol. 382 · *DNB* · will, 1663, Norfolk RO, Norwich consistory court · Venn, *Alum. Cant.* · parish register, Long Melford, 16 June 1583, Suffolk RO, 16 June 1583 [baptism]

Mayer, Joseph (1803–1886), collector of antiquities and works of art, was born on 23 February 1803 at Thistlebury House, Newcastle under Lyme, Staffordshire, fourth son and the sixth of eleven children of Samuel Mayer (1767–1838), tanner, currier, and mayor of Newcastle under Lyme, and his wife, Margaret (1773–1859), daughter of John Pepper, architect.

Having attended Newcastle under Lyme grammar school, Mayer moved to Liverpool in October 1821 at the age of eighteen. He commenced an informal apprenticeship as a silversmith under his brother-in-law, James Wordley (*fl.* 1817–1861), entering into partnership with him in 1834, and setting up on his own as a jeweller and

Joseph Mayer (1803–1886), by William Daniels, 1843

goldsmith in 1844. He demonstrated a remarkable flair for business and the financial success he achieved enabled him to indulge a passion for archaeology and collecting which he had had since childhood. This had first manifested itself when he was eight when he acquired a small hoard of Roman coins and pottery sherds whose unearthing he had witnessed—a minuscule foreshadowing of the scale and comprehensiveness of the collections he later amassed, displayed to the public, and finally bestowed on the city of Liverpool.

Born into a radical and nonconformist family, Mayer was a natural patriot, and realized the value of cultivating learning and the arts among all classes in Britain. From his twenty-fifth year he contributed readily to loan exhibitions and made gifts to mechanics' institutes. He was an exhibitor at the Great Exhibition of 1851 and at the 1857 Manchester Art Treasures Exhibition. He was sustained in his endeavours by the support of a wide circle of friends, distinguished by their contributions to archaeology, to historical studies, and as influential moulders of opinion in the decorative arts. The development of his collection was greatly furthered by a close collaboration, in particular, with Charles Roach Smith and Augustus Wollaton Franks. Mayer's acquisition, in 1854, of the collection of Kentish antiquities excavated by the Revd Bryan Fausset was an outstanding event in the history of British archaeology, and his purchase in 1855 of the Byzantine and medieval ivories of Baron Gábor Fejérváry was an equally invaluable contribution to art collecting in Britain.

Mayer regarded his collections as a public resource which he willingly made available to those able to employ them to positive ends, and also funded several scholarly publications and sponsored archaeological excavations.

His own contributions to literature were more modest, constituting a series of articles in the *Transactions* of the Historic Society of Lancashire and Cheshire, of which he was one of the three founding members, on 20 March 1848. In 1855 he contributed a paper, 'History of the art of pottery in Liverpool' (revised edn, 1873), which remains fundamental to the study of the subject. Mayer was one of the earliest systematic collectors of ceramics, with important holdings of Liverpool porcelain and pottery, and a notable collection of Wedgwood wares. His most striking achievement in this connection was his discovery and acquisition of the vast hoard of documents of Josiah Wedgwood, the foundation deposit of the Wedgwood archive collection now at the University of Keele. Mayer generously put these papers at the disposal of Eliza Meteyard and advised, and assisted financially, in the completion of her *Life of Josiah Wedgwood* (1865). Mayer's collection was first made accessible to the general public in May 1852, when he opened an Egyptian Museum (later the Museum of National and Foreign Antiquities) in Colquitt Street, Liverpool. In 1867 he presented the collection, then valued at £75,000, to the Liverpool Free Library and Museum. In recognition of the munificence of his gift and other services to the town, the corporation of Liverpool commissioned the life-size statue of Mayer by Giovanni Fontana in St George's Hall, Liverpool. As with other surviving portraits, it reveals him to have been throughout his life a person of distinguished appearance, with an authoritative but sympathetic bearing. The Mayer collection continues as a significant constituent of the collections of the National Museums and Galleries on Merseyside.

The honour which Mayer most valued, however, was the fellowship of the Society of Antiquaries of London, awarded in 1850. In 1860 he was appointed captain of the Liverpool volunteer borough guard, and in 1864 captain of the 4th Bebington company of the 1st Cheshire rifle volunteers, a unit he had raised at his own expense. He had moved in 1860 to Pennant House, Bebington, Cheshire, where he continued his benefactions, endowing the borough with a well-stocked lending library, public gardens, and a lecture hall and picture gallery. Retiring from business in 1873, he applied himself, inconclusively, to writing a history of art in England, amassing more than 20,000 drawings, prints, and autograph letters, as well as continuing to collect works of art and antiquities. This collection, with an estimated value of £10,000, was dispersed by auction in Liverpool on 15–16 December 1887. He also collaborated with his nephew Frederick Boyle in the publication of two works which remain of permanent value in the study of the life and work of George Stubbs (1724–1806): *Early Exhibitions of Art in Liverpool with some Notes for a Memoir of George Stubbs RA* (1876), and *Memoirs of Thomas Dodd, William Upcott, and George Stubbs RA* (1879). In his retirement he pursued an interest in gardening, having in 1870 successfully cultivated in the open air the giant Victoria Regia water lily. He died unmarried at Pennant House on 19 January 1886, aged eighty-two, and was interred on 23 January 1886, at St Andrew's Church, Bebington.

Mayer's benevolence and commitment to public enlightenment ensure his position as an important civic figure of the nineteenth century.

C. W. SUTTON, *rev.* LIONEL BURMAN

Sources M. Gibson and S. M. Wright, eds., *Joseph Mayer of Liverpool, 1803–1886* (1988) · S. Nicholson and M. Warhurst, *Joseph Mayer, 1803–1886* (1983) · L. Burman, 'Joseph Mayer and the progress of "The art of pottery"', *Riches into art: Liverpool collectors, 1770–1880, essays in honour of Margaret T. Gibson*, ed. P. Starkey (1993), 27–44 · S. M. Nicholson, *Catalogue of prehistoric metalwork in Merseyside County Museums* (1980) · *Inventorium sepulchrale*, ed. C. R. Smith (1856) · E. Meteyard, *A group of Englishmen* (1871), ix–xiii · C. T. Gatty, *The Mayer collection in the Liverpool Museum, considered as an educational possession* (1878) · J. Mayer, 'Address to the members of the Historic Society of Lancashire and Cheshire', *Transactions of the Historic Society of Lancashire and Cheshire*, new ser., 7 (1866–7), 1–12; new ser., 9 (1868–9), 1–18 · J. Culme, *The directory of gold and silversmiths, jewellers and allied traders, 1838–1914*, 1 (1987), 320, 498 [list of Mayer's exhibits in the 1851 Exhibition] · *Liverpool Daily Post* (20 Jan 1886) · *Liverpool Mercury* (20 Jan 1886) · *Birkenhead News and Advertiser* (25 Jan 1886) · Lpool RO, Mayer papers · Mayer MSS, Liverpool Central Library, 920MAY · Mayer collection, National Museums and Galleries on Merseyside, Liverpool Museum, departments of antiquities and decorative art

Archives Bebington Central Reference Library, Wirral, Cheshire · BL, corresp. relating to his papyri, Add. MS 34098 · BL, Add. MS 33963, fols. 76–83 · JRL, verses and papers · Liverpool Museum, collection · Lpool RO, MSS and autograph collection relating to Liverpool art; collection relating to the history of Liverpool | Keele University, A. W. Franks MSS · Keele University, Wedgwood archive · NL Wales, Gibson MSS · Swiss Cottage Library, London, Meteyard MSS · U. Lpool, corresp. relating to Sprott's Chronicle

Likenesses W. Daniels, oils, 1843, Walker Art Gallery, Liverpool [*see illus.*] · G. Freizor, engraving, 1851, Bebington public library, Wirral · G. Fontana, marble relief medallion, 1856, Walker Art Gallery, Liverpool · J. Harris, oils, 1856, Williamson Museum and Art Gallery, Birkenhead · G. Fontana, marble bust, 1868, Walker Art Gallery, Liverpool · G. Fontana, marble statue, 1869, St George's Hall, Liverpool · engraving, repro. in Smith, ed., *Inventorium sepulchrale*

Wealth at death £9762 15*s.*: probate, 1 March 1886, *CGPLA Eng. & Wales*

Mayer, Matthew (1740–1814), Methodist preacher and promoter of the Sunday school movement, was born on 4 November 1740 at Portwood Hall estate, near Stockport, Cheshire, the son of John Mayer, yeoman farmer (*d.* 1775), and his wife, Hannah. Educated at a good country school, Matthew had a strictly moral Anglican upbringing. In 1759, affected by illness and the death of an uncle, he became seriously religious, heard John Wesley preach, and joined the Methodists. After three years' struggle he was converted on 1 August 1762 while taking communion. He participated in newly created public prayer meetings around Manchester and began preaching, one of his converts being John Whitehead, a future biographer of Wesley.

In June 1763 Wesley took Mayer to Birmingham and left him in charge of the Methodist circuit for a week, which resulted in conversions and confirmed his call to preach. He resolved not to be an itinerant or local preacher but to

accept calls to evangelize new places. For twenty years he preached far afield at weekends and pioneered many causes in Cheshire, Staffordshire, Derbyshire, south Lancashire, and west Yorkshire. He faced mob violence and had 'providential' experiences of facing down mob leaders and 'judgements' on opponents. Though some envied his freelance preaching and popularity, he acquired close friendships with Wesley and leading preachers including Thomas Rankin and Joseph Benson. On 1 August 1771 he married Sarah Flower (1748–1825), a devout Methodist and only daughter of Joseph Flower (*d.* 1785), a Bristol potter. They had at least four children, of whom two survived him. In 1783 he moved to Cale Green near Stockport and thereafter preached mainly in the Stockport area, monthly in Manchester, and occasionally further afield.

Mayer was a leading founder and manager of Stockport Sunday school, later the country's largest institution of this type, which moved into its own premises in 1805. His son Joseph (1773–1857), a pioneer cotton manufacturer in Stockport, was a major force in the school and a public defender of its work and policy. Though originating on Methodist premises the school was undenominational, and taught writing and arithmetic as well as reading. In 1808 Matthew led a formal protest against the Methodist conference's attempt to restrict Sunday schools under Methodist control to reading only. The school became a centre for religion and culture for all ages and a kind of people's church.

Mayer approved of Anglican liturgy and doctrine despite his Methodism and followed the biblical maxims 'Fear God and honour the king' and 'not to meddle with those who are given to [political] change'. Though supporting Wesley's doctrine of 'Christian perfection' he was critical of the claims of some perfectionists. He was respected for honest business dealings, benevolence, and charity. He was a notable example of a local Methodist preacher who nevertheless had a major role as a regional creator of societies. His Sunday school policy exemplified the earlier Methodist tradition of undenominational openness against the growth of tighter denominationalism. Mayer died on 5 November 1814 in Cale Green and was buried in Stockport, where Benson preached memorial sermons in the Methodist chapel and Sunday school.

HENRY D. RACK

Sources 'Memoir of Matthew Mayer', *Methodist Magazine*, 39 (1816), 3–11, 161–70, 241–51 · Stockport Library, Stockport, Stockport Sunday school MSS, MSS B/T/3/21; B/S/6/1, 2; B/S/2/18 · W. R. Ward, *Religion and society in England, 1790–1850* (1972) · T. W. Laqueur, *Religion and respectability* (1976) · W. I. Wild, *History of Stockport Sunday school* (1891) · JRL, Methodist Archives and Research Centre · parish register, Bristol, St Nicholas, 1 Aug 1771 [marriage] · W. J. Pountney, *Old Bristol potteries* (1920) · L. Tyerman, *The life and times of the Rev. John Wesley*, 3 vols. (1870–71) · *The letters of the Rev. John Wesley*, ed. J. Telford, 8 vols. (1931) · parish records (baptism), Stockport, St Mary's, 25 Nov 1740

Archives JRL, Methodist Archives and Research Centre, Methodist church MSS · Stockport Library, Stockport, Stockport Sunday school MSS

Wealth at death assets of £1016 10s. 6d. (cash, household goods, farm stock, debts due, and rents); liabilities, £1145 11s. 6d.: Stockport Library, Stockport, Stockport Sunday school MS B/T/3/21/2

Mayer, Sir Robert (1879–1985), patron of music and philanthropist, was born on 5 June 1879 at Mannheim, Germany, the third of the four sons (there was no daughter) of Emil Mayer, hop merchant and later brewer, of Mannheim, and his wife, Lucie Lehmaier of Frankfurt. He was educated at Mannheim Gymnasium and conservatoire. He displayed musical gifts from his earliest years, and was encouraged by an encounter with Johannes Brahms. Increasing distaste for Prussian militarism led Mayer's father to send him in 1896 to settle in Britain, where his first job was with a firm of stockbrokers. On leaving that he went into the non-ferrous metal business, in which he remained until 1929. He became a naturalized British citizen in 1902, and from 1917 to 1919 served in the British army.

In 1919 Mayer married Dorothy Moulton (d. 1974), the daughter of George Piper OBE, civil servant at the War Office, of London. They had a daughter and two sons, the elder of whom died in 1983. Dorothy was a soprano singer of considerable distinction who was notable for introducing to the public the work of young composers (particularly English ones) while they were still unknown. She encouraged Mayer to support music and in particular to promote the musical development of children. Following the example of Walter Damrosch's special concerts for children in America, they instituted the Robert Mayer concerts for children, the first of which was given in the Central Hall, London, on 29 March 1923. Mayer chose his conductors well: the first season was conducted by Adrian Boult; and most of the seasons thereafter until 1939, when the concerts had to be suspended, were directed by Malcolm Sargent. The combination of Sargent's musicianship and skill with the young audience, Dorothy's enthusiasm, and Robert's generosity and determination ensured that the Robert Mayer concerts became and remained an important institution in the musical life of London. They spread to a large number of provincial centres in the 1930s and made a significant contribution to the renaissance of music in England, as well as later in Ireland where Mayer supported his wife's foundation for the promotion of music.

In 1929 Mayer retired from a formal business career, his means being by now sufficient to fund his work for music. He was co-founder with Sir Thomas Beecham of the London Philharmonic Orchestra in 1932. In 1939 he was knighted for his services to music.

The concerts for schoolchildren started again after the war, which Mayer spent in the United States, and in 1954 Mayer established Youth and Music, an organization modelled on the continental Jeunesses Musicales and catering for young people from fifteen to twenty-five. Its main activity was to take blocks of seats at concerts and opera performances and make them available at affordable prices to groups formed in places of education and work. Thus many who had been introduced to orchestral music by the children's concerts were enabled to develop their appreciation of music in the years after they had left school.

In addition to these activities Mayer supported talented musicians in various ways: he would, for example, assist groups of players or singers to undertake concert tours abroad, or help promising students to continue a course of training when other support was not available.

In later years Mayer's philanthropy was not confined to musical causes. There were three threads that ran through it—music, young people, and the improvements of relations with citizens of other countries—and they were related in his mind: he saw music as a civilizing force in society and in international relations. He became interested in the problems of juvenile delinquency, and in 1945 published a book, *Young People in Trouble*. He supported the Elizabeth Fry Fund, the International Student Service, the Children's Theatre, the Transatlantic Foundation, the Anglo-Israel Foundation, and many other such causes. In his nineties he was a strong supporter of the movement for British membership of the EC.

Mayer's wife died in 1974, when he was ninety-five. It seemed at first as if all the light had gone out of his life. But his irrepressible energy and vitality triumphed over age and bereavement, and within a few months his small, brisk, neat—almost dapper—figure was to be seen in London concert halls and opera houses as often as ever, and his imagination was once again at work on plans for expanding the scope of Youth and Music. His hundredth birthday was celebrated by the publication of an autobiography confidently entitled *My First Hundred Years* (1979) and by a gala concert at the Royal Festival Hall in the presence of Elizabeth II, who afterwards bestowed upon him the insignia of KCVO.

Mayer was appointed CH in 1973. He was an honorary fellow or member of the Royal Academy of Music, the Royal College of Music, the Guildhall School of Music, and Trinity College of Music, London, and was given honorary doctorates at Leeds (1967), the City University, London (1968), and Cleveland, Ohio (1970). He was awarded the Albert medal of the Royal Society of Arts in 1979. The international dimension of his activities was recognized by the award of the grand cross in the order of merit in the Federal Republic of Germany (1967) and membership of the order de la Couronne in Belgium (1969).

In 1980 Mayer married Jacqueline Noble (née Norman), who cared for him with devotion through his last years of increasing frailty and withdrawal from public activity until he died in London on 9 January 1985 at the age of 105. ROBERT ARMSTRONG, *rev.*

Sources *The Times* (15 Jan 1985) · personal knowledge (1990) · private information (1990) · F. Aprahamian, 'Mayer, Sir Robert', *New Grove* · R. Mayer, *My first hundred years* (1979) · *CGPLA Eng. & Wales* (1985)

Archives FILM BFI NFTVA, 'Robert Mayer – a debt repaid', 14 June 1983

Likenesses W. Stoneman, photograph, 1946, NPG · W. Bird, photograph, 1967, NPG · D. Hill, oils, c.1970, Royal College of Music, London · H. Freibusch, bronze bust, 1979, BBC Broadcasting House, London · J. Epstein, bronze bust, Royal Festival Hall,

London · photographs, Youth and Music Ltd, London · photographs, Royal College of Music, London

Wealth at death under £40,000: probate, 11 April 1985, *CGPLA Eng. & Wales*

Mayer, Samuel Ralph Townshend (1841–1880), founder of the Free and Open Church Association and writer, second son of Samuel Mayer, solicitor, of Gloucester, was born at Gloucester in August 1841. As he grew up he is said to have borne a remarkable resemblance to the poet Keats, not least in his poor health. He was for several years a frequent contributor to the Gloucester newspapers, and to many serial publications. In 1859 he published a novelette, *Amy Fairfax*. Moving to London, he founded and, from 1866 until February 1872, was secretary of the Free and Open Church Association, advocating the abolition of pew-rents. He edited the *Churchman's Shilling Magazine*, the *Illustrated Review* from January to June 1871, the *Free and Open Church Advocate* (3 vols., 1872–7), and was proprietor and editor of the *St. James's Magazine* for a short period in 1875. In 1868 he was the editor of the first report of the Metropolitan Conservative Working Men's Association, and in 1870 he established the Junior Conservative Club, in conjunction with J. B. Payne. In *The Origin and Growth of Sunday Schools in England* (1878), and *Who Was the Founder of Sunday Schools? Being an Inquiry* (1880), he attempted to prove that whatever credit belonged to Robert Raikes as the founder of those institutions should be shared with the Revd Thomas Stock. With J. C. Paget he published *Afghanistan* in 1878, examining its history, geography, and ethnography.

Mayer died at his home in Crown Terrace, Mortlake Road, Richmond, Surrey, on 28 May 1880 and was buried in Gloucester cemetery. His wife, Gertrude Mary (1839–1932), daughter of John Watson Dalby, whom he married in 1868, was a friend of Leigh Hunt and B. W. Procter (Barry Cornwall). She wrote a number of novels, including *Sir Hubert's Marriage* (3 vols., 1876), and in 1894 she published *Women of Letters* (2 vols.), essays which had previously appeared in *Temple Bar*. She and Mayer had been contributors to the journal, of which she subsequently became the editor.   G. C. BOASE, *rev.* K. D. REYNOLDS

Sources Boase, *Mod. Eng. biog.* · J. Stratford, *Gloucestershire biographical notes* (1887) · Blain, Clements & Grundy, *Feminist comp.* · *Gloucester Chronicle* (5 June 1880) · *Gloucester Journal* (5 June 1880) · *CGPLA Eng. & Wales* (1880)

Archives BL, letters to William Hazlitt, Add. MSS 38900–38902

Wealth at death under £400: probate, 25 Aug 1880, *CGPLA Eng. & Wales*

Mayerl, William Joseph [Billy] (1902–1959), pianist and composer, was born on 31 May 1902 at 53 Tottenham Court Road, London, the second of three children of Joseph Mayerl (1871–1937), violinist, and his wife, Elise (1881–1938), daughter of Adam August Umbach from Holland. His paternal grandfather was Anton Mayerl, probably from Bohemia. There were professional musicians on both sides of Mayerl's family but his only formal study was on a scholarship in the junior department at Trinity College of Music, London, from 1911 to 1914. He was a child prodigy, apparently playing Grieg's piano concerto in the

William Joseph [Billy] **Mayerl** (1902–1959), by unknown photographer, 1940s

Queen's Hall at the age of nine. But before he had finished even these minimal studies he was employed in cinemas, in the days of silent films, billed as the 'Wonder boy pianist'. He was fascinated by American popular music, learning the tunes from the mechanical penny-in-the-slot machines. In 1919 Mayerl became a published composer but, in spite of his own energetic promotion, he was mortified when his *Egyptian Suite* was not a success. But success was to come. He graduated from cinemas to playing in dance bands. It was probably in 1921 that he was heard in Southampton by the American saxophonist and bandleader Bert Ralton, who was building up a band at the Savoy Hotel in London, and made him an immediate offer. The Savoy Havana and the Savoy Orpheans became the most famous of all dance bands through their regular appearances on BBC radio in the earliest days of broadcasting. As pianist in the Savoy Havana, Mayerl was in a unique position to present his own dazzling piano playing, including his compositions such as *The Jazz Master*, *The Jazz Mistress*, and *Jazzaristrix*. These titles suggested jazz but the genre was novelty piano since Mayerl was never an improvising player. His effortless high-speed playing caused him to be known as 'the pianist with the lightning fingers' and he was filmed in slow motion to try to see how it was done. Mayerl was an admirer of George Gershwin and gave the first British public performance of *Rhapsody in Blue* at the Queen's Hall on 28 October 1925.

On 19 April 1923 Mayerl married a fellow cinema pianist, Ermenegilda (Gilda, Gil, and later Jill; 1896–1984), daughter of Isidoro Bernini, a tailor, who had come to this country from Italy as a child. There were no children. This was a particularly happy marriage and it gave Mayerl the stability to launch into three simultaneous careers when he left the Savoy in 1926. He became a celebrity on the music halls; he worked in the musical theatre; and, along with the businessman novelist Geoffrey Clayton, he started the Billy Mayerl School of Music, where the teaching was done by post supported by 78 r.p.m. recordings. Between the wars syncopated piano playing was all the rage and both amateurs and professionals wanted to learn how to update their style. The Billy Mayerl School had thirteen branches in England and five abroad; it issued the *Billy Mayerl Club Magazine* every month from 1934 until the war, and the club enrolled almost 2000 members. Mayerl had some famous pupils and the prince of Wales (later Edward VIII) was a fan who used to enjoy accompanying him on drums. In the theatre Mayerl's first full-length show was *Nippy*, about a waitress in a café which belonged to the popular chain of Lyons Corner Houses. The title role was taken by the glamorous Binnie Hale and the show contained 'A couple of fine old schools', which turned out to be a song about Eton College and Borstal prison. Throughout the 1930s, with extraordinary energy, Mayerl composed and conducted musical comedies designed as vehicles for some of the most celebrated actors of the period, went on broadcasting regularly, and appeared on the early pre-war television broadcasts. When the war came this world collapsed. Mayerl's school went into liquidation and, turned down for active service, he took a routine job directing the band at the Grosvenor House Hotel on Park Lane. Increasingly Mayerl felt at home in the field of British light music, helping to start the Light Music Society in 1957 and editing its magazine until his death.

Mayerl's stunning pianism is preserved in many recordings, but he left a unique body of piano music, consisting of some 300 piano solos and more than 100 transcriptions of popular songs. Mayerl encapsulated the mood of the 1920s perfectly in his *Six Pianolettes* and *Four Piano Exaggerations* which demand a virtuosity few pianists have been able to match. In the 1930s the *Four Aces Suite* and the *Aquarium Suite* reflected two of his enthusiasms—playing cards and fish—and Mayerl also developed what he called syncopated impressions. He was a keen gardener so these lyrical pieces often had floral titles. For millions his name has always been synonymous with one of these in particular—Marigold (which he used as the name of his house). But he also thought of himself as a more serious composer in orchestral works such as *Sennen Cove* and *The Forgotten Forest*. By the 1990s, thanks to Eric Parkin's series of recordings and reissues of Mayerl himself, his attractive music was being recognized in a category somewhere between classical music and jazz. Mayerl enjoyed his friends and his success but his later years were dogged by ill health exacerbated by overwork since early youth. A heavy smoker, he died of coronary thrombosis and arteriosclerosis at Marigold Lodge, Pyebush Lane, Beaconsfield, on 25 March 1959, and was cremated at Golders Green on 31 March.   PETER DICKINSON

Sources P. Dickinson, *Marigold: the music of Billy Mayerl* (1999) • M. Harth, ed., *Lightning fingers: Billy Mayerl, the man and his music* (1995) • b. cert. • m. cert. • d. cert. • b. cert. [Ermenegilda Bernini] • d. cert. [Ermenegilda Mayerl] • *CGPLA Eng. & Wales* (1959)
Archives Billy Mayerl Society, St Leonard's Road, Thames Ditton, Surrey | FILM BFI NFTVA, performance footage | SOUND BL NSA
Likenesses photograph, 1940–49, NPG [*see illus.*] • photographs, Billy Mayerl Society, Thames Ditton, Surrey
Wealth at death 20,329 10s. 8d.: probate, 28 May 1959, *CGPLA Eng. & Wales*

Mayerne, Sir Theodore Turquet de (1573–1655), physician, the eldest son of Louis Turquet and his wife, Louise, daughter of Antoine le Maçon, treasurer-at-war to François I and Henri II of France, was born at Geneva on 28 September 1573. He was christened Théodore after his godfather, Theodore Beza. The family had long been settled at Chieri in Piedmont; his grandfather, Étienne Turquet, had emigrated to Lyons and founded a silk industry there. In 1572, when the St Bartholomew's day massacre spread to Lyons, Louis Turquet, who had become a protestant, fled with his wife to Geneva. Louis Turquet was an active supporter of Henri of Navarre, afterwards Henri IV of France. He assumed the name of de Mayerne-Turquet, allegedly from a former property in Piedmont. Under that name he published translations of Latin and Spanish works, and political pamphlets, one of which, *De la monarchie aristo-démocratique* (1611), was banned as seditious by the regency of Marie de Médici.

Huguenot physician After school in Geneva, Théodore Turquet studied philosophy at the University of Heidelberg and then medicine at the University of Montpellier, where he graduated MB in 1596. While a student at Heidelberg he compiled a handbook for travellers in Europe which his proud father published in Geneva as *Sommaire description de la France, Allemagne, Italie et Espagne* (1591). In his doctoral thesis at Montpellier (1597), he defended chemical remedies. This reflected, above all, the influence of his father's friend, a fellow Huguenot, who had also emigrated from Lyons to Geneva: Joseph du Chesne, alias Quercetanus, the most famous Paracelsian and Hermetic physician of the time. From Montpellier Turquet moved to Paris and joined du Chesne, who was now established there as *médecin ordinaire* to Henri IV, working under the king's *premier médecin*, Jean Ribit, sieur de la Rivière, another Huguenot from Geneva. Through them he entered the royal service as *médecin ordinaire par quartier*—that is, on duty for three months in the year. In 1599 the king assigned him as physician to his kinsman Henri, duc de Rohan, who, with other young Huguenot nobles, was making a grand tour of Europe. Turquet accompanied Rohan through Germany and Italy as far as Naples. Rohan remained, for the rest of his life, Turquet's friend and hero, his model of austere, aristocratic, Huguenot virtue.

Back in Paris, Turquet rejoined la Rivière and du Chesne, becoming an enthusiastic alchemist in du Chesne's esoteric Hermetic circle. The medical successes of this trio—three Paracelsian Huguenots from heretical Geneva, none of them a doctor of the University of Paris—alarmed the orthodox Galenists of the faculty of medicine, which in 1603 formally and intemperately condemned du Chesne and Turquet as charlatans, and forbade them to practise in the city. The ban was completely ineffective, but led to a long and bitter controversy, to which Turquet contributed a restrained *Apologia* (1603).

Chief physician to James I Meanwhile Turquet achieved a spectacular success. In 1605 Lord Norreys of Rycote, a young kinsman of Robert Cecil, earl of Salisbury, returning from a special embassy to Spain, had been struck

Sir Theodore Turquet de Mayerne (1573–1655), by Sir Peter Paul Rubens, 1630–31

down in Paris by an epidemic then raging. Several other physicians having failed, the king sent Turquet to treat him and he recovered. Next spring, with the king's permission, Norreys took Turquet to England to treat Queen Anne, wife of James I. There, on a visit to Oxford, he found himself welcomed as 'the queen's physician' and suddenly made a doctor of the university. He also made other useful contacts which, on his return to Paris, he improved.

In 1611 Turquet decided to use them. By then the Paris partnership had broken up. La Rivière had died in 1605, du Chesne in 1609. Henri IV had wished in 1609 to make Turquet his *premier médecin*, but under clerical pressure had insisted that he become a Roman Catholic, which he refused to do. The king was assassinated the following year, the Catholic *dévots* took over, and Turquet decided to act. Having negotiated excellent terms, he accepted the post of chief physician to James I. At the same time he contrived to keep his formal appointment and pension at the French court, relying on periodic visits and a deputy. Having been recognized as 'noble' in 1609, he now dropped altogether the plebeian name Turquet, and would sign himself only as Theodore de Mayerne.

Despite initial jealousies—the death of Prince Henry in 1612 was particularly exploited against him, but the king supported him throughout—Mayerne soon became the most successful (and the most expensive) physician in London. In 1616 he was elected fellow of the College of Physicians and supported the now resumed project of a London pharmacopoeia which some members of the college, and particularly the Paracelsian Thomas Moffett,

had advocated under Elizabeth. He acquired Moffett's papers, including his unpublished compilation on insects (*Insectorum theatrum*), which he would publish, and dedicate to the college, in 1634. This project was now completed: the *London Pharmacopoeia* was published in 1618, with an introduction by Mayerne, and a special section on chemical and metallic remedies. Mayerne also supported the London apothecaries in the campaign which led to their separation from the grocers and their incorporation under charter in 1620. Although he seldom attended the regular meetings of the college and was to decline the position of elect in 1627, he had by now won the respect and friendship of the fellows. King James knighted him in 1624.

Mayerne served James I as a confidential agent in various literary, diplomatic, and political affairs. Through his marriages and his cosmopolitan family he had contacts in the Netherlands, the Palatinate, Switzerland, and Savoy. Almost all British and several foreign ambassadors were his patients; so were the Huguenot leaders Bouillon, Rohan, and Soubise. Recognizing his influence, the city of Geneva and the canton of Bern, the head of the Swiss confederation, appointed him their agent at the English court. In 1620 he bought the barony, castle, and estate of Aubonne in the Pays de Vaud—subject to Bern and conveniently close to Geneva. He spoke of retiring there to write a great work on medicine and hoped to plant a noble dynasty in Switzerland. Meanwhile it was useful as a listening post in the early years of the Thirty Years' War.

The French court was very suspicious of these activities, and especially of Mayerne's connections with the malcontent Huguenot grandees. It therefore watched him closely. In 1618—a delicate time in both internal and international affairs—he arrived in Paris, only to be summarily, and without explanation, ordered out of the country. This caused great umbrage, loud expostulations, and a breach in diplomatic relations. During the Anglo-French war of 1627–9 the French court seized the opportunity to cancel his office and his pension; which caused further umbrage and expostulation.

At the Caroline court Mayerne was abroad, visiting Aubonne, when James I died in March 1625. Before leaving England he had written, for the other royal doctors, a valuable psychosomatic portrait of the king. On his return he found a changed court. His appointment and privileges were continued, but the new king clearly preferred William Harvey, and Mayerne became, in effect, the queen's doctor only. Fortunately she became devoted to him and resisted Richelieu's attempt to have him replaced by another French physician, to be nominated by himself, who would certainly have been a spy. There were other ominous changes too. The following year, when Mayerne sought permission to revisit Aubonne, it was refused: his services at court, he was told, were too valuable. Year after year he tried again, with the same reply. Finally he was told never to raise the matter again: the ban on all foreign travel was permanent; and he was ultimately compensated (together with the queen's other doctor, Sir Thomas

Cadyman) with a patent for distilling (1636). Meanwhile, his frustrated energies were redirected into potentially lucrative chemical and mineral experiments, and a new interest (appropriate to the aestheticism of the new court) in the technology of the arts. He patronized the medallist Nicolas Briot, cross-examined Rubens while sitting for his portrait, supplied colours for the enamels of Jean Petitot, and encouraged Edward Norgate to write his treatise on miniatures. His house in St Martin's Lane, London, became the resort of immigrant artisans, whom he found more congenial than English courtiers.

Why did Charles I so firmly forbid Mayerne to travel? After all, he would allow Harvey to accompany the earl of Arundel to Austria, Bohemia, and Italy. But Mayerne was a political doctor, perhaps a political busybody, deeply involved in the protestant interest in Europe and the Huguenot cause in France, both of which Charles I would decisively abandon. Mayerne did not abandon them. During the 1630s he intervened in favour of Palatine or Vaudois refugees, the protesting ministers of Geneva, and the Dutch and French churches in England, now harassed by Archbishop Laud. Laud was not his patient, and their relations, understandably, were cool.

So, behind the mask of courtly deference, the fashionable court physician moved mentally away from the court. The ban on travel was a standing grievance. Aubonne, Mayerne complained, had become 'a hole' in his enforced absence, and his prodigal son, who lorded it there as 'Henry d'Aubonne', the young baron, was wasting his father's hard-earned substance with riotous living and harlots. An overbearing father, Mayerne worked off his resentments in furious letters to his son, who had reacted against the Huguenot austerity of his father and of his godfather, the duc de Rohan, and would soon die of his dissipations. In private letters to foreign friends Mayerne complained that the life at court to which he was now committed was one of servitude: how different from his happy association with the easy-going King James, 'mon bon maistre', whom he always remembered with affection.

In the summer of 1642 the mask fell. The king, having left London to prepare for civil war, then summoned the royal doctors to join him at York. Harvey obeyed; Mayerne did not. Pleading age and corpulency, he stayed in London to concentrate on his private practice and his chemical experiments in his new house in Chelsea. Royalists regarded him as a deserter. In fact, he maintained his Huguenot independence and self-sufficiency. He received no salary from the king after 1642, but in March 1644 the parliament entrusted him with the health of those of the king's children who had been left in London; and in May 1644—age and corpulency notwithstanding—he obeyed an urgent appeal from the king in Oxford to travel to Exeter and attend the queen, then ill and expecting her youngest child, Henrietta, afterwards duchess of Orléans.

Throughout the civil wars Mayerne hoped for a 'Presbyterian' compromise, and it was even suggested that, through his influence in Switzerland, he could mediate it.

But in 1643, and again in 1645, when the parliament proposed to tax him, he ostentatiously prepared to emigrate, with his whole family, to the Netherlands. The threat sufficed: the parliament agreed that 'a man whose extraordinary abilities would make him welcome in any part of Christendom' deserved special treatment; and he stayed in London until his death.

Mayerne was twice married: first, in 1606, to Margaretha Elburg van den Boetzelaer, of a noble Dutch family, who died on 17 November 1628; secondly, on 14 August 1630, to Isabella, daughter of Albert Joachimi, Dutch ambassador to England from 1625 to 1651. She survived him by seven months only, dying early in November 1655. Of the four sons and five daughters of these two marriages, all but the two youngest daughters died young and unmarried. Of these two, the elder, Elizabeth, married in 1652 Pierre de Caumont, marquis de Cugnac, son of the Huguenot duc de la Force, but died childless on 10 July 1653; the younger, Adriana, who alone survived her father, married Cugnac's brother Armand de Caumont, marquis de Montpouillan, in 1659, but died childless at The Hague in 1661.

Mayerne died at Chelsea on 22 March 1655, aged eighty-two, in full possession of his faculties and fortune. He was buried with his wife, mother, and five of his children, at the church of St Martin-in-the-Fields, London, where a monument was erected on the north wall of the chancel, with a Latin inscription written by his godson and former amanuensis Sir Theodore de Vaux. Thomas Hodges' funeral sermon for Mayerne, *Inacessible Glory*, was published in 1655.

Reputation and achievement Mayerne's reputation as a physician, in his own time, was immense throughout Europe, but he was not, like his colleague Harvey, an original thinker. He and Harvey had indeed little in common, Harvey being as dismissive of chemistry as Mayerne was of the doctors of Padua. He was essentially an eclectic, who sought to incorporate Paracelsian and Hermetic ideas in a basically Galenic system. He was far more tolerant of the Galenist doctors of Paris than they of him, and sent his second son, James, to Paris to learn 'the solid foundations of medicine' from the men who had previously vituperated him. His proclaimed masters were, among the ancients, Hippocrates and Hermes Trismegistus; among the moderns, Fernel and du Chesne. His great contribution lay in his therapeutic practice, his careful and continuous observation of his patients, and his flexible response to their condition. This is recorded in his 'Ephemerides', a regular record, which shows him as an open-minded, rational, objective practitioner, not tied to any theoretical system.

On one occasion during the personal reign of Charles I Mayerne came forward as a constructive medical reformer. In 1631, alarmed by the great plague of 1630, the privy council solicited advice from both the College of Physicians and the royal doctors. The recommendations of the latter (written in French) were clearly the work of Mayerne. He proposed the establishment of a centralized 'office of health' with wide coercive powers to prevent and control outbreaks of plague, a corps of trained officials, and special hospitals modelled on those which he had known in France and Italy. The government at first took this bold and costly project seriously but afterwards allowed it to lapse.

Mayerne was a colourful personality, larger than life in all respects. Though he lived for forty-four years in England, he never became English. He refused to own land in England or, unless pressed, to speak or write English. His letters, written in a majestic, sometimes flamboyant hand, are lively and robust; though sometimes grandiose and self-important, they are never dull and often humane. Though notoriously fond of money, he kept a liberal and hospitable table, at which he indulged himself freely: in his last years he was immobile through obesity, which he did nothing to correct. To Lord Conway, who sent him a recipe 'to make fat men lean', he replied that the recipe was good, but that he would never use it, 'having been long aware that an evil soul never—or rarely—dwells in a fat body'. He compiled a cookery book, collected foreign recipes, kept deer, and grew medicinal herbs at Horne Park, near Eltham in Kent, of which he was ranger. He invented a cordial, the secret of which remained the valuable property of his sister's family in Geneva and which would be offered to Napoleon when he entered Geneva as conqueror.

After his death, and protracted litigation, Mayerne's books and papers passed to his niece, Aimée de Frotté, and her husband, his long-serving Genevan assistant, Jean (afterwards Sir John) Colladon; and then to their son, Mayerne's godson, Sir Theodore Colladon, physician of Chelsea Hospital. Since the Colladons had published nothing Sir Theodore de Vaux, using his own copies and supported by the Royal College of Physicians, published his *Praxis Mayerniana* in two volumes (1690–96). This roused Sir Theodore Colladon to supply the originals to Joseph Browne, a bookseller's hack, who then published *Mayernii opera medica* (1700), a hasty and inaccurate compilation prefaced by attacks on Vaux and the Royal College.

HUGH TREVOR-ROPER

Sources Mayerne's personal records, BL, Add. MS 20921 · I. Scouloudi, 'Sir Theodore Turquet de Mayerne, royal physician and writer, 1573–1655', *Proceedings of the Huguenot Society*, 16 (1938–41), 301–37 · T. Gibson, 'Letters of Sir Theodore Turquet de Mayerne to the syndics and executive council of the republic of Geneva', *Annals of Medical History*, new ser., 9 (1937) · H. Trevor-Roper, 'Mayerne and his manuscript', *Art and patronage in the Caroline courts: essays in honour of Sir Oliver Millar*, ed. D. Howarth (1993), 264–93 · DNB
Archives BL, corresp. and papers, 777 i 11, 777 k 7, Add. MSS 20921, 46378 · Bodl. Oxf., antidotarium · CUL, notebooks, journal, and papers · PRO, corresp. and papers, SP 14–18 · RCP Lond., casebook · RCS Eng., papers | BL, Sloane MSS
Likenesses P. van Somer?, portrait, c.1620, NPG · N. Briot, medallion, 1625, BM · P. P. Rubens, oils, 1630–31, North Carolina Museum of Art, Raleigh [*see illus.*] · portrait, 1635–6, Longleat House, Wiltshire · oils, c.1650 (after P. P. Rubens), Royal Collection · line engraving, 1731 (after F. Diodati), Wellcome L. · F. Diodati, portrait, Public Library, Geneva · W. Elder, line engraving (aged eighty-two), BM, NPG, Wellcome L. · J. Petitot, miniature, NPG · W. Read, stipple engraving, Wellcome L. · P. P. Rubens, oils, copy, NPG · P. P. Rubens, portrait, Art Institute of Chicago · J. Simon, mezzotint (after P. P. Rubens), Wellcome L. · portrait, RCP Lond. · Wellcome L.

Mayers, William S. Frederick (1831–1878), Sinologist, was born on 7 January 1831 in Van Diemen's Land, the son of the Revd Michael John Mayers, colonial chaplain. After being educated at Marseilles, where his father became consular chaplain, Mayers spent some years as a journalist in New York. On 7 February 1859 he gained a position as a British Foreign Office student interpreter and was sent to Canton (Guangzhou) on 13 June 1859, after travelling with Lord Elgin to Peking (Beijing). He was interpreter to the allied commission administering Canton from January 1860 until October 1861 and acting interpreter at Shanghai from June 1863 to April 1864. He was acting vice-consul at Canton from May 1870 to March 1872. He was appointed vice-consul at Kiukiang (Jiujiang) in August 1871, and Chinese secretary of legation at Peking in November 1871. He returned to Britain for a short period in 1872 and presented various papers to learned societies on Chinese subjects. Mayers was an accomplished Chinese scholar and wrote many lengthy works on Chinese government and society. His official report on the famine in the northern provinces of China was published as a parliamentary paper in 1874 (*Parl. papers*, 1874, 68). In 1861 he became a fellow of the Royal Geographical Society; he was also a member of the Royal Asiatic Society of Great Britain and Ireland. He was a constant contributor to periodical publications, especially the *China Review*. He died on 24 March 1878 at Shanghai of typhus fever. He was survived by his wife, Jannie Cecilia.   A. F. POLLARD, *rev.* JANETTE RYAN

Sources FO List (1878) · *The Times* (6 May 1878) · Crockford (1870) · R. Alcock, *Proceedings* [Royal Geographical Society], 22 (1877–8), 326–7 · Allibone, *Dict.* · Boase, *Mod. Eng. biog.* · *Journal of the Royal Asiatic Society of Great Britain and Ireland*, new ser., 10 (1878), xii–xiv · CGPLA Eng. & Wales (1878)
Wealth at death under £1500: administration, 3 Sept 1878, CGPLA Eng. & Wales

Mayett, Joseph (1783–1839), agricultural labourer and autobiographer, was born on 12 March 1783 at Quainton, Buckinghamshire. He was the second of the eight children born to Mary (c.1749–1829/30), the wife of Joseph Mayett (1743/4–1826), a day labourer, though his father had had two children from a previous marriage. Most of these ten children died in their infancy, and 'four was the most that ever was living at one time' (*Autobiography*, 1). It was a nonconformist family whose house in Quainton was licensed for preaching first by the Methodists and after 1801 by the Baptists, though until the second decade of the nineteenth century the family attended the Particular Baptist Chapel at Waddesdon Hill.

Mayett was taught to read by his mother at about the age of four from a chapbook—*The Reading Made Easy in a Variety of Useful Lessons*—and later from the Bible, *Pilgrim's Progress*, and Isaac Watts's *Hymns*. His education continued from 1794 onwards at Sunday school, though he was still trying to perfect his writing and to grasp punctuation in the militia when he was twenty-three. He learned lace making at the age of seven, but then followed his father as a labourer and farm servant for various masters in Buckinghamshire and Oxfordshire. His autobiography depicts a young man trying to square the competing claims, in a poor rural community, of a fundamentalist religion and the desire for physical pleasure, and, feeling himself often misunderstood or misrepresented, he enlisted in 1803 in the Royal Buckinghamshire militia.

For the next twelve years Mayett saw service in various parts of England. He experienced the Luddite riots in Nottinghamshire and Lancashire in 1812, and served in Ireland from 1812 to 1814. He survived smallpox, suffered permanent eye damage, and, according to the autobiography, veered from periods of religious rectitude to those of licentiousness. In May 1815 he obtained his discharge as the oldest soldier in the regiment and returned to Quainton, where, despite initial prosperity and happiness, he was soon on hard times again, scraping a living as a pedlar, gathering rags, and selling tapes and laces. He married, on 18 December 1815, Sarah Slade (*bap.* 1784, *d.* 1844), another member of the Waddesdon Hill church, and he was formally accepted into the congregation there in May 1816. Five months later, however, seventeen members formed a separate church at Quainton with Joseph Mayett as deacon. They built a new chapel, and later Mayett and his wife began a Sunday school, which was initially very successful. Numbers fell away, however, when they could no longer offer cash prizes for good work to match those at the rival church school.

The last twenty years of Mayett's life were a struggle to find work and keep it, to obtain parish relief when out of work, and, when unable to work through sickness, to obtain payment from his friendly society. He was also constantly in dispute over family and church matters with his brother William (*b.* 1786) and his wife and then, after William's death in 1827, with his remaining brother Thomas (*b.* 1790), who subsequently emigrated to America. His father's death in 1826 is unrecorded in the autobiography though that of his mother, in 1830, is. He continued to live in Quainton, in declining health, and died there, childless, on 17 February 1839. His wife died on 18 August 1844.

The autobiography records the principal events in Mayett's life until the end of 1830, and seems to have been written up between 1828 and 1831, perhaps from a journal or notes made earlier. It was published by the Buckinghamshire Record Society in an edition by Ann Kussmaul in 1986. A rare survival from a level of rural society not frequently documented, its naïve and misspelt narrative, described by Kussmaul as a 'late example of confessional writing, in the Puritan tradition' (*Autobiography*, xv), provides a picture of a man struggling to survive and to find salvation at a time of rural economic depression.

DAVID VAISEY

Sources *The autobiography of Joseph Mayett of Quainton (1783–1839)*, ed. A. Kussmaul, Buckinghamshire RS, 23 (1986) • D. Souden and D. Starkey, *This land of England* (1985) • church book of the Particular Baptists, Bucks. RLSS, NB/15/1 • parish records, Quainton, Buckinghamshire, Bucks. RLSS, 6 April 1783 [baptism]
Archives Bucks. RLSS, autobiography MS, DX/371 | Bucks. RLSS, church book of the Particular Baptists, NB/15/1

Mayhew, Arthur Innes (1878–1948), educationist, was born at 18 Bradmore Road, Oxford, on 27 September 1878, the third son and sixth in the family of seven children of the Revd Anthony Lawson Mayhew (1842–1916), chaplain of Wadham College, Oxford, and a noted lexicographer of the English language, and his wife, Jane Innes (1843–1915), the daughter of John Griffen, a doctor in Banbury. He attended the Oxford preparatory school (1888–91) before winning an open scholarship to Winchester College in 1891. Six years later he won a further scholarship to New College, Oxford, from where he graduated in 1901 with firsts in classical moderations and *literae humaniores*. By his own admission he was fascinated by Plato's insistence on the state's responsibility for the education of its citizens and this eventually led him, after travel in Europe, Ceylon, and Burma, to join the élite Indian education service in 1903. He was to spend almost twenty years in India, during which time he met his future wife, raised a family of three children, and achieved high office in the educational bureaucracy.

Mayhew's first appointment was as a school inspector in Madras. Within four years he was deputy director of public instruction and two years later inspector of European and teacher-training schools. In 1909 his career took an unusual turn when he was seconded for two years as the educational adviser to the nizam of Hyderabad. In 1914, at the age of thirty-six, he was appointed acting director, and two years later director, of public instruction in the Central Provinces. As acting director he presided over a committee whose report subsequently led to the establishment of Nagpur University. In 1919 he was made CIE for his services to Indian education. Prior to his departure from India in 1922 he also presided briefly over the newly created central advisory Board of Education.

In September 1908 Mayhew married May Catherine (1882–1954), the daughter of Sir James Davies, a judge of the high court of Madras. They had two sons and a daughter. Mayhew left India partly for family and health reasons but also because he was opposed to the transfer of education to local Indian control in 1921. He feared that this would lead to increasing political interference, especially in universities, with appointments being made in return for political favours and a further decline in already dubious academic standards.

Upon his return to England Mayhew taught classics at Eton College and wrote two books, *The Education of India* (1926) and *Christianity and the Government of India* (1929), which established him as a leading scholar on British rule in India. By the late 1920s he was seeking a new career opening; he was selected in 1929 as one of the two joint secretaries of the revamped and enlarged Colonial Office advisory committee on education in the colonies.

Mayhew was fifty years old when he started sharing an office with Hanns Vischer, the other joint secretary, at 2 Richmond Terrace, situated on the southern side of Whitehall, London. During the next ten years he travelled widely. In 1931 he visited the West Indies and, together with F. C. Marriott, wrote a report on education in Trinidad, Barbados, and the Leeward and Windward islands. In

1932 he visited the Gold Coast as a member of the first inspection team of Achimota College. He attended two major overseas conferences on colonial education, at Yale (1934) and Hawaii (1936), and thereafter visited Fiji to prepare a report on education (1937). Throughout the 1930s he was also known personally to dozens of officers in the colonial education service; he edited *Oversea Education*, a successful journal about colonial education; he was closely involved in the ever expanding activities of the advisory committee; he lectured on British education policy in India and the colonies at the London Institute of Education; and he also wrote a third book, *Education in the Colonial Empire* (1938), which established his reputation as the leading authority on the subject. His experience in India had made him acutely aware of the practical problems which confronted men and women working in schools in tropical Africa and elsewhere and enabled him to empathize with teachers and administrators.

Mayhew's was the major voice on colonial education in Whitehall in the 1930s, and his advice was always sought. His successor at the Colonial Office, Sir Christopher Cox, spoke of his selfless character, his unassuming and modest, but far from diffident, personality, and his depth of knowledge, sanity, clarity, and accuracy, to which he sometimes added irony and a salty wit (PRO, CO 1045/1483). As an educationist he was highly critical of British education policy in India. He recognized the value of Western knowledge and the English language in helping India and the colonial empire to relate to the modern world but he was equally insistent that the education system of any country must be closely linked to its own unique history and culture. Throughout his life he retained strong Anglican beliefs derived from his family background and these helped him to win the trust and respect of the Christian missions; his close and friendly links with protestant missions raised his influence within the Colonial Office. He was made a CMG in 1936.

The onset of war in 1939 gave Mayhew few opportunities to enjoy retirement. He continued to edit *Oversea Education* until 1946 and remained an active member of the advisory committee on education in the colonies besides doing war-work of a non-educational kind in Whitehall. He was also a member of the council of Radley College, and in 1940 he wrote a series of articles for the *Times Educational Supplement* entitled 'Educating the colonies'. He died unexpectedly in his sleep at his home, Normanhurst, Slough Road, Datchet, Buckinghamshire, on 16 March 1948, and was cremated on 18 March at Woking.

Mayhew's career epitomized the Platonic ideal of the guardians that so interested him as a student at Oxford at the turn of the century. He never consciously sought the limelight—he remained a relatively obscure figure in British colonial education—and his outstanding intellect was best suited to those behind-the-scenes activities traditionally associated with the drafting of memoranda and official correspondence but, as Cox suggested, there was also a warm human side to his personality. W. E. F. Ward wrote soon after his death:

There are probably many of us in the Colonial Education Service to whom for many years the Colonial Office meant simply Arthur Mayhew. In our timidity we never ventured to approach the frowning portals of Downing Street; but on the other side of the Cenotaph, in the sunny seclusion of Richmond Terrace, we were sure to find a ready welcome from a professional colleague. Mayhew was a man of two worlds: a man of Kipling's India and, though he never served in the Colonies, a man of the Colonial Empire. (Ward, 755)

CLIVE WHITEHEAD

Sources private information (2004) · C. Whitehead, 'The Nestor of British colonial education: a portrait of Arthur Mayhew CIE, CMG (1848–1948)', *Journal of Educational Administration and History*, 29 (1997), 51–76 · Arthur Mayhew's memoirs, priv. coll. · SOAS, Archives of the Joint International Missionary Council and Conference of British Missionary Societies · PRO, Sir Christopher Cox MSS, CO 1045/1483 · W. E. F. Ward, *Oversea Education*, 19/4 (1948), 755 · *The Draconian* (1948), 10943–5 · *India Office List* (1918), 497–8 · *The Times* (17 March 1948) · *The Times* (30 March 1948) · C. K. Williams, *Achimota: the early years, 1924–1948* (1962) · J. D'E. Firth, *Winchester College* (1949) · A. K. Boyd, *The history of Radley College, 1847–1947* (1948)
Archives Bodl. RH, corresp. with Lord Lugard
Likenesses group photograph (Radley College Council and staff), repro. in A. K. Boyd, *The history of Radley College, 1847–1947* (1948), following p. 352
Wealth at death £16,156 18s. 0d.: probate, 9 July 1948, *CGPLA Eng. & Wales*

Mayhew, Augustus Septimus (1826–1875), writer, was born in London on 27 September 1826, the seventh and youngest son of Joshua Dorset Joseph Mayhew (*d.* 1858), attorney, of 26 Carey Street, Lincoln's Inn Fields, London, and Mary Ann Fenn, about whom nothing else is known. When the sons were living at home, the family lived at 7 Fitzroy Square. Augustus was the brother of Henry *Mayhew (1812–1887) and Horace *Mayhew (1816–1872). Like his brothers Augustus devoted himself to literature and journalism from an early age, and he collaborated with Henry in several literary projects. As 'the brothers Mayhew' they produced six comic novels between 1847 and 1850 illustrated by George Cruikshank, Kenny Meadows, and Hablot Browne or 'Phiz'. Most of these satirized the pretensions of the middle classes, the best-remembered being *The Greatest Plague of Life, or, The Adventures of a Lady in Search of a Good Servant* (1847), which displays strong powers of social observation. It apparently sold more copies than any other serial since *Pickwick*. Other titles include *Whom to Marry and How to Get Married* (1848) and *Fear of the World, or, Living for Appearances* (1850), which includes a very effective portrayal of a family going bankrupt.

During the 1840s and 1850s Augustus Mayhew was also involved with his brother Henry in several other projects: he did illustrations and some writing for the *Comic Almanac* from 1848 to 1850, when Henry was editing it, and the two collaborated in several schemes to make money, one of which was a scientific lecture tour in 1849 which failed and resulted in Augustus being imprisoned for debt in Jersey. Indeed, the two shared rustication to avoid creditors several times in the 1840s and 1850s. Augustus also spent a few years in Paris as an art student.

More importantly, between 1849 and 1852 Augustus

assisted Henry in the investigations both for the 'Labour and the poor' series in the *Morning Chronicle* and the subsequent *London Labour and the London Poor*. He served as one of Henry's stenographers when Henry interviewed various workers and street sellers, but Augustus did some interviews himself and also wrote them up, in particular the section on crossing-sweepers, in volume 2 of *London Labour and the London Poor*, and 'The night at rat catching' in volume 3. These interviews led to his best novel, *Paved with Gold, or, The Romance and Reality of the London Streets*, in 1858, which began as a joint project with Henry but which, after four numbers, was Augustus's alone. This novel traces the life of a young boy from the streets to a respectable life. His other novels include *Kitty Lamere, or, A Dark Page in London Life* (1855), another product of his contributions to *London Labour and the London Poor*, and *Faces for Fortunes* (1861); *The Finest Girl in Bloomsbury*, a comic tale of ambitious love (1861); and *Blow Hot, Blow Cold*, a love story (1862).

With Henry Sutherland Edwards Mayhew was joint author of six convention farces and comic dramas, among them *The Poor Relation* (1851), *My Wife's Future Husband* (1851), *A Squib for the Fifth of November* (1851), *The Goose with the Golden Eggs* (1859), and *The Four Cousins* (1871). He was on the staff of the *Illustrated Times* in the 1850s, and served as a somewhat unconventional special correspondent for the William Palmer poisoning trial in 1856.

In 1858 Mayhew made a trip to Germany with George Augustus Sala and Henry Vizetelly, as charmingly recounted by Sala in *Make your game, or, The adventures of the stout gentleman, the slim gentleman, and the man with the iron-chest* (1860) and illustrated with several sketches of Mayhew as 'the stout gentleman'. Sala also wrote an affectionate dedication of his *Twice around the Clock* (1864) to Mayhew. In fact, all contemporary accounts of Mayhew are affectionate—he was known as 'the dear child'—noting his high spirits, his light-heartedness, and his sense of fun, qualities that did not appear to lessen as he grew older. He was, Vizetelly said, 'the merriest of men and pleasantest of companions' (Vizetelly, 2.48).

When his father died in 1858 Mayhew was left financially secure, though contemporary accounts indicate that he ran through much of his money fairly thoroughly. He married Laura Stanton, daughter of George Stanton, at St Giles and St George on 15 July 1858, almost immediately after his father's death in January—though according to Mayhew's will his family remained opposed to his wife. They had one son, Reginald Frederick, born on 15 December 1861.

At the time of his marriage Mayhew lived at 8 South Crescent off Tottenham Court Road, and at his death at 7 Montpelier Row, Twickenham. He died aged forty-nine on 25 December 1875 in the Richmond Infirmary, where he had gone for an operation for a hernia. He was buried in Barnes cemetery on 30 December and was survived by his wife. ANNE HUMPHERYS

Sources H. Vizetelly, *Glances back through seventy years*, 2 (1893) · H. S. Edwards, *Personal recollections* (1900) · A. Humpherys, 'Introduction', in A. Mayhew, *Paved with gold* (1971) · G. A. Sala, *Make your game* (1860) · *The Era* (2 Jan 1876) · *The Academy* (1 Jan 1876) · *The Times* (28 Dec 1875) · *The Times* (30 Dec 1875) · application to the Royal Literary Fund, 9 June 1849, BL, 1077/43, #96 · private information (2004) [L. M. Coumbe, 'The Mayhew brothers', unpublished MS] · *Men of the time* (1856) · A. Humpherys, *Travels into the poor man's country: the work of Henry Mayhew* (1977) · G. Hodder, *Memories of my time* (1870) · m. cert. · d. cert.
Archives BL, application to Royal Literary Fund, MS 1077/43
Likenesses sketches, repro. in Sala, *Make your game*
Wealth at death £450: will, 26 July 1873

Mayhew, Christopher Paget, Baron Mayhew (1915–1997), politician, was born on 12 June 1915 in London, the eldest of three sons and second of six children of Sir Basil Edgar Mayhew (1883–1966), accountant and company director, and his first wife, Dorothea Mary (Mollie; 1890–1931), the daughter of Stephen *Paget, writer and founder of the Research Defence Society, and granddaughter of Sir James Paget, surgeon-extraordinary to Queen Victoria. His mother's altruistic social work in North Kensington was an early influence on Mayhew's political outlook. Schooled at the Manor School, Horsham (1924–9), and Haileybury, he went up to Christ Church, Oxford, in 1934. He gained a second in philosophy, politics, and economics, spending much of his time engaged in university politics. He was president of the union in 1937 and was an active opponent of communism within the Oxford University Labour Club, a stance reinforced by a visit to the Soviet Union in 1935. On graduating he worked for the New Fabian Research Bureau, publishing a volume on economic planning, before enlisting as a gunner with the Surrey yeomanry before war broke out. He served in France in the early months of the Second World War but was invalided back to England before the Dunkirk evacuation. He was commissioned as an officer, whereupon Hugh Dalton invited him to be his personal link with Special Operations Executive, which was responsible for organizing resistance to and sabotage of axis forces in Europe. Seeking action he soon joined Phantom, a small force of officers intended to form a link between commanders and the front. He later pioneered the infiltration of allied agents behind German lines following the Normandy landings. He was mentioned in dispatches and promoted to major; his wartime letters were published by his brother Patrick in 1986.

Mayhew had been adopted as Labour candidate for South Norfolk in 1938 and, as a consequence, he was demobilized immediately at the end of the war in order to fight the general election. He was swept into parliament with a 6000 majority and was soon appointed Herbert Morrison's parliamentary private secretary. In 1946 he was promoted to become under-secretary of state at the Foreign Office, serving under Ernest Bevin. At the Foreign Office he promoted a more proactive approach to combating Soviet propaganda, establishing the information research department which briefed journalists, diplomats, and MPs about the deficiencies of the communist regime and the threat that the Soviet Union posed to the West. The department employed Guy Burgess for a time, before Mayhew dismissed him for being 'dirty, drunken and idle' (Mayhew, *War*, 24). While at the Foreign Office Mayhew married, on 8 December 1949, Cicely Elizabeth

Christopher Paget
Mayhew, Baron
Mayhew (1915–
1997), by Godfrey
Argent, 1970

Ludlam (b. 1924), the second woman ever to be accepted for the diplomatic service. They had two sons and two daughters.

After losing his seat in the general election of 1950 Mayhew wrote a television play based on his experiences of East–West diplomacy and became a respected documentary maker for the BBC, publishing several books related to the subjects of his documentaries. He continued his television work when re-elected to parliament for the Woolwich East constituency at a by-election in June 1951 following Ernest Bevin's death. Although, as Labour's spokesman on broadcasting, he campaigned against the introduction of commercial television, his main interest remained the communist threat and he chaired the British Council's British–Soviet relations committee. A posthumous memoir of his campaign against Soviet communism was published in 1998. He was unpopular with the left of the Labour Party as a result of his attitude to communism, leading Emrys Hughes MP to comment that 'the trouble with Christopher Mayhew is, he sees a Communist under every bed' (Mayhew, Time, 110).

Mayhew hoped to become minister of state at the Foreign Office when Labour won the 1964 general election but was instead made minister for the navy, a decision he attributed to Harold Wilson's opposition to Mayhew's prominent anti-Zionism. Mayhew campaigned vigorously for Arab causes, launching the magazine Middle East International in 1970 and co-authoring Publish it Not … the Middle East Cover-Up in 1975. He resigned (with the first sea lord, Sir David Luce) in February 1966 over the decision by the minister of defence, Denis Healey, to discontinue Britain's aircraft-carrier programme. Mayhew did not dispute the need for defence cuts—indeed, he argued that Britain should withdraw from its commitments east of Suez, without waiting for the sterling crisis which eventually forced the Wilson government to agree, the following year—but he argued that the cuts made it all the more necessary to maintain a flexible defence force, as represented by the disputed carriers. He published his own views on this issue in Britain's Role Tomorrow (1967).

Following his resignation Mayhew organized the 1963 club of Labour right-wingers who wished to see Harold Wilson replaced as Labour leader by Roy Jenkins, many of whom later joined the Social Democratic Party. Mayhew's dissatisfaction with adversarial two-party politics was set out in Party Games (1969), and his unhappiness increased during the 1970 parliament when he disagreed with Labour's opposition to the industrial relations and European Communities bills. He became the first sitting Labour MP to join the Liberal Party, in July 1974, and narrowly lost at Bath in the October 1974 election. He lost again at Bath, and lost two European parliamentary election contests, in 1979.

As a Liberal Mayhew urged former Labour colleagues to join him and was an enthusiastic supporter of the alliance of Liberal and Social Democratic parties. He chaired the mental health charity MIND, drawing on his own experiences of psychiatry in the 1940s and of his television work, including a series of programmes on mental health and an innovative television documentary into the mental effects of hallucinogenic drugs in 1955. He was elevated to the peerage as Baron Mayhew of Wimbledon in 1981, serving as Liberal defence spokesman in the Lords, where he resumed battle with unilateralists in both the Labour and Liberal parties, and with Zionists in all parties. He published a volume of autobiography, Time to Explain, in 1987. He died in London on 7 January 1997 and was buried at Roehampton three days later; he was survived by his wife and four children.   ROBERT INGHAM

Sources C. P. Mayhew, *Time to explain* (1987) · C. P. Mayhew, *A war of words: a cold war witness* (1998) · *The Times* (24 April 1931) · *The Times* (8 Jan 1997) · *The Independent* (9 Jan 1997) · *Daily Telegraph* (9 Jan 1997) · *The Guardian* (14 Jan 1997) · private information (2004) [Lady Mayhew] · *WWW*, 1961–70 · *People of Today* · D. Brack and M. Baines, eds., *Dictionary of liberal biography* (1998)
Archives King's Lond., Liddell Hart C., papers relating to his career · NRA, papers and diary | BLPES, letters to John Parker · King's Lond., Liddell Hart C., corresp. with Sir B. H. Liddell Hart
Likenesses G. Argent, photograph, 1970, NPG [*see illus.*] · photograph, repro. in *The Times* (8 Jan 1997) · photograph, repro. in *The Independent* · photograph, repro. in *Daily Telegraph* · photograph, repro. in *The Guardian* (9 Jan 1997) · photographs, repro. in Mayhew, *Time to explain* · photographs, repro. in Mayhew, *War of words*
Wealth at death £917,391: probate, 21 Feb 1997, *CGPLA Eng. & Wales*

Mayhew, Henry (1812–1887), author and social reformer, was born in London on 25 November 1812, the son of Joshua Dorset Joseph Mayhew (d. 1858) and Mary Ann Fenn. He was educated at Westminster School from 1822 to 1827, and began his writing career shortly thereafter, at the age of sixteen, according to his son Athol.

One of seventeen children and the fourth of seven sons (among his siblings were Horace *Mayhew and Augustus *Mayhew), Mayhew failed to live up to his father's expectations; a prominent solicitor and a rigid patriarch, Joshua Mayhew apprenticed each of his sons to the law, and each, except one, eventually pursued other interests. Almost all of them, including Henry, were disinherited as a result (after his father's death, Henry received a legacy of £1 per week). Henry was particularly ill-suited to legal study, and

Henry Mayhew (1812–1887), by unknown engraver, pubd 1851 (after Richard Beard)

nearly caused Joshua's arrest by neglecting to file some important documents. This débâcle led to expatriation in Paris for a period, where he formed a close circle with Douglas Jerrold and William Thackeray.

Back in London in the late 1820s Mayhew and his friend Gilbert À Beckett conceived and edited the popular weekly *Figaro in London*, a journal based on the French *Le Figaro*. About this time Mayhew also began to explore writing for the stage; he is responsible for the well-received—and, even by today's standards, funny—farce *The Wandering Minstrel* (1834), and he co-wrote plays with Henry Baylis (*But However*—, 1838), and others. In fact, Mayhew may be considered a significant contributor to the Victorian theatre, although little critical attention has been paid to his plays in the twentieth century.

In 1841 Mayhew embarked on one of his most important journalistic ventures: the hugely successful magazine *Punch*. Co-edited by Mayhew, Mark Lemon, and Stirling Coyne, *Punch* solicited and printed articles by talented young writers such as Jerrold, Thackeray, Henry's brother Horace Mayhew, and À Beckett. In 1842 Lemon became sole editor, and Mayhew increasingly drifted away from the magazine. That same year he began serial publication of *What to Teach, and How to Teach It*, followed in 1844 by *The Prince of Wales's Primer*. Neither serial was completed.

This faltering energy was typical of Mayhew, who was indolent and undirected, if prolific. Even his marriage, on 20 April 1844, to Douglas *Jerrold's daughter Jane Matilda

(1825–1880) was uneven, interrupted periodically by separations, and ended, practically speaking, by a final separation in the late 1860s, at which point Jane moved in with their daughter, Amy. The first of these separations may well have been instigated by his 1846 bankruptcy, a result of lavish housekeeping and the failure of the journal devoted to railway news, *Iron Times*, he had started with the publisher Thomas Lyttleton Holt.

In spite of the personal and financial difficulties which plagued him throughout his life, Mayhew produced some important work. His *London Labour and the London Poor* (2 vols., 1851; reissued with additions, 1861, 1862, 1864, 1865) remains a seminal study of London street life in the middle of the century, and has been often reprinted. It is required reading for anyone interested in the minutest details of Victorian lower-class life, such as what kinds of foods were sold on the streets, how financial transactions with street-sellers were conducted, and how vendors 'cried' their wares. Mayhew provided 'in embryo at least … a theory of the specificity of the London economy which in turn made intelligible the economic behaviour of the London poor' (Jones, 263). The study had its origin in a series of eighty-two articles, published from October 1849 through December 1850, entitled 'Labour and the poor', in the *Morning Chronicle* (Mayhew was its metropolitan correspondent). The series was hugely popular, attracting enthusiastic letters from readers and resulting in the establishment of a special Labour and the Poor Fund.

In late 1850 Mayhew left the *Chronicle* over a political dispute; according to a recent biography, the magazine strongly supported free trade, while the radical Mayhew, probably as a result of his two years among the working class, opposed it on the grounds that international competition compromised workers' wages. When the *Chronicle* published articles promoting its position, Mayhew walked out. His friend H. Sutherland Edwards tells a different story: that, according to Mayhew, the *Chronicle's* editor refused to expose the sub-standard working conditions in a Regent Street tailor's establishment on the grounds that the business advertised regularly in the *Chronicle*. In any case, it was only after leaving the newspaper that he developed his earlier work and produced, initially as a serial from December 1850 to February 1852, the study that became *London Labour and the London Poor*.

Mayhew's journalistic achievements were considerable. He edited several publications, including *Figaro in London* (1835–8), *Punch* (1841–2), the *Comic Almanack* (1850–51), and the *Morning News* (1859). He also, of course, contributed to the periodical press, writing articles for the *Morning Chronicle*, *Bentley's Miscellany*, and the *Edinburgh News and Literature Chronicle*. Among his fiction works are several novels, co-authored with his brother Augustus and published under the name the Brothers Mayhew. These include the notably titled *Whom to Marry and How to Get Married, or, The Adventures of a Lady in Search of a Good Husband* (1848) and *The image of his father, or, One boy is more trouble than a dozen girls, being a tale of a young monkey* (1848). He also wrote travel literature, including several titles on Germany that achieved wide contemporary notice, and children's books, such as *Young Benjamin Franklin* (1861).

Mayhew's work influenced contemporary literature and popular entertainments as readily as it helped to shape Victorian social theories. Many literary representations of the working class were indebted to Mayhew's sketches; Dickens's certainly were, and the same might be said for any number of novels with lower-working-class characters produced during and after the 1840s. Equally indebted was the stage: plays such as J. B. Johnstone's *How we Live in London* (1856) and J. Elphinstone's *London Labour and the London Poor, or, Want and Vice* (1854), to name only two, drew liberally on Mayhew's characterizations, as did legions of music-hall patter singers and songs. It is also possible, however, that Mayhew himself drew on English popular entertainments as well as on the testimonies of his subjects in creating the personae in *London Labour*. Lower-class characters had been represented on the stage as comic, loose, or slick talkers for centuries prior to Mayhew's day, and this at least complicates his affiliation of street folk with these eccentric idioms. However he derived them, the subjects of *London Labour* are vivid and unforgettable.

Mayhew's corpus of published works was extensive. He wrote to instruct and entertain, producing not only popular farces and comic novels but educational children's books and serious journalistic prose as well. He contributed richly to the Victorian cultural scene, continuing to write well into his later years. He died at 8 Tavistock Street, Holborn, London, on 25 July 1887, leaving a very modest personal estate, and was buried at Kensal Green cemetery. DEBORAH VLOCK

Sources A. Humpherys, *Henry Mayhew* (1984) · H. S. Edwards, *Personal recollections* (1900) · M. H. Spielmann, *The history of 'Punch'* (1895) · G. Himmelfarb, 'Mayhew's poor: a problem of identity', *Victorian Studies*, 14 (1970–71), 307–20 · R. J. Dunn, 'Dickens and Mayhew once more', *Nineteenth Century Fiction*, 25 (1970), 348–53 · G. S. Jones, *Outcast London* (1971) · E. P. Thompson, 'The political education of Henry Mayhew', *Victorian Studies*, 11 (1967–8), 41–62 · R. Maxwell, 'Henry Mayhew and the life of the streets', *Journal of British Studies*, 17/2 (1977–8), 87–105

Archives BL, Lord Chamberlain collection · BL, letters to Royal Literary Fund, Loan 96 · NL Scot., corresp. with Blackwoods

Likenesses woodcut, 1851 (after daguerreotype by R. Beard), NPG · R. T., wood-engraving (after photograph by Bedford Lemere & Co.), NPG; repro. in *ILN* (6 Aug 1887) · engraving (after R. Beard), NPG; repro. in H. Mayhew, *London labour and the London poor*, 1 (1851) [*see illus.*]

Wealth at death £90 10s. 0d.: Humpherys, *Henry Mayhew*

Mayhew, Horace (1816–1872), writer, was born in London, the son of Joshua Dorset Joseph Mayhew (d. 1858) and Mary Ann Fenn, and the brother of Henry *Mayhew (1812–1887) and Augustus Septimus *Mayhew (1826–1875). Like all the seven Mayhew brothers, he was articled to his father, a London attorney, but he chose to pursue other professional interests. He had a lengthy career in journalism, serving as sub-editor of *Punch* with Douglas Jerrold and William Makepeace Thackeray and as editor of the *Comic Almanac*. In 1845 he was on the staff of contributors to George Cruikshank's *Table Book*, and was an early contributor to the *Illustrated London News*. He was the author of

one play, *Plum Pudding Pantomimes*, which was produced at the Olympic Theatre, London, in December 1847. His publications include the humorous sketches 'Change for a Shilling', 'Model Men', and 'Model Women and Children' (all 1848; published in 1872 in one volume entitled *Wonderful People*); 'Whom to Marry and How to Get Married' (1848); 'A Plate of Heads', with drawings by Gavarni (1849); 'The Toothache' (1849); 'Guy Faux' (1849); and 'Letters Left at the Pastry-Cook's' (1853). A good-natured man, Ponny (as he was called) is said to have been deeply hurt by harsh criticism of his work. The death of his father in 1858 left him in easy circumstances and he wrote little in later years. He had been engaged to one of Douglas Jerrold's daughters—his brother Henry's sister-in-law—but Jerrold is reported to have ended the affair, stating that 'one Mayhew in the family is enough' (Spielmann, 329). He was married late in life, on 7 September 1868, to Emily Sarah Fearer, the widowed daughter of William Slade, an army officer.

Mayhew was a handsome, captivating man—though reputedly the model for Sir John Tenniel's not-so-handsome white knight in the illustration for Lewis Carroll's *Through the Looking Glass*. He was also a bon vivant and, according to Spielmann, 'scorned to seek repose before the milkman started on his rounds' (Spielmann, 328). His politics, at least in the context of the important Reform Bill of 1867, were Conservative, and in a reputed debate at *Punch*'s table he firmly rejected the premises of the bill, noting that as many working writers as labourers were suffering from want of work and money. On 30 April 1872 Ponny Mayhew died suddenly of a ruptured blood-vessel at his home, 33 Addison Gardens, South Kensington, London. He was survived by his wife. *Punch* published a moving obituary shortly after. DEBORAH VLOCK

Sources H. S. Edwards, *Personal recollections* (1900) · M. H. Spielmann, *The history of 'Punch'* (1895) · M. Hancher, 'John Tenniel, Horace Mayhew, and the white knight', *Jabberwocky*, 8/4 (1979), 98–107 · A. Humpherys, *Henry Mayhew* (1984) · J. Ellis, J. Donohue, and L. A. Zak, eds., *English drama of the nineteenth century: an index and finding guide* (1985) · H. R. Fox Bourne, *English newspapers: chapters in the history of journalism*, 2 (1887) · *DNB* · m. cert. · d. cert. · *CGPLA Eng. & Wales* (1872)

Archives BL, letters to Royal Literary Fund, loan 96 · Bodl. Oxf., letters to F. M. Evans

Likenesses Bassano, photograph, repro. in Spielmann, *History of 'Punch'* · R. Doyle, caricature sketch, repro. in Spielmann, *History of 'Punch'* · J. Leech, caricature, sketch, repro. in Spielmann, *History of 'Punch'* · R. and E. Taylor, woodcut (after photograph by Bassano), NPG; repro. in *Illustrated Review* (1 June 1872) · J. Tenniel, caricature, repro. in L. Carroll [C. L. Dodgson], *Through the looking glass and what Alice found there* (1872)

Wealth at death under £9000: resworn probate, July 1881, *CGPLA Eng. & Wales* (1872)

Mayhew, Jonathan (1720–1766), Congregationalist minister in America, was born on 8 October 1720 at Chilmark, Martha's Vineyard, Massachusetts, the youngest child of Experience Mayhew (c.1674–1759), a missionary to the American Indians, and his wife, Remember Bourne (c.1682–1722). Jonathan's father and three generations of Mayhews before him had been missionaries to the island's American Indians. He received his education on the island until he entered Harvard College in 1740. Having heard his father preach a practical Christianity to the American Indians, he was ready to read the works of the rationalistic archbishop of Canterbury John Tillotson and the liberal English clergyman Samuel Clark. Upon graduation with honours in 1744 he received grants from the Saltonstall Foundation which enabled him to continue his studies at Harvard for another three years; he gained a master of arts degree in 1747.

When Mayhew left Harvard he was called to Boston's ten-year-old West Congregational Church, which he served for the rest of his life. His parishioners were primarily upper- and middle-class merchants whom his predecessor had accustomed to hearing presentations of liberal theology. In this setting Mayhew preached his rational religion at Sunday morning and afternoon services. Although Boston's Congregational clergy often exchanged pulpits, Mayhew's unorthodoxy prevented most others from inviting him. About 1756 he married Elizabeth Clarke (c.1734-1777).

Always controversial, Mayhew undermined the pillars of Calvinistic puritanism. Although he emphasized the ultimate power of God, his was a reasonable and benevolent deity. He rejected the doctrines of original sin and predestination, explaining that God did not create people in his own image and then condemn some to perdition. According to Mayhew, people had free will to act morally or otherwise. He preached the ethics of Jesus but insisted that God-given reason reinforced them. His belief that Jesus derived his authority from God but was not co-equal with God led him to view the doctrine of the Trinity negatively. The Bible taught Mayhew that there was but one God, the Father, who could not be divided into Son and Holy Spirit. The publication of Mayhew's *Seven Sermons* in 1749 and their circulation in Great Britain gained for him the degree of doctor of divinity from the University of Aberdeen in 1750. The intense opposition of clerical colleagues failed to silence him.

Mayhew believed that his mission was to 'proclaim liberty' from all forms of tyranny. In response to the attempts of high-church Anglicans to make a martyr of Charles I, in 1750—101 years after that monarch's execution—Mayhew preached a 'Discourse concerning unlimited submission … to the higher powers'. He charged that rulers had no authority from God to govern unjustly. His sermon was published immediately and distributed widely. It made Mayhew a leading advocate of religious freedom. When members of the Church of England in the 1750s and 1760s urged the appointment of a bishop for the American colonies, Mayhew vigorously opposed this. What he feared was the imposition of religious qualifications for voting and office-holding that would exclude dissenters, the levy of taxes to support Church of England clergy and bishops, as well as episcopal political influence as prevailed in Britain. The passage by the British parliament of the Stamp Act in 1765, which imposed controversial direct taxes on internal American trade, provided him with another opportunity to warn against the abuse of power. He announced to his congregation that laws imposed without the people's participation reduced them to slavery. When parliament repealed the act in 1766 Mayhew preached a 'Thanksgiving' sermon, 'The snare broken', in which he likened the American colonists to birds who had escaped the hunters. He optimistically expressed the hope that now God would permit his children to enjoy liberty for ever. In a letter to James Otis he cautioned, however, that vigilance would be necessary to maintain the colonists' freedom.

A short time later Mayhew served as scribe for a pastors' council that had gathered to hear a neighbouring congregation's complaints against its minister. The journey and the meeting left him exhausted. He suffered either a stroke or a cerebral haemorrhage that led to his death on 9 July 1766. He was buried two days later. He was survived by his wife, who later married his successor, Simeon Howard, and a daughter. Another daughter and a son had died in infancy.

Mayhew's thoughts and actions were precursors of what was to come. His political and religious beliefs were those of the Enlightenment, which was becoming increasingly influential among colonial American intellectuals. Although others, such as Mayhew's Boston colleague Charles Chauncey, endorsed the theories of Isaac Newton and John Locke, no one advocated them more forcefully than Mayhew. He was the forerunner of American Unitarianism. By resisting arbitrary rule in church and state, he contributed to the coming of the American War of Independence.   JOHN B. FRANTZ

Sources C. W. Akers, *Called unto liberty: a life of Jonathan Mayhew, 1720–1766* (1964) • C. K. Shipton, *Sibley's Harvard graduates: biographical sketches of graduates of Harvard University*, 17 vols. (1873–1975), vol. 10, pp. 440–72 • C. Wright, *The beginnings of Unitarianism in America* [1955] • C. Bridenbaugh, *Mitre and sceptre: transatlantic faiths, ideas, personalities, and politics, 1689–1775* (1962) • C. Rossiter, 'The life and mind of Jonathan Mayhew', *William and Mary Quarterly*, 7 (1950), 530–58 • W. B. Sprague, *Annals of the American pulpit*, 8 (1865); repr. (New York, 1969), 22–9

Archives Boston University • Hunt. L. | Mass. Hist. Soc., Thomas Hollis MSS

Likenesses J. Greenwood, portrait, 1747–52, Congregational Library, Boston • T. Hollis, etching, 1767 (after portrait by J. Singleton Copley (?)), Mass. Hist. Soc.

Wealth at death bequeathed to widow £800: Akers, *Called unto liberty*, 111–12

Mayhew [Mayew], **Richard** (1439/40–1516), bishop of Hereford, was born at Edmundsthorp, Kingsclere, Hampshire, to unknown parents. He was educated at Winchester College, where he was admitted in 1455, and then at New College, Oxford, from 1457, where he became a fellow in 1459. He had proceeded MA by 1467, BTh by 1475, and DTh by 1478. In 1500 his doctorate was incorporated at Cambridge. Principal of Hart Hall between 1468 and 1471, Mayhew was senior proctor of the university in 1469–70 and chancellor's commissary by 1485. By December 1503 he had become chancellor of Oxford University, holding that office until 28 May 1506. Meanwhile Bishop William Waynflete, the founder of Magdalen College, had appointed Mayhew its president on 28 August 1480; he retained that position until his resignation in 1507.

Mayhew was ordained deacon on 28 March 1467 and

priest on 23 May following. By then he was already rector of Wolverton, Buckinghamshire, and subsequently received numerous other preferments, including prebends in Wells Cathedral and in York and Beverley minsters. Recorded as chaplain to William Smith, bishop of Lincoln, in 1488, he was also a royal chaplain under Richard III and Henry VII. As president of Magdalen he attended the latter's coronation, and probably came to the king's notice at that time. On 23 September 1490 he was an envoy to Spain to ratify the marriage between Prince Arthur and Katherine of Aragon, and by 1497 he was the king's almoner. He also became a royal councillor, and is recorded as sitting in Star Chamber and the court of requests in the mid-1490s.

Mayhew was made bishop of Hereford in 1504, when he was recorded as having completed his sixty-fourth year. Papal provision was granted on 9 August, he was consecrated on 27 October, and the temporalities were restored on 1 November. Having been installed by proxy he was received in his cathedral on 15 August 1505. Although he seems to have resigned all his ecclesiastical benefices Mayhew remained president of Magdalen, and at first ran his diocese through vicars-general while conducting ordinations at Oxford. But his elevation led to problems of discipline and thence to divisions within the college as to whether he should continue in office there, and eventually he was obliged to resign, a decision ratified by Bishop Richard Fox of Winchester, Magdalen's visitor, in 1507.

Mayhew began his primary visitation of his diocese on 13 March 1507, and conducted two more triennial visitations. His register suggests that he was a conscientious bishop, who usually resided at the episcopal manor of Whitbourne, north-east of Bromyard, and at Hereford, conducting ordinations in person at both places, though he often also delegated the task to his suffragan, Thomas Fowler. In 1511 he presided at the trial for heresy of Thomas Hygons, who subsequently did penance, and he endeavoured to maintain discipline within the monasteries of his diocese; in 1513, for instance, he issued injunctions for Wigmore Abbey, albeit to little effect, after his visitation had found much amiss there. His effectiveness was probably reduced, however, by the effects of old age, which increasingly led to his being excused attendance at parliament and convocation, and even to his receiving a papal dispensation in 1511 from saying mass in his own cathedral on the greater festivals.

In his will, which he drew up on 24 March 1516, Mayhew requested burial in his cathedral, at the feet of the image of St Ethelbert (Æthelberht), and made bequests to it which included his mitre and pastoral staff, a silver-gilt holy water sprinkler given to him by Katherine of Aragon, and the organs he had recently bought for the chapel of the Virgin and St Thomas (Cantilupe). He also remembered Oxford, leaving money for priests there who should pray for him, and books to New and Magdalen colleges. He died on 18 April his will was proved on 10 May. Mayhew's tomb survives, with his effigy, on the south side of the high altar of Hereford Cathedral, where his episcopal ring is also preserved.   D. G. NEWCOMBE

Sources Emden, *Oxf.*, 2.1247–9 • M. Bateson, ed., *Grace book B*, 2 (1905) • *CPR, 1494–1509* • T. F. Kirby, *Winchester scholars: a list of the wardens, fellows, and scholars of … Winchester College* (1888) • *Registrum Ricardi Mayew, episcopi Herefordensis, AD MDIV–MDXVI*, ed. A. T. Bannister, CYS, 27 (1921) • H. Anstey, ed., *Epistolae academicae Oxon.*, 2, OHS, 36 (1898) • H. E. Salter, ed., *Registrum annalium collegii Mertonensis, 1483–1521*, OHS, 76 (1923) • H. E. Salter, ed., *Registrum cancellarii Oxoniensis, 1434–1469*, 2, OHS, 94 (1932) • *Fasti Angl., 1300–1541*, [Hereford] • I. S. Leadam, ed., *Select cases in the court of requests, AD 1497–1569*, SeldS, 12 (1898) • I. S. Leadam, ed., *Select cases before the king's council in the star chamber, commonly called the court of star chamber*, SeldS, 16 (1903), • G. Aylmer and J. Tiller, eds., *Hereford Cathedral: a history* (2000) • J. A. F. Thomson, *The later Lollards, 1414–1520* (1965)

Likenesses tomb effigy, repro. in Aylmer and Tiller, eds., *Hereford Cathedral*, 327

Mayhew, Thomas (*bap.* 1593, *d.* 1682), colonial governor and missionary in America, was baptized on 1 April 1593 at St John the Baptist parish, Tisbury, Wiltshire, the son of Matthew Mayhew (*d.* 1612?), farmer, and Alice Barter. Thomas was apprenticed to a mercer in Southampton, and completed his apprenticeship in 1621. About 1619 he married (according to tradition) Abigail Parkus or Parkhurst; they had one son, Thomas jun. In 1631 he agreed to go to Massachusetts Bay and work as the agent of Matthew Cradock, a former governor of that colony and then a prominent London merchant who owned (among other enterprises) a plantation at Medford. Mayhew settled there, managed Cradock's plantation, mill, trading house, shipbuilding, and fishing fleet, and became friends with John Winthrop jun., governor of Connecticut. About 1636, following a visit to England during which he married his second wife, Jane Gallion Paine (with whom he had four daughters), he left Cradock's employ and moved to Watertown. His extensive merchant connections made him one of the wealthiest men in town, and he was elected selectman and delegate to the general court.

In 1641 Mayhew purchased, from Ferdinando Gorges and Henry Alexander, third earl of Sterling, competing patents to Martha's Vineyard, Nantucket, and the Elizabeth Islands. His son and a group from Watertown settled on the Vineyard at what is now Edgartown. Mayhew himself did not move to the island until 1646. By that time his son was already an active missionary among the Wampanoag Indians on the islands, becoming their doctor, minister, and teacher. Mayhew followed his son in becoming fluent in the Wampanoag language and extended his influence among them. In 1657, after his son was lost on a voyage to England, Mayhew took over the missionary work, preaching at least one day a week and often acting as a judge or adviser to American Indian communities and converts. Backed by the Boston-based Society for the Propagation of the Gospel, he followed a policy of recognizing the American Indian leaders' traditional authority while gradually building Christian Indian communities. It is this policy, and the Mayhews' ability to maintain good relations with the Vineyard natives, which still draw the admiration of historians. The peace on the island may, however, have cloaked a muted conflict between the Christian Indians and Mayhew's support for traditional native rules and polity.

Within a few years of his arrival on his island Mayhew exercised extensive executive power over that tiny English community, governing with a small advisory council. In the wake of his son's death he became even more autocratic, as a sole ruler in both magisterial and executive capacities. But in the 1660s he confronted various challenges to his proprietary authority. First, in 1661, he noticed enough discontent to feel it necessary to have some settlers sign a form that acknowledged his rule. Several years later two powerful Englishmen pressed competing patents: James, duke of York (whose brother Charles II had rolled the Vineyard and Nantucket into his rights to New Netherland), and the heir to Gorges's patent—also confirmed by the king. For the rest of the decade Mayhew waited resolution of the issue (and tried to ignore the letters from James's representative, the governor of New York) while maintaining daily control of the island. In 1671 he was summoned to New York by a new governor, Francis Lovelace, to defend his claims. At the hearing Mayhew and Lovelace worked out an arrangement by which the island ruler would acknowledge York's sovereignty in exchange for a lifetime appointment as governor of Martha's Vineyard. While the English on the islands would elect magistrates and a general court, Mayhew retained effective control by presiding over both. He even persuaded the governor to grant him a manor—the only one in New England—incorporating the Elizabeth Islands and the current boundaries of the towns of Chilmark and Tisbury.

In 1673, after receiving word that the Dutch had retaken New York, a group of Vineyard settlers challenged Mayhew's domination. They set up their own government, and applied to Massachusetts for recognition, but without success. After the English regained control in October 1674 and reconfirmed Mayhew's rule, he took revenge by seizing the estates of his wealthier antagonists, and imposing fines and disfranchising his opponents. But the rumblings of dissatisfaction continued, even after Thomas Mayhew's death on 25 March 1682 at Edgartown, Martha's Vineyard. His grandson Matthew, who had been his steadfast assistant, succeeded him and continued the family's control until 1691, when the island was incorporated into Massachusetts by a new charter. The family would also continue as missionaries to the Indians on the Vineyard, a role that was apparently a key support for their authority on the island. While the Mayhew family lost much of their political power, Thomas's legacy allowed them to dominate the island's society and economy for several generations.   DANIEL R. MANDELL

Sources C. E. Banks, *The history of Martha's Vineyard, Dukes county, Massachusetts*, 3 vols. (1911), 1.104–81 • L. C. M. Hare, *Thomas Mayhew: patriarch to the Indians* (1932) • C. Mather, 'A brief narrative of the success which the gospel hath had among the Indians of Martha's Vineyard, and the places adjacent in New England', *Magnalia Christi Americana*, 2 (1853), 422–46, esp. 422–37 • M. Mayhew, *A brief narrative of the success which the gospel hath had among the Indians* (1694) • L. Travers, 'John Cotton, Jr., among the Indians: Martha's Vineyard, 1664–1667' [presented at 'Microhistory: advantages and limitations for the study of early American history', 15–17 Oct 1999, University of Connecticut]

Maynard, Constance Louisa (1849–1935), college head, was born on 19 February 1849 at 17 Park Terrace, Highbury, Middlesex, the youngest of the four surviving daughters (there were also two surviving sons and two children who died in infancy) of Henry Maynard (1800–1888), South Africa merchant, and his wife, Louisa (1806–1878), *née* Hillyard, who was of Huguenot descent. She grew up in the Kent village of Hawkhurst, in the house, Oakfield, set in spacious surroundings to which the family moved in 1854, and was educated at home, apart from one year at Belstead School in Suffolk. The lives of Constance and her sisters were regulated by their mother in accordance with strongly held evangelical principles. Worldly amusements, dancing, novel reading, and the like were banned, but so was idleness. When her formal education was deemed complete, Constance took up astronomy and New Testament Greek, developed the artistic skills which produced her clear, unmistakable handwriting, and endeavoured to bring material and spiritual comfort to the neighbouring poor.

At the age of twenty-three, still dutiful but inwardly dissatisfied with the life prescribed for her (to be varied, if at all, only by marriage), Constance Maynard heard while visiting cousins in St Andrews much talk of the Cambridge education for women and in particular of a college for women at Hitchin. The whole notion came as a revelation, filling her with 'an overwhelming desire' to enrol as a student. Brushing aside her mother's fears that the college might be worldly, filled with people 'not at all our sort' (Maynard MS autobiography, bundle 8, 1915, Westfield College Archives) and undeterred by her father's insistence that paid employment must not be the outcome, Constance Maynard entered Hitchin in the autumn of 1872, moved with the college to Girton in 1873, and became the first Girtonian to sit for the moral sciences tripos, in which she achieved in 1875 the equivalent of a second-class honours degree. At Girton, her intellectual powers were at last fully engaged and her social horizons expanded by daily contact with women contemporaries who were indeed 'not of our own sort', in the sense that they dismissed, some casually, some scornfully, the truths she held sacred; still more disturbing, the most outspoken were also the students she most admired. She came away from Girton cherishing the vision of a college 'just like it in the scope and energy of learning, the freedom of action in the present and high aims for the future, but where the Name of Christ should be loved and honoured' ('The Inception of Westfield College', 1927, Westfield College Archives).

Back at Oakfield, trying to readjust to the old routines, Constance Maynard responded with alacrity to an invitation to join the staff of Cheltenham Ladies' College which, because of a temporary crisis in her father's business affairs, she had a valid reason to accept. Her immediate superior there was Louisa Innes Lumsden, a fellow Girtonian with whom she departed in 1877 to start up St Leonards School, St Andrews, where her older and more experienced friend had been appointed head. Three unsatisfying years (1877–80) at St Leonards convinced Constance Maynard that her vocation did not lie in schools, and offers of headships were steadfastly declined. She also rejected, with some hesitation, an offer of marriage from a Scots minister, being unwilling, as she told her eldest sister, to take an 'irretrievable step into bondage' (Firth, 162). Moving in 1880 to London, where she shared lodgings with her younger brother and enrolled as a part-time student at the Slade School of Art, she focused more sharply than before on the idea of a 'Christian college' and began to promote it in the evangelical circles whose support would be essential to success. Introduced via this network to Ann Dudin Brown, an elderly spinster of independent means interested in starting a training college for women missionaries, Constance Maynard persuaded this virtual stranger to adopt instead her own plan, which was now geared on the academic side to preparation for London University degrees, open since 1878 to women on equal terms with men; the life of the collegiate household was to be governed by 'the truths of living Christianity', but the future vocation of the students was left open. Events moved fast. Constance Maynard had her first formal meeting with Ann Dudin Brown and her advisers (shortly to become founding members of the college council) in February 1882; in May she was appointed mistress, a title borrowed from Girton. In October, with one lecturer and five students, Westfield College opened in two private houses in Hampstead, just off the Finchley Road.

Constance Maynard, mistress of Westfield for thirty-three years, made the title so much her own that it did not pass to her successors. When first appointed she appeared little older than her students; yet she rarely found it necessary to stand on her dignity with them: when a public swimming bath opened in the vicinity, she was the first to take the plunge. Photographs of this era show a serious, good-looking young woman; later, people were struck in particular by her 'big clear grey eyes, kindly and humorous, but very searching' (The Times, 27 March 1935). When Westfield moved in 1891 to larger premises of a more collegiate style, she endeavoured to preserve its family atmosphere. She wished to know and guide the students—sixty was her limit—as individuals.

The religious life of the college revolved around Constance Maynard's weekly Bible classes and the less formal Sunday evening 'Function' at which attendance was voluntary; in her time there was neither a chapel nor a chaplain. She noticed that, while the students were interested in philosophy, 'simple religious teaching' fell flat, and reworked her material accordingly.

When Constance Maynard retired in 1913, Westfield was securely established as a school of London University, and its graduates, numbering about five hundred, were much sought after by schools, colleges, and missionary organizations in the UK and abroad. But mastery of her 'complex profession', as she termed it on her sixtieth birthday, had been achieved at a high cost. For years she lived under a heavy cloud of depression, brought on by a mixture of overwork, loneliness, and inner religious turmoil as she struggled 'to find the true relationship between thought and faith' (Girton Review, Easter term 1949, 17). Rightly or wrongly, she felt undervalued by the college council, which hedged her about with petty restrictions and whose meetings she attended, if at all, only by invitation. For sympathy and support she came to rely on intimate friendships with favoured students and close colleagues (principally Frances Ralph *Gray and Anne Wakefield Richardson) which while they lasted detracted from the supposed impartiality of her office; when they collapsed, her isolation was the harder to bear. Her legal adoption in 1888 of Effie, an abandoned six-year-old of Italian extraction, gave no real joy to either party and ended most unhappily. These experiences, indeed the whole of her life from 1866 onward, are recorded in diaries (unpublished) which shed light both on their author, revealed as an acute observer with a gift for thumbnail portraits, and on people and movements of the day. Religious movements, from the Salvation Army to the Modern Churchmen's Union, figure prominently. She supported women's suffrage but played no active part in the suffrage movement. She was elected as old students' representative to the governing body of Girton and served from 1897 to about 1905 on the council of the Church Schools' Society. Separate notebooks describe her travels, to South Africa, the Holy Land, Canada, Europe, and by bicycle throughout the British Isles.

In retirement, Constance Maynard continued to keep in touch with her Westfield 'flock' through a correspondence network, 'the Budget', she had instituted as early as 1887. The money they collected as a parting gift she donated to the college; some was used as a hardship fund, the remainder as endowment for the Maynard divinity lectures. Constance Maynard died at her home, The Sundial, Marsham Way, Gerrards Cross, Buckinghamshire, on 26 March 1935, and was buried at Gerrards Cross parish church on 29 March. Under her will the college received £1500 to fund an entrance scholarship.

Constance Maynard's published works include Between College Terms (1910); The Life of Dora Greenwell (1926); 'From an early Victorian schoolroom to the university', Nineteenth Century, November 1914; contributions to The Hibbert Journal and other religious periodicals; and numerous tracts and pamphlets. Her unpublished writings include an unfinished autobiography, composed at intervals between 1915 and 1927, which with her diaries, supplemented by personal knowledge, form the basis of C. B. Firth's biography (1949). These intimate records have been given a more detached interpretation by M. Vicinus (1985). JANET SONDHEIMER

Sources Queen Mary College, London, Constance Maynard archives • Queen Mary College, London, Westfield College Archives • C. B. Firth, Constance Louisa Maynard (1949) • J. Sondheimer, Castle Adamant in Hampstead: a history of Westfield College, 1882–1982 (1983) • The Times (27 March 1935) • The Times (30 March 1935) • K. T. Butler and H. I. McMorran, eds., Girton College register, 1869–1946 (1948) • M. Vicinus, Independent women: work and community for single women, 1850–1920 (1985) • b. cert. • d. cert.
Archives Queen Mary College, London, diaries, notebooks, and MS of unfinished autobiography | PRO NIre., corresp. with Miss A. W. Richardson

Likenesses photographs, 1880–1913, Queen Mary College, London, Constance Maynard archive · portraits, 1880–1913, Queen Mary College, London, Constance Maynard archive · G. Jay, oils, 1907, Queen Mary College, London · A. Footner, photograph, c.1930, Queen Mary College, London, Constance Maynard archive
Wealth at death £23,230 11s. 10d.: probate, 10 May 1935, CGPLA Eng. & Wales

Maynard, Edward (1654–1740), Church of England clergyman, was born on 23 August 1654 at Daventry, Northamptonshire, the son of William Maynard of that town. He matriculated from Wadham College, Oxford, on 21 October 1670, aged fifteen, and became a demy of Magdalen College, Oxford, in 1672. He graduated BA in 1674 and proceeded MA in 1677.

In 1678 Maynard became a fellow of Magdalen, and was college bursar in 1687–8. He was inevitably involved in the conflict between the fellows and the crown which followed the death of the college president, Henry Clerke, on 24 March 1687. When the fellows chose John Hough as president in defiance of the king's nomination of the Catholic Anthony Farmer, Maynard stood as the second candidate required by the college's election process and formally presented the successful Hough to the college visitor. During the assault on the autonomy of the college which ensued Maynard took refuge at Coleshill, the Warwickshire seat of William Digby, fifth Baron Digby of Geashill. When in November 1687 most of the fellows refused to submit to the king's new choice, Samuel Parker, Maynard escaped expulsion because he had formal leave of absence to serve as Digby's chaplain. In August the following year Maynard and the handful of remaining Anglican fellows were expelled by Parker's Catholic successor Bonaventure Gifford on the formal grounds of non-residence but in reality because of their refusal to acknowledge him as their lawful president. Maynard was restored with his colleagues to his fellowship in October 1688, following the beleaguered James's reversal of policies. Maynard proceeded BD in 1688 and DD in 1691.

However, Maynard does not seem to have spent much time at his college following his restoration, continuing to spend much of his time at Digby's. In November 1691 he was appointed preacher at Lincoln's Inn, a position which required his attendance in London except during the four summer months of the long vacation. He finally resigned his fellowship in July 1694 following his marriage on 10 April to Barbara Harris (1661/2–1704), daughter of Thomas Harris of Worcester, who had been a judge on the Welsh circuits. In 1696 Maynard was presented by the earl of Sunderland to the rectory of Boddington, Northamptonshire, a living which he held until his death forty-four years later. He continued to serve at Lincoln's Inn during term time until relinquishing the post in May 1699 for health reasons.

In 1738 Maynard looked back on his Northamptonshire pastorate in Memoirs Concerning Parsons and the Parsonage of Bodington, which combined an account of his predecessors with elements of autobiography and in particular of the tangible aspects of his four decades in the parish. He discussed, for instance, tithes, his repairs to the chancel of the church and to the rectory, and the causeway that he had built out of his own pocket because the village's roads were so dirty and broken 'that I could not see how they could safely bring up corpses to Church' (Maynard, Memoirs, 13). He recalled how he decided against challenging the dubious claim of the parishioners of the lower part of the town that they only owed him 9s. a year for the tithe on milk. Considering both the legal advice of his friends at Lincoln's Inn and 'my great love to peace added to all, I was not long in concluding not to make my whole life uneasy and my ministry most unprofitable amongst them by engaging in an endless suit' (ibid., 19–20).

From 1701 until his resignation in 1706 Maynard was also rector of Passenham, Northamptonshire. From 1700 until his death Maynard was canon and precentor of Lichfield Cathedral. There his first wife, who died on 25 March 1704, aged forty-two, was buried. By licence dated 10 April 1705 he married at Woodford, Northamptonshire, Elizabeth Archer, née Hastings (1664/5–1736), daughter of William Hastings of Hinton, in Woodford. From 1719 until his death Maynard was master of the hospital of St John, Lichfield, undertaking repairs and alterations to the then derelict buildings, which improvements remained for the next 240 years.

Maynard maintained his connection with the Digby family, and it was a meeting at Lord Digby's house which led Maynard to edit and publish a second edition of Sir William Dugdale's History of St Paul's in 1716. In the preface Maynard explained how Dugdale's grandson had shown him there the manuscript that Sir William had been preparing for a second edition at the time of his death. Maynard undertook to find a printer and to have some of the worn plates restored. In the preface Maynard prided himself on having 'done a service acceptable to the Publick, and obliged the Lovers of Antiquity'. Maynard's edition included a continuation of the history of the cathedral down to 1685 and an addition concerning cathedrals and collegiate churches in the province of York. In 1722–24 Maynard published some of the sermons that he had preached at Oxford and Lincoln's Inn many years before, including 'two discourses on natural and reveal'd religion'. The latter, he claimed, were the first sermons he had preached at Oxford, heavily revised during his Warwickshire sojourn in 1687–8 in the light of the 'Ancient Moralists' he had then been studying so that they now read more like tracts than sermons (Maynard, Sermons, preface). He had developed a sermon which he had first delivered in Oxford in 1686 on the resurrection into four which he had preached at Lincoln's Inn in the 1690s, 'with a particular Eye to the Socinians' (ibid.)—now published over a quarter of a century since the council of Lincoln's Inn had urged him to publish one of them.

Maynard died on 13 April 1740 at Boddington and was buried in Boddington church. With no surviving children his will mixed bequests to kin and friends, including portraits of the late Lord and Lady Sunderland and of St Peter left to Lord Digby, and to charitable purposes. He left his library and £500 to Magdalen, 'the beloved place of my Education'; those books not absorbed into its library were to be sold towards its rebuilding fund (PRO, PROB 11/703, fol. 123*v*). The Lincoln's Inn flagon given to Magdalen is not mentioned so must have been given during his lifetime. Any of his unpublished writings were to be destroyed—except for the accounts. He left money to the poor of Boddington ('choosing not so much those that are most wanting, but chiefly those that are and have been most deserving') and of Lichfield (PRO, PROB 11/703, fol. 124*r*). He gave shirts and money to the men of St John's and money to the women of a sister hospital. To Daventry he left £300 to found a charity school and £200 to augment the living, and he left a further £200 to the Society for the Propagation of the Gospel. On hearing of the death his old friend John Hough, now bishop of Worcester, wrote that, 'He was a learned man, a sincere Christian, unblameable in the whole course of his life, who lived inoffensively and died quietly' (Maynard, *Memoirs*, 21).   PAT BANCROFT

Sources E. Maynard, *Memoirs concerning parsons and the parsonage of Bodington*, ed. S. J. W. Bromet (1968) · J. R. Bloxam, *A register of the presidents, fellows … of Saint Mary Magdalen College*, 8 vols. (1853–85) · H. I. Longden, *Northamptonshire and Rutland clergy from 1500*, ed. P. I. King and others, 16 vols. in 6, Northamptonshire RS (1938–52), 9.189–91 · will, PRO, PROB 11/703, sig. 176 · private information (2004) [Dr Robin Darwall-Smith] · H. Clayton, 'St John's Hospital Lichfield', Lichfield Cathedral Library · *VCH Staffordshire*, 3.284–8 · chapter act books, Lichfield Cathedral Library · 'Lost heraldry and inscriptions of Lichfield Cathedral', Lichfield Cathedral Library [typescript] · W. Dugdale, *The history of St Paul's Cathedral in London*, 2nd edn (1716) · E. Maynard, *Sermons preach'd before the University of Oxford: or before the honourable society of Lincoln's Inn* (1722–4) · J. R. Bloxam, ed., *Magdalen College and James II, 1686–1688: a series of documents*, OHS, 6 (1886) · L. Brockliss, G. Harriss, and A. Macintyre, *Magdalen College and the crown: essays for the tercentenary of the restoration of the college, 1688* (1988) · W. P. Baildon, ed., *The records of the Honorable Society of Lincoln's Inn: the black books*, 3 (1899) · IGI
Likenesses portrait; formerly at Boddington vicarage
Wealth at death considerable in available money, plus books: will, PRO, PROB 11/703, sig. 176

Maynard, Harry Russell (1873–1954), charity administrator, was born on 5 January 1873 at Milton House, Harringay Park, Crouch End, Middlesex, the third son of Robert Russell Maynard, East India agent, and his wife, Jessie Carter. He attended Amersham Hall School and Oxford University, where he took a first in modern history in 1901. He later attended classes at the London School of Economics. With a lively social conscience, he became a resident of Toynbee Hall in 1903. A gifted statistician with a capacity for hard work, he served as honorary secretary to the Mansion House Unemployed Committee (1903–4), as secretary to the London Unemployed Fund (1904–5), and then as clerk to the Central (Unemployed) Body for London (1905–6). In 1906 he joined the King Edward's Hospital Fund for London (King's Fund), at a salary of £500 p.a., not an inconsiderable sum for a man of thirty-three trained as an economic historian. On 22 June 1907 he married Mabel Esther Carter (*b.* 1869/70), daughter of Thomas Carter, a physician and surgeon of Richmond, Yorkshire. Maynard spent the remainder of his career with the fund, apart from a brief period at the end of the First World War when he was seconded to the Ministry of Food as a result of a request for his services from William Beveridge, a former colleague from his days at Toynbee Hall.

The King's Fund, which started life in 1897 as the Prince of Wales's Hospital Fund for London, was a leading medical charity which sought to defend the voluntary principle in hospital provision. Its aims were to ensure the financial stability of the capital's charitable hospitals and to improve their performance through the co-ordination of their services. As the fund's leading administrator, Maynard built up an encyclopaedic knowledge of hospital administration and was a principal reason for the institution's great prestige in the early decades of the century. During the hospital funding crises in the inter-war years he was deeply involved in appeals which helped to stave off government intervention; and in 1921 he provided information to the Cave committee, which had been appointed by the Ministry of Health to inquire into the finances of the voluntary hospitals.

Maynard always preferred the statistical to the political side of the fund's work and was chiefly responsible for the annual publication of the *Statistical Report*, which drew on information from the 150 or so voluntary hospitals in London. Elegantly and formally presented, it provided administrators with detailed information on everything from income and expenditure to the cost of cod-liver oil and scrubbing-brushes. It was an invaluable guide to reform. Maynard kept a firm hand on the affairs of the fund, which by the 1930s served as an innovative central board for London's voluntary hospitals. But with the years he grew increasingly irritable. He often communicated with his staff by notes brought in by an office boy and when someone once asked him for two hours' leave to attend a funeral, he was told that one hour would do. In 1938 the management committee decided to make a change, but asked Maynard to stay on as clerk of the general council. Upon his retirement in 1941 he was elected to the council. At the time, the institution paid him formal tribute: 'the present position and prestige of the Fund is largely due to Mr Maynard's disinterested service' (management committee minutes, 23 Sept 1941, King's Fund archive, LMA). Maynard had turned down a knighthood, but he was appointed CVO in 1932. He died after a long illness on 8 February 1954 at 26 Thurlow Road, Hampstead, London.   FRANK PROCHASKA

Sources F. K. Prochaska, *Philanthropy and the hospitals of London: the King's Fund, 1897–1990* (1992) · LMA, King's Fund archives · *The Times* (11 Feb 1954) · *WWW*, 1951–60 · King's Fund annual reports, LMA, King's Fund archives · *CGPLA Eng. & Wales* (1954) · b. cert. · m. cert. · d. cert.
Archives Bodl. Oxf., corresp. with Henry Burdett · LMA, King's Fund archives
Wealth at death £987 16*s.* 5*d.*: probate, 8 May 1954, *CGPLA Eng. & Wales*

Maynard, Sir Henry (*b.* after **1547**, *d.* **1610**), administrator, was the eldest of two sons and a daughter of John Maynard (1508/9–1556), MP and steward of St Albans, Hertfordshire, and his second wife, Dorothy, widow of John Bridge (or

Sir Henry Maynard (b. 1547, d. 1610), by unknown artist, after 1610 [nearer recumbent figure]

Bridges) and daughter of Robert Perrot and his wife, Margaret. Maynard's will testified to his protestant convictions (probably derived from his father), but little else is known of his childhood and education: he did not enter the Middle Temple until 26 May 1581, following the request of Sir John Popham, the inn's treasurer.

It has been argued that Maynard was secretary to Sir Nicholas Bacon, the lord keeper of the great seal, until Bacon's death in 1579; but Maynard's handwriting is found throughout letters and memoranda in Lord Burghley's archive from the late 1570s, including diplomatic issues, normally the preserve of the principal secretary. This suggests Maynard's service as William Cecil's chief secretary predated Bacon's death, or that he was employed by the privy council for important issues. He was officially listed as Burghley's secretary in 1581. Maynard may have entered Burghley's household through connections his father had established earlier with Burghley, especially as steward of St Albans.

Maynard was chief secretary, concerned with 'matters of state' (meaning issues of domestic and foreign policy rather than petitions for office, pensions, and wardships) until Burghley's death in 1598. He drafted memoranda, instructions for envoys to foreign courts, and some of Burghley's letters; and he organized supplies of ordnance and money to the Netherlands and Ireland and endorsed incoming letters and filed them away. He also took over the duties of Burghley's other secretaries when they were ill or on holiday; they did the same for him. During this time Maynard was made surveyor of crown lands in Hertfordshire (c.1594) and Essex (1596) and general overseer of the musters in Ireland (1597). He was MP for St Albans between 1584 and 1597 and sat for the county seat of Essex in 1601. His St Albans seat has been attributed to Burghley's influence, but Maynard's family had solid connections with the town: his father had been MP in 1553. According to parliamentary records, Maynard made no contribution to debates in the Commons but he was active in committees from 1593. He was appointed to a variety of committees, including those on recusancy (1593) and

monopolies (1601). After heated debate in the subsidy committee in 1601 Maynard was requested by the whole house to draft the committee's orders.

After Burghley's death it was rumoured Maynard would be appointed principal secretary if Robert Cecil was promoted to the lord treasurership, but this never materialized. Instead Maynard was appointed secretary to Lord Admiral Nottingham (1599). He was knighted by James VI and I (7 May 1603) and made sheriff and deputy lieutenant of Essex (1603). John Chamberlain expected Maynard to be appointed ambassador to France in 1604, but this post eluded him; he was appointed muster master general of Ireland instead.

At some date before 1592 Maynard married Susan (d. in or after 1612), the second daughter and coheir of Thomas Pearson (or Pierson), gentleman usher of Star Chamber. They had eight sons and two daughters, of whom two sons predeceased their father. Maynard's heir was Sir William Maynard (d. 1639), who became Lord Maynard of Wicklow (30 May 1620) and Baron Maynard of Little Easton (14 March 1628). His other sons were Charles (d. 1665), Francis, Henry, and Sir John *Maynard, and one unidentified; his daughters were Elizabeth and Mary.

Though Maynard received no formal salary as secretary, he was able to build up a landed estate in Essex through gratuities, wardships, and privileges obtained during Burghley's service. His estate surrounded his house, Easton Lodge, in Little Easton, Essex, and included manors, parks, woods, and messuages in nearby parishes. He also owned or leased land and houses in London, St Albans, and Warwickshire. These were acquired through inheritance from his stepfather, Francis Rogers, and purchases from Thomas Howard and Sir Thomas Cromwell. Maynard had sufficient funds to lend £5000 to Sir Horatio Palavicino in 1593; Francis Bacon approached him for a loan the same year.

Maynard died on 11 May 1610 leaving £2000 to each of his daughters, of which part was to be drawn from the revenue accruing from a wardship. Property or money was left to Charles and Francis; John and Henry were not mentioned. His widow was given a life interest in the west part of Easton Lodge, and Sir William was left his father's household stuff 'which lyethe from the kitchin towardes the Easte' (PRO, PROB 11/115, fols. 312v–313v). Maynard left £45 to the poor of Little Easton and neighbouring parishes. He was buried in the family chapel in the parish church of St Mary the Virgin, Little Easton, where there is a fine alabaster monument with effigies of him and his wife.

NATALIE MEARS

Sources R. C. Barnett, *Place, profit and power: a study of the servants of William Cecil, Elizabethan statesman* (1969) · A. G. R. Smith, *Servant of the Cecils: the life of Sir Michael Hickes, 1543–1612* (1977) · F. Chancellor, *The ancient sepulchral monuments of Essex* (1890) · R. Clutterbuck, ed., *The history and antiquities of the county of Hertford*, 3 (1827) · A. G. R. Smith, 'The secretariats of the Cecils, c.1580–1612', *EngHR*, 83 (1968), 481–504 · *An inventory of the historical monuments in Essex*, Royal Commission on Historical Monuments (England), 1 (1916) · C. Demain-Saunders, 'The early Maynards of Devon and St Albans', *The Genealogists Magazine*, 6 (1934), 591–641 · P. Morant, *The history and antiquities of the county of Essex*, 2 (1768); repr. (1816) · *The letters of*

John Chamberlain, ed. N. E. McClure, 2 vols. (1939) · *Calendar of the manuscripts of the most hon. the marquis of Salisbury*, 24 vols., HMC, 9 (1883–1976) · *CSP dom.*, 1596–1601; 1603–10 · *CSP Ire.*, 1600–01 · G. R. Morrison, 'The land, family, and domestic following of William Cecil, Lord Burghley, *c.*1550–1598', DPhil diss., U. Oxf., 1990 · will, PRO, PROB 11/115, fols. 312*v*–313*v*

Archives Hatfield House, Hertfordshire, Cecil MSS · PRO, state papers, domestic, Elizabeth, SP12 · PRO, state papers, Ireland, SP63 · PRO, state papers, domestic, James VI and I, SP14

Likenesses alabaster effigy on monument, after 1610, parish church of St Mary the Virgin, Little Easton, Essex [*see illus.*]

Wealth at death £2000 each to two daughters on marriage or eighteenth birthday (whichever sooner) from wardship; £500 and £45 left to individuals and the poor; also estate and goods: will, PRO, PROB 11/115, fols. 312*v*–313*v* · bought much land, lent large sums

Maynard, (Vera) Joan (1921–1998), trade unionist and politician, was born on 5 July 1921 at Brooklands, Easingwold, Yorkshire, the daughter of Matthew Maynard, a small farmer trying to scratch a living from 17 acres of land, and his wife, Effie Eliza, *née* Wright. She was educated at a local village school in Ampleforth, leaving at the age of fourteen. In the late 1930s the family abandoned the struggle with the farm and moved to Thornton-le-Street, where they took over the post office and Joan did a postal round. She later recalled it as her first lesson in economics that she was paid less than the men for doing the same job.

In 1945 Maynard and a handful of others met in Thirsk to found a Labour Party branch and challenge the hegemony of the local squire. She was elected secretary and electoral agent of the Thirsk and Malton branch, which grew from its tiny beginnings to become one of the biggest in the country. She was appointed a magistrate in 1950, in 1952 she stood successfully for the South Kilvington district council, and in 1956 she became a North Riding county councillor. She became Yorkshire county secretary of the National Union of Agricultural and Allied Workers (subsequently the Agricultural and Allied Workers Trade Group of the Transport and General Workers' Union) in 1956. It was a post she held for twenty-two years, including a period as national vice-president from 1966 to 1972, a position in which she is said to have so irritated the leadership of the union that, unable to stop her being repeatedly elected, they simply abolished the post.

Maynard took a seat on the Labour Party's national executive in 1972 after a conference speech calling for the nationalization of land, and in 1974 successfully stood for the parliamentary seat of Sheffield Brightside, thus becoming one of the few working-class women ever to be elected to parliament. In her maiden speech she declared her pride at being 'the only sponsored Member for farm workers … I speak for one of the lowest-paid groups' (*Hansard 5C*, vol. 880, 6 Nov 1974, col. 1135). Within hours of taking her seat she was lobbying ministers for a bill to secure tenure for farmworkers, to end the tied-cottage system which caused misery for many rural workers and their families who would lose their homes if they lost their jobs. She got 180 MPs to sign an early day motion on the issue and spoke about it at the first meeting of the Parliamentary Labour Party that she attended. Within two years the Rent (Agriculture) Act was law.

Maynard always spoke for the crusading spirit of the Labour Party, which made her more popular with the membership than with most of her parliamentary colleagues. She espoused a wide range of left-wing causes, being in favour of Britain's withdrawal from Northern Ireland and an extension of public ownership; and against nuclear weapons, the Common Market, the Falklands War, and Labour's 'tinkering with capitalism'. She was at odds with the Labour leadership in the turbulent 1970s and early 1980s, when she stood for traditional Labour values against those who called themselves modernizers but whom she saw as betrayers of the working class. Nevertheless her membership of the select committee on agriculture for twelve years from 1975 saw her forming an unlikely alliance with the Conservative Sir Richard Body to oppose the excesses of factory farming. She also found unexpected allies in her opposition to the common agricultural policy and the fight to save her beloved Hambleton Hills from electricity pylons.

Maynard became chair of the Campaign Group of MPs, formed to represent the left in 1981 following Tony Benn's failure to be elected deputy leader of the Labour Party, but the tide had already turned against them and Maynard lost her seat on the national executive committee in the following year. She regained her position on the national executive committee in 1983 but the left was no longer a powerful force, and the actions of Maynard and like-minded colleagues were now limited to such protests as a walkout in 1986 to cause the collapse of disciplinary hearings against members of the Marxist militant group. Her advancing age but continued championship of socialist causes acquired her the nickname 'Stalin's Grandmother' (her response to which was that Stalin's grandmother was probably a pillar of the Russian Orthodox church in Georgia, and therefore rather more conservative than herself).

Despite Maynard's trenchant political views, she was known to be kind and gentle. She bore the burden of caring for her elderly parents until their deaths, then cared for her elder sister who developed Alzheimer's disease, then for an elder brother. She retired from the House of Commons and lost her seat on the national executive in 1987. She died at her home, Lansbury House, 76 Front Street, Sowerby, Thirsk, on 27 March 1998, of stomach cancer, and was buried at St Oswald's, Sowerby, on 3 April. She was unmarried.   JAD ADAMS

Sources *The Guardian* (30 March 1998) · *The Independent* (30 March 1998) · *Daily Telegraph* (30 March 1998) · *The Times* (30 March 1998) · private information (2004) [C. Mullin] · *WWW* · A. Benn, *Conflicts of interest: diaries, 1977–80* (1990) · A. Benn, *The end of an era: diaries, 1980–90* (1992) · b. cert. · d. cert.

Archives NRA, priv. coll., papers · Sheff. Arch., corresp. and papers

Likenesses photograph, repro. in *The Times* · photograph, repro. in *Daily Telegraph* · photograph, repro. in *The Guardian* · photograph, repro. in *The Independent*

Wealth at death £450,334: probate, 1 June 1998, CGPLA Eng. & Wales

Maynard, John (*bap.* 1577, *d.* in or before 1633), lutenist and composer, was baptized on 5 January 1577 at St Albans

Abbey, Hertfordshire, the third son of Ralph Maynard (d. 1614) of St Julian's, a former leper hospital in St Michael's parish, St Albans, and his wife, Margery, daughter of Robert Seale. In March 1600 he was one of two commissaries appointed by his uncle Henry (later Sir Henry) Maynard, surveyor of musters in Ireland. Perhaps the Irish position was a sinecure; a bass singer, Johan Meinert, and a bass violist, Daniel Norcum, possibly Dowland recruits, were at the Danish court in 1599, but absconded without leave in 1601. Unsuccessfully pursued, they were spotted in Venice a year later; an extradition request was refused and they were never caught. A bass singer, John Miners (Mynars), was active in England between 1607 and his death in 1615. However, Meinert is a common surname in north Germany and the confusion of dates and names makes certain identification of these two men with John Maynard impossible. None the less, although he was in Ireland at the time his father drew up his will (proved in 1614), the will hints at his having lived or having intended to live elsewhere abroad.

Maynard's only known publication, *The XII Wonders of the World* (1611), describes him as 'Lutenist at the most famous Schoole of St Julians in Hertfordshire'. His dedication to Joan, Lady Thynne, of Caus Castle in Shropshire, states: 'This poore play-woorke of mine, had its prime originall and birth-wrights in your own house, when by nearer service I was obliged yours', and mentions her daughter Dorothy, 'who once laboured me to that effect', implying that he once taught music in the household. The words of *The XII Wonders* were written about 1600 by Sir John Davies, then solicitor-general for Ireland. Published in the 1608 edition of Davison's *Poetical Rhapsody*, the poems poked fun at stock figures of the time. Maynard's music is for voice, lute, and bass viol, 'all three ioyntly, and none seuerall', and treats the two instruments more independently than was usual at the time. Six duets for lute and bass viol follow, the first three forming a thematically related suite: pavan, galliard, and 'An almond to both'. The following pavan and galliard require special tunings for both instruments, but the final 'Adew' returns to normal. The book concludes with seven pavans in tablature for the lyra viol with optional bass viol 'to fill up the parts'.

Maynard may have had a London house: 'Joane, wife of John Maynard', was buried on 6 June 1619 at St Dunstan-in-the-West, a parish where many musicians lived at that time. However, for some periods at least he lived at St Julian's, apparently inherited from his elder brother Robert: in 1611 he paid tithes there, and in 1633 the property was described as 'late' in his occupation. Maynard died before November 1633.   IAN HARWOOD

Sources J. Maynard, *The XII wonders of the world* (1611); facs. edn, ed. I. Harwood (1970) · I. Harwood, 'John Maynard and *The XII wonders of the world*', *Lute Society Journal*, 4 (1962), 7–17 · J. Traficante, 'Music for the lyra viol: the printed sources', *Lute Society Journal*, 8 (1966), 7–25 · *New Grove* · parish register, St Albans Abbey, Herts. ALS · parish register (burial), St Dunstan-in-the-West, London · tithes, parish of St Michael's, St Albans

Maynard, Sir John (1592–1658), politician, was the second son of Sir Henry *Maynard (b. after 1547, d. 1610) of Little Easton, Essex, secretary to Lord Burghley, and Susan (d. in or after 1612), second daughter of Thomas Pierson (or Pearson), gentleman usher of Star Chamber. His elder brother was William, first Lord Maynard (b. in or before 1589, d. 1640). There is no certain record of him attending a university, but it is known that he entered the Inner Temple in 1610.

By 1619 Maynard had come to the notice of the marquess of Buckingham and had become a member of his circle at court. His participation in court masques in January 1619 and January 1620 was noted by John Chamberlain, who commented on the first occasion that 'young Maynard … beares away the bell for dauncing, and were otherwise a very proper man but that he is extreme poreblind' (*The Letters of John Chamberlain*, ed. N. E. McClure, 1939, 200). Maynard reported to Buckingham from the siege of Bergen-op-Zoom in July 1622, and sent him news from the English court when the duke was with the prince of Wales in Spain in 1623. In October that year he was chosen to carry the king's condolences to the French ambassador following the collapse of the chapel at the latter's residence, and in the following November his masque congratulating Prince Charles on his return from Spain was performed at York House. The masque was reported to have offended the Spanish ambassador, in whose presence it took place. A masque of Maynard's was also performed at Burley on the Hill in August 1624.

Maynard served as member for Chippenham, Wiltshire, in the 1624 parliament, and represented the borough again in 1625. In the 1628–9 parliament he sat for Calne in the same county. At the coronation of Charles I Maynard was made knight of the Bath and a servant of the privy chamber. On 25 November 1624 he married Mary (d. c.1680), daughter of Sir Thomas *Myddelton (1549×56–1631) of Stansted Mountfichet, a former mayor of London, through whom he gained significant political contacts in the City. Maynard made his principal home at Tooting in Surrey, but also acquired estates at Isleham in Cambridgeshire and Bradford in Yorkshire.

By 1628 Maynard had become an effective agent and propagandist for Buckingham, working to advance his patron's interests in parliament and the City while defending him against the charge that he favoured Arminianism and popery. One product of this work for Buckingham was a forged letter, widely circulated before parliament sat in 1628, which purported to be written by an English Jesuit to the father rector in Brussels and which identified Buckingham as the Jesuits' most formidable enemy in England. The letter angered Buckingham, however, as did Maynard's speech in parliament attacking the use of foreign mercenaries by the English crown, and it is possible that Maynard was still out of favour when the duke was assassinated in August 1628. His involvement in court affairs was much reduced following the death of his patron, and an incident in 1637, when he attacked John Craven on the bowling green at Whitehall over a debt, and struck Lord Powis when he tried to intervene, cannot have helped his ambitions.

Maynard sided with parliament on the outbreak of civil

war. He lent at least £700 to parliament on the propositions in the autumn of 1642, and in November he was appointed a Surrey deputy lieutenant. In the following August he was involved in moves to secure the arrest of MPs close to the earl of Northumberland who were suspected of planning to go over to the king. In the same month he emerged as a leading figure on the committee for the safety of Surrey, a new committee set up by parliament to take over the control of military affairs from the county's deputy lieutenants. Maynard used his influence on this committee to support his kinsman Colonel Samuel Jones, who had been appointed governor of Farnham Castle in August 1643. Between April 1644 and April 1645 Maynard was engaged in a series of disputes with the Surrey politician Sir Richard Onslow and his allies, who sought to reduce the costly Farnham garrison and return the control of the Surrey forces from the committee to the deputy lieutenants. Although Maynard benefited from the support in print of the poet George Wither in his conflicts with Onslow, and from the support of militant parliamentarians in London and the south-east, it was Onslow who won the backing of parliament in April 1645 when a new county committee was established from which Maynard and his supporters were excluded. Maynard continued to serve on the Surrey subcommittee of accounts, which clashed regularly with the county committee, but his involvement in Surrey affairs had ceased by December 1646.

Sir John was elected as MP for Lostwithiel, Cornwall, in January 1647, and quickly became identified as an outspoken opponent of the army and ally of the presbyterian leadership in the Commons. He had, two years before, supported the creation of the New Model Army, but his doubts about the trustworthiness of leading Independents were evident as early as June 1645, when he was suspected of spreading rumours that the earl of Northumberland, Viscount Saye and Sele, Sir Henry Vane, Oliver St John, and Oliver Cromwell were engaged in secret negotiations with the king to end the war and 'bring in all manner of religions' (House of Lords RO, main papers series, 1645, 24 June–9 July, fol. 211). Maynard was an active member of parliament, being appointed to several committees including the indemnity committee and committee for the fens. On the latter committee, before which he had appeared on behalf of fenland inhabitants in June 1646, he soon became known as a vigorous opponent of drainage undertakings. In June 1647 he was one of the eleven members singled out for impeachment by the army. When details of the particular charges were published it was clear that no specific charge could be levelled against Maynard, whose name was included only in the general charges laid against the group as a whole. His hostility towards the army leadership was no doubt the main reason why he was accused with the rest, but at least one commentator suggested that his name was on the list only because he had opposed the fen drainage schemes in which Cromwell was 'so deeply engaged' (W. Prynne, *A Declaration of the Officers and Armies illegall, Injurious Proceedings & Practices Against the XI impeached Members*, 1647, 5).

Maynard withdrew from parliament after 26 June 1647, when the Commons granted the eleven members leave of absence. Although reports from London in early July suggested that he was openly accusing the army of being all 'rebelles and traytors' (C. H. Firth, ed., *The Clarke Papers*, 1891, 1.150), there is no evidence that he was involved in planning the apprentices' assault on parliament on 26 July. After the speakers and several members of both houses fled to the army following the riots Maynard resumed his seat in the Commons, and by 3 August he was signing warrants as a member of the revived committee of safety. In an intercepted letter he reiterated his earlier claims about the duplicity of Independent politicians, on this occasion accusing Lord Saye and several of his allies in the House of Commons of being the true authors of the army's *Heads of Proposals*.

Maynard was, with John Glynn, one of only two of the eleven members to obey the summons to attend the House of Commons following the army's march on London and the return of the speakers and fugitive members. On 7 September 1647 he appeared before the house and, having refused to answer the charges against him, was committed to the Tower. On 28 October articles of impeachment against him were read in the house and assented to. By 3 November he had made contact with his fellow prisoner in the Tower, John Lilburne, who became an important friend and ally. When Maynard was brought before the House of Lords on 5 February 1648 he refused to listen to the charges made against him or to answer them, and was fined £500. His insistence that the Lords had no right to proceed against him drew comparisons in the press with Lilburne, and in the following two months not only Lilburne but his allies John Wildman and John Harris published pamphlets in support of his cause.

Maynard's impeachment was discharged on 3 June 1648 and he was allowed to resume his seat in the Commons. On 27 June he spoke in favour of the City of London petition for an accommodation with the king, and denounced those he called 'Royal Independents' and 'Royal Presbyterians', terms which had first appeared in print in February in *The Royall Quarrell*, the pamphlet published on his behalf by John Harris. On 1 August his persuasive speech in the Commons in favour of Lilburne helped secure the latter's release from imprisonment.

Sir John supported the treaty of Newport and was secluded from the Commons at Pride's Purge. Although his name does not appear alongside those accused of involvement in presbyterian plots against the new regime, he continued to act with Lilburne in opposing the activities of drainage undertakers in the fens, who in the Great Level included several prominent supporters of the government. In 1649 he argued before the parliamentary committee for the Great Level that the drainage scheme was chiefly the work of courtiers whose disregard for property rights in the 1630s had been a principal cause of civil war. His continuing activities in 1653 against the scheme led to complaints about the interference in these matters of 'discontented busy persons' (BL, Add. MS

25302, fol. 130), and one supporter of the scheme suggested to Secretary Thurloe that 'we are in the same danger of him that the State is of Lilburne' (*CSP dom.*, 1653–4, 120).

Little is known of Maynard between late 1653 and his death in Tooting on 29 July 1658. He was buried at Tooting; he was survived by his wife and was succeeded by his son John, who was knighted on 7 June 1660 and died on 14 May 1664.

JOHN GURNEY

Sources J. Gurney, 'The county of Surrey and the English revolution', DPhil diss., U. Sussex, 1991 · J. Gurney, 'George Wither and Surrey politics, 1642–1649', *Southern History*, 19 (1997), 74–98 · *The picklock of the olde fenne projects* (1650) · J. Howldin [J. Wildman], *The lawes subversion* (1648) · Sirrahniho [J. Harris], *The royall quarrell, or, England's lawes and liberties vindicated* (1648) · *A speech spoken in the honourable House of Commons (July 27, 1648) by Sir John Maynard* (1648) · *A speech by an honourable knight [Sir John Maynard] in the House of Commons upon the delivery of the City petition* (1648) · *JHC · JHL · DNB* · K. Lindley, *Fenland riots and the English revolution* (1982) · R. C. Johnson and others, eds., *Commons debates, 1628*, 4 (1978); 6 (1983) · R. C. Johnson and others, eds., *Commons debates, 1628*, 1 (1977); 4 (1978); 6 (1983) · *State trials*, vol. 4 · PRO, SP 14; SP 16; SP 18 · will, 13 April 1655, PRO, PROB 11/280, fol. 226 ff. · J. Aubrey, *The natural history and antiquities of the county of Surrey*, 5 vols. (1718–19) · O. Manning and W. Bray, *The history and antiquities of the county of Surrey*, 3 vols. (1804–14) · P. Morant, *The history and antiquities of the county of Essex*, 2 vols. (1768) · W. M. Myddelton, ed., *Chirk Castle accounts, AD 1605–1666* (privately printed, St Albans, 1908) · W. H. Cooke, ed., *Students admitted to the Inner Temple, 1547–1660* [1878] · J. L. Chester, ed., *The registers of St Mary Aldermary ... 1558–1754* (1880) · W. A. Shaw, *The knights of England*, 2 vols. (1906) · BL, Lansdowne MS 92 · Venn, *Alum. Cant.* · *VCH Cambridgeshire and the Isle of Ely*
Archives PRO, state papers, domestic, Charles I, SP 16 · PRO, state papers, domestic, James I, SP 14
Wealth at death estates at Tooting, Surrey, Isleham, Cambridgeshire and Little Horton in Bradford, Yorkshire: will, PRO, PROB 11/280, fols. 226 ff.; widow's correspondence, 1658

Maynard, John (1600–1665), clergyman and ejected minister, was born at Rotherfield, Sussex, and baptized at Mayfield in the same county, on 8 March 1600, the son of a wealthy yeoman. He entered Queen's College, Oxford, on 21 June 1616, and graduated BA on 3 February 1620 as a 'grand compounder'. He transferred to Magdalen Hall, and proceeded MA on 26 June 1622.

At that time Maynard owned 19 acres in the manor of Sharendon, Mayfield. On 12 August 1624 he took up the living there, and on 9 February the next year married Margaret, daughter of the previous incumbent, John Luck. Together they had seven children—two sons, John and Richard, and five daughters, most of whom died young. Margaret died on 2 October 1635 after giving birth to twins. Maynard then married, on 28 June 1637, the widowed Mary Withers of St Edmund's parish, Lombard Street, London. Mary was buried at Mayfield on 6 May 1640. She too may have died following childbirth, since a tablet in Southwark Cathedral records the death of her daughter, Margaret, on 14 March 1653, aged thirteen. On 1 April 1642 at St Margaret Moyses, Friday Street, London, Maynard was again married, this time to Mary Wood, of Hackney, Middlesex.

At the opening of hostilities between the king and parliament, according to Wood, Maynard 'preached with more liberty' (Wood, *Ath. Oxon.*, 3rd edn, 3.892). He took the covenant and on 14 September 1643 was selected as a representative of Sussex to the Westminster assembly of divines, which he regularly attended. On 26 February 1645 he preached before the House of Commons on a fast day and his sermon was subsequently published. At another fast on 28 October 1646 Maynard again addressed the Commons. In this sermon, entitled *A Shadow of the Victory of Christ* (1646), he professed his belief that 'we are under the seventh trumpet [of Revelation] ... Now is the time when Christ shall conquer Kingdoms ... to reign over them, forever' (p. 10).

Maynard was appointed vicar of Camberwell, Surrey, on 21 November 1646. His parishioners petitioned against him on account of his having another living in Sussex, but they were overruled in December. In an undated entry Maynard recorded in the Mayfield parish register that he had offered to give up the tithes of the parish for the maintenance of a minister in his absence, but since no fit person was appointed, 'there was no constant minister for sometime, and afterwards divers changes, so that the register was neglected for divers years' (Lower, 234). However, Maynard deputed Elias Paul D'Aranda, later pastor of the Walloon church in Canterbury Cathedral, to act as a curate with full benefit of the parish tithe. In 1654 Maynard was appointed one of the assistants to the commissioners of Sussex for the ejection of scandalous ministers and schoolmasters. In the late 1650s Maynard is said to have preached out of his home in Camberwell and to have erected a meeting-house there in 1657 after apparently resigning his living.

In 1662 both Maynard and his curate were ejected from Mayfield. He subsequently lived at Cranesden, a farmhouse in Mayfield, until his death on 7 June 1665. He was buried in the churchyard in Mayfield. He was survived by his fourth wife, Ann, daughter of Henry Engham, whom he had married before 7 June 1665; she died on 7 September 1670, and was buried beside her husband. Maynard's *The Young Man's Remembrancer and the Old Man's Monitor* had appeared the previous year and a number of his Mayfield sermons were published in 1674, with the encouragement of his son-in-law.

MARK ROBERT BELL

Sources *Calamy rev.*, 346 · R. W. Blencowe, 'Extracts from parish registers and other parochial documents of east Sussex', *Sussex Archaeological Collections*, 4 (1851), 243–90, esp. 258–9 · W. D. Cooper, 'Mayfield', *Sussex Archaeological Collections*, 21 (1869), 1–23, esp. 18–19 · J. R. Daniel-Tyssen, 'Parliamentary surveys of the county of Sussex [pt 2]', *Sussex Archaeological Collections*, 25 (1873), 23–61, esp. 25 · M. A. Lower, *The worthies of Sussex* (1865), 234–5 · *DNB* · Wood, *Ath. Oxon.*, new edn, 3.892–3 · Foster, *Alum. Oxon.* · E. M. Bell-Irving, *Mayfield: the story of an old wealden village* (1903) · *JHL*, 6 (1643–4), 216 · *JHC*, 4 (1644–6), 39, 46 · *JHC*, 6 (1648–51), 12 · J. F. Wilson, *Pulpit in parliament: puritanism during the English civil wars, 1640–1648* (1969) · A. R. Bax, 'The plundered ministers of Surrey', *Surrey Archaeological Collections*, 9 (1888), 233–316, esp. 249–52

Maynard, Sir John (1604–1690), lawyer and politician, was born on 18 July 1604 at the Abbey House in Tavistock, Devon, eldest son of Alexander Maynard (b. c.1567) and Honora, daughter of Arthur Arscott of Tetcott, Devon. Maynard followed his father's profession and entered his

Sir John Maynard (1604–1690), after John Riley?

father's inn, the Middle Temple, after taking his BA from Exeter College, Oxford, on 25 April 1621. He came to the bar in 1626 and became a bencher of his inn in 1648.

Maynard married Elizabeth (*d.* 1654/1655), daughter of Andrew Henley of Taunton, by 1631, by which time he was well advanced in his legal career. He first appears in the records and reports of the courts at Westminster Hall in 1628, where he continued to plead in the 1630s, aided in part by the patronage of Attorney-General Sir William Noy. He represented Totnes in both parliaments seated in 1640. Throughout the controversies of that decade Maynard remained close to his native county. Plymouth made him their recorder in 1640, as did Totnes in 1645, and he served in various county commissions during those years. But it was at Westminster that he made his name. Maynard, with John Glynn and his old friend Bulstrode Whitelocke, served as counsel prosecuting the earl of Strafford in parliament in 1641. Maynard later played the same role in the impeachment of Archbishop William Laud. Though he helped to destroy the king's servants, as late as Hilary term 1642 Maynard continued to present briefs for the crown in king's bench, as he had done for years.

In parliament Maynard actively engaged in the regulation of the church, reporting the work of a committee in 1641 to examine irregularly composed church canons. In the debate on the grand remonstrance later that year, Maynard spoke in favour of requiring privy councillors to receive parliamentary approval. Maynard remained at Westminster throughout the civil war. He participated in the Westminster assembly of divines and took the covenant. His commitment to presbytery and his willingness to work with the Scots put him in league with those who

sought a peaceful resolution of the conflict. In February 1648 Maynard argued that parliament's decision to make no more addresses to the king in effect dissolved the parliament. He then withdrew from parliament and remained at a distance during the trial and execution of the king.

Maynard may have withdrawn from Westminster Hall as well during the second half of 1648 and early 1649: he made no appearances in king's bench, in which he had pleaded often during the previous twenty years. But he took the engagement to the Commonwealth, returned to his lucrative practice, and maintained an active public presence. In December 1650 Maynard was one of the principal defenders of the corporation of London against the Leveller Major John Wildman, who argued that the City's government should be re-established by popular assent. Maynard condemned 'popularity': 'certainly the experience of all generations in the world evidences this truth, that there may be just subjection without assent' (*London's Liberties*, 13). Perhaps this helps explain Maynard's initial reluctance to provide counsel to John Lilburne in 1653. When he at last did so, he helped Lilburne undermine the indictment against him. Much of Maynard's legal work in the 1640s and 1650s came on writs of habeas corpus and mandamus, related devices used to constrain the actions of lesser courts and administrative officers. Having pleaded numerous times in habeas corpus cases since the 1630s, the conflicts of civil war and interregnum created only more chances for Maynard to do so. In 1655 Maynard argued the habeas corpus for a London merchant imprisoned by the council of state for refusing to pay a duty. Maynard and his co-counsel were committed when they argued that the duty was illegal; they were soon released after making their submission to the council. Maynard played an even more important role in cases on mandamus, by which people purged from local office during the recent turmoil could win back their places. In 1643 he used the writ to try to regain a schoolmaster's lost place, and in 1647 he argued successfully for the restoration of two London common councilmen.

Support for monarchy According to Bishop Burnet, Maynard had become one of a handful of prominent lawyers desiring a restoration of monarchy as early as the mid-1650s. In 1656 Maynard was chosen to parliament for Plymouth, though he was not allowed to sit. Otherwise he continued to enjoy preferment. In 1654 he was made serjeant-at-law, and in May 1658 he became a protector's serjeant. In 1659 he was again chosen as a member of parliament, for Newtown, Isle of Wight. Maynard prospered during the 1650s: by 1654 he had purchased the manor of Bere Ferrers, between Plymouth and Tavistock, from the royalist earl of Newport. His wife died around this time, but by 1658 he was building a new house at Gunnersbury, Middlesex, on a property once belonging to the bishop of London. This project may well have been connected to his second marriage, in February 1657, to a Kent widow, Jane Selhurst. Maynard would marry twice more after her death in early 1668. Margaret (*d.* 1679), daughter of Edward, Lord Gorges and twice widowed herself, became his third wife by 1671. Mary Upton (d. 1721), daughter of a canon of Christ Church, Oxford, and widow of Dr Charles Vermuyden, married Maynard on 2 June 1680. Maynard had seven children with his first wife, though no children followed from his later marriages.

Both Plymouth and Exeter chose Maynard for the Convention of 1660, though he ultimately sat for Exeter. Like many, Maynard was ready to do everything possible to help the nation forget the preceding two decades. The Commons asked Maynard and William Prynne to see that all orders relating to the engagement were expunged. Maynard sat on the committee charged with promoting Charles II's tolerationist declaration of Breda and on another that prepared the bill for continuing judicial proceedings; he took the lead in preparing the Indemnity Bill and helped to draft the acceptance of the king's pardon. The king too seemed ready to forget recent events; among other acts of forgiveness, he again made Maynard a serjeant-at-law. In November 1660 Charles knighted him and promoted him to king's serjeant.

In 1661 Maynard was seated for Bere Alston, his own pocket borough given his ownership of the manor of Bere Ferrers. He chaired or sat on numerous committees, especially those concerned with proposed changes to the law. He thus assisted with an unsuccessful bill for setting up a land registry and another concerning delays in legal process. In December 1666 Maynard served on the committee that drew up the charges on which Lord Mordaunt was impeached, and he helped to manage the conference with the Lords on the same matter. Maynard took the other side in the impeachment of the earl of Clarendon in 1667, and made a valiant attempt to fend off his attackers: 'where life is concerned, you ought to have a moral certainty of the thing' (State trials, 6.330). Saying this in a proceeding so like the impeachments of Strafford and Laud must have started tongues to wag against the now venerable lawyer.

Maynard was widely seen as a supporter of the crown throughout the 1660s, particularly in matters affecting royal revenues. The privy council and royal officers turned to him for legal advice and for help mediating disputes. As a king's serjeant, Maynard pleaded often for the king as he continued his practice as one of the leaders in the courts at Westminster. He maintained his prominence in arguments on mandamus, including those used in efforts to restore dismissed university fellows, cases that proved crucial for defining king's bench's purview on the writ. Similarly, Maynard presented the king's case in a 1663 mandamus sent to the New River Water Company, successfully contending that a dismissed company officer should have the writ because expulsions from companies with royal charters 'concerned the king' (1 Levinz 123, 83 ER 329). Maynard premised his arguments on the idea that the king should superintend the conduct of all lesser authorities; acting through this court and using these writs, the king protected his subjects' liberties and privileges. Maynard applied much the same reasoning in 1668 during the Commons' dispute with the House of Lords in the case of Thomas Skinner v. the East India Company. When the Lords heard the matter and found for Skinner, the Commons complained that the Lords had exceeded their jurisdiction. As Maynard explained at a conference with the Lords, 'all justice flows from his Majesty' (Hart, 246). Conflict between the two houses continued until the king intervened, ordering the proceedings of both houses to be erased from their journals.

Among those who had been imprisoned and fined by order of the Lords in Skinner's case was Sir Samuel Barnardiston, the company's deputy governor. In 1674 Maynard served as one of Barnardiston's counsel against Sir William Soame, who as sheriff of Suffolk in 1674 had, according to Barnardiston, wrongly made a double return in his contest for a parliamentary seat. This was another crucial test of the Commons' privilege to decide disputed elections. Maynard now took the other side, arguing that this was not properly a parliamentary matter since the events in question occurred outside the house. More important was the legal device Maynard employed: an action on the case for a false return, the same device used in testing the propriety of returns to writs of mandamus. Maynard admitted in court that this was a novel way to proceed, but successfully argued that only with this most flexible of procedural instruments could one have a wrong righted when it involved circumstances that were new to the law. The decision went for Barnardiston, though it was later reversed in exchequer chamber when it was presided over by Sir Francis North, who had earlier represented Soame. In 1679 Maynard would serve on a committee charged to propose electoral reform and to consider a parliamentary reversal of the judgment in Barnardiston's case.

Law in parliament As one of the kingdom's most important lawyers, Maynard consistently took centre stage in parliamentary discussions of changes to the workings of the law. Thus he sat with other prominent lawyers on a committee appointed in February 1677 to consider the inroads made by courts of equity on common law jurisdiction. Perhaps owing to his experience arguing writs of habeas corpus, he was also among those charged in 1668 and again in the mid-1670s with preparing a bill to improve the writ's effectiveness. On the other hand, in 1670 Maynard had argued unsuccessfully for the king in Bushell's case that habeas corpus might not be used to free jurors imprisoned for returning a verdict against the evidence. And for Maynard, the writ did not extend to the inspection of commitments by parliament. Thus when the earl of Shaftesbury was imprisoned by the House of Lords in 1677, it was Maynard who argued against his release. Astonishingly—given his contentions in Skinner's case—Maynard contended in Shaftesbury's case 'that the House of Lords is the supreme court of the land' (State trials, 6.1290); thus the writ could not run from king's bench to a superior court. Maynard's view now prevailed. Despite these courtroom appearances in which he argued to limit the writ, Maynard proved one of the central figures when the Habeas Corpus Act—which dramatically expanded the writ's ambit—finally passed in 1679.

Maynard served for Plymouth in the parliaments of

1679–81, where he eagerly joined his Commons colleagues in believing the tales of a 'popish plot'. Depending largely on the evidence of Titus Oates, Maynard prosecuted Edward Coleman; he participated in other trials of accused plotters throughout 1679 to destroy what he called the 'abominable conspiracy against the king, the nation, the religion, and the law' (*State trials*, 7.768). He also helped to manage the Commons' evidence against Viscount Stafford. Many sympathetically noted Stafford's advanced age, suspecting that this explained why he was the first of the five 'popish lords' to be tried in parliament. But Maynard, his prosecutor, was ten years older; he could look back now on a lengthy career in parliamentary impeachments. In 1667, while defending Clarendon, Maynard had argued that 'when a case comes that is the sheet-anchor of life, and estate, you should be wary; for by wit and oratory that may be made treason which is not' (ibid., 6.345). But with the attack on Stafford and on the earl of Danby, Maynard argued for a dramatically expanded reading of the law of treason; he later served on the committee which drew up the articles for Danby's impeachment. Likewise, Maynard justified impeaching Chief Justice Sir William Scroggs by broadening treason to include anything the Commons might choose: 'Whatever offence deserves the punishment of a traitor, the Parliament may impeach' (ibid., 8.202).

Maynard also argued for impeaching Edward Fitzharris. When the House of Lords refused to try him, Maynard insisted that this was a breach of the Commons' privilege to impeach. None the less, Maynard joined the team of prosecutors once Fitzharris was brought for trial in king's bench. Fitzharris pleaded against king's bench's jurisdiction, claiming that an impeachment still pended against him in parliament, thus barring process in a lesser court. Ironically Maynard, who had previously defended parliament's jurisdiction, now tossed Fitzharris's complaint aside. After convincing the court that it could proceed to trial, Maynard then helped manage the evidence which ultimately produced Fitzharris's execution for treason.

Maynard joined in some of the other prosecutions of plotters and libellers of the early 1680s, but, given his prominence in court and Commons, Maynard slipped surprisingly far from view in the years after 1682. He played no part in formulating London's defence against the *quo warranto* adjudged against the City in 1683, though in 1684 he advised Plymouth against giving up its charter when threatened by a *quo warranto*, saying that the charter was 'a trust that could not be surrendered' (M. Landon, *The Triumph of the Lawyers*, 1970, 128). He thus promoted a view that had been demolished by the London judgment, a view that would not be revived after 1688, and one Maynard himself had condemned in his 1650 debate with John Wildman when he observed that 'no doubt but there is forfeiture of charters' (*London's Liberties*, 38). Maynard lost his recorderships when Plymouth and Totnes received new charters in 1684, and he fared worse in the next reign when he was put out of the many county commissions of the peace on which he had served. But Maynard sat for Bere Alston in James II's parliament,

where he opposed the grant of supply on grounds that it might be used to build a royal army officered by Catholics.

In October 1688 Maynard was one of the legal luminaries appointed to the special commission for investigating the birth of the prince of Wales. In December the provisional government consulted Maynard about how to proceed in the king's absence; later he helped to draw up the address of thanks to the prince of Orange. Maynard represented Plymouth in the convention in 1689 and again in the parliament convened in 1690. Though in 1650 he had argued that 'to say that no man nor people shall be governed but by assent, we deny' (*London's Liberties*, 13), he now provided a remarkably contractarian explanation of the meaning of James II's departure.

> I am of opinion that the King has deposed himself. … All government had at first its foundation from a pact with the people: & here no one can say but that pact has apparently been broken by the king's invading and violating our laws, property, liberty, and religion.   (Lewis Jones, 242)

In the weeks following Maynard helped draft the declaration of rights and supported further restrictions against Catholics. As one of England's most eminent and long-lived lawyers, Maynard was appointed with two others in February 1689 to serve as commissioner of the great seal, a post he retained until late May 1690. By September of that year, Maynard was reportedly on his deathbed. He died on 8 October 1690 at his magnificent home at Gunnersbury, in Ealing parish, where he was buried on 25 October. Having survived nearly all his family, Maynard left his property to his grandchildren in a will so tangled by the remainders he appointed that it required a private act of parliament and litigation to unravel.

Reputation Maynard demonstrated strong presbyterian commitments throughout the 1640s and 1650s. Though he later moderated these tendencies, he employed at least three chaplains ejected from their livings after 1660, gave financial support to other nonconformist clergy, and permitted them to preach in Tavistock Abbey, whose lease he held. But Maynard might be best characterized as an Anglican who retained dissenting sympathies. By at least 1680, his views were even more clearly of a conforming variety. In the debate on a bill for uniting protestants in December 1680, Maynard spoke eloquently against the dangers of permitting innovations in liturgy or in clerical vestments. But Maynard continued to promote the acceptance of presbyterian methods of ordination. He also favoured elimination of the oaths of allegiance and supremacy and the requirement that urban office-holders subscribe the declaration against the covenant, which oaths and subscription Maynard himself would have performed in order to retain his various local offices. As one Devon cleric noted, he 'never failed to conform to all things required of him in public, as oaths and tests' (Croissette).

The dissenter Roger Morrice thought Maynard 'the greatest lawyer in England' (Lacey, 423), and many agreed. Roger North suspected Maynard of presbyterian loyalties, calling him 'an anti-restoration lawyer … true as steel to the principles of the late times' (North, 1.237); but North also admired him for his professional ability, calling him 'the best old book-lawyer of his time' (ibid., 27). A constant reader of yearbooks, Maynard gathered an impressive collection of manuscript law reports and readings which was deposited in Lincoln's Inn; he edited a large body of yearbook reports, which he published in 1678. For one of his learning and ability, it is remarkable that he reached the bench only when he was in his eighties. Presiding in chancery as one of the great seal commissioners for just over a year, Maynard's time there was too brief to have any effect on that court's doctrine and practice.

As Maynard noted, 'laws are edged tools; those that understand them, make good use of them; and those that do not understand them, will find that they are sharp, and will cut' (*London's Liberties*, 14). One area of the law Maynard understood better than anyone concerned impeachments. From Strafford's trial to Stafford's, there was not a significant impeachment in which Maynard was not directly, and controversially, involved. One of his last recorded speeches in the Commons, in 1689, concerned his opposition to the impeachment of Sir Adam Blair for publishing a paper proclaiming James II. Perhaps for his support of the Commons' power to impeach and for his charity to nonconformists, Maynard is often labelled a whig. But though he felt sympathy for dissent and bigotry against Catholics, his support of monarchy was just as clear. Maynard saw the king standing at the heart of the law he knew so well. Thus he could join with notable supporters of the prerogative such as Sir George Jeffreys and Sir Robert Sawyer in some of the major prosecutions of the 1680s. In 1673 he spoke in parliament in support of the king's power to dispense with statutes, if not to suspend them altogether, and in 1667 he made the strongest defence of the king's embattled minister the earl of Clarendon. Thus Maynard rejected simplistic juxtapositions of 'the king's prerogative and the people's liberty', and was always more suspicious of the latter than he was of the former (HoP, *Commons, 1660–90*).

PAUL D. HALLIDAY

Sources J. S. Croissette, 'Maynard, Sir John', HoP, *Commons, 1660–90*, 3.38–44 • D. R. Lacey, *Dissent and parliamentary politics in England, 1661–1689* (1969) • Foss, *Judges*, 7.325–34 • ER, Croke Car.; Keble; Ventris; Levinz; Freeman;Vaughan • *London's liberties, or, A learned argument of law and reason* (1651) • CSP dom., addenda, 1660–85; 1680–84; 1689–91 • *Ninth report*, 1, HMC, 8 (1883) • *The manuscripts of the duke of Beaufort ... the earl of Donoughmore*, HMC, 27 (1891) • *The manuscripts of S. H. Le Fleming*, HMC, 25 (1890) • Foster, *Alum. Oxon., 1500–1714*, 3.995; 4.292–6 • *State trials*, vols. 3–9 • *The diary of Bulstrode Whitelocke, 1605–1675*, ed. R. Spalding, British Academy, Records of Social and Economic History, new ser., 13 (1990) • *The life and times of Anthony Wood*, ed. A. Clark, 2, OHS, 21 (1892); 3, OHS, 26 (1894) • S. R. Gardiner, *History of England from the accession of James I to the outbreak of the civil war, 1603–1642*, 10 vols. (1883–4) • S. R. Gardiner, *History of the Commonwealth and protectorate, 1649–1656*, new edn, 4 vols. (1903) • J. Hart, *Justice upon petition* (1991) • N. Luttrell, *A brief historical relation of state affairs from September 1678 to April 1714*, 6 vols. (1857) • R. North, *The lives of ... Francis North ... Dudley North ... and ... John North*, new edn, 3 vols. (1826) • J. Bruce, ed., *Verney papers: notes of proceedings in the Long Parliament*, CS, 31 (1845), (for 1844) • JHC, 2 (1640–42); 9 (1667–87) • Sainty, *King's counsel* • *The autobiography of Sir John Bramston*, ed. [Lord Braybrooke], CS, 32 (1845) • *Burnet's History of my own time*, ed. O. Airy, new edn, 2 vols. (1897–1900) • E. M. Thompson, ed., *Correspondence of the family of Hatton*, 2 vols., CS, new ser., 22–3 (1878) • J. Granger, *A biographical history of England, from Egbert the Great to the revolution*, 2 vols. (1769); suppl. (1774) • *Le Neve's Pedigrees of the knights*, ed. G. W. Marshall, Harleian Society, 8 (1873) • D. Lewis Jones, ed., 'Debate in the Convention Parliament on the status of the crown', *A parliamentary history of the glorious revolution* (1988)

Archives Lincoln's Inn, London, legal MS collections, reports, commonplace books | Cornwall RO, corresp. with Edward Nosworthy

Likenesses oils, *c*.1680, Blickling Hall, Norfolk; versions in Inner Temple, London • G. Kneller, oils, Harvard U., law school • oils (after J. Riley?), NPG [*see illus.*]

Mayne, Cuthbert [St Cuthbert Mayne] (*bap.* **1544**, *d.* **1577**), Roman Catholic priest and martyr, was baptized in Youlston, near Barnstaple, north Devon, on the feast of St Cuthbert, 20 March 1544, the son of William Mayne, a farmer employed by Sir John Chichester. He was educated at Barnstaple grammar school. Under Chichester's patronage, he was installed as rector of Huntshaw, Devon, on 11 December 1561. At the time he was only seventeen 'not knowing what religion and ministry meant' (Boyan and Lamb, 39). His uncle sent him to St Alban Hall, Oxford, in 1565. Having graduated BA in 1566 he was appointed a chaplain at St John's College and he proceeded MA in 1570.

At St John's College Mayne met two scholars, Gregory Martin and Edmund Campion, who persuaded him to embrace the Roman Catholic faith. He was forced to leave Oxford, and set sail from Cornwall to the English College at Douai, where he was admitted in 1573. He was ordained priest in 1575 and was awarded his BTh at Douai in 1576. That same year he returned to England and became chaplain to Francis *Tregian of Golden Manor, Probus, Cornwall. Acting as steward to Tregian, Mayne was able to celebrate the mass freely throughout Cornwall on the extensive family estates. At the same time the bishop of Exeter, William Bradbridge, had been instructed to deal severely with the Catholics in Cornwall. He met the sheriff of Cornwall, Richard Grenville, in nearby Truro and endorsed Grenville's wish to search Golden Manor. On Corpus Christi day, 8 June 1577, Grenville surrounded Golden with a hundred armed men and at least eight JPs. After forcing their way in, they arrested Cuthbert Mayne who was wearing the waxen Agnus Dei, prohibited under Elizabethan law. Mayne's books and papers, which included a papal bull, were rushed to the bishop waiting in Truro.

Mayne was humiliatingly paraded through the villages of Cornwall to Launceston Castle. He was clapped in irons and held in a filthy dungeon for three months. At the Michaelmas assizes he was tried before Sir Roger Manwood and Sir John Jeffreys. There were six charges. He was accused of traitorously obtaining a bull from Rome on 1 October 1576, and of publishing this bull at Golden. The third charge was that he had strongly defended the authority of the bishop of Rome on 14 February at Launceston. The next two charges related to his purchase of Agnus Deis; he was accused of delivering one to Tregian and a second to eleven other people in September 1576.

The final charge was that he had celebrated mass in the papal manner, assisted by Francis Tregian, on 1 June 1577. Although Judge Jeffreys argued that Mayne had never been to Rome and that the jubilee bull was out of date, Manwood declared Mayne a traitor and sentenced him to death. Tregian was to forfeit all his property and lands and was sentenced to imprisonment for life.

On 29 November 1577 Mayne was examined from early morning until dusk. He was assured of his life if he would swear on the Bible that the queen was the supreme head of the church in England. 'Upon this he took the Bible into his hands. Made the sign of the cross on it and said, "The Queen neither ever was, nor is, nor ever shall be the head of the Church in England"' (Boyan and Lamb, 58). Following this admission a form was drawn up for him to sign where he asked for clemency for his servant John Hodges, refused to name any of his friends, and admitted that he believed that if a Catholic prince should invade the realm to restore the Catholic faith then the Catholics in that realm should assist and help them. The document is signed in his own hand, 'These things affirmed by me Cuthbert Mayne I think to be trewe' (PRO, SP 12/118, 46). Mayne was sentenced to be hanged, drawn, and quartered at Launceston on 30 November 1577. He was dragged through the streets on a hurdle and was hanged in the market place. While still alive he was cut down, falling with such force that his eye was driven out. His members were severed and his heart held up to the people. His head was placed on the gate of Launceston Castle, and quarters of his body were sent to Bodmin, Barnstaple, Tregony, and Wadebridge. His skull is still publicly displayed in Launceston on a special pilgrimage day each June.

The first seminary priest to be martyred, Cuthbert Mayne was canonized by Pope Paul VI on 15 October 1970 as one of the forty martyrs of England and Wales. His saint's day is 30 November.

RAYMOND FRANCIS TRUDGIAN

Sources R. F. Trudgian, *Francis Tregian, 1548–1608: Elizabethan recusant* (1998) · P. Boyan and G. Lamb, *Francis Tregian (Cornish recusant)* (1955) · A. L. Rowse, *Tudor Cornwall: portrait of a society* (1941), 342–79 · G. H. Bushnell, *Sir Richard Grenville* (1936), 107–25 · G. Anstruther, *The seminary priests*, 1 (1969) · *The letters and memorials of William, Cardinal Allen (1532–1594)*, ed. T. F. Knox (1882), vol. 2 of *Records of the English Catholics under the penal laws* (1878–82) · J. Morris, ed., *The troubles of our Catholic forefathers related by themselves*, 1 (1872)
Likenesses D. Fournier, mezzotint, NPG · D. Fournier, portrait, AM Oxf.

Mayne, Jasper (1604–1672), Church of England clergyman and poet, was born in Hatherleigh, Devon, in November 1604, and baptized in the parish church there on 23 November, the fourth of five children of Jasper Maine and his wife, Mary (d. 1632). Cuthbert Mayne, the Roman Catholic seminary priest executed in 1577, came from Youlston, about 10 miles away, but Jasper Mayne's family cannot definitely be connected to the martyr. However, the Hatherleigh Maynes were local prominent Roman Catholic gentry, their once considerable property gradually wasted away by recusancy fines during the first half of the seventeenth century. By 1648 Jasper's eldest brother, John, suffered sequestration of the family's estate and was listed with other Devon papists as 'delinquent, notorious, poor' (Abell, 260).

Mayne himself conformed, if not when he was admitted to Westminster School, at least in 1623 when he proceeded to Christ Church, Oxford, as a servitor. When he matriculated on 10 October 1624 it was as a student: his election that year was for him the defining achievement of his career; ever after his signature was 'Jasper Mayne, Student'. He graduated BA on 21 October 1628 and proceeded MA on 18 June 1631. Favoured by deans Richard Corbett and (from 1628) Brian Duppa, he became 'a quaint preacher and a noted poet' (Wood, *Ath. Oxon.*, 3.971). Among his contemporaries at both Westminster and Christ Church were the poet Thomas Randolph, John Donne the younger (son of the dean of St Paul's), and the poet William Cartwright, with whom Mayne joined in an effort to retain threatened privileges traditionally enjoyed by Westminster scholars at Christ Church, the Westminster suppers. With Cartwright and others Mayne also contributed his earliest poems to collections of Latin and English commemorative verse instigated by Corbett and Duppa, verses chiefly composed on various occasions in the lives of the royal family. In such trivial academic flattery Mayne showed himself no worse and sometimes better than other contributors.

Mayne applied his poetic talent to much better effect in several commendatory poems contributed to editions of poetry by some of the finest English writers of his time. Earliest among these was 'On Worthy Master Shakespeare and his Poems', prefaced to the second folio edition of the plays (1632), in which Mayne, with critical originality, praised the playwright for his ability to make ancient and medieval history vibrant on the stage. Mayne also wrote 'On Dr. Donne's Death' for the 1633 edition of John Donne's *Poems*. Here Mayne recalled being present when Donne preached, contrasting Donne's sermons to those of puritan divines. 'To the Memory of Ben. Jonson' was Mayne's contribution to *Jonsonus virbius*, the 1638 collection of poems by various hands published after Jonson's death. Mayne praised the runic toughness of Jonson's poetry, faithful to classical models. In all three poems Mayne honoured his subjects with discriminating parody of each characteristic style, a wit of imitation combining poetic skill with critical acumen. Mayne's reputation as a poet is virtually nil; he has been best known for his plays, which are amusing. His more noteworthy poems and translations, rarely republished, have on insufficient grounds been slighted, ignored as misattributions, or branded as forgeries. But if some of his work was mediocre, Mayne was capable and did on several occasions rise to first-rate poetry.

Diversifying his literary production, in 1639 Mayne published (anonymously) his play *The Citye Match*, which had been performed before the king and queen at Whitehall the same year. His translation of some dialogues of Lucian in 1638, under the patronage of William Cavendish, earl of Newcastle, remained unpublished for years, Newcastle having turned from patronage of the arts to defence of the monarchy in the civil war. It was eventually published in

1664, dedicated to Cavendish as, by then, duke of Newcastle. Mayne also preached a Good Friday sermon at Christ Church in 1638, evidently without sufficient regard to royal regulations, an offence for which he submitted to censure by Archbishop William Laud, chancellor of the university.

In 1639 Mayne succeeded Richard Corbett as vicar of Cassington, a Christ Church benefice near Oxford, and on 1 or 2 November 1642 he proceeded BD. He continued to publish occasional poems in Oxford collections of commemorative verse through the 1640s, but the circumstances of civil war gradually prompted his withdrawal from literary pursuits to take part in ideological struggle for the cause of royalism. Following the king's arrival in the city in October 1642 and the setting up of his headquarters at Christ Church, Oxford became a garrison. It is not clear whether, like his fellow student Cartwright, Mayne formed part of the band of 'loyal schollers' (*Life and Times of Anthony Wood*, 1.55) who took up training in arms for the defence of the university, but he certainly engaged in the propaganda war. Having proceeded DD on 17 June 1646 during the last weeks of royalist occupation, following the city's surrender to the parliamentarian army Mayne preached 'shortly after' at St Mary's *A Sermon Against False Prophets* (not published until 1647) and on 9 August at Carfax church *A Sermon Concerning Unity and Agreement* (1646); peacemaking was the avowed intent of his other publication of that year, *The Difference about Church Government Ended*, which argued for civil rather than ecclesiastical governance of the church. *Ochlomachia, or, The Peoples War* (1647) opposed the taking up of arms against the king.

Having failed to answer a summons to appear before the parliamentary visitors to the university in May 1648, Mayne abandoned Oxford and Cassington for a second Christ Church living at Pyrton, given to him just two months previously. In November he was expelled from his scholarship at Christ Church. While living at Pyrton, Mayne again anonymously published a play—*The Amorous Warre* (1648), a very complicated piece of plotting that apparently was never produced on the stage. In 1651 he published another of his commemorative elegies on deceased poets, this time for a posthumous edition of Cartwright's poetry. 'To the deceased author of these poems' is as much an elegy for Mayne's own career in literature as for Cartwright, who emerges here the lamented embodiment of Mayne's aspirations as a poet, scholar, and preacher. The desolation Mayne felt, surrounded by the evident demise of his own war-torn career, is here assimilated to his grief for Cartwright.

In 1652 Mayne was ejected from his Cassington living. His predicament under the Commonwealth is illustrated by an incident when, about this time, he engaged in a futile disputation at nearby Watlington parish. Wood records that one John *Pendarves, whom he describes as an Anabaptist 'preaching in houses, barns, under trees, hedges, &c.', but who was at that time actually vicar of St Helen's, Abingdon and minister of Wantage, had provoked Mayne to preach at Watlington to a largely hostile congregation. Mayne's eloquent and learned sermon addressed the needs of that small portion of the auditory who felt inundated by the followers of Pendarves and craved the traditional ministrations of the Church of England. However, the sermon was brutally interrupted, Wood alleged, by 'a great party of anabaptists and the scum of the people' (Wood, *Ath. Oxon.*, 3.419). Mayne published his full text as *A Sermon Against Schisme, or, The Separations of these Times* (1652); preached in the style of Cartwright and Donne it bemoaned the losses for English society caused by the civil war. The same year he also published his translations of Donne's Latin epigrams in a volume of Donne's fugitive prose and poetry edited by Mayne's college friend John Donne the younger. The Latin epigrams seem to have been translated earlier, probably before 1632, although no earlier edition of the poems is extant. Since the original Latin poems have been lost, Mayne's translations constitute the only surviving record of Donne's earliest work as a poet.

In 1653 Mayne published *Certaine sermons and letters of defence and resolution, to some of the late controversies of our times* and wrote a prose letter to preface Richard Whitlock's *Zootomia, or, Observations on the Present Manners of the English*, published in 1654. In his letter he explained why he could no longer muster commendatory verse: 'the *Rudeness* of the *place* where I dwell, and my weekly *Thoughts* compelled to *size themselves* to a plain *Countrey Congregation*, have abated much of that *Fancie* which should do honour, either to your *Book* or my self'. He went on to complain in addition that 'all my *publike Poetry* hath and still is, *objected* to me as a piece of *Lightnesse*, not befitting the *Profession* or *Degree* of' a clergyman (R. Whitlock, *Zootomia*, 1654, sig. A4v).

Finally deprived of his Pyrton living, before 21 May 1656, Mayne retreated to Chatsworth, the estate of a second William Cavendish, third earl of Devonshire, where he served as a chaplain and renewed his old acquaintance with the earl's secretary, the philosopher Thomas Hobbes. According to Wood, 'between them there never was a right understanding', presumably in theological if not in political discussions (Wood, *Ath. Oxon.*, 3.972).

At the Restoration in 1660 Mayne was reinstated in his college benefices at Cassington and Pyrton and was also appointed canon of Christ Church Cathedral, archdeacon of Chichester, and a chaplain-in-ordinary to the king, in which capacity he preached at the consecration of Herbert Croft as bishop of Hereford a sermon which was later published. He could never reconcile himself to the changes a decade of parliamentary domination had brought to Oxford. In *Concio ad academiam Oxoniensem*, preached on 27 May 1662, he blasted the faculty as dull, leaden politicians: '"*plumbeos aldermannos*" and "*aldermannos plumbeos*" all one' (*Life and Times of Anthony Wood*, 1.441). Nevertheless he supported the activities of students, such as a play of 1664 after which the actors seem to have caroused excessively with the encouragement of Mayne and some other dons. According to Wood 'Dr. Mayne spoke them a speech commending them for their ingenuity, and told them he liked well an acting student' (ibid., 2.2).

Mayne now became a rich man, and contributed money for restoring a building at Christ Church. At his death in Oxford, unmarried, on 6 December 1672 he willed a large sum for the rebuilding of St Paul's Cathedral and additional bequests to the poor people of his parishes at Cassington and Pyrton, but he left nothing to Christ Church, whose atmosphere and administration on the whole he had come to find offensive. A related gesture perhaps was Mayne's promise to one of his servants at the college of '*Somewhat* (as he said) *that would make him Drink after his Death*' (Langbaine, 338). The bequest turned out to be a salted herring (not mentioned in the will). Mayne was buried in Christ Church Cathedral. DENNIS FLYNN

Sources Foster, *Alum. Oxon.* · Walker rev., 298 · Wood, *Ath. Oxon.*, new edn, 3.971 · *The life and times of Anthony Wood*, ed. A. Clark, 1–2, OHS, 19, 21 (1891–2) · J. Prince, *Danmonii orientales illustres, or, The worthies of Devon*, 2nd edn (1810) · G. B. Evans, *The plays and poems of William Cartwright* (1951) · E. T. Abell, 'A note on Jasper Mayne', *Report and Transactions of the Devonshire Association*, 57 (1925), 257–65 · M. Burrows, ed., *The register of the visitors of the University of Oxford, from AD 1647 to AD 1658*, CS, new ser., 29 (1881) · G. Langbaine, *An account of the English dramatick poets* (1691) · *The works of the most reverend father in God, William Laud*, 5, ed. J. Bliss (1853), 191 · *Hist. U. Oxf.* 4: *17th-cent. Oxf.* · probate act proved in court of the university, 28 Feb 1673, Oxf. UA · J. Donne, *Paradoxes, problemes, essayes, characters* (1652) · J. Mayne, *A sermon against false prophets* (1647)

Mayne, John (1759–1836), poet, was born at Dumfries, on 26 March 1759. Having been educated in the local grammar school he became a printer in the office of the *Dumfries Journal*. In 1782 he accompanied his family to Glasgow, where he was engaged for five years in the publishing house of the brothers Foulis. In 1787 he settled in London, first as a printer and then as proprietor and joint editor of *The Star*, an evening paper in which he inserted several of his poems. He married, but it is unclear when or to whom. He had written poetry while in Dumfries, and after 1777 he occasionally contributed poems to *Ruddiman's Weekly Magazine* in Edinburgh. Sher notes that 'Robert Fergusson was certainly a great influence. It is said that they met in Dumfries when Mayne was just 14 … and Fergusson at most 23' (Sher, 193). Between 1807 and 1817 several of Mayne's lyrics appeared in the *Gentleman's Magazine*.

Mayne's *Siller Gun* (1777) describes the celebration of an ancient Dumfries custom, first instituted by James VI and revived in 1777, of shooting for the prize of a silver gun on the king's birthday. Enlarged to two cantos in 1779, and to three and four in 1780 and 1808 respectively, it took final shape in five cantos, with notes, in 1836. Scott considered it superior to anything of Fergusson's and approaching the excellence of Burns (*The Poetical Works of Sir Walter Scott*, 1894, 307). Mayne's *Hallowe'en*, published in November 1780, probably stimulated Burns's brilliant treatment of the same theme. 'Logan braes', which appeared in *The Star* (23 May 1789), fooled Burns into thinking it a vagrant of an early master and he appropriated two of its lines in a 'Logan braes' of his own. 'Glasgow', a poem of description and characterization published in the *Glasgow Magazine* in

December 1783, is described by Sher as 'subtle and genuine' (Sher, 199); it was enlarged and issued, less successfully, in 1803. In the same year Mayne published a patriotic address entitled 'English, Scots, and Irishmen'. Though Mayne expressed a desire to revisit Dumfries he never realized this ambition and he died at his home 2 Lisson Grove, Marylebone, Middlesex, on 14 March 1836. He was buried in Paddington churchyard. Much admired by contemporaries, on his death he was (surely over-) praised by the *Gentleman's Magazine* as being second only to Burns among Scottish poets. T. W. BAYNE, *rev.* JAMES HOW

Sources R. B. Sher, 'Images of Glasgow in late eighteenth-century popular poetry', *The Glasgow Enlightenment*, ed. A. Hook and R. B. Sher (1995), 190–213 · Chambers, *Scots.*, rev. T. Thomson (1875) · '"Glasgow": a poem by John Mayne', *Glasgow, past and present: illustrated in dean of guild court reports and in the reminiscences and communications of Senex, Aliquis, J.B., &c*, rev. D. R. [D. Robertson], 1 (1884), 442–54 · Anderson, *Scot. nat.* · Irving, *Scots.* · H. R. Plomer and others, *A dictionary of the printers and booksellers who were at work in England, Scotland, and Ireland from 1726 to 1775* (1932) · W. D. Adams, *Dictionary of English literature*, 2nd edn [1878] · J. D. Ross, *Who's who in Burns* (1927) · W. McDowall, *History of the burgh of Dumfries* (1867) · R. Chambers, ed., *The songs of Scotland prior to Burns* (1862)
Archives NL Scot., literary MSS and letters

Mayne, Perry (*c*.1700–1761), naval officer, was the son of Covill Mayne (*c*.1675–1746), captain in the navy. He entered the service in August 1712 in the *Dolphin*, then commanded by his father, and served, according to his passing certificate, briefly in the *Lynn*, and then (again with his father) in the *Prince Frederick*, in the Baltic, and the *Guernsey*; a John Mayne also accompanied them and was probably a relation. Perry passed for lieutenant on 21 June 1720 and was soon appointed to the *Ipswich*; in June 1721 he moved to the *Falkland*, going out to Jamaica with the broad pennant of Commodore Barrow Harris, who, on 22 March 1725, promoted him to command the sloop *Spence*. He was with her until appointed captain of the *Dragon* on 24 September 1725.

On his return home Mayne was appointed in March 1727 to the *Seaford*, going to the Sound with Sir John Norris's fleet, and in 1729, after home service, he went to Jamaica. In December 1730 Mayne exchanged with Captain Berkeley of the *Lion*, in which he returned home in June 1732. His next appointment was to the *Worcester* in July 1738, and he joined Edward Vernon's fleet for the West Indies, taking an important part in the attack on Portobello, bombarding the Gloria Castle. Later, as one of the senior captains of the fleet, he was put in charge of such important tasks as the landing at Cartagena. He moved to the *Princesa* in 1742, and later to the *Orford*, but she was wrecked on the voyage home, though without loss of life.

Mayne reached flag-rank on 23 April 1745, and was employed in the Channel Fleet until ordered to be a member of the court martial of Vice-Admiral Richard Lestock, and later at that of Admiral Thomas Mathews. Although appointed commander-in-chief at the Nore on 10 March 1746 he was engaged for much of that year, and for most of 1747, with Lestock's and Mathews's courts martial, of which he became president after the withdrawal through illness of Sir Chaloner Ogle. During Lestock's trial Mayne was himself accused of false imprisonment by a Lieutenant Frye who had been sentenced by a court martial on which Mayne had sat. The accusation brought the members of Lestock's court martial into confrontation with the chief justice of common pleas, and alarmed the Admiralty, who feared the collapse of order and government in the navy. Mayne's position was further complicated since his presidency required him to try officers of greater seniority; the final verdicts were very controversial, and were clearly heavily influenced by political pressure.

Although he seems to have been in good standing, and was mentioned for possible commands, Mayne did not serve again. He was superannuated in 1757 and died at home at Mortlake on 5 August 1761. Mayne apparently never married, leaving bequests to a sister and the residue to a schoolmaster friend. He was evidently in comfortable circumstances.   A. W. H. PEARSALL

Sources DNB · The Vernon papers, ed. B. McL. Ranft, Navy RS, 99 (1958) · H. W. Richmond, The navy in the war of 1739–48, 3 vols. (1920) · R. F. Mackay, Admiral Hawke (1965) · GM, 1st ser., 31 (1761), 382 · J. Charnock, ed., Biographia navalis, 4 (1796), 137 · R. Beatson, Naval and military memoirs of Great Britain, 3 vols. (1790) · pay books, PRO, ADM 33/299; 33/311 · logs, PRO, ADM 51/877, 4241 · passing certificate, PRO, ADM 107/3

Mayne, Sir Richard (1796–1868), police officer, fourth son of Edward Mayne, a judge of the court of king's bench in Ireland, was born in Dublin on 27 November 1796. He graduated BA from Trinity College, Dublin, in 1818, proceeding to Trinity College, Cambridge, from where he received his MA in 1821. He was called to the bar at Lincoln's Inn on 9 February 1822, and practised on the northern circuit for seven years. In the summer of 1829 Robert Peel, the home secretary, was looking for a barrister to serve as joint commissioner of his planned Metropolitan Police. Prompted by the home secretary's cousin, also a barrister on the northern circuit, Mayne applied for the position. He was offered it without interview and accepted with alacrity. He had fallen in love with Georgina Marianne Catherine, eldest daughter of Thomas Carvick of Wyke, Yorkshire; his salary of £800 as police commissioner enabled him to propose, and the couple were married in 1831. Mayne first met his fellow commissioner, Colonel Charles Rowan, in the home secretary's office on 6 July 1829; twelve weeks later, on 29 September, the first Metropolitan Police constables began patrolling the streets of London.

Rowan and Mayne had the formidable task of recruiting, training, and organizing the new force, whose principal task, according to the instructions written by the commissioners, was 'the prevention of crime'. Mayne was the more articulate and imaginative of the two; but he was, as later events were to prove, less skilled at managing men. The commissioners dealt carefully and conscientiously with criticism from parliament, the press, and the public. However, they shared the prejudices of early nineteenth-century Englishmen against spies, and this impeded growth of a detective branch. Mayne's services were rewarded on 29 April 1848 when he was created a CB; on 25 October 1851, at the close of the Great Exhibition, he was promoted to KCB. When Rowan retired on 5 January 1850 Mayne expected to assume sole command of the force, but Captain William Hay was appointed joint commissioner. Hay and Mayne differed seriously over a variety of issues, and the situation was resolved only with Hay's death in August 1855; the following February a short Police Act was passed establishing one commissioner with two assistants.

Mayne's period as sole commissioner was increasingly unhappy. He grew more and more remote from his men, issuing pettifogging orders and insisting on the enforcement of trivial street regulations. At the same time the police had little success against violent street robbers known as 'garotters'. All this prompted a critical press campaign, which worsened following the Hyde Park riot of June 1866 and the failure to act on information which might have prevented the explosion at Clerkenwell prison on 13 December 1867. Mayne offered his resignation on these occasions, but it was refused on the grounds of his long public service. He died while still in office, at his London residence, 80 Chester Square, on 26 December 1868, and was buried four days later in Kensal Green cemetery. Initially tributes were muted, but his widow was granted a civil-list pension of £150 on 21 April 1870, and a monument to Mayne's memory was unveiled in Kensal Green cemetery on 25 January 1871.

Mayne's son, **Richard Charles Mayne** (1835–1892), naval officer, was educated at Eton College; he joined the navy in 1847. He served in the three naval theatres of the Crimean War (1854–6), in Vancouver Island and British Columbia (1857–61), about which he wrote a memoir, and in New Zealand (1863–4), where he was wounded. Between 1866 and 1869 he commanded the survey expedition to the Strait of Magellan, subsequently publishing sailing instructions for the region. In 1870 he married Sabine, the daughter of Thomas Dent. He retired from the navy on 27 November 1879 with the rank of rear-admiral, and was made a CB; on 26 November 1885 he was gazetted a retired vice-admiral. In 1885 he contested Pembroke and Haverfordwest as a conservative, but was narrowly beaten; the following year, as a Liberal Unionist, he was successful. He died suddenly, at his home, 101 Queen's Gate, London, after attending a banquet at the Mansion House, London, on 29 May 1892.   CLIVE EMSLEY

Sources Boase, Mod. Eng. biog. · S. H. Palmer, Police and protest in England and Ireland, 1780–1850 (1988) · B. Cobb, The first detectives and the early career of Richard Mayne, commissioner of police (1957) · P. T. Smith, Policing Victorian London: political policing, public order, and the London Metropolitan Police (1985) · D. Ascoli, The queen's peace: the origins and development of the Metropolitan Police, 1829–1979 (1979) · The Times (29 Dec 1868) · Kelly, Handbk [Richard Charles Mayne]
Archives PRO, MEPO files, corresp. and orders | W. Sussex RO, letters to duke of Richmond
Likenesses T. Langer, line engraving (after photograph by J. Watkins), NPG · Russell & Sons, photograph (Mayne, Richard Charles), repro. in The Graphic (4 June 1892), 655 · engraving (Mayne, Richard

Charles; after Russell & Sons), repro. in *ILN* (4 June 1892), 683 · portrait, repro. in Ascoli, *Queen's peace* · wood-engraving (after photograph by J. Watkins), repro. in *ILN* (9 Jan 1869)

Wealth at death under £5000: probate, 19 Jan 1869, *CGPLA Eng. & Wales* · £10,934 7s. 11d.—Richard Charles Mayne: probate, 16 Aug 1892, *CGPLA Eng. & Wales*

Mayne, Richard Charles (1835–1892). *See under* Mayne, Sir Richard (1796–1868).

Mayne, Robert Blair (1915–1955), army officer, was born on 11 January 1915 in Newtownards, co. Down, the third son in the family of four sons and three daughters of William Mayne, who ran the family's prosperous wine and grocery business, and his wife, Margaret Vane. He was educated at Regent House School and was later articled to a solicitor, while reading law at Queen's University, Belfast. An outstanding sportsman, he became in 1936 Irish universities' heavyweight boxing champion, and in 1938 he received the first of six rugby international caps for Ireland and toured South Africa with the British Lions.

At the outbreak of the Second World War Mayne served with various units, including the Royal Ulster Rifles. When the Special Air Service (SAS) was formed in north Africa in 1941 by Captain David Stirling, Mayne volunteered to join it. Initially known as L detachment SAS brigade, this force consisted of seven officers and sixty other ranks. Its aim was to disrupt axis lines of communication in the desert, in particular by attacks on enemy airfields. The first operation in which the new unit was engaged and in which Mayne participated—parachute raids on two German airfields in November 1941—was a disastrous failure, owing to atrocious weather conditions. After this Stirling decided the approach must be made by land through the desert. Mayne quickly established himself as the most exceptional officer in Stirling's rapidly expanding SAS force, which became the 1st Special Air Service regiment in September 1942, with Stirling in command as lieutenant-colonel. Mayne received the DSO for a raid on Tamet airfield, only three weeks after the initial disaster, destroying fourteen enemy aircraft and damaging ten others. Three weeks later he again raided this airfield, destroying another twenty-seven aircraft. Mayne personally, together with the patrols which he led with such skill and dash, almost certainly destroyed, during some fourteen months of constant raids from desert bases deep behind enemy lines, more aircraft than any fighter ace on either side in the Second World War.

Following Stirling's capture in early 1943, the SAS was reorganized into two parts, with Mayne in command of the special raiding squadron (SRS), 1 SAS. The SRS played a notable part in the invasion of Sicily. On the night of 9–10 July 1943, landing from the sea, it put out of action two Italian coastal batteries at Cape Murro di Porco, and two days later it followed this by a daylight landing and attack on Augusta, which was strongly defended by troops of the Hermann Goering division. For his part in these attacks Mayne received his first bar to a DSO. Later, on 4 September, the SRS attacked Bagnara Calabria, capturing a vital bridge, thus facilitating the advance of the Eighth Army. A month later the SRS, together with 3 and 40 commandos,

captured Termoli, albeit incurring serious casualties. This was Mayne's last action in Italy.

On his return to England the SRS was expanded, becoming 1st SAS regiment, with Mayne, promoted lieutenant-colonel, forming part of the SAS brigade. The strategic function of the brigade was deep penetration by parachute and jeep behind the enemy lines, during and after the opening of the second front. In August 1944 Mayne was parachuted into France, west of Dijon. He subsequently played a notable part, harassing the enemy behind the lines, and was awarded a second bar to his DSO.

During the later stages of the campaign in Europe, the role of the SAS became more tactical. Mayne took command of two jeep-borne SAS squadrons which helped to clear the way, working with 4 Canadian armoured division, for the capture of Kiel and Wilhelmshaven. In these operations, often in close and difficult country, 1st SAS incurred serious casualties. But its success, as always, owed much to the presence right forward of Mayne, who received a third bar to his DSO, an almost unprecedented award, and a recognition of Mayne's prowess as an officer of rare quality. Although the SAS owed its inception and early inspiration to Stirling, the run of successes which Mayne achieved in its early formative months assured its immediate future. The unit's subsequent successes in Italy, France, and Germany made the post-war renaissance of the SAS, as a permanent part of the British defence forces, that much easier to achieve.

Mayne was an unusual and complicated person. He was cool and fearless in wartime, and an excellent leader. He could be ruthless and on rare occasions callous. The life of this normally gentle giant of a man was also punctuated from time to time by acts of sudden, often inexplicable, violence—usually associated with an over-generous intake of alcohol. He had a deep concern for the welfare of his men and their families, and in his later years lavished much care on his invalid mother. He never really adjusted to peacetime routine, suffering much in his later years, as secretary to the Incorporated Law Society of Northern Ireland, from wartime injuries. He was unmarried. He died in a car accident in Mill Street, Newtownards, on 14 December 1955.   JELLICOE, *rev.*

Sources R. Bradford and M. Dillon, *Lt.-Col. Paddy (Blair) Mayne D.S.O.* (1987) · W. Seymour, *British special forces* (1985) · J. Strawson, *A history of the SAS regiment* (1984) · private information (1993) · personal knowledge (1993) · *CGPLA Eng. & Wales* (1956) · *The Times* (15 Dec 1955) · *The Times* (24 Dec 1955)

Archives SAS Regimental Association Holdings | FILM IWM FVA, actuality footage

Wealth at death £1896 18s. 5d. in England: Northern Irish probate sealed in England, 26 July 1956, *CGPLA Eng. & Wales*

Mayne, Symon [Simon] (*bap.* 1612, *d.* 1661), regicide, was baptized at Dinton, Buckinghamshire, on 17 February 1612, the son and heir of Symon Mayne (1576/7–1617) of Dinton Hall, near Aylesbury, and his wife, Coluberry (*d.* 1629), daughter of Richard Lovelace of Hurley, Berkshire, sister of the first Lord Lovelace and widow of Richard Beake of Haddenham, who died in 1606. The elder Symon

Mayne died on 13 July 1617, aged forty, and was buried in Dinton church, where a large monument was erected in his memory. His will reveals a prosperous and generous man: it includes legacies of £20 each to a niece and a nephew, to his two godsons and to seven stepchildren, with smaller sums to all his servants and to poor people in three parishes. His wife inherited the Dinton estate, with reversion to their son on her death, which occurred on 10 January 1629; she too was buried in Dinton church. The family's long lease from the dean and chapter of Rochester for the nearby parishes of Haddenham, Cuddington, and Kingsey was left to their daughter, another Coluberry (or Celiberry), who married Thomas Boulstrode (or Bulstrode) of Upton, Buckinghamshire, with reversion to her young brother after fifteen years.

In November 1630 Mayne enrolled as a student at the Inner Temple. His first marriage, on 23 May 1633, was to Jane Burgoine (1613/14–1641), then aged nineteen, eldest daughter of John Burgoine of Sutton, Bedfordshire, and his wife, Jane, daughter and heir of William Kempe of Finchingfield, Essex. After her death he married Elizabeth (née Woodward), perhaps the widow of someone called Tow, of Essex. They had three sons, Symon, Edward, and Samuel, a mercer. Mayne was related to many families who supported the cause of parliament in the civil war, including his near neighbours Arthur Goodwin and Sir Richard Ingoldsby. He threw in his lot with them and served on the grand jury of Buckinghamshire, which apparently presented an address to Charles I for the dismissal of his army in 1642. On 14 June 1645, after the battle of Naseby, Cromwell is said to have stopped at his house, Dinton Hall. About September 1645 he was returned as a recruiter MP for the nearby borough of Aylesbury. He was a prominent figure in the parliamentarian government of Buckinghamshire, the author of the *Mystery of the Good Old Cause* (1660) describing him as a 'great committee man, wherein he licked his fingers'. Certainly, as early as October 1643 he had secured the sequestered lands he had formerly held under lease from the dean and chapter of Rochester. In 1648 he helped sponsor a petition from Buckinghamshire in support of the radical vote of no addresses ending parliament's approaches to Charles I for a settlement. Local power was emphasized when, in September 1648, he and his cousin Henry Beake, George Fleetwood, and others signed a defiant reply to the treasurers of sequestration, following demands for a speedy account of profits from sequestrations for the county in their charge. In 1649 he was appointed one of the judges for the trial of Charles I, attended on most days, and signed the warrant for the king's execution [*see also* Regicides]. Not active in parliament, he served during the protectorate on the committee for Buckinghamshire.

After the Restoration Mayne, as a regicide, was excepted from the general act of pardon. What is believed to have been his temporary hideout was discovered in 1804 during restoration work on Dinton Hall. In June 1660 he surrendered to a serjeant-at-arms and was tried at the Old Bailey on 13 October. Bulstrode Whitelocke recorded that Mayne's wife retained him as counsel to prepare a petition

to the king. At his trial Mayne made an inaccurate and incoherent defence: 'I knew not of the King's bringing up [to London], I was never at any Committee'. When asked, of the death warrant, 'see if your hand and seal be not upon it', he replied 'I acknowledge it is my hand, ... there was a gentleman told me I should be sequestered as a delinquent ... saith he, you will rather lose your estate than take away the king's life' (*State trials*). He was found guilty and sentenced to death.

Mayne's health may never have been robust. As early as 1635 and 1636 he and his wife had received licences 'for notorious sickness' to eat flesh on fish days. After his committal to the Tower his illness became fatal and he died there on 13 April 1661 'from gout, with fever and convulsion-fits'. An inquest was held next day, and Sir Edward Nicholas gave the lieutenant of the Tower a warrant for delivery of the corpse to the widow 'for interment in the country without ostentation'. Mayne was buried in Dinton church on 18 April 1661. The lands sequestered from the dean and chapter of Rochester had been restored to them (and leased to a member of the royal household) but the Dinton estate, forfeited by Mayne, was regained by his widow in 1664, the conveyance being made by Christopher Egleton of nearby Ellesborough, who had known Mayne, and George Goswell of Beaconsfield. Elizabeth Mayne died in 1694 and was buried at Dinton on 10 August. The Dinton estate remained in the family until well into the next century.

W. P. COURTNEY, rev. RUTH SPALDING

Sources W. H. Rylands, ed., *The visitation of the county of Buckingham made in 1634*, Harleian Society, 58 (1909) · Bucks. RLSS, Dinton Hall estate records, D63 · PRO, PROB 11/130, fols. 189–90 · Medway Archives and Local Studies Centre, Rochester, Kent, dean and chapter archives (Haddenham, Cuddington, and Kingsey, Buckinghamshire) · *JHC*, 3 (1642–4), 291 · *JHC*, 6 (1648–51), 87 · BL, Add. MS 5497, fol. 91 · BL, Add. MS 5494, fols. 28–9 · BL, Sloane MS 856, fol. 23v · *The manuscripts of the duke of Leeds*, HMC, 22 (1888), 1, 2, 4 · *CSP dom., 1660–61* · S. Mayne, 'Considerations humbly tendered by Simon Mayne, to shew that he was no contriver of that horrid action of the death of the late king, but merely seduced into it by the persuasion of others', *A collection of scarce and valuable tracts ... Lord Somers*, 2 (1751), 196–7 · C. V. Wedgwood, *The trial of Charles I* (1964) · D. Underdown, *Pride's Purge: politics in the puritan revolution* (1971) · G. Lipscomb, *The history and antiquities of the county of Buckingham*, 4 vols. (1831–47), vol. 2, pp.138–40, 147–52 · *State trials*, 5.947–8 · family tree by Broune Willis, Bodl. Oxf., MS Rawl. B. 263, fol. 69 · M. Noble, *The lives of the English regicides*, 2 vols. (1798)
Wealth at death estate forfeited but restored to widow in 1664: Bucks. RLSS, Dinton Hall estate records D63 1/14

Mayne, William (1818–1855), army officer in the East India Company, was born on 28 October 1818, the second surviving son of the Revd Robert Mayne of Limpsfield, Surrey, and his wife, Charlotte Cuninghame Graham, daughter of Colonel Graham of St Lawrence House, near Canterbury. William Mayne, Baron Newhaven, was his father's brother. He attended Addiscombe College in 1836 and 1837, and was appointed ensign on 15 December 1837, serving with the 4th and later the 49th Bengal native infantry.

In November 1838 Mayne was appointed to serve in the invasion of Afghanistan by the army of the Indus, and was appointed detachment adjutant to the detachments of the 27th and 37th Bengal infantry. He distinguished himself at the unsuccessful attack on the fort of Jalgah on 3 October 1840, and became lieutenant on 2 November 1841. As lieutenant in command of a *ressalah* (squadron) of the 2nd Shah Shuja's irregular cavalry, or Anderson's Horse, he fought in various actions under Brigadier John Shelton and Sir Robert Sale. He went with Sale's brigade to Jalalabad, where he distinguished himself in the siege and was mentioned in dispatches. Following General Pollock's relief of Jalalabad he served with his quartermaster-general's department and at the capture of Istalif on 29 September 1842 by Major-General McCaskill's division. Lord Ellenborough, who favoured the 'illustrious garrison' of Jalalabad, praised Mayne and appointed him adjutant of the governor-general's bodyguard. While second in command of it he had a horse killed under him at Maharajpur on 31 December 1843. He was not engaged in the Anglo-Sikh wars, being in command of the 5th irregular horse at Bhawanipur during the first war, and commandant of Lord Dalhousie's bodyguard at the time of the second. In 1844 Mayne married Helen Cunliffe, daughter of Thomas Reed Davidson, Bengal civil service, and niece of Lieutenant-General Sir Robert Cunliffe.

In 1851, while still a captain in the 37th Bengal infantry, Mayne was selected by Lord Dalhousie to command the Hyderabad contingent of the nizam's forces, and retained this command until his death. With 6000 of these troops he suppressed disturbances in the Deccan. The rapidity of his marches and the success of his operations attracted favourable notice. He was repeatedly thanked by the governor-general in council, particularly for the defeat of a large force of Arabs near Aurangabad on 20 September 1853 and for his conduct on 22 September 1854 when, while besieging the fort of Saila, near Hyderabad, he charged and annihilated a force of Rohillas, who sallied out at night.

On his return to England at the close of 1854 Mayne was made a brevet colonel and aide-de-camp to the queen. He had just returned to India when an attack of dysentery sent him home again. He died at Cairo on 23 December 1855, survived by his wife and one son.

H. M. Chichester, *rev.* James Lunt

Sources J. W. Kaye, *History of the war in Afghanistan*, rev. edn, 3 vols. (1857–8) · P. Macrory, *Signal catastrophe: the story of a disastrous retreat from Kabul, 1842* (1966) · J. C. Pollock, *Way to glory: the life of Havelock of Lucknow* (1957) · G. R. Gleig, *Sale's brigade in Afghanistan: with an account of the seisure and defence of Jellalabad* (1846) · J. W. Kaye and G. B. Malleson, *Kaye's and Malleson's History of the Indian mutiny of 1857–8*, 6 vols. (1888–9) · T. Seaton, *From cadet to colonel: the record of a life of active service*, 2 vols. (1866) · Fortescue, *Brit. army*, vols. 11–13 · R. G. Burton, *A history of the Hyderabad contingent* (1905) · W. A. Watson, *The central India horse* (1930) · *GM*, 2nd ser., 45 (1856), 185 · H. M. Vibart, *Addiscombe: its heroes and men of note* (1894)

Likenesses G. S. Shury, mezzotint, pubd 1856 (after K. Hartman), NPG

Mayne, Zachary (1631–1694), religious writer, son of Richard Maine, was born at Exeter and baptized at St Petrock's Church there on 1 January 1632. He entered Christ Church, Oxford, on 15 October 1649, but by favour of the parliamentary visitors was soon made a demy of Magdalen College. On 6 May 1652 he graduated BA, although his period of residence was less than the regulations required. The indulgence was granted him at Oliver Cromwell's request on the recommendation of Thomas Goodwin, then president of Magdalen College. Mayne was described by Cromwell as 'eminently godly, of able parts, and willing to perform all his exercises' (Wood, 4.411). He was senior student in his class the following Lent, elected fellow of Magdalen in 1652 and proceeded MA on 6 July 1654.

A member of the Independent church gathered at Magdalen by Goodwin, Mayne preached regularly in and around Oxford, and became lecturer at Abingdon, Berkshire, on 3 April 1657. He regarded Goodwin as a very good friend and it was through the latter's influence that he was appointed lecturer at St Julian's Church in Shrewsbury on 24 March 1658. Here he was received very favourably by both the church and the town, and was inclined to accept ordination from the bishop of Bangor, but Cromwell's death in 1658 interrupted the plan.

On preaching 'Concerning the salvability of the heathen and of universal redemption' in St Mary's Church, Oxford, in February 1660, Mayne was summoned before the vice-chancellor and threatened with expulsion, whereupon he retired to London until the following May. His religious opinions vacillated, but he is said to have been an Arian with leanings towards Socinianism. His published works show him to have held Arminian views. Scruples as to authority prevented him from administering the sacraments when he was an Independent preacher.

At the Restoration Mayne was ejected from his fellowship and retired to Dalwood in east Devon. However, he did not renounce controversy; his *St Paul's Travailing Pangs … or, A Treatise of Justification* appeared in 1662. Having expounded at length in a letter of 8 October 1669 to John Newburgh of Wooth Francis, near Bridport, his views on education—'I doe look upon teaching to be the highest work upon earth' (*GM*, 1.11)—by about 1671 he had become a schoolmaster, and in 1672 was licensed at his house. About this time he married Katharine; the couple had a daughter, Elizabeth, and three sons, Gabriel, Samuel (c.1677–1750), who, after graduating from Exeter College, Oxford, in 1698, proceeded BM from New Inn Hall in 1708 and practised medicine in Northampton, and Joel.

In another letter to Newburgh of 3 May 1671 Mayne revealed that he was raising money in his parish to fund a preaching minister, and about to hear a candidate preach, but some time before 19 January 1690, when he was made master of Exeter grammar school, he had conformed to the Church of England, probably as a layman. He enthusiastically welcomed the revolution of 1688–9. In his *The Snare Broken*, published anonymously in Oxford in 1692, and written several years previously, he recanted Socinian and Arian views, and tried to confute various calumnies. This was reinforced by *Sanctification by Faith Vindicated* (1693), which contained a preface by the rector of Totnes and conformist controversialist Robert Burscough.

On 7 August 1694 Mayne witnessed a waterspout at Topsham near Exeter, and sent a description to the Royal Society. Four months later, on 11 November 1694, he died in Exeter, and was buried in the north aisle of St Peter's Church, Dalwood, Devon.

BERTHA PORTER, rev. H. J. MCLACHLAN

Sources Wood, *Ath. Oxon.*, new edn, 4.411 · *Calamy rev.*, 346–7 · *GM*, 1st ser., 64 (1794), 11

Maynwaring, Arthur (1668–1712), politician and author, was born at Ightfield, Shropshire on 9 July 1668, the son of Charles Maynwaring (*bap.* 1636, *d.* 1690) and Catherine (*d.* 1702), a daughter of Charles Cholmondeley. After attending grammar school in Shrewsbury he went up to Christ Church, Oxford, in 1683, but left before graduating. From Oxford he went to Cheshire, where he spent several years with his maternal uncle Francis Chomley, and visited regularly another relative, Sir Philip Egerton. Both men were nonjurors, and in his early years he followed their views, extolling the tories in his earliest satires in 1689. *Tarquin and Tullia* was attributed to John Dryden, but Dryden revealed the true author, which gave Maynwaring early celebrity. From Cheshire he went to his parents' lodgings in Essex Street, London, while he studied law at the Inner Temple. Through the earl of Cholmondeley he became acquainted with the leading whig grandees and gradually converted to their political principles. Through Dryden he became acquainted with William Congreve, whose play *The Double-Dealer* he edited and revised (1693). He quickly developed a reputation as a critic and wit. About 1700 his whig and literary credentials earned him entry into the Kit-Cat Club, and he became one of its chief ornaments. His father died in 1690 leaving his estate heavily encumbered. Maynwaring raised some £4000 upon it and lived for a time as a man of fashion, travelling to Paris in 1697 after the treaty of Ryswick, where he met Boileau and La Fontaine. On 18 November 1701, through the intercession of Charles, Lord Halifax, he was appointed a commissioner of the customs, where he distinguished himself by his ability and probity.

Not long after the accession of Queen Anne, Maynwaring met Anne Oldfield (1683–1730) through a fellow Kit-Cat member, John Vanbrugh, who had discovered her dramatic talents. Oldfield, who first went on the stage at the age of sixteen, was barely twenty when Maynwaring became her admirer and then lover. Her later success was attributed by her anonymous biographer to his grooming and teaching. Her career also prompted Maynwaring to write more than a dozen epilogues and prologues to be spoken by her. In 1703 he was credited with writing *The Golden Age Restored*, which was actually by his friend William Walsh. It nearly cost him his place when the tory secretary of state, the earl of Nottingham, complained to Lord Treasurer Godolphin. Godolphin, respecting Maynwaring's ability and integrity, assured him he could keep his place but found him a better one: in May 1705 the treasurer purchased for Maynwaring the office of an auditor of the imprests, an accounting office in the exchequer,

which he retained until his death. Befitting his new eminence, at the end of 1706 he was elected in a by-election to parliament for Preston and was re-elected in 1708. He lost his seat in the tory landslide of 1710 but was returned for West Looe, a seat controlled by Bishop Trelawny, for which he sat until his death.

By 1704 Maynwaring had begun writing whig attacks on the tories, although only one, a poem, *The History and Fall of the [Occasional] Conformity Bill* (1704), has been identified in print. At some stage in the early years of the century he was admitted into the circle of friends of Sarah, duchess of Marlborough. It may have been in the summer of 1704, which he spent with Anne Oldfield at Windsor; the duchess was ranger of Windsor Great Park and the lodge there her favourite residence. Over the next several years Maynwaring became her confidante and aide, and was eventually rewarded with the title of her secretary. The earliest surviving letter from Maynwaring to the duchess dates only from 4 September 1707, but thereafter more than 200 survive, including a few from her, that continue right up until his death. The duchess, for several decades Queen Anne's closest friend, had isolated herself from the court after the death of her only surviving son in 1703. Moreover, her outspoken championing of the whigs gradually estranged her from the tory-inclined sovereign and led by 1707 to a complete alienation. The whig leaders assumed she could influence the queen in their favour, not recognizing the growing bitterness between the two women. Maynwaring gradually entered into an ever more critical relationship with the duchess, who depended upon him and his friends for companionship and entertainment. He encouraged her to lobby for the whigs with the duke of Marlborough and Godolphin, and drafted letters for her to send to the queen and even to her husband.

In 1708 Maynwaring's writings began to take a more serious turn. His *Advice to the Electors of Great Britain*, written in conjunction with the duchess, was highly successful; no other tract survives for that year. He was indifferent to literary success, and much of his earlier material probably circulated only in manuscript. But the political crises of 1710 turned him from an occasional writer into a dedicated pamphleteer and propagandist. The queen resented the importunities of the whig leaders and their insistence on a growing presence in the ministry. At the impeachment of Dr Henry Sacheverell, a high-flying tory cleric, the strong show of public support for Sacheverell, and the growing disenchantment with the government for the long-drawn-out and expensive war with France, emboldened the queen, acting on the advice of Robert Harley and his confederates, to begin turning out the whigs. The dismissals became a rout, capped by the removal of Godolphin in August and the dissolution of parliament in September. Maynwaring gradually assumed the role of director of the press for the whigs and devoted the remaining two years of his life to defending their policies and those of Marlborough and leading the attack on the now dominant tories led by Harley.

Maynwaring's first important effort was *Four Letters to a Friend in North Britain*. Appearing in August 1710, it branded the high-church party with Jacobitism and popery. It was followed by *A letter from Monsieur Pett[ecu]—to Monsieur B[uy]s*, which warned against a change of the ministry as it would lead to Marlborough's resignation and a decline in support for the war. The latter tract was the focus of the first three issues of a new ministerial organ, *The Examiner*, soon to be directed by Jonathan Swift. Maynwaring rebutted by starting first the *Whig Examiner*, written by Joseph Addison, and, when that proved ineffectual, recruiting John Oldmixon to produce *The Medley*, much of which was written by Maynwaring. A flood of poems, broadsides, tracts, and books followed. It is impossible to identify all his handiwork, but Oldmixon, who had possession of his papers after his death, is the best authority in his *The Life and Posthumous Works of Arthur Maynwaring* (1715). *The Medley* succeeded in fulfilling his aim, for *The Examiner* suspended publication in July 1711, prompting Maynwaring to terminate *The Medley* soon afterwards. Towards the end of the year illness brought on by the consumption from which he had suffered for over a decade sapped his energies. Somehow he was able to edit two sets of tracts by Francis Hare, Marlborough's chaplain-general, who had accompanied the duke on his marches since 1704 and was privy to his thoughts. Four *Letters on the Management of the War* appeared during the winter of 1711–12, followed by a second set of four, *The Allies and the Late Ministry Defended*. In late 1711 the government made a sweep of the opposition press, incarcerating fourteen printers and publishers for seditious writing. Maynwaring had close connections with virtually every one, and he had no doubt that he was a principal target in the government's efforts to stamp out its opponents. Indeed, he was so informed, directly and indirectly by Harley, now lord treasurer and earl of Oxford. Several vindications and defences of Marlborough written by Hare or Maynwaring himself appeared early in 1712. Maynwaring answered Swift's *British Academy*; he wrote a statement of the conditions behind the controverted election in Bewdley.

After Marlborough was cashiered by Oxford at the end of 1711, the duke, fearing for his life, contemplated exile, and the death of Godolphin on 15 September 1712 only confirmed him in his decision. Maynwaring, now gravely ill, performed one last service for the Marlboroughs, interceding with Oxford for passes to permit them to go abroad. His petition was successful and the duke, to be followed by the duchess, departed on 28 November, shortly after Maynwaring's death in London on 13 November 1712. He was buried with his forebears at Chertsey, Surrey. Owing to the heavy debts of his father, which he had been repaying, and his own lack of attention to money matters until late in his life, his estate was small. What remained was divided between a sister, Grizel, and Anne Oldfield, who used it to bring up their son, Arthur.

Although his production was small, Maynwaring's influence among both politicians and writers was great. He befriended and promoted Congreve, Richard Steele, Robert Walpole, and a host of actors, writers, and minor politicians. He was part of the inner circle of the Godolphin ministry, and his influence with the duchess was extraordinary. It was largely Maynwaring who persuaded her to remain in office until she was forced to resign at the end of 1710. The draft biography and apologia of Marlborough he was working on at the time of his death was turned over, along with his correspondence and literary remains, to Steele by the duchess after his death. Steele completed the draft, coupled it with a life of Prince Eugene, and published it in 1714 as *The Lives of Two Illustrious Generals*. Maynwaring was an accomplished classicist (the catalogue for the auction of his books in 1713 testifies to his love of the classics and the breadth of his knowledge), a poet, a musician who sang and accompanied himself at the harpsichord, and a famous wit and conversationalist. But he was also a devoted lover, friend, and patron of men of letters and the stage.

HENRY L. SNYDER

Sources J. Oldmixon, *The life and posthumous works of Arthur Maynwaring* (1715) · H. L. Snyder, 'Arthur Maynwaring and the Whig press, 1710–1712', *Literature als Kritik des Lebens*, ed. R. Haas, H.-J. Müllenbrock, and C. Uhlig (1974), 120–36 · F. H. Ellis, *Swift vs Mainwaring: The Examiner and The Medley* (1985) · H. L. Snyder, 'Prologues and epilogues of Arthur Maynwaring', *Philological Quarterly*, 50 (1971), 610–9 · G. de F. Lord and others, eds., *Poems on affairs of state: Augustan satirical verse, 1660–1714*, 7 vols. (1963–75) · H. L. Snyder, 'Daniel Defoe, the duchess of Marlborough, and the *Advice to the electors of Great Britain*', *Huntington Library Quarterly*, 29 (1965–6), 53–62 · *Private correspondence of Sarah, duchess of Marlborough*, 2 vols. (1838) · F. Harris, *A passion for government: the life of Sarah, duchess of Marlborough* (1991) · H. L. Snyder, 'Richard Steele, Arthur Maynwaring, and the *Lives of two illustrious generals*', *Studies in Bibliography*, 24 (1971), 152–62 · H. L. Snyder, 'Daniel Defoe, Arthur Maynwaring, Robert Walpole, and Abel Boyer', *Huntington Library Quarterly*, 33 (1969–70), 133–53 · *Biographia Britannica, or, The lives of the most eminent persons who have flourished in Great Britain and Ireland*, 5 (1757), 3074–7, 3262–5 · parish register (birth), 9/7/1668, Chertsey, Surrey · parish register (baptism), 18/1/1636, Chertsey, Surrey [father]

Archives BL, corresp. with Sarah Churchill, duchess of Marlborough, Add. MSS 61101–61710 · BL, Egerton MSS · U. Nott. L., Cavendish Bentinck MSS

Likenesses G. Kneller, oils, *c*.1705–1710 (*Kit-Cat Club*), NPG · J. Simon, mezzotint, before 1715 (after oil painting by G. Kneller), BM, NPG

Wealth at death see will, E. Curll, *Faithful memoirs of … Ann Oldfield, by William Egerton*, 1731

Maynwaring, Everard (*b.* 1627/8), physician, born at Gravesend, Kent, was the son of Kenelm Maynwaring, rector of Gravesend, and was educated at Gravesend grammar school, his tutor being a Mr Chandler. On 21 June 1645 he was admitted a sizar at St John's College, Cambridge, at the age of seventeen, and graduated MB on 1 July 1652. In 1652 Maynwaring practised at Norton, near Sheffield, Yorkshire, and from 1653 until the end of the decade was practising in Chester, Cheshire. In the mid-1650s Maynwaring travelled to America, where he developed a lasting friendship with Christopher Lawrence MD of Dublin. On 17 August 1655 Maynwaring was created MD of the University of Dublin, 'after performing such exercises as the Statutes of the University required', as his diploma reads. By 1663 Maynwaring had moved to London, where he established himself next to the Blue Boar, on Ludgate Hill as a 'doctor in physic and hermetick phylosophy'. An advocate of chemical medicine, Maynwaring dedicated his first works to two prominent patrons of Helmontian medicine: *Tutela sanitatis* (1663) to Prince Rupert, and *Solamen aegrorum, sive, Ternarius medicamentorum chymicorum* (1665) to George Villiers, duke of Buckingham.

In 1665 Maynwaring was entrusted with the care of the pest-house of the society for employing the poor in Middlesex. His treatment of patients seems to have been successful, as he claimed that out of the eighty patients in his care, fifty-six recovered. In the same year Maynwaring was among the proponents of the Society of Chymical Physicians, which was meant to challenge the authority of the College of Physicians. Maynwaring adopted Jean Baptiste van Helmont's medical theories, favourably quoted from the works of Helmontians such as George Thomson, and became acquainted with George Starkey. He accepted van Helmont's view that the *archeus* or vital spirit was responsible for the main functions in the human body, and endorsed the Helmontians' criticism of the doctrine of the chemical principles. He singled out Thomas Willis's version of this theory as his target. An anonymous pamphlet (possibly written in 1668–9) attacked Maynwaring together with Robert Boyle and Christopher Merrett as enemies of learned medicine and of the College of Physicians. None the less Maynwaring never participated in the Helmontians' violent attacks on traditional medicine, and often censured unlearned chemists as well as empirics. In addition, unlike most of the Helmontians, he did not entirely rule out the use of phlebotomy. Like other advocates of chemical medicine Maynwaring defended the respectability of chemistry by arguing that it was part of the ancient learning which originated in Egypt with Hermes Trismegistus.

Maynwaring also engaged in a series of polemics against apothecaries, claiming that physicians should prepare their own medicines, and not have them made up by apothecaries. In the dispute between members of the College of Physicians and the Society of Apothecaries Maynwaring in his *Praxis medicorum* (1671) explicitly supported Christopher Merrett's attacks on apothecaries. Throughout his career, Maynwaring took an interest in the cure of scurvy, which he regarded as a disease endemic in northern countries. He made and sold his own remedies against scurvy and recommended oranges and lemons as antidotes against this disease. He condemned tobacco smoking as one of the causes of scurvy. In his late works Maynwaring advertised his pills and a 'catholic' (that is, universal) medicine. As an answer to those who regarded him as an empiric, Maynwaring published a copy of his academic diplomas in his last work, *Ignota febris* (1698). There is no evidence that Maynwaring was married, and the date of his death is unknown.   ANTONIO CLERICUZIO

Sources Venn, *Alum. Cant.* · E. Maynwaring, *Ignota febris* (1698) · H. Thomas, 'The Society of Chymical Physitians: an echo of the great plague of London, 1665', *Science, medicine and history*, ed. E. A. Underwood, 2 (1953), 56–71 · H. J. Cook, *The decline of the old medical regime in Stuart London* (1986) · P. M. Rattansi, 'The Helmontian-Galenist controversy in Restoration England', *Ambix*, 12 (1964), 1–23 · BL, Sloane MS 1786, fols. 116–28 · *DNB*

Archives BL, Sloane MS, 1786

Likenesses portrait, 1668, repro. in E. Maynwaring, *Medicus absolutus* (1668) · R. White, line engraving (aged thirty-eight), NPG, Wellcome L.

Maynwaring [Manwaring], **Roger** (1589/90?–1653), bishop of St David's, was born at Stretton, Shropshire, into a Cheshire gentry family, according to David Lloyd on 9 November and, if the age at death recorded in his epitaph is accurate, in 1589 or 1590. He attended the King's School, Worcester, before going early in 1604 to Oxford, where he became a bible clerk at All Souls College. He graduated BA in February 1608 and proceeded MA on 5 July 1611. While his 'critical skill in Greek and rational head' recommended him to the college, his 'discreet carriage, and observing head' (Lloyd, 271) prompted the unknown 'noble lord' who was his patron to make him his chaplain and help him to the perpetual curacy of St Katharine Cree, London, where the advowson was owned by Magdalene College, Cambridge, and where he was admitted on 11 July 1611. Five years later he resigned and on 3 June 1616 was instituted as rector of St Giles-in-the-Fields, also in London. Although Lloyd says that he kept three diaries, for personal life, for recording public affairs, and for noting 'the most remarkable passages of Providence in the World' (ibid., 272), none appears to have survived and much about his private affairs is uncertain. He probably married during his earlier years at St Giles, since three daughters named in his will were apparently themselves married, but the identity of their mother and his first wife is unknown.

On 2 July 1625 Maynwaring proceeded BD and DD, and about the same time was appointed a chaplain-in-ordinary to the king. When the imposition of forced loans to fund government policy aroused discontent in 1626–7 he was one of several royal chaplains to heed Bishop William Laud's direction to preach on the theme of subjects' duty of obedience to their king. A sermon by Robert Sibthorpe and his own delivered at Oatlands on 4 July 1627 and at Alderton on 29 July attracted both controversy and the enthusiastic approval of Charles I. Ignoring Laud's advice 'to think better of it that there were many things therein which will be very distasteful to the people' (Cust, 62), the king ordered that Maynwaring's be printed with the inscription 'by his Majestie's special command'. *Religion and Alegiance*, which appeared in August, contained much commonly accepted divine right theory: to assert that 'lawfull Soveraignes are no lesse then Fathers, Lords, Kings and Gods upon earth' (vol. 1, p. 4) was to uphold mainstream political thinking. However, the sermons transgressed the boundaries of that thinking in two respects: instead of vague generalizations they applied theory to particular circumstances and policies, and they extended the religious obligation of obedience in such a way as to ignore the claims of common law and parliamentary precedent. 'To Kings … nothing can be denied that may further the supply of their Urgent Necessities', stated Maynwaring, who outlined what these were. Although in one breath he seemed to concede that kings might command only 'what stands not in any opposition to the originall Lawes of God, Nature, Nations and the

Gospell', in the next he asserted that the subject was bound to obey unquestioningly, 'though it be not correspondent in every circumstance, to Lawes Nationall, and Municipall', on 'hazard of his own Damnation in rebelling against God' (vol. 1, pp. 19–20). Assemblies such as parliament were instituted not as consultative bodies, 'to contribute any Right to Kings, whereby to challenge Tributary aydes and subsidiary helpes', but as executive bodies, which fine-tuned the details, 'for the more equall Imposing, and the more easie Exacting of that, which, unto Kings doth appertaine' (vol. 1, p. 26). Christ himself had shown the way. In unhesitatingly affirming that one should render to Caesar what was Caesar's, 'our blessed Lord did with that Readinesse, not expecting any Parliament, at Rome, or in Judea, to bee first assembled' (vol. 2, p. 37). Even though, unlike the current situation, this question was put in peacetime, 'no sooner was He demanded, but … Pay hee did' (vol. 2, p. 38).

When the next parliament opened in March 1628 Maynwaring was one of several preachers and writers associated with unpopular policies whose books were investigated by the committee for religion. Its initial report to the house on 31 March observed that 'they say he disavowes' his sermon, 'owning it only so far as a way to get preferment, wherein nevertheless he says he hath failed' (Johnson and others, 2.219), but on 4 May he reiterated his views in his own pulpit at St Giles. Subsequent committee reports relayed by Francis Rous and John Pym were damning. Ready to believe that he aimed at promotion they none the less took his arguments seriously: he had invested the king with absolute power unbound by law, supported illegal action, deprived subjects of private property, and defamed parliament; in so doing he was on the verge of both blasphemy and treason. The Commons' official charge on 4 June alleged 'a wicked and malicious intention to seduce and misguide the conscience of the king … touching the observation of the laws and custome of this kingdom, and the rights and liberties of subjects', as well as to incite the king against those who refused the loan and 'to avert his Majesty's mind from calling of parliaments' (ibid., 4.102). Answering before the Lords on 13 June Maynwaring expressed sorrow and contrition, but rejected any seditious or malicious motivation, protesting that his views on divine right monarchy went no further than the scriptures or John Calvin, and did not go against law. The submission mollified the Lords slightly, but the judgment announced the following day was still severe: imprisonment during the pleasure of the house; a £1000 fine to the king; formal acknowledgement of his offences before parliament; suspension for three years from the exercise of his ministry; and permanent disablement from holding any ecclesiastical dignity or secular office.

Brought from the Fleet prison on 21 June to make his submission Maynwaring did so, according to several accounts, with tears. However, although the king had formally expressed his concurrence on 18 June and Maynwaring's sermons were called in on 24 June to be burnt, the limits of parliamentary power to impose on Charles something so contrary to his real will rapidly became apparent.

On 30 June Sir Francis Nethersole wrote in disbelief to Charles's sister the queen of Bohemia of rumours that Maynwaring would be absolved from his suspension. On 6 July Charles ordered a pardon, issued on 8 July; on 18 July he presented Maynwaring to the rectory of Stanford Rivers, Essex; and on 28 July he issued him with a dispensation to hold it *in commendam* with St Giles-in-the-Fields. If Maynwaring had suffered any loss of confidence it was soon restored. Later that year, pointing to the fact that he had been 'so lately bruised only for his devotion to the king' (*CSP dom.*, *1628–9*, 421), he appealed to the latter for support in a St Giles tithe dispute which had escalated into a Star Chamber case. By late December Laud, now bishop of London, had received a paper in which he specified particularly reverential behaviour towards the king by a proposed lecturer and in the service by parishioners. Early in 1629 he lobbied Laud to oppose a move in parliament to abolish fees for burials. His confidence was well placed: awarded the additional rectories of Muckleton, Staffordshire (1630), and Mugginton, Derbyshire (1631), on 28 September 1633 he was presented by the king to the deanery of Worcester, although he was not installed until 5 September 1634.

There is no direct evidence that Maynwaring was or became a doctrinal Arminian, but his championing of clerical rights and his liturgical innovations reveal him to have been an enthusiastic proponent of a strong and authoritarian church and of order and ceremonial in worship. The exaction of fees at St Giles continued to cause litigation in the 1630s. By September 1635, as he reported to Archbishop Laud, whom he evidently considered his patron, he had effected significant changes in Worcester Cathedral: he had erected, decorated, and railed in a marble altar, regulated the unseemly behaviour of the choir, destroyed vestments and other ornaments debased through the misuse of the organist, Nathaniel Tompkins, and had beautified the king's audit hall. A final reward, and defiance of the 1628 sentence against Maynwaring, followed quickly. On 28 February 1636 he was consecrated by Laud as bishop of St David's in the only such ceremony of the reign attended by members of the royal family. Little is known of his episcopate, but a letter of 18 October 1637 to secretary of state Francis Windebank suggests a loyal servant of the king, and he was later accused of 'popish innovations'.

With the opening of the Short Parliament in 1640 Maynwaring evidently expected retribution. On 6 April the king licensed his absence from the Lords, and he did not appear in convocation, but his original offence and later preferment were prominently remembered in debates on breaches of parliamentary privilege. The 1628 declarations against him were rehearsed, and despite a royal order on 29 April to halt proceedings, the Lords were not silenced. His name resurfaced in the Long Parliament. In February 1641 the Commons deputed a committee to review the case against him, both old scores and new allegations of his conduct at Worcester, and to draft a reversal of his pardon; his arrest was also agreed. On 25 August it was recorded in the Lords that those serving a formal summons had not found him at home, and the seizure of his temporalities was ordered. The next day, according to one diarist, John Williams, bishop of Lincoln, doubtless no friend, 'affirmed that he roved from alehouse to alehouse in disguise' and 'moved his bishopric might be sequestered' (Russell, 232).

At some point Maynwaring had fled his diocese and seems to have gone to Ireland. In his *A True Relation of the Taking of Roger Manwering* (1642), Captain John Pointz described recognizing and apprehending him on board the *Eagle* as he made a return voyage on 28 June 1642. With him was his wife, 'a very neere kinswoman to him before he married her, being of the age of 22 year', but he had left 'his sister poore and lying in the parish where he formerly lived', and 'his children by his former wife to shift for themselves' (p. 2). Having landed at Minehead, Somerset, he was examined before a magistrate, Thomas Lutterall, and 'confessed that he departed … into Ireland, for preferment upon the Kings promise' (p. 3).

After a period in custody Maynwaring retired to Wales, where he lived on the income from a small estate. When he drew up his will on 29 June 1653 he was living at the college of Brecon. Leaving 5s. each to his 'eldest son' Thomas and daughters Elizabeth Stevens, Mary Brooke, and Sarah Mellyn, and 20s. to his sister Susanna Stevens, he bequeathed the residue of his estate to his wife, Jane, whom he made the sole executor and guardian of 'my children'. He died within hours, aged sixty-three or in his sixty-third year, and was buried on 1 July by the altar in Brecon collegiate church. For David Lloyd, royalist memoirist, this was an orderly and stern but sociable and jovial man, an improving landlord eventually hounded to his death by plunder and continual persecution. Anthony Wood stressed his zeal for the church and his keenness to bring both Catholics and sectaries to conversion and inclusion. The motivations of this most infamous of proponents of royal absolutism remain obscure.

VIVIENNE LARMINIE

Sources Foster, *Alum. Oxon.* · Wood, *Ath. Oxon.*, new edn, 4.810–12 · *Fasti Angl., 1541–1857*, [Ely], 111 · will, PRO, PROB 11/229, sig. 238 · H. F. Snapp, 'The impeachment of Roger Maynwaring', *Huntington Library Quarterly*, 30 (1966–7), 217–32 · [J. Pointz], *A true relation of the taking of Roger Manwering* (1642) · R. C. Johnson and others, eds., *Commons debates, 1628*, 6 vols. (1977–83) · *CSP dom., 1628–40* · D. Lloyd, *Memoires of the lives … of those … personages that suffered … for the protestant religion* (1668), 270–76 · *JHL*, 4 (1628–42), 376 · W. Prynne, *Canterburies doome, or, The first part of a compleat history of the commitment, charge, tryall, condemnation, execution of William Laud, late arch-bishop of Canterbury* (1646), 81, 252–3 · T. Jones, *A history of the county of Brecknock*, 2 (1809), 742–5 · G. Hennessy, *Novum repertorium ecclesiasticum parochiale Londinense, or, London diocesan clergy succession from the earliest time to the year 1898* (1898), 118 · C. Russell, 'The authorship of the bishop's diary of the House of Lords in 1641', *BIHR*, 41 (1968), 229–36 · R. P. Cust, *The forced loan and English politics, 1626–1628* (1987) · J. Davies, *The Caroline captivity of the church: Charles I and the remoulding of Anglicanism, 1625–1641* (1992) · K. Fincham, 'William Laud and the exercise of Caroline ecclesiastical patronage', *Journal of Ecclesiastical History*, 51 (2000), 80 · N. Tyacke, *Anti-Calvinists: the rise of English Arminianism, c.1590–1640* (1987), 189, 216 · G. Burgess, *The politics of the ancient constitution: an introduction to English political thought* (1992) · G. Burgess, *Absolute monarchy and the Stuart constitution* (1996)

Mayo. For this title name *see* Bourke, Richard Southwell, sixth earl of Mayo (1822–1872).

Mayo, Charles (1750–1829), historian and Church of England clergyman, was born on 7 December 1750 at Beechingstoke, Wiltshire, the son of the Revd John Mayo, rector of Beechingstoke and vicar of Wilcot, and grandson of the Revd John Mayo, vicar of Avebury, brother of Charles Mayo of Hereford. He was the second cousin of Paggan William Mayo (1766–1836), physician, and of the Anglo-Saxon scholar Charles Mayo (1767–1858). He was educated at the Queen's College, Oxford, where he matriculated on 27 April 1767 and graduated BA (1771), MA (1774), and BCL (1779). Mayo later provided funds for two sons of Wiltshire clergymen to study at any Oxford college. He held the livings of Huish in Wiltshire from 1775, and of Beechingstoke from 1779, and was chaplain to the Somerset Hospital in Froxfield, Wiltshire, in whose trustees he vested the patronage of his Oxford benefaction. Mayo was the author of *A Chronological History of European States, 1678–1792* (1793) and a *Compendious View of Universal History, 1753–1802* (1804). In addition he published two theological discourses, one on principles of religious worship (1818) and the other on the internal evidence of Christianity (1824). He died, unmarried, at Beechingstoke on 27 November 1829.

C. H. MAYO, *rev.* PHILIP CARTER

Sources C. H. Mayo, *A genealogical account of Mayo and Elton families* (privately printed, London, 1882) · Foster, *Alum. Oxon.*

Mayo, Charles (1767–1858), literary scholar and university teacher, born in London on 24 March 1767, was the younger son of **Herbert Mayo** (1720–1802), Church of England clergyman, and his wife, Mary (1732/3–1824), daughter of George Coldham, surgeon-extraordinary to the prince of Wales. Herbert Mayo was the son of Charles Mayo of Hereford; he matriculated in April 1739 at Brasenose College, Oxford, and was elected fellow in 1740 (BA, 1742; MA, 1745; DD, 1763). After curacies in the east of London he was presented in 1764 to the living of Middleton Cheney, Northamptonshire, but left the same year to return to the East End of London as rector of St George-in-the-East, Stepney. He married Mary Coldham on 15 January 1765, and served as JP for Middlesex and treasurer of Raine's Hospital. Herbert Mayo was an exemplary parish priest, and cared for the poor and took an interest in the welfare of black people. He died in London on 5 January 1802, and was buried in the churchyard of St George-in-the-East on 13 January.

Charles Mayo was admitted to Merchant Taylors' School in 1776, and was elected to St John's College, Oxford, in June 1785, becoming a fellow in 1788. He graduated MA in 1793 and BD in 1796. In 1795 he was elected by the university as professor of Old English (a chair founded by Dr Rawlinson); he was the first to hold that office, which he occupied for the allotted period of five years. According to Dr Samuel Parr his lectures were well received. Mayo was ordained in 1791 and was Whitehall preacher in 1799–1800. On 2 June 1801 he married Louisa (1774–1852), the youngest daughter of James Landon; they had no children. Mayo also served as morning lecturer at the old chapel of St Michael, Highgate, from 1803 to 1833. He was elected FSA in 1820, FRS in 1827, and a governor of Sir Roger Cholmeley's School in Highgate in 1842. He was proud to be an examiner of his old school, Merchant Taylors'. He lived for most of his life at Cheshunt, Hertfordshire, where in 1824 he inherited the manor of Andrewes and Le Motte from his grandmother Rebecca, daughter of Sir John Shaw, baronet. Charles Mayo died on 10 December 1858 at Cheshunt, where he was buried.

Charles's elder brother, **Paggen William Mayo** (1766–1836), physician, was born on 11 January 1766, and was baptized on 7 February at St George-in-the-East, Stepney, his father's parish. He was educated at Merchant Taylors' School and St John's College, Oxford, and was elected to a medical fellowship at St John's on 6 July 1792; he graduated DM in 1795. Having been elected physician to the Middlesex Hospital on 23 August 1793, he was admitted FRCP on 30 September 1796, and was censor in 1797, Goulstonian lecturer in 1798, and Harveian orator in 1807. He resigned his hospital appointment in 1801, and moved from Conduit Street, Hanover Square, London, to Doncaster, and eventually to Bridlington. He married on 8 February 1798 Charlotte (d. 1828), daughter of the Revd Stephen Buckle LLD of Norwich. They had six children. Paggen William Mayo died at Bridlington on 6 July 1836, and was buried in the churchyard there.

C. H. MAYO, rev. JOHN D. HAIGH

Sources C. H. Mayo, *A genealogical account of Mayo and Elton families* (privately printed, London, 1882) · *GM*, 3rd ser., 6 (1859), 210 · Munk, *Roll* [Paggen William Mayo] · [E. Wilson], ed., *The history of the Middlesex Hospital* (1845) · Foster, *Alum. Oxon.* · *IGI* [Paggen William Mayo]

Likenesses Grimaldi, etching, 1800 (Mayo, Paggen William; after minature), repro. in Mayo, *Genealogical account*, 91 · engraving (after miniature), repro. in Mayo, *Genealogical account*, 89

Wealth at death under £7000: probate, 13 Jan 1859, *CGPLA Eng. & Wales*

Mayo, Charles (1792–1846), educational reformer, was born at 1 Hammett Street, Aldgate, London, on 9 June 1792, the eldest son in the family of four sons and one daughter of Charles Mayo (1754–1814), a solicitor who practised in London, and his wife, Elizabeth (d. 1837), daughter of William Knowlys and sister of Newman Knowlys, recorder of London. Elizabeth *Mayo was his sister; Charles *Mayo (1767–1858), the Anglo-Saxon scholar, was his cousin. Educated at Henley-on-Thames grammar school and Merchant Taylors' School, he proceeded to St John's College, Oxford, where he held a scholarship from 1810 to 1813. Taking second class honours in classics, he was elected to a law fellowship in 1813, graduating BA in 1814, BCL in 1817, and DCL in 1822. He was admitted at Gray's Inn in 1814 but deafness forced him to give up his intention to read for the bar. In August 1817 he became headmaster of Bridgnorth grammar school, Shropshire. He was ordained deacon by the bishop of Oxford later in that year and priest in June 1819, resigning from his headmastership in July 1819.

A friendship with John Synge of Glanmore Castle, co. Wicklow (1788–1845), an Irish landowner and, like Mayo, an evangelical in religion, was to be crucial in forming Mayo's life's work. Synge's favourable impression of the model school run by the Swiss educationist Pestalozzi, which he had visited during his grand tour, encouraged Mayo to see the establishment for himself. In 1819 he joined Pestalozzi at Yverdun, near Lake Geneva, as English chaplain, bringing with him a number of pupils. Although Pestalozzi's school was then past its peak, the experience convinced Mayo of the value of both the man and his methods. He returned to London in 1822 determined to promote Pestalozzi's ideas in England. An early subscriber and committee member of the London Infant School Society (founded in 1824), he delivered two lectures at the Royal Institution in May 1826 on the life of Pestalozzi (later published as a memoir, 2nd edn 1828) and on infant schools, *Observations on the Establishment and Direction of Infants' Schools* (1827). In the latter he commented that 'infancy is a rich but unclaimed waste'; learning began with the child's own experiences and could be developed before children entered the monitorial schools which at that time provided elementary education. Object lessons, a method widely popularized by his sister, were central to his principles for teaching young children, which he later described in a treatise produced in collaboration with his sister, *Practical Remarks on Infant Education for the Use of Schools and Private Families* (1837).

In 1822 Mayo opened a school in Epsom, which his mother helped him to run, to demonstrate how Pestalozzi's ideas could be applied to the teaching of children from the upper classes. In September 1826 he became headmaster of Cheam School, a well-established private boarding-school for boys aged between seven and eighteen, in succession to James Wilding (1781–1863). Mayo initially ran the school in association with his mother and sister as a family enterprise; the creation of a domestic environment, headed by a father figure, was regarded as a necessary aspect of moral education. In the early years of his headmastership he was remembered as a kindly figure who maintained affectionate, informal relations with the boys, admitting them to his family circle. 'The method of Pestalozzi is, in essence, the application of Christianity to the business of education', Mayo stated (Mayo, *Memoir of Pestalozzi*, 1828, 28), and religious instruction was an essential part of the curriculum. During the late 1820s and early 1830s Cheam School enjoyed notable patronage from aristocratic parents of evangelical views, who disliked the absence of vital religion in the traditional public schools. Among those who sent sons there were the Glyn, Pakenham, Ryder, and Waldegrave families. Opposing the mere mechanical inculcation of factual knowledge, Mayo tried to carry out Pestalozzi's ideal of developing all the faculties. Gymnastics, which he considered essential to physical health, were part of the curriculum. A school magazine established in 1832 testified to the self-expression which was encouraged among the boys. Charles Reiner, a German and former assistant to Pestalozzi, who taught at Cheam until 1849, was mainly responsible for the innovative teaching of mathematics and natural sciences.

In June 1831 Mayo married Mary Shepheard (1799–1877), who with her younger sisters ran a school for girls in Notting Hill after the death in 1824 of their father, Edward Walwyn Shepheard, left them in straitened circumstances. Soon after his marriage Mayo's mother and sister left Cheam, the latter going on to run the Home and Colonial Infant School Society's training college, in which Mayo took a close interest. Either through poor health or, it was said, the influence of his wife, Mayo presented a sterner figure to the boys in the later years of his headmastership. There had always been an inherent conflict between Pestalozzi's optimistic view of young children and the evangelical sense of their sinfulness. Mayo's free use of the cane was remarked upon by later generations of his pupils; and Hugh Childers, who entered the school in 1836, remembered a regime whose obsession with the wickedness of boys promoted sneaking and spying among them. It was suggested that he was not always a good judge of assistant masters. The choice of his brother-in-law, Henry Shepheard (1809–1878), as his successor was not a fortunate one. Mayo died at Cheam on 23 February 1846, leaving a widow, daughter, and two sons. He was buried at Cheam, and a tablet erected by his pupils and friends described his work as illustrating 'both in theory and practice, the blessings of an education based upon Intellectual Development, Scriptural Teaching, and Christian Influence'. M. C. CURTHOYS

Sources GM, 2nd ser., 26 (1846), 213–14 · C. H. Mayo, A genealogical account of the Mayo and Elton families, 2nd edn (1908) · V. Sillery, St John's College biographical register, 1775–1875 (1987) · E. Peel, Cheam School from 1645 (1974) · W. A. C. Stewart and W. P. McCann, The educational innovators, 2 vols. (1967–8) · PRO, PROB 11/2034, fol. 287 · K. Silber, Pestalozzi (1960) · Foster, Alum. Oxon.
Archives Cornwall RO, letters to John Hawkins · W. Sussex RO, John Hawkins MSS
Likenesses portrait, repro. in Peel, Cheam School, facing p. 114
Wealth at death under £20,000: will, PRO, PROB 11/2034, fol. 287

Mayo, Charles (1837–1877), army medical officer, born at Winchester on 13 January 1837, was the elder son of Charles Mayo (1788–1876), senior surgeon at Winchester County Hospital. He was elected on the foundation of Winchester College in 1847, and of New College, Oxford, where he became fellow in 1858. He graduated BA in 1859, BM in 1865, and DM in 1871; and he became MRCS in 1861 and MRCP in 1869. In October 1862 he travelled to the United States, where he was staff surgeon-major and medical inspector of the 13th US army corps with Grant's army at the siege of Vicksburg. He later published an account of his experiences in America, in Francis Galton's Vacation Tourists (1864).

The next few years Mayo spent partly at Oxford, where he was coroner of the university (1865–9) and dean of New College, and partly in London as physician to the General Dispensary in Bartholomew Close. On the outbreak of the Franco-Prussian War in 1870 Mayo joined the medical service of the German army as staff surgeon-major, and he was appointed director of the Alice Hospital at Darmstadt, which was built under his supervision. In the nine months of its existence, about 700 German and 250 French soldiers were treated, and only fifty-one died. At the close of the war Mayo received five decorations, and the thanks of the German ministry of war. He was also made a knight of the Hessian order of Philip the Generous. During the campaign in Atchin he served with the Dutch medical service, and he went with the expedition from the Netherlands to Sumatra in 1873–4, his account of which appeared in The Times of 19 October 1874.

Being unwilling to settle in England Mayo sailed for Fiji as one of the government medical officers in 1875. Here, he had an acute attack of dysentery, and he died on the voyage to Sydney. Mayo was buried at sea on 15 July 1877. He was unmarried. C. H. MAYO, rev. JAMES MILLS

Sources T. F. Kirby, Winchester scholars: a list of the wardens, fellows, and scholars of … Winchester College (1888) · Foster, Alum. Oxon. · CGPLA Eng. & Wales (1878)
Likenesses brass, Winchester Cathedral
Wealth at death under £800: probate, 17 June 1878, CGPLA Eng. & Wales

Mayo, Daniel (1672–1733), Presbyterian minister, was born probably at Kingston, Surrey, the son of Richard *Mayo (c.1630–1695), the ejected vicar of Kingston, and his wife, Jane Smyth (d. 1713). His father was the Presbyterian minister at Kingston, and Daniel was 'strongly inclined to the ministry from early youth, but was diverted from it, for some years, by the difficulties of the times' (Harris, 34–5). His elder brother took orders in the Church of England, but Mayo maintained his father's Presbyterianism all his life. His early education was probably undertaken by his father. He obtained the degree of MA, probably from Glasgow, and finished his studies at the University of Leiden under Hermann Witsius. On his return he preached occasionally in and about London. He was appointed assistant minister at the Tothill Street meeting, Westminster, in 1696, but moved in 1698 to Kingston, where he became the pastor of the Presbyterian congregation formerly served by his father. He was married about this time to Honour, who outlived him.

The congregation increased greatly under Mayo's care, and he was a popular preacher. He kept a school for dissenters at which Philip Doddridge was a pupil from 1712 to 1715. In his Sermons on the Education of Children, Doddridge acknowledges with gratitude the excellent instruction he received from Mayo. Mayo's 'heart and soul was in his preaching which was practical and serious, with great gravity and warm affection' (Harris, 36). He was a lively conversationalist and was considered 'a minister of considerable talents and exerted them with great success, both from the pulpit and the press' (Wilson, 3.62). He was one of the group of scholars who continued Matthew Henry's Exposition, contributing the notes on 2 Corinthians and 1 and 2 Thessalonians.

Mayo candidated in 1714, on the death of Matthew Henry, for the important Presbyterian pulpit at Mare Street, Hackney, in competition with John Barker. Barker was appointed, but this caused a split in the congregation. The seceders built a new meeting-house for Mayo at the

Gravel Pit, Hackney. He preached alternate weeks at Kingston and Hackney, with George Smith as his colleague in both places. In 1723 he resigned from Hackney to become one of the two ministers at Silver Street meeting in London, where he remained until his death.

Mayo was recognized as one of the leading Presbyterians of his time, and his sermon *The Necessity of Regular Mission to the Ministry*, delivered at Chertsey in 1705, expressed its traditional principles by deploring a drift to radical thinking on the one hand and extreme Calvinism on the other. He affirmed the right to private judgment, which must be open to all. He died at Kingston on 13 June 1733, his son Daniel later succeeding him as minister at the church where he had followed his own father. Another son became a vicar in the established church, so the family split between the two denominations continued in succeeding generations.   ALAN RUSTON

Sources W. Harris, *Diligence in the Christian life to be found in peace: a sermon occasioned by the death … of D. Mayo* (1733), 34–8 · W. Wilson, *The history and antiquities of the dissenting churches and meeting houses in London, Westminster and Southwark*, 4 vols. (1808–14), vol. 2, pp. 9–12; vol. 3, pp. 60–64 · A. Sturney, *The story of Kingston Congregational Church* (privately printed, Kingston, 1955), 12–15 · *Calamy rev.*, 347 · A. R. Ruston, *Unitarianism and early presbyterianism in Hackney* (1980), 7–9 · *Protestant Dissenter's Magazine*, 4 (1797), 472 · *Protestant Dissenter's Magazine*, 6 (1799), 429 · T. Bures, *A funeral sermon occasioned by the death of the Revd Mr Daniel Mayo* (1733), 30–32 · W. D. Jeremy, *The Presbyterian Fund and Dr Daniel Williams's Trust* (1885), 124–5 · *DNB* · *IGI* · C. Surman, index, DWL · administration, Surrey (Welham), July 1733, PRO, PROB 6/109, fol. 109
Wealth at death see administration, PRO, PROB 6/109, fol. 109

Mayo, Elizabeth (1793–1865), educational reformer and evangelical writer, sister of the educationist Charles *Mayo (1792–1846), was born at 1 Hammet Street, Aldgate, London, on 18 June 1793, daughter of Charles Mayo (1754–1814), a solicitor, and his wife, Elizabeth Knowlys (*d.* 1837). In 1822 Elizabeth joined her brother to help run an evangelical school, first at Epsom and later at Cheam, based on ideas Charles had acquired from the Swiss educationist Pestalozzi.

Under Charles's influence Elizabeth acquired a lifelong interest in infant education, with a particular concern to develop teacher training. She adopted the Pestalozzian method of developing observation through the examination of objects. At Cheam Elizabeth produced her two most successful works, *Lessons on Objects* (1830) and *Lessons on Shells* (1832). The first books of their kind in England, they popularized the use of the object lesson, influencing generations of teachers. They were frequently reprinted, both in England and abroad, with *Lessons on Objects* reaching a sixteenth edition by 1859. However, although Elizabeth was keen to counteract the dullness of contemporary teaching styles, her lesson plans tended to be artificial and mechanical. *Lessons on Objects* is a simple analysis of the properties of 100 common objects and shows a limited understanding of Pestalozzi's claim that good observation can lead to verbalization and subsequent concept formation.

In 1834, following her brother's marriage, Elizabeth moved to Hampstead, where she continued to write about infant methodology, both separately and with Charles. The Mayos differed from other infant school pioneers, Robert Owen, David Stow, and Samuel Wilderspin, because they attempted to combine Pestalozzian philosophy with a passionate religious conviction. They became the most widely known contemporary evangelical writers on early years education. Both stressed the importance of making infant education a 'sacrifice to the Lord', and of ensuring children were on 'the side of religion and morality' (C. and E. Mayo, *Practical Remarks on Infant Education*, 1837, 47). Elizabeth was, if anything, more zealous and single-minded than Charles. Teachers had a duty to inculcate religion in the next generation simply because 'it is written' (E. Mayo, *Lessons on Objects*, 1852, v).

In 1843 Elizabeth became the first woman in England to be employed in teacher training. She undertook supervisory work at the Home and Colonial Infant School Society in Gray's Inn Road, London, the first specific institution dedicated to the training of infant teachers. Her exact position is unclear, but it is evident she devised and presented model lessons, supervised and reviewed programmes of work, and acted as a general consultant. Students were trained to teach grammar, arithmetic, geography, drawing, singing, physical education, and sensory discrimination through the examination of objects. Priority was given to the inculcation of religious and moral beliefs. Members of the public were invited into the institution to observe the teaching process for themselves.

Under Elizabeth's guidance the Home and Colonial Society provided not only teachers but lesson plans, pictures, and objects specifically designed for young children (see her *Model Lessons for Infant School Teachers*, 1838). By 1846 Joseph Fletcher, an inspector of schools, reported that the society was supplying teachers for nearly all the country's infant teaching vacancies. In 1848 and 1849 Elizabeth also edited the society's *Quarterly Educational Magazine and Record*. Although ill health forced her to relinquish this post, she continued to make regular contributions to society publications (see *The Educational Paper of the Home and Colonial Society*, vols. 1–5, 1859–63) until her death.

Elizabeth's emphasis on structure, at a time when early years teaching tended to be unsystematic, secured her importance in the history of infant education. A plaque at the Home and Colonial Society buildings commemorated her 'hearty sympathy, wise counsel and friendly aid', and praised her attempts to combine the 'principles of Pestalozzi … with evangelical truth'. A £500 bequest from Elizabeth was subsequently used for a Mayo Schoolroom in Gray's Inn Road. In 1861 her approach was adopted at Oswega, America's foremost teacher training institution. Elizabeth Mayo died at Great Malvern, Worcestershire, on 1 September 1865, and was buried on 8 September in her mother's grave in Kensal Green cemetery, London.

JANET SHEPHERD

Sources 'Committee of council on education: minutes', *Parl. papers* (1847), 45.553–573, no. 866 [schools of the home and colonial infant and juvenile school society] · C. H. Mayo, *A genealogical account of Mayo and Elton families* (privately printed, London, 1882) · F. E. Baines, ed., *Records of the manor, parish and borough of Hampstead,*

in the county of London, to December 31st, 1889 (1890) · P. McCann and F. A. Young, *Samuel Wilderspin and the infant school movement* (1982) · N. Whitbread, *The evolution of the nursery infant school* (1972) · K. Silber, *Pestalozzi: the man and his work* (1960) · d. cert.
Wealth at death under £25,000: probate, 27 Sept 1865, *CGPLA Eng. & Wales*

Mayo, Henry (1733–1793), Independent minister, was probably born in Plymouth; nothing is known of his parentage. He moved to London in 1756, when he was admitted to the Independent academy at Mile End Road. Having preached for a short time at Philip Doddridge's former chapel at Castle Hill, Northampton, he became, on 30 November 1762, the pastor of the Independent congregation in Nightingale Lane, Wapping, where he remained until his death. He was awarded the degree of MA by King's College, Aberdeen, in 1764, and LLD by Marischal College in 1772. He was twice married, first in 1764 to Jane Marder (d. 1766), a member of a Dorset family and the widow of Mr Martin, a West India merchant; they had one daughter. Mayo married again on 17 June 1766 at St George-in-the-East, London; his second wife was Jane Belpur, who died in or before 1796. They had three daughters. In 1785 he was chosen tutor in oratory and elocution at the Homerton Academy on the death of Thomas Gibbons, a post he held until his death, when it was discontinued.

Mayo took a prominent, if controversial, part in the dissenters' attempts to alter the terms of subscription required by the Toleration Act between 1772 and 1779. The London dissenting ministers, under the leadership of Edward Pickard, were prepared to accept a declaration of belief in scriptures as an alternative to subscription to the doctrinal part of the Thirty-Nine Articles required by the act. Mayo took the view that a government did not have the right to lay down religious tests as a condition for toleration and preferred a complete repeal of the penal laws against dissenters. He was in a minority of one, and so resigned as secretary of the committee charged with the application and became a vociferous critic of the campaign, suggesting that the ministers had been bought off with the promise of a partial relief acceptable to the administration. He was especially critical of the involvement of some of them in the administration of the *regium donum*, an annual grant to poor ministers and their widows, partly on the grounds of its secrecy but principally because he saw it as a means of ensuring that the ministers involved did the government's bidding. His anonymous accounts of these matters in the *London Magazine* in 1774 and 1775 are important, if partisan.

Mayo was the editor of the *London Magazine*, in which Edward Dilly and James Boswell were partners, from about April 1775 until the ownership changed about June 1783, and used the position to give extended coverage to a radicalism that was not confined to dissenting politics. He was interested in literary matters and was closely involved with Edward and Charles Dilly, the radical booksellers in the Poultry, at whose dinners he was a frequent guest and for whom he seems to have acted in an editorial capacity. Boswell, who had disapproved of Mayo's alterations to his

Account of Corsica, first met him in this context in 1768 and records a number of subsequent encounters, including several with Samuel Johnson, at one of which in 1773 the two had a heated argument on toleration which led Boswell to dub him Johnson's literary anvil.

Mayo appears to have been a dogged, no-nonsense character, intolerant of compromise or evasion but nevertheless sociable. Boswell records that he gave a dinner for his friends once a week and dined abroad the other days. Theologically he was an orthodox Calvinist: he wrote against John Gill on infant baptism in 1766 and published an abridgement of a work of John Owen in 1768. He died at his house in Wellclose Square, London, 'after a long and painful illness' (GM, 379) on 4 April 1793, and was buried in Bunhill Fields.   JOHN STEPHENS

Sources J. Stephens, 'The London ministers and subscription, 1772–1779', *Enlightenment and Dissent*, 1 (1982), 43–7 · T. Rees, *A sketch of the history of the regium donum* (1834), 53ff. · *The journals of James Boswell, 1760–1795*, ed. J. Wain (1990) · Boswell, *Life*, 2.249ff. · P. J. Anderson, ed., *Officers and graduates of University and King's College, Aberdeen, MVD–MDCCCLX*, New Spalding Club, 11 (1893) · P. J. Anderson and J. F. K. Johnstone, eds., *Fasti academiae Mariscallanae Aberdonensis: selections from the records of the Marischal College and University, MDXCIII–MDCCCLX*, 3 vols., New Spalding Club, 4, 18–19 (1889–98) · H. McLachlan, *English education under the Test Acts: being the history of the nonconformist academies, 1662–1820* (1931) · C. H. Mayo, *A genealogical account of the Mayo and Elton families*, 2nd edn (1908), 294 · GM, 1st ser., 63 (1793), 379 · parish register, St George-in-the-East, London [marriage], 17/6/1766 · R. B. Barlow, *Citizenship and conscience: a study in the theory and practice of religious toleration in England during the eighteenth century* (1962), 171ff. · will, proved, 8 April 1793, PRO, PROB 11/1231, sig. 213 · administration, PRO, PROB 6/172 [Jane Mayo], fol. 269 · *DNB*
Archives DWL, Mercy Doddridge MSS, L/1/7/98–99

Mayo, Herbert (1720–1802). *See under* Mayo, Charles (1767–1858).

Mayo, Herbert (1796–1852), physiologist and anatomist, third son of John *Mayo (1761–1818), physician, and his wife, Ann, daughter of Thomas Cock, was born in Queen Anne Street, London, on 3 April 1796. His brother, Thomas *Mayo, became president of the Royal College of Physicians. Mayo entered the Middlesex Hospital, London, as a surgical pupil on 17 May 1814. He was also a pupil of Charles Bell between 1812 and 1815. He studied medicine at Leiden; his MD thesis, 'De urethra ejusque constrictione', was published in Leiden in 1818. In 1818 he became house-surgeon at the Middlesex Hospital; in 1819 he became a member of the Royal College of Surgeons. He was a surgeon at the Middlesex Hospital from 1827 until 1842, was professor of anatomy and surgery at the Royal College of Surgeons in 1828 and 1829, became a fellow of the Royal Society in 1828, was a professor of anatomy at King's College in 1830, became professor of physiology and pathological anatomy at King's College in 1836, and became a fellow of the Royal College of Surgeons in 1843. He is credited with founding the medical school at Middlesex Hospital. He married Jessica Matilda, daughter of Samuel James *Arnold, dramatist. They had a son and two daughters.

Mayo discovered that the seventh cranial nerve is the nerve the activity of which causes the muscles of the face to move—that is, it is the motor nerve of the face. He also discovered that the fifth cranial nerve is the nerve that conveys sensation from the face to the brain—that is, it is the chief sensory nerve of the face. Beyond that, he showed that the fifth cranial nerve has two connections to the brain (roots), and that one root is motor and that the other, sensory, root has a ganglion (a collection of nerve cells). In his report of those findings (*Anatomical and Physiological Commentaries*, 1822, 107–20), Mayo remarked that he had been led to perform his experiments by reading Charles Bell's report of similar experiments, and added eight pages of unsparing criticism of Bell's methods and conclusions. Bell was later to claim that he had correctly described the function of the nerves of the face and that he had shown that only sensory nerves have a ganglion.

In 1823 Mayo published the second part of the *Anatomical and Physiological Commentaries*, in which he reported that stimulation of the optic nerve (the nerve that conveys visual sensation from the eye to the brain) resulted in narrowing of the pupil of the eye, even if the optic nerve and the nerve to the pupil were connected only by that small part of the central nervous system to which the optic nerve travels and from which a nerve travels to the pupil (*Commentaries*, 1823, 1–21). In a later generalization he said that 'an influence may be propagated from the sentient nerves of a part, to their correspondent nerves of motion, through the intervention of that part alone of the nervous centre, to which they are mutually attached' (*Commentaries*, 1823, 135). Mayo was thus not only the first to discover what we would now call reflex action, but also the first to point out its general significance for the function of the nervous system. Charles Sherrington, perhaps the greatest neurophysiologist of all time and certainly the greatest authority on the reflex, referred to 'Mayo's celebrated experiment', and said that it went far 'to draw attention to the fractional powers of the cerebro-spinal organ' (Sherrington, 786).

Mayo's *Commentaries* also contain useful translations from the German of the anatomical studies of the brain by J. C. Reil, as well as reporting other important findings made by Mayo, including his discovery that the walls of arteries contain muscle fibres, the contraction or relaxation of which changes the diameter of the artery. Mayo published several other books and pamphlets, including *Outlines of Human Pathology*, which was published in London in 1835, in Philadelphia in 1841, and in translation in Germany in 1838–9.

Following in the footsteps of James Braid, James Esdaile and John Elliotson, Mayo became convinced of the reality and clinical usefulness of mesmerism. His views, like those of his predecessors, were often greeted with scorn and contempt; the author of the entry on Mayo in the *Dictionary of National Biography* spoke of Mayo as having 'thrown himself in the hands of the mesmerists'. In his *Letters on the Truths Contained in Popular Superstitions* (1849) Mayo wrote that 'As it is certain that there is no disease, which the nervous system is not primarily or secondarily implicated in, it is impossible to foresee what will prove the limit of the beneficial application of mesmerism in

practice' (Mayo, *Letters on the Truths*, 138). By 1842 Mayo was disabled by rheumatic gout, sought and found relief in hydropathy, and ended his career as a physician at Bad Weilbach, Germany, where he died on 15 May 1852.

Mayo was a distinguished scientist who made discoveries of great importance and was a major figure in British medicine during the nineteenth century. During his lifetime his reputation unquestionably suffered from Charles Bell's temporarily successful effort to claim that he had made certain discoveries that were in fact made by Mayo and by François Magendie. Mayo's later reputation was not enhanced by his entry in the *Dictionary of National Biography* which is curiously defensive and ambivalent.

PAUL F. CRANEFIELD

Sources Mayo, Herbert, anatomical and physiological commentaries, 2 vols. (1822–3); repr. with introduction by P. F. Cranfield (1975) · P. F. Cranefield, *The way in and the way out: François Magendie, Charles Bell and the roots of the spinal nerves* (1974) · C. Sherrington, 'The spinal cord', *Textbook of physiology*, ed. E. A. Schäfer, 2 (1900), 783–883 · *DNB* · H. Mayo, *Letters on the truths contained in popular superstitions* (1849)
Archives RS · Wellcome L., copy of his book on popular superstitions with his MS additions
Likenesses D. Lucas, mezzotint (after J. Lonsdale), Wellcome L.

Mayo [*née* Fyvie], **Isabella** [*pseud.* Edward Garrett] (1843–1914), novelist and essayist, was born on 10 December 1843 at 2 Bedford Street, London, in the West End bakery of her Scottish parents Margaret Thomson and George Fyvie. Of the couple's eight children five died, including all four sons; George Fyvie died in 1851. According to Isabella's autobiography, *Recollections of Fifty Years* (1910), her mother had 'little business acumen' (Mayo, *Recollections*, 66) and her inability to manage the financial aspects of the family business led to its failure. From the 1860s onwards Isabella Fyvie began her 'battle of life'—a struggle to survive and pay off the family debt of £800 (ibid.).

Fortunately her education at a private co-educational school in London enabled Fyvie to take advantage of the city's growing number of female employment agencies and to survive what she termed 'the School of Life' (Mayo, *Recollections*, 65). She earned a meagre living by working as a secretary and law writer from 1860 to 1869, as an amanuensis to an employer she calls 'Miss Y', and spent a short period of time in Bessie Parkes's Office for the Employment of Women at Langham Place, London. One of her first assignments was to address envelopes for the sum of 3 *s.* per 1500 (ibid., 74–5).

Nevertheless Fyvie found time to write poems and stories, and through the efforts of literary patrons such as Isa Craig, Mrs S. C. Hall, and Edwin Arnold, had her first novel serialized by Alexander Strahan in 1867. *The Occupations of a Retired Life* is the evangelical tale of siblings Ruth and Edward Garrett and provided Isabella Fyvie with her *nom de plume* as well as the large sum of £300. On 9 July 1870 Fyvie married John Ryall Mayo (1844/5–1877), a solicitor. By this time she had cleared the family debt and had won what she termed 'My life-and-death fight for bread and independence'—a struggle she says lasted from 1860 to 1869 (Mayo, *Recollections*, 116). In the next two decades Isabella Mayo edited a collection of Aesop's fables and wrote

By Still Waters (1874), *The Capel Girls* (1874), *Family Fortunes* (1881), *Thoughts and Stories for Girls* (1884), and *Her Object in Life* (1884), this last the tale of Faith Alleyne, a hard-working young woman whose efforts to secure financial independence are repeatedly undermined by the actions of her feckless brother, Denzil. *A Black Diamond, or, The Best and the Worst of It* (1894) was possibly inspired by the experiences of an elderly black servant of the Fyvies' who had escaped from slavery in America. Mayo believed that memories of his sufferings ultimately caused him to commit suicide (ibid., 18). In the preface she states that the novel is 'derived from the best authorities or from personal knowledge' and argues that: 'We can be saved from race prejudice only by faithful practice of the great Christian doctrine of the Brotherhood of Man' (Garrett, *Black Diamond*, 5–6). The novel is set in Canada, a country Mayo visited, and conveys her work ethic as well as her abolitionist views.

Mayo lived much of her life in Aberdeen, while travelling extensively, visiting Quebec, the Holy Land, Egypt, and Greece. Her charitable ethic was not limited to humankind, and Mayo worked for the Scottish Society for the Prevention of Vivisection, editing the society's publication *Our fellow mortals*. Mayo was a lifelong non-sectarian Christian; she believed that 'the best expression of vital Christianity' was 'the brotherhood of races of men, the cause of international peace, and the recognition of the rights of animals' (Mayo, *Recollections*, 170). In later life she continued to be productive, publishing a six-volume collection of stories and sayings from Great Britain and the Near East, *Old Stories and Sayings of many Lands* (1910–11), and she was among the first to translate Tolstoy. She continued to write reviews, articles on history and travel, and biographical essays for a number of magazines until her death at Bishop's Gate, Don Street, Old Aberdeen on 13 May 1914.   EMMA PLASKITT

Sources I. Mayo, *Recollections of fifty years* (1910) · B. P. Kanner, *Two hundred years of British women autobiographers* (1977), 579–81 · Blain, Clements & Grundy, *Feminist comp.* · J. Sutherland, *The Longman companion to Victorian fiction* (1988) · I. Mayo, *Thoughts and stories for girls* (1884) · E. Garrett [I. Mayo], *A black diamond, or, The best and worst of it* [1894] · *WWW, 1897–1915* · b. cert. · m. cert. · d. cert.
Likenesses photographs, repro. in Mayo, *Recollections*, frontispiece and facing p. 116
Wealth at death £1364 3s. 11d.: probate, 1914, CGPLA Eng. & Wales

Mayo, John (1761–1818), physician, son of Thomas Mayo, was born in Hereford on 10 December 1761. He matriculated at Oxford in 1778 from Brasenose College, graduated BA in 1782, was elected fellow of Oriel College on 16 April 1784, and proceeded MA in 1785, MB in 1787, and DM in 1788. He became FRCP on 30 September 1789, and was censor in 1790, 1795, 1804, and 1808; he was Harveian orator in 1795, elect on 10 April 1807, and resigned this last position on 6 October 1813. He served in London as physician to the Foundling Hospital from July 1787 to 1809 and as physician to the Middlesex Hospital from 6 November 1788 until 11 January 1803, and he was also physician-in-ordinary to the princess of Wales. At a meeting of the board of the Middlesex Hospital in December 1802, it was

resolved that Mayo, 'who had been physician to this hospital with equal advantage to the charity and honour to himself for fourteen years, be solicited to attend the cancer ward as physician extraordinary' (Wilson, 200). With his first wife, Ann, daughter of Thomas Cock of Tottenham, whom he married on 5 February 1789, he had three sons: Thomas *Mayo (1790–1871), subsequently president of the Royal College of Physicians; John, who took holy orders; and Herbert *Mayo (1796–1852), physiologist. His second wife was Frances Lavinia, daughter of William Fellowes of Ramsey Abbey, MP for Ludlow and Andover.

Mayo habitually divided his time between London and Tunbridge Wells, practising at the latter during the summer months. There he enjoyed 'the undisputed lead in medical business and emoluments' (Munk, 395). After resigning his hospital appointments in 1817, he lived wholly at Tunbridge Wells, where he died on 29 November 1818; he was buried at Speldhurst, Kent. His eldest son published *Remarks on Insanity, Founded on the Practice of J. Mayo, M.D.* (1817).   C. H. MAYO, rev. MICHAEL BEVAN

Sources GM, 1st ser., 59 (1789), 177 · B. Murphy, 'Fellowes, William', HoP, *Commons, 1790–1820*, vol. 3 · [E. Wilson], ed., *The history of the Middlesex Hospital* (1845) · Foster, *Alum. Oxon.* · Munk, *Roll* · *History of Mayo family* (1882)

Mayo, Paggen William (1766–1836). *See under* Mayo, Charles (1767–1858).

Mayo, Richard (c.1630–1695), clergyman and ejected minister, was the son of Richard Mayo (d. 1660) of St Giles Cripplegate, London. His father was said to be a man of some property, and Richard was educated in London under the puritan Thomas Singleton. On 2 December 1652, after serving a few months as ship's chaplain aboard the *Sovereign* and perhaps attending Wadham College, Oxford, Mayo was ordained by the fourth London classis as lecturer at Whitechapel. By the time of his marriage to Jane Smyth (d. 1713x15), of St Mary, Somerset, in January 1654, Mayo had begun to officiate at Kingston, Surrey, in the absence of the vicar, Dr Edmund Staunton, whom the parliamentary visitors had appointed president of Corpus Christi College, Oxford, in 1648. Staunton eventually resigned the living to Mayo in 1658. His ministry at Kingston, long a hotbed of radical agitation, was not without its trials. While he succeeded in having the Quaker missionary Edward Burrough imprisoned and fined £100 for slander in 1658, Burrough and his supporters published two pamphlets decrying Mayo's 'damnable doctrine', and denouncing the 'priest's' cruelty in prosecuting him 'for speaking the truth' (Cooke, 8; Burrough, 5, 3).

Following his ejection for nonconformity in 1662 Mayo continued to preach in conventicles. In 1669, according to episcopal returns, he preached not only at Kingston, but at Guildford, 'to sometimes one-hundred Anabaptists', and at Henley-on-Thames, Oxfordshire, to former 'officers and soldiers in the parliamentary army' (Gordon, 310–11). In April 1672 he obtained a licence as presbyterian teacher at Kingston but by the early 1680s he had settled in Upper Thames Street, London, as pastor of a presbyterian congregation. About 1689 his people built him a new meeting-house in Salters' Hall Court. An advocate of the 'Happy Union' (1691) between city Independents and presbyterians, Mayo served as one of the original managers of the Common Fund, which supported deserving candidates for the ministry, and himself contributed £100 to the fund in 1690. When the union collapsed in 1694, the presbyterians John Howe, William Bates, Vincent Alsop, and Daniel Williams withdrew from the merchants' lecture at Pinners' Hall and set up their own at Salters' Hall, to which Samuel Annesley and Mayo were added.

In the midst of this rancour Mayo urged dissenters to seek peace in two sermons, published as *The Cause and Cure of Strife and Division* (1695). But he had first established his reputation as an author three decades earlier, with his best-selling *Plain Answer* (1664), which encouraged readers to attend to the 'neglected duty of secret prayer'. He offered practical 'hints' so that Christians would go to prayer 'not as sick persons to their meals, because they must', but with a suitably 'quickened and enlarged heart' (*Plain Answer*, foreword). Under the initials N. H., Mayo published *A Conference betwixt a Papist and a Jew* (1673) and *Two Conferences* (1677); the latter enjoyed at least six editions, that of 1754 bearing the title *Two Disputations Concerning the Messiah*. In both Mayo argued that the Church of Rome, with its 'lying wonders and feigned miracles', gave a 'stab to the Christian Faith' by discrediting the best evidence that Jesus was the Messiah, the miracles he and his immediate followers performed (*Two Conferences*, 1679, 28). His *Life* of his predecessor, Edmund Staunton, (1673), was reprinted in Clarke's *Lives* (1683). In addition to several sermons published in the *Morning-Exercise* collections, Mayo also wrote the commentary on Romans in Matthew Poole's *Annotations* (1683–5).

Mayo and his wife, Jane, had six children. Of their three sons the eldest, Richard (b. 1661), became vicar of Great Kimble, Buckinghamshire, through the patronage of the presbyterian Richard Hampden. Mayo's youngest son, Daniel *Mayo (1672–1733), was pastor of his father's congregation in Kingston and of the Gravel-Pit meeting in Hackney, Middlesex. After a six-week illness, Richard Mayo died on 8 September 1695 and was buried three days later on 11 September at Kingston. His assistant, Nathanael Taylor (d. 1702), preached his funeral sermon, in which he stated that Mayo was about sixty-five on his death. He left property worth almost £1000 to his wife and children.   JIM BENEDICT

Sources N. Taylor, *A funeral sermon on the decease of Revd. Richard Mayo* (1695) • *Calamy rev.*, 347, 368, 444, 460 • E. Calamy, ed., *An abridgement of Mr. Baxter's history of his life and times, with an account of the ministers, &c., who were ejected after the Restauration of King Charles II*, 2nd edn, 2 vols. (1713), vol. 2, pp. 15, 668 • A. Gordon, ed., *Freedom after ejection: a review (1690–1692) of presbyterian and congregational nonconformity in England and Wales* (1917), 160, 164, 168, 310–11 • W. Wilson, *The history and antiquities of the dissenting churches and meeting houses in London, Westminster and Southwark*, 4 vols. (1808–14), vol. 2, pp. 9–12 • will, PRO, PROB 11/429, fol. 131 • E. Calamy, *An historical account of my own life, with some reflections on the times I have lived in, 1671–1731*, ed. J. T. Rutt, 1 (1829), 351, 370 • E. Burrough, *To Charles Fleetwood … The state of the old controversie … between Richard Mayo … and Edward Burrough* (1659) • E. Cooke, *A short account of the unjust proceedings … in a tryal between Richard Mayo, priest, and E. Burrough*

(1658) • W. A. Shaw, *A history of the English church during the civil wars and under the Commonwealth, 1640–1660*, 2 (1900), 595 • C. Hill, *The world turned upside down: radical ideas during the English revolution* (1972), 111–13 • Foster, *Alum. Oxon.* • *The life and errors of John Dunton*, [rev. edn], 1, ed. J. B. Nichols (1818), 174 • G. H. Pike, *Ancient meeting-houses, or, Memorial pictures of nonconformity in old London* (1870), 378 • J. Sampson, *The story of Kingston* (1972), 88, 95 • *IGI* • R. Mayo, *Plain answer* (1664) • N. H. [R. Mayo], *Two conferences* (1679)
Likenesses oils, DWL
Wealth at death £1000 in legacies to his children, to be paid out of the rest of estate, real and personal, left to wife: will, PRO, PROB 11/429, fol. 131

Mayo, Thomas (1790–1871), physician, eldest son of John *Mayo (1761–1818) and his wife, Ann, the daughter of Thomas Cock, was born in London on 24 January 1790. He was the brother of the physiologist Herbert *Mayo (1796–1852). He began his education under the Revd John Smith of Eltham, and then after eighteen months at Westminster School he was transferred to the private tuition of the Revd George Richards, vicar of Bampton, Oxfordshire. He entered Oriel College, Oxford, in 1807, and obtained a first class *in literis humanioribus* in 1811. He was elected a fellow of Oriel on 23 April 1813:

> to the attainment of which honour I had pledged myself to my father, provided he would permit me to escape the Foundation of Westminster and its peculiar training, which combined with a very fair proportion of Latin and Greek occasional aerostation in a blanket. (Munk)

Mayo graduated MA in 1814, BM in 1815, and DM in 1818.

On his father's death Mayo succeeded to his lucrative practice at Tunbridge Wells. In 1835 he settled in London, where he lived at 56 Wimpole Street. He became FRCP in 1819 and censor of the Royal College of Physicians in 1835, 1839, and 1850. He delivered the Lumleian lectures in 1839 and 1842, the Harveian oration in 1841, and the Croonian lectures in 1853, and he was named an elect in 1847. In 1835 he became FRS, and in 1841 physician to the Marylebone Infirmary. He was also physician-in-ordinary to the duke of Sussex. On 5 January 1857 he was elected president of the Royal College of Physicians, a post to which he was annually re-elected until 1862. Mayo was therefore president during the passing of the Medical Act of 1858, and in his colleges offices had been closely concerned with questions of reform for a number of years.

Mayo was the last president chosen by the ancient system, and the last elect chosen by his brother-elects (Clark, 725). In his pamphlet *Medical Examinations and Physicians' Requirements Considered* (1857), published soon after his election as president, Mayo stressed the value of a classical education and warned against competitive examinations 'as likely to produce a knowledge which was neither lasting nor sufficiently wide' (Clark, 725).

Mayo was also something of an authority on mental illness, and he published *An Essay on the Relation of the Theory of Morals to Insanity* (1831) and *Elements of Pathology of the Human Mind* (1838). His Croonian lecture, 'Medical testimony in cases of lunacy' was published in 1854. Mayo repeatedly rejected medico-psychological attempts to reform the law and opposed the insanity plea. After one case *The Lancet* criticized him for propounding 'not evidence but metaphysical speculations; and to apply to a living fellow-creature his famous doctrines of abstract mental disease, of insane responsibility, and the propriety of making madmen the subject of criminal punishment' (Smith, 138). In 1860 Mayo delivered a remarkable address at the Royal Institution, entitled 'Relations of the public to the science and practice of medicine'.

Mayo was twice married; first, to Lydia, daughter of John Bill MD of Farley Hall, Staffordshire; and second to Susan Mary, widow of Rear-Admiral Sir William Symonds, and daughter of the Revd John Briggs, fellow of Eton College. He had seven children (by his first marriage only), including Augustus Frederick Mayo, barrister; the Revd Robert Mayo; and Charles Thomas Mayo of Corsham, Wiltshire. In 1862 Mayo retired from practice, to live first at Yarmouth, on the Isle of Wight, and then with his son Charles at Corsham, where he died on 13 January 1871, and where he was buried.   C. H. MAYO, rev. MICHAEL BEVAN

Sources Munk, *Roll* · Foster, *Alum. Oxon.* · Boase, *Mod. Eng. biog.* · *The Lancet* (21 Jan 1871), 101 · *BMJ* (21 Jan 1871), 79 · J. Alderson, 'Annual address', *BMJ* (15 April 1871), 387–8 · G. Clark and A. M. Cooke, *A history of the Royal College of Physicians of London*, 2 (1966) · R. Smith, *Trial by medicine: insanity and responsibility in Victorian trials* (1981)
Likenesses G. Richmond, chalk drawing, 1862, RCP Lond.
Wealth at death under £70,000: probate, 10 Feb 1871, *CGPLA Eng. & Wales*

Mayor, Flora Macdonald (1872–1932), novelist, was born on 20 October 1872 at Queensgate House, Kingston Hill, Surrey, the youngest of the four children of the Revd Joseph Bickersteth *Mayor (1828–1916), professor of classics and later of moral philosophy at King's College, London, and his wife, Alexandrina Jessie (1831–1927), daughter of Andrew Grote of the Indian Civil Service and his wife, Isabella. Flora's mother was a remarkable linguist, and Flora is said to have spoken thirteen languages. The family was comfortably off: like her character Henrietta Symons, Flora 'was always cursed with her tidy little income'. Flora was educated with her identical twin Alice at Surbiton high school and in Switzerland, then read history at Newnham College, Cambridge (1892–6). A lively girl, she threw herself so fervently into Cambridge pleasures that despite earlier academic achievement at school, she got only a third. For the next seven years she thrashed about in search of an occupation. Despite having asthma, and to the horror of her family who wanted her to be a 'daughter at home', she attempted to become an actress. Her experiences in the theatre were unpleasant and degrading, and she got only tiny parts. She also published a novel, *Mrs Hammond's Children* (1901), under her stage name of Mary Strafford.

In March 1903 Flora became engaged to an old friend, Ernest Shepherd (1871/2–1903), but they had only a few weeks together. Ernest had accepted a job with the architectural survey of India so that he could afford to marry, and Flora allowed him to go there ahead of her. He died of fever at Simla on 22 October 1903, aged thirty-one. The shock made her a semi-invalid for years. Flora wrote that

up to then, 'I instinctively put happiness as what I was aiming for and expecting as my right in life. Since then I have also quite instinctively given up expecting it' (Oldfield, 136). Outwardly the second half of her life appeared a long sad postscript to the adventurous years. She never again attempted to leave her family, living at various times with her brothers in London, or Bristol, or with her elderly parents at Kingston Hill. Inwardly she was preparing to write two great novels about the buried, intense emotions of spinsters like herself.

About one in four women never married, and there was much discussion before 1914 about what society should do with them. Flora's contribution to this debate was *The Third Miss Symons* (1913), a novel about an unloved and useless woman. It carried a preface by John Masefield, and narrowly missed winning the Polignac prize. The war years were spent unhappily keeping house for her brother Henry, a master at Clifton College. She then began work on her masterpiece, *The Rector's Daughter* (1924). This is a longer and more complex novel, concentrating on the inner life of a middle-aged spinster, Mary Jocelyn, her unconsummated love for a married clergyman, and her lonely death. With such unfashionable subject matter she had difficulty finding a publisher, until Leonard Woolf and Virginia Woolf offered to take it on a commission basis for the Hogarth Press. It was modestly successful and won praise from Masefield, E. M. Forster, and Rebecca West, but Flora Mayor was never recognized as an important novelist.

Afterwards Flora's health and powers declined. Her mother died in 1927 and she moved with Alice to Hampstead. She wrote some supernatural and other stories and an inferior novel, *The Squire's Daughter* (1929), which laments the decay of post-war England. She died at her home at 7 East Heath Road, Hampstead, on 28 January 1932 of pneumonia complicated by influenza, and is buried in Hampstead cemetery. A collection of stories, *The Room Opposite*, appeared posthumously in 1935.

Flora Mayor was undervalued during her life and for many years after her death because she appeared to have been born out of her time. She belonged in the tradition of Jane Austen, Charlotte Brontë, and Mrs Gaskell—her work was described by Sylvia Lynd as 'a bitter *Cranford*' (Oldfield, 241)—but unlike them, she did not allow her spinsters to achieve happiness, and was a woman of the early twentieth century, very much aware of feminism, agnosticism, and the lifestyle of Bloomsbury. Her novels are valuable as the only serious, full-length studies of a vast group of despised and rejected women, English spinsters. Celibacy, damaged family relationships, and the tension between modernism and tradition are the materials from which she built two extraordinary books. *The Rector's Daughter* was reprinted in 1973, *The Third Miss Symons* in 1980.   MERRYN WILLIAMS

Sources S. Oldfield, *Spinsters of this parish* (1984) · Trinity Cam., Mayor MSS · priv. coll. · b. cert. · *The Times* (1932)
Archives Newnham College, Cambridge · priv. coll. · Trinity Cam., corresp.

Likenesses group photograph (with fellow students), Newnham College, Cambridge · photograph, Trinity Cam., Wren Library
Wealth at death £12,328 1s. 10d.: probate, 30 March 1932, *CGPLA Eng. & Wales*

Mayor, John Eyton Bickersteth (1825–1910), classical scholar and Church of England clergyman, third son of the Revd Robert Mayor (1791–1846), was born on 28 January 1825 at Baddegama in Ceylon, where his father was a missionary of the Church Missionary Society from 1818 to 1828. His mother was Charlotte (1792–1870), daughter of Henry Bickersteth, surgeon, of Kirkby Lonsdale, and sister of Henry Bickersteth, Baron Langdale, and Edward Bickersteth, rector of Watton. He was named John Eyton in memory of his father's friend, the Revd John Eyton (d. 1823), rector of Eyton in Shropshire, who had prompted the elder Mayor to abandon the medical profession and to become a missionary.

From his early boyhood Mayor delighted in books. At the age of six he enjoyed English prose versions of Homer and Virgil. After attending in 1832 the grammar school of Newcastle under Lyme as a day boy, he was from 1833 to 1836 at Christ's Hospital, but was removed owing to an attack of scarlet fever. For several years he was at home, learning Greek, as well as Latin, with his mother, who leant the languages in order to help her sons. In 1838, with the aid of his uncle, Robert Bickersteth, a successful surgeon in Liverpool, he was sent to Shrewsbury, the school which won his lifelong devotion. He read much out of school, for his own improvement. He later recalled that he 'nearly knew by heart' all Milton's verse, English and Latin.

In October 1844 Mayor began residence at St John's College, Cambridge. His college tutor was the mathematician John Hymers, his private tutor William Henry Bateson, ultimately master of St John's. He also read classics with the famous coach, Richard Shilleto. In the classical tripos of 1848 he was third in the first class. An elder brother, Robert Bickersteth (1820–1898), was third wrangler in 1842; his younger brother, Joseph Bickersteth *Mayor (1828–1916), was second classic in 1851. All three brothers were elected fellows of the college, John being admitted as fellow on 27 March 1849.

From 1849 to 1853 Mayor was master of the lower sixth at Marlborough College, and there he prepared his edition of *Thirteen Satires of Juvenal*. This important work, a remarkable achievement for a scholar of twenty-eight, shows both the strengths and the weaknesses of Mayor's editorial method. He was not primarily concerned with the emendation of the text, but rather with the history and use of words and the amassing of illustrative material. The note on the word *hortus* in satire 1 runs for over 150 lines. The commentary expanded considerably over four editions. Mayor did not enjoy his years at Marlborough. The school was at its lowest ebb: in 1851 came the 'great rebellion' which dislodged the headmaster and nearly destroyed the school, and Mayor's letters refer to the low level of discipline and behaviour.

In 1853 Mayor returned for life to St John's, at first as an assistant tutor or lecturer in classics, but the vastness of his learning prevented him from being a good lecturer. One obituarist recalls that he delivered his final set of lectures to a solitary MA: 'The subject announced was Minucius Felix; but at the suggestion of the auditor, who had heard him before on this writer, he changed it in a twinkling to Seneca's *Epistles*' (Stewart, xliv). He was, however, one of the group of younger fellows who brought about much needed changes in the organization and methods of college teaching in the 1850s. He was ordained deacon in 1855 and priest in 1857. He subsequently kept the act for the BD degree (taking the subject of vernacular services *versus* Latin), preached a Latin and an English sermon, but never took the degree. To the *Journal of Classical and Sacred Philology*, founded by Hort, Lightfoot, and Mayor in 1854, he contributed two learned and comprehensive articles on Latin lexicography (November 1855 and March 1857).

Throughout life Mayor applied himself with exceptional ardour to various forms of literary and antiquarian research, and he proved indefatigable in amassing information. He brought together an immense library, which he stored until 1881 in his college rooms over the gateway of the second court. In that year he acquired a small house in Jordan's Yard to make room for the overflow of books and papers. An accomplished linguist, he was familiar not only with Latin and Greek but with French, Italian, and Spanish, and notably with German and Dutch. To the collecting of biographical material he devoted immense energy, and in later life he placed his biographical notes at the disposal of contributors to the *Dictionary of National Biography*.

Mayor's early publications include a number of historical biographies, as well as an edition of Roger Ascham's *Scholemaster* (1863; new edn, 1883). But the history of his own university was one of his most absorbing interests, and he emulated the antiquarian zeal of Thomas Baker, the ejected fellow of the eighteenth century. He printed the four earliest codes of the college statutes (1859). He transcribed the admissions to the college from 1630, and his transcript was edited as far as 1715 by himself (1882–93), and as far as 1767 by R. F. Scott (1903). He calendared Baker's voluminous MSS in the university library. He supplied material to Professor R. Willis and John Willis Clark for their *Architectural History of Cambridge*, and he gave every aid and encouragement to Charles Henry Cooper in his labours on Cambridge history and biography, and accumulated manuscript notes for a continuation of Cooper's *Athenae Cantabrigienses*. Mayor foretold that his own biographical collections would survive with the manuscripts of Baker and Cole. In 1869 Mayor published for the first time Baker's *History of St John's College*, a solid work in two large volumes; he continued Baker's text, and added abundant notes to the lives of all the masters of the college and of the bishops trained within its walls.

In 1864 Mayor was elected without a contest university librarian. He held the post for three years, and was never absent from his duties for more than eight days together. During his tenure of office the catalogue of MSS was completed, and he substituted for the various series of classmarks a single series of Arabic numerals (a reform which was subsequently abandoned). Not all his activities met with the approval of the syndics. He managed to spend in three months the library's annual allowance for buying books, and sold large numbers of duplicates for very low prices. Although his energy increased the life and vigour of the library, all his literary and antiquarian projects were in his own words put 'out of gear' by his duties, and in 1867 he withdrew to resume his private work. In 1872 he was elected professor of Latin in succession to Hugh Andrew Johnstone Munro. He remained professor until his death. His favourite subjects for lectures were Martial and the letters of Seneca and the younger Pliny, with Minucius Felix and Tertullian. But, like his college lectures, those delivered before the university were too closely packed with references to parallel passages to be appreciated by the ordinary student. His lectures on Bede bore fruit in 1878 in a joint edition (with Dr J. R. Lumby) of the *Ecclesiastical History* (bks 3 and 4), in which the learned and multifarious commentary fills a little more space than the text.

Mayor pursued his studies unremittingly, 'taking no exercise for its own sake' and rarely going abroad except on academic or learned business. In 1875 he represented Cambridge University at the tercentenary of Leiden, where he met Madvig and Cobet. In the same year he paid his only visit to Rome, where, apart from its ancient associations, he was mainly interested in the modern schools, where the boys learnt by heart whole books of Virgil and Tasso. A keen interest in the Old Catholics led him to attend the congress convened at Constance in 1873, when he delivered a German as well as an English speech.

Mayor's physical constitution was remarkably strong. He attributed the vigour of his old age to his strict adherence to vegetarian diet, which he adopted in middle life and thenceforth championed with enthusiasm. He set forth his views on diet first in *Modicus cibi medicus sibi, or, Nature her Own Physician* (1880), and subsequently in the selected addresses published in *Plain Living and High Thinking* (1897). In 1884 he became president of the Vegetarian Society, and held office until his death. Throughout that period he was a frequent contributor to the *Dietetic Reformer and Vegetarian Messenger*, and the Vegetarian Society in 1901 printed selections by him from the Bible and from English poets under the title of *Sound Mind in Body Sound: a Cloud of Witnesses to the Golden Rule of Not Too Much*. He was also keenly interested in missionary work at home and abroad, and especially in the St John's College mission in Walworth.

Mayor became president of his college in October 1902, and at the fellows' table he charmed visitors of the most varied tastes by his old-fashioned courtesy, and by his learned and lively talk. His interests within their own lines remained alert to the last. When the National Library of Turin was partly destroyed by fire on 26 January 1904, he promptly sent the library no fewer than 710 volumes. In 1907 he easily mastered Esperanto. He offered to resign his chair in 1904 but the offer was not accepted, chiefly because the university would have had to pay a far higher stipend to his successor than Mayor ever received.

Mayor's wide learning received many marks of respect in his later years. He received the honorary degree of DCL from Oxford in 1895, that of LLD from Aberdeen in 1892 and from St Andrews in 1906, and that of DD (an honour of which he was particularly proud) from Glasgow in 1901. He was one of the original fellows of the British Academy (1902). In 1905, on his eightieth birthday, a Latin address of congratulation written by Professor J. S. Reid and signed by 173 scholars was presented to him at a meeting held in the combination room of St John's, under the presidency of Sir Richard Jebb. Until 1908 he preached in the college chapel and occasionally in the university church. He printed his sermons immediately after delivery, without his name, but with the date and place, and with an appendix of interesting notes. His style in the pulpit reflected the best seventeenth- and eighteenth-century examples, and his sermons dealt exhaustively with aspects of church history and doctrine in which he had become interested. Mayor, who was unmarried, died suddenly of heart failure within two months of completing the eighty-sixth year of his age, on 1 December 1910, while he was preparing to leave his Cambridge residence with a view to reading prayers in the college chapel. He was buried in St Giles's cemetery, on the Huntingdon Road, Cambridge.

Mayor possessed an unusual power of accumulating knowledge. He had far less ability at construction, and much of the work that he designed was not attempted, or if attempted was uncompleted. A projected commentary on Seneca never appeared. A Latin dictionary, which might have been his *magnum opus*, was never seriously begun. Contemplated editions of Milton and of Boswell's *Life of Johnson*, and an ecclesiastical history of the first three centuries came to nothing. Yet his publications were very numerous and covered a wide range. His scholarly reputation mainly rests on his edition of Juvenal. Apart from this, his chief contributions to classical learning were an edition of Cicero's *Second Philippic*, founded on that of Halm (1861); a bibliography of Latin literature, founded on that of Hübner (1875); and an independent edition of the *Third Book of Pliny's Letters* (1880). In 1868 he published an excellent *First Greek Reader*, with a vigorous preface on classical education, interspersed with interesting touches of autobiography. Miscellaneous works included an edition of Richard of Cirencester's *Speculum historiale de gestis regum Angliae* for the Rolls Series (2 vols., 1863–9), in which Mayor devoted many pages of the preface to indicating the exact sources of all the borrowed erudition of the forger of the treatise *De situ Britanniae*, which its first editor (and, indeed, author), Charles Bertram of Copenhagen, had falsely attributed to Richard of Cirencester. In 1874 Mayor edited Cooper's *Memoir of Margaret Countess of Richmond and Derby*, and in 1876 published, for the Early English Text Society, *The English Works of Bishop Fisher*. His latest work was a *First German Reader, with Translation and Notes*, which he had printed for himself and published at the Cambridge University Press in January 1910 with the title *Jacula prudentum, Verse and Prose from the German*.

Mayor's annotated copies of Juvenal and Seneca were among the books presented by his executors to the library of his college, and his interleaved Latin dictionaries were among those presented to the university library, which he named as the ultimate destination of his biographical collections. Of the rest of his library more than 18,000 volumes were sold in Cambridge after his death.

J. E. Sandys, *rev.* Richard Smail

Sources J. E. Sandys and others, *The Eagle*, 32 (1910–11), 188–232 [memoirs, incl. repr. extracts of obits.] · H. F. Stewart, 'Memoir', in J. E. B. Mayor, *Twelve Cambridge sermons*, ed. H. F. Stewart (1911) · E. Miller, *Portrait of a college: a history of the College of Saint John the Evangelist, Cambridge* (1961) · P. G. Naiditch, *A. E. Housman at University College, London: the election of 1892* (1988)
Archives St John Cam., annotated editions etc. · Trinity Cam., corresp. and papers | BL, corresp. with Philip Bliss, Add. MS 34582 · BL, corresp. with Samuel Butler, Add. MSS 44033–44037 · CUL, department of manuscripts and university archives, annals of Cambridge University and biographical notes on Oxford and Cambridge men · Dorset RO, George Bell MSS · U. Reading L., letters to George Bell
Likenesses H. von Herkomer, oils, 1891, St John Cam. · H. von Herkomer, etching, repro. in *Minerva* (1903–4) · H. von Herkomer, etching, repro. in *The Eagle*, 25 (1904), 129 · J. Russell, photograph, repro. in Stewart, 'Memoir' · portrait, repro. in Stewart, 'Memoir'
Wealth at death £3220 6s. 8d.: resworn administration, 27 March 1911, *CGPLA Eng. & Wales*

Mayor, Joseph Bickersteth (1828–1916), philosopher and classical scholar, was born on 24 October 1828 at the Cape of Good Hope, as his parents were returning from Ceylon. He was the eighth of the twelve children of Robert Mayor (1791–1846), missionary and cleric, and his wife, Charlotte (1792–1870), daughter of Henry Bickersteth, surgeon apothecary of Kirkby Lonsdale, and his wife, Elizabeth. The family on the father's side was descended from the lord chief justice of England, Sir Matthew Hale (1608–1679). The mother's brothers included Henry Bickersteth, master of the rolls and friend of Jeremy Bentham, and Edward Bickersteth (1786–1850), a missionary. Several of Mayor's brothers and sisters followed their parents into evangelicalism.

Mayor attended Rugby School under Thomas Arnold and later joined the school governors. In 1847 he entered St John's College, Cambridge, on a scholarship, joining his elder brothers Robert, a mathematician and author, and John Eyton Bickersteth *Mayor, classical scholar and vegetarian. By networking and diligence they all achieved high honours, fellowships, and brilliant careers: Robert became a master at Rugby and rector of Frating; and John Eyton became president of college, university librarian, professor of Latin, and FBA. Joseph was placed second in the first class in classics in 1851 behind his great friend, Trinity fellow and author Bishop Joseph B. Lightfoot. He proceeded MA in 1854, and was ordained deacon in 1859 and priest in 1860.

Mayor's network involved many of the best minds in mid-century Cambridge, including: George Downing Liveing, professor of chemistry; Edwin Abbott, philologist and author; Henry Roby, educational reformer, professor of jurisprudence and MP for Eccles; Fenton John Hort, author and Hulsean professor of divinity; Henry Sidgwick, philosopher; Sir John Seely, who with Sidgwick established political science at Cambridge; and John Venn, logician and historian. He was drawn into a philosophical network, the precursor of the Moral Sciences Club, called the Grote Society after its leader, Professor John Grote, brother of the historian George Grote, whose adopted niece Alexandrina Jessie Grote (1831–1927), daughter of Andrew Grote of the Indian Civil Service, Mayor married on 29 December 1863. Members included Sidgwick, Venn, John Rickards Mozley, W. Aldis Wright, and John Batteridge Pearson. Friendship, discussion, and judicious criticism, the hallmark of later Cambridge philosophy, were developed here and earlier in The Society, whose members included Leslie Stephen, Henry Fawcett, Sidgwick, and Roby. These networks lasted for life, with the exception of Stephen, who engineered the election of Fawcett over Joseph Mayor for the chair in political economy in 1862. The Mayors, Grote, Sidgwick, Venn, Roby, Hort, and Stephen were among the great Cambridge college and syllabus reformers of the period. They helped establish the moral sciences and became the subject's college tutors, with Mayor writing the famous 'The moral sciences' in the *Student Guide to the University of Cambridge* (1862).

Mayor had to surrender his college living on marriage, and left Cambridge in 1862 to become master and then headmaster of Kensington School (1862–8) before moving to Twickenham and then becoming professor of classical literature (1870–79) and later professor of moral philosophy (1879–83) at King's College, London. His major contribution to philosophy was his lifelong endeavour to publish the work of his mentor John Grote. He edited three of Grote's major philosophical works (1870, 1876, 1900), a collection of *Sermons* (1872), and eight articles, assisted by Sidgwick and Hort. Here, as in his own life, he displayed a conversational style, acute criticism, and care for the truth, shared with his network and revealed further in his *Sketch of Ancient Philosophy* (1881). Informed by German scholarship, he favoured idealist philosophy and opposed in particular positivism, materialism, scepticism, and the utilitarianism of Jeremy Bentham and John Stuart Mill. Like Grote, he moved with the romantic current, but he favoured an eclectic moral philosophy, built an ethics around duty, and embellished the Stoic qualities and philosophy of Cicero, whose work *De natura deorum* he edited in three volumes (1880–85). He published several classical books, including *Greek for Beginners* (1869), *Guide to the Choice of Classical Books* (3rd edn, 1885; suppl. 1896), and *Virgil's Messianic Eclogue* (1907) with R. S. Conway and W. Warde Fowler. His interest in philology and a desire to counter the corruption of language led to several books, including *Chapters on English Metre* (1896; rev. 2nd edn, 1901) and *A Handbook of Modern English Metre* (1903; rev. 2nd edn, 1912). His efforts to use critical and liberal Anglican scholarship for restoring credibility to Christianity led to *The Epistle of St James* (1892; rev. 3rd edn, 1910), *Clement of Alexandria: Seventh Book of the Stomaties* (1902), *Epistle of St. Jude and Second Epistle of St. Peter* (1907), *Selected Readings from the Psalms, with an Essay on the Growth of Revelation* (1908), *The World's Desire, and other Sermons* (1906), and a revealing sermon, *The End of the Century* (1901). He took a leading role in founding and running the *Classical Review* and was made FBA and honorary fellow at St John's in 1902.

Mayor was grave, serious, and strict as a tutor and parent, but like his friend William Whewell he used his charm, empathy, a sense of justice, reading sessions, and invitations to walk in the Lakes, to find men out and bring them into intellectual networks. He became the fellow editor at the founding of *The Eagle*. His children included a brilliant King's College scholar and Apostle, Robert John Grote Mayor, who was a pioneer of teacher training and a friend of Moore, Russell, Keynes, and McTaggart. Of his other three children, Henry Bickersteth Mayor (1870–1948) was a master at Clifton College, Flora Macdonald *Mayor (1872–1932) went to Newnham College and wrote several novels, and Alice (1872–1961) kept the family archive. A granddaughter, Teresa Georgina Rothschild, played a significant role in MI5. Of her three children, Amschel became a banker, Victoria a university lecturer, and Emma a fellow at King's College, Cambridge, and the wife of the economist and master of Trinity College, Cambridge, Armatya Sen. Little is written about the Mayor network though extensive archive material, notebooks, letters, and photographs of them all are now in the Mayor papers in the Wren Library, Trinity College, Cambridge. Mayor died at Kingston upon Thames on 29 November 1916.

JOHN R. GIBBINS

Sources J. R. Gibbins, 'John Grote and modern Cambridge philosophy', *Philosophy*, 73 (1998), 453–77 · S. Oldfield, *Spinsters of this parish: the life and times of F. M. Mayor and Mary Sheepshanks* (1984) · Trinity Cam., Mayor MSS · H. J. Roby, 'Reminiscences of my life and works', 1904, St John Cam. · *The Eagle*, 38 (1916–17), 323–9 · *The Times* (1 Dec 1916) · J. R. Gibbins, 'John Grote, Cambridge University and the development of Victorian ideas', PhD diss., U. Newcastle, 1988 · m. cert.

Archives Trinity Cam., corresp. and papers | Newnham College, Cambridge, Flora Mayor MSS

Likenesses double portrait, cabinet photograph, 1871 (with his son), Trinity Cam., Mayor MSS · W. Orpen, oils, 1928, St John Cam. · Eddis, double portrait (with Alexandrina); [now lost] · Stewartson, portrait; [now lost] · carte-de-visite, CUL, C. A. S. Portrait Collection, H106 · two cabinet photographs (as young man), Trinity Cam., Mayor MSS · two cabinet photographs, Trinity Cam., Mayor MSS, 66, 67 · two cabinet photographs (as older man), Trinity Cam., Mayor MSS · two cabinet photographs (as old man), Trinity Cam., Mayor MSS, 23, 30

Wealth at death £8296—gross: probate, 24 May 1917, *CGPLA Eng. & Wales* · £3132—net: probate, 24 May 1917, *CGPLA Eng. & Wales*

Mayow [Mayer, Mayo], **John** (*bap.* 1641, *d.* 1679), physiologist and chemist, was born in the manor house of Brae, in the parish of Morval, near Looe, Cornwall, and baptized at Morval on 21 December 1641, the second son and third child of Phillip Mayow, gentleman, and Frances, daughter of John Stuckley of Afton. He was received as a commoner at Wadham College, Oxford, on 2 July 1658 (under the name John Mayouwe), and admitted scholar on 23 September 1659. On the recommendation of Henry Coventry, a former fellow of the college, he was elected on 3 November 1660 to a jurist's fellowship at All Souls College from which he resigned in 1678. He graduated BCL on 30 May 1665, and DCL on 5 July 1670. Mayow obtained the further privilege of studying medicine, which exempted him

John Mayow (*bap.* 1641, *d.* 1679), by William Faithorne the elder, pubd 1674

from taking holy orders. Although he never took a medical degree he practised as a physician, his knowledge probably being acquired through his friendship with the physician Thomas Millington. Other important scientific contacts at Oxford included John Castle, Thomas Guidott, Robert Plot, John Ward, and Christopher Wren, all of whom were interested in anatomy, physiology, chemistry, and the new experimental philosophy. He almost certainly knew Richard Lower, a fellow Cornishman, who was working on the function of respiration with Thomas Willis, Sedleian professor of natural philosophy. His writings indicate a close familiarity with the mechanical philosophy of René Descartes. Mayow took his facts from great observers like Robert Boyle, Marcello Malpighi, Nicolaus Steno, Willis, and Lower, but above all from his personal dissections, observations, and experiments.

The details of Mayow's career between 1670 and 1679 remain in shadow. He visited London on several occasions, where he shared with Robert Hooke his interest in respiration and combustion, but spent most of the teaching year in residence at All Souls. During the summer season he practised medicine at Bath, where he made a careful study of the spa waters, and published the results in a tract 'De sal-nitro'. In his *Discourse of Bath* (1676), Mayow's former Oxford colleague Thomas Guidott denounced his chief conclusion that there was no nitre (potassium nitrate) in Bath waters, and suggested jealously that Mayow 'ploughed with my Heifer' (T. Guidott, *Discourse of Bath*, 1676, 6). Mayow was elected FRS on 30 November 1678 on the recommendation of Hooke, who clearly thought highly of his experimental talents.

Mayow began the study of chemistry about 1667 with the Oxford chemist William Wildan, with whom he learned to prepare mineral acids, the art of distillation, the purification of metals, and the preparation of medicines. At the same time he appears to have acted as an occasional assistant to Boyle and Lower in their pneumatic experiments, some of which were devoted to the possibility of blood transfusion. In October 1667 Hooke and Lower performed a pulmonary insufflation procedure whereby an incision was made in the lungs of a dog while it was kept alive by air being artificially pumped into the lungs with bellows. Hooke believed this to be a crucial demonstration disproving the mechanical theory of respiration in favour of a chemical particulate theory that something extractable from the air powered the normal motions of respiration. The success of this brutal experiment in London inspired Mayow to write an essay on the mechanism of respiration, to which he coupled a medical essay on rickets. The *Tractatus duo, de respiratione et de rachitide* was published at Oxford in 1668 and was favourably received by contemporaries. The second tract on rickets complemented Francis Glisson's comprehensive treatise on the disease published in 1650. It provided a clear clinical description of the disease and attributed the deformed limbs and pointed chests of victims to muscles failing to grow in the same proportion as the bones to which they were attached. The subject of the first essay, respiration, determined the work of Mayow's life. Both essays were republished at Leiden in 1671, and an English translation of *De rachitide*, by W. Sury, appeared under the title *Rhachitidologia* at Oxford in 1685. The two tracts were meanwhile revised and republished at Oxford in 1674 (with the vice-chancellor's imprimatur, 17 July 1673), together with three new essays ('De sal-nitro', 'De motu muscularis', and 'De respiratione foetus') under the title *Tractatus quinque medico-physici*. This contains the only known portrait of Mayow. The book was dedicated to his patron, Coventry, and republished at The Hague in 1681 under the title *Opera omnia*, and at Geneva in 1685. They were also translated into Dutch (1684), German (1799), French (1840), and English as *Medico-Physical Works*, by A. Crum Brown and L. Dobbin for the Alembic Club of Edinburgh in 1907.

In the tract on respiration (1668, revised 1674) Mayow described perfectly its mechanism, with the movement of ribs and diaphragm. He understood that the lungs were moved by the action of the diaphragm, and suggested that the internal and external intercostal muscles brought about the inspiration of air, which then expanded naturally into the enlarged space produced in the chest cavity. The function of breathing was not to cause the lungs to expand or to cool the blood, as William Harvey had thought, but to bring air in contact with the blood, to

which it gave up its 'nitrum hoc aerium' ('aerial nitre'), and from which it carried off the vapours produced by the heating of the blood. He argued that the heart could not possibly be dilated by the blood fermenting in its cavity (as Descartes had suggested in *L'homme*, 1664), but that it is a muscle, whose function is to drive the blood through the lungs and over the body, a view proved experimentally the following year by Lower (*Tractatus de corde*, 1669). The blood carried the aerial nitre constituent to the muscles, and their motion resulted from the chemical reaction (fermentation) with the combustible matter (sulphur) contained in them. The heart, like any other muscle, ceased to act when the nitro-aerial particles were no longer supplied to it. Air deprived of aerial nitre necessarily produced death. The tract clearly demonstrated awareness of ideas current in chemistry as well as physiology, especially those of Willis, but does not appear to be based on personal experiments.

Experiments with the new air pump in the early 1660s with birds, mice, and candles had led Boyle to conclude that the air acted as a transporting agent to remove impurities from the lungs to the external air. In the *Micrographia* (1665), Hooke developed a theory of combustion that owed much to a widely known contemporary meteorological theory that was based upon a gunpowder analogy. According to this nitro-aerial theory, thunder and lightning were likened to the explosion and flashing of gunpowder, whose active ingredients were known to be sulphur and nitre. Since it was also known that nitre lowered the temperature of water and fertilized crops, it could be supposed that the nitrous particles of air were probably responsible for snow and hail and the vitality of vegetables. Such ideas can be traced directly to the work of the Polish alchemist Michael Sendivogius, especially his *Novum lumen chymicum* (*New Light of Alchemy*, 1604), in which he had identified *sal nitrum* (nitre) as a universal salt and a component of the atmosphere. It was Mayow who developed this nitro-aerial theory to its fullest extent in 1674 in the tract 'On sal nitrum and the nitro-aerial spirit' in which he explored the physico-chemical properties of this 'vital, igneous and highly fermentative spirit' (Mayow, 1). He used the theory to explain a very wide range of phenomena, including respiration, the heat and flames of combustion, calcination, deliquescence, the maintenance of body heat, the scarlet colour of arterial blood, plant growth, and, once more, meteorological phenomena. He recognized saltpetre as containing a base and an acid, and that (following Sendivogius), the acid part was formed from one of the air's constituents, the air being composed of these nitrous particles and other materials that were left behind after respiration and combustion. He showed that when a candle burned in an inverted round bottomed glass flask submerged in water, it consumed the nitrous part of the air, which thereupon lost its elasticity, causing the water to rise. The same thing happened when a live mouse replaced the candle. 'Hence', he concluded, 'it is manifest that air is deprived of its elastic force by the breathing of animals very much in the same way as by the burning of flame' (Mayow, 75). Calcination involved the mechanical addition of nitro-aerial particles to a metal (such as antimony) which, he knew from some of Boyle's findings, brought about an increase in weight. This explanation seemed confirmed by the fact that antimony produced the same calx when it was heated in air as when it was dissolved in nitric acid and heated. The rusting of iron and the conversion of iron pyrites into vitriol (sulphuric acid) were due to the same cause. Combustion was possible only when sulphurous (that is, inflammable) matter came into contact with nitro-aerial particles.

The older tract, 'De respiratione', revised, followed 'De sal-nitro' and Mayow next extended his explanation of respiration to the foetus in the uterus and the chick in the egg. The maternal blood supplied the foetus not only with nutrition but also with nitro-aerial particles. The egg, he believed, contained 'pure or vital air', and not ordinary air (Mayow, 219). Moreover, as the egg is kept warm and the chick itself does little work, it needs little respiration. In the tract 'Muscular motion and animal spirits' he modified Descartes's explanation of muscular action, and his own account of 1668, by suggesting that animal spirits were the nitro-aerial particles that, separated from the blood in the brain, travelled along the nerves to the muscles, where they combined with sulphurous matter and caused the muscles to contract by the vehement motion set up in the fibres. Although divided into tracts, the *Tractatus quinque* is given unity of form by the way the nitro-aerial particles are deployed to develop a coherent physiological system. While he carefully qualified his assertions when they were not fully rooted in experience and logic, the book was less favourably received than the *Tractatus duo*. Henry Oldenburg, secretary of the Royal Society, and a friend of Boyle's, was particularly hostile—no doubt because Mayow seemed closer to Hooke than Boyle in the debates over combustion and respiration.

Mayow died in an apothecary's house bearing the sign of the anchor in York Street, Covent Garden, 'having a little before been married, not altogether to his content' (Wood, *Ath. Oxon.*, 1119). Mayow's will, dated 24 May 1679, leaves bequests to his wife and son, John, as well as to his mother, brother, and sisters. He was buried in the church of St Paul, Covent Garden, on 10 October 1679.

Mayow's two books were widely read and quoted both by contemporaries and by later writers. Early historians of chemistry liked to find a close resemblance between Mayow's aerial nitre and the late eighteenth-century oxygen theory of combustion and respiration, and this interpretation caused much controversy among twentieth-century historians of science concerned with Mayow's originality. But it is only the transference properties that are similar. Quite apart from different theoretical entities being used by Mayow and Lavoisier, Mayow's theory was essentially a Cartesian mechanical, not chemical, theory of combustion and respiration. It also remained locked into a dualistic and panvitalistic world of powers and principles. Nevertheless, despite the speculative character of

the nitro-aerial theory, there is much to admire concerning Mayow's experimental ingenuity. Although he did not develop the pneumatic trough for collecting gases, he devised a method for capturing the 'wild spirits' (gases) that his contemporaries found so elusive by arranging for pieces of iron to be lowered into nitric acid inside an inverted cupping glass. His method of transferring an air (gas) from one vessel to another was original and influential. He must be classed with Hooke and Boyle, possessing the scientific imagination of the one, the tenacity of the other. Mayow was a major figure in the Restoration school of Oxford experimentalists who took Harvey's discovery of the circulation of the blood as the basis for further experimental investigations. Mayow had the genius to perceive exactly the problems that had to be solved before any great advance in chemistry or physiology could be made; to guess at and partly to discover their solutions; and he showed a critical faculty in theory and experiment that was not to be met with in these two sciences until the time of Lavoisier. W. H. BROCK

Sources D. McKie, 'The birth and descent of John Mayow', *London, Edinburgh, and Dublin Philosophical Magazine*, 7th ser., 33 (1942), 51–60 · J. R. Partington, 'The life and work of John Mayow', *Isis*, 47 (1956), 217–30, 405–17 · J. R. Partington, *A history of chemistry*, 2 (1961), 577–613 · R. G. Frank, *Harvey and the Oxford physiologists* (1980), chaps 9 and 10 · H. Guerlac, 'The poet's nitre: studies in the chemistry of John Mayow', *Isis*, 45 (1954), 243–55 · Z. Szydlo, *Water which does not wet hands: the alchemy of Michael Sendivogius* (1994), chaps 9 and 10 · J. Mayow, *Medico-physical works*, Alembic Club Reprints, 17 (1907) · Wood, *Ath. Oxon.*, new edn, 3.1119 · *IGI* · T. K. Brown, 'Mayow, John', *DSB* · will, PRO, PROB 11/363, sig. 83 · *DNB*
Likenesses stipple, 1798 (after D. Loggan), Wellcome L. · J. Caldwell, line engraving, 1799 (after D. Loggan), Wellcome L. · A. Gajani, line engraving, 1815 (after A. Gajani), Wellcome L. · W. Faithorne the elder, line engraving, BM, NPG, Wellcome L.; repro. in J. Mayow, *Tractatus quinque medico-physici* (1674) [see illus.] · coloured stipple, Wellcome L. · engraving, BM; repro. in Mayow, *Tractatus* (1674)
Wealth at death see will, 1680, PRO, PROB 11/363, sig. 83

Maze, Sir Frederick William (1871–1959), civil servant and customs official in China, was born on 2 July 1871 at 11 Abercorn Terrace in Belfast, the younger son of James Maze, linen merchant, of Ballinderry, and Mary, one of two daughters of Henry Hart of Lisburn. He was educated privately and at Wesley College, Dublin. He followed his uncle, Sir Robert *Hart, into the Chinese imperial maritime customs service in 1891 and was appointed in 1899 as acting audit secretary at the inspectorate-general in Peking (Beijing). During the Boxer uprising, 1900, he was acting commissioner at Ichang (Yichang). There followed numerous appointments as deputy commissioner and then commissioner in various provinces, and consequent responsibility for the opening of new customs houses. Maze married, in 1917, an Australian, Laura Gwendoline (1888–1972), younger daughter of Edward Bullmore of Oakwood Station and Ipswich, Queensland. Three times in 1927 Maze was offered and refused the post of southern inspector-general by the Nationalist government, but in 1928 he accepted an appointment as adviser to the national board of reconstruction. In 1929 he became inspector-general of the maritime customs service. In

1932 he was a member of the national loans sinking fund commission. In 1937 he was appointed counsellor to accompany Dr Kung, envoy-extraordinary, to London for the coronation of George VI.

Maze worked in the customs service through a period of great political upheaval: the fall of the Ch'ing dynasty (China's last) in 1911; the breakdown of the republic; the attempts of the Nationalist Party to unite the country; and the splitting away of the communists and invasions by Japan in the 1930s. However, with great skill and diplomacy, recognized by his creation as KBE in 1932, he was able to keep the service together, particularly during the war with Japan, which controlled many of China's main ports. He preserved the integrity and efficiency of the service by treading a careful line between loyalty to the recognized Chinese government on the one hand and maintaining good relations with the Japanese on the other.

Maze was interested in, and helped to promote, many aspects of Chinese life and culture, in particular its maritime architecture. He assembled an unrivalled collection of scale models of Chinese junks and sampans, built in Hong Kong and Shanghai by Chinese craftsmen under expert supervision. He presented the collection to the British nation by depositing it with the Science Museum in London in 1938. He was also an honorary member of l'Association des Amis du Musée de Marine, Paris.

As the Sino-Japanese War was swallowed up by the Second World War the situation in China became impossible. Soon after the attack on Pearl Harbor Maze was one of almost two hundred Britons and Americans held captive at the 'Bridgehouse', once the New Asia Hotel, in Shanghai. On his release the following year he was repatriated to Portuguese East Africa, but he returned to China in an effort to help his staff imprisoned there. He resigned from the service on health grounds in 1943 and was made KCMG in 1944. Foreign governments, to which he had rendered great service over many years, also honoured him; in addition to numerous honours from the Chinese, he received notable distinctions from Japan, Belgium, Portugal, Norway, Denmark, France, and Germany, and was made knight commander of the order of Pius IX by the Holy See.

After serving briefly as adviser to the ministry of finance, Maze joined his wife in retirement in Cape Town, South Africa, moving to Victoria, British Columbia, in Canada in 1948. They were founder members of the Victoria branch of the English-Speaking Union in 1955. Maze died at the Royal Jubilee Hospital, Victoria, on 25 March 1959 and was buried at Royal Oak burial park on 28 March.   ROBERT SHARP

Sources WWW · *The Times* (30 March 1959) · *The Times* (2 April 1959) · *Daily Colonist* (27 March 1959) [Canadian journal, Victoria] · *Victoria Times* (28 March 1959) [Canadian journal] · *Daily Colonist* (17 Dec 1972) [Canadian journal, Victoria] · Sci. Mus., file no. 3699 · register, PRO NIre., book 22, urban no. 3 [birth]
Archives NMM, memoirs and papers · Sci. Mus., collection of models of Chinese junks and sampans · Sci. Mus., corresp. · SOAS, corresp. and papers

Mazzinghi, Joseph, Count Mazzinghi in the papal nobility (1765–1844), composer, descended from an ancient Florentine family, was born, probably in London, on 25 December 1765, the eldest son of Tommaso Mazzinghi, a wine merchant who played the violin at Marylebone Gardens and, in 1763, had published six solos for that instrument. Tommaso went bankrupt in 1771 and died in 1775. Joseph was trained as a musician by his mother's sister, Cassandra Frederich (or Friedrich; afterwards Mrs Wynne), and later by Johann Christian Bach. At the age of ten he became organist to the Portuguese Chapel.

In 1779 Mazzinghi was apprenticed to Leopoldo De Michele, chief copyist to the Italian Opera at the King's Theatre, and acted as orchestra librarian. This led to his appointment, from the 1784–5 season, as composer, arranger, and concertmaster (directing rehearsals and playing continuo from the harpsichord) under the management of John Gallini. The London system of presenting most operas as pasticcios meant that he 'became nearly as important a member of the company as the foreign [visiting] house composers' (Price and others, *Italian Opera*, 1.336). Even though recognition of recent continental opera as an integral whole was beginning to creep in, he adapted works by Sarti, Cimarosa, and Paisiello, sometimes adding arias of his own. He was not above publishing as his two of the most popular pieces in Martín y Soler's *Una cosa rara*; on the other hand a substitute aria for Cimarosa's *L'Olimpiade* improved on the original. He also composed original music for at least nine ballets, some of them by the innovative choreographer Jean-Georges Noverre. This, however, was regarded as a task for a second-rate composer, and some of the music has been judged 'frankly dull'.

Mazzinghi remained at his post until the King's Theatre was burnt down on 17 June 1789. He was then taken on at a salary of £300 as director of the 1790–91 season at the Pantheon, the aristocratic managers of which had secured the one licence granted for Italian opera. His appointment may have been influenced by his closeness to the prince of Wales, who entrusted him with running the Carlton House concerts; he later taught the princess the piano. The Pantheon was, in its turn, destroyed by arson on 14 January 1792. Mazzinghi's duties were wide and included the composition of an opera; he apparently set out to write yet another pasticcio, but it was never performed. He and the company finished the 1792 season at the Little Theatre in the Haymarket, but when the rebuilt King's Theatre opened for Italian opera under new direction in 1793 Mazzinghi was no longer employed.

Meanwhile Mazzinghi had taken advantage of the wide terms of his contract to compose English operas for Covent Garden, and went on doing so until 1810. Among them was *Ramah Droog* (1798), written in collaboration with William Reeve, with a 'spirited and inventive' overture (Fiske). Mazzinghi's miscellaneous piano compositions were popular; he was a fashionable teacher and arranged the 'nobility concerts', established in 1791 and held on Sunday evenings at private houses.

Mazzinghi had married, at an unknown date, a woman

with whom he had a son. After her death he married a daughter of the distiller Benjamin Hodges, who also predeceased him; they had a daughter. During a trip to Italy in 1834 he was made a count by Pope Gregory XVI, and recognized as a patrician of Florence by the grand duke of Tuscany. In his last years he retired to Bath while keeping on a house in Cadogan Place, Chelsea. He died on 15 January 1844 of a cerebral haemorrhage while on a visit to his son at Downside College, and was buried in the vault of the Chelsea Catholic church on the 25th.

Besides his stage pieces, Mazzinghi published between seventy and eighty piano sonatas, upwards of 200 other works for piano and as many for harp and other instruments, as well as about thirty-five vocal trios and a number of songs. Much of this mass of work, produced with apparent ease, was musicianly, but the flowing melodies were seldom strikingly original. JOHN ROSSELLI

Sources C. Price, J. Milhous, and R. D. Hume, *Italian opera in late eighteenth-century London*, 1: *The King's Theatre, Haymarket, 1778–1791* (1995) · C. Price, 'Italian opera and arson in late eighteenth-century London', *Journal of the American Musicological Society*, 42 (1989), 55–107 · R. Fiske, *English theatre music in the eighteenth century*, 2nd edn (1986) · *GM*, 1st ser., 41 (1771), 524 · *GM*, 2nd ser., 21 (1844), 322 · *Musical World* (25 Jan 1844), 30 · *The Times* (18 Jan 1844) · F. T. Cansick, *St Pancras epitaphs* (1869)

Wealth at death 'It is supposed that the count died very wealthy': *Musical World*

Giuseppe Mazzini (1805–1872), by John Andrews, 1852

Mazzini, Giuseppe (1805–1872), politician, thinker, and teacher, was born in Genoa on 22 June 1805, but spent most of his adult life in England as an impoverished exile. His father, Giacomo, was professor of medicine at Genoa University and married Maria Drago; they also had three daughters. Mazzini himself never married, though most of his close friendships were with women.

Mazzini's primary political objective—the creation of a united Italian nation—made him a lifelong enemy of the French and Austrian empires that occupied various regions of his country. Patriotism, not aggressive nationalism, was his ideal, and he even hoped that a united Italy would one day take the lead in creating a European common market inside a federal union of free peoples.

After graduating in law at Genoa University, Mazzini at first hoped to become a literary critic. But in 1827 he enrolled in the secretive carboneria as a political revolutionary and in 1831 was exiled by King Charles Albert of Sardinia. Soon afterwards, as a persistent and dangerous rebel, he was sentenced to death in his absence. Together with other exiles in Marseilles he founded Young Italy, a society whose patriotic and revolutionary aims quickly found adherents in the eight Italian states. Occasionally he hoped that Charles Albert or Pope Pius IX might lead a national movement, but their refusal confirmed his strong personal preference for republicanism.

Expelled from France and Switzerland, in January 1837 Mazzini arrived in England where he was in close touch with the Chartists, and earned a precarious income from literary journalism. He wrote on Dante, Lammenais, Carlyle, and Sismondi, and his ideas were enthusiastically welcomed by John Stuart Mill as a corrective of British cultural insularity. In 1840 he started a mutual aid society among Italian artisans in London, producing for them *Apostolato Popolare*, one of a dozen periodicals he published at various times. The following year, with funds provided by Scottish and English friends, he opened a free school in Hatton Garden where two hundred abandoned or deprived Italian children received a rudimentary education. This school, opposed by the Piedmontese embassy and by the employers of the children, gave him some notoriety. So, even more, did the fact that, at Metternich's request in 1844, letters addressed to him were opened and used by Lord Aberdeen to inform Austria about the patriotic movement. Under British law he had committed no offence, and Macaulay was one of many to protest against this violation of personal liberty. Parliamentary debates on the issue filled over 500 pages of Hansard, and Carlyle wrote indignantly to *The Times* describing Mazzini as a man of genius and nobility.

In 1847 Young Italy was replaced by a broader-based National Association, once again in a vain hope that the rulers of Italy would combine to expel the Austrians from Lombardy and Venice. The next year Mazzini joined Garibaldi in an unsuccessful guerrilla campaign against Austria, and in 1849 he was chosen by popular vote as ruler of a republican government in Rome. Here the two patriotic leaders held out for three months against armies from France, Austria, Naples, and Spain. This Roman republic gave Mazzini his only experience in government, and his ability in administration was much admired by liberals throughout Europe.

Back in England, moving from one shabby bed-sittingroom to another, Mazzini spent the 1850s organizing a succession of minor insurrections throughout Italy.

None of these had much chance of success, but he was determined to keep up the revolutionary momentum in order to disseminate ideas of patriotism and to perhaps persuade the Piedmontese government to give material support. For ten years he also tried to persuade Garibaldi to invade Sicily with 1000 volunteers, and in 1860 the latter eventually agreed. Garibaldi's conquest of Sicily and Naples then compelled an at first reluctant Cavour to send the Piedmontese army and annex the southern half of Italy.

The new rulers of a united kingdom showed no gratitude to someone they feared as a revolutionary, a democrat, a republican, and a believer in extravagant causes such as universal suffrage, free education, freedom of conscience, women's liberation, and labour unions. Indeed Cavour's followers positively needed Mazzini's enmity in order to win acceptance by other conservative and reactionary governments. He was therefore quite inaccurately depicted as an assassin, a communist, an enemy of religion, and all of these falsehoods were later deliberately perpetuated by the historians of liberal Italy. Equally hostile were Catholic historians who, despite Mazzini's profound religious faith, condemned him as a heretic or unbeliever. Nor could socialist historians accept his fierce criticism of Marxism and the class struggle.

Mazzini's last years were therefore spent mostly in England where he could live and publish freely, so becoming far better known than in Italy. In London he was much admired not only for unselfish idealism, but also for his brilliant conversation and great personal beauty; also for what *The Spectator* (16 March 1872) called a lovability 'in which he surpassed almost all living men'. Many Englishmen and Scots helped to finance his conspiracies. He appeared in novels by Meredith, Disraeli, and Swinburne; was befriended by Dickens, George Eliot, and J. S. Mill; admired by Benjamin Jowett, John Morley, and T. H. Green. Of his best-known writing, *The Duties of Man* (trans. Mrs E. A. Venturi) was first published in England in 1862 before being translated all over the world. This book was unusual in stressing the need for morality in politics and for individual rights to be always balanced by duties towards society.

In 1872 Mazzini returned secretly and under a false name to Italy, where he died at Pisa on 10 March and was buried in the magnificent cemetery of Staglieno at Genoa. An obituary notice in the London *Times* (12 March 1872) was longer than that given to any other Italian of the century. Only in 1947 was he accorded the honour of a national monument in Rome. An edition of his letters and writings has been published in over 100 volumes.

DENIS MACK SMITH

Sources D. Mack Smith, *Mazzini* (1994) · B. King, *Mazzini* (1903) · G. O. Griffith, *Mazzini, prophet of modern Europe* (1932) · *Scritti editi ed inediti di Giuseppe Mazzini*, 108 vols. (1903–86) · *The Times* (12 March 1872) · M. C. W. Wicks, *The Italian exiles in London, 1816–1848* (1937) **Archives** BL, corresp. with Karl Blind, Add. MS 40123 · BL, letters to Aspasia Fletcher, Add. MS 46875 · BL, letters to Antonin Roche, Add. MS 63594 · Co-operative Union, Holyoake House, Manchester, archive, letters to George Holyoake · U. Glas. L., letters to John McAdam · V&A NAL, letters to John Forster

Likenesses J. Andrews, portrait, 1852, priv. coll. [*see illus.*] · Earl of Carlisle, drawing, Balliol Oxf. · S. Lega (Mazzini on his deathbed), Rhode Island Museum of Art · lithograph, NPG · portrait, priv. coll.

Mboya, Thomas Joseph (1930–1969), labour leader and politician in Kenya, was born at Kilima Mbogo, near Thika, north of Nairobi, on 15 August 1930, the eldest of the six children of Leunadus Ndiege, a sisal worker from Rusinga Island, Lake Victoria, and his wife Marsella Awuor. Mboya's parents were Suba Luo by ethnic identity and Roman Catholic by religious conversion. Mboya was baptized a Catholic, and between the ages of seven and seventeen attended Irish-run Catholic schools in Kikuyu, Kamba, and Luo districts. By his own account, his non-tribal outlook in later life owed much to his unusually travelled childhood.

Mboya spent the years 1948–50 at the Jeanes School, Kabete, where he studied sanitation and was president of the student council. In 1951 he began work with the Nairobi city council as a sanitary inspector. Politicized, confident, and ambitious, he plunged into labour organization. Despite his employers' resistance he converted the African Municipal Workers' Staff Association into the Kenya Local Government Workers' Union, with himself as secretary. In October 1952, immediately following the declaration of the Mau Mau emergency, he defiantly joined the Kenya African Union, the main nationalist party, and in the absence of its incarcerated leadership served as director of information and then as treasurer until the party's proscription in June 1953. Two months later he quit his city council job and in September took his union into the fledgeling Kenya Federation of Registered Trade Unions, becoming general secretary of the federation shortly afterwards. He would hold this post for almost a decade. During the early years of the emergency, when political activity by Africans was banned, Mboya used the federation (renamed Kenya Federation of Labour in 1955) as a vehicle for social, economic, and political protest. His co-operation with the government on labour matters helped him to survive unarrested. So too perhaps did the support he was garnering abroad, notably from the International Confederation of Free Trade Unions. His achievement in settling the Mombasa Dock strike of March 1955 confirmed both his dominance in labour affairs and his extraordinary political skills.

In 1955–6, armed with a scholarship provided by the Trades Union Congress and the Colonial Office, Mboya studied at Ruskin College, Oxford. He went on to make a speaking tour of the United States, where he established ties with various businessmen, politicians, and labour leaders. These American connections bore much subsequent fruit; his student airlift scheme of 1959–61, for example, was partly funded by the Kennedy Foundation. In March 1957 he won the seat of Nairobi in the first African elections to the legislative council. With Kenyatta and other Kikuyu leaders still in detention, Mboya could use his position in Legco to assume *de facto* leadership of the nationalist movement. The British authorities sought a multiracial dispensation for Kenya. By contrast, Mboya's

Thomas Joseph Mboya (1930–1969), by unknown photographer, 1960

agenda was to break settler power and press for majority rule. Blending lawyerly finesse with implacable non-co-operation, he extracted a series of concessions from the government. He also joined forces with his political rival Oginga Odinga in campaigning for Kenyatta's release. On the wider African stage, he chaired the historic All-African Peoples' Conference in Accra in 1958.

Mboya was a key participant at the 1960 Lancaster House conference at which the principle of majority rule for Kenya was conceded. Nationwide parties were then established: the Kenya African National Union (KANU) and the Kenya African Democratic Union (KADU). Mboya mobilized the alliances he had created between his Nairobi People's Convention Party and political associations in other districts in order to secure the general secretaryship of KANU, thus maintaining a position of organizational power even after the return of the detainees. Mboya was strong-willed, single-minded, and acutely intelligent. In appearance he was distinctively round-faced. He married twice: his first, short-lived, marriage in the early 1950s to Ogweni was contracted under Luo custom, his second, to Pamela Odede (b. 1939) on 20 January 1962, within the church. From the first marriage there was a daughter, from the second two sons and two daughters.

In April 1962 Mboya entered government, serving in the KANU–KADU coalition of 1962–3 as minister of labour.

After the election of June 1963, which was followed by independence in December, KANU ruled alone under Kenyatta's leadership, with Mboya holding the portfolios of justice and constitutional affairs (June 1963 to December 1964) and economic planning and development (December 1964 to July 1969). In the former portfolio he engineered Kenya's presidential constitution; in the latter he was an orthodox developmentalist of his time, relying on state planning and foreign investment to stimulate growth. He was also indispensable to Kenyatta as a tactician, first in marginalizing KADU, later in forcing Odinga's radical faction out of KANU, tasks accomplished by 1966.

Tom Mboya's talents, achievements and sophistication won him fame abroad, his rapport with the common people, popularity at home. Within KANU, however, he had enemies; men who had been outmanoeuvred by him politically and resented his arrogance towards them. The ethnic variable was probably relevant; by the later 1960s he was the only Luo in the higher reaches of a Kikuyu-dominated government. He was assassinated by gunshot in Government Road, Nairobi on 5 July 1969, dying on the way to hospital. His death precipitated widespread civil strife, including anti-Kikuyu riots by Luo crowds. On 11 July he was buried on Rusinga island, Nyanza. A Kikuyu suspect was arrested, tried, convicted, and executed. Rumour had it that the assassin had been hired by one or more of Mboya's political antagonists, intent, perhaps, on ensuring that he would never succeed to the presidency.

DAVID GOLDSWORTHY

Sources D. Goldsworthy, *Tom Mboya* (1982) · D. Goldsworthy, 'Tom Mboya: a bio-bibliography', *Africana Journal*, 8 (1977), 7–20 · A. Rake, *Tom Mboya: young man of new Africa* (1962) · T. Mboya, *Freedom and after* (1963)
Archives Bodl. RH, Perham MSS, box 343, files 1–2 · PRO, CO 822/824 · PRO, CO 822/1303 · PRO, CO 822/2020 | FILM BFI NFTVA, news footage · IWM FVA, documentary footage
Likenesses photograph, 1960, East African Newspapers (Nation) Ltd [*see illus.*] · photographs, repro. in M. Amin, *Tom Mboya: a photographic tribute* (1969)

Mc. Names starting Mc— are alphabetized as though they started Mac—.

Meacham [*married name* Cuthbert], **Gwendoline Emily** [*pseud.* Wendy Wood] (1892–1981), Scottish nationalist, was born on 29 October 1892 at 62 Earl Street, Maidstone, Kent, one of three daughters of Charles Stephen Meacham, a scientist, and his wife, Florence Wood. Her Scottish ancestry was on her mother's side, and her mother was herself a Scottish patriot whose father had been involved in Garibaldi's uprising and who told Meacham tales of Wallace as a child. Her father, however, was always an 'empire man' (Wood, *Yours Sincerely*, 9). In 1899 her father was offered a senior position in a brewing firm, as a result of which the family emigrated to South Africa. Later he inaugurated the South African Society of Artists, and his daughter first exhibited her own art in the colony under the society's auspices. Later in life she exhibited regularly at the Royal Scottish Academy and Society of Scottish Artists. Her mother was a still-life painter, her

Gwendoline Emily Meacham [Wendy Wood] (1892–1981), by David Foggie, 1932

grandfather Samuel Wood was a sculptor, and her great-uncle Thomas Peploe Wood was a painter, so an affection for art clearly ran deep in the family.

Meacham's childhood experience of Boer attitudes to the British seems to have helped to form her later political opinions, and indeed Scottish nationalists of the 1890s, such as Theodore Napier, drew a strong analogy between the Scots and the Boers. In 1902 Meacham was sent to Hamilton House School, Tunbridge Wells, and later she went to London to study art under Walter Sickert in Chelsea, dividing her time between her older sister in the capital and the family home, Scaur Topp, near Dumfries, which had been designed by her father; later she went to the Westminster School of Art, and gained the certificate of the Royal Drawing Society in 1909. Sympathetic to the suffragettes, she joined the Women's Volunteers. In 1913 she married Walter Robertson Cuthbert, a shoe manufacturer. She and her husband went on honeymoon to Basutoland, where their guide was Roger Casement's brother Tom. Subsequently they went to Scotland to live in Ayr, where her husband built her a studio, as he did later in Dundee. Their first daughter, Cora, was born in 1915. Her husband was unsympathetic to her artistic ambitions, and by this time she was beginning to be politically active.

A home-rule Liberal in 1912, in 1916 she joined the Scottish League and in 1918 the Scottish Home Rule Association. In her autobiography, *Yours Sincerely for Scotland*, she claims that she experienced some kind of nationalist epiphany at the Wallace monument in 1913.

In 1914 Meacham's husband worked at a munitions factory then went into the artillery. After suffering a miscarriage, she gave birth to a second daughter, Irralee, in 1918, and she went to London to explore an acting career before returning to Ayr. Owing to financial difficulties the family moved to Dundee in the early 1920s where she gave art lessons. In 1923 she obtained a job with BBC radio in Glasgow, and from 1924 was 'lady organizer' in Dundee responsible for *Children's Hour* and *Woman's Hour*. From 1926 she featured on *Children's Hour* as Auntie Gwen. Reading aloud to children was one of her fortes: in later life she gave public readings in Edinburgh city libraries, and as late as the 1970s she was the storyteller in *Jackanory*. During the 1920s she also worked as a talented if somewhat sentimental illustrator for the children's comic *Little Dots*. In 1927 she joined Lewis Spence's Scottish national movement. She made her own friends, and she and her husband separated, and eventually divorced. At this stage Wendy Cuthbert joined the National Party of Scotland, which had recently been founded (1928), and took her mother's maiden name for her writing, becoming henceforth Wendy Wood. Rather like a Scottish version of Maud Gonne, Wood, 'the queen of demagogues' (Wood, *Yours Sincerely*, 198), raised nationalist consciousness through repeated addresses at public meetings: she averaged thirty-two of these a year, and in 1957 spoke at no fewer than seventy-three.

In 1931 Wood started Scottish Watch, a youth movement which at one time claimed more members in Scotland than the Scouts. Leading Scottish intellectuals such as Sir James Frazer were asked to act as patrons to the movement, which gained the support of the *Daily Record*. In 1932, at the Bannockburn rally, Wood led a group of nationalists into Stirling Castle to pull down the union flag and put up a lion rampant in its stead. This direct action offended many in the National Party of Scotland, with whom Wood's relations became steadily more strained. The following year she started an anti-conscription league. In 1939 she met a fellow patriot called Mac, who had connections with Irish nationalism. She spent the war with him in a croft on Glen Uig in Moidart and when the relationship broke up, she moved to another croft. In *Mac's Croft* (1946) he is described as her 'husband' (p. 13), but this appears to have been a euphemism. In 1947 she made a fundraising and publicity trip to the United States, and was appointed to an official position in the Scottish National Party (founded in 1934 from the merger of the National Party of Scotland and the Scottish Party). However, like her contemporary the writer Hugh MacDiarmid, she could not endure the demands of party discipline, and drifted away to form the Scottish Patriots, an organization dedicated to the cultural nationalism Wood saw the Scottish National Party as neglecting.

Wood stood twice for election for Edinburgh town council in 1935 and at the Glasgow Bridgeton by-election in 1946, where she gained 14 per cent of the vote. She was arrested and detained in the 1930s for disrupting a blackshirt rally, and was twice in prison: in 1951, when she was found guilty of inciting the crowd in Trafalgar Square on the day of a Scotland v. England football match, and for non-payment of national insurance as a protest against the state of women's prisons. That same year she showed a side of her policy of direct action not likely to appeal to either the British government or the Scottish National Party by speaking at an old IRA rally in co. Kildare, where 'her speech … was given with such sincerity and earnestness that it evoked a storm of applause from … hundreds of IRA veterans' (Wood, *Yours Sincerely*, 184).

After moving to 31 Howard Place, Edinburgh, at the end of the 1950s, Wood's nationalist activities entered a new phase. Following her address to its general assembly in 1961, the Church of Scotland accepted the policy of home rule. In 1966 her pressure was instrumental in persuading the Post Office to issue Robert Burns stamps and in 1972 the Post Office in Scotland also advised against the use of E2R on the silver wedding stamps (NL Scot., Wood folder 26). In December 1972 she commenced a hunger strike for Scottish home rule. Jim Sillars (then a Labour MP) made a television plea to her to end the strike, and she conceded after the secretary of state, Gordon Campbell (who lost his seat to the Scottish National Party in 1974), 'repeated undertakings' to publish a green paper 'after the Royal Commission had reported' (Kemp, 118). She placed a union flag under the staircarpet of her Georgian villa in Howard Place so that she could tread on it every day: towards the end of her life she gave fragments of the flag away as trophies to her younger supporters. She also grew a cutting in the garden from the rose at Fassifern in Lochaber said to be the very one from which Prince Charles had taken his white rose badge in 1745. In her later years she appeared increasingly interested in Jacobitism, and along with her supporters entertained the claims of 'Prince' Michael, a Belgian citizen, to be the 'direct and lawful heir' of the Stuarts. Wood herself always supported direct action and civil disobedience, and stated that 'Patriots finding themselves in trouble with the law would be supported completely … providing their offence was not of a serious criminal nature and directly against Patriots' policies' (minutes of the group meeting, 8 July 1979, priv. coll.). She died on 30 June 1981 in the Western General Hospital, Edinburgh.

Wood had a striking appearance, with piercing blue eyes and a rugged, purposeful look. She was a poet and illustrator of some talent, and published a number of books on her own life, and on folklore, lifestyle, and travel; these included *The Baby in the Glass* (1918), *The Chickabiddies Book* (1927), *The Secret of Spey* (1930), *I Like Life* (1938, her first autobiography), *Mac's Croft* (1946), *From a Highland Croft* (1952), *Legends of the Borders* (1973), and *The Silver Chanter* (1980). Her liking for folklore no doubt had some connection to her reputed gift of second sight. Her

final autobiography, *Yours Sincerely for Scotland*, was published in 1970; in 1985 Joy Hendry edited a posthumous collection of her poems and illustrations under the title *Astronauts and Tinklers* (1985).

Whatever Wood's limitations and excesses, her determined impossibilism helped to put Scottish nationalism on the map. The Patriots' policy of recalling the Scottish estates had something in common with the constitutional convention of the late 1980s and early 1990s: indeed, the Patriots were in essence an oddball 'cross-party campaigning organisation' (Mitchell, 99). Though given to inflammatory posturing, they were never dangerous, and through the indefatigable activity of their leader played a significant role in defining a distinctive Scottish politics, though in their day their extremism rendered them marginal.   MURRAY G. H. PITTOCK

Sources I. McKemmie, 'Wendy Wood: Scottish patriot: biographical notes', unpublished paper, Saltire Society, Balcurvie Lodge, Balcurvie, Windygates, Fife • J. Mitchell, *Strategies for self-government* (1996) • NL Scot., Wood MS Acc. 7980 • minutes of the Scottish Patriots group meeting, 8 July 1979, priv. coll. • *Yours sincerely for Scotland* (1993) [exhibition catalogue, Edinburgh] • W. Wood, 'Yours sincerely for Scotland', NL Scot., Acc. 8197 • *Wendy Wood: illustrator* (1999) [Museum of Childhood exhibition, Edinburgh] • W. Wood, *Astronauts and tinklers*, ed. J. Hendry (1985) • K. Webb, *The growth of nationalism in Scotland* (1977) • A. Kemp, *The hollow drum* (1993) • F. W. S. Craig, *British parliamentary election results, 1918–1949*, 3rd edn (1983) • private information (2004) [Cora Cuthbert, daughter; Irralee Scott-May, daughter] • private information (2004) [conversation with Patriot and Siol Nan Gaidheal member who knew Wendy Wood] • W. Wood, *Yours sincerely for Scotland: the autobiography of a patriot* (1970) • d. cert.

Archives Edinburgh Museums and Galleries, 'Yours sincerely for Scotland' MSS • NL Scot., corresp. and papers

Likenesses S. Carmichael, watercolour, 1923, Scot. NPG • D. Foggie, chalk drawing, 1932, Scot. NPG [*see illus.*] • F. St. John Cadell, oils, 1959, Scot. NPG • W. G. B. Murdoch, crayon drawing, Scot. NPG • W. Wood, self-portrait, chalk drawing, Scot. NPG • photograph, Edinburgh Museums and Galleries • photograph, repro. in *The Observer*

Wealth at death £11,776.03: confirmation, 15 Dec 1981, NA Scot., SC 70/1/3659, 183–91

Mead, Charles Philip (1887–1958), cricketer, was born on 9 March 1887 at 10 Ashtons' Buildings, Battersea, London, the eldest son and second child in the family of four daughters and three sons of Matthew Orlando Mead, wharf labourer, and his wife, Louisa Hannah Mann of Battersea. The family moved to accommodation on the Shaftesbury Park estate in Battersea, where he was brought up. After elementary schooling, and having found little chance of advancement with his native Surrey county club, he opted to qualify by residence for Hampshire. He made his début in 1905 against the touring Australians, and then played first in the county championship in 1906.

Almost immediately Mead became the anchor of the Hampshire batting and he was to score over 1000 runs in a season twenty-seven times, including twice when he passed the 3000 mark, and nine times when he exceeded 2000. He did not leave Hampshire until 1936, during which lengthy spell he played 700 matches—a record—

for them. He scored 48,892 runs for Hampshire at an average of 48.84, and in all first-class cricket he accumulated no fewer than 55,061 runs (average 47.67), leaving him with the fourth highest aggregate in the world rankings. This is the largest number of first-class runs ever scored for a single club in cricket history. With 153 centuries and a highest score of 280 not out, against Nottinghamshire in 1921, it is fair to describe him as one of the most acquisitive bats of all time, and as Hampshire's most successful cricketer. Strangely, he played only seventeen times for England, and his 182 not out in 1921 remained for seventeen years the highest test score against Australia in England. He scored 1185 runs (average 49.37) in test cricket. A nimble slip fielder and occasional spin bowler, he played for Suffolk in 1938 and 1939 after leaving Hampshire.

Of large build and possessed of ritual mannerisms when facing the bowling, Mead's technique was founded on the securest of defence, and, although he was a shrewd placer of the ball, it was perhaps his seeming doggedness that left him out of the international reckoning at a time when England possessed several middle-order batsmen of sterling class. None the less, he proved to be a left-hand bat of the highest possible calibre, and a character much respected as well as affectionately regarded for what John Arlott called his 'pin-toed toddle' (*John Arlott's 100 Greatest Batsmen*, 1986, 180). His drooping shoulders, bowed legs, and solemn demeanour certainly made him an easily recognizable, if rather ungraceful, figure.

On 19 September 1908 Mead married Beatrice (*d.* 1949), daughter of George Henry Englefield, bootmaker, of Southampton. They had two sons and one daughter. He was twice rejected on medical grounds (varicose veins) for active service in the First World War. For the last ten years of his life he was blind, but his interest endured in the game to which he had brought such commitment and talent. He died on 26 March 1958, following an operation for an internal haemorrhage at the Royal Victoria Hospital, Boscombe, Bournemouth.　ERIC MIDWINTER

Sources N. Jenkinson, *C. P. Mead: Hampshire's greatest runmaker* (1993) · N. Cardus, *The 'Playfair' Cardus* (1963), 119–22 · *The Times* (27 March 1958) · B. Green, ed., *The Wisden book of obituaries* (1986) · b. cert. · *CGPLA Eng. & Wales* (1958)
Archives SOUND BBC WAC
Likenesses photographs, Hampshire County Cricket Club, Southampton · photographs, Lord's Cricket Ground, London, MCC Library · portrait, repro. in Jenkinson, *C. P. Mead*
Wealth at death £390 1s. 11d.: administration, 25 April 1958, *CGPLA Eng. & Wales*

Mead, George Robert Stow (1863–1933), theosophist and writer on gnosticism and Christian origins, was born on 22 March 1863 at 2 Montague Cottages, Albert Grove, Peckham, London, the son of Robert Mead, then a lieutenant with the Military Staff College, and his wife, Mary Stowe. He was educated at King's School, Rochester, and St John's College, Cambridge, where he first read mathematics but changed to classics, in which he obtained a BA in 1884. After graduation he studied oriental philosophy at Oxford and then taught classics at various minor public schools until 1889.

Mead had joined the Theosophical Society in 1884 and

determined to devote his life to the cause of theosophy. In 1889 he became Madame H. P. Blavatsky's private secretary, and after her death in 1891 he edited many of her works—notably the revised edition of *The Secret Doctrine* (1897). He had been appointed general secretary of the European section of the Theosophical Society in 1890, and for almost twenty years his ability to balance objective scholarship with a sympathetic approach to spiritual reality ensured that the society maintained at least the semblance of academic respectability. Even more important, in terms of the society's survival, was Mead's genuine tolerance of dissenting beliefs that enabled him to steer the society through its first internal crisis. This arose in 1894 when a prominent theosophist, William Quan Judge, was accused of self-promotion by sending fraudulent 'Mahatma' letters (letters containing doctrinal teachings and practical instructions from allegedly supernatural beings) to selected influential members of the society. Compromise between the pro- and anti-Judge factions proved impossible and although Mead came down against Judge, his skill in handling the situation prevented the inevitable split from being a fatal wound.

Mead was now seen as one of the Theosophical Society's foremost members, a view that became entrenched as he poured out a stream of books and articles, some of which had a lasting influence beyond the narrow confines of the society itself. Thus in 1896 Mead's *Orpheus*, his study of 'the theosophy of the Greeks', greatly impressed W. B. Yeats and led him to revise his earlier opinion that Mead's intellect resembled that 'of a good-sized whelk' (Yeats, *Memoirs*, 282). In the same year Mead published his version of *Pistis Sophia*, the first translation into English of any significant or complete gnostic text. This was followed in 1900 by *Fragments of a Faith Forgotten*, a general survey of gnosticism, and in 1906 by *Thrice-Greatest Hermes*, an outstanding translation and critical commentary on the hermetic texts of the Hellenistic era. With these works Mead established himself as an authority in the field of Christian origins, although his reputation was severely dented by his admission in 1903 that in his book *Did Jesus Live 100 B.C.?* he had considered (but had not accepted) evidence on the question obtained by clairvoyant means.

Mead's critical approach can be clearly seen in the contents of the *Theosophical Review*, which he edited from 1898 to 1909, and in the eyes of the Theosophical Society Mead was now proving to be too honest a scholar. But it was not to be academic differences that drove him to resign from the society—it was a matter of sexual morality. Mead had been happily married since 12 July 1899 to Laura Mary Cooper (1855/6–1924), an author and fellow theosophist, the daughter of the late Frederick Henry Cooper, an Indian civil servant. He unquestioningly accepted the sexual mores of his day and was profoundly shocked when in 1906 the paedophile activities of C. W. Leadbeater came to light. Leadbeater was one of the most respected theosophists of his day and the uproar was great, but public scandal was avoided when Mead secured his resignation from the society. The real problem arose two years later when

Annie Besant, by now president of the Theosophical Society, performed a volte-face and early in 1909 brought an unrepentant Leadbeater back into the fold. Mead had fought vigorously and publicly against Leadbeater's reinstatement, and having failed to keep him out, promptly resigned, taking 700 fellow theosophists with him.

Mead was determined to provide a forum for all those who wished, as he did, 'to promote investigation and comparative study of religion, philosophy and science, on the basis of experience' (Mead and Waite, 3) and in March 1909, with the aid of A. E. Waite, he established the Quest Society and a journal of the same name. Both *The Quest* and its parent society survived for twenty years, fulfilling their purpose with the aid of writers and speakers as diverse as Martin Buber, Ezra Pound, Ananda Coomaraswamy, Arthur Machen, Tagore, and Yeats. The success of *The Quest* also ensured Mead's return to academic respectability: in 1917 he supplied the entry on occultism for James Hastings's *Encyclopaedia of Religion and Ethics*.

Mead's last important work, *The Gnostic John the Baptizer*, appeared in 1924 but after the death of his wife in the same year Mead wrote little of any significance, and when *The Quest* came to an end in 1930 his career as a scholar effectively ended with it. By this time he had become increasingly preoccupied with psychical research and he continued to wrestle with the question of survival until his death on 28 September 1933 at his home, 21 Ovington Street, Chelsea, London. He was cremated at Golders Green two days later. His works on Christian origins have since been superseded, but while he was not the only pioneer in the study of gnosticism, he was the first scholar to present a sympathetic view of gnostic and hermetic texts and the first to bring them before a wider public.

R. A. GILBERT

Sources G. R. S. Mead, 'The Quest' — old and new: retrospect and prospect (1926) • B. De Zirkoff, 'Biographical sketch of G. R. S. Mead', in H. P. Blavatsky, *Collected writings*, ed. B. De Zirkoff, 13: 1890–1891 (1982), 393–7 • R. A. Gilbert, 'The idol with feet of clay: G. R. S. Mead in the Theosophical Society', unpublished paper delivered to the Theosophical History Conference, London, 1986 • G. R. S. Mead, 'Facts about "The secret doctrine"', *Occult Review*, 45/4 (1927), 247–52 • G. Tillett, *The elder brother: a biography of Charles Webster Leadbeater* (1982) • A. H. Nethercot, *The first five lives of Annie Besant* (1961) • W. B. Yeats, *Memoirs*, ed. D. Donoghue (1973) • D. Gow, *Light*, 53 (1933), 637 • D. Stocker, 'Recollections', *Light*, 53 (1933), 655 • G. R. S. Mead and A. E. Waite, *The Quest Society: constitutions, rules and regulations* (1909) • b. cert. • m. cert. • d. cert. • *CGPLA Eng. & Wales* (1933)

Archives Stanstead Hall, Essex, Arthur Findlay collection

Likenesses photograph, 1891, Theosophical Society, Gloucester Place, London • photograph, c.1892, repro. in H. S. Olcott, *Old diary leaves: the true story of the Theosophical Society* (1895), vol. 4 • H. Donald-Smith, oils, 1929, College of Psychic Studies, Queensberry Place, London • Elliott & Fry, photograph, repro. in *The Quest*, 17 (1926)

Wealth at death £930 16s. 2d.: probate, 13 Nov 1933, *CGPLA Eng. & Wales*

Mead, Joseph. *See* Mede, Joseph (1586–1638).

Mead, Matthew. *See* Meade, Matthew (1628/9–1699).

Mead, Richard (1673–1754), physician and collector of books and art, was born at Worcester House, Stepney, Middlesex, on 11 August 1673, the eleventh child of thirteen of Matthew *Meade (1628/9–1699), a nonconforming minister, and his wife, Elizabeth Walton (d. 1707). Matthew Meade had been ejected for nonconformity in 1662, but apparently had a private income. He educated his children at home, hiring John Nesbitt, another dissenter, to tutor them in Latin. Matthew Meade's involvement in the Rye House plot in 1683 led to his temporary exile to the Netherlands, at which time he sent his son Richard to the private school, in Clerkenwell Close, of the dissenter Thomas Singleton, a former second master at Eton. Richard Mead excelled in the classics, and in 1689 he followed his elder brother Samuel (1670–1734) to the University of Utrecht, where he studied with Johann Georg Graevius (1632–1703), a noted scholar of classical culture, whose *Thesaurus antiquitatum Romanorum* helped form Mead's taste for collecting antiquities.

Early career Mead decided to study medicine, and registered on 18 April 1693 at the University of Leiden. It is likely that he arrived in Leiden several months earlier because he became a close acquaintance of Archibald Pitcairne, who had arrived in Leiden as professor in the spring of 1692 and left abruptly in the summer of 1693. Mead lived in Pitcairne's house for a time, along with Hermann Boerhaave, then also a student. Pitcairne's iatromechanics strongly influenced Mead, as his subsequent works in physiology attest, and the two remained friends. Mead also studied botany with Paul Hermann.

Mead left Leiden early in 1695 without taking a degree, and accompanied his brother Samuel, David Polhill, and Thomas Pellett, another medical student, on a tour of Italy. Their first stop was Turin, where a plausible story about Mead (with some variations) later arose. According to the story Mead inquired about the so-called Tabula Isiaca, a bronze tablet inlaid with silver depicting the Egyptian goddess Isis. It had been found in Rome in 1525 and eventually reached Turin, where it was then lost. Mead asked permission to search for it and found it in storage (some versions of the story say he found it in Florence), and it was duly put on exhibit at the royal museum in Turin. Although at the time the tablet was believed to originate in ancient Egypt it has since been proved to be a Roman forgery. The story is notable for indicating Mead's early interest in antiquities.

From Turin the party travelled to Florence and then Padua, where Mead received the degree of MD on 26 August 1695 after a short period of residence. The tour continued to Rome and Naples, and the group returned to England in the summer of 1696. Mead set up a medical practice out of his father's house in Stepney. He did not obtain a licence from the Royal College of Physicians of London, but a dissenting physician in Stepney was probably below the consideration of the college. Certainly Mead made no effort at concealment, and his father, Matthew, who had returned from the Netherlands in 1687, promoted his son's practice to his congregation. In July 1699 Mead married Ruth Marsh (1683–1720), the daughter

Richard Mead (1673–1754), by Allan Ramsay, 1747

of a Bristol and London merchant, and his father gave him the Stepney house (which he had been given by the trustees of the Stepney meeting-house). Matthew Meade died on 16 October 1699, and soon after his death Richard Mead left the Stepney meeting-house (of which he was a deacon) and joined the Church of England. Mead had eight children with his wife Ruth, of whom three daughters and a son reached adulthood.

In 1702 Mead published his first work, *A Mechanical Account of Poisons*, which fully displayed his commitment to Pitcairne's style of iatromechanics, stating that mathematical learning would soon distinguish a physician from a quack. However, Mead was never known as a mathematician, and his book contained very little mathematical analysis. His emphasis was rather on mechanical chemistry, which explained phenomena in terms of particles of differing sizes and shapes. Mead added an attractive force to this chemistry which he identified with gravity, thus placing himself among the Newtonians. His most original contribution was his discussion of venomous snakes, which had been instigated by his studies with Paul Hermann at Leiden. Mead dissected several vipers and accurately described the mechanism of the fang and its operation. He also confirmed Galen's observation that a

puncture wound was necessary for the venom to take effect, in part by swallowing a sample of venom without ill effect. *A Mechanical Account of Poisons* also discussed, among other topics, noxious airs, citing the Grotta de' Cani near Naples, which Mead had visited in 1695. For therapies he recommended either a substance to neutralize the excess acidity of the poison or an external stimulant such as a cold bath which would keep the blood moving and prevent the formation of coagulated clusters of blood which he believed caused the symptoms in poisoning cases.

The *Mechanical Account* was a success, and it placed Mead at the centre of a highly competitive group of young physicians and natural philosophers who sought the approbation of Isaac Newton. Mead was ambitious, and his combination of Newtonian (but not mathematical) theory, classical allusion, and practical therapies won him attention. He was elected to the Royal Society in 1703, and the *Philosophical Transactions* favourably summarized his book. In the same year the *Transactions* published his translation of a letter from Giovanni Cosimo Bonomo to Francesco Redi of 1687, in which Bonomo described his discovery of the mite, *Acarus* or *Sarcoptus scabiei*, which caused the common skin disease known as scabies or 'the itch'.

Mead was elected physician to St Thomas's Hospital in Southwark on 5 May 1703, and left Stepney with his young family to settle in Crutched Friars in the City of London, where he lived until 1711. A hospital physician, while not usually paid, gained clinical experience with a wide variety of patients as well as access to the wealthy and influential individuals who formed the governing board of the hospital and whose patronage could significantly advance a medical practice. At about the same time Mead was appointed one of the readers in anatomy by the London Company of Barber–Surgeons. The readers delivered the lectures which accompanied the annual public dissection for the benefit of the surgical apprentices. Each reader commented upon one part of the body but did not himself perform the dissection. It is not known where Mead might have gained his knowledge of dissection and anatomy. The professorship of anatomy was vacant at Leiden during his time there, but Boerhaave held private dissecting sessions and Mead may have joined him. The readership paid well, and Mead continued in this position until 1715.

Mead continued his efforts in Newtonian physiology with his next publication, *De imperio solis ac lunae in corpora humana et morbis inde oriundis* (*On the Influence of the Sun and Moon on Human Bodies and the Diseases Arising Thence*), published in 1704. Here Mead joined Hippocratic climatic theory with Newton's theory of the tides, claiming that a tidal flux of the air caused many ailments. This account has variously been termed the last gasp of astrological medicine and one of the first works of Newtonian medicine. The lack of any mathematical foundation makes Mead's claims to Newtonianism unconvincing, but the case histories he cites, many from Pitcairne, are of interest. Mead's puritan upbringing is evident in his accounts of providential interventions in the weather, such as the storms which accompanied Cromwell's death in 1658.

This work was also a great success: Halley reprinted it in his *Miscellanea curiosa* (1708), and an English translation appeared in 1712.

Mead was elected to the council of the Royal Society in 1705, and again in 1707, serving continually from the latter date until his death nearly half a century later. He was appointed a vice-president by Newton on 17 December 1713. On 4 December 1707 Mead was made DM at Oxford, and the Royal College of Physicians admitted him as a candidate on 25 June 1708. He was elected a fellow on 9 April 1716, the same day as his close friend Dr John Freind, and they 'ate sweet cakes together as censors' (*DNB*). Despite their differences in politics, for Mead was as strong a whig as Freind was a tory, they remained the best of friends, sharing interests in classical literature as well as in Newtonian natural philosophy.

As Mead progressed in his profession his residence moved west: from Stepney to Crutched Friars, and then to Austin Friars in 1711, where he occupied the house of the recently deceased physician George Howe, inheriting many of his patients. Here he made the acquaintance of John Radcliffe, one of the most successful physicians of his generation. An anecdote relates that Radcliffe, encountering Mead reading Hippocrates in Greek, commented, 'When I am dead, you will occupy the throne of physic in this town,' Mead is said to have replied, 'Sir, your empire, like Alexander's, will be divided among many successors' (Macmichael, 23), an answer which well pleased Radcliffe and which reveals something of Mead's character. While Radcliffe prided himself on his lack of theory, on the model of Sydenham, Mead had made his mark in part by writing about theory. None the less, Radcliffe chose Mead as his successor, bequeathing to him not only his gold-headed cane but his house in Bloomsbury and his substantial medical practice. Mead attended Queen Anne on her deathbed in 1714 and accurately predicted her imminent demise, although this was not a politically expedient view. Radcliffe died a few months later. Mead resigned as physician at St Thomas's on 5 January 1715 and was named a governor. While at St Thomas's he had devised a method of tapping for dropsy which involved applying pressure to the abdomen while tapping occurred. This greatly reduced the incidence of syncope during the procedure. Mead's patients included Gilbert Burnet, Robert Harley, and the princess of Wales.

At the height of his profession The publication in 1717 of John Freind's *Commentarium novem de febribus* (*Nine Commentaries on Fevers*), appended to his edition of Hippocrates' *De morbis popularis*, engaged Mead in a long controversy about smallpox therapy. Freind included a letter from Mead about his use of purgatives in confluent smallpox. Mead's letter was attacked by John Woodward in his *State of Physick and Diseases* (1718), leading to a pamphlet war which lasted for several years. Mead did not write any pamphlets, but he was ably supported by Freind and others. According to *Mist's Journal* for 13 June 1719 Mead and Woodward came to blows on the night of 10 June in front of Gresham College. Various accounts of the so-called duel exist, and Woodward and Mead are said to be the figures by the gate of the stable yard in the engraving by Vertue of Gresham College in John Ward's *Lives of the Professors of Gresham College* (1740). Mead maintained a lifelong enmity toward Woodward.

Mead's wife, Ruth, died on 31 January 1720, and shortly thereafter Mead moved to a house on Great Ormond Street in Bloomsbury later occupied by the Hospital for Sick Children. He lived in this house for the rest of his life. He also owned property in Chelsea, and is said to have lived between 1715 and 1718 at Gorges House there.

The outbreak of plague in Marseilles in 1719 led Craggs, the secretary of state, to ask Mead to draw up a statement concerning its prevention. Mead's *Short Discourse Concerning Pestilential Contagion and the Methods to be used to Prevent it* appeared in 1720, and seven editions appeared within a year. An enlarged eighth edition was published in 1722. Mead argued that plague was contagious, caused by a 'volatile active spirit' (p. 11) which acted chemically to corrupt the blood. He had no notion of living contagious particles, however. He recommended separating the sick from the well (against the usual practice of quarantining entire households), and noted especially the role of soft goods such as fabrics in the transmission of plague, which would indeed provide transport for plague-carrying fleas. Mead's *Discourse* was credited with alleviating local panic, and in 1721 he, Sloane, and Arbuthnot were ordered by the privy council to investigate measures to be taken in case of an outbreak of plague.

Mead also joined Sloane in 1721 to conduct trials of smallpox inoculation among some condemned prisoners at Newgate. While Sloane instigated the trials Mead enthusiastically supported them, and described them two decades later in his *De variolis et morbillis liber* (*Discourse on the Small-Pox and Measles*, 1747). Mead was especially interested in the Chinese method of introducing the infectious material nasally, and this was tried on one prisoner. All recovered, and this success helped to establish the practice of inoculation, although it remained controversial.

In the spring of 1723 John Freind was confined to the Tower for his role in the Atterbury plot, and Mead was instrumental in securing his release (according to one story, by threatening to withhold his services from Robert Walpole). Mead brought Freind, while in prison, a copy of Daniel LeClerc's history of medicine, which inspired Freind to write his own history. He is said to have presented Freind upon his release with the fees he had received from Freind's patients, although the sum usually given of £5000 is wildly exaggerated, since Freind had been in prison for only three months. Mead also helped obtain a pardon for George Kelly, an Irish clergyman implicated in the plot. Despite his whig politics Mead seems to have enjoyed aiding the opposition; he also helped the nonjuror Thomas Hearne regain his position at Oxford, and he helped secure the release from prison of Pitcairne's son, who had participated in the 1715 Jacobite rising.

On 18 October 1723 Mead delivered the Harveian oration at the Royal College of Physicians, combining his antiquarian and medical interests in an address on the status of physicians in ancient Greece and Rome. Mead, himself very conscious of status, concluded that physicians held a high place in ancient society. This view was attacked by Conyers Middleton, and a pamphlet war ensued, with John Ward defending Mead's position. Mead was elected a censor of the College of Physicians in 1716, 1719, and 1724.

Mead married Anne, daughter of Sir Rowland Alston of Odell, Bedfordshire, on 14 August 1724. The union produced no children. Mead was now at the height of his profession. He was named a governor to Bridewell, Bethlem, and St Bartholomew's hospitals in 1720, and was instrumental in persuading Thomas Guy, one of his patients, to use some of his enormous profits from South Sea stock to endow a new hospital. In 1727 Mead was appointed physician to George II, and in the same year he attended Sir Isaac Newton in his final illness. Mead's income surpassed even that of his mentor Radcliffe, amounting to £5000 or £6000 a year. From his post at a coffee house—usually Batson's near the Royal Exchange, or Tom's on Great Russell Street—he received reports in the mornings from apothecaries about patients, and wrote up prescriptions which the apothecaries would then fill. This service was by no means uncommon among physicians but it subjected Mead to some criticism and satire. At other times of the day he might be found at Rawthmell's coffee house in Henrietta Street, Covent Garden, or Child's in St Paul's Churchyard. He owned a coach, and his wealth is indicated by the six horses he used to drive out to his country house near Windsor. Through his second wife he also had possession of Harrold Hall in Bedfordshire.

Mead as patron and collector To his contemporaries Mead was as well known a patron and collector as he was a physician. He subscribed to an enormous number of books from 1710 onward, including such varied titles as Burnet's *History of his Own Time* (1724), Henry Pemberton's *View of Sir Isaac Newton's Natural Philosophy* (1728), John Quinton's *Treatise of Warm Bath Water* (1733), and John Ward's *Lives of the Professors of Gresham College* (1740; Mead took ten copies, five on large paper). A number of books were dedicated to Mead, including William Cheselden's *Anatomy of the Humane Body* (1713), Michael Maittaire's edition of Lucretius (1713), William Baxter's *Glossarum antiquitatum Britannicarum* (1719), John Blackbourne's edition of the works of Francis Bacon (1730), a volume of Eleazar Albin's *Natural History of Birds* (1738), and Robert James's *Medicinal Dictionary* (1742). Others were dedicated to him without his consent in the hope of gaining his patronage, which he dispensed generously to natural philosophers, naturalists, and antiquarians. He sponsored the elaborate new edition of William Cowper's *Myotomia reformata* which appeared in 1724 with a new introduction by Mead and Henry Pemberton who explained muscular motion in Newtonian terms. Hearne called it 'the most beautiful

book … ever printed in England' (*Remarks and Collections of Thomas Hearne*, 7, Oxford Historical Society, 48, 1906, 271). Mead gave financial assistance to the naturalists George Edwards and Mark Catesby, the latter of whom named a flower, the *Dodecathon meadia* or American cowslip, after him.

Mead championed the invention for ventilating ships of Samuel Sutton over the rival invention of Stephen Hales and read a paper on Sutton's principles to the Royal Society on 11 February 1742. Mead wrote his *Discourse on the Scurvy* (1749) to support Sutton's cause. Mead based much of his argument on the evidence of Lord Anson's voyage around the world between 1740 and 1744, during which 90 per cent of his men succumbed to scurvy, which Mead attributed in part to corrupted air. Mead's work was soon superseded by James Lind's *Treatise of the Scurvy* (1753). While Sutton's invention enjoyed the favour of the navy for a time, Hales's invention ultimately was adopted in 1756.

Mead sponsored the printer Samuel Palmer to write his *History of Printing* (1732), and between 1722 and 1733 he provided the means to publish a complete edition of Jacques-Auguste de Thou's *Historia sui temporis*. He supported the research in France of the Jacobite exile Thomas Carte, purchasing Carte's materials from him in 1724, and hired the printer Samuel Buckley to edit and print de Thou's work, which appeared in seven folio volumes in 1733. Mead also assisted the Shakespearian scholar Lewis Theobald and the physician Samuel Jebb, whose edition of the works of Roger Bacon appeared in 1733, as well as the forger William Lauder, who wrote Mead a letter defending himself on 9 April 1751. Mead was also one of the subscribers to the Society for the Promotion of Learning, founded in 1736 to assist in the publication of scholarly works deemed unprofitable by publishers. He was a noted scholar of the classics, and Richard Bentley, his closest friend after Freind, often consulted him about classical texts. John Davies DD bequeathed to Mead his papers on Cicero, which Mead gave to Bentley's nephew Thomas to complete an edition of the *Offices*. The papers were destroyed in an accidental fire at Thomas Bentley's lodgings, as Mead stated in a letter prefixed to the third edition of Davies's *Cicero de natura deorum*. Mead also sponsored the translation from Arabic into Latin of the treatise on smallpox of the medieval Arabic physician Rhazes (Abu Bakr Muhammad ibn Zakariyya al-Razi 850–923). He procured a copy of the Arabic version from Boerhaave in Leiden, and Thomas Hunt, the professor of Arabic and Hebrew at Oxford, edited the final translation from two versions by Solomon Negri (a Greek Orthodox priest from Damascus) and John Gagnier (reader in Arabic at Oxford). The essay was appended to Mead's *De variolis et morbillis liber*.

A number of individuals, including Martin Folkes and Nathaniel Cotton, consulted Mead about antiquities. Mead was a major collector of both books and art. He had a separate room built at the foot of the garden of his house on Great Ormond Street which housed his library and collections, which were among the largest of his time. The room also served as a meeting place for physicians, natural philosophers, and men of letters. Mead had an extensive collection of antique medals and coins (some of which had provided evidence for his Harveian oration), as well as other antiquities, including an Egyptian mummy and other Egyptian and Etruscan pieces. His collection of antique paintings had been acquired at great expense, the most famous being the *Court of Augustus*, which had been brought to Mead from Rome by Sir Alexander Dick in 1737. In keeping with the style of the cabinets of the time, Mead's collection also included a miscellaneous assortment of fossils, scientific instruments, anatomical specimens, and curiosities.

Mead owned about 150 paintings, including landscapes by Rembrandt, Claude Lorrain, and Brueghel, and architectural pictures by Nicolas Poussin and Canaletto. He had many portraits, including the physicians Mayerne (by Rubens) and Vesalius (by Titian), scientists such as Boyle (by Kerseboom) and Halley (by Kneller), and the famous Holbein portrait of Erasmus, as well as portraits of contemporary men of letters, including Swift and Richardson. His collection of miniatures was especially noted. He also owned thousands of engravings and drawings by such artists as Durer, Holbein, Michelangelo, and Raphael, as well as Hogarth and Vertue. Mead was a patron of art as well as a collector. He commissioned the bust of William Harvey by Peter Scheemakers, later displayed at the Royal College of Physicians, and the French artist Watteau, who came to consult Mead in the early 1720s, painted for him *L'amour paisible* and *Italian Comedians*. Mead opened his gallery to interested artists to copy, and he even loaned paintings for copying. In this era before public galleries Mead played an important role in the advancement of art. He was one of the promoters of the Foundling Hospital, which housed the first public gallery in London in the 1740s.

Mead's collection of books and manuscripts was second only to that of Hans Sloane. His books numbered some 10,000 volumes, including 146 incunabula and many fine bindings. His library was especially rich in the classics and in works of medicine and natural philosophy. Mead aimed to find the best editions of canonical works. One example is his fine collection of medical works, dominated by anatomy. This included a first edition on vellum of Vesalius's *Epitome* of his *De fabrica* (1543), which is now in the British Library, as well as several editions of Mondino de' Luzzi and Berengario da Carpi. Mead possessed a very rare copy of Michael Servetus's *Christiani restitutio* (1553), in which Servetus explained the pulmonary circulation. Mead gave this book to M. de Boze, secretary of the Academy of Inscriptions and Belles-Lettres in Paris, with whom he shared a long correspondence; de Boze gave him in turn some medals. The book, one of only three copies in the world, is now at the Bibliothèque Nationale in Paris. Mead's anatomy books also included an extensive collection of seventeenth- and eighteenth-century authors. He also owned most of the canonical works of the scientific revolution. Mead collected books on fine art and architecture, and owned a second-folio Shakespeare which had once belonged to Charles I (and is now in the Queen's Library at Windsor). However, he was little interested in contemporary fiction, and only one novel, Fielding's *Tom Jones* (1749), was in his collection. He owned a fine collection of Latin and Greek manuscripts which he sold to his friend Anthony Askew for £500.

Family life and final years When Mead's first wife, Ruth, died in 1720 he was left a widower with six children in their teens or early twenties: four daughters, Sarah, Bathsheba, Elizabeth, and an unnamed daughter who died of smallpox in 1725 aged fifteen; and two sons, John and Richard. John died in the Canary Islands in 1721. Another son had died in 1716. Sarah Marsh Mead, the eldest daughter, born about 1702, married the physician Edward Wilmot. Probably through the influence of Mead he was named a physician to St Thomas's in 1729. They had three children. Sarah Wilmot died on 11 September 1785, aged eighty-three. The second daughter, Bathsheba, married Charles Bertie of Uffington, Lincolnshire, and had four children; she died before 1754. The youngest daughter, Elizabeth, born about 1705, also married a physician, Frank Nicholls. They had five children. Elizabeth Nicholls was still alive in 1798, aged ninety-two; her grandson was John Nicholls, the literary historian. Little is known about Mead's son Richard. *Biographia Britannica* stated that he inherited £30,000 from his uncle, Samuel Mead, who died in 1734, but this is not corroborated by Samuel Mead's will. Richard did receive an income of £800 per annum from the estate of Sir Thomas Reeves, lord chief justice of the common pleas. The younger Richard Mead married Anne, daughter of William Gore of Tring, Hertfordshire, in 1741. They had a daughter in 1742 who did not reach adulthood, and he died in 1762 without heirs.

Mead wrote little in the later 1720s and 1730s, but in the 1740s he seems to have been compelled to establish his intellectual legacy. He rewrote many of his earlier works, discarding the Newtonianism of attracting particles in favour of the new Newtonian orthodoxy of ethers. New works in this period included the books on smallpox and scurvy already mentioned. He also published in 1749 *Medica sacra*, a commentary on diseases in the Bible, which he explained in naturalistic rather than supernatural terms. From the intense puritan piety of his youth Mead seems to have travelled to a more deistic religion. His later edition of *De imperio solis ac lunae* omits mention of the storms on Cromwell's death or any supernatural intervention. Mead's final work, *Monita et praecepta medica* (1751) consisted of aphorisms drawn from his medical practice. Mead did not keep detailed case records, and while celebrated in its time, the book's lack of specificity makes it less interesting now.

Mead was visibly declining in health by the early 1750s, as he neared eighty. He outlived many of his friends and contemporaries, including Freind, Arbuthnot, and Bentley. He took to his bed on 11 February 1754 and died on 16 February in his house on Great Ormond Street, of unknown causes, but without visible pain. On 23 February Mead was laid to rest in the Middle Temple vault of the

Temple Church, next to his brother Samuel. His son Richard erected a monument to him in the north aisle of Westminster Abbey, consisting of a bust of the doctor by Scheemakers above a long Latin epitaph by John Ward.

Legacy In the last years of his life rumours circulated that Mead was in financial difficulties, and the sale of his ancient manuscripts to Askew only fanned the flames of rumour. Although his income during the years of his greatest success was high, he was known for his extravagance, both as a patron and in his household: Horace Walpole claimed that Mead spent £70 a week on his table. His charities were also notable. Mead's financial legacy was less than might have been expected for someone of his eminence. His will, written on 16 August 1753 and proved on 26 February 1754, is relatively modest in its bequests. Mead's widow, Anne, is given £5000, some plate, jewels, portraits, and household goods. A few particular books and manuscripts are bestowed on Mead's son, his son-in-law Nicholls, and grandson Robert Wilmot, and the younger Richard Mead is given the use of the house at Windsor and its contents. He set up modest trust funds for the benefit of his Mead, Nicholls, and Wilmot grandchildren, and directed that a debt owed him by his third son-in-law, Charles Bertie, become, if paid, a trust fund for the Bertie children. But most of Mead's assets were in his collections. Unlike Sloane, to whom he is often compared, Mead desired that his collections be scattered. The auction of his goods over several weeks in 1754–5 was a major event. The books were auctioned in November 1754 and April 1755, and the catalogue, *Bibliotheca Meadiana*, is itself an important source for Mead and for eighteenth-century collecting. Bidders came from across Europe; Louis XV of France acquired Mead's copy of the 1469 Pliny *Historia naturalis*. Anthony Askew purchased many volumes. The book collection sold for over £5500, and the pictures, medals, and antiquities (catalogued in *Museum Meadianum*), auctioned at the same time but in a different location, produced almost £11,000. When Mead's debts were paid he left a total of about £20,000 to his son Richard—a handsome sum, but not a fabulous one.

Samuel Johnson said of Mead that he 'lived more in the broad sunshine of life than almost any man'. He had many friends; Woodward, his chief antagonist, was known to be a contentious person, and although Mead disliked George Cheyne, his enmity was not returned. Mead was the subject of satires and pamphlets, but this was itself an indication of his fame. A popular practitioner in an age when bedside manner was at least as valuable as medicines, he was successful both professionally and financially. He loved the life of the intellect, and relished books and pictures and learned conversation. Mead was a good classical scholar but was less skilled in natural philosophy. His practical works, such as the *Short Discourse Concerning Pestilential Contagion*, are clear and straightforward in advice, but muddled in theory, while his purely theoretical works are highly derivative. Mead was very ambitious, and sought to enter the community of Newtonians as a way to advance his career. His stratagem worked, but he did not leave a lasting intellectual legacy as a medical theorist. Mead's main legacy in the eighteenth century was as a collector, an activity perfectly suited to his temperament.

ANITA GUERRINI

Sources A. Zuckerman, 'The life and works of Richard Mead', PhD diss., University of Illinois, 1965 · R. H. Meade, *In the sunshine of life* (1974) · *Biographia Britannica, or, The lives of the most eminent persons who have flourished in Great Britain and Ireland*, 5 (1757) · Munk, *Roll* · *DNB* · W. Macmichael, *The gold-headed cane*, 5th edn, ed. G. C. Peachey (1923) · A. Guerrini, 'Newtonian matter theory, chemistry, and medicine, 1690–1713', PhD diss., Indiana University, 1983 · *IGI*

Archives RCP Lond., corresp. and MSS · RCP Lond., notes on materia medica; prescriptions; Padua diploma · Wellcome L. | BL, Sloane MSS, corresp.

Likenesses B. Lens, miniature, 1726, RCP Lond. · J. Richardson, drawing, 1738, BM · J. Richardson, oils, *c*.1738, NPG · J. Richardson, drawing, 1739, AM Oxf. · attrib. W. Hoare, oils, *c*.1740, RCP Lond. · A. Ramsay, oils, 1740, NPG · studio of A. Ramsay, oils, 1740, NPG · A. Pond, oils, 1743, RCP Lond.; copy, RCP Lond. · A. Ramsay, oils, 1747, Foundling Hospital, London [*see illus.*] · attrib. A. Ramsay, oils, 1748, Society of Apothecaries, London · P. Scheemakers, marble bust on monument, 1754, Westminster Abbey · L. F. Roubiliac, marble bust, *c*.1756, RCP Lond. · M. Dahl, priv. coll. · R. Houston, engraving, repro. in Mead, *The medical works of Richard Mead* (1762), frontispiece · A. Ramsay, oils, RCP Lond. · attrib. J. Richardson, oils, Bodl. Oxf. · W. Stukeley, wash drawing, RCP Lond.

Wealth at death approx. £30,000; plus property in London and Windsor: will, PRO, PROB 11/807

Mead, Robert (1615/16–1653), poet and playwright, was born at the Black Lion, Fleet Street, London, the son of Robert Mead (*d.* 1658), who was later four times master of the Stationers' Company (1644–5, 1645–6, 1649–50, and 1656–7). The younger Mead was educated at Westminster School, where he became a king's scholar in 1630. In 1633 he contributed a commendatory sonnet to his schoolfellow Abraham Cowley's *Poetical Blossomes*. In the following year, at the age of eighteen, he was elected to Christ Church, Oxford, from where he graduated BA on 11 April 1638 and proceeded MA on 22 May 1641.

While at Oxford Mead wrote a comedy entitled 'The combat of love and friendship'. The play was acted by the students at Christ Church, but was not printed until after Mead's death. The address to the reader prefixed to the 1654 edition indicates that Mead wrote the play 'when his youth was willing to descend from his then higher Contemplations' (Mead, sig. A2*r*), which implies a date of composition between 1634 and 1638. The comedy details the struggle of Lysander to remain loyal to his best friend and faithful to his mistress. Forced to choose between the two, the hero opts to deceive his mistress, but is then betrayed by his friend. The play ends happily when the hero himself proves unfaithful, allowing a series of pragmatic marriages to take place. In 1638 a poem by Mead was included in *Death Repeal'd*, a volume of verse published by Christ Church students in remembrance of Viscount Bayning of Sudbury. The same year Mead contributed a further elegy, 'Our bayes (me thinks) are withered', to *Jonsonus virbius*, a poetical miscellany published as a tribute to the late Ben Jonson.

From 1639 Mead appears to have relinquished literature. In 1640 he was made a captain in Charles I's army. He later distinguished himself at the siege of Oxford, took part in the assault on Abingdon in the spring of 1646, and was one of the commissioners for negotiating the surrender of Oxford to parliament in May 1646. He was created MD on 23 June 1646, the day before the surrender, but was later expelled from his studentship by the parliamentary commission of 1648. Eager to continue in the king's service, Mead travelled to Ireland, where he served briefly in the Munster forces under Lord Inchiquin. Following the defeat of Inchiquin's troops, Mead travelled to Jersey, and soon afterwards proceeded to Göteborg in Sweden as Charles II's agent. From there he wrote to Sir Edward Nicholas in February 1650, expressing Queen Kristina's dissatisfaction at hearing so little of the king's activities. He subsequently submitted a diplomatic note from Charles to the queen, and entered into Charles's project of visiting Stockholm. In 1651 Lord Inchiquin appears to have appointed Mead his son's tutor. In 1652 Mead travelled up the Rhine into Switzerland, and then via Strasbourg, Speyer, Heidelberg, Frankfurt, and Mainz to Cologne. In a letter to Edgeman dated September 1652, but wrongly transcribed as 1654 in the Clarendon state papers, Mead offers a brief account of his travels. He next sailed from Amsterdam to England, where he lodged at his father's house in Fleet Street. There Mead himself fell victim to a malignant fever. He died on 21 February 1653 and was buried two days later in the church of St Dunstan-in-the-West, Fleet Street.

Mead's friends attempted to secure for him a posthumous reputation as a gifted poet and playwright. Removed from the historical context of late Caroline England, Mead's published writings fail to substantiate this claim. However, for his contemporaries at Oxford, Mead's reputation for talent and discernment may well have owed as much to his political allegiance as his literary ability. As the anonymous publisher of Mead's *The Combat of Love and Friendship* (1654) explains, Mead was 'a stout and learned man, and excellent in the faculty of poetry and making plays. His eminent general abilities were also such that they have left him a character precious and honourable to our nation' (Mead, sig. A2r).

CHARLES BRAYNE

Sources Wood, *Ath. Oxon.*, new edn, 3.342–4 · Foster, *Alum. Oxon.*, 1500–1714, 3.997 · R. Mead, *The combat of love and friendship* (1654) · Bodl. Oxf., MSS Clarendon 43, 49 · *Calendar of the Clarendon state papers preserved in the Bodleian Library*, 2: 1649–1654, ed. W. D. Macray (1869) · *Jonsonus virbius, or, The memorie of Ben Johnson revived by the friends of the muses* (1638) · *Death repeal'd by a thankfull memoriall sent from Christ-Church in Oxford … celebrating … Paule, late Lord Viscount Bayning of Sudbury* (1638) · A. C. [A. Cowley], *Poetical blossomes* (1633) · *CSP dom.*, 1649–50 · M. Burrows, ed., *The register of the visitors of the University of Oxford, from AD 1647 to AD 1658*, CS, new ser., 29 (1881) · J. Mills, *One soul in bodies twain: friendship in Tudor literature and Stuart drama* (1937) · *The manuscripts of the marquis of Ormonde*, [old ser.], 3 vols., HMC, 36 (1895–1909), vol. 1, p. 215 · private information (2004) [I. Gadd] · *IGI*

Mead, William (*c*.1627–1713), Quaker patron and merchant, lived in London, where he became a prosperous linen draper and merchant; he was also a member of the Company of Merchant Taylors. He served as captain of a trained band and was a Seeker in religion, joining the presbyterians and Independents among others before finally becoming a Quaker early in 1670. Later that year, on 14 August, he was present at a large and crowded meeting in Gracechurch Street at which William Penn was the chief speaker. Soldiers arrived with orders to break up the meeting, and in order to keep the peace Penn volunteered to give himself up when the meeting had ended. When he did so, Mead accompanied him; both were arrested and committed to Newgate. Accused of unlawful assembly and disturbing the peace Penn and Mead were tried at the Old Bailey, and when the jury found them not guilty the jury were imprisoned by the judge without food or water until they returned a verdict with which he agreed. However, the jury refused to be intimidated, and so the case, and in particular the jury's foreman, Edward Bushell, became famous in legal history. Eventually all parties were released, and a detailed account of the trial under the title *The Peoples Ancient and Just Liberties Asserted* was published by Penn and Mead later the same year.

Mead now put his energies and his wealth at the disposal of London Friends and the Quaker leadership. He bought flax which poor Friends were employed to spin and was involved in buying land on which to erect workhouses for the poor. He often advanced money for Friends' projects, although he was careful to claim it back again in due course. He gave hospitality to travelling Friends, and his house was often used as an address to which Friends' letters could be directed. George Fox, who had no permanent home in London, often stayed with him in Fenchurch Street and later in Highgate. Mead was not averse to using his position in London society to advance the Quaker cause and to assure those in power that Quakers were respectable and posed no threat. In 1672 he is quoted as being 'confident his Majesty cannot be safe from any of the Dissenters but the Quakers' ('Present state of the nonconformists').

Mead was of mature years and a settled and prosperous position when he first married in 1679, but his wife, Mary Lawrence, died the same year, and their son, Jonathan, died in 1680. In 1681 William Mead married Sarah Fell (1643?–1714), the fourth daughter of Margaret Fell, the wife of George Fox. Sarah was confident, capable, and well educated, a prominent member of Quaker women's meetings and the efficient manager of the large household at Swarthmoor Hall. In 1684 William Mead bought an additional country property at Gooses, near Romford in Essex, and in the same year their only son, Nathaniel (*d.* 1760), was born. Mead was now at the centre of the Quaker leadership in London. His house, his coach, and his business acumen were at the service of his father-in-law, George Fox. He looked after Fox's business papers and his library of more than 300 books, and in time became his literary executor. It was Mead's money that ensured the printing of Fox's *Journal* in 1694, but this also gave Mead the power to object to William Penn's preface which, as a result, was printed only in later editions; Mead and Penn had become estranged over politics, Penn appearing to be too much of a friend to James II while Mead remained a staunch whig.

Mead was a man of strong opinions and quick decisions, downright in speech and behaviour. His wealth made it possible for him to help Friends and to keep in contact with London society, but some accused him of a lack of Quaker simplicity, and there may be some grounds for this. William and Sarah's son, Nathaniel, was sent to the Middle Temple at sixteen, a 'worldly' employment which caused some unease to his relatives if not to his parents: he prospered, was knighted, and did not remain a Quaker.

William Mead died at his house, Gooses, on 3 April 1713, when he was said to be aged eighty-six, and was buried in the Quaker burial-ground at Barking. His wife, Sarah, died on 9 June 1714 and was buried with him. William's grave is marked by a headstone which, most unusually for a Quaker, describes him as 'William Mead Esq.'.

GIL SKIDMORE

Sources W. C. Braithwaite, *The beginnings of Quakerism* (1912) • W. C. Braithwaite, *The second period of Quakerism* (1919) • *The journal of George Fox*, ed. J. L. Nickalls, rev. edn (1952); repr. (1975) • W. M. White, *Six weeks meeting, 1671–1971* (1971) • *Journal of the Friends' Historical Society*, 1–54 (1903–77) • H. L. Ingle, *First among Friends: George Fox and the creation of Quakerism* (1994) • 'Dictionary of Quaker biography', RS Friends, Lond. [card index] • 'The present state of the nonconformists', 1672, BL, Stowe MS 186, fol. 16

Meade [*married name* Toulmin Smith]**, Elizabeth Thomasina** (1844–1914), children's writer and novelist, was born on 5 June 1844 in Bandon, co. Cork, Ireland, one of six children of the Revd Richard Thomas Meade (1815–1888), rector of Kilomen and subsequently of Nohoval, and his first wife, Sarah, *née* Lane (*c*.1814–1874). Educated at home by a governess, she moved to London during the mid-1870s, following her mother's death and her father's remarriage, and quickly learned to craft stories that publishers would readily purchase. Even with marriage, on 20 September 1879, to solicitor, Alfred Toulmin Smith and the birth of three children, she continued an active career, choosing to be known as L. T. Meade not only as an author but also in all other aspects of her public life.

An exceptionally prolific writer, Meade produced some 280 books for more than thirty different publishers. Her short stories and essays appeared in a range of periodicals including *Atalanta*, *Little Folks*, *Young Woman*, *Sunday Magazine*, *Harmsworth Magazine*, *Chambers's Journal*, *Cassell's Family Magazine*, the *Daily Mail*, *The Quiver*, and the *Strand Magazine*. Interviewed in *Young Woman* in 1893, she cast herself as a consummate professional who never waited for inspiration, could 'write to order' whatever book her publisher wanted, and, by dictating to a stenographer, turned out an average of 2000 words per day over the course of a year.

L. T. Meade worked in a wide variety of popular genres, some of which she apparently invented. Most of her early stories were pathetic tales of East End children using 'city arab' conventions. For adults, she wrote sensation fiction, romances, stories of aristocratic life, and problem novels about topics such as vivisection and drug addiction. As a writer who knew her public, she responded to current issues and popular trends. During the 1890s, when Arthur Conan Doyle's Sherlock Holmes stories were regularly featured in its pages, the *Strand Magazine* also had detective fiction by L. T. Meade and two collaborators. *Stories from the Diary of a Doctor* (1893–6) apparently originated the subgenre of medical mystery, and the stories collected as *The Brotherhood of the Seven Kings* (1899) featured a woman master criminal who headed a sinister Italian organization. Also during the 1890s she collaborated on short stories with the orientalist Robert Kennaway Douglas.

Meade is best remembered, however, as a writer for older girls. From 1887 to 1893 she edited the magazine *Atalanta*, turning it into a vehicle for good fiction and thoughtful articles about schooling, careers, and women's history. In addition, Meade popularized several genres of girls' fiction which remained in vogue throughout the twentieth century. *A World of Girls* (1886) established many conventions of the school story. *A Sweet Girl Graduate* (1891) made college life attractive. *A Sister of the Red Cross* (1900) followed a heroic nurse to the Second South African War. Career novels about medicine, art, market gardening, typing, and other fields gave advice about training as well as tracing the adventures of young women living on their own in shared flats. *Ruffles* (1911) was about a girl who solved mysteries and drove her family's car.

A writer as prolific and popular as Meade inevitably drew on contemporary stereotypes that prevented her work from surviving beyond her own generation. Although she did not use the term, L. T. Meade in interviews presented herself as a 'new woman' who could capably manage a home, raise children, commute into London for editorial work, write thoroughly professional fiction, and enjoy a public life. She served on the managing committee of the Pioneer Club, where independent women of the 1890s met for social events and debates on contemporary issues. Her photographs show a vigorous if not handsome woman; the biographical note on book jackets often described her as fond of outdoor sports.

L. T. Meade and Alfred Toulmin Smith lived in the London suburb of Dulwich for most of their married life but later moved to 20 Lathbury Road, Oxford, where she died on 26 October 1914. She was buried in Wolvercote cemetery, north Oxford. She was survived by her husband and by her children, Alfred Kendal Toulmin Smith, Hope Douglas, and Lucy Lilian Joy Grieve.

SALLY MITCHELL

Sources M. Reimer, 'L. T. Meade', *British children's writers, 1880–1914*, ed. L. M. Zaidman, DLitB, 141 (1994), 186–98 • 'How I write my books: an interview with Mrs L. T. Meade', *Young Woman*, 1 (1892–3), 122–3 • H. C. Black, 'Mrs L. T. Meade', *Pen, pencil, baton and mask: biographical sketches* (1896), 222–9 • L. T. Meade, 'How I began', *Girls' Realm* (Nov 1900), 57–60 • *The Times* (28 Oct 1914) • S. Mitchell, *The new girl: girls' culture in England, 1880–1915* (1995) • Meade's tombstone, Wolvercote cemetery, Oxford • d. cert.

Likenesses four photographs, 1863–98, repro. in *Strand Magazine*, 16 (Dec 1898), 674 • Window & Grove, photograph, 1892–3, repro. in 'How I write my books', 1 (1893), 122

Meade, James Edward (1907–1995), economist, was born on 23 June 1907 at Broome, Swanage, Dorset, the second

James Edward Meade (1907–1995), by Walter Stoneman, 1951

child and only son of Charles Hippisley Meade (b. 1866/7?) and his wife, Kathleen Cotton (Kitty), née Stapleton (b. 1884), daughter of George Cotton Stapleton. He was brought up at 6 Lansdown Crescent, Bath, Somerset, where his father, an Oxford graduate and the descendant of a long line of country parsons, lived the quiet and unostentatious life of a gentleman. Socially, religiously, and politically conservative, he was not an encouraging role model for his son, but, a fine woodworker, he did teach him carpentry. He sent his son at the age of ten to Lambrook School, a preparatory school, and four years later to Malvern College. Meade disliked the emphasis on games at Malvern but two masters, the left-wing classics master and the music master, who took some of his pupils to the Salzburg festival, 'kept [him] sane'. Another element of sanity was provided by his paternal aunt Sybil, an eccentric in a family with more than its fair share of eccentrics, whom he visited often during his holidays from school. He left Malvern in 1926 with a love of music, many prizes, for English verse and Latin prose among others, and a classical scholarship to Oriel College, Oxford. He switched from Greats to the newly established course in philosophy, politics, and economics at the end of his second year. In the summer of 1930 he gained an outstanding first-class degree and was elected to a fellowship in economics at Hertford College.

A young economist Oxford was a welcome liberation from Bath society. Meade joined the Labour Club and became a member of the 'Cole group' of young socialists (gathered around G. D. H. Cole, then a fellow of University College). His switch to economics was motivated by concern with the serious unemployment problem in Britain in the 1920s; in 1928 he also thought it could easily be cured, his aunt Sybil having introduced him to the writings of the monetary crank Clifford (Hugh) Douglas. He soon shed this belief but throughout his career his main concern was with the contribution which economic analysis had to make to the solution of problems of practical economic policy. He was one of several young Oxford economists advising the Labour Party in the 1930s; then and later he described himself as a liberal socialist, who believed in using the market mechanism for egalitarian ends. A convinced internationalist, he was also active in the League of Nations Union.

Meade spent the academic year 1930–31 in Cambridge. Hertford had allowed him a postgraduate year to learn more economics (and some mathematics); Dennis Robertson, whom he had met in Bath through Robertson's aunts, who were neighbours in Lansdown Crescent, had invited him to Trinity College. Meade was both a pupil of Robertson and a member of the 'Cambridge circus', the group of young economists including Richard Kahn, Piero Sraffa, Austin Robinson, and Joan Robinson, who gathered together to analyse and criticize the recently published *Treatise on Money* (1930) of John Maynard Keynes. He worked closely with Kahn, whose employment multiplier showed that an exogenous increase in investment would lead to successive increase in aggregate demand and so in incomes; Kahn gave the name 'Mr Meade's relation' to Meade's finding that these increases in income would bring desired savings into equality with the initial exogenous increase in investment. These relations, which implied that adjustments in aggregate demand and income would bring about macroeconomic equilibrium, were essential ingredients of the theoretical system of Keynes's *General Theory of Employment, Interest and Money* (1936). Meade, having fallen under the spell of the 'magician' Keynes, returned to Oxford already a Keynesian in the modern (post-1936) sense.

Back in Oxford in the Michaelmas term 1931, Meade set his first students to read Keynes's work. They remembered him as a dry but lucid lecturer and an excellent tutor whose enthusiasm for his subject was contagious. He continued his research in monetary theory, publishing his first book, *The Rate of Interest in a Progressive State*, in 1933. At the same time, in a Fabian pamphlet, *Public Works in their International Aspect*, he used the idea of the multiplier (and his 'relation') to argue for countercyclical government expenditure on public works, accompanied by the appropriate monetary policy, to prevent unemployment in slumps and inflation in booms, and for international monetary co-operation to avert the balance-of-payments problems of domestically orientated macroeconomic policies. Advising Hugh Dalton, a future Labour chancellor of the exchequer, he advocated the removal of barriers to trade, a flexible (but managed) exchange rate for sterling, and the use of exchange controls to regulate the capital account of the balance of payments, in order to permit the adoption of a macroeconomic employment policy by a Labour government.

In the spring of 1932 Albert Einstein visited Oxford. Gilbert Murray asked the new secretary of the Oxford branch of the League of Nations Union, (Elizabeth) Margaret Wilson (b. 1908), daughter of Alexander Cowan Wilson, a civil engineer, to get together a group of young dons to meet him. She invited Meade, whom she had met once before through her younger brother, who had rowed in the same Oriel boat as Meade when an undergraduate. They married on 14 March 1933, setting up house at 11 Holywell Street. In their long and happy life together they were to have a son and three daughters.

Meade wrote the first modern Keynesian textbook, *An Introduction to Economic Analysis and Policy*, in 1936. He tried 'to expound the whole corpus of Economic Theory without taking any knowledge of technical terms for granted and with full use of the more recent developments' (Preface) and to include every piece of theory with an application to current economic problems, beginning with the problem of unemployment. The book was immediately successful and had gone into a third, American edition and a French translation by 1939.

By 1937 Meade was looking for the opportunity to devote more time to (policy-orientated) research. When he and Margaret took a holiday on the Riviera they disliked it so much that Margaret suggested they go on to Geneva, which she knew well from her parents living there and her work for the League of Nations Union. In Geneva they met Dennis Robertson, who introduced them to Alexander Loveday, director of the financial section and economic intelligence service of the League of Nations. Loveday invited Meade to join the economic intelligence service to write its *World Economic Survey*, and Meade's college gave him leave of absence for four years from December 1937. Meade wrote two excellent surveys but he did not return to Oxford because of the Second World War.

War service In 1940 Meade was offered wartime employment with the British government. He and his wife with their three small children undertook a nightmare journey by car across France in May, arriving exhausted at Nantes only to find themselves stranded on board ship without an escort: all available craft were evacuating the British army from Dunkirk. When they reached England in June they had no home; soon after Meade took up his job in Whitehall, Margaret and the children very reluctantly sailed to America. Fortunately they were able to return in November 1942.

Meade's first assignment in what was to become the economic section of the war cabinet offices in 1941 was to prepare estimates of national income and expenditure as part of a survey of resources available for the war effort. He drew up a complicated and comprehensive system of balancing tables; a young Cambridge graduate in the Ministry of Economic Warfare, Richard Stone, was sent over to help him with the statistics. Meade's description of what happened next characteristically downplays his own initial contribution: Stone joined Meade in his tiny room with its single desk, established himself on a corner of the desk with a quill pen and a hand calculator, and gradually moved from the corner of the desk to the centre, while Meade turned the handle of the calculator. With the active encouragement of Keynes in the Treasury, their calculations, the first modern double-entry social accounts for any country, were utilized in the 'Keynesian' budget of April 1941 and published with it; they also published, jointly, academic and popular accounts of their methods (notably *National Income and Expenditure*, 1944).

In February 1941 Meade wrote the first of a long series of memoranda on the subject of post-war reconstruction, identifying four problems: unemployment, the standard of living and the distribution of income, the form of industrial structure, and the re-establishment of international trade and finance. His proposals for post-war employment policy included measures for influencing consumption expenditure countercyclically along the lines of his *Consumers' Credits and Unemployment* (1938), which he had written before he left Oxford. The Beveridge committee on social insurance and allied services provided him with an opportunity to put forward a detailed scheme for variations in the rate of social security contributions as a means of stabilizing the demand for labour. He tried it out first on Keynes, who had sympathetically reviewed his book in the *Economic Journal*, before submitting it to the committee. Although Meade's scheme did not appear in the Beveridge report, it was included as an appendix to the white paper *Employment Policy* in May 1944.

Meade wrote the first draft, in March 1943, of what eventually became the employment white paper. Adverse Treasury reaction meant it had a long and circuitous route to travel. Keynes, less pessimistic than Meade about the possibility of post-war depression, was not entirely sympathetic either, but he endeavoured to educate his Treasury colleagues to the necessity of a macroeconomic employment policy. When a small steering committee, including the permanent secretary of the Treasury, Sir Richard Hopkins, and the director of the economic section, Lionel Robbins, managed at last to produce an agreed report, Keynes commented that it was 'indeed an outstanding State Paper which, if one casts one's mind back ten years or so, represents a revolution in official opinion' (*The Collected Writings of John Maynard Keynes*, 27, 1980, 364).

Meade was also a founding father of the General Agreement on Tariffs and Trade (later the World Trade Organization). Early in the war, before he left Geneva, he had written a short book, *The Economic Basis of a Durable Peace* (1940), dedicating it at Christmas 1939 to his children. Believing that a satisfactory peace settlement would require the existence of an international organization, he considered the economic role that such an organization would need to play in the post-war world. He favoured an international bank with the power to issue an international currency against which individual countries would peg their exchange rates but be able to adjust the pegs if the pursuit of high employment policies threatened persistent losses of reserves. The countries adhering to these international arrangements would have to commit themselves to multilateral free trade and payments arrangements. Hence when Keynes produced his 'clearing union' plan for the post-war international currency system, Meade proposed a complementary 'international commercial union' to restore multilateral trade and remove trade restrictions after the war. Dalton, now president of the Board of Trade in the wartime coalition government, took this up enthusiastically, and arranged for Meade to be seconded part-time to his department. The Keynes and the Meade plans formed the basis of the British contributions to the wartime Anglo-American discussions on the post-war international economic order; Meade crossed the Atlantic for the first time to take part in the talks in Washington in September–October 1943.

Further discussions led to the Anglo-American *Proposals for Consideration by an International Conference on Trade and Employment*, published in December 1945. Meade served as a British representative on the preparatory commission for the conference, which met in London in 1946 and in Geneva in 1947 to produce a draft charter for an International Trade Organization. The ITO Charter adopted at the Havana conference in March 1948 was not ratified, but its main principles were incorporated in the General Agreement on Tariffs and Trade negotiated in Geneva in 1947.

In November 1944 Meade had been persuaded to succeed Robbins as director of the economic section at the end of the war; he took over officially in January 1946. When he agreed to serve, he had high hopes of what government economists could achieve on both domestic and international economic policy fronts; he also thought he might be able to pursue his academic ambitions by writing a new edition of his *Economic Analysis and Policy*. But in the event his position did not give him the chance to influence domestic economic policy in the directions he wished it to go. Dalton, chancellor of the exchequer in the first majority Labour government, decided to pursue a policy of low interest rates much further than Meade thought safe. This was only one of several issues on which they disagreed—and on which Dalton did not heed Meade's advice. Meade's macroeconomic conception of 'economic planning', which was essentially the use of financial policy to influence aggregate demand, was adopted by Dalton's successor Stafford Cripps, several months after Meade had resigned in frustration and ill health in the spring of 1947. As two of his former colleagues put it, Meade

> was advising the wrong minister at the wrong time. ...
> Moreover, he was uncomfortable in a world of physical
> controls when his vision was of a world of financial controls.
> ... Meade, more than any man—more than Keynes—was the
> prophet of demand management when the world was not
> yet ready for demand management. (Cairncross and Watts,
> 130)

London School of Economics Meade returned to academic life, this time to the London School of Economics (LSE), where Lionel Robbins had suggested he take the Cassel professorship of commerce with special reference to

international trade. Here, as a direct result of his wartime work on economic policy, he was to make his most lasting contributions to economic *theory*. His plan was to produce a '"Treatise on Economic Policy" (probably in five or six volumes)' which would cover much the same ground as his pre-war textbook but reflect his experience in government (Meade to Robbins, 3 June 1947, BPLES, Robbins MSS). Since he had been hired to teach international economics, he began on his planned last volume, on international economic policy.

Meade did not follow the conventional order of writing on trade before finance. He began by constructing a general-equilibrium comparative static model for an economy open to trade and capital flows, synthesizing Keynesian and classical theory and extending it in order to analyse the effects of different policy instruments and other variables on internal and external balance. Since his 'method of work ... [was] to make a simple mathematical model of most of the problems before writing about them' in simple prose, the result appeared in a book, *The Theory of International Economic Policy, Volume 1, The Balance of Payments* (1951), with a separate mathematical supplement containing the model, which also appeared in journal articles. The first systematic exploration of the relationship between domestic and international equilibrium, Meade's model became 'part of the baggage of every economist' (Corden and Atkinson, 529), the most important single influence behind the development of open economy macroeconomics in the next four decades.

The Theory of International Economic Policy, Volume 2: Trade and Welfare (1955) was equally pathbreaking. It made at least three major and lasting contributions to economics: a fundamental reformulation of the theory of economic welfare to make it both operational and more widely applicable; the use of this new theory to analyse controls on factor movements as well as controls on trade; and the extension of the analysis from two-country models to a many-country world, including its application to the theory of customs unions. Meade originally drafted much of the book on the basis of the 'new welfare economics' of the late 1930s but he rewrote it to utilize (and expand on) the method of his former wartime colleague Marcus Fleming's 'On making the best of balance of payments restrictions on imports' (published in the *Economic Journal*, 1951).

> It was a brilliant feat of imagination ... to realize ...
> [Fleming's method] was capable of large-scale generalization
> into a powerful tool for welfare analysis of practical policy
> problems, and an act of great intellectual honesty and
> courage for him to scrap his existing draft and rework the
> whole problem on the new approach. (Johnson, 73)

Meade was awarded the Nobel memorial prize in 1977, jointly with the Swedish international economist Bertil Ohlin, for the work in the two volumes.

Throughout his LSE years Meade wrote extensively on topical issues of economic policy. To the public debate in England on planning he contributed *Planning and the Price Mechanism: the Liberal-Socialist Solution* (1948): he argued persuasively for the restoration of the market system and the use of financial policy instruments which work through the price mechanism for the control of inflation and deflation. He also urged the use of taxation, including if necessary and feasible a capital levy, to promote a more egalitarian distribution of income and wealth. In several papers on current international economic arrangements he made clear his then unfashionable preference for flexible exchange rates as the best way to reconcile free trade, domestic full employment, and external balance.

Cambridge and retirement In 1957 Meade succeeded Dennis Robertson as professor of political economy in Cambridge. He and his family now made their home in a Cambridgeshire village, first Hauxton and then Little Shelford. In his first Cambridge decade, as well as making important contributions to the theory of economic growth and income distribution, he recommended his ambitious project of a multi-volume treatise on economic policy. He had completed two volumes of his *Principles of Political Economy* (1965 and 1968) before he decided to resign the chair in 1968. He had not been made welcome by the Cambridge Keynesians, for whom he was too 'neo-classical'—being prepared, as he told students, to use 'Classical and Keynesian analysis and any old tools which seem to be relevant' to economic problems (personal knowledge). With a research fellowship from his college, Christ's, and the continuing intellectual support of younger Cambridge colleagues, he produced two more volumes of *Principles* (1972 and 1976) before the temptations of policy-orientated collaborative research made him less single-minded about the theoretical project. What might have formed the fifth volume appeared as a political tract, *The Intelligent Radical's Guide to Economic Policy* (1975), dedicated like *Planning and the Price Mechanism* to his wife.

Meade returned to macroeconomics in 1978 to lead a major research project on 'stagflation' in the department of applied economics at Cambridge. He had long been concerned with the inflation problem in a fully employed economy (his well-known Cambridge inaugural lecture had been on the subject), and had reconsidered the concept of internal balance he had used in *The Balance of Payments*. He now had three policy targets in mind: the balance of payments, full employment, and price stability. He proposed a 'New Keynesian' assignment of policy instruments to these targets: monetary and fiscal policy to maintaining total money expenditure (nominal GDP [gross domestic product]), reform of wage-fixing arrangements to full employment, and exchange rate policies to the balance of payments. While his younger collaborators worked on the design of the appropriate demand-management policies, he concentrated on the reform of wage-fixing arrangements.

On the wage-fixing front Meade explored several avenues over two decades. From the outset he rejected the extreme 'solutions' of incomes policies and union bashing. He came eventually to advocate the system he found in Agathotopia. As he explained:

I recently set sail to visit the island of Utopia … But, alas, I could find the island Nowhere. However on my way home I chanced to visit the island of Agathotopia. The inhabitants made no claim for perfection in their social arrangements, but they did claim the island to be a Good Place to live in. I studied their institutions closely, came to the conclusion that their social arrangements were indeed about as good as one could hope to achieve in this wicked world, and returned home to recommend Agathotopian arrangements for my own country. (Meade, *Liberty, Equality and Efficiency*, 1993, 104)

Agathotopia had a widespread structure of labour–capital partnerships rather than capitalist firms; it also had a government committed to maintaining the desirable rate of growth of money GDP; and an ingenious set of arrangements for encouraging a more equal distribution of income and wealth. As Meade had realized at least thirty years earlier, the use of flexible factor prices to ensure efficient employment of all resources could lead to unacceptably low wages; it was necessary deliberately to separate the problem of employment from the problem of distribution by providing, for instance, a basic income or 'social dividend' to all citizens, as well as a more equal distribution of property. Agathotopia was the closest Meade came to the solution of the problem of the dual function of the price mechanism, which means that the prices of goods and factors of production that promote the most efficient use of resources might well produce an unacceptably unequal distribution of income from those resources. His concern for both efficiency and equality, spelt out most clearly in *Efficiency, Equality and the Ownership of Property* (1964), was a feature of the two 'Meade reports', *The Economic and Social Structure of Mauritius* (1961) and *The Structure and Reform of Direct Taxation* (1978).

Meade was always youthful in appearance as well as in spirit. In old age he looked more youthful than in photographs of his middle age: the abandoning of thick-rimmed glasses meant that the eyes sparkling with intelligence, good humour, and tolerance were more readily seen. He was a man of integrity and optimism, and cynicism was foreign to his nature; in spite of his experiences in Whitehall he never abandoned his belief in the ability of men and women to make for themselves a better society. A modest man—though justifiably proud of his achievements—he disliked honours and declined a knighthood on leaving government service; he was made a companion of the Bath in 1947. Elected a fellow of the British Academy in 1951, he served as chairman of section F in 1957, and as president of the Royal Economic Society in 1964–6. Among his many talents were a fine baritone singing voice and his woodworking skills, which he put to good effect in making ingenious mechanical toys for his children and grandchildren. He died at his home, 40 High Street, Little Shelford, Cambridgeshire, on 22 December 1995, of multiple myeloma, and was cremated at Cambridge on 29 December. He was survived by his wife and four children.   SUSAN HOWSON

Sources private information (2004) · personal knowledge (2004) · *WWW*, 1991–5 · H. G. C. Salmon, ed., *The Malvern College register, 1865–1924* (1925) · A. Deaton, 'John Richard Nicholas Stone, 1913–1991', *PBA*, 82 (1993), 475–92 · A. Cairncross and N. G. M. Watts, *The economic section, 1939–1961: a study in economic advising*

(1989) · W. M. Corden and A. B. Atkinson, 'James E. Meade', *International encyclopaedia of the social sciences, biographical supplement, volume 18*, ed. D. L. Sills (1979), 528–32 · S. Howson, *British monetary policy, 1945–51* (1993) · H. G. Johnson, 'James Meade's contribution to economics', *Scandinavian Journal of Economics*, 80 (1978), 64–85 · J. Meade, 'Impressions of John Maynard Keynes', *Keynes and the modern world: proceedings of the Keynes Centenary Conference, King's College, Cambridge* (1983), 263–6 · *The collected papers of James Meade*, ed. S. Howson, 1–3 (1988); 4: *The cabinet office diary, 1944–46*, ed. S. Howson and D. Moggridge (1990), vols. 1–3 · *The wartime diaries of Lionel Robbins and James Meade, 1943–45*, ed. S. Howson and D. Moggridge (1990) · L. S. Pressnell, *External economic policy since the war*, 1: *The post-war financial settlement* (1986) · D. Vines, 'Meade, James Edward', *The new Palgrave: a dictionary of economics*, ed. J. Eatwell, M. Milgate, and P. Newman, 4 vols. (1987) · W. Young and F. S. Lee, *Oxford economics and Oxford economists* (1993) · *The Times* (28 Dec 1995) · *The Guardian* (28 Dec 1995) · *Financial Times* (28 Dec 1995) · *New York Times* (28 Dec 1995) · *The Independent* (29 Dec 1995) · *Daily Telegraph* (29 Dec 1995) · *International Herald Tribune* (29 Dec 1995) · *The Economist* (6 Jan 1996), 72 · W. M. Corden, 'James Meade, 1907–1995', *Economic Record*, 72/217 (June 1996), 173 · D. Greenaway, 'The intelligent radical on economic policy: an essay on the work of James Edward Meade', *Scottish Journal of Political Economy*, 37 (1990), 288–98 · S. Howson, 'James Meade', *Economic Journal*, 110 (2000) · b. cert. · m. cert. · d. cert.

Archives BLPES, diaries, corresp. and papers · PRO, Treasury MSS, 7230 | BLPES, Dalton MSS · BLPES, Durbin MSS · BLPES, corresp. with the editors of the *Economic Journal* · BLPES, Robbins MSS · BLPES, comments on papers by Z. A. Silberston relating to the Scitovsky Paradox · BLPES, corresp. with Lady Rhys Williams · King's Cam., Keynes MSS · Trinity Cam., Robertson MSS · United Nations Library, Geneva, League of Nations archives | SOUND BL NSA, recorded lecture

Likenesses W. Stoneman, photograph, 1951, NPG [*see illus.*] · L. Woon, cibachrome print, 1990, NPG · photograph, repro. in *The Times* · photograph, repro. in *The Guardian* · photograph, repro. in *The Independent* · photograph, repro. in *Daily Telegraph* · photographs, priv. coll.

Wealth at death £648,760: probate, 1996, *CGPLA Eng. & Wales*

Meade [Mead], **Matthew** (1628/9–1699), clergyman and ejected minister, was born at Leighton Buzzard, Bedfordshire, the second son of Richard Meade of Mursley, Buckinghamshire, and his wife, Joane. After studying at Eton College (1645–8), he was elected a scholar at King's College, Cambridge, where he was admitted as a fellow on 6 August 1649. He resigned on 6 June 1651, possibly to avoid expulsion for refusing to take the engagement to the Commonwealth. Between 1653 and 1657 he was involved in a dispute over the rectory of Great Brickhill, Buckinghamshire, which (despite support from within the parish and from the triers, who dispatched a troop of horse to back up their presentation of him to the living) he ultimately lost.

Meade married Elizabeth Walton (d. 1707) of All Hallows parish, Lombard Street, London, on 3 January 1655 at St Mary Woolnoth, London. The same year he became morning lecturer at St Dunstan and All Saints, Stepney, where he associated with William Greenhill, the vicar, and on 28 December 1656 he joined the gathered congregation of which Greenhill was pastor. About August 1656 Meade wrote to Richard Baxter, whom he did not know, expressing his admiration for *Gildas Salvianus* and asking Baxter's advice on which books of philosophy and divinity to read,

Matthew Meade (1628/9–1699), by Robert White, 1683

subjects where he admitted his knowledge did not match his competence in Hebrew, Latin, and Greek. Meade became an assistant to the Buckinghamshire commission on 29 September 1657 and the Middlesex commission on 24 October 1657. Cromwell appointed him curate of New Chapel, Shadwell, near Stepney, in January 1658, and on 1 February 1659 he became a lecturer at St Bride's, Fleet Street. After the army dissolved the restored Rump Parliament in October 1659, on the 31st, Meade, Greenhill, John Owen, and sixteen other Independents sent a delegation to ascertain George Monck's intentions. Appointed preacher to the council of state on 16 January 1660, Meade was assigned lodgings at Whitehall on the 31st.

Ejected from his positions at the Restoration, Meade continued to preach. In his prefatory epistle to *Spiritual Wisdom Improved Against Temptation*, a sermon preached at Stepney on 16 September 1660, he indicated he had been accused of sedition for having averred that worship according to the Book of Common Prayer was sinful. Following Thomas Venner's Fifth Monarchist uprising in January 1661, Meade and Greenhill had to take out recognizances of £300 each for their good behaviour. With William Dell, George Cokayne, and five other nonconformist ministers, Meade published *An English-Greek Lexicon* in the same year. That summer, as lecturer at St Sepulchre, Holborn, he preached seven sermons on Acts 26: 28, seeking to unmask hypocrites and awaken 'the formal sleepy professor'; the sermons were published as *En oligōi Christianos: the Almost Christian Discovered* (1662). The informer Edward Potter deemed Meade one of the 'Chief Ringleaders' among London nonconformists (PRO, SP 29/43/107). Ejected from his lectureship at St Sepulchre in 1662, Meade preached his farewell sermon, *The Pastors Valediction* (1662), on 1 Corinthians 1: 3, exhorting his audience to suffer rather than conform.

Meade subsequently visited the Netherlands, but he was apparently back by 1665. In *Solomon's Prescription* (1666) he depicted the plague as 'Medicine for a distempered Nation' (sig. A3r) and vowed to preach despite the government's efforts to silence him. The following year, in *An Appendix to Solomon's Prescription*, he blamed England's calamities on the restraints imposed on dissenting clergy and called for an indulgence and protestant unity. On 21 February 1669 he became Greenhill's assistant at Stepney, and the same year they preached to a conventicle of 300 in Meetinghouse Alley, Wapping. Archbishop Gilbert Sheldon's survey also linked him to an Independent church at Woburn, Bedfordshire, and a congregation of presbyterians, Independents, and Baptists at Sibson, Leicestershire. His reputation reached to Massachusetts, where on 21 August 1671 a group of magistrates and clergy wrote to him, Greenhill, Owen, and sixteen others seeking help for Harvard College.

Following Greenhill's death the Independent church at Stepney called Meade as its pastor on 13 October 1671, and on 14 December Owen, Joseph Caryl, George Griffith, and John Collins ordained him. The church inaugurated a new meeting-house on 13 September 1674, complete with four pine columns donated by the Dutch states general. Earlier that year he preached the first of what would become annual May day sermons for young people. Found guilty in king's bench of violating the Five Mile Act and fined £40 in 1678, he filed a writ of errour, which the court rejected because the judgment had not been entered on the plea roll. When he sought relief from the king, the House of Lords upheld the verdict on 10 July.

Undeterred Meade continued to preach and in November 1681 he, Owen, and nine other dissenters were fined a total of £4840 for recusancy and violating the Five Mile Act. At Tunbridge Wells in July 1682 the printer Henry Hills heard Meade, Griffith, and other nonconformist ministers denounce popery and arbitrary government. For preaching to five conventicles at his house in October and November 1682, Meade was fined £180 at the Middlesex sessions, and in December a magistrate and his guards damaged Meade's meeting-house and distrained his goods, though Meade escaped. In the ensuing days he completed an expanded version of his 1681 and 1682 May day sermons, *The Good of Early Obedience* (1683), with an epistle, dated 15 November 1682, to Lady Diane Alington.

Following the disclosure of the Rye House Plot the government issued a warrant for Meade's arrest on 27 June 1683. With the dissenting minister Walter Cross and the conspirator Zachary Bourne he was apprehended as he attempted to flee the country; one E. M. provided an account of his capture in *A Copy of a Letter* (1683). Examined by the privy council in July, Meade admitted having used the alias Matthew Richardson to avoid arrest, acknowledged that John Nisbet, an agent of the radical covenanters known as the United Societies, had lived in his home eight or nine months, and confessed having had contact with the plotter Robert Ferguson. Meade was suspected of having administered a 'sacramentall Oath of Secrecy to diverse persons in Wapping' (U. Nott. L., MS PwV95, fol. 250), but he almost certainly knew nothing of the conspiracy of Robert West and others to assassinate Charles and James, a point confirmed by Bourne. Meade claimed he had criticized Ferguson for writing in opposition to the government. However, he apparently knew about the plans of the Monmouth cabal for an insurrection, as the duke, West, and (under torture) William Carstares testified. In mid-July Meade, suffering from a stone, petitioned Charles for pardon and release, expressing remorse for having opposed the government. A warrant for his release dated 27 July stipulated that he appear in king's bench in Michaelmas term, and he was freed on the 30th after being bound over on his recognizance of £2000 and providing two sureties.

Following Owen's death, Meade succeeded him as lecturer at Pinners' Hall, London, in September 1683, a position which he held until his own death. Charged at the Middlesex sessions in December 1683 with recusancy and attending conventicles, Meade was ordered to conform and publicly confess. In October 1684 he was among 111 dissidents in London and Westminster targeted for arrest. The following year Ferguson recruited him to help raise London for Monmouth. The duke wanted Meade, John Wildman, and Henry Danvers to launch an insurrection as soon as royalist troops left for the south-west but Meade, now increasingly cautious, was dilatory in returning from Essex and failed to assist Monmouth. He evaded arrest by fleeing to the Netherlands in October with the help of Sir John Thompson, the former whig MP.

At first Meade was openly hostile to James's regime, proclaiming in Amsterdam 'that Babylon might be destroyed in England & her brats dasht against the walls' (BL, Add. MS 41818, fol. 125v). However, by April 1686 he had repudiated his militancy and was defending the royal prerogative and dissuading English merchants from settling abroad. This probably explains why the exiled Monmouth rebel Joseph Tiley opposed his appointment as minister to the English clothworkers in Leeuwarden. Before moving to Utrecht in June, Meade preached a farewell sermon in Amsterdam criticizing the use of violence to oppose princes or reform the church. That summer he sought the assistance of the English envoy Bevil Skelton in obtaining a pardon, manifesting his loyalty by praying for James II so fervently 'that all the whiggish auditory were amazed' (BL, Add. MS 41813, fol. 233v).

Pardoned on 19 March 1687, Meade returned to England, and in November preached before the lord mayor at Grocers' Hall. On 31 January 1689 he preached thanksgiving sermons for William's victory in the merchants' lecture at Broad Street and to the Independent church at Stepney.

Published as *The Vision of the Wheels* (1689), the sermons described the revolution as a work of providence. His return to Stepney prompted the congregation to add galleries to their meeting-house in March 1689 and give him an adjoining house and garden in July. He wrote an epistle for Cotton Mather's funeral sermon commemorating his brother, *Early Piety, Exemplified in the Life and Death of Mr. Nathanael Mather* (1689).

Meade devoted his final years to the cause of nonconformist unity. In 1690 he joined the presbyterian minister John Howe in promoting the Happy Union of Independents and Presbyterians, and the Common Fund to assist needy ministers, subscribing £100 and serving as correspondent for Bedfordshire, Gloucestershire, Kent, Leicestershire, Middlesex, Oxfordshire, and Lancashire. On 6 April 1691 he preached the inaugural sermon for the Happy Union in his meeting-house on Ezekiel 37: 19. Published as *Two Sticks Made One* (1691), it included his argument that 'Divisions are very dishonourable to Jesus Christ' (p. 15). His ecumenical outlook was also reflected in the fact that two of the young men who had lived and studied with him, John Nesbit and James Peirce, became Independent and presbyterian ministers respectively. In 1692 Meade published *A Funeral Sermon* for Thomas Rosewell, minister at Rotherhithe. Theological differences led to the disintegration of the Happy Union in 1694, but in December 1695 Meade helped found the Congregational Fund Board to aid needy clergy. With Howe, he wrote an epistle to David Clarkson's *Sermons and Discourses* (1696), and he preached the funeral sermon for the London minister Timothy Cruso, published as *Comfort in Death* (1698).

Meade died on 16 October 1699, aged seventy, and was buried in Stepney churchyard—Howe's sermon on the occasion was published as *A Funeral Sermon for … Matthew Mead* (1699). Meade was survived by his widow and seven of their thirteen children, Matthew, Samuel, Robert, Richard *Mead (a physician), James, Rebecca (Shrimpton), and Elizabeth. In his will, dated 28 September 1699, he bequeathed more than £2800, houses in London, property in Buckinghamshire, stock in the East India Company, and part-ownership of a ship to his wife, children, grandchildren, and three servants. An anonymous elegy also marked his death: *Tristiae Christianae* (1699). Several of his works were posthumously published: *The Young Man's Remembrancer, and Youth's Best Choice* (3rd edn, 1701), his last two May day sermons, and *Original Sermons on the Jews; and on Falling into the Hands of the Living God* (1836). An uncompromising nonconformist for nearly four decades, Meade was deeply concerned for protestantism's future in England. His support for Monmouth, his enthusiastic embrace of William, and his efforts on behalf of nonconformist unity were manifestations of that concern.

RICHARD L. GREAVES

Sources PRO, SP 29/43/107, 57; 29/427/25, 98; 29/428/137; 29/429/168; 29/431/108; 44/54, 185 · *Calamy rev.*, 347–8 · BL, Add. MS 4107, fol. 39a · BL, Add. MS 41803, fol. 337r–v · BL, Add. MS 41812, fol. 208v · BL, Add. MS 41813, fols. 113v–114r, 233v, 249v · BL, Add. MS 41818, fols. 103r, 108r · BL, Add. MS 41819, fols. 162v, 240r–v · *CSP dom.*, 1655–6, 34, 60–61; 1659–60, 310, 338, 350; 1660–61, 471; *Jan–June 1683*, 357; *July–Sept 1683*, 14–15, 31, 53–4, 57, 63, 80, 129, 164, 191, 195, 198; *1684–5*, 146; *1686–7*, 393 · R. L. Greaves, *Secrets of the kingdom: British radicals from the Popish Plot to the revolution of 1688–89* (1992) · [T. Sprat], *Copies of the informations and original papers relating to the proof of the horrid conspiracy against the late king, his present majesty and the government*, 3rd edn (1685) · *JHL*, 13 (1675–81), 243–4, 254, 281 · *Ninth report*, 2, HMC, 8 (1884), 116 · *Report on the manuscripts of the marquis of Downshire*, 6 vols. in 7, HMC, 75 (1924–95), vol. 1, p. 276 · A. Gordon, ed., *Freedom after ejection: a review (1690–1692) of presbyterian and congregational nonconformity in England and Wales* (1917) · *Calendar of the correspondence of Richard Baxter*, ed. N. H. Keeble and G. F. Nuttall, 1 (1991), 221 · *Journal of the Hon. John Erskine of Carnock*, ed. W. Macleod, Scottish History Society, 14 (1893) · J. C. Jeaffreson, ed., *Middlesex county records*, 4 vols. (1886–92), vol. 4, p. 182 · *The correspondence of John Owen (1616–1683)*, ed. P. Toon (1970), 149–51 · *DNB* · G. F. Nuttall, 'Stepney Meeting: the pioneers', *Transactions of the Congregational Historical Society*, 18 (1956–9), 17–22 · Greaves & Zaller, *BDBR*, vol. 2 · will, PRO, PROB 11/453, sig. 192 · [J. Howe], *A funeral sermon [on 1 Tim. IV. 16] for … M. Mead* (1699)
Archives Bodl. Oxf., sermon notes, MS Rawl. E.120 | BL, Add. MSS 4107, 10600–10601, 41803, 41812, 41818, 41819 · DWL, Baxter corresp. MS 59, vol. v, fol. 59 · PRO, state papers, domestic, ser. 29 and 44 · U. Nott., Portland MSS PwV 95
Likenesses R. White, line engraving, 1683, BM, NPG [*see illus.*] · R. White, line engraving, *c.*1689, BL · J. Nutting, line print, 1699, NPG
Wealth at death over £2800; houses in London (probably in Buckinghamshire); stock in the East India Company; part ownership of a ship: will, PRO, PROB 11/453, sig. 192

Meade, Richard Charles Francis Christian, third earl of Clanwilliam (1795–1879), diplomatist, was born in Dublin on 15 August 1795, the only son of Richard Meade, second earl of Clanwilliam (1766–1805), and his first wife, Caroline (d. 1800), third daughter of Joseph, Count Thun, and his wife, Wilhelmina. He succeeded to the title in September 1805. After education at Eton College he entered the diplomatic service at an early age. In August 1814 he attended Lord Castlereagh, plenipotentiary at the Congress of Vienna, and in February of the following year was there with Castlereagh's half-brother, Lord Stewart. He was private secretary to Castlereagh at the Foreign Office from 5 January 1817 to 11 July 1819, and acted as undersecretary for eighteen months before being formally appointed to the office on 22 January 1822. On 12 August of the same year he resigned in order to become *chef de chancellerie* to the mission at the Congress of Verona of the duke of Wellington, with whom he became quite closely associated. Clanwilliam served as envoy-extraordinary and minister-plenipotentiary at Berlin from 1 February 1823 to 25 December 1827, and was created grand cross of the Royal Guelphic Order (GCH) in 1826. In a letter dated 14 August 1827, from Sir Henry Hardinge to the duke of Wellington, Clanwilliam was described as 'up to his neck' in the preliminary arrangements for the formation of the Goderich ministry, but incredulous as to its duration. On 28 January 1828 he became a peer of the United Kingdom by the title of Baron Clanwilliam of Tipperary. He took little part in public affairs after this date, though he followed Wellington in supporting Catholic emancipation in 1829. The degree of DCL was conferred on him by Oxford University on 11 June 1834, at the start of Wellington's chancellorship.

Clanwilliam married, on 3 July 1830, Lady Elizabeth Herbert (1809–1858), daughter of George Augustus *Herbert, eleventh earl of Pembroke; they had four sons and one daughter. The eldest son, Richard James *Meade (1832–1907), succeeded to the peerage, and was a distinguished naval officer; another son, Sir Robert Henry *Meade (1835–1898), was an eminent civil servant. Clanwilliam died at his house, 32 Belgrave Square, London, on 7 October 1879, having lately returned from Deal Castle, of which he was captain.

G. Le G. Norgate, *rev.* H. C. G. Matthew

Sources *Morning Post* (8 Oct 1879) · *ILN* (18 Oct 1879) · GEC, *Peerage* · *Despatches, correspondence, and memoranda of Field Marshal Arthur, duke of Wellington*, ed. A. R. Wellesley, second duke of Wellington, 8 vols. (1867–80)
Archives PRO NIre., diaries, corresp., and papers | BL, corresp. with third Viscount Melbourne, Add. MSS 60411–60415 · NL Scot., letters to Lord Stuart de Rothesay · PRO, corresp. with Stratford Canning, FO 352 · RA, corresp. with Thomas Lawrence · U. Southampton L., letters to duke of Wellington · U. Wales, Swansea, letters to Sir Robert Meade
Likenesses G. Hayter, group portrait, oils (*The trial of Queen Caroline, 1820*), NPG · attrib. Lawrence, oils (as a young man), Pen-y-Ian, Meifod, Montgomeryshire · G. F. Watts, oils, Uppark, West Sussex
Wealth at death under £250,000: probate, 15 Jan 1880, *CGPLA Eng. & Wales*

Meade, Richard James, fourth earl of Clanwilliam (1832–1907), naval officer, born on 3 October 1832, was the eldest son in the family of four sons and a daughter of Richard Charles Francis Christian *Meade, third earl of Clanwilliam (1795–1879), and his wife, Lady Elizabeth (1809–1858), the eldest daughter of George Augustus Herbert, eleventh earl of Pembroke. After Eton College he entered the navy (17 November 1845); he passed his examination in November 1851 and was promoted lieutenant on 15 September 1852. In December of that year he was appointed to the frigate *Impérieuse*, in which he served during the whole of the Crimean War. The *Impérieuse* was senior officer's ship of the advanced squadron and followed up the ice and established the blockade of the Gulf of Finland as early in the spring as possible, and before the navigation was thought safe for heavy ships. In September 1856 Lord Gillford (as he was known until 1879) was appointed to the *Raleigh* bound for the China station, and when the *Raleigh* was wrecked near Hong Kong on the passage out he joined Captain Keppel and with him took part in the boat actions of Escape Creek on 25 May 1857 and of Fatshan (Foshan) Creek on 1 June. In August he was appointed to the *Calcutta*, flagship of Sir Michael Seymour, and in December he landed with the naval brigade before Canton (Guangzhou). At the storming of Canton on 29 December Gillford was severely wounded in the left arm by a bullet fired from a gingal; he was mentioned in dispatches, and on 26 February 1858 was promoted commander and appointed to the *Hornet*, which he took to England.

On 22 July 1859 Gillford was promoted captain. From 1862 to 1866 he commanded the *Tribune* in the Pacific, and from October 1868 to 1871 the battleship *Hercules* in the channel. He married on 17 June 1867 Elizabeth Henrietta (d. 31 March 1925), the eldest daughter of Sir Arthur Edward *Kennedy, governor of Queensland; they had four

sons and four daughters. In 1872 he became an aide-de-camp to Queen Victoria, and was given the command of the steam reserve at Portsmouth. On the formation of Disraeli's ministry in 1874 he joined the Board of Admiralty as junior sea lord, and continued at Whitehall until the change of government brought in a new board in May 1880. He was promoted to flag rank on 31 December 1876, received the CB in June 1877, and succeeded to the earldom on 7 October 1879. From 1880 to 1882 Clanwilliam had command of the flying squadron. He was appointed vice-admiral on 26 July 1881 and made KCMG in March 1882. From August 1885 to September 1886 he was commander-in-chief on the North America and West Indies station, laying down the command in consequence of his promotion to admiral on 22 June 1886. In June 1887 he was raised to KCB, and in 1888 he became a commissioner of the Patriotic Fund. He was commander-in-chief at Portsmouth from June 1891 to June 1894, was promoted admiral of the fleet on 20 February 1895, received the GCB in May 1895, and reached retirement age on 3 October 1902. He was a Conservative in politics.

According to one of his messmates, Clanwilliam throughout his life was before everything a sailor, and probably valued his admiral's rank much more than his title. He 'affected the tight, very short jacket' of an earlier naval age and had 'a certain roughness of manner, which was at times rather puzzling to his subordinates' (*The Times*, 5 Aug 1907). He died of pneumonia on 4 August 1907 at Badgemore, Henley-on-Thames, and was buried on 8 August in the family vault at Wilton, near Salisbury. Clanwilliam's eldest son, Richard Charles, Lord Gillford (1868–1905), entered the navy, was made lieutenant in 1891, was flag lieutenant to Sir George Tryon in the *Victoria* in 1893, but left the navy shortly afterwards. The second son, Arthur Vesey Meade, Lord Dromore (1873–1953), succeeded to the earldom; the third, Herbert Meade-*Fetherstonhaugh (1875–1964), entered the navy and reached the rank of commander in 1908; and the youngest, Edward Brabazon, was a captain in the 10th hussars.

L. G. C. Laughton, *rev.* Roger Morriss

Sources *The Times* (5 Aug 1907) · *The Times* (9 Aug 1907) · Burke, *Peerage* · *WWW*, 1897–1915 · G. S. Graham, *The China station: war and diplomacy, 1830–1860* (1978) · GEC, *Peerage*
Archives PRO NIre., journal, corresp., and papers
Likenesses R. Lehmann, portrait, exh. RA 1899 · V. Prinsep, oils, c.1899 (after R. Lehmann), Uppark, West Sussex · oils, c.1899 (after R. Lehmann), HMS *Mercury* · Spy [L. Ward], chromolithograph cartoon, repro. in *VF* (22 Jan 1903) · engraving
Wealth at death £249,730 18s. 8d.: probate, 12 Oct 1907, *CGPLA Eng. & Wales* · £2117 13s. 5d.—in Ireland: probate, 29 May 1908, *CGPLA Ire.*

Meade, Sir Robert Henry (1835–1898), civil servant, second son of Richard *Meade, third earl of Clanwilliam (1795–1879), and of his wife, Lady Elizabeth (d. 1858), daughter of George *Herbert, eleventh earl of Pembroke, was born on 16 December 1835, and educated at Harrow School and at Exeter College, Oxford, where he matriculated on 7 December 1854, graduating BA in 1859 and MA in 1860. On 1 June 1859 he entered the Foreign Office with the encouragement of his uncle, Sidney *Herbert. He was dispatched to Syria with Lord Dufferin's special mission on 31 July 1860; on his return in September 1861 he was selected to accompany the prince of Wales in his tour through Palestine and eastern Europe in 1861–2. In the autumn of 1862 he accompanied Earl Russell to Germany in attendance upon the queen. On 27 November 1862 he was appointed a groom of the bedchamber to the prince of Wales. In 1863 he accompanied Earl Granville abroad with the queen.

In June 1864 Meade became private secretary to Earl Granville as president of the council, and was with him until July 1866; he then resumed his work in the Foreign Office. When Lord Granville became, on 10 December 1868, secretary of state for the colonies, Meade accompanied him as private secretary to the Colonial Office. On 21 May 1871 Meade was appointed to an assistant under-secretaryship of state in the Colonial Office; from this time he devoted himself to the duties of his post which chiefly concerned colonies not possessing responsible government, the supervision of the West Indian and Eastern department, as well as financial and defence issues. In March 1883 he was offered, but declined, the position of permanent under-secretary at the Irish Office. He was a British delegate to the Berlin conference in December 1884. He there entered into negotiation with the German foreign ministry and with Prince Bismarck over African and Pacific issues. In 1885 he helped establish the interdepartmental colonial defence committee and later served on and sustained it.

In February 1892 Meade became permanent under-secretary for the colonies under Lord Knutsford, and subsequently served under Lord Ripon and Joseph Chamberlain. Later his health became indifferent; he was anxious to retire in 1895, but stayed on at the request of the secretary of state for a year longer. This was the period of the Jameson raid in South Africa which caused much work and worry. However, towards the end of 1896 he fell and broke his leg one evening while boarding a bus after leaving his office. He never returned to his work. Ill health and the sudden death of his daughter, Mary, in 1897 broke him down completely. She was the only child of his first marriage, on 19 April 1865, to Lady Mary Elizabeth, daughter of Henry Lascelles, third earl of Harewood. Mary Elizabeth died on 7 February 1866. Meade was married again, on 13 April 1880, to Caroline Georgiana, daughter of Charles William Grenfell MP, of Taplow Court, Maidenhead. She, too, died within a year of their marriage, on 5 March 1881, following the birth of a son, Charles Francis. Meade died on 8 January 1898 at the Grand Central Hotel, Belfast. He was buried at Taplow, near Maidenhead. He became CB on 21 March 1885, KCB in 1894, and GCB in 1897.

Meade had considerable practical common sense and much tact, and was also a man of peculiar charm, greatly liked by all who knew him. He was one of a knot of official Liberals who formed a little coterie in the service of the crown from about 1870 to 1890.

C. A. HARRIS, rev. LUKE TRAINOR

Sources *The Times* (10 Jan 1898) · Boase, *Mod. Eng. biog.* · *FO List* (1895) · *Colonial Office List* (1895) · Burke, *Peerage* · personal knowledge (1901) · L. Trainor, 'Policy making at the colonial office: Robert Meade, the Berlin conference, and New Guinea', *Journal of Imperial and Commonwealth History*, 6 (1977–8), 119–43 · L. Trainor, *British imperialism and Australian nationalism: manipulation, conflict, and compromise in the late nineteenth century* (1994) · private information (2004) · *Daily Free Press* (12 Jan 1898) · L. Trainor, 'The liberals and the formation of imperial defence policy, 1892–5', *BIHR*, 42 (1969), 188–200

Archives PRO, Colonial Office records · PRO NIre., diaries, corresp., and papers · U. Wales, Swansea, corresp. and papers | Balliol Oxf., corresp. with Sir Robert Morier · BL, corresp. with Lord Carnarvon, Add. MS 60796 · BL, Gladstone MSS · BL, corresp. with Lord Ripon, Add. MSS 43556–43558 · Bodl. Oxf., corresp. with Lord Kimberley · National Library of South Africa, Cape Town, letters to Sir Graham Bower · PRO, Granville MSS · PRO NIre., Blackwood MSS · PRO NIre., letters to Lord Dufferin · U. Birm. L., corresp. with Joseph Chamberlain

Likenesses attrib. Hills & Saunders, photograph, 1863, NPG · prints, repro. in *ILN* (15 Jan 1898) · prints, repro. in *London Figaro* (6 Jan 1892), 10

Wealth at death £53,825 16s. 11d.: probate, 31 March 1898, *CGPLA Eng. & Wales*

Meades, Anna (*bap.* 1734, *d.* in or before 1779?), novelist, was baptized in Fordingham, Hampshire, on 18 October 1734, the daughter of Frances Blachford (*d.* 1780) and the Revd William Meades (1700–1780), rector of All Saints' Church, Rampton, Cambridgeshire. Her brother William was baptized in Rampton on 12 March 1738. In her early youth Meades travelled frequently between her home in Cambridgeshire and London and Bath. Between the ages of nineteen and twenty-two she continued to travel frequently, living in such places as Lombard Street, London, Rampton, and Northaw, Hertfordshire. During these years she wrote two novels: *The history of Cleanthes, an Englishman of the highest quality and Celemene, the illustrious Amazonian princess*, published anonymously in 1757, and *The History of Sir William Harrington*, published anonymously and perhaps posthumously in 1771, which she originally planned to entitle 'A Description of Modern Life'.

Meades wrote to Samuel Richardson on 19 January 1757, signing herself Cleomira and asking him to sell her book, written in imitation of his works. Richardson declined the request, explaining that he was a publisher, not a bookseller, but the letter marked the beginning of a correspondence (that lasted until August 1758) in which they discussed Meades's two novels as well as her personal life. At Meades's request Richardson read and commented on her first novel, *The History of Cleanthes*; written in imitation of old romances it contains histrionic accounts of shipwrecks, royalty, slavery, and romance. Richardson praised her 'fine imagination' but predictably censured the novel because 'a due attention is not always given to Nature & Probability'. Meades apologized for her youthful excesses, explaining that she had been only nineteen when she wrote it. She visited Richardson at least twice, and by 18 August 1757 was on friendly enough terms with him to sign herself 'your Anna'.

In May 1757 Richardson read and offered editorial suggestions on Meades's second novel, *The History of Sir William Harrington*. This epistolary novel, about virtuous women who reform their rakish paramours, is certainly imitative of Richardson in both style and content but the extent to which Richardson's revisions were incorporated into the final version has been a subject of controversy since its initial publication. The title-page to the first edition presented the novel as 'revised and corrected by the Late Mr. RICHARDSON', and the *Monthly Review* (March 1771) likewise described it as 'written some years since, and revised and corrected by the late Mr. Richardson'; but Richardson's daughters placed a newspaper advertisement claiming that they held all of his correspondences and that he had not participated in its composition. However, the editor of the novel's second edition reasserted Richardson's influence on its composition, stating that his 'notes and emendations, in his own handwriting, were left for many months with Mr. Bell the bookseller, for general inspection'. In 1935 William Sale used Richardson's manuscript notes and letters to prove for the first time that Anna Meades had been the novel's author; he further argued that the notes indicated Richardson's influence on the novel's composition. However, Richardson's 1971 biographers, Eaves and Kimpel, found no evidence that Richardson's remarks were actually used by Meades or the editor who published the book. Against this view John Dussinger argued in 1996 that, although Meades was perhaps unable to complete Richardson's emendations (either because she had married or because she had died), her editor—probably Thomas Hull, first thought to be the novel's author—incorporated many of Richardson's suggestions into his own substantial revisions, perhaps after her death. He suggested that the Ann Meeds, aged twenty-five, who married James Stamp, a mariner aged twenty-six, at St Botolph, Aldersgate in London in 1762 was in fact Anna Meades. Her absence from her father's will of 1779 suggests that she was dead by that date.

ANNA LOTT

Sources J. Dussinger, 'Anna Meades, Samuel Richardson and Thomas Hull: the making of *The history of Sir William Harrington*', *New essays on Samuel Richardson*, ed. A. J. Rivero (New York, 1996) · letters between Samuel Richardson and Anna Meades, BL, Add. MS 28097 · T. C. D. Eaves and B. D. Kimpel, *Samuel Richardson: a biography* (1971) · A. D. McKillop, *Samuel Richardson: printer and novelist* (1936) · W. M. Sale, *Samuel Richardson: a bibliographical record of his literary career with historical notes* (1936) · *Critical Review*, 31 (1771) · J. Todd, ed., *A dictionary of British and American women writers, 1660–1800* (1984) · *Monthly Review*, 44 (1771), 262–3 · IGI

Archives BL, corresp. with Samuel Richardson, Add. MS 28097 · BL, Richardson's critical remarks on *The history of Sir William Harrington*, Add. MS 28097

Meadley, George Wilson (1774–1818), biographer, was born at Sunderland, co. Durham, on 1 January 1774, the only son of Abraham Meadley and Alice Wilson. His father died in 1775, and his mother soon afterwards moved with her five children to the adjoining town of Bishopwearmouth where Meadley resided for the rest of his life. In 1783 he was placed at the grammar school of Witton-le-Wear, under the Revd John Farrer; he had a remarkable memory and a turn for rhyme, which he cultivated until 1791. At the end of 1788 Meadley was apprenticed to a Mr Chipchase (afterwards alderman), a banker and general dealer at Durham, where he spent his spare time writing poetry (some of which was published in provincial papers), and became involved in debates about abolition of the slave trade and the French Revolution. These inspired him to become an ardent liberal in politics.

After leaving Durham in 1793 Meadley remained at home, learning Italian, improving his French, and founding a subscription library at Sunderland (1795) with the help of his old schoolmaster, now rector of Sunderland. In March 1795 he made the acquaintance of William Paley DD, then made rector of Bishopwearmouth. Next year Meadley went on a mercantile voyage to the Levant. He visited Naples, Smyrna, and Constantinople, collected a library of books, fell into the hands of the French on his return voyage, and was for some time a prisoner in Spain. On his return to England he learned German, and made further mercantile voyages to Danzig (1801) and Hamburg (1803), travelling thence on foot with a friend through north Germany (see accounts in *Monthly Magazine*, 14, 127 ff., 218 ff., 412 ff.). By now disgusted with trade he devoted himself to a literary life.

Three years after Paley's death (1805) Meadley began to collect materials for his biography, applying, among others, to John Disney DD, who introduced him to Thomas Jervis. His association with these men led to his adoption of Unitarian views. The first edition of his *Memoirs* of Paley was entirely rewritten before publication, on the advice of a friend who criticized its florid style. When bringing out a second and amended edition he spent the winter (1810–11) in Edinburgh to see it through the press. Here he attended the moral philosophy lectures of Thomas Brown. In 1812 he published *A Sketch of … Proposals for … Reform in Parliament*, which was printed without his knowledge and with some amendments in Wooler's edition of Bentham's catechism. A biography of Algernon Sydney, a work in keeping with his political principles, followed. He also produced short memoirs of his friends Mrs Jebb and the Revd Robert Waugh, and of Robert Clark, a Sunderland surgeon, for the *Monthly Repository*. In 1814 Meadley publicly announced his secession in *A Letter to the Bishop of David's*. He wrote a second letter in 1816 after he was mistakenly thought to be becoming a deist.

In 1818 Meadley returned from literary researches in London and the south of England suffering from a 'hepatic affection'. It was said that he was a large man, and that his 'natural inactivity and his studious habits had led him to indulge' (*Monthly Repository*, March 1819, 141). He was working on biographies of John Hampden and Disney, and had ready for press a sketch of the political character of Sir William Jones, and a parallel between Bonaparte and Rienzi when he died at Bishopwearmouth on 28 November 1818. He had never married. He was buried in the churchyard of Holy Trinity, Sunderland, and a marble tablet to his memory was placed in the Sunderland Subscription Library. An attempt at the annual meeting (2 February 1819) to have this tablet removed, because of Meadley's religious views, led to an angry local controversy.

Meadley is remembered as unprepossessing but 'cheerful ... and affectionate' with strong ethical and religious convictions (*Monthly Repository*, March 1819, 142). His immediate posthumous reputation suffered; a reader of the *Monthly Repository* felt that Meadley's 'claims to literary eminence' had been overemphasized and some critics judged his memoirs as 'not abundant in novelty' (*Monthly Repository*, August 1819, 465; January 1819, 121). But he has recently been praised by Paley scholars (see LeMahieu) and his biography of Paley served as the basis for subsequent work.

ALEXANDER GORDON, *rev.* CLARE L. TAYLOR

Sources *Monthly Repository*, 14 (1819), esp. Jan, March and Aug issues · D. L. LeMahieu, *The mind of William Paley: a philosopher and his age* (1976) · IGI

Archives CUL, interleaved copy of *Memoirs of William Paley*, with annotations · N. Yorks. CRO, corresp. with Christopher Wyvill

Meadowbank. For this title name *see* Maconochie, Allan, of Meadowbank, Lord Meadowbank (*bap.* 1748, *d.* 1816); Maconochie, Alexander, Lord Meadowbank (1777–1861).

Meadowcourt, Richard (*c.*1695–1760), Church of England clergyman and literary critic, the son of Richard Meadowcourt, was born at Worcester. He matriculated at Merton College, Oxford, on 9 March 1710, graduated BA in 1714, and proceeded MA in 1718. He was also elected one of six whig fellows at Merton College in 1718. This happened at a time when there was great pressure to elect tories as fellows (Ward, 99–100).

Meadowcourt's university experience included membership of the whig-orientated Constitution Club, in which he served as the club steward. Founded by students with whig proclivities, the club sought to oppose perceived treasonous attitudes at the university on the part of the tories, then dominant at Oxford. Meadowcourt's involvement with the group led to a two-year delay in the granting of his MA. Nicholas Amhurst's *Terrae filius* (1726) alleged that Meadowcourt was disciplined for fomenting rebellion against the university. He was fined 40s. for being out after 9.00 p.m., and also had his name placed in the proctor's black book, which meant that he would not receive his degree until giving satisfaction to the proctor. Allegedly these actions were taken because he drank to the health of King George I. He finally received his degree in 1718 on the basis of a royal decree of grace (Amhurst, 116–20, 130–1, 284).

Meadowcourt's political and religious positions, including his flirtation with Bangorianism, delayed his long-sought preferment in the church. His ecclesiastical career began only in 1727, when he was appointed vicar of Oakley, Buckinghamshire. He was passed over for the nomination as warden of Merton College in 1734, but on 15 October 1735 he was instituted a canon of the cathedral at Worcester. Following this appointment Meadowcourt was able to add to his preferments the vicarage of Quinton, Gloucestershire, in 1738 and the rectory of St Martin's, Worcester, in 1738. In 1751 he received his final preferment, as vicar of Lindridge, Worcestershire. He resided at

Lindridge until he died, apparently unmarried, on 8 September 1760.

Meadowcourt's literary career was marked by the publication of eleven sermons, including *The Nature of Truth Defin'd, and it's Definition Apply'd to the Holy Scriptures* (1724; 2nd edn, 1725), and *Popery disarmed of those weapons of force, and those instruments of fraud, in which it chiefly trusts* (1740). The latter sermon was preached at the cathedral at Worcester on 5 November 1739. He also devoted attention to the literary world, especially John Milton. His *Critique of Milton's 'Paradise Regain'd'* (1732; 2nd expanded edn, 1748) is considered by modern scholars to be the first critical study of Milton's epic poem, precipitating a 're-evaluation of the brief epic' (Wittreich, vi, xiv). In Bishop Thomas Newton's edition of *Paradise Regain'd* (1752), Meadowcourt provided manuscript remarks and explanations for several difficult lines in the poem. Although he was an early Milton scholar, modern scholars have questioned his insight into the work. One has suggested that 'there is little penetration in Meadowcourt's analysis of the characters of the poem', and has concluded that the 'frankness and outspokenness of this artistic utilitarianism and classicism is that of a clergyman apparently more intent on professional sermonizing and instruction than on the study of literary subtleties' (Oras, 221).   ROBERT D. CORNWALL

Sources Foster, *Alum. Oxon.* · N. Amhurst, *Terrae Filius, or, The secret history of the University of Oxford*, 2nd edn (1726) · J. Wittreich, ed., *Milton's 'Paradise regained'* (1971) · W. R. Ward, *Georgian Oxford: university politics in the eighteenth century* (1958) · A. Oras, *Milton's editors and commentators from Patrick Hume to Henry John Todd, 1695–1801* (1931); repr. (New York, 1964) · *Fasti Angl., 1541–1857*, [Ely] · P. Langford, 'Tories and Jacobites, 1714–1751', *Hist. U. Oxf.* 5: *18th-cent. Oxf.*, 99–127 · *GM*, 1st ser., 30 (1760), 443

Meadowes, John (1675/6–1757). *See under* Meadows, John (1622–1697).

Meadows, Alfred (1833–1887), obstetric physician, was born at Ipswich on 2 June 1833, the fourth child of Charles Meadows. After attending Ipswich grammar school Meadows began his medical career as an apprentice to Mr William Elliston, of Ipswich. In 1853 he matriculated at the University of London and entered King's College medical school, where he was first associate, and then fellow. In 1856 he became MRCS and LRCP; he also obtained the midwifery licence of the Royal College of Surgeons. In 1857 he graduated MB of the University of London; he became MD in 1858, MRCP in 1862 and FRCP in 1873. On 29 April 1858 he married Sara Stirling Davidson (*b.* 1832/3), daughter of Major James Davidson; they had one daughter.

On qualifying Meadows was appointed to the posts of house physician and resident midwifery assistant at King's College Hospital, and he spent the winter of 1857 in Paris. He subsequently held a large number of appointments, achieving a degree of celebrity which earned for him a long list of honorary memberships of foreign societies. The more important appointments were at King's College Hospital, where he was elected assistant physician for diseases of women and children in 1860, and at the Hospital for Women, Soho Square, to which he was physician from 1865 until his resignations in 1874; he was also physician accoucheur to the General Lying-in Hospital. His career reached its zenith in 1871, when he was elected physician accoucheur and lecturer on the diseases of women and children at St Mary's Hospital; he held this post until his death.

Meadows was an active fellow of the Obstetrical Society of London: he held several of the various appointments on council and won general praise for his work as secretary. However, he left the society after failing to be elected president in 1884 as a result of his belief that ovariotomies ought to be performed by obstetricians rather than left to general surgeons. Meadows considered that the removal of healthy ovaries was a useful sterilization procedure in cases where childbirth would endanger a woman's life. He also thought it preferable to mechanical methods of contraception. The dispute over ovariotomy led to the establishment of the British Gynaecological Society in December 1884, and Meadows was elected its first president. He was also corresponding member of the German, Swedish, and Boston gynaecological societies. In 1878 he attended the crown prince of Sweden while he visited England: in recognition of his services, the king of Sweden in 1881 made him a commander of the second class of the order of Vasa.

Meadows was the author of the *Prescriber's Companion* (1864), a work that went through many editions, and of a *Manual of Midwifery* (1870), well known to a generation of students and teachers; the second edition of this text was translated in 1875 into Japanese. He revised and enlarged Thomas Hawkes Tanner's *Practical Treatise on the Diseases of Infancy and Childhood* (1870) and published *Clinical Memoirs on the Diseases of Women* (2 vols., 1866–7), translated for the New Sydenham Society from the work by Gustave Bernutz and Ernest Goupil, thus making accessible to the British profession one of the most important contemporary works on inflammatory and other diseases of the pelvic peritoneum in women. He also founded and edited the short-lived *London Medical Review* in 1860.

Meadows was a skilful practitioner and had a kindly nature, and was much respected by patients and colleagues alike. His personal and professional qualities ensured his professional success, and he built up a lucrative private practice. A Conservative in politics, he held his religious beliefs with conviction and actively promoted the Guild of St Luke, of which he was provost. He was JP for Buckinghamshire, where he owned a house, Poyle Manor, near Colnbrook. A well known and energetic freemason, Meadows took a leading part in founding the University of London lodge and was an officer of the grand lodge of England, of which he became master.

Meadows died suddenly on 19 April 1887, of enteritis, at his home, 27 George Street, Hanover Square, London, and was buried at Colnbrook on 23 April. He was survived by his wife.   D'A. POWER, *rev.* ORNELLA MOSCUCCI

Sources *BMJ* (23 April 1887), 914 • *The Lancet* (30 April 1887), 908 • *British Gynaecological Journal*, 3 (1887–8), 343–5 • *DNB* • m. cert. • d. cert. • O. Moscucci, *The science of woman: gynaecology and gender in England, 1800–1929* (1990), 149–50, 171–2 • CGPLA Eng. & Wales (1887)

Likenesses Barraud & Jerrard, photograph, 1873, Wellcome L. • photograph, repro. in *British Gynaecological Journal*, 343
Wealth at death £15,416 2s. 5d.: administration with will, 11 June 1887, CGPLA Eng. & Wales

Meadows, Drinkwater (1793×9–1869), actor, is said to have been born in Yorkshire in 1799, though his gravestone suggests that he was born in 1793 or 1794. He was intended for the navy but joined a theatrical company established in Kendal, and played in various towns in Westmorland and Yorkshire. Subsequently he became a member of another company, playing in Lincoln, Leicester, Peterborough, and Birmingham, in which town he was seen and engaged by Charlton, the manager of the Bath theatre. Meadows made his first appearance at Bath in November 1817 as Fogrum, in Morton and Bishop's musical drama *The Slave*. He later played a wide variety of roles, including Scrub in *The Beaux' Stratagem*, Adam Winterton in *The Iron Chest*, Solomon Lob in *Love Laughs at Locksmiths*, and in 1819–20, Ratcliffe in *The Heart of Midlothian*, First Gravedigger in *Hamlet* to Kean's Hamlet, and Slender in *The Merry Wives of Windsor*. In September 1821 he made his first appearance in London, at Covent Garden, as Scrub. Here he played his old characters, and was also seen as Crabtree in *The School for Scandal* and Filch in *The Beggar's Opera*. In following seasons he was given plenty of opportunities to play original roles, such as Timothy Quaint in Howard Payne's *The Soldier's Daughter* and Raubvogel in Planché's *Returned Killed*, as well as such parts in revivals as Launcelot Gobbo in *The Merchant of Venice*, Shallow in *The Merry Wives of Windsor*, Stephen in Jonson's *Every Man in his Humour*, and Squire Richard in Cibber's *The Provoked Husband*.

Meadows remained at Covent Garden until 1844, being the original Fathom in Sheridan Knowles's *The Hunchback* in 1832 and the following year the original Bartolo in *The Wife* by the same author. In 1836 he was the original Philippe in George W. Lovell's *The Provost of Bruges* at Drury Lane, but then returned to Covent Garden, where in September 1842 he made a success as a miserly old clerk in Lovell's *Love's Sacrifice* and played one of the witches in *Macbeth*. On 18 July 1842 he married, at the British embassy in Paris, Georgina Caroline Pridham, the youngest daughter of Admiral Pridham; they had two sons. In 1844 Meadows acted under the management of the Keeleys at the Lyceum (1844–7), and remained there under the succeeding management of C. Mathews. After joining the Kean and Keeley management at the Princess's he was Boaz in Douglas Jerrold's *The Prisoner of War*, first given at Windsor Castle, under Charles Kean's direction, in January 1851; and the original Joe Harrup, a toothless old huntsman, in Boucicault's *Love in a Maze*. He remained at the Princess's under Harris until his retirement in 1862. He died at his home, Prairie Cottage, The Green, Barnes, on 12 June 1869, and was buried in Barnes cemetery on 17 June. A careful, retiring man, shunning publicity, he was much respected but little noticed. While he was a careful, conscientious, and trustworthy actor, he was lacking in inspiration, homely, dry, and quaint in style. He was seen to most advantage in eccentric comedy. For thirty-four years he was secretary to the Covent Garden Theatrical Fund. He occasionally contributed some recollections and other articles to the press.

JOSEPH KNIGHT, rev. NILANJANA BANERJI

Sources The Era (20 June 1869) · Hall, Dramatic ports. · The Athenaeum (19 June 1869), 832 · J. W. Cole, The life and theatrical times of Charles Kean … including a summary of the English stage for the last fifty years, 2 vols. (1859) · Genest, Eng. stage
Likenesses R. J. Lane, lithographs, NPG · R. J. Lane, two engravings, NPG · W. Meadows, lithograph, NPG · H. Meyer, oils (as Raubvogel in Returned killed), Garr. Club · portrait, repro. in Oxberry's Dramatic Biography
Wealth at death under £1500: probate, 8 July 1869, CGPLA Eng. & Wales

Meadows, John (1622–1697), clergyman and ejected minister, was born at Chattisham, near Ipswich, Suffolk, on 7 April 1622, the second son of Daniel Meadowe (1577–1651) of Chattisham and his wife, Elizabeth Smith of Wickham Market (d. 1678); Sir Philip *Meadows (bap. 1626, d. 1718) the diplomat was his younger brother. On 26 February 1640 he was admitted at Emmanuel College, Cambridge, and graduated BA early in 1644. He moved to Christ's College on 23 December that year, taking up one of the fellowships made vacant there by the parliamentary commissioners, and proceeded MA in 1647. Following the death of his father in 1651 Meadows inherited substantial property, including the manor and advowson of Witnesham, and that year he resigned his fellowship.

In 1653 Meadows married Anne, daughter of Roger Rant of Swaffham Prior, Cambridgeshire, who brought him an estate at Exning, Suffolk. On 26 August that year he settled at Ousden Hall, the home of his patron Humphrey Mosely, where he was provided with a study. Meadows was ordained to the ministry at Ousden on 17 April 1657 by three ministers of the county, William Pickering of Denham, Jonathan Jephcot of Swaffham Prior, and Abraham Wright of Cheveley, and was approved by the commissioners for approbation (or triers) at Whitehall on 7 May 1658. Ejected on 24 August 1662 under the Act of Uniformity, he was soon forced to vacate the parsonage, recording on 1 October that his wife had gone to live at Ousden Hall. The death of his patron did not result in any abrupt change for Meadows, and John Greene, his successor in the rectory, inducted on 8 August 1663, was friendly (or circumspect) enough to store property for him as late as July 1665. Meadows was joined at Ousden Hall by his mother, who was permitted to stay until her death, aged almost eighty, in 1678. Meadows himself lived there (at a rent of £3 per annum paid from 1665) only until 21 October 1670, when he and Anne went to lodge with a Mr Crane, Anne Meadows died soon afterwards.

By 1672 Meadows had moved to Stowmarket where the sympathetic merchant Thomas Blackerby had his business. There, under the indulgence of that year, he took out licences as a presbyterian teacher, both at his own house and that of Elizabeth Nelson. In 1675 he married Sarah (1654–1688), daughter of Benjamin Fairfax (d. 1708) of Halesworth, Suffolk, and granddaughter and niece of three ejected ministers, Benjamin Fairfax (1592–1676),

John *Fairfax (1623/4–1700), and Nathaniel *Fairfax (1637–1690).

In 1680 Meadows was prosecuted for nonconformity and bound over by the judges of the sessions. About 1688, perhaps on the death in that year of his wife, Sarah, he moved to Bury St Edmunds, where (it must be supposed) he married his third wife, Hannah Beaumont (d. 1707). At Bury he was an occasional conformist and friend of Samuel Bury, the Presbyterian minister. Meadows used part of his considerable wealth to assist less fortunate Independent and Presbyterian ministers. He died at Bury St Edmunds in 1697 and was buried in the churchyard at Stowmarket on 1 March. In his will (proved 7 April 1697) he left property in fourteen Suffolk parishes, including the advowsons of Witnesham and Exning. His second marriage had produced seven children, notably Philip (1679–1752), mayor of Norwich in 1734, and **John Meadowes** (1675/6–1757), Presbyterian minister, who was born at Stowmarket and attended schools at Stowmarket and at Bury St Edmunds before being admitted, aged eighteen, to Gonville and Caius College, Cambridge, on 25 May 1694. Although a scholar between 1694 and 1698, there is no record of his taking a degree. He married Sarah, daughter of Robert Chaplin. Ordained to the Presbyterian church at Needham Market, Suffolk, on 26 August 1702, he served there for the rest of his life. His The Apostolic Rule of Ordination appeared in 1738. He died on 10 April 1757 and was buried at Barking.

ALEXANDER GORDON, rev. STEPHEN WRIGHT

Sources Calamy rev., 348, 189–90 · E. Taylor, The Suffolk Bartholomeans: a memoir of the ministerial and domestic history of John Meadows (1840) · Venn, Alum. Cant. · A. Gordon, ed., Freedom after ejection: a review (1690–1692) of presbyterian and congregational nonconformity in England and Wales (1917) · G. Hollingsworth, The History of Stowmarket (1844) · will, Suffolk RO, R 2/73/190 (JS 45/46–190)
Likenesses A. Fox, portrait, repro. in Taylor, Suffolk Bartholomeans

Meadows, (Joseph) Kenny (bap. 1790, d. 1874), illustrator and caricaturist, was born at Cardigan in south Wales and baptized on 1 November 1790, the son of James Meadows, a retired naval officer. He grew up living simply in a lighthouse; always hungry, he 'used to devour [his] food like a ravening wolf' (Dalziel and Dalziel, 38). His family's slender means prevented him from obtaining much education. Self-taught and learning from the 'wishy-washiness' of the likes of Finden's Book of Beauty (Linton, 72), he was handicapped by his poor training and sometimes resented it. Like many other black and white artists of his day, Meadows preferred to draw from his imagination rather than from models: 'Nature puts me out', he told the Dalziel brothers (Dalziel and Dalziel, 41). By 1823 he had moved to London, where that year he collaborated with George Scharf in designing and lithographing the plates for James Robinson Planché's five-part edition illustrating the costume of six of Shakespeare's plays (1823–5). Meadows was one of the first to introduce wood-engraving among English publishers as a means of cheap and popular illustration, and he became a useful, unostentatious workman who supplied many cuts for newspapers, especially Herbert Ingram's Illustrated London News.

The publisher Henry Vizetelly described Meadows as 'a slow and not very regular worker', needing help at first from other artists in drawing landscapes (Vizetelly, 1.153). Often unoriginal, he none the less sometimes invented epigrammatic and witty images, such as 'Peace' represented by a butterfly at the mouth of a cannon (*Punch*, February 1844). He dropped his first name for reasons of 'professional distinction' (Spielmann, 447) and was known throughout his career as Kenny Meadows.

Meadows collaborated with Isaac Robert Cruikshank on *The Devil in London* (1832), and in the late 1830s he produced portraits of Dickens's characters (*Bell's Life in London*, 1838) and twenty-four portrait heads of characters in *Nicholas Nickleby* 'from drawings by Miss La Creevy' (6 parts, 1839). *The Heads of the People, or, Portraits of the English*, published in 1838–40, to which William Makepeace Thackeray, Douglas Jerrold, Laman Blanchard, and Leigh Hunt contributed letterpress, increased his popularity. The images range from the highest society ('The Young Lord') to the lowest ('The Farmer's Daughter'), and, while devoid of originality, they sold well and were republished in Paris in 1839 under the title *Les Anglais peints par eux-mêmes*, running in tandem with Paul Gavarni's superb *Les Français peints par eux-mêmes*. Thereafter he was much in requisition for portraits; for the *Illustrated London News* he drew the principal actors in Dickens's amateur theatrical company (22, 29 November 1845) and a memorable 'Old Father Christmas'.

The chief ambition of Meadows's life was to produce a complete illustrated Shakespeare. This he accomplished between 1839 and 1843 by designing upwards of 1000 plates for Barry Cornwall's three-volume edition (1843). His wit and graceful fancy here had free rein, and his designs were masterfully cut by W. J. Linton, John Orrin Smith, and his best pupil, Alfred Harral. Some found a few designs eccentric: in the late nineteenth century Graham Everitt complained that Richard III seemed to suffer 'from an attack of tetanus instead of an accession of mental terror' (Everitt, 361). But Meadows's contemporaries praised the work: 'almost poetical', the painter William Powell Frith called the pictures for *A Midsummer Night's Dream* (Frith, 2.103). And subsequent commentators in Britain and Germany have judged his Shakespeare plates 'astonishing', 'not to be missed', 'the best in the whole of the 19th century' (Muir, 54–5). So popular was his conception of Falstaff that a bronze statuette modelled after it in Germany sold in large numbers.

Thereafter Meadows's services were eagerly sought as an illustrator of holiday stories and children's books. Among his later productions, Percy Muir singles out the drawings for a nursery classic, Frances Browne's *Granny's Wonderful Chair* (1856), as deserving of a 'very special place' in book illustration (Muir, 133), and Everitt calls the wood-engravings for D. W. Jerrold's 'Chronicles of Clovernook' 'probably the finest designs he ever executed' (Everitt, 362). Meadows painted a few oil portraits; between 1830 and 1838 he exhibited once at the Royal Academy and on four occasions at the Suffolk Street gallery of the Society of British Artists. It is said that necessity forced him to paint a butcher's wife in order to pay off his bill, and that he added bits of jewellery on the barter system: a brooch for so many ribs of beef, a watch for chops and steaks, and so forth (Price, 43). In later life Meadows became an accomplished watercolourist.

Meadows associated intimately with the early *Punch* circle. His wife, Agnes (*bap.* 19 Aug 1800), the daughter of the eminent sculptor John *Henning, was 'a quiet, thrifty woman' (Spielmann, 447). Her brother was Archibald S. Henning, who designed the first *Punch* cover; Meadows provided the fifth. For the first seven years of *Punch*'s existence he supplied unoriginal but competent drawings; his landscapes were often better than his figures, which tended to 'puffy faces and straight arms' (Houfe). R. G. G. Price judged Meadows's best work to be 'more delicately fanciful than either [John] Leech's or [Richard] Doyle's' (Price, 42), but Meadows received little encouragement from Mark Lemon, the editor, perhaps because his humour was more poetic than robustly pointed. When the magazine developed a small stable of house artists Meadows was no longer employed.

Meadows was a genial, if sometimes temperamental, drinking companion. While working on Samuel Carter Hall's *Book of British Ballads* (1842), he and the other artists would gather at the Halls' home, The Rosery, Brompton, for 'small talk and smaller Marsala' and afterwards repair to a neighbouring tavern for a night-long carouse (Linton, 74). Despite his slight frame and chronic rheumatism, he was known as Iron Jack for his stamina and capacity to hold his liquor. Among Meadows's many friends were Blanchard, Dickens, John Gilbert, George Hodder (a nephew by marriage), Hunt, Jerrold, Charles and Edwin Landseer, Daniel Maclise, David Roberts, Clarkson Stanfield, Frank Stone, and Thackeray.

Meadows lived for some years in Cottage Place, Camden Town, and enjoyed afternoon rambles up to Highgate and Hampstead. Constantly in financial difficulties, in June 1864 he was granted a civil-list pension of £80 'in acknowledgment of his merit as an artist, more especially shown by his illustrations of Shakespeare' (*DNB*). He spent 'a hale and vigorous' old age (Heaton), outliving his reputation, as the obituarists noted ruefully. He died at 458 King's Road, Chelsea, on 19 August 1874; five days later he was buried, near his father-in-law, in the St Pancras cemetery at Finchley.

ROBERT L. PATTEN

Sources G. Everitt, *English caricaturists and graphic humourists of the nineteenth century* (1893) · R. K. Engen, *Dictionary of Victorian wood engravers* (1985) · S. Houfe, *The dictionary of British book illustrators and caricaturists, 1800–1914* (1978) · P. Muir, *Victorian illustrated books* (1971) · W. J. Linton, *Threescore and ten years, 1820–1890: recollections* (1894) · M. H. Spielmann, *The history of 'Punch'* (1895) · [G. Dalziel and E. Dalziel], *The brothers Dalziel: a record of fifty years' work … 1840–1890* (1901) · *DNB* · H. Vizetelly, *Glances back through seventy years*, 2 vols. (1893) · G. Hodder, *Memories of my time* (1870) · W. P. Frith, *John Leech*, 2 vols. (1891) · R. G. G. Price, *A history of Punch* (1957) · Graves, *Artists*, new edn · Boase, *Mod. Eng. biog.* · M. M. Heaton, *The Academy* (26 Sept 1874), 360 · *The Athenaeum* (5 Sept 1874), 326 · *Art Journal*, 36 (1874), 306–7 · Bryan, *Painters* (1930–34) · F. G. Kitton, *Dickens and his illustrators* (1899) · *The letters of Charles Dickens*, ed. M. House, G. Storey, and others, 12 vols. (1965–2002) · W. J. Linton, *The masters*

of wood-engraving (1889) · *The letters and private papers of William Makepeace Thackeray*, ed. G. N. Ray, 4 vols. (1945–6)
Likenesses L. B. Smith, oils, NMG Wales · L. B. Smith, watercolour, repro. in Spielmann, *History of 'Punch'*, 447

Meadows, Sir Philip (*bap.* 1626, *d.* 1718), diplomat, was baptized at Chattisham, Suffolk, on 4 January 1626, the fifth son of Daniel Meadows (1577–1651) of Chattisham and Elizabeth (*d.* 1678), daughter and coheir of Robert Smith of Wickham Market, and the grandson of William Meadows (*d.* 1588) of Witnesham. His grandfather's elder son, William Meadows, married the heir of Witnesham Hall, and his father bought the lordship of the manor in 1630. Philip was admitted to Emmanuel College, Cambridge, on 18 February 1642 and graduated BA in 1646. He proceeded MA from Queens' College, Cambridge, in 1649 and became a fellow.

Early career In 1653, on the recommendation of John Thurloe, Meadows was recruited as Latin translator to the council of state to assist the blind John Milton—Milton's preference for Andrew Marvell was overridden. On 17 October Meadows was chosen to assist Thurloe in foreign affairs as well, his salary doubled to £200 per annum, and he gave enough satisfaction to be confirmed as full 'Latin Secretary', Milton remaining 'Latin Secretary Extraordinary', in Thurloe's list of officials to the protectoral council of state on 3 February 1654 (*CSP dom.*, 1653–4, 386).

Meadows's growing knowledge of foreign affairs as Thurloe's assistant and his expertise in Latin were such that on 19 February 1656 the council advised Oliver Cromwell to appoint him envoy to Portugal to seek the ratification of the Anglo-Portuguese treaty of 1654. England's conflict with Spain, with which Portugal was also at war, meant that English warships needed access to Portuguese ports and that merchants excluded from Spain sought Portuguese markets. However, the treaty was contentious in Portugal as Cromwell had required the fervently Catholic government to accept the open practice of protestantism by English residents and had sought compensation for Portuguese aid to royalist privateers. Tension had been increased by the execution in London, following conviction for murder, of the Portuguese ambassador's brother, Dom Pantaleon de Sa, in defiance of his diplomatic immunity. Meadows was required to secure an immediate payment of £50,000 damages on penalty of attack, and sailed from Plymouth on the *Phoenix* on 11 March. However, King João VI proved obstinate, over both compensation and the opening of a protestant church in Lisbon, and in order to intimidate him Cromwell duly ordered his navy to seize the Portuguese 'plate fleet', en route for Lisbon. Vengeful relatives of Dom Pantaleon tried to shoot Meadows as he left the palace on 1 May; as it happened, he was only slightly injured in the hand, but the perpetrators were not arrested. Given Cromwell's high-handedness and the previous murders of Commonwealth ambassadors in Madrid and Holland, a violent English reaction and subsequent collapse of the treaty was probable. Meadows was instructed to give João five days to sign and then, if he refused, to join the English fleet, but in order to continue negotiations he delayed departing until the fleet anchored at Cascaes on 30 May. When Meadows then requested a farewell audience, the king promptly signed and provided the compensation. The envoy's gamble paid off, but he faced criticism from Admiral Robert Blake and his assistant Edward Mountagu for not leaving earlier. The money delivered, Meadows arrived on Mountagu's ship to be told Whitehall would have preferred him to cancel the negotiations. He wrote to Thurloe that the risks entailed in trying to find the plate fleet to retaliate outweighed the pecuniary advantage of capturing it, and that the personal insult to himself of the attack was better dealt with separately from national-level negotiations. His success was duly commended in England, and on 15 July the council voted him a ninety-nine-year lease on lands worth £100 'in consideration of the maim received … in execution of his duty' (*CSP dom.*, 1656–7, 22). There was, however, difficulty in finding lands, though confiscated episcopal estates were considered, and the case was still outstanding in August 1657. The money presumably helped Meadows in his subsequent purchase of an estate at Bentley, Suffolk.

Baltic diplomacy Meadows returned to England in November and resumed his duties as Thurloe's deputy; Marvell replaced him as Latin secretary in 1657. His diplomatic success led to the council's selecting him on 24 February 1657 for the equally difficult role of ambassador to Denmark at a time when Cromwell was endeavouring to keep the peace between the two leading protestant powers in the Baltic, Denmark and Sweden, to secure access to shipping supplies and to divert Charles X of Sweden's aggressiveness against exclusively Catholic targets. Meadows's allowance was to be an impressive £1000 per annum, but his departure was delayed by pressure of council business and the kingship debate, and in June Frederick III of Denmark declared war on Sweden. When Meadows was finally given his instructions, he was told to try to persuade Frederick that war only assisted Habsburg plans to weaken protestantism and endangered commercial access to the Baltic; he was to offer to mediate with Sweden to prevent Charles seizing more Danish territory. He sailed on the *Assistance* in August, a Mr. Sterry taking on his council duties, and was received honourably by Frederick at Copenhagen about 20 September. Frederick declared that he would accept 'equal and honourable terms' (Thurloe, *State papers*, 6.533), but Cromwell did not send Meadows detailed instructions, and when the Sound froze Charles was able in February 1658 to march his army over the ice on Copenhagen. Cromwell was personally sympathetic to Charles, but Meadows proceeded to the king's camp with the Dutch and French ambassadors to endeavour to moderate his demands. He shuttled between the Danish and Swedish commissioners, whose initial demands he reckoned 'both monsters, the one *in defectu* and the other *in excessu*' (ibid., 802–03), while Charles continued to advance, and claimed 'unless I make a peace, adieu Denmark' (Meadows, *A Narrative*, 59). Meadows rejected Charles's proposal to occupy all Norway on the grounds that it would give the Swedish king control of shipping materials vital to England, 'too great a treasure to be entrusted to one hand' (ibid.). The threat of England's combining with the Dutch finally persuaded Charles to accept at Roskilde on 8 March a peace founded on Sweden's occupation of both the Trondheim province (thus cutting Norway in two) and Denmark's last possession east of the Sound, Scania. Crucially, at Meadows's insistence, 'hostile' (ibid., 62) warships were banned from the Sound, rather than all foreign warships, a proposal which 'though immediately levelled against Holland, yet obliquely and remotely reflected upon England' (ibid.). Charles had allegedly paid Meadows 9000–10,000 rixdollars in an attempt to influence him, evidently without effect.

The treaty of Roskilde was Meadows's greatest achievement, but it only served as a temporary brake on Charles X's ambitions; Meadows commented that the sword which he presented to the king to use against the Habsburgs could easily be wielded against Brandenburg. He vainly begged Thurloe to send the outstanding £30,000 in aid promised to Sweden. In April he was sent to Charles's peace conference with Poland at Braunsberg to prevent any terms to England's disadvantage and to promote war against the Habsburgs. Charles used the peace to attack Denmark again in August, and Cromwell's death weakened England's position. Still attending the Swedish court as Charles attacked Copenhagen again that winter (while the Dutch and Brandenburg assisted Denmark), Meadows found Charles appealing for assistance which he could not give. In April 1659 Mountagu brought the English fleet out to join the Dutch, and Meadows sought to mediate on the basis of the Roskilde settlement. This foundation was accepted at The Hague negotiations in June, but the upheavals in England, illustrated by the dispatch of Algernon Sidney and other commissioners to watch Mountagu, diminished England's potential role, and in August the recall of most of the fleet undermined Meadows's bargaining position. He requested his recall, which the council of state granted on 23 August; the eventual peace of Copenhagen in 1660 was reached without him.

Restoration author Meadows had been knighted by Cromwell in the spring of 1658 in recognition of Roskilde and had been made knight marshal of the household, while Frederick III had knighted him in the order of the Elephant. However, Meadows returned to England to be evicted from his Whitehall lodgings (7 February 1660), though he was unmolested at the Restoration. On 4 April 1661 he was granted a licence to marry Constance Lucy, second daughter and eventual coheir of Francis Lucy of Westminster (from the Charlecote family). He retired to his new estate at Bentley, and had sufficient reputation to be knighted by Charles II on 24 November 1662; on 15 January 1664 the king granted him an augmentation to his arms in return for surrendering that assumed through his Danish knighthood. In 1669 Meadows was advising the deputy secretary of state, Joseph Williamson, on his recollection of the terms of the treaty of Copenhagen in 1660, saying that he had copies of all the treaties involving

France and the Dutch since 1621 in his possession. This collection was useful when he utilized his leisure to write on diplomacy; in 1677 he published *A narrative of the principal actions in the wars betwixt Sweden and Denmark before and after the Roskilde treaty*, including a view of the current Swedish involvement in Germany as it affected England. In 1681 he published *A Brief Enquiry into Leagues and Confederacies Made betwixt Princes and Nations*, with particular reference to England's abandoning the triple alliance to combine with France in destroying their confederate, Holland, and then abandoning France to make peace. He concluded that man was 'bound to the true and just performance' of contracts as 'declarative testimony' (*Scarce and Valuable Tracts … Lord Somers*, ed. Scott, 8.21–8) of private intentions, while accepting that princes could alter decisions as circumstances changed to protect their subjects; criticism of Charles II's vacillations was implied. In 1689 followed *Observations Concerning the Dominion and Sovereignty of the Seas*, a work influenced by John Selden, in which Meadows considered England's claim to salutation of the flag (with its inconsistencies and dangers), marine jurisdiction, and the theory of dominion of the seas.

Last years Having lived from 1666 partly in Newport Street, Covent Garden, in 1685 Meadows acquired a house in the new Gerrard Street development, and that April joined the commission set up to hasten the building of the parish church, St Anne's, Soho. In 1675 Danby reckoned that Meadows exercised influence on two Lucy relatives in parliament but he was not otherwise politically prominent. The revolution of 1688 brought him greater favour, and on 28 January 1692 he became a commissioner for public accounts. On 19 December 1695 he also became a commissioner for trade and the plantations, and remained active in the role into his eighties; in March 1696 he joined the commission for excise. In 1696 he advised the suspected Jacobite plotter Thomas, Lord Ailesbury, to give himself up to the secretaries of state; Ailesbury called him 'grave and ancient and formal, but he had a good and solid judgement' (*Memoirs of … Ailesbury*, 373). Meadows also concluded an important marriage alliance for his eldest son, Philip, with a niece of Sidney Godolphin. He resigned from the excise commission in November 1702 but remained a commissioner for trade, as of 1697 at a salary of £1000 per annum, until December 1715.

Meadows died at Hammersmith on 16 September 1718, his age variously given as ninety-three or ninety-four, and was buried at Hammersmith Chapel on 18 September; the menfolk of his family were frequently long-lived. Of his three daughters, Elizabeth married Sir Thomas Powis, Constance married Joseph Craggs, and the third married Richard Dyott, commissioner of stamp duties in 1708–10. A skilled, pragmatic diplomat, Meadows had played a major role in protectoral foreign relations in mitigating the effects of Cromwell's and Mountagu's desire to intimidate Portugal in 1656, helping to secure vital naval bases, and Cromwell's naive belief in Charles X's potential as an anti-Habsburg weapon in 1657–8. His success at Roskilde would have been impossible without French and Dutch backing and did not bind Charles X to Cromwell, but both there and with Portugal Meadows showed more realism than his master and his subsequent writings show a professional expertise in the subjects of international relations and naval power from which the Stuarts could have benefited.

Meadows's eldest son, **Sir Philip Meadows** (1662?–1757), diplomat and politician, was born almost certainly in 1662. On 30 August 1696 he married Dorothy (c.1675–c.1749), sister of Hugh Boscawen and niece of Lord Godolphin, at Lambeth, with Archbishop Thomas Tenison officiating; John Evelyn, congratulating Meadows senior, reckoned them 'a most virtuous discreet young virgin and as hopeful a young gentleman' (Evelyn, *Diary*, 5.258). On 4 August 1698 Meadows joined his father as a commissioner of excise (until March 1700), and on 27 June 1700 was appointed knight marshal of the king's household (a post held by his father under Cromwell) and marshal of the Marshalsea for life. Lord Jersey, who had disposed of the offices, was reckoned to have been paid about £5000. On 23 December Meadows was knighted at Hampton Court, and in 1703 added the clerkship of the green cloth to his emoluments.

In 1702 Meadows entered parliament as MP for Truro, a seat controlled by his brother-in-law Hugh Boscawen. As in his father's case, Whitehall office was the precursor to diplomacy and in January 1704 he became ambassador to Holland, an important position at a critical point in the war of Spanish Succession when William III's death had put the onus of maintaining the alliance on officials. At the 1705 general election Meadows was elected in his absence MP for Tregony, another Boscawen borough. In December 1706, having reportedly at first declined the honour, he was appointed special envoy to Vienna to maintain relations with another crucial ally, Emperor Josef I, and was awarded £500 for his equipage and £720 per quarter in his dual role as envoy and plenipotentiary. In this capacity he not only worked to maintain the military alliance but, as his father had, kept a watchful eye on protestant interests, making a determined protest to Josef in November 1708 against Habsburg persecution of Silesian protestants.

In June 1708, while he was still abroad, Meadows was appointed joint commissioner for army accounts; Richmond House in the Privy Garden, Whitehall, was fitted up as an office. He was replaced as ambassador by Lord Raby in August 1709, and on his return to London on 16 October took up his new duties. He also acquired the lease of a house between Richmond House and the Thames, and in January 1714 became a governor of the Royal Hospital, Chelsea. He was retained in office by George I with James Bruce as his colleague; Narcissus Luttrell reckoned him 'a worthy person, but not so vigilant as the other' (Luttrell, *Brief Relation*, 6.648). Clearly benefiting from nepotism but politically inoffensive to any of the whig factions, he remained in position until his death, living in Whitehall

until some time prior to 1738 and subsequently at Richmond and Brompton. He died at Brompton on 3 December 1757, aged ninety-five, leaving three sons and five daughters. His eldest son, Sydney (d. 1792), succeeded him as marshal of the household; his third son, Philip (d. 1781), deputy ranger of Richmond Park, married Frances Pierrepoint, through which arrangement their sons Evelyn and Charles became heirs to the extinct dukedom of Kingston.

TIMOTHY VENNING

Sources Thurloe, *State papers* · P. Meadows, *A narrative of the principal actions in the wars betwixt Sweden and Denmark before and after the Roskilde treaty* (1677) · *CSP dom.*, 1653–1702 · W. A. Shaw, ed., *Calendar of treasury books*, [33 vols. in 64], PRO (1904–69), vols. 9–11, 19–31 · N. Luttrell, *A brief historical relation of state affairs from September 1678 to April 1714*, 6 vols. (1857) · M. H. Cox and G. T. Forrest, eds., *The parish of St Margaret, Westminster*, 1–2, Survey of London, 10, 13 (1926–30) · *The parish of St Anne, Soho*, 2 vols., Survey of London, 33–4 (1966) · Venn, *Alum. Cant.* · Evelyn, *Diary*, vol. 5 · J. L. Chester and G. J. Armytage, eds., *Allegations for marriage licences issued by the bishop of London*, 2 vols., Harleian Society, 25–6 (1887) · BL, Harley MS 2263; Add. MSS 5131, 5132, 30211 · Burke, *Gen. GB* (1886), vol. 2 · *GM*, 1st ser., 27 (1757) [Sir Philip Meadows, d. 1757] · Burke, *Gen. GB* (1835) [Sir Philip Meadows, d. 1757] · Burke, *Peerage* (1907) [Sir Philip Meadows, d. 1757] · *Papers illustrative of the origin and early history of the Royal Hospital at Chelsea* (1872) [Sir Philip Meadows, d. 1757] · W. A. Shaw, *The knights of England*, 2 vols. (1906) [Sir Philip Meadows, d. 1757] · W. T. Lawrence, *Parliamentary representation of Cornwall* [n.d.] [Sir Philip Meadows, d. 1757] · D. Lysons, *Environs of London*, 2, vol. 2 · T. Faulkner, *Historical and topographical account of Fulham* (1813) · W. E. Buckley, *Memoirs of Thomas, earl of Ailesbury*, 2; Roxburghe Club, 122 (1890) · G. E. Aylmer, *The state's servants: the civil service of the English republic, 1649–1660* (1973) · *The manuscripts of the Marquess Townshend*, HMC, 19 (1887) · *The manuscripts of the House of Lords*, 4 vols., HMC, 17 (1887–94), vol. 3 · W. Scott, ed., *A collection of scarce and valuable tracts … Lord Somers*, 2nd edn, 8 (1812)

Archives BL, legal, diplomatic, naval tracts, Add. MSS · Bodl. Oxf., legal, diplomatic, naval tracts · Bodl. Oxf., pedigree, Tanner MS vol. CLXXX

Wealth at death house and estate at Bentley, Suffolk; house at 33 Gerrard Street, London; salary of £1000 p.a. in 1695–1715 · house at Brompton, Middlesex; Sir Philip Meadows: *GM*

Meadows, Sir Philip (1662?–1757). *See under* Meadows, Sir Philip (*bap.* 1626, *d.* 1718).

Meager, Leonard (c.1624–c.1704), gardener and writer on gardening, worked for Philip Hollman of Warkworth, Northamptonshire, and later at the Brompton Park nursery. His most popular work, which ran to eleven editions between 1670 and 1710, was *The English Gardener, or, A Sure Guide to Young Planters and Gardeners, in Three Parts*. This deals with fruit trees and the kitchen garden, and arranges plants in categories such as 'Herbs for setting knots' and 'Florist's flowers'. *The New Art of Gardening; with the Gardener's Almanack* (1697) was followed by *The mystery of husbandry, or, Arable, pasture, and wood-land improved; to which is added, the countryman's almanack* (1697), with 61 chapters in 61 pages on how to improve the soil. Meager died about 1704.

W. A. S. HEWINS, rev. ANNE PIMLOTT BAKER

Sources G. E. Fussell, 'Leonard Meager and the "Mystery of husbandry", 1697', *Journal of the Ministry of Agriculture*, 37/no. 9 (Dec 1930), 879–85 · J. Donaldson, *Agricultural biography* (1854), 38–40 ·

Desmond, *Botanists* · R. Girling, *The making of the English garden* (1988)

Meagher, Thaddeus de (1690–1765). *See under* Meagher, Thomas Francis (1823–1867).

Meagher, Thomas Francis (1823–1867), Irish nationalist and soldier, was born in the city of Waterford, at what is now the Granville Hotel, Meagher Quay, on 3 August 1823. Little is known of his mother apart from the fact that she was a member of the Quan family of Waterford. His father, Thomas Meagher (1796–1874), was, however, quite prominent. A prosperous merchant engaged in the New-foundland provision trade, he was elected mayor of Waterford in 1843 and 1844, and later represented the city in the British House of Commons, 1847–57. The marriage produced two other children, Henry Meagher JP (*d.* 1875) and Mary Agnes Meagher, who became a nun.

The Meaghers were a prominent family who had long held lands in the barony of Irrekin, Tipperary. They were gradually dispossessed, and the process was escalated after their open support for James II in 1689. Following the treaty of Limerick, 1691, many Meaghers left Ireland for service in Catholic Europe and distinguished among these was **Thaddeus** [Thadée] **de Meagher** (1690–1765). Sometimes referred to as Chevalier de Maar, he served in the French army and in 1734 was commissioned in the Saxon lifeguards of Frederick Augustus II, king of Poland and elector of Saxony. Appointed the king's chamberlain in 1739, he was promoted to colonel, 1740, appointed captain-proprietor of the Swiss guards, 1742, and advanced to the rank of major-general, 1744, and later lieutenant-general, May 1752, in the Polish army. At the beginning of the Seven Years' War, 1756, Frederick the Great of Prussia invaded Saxony, and de Meagher was dispatched to Wilsdruf to negotiate Saxony's neutrality with Frederick. General de Meagher died in Dresden on 22 May 1765.

Educated by the Jesuits at Clongowes Wood College, co. Kildare (1833–9), Thomas Francis Meagher later attended their college at Stonyhurst, Lancashire (1839–43). He returned to Waterford in 1843 with a lisping English upper-class accent, affected manners, and a taste for fine clothes. In 1844 he was sent to Queen's Inn, Dublin, to study law but quickly abandoned his studies for politics. He attached himself to the radicals of the Repeal Association, Young Ireland, who advocated a physical force solution to end the union with Britain. At an emotional meeting in Conciliation Hall, Dublin, on 28 July 1846, he made an impassioned speech asking the members not to 'abhor the sword' nor 'stigmatize the sword' but to view it as an instrument of liberation. When moderate members called for his expulsion from the association, he and other radicals left the meeting and the organization. William Makepeace Thackeray sarcastically labelled him Meagher of the Sword, a name Meagher proudly used for the rest of his life.

In January 1847 Meagher was a founder member of the

Thomas Francis Meagher (1823–1867), by George Mulvany

Irish Confederation, a new organization dedicated to raising revolution in Ireland. In February 1848 he unsuccessfully contested, much to his father's annoyance, a by-election in the city of Waterford and in the following March made a violent speech which attracted the attention of the authorities. Arrested for sedition, he travelled to Paris while on bail to congratulate the new French provisional government on its own successful revolution. The day before his trial, 15 April 1848, he presented the citizens of Dublin with a new Irish tricolour. Arraigned before Lord Chief Justice Blackburne on 16 April 1848, he was later released when the jury failed to agree on a verdict.

As a member of the Irish Confederation's war directory, Meagher toured Ireland in the summer of 1848 attempting to stir up rebellion. The activity of Meagher and his confederates so alarmed the government in Dublin that in July 1848 a warrant and a reward were posted for his arrest. Following a somewhat pathetic clash with the police in Ballingarry, co. Tipperary, Meagher and others were taken into custody. In October 1848 he was tried before a special commission headed by Lord Chief Justice Blackburne in Clonmel. He was found guilty of high treason and sentenced to be hanged, drawn, and quartered, but his sentence, because of his youth, was reduced to penal servitude and exile for life in Tasmania. He was transported in July 1849.

Allowed a considerable liberty upon a ticket of leave, Meagher farmed, and in February 1851 married Catherine Bennett (1832–1854), the daughter of another Irish political exile. The marriage produced two sons but only the younger, Thomas junior, survived; in 1872 he became a US army cadet at West Point. Thomas senior planned his escape. On 3 January 1852 he notified the magistrate at Campbelltown that he intended to break his parole, rode to the coast, and by pre-arrangement was picked up by Captain Betts of the *Elizabeth Thompson*. Transferred to the *Acorn*, he arrived in New York on 26 May 1852. His revolutionary reputation, good looks, and daring escape made him an instant hero among the Irish Catholic population of New York. In 1853 he published his *Speeches on the Legislative Independence of Ireland*. But he proved as restless in the United States as he had in Ireland. Having become an American citizen, and a popular public lecturer, he helped to create the *Citizen* newspaper in 1854; he studied law and was called to the New York bar in September 1855. In November, following the death of his first wife the previous year, he married Elizabeth Townsend, daughter of Peter Townsend, a successful New York businessman. In April 1856 he was a co-founder of the *Irish News*, a New York newspaper which became noticeably pro-southern, toured Central America in 1857, and became a strong supporter of the Democratic Party. Regarding the slavery issue, Meagher identified with the south, and even after the Confederate attack on Fort Sumter, April 1861, he initially remained pro-southern. However, following President Lincoln's call for volunteers, Meagher decided to fight for the union.

Meagher raised a company of Irish zouaves, which became company K of the Irish 69th New York volunteers, and became its captain. With the regiment, he fought at the first battle of Manassas, 21 July 1861, where he had his horse shot from under him. Responding to nativist attacks on the bravery of the Catholic Irish, he published *The Last Days of the 69th in Virginia* (New York, 1861). When the regiment, a thirty-day militia unit, volunteered for the duration of the war, it became the nucleus for an American Irish brigade seen by Meagher as a unit he hoped would emulate the eighteenth-century 'wild geese' brigades in European armies. Elected the colonel of the brigade's first regiment, Meagher proved tireless in raising the command, and when James Shields, an Irish-born veteran of the Mexican War, refused command, Meagher was commissioned the unit's first brigadier-general, 3 February 1862. He proved to be a courageous commander who helped shape the brigade into one of the army of the Potomac's finest combat units.

The brigade distinguished itself during the seven days' campaign in Virginia, 25 June to 1 July 1862, and during the battle of Antietam, September 1862, where it launched a heroic charge against a strong Confederate position known as the Bloody Angle. During the battle of Fredericksburg, 13 December 1862, Meagher led an even more heroic, but hopeless, charge against Mary's Heights. Decimated by this action, the brigade was little more than a skeleton command during the battle of Chancellorsville, May 1863. When he was refused permission to return to New York to raise new volunteers for the brigade, he resigned his commission, which was accepted on 14 May 1863. As a democrat, Meagher had made political enemies who suggested the high casualty rate among

his command was due to his heavy drinking. Returning to New York, he was accorded another hero's welcome. Frustrated by inactivity, he petitioned constantly for reappointment. Political reasons led to his being recommissioned a brigadier-general in December 1864. Ordered to Nashville, he was placed in command of the military district of Etowah. When directed to transport his command to Savannah, January 1865, to support General Sherman's Georgia campaign, he so mismanaged the transportation—due, so his critics believed, to his heavy drinking—that he was relieved by General Grant and ordered home to await orders. Inactive, he resigned his commission on 12 May 1865.

Political reasons led to Meagher's appointment by President Andrew Johnson as secretary to the territory of Montana. Arriving in the territory in September 1865, he became *de facto* governor in September 1866. Faced with disorder and the hostility of the Sioux under Red Cloud, Meagher raised a militia unit, the Montana Volunteers. While awaiting a shipment of arms for the unit at Fort Benton, he fell off the deck of the *G. A. Thompson* into the Missouri River and drowned on 1 July 1867. His body was never recovered, nor his death adequately explained.

If considered by some, such as Thackeray, as an impulsive and reckless Irishman, Meagher was none the less a brave soldier and was considered a national hero by both the Irish and Irish-Americans alike. In Waterford he is remembered by a plaque outside the Granville Hotel, and a fine equestrian statue outside the Montana state capital in Helena. He was survived by his second wife, Elizabeth, who presented his ceremonial swords and portrait of him in his federal uniform to the city corporation of Waterford in 1886.   RORY T. CORNISH

Sources R. G. Athearn, *Thomas Francis Meagher: an Irish revolutionary in America* (1949) · J. C. O'Meagher, *Some historical notices of the O'Meaghers of Ikerrin* (1890) · M. Cavanagh, *Memoirs of General Thomas Francis Meagher* (1892) · *My life in the Irish brigade: the civil war memoirs of Private William McCarter, 116th Pennsylvania infantry*, ed. K. E. O'Brien (1996) · W. F. Lyons, *Brigadier General Thomas Francis Meagher: his political and military career* (1870) · J. G. Bilby, *The Irish brigade in the civil war: the 69th New York and other Irish regiments of the army of the Potomac* (1998) · *DNB*
Likenesses J. Hayes, watercolour drawing, 1848, President's Residence, Dublin · T. F. Gallagher, portrait, priv. coll. · G. Mulvany, oils, NG Ire. [*see illus.*] · H. O'Neill, lithograph, BM · photographs, Michael J. McAfee collection; repro. in Bilby, *Irish brigade in the civil war* · portraits (in youth), repro. in Athearn, *Thomas Francis Meagher*

Meakin, James Edward Budgett (1866–1906), historian, was born at Ealing Park, London, on 8 August 1866, the eldest son in a family of three sons and two daughters of Edward Ebenezer Meakin, then a tea planter in Almora, India, and his wife, Sarah, only daughter of Samuel Budgett of Bristol. He was educated first at Mr Hill's Preparatory School, Redhill, then at Reigate grammar school.

Meakin's father, who was keenly interested in oriental peoples and religion, visited Morocco and founded there on 15 July 1884 the first English newspaper, the *Times of Morocco*, which urged sympathetic consideration of native interests. James joined his father in Morocco for reasons of health and worked on the paper, first as assistant editor and later as editor, from 1884 to 1893. He immersed himself in the customs and language of the Moorish people and by adopting local dress and the native name Tahar bil Mikki mixed freely with all classes. He soon mastered the Moorish dialect of Arabic and in 1891 published *An Introduction to the Arabic of Morocco*, an English–Arabic vocabulary with notes on grammar. In 1890 he returned to England to explore the means of preparing a work on Morocco that he intended should be as authoritative as Edward William Lane's *Modern Egyptians* (first edn, 1836) on Egypt. But he could not find a publisher and he later complained 'all they wanted was something light and picturesque' (Meakin, vii). Nor would either the Royal Geographical or the Scottish Geographical Society support his proposal to explore, under their auspices, the mountainous district of the central Atlas behind Morocco. He felt a lasting disappointment at these reverses.

After another year in Morocco, 1892, Meakin began a journey visiting all the important Muhammadan settlements in Asia and Africa, travelling by way of Turkey and Persia. He returned to Morocco for some months in 1897 but afterwards settled permanently in England, where he was occupied in journalism and public lecturing. In 1900 he married Kate Alberta, daughter of C. J. Helliwell, sometime of Liverpool and afterwards of Vancouver; they had one son. During this time he kept alive his plan for a definitive work on Morocco and the result of many years of labour was a 'comprehensive and painstaking trilogy' (*Athenaeum*, 14), which began with *The Moorish Empire* (1899), 'a historical epitome' covering 500 BC to the present. Next came *The Land of the Moors* (1901), a description of the natural, physical, and political characteristics of the region; originally published by Sonnenschein of London, it was reissued in a facsimile edition in 1986. The final work was *The Moors* (1902), a detailed account of the manners and customs of the Moorish people. Though Meakin could not claim any particular gifts of style, the three volumes were thoroughly researched and established him as the leading English authority in the field. A fourth book, *Life in Morocco* (1905), subsequently appeared, but it was described by one reviewer as 'something of a scrapbook of notes' left over from the trilogy (*Athenaeum*, 14). With his wife, Kate, who helped him in many of his works, Meakin also wrote the article on Morocco in the eleventh edition of *Encyclopaedia Britannica*.

Besides his work on Morocco, Meakin made questions of social reform in England a special subject of study. In 1901 he organized the Shaftesbury Lectures, devoted to raising the standard of health and comfort among the working classes and to exposing the conditions of city slums. The lectures took place throughout the country and Meakin often lectured himself. In 1905 he took a leading part, with Dr John Brown Paton, in forming the British Institute of Social Service, under whose auspices the Shaftesbury Lectures were continued. In connection with this work he published *Model Factories and Villages* (1905). In 1906 he acted as a special correspondent at the Algeciras conference for *The Tribune*, a short-lived London daily newspaper.

He received the Turkish order of the Mejidiye in 1902 in recognition of his studies of Islam. Meakin died in Hampstead Hospital, London, after a brief illness, on 26 June 1906 and was buried at Highgate cemetery. His wife survived him. S. E. FRYER, *rev.* MARK POTTLE

Sources *The Times* (30 June 1906) · J. E. B. Meakin, *The Moors: a comprehensive description* (1902) · *Athenaeum* (June 1906) · *WWW* · *Progress* (Oct 1906) · private information (1912) · *CGPLA Eng. & Wales* (1906)

Wealth at death £2142 8s. 10d.: probate, 10 Aug 1906, *CGPLA Eng. & Wales*

Mealmaker, George (1768–1808), weaver and radical, was born on 10 February 1768, the son of John Mealmaker, weaver, of the Seagate, Dundee, and Alison Auchinleck. Of Mealmaker's early life and education there is no direct information. Similarly, it is possible only to speculate about the sources of his political radicalism. A description of him from 1793 as 'a common unlettered weaver' reflects more the patronizing assumptions of the writer than reality. Dundee was an important centre for the linen trade in Scotland by the later eighteenth century, and the weavers were an increasingly prosperous, literate, and culturally aware part of the Scottish labouring classes. That Mealmaker was reasonably successful and competent as a weaver is suggested by his later important contribution to an attempt to establish a weaving industry in New South Wales. (He was also described as a 'manufacturer' in the local parish register, OPR S3 282/9, p. 214.) The other roots of his radicalism may have been religious. Dundee and its environs were relatively unusual in Scotland in this period in that their radicalism was fed by strong religious currents. Local ministers who made an important contribution to radicalism included Thomas Fysshe Palmer, the Unitarian. Mealmaker was himself a member of the Relief congregation, and was almost certainly the author of a radical sermon from Dundee published in London in 1795. This sermon drew on, and gave violent expression to, a radical and apocalyptic tradition in Presbyterianism which resurfaced under the impact of the French Revolution among some (but far from all) Secessionist and Independent congregations. In addition, in November 1793, as the Dundee delegate to the third Edinburgh convention of Scottish radicals, he strongly supported an unsuccessful motion for a general fast and day of humiliation. His speech was lengthy and described by one observer as in the style of a 'Tent Sermon' (Brims, 58).

Mealmaker's role in radical politics in Scotland in the 1790s was that of a committed and articulate activist. He joined the local Friends of Liberty society at its inception in early 1791. In 1793 he was the author of a broadsheet entitled *Appeal to their Fellow Citizens*, issued by the society, which sought to exploit the hardship and downturn in trade caused by the outbreak of war against revolutionary France to draw support to the radicals. This broadsheet, which came very close to accusing the government of tyrannical intentions and advocated democratic elections, was the tool which the ministry used to convict and transport Palmer, as a leading radical of some social standing, for sedition in September 1793. Mealmaker also became caught up in the aftermath of the exposure of the Watt plot to seize Edinburgh Castle of the following spring, having his house raided and papers seized, and, after fleeing to Arbroath, being arrested and taken to the Scottish capital for examination. On this occasion he was fortunate, the authorities believing his story that he knew nothing of Watt's plans for an armed rebellion.

Mealmaker's career thereafter mirrors the course described by Scottish radicalism in the mid- to later 1790s. In 1795 he was responsible for the re-establishment of the Dundee Friends of Liberty, which had ceased to meet following the severe repression of 1793–4. He was also, from 1796, an early member of the clandestine Society of United Scotsmen. Mealmaker's role in this society was an important one, especially among the Fife and Forfarshire weaving villages. Henry Dundas was to describe him as one of the 'Ringleaders' of the society (NA Scot., RH 2/4/83, fols. 21–2). He was also the United Scotsmen's principal ideologue, writing and causing to be published and circulated *The Moral and Political Catechism of Man*. It was also under his direction that the *Resolutions and Constitution of the Society of Scotsmen*, which followed closely those of the more numerous and menacing United Irishmen, were printed and distributed in the counties of Forfar, Perth, and Fife. A meeting of four delegates of the society from Cupar, Kirriemuir, Brechin, and Coupar Angus was held in his house in 1797, and Mealmaker was appointed to represent them on a national committee. From the fragmentary and unilluminating sources which survive, it appears that he also played an important strategic role in a network of radical printers, booksellers, and activists which kept the flame of radicalism and radical political argument alive in Scotland in difficult and often dispiriting conditions in the later 1790s.

Arrested in November 1797, Mealmaker was the principal victim of the inevitable wave of repression which followed the authorities' growing concern, fuelled by fears that the violence and disorders in Ireland would spread to Scotland, over the activities and threat posed by the United Scotsmen. Refusing to reveal anything significant to the authorities, protesting his innocence of any ambition other than the pursuit of parliamentary reform, and before a hostile court, Mealmaker was found guilty in 1798 of sedition and administering illegal oaths under legislation passed in 1797. He was sentenced to fourteen years' transportation. The conviction brought to an end Mealmaker's brief married life with Marjory Thoms (*d.* 1843?), a Dundee woman whom he had married on 23 November 1795 and with whom he had two daughters.

In New South Wales, Mealmaker may have made contact with fellow radical 'martyrs', including Palmer. On two occasions in the eighteen months after his arrival, he clashed with the authorities. In 1803, however, he received a conditional pardon, and became involved, as manager, of an attempt to develop a weaving industry in the colony at Parramatta. The attempt ended in failure when the factory was burnt down in 1807. Mealmaker

died at Parramatta on 30 March the following year in poverty—he did not leave any property or money to pay his funeral expenses. His end was a sad one, caused, apparently, by him suffocating by 'drinking spirits'. From 1805 communication between Mealmaker and his wife appears to have lapsed. She was to learn of her husband's death only in 1811.

Mealmaker's committed and principled radicalism was forged through a lively tradition of discussion and self-education which flourished among some skilled sections of the labouring classes in the 1790s. His political commitment started amid his books and papers—he described these on one occasion as the 'labour of years, which I accounted more valuable than their weight in gold' (Roe, 286)—and he looked to political education as the best means of effecting reform. His political ideology and outlook, which were formed from an amalgam of Paineite republicanism, radical Presbyterianism, and a commitment to religious freedom and democratic parliamentary reform, distanced him from the mainstream of Scottish radicalism of this period, which was more moderate in tone and aims. What changed during the 1790s, and what shaped his political activities, was not so much his stance but the political conditions and possibilities confronting radicals.   BOB HARRIS

Sources M. Roe, 'George Mealmaker, the forgotten martyr', *Royal Australian Historical Society Journal and Proceedings*, 43 (1957), 284–98 · *State trials*, vols. 23–4 · NA Scot., JC 26/281 · NA Scot., RH 2/4/83 · NA Scot., S4/282/5, p. 178 · NA Scot., S3/282/13, p. 168 · *The moral and political catechism of man, or, A dialogue between a citizen of the world and an inhabitant of Britain. By George Mealmaker, M.B. C—N. To which is added, a narrative of the arrest, examination, and imprisonment of the author, for supposed treasonable and seditious practices; with copies of two letters written by him to the magistrates of Arbroath, during and after his confinement* (1797) · *A sermon: delivered in Dundee, Febuary 26th, 1795. By G M — M... B... C... N* (1795) · H. W. Meikle, *Scotland and the French Revolution* (1912) · N. J. Gossman, 'Mealmaker, George', *BDMBR*, vol. 1 · J. Brims, 'The convenanting tradition and Scottish radicalism in the 1790s', *Covenant, charter and party: traditions of revolt and protest in modern Scottish history*, ed. T. Brotherstone (1989), 50–62 · *The Dundee register of merchants and traders* (1782), 26 · PRO, CO 201/54
Archives NA Scot.

Meaney, Sir Patrick Michael (1925–1992), businessman, was born on 6 May 1925 at 66 Bodmin Street, Wandsworth, London, the youngest in the family of two sons and two daughters of Joseph Francis Meaney, a tram driver, and his wife, Ethel Clara Martin. He was at first named Patrick Henry. Brought up in London, he was educated at Wimbledon College and the Northern Polytechnic. He served in the armed forces during the Second World War, remaining from 1941 until 1947; he was with the 6th airborne division at Arnhem. Meaney was married twice. His first marriage having ended in divorce, his second marriage, on 9 July 1968, was to Mary June Connell (*b.* 1927/8), the daughter of Albert William Kearney, a company director. He had a son, Adam, and a stepson and stepdaughter from his second marriage.

In 1951 Meaney joined the haulage group Thomas Tilling Ltd. He rose in the company to become a director in 1961 and managing director and chief executive in 1973;

under his management the group developed a strong building-product division and took over a number of companies in order to expand and diversify its activities. Following the recession of 1980–81, and the slump in profits, Meaney was unable to prevent the hostile takeover of Thomas Tilling by BTR in 1983: as a result of this, he was ousted from his job.

Meaney had been a director of the Rank Organization since 1979, and at the end of 1983 he replaced Sir John Davis as chairman. The Rank Organization, founded in 1933 by the Methodist J. Arthur Rank as the Religious Film Society to make films for Sunday schools and Methodist halls, had developed into a large film-making company; it diversified in the 1950s, when Rank took over the family flour business in 1952 and set up Rank Xerox Ltd in 1956 to manufacture photocopying equipment. By the late 1960s, when the Rank Organization stopped making films, Rank Xerox was contributing over 90 per cent of the group's overall profit, and Meaney saw his main task as developing the group's other activities in order to lessen its dependence on Rank Xerox. He appointed Michael Gifford, from Cadbury Schweppes, as his chief executive, and together they built up the cinema chain and film-distribution side of the group and modernized the Top Rank bingo clubs. By 1992 the Rank Organization had a stock market value of £1.8 billion and a workforce of 45,000.

Meaney was also on the boards of several other companies, including Cable and Wireless from 1978 to 1984, ICI from 1981, and Tarmac from 1989, and he was chairman of the Mecca Leisure Group from 1990. Keenly interested in horse-racing, from 1985 he was a director of Racecourse Technical Services Ltd and Metropolitan and Country Racecourse Management Holdings Ltd and deputy chairman of the Horserace Betting Levy Board. A director of Midland Bank from 1980, he was appointed deputy chairman in 1984 and served as chairman of the remuneration committee. He played a crucial part in the merger negotiations with the Hongkong and Shanghai Banking Corporation (HBSC) at the beginning of 1992, when his negotiating skills ensured that a likely takeover bid from Lloyds Bank was deflected.

Meaney was much in demand for membership of trade and industry committees, and served on the councils of the Confederation of British Industry and the London chamber of commerce and industry, and on the stock exchange listed companies advisory committee. He was president of the Chartered Institute of Marketing from 1981 to 1991: during his presidency the membership grew to 50,000, and the institute developed a relationship with the Department of Trade and Industry that led to the successful marketing initiative, while he helped to make contact with influential people interested in business development and built up a panel of vice-presidents from the leaders of British industry. He was asked by the government to chair the review committee on the shipbuilding company Harland and Woolf in 1980. He also chaired the commerce and industry committee of the Great Ormond Street Hospital's wishing well appeal.

A jovial and friendly man, Meaney was widely respected in the City for his energy and his ability to grasp the essentials of every situation and problem. A keen rugby player, he belonged to Harlequins Rugby Club. He was also a great opera lover and a Francophile. He was knighted in 1981. He died of heart failure at 27 Circus Road, Westminster, on 16 July 1992, survived by his wife, Mary, his son, Adam, and his stepson and stepdaughter. There was a memorial service on 7 October 1992 at the church of the Immaculate Conception, Farm Street, London.

ANNE PIMLOTT BAKER

Sources G. Macnab, *J. Arthur Rank and the British film industry* (1993) · *The Times* (20 July 1992) · *The Times* (24 July 1992) · *The Independent* (30 July 1992) · WWW · b. cert. · m. cert. · d. cert. **Likenesses** T. Pilston, photograph, repro. in *The Independent* · photograph, repro. in *The Times* (20 July 1992) **Wealth at death** £1,630,472: probate, 1992, *CGPLA Eng. & Wales*

Means, Joseph Calrow (1801–1879), General Baptist minister, was born in London on 20 May 1801, the only surviving child of John Means, a wine merchant in Rood Lane, London, and his wife, Phillis Simpson (*d.* 1814), the third daughter of John Simpson, preacher to the afternoon congregation of General Baptists at Worship Street. From 1809 he was educated in a day school, but on his mother's death he was enrolled at the boarding-school of the Revd John Evans (1767–1827). He left this school in 1818 and entered his father's business as a clerk. Unhappy in commercial life, he became one of the original teachers of the Worship Street Sunday school. In 1822 he was baptized at Deptford and in 1823 he was elected to the committee of the General Baptist assembly. Turning his thoughts towards the ministry, he entered the classics and mathematics classes of the newly opened University College, London, in 1828, and at the same time studied theology in the General Baptist Academy under Benjamin Mardon.

In 1829, while still pursuing his studies, Means became preacher to the afternoon congregation at Worship Street. His ministry was successful, and his congregation moved later that year to Trinity Place, and subsequently to Coles Street, Southwark. In 1831 he was appointed secretary to the General Baptist assembly, a post he held with only two short breaks until 1872. He edited the organ of his denomination, the *General Baptist Advocate*, from 1831 to 1836. In 1834 he was elected a messenger, a quasi-episcopal office held for life. In 1836 he preached the annual sermon before the assembly, and caused a sensation by blaming the perceived decline among the Old Connexion of General Baptists on their repudiation of the atonement. The position which he held, and made clear during the sermon, was an evangelical one, and totally unacceptable to the majority of the assembly, who were inclined towards unitarianism. The strength of the reaction against him led Means to retire from his editorship of the *General Baptist Advocate*. After the publication of his volume on the atonement, *Jesus the Mercy Seat, or, A Scriptural View of Atonement* (1838), his connection with his congregation was severed in 1839. He formed a small evening congregation at Worship Street to which he ministered without stipend, supporting himself by literary work and by taking in boarders. He remained outside the denomination for four years.

In 1843 Means became minister of the General Baptist congregation at Chatham, Kent; his settlement was in the face of great opposition, but proved a very happy one. He was elected headmaster of the Chatham proprietary school, and kept it on when it was relinquished by the proprietors. In 1855 he succeeded Mardon as minister at Worship Street, and from this time he exerted a paramount influence on the counsels of his denomination. Means ceaselessly advocated closer union between the Old and New Connexions of General Baptists. His campaigning bore some fruit: the two bodies exchanged delegates over a period of about twenty years, beginning in 1868.

In 1837 Means married Louisa (d. 1878), daughter of Lieutenant-Colonel Hugh Robert Alcock; they had no children. He was never robust, and in later life he suffered greatly from asthma. He retired from the pastoral charge in October 1874, but returned again to many of its duties, preaching the last sermon (23 June 1878) at Worship Street before the removal of the congregation to new premises in Bethnal Green. He died on 6 February 1879 in his home at 21 New North Road, Hoxton.

Means's lucid contributions to theology were undervalued by his co-religionists; his position was a modified Arianism. His general literary work began in the *Penny Cyclopaedia*, to which he contributed topographical and other articles, including a biography of the Unitarian minister Lant Carpenter. He published a few separate sermons, and his addresses as messenger, often valuable for their historical details, are included in the *Proceedings* of the assembly. He wrote frequently on theological topics in the *Christian Reformer*, *The Inquirer*, and in Baptist periodicals. He also contributed to the *Biographical Dictionary* (4 vols., 1842–4) published by the Society for the Diffusion of Useful Knowledge and to William Smith's *Dictionary of Greek and Roman Biography* (3 vols., 1844–9).

ALEXANDER GORDON, *rev.* L. E. LAUER

Sources E. C. Starr, ed., *A Baptist bibliography*, 15 (1970), 232–3 · *Proceedings of the general assembly of General Baptist churches* (1880), 26–34 · J. H. Y. Briggs, *The English Baptists of the 19th century* (1994), 125–7 · *Christian Life* (15 Feb 1879), 78 · *The Inquirer* (15 Feb 1879), 98 · *Unitarian Herald* (27 April 1866), 137 · *Monthly Repository*, 9 (1814), 506–7 [obit. of Mrs Phillis Means] · personal knowledge (1894) · CGPLA Eng. & Wales (1879)
Archives NL Wales, diary | UCL, letters to Society for the Diffusion of Useful Knowledge
Wealth at death under £3000: probate, 3 March 1879, CGPLA Eng. & Wales

Meara, Dermod. *See* O'Meara, Dermot (*fl. c.*1614–1642).

Meara, Edmund. *See* O'Meara, Edmund (*c.*1614–1681).

Meares, John (1756?–1809), naval officer and entrepreneur, is of unknown origins. Nothing is known of his early years until he entered the navy in 1771 on board the *Cruiser*, in the rating of 'captain's servant'. After serving for nearly seven years, mostly in small ships, he passed his examination on 17 September 1778, when he was said to be more than twenty-two (passing certificate); the next day he was promoted to the rank of lieutenant. After the peace of 1783 he entered the merchant service and obtained command of a ship for a voyage to India. At Calcutta he was inspired, like many others in India and Britain, by news of Cook's discoveries in the north Pacific and he formed a company for opening or developing a trade with north-west America. On 12 March 1786 he sailed in the ship *Nootka* of 200 tons, not knowing that two other expeditions were being mounted at the same time. On 25 September he arrived in Prince William Sound, where he wintered in extremely harsh conditions. Most of the crew of the *Nootka* were dead by the time George Dixon and Nathaniel Portlock arrived in the sound in the *Queen Charlotte* and the *King George* the following spring. As an officially sanctioned expedition sent from London, they were surprised to find Meares already on this coast, and they only offered to help him in his difficult situation if he undertook to leave at once. This later prompted a bitter dispute between the two parties which became known as the Dixon–Meares controversy.

When Meares reached Macao in October 1787, he at once began to lay plans for a return to the coast of north-west America and a small group of interested entrepreneurs funded two ships for a voyage. In January 1788 he sailed for Nootka Sound in the ship *Felice*, arriving there in May. In June he was joined by the *Iphigenia*, with William Douglas as master; and after some traffic with the indigenous people, land was bought and a trading post was established. Having obtained a promise of free and exclusive trade, Meares sailed for China in the *Felice* in September, leaving the *Iphigenia* and her tender, the *North-west America*, with orders to winter in the Hawaiian Islands.

In Macao, Meares formed a consortium with a rival group of businessmen led by John Cadman Etches (whose partners ironically included George Dixon and Nathaniel Portlock). Meares, whose position was vulnerable as an interloping trader, believed that this merger under a joint trading account would allow him the official recognition that had previously been granted to Etches's organization, the King George's Sound Company. In 1789 Meares and his partners at Canton (Guangzhou) dispatched two ships, the *Argonaut* in April, and the *Princess Royal* in May, to join the *Iphigenia* in Nootka Sound. Their instructions from the consortium were to establish a permanent factory there. The *Iphigenia* was in the sound on 6 May when the Spanish frigate *Princesa* of twenty-six guns came in. On the 13th the *Princesa* was joined by the sixteen-gun corvette *San Carlos*; and on the 14th the Spaniards seized the *Iphigenia* and the *North-west America*, making Douglas and all his men prisoners. On their arrival later on, the *Argonaut* and *Princess Royal* were also seized, the grounds of the aggression being the allegation that the coast was in the possession of Spain, and that any foreign ships trading and establishing settlements there were violating Spanish rights. When fragmentary news of these events reached London, in January 1790, a demand for compensation and the return of British property was made to the Spanish. Only then, it was declared, would the larger issue of territorial rights be discussed. Simmering tension, however, became a deep international crisis when Meares entered on the scene.

As soon as news of the incident in Nootka Sound had reached Meares in China, he had returned to Britain, and in a memorial dated 30 April 1790 he laid the details of the case before the government. He presented ministers with a colourful and far from accurate account of what had happened the previous year and during his earlier voyages to the sound. In particular, there was great uncertainty as to whether or not the British had ever established permanent settlements which had then been taken into the possession of the Spanish crown. After the cabinet had assessed the information from Meares, a message from the king (drafted by Pitt) was laid before parliament on 5 May noting that two ships flying British flags (the other ships had been operating under Portuguese colours) had been taken by the Spanish and that Spain had established an exclusive right to trade on that coast. This provoked a great public uproar and a clamour for war against Spain. A fleet of forty ships was assembled, under the command of Lord Howe, which became known as 'the Spanish armament of 1790'. In the face of this threat, the Spanish government eventually acceded to British demands in August, and the Anglo-Spanish Convention of 28 October 1790 saw the restoration of all land taken from British subjects and the opening of trade on the north-west coast of America to all nations. The political excitement created great interest in Meares's voyages and mercantile schemes, and encouraged him to publish a number of books and pamphlets relating to his travels and the exploration of the coast of north-west America, in addition to items associated with his dispute with George Dixon. As the crisis passed, however, Meares disappeared from public view. It does not appear that he had any further service in the navy; but on 26 February 1795 he was promoted to the rank of commander. He died in 1809.

J. K. LAUGHTON, rev. H. V. BOWEN

Sources V. T. Harlow, *The founding of the second British empire, 1763–1793*, 2 (1964), 419–81 · J. M. Norris, 'The policy of the British cabinet in the Nootka crisis', *EngHR*, 70 (1955), 563–80 · F. W. Howay, ed., *The Dixon–Meares controversy* (1929) · 'Significance of the memorial presented by Lieut. Mears to the Rt. Hon. W. Wyndham Grenville', *GM*, 1st ser., 60 (1790), 487–90 · J. Meares, *Voyages made in the years 1788 and 1789 from China to the north-west coast of America …* (1790) · G. Dixon, *Remarks on the voyages of John Meares, esq.* (1790) · *An answer to Mr. George Dixon, later commander of the Queen Charlotte, by John Meares, esq.* (1791) · G. Dixon, *Further remarks on the voyages of John Meares, esq.* (1791)

Mearne, Samuel (1624–1683), publisher and bookbinder, was born at Reading at 11 a.m. on 20 April 1624, the son of Henry Mearne, yeoman. In 1637 he was apprenticed to Robert Bates, a member of the Stationers' Company, subsequently turned over to John Arnold, bookseller, and in July 1646 freed by both Arnold and Bates. In 1653 Mearne took the first of his twelve apprentices. Two years later, when he bound a book for one Cor: Pigeon, his address is given as 'Pellecan Courte, in Littill Brettin'. He lived in Little Britain, in the parish of St Botolph, Aldersgate, all his working life.

In 1655 a pass was granted for Cornelius Bee, Samuel Mearne, and William Minshaw to go to the Netherlands. He may there have been of service to Charles II, who was at Middelburg. In any event, he was speedily rewarded at the Restoration by being granted, by letters patent of 20 June 1660, the office of bookbinder to the king at a fee—which he seldom received—of £6 per annum. Mearne was already referred to as a bookseller in 1655 and his first publication also dates from that year. Only two other books survive which he issued before 1670, but from then onwards until his death in 1683 he published regularly. He was not himself a printer, but he had a share in the king's printing house, as one of the assigns of John Bill and Christopher Barker. His success as a businessman was partly due to keeping on good terms with the establishment as a zealous seeker-out of illegal presses, an activity which helped the government to suppress seditious pamphlets and helped the leading members of the book trade, such as Mearne himself, to suppress possible competitors. In 1668 the king requested the Stationers' Company to admit, as member of the court, among a number of other royal servants, 'Samuel Mearne, our bookbinder'. Mearne subsequently served as warden and master of the company and continued to be concerned about illegal printing for the rest of his life.

Mearne is, however, best known as a bookbinder. His first surviving binding in blind-tooled brown calf was that made for Cor: Pigeon in 1655. At this time he married; his eldest child, Anne, named after her mother, was born on 3 January 1656, but she did not live long and her burial is recorded on 3 March of the same year. On 2 January 1657 his eldest son, Samuel, was born, followed by Charles (*b.* February 1658) and Anne (*b.* 26 May 1665). Another son, James, was buried on 29 May 1664.

From 1660 onwards, Samuel Mearne the elder was much too important a figure in the book trade to have worked at the bench himself, but he did have a bookbinding shop on the premises of his bookselling business and the Mearne bindery was responsible for the most splendid gold-tooled and onlaid bindings produced during the reign of Charles II. Mearne also carried out all the standard binding for the royal library, mainly in red turkey leather, decorated with gold fillets, the royal arms block, a conventional flower, or, later and most frequently, with Charles II's cipher. More elaborate bindings were supplied for use in the various royal chapels, for members of the royal household, for presentation to ambassadors and plenipotentiaries, and for the ceremonies of the Order of the Garter. Several sets of Bibles and prayer books survive, bound for the chapel and the closet at Whitehall, the set for the king's own use the most elaborate and costliest of all in red turkey leather, decorated with black paint, and lavishly tooled in gold to a cottage roof design with small massed floral and curling tools and the king's cipher, their foredges painted beneath the gold with the royal arms or ciphers. The Mearne bindery also supplied a considerable number of other Bibles and prayer books for use in the royal chapels, the most elaborate of which, in gold-tooled and onlaid black, olive, or red turkey with painted foredges, may have been for the altar. Although Mearne's favourite style was the 'cottage roof', he occasionally produced a design based on the French 'fanfare' style, as well as simpler panel designs. He also supplied books to the dean of Windsor as register of the Order of the Garter, the registers bound in velvet, and the manuscript copies of the statutes for the newly installed knights in very dark blue turkey leather.

In 1674, on the death of Francis Bowman, Mearne had become stationer in ordinary to the king and in May 1675 a new grant of the offices of bookbinder, bookseller, and stationer to the king was made to Samuel Mearne and his son Charles for their lives and the life of the survivor. Mearne died at Little Britain in May 1683 and was buried at St Botolph, Aldersgate, on 16 May of that year. On 9 July, Mr Secretary Jenkins wrote to the lord mayor: 'The late Mr Mearne was so zealous in the King's service that I think myself obliged to remember it on every opportunity of doing a good office to his son.' Charles Mearne, who was apprenticed to his father and freed by patrimony on 24 June 1682, but who had been working in partnership with his father since 1678, continued as royal bookbinder, bookseller, and stationer to supply the Bibles and prayer books to the closet. He survived his father by only three years, when his elder brother, Samuel junior, was appointed royal bookbinder, an office he held until the revolution in 1688.   MIRJAM M. FOOT

Sources H. M. Nixon, *English Restoration bookbindings* (1974), 10–23 · H. M. Nixon and M. M. Foot, *The history of decorated bookbinding in England* (1992), 62–71 · E. G. Duff, 'The great Mearne myth', *Papers of the Edinburgh Bibliographical Society*, 2 (1918), 47–65 · *Catalogue of bookes*, Longleat House, Wiltshire, Thynne MSS [belonging to the King's Library at St James's], vol. 83, fols. 23r–31v · Lord Chamberlain's bill books, PRO, LC 5/39; LC 5/40; LC 5/43; LC 5/138; LC 9/271; LC 9/273; LC 9/274; LC 9/278 · Bagford fragments, BL, MS Harl. 5943, fol. 3r · D. F. McKenzie, ed., *Stationers' Company apprentices*, 3 vols. (1961–78), vols. 1–2 · C. Davenport, *Samuel Mearne* (1906) · Sloane MS, BL, 1707, fols. 23v, 25v · parish register (births), London, St Botolph, Aldersgate, 3 Jan 1656 · parish register (burials), London, St Botolph, Aldersgate, 16 May 1683

Archives BL, bindings · Bodl. Oxf., bindings · Brasenose College, Oxford, bindings · Hunt. L., bindings · Keble College, Oxford, bindings · Lincoln College, Oxford, bindings · Morgan L., bindings · PRO, bindings · St George's Chapel, Windsor, bindings · St John's College, Oxford, bindings · U. Durham, bindings | Longleat House, Wiltshire, Thynne MSS, bills · PRO, lord chamberlain's bill books, bills

Mearns, Andrew (1837–1925), Congregational minister and author, son of John Mearns and his wife, Agnes, *née* Hyslop, was born on 4 July 1837 in Burnside, New Cumnock, Ayrshire, and educated at the Glasgow normal school and Glasgow University. After an early career as a pupil teacher at the Glasgow normal school and an assistant master, first at the Royal Grammar School, Newcastle upon Tyne, and then at a school in Maidenhead, Mearns entered the Theological Hall of the United Presbyterian church in Edinburgh in 1860. On completing his training there in 1863, he accepted the co-pastorate of the Congregational church in Great Marlow. From 1866 to 1879 he served as pastor of the new Congregational church in Markham Square, Chelsea.

In 1876 Mearns was elected secretary of the London Congregational Union, Congregationalism's overseeing and co-ordinating body for the capital, and three years later he gave up active ministry (although in 1884 he served as pastor of the Bishopsgate church) to become the union's full-time 'secretary without pastoral care', a post he held for over a quarter of a century. It was in that capacity that he initiated an inquiry into the physical and moral condition of the London slums that resulted in the reform tract *The Bitter Cry of Outcast London. An Inquiry into the Condition of the Abject Poor* (October 1883), a twenty-page penny pamphlet that has been called 'perhaps the most influential single piece of writing about the poor that England has ever seen' (Gilbert, 67). The pamphlet, with its dramatic emphasis upon the physical and moral consequences of overcrowding (including incest), created a furore. The Congregational and other churches responded by immediately establishing missions in the East End, and the government responded by appointing the royal commission on the housing of the working classes (1884–5). The pamphlet inspired the settlement house movement and encouraged a widespread, fresh examination of the social consequences of urbanization and unregulated capitalism, and what the Congregational assembly in 1885 termed 'the inequalities which unjust laws and customs produce' (*Congregational Year Book*, 1886, 17).

The Bitter Cry, issued by the London Congregational Union, was anonymous, and soon after its appearance Congregational minister, W. C. Preston, in a series of letters to the *Daily News*, claimed authorship. Mearns hotly disputed the claim in the same newspaper and in the pages of the *Contemporary Review*, and when he was called as a witness before the royal commission on the housing of the working classes, Mearns laid claim to being the 'responsible author' ('Royal commission', 30.175, 180). When Mearns offered to bring forward the co-workers on *The Bitter Cry* as witnesses on his behalf, Preston did not press his claim. It would appear that the initial conception of the inquiry came from Mearns, and that he gathered the information and compiled the social and economic statistics, and, although he handed over his materials and drafts to be written up by Preston, Mearns wrote much of the text, keeping a firm editorial grip on the whole, and revised the final draft. *The Congregationalist* argued, 'It is but common justice to say the credit of this entire work belongs to Mr Mearns' (12, 1883, 908). In 1906 Mearns, who had lived in Chelsea, Bishopsgate, Brixton, and Upper Norwood, retired as secretary of the London Congregational Union and left London to live at 35 The Esplanade, Burnham-on-Sea, near Weston-super-Mare, Somerset, where, vigorous to the end, he died on 25 August 1925.   ANTHONY S. WOHL

Sources *The Times* (26 Aug 1925) · *Congregational Year Book* (1926), 170 · *The Congregationalist*, 10 (1881), 889–94 · *The Congregationalist*, 12 (1883), 907–8 · *Daily News* (8 April 1884) · *Daily News* (10 April 1884) · *Daily News* (12 April 1884) · *Daily News* (15 April 1884) · A. Peel, *These hundred years: a history of the Congregational Union of England and Wales, 1831–1931* (1931) · A. S. Wohl, ed., *The bitter cry of outcast London* (1970) · P. D'A. Jones, *The Christian socialist revival, 1877–1914* (1968) · K. S. Inglis, *Churches and the working classes in Victorian England*

(1963) • A. Mearns, 'The outcast poor, II: outcast London', *Contemporary Review*, 44 (1883), 924–33 • 'Royal commission to inquire into the housing of the working classes', *Parl. papers* (1884–5), 30.75ff., C. 4402-I • A. Porritt, *The best I remember* [1923] • B. B. Gilbert, *The evolution of national insurance in Great Britain: the origins of the welfare state* (1966) • b. cert. (Scotland) • CGPLA Eng. & Wales (1925)

Likenesses London Stereoscopic Co., photograph, repro. in *The Congregationalist*, 10 • photograph, repro. in Peel, *These hundred years*

Wealth at death £1348 7s. 5d.: probate, 19 Sept 1925, *CGPLA Eng. & Wales*

Mearns, Duncan (1779–1852), university professor, was born on 28 August 1779, the elder of two children, at the manse of Towie, Aberdeenshire, where his father, Alexander Mearns (1745–1820), was parish minister. His mother was Anne (*d.* 1823), daughter of James *Morison of Disblair and Elsick, lord provost of Aberdeen; she was the widow of John Farquhar (1732–1768), minister of Nigg in Kincardineshire, with whom she had had three sons. At the age of twelve Mearns entered Marischal College, Aberdeen, gaining the first bursary. He graduated MA in 1795 and went on to study divinity under Gilbert Gerard and George Campbell. He was licensed by the presbytery of Kincardine O'Neil in June 1799, and in November of that year he was ordained assistant in the parish of Tarves, Aberdeenshire, to which he succeeded soon after. On 11 August 1808 he married Elizabeth Forsyth (*d.* 1830), with whom he had eight daughters and two sons, the younger of whom, William (1814–1891), became minister of Kinneff. His eldest daughter, Anne, married Robert Macpherson, Mearns's successor in the divinity chair, while his second daughter, Jane, married Hercules Scott, professor of moral philosophy in Aberdeen University.

Mearns was admitted to the chair of divinity in December 1816; while not in principle opposed to the practice, he declined to follow his predecessor's example in holding the chair in plurality. In 1818 he was awarded a DD by St Andrews University. A leading figure in the moderate party in the Church of Scotland, he served as moderator of the general assembly in 1821, becoming a royal chaplain in 1823. He took a prominent part in the events leading up to the Disruption of 1843, showing a particular interest in the suspended moderate ministers in the presbytery of Strathbogie. Mearns was always deeply studious and retiring; in the words of his obituary in the *Aberdeen Journal* he was 'plain to a degree of earnestness in his own tastes and habits, he let the vain show of the world pass with contempt'. For a scholar of such repute he published little: his *Principles of Christian Evidence Illustrated* (1818) was, perhaps significantly, as much a polemical as a theological work, with Thomas Chalmers as its intended target. After his death, his Murtle lectures appeared in two volumes as *Lectures on Scripture Characters* (1853), edited by his son William. He died, after a long and painful illness, at Chanonry, Old Aberdeen, on 2 March 1852, and was buried in the churchyard of St Machar's, Aberdeen, on 5 March.

LIONEL ALEXANDER RITCHIE

Sources *Aberdeen Journal* (10 March 1852) • *Fasti Scot.* • personal knowledge (1894) [*DNB*] • W. E. McCulloch, ed., *Viri illustres*

universitatum Abredonensium, Aberdeen University Studies, 88 (1923), 81–2

Wealth at death £10,250 6s. 1d.: inventory, 1852, Scotland

Mears [*née* Loudon], **Eleanor Cowie** [Ellen Cowie] (1917–1992), medical practitioner and campaigner, was born on 9 December 1917 at Willowbank, Cleland, Lanarkshire, the second of three children of William Loudon (1888–1958), builder, and his wife, Helen Cowie, *née* Robertson (1893–1983). Her parents intended to christen her Ellen, but the name was evidently misheard: her birth certificate names her Helen. She went to school in Cleland from 1924 to 1930, and attended Wishaw high school until 1935. Her father disapproved of women being educated beyond their conventional role, and it was against his wishes that she went to Edinburgh University to study medicine. There, she was a prominent and popular student. Her political views were to the left, but she was a member of the Student Christian Movement, sometimes preaching in the Royal Infirmary, and she played hockey and golf for the university. She also met a fellow medical student, Kenneth Patrick Geddes Mears (*b.* 1916), eldest son of a distinguished Edinburgh architect, Sir Frank Mears. Ellen found Kenneth, the product of a cultivated but unconventional family, hugely stimulating, and, audaciously, she and Kenneth married in the spring of 1940, a few months before their finals.

That summer they duly graduated MB ChB. Kenneth joined the RAF as a medical officer, and was posted to an East Anglia bomber squadron. Ellen bought a practice at 374 St Helier Avenue, Morden, Surrey. She was twenty-three, inexperienced with patients, and to acquire authority, dressed her hair in a bun and took the name Eleanor. But she swiftly discovered that women patients would bring her problems of a sexual nature which they would never have discussed with a male doctor; she began to take a special interest in women's medicine.

Kenneth had been posted to India in 1944. His wartime experiences had been deeply disturbing, and when he was demobilized in 1946 he had the chance to emigrate to New Zealand, where the national health service was much more to his liking than the scheme proposed for Britain. Eleanor joined him, with their children, and they settled in Sumner Road, Christchurch. She set up in practice as a gynaecologist and her sojourn there lasted ten years.

When Ellen became pregnant a fourth time, she aborted the baby herself. With three children to bring up, and a husband by now in so severe a depression that at times he could not work, a new baby would have been a ruinous handicap. But the experience of abortion and the ordeal of unwanted pregnancy profoundly influenced her professional life. It gave her a deep understanding of a dilemma familiar to women, committed her to the cause of abortion law reform, and strengthened her conviction that women were entitled to a reliable method of birth control. With two women colleagues Eleanor set up the Christchurch Marriage Guidance Council; she also won a reputation as a lecturer and radio broadcaster, and was asked by both main political parties to stand at the same election for parliament.

But her marriage was in crisis: Kenneth moved out in 1954. Wanting greater professional opportunities, she arranged a four-month exchange of practices with Dr Joan Malleson (wife of the actor Miles Malleson), who practised privately as a gynaecologist in London. But, the four months over, Dr Malleson died on the way back; whereupon Eleanor took over her practice and moved to 2 Kent Terrace, Park Road, London, with her children. Her interest in women's problems had become paramount, and in 1958 she became the first medical secretary of the Family Planning Association, and soon afterwards medical secretary of the Planned Parenthood Federation. Contraception was still a delicate subject; Mears strove to dispel the prejudice surrounding it. Meanwhile, under trial in America was 'the pill'. Mears was already prescribing Conovid to patients and was well placed to organize the first British trial, in Birmingham in 1959, under Family Planning Association auspices; she was able to co-ordinate and monitor the results of this trial, and others implemented by the pharmaceutical companies. Mears now believed passionately that a woman should be able to control her own fertility, championing oral contraceptives in the teeth of often formidable opposition from many of her profession. When she edited the *Handbook on Oral Contraception* (1965), it was welcomed for its trustworthy, evidence based approach.

All through these years Mears had been a single mother, bringing up her two daughters and a son at Kent Terrace. Then in 1968 she found a second husband, a Grimsby fish wholesaler, Francis Frederick Smith (1910–1996); it seems they met through a matrimonial agency. At his instigation Mears moved to End House, Augusta Close, Grimsby, Lincolnshire, at first maintaining consulting rooms in Harley Street; she set up a small practice from End House and ran a clinic for psychosexual problems for the Lincolnshire Health Authority. Then in 1977 she and her husband moved to 71 London Road, Sleaford, where she lived, in worsening health, until 1989, when she was admitted to Rauceby Mental Hospital, Sleaford, by now seriously ill with dementia. She died at the hospital on 18 May 1992, and was buried eight days later at Grantham.

Mears was a leading figure in the struggle for female equality through her position with the Family Planning Association, in a period when British attitudes towards sex were undergoing radical change. She was a founder of the Institute for Psycho-Sexual Medicine (she underwent Jungian analysis earlier in her life); was a fellow of the Royal Society of Medicine and the Society of Endocrinology; and the author or part author of numerous papers contributed to medical journals. She also advised the World Health Organization on matters of population control and was a member of the Medical Advisory Council for the Investigation of Fertility Control and the Marriage Guidance Council. She was a highly professional organizer and gatherer of data and a zealous advocate of oral contraception to doctors, patients and, critically, the press, to whom she was always available for an authoritative opinion. She had a pioneering energy, much of it derived from her private experiences and as the daughter of a conservatively principled father and his chilly, strait-laced wife.

Mears was a woman of strong character: fair haired, angular, nearly 6 feet tall, inclined to the brusque. Yet if colleagues found her outspoken and peremptory, she could be humorous, jolly, and gregarious, outstanding at family parties. But it is a paradox that in 1960 her 90-page book of advice for newly weds, *Marriage, a Continuing Relationship*, suggested a conventionally meek role for women, avoided promoting any radical view of their rights, and, not so surprisingly, revealed nothing of her own failed marriage. It is a further paradox that in her second marriage she seemed ready to bow to the wishes of a husband with whom, intellectually, she had little in common. Yet she made a substantial, even crucial contribution to the altered condition of her sex. She was fallible in personal relationships, perhaps, but that she was a woman of courage and spirit there can be no doubt. PAUL VAUGHAN

Sources private information (2004) [Roger Mears] · *Medical Register* · *Medical Directory* · BMA Library, index medicus · *The Times* (22 May 1992) · *The Independent* (22 May 1992)
Archives British Medical Association, London
Likenesses photograph, repro. in *The Times* · photograph, repro. in *The Independent*

Mears, John (1695–1767), non-subscribing Presbyterian minister, was born in Loughbrickland, co. Down, one of at least two sons of John Mears (d. 1718), Presbyterian minister successively at Colydon, Ayrshire (1689), Longford (1697), and Newtownards (1707), and his wife, Margaret Gilchrist (d. 1716) of Antrim. He entered Glasgow University in 1710, graduated MA in 1713, and studied divinity under John Simson, whose teaching shook his orthodoxy. Early in 1718 he was licensed by the Down presbytery and on 10 February 1720 he was ordained at Newtownards, in succession to his father.

On the outbreak of the subscription controversy in 1720 Mears, who was clerk of Down presbytery, sided strongly with the non-subscribers. In 1722 he made overtures to Francis Hutchinson, bishop of Down and Connor, offering to conform to the Church of Ireland. On 22 November 1722 the matter came before the Down presbytery, to whom Mears apologized; blaming his actions on a 'temptation of Satan', he declared that 'he was now more fixed in his former faith and Presbyterian principles, and hoped this step of his weakness should have a good effect upon him in making him a more able advocate for the Presbyterian cause' (Reid and Killen, *History of the Presbyterian Church*, 3.166n). As some of his congregation remained dissatisfied and suspicious of his non-subscribing principles the presbytery moved them into a separate congregation in May 1723. In 1724 Mears supported his fellow non-subscriber Thomas Nevin, minister of Downpatrick, who had been accused of Arianism and excluded from ministerial communion. Mears had to defend himself from the charge of Arianism made by Gilbert Kennedy, of Donacloney and Tullyish, and anonymously vindicated himself in Samuel Haliday's *Letter to the Revd Mr G. Kennedy* (1725). In June 1725 Mears and his congregation were transferred to the Antrim presbytery, which formally separated from the general synod in the following year. In 1732 he published a catechism for adults that became the standard 'shorter catechism' in Irish non-subscribing congregations until the nineteenth century; as a consequence it was frequently reprinted.

In 1735 Mears resigned Newtownards to take charge of the Presbyterian congregation at Clonmel, co. Tipperary, where he was installed on 9 April. In 1738 it was recorded that he had between seventy and eighty communicants. On 9 January 1740 he was installed minister of a small congregation in Stafford Street, Dublin, which had separated from Capel Street congregation on 10 October 1738. In December 1740 he preached the funeral sermon for John Abernethy, at Wood Street Chapel, and in 1762 his congregation amalgamated with that in Wood Street. A new meeting-house was built for the united congregation in Strand Street, where Mears preached the opening sermon on 22 January 1764. He wrote a short explanation of the Lord's supper that was published in 1758 and incorporated in *Forms of Devotion* (1766) by John Leland, James Duchal, and Isaac Weld.

Mears died on 11 October 1767, leaving a son, who settled in Calcutta, and a daughter, who married John Brown, Presbyterian minister at Waterford.

ALEXANDER GORDON, rev. S. J. SKEDD

Sources J. Armstrong, 'An appendix, containing some account of the Presbyterian churches in Dublin', in J. Armstrong and others, *Ordination service … of the Rev. James Martineau* (1829) • J. S. Reid and W. D. Killen, *History of the Presbyterian church in Ireland*, new edn, 3 (1867), 131, 166, 184, 191 • J. S. Reid, *History of congregations of the Presbyterian church in Ireland*, ed. W. D. Killen (1886), 104, 185, 207 ff. • T. Witherow, *Historical and literary memorials of presbyterianism in Ireland, 1731–1800* (1880), 26–33 • C. H. Irwin, *A history of presbyterianism in Dublin and the south and west of Ireland* (1890), 286ff. • *Records of the General Synod of Ulster, from 1691 to 1820*, 1 (1890), 456, 486, 558 • J. McConnell and others, eds., *Fasti of the Irish Presbyterian church, 1613–1840*, rev. S. G. McConnell, 2 vols. in 12 pts (1935–51), 77–8, 117 **Likenesses** J. Macardell, mezzotint (after R. Hunter), NG Ire. • mezzotint (after R. Hunter), BM, NPG

Mears, William (*bap.* **1686**, *d.* **1739**). *See under* Meres, John (1698–1761?).

Meath. For this title name; *see* Brabazon, Reginald, twelfth earl of Meath (1841–1929); Brabazon, Mary Jane, countess of Meath (1847–1918) [*see under* Brabazon, Reginald, twelfth earl of Meath (1841–1929)].

Meath, saints of (*act. c.*400–*c.*900), holy men and women who were subjects of a cult within the lands of the southern Uí Néill, flourished mainly between the fifth century and the early seventh. The area (the early medieval Brega, Mide, and Tethbae) is approximately represented by the modern counties of Meath, Westmeath, the part of the old co. Dublin north of the Liffey (more recently co. Fingal and the northern part of Dublin itself), co. Longford, and parts of co. Offaly and co. Louth. In the case of saints who had churches both within and without the lands of the southern Uí Néill, only those who were probably buried within the area are included. The saints can be divided into three groups: early saints, generally associated, often falsely, with St Patrick; those saints who, in the mid- and late sixth

century, were the founders of the principal monastic churches of the area; and, finally, the smaller group of seventh-century and later saints. The first group is known from the Patrician material, chiefly Tírechán's *Collectanea* in the late seventh century and the tripartite life of St Patrick in the tenth; the main saints of the second group are the subject of lives and are all recorded in the ninth-century martyrologies; those in the third group are usually known only from the martyrologies and the annals (for more on these sources, *see* Munster, saints of).

Saints attributed to the fifth and early sixth centuries The evidence for the early saints is predominantly from the Patrician texts, beginning with Tírechán's *Collectanea*, written in the last quarter of the seventh century, but **Mél** (*fl.* 5th–early 6th cent.) of Ardagh (Ardachad) in modern co. Longford, is also a character of some importance in what has been claimed as the earliest life of Brigit, the so-called *Vita prima*, and in her mainly vernacular life, *Bethu Brigte*. The heirs of these saints, Patrick and Brigit, were competing for influence within the kingdom of southern Tethbae; Ardagh was the episcopal church of southern Tethbae, and the competition naturally centred on the principal church of the kingdom. Although there is no life of Mél, his cult seems to have been resilient. In the ninth century his feast day, 6 February, is recorded in the martyrology of Tallaght, and also in the text of the *Félire Óengusso*: the *Félire* chose the most important saints to include within its brief verses, one to each day of the year, and it is thus significant that the Irish saint chosen for 6 February was Mél. The connection between Mél and Patrick seems to have strengthened in the viking period: according to the saints' genealogies, his mother, Dar Erca, was Patrick's sister.

Lommán mac Dalláin (*fl.* 5th–early 6th cent.) of Trim, whose feast day was celebrated on 17 February, but also on 11 October, is one of the clearest cases of an early British saint being drawn into a subordinate position within the cult of St Patrick. This appears to have happened for reasons of dynastic politics within the kingdom ruled by the dynasty of Cenél Lóegairi, in which Trim was the principal church. Up to the early eighth century, the church of Trim belonged to a cadet branch of the dynasty; in the early eighth century, however, their position came under threat from the ruling branch. The subjection of Lommán, the patron saint of the church, to St Patrick first appears at that date, in a text included in the Book of Armagh; it seems to have been a defensive measure by the cadet branch, seeking to gain the influence of Armagh in order to defend its control. The text also asserts that Lommán was related through his mother, not just to Patrick, but to a string of minor local saints across Meath and into Connacht, all of presumed fifth-century date, including **Munis** (*fl.* 5th cent.?), bishop, 'in Forgnaide among the Cuircne', that is, buried at Forgney in the modern barony of Kilkenny West, Westmeath (feast day 18 December), and **Mo Genóc** (*fl.* 5th cent.?) in Cell Dumai Glinn in southern Brega (Kilglinn, Meath; feast day 26 December). Although the manoeuvre failed to defend the cadet branch of Cenél Lóegairi, in that the ruling branch took control of Trim, the subordination of Lommán to Patrick is still there in the tenth-century tripartite life of Patrick. Once this hagiographical weapon had been given to Armagh, it was retained for possible use.

Cairnech (*fl.* 5th–early 6th cent.) of Dulane (Tulén, or Tuilián), Meath, another early saint of probable British origin, is with little doubt identical with the British saint, Carannog (Carantocus). They have the same feast day, 16 May, and the first life of the latter explicitly identifies the two saying that 'he changed his name in their [the Irish] language to Cernach' (*Vita prima*, ed. Wade-Evans, chap. 2). It also admits that Carannog was buried in his chief Irish monastery. On the other hand, the first life's understanding of the geography of Cairnech's Irish cult is limited: it plainly thinks that he was primarily a Leinster saint, probably being led astray by the proximity of Leinster to Ceredigion in Wales, where the life appears to have been written. In one of the notes to the *Félire Óengusso* he was said to be of the Cornishmen, but the Welsh lives associate him with Ceredig ap Cunedda, the eponymous founder of the kingdom of Ceredigion. They thus connect him with his principal Welsh church at Llangranog, Cardiganshire; on the other hand, the first life also makes him the saint of Carhampton, 3 miles south-east of Minehead in Somerset, although it fails to mention Crantock (from 'Carantoc'), just to the west of Newquay on the north coast of Cornwall. The *Félire Óengusso*'s notion that Carannog was a Cornishman may stem from some link between Ireland and Crantock. In Brittany a parish in Finistère was dedicated to Carantec; so also Tregarantec in Léon. The cult was, therefore, widespread by the twelfth century, the latest possible date for the Welsh life and the date also of the Irish saga of the triple death of Muirchertach mac Erca, king of Tara, in which Cairnech is a principal character (*Aided Muirchertaig meic Erca*). It is likely that this saga was written at Cairnech's main Irish church, Dulane.

Cairnech was already, however, a saint of some importance in Ireland by the ninth century. In the later, probably ninth-century, prologue to the *Senchas Már*, the principal early Irish law book, it was claimed that a panel of bishops, poets, and lawyers compiled the book; the three bishops were Patrick, his successor, Benén, and Cairnech. The origins of Cairnech's role as lawgiver may perhaps lie in local ecclesiastical rivalries. At much the same period, another Patrician text, the tripartite life, claimed that **Erc mac Dega** (*d.* 513), the patron saint of Slane (about 12 miles east and a little south of Dulane), whose feast day was 2 November, was Patrick's judge. The ninth-century collection of monastic anecdotes about Céili Dé reformers known as 'The monastery of Tallaght' mentions Slane as a particularly, even discreditably, wealthy church. Erc's, and thus Slane's, connection with Patrick and Armagh goes back at least to the late seventh century, so that Dulane may have been making an attempt in the ninth century to supplant Slane as an ally of Armagh. Such a policy might have something to do with the construction, at the beginning of the ninth century, of the new Columban monastery of Kells, only 2 miles to the south of Dulane. As Kells enjoyed the favour of the kings of Mide (Meath), so Dulane might be led to look with hope at the rival power

of Armagh. A possible corollary may be that Dulane was where the later prologue was composed.

Both Dulane and Slane lay within the immediate territories of the Uí Néill rulers of Brega (the eastern part of modern Meath), namely Síl nÁeda Sláine. Duleek, however, the church of **Cianán mac Sétnai** (*d.* 489), although close to Slane, was one of the three principal churches of the Ciannacht Breg, perhaps the most powerful client kingdom within Brega. Cianán, whose feast day was 24 November, is attributed to the Ciannachta in the saints' genealogies, a connection suggested by his name (the Ciannachta were thought to be descended from Cian, while Cianán means 'little Cian'). The tripartite life of St Patrick has Patrick blessing Cianán in the northern kingdom of Ciannacht Glinne Geimin (around Dungiven, Dún Geimin, in modern co. Londonderry), although his church Duleek was in the southern kingdom of Ciannacht Breg. Although the leading saint of Ciannacht Glinne Geimin came to be *Cainnech moccu Dálann [*see under* Munster, saints of], Cianán's cult had a minor role in binding together the two Ciannacht kingdoms. His obit in the annals of Ulster is also found in the annals of Tigernach and thus goes back to the chronicle of Ireland, the hypothetical parent text compiled in or soon after 911. It connects him with St Patrick by saying that he received his gospels from the saint of Armagh.

The second major church of the Ciannacht Breg was Monasterboice (Mainister Buíte), the monastery of **Buíte** [Boetius] **mac Brónaig** (*d.* 519/20), whose feast day was celebrated on 7 December. This lay north of the River Boyne in an area which remained under Ciannacht control even after, in the early eighth century, the territory around Duleek was taken from them by the Uí Néill of Brega. A cadet branch of the ruling dynasty of the Ciannacht Breg held the abbacy of Monasterboice for much of the eleventh century and included the important Middle Irish poet *Flann Mainistrech (Flann of Monasterboice). The strength of the church in the post-viking period is also demonstrated by the surviving high crosses. The annals fix Buíte's obit by asserting that it occurred in the same year as the birth of St Columba; the information may, therefore, have been part of the Iona annals which seem to have covered the period from the sixth century up to the 740s. His genealogy attributes Buíte to the Ciannacht Breg. The Latin life is post-Norman, seeking to associate Buíte with Mellifont, the Cistercian monastery founded close to Monasterboice in 1140. Unusually for an Irish saint, there is special mention of the finding of his relics, both in the twelfth-century martyrology of Gorman and also in the Latin life. The first part of the life ends, first, with Buíte being taken up to heaven 'like a second Elijah' on 1 May (Plummer, *Vitae sanctorum Hiberniae*, vol. 1), then being returned to earth after unusual divine attention had been paid to the complaints of the brethren; finally, the saint died on 7 December having thus been enabled to live to see and declare the day on which Columba was born. The life further claims, via prophecy on the part of Buíte, that, thirty years after Buíte died, Columba came to Monasterboice, revealed the site of the saint's burial and prescribed the bounds of the cemetery. The life's version suggests, therefore, that the saint's body remained buried in the cemetery but was indicated by some sign. The treatment would thus be the same as that accorded to Columba himself in the time of Adomnán (d. 704) and would not reflect the growing practice of elevation and enshrinement found in the eighth century. It is possible that the appearance of a second feast day, 16 May, in the martyrology of Tallaght, may indicate that a form of this story was already current in the ninth century, even though the days do not agree (1 and 16 May).

The third principal church of Ciannacht Breg was Lusk, north-east of Dublin, said to be the episcopal see of **Mac Cuilinn mac Cathmoga** [Maculinus, Cuindid] (d. 496). He himself is given a Ciannacht pedigree in the genealogies of the saints; moreover, the close identification of church and dynasty is indicated by the consequences of the loss of royal status by the local branch of the Ciannachta in the early eighth century: they reinvented themselves as the kindred controlling the church of Lusk. The amenities of Mac Cuilinn's feast day (6 September) appear to have included horse-racing, since in 800 a king of southern Brega was thrown from his horse in a race on the feast day and died immediately. The only life of Mac Cuilinn to survive was described by Charles Plummer (d. 1927) as an impudent forgery, having been lifted from a life of Finnbarr.

The cults of the Ciannacht saints may sometimes, as in the case of Lusk, have gained in significance from the decline of local dynasties. They offer a striking contrast with the cults of the saints associated with churches closer to the centres of royal power among the southern Uí Néill themselves. It is broadly true of the midlands that the greatest churches were to be found in the minor kingdoms. The exception is Kells, and that church was not founded until the early ninth century, after the first viking attacks on Iona. The principal 'seat of kingship' among the rulers of southern Brega in the eighth and ninth centuries, one of whom suffered the unfortunate riding accident on 6 September 800, was the crannóg—or lake-fort—of Lagore. Three churches were ringed around this royal seat: the old church of Domnach Sechnaill (Dunshaughlin), 2 miles to the west; Treóit (Trevet), just over 2 miles to the north-west; and Cell Fhoibrig (Kilbrew), just over 2 miles to the north-east. None of these churches was insignificant: bishops and scholars are recorded for Trevet in the eighth century and for Kilbrew in the ninth, while an obit of an abbot of Domnach Sechnaill is recorded in 833. Yet their cults were relatively weak: no saint was attributed to Cell Fhoibrig in the martyrologies; **Lonán mac Talmaig** (fl. 5th–6th cent.) of Trevet, whose feast day was 1 November, is said to have been of British descent on his mother's side, but there is no surviving paternal pedigree and no life. Domnach Sechnaill may well have been the principal early church of the region, as suggested by the term domnach, borrowed from the early Latin word for a church, dominicum; its saint, **Sechnall mac Restitiúit** [Secundinus] (fl. 5th cent.), bishop, whose feast day was celebrated on 27 November, was said by the tenth century

to be the son of Restitutus and Culmana, who was identified as one of Patrick's sisters. Sechnall was of secure reputation as one of the principal episcopal assistants of St Patrick. Yet the only surviving life was copied in the seventeenth century from a humanist compilation in the possession of an Irish Jesuit exile, Henry FitzSimon. This contained some plausibly medieval material, but nothing to demonstrate an especially active cult. It is likely that Sechnall's connection with Patrick was created by the development of the Patrician legend; he may have been the principal bishop of the northern province of what, in the fifth century, was still a greater Leinster including most of Brega; and, if he was anyone's assistant, he was more likely to have been Palladius's rather than Patrick's. His cult, therefore, may have been damaged by being made dependent on that of Patrick, and yet, given his new role as Patrick's lieutenant, his cult was never likely to decline beyond that of a second-rank local saint.

Sechnall may be contrasted with **Mochtae** [Mauchteus] (d. 535) of Louth, whose feast day was 24 March. He was always considered to be both a Briton and a disciple of St Patrick, as in Adomnán's second preface to his life of St Columba. The annals of Ulster, in his obit s.a. 535, quote the beginning of a letter purporting to have been written by him, in which he describes himself as 'Mauchteus, a sinner, priest, disciple of the holy Patrick'; and there is a reasonable chance that the letter is genuine, given the relationship between Mochtae and Columba disclosed by Adomnán and the Iona provenance of the early annals. There is an apparently abbreviated life preserved in the part of Codex Salmanticensis that contains a string of lives of northern saints for August and September, arranged in the order of their feast days. The church of Louth was one of the principal churches of the client kingdom of Conailli Muirthemne; it was sometimes linked to Slane, and even to Lusk, by joint abbacies; and it may have been the Irish monastery of *Fursa of Péronne.

The major churches of the southern Uí Néill The most important churches of the southern Uí Néill were, however, strung out along their southern frontier, from Finglas just north of Dublin to Clonmacnoise on the Shannon. Finglas had three saints in the martyrology of Tallaght, of whom one is of historical importance, **Dublitter** (d. 796), abbot, scriba (principal scholar and teacher), and probably also bishop, whose feast day was 15 May. Dublitter was one of the main leaders of the Céili Dé reform movement in the late eighth century, a movement given a major impulse by the 'assembly of the synods of the Uí Néill and the Leinstermen in the oppidum of Tara, where there were many anchorites and scribae, whose leader was Dublitter' (Ann. Ulster, s.a. 780). His name, which means 'Black Letter', was evidently a religious name, following a characteristic practice of the Céili Dé. He is not included, under that name at least, in the genealogies of the saints.

Clonard lay on the very frontier between Leinster and Mide. Indeed, it may have belonged more to Leinster in the lifetime of its founder, **Finnián mac Findloga** [Finnio moccu Thelduib, Vinniauus] (d. 549/551), whose feast day is celebrated on 12 December. His pedigree, as given in the genealogies of the saints, attached him to the descendants of Celtchair mac Uithechair, one of the Ulster heroes who provided popular ancestors for saints of uncertain lineage. His obit's ascription of him to a group (what Adomnán called a *gens*) Dál or Corcu Thelduib is paralleled in the ascription of Bishop Colmán moccu Thelduib, abbot of Clonard (*d*. 654) to the same people. If the Finnián of Clonard were merely one local manifestation of the Ulster saint *Findbarr moccu Fiatach [*see under* Ulster, saints of], as has been argued, it would be necessary to suppose that he was called 'moccu Thelduib' as a consequence of later connections, illustrated by the obit of Bishop Colmán, between Clonard and Dál Thelduib.

It has been argued that the Latin lives of Finnián go back to an Anglo-Norman text, whereas the two, closely related, Irish lives contain material of ninth-century date. The lost Irish life that was the parent of the two surviving versions was apparently written by a Leinsterman and thus stresses the saint's early connections with that province. A corollary of the view that Clonard was originally a Leinster house is that the annal entry recording the violent imposition of his authority over the monastery in 775 by Donnchad mac Domnaill, southern Uí Néill king of Tara, caused a decisive change of allegiance: from then on Clonard looked to the Cland Cholmáin kings of Mide. Yet Clonard was already by 775 a house of wide connections and considerable wealth. When, in 788, 'Dub dá Bairenn, abbot of Clonard, visited the *paruchia* of the land of Munster' (*Ann. Ulster*, s.a. 788), he appears to have been going on a visit round the churches and other property subject to Clonard in Munster. The tripartite life of Patrick mentions a church claimed by Armagh being exchanged by Clonard for other churches belonging to Clonmacnoise: by the ninth century there was a market in minor churches and the great monasteries such as Clonard might seek to rationalize their holdings. In the mid-ninth century, during the reign as king of Tara of the Cland Cholmáin king Máel Sechnaill mac Máele Ruanaid, Clonard seems to have occupied a position as head of the churches of Meath on a level with the pre-eminence of Armagh among the churches of the north, the kingdoms subject to Cenél nEogain. At the period, therefore, when the earliest materials detected within the Irish lives may have been written—materials concerned especially with the monastery's property interests in Leinster—Clonard was already firmly part of the Cland Cholmáin kingdom of Mide. Just as Dub dá Bairenn's 788 visit to Munster was probably designed to protect the material interests of Clonard in that province, so the hypothetical ninth-century hagiographical material may have played a role in protecting Clonard's rights in Leinster.

The hagiography of Clonard contains two further significant themes: the first is the reputation of Finnián as the teacher of many of the most famous Irish saints, including *Brendan of Clonfert [*see under* Connacht, saints of], Brendan of Birr [*see below*], and *Columba of Iona. In the last case, at least, there is evidence to suggest that the claim is false, but it does imply the continuing

intellectual aspirations of Clonard. If the later ascription of the scholar Ailerán (*d*. 665) to Clonard were correct, it would show that the monastery was already a centre of scholarship in the seventh century. The other major theme is the link between Finnián and the Welsh saint *Cadog of Llancarfan in Glamorgan. The latter's importance for the Irish is suggested by the early life of St Cainnech, where he is mentioned as a teacher of the saint. The late eleventh-century Welsh life of St Cadog itself appeals to the authority of the scholars of Clonard.

Immediately to the west of Clonard, the borderlands between Leinster and Meath were an area in which the cult of St *Brigit of Kildare was solidly entrenched, both in the north-western part of the medieval Leinster kingdom of Uí Fhailgi and in the neighbouring kingdom of Fir Thulach subject to the Uí Néill. Beyond this cross-frontier extension of the cult of Brigit, further south-west, came two kingdoms dotted with major churches, Cenél Fiachach and Delbnae Bethra. Cenél Fiachach was a once-powerful branch of the Uí Néill, victim of more successful cousins, while Delbnae Bethra, in the low-lying lands of the River Clodiagh, was a lowly client kingdom. Their fate is demonstrated by the later name of much of the kingdom of Cenél Fiachach, Tír Cell or Fir Chell, 'the land [or men] of churches'.

The great saint of Cenél Fiachach was **Áed mac Bricc** (*d*. 589), bishop, of Rahugh and Killare in the midlands, and Slieve League on the south-west coast of modern co. Donegal, whose feast day was 10 November. The site of the church of Killare, close to the legendary centre of Ireland and of Mide at Uisnech, is an indication of the earlier power of Cenél Fiachach. His more important church, however, was Rahugh, a few miles to the east of the Columban monastery of Durrow. In spite of having a neighbouring house which was favoured by the Cland Cholmáin kings of Mide, Rahugh retained enough importance to be the church of an abbot who was also a bishop, Dub dá Thuath (*d*. 788), and to be chosen as the site of a major royal assembly in 859 at which Osraige was alienated to Leth Cuinn (effectively, the Uí Néill) by the king of Munster. Áed mac Bricc's life in the Codex Salmanticensis is early, probably eighth-century. Its political stance is ambiguous: on the one hand, it presents Áed as a peacemaker between Munster and the Uí Néill and between Mide and Tethbae, befitting his cross-border descent through his mother, Eithne, from the neighbouring Munster people of Múscraige Tíre (north-west co. Tipperary) and his foundation of a church, Enach Midbren, in their kingdom; it also declares that 'kings were always hostile to him and used to be compelled by divine power to be obedient to him' (*Vita sanctorum*, ed. Heist). However, the life also glosses over Áed's descent on his father's side from Fiachu mac Néill, ancestor of Cenél Fiachach, preferring to say, more generally, that he belonged to the Uí Néill. That Áed mac Bricc was influential among the Uí Néill is suggested by his having founded a church by Slieve League in the lands of Cenél Conaill in the far north-west. Although the life borrows from Adomnán's life of Columba, a copy of which may have been obtained from the nearby monastery of Durrow, it is more small-scale in scope: its central concerns are with local violence and with the poverty and insecurity of women, especially nuns, but it also gives Áed a special role as a healer of headaches. An episode in the life in which he heals Brigit of headache is echoed in the ninth-century Irish life of Brigit. A stone close to the existing church is still associated with the curing of headaches; it may be the stone mentioned in the Irish life of Brigit in association with Áed mac Bricc.

Durrow was probably the burial place of **Cormac ua Liatháin** (*fl.* late 6th cent.), whose feast day was 21 June. He belonged to the royal kindred of the kingdom of the Uí Liatháin in the east of modern co. Cork (where Castlelyons is Caisleán ua Liatháin). No life of Cormac survives but he is an important character in Adomnán's life of Columba. He was included together with three other 'holy founders of monasteries', Comgall moccu Araidi of Bangor, Cainnech moccu Dalonn of Aghaboe, and Brendan of Clonfert, who together visited Columba on the island of 'Hinba' (*Life of Columba*, 3.17), but his best-remembered role was as a navigator, 'a holy man who sought with great labour not less than three times a desert in the ocean, and yet found none' (ibid., 1.6). By Adomnán's time, it is quite likely that some of the settlements of Irish monks in the Atlantic (Faeroes and Iceland), recorded by the geographer Dícuil in the early ninth century, had already been established. Adomnán, therefore, may have had good reason to believe that none of the land discovered in the Atlantic was inhabited. One detail given by Adomnán, however, raises the question whether Cormac sailed in the same frame of mind. Cormac sailed from Eirros Domno (Erris) beyond the River Moy, namely from the north-western part of Mayo. This included the district in which Patrick lived as a slave, by the 'Silva Vocluti'. Moreover, Patrick is likely to have included that district in those lands beyond which there was only the ocean, the western edge of the inhabited world, to which he was proud to have brought the Christian faith, in fulfilment of an eschatological passage in Paul's epistles implying that once the inhabited world had all been evangelized the last Judgment would come. By Cormac's time it would have been apparent that, though Ireland was on the edge of the world, 'a pimple upon the face of the world', as Cummian (possibly Cumméne Fota) was to call it in his letter to Ségéne, abbot of Iona, and Béccán the anchorite, the last Judgment had not come. Some may well have concluded that there might be inhabited land to the west still unevangelized, land which it was their Christian duty to discover. Cormac, who came from Munster and had no connection with north-western Connacht, may have chosen to sail from Erris, in Mayo, because it was perceived as the western edge of the known world, from which a voyage to discover if there were any more land in the Atlantic might properly begin.

Beyond Durrow, a few miles further south-west, lay Lynally (Lann Elo), the monastery of **Colmán Elo** [Colmán moccu Sailni, Colmán mac Beognai] (*d.* 611), whose feast day was 26 September. He came from an Ulster people to which the founder of the church of Connor, Mac Nisse, also belonged. Colmán himself was described in one of his

lives as the second patron of Connor. In his Salmanticensis life, however, although it is probably eighth-century, it is claimed that he belonged to the Uí Néill. No doubt this reflects the situation of Lynally within the lands of the Uí Néill, but it is also paralleled by the generalized reference in the life of Áed mac Bricc to his descent from Niall. Both churches, under the shadow of the Cland Cholmáin kings of Meath, were tending to conceal other loyalties. Yet, in spite of the life, Colmán's membership of Dál Sailni, attested in Adomnán's life of Columba, remained well-known: not only is there the reference in the life of Mac Nisse to his kinship with that saint, but his pedigree in the genealogies of the saints reveals his northern origins and his kinship both with Mac Nisse of Connor and with Senán of Láthrach Briúin, near Maynooth (both also attested by joint abbacies). The claim in the martyrology of Donegal that his mother was Mór, sister of Columba of Iona, is demonstrably late, since neither Colmán nor Mór is mentioned in the account of Columba's sisters' sons written *c*.700; presumably it reflects the proximity of Lynally to Durrow and the association with Columba revealed by Adomnán, from whose work the life of Colmán Elo borrowed incidents. The same concerns governed the account of the foundation of Lynally. According to the life, the decision was taken at an assembly of the kings of the Uí Néill, including Áed Sláne of Brega and Áed mac Ainmirech of Cenél Conaill, Columba's cousin. At this assembly were also present Columba, Cainnech of Aghaboe, and Colmán Elo. Áed Sláne's gift of land 'in the Wood of Ail [*Fid Elo*]' on his southern frontier was dictated by Columba. Moreover, the site for the monastery was chosen jointly by Colmán Elo himself and Columba's disciple Laisrán, presumably the *Laisrén or Laisrán [see under Iona, abbots of] of whom Adomnán relates that he was the head of Durrow during Columba's lifetime and who was also third abbot of Iona. Otherwise the prevailing theme of the life is Colmán Elo's friendship with neighbouring saints, notably *Mo Lua moccu Óche [see under Munster, saints of], the founder of Clonfertmulloe on the southern side of Slieve Bloom, and with Mo Chutu of Rahan, just over 2 miles to the west of Lynally (see further below). The concentration of major churches within a few miles of each other, with the supply of good land limited by surrounding bogs, determined the concerns of the life.

There is good manuscript evidence in favour of Colmán Elo's authorship of the *Apgitir Chrábaid* ('Alphabet of piety'), a vernacular text in verse and prose, both an exceptionally polished piece of writing and one of the central texts within the early Irish tradition of spiritual and moral teaching. If the text is indeed by Colmán Elo, he would appear to have deliberately avoided the archaisms of language found in early legal texts, while at the same time employing most of the stylistic artifices, other than archaism, to be found in the laws. It has also been suggested that he may have been the author of the Latin hymn on St Patrick ascribed to Secundinus.

Further south-west, on the southern boundary of the kingdom of Cenél Fiachach, was Kinnitty (Cenn Etig), the church of **Fínán Cam mac Móenaig** (*fl.* late 6th–early

7th cent.), whose feast day is 7 April. Although Kinnitty was on the north side of Slieve Bloom, it was said to have been on the very border between Munster and the lands of the Uí Néill. Fínán Cam himself came from the Corcu Duibne, the ruling group of the Dingle peninsula in west Munster. His mother is named as Bécnat, daughter of Cian, but it is not said to what kindred she belonged. In the West Munster Synod, a propaganda text written in west Munster *c*.800, in which particular saints were so closely identified with their peoples that they could swear on their behalf, Fínán Cam swore allegiance to the alliance on behalf of Corcu Duibne. Like Áed mac Bricc and Colmán Elo, Fínán Cam was the subject of an early, probably eighth-century, life in the Codex Salmanticensis. The life portrays him as the defender and representative of his people: he protects them from the attacks of the Uí Fhidgeinte (modern co. Limerick) and secures a remission of tribute from Faílbe Flann, king of Munster (*d*. 637). He was a disciple of Brendan of Clonfert and Ardfert, but it is not made clear whether this was in the southern church, Ardfert, or in Connacht, Clonfert being much closer to Kinnitty, Ardfert to Corcu Duibne. The principal surviving physical testimony to the church of Kinnitty is the high cross, now in the grounds of a hotel.

A distance of 8 miles west of Kinnitty is Birr, the site of the church of **Brendan mac Nemainn** (*d*. 565/573), whose feast day is 29 November, and who was an older contemporary of Brendan of Clonfert. In the West Munster Synod, Brendan of Birr swore on behalf of the Cuirigi, an exceedingly obscure group of peoples; in a genealogy he is assigned to Dál nAuluimm to whom Erc of Slane is also assigned. In the genealogies of the saints he is attributed to the widely distributed but politically weak descendants of the Ulster hero, Fergus mac Róich. No life survives, though apparently a fragmentary text still existed in the seventeenth century. Yet in spite of his undistinguished and uncertain lineage and the lack of a surviving life, Brendan of Birr came to be reckoned in the post-viking period as one of 'the twelve apostles of Ireland'. Much earlier, in Adomnán's life of Columba, Brendan was the only person to rise up as Columba approached a synod at Tailtiu (Teltown) that was all set to condemn him; Adomnán also devoted a chapter to Columba's miraculous perception of the angelic welcome given to Brendan's soul: 'in this past night I have seen the sky suddenly opened, and companies of angels coming down to meet the soul of the holy Brendan' (*Life of Columba*, 3.11). The chapter demonstrates that it was the day of death and not the day of burial that was commemorated as the (celestial) birthday of the saint.

North of Birr and Kinnitty lay the three major monasteries of Delbnae Bethra: Rahan, Lemanaghan, and Clonmacnoise. The principal saint of Rahan, *Mo Chutu [see under Munster, saints of], died at his Munster monastery of Lismore on 14 May 637, having the previous year been expelled from Rahan on account of his paschal views. He was, however, largely to displace an earlier saint, **Camulacus** (*fl*. 5th cent.?), who is attested in the late seventh-century *Collectanea* of Tírechán and in the hymn in his

honour preserved in the antiphonary of Bangor. Camulacus must, on the evidence of his name, have been a Briton, and Rahan thus offers an unusually well-attested example of the submerging of an early cult of a British saint in Ireland. Unless he is the Mo Chamal of 16 May, Camulacus was not included in the martyrologies.

Ciarán mac int Shaír (*c*.515–548/9) of Clonmacnoise (feast day 9 September), was described as *mac int shaír* ('son of the wright'), but his father's name was Béoán; he came from the Cruithnian people of Latharnae, who gave their name to the modern town of Larne; his mother, Dar Erca, was later said to be Patrick's sister, but this was Patrician propaganda of a familiar kind. The monastery of Clonmacnoise (Cluain Moccu Nois) was founded a year before his death. Its border location on the east bank of the Shannon and the comparatively humble, and distant, situation of the Latharnae were exploited in two directions. First, as with the monastery of Clonfertmulloe in the north of Munster, the abbacy was not attached to any one family. Abbots were recruited from a wide variety of kindreds, so creating links with many kingdoms. Second, Clonmacnoise extended its influence not just in Meath but also, and especially, in Connacht. In the Middle Irish genealogies of the saints, it is said that the Connachta followed Ciarán, the Uí Néill Columba. The acquisition of lordship over Connacht churches by Clonmacnoise was said by Tírechán, writing *c*.690, to have spread in the recent past. The prestige of Clonmacnoise within Connacht is demonstrated by the ecclesiastical edicts, *cánai*, promulgated in the province in the name of Ciarán in the eighth century. But the monastery was also patronized by the Uí Néill and especially by Cland Cholmáin; the west cross was put up at the expense of a late ninth-century king of Tara, Flann Sinna, who is very probably represented, together with the abbot, on one of its panels.

None of the three Latin and one Irish lives of Ciarán is early. They fall into three main sections: first comes the saint's origins and education; then his period at Inis Aingin (Hare Island at the southern end of Lough Ree); and finally his foundation of Clonmacnoise and, only one year later, his death. The first section was mainly designed to buttress alliances between Clonmacnoise and other great churches; Ciarán was thus among the pupils of Énda of Aran and Finnián of Clonard. But the version edited by Charles Plummer, a thirteenth-century reworking of older materials, also reveals a political allegiance. Ciarán's father, initially working as a wright in Meath, left that province for Connacht because of the heavy taxes imposed by a king of Tara, Ainmire mac Sétnai. This early tax exile then established himself in Mag nAí, where Ciarán was born. Ainmire, of Cenél Conaill in the north, was not king of Tara until well after Ciarán's death. He may have been chosen as a king associated both with Columba of Iona and Durrow, and therefore with the new monastery of Columba at Kells, to make tactfully coded suggestions to Cland Cholmáin, the royal dynasty of Meath. The implication is, presumably, that the kings of Meath (Cland Cholmáin) should forbear to impose heavy taxes, or perhaps taxes at all, on Clonmacnoise. The second section is centred on Inis Aingin, his first monastery, situated in Lough Ree (much favoured by monastic founders) and thus between Connacht and Meath. Finally, in the third section, with the foundation of Clonmacnoise, the saint returned to Meath from where his father had been driven by the tax collector.

Plummer rightly noted the sentiments expressed by Ciarán before death as unusual for Irish saints. Many of the latter saw their own sanctity from afar, with angels anxious to escort them to heaven. Not so Ciarán for whom death was a subject of anxiety about the unknown and trepidation at the judgment of God. It is possible, as Plummer guessed, that this is a fragment of early, unformulaic material which survived into the late medieval text. Much of the matter in the lives, however, had more to do with the history of Clonmacnoise than with Ciarán; in placing the saint's birth in Mag nAí, they were probably seeking to align the monastery with the dominant dynasty of Connacht from the eighth century, the Uí Briúin Aí.

Ciarán's first foundation, Inis Aingin, remained within the jurisdiction of Clonmacnoise to judge by an annal entry recording the profanation and insulting of the island in 899, where a synod was being held, headed by **Coirpre Crom mac Feradaig** (d. 904), bishop of Clonmacnoise, whose feast day was 6 March. A story probably put into circulation by Clonmacnoise declared that this Coirpre, who was himself included in the martyrologies as a saint, had succeeded in bringing to heaven, by dint of prolonged and intense prayer, the soul of Máel Sechnaill mac Máele Ruanaid, king of Tara. Although, therefore, Clonmacnoise flourished by dint of good relations, genuine and fictional, with the most powerful kings of both Meath and Connacht, it also sustained a reputation as the home of holy men and scholars, such as Coirpre and also **Colcu ua Duinechda** (d. 796), *scriba* and probably bishop of Clonmacnoise, whose feast day was 20 February. He has been identified with the Colcu who was Alcuin's correspondent and teacher of Alcuin's pupil, *Joseph Scottus, but this is improbable: Alcuin's friend was evidently resident in England. The martyrology of Donegal ascribes to him 'the kind of prayer that is called the Broom of Devotion' (Scuab Crábhaidh), referring to the litanies of Jesus (nos. 4 and 5 in Plummer's *Irish litanies*). His inclusion in the martyrology of Tallaght suggests that he was venerated by the Céili Dé reformers of the late eighth century, although they had little time for many of the wealthier and more secularized 'old churches'; he may, therefore, be the Colcu referred to, in terms of respect, in 'The monastery of Tallaght'. Such houses as Clonmacnoise were probably tending to divide between an abbatial administration, set upon defending and expanding the material interests of the monastery, and the *scribae* (leading scriptural scholars), anchorites, and bishops whose concerns were more spiritual. Yet the split was not complete, for some abbots were also venerated for their religious manner of life and scholarship.

As the most important churches of the midlands were in the client kingdoms to the south of the main lands held by Cland Cholmáin, so the church of **Caillín** [Caillén] **mac Niataig** (*fl.* 6th cent.?) lay to the north of the heartlands of Mide, at Fenagh, in modern co. Leitrim. Fenagh is in the drumlin belt, in an area of poor lands and, in the early period, marginal dynasties. Once the area had been conquered by what claimed to be a cadet branch of the Uí Briúin of Connacht—a branch that became the Ó Ruairc (O'Rourkes) of Bréifne—however, the fortunes of Fenagh and of St Caillín improved. The main information comes from the Book of Fenagh, written in 1516 for the family regarded as the heirs of Caillín, the Uí Ródaigh (O'Roddys). Its concern is with the dues and fees paid to Fenagh; stories about Caillín serve to justify such claims. His feast day was celebrated on 13 November.

Later foundations The saint of Lemanaghan, **Manchán mac Silláin** (d. 665), whose feast day was 24 January, was not the subject of a life; his church, a late arrival in the kingdom of Delbnae Bethra, was apparently overshadowed by its neighbour to the west, Clonmacnoise. There are only two obits of abbots during the eighth and ninth centuries. On the other hand, there are six early gravestones and there is the twelfth-century tomb-shaped shrine containing Manchán's relics, which seems never to have left the district and is preserved in a neighbouring Catholic church at Boher.

Although it is a general rule that the more important churches of Meath lay on its borders, a partial exception is the monastery of Fore, to the north-east of Lough Leane in Westmeath, and within a client kingdom close to the centre of power of the Cland Cholmáin kings. Fore (Fobar) was the monastery of **Féchín moccu Cháe** [Mo Fhéccu mac Caílcharna] (d. 665), whose feast day was 20 January. The genealogies contain rival claims associating him with the Gailenga (of Meath and northern Connacht) and the Fothairt (mainly of Leinster). The latter claim may be connected with his church of Láthrach Caín, probably one of the places named Laragh in Leinster. The first Irish life (the printed text, from a single fourteenth-century manuscript, is a combination of two earlier lives) associated him with the Luigne of Connacht and, in particular, with the church of Achonry and its patron saint, Nath Í. Similarly, Fore itself is said to have been within the bounds of the Luigne of Meath. Just as Cianán of Duleek linked together the Ciannachta of Brega and of Glenn Geimin, so Féchín linked together the Luigne of Connacht and Meath. As befitted the saint of an important client kingdom, Féchín was shown as taking a firm line with overkings, such as Diarmait mac Áeda Sláne, king of Tara. The second Irish text shows rather more interest in Leinster and provides a story of a usual kind to justify the payment of rents of Féchín from Leinster. In the Latin and Irish lives his mother was called Lassair; according to the first Irish life, she was of the royal family of Munster. Féchín also founded a monastery on the island of Omey near Clifden in Connemara, confirming his Connacht connections, but Fore was his principal church and 'the place of his resurrection'.

A saint similarly closely identified with a client people was **Ultán moccu Chonchobair** (d. 657), bishop of Dál

Conchobair (Conchuburnenses) and abbot of Ardbraccan, whose feast day was 4 September. An addition to his pedigree in the genealogies of the saints says that his mother, Collo (Colla) ingen Dímmai, was of the Gailenga (a neighbouring client kingdom), and thus Ultán (that is, Ardbraccan) was entitled to a share of dues from them. In the Rheims prologue of the ninth century, Ultán was the first named hagiographer of Brigit, preceding Ailerán and Cogitosus. A hymn to Brigit, *Brigit bé bithmaith*, was ascribed to him (the ascription is probably of the eleventh century, and, although almost certainly false, it attests his continuing reputation as a supporter of the cult). He also, however, possessed a book from which Tírechán, in the late seventh century, took his information about the four names of Patrick. The Latin phrase used by Tírechán may imply that Ultán was the author of the book. In any case, Ultán was certainly an oral source for Tírechán and was also his teacher. Ultán is thus important in that he demonstrates that a bishop of a client people within the lands of the southern Uí Néill could be concerned with the hagiography of both Patrick and Brigit.

The only important female saint within the lands of the southern Uí Néill, and also one of the later saints to be given a cult, was **Samthann ingen Díaráin** (*d.* 739) of Clonbroney (Cluain Brónaig) in the northern Tethbae kingdom of Cenél Coirpri, whose feast day was 19 December. Samthann was not the founder of Cluain Brónaig. In her Latin life that honour is reserved for **Funech** (*fl.* late 7th cent.), whose feast day was 11 December. Funech, however, is made responsible for bringing Samthann to Cluain Brónaig; the suggestion, therefore, is that Cluain Brónaig was founded in the second half of the seventh century. In the tripartite life of Patrick, however, it was claimed that the founders were two sisters of **Guasacht maccu Buáin** (*fl.* late 5th cent.), bishop of Granard, and thus of the kingdom of Cenél Coirpri in northern Tethbae to which Cluain Brónaig belonged, whose feast day was celebrated on 24 January. This is coupled with a claim that the head of the church of Granard had the right to veil all the nuns. There may be some connection, not easy to decipher, between this claim and the pedigree given to Samthann in the genealogies of the saints, namely that she was great-granddaughter of Díchu mac Trichim, the founder of the ecclesiastical family of Saul in co. Down (Patrick's claimed burial place). Both claims are made within the language of Patrician hagiography, specifically its Ulster branch; the connection with Díchu is quite impossible chronologically, but what it probably signifies is a rejection of the story in the tripartite life, the latter being favourable to Granard. In the Patrician legend, Díchu was Patrick's friend while Míliucc maccu Bóin was his owner when he was a slave and refused to be converted. The pedigree thus aligned Samthann with the church of Saul and with the Dál Fiatach of co. Down, and was opposed to the kindred of Guasacht maccu Buáin of Granard. The pedigree is echoed by the life's assertion that Samthann came from the Ulaid. It neatly gets her to the right part of Ireland by going on to say that her foster father was Cridán, king of Cenél Coirpri.

The broad lines of her career as a nun are set out in the life. Samthann was given to a man in marriage by her foster father, put up stern resistance, and thus compelled him to accept that she should be betrothed to God. She thereupon entered the monastery of 'Airnaide' (perhaps the Urney near Lifford, modern co. Donegal, or the Urney of co. Cavan), where she was in charge of the material sustenance of the monastery. From there she was summoned by Funech to succeed her at Cluain Brónaig. Perhaps the most striking point made by the life is that Niall mac Fergaile (Niall Frossach), king of Tara (*d.* 778), was so attached to her memory that he enshrined her staff. Niall was from Cenél nÉogain, while Cluain Brónaig was within a client kingdom of Cland Cholmáin of Mide. It suggests that a northern Uí Néill king of Tara might extend his power in the midlands, not his normal sphere of influence, by patronage of churches.

NATHALIE STALMANS and T. M. CHARLES-EDWARDS

Sources *Ann. Ulster* · S. Mac Airt, ed. and trans., *The annals of Inisfallen* (1951) · *AFM* · W. M. Hennessy, ed. and trans., *Chronicum Scotorum: a chronicle of Irish affairs*, Rolls Series, 46 (1866) · D. Murphy, ed., *The annals of Clonmacnoise*, trans. C. Mageoghagan (1896); facs. edn (1993) · W. Stokes, ed., 'The annals of Tigernach [8 pts]', *Revue Celtique*, 16 (1895), 374–419; 17 (1896), 6–33, 119–263, 337–420; 18 (1897), 9–59, 150–97, 267–303, 374–91; pubd sep. (1993) · R. I. Best and H. J. Lawlor, eds., *The martyrology of Tallaght*, HBS, 68 (1931) · *Félire Óengusso Céli Dé / The martyrology of Oengus the Culdee*, ed. and trans. W. Stokes, HBS, 29 (1905) · W. Stokes, ed., *The martyrology of Gormán*, HBS, 9 (1895) · J. H. Todd and W. Reeves, eds., *The martyrology of Donegal* (1864) · K. Meyer, ed., 'The Laud (610) genealogies and tribal histories', *Zeitschrift für Celtische Philologie*, 8 (1911), 291–338, 418–19 · M. A. O'Brien, ed., *Corpus genealogiarum Hiberniae* (Dublin, 1962) · P. Ó Riain, ed., *Corpus genealogiarum sanctorum Hiberniae* (Dublin, 1985) · W. W. Heist, ed., *Vitae sanctorum Hiberniae ex codice Salmanticensi nunc Bruxellensi* (Brussels, 1965) · C. Plummer, ed., *Vitae sanctorum Hiberniae* (1910) · C. Plummer, ed. and trans., *Bethada náem nÉrenn / Lives of Irish saints*, 2 vols. (1922) · W. Stokes, ed., *Lives of the saints from the Book of Lismore*, 2 vols. (1890) · F. J. Byrne, *Irish kings and high-kings* (1973) · A. Gwynn and R. N. Hadcock, *Medieval religious houses: Ireland* (1988) · E. Hogan, ed., *Onomasticon Goedelicum, locorum et tribuum Hiberniae et Scotiae* (1910) · J. F. Kenney, *The sources for the early history of Ireland* (1929); repr. (1979) · Lord Killanin and M. V. Duignan, *Shell guide to Ireland* (1962) · T. W. Moody and others, eds., *A new history of Ireland*, 9: *Maps, genealogies, lists* (1984) · C. Plummer, 'A tentative catalogue of Irish hagiography', *Miscellanea Hagiographica Hibernica* (1925) · R. Sharpe, *Medieval Irish saints' lives: an introduction to the 'Vitae sanctorum Hiberniae'* (1991) · M. Herbert, *Iona, Kells and Derry: the history and hagiography of the monastic families of Columba* (1988) · *Adomnán's life of Columba*, ed. and trans. A. O. Anderson and M. O. Anderson, 2nd edn (1991) · W. Stokes, ed. and trans., *The tripartite life of Patrick, with other documents relating to that saint*, 2 vols., Rolls Series, 89 (1887) · D. N. Dumville and others, *Saint Patrick, AD 493–1993* (1993) · J. Ryan, *Irish monasticism: origins and early development* (1931); 2nd edn (1972), repr. (1992) · A. W. Wade-Evans, ed., *Vitae sanctorum Britanniae et genealogiae* (1944) · *Senchas Már, Corpus iuris Hibernici*, ed. D. Binchy (1978) · C. Plummer, *Irish litanies*, HBS, 62 (1925) · F. E. Warren, *The antiphonary of Bangor*, 2 vols., HBS, 4 and 10 (1893–5) · S. H. O'Grady, *Silva Gadelica*, 2 vols. (1892)

Meautys, Sir Thomas (*c.*1590–1649), government official, was the third son of Thomas Meautys (*d.* 1614) of West Ham, Essex, and St Julian's Hospital, Hertfordshire, and Elizabeth (*d.* 1641), daughter of Sir Henry Coningsby of North Mimms, Hertfordshire. The family was descended from John Meautas (or Meautis), a native of Calais and secretary of the French tongue to Henry VII. Thomas Meautys's great-great-grandfather, Philip, was a clerk of the privy council under Henry VII and Henry VIII. His great-grandfather, Sir Peter, gentleman of the privy chamber to Henry VIII, undertook delicate continental missions for the king and acquired the family's Essex estates, former monastic property.

Meautys attended Lincoln's Inn and as a young man was employed by Robert Cecil, first earl of Salisbury. Salisbury's secretary, Sir Thomas Wilson, his uncle by marriage, probably introduced him to Sir Francis Bacon, later lord chancellor and by 1616 he was in Bacon's employment, as were two of his brothers, while a third was employed by Bacon's protégé Sir John Finch. Meautys and his brothers benefited from their association with Bacon through holding a series of administrative offices in chancery. In 1619 he became an extraordinary clerk of the privy council. He was elected to the parliament of 1621 for the Cambridge borough through the lord chancellor's patronage and would also represent it in every Caroline parliament up to the Short Parliament, though usually as an inactive member.

In 1621, however, Meautys was a vocal and vehement defender of Bacon, accused of using his office to solicit bribes. He said he could see the proceedings were already 'chalked out' and demanded hard evidence of his patron's offences. Ultimately he was accused by the house of having served as middleman in the lord chancellor's misconduct, but seems to have escaped punishment when Bacon submitted to the charges. This trial infused him with a bitterness and cynicism toward politics and government, attitudes especially evident in the long series of letters he wrote to his cousin and future mother-in-law, Jane, Lady Bacon.

Whether involved in misconduct or not, Meautys did serve as middleman for Bacon in numerous financial and political transactions. He negotiated Bacon's transfer of a lease on York House to the lord treasurer Sir Lionel Cranfield in hope of obtaining his assistance in Bacon's quest for restoration. It was also through Meautys that Bacon approached the king and the royal favourite, the duke of Buckingham, on matters ranging from approval for the publication of Bacon's life of Henry VII to his return to court. Buckingham defended the offices and reversions held by Meautys in chancery when they were attacked by the new lord keeper, John Williams. When he attempted to redeem a reversion to a mastership of requests, however, Sir John Coke approached Buckingham for that office. He suggested Meautys be given one of the two council clerkships about to become vacant and Buckingham agreed, though he upheld incumbent clerk Sir Francis Cottington's wish to be paid £450 for the office. Meautys was later allowed to recoup the money from the making of a baronet, for which he preferred his cousin, Sir Frederick Cornwallis.

In 1626 Buckingham aided Meautys in his attempt to add the clerkship of writs and processes in Star Chamber to his collection of offices. Meautys borrowed £600 of the

£900 it cost him from Jane, Lady Bacon. Sir Francis Bacon died in April 1626 and the probate of his will a year later made Meautys, along with the other chief creditor, Sir Robert Rich, co-administrator of his patron's debt-ridden estate. He funded a marble monument with an epitaph composed by his cousin Sir Henry Wotton to be erected over the grave of his beloved master in St Michael's, Gorhambury, Hertfordshire, and seems to have done quite well for himself out of Bacon's estate. Gorhambury was conveyed to trustees for the use of Meautys, who leased it to his cousin-by-marriage, the earl of Sussex, and then to the earl's widow and her new husband.

In June 1626 Meautys was admitted to Gray's Inn and took up residence in Bacon's old chambers there. The following September he purchased the crown manor of Redbourne, Hertfordshire, once held by Bacon. His combined income from land and the offices he held has been estimated at between £1000 and £1200 per annum, a comfortable sum despite his complaints that the demands of continual service deprived him of any free time. Some of his colleagues in the council office believed him expert at 'slipping his neck out of the collar' of his service in the post, undertaken in rotation. After Bacon's death he apparently conducted occasional business for members of the nobility such as Bacon's old friend Edward Sackville, earl of Dorset, and Thomas Wentworth, earl of Cleveland, of whose family Meautys counted himself a member.

Twice during the 1630s Meautys applied for a licence to remove butcher's offal from London, but was denied both times. On the basis of his council clerkship, he was appointed muster master general in March 1636. In 1638 Meautys and his heirs were granted a weekly market and three annual fairs at Redbourne, and that same year he became treasurer for life to the Company of Starchmakers. The next spring he was one of two council clerks designated to attend the king on his journey to York, but he fell ill and returned to London to recover. He was elected to the Short Parliament for Cambridge on the lord keeper's nomination, alongside Oliver Cromwell, but despite his provision of money and venison for feasting the corporation at the spring election, he lost the seat in the Long Parliament to town councillor John Lowry.

In February 1641, the same month he was knighted by the king at Whitehall, Meautys arranged for his Coningsby nieces to inherit Redbourne, but changed his mind on his marriage three months later, settling the manor on his young bride, Anne (bap. 1615, d. 1680), daughter of Jane, Lady Bacon. He was reportedly very ill again in 1642: 'pore man he lokes miserably', one of his cousins wrote (Verney, 1.254). He effectively retired and was living at Gorhambury when he was lightly taxed by the parliamentarian commissioners in 1645. He died at Gorhambury and was buried at Bacon's feet in St Michael's Church on 31 October 1649. His infant daughter Jane was his sole heir but his estate passed to his brother Henry at the child's premature death in 1652. His widow married Sir Harbottle Grimston, an old business acquaintance and later speaker of the Convention Commons, who purchased Redbourne and Gorhambury.   S. A. BARON

Sources *CSP dom.* • PRO, state papers domestic, Charles I, SP16 • PRO, state papers domestic, James I, SP14 • *The Fortescue papers*, ed. S. R. Gardiner, CS, new ser., 1 (1871) • R. Clutterbuck, ed., *The history and antiquities of the county of Hertford*, 3 vols. (1815–27) • A. Chambers Bunten, *Sir Thomas Meautys, secretary to Lord Bacon, and his friends* (1908) • *The works of Francis Bacon*, ed. J. Spedding, R. L. Ellis, and D. D. Heath, 14 vols. (1857–74) • G. E. Aylmer, *The king's servants: the civil service of Charles I, 1625–1642*, rev. edn (1974) • *The private correspondence of Jane, Lady Cornwallis, 1613–1644*, ed. Lord Braybrooke (1842) • F. P. Verney and M. M. Verney, *Memoirs of the Verney family*, 4 vols. (1892–9), vols. 1–2 • A. F. Upton, *Sir Arthur Ingram, c.1565–1642: a study in the origins of an English landed family* (1961) • *Calendar of the manuscripts of the most hon. the marquess of Salisbury*, 24, HMC, 9 (1976) • W. C. Metcalfe, ed., *The visitations of Hertfordshire*, Harleian Society, 22 (1886) • PRO, PC2 • APC

Archives Herts. ALS, Gorhambury MSS
Likenesses attrib. Van Somer, portrait, probably Gorhambury House
Wealth at death exact sum unknown: administration, Herts. ALS

Mechi, John Joseph (1802–1880), agriculturist, was born on 22 May 1802 in London, the third son of Giacomo Mechi, of Bologna, and of Elizabeth, daughter of J. Beyer of Poland Street, London. He passed much of his childhood in Kensington, where his father is said to have held a position at the palace, taking holidays in the countryside of Essex and Suffolk, and he finished his education in France. He entered the City at sixteen, as a clerk in a house in Walbrook in the Newfoundland trade. He married first, in 1823, Fanny Frost, who died in 1845 after giving birth to a son named after him, who also predeceased him. Second, in 1846, he married Charlotte, daughter of Francis Ward of Chillesford, Suffolk, with whom he had four daughters.

In 1827 Mechi was able to set up on his own account as a retail cutler in small premises at 130 Leadenhall Street; he moved to no. 4 in 1830. In that year he regularized his position by being admitted to the Loriners' Company (of which he was master in 1860–63), and by becoming a freeman in the City of London (he had to petition the court of common council because his father was not naturalized). His business prospered between 1830 and 1840; 'he set and ground razors with more than ordinary skill' (*City Press*, 29 Dec 1880) and supplied scientific instruments, pencils, and quill-cutting penknives. 'Mechi's magic razor strop' was heavily advertised and may have been based on a purchased patent. His own two patents, of 1840, were both concerned with lighting improvements—to illuminate shop window fronts and to modify oil and gas lamps so that the heat and the combustion vapours were carried off, thus improving room ventilation.

From 1840 Mechi turned his attention to farming and after an intensive study of the earlier English farming writers he resolved to practise, and especially to publicize, improvements in agriculture. Accordingly in 1841 he purchased, for £3400, Tiptree Hall Farm, said to be of 130–170 acres at Tiptree Heath, an area of poor clay soil in Essex. Mechi established a model farm with a large capital input for drainage and irrigation; the farm also had a 6 hp fixed steam-engine to provide power for driving barn machinery and for pumping water and liquid manure. The essence of his practice was to use the manure from sheep, pigs, and bullocks, expensively stall-fed on bought concentrates, to fertilize crops of wheat, pulses, and sown grasses. He held annual gatherings in July to which 'he invited men of talent and skill to witness the combined results of capital and science' (*ILN*, 11 April 1857), and he encouraged visitors, who came from all over the world and who recorded their comments in the visitors' book, kept from 1846 to 1878. The farm was the scene of the reaping machine trials of the 1851 Great Exhibition and of the 1855 trial of Robert Romaine's steam cultivator.

Above all Mechi used the spoken and written word to spread his views on scientific farming, with talks (many subsequently published) to farmers' clubs and agricultural societies, with letters to the agricultural press, and with his best-selling publications, notably the three main versions of *How to Farm Profitably* (1859, 1872, and 1878); included in these were the Tiptree Hall Farm balance sheets. Among the improvements he advocated were deep cultivation, farm steam power, and the use of town sewage. Although many were impressed by Mechi's achievements, others criticized his intensive husbandry for requiring a massive capital input beyond the reach of ordinary farmers.

Gradually Mechi's enterprises ceased to prosper. He had operated his business as a cutler with Charles Bazan (1859–69) and had moved to 112 Regent Street, London, but sales of the 'magic razor strop' and penknives declined. Certainly since 1840 Mechi had ceased to direct his creative energy into the City concerns which helped to underpin his farm financially. Nevertheless he was elected sheriff of London and Middlesex in 1856–7 (receiving a grant of arms in 1856), and alderman of the ward of Lime Street in the City in 1858. However, he resigned this post in 1866 to avoid the expensive prospect of becoming lord mayor, after heavy losses in companies that he had founded. The Unity Joint Stock Bank, of which he was a governor, failed in 1866, and the Unity Fire and General Life insurance companies were torn apart by internal dissension. Mechi was a juror in the department of art and science at the Great Exhibition of 1851 and also in the Paris Universal Exhibition of 1855. He was a member of the council of the Royal Agricultural College, Cirencester, from 1845, and of its committee of management from 1847, and he was regarded as the founder of the Royal Agricultural Benevolent Institution in 1860. Mechi was elected a member of the Farmers' Club, London in 1846, was a prominent speaker at meetings, and served as chairman 1877–8.

The decline of all Mechi's enterprises continued inexorably, that of Tiptree Farm being accelerated by the bad seasons of the 1870s which culminated in the disastrous year of 1879. Mechi became ill with diabetes and was forced to place his affairs into liquidation on 14 December 1880. He died at Tiptree Hall on 26 December 1880 and was buried in Tiptree Heath church on 1 January 1881.

Mechi's early farming success had coincided with the 'golden age' of English agriculture but it was doubtful whether his intensive method of mixed farming was appropriate to the heavy Essex clays or even to the more general run of English soils. His more lasting reputation must remain that of an enthusiastic publicist of scientific agriculture in an era of high farming.

JOHN S. CREASEY

Sources *City Press* (29 Dec 1880) · J. A. S. Watson and M. E. Hobbs, *Great farmers*, 2nd edn (1951), 86–97 · 'Mr Sheriff Mechi', *ILN* (11 April 1857), 337–8 · 'The Mechi testimonial', *ILN* (26 Sept 1857), 317–18 · *ILN* (8 Jan 1881), 37 · J. Caird, *English agriculture in 1850–51* (1852), 140–42 · G. E. Fussell, 'John Joseph Mechi of Tiptree Hall farm', *N&Q*, 149 (1925), 39–40 · E. Burritt, *A walk from London to John O'Groat's* (1864), 9–28 · L. de Lavergne, *The rural economy of England, Scotland, and Ireland* (1855), 221–3 · C. S. Orwin and E. H. Whetham, *History of British agriculture, 1846–1914*, 2nd edn (1971), 126–30 · *The Insurance Guardian* (24 Jan 1881) · A. B. Beaven, ed., *The aldermen of the City of London, temp. Henry III–[1912]*, 2 vols. (1908–13) · R. Sayce, *The history of the Royal Agricultural College, Cirencester* (1992) · d. cert. · *CGPLA Eng. & Wales* (1881) · F. W. Boot, *St Luke, the parish church of Tolleshunt Knights with Tiptree: a short history* (1988) · C. C. Spence, *God speed the plow* (1960) · J. Haining, *Ploughing by steam* (1970) · P. Pusey, 'On agricultural implements, class IX', *Journal of the Royal Agricultural Society of England*, 12 (1851), 611–16, 644–8

Archives BL, list of visitors to Tiptree Hall farm, 1846–78, Add. MS 30015 · CLRO, freedom rolls (City freedom admission papers), CFI/1582 [December 1830] · Essex RO, grant of arms, 12 July 1856 · UCL, corresp. with E. Chadwick

Likenesses stipple, pubd 1877, NPG · engraving, repro. in J. J. Mechi, *How to farm profitably*, 1st–4th edns (1859–64), frontispiece · engraving (after photograph), repro. in *ILN* (8 Jan 1881), 37 · lithograph, BM · wood-engraving (after photograph by London Stereoscopic Co.), repro. in *ILN* (11 April 1857), 338

Wealth at death under £2000: probate, 7 Jan 1881, *CGPLA Eng. & Wales*

Medawar, Sir Peter Brian (1915–1987), biologist, was born on 28 February 1915 in Rio de Janeiro, the elder child and only son of Nicholas Agnatius Medawar, a Brazilian businessman of Lebanese extraction, and his British wife, Edith Muriel Dowling. He was educated at Marlborough College and Magdalen College, Oxford, where he took a first-class degree in zoology in 1935 and a DSc in 1947. At Oxford he was successively a Christopher Welch scholar and senior demy of Magdalen (1935), a senior research fellow of St John's (1944), and a fellow by special election of Magdalen (1938–44 and 1946–7). From 1947 to 1951 he was Mason professor of zoology in the University of Birmingham, from 1951 to 1962 Jodrell professor of zoology and comparative anatomy in University College, London, and from 1962 to 1971 director of the National Institute for Medical Research, Mill Hill. From 1971 to 1986 he was head of the transplantation section of the Medical Research Council's clinical research centre, Harrow.

Medawar created a new branch of science, the immunology of transplantation. During the battle of Britain in 1940 a plane crashed near Oxford, and Medawar, engaged there in research on tissue growth and repair, was asked whether he could help the badly burnt pilot. Although he had nothing to offer at the time, this awoke in him an interest in transplantation of skin, which was to form the core of his scientific achievement. With the Glasgow surgeon Thomas Gibson he discovered the 'homograft reaction', the process whereby an immunological response causes the rejection of tissue that has been transplanted

between unrelated individuals. It took another two decades and the work of many people to find ways of overcoming this reaction by means of immunosuppressive drugs, but it was Medawar's first decisive step that made possible organ transplantation as it was later known.

Along the way he and his small research group, especially Leslie Brent and Rupert Billingham, made other important discoveries, most notably of immunological tolerance in 1954. The immune system discriminates efficiently between skin grafts of foreign and self-origin, and under certain experimental conditions, which Medawar and his colleagues first defined, it can be misled into treating as self what is in fact foreign. Just as a new branch of surgery sprang from Medawar's seminal work on the homograft reaction, so also a new branch of developmental biology sprang from his work on tolerance. For this discovery he was awarded the Nobel prize for medicine in 1960, jointly with Macfarlane Burnet.

It must not be thought that a scientist as clear-minded and creative as Medawar was never wrong. Indeed, it is precisely those qualities which make his few mistakes easy to identify. A conspicuous example was his idea, during the early 1950s, that pigment spreads in the skin by cell-to-cell passage of infective particles.

To a wider public Medawar was known for his eloquent projection of ideas in and about biology. He was passionately convinced of the power of the scientific method not only to create what he called a magnificent 'articulated structure of hypotheses', but also to solve human problems. His deepest contribution was to expound the deductive view of scientific activity. For Medawar the place of honour is occupied by the 'act of creation', in which a new idea is formulated; experimentation has the humbler (but entirely necessary) role of verifying ideas. He happily accepted the consequence that an idea can never formally be proved true. Even the faintest whiff of induction was dismissed with contumely. He took pleasure in searching out the roots of this position in the English thinkers of the last three centuries. In all of this he was much influenced by his friends the philosophers T. D. ('Harry') Weldon, Sir Alfred Ayer, and Sir Karl Popper. He conveyed these convictions with eloquence, elegance, and an unfailing sense of humour in ten books published between 1957 and 1986—including *The Uniqueness of the Individual* (1957), *The Future of Man* (1960), *Advice to a Young Scientist* (1979), and *The Limits of Science* (1984)—and in some 200 articles and reviews. His Reith lectures (1959) on the future of man powerfully rejected the gloom-and-doom view of the impact of science on ordinary life. 'Is the scientific paper a fraud?' (BBC Third Programme, 1963, reprinted in his *The Threat and the Glory*, 1990) was much enjoyed in scientific circles.

His autobiography, *Memoir of a Thinking Radish* (1986), relates that the Oxford senior common rooms taught him to regard no subject as intellectually beyond his reach. Throughout his life he was quick to respond to the ideas of those around him: colleagues, students, friends, and family. How delighted were the undergraduates who attended his tutorials to find themselves acknowledged in his profound review in 1947 of cellular inheritance and transformation. He never ran a large laboratory, and even as director of the National Institute for Medical Research he and two or three junior colleagues occupied just two rooms (where he continued to do his own research and his own washing up, on the Tuesdays and Thursdays that he kept free of administrative duties). He laughed at gigantic research programmes, and at the possibility that government might perceive the practical benefits of research better than the individual scientist who carried it out. In his own experimental work, and above all in his writing, he set a standard which inspired the post-war flowering of immunology.

Medawar needed and received the total love and support of his wife, whom he married on 27 February 1937, from their first meeting as undergraduates at Oxford to his last paralysing illness. She was Jean (b. 1912/13), daughter of Charles Henry Shinglewood Taylor, surgeon; they had two sons and two daughters. Jean entered fully into his professional life, filling first their house in Edgbaston, and then successively Lawn House and Holly Hill, their large houses in Hampstead, with his students and colleagues, many of whom became her own friends. They had a wide circle of friends in the media, in music, and especially in opera, which he enjoyed intensely. A sudden visit to Covent Garden or Glyndebourne was one of the joys of his University College days. His wife collaborated in his later writings, and maintained a strong interest in birth control and in the environment.

Medawar was tall, physically strong (an excellent cricketer), with a voice which could hold a lecture theatre in suspense or reassure a doubting student. Always accessible and open to argument, he had no doubts about his own capacity: sitting at his typewriter in University College, cigarette in his mouth, he told James Gowans that 'It takes an effort to write undying prose'. His books are lucid and beautifully written.

Medawar was elected a fellow of the Royal Society (1949), appointed CBE (1958) and CH (1972), knighted (1965), and admitted to the Order of Merit (1981). He became an honorary FBA in 1981. He was an honorary fellow of many colleges and was awarded numerous honorary degrees.

During Medawar's last fifteen years at the clinical research centre at Harrow he was partially paralysed from a stroke suffered in 1969, while reading the lesson in Exeter Cathedral at the British Association for the Advancement of Science (of which he was president in 1968–9), but his ideas continued to flow, and he both inspired and received support from devoted colleagues. He suffered several more strokes and eventually died from one on 2 October 1987, in the Royal Free Hospital, London.

AVRION MITCHISON, rev.

Sources P. B. Medawar, *Memoir of a thinking radish* (1986) · N. A. Mitchison, *Memoirs FRS*, 35 (1990) · personal knowledge (2004) · *The Times* (5 Oct 1987) · *The Independent* (5 Oct 1987) · *The Guardian* (9 Oct 1987) · m. cert. · *CGPLA Eng. & Wales* (1988)

Archives Wellcome L., corresp. and papers | Rice University, Houston, Texas, Woodson Research Center, corresp. with Sir Julian Huxley
Likenesses photograph, 1960, Hult. Arch. · photograph, repro. in *The Times* · photograph, repro. in *The Independent*
Wealth at death £385,982: probate, 1988, *CGPLA Eng. & Wales*

Medbourne, Matthew (*bap.* 1637?, *d.* 1680), actor and playwright, may have been the Mathew Medburne, son of George Medburne, who was baptized at St Margaret's, Westminster, London, on 17 June 1637. He performed with the Duke's Company, London, from 1661, and is the author or translator of at least one play. His earliest documented appearance on stage was as Delio in John Webster's *The Duchess of Malfi* on 30 September 1662, though he was active in the company before that date. Medbourne played many secondary roles for the Duke's Company throughout his career: Lennox in *Macbeth*, the Ghost in *Hamlet*, Morat in Elkanah Settle's *Ibrahim the Illustrious Bassa*, and Don Pedro in Aphra Behn's *The Rover*. He played the count of Blamount in Roger Boyle's *History of Henry V*, and John Downes notes that Medbourne played Clermont, though no role by that name appears in the play.

Medbourne may have been the author of *Saint Cecily, or, The Converted Twins*, which was licensed on 11 June 1666, during the time when the theatres were closed because of the plague. The play's title-page assigns authorship to 'E. M.', but Medbourne's name appears at the end of the dedication. Lori Sonderegger makes a convincing case for attributing the play to him. Medbourne's other known literary effort was a translation of Molière's play entitled by Medbourne as *Tartuffe, or, The French Puritan*. Judith Milhous and Robert D. Hume date this play as being performed in autumn or winter 1669–70 (Milhous and Hume, 'Dating play premieres'). Gerard Langbaine repeats the author's claim that it 'was receiv'd with universal Applause on our English Stage' (Langbaine, 367), but we have record of only one performance. An epilogue by Charles Sackville, earl of Dorset, from March 1670, credits Medbourne with ten plays, but only the two mentioned survive. His engagements with the Duke's Company are fairly steady throughout his career, though after the reopening of the theatres in autumn 1666 he is not listed in the company roster until 1668. He seems to have worked for the rival King's Company in the season 1669–70, since he appears to have spoken the epilogue to *Tartuffe*, which was performed at the King's Bridges Street Theatre. He appears to have returned to the Duke's Company for the 1670–71 season.

Medbourne's career was marred, however, by legal and political difficulties. On 18 July 1662 he was fined 3*s*. 4*d*. for assaulting a messenger from the office of the revels on 4 July. The bill states that he and eleven others, 'all twelve late of St. Clement's Danes' … with divers unknown disturbers of the peace, riotously assembled together and assaulted Edward Thomas, gentleman, and beat and maltreated him, and held him their prisoner for the space of two hours' (Jeaffreson). On 9 December 1669 an arrest warrant was issued for Medbourne and his fellow actor Samuel Sandford for 'refractory & disorderly' conduct

(Milhous and Hume, *Register*, vol. 1, p. 110). Medbourne's greatest trials were ahead. In November 1678 he played Agamemnon at Dorset Garden Theatre in John Banks's *The Destruction of Troy*. This was his last known stage role, for he was arrested, charged with high treason, and sent to Newgate prison on 26 November. As a Roman Catholic and an acquaintance of Titus Oates from at least 1676, he became swept up in the Popish Plot. A man named Phillips 'in Black Friars at the Wonder Tavern' swore on 3 February 1679 that 'Medbourne's wife, in the presence of another woman, offered in her husband's name to make him a man forever, if he could invalidate Oates' testimony' (*CSP dom.*). On 7 February Phillips maintained that 'a certain woman brought to him by Mrs. Medbourne offered him money to swear that Oates offered him money to bring witnesses against Medburne' (ibid.). Medbourne remained in Newgate until his death on 19 March 1680. In May 1679 he made out his will to 'give all that I have unto my wife', Catherine. Langbaine wrote that Medbourne was 'One, whose good parts deserv'd a better fate than to die in prison, as he did in the time of the late *Popish-Plot*; thro' a too forward and indiscreet Zeal for a mistaken Religion' (Langbaine, 366).   CHERYL WANKO

Sources Highfill, Burnim & Langhans, *BDA*, 10.164–5 · W. Van Lennep and others, eds., *The London stage, 1660–1800*, 5 pts in 11 vols. (1960–68) · J. Milhous and R. D. Hume, eds., *A register of English theatrical documents, 1660–1737*, 2 vols. (1991) · *CSP dom.*, 1645–7, 69 · J. C. Jeaffreson, *Middlesex county records*, Middlesex County Records Society (1888), vol. 3, pp. 322–3 · L. Sonderegger, 'Sources of translation', *Papers on French Seventeenth Century Literature*, 27 (2000), 553–72 · J. Downes, *Roscius Anglicanus*, ed. J. Milhous and R. D. Hume, new edn (1987) · G. Langbaine, *An account of the English dramatick poets* (1691); repr. (New York, Burt Franklin, 1967) · J. Milhous and R. D. Hume, 'Dating play premieres', *Harvard Library Bulletin*, 22 (1974), 383 · J. Kenyon, *The Popish Plot* (1972), 47 · P. Danchin, ed., *The prologues and epilogues of the Restoration, 1660–1700*, 7 vols. (1981–8), vol. 1, pp. 304–5, 354–5 · will, GL, Archdeaconry court of London, GL MS 9051/10, fols. 758v; MS 9050/1/2, fols. 28r, 47v · IGI

Medd, Peter Goldsmith (1829–1908), Church of England clergyman and ecclesiastical historian, was born on 18 July 1829, the eldest son of John Medd FRCS of Leyburn, Yorkshire, who practised at Stockport, and his wife, Sarah, daughter of William Goldsmith. After education at King's College, London, where he became an associate in theology in 1849 (and subsequently an honorary fellow), Medd matriculated at St John's College, Oxford, on 1 March 1848, from where he migrated as scholar to University College. He graduated BA there in 1852, and proceeded MA in 1855. He was a fellow of University College from 1852 to 1877, bursar in 1856, dean and librarian in 1861, and tutor from 1861 to 1870. After taking holy orders in 1853, he served a curacy at St John the Baptist, Oxford (1858–67); he left Oxford in 1870 to become rector of Barnes, Surrey, where he remained until 1876. In 1875 he declined an offer of the bishopric of Brechin; from 1876 until his death he was rector of North Cerney, near Cirencester. He married on 19 January 1876 Louisa, daughter of Alexander Nesbitt of Byfield House, Barnes. In 1877 he was made honorary canon of St Albans Abbey. In 1883 he was

proctor in convocation for the diocese of Gloucester and Bristol.

Medd played a leading part in the establishment of Keble College, Oxford, of whose council he was senior member in 1871. He was select preacher at Oxford in 1881 and Bampton lecturer in 1882. His Bampton lectures, published as *The One Mediator* (1884), were erudite, if terse. Medd's major interest was in the history of liturgy, on which he was an authority. In 1865 he edited, with William Bright, the *Liber precum publicarum ecclesiae Anglicanae*, the Latin version of the prayer book. He contributed in 1869 a historical introduction to Henry Baskerville Walton's edition of the first prayer book of Edward VI and the ordinal of 1549 (no longer, however, a standard edition). In 1892 he edited Lancelot Andrewes's *Greek Devotions*, from a manuscript annotated by Andrewes himself, which had been rediscovered by Robert George Livingstone, a tutor at Pembroke College; this was an earlier and more authentic transcript than the one on which all previous editions had been based. Medd also published a number of sermons and devotional works, which reflected his mildly Tractarian views, and contributed an introductory memoir to the *Selected Letters of William Bright* (1903).

Medd took a keen interest in the higher education of women, and represented his university on the council of Cheltenham Ladies' College. He died, after a long illness, at North Cerney on 25 July 1908, and was buried there. His wife, and their six sons and two daughters, survived him.

W. B. OWEN, *rev.* DONALD GRAY

Sources *The Times* (28 July 1908) · *WWW*, 1897–1915 · G. J. Cuming, *A history of Anglican liturgy*, 2nd edn (1982) · private information (1912) · *CGPLA Eng. & Wales* (1908)
Wealth at death £6555 9s. 8d.: probate, 27 Aug 1908, *CGPLA Eng. & Wales*

Mede [Mead], **Joseph** (1586–1638), Hebraist and biblical scholar, was born in October 1586 at Berden, Essex, of unknown parents 'of honest rank', according to the 'Life' contained in his collected works, and was related through his father to Sir John Mede (or Mead) of Wenden Lofts, near Bishop's Stortford. When Mede was ten his father died of smallpox, and his mother married a Gower of Naseing, Essex, by whom he was sent to school, first at Hoddesdon, Hertfordshire, and later at Wethersfield, Essex. While at Wethersfield, and on a trip to London, he purchased a copy of Bellarmine's *Institutiones linguae Hebraicae* and by the time he left school had, without any instruction, obtained a considerable working knowledge of Hebrew. In 1603 he matriculated as sizar at Christ's College, Cambridge, where he studied first under Daniel Rogers and then under William Addison, before graduating BA in 1607 and proceeding MA in 1610. In 1613 he was elected to succeed Hugh Broughton to the King Edward VI fellowship through the influence of Lancelot Andrewes, then bishop of Ely, after having been passed over several times on suspicion of having 'too much … tenderness to the Puritan faction' (Mede, 850). Valentine Cary, master of Christ's, may eventually have been disposed to view him more favourably on account of his friendship with Sir Martin Stuteville of Dalham, who was also a friend of

Mede. In 1618 Mede was appointed Mildmay Greek lecturer, holding both fellowship and lectureship for the rest of his life. He did not marry, and lived modestly in a chamber at ground level beneath the college library.

Mede was a man of wide interests and considerable attainment. In addition to his skills in Hebrew, Greek, and Latin and his knowledge of the biblical text in English and the original languages, he was proficient in several other disciplines. His early biographer describes him as 'an acute logician, an accurate philosopher, a skilful mathematician, a great philologer, and an excellent anatomist' (Worthington, ii). By invitation he frequently attended dissections at Gonville and Caius College. He was also proficient in botany, physics, and history, and was interested in astrology. He is said to have been as deeply versed in ecclesiastical antiquities and knowledge of the Greek and Latin fathers 'as any man living' (Brook, 429). His pursuit of knowledge and his scholarly achievements, including his biblical studies, were marked by a love of truth for its own sake. 'I cannot believe', he is reported as saying, 'that truth can be prejudiced by the discovery of truth' (ibid., 431). A period of scepticism early in his reading of philosophy, which led towards Pyrrhonism, gave way to devout belief. As has been observed, 'escaping the jaws of atheism, he fled towards faith' (Firth, 214).

Despite his profound erudition, Mede was a man of great modesty and humility. John Worthington, who is generally credited with the 'Life' of Mede prefixed to later editions of his *Works*, says he was 'studiously regardless' of formal academic attainment, ecclesiastical preferment, and worldly advantage (Worthington, xv). He eschewed higher degrees beyond the BD, which he took in 1618, and in 1627 and again in 1630 declined the provostship of Trinity College, Dublin, an opening made possible on the recommendation of Archbishop James Ussher, who is said to have sought Mede's assistance in the determination of his own great work on sacred chronology. Among Mede's pupils, whom he treated with great consideration, were several who achieved distinction, including John Milton and Henry More. Although his income was meagre Mede regularly gave one-tenth to charitable causes. He maintained good personal relationships and was known for his openness and generosity towards those who opposed him. He suffered throughout life from a speech impediment which, particularly in the early years, led him to decline many invitations to speak in public. He persevered with the defect, however, and was able to preach without noticeable hesitation.

Mede's theological and ecclesiological allegiance was finally settled in favour of moderation and episcopacy, although he was included in Benjamin Brook's *The Lives of the Puritans* (1813) and had some puritan sympathies. Worthington notes his 'reverential regard to the established government and discipline of the Church' (Worthington, xxx), and Ussher's support and, more strikingly, Andrewes's invitation to him to become his chaplain cannot be ignored. Brook refers to Mede's correspondence with several eminent nonconformists and his fear that

Roman rites would prevail again in the Church of England. Mede's view of Rome as the Antichrist and his conviction of the necessity of a godly life were both puritan emphases. They were balanced, however, by his concern that some puritan arguments opened the door to Socinianism and by his condemnation of a book by John Bastwick in a letter to Samuel Hartlib. He also opposed presbyterian discipline and practice. It would be incorrect to denominate him a party man in any strict sense, since a spirit of fraternal ecumenicity marked his outlook. He sought charity and mutual forbearance, 'the owning of each other as brethren and members of the same body whereof Christ is the head' (ibid., xvii). Remaining loyal to the Thirty-Nine Articles and prayer book liturgy, he expected that more would be achieved from mutual respect and toleration than by any attempt to legislate or impose uniformity.

Mede is notable for his works on biblical eschatology, and especially for *Clavis Apocalyptica* (1627), translated into English posthumously by Richard More and published as *The Key of the Revelation* (1643). It enjoyed the almost universal praise of contemporaries in England and on the continent and deeply influenced the development of eschatological thought in seventeenth-century England. Despite being intended originally only for private circulation among a select academic audience, it was published three times in Latin and in English between 1627 and 1650. The second Latin (1632) and subsequent English editions included Mede's *In sancti Joannis Apocalypsin commentarius*, a commentary on the Apocalypse, and the *Key* and the commentary, together with his other eschatological works, sufficiently emphasized the coming millennium to justify Mede being regarded as the father of English millenarianism. Given the radical nature of much of the ensuing millenarian activity, it was a reputation that Mede would have sought to avoid almost at any cost. He claimed to have reached his own moderate millenarian convictions with reluctance, having honestly endeavoured to locate the millennium in the past as had other interpreters, including Thomas Brightman and Hugo Grotius. His study of the biblical text, however, would not permit that conclusion. In anticipating a future millennium Mede did not consider that he was proposing extreme or heretical doctrine, but rather a return to the belief of the early church. The view that Mede derived his millenarianism from continental sources, particularly Alsted and Pareus, is outweighed by his own testimony and that of contemporaries. His biographer comments, 'He proceeded upon grounds never traced by any, and infinitely more probable than any laid down by those who before him undertook that task' (Worthington, vii). Fuller remarked that the Fifth Monarchists had driven the nail 'which Master Mede did first enter further than he ever intended it' (Fuller, 335). It remains fair comment on Mede's own millenarian position, and is supported by the later view that it was due to the efforts of others after his death that Mede was 'transformed from scholar to prophet' (Firth, 228). Most of his works were first published posthumously.

The distinctive element of the *Clavis Apocalyptica*, and

Mede's unique contribution to contemporary and subsequent prophetic studies, was the noted synchronisms, which he argued were essential to a correct understanding of the book of Revelation. Within the context of the prevailing historicist interpretation of apocalyptic prophecy, the thesis underlying the synchronisms was that the major prophetic outlines in the books of Daniel and the Revelation were inter-related, contingent on each other, and that at many points they overlapped in scope, depicting the same era or events with different emphases. This was Mede's 'Law of Synchronistical necessity' (Mede, 583). It proposed to unlock the mysteries of apocalyptic prophecy making them accessible and relevant to the present age. Mede's standing as a careful scholar ensured that it was to have a profound effect on the religious life and outlook of the time and on the immediate course of English history over the next three decades. In addition to placing the millennium firmly in the future, thus opening the way for speculative interpretations and extreme millenarianism, Mede's exegetical scheme had at least two further consequences: it confirmed historicism as the fundamental principle of prophetic interpretation in English eschatological thought for several succeeding generations, and it unhesitatingly identified Rome as the Antichrist and the predicted latter-day apostasy. In an age which vividly remembered the Gunpowder Plot and its associated fears, Mede's considered and clearly articulated view of Rome as 'the unfaithful and treacherous spouse, the Christian Jezebel' (J. Mede, *The Apostasy of the Latter Times*, 1641) was staple diet for English minds which cherished protestantism and valued their religious freedom. Mede's work underpinned such intrinsic aspects of the religious outlook which prevailed in English post-Reformation thought for another 300 years or so.

Chronology and eschatology formed the basis for much of Mede's extensive correspondence, published in the later definitive editions of his works, edited by John Worthington (3rd edn, 1672; reprinted, 1677). Between 1626 and 1638 Mede's correspondents included Samuel Hartlib and John Dury, and his friends William Ames, professor of theology at Franeker in the Netherlands, and Sir William Boswell, ambassador to The Hague, each of whom was instrumental in bringing Mede and the *Clavis Apocalyptica* to the attention of potential readers abroad, and conveyed to Mede the comments and criticisms of some of his overseas readers. He also corresponded with James Ussher, William Twisse—later prolocutor of the Westminster assembly, who provided the preface for *The Apostasy of the Latter Times*—and Samuel Ward, master of Sidney Sussex College, Cambridge. Between 1620 and 1631 Mede also wrote regularly and at length to his friend Sir Martin Stuteville. This extensive series of letters, filling two folio volumes in the British Library (Harleian MSS 389 and 390), deals largely with current university issues and matters of local and public interest in England and abroad, throwing additional light on Mede as a man of his time, willing and able to comment on contemporary issues. The correspondence was brought to an end by Sir Martin's death in 1631.

Mede himself died prematurely, and in some discomfort, on 1 October 1638 at Christ's College, his death precipitated by the application of inappropriate medication which caused an internal blockage. His will, drawn up the day before his death, reveals that he was a man of only modest means, worth in all no more than £500. He left £100 to 'the master and fellows' of Christ's College, £100 to the poor of Cambridge, and, after various smaller bequests to his sister and her children, to the children of a deceased sister, and to a pupil, the residue of his estate to Christ's College, 'towards the adorning of the College Chapel', where he was buried on 2 October. A delayed memorial service was held at Great St Mary's in February 1639 at which the preacher was John Alsop, also a fellow of Christ's and Mede's executor. A monumental inscription to Mede in Christ's College chapel, preserved in Latin (Mede, 35) and English, recalls his interest in philosophy, mathematics, chronology, history, and Near Eastern antiquities, and contains the words,

> He studied all languages, cultivated all the arts, … and above all things, theology, the queen of all sciences. … He was a bigot to no party, but loving truth and peace, he was just to all; candid to his friends, benignant to others: holy, chaste, and humble in his language, wishes, and habits. (Brook, 433)

It remains a fitting tribute to one of the more notable English scholars of the seventeenth century.

BRYAN W. BALL

Sources J. Peile, *Biographical register of Christ's College, 1505–1905, and of the earlier foundation, God's House, 1448–1505*, ed. [J. A. Venn], 1 (1910) · J. Mede, *The works of the pious and profoundly-learned Joseph Mede* (1677) · J. Worthington, 'The life of the reverend and most learned Joseph Mede', in *The works of … Joseph Mede*, ed. J. Worthington, 4th edn (1677) · B. Brook, *The lives of the puritans*, 2 (1813) · Venn, *Alum. Cant.*, 1/3 · E. Middleton, ed., *Biographia evangelica*, 4 vols. (privately printed, London, 1779–86), vol. 3 · D. Neal, *The history of the puritans or protestant nonconformists*, ed. J. Toulmin, new edn, 2 (1822) · K. R. Firth, *The apocalyptic tradition in Reformation Britain, 1530–1645* (1979) · B. W. Ball, *A great expectation: eschatological thought in English protestantism to 1660* (1975) · Fuller, *Worthies* (1662) · J. van den Bergh, 'Continuity within a changing context: Henry More's millenarianism, seen against the background of the millenarian concepts of Joseph Mede', *Pietismus und Neuzeit*, 14 (1988), 185–202 · J. van den Bergh, 'Joseph Mede and the Dutch millenarian Daniel van Laren', *Prophecy and eschatology*, ed. M. Wilks (1994), 111–22 · J. Hunt, *Religious thought in England from the Reformation to the end of the last century*, 1 (1870) · D. A. Cockburn, 'A critical edition of the letters of the Reverend Joseph Mead, 1626–27, contained in British Library Harleian MS 390', PhD diss., U. Cam., 1994 · *DNB* · will, PRO, PROB 11/179, fol. 142r · J. Heywood and T. Wright, eds., *Cambridge University transactions during the puritan controversies of the 16th and 17th centuries*, 2 (1854) · A. J. Gilsdorf, 'The puritan apocalypse: New England eschatology in the seventeenth century', PhD diss., Yale U., 1965 · F. S. Plotkin, 'Sighs from Sion: a study of radical puritan eschatology in England, 1640–1660', PhD diss., Columbia University, 1966

Archives BL, Harley MSS 389, 390 · BL, Harley MSS, letters to Sir Martin Stuteville · BL, Add. MSS 4276, 4254, 4179

Wealth at death approx. £500: will, PRO, PROB 11/179, fol. 142r

Medhurst, George (bap. 1759, d. 1827), mechanical engineer, was baptized on 11 February 1759 at Shoreham, Kent, the son of George and Anne Medhurst. He was in business as a clockmaker at Pleasant Row, Clerkenwell, London, until the imposition in 1797 of a duty on clocks depressed trade. He then turned to engineering, working at Battle Bridge, Clerkenwell. His first patent, filed in 1799 (no. 2299) was for a windmill and pump for compressing air to obtain motive power. The sails of the windmill were arranged in the manner which became commonplace for pumping windmills, while his machinery showed great ingenuity, with a governor attached to vary the length of stroke to the pump, according to the wind strength and the pressure of air in the reservoir. The specification included a description of a small rotary engine to be worked by compressed air. Medhurst pursued the idea of taking advantage of the available wind to compress large bodies of air, as an energy source for use when required, throughout his life.

The following year Medhurst patented his Aeolian engine (no. 2431 of 1800), by which a carriage could be propelled by compressed air contained in a reservoir beneath the vehicle. In an undated pamphlet he proposed the establishment of regular coach services, with pumping stations along the route, to replenish the reservoirs. He also described an engine worked by gas produced by exploding small quantities of gunpowder at regular intervals in the cylinder. In 1801 he patented a compound crank for converting rotary into rectilinear motion (no. 2467) and in the same year he took over the patent rights for a washing and wringing machine devised by James Wood in 1790.

By about 1800 Medhurst had established himself at 1 Denmark Street, Westminster, as a maker of scales and weighing machines, machinist, and ironfounder. He was the inventor of the equal balance weighing machine, patented in 1817 (no. 4164), which found a place on the counter of most retail shops, and he also made heavy duty platforms for weighing goods in sacks, cases, or carts, and for weighing jockeys.

Medhurst was the first to suggest pneumatic dispatch, as it was later called, whereby letters and small packages were propelled along a tube by compressed air. This idea was not patented; Medhurst published a description in 1810, followed in 1812 by proposals for a pneumatic passenger railway. His plan specified brick tunnels of 30 feet cross-section, through which closely fitting passenger or goods carriages ran on rails. The carriages might, he thought, reach a speed of 50 m.p.h., with goods conveyed at the low cost of a penny per ton per mile, passengers at a farthing per mile. Recognizing that people might not be willing to be propelled through a tube, Medhurst also proposed carriages running on rails on the roadway, connected to a piston driven through a continuous tube beneath the rails. He did not put these plans into action. Like others with similar ideas at this time, he could not devise a practical method of sealing the longitudinal slit in the pressurized tube while permitting the tow bar to pass along.

Medhurst's steam carriage met with more success;

carrying one man it ran between Paddington and Islington on 3 April 1820 and again on 6 July. A year later his more substantial carriage ran up and down Paddington Hill at 5 m.p.h.. By 1827 Medhurst was offering to sell a carriage able to carry four persons at 7 m.p.h.. At this time he was also advertising his patent canal lock, to prevent loss of water, and a leak proof lock gate, though no patents were filed under his name. Medhurst died early in September 1827 and was buried at the church of St Peter and St Paul, Shoreham, on 10 September. He left a widow, Ann, four sons, who inherited his Denmark Street workshop, and five daughters.

R. B. PROSSER, rev. ANITA MCCONNELL

Sources private information (1894, 2004) · H. Clayton, *The atmospheric railways* (1966), 5–7 · G. Clifton, *Directory of British scientific instrument makers, 1550–1851*, ed. G. L'E. Turner (1995), 186 · PRO, PROB 11/1730, sig. 549 · death duty register, PRO, IR 26/1135 fol. 790 · G. Medhurst, *A new method of conveying letters and goods with great certainty and rapidity by air* (1810) · G. Medhurst, *Calculations and remarks tending to prove the practicability, effects and advantages of a plan for the rapid conveyance of passengers upon an iron railway, through a tube of thirty feet in area, by the power and velocity of air* (1812) · G. Medhurst, *A new system of inland conveyance for goods and passengers capable of being applied and extended throughout the country and of conveying all kinds of goods and passengers with the velocity of sixty miles in an hour* (1827)

Wealth at death £6000: will, 1827, PRO, PROB 11/1730, sig. 549

Medhurst, Walter Henry (1796–1857), missionary, was born in London on 29 April 1796, the son of William Medhurst, an innkeeper of Ross, Scotland. He attended St Paul's School (1807–12), and after leaving was apprenticed as a printer to Joseph Wood at the *Gloucester Herald* office. There he joined the Congregational church at Southgate Chapel in December 1813. In 1816 he began work for the London Missionary Society (LMS). Following a short period of study at Hackney College he left Britain for Malacca in September 1816 as a missionary printer at the Anglo-Chinese College. On the way he broke his journey at Madras from 11 February to 20 May 1817, and there he married Mrs Elizabeth Braun, *née* Martin (1794–1874), the day before he sailed. From June 1817 he worked at the printing press and also made rapid progress in Malay and Chinese, and began preaching in Hokkien. He was ordained by William Milne at Malacca on 27 April 1819.

Of wiry frame, good health, and unfailing cheerfulness, Medhurst proved an efficient if independently minded missionary. He was too energetic to be confined to the college and, after a disagreement, left in September 1820 for Penang, and began his own mission station. At the end of 1821 he moved to Batavia, where his only surviving son, Walter Henry *Medhurst, was born in 1822. There were also four daughters from the marriage. In 1829–30 Medhurst journeyed in Java and Bali, and in 1835 along the Chinese coast and even to Shanghai, then still a closed port. In 1836 he returned to Britain, where he wrote *China, its State and Prospects*, published in 1838, with a view to stimulating interest in Chinese missions, and especially in a new translation of the Bible into Chinese, later known as the Delegates' Version, a work he accomplished with the co-operation of friends between 1847 and 1850. In November 1838 he returned to Java. When Shanghai and four other ports were opened to British merchants in 1842 under the Anglo-Chinese treaty of Nanking (Nanjing), he seized his opportunity and established an LMS mission there, largely on his own initiative. His family joined him the following year. Medhurst became the dominant figure in this, the most important station of the LMS in China, and also in the steadily growing British community in Shanghai, where he served on the first municipal council in 1854–5.

Medhurst was by no means genial, or an easy man to get on with, and was the object more of respect than affection. In Shanghai he established the mission press (the first modern one in China) and published a steady stream of works in English and in Chinese, many of them his own. His works were numerous, and included thirty-four Chinese and some sixty-two Malay volumes, as well as translations from the Chinese and his English writings. They exhibit unceasing activity of mind, a remarkable gift for languages, and an intellect not shackled by the disciplinary barriers between sacred and secular learning. Medhurst also had the energy to undertake proselytizing trips into the Chinese interior almost immediately, most notably a courageous clandestine journey in 1845, engagingly written up that year as his *Glance at the Interior of China*. On 8 March 1848, on a less secretive trip, he was badly beaten in what became known as the 'Tsingpu outrage'.

On 19 March 1853 Medhurst wrote that he had seen a 'most extraordinary document'. This was a religious pamphlet, apparently Christian, issued by the Chinese Taiping insurgents. The excitement thus generated cannot be overestimated, even though it was ultimately disappointed. The following month Medhurst accompanied George Bonham on a delegation to meet the Taiping leadership in their capital, Nanjing. There he collected a large number of rebel pamphlets which he translated and published.

The strain of the past decade's pioneering work began to show. During the occupation of Shanghai by the rebel Small Sword Society (1853–4) Medhurst was assaulted by Qing soldiers, and in 1855 his son implored the LMS to recall him, as he had aged appreciably in the previous two years. On 10 September 1856 he sailed with his wife and family for Britain. The voyage was hardly a restful affair and he died in London on 24 January 1857, just three days after reaching the country. He was buried in Abney Park cemetery on 30 January.   ROBERT BICKERS

Sources A. Wylie, *Memorials of protestant missionaries to the Chinese* (1867) [incl. work list] • W. C. M. [W. C. Milne], 'Memoir of the late Dr. Medhurst', *Evangelical Magazine and Missionary Chronicle*, new ser., 35 (1857), 524–9 • *Congregational Year Book* (1858), 215 • Annotated register of missionaries, 1796–1923, London Missionary Society • SOAS, Archives of the Council for World Mission (incorporating the London Missionary Society) • B. Harrison, *Waiting for China: the Anglo-Chinese college at Malacca, 1818–1843, and early nineteenth-century missions* (1979) • J. K. Leonard, 'W. H. Medhurst: rewriting the missionary message', *Christianity in China: early protestant missionary writings*, ed. S. W. Barnett and J. K. Fairbank (1985), 47–59 •

R. Nelson, *An address by the Rev. Dr. Nelson … on the occasion of his leaving the old mission house in Hongkew* (Shanghai, 1879)
Archives SOAS, Council for World Mission archives, London Missionary Society MSS
Likenesses lithograph, repro. in D. Roberts, *Egypt and Nubia*, 3 (1849) • portrait, repro. in W. H. Medhurst, *China, its state and prospects* (1838)

Medhurst, Sir Walter Henry (1822–1885), consul in China, was born in Batavia, Java, the son of the missionary Walter Henry *Medhurst (1796–1857) and his wife, Elizabeth Braun, *née* Martin (1794–1874). Educated at Macao, he was appointed Chinese secretary to the British superintendent of trade in China in October 1840. Britain's consular officials in the Far East in the mid-nineteenth century generally owed more to government patronage than to their knowledge of China or the Chinese language. Almost by accident, some of the appointees turned out to be men of great ability. W. H. Medhurst was one of those few. He proved to be a capable, energetic, and willing official, who spoke with ease Dutch, Chinese, and Malay. His career spanned a crucial period in the history of China; a period which saw the gradual, though reluctant, opening of the country to Western influence. Indeed, Medhurst entered the consular service at a critical moment, just after the outbreak of the First Opium War.

In February 1841 Medhurst accompanied Captain George Elliot, Britain's outgoing plenipotentiary to China, to take possession of and inspect the newly acquired Hong Kong, then a small, barren island, but also the centre of opium smuggling into China. In August 1841 he joined the suite of Colonel Sir Henry Pottinger, the new plenipotentiary to China, moving north with him as the third phase of the war began. He was present when Amoy (Xiamen) was occupied at the end of the month and later, in October, when Chushan was taken. Medhurst's linguistic skills soon attracted Pottinger's attention, and he was attached to the garrison at Chushan as interpreter between October 1841 and December 1842. He was later decorated with the Opium War medal for the services he rendered to the Chushan garrison.

Medhurst's knowledge of Chinese continued to stand him in good stead: in October 1843 he was appointed consular interpreter at Shanghai, just after that place, along with four other ports, was first opened to foreign trade under the treaty of Nanking (Nanjing) of August 1842. He continued to serve in his new function for seven years. Having also been acting vice-consul at Amoy between 1848 and 1849, he became Chinese secretary to the British superintendency of trade in China in August 1850. In November 1854 he was promoted to the consulship at Foochow (Fuzhou) in Fukien (Fujian) province, where he remained for four years. Medhurst's next posting was to Hangchow (Hangzhou) in December 1858, though he was repeatedly left in charge of Foochow and Shanghai as well. His linguistic services were called upon again in 1861 when he was attached to the British contingent of the Anglo-French expeditionary corps at Shanghai, which was sent to China in response to the Taiping uprising.

Life in China was notoriously difficult for European

women. Medhurst married three times. On 20 October 1847, while in London, he married the sixteen-year-old Ellen Gilbert, daughter of James Woodward Cooper; she died in China in December 1848. His second wife, whom he married in February 1854, was the daughter of the US consul in Macao; she too died after a year, in February 1855. In 1858 he married Juliana Tryphena, daughter of Henry Burningham, who survived until 1881, and with whom he had a son and two daughters.

In January 1864 Medhurst was transferred to Hankow (Hankou), a major treaty port on the Yangtze (Yangzi) River in Hupeh (Hubei) province. In his new post he fought staunchly for British treaty rights, and was contemptuous of Mandarin officials, but never anti-Chinese, as so many Westerners were at that time. Medhurst was one of the 'warrior consuls', an advocate of gunboat diplomacy, the method much preferred by Britain's minister-plenipotentiary to China, Sir Rutherford Alcock, of exerting pressure locally to solve disputes with local authorities in the absence of a strong Chinese central government. In August 1868 the minister at Peking (Beijing) dispatched Medhurst on such a mission. With four gunboats the consul sailed down the Yangtze to Nanking, the provincial capital of Kiangsu (Jiangsu), to pressurize the governor-general to cashier some Chinese officials at Yangchow (Yangzhou) who had condoned the plundering and burning of a missionary station there. Medhurst's mission was successful and compensation was duly paid; but the British government later condemned the action as rash and contrary to Britain's established China policy. None the less, later in 1868 Medhurst was sent to Shanghai as acting consul. When his posting to Shanghai was made permanent in January 1871 Medhurst had reached the peak of the Chinese consular service. Six years previously, when that same post had fallen vacant, Medhurst failed to secure promotion to the much coveted Shanghai consulship. Aggrieved, he considered resigning from the service, only to stay on after the Treasury disputed his pension rights.

Medhurst eventually retired from the service on 1 January 1877 on grounds of ill health, and was knighted in March of the same year. He returned to south-east Asia in 1881 to take part in the formation of the British North Borneo Company. From 1882 he resided for two years in Hong Kong to organize the emigration of Chinese labourers to the new company's territories. In 1884 Medhurst finally returned to England to live at Formosa, Torquay, where he died of apoplexy on 26 December 1885. In 1872 Medhurst had published *The Foreigner in Far Cathay*.

C. A. HARRIS, *rev.* T. G. OTTE

Sources *The Times* (30 Dec 1885) · *FO List* (1877) · *FO List* (1885) · PRO, FO China Files, FO 17 · P. D. Coates, *The China consuls: British consular officers, 1843–1943* (1988) · m. cert. (to E. Cooper) · d. cert. · will · *CGPLA Eng. & Wales* (1886)
Archives PRO, FO 17, 228
Wealth at death £2667 17s. 3d.: probate, 12 March 1886, *CGPLA Eng. & Wales*

Medina, John (1721–1796). *See under* Medina, Sir John Baptiste de (1659–1710).

Medina, Sir John Baptiste de (1659–1710), painter, was born in Brussels, the son of a Spanish officer serving in the Southern Netherlands whom George Vertue calls 'Captain Medina de L'Asturias'. His mother's identity is unknown. Little is known of his training, beyond an apprenticeship with François Duchatel. In this workshop Medina would have acquired the technique and the rather formal manner of later Flemish portrait painting, although at some stage his style acquired the more painterly breadth associated with Sir Godfrey Kneller, whose origins were Dutch rather than Flemish.

At some time about 1686 Medina was attracted by the possibilities of the London market, where Kneller was already firmly established. There is no evidence that he ever rivalled Kneller during the period of eight or nine years that he spent in London before eventually settling in Scotland. This is confirmed by a comparison of their prices, Medina's being only one-third of Kneller's—for example, £8 as opposed to £24 for a three-quarter length portrait. Although Medina was primarily a portrait painter, among his earliest recorded works in London was a series of eight illustrations (V&A) for an illustrated edition of Milton's *Paradise Lost*, published in 1688 by Jacob Tonson in association with the barrister John Somers. These wash drawings are slight, and derivative, vaguely Rubensian in manner. Throughout his career Medina also produced a number of subject paintings, usually small in scale, which have a higher quality of draughtsmanship than his portraits. These include *Prometheus*, *Cain and Abel* (priv. coll.), and, the finest of those known, *Apelles and Campaspe* (priv. coll.). By the early 1690s Medina was running a productive portrait workshop in Drury Lane. Among his clients were members of the Scottish nobility, no doubt attracted by his reasonable prices. One of these was George Melville, first earl of Melville, whose cousin Margaret, countess of Rothes, was instrumental in persuading Medina to move to Edinburgh to fill the void in the Scottish portrait market. After a temporary visit with an array of partially completed canvases he finally settled there, along with his wife, Jeanne Marie Vandale, and their children—John (who became a painter), William, Gisberta, Katherine, Elizabeth, and Anne. Two of these are the subjects of an intimate and lively double portrait (priv. coll.).

Medina's earliest commissions in Scotland were from members of Melville's family, including his son David, third earl of Leven, whose three-quarter length portrait of 1691 has a not unconvincing baroque panache (Scot. NPG). The circle of Melville and his son encompassed a wide spectrum of Scottish society and provided Medina with the basis of a highly lucrative practice. There is a slightly mechanical air to many of these portraits, as might be expected in a virtual monopoly, lively heads not always convincingly attached to draped or armoured bodies. However, a less contrived head and shoulders portrait of the learned Sir John Clerk of Penicuik (priv. coll.) shows Medina working in a fresh, observational manner not much inferior to Kneller.

About the turn of the century Sir John Clerk's cousin

William Aikman, a minor landowner who wished to become a painter, joined Medina to learn the craft, although he was not formally apprenticed. He may have been involved in a major project that Medina accomplished between about 1697 and 1708—a series of twenty-nine portraits of members of the Royal College of Surgeons. At the request of the surgeons, Medina added his self-portrait to the group, as explained in detail in a *cartellino* within the painting (Royal College of Surgeons, Edinburgh). This inclusion was evidence of the status Medina had gained within Scottish society, and it was further confirmed by a grant of naturalization by the soon to be dissolved Scottish parliament. Shortly afterwards he received the rare honour of a knighthood, the last, as it happened, to be granted in an independent Scotland. Despite the relative artificiality of much of his portraiture, and its uneven quality, Sir John Medina created an image of Scotland around the years of the union that remains historically significant.

Medina died in Edinburgh on 5 October 1710 and was buried the following day in Greyfriars churchyard. He left considerable wealth to his widow, and his elder son, John (*d.* 1764), carried on the business. The latter's son, **John Medina** (1721–1796), who was born in Edinburgh was also a portrait painter. He restored the pictures at Holyrood Palace and made several copies of the 'Ailsa' portrait of Mary Queen of Scots. He resided in London for a short time, and exhibited portraits at the Royal Academy in 1772 and 1773. He died at Edinburgh on 27 September 1796, in his seventy-sixth year. Examples of his work are in the Scottish National Portrait Gallery.

DUNCAN THOMSON

Sources R. K. Marshall, *John de Medina, 1659–1710* (1988) · W. Brotherston, 'Sir John Baptiste Medina', diss., U. Cam., 1965 · Vertue, *Note books*, vols. 1–4 · J. Holloway, *Patrons and painters: art in Scotland, 1650–1760* (1989) [exhibition catalogue, Scot. NPG, 17 July – 8 Oct 1989] · J. Brown, *The epitaphs and monumental inscriptions in Greyfriars churchyard, Edinburgh* (1867) · register of testaments, NA Scot., 16 March 1711
Likenesses J. B. Medina, self-portrait, oils, *c.*1690–1700, Rhode Island School of Design, Providence · J. B. Medina, self-portrait, oils, *c.*1695–1700, Uffizi, Florence · J. B. Medina, self-portrait, oils, 1708, Royal College of Surgeons, Edinburgh · J. B. Medina, self-portrait, oils, Scot. NPG · J. B. Medina, self-portrait, oils, priv. coll.
Wealth at death £14,180 Scots: 16 March 1711, NA Scot., Edinburgh register of testaments

Medina, Sir Solomon de [*formerly* Diego de Medina] (*c.*1650–1720), merchant and financier, was born in Bordeaux, a younger son of Francisco de Medina, merchant, and his wife, Gracia Pereira, who were both of Portuguese Jewish origin. In 1662 the family moved to Middelburg in the Netherlands, where they openly professed Judaism. Medina trained as a merchant in Amsterdam, moved to London in 1670, and from 1672 until 1677 lived in St Helens, where he became well established as a merchant. In 1686 he supplied imported silks and other luxury textiles to the duchess of Somerset and in 1689–90 to Mary II. By 1696 he had moved to Pall Mall, near to the court.

From 1689 onwards Medina acted as London factor for Antonio (or Moses) Alvarez Machado and Jacob Pereira, the *providiteurs généraux* to the Dutch army in England and to the land forces of the allies in the Low Countries. Medina's function was to collect sums owing to the partnership from the English crown and, when necessary, to provide short-term loans to both parties. This led on to contracts for shipping grain to Flanders. On 18 November 1699 William III dined at Medina's house in Richmond and, on 23 June 1700, in recognition of his services, the king knighted him at Hampton Court. He was the first professing Jew to be knighted in England.

In 1702, after the king's death, Medina settled in the Netherlands, where he continued to work in close collaboration with Machado and Pereira. When Machado died in 1706, Medina succeeded him as contractor for supplying bread and wagons to the land forces of the grand alliance, initially on his own and later in partnership with his older brother, Joseph de Medina of Amsterdam, and with Joseph's son, Moses. As commissary-general, he fed the allied troops throughout the campaigns of John Churchill, first duke of Marlborough. He handled large sums of money but lost much of his wealth on the 1709 contract, when the price of corn rose unexpectedly. In 1711 he was summoned before the parliamentary commissioners for examining and stating the public accounts and testified that he and his predecessor had regularly paid commission on their contracts to the duke of Marlborough, amounting to some £6000 a year. The duke claimed that this was a customary perquisite of the commanding general. Medina's evidence was used by the tories to bring about Marlborough's downfall.

Medina comes across as an able and honest merchant, who gave important services to the grand alliance. When questioned under oath he told the truth without shame or political motivation. His wife, Esther Azevedo, survived him by eight months. Their only surviving child, Deborah, married his nephew, Moses de Medina. He died in The Hague on 15 September 1720, leaving an estate of under £20,000, and was buried in the Jewish cemetery at Ouderkerk.

EDGAR SAMUEL, *rev.*

Sources O. K. Rabinowicz, *Sir Solomon de Medina* (1974) · L. Wolf, *Jews in the Canary Islands* (1926) · D. De Marly, 'Sir Solomon de Medina's textile warehouse', *Miscellanies of the Jewish Historical Society of England*, 12 (1982), 155 · L. D. Barnett, trans., *El libro de los acuerdos: being the records and accompts of the Spanish and Portuguese synagogue of London from 1663 to 1681* (1931) · will, PRO, PROB 11/640, sig. 273
Wealth at death under £20,000: Rabinowicz, *Sir Solomon*

Medland, Thomas (*c.*1765–1833), engraver and draughtsman, of unknown parentage, resided in Westminster for many years. His education is largely unknown but it appears from his inclusion in a drawing by Alfred Edward Chalon entitled *Students at the British Institution* (1807) that he did undertake some training or teaching there. He practised both in the line manner and in aquatint and excelled in landscape work; his skill in this field led to many commissions for topographical work, and it is this for which he is now chiefly known. He engraved many plates for Farington's *Views of the Lakes in Cumberland and Westmoreland* (1789) and *Cities and Castles of England* (1791);

Harding's *Shakspeare Illustrated* (1793); the *Copperplate Magazine*; Sir G. Staunton's *Embassy of the Earl of Macartney to China* (1797), three engravings from which, including a *View of the Great Wall of China*, are in the department of prints and drawings at the Victoria and Albert Museum; Seeley's *Stowe: a Description of the House and Gardens* (1797); *Select Views in London and Westminster* (1800); and Sir W. Gell's *Topography of Troy* (1804). Among Medland's most successful early works was a set of illustrations to *Robinson Crusoe*, from designs by Stothard (1790), and his largest plate was *Evening of the Glorious First of June*, after R. Cleveley.

Medland was also well known for his aquatints, especially those of topographical scenes. His finest examples are possibly those after drawings by Colonel Garstin in *An Account of the Hindoo Temple of Vissvisshoor, or Bissinant, at Benares* (1801), which included an impressive elevation of the temple, and those after drawings of W. Alexander in *Egyptian Monuments from the Collection Formed by the National Institute … Deposited in the British Museum* (1805–7), notably an important depiction of *The Sarcophagus in which the Enbalmed Body of Alexander the Great was Deposited, Taken from the Mosque of St Athandonis*. In other collections he depicted parts of Scotland, Ireland, and China. In addition Medland executed a few aquatints of hunting scenes, such as *Pheasant Shooting with Pointers* for Thornhill's *The Shooting Directory* (1804). His skill in this field enabled him to convey a heightened atmosphere and depth in his works. A few engraved portraits survive, among them those of George Cartwright and Daniel Defoe (in the British Museum department of prints and drawings), but these seem to be unusual among his output.

Medland also practised watercolour painting and exhibited views of London at the Royal Academy, such as *A View in Hyde Park* and *A View on Millbank, Westminster* in 1777, and *A View of Aylesford Priory in Kent* in 1779. He later made many transcripts of English scenery. An oil painting by him of *The Panshanger Oak* survives (Christies, 16 October 1956), but is a rare example of his work in this medium.

When Haileybury College was founded by the East India Company in 1806 Medland was appointed drawing and oriental writing-master there, and thereafter he resided near Hertford. He continued to send drawings to the Royal Academy up to 1822, among them one of the west front of Haileybury College (1808), a view of St Albans Abbey in 1810, and of Windsor Castle, seen from the Great Park, in 1814. He died at Hertford on 30 October 1833 and asked to be buried in All Saints, his parish church. Medland's wife is unidentified, but he left a will bequeathing his household goods and furnishings to his unmarried daughter, Anne, his clothing to his youngest son, Henry, and to his eldest son, William, the choice of a picture, drawing, book, or proof. **ELEANOR TOLLFREE**

Sources Redgrave, *Artists*, 291 · Graves, *RA exhibitors*, 6 (1906), 224–5 · *GM*, 1st ser., 103/2 (1833), 476 · L. Binyon, *Catalogue of drawings by British artists and artists of foreign origin working in Great Britain*, 1 (1898), 204–6 · *Engraved Brit. ports.*, 4.652 · will, PRO, PROB 11/1826, sig. 38

Likenesses A. E. Chalon, Indian ink, pen, and watercolour drawing, 1807 (*Students at the British Institution, 1807*), BM
Wealth at death see will, PRO, PROB 11/1826, sig. 38

Medley, Henry (d. 1747), naval officer, was the son of Robert Medley (1650–1708), lawyer, and Dorothy, *née* Grimston (d. 1691). He married Anne Gooch (d. 1733). Medley entered the navy in 1703 and three years later was a midshipman of the *Somerset* with Captain Price at the relief of Barcelona. He passed his examination on 8 February 1710, was promoted lieutenant of the *Fame* by Sir John Norris on 5 September, and was moved into the *Stirling Castle* a few months later. In 1717 he was a lieutenant of the *Barfleur*, flagship of Sir George Byng in the Baltic. Early in 1720 he was promoted to the command of the fireship *Poole*, and on 17 February 1721 he was posted into the *York*. In 1722, while commanding the *Leopard* in the Mediterranean, he seized a ship named the *Revolution*, lying within the mole of Genoa, on information that she was in the service of James Francis Edward Stuart, the Old Pretender. Medley afterwards commanded the *Leopard* on the coast of Portugal and in the channel until the end of 1728. On 5 May 1730 he was given command of the *Diamond*; on 19 May 1731 he moved to the *Romney*, and on 12 May 1732 he was appointed captain of the *Gibraltar* which he took to Virginia and Maryland. On 8 August 1734 he arrived back at Spithead; he was then sent cruising, and during this period retook a British brigantine from Barbary corsairs. On 8 November 1734 Medley assumed command of the *Dreadnought*. He served in Sir John Norris's squadron at Lisbon from 1735, becoming at one point after Norris's departure in 1737 the senior officer of the force. In September 1737 the *Dreadnought* was ordered to be paid off. Medley was then moved to the *Romney*. During 1739 and 1740 he convoyed the Newfoundland fishing fleet to the fishing grounds and to the Lisbon market. On 29 January 1741 he took command of the *Nassau* in the Channel Fleet under Norris, and in 1742–4 he was with Norris as captain of the fleet. On 19 June 1744 he was promoted rear-admiral of the white, and in the following winter he commanded a squadron cruising in the Soundings for the protection of trade. On 23 April 1745 he was promoted vice-admiral of the blue, and sent out as commander-in-chief in the Mediterranean. The service was one of blockade and co-operation with the Austro-Sardinian armies which, in the winter of 1746–7, drove the French out of Italy, and then invaded Provence. Medley's squadron closely supported the invading armies but, after an unsuccessful attack on Antibes, the Austro-Sardinians were obliged to retire. Medley continued to maintain support to the allied armies. On 15 July 1747, he was advanced to vice-admiral of the red, but he died of fever at Vado on 5 August 1747, probably in ignorance of his last promotion. His body was taken back to England and buried at St Michael-le-Belfrey church in York on 10 December. A monument to Medley was placed in the north choir aisle of York Minster.

J. K. LAUGHTON, *rev.* RICHARD HARDING

Sources East Riding of Yorkshire Archives Service, Beverley, Grimston MSS, DDGR/39 · bundles of correspondence 1721–45;

correspondence 1746; correspondence 1746–7, East Riding of York-shire Archives Service, Beverley, Vice-Admiral Medley MSS [other vols.—assorted correspondence not used] · PRO, SP 42/97 [commander-in-chief Mediterranean to admiralty 1745–7] · PRO, ADM 1/2098 [captain's letters, 1729–40] · PRO, ADM 6/11, 219 [commissions and warrants] · PRO, ADM 6/12, 193 · PRO, ADM 6/13, 31 · PRO, ADM 6/14, 48v, 76, 107, 196v · PRO, ADM 6/15, 97, 375, 482 · PRO, ADM 8/19 [fleet disposition lists] · Anson correspondence, Shugborough-Anson, April 1747, BL, Add. MS 15955 · E. M. Ingram, *Leaves from a family tree* (1951), 1–20 · J. Charnock, ed., *Biographia navalis*, 4 (1796), 93

Archives East Riding of Yorkshire Archives Service, Beverley, corresp. and papers · PRO, SP 42/97 · PRO, ADM 6/11, 219; 6/12, 193; 6/13, 31; 6/14, 48v, 76, 107, 196v; 6/15, 97, 375, 482

Likenesses J. Faber junior, mezzotint, 1745 (after J. Ellys), BM, NPG · H. Cheere, monumental bust, 1747, York Minster · line engraving, NPG

Wealth at death probably over £13,000: will, PRO, PROB 11/760/342

Medley, John (1804–1892), bishop of Fredericton, was born on 19 December 1804, in Grosvenor Place, London, the home of his father, George Medley (who died while his son was still young), and his wife, Henrietta, who, having greatly influenced her son's choice of vocation, was killed in a carriage accident at Oldridge, near Exeter, in September 1844. Medley graduated from Wadham College, Oxford, in 1826, in which year he married, on 10 July, Christina Bacon. They had five sons and two daughters before her death from tuberculosis in 1841; her effigy was placed in the chancel of St Thomas's Church, Exeter.

Medley was ordained deacon in 1828 and priest in 1829, and served as curate of Southleigh, Devon, from 1828 to 1831; he was perpetual curate of St John's, Truro, from 1831 to 1838, and vicar of St Thomas's, Exeter, from 1838 to 1845. In 1842 he was made a prebendary of Exeter Cathedral. He assisted in the translation of the *Homilies of St John Chrysostom on the Corinthians* (1838), and at the request of his friends he published a volume of his sermons in 1845. At Lambeth Palace on 4 May 1845 he was consecrated bishop of Fredericton, New Brunswick, Canada, and on 11 June 1845 he was installed as the first bishop of the new diocese in the parish church there. This church served as his pro-cathedral until the cathedral church, Christ Church Cathedral, begun in that year, was completed and consecrated in 1853.

John Medley embodied the Tractarian understanding of the episcopate. From its beginning he was an active supporter of the Oxford Movement and a close friend of John Keble, E. B. Pusey, and W. E. Gladstone. With his appointment to the see of Fredericton he became the first Tractarian bishop and was able to put into practice his understanding of the role of a bishop in the life of the church. His views had already been expressed in *The Episcopal Form of Church Government*, which he had published in 1835. The charges that he delivered to his clergy in the course of his episcopate reflect a deep understanding of the work of the priest, and of his view of the bishop as shepherd. In spite of his argumentative nature, by perseverance he was able to unite a divided diocese and to gain the respect and support of the majority of those who served under him. Although he was a vocal supporter of Catholic principles,

as his sermons and writings demonstrate, he showed tolerance towards his opponents.

Medley sought to improve the standard of worship in the diocese and used his cathedral to reflect his understanding of the uses of music and ritual in public worship. The hymns that he wrote reflected his scholarship and are a testament to his musical ability: although no longer in general use, his settings of the canticles were revived for the celebrations in 1995 of the 150th anniversary of the founding of the diocese. In his sermons he spoke out against the materialism of the age. His own simple life reflected a devotion to the principle of charity: it was his sincerity as much as his scholarship that swayed the opposition to his understanding of the church and churchmanship.

Medley's interest in church architecture dated at least from his time as vicar of St Thomas's, Exeter. He was supported by the Camden Society, Cambridge, in his building projects both in his Canadian parish and in his diocese. The cathedral, modelled on St Mary's, Snettisham, and St Anne's Chapel, Fredericton (begun in 1846 and consecrated in 1847), the precursor of which he had built as St Andrew's, Exeter, were to serve as examples of design for his diocesan churches. In these and other projects he was assisted by the architects Frank Wills and William Butterfield, and the impact which these two churches were to have on Canadian ecclesiastical architecture was profound. Because of the lack of experienced craftsmen and of stone for building, Medley supported the development of a type of wooden structure, in Gothic style. Within his lifetime the Gothic revival, its roots in Fredericton, had swept North America, its influence extending to secular as well as ecclesiastical design throughout the continent.

Over twenty years after the death of his first wife, Medley married Margaret Hudson (d. 26 Feb 1905), of Exeter, on 16 June 1863, at Campobello island, New Brunswick. He was elected metropolitan of Canada in January 1879, and in 1889 he attended the Lambeth conference, causing an uproar by speaking against the Public Worship Regulation Act of 1874 and in favour of the ritualists. He died on 9 September 1892 at his home, Bishop's Cote, 97 Church Street, Fredericton, and was buried outside Christ Church Cathedral, on 13 September, having served as bishop for forty-seven years.

DAVID E. MERCER

Sources W. Q. Ketchum, *The life and work of the Most Reverend John Medley* (1893) · J. Medley, 'Annals of the see, 1845–1892', Christ Church Cathedral Archives · A. G. Finley, 'New Brunswick's Gothic revival: John Medley and the aesthetics of Anglican worship', PhD diss., no. 4532, University of New Brunswick, Harriet Irving Library, Fredericton, New Brunswick · E. R. Fairweather, 'A Tractarian patriarch', *Canadian Journal of Theology*, 6/1 (1960), 15–24 · M. Ross, 'Medley, John', *DCB*, vol. 12 · L. N. Harding, *Citizens with the saints* (1994) · J. Medley, *Sermons* (1845) · J. Medley, *The episcopal form of church government* (1835) · C. Headron, 'Unpublished correspondence between John Medley and E. B. Pusey', *Journal of Canadian Church Historical Society*, 16

Archives Christ Church Cathedral Archives | BL, Gladstone MSS · LPL, letters to Cecil Wray · New Brunswick Legislative Library, letters to Sir Edmund Walken Hunt · Sheff. Arch., letters to the Gatty family

Likenesses J. Bridges, oils, 1847, Wadham College, Oxford; on loan to diocese of Fredericton, New Brunswick, 1994 · marble tomb effigy, Christ Church Cathedral, Fredericton, New Brunswick · photograph (in old age), repro. in Ketchum, *Life*

Wealth at death £4470 4s. 1d.: resworn probate, Feb 1894, CGPLA Eng. & Wales (1892)

Medley, Mat. *See* Aston, Anthony (c.1682–1753?).

Medley, (Charles) Robert Owen (1905–1994), artist, was born on 19 December 1905 at 11 Edith Grove, London, the second child in the family of four sons and two daughters of Charles Douglas Medley, lawyer, and his wife, Anne Gwendoline (Nancy), *née* Owen. The Medleys traced their roots to Yorkshire, and the Owens were a Welsh family who moved in the Holland Park circle around the Greek shipping family of Ionides. Charles Medley was an authority on authors' copyright who acted for Somerset Maugham, George Bernard Shaw, and Noël Coward, among others, and who numbered George Moore and Harley Granville-Barker among his closest friends.

A happy childhood was marred by inadequate early schooling, and Medley found his feet only when he enrolled at Gresham's School at Holt, Norfolk in 1919. It was there that he decided to become a painter, after seeing a reproduction of a Glyn Philpot painting. In 1921 he was severely injured in a cycling accident (his left arm was broken in five places), and was sent to his aunt and uncle Christine and Cecil Pilkington in Lancashire to recuperate. This sojourn with people of deep sophistication formed an important part of Medley's education, augmented when he returned to Gresham's and struck up a friendship with the young W. H. Auden. It was Medley who encouraged Auden to start writing poetry, and who became the subject of many of Auden's first poems; they remained lifelong friends.

Meanwhile, Medley's ambition to paint won his mother's support, and she took him to the studio of her friend the principal of the Byam Shaw School of Art, F. E. Jackson. Medley duly attended the Byam Shaw in 1923, followed by a brief spell of further training at the Royal Academy Schools (1924), before settling at the Slade School of Fine Art (1924–6). Among his Slade friends and contemporaries were Rex Whistler, Oliver Messel, and Stephen Tennant. Through Richard Carline, Medley met Stanley Spencer, and was soon inducted into the Bloomsbury group via the Stracheys in Gordon Square. The influence of Roger Fry and Clive Bell, of Duncan Grant and Vanessa Bell, was to be formative on Medley's early development as a painter. But even more fundamental was meeting the dancer and theatre director Rupert Doone (Reginald Ernest Woodfield; 1903–1966) in November 1925, shortly after Medley had come to terms with his own homosexuality. A permanent relationship was established between Medley and Doone which lasted for forty years, until Doone's death.

In May 1926 Medley and Doone left London for Paris, and spent much of the next three years there. Medley pursued his studies in the various art academies and through copying in the Louvre, and Doone danced. They moved in a circle which included Cocteau, Duchamp, and Djuna

Barnes, which helped to educate Medley's eye and mind, and liberate him from Bloomsbury provincialism. Back in London by 1930, Medley helped Doone to found the Group Theatre (1932–53), a play-producing society that advocated 'realistic fantasy' through creative co-operation between artists, performers, and technicians. Doone was the driving force behind this initiative, with the active involvement of such major talents as Benjamin Britten and John Piper. The writing was of equally high quality: Auden and Isherwood wrote *The Dog Beneath the Skin* and *The Ascent of F6* for the Group Theatre, Stephen Spender wrote *The Trial of a Judge*, and in 1934 T. S. Eliot's *Sweeney Agonistes* was staged. Throughout the 1930s Medley's involvement with the theatre was intense, in part because he and others questioned the relevance of painting to the social issues of the day.

The Second World War disrupted Medley's career at a crucial moment, but service in the camouflage corps in the Middle East entailed a further sensual liberation through the commonplace promiscuity of wartime, while awakening in him a sense of the numinous. He returned to Britain eager to prove himself as the conceptual and philosophical painter he now knew himself to be. He began working more from the imagination, employing allegory and myth, though retaining his deep involvement with the human figure. His work became lyrical and decorative in the best Matissean sense, evolving through ambiguous biomorphic imagery done in a 'tachiste' style, to the hard-edged abstraction he embraced in order to cope with the death of Rupert Doone in 1966. His masterpiece in this manner was his series of illustrations for Milton's *Samson Agonistes*, published in book form in 1979. In later years he returned to a form of evocative and open-ended figuration characterized by sensitive draughtsmanship, acute intelligence, and deep feeling. He enjoyed considerable success in commercial exhibitions and at the Royal Academy.

The concept of public service was strong in Medley, a need which was at least partially fulfilled by a long and distinguished career in art education. He taught at Chelsea Art School from 1932 to 1939, and again from 1945 to 1949; he ran the department of theatre design at the Slade (1949–58); he was head of fine art at Camberwell School of Arts and Crafts (1958–65); and he served on the faculty of painting, the British School of Rome, latterly as chairman (1961–77). Among his best-known students were Elisabeth Frink, John Berger, Derek Jarman, and Maggi Hambling.

Medley was appointed CBE in 1982, and elected a Royal Academician in 1986. He had retrospectives at the Whitechapel Art Gallery, London, in 1963, the Museum of Modern Art, Oxford (and on tour), in 1984, and the Coram Gallery, London, in 1994. Also in 1994 he won the Charles Woolaston prize of the Royal Academy for the most distinguished work at its summer exhibition. In 1983 he published an autobiography, *Drawn from the Life*, which started as an account of the Group Theatre. He continued painting almost until his death, of heart failure, at St Bartholomew's Hospital, London, on 20 October 1994. He was cremated at Golders Green crematorium, London, on 27 October. A celebration of his life was held at St James's, Piccadilly, on 18 January 1995.   ANDREW LAMBIRTH

Sources R. Medley, *Drawn from the life: a memoir* (1983) · *The Times* (24 Oct 1994) · *The Independent* (28 Oct 1994) · *WWW*, 1991–5 · personal knowledge (2004) · private information (2004)
Archives Tate collection, corresp. and papers │SOUND BL NSA
Likenesses R. O. Medley, self-portrait, oils, *c*.1935, priv. coll. · photograph, 1938, repro. in *The Independent* · R. O. Medley, self-portrait, oils, 1980–89, priv. coll. · R. O. Medley, self-portrait, oils, *c*.1983, priv. coll. · D. Santini, photograph, repro. in *The Independent* · photograph, repro. in *The Times*
Wealth at death £291,535: probate, 7 March 1995, *CGPLA Eng. & Wales*

Medley, Samuel (1738–1799), Particular Baptist minister and hymn writer, was born at Cheshunt, Hertfordshire, on 23 June 1738, the second son of Guy Medley (*d*. 1760), tutor, and Elizabeth, the youngest daughter of William Tonge, schoolmaster in Enfield, Middlesex. His grandfather, Samuel Medley, had been a diplomatist, and his father, who was a considerable linguist, had served as attorney-general of St Vincent before settling in Cheshunt, where he kept a school. His father was a deacon at Eagle Street Particular Baptist Church, Holborn, where the pastor was Andrew Gifford, and corresponded frequently with the religious writer James Hervey, offering loving criticism on his works.

After being educated at William Tonge's school in Enfield, at the age of fourteen Samuel Medley was apprenticed to an oilman of the city of London, but in 1755 secured his freedom in order to follow his brothers into the navy. During his naval years he confesses 'he had neither the fear of God nor man' (*Memoirs*, 66). Severely wounded, with incipient gangrene threatening the need for amputation of a limb, he turned to prayer, and an apparently miraculous cure ensued. However, as his health improved, so his new-found seriousness declined. Invalided out of the navy, he lived with his grandfather and was convinced of sin under a grand-paternal reading of a sermon by Isaac Watts. Attendance on the preaching of Whitfield and Gifford led to his conversion in July 1760, just before the death of his father. He sealed this by joining the Eagle Street church, which practised strict communion, by public profession of his faith in baptism in December 1760. Using his grandfather's excellent library he equipped himself in biblical languages and the study of the sacred text.

Following his marriage to Mary, daughter of William Gill, a hosier from Nottingham, on 17 April 1762, Medley started a school in Soho. However, under the tutelage of Gifford, he discovered a call to the ministry to which he was set aside by the Eagle Street Church on 29 August 1766, with his first endeavours exercised at Harlington, near Hounslow. Ivimey says that Gifford had hoped Medley might have become his assistant, but in June 1767 he accepted a call to the church at Watford which had been pastorless for five years. He was ordained on 13 July 1768, Gifford presiding, with Robert Robinson of Cambridge offering the ordination prayer. Because of the financial deficiencies of the congregation Medley combined the pastorate with running a school.

The Particular Baptist church in Liverpool, which practised closed communion, was in 1771 facing severe difficulties consequent on the revelation of the moral lapses of its then pastor. John Livesley, a senior deacon, on a visit to London discovered that Medley might be persuaded to take a northern pastorate, and accordingly Medley was invited to preach in Liverpool for two Sundays in December 1771. The impression was such that he was immediately invited to the vacant pastorate, and the family accordingly moved to Liverpool in April 1772, where Medley was able to devote all his energies to the pastorate. Within a year the church needed to be enlarged, and in 1789 new and commodious premises were opened on Byrom Street. In addition to his normal pastoral duties he took a special interest in the Liverpool seamen.

In 1786 a group of northern Baptist leaders met in Preston and determined to break the spell of hyper-Calvinism and reshape their association on the model of what was happening within the Northamptonshire Association. Much of the leadership fell to Medley in association with his good friend John Fawcett of the Wainsgate church at Hebden Bridge, both of them successful hymn writers. Of Medley's hymns, only 'I know that my Redeemer lives' remains in regular use, though it has been suggested that Thomas Kelly's 'We sing the praise of him who died' is really Medley's. By contrast to the urbane Medley, Fawcett was a rough-hewn northern autodidact. That Fawcett became a successful schoolmaster was partly due to instruction he received from Medley.

With his well-kept wigs and cultivated southern education, Medley suggested a very different appearance from the other northern Baptist leaders, but commitment and faith soon brought them together. Sellers argues that Medley 'preached a warm Evangelical Calvinism' but, out of deference to the narrower 'walled garden' mentality of the staunch Calvinists of the north-west, never avowed himself a Fullerite (Sellers, 114). The extent to which Medley shared the views of Joseph Ivimey, Gifford's successor at the Eagle Street Church from 1805, in criticizing those who 'preached upon the non-application, non-invitation scheme' of higher Calvinism has been contested. Some claim that he did not, but implicit invitation seems very evident in the way in which the attractions and admonitions of the gospel were placed before 'Christless sinners'. Medley exhorted in a sermon preached at Moorfields in October 1777

> let me intreat you to consider what will all your worldly wealth do for you in a dying hour … Oh, sirs, the unsearchable and inexhaustible riches of Christ are the one thing needful, to make poor sinners rich, and miserable sinners happy. May the Lord help you to consider this to your soul's eternal welfare and salvation. (*Memoirs*, 196)

Halley, who speaks of the Lancashire Baptists being 'neither very general nor very particular, neither low Arminians nor high Calvinists', ranks Medley as 'a great preacher' (Halley, 2.478, 480). Medley exercised an 'earnest, popular and prolonged ministry', while displaying 'his liberal and catholic spirit' in forming happy associations with the Liverpool Independents (ibid., 2.480). He was certainly one of those who readily gave support to the infant missionary society in which his son, Samuel *Medley (1769–1857), painter, took a particular interest.

Medley maintained close contact with metropolitan revivalist Calvinism, and regularly supplied the pulpit at Whitfield's chapels at Moorfields Tabernacle and Tottenham Court Road. Indeed it was on a visit to these churches that his final illness began upon its critical progress. With difficulty he returned to Liverpool, where he died on 17 July 1799, anxious to clarify that he was no Arminian, Arian, or Socinian. He was buried in Liverpool on 24 July.

J. H. Y. BRIGGS

Sources *Memoirs of Samuel Medley* (1800) • R. Halley, *Lancashire: its puritanism and nonconformity*, 2 vols. (1869) • W. Urwick, *Nonconformity in Hertfordshire* (1884) • J. Ivimey, *A history of the English Baptists*, 4 vols. (1811–30), vols. 3–4 • I. Sellers, 'Liverpool nonconformity, 1786–1914', PhD diss., Keele University, 1969 • W. T. Whitley, *Baptists of north-west England, 1649–1913* (1913) • I. Sellers and E. F. Clipsham, eds., *Our heritage: the Baptists of Yorkshire, Lancashire and Cheshire, 1647–1987* (1987) • B. A. Ramsbottom, *Samuel Medley* (c.1978) • *DNB*
Archives Regent's Park College, Oxford, Angus Library, MSS, hymns, sermons
Likenesses J. Fittler, line engraving, pubd 1793 (after S. Medley), BM, NPG • engraving (after S. Medley junior), repro. in *Memoirs of Samuel Medley* • line engraving, BM, NPG; repro. in *Gospel Magazine* (1776)

Medley, Samuel (1769–1857), painter, was born on 22 March 1769, probably at Watford, Hertfordshire, the son of Samuel *Medley (1738–1799), the Baptist minister, and his wife, Mary, *née* Gill. He entered the Royal Academy Schools on 14 October 1791 aged twenty-two, and exhibited there for the first time in 1792 sending *The Last Supper*. On 2 October 1794 Joseph Farington mentioned that Medley 'has been at Leigh, employed somehow by Taylor' (Farington, *Diary*, 1.248). He painted religious and historical subjects, but subsequently devoted himself chiefly to portraiture, in which he gained considerable practice and reputation. Between 1792 and 1805 he exhibited twenty-eight pictures at the Royal Academy. In 1805, however, he found his profession injurious to his health, so he abandoned it, and went to work on the stock exchange, where he made a comfortable income, continuing to paint in his leisure hours.

Medley was a member of a large Baptist community in Hackney, Middlesex, under the Revd F. A. Cox, with whom, Lord Brougham, and some leading dissenters of education and position, he was associated in founding University College, London, in 1826. Medley married, first, in 1792 Susannah, daughter of George Bowley of Bishopsgate Street, London; second, in 1818, he married Elizabeth, daughter of John Smallshaw of Liverpool. With his first wife he had three sons, William, Guy, and George, and three daughters, of whom the eldest, Susannah, married Henry Thompson of Framlingham, Suffolk, and was mother of Sir Henry Thompson, the eminent surgeon.

A large group portrait by Medley, *The Medical Society of London*, hangs in the rooms of that society in Chandos Street, Cavendish Square, London. A portrait of Joseph Warner is in the collection of the Royal College of Surgeons and his work is also represented in the National Maritime Museum, Greenwich. Medley lived the latter years of his life at Chatham, Kent, and it is there that he died on 10 August 1857.

L. H. CUST, rev. JILL SPRINGALL

Sources S. Medley, *Memoir of Rev. S. Medley* (1800) • private information (1894) • B. Stewart and M. Cutten, *The dictionary of portrait painters in Britain up to 1920* (1997) • Farington, *Diary*, 1.183, 248, 269; 3.868–9, 876 • Graves, *RA exhibitors* • S. C. Hutchison, 'The Royal Academy Schools, 1768–1830', *Walpole Society*, 38 (1960–62), 123–91, esp. 153 • *Concise catalogue of oil paintings in the National Maritime Museum* (1988) • will, 1857, PRO, PROB 11/2256, sig. 634 • D. M. Lewis, ed., *The Blackwell dictionary of evangelical biography, 1730–1860*, 2 vols. (1995)
Wealth at death left property and household goods to sons on death of wife, to whom he left £50 and use of his property until her death at 54 Lisson Grove, Paddington, Middlesex, which he leased for £7 10s. p.a.: will, PRO, PROB 11/2256, sig. 634

Medlicott, Henry Benedict (1829–1905), geologist, was born on 3 August 1829 at Loughrea, co. Galway, Ireland, the second of three sons of Samuel Medlicott (1796–1858), rector of Loughrea, and his wife, Charlotte (d. 1884), daughter of Colonel Henry Benedict Dolphin CB. His eldest brother, Joseph G. Medlicott (d. 1866), of the geological survey of Ireland and then India, was afterwards inspector of schools in the Bengal education department. His youngest brother, Samuel (c.1831–1889), also worked for the geological survey of Ireland before becoming rector of Bowness in Cumberland in 1877.

Medlicott received his early education in France and Guernsey, and then entered Trinity College, Dublin, where he attended the geology classes of Thomas Oldham (1816–1875). He graduated BA in 1850, with a diploma and honours in the school of civil engineering; he proceeded MA in 1870. In October 1851 he joined the geological survey of Ireland as a general assistant, and worked for two years under Joseph Beete Jukes (1811–1869), after which he was transferred, at his own request, to the English staff and was engaged from September 1853 in fieldwork in Wiltshire. On 31 December of that year he resigned the British survey, having accepted an appointment with the geological survey of India which he joined on 24 March 1854. However, before beginning fieldwork, on the recommendation of Sir Henry De la Beche (1796–1855), he was appointed by the directors of the East India Company to the post of professor of geology at the Thomason College of Civil Engineering at Roorkee. He held this position from 15 August 1854 until he rejoined the survey as deputy superintendent for Bengal on 1 October 1862. During his vacations at Roorkee he carried out valuable geological fieldwork for the survey under an arrangement with its superintendent, Thomas Oldham. On 27 October 1857 he married at Landour, near Mussooree, Louisa (b. 1830), second daughter of the Revd Daniel Henry Maunsell. They had four sons and two daughters. On the outbreak of the rebellion of 1857 he joined the garrison of Roorkee as a volunteer and was awarded the Indian mutiny medal for his services.

Medlicott travelled extensively in northern and central India, making important contributions to Indian geology. During his early years in India, together with his brother Joseph, he investigated the stratigraphical position of the Vindhyan series, which he distinguished from the later Gondwana formations, the name Gondwana being proposed first by him in 1872. In a classic *Memoir* published by the survey in 1864 Medlicott dealt with the structure and stratigraphy of the southern portion of the Himalayan ranges. Here he expressed the view that the elevation of the mountains did not commence before Tertiary times. He instituted some comparisons between the structure of the Alps and the Himalayas in a contentious paper published by the Geological Society in 1868. In general, he was a proponent of uniformitarian as opposed to catastrophist views.

On 1 April 1876 Medlicott succeeded Oldham as superintendent of the geological survey of India, the title being altered to director in 1885. Following this appointment his wife returned to England, and until his eventual retirement on 27 April 1887 Medlicott lived alone at the Geological Museum in Calcutta where he adopted an increasingly ascetic and retiring lifestyle, walking barefoot and shunning social pursuits. During this time he devoted himself to editing the survey publications and to writing, with William Blanford (1832–1905), an extended general account of Indian geology, the *Manual of the Geology of India* (1879), which remained the standard work for the next fifty years. Nevertheless, he was not a fluent writer, and his style was regarded as rather intemperate by his contemporaries. As superintendent he allowed his subordinates free expression in print (a policy which caused some friction among the staff), but adopted a generally hostile policy towards the promotion of Indian geologists. On his retirement he returned to England and lived quietly at Clifton, Bristol, devoting his time mainly to his philosophical and theological interests. He suffered from a serious heart condition in his last years and died, probably from a heart attack, at his home, 43 St John's Road, Clifton, on 6 April 1905. His wife, two sons, and two daughters survived him.

Medlicott was elected a fellow of the Geological Society of London in 1856, and of the Royal Society in 1877. In 1888 he was awarded the Wollaston medal by the Geological Society. He was president of the Asiatic Society of Bengal in 1879–81, and was a fellow of Calcutta University. His eighty-six publications included fifty-three in the *Memoirs* and *Records* of the Indian survey, seven in British and European journals, thirteen in the *Journal* and *Proceedings of the Asiatic Society of Bengal*, and two pamphlets, written during his retirement, on philosophical and theological topics.

ANDREW GROUT

Sources W. T. Blanford, *PRS*, 79B (1907), xix–xxvi · W. T. Blanford, 'H. B. Medlicott', *Records of the Geological Survey of India*, 32 (1905), 233–41 · R. L., *Quarterly Journal of the Geological Society*, 62 (1906), lx–lxi · G. L. Herries Davies, *Sheets of many colours: the mapping of Ireland's rocks, 1750–1890* (1983), 168 · D. Kumar, *Science and the raj, 1857–1905* (1995) · L. Leigh Fermor, *First twenty-five years of the Geological Survey of India* (New Delhi, 1976) · *A short history of the first hundred years*, Geological Survey of India (Calcutta, 1951), 30–35 · W. King, 'The retirement of Mr Medlicott', *Records of the Geological Survey of India*, 20 (1887), 121–2 · *Geological Magazine*, new ser., 5th decade, 2 (1905), 240 · *Nature*, 71 (1904–5), 612–13 · T. H. D. La Touche, *A bibliography of Indian geology and physical geography*, 5 vols. (1917–26) · private information (2004)

Archives BGS, archives · Geological Survey of India, Calcutta · Geological Survey of Ireland, Dublin | NHM, specimens presented on behalf of Geological Survey of India

Likenesses group photograph, c.1867, Geological Survey of India, Calcutta; repro. in *A short history*, Geological Survey of India (1951), 5 · group photograph, c.1870, Geological Survey of India, Calcutta; repro. in *A short history*, Geological Survey of India (1951), 20 · photograph, c.1880, Geological Survey of India, Calcutta; repro. in *A short history*, Geological Survey of India (1951), 30

Wealth at death £6577 8s. 6d.: probate, 10 May 1905, CGPLA Eng. & Wales

Medlicott, William Norton (1900–1987), historian, was born at 3 Quarry Road, Wandsworth, London, on 11 May 1900, the eldest son of William Norton Medlicott (d. 1923), a religious journalist and editor of the *Church Family Newspaper* (1905–11), and his wife, Margaret Louise McMillan. He was educated at Haberdashers' Aske's School, Hatcham, and at University College, London, where he took a first-class degree in history and graduated PhD working under Professor R. W. Seton-Watson, who was then among the leading historians of British nineteenth-century foreign policy. His first post was as lecturer at University College, Swansea (1926–45). On 18 July 1936 he married a Swansea colleague, Dr Dorothy Kathleen Coveney (1904/5–1979), a historian and palaeographer, daughter of James Richard Coveney, a printer's reader. During the Second World War he served for two years as a principal in the Board of Trade before being appointed official historian of the Ministry of Economic Warfare (1942–58). In 1946 he was appointed to the chair of history at the University College of the South-West.

In 1953 Medlicott succeeded Sir Charles Webster as the second occupant of the Sir Daniel Stevenson chair of international history at the London School of Economics and Political Science (LSE). He held the chair until his retirement in 1967.

Medlicott's first published work was on Bismarck's foreign policy and British relations with Bismarckian Germany. *The Congress of Berlin and after* (1938), *Bismarck, Gladstone and the Concert of Europe* (1950), and his later pamphlet *Bismarck and Modern Germany* (1965) put him squarely in the mainstream of British historiography of foreign policy, in the tradition created by G. P. Gooch, Harold Temperley, Sir Charles Webster, and others. His books were well received in America, France, and, once Nazism had died, in Germany and Italy. His work was distinguished by what he said and the scholarship which underlay it, rather than by his manner. He revealed himself as concerned to understand rather than to condemn, reserving for private conversation among his colleagues and students his often sulphurous comments on those whose policies he studied. His defence of British foreign policy in the inter-war years, *British Foreign Policy since Versailles* (1940), against both the right-wing Churchillians such as Sir Lewis Namier and the para-popular frontists of the left for whom any attempt to reach an accommodation with Hitler was ideological treason, revealed that he was not afraid to apply his historical principles to contemporary controversy. But it was his two-volume history of British economic warfare (1952, 1959), completed as part of the Cabinet Office series of official histories presided over by Sir Keith Hancock, which was to prove his outstanding memorial; although his return to his pre-war argument in a series of pamphlets in the 1960s, *The Coming of War in 1939* (1963), *Britain and Germany: the Search for an Agreement, 1930–1937* (1969), and in the second edition of his 1940 work (1968), in which he depicted the dilemmas of Britain's cabinets faced with military threats from Germany in Europe, Italy in the Mediterranean and Middle East, and Japan in the Pacific, would now command widespread acceptance. If historians of British foreign policy passed from vilifying the characters of MacDonald, Baldwin, and Neville Chamberlain to analysing the disparity between their obligations, the unreal expectations both of their allies and of their enemies, and the obvious gap between their military and financial commitments and the resources available to meet them, it was Medlicott's quiet influence which had as much to do with this as anything. His final work, *Contemporary England, 1914–1964* (1967), enshrined his views.

Medlicott became the leader in Britain of that transformation of the history of foreign policy and of diplomatic history into the discipline of international history (*anglice* the history of international relations), embodied in the title of his LSE chair. He was a pioneer in the widening of old-style diplomatic history to include issues of trade, strategy, and economic warfare. The first work on the Nazi economic organization of Europe was undertaken under his supervision. From 1965 until the completion of his task in 1977, he served in the Foreign and Commonwealth Office as editor of the official publication of Foreign Office documents covering the inter-war years, *Documents on British Foreign Policy, 1919–1939* (1969–84), with responsibility for completing Series II, covering the years 1932–8, revealing himself as both efficient and speedy in his task. He can be counted among the great editors of historical documents.

During his period at the LSE Medlicott both created and built up its department of international history until it became one of the leaders in the field internationally with a graduate school, more than 150 of whose students were to fill academic posts worldwide at the time of his retirement. He made sure that its staff included expertise in Japanese foreign policy. His attempt to build up similar expertise in the diplomacy of imperialism in Africa and India failed for lack of any interest among the products of the new universities in those two parts of the world in advancing their knowledge of the contribution made by European diplomacy to their frontiers and political development.

Medlicott suffered all his life (and was sensitive on the point) from not having been a product of the universities of Oxford or Cambridge and from having no links with them. Indeed there were a number of snide comments made in Oxford and Cambridge common rooms at his success in winning appointment to the Stevenson chair against the competition of A. J. P. Taylor and E. H. Carr. He was certainly aided in his appointment by the prejudice of the director of the LSE, Sir Alexander Carr-Saunders, against university figures who wrote regularly for the daily press. It was a prejudice based on the difficulties LSE graduates encountered in obtaining jobs as a result of the public role which its leading professors of politics and economics had played in the 1930s in creating that institution's reputation for being a hotbed of left-wing views. But the committee appointing Medlicott was also influenced by the strong support given him by Sir Llewellyn Woodward, Sir Keith Hancock, and other historians familiar with Medlicott's work as an official historian in the wartime Cabinet Office. In the event his appointment was thoroughly justified. By comparison with his rivals Medlicott was a consummate university politician; he was also an excellent judge of the new generation of post-war historians, and a first-class teacher of graduate and undergraduate students alike, providing they impressed him as serious in their scholarship. He was impeccable in his exercise of scholarship, leading as much by example as by exhortation.

Medlicott compensated for his lack of Oxford and Cambridge connections by tireless work in the Historical Association (which he served successively as secretary and president), on the council of the Royal Institute for International Affairs, the editorial board of the *Annual Register*, as chairman of the co-ordinating committee for international studies, and as historical adviser to the leading firm of academic publishers of history, Longmans, Green. It was his intervention which prevented the history department of King's College, London, from ridding itself of the lectureship in military history founded with War Office support in 1927, and in transforming it into a chair of war studies. Out of this was to develop the department of war studies now widely recognized as a leading international institution in the field.

Medlicott collaborated with his wife in two works published in 1971, *Bismarck and Europe*, and *The Lion's Tale*, the latter an often amusing collection of comments made over the past three centuries by distinguished foreign visitors to England. He died at Kings Ride Nursing Home, 289 Sheen Road, Richmond, Surrey, on 7 October 1987 and was buried in Richmond cemetery.   D. CAMERON WATT

Sources *The Times* (9 Oct 1987) · *WWW* · K. Bourne and D. C. Watt, *Studies in international history in honour of Professor W. N. Medlicott* (1967) · personal knowledge (2004) · b. cert. · m. cert. · d. cert.
Archives University of Calgary Library, letters to Erich Eyck
Likenesses photograph, in or before 1967, London School of Economics
Wealth at death £263,502: probate, 6 June 1988, *CGPLA Eng. & Wales*

Medows, Sir William (1738–1813), army officer and colonial governor, was born on 31 December 1738, the third son of Philip Medows (1708–1781), deputy ranger of Richmond Park, and his wife, Lady Frances Pierrepont, the daughter of the duke of Kingston. As a youth he is thought to have attended Eton College (1755–6) before entering the army as an ensign in the 50th foot on 26 February 1757; he was promoted lieutenant on 20 November 1757 and campaigned with his regiment in Germany between 1760 and 1762. Commissioned a captain in the 4th horse on 6 March 1764, he was promoted major in 1766, and appointed lieutenant-colonel of the 5th foot on 31 December 1769. When stationed with his regiment in Ireland he married, in 1770, Frances Augusta (1747/8–1827), the daughter of Robert Hammerton, of Hammerton, co. Tipperary. Medows then completed two years as lieutenant-colonel of the 12th light dragoons before exchanging into the 55th foot on 20 September 1775. He took his regiment to America the same year and was given command of a composite battalion of grenadiers during the New York campaign of 1776. In September 1777 he was wounded while leading his grenadiers at the battle of Brandywine. He then returned to the lieutenant-colonelcy of the 5th foot (16 October 1777).

In November 1778 Medows accompanied, as a brigadier-general, the expedition led by General James Grant which sailed from New York to the West Indies. During the landings on the French-held island of St Lucia he commanded the reserve, some 1300 men, which consisted of his own regiment, the 5th, and the expedition's combined grenadier and light infantry companies. St Lucia had no sooner been captured, however, when a vastly superior French armament under the command of the marquis d'Estaing appeared, and Medows's position on the Vigie peninsula—the key to the British defences—was assaulted by 5000 troops. Notwithstanding the odds, the battle-hardened British veterans beat off the enemy attacks and inflicted 1600 casualties, and in so doing established Medows's reputation.

Medows returned to England in 1780 and was made colonel of the 89th foot. In March 1781 he commanded the troops which sailed for the Cape of Good Hope with Commodore George Johnstone's squadron. The French, however, beat the British to the Cape, reinforced the Dutch garrison, and rendered a landing by Medows's troops impracticable. Dismissing Johnstone's suggestion that their expedition divert to the River Plate, Medows interpreted his instructions positively and continued on to India, where his reinforcement, which arrived in February 1782, proved crucial in the struggle against Haider Ali of Mysore and the French. Medows himself, although carrying the rank of major-general, played only a minor part in the unfolding conflict. Dismayed by the antagonism between the civil and military authorities at Madras, he refused the overall command which a disgruntled Eyre Coote attempted to thrust upon him and elected instead to serve as a volunteer aboard Admiral Hughes's fleet.

In 1788 Henry Dundas sent Medows back to India as governor and commander-in-chief of Bombay. The governor-general of Bengal, Lord Cornwallis, was given to understand that Medows would ultimately be his successor. After two years in post at Bombay, during which time Cornwallis first came to doubt his intended replacement's

judgement and application to business, Medows succeeded to the governorship of Madras and immediately took command of the forces assembling to fight the Third Anglo-Mysore War against Tipu Sultan. Throughout the ensuing campaign, however, Medows proved incapable of getting to grips with his elusive foe. Not only were his movements, burdened by a long supply train, too slow, but by splitting his army into detachments he risked defeat in detail. In the end all Medows had to show for his efforts was the capture of Coimbatore: he had not penetrated the Mysore heartlands, and Tipu Sultan had been left free to ravage the Carnatic. Medows admitted to Cornwallis that he felt unequal to his responsibilities, and the governor-general, having by now lost patience, sailed from Bengal in December 1790 to take personal charge. Thereafter, as second in command, Medows was happier. Leading the stormings of Bangalore and Nandidroog was more to his taste than accepting the reversion of the governor-generalship, which, when formally offered him, he declined. Medows relished also the prospect of leading the right-hand of three assault columns against Tipu Sultan's capital of Seringapatam. But faulty staff work led his column to turn in the wrong direction during the night attack of 6–7 February 1792; Medows succeeded in reuniting with Cornwallis's centre column only after the decisive combat had already been won. While he was not exclusively to blame, Medows allowed the error to disturb his mind; and when Tipu Sultan's decision to sue for peace denied him the opportunity to atone in battle for his mistake he shot himself. Fortunately the suicide attempt was bungled and Medows speedily recovered.

Medows was kindly received on his return to England; he was made a KB on 14 December 1792 and was offered command of an expedition (which never sailed) to capture Mauritius and the Isle de Bourbon. George III considered him 'eccentrick though worthy' (*Later Correspondence of George III*, 2.74). Medows was promoted lieutenant-general on 12 October 1793, was made colonel of the 7th dragoon guards on 2 November 1796, and became a full general in 1798; the same year he was appointed lieutenant-governor of the Isle of Wight. Between June 1801 and May 1803 he served as commander of the forces in Ireland. He settled afterwards at Conholt Park, near Andover, Wiltshire. His last appointment was as governor of Hull in 1808, a post which he held until his death, at Bath on 14 November 1813.

Medows lacked the self-belief necessary to high command but he was a notable fighting general. In moments of danger he always had well-chosen words of encouragement to offer his men and they admired him wholeheartedly. It was entirely characteristic that he should have resigned to the troops his share of the Seringapatam prize money, worth nearly £5000.   ALASTAIR W. MASSIE

Sources letters from Lord Cornwallis to W. Medows, 1788–92, PRO, PRO 30/11/174 • *Royal Military Panorama*, 4 (1814), 201–17 • S. R. Lushington, *The life and services of General Lord Harris* (1840) • J. W. Kaye, *Lives of Indian officers*, new edn, 1 (1904) • M. Wilks, *Historical sketches of the south of India, in an attempt to trace the history of Mysoor*, 3 vols. (1810–17), vols. 2–3 • *Correspondence of Charles, first Marquis Cornwallis*, ed. C. Ross, 3 vols. (1859) • will, 1792, PRO, PROB 11/1550,

609 • *The later correspondence of George III*, ed. A. Aspinall, 5 vols. (1962–70), vols. 1, 2 • 'Proposed attack on the French islands of Mauritius and Bourbon', 1785–93, BL OIOC, MSS Eur D707 • *GM*, 1st ser., 9 (1739), 46 • *GM*, 1st ser., 83/2 (1813), 624 • *GM*, 1st ser., 97/1 (1827), 382 • Fortescue, *Brit. army*, 2nd edn, vol. 3 • T. Pasley, *Private sea journals, 1778–1782*, ed. R. M. S. Pasley (1931) • *Army List* • *DNB* • R. A. Austen-Leigh, ed., *The Eton College register, 1753–1790* (1921) • W. A. Shaw, *The knights of England*, 2 vols. (1906)
Archives BL OIOC, papers, MS Eur. D 707 | BL, corresp. with Lord Hardwicke, etc., Add. MSS 34728–34758 • Bodl. Oxf., corresp. with Lord Macartney • PRO, corresp. with Lord Cornwallis, PRO 30/11
Likenesses Orme, stipple, pubd 1794 (after Smart), NPG • H. R. Cook, stipple, 1814 (after W. Haines), BM, NPG; repro. in *Royal Military Panorama* (1814) • R. Home, portrait (*The death of Colonel Moorhouse at the Siege of Bangalore*), NAM
Wealth at death £64,815—legacies: PRO, death duty registers, IR 26/586, 802

Medwall, Henry (*b.* 1462, *d.* after 1501), playwright, was evidently born on 8 September 1462. His father, John Medwall (*d.* 1491), was a resident of St Margaret's parish, Southwark, by 1449, where he served as clerk, organist, churchwarden, and provider of banners and prick-song books. An Emma Medwall who died in 1498 may have been his mother. In 1475 Henry followed his elder brother John to Eton College, whence he entered King's College, Cambridge, in 1480. He left King's College precipitately in June 1483, at almost exactly the time his future patron John Morton, then bishop of Ely, was sent to the Tower. Following the accession of Henry VII, Medwall served as a notary (by 18 August 1489), and entered minor orders (1490). In 1491 he was granted a degree in civil law from Cambridge. In 1492 he was appointed to the living of Balinghem in the district of Calais, but was almost certainly non-resident, dwelling rather at Lambeth Palace, where he served Morton as chaplain and factotum. Following Morton's death on 12 October 1500 Medwall's name can be traced for one further year. He was separated from various benefices, and after 1501 disappears from the records.

Medwall is the first English vernacular playwright known by name. While a student at King's College, and during subsequent visits, he witnessed and perhaps participated in college disguisings. His service under Morton overlapped with that of young Thomas More (1491–2), who, according to his biographer William Roper, would 'at Christmas tyde sodenly sometimes steppe in among the players, and neuer studyeng for the matter, make a parte of his owne there presently among them' (Roper, 5). The two interludes that survive under Henry Medwall's name were probably written for Morton's household at Lambeth in the 1490s (a proposed date of 1497 depends on the doubtful supposition that one or both interludes were written for the reception of ambassadors from Spain or the Low Countries). *Fulgens and Lucres*, the earliest full-length secular play in English, draws its plot from Buonaccorso da Montemagno's humanist Latin treatise *De vera nobilitate* (*c.*1428), translated into English *c.*1460 by John Tiptoft, earl of Worcester, and printed in 1481 by Caxton: in Medwall's play, Lucrece, daughter of the Roman senator Fulgens, chooses for a husband not the debauched noble Publius Cornelius, but the virtuous commoner

Gaius Flaminius; meanwhile, in a sub-plot, her wily maid Joan outwits two servant-wooers identified only as A and B. *Nature*, by contrast, conforms to the structure of a typical English morality play: Reason tries in vain to protect Man from Sensuality; Worlde introduces Man to Worldly Affeccyon, and thence to Pryde, Bodyly Lust, and other sins. Rescued by Reason, Man lapses into sin once more, but as Age renders him incapable, he finally faces death as a penitent, confident of salvation. Both interludes were published posthumously, *Fulgens and Lucres* *c.*1512–16 by John Rastell (*STC*, 1475–1640, 17778), *Nature* *c.*1530 by William Rastell (ibid., 17779). A third play, *Of the Finding of Truth*, for which no text survives, is probably an invention of the nineteenth-century forger J. Payne Collier.

ALAN H. NELSON

Sources *The plays of Henry Medwall*, ed. A. H. Nelson (1980) • A. H. Nelson, 'Life records of Henry Medwall', *Leeds Studies in English*, 11 (1979), 111–15 • S.-B. MacLean and A. H. Nelson, 'New light on Henry Medwall', *Leeds Studies in English*, 28 (1997), 77–98 • *The plays of Henry Medwall: a critical edition*, ed. M. E. Moeslein (New York, 1981) • W. Roper, *The lyfe of Sir Thomas Moore, knighte*, ed. E. V. Hitchcock, EETS, 197 (1935) • *STC*, 1475–1640, no. 17778–9 • W. Sterry, ed., *The Eton College register, 1441–1698* (1943)

Medwin, Thomas (1788–1869), writer and biographer, was born on 20 March 1788 in Horsham, Sussex, the second child of Thomas Charles Medwin (1752/3–1829), a solicitor and steward to the duke of Norfolk, and his wife, Mary (*c.*1760–*c.*1850), daughter of John Pilfold and first cousin to Shelley's mother, Elizabeth Pilfold. Like Shelley, who was four years younger, Medwin attended Syon House Academy, entering about 1798 and leaving in 1804 to attend an unidentified 'public' school before matriculating at Oxford on 2 December 1805. Although Medwin's veracity as a biographer has been questioned, his close relationship with his young cousin in these early years is attested to by Shelley's earliest extant letter and by later correspondence showing the poet's continuing respect and affection for his 'old friend and fellow-townsman' (*Letters of Percy Bysshe Shelley*, 2.240).

In 1807 or 1808 Medwin visited Wales, where he met the fourteen-year-old Felicia Dorothea Browne (later Hemans). On his return he incited Shelley's interest in Felicia's poetry, initiating a brief correspondence between the two young poets. During this period the boys collaborated on a novel, 'The Nightmare' (no longer extant). Before Shelley's arrival at Oxford in October 1810, Medwin had left the university without a degree and was living at Lincoln's Inn, perhaps studying law independently at his father's behest. Whether he or Shelley or anyone really picked up a scrap of German poetry in Lincoln's Inn Fields and whether that scrap later became the seed of 'The Wandering Jew' remains a subject of heated debate among Shelley biographers and critics, along with the extent of Medwin's contribution to the poem. But, as Medwin remembered vividly thirty-six years later, Shelley's career at Oxford was about to come to an abrupt and unpleasant end. At four o'clock in the morning of 27 March 1811, Medwin was awakened by Shelley's high-pitched voice excitedly crying out that he had been expelled for atheism. After Shelley's elopement with Harriet Westbrook in August 1811 (during which time he borrowed money from Medwin's father and sought his legal advice), the lives of the two young men diverged and they did not meet again until 1820.

Meanwhile, Medwin incurred his father's displeasure by rejecting a legal career. According to his biographer Ernest J. Lovell jun., his father's affluence and his mother's connections with the Sussex gentry had bred in Medwin expensive tastes and an aversion to earning his living. Now the eldest surviving son, his brother John having died in a fall in 1806, he persuaded his father to purchase him first a cornetcy and then a lieutenantcy in the army. Sent to India, he joined the 24th light dragoons on 12 November 1813, arriving at Cawnpore after a 1200-mile journey up the Ganges. Less than a year after his arrival, probably in June 1814, he contracted dysentery, resulting in lifelong disease of the liver. Of his four and a half years with the regiment, twelve months were spent on leave of absence. Although Medwin spent much of his tour of duty hunting, attending parties, and writing in his journal, he probably participated in the siege of the fort at Hathras in February–March 1817. At some point during his enlistment, he met and befriended Edward Ellerker Williams, then serving in another regiment.

On 8 May 1818 Medwin received permission to return to England on an eighteen-month leave of absence. Despite his ill health, however, he did not leave India until October. The day before he sailed, Medwin felicitously discovered a copy of Shelley's *Revolt of Islam* 'at a Parsee bookstall' (Medwin, ed. Buxton Forman, 230), rekindling his interest in the young genius he had half forgotten. On 24 May 1819 the 24th light dragoons disbanded, and in July Medwin went on the half-pay of a lieutenant. (Though he is frequently referred to as Captain Medwin, Mary Shelley disputed his claim to this title and the issue remains unresolved.)

After a brief stay in England, Medwin travelled to the continent, still sporting a magnificent military moustache lubricated with bear grease. He arrived in Geneva on 20 September 1819 and was soon joined by Edward Williams and Jane Cleveland Johnson (who was known as Jane Williams though the couple were not married). In the autumn of 1820 Medwin accepted Shelley's invitation to join him in Italy and spent many contented hours reading, writing, and conversing with Shelley and Lord Byron. After the deaths of Shelley and Williams in July 1822 and of Byron two years later, these conversations, which Medwin had recorded in his journal, became the basis for the highly popular but controversial *Conversations of Lord Byron* (1824).

Medwin's reputation and social position were sufficient to enable him on 2 November 1824 to marry Anne Henrietta Starnford, countess of Starnford (1788–1868), born Baroness Hamilton of Sweden. At first the marriage was happy and Medwin lived in high style, 'moving in the most exclusive circles' (Lovell, 220). Their first daughter, ostentatiously baptized Catherine Mary Anne Pilfold Hamilton Medwin, was born in Florence on 3 November

1825. But before the birth of his second daughter, Henriette, in 1829, lavish spending coupled with speculation in art had resulted in financial ruin. In September 1829 the destitute Medwin hurried to England for the reading of his father's will, only to find that the elder Medwin, exasperated by his son's extravagance, had left him only 10 guineas for a memorial ring. Unable to support the wife whose fortune he had squandered, Medwin returned to Italy determined to live alone and supplement his scanty income through his writing, leaving his wife and their two small daughters in Florence. In 1831 he returned to England where he sold his commission (apparently at a profit) and, according to Lovell, 'set about again trying to clear his name' of the attacks on the authenticity of his *Conversations* (ibid., 252). The publication in *The Athenaeum* of his 'Memoir of Shelley' (1832) and 'The Shelley papers' (1832–3) established him (along with Thomas Jefferson Hogg, whose 'Shelley at Oxford' articles appeared almost simultaneously) as one of the few living authorities on the poet (the articles were published together in 1833 as *The Shelley Papers. Memoir of Percy Bysshe Shelley*). Medwin also published a substantial amount of literary criticism and poetry; one play; a novel, *Lady Singleton*, attacking England's stringent divorce laws; and the semi-autobiographical *Angler in Wales* (1834), incorporating material from his Indian journals. In 1846 he returned to England to visit his ageing mother and to obtain letters for his most important work, *The Life of Percy Bysshe Shelley* (2 vols., 1847), the first full-length biography of the poet.

Though Medwin was working abroad from limited sources and his faulty memory sometimes led to misquotations or errors in dates, he seems to be guilty of only two deliberate distortions in his writings on Shelley: the implication in the *Conversations* that he had been present at Shelley's cremation and the conflation in the 'Memoir of Shelley' of two trips abroad into one to disguise the married poet's elopement with young Mary Godwin.

Well aware that such mendacity was no longer feasible and fearful of adverse publicity, Mary Shelley strenuously opposed the publication of Medwin's biography and condemned it unread, interpreting Medwin's request for reimbursement of his expenses in exchange for withdrawal from publication as an attempt at blackmail. Her reaction, perpetuated in Lady Jane Shelley's *Shelley Memorials* and in H. Buxton Forman's introduction to the 1913 edition of Medwin's *Life*, is largely responsible for the general disrepute in which Medwin's biography has long been held. Admittedly the book is riddled with small inaccuracies such as his reference to Claire Clairmont as Mary Shelley's 'half sister' (p. 129), but his depiction of Shelley is straightforward, undistorted by the conflicting emotions that led Hogg to exaggerate Shelley's eccentricities and even deliberately to alter documents. An ardent admirer and astute critic of Shelley's poetry, Medwin had neither the motive nor the inclination to harm his cousin's reputation as Mary Shelley feared.

Medwin's last years were spent in the company of fellow poet Caroline Champion de Crespigny, *née* Bathurst (1798–1858x62), whom he had met about 1843. Accepted into élite social circles in Germany and elsewhere, he seems to have been respected as a critic and forgiven, at least on the continent, for the abandonment of his wife. He returned to England in 1862 and continued to write and to annotate his *Life of Shelley*. After an extended illness that prevented him from accepting Sir Percy Shelley's invitation to visit Boscombe Manor, he died on 2 August 1869 in the Carfax, North Horsham, aged eighty-one. He was buried a few days later in Denne Road cemetery, also in the Carfax.

CAROL L. THOMA

Sources T. Medwin, *The life of Percy Bysshe Shelley*, 2 vols. (1847) · T. Medwin, *The life of Percy Bysshe Shelley*, new edn, ed. H. B. Forman (1913) · E. J. Lovell jun., *Captain Medwin: friend of Byron and Shelley* (1962) · *The letters of Percy Bysshe Shelley*, ed. F. L. Jones, 2 vols. (1964) · K. N. Cameron, D. H. Reiman, and D. D. Fischer, eds., *Shelley and his circle, 1773–1822*, 10 vols. (1961–2002), vols. 1–4 · T. Medwin, '*Oswald and Edwin*', '*Sketches in Hindoostan*', '*Ahasuerus*', ed. D. H. Reiman (1978) · N. I. White, *Shelley*, [2nd edn], 2 vols. (1947) · *The letters of Mary Wollstonecraft Shelley*, ed. B. T. Bennett, 3 vols. (1980–88) · H. Taylor, 'Thomas Medwin: intermediary of German literature and culture', *Anglo-German and American-German crosscurrents*, ed. A. O. Lewis, W. L. Kopp, and E. J. Danis, 4 (1990) · C. R. Zimansky, 'Shelley's *Wandering Jew*: some borrowings from Lewis and Radcliffe', *Studies in English Literature, 1500–1900*, 18 (1978), 597–609 · G. M. Rosa, 'A Stendhal *inédit*: Stendhal, Medwin, and Edward John Trelawny', *French Studies Bulletin: a Quarterly Supplement*, 52 (autumn 1994), 4–6

Archives Bodl. Oxf., letters · Horsham Museum, West Sussex, notes to his biography of Shelley | Bodl. Oxf., letters to James Ingram · Bodl. Oxf., MS Shelley adds. and Abinger collection · Horsham Museum, West Sussex, corresp. with his brother Pilfold

Likenesses E. Walker, photogravure (after oil painting by unknown artist), repro. in White, *Shelley*, vol. 2

Medwyn. For this title name *see* Forbes, John Hay, Lord Medwyn (1776–1854).

Mee [*née* Foldsone], **Anne** (*c*.1770–1851), miniature painter, was the eldest daughter of John *Foldsone (*d*. 1784), portrait painter of small whole-lengths, for which 'a guinea the piece, or less, rather than lose the sitter was taken' (*Court and Private Life*, 2.144). He lived in 1770 in Little Castle Street, Oxford Market, London, though his occupation took him to fashionable resorts during the summer months. Anne attended Madame Pomier's school in Queen Square, Westminster, where her artistic, poetic, and musical skills became evident at an early age. She mixed colours for her father, prepared his palette, and 'put in the background to the canvas, ready for his portraits' (ibid.). Basil Long notes that she began painting at the age of twelve and became a pupil and protégée of the portrait painter George Romney, under whom she made copies of works by Gainsborough and Reynolds. After her father died she was noted to have been the sole support of her mother and her eight brothers and sisters, though her mother's acknowledgement in a letter of 1792 to Sir Thomas Lawrence that 'your goodness to me and my poor children has been unbounded' suggests that the painter gave them substantial financial assistance (Layard, 19). This led to rumours that he had 'in the common phrase, paid [his] addresses to Miss Anne Foldsone' but in a draft of a letter he described himself, rather, as 'a friend of the lady' (ibid.). The poet William Hayley, who sat to her in

Anne Mee (*c*.1770–1851), self-portrait

1788, described her as a 'young female genius in miniature' and 'a pretty, modest and sensible girl' (Long, 218). Walpole on the other hand called her 'a prodigy of dishonest impertinence' (Walpole, *Corr.*, 11.193).

Miss Foldsone was introduced to Queen Charlotte by Lady Courtown through Lady Cremorne. With her sister she was placed to board with Madame de Lafitte, a Dutch emigrée under the protection of the queen who lived in a house in the cloisters at Windsor. When Madame de Lafitte visited the lodge to read German with the princesses she was accompanied by Miss Foldsone, to whom the princesses and the queen herself sat for their miniatures. In his letters to Miss Berry of 1790 and 1791 Walpole had noted that Miss Foldsone was occupied with commissions at Windsor—commenting that they were 'not the work of a moment'—instead of completing her commission to paint miniatures of the misses Berry for him (Walpole, *Corr.*, 11.145). Miniatures of the princesses Sophia, Amelia, and Charlotte by Miss Foldsone remain in the Royal Collection. The portraits of the misses Berry (priv. coll.) were eventually completed and one was engraved as the frontispiece to the second volume of Lady Theresa Lewis's edition of Miss Berry's journals and correspondence (1865).

Miss Foldsone married at St Marylebone on 15 May 1793 Joseph Mee (*d*. 1849), a barrister of Mount Anna, Armagh, with whom she had six children by 1833. Joseph Mee owned a fairly large estate in co. Armagh, and on his death left a substantial amount of property. In his diary Joseph Farington recorded a comment made by Lady Smith Burgess, a distant relative of Joseph Mee whose miniature portrait Mrs Mee had painted:

> Mr. Mee had consented to let Her paint *Ladies Only* who were never to be attended by gentlemen.—She sd. She gave Mrs. Mee 40 guineas for [her] picture, & that she had 18 guineas for pictures of a certain size. (Farington, *Diary*, 26 April 1804)

Mrs Mee exhibited at the Royal Academy and at the British Institution from 1804 to 1837.

Mrs Mee had also obtained the patronage of George IV,

when prince regent, and it was from him that she received her most important commission, completed in 1814, to paint a series of large miniature portraits of fashionable ladies, seventeen of which remain in the Royal Collection. When serial publication of engravings from these miniatures was begun in 1812 they were entitled *The Gallery of Beauties of the Court of … George the Third*, an intended reference to two previous series of portraits of court beauties, the 'Windsor Beauties', painted by Sir Peter Lely for Mary II, and the 'Hampton Court Beauties', by Sir Godfrey Kneller for Anne Hyde, duchess of York. The account from the silversmiths Rundell, Bridge, and Rundell 'For setting 19 portraits of Ladies in richly chased Frames, antique scroll honey suckle, richly gilt … with chased coronets &c' (Walker, 357) conveys an opulence that 'suggests that the Prince Regent intended his "Gallery of Beauties" to be displayed in an area of some importance' (Lloyd and Remington, 190). Indeed the *Ladies Monthly Museum* recorded that the prince regent was 'forming a superb boudoir for their reception' (ibid.). Basil Long considered that 'Mrs Mee's miniatures are rarely satisfactory … often the eyes are of an exaggerated size … [and] her colouring is often displeasing' (Long, 48) and Walker held that 'The Beauties of 1812–13 incline to be flashy, affected and melodramatic, all with large soulful eyes and melodramatic colouring' (Walker, 354). Compared with the series of full-size portraits of court beauties by Lely and Kneller, Mrs Mee's large miniatures (about 8 inches x 9) lack subtlety of execution. In their attributes and settings, however, they constitute an original development from the earlier series of beauties. While some of the sitters' attributes are those traditionally associated with female portraiture others are highly contemporary in their reference to literary, especially poetical, sources. The decision to place some sitters within Gothic architectural settings increases the sense of a move away from the classicizing effect of introducing the attributes of goddesses into female portraiture. In this context the rich and sometimes brilliant colouring conveys an intensity of vision that is essentially Romantic. In addition to the engravings published in *The Gallery of Beauties* others were engraved and illustrated in the *Court Magazine*, *La Belle Assemblée*, and the *Ladies Monthly Museum*.

Lord Byron sent privately to the sitter a 'Condolatory address to Sarah countess of Jersey on the prince regent's returning her picture to Mrs Mee', which was subsequently published, without his leave, in *The Champion* (31 July 1814) and in the *Morning Chronicle* (1 August 1814). A miniature by Mrs Mee of Lady Jersey, a noted court beauty, was given by the prince regent to the duke of Cumberland and remains in the Hanoverian collection (Calenberg, Hanover). Mrs Mee had earlier painted for Byron a miniature portrait of Lady Oxford, by whose 'autumnal charms' he was soothed following the débâcle of his affair with Lady Caroline Lamb in 1812.

Towards the end of her life Mrs Mee lived at 3 Woodman's Cottages, The Grove, Hammersmith, where she died on 28 May 1851, leaving her son Arthur Patrick Mee, who was articled to the architect Sir John Soane, sole beneficiary and executor of her will. A self-portrait in watercolour on ivory is in the Victoria and Albert Museum, London, together with her miniature of William Grimaldi. ANNETTE PEACH

Sources A. Mee, *The gallery of beauties in the court of his most excellent majesty George the Third* (1812) · R. Walker, *The eighteenth and early nineteenth century miniatures in the collection of her majesty the queen* (1991) · B. S. Long, *British miniaturists* (1929) [V&A copy with MS annotations] · C. Lloyd and V. Remington, *Masterpieces in little* (1996) [exhibition catalogue, Queen's Gallery, Buckingham Palace, 23 July – 5 Oct 1997] · MS records, V&A · records and sales catalogues, NPG, Heinz Archive and Library · IGI · will, PRO, PROB 11/2136, fol. 211*v* · *Court and private life in the time of Queen Charlotte, being the journals of Mrs Papendiek*, ed. V. D. Broughton, 2 vols. (1887) · Farington, *Diary* · *Byron's letters and journals*, ed. L. Marchand, 3–4 (1974–5) · Graves, *RA exhibitors* · *Ladies Monthly Museum* (1814–16) · E. C. Clayton, *English female artists*, 2 vols. (1876) · G. S. Layard, *Sir Thomas Lawrence's letter bag* (1906) · D. Foskett, *Miniatures: dictionary and guide* (1987) · *GM*, 2nd ser., 36 (1851), 102 · *DNB*

Likenesses H. R. Cook, engraving, repro. in *Ladies Monthly Museum* (1814) · A. Mee, self-portrait, watercolour on ivory miniature, V&A [*see illus.*] · H. Meyer, stipple (after A. Mee), BM, NPG; repro. in Mee, *Gallery of beauties*

Wealth at death left all property to son

Mee, Arthur Henry (1875–1943), journalist and children's writer, was born on 21 July 1875 in a cottage (now demolished) behind the west front of St Helen's Church in Stapleford, Nottinghamshire. He was the second of the ten children of Henry Mee (*b.* 1852), railway fireman, and his wife, Mary, *née* Fletcher (*b.* 1853), both pious Baptists. The Mees moved to 7 Pinfold Lane, Stapleford, shortly after his birth and to 237 Woodborough Road, Nottingham, in 1889.

After attending the Stapleford board school, on Church Street, Stapleford, Mee began his long writing career (he celebrated fifty years in journalism in 1941) at the age of fourteen as a copy holder on the *Nottingham Evening Post*; at sixteen he was articled to the *Nottingham Daily Express* for four years. By the age of twenty he was editing the *Express's Evening News* for John Hammerton, and contributing regularly to *Tit-Bits*. A year later (1896) Mee was working in London, first for *Tit-Bits* followed by three years editing *Black and White*. In 1898 Mee was invited by Alfred Harmsworth to join the staff of the *Daily Mail*, becoming its literary editor in 1903. This led to a series of Harmsworth publications, among them the *Self-Educator* (1905–7), the first of many collaborations with John Hammerton; it was followed by *The History of the World* (1907–9), *Natural History* (1909–11), and *The World's Great Books*. Each work relied on Mee's talent for organizing vast and diverse amounts of information and popularizing general knowledge. He was famous for his collection of 250,000 cross-referenced articles on all manner of subjects.

Mee married Yorkshire-born Amelia (Amy) Fratson (*b.* 1877) on 6 March 1897, and they had one child, born in 1901. Mee claimed that listening to seven-year-old Marjorie ceaselessly questioning her mother gave him the idea of producing a book which would answer the most common questions asked by children. The resulting *Children's Encyclopedia* (1908–10) was published in fifty fortnightly parts. The combination of Mee's accessible style,

Arthur Henry Mee (1875–1943), by Frank O. Salisbury, 1940

the breadth of information covered, and effective use of illustrations made the *Encyclopedia* popular with children, parents, and educationists. By 1910 it was being marketed in the USA as the hugely successful *Book of Knowledge*; during Mee's lifetime it was translated into many languages, including Chinese.

Mee followed up the *Children's Encyclopedia* with two publications: the monthly *My Magazine* (1910–35) and the weekly *Children's Newspaper* (1919–64)—Mee edited it until his death. His declared aim was to educate the next generation, 'which is going to save the world from the sins and follies and blunders of this' (Hammerton, 176). The *Children's Newspaper* was read throughout the empire; Mee used it shamelessly as a platform for his personal views. While in many ways a liberal—at times radical—writer, he inevitably saw the world from his position as a white, middle-class, successful, Christian Englishman; his faith and patriotism particularly inform his interpretation of facts, history, and events. Though he was prepared to question individuals and institutions, his belief in the universally beneficial effects of empire was total. This now makes his work look dated—even offensive. It is important, however, not to let these qualities obscure the frequently stirring (if somewhat gushing and self-absorbed) quality of his prose.

By the First World War Mee was a wealthy man, living in comfort first at Uplands, Hexable, Kent, and later in the home he had built at Eynsford, near Sevenoaks, Kent. He was a short, slightly built man who eschewed physical exercise. The 'little champion of the Nonconformist Conscience' (Hammerton, 140), as Lord Northcliffe referred to

him, attempted to use his influence in the service of faith and country by involving himself in a temperance campaign, the Strength of Britain movement. Although itself a failure, this culminated in *Who Giveth us the Victory* (1918), the work which most clearly explains the faith which underpinned all Mee's work.

Arthur Mee's last project was *The King's England*, a guide to the counties of England in forty-one volumes. It was nearing completion when, during an operation at King's College Hospital, Lambeth, London, he died on 27 May 1943. He was cremated at Golders Green, Middlesex; his ashes were scattered at Eynsford, Kent.

KIMBERLEY REYNOLDS

Sources J. Hammerton, *Child of wonder: an intimate biography of Arthur Mee* (1946) · *DNB* · *The Times* (29 May 1943) · G. Elias, *Arthur Mee* (1993) · private information (2004) [Andrea Lowe, Area Librarian, Nottinghamshire County Council] · b. cert. · m. cert.
Archives JRL, Methodist Archives and Research Centre, corresp. · Stapleford Library, Church Street, Stapleford | BL, corresp. with Lord Northcliffe, Add. MS 62183 · U. Reading L., letters to John Derry
Likenesses F. O. Salisbury, oils, 1940, priv. coll. [*see illus.*] · photographs, repro. in Hammerton, *Child of wonder*
Wealth at death £43,507 10s. 9d.: probate, 3 Aug 1943, *CGPLA Eng. & Wales*

Mee [*née* Brown; *other married name* Bartlett], **Margaret Ursula** (1909–1988), political activist and botanical artist, was born on 22 May 1909 at The Crest, White Hill, Chesham, Buckinghamshire, one of three daughters of George John Henderson Brown (*d.* 1938), insurance clerk, and his wife, Elizabeth Isabella, formerly Churchman. Her early interest in art was fostered by an aunt who illustrated children's books, that in nature by her father, an amateur naturalist. Educated at Dr Challoner's Grammar School, Amersham, and the School of Art, Science and Commerce in Watford, she taught briefly at Liverpool before deciding to travel. She spent several months in Germany, at a time of active and highly visible persecution of socialists and Jews; in February 1933 she witnessed the Reichstag fire in Berlin and the succeeding Jewish boycott day, events which reinforced her own left-wing views. Margaret married, on 11 January 1936, Reginald Bruce Bartlett (*b.* 1905), son of Herbert William Bartlett, a clerk. Bartlett was a trade union activist, and Margaret herself became an ardent trade unionist. A passionate speaker at meetings she was a delegate for the Union of Sign, Glass and Ticket Writers to the Trades Union Congress of 1937, where she proposed a resolution for raising the school-leaving age.

The marriage was not successful, and after her father's death Margaret went to France, having to flee the country fifteen days after the outbreak of war. She spent the war years first as a machinist, then as a draughtswoman in the De Havilland aircraft factory at Hatfield, and divorced Bartlett in 1943. When peace returned she enrolled as an evening student at St Martin's School of Art, Westminster, where she met Greville Ronald Bosworth Mee (*b.* 1909), a fellow student who became her lifelong partner. He was the son of Albert Alexander Mee, painter. The portfolio she built up at St Martin's gained her a place, and a post-war grant, at the Camberwell School of Arts and Crafts in south London, 1947–9. Under the tuition of Victor Pasmore she learned the attention to detail and developed the style which was to characterize her later work.

In 1952, by which time Margaret had changed her name to Mee by deed poll, the Mees went to São Paulo, Brazil, where Margaret's sister was living, intending to stay for three or four years. She taught art at St Paul's, the British School, while Greville found work as a commercial artist. Margaret soon became captivated by the luxuriant tropical flora of the forests of the Serra do Mar in south-eastern Brazil; she began seriously to collect and paint, taking detailed notes and working in gouache, and in this wealth of subject material found her true vocation as a botanical artist. Before long she yearned to see the plants of the tropical forests, and, with a friend from the school, she set out in 1956 for Belém and her first experience of the Amazonian flora. It was the first of many expeditions which led her through most of the vast Amazon basin, relying on local guides, surviving the hazards of canoe travel, the local food or lack of it, the often dangerous and always troublesome insect life, and the occasional hostility towards a solitary white woman.

The São Paulo Botanical Institute encouraged Margaret's obsession for accuracy in botanical detail and colour, and sent her to the Mato Grosso, where she collected several plants new to science. She exhibited in Rio in 1958 and in London's Royal Horticultural Society, receiving the Grenfell medal, and henceforth worked as a freelance artist. Other exhibitions followed: São Paulo in 1964, and then Washington, which brought her support from the National Geographic Society for an expedition in 1967 to the 3000 metre Pico de Neblina, on the border of Brazil and Venezuela. She was the first woman to make the southern approach to this peak, but the route being badly eroded, the party was obliged to turn back at 1000 metres.

Unlike Amazon botanical artists before her, Margaret worked entirely from living plants. Her fifteen expeditions into the interior, mostly to Amazonia, involved travelling and living under the most primitive conditions. She would draw at night by torchlight to capture rare nocturnal flowers, and this immediacy gave her paintings an accuracy, depth, and colour unrivalled by her predecessors. Her travels coincided with the beginning of the commercial exploitation of the forest, and she expressed her fury at the damage caused to the land and its peoples. Margaret was back in London in January 1968 for the exhibition and launch of her book, *Flowers of the Brazilian Forests*, a folio edition of thirty-one paintings, for which the duke of Edinburgh was the patron. She returned to Brazil, fired by a fresh ambition to confront the threat to the Amazon Forest caused by the government's road building and mining programme. The Mees moved to Rio de Janeiro, where Margaret was able to paint from the living plants which she had sent back from her explorations.

A Guggenheim fellowship paid for two further expeditions to the lower Amazon, which yielded more new species. Margaret wrote a report for the Forestry Development Institute, drawing attention to the devastation around Manaus and the damage caused by unregulated trade in forest products. Her work was now internationally acclaimed. Honours accrued: in 1975 honorary citizenship of Rio, on 1 January 1976 the British MBE for services to Brazilian botany, in 1979 the Brazilian order of Cruzeiro do Sul, fellowship of the Linnean Society, 1986. The Brazilian government supported her travels in order to produce another book, *Flowers of the Amazon*, launched in Brazil in 1980, with an exhibition in London's Natural History Museum. During this visit, Margaret and Greville married, on 8 October.

Margaret's campaign against the environmental damage, with its pollution and loss of species, voiced on Brazilian television, was repeated in the USA when her Amazon Collection of sixty paintings, many of plants new to science, was exhibited at the Missouri Botanical Garden in 1986. This publicity led to an invitation to visit an opencast bauxite mine near Manaus, which she found far more destructive than the mining company had claimed, and an upstream botanical reserve, which yielded new species. Her ambition now was to paint the rare night flowering *Selenicereus* (*Strophocactus*) *witterii*, the Amazonian moonflower. The plant does not flower every year, and when it does, the flowers open for a single night. Near Manaus she located a plant with buds, and with a companion, waited through the night until it opened. She then sketched by the light of a fluorescent torch, taking the colours the following day from the now closed flower.

In November 1988 the Mees came to England for the launch of a book based on Margaret's diaries, *Margaret Mee in Search of Flowers of the Amazon Forest* (1988), and a major exhibition of her paintings at the Royal Botanic Gardens, Kew. Meanwhile she was setting up the Margaret Mee Amazon Trust, based at Kew, to assist Brazilian botanical students to study in the UK. On 30 November the Mees were travelling by car when they were involved in an accident at Seagrave crossroads, Leicestershire; Margaret suffered severe chest injuries and died later that day in Leicester Royal Infirmary. Although she subscribed to no religion beyond a respect for nature, a memorial service was held at Kew on 16 January 1989, with representatives of the duke of Edinburgh, the Brazilian government, and the world of botany attending. She was survived by her husband.

ANITA MCCONNELL

Sources S. Mayo, *Margaret Mee's Amazon: paintings of plants from Brazilian Amazonia* (1988) · *Margaret Mee, uma visão da Amazonia* [leaflet] · *The Times* (2 Oct 1980), 17c · *The Times* (3 Dec 1988), 12f · M. Mee, *Margaret Mee in search of flowers of the Amazon forests*, ed. T. Morrison (1988) · private information (2004) · personal knowledge (2004) · R. Stiff, *Return to the Amazon* (1966) · b. cert. · m. cert. · d. cert.
Likenesses photographs, repro. in Mayo, *Margaret Mee's Amazon*

Meehan, Charles Patrick (1812–1890), writer and translator, was born at 141 Great Britain (now Parnell) Street, Dublin, on 12 July 1812. He received his early education at his parents' native town, Ballymahon, co. Longford, and in 1828 went to the Irish College in Rome, where he was ordained priest in 1834. He also acquired a good knowledge of Italian, German, French, and Spanish there. After nine months' work as a curate at Rathdrum, co. Wicklow, he was transferred to a curacy at the parish church of Sts Michael and John, Exchange Street, Dublin, in 1835. He remained there all his life. He was well known for his charity and temperance activity.

As a member of the Romantic nationalist group Young Ireland, Meehan contributed to *The Nation*. His first poem, 'Boyhood's Years', appeared in the journal on 5 November 1842 under the pseudonym Clericus. A few more poems, translations of continental poetry, and articles followed. Meehan was known for his wit, and Young Irelanders often gathered in his presbytery. He was close friends with John Mitchel, Father Kenyon, T. D. Reilly, and James Clarence Mangan.

Meehan prominently defended Young Ireland from accusations of atheism, and also spoke in favour of mixed education. He seceded with Young Ireland from Daniel O'Connell's repeal movement in 1846, and became an active member of the Irish confederation. He wrote *History of the Confederation of Kilkenny* (1846) and a translation from the Latin of Dominic O'Daly, *The Geraldines, Earls of Desmond* (1847) for the Library of Ireland.

In 1847 Meehan was president of St Patrick's Confederate Club, which met in Bishop Street, Dublin, but retired in the hope for an appointment at one of the new queen's colleges. He published *The life and death of Most Rev. Francis Kirwan, bishop of Killala, from the Latin of John Lynch, archdeacon of Tuam, author of Cambrensus eversus* in 1848.

After the failed rising of 1848 Meehan appears to have taken no further part in public life, but focused on his parish duties and his literary work. He gave occasional lectures, and visited famous libraries on the continent in search of unpublished manuscripts dealing with Ireland. In 1865 he was elected member of the Royal Irish Academy, and he was known in Irish literary circles. He wrote many articles in Irish periodicals, mainly translations and historical works. His chief compilations were *Rise and fall of Irish Franciscan monasteries, and memoirs of the Irish hierarchy in the seventeenth century* (1869) and *Fate and Fortunes of Hugh O'Neill, Earl of Tyrone, and Rory O'Donell, Earl of Tyrconnel* (1870); the latter was popularly known as 'The flight of the earls'. He also edited Thomas Davis's essays (1883) and selections of Mangan's poetry (1884), and re-edited Richard R. Madden's *Literary Remains of the United Irishmen* (1887).

In his old age Meehan was regarded as an eccentric. He was 'slightly under medium height, always wore a monocle, attached to a silk ribbon, a tall silk hat, and a stout blackthorn stick' (O'Sullivan, 314). He died on 14 March 1890 in the presbytery of Sts Michael and John, Lower Exchange Street, Dublin, and was buried in Glasnevin cemetery, Dublin. His parishioners erected a mural tablet to him in the church of Sts Michael and John.

J. T. GILBERT, *rev.* BRIGITTE ANTON

Sources T. F. O'Sullivan, *The Young Irelanders* (1945) · M. Russell, 'Sketches in Irish biography no. 16—the Rev. Charles Patrick Meehan', *Irish Monthly*, 17 (Aug 1889), 427–38 · M. Russell, 'Rev. C. P. Meehan', *Irish Monthly*, 18 (April 1890), 218–19 · 'Centenary of Father Meehan', *Irish Book Lover*, 4 (1912–13), 25–7 · C. G. Duffy, *Young Ireland: a fragment of Irish history, 1840–1845*, rev. edn, 2 vols. (1896) · R. J. Hayes, *Manuscript sources for the history of Irish civilisation*, 3 (Boston, 1965) · *Manuscripts sources for the history of Irish civilisation*, first supplement: 1965–1979 (Boston, 1979), vol. 1 · R. Davis, *The Young Ireland movement* (1987) · *DNB* · J. S. Crone, *A concise dictionary of Irish biography*, rev. edn (1937)

Archives Bodl. Oxf., R. Caulfield corresp., MS Eng. Misc. e. 108 · NL Ire., John Keegan Casey corresp., MS 8260 · NL Ire., W. J. Fitzpatrick papers, MS 15499 · NL Ire., T. Lee papers, MS 4184 · NL Ire., Maurice Lenihan corresp., MS 133 · NL Ire., (Thomas) Wyse papers, MS 15026 · Royal Irish Acad., John Hardiman corresp., MSS 12 N. 20–21

Likenesses photograph, repro. in Duffy, *Young Ireland*, vol. 2, p. 157

Wealth at death £390: probate, 24 April 1890, *CGPLA Ire.* (1890)

Meek, Charles Kingsley (1885–1965), anthropologist and colonial administrator, was born on 24 June 1885 in Ballyloran, Larne, co. Antrim, the son of James Brady Meek, a Presbyterian minister, and his wife, Mary Elizabeth McCarter. Educated first at Rothesay Academy and Bedford School, he went up to Brasenose College, Oxford, as a Colquitt exhibitioner at the relatively late age of twenty-one. Seemingly his undergraduate days were remarkable only for a decision to switch his career: having graduated BA in theology in 1910, he decided to join the colonial administrative service and in 1912 was posted to the northern provinces of Nigeria.

This was the moment when the new governor-general, Sir Frederick Lugard, was about to embark on extending his policy of indirect rule from a successful north to a suspicious south. Fundamental to such a policy was a systematic understanding of traditional institutions. In such knowledge much of Nigeria still remained something of a *tabula rasa*. As commissioner of the decennial census of 1921, Meek was able to exploit the interest he had developed, on his own initiative, in the social institutions of the peoples he administered in the northern provinces. With the publication of *The Northern Tribes of Nigeria* (1925), an ethnological account which, by its novel and deliberate inclusion of substantial social and cultural data, became far more important than the bald population count it was conventionally intended to be, he introduced to the outside world an awareness of the social dynamics of a large number of tribal groups of whose existence it had hitherto been unaware.

Meek's research talents had already been recognized by his appointment to one of the two posts of government anthropologist established in Nigeria in 1924. An early fruit of this happy selection was the appearance of his *A Sudanese Kingdom* (1931), a study of 'divine kingship' among the Jukun-speaking peoples. This was followed in the same year by *Tribal Studies in Northern Nigeria*, long to be an ethnographic work of first reference on many of the less-studied peoples of the region. Meek, who had been promoted to the rank of resident and transferred to the southern provinces of Nigeria in 1929, resigned from the colonial service because of ill health in 1933. He had married Helen Marjorie, daughter of Lieutenant-Colonel C. H.

Innes Hopkins, in 1919. They had two sons, the elder of whom was to follow his father into the colonial administrative service and became head of the civil service in Tanganyika.

Meek devoted the second half of his life to the scholarly study of the field in which he had acquired such an extensive experience in his first career. In view of the fact that he was 'Largely self-taught in ethnological science' (*The Times*), for Meek to have written *A Sudanese Kingdom*—albeit with some help from the anthropologists R. R. Marett and C. G. Seligman—was a notable achievement. In recognition of this and his established record of research, he was granted leave by Oxford University in 1934 to supplicate for the degree of DSc. Two years later the Royal Anthropological Institute (he was a fellow both of that institute and of the Royal Geographical Society) awarded him its Wellcome medal.

Following the appearance in 1937 of Meek's major testimony to his practical anthropological work while in the Nigerian service, *Law and Authority in a Nigerian Tribe: a Study in Indirect Rule*—a meticulous analysis, undertaken in the aftermath of the Aba 'women's' riots of 1929, of the legal and political institutions of the highly individualistic Ibo people of south-eastern Nigeria in which he sympathetically disproved the apparently anarchic nature of their acephalous (leaderless) society—he was appointed to the Heath Clark lectureship in the University of London for 1938–9. These lectures—delivered by Meek, W. M. Macmillan, and E. R. J. Hussey at the London School of Hygiene and Tropical Medicine—were published as *Europe and West Africa* (1940).

In 1943 Meek was elected to a senior research fellowship at his old college, Brasenose, Oxford. His experience and advice were valuable to the Colonial Office, then engaged in designing a fresh style of training course for its putative post-war administrative cadets, and when these 'Devonshire' courses started in 1947 he was appointed to the university lectureship in anthropology earmarked for this programme. Meek's long association with the International Institute of African Languages and Cultures meant that he was also closely involved in plans for its ethnographic survey. In 1946 he published *Land Law and Custom in the Colonies*, a work he subsequently revised in the series Colonial Research Studies as *Land Tenure and Land Administration in Nigeria and the Cameroons* (1957). He also produced *Colonial Law* (1948), a bibliography of African land law and tenure.

On the expiry of his research fellowship in 1947, Meek's college paid him the rare tribute of electing him tutor and supernumerary fellow, with continuing membership of the governing body. Modest to a fault—he used to deprecate his own contributions when set beside those of his younger, professionally trained colleagues—and a favourite among dons and pupils alike, he found life in the common room 'as congenial as his colleagues found his presence there' (*Brazen Nose*, 33). He took an interest in all members of the college and their families and was always ready for a round of golf. He retired in 1950.

Meek's kind of applied anthropology declined in importance over the years, and it later became fashionable to denigrate it as merely an illustration of the subservience of the discipline to the needs of colonial administration, yet he long enjoyed a reputation as the leading practitioner of anthropological studies in Nigeria. He belonged to no mainstream 'school' of anthropology. For Kuper, he was no more than 'an administrator with some anthropological training' (Kuper, 128), though his erstwhile boss, Lugard, saluted him as a pioneer of African sociological research. Primarily a meticulous ethnographer, Meek represented for countless field administrators in inter-war Nigeria the *beau idéal* government anthropologist. Along with the work of P. A. Talbot and R. S. Rattray, his was the first detailed scholarly account of the diverse peoples of west Africa. Writing in 1995, George Stocking suggested that while his earlier work was backward-looking and derivative, Meek's later study of the Ibo took account of current developments in anthropological theory such as Radcliffe-Brown's writings on social structure. Meek's documentation of vernacular institutions strikes a chord with later research on what came to be called 'African civil society'.

On leaving Oxford, Meek moved to Tunbridge Wells. He did not lose his interest in Africa, and it was a compliment to his standing among the new phenomenon of academic Africanists that he was invited to contribute the opening article to the inaugural issue of the *Journal of African History* (1960). His last years were marred by ill health, and he died at St Mary's Hospital, Eastbourne, on 27 March 1965.

A. H. M. KIRK-GREENE

Sources *Brazen Nose*, 14 (1965–8) · *The Times* (14 April 1965) · C. K. Meek, *Law and authority in a Nigerian tribe* (1937), i–xvi · A. Kuper, *Anthropologists and anthropology: the British school, 1922–1972* (1973) · T. Asad, *Anthropology and the colonial encounter* (1973) · H. Kuklick, *The savage within: the social history of British anthropology, 1885–1945* (1991) · A. E. Afigbo, *The warrant chiefs* (1972) · N. O. Ita, *Bibliography of Nigeria: a survey of anthropological and linguistic writings … to 1966* (1971) · G. W. Stocking, *After Tylor: British social anthropology, 1888–1951* (1995) · d. cert.

Archives BLPES, notes on Gbari and Hausa relationship terms | Bodl. RH, corresp. with M. Perham and related papers · International African Institute, London, Nigerian intelligence reports, 1931–4, IAI 25/1, 25/56, 25/67

Wealth at death £1062: probate, 26 May 1965, *CGPLA Eng. & Wales*

Meek, Sir James (1778–1856), civil servant, was born at Astbury, Cheshire, where he was baptized on 13 September 1778, the son of John Meek and his wife, Sarah. He entered the public service in the commissariat department in 1798, and was employed by Lord Keith in collecting supplies in Sicily for the Egyptian expedition of 1800. He was appointed a paymaster in the Royal Navy on 25 July 1800 and became secretary to several flag-officers on the Mediterranean station between 1803 and 1814. In June 1830 he was made a commissioner of the victualling board, and after Sir James Graham's reorganization of naval administration was appointed in 1832 comptroller of the victualling and transport services at the Admiralty.

In November 1841 Meek was employed by government,

on Gladstone's instructions, to undertake a special mission to the ports of northern Europe, to establish the price of agricultural produce, the quantity available for export, and the current freight charges. His report was printed by command of parliament in February 1842, and formed part of the material upon which Sir Robert Peel based his free-trade measure of 1846.

On his retirement from the public service Meek was knighted (3 February 1851). He was married twice: first to a daughter (d. 1851) of Edward Down, lieutenant RN, and second, in 1853, to Mary Anne, daughter of Dr Grant of Jamaica. He died at his home in Ilfracombe, Devon, on 18 May 1856. M. C. CURTHOYS

Sources GM, 2nd ser., 45 (1856), 245–6 · Annual Register (1856) · Boase, Mod. Eng. biog. · Gladstone, Diaries · IGI · DNB

Archives BL, letters to Sir Charles Napier, Add. MSS 40028–40030 · NMM, essay on surrender of Bonaparte

Meek, Robert George [Joe] (**1929–1967**), record producer, was born on 5 April 1929 at 8 Market Square, Newent, Gloucestershire, the second son of Alfred George Meek (d. 1950), a fish merchant, and his wife, Evelyn Mary (née Birt). His mother had hoped for a daughter and dressed him as a girl until he was four. Meek attended Picklenash School, which he left at fourteen to work on the family farm. But his main fascination was with constructing radio equipment, and he would rig up speakers in trees to play music to the cherry-pickers on the farm. This interest was furthered by his national service as an RAF radar mechanic. After working in television shops in Gloucester and recording local dance bands in his spare time Meek moved to London in 1954 and joined the Independent Broadcasting Company as an engineer. He took advantage of the freedom he enjoyed in his studio to develop what became known as the Meek sound, which made heavy use of echo, reverb, and distortion. Among the hit records on which he stamped his style were 'Bad penny blues' by Humphrey Lyttelton, 'Lay down your arms' by Anne Shelton, and 'Green door' by Frankie Vaughan.

After a spell with Lansdowne studios Joe Meek (as he was invariably known) established his own Triumph record label in 1960, but it did not prosper. He was saved by a refinancing deal from a mysterious backer named Major Wilfred Alonzo Banks, a manufacturer of Christmas decorations. With Banks's support Meek set up RGM Sound—the name derived from his own initials—establishing a studio in his north London flat, 304 Holloway Road, above Shenton's leather goods shop. Here he engaged in frenetic bursts of musical creativity—he made 350 records in the course of his career—punctuated by sudden violent tantrums in which he was known to attack session musicians. Working in cramped, chaotic conditions and using, by later standards, extremely primitive overdubbing techniques, Meek applied ingenuity and improvisation to enhance the sounds on his records—for example, putting drawing pins into a piano's hammers to achieve a brighter tone. Another now conventional technique that he pioneered was the direct inputting ('Di-ing') of guitars into the mixing desk to give a cleaner sound.

Meek's first big success came when he discovered Geoff Goddard, whom he initially attempted to launch as a singer under the stage name Anton Hollywood. But Goddard's real talent was as a writer, and in 1961 he penned 'Johnny remember me', a melodramatic song about a man hearing the voice of his dead lover, to which Meek added a characteristically eerie set of sound effects evoking the whistling of the wind. 'Johnny remember me' was a number 1 hit for John Leyton for fifteen weeks.

Meek recorded other songs in this 'death disc' genre, as well as morbid offerings such as the Moontrekkers' 'Night of the vampire' and Screaming Lord Sutch's 'Til the following night'—both banned by the BBC as unsuitable for those of a nervous disposition. (It was to promote his singles that Sutch inaugurated his political career by standing in the Stratford by-election of 1963.) Meek was obsessed with the occult, frequently resorting to séances. He claimed that during a tarot session he had a premonition that Buddy Holly would die on 3 February 1958 and that he unsuccessfully tried to alert the singer to this danger. Meek had got the year wrong, but the date was right: Buddy Holly died on 3 February 1959.

Meek's greatest hit was with his own instrumental composition 'Telstar', which he wrote after watching the first transatlantic broadcasts from the Telstar satellites on television. He used a Clavioline, a precursor of the synthesizer, to evoke the excitement of the space age. 'Telstar' was performed by the Tornados, one of several bands which Meek manufactured and backing band for the singer Billy Fury. 'Telstar' was a number 1 hit in 1962 in Britain and the United States, selling over 4 million copies and making the Tornados the first all-British band to reach number 1 in the USA. Margaret Thatcher later revealed that 'Telstar' was one of her favourite records.

As lead singer of the Tornados, Meek had recruited Heinz Burt (d. 2000), who had hitherto worked on the bacon counter for a Southampton grocer. Inspired by the horror film Village of the Damned, Meek arranged for Heinz, born in Germany, to have his hair peroxided. Meek was infatuated with Heinz and moved his protégé into his flat, though Heinz was later at pains to deny that they were lovers. When Heinz left the Tornados in 1963, Meek attempted to launch him as a solo artist and scored a number 5 hit with another Geoff Goddard composition, 'Just like Eddie', a tribute to Eddie Cochran which featured a guitar solo by Ritchie Blackmore, later of Deep Purple. But Meek became extremely jealous when Heinz acquired a girlfriend and punished his protégé by sending him on endless tours. Dispatched to Birmingham, Alabama, to perform with Jerry Lee Lewis and Gene Vincent, the luckless Heinz was pelted with Heinz baked beans by a disaffected audience.

It was Meek's misfortune that by 1963 his career had been overtaken by Beatlemania. He enjoyed a further number 1 hit with 'Have I the right' by the Honeycombs in August 1964, but a dispute over the ownership of this song led to a feud with Geoff Goddard, who subsequently withdrew from the music business and spent the rest of his career in the catering department at Reading University.

Beset by legal and drug problems, Meek became increasingly paranoid and convinced that his rivals in the record business were bugging his flat. In November 1963 he was fined £15 for importuning in a men's toilet in Madras Place, north London (also a haunt of Joe Orton), and thereafter he was a target for blackmailers. He was also deeply troubled when in January 1967 the police discovered the dismembered body of a seventeen-year-old acquaintance, Bernard Oliver, in two suitcases in a Suffolk farm. Meek became certain that he would be falsely accused of Oliver's murder.

On 3 February 1967, following a dispute about his rent, Meek shot dead his landlady, Violet Shenton, at 304 Holloway Road and then turned the gun on himself. At his inquest, which recorded a suicide verdict, it was revealed that traces of amphetamines had been found in his body. He was buried in Newent cemetery on 10 March.

The circumstances of Meek's death and the fact that it occurred on the anniversary of Buddy Holly's death gave conspiracy theorists a field day. This circus has unfortunately tended to overshadow his status as a musical pioneer: a late twentieth-century history of record production called him 'an enigmatic visionary who was years ahead of his time' (Cunningham, 77). At a time of American preeminence in popular music the strange and colourful sounds that emanated from Meek's small independent studio blazed a trail for the British 'psychedelic' music of the later sixties. The memory of this achievement is perpetuated in the brand name of the Joe Meek range of recording studio equipment.   MATTHEW GRIMLEY

Sources J. Repsch, *The legendary Joe Meek* (1989) · *The Sun* (4 Feb 1967) · *Evening Standard* (3 Feb 1967) · *Evening Standard* (9 March 1967) · J. McCready, 'Room at the top', *Mojo*, 90 (May 2001), 60–65 · *Rough guide to rock* (1999) · *The Independent* (11 April 2000) [obit. of Heinz Burt] · *The Independent* (26 May 2000) [obit. of Geoff Goddard] · *The Guardian* (11 April 2000) [obit. of Heinz Burt] · www.concentric.net/~meekweb/telstar.htm, 1 Sept 2001 · www.joemeek.com, 1 Sept 2001 · 'Meek, Joe', *Virgin encyclopaedia of rock music*, ed. C. Larkin (1999) · M. Cunningham, *Good vibrations* (1996) · b. cert. · d. cert.

Archives FILM BFI NFTVA, *Cue the music*, 28 Feb 1994 | SOUND BL NSA, *Arena*, 1991, V421/1 · BL NSA, performance recordings

Meek, Ronald Lindley (1917–1978), economist, was born on 27 July 1917 in Wellington, New Zealand. He never lost his affection for his country of origin, and insisted on keeping his New Zealand passport throughout his life. He was the only son of Ernest William Meek, a company secretary and orchardist, and his wife, Matilda Isabel Williams. From 1922 to 1934 he attended the Hutt Valley high school before entering Victoria College of the University of New Zealand at Wellington, where he graduated with first-class honours in law in 1939.

Ineligible for active service as a result of losing an eye when playing cricket, Meek worked in the public service between 1939 and 1946. During this period his interests changed from law to economics. He studied for a degree in the subject at night school and graduated, again with first-class honours, in 1946. In that year he was able to take up a Strathcona scholarship, which enabled him to enrol as a research student at St John's College, Cambridge, where he was supervised by Maurice Dobb and came into contact with Piero Sraffa. He graduated with the degree of PhD in 1948 and was appointed to a lectureship in economics in the University of Glasgow. He was promoted, belatedly, to a senior lectureship in 1960. On 21 October 1951 he married Dorothea Luise Schulz (*b.* 1926/7), secretary, a colleague in what was to become the Institute of Russian and East European Studies in the University of Glasgow, and daughter of Professor Fritz Heinrick Schulz. There were two children. On their marriage certificate Meek is described as divorced, but nothing is known about his first wife.

In 1963 Meek moved to Leicester as the Tyler professor of economics. At Leicester he was largely responsible for the introduction of the BSc degree course in economics and also for the inception of the Public Sector Economics Centre, an area to which he made a distinguished contribution.

Meek's work on the history of economic thought, for which he will be best remembered, began with his thesis on the concept of surplus in classical political economy, much of which went into his *Studies in the Labour Theory of Value* (1956), a work which was considerably revised in 1973. Research begun in this field led him to a closer study of the eighteenth century, with particular reference to the physiocrats, for whom he showed a rare sympathy. This part of his career as a researcher culminated in his distinguished translation of the works of Mirabeau and Quesnay as contained in *Economics of Physiocracy* (1962) and *Quesnay's tableau économique* (with M. Kuczynski, 1972); it was completed with *Turgot on Progress, Sociology and Economics* (1973). Meek's major papers are included in his book *Physiocracy*, in *Economics, Ideology, and other Essays* (1967), and in *Smith, Marx and after* (1977).

Meek was one of the major pioneers working on the philosophical historians of the eighteenth century, notably in an extremely influential paper, 'The Scottish contribution to Marxist sociology', published in 1954. His interest in the relationship between economic and social order, and a growing preoccupation with what he called the 'stadial' thesis, are also reflected in his *Social Science and the Ignoble Savage* (1976). The same interest features in *Adam Smith: Lectures on Jurisprudence* (1977), a work which he edited, and introduced, in conjunction with P. G. Stein and D. D. Raphael. Those who worked with him on a project which was so long in the execution can attest to the enthusiasm and skill which he brought to a particularly difficult editorial task.

Meek was a Marxist who later described himself as a 'Meeksist'. He was at one time a member of the Communist Party but was deeply affected by events in Hungary in 1956. In addition to his output on economics he wrote a successful book *Hill Walking in Arran* (1963; 2nd edn, 1972) as well as a popular study *Figuring out Society* (1972). In addition to his wide-ranging interests in the arts and his excellence as a scholar he was an inspiring teacher, formidable and stylish in the best tradition of his adopted country. He died of a pulmonary embolism at the Royal Infirmary, Leicester, on 18 August 1978; he was survived by his wife.

ANDREW S. SKINNER

Sources A. S. Skinner, 'Ronald Lindley Meek: in memoriam', *History of Political Economy*, 11 (1979), iv–vi • J. Eatwell, M. Milgate, and P. Newman, eds., *The new Palgrave: a dictionary of economics*, new edn, 4 vols. (1998) • I. Bradley and M. Howard, eds., *Classical and Marxian political economy: essays in honour of Ronald L. Meek* (1982) [incl. bibliography of Meek's writings] • private information (2004) [Dorothea Meek] • m. cert. • d. cert. • *CGPLA Eng. & Wales* (1978)
Likenesses portrait, repro. in Bradley and Howard, eds., *Classical and Marxian political economy*
Wealth at death £13,960: probate, 14 Dec 1978, *CGPLA Eng. & Wales*

Meeke, Mary [*pseud.* Gabrielli] (*d.* 1816?), novelist, seems to have been the wife of the Revd Francis Meeke (*d.* 1801) of Johnson Hall, Staffordshire (BA Cantab. 1773 and MA 1776), who published a volume of poems in 1782 (*N&Q*, 3rd ser., 2.229). She is believed to have produced more than thirty-four novels, many of which were published under the pseudonym Gabrielli. She began her prolific career as a novelist in 1795 when she published *Count St Blancard*, in three volumes, and carried on writing for more than twenty years.

In the preface to her *Midnight Weddings* (1802) Mary Meeke recommends that novelists, before planning a work, consult their publisher on how best to satisfy the prevailing public taste. She apparently followed this plan herself with some success. Although her literary style is poor and her characters only faintly reflect contemporary manners, 'she won popularity because she cultivated middle-class Cinderella stories in modish sentimental gothic narratives' (Todd, 218). Her novels were marked by melodramatic plot turns (including contrived recognition scenes) and prevalence of the sentimental. And yet she had some distinguished readers. According to Lady Trevelyan, Macaulay 'all but knew Mrs. Meeke's romances by heart', but, despite his liking for them, he relegated Mary Meeke to the position of his favourite among bad novelists and agreed in his sister's criticism that her novels 'were one just like another, turning on the fortunes of some young man in a very low rank of life who eventually proves to be the son of a duke' (Trevelyan, *Life of Macaulay*, 1.129). Mary Mitford was also a reader of Mary Meeke's works in her youth, and in her old age reread at least six of them.

Mary Meeke's novels include: *Count St Blancard, or, The Prejudiced Judge* (1795), *The Abbey of Clugny* (1795), *Palmira and Ermance* (1797), *Matrimony the Height of Bliss or Extreme of Misery* (1811), and *Spanish Campaigns, or, The Jew* (1815). *Murray House* (1804) has been attributed both to Mary Meeke, and to another prolific Gothic novelist, Eliza Parsons. Probably posthumously published were *The Veiled Protectress, or, The Mysterious Mother* (1818) and *What Shall Be, Shall Be* (1823).

Meeke also translated works from the French under the titles *Lobenstein Village* (1804), from Isabelle de Montolieu's 1802 version of a book by August Heinrich Julius Lafontaine, *Julian, or, My Father's House*, originally by Ducray

Dumenil (1807), *The Unpublished Correspondence of Madame Du Deffand* (1810), and *Elizabeth, or, The Exiles of Siberia*, from the work by Madame de Cottin (1817). In 1811 she completed the translation by Mrs Collyer of Klopstock's *Messiah* (another edn 1821). Mary Mitford attributed *Anecdotes of the Altamont Family* to her. Mary Meeke, widow of the Revd Francis Meeke, and possibly the same person as the novelist, died in October 1816 at Johnson Hall, Staffordshire. ELIZABETH LEE, *rev.* REBECCA MILLS

Sources Blain, Clements & Grundy, *Feminist comp.* • J. Shattock, *The Oxford guide to British women writers* (1994), 289–90 • *N&Q*, 3rd ser., 2 (1862), 229 • *N&Q*, 2nd ser., 1 (1856), 133–4 • Allibone, *Dict.* • Watt, *Bibl. Brit.*, vol. 2 • *IGI* • J. Todd, ed., *A dictionary of British and American women writers, 1660–1800* (1984) • D. Blakey, *The Minerva Press, 1790–1820* (1939) • G. O. Trevelyan, *The life and letters of Lord Macaulay*, 2 vols. (1876)

Meen, Henry (1744–1817), classical scholar and Church of England clergyman, was born on 2 December 1744 at Harleston, Norfolk, the son of Henry Meen, a local apothecary. He was educated at Mr Colling's school, Bungay, and entered Emmanuel College, Cambridge, on 9 October 1761. He graduated BA (1766), MA (1769), BD (1776), and became a fellow of the college. As an undergraduate he published *Happiness, a Poetical Essay* (1766), which brought him little when reread as an adult. Having been ordained into the Anglican church, on 30 April 1792 he was appointed to a minor canonry in St Paul's Cathedral, instituted to the rectory of St Nicholas Cole Abbey, with St Nicholas Olave, London. On 13 November 1795 he was collated as prebendary of Twyford in St Paul's Cathedral, where he also held the office of lecturer. He obtained no other preferment, and these posts left him ample time for literary pursuits.

In 1780 Meen 'revised, corrected, and completed, as coadjutor and editor', the unfinished translation of Apollonius Rhodius, by the Revd Francis Fawkes, and superintended its publication for his widow's benefit. To it he annexed his own independent version of Coluthus's *Rape of Helen, or, The Origin of the Trojan War*. His other works were *A Sermon before the Association of Volunteers* (1782), *Remarks on the Cassandra of Lycophron* (1800) and *Succisivae operae, or, Selections from Ancient Writers, with Translations and Notes* (1815). The biblical scholar Gilbert Wakefield believed that Meen had studied the writings of Lycophron more than any man living. When Meen told Samuel Parr that he proposed to undertake an edition of Lycophron's works, Parr encouraged him with the remark that 'many books have been well edited by men who were no scholars'. Meen's criticisms on Lycophron appeared in the *European Magazine* from 1796 to 1813, but his complete translation was never published. Meen's additional literary activities included proof-reading Bishop Percy's 'Blank verse before Milton' (a work which was destroyed in the fire at the printing office); their correspondence is reprinted in John Nichols's *Illustrations of ... Literary History* (1817–58, 7.38–68). He was also employed to collect and pass through the press *Alonzo and Cora* (1801) by the Edinburgh poet Elizabeth Scot. The literary commentator George Steevens dubbed Meen 'Little Meen' on account of his confused and haphazard working practices, with the result that he was 'always employed without doing anything'. Gilbert Wakefield more charitably described him as 'pacific, gentle, unassuming'. Henry Meen died, unmarried, aged seventy-two, at the rectory, Bread Street Hill, London, on 3 January 1817. Several months later (17–21 March) his manuscript translation of Lycophron and other books were sold at Sothebys.

W. P. COURTNEY, rev. PHILIP CARTER

Sources GM, 1st ser., 87/1 (1817), 86–7 • Fasti Angl., 1541–1857, [St Paul's, London] • Nichols, Illustrations, 7.6–68 • Venn, Alum. Cant. • J. P. Malcolm, Londinium redivivum, or, An antient history and modern description of London, 4 vols. (1802–7), vol. 1, pp. ii, iv, 546–8 • will, PRO, PROB 11/1588, fol. 238v • Parriana, or, Notices of the Rev. Samuel Parr, ed. E. H. Barker, 2 vols. (1828–9), vol. 1, p. xxxi; vol. 2, pp. 636–7
Archives UCL, MS of Lexicon Lycophronicum

Meer Hassan Ali, Mrs (fl. 1832), author, was remarkable for being the first educated British woman known to have lived in India as the wife of an Indian and to describe, in her Observations on the Mussulmauns of India (1832), the social and religious customs of Muslims, about which there was little firsthand knowledge in Europe, particularly those relating to women. The details of her life, including her maiden name, remain unknown, though it was reported that at some period she worked in the household of Princess Augusta, to whom her book was dedicated. Her husband, who came from a well-connected Muslim family in Lucknow, was assistant teacher in the oriental department at Addiscombe, the East India Company's military college, from 1810 to 1816, when he resigned, disappointed by lack of professional progress and increasing ill health. In 1817 he returned with his wife to northern India, where she spent the next twelve years, largely in Lucknow, with short periods in Fatehgarh and Kanauj.

Mrs Meer Hassan Ali was a well-educated and broad-minded woman who shared her husband's scholarly tastes and took a keen interest in life in India. Her task was to explain and not to judge: 'It is not my province either to praise or condemn, but merely to mark out what I observe of singularity in the habits, manners, and customs of the Mussulmauns …' (Mrs Meer Hassan Ali, Observations, 1832, 54). This was true even of religion, though she was a devout Christian who regretted her failure to make any converts. She paid warm tribute to the genuine faith and devotion of those among whom she lived, and enjoyed long religious discussions with her husband and father-in-law, to whom she was devoted. Her work contains many anecdotes of Muslim religious history, and she gives lively descriptions of religious ceremonies in Lucknow, some of the details of which were not readily comprehended by foreigners. She also recorded in detail the life around her in India, its natural world, and the daily occupations of those among whom she lived, whose relationships she found to be marked by charity and affection. But it was her insight into the secluded life of women in the zenana, which was impenetrable to foreign men and had been glimpsed only superficially by other Englishwomen, which was the main interest of her book. She described

every aspect of their lives, the customs of marriage and childbirth, their social organization and pastimes, and their participation in religious observance.

Toleration on both sides marked Mrs Meer Hassan Ali's life in Lucknow. While she continued to wear European clothes and follow her own faith, she spoke fluent Hindustani, observed the intricacies of local etiquette, and was invited to play an intimate role in society. Her unique position enabled her to explain each world to the other. While admitting the limitations of Indian women's lives from the point of view of an educated Englishwoman, she nevertheless depicted them as happy and fulfilled in their own terms—and also pointed to Muslim women's property laws, which were much in advance of similar laws in Britain. In addition, she sought to create a more tolerant attitude towards religion, explaining to Christians that Muslims venerated Christ as a prophet, while assuring Muslims that Christians were not idolaters.

Although she gives no hint of unhappiness in her writing, and was reported to have been admired by both the British and Indian community, she left India about 1829 and did not return. Her husband had adopted the permitted custom of additional wives, possibly because their marriage was childless; despite her non-judgemental attitude to polygamy in her book, it was suggested by contemporaries that she could not tolerate it in practice. In the early 1840s she was rumoured to be the matron of a boys' school in England. Her subsequent career remains unknown.

The uniqueness of the information contained in her work was widely recognized at the time, and it became a standard reference book on India: her readers included Emma Roberts and W. E. Gladstone.

ROSEMARY CARGILL RAZA

Sources Mrs Meer Hassan Ali, Observations on the Mussulmauns of India descriptive of their manners, customs, habits and religious opinions made during a twelve years residence in their immediate society (1832) • Mrs Meer Hassan Ali, Observations on the Mussulmauns of India, ed. W. Crooke (1917) • Calcutta Review, 2 (1844), 387 • W. Knighton, The private life of an eastern king (1857), 173 • The journals of Honoria Lawrence: India observed, 1837–1854, ed. J. Lawrence and A. Woodiwiss (1980), 139

Meeson, Alfred (1808–1885), architect and engineer, was born on 4 April 1808 at 67 Aldermanbury, London, the son of Edward Meeson and his wife, Elizabeth, née Collins. He was educated in London, and spent the earlier part of his life in private practice as architect and surveyor in Wakefield, Yorkshire. In 1842 he moved to London at the request of Sir Charles Barry to superintend the constructional and engineering details of the new Houses of Parliament; he continued to act as Barry's confidential assistant until the completion of the work. In 1853 he was appointed building services engineer at the Houses of Parliament, with a residence in the building. On the abolition of that post Meeson continued in private practice at 58 Pall Mall. His principal tasks as a surveyor and consulting engineer were on the international exhibitions buildings of 1851 and 1862, and on the erection of Covent Garden Theatre, and of the Royal Albert Hall. He was architect to the first Alexandra Palace on Muswell Hill (1867–73), in the construction of which he reused materials from the 1862 exhibition building in Kensington. The distinctive building with five domes was almost destroyed by fire in 1873; Meeson worked on the new building with the architect John Johnson. Meeson died unmarried, aged seventy-six, on 12 January 1885, at his home, 4 Harley Road, South Hampstead, London. His nephew Frederick Meeson lived next door and was also an architect.

L. H. CUST, *rev.* SUSIE BARSON

Sources biography file, RIBA BAL · *The Builder*, 48 (1885), 118 · *The museums area of South Kensington and Westminster*, Survey of London, 38 (1975), chap. 10 · *CGPLA Eng. & Wales* (1885)
Wealth at death £437 4s. 6d.: probate, 18 March 1885, *CGPLA Eng. & Wales*

Meetkerke, Adolf van (1528–1591). *See under* Meetkerke, Edward (1590–1657).

Meetkerke, Edward (1590–1657), Church of England clergyman, was born in the parish of St Botolph, Aldersgate, London, and baptized at the Dutch church, Austin Friars, on 29 September 1590, the only son (of three children) of **Adolf van Meetkerke** (1528–1591) and his second wife, Margaret (1548/9–1594), daughter of John Lichtervelde, sometime president of Flanders. Adolf, who was born in Bruges and who had published there in 1565 a work on Greek pronunciation, had himself been president of Flanders. He had presided over the states general of the United Provinces (as whose ambassador to England he served) in the immediate aftermath of the assassination of William the Silent in 1584. One of the few trusted supporters of the earl of Leicester on the Dutch council of state in 1585, with his friend Adrian Saravia and with English support he was a leader of the abortive attempt to stage a coup in Leiden in 1587. Like Saravia, a few months later he escaped to England, where he may have received payment from the privy purse. In December 1588 he was placed first in a list of householder members of the Dutch church in London.

Meanwhile, Adolf's four sons with his first wife, Jacoba Cervina, Adolf, Nicolaas, Anthony, and Baldwin, continued to distinguish themselves in Anglo-Dutch military service. Nicolaas van Meetkerke fought valiantly at the battle of Sluys in 1587, took 500 troops levied by refugee protestants in England to the Netherlands in 1588, commanded the Dutch regiment that Sir John Norris recruited for the unsuccessful expedition to Portugal in 1589, and commanded a company in the English army in 1590–91. He was killed at Deventer. The earl of Leicester paid for the education of Baldwin van Meetkerke, who joined other young men of his circle at Christ Church, Oxford, where he matriculated on 11 March 1587, aged nineteen. Between 1591 and 1596 he served in the English army in the Low Countries. He was knighted by the earl of Essex after the storming of Cadiz, probably on 22 June 1596, but died of his wounds and was buried eight days later at sea.

Adolf van Meetkerke died in London on 6 October 1591 and his widow in November 1594; both were buried at St Botolph, Aldersgate. The infant Edward was brought up, as his will reveals, by Mary du Bois of London. He attended Westminster School, being taught Hebrew there by Saravia, before matriculating from Christ Church, Oxford, on 16 January 1607, aged sixteen. He graduated BA on 21 June 1610 and, having declined an offer from the Dutch church of a scholarship to study theology in Leiden, proceeded MA on 10 June 1613. He became a tutor of his college and provided private instruction in Hebrew. In 1616 he published *A Declaration and Manifestation, of the Chief Reasons … of Master M. Du Tertre* and *A Declaration of Henri Marc de Gouffier, Marquise of Boniuet*, translations from the French of two conversion testimonies given respectively at Saumur and La Rochelle. He later contributed some Latin and Greek verses to Oxford poetical collections. He proceeded BD and was licensed to preach on 19 June 1620, and on 8 November that year was elected to succeed Edward Kilbye as professor of Hebrew. On 26 May 1625 he proceeded DD and was made a canon of Christ Church.

That year Meetkerke's career took a new turn, however, when he was made rector of Easton, Hampshire, and by 1626 he had resigned his professorship. On 9 January 1631 he was installed as a prebendary of Winchester, and about this time he married Barbara, daughter of fellow prebendary Robert More (1568–1640). Deprived of his prebend during the 1640s, he retained his rectory, 'my only Pastorate charge that I ever had' (PRO, PROB 11/267, fols. 88–9). He died at Easton on 10 August 1657 and was buried there, having expressed the desire to be buried in the chancel 'under the communion table as it now standeth'. In his will, drawn up on 7 December 1654, and proved by his widow on 24 September 1657, he repeated, 'as bound in duty to hir memory', the 'hearts desire for my children, and childrens children' enunciated in his mother's testament. This was that they might all:

be brought up in the true reformed Christian Protestant Religion, and not led away by any sects, schismes or heresies of the times … and that for no temporall advancement or preferment they be enticed from the same to the profession of Popery, it being better that they should for want be forced to beg their bread, then ever to have such nurture. (PRO, PROB 11/267, fols. 88–9)

Property in Hampshire and an outstanding loan of £540 were to go to his widow and their son Adolf (who had followed Meetkerke to Christ Church and graduated in 1654); other beneficiaries included his daughter Frances, her husband Nathaniel Napper, their children, and four godsons—Robert Moore, Adolf Balgnymy, Richard Glyd of New College, Oxford, and Thomas Newcomen. Meetkerke's apparently wide circle of friends is further attested by the identities of the overseers—John Harris, warden of Winchester College and Edward Appleford of Winchester, common lawyer—and of the witnesses, Robert Fishwick, minister of Hideburne Worthy, and Lancelot Addison.

VIVIENNE LARMINIE

Sources Foster, *Alum. Oxon.* · *Old Westminsters*, 1.639 · W. J. C. Moens, ed., *The marriage, baptismal, and burial registers, 1571 to 1874, and monumental inscriptions of the Dutch Reformed church, Austin Friars, London* (privately printed, Lymington, 1884), 49 · R. Clutterbuck, ed., *The history and antiquities of the county of Hertford*, 3 (1827), 572–3 · *Hist. U. Oxf. 4: 17th-cent. Oxf.*, 455 · PRO, PROB 11/267, fols. 88–9 [Edward Meetkerke's will] · *Fasti Angl.* (Hardy), 3.514 · *Fasti Angl.*,

1541–1857, [Canterbury], 98 · *Walker rev.*, 187 · O. P. Grell, *Calvinist exiles in Tudor and Stuart England* (1996), 224, 237 · R. E. G. Kirk and E. F. Kirk, eds., *Returns of aliens dwelling in the city and suburbs of London, from the reign of Henry VIII to that of James I*, Huguenot Society of London, 10/2 (1902), 410 · P. Geyl, *The revolt of the Netherlands, 1555–1609*, 2nd edn (1958) · R. B. Wernham, *After the Armada: Elizabethan England and the struggle for western Europe, 1588–1595* (1984) · W. A. Shaw, *The knights of England*, 2 (1906), 93 · *The works of Sir Roger Williams*, ed. J. X. Evans (1972) · P. E. J. Hammer, *The polarisation of Elizabethan politics: the political career of Robert Devereux, 2nd earl of Essex, 1585–1597* (1999), 301 · *CSP dom.*, 1581–90, 555

Meggott [Meggot], **Richard** (*d.* 1692), dean of Winchester, was born in St Olave, Southwark, the son of a brewer; nothing more of his parentage is as yet known. He was a scholar at St Paul's School, London, where he was a contemporary of Samuel Pepys, who on Christmas day 1664 heard 'a good sermon of one that I remember was at Pauls with me, his name Maggett' (Pepys, *Diary*, 5.356). Meggott was admitted pensioner to Queens' College, Cambridge, on 4 March 1650, graduating BA in 1653 and proceeding MA in 1657 and DD in 1669. He was appointed by Oliver Cromwell to the Sussex livings of Ford (9 June 1654) and West Tarring (15 November 1655). He held the latter living until 1657, and in June 1656 was also installed as vicar of Fermy in the same county. In 1656 he published *The Rib Restored, or, The Honour of Marriage*, a wedding sermon he had delivered the year before at St Dionis Backchurch, London.

Meggott conformed at the Restoration and was collated to the rectory of Ford on 6 August 1661. From 1662 he was rector of St Olave, Southwark, but it seems that the effort of ministering to a large urban parish badly affected his health. To lessen the strain on his constitution Meggott was appointed to the vicarage of Twickenham, Middlesex, on 17 November 1668, a living he held until 1687. He was appointed a canon of Windsor on 18 July 1677 and on 9 October 1670 was installed dean of Winchester. In spite of his supposed ill health Meggott still seems to have passed much of his time in London. In 1672 he was appointed chaplain-in-ordinary to Charles II and preached several times before the court during the 1670s and 1680s. When James II visited Winchester in September 1685, John Evelyn records, he stayed at Dean Meggott's lodgings.

Although, as the editor of a posthumous collection of his sermons admitted, Meggott had on occasion preached in favour of 'the Lineal Succession' with much 'warmth' (Meggott, *Ten Sermons*, 'To the reader'), Meggott conformed at the revolution of 1688. His earlier support for James did not prevent Meggott from remaining a popular court preacher and he delivered many sermons before William and Mary. He remained in these court sermons a staunch defender of the Anglican church. One sermon in particular, delivered on 14 July 1689 before the king and queen at Hampton Court, provoked controversy. Here Meggott urged that, in spite of the Toleration Act, dissenters who remained outside the communion of the Church of England were schismatics. This received a reply in *The Charity and Loyalty of some of our Clergy* (1689), in which the author both refuted the charge of schism and attacked the conformist Anglican clergy (among whom, by implication, he included Meggott) for offering William only *de facto* allegiance.

Meggott died at Twickenham on 7 December 1692. His Williamite political inclinations are underlined by the fact that it was William Sherlock, dean of St Paul's and advocate of King William's providential divine right, who delivered his funeral sermon at Twickenham three days later. Sherlock praised Meggott's learning and abilities as a preacher, accurately describing him as a 'hearty and zealous assertor of the doctrine, worship, government and discipline of the Church of England' (Sherlock, 21). Though no details of his wife are as yet known, he had at least one son, born in 1673 or 1674.

Sir Godfrey Kneller twice painted Meggott's portrait, engraved copies of which were made by Thomas White and David Loggan.   EDWARD VALLANCE

Sources *DNB* · Venn, *Alum. Cant.* · R. Meggott, *Ten sermons upon several occasions* (1696) · R. Meggott, *The rib restored, or, The honour of marriage* (1656) · E. H. W. Dunkin, 'Admissions to Sussex benefices', *Sussex Archaeological Collections*, 33 (1883), 213–24 · R. Meggott, 'The new-lived criples caveat' (1662) · *The charity and loyalty of some of our clergy* (1689) · W. Sherlock, *A sermon preached at the funeral of the Reverend Richard Meggott* (1693) · M. McDonnell, ed., *The registers of St Paul's School, 1509–1748* (privately printed, London, 1977)
Archives Winchester Cathedral, letters
Likenesses R. White, two line engravings (after G. Kneller), BM, NPG · T. White, engraving (after G. Kneller), repro. in Meggott, *Ten sermons*

Mehemet von Königstreu, (Georg) Ludwig Maximilian

(*c.*1660–1726), royal administrator, may have been the son of a Turkish pasha who governed Peloponnesian Greece for the Ottoman empire. His Muslim name was Mehemet, by which he is usually known to posterity.

The legend that he and his fellow royal servant Mustapha had been captured by Prince Georg Ludwig of Hanover, later George I of Great Britain, during the prince's campaigns in Hungary against the Turks, has been discredited. Rather, Mehemet was probably brought to Hanover as a war captive by an officer under Georg Ludwig's command about 1686, and only thereafter entered Georg Ludwig's household, where he seems to have served for over a quarter-century prior to 1714. At some point following his arrival in Germany, he converted to Christianity, presumably becoming a Lutheran like his employer Georg Ludwig, and was baptized with the forenames Ludwig Maximilian (in some accounts Georg Ludwig Maximilian). This took place no later than 13 April 1706, when he married Hedwig Wedekind (*c.*1689–1729), the daughter of a wealthy Hanoverian burgher and brewer. During the years 1707 to 1720 the couple produced seven children, many of whom were baptized with names paying homage to the Hanoverian dynasty, such as Sophia, Georg August, and Georg Ludwig. At least two of the children survived infancy.

Following the accession of Georg Ludwig to the British throne as George I, Mehemet was among the approximately seventy-person entourage which arrived in England in the last months of 1714, and the member of an even more select group of twenty-five key 'Hanoverians' who remained in England after 1716. A chamber-attendant (*Kammerdiener*) on George I, he began his career with the title of bodyservant (*Leibdiener*), but was eventually granted the English title of 'keeper of the king's closet'. Because of the rarity of Turks in England in 1714, Mehemet and his counterpart Mustapha were often perceived as oddities in George I's court, which included in its assortment of unusual people the dwarf court jester Christian Jorry and Peter the Wild Boy. Perversely, his efforts at assimilation, such as his conversion to Christianity, marriage and children in Germany, and acquisition of languages such as French and English, only underlined his exoticism, no doubt accentuated by the presence of his mother in England. This foreign quality was captured in the best-known portrait of Mehemet, in William Kent's grand staircase hall mural at Kensington Palace, where he appears in semi-Turkish dress. Like George I, although he wrote most extensively and easily in French, Mehemet learned some English, and after his arrival in England in 1714 employed English words and phrases in his official accounts. He also apparently understood the printed and manuscript English documents which he compiled for the king's private accounts.

Owing to the opposition's suspicion of the sexual ethics and fiscal intentions of the Hanoverian court in England, and on account of the images of oriental despotism conjured up by Turks in the ruler's household, Mehemet quickly accreted rumours and legends to his little-known person. As a consequence of his exercise of control over personal access to George I, lewd rumours began to circulate about Mehemet's actual function. Sir John Perceval's diary repeated the gossip that 'the King keeps two Turks for abominable uses' (26 Jan 1715; BL, Add. MS 47028, quoted Hatton, 333). Later works long perpetrated the old myth that Mehemet was one whose 'backstairs duty' was 'to organise the King's strenuous sex life' (P. Howard, *The Royal Palaces*, 1970, 155).

In truth Mehemet's duty was far more domestic and fiscal than sexual. When in his role as *valet de chambre* of George I, he dealt with chamber duties which by the conventions of the English court would have been left to the English bedchamber staff. In his daily household duties, he has been described variously and accurately as a groom of the king's chamber, a keeper of the closet, and was arguably the closest servant of the king, with his personal apartments near the royal ones. As manager of the king's private accounts (*Schatullrechnungen* or *Hofhaltung Quittungen*) from 1699 to 1726, he reconciled various royal books, and functioned as a personal treasurer. He was George I's *de facto* keeper of the privy purse, although he never formally held that office. Mehemet's management of the *Schatullrechnungen* included duties which would ordinarily have been handled by the master of the robes: ordering of and payment for wigs, hats, and suits. He provided the moneys for the master of the horse to dispense as royal bounty during the peregrinations of the court, and also paid incidentals such as theatre subscriptions. He seems to have played a role in the supervision of the king-elector's health, as in his recommendation of a medical examination on one occasion. He was also granted the ecclesiastical title of 'Kanonikus in Wunstorf'. On George's nomination, Mehemet was ennobled by the holy Roman emperor, Charles VI, in 1716, and took a (hypothetical) toponym, von Königstreu, meaning true or loyal to the king.

Mehemet's importance in the Anglo-Hanoverian court was clear: he preserved George I's fiercely guarded privacy against the intrusive demands of the native British ceremonial and retainers. As with the Roman empire's imperial freedmen, or the Ottoman empire's imperial civil servants, Mehemet's identity and life were not centred in the wider world outside the court, but were chiefly lived with reference to the king. Ironically it was precisely the valued mix of confidentiality, isolation, secrecy, and protection from accountability with which Mehemet provided George that made Mehemet a suspect character in the eyes of the world outside the court. Owing to his years of close royal access, he was able to provide contemporaries at court, to whom the king remained enigmatic, with insightful anecdotes. One, George's anguished reaction to his sister's death in 1705, he described to Mary, Countess Cowper, after George's accession to the British throne.

Mehemet died at Kensington Palace on 1 November 1726, thus predeceasing George I whom he had served for nearly forty years. He was buried in the Savoy Church, London. His wife was buried on 24 March 1729.

J. J. CAUDLE

Sources H. Funke, ed., *Schloss-Kirchenbuch Hannover, 1680–1812*, 2 vols. (Hannover, 1992) · R. Hatton, *George I: elector and king* (1978) · J. M. Beattie, *The English court in the reign of George I* (1967) · E. H. Kneschke, *Neues allgemeines Deutsches Adels-Lexikon im Vereine mit Mehreren Historikern*, 5 vols. (Leipzig, 1859–70) · O. Millar, *The Tudor, Stuart and early Georgian pictures in the collection of her majesty the queen*, 2 vols. (1963)
Archives Niedersächsisches Hauptstaatsarchiv, Hanover, König Georg Archiv · Niedersächsisches Hauptstaatsarchiv, Hanover, Calenberg Brief Archiv 22–23
Likenesses Göhrde, group portrait, 1725, Royal Collection; repro. in J. Prüser, *Die Göhrde: ein Betrag zur Geschichte des Jagd- und Forstwesens in Niedersachsen* (1969) · W. Kent, mural, 1725–7, Royal Collection

Mehmet Ali (*c.*1769–1849), Ottoman viceroy and founder of the Egyptian royal family, was born in the Macedonian port of Kavalla, though the actual date of his birth has been obscured. Mehmet Ali himself often gave the date as 1769, the year in which both Napoleon and Wellington were born. Son of Ibrahim Agha, commander of a detachment of infantry irregulars and part-time tobacco merchant, and Khadra, a colonel's daughter in Kavalla, there is no record of Mehmet Ali's siblings. His father is said to have been of Albanian extraction, his mother a native of Kavalla. As Ottoman governor of Egypt (1805–48) Mehmet Ali oversaw a radical restructuring of the province's administration and economy which transformed Egypt into a regional power. At its height, Mehmet Ali's empire embraced the Red Sea coast of Arabia, the Sudan, Crete, and all of greater Syria. His expansionism led him into direct conflict with Lord Palmerston in the two Syrian campaigns (1831–3 and 1840), defining moments of British policy towards the Eastern question. Though ultimately

Mehmet Ali (*c*.1769–1849), by Thomas Brigstocke, exh. RA 1849

divested of his holdings beyond the frontiers of Egypt and the Sudan, Mehmet Ali succeeded in establishing a hereditary governorship which set Egypt on a course of autonomy from the Ottoman empire.

There is little in his upbringing to recommend Mehmet Ali for such greatness. His early training in the tobacco trade was combined with a military career, much like his father. He entered state service against Aegean corsairs at seventeen, and married his only wife, Amina, soon after. The couple had three sons and two daughters: Ibrahim (*b.* 1789/90), Ahmad Tosun (*b.* 1793), Isma'il Kamil (*b.* 1795), Tevhide (*b.* 1797), and Nazli (*b.* 1799). He never took another wife, but Mehmet Ali had a further seventeen sons and thirteen daughters with a series of concubines— the last when he was in his sixties—yet he was survived by only three sons and one daughter.

In March 1801 Mehmet Ali landed in Egypt as second in command of an Albanian detachment with the Anglo-Ottoman force dispatched to evacuate the survivors of Napoleon's ill-fated French expedition of 1798 to 1801. He took command of the Albanian force and entered the political struggle between the Ottoman governor and the Mamluk households. With the support of the notability of Cairo he ultimately won the governorship of Egypt in May 1805, a post he would retain for the next forty-three years. In his first six years in office he faced opposition from the Mamluk military households that had been displaced by the French, and from the British government who feared the return of the French and considered the Mamluks as

the only basis for effective local government. A British force landed in Alexandria to support a sympathetic Mamluk coalition in a bid to overthrow Mehmet Ali in March 1807. A column of 1400 soldiers under the command of General Fraser moved on Rosetta where, abandoned by their Mamluk allies, they met strong local resistance and were forced to retreat. Mehmet Ali dispatched troops to engage the British forces in a second attempt on Rosetta in April in which some 400 British soldiers were killed and a similar number taken prisoner. The survivors retreated to Alexandria, whence they entered into negotiations for a release of prisoners in exchange for the withdrawal of the British force from Alexandria, which was concluded on 14 September 1807.

This victory strengthened Mehmet Ali's domestic position and by 1811 he was sufficiently confident to attempt campaigns abroad. That year, at the request of Sultan Mahmud II, he sent an army headed by his son Tosun to Arabia to restore the holy cities of Mecca and Medina to Ottoman rule, and in 1820 he sent a campaign force to occupy the Sudan. In 1822 the sultan turned to his governor in Egypt for assistance in suppressing the Greek insurrection. The Egyptian army was first sent to occupy Crete (1822–4), and then to quell the rebellion in Morea. The campaign force of 30,000 men and 200 vessels reached Athens by 5 June 1827, and both Crete and Morea were added to Mehmet Ali's domains.

Britain and France were divided in their policies towards Mehmet Ali. Extensive French technical assistance to Egypt led Britain to view Mehmet Ali as a French client astride a strategic route between the Mediterranean and the Indian Ocean. British policy towards the Egyptians in Greece was also coloured by philhellenism at home, which had been intensified by the poetry (and death) of Lord Byron. These differences would prove an enduring tension in Anglo-French relations, though in 1827 the powers agreed to take joint action in Greece. A fleet was dispatched, led by Admiral Codrington, which destroyed the Egyptian and Ottoman ships anchored at Navarino (20 October 1827) and negotiated the repatriation of the surviving forces of Mehmet Ali's eldest son, Ibrahim Pasha, to Egypt. Mehmet Ali sought compensation for his sacrifices in Greece with new territory in Syria. When this was denied him by Mahmud, the viceroy re-equipped his armed forces and sent an expedition up the Palestine coast in October 1831, again under Ibrahim Pasha's command. The Egyptian army not only conquered all of greater Syria over the next ten months, but also swept across Anatolia to within 100 miles of the Ottoman capital of Constantinople. The first 'Syrian crisis' revealed the vulnerability of Ottoman territorial integrity and was instrumental in shaping British policy towards the Eastern question. Secretary of state Palmerston, faced with French support for Mehmet Ali and Russian interests in gaining access to the Dardanelles, feared that European ambitions in Ottoman territories could provoke conflict between the powers.

In May 1838 Mehmet Ali informed the British and French consuls of his intention to seek independence from the Ottoman empire, prompting the Ottoman army to move against the Egyptians at Nasib (24 June 1839). The Ottoman army was defeated, the sultan died suddenly before hearing the news, and the Ottoman fleet reacted to the power vacuum by defecting to the Egyptian navy. Palmerston rallied Austria, Russia, and Prussia to back the young Sultan Abdul Mejid, who offered Mehmet Ali hereditary rule over Egypt and southern Syria in exchange for a withdrawal from northern Syria. Mehmet Ali refused the terms, and Palmerston responded by ordering a blockade of Syrian ports and inciting local rebellions against Egyptian rule. The British fleet, under Admiral Napier, then bombarded Egyptian forces in Beirut (11 September 1840), and an Anglo-Ottoman force landed to force an Egyptian retreat. Egypt's relations with the Ottoman empire were regulated in an imperial decree (1 June 1841) conferring hereditary rule over Egypt to Mehmet Ali's line, and stripping him of all other possessions except the Sudan.

Mehmet Ali, now in his seventies, attempted no further reforms. His physical and mental health deteriorated until, in 1847, his son Ibrahim assumed control over Egypt. Ibrahim, who was terminally ill, died, passing the succession to his nephew, Mehmet Ali's grandson Abbas, in December 1848. Mehmet Ali himself died in Alexandria on 2 August 1849 and was buried in the Cairo Citadel in the mosque which bears his name.   EUGENE ROGAN

Sources A. L. al-Sayyid Marsot, *Egypt in the reign of Muhammad Ali* (1984) · H. Dodwell, *The founder of modern Egypt: a study of Muhammad 'Ali* (1931) · M. Sabry, *L'empire égyptien sous Mohamed-Aly et la question d'Orient* (1930) · *'Abd al-Rahman al-Jabarti's history of Egypt*, ed. T. Philipp and M. Perlmann, 4 vols. (Stuttgart, 1994) · K. Cuno, *The pasha's peasants: land, society and economy in lower Egypt, 1740–1858* (1992) · H. A. R. Rivlin, *The agricultural policy of Muhammad Ali in Egypt* (1961) · A. al-Rahman al-Rafi'i, *'Asr Muhammad' Ali* (Cairo, 1951)
Archives Egyptian National Archives, Cairo, corresp.
Likenesses T. Brigstocke, portrait, exh. RA 1849; Sothebys, 22 May 1990, lot 254 [*see illus.*] · D. Roberts, group portrait · lithograph, repro. in D. Roberts, *Egypt and Nubia*, 3 (1849)

Mehta, Sir Pherozeshah Merwanjee (1845–1915), politician and Indian nationalist, was born on 4 August 1845 in Bombay, the son of Merwanjee Mehta, a successful Parsi merchant. He attended Ayrton's School and, from 1855, Branch School in Bombay. A brilliant student at Elphinstone College of the University of Bombay, Pherozeshah graduated BA in 1864 and won a Dakshina scholarship for an MA which he was permitted to complete in six months, becoming the first Parsi MA and one of the first MAs of the university. He accepted a Rustomjee Jamsetjee Jeejeebhoy scholarship to keep terms at Lincoln's Inn in London from 1865 and was called to the bar in 1868. In London he established contact with expatriate Indians, some later to be leading nationalists, including Dadabhai Naoroji, in whose East India Association Mehta became involved. When he returned to India in 1868 Mehta maintained a similar involvement in its Bombay branch as well as in the reformist Bombay Association following its revival in 1867.

Sir Pherozeshah Merwanjee Mehta (1845–1915), by unknown photographer, 1911

On his return to India Mehta won quick success on the appellate side of the Bombay bar and earned rich rewards from representing Indian princes from Gujarat. His lucrative practice supported an aristocratic lifestyle and funded his lifelong commitment to politics. In his chambers opposite the University of Bombay he held regular evening court to discuss current events and devise campaign strategies. In attendance were the cream of the city's established lawyers and politicians, and the most talented younger men, notable among whom in the first decade of the twentieth century was M. A. Jinnah, then a rising lawyer and Congress politician. In private life he had five sons and one daughter from his marriage with Dinbai Behramji Marzban, a granddaughter of Fardoonji Marzban, who started Bombay's first Gujarati newspaper. Immediately after her death in 1907 he married a longtime friend, Aimai Shroff, who survived him by many decades, serving as patron of various Parsi and other charities.

It was in the field of municipal reform that Mehta first made his public mark, when he joined in the agitation for representative municipal government, which led to a new municipal constitution in 1872. He was elected to the Bombay corporation in 1873 and served on it until his death, acting as president or chairman in 1884–6 and 1905–6. His role in municipal politics was such that he was sometimes called the 'Uncrowned King of Bombay', while his brilliant rhetoric and his pugnacious debating style earned him the nickname Pherozeshah the Ferocious. Although he was a significant figure in Bombay life he was on occasion in conflict with the orthodox or more conservative members of his own Parsi community. His attempts to build bridges included his membership of the Parsi masonic lodge, the Lodge Rising Star of Western India, Bombay, and his establishing of the Ripon Club in 1884 as a social link between various sections of the community.

In 1883 Mehta became involved in co-ordinating Indian support for the Ilbert Bill (which enabled Indian judges in the countryside to try cases against Europeans), countering vigorous British opposition throughout India. With two other Bombay luminaries, K. T. Telang and Badruddin Tyabji, he founded the Bombay Presidency Association in 1885. His dominance both of the association and of municipal politics ensured him a voice in Indian political arenas outside the city, in the presidency and elsewhere in India. He was among those instrumental in organizing the first session of the Indian National Congress in Bombay in 1885 and was its president in 1890. Thereafter he dominated Congress politics until the early twentieth century, when political challenges from a new party, popularly known as the extremists, led by B. G. Tilak and others, split Congress in 1907. Mehta's group, the moderates, which included G. K. Gokhale, retained control of the organization until the early years of the First World War, when new political forces moved towards unifying the factions. Mehta died of a heart attack on 5 November 1915 in Bombay before the unification he opposed took place. His political support in the municipality had also been challenged in 1907–8 by a so-called 'caucus' led by expatriate Englishmen who objected to his predominance and supported the Bombay municipal commissioner, a European nominee of the government. Mehta survived the challenge in the municipal elections in 1907, as he survived the challenge in Congress, but his power base was weakened. The major political act of his final years was the founding in 1913 of an English-language daily newspaper, the *Bombay Chronicle*, to promote a Congress—and Indian—viewpoint.

Though one of India's leading nationalists, Mehta served on the Bombay legislative council from 1886 until his death and on the central legislative council from 1894 to 1896. He was potent as a kind of unofficial opposition in the councils and represented causes other than those of his immediate power bases. Made a CIE in 1895 he was promoted KCIE in 1904. He favoured the constitutional changes initiated by Lord Morley, the secretary of state for India, from 1905 and influenced the negotiations. Mehta's activities have been somewhat overshadowed by later nationalist struggles, but his was a powerful voice which could vigorously oppose British policies and actions and equally energetically lead his fellow Indians in the direction of anti-communal and constitutional politics. He influenced a subsequent generation of politicians and gave strong support in the last decade of his life to M. K.

Gandhi and his South African campaigns. He also ensured the successful working of municipal self-government and its impact upon the quality of urban life.

JIM MASSELOS

Sources H. P. Mody, *Sir Pherozeshah Mehta: a political biography*, 2 vols. (1921) · *Famous Parsis: biographical and critical sketches* (1930), 330–400 · *Some unpublished and later speeches and writings of the Hon. Sir Pherozeshah Mehta*, ed. J. R. B. Jeejeebhoy (1918) · *Speeches and writings of the Hon. Sir Pherozeshah Mehta*, ed. C. Y. Chintamani (1905) · E. Kulke, *The Parsees in India: a minority as agent of social change* (1974) · J. C. Masselos, *Towards nationalism: group affiliations and the politics of public associations in nineteenth century western India* (1974) · B. Nawaz and B. Mody, eds., *Pherozeshah Mehta: maker of modern India* (1997)
Archives National Archives of India, New Delhi
Likenesses photograph, 1911, repro. in Mody, *Sir Pherozeshah Mehta* [*see illus.*] · portrait, 1917, Bombay Presidency Association rooms · metal statue, 1923, near Mumbai municipal corporation offices

Meidel, Christopher (*b. c.*1659, *d.* in or before **1715**), Quaker minister and translator, was born probably in Skien, Norway, one of three or more children of Gert Meidel (*c.*1606–1696), a shipowner of Langesund, and his wife, Elen, whose surname was probably Winge. He was educated at the University of Roskilde and may have come to England about 1683 as chaplain to Prince George of Denmark. In 1687 he was appointed minister of the Danish congregation in Wellclose Square, Ratcliffe, London, but he was soon troubled in his conscience by the fact that he 'administered the sacrament to persons who were no way bettered thereby', and consequently, about 1690, he relinquished the charge. About 1696 he began preaching to an Independent congregation in Nightingale Lane, East Smithfield, but after holding the post for a few years his doubts were confirmed and eventually he joined the Quakers. At the time he was living at Stratford in Essex, and supported his family by manual labour.

With the approval of Friends Meidel travelled to Norway in 1700 to visit his brother and other relatives. He ran into difficulties and was arrested in Skien. English Friends intervened and Prince George of Denmark persuaded the Danish ambassador to write to the king of Denmark, thus securing his release. On 24 February 1701 Meidel took part in a notable dispute at Green's Coffee House, Finch Lane, in the City, between Benjamin Keach, a Baptist, and the Quaker minister Richard Claridge. In November of the same year he accompanied Claridge on a series of visits to meetings in Hertfordshire and Buckinghamshire. In September 1705 he and Claridge attended the burial of a Quaker, by direction of her son at Barking churchyard, and protested that she, being unbaptized, or excommunicate, had no need of ceremonies. Meidel addressed a large crowd over her grave but the vicar's son thrust him out of the churchyard. In the same year, 1705, Meidel issued *An address to my neighbours and others in and about Stratford, near Bow, Essex, assembled to dance on the 1st of the 3rd month, called Mayday*.

Meidel was soon afterwards imprisoned. On 4 July 1706 he wrote, from Chelmsford gaol, *An Address to the Danish and Norwegian Lutheran Church in London*, which was printed in a Danish translation by himself in his Danish edition of

William Dell's *Treatise on Baptism* (1706); an English version later appeared in *The Irish Friend* (2/5 1837, 36). Meidel's address gives his reasons for joining the society and takes affectionate leave of his former congregation. He was imprisoned again, in 1707, in Truro and in Launceston, after disturbing the Anglican incumbent of Liskeard's services and for preaching in the streets. He was responsible for the Danish version of William Penn's *Key Opening the Way … to Discern the Difference* (1705) as well as the Danish translations of Robert Barclay's *Apology for the True Christian Divinity*, a major undertaking published posthumously in 1738, and Barclay's *Catechism and Confession of Faith* (1717).

Meidel also travelled on the continent. In 1704 he attended the yearly meeting of Friends in Amsterdam, and in 1705 made another journey to visit Friends in the Netherlands. As a Quaker minister, in 1708 he visited Friedrickstadt and other towns in Holstein, where the Friends were suffering persecution. Travelling through France he was arrested, detained at Pont and at St Lys, and finally taken to Paris. There he was brought through the streets, chained to other prisoners, and preached repentance to the people standing by, who freely offered him money which he refused. On 22 August 1708 he wrote to William Sewel from the Grand Châtelet, asking for money to be sent. Meidel appears to have died, presumably in Europe, by 1715, when his brother Gerhard acted on behalf of his son, who was in London, in the matter of a family inheritance. Nothing further is known of his wife and family.

CHARLOTTE FELL-SMITH, *rev.* DAVID J. HALL

Sources 'Dictionary of Quaker biography', RS Friends, Lond. [card index] · H. J. Cadbury, 'Christopher Meidel and the first Norwegian contacts with Quakerism', *Harvard Theological Review*, 24 (1941), 7–23 · J. Smith, ed., *A descriptive catalogue of Friends' books*, 2 (1867), 2 · W. I. Hull, *Willem Sewel of Amsterdam* (1933) · J. G. Bevan, *Piety promoted … the tenth part*, 2nd edn (1811), iii–vii

Meidner, Ludwig Baruch (1884–1966), painter and graphic artist, was born on 18 April 1884 in Bernstadt, Silesia, one of four children of Gustav Georg Meidner (*b.* *c.*1818), a textile merchant, and his wife, Rosa Glogauer (*d.* 1942). Meidner grew up in a Jewish family who owned a textile shop. In 1901 he started training as a bricklayer in preparation for the study of architecture. Two years later he began studying drawing at the Königliche Kunst- und Gewerbeschule in Breslau, Silesia. In 1905 he left the school and moved to Berlin; from there he went to Paris in 1906 to take painting lessons at the renowned academies Julian and Cormon. He became close friends with Amadeo Modigliani, whom he later commemorated in an article ('The young Modigliani: some memories', *Burlington Magazine*, 82, 1943, 87–91). In 1907 he returned to Berlin, where he lived, with some intervals of absence, until 1935. In the years from 1907 he produced many works on paper for his finances hardly allowed him to paint in oil, a situation which changed in 1911 when he received a scholarship, largely owing to a testimonial from Max Beckmann. In 1912 he co-founded the group Die Pathetiker, which dissolved after its only exhibition at Der Sturm Gallery,

Berlin, in the same year. About this time his style became more expressive and he produced urban landscapes such as *Apokalyptische Landschaft (Beim Bahnhof Halensee)* (1913; Los Angeles County Museum of Art), in which people run in several directions, houses seem to hang on to one another, and clouds scud across the sky, echoing the cubists' agitation of form and the futurists' dynamism. These works established Meidner's reputation as a central figure within the expressionist movement. Additionally he produced self-portraits, a genre which ran through his entire output, giving him the reputation of being the most frequently portrayed twentieth century artist.

From 1916 to 1918 Meidner served in the infantry and as a French interpreter in prisoner of war camps in Merzdorf, near Cottbus, Germany. Concurrently he wrote expressionist prose, including *Septemberschrei* (1920). In February 1918 he had his first solo exhibition at the Paul Cassirer Gallery, Berlin, which then went to the Kestner Society, Hanover. A year later he co-founded the Novembergruppe. From 1919 his expressionistic style became more relaxed and baroque, while Jewish and Bible themes replaced his earlier urban landscapes. At this time Meidner converted to Orthodox Judaism. From 1924 to 1926 he taught at the studios for painting and sculpture in Berlin-Charlottenburg, where he met his future wife, the painter and graphic artist Else Meyer (1901–1987), whom he married in 1927 and with whom he had his only child, David (*b.* 1929). After the Nazis' rise to power Meidner was condemned as a degenerate artist and forbidden to work or exhibit because of his earlier expressionist style and his adherence to Judaism. The only employment he could find was at a Jewish institution, the Gymnasium Jawneh in Cologne, Germany, where he taught drawing between 1935 and 1938. Many of his works were confiscated from museums, such as the Nationalgalerie Berlin, and included in the Munich Degenerate Art Exhibition of 1937.

Because of these events, in August 1939 Meidner and his family left Germany for Britain with the help of Augustus John and Thomas Tufton, who acted as personal guarantors. Meidner went to London, where he lived throughout his time in Britain except for his internment as an enemy alien on the Isle of Man between June 1940 and January 1942. Strangely enough this was his happiest time in exile as he was stationed with other kindred German artists. In Britain he had little artistic recognition and, as a result, became impoverished; the only gallery to mount an exhibition of his (and his wife's) work was the Ben Uri Gallery, London, in 1949. Despite the paucity of artistic acceptance he produced numerous works, including charcoal, chalk, and watercolour series, ranging from political themes, such as *Massacres in Poland* (1942–5, Stadtarchiv Darmstadt, Germany), to burlesque prints, for example, *Cafés, Theater, Varieté (und Comics)* (1951; priv. coll.). These series reflect the influence of William Blake, who, as Meidner felt, was a kindred spirit in visionary painting and writing.

Since he never felt at home in Britain Meidner returned to Germany, without his wife, in 1953. For the first two years he lived in a Jewish old people's home in Frankfurt and then in Marxheim (near Hofheim). He stayed there until 1963, when the town of Darmstadt provided him with a studio flat at the same time as holding a large retrospective of his work. He died on 14 May 1966, of a heart attack in Darmstadt (where he was buried at the Jewish cemetery), and so he could only briefly experience recognition as one of the most important German artists of the twentieth century. He received decorations such as the Grosses Bundesverdienstkreuz of the Federal Republic of Germany in 1964, and had national and international exhibitions, including the 1991 retrospective at the Institut Mathildenhöhe Darmstadt, where thirty-five oils and numerous works on paper were shown. Besides his main archive, held at the Stadtarchiv Darmstadt, his works appear in the collections of, among others, the Städtische Kunstsammlungen in Darmstadt, the Marvin and Janet Fishman collection in Milwaukee, USA, and the Deutsches Literaturarchiv in Marbach, Germany.

JUTTA VINZENT

Sources L. Meidner, *Septemberschrei: Hymnen, Gebete, Lästerungen* (Berlin, 1920) · L. Meidner, 'The young Modigliani: some memories', *Burlington Magazine*, 82 (1943), 87–91 · G. Breuer and I. Wagemann, eds., *Ludwig Meidner: Zeichner, Maler, Literat, 1884–1966*, 2 vols. (Stuttgart, 1991) [exhibition catalogue, Mathildenhöhe Darmstadt, 15 Sept – 1 Dec 1991] · T. Grochowiak, *Ludwig Meidner* (Recklinghausen, 1966) · *Ludwig Meidner, 1884–1966, das druckgraphische Werk: ein Überblick* [exhibition catalogue, Stadtmuseum, Hofheim am Taunus, 20 Sept – 20 Oct 1991] · C. S. Eliel, ed., *Ludwig Meidner: apokalyptische Landschaften* (Munich, 1990) · E. Scheid, ed., *Ludwig Meidner, 1884–1966: Kneipe und Café, Aquarelle, Zeichnungen, Druckgrafik* (Hofheim am Taunus, 1994) [exhibition catalogue, Stadtmuseum Hofheim am Taunus, 4 Nov 1994 – 8 Jan 1995] · L. Kunz, ed., *Ludwig Meidner: Dichter, Maler und Cafés, Erinnerungen* (Zürich, 1973) · H. Haindl and others, *Ludwig Meidner in Marxheim* (1991) [exhibition catalogue, Stadtmuseum, Hofheim am Taunus, 20 Sept – 20 Oct 1991] · F. Whitford, 'The work of Ludwig Meidner', *Studio International*, 183 (1972), 54–9 · J. P. Hodin, *Ludwig Meidner: seine Kunst, seine Persönlichkeit, seine Zeit* (Darmstadt, 1973) · H. A. Strauss and W. Röder, eds., *Biographisches Handbuch der deutschsprachigen Emigration nach 1933 / International biographical dictionary of central European émigrés, 1933–1945*, 3 vols. (1980–83)

Archives Berlinische Galerie, Berlin, Germany · Deutsches Literaturarchiv Marbach, Germany · priv. coll. · Städtische Kunstsammlungen, Darmstadt, Germany, MSS · Stadtarchiv Darmstadt, Germany, MSS

Likenesses L. B. Meidner, self-portrait, oils, 1912, Hessisches Landes Museum, Darmstadt, Germany · L. B. Meidner, self-portrait, oils, 1913, priv. coll. · L. B. Meidner, self-portrait, oils, 1915, Nationalgalerie, Berlin, Germany · L. B. Meidner, self-portrait, oils, 1923, priv. coll. · L. B. Meidner, self-portrait, oils, 1937, Städtische Kunstsammlungen, Darmstadt, Germany · L. B. Meidner, self-portrait, oils, 1962, Gallery of the Friedrich-Ebert-Stiflung, Bonn, Germany

Meiggs, Russell (1902–1989), classical historian, was born on 20 October 1902 in Balham, London, the only son and younger child of William Herrick Meiggs, of no fixed occupation but who described himself on his son's birth certificate as 'general merchant', and his wife, Mary Gertrude May, of Brantham, Suffolk. William Meiggs abandoned his family when his children were young, and they

Russell Meiggs (1902–1989), by Michael Noakes, 1972

were brought up in great poverty. Russell Meiggs was educated at Christ's Hospital and at Keble College, Oxford, taking first classes in both classical honour moderations (1923) and *literae humaniores* (1925). He then began to work on Ostia, the ancient port of Rome, as Pelham student at the British School at Rome. On his return he taught at his old school for two years; then in 1928 he was elected to a tutorship at his former college, becoming a fellow in 1930 and dean in 1935.

This smooth progress was interrupted when, in 1939, Meiggs left Keble and became a fellow of Balliol College, Oxford. Balliol's classical teaching had declined alarmingly, and Meiggs later described his move as 'like a First Division team needing to bring in a goalkeeper from a Third Division side'. He remained at Balliol until his retirement in 1970, and became profoundly identified with the college. During this period he was university lecturer in ancient history. Meiggs married in December 1941 the historian Pauline Gregg, daughter of Thomas James Nathaniel Gregg, Post Office sorter. They had two daughters.

For many years Meiggs published little. He lavished his great energies on teaching, college activities, and that wide range of contacts which often enabled him to place a pupil. It was typical of his attitude to scholarship that he put so much energy into co-operative ventures and the revision of standard works. In 1951, with Antony Andrewes, he published a thoroughly revised version of Sir George Hill's *Sources for Greek History* (1897). He also revised the *History of Greece* by J. B. Bury (third edn, 1951;

fourth edn, 1975). *Roman Ostia* (1960; revised edn, 1973), his first major book, sprang from thirty-five years of work and reflection. It combines mastery of the evidence with a synthesis of archaeology, social history, economics, and religion, which goes far beyond most local histories. It anticipates interests which historians were to find increasingly central in the next thirty years. Meiggs was elected FBA in 1961. In 1969 he edited *A Selection of Greek Historical Inscriptions* with David M. Lewis. In 1972 appeared his second main work, *The Athenian Empire*. It handled the complex and controversial evidence without the violent disagreements which had infected that area of scholarship, and the book is almost surprisingly cool. The mastery of detail is impressive; the work is a judicious account of the views of its period.

The later years of Meiggs's retirement were darkened by increasing ill health, immobility, and, at the end, loss of sight. With great courage he battled to finish *Trees and Timber in the Ancient Mediterranean World* (1982). Meiggs had served in the Second World War as chief labour officer in the Ministry of Supply, home timber production, and had published *Home Timber Production, 1939–1945* (1949). His last major work was a pioneering one on a fundamental feature of ancient society: all the uses of timber and the history of forestation of the Mediterranean area. The work displayed so high a level of technical expertise that most classical scholars were daunted, and disappointingly few reviews appeared. It points forward to interests which are increasingly attracting historians. Meiggs continued to talk of finishing his long projected and much desired book on Herodotus, but ill health prevented him.

Meiggs was one of the great Oxford tutors. Amid growing specialization he taught both Greek and Roman history; he was an authority on Greek epigraphy who worked closely with archaeologists. His striking exterior, the mane of hair, the Aztec profile apparently hewn from some hard wood, the long shorts, and the uniquely shaped grey flannel trousers, made him a magnet for the cameras of tourists, especially as he tramped to and from his allotment with spade and wheelbarrow. His manner, much imitated, was no less individual. Challenging questions were accompanied with a piercing gaze under eyebrows of matchless bushiness, and he loved to disconcert with his rather ferocious geniality. In tutorials he liked pupils to put up a fight. Slipshod argument or carelessness over details did not pass unmauled, but he never had a 'line' for pupils to follow, nor a narrow or exclusive conception of history.

Meiggs suffered all his life from the alternation of periods of great elation with others of crippling depression. Physically he was robust and Spartan, famous for rolling in the snow in his bathing costume. He was a gardener, a Christian, a family man; quick to assess people and usually right about them. He did not aspire to promotion, and he published his first important book at the age of fifty-eight, giving his energies without reservation to pupils and college; British universities will see few such careers hereafter. He went his own way, choosing widely different subjects to work on, without regard to fashion.

In some ways a traditionalist, Meiggs welcomed the coming of co-education to Balliol, and he sympathized with the rebellious students of 1968. From 1945 to 1969 he was praefectus of Holywell Manor, the annexe of the college in which most students from overseas lived. He had many connections in North America and was frequently a visiting professor at Swarthmore. Meiggs died on 24 June 1989 at his home, the Malt House, Pettiwell, Garsington, Oxfordshire. JASPER GRIFFIN, *rev.*

Sources K. Dover, 'Russell Meiggs, 1902–1989', *PBA*, 80 (1993), 361–70 · personal knowledge (1996) · private information (1996) · *The Guardian* (28 June 1989) · b. cert. · *CGPLA Eng. & Wales* (1989)
Archives Bodl. Oxf., corresp. with J. L. Myres
Likenesses M. Noakes, drawing, 1972, Balliol Oxf., Holywell Manor [*see illus.*] · photograph, repro. in J. Jones, *The portraits of Balliol College: a catalogue* (1990)
Wealth at death under £100,000: probate, 17 Oct 1989, *CGPLA Eng. & Wales*

Meighen, Arthur (1874–1960), prime minister of Canada, was born at Anderson, Perth county, western Ontario, on 16 June 1874, the second child and eldest son of Joseph Meighen (*b.* 1846), a farmer, and his wife, Mary Jane Bell, a farmer's daughter. The boy went to a country school, his path winding along a creek, a contemplative route where he watched water and fish. He was solitary, studious, serious, with no love for sports or much proficiency in them. He liked his own company. After school there were always farm chores; he was not much good at milking cows, and, once he had learned to read, books became his passion. His parents, mercifully, entirely approved his studiousness. Neither had had much schooling, but both knew its importance. Indeed, in 1886 they moved into the town of St Mary's in order that their family could go to St Mary's High School. Mary Meighen had a literary bent and encouraged her eldest son's reading of Gibbon, Shakespeare, and her favourite, Carlyle. He learned debating from his father across the kitchen table at home. Joseph Meighen would take positions he did not believe in just to provoke debate with Arthur.

Having graduated from high school with high marks in English, Latin, and mathematics, young Meighen went to the University of Toronto, where in 1896 he graduated with a first in mathematics. He had in mind to go into business, but the summer of 1896, running a general store in a little hamlet, made him decide against that venture. His mother dearly wanted him to be a schoolteacher, and he began teaching in a high school in southern Ontario. But a few months into the job he had a row with the chairman of the school board, in which he was entirely in the right; he defeated the chairman in round one but lost round two, and resigned his post rather than accept arrangements that contradicted his principles.

As many were doing, Meighen headed west and became articled in Winnipeg to a lawyer. Law was intrinsically more interesting than going over Euclid year after year or trying to teach adolescents the delights of the ablative absolute. He ended up with a legal practice in Portage la Prairie, an aggressive little town 50 miles west of Winnipeg. Two years later, in 1906, he won his first major law

Arthur Meighen (1874–1960), by Bassano, 1918

case. It was a murder trial, and the defendant was clearly guilty as charged. The only defence was insanity, which Meighen was indeed able, with hard work and pertinacity, to prove to the jury. It made his reputation.

On 1 June 1904 Meighen married Isabel Cox, a schoolteacher from Birtle, 150 miles distant. He was still an unsocial animal; fun to Meighen was irrelevant—worse, for it wasted time and achieved nothing. His wife, with whom he had three children, was the social centre of the family. His talent, legal and political, was manifest, however, and in 1908 he was elected to the Canadian House of Commons for Portage la Prairie. He was there for the next eighteen years.

Meighen soon became a formidable parliamentarian. Industrious, knowledgeable, courageous—there was nothing, it seemed, that he couldn't master. When the Conservative Party took over the government in 1911, his value was soon recognized by the Conservative prime minister, Robert Borden. Appointed solicitor-general in 1913, Meighen became indispensable. The First World War forced the Borden government to make several unpopular decisions, many of them pushed through parliament by Meighen: in 1917 conscription and changing the franchise for the election that year to make sure the government won; and at the end of the war the creation of the Canadian National Railways, merging two very big and moribund transcontinental railways with a third government one.

These difficult measures were put through parliament by Meighen's knowledge, advocacy, and forensic power.

In 1920 Sir Robert Borden retired, worn out by war, diplomacy, and politics. Not all of Meighen's colleagues in cabinet wanted him as prime minister, as they considered him too strong, too outspoken, and too much a law unto himself. However, the back-benchers of the party liked him: he was a strong horse who could pull the party out of difficulties.

There were plenty of those; not even Meighen could overcome the legacies of the war. Under the stress of the war, its terrible casualties, and the resulting conscription, the Liberal Party had split, some joining the Borden government until the war was over. Conscription had seriously alienated voters in French Canada and farmers in Ontario and in the west. Meighen was the ogre who had done that. He too had forced the franchise changes of December 1917. By 1920 the Conservative Party was finding it difficult to recover that ground lost in the war; the Liberal Party was healing quickly, based as it was in French Canada.

The election of December 1921 was a Conservative disaster: of 235 seats the Conservatives won only fifty: none in Nova Scotia, none in Quebec, none in any of the three prairie provinces. Meighen himself was defeated in Portage la Prairie and had to be re-elected for an Ontario riding. Mackenzie King was now prime minister, and he was very different in style, manner, and substance from Meighen.

King had useful political qualities, but Meighen admired none of them: he had timorousness when Meighen admired courage, obfuscation where Meighen liked clarity, long-windedness in parliament where Meighen loved brevity. Meighen was a parliamentary warrior, armed at all points: his mastery of facts, his ability to use them, his control of himself and his language were intimidating. And there was more than a touch of ferocity in him; he could ridicule and taunt without mercy. Those on the Liberal side of the house feared him, feared that whiplash tongue, those fierce denunciations. The Liberal front benches seemed at times positively to cringe. There he would stand, lean, hard, unrelenting, totally in control, while Liberals writhed with anger and frustration. He would say, 'What are you people on that side growling about? Speak up. If you've anything to say, *say* it' (Graham, 2.199). If they did they would soon be chopped down. King hated Meighen for these humiliations.

It is possible that Meighen made a better leader of the opposition than prime minister. The King government drifted, and the opposition became stronger. In the election of 1925 King got only 99 of 245 seats; Meighen and the Conservatives took 116. King did not resign, however; the plunge into the cold water of opposition was too awful to contemplate. He decided that he could carry on provided he could count on the support of twenty-four members of the Progressive Party, mostly westerners, mostly anti-Meighen. Meighen was furious over King's abuse of power, and he regarded King's conduct as pure trickery. When parliament met early in 1926 Meighen did his utmost to unhinge King's alliance with the Progressives, but King carried on in government until June 1926. Then there developed a malodorous scandal in the customs department. It was centred in Montreal, but the maritime provinces were not free of rum-running either, often winked at by customs officials in Quebec and Nova Scotia for a consideration. A motion of censure was put in the House of Commons; Mackenzie King feared that the Progressives would desert him and he would be defeated. Before the censure motion could be voted on, King went to Lord Byng, the governor-general, and asked for dissolution of parliament. In vain did Lord Byng point out that after the 1925 election he had told King he could not promise him a dissolution if the government were defeated, to say nothing of the impropriety of King's asking for a dissolution when a motion of censure was pending in the House of Commons. King insisted. When Lord Byng stood firm, King abruptly resigned.

Meighen was asked to form a government and did, but within a few days, in a vote that included a broken pair by one of the Progressives, he was defeated by one vote. He resigned and Lord Byng gave him a dissolution of parliament. In the election of September 1926 that followed, King made his theme the 'constitutional issue', Lord Byng having previously refused King, his prime minister, a dissolution (though constitutional experts have subsequently sided with Meighen in the so-called King–Byng affair). Meighen made it the customs scandal. King won 128 seats to Meighen's ninety-one, the Progressives having twenty. Thus defeated, beset by powerful interests within his own party, Meighen resigned as prime minister and as party leader, and, having been defeated in Portage la Prairie (where he had again been MP), was out of politics completely. He was fifty-two.

Meighen had several offers of positions. He accepted that of vice-president and general counsel to Canadian General Securities in Toronto. It was a much quieter life. He lived 3 miles north of his Bay Street office, and would walk to work every morning, lunch at the Albany Club downtown, and walk home every evening. He used to say that walking allowed him to think. In 6 miles one can do some thinking! He needed it to help deal with the financial shocks, both to himself and to his firm, stemming from the stock market crash of October 1929.

Then in January 1932 the Conservative prime minister, R. B. Bennett, who had defeated King in the general election of 1930, invited Meighen to join the cabinet and be government leader in the senate, Canada's upper house. Senators were appointed for life. Meighen accepted. There was approval from both sides of politics. He was too valuable to be left on the sidelines. Parliamentary reporters now requested space in the senate press gallery—a place not hitherto thronged with them. Some even regarded it as a measure of senate reform to have such an able man as government leader. In some ways that was true. Meighen believed the senate ought to be a workshop, not a theatre, and over the next three and a half years he endeavoured to make it so.

After Bennett's defeat by Mackenzie King in October 1935 Meighen was no longer government leader in the senate, but he carried on his senate work, anxiously watching the Conservative Party. Bennett continued at its head, an even better leader of the opposition than Meighen had been; but Bennett's weakening health—his years in office had overstrained his heart—compelled him to give up the leadership in March 1938. The party called a convention to decide on a new leader, and Meighen was asked to consider it. He declined to stand, and Dr Robert Manion, an amiable Roman Catholic, was elected. The Manion leadership did not go well; he was defeated in the 1940 general election and in November 1941 he resigned, with R. B. Hanson of New Brunswick party becoming leader pro tem.

The Conservative Party now agreed to try to persuade Meighen to come back and accept the leadership. He did not want it and fought off reiterated persuasion as long as he could. Finally even Isabel Meighen, hitherto opposed, thought he had no option but to accept. It is possible that he expected to be swept to power on the issue of conscription, though it is more probable that his re-entry into politics stemmed from his high-minded concept of duty.

Resigning his senate seat on 16 January 1942, Meighen stood for a by-election in South York. His opponent was not a Liberal; the Liberal Party carefully avoided putting up a candidate, wanting to combine all votes possible against Meighen. The last person King wanted back in the House of Commons was Meighen, whom King had happily seen the last of in 1926. Meighen's opponent in South York was J. W. Noseworthy of the Co-operative Commonwealth Federation, a socialist party. Noseworthy pulled out the socialist shibboleths: Meighen, a minion of Canadian big business, represented the Conservative old guard. Noseworthy won, on 9 February 1942, and it was not a narrow victory. It was, said Meighen, the triumph of the 'nurse-maid state'. He deplored it and it plunged him into gloom, not just for himself and the Conservative Party, but for the country.

What to do now? Meighen was still the leader of the Conservative Party, but without a seat in parliament. He called a Conservative convention for Winnipeg in December 1942 and picked his man: John Bracken, an able agronomist who was premier of Manitoba, whom the convention duly accepted. Bracken's one condition was changing the name of the party to Progressive Conservative, which created an effect similar to that, as Grant Dexter remarked, of dynamite at a Sunday school picnic. But in the end it prevailed. Meighen could now make his exit.

Meighen was now nearly seventy. Manion's unsuccessful campaign of 1940 and his own loss in South York left him exhausted and discouraged. He went back to his financial business on Bay Street. He still walked to work. The car was to him at best a nuisance, at worst an abomination; he was a terrible driver anyway. Absent-minded, on one occasion he went through three red lights in the space of a 3 mile drive, at the last of which, a major intersection, a policeman flagged him down and lectured him on bad driving. A friend told him once: 'You're like the Irish, you want to make and enforce laws, but you hate like hell to obey them' (Graham, 3.169).

In June 1953 Meighen was afflicted with Ménière's disease, which affected his balance and hearing; he fought the worst of it off but he did not fully recover his health and could no longer walk to work. But there were consolations: the Canadian Club of Toronto celebrated its sixtieth anniversary in December 1957 by giving a testimonial dinner to him. The official address was delivered by the new Conservative prime minister, John Diefenbaker, who twenty years previously had worked hard in Saskatchewan politics for both Meighen and R. B. Bennett. In 1960 Meighen's health began seriously to fail, and he died quietly in his sleep of heart failure during the night of 4–5 August 1960. He was buried on 8 August at St Mary's, Ontario, where he grew up.

The *Winnipeg Free Press*, long Meighen's enemy, remarked on 17 September 1926 that Meighen frightened listeners more than he convinced them: 'venom is poor stuff to win public approval'. Nevertheless, it said, in their boots westerners were proud of him, even if they did not always vote for him. There was reason for that pride: Meighen's strength, his dislike of pretence, his strong sense of duty, and above all his marvellous power as parliamentarian have made him one of the great, if flawed, men in Canadian history. P. B. WAITE

Sources R. Graham, *Arthur Meighen*, 3 vols. (1960–64) · J. L. Granatstein, *The politics of survival: the conservative party of Canada, 1939–1945* (1967) · J. M. Beck, *Pendulum of power: Canada's federal elections* (1968) · *A party politician: the memoirs of Chubby Power*, ed. N. Ward (1966) · A. Meighen, *Unrevised and unrepentant: debating speeches and others* (1949)

Archives NA Canada, papers, MG 26 (I) | HLRO, corresp. with Lord Beaverbrook · NA Canada, Borden papers, MG 26 (H) · NA Canada, R. J. Manion papers, MG 27 III B.7 · University of New Brunswick, Fredericton, R. B. Bennett papers | FILM BFI NFTVA, news footage

Likenesses Bassano, photograph, 1918, NPG [*see illus.*] · portrait, House of Commons, Ottawa, Ontario

Meikle, Andrew (1719–1811), millwright and inventor of the threshing machine, was born on 5 May 1719, probably at Saltoun, Haddingtonshire. He was one of at least two brothers. His father, James Meikle, wright in Nether Keith, Haddingtonshire, working on behalf of Henry Fletcher, brother of Andrew Fletcher of Saltoun, visited the Netherlands in 1710 and brought back knowledge of pot barley making.

Between the late 1740s and late 1760s Meikle worked on a number of projects, mostly textile mills, with his brother, Robert (*d.* 1780), whose surname was sometimes rendered Mackell. In 1751 they were appointed as consultants to the board of trustees for manufactures, who allowed them £20 per annum to train apprentices and in 1754 granted them a premium for improvements to bleaching machinery. They surveyed mills for the forfeited estates commission and in 1768 obtained a patent (no. 896) for a grain winnowing machine. In 1772 Andrew Meikle took out a second patent, for spring-regulated windmill sails. In addition to Scottish projects and commissions, his work took him to the north of England, East Anglia, and London.

By the early 1750s Meikle had settled at Houston Mill,

Andrew Meikle (1719–1811), by A. Reddock, *c.*1790–1800

near East Linton on the Haddingtonshire Tyne. John Rennie, the engineer, lived at the nearby farm of Phantassie and spent two years working with Meikle in the early 1770s before completing his formal education. From about 1780 onwards, Meikle was also associated with Knowes Mill, a mile or so further downstream.

Meikle was married to Marjorie Mirrilees, who predeceased him. They are known to have had at least eight children. Of these, James (the eldest, *d.* before 1807), Andrew (1760–1839), Mary, and Marion remained in Haddingtonshire; George [*see below*] followed his father's trade and was best-known as the inventor in 1787 of an ingenious water-lifting wheel, which was used to float peats from Blairdrummond Moss, Perthshire; Robert and John lived and worked in the West Indies, at Berbice, Demerara, and Grenada, where John was reputed to have made a considerable fortune from building sugar mills; and another son, David, died at Houston Mill before he could make the passage to Grenada.

Meikle's work on the threshing machine first comes to light with a machine for threshing grain and 'scutching' (that is, beating) flax, and which consisted of five flails driven by a water-wheel at Knowes Mill. A demonstration on 14 February 1788 impressed a number of Haddingtonshire gentlemen, who drew it to the attention of the board of trustees for manufactures. Meikle did not persist with this design, but instead worked on machines based on a revolving drum, which had originated in Northumberland in the early 1770s and had been brought to Scotland in model form by Sir Francis Kinloch of Gilmerton. Kinloch sent a model, incorporating his own improvements, to Meikle, who tested it to destruction at Houston Mill in 1784. When in 1785 Meikle worked on a new design, this incorporated a revolving drum.

George Meikle (*d.* 1811), working from Alloa, Clackmannanshire, almost certainly knew of another early design, initiated by Michael Stirling, farmer at Craighead, Dunblane, in 1748 or 1758. This machine had revolving wooden 'scutchers' (beaters) of a type already used in flax-preparing lint mills. Meikle's prototype machine, erected at Knowes Mill, used short scutchers mounted on a revolving drum. When in 1786 George Meikle installed the first complete machine for James Stein at Kilbagie, Clackmannanshire, he added a pair of fluted feed-rollers, another feature of lint mills. The patent (no. 1645), granted to Andrew and George Meikle in 1788, incorporated all of these elements, but could not apply in Scotland as the machine had already been publicly used there.

The patent proved troublesome. There were competing claims from proponents of the Northumbrian and Dunblane machines and from Sir Francis Kinloch. During the first ten years so many unlicensed machines were erected that attempts to enforce the patent were abandoned. In 1809 Sir John Sinclair established a subscription fund which raised £1500 on Andrew Meikle's behalf. Andrew Meikle died on 27 November 1811 at Houston Mill, near East Linton, and was buried at the kirk of Prestonkirk, East Linton, where there is a tombstone to his memory. His son George died just two days later.

JOHN P. SHAW

Sources J. Sinclair, *General report of the agricultural state and political circumstances of Scotland*, 1 (1814) · S. Smiles, *Lives of the engineers*, new edn, 2 (1874) · C. T. G. Boucher, *John Rennie, 1761–1821: the life of a great engineer* (1963) · J. Sinclair, *Statistical account of Scotland*, 20–21 (1798–9) · A. Wight, *Present state of husbandry in Scotland*, 2 (1778) · J. P. Shaw, *Water power in Scotland, 1550–1870* (1984) · *DNB*
Archives NRA, priv. coll., notebooks and cash book, corresp. | NA Scot., records of the forfeited estates commission, E769 · NA Scot., records of the board of trustees for fisheries, manufactures and improvements, NGI · Signet Library, Edinburgh, Old Court of Session MSS, OSP 485:25
Likenesses A. Reddock, oils, *c.*1790–1800, NPG [*see illus.*] · I. D. Scott, engraving (after A. Reddock), repro. in Smiles, *Lives of the engineers*
Wealth at death £1440 13*s.* 9*d.*: Edinburgh register of testaments, NA Scot., SC 70/1/8

Meikle, George (*d.* 1811). *See under* Meikle, Andrew (1719–1811).

Meikle, James (1730–1799), surgeon and religious writer, was born at Carnwath, in the upper part of Clydesdale, on 19 May 1730, the fifth child of George Meikle (*d.* 1748), a surgeon and druggist. James, a delicate boy, received little regular education; but he was religiously brought up by his parents, and when about sixteen years old joined the 'Secession' church, a body which had separated from the established church of Scotland in 1732.

Meikle's wish to study at Edinburgh for the ministry remained unfulfilled owing to his poverty and the death of his father in February 1748, which left his mother and two sisters dependent on his earnings. He managed to attend some medical lectures at Edinburgh, and returned to Carnwath in 1750, intending as a temporary expedient to practise as a surgeon before becoming a minister. But his difficulties grew, and in December 1757 he decided to join the Royal Navy.

After passing the examination at Surgeons' Hall in London Meikle was appointed second surgeon's mate to the *Portland*, a 50-gun ship, in April 1758. Although he was distressed by the loose conduct both of the officers and the crew, writing at one point that their 'wickedness made me weary of my life' (Peddie, lx), they grew to respect him. Meikle spent much of his time reading and writing; many of the 'Meditations', which afterwards appeared in *The Traveller* and in *Solitude Sweetened*, were written at this time. After cruising off the western coast of France and in the Mediterranean, the *Portland* was ordered to join the fleet under Admiral Boscawen, and took part in the victory off Cape Lagos on 18 August 1759. His ship being ordered home with the prisoners and for repairs, Meikle reached Spithead on 16 September. An application to the Admiralty for his release from the service was refused, but he was promoted to the rank of first mate, and put to sea again on 22 October. He joined the fleet under Admiral Hawke, and took part in the victory off Belleisle on 20 November.

After repeated applications Meikle finally obtained his discharge in February 1762, and immediately returned to Carnwath. He went to Edinburgh for some months in the summer of 1764 to continue his medical studies. In 1779 he married his first wife Agnes Smith, who died in 1781; he married again in November 1785. In July 1789 he was ordained to the eldership in the congregation of Biggar, and continued his devotional writings to the last week of his life, dying rather suddenly on 7 December 1799, leaving a widow and five children.

Meikle was a man of earnest religious feeling, and at the same time of great cheerfulness, a characteristic one would scarcely expect from the author of such works as 'The house of mourning' and 'The monthly memorial, or, A periodical interview with the king of terrors'. In 1797 he published a small volume entitled *Metaphysical Maxims*, which was reprinted in 1805 and 1807. In addition to his several published collections of religious writings, he left a large number of religious meditations in prose and verse, a selection from which was published by subscription for the benefit of his widow under the title of *The Select Remains* (1803), which contains both 'The house of mourning' and 'The monthly memorial'.

W. A. GREENHILL, *rev.* PATRICK WALLIS

Sources [J. Peddie], 'A life of the author', in J. Meikle, *The traveller*, 4th edn (1816) · Watt, *Bibl. Brit.*, 2.662 · *Christian Magazine* (Feb 1800)

Meiklejohn, Andrew (1899–1970), physician, was born on 30 April 1899 at 56 Drungan Row, Ochiltree, Ayrshire, the son of Andrew Meiklejohn, journeyman joiner, and his wife, Mary Jane, *née* Hewitson. After being educated at Bellahouston Academy in Glasgow, he joined the Royal Scots in 1917 and served in France, where he was wounded at Armentières, in April 1918. He returned to Scotland and entered Glasgow University to study medicine; there he graduated with commendation in 1923. While at Glasgow University, he met Gertrude Rebecca Simpson Gregor Smith (b. 1898/9), daughter of Richard Smith, a tubework manager, and his wife, Euphemia; a fellow medical student, he married her in 1930. They had one daughter, Mary, who trained as a nurse. Following graduation Meiklejohn trained for a further two years in hospital and another two years in general practice, before entering the tuberculosis service about 1927. He worked first in Sheffield and then in Manchester, where in 1930 he was awarded the university's diploma in public health. He became MD in the same year. Meiklejohn was elected member of the Royal College of Physicians in 1950 and a fellow of the college in 1963. He was also elected FRSE in 1957 and honorary DIH of the Society of Apothecaries in 1959.

Meiklejohn's experience in the tuberculosis service stimulated his interest in respiratory disease, particularly pneumoconiosis. In 1930 he was appointed to the silicosis medical board (forerunner of the pneumoconiosis medical panels) at Newcastle upon Tyne, and in 1931 he joined the Stoke-on-Trent silicosis board. While at Stoke he undertook research into both lead poisoning and pneumoconiosis, the two principal industrial diseases of pottery workers. He was especially concerned with how pneumoconiosis could be prevented within the industry. During the 1930s, Meiklejohn pioneered the substitution of alumina for silica in certain branches of the pottery industry, thereby reducing exposure to silica dust. He also encouraged employers to provide their workers with protective clothing of better quality. He was given the opportunity to put his ideas about preventive measures into practice when he was invited to visit the copperbelt in Africa, where for many years he acted as medical referee for the Pneumoconiosis Medical Bureau, the body which oversaw the routine examination of workers. In 1946 Meiklejohn returned to Glasgow University as a senior lecturer in industrial health; he remained there until his retirement in 1964. He was president of the Association of Industrial Medical Officers (later the Society of Occupational Medicine) from 1951 to 1953; and he was a member of the pulmonary diseases committee of the Medical Research Council from 1947 until the committee was disbanded in 1962. He was an adviser for the World Health Organization in Scandinavia (in 1954), and in Egypt (in 1960), and, following his retirement, he worked between 1964 and about 1968 as consultant for the International Labour Office in Geneva, despite suffering from ill health. His interest in workers' welfare was reflected in appointments as honorary adviser to both the Trades Union Congress and the National Union of Mineworkers. His contribution to the occupational health service in north Staffordshire was acknowledged in 1966 when he was made honorary president of the Arlidge section of occupational health at the North Staffordshire Medical Institute.

Meiklejohn published widely on the issue of pneumoconiosis and its prevention, drawing mainly on his own experience of the disease among pottery workers. He was a frequent contributor to, and member of the editorial board for, the *British Journal of Industrial Medicine*, the *Transactions of the Association of Industrial Medical Officers*, and the *Journal of Occupational Health Nurses*. He also published works on the history of occupational medicine, including two articles on potters' diseases which were based on his Milroy lectures for 1963, presented to the Royal College of Physicians. In 1957 he presented a monograph to the Thackrah Club entitled *The Life, Work and Times of Charles Turner Thackrah*. He declared his own favourite book to be the Bible, and his devout Church of Scotland faith influenced his career and writings. He was well respected by his medical colleagues, particularly for his dedication to workers' health and welfare. Meiklejohn died of heart failure in the Western Infirmary, Glasgow, on 27 October 1970. He was survived by his wife and daughter.

CLARE HOLDSWORTH

Sources R. Murray, 'Whither occupational medicine? The first Meiklejohn lecture' (North Staffordshire Medical Institute, 1971) · *BMJ* (7 Nov 1970), 371 · Munk, *Roll* · L. A. Fearfield, 'Andrew Meiklejohn, 1899–1970, and his views on silicosis', BSc diss., U. Oxf., Wellcome Unit for the History of Medicine · b. cert. · d. cert.
Likenesses photograph, North Staffordshire Medical Institute

Meiklejohn, John Miller Dow (1836–1902), writer of school books, born in Edinburgh on 11 July 1836, was the son of John Meiklejohn, an Edinburgh schoolmaster. Educated at his father's private school (7 St Anthony Place, Port Hopetoun), he graduated MA at Edinburgh University on 21 April 1858, when he was the gold medallist in Latin. At an early age he studied German philosophy, and when still under twenty produced for Bohn's Philosophical Library a translation of Immanuel Kant's *Critique of Pure Reason*.

Meiklejohn became a private schoolmaster, running preparatory schools first in the Lake District and then in Orme Square and York Place, London. He also lectured and engaged in journalism. His ability to speak foreign languages and his general interest in affairs led him in 1864 to act as a war correspondent in the Danish-German war, when he was arrested as a spy. But he was already busy writing useful school textbooks. Between 1862 and 1866 he issued, in four parts, *An Easy English Grammar for Beginners, being a Plain Doctrine of Words and Sentences*. Dissatisfied with his publishers, he published his school books for himself in Paternoster Square. In 1869 he issued (jointly with Adolf Sonnenschein) *The English Method of Teaching to Read*, and this was followed in 1870 by *The Fundamental Error in the Revised Code, with Special Reference to the Problem of Teaching to Read*. By this time he was married, to Jane Cussans (or de Cusance).

In 1874 Meiklejohn was appointed an assistant commissioner to the endowed schools commission for Scotland, contributing valuable educational suggestions to its report. In 1876 Dr Andrew Bell's trustees used the surplus of the Bell endowment to found chairs of the theory, history, and practice of education at Edinburgh and St Andrews universities, the first professorships of education in Scotland. Meiklejohn was appointed as the first holder of the St Andrews chair. Although his inaugural address outlined ambitious ideas for extending the science of pedagogy (see *The Study of Education: a Collection of Inaugural Lectures*, vol. 1, ed. P. Gordon, 1980), he encountered the problem that the chair had no obvious function (the universities did not provide teacher training) and was from the outset under-endowed. He lacked even a lecture room and sometimes had to hold classes in his own drawing-room.

Either through financial necessity or through a belief that this was a practical way of raising standards of teaching, Meiklejohn spent much of his time as professor compiling and editing school textbooks on history, geography, and literature. His works, apart from numerous school texts and reading books for Blackwood's educational series (1883–7) and the like, included *The Book of the English Language* (1877), *The English Language: its Grammar, History, and Literature* (1886), and *The British Empire: its Geography, Resources, Commerce, Land-Ways, and Water-Ways* (1891). His numerous geographical manuals updated the work of James Cornwell. Meiklejohn's series of school books, which was inaugurated in 1894, included a book on Australasia (1897) and *The Art of Writing English* (1899; 4th edn, 1902). There followed *English Literature: a New History and Survey from Saxon Times to the Death of Tennyson* (1904). Although his contribution to making better school books available was acknowledged, Meiklejohn attempted to cover too broad a field: 'His text-books are often inaccurate and defective, but they are never dull' (*Journal of Education*, May 1902, 354). He was also the biographer of two pioneering Scottish educationists, Andrew Bell (1881) and W. B. Hodgson (1883).

Meiklejohn was a regular commentator on educational matters, writing for the *Journal of Education*. He was known as a fair and humorous controversialist. He was a strong Liberal in politics, unsuccessfully contesting the Tradeston division of Glasgow as a Gladstonian Liberal in July 1886. He died at his home, Highworth, Ashford, Kent, on 5 April 1902, and was buried in Ashford. Of his sons and daughters, Matthew Fontaine Maury Meiklejohn (1870–1913) of the Gordon Highlanders was awarded the Victoria Cross for gallantry at the battle of Elandslaagte (October 1899) in the Second South African War.

J. E. G. DE MONTMORENCY, rev. M. C. CURTHOYS

Sources *The Times* (7 April 1902) · *Journal of Education*, new ser., 24 (1902), 354 · *The Post Office Edinburgh and Leith directory* (1846–7) · WWW · W. M. Humes and H. M. Paterson, *Scottish culture and Scottish education, 1800–1980* (1983) · R. D. Anderson, *Education and opportunity in Victorian Scotland: schools and universities* (1983)
Archives Bodl. Oxf., papers relating to claim for salary as professor of teaching at St Andrews, Asquith MSS | NL Scot., corresp. with Blackwoods and papers; corresp. with W. and R. Chambers
Wealth at death £2013 2s. 6d.: administration, 26 April 1902, CGPLA Eng. & Wales

Meilan, Mark Anthony (*b. c.*1743, *d.* in or after **1809**), writer, was born apparently in England. His family was possibly of Swiss protestant or French origin. Meilan left a position in the Post Office to become, in his own words, an 'indefatigable Labourer in the Vineyard of Instruction' (*Holy Writ Familiarized to Juvenile Conceptions*, 1791, 1.i) who,

for over forty years, offered private instruction in languages, arts, mathematics, and sciences. In 1776 he was keeping an academy in Charles Square, Hoxton, London. Meilan was an equally indefatigable author of works on English grammar and shorthand, drama and poetry, as well as moral and didactic books for children that reflected his wish to 'convert instruction into pastime, and seduce them as it were to virtue' (*The Friend of Youth*, 1788, 1.ii).

His first work, *Stenography, or, Short-Hand Improved* (1764), was a more curvilinear—and at 3s. cheaper—version of Thomas Gurney's shorthand (based on that of William Mason), the best system then extant, according to Meilan, who employed a simplified alphabet, used different symbols for five letters, and altered Gurney's method for writing vowels. On 4 October 1768 Meilan married Elizabeth Newton in the parish church of St Dunstan-in-the-West, London, he at that time being resident in that parish and she in the parish of St Andrew Holborn. They had a large family.

Having from youth nursed the ambition to be a playwright, Meilan submitted in turn three tragedies (*Northumberland*, *Emilia*, and *The Friends*—derivative of plays by Shakespeare and Nicholas Rowe and stories in *The Spectator* and the *Gentleman's Magazine*) to David Garrick and George Colman. They were not accepted, but subscription allowed their publication as *The Dramatic Works of Mark Anthony Meilan* (1771?), with a preface containing a sharp but entertaining rebuttal to the 'despots of the drama'. The published plays met no happier fate: 'Such pieces ... would have been dismissed with contempt even by the manager of a company of strollers acting in a barn' (*Critical Review*, 31.228). In prefaces to his later works Meilan attacked those who 'exercise the tooth of surly criticism' (*The Book of Righteousness*, 1800?, vii). Better, if mixed, reception met his verse adaptation of Fénelon's *Les aventures de Télémaque* (*The Adventures of Telemachus, an Epic Poem*, 4 vols., 1776; 2nd edn, 2 vols., 1792–4).

Meilan was ordained deacon in the Church of England in 1778 and in the following year the bishop of London ordained him priest and licensed him as curate to the rector of Ilford Parva, Essex, at a salary of £30 per annum. He later served as curate of St John-at-Wapping, and, from 1809, was assistant minister of St Mary's Newington, London. He is listed in *A Biographical Dictionary of the Living Authors* (1816). It is not known when he died.

The popularity in England of French moral and didactic literature for children inspired Meilan to direct his literary ambitions towards what he often termed the 'rising generation', producing between 1786 and 1800 five works (a total of forty-four volumes) on this and religious subjects. *The Children's Friend, Consisting of Apt Tales, Short Dialogues, and Moral Dramas* (24 vols., 1786), in small format 'suited to the little hands of children' (24.163), was Meilan's translation and adaptation of the popular *L'ami des enfans* (1782–3) by Arnaud Berquin. PAGE LIFE

Sources GL · D. E. Baker, *Biographia dramatica, or, A companion to the playhouse*, rev. I. Reed, new edn, 1 (1782) · *Critical Review*, 31 (1771),

228–9; 32 (1771), 314–16; 36 (1773), 69–70; 65 (1788), 157 • *Monthly Review*, 44 (1771), 343; 47 (1772), 72–3; 48 (1773), 408–9; 78 (1788), 71–2; 79 (1788), 269–70 • P. Demers, *Heaven upon earth: the forms of moral and religious children's literature to 1850* (1993) • R. C. Alston, *A bibliography of the English language from the invention of printing to the year 1800*, 8: *Treatises on shorthand* (1966) • J. H. Lewis, *An historical account of the rise and progress of short hand* (privately printed, London, c.1825) • I. Pitman, *A history of shorthand*, 3rd edn (1891) • *DNB*

Archives GL, MSS 9535/3/405; 9549, fol. 36; 10326/110; 10354, fol. 172

Likenesses line engraving, 1792?, NPG

Meiler fitz Henry (*d.* 1220), soldier and justiciar of Ireland, was the son of Henry, illegitimate son of *Henry I and *Nest, daughter of Rhys ap Tewdwr, king of Deheubarth (south Wales), who also had children with Gerald, constable of Windsor, and Stephen, constable of Cardigan. Meiler was thus a first cousin of Henry II and related also to prominent Cambro-Normans of south Wales, including *Robert fitz Stephen, Maurice fitz Gerald *Fitzgerald (*d.* 1176), *David fitz Gerald (*d.* 1176), bishop of St David's, who were his uncles, and Raymond *Fitzgerald le Gros and *Gerald of Wales, who were his cousins. His father, who had acted as steward (*dapifer*) of the lordship of Pebidiog, which had been granted by Henry I to Bernard, bishop of St David's, was slain in 1157 during Henry II's campaign in Wales. Meiler, then quite young, succeeded to his father's interests in Pebidiog and Narberth in Dyfed, the precise nature of which is unknown, but was exaggerated by Gerald of Wales; certainly, the stewardship of St David's subsequently was granted by David fitz Gerald, as bishop of St David's, to Maurice Fitzgerald.

Role in the conquest of Ireland In 1169 Meiler accompanied his uncle, Robert fitz Stephen, on his first expedition to Ireland where Gerald of Wales and the so-called 'Song of Dermot and the Earl' depict Meiler distinguishing himself in military engagements between 1169 and 1176. In 1171, before his departure from Ireland, Henry II left Meiler under the constableship of Hugh de Lacy at Dublin. About 1173–4 Meiler departed for Wales with Raymond le Gros, but, when the latter returned to Ireland, Meiler went with him and received a grant of the cantred of Conall in Uí Fáeláin from Richard de Clare, earl of Pembroke (Strongbow), as well as the cantred of Cairpre. In October 1175 he accompanied Raymond le Gros on his expedition to Limerick, and, alongside his cousin, David of Barry, withstood the Irish attack until the Anglo-Norman party had crossed the River Shannon. Following Strongbow's death in 1176 William fitz Aldelin, a royal official, arrived to administer the lordship of Leinster during the minority of Strongbow's heirs. Gerald of Wales depicted fitz Aldelin as harassing Meiler and his Geraldine relatives. In 1181 two other royal administrators, John the Constable and Richard de Pec, exchanged Meiler's custody of the castle of Kildare in the cantred of Conall in Uí Fáeláin for the border territory of Laigis. About 1182 Hugh de Lacy, lord of Meath (at that time also Henry II's agent in Ireland), built a castle for Meiler at Timahoe and gave him his niece as a wife. It may have been on the same occasion that Hugh

enfeoffed him with the cantred of Ardnurcher (Westmeath). In 1192 a castle was erected at Ardnurcher.

Justiciar of Ireland On John's accession as king of England, when documentary evidence on Angevin lordship in Ireland increases, Meiler is named as justiciar on 4 September 1199. He witnessed a charter (without title of justiciar) of John on 25 June 1200 at Chinon. On 28 October 1200 the king granted him (without title of justiciar) two cantreds in Ciarraige, Tricha Cét an Aicme and Uí Ferba, and Eóghanacht Locha Léin (Kerry) in the kingdom of Cork, to be held for the service of fifteen knights. No later than 2 November 1201 he was reappointed to the custody of Ireland, John reserving to himself pleas touching the crown, the mint, and exchange. On 22 December 1201 the king threatened to remove him from the justiciarship unless he acted as instructed in 'the affair of William de Briouze', who had been granted the honour of Limerick on 12 January 1201 (*Calendar … Ireland*, 1, no. 160). About 30 August 1204 he was directed by the king to build a castle in Dublin 'to administer justice to the city', as well as for defence (*Calendar … Ireland*, 1, no. 226); he was also to compel the citizens of Dublin to fortify their city. On 2 November 1204 the king ordered that Meiler's writs as justiciar should run throughout his land of Ireland.

Meiler's actions as justiciar, while also a tenant of the lords of Leinster and of Meath, were to create serious tensions among the Anglo-Norman baronage in Ireland. In January 1204 he took the lordship of Uí Failge into his own hands, following the death of Gerald fitz Maurice Fitzgerald, thereby encroaching on the rights of William (I) Marshal, as lord of Leinster. He was also in dispute with the Marshal over custody of the castle of Dunamase in Laigis, a situation to which King John had contributed by confirming to Meiler, on 6 November 1200, Laigis and Uí Chremthannáin to be held of the king for the service of five knights; this grant also encroached on the rights of the Marshal as lord of Leinster. On 26 March 1204 the king appointed commissioners, authorizing them to act with the powers of justiciar, to hear the actions and plaints which Meiler fitz Henry had against William de Burgh. On 12 February 1207 King John wrote to Meiler concerning William (III) de Briouze's complaints against Meiler and his son, in relation to custody of Limerick city. In the same year Meiler contrived the recall from Ireland of William Marshal, and, in his absence, Meiler's followers invaded Leinster; but the tenants of Walter de Lacy's lordship of Meath supported the Marshal's men against the justiciar's army. Meiler's castle of Ardnurcher was besieged for five weeks and eventually captured by Walter and Hugh de Lacy. During November 1207 Meiler persuaded King John to recall William Marshal's seneschal in Leinster so as to weaken his position in Ireland. By 20 March 1208, however, John had reached an accommodation with the Marshal and subsequently withdrew support for his justiciar, electing to settle the dispute between him and the Marshal by authorizing the latter's recovery of Uí Failge and removing Meiler from office. The latest writ addressed to him as justiciar was dated 19 June 1208.

Later years, religious patronage, and death In 1211–12 the cantreds of Laigis, Conall, and Cairpre, the land which Meiler held in the cantred of Aghaboe, and the castle of Dunamase in Laigis, were accounted by William (I) Marshal as being in the king's hand, probably resulting from John's expedition to Ireland. About 1212 Meiler's name appeared immediately after that of the Marshal in the declaration of loyalty offered by the Irish barons to John against his threatened deposition by the pope. In August 1219 the expenses he had incurred during his justiciarship were defrayed from the exchequer. On 24 November 1219 the citizens of Dublin offered half of the debt owed them by Meiler to the king, the other half to be deployed for the fortification of the city, an arrangement which was reiterated on 28 September 1220. Meiler must by that date have been a very old man. Already in 1216 it was thought likely that he might die, or at least retire into a monastery; in the same year, his lands in Ciarraige and Eóghanacht Locha Léin were granted to his Leinster feoffee, John de Clahull. On 28 May 1216 King John commanded Geoffrey de Marisco, justiciar of Ireland, to cause William Marshal to have all his fees in the lands held by Meiler fitz Henry. On 2 December 1219 Henry III restored to William Marshal, by then acting as regent, the service due from Meiler which King John had taken into his hand and ordered Meiler to render that service to the Marshal and to be attentive to him as his lord.

About 1202 Meiler had founded the Augustinian priory of Greatconnell (Kildare), affiliated to the Augustinian house of Llanthony Prima in Glamorgan, and which he endowed with the churches and benefices of his lands in Ireland, and with a tenth of his household expenses, rents, and produce. From the royal confirmation to Greatconnell, 10 September 1205, it is apparent that Meiler also held five burgages in Dungarvan. About July 1203 the king had issued letters of presentation to the bishop of Waterford directing that David, clerk of Meiler fitz Henry, be admitted to the church of Dungarvan and on 19 October 1204 the king gave his assent to the promotion of David, clerk and cousin of Meiler fitz Henry, to the see of Waterford (David was to be murdered in 1209). Meiler granted to Llanthony prima the churches and tithes of his land in Wicklow, where he held Kilpool and Killoughter of Gerald fitz Maurice Fitzgerald (d. 1204). He died in 1220 and was buried in Greatconnell. He had no legitimate heirs, a punishment, according to Gerald of Wales, writing in 1210, for the fact that he had not been sufficiently generous to the church. His brother, Robert fitz Henry, had died about 1180; of his other brother, Morgan, who witnessed his charter in favour of Llanthony, nothing more is known. The same charter refers to his heirs; if the son, Meiler, mentioned in 1206, was legitimate, he must have been dead before 1210, when Gerald stated that Meiler had no legitimate heirs. M. T. FLANAGAN

Sources Giraldus Cambrensis, *Expugnatio Hibernica* / *The conquest of Ireland*, ed. and trans. A. B. Scott and F. X. Martin (1978), 136–7, 142–3, 150–51, 154–5, 168–9, 194–5 • H. S. Sweetman and G. F. Handcock, eds., *Calendar of documents relating to Ireland*, 5 vols., PRO (1875–86) • G. H. Orpen, ed. and trans., *The song of Dermot and the earl* (1892), lines 447–8, 747, 765–7, 930, 1551, 1945–6, 2001–14, 2721, 3084–5, 3138–41, 3425–55 • P. Meyer, ed., *L'histoire de Guillaume le Maréchal*, 3 vols. (Paris, 1891–1901), lines 13430–48, 13554–784, 14091, 14123–31 • W. M. Hennessy, ed. and trans., *The annals of Loch Cé: a chronicle of Irish affairs from AD 1014 to AD 1590*, 1, Rolls Series, 54 (1871), 186–7, 228–31, 236–9 • E. St J. Brooks, ed., *The Irish cartularies of Llanthony prima and secunda*, IMC (1953), 254–7 • O. Davies and D. B. Quinn, eds., 'Irish pipe roll of 14 John, 1211–1212', *Ulster Journal of Archaeology*, 3rd ser., 4 (1941), 16–19, 34–5 [suppl.] • J. Mills and M. J. McEnery, eds., *Calendar of the Gormanston register* (1916), 165–6, 203–4 • S. Mac Airt, ed. and trans., *The annals of Inisfallen* (1951), s.a. 1209 • J. T. Gilbert, ed., *Chartularies of St Mary's Abbey, Dublin: with the register of its house at Dunbrody and annals of Ireland*, 2, Rolls Series, 80 (1884), 314 • *Gir. Camb. opera*, 1.59; 6.130 • J. Williams ab Ithel, ed., *Annales Cambriae*, Rolls Series, 20 (1860), 47 • *The annals of Ireland by Friar John Clyn and Thady Dowling: together with the annals of Ross*, ed. R. Butler, Irish Archaeological Society (1849), 7–8 • Dugdale, *Monasticon*, new edn, vol. 6

Meilyr Brydydd (*fl.* 1081–1137), poet, was perhaps the son of Mabon ab Iarddur ap Môr, and, we may assume, dwelt at Trefeilyr in the parish of Trefdraeth, Anglesey, an estate which doubtless took its name from him; his wife was Tandreg ferch Rhys ap Seisyllt. Three poems preserved in the Hendregadredd manuscript (NL Wales, MS 6680B) have been attributed to him, namely: an elegy on Gruffudd ap Cynan (d. 1137); the poet's death lay, in which he prays that his bones may be laid in Enlli (Bardsey Island); and a short poem on the battle of Mynydd Carn (1081), which professes to foretell the deaths of Trahaearn ap Caradog, Meilyr ap Rhiwallon, and Caradog ap Gruffudd ap Rhydderch (who is not named) in that battle. His authorship of the last has been disputed on chronological grounds.

Meilyr (whose name means Meilyr the Poet) is among the first of the *Gogynfeirdd, the medieval professional poets whose poems can be approximately dated, as distinguished from the *cynfeirdd*, the poets of the later sixth and earlier seventh centuries, whose verse, in the main, celebrates the exploits of north British kings and warriors. He is the herald of the poetic revival which contact with Norman civilization and success in arms brought about among the Welsh towards the middle of the twelfth century. From his elegy for Gruffudd ap Cynan it is apparent that he was *pencerdd* (chief poet) under that prince. On at least one occasion, according to the same source, he acted as envoy for the court of Aberffraw. His son, Gwalchmai, and his grandsons, Einion, Meilyr, and Elidir Sais, also won renown as poets, and the family was for generations of consequence in Anglesey.

J. E. LLOYD, rev. R. GERAINT GRUFFYDD

Sources *Gwaith Meilyr Brydydd a'i Ddisgynyddion*, ed. J. E. Caerwyn Williams, P. I. Lynch, and R. G. Gruffydd (1994)
Archives NL Wales, MS 6680B

Meinertzhagen, Daniel (V) (1801–1869), merchant and merchant banker, was born at Bremen, Germany, on 8 December 1801, the eldest of at least four sons and four daughters of Daniel (IV) Meinertzhagen (1772–1859) and his wife, Meta Rebecca, daughter of George von Groning, who married in December 1800. The name of Daniel was traditionally given to the eldest son, one being differentiated from another by the addition of a roman numeral. Thus Meinertzhagen was known as Daniel (V).

The Meinertzhagens were a leading, if not prosperous, Bremen family. Daniel (I), a merchant, originally from Cologne, had settled there at the end of the seventeenth century and had become a senator in Bremen's legislative council; both his son and his grandson, Daniel (II) and Daniel (III), were to follow him in this office. Daniel (V)'s father was a Bremen merchant and at least two of his brothers held important positions in the city, George as a clergyman and Emile as a lawyer. Three of his sisters were still unmarried by 1859; a fourth was the wife of a local merchant, Johannus Tibeman. Daniel (V) followed his father into merchanting and in 1820 took up a clerkship at Nantes; in 1822 he moved to Bordeaux, which did more trade with Bremen than any other French port. A third brother, Heinrich Albrecht (known outside Germany as Henry Albert), also became a merchant; by 1859 he had settled at Melbourne, Australia, and appears to have been linked in business with Daniel, who by then had lent him £3000.

When the family firm, along with many others, failed during the economic downturn of 1826, Meinertzhagen moved to London and sought employment with Frederick Huth & Co., merchants, where a contact of his mother and grandmother, John Frederick Gruning, was a partner and where a friend from Nantes, Jules Dufou, was a clerk. Four years earlier, Dufou had written to Meinertzhagen telling him that 'for learning commerce, London is without exception the best school' (Meinertzhagen, 252). Huths recruited Meinertzhagen as a clerk and his rapid progress was consolidated when in June 1833 he married Amelia Huth (1810–1887), daughter of Frederick *Huth, at St John's Church, Hackney, Middlesex. They had eight daughters and three sons, the eldest of whom was Daniel (VI), born in 1842. His betrothal resulted in his admission to the Huth partnership in January 1833, despite his modest wealth; by 1836 he still contributed only £4200 of his firm's capital of £123,000. In 1837 he became a naturalized British subject.

The Huth business had been formed by Frederick Huth in London in 1809. He had come from Hamburg via Spain and initially his firm, widely recognized as a leading 'German' house, did business with Europe and especially with Germany, Spain, and the Baltic. Its interests were extended to the west coast of South America in the mid-1820s, when local houses were established at Lima and Valparaiso. By the time of Meinertzhagen's admission, Huths was a major London merchant bank, ranking immediately below firms such as Barings and Rothschilds. Barings recorded in the 1820s that 'there is no doubt that their means are most complete for anything they may undertake' and that 'Mr Huth is a most prudent & circumspect man and thought highly of' (Baring Brothers & Co. archives, HC16.1).

Frederick Huth, who retired in 1850 aged seventy-three, and who died in 1864, almost outlived Meinertzhagen, which makes distinction of their individual achievements difficult. However, Meinertzhagen, who succeeded as senior partner of a partnership largely comprising Huth's sons, appears to have had little regard for the entrepreneurial skills of the junior Huths. 'I often wish the counting house was again in our house and that you could come sometimes and be by my side ... so as to gain an interest in the business', he confided to his wife in 1843, but adding 'it is not in your family and [I] do not like to talk about it then' (Meinertzhagen, 277). Under Meinertzhagen's leadership, the Huth business made steady progress; by 1845 its capital was £312,000, and it rose to about £500,000 by 1870.

It seems fair to attribute Huths' important diversification into North American trade and finance to Meinertzhagen, though he came to this with no obvious qualification. As a major accepting house, in 1839 Huths established a Liverpool firm to handle its cotton finance business and in 1837 it became co-financier, with Barings, of the Bank of the United States; later, however, unlike Barings, it made substantial losses when the bank collapsed. By the 1850s important business was done in financing the export of railway materials to the United States.

If accepting was one leg of Huths' business in the USA, then trading in securities was the second. The firm became a major conduit for the flow of United States securities to Europe, but it specialized in placing them privately, often among rich continental investors, rather than making public issues. By the mid-1830s, important positions were taken in Morris Canal and Banking Company bonds, New Orleans City stock, and New York 5 per cents. In 1839 Meinertzhagen reached agreement with the Bank of Missouri for the sale of Missouri state and bank bonds.

When financial crisis overwhelmed the United States in 1841, Huths was badly damaged and Meinertzhagen, along with the young Louis Huth, was dispatched to rescue what he could. Despite having 'hardly anything but bad business to attend to, constant discussions with debtors and lawyers, and nothing very cheering from London', he appears to have done well, and stated that in Florida 'I have been rather fortunate in settling one of our heaviest claims. ... In Texas I have also secured a small claim which we had considered as lost' (Meinertzhagen, 291).

In extending Huths' securities business to Europe in 1863, Meinertzhagen 'was much in favour' of joining a consortium of seven of London's second-division houses to form the International Financial Society, but in doing so he had to overcome the opposition of 'old Huth' who had 'said nay' (Kynaston, 221). This combination aimed to compete with more powerful forces in winning a share in arranging finance for infrastructure projects and governments largely in central Europe.

Throughout his life Meinertzhagen maintained close links with his native Bremen, where his wider family continued to live. By 1859 he had provided a house and land at nearby Grohn for use by his mother and three unmarried sisters, and in the same year Bremen granted him its freedom in recognition of his assistance during the financial crisis of 1857. In London Meinertzhagen's leading role in the German community was illustrated by his treasurership, taken up by 1862, of the German Hospital. His daughter-in-law described him as 'a delightful personality, a hard worker, enterprising and far seeing and generous almost to a fault' (Meinertzhagen, 16).

Early on Meinertzhagen lived above Huths' City offices in South Place, but later he settled at Devonshire Place in London's West End. Later still he acquired Belmont House, a country home at Wimbledon, where he died on 12 July 1869; he was buried in Mottisfont churchyard, Hampshire. Daniel (VI) succeeded him as a partner at Huths, and subsequent generations of Meinertzhagens played a prominent role both in the affairs of Huths, until their winding up in 1936, and in the City of London generally.

Although few details of his achievements are now known, Meinertzhagen was one of London's greatest merchants during the mid-nineteenth century. On his death, *The Times*, then not noted for carrying obituaries of merchants, described him as 'a leading and greatly esteemed member of the mercantile world' (*The Times*, 13 July 1869).   JOHN ORBELL

Sources G. Meinertzhagen, *A Bremen family* (1912) · A. J. Murray, *Home from the hill: a biography of Frederick Huth*, *'Napoleon of the City'* (1970) · M. Wilkins, *The history of foreign investment in the United States* (1989), 56 · D. Kynaston, *The City of London*, 1 (1994), 221 · *The Times* (13 July 1869), 10c · Burke, *Gen. GB*
Archives GL, Frederick Huth & Co. MSS · UCL, Frederick Huth & Co. MSS
Likenesses portrait, repro. in Meinertzhagen, *Bremen family* · portrait, repro. in Murray, *Home from the hill*
Wealth at death under £140,000: probate, 19 Aug 1869, CGPLA Eng. & Wales

Meinertzhagen, Daniel (1915–1991), merchant banker, was born on 2 March 1915 at Blundell House, Campden Hill, Kensington, London, the eldest of the three sons of Louis Ernest Meinertzhagen, a merchant banker, of Theberton House, Leiston, Suffolk, and his wife, Gwynedd Marion, the daughter of Sir (Samuel Henry) William *Llewellyn, portrait painter and president of the Royal Academy from 1928 to 1938. His father's family was of Danish origin, and had settled in Bremen, but this branch of the family had lived in England for several generations. His grandmother was a sister of Beatrice Webb, his uncle was the ornithologist and traveller Richard *Meinertzhagen, and both his brothers went into the City: Luke became senior partner of the stockbroking firm Cazenove & Co. and Peter was general manager of the Commonwealth Development Corporation.

After Eton College and New College, Oxford, where he was awarded a third in philosophy, politics, and economics in 1936, Meinertzhagen joined Lazard Brothers, a leading City merchant bank, and began by working in the gilt-edged department. During the Second World War he served with the Royal Air Force Volunteer Reserve and reached the rank of wing commander. On 12 November 1940 he married Marguerite Josephine (*b*. 1913/14), the daughter of Albert Edward Leonard, a solicitor. They had two sons.

After the war Meinertzhagen went back to Lazards, where he was appointed managing director in 1954 and a partner in 1955. In January 1957 he organized the sale of the *Financial Times* to S. Pearson & Son Ltd, after his brother

Luke advised Oliver Crosthwaite-Eyre, whose family controlled the *Financial Times*, and who was involved in a dispute with the chairman, Brendan Bracken, to sell the paper and spread his capital over a wider range of investments. Lazards was the merchant banking arm of Pearsons, and Meinertzhagen was able to arrange for Pearsons to buy a controlling interest in the *Financial Times* before it was generally known that the paper was for sale.

Meinertzhagen became director of a number of City companies and companies for which Lazards acted, including Trolloppe and Colls, the Costain Group, and Alexanders Discount. He advised Rootes Motors on its merger with Chrysler in the 1960s, and when Lord Poole, chairman of Lazards, suffered a stroke in 1973, Meinertzhagen succeeded to his post. The following year he was appointed non-executive chairman of Royal Insurance, a client of Lazards. He was also chairman of Mercantile Credit, a prominent hire-purchase company. During the secondary banking crisis of 1974–5, and the collapse of the stock market, Meinertzhagen played an important part in the restoration of confidence in the secondary banks through the recovery operation mounted by the big banks: Mercantile Credit was one of the financial institutions to be helped through the crisis, with support loans to the value of £167 million. Meinertzhagen retired from the chairmanship of Lazards in 1980, but continued to advise Pearsons. He was chairman of Alexanders Discount from 1981 to 1984 and remained chairman of Royal Insurance until 1985.

Meinertzhagen was a leading figure in the financial world from the mid-1950s until his retirement, highly respected for his wisdom and sound judgement. He loved gardening at his home in Bramshot, Hampshire, and had a fine collection of porcelain. He died of pneumonia and chronic lymphatic leukaemia at the Cromwell Hospital, Kensington, London, on 22 March 1991, survived by his wife and their two sons—one of whom, Peter Meinertzhagen, was chairman of the stockbrokers Hoare Govett.

ANNE PIMLOTT BAKER

Sources M. Reid, *The secondary banking crisis, 1973–1975* (1982) · D. Kynaston, *The Financial Times: a centenary history* (1988) · *The Times* (25 March 1991) · *The Independent* (19 April 1991) · *Financial Times* (25 March 1991) · WW · b. cert. · m. cert. · d. cert.
Likenesses photograph, repro. in *The Times* · photograph, repro. in *The Independent*
Wealth at death £1,448,503: probate, 1991, CGPLA Eng. & Wales

Meinertzhagen, Richard (1878–1967), naturalist and army officer, was born on 3 March 1878 at 10 Rutland Gate, Knightsbridge, London, the second son and third child in the family of four sons and five daughters of Daniel Meinertzhagen, a London merchant banker whose German family had long settled in Bremen, and his wife, Georgina, an elder sister of Beatrice Webb, the daughter of Richard Potter, railway and industrial magnate. Though registered as Oliver, he was christened Richard, and called Dick by his intimates. He was at two preparatory schools: Aysgarth, where he learnt self-reliance, and Fonthill, where he was sadistically beaten by a master—until he hit back.

posted to the intelligence branch of the general headquarters in France, commanded by Sir Douglas (later first Earl) Haig. Never one to sit behind a desk if he could help it, he tried to see the battle front for himself, and was severely wounded. He recovered in time to join, as a colonel, the staff of 400 that A. J. Balfour took to the Paris peace conference, where he watched politicians disputing over Levantine problems. After a short spell as chief political officer in Palestine and Syria he spent 1921–4 as military adviser to the Colonial Office, sharing a room there with his friend T. E. Lawrence. In 1921 Anne Constance (*d.* 1928), daughter of Major Randle Jackson of Swordale, Easter Ross, became Meinertzhagen's second wife. They had a daughter and two sons.

By now Meinertzhagen had become a convinced Zionist. This conviction did not sit well either with regimental soldiering or with Whitehall. In 1925 he resigned from the army, and spent most of the rest of his long life travelling—mainly in western and central Asia—and studying birds, partly as cover for observing international politics. He returned to the War Office in the winter of 1939–40, and was wounded again off Dunkirk in June 1940, when he took a small boat across to join the rescue. For the rest of the war he was in the Home Guard. After it he rejoiced in the creation of the state of Israel in 1948; he was an active eyewitness. While on his way to watch birds he slipped ashore during a skirmish at Haifa, disguised as a Coldstream private, and shot several men.

He was a lifelong diarist, and published some of the results: *Kenya Diary, 1902–1906* (1957), *Middle East Diary, 1917–1956* (1959), *Army Diary, 1899–1926* (1960), and *Diary of a Black Sheep* (1964). Apart from many articles in *Ibis*, he wrote *Nicholl's Birds of Egypt*, 2 vols. (1930), *Birds of Arabia* (1954), and *Pirates and Predators* (1959). In 1951 he received the Godman Salvin medal of the British Ornithologists' Union, and in 1957 he was appointed CBE for services to ornithology. Subsequently doubts have been cast on the authenticity of some of his ornithological discoveries.

Meinertzhagen's elder son was killed, aged nineteen, in the guards armoured division on the Dutch–German border in 1944. Of him he wrote a memoir, *The Life of a Boy* (1947). Meinertzhagen died at 17 Kensington Park Gardens, Kensington, London, on 17 June 1967.

M. R. D. FOOT, *rev.*

Sources J. Lord, *Duty, honour, empire: the life and times of Col. R. Meinertzhagen* (1971) · *The Times* (19 June 1967) · *The Times* (31 Dec 1997) · d. cert. · b. cert. · *CGPLA Eng. & Wales* (1967)
Archives Bodl. RH, diaries and papers · NHM, notes and catalogues · NHM, papers and drawings · NL Scot., Kenya diary [typescript] | BL OIOC, corresp. with F. M. Bailey · King's Lond., Liddell Hart C., corresp. with Sir B. H. Liddell Hart · St Ant. Oxf., Middle East Centre, corresp. with Harry Philby · U. Oxf., Edward Grey Institute of Field Ornithology, corresp. with David Lack · U. Oxf., Edward Grey Institute of Field Ornithology, corresp. with Reginald Moreau
Likenesses photograph, 1906, Bodl. RH [*see illus.*]
Wealth at death £108,834: probate, 14 Aug 1967, *CGPLA Eng. & Wales*

Richard Meinertzhagen (1878–1967), by unknown photographer, 1906

Much of Meinertzhagen's childhood was spent at Mottisfont Abbey, on the River Test above Romsey; there he began his lifelong study of birds. He continued his education at Harrow School, from where he went for a few months into his father's City office, which he hated; and he spent a term in Göttingen, learning German. A subaltern's commission in the Hampshire yeomanry in 1897–8 gave him a liking for army life, and in January 1899 he was commissioned into the Royal Fusiliers. He missed the Second South African War, as he was serving in south Asia. In 1902–6 he had four adventurous years' attachment to the King's African rifles, serving up-country in Kenya, where he discovered a new species (*Hylochoeros meinertzhageni*, the giant forest hog). He was wounded, mentioned in dispatches, and promoted captain; he saved most of his pay. In 1911 he married Armorel, daughter of Colonel Herman le Roy-Lewis of Westbury House, Petersfield.

Meinertzhagen's regiment released him again to pass through the Staff College in Quetta, and at the start of the First World War in 1914 he was made intelligence officer to the Tanga expeditionary force. In 1916 he was appointed DSO for exceptionally valuable work with this force. He then became chief intelligence officer to the Egyptian expeditionary force that advanced into Palestine. In October 1917 the Turks held an entrenched front from Gaza to Beersheba. Sir E. H. H. Allenby (later first Viscount Allenby of Megiddo) misled them as to which flank he was about to attack, in part through a bloodstained haversack full of papers dropped by Meinertzhagen on reconnaissance: a classic of practical deception.

After a brief spell at the War Office Meinertzhagen was

Meitner, Lise (1878–1968), physicist, was born on 7 November 1878 at 27 Kaiser Josefstrasse, Vienna, the third of the

Lise Meitner (1878–1968), by Lotte Meitner-Graf

eight children of Philipp Meitner (d. 1910), a lawyer, and his wife, Hedwig Skovran (1850–1924). Both parents were of Jewish descent, yet Meitner accepted baptism as a protestant in 1908. As a woman scientist, Lise Meitner had to struggle to launch a career. She trained as a French teacher yet, crucially, her family backed her decision to pursue a higher education when in 1897 women were granted access to the philosophical faculties of Austrian universities. After training privately to take the required examination she entered the University of Vienna in 1901. She studied physics and mathematics with the renowned Ludwig Boltzmann, and in 1906 took her PhD under Franz Exner, on heat conduction in inhomogeneous solids. She then turned to the new field of radioactivity, to which she was to devote her scientific work.

The study of radioactivity thrived in Vienna yet chances to get a position were slim. In 1907, with her family's continued financial support, Meitner moved to Berlin. She attended Max Planck's lectures at the university and met an assistant at Emil Fischer's chemistry institute, Otto Hahn, an early advocate of radioactivity in Germany. In the years leading to the First World War Meitner collaborated with Hahn on the identification and separation of new radioactive substances, and entered the German academic system: in 1912, at thirty-five, she obtained her first paid position, as Planck's assistant, and that same year she moved with Hahn to the radioactive section of the new Kaiser Wilhelm Institut für Chemie, one in a series of research centres funded by German industrialists. In 1913

she became an associate at the institute, and in 1917, after a year serving as an X-ray nurse–technician with the Austrian army, she was appointed director of its physics section. During the war she managed to complete, with Hahn's occasional assistance when on leave, the search for the precursor of actinium—protactinium (Pa, element 91). Meitner secured the necessary pitchblende residues from the chemical firm Buchler's industrial laboratory in Brunswick, where part of the treatment was also carried out.

Meitner built her prestige as a physicist during the Weimar years (1918–33)—her best both professionally and personally. In 1922 she received the *venia legendi*, which qualified her for teaching at the university, and in 1926 she was appointed extraordinary professor. The human and material resources of her laboratory at the Kaiser Wilhelm Institut grew steadily after temporary setbacks during the 1922–3 inflation, making it, together with Hahn's chemical section, Germany's most important radioactive research centre.

During this period Meitner studied the relationship between beta and gamma rays, with important implications for nuclear structure. In the context of a long-standing controversy with C. D. Ellis, from the Cavendish Laboratory in Cambridge, she established in 1925 that gamma-ray emission followed, rather than triggered, radioactive transformations, though she later confirmed Ellis and W. A. Wooster's result that the primary beta-spectrum was continuous. Beginning in 1929, a substantial mesothorium (^{228}Ra) and radiothorium (^{228}Th) loan from the Kaiser Wilhelm Gesellschaft allowed her and her co-workers to study the absorption of high-energy gamma rays in matter—a topic of relevance for the physics of the nucleus and cosmic rays. In these experiments Meitner used the newly developed Geiger-Müller counter; as with the cloud chamber before, she was quick in adapting new instruments. By virtue of its technical expertise and its stock of radioactive sources Meitner's section also played a substantial role in the study of the new particles of the early 1930s, the neutron and the positron.

As an Austrian citizen and non-state employee, Meitner was spared the Nazis' first racial laws (introduced in 1933). She considered leaving Germany at the time, yet the excellent work conditions at the institute prevailed. The removal of her *venia legendi* and increasing isolation may have conditioned her resuming collaborative work with Hahn. For four years, with a younger researcher, Fritz Strassmann, they studied the radioactive elements formed in the bombardment of uranium nuclei by neutrons, some of which were presumed to be heavier than uranium itself (to have an atomic number over 92).

In July 1938, three months after the annexation of Austria by the Reich, Meitner fled Germany. From her exile in Sweden she learned firsthand of Hahn and Strassmann's result that barium (an element about half the atomic weight of uranium) was among the products of the collision of a neutron with an uranium nucleus. This seemed very implausible physically. Her nephew, the physicist Otto Robert *Frisch, was visiting; over Christmas they arrived at an explanation in terms of the excessive electric charge of the nucleus, and estimated the energy released in the process, for which Frisch proposed the term 'fission'.

Meitner spent twenty years in Sweden, becoming a Swedish citizen in 1949. During the war she tried to pursue fission research at Magne Siegbahn's research institute in Stockholm. Her situation improved in 1947, when together with Sigvard Eklund she was assigned the creation of a nuclear physics section at the Swedish Royal Institute of Technology. She retired in 1954, was elected a fellow of the Royal Society of London the following year, and in 1960 moved to Cambridge, where Frisch lived. She died at Cambridge on 27 October 1968 and was buried at Bramley in Hampshire.

Meitner's share in the discovery of fission continues to dominate judgements of her stature as a scientist. In 1945 Hahn alone was controversially awarded the 1944 chemistry Nobel prize for this discovery. Recent work has made clear that Meitner contributed decisively to the discovery, that the Nobel committee's decision was characteristically open to question, and that Hahn did not do much to clarify Meitner's role. The historiographical dominance of this issue has unfortunately prevented many from arriving at a balanced view of Meitner's achievements as a physicist, particularly with regard to her prominent role in the development of radioactivity and the rise of nuclear physics in Germany. XAVIER ROQUÉ

Sources R. L. Sime, *Lise Meitner: a life in physics* (1996) · O. R. Frisch, *Memoirs FRS*, 16 (1970), 405–20 · E. Crawford, R. L. Sime, and M. Walker, 'A Nobel tale of wartime injustice', *Nature*, 382 (1996), 393–5 · S. Ernst, ed., *Lise Meitner an Otto Hahn: Briefe aus den Jahren 1912 bis 1914* (1992) · *CGPLA Eng. & Wales* (1969) · E. Scheich, 'Science, politics, and morality: the relationship of Lise Meitner and Elizabeth Schiemann', *Osiris*, 2nd ser., 12 (1997), 143–68
Archives CAC Cam., personal and scientific papers | Archiv zur Geschichte der Max-Planck-Gesellschaft, Berlin, O. Hahn Nachlass · Archiv zur Geschichte der Max-Planck-Gesellschaft, Berlin, Kaiser-Wilhelm-Institut für Chemie · Royal Swedish Academy of Sciences, Stockholm, Nobel archives · Trinity Cam., O. R. Frisch collection · University of Chicago, Joseph Regenstein Library, James Franck MSS | FILM BBC Archive, London · CAC Cam., Meitner Collection | SOUND CAC Cam., Meitner Collection
Likenesses L. Meitner-Graf, photograph, RS · L. Meitner-Graf, photograph, Österreichische Nationalbibliothek, Vienna [*see illus.*] · L. Meitner-Graf, portraits, CAC Cam., Meitner collection · likeness, Archiv zur Geschichte der Max-Planck-Gesellschaft, Berlin · portrait, CAC Cam., Meitner collection · portrait, Bildarchiv der Österreichischen Nationalbibliothek, Vienna
Wealth at death £15,232: probate, 24 Jan 1969, *CGPLA Eng. & Wales*

Mél (*fl.* 5th–early 6th cent.). *See under* Meath, saints of (*act. c.*400–*c.*900).

Melachrino, George Miltiades (1909–1965), conductor and composer, was born at 57 Albany Street, London, on 1 May 1909, the eldest son of John Melachrino, a tobacco merchant, and his wife, Ellen Emms. The very versatile musician who was to have a great influence on British light music was something of a child prodigy and was playing on a small-sized violin when he was only four and performed in public when he was thirteen. He went to Trinity College of Music, London, at the age of fourteen, where he led a band, emerging four years later as an accomplished exponent of the violin, viola, oboe, alto and tenor saxophone, and clarinet, and as pianist and singer. He was one of the first musicians to broadcast from 2LO at Savoy Hill and became a leading light in British dance music, working with bands led by Mantovani, Ambrose, Jack Jackson, Jay Wilbur, and Carroll Gibbons at various times. He was given the opportunity to lead his own orchestra at the Café de Paris in London just before the outbreak of war in 1939. If, at first, it looked as if the war might be cutting short a promising career, it became a golden opportunity when, after touring with the Stars In Battledress company, he was chosen to lead 'The orchestra in khaki', which was made up of top professional musicians serving in the army. This became, in 1944, the fifty-piece British Band of the Allied Expeditionary Forces. As a result, and through regular wartime broadcasts that brought his music to the general public as well as the forces, he became known as one of the top British arranger–conductors. He also sang with the equivalent United States and Canadian forces bands led by Glenn Miller and Robert Farnon.

After the war the band remained together, operating as two separate musical units, the full-scale Melachrino Orchestra and the Melachrino Strings, which tapped the same demand for mood music that helped Mantovani to his similar success. Melachrino achieved a worldwide reputation through regular broadcasts and recordings, and such albums as *Music for Dining*, *Music for Relaxation*, and *Music for Two People Alone* became best-sellers on the Decca, HMV, and RCA labels. There were later stereo LPs on ABC Paramount. He appeared with his full orchestra in the London Hippodrome show *Starlight Roof* (1947), which introduced Julie Andrews as a budding young singer. He wrote the score for this show including the novel and high spirited 'Starlight Roof' waltz. He also ran the Melachrino Organization, one of the largest agencies for bands and orchestras in the country, and the provider of stage shows for MGM's Empire cinemas in the 1950s. He helped to found the Arcadia Publishing Company which promoted his own works as well as those of contemporaries like Ernest Tomlinson.

Melachrino's popularity was founded on the distinctive sound of the Melachrino Strings, an expanded orchestral form of the typical dance band score, breaking away from the usual classically orientated light music sound with scores that used the various tones of musical sections in a clearly spotlighted way, with distinctive harmonies, above a regular dance band type of rhythm. He was also a gifted composer in this same field and the traits outlined above were well demonstrated in the 'Starlight Roof' waltz, as in 'Winter Sunshine', 'Woodland Revel', and his theme tune 'First Rhapsody'. He also wrote film music, including that for *No Orchids for Miss Blandish* (1948) which the *Daily Express* critic branded as the worst film he had ever seen.

Melachrino's career was sadly cut short at the age of

fifty-six, when he drowned in his bath on 18 June 1965 at his home at 11 Gordon Place, Kensington. The coroner pronounced a verdict of accidental death.

PETER GAMMOND

Sources b. cert. · d. cert. · P. Gammond, *The Oxford companion to popular music* (1991) · D. Clarke, ed., *The Penguin encyclopedia of popular music* (1989) · *The Times* (19 June 1965) · *New Grove* · *CGPLA Eng. & Wales* (1965)
Archives SOUND BL NSA, documentary recordings · BL NSA, performance recordings
Wealth at death £53,472: probate, 5 Nov 1965, *CGPLA Eng. & Wales*

Melba, Dame Nellie [*real name* Helen Porter Mitchell] (1861–1931), singer, was born on 19 May 1861 in Richmond, Australia, the eldest of seven children of David Mitchell and his wife, Isabella Ann Dorn, both of Scottish descent. Her father had emigrated to Australia in the gold rush of 1852 and became a successful builder. Nellie (as she was known from childhood) learned to play the piano and first sang in public at an age which in her memoirs she gave as six. She was educated at a local boarding-school and then at the Presbyterian Ladies' College in Richmond. Her first professional teacher of singing was Mary Ellen Christian, a former pupil in England of Manuel García. The second, Pietro Cecchi, an Italian tenor with a high reputation as a teacher in Melbourne, she somewhat belatedly acknowledged as the one who did most to lay the foundations of her career.

That honour has been most widely given to Mathilde Marchesi, who took Nellie as a pupil at her Paris studio in 1886. Nellie had left Australia after a failed marriage in December 1882 to an adventurer, Charles Armstrong; they separated by mutual consent after little more than a year of marriage, during which their only child, a son, was born (they were divorced in 1900). She had then begun to study singing in earnest with the fixed idea of becoming a professional. Cecchi believed she had a great future, and after some concerts in Melbourne several discerning listeners expressed their high opinion. Unfortunately, this was not shared at first by experienced British musicians, including Sir Arthur Sullivan, for whom she auditioned in 1885 shortly after arriving in London. Sullivan offered the prospect of a small part in *The Mikado* after a further period of study. Instead, she went to Paris with a letter of introduction to Marchesi, reputedly the best and most influential teacher of the day.

The story of Nellie's audition has become famous. 'Salvatore!' the teacher cried out to her husband, 'J'ai enfin une étoile!' Apparently, the pupil's brilliance was such that she went straight into the advanced opera class and was then sent out to launch her career after no more than nine months of tuition. Her professional name was to be Nellie Melba (partly in honour of Melbourne, the city close to her birthplace). Her operatic début occurred on 13 October 1887 at the Théâtre Royale de la Monnaie in Brussels. Her performance as Gilda in *Rigoletto* won enthusiastic reviews and was followed by appearances in *La traviata* and *Lucia di Lammermoor*. All three roles of this first season

Dame Nellie Melba (1861–1931), by H. Walter Barnett, in or before 1903

were to remain central to her career. The success in Brussels led to an engagement at the Royal Opera House, Covent Garden, where her introduction to the London public on 24 May 1888 in the title role of *Lucia di Lammermoor* gave little indication of the illustrious career she would eventually have in that house.

Melba's début at the Paris Opéra was a different matter. Here, on 8 May 1889, she sang the role of Ophélie in Ambroise Thomas's *Hamlet* and enjoyed an ovation that made her famous overnight. Her reviews told of an incomparably lovely voice with exceptional resonance in the middle register; the brilliance of her technique in florid work was admired, so too the touching simplicity of her manner and enunciation. After that, she returned in triumph to Covent Garden where she had acquired a powerful friend in Lady Gladys de Grey, later marchioness of Ripon, who had influence with leading figures at the opera house and in London society. In this second season Melba opened with Gounod's *Roméo et Juliette*, singing with the brothers Jean and Edouard de Reszke. This association flourished throughout the 1890s, which in both London and New York were subsequently dubbed 'the golden age of opera'. The three singers also appeared together at St Petersburg by invitation of the tsar in 1891. In these years Melba also sang at La Scala, Milan, and in the opera houses of Palermo, Monte Carlo, Berlin, Vienna, and Stockholm and elsewhere in Europe. More important for the development of her career was her American début with the Metropolitan company on 4 December 1893. The event itself appears to have been a *succès d'estime* rather than a popular sensation, and it was a performance of *Roméo et Juliette* a little later in the season that established Melba in succession to Adelina Patti as the leading prima donna of the time. The performances she gave in these years of her absolute prime were recalled by one of New York's sharpest and most respected critics, W. J. Henderson, when he wrote of Melba shortly after her death. The quality which distinguished her from other sopranos singing in her repertory, he said, was 'splendour': 'The tones glowed with a star-like brilliance. They flamed with a white flame. And they possessed a remarkable force which the famous singer always used with continence. She gave the impression of singing well within her limits' (*New York Sun*, 28 Feb 1931).

An exception to that last point of Henderson's was Melba's single appearance, on 30 December 1896, as Brünnhilde in Wagner's *Siegfried*. The role, written for a powerful dramatic soprano, lay beyond her capabilities. The experiment was potentially ruinous, and, though the reviews were by no means uniformly bad, Melba herself was unsparing: 'I've been a fool,' she said. The 'case' became a famous one (in some quarters Jean de Reszke was wrongfully blamed as having provided encouragement), and yet the folly may not have been so unaccountable as it seemed. Melba had sung other Wagnerian roles, Elsa in *Lohengrin* and Elisabeth in *Tannhäuser*, with considerable success. Her voice at this time, by all accounts, was ample in volume with strong middle notes. In London she had sung the heavy role of Verdi's *Aida*, and the critics observed that her voice easily dominated the great ensembles. The *Siegfried* Brünnhilde, whose appearance is confined to the third act and for whom the writing lies higher in the voice than in *Die Walküre* and *Götterdämmerung*, may quite reasonably have seemed to provide an attractive, almost cautious, way into the repertory. It was not one she tried a second time.

Melba's most frequent role at the Metropolitan was that of Marguerite in Gounod's *Faust*, and her last appearance in the house was as Violetta in *La traviata*. The other major contribution she made to opera in New York was to give a needed boost to Oscar Hammerstein's venture with his Manhattan Company as a rival to the Metropolitan in 1907. Melba sang in sixteen performances, and on her last appearance was called before the curtain twenty-three times with applause continuing for forty minutes.

The opera that evening was Puccini's *La Bohème* (which, incidentally, was followed by the mad scene from *Lucia di Lammermoor* sung by Melba alone, who then had a piano brought on stage and accompanied herself in Tosti's 'Mattinata'). The role of Mimì in *La Bohème* became closely identified with her throughout the remainder of her career. She sang it first in 1899 at Covent Garden, having argued strongly in its favour with a management opposed to the inclusion of such a new and plebeian opera into the 'grand' (summer) season. Increasingly in the new century

she was criticized as a reactionary force in music. Yet she had taken part in several British premières (Goring-Thomas's *Esmeralda*, Bemberg's *Elaine*, Leoncavallo's *Pagliacci*, Mascagni's *I Rantzau*, and *Hélène*, the title role of which was written for her by Saint-Säens), and *Bohème* itself was still struggling for recognition when she took it up. She studied her role with Puccini in Italy (as she had previously done with Verdi for her Desdemona in *Otello*, and with Gounod, Massenet, and Delibes in Paris). It is doubtful whether she ever endowed her Mimì with the emotional warmth and fragile youthfulness the part needs, but always, even into her sixties, she brought her special purity of tone and an unforgettable top C from offstage at the end of act I.

That note is preserved on a gramophone record of 1907, the only one Melba made with the great tenor Enrico Caruso, her partner in many stage performances. Exquisite in itself it is part of a recording in which the listener may be, initially at least, at a loss to see how it, and many of her other records, can support Melba's reputation. She recorded a repertory that for those times was quite extensive, from 1904 to 1926, though with varying success. The fine definition, purity of tone, and technical accomplishment can be recognized easily enough, but the terms of Henderson's memoir, quoted above, and especially his word 'splendour', may not be the first that come to mind. Even so, her records exercise a fascination and bring flashes of understanding. It is even possible, with modern reproduction, to sense something of the house-filling power that she reputedly had at her command. They can even breed affection. Tosti's 'Serenata', recorded in 1904, gives some notion of the thrill, in quality and 'attack', that her high notes could create. She can be unexpectedly moving in a simple song such as 'Come back to Erin'; and a strangely preserved 'distance test' made for a recording session in 1910 suggests how excitingly full the voice could have sounded on record had the conditions been more propitious. Limitations of sensibility and in the range and depth of vocal colouring are evident too, yet it remains one of the paradoxes of the gramophone's history that this artist, so often characterized as coldly perfect, should exhibit evident faults and yet surprise her listeners by something so strongly individual, and beautiful in its individuality, that the response is emotional and warm.

Melba's personal reputation was more equivocal. An astute businesswoman, driving hard bargains with management and ruling the roost to the detriment of all foreseen rivals at Covent Garden, she could also be generous to needy causes and individuals, and she raised over £100,000 for the Red Cross during the First World War. In his memoirs, the singer Peter Dawson, a compatriot, writes that she was known in the profession as 'Madame Sweet and Low' (referring to 'a sweet voice but low language') (Dawson, 138). Honoured by people of wealth and title, she was a shameless snob, yet she would remember a flower-seller from years ago and would ask the stage hands at the opera house in Sydney, 'Like to hear me sing, boys?' (Hetherington, 171). Pathologically critical of other sopranos, she wrote to the choirboy Ernest Lough a letter saying that she had been trying all her life to sing 'O for the wings of a dove' as well as he had done at the age of fourteen.

Though her personality was too hard to be the subject of popular romantic fiction, much was made by gossip-writers of Melba's affair with Louis Philippe, duke of Orléans, who was her lover from 1890 until scandal threatened to ruin both of them two years later. A film of her life, *Melba* (1953), starred the young American soprano Patrice Munsel; and, more memorably, her private secretary, Beverly Nichols, wrote an infamous novel called *Evensong* (1932), made the following year into a film with Evelyn Laye as the vain and vindictive ageing prima donna, Irela, clearly based on his employer. But such was Nellie Melba's popularity that a number of dishes were named after her. These include Melba toast, Melba sauce (a raspberry sauce for desserts), and peach Melba. The third of these, involving both peaches and ice-cream, was created in 1892 by Escoffier, then the chef at the Savoy Hotel in London, for a party in her honour.

In the later years of her career Melba became an artistic anachronism. She enriched her concert repertory by the addition of a few French art songs, but her programmes still resorted predictably to the jewel song from *Faust* and 'Home, sweet home'. In 1921 a newspaper headline 'The diva to go home' was gleefully greeted in the *Musical Times*. Feste, a pseudonym of the editor Harvey Grace, quoted the words and wrote: 'By all means. Why not? As the Diva has melodiously declared (only too often), there's no place like it' (*MT*, 409). She retired from opera eventually with a performance at Covent Garden on 8 June 1926, singing in scenes from *Roméo et Juliette*, *Otello*, and *La Bohème*. Some of this was recorded, including her farewell speech, in which she declared that Covent Garden was her artistic home and thanked Mr Austin, the doorman. On her return to Australia she settled at Coombe Cottage, Coldstream, near Lilydale, where she taught privately for a while, struggling courageously with illness. She died in Sydney on 23 February 1931; her death was front-page news. In Britain, where she had become a national institution and had been made a DBE in 1918 for contributions to the war effort, *The Times* devoted a leading article to her. In Australia, where relations had not been altogether smooth despite her bringing over an opera company of her own for several seasons, her funeral was grandly Victorian. The cortège travelled from Sydney to Melbourne where more than 5000 people passed before her coffin in the Scots church and more than 500 wreaths covered the catafalque.

J. B. STEANE

Sources N. Melba, *Melodies and memories: the autobiography of Nellie Melba* (1925) · J. Hetherington, *Melba: a biography* (1967) · W. R. Moran, ed., *Nellie Melba: a contemporary review* (1985) · W. J. Henderson, *The art of singing* (1938) · J. P. Cone, *Oscar Hammerstein's Manhattan Opera Company* (1964) · H. Rosenthal, *Two centuries of opera at Covent Garden* (1958) · G. Fitzgerald, ed., *Annals of the Metropolitan Opera* (1989) · private information (2004) · *The Times* (24 Feb 1931) · *MT*, 62 (1921), 409 · P. Dawson, *50 years of song* (1951) · R. Fawkes, *Opera on film* (2000) · *New York Sun* (28 Feb 1931) · J. A. Simpson and E. S. C. Weiner, eds., *The Oxford English dictionary*, 2nd edn, 20 vols. (1989) · *DNB* · *CGPLA Eng. & Wales* (1931)

Archives FILM BFI NFTVA, documentary footage |SOUND BL NSA, performance recordings · BL NSA, documentary recording · BL NSA, news recording · BL NSA, oral history interview

Likenesses B. Mackennal, bust, 1899, National Gallery of Victoria, Melbourne · H. W. Barnett, photograph, in or before 1903, Royal Opera House, London [*see illus.*] · R. Tuck & Sons, postcard, *c.*1904, NPG · R. Bunny, portrait, repro. in Hetherington, *Melba*, frontispiece · photographs, Royal Opera House, London · photographs, Metropolitan Opera House, New York · photographs, NL Aus. · postcard, NPG

Wealth at death £43,095 19*s*. 9*d*.: Australian probate sealed in England, 22 Aug 1931, *CGPLA Eng. & Wales* · approx. $1,000,000: wire service

Melbancke, Brian (*d.* 1600), writer, was probably born in Yorkshire, where he attended Sedbergh School. Later he went to St John's College, Cambridge, where he matriculated in the same term as the playwright Robert Greene (Michaelmas 1575) and graduated BA in 1580. He is identified in his own book, entitled *Philotimus* (1583), as 'Student in Graies Inne' and the book is prefaced by an epistle to the gentlemen of the inns of court. Nevertheless Melbancke's admission to Gray's Inn is not officially recorded.

Philotimus, subtitled 'The Warre betwixt Nature and Fortune', is an obvious imitation of John Lyly's *Euphues*. It contains many proverbs and pieces of verse, including an allusion to the story of Romeo and Juliet. One part of the dedication—to Philip Howard, earl of Arundel—might allude to Howard's time as a student at St John's. The other part of the dedication—to the 'Gentleman Students in the Inns of Court and Chancerie, and the University of Cambridge'—is clearly an attempt to solidify whatever ties Melbancke had to Gray's Inn and Cambridge. It has been hypothesized that 'George Wastnes Esquire', who contributed some verses to Melbancke's collection, was a relative of Gervase Wastenys, student of Gray's Inn in 1571.

'Brian Mullebanke and Sara Baker' were married on 3 June 1583 at St Olave's, Southwark. Melbancke had buried a daughter named Margaret on 9 December 1582 in the parish of St Mary Magdalene, Bermondsey, but the identity of her mother is unknown. All the subsequent life events of Melbancke's immediate family were recorded in the parish registers of St Mary Magdalene, where he and his wife seem to have lived following their marriage. The registers include baptismal and burial records for eight other children, from 1584 to 1595, as well as Melbancke's own burial (20 June 1600) and what is probably that of his widow (13 August 1603). How Brian Melbancke made a living remains a mystery. *Philotimus* (now extant in only a few copies) appears to have been printed only once, in 1583 by R. Warde (although some title-pages bear the date 1582), and there were seemingly no subsequent printings of it or other publications bearing Melbancke's name.

The Milbankes of Yorkshire, who possibly were relatives, were distinguished by a long line of baronets and famous aristocrats, including Admiral Mark Milbanke and Anne Isabella Milbanke, Lady Byron.

S. P. CERASANO

Sources M. Eccles, *Brief lives: Tudor and Stuart authors* (1982), 94 · *DNB* · R. Maud, 'The date of Brian Melbancke's *Philotimus*', *The Library*, 5th ser., 11 (1956), 118–20 · H. Rollins, 'Notes on the source of

Melbancke's *Philotimus'*, *Harvard Studies and Notes in Philology and Literature*, 18 (1935), 177–98 · parish register, Southwark, St Olave [marriage], 3 June 1583 · parish register, Bermondsey, St Mary Magdalene [burial], 20 June 1600 · parish register, Bermondsey, St Mary Magdalene [burial, Sara Baker], 13 Aug 1603

Melbourne. For this title name *see* Lamb, Elizabeth, Viscountess Melbourne (*bap.* 1751, *d.* 1818); Lamb, William, second Viscount Melbourne (1779–1848); Lamb, Frederick James, Baron Beauvale and third Viscount Melbourne (1782–1853).

Melchebourne, Thomas (*d.* 1356), merchant and financier, was a native of Bishop's Lynn, for which he sat in the parliaments of 1319, 1328, 1330, 1336, 1337, and 1340, and of which he was mayor in 1338. Between 1319 and the beginning of the Hundred Years' War he is often mentioned in connection with mercantile or administrative affairs. He exported wheat and cloth to Gascony, and wool to Flanders, and his ships also traded with Norway and carried victuals for the king's forces in Scotland. In 1333 he was collector of customs on wine and wool at Bishop's Lynn.

With the beginning of the war in 1337 Melchebourne had other opportunities, and from this time was described as 'king's merchant'. In 1336 he and his brother were already building a barge with sixty oars for the king at Bishop's Lynn, and in 1337 he was commissioned to make anchors. In 1338 he was collecting wool for the king in Norfolk, and was again a collector of customs at Bishop's Lynn and deputy chief butler. He purveyed victuals for the king's use, and in 1339 was one of those appointed to collect the moiety of wool in Norfolk. He sent ships carrying the king's envoys to Holland and Zeeland, and was empowered in 1341 both to arrest ships illegally exporting corn to Scotland, and to search for wool exported without payment of customs.

The opportunity for Melchebourne's major step into prominence, in connection with Edward III's financial schemes involving wool export and customs duties, came in 1343. On 2 June Melchebourne was elected mayor of the staple of Bruges by the community of English merchants, a position which he held until at least March 1345. On 8 July the king set up the English Company, replacing the aliens who had hitherto played a large part in war finance, with a moderately large group of merchants, who were entrusted with the farming of the customs and subsidies from midsummer 1343 until Michaelmas 1346. In return they were obliged to pay the wardrobe 1000 marks a month, and also to lend the king 10,000 marks per annum—in all 22,000 marks a year, a sum easily obtainable from the normal yield of customs. Later documents show that the leading member of the English Company was William de la Pole (*d.* 1366), but he remained in the background, with Melchebourne as the most prominent representative of the company, and Melchebourne was still present when it was reorganized in 1344 as a smaller group of six members. The company did in fact advance more than £60,000 to the crown between 1343 and 1345, but it was wound up in August 1345. Melchebourne was one of those involved in redeeming the king's small crown in 1343, and Queen Philippa's crown in March 1344, after these had been pledged for loans at Cologne.

For the years 1343–5 Melchebourne had been in an absolutely central position in trade with the Netherlands and in war finance. After the winding-up of the company, apparently because it was unable to make the payments required, Melchebourne appears to have retained royal favour. In 1347 the king granted him and his brother three inns at Calais, and in 1349 he was exporting corn to Norway. He died in 1356, when he owned houses at Stokfysshrowe and Briggegate at Bishop's Lynn and land at Melchbourn and Beccles. His wife's name was Johanna, and he had a son, Peter, who also became a prominent merchant, and a daughter, Alice.

William Melchebourne (*d.* 1360×62?), the brother of Thomas, was also an important merchant of Bishop's Lynn, who was associated with his brother in the business of exporting grain to Norway and wool to the Netherlands, in supplying the royal army's needs for victuals in the north, and as a member of the English Company of 1343. He is also sometimes named independently as carrying out these trading or financial functions. Likewise given the designation of king's merchant, William was appointed weigher of wools in the port of London in 1341, and collector of tunnage at Bishop's Lynn and butler at Boston in 1342. In 1344 he was rewarded for helping to recover the king's great crowns from Flanders, where they had been left as pledges for debts. His brother left him a house in Stokfysshrowe, Bishop's Lynn, for life. William died apparently between December 1360 and May 1362, leaving a widow named Deruegolda and a son, John.

GEORGE HOLMES

Sources *Chancery records* · E. B. Fryde, *Studies in medieval trade and finance* (1983) · E. B. Fryde, *William de la Pole merchant and king's banker, 1366* (1988) · C. Ingleby, ed., *A supplement to Blomefield's Norfolk* (1929) · D. M. Owen, *The making of King's Lynn*, British Academy Records of Social and Economic History, new ser., 9 (1984) · G. Sayles, 'The "English Company" of 1343 and a merchant's oath', *Speculum*, 6 (1931), 177–205 · *CClR, 1360–64*, 405
Archives PRO, Exchequer records

Melchebourne, William (*d.* 1360×62?). *See under* Melchebourne, Thomas (*d.* 1356).

Melchett. For this title name *see under* Mond family (*per.* 1867–1973) [Mond, Alfred Moritz, first Baron Melchett (1868–1930); Mond, Henry Ludwig, second Baron Melchett (1898–1949); Mond, Julian Edward Alfred, third Baron Melchett (1925–1973)].

Melcombe. For this title name *see* Dodington, George Bubb, Baron Melcombe (1690/91–1762).

Meldola, Raphael (1754–1828), rabbi, was born in Leghorn, Italy, the son of Hezekiah Moses Meldola (1725–1791), a professor of oriental languages at the University of Paris. He came from a line of rabbinical scholars taking their family name from Meldola, near Forli, in north-east Italy. The first to attain some prominence was Jacob Meldola in the sixteenth century; a family tradition of earlier

Spanish origins, though not improbable, cannot be proved. Raphael Meldola's paternal grandfather (1684–1748), also named Raphael, was rabbi in Pisa and Bayonne. At Leghorn, Meldola received a secular education, alongside a thorough training in talmudic and wider rabbinic literature. After employment as a preacher he attained rabbinical qualification in 1796, by which date he was married to Stella (Estrella) Bollaffi (d. 1851); they had eight children. He was appointed *dayyan* (a member of the rabbinical court) in 1803. In October 1804 he was invited to become ʿ*hakham* (chief rabbinical authority) of the Sephardic Jews in London, where he worked congenially with his Ashkenazic counterpart, Solomon Hirschell. Although he presumably knew some French, he never mastered English properly and may have preached in Spanish, of which his command was indifferent. Relations with his lay leadership were difficult and sometimes stormy; coming from a large Italian Jewish community, long integrated socially, he probably failed to appreciate the need for a strong lay leadership to steer British Jews towards Anglicization.

Meldola's activity was naturally limited to his own (and the wider) Jewish community. He proved energetic in combating missionary attempts at attracting children of the Jewish poor to a locally established school and addressed himself, on arrival, to securing co-operation with the Ashkenazic community regarding control of the butchery trade in accordance with Jewish religious requirements. The emergence of a joint board for *shehitah*, to implement this, owed much to him. For the re-opening of the Bevis Marks Synagogue in 1825, following its redecoration, he composed a Hebrew hymn which was rendered, innovatively, by a choir—a feature that would later become a regular congregational institution.

Meldola's published legacy included two significant Hebrew texts. The first, a commentary on the entry of the high priest into the holy of holies in the temple, as described in the liturgy for the Day of Atonement, was included in a prayer book published at Leghorn in 1791. His manual regarding marital conduct (ʿ*huppath* ʿ*hatanim*) appeared, likewise at Leghorn, in 1797. Unpublished Hebrew works were said to survive him. Fourteen other pieces have been traced (Barnett, 13–14), mainly special prayers or sermons for national occasions, such as the peace of 1814. He attended Nelson's funeral and subsequently preached a commemorative sermon (which does not survive), as he did in 1817, on the death of Princess Charlotte, which was perhaps the occasion of his being introduced to George III by the archbishop of Canterbury.

During his latter years Meldola suffered from ill health. He died on 1 June 1828 and was buried two days later in the Sephardic Jewish cemetery at Mile End, London; his wife survived him. He cannot be said to have been a national figure, but it is notable that the bells of Aldgate church tolled while his funeral procession passed. Of his sons, David (1797–1853), also a rabbi, was his *de facto* successor, although he did not bear the title ʿ*hakham*. Through his daughter Rebecca, married in 1819 to David de Sola, the

reader (ʿ*hazzan*) in his own synagogue, a number of leading Sephardi families in England, Canada, and the United States were descended from him. RAPHAEL LOEWE

Sources R. D. Barnett, 'Haham Medola and Hazan de Sola', *Transactions of the Jewish Historical Society of England*, 21 (1962–7), 1–38 [incl. list of pubns] · *GM*, 1st ser., 98/2 (1828), 377–8 · *Sunday Herald* (3 June 1828) · A. M. Hyamson, *The Sephardim of England: a history of the Spanish and Portuguese Jewish community, 1492–1951* (1951) · M. Gaster, *History of the ancient synagogue* (1901) · *DNB* · burial register, Spanish and Portuguese Jews' Congregational archives, 2 Ashworth Road, London

Archives Spanish and Portuguese Jews' Congregational archives, 2 Ashworth Road, London, Meldola and de Sola MSS, Mahamad minutes

Likenesses J. Lopez, engraving, 1806 (after F. B. Barlin), repro. in A. Rubens, *Anglo-Jewish portraits* (1935), 70, n. 180 · J. Lopez, stipple, pubd 1806 (after F. B. Barlin), NPG · F. B. Barlin, oils, Spanish and Portuguese Jews' Congregation, London · portrait, repro. in C. Roth, ed., *Encyclopedia Judaica* (1971), vol. 11, p. 1290

Meldola, Raphael (1849–1915), chemist, was born on 19 July 1849 in Islington, London, the only son of Samuel Meldola, printer, and grandson of Raphael *Meldola, formerly chief rabbi to the London Sephardi community. He was educated at private schools in Kew and Maida Vale, and in 1866 entered the Royal College of Chemistry, presided over by Edward Frankland (1825–1899). After two years he received the certificate of the college for proficiency in chemistry. From 1868 until 1871 he was assistant to Dr John Stenhouse, assayer to the Royal Mint. He then entered industrial chemistry at Williams, Thomas and Dower, manufacturer of coal-tar dyestuffs, at Brentford. He left the firm in 1873, and returned to the Royal College of Chemistry, which had recently transferred to South Kensington. Studies on spectrum analysis led to his taking charge of the Royal Society's expedition to the Nicobar Islands to observe the total eclipse of the sun (6 April 1875). At this time he developed a deep interest in photography, which later led to a textbook on the subject (1889) and a series of Cantor lectures before the Society of Arts (1891). In 1877 he joined the laboratories of Brooke, Simpson, and Spiller at the Atlas works, Hackney Wick, another manufacturer of dyestuffs. During this period Meldola discovered the first oxazine dyestuff, Meldola's blue, though it was not manufactured to any extent, if at all, in England, and also the first alkali green, viridine. In 1883 he discovered alkali blue XG, an important cotton dye. Apart from laboratory research, he became familiar with all aspects of the manufacture of dyes, and particularly of the general situation of the industry in England and elsewhere. He left the firm in 1885, amid circumstances that for over thirty years fuelled the debate on why England lost the dye industry to Germany. The reasons put forward included his employer's reluctance to exploit his products or to file patents for them, and a tendency not to reinvest profits in the business. If nothing else, this raised his status as a leading expert in the then important field of dyestuff chemistry.

In 1885 Meldola became professor of chemistry at Finsbury Technical College. He was one of the original fellows

Raphael Meldola (1849–1915), by Solomon Joseph Solomon

of the Institute of Chemistry (founded in 1877) and ultimately became its president (1912–15). On 8 July 1886 he married Ella Frederica, daughter of Maurice Davis, surgeon. In the same year, with a lecture to the Society of Arts, he began to draw attention to the failings of the British dye industry and the general lack of interest in scientific research, and its application, in England. In particular, he held up the example of the BASF company of Ludwigshafen as an example of what science had done for industry and vice versa. In 1886, also, he was elected FRS, although he had no academic degree until 1910, when he delivered the Herbert Spencer lecture at Oxford and the university conferred on him an honorary DSc. In 1911 he received an honorary LLD from St Andrews, and in 1913 the Royal Society awarded him the Davy medal. From about 1870 he began to publish on aspects of natural history, and as secretary of the Entomological Society (1876–80) he became very friendly with Charles Darwin. Meldola himself was much interested in protective colouring and mimicry of moths.

During his first twenty years at Finsbury, Meldola published more than 250 papers and reports, and during his presidency of the Institute of Chemistry he did much work for the development of all aspects of its activities. He was chairman of the executive committee of the events in London that in 1906 marked the jubilee of the discovery of the first aniline dye, mauve, by William H. Perkin. In 1915 he became chairman of the advisory council of British Dyes Ltd. He also served on the advisory council set up under an order in council of 28 July 1915, for the 'organization and development of scientific and industrial research' (forerunner of the Department of Scientific and Industrial Research, 1916). Meldola was by now an ailing and weary man, overcome by excessive worry and work for the growing war effort.

Meldola died suddenly at his home, 6 Brunswick Square, London, on 16 November 1915 and was buried in the Sephardi Jewish cemetery at Hendon. In his prime he was described as a small, trim, wiry figure of somewhat severe appearance, but with a whimsical sense of humour and ready wit. The Meldola medal of the Institute of Chemistry, first awarded in 1921, was named in his honour and sponsored by the Society of Maccabaeans, a Jewish organization of which Meldola was a former president (1911–15). Memorial funds were set up for a reference library of chemical books at Finsbury College (1917).

K. R. WEBB, *rev.* ANTHONY S. TRAVIS

Sources E. B. Poulton, 'Raphael Meldola', *PRS*, 93A (1916–17), xxxii–xxxvii · W. A. Tilden, *JCS*, 111 (1917), 349–53 · J. V. Eyre and E. H. Rodd, 'Raphael Meldola', *British chemists*, ed. A. Findlay and W. H. Mills (1947), 96–125 · J. Marchant, ed., *Raphael Meldola: reminiscences of his worth and work by those who knew him, together with a chronological list of his publications, 1869–1915* (1916) · K. R. Webb, 'Raphael Meldola, 1849–1915', *Chemistry in Britain*, 13 (1977), 345–8 · M. Tordoff, *The servant of colour: a history of the Society of Dyers and Colourists, 1884–1984* (1984) · M. R. Fox, *Dye-makers of Great Britain, 1856–1976: a history of chemists, companies, products, and changes* (1987) · R. Meldola, A. G. Green, and J. C. Cain, eds., *Jubilee of the discovery of mauve and of the foundation of the coal-tar colour industry by Sir W. H. Perkin* (1906) · *Journal of the Society of Dyers and Colourists*, 31 (Dec 1915), 260–62 · *Journal of the Society of Chemical Industry* (30 Nov 1915), 1131 · E. B. Poulton, *Nature*, 96 (1915–16), 347 · d. cert. · m. cert.

Archives ICL, corresp. and notebooks · Newham Heritage Centre, Plaistow, London, MSS · Oxf. U. Mus. NH, Hope Library, notes · Royal Society of Chemistry, London · RS | Deutsches Museum, Munich, Caro Nachlass · Oxf. U. Mus. NH, corresp. with C. R. Darwin [some copies]; corresp. and papers

Likenesses J. Lopez, print, 1906, NPG · group photograph, 1906, Zeneca Archives · portrait, 1907, repro. in Eyre and Rodd, 'Raphael Meldola', facing p. 96 · F. Bowcher, bronze plaque (posthumous), NPG · S. J. Solomon, oils, RS · S. J. Solomon, oils, NPG [*see illus.*] · S. J. Solomon, portrait, Institute of Chemistry · photograph, repro. in Poulton, 'Raphael Meldola', 32 · photograph (after portrait, 1907), repro. in Fox, *Dye-makers of Great Britain*, 142–3

Meldrum, Charles (1821–1901), meteorologist, was born at Kirkmichael, near Tomintoul, Banffshire, on 6 November 1821, the second son of William Meldrum, farmer, and his wife, Isobel McPherson. Educated at Marischal College, Aberdeen, 1840–44, he was lord rector's prizeman and graduated MA (with honours). In 1846 he was appointed to the education department, Bombay, and in 1848 to the Royal College of Mauritius as professor of mathematics. In 1851 he founded the Mauritius Meteorological Society, which he served as secretary for many years. In 1861 Meldrum was appointed government observer, and from 1862 he had charge of the small meteorological observatory at Port Louis. There he continued work he had done for the Meteorological Society, collecting and analysing meteorological observations extracted from the logs of all ships using the harbour. By 1865 he had over 160,000 records.

At that time the relationship between wind and the distribution of atmospheric pressure was only just being clarified in the northern hemisphere. From his outpost Meldrum produced the first recognizably modern weather maps for the Southern Ocean at about the same time as Alexander Buchan in Edinburgh was doing so for the Atlantic. Meldrum determined the frequency and behaviour of cyclones in the Indian Ocean. Thus he confirmed earlier hypotheses that the earth's rotation causes winds around weather systems to flow in opposite directions in the two hemispheres. When sailing ships carried the world's trade and had no communication with the land his work was of immeasurable practical benefit. He also detected the curving low level inflow which leads to the ascent of air, and consequent formation of clouds and rain. Meldrum exploited his remote situation and made a defining contribution to meteorology.

The site at Port Louis was convenient for the harbour but the surrounding hills made it unsuitable for a meteorological observatory. With the support of Sir Edward Sabine, president of the Royal Society in London, and Sir Henry Barkly, governor in Mauritius, Meldrum obtained approval for a new observatory not far from Port Louis, at Pamplemousses—a site he chose on meteorological grounds, but which was struck when fever broke out widely in 1866–7. Meldrum was in Great Britain in 1867–9. He visited Kew observatory and others, refreshed his scientific contacts, was elected a fellow of the British Meteorological Society, and presented a paper on Mauritius rainfall. After returning to Mauritius he married, on 3 February 1870, Charlotte, daughter of Dr Percy FitzPatrick. Three months later Queen Victoria's second son, the duke of Edinburgh, laid the foundation stone of the Royal Alfred Observatory. The new observatory became fully operational in 1875 with Meldrum as superintendent until 1896. The principal work was both meteorological and magnetic. Work continued on rainfall, including its apparent variation during sunspot cycles, and on the behaviour of Indian Ocean storms. In 1876 Meldrum presented a controversial paper to the Royal Society showing similarities in meteorological data and the sunspot cycle; in the same year he was elected a fellow of the society and received an LLD from Aberdeen. Sir Walter Besant, senior professor at the Royal College of Mauritius, 1861–7, described Meldrum as 'a great light in meteorology—he was made a Fellow of the Royal Society, to his infinite gratification' (Besant, 138). Meldrum loved sport, especially riding. During one of his favourite afternoon rides in Mauritius, he fell from his horse and broke a collarbone.

From 1880 the observatory photographed the sun daily to complement records maintained at Greenwich and Dehra Dun, India, of the number of sunspots. In 1886 Meldrum was made CMG. He served on the governor's council from 1886 until his retirement in 1896, when he returned to England in very failing health and settled at Southsea. He died in his eightieth year in his native Scotland, at 21 Colinton Road, Edinburgh, on 28 August 1901. He was buried three days later.   A. R. HINKS, rev. S. G. CORNFORD

Sources W. Besant, *Autobiography of Sir Walter Besant* (1902), 138 · *Yearbook of the Royal Society* (1902), 151–2 · R. H. S., *PRS*, 75A (1905), 151–2 · A. M. Munro, ed., *Records of old Aberdeen*, 2 vols., New Spalding Club, 20, 36 (1899–1909), vol. 1, p. 510 · C. Meldrum, 'A meteorological journal of the Indian Ocean for the month of March 1853', *Contributions to the meteorology and hydrography of the Indian Ocean* (1856) · C. Meldrum, 'Rainfall in Mauritius', *Proceedings of the British Meteorological Society*, 4 (1868), 173 · S. G. Cornford, 'Some early synoptic charts for the Indian Ocean', *Colonial observatories and observations*, ed. J. M. Kenworthy and M. Walker (1997), 177–212 · *Proceedings of the British Meteorological Society*, 4 (1869), 139, 171–93, 203, 214, 283–6, 392–4 · *Proceedings of the British Meteorological Society*, 5 (1871), 16, 54 · C. Meldrum, 'Report on the storm', *Quarterly Journal of the Meteorological Society*, 5 (1879), 222–5 · C. Meldrum, 'On a secular variation in the rainfall in connexion with the secular variation in amount of sun-spots', *PRS*, 24 (1876), 379–87 · council minutes, April–June 1876, RS, MC. 7.165; MC. 8.155 · R. H. Scott, *Cyclone tracks in the south Indian Ocean, from information compiled by Dr Meldrum* (1891) · *The Times* (30 Aug 1901) · election certificate, RS, Sa.856–72 · lists of candidates, 1868–87, RS, MM.17.27 · private information (2004) · E. Michaud, 'Meteorologist's profile – Charles Meldrum', *Weather*, 55 (2000), 15–17

Archives Meteorological Office, Bracknell, Berkshire, National Meteorological Library · RS

Likenesses photograph

Meldrum, George (1634?–1709), Church of Scotland minister and religious controversialist, was the fourth son of Andrew Meldrum, dyer and baillie of the city of Aberdeen. He studied divinity at Marischal College, Aberdeen, and in 1651 graduated MA. His prodigious intellect and undoubted ability as a teacher were quickly recognized, and in 1653 he was appointed as one of the regents, or bursars, of the college. He sat upon the ecclesiastical committee, which investigated irregularities in the administration of the parish of Turriff, Aberdeenshire, from April 1653 to April 1657, and in March 1658 served as the moderator of the synod of Aberdeen. Unanimously elected by the town council, on 1 December 1658, to the ministry of the East parish of Aberdeen, he was ordained on 2 February 1659.

However, Meldrum was deprived of his charge by act of parliament and privy council in October 1662, and retired to the country after being relieved of his pastoral duties by the express order of the bishop of Aberdeen. Unable, in his own words, to distinguish 'the Difference betwixt the State of Things Anno. 1662 and before the 1638', he decided to bide his time and to accept tacitly the return of episcopacy to the church (Wodrow, *Sufferings*, 1.148). Accordingly he appeared before the Scottish privy council on 16 December 1662 and subscribed to the oath of allegiance. Promptly restored to his ministry he distinguished himself through his zeal in combating the influence of both the Quakers and the Jesuits within the parish, and on one occasion was said to have only narrowly escaped assassination at the hands of a Roman Catholic after being called out at night to visit the sick. In his posthumously published pamphlet, *The Danger of Popery Discovered* (1714), Meldrum sought to demonstrate to those 'who have not Money to buy, or time to read larger Books' that Roman Catholicism was deceitful, corrupt and idolatrous, destroying 'faith and truth among Men' (39).

In 1663 Meldrum was elected rector of Marischal College, but he declined the offer of a DD in 1679. In 1681 he was deprived of all of his offices on account of his refusal to take the Scottish Test Act, and 'continued silent till King James Toleration' (Wodrow, *Analecta*, 1.176). Admitted to Kilwinning parish, Ayrshire, before 21 March 1688, he accepted the ministry of the Tron Kirk at Edinburgh on 11 February 1692. Thereafter his rise in the hierarchy of the Church of Scotland was both steady and assured. He was elected as the moderator of the general assembly of the Church of Scotland on 11 January 1698, and accepted the position of professor of divinity at Edinburgh University on 24 December 1701. Unwilling to abandon his charge of the Tron Kirk he initially agreed to serve for only one year but on the appointment of an assistant, who assumed the more onerous and time-consuming aspects of his pastoral work, he consented to accept the appointment upon a permanent basis.

Elected moderator of the general assembly for a second time on 10 March 1703 Meldrum used a sermon preached before the duke of Queensberry on 16 May (later published) as a set piece in which to attack the episcopal wing of the Church of Scotland, which had been gaining ground, and to refute moves aimed at the granting of toleration and the restoration of lay patronage. The impact of the closing words of a sermon, which had otherwise consisted of an unremarkable exposition of Psalm 122: 6 upon peace, was both immediate and electrifying. Meldrum was mercilessly attacked by his adversaries in a paper war between rival pamphleteers who published *A Vindication and Defence of Mr. George Meldrum's Sermon* (1703); *Toleration Defended*, (1703); *Reasonableness of a Toleration to those of Episcopal Perswasion*, (1704); and *Reasonableness of a Toleration, Enquir'd into* (1705). He more than managed to hold his own and did much to unite the core membership of the Church of Scotland around a common system of presbyterian self-government.

Famed for his many charitable bequests and personable demeanour, Meldrum died unmarried at Edinburgh on 18 February 1709 after suffering a succession of strokes.

T. F. HENDERSON, *rev.* JOHN CALLOW

Sources R. Wodrow, *Analecta, or, Materials for a history of remarkable providences, mostly relating to Scotch ministers and Christians*, ed. [M. Leishman], 1, Maitland Club, 60 (1842) · *Fasti Scot.*, new edn, vols. 1, 3, 6–8 · J. Stuart, ed., *Selections from the records of the kirk session, presbytery, and synod of Aberdeen*, Spalding Club, 15 (1846) · [G. Meldrum], *A letter from a friend in the city to a member of parliament anent. patronages* (1703) · R. Wodrow, *The history of the sufferings of the Church of Scotland, from the Restauration to the revolution*, 1 (1721) · A. Bower, *The history of the University of Edinburgh*, 2 (1817), 9–11 · *A letter to a friend, giving an account of of all the treatises that have been publish'd with relation to the present persecution against the Church of Scotland* (1692) · T. Boston, *Memoirs of the life, time, and writings of the reverend and learned Thomas Boston* (1776) · A. M. Munro, ed., *Records of old Aberdeen* (1909), 2. 148 · *A brief examination of some things in Mr. Meldrum's sermon preach'd against a toleration to those of the episcopal perswasion* (1703)
Archives U. Edin., Wodrow's corresp. and papers, Dc 8 1 110; la ii 690, iii 116 263 355 · U. Glas. L., Wodrow's MS collections, incl. Meldrum's own testament about his deposition in 1662, MS Gen 1197–1218

Meldrum, Sir John (*b.* before 1584?, *d.* 1645), parliamentarian army officer, came of obscure Scottish origins. Nothing is known of his parents and all that is known of his date of birth is the statement by an adversary that he was over sixty in the year of his death, a plausible claim in the light of what is known of his early career. In April 1611 he was described as a captain in the Irish army; in 1642 he was to remind the king of his thirty-six years' service to the crown, and of his 'zeal to your majesty's father's service in settling the province of Ulster' (Rushworth, 4.627–8). As a result of his Irish service he was granted lands in co. Fermanagh in 1617. The following year he and Sir William Erskine purchased a monopoly to build and maintain a lighthouse at Winterton Ness on the Norfolk coast, for which they were entitled to levy a penny per ton of cargo on every ship passing; this patent set them at odds both with Trinity House and—for the charges it imposed on the east coast coal trade—with the hostmen of Newcastle and the City of London. The monopoly was complained of to the privy council and in every parliament from 1621 to 1626. Meldrum retained the patent and acquired another for a lighthouse at Orford Ness on the Suffolk coast.

After fighting as a mercenary in the Low Countries, Meldrum returned to England where James I, who evidently liked his fellow Scot, knighted him on 6 August 1622. In 1627 Meldrum was collecting weapons and recruits for the Ré expedition, in which he took part and was generously paid £600 for his services. During the early 1630s Meldrum returned to the continent, in Swedish service under Gustavus Adolphus: in 1632 he was serving in east Prussia as a colonel of foot. By 1635 he was back in England, defending another lighthouse patent, for three lights at the North Foreland and South Foreland to guide ships passing by the Goodwin Sands. A royalist opponent later taunted Meldrum that his desire to protect his monopoly—those 'lights you study to preserve' rather than 'the dazeling lighte of Reformation' had 'misled you out of the way of obedience' and prompted him to become one of the first mercenary officers to side with parliament (*Abergavenny MSS*, 156).

In June 1642 Meldrum commanded a force of 1500 men sent from London to reinforce the arsenal at Hull. Early that month Meldrum explained his choice of allegiance in an open letter to Charles I. He reminded the king of their conversation in Newcastle the previous November, when the veteran of the Thirty Years' War warned of the 'inhuman Butcheries of an intestine war'. Blaming the failure of the king's policies on 'Court parasites', Meldrum begged Charles to heed the advice of parliament. 'I could find no better way to do your majesty a more general service than by stopping the course of the civil war' he concluded, 'as to cast myself into Hull' (Rushworth, 4.627–8). The contradictions of the argument that he was going to war to stop a war may suggest other motivations. The Scottish mercenary may have felt poorly done by. Without mentioning the land in Ireland and the lighthouse monopoly, Meldrum complained that during his thirty-six years of royal service he had incurred debts of £3000.

There was no more vigorous defender of Hull than Sir John Meldrum. In early July at the head of 500 men he ambushed an approaching royalist column of some 3000 under the king's command, driving them back to Beverley. This was 'the first blood', reported a news sheet, 'that was shed in these unnatural wars' (Rushworth, 4.610). A couple of weeks later he led a night attack against the royalists at Anlaby, capturing some fifteen cannon, as well as a 36 lb mortar called 'the Queen's pocket pistol' (which the parliamentarians immediately renamed 'Sweet Lips' after Hull's most celebrated prostitute). It was reported that the king 'was much incensed at the news thereof' (Cooper, 4). Certainly Meldrum's vigorous defence of Hull persuaded Charles to lift the siege.

After helping Sir William Waller capture Portsmouth in September 1642, Meldrum commanded an infantry brigade on the parliamentarian right at the battle of Edgehill on 23 October. Lord Saye, who had raised most of the troops from his north Oxfordshire estates, had sense enough to let the Scots veteran lead them. One regiment panicked, but the other two stood their ground and acquitted themselves with credit. After the battle Meldrum was one of six parliamentarian officers who sent John Pym a report of the battle, which was published five days later on 28 October (*An Exact and True Relation of the Dangerous and Bloody Fight*, 1642).

During 1643 parliament employed Meldrum, who had gained the reputation as 'a Scot of good capacity', as a trouble-shooter in the midlands (*CSP Venice*, 1642–3, 292). In June he arrested Captain John Hotham, his old commander from Hull, for treachery. In October he reinforced the besieged garrison at Hull with 400 men, and as a result of the sally he led on 9 October, in which he was wounded, forced the royalists to lift the siege. He took part in the capture of Gainsborough in December 1643, and expelled the royalists from the Isle of Axholme the following February.

After laying siege to the important garrison of Newark in late February 1644, Meldrum complained to his good friend Colonel John Hutchinson 'of the envyings, heart-burnings and dissensions' of his officers. Recruited from several counties, the garrison would not co-operate. 'It galled the poor old gentleman to the heart', recalled the colonel's wife, Lucy Hutchinson, 'who having commanded abroad, and been used to deal with officers that understood the discipline of war, was confounded among those who knew not to obey any orders' (Hutchinson, 173). On 22 March 1644 Meldrum was forced to surrender Newark to Prince Rupert's relieving force and give up a large quantity of arms: eleven brass cannon, two mortars (including 'Sweet Lips'), fifty barrels of gunpowder, and 4000 muskets. Although the royalists had agreed to let Meldrum's troops march away with colours flying, they plundered the troops to their shirts, 'and sent many captains quite naked away' (ibid., 177). The surrender had a tremendous effect on the morale of both sides. 'Even the most zealous were cast down and gave up all for lost', remembered the parliamentarian Lucy Hutchinson. Edward Hyde the royalist historian crowed that Meldrum's capitulation was 'a victory as prodigious as any happened throughout the war' (ibid.; Clarendon, *Hist. rebellion*, 3.327).

Over the next eight months Meldrum learned much from his defeat, admitting in November 1644 that 'I have passed an apprenticeship' (*CSP dom.*, 1644–5, 129). He now thought of the royalists as 'This potent and vigilant enemy, which is now … wasting and spoiling'. He recognized that Prince Rupert was their most dangerous leader, telling the committee of both kingdoms in August that he would follow up his victory at Ormskirk, 'If Prince Rupert does not enter upon the stage and interrupt the game' (ibid., 1644, 180, 442). On 9 September he and Sir William Brereton captured Montgomery Castle, killing 500 royalists and taking 1200 prisoners. At the end of the month Meldrum started the siege of Liverpool. 'The enemy is stronger in the town', he reported, 'than we are without, beside the advantage of very strong works' (ibid., 1644, 543–4). Yet by 1 November he persuaded the garrison to surrender, granting clemency to the Irish troops, whom he paroled home.

The following February, Meldrum besieged Scarborough, the royalist stronghold on the north Yorkshire coast, which was defended by Sir Hugh Cholmley. Meldrum bombarded the castle with a 57 lb cannon and two 27-pounders. He nearly died when he fell down a 200 foot cliff, but was saved by his cloak, which acted as a parachute. 'Yet hee is taken up for dead', Cholmley admiringly recorded:

> lyes 3 dayes speachless, his head opened and the bruised blood taken out [i.e. he was trepanned], though a Man above three score yeare old, recovered thus soe perfectlie that within six weekes hee is on foote againe, and begins to batter the Castle. (*Memoirs and Memorials*, 156)

Soon afterwards he suffered a 'shot through the Codds' (ibid., 158) which so discouraged him that the committee of both kingdoms wrote saying how much they appreciated his fine service, and that the House of Commons had voted him £1500. Leading an assault on the castle on 11 May, Meldrum was shot in the stomach. Cholmley is probably wrong in asserting that he 'dyed with in six dayes of this wound' (ibid.), as the date on the preserved copy of his will, 24 May, suggests an even more horribly prolonged death. By it he appointed his nephew Robert Meldrum executor, the only kin named, though the will alluded to legacies which Robert was to pay. The will proclaimed Meldrum's commitment to the parliamentarian cause:

> since theis unhappie troubles began, God is my witnes I have denied myselfe and all private ends, and followed the publicke cause with a single hearte and unwearied spirite, and am nowe readie to give up my life in a willinge sacrifice for the honour of God and welfare of these Kingdomes.

However, he was hard-headed enough to remember orders made by the Commons for his arrears of pay, 'which I have not yet receaved' and 'for the establishing in my Person the Pattent of Goodwin Lights, which is a necessarie service for the good of the Navigation' (will, PRO, PROB 11/200, fol. 494r). He was buried with full military honours on 4 June at the church of the Holy Trinity, Hull. His death so demoralized the troops that they ceased offensive operations, starving the royalists into surrender on 21 July 1645.

Had Meldrum lived he might have gone on to become

one of the parliament's leading generals, who as a Scot in English employ might have helped deal with the covenanters. As it was, Meldrum was a fine soldier who learned from his mistakes. He had a firm understanding of his profession and of European affairs, and a sincere reluctance to take up arms against his sovereign. He alerted parliament to the dangers of getting bogged down in sieges which could 'rather forment than finish a war', and urged them to treat their troops fairly, since such will be 'to the advancement of the public service' (*CSP dom.*, 1644, 91, 523–4). Historians have assessed Meldrum positively. S. R. Gardiner described Meldrum as 'A Scottish Officer of tried ability and character' (Gardiner, 1.190). J. P. Kenyon thought him to be 'one of Parliament's most enterprising and successful generals' (Kenyon, 45). The last word, however, must go to his fatal adversary, Sir Hugh Cholmley, who called him 'a bold Scot' (Rushworth, 4.627).

CHARLES CARLTON

Sources *CSP dom., 1618–45* · J. Rushworth, *Historical collections*, 5 pts in 8 vols. (1659–1701) · L. Hutchinson, *Memoirs of the life of Colonel Hutchinson*, ed. J. Sutherland (1973) · Clarendon, *Hist. rebellion* · S. R. Gardiner, *History of the great civil war, 1642–1649*, new edn, 4 vols. (1893) · J. P. Kenyon, *The civil wars of England* (1988) · *CSP Venice, 1618–45* · *Munro: his expedition with that worthy Scots regiment called MacKeys*, ed. W. E. Brockington (1999) · A. Cooper, *A speedy post with more news from Hull* (1642) · *An exact and true relation of the dangerous and bloody fight* (1642) · J. Binns, *A place of great importance: Scarborough in the civil wars, 1640–60* (1990) · J. Sykes, 'Extracts from the registers of the church of holy trinity, Hull', *The Yorkshire Archaeological Journal*, 14 (1898), 185–219 · will, PRO, PROB 11/200, sig. 125, fol. 494r and v · *The memoirs and memorials of Sir Hugh Cholmley of Whitby, 1600–1657*, ed. J. Binns, Yorkshire Archaeological Society, 153 (2000) · W. Notestein, F. H. Relf, and H. Simpson, eds., *Commons debates, 1621*, 7 (1935) · *The manuscripts of the marquess of Abergavenny, Lord Braye*, G. F. Luttrell, HMC, 15 (1887)
Archives Suffolk RO, Ipswich, corresp. with the bailiffs of Ipswich
Likenesses line engraving, BM, NPG; repro. in J. Ricraft, *A survey of England's champions and faiths truthful patriots* (1647)

Meldrum, Thomas (*c*.1605–1693), army officer in the Danish service, was born in Scotland about 1605. There is very little information on his early life and indeed confusion surrounds his early military career. Danish archival sources refer to a Thomas Meldrum in service at a time when Denmark was involved in the Thirty Years' War (1625–9). However, there is disagreement about his rank and the regiment in which he served. A Thomas Meldrum joined the Sjælland knight's regiment on 1 August 1627 as a private and departed from Danish–Norwegian service on 12 June 1628 (Lind database). There was also a Captain Thomas Meldrum in command of a company of the Sjælland national foot by February 1628, who departed from Danish service in June 1629 (Riis, 2.115). It is not implausible that these are the same man, given the chaotic state of the Danish army during this period.

In 1629 Denmark–Norway signed the treaty of Lübeck and withdrew from the war against the Habsburg empire. Many Scottish officers and soldiers then transferred from the army of Christian IV to serve in the Swedish army of Gustav II Adolf. It appears that Thomas Meldrum was one of these men. Certainly a Captain Thomas Meldrum

fought for the Swedish army in Germany as a member of Alexander Cunningham's Scottish infantry regiment in 1632. This is the same man who re-enlisted into Danish service for their wars against Sweden between 1657 and 1660.

From this point on, Meldrum's military service can be traced more easily. He re-entered the Danish service from that of Brandenburg in January 1657. Meldrum initially served as a captain in the infantry regiment of the Scot Major-General John Henderson. He did not stay with the unit long, which allowed him to avoid capture when Henderson surrendered the garrison of Hindsgavl in January 1658. Meldrum temporarily became a dragoon captain in October 1657, departing from his usual capacity as an infantry officer. He later returned to foot service when he served as a captain of the students' regiment during the siege of Copenhagen in April 1658. Meldrum served as a captain in Krag's infantry regiment in 1659 and remained an infantry captain until 1663. Some time after 1670 he gained his promotion to lieutenant-colonel of infantry stationed in Copenhagen.

War broke out between Denmark–Norway and Sweden in 1675 as the Danes sought to recover their former territories east of the Sound. The treaty of Copenhagen had ceded these to the Swedes in 1660. Meldrum took an active part in the Danish campaign and earned the titles commander and full colonel at the battle of Lund. By 1677 he was vice-commander of the newly captured Swedish town of Landskrona, and later military governor of the castle. It was from this strategic position commanded by Meldrum that Christian V conducted his devastating campaign against Swedish Skåne. Yet despite Danish success in the campaign the French brokered the peace of Lund in 1679, which ensured that Sweden retained the former Danish provinces. Thereafter Meldrum returned to Denmark, where he remained on active military service. In 1684 he was promoted brigadier. Thomas Meldrum died with the rank of general in 1693, aged about 88. In a career which spanned nearly sixty years he had risen from a common soldier to a respected commander.

STEVE MURDOCH

Sources J. C. W. Hirsch and K. Hirsch, eds., 'Fortegnelse øver Dansu ou Norske officerer med flere fra 1648 til 1814', 12 vols., unpublished MS, 1888–1907, Rigsarkivet, Copenhagen, vol. 2 · G. Lind, *Danish officers, 1614–1662* [computer database, Danish data archives 1573] · military muster rolls, Krigsarkivet, Stockholm, 1632/30 · T. Riis, *Should auld acquaintance be forgot … Scottish–Danish relations, c.1450–1707*, 2 (1988), 92, 115 · Copenhagen Rigsarkivet, Kanc B 150, fol. 116r, no 115

Melfort. For this title name *see* Drummond, John, styled first earl of Melfort and Jacobite first duke of Melfort (1649–1714).

Melhuish, Sara (1861–1939), educationist, was born on 28 April 1861 at Oxton, Cheshire, the daughter of Charles Melhuish (*d*. before 1891), general merchant, and his wife, Emily Martha Hull. Little is known of her early life until 1885, when she appeared as a day student at University College, Liverpool, residing in Birkenhead. She was an excellent student, earning a scholarship and a first-class honours degree in history in 1890 from the Victoria University, of which University College, Liverpool, was a constituent school. Upon graduation she received the Charles Beard fellowship, enabling her to remain at the college as an assistant to the professor of history from 1890 to 1891. She was granted an MA degree from the Victoria University in 1905. In 1891 she received a scholarship to attend Somerville College, Oxford, where, after only one year of reading, she received second-class honours in the second public examination of the school of modern history.

Sara Melhuish had extremely varied experiences as a teacher. From 1892 to 1895 she remained at Somerville as a lecturer and tutor in history. From 1895 to 1900 she was principal of the Mount Vale School, a private school in York. For the next four years she served as head of College Hall, the residence for women students attached to University College, London. In order to improve her knowledge of pedagogy she spent a term at the Maria Grey Training College in London and acted as a supervisor of teaching practice at the London Day Training College. She also taught in a county council school in Essex and as an occasional teacher in elementary and continuation schools. During this period she earned the London postgraduate teacher's diploma.

In 1907 Sara Melhuish returned to Liverpool, taking a post as lecturer in education and tutor to women students in the university's training college. She was responsible for the training of both elementary and secondary school teachers, for the organization and supervision of the practical work of all the women students and of some of the men students, and for lecturing on the history of education and principles of teaching. She also served as an examiner in education for the undergraduate degree and for the postgraduate diploma, and was a member of the faculty of arts, the training college board, the philosophy and education board, and other university committees. She even found time to teach a history form at Liverpool high school. Her colleagues praised her knowledge of the interrelationship of theory and practice, her familiarity with many types of schools, including elementary schools and their relationship with secondary schools, and her skill in maintaining relations with other university departments and with outside authorities such as heads of schools and local officials.

In 1910 Sara Melhuish took a position as head of the training department at Bedford College, University of London. The Bedford College training department, which had been founded in 1891, was a leading centre for training women graduates to be secondary school teachers. Supported by Department of Education grants, the department reached its height during Melhuish's tenure, with sixty students and a staff of four specialists. Melhuish was appointed university reader in education in 1915. A colleague recalled the Oxford-educated Melhuish's high standards:

Miss Melhuish demanded of the students under her a standard of academic and professional excellence to which not all could attain, but which gave to the department a quality of its own in keeping with its position as belonging to a school of the university. (Tuke, 260)

The training department, renamed the department of education in 1920, began to decline in the latter years of the First World War, and was closed for financial reasons in 1922, the year in which Melhuish retired. In 1930 she was appointed a governor of Bedford College. She died from a coronary thrombosis in German Street, Winchelsea, Sussex, on 23 October 1939 and was buried at Conduit Hill, Rye, Sussex, on 25 October.

Sara Melhuish was a well-respected proponent and practitioner of teacher education, as was shown in 1920 by her being given the opportunity to visit 'People's High Schools and rural technical schools for girls and young women' in Denmark with the intention of possibly applying their methods to elementary schools in Britain. She was also something of a scholar, or at least an interpreter of historical scholarship. During the First World War she did part-time work in the historical section of the Foreign Office. She was the author of *English History Illustrated from Original Sources from the Earliest Times* (1911), part of A. C. Black's School History series, and was a contributor to the Victoria county history on the ecclesiastical history of Lincolnshire. FERNANDA HELEN PERRONE

Sources *Somerville College register, 1879–1971* [1972] · b. cert. · d. cert. · S. Melhuish staff file, Royal Holloway College, Egham, Surrey, archives, AR150/D143 · old students association report, 1940, Royal Holloway College, Egham, Surrey, archives AS/903/3/3 · M. J. Tuke, *A history of Bedford College for Women, 1849–1937* (1939) · day student address book, 1885–90, U. Lpool L., special collections and archives · J. B. Thomas, 'The day training college', *British Journal of Teacher Education*, 4 (1978), 249–61
Archives Royal Holloway College, Egham, Surrey, staff files
Wealth at death £3049 6s. 10d.: probate, 11 Jan 1940, CGPLA Eng. & Wales

Melia, Pius (1800–1883), Roman Catholic priest, was born in Rome and joined the Society of Jesus at the age of sixteen. He became professor of literature at the Jesuit college in Rome, and afterwards served as a missionary priest in Corsica, Tuscany, and elsewhere. In 1848, when the society was dispersed, he went to England at the invitation of Cardinal Wiseman to minister to immigrant Italians and to act as confessor to the cardinal. He became a naturalized British subject on 13 September 1849.

After officiating at Lincoln's Inn, Melia was in charge of the mission at Hastings and St Leonards from 1850 to 1853. He then moved to Walthamstow, where he was missioner from 1855 to 1861, residing at 14 Gray's Inn Square, where he lived for the rest of his life. About 1853 he was appointed almoner to the Italian Benevolent Society, a post which he held until his death. He was Wiseman's private chaplain until the cardinal's death in 1865, after which he continued to preach the Sunday morning sermons at Brentwood, Essex.

Melia was closely associated with the Pallottini Fathers, in which society his brother Raphael Melia (b. 1804) served as rector-general from 1856 to 1862 and again from 1869. The Pallottines (known from 1854 to 1947 as the Pious Society of Missions) were founded in 1835 and were devoted to the spiritual welfare of Catholic emigrants, particularly from Italy. The society had gone to London in 1844, founding the Italian church of St Peter at Hatton Garden. Pius Melia helped to collect money for the building of the church, and regularly preached in Italian there. In 1863 he bought an action against the builder's solicitor, Neate, for false imprisonment; the builder, claiming that he had not been fully paid for his work, had had Melia imprisoned on the grounds that he was about to travel abroad.

In the late 1860s Melia spent some time in Italy. He read a laudatory article on the Waldensian sect in the *Daily Telegraph* in April 1868, which provoked him to write *The Origin, Persecution, and Doctrines of the Waldenses* (1870). Based on original documents which Melia had read in Roman libraries, the king's library at Turin, and elsewhere, it was a scholarly work which was 'regarded by competent judges as the standard work on the subject' (*Annual Register*). He also published *Doctrines of St Thomas Aquinas on the Rulers and Members of Christian States* (1860) and *Hints and Facts on the Origin of Man* (1872).

Melia died on 25 May 1883, after an operation, at the University College Hospital, London, and was buried at Kensal Green cemetery on 30 May.   ROSEMARY MITCHELL

Sources Gillow, *Lit. biog. hist.* · Boase, *Mod. Eng. biog.* · *The Tablet* (2 June 1883), 873 · *The Times* (1 June 1883) · *Annual Register* (1883), pt 2, p. 152 · C. Fitzgerald-Lombard, *English and Welsh priests, 1801–1914* (1993) · *DNB*

Wealth at death £73: probate, 9 June 1883, *CGPLA Eng. & Wales*

Meliton, William of. *See* Milton, William of (*d.* 1257x60).

Mell, Davis (1604–1662), violinist and clockmaker, was born on 15 November 1604 at Wilton near Salisbury, where his father, Leonard Mell (*d.* 1641), was in the employ of William Herbert, third earl of Pembroke. Although not appointed to a place in the court musical establishment until late in 1626, Mell was apparently associated with the violins at least since May of the preceding year (when he received livery for the funeral of James I). He was heavily involved with the inns of court masque *The Triumph of Peace* (1634): he not only played with the violin band for the performances but also composed some of the antimasque dances and accompanied the masquers' rehearsals.

When the court music was disbanded in 1642, Mell remained in London earning a living from teaching and playing. Playford listed him in *A Musicall Banquet* (1651) among the 'excellent and able Masters … For the Voyce or Viole'. Mell was one of the five musicians employed by Cromwell from *c.*1654. Early in 1657 these five petitioned Cromwell to re-establish a Musicians' Company as a way of trying to offset the damage to the profession caused by the breakup of court and ecclesiastical musical establishments. Mell walked in Cromwell's funeral procession.

At the Restoration, Mell took up his old place in the court violins and was appointed to a place in the private music. In May 1661 (less than a year before his death) he was given joint authority (with George Hudson) over the violins.

All the accounts of Mell's violin playing suggest that he was a fine musician. Lodewijck Huygens recorded in his

journal for March 1652 that he played 'admirably well'. Four months later, on 1 August, John Evelyn described Mell in his diary as a 'rare musician'. Anthony Wood, who heard him in Oxford in March 1658, reported that 'The Company did look upon Mr Mell to have a prodigious hand on the violin, and they thought that no person, as all London did, could goe beyond him' (*Life and Times*, 1.242). This group were to revise their notions of Mell's supremacy when, just four months later, they first heard Thomas Baltzar's technical virtuosity. Even then, however, Mell's playing was judged 'farr sweeter than Baltsar' (ibid.).

Mell's compositions are well represented in John Playford's publications, especially *Courtly Masquing Ayres* (1662), which contains a total of fifty-four dances grouped by key into suites, and *The Division Violin* (1684). Oxford, Christ Church, MS 433 is an autograph manuscript containing versions of the violin suites without an accompanying bass line. In comparison with other English violin compositions of the period, at least, they show quite a sophisticated technique.

Presumably because of the precariousness of the music profession during the Commonwealth, Mell developed an alternative career as a clockmaker. The first mention of his horological skills occurs in Samuel Hartlib's 'Ephemerides' of 1649:

> Mr Mell one of the king's Musitians very excellent in his Art and of a very inventive genius. Hee hath made a most admirable Clocke of 50 lb. or more price which should bee sent for a present to some king in the Indies.

Mell was admitted as a free brother to the Clockmakers' Company in 1655 and four years later was made an assistant of the company (a status which implied some responsibility for the governance of the guild). According to Aubrey (*Miscellanies*, 1696), Mell 'made a great name for the goodness of his work', and the few surviving examples of his work (including one with statuettes of musicians revolving in a little gallery above the clock face) seem to be beautifully made. After the Restoration, when Mell was once again fully occupied as a musician, he apparently abandoned clockmaking. He no longer attended company meetings, and in 1661 his one remaining apprentice was transferred to another maker.

Mell married Alice Comey on 30 April 1635, and their first daughter, Dorothy, was born exactly nine months later (she appears not to have survived beyond infancy). A son, Richard, born in 1637, died at the age of three. But two daughters, Abigail and Elizabeth (*b.* 1641), reached adulthood and were named as executors of Mell's will, written in 1662, which provides for a second wife, Ann (*née* Allen). Mell died on 27 April 1662.   PETER WALLS

Sources A. Ashbee, ed., *Records of English court music*, 9 vols. (1986–96) · A. Ashbee and D. Lasocki, eds., *A biographical dictionary of English court musicians, 1485–1714*, 2 vols. (1998) · B. Bellingham, 'The musical circle of Anthony Wood in Oxford during the Commonwealth and Restoration', *Journal of the Viola da Gamba Society of America*, 19 (1982), 6–70 · F. J. Britten, *Old clocks and watches and their makers*, 5th edn (1932) · G. Dodd, *Thematic index of music for viols* (1980–92) · Evelyn, *Diary* · M. P. Fernandez and P. C. Fernandez, 'Davis

Mell, musician and clockmaker and an analysis of the clockmaking trade in 17th-century London', *Antiquarian Horology and the Proceedings of the Antiquarian Horological Society*, 16 (1986–7), 602–17 · P. Holman, *Four and twenty fiddlers: the violin at the English court, 1540–1690* (1993) · *Lodewijck Huygens: the English journal, 1651–1652*, ed. A. G. M. Babrach and R. G. Collmer (Leiden, 1982) · F. Madan and others, *A summary catalogue of Western manuscripts in the Bodleian Library at Oxford*, 7 vols. (1895–1953) · J. D. Shute, 'Anthony A Wood and his manuscript Wood D 19 (4) at the Bodleian Library, Oxford: an annotated transcription', PhD diss., International Institute of Advanced Musical Studies, Clayton, Missouri, 1979 · I. Spink, ed., *The seventeenth century* (1992) · P. Walls, *Music in the English courtly masque, 1604–1640* (1996) · *The life and times of Anthony Wood*, ed. A. Clark, 5 vols., OHS, 19, 21, 26, 30, 40 (1891–1900) · will, PRO, PROB 11/308, sig. 68

Likenesses attrib. J. B. Medina, group portrait (*The Cabal*), Nostell Priory, Yorkshire

Wealth at death see will, PRO, PROB 11/308, sig. 68

Mellanby, Sir Edward (1884–1955), medical scientist and administrator, was born at West Hartlepool, co. Durham, on 8 April 1884, the youngest of the four sons and six children of John Mellanby, manager of the shipyard of the Furness-Withy Company, and his wife, Mary Isabella Lawson. Elder brothers were John *Mellanby (1878–1939), the physiologist, and Alexander Lawson Mellanby (1871–1951), who became professor of civil and mechanical engineering at the Royal Technical College, Glasgow. From Barnard Castle School, where he was head boy and captain of cricket and football, Mellanby gained an exhibition to Emmanuel College, Cambridge. Having been placed in the second class in part I of the natural sciences tripos (1904), and the first class with physiology as his special study in part II (1905), he obtained a research studentship at Emmanuel, which he held until 1907, working under the guidance of Frederick Gowland Hopkins, his former tutor, whose influence largely determined the rest of Mellanby's career. He completed his medical studies at St Thomas's Hospital, London, where between 1909 and 1911 he was a demonstrator in physiology, and during 1910–12 held a Beit memorial fellowship for medical research. In 1913 he became a lecturer in and later professor of physiology at King's College for Women, London, where he remained until 1920. He maintained a distinguished association with Cambridge, where he graduated MD in 1915 and was awarded the Walsingham medal (1907) and the Gedge (1908) and Raymond Horton-Smith (1915) prizes.

In 1914 Mellanby married May Tweedy, who had been a fellow student at Cambridge, and was herself engaged in physiological research at Bedford College, London; they had no children.

The research work for which Mellanby was perhaps best known was his investigation of rickets, begun in 1914 at the request of the Medical Research Committee. His first major publication on the subject was 'An experimental investigation on rickets' (*Lancet*, 196, 15 March 1919, 407–12). Mellanby established that the main cause of the disease was deficiency of a fat-soluble vitamin, which came to be known as vitamin D. At a later stage he demonstrated the rachitogenic action of certain cereals. His researches,

however, extended over a wide range and he was recognized as an outstanding expert in the biochemical and physiological field.

Mellanby was appointed in 1920 to the newly founded chair of pharmacology at the University of Sheffield and as honorary physician to the Royal Infirmary. In 1931 he was appointed chairman of an international conference for the standardization of vitamins. In 1933 he succeeded Walter Fletcher as secretary of the Medical Research Council, having been a member of the council for two years; and shortly after this appointment he accepted the Fullerian professorship of the Royal Institution (1936–7). He was also the chairman of the international technical commission on nutrition in 1934, and in the same year published *Nutrition and Disease: the Interaction of Clinical and Experimental Work*. Before and during the Second World War he was involved in schemes concerning wartime diet, as well as the welfare of service personnel and civilians, and was chairman of the royal naval and the flying personnel research committees, a member of a similar committee relating to the army, a member of the scientific advisory committee of the cabinet, and chairman of the colonial medical research committee. The Medical Research Council, under Mellanby's direction, and the Ministry of Health were jointly responsible in 1939 for the setting up of an Emergency Public Health Laboratory Service, which after the war became the Public Health Laboratory Service. He retired from the Medical Research Council in 1949. The previous year the new Institute for Medical Research, with the planning of which Mellanby had been closely concerned, opened at Mill Hill, London.

Mellanby was appointed KCB in 1937 and GBE in 1948 and received a number of foreign decorations. From 1937 to 1941 he was an honorary physician to George VI. He was elected FRS in 1925, FRCP in 1928, and honorary FRCS Edinburgh in 1946. In 1935 he and his wife were jointly awarded the Charles Mickle fellowship of Toronto University.

Among Mellanby's other awards were the Royal and Buchanan medals from the Royal Society and the Bissett-Hawkins, Moxon, and Baly medals from the Royal College of Physicians; the Halley-Stewart prize for medical research from the British Medical Association; and the Cameron prize from Edinburgh University. He was elected an honorary fellow of Emmanuel College, Cambridge (1946), and received honorary degrees from a number of universities. He gave many special lectures on medical and scientific subjects, including the Croonian lecture of the Royal Society; the Oliver Sharpey and Croonian lectures and the Harveian oration of the Royal College of Physicians; the Linacre and Rede lectures of Cambridge University, published as *Recent Advances in Medical Science: a Study of their Social and Economic Implications* (1939); the Ludwig Mond lecture (Manchester University); a special bicentenary lecture at the Royal College of Surgeons; and the Robert Boyle, Stephen Paget, and Hopkins memorial lectures. In 1947 he held the Abraham Flexner lectureship at Vanderbilt University, Nashville, Tennessee, which involved a period of three months' residence in Nashville.

During the last year or two of his secretaryship of the Medical Research Council, Mellanby attended meetings abroad on behalf of the British government and the Colonial Office and at the invitation of the South African Council of Scientific and Industrial Research. After his retirement he undertook two further advisory missions, the first to India (where he played a significant part in the establishment of the Central Drug Research Institute at Lucknow and was its first director for a few months in 1950–51) and the second to Australia and New Zealand. For the most part, however, he spent his retirement at work in his laboratory at Mill Hill and it was there that he died, quietly and unexpectedly, on 30 January 1955.

Mellanby was tall and handsome, friendly and unaffected, with a great sense of fun and a certain boyishness. To those who did not know him well, his more endearing personal qualities were sometimes masked by his brusque, forthright manner; generally, however, this was due to a wish to stimulate argument and, if his help was being sought, to find out what was in the mind of his inquirer, so that he could advise to the best of his ability.

Mellanby's wife, **May Mellanby**, Lady Mellanby (1882–1978), physiologist, was born in London, the eldest daughter of George Tweedy, a businessman, and his wife, Rosa. She spent part of her childhood in Russia, where her father was involved in the development of the oil industry and, after being educated at Hampstead and Bromley high schools, went up to Girton College, Cambridge in 1902. She sat both parts of the natural sciences tripos in 1905 and 1906, achieving the equivalent of a second-class degree. Appointed a research fellow and then a lecturer at Bedford College for Women, London University, she held the latter post until her marriage in 1914.

While at Bedford College, May worked with her future brother-in-law J. S. Edkins on gastric secretion. Following her marriage, she collaborated with her husband on a range of nutritional studies, but also developed her own research on the nutritional influences on dental development which was carried out for the Medical Research Committee and its successor body, the Medical Research Council. May published a number of research papers, which were summarized in a chapter of her husband's *Nutrition and Disease* (1934), as well as three Special Reports for the MRC (1929, 1930, 1934). She was awarded the honorary degree of DSc by the universities of Sheffield (1933) and Liverpool (1934) and was elected to the Physiological Society in 1956. She died in London on 5 March 1978.

B. S. PLATT, *rev.* MICHAEL BEVAN

Sources H. H. Dale, *Memoirs FRS*, 1 (1955), 193–222 · *BMJ* (5 Feb 1955), 355–8 · *BMJ* (12 Feb 1955), 421–2 · *Annual Review of Biochemistry*, 25 (1956), prefatory chapter · private information (1971) · personal knowledge (1971) · L. Bindman, A. Brading, and T. Tansey, eds., *Women physiologists: an anniversary celebration of their contributions to British physiology* (1993) · WWW · *CGPLA Eng. & Wales* (1955)
Archives RS · Wellcome L., corresp. and papers | CAC Cam., corresp. with A. V. Hill · Nuffield Oxf., corresp. with Lord Cherwell · PRO, corresp. with Sir Henry Dale, CAB127/216 · RCS Eng., corresp. with Lord Webb-Johnson · University of Sheffield Library, corresp. with Hans Krebs
Likenesses Elliott & Fry, photograph, 1927, repro. in Dale, *Memoirs FRS* · W. Stoneman, photograph, 1931, NPG · H. A. Freeth, chalk drawing, 1946, IWM · J. Gunn, portrait; in family possession, 1971
Wealth at death £46,122 10s. 3d.: probate, 2 May 1955, *CGPLA Eng. & Wales* · £184,213—May Mellanby: probate, 30 May 1978, *CGPLA Eng. & Wales*

Mellanby, John (1878–1939), physiologist, was born at West Hartlepool on 12 June 1878, the second of the four sons (there were six children) of John Mellanby, manager of a shipbuilding yard at West Hartlepool, and his wife, Mary Isabella Lawson, of Edinburgh. Sir Edward *Mellanby, also a physiologist, was his brother. From Barnard Castle School he won a scholarship at Emmanuel College, Cambridge, in 1896; he was placed in the first class in both parts of the natural sciences tripos (1899 and 1900, physiology). In 1902, after a year's postgraduate work, he was put in charge of the new research laboratories of Burroughs Wellcome at Brockwell Park, Herne Hill, London. After three years he went to Manchester in order to do the clinical work for the medical degree; he took his MD (Cantab.) in 1907.

Mellanby then worked as a G. H. Lewes research student at Cambridge until in 1909 he was appointed lecturer in charge of the physiological department at St Thomas's Hospital medical school, a post which became a professorship in the University of London in 1920; there he stayed until he was appointed Waynflete professor of physiology in the University of Oxford in 1936, becoming a fellow of Magdalen College. In 1911 he married Alice Mary, daughter of Joseph Watson, solicitor, of Barrhead; they had a daughter.

Mellanby's work is contained in some sixty papers, mostly in the *Journal of Physiology* and the *Proceedings of the Royal Society*. The most important deal with the proteins of the blood, coagulation, and the secretion of the pancreas. His duties at Brockwell Park, connected with the preparation of diphtheria antitoxin, provided him with ample supplies of horses' blood and while there he laid the foundation of work to which he returned again and again throughout his life.

In Mellanby's first paper, on globulin (1905), he demonstrated a number of important points. First, he showed that in the solution of globulin by electrolytes bivalent ions are four times as efficient as univalent; and secondly, that the conductivity due to the ions is not diminished by the presence of the globulin. His third point was that the long-current belief that globulin could be separated from albumin by fractional precipitation with neutral sulphates was mistaken: much more albumin than globulin is thrown down in serum by half saturation, for instance, with ammonium sulphate and also at lower concentrations. Finally, he showed that some 80 per cent of the protein in serum is compounded with un-ionized salts; for if serum was frozen in a long vertical tube, then thawed and removed in a number of layers, each layer contained more solids than the layer next above it, protein and salts in the same proportion, the lowest perhaps ten times as much as the uppermost. If the protein was coagulated and removed, the conductivity at the original temperature increased in proportion to the amount of protein removed.

In work on coagulation Mellanby devised a method for isolating prothrombase, finally (1930) as a dry white powder that could be kept and retain its properties for months; and by a related method obtained refined preparations of thrombase (1933). With these purified products the study of coagulation was put on a surer basis, as his own work showed.

In work on the pancreas Mellanby showed that the curdling of milk in the stomach is due to pepsin, thus explaining the secretion of 'rennet' by fish, and that the curdling by pancreatic juice is due to trypsin. As this action on milk can be demonstrated with far smaller amounts of trypsin than any other action on proteins, he used it for a delicate method of estimating the amount of trypsin, which has proved valuable. He also added to exact knowledge of the other enzymes secreted by the pancreas. He corrected many errors in the original description of secretin's properties, formation, and mode of action, and especially showed that the secretion which it induced consisted of little more than an alkaline fluid, the appropriate medium for the action of the pancreatic enzymes, and contained none of those enzymes themselves. Finally in 1932 he succeeded in obtaining preparations of secretin as a fine white powder of which 1/40 of a milligram injected into the bloodstream of a cat gave unmistakable evidence of activity. One of his latest publications (1938) dealt with the action of secretin on the liver. In this work he described interesting observations on the formation and circulation of bile salts.

Mellanby was elected FRS in 1929. He was editor of *Physiological Abstracts* for many years and a member of the Medical Research Council from 1936. He had a happy disposition, but shrank from accepting any responsibility outside his own department. He died in the Acland Nursing Home, Banbury Road, Oxford, on 15 July 1939.

J. B. LEATHES, *rev.* RACHEL E. DAVIES

Sources *The Times* (17 July 1939) · *BMJ* (29 July 1939), 256–7 · *The Lancet* (22 July 1939), 226–7 · J. B. Leathes, *Obits. FRS*, 3 (1939–41), 173–95 · 'Mellanby, Sir Edward', *DNB* · *CGPLA Eng. & Wales* (1939)
Likenesses W. Stoneman, photograph, 1930, NPG · J. Russell & Sons, photograph, Wellcome L. · photograph, repro. in *Obits. FRS*
Wealth at death £7610 18s. 1d.: probate, 6 Oct 1939, *CGPLA Eng. & Wales*

Mellanby, Kenneth (1908–1993), ecologist, was born on 26 March 1908 at Chapellfield, Barrhead, Renfrewshire, the son of Alexander Lawson Mellanby (1871–1951), professor of mechanical engineering at the Royal Technical College, Glasgow, and his wife, Annie, formerly Maundel. His uncle John *Mellanby (1878–1939) was Waynflete professor of physiology at Oxford; another uncle, Sir Edward *Mellanby (1884–1955), directed the Medical Research Council. Mellanby was educated at Barnard Castle school, then read natural sciences at King's College, Cambridge, when his interest in medical entomology began. He

moved in 1930 to the London School of Hygiene and Tropical Medicine where he studied for a PhD on the susceptibility of human parasites to desiccation and overheating, and became interested in cockroaches and bedbugs. He married on 2 October 1933 Helen Neilson (*b.* 1910/11), daughter of George William Dow, a retired accountant. A daughter, Jane, was born but the marriage ended in divorce.

Between 1936 and 1941 Mellanby was Sorby fellow of the Royal Society, which directed him to research in Sheffield. From October 1939, following advice from Patrick Buxton of the London School of Hygiene, Mellanby conducted research on head lice. He found that possibly 50 per cent of girls aged up to fourteen were infested with head lice. He correlated the incidence of head lice with poverty and with family size. At the prompting of medical officers, in December 1940 he set up a research unit to study the effects of scabies infestations. He gathered a group of conscientious objectors to serve as his human guinea-pigs. Among these was Walter Bartley, then a laboratory technician but destined to become professor of biochemistry and vice-chancellor of the University of Sheffield. Mellanby placed scabies in bedding to study how long it would take for persons to be infected, and was surprised to find that this took months. However, when a bed was shared, infestation took place. In order to make greater use of his volunteers he suggested dietetic experiments and he collaborated with Hans Krebs, the refugee biochemist, in research on the properties of 'national wheatmeal' flour.

The scabies work led to extensive observation and treatment of military personnel in a special hospital for infested soldiers, and to the instruction of army medical officers. Mellanby kept volunteers (numbering forty-seven by May 1942) infested for months at a time, and he devised a successful treatment. The Ministry of Information produced a film on the experiments to advise on treatment of scabies. He conducted experiments on water deprivation in 1942, and on vitamins. He went on to propose infecting his volunteers with malaria in 1943, and at one stage suggested infecting them with typhus, albeit with their consent. The Medical Research Council prohibited what would have been a dangerous and unnecessary human experiment. He wrote up his experiences in *Human Guinea Pigs* (1945), and concluded by proposing a permanent institute for human experiments. He was made an OBE for his scabies work. In 1945 Mellanby turned to scrub typhus research, which was relevant for the continuing war in the Far East. For this he went to Burma and New Guinea. In December 1946 Mellanby went to Germany for three weeks to hunt for medical documents, and attended the trials of Nazi doctors at Nuremberg and Dachau. It appears that he sifted through the reports of British intelligence officers at Frankfurt (presumably of the British branch of FIAT), and visited some former concentration camps. The exact documents which he brought to Britain have never been identified. He was accredited as correspondent of the *British Medical Journal* with the brief of observing the Nuremberg medical trial. He published in *The Lancet* on 7 December 1946 and in the

BMJ, drawing attention to the scientific quality of some experiments, particularly those of the malariologist Claus Schilling, who was tried at Dachau in 1945, and to the typhus experiments of Erwin Ding at Buchenwald. Both sets of experiments involved deliberate infection of victims. While Mellanby roundly condemned Nazism, and the sadism of many of the experiments, he identified a legitimate scientific component and asserted (without providing a source) that Schilling had obtained prisoners' consent at Dachau. He also commended the typhus work as a 'useful evaluation of the various vaccines', overlooking the fact that about 1200 Russian, Gypsy, and French prisoners were killed in the experiments. Mellanby strongly believed that Gerhard Rose, a professor of tropical medicine whom he knew personally, was innocent, as were a number of the defendants, for example Handloser. The defence counsel of Becker-Freyseng cited Mellanby in the document book no. 20. The *Daily Telegraph* of 11 February 1947 cited Mellanby in its report on Nazi medical experiments, quoting its correspondent as saying that Mellanby '"told me yesterday that some of the results of experiments by Nazis on inmates of concentration camps could be of great value to medical science"'. Mellanby believed that the results should be made available to bona fide investigators.

There followed a succession of appointments as academic administrator. Mellanby's work as principal of University College, Ibadan, from 1947 to 1953 confirmed his abilities as an academic organizer. He was appointed CBE in recognition of his achievements. On 17 May 1949 he remarried; his second wife was Jean Louie Copeland (*b.* 1915/16), who, with their son Alexander Robert Mellanby, survived him. In 1955 Mellanby became head of the department of entomology, Rothamsted Experimental Station. From 1961 to 1974 he was director of the Nature Conservancy's new experimental station at Monk's Wood in Hertfordshire. Mellanby was no conventional bureaucrat: he reflected on his own career:

> Ideas for practical research are more likely to come from active young scientists than from learned councils and committees. We need to find ways of encouraging such work and of interfering with its progress as little as possible. I was lucky; there was a war on, and the red tape that strangles so much initiative could be cut in a way that would be more difficult today.

He was drawn into controversy, first advocating environmentalist views but increasingly defending the use of chemicals in farming. He found some time for research, particularly on moles. He shifted to a defence of modern farming techniques. He was awarded an honorary DSc in 1970 from the University of Essex.

In the 1970s Mellanby took a leading role at the International Conferences on the Unity of the Sciences, founded by Sun Myung Moon in 1972. He co-chaired with R. V. Jones the third conference held in London in 1974, and chaired committees at the fourth conference, on science and absolute values, in New York in 1975, at the sixth in San Francisco in 1977, and at the seventh conference in Boston in 1978.

In retirement Mellanby continued to act as scientific consultant (as for the development of Gomera in the Canaries) and as a scientific author. He wrote eloquently on environmental issues, defending the use of pesticides and modern farming techniques, while also calling for a greater ecological awareness.

Mellanby was a determined researcher, and a headstrong character, as when he was the only British delegate who attended a conference on 23 August 1939 in the Netherlands despite imminent war. He was talented as an organizer of research, and in presenting lucid analyses of scientific issues. His instincts were conservative, and he generally sided with the scientist as a dispassionate arbiter of biological and social problems. While major scientific awards and honours eluded him, he carved an outstanding career in applied biological research, and stirred some hornet's nests on controversial issues such as pesticides and experiments on human beings. He died at his home, 13 Wonford Road, Exeter, Devon, on 23 December 1993.   PAUL WEINDLING

Sources *The Times* (24 Dec 1993) · *The Independent* (11 Jan 1994) · *WWW* · P. Weindling, 'Human guinea pigs and the ethics of experimentation: the *BMJ*'s correspondent at the Nuremberg medical trial', *BMJ* (7 Dec 1996), 1467–70; rev. in *Informed consent in medical research*, ed. L. Doyal and J. S. Tobias (2001), 15–19 · personal knowledge (2004) · private information (2004) · b. cert. · m. cert. [Helen Neilson Dow] · m. cert. [Jean Louie Copeland] · d. cert.
Archives Bodl. Oxf., corresp. with T. R. E. Southwood
Likenesses photograph, repro. in *The Times*
Wealth at death £212,083: probate, 28 March 1994, *CGPLA Eng. & Wales*

Mellanby, May, Lady Mellanby (1882–1978). *See under* Mellanby, Sir Edward (1884–1955).

Mellis, John (*fl. c.*1564–1588), writer on arithmetic and bookkeeping, came from Norwich, but few details of his life are known and there is no record of his death. He had (according to himself) a natural genius for drawing proportions, maps, cards, buildings, and plates. He attended a Dr Robert Forth at Trinity Hall, Cambridge, and went to the arithmetic lecture in the common school. He left the service of Forth, who afterwards became a master in chancery, about 1564. Subsequently he kept a school for writing and arithmetic at Mayes Gate, near Battle Bridge, in the parish of St Olave, Southwark.

In 1582 Mellis published an edition of Robert Recorde's *Grounde of Artes*, which he dedicated to Robert Forth and to which he added his own 'Brief rules, called rules of practize, of rare, pleasant, and commodious effect, abridged into a briefer method than hitherto hath bene published. With diuers other very necessarie rules, tables, and questions, not only profitable for merchants, but also for gentlemen and all other occupiers whatsouer'. His other main work, *A briefe instruction and maner how to keepe bookes of accompts after the order of debitor and creditor, and as well for proper accompts partible* (1588), was described by Mellis as a reissue 'of an auncient old copie printed here in London the 14 of August, 1543', from the pen of 'Hugh Oldcastle, Scholemaster'. No copy of Oldcastle's original is known to be extant but there is some independent evidence that it existed, and it would have been the first printed book in the English language on double-entry bookkeeping. Mellis's *A Briefe Instruction* was only the sixth book of its kind.

THOMPSON COOPER, *rev.* H. K. HIGTON

Sources R. Recorde, *The grounde of artes* (1582) · A. De Morgan, *Arithmetical books from the invention of printing to the present time* (1847) · W. T. Lowndes, *The bibliographer's manual of English literature*, ed. H. G. Bohn, [new edn], 6 vols. (1864) · W. Massey, *The origin and progress of letters: an essay in two parts* (1763) · B. S. Yamey, H. C. Edey, and H. W. Thomson, *Accounting in England and Scotland, 1543–1800* (1963)

Mellish [*née* da Costa; *other married name* Villareal], **Catherine Rachel** [Kitty; *known as* Kitty da Costa Villareal] (1710–1747), breach of promise defendant, was born in London in the summer of 1710, probably in the Budge Row house of her paternal grandfather, Alvaro da Costa. She was the eldest child of Joseph da Costa (1683–1753), a rich Anglo-Jewish merchant, trader, and financier, and of his wife and first cousin, Leonora Sara Mendes (*d.* 1767). Kitty was brought up in Budge Row and also, from about 1722, in her father's much admired mansion, Copped Hall, Totteridge, Hertfordshire. Her upbringing was that of a rich and well-educated English lady.

About 1724 a match was mooted between a willing Kitty and her eager first cousin, Philip Jacob Mendes da Costa (1708–1780), but the young man was unacceptable to Kitty's parents on moral grounds. On 24 May 1727 the reluctant Kitty, 'at the age of almost seventeen' ('Proceedings'), married the wealthy but 54-year-old Joseph Isaac Villareal (1673–1730), son of the former comptroller-general of the armies of the king of Portugal, who with his family had arrived in London in 1726, fleeing Lisbon to escape charges of Judaizing. Kitty and Joseph had two children, Sarah and Abraham, born on 10 June 1728 and 15 May 1729. On 27 December 1730 Joseph Villareal died leaving Kitty, at twenty, a rich, beautiful, and by no means inconsolable widow.

Only three weeks after her husband's death the seemingly besotted Kitty was promising to marry her former suitor as soon as her year of mourning was ended. Love-tokens of a ring and a miniature were exchanged; indiscreet assignations took place in Kitty's own house in College Hill in the City of London; Philip's letters to Kitty were pressing, Kitty's to him passionate, and virulent about alleged machinations on the part of members of her family to gain control of her fortune. There was an abortive elopement from Copped Hall, and a feigned illness on her part designed to persuade her father to accept Philip. But eventually Philip, probably a libertine and certainly a fortune-hunter, was sent packing. Furious, he ill-advisedly sued Kitty for breach of promise in the ecclesiastical court of arches on 11 January 1732 (the first time a Jew had done such a thing), demanding fulfilment of the alleged contract or damages of £100,000. On 25 June 1733 judgment went against him on the grounds that Kitty's promise of marriage had not been absolute but conditional on her father's consent. In February 1734 Philip

brought a civil suit in the court of king's bench for damages, but lost it on the same grounds as before. Later that year he published an embittered and venomous account of the court of arches proceedings, bringing additional shame on the Sephardi community.

Kitty, by no means blameless and undoubtedly headstrong, finally broke with her family and Judaism on 27 February 1735 by marrying a Christian, William *Mellish (*c.*1710–1791) [*see under* Mellish, William (1764?–1838)], of Blyth, Nottinghamshire, the younger son of a good local family who had made their fortune in trade with Turkey and Portugal. William was a barrister, educated at Eton and at Cambridge. A month after the wedding Kitty was baptized at St George's, Bloomsbury. Her children from her first marriage, by agreement under the tutelage of her father, were returned to her after a protracted legal battle and also baptized, as Elizabeth and William, on 11 April 1738 at St Anne's, Soho. Kitty and William Mellish had one surviving son, Charles, born on 16 July 1737, who became recorder of Newark, and an MP in 1774, only the second man of Jewish blood to enter parliament. Elizabeth married the future second Viscount Galway in 1747 and thus became the first person of Jewish birth to marry into the peerage. Her brother, William, married the sister of a future English bishop. Possibly with the help of his wife's fortune, William Mellish himself had been returned to parliament as member for Retford from 1741 to 1751, and then became commissioner of excise, then receiver-general of customs. Kitty's younger brother, Benjamin (1712–1782), also converted to Christianity and married a gentile.

Kitty died, still young, at Blyth on 19 March 1747, and was buried on 27 March at Blyth church, leaving her entire estate to her 'dear and loving husband'. She and her kin were striking early examples of defection or drift from Judaism by Anglo-Jews and of assimilation into mainstream English society.

NORMA PERRY

Sources E. Mendes da Costa, 'Genealogical notes', *GM*, 1st ser., 82/1 (1812), 21–4 [BL, Add. MS 29867] · A. Mendes da Costa, 'Genealogical tables of the Mendes da Costas', priv. coll. · 'Proceedings … between Mr Jacob Mendes da Costa and Mrs Catherine da Costa Villareal … relating to a marriage contract', process books of the court of arches, LPL, MSS EE9 187/1, EEE 13 · J. Mendes da Costa, *The proceedings at large … between Mr Jacob Mendes da Costa and Mrs Catherine da Costa Villa Real … relating to a marriage contract* (1734) · M. J. Landa, 'Kitty Villareal, the Da Costas and Samson Gideon', *Transactions of the Jewish Historical Society of England*, 13 (1932–5), 271–91 · N. Perry, 'City life in the 1720s: the example of four of Voltaire's acquaintances', *The secular city: studies in the Enlightenment, presented to Haydn Mason*, ed. T. D. Hemming, E. Freeman, and D. Meakin (1994), 42–56 · T. M. Endelman, *Radical assimilation in English Jewish history, 1656–1945* (1990), 12–17 · C. Roth, ed., *Anglo-Jewish letters (1158–1917)* (1938), 99–102 · P. H. Emden, *Jews of Britain: a series of biographies* (1944), 17–21 · G. Landa and M. J. Landa, *Kitty Villareal: an historical romance* (1934) · D. S. Katz, *The Jews in the history of England, 1485–1850* (1994)

Archives LPL, process books of the court of arches, MSS EE9, EEE 13

Likenesses J. Ellys, group portrait; formerly priv. coll., 1935 · engraving (after miniature), repro. in *The proceedings at large*

Wealth at death £35,000 in 1735 (seemingly understated): *GM*, 5, 107

Mellish, Sir George (1814–1877), judge, was born on 19 December 1814 at Tuddenham, Norfolk, the second son of Edward Mellish, rector of East Tuddenham (afterwards dean of Hereford), and his wife, Elizabeth Jane, daughter of a prior dean of Hereford, William Leigh of Rushall Hall, Staffordshire. His godfather was George Canning, who was his mother's first cousin. He was educated at Eton College, where he was in the middle division in 1829 and the sixth form in 1832, but did not distinguish himself either as a scholar or as an athlete, though he was a good sculler and took part in the school's debating society. In 1833 he entered as a commoner at University College, Oxford, but soon won an open scholarship on Sir Simon Bennet's foundation. He was a member of the undergraduate debating society, the Oxford Union, and took a second class in *literae humaniores* in 1836. He graduated BA on 26 January 1837, proceeding to an MA on 24 October 1839. He became an honorary fellow of University College in 1872, and received an honorary DCL degree on 17 June 1874.

On 6 November 1837 Mellish joined the Inner Temple where he read in the chambers of Spencer Walpole, John Unthank, and Crompton. For eight years he practised as a special pleader and on 9 June 1848 was called to the bar, joining the northern circuit. He rapidly built up a good commercial practice, became a queen's counsel in 1861, and left the lead of his circuit after a few years to concentrate on what had become a substantial leading practice in London.

Neither his mind nor his health suited Mellish for the strain of *nisi prius* work. His strength lay in arguments *in banco*, in chancery, and in the House of Lords. More than once he refused a High Court judgeship, but in 1870, on the death of Sir George Giffard, he was appointed a lord justice of appeal in chancery, was knighted, and sworn of the privy council. It was a bold move to appoint a mere common-law practitioner to such an important post in chancery, but it proved a success, and the court, which consisted of him and Lord Justice James, continued for some years to give judgments which were considered excellent, although Mellish was often criticized for interrupting the arguments of counsel. Mellish suffered from severe gout, and was often in severe pain in court and frequently unable to work. He died unmarried at his house, 33 Lowndes Square, London, on 15 June 1877.

J. A. HAMILTON, *rev.* HUGH MOONEY

Sources Law Magazine, 4th ser., 3 (1877–8), 55–65 · Solicitors' Journal, 21 (1876–7), 652 · CGPLA Eng. & Wales (1877)
Likenesses Spy [L. Ward], caricature, watercolour study, NPG, repro. in VF (30 Dec 1876) · wood-engraving (after photograph by J. Watkins), NPG; repro. in ILN (5 Nov 1870)
Wealth at death under £120,000: probate, 21 July 1877, CGPLA Eng. & Wales

Mellish, Robert Joseph, Baron Mellish (1913–1998), politician, was born on 3 March 1913 at 63 Giffin Street, Deptford, the thirteenth of fourteen children (of whom only six survived) of John Mellish, docker, and his wife, Mary, *née* Carroll. Close proximity to death in childhood was the trigger for a crusade to improve conditions for families in east London, and one of Mellish's causes in later life was

Robert Joseph Mellish, Baron Mellish (1913–1998), by Walter Bird, 1964

the North-East Metropolitan Regional Hospital Board: 'half my brothers and sisters died from scarlet fever and meningitis' (personal knowledge). His father had taken a prominent part in the dock strikes of 1889 and 1912 and was a founder member of the Labour Party. Mellish himself joined the party at sixteen, two years after he had left St Joseph's Roman Catholic School, Deptford, to work as a clerk in the docks. He was active in the Transport and General Workers' Union, and in 1938 became a full-time official in its docks section. On 15 October in the same year he married Annie Elizabeth (*b.* 1912/13), daughter of George Warner, docker; they had five sons.

In 1940 Mellish was enlisted in the dockworkers' battalion of the Royal Engineers and served for much of the war in Burma as part of the 'forgotten' Fourteenth Army. He ended the war as captain. One of the reasons for his later good relations with the tories in the House of Commons—despite colourful verbal abuse in east London vernacular—was that the knights of the shires saw him as exactly the genre of Londoner who fitted their idea of the quintessential working-class Labour MP. But another part of the tory acceptance of him was that decorated guards, cavalry, and naval officers such as William Whitelaw, Francis Pym, and Humphrey Atkins, successively his opposite number as tory chief whip, recognized that he and they had fought in the same war, side by side, against the same enemy.

On the unexpected resignation of the minister for food, Sir Ben Smith, in May 1946 and his decision subsequently to leave the House of Commons, Mellish was selected as Labour's standard-bearer in Rotherhithe, a constituency that had shrunk to a 22,000 electorate as a result of the blitz. He won the ensuing by-election, on 19 November 1946, by 7265 votes to 2821 for the Liberal Fred Martell and 1084 for the Conservative Freddy Burden, later MP for Gillingham. He held the seat (expanded in 1950 to Bermondsey) as a fiefdom for the next thirty-six years. His maiden speech, on 16 December 1946, was in support of the government's plans to nationalize transport. After the Labour losses in the general election of 1950 he got his foot on the ladder by being appointed parliamentary private secretary to George Strauss, minister of supply, and then, from January to November 1951, to George Isaacs, minister of pensions. Years later he would say: 'What matters is bleeding loyalty, especially when you know that the Minister is wrong!' (personal knowledge). He was also active in the London Labour Party, a raucous organization of which he became chairman in 1956 at the behest of Herbert Morrison.

In October 1964 Harold Wilson, as incoming prime minister, had the inspiration of teaming up Mellish with the Oxford intellectual Richard Crossman at the Ministry of Housing. Mellish was described as 'the best thing that ever happened to Crossman' (*The Times*). The kind of issue that mattered to him was protection from eviction to deal with the Rachmanism of the time. Both at Housing and later as minister of public building and works, from August 1967, he supported the work of the Building Research Station, to combat dampness and hasten slum clearance. For seven eventful years from April 1969 he was Labour chief whip—first in government, then from 1970 to 1974 in opposition, and again in government. As *The Times* obituarist put it, 'His appointment proved a master-stroke; his combination of warmth … and toughness gained the respect of Members throughout the parliamentary party and particularly among left-wingers'. The truth was that the left felt inhibited with having a sustained animosity against a man with impeccable union working-class credentials. On several occasions he asked Wilson to move him to another post but each time he was persuaded to stay. He finally resigned in April 1976, having supported Michael Foot in the leadership contest following Wilson's resignation.

Mellish's final years in the Commons were dogged by controversy and beset with troubles in Bermondsey from hard-left 'yuppie' incomers and the Militant Tendency, people who were moons apart from the dockers who had selected him four decades earlier. When Mellish announced in 1981 that he would not stand again for election Peter Tatchell, a leading figure on the hard left, was chosen by the local party as prospective candidate. Labour's National Executive Committee initially refused to endorse Tatchell's candidature but in the following year acquiesced. Mellish—who was already facing disciplinary proceedings for supporting unofficial or independent labour candidates against left-wing official candidates at local elections—resigned from the Labour Party and from the House of Commons, precipitating a by-election

which was won by Simon Hughes, for the Liberal and Social Democrat Alliance.

Mellish was deputy chairman of the London Docklands Development Corporation from 1981 to 1985; it was his determination to devote himself full-time to this post that had led to his decision to leave the House of Commons. Following his retirement he was made a life peer, as Baron Mellish of Bermondsey. He sat as an independent, but according to one critic 'always voiced Thatcherite views' (*The Guardian*). Nevertheless he was (as he had been throughout his career) an outspoken pro-European. He was a keen supporter of Millwall Football Club, becoming its president. A leading Roman Catholic, he was made a papal knight of the order of St Gregory the Great in 1959. He was a devoted family man. In his last years he suffered from cancer and Parkinson's disease. He died at his home, Rectory House, West Street, Sompting, Sussex, on 9 May 1998; his remains were cremated. He was survived by his wife, Annie, and four of their five sons.　　　TAM DALYELL

Sources *The Independent* (11 May 1998) · *The Times* (11 May 1998) · *Daily Telegraph* (11 May 1998) · *The Guardian* (11 May 1998) · *WWW* · *Debrett's Peerage* · personal knowledge (2004) · private information (2004) · b. cert. · m. cert. · d. cert.
Archives SOUND [Hansard]
Likenesses W. Bird, photograph, 1964, NPG [*see illus.*] · Moore, photograph, 1964, Hult. Arch. · photograph, 1964, repro. in *The Independent* · photograph, 1964, Hult. Arch. · photograph, 1969, repro. in *The Times* · photograph, 1976, repro. in *Daily Telegraph* · photograph, repro. in *The Guardian*

Mellish, William (*c*.1710–1791). *See under* Mellish, William (1764?–1838).

Mellish, William (1764?–1838), banker and politician, was the third son of **William Mellish** (*c*.1710–1791), landowner and politician, of Blyth, Nottinghamshire, and his second wife, Anne, the daughter of John Gore, a leading government financier.

Mellish's father was the second son of Joseph Mellish, landowner and politician, and his wife, Dorothy, the daughter of Sir William Gore, lord mayor of London. The elder William Mellish was educated at Eton College and at Peterhouse, Cambridge, of which he became a fellow. Originally intended for the bar, he was admitted to Lincoln's Inn in 1725 and to the Inner Temple in 1734. In the following year he married Catherine [*see* Mellish, Catherine Rachel (1710–1747)], the daughter of Joseph da Costa (1683–1753) and the widow of Joseph Isaac Villareal of Edwinstowe, Nottinghamshire. Both her father and first husband were wealthy Portuguese Jews. The couple had two sons. In 1762 Mellish married again; his new wife was Anne, daughter of John Gore, himself the son of Sir William Gore.

Keen to hold office, Mellish was appointed lord treasurer's remembrancer, a minor sinecure office in the exchequer, in 1753, and continued to hold this office until 1754. He was elected MP for East Retford in 1741, but gave up his seat in 1751 upon his appointment as a commissioner of excise. He became receiver-general of customs in 1760, but was dismissed in January 1763. He owed all his appointments to the patronage of the duke of Newcastle.

An uninspired politician, Mellish's name appeared in Lord Egmont's list of 1749–50 as one of 'the most obnoxious men of an inferior degree', and also as one of the twelve 'worst cast for us in the whole House' (HoP, *Commons, 1715–54*, 2.252). He succeeded to the Blyth estate in 1757 upon the death of his elder brother. He died on 16 December 1791.

The younger William Mellish and his elder brother John each inherited £10,000 as well as the business of John Gore (including £12,000 of capital stock in trade); in 1798 William secured sole control upon the death of his brother, murdered by highwaymen. There appears to have been in practice two firms, John Gore & Co., and J. and W. Mellish & Co., and in addition to being contractors in government loans, both firms seem to have been general mercantile houses, trading in cotton and copper to the Baltic, to Lisbon, and to Hamburg in 1807. William Mellish became a director of the Bank of England in 1792, and so continued until his death. He was deputy governor in 1812 for two years, then governor, again for two years. He became captain of the grenadier company of the Bank of England Volunteers in 1798, and major in 1805.

Mellish was elected MP for Grimsby in 1796, and again in 1803, ostensibly as a supporter of William Pitt. He was returned for Middlesex in 1806, and held this seat until defeated in 1820. He usually supported the ministries of the duke of Newcastle and the earl of Liverpool, and was always opposed to any measure of Roman Catholic relief. He spoke on several occasions in defence of the Bank of England, and voted in 1810 against parliamentary reform.

At the time of his death in 1838 Mellish, a wealthy man, owned a house in Bishopsgate, London, and a country estate at Bush Hill, Edmonton, which he had inherited from an aunt. This latter was a well-managed agricultural undertaking. Mellish died on 8 June 1838, at Bishopsgate, in his seventy-fifth year, and was buried in the church of All Saints, Edmonton. He does not appear to have married. MICHAEL REED

Sources HoP, *Commons, 1790–1820* · HoP, *Commons, 1715–54*, 2.252–3 · executors' vouchers, U. Nott., Mellish MSS, Me E 68 · account of real and personal estate, U. Nott., Mellish MSS, Me B2/6/1 · U. Nott., Mellish MSS, Me B2/6/3 [brief obit. notice] · account with John Gore & Co., and J. and W. Mellish & Co., U. Nott., Mellish MSS, Me B2/3/1 · bad and doubtful debts of J. and W. Mellish & Co., U. Nott., Mellish MSS, Me B2/1/1–10 · W. M. Acres, *The Bank of England from within, 1694–1900*, 2 vols. (1931) · J. Clapham, *The Bank of England: a history*, 2 vols. (1966)
Archives U. Nott., Mellish MSS
Wealth at death approx. £110,670; debts of approx. £50,059; U. Nott., Mellish MSS, Me B2/6/1

Mellitus (d. 624), archbishop of Canterbury, was the leader of the group of missionaries sent by Pope Gregory I in 601 to reinforce Augustine at Canterbury and he subsequently became the first known bishop of London (604–616/618) and later the third archbishop of Canterbury (619–24). According to Bede, he was of noble birth and when first encountered in Gregory's letters for the mission he is already styled 'abbot'—an office perhaps intended to confer leadership of the missionary expedition rather than one already held in Gregory's monastery of St Andrew, on

the Caelian Hill, or some other Roman house. On 22 June 601 the pope provided the mission with a series of commendatory letters to the Frankish kings Theuderic II of Burgundy and Theudebert II of Austrasia, and to their powerful mother, Brunhild, as well as to King Chlothar II of Neustria and a number of Frankish bishops. From these letters the group's expected route and possible diversions may be deduced: Toulon, Marseilles, Arles, Gap, Vienne, Lyons, Chalon-sur-Saône, Metz, Paris, and Angers. Mellitus also brought with him letters from Gregory, issued on the same day, with detailed guidance for Augustine, for King Æthelberht, and for his queen, Bertha. Accompanying Mellitus were Laurence, who had reported news of Augustine's mission back to Rome, and also Justus, Paulinus, and Rufinianus. According to Bede they took to Kent everything 'necessary for divine worship ... sacred vessels, altar cloths, church ornaments, vestments for priests and clerks, relics of the holy apostles and martyrs, and many books [*codices*]' (Bede, *Hist. eccl.*, 1.29). In the fifteenth century Thomas of Elmham claimed that several of the oldest altar-books in the possession of the monks of St Augustine's had been among the volumes brought by the missionaries. Most of those manuscripts in the list which can be identified are in fact of much younger date, but the claim is plausible with regard to the Canterbury gospels, a sixth-century Italian gospel book that is now Cambridge, Corpus Christi College, MS 286. After their departure from Rome, Gregory had sent to Mellitus 'in Francia' a further letter for Augustine, authorizing the reuse of pagan temples as churches after they had been purified and permitting feasting in lieu of animal sacrifice—practices designed to ease the transition from paganism to Christianity.

Mellitus's party had certainly reached England by 604, for in that year he was consecrated by Augustine as bishop of the East Saxons with his see at London. The extension of the mission was due to the influence of King Æthelberht of Kent. The East Saxon king, Sæberht, was Æthelberht's nephew (being the son of his sister Ricula) and the construction of an episcopal church, dedicated to St Paul, in London is attributed to Æthelberht rather than to Sæberht. The choice of London for the East Saxon see reflects its position at the focus of the road system of southern Britain and the mission's preference for former Roman towns. In 601 Gregory had intended London to be one of the two metropolitan sees of the English church; but after Augustine's death it seems to have been Laurence at Canterbury, rather than Mellitus at London, who exercised metropolitan authority, perhaps because Æthelberht was unwilling that the metropolitan see should be outside his Kentish kingdom. Bede tells that Æthelberht bestowed gifts and lands on Mellitus to support his household, but a charter purporting to be Æthelberht's grant of Tillingham, Essex, to Mellitus and St Paul's is shown by its spurious witness list and its formulation to be a forgery.

Mellitus was associated with Laurence and with Bishop Justus of Rochester in sending a letter to the bishops and abbots of the Irish church in the hope of inducing them to accept Roman practices and he was sent back to Rome to take part in Pope Boniface IV's synod (27 February 610) which sought to harmonize monastic practices. He brought back to England the decisions of that council as well as two letters, which were addressed to Archbishop Laurence and all the clergy, and to King Æthelberht and the English people, respectively. No authentic texts either of the canons or of the letters survive, though spurious privileges attributed to Boniface were concocted for both the Canterbury houses, Christ Church and St Augustine's, in the 1060s or 1070s. In 616 or 618 the deaths of kings Æthelberht of Kent and Sæberht of Essex at much the same time produced a crisis for the Roman mission. Mellitus had not converted Sæberht's three sons, who ruled jointly after his death; Bede recounts how Mellitus's refusal to let them receive the eucharist, on the grounds that they had not been baptized, led them to expel the bishop. He fled to Kent, but the succession there of (the similarly still pagan) Eadbald caused Mellitus to flee to Frankish Gaul with Justus. Although they were able to return to Kent within a year after Eadbald's conversion, Mellitus could not recover his see since the East Saxons remained pagan and the Christian Eadbald had no authority beyond Kent.

Early in 619, following the death of Archbishop Laurence, Mellitus succeeded to the see of Canterbury in his place. According to Bede he suffered severely from gout, but was active in mind and exalted in spirit. Both Mellitus and Justus are said to have received letters of encouragement from Pope Boniface V (r. 619–25), doubtless to congratulate them on securing Eadbald's conversion and perhaps also on the marriage of King Edwin of Northumbria to the Christian Kentish princess, Æthelburh, which seems to be placed several years too late by Bede (who recounts it after July 625). It is not known whether or not the pope sent Mellitus a pallium with his letter. Just two acts are known from his tenure of the archiepiscopal see; both derive from the traditions of the monastery of St Peter and St Paul (later St Augustine's) in Canterbury, as transmitted by Bede: first his consecration of the church of St Mary, which had been constructed by King Eadbald in that monastery, and second the miraculous saving from destruction by fire of the Canterbury church of the Four Crowned Martyrs, and indeed of the whole city, when his prayers reversed the direction of a strong south wind that was fanning the flames. Mellitus died in 624 and was buried in the monastery of St Peter and St Paul on 24 April. After the Norman conquest the wish of the monks of St Augustine's to develop the cult of the early archbishops buried in their church led to the production of a series of short lives but neither the first, written by Goscelin, nor those of later date add anything to our knowledge of Mellitus, though they do reveal that sufferers from gout were directed to his tomb.   N. P. BROOKS

Sources Bede, *Hist. eccl.*, 1.29–30; 2.3–8; 3.22 · *S. Gregorii magni registrum epistularum*, ed. D. Norberg, 2 vols. (1982), 922–3, 938, 946–7, 950–51 [letters 34, 41, 48, 51] · N. Brooks, *The early history of the church of Canterbury: Christ Church from 597 to 1066* (1984), 9, 11–13, 30, 66, 265 · T. D. Hardy, *Descriptive catalogue of materials relating to the history of Great Britain and Ireland*, 1, Rolls Series, 26 (1862), nos. 591–4 · H. Mayr-Harting, *The coming of Christianity to Anglo-Saxon England*,

3rd edn (1991) · S. Kelly, 'Some forgeries in the archives of St Augustine's Abbey, Canterbury', *Fälschungen im Mittelalter*, MGH Schriften, 33/4 (Hanover, 1988), 347–69

Mellon, Alfred (1820–1867), conductor and composer, was probably born in London on 7 April 1820, although his early years were spent in Birmingham, his parents' home town. He became a violinist and played in the opera and other orchestras, and was later appointed leader of the orchestra at the Royal Italian Opera, Covent Garden. He then held the post of music director at the Haymarket and Adelphi theatres, and afterwards of the Pyne and Harrison English opera company, by whom his opera *Victorine* was produced at Covent Garden in 1859. He was conductor of the Musical Society and also of the Promenade Concerts, which for several seasons were given under his name at Covent Garden. In September 1865 he became conductor of the Liverpool Philharmonic Society. Among his compositions were the opera *The Irish Dragoon* (1845), a glee, 'Crown'd with clusters of the vine' (1850), numerous songs for farces and plays, and ballads and piano pieces. He died on 27 March 1867 at his home at The Vale, Chelsea, London, and was buried in Brompton cemetery. He left a widow, Sarah Jane *Mellon, née Woolgar (1824–1909), a well-known actress, whom he had married on 28 July 1855, and two daughters, of whom the younger, Mary Woolgar Mellon, also became an actress. He was considered an excellent practical musician. An obituary refers to his death as leaving 'a blank in the list of English conductors which will not be easily filled up' (*MT*).

J. C. HADDEN, *rev.* DAVID J. GOLBY

Sources *MT*, 13 (1867–9), 58 · Grove, *Dict. mus.* · Brown & Stratton, *Brit. mus.* · *CGPLA Eng. & Wales* (1867)
Likenesses C. Baugniet, lithograph, 1854, BM · H. Watkins, albumen print photograph, 1855–9, NPG · wood-engraving (after photograph), NPG; repro. in *ILN* (13 April 1867) · woodcut, Harvard TC; repro. in *Entr'acte* (30 June 1877), supplement
Wealth at death under £1500: probate, 30 April 1867, *CGPLA Eng. & Wales*

Mellon, Harriot. *See* Beauclerk, Harriot (1777?–1837).

Mellon, Paul (1907–1999), philanthropist and art collector, was born on 11 June 1907 at 5052 Forbes Street, Pittsburgh, Pennsylvania, USA, the only son and second of the two children of Andrew William Mellon (1855–1937), banker and statesman, and his wife, Nora (1879–1973), daughter of Mr and Mrs Alexander McMullen of Hertford, England. His childhood was marred by his parents' incompatibility and by their heavily publicized divorce, granted in 1912. On the other hand it was marked by happier memories of summers in rural England in stark contrast to the rest of the year in industrial Pittsburgh. At the age of twelve Mellon was sent to Choate School in Wallingford, Connecticut, and from there, in 1925, he went to Yale University. Unsurprisingly, given his ties to England, he fell under the spell of Yale's great teachers of English literature, men to whom he later ascribed his love of English literature, life, and art. After graduating in 1929, he spent two years reading English history at Clare College, Cambridge. After Yale he 'found Cambridge lectures dull and dry', but discovered other attractions, including 'lovely Newmarket,

Andrew Mellon in 1937 placed a heavy burden of responsibility on the shoulders of his only son, not least for his father's gift to the nation of the National Gallery of Art in Washington, DC, on which construction had begun in the same year. In 1941 he presented the finished building, designed by John Russell Pope, to President Roosevelt, who accepted it on behalf of the American people. Within weeks of the ceremony Mellon was in uniform as a volunteer under selective service. He served as an instructor at the US army's cavalry training centre at Fort Riley, Kansas, from 1941 to 1943, and was then posted to the office of strategic services in London. After D-day he served in France and Belgium before returning to the United States with the rank of major in 1945. Before the war Mary Mellon had persuaded her husband to join her in undergoing analysis with C. G. Jung; they were on one of their extended visits to Zürich when Hitler invaded Poland on 1 September 1939. In 1945, in what Mellon described as the most significant result of their association with Jung, he and his wife established the Bollingen Foundation. A year later Mary Mellon died as a result of chronic asthma, and on 1 May 1948 Mellon married Rachel 'Bunny' Lloyd, *née* Lambert (*b.* 1910), a horticulturalist whose interest in French art complemented his own growing attachment to that of England.

Mellon concentrated after the war on the task he once described as 'giving away a fortune wisely'. In 1941 he set up the Old Dominion Foundation to which he contributed more than $90 million before merging it with his sister's Avalon Foundation, following her death in 1969, to form the Andrew W. Mellon Foundation. He rejoined the board of the National Gallery of Art in 1945 and served as president from 1963 to 1979 and as chairman from 1979 to 1985. He oversaw the building of the east wing, designed by I. M. Pei, funded largely by the Andrew W. Mellon Foundation and accepted on behalf of the nation by President Carter in 1978. To his father's collection of old masters, he and his wife added works by the impressionists and post-impressionists, along with a selection of their British paintings.

Mellon bought his first painting by George Stubbs (1724–1806) in 1936, a profound study of humane sportsmanship entitled *Pumpkin with a Stable-Lad* and an augury of the controlled passion with which, from 1959 onwards, he was to collect and promote the study of British art. Advised initially by the critic and broadcaster Basil Taylor, he acquired some 1600 paintings and many thousands of prints and drawings, the great majority of which he gave or bequeathed to the Yale Center for British Art, the museum and research centre he established in 1966, and to which he attached his London foundation, known from 1970 onwards as the Paul Mellon Centre for Studies in British Art. The Yale Center, housed in a landmark building by Louis I. Kahn, opened in 1977. Meanwhile Mellon recognized the claims of the state in which he had made his home by giving parts of his British and French collections to the Virginia Museum of Fine Arts and contributing to the cost of a new wing to house them there.

Mellon held honorary degrees from the universities of

Paul Mellon (1907–1999), by John Ward, 1980s?

its long straight velvet training gallops, its racecourse, (to me) the most beautiful one anywhere' (Mellon and Baskett). When the self-styled 'galloping Anglophile' was given a chestnut mare in 1930, he named her Lady Clare.

The following decade was one of uncertainty. Unsure of his ability to live up to his father's expectation that he would succeed him as the head of an international business empire, Mellon sought other outlets for his energies. In 1933 he bought his first racehorse, fully aware of his father's opinion that 'any damn fool knows that one horse can run faster than another'. But encouraged by the success of his horses, Mellon in 1936 bought from his mother the 400 acre Rokeby Farm in Upperville, Virginia, where he centred his highly successful racing and breeding operations. Determined to run them profitably, he decided after the war to switch from steeplechase to flat racing and each year to send selected yearlings to England to train with Peter Hastings-Bass and, from 1964, with Ian Balding at Kingsclere, Berkshire. From these arrangements came a succession of winners on both sides of the Atlantic, including the legendary Mill Reef, winner in 1971 of the Epsom Derby, the Eclipse stakes at Sandown, the King George VI and Queen Elizabeth at Ascot, and the Prix de l'Arc de Triomphe at Longchamp. In the same year Run the Gantlet won the Washington DC International and was voted America's champion turf horse. Twenty-two years later, in 1993, it was Sea Hero who realized his owner's ambition to add the Kentucky Derby to his trophies.

On 2 February 1935 Mellon married Mary Elizabeth Brown, *née* Conover (1904–1946). A daughter, Catherine, was born in 1936 and a son, Timothy, in 1942. The death of

Cambridge and Oxford, Yale University, the Carnegie Institute of Technology, Pittsburgh, and the Royal Veterinary College, University of London. In 1974 he received an honorary knighthood for his services to British art and his generosity to many UK institutions. He was awarded the Benjamin Franklin medal of the Royal Society of Arts in 1965, he was a fellow of the British Academy, and he became a corresponding member of the Royal Academy of Arts in 1977. Among the awards he received in the United States were the national medal of arts (1985), the American Philosophical Society Benjamin Franklin award, and the World Monuments Fund Hadrian award (1989). By 1992 his philanthropic contributions were valued at more than $600 million, excluding grants made by the Andrew W. Mellon Foundation. To that sum his charitable bequests added more than $300 million, excluding the value of the works of art he gave or bequeathed to the National Gallery of Art, the Yale Center for British Art, the Virginia Museum of Fine Arts, and other institutions. Paul Mellon died on 1 February 1999 at his home, Oak Spring, Upperville, Virginia, and was buried on 8 February at Trinity Episcopal Church, Upperville. His wife, Rachel, survived him. His testamentary provisions followed his lifetime commitments to the museums and galleries he supported, Cambridge, Carnegie Mellon, and Yale universities, and his school, known latterly as Choate Rosemary Hall. They also reflected his wider interests in art and architecture, conservation, education, environmental protection, sport, and veterinary medicine.

In 1992 Mellon published the memoir he wrote with the help of his friend and adviser, John Baskett. He ended *Reflections in a Silver Spoon* with a typically modest self-assessment:

> I have been an amateur in every phase of my life; an amateur poet, an amateur scholar, an amateur horseman, an amateur farmer, an amateur soldier, an amateur connoisseur of art, an amateur publisher, and an amateur museum executive.

It would never have occurred to this unassuming man that he was widely regarded as the greatest philanthropist of the twentieth century.   DUNCAN ROBINSON

Sources P. Mellon and J. Baskett, *Reflections in a silver spoon: a memoir* (New York and London, 1992) · P. Mellon, 'A collector recollects', in *Selected paintings, drawings and books*, Yale U. CBA (1977) [excerpts from a speech delivered at the opening of the exhibition 'Painting in England 1700–1850' at the Virginia Museum of Fine Arts, Richmond, Virginia, 20 April 1963] · *The Independent* (3 Feb 1999) · *The Times* (3 Feb 1999) · *Daily Telegraph* (3 Feb 1999) · *The Guardian* (4 Feb 1999) · personal knowledge (2004)

Archives National Gallery of Art, Washington, DC · Yale U. CBA
Likenesses W. Orpen, oils, 1925, Yale U. CBA · A. Munnings, oils, 1932–3, Yale U. CBA · J. Ward, pencil and watercolour drawing, 1980–1989?, NPG [*see illus.*] · T. Pullan, bronze bust, 1984, NPG · K. Draper, oils, National Gallery of Art, Washington, DC · K. Draper, oils, Yale U. CBA · K. Draper, oils, Choate Rosemary School, Wallingford, Connecticut · T. Pullan, bronze head, Yale U. CBA; casts, Paul Mellon Centre for Studies in British Art, London; Clare College, Cambridge

Mellon [*née* Woolgar], **Sarah Jane** (1824–1909), actress, was born on 8 July 1824 at Gosport, Hampshire, the daughter of William Woolgar, a tailor and actor. The *Dictionary of*

Sarah Jane Mellon (1824–1909), by Fradelle & Marshall

National Biography condemned him as an 'indifferent tragedian'—unsurprising, as his daughter's marriage certificate describes him as a comedian. He trained his daughter, and guided her career. She made her first appearance at Plymouth in May 1836, as Leolyn in *The Wood Demon*, and quickly acquired a reputation as a 'young phenomenon' on the Worcester and York circuits. She then studied music, and at Birmingham in 1841, during the visit of the opera singers Mary Ann Wood (*née* Paton) and Joseph Wood, she sang for five nights as Adalgisa in Bellini's *Norma*. In 1842 she appeared in *Guy Mannering* at Edinburgh, and later that year was Ophelia at the Theatre Royal, Manchester. Her increasing popularity was reflected in a benefit early in 1843, which brought her £170.

On 9 October 1843 Sarah Woolgar made her London début at the Adelphi, in Charles Selby's burletta *Antony and Cleopatra*; she was to be associated with this theatre for many years. Her first original role there was in T. Egerton Wilks's *The Roll of the Drum* on 16 October. She joined the Keeleys at the Lyceum for a time in 1844, her parts there including Mercy in Edward Stirling's version of *Martin Chuzzlewit*. In the autumn of 1844 the Adelphi reopened under the management of Benjamin Webster and Madame Celeste, and the golden period of the career of 'La Belle Woolgar' at that theatre began. On 14 October she showed dramatic feeling as Lazarillo in Dion Boucicault's *Don Cesar de Bazan*. At the Haymarket on 18 November (owing to the sudden illness of Madame Vestris) she played Lady Alice Hawthorn, on half a day's notice, in the same author's new comedy *Old Heads and Young Hearts*. She returned to the Adelphi at Easter 1845, and afterwards fulfilled some provincial engagements with her father. At the Adelphi on 11 March 1847 she was the original Lemuel in J. B. Buckstone's melodrama *The Flowers of the Forest*. Dickens spoke of this performance as the most remarkable and complete piece of melodrama he had seen. Appearances in a variety of unimportant dramas, farces, and burlesques followed. After a severe illness she reappeared at the Adelphi on 1 March 1852 as Phoebe to Edward Richard Wright's Paul Pry. Among her original characterizations in 1854 was Anne Musgrave in Tom Taylor and Charles Reade's *Two Loves and a Life* (20 May).

On 28 July 1855 Sarah Woolgar married Alfred *Mellon (1820–1867), the leader of the Adelphi orchestra, and subsequently acted under her married name. In 1856 Mrs Mellon joined the Lyceum company under Charles Dillon, and appeared there on 15 September as Florizel in the burlesque *Perdita* opposite Marie Wilton (Lady Bancroft), who was then making her metropolitan début. In March 1857 she gave a notable rendering of Ophelia, and the following Christmas she sustained a leading character in the oriental pantomime *Lalla Rookh*. On 20 January 1858 she was the original Countess de Montelons in Leigh Hunt's comedy *Lovers' Amazements*. Following the opening of the new Adelphi Theatre in December 1858, her finest original role was Catherine Duval in Watts Phillips's *The Dead Heart* (10 November 1859). In January 1860 her Mrs Cratchit in *A Christmas Carol* was highly praised by Henry Morley. On 29 March 1860, at Covent Garden, in aid of the funds of the ill-fated dramatic college, she played Black-Eyed Susan in Douglas Jerrold's drama to T. P. Cooke's William, notable as Cooke's last appearance on the stage. At the Adelphi on 10 September 1860 she had a great success as Anne Chute in the first English performance of Boucicault's *The Colleen Bawn*.

On 5 October 1867 the Adelphi was reopened under Mrs Mellon's supervision (but not responsible management). She then demonstrated her versatility by playing Peg Woffington in Reade and Taylor's *Masks and Faces* and Tom Croft in Mark Lemon's *The School for Tigers*. On 26 December 1867 she was the original Sally Goldstraw in Charles Dickens and Wilkie Collins's drama *No Thoroughfare*. She continued to perform, but, failing to keep step with the steady march towards 'naturalness', she came to be considered stilted, and she gradually lost caste. On 15 May 1878 a testimonial performance of Buckstone's *The Green Bushes* was given on her behalf at Drury Lane, when Madame Celeste made her last appearance on the stage. On 14 May 1879 she reappeared at the Adelphi as Mrs Candour in a revival of *The School for Scandal*, and there on 24 April 1880 she played Mrs O'Kelly in the first performance given in England of Boucicault's *The Shaughraun*. On 2 August following, at the Haymarket, she was the original Miss Sniffe in the same author's comedy *A Bridal Tour*. She finally retired in 1883.

Sarah Mellon died at her residence, 32 Vardens Road, Wandsworth Common, after a very brief illness, on 8 September 1909, and was buried in Brompton cemetery beside her husband, whom she survived forty-two years. She left two daughters, of whom the younger, Mary Woolgar Mellon, became an actress.

W. J. LAWRENCE, *rev.* J. GILLILAND

Sources T. Marshall, *Lives of the most celebrated actors and actresses* [1846–7] · *Daily Telegraph* (10 Sept 1909) · *Tallis's drawing room table book of theatrical portraits, memoirs and anecdotes* (1851) · H. Morley, *The journal of a London playgoer from 1851 to 1866* (1866) · GM, 265 (1888), 391–410, esp. 409 · *The Athenaeum* (18 Sept 1909), 340 · M. E. Bancroft and S. Bancroft, *The Bancrofts: recollections of sixty years* (1909) · T. E. Pemberton, *Charles Dickens and the stage* (1888) · m. cert. · d. cert. · personal knowledge (1912)
Archives Theatre Museum
Likenesses T. H. Wilson, lithograph, 1849, NPG · R. Clothier, double portrait, oils, 1869 (with Toole); Sothebys, November 1906 · T. H. Wilson, watercolour, 1897 · A. E. Chalon, watercolour (as the Countess in *Taming of a Tar Tar*); Sothebys, November 1906 · Fradelle & Marshall, woodburytype carte-de-visite, NPG [*see illus.*] · G. Graetbach, stipple and line engraving (as Rosalind in *As you like it*; after daguerreotype), BM, NPG; repro. in Tallis, *Drawing room table book* (1851) · J. T. Wigney, carte-de-visite, NPG · five prints, Harvard TC
Wealth at death £815 19*s.* 6*d.*: probate, 1 Oct 1909, CGPLA Eng. & Wales

Mellor, George (*c.*1790–1813), machine breaker and assassin, lived at Longroyd Bridge, Huddersfield, where he was employed by his stepfather, John Wood. His parentage is unknown as are the exact date and place of his birth, but he is presumed to have been born in Huddersfield and to have spent his entire life there. He worked as a cloth-dresser or cropper, in charge of apprentices and superintending the work of the cropping shop.

In 1811–12 newspaper reports of successful frame breaking in the east midlands hosiery and lace trades supposedly inspired Mellor to apply Luddite tactics against cropping frames and gig mills in the West Riding, where there was already a history of machine breaking in the woollen industry. After the failure of the attack on Rawfolds mill on 12 April, in which he was clearly a leader and for which he was later charged, he sought to avenge the dead by persuading his fellow workers to abandon their traditional methods of industrial protest, and instead arm themselves, and assassinate the masters, a tactical switch that cost them much community support. Mellor, with three associates, shot and killed the Marsden mill owner, William Horsfall, on 27 April, and tried to protect the participants by requiring an oath of secrecy from all involved. After six months of investigation he was arrested on 12 October, tried by special commission, convicted, and hanged at York on 8 January 1813. He was unmarried.

Vilified in his lifetime and beyond, Mellor was eventually raised to heroic status by E. P. Thompson in 1963, but neither reputation was gained without straining the evidence. It suited the terror tactics of the government to exaggerate his leadership role and influence, as the alleged Luddite captain of the district, an exaggeration sustained by the imaginative writing of the Spen valley historian Frank Peel, who in 1880 retrospectively created from oral tradition a character for his villain, at once a domineering, audacious, reckless, passionate, determined, and violent bully, yet also a naturally gloomy and reserved introvert when not suffering from fits of uncontrolled passion. The contemporary *Leeds Mercury*, also hostile, eschewed the character analysis but noted his respectable appearance and fervour in prayer, while reaching the extraordinary conclusion that Mellor's failure to confess his guilt before death confirmed the correctness of the verdict. Almost everything written about him is extrapolated from the few facts that emerged at the trial and is an inference of what his political beliefs actually were, though it is known that he supported a petition for parliamentary reform from his cell. His importance lies less in what he actually did, thought, or achieved than in the way the authorities selected him as an example to law-breakers and as reassurance to the law-abiding.

Although there is little doubt that Mellor was guilty as charged, despite his insistence on his innocence, the case has become a notorious example of all that was wrong in the way that early nineteenth-century law was administered. Mellor's prosecutors abducted and intimidated possible witnesses, offering massive financial inducements (never paid) for evidence, and there were many irregularities in the treatment of the accused and their counsel, and the conduct of the trial, including the partial behaviour of the judge. Mellor's almost immediate execution, along with two co-defendants, the third having turned king's evidence, was a political act to establish the government's authority. The traditional indignity of dissection by surgeons was also carried out on his corpse. The significance of Mellor's life and death is not in his contribution to the ideology, organization, or tactics of working-class industrial or political action but in their use by the government of the day to make a point to the governed.

MALCOLM I. THOMIS

Sources B. Turner, 'Luddism and the law', PhD diss., University of Queensland, 1993 · F. Peel, *The risings of the Luddites* (1880) · *Leeds Mercury* (May 1812–Jan 1813) · E. P. Thompson, *The making of the English working class* (1963) · J. L. Hammond and B. Hammond, *The skilled labourer, 1760–1832* (1919) · Leeds Public Library, Radcliffe MSS · Fitzwilliam papers, Sheff. Arch., Wentworth Woodhouse muniments · *Leeds Intelligencer* (May 1812–Jan 1813)

Mellor, Sir John (1809–1887), judge, was born on 1 January 1809 at Hollinwood House, Oldham, Lancashire, the son of John Mellor and his wife (of whom little is known). His father came from an old south Lancashire family and as well as being a partner in the firm of Gee, Mellor, Kershaw & Co., was mayor of the borough of Leicester and justice of the peace there. Mellor was educated at the Leicester grammar school, and afterwards under Charles Berry, a Unitarian minister of Leicester. His schooling caused him to consider the merits of religious belief at an early age and, as a young man, he followed the Unitarian notion in rejecting the idea of subscription to any religious dogma. As a result, he was unwilling to subscribe to the Thirty-

Nine Articles and so had to abandon his plan to attend university at Lincoln College, Oxford. Instead, he read for some time in the office of a Leicester attorney and was admitted as a student to the Inner Temple on 5 June 1828. He then read in the chambers of Thomas Chitty for four years, attended Austin's lectures at University College, London, and was called to the bar on 7 June 1833. On 24 September of the same year he married Elizabeth Cooke Moseley; they had eight sons.

Mellor joined the midland circuit, and practised at the parliamentary bar, at assizes, and (both civil and criminal cases) at Leicester borough and Warwick sessions. After taking silk in 1851 he became leader of the circuit. From 1849 to 1852 he was recorder of Warwick, and from 1855 to 1861 recorder of Leicester. After unsuccessful attempts to be elected as a Liberal for Warwick (1852) and Coventry (1857), in 1857 he was elected for Great Yarmouth, and at the general election of 1859 was returned for Nottingham, but tended to speak little in parliament.

On 3 December 1861 Mellor succeeded Mr Justice Hill in the queen's bench; he was knighted on 11 June 1862. He was a member of the special commission which tried Fenian prisoners at Manchester in 1867 and of the court which tried Arthur Orton, alias Castro, for perjury in claiming to be the long-lost Roger Tichborne in the highly celebrated Tichborne case of 1873. During this unusually protracted trial Mellor often amused the jury with his dry humour, and concluded the proceedings by reading out the long sentence of guilt. Deafness led him to retire in June 1879 when he was given a pension and was sworn of the privy council; he settled on the Kent coast at this time. Although retired, he often attended the judicial committee, went the northern circuit once as commissioner of assize, and frequently acted as an arbitrator in important cases. He also pursued his interest in the activities of his local lifeboat. He died at his London house, 16 Sussex Square, Hyde Park, on 26 April 1887, and was buried on 30 April in Kingsdown churchyard, near his home in Kent. Mellor wrote several papers dealing with religious issues and the question of the oath in court and in parliament.

J. A. HAMILTON, *rev.* SINÉAD AGNEW

Sources J. Foster, *Men-at-the-bar: a biographical hand-list of the members of the various inns of court*, 2nd edn (1885) · Foss, *Judges* · *Law Times* (7 May 1887), 15 · *Solicitors' Journal*, 31 (1886–7), 429 · J. E. Martin, ed., *Masters of the bench of the Hon. Society of the Inner Temple, 1450–1883, and masters of the Temple, 1540–1883* (1883), 110 · Allibone, *Dict.* · Boase, *Mod. Eng. biog.* · *Men of the time* (1875), 718 · *The Times* (25 April 1887) · E. Kilmurray, *Dictionary of British portraiture*, 3 (1981), 141 · J. D. Woodruff, *The Tichborne claimant: a Victorian mystery* (1957), 255, 299, 303, 309, 366–9

Likenesses E. G. Papworth, marble bust, 1870, Gov. Art Coll. · Spy [L. Ward], caricature, watercolour study, 1873, NPG; repro. in *VF* (24 May 1873) · Faustin, chromolithograph caricature, NPG · Lock & Whitfield, woodburytype photograph, NPG; repro. in T. Cooper, *Men of mark: a gallery of contemporary portraits* (1880) · J. Napier, oils, Leicester Museum · woodcut, repro. in *Harper's Weekly*, 18 (1874), 261

Wealth at death £97,071 6s. 5d.: probate, 8 June 1887, CGPLA Eng. & Wales

Mellor, Joseph William (1869–1938), chemist, was born on 9 July 1869 at Lindley, Huddersfield, the son of Job

Mellor, a draper, and his wife, Emma Smith. When he was ten years old, the family emigrated to New Zealand, where his father found work in the woollen mills of Kaiapoi and later Dunedin on the South Island. His working-class background ruled out any thoughts of higher education, and at the age of thirteen he left school to take employment in boot manufacturing. In the evenings, however, by light of a kerosene lamp, he read second-hand or borrowed books and performed some chemical experiments.

Mellor's remarkable efforts at self-education eventually came to the attention of the director of the local technical school, who arranged for him to attend classes. In 1892 he was assisted by his school director to become a part-time student at the University of Otago in Dunedin. In 1898 he graduated with first-class honours and then took a teaching post at Lincoln Agricultural College. In the same year he married the organist at Mornington Methodist Church, Emma Cranwell Bakes. A few months later he resigned his post at the agricultural college and sailed from Port Chalmers to take up an 1851 Exhibition scholarship in Manchester, England.

In 1902 Mellor obtained the degree of DSc from the Victoria University, Manchester. He then accepted a teaching position at Newcastle under Lyme, Staffordshire. In 1904, the local pottery industry started a pottery school which soon became part of the North Staffordshire Technical College. Mellor lectured there and later became the principal. He was also secretary of the newly formed Ceramic Society. During the First World War he directed a modest research programme on refractories, which became the first stage in the formation of the British Ceramic Research Association. In 1921 the British Refractories Research Association was formed with Mellor as director. In 1927 he was elected a fellow of the Royal Society.

The Mellors had no children but he had four sisters in New Zealand and several nieces and nephews. He used to write to them amusing letters, illustrated with cartoons. Some of these were collected together by friends and published in 1934 under the title *Uncle Joe's Nonsense*. In addition he described his trip to the United States in 1929 (when the Ceramic Society travelled to New York on board the Cunard Line *Laconia*) in a 36-page brochure illustrated by witty cartoons and comments; three of the cartoons were also published in the *Journal of Chemical Education*. Two more cartoons were published a few years later in the same journal, in which Mellor showed himself fainting on the floor, and then recovering in hospital.

Mellor published 116 papers and obtained six patents, nearly all of which were on clays, ceramics, and refractories. He also published five books on inorganic chemistry (1912–30), and pioneering texts on mathematics for chemists (1902) and chemical kinetics (1904), as well as on quantitative chemical analysis (1914), clay and pottery (1914), and metallography (1916). His major work, however, is a monumental sixteen-volume book on inorganic chemistry entitled *Comprehensive Treatise on Theoretical and Inorganic Chemistry* published between 1927 and 1937 in 15,320 pages, complete with extensive references to the original literature—a characteristic of all Mellor's books. The book also contains numerous quotations from famous writers and poets. It is difficult to believe that a work of this scale was produced by one person working alone. He dedicated it to: 'the privates in the great army of workers in chemistry … [whose] names have been forgotten, [but whose] work remains'. In his 1927 election certificate for the Royal Society his proposers for membership described this reference work as 'so valuable to chemists that its importance can hardly be over-estimated'. Mellor himself was described as 'the leading authority on the scientific principles underlying the Pottery Industry'.

Mellor retired in 1934 and died four years later at his home, 132 Highlands Heath, Portsmouth Road, Putney, on 24 May 1938. He was cremated in London. Some pieces from his pottery collection and other archive material were donated by his widow to the University of Otago. He left behind a wealth of books that form an important source for research in the history of chemistry, and which his widow donated to the public library in Dunedin. In 1949 the New Zealand Institute of Chemistry created an annual Mellor lecture in his honour and in 1954 a plaque in his memory was unveiled at the University of Otago in the presence of the duke of Edinburgh.

FATHI HABASHI

Sources F. Habashi, 'Joseph William Mellor, 1869–1938: a tribute to the master textbook author of all times', *Bulletin for the History of Chemistry*, 7 (1990), 13–16 · M. Rose, 'Joseph Mellor: Otago's brilliant chemist who took the British ceramics industry into the twentieth century', *New Zealand Potter*, 1 (1985), 8–10 · A. Silverman, 'Mellor's nonsense', *Journal of Chemical Education*, 29 (1952), 187; 31 (1954), 17 · A. T. Green, *Obits. FRS*, 2 (1936–8), 573–6 · A. H. Reed, *Joseph William Mellor: Dunedin boy who became the world's greatest authority on inorganic chemistry* (privately printed, Wellington, New Zealand, 1957) · b. cert. · d. cert.
Archives University of Otago, Dunedin, New Zealand, papers, archive material, and a small collection of pieces of pottery
Likenesses photograph, University of Otago, Dunedin, New Zealand
Wealth at death £14,689 7s. 1d.: probate, 16 Dec 1938, *CGPLA Eng. & Wales*

Melmoth, Courtney. *See* Pratt, Samuel Jackson (1749–1814).

Melmoth, William, the elder (1665/6–1743), lawyer and religious writer, was admitted to Clifford's Inn on 15 April 1686 and to the Inner Temple on 30 May 1689. Nothing is known of his background beyond the fact that the Inner Temple admitted him as a gentleman. He was called to the bar at the Inner Temple on 29 May 1693.

Melmoth's religious beliefs caused him some unease about taking the oaths to William and Mary on his call to the bar, and prompted him to write for advice to the clergyman and philosopher John Norris, then rector of Bremerton, Wiltshire, though at the time he knew Norris only through his work. Their brief epistolary exchange between March and May 1693 suggests that Melmoth had nonjuring sympathies; his son wrote that 'he may seem, perhaps, in his early youth, to have been inclined to give a cast of superstition to the colour of his religion' (Melmoth, *Memoirs*, 15–16). In one letter he asked Norris 'whether swearing allegiance to an usurper, who is established and firmly settled on the throne, is not only supporting an unjust power, but approving of all he has done, and thereby becoming *particeps criminis*?' (ibid., 20). However, he was sufficiently persuaded of the government's legitimacy to take the oaths. On 25 April 1699, described as 'of Middlesex' (*Lincoln's Inn Admission Register*, 1.356), he migrated to Lincoln's Inn. His first wife, whose maiden name was Sambroke and whose given name may have been Sarah (a William Melmoth, son of William and Sarah Melmoth, was baptized at St Andrew's, Holborn, on 17 May 1696), died about this time, reputedly leaving him some property. By 1710 he had married Catherine, daughter of Samuel Rolt of Bedford, and granddaughter, on her mother's side, of Thomas Coxe, physician-in-ordinary to Charles II. They had four daughters—Constantia, Sophia, Catherine, and Jane—and two sons: the author William *Melmoth the younger (*bap.* 1710, *d.* 1799) and Thomas. Before their marriage Melmoth had to assure himself that an estate to be settled on him as part of his wife's jointure 'was so absolutely his property as to render it a sufficient security' (Melmoth, *Memoirs*, 44), presenting him with a clash between his love, his ambition, and his conscience.

Melmoth welcomed the accession of Queen Anne and the formation of a government with high-church sympathies, and hoped that it would prepare the way for a general reformation of manners. Melmoth viewed the stage with particular concern. In 1703 he brought playbills for a new version of *The Tempest* to a meeting of the SPCK, where he described them as a flaunting of God's judgment. He entered into an anonymous correspondence with Thomas Tenison, archbishop of Canterbury, in which he urged that 'nothing would soe effectively contribute to check the debauchery of the present age, as the suppressing the theatre, or at least a due regulation of it' (Melmoth, *Memoirs*, 53), as the stage encouraged the young into 'false notions of virtue and vice' (ibid.). He wrote in a similar strain to Daniel Defoe, to whom he sent a copy of Arthur Bedford's *The Evil and Danger of Stage Plays* (1706). He explained to Defoe that he was not opposed to plays in principle, as they could be morally useful, but that he considered the current London theatre corrupting.

Melmoth's increasing celebrity as a chancery counsel robbed him of time for writing, and according to his son he composed *The Great Importance of a Religious Life Consider'd* 'every Sabbath, after joining in the sacred and established functions of the day' (Melmoth, *Memoirs*, 58). The treatise concentrated less on the moral decay of society than on instilling in the individual 'a serious sense of religion and a true concern for the interest of their immortal souls' (Melmoth, *The Great Importance*, 1849, 37). An example of a religious life was that of the nonjuring clergyman John Kettlewell; Archbishop John Sharp's words on the distinction between worldly pleasures and communion with God were also quoted with approval. Melmoth's book was published anonymously in 1711 and became extremely popular. It was translated into Welsh and French, and Melmoth added to later editions a collection of morning and evening prayers and an essay on the

sacrament. Melmoth did not claim *The Great Importance* as his own during his lifetime; it was generally regarded as the work of John Perceval, first earl of Egmont, and listed as such by Horace Walpole in his *Catalogue of the Royal and Noble Authors of England*. The identity of the author was revealed by the younger William Melmoth only in 1797.

In 1719 Melmoth became a bencher of Lincoln's Inn; in the next year he was one of the leading chancery counsel, making 220 motions. Following the death of Thomas Vernon, MP for Worcestershire, in 1721, he and William Peere Williams were entrusted by Lord Chancellor Macclesfield with editing Vernon's chancery reports; Melmoth planned to publish his own reports but they remain in manuscript at the British Library. In 1730 he held the office of treasurer of Lincoln's Inn, and in 1741 he received a legacy from a friend, the tory MP John Hungerford, on the death of Hungerford's widow, towards the erection of posts and lamp irons around the inn. Melmoth's will shows that by 1742 he and his wife were living in a house in the passage between Fetter Lane and Bartlett's Buildings, in the parish of St Andrew, Holborn, and that he had property elsewhere in London and a country residence at Ealing, Middlesex.

In 1743 Melmoth was 'suddenly attacked with the strangury' (Melmoth, *Memoirs*, 72) but he continued to work until a few days before his death on 6 April 1743. He was buried in the cloister under the chapel at Lincoln's Inn on 14 April. *The Great Importance* continued to sell well throughout the eighteenth century and the first half of the nineteenth. It had reached thirty editions by 1797, selling 42,000 copies between 1766 and 1784 alone, and an edition published early in the 1840s claimed that 150,000 copies had been sold in the first forty years of the nineteenth century. Charles Purton Cooper, who edited *The Great Importance* for an edition published in 1849, claimed that Archbishop William Howley had related that it 'had been deemed by Queen Charlotte a book proper to be used in the education of the Princesses her daughters' (Melmoth, *The Great Importance*, 1849, 148). Princess Sophia's copy of the 1790 edition was placed in Lincoln's Inn Library, and in 1910 was given to Lambeth Palace Library, where it remains. Melmoth's thoughts on how a Christian society could be achieved by the self-examination and self-discipline of each individual endured well beyond the controversy that had given them form.

EMMA MAJOR and NICOLE POHL

Sources W. Melmoth, *Memoirs of a late eminent advocate and member of the honourable society of Lincoln's Inn* (1796) • will, PRO, PROB 11/725, sig. 125 • ESTC • DNB • W. Melmoth, *The great importance of a religious life consider'd* (1711); 30th edn (1797) • *A biographical history of England, from the revolution to the end of George I's reign: being a continuation of the Rev. J. Granger's work*, ed. M. Noble, 3 vols. (1806) • *A catalogue of the royal and noble authors of England, Scotland and Ireland … by the late Horatio Walpole*, ed. T. Park, 5 vols. (1806) • W. T. Lowndes, *The bibliographer's manual of English literature*, ed. H. G. Bohn, [new edn], 6 vols. (1864) • W. Melmoth, *The letters of Sir Thomas Fitzosborne* (1795) • *GM*, 1st ser., 67 (1797), 586–7 • W. Melmoth, *The great importance of a religious life considered*, new edn (1849) • W. P. Baildon, ed., *The records of the Honorable Society of Lincoln's Inn: the black books*, 3 (1899) • D. Lemmings, *Professors of the law* (2000) • J. Barry, 'Hell upon earth, or, The language of the playhouse', *Languages of* *witchcraft: narrative, ideology and meaning in early modern culture*, ed. S. Clark (2001), 139–58 • private information (2004) [Inner Temple; Lincoln's Inn]

Archives BM, reports, Add. MS 8127

Likenesses N. Schiavonette junior, stipple, BM, NPG; repro. in Melmoth, *Memoirs*

Wealth at death £5500—in shares and savings, plus property in London: will, PRO, PROB 11/725, fols. 239*v*–243*r*, sig. 125

Melmoth, William, the younger (*bap.* 1710, *d.* 1799), author and translator, was probably born in London, one of the seven children and elder of the two sons of William *Melmoth the elder (1665/6–1743), barrister, and his second wife, Catherine, daughter of Samuel Rolt of Milton Erneys in Bedfordshire and his wife, Mary, the daughter of Dr Thomas Coxe. He was educated first at a private school in Westminster, under the tutelage of a Mr Philips, before being admitted to Lincoln's Inn on 26 June 1724, and admitted pensioner at Magdalene College, Cambridge, on 24 June 1726, aged seventeen. Early sources suggest that he was also attached to Emmanuel College, but he seems not to have stayed long in Cambridge since he was called to the bar on 9 June 1732. In 1756 Sir John Eardley-Wilmot appointed Melmoth a commissioner of bankrupts.

According to earlier biographical sources, by 1739 Melmoth had left London and settled near Shrewsbury, but it is clear from surviving letters to his friend and publisher Robert Dodsley that he was based in Ealing until 1762. He seems to have abandoned the law at an early stage. Melmoth's first wife, Dorothy, daughter of William King (1685–1763), died on 20 June 1761, and in the autumn of 1762 he settled in Bath with his second wife, a Miss M. Ogle. He had no children of his own, but adopted and educated Sophia Skynner, daughter and coheir of the Revd John Skynner and granddaughter of Melmoth's uncle, and later the mother of a son named Melmoth Walters.

Melmoth's earliest publication, 'Of an Active and Retired Life', a poetic epistle to Henry Coventry (*d.* 1752), first printed in 1735, was later included in Dodsley's *Collection*. He is supposed the author of imitations of two epistles of Horace (i.18 and ii.1) published by T. Cooper in 1736. The first volume of his *Letters on Several Subjects* appeared in 1748, under the pseudonym Sir Thomas Fitzosborne; a second volume was added in 1749. The letters are fictionalized but have generally been held to have some autobiographical reference, and they certainly illustrate Melmoth's own favourite themes of retirement, friendship, and rhetorical style. 'Fitzosborne's letters' were to become one of Dodsley's best-sellers, going through ten editions by 1795; the eleventh edition, published in 1805, included an anonymous prefatory memoir which is usually attached to later printings of the work.

Melmoth actively contributed to various literary projects such as Edward Moore's *World* (1753–6) and Dodsley's *Fables* (1761), but otherwise occupied himself chiefly as a translator from Latin. The letters of Pliny the younger appeared in 1746, with a second edition in 1747 and a third in 1748. In 1753 Dodsley paid Melmoth £600 for his translation of Cicero's *Ad familiares* (as compared with £50 for Pliny's letters). Further translations from Cicero (*Cato, or,*

An Essay on Old Age and *Laelius, or, An Essay on Friendship*) appeared in 1773 and 1777. All these translations are accompanied with Melmoth's own extensive and learned 'remarks'.

The *Travels in Switzerland* of William Coxe consists of letters addressed to Melmoth, between 1776 and 1779, and in the edition of 1801 Coxe pays warm tribute to him as 'an affectionate and kindly instructor' ('Advertisement', viii). In 1793 Melmoth published a pamphlet vindicating himself against an attack by Jacob Bryant two years earlier on the view expressed in his notes on Pliny on Trajan's attitude towards the Christians. His last work, the brief *Memoir of a Late Eminent Advocate*, published in 1796, had been intended some five years earlier to accompany an edition he was planning of his father's chancery reports. His reputation quickly faded after his death, and in an acerbic note in the *London Magazine* (vol. 10, July 1824, 28) De Quincey describes his reluctance to take up the opportunity even to inspect a trunk full of Melmoth manuscripts. On the other hand Melmoth's version of Pliny's letters survived as the basis of the Loeb translation until 1969.

Although something of a recluse, Melmoth did have some dealings with Bath literary society. Mrs Thrale met him at Mrs Montagu's in 1780, reporting him to Johnson as 'just Tory enough to hate the Bishop of Peterborough for Whiggism, and Whig enough to abhor you for Toryism' and eliciting from Johnson the response: 'From the author of Fitzosborne's letters I cannot think myself much in danger. I met him only once about thirty years ago, and in some small dispute reduced him to whistle' (*Boswell's Life of Johnson*). Despite his longevity his health seems generally to have been poor, and a posthumous difficulty over the disposal of his father's manuscripts suggests that by the 1790s he had become somewhat erratic in his dealings with others. Melmoth was of middle height, spare, with bright, quick eyes and a deeply lined face. He died at his home, 12 Bladud's Buildings, Bath, on 13 May 1799, and was survived by his second wife. There is a Latin epitaph on a tablet in Bath Abbey, but he was buried at Batheaston.   PENELOPE WILSON

Sources 'A brief memoir of the life and writings of the author', W. Melmoth, *Fitzosborne's letters on several subjects*, 11th edn (1805) • *Universal Magazine of Knowledge and Pleasure*, 107 (1800), 100 • *GM*, 1st ser., 64 (1794), 550, 824, 989 • *GM*, 1st ser., 67 (1797), 586–7 • *GM*, 1st ser., 69 (1799), 261 • R. E. M. Peach, *Historic houses of Bath and their associations*, 2 (1884), 52–3 • T. De Quincey, 'Manuscripts of Melmoth', *London Magazine*, 10 (1824), 28 • *The correspondence of Robert Dodsley, 1733–1764*, ed. J. E. Tierney (1988) • Venn, *Alum. Cant.*, 1/3.175 • admission register, Magd. Cam., B/424 • J. E. Wilmot, *Memoirs of the life of the Right Honourable Sir John Eardley Wilmot* (1802), 9–10 • *Monthly Review*, 8 (1753), 430–56 • *Monthly Review*, 49 (1773–4), 109–15 • *Monthly Review*, 57 (1777), 461–6 • *Monthly Review*, enlarged ser., 15, 251–2 • *Monthly Review*, enlarged ser., 23, 269–70 • *ESTC* • Nichols, *Lit. anecdotes*, 2.193–4, 251; 3.40–42; 4.163; 5.414 • Nichols, *Illustrations*, 1.613–16 • notice of death of Melmoth's wife, *Public Advertiser* (24 June 1761) • J. Bryant, *The authenticity of the scriptures* (1791), 118–25 • T. J. Mathias, *The pursuits of literature: a satirical poem in four dialogues*, 5th edn (1798), 355 and n. • *Boswell's Life of Johnson*, ed. G. B. Hill, 3 (1887), 422–4 • 'Advertisement', W. Coxe, *Travels in Switzerland*, 4th edn (1801) • W. P. Baildon, ed., *The records of the Honorable Society of Lincoln's Inn: the black books*, 3 (1899), 300–01 [see entry for 25 June 1724] · W. P. Baildon, ed., *The records of the Honorable Society of Lincoln's Inn: the black books*, 4 (1902), 78–82, 192–3 [see entry for 25 June 1724] · *DNB*

Archives BL, commonplace books and letters on astronomy, Add. MSS 27463–27465 | BL, letters to Robert Dodsley and James Dodsley, Add. MS 35338 · BL, letters to Mrs S. Walters, Add. MS 22171 · Wilts. & Swindon RO, letters to Lord Ailesbury

Melrose. For this title name *see* Hamilton, Thomas, earl of Melrose and first earl of Haddington (1563–1637).

Melton, Geoffrey (*d.* in or before 1411), priest and physician, was one of several Oxford physicians who made a career out of university service, incomes from the church, and royal patronage. First mention of him occurs in February 1377, when, as master of arts, he was admonished not to carry arms in a university conflict. No other university degrees are recorded beyond this, although Melton practised medicine in royal circles. University-educated clerics commonly served élite patrons, without formal medical qualification, implying that reputation, clerical status, and arts education were more important than a medical degree in the later middle ages. Melton seems to have resided in Oxford for most of the rest of his life, probably teaching. He rented Little Black Hall in 1387 and in 1406 rented Staple Hall next door.

Melton's career in the church illustrates well why the church objected to the clerics it had educated serving as physicians. He was ordained subdeacon on 6 March 1395 and priest on 26 May 1396, but before that he held several incomes from the church. In 1389 he was canon of Westbury-on-Trym, Gloucestershire, and became prebendary of Woodford in Wiltshire. That same year he was imprisoned in Gloucester Castle in a dispute with the dean of Westbury, Wiltshire, only to be released by order of Richard II on 23 August 1389, after Richard had reasserted his authority. He received other benefices in 1393 and 1394.

Melton is first recorded as a doctor in 1388, when Master Geoffrey Melton 'medicus' was summoned from Oxford to Kenilworth to attend the earl of Derby, later Henry IV, 'because of the lord's infirmity'. The patent rolls record that on 17 June 1399 Richard II granted Melton an annuity of 40 marks a year for life from the exchequer until he received a benefice of equal value without cure of souls, or one of 100 marks a year with cure. He is there named king's clerk and physician. The new king, Henry IV, confirmed these letters patent for his former physician in November 1399. In 1400 Melton was in service as physician to Richard's second wife, Isabella, daughter of Charles VI of France. Toward the end of his life, in 1405, he was appointed canon of St George's Chapel, Windsor, whose records state that he left it a copy of the *Summa summarum* of Master William de Paul and a silk girdle with a silver gilt buckle and pendants in the image of the Virgin Mary. Melton was dead by 1411. A manuscript in the British Library (BL, Sloane MS 3153, fols. 19*v*–20) preserves a uroscopy 'secundum modernos per magistrum Galdfridum Mediltoun doctorem'.   FAYE GETZ

Sources C. H. Talbot and E. A. Hammond, *The medical practitioners in medieval England: a biographical register* (1965) · H. E. Ussery, *Chaucer's physician: medicine and literature in fourteenth-century England* (1971) · F. Getz, 'Medical practitioners in medieval England', *Social History of Medicine*, 3 (1990), 245–83 · BL, MS Sloane 3153, fols. 19*v*–20

Archives BL, Sloane MS 3153, fols. 19*v*–20

Melton, Sir John (*d.* 1640), author and politician, the son of Evan Melton, was born in Bampton parish, Devon, although it is possible that his family came from Yorkshire. He might be the John Melton who was admitted pensioner at Sidney Sussex College, Cambridge, on 25 June 1608; the following year he was reading law in chambers. In August 1626 he obtained a grant of arms and in 1634 he was admitted to Gray's Inn, perhaps as an honorary member. He was married three times and fathered six children who survived infancy. His first marriage, in January 1624, was to Elizabeth (*née* Moore), widow of Sir Ferdinando Heyburne and mother to Francis and Elizabeth. In 1634 he married Catherine Currance (*d.* 1635), who brought him land in Kent, and who produced Edward, John, Richard, and Anne from two pregnancies in 1634–5. Melton's third wife, Margaret Aldersley, outlived him.

Melton was the author of a single published poem, 'In laudem authoris', written in support of William Fennor's work, *Descriptions*, and two books—*A Sixe-Folde Politician: together with a Sixefolde Precept of Policy* (1609) and *Astrologaster, or, The Figure-Caster* (1620). 'Unlike the learned treatises, which sound as though they had been addressed to men of the twelfth century', *Astrologaster* 'is shot through with bright threads drawn from the life of Jacobean England' (Dick, iii–iv). It was sufficiently well known to be incorporated by William Rowland into his *Judicial Astrologie, Judicially Condemned* (1652), an attack on parliament's use of astrologers. Both books contain anti-Catholic rhetoric.

By 1624 Melton was secretary to Henry Percy, ninth earl of Northumberland, and the continued patronage of the Percy family brought him wealth and furthered his career. By 1632 he was serving Northumberland as receiver of rents and it might have been this that in 1628 gained him membership of a commission for levying debts due to the crown. His work for Northumberland brought him to the attention of Sir Thomas Wentworth, who in May 1625 asked Melton to gain for him the votes of the earl's freeholders in the Yorkshire election. Melton was Wentworth's replacement for Sir Arthur Ingram in the office of secretary to the council of the north. He bought the office in April 1632 and held it until his death, exercising it in person. On 11 September 1632 he was knighted at Wanstead, and the next year Wentworth took him on to the northern recusancy commission, where he supported the vice-president of the north, Sir Edward Osborne, in the face of several threats to the commission's work. Most of his letters to Wentworth refer to the commission's business, but he penned one letter in May 1635 to encourage Wentworth to bid for the post of lord treasurer.

Melton's commercial interests in saltpetre and coal appear to have been of significant financial benefit to him. By 1631 he was deputy saltpetreman for Yorkshire, Durham, and Northumberland, and during the 1630s he leased several mines from the earl of Northumberland and traded in coal, enabling him to leave manors in several counties, mining interests, and jewellery, in all worth about £2000, and more than £6000 in money to his family. He was elected as MP for Newcastle upon Tyne in the autumn of 1640, gaining the seat through Northumberland's patronage. He died in December, before his disputed return was handled by the committee for privileges, probably at Tottenham, for he was buried there, rather than at York Minster, his chosen resting-place. A monument to his memory was placed in Tottenham church.   FIONA POGSON

Sources DNB · Keeler, Long Parliament · H. G. Dick, 'Introduction', in J. Melton, Astrologaster, or, The figure caster, repr. 1975 (1620) · will, PRO, PROB 11/185, sig. 29 · The manuscripts of the Earl Cowper, 3 vols., HMC, 23 (1888–9) · The manuscripts of his grace the duke of Rutland, 4 vols., HMC, 24 (1888–1905), vol. 1 · Strafford papers, Sheff. Arch., Wentworth Woodhouse muniments, 2–3, 13–15 · J. Pory, letter to Viscount Scudamore, 28 April 1632, PRO, C115/M5/8404 · CSP dom., 1631–3; 1638–9 · The letters of John Chamberlain, ed. N. E. McClure, 2 vols. (1939) · J. Melton, letter to earl of Carlisle, 2 Dec 1633, BL, Egerton MS 2597, fol. 166 · renewal of northern recusancy commission, 1633, PRO, Chancery 66/2615 [unfol.] · R. Howell, Puritans and radicals in north England (1984) · R. R. Reid, The king's council in the north (1921) · Venn, Alum. Cant. · J. Le Neve, Monumenta Anglicana, 5 vols. (1717–19), vol. 4

Wealth at death approx. £8000; incl. £6000 in money, plus approx. £2000 in jewellery, land, and mining interests: PRO, PROB 11/185, sig. 29

Melton, William (d. 1340), archbishop of York, was the son of undistinguished parents from Melton in the parish of Welton near Hull, where he later established a chantry for them. However, he had a brother named Henry, whose grandsons he sent to be educated in Newark at his own cost, and this family became established among the gentry of Yorkshire. In his youth Melton spent some time in the University of Oxford, but no details of this are known, although he continued to help the university financially. By 1297 he had entered royal service in Prince Edward's household, of which he later became controller. He was extensively beneficed, probably (and quite lawfully) to pay his salary during the period of his employment in the king's service, since he owed most of his advancement to royal patronage. He was rector of Reepham, Lincolnshire, from 1299 and of six other places at times thereafter, as well as being a prebendary of Southwell Minster and of Dublin, Lincoln, York, and Salisbury cathedrals. He also held a prebendal position in the royal free chapel in Hastings (1314) and was provost of Beverley (1309), dean of St Martin's le Grand (1308–16), and archdeacon of Barnstaple (1308–9). His principal patron was Edward II, for whom he seems to have had a genuine and lasting affection.

Melton's outstanding ability in finance led to his rapid advancement when Edward became king. Already in 1301 he had been responsible for paying the wages of the Welsh infantry enrolled in the prince's army. From 8 July 1307 to 18 September 1312 he was keeper of the privy seal, and from 8 July 1307 to 30 November 1314 treasurer of the wardrobe. In 1308 he accompanied the king to his wedding with Isabella of France, having temporary charge of

the great seal, which he held again in 1310. In June 1308 he had witnessed the king's appointment of Gaveston as lieutenant of Ireland. He seems to have avoided committing himself either to the ordainers in 1312 or to the party of Thomas, earl of Lancaster, in 1322, again probably out of personal loyalty to the king, although he allowed his clergy to give an aid to Lancaster, and eventually, after some hesitation, supported the plea for the earl's canonization. In 1312 he was one of the proctors of the northern convocation that refused an aid to the king, but this was not held against him, for in the same year he was a commissioner to deal with the Cinque Ports, and in 1313, and again in 1319 and 1321, he was commissioned to treat with the Scots. In 1323 he was appointed to head a commission investigating abuses by commissioners of array in Nottinghamshire, while from 3 July 1325 to 14 November 1326 he was treasurer.

After Edward II's death Melton seems to have avoided royal appointments so far as he could. He did not attend Edward III's coronation, although he married the king to Philippa of Hainault in York Minster in 1328. In 1329 he was accused of complicity in Edmund of Woodstock's plot against Mortimer and Isabella, started in the belief that Edward II was still alive. He succeeded in clearing himself, and later was again treasurer (1330–31) and temporary keeper of the great seal (1333–4).

On 21 January 1316 Melton was through royal influence elected archbishop of York. He went to Avignon for his consecration, but despite repeated appeals from the king, this was delayed until 25 September 1317 by an interregnum in the papacy. On his return to England, Melton had his cross carried erect before him in Kent and London, to uphold the claims of the northern province against Canterbury, and on a later occasion seems to have imposed an interdict on any place where the archbishop of Canterbury trespassed with erect cross in the province of York, though an agreement was afterwards reached at the instance of the king. His relations with his suffragans were not always easy, and he once excommunicated Bishop Beaumont of Durham (d. 1333) for resisting his rights of visitation.

The years of Melton's tenure at York were greatly disrupted by Scottish invasions. Already in 1314 he had been empowered to raise money for the defence of the border, and after 1318 the raids of the Scots became more extensive and ferocious. They penetrated as far south as Preston and Boroughbridge, and exposed the archbishop himself to considerable danger in the course of his visitations. In 1319 a raid led by Sir James Douglas threatened York itself, and caused Melton to collect a scratch force of clerics and townsmen to resist the Scots at Myton-on-Swale. On 20 September he was heavily defeated and lost most of his army, with his armour, horses, and silver plate, but York did not fall. Between this date and the treaty of Edinburgh in 1328 Melton's province suffered more or less continuously from raids which left the country ravaged and the religious houses particularly impoverished. As late as 1339 the northern convocation was pleading poverty as an excuse for non-payment of taxation. His register also shows that Melton was heavily involved in the papal attempts to deal with Robert I. Repeated emissaries (often unfortunate friars) were sent north, either to publish Robert's excommunication or to urge him to a settlement, but these were invariably unsuccessful, either because of Robert's highly intelligent diplomacy or the terror inspired by his army.

There was also trouble from France, Scotland's traditional ally. During the War of St Sardos (1324–6) Edward II ordered Melton to banish foreign incumbents of English livings to 'rather remote places' where they could do no harm—an order to which the archbishop replied that he could not find any such persons (Hill and Robinson, 3, nos. 127–8). Edward III charged Melton, among others, to summon the army to resist a French invasion in 1339.

Melton's personal reputation in the civil service stood high in an age of considerable corruption. In 1316 the king, in granting him a quitclaim for any responsibilities he had incurred, mentioned his 'good service and fidelity in converting to the King's profit all the money and other goods which fell into his hands and custody' (CPR, 1313–17, 432). T. F. Tout wrote that Melton 'preserved his reputation unblemished throughout a long life. Many years of court service did not corrupt his fidelity or diminish his piety and charity' (Tout, 21–2). His practical knowledge of finance stood him in good stead as an archbishop. His register shows that, in a period when most officials were in debt, he was able to make extensive loans to the king, to the northern barons, and to poor religious houses, and even to the Italian banking house of Bardi, as well as building up his private estates. He contributed £700 to the fund for rebuilding York Minster, and restored at his own expense the tomb of St William. Not surprisingly, he took particular care to check the credentials of pardoners and collectors for good causes, giving special encouragement to those whom he found responsible.

In his diocese Melton was remembered as a good man who lived honestly and chastely. His household noted his habit of early rising and assiduous attendance at divine service, and seem to have received new outfits from him twice a year. He was sparing to himself and generous to the poor, often forgiving debts when they were owed by the needy. He was particularly careful in carrying out visitations (often in considerable personal danger) and enforcing subsequent injunctions. He was thorough in performing all the normal duties of his office, maintaining good order and discipline in parishes and non-exempt religious houses, supervising clerical appointments, and granting licences, dispensations, and testimonials. He dealt with some exceptional problems, such as a heretical preacher who was upsetting his female congregations, and a man addicted to necromancy. He had also to deal with the reallocation of the templars, whose order was dissolved in 1312, to other religious houses, and the regular payment of their pensions, a process that seems to have caused both him and the templars much trouble and distress. He dealt very mercifully with Joan Picot, a widow from Wigan, whose husband had burdened her with unreasonable conditions and heavy debts. Melton seems to have spent the last years of his life at Cawood and died there on 5 April 1340, to the general grief of his people. When his tomb was excavated it was found that he had been a very tall man. He had been buried with his chalice and paten. The statue in the niche over the west door of the minster is said to represent him, but too much reliance cannot be placed on portraiture in stone at this period.   ROSALIND HILL

Sources *The register of William Melton, archbishop of York, 1317–1340*, ed. R. M. T. Hill and D. Robinson, 1–3, CYS, 70–71, 76 (1977–88) · *Chancery records* · F. Palgrave, ed., *The parliamentary writs and writs of military summons*, 2 (1830–34) · *RotP*, vol. 2 · Rymer, *Foedera* · L. H. Butler, 'Archbishop Melton, his neighbours, and his kinsmen, 1317–1340', *Journal of Ecclesiastical History*, 2 (1951), 54–68 · S. Brown, 'A dispute between Archbishop Melton and the dean and chapter of York, c.1336–8', *BIHR*, 54 (1981), 110–19 · *Fasti Angl., 1300–1541*, [York] · J. Barbour, *The Bruce*, ed. W. W. Skeat, 2 vols., STS, 31–3 (1894) · T. F. Tout, *The place of the reign of Edward II in English history: based upon the Ford lectures delivered in the University of Oxford in 1913*, rev. H. Johnstone, 2nd edn (1936) · W. Stubbs, ed., *Chronicles of the reigns of Edward I and Edward II*, 2 vols., Rolls Series, 76 (1882–3) · J. Raine, ed., *Historical papers and letters from the northern registers*, Rolls Series, 61 (1873)

Archives Borth. Inst., register

Likenesses statue (of Melton?), York Minster

Wealth at death considerable: Hill and Robinson, eds., *Register*

Melton, William (*d.* 1528), theologian and Catholic priest, originated in the north of England and was educated at Cambridge (BA, 1476; MA, 1480; BTh, 1491; DTh, 1496), where between 1485 and 1495 he was a fellow of Michaelhouse (college records do not bear out the claim, first made in the Tudor biography of John Fisher, that he was master of Michaelhouse). At Cambridge he was a central figure in a group of reforming scholars which included John Fisher, John Constable, Ralph Collingwood, and John Colet, a group closely involved with the first stirrings of humanism in the Cambridge curriculum. Fisher treasured fond memories of Melton's lectures on Euclid. Ordained priest on 23 September 1486, Melton was instituted to the rectory of Clayworth, Nottinghamshire, on 18 May 1490, presented by George Fitzhugh, dean of Lincoln (whom he doubtless knew from Cambridge, and by whom he was appointed an executor in 1506). On 6 June 1496, by now papally dispensed for plurality, he was presented to the rectory of Aston, Yorkshire (which he resigned in 1517), by Sir John Melton, the head of the family. Archbishop Rotherham of York collated him to the prebends of Thockrington (1493–4) and then Laughton-en-le-Morthen (1498–1528) in York Minster, making him chancellor of York in 1496, a position he retained until his death. In this capacity he figured as executor and beneficiary of many prominent York churchmen over the following thirty years.

Melton retained his scholarly interests after leaving Cambridge. His impressive library, recorded in the inventory of his goods, numbered over 100 items, including many patristic, classical, and humanist texts. Particularly noteworthy are his copies of Plato and of More's *Utopia*, as well as works by such leading humanists as Pico della Mirandola, Jacques Lefèvre d'Étaples, and Erasmus (who was aware of Melton's support for his use of humanist techniques in theology). Besides these, he had an almost complete set of the works of his former pupil John Fisher against Luther and Oecolampadius. These were probably gifts from the author, who had certainly sent him a copy of an earlier work on St Mary Magdalen in 1519. He was clearly adding to his library until the onset of his final illness in 1528. Fisher praised him as an 'outstanding theologian', and recorded that Melton had written unpublished tracts against Luther. Melton contributed prologues to some devotional writings of John Norton, prior of the Yorkshire Charterhouse of Mount Grace, and was probably the author of a continuation of a chronicle of the archbishops of York. He did publish, with the seal of approval of his friend John Colet—the inventory attached to Melton's will included 'A little table that was Mr Doctor Colette's'—*Sermo exhortatorius* (c.1510), an address to ordinands urging them to piety and study. Like Colet, Fisher, and other leading churchmen around the turn of the century, he was particularly attached to the cult of the name of Jesus, and was committed to the reform of the clergy through education. Melton was struck down with 'a palsy' in May 1528, and died at Acklam, Yorkshire (a living in his gift), on 25 October 1528.   RICHARD REX

Sources S. M. Leathes, ed., *Grace book A* (1897) · M. Bateson, ed., *Grace book B*, 2 vols. (1903–5) · E. E. Barker, ed., *The register of Thomas Rotherham … 1480–1500*, CYS, 69 (1976) · J. Fisher, *De veritate corporis et sanguinis Christi in eucharistia* (1527), sig. BB4r and fol. cxxxiiiir, prefaces to bks 1 and 5 · *CEPR letters*, 16.646 · Lincoln Cathedral Library, MS A.6.8 [devotional writings of John Norton] · J. Raine, ed., *The historians of the church of York and its archbishops*, 2, Rolls Series, 71 (1886), xxv, 422–55 · letters, 29 March 1519, St John Cam., Archives, D.56.14, D.56.45 [relating to Fisher's friendship with Melton] · Erasmus, *Adversus Petri Sutoris … debacchationem apologia* (1525), sig. K2 · Emden, *Cam.*, 400–01 · [J. Raine], ed., *Testamenta Eboracensia*, 5, SurtS, 79 (1884), 251–63 · *LP Henry VIII*, 4/2, nos. 1887–8

Melun, Robert de (c.1100–1167), theologian and bishop of Hereford, was of obscure origins; nothing is known of his parentage or place of birth, save that he was English. According to William fitz Stephen he taught in the schools of France for over forty years; his birth, therefore, has usually been dated to c.1100. Robert made his reputation as a teacher of dialectic and theology. He studied in Paris under Hugh of St Victor and, probably, Peter Abelard. John of Salisbury (d. 1180), Henry II's cousin Roger (later bishop of Worcester, d. 1179) and, perhaps, Thomas Becket were numbered among his pupils. Herbert of Bosham describes him as a great luminary, 'who sent forth from himself, like rays of his light, a great and learned host of students' (Robertson and Sheppard, 3.260). The best portrait of Robert in these years comes from John of Salisbury, who considers him to be one of the great dialecticians of his time. Robert, he says, was a perceptive scholar who always had a ready response to the propositions laid before him; however, he 'never ended a discussion without first setting forth opposing arguments', maintaining that there was no single answer to a question (*Metalogicon*, 79). Modern commentators have concurred in this assessment of Robert's scholarly technique.

Robert was active in the schools of Paris from 1137, when John of Salisbury studied under him, until 1142, when he moved to Melun, whence he took the name under which he has since been known. By 1147 he had returned to Paris to join Peter Lombard's attack on Gilbert de la Porrée, bishop of Poitiers; it is likely that he attended Gilbert's trial at the Council of Rheims in 1148. Precise dating of Robert's three extant theological works remains a matter of controversy. His *Questiones de epistolis Pauli* was probably written between 1145 and 1157; a similar range of dates has been suggested for his *Questiones de divina pagina*, 125 questions focusing on the gospel according to St Matthew. The unfinished *Sententie* which was revised twice, dates from the 1150s or 1160s. Robert's editor, R. M. Martin, has identified eight extant manuscripts of the *Sententie*, none of which is complete, and four abbreviations. Annotations in several of these manuscripts, and direct or indirect references to Robert's work in the texts of twelfth- and thirteenth-century authors, suggest that Robert did have some influence on his contemporaries, although it was clearly not as great as that exerted by Peter Lombard.

Robert de Melun was a scholar of independent mind. He joined Peter Lombard in condemning Gilbert de la Porrée, but opposed Lombard's Christology. A proponent of Abelard's methodology, Robert explored many of the questions Abelard had raised, and defended him against the charge of heresy, but he did not adopt all of Abelard's doctrinal positions. Like many of his contemporaries, Robert was interested in harmonizing apparently conflicting authorities. In the introduction to his *Sententie*, he announced his intention to reconcile the works of 'two pre-eminent authors' (*Oeuvres*, 3, pt 1, 45), unnamed in the text, but identified by modern scholarship as Abelard and Hugh of St Victor. Robert, who claims to have heard both authors *viva voce*, argues that there is an underlying unity in their work, despite their apparent difference. Combining them, therefore, will produce 'one most distinguished book of sentences' (ibid., 3, pt 1, 47–8).

However, the independence of thought, commitment to understanding all sides of the issues, and interest in reconciling conflicting opinions, that characterized Robert's scholarly career, did not stand him in good stead when his elevation to the bishopric of Hereford forced him into the volatile arena of English ecclesiastical politics. Some time between 1160 and 1163 Henry II summoned Robert to England, probably at the suggestion of Thomas Becket. He was nominated to the see of Hereford in 1163 and was consecrated on 22 December by Becket, to whom he swore obedience.

Little can be said of Robert de Melun's tenure of the see of Hereford—only five certain *acta* survive from its three years and two months. In 1165 he is recorded as acting as a papal judge-delegate, and he confirmed the grants of his two immediate predecessors to Llanthony Priory, himself adding to these a grant of tithes from the episcopal demesne at Prestbury, Gloucestershire. His apparent inactivity is doubtless attributable to the conflict between Becket and Henry II, which bedevilled his episcopate.

Indeed, even before his consecration Robert found himself caught in a tug-of-war between the archbishop, the king, and the pope. In October 1163 Alexander III sent Robert to Canterbury as part of a mission urging Becket to come to terms with Henry. Becket's subsequent submission was ephemeral, and by October 1164 he was on trial at Northampton. Nevertheless, Robert continued to play a moderating role. When Becket arrived at court bearing his episcopal cross before him, a dramatic reminder of his spiritual power, Robert, with all deference, tried to take it from him, perhaps in an attempt to defuse the situation. At the trial's conclusion it was Robert, according to William fitz Stephen (Robertson and Sheppard), who urged the king to issue orders protecting Becket, and Robert, along with the bishops of Worcester and Rochester, whom Becket sent to Henry to ask for a safe conduct from the court.

Robert's role as intermediary became increasingly untenable as Becket's escape to France and subsequent exile further estranged the king and his archbishop. In June 1165 Alexander III ordered him to accompany Gilbert Foliot (d. 1187) on a mission to rebuke Henry for his mistreatment of Becket and the church. The mission was unsuccessful, and Robert was chastised by the pope for his failure to advance Becket's cause, and enjoined to offer him full support; the letter ended, however, with an admonition to keep this command secret until the king and the archbishop had been reconciled.

Throughout 1165–6 Robert de Melun was plagued by conflicting demands from Becket, who implored him to support his cause, and Henry, who demanded that his bishops join him in appealing against the sentences of excommunication pronounced by Becket at Vézelay in June 1166. Robert was one of three bishops whose seals were appended to the appeal. Yet at the same time he was criticized with increasing vehemence by the archbishop's supporters. In August 1166, Abbot Ernisius and Prior Richard of St Victor wrote to him at John of Salisbury's instigation, urging him to support Becket and accusing him of hypocrisy; Robert, they said, did not practise what he had preached as a schoolmaster. John of Salisbury, once so effusive in his praise, now affirmed that Robert was 'believed to be a man of letters by those who know nothing of letters, or of him' (*Letters of John of Salisbury*, 2.156–7).

An event recounted by William fitz Stephen suggests that Robert de Melun's approach to the conflict was conditioned by his scholarly training. The bishop, he says, 'tearfully' proposed a question to a group of bishops and priests: if the archbishop should be killed in the cause of defending the liberties of the church, could he be considered a martyr? No, Robert concluded, a martyr was one who died for the faith. The story may be apocryphal, but conforms to Robert's character and reflects his interest in precise definitions. By distinguishing between 'ecclesiastical liberties' and 'faith', Robert could justify his tepid support of Becket; in matters of faith, compromise was not possible, but Becket's cause was no such matter. It was

Robert's tragedy, perhaps, to be intellectually and temperamentally committed to compromise at a time when compromise was no longer possible.

In October 1166 Becket ordered Robert de Melun to join him in France; Henry forbade him to go, swearing that if he left he would not be allowed to return. When Becket's third summons came, Robert tried to leave England secretly, but was caught at Southampton on 2 February and ordered to turn back. He died at Hereford less than a month later, on 27 February 1167—of a broken heart, William fitz Stephen claims—and was buried in his cathedral. M. L. RAMPOLLA

Sources *Oeuvres de Robert de Melun*, ed. R. M. Martin, 4 vols. (1932–52) · D. E. Luscombe, 'Robert of Melun', *The school of Peter Abelard: the influence of Abelard's thought in the early scholastic period* (1969), 281–98 · B. Smalley, 'Robert Pullen and Robert of Melun', *The Becket conflict and the schools* (1973), 51–8 · J. C. Robertson and J. B. Sheppard, eds., *Materials for the history of Thomas Becket, archbishop of Canterbury*, 7 vols., Rolls Series, 67 (1875–85) · M. L. Colish, 'Roland of Bologna, Robert Pullen, Robert of Melun', *Peter Lombard*, 2 vols. (1994), 1.65–77 · *Ioannis Saresberiensis episcopi Metalogicon libri IIII*, ed. C. C. I. Webb (1929) · *The letters of John of Salisbury*, ed. and trans. H. E. Butler and W. J. Millor, rev. C. N. L. Brooke, 2 vols., OMT (1979–86) [Lat. orig. with parallel Eng. text] · F. Barlow, *Thomas Becket* (1986) · D. Knowles, *The episcopal colleagues of Archbishop Thomas Becket* (1951) · J. Barrow, ed., *Hereford, 1079–1234*, English Episcopal Acta, 7 (1993)

Melvill, Henry (1798–1871), Church of England clergyman, fifth son of Philip Melvill (1760–1811), an officer in the army, who was lieutenant-governor of Pendennis Castle from 1797 until 1811, and his wife, Elizabeth Carey (1770–1845), daughter of Peter Dobree of Beauregard, Guernsey, was born in Pendennis Castle, Cornwall, on 14 September 1798, and became a sizar of St John's College, Cambridge, in October 1817. After migrating to Peterhouse he passed as second wrangler in 1821, and was a fellow and tutor there from 1822 to 1829. He graduated BA in 1821, MA in 1824, and BD in 1836. From 1829 to 1843 he served as incumbent of Camden Chapel, Camberwell, Surrey, and was appointed by the duke of Wellington chaplain to the Tower of London in 1840. Early in 1844 he became principal of the East India College, Haileybury, holding the post until the college was closed, by the legislation which followed the Indian mutiny, on 7 December 1857. By then, Melvill was already (from 21 April 1856) a canon residentiary of St Paul's Cathedral; he was also rector of Barnes, Surrey, 1863–71. He was, in addition, Golden lecturer at St Margaret's, Lothbury, 1850–56, and one of the chaplains to Queen Victoria from 13 June 1853.

Melvill for many years had the reputation of being 'the most popular preacher in London' and one of the greatest rhetoricians of his time. First at Camden Chapel, then at St Margaret's, and later at St Paul's, large crowds of people attended his sermons. These generally occupied three-quarters of an hour, but such was the rapidity of his utterance that he spoke as much in that time as an ordinary preacher would have done in an hour. His delivery was earnest and animated, without distinctive gesticulation; his voice was clear and flexible, while his emphatic pronunciation and his hurried manner of speaking impressed the hearers with a conviction of his sincerity. He had a 'wonderful faculty of what may be called magnetizing or fascinating the ear' (Prestige, 154), and he was known as the evangelical Chrysostom. But his sermons lacked simplicity and directness of style, and his ornate phraseology, happy analogies, and smoothly balanced sentences appealed more directly to the literary than to the spiritual sense. His views were evangelical, and he was a zealous parish priest. Melvill published many volumes of his sermons, several of which went through numerous editions. These were chiefly of his Cambridge sermons and those delivered at St Margaret's, Lothbury (one volume of the latter, *Forty Eight Sermons* (1850), was published without his permission).

Melvill died, rather rich, at 2 Residentiary Houses, Amen Corner, London, on 9 February 1871, and was buried in St Paul's Cathedral on 15 February. His widow, Margaret Alice, daughter of Captain Richard Jennings RN, died on 18 April 1878, aged seventy-three, leaving a daughter Edith, who married Clement Alexander Midleton.

G. C. BOASE, *rev.* H. C. G. MATTHEW

Sources Venn, *Alum. Cant.* · Crockford (1870) · J. Grant, *The metropolitan pulpit*, 2 vols. (1839) · J. E. Ritchie, *The London pulpit* (1854) · J. Johnson, *Popular preachers of our time* (1864) · *Memoirs of … Philip Melvill … selected by a friend* (1812) · W. H. Blanch, *The parish of Camberwell* (1875) · F. C. Danvers and others, *Memorials of old Haileybury College* (1894) · G. L. Prestige, *St Paul's in its glory: a candid history of the cathedral, 1831–1911* (1955)
Archives U. Southampton L., Wellesley MSS
Likenesses C. Turner, mezzotint, pubd 1835 (after J. Rand), BM · R. Artlett, stipple (after Rand), NPG · portrait, repro. in *ILN*, 4 (1844), 48 · portrait, repro. in Danvers and others, *Memorials*, 152 · portrait, repro. in *Illustrated News of the World* (6 Sept 1862)
Wealth at death under £60,000: probate, 31 March 1871, *CGPLA Eng. & Wales*

Melvill, Sir James Cosmo (1792–1861), East India Company servant, was born at Guernsey, the third son of Captain Philip Melvill (1760–1811), afterwards lieutenant-governor of Pendennis Castle, Cornwall, and his wife, Elizabeth Carey (1770–1845), youngest daughter of Peter Dobree of Beauregarde, Guernsey. Their fifth son, Henry *Melvill, was principal of Haileybury College and canon of St Paul's. Their fourth son, Lieutenant-Colonel Peter Melvill, was military and naval secretary to the government of Bombay.

Melvill entered the home service of the East India Company as a clerk in February 1808. In March 1815 he married Hester Jane Frances (d. 1864), youngest daughter of William Marmaduke Sellon of Harlesden, Middlesex; they had nine children. In 1824 he was promoted to auditor of Indian accounts, in which capacity he appeared before several parliamentary committees. In 1834 he became financial secretary to the company and in 1836 chief secretary.

As chief secretary Melvill corresponded with many of the company's principal servants in India and with friends and critics alike of the company at home. Often, as at the time of Lord Ellenborough's recall, he was required to soften and deflect opposition to the company's more controversial decisions. His friendly diplomacy won over even the notoriously unforgiving critic of the company, Joseph Pease, the anti-slavery campaigner, who came to look upon him as a fellow fighter in the cause of humanity and a personal friend.

Politically, Melvill was a traditionalist, opposed to the territorial acquisitions of the 1840s and 1850s and keen to preserve the independence and prestige of India's remaining princes. In spite of his financial background, he did not hesitate to criticize acts of economy which he thought to be politically harmful. For example, he deplored as short-sighted the company's periodic bouts of military retrenchment, correctly observing that such cutbacks were generating a smouldering resentment among Indian soldiers and their families.

In 1853 Melvill was created KCB. In February 1858, after fifty years of service, he retired, although he continued for some months as *ex officio* government director of Indian Railways. He was the last chief secretary of the company. He was elected a fellow of the Royal Society in 1841 and became a commissioner of lieutenancy for the city of London in 1847.

Melvill died at his home, Tandridge Court, near Godstone in Surrey, on 23 July 1861. His widow survived him by three years. Their second son, James Cosmo (1821–1880), followed his father into the home administration of British India and in 1859 was appointed assistant undersecretary of state for India.

E. I. CARLYLE, *rev.* KATHERINE PRIOR

Sources BL OIOC, Melvill MSS · *ILN* (3 Aug 1861), 124 · J. H. Bell, *British folks and British India fifty years ago: Joseph Pease and his contemporaries* [1891] · BL OIOC, Clerk MSS · *DNB* · *GM*, 3rd ser., 11 (1861), 334 · *CGPLA Eng. & Wales* (1861)
Archives BL OIOC, papers, MS Eur. B 137 · priv. coll., family papers | BL OIOC, corresp. with Sir George Russell Clerk, MS Eur. D 538 · BL OIOC, letters to Lord Tweeddale, MS Eur. F 96 · NL Scot., corresp. with Sir Charles Malcolm · W. Sussex RO, corresp. with Moulree Museeh-Ooddeen Khan Bahador [copies]
Likenesses J. J. Napier, portrait, exh. 1858, NPG
Wealth at death £60,000: probate, 16 Aug 1861, *CGPLA Eng. & Wales*

Melvill, Thomas (1726–1753), natural philosopher, was born in Monimail, Fife, the son of the Revd Andrew Melvil (d. 1736) of Monimail and his wife, Helen, formerly White, and the younger brother of Robert *Melville (1723–1809), army officer. He matriculated at Glasgow University in 1739 and graduated MA in 1744. In 1748–9, as a student of divinity at the university, he became friends with Alexander Wilson, later the first professor of astronomy at Glasgow. Together they decided to explore the temperature of the upper air by raising a string of kites, each of which bore a thermometer. In July 1749 and again the following summer they sent up kites. It was arranged that the thermometers, wrapped in bundles of protective paper, should be detached by setting a slow match to burn through the strings that held them, and fall to the ground (the registering thermometer had yet to be invented). As these experiments were done in fine weather, they did not anticipate Franklin's discovery of atmospheric electricity.

Melvill then studied optics, intending to verify Newton's theories. In his 'Observations on light and colours', delivered to the Medical Society of Edinburgh on 3 January and 7 February 1752, Melvill described his use of a prism to examine an alcohol flame coloured by various salts. He remarked on a yellow line always seen at a constant place in the spectrum. This yellow line was in fact derived from sodium, which was present as a constituent or impurity in all the salts that he was testing; hence Melvill is sometimes seen as the father of flame spectroscopy, though there is no evidence that he thought of his experiments as a method of analysis.

In a letter sent from Geneva on 2 February 1753 to the astronomer royal, James Bradley, Melvill discussed whether light rays of differing colours travelled at different velocities, which might account for their differing refraction through a prism. He proposed that this could be confirmed if the satellites of Jupiter were seen to change slightly in colour as they occulted and emerged. This letter was read before the Royal Society on 8 March and the telescope maker James Short was instructed to make the necessary observations, but he reported that no such effect could be seen. In a second letter to Bradley, dated 2 June, Melvill suggested that the rate of light travel concerned in aberration might be affected by the humours of the eye itself. Melvill died in Geneva in December 1753 at the age of twenty-seven.

A. M. CLERKE, rev. ANITA MCCONNELL

Sources P. Wilson, 'Biographical account of Alexander Wilson, MD, late professor of practical astronomy in Glasgow', *Transactions of the Royal Society of Edinburgh*, 10 (1824), 279–97 · W. I. Addison, ed., *The matriculation albums of the University of Glasgow from 1728 to 1858* (1913), 23 · J. C. D. Brand, *Lines of light: the sources of dispersive spectroscopy, 1800–1930* (1995), 58 · J. Priestley, *The history and present state of discoveries relating to vision, light and colours*, 1 (1792), 359 · Monimail, parish register, 1726

Melville. For this title name *see* individual entries under Melville; *see also* Dundas, Henry, first Viscount Melville (1742–1811); Dundas, Robert Saunders, second Viscount Melville (1771–1851); Dundas, Henry, third Viscount Melville (1801–1876).

Melville, Andrew (1545–1622), university principal and theologian, was born at Baldovy, near Montrose, Angus, on 1 August 1545, the youngest of nine sons of Richard Melville of Baldovy (d. 1547) and Giles Abercrombie, daughter of a burgess in Montrose. Andrew's eldest brother, Richard, who inherited the family's estate, studied at the Lutheran University of Greifswald, where he matriculated in 1546; as tutor to James Erskine, the laird of Dun's son, he accompanied the latter to Wittenberg, where they studied for two years under Philip Melanchthon before proceeding to Copenhagen and meeting John Macalpine, who taught theology in the university there. By 1560 Richard was authorized by the general assembly of the kirk in Scotland to undertake service in the reformed church, and he became minister of the neighbouring parish of Maryton. Of the other brothers, Thomas visited France and Italy, became a civil servant, and

attained high office; Walter settled in Montrose and was a magistrate; Roger became a burgess of Dundee; James became minister of Arbroath; John served as minister of Crail; and Robert and David both became craftsmen.

Education Brought up by his brother Richard, Andrew Melville attended Montrose grammar school, where Thomas Anderson was schoolmaster. According to his nephew, Andrew was a 'seiklie tender boy' who 'tuk pleasur in na thing sa mikle as his buik'. He remained in Montrose for a further 'year or twa', at his own expense, to be taught 'the Greek grammar and something of that language' by the Frenchman Pierre de Marsiliers, whom the reforming provost, John Erskine of Dun, had attracted to the burgh (*Autobiography and Diary*, 39). In 1559 he enrolled at St Mary's College in St Andrews University and was befriended by its provost, John Douglas, who conformed at the Reformation and contributed in 1560 to the reformers' Book of Discipline. Among his fellow students in the class of 1559–60 was James Lawson, who eventually aspired to the presbyterian leadership as Knox's chosen successor as minister in Edinburgh. After he had 'past his cuirse' and graduated MA probably in 1563, with the reputation of being 'the best philosopher, poet, and Grecian, of anie young maister in the land' (ibid., 39), Melville sailed first to England and then to France. He visited Bordeaux and Dieppe before finally reaching Paris, 'whar he remeanit in the Universitie twa yeiris at his awin studies' (ibid., 39–40).

In Paris, Melville attended the public lectures given in the Collège de France, the royal trilingual college founded by François I in 1530, primarily for the study of Latin, Greek, and Hebrew. He heard Jean Mercier and Jean de Cinquarbres on Hebrew; Pierre de la Ramée (Peter Ramus), the great critic of Aristotelianism, and his great opponent Adrien Turnèbe, on Greek and Latin philosophy; Pierre Forcadel, Jacques Charpentier, and Pascal Duhamel on mathematics; and Louis Duret on medicine. He also heard the Italian protestant scholar Joseph Justus Scaliger on Hebrew and François Baudouin on law. By 1566 Melville had decided to further his legal studies by proceeding to Poitiers, a Roman Catholic town held by the duke of Guise and besieged by protestant forces under Admiral Coligny, where he tutored privately and taught in the university for three years.

In 1569 the religious wars led Melville to seek refuge in Geneva, where his kinsman Henry Scrimgeour was a professor of law. Melville travelled on foot, 'as he haid done befor from Deipe to Paris, and from that to Poicteors' and 'caried na thing with him bot a litle Hebrew Byble in his belt', to study theology, 'wherto he was dedicat from his mother's wombe' (*Autobiography and Diary*, 40–41). He did, however, take letters of introduction to Theodore Beza. He attended Beza's 'daylie lessons and preatchings' and made divinity 'his cheiff studie' (ibid., 42). At Geneva he gained a knowledge of the Chaldaic and Syriac tongues from Bertram, the professor of Hebrew, and Beza secured his appointment in November 1569 to teach Latin in the *collège*. Melville was bold enough to question the pronunciation of Portus, the professor of Greek, probably following the new pronunciation of the language fostered by Ramus in Paris.

Also resident in Geneva by 1571 were two future leaders of English presbyterianism, Thomas Cartwright and Walter Travers, the latter of whom produced during his Genevan stay his *Ecclesiasticae disciplinae … explicatio* (1574). Melville's interest in the work was such that he later presented a copy of the treatise to a fellow Calvinist, Alexander Arbuthnot, principal of King's College, Aberdeen. Following the influx of further Huguenot exiles to Geneva after the massacre of St Bartholomew's day in 1572, Melville had the opportunity to hear François Hotman, the French lawyer and political theorist, whose *Franco-Gallia* (1573) reasserted the ultimate sovereignty of the people over their king. He also maintained a lasting friendship with another exile from France, Joseph Scaliger, who taught philosophy. In 1570 Melville heard Ramus lecture on Cicero and followed him to Lausanne to attend his lectures in July the same year. Ramus then returned to Paris, and Melville went back to Geneva.

Return to Scotland and university reform at Glasgow Persuaded by his fellow countrymen to go home, so that his native land might benefit from the services of a distinguished scholar at a politically critical time, Melville left Geneva in April 1574 after five years' residence. He travelled in the company of Alexander Campbell, titular bishop of Brechin, and Andrew Polwarth, later minister at Paisley. In Paris he engaged in debates at the Jesuit college, where the archbishop of Glasgow, then resident, made 'sum minassing speitches'; aware of the dangers, he made for Dieppe (*Autobiography and Diary*, 44). After spending some time in London he arrived home in July with testimonials from Beza, as moderator of the Venerable Company of Pastors, and from Jean Pinaud, rector of the *collège*, in which they warmly praised his abilities and recommended him to the Scottish church. According to Melville's nephew, Beza considered that 'the graittest tak*en of affection the Kirk of Genev could schaw to Scotland' was 'that they had suffered tham selves to be spuiled of Mr Andro Melvill, wherby the Kirk of Scotland might be inritched' (ibid., 42–3).

From Edinburgh, Melville set out for Baldovy, where he sought 'to repose a whyll with his frinds' (*Autobiography and Diary*, 45) and tutored his nephew James *Melville (1556–1614). News of his return resulted in competition for his services, but as he 'lyked nocht to be in Court bot rather to be in sum Universitie' (ibid.), he declined the offer to become court chaplain to the regent, James Douglas, fourth earl of Morton. His candidature as principal of St Mary's College in St Andrews, in succession to John Douglas, the archbishop, who had died in July, was canvassed in the general assembly in August 1574. In the end, however, he accepted the invitation to become principal of Glasgow University at the behest of Archbishop Boyd, the university chancellor, and Andrew Hay, university rector and commissioner of churches in the west. Before taking up his appointment, which took effect in November

1574, Melville visited Stirling where he 'conferrit at leynthe' with George Buchanan, then tutor to King James, and met the young king, 'the sweitest sight in Europe that day, for strange and extraordinar gifts of ingyne, judgment, memorie and langage' (ibid., 48).

Once installed in Glasgow, Melville set about revitalizing teaching. As an admirer of the anti-scholastic philosophy of Ramus, he introduced Ramist texts in logic, rhetoric, geometry, and arithmetic, and initiated specialist teaching in place of the outmoded practice of regenting, the system of conducting students through their entire course of study. Greek, Hebrew, and the unfamiliar Syriac and Chaldaic languages, necessary for scholarly biblical exegesis, took their place in the curriculum alongside classes in history, geography, and astronomy, but not metaphysics, which was discarded as unprofitable.

Melville's emphasis was on the *studia humanitatis*, the liberal arts, and epitomized the new humanist values designed to replace the old scholasticism. At table after meals in college, he was apt to demonstrate informally how 'Aristotle could err and haid erred' (*Autobiography and Diary*, 67). His drastic reconstitution of the curriculum and a realistic benefaction by King James in 1577 strengthened Glasgow's reputation, and soon St Andrews and Aberdeen universities, followed by the town college in Edinburgh, adopted features of his successful experiment in Glasgow.

Reform in the church As theology professor and biblical scholar Melville also exercised a powerful influence within the church, which stood in the tradition of the 'best reformed churches' on the continent. Unlike the universities, the church had experienced a thorough reformation on Calvinistic lines. After his homecoming Melville attended meetings of the general assembly and, by applying Reformation principles, sought to correct perceived defects in the church's operation. He offered attractive solutions to outstanding problems and was keen to integrate the universities more fully in the wider work of the reformed church. He saw himself as holding the ecclesiastical office of doctor, which according to Calvin was one of the four essential offices in the church, and with a seat in church courts he saw it as his duty to interpret scripture aright by applying the tools of philology to exegesis. He also lent his support to the general assembly's determination to resist Regent Morton's policy of conforming the Scottish church with that of England.

When appointed by the general assembly in 1575 to two committees for examining the aptitude of the bishop of Moray and the bishop-elect of Dunblane, Melville seems to have expressed no disapproval of the episcopal office. He was concerned not with ending episcopacy but with recommending how the examination and election of bishops could be made more effective. His attitude to bishops was based at least as much on observation and experience of Scottish practice as on any doctrinaire argument inherited from Geneva. Yet his introduction to the episcopate through the bishops of Moray and Dunblane, two improper promotions criticized by the assembly as neither had first served as a minister, provided Melville with ample ammunition when prevailing dissatisfaction over episcopal appointments led to a critical appraisal of bishops 'as they are now in the Kirk of Scotland'.

In the assembly of 1575 Melville is said to have supported opponents of the Leith episcopacy by illustrating how the New Testament bishop was 'not to be taken in the sense that the common sort did conceive, there being no superiority allowed by Christ among ministers' (Spottiswoode, 2.200). He affirmed (as Beza had earlier warned John Knox) that the church could not remain in purity unless the corruption that had crept into the estate of bishops was completely removed. The assembly certainly appointed him to a committee to debate whether diocesan episcopacy had scriptural validity and whether the electoral chapter could be tolerated in a reformed church. The committee's verdict was that the name 'bishop' was applicable to all ministers of the word and sacraments, though some might still be chosen to act as visitors while retaining their congregational charges. Melville's nephew claimed that ministers were 'informed mair throwlie be Mr Andro of the unlawfulnes of Bischopes, and the right maner of governing of the Kirk be Presbyteries', which suggests that his uncle's ideas were already shared by others, and Andrew Hay is named as one minister 'wha lyked never those bischopries and wha specialie was the ernest suttar for Mr Andro Melvill' (*Autobiography and Diary*, 48, 56).

The arguments advanced by Melville and his colleagues, so familiar to readers of Calvin's *Institutes*, seem to have been that the New Testament bishop was not a great diocesan prelate who sat in parliament and council, the 'lord-like bishop' for whom Knox had shown such distaste, but rather an overseer and shepherd of the flock. Melville was determined to ensure that power continued to lie with assemblies of the church, which Regent Morton's policy threatened to subvert, and not with a new order of bishops. He was a member of the assembly's committee of more than thirty members charged with preparing the second Book of Discipline (1578). Of his 'exceiding grait peans' in regularly 'keiping Assemblies and dyettes of conference, reasoning and advysing with brethring anent that wark', there is sufficient testimony (*Autobiography and Diary*, 52); yet he was not the chief author, and even his admiring nephew assigned no greater role to him than to the other participants. Nevertheless, the whole thrust of the programme outlined in the second Book of Discipline was entirely consistent with Melville's ideas.

Melville was elected moderator of the general assembly in April 1578, which ratified the presbyterian polity of the second Book of Discipline; and his prominence in the councils of the church led to his re-election as moderator of the assembly in April 1582, his retention in June 1582, re-election in June 1587 and May 1594, and election to a convention in January 1590. The spiritual jurisdiction and government granted to the church by God through Christ the mediator was understood to be exercised not by the membership at large but by those appointed by the Word to specialized functions within the congregation of the faithful. The church was not deemed to have received its

jurisdiction from God intermediately through the prince, as was claimed in England. Any notion of intermediate, earthly headship of the church, either papal or princely, was denounced as 'ane title falslie usurpit be antichryst', which 'aucht not to be attributit to angell or to mane of quhat estait soevir he be, saiffing to Chryst, the heid and onlie monarche in this kirk' (second Book of Discipline, 167). The prince and civil magistrate, as members of the church, ought to be willing to hear God's word revealed through his messengers and ambassadors, the ministers of the word, and so 'reverence the majestie of the sone of God speiking be thame' (ibid., 216). From doctrine, discipline, and distribution, there arose a fourfold permanent order of ministers or bishops, doctors or teachers, elders or governors, and deacons or distributors of the church's revenues. The office bearers were responsible for governing the church through a series of councils from congregational elderships to the general assembly, and were empowered to convene without tarrying for the magistrate's permission. All of this, however, amounted to little other than a succinct summary of earlier strands of Reformation thought, which it was deemed advisable to restate and reinforce, at a point when the crown sought to dictate policy and control the church through its bishops.

St Mary's College His nephew James attributed Melville's negligible published output to his 'grait occupationes and distractiones' (*Autobiography and Diary*, 63) in promoting the work of the ministry and schools. This received a fresh stimulus in 1580 with Melville's appointment at St Andrews University as principal of St Mary's College, reconstituted as a divinity college after the university's reorganization in 1579. Melville himself had been an early advocate of establishing 'an anti-seminarie to be erected in St Androis to the Jesuit seminaries for the course of theologie' (ibid., 76), and had tried, without success, to secure the services of his Geneva acquaintances Thomas Cartwright and Walter Travers as theology professors for St Andrews.

Leaving Glasgow 'sear against his will', Melville saw his work in St Andrews as professing the 'learned tongues and theologie against the seminaries of Rems and Rome' (*Autobiography and Diary*, 83). Yet he soon encountered opposition to his reforms from more conservative colleagues. The course he devised was an expansion of his theology course at Glasgow, based on an intensive study of the tongues and biblical exegesis. He resisted the influence of scholastic philosophy on theology and in 1583 helped to secure the general assembly's condemnation of those aspects of Aristotle's 'doctrine directlie impugning the grounds of religioun' (Thomson, pt 2, 640–41). Favouring Ramus's anti-metaphysical approach, which offered clarity and order in analyses of scripture, Melville saw the biblical text as 'perfect, clear in itself, its own interpreter' and 'the supreme judge of all controversies' (*Scholastica diatriba de rebus divinis*, 1599). But within a year of his arrival his opponents attempted to fight a rearguard action. If Ramus were right and Aristotle wrong, the implications were clear enough to Melville's opponents:

'thair breadwinner, thair honour, thair estimation, all was gean, giff Aristotle sould be sa owir-harled in the heiring of thair schollars; and sa dressit publict orationes against Mr Androe's doctrine' (*Autobiography and Diary*, 123–4). The same domineering attitude which he had displayed at Glasgow was brought to bear at St Andrews, where 'Mr Andro insisted mightelie' against the exponents of the old scholastic philosophy 'in his ordinar lessones' until they finally 'acknawlagit a wounderfull transportation out of darkness unto light'. Despite 'mikle feghting and fascherie', he made his views prevail (ibid.), and for three decades he remained the dominant figure in Scottish theological education.

In St Andrews, Melville also sat as an elder on the kirk session for several years and, on occasion, preached from the pulpit of Holy Trinity parish church. He took part in the general assembly's proceedings against Patrick Adamson and Robert Montgomerie, the recalcitrant archbishops of St Andrews and Glasgow, and was chosen to help with the work of establishing presbyteries in east Fife. In an address to the assembly of which he was moderator in 1582, he condemned the crown's exercise of that 'absolute authoritie whereby men intended to pull the crown off Christ's head and to wring the sceptre out of his hand' (Calderwood, 3.622). As a leading presbyterian he was of considerable interest to English diplomats in Scotland: Stephan Pole, a student at St Andrews, acted as informant to the English envoy, from whom he received £50 for his services.

Political confrontation and exile in England Following the rise to power of James Stewart, earl of Arran, and the inauguration of an administration which was hostile to the presbyterians, in 1584 Melville was summoned to appear before the privy council for uttering in a sermon on Daniel allegedly seditious and treasonable speeches from the pulpit, in which he was said to have compared the king to Nebuchadnezzar. Taking with him testimonials in his favour from the staff of St Andrews University, he denied the charge and affirmed subjects' duty to obey the king whom 'God in his mercie hath placed lawfull king and supreme magistrat in the civill government of this countrie' (Calderwood, 4.4), but declined the privy council's jurisdiction in matters of doctrine and 'planlie tauld the King and Counsall that they presumed ower bauldlie' to 'judge the doctrin and controll the ambassators and messingers of a King and Counsall graitter nor they, and far above tham'. Unfastening his little Hebrew Bible from his belt, he clanked it down on the table before the king and chancellor, declaring that this was his warrant, for 'with all ernestnes, zeall and gravitie, I stand for the cause of Jesus Chryst and his Kirk' (*Autobiography and Diary*, 142).

When charged to enter ward in Blackness Castle, Melville took flight with his brother Roger and sought refuge in England, where others had also fled for safety. With his departure from St Andrews, along with 'ane number of maisters and regentis thairof', the government declared the principalship of St Mary's vacant and proceeded to appoint John Robertson as Melville's successor. From the safety of Berwick, Melville contemplated resuming his academic life on the continent and as a preliminary went to London, where in June 1584 with other exiles he had an interview with the secretary of state Sir Francis Walsingham. In July he visited Oxford and Cambridge universities, where he 'conferrit with the most godlie and lernit ther' (*Autobiography and Diary*, 219). At Oxford the debate concerned the contentious issue of whether the minister in exercising his office need tarry for the civil magistrate. In London puritan ministers conferred with Melville and the Scottish exiles about creating a presbyterian polity.

To counteract the effect of propaganda by Patrick Adamson, archbishop of St Andrews, directed to the reformed churches abroad, Melville wrote on 1 July 1584 to the churches of Geneva and Zürich with his version of events in Scotland. He was also able to lecture in the chapel of the Tower of London, which was exempt from the bishop of London's jurisdiction. In October he attended the funeral in London of James Lawson, the exiled minister of Edinburgh. In November 1585 he joined the banished lords in returning home as Arran's administration collapsed.

Clashes with James VI From 1586 presbyterianism made headway again, and Melville urged ministers to unite in opposing the Black Acts of 1584, legislation which had asserted the crown's supremacy and the authority of bishops and had deprived the church of free assemblies. Unable to return to St Andrews, where plague had broken out, Melville spent the winter in Glasgow and was invited to visit the university which he called 'his eldest bern'. In March 1586 he resumed teaching at St Andrews, but in May, on being summoned to court, he was informed by the king, displeased by his continued opposition to Archbishop Adamson, that his services in the university would be dispensed for a season and that he would be warded at Baldovy until such time as James would recall him. When the university petitioned for Melville's return, James relented, providing Adamson were treated 'reverendlie' (*Autobiography and Diary*, 251).

Forbidden by the king in 1587 from preaching to the people in English on Sundays, Melville further angered James VI in 1592 by defending the views of John Knox and George Buchanan, who had 'sett the crowne upon his head'. James considered them defensible only by 'traterous and seditious theologues', and asserted that he had received his crown 'by successioun and not by anie man'. This led Melville to deliver to the king 'a maiste scharpe and frie admonition concerning his evil thinking and speaking of the best frinds of Chryst and him selff'. In 1593 he also 'gave the king a sharpe reprooffe for his favour borne to Papists', especially to the earl of Huntly (*Autobiography and Diary*, 313), and when the king marched north with an army to secure the submission of Huntly and the northern earls Melville accompanied him.

Melville had attended the coronation of Anne of Denmark in May 1590 and, much to the king's satisfaction, contributed an oration in Latin verse for the occasion, printed as *Stephaniskion* by Waldegrave, at the king's request. Both Joseph Scaliger and Justus Lipsius congratulated him, as copies of the work 'past throw all Europe'

(*Autobiography and Diary*, 279). Melville penned a further poem in 1594 to mark the birth of James's son and heir, Prince Henry, who he predicted would unite the crowns of Scotland and England and humble the pride of Spain and Rome.

In 1594 Melville was suspected by the king, apparently without foundation, of favouring the earl of Bothwell, when the latter for a time supported presbyterian objections to the king's leniency towards Huntly. In 1595, and again in 1596, he made his famous 'two kingdoms' speech on the separate nature of the ecclesiastical and civil jurisdictions. At Falkland Palace he sharply reminded the king that he was 'God's sillie vassall'. There were two kings and two kingdoms in Scotland with overlapping spheres: the kingdom of 'Chryst Jesus the King' was the kirk, 'whase subject King James the Saxt is', and in that realm there were no lords or heads, but only members. Those who had a special commission from Christ 'to watch over his Kirk and governe his spirituall kingdome', that is, ordained ministers, 'hes sufficient powar of him, and authoritie sa to do, bathe togidder and severallie; the quhilk na Christian King nor Prince sould controll and discharge, but fortifie and assist, utherwayes nocht fathfull subjects nor members of Chryst' (*Autobiography and Diary*, 370).

Excluded by the king from attending presbyteries, in 1597 Melville was also deprived of his office as rector of St Andrews University, though in 1599 he still remained dean of the faculty of divinity. Opposed to ecclesiastical representation in parliament, he was ordered by the king to leave the general assembly meeting at Dundee in 1598; and though commissioned by his presbytery to attend, he was again forbidden by the king from participating in the Montrose assembly of 1600. In vain he protested that 'he had a calling in the Kirk of God, and of Jesus Chryst, the King of kings, quhilk he behovit to dischairge at all occasiounes' (*Autobiography and Diary*, 542). In 1602 he was warded in his college for making the exercise on the text Ephesians 5: 11 and touching upon 'the present corruptions of the kirk' (ibid., 545). Yet he welcomed James's accession to the English throne in 1603, which he celebrated in verse, and favoured a legislative union of the two kingdoms.

England and final exile After James suspended meetings of the general assembly in 1604, the following year Melville and others made a stand and held an assembly at Aberdeen in defiance of the king, who resorted to severe measures against the ringleaders. In 1606, after heading the list of forty-two signatories to a protest against episcopacy, Melville was summoned to London. He arrived by the end of August, and in meetings with the king at Hampton Court during September he defended the freedom of general assemblies and the meeting of the Aberdeen assembly. Accused by the English privy council in November of writing some verses 'tending to the scandall and dishonour of the Church of England', he admitted to 'being muche moved with indignatioun to see suche vanitie and superstitioun in a Christian church under a Christian king'. Shaking the sleeves of the archbishop of Canterbury's rochet he branded them 'Romish ragis', a

'pairt of the beastis marke', and their wearer, Richard Bancroft, 'the capitall enemie of all the reformed kirks in Europ' (Calderwood, 6.597–8). Melville also disapproved of the 'great superstitioun and vanitie' displayed at court on St George's day and wrote some verses in Latin, translated as:

> Saint Andro, Chrystis Apostle trew,
> Does sign the Scotismenes rites;
> St George, Armenian Heresiarch,
> The Inglischmenes delytis.
> Let Scotismen, thane, hauld fast the faith!
> That is holie Appostolicke,
> Howbeit that Ingland keipes the cours
> That Papistis Apostaticke.
> (*Autobiography and Diary*, 706)

Confined first in the house of the dean of St Paul's, Melville was finally committed to the Tower of London in April 1607. The principalship of St Mary's in St Andrews was then declared vacant. From the Tower he wrote a reply to George Downame's sermon in defence of episcopacy. His services as divinity professor were sought in vain by the protestant academy at La Rochelle. Melville was initially denied visitors and the use of writing materials, but after a year some relaxation was permitted through the intercession of Sir James Sempill of Beltrees. When his room was examined, its walls were found covered with verses which he had engraved with the tongue of his shoe buckle.

By 1608 Melville was persuaded to address some conciliatory verses to the king and an apologetic letter to the privy council, on the advice of Archbishop John Spottiswoode, once his student at Glasgow. In 1610 the English ambassador to France received a request from the protestant duc de Bouillon that James release Melville and allow him to become professor of biblical theology in the Huguenot enclave at Sedan. Released from the Tower in 1611 but forbidden to return to Scotland, he debated the merits of the post in Sedan. 'I am in a state of suspense as to the course which I ought to take. There is no room for me in Britain', he wrote, 'on account of pseudo-Episcopacy—no hope of my being allowed to revisit my native country'. He had pondered the thirty-six years of active life in Scotland and 'the idle life which I have been condemned to spend in prison', a miserable reward for all his efforts 'taken in connection with the disgraceful bondage of the Church and the base perfidy of men'. The choice before him was an unpalatable one. 'Shall I fly from my native country, from my native Church, from my very self? Or, shall I deliver myself up, like a bound quadruped, to the will and pleasure of men?' (M'Crie, 314–15). In the end he accepted the invitation and left for France on 19 April 1611.

At Sedan, Melville found himself in controversy with David Tilenus, his fellow professor of theology, a critic of Calvinism and inclined toward the views of Arminius. He showed sympathy, however, towards Johannes Piscator, a prominent Ramist and theologian at Herborn in the Rhine palatinate, whose teaching on the doctrine of justification caused considerable controversy in both France and Switzerland. Yet Melville remained resolute in his defence of the absolute decree of reprobation and was vigorous in his opposition to all who deviated in the direction of Arminianism. He died in Sedan, unmarried, in 1622.

As a champion of ecclesiastical independence and a redoubtable opponent of royal supremacy, Melville proved a worthy successor to John Knox in defending Reformation principles. Yet his intransigence, his explosive temper, and his unwillingness to compromise led to open conflict with King James who, taking up Melville's challenge, succeeded in outmanoeuvring him by remodelling the church to suit his own preferences along English lines. Beyond his contribution as presbyterian leader within the church, Melville exerted a powerful influence in revitalizing university education. In neither field did James VI manage to expunge his achievement. Although his published works were slender, his beliefs helped to shape the covenanting struggle in the seventeenth century. They also permeated thinking both within the presbyterian establishment after the revolution settlement in 1690 and within the ranks of presbyterian seceders in the eighteenth century.   JAMES KIRK

Sources *The autobiography and diary of Mr James Melvill*, ed. R. Pitcairn, Wodrow Society (1842) • D. Calderwood, *The history of the Kirk of Scotland*, ed. T. Thomson and D. Laing, 8 vols., Wodrow Society, 7 (1842–9) • *CSP Scot.* • T. Thomson, ed., *Acts and proceedings of the general assemblies of the Kirk of Scotland*, 3 pts, Bannatyne Club, 81 (1839–45) • J. Spottiswoode, *History of the Church of Scotland*, ed. M. Napier and M. Russell, 3 vols., Spottiswoode Society, 6 (1847–51) • J. Kirk, *The Second Book of Discipline* (1980) • J. Durkan and J. Kirk, *The University of Glasgow, 1471–1577* (1977) • J. Kirk, *Patterns of reform: continuity and change in the Reformation kirk* (1989) • T. M'Crie, *The life of Andrew Melville*, new edn (1899) • J. Kirk, '"Melvillian" reform in the Scottish universities', *The Renaissance in Scotland: studies in literature, religion, history, and culture offered to John Durkan*, ed. A. A. MacDonald and others (1994), 276–300 • R. G. Cant, *The University of St Andrews: a short history*, rev. edn (1970)
Archives U. Edin. L., Melvini Epistolae
Likenesses engraving, U. St Andr., archives

Melville, Andrew (1624–1706), army officer, was born in Scotland in May 1624, the son of John Melville, minister of Newton in Edinburghshire, and grandson of the leading Presbyterian divine, and diarist, James *Melville; his mother was Joannetta Kellie, whose brother Melville was later described as chamberlain to Charles I. Sent to Königsberg at thirteen to study the languages of northern Europe, Melville escaped to Poland, having joined a regiment levied for Polish service, but, seeing no prospect of active employment, he returned to Scotland in 1639. There he learned that his parents, ruined by his uncle's debts, had died, and that creditors had seized the entire property. He joined the covenanter forces and served in the bishops' wars, and in England from 1644. Lord Grey of Werke, who had already taken his brother into his service, promised Andrew a cornetcy, pending which, at the head of other young men also waiting for appointments, he lived by plunder until captured by countrymen in the north of England and imprisoned for some months. On his release he accompanied the army as it withdrew to Scotland in 1647. He then went to France, served with the Scots guards in the French army in Flanders, and was seriously wounded at the siege of Lens. After a variety of

adventures he waited on Charles II at Breda, and agreed to join him in Scotland. He was part of the army which entered England in 1651, and he fought at the battle of Worcester, was shot in the arm, stripped, and left for dead, but was sheltered for three months by villagers until he recovered from his wounds. He then repaired in disguise to London, and was assisted by a kinsman in escaping to Holland. After further privations and perils he joined the Scottish bodyguard of Cardinal de Retz, and served under the duke of York in French pay. Eventually he linked his fortunes with those of Count Josias Waldeck, with whom he fought for the elector of Brandenburg, the king of Sweden, the elector of Cologne, and the duke of Celle (Brunswick-Luneburg). The duke sent him to London in 1660 to compliment Charles II on his restoration, and Melville paid a second visit on his own account in 1667; but the king, while very affable, professed inability to do anything for him. In 1680–81 Melville accompanied the prince of Hanover (afterwards George I) to England, and received the degree of MD at Oxford, whither he went with the prince. By 1678, retiring from active service, Melville had been appointed drost (governor or commandant) of Gifhorn with the rank of brigadier. He had married, in Germany about 1667, a Mlle Lamotte, a lady of the household of the Electress Sophia, and had a son, who predeceased him, and a daughter, Charlotte Sophia Anna (1670–1724), who in 1690 became the wife of Alexander von Schulenburg-Blumberg, a Hanoverian general.

Melville was author of an autobiography published as *Mémoires de Monsieur le Chevalier de Melvill* in Amsterdam in 1704, at the request of the Electress Sophia of Hanover, who dubbed him a 'soldier of *ill*-fortune'. He died at Gifhorn in 1706, his career having 'typified the life of the mercenary soldier in the Thirty Years' War—except for his survival' (Stevenson, 1–2).
                              J. G. ALGER, *rev.* TIMOTHY HARRISON PLACE

Sources Poten, 'Melville, Andreas', *Allgemeine deutsche Biographie*, ed. R. von Liliencron and others, 21 (Leipzig, 1885) • A. Melville, *Mémoires de monsieur le chevalier de Melvill, général major des troupes de S. A. S. Monseigneur le duc de Cell, et grand ballif du comté de Giforn* (Amsterdam, 1704) • Wood, *Ath. Oxon.: Fasti* (1820), 379 • D. Stevenson, *King or covenant?* (1996), 1–16 • A. Melville, *Memoirs*, trans. T. Ameer-Ali (1918)

Melville, Arthur (1855–1904), watercolour painter, was born on 10 April 1855 at Loanhead of Guthrie, Forfarshire, the fourth son of Arthur Melville (*b.* 1821/2), a coachman, and his wife, Margaret Wann (*b.* 1823/4). When Melville was quite young, his father gained a position at Smeaton Hepburn near East Linton. He was educated locally and then apprenticed to the local grocer as a bookkeeper. Melville also established a gymnasium at Dalkeith where he gave instruction. This early business acumen proved useful, as by this time he had also assumed responsibility for funding his younger brother George's medical studies.

However, Melville gave up his position in Dalkeith and moved to Edinburgh. In 1875 he entered the life school of the Royal Scottish Academy, where he encountered the established painters John R. Reid and Robert McGregor. He was a pupil of J. Campbell Noble, who offered him much encouragement, and he received occasional instruction from William McTaggart. These four artists were formative influences on Melville's work. His first exhibit at the Royal Scottish Academy, also in 1875, was a subject of rustic naturalism entitled *Scotch Lassie*. In 1878 he exhibited *Cabbage Garden*, an ambitious oil painting featuring a dominant, almost abstract foliage dramatically tilted toward the viewer. Thematically, it may be one of the first notable examples of the 'kailyard' genre in Scottish culture.

Melville enjoyed early success as an exhibitor at the Royal Scottish Academy and sold a number of his paintings to J. H. Annandale of Polton Vale paper mill (including *Cabbage Garden*), and to the Glasgow interior decorator R. J. Bennett. Such a strong financial and artistic position enabled Melville to visit France between 1878 and 1880. There he met with the painter R. W. Allan, who encouraged Melville's distinctive 'blottesque' watercolour technique of applying pigment to a wet ground. However, it was the paintings Melville encountered at the Universal Exhibition in Paris in 1878 that had the most profound effect on his output. Although he had already begun to explore the effects of full sunlight during a painting trip to Surrey in 1878, his time in France undoubtedly encouraged his exploitation of such effects. Between 1878 and 1879 Melville stayed at Grez-sur-Loing, his time there coinciding with that of the Irish painter Frank O'Meara and Robert Louis Stevenson. *Paysanne à Grez*, dated 1880 (priv. coll.), features a figure in full sunlight against a whitewashed wall and represents a significant departure from the consistent predilection towards naturalism evident in contemporary Scottish painting. The innovative, geometric design utilized areas of flat colour in the wall and blue shutter, interacting with the stripes of the blouse and abstracted forms of the head-dress and vines to create a decorative whole.

Melville's representations of Paris, which he visited between 1878 and 1880, mostly comprise suburban river scenes. However, he also executed subjects consistent with impressionist themes such as his studies of Moulin Rouge dancers, cafés on the boulevard des Italiens, and *Interior of a Turkish Bath* (1881; priv. coll.). This watercolour, executed in rich sombre tones, imbues a mock-Oriental setting with the resonance of a bourgeois men's club.

The Universal Exhibition was also instrumental in introducing Melville to the Orientalism of J. L. Gérôme, A. Pasini, and M. Fortuny. These artists, who fuelled contemporary taste at the Salon, doubtless inspired Melville's subsequent odyssey from Egypt round the Gulf, through Persia and home via Constantinople during 1881–2. However, his reactions to Islam contrast directly with his peers, whose choice and treatment of themes reveal contemporary sexual, racial, and imperialist attitudes. Melville's work is altogether more neutral. His use of the watercolour medium stresses the immediacy of the work, presenting the East in the form of an observational journal which focuses on architecture and topography. Figure studies are almost exclusively of adult males and have an

ethnographic element, for example *Abdullah the Snake Charmer* (1883; priv. coll.).

Melville's redefinition of Orientalism can be attributed to the particular social, religious, and moral codes he absorbed during his formative years—a presbyterian conditioning which ensured that his patrons were in sympathy with his approach. These were principally self-made businessmen such as John Tullis, a Glasgow leather manufacturer, or the Edinburgh distiller Arthur Sanderson—wealthy men who had experience of foreign trade and were accruing major collections of Scottish painting. Like Melville, however, many of his patrons were only one or two generations removed from the land, and retained sober, modest values that were reflected in their artistic tastes.

During his journey to the Middle East, Melville was shot at, robbed, and abandoned naked by bandits in the desert, yet still managed to amass sufficient material for his most important works. *Fringe of the Desert* (1881; Dundee Museums and Art Galleries), *Awaiting an Audience with the Pasha* (c.1883–7; priv. coll.), and in particular *Grand Bazaar, Muscat* (1882) and *Gateway at Kirkuk* (1882), define the modern, decorative concerns of his best watercolours reconciled with traditional themes. They employ the optical properties of pure primary colour dropped on to paper, combined with the tension between areas of resolved form and void, to create shimmering movement and space. His best work was executed between 1878 and 1883, and encapsulates a swift transition from naturalism towards the abstract, where the effects of pure colour, light, and movement outstrip representational concerns.

After he returned to Edinburgh in 1882, Melville's vision, vigour and style were brought to bear on the Glasgow school of painters known as the *Glasgow Boys. This influence was especially pronounced when he and George Henry, James Guthrie, and E. A. Walton, among others, worked together around the village of Cockburnspath in 1884. *Audrey and her Goats* (1884–9; Tate Collection), begun at Cockburnspath, utilizes themes and motifs later explored by Henry, E. A. Hornel, and Walton. However, in 1888 Melville moved to London and devoted his energies to elegant yet derivative society portraiture and fruitful trips to north Africa and Spain, the latter of which he visited with Frank Brangwyn in 1892. A visit to Venice in 1894 produced stunning watercolours of the lagoon and canals.

Melville was elected an associate of the Royal Scottish Academy in 1886 and a member of the Royal Watercolour Society in 1890. On 18 December 1899 he married Ethel, daughter of David Croall, a coachbuilder, of Southfield, Liberton, with whom he had one daughter, Marion. He contracted typhoid fever while in Spain, and died at his home, Redlands, in Witley, Surrey, on 28 August 1904. He was buried at Brookwood cemetery.

CHRIS BRICKLEY

Sources C. Brickley, 'Arthur Melville and Presbyterian realism', PhD diss., U. St Andr., 1996 · *DNB* · A. E. MacKay, *Arthur Melville: Scottish impressionist* (1951) · I. Gale, *Arthur Melville* (1996) · *Arthur Melville (1855–1904)* (1977) [exhibition catalogue, Dundee Museums and

Art Galleries, 12 Nov – 10 Dec 1977] · R. Billcliffe, *The Glasgow Boys: the Glasgow school of painting, 1875–1895* (1985) · b. cert. · d. cert.
Archives NL Scot., Eastern journal
Likenesses photograph, repro. in G. B. Brown, *The Glasgow school of painters* (1908) · photograph, repro. in sale catalogue (Christies, Edinburgh, 8 June 1995)
Wealth at death £2853 15*s*.: administration, 14 Dec 1904, *CGPLA Eng. & Wales*

Melville, David, third earl of Leven and second earl of Melville (1660–1728), army officer and politician, was born on 5 May 1660 at Monimail, Fife, third son of George *Melville, first earl of Melville (1636–1707), and Lady Catherine Leslie (1639–1713), daughter of Alexander Leslie, Lord Balgonie and second earl of Leven. In 1677, after the death of his maternal grandfather, the second earl, and of his two aunts, Catherine and Mary (both of whom held the title as countesses in their own right), David Melville claimed the right to succeed as third earl. He was opposed by his kinsman the earl of Rothes who, as lord chancellor, pursued the claim in the court of session until his death and a favourable judgment from Charles II in July 1681. Thereafter David Melville took a seat in the Scottish parliament with a rank equal to that of his father.

When Leven's father fell under suspicion for the Rye House plot, Leven fled with him to the United Provinces in 1683. From there, Leven travelled to Kiel, Hamburg, and Berlin, eventually entering the service of the elector of Brandenburg through the patronage of Sophia, electress of Hanover, accepting the rank of colonel. Leven also acted as the envoy of William of Orange in Berlin, arranging a meeting between the prince and the elector of Brandenburg at Cleves. In 1688 he was granted permission to raise a regiment (the 25th regiment) of Scottish refugees living in the German states and United Provinces, which was used to garrison Plymouth during the prince of Orange's invasion. Subsequently, William sent Leven to Edinburgh as his envoy to the Scottish convention in March 1689.

As part of his mission to Scotland, Leven was commissioned to raise a force of 800 to defend the capital until regular troops arrived from England. Following the departure of Viscount Dundee from the convention, and the declaration of the duke of Gordon that he held Edinburgh Castle for James II, Leven successfully summoned a force which, until the arrival of his own men from Plymouth, calmed the convention and the populace. Having joined General Hugh Mackay to fight against Dundee, Leven raised more troops and was awarded the power to treat with those who surrendered.

At the battle of Killiecrankie (17 July 1689) Leven's regiment, on the far right of the battlefield, held fast while other regiments, including Mackay's, broke and ran in the face of a highlander charge. The composure and courage of the regiment under fire won great respect for Leven, who held them together as they covered the army's retreat to Stirling. When the duke of Gordon surrendered Edinburgh Castle in June 1689, Leven was appointed its keeper, as well as acting as a privy councillor, and as commissioner for forfeiture of estates, for plantation of kirks, and of supply for Perth and Fife. During this period he also

David Melville, third earl of Leven and second earl of Melville (1660–1728), by Sir John Baptiste de Medina, 1691

spent time on campaign in Flanders with William of Orange, paying his regiment out of his own pocket.

On 3 September 1691 Leven married his first cousin, Anne Wemyss (1675–1702), who joined him in living in Edinburgh Castle. While there, he acquired a seat in the Tron Church and became a patron of local horse-racing. One of his most trying duties, however, was the keeping of Jacobite prisoners, among them lords Seaforth, Breadalbane, and Strathmore. Leven also quarrelled incessantly over castle appointments with the commander-in-chief in Scotland, Sir Thomas Livingstone. Perhaps because of this, and despite his active opposition to the Act of Security and promotion of the succession of Queen Anne, he was removed from the keeping of the castle in December 1702 and instead named major-general of the Scottish forces. Rewarded in 1704 with the wards that had been in the hands of the crown since 1689, he was also called to London to advise on Scottish affairs. While there he was caught up in the Queensberry plot, in which the second duke of Queensberry, working with Simon Fraser, Lord Lovat, alleged that Leven and others, including lords Seafield, Cromarty, and Tweedale, had through him been in communication with James Stuart, the Jacobite Pretender. Although disproven, this allegation later returned to haunt Leven. In 1705 he returned to Scotland as keeper of Edinburgh Castle, although this time without his wife, who had died on 9 January 1702. This was followed by his appointment as master of ordinance (1705) and commander-in-chief in Scotland (1706). An enthusiastic promoter of the union, in the following year he was chosen as a representative peer, a position he held until

1710. In 1707 he also inherited the title second earl of Melville upon the death of his father and the prior death of his elder brothers. During the Jacobite attempts of 1708 Melville once again had the custody of high-ranking Jacobites in Edinburgh Castle, a job he handled with such discretion that even George Lockhart of Carnwath admitted that he had treated the prisoners civilly and fairly. Melville, however, was a harsh critic of the government's neglect of Scottish fortifications and ordinance, and was stripped of his position as commander-in-chief and governor of the castle in 1712, with considerable arrears in pay.

Melville eagerly greeted the accession of George I, to whom he was known from his time in Brandenburg and through the Electress Sophia. The new king briefly returned his friendship upon his arrival at Greenwich, but this action aroused considerable envy among other courtiers. That same year Simon Fraser revived suspicions first raised during the Queensberry plot when he suggested to Lord Ilay, brother of the duke of Argyll, that, in France, he had had contact with Melville through Jacobite messengers and had sent him medals from the Pretender. Although Melville proved his innocence, suspicion stalled his career. During the rising of 1715 Jacobites seized Melville's house at Balgonie, while government troops rudely searched his Edinburgh house.

With no further royal preferment, Melville fell into debt sufficient to force the sale of family lands and his retirement to Markinch, where he died on 6 June 1728 and was buried six days later. Melville had two sons: George, who married Margaret Carnegie, daughter of the fourth earl of Northesk and predeceased his father, producing a son, David, who became fourth earl of Leven and third earl of Melville; and Alexander, who succeeded his nephew as fifth earl of Leven and fourth earl of Melville. He also had two daughters, Mary, who married William, second earl of Aberdeen, and Margaret, who died in infancy.

MARGARET D. SANKEY

Sources DNB · GEC, Peerage · W. H. L. Melville, ed., Leven and Melville papers: letters and state papers chiefly addressed to George, earl of Melville … 1689–1691, Bannatyne Club, 77 (1843) · W. Fraser, ed., The Melvilles, earls of Melville, and the Leslies, earls of Leven, 3 vols. (1890) · BL, Harley MS 6584
Archives NA Scot., corresp. and papers · NA Scot., Leven and Melville papers | Hunt. L., letters to earl of Loudon · NA Scot., corresp. with earl of Mar · NA Scot., letters to duke of Montrose · NL Scot., letters to Lord Godolphin
Likenesses G. Kneller, oils, 1691, Scot. NPG · J. B. de Medina, oils, 1691, Scot. NPG [see illus.]

Melville, Elizabeth (fl. 1599–1631), writer, was the daughter of Sir James *Melville of Halhill (1535/6–1617), privy councillor and author of memoirs, and Christine Boswell. Elizabeth married John Colville, who became commendator of Culross in 1597 until 1609; he appears to have become a minister in the parish of Culross until his death. She had three sons: Samuel Colville, who sustained the literary preoccupations of the Melville family—he was the author of The Scots Hudibras, or, The Whig's Supplication; James Colville; and Alexander *Colville, who became professor of divinity at St Andrews. The date of her death is

unknown, but she may have died in 1640, or possibly later.

Elizabeth Melville's life and art are inextricable: the spiritual homiletic voice of her major work, Ane Godlie Dreame (first published by Robert Charteris in 1603), is mirrored in her probable vocation as a preacher; her faith was publicly manifest in political gestures of support for exiled and excommunicated presbyterian ministers such as William Ridge of Adderny, John Welsh, Robert Blair, and John Livingstone. 'A Sonnet Sent to Blackness to Mr John Welsch, by the Lady Culross' (c.1606) confirms Melville's pragmatic faith. Welsh belonged to the faction of dissenting ministers who opposed the ecclesiastical reforms of James VI and I. At Aberdeen in July 1605 Welsh was accused of treason; from the Tolbooth in Edinburgh he was sent to Blackness on 26 July of the same year. Melville's poem communicates spiritual support and courage to a religious ally.

Melville's life is largely recreated through witnesses in the Calvinist and covenanting communities. In the early 1600s Livingstone's autobiography refers to 'the lady Culross' as an exemplar of 'sundry gracious Christians who used to resort to my father's house [that of William Livingstone, minister at Monyabrook], especially at times of, the communion' (Livingstone, 'Memorable characteristics', 346). In 1599 the protestant minister Alexander Hume dedicated his Hymnes, or, Sacred Songs to Melville, his 'sister' in Christ and 'a Ladie chosen of God to bee one of his saincts' (Poems, 3). Hume instructs the young woman to sustain and nurture her vocation as a spiritual daughter, and praises her 'compositiones so copious, so pregnant, so spirituall' (five years before the publication of her major work). Hume's adoration of Melville's affective piety, 'sighing & weepinge … in murmuring and in paine' (ibid., 3–4), is echoed in the much later account of Melville at a devotional meeting in Shotts in June 1630:

> William Ridge of Adderny coming into the room, and hearing her have great motion upon her, although she spake not out, he desired her to speak out, saying, that there was none in the room but him and her woman … She did soe, and the door being opened, the room filled full. She continued in prayer, with wonderfull assistance, for large three hours time. (Livingstone, 'Memorable characteristics', 347)

It seems that she may have received formal spiritual instruction, according to Livingstone, from 'the godly and able ministers and professors of Scotland' ('Brief historical relation', 138).

Melville's faith is enshrined in her own extant letters to Livingstone and to her son James. The former, written c.1626–31, convey her anxiety that the minister communicate with her regularly; she confesses her own fragility at times (through events in her family and the parish), yet exhorts Livingstone in a powerful, scriptural prose to have courage throughout the period of his excommunication in Ireland: 'mak gude that new covenant', she urges (Livingstone, 'Memorable characteristics', 364). Her letters serve as meditations on her relationship with God, the nature of suffering and endurance through devotion, as well as the earthly trials afforded by her errant son at court.

Melville's *Ane Godlie Dreame*, composed 'at the request of friends', reflects medieval and Renaissance conventions of female spiritual 'autobiography', but is an allegory moulded by the doctrinal exigencies of Melville's Calvinism. Structured literally and metaphorically as a pilgrimage or journey, the poem depicts the visitation of Christ, who leads the dreamer through a variety of physical trials; on wakening, the dreamer expounds the allegorical significance of the journey. Melville's language is a complex weave of scriptural quotations, while the intimacy of faith is embodied in the dreamer's relationship with Christ, guide and bridegroom. The number of reprintings of Melville's poem throughout the seventeenth century, and its Anglicization, attest its popularity. Melville's life affords insight into a spiritual community, and the role of women within that; she stands as one of the most important religious writers in Renaissance Scotland.

S. M. Dunnigan

Sources U. Edin. L., MS La.III.347 • U. Edin. L., MS De.3.70 • E. Melville, 'A sonnet sent to Blackness to Mr John Welsh', NL Scot., Wodrow MS 29, no. 4, fol. 11r • E. Melville, *Ane godlie dreame* (1603) • J. Livingstone, 'A brief historical relation of the life of Mr John Livingstone', *Select biographies*, ed. W. K. Tweedie, 1, Wodrow Society, 7/1 (1845), 127–97, 293–348, 351–70 • J. Livingstone, 'Memorable characteristics', *Select biographies*, ed. W. K. Tweedie, 1, Wodrow Society, 7/1 (1845), 293–348 • D. Laing, *Early popular poetry of Scotland and the northern border*, 2 vols. (1822) • D. Laing, *Early metrical tales including 'The history of Sir Eger, Sir Gryme and Sir Greysteill'* (1826) • *The poems of Alexander Hume*, ed. A. Lawson, STS, 48 (1902), 184–98 • W. Fraser, ed., *The Melvilles, earls of Melville, and the Leslies, earls of Leven*, 3 vols. (1890) • S. M. Dunnigan, 'Scottish women writers, c1560–c1650', *A history of Scottish women's writing*, ed. D. Gifford and D. Macmillan (1997), 15–43 • G. Greer et al., ed., *Kissing the rod: an anthology of seventeenth century women's verse* (1988), 79–82 • B. Travitsky, ed., *The paradise of women: writings by Englishwomen of the Renaissance* (1981), 139–41 • M. Bell, G. Parfitt, and S. Shepherd, eds., *A biographical dictionary of women writers, 1580–1720* (1900), 148 • J. Todd, ed., *A dictionary of British and American women writers, 1660–1800* (1984) • *Scots peerage*

Melville, Frances Helen (1873–1962), promoter of higher education for women in Scotland and suffragist, was born at 4 Abbotsford Park, Merchiston, Edinburgh, on 11 October 1873, elder daughter of Francis Suther Melville (1815–1895), depute clerk of the Court of Session, and his second wife, Helen Alexandrina Kerr (1841–1910). She was one of a family of five brothers and two sisters. Her early years were spent in Edinburgh, where she was educated at George Watson's Ladies' College. She went abroad as a music student to Germany for a year, but returned to be one of the first women to matriculate in 1892 at Edinburgh University after the Universities (Scotland) Act of 1889 permitted women to matriculate and graduate from the Scottish universities. Her academic ability was reflected in her first-class honours MA degree in philosophy in 1897. From 1896 to 1899 she was a tutor in Professor Pringle Pattison's classes in logic, psychology, and metaphysics.

As one of the new band of women students Frances Melville made her mark. She was president of the first Women's Representative Committee at Edinburgh University, a forerunner of the Women's Union, at a time when the voice of women in the university was very tentative. She was present at the first meeting of the Edinburgh University Women's Debating Society and chaired the society in its first year. She took part in one of the early debates on whether women should have the franchise, signifying her interest in women's suffrage, which was to be a lifelong commitment.

In 1899 Melville became a lecturer in mental and moral science at the Cheltenham Ladies' College, but this proved a brief appointment because in 1900 she was appointed warden, in succession to Louisa Lumsden, of University Hall, St Andrews University, a hall of residence for women students. Under Louisa Lumsden the aim of creating a Scottish Girton at University Hall, where residential and corporate spirit would embody the ideals of women's education, had created conflicts over the relationship of hall students to other women students in the university and also in terms of the relationship of University Hall to the university itself. During her wardenship Melville did much to reduce the tensions arising from the perception of the hall as being élite and separate, although she recognized the benefits of residential academic life. She saw to the day-to-day running of the hall and the management of its accounts and correspondence, as well as giving guidance and advice to students. She was a woman of strong, even stern, features and one student later recalled her as rather remote:

> In her earlier days young students were too much awed by her stately figure and carriage to recognise the warmth of her heart, the love of fun and the need for sympathy and affection which underlay a dignified and reserved manner. (*Alumnus Chronicle*, 45–6)

She also studied for the degree of bachelor of divinity, which she was awarded in 1910, and had the distinction of becoming the first woman to receive this degree at a Scottish university.

Frances Melville left St Andrews in 1909 on her appointment as mistress of Queen Margaret College, Glasgow University, following the death of Janet Ann Galloway. Once again she was moving into an area of university life where pioneering roots were strong. Queen Margaret College had been founded by the Glasgow Association for the University Education of Women in 1883 and had become a separate college for women within Glasgow University in 1892. Most women students at the university were taught in separate classes at the college. As mistress of the college she brought to the post her wide experience of university life and her interest in the cause of women students. Her views on women's education were set out in her contribution to a collection of essays, *The Position of Woman: Actual and Real* (1911). She argued that women's education had been influenced to a damaging extent by preconceived ideas about women's capacities and prospects in life, and in particular by the artificial tension between the two ideals: of domesticity, for those intending to marry; and of professionalism, for those who were likely to be self-supporting. She favoured a general education for all women to develop their intellectual and critical faculties in the way that education for men was intended to do, but not necessarily by the same curricula and methods as were traditionally used in boys' schools and universities.

At Glasgow the effect of the First World War, wider social changes, and the sheer increase in numbers of women students gradually saw the full integration of women students into mixed university classes. It became impractical to run duplicate classes and the college closed in 1935. The university gave up the college buildings and Frances Melville retired to Dalry, Kirkcudbrightshire. In 1927 she was awarded an LLD by Glasgow University, the first Scottish woman graduate to receive this distinction. An appointment as OBE followed in 1935.

Frances Melville was deeply involved in the cause of women's suffrage and a range of women's issues throughout her life. She played a prominent role in the Edinburgh National Society for Women's Suffrage and the Scottish Universities Women's Suffrage Union. She frequently gave talks or wrote papers on women's topics; in October 1902 she gave a talk in Edinburgh to the National Union of Women Workers of Great Britain entitled 'University education for women in Scotland: its effects on social and intellectual life'. In an obituary appreciation of her it was suggested that 'it cost her some effort to make the public appearance that was expected of her', yet the listings of her activities and appointments suggest that she overcame this (*Glasgow Herald*, 10 March 1962).

Frances Melville was directly involved in the 'Scottish women graduates' case' from 1906 to 1908. Since the Representation of the People (Scotland) Act of 1868, the universities in Scotland had returned two members of parliament, elected by graduates, as members of the general councils of the universities. As an election loomed in 1906 a group of women graduates applied to receive voting papers as members of the general council. Among these women was Frances Melville. The others were Margaret Nairn, Chrystal MacMillan, Frances Simson, and Elsie Inglis. They took the universities of St Andrews and Edinburgh to the Court of Session in a case which argued that as graduates they were entitled to receive voting papers and that under the 1868 act 'person' did not mean only male voters. They lost the case on appeal in 1907 and took it to the final court of appeal, the House of Lords, in November 1908. The case aroused great national interest, giving these suffragists an arena for their arguments to be presented and to demonstrate their ability and worthiness of receiving the vote. Although present, Frances Melville did not speak during the House of Lords case, leaving it to Chrystal MacMillan, who had been their eloquent spokeswoman throughout. The appeal, as expected, was lost.

Frances Melville was later honorary president of the Glasgow Women Citizens' Association and was also a member of the Glasgow Society for Equal Citizenship. She remained active in the political field and in 1938 stood as an independent candidate for a Scottish universities by-election caused by the death of Ramsay MacDonald. Sir John Anderson was elected, but she came second in the poll (ahead of a Scottish nationalist and another independent candidate) with 5618 votes. During her time in Glasgow she served as a justice of the peace, and was a member of the Royal Philosophical Society of Glasgow, the Lady Artists' Club, and the Glasgow Archaeological Society. During both world wars she was involved in a wide range of volunteer work.

From early on Frances Melville recognized the importance of women grouping together to promote a cause, thus creating a unity of purpose and network of support. This was most evident in the support she gave to the British Federation of University Women, an organization formed in 1907 in Manchester to create such a network of shared experience and support for the many associations of university women which had been set up throughout the country. She was responsible for the setting up of the St Andrews Association of University Women in 1909 and later served in 1935 as president of the British Federation of University Women, writing an unofficial history of the organization in 1949 and becoming honorary vice-president. In her honour a room in the headquarters at Crosby Hall was named after her. Frances Melville died at her home, 16 Merchiston Place, Edinburgh, on 7 March 1962, and was buried in Warriston cemetery, Edinburgh, on 9 March. Her obituarist noted that 'it was by the graces, no less than the strengths of her indefatigable encouragement and guardianship of women's interests that thousands of her students were equipped for later life and work' (*Glasgow Herald*, 8 March 1962).

SHEILA HAMILTON

Sources *Alumnus Chronicle* [U. St Andr.], 53 (1962), 45 · B. L. N., 'Melville, Frances Helen', *College Courant: Journal of the Glasgow University Graduates Association*, 14/28 (1962), 143–4 · *Glasgow Herald* (8 March 1962) · *Glasgow Herald* (10 March 1962) · *The Scotsman* (8 March 1962) · *The Times* (14 March 1962), 15b · *WWW* · *Scottish biographies* (1938) · F. Melville, 'Queen Margaret College', *College Courant: Journal of the Glasgow University Graduates Association*, 1/2 (1948), 99–107 · S. Hamilton, 'Women and the Scottish universities, *circa* 1869–1939: a social history', PhD diss., U. Edin., 1987 · O. Checkland, *Queen Margaret Union, 1890–1980* (1980) · L. Walker, ed., *Celebrating a centenary* (1996) · Edinburgh University Women's Debating Society, minutes, 1893–1914, U. Edin. L., special collections division, GEN 160–163 · Women's Representative Committee minutes, U. Edin. L., special collections division, Masson Hall MSS, Da 64MAS/39 · F. H. Melville, 'British Federation of University Women: a history', 1949 · C. Dyhouse, *No distinction of sex? Women in British universities, 1870–1939* (1995) · b. cert. · d. cert. · census returns, 1871, 1881, 1891 · gravestone, Warriston cemetery · Edinburgh directories
Archives U. Glas., Archives and Business Records Centre, corresp. and papers | U. St Andr., University Hall records
Likenesses four photographs, U. Glas., Archives and Business Records Centre
Wealth at death £5956 1s. 4d.: confirmation, 8 June 1962, CCI

Melville, George, fourth Lord Melville and first earl of Melville (1636–1707), politician, was the eldest son of John Melville, third Lord Melville (*d.* 1643), and Anna (*d.* after 1643), elder daughter and coheir of Sir George Erskine of Innerteil.

George Melville, fourth Lord Melville and first earl of Melville (1636–1707), by Sir John Baptiste de Medina, 1691

On 6 May 1651 the king wrote to Melville from Dunfermline, seeking money on behalf of Melville's kinsman Sir George Melville of Garvock, who had obtained the position of under-master of the household to the king in Scotland. The following year the king wrote on his own behalf to Melville seeking financial aid. On 3 January 1654, in the aftermath of the abortive Glencairn rising, English troopers arrested Melville and one Sir John Carstairs in St Andrews. Although they had taken no part in the rising they were suspected of implication in the stealing of horses by some of Glencairn's men. Taken to Burntisland, they were briefly imprisoned.

By contract dated 17 January 1655 Melville married Catherine (1639–1713), only surviving daughter of Alexander Leslie, Lord Balgonie, and granddaughter of the famous covenanting general Alexander *Leslie, first earl of Leven (c.1580–1661); they had eight sons, including David *Melville, third earl of Leven and second earl of Melville (1660–1728), and four daughters. Following his marriage, Melville's political profile increased. In 1656 he was a justice of the peace for Fife and Kinross-shire. That autumn he was named as a commissioner in Fife and Kinross for raising the counties' contribution to Cromwell's war with Spain and other Commonwealth expenses. He served again as a commissioner of assessment in the area in 1659. In May 1660 he was among the Scots who went to London to greet Charles II following his return to England, but stayed for only ten days, and 'haveing kissed the Kings Maj. hand' (*Diary of Mr John Lamont*, 122), returned home to Scotland on 12 June 1660. He attended the first session of the Restoration parliament in Scotland from 1 January to 12 July 1661, and served as a commissioner of supply for Fife and Kinross-shire.

In February 1663, Melville returned to London, possibly remaining there until after the marriage on 20 April of his wife's younger stepsister Anna Scott, countess of Buccleuch, to James, duke of Monmouth. Appointed one of the duchess of Buccleuch's curators, Melville afterwards managed her affairs efficiently in Scotland, obtaining the approval of the duke and duchess as well as that of Charles II. In September 1678 he received a special commission over the Buccleuch estates, probably as the result of a visit to London earlier that spring at the request of the duke. By 1681 Melville wanted to resign his position of curator, but he was persuaded to retain it until 1683.

During the Pentland rising of 1666 Melville was one of the Fife landowners summoned by the privy council to defend Edinburgh. Twelve years later, in the context of growing covenanting tensions and activities, on 29 January 1678 Melville was listed among those in the presbytery of Cupar who had not signed the bond for keeping the public peace; neither, it seems, had he signed the bond against conventicles. However, following the duke of Monmouth's appointment the following year as captain-general of the royal forces in opposition to the covenanters in Scotland, while at court in London Melville offered his services to the cause and the king accepted them. Melville joined Monmouth's forces the day before the battle of Bothwell Bridge on 22 June 1679. Monmouth later certified that then 'I did direct and authorize the Lord Melvill to send propositions to the rebels, and receive some from them, in order to laying downe their armes, and submitting to the king's mercy' (Fraser, 2.27).

A few years later Melville's association with Monmouth made him more vulnerable. In 1683 orders were issued for his arrest on suspicion of being involved in the Rye House plot, but by 28 July he had escaped to the Netherlands, where he attached himself to the court of the prince of Orange. In January 1684 Melville was summoned to appear before the privy council on 8 April, but when he was expected medical evidence was submitted by doctors in Rotterdam stating that he was too ill to travel. By 13 November 1684 Melville was being referred to by the privy council as 'a declared fugitive' (*Reg. PCS*, 10.26). Yet he was not an active participant in the Argyll and Monmouth rebellions of 1685. In a vindication of his conduct written in 1703 he stated that he was opposed to both expeditions, although he had reluctantly granted a bond for £500 to one James Stewart in support of the Argyll expedition, in ignorance that it had already sailed. The Scottish parliament none the less declared Melville a rebel and on 16 June 1685 his estates were forfeited and annexed to the crown. Punishment was modified by James VII in January 1687: the estates were granted to Melville's eldest son, the master of Melville. In return, Melville paid compensation of £3000 sterling (£36,000 Scots) and a yearly rent of £200 sterling (£2400 Scots). Nevertheless, he remained in the Netherlands until after William and Mary had been proclaimed king and queen in 1688.

Melville was summoned to the convention of estates which met on 14 March 1689 but did not subscribe the act of 16 March which declared it to be a free and lawful meeting of the estates. On 27 March he was appointed to the parliamentary committee for settling the government, and on 30 March as a commissioner of the militia in Fife and Kinross; on 23 April he was also appointed as a commissioner to treat for a union with England. Melville was in London when William and Mary were crowned as king and queen of Scotland. On 13 May 1689 he was appointed sole secretary of state for Scotland, securing the position from his rival Sir James Montgomerie of Skelmorlie, a militant presbyterian and the leader of the 'Club'. Melville's moderate presbyterianism appears to have satisfied episcopalians, who were wary of Montgomerie's more militant stance. He took the oath at Hampton Court on 23 September 1689. On 21 January 1690 Melville was named as an exchequer commissioner in Scotland, and on 26 February he was appointed high commissioner to the forthcoming second session of William's and Mary's parliament in Scotland. Returning to Edinburgh between 8 March and 10 March 1690, he first attended the privy council on 10 March. On 8 April 1690 he was created earl of Melville, viscount of Kirkcaldy, and Lord Raith, Monymail, and Balwearie.

Melville continued as a high commissioner in the second session of the Williamite parliament in Scotland, apparently to the satisfaction of both people and king. His speech to the assembled estates on 15 April 1690 referred to William as 'the Instrument in the Hand of God' who 'did so magnanimously expose Himself for the Rescuing you from the greatest of evils, Popery and Slavery; and Delivering you from the Fears you were ready to sink under' and expressed his own 'intire Faithfulness to the King my Master, a sincere respect to you, and a zealous application for promoting of the true Religion, and Common good of all' (APS, 9, appx, 38). The strident demands of the 'Club' for constitutional reform and a presbyterian church made the securing of a settlement for the king difficult, but Melville presided over the abolition of the controversial lords of the articles (8 May) and the legislation re-establishing presbyterian church government of the church of Scotland (7 June). Legislation passed in July rescinding forfeitures and fines resulted in Melville, among others, receiving back his land and estates. However, King William was displeased at the Scottish religious settlement with its concentration of power in the hands of a militant minority of presbyterian ministers and its failure to grant liberty to conscience. Although Melville had probably done the best he could, given the atmosphere in the Edinburgh parliament, his position was weakened, especially at the English court. None the less, he continued as secretary of state and he was high commissioner to the short parliamentary session of 3–10 September 1690.

However, Melville soon suffered a political eclipse. In January 1691 Sir John Dalrymple of Stair was appointed as joint, and apparently senior, secretary of state, residing near the king and accompanying William to Flanders. On 29 December Melville exchanged his post as joint secretary for the lesser office of lord privy seal. He appears to have got on with the duties of this position and he remained in close contact with William Carstares, then one of the royal chaplains. He attended the parliamentary sessions of 1693 (18 April to 15 June) and 1695 (9 May to 17 July) as lord privy seal. Anxiety about the permanence of the 1690 restoration of his estates was allayed by the passing of an act of ratification in his favour on 12 June 1693. When the 1695 parliamentary session debated the 1692 massacre of Glencoe, Melville refused to vote either against Dalrymple, his erstwhile rival, or for the imprisonment of John Campbell, first earl of Breadalbane, on the grounds that the king should be consulted before any summary action was taken. On 28 June 1695 parliament was presented with a petition from the city of Edinburgh reclaiming from Melville a bond of £3000 sterling (£36,000 Scots) assigned to him when he was high commissioner. The case was remitted to the lords of session, but the dispute was not settled in Melville's favour until 1698 when the king endorsed the assignment. Meanwhile, on 17 July 1695, parliament granted to Melville the right to hold two yearly fairs, in May and October, in the parish of Monimail at Letham in Fife.

In October 1695 Melville received a letter from Carstares suggesting that if he were to come to London then the king would not be displeased. Melville's return to political favour was apparent by May 1696 when he was offered the position of president of the privy council. He initially declined but persuasion from Carstares and William Bentinck, first earl of Portland, eventually changed his mind, and he took up the position about the middle of August 1696. Attending parliament in this capacity, on 10 September he became president of, and an important influence on, the committee for the security of the kingdom; he also signed the association in defence of King William on the same day. During the 1698 parliamentary session (19 July to 1 September) he was a member of the same committee but Archibald Campbell, tenth earl of Argyll, wrote to Carstares that 'Our friend Melvill has not opened his mouth scarce all this session' (Fraser, 2.237). However, he continued as president of the privy council until December 1702, when he was deprived following the accession of Queen Anne.

Melville was not closely associated with the Darien project and, unlike his sons, he was not a stockholder in the Company of Scotland. Having attended the parliamentary session of May 1700 he went to Bath in an attempt to relieve his health problems and thereafter to London. Back in Scotland to attend the parliamentary session which sat from 29 October 1700 to 31 January 1701, on 16 January he voted in favour of a parliamentary address, as opposed to a full act, being presented to William over the legality of the Darien enterprise. In the 1702 parliamentary session he was again a member of the committee for the security of the kingdom. Although an attender at the majority of the sessions of the new parliament of 1703–7, he was not present from 3 October 1706 to 25 March 1707 and therefore he did not vote on the articles of the treaty of union. In his absence, on 12 February 1707, he was voted recompense for money advanced from him in 1689–90 for the payment of officers' commissions and to help maintain troops who had not been paid. Melville died on 20 May 1707 and was buried in the parish church of Monimail, Fife. His widow died on 2 April 1713. Writing in the early eighteenth century, Macky wrote of Melville in old age:

> He hath neither Learning, Wit, nor common Conversation; but a Steadiness of Principle, and a firm Boldness for Presbyterian Government, in all Reigns … He makes a very mean Figure in his Person, being low, thin, with a great Head, a long Chin, and little Eyes.   (*Memoirs of the Secret Services*, 203)

JOHN R. YOUNG

Sources W. Fraser, ed., *The Melvilles, earls of Melville, and the Leslies, earls of Leven*, 3 vols. (1890) • *Scots peerage*, vol. 6 • *APS, 1648–1707* • *Reg. PCS*, 3rd ser., vols. 11–16 • E. W. M. Balfour-Melville, ed., *An account of the proceedings of the estates in Scotland, 1689–1690*, 1, Scottish History Society, 3rd ser., 46 (1954) • T. B. Macaulay, *The history of England from the accession of James II*, new edn, 2 vols. (1889) • *The diary of Mr John Lamont of Newton, 1649–1671*, ed. G. R. Kinloch, Maitland Club, 7 (1830) • *Memoirs of the secret services of John Macky*, ed. A. R. (1733) • W. H. L. Melville, ed., *Leven and Melville papers: letters and state papers chiefly addressed to George, earl of Melville … 1689–1691*, Bannatyne Club, 77 (1843) • *State papers and letters addressed to William Carstares*, ed. J. M'Cormick (1774) • *Bishop Burnet's History* • P. W. J. Riley, *King William and the Scottish politicians* (1979)
Archives NA Scot., Leven and Melville muniments, GD.26 • NRA, priv. coll., corresp.
Likenesses J. B. de Medina, oils, 1691, priv. coll. [see illus.] • J. B. Medina, oils, Scot. NPG • R. White, line engraving (after J. B. Medina), BM, NPG • portrait, repro. in Fraser, ed., *Melville*, 1

Melville, George John Whyte- (1821–1878), novelist and poet, was born on 19 June 1821 at Strathkinness, Fife, the eldest son of Major John Whyte-Melville (1796/7–1883) of Strathkinness, convenor of the county of Fife, and his wife, Catherine Anne Sarah Osborne (1791/2–1878), youngest daughter of Francis Godolphin *Osborne, fifth duke of Leeds. Robert Whytt (1714–1766) was his great-grandfather. He was educated at Eton College under John Keate, and in 1839 received a commission in the 93rd highlanders. He exchanged into the Coldstream Guards in 1846, was made captain, and retired in 1849. He married, on 7 August 1847, Charlotte, daughter of William Hanbury, first Lord Bateman; they had a daughter, Florence Elizabeth, who became the Viscountess Massareene. However, he did not have a happy relationship with his wife, and she eventually remarried bigamously.

When the Crimean War broke out in 1854, Whyte-Melville volunteered for active service and was appointed major of Turkish irregular cavalry. After peace was restored two years later, he devoted himself to literature and field sports, especially fox-hunting, on which he soon came to be regarded as an authority. He lived for some years in Northamptonshire after his marriage and then moved to Tetbury in Gloucestershire. He published some translations of Horace in 1850, and in 1853 his first novel appeared, *Captain Digby Grand: an Autobiography*, which was initially serialized in *Fraser's Magazine*. It was, arguably, semi-autobiographical: its hero leaves Eton and joins the army, sees service in North America, and, after a period of dissipated living, inherits, marries, and goes hunting. The book was popular.

Over the next twenty-five years, Whyte-Melville wrote twenty-five more novels, some of contemporary life and some historical romances. He was particularly concerned with the military and sporting life. He drew on his experiences of the Crimean War for *The Interpreter: a Tale of the War* (1858). The title of *Riding Recollections* (1875) is self-explanatory, while John Sutherland notes *Katerfelto* (1875) for its 'vivid stag-hunting scenes' (Sutherland, 672). On the other hand, it was with a romance set during the English civil war, *Holmby House: a Tale of Old Northamptonshire* (1860), that he established his name.

Despite Whyte-Melville's devotion to literature, he did not seem to regard himself as a professional, or even as a particularly good, novelist. All his earnings from writing he gave to projects such as the provision of reading-rooms for grooms and stable-boys in hunting-quarters. Nor, according to his friend Frederick Locker-Lampson, did he seek out overtly literary society, preferring the company of soldiers, hunters, and country gentlemen (Locker-Lampson, 382). The plots of his novels were sometimes incredible and always exciting; *The Times* (4 January 1871) remarked on his 'light and rapid style, which seems to run on wheels'. However, his concerns were not necessarily light-hearted. For example, his long religious poem *The True Cross* (1873) delineates a punitive God and, with great ambivalence, a proud, noble yet damned hunter and his lady.

Given his reputation, Whyte-Melville's death was ironic. On 5 December 1878 he was hunting near the White Horse, in the Vale of Pewsey; the hounds had found a fox, and he was galloping along the grass headland of a ploughed field. His horse fell, and he broke his neck and was killed outright. He was buried at Tetbury. His friends commissioned R. W. Edis to design both a large marble cross, placed over his grave, and a memorial fountain at St Andrews in Scotland. Joseph Edgar Boehm designed a portrait medallion to adorn the fountain. Whyte-Melville's father survived him, and at his death in 1883 Strathkinness passed to his kinsman, James Balfour, who assumed the name of Melville in addition to his own.

JESSICA HININGS

Sources J. Sutherland, *The Longman companion to Victorian fiction* (1988), 671–2 • P. N. Lewis and A. D. Morrison, *A grand man and a golfer: the novelist George Whyte Melville and his memorials* (1999) • F. Locker-Lampson, *My confidences: an autobiographical sketch addressed to my descendants*, ed. A. Birrell, 2nd edn (1896), 379–82 • *The Times* (18 Sept 1878) • *The Times* (6 Dec 1878) • *The Times* (24 Dec 1878) • *The Times* (24 Jan 1879) • *The Times* (10 Feb 1880) • *The Times* (17 July 1883) • Burke, *Peerage* • *DNB* • *CGPLA Eng. & Wales* (1879)
Archives JRL, letters from him, received or collected by R. E. E. Warburton
Likenesses J. E. Boehm, marble bust, 1879, NPG • J. E. Boehm, medallion on fountain, St Andrews • J. Brown, stipple (after photograph by Mayall), BM; repro. in *Baily's Magazine* (1867) • Judd & Co., lithograph, NPG; repro. in *Whitehall Review* (11 Jan 1879) • T. Rodger, carte-de-visite, NPG • chromolithograph caricature, NPG; repro. in *VF* (23 Sept 1871) • oils, Royal and Ancient Golf Club of St Andrews • wood-engraving, NPG; repro. in *ILN* (28 Dec 1878)

Wealth at death under £70,000: probate, 2 Jan 1879, *CGPLA Eng. & Wales*

Melville, Sir Harry Work (1908–2000), chemist, was born on 27 April 1908 at 233 Dalkeith Road, Edinburgh, the son of Thomas Melville, a brewer's clerk, and his wife, Esther Cumming Burnett, *née* Nicol. He was educated at George Heriot's School and read chemistry at the University of Edinburgh; after graduating with a first-class degree, he continued as a Carnegie research scholar and was awarded his PhD. The first of his many scientific papers was written after only six months' research. Much of his early work was concerned with the oxidation of phosphorus in the gas phase. He devised procedures to measure quantities very difficult to access, and, indeed, throughout his scientific career he was famed for his novel and ingenious experimental approaches. In 1933 he moved to Trinity College, Cambridge, where he was an 1851 Exhibition scholar; he was elected to a fellowship at the early age of twenty-five. His work on reactions in the gas phase continued in the prestigious Colloid Science Laboratory under Professor Eric Rideal. It was a time of great developments in the theory of chain reactions, and Melville's contributions were notable, receiving most favourable comments in Semyonov's book. He was awarded the Meldola medal of the Institute of Chemistry in 1936, and he was later appointed assistant director of research in the Colloid Science Laboratory.

The book written by Melville with A. Farkas, *Experimental Methods in Gas Reactions* (1939), was described in Benson's *The Foundations of Chemical Kinetics* as an excellent treatise—praise indeed from that author; a new version with B. G. Gowenlock was published in 1964. Alongside his research on reactions of gases, Melville became increasingly involved with synthetic polymers and the processes of polymerization. The change of emphasis may well have resulted from his contacts in Cambridge with F. R. Eirich, a refugee from Austria, and a meeting with Hermann Staudinger during a conference at Cambridge in 1936. Melville realized that much could be done to unravel and characterize the processes leading to giant molecules and to understand the relationships between the structures and properties of polymers; his publications reveal that he was also fully aware of the tremendous practical importance of the new synthetic materials. The citation leading to his election as fellow of the Royal Society in 1941 referred to his developing interest in polymerizations, although emphasis was placed on his work on gaseous reactions.

During the Second World War Melville served as scientific adviser on chemical defence. While stationed at Porton and living in Salisbury, he married, on 8 August 1942 in St Columba's Church, Dollar, Janet Marian Cameron (1917/18–2001), a physiotherapist at Guy's Hospital. There have been many references to their happiness together. Between 1943 and 1945 Melville held the very responsible post of superintendent at the radar research station at Malvern. He did not talk or write about his wartime activities, but evidently he must have impressed those with influence because he was appointed chief scientific adviser for civil defence in the midland region in 1952, when there was great concern about possible dangers to civilians from atomic, biological, and chemical weapons, including the so-called nerve gases.

Melville had been appointed to the chair of chemistry at Aberdeen in 1940, but he could not become active there until the end of the war. He then quickly established research activities in the department and gathered an enthusiastic and able group of students. He was in great demand for service on various committees in London and spent much time travelling. That problem was eased in 1948 when he took up his appointment to the Mason chair of chemistry at Birmingham as successor to Sir Norman Haworth, Nobel laureate. The contingent of research workers with his apparatus and equipment moved *en masse* from Aberdeen. The group at Birmingham grew in size, scope, and reputation in the field of polymer science. Melville originated a wide range of projects and the results were described in an extensive set of published papers, several of them in the *Proceedings of the Royal Society*. Many of those who worked under his direction subsequently achieved success in academia and in industry. It was a very productive period in Melville's scientific career. While it was inevitable that he should delegate some of the day-to-day supervision of research students to his lieutenants, he maintained close contact and provided direct support and advice. While at Birmingham he continued to serve on many official committees, and he was still in great demand to speak at conferences at home and overseas. He was selected to deliver the Bakerian lecture of the Royal Society in 1956. Melville was not a flamboyant lecturer but he was clear and authoritative, stimulating great interest in polymer science. His Christmas lectures at the Royal Institution in 1958 under the title 'Big molecules' were very well received. He also gained a reputation as an accomplished after-dinner speaker.

In 1956 Melville was persuaded to take charge of the Department of Scientific and Industrial Research with its many and varied activities. The family moved from Moseley in Birmingham to Chalfont St Giles in Buckinghamshire. Two years later he was knighted. The *New Scientist* of 7 February 1957 paid him a tribute by stating that the department was being run by a scientist not by an ex-scientist. Melville supervised the profound change from the Department of Scientific and Industrial Research to the Science Research Council and he was the first chairman of the new body, from 1965 to 1967. He was responsible for establishing sound foundations, and the basic structure of the council changed little for about twenty years. He confronted and resolved the many financial problems facing an organization depending upon funding from the government at a time of economic difficulties, and he dealt effectively with competing and conflicting demands, never seeming flustered and always listening attentively to submissions. He was not slow in reaching decisions.

In 1967 Melville became principal of Queen Mary College in the University of London, a post he held for nine years. During that period he maintained many of his scientific interests; he was president of the Chemical Society and held high office in other scientific societies. He served on many official bodies, including the parliamentary scientific committee and the nuclear safety committee, and he had strong connections with several industrial concerns. To many members of Queen Mary College he may have seemed remote, but he served the college well during a critical period of development and growth. He was chairman of the council of Westfield College from 1977 to 1980.

Melville was the moving spirit in the founding in 1960 of the High Polymer Research Group, and for more than twenty years he chaired its annual meetings at Moretonhampstead; he frequently ventured on to the golf course there. Cambridge University has a well-endowed laboratory named after him and dedicated to the study of polymers. There are also annual Melville lectures at Cambridge, delivered by persons of international renown.

Melville died at Austenwood Nursing Home, 29 North Park, Gerrards Cross, on 14 June 2000; he was very properly described on the death certificate as a scientist. He was survived by Janet, who died on 4 November 2001, their two daughters, and five grandchildren; a greatgranddaughter was born a few days after his death. His name will long appear in the references cited in publications, and he will be remembered with admiration, gratitude, and affection by those whom he taught and by those who had the privilege of collaborating with him. He was an unassuming but truly great man who never lost the human touch.   JOHN BEVINGTON

Sources J. C. Bevington and B. G. Gowenlock, *Memoirs FRS* [forthcoming] · *The Independent* (22 July 2000) · *The Independent* (21 July 2000) · *The Guardian* (23 June 2000) · *The Times* (4 July 2000) · *The Scotsman* (6 July 2000) · WWW · personal knowledge (2004) · private information (2004) · b. cert. · m. cert. · d. cert.
Likenesses Godfrey Argent studio, photograph, repro. in *The Independent* · photograph, repro. in *The Guardian* · photograph, repro. in *The Times*
Wealth at death £1,042,501: probate, 2000, *CGPLA Eng. & Wales*

Melville, James, of Carnbee (*d.* in or before **1550**). *See under* Castilians in St Andrews (*act.* 1546–1547).

Melville, Sir James, of Halhill (**1535/6–1617**), diplomat and autobiographer, was the third son of Sir John *Melville, fourth laird of Raith (*d.* 1548), and his second wife, Helen (*d.* in or after 1584), daughter of Sir Alexander Napier of Merchiston and his wife, Janet, daughter of Edmund Chisholm of Cromlix. Born into a family that had long been prominent in Fife, at the age of fourteen James Melville was sent to France by Mary of Guise 'to be placit paige of honour with the Quen hir dochter' (*Memoirs of His Own Life*, 9). He left Scotland in the entourage of Jean de Montluc, bishop of Valence, the French ambassador to the Scottish court, and in April 1550 arrived in Paris, where he spent the next three years in the bishop's household continuing his education—learning French, dancing, fencing, and playing the lute, as well as acquiring knowledge of current European affairs. He then entered the service of Anne, duc de Montmorency, great constable of France and

chief minister to Henri II, and from May 1553 he saw military service in the war against the emperor, Charles V. In August 1557 Melville was wounded at St Quentin and narrowly escaped capture.

Following the treaty of Cateau Cambrésis in April 1559, Henri II sent Melville to Scotland on a special mission to discover the real intentions of Lord James Stewart, halfbrother of Mary, queen of Scots, whom Mary of Guise suspected of aiming at her daughter's crown. Melville achieved a meeting with Lord James through the good offices of Henry Balnaves, 'a godly, learnit, lang experimented, wyse consellor' (*Memoirs of His Own Life*, 81), and was satisfied as to his intentions.

On Montmorency's recommendation Melville moved to the court of the elector palatine, Friedrich III, where he learned German, and from where he was able to visit the main cities of Italy. He returned to Paris to offer condolences to Mary, left a widow by the death of François II on 5 December 1560, and to present a commission regarding the proposed marriage of Charles IX to the emperor Maximilian's daughter. The French queen dowager, Catherine de' Medici, offered to make Melville a gentleman of the king's chamber and an ambassador to Germany, England, and Flanders, but in the meantime he received letters on behalf of Mary calling him home to Scotland to be employed in her service. Melville returned via England, where he had an interview with Queen Elizabeth regarding a proposal of marriage to the elector palatine's son, Johann Kasimir. Elizabeth, however, was more interested in Mary's choice of husband and proposed Lord Robert Dudley, later earl of Leicester, as one of two men she had in mind to offer Mary—the other being Darnley, 'a lusty yong prince' (*Memoirs of His Own Life*, 108).

On 5 May 1564 Melville presented himself to Mary at Perth and was well received. Melville 'thocht her mair worthy to be servit for litle proffet, then any uther prence in Europe for gret commodite' (*Memoirs of His Own Life*, 111). He was appointed a privy councillor and gentleman of the bedchamber, and on 20 July 1564 was granted a yearly pension of £100 Scots. He also received 1000 merks yearly out of Mary's revenues in France, together with lands in Auchtermuchty. In September 1564 he was sent to England to win the confidence of Elizabeth, to assess her opinions concerning Mary's marriage, and to secure her position as heir to the English throne. Melville worked hard to ingratiate himself with Elizabeth, but admitted that he did not trust her.

On 22 January 1565 Melville was granted the lands of Drumcorse in Linlithgowshire for his services, and on 18 November 1565 he was given all the goods, debts, and rights pertaining to his elder brother, Robert *Melville, escheated to the crown for Robert's support to the rising known as the chaseabout raid. James Melville was staying at Holyrood on the night of 9 March 1566, and, though he was not a witness to Rizzio's murder, he exploited it to bring about the reconciliation of Mary and Moray. On 16 April 1566 he was granted a life pension of 500 merks Scots a year. Following the birth of Prince James on 19 June 1566 Melville was sent to relay the news to Elizabeth. He requested her to be a godmother to the prince, and she agreed.

Melville was in Mary's entourage when she was abducted by Bothwell on 24 April 1567. But although he blamed Bothwell as the chief source of Mary's ruin, the prime suspect in Darnley's murder, and the bringer of 'gret trouble and mischeif into the contre' (*Memoirs of His Own Life*, 170), he was nevertheless present at their marriage on 15 May. After Mary had abdicated, on 24 July, Melville was sent by the nobles in August to offer the regency to the earl of Moray. In politics and religion Melville favoured Moray, but he was loyal to Mary and hoped that she and her opponents could be reconciled. This was prevented, however, by Mary's escape from Lochleven in May 1568, followed quickly by her defeat at Langside and her flight into England.

On the death of Henry Balnaves in February 1570, Melville inherited the estate of Halhill in Fife. Balnaves was a senator of the college of justice and an active reformer. Having no children of his own he had adopted Melville as his son and sole executor, and left him the whole heirship of Halhill. Balnaves's will, dated 3 January 1570, contains a bequest to his 'sones wyffe' of a damask gown lined with velvet showing that Melville was now married (Fraser, 3.117–20). Melville's wife, Christine Boswell, with whom he had two sons and two daughters, (including Elizabeth *Melville, the writer) is identified in a charter of 24 February 1576 confirming Melville's grant to her in liferent of the half-lands of Easter Collessie (called Halhill) and of Murefield, in the sheriffdom and county of Fife.

During the minority of James VI, Melville was entrusted with diplomatic missions by all four regents, before choosing to retire from court life. But having been recommended by Mary, queen of Scots, for his good counsel and services, he returned during James VI's reign, when he offered advice and support to the young king and received foreign ambassadors. However, 'hindered by want of health' (*CSP Scot.*, 1581–3, 652), he was reluctant to act as ambassador himself, and declined missions to England, Denmark, and Spain, in spite of being commended in 1590 for his knowledge of Latin, Italian, and German, and his diplomatic experience. Appointed a member of the privy council and of the exchequer, and also made gentleman of the bedchamber to Queen Anne, Melville was knighted at her coronation on 17 May 1590. He was present at Holyrood on 27 December 1591, and again at Falkland on 28 June 1592, when the first earl of Bothwell tried to kidnap the king, and he commented at length on Bothwell's association with witches.

Following the death in 1594 of his brother David Melville of Newmill, Melville was retoured his heir in the lands of Prinlaws. He was called to parliament on 30 May 1594, as one of four representatives for Fife, and in December 1597 his annual pensions of £100 and 500 merks were ratified by the king in parliament, with an augmentation fee of £300. In July 1599 Melville was named to a commission for raising men for military service, and on 14 July 1600 he was received and admitted to the privy council (as reconstituted in 1598).

Melville declined James VI's request to accompany him to England in 1603, though he did subsequently make one visit to London. His later years were spent quietly at Halhill, where he wrote his memoirs. Intended mainly as a guide for his son James, they are among the most important sources for British history in the second half of the sixteenth century, through the light they shed on the human qualities of the leading actors on the public stage. They did much to justify Sir Walter Scott's verdict that they may 'justly be compared with the most valuable materials which British history affords' (Scott, *History of Scotland*, 1850, 2.93). Melville based his judgements on Mary, Elizabeth, Darnley, Moray, and others on his personal observation. It was to Melville that Queen Elizabeth uttered her famous cry of distress, when told of the birth of Prince James: 'The queen of Scots is this day leichter of a fair son, and I am but a barren stock' (*Memoirs of His Own Life*, 159). Likewise it is to Melville that posterity owes such vignettes of the great as Mary praising Darnley's good looks, Elizabeth tickling Robert Dudley's neck while creating him earl of Leicester, and Bothwell's disgusting language. The memoirs were not published until 1683. Several further editions followed in the eighteenth century and later, notably those of Thomas Thomson in 1827 and Gordon Donaldson in 1969.

Melville owed his ability to record people and events primarily to his employment as a diplomat. In that role he seems to have been fairly impartial, avoiding direct involvement in political and religious intrigue, and remaining free from links to any of the leading families. When setting down his opinion that the main figures of his time would have been better off if they had listened to his advice, Melville may well have been exaggerating his own importance. But his very lack of bias and self-interest did at least make it easier for him to speak freely. As both courtier and ambassador he earned the respect he won during the reigns of two monarchs and four regents. Melville died on 13 November 1617, aged eighty-two, and was buried in the churchyard of Collessie.

ELAINE FINNIE GREIG

Sources *Memoirs of his own life by Sir James Melville of Halhill*, ed. T. Thomson, Bannatyne Club, 18 (1827) • W. Fraser, ed., *The Melvilles, earls of Melville, and the Leslies, earls of Leven*, 3 vols. (1890) • *CSP Scot.*, 1547–1603 • J. M. Thomson and others, eds., *Registrum magni sigilli regum Scotorum / The register of the great seal of Scotland*, 11 vols. (1882–1914), vol. 4 • M. Livingstone, D. Hay Fleming, and others, eds., *Registrum secreti sigilli regum Scotorum / The register of the privy seal of Scotland*, 5 (1957) • *Reg. PCS*, 1st ser., vol. 6 • *The memoirs of Sir James Melville of Halhill*, ed. G. Donaldson (1969)

Archives BL, memoirs, Add. MS 37977 • NA Scot., family papers of the earls of Leven and Melville, GD26

Melville, James (1556–1614), Church of Scotland minister and diarist, was the son of Richard Melville of Baldovy, minister of Maryton near Montrose, Angus, and his wife, Isabell Scrimgeour (d. 1557/8), sister of the laird of Glasswell. He was born on 25 July 1556, though his uncle, the presbyterian leader Andrew *Melville, considered that he was born in 1557 (*Autobiography and Diary*, 1.13). Taught first by the minister of Logie-Montrose, James was sent to school in the nearby burgh of Montrose and learned the rudiments of Latin and some French, before entering St Leonard's College, St Andrews, where he matriculated in 1570. He appreciated the value of education, was promised a bursary, and 'lyked the schollar's lyff best' (ibid., 23). Yet on arrival at university he found himself 'nather being weill groundet in grammar, nor com to the yeirs of naturall judgment', burst into tears when he failed to follow the Latin lectures, and was ready to return home (ibid., 25). He persevered, however, and benefited from private tuition in the evenings. Also in St Andrews he heard the preaching of John Knox, whose powerful oratory made him shudder and tremble to such an extent that he found himself unable to 'hald a pen to wryte'; he nevertheless became accustomed to hear the reformer, who was apt to call 'us schollars unto him and bless us, and exhort us to knaw God and his wark in our contrey, and stand be the guid cause' (ibid., 26). Melville's father hoped that he would become a lawyer, but James's thoughts turned to the ministry, and after graduating BA on 9 February 1572, he was invited by Andrew Melville, on the latter's appointment as principal of Glasgow University, to undertake teaching in arts.

At Stirling, as he travelled west to Glasgow, Melville met the eight-year-old James VI, 'the sweitest sight in Europe that day, for strange and extraordinar gifts of ingyne, judgment, memorie and langage' and heard him discourse on knowledge and ignorance, 'to my grait mervell and estonishment' (*Autobiography and Diary*, 48). Melville's teaching at Glasgow began in 1575 with the Greek authors, Ramus's *Dialecticae*, and Talon's *Rhetorica*, followed in 1576 with instruction in arithmetic, mathematics, logic, and moral philosophy. In private study, however, Melville pursued Hebrew and theology, and participated in the 'exercise' or 'prophesying' organized by the ministers of the area for biblical exposition and homiletical training. According to his own account, his exhortation in church before the congregation, when his turn came round, 'pleasit and confortit guid peiple verie mikle, sa that they resorted verie frequentlie' (ibid., 55–6).

When his uncle left Glasgow for St Andrews in 1580 to become principal of St Mary's College, James Melville, who had proposed to go to France, was persuaded to accompany his uncle to St Andrews and teach Hebrew grammar there. The town of Stirling petitioned in 1582 to have him as their minister, but neither the general assembly nor Andrew Melville granted approval for his translation. On 1 May 1583 he married Elizabeth (d. 1607x10), daughter of John *Durie (1537–1600), the radical minister in Edinburgh who had initiated the debate on episcopacy in the general assembly in 1575. They had six children: Ephraim (b. 1585, d. in or before 1629), later minister of Pittenweem; Andrew (1586–1588); Andrew (b. 1588, d. in or before 1613); Margaret (1593–1594); John (1595–1649), later minister of Newton; Issobel; and Anna (b. c.1598).

Following the promulgation in 1584 of the Black Acts asserting the royal supremacy and authority of bishops, Melville heard that the archbishop of St Andrews intended to have him arrested. He made for Dundee and

sailed for the safety of Berwick upon Tweed disguised as a 'shipbroken sie-man' (*Autobiography and Diary*, 168), as his house and papers were searched by the authorities. His eldest son was born in the town on 15 January 1585. Prohibited from preaching in public at Berwick, Melville served as minister to the banished ultra-protestant lords who had congregated at Newcastle upon Tyne and drew up an order of discipline to be observed. He announced there would be four sermons a week, with common prayers twice daily, and thanksgiving at every meal, with a chapter read from the Bible and a psalm sung. A week each month was to be set aside for fasting and meditation, followed by the celebration of the Lord's supper. Provision was also made for lectures and for lessons on the catechism. All who could read were to possess copies of the Bible and Psalm Book. The elders and deacons elected from the congregation were to meet weekly. The nobles dutifully agreed to these terms, which they observed for the duration of their exile.

From the safety of England, Melville wrote a lengthy letter condemning 'this present intolerable tyrannie of the fals Bischopes' and censuring those ministers who had obeyed the king's requirement and signed the subscription of 1584 in favour of bishops and the royal supremacy (*Autobiography and Diary*, 200). In November 1585 he returned home along with other presbyterian exiles. He and his uncle soon became embroiled in disputes with Archbishop Patrick Adamson, partly because the archbishop had reconverted St Mary's College into an arts school in their absence. A fierce attack on Adamson by James Melville at a meeting of the synod of Fife in the spring of 1586 led the assembled body to excommunicate the archbishop. The latter then retaliated by having an excommunication of the Melvilles proclaimed in Edinburgh. Uncle and nephew were called before the privy council in May, and the dispute was resolved by all parties being assigned teaching duties. In October 1586 James Melville was appointed minister of Anstruther and Kilrenny in Fife. Two years later he had the unusual experience of interviewing an admiral of the Spanish Armada whose ship found its way to Anstruther harbour after the fleet had been damaged in storms off Fair Isle in the far north.

Melville acquired further charges in Fife, but kept them only briefly. Active in collecting for the relief of exiled French protestants in England and for the city of Geneva, he consulted with nobles, lawyers, burgesses, and ministers in 1588 on the threat posed by the activities of Jesuits and seminary priests at home. In 1590 he was appointed by the privy council as a commissioner for preserving and promoting protestantism in Fife. During the following decade he published *The description of the Spainyart's naturall, out of Julius Scaliger, with sum exhortations for warning of kirk and countrey* (1592) and a devotional work, *Ane fruitful and comfortable exhortatioun anent death* (1597). In 1598 he issued *A Spiritual Propyne of a Pastor to his People*, a catechism 'for the profit of my peiple' (*Autobiography and Diary*, 12). His proposition that prayer makes 'us hamely with God' (*A Spiritual Propyne*, 5) reveals his ability to appreciate his parishioners' needs, and he underlined the value of music in enhancing family devotions. Sensitive to nature in his writings, he wrote poetry as well as prose, including a lament on the kirk in Greek verse.

Moderator of the general assembly in June 1589, Melville preached against attempts at introducing conformity with the Church of England. After obtaining Archbishop Adamson's repentance in 1591, he recommended to the synod of Fife the archbishop's release from excommunication. In 1594, with his uncle Andrew, he accompanied King James on an expedition against the northern Roman Catholic earls but at an interview with the king at Falkland Palace in 1595 he defended his fellow minister David Black whom the king had accused of preaching politics. In 1598 he opposed the king's plans for ecclesiastical representation in parliament as a device for reviving episcopacy. While he was prepared to give a public thanksgiving for the king's deliverance from the Gowrie conspiracy in 1600, he refused thereafter to celebrate the anniversary, as commanded by king and parliament. After his uncle had been warded in 1602, he continued to attend assemblies of the kirk and to speak out forcefully. By 1604 it was said that 'the king hated him most of anie man in Scotland, becaus he crossed all his turnes and was a ring-leader to others' (Calderwood, 6.261–2).

In September 1605 Melville wrote an apology on behalf of the warded ministers who had offended the king by holding a general assembly at Aberdeen in defiance of his wishes, and in 1606 he signed the protest against episcopacy. As one of the presbyterian ministers invited by the king to London to attend a meeting at Hampton Court in 1606, he rejected any notion of royal supremacy in matters ecclesiastical, and was warded with the bishop of Durham. Permitted to leave London on 6 May 1607, he was ordered to remain within ten miles of Newcastle. However, following the death of his wife some time between 1607 and 1610 he was allowed to return briefly to Scotland to settle his affairs. According to David Calderwood, in October 1607 the king deputed Sir John Anstruther to go to Newcastle and offer Melville a bishopric, which he firmly declined; and in 1608 Melville declared that episcopacy 'was poprie' (Calderwood, 6.732). From Newcastle Melville published another devotional work, *A Morning Vision* (1609). In 1612 he married Deborah, the nineteen-year-old daughter of Richard Clerke, vicar of Berwick; they had no children. Melville seems to have contemplated moving to France, but he died in Berwick on 19 January 1614, and was buried there on 21 January.

To the sympathetic Calderwood, Melville was 'one of the wisest directors of kirk affaires that our kirk had in his tyme' (Calderwood, 7.190). With John Forbes and Robert Bruce he was a central figure in the ongoing Reformation and played a key role of spiritual father to men only a little younger than himself. For Archbishop John Spottiswoode, once his student at Glasgow, he was 'a man of good learning, sober and modest', but 'a crafty, biding man' and 'so addicted to the courses of Mr Andrew Melvill, his uncle, as by following him he lost the king's favour, which he once enjoyed in a good measure, and so made himself

and his labours unprofitable to the Church' (Spottiswoode, 3.190). Yet his writings have made a profound impression on the historiography of the kirk. His *Diary*, completed in 1602 and published in the nineteenth century, paints an admiring picture of one of its leading figures, his uncle Andrew, and presents a vivid and intimate portrait of church life which is generally faithful to the facts. His *True Narratioune of the Declyneing Aige of the Kirk of Scotland*, composed in 1610, also heavily influences an anti-episcopalian perspective, and other posthumously published works such as *The Black Bastel* (1634) and *A Short Relation of the Kirk of Scotland since the Reformation* (1638), have served to enhance it.　　JAMES KIRK

Sources *The autobiography and diary of Mr James Melvill*, ed. R. Pitcairn, Wodrow Society (1842) · T. Thomson, ed., *Acts and proceedings of the general assemblies of the Kirk of Scotland*, 3 pts, Bannatyne Club, 81 (1839–45) · D. Calderwood, *The history of the Kirk of Scotland*, ed. T. Thomson and D. Laing, 8 vols., Wodrow Society, 7 (1842–9) · *CSP Scot., 1581–1603* · J. Spottiswoode, *History of the Church of Scotland*, ed. M. Napier and M. Russell, 3 vols., Spottiswoode Society, 6 (1847–51) · J. Kirk, *The Second Book of Discipline* (1980) · J. Durkan and J. Kirk, *The University of Glasgow, 1451–1577* (1977) · R. G. Cant, *The University of St Andrews: a short history* (1946); rev. edn (1970) · T. M'Crie, *The life of Andrew Melville*, new edn (1899) · J. M. Anderson, ed., *Early records of the University of St Andrews*, Scottish History Society, 3rd ser., 8 (1926) · *Reg. PCS*, 1st ser., vols. 3–10 · A. R. MacDonald, *The Jacobean kirk, 1567–1625: sovereignty, polity and liturgy* (1998) · D. G. Mullan, *Scottish puritanism, 1590–1638* (2000)

Archives NL Scot., diary and poems · U. Edin. L., MSS

Wealth at death £137 6s. 10d.: will, 24 Feb 1614, repr. in *Autobiography and diary of Mr James Melville*, ed. Pitcairn, li–lv

Melville, Sir John, of Raith (d. 1548), landowner, was the elder son of John Melville of Raith (d. c.1494), and his wife, Janet Bonar (d. in or after 1506). In 1502 he succeeded his grandfather William Melville as laird of Raith, and by 1506 he had been knighted (perhaps at James IV's wedding celebrations in 1503). He married twice. With Margaret Wemyss, whom he married about 1503, he is known only to have had a daughter, Janet, who married Sir James Kirkcaldy of Grange. With Helen Napier (d. in or after 1584), whom he probably married about 1525, he had nine sons and two daughters. He also had an illegitimate son, John, begotten in England.

A handsome and plausible man, able to frame his face to all occasions, Melville is said to have fought at Flodden in 1513. Having survived the Scottish defeat, in the 1520s he charmed the sixth earl of Angus, who in October 1526 appointed him master of the Royal Artillery for life, even though a month earlier Melville had joined the earl of Lennox in trying to release the young James V from Angus's custody. After the coup failed Melville had to plead for a pardon, which he obtained on 14 August 1527. A year later Angus was banished by James, who clearly did not regard Melville as seriously compromised by his links with the fallen regime, for he several times employed him on justice ayres. A more serious handicap was probably an extended feud, beginning in 1527, with John Moultray of Markinch and Seafield, whose father had been killed by Melvilles, causing much violence and several deaths. The quarrel was eventually settled in 1534 after the king's intervention. In 1533 Melville had accompanied James to the borders when war with England threatened, and he also served on the assizes which condemned Lady Glamis in 1537 and Sir James Hamilton of Finnart in 1540. Described in the latter year as the king's 'lovit familiar servitour' (Fraser, 1.53), he was made captain of Dunbar Castle, the greatest strength north of the border at this time, and in that capacity had custody of highland chiefs arrested on James's expedition to the Western Isles.

Like many other Fife gentry, including his own son-in-law Kirkcaldy of Grange, Melville was won over to the cause of religious reform, so much so that he features among the martyrs in John Johnston's *Heroes ex omni historia Scotica lectissimi* (1603). In 1540 he was named in the list of heretics that Cardinal David Beaton presented to the king, recommending that James confiscate their lands and goods. No action followed, and Melville remained captain of Dunbar until about the end of 1542, after the king's death. Melville was later one of the landowners whose support the cardinal tried to buy with grants of church land, and in 1544 Mary of Guise appears to have regarded him as at least a potential supporter. There is no evidence that Melville was involved in Beaton's assassination, on 29 May 1546, though he was later suspected of gaining possession of some of the dead cardinal's valuables. In the meantime he had travelled widely, in England as well as in Scotland. He clearly favoured an English marriage for Mary, queen of Scots, and appears to have worked for an English victory.

Melville's bastard son John had been involved in the plot against Beaton, and subsequently withdrew to England, where he became an agent for Protector Somerset. He received letters from his father, in one of which, sent in January 1548, Sir John gave information of Scottish military affairs, telling how the fourth earl of Argyll was advancing on Dundee, which was then in English hands. A month later this letter, and perhaps others, fell into the hands of the governor of Scotland, the second earl of Arran, when Arran captured the tower-house of John Cockburn of Ormiston. Arran sat on this highly incriminating evidence for months and then struck, at the beginning of December. Melville was arrested by servants of the Scottish treasurer, John Hamilton, abbot of Paisley, and taken to Edinburgh, where he was tried and condemned on 13 December. The charge sheet stretched far and wide. Melville's 'lese maiestie' included aiding the 'evill and mischevous purpois and effaris of … Henrie the aucht King of Ingland'. He had allegedly behaved traitorously since the end of 1542 ('continewalie sen the deceis of oure said ladiis umquhile derrest fader'). In particular he had revealed the 'secretis' of the realm in the first half of 1546, and had also given warning of Argyll's 'starklie' descent upon Dundee at the end of the following year.

Executed by hanging on the day of his trial, Melville's head was set 'upoun ane prik upoun the tolbuith' and his body was dismembered, with 'every quarter put upoun ane port of the said burgh of Edinbur, to the sycht of the peple' (Fraser, 3.103–4). On 14 December all his possessions were escheated to the crown, but on 4 June 1563 his

forfeiture was rescinded, enabling his widow and children to recover their inheritance. His sons included Robert *Melville, who was made first Lord Melville in 1616, the memoirist Sir James *Melville of Halhill, Sir Andrew Melville of Garvock, who became master of Queen Mary's household and accompanied her to England, and William, commendator of Tongland.

Marcus Merriman

Sources W. Fraser, ed., *The Melvilles, earls of Melville, and the Leslies, earls of Leven*, 3 vols. (1890) · *Scots peerage*, 6.85–95 · M. Merriman, *The rough wooings: Mary queen of Scots, 1542–1551* (2000) · G. Donaldson, *Scotland, James V to James VII* (1965) · M. H. B. Sanderson, *Cardinal of Scotland: David Beaton, c.1494–1546* (1986)

Melville, Leslie Melville Balfour- (1854–1937), sportsman, was born in St Andrews on 9 March 1854, the son of James Balfour, writer to the signet, and his wife, Eliza Ogilvie Heriot Maitland. His father, who was twice winner of the gold medal of the Royal and Ancient Golf Club, assumed the additional name of Melville in 1883 on inheriting from his kinsman John Whyte-Melville the property of Mount Melville, Strathkinness, St Andrews. Leslie Balfour was educated at Edinburgh Academy (1865–71), where he captained the football fifteen, but made his mark particularly at cricket. While still at school, he played for twenty-two of Edinburgh against George Parr's All England eleven. While studying law at Edinburgh University (1871–5), he was an enthusiastic rugby player and in 1872 he played for Scotland against England. He was admitted a writer to the signet in 1879, and married on 29 November 1879 Jeanie Amelia, daughter of Dr William Wilson of Florence.

In professional life Balfour-Melville, who belonged to the law firm of Balfour and Scott, was for many years clerk to the income tax commissioners for the county of Midlothian. But he was best-known as Scotland's leading amateur player of summer sports. On leaving school in 1872 he began his long career with the Grange cricket club and made an impressive début against Glasgow by scoring 150 runs. His highest score was 207 against Drumpellier in 1893. He played for the MCC and captained the Gentlemen of Scotland against the Gentlemen of Ireland in 1909. He joined the Royal and Ancient Golf Club, St Andrews, in 1873, and in 1875 won the King William IV medal, which before the introduction of the amateur championship was regarded as the highest award open to an amateur golfer. In 1879 he became Scottish lawn tennis champion.

Balfour-Melville was captain of the Honourable Company of Edinburgh Golfers in 1902–3 and of the Royal and Ancient in 1906–7. His record in the amateur championship was equally impressive: he won in 1895, was runner-up to J. E. Laidlaw at St Andrews in 1889, and made four semi-final appearances. He represented Scotland in 1902 and 1903 in golf internationals against England. Billiards, curling, and skating were among his other sports; when his cricket career ended, at the age of seventy, he could be seen at the Edinburgh dance-halls.

Balfour-Melville married a second time, in 1923, Harriet Maud Carey MBE. In politics he was a unionist; in religion, a member of the established Church of Scotland. He died on 16 July 1937 at his home, 35 Westgate, North Berwick. He left at least one son. WALTER ALLAN

Sources WWW · *Burke's Who's who in sport* (1922) · *Scottish Law Review*, 53 (1937), 254 · d. cert. · parish register (birth), St Cuthbert's, Edinburgh
Archives NA Scot., family and estate MSS

Melville, Robert, first Lord Melville (1527/8–1621), administrator and judge, was born in Fife, the second son of Sir John *Melville of Raith (*d.* 1548), and his second wife, Helen Napier of Merchiston (*d.* in or after 1584). Raised in the international tradition of noble service, he was not university trained but was entered into the service of Mary of Guise, queen dowager of Scotland, in his youth. His famous younger brother, the statesman Sir James *Melville of Halhill, had an almost identical early career. Robert was afterwards at the French court in the service of Henri II, on whose death in 1559 he returned to Scotland. He was usually known as Melville of Murdocairny. Throwing in his lot with the lords of the congregation, who were then in conflict with Mary of Guise, Melville was sent by them, along with William Maitland of Lethington, to beg the assistance of Queen Elizabeth of England. He was admitted a privy councillor in 1562. Later he was employed in other diplomatic missions to England, one of which had for its object the marriage of Elizabeth to the third earl of Arran. Melville joined the opposition to Mary's marriage with Darnley in 1565, and in the autumn played a small part in the rebellion led by Moray known as the Chaseabout raid. For a time he took refuge in England, but Mary granted him an early pardon and sent him as her resident ambassador to the English court, whose projects he faithfully reported. He was instrumental in making peace between Mary and the earl of Moray, but the murder of Darnley (9 February 1567) disgusted him, and he withdrew from politics.

Mary, however, after marrying the fourth earl of Bothwell (15 May 1567), sent Melville back to Queen Elizabeth to make the most plausible representation of her actions. But Melville, who thoroughly disliked Bothwell, acted more in the interests of the Scottish nobles who were opposing Mary than in those of his queen. In 1567 she made him keeper of her palace of Linlithgow, and he held this office until 1587. When Melville returned to Scotland in July 1567 Mary was a captive in Lochleven Castle, but he was permitted to visit her there. Bishop Robert Keith records that he then delivered her a ring as a pledge of Elizabeth's protection—a promise that Mary would later rue. Melville used all his persuasive energy to induce Mary to renounce Bothwell, and so save herself and the country. Mary was obdurate, and the nobles, resolving to force her to abdicate, selected Melville to intimate to her their intention. He declined the mission, but seeing their determination he visited Mary privately and advised her to acquiesce.

When Queen Mary effected her escape in 1568, Melville joined her at Hamilton, and he was present when she publicly revoked her deed of abdication. At the battle of Langside (13 May), Mary's last stand, he was taken prisoner by Regent Moray, but having been a non-combatant, and with many friends in the regent's party, he was speedily released and employed in further diplomatic negotiations with Elizabeth. While Mary was a prisoner in England, Melville, who maintained his attachment to her to the end and was trusted by her, laboured to bring about a reconciliation of all parties. His efforts failed, and when hostilities broke out between her supporters and the friends of the young James VI, Melville joined with Kirkcaldy of Grange in his attempt to re-establish the authority of the Scottish queen. He was prominent among the many Fife lairds, sometimes characterized as the 'loyal Melvilles', who maintained a remarkable personal loyalty to Mary despite many misfortunes (Donaldson, 106). During the siege of Edinburgh Castle, Melville was declared a traitor and forfeited, and when the castle surrendered in April 1573 he fell into the hands of Regent Morton, who would have put him to death, as he did other prominent prisoners, had not Queen Elizabeth and Henry Killigrew, the English ambassador, interposed in his favour. After a year of captivity, spent partly in Holyrood and partly at Lethington, near Haddington, Melville was liberated. He lived in retirement during the remainder of Morton's government and was not fully restored to his estates until 1579.

In 1580 the influence of Esmé Stewart, soon to be duke of Lennox, became paramount at court, and Melville was recalled, his forfeiture rescinded. He was knighted on 20 October 1581, at the same time as Lord Ruthven was created earl of Gowrie. Gowrie was already treasurer of Scotland, and Melville was appointed his clerk and treasurer-depute in August 1582. Melville did not participate in the Ruthven raid that same month, but he assisted James in his escape from Gowrie. Melville was reappointed a privy councillor in 1583. When Queen Mary was lying under sentence of death, James sent Melville, along with the master of Gray, to entreat Elizabeth on 7 December 1586 to spare Mary's life. Melville discharged his mission so fearlessly that Elizabeth threatened his life and but for Gray would have deprived him of his liberty. After his return on 7 February 1587 Melville was commended, and as a reward received from James the gift of a wardship worth £1000 Scots.

Two English lists of 1585 assessing the religious inclinations of Scottish nobles support the conclusion that Melville was a protestant. However, they also indicate that he was inclined toward a political alliance with France, and thus was not wholly friendly to English purposes. Melville was certainly supportive of a church subservient to the polity of the state and appears to have urged presbyterian conciliation in such affairs. James Melville records in his autobiography that Sir Robert came to St Andrews in 1583 to persuade the doctrinaire presbyterian minister Andrew Melville to make peace with the king. In July 1584 Sir Robert lobbied Patrick Galloway on behalf of the government to abandon certain policies being proposed at the general assembly. Yet he apparently enjoyed the confidence of some sections of the kirk, for in February 1588 the assembly adopted a resolution to draw up of a list of known Jesuits, which was to be delivered to him on the premise that he would issue summonses against the named individuals.

On the departure of King James for Scandinavia in October 1589 to bring home his bride, Princess Anne of Denmark, Melville was deputed to act as chancellor. He was afterwards sent to pacify disorderly districts in the north and on the borders. From the 1590s until his retirement, Melville was one of few men not trained in law who was regularly appointed one of the lords of the articles, important officials selected before each parliament to prepare its legislation. He purchased the lands and castle of Monimail, Fife, an old residence of Cardinal David Beaton, from Sir James Balfour in 1592. In 1593 he again went to England to negotiate with Elizabeth about the relations of the two kingdoms with Spain. On 11 June 1594 he was admitted a judge-extraordinary of the court of session, the highest civil court in Scotland, by the title of Lord Murdocairny, the name of his seat in Fife. The same year he accompanied King James to the north, opposing the sixth earl of Huntly, and remained there for some time with the second duke of Lennox to restore order. Melville remained treasurer-depute until 1596. After Gowrie's downfall his successors as treasurer (the third earl of Montrose, from 1584 to 1585; Thomas Lyon, master of Glamis, from 1585 to 1596) usually had only a nominal connection with their office. It was Melville who handled the money, submitted the accounts, and took responsibility for the growing deficit caused by the establishment of a royal court on inadequate revenues. On the appointment in 1596 of the Octavians, eight commissioners who undertook to manage the national finances, he ceased to be treasurer-depute, but before a year was past the Octavians petitioned for assistance, and Melville was among those directed to help them. When he quitted the office of treasurer-depute Melville was so much out of pocket (he was superexpended by £35,656 Scots) that he could not meet his own creditors and had to be protected from them by a special act of parliament, while the court of session was forbidden to entertain any action at law against him. In 1605 he and his son were granted discharge for their lifetimes of feu-duties due to the crown for the lands of Murdocairny for his service 'albeit as yet dewlie recompansit' (*APS, 1593–1625*, 4.264, 455). The king did not repay him until well after 1610, and possibly not even then.

By 1600 old age was telling upon Melville, and in December that year he resigned both his offices of privy councillor and judge in favour of his son; from time to time he still attended the council meetings, notwithstanding a special dispensation from the king in February 1604, because of his age and infirmity. He accompanied James to London in 1603, and when steps were being taken in 1605 for uniting the kingdoms, the Scottish parliament appointed him one of their commissioners. A draft treaty of union was prepared, which Melville signed, but it was not then carried into effect.

Melville's long services were recognized on 1 April 1616 by his creation as a lord of parliament, with the title of Lord Melville of Monimail. He was thrice married, first to Katherine, daughter of William Adamson of Craigcrook, a burgess of Edinburgh; second, before 1593, to Lady Mary Leslie (*d.* 1605), daughter of Andrew, fifth earl of Rothes; and third to Lady Jean Stewart (*d.* after 1642), daughter of Robert, earl of Orkney (a natural son of King James V), and widow of Patrick Leslie, first Lord Lindores. Melville died in December 1621, aged ninety-four. His son Robert, who succeeded him as second Lord Melville, was the son of his father's first marriage. Melville also had a natural daughter, Christian, married to Thomas Oliphant, portioner of Hilcairny.   R. R. ZULAGER

Sources *APS, 1593–1625* · J. Row, *The history of the Kirk of Scotland, from the year 1558 to August 1637*, ed. D. Laing, Wodrow Society, 4 (1842) · *CSP Scot., 1547–1603* · T. Thomson, ed., *Letters and papers relating to Patrick, master of Gray, afterwards seventh Lord Gray*, Bannatyne Club, 48 (1835) · *Memoirs of his own life by Sir James Melville of Halhill*, ed. T. Thomson, Bannatyne Club, 18 (1827) · *The autobiography and diary of Mr James Melvill*, ed. R. Pitcairn, Wodrow Society (1842) · A. Hay, *Estimate of the Scottish nobility during the minority of James the Sixth*, ed. C. Rogers, Grampian Club (1873) · W. Fraser, ed., *The Melvilles, earls of Melville and the Leslies, earls of Leven*, 1 (1890), 82–124 · R. Keith, *History of the affairs of church and state in Scotland from the beginning of the Reformation to the year 1568*, ed. J. P. Lawson and C. J. Lyon, Spottiswoode Society, 1 (1844) · G. Donaldson, *All the queen's men: power and politics in Mary Stewart's Scotland* (1983) · *Scots peerage*, 6.86–99

Melville, Robert (1723–1809), army officer and colonial governor, was born in Monimail, Fife, on 5 October 1723, the son of the Revd Andrew Melvil (*d.* 1736), the minister of Monimail, and his wife, Helen, daughter of Robert Whytt or White, an advocate. His younger brother was the natural philosopher Thomas *Melvill (1726–1753). Through both maternal and paternal lines Melville was descended from a cadet branch of the family headed by the earls of Leven and Melville. Owing to the early death of both parents, his education was entrusted to a maternal uncle, Dr Robert *Whytt (1714–1766), a professor of medicine at the University of Edinburgh. Educated at Leven grammar school, Melville matriculated at the University of Glasgow in 1737, continued his medical studies at the University of Edinburgh, but left university without graduating to follow a military career.

Commissioned an ensign in the 25th regiment of foot in March 1744, Melville served in Flanders during the War of the Austrian Succession, from 1744 to 1748. Present at Fontenoy (April 1745) he returned with the regiment to Scotland during the Jacobite rising. Part of the garrison of Blair Castle, Perthshire, he may have been present at Culloden (April 1746). Having returned to Flanders, he was present at Rocoux (September 1746) and at Laffeldt (June 1747). At the latter battle his conduct won him promotion to lieutenant. Following the war he served in Ireland from 1749 to 1755 and was promoted to captain in August 1751. He then returned to Scotland to recruit for the regiment. Appointed an aide-de-camp to William Maule, earl of Panmure, he was promoted to major of the 38th regiment of foot, then stationed in Antigua, in January 1756.

During the Seven Years' War (1756–63) Melville's service was limited to the West Indies. Between January and May

1759 he commanded the light infantry during the reduction of Guadeloupe. Appointed the lieutenant-governor of the island, he was promoted to lieutenant-colonel in June 1759; following the death of Brigadier Bryan Crump in February 1761 he was appointed temporary governor of Guadeloupe. He took part in the capture of Dominica by Andrew, fifth Lord Rollo, and having been promoted to brigadier in September 1761, he commanded a division in General Robert Monckton's reduction of Martinique in February 1762.

During these amphibious campaigns Melville continued the studies in ordnance and shell delivery that he had begun while at Blair Castle. By 1759, at the earliest, he had developed a naval gun carriage without trunnions that could mount a new type of naval gun which he had invented. A short seven-calibre weapon, the gun delivered a slow-moving, heavy shot which upon impact with timber caused a large irregular hole and massive splintering. Initially nicknamed 'the smasher', the weapon was finally put into production at the Carron Iron Works, Falkirk, in 1779, and was renamed the carronade. Although the larger version, the melvillade, was rarely used, the carronade became one of the most important innovations in naval warfare in the second part of the eighteenth century. The gun, whose elevation and angle of fire were governed by a screw on its gun carriage, suited the British style of close-in fighting and by 1781 over 600 guns had been mounted by the Royal Navy. The carronade proved decisive in Admiral Rodney's victory over the French at the battle of the Saints on 12 April 1782.

Melville returned to Britain in September 1762, and following the treaty of Paris (1763) his appointment as the new governor of the Ceded Islands (Grenada, the Grenadines, Tobago, Dominica and St Vincent) was announced in July that year. He arrived at his administrative capital, Port Royal, Grenada, in December 1764, and his seven-year governorship was largely successful. Regional economic growth was generated largely by the concentration of land into bigger plantations and the increased importance of African slaves to work them: over 10,000 between 1746 and 1764 alone. He was promoted to major-general in August 1766. Regional prosperity was reflected in Melville's own rising wealth: in 1770 his island properties were estimated to value £45,000—including a large plantation, Melville Hall, on Grenada and another, Carnbee, on Tobago. Like most colonial governors in America, however, Melville experienced problems with his regional assemblies. Transplanted British planters especially opposed Melville's policy of allowing the French Catholic landowning subjects the vote and a share in administration. Recalled in 1768 to defend his actions, Melville's presence in London generated a pamphlet exchange and hostile comments in the opposition press, especially the *Political Register*. Melville's policies were supported by the imperial government and were later implemented on Grenada by his lieutenant-governor, Ulysses Fitzmaurice, in 1769.

Melville resigned his commission as governor in July 1771 and between 1774 and 1776 he travelled extensively in Europe, pursuing his interest in Roman history. He visited many important sites of antiquity and suggested an alternative route for Hannibal's crossing of the Alps to that favoured by historians of the day. With the outbreak of the American War of Independence he returned to Britain and was promoted to lieutenant-general in August 1777, but took no active part in the war itself. When Tobago was ceded to France at the end of the conflict, Melville undertook a successful diplomatic mission to Paris in 1783 to protect the property rights of the British subjects remaining on the island.

A prominent freemason and an energetic supporter of the Scots Corporation in London as well as other Scottish charities, Melville was a member of the Royal Society and the Society of Antiquaries of London, and of the Royal Society of Edinburgh. Awarded an honorary LLD by the University of Edinburgh, he was, despite being totally blind in later life, advanced to full general in October 1793. At the time of his death at his house in George Street, New Town, Edinburgh, on 29 August 1809, he was the second oldest general in the British army. A bachelor, Melville left his property, including an estate at Strathkinness, Fife, to his cousin John Whyte, son of Robert Whytt, his mother's brother, who had taken the name Melville in 1797.

RORY T. CORNISH

Sources E. W. M. Balfour-Melville, ed., 'A biographical sketch of General Robert Melville of Strathkinnes, written by his secretary', *SHR*, 14 (1916–17), 116–46 • *A narrative to the proceedings upon the complaint against Governor Melville* (1770) • *A letter to the Right Hon. the earl of Hillsborough … on the present situation of the island of Grenada* (1769) • S. C. Tucker, 'The carronade', *Naval Institute Proceedings*, 99 (1973), 65–70 • L. H. Gipson, *The British empire before the American revolution*, 9: *The triumphant empire: new responsibilities within the enlarged empire, 1763–1766* (1956) • *Political Register*, 4 (1769), 258–73 • *Political Register*, 5 (1769), 79–81, 119–24 **Archives** NA Scot., journals, corresp., and papers • NL Scot., corresp. • PRO, commission and instructions, Co., vol. 102, vol. 5 | BL, corresp. with first earl of Liverpool, Add. MSS 38201–38210, 38304–38309 • RSA, letters to the RSA relating to botanical gardens in St Vincent • U. Edin. L., letters to M. de Valmont [copies] • U. Mich., Shelburne papers, accounts and corresp., vols. 48, 49, 52 **Likenesses** plaster medallion, 1791 (after J. Tassie), Scot. NPG • H. Raeburn, oils, Scot. NPG **Wealth at death** property in ceded islands valued at approx. £45,000 in 1770; an estate in Scotland: Balfour-Melville, ed., 'A biographical sketch'

Melvin, James (1795–1853), Latin scholar, was born in Aberdeen, of poor parents, on 21 April 1795. He passed through the grammar school a few years after Byron had left it, during Mr Cromar's rectorship, and was the first bursar of his year at Marischal College, whence he graduated AM in 1816. After acting successively as usher at a private school kept by Bisset at Udny, and at Old Aberdeen grammar school under Ewen Maclachlan, he became in 1822 a master at the Aberdeen grammar school, and in 1826 he succeeded Mr Cromar as rector. He also became 'lecturer on humanity' (Latin) at Marischal College, and was created LLD by the college in 1834. He formed a wonderful collection of classical and medieval Latin literature (he was said to own a copy of Horace for every day of the year), and became probably the most accomplished Scottish Latinist of his day. He has been identified as one of the last representatives of a distinctive tradition of Scottish Latin scholarship, combining an enthusiasm for classical literature with a deep knowledge of the philology and literature of the Scottish language. He was one of the volunteers who assisted John Jamieson in preparing the two-volume supplement (1825) to his dictionary of the Scottish language. An appreciative account of his teaching and personality was contributed to *Macmillan's Magazine* for January 1864 by a former pupil, Professor David Masson, who compares Melvin as a ruler and inspirer of boys to Thomas Arnold. His method of instruction was minute and punctilious, with a heavy emphasis on philology, but also led his students to a literary appreciation of classical works. He was twice an unsuccessful candidate for the professorship of Latin at Marischal College, first in 1839 when he was defeated by J. S. Blackie in controversial circumstances, and second in 1852. On 18 June 1853 a testimonial in the shape of £300 in a silver snuff-box (souvenir of an inveterate habit) was presented to him by old pupils. Severe application had told upon his health, and he died at his house in Belmont Street, Aberdeen, on 29 June 1853. He was publicly buried in the town churchyard on 5 July.

Latin exercises as dictated by the late James Melvin, LL.D., to which are prefixed dissertations on a variety of Latin idioms and constructions, was published by the Revd Peter Calder, rector of Grantown grammar school, in 1857. A supplementary volume or key appeared in 1858, and a third edition, revised by the Revd J. Pirie, Edinburgh, in 1873. Melvin also wrote for use in his school a Latin grammar, which first appeared in 1822, and passed through three editions, and a number of grammatical 'Melviniana' were appended by W. D. Geddes, professor of Greek in Aberdeen University, to his *Principles of Latinity* (1860).

Melvin was said to have been long occupied with a large Latin dictionary, but does not appear to have left any materials. His books (6984 in number) were presented to Marischal College in September 1856 by his sister and executor, Agnes Melvin. A stained-glass window was erected in the university library, Aberdeen, representing Melvin in his rectorial robes, in association with George Buchanan (whose Latin versions of the psalms he greatly admired), Arthur Johnston, and Thomas Ruddiman. The device was a beehive and grapes, and the inscription, 'Melvinum Natura dedit, gaudete Camenae' ('Nature gave us Melvin'—the name in Latin means 'honey-wine'— 'Rejoice, Muses').

THOMAS SECCOMBE, *rev.* RICHARD SMAIL

Sources D. Masson, 'Dr James Melvin', *Macmillan's Magazine*, 9 (1863–4), 225–39 · *GM*, 2nd ser., 40 (1853), 318 · W. E. McCulloch, ed., *Viri illustres universitatum Abredonensium*, Aberdeen University Studies, 88 (1923) · *Aberdeen Herald and General Advertiser* (2 July 1853) · *Aberdeen Herald and General Advertiser* (9 July 1853) · *The Athenaeum* (16 July 1853), 861–2 · P. J. Anderson and J. F. K. Johnstone, eds., *Fasti academiae Mariscallanae Aberdonensis: selections from the records of the Marischal College and University, MDXCIII–MDCCCLX*, 3 vols., New Spalding Club, 4, 18–19 (1889–98) · W. D. Geddes, *The Melvin memorial window* (1885) · private information (1894) · G. E. Davie, *The democratic intellect: Scotland and her universities in the nineteenth century* (1961) · Boase, *Mod. Eng. biog.*

Likenesses memorial stained-glass window; U. Aberdeen L. in 1894

Menahem, Elijah [*known as* Master Elias] (*b.* in or before 1232?, *d.* 1284), financier and rabbi, known in royal records as Master Elias, son of Master Mosse of London, was probably born in London not later than 1232. He was one of the six sons of Rabbi Moses of London, who was active in business and in communal affairs from about 1240 onwards, and the writer of an authoritative work on biblical punctuation, and of his wife, Antera, the daughter of Jacob. Elijah Menahem may have been educated in France, perhaps at Sens.

Before the Statute of Jewry of 1275 Menahem was one of the major moneylenders in the Jewish community. Thereafter he may have been engaged in wholesale dealing in corn and wool, though it is more probable that he continued to lend money under the guise of advancing money against future payment of commodities. He could trace descent from the late tenth-century Rabbi Simeon ben Isaac ben Abun the Great, of Mainz, and his family had produced rabbinic scholars for generations. From 1266 onwards Menahem is regularly described as *magister* in official records, indicating that he, too, was recognized as a rabbi within the Jewish community. There are many references to his opinions and jurisprudential decisions in medieval rabbinic literature, and commentaries survive on the first Mishnaic tractate of the Talmud (*Berakhoth*, 'Benedictions'), and on the domestic service (Haggadah) for Passover eve, which were written by him. These are in Hebrew, but the opinions include occasional lexical items in Anglo-Norman—'rissoles' and 'pastides' (pies), for example. He was also active as a physician, and in 1280 went to Flanders to treat the nephew of the count.

Menahem lived in a large stone-built house in the parish of St Nicholas Candlewick Street, in London. He seems to have enjoyed friendly relations with successive kings and queens of England, and even with the papal legate, Ottobuono Fieschi. He also got on well with the justices of the Jews, and may for a brief period have enjoyed some sort of official position in the exchequer of the Jews. Nevertheless, in 1279 he was caught up in the nationwide accusations of coin-clipping brought against Jews, and had to pay 1000 marks for a pardon. There may have been a more sinister side to his friendly relationship with the justices of the Jews. Shortly after Menahem's death it was alleged that they had co-operated with him in altering entries on their own plea rolls at his house. These entries related to royal debts assigned to Elijah by way of compensation for debts pardoned by the crown in favour of the abbey of Stratford, and the alterations allegedly had the effect of enriching Elijah at the crown's expense. These allegations led to the dismissal and disgrace of the two justices concerned (Hamon Hauteyn and Robert of Ludham).

Elijah Menahem was married by 1253 to a wife named Pucelle, of whom no more is known. His second wife,

Fluria, the widow of Sampson of Northampton, was married to him by 1267. He had at least six sons. Elijah Menahem probably died in London not long before 13 June 1284. His total estate was worth over £1000.

PAUL BRAND, *rev.*

Sources C. Roth, 'Elijah of London: the most illustrious English Jew of the middle ages', *Transactions of the Jewish Historical Society of England*, 15 (1939–45), 29–62 · C. Roth, *The intellectual activities of medieval English Jewry*, British Academy supplemental papers, no. 8 (1949) · M. Y. L. Sachs, *The writings of Rabbi Elijah of London* (1956) · H. G. Richardson, *The English Jewry under Angevin kings* (1960) **Wealth at death** approx. £1000: Roth, 'Elijah of London'

Menasseh ben Israel (1604–1657), rabbi and campaigner for the readmission of Jews to England, was born in Portugal. His parents, Joseph (ben Israel) Soeiro and Rachel Abrabanel, were Marranos (secret Jews) and they emigrated to Amsterdam while Menasseh was still a child. He studied with the celebrated Rabbi Isaac Uziel, but never really succeeded in establishing himself as a respected and financially secure scholar in the Jewish community at Amsterdam. His first appointment came in 1622, as rabbi of the Neveh Shalom congregation, the 'poor relation' of Amsterdam's three synagogues. About this time, or within the next few years, he married Rachel, whose other name is unknown. His salary was extremely low, so Menasseh supplemented his income by establishing the city's first Hebrew printing house, enjoying a monopoly until about 1633, and continuing to publish Hebrew books until he left for England over twenty years later. Menasseh was the only Jew to take part in the Frankfurt bookfair in 1634, and one of his booklists from the 1640s survives among the papers of John Selden, noting the names of eight used books and the prices paid for them. When Menasseh's congregation was united with that of the other two synagogues in 1639, he was relegated to the task of teaching the primary school, with the face-saving perk of a monthly sermon to the newly organized community.

Yet Menasseh's lack of success in Amsterdam's Jewish world stood in stark contrast to his high reputation outside it. Indeed, after his first book, published in Hebrew in 1628, Menasseh wrote only one more work in that language, which in any case was dedicated to a Christian sovereign and had an argument in Latin. Most of the rabbi's books were published in Spanish or Latin, and sometimes simultaneously in both. His most famous early work was undoubtedly his *Conciliador*, published in Spanish in four parts between 1632 and 1651. Part one was an analysis of 180 discrepancies in the Pentateuch, achieved by the citation of 221 Jewish and 54 gentile authorities. The other parts of the work dealt with the rest of the Old Testament in turn. The *Conciliador* was an overnight success among non-Jewish theologians, in no small measure because it was a learned Jewish work that contained not a single attack against Christianity. His entry into the bibliographies of Christian theology assured, Menasseh followed his advantage with several other learned works. *De creatione problemata XXX* appeared in 1635, followed by *De resurrectione mortuorum* in 1636, and *De termino vitae* in 1639. Only the appearance of his *Dissertatio de fragilitate humana*

in 1642 in Spanish and Latin marked some measure of acceptance by Jews as well as Christians. Menasseh also published a Portuguese compendium of Jewish law for returning Marranos, which must have found its way into the hands of Christians seeking a concise outline of Hebrew customs.

By the 1640s Menasseh ben Israel had very nearly become the ambassador of western Jewry to European Christendom. His correspondents included G. J. Vossius, his son Isaac Vossius, Hugo Grotius, John Dury, and many others. Nevertheless, Menasseh's reputation among Christian scholars was not matched either by his financial or intellectual standing among the Jews of Amsterdam, a fact underscored in May 1640 when he was actually excommunicated for one day, and a fine (valued at nearly half of his annual salary) levied against him as punishment for an overly heated defence of his brother-in-law at a synagogue meeting. Menasseh made preparations to emigrate to Brazil, to the astonishment of Grotius and others, but in the event managed to obtain a position in Amsterdam as director of the community school and a lecturer at the *yeshivah* (religious academy). In 1644 he was appointed principal of the newly established Talmudic academy founded by the affluent Pereira brothers, Abraham and Isaac, who had just arrived from Venice.

Despite having achieved a measure of financial security, Menasseh carried on with the business contacts that he had already established during the lean years. Both of his sons were involved in the family printing house, and the elder one, Joseph, acted as Menasseh's personal emissary to agents in Poland. It was there, in Lublin, that Joseph ben Israel died in 1648, consigning to oblivion the large quantity of goods and cash that he had in his possession. This was the final blow for Menasseh's foreign investments: he shared commercial interests with his brother Ephraim Soeiro in the Dutch port of Pernambuco (Recife) which was under Portuguese siege from 1645, and by the time Joseph died Menasseh was out of business in the New World as well as the Old.

Menasseh's mission to secure the readmission of the Jews to England began when a Jew by the name of Antonio Montezinos returned to Amsterdam in 1644 from South America, claiming that he had made contact there with Hebrew-speaking remnants of the lost ten tribes of Israel. Menasseh was entranced by this revelation, and saw it as fulfilling another part of the messianic precondition of the scattering of the Jews to all corners of the globe. A Jewish presence in England would complete the square, but they had been expelled by Edward I in 1290. When an English trade delegation led by Oliver St John visited Menasseh in his synagogue in 1650, the question of Jewish readmission was broached, and the rabbi's campaign was launched.

Menasseh received a passport and permission to visit England in 1650 and in every year until his arrival in September 1655, after the end of the trade war between England and the Netherlands. He became well known to the English public with the appearance of his book about the

Montezinos affair, *The Hope of Israel* (1650). Menasseh himself spent the years 1650–55 in an effort to win a place at the court of Queen Kristina of Sweden, hoping to turn himself into the Jewish Descartes of the north. When Kristina abdicated in June 1654 she left unpaid a large book bill owed to Menasseh, and he took the bold and quite illegal step of travelling to her retreat at Antwerp, where she received him favourably and eventually gave him his due. Menasseh was now free from the distractions of this troublesome side-show and could concentrate on the readmission.

Menasseh's son Samuel ben Israel came to England in October 1654 in order to test the waters, accompanied by another Jew named Manuel Martinez Dormido, who immediately petitioned Oliver Cromwell for the recovery of lands lost in the Portuguese conquest of Dutch territory. On 26 February 1655 the protector did indeed write to the king of Portugal on Dormido's behalf, perhaps an indication of Cromwell's favourable disposition to the Jews at that moment. Samuel also reported to his father that he had received a doctorate from Oxford University in the dual fields of medicine and philosophy. The document was forged, but Menasseh was unaware of this. Moved by his son's report, in September 1655 Menasseh addressed an open letter to the Jewish people, informing them of his mission and recent favourable messianic developments. By the Jewish new year (22 September 1655) Menasseh was in London, and on 31 October he formally submitted a petition for the readmission of the Jews to England.

The council of state received Menasseh's requests, and on 13 November 1655 appointed a subcommittee, which seems to have returned its favourable report on the very same day, consisting as it did of seven of the eleven members of the council physically present. They also adopted Cromwell's strategy of spreading the political risk by appointing a conference to meet at Whitehall, directed to thrash out the pros and cons of readmitting Jews to England. The conference was opened by Cromwell himself on 4 December near the chambers of the council of state. The delegates were theologians, politicians, and merchants, and they held further sittings on 7, 12, 14, and 18 December. Menasseh ben Israel was not invited, and did not attend even the final, public session. In the event, Cromwell was unable to obtain an unequivocal endorsement of readmission, so he dissolved the conference rather than suffer a formal rejection of the proposal.

The irony of Menasseh's mission was that there already were a number of secret Jews in England, pretending to be Roman Catholic Spanish and Portuguese, and his campaign cast an unwelcome spotlight on their affairs. Most probably they would have continued in this clandestine Marrano fashion for much longer had not England gone to war with Spain at the beginning of 1656, rendering their goods and property liable to confiscation as belonging to enemy aliens. The denunciation of one of their leaders forced England's secret Jews to throw off their Spanish disguises and to jump on Menasseh's tarnished bandwagon.

The famous petition of England's Jewish community was received by Cromwell on 24 March 1656. Little choice had been left to them but to request readmission and to throw themselves on the mercies of the protector, whose sympathetic views had already been amply revealed. Menasseh ben Israel was the first signatory, and within a few weeks had completed his *Vindiciae Judaeorum*, his powerful refutation of slanders against the Jewish people, which has been translated and reprinted many times during the past three centuries.

But Cromwell never gave a formal answer to the Jews' petition, preferring to turn a blind eye to their presence. After the failure of the Whitehall conference he could hardly do otherwise. Yet Menasseh ben Israel failed to realize that a new era had begun for Jews in England. His single-minded dedication to obtaining a formal declaration of Jewish toleration and freedom of worship blinded him to the substantial benefits which had been achieved informally, and to the practical determination of the English government to allow the Jews to continue living in England unmolested. Menasseh thus alienated the leaders of Anglo-Jewry, who were anxious to effect a smooth transition to toleration, and they turned their backs on him. Sometime during 1656 they agreed to bring over Rabbi Moses Athias from Hamburg to lead their congregation. Menasseh may have been considered for the post, but there is no evidence that his name was put forward at all. He seems to have been ill for some time in any case, and was forced to turn to Cromwell for assistance. The protector granted him a state pension of £100 per annum, payable quarterly and commencing from 20 February 1657. At least two payments of £25 each were made to Menasseh between Michaelmas 1656 and Michaelmas 1658.

By the middle of September 1657 Menasseh's hopes and patience were finally exhausted. His son Samuel having recently died, Menasseh turned to Cromwell once again for financial help to enable him to carry the body back to the Netherlands. Menasseh offered to surrender his pension seal for £300, and to cease troubling Cromwell with his millennial dreams and pleas for aid. Menasseh apparently was willing to renounce his pension for even £200 because of the intense pressure of his debts and his need to return to the Netherlands immediately. The sum seems not to have been paid, and in November Menasseh was forced to return empty-handed, but he never reached Amsterdam, and died *en route* in Middelburg on about 20 November. Samuel ben Israel was buried there, but Menasseh's body was carried to the Jewish cemetery at Ouderkerk near Amsterdam, where he was laid to rest.

Menasseh's widow, Rachel, was left destitute and was forced to rely on charity. Before Cromwell's death in September 1658 she sent him several begging letters, which were entrusted to John Thurloe and John Sadler, long a friend of the Jews. By the beginning of January 1659 she had persuaded Sadler to plead her case before Richard Cromwell. Sadler asked the new protector to pay the £200 'to the said Widow, & Relations of a Man so Eminent &

ffamous in his owne & many other Nations; & for the honour of Christian Religio with many other Reasons'. It is not known whether Richard Cromwell honoured his father's debt.   DAVID S. KATZ

Sources D. S. Katz, *Philo-Semitism and the re-admission of the Jews to England, 1603–1655* (1982) · D. S. Katz, *The Jews in the history of England, 1485–1850* (1994) · D. S. Katz, 'Menasseh ben Israel's mission to Queen Christina of Sweden', *Jewish Social Studies*, 45 (1983–4), 57–72 · C. Roth, *A life of Menasseh ben Israel* (Philadelphia, PA, 1934) · M. Kayserling, *The life and labours of Manasseh ben Israel* (1877) · L. Wolf, *Menasseh ben Israel's mission to Oliver Cromwell* (1901)
Likenesses S. A. Hart, portrait (*Manasseh ben Israel before Cromwell and his council*) · Rembrandt, portraits

Menchik [*married name* Stevenson], **Vera Frančevna** (1906–1944), chess player, was born in Moscow on 16 February 1906, the daughter of Franz Mencik (*d.* in or before 1937), a mill owner, who was of Czech origin. Her mother was English. The family moved to Hastings in 1921 and the young Vera, who had been playing chess since the age of nine, became a pupil of Géza Maróczy a year or so later.

In 1927 the Fédération Internationale des Echecs (FIDE) organized both the first chess Olympiad and the first world championship for women; both events ran concurrently, apart from 1928, until the outbreak of the Second World War. Menchik won every one of the women's competitions, in London (1927), Hamburg (1930), Prague (1931), Folkestone (1933), Warsaw (1935), Stockholm (1937), and Buenos Aires (1939). Such was her domination of the women's game that in these seven tournaments she won seventy-eight games, drawing four and losing only one. She also put her title at stake in two privately arranged matches against her closest rival, Sonja Graf, defeating this German-born opponent in 1934 and 1937.

Menchik played her first championship tournament as a Russian, the next five as a Czech, and the last as a Briton, having married Rufus Henry Streatfield Stevenson (1877/8–1943), secretary of the British Chess Federation, on 19 October 1937. Her husband, a pharmacist, was a widower twenty-eight years her senior. She also played in such men's tournaments as did not exclude women. Although she usually finished in the second half of the score in these contests, her positional style and mastery of the endgame occasionally brought her victories over the greatest masters of the day. Men she defeated were granted the dubious honour of membership of the 'Menchik Club'. Among these were the Dutchman Max Euwe and the American Samuel Reshvsky. Another victim was the 77-year-old Jacques Mieses, whom she beat in 1942, but this victory was not widely reported, to lessen the veteran's indignity at defeat at the hands of a mere woman.

Vera Menchik was not only the foremost woman player of all time: she devoted her life to the game. A professional player, she also wrote articles for chess magazines, gave lessons, and undertook lecture tours. In 1939 she was appointed manager of the National Chess Centre, which had been set up largely at the instigation of herself and her husband. In 1940 the building was totally destroyed in an air raid. She herself died along with her mother and her sister Olga, also a chess player, on 26 June 1944, when her home, 47 Gauden Road, Clapham, London, was hit in a German V1 flying bomb raid. She was immortalized in 1957, when FIDE inaugurated the women's Olympiad. The trophy for the winning team was called the Vera Menchik cup.   TONY RENNICK

Sources D. Hooper and K. Whyld, *The Oxford companion to chess*, 2nd edn (1992) · N. Divinsky, *The Batsford chess encyclopedia* (1990) · R. Eales, *Chess: the history of a game* (1985) · P. Matthews and I. Buchanan, *The all-time greats of British and Irish sport* (1995) · *The Times* (4 July 1944) · m. cert. · d. cert.
Likenesses photographs, 1936, Hult. Arch.
Wealth at death £5252 3s. 7d.: probate, 25 Jan 1945, *CGPLA Eng. & Wales*

Mendelsohn, Eric (1887–1953), architect, was born in Allenstein, East Prussia, on 21 March 1887, of German-Jewish parents; he was the fifth of the six children of David Mendelsohn, who kept a store in the town, and his wife, Emma Jaruslawsky. Among the important influences of his childhood was his mother's enthusiasm for music (she was a gifted musician) and her love of plants and flowers. Mendelsohn was educated at the *Gymnasium* in Allenstein and early entertained an ambition to be an architect; but—by his father's wish—he was apprenticed to a Berlin firm of merchants. He soon abandoned this career and studied architecture for four years, first at the Technische Hochschule in Berlin–Charlottenburg, and then at Munich University, where he graduated in architecture in 1912. At the outset of his career he was engaged in stage designing and during this period he became interested in the German expressionist movement. Shortly after the outbreak of the First World War he enlisted with the engineers and served first on the Russian, later on the western, front. In 1915 he married Luise Maas, a cellist, daughter of Ernst Maas, a tobacco merchant in Baden; they had one daughter.

In 1919, at Paul Cassirer's galleries in Berlin, Mendelsohn held an exhibition of his sketch designs which he called Architecture in Steel and Reinforced Concrete. This represented the work of several years, since a large number of the drawings had been made while he was on military service. They were projects for a wide variety of buildings in which steel and concrete partly determine the character of the buildings, and where purpose was partly expressed by symbolic forms, thus showing the influence of expressionism. The most famous of Mendelsohn's early buildings is the Einstein Observatory, at Potsdam (1920) which, although conceived in reinforced concrete, was built mainly in brick owing to the shortages of materials. The rounded shapes which compose the buildings are expressive of optical instruments, and these forms, together with the deep window recesses on the curved surfaces, allow a dramatic play of light and shadow, and convey a sense of mystery particularly appropriate to the purpose of the building.

After the Einstein Observatory Mendelsohn built up a very extensive practice. He was the architect of a large number of buildings, among them a hat factory at Luckenwalde, the Herpich fur store in Berlin, the Petersdorff store at Breslau, and the Schocken stores at Stuttgart and

Chemnitz. In Berlin he designed a group of buildings adjoining the Kurfürstendamm which included houses, a block of flats, a cinema, and a cabaret theatre, and Columbus House in the Potsdamerplatz, a large block of offices with shops below. In all these buildings the newer materials of steel and concrete were used expressively, and the designs of the façades exhibited a strong horizontal emphasis with large alternating bands of fenestration and opaque panelling. In the Schocken store at Chemnitz and in Columbus House an effect of lightness was achieved by cantilevering which thrust the walls forward beyond the structural supports.

After Hitler came to power in 1933, Mendelsohn moved to London, where he began practice in partnership with Serge Chermayeff: their first work in Britain was a house at Chalfont St Giles in 1933. Early in the next year they won the competition for a municipal social centre at Bexhill, which was named the De La Warr Pavilion and was opened by the duke of York. The long low mass of this building in steel and concrete with horizontal emphasis accorded well with its position by the sea, and the glass wall terminating in the semicircular glass projection of the stairway was reminiscent of a similar feature in the famous Schocken store at Stuttgart. Another work in England was a house at 64 Old Church Street, Chelsea, while the partners were responsible also for several projects: a large scheme for flats and exhibition centre at the White City, and large hotels at Southsea and Blackpool.

Mendelsohn's original permit to stay in Britain for five weeks was extended to five years as a result of the representations of the Royal Institute of British Architects, which elected him a fellow in February 1939 after his naturalization in the previous year. In the meantime the partnership with Chermayeff, which was not a happy one, had been dissolved in 1936. Thereafter Mendelsohn's principal work was in Palestine, to which he made long and frequent visits. He became the architect for houses for Chaim Weizmann and Salman Schocken, the Hadassah University medical centre on Mount Scopus, Jerusalem, the Anglo-Palestine Bank, Jerusalem, and the research laboratories and agricultural college at Rehoboth.

In June 1939 Mendelsohn finally left Britain and after two years in Palestine, and unsuccessful attempts to join the British army, he went to America. In 1945 he started afresh in San Francisco and such was his reputation that he quickly built up a considerable practice. He was the architect of the Maimonides Hospital in San Francisco and of a series of large combined synagogues and community centres. Those completed during his life were at St Louis, Missouri, at Cleveland, Ohio, which includes a dome 100 feet in diameter, at Grand Rapids, Michigan, and at St Paul, Minnesota. He was also the architect of laboratories for the atomic energy commission in California. Among his projects was an impressive design for a memorial in New York to the 6 million Jews killed in the Holocaust.

Mendelsohn's architecture was characterized by an expression of purpose partly by means of symbolic forms. He was one of the first architects to realize the architectural potentialities of steel, concrete, and glass. His designs were always actuated by the principles of organic structure so that each part by its character denotes its relation to the whole; he also aimed at the integration of the building with the site and the surroundings. He attempted to imitate natural forms in his architectural designs; in most of his buildings there is a sense of organic rhythm and unity. His work has been one of the vital architectural influences of the century. In the period of austere building in Britain after the Second World War his reputation suffered something of an eclipse, but in the late 1950s there was a revival of interest with a renewed appreciation of the value of architectural expression of a more positive and symbolic character.

Mendelsohn was a man of wide cultural interests. Probably his chief enthusiasm after architecture was music, and he had a particular fondness for Bach, whose music he liked to hear while he worked. He often said that music gave him ideas for designs, and many of his sketch projects bear the titles of musical compositions. Physically he was a man of medium height, rather thickset. A dynamic personality and a tireless worker, he rarely took a holiday. He had a remarkable intuitive faculty of quickly grasping the essential significance of relationships and situations, revealed in his masterly analysis of the relation of the Jews to modern society in a pamphlet which he wrote in 1933 on the political, economic, and social conditions of the world. Mendelsohn died in San Francisco on 15 September 1953. His wife survived him.

ARNOLD WHITTICK, *rev.* CATHERINE GORDON

Sources O. Beyer, *Eric Mendelsohn: Briefe eines Architekten* (1961) • W. von Eckardt, *Eric Mendelsohn* (1960) • M. F. Raggero, *Il contributo di Mendelsohn alla evoluzione dell'architettura moderna* (1952) • A. Whittick, *Eric Mendelsohn*, 2nd edn (1956) • M. Emanuel, ed., *Contemporary architects*, 3rd edn (1994), 537–9 • A. K. Placzek, ed., *Macmillan encyclopedia of architects*, 3 (1982), 158–9 • *The Builder*, 185 (1953), 473 • *Architect and Engineer*, 195 (Oct 1953), 26–7 • *RIBA Journal*, 60 (1952–3), 507 • *Architectural Record*, 114 (Nov 1953), 10–11
Archives RIBA BAL, lectures [typescript]

Mendelssohn, Kurt Alfred Georg (1906–1980), physicist, was born on 7 January 1906 in Berlin, Germany, the only child of Ernst Moritz Mendelssohn, a clothing agent with distinguished Jewish ancestors, and his wife, Elizabeth Ruprecht. His father aroused his scientific interests, which he pursued from 1912 to 1925 at the Goethe School, Berlin. In 1925 he entered the University of Berlin where he graduated in physical sciences in 1927. He then began research on low temperature physics at the Physikalisch Chemische Institut, Berlin, under his cousin, Franz Simon, who was twelve years his senior and a leading expert on attaining very low temperatures through new techniques for the liquefaction of helium. Completing his doctorate in 1930, Mendelssohn became chief assistant to Simon and, when Simon moved in April 1931 to a chair at the Breslau Technische Hochschule, Mendelssohn followed him in June as a research associate.

While at Berlin, Mendelssohn had demonstrated a hydrogen liquifier to Lindemann, professor of physics at Oxford, who wished to develop low temperature physics in the Clarendon Laboratory there. Lindemann soon had a hydrogen liquifier working at Oxford and in spring 1932 turned again to Mendelssohn, who was in charge of the Breslau laboratory while Simon was on leave abroad, for a helium liquifier which gave even lower temperatures than the hydrogen one. Keen to secure the services of Mendelssohn, who had spent several years under Simon designing and making various types of miniature helium liquifiers, Lindemann invited him to Oxford to install one. Mendelssohn went to Oxford in the Christmas vacation 1932–3 and in early January 1933 became the first in Britain to produce liquid helium. He returned to Breslau but in April 1933 sought sanctuary from Nazi violence in Oxford where Lindemann soon secured funding for him from Imperial Chemical Industries (ICI). Impressed by Mendelssohn's achievement, Lindemann quickly brought to Oxford, with Mendelssohn's help, two of his Breslau colleagues (Simon and N. Kurti) to develop cryogenics.

Having married Jutta Lina Charlotte Zarniko in 1932, Mendelssohn had a family and subsequently his parents to support in Oxford. Until the war he existed on grants provided by ICI and Sir Robert Mond. Although Mendelssohn had successfully launched cryogenics at Oxford and was the first of the Breslau cohort to settle there, he soon found himself number two to Simon. Inclined to be awkward and paranoiac, he became jealously resentful of Simon. To avoid conflict between them it was agreed that Mendelssohn's research group should concentrate on superconductivity (the mysterious disappearance of electrical resistance at very low temperatures). His most spectacular discovery (1938) was that any surface in contact with liquid helium develops a frictionless and flowing thin film which is analogous to superconductivity.

Having become a naturalized British subject in March 1939, Mendelssohn's instrumental ingenuity was fruitfully deployed during the war in medical physics. At the request of Professor Macintosh he joined the department of anaesthetics, Oxford, where he took a leading role in devising an ether vaporizer which was widely used, but it led to a priority dispute with Macintosh, who ejected Mendelssohn in 1942. He then worked mainly in the Clarendon Laboratory on devices concerned with the medical effect of burns and on a semi-automatic recorder of blood pressure. Having subsisted during the war on grants from the university's higher studies fund and the Medical Research Council, he later resumed research on cryogenics supported by an ICI fellowship. Only in 1947 did he gain financial security when he became a university demonstrator. Elected FRS in 1951, he became reader in physics at Oxford in 1955 and a founding fellow of Wolfson College, Oxford, in 1966. His prowess as a researcher and as a driving supervisor of successful doctoral candidates (forty-nine all told) led to his election as a vice-president of the Physical Society (1957–60) and the awards of the Hughes medal of the Royal Society of London (1967) and the Simon medal of the Institute of Physics (1968).

In the 1960s Mendelssohn extended his interests. He promoted cryogenic engineering by founding, in 1960, and editing a new journal, *Cryogenics*, by editing *Progress in Cryogenics* (1959–64), and by establishing, in 1969, and

chairing the international cryogenic committee. Though he was a consultant to the Atomic Energy Research Establishment, Harwell, from 1962, he rejoiced more in visiting and advising scientists in China, India, Japan, and Ghana. From 1943 to about 1960 he learned how to popularize science as a teacher in adult education. His vivid fluency led to broadcast talks, much journalism, and several books. After *What is Atomic Energy?* (1946) there was a lull until *Cryophysics* (1960) and *The Quest for Absolute Zero* (1966) which was translated into thirteen languages. He took an optimistic view of the cultural revolution in his *In China now* (1969). *The World of Walter Nernst* (1973) delineated the rise and fall of German science. *The Riddle of the Pyramids* (1974) advanced novel ideas about their construction and uses. *Science and Western Domination* (1976) explained why Europe developed modern science and technology.

Mendelssohn was a dedicated and hard worker: he left his own wedding celebrations after lunch to finish an experiment before leaving later for his honeymoon. He was a gifted if prickly researcher who was determined to outwit nature and his competitors. Though he helped to make the Clarendon Laboratory internationally famous for low temperature physics, he was not always happy there and on several occasions between 1935 and 1958 tried to leave. He loved travel, oriental art, and photography. Happily married and proud of his four daughters and a son, Mendelssohn retired in 1973 only to be afflicted about 1976 by Parkinson's disease, from which he died on 18 September 1980 in Oxford, where he was buried on 24 September 1980. He was survived by his wife.

JACK MORRELL

Sources D. Shoenberg, *Memoirs FRS*, 29 (1983), 361–98 · J. B. Morrell, 'Research in physics at the Clarendon Laboratory, Oxford, 1919–1939', *Historical Studies in the Physical and Biological Sciences*, 22 (1991–2), 263–307 · Bodl. Oxf., Mendelssohn MSS · D. F. Brewer, 'Mendelssohn', *Physics Bulletin*, 32 (1981), 115–16 · private information (2004) · *The Times* (19 Sept 1980) · *CGPLA Eng. & Wales* (1980)
Archives Bodl. Oxf., corresp. and papers; Society for the Protection of Science and Learning and Home Office files | Nuffield Oxf., corresp. with Lord Cherwell
Likenesses photograph, 1933–7, Bodl. Oxf. · E. Frank, photograph, c.1952, RS · Ramsey and Muspratt, photograph, 1975, repro. in Shoenberg, *Memoirs FRS* · photograph, repro. in Shoenberg, *Memoirs FRS*
Wealth at death £87,621: probate, 3 Dec 1980, *CGPLA Eng. & Wales*

Mendelssohn Bartholdy, (Jacob Ludwig) Felix (1809–1847), composer, was born on 3 February 1809 at Hamburg, Germany, the second of four children of the Jewish banker Abraham Mendelssohn (1776–1835) and his wife, Lea, *née* Salomon (1777–1842). In 1811 the family moved to Berlin, where the precocious musical gifts of Felix and his elder sister Fanny (1805–1847) soon became evident. The children were baptized as protestants in 1816, and Bartholdy was added to the family name, although it was not used until 1822, when the parents also converted.

Mendelssohn's early contacts with Britain Mendelssohn's association with Britain began in 1829, by which time his reputation as a composer was already securely established, with an output which included the masterpieces of

(Jacob Ludwig) Felix Mendelssohn Bartholdy (1809–1847), by Eduard Magnus

the octet (1825) and the overture to *A Midsummer Night's Dream* (1826), the latter inspired by recent acquaintance with Shakespeare's works through the German translation of A. W. Schlegel. Following his famous revival of Bach's St Matthew passion with the Singakademie in Berlin in March 1829, he embarked upon the first stage of a three-year grand tour to complete his education, and arrived in England on 21 April. A rudimentary knowledge of the English language was soon transformed into complete fluency, both spoken and written. In London he renewed acquaintance with three German friends, Karl Klingemann, secretary at the Hanoverian chancery, the composer and pianist Ignaz Moscheles, and the orientalist Friedrich Rosen. Through Moscheles he gave his first concert with the Philharmonic Society, on 25 May, when he conducted his symphony no. 1 in C minor, replacing the original minuet movement with an orchestrated version of the scherzo of the octet. The symphony was subsequently published with a dedication to the society, to whom Mendelssohn also presented the autograph score; in return he was made an honorary member on 29 November 1829. The association with the Philharmonic Society, where he was always enthusiastically received, was to become the principal reason for many of his later visits to the country. Conducting with a white baton, still a novelty at the time, he was to produce a wholly beneficial impact on orchestral discipline in the capital.

Mendelssohn was fêted by London musicians and society; lasting friendships were formed with families such as

the Alexanders, the Attwoods, and the Horsleys, and the congenial musical, political, and social atmosphere of England was to prove a lifelong attraction. Time was also found to study the Handel autograph scores in the Royal Music Library, and to play the organ at St Paul's Cathedral. Performances on the organ, often to large audiences, were to become a regular feature of his English visits, and his playing of Bach and improvisation in particular brought wide admiration from fellow musicians, and exerted an important influence in a country where the provision and use of a pedal division on the instrument was still in its infancy. In July 1829, following the end of the London season, he embarked upon a tour of Scotland with Klingemann, which took them via York and Durham to Edinburgh, and then, after a brief inconsequential meeting with Sir Walter Scott at Abbotsford—the Mendelssohn family were devotees of his novels—on up to Stirling, Perth, and Blair Atholl before crossing to Crianlarich, Glencoe, and Fort William, from where they took a steamer to Oban. At Tobermory on Mull on 7 August came the first inspiration for *The Hebrides* or 'Fingal's Cave' overture, while they visited Staffa and the cave itself the following day, when Mendelssohn suffered badly from seasickness. After returning south by way of Inveraray and Glasgow to Liverpool, Mendelssohn continued alone into Wales as far as the Menai Strait, and then stayed for a week with the family of John Taylor at Coed-du near Holywell. Back in London in early September, he suffered a severe knee injury on falling from a carriage, which delayed his departure for Berlin until the end of November.

Further visits to Britain At the end of his two-year stay in Italy, Switzerland, and France, Mendelssohn was in England again from April to June 1832, and *The Hebrides* overture received its first performance at the Philharmonic Society on 14 May, as did the *Capriccio Brilliant* for piano and orchestra, played by the composer at a concert of Nicholas Mori's on 25 May. Back in Berlin, Mendelssohn received a commission worth 100 guineas from the society in November 1832 for three new works, 'a symphony, an overture and a vocal piece' (Foster, 111). The 'Italian' symphony in A major (in progress since the winter of 1830–31), and the 'Trumpet' overture (a revision of an 1826 work) were ready for the following year, when Mendelssohn paid two visits to London (April–May and June–August), separated by a journey to Düsseldorf for the lower Rhine music festival, from which he returned accompanied by his ageing father. The third part of the commission, the first version of the scena *Infelice*, was completed only later in the year, and received its première in Mendelssohn's absence in 1834. In addition, several of the composer's other works owed their origins to English performers or music publishers, of which Novello, Mori and Lavenu, Ewer, and Coventry and Hollier were the principal ones. The works included the Morning and Evening Service, the motet 'Hear my prayer', the Ossianic scena *On Lena's Gloomy Heath*, and the six organ sonatas.

The demands of his posts as music director in Düsseldorf (1833–5) and conductor of the Gewandhaus orchestra in Leipzig (from 1835) delayed another English visit until

1837, the year in which he married (on 28 March) Cécile Sophie Charlotte Jeanrenaud (1817–1853). He had accepted an invitation to conduct his oratorio *St Paul* at the Birmingham music festival, and, reluctantly leaving his new bride (expecting the first of their five children), he travelled to London at the end of August before proceeding to Birmingham in September, where besides *St Paul* he also gave the première of his second piano concerto and played the large organ of the new town hall. In the same year the music publisher Chappell commissioned an opera to a specially written libretto by J. R. Planché on the theme of the siege of Calais, but Mendelssohn's initial enthusiasm, as so often with his adult operatic ventures, waned and it came to nothing. The Birmingham festival was also the reason for his next brief visit in September 1840, when he conducted the first British performances of the *Lobgesang* ('Hymn of Praise') and his setting of Psalm 114.

Mendelssohn returned to England in June and July 1842, accompanied for the first and only time by his wife. On this occasion the main event was the British première on 13 June of the newly completed A minor symphony ('Scottish'), the initial inspiration for which had occurred in the chapel of Holyrood Palace back in 1829. This visit also saw his first audiences with Queen Victoria and Prince Albert at Buckingham Palace, when he obtained permission to dedicate the symphony to the queen, one of his great admirers. An excursion was also made to see Cécile's relatives in Manchester.

In 1844, increasingly frustrated by the musical situation in Berlin, where he had been Kapellmeister to the king of Prussia since 1841, Mendelssohn readily accepted another invitation from the Philharmonic Society, and arrived in May to conduct the last five concerts of the season. London heard the incidental music to *A Midsummer Night's Dream*, and *Die erste Walpurgisnacht* for the first time, and on 27 May Mendelssohn conducted Beethoven's violin concerto with his protégé the twelve-year-old Joseph Joachim as soloist. In addition he was involved at this time with the Handel Society, for whom he edited *Israel in Egypt* (published in 1845). Mendelssohn's intense musical and social activities during this trip also included conducting two performances of *St Paul* for the Sacred Harmonic Society, a meeting with Dickens, and a further visit to Manchester before finally leaving London on 10 July.

The first performances of *Elijah*, 1846–1847 In June 1845 the Birmingham music festival committee issued an invitation for Mendelssohn to act as chief conductor of the 1846 festival, together with a request for 'a new oratorio, or other music for the occasion' (Edwards, 29). Mendelssohn, already at work on *Elijah*, offered them its première, but declined to conduct the whole festival. In the event the oratorio was only just ready in time, thanks to the prompting of the translator William Bartholomew and his English publisher, Edward Buxton of Ewer & Co. Mendelssohn arrived in England a week before the performance on 26 August, which was greeted with enormous acclaim. After returning to London he went to Ramsgate for four days with his Benecke cousins, and crossed the channel again on 6 September. Despite the favourable reception of *Elijah*,

Mendelssohn, as so often with his works, decided it needed revision before publication, and this he undertook over the following winter. During this time he was also in negotiation with Benjamin Lumley of Her Majesty's Theatre over an opera based on *The Tempest* with a libretto by A. E. Scribe, but once again Mendelssohn found the text unsatisfactory. He returned to England for the tenth and last time in April 1847 and conducted four London performances of the revised *Elijah* for the Sacred Harmonic Society, the second of which (23 April) was attended by the queen and Prince Albert, as well as single performances in Manchester (20 April) and Birmingham (27 April). After further concerts and visits to Buckingham Palace he returned to Frankfurt in the middle of May in an exhausted condition. The news of the sudden death of his sister Fanny on 14 May further weakened his health, which even a period of recuperation in Switzerland over the summer did not fully restore. Further requests for new compositions continued to come from England that year—the Philharmonic Society wanted a symphony, and Liverpool a piece for the opening of the Philharmonic Hall—but back in Leipzig a series of strokes in October led to Mendelssohn's death on 4 November 1847 at Königstrasse 3. He was buried in Dreifältigkeitskirche cemetery, Berlin, on 8 November.

Mendelssohn's influence in Britain To honour his memory, fund-raising for a Mendelssohn scholarship was instituted in London in 1848, and the first scholar, Arthur Sullivan, was elected in 1856. Enthusiasm for his music in Britain, always warm in his lifetime and furnished with the seal of royal approval, reached its apogee in the decade following his death. Of his pupils, William Sterndale Bennett was to prove the most outstanding, possessing enough individuality to avoid wholesale subservience to his master's style. Mendelssohn's influence on other English composers, although it inevitably produced second-rate imitators, particularly in the field of oratorio and piano music, was not as dominant as sometimes claimed, being only one of many influences (including Mozart and Spohr) discernible in the more conservative aspects of mid-Victorian musical style. Mendelssohn's own two oratorios breathed new life into the Handelian inheritance, and, together with the *Lobgesang*, became part of the staple fare of the burgeoning amateur choral movement in the second half of the nineteenth century. This, and the enduring appeal of the *Songs without Words* to the vast army of Victorian pianists, led, however, by the end of the century to a derogatory view of the composer in certain circles as a panderer to bourgeois tastes—most famously articulated by Bernard Shaw when he mocked 'his kid-glove gentility, his conventional sentimentality, and his despicable oratorio mongering' (*The Star*, 23 Feb 1889). A considerably more appreciative assessment of Mendelssohn's many-sided genius has begun to prevail in recent times.

PETER WARD JONES

Sources G. Grove, 'Mendelssohn', Grove, *Dict. mus.*, repr. in *Beethoven, Schubert, Mendelssohn* (1951) • S. Hensel, ed., *Die Familie Mendelssohn, 1729–1847: nach Briefen und Tagebüchern*, 3 vols. (1879) • M. B. Foster, *History of the Philharmonic Society of London: 1813–1912* (1912) •

F. G. Edwards, *The history of Mendelssohn's oratorio 'Elijah'* (1896) • N. Temperley, 'Mendelssohn's influence on English music', *Music and Letters*, 43 (1962), 224–33 • R. Fiske, *Scotland in music: a European enthusiasm* (1983) • K. Klingemann, ed., *Felix Mendelssohn-Bartholdys Briefwechsel mit Legationsrat Karl Klingemann in London* (1909) • P. Ward Jones, 'Mendelssohn and his English publishers', *Mendelssohn studies*, ed. R. L. Todd (1992), 240–55 • G. B. Shaw, *Shaw's music: the complete musical criticism*, ed. D. H. Laurence, 3 vols. (1981) • *Mendelssohn and his friends in Kensington: letters from Fanny and Sophy Horsley, written 1833–36*, ed. R. B. Gotch (1934) • J. Benedict, *Sketch of the life and works of the late Felix Mendelssohn Bartholdy*, rev. 2nd edn (1853) • N. Thistlethwaite, 'Bach, Mendelssohn, and the English organist, 1810–1845', *BIOS Journal*, 7 (1983), 34–49 • F. Krummacher, 'Composition as accommodation? On Mendelssohn's music in relation to England', *Mendelssohn studies*, ed. R. L. Todd (1992), 80–105

Archives BL, Add. MSS • Bodl. Oxf., corresp. and papers • NYPL • Staatsbibliothek, Berlin • U. Wales, Aberystwyth, manuscripts | Bodl. Oxf., corresp. with Karl Klingemann • Bodl. Oxf., letters to Charles Coventry

Likenesses E. Begas, oil sketch, 1821, Bodl. Oxf. • J. W. Childe, watercolour, 1829, Staatsbibliothek, Berlin, Mendelssohn-Archiv • T. Hildebrandt, oils, 1835, Staatsbibliothek, Berlin, Mendelssohn-Archiv • W. von Schadow, oils, 1835, repro. in W. Blunt, *On wings of song* (1974) • W. Hensel, pencil, 1837, Nationalgalerie, Berlin • E. Bendemann, pencil, 1847, Staatsbibliothek, Berlin, Mendelssohn-Archiv • W. Hensel, pencil, 1847, Bodl. Oxf. • H. Knaur, death mask, 1847, Bodl. Oxf. • C. Cook, stipple and line engraving (after Leighton), NPG • E. Magnus, oils, Staatsbibliothek, Berlin, Mendelssohn-Archiv [*see illus.*]

Mendes, Fernando Moses (1647–1724), physician and entrepreneur, was born at Trancoso, Beira Alta, Portugal, into a wealthy family of New Christian merchants and officials. He was one of the ten children of António Jacob Mendes da Costa (*d.* 1716), a merchant, and Joana, *née* da Silva, who fled to France in the 1650s or early 1660s for fear of the Inquisition, and settled temporarily in Rouen. Alvaro da Costa was Fernando's cousin. Fernando (originally Fernão) studied medicine, registering at the University of Montpellier on 27 July 1666; he was awarded his doctorate on 11 January 1668. He specifically stated (incorrectly) that he was from Trancoso in 'Castille', to avoid admitting that he was Portuguese, a term which in the France of the day was virtually synonymous with 'Jew'. No Jew could enter a French university. He was 'consiliarius', one of four senior students in medicine elected by the professors as heads of the student body. His thesis was published in Lyons later in 1668, prefaced by his portrait, that of a handsome gentleman in a periwig, with a thin moustache. It is dedicated to Dom Francisco de Mello, the poet and diplomat who accompanied Catherine of Braganza to England in 1662 and was later ambassador to the Netherlands, France, and England.

Mendes's family was by now in London, where he joined them on 25 October 1669. Publicly, at least, Mendes remained a Roman Catholic, although in 1675 he married a professing Jew, Isabel Rachel Marques (*d.* 1695) with whom he had six children. His elder daughter, Catherine Rachel (*c.*1678–1756) [*see* Costa, Catherine da], is said to have been the queen's god-daughter and was the first Anglo-Jewish portraitist. She married Alvaro's son, Anthony Moses da Costa. Mendes's sons were all wealthy merchants or stockbrokers. One, James Mendes, was the father of Moses Mendes, the dramatist. Mendes's wife was one of the heirs of her uncle, Abraham Rodrigues Marques, a rich merchant and devout Jew, who in his will of 1688 referred bitterly to Mendes's refusal to be circumcised and disinherited him and his sons if they were not circumcised within two years. Mendes proved obdurate and his Roman Catholicism injured him both professionally and financially.

Possibly through the influence of his family and of his patron, Dom Francisco, Mendes entered the household of Queen Catherine. On 25 March 1678 he was appointed one of her physicians, 'in consideration of good and faithful services', and sworn in on 10 September. His emoluments were £100 a year for life, the customary 12s. a day board-wages, and one horse-livery a year. He attended Charles II during his last illness, and was physician to the queen until 1692, when the dowager returned to Portugal; he continued to receive his emoluments until her death in 1705, when with her other staff he received a legacy equal to one year's salary.

Mendes was admitted as fellow to the Royal College of Physicians on 12 April 1687, after a reform of the college charter, approved by James II, who wished religious minorities, especially Roman Catholics, to be admitted to closed institutions and offices. After James's flight in 1688, the House of Lords ordered the college to return the names of such of its members as were 'Papists, reputed Papists and criminals'; the names were reluctantly provided on 1 July 1689 and included that of Mendes. He was duly struck off the rolls on 1 October 1689.

Mendes had become endenizened, together with his younger brother, John Joseph Mendes da Costa, a professing Jew, on 16 December 1687. Both brothers and their families shared Cromwell House, Highgate Hill, with its owner, their cousin Alvaro. Mendes also had apartments in Somerset House, Queen Catherine's palace, and probably had a house in the City. He was wealthy, perhaps partly through a business partnership with his cousin Alvaro. On 22 June 1694 he was able to invest £1000 in Bank of England stock, which he held until his death. He was involved in the London manufacture of scientific instruments intended to encourage Portuguese cartography, and had close contacts not only with Portuguese diplomats in London but, even more unusually for a refugee *converso*, with the royal court at Lisbon. In 1706 he was consulted about the health of Pedro IV, which he would not have been had he been suspected of judaizing, and in 1723 he seconded the (fruitless) attempts of the Portuguese minister in London, Castello Branco, to purchase the fine library of the late Charles Spencer, third earl of Sunderland. He was appreciated in the highest Lisbon circles for his quinine-based elixir, 'Agua de Inglaterra', which was apparently exported to Lisbon by his four sons.

Mendes was a highly respected physician, who lived on the best of terms with his family and with the Sephardi community. His refusal to renounce Roman Catholicism may have been due to self-interest, possibly compounded by loyalty to his queen, and to religious cynicism. What his true beliefs were, if any, is unknown. However, in his will he left £100 to the Sedaca (charity fund) of the synagogue; he asked to be buried next to his wife, who lay in the Jewish burial-ground at Mile End. Mendes died on 15 November 1724. Although his ties with the Jewish community seem mainly based on ethnic identity and family solidarity, he is considered one of the founding fathers of English Jewry, and his portrait, in full doctoral robes and painted by his daughter in 1721, was hung in the Spanish and Portuguese Synagogue, Ashworth Road, London.

NORMA PERRY

Sources A. Mendes da Costa, Genealogical tables of the Mendes da Costas, private information · *Stadium Apollinare sive progymnasmata medica, ad Monspeliensis Apollinis laurum consequendam: habita, propugnataque a Ferdinando Mendez Hispano Trancozensi eiusdem universitatis consiliario* (1668) [incl. portrait] · H. Friedenwald, 'Dr Ferdinand Mendez: a comedy of errors', *Medical Press and Calendar*, 201 (1939), 523–5 · J. Mackay, *Catherine of Braganza* (1937) · G. Clark and A. M. Cooke, *A history of the Royal College of Physicians of London*, 1 (1964) · N. Perry, 'Anglo-Jewry, the law, religious conviction and self-interest (1655–1753)', *Journal of European Studies*, 14 (1984), 1–23 · N. Perry, 'Voltaire and the Sephardi bankrupt', *Jewish Historical Studies*, 29 (1982–6), 39–52 · N. Perry, 'Voltaire's first months in England: another look at the facts', *Studies on Voltaire and the Eighteenth Century*, 284 (1991), 115–38 · L. Wolf, 'The Jewry of the Restoration, 1660–1664', *Transactions of the Jewish Historical Society of England*, 5 (1902–5), 5–33 · 'Dr Fernando Mendes', *Transactions of the Jewish Historical Society of England*, 16 (1945–51), 226–7 · J. Veríssimo Serrão, *Les Portugais à l'université de Montpellier (xiie–xviiie siècles)* (1971) · J. A. Giuseppi, 'Sephardi Jews and the early years of the Bank of England', *Transactions of the Jewish Historical Society of England*, 19 (1955–9), 53–63 · PRO, PROB 11/1724, sig. 278 · *The historical register*, 9 (1724), 48 · BL, Add. MS 29868, fol. 20 · PRO, LS13 253 (151, 158) · PRO, LC3 24 · PRO, LC3 28 (80)
Archives Bibliothèque Nationale, Paris, doctoral diss., 4ᵉT (3) 264 · BL, Add. MS 29868, fol. 1
Likenesses N. Reguessen, engraving on medallion, 1667, repro. in F. Mendes, *Stadium Apollinare, sive, Progymnasmata medica*, frontispiece · C. da Costa, watercolour, 1721, Spanish and Portuguese Synagogue, London
Wealth at death very rich; £10,000 in bequests, the rest of his estate divided among his four sons: will, PRO, PROB 11/1724, sig. 278

Mendes, Moses. *See* Mendez, Moses (1690?–1758).

Mendes da Costa, Benjamin (1704–1764), philanthropist and merchant, was born in Amsterdam, the son of Luis (Abraham) Henriques Mendes da Costa (1652–1724), merchant, and his wife, Theresa (Judith) Salazar. His parents were the descendants of Iberian Jews who had converted to Christianity in the late middle ages and later found refuge from inquisitorial persecution in St Esprit de Bayonne in south-western France. About 1700 they migrated to Amsterdam, then the hub of the western Sephardi diaspora. Benjamin later moved to London, becoming an endenizened citizen in 1725. His first wife was Judith (*d.* 1736), the daughter of Raphael Mendes da Costa, with whom he had two sons, Abraham and Raphael, both of whom predeceased him. After Judith died in 1736, he married Rebecca Alvares Pereira.

A successful overseas merchant, Mendes da Costa was a leader of the Spanish and Portuguese Jewish community of London in the mid-eighteenth century. He was elected to the *mahamad* (council) of the synagogue in Bevis Marks five times between 1730 and 1762. In 1746, following the

defeat of a Jewish naturalization bill in the Irish parliament in two consecutive years (1745 and 1746), the *mahamad* appointed a five member 'committee of diligence' to monitor legislative efforts to regulate the legal status of Jews in Great Britain; the committee, in turn, made Mendes da Costa its president. When George III ascended the throne in 1760, the congregation chose seven members, including Mendes da Costa, to offer its congratulations and to request a continuation of the Hanoverian policy of toleration. The *deputados*, as they were known, drafted a congratulatory address, which Mendes da Costa and three other members of the committee presented in November 1760. The committee did not disband afterwards but, with the addition of delegates from the Ashkenazi synagogues, evolved slowly into a permanent representative body, the Board of Deputies of British Jews.

In addition to serving as a communal leader, Mendes da Costa was also a generous benefactor, primarily but not exclusively of the Spanish and Portuguese Jewish community. He established two funds to support students at the congregational school, one in memory of his deceased son Raphael. He supported the establishment of Jewish communities in British North America, promoting the settlement of Jews in South Carolina and contributing to the erection of a new synagogue building in New York. In 1747 he purchased and donated to his own congregation the remainder of the lease on the congregation's building. Toward the end of his life, his annual benefactions totalled £3000. In his will he left bequests to Sephardi and Ashkenazi charities as well as to the Christian poor of St Katharine Cree.

Mendes da Costa was a member of a far-flung, complex clan of New Christian origin whose various branches used either or both of the surnames da Costa and Mendes. Its most prominent English members included the wealthy widow Catherine Mendes da Costa, who married into the landed gentry; the rake Philip Mendes da Costa; and the mineralogist and conchologist Emanuel *Mendes da Costa, a brother of Philip.

Benjamin died on 28 March 1764 at his home in Bury Street, St Mary Axe, London, and was buried in the city's Spanish and Portuguese Jewish cemetery on Mile End Road.

TODD M. ENDELMAN

Sources A. M. Hyamson, *The Sephardim of England: a history of the Spanish and Portuguese Jewish community, 1492–1951* (1951) · J. Picciotto, *Sketches of Anglo-Jewish history* (1875) · Jewish Museum, London, Colyer-Fergusson MSS · R. D. Barnett, 'Diplomatic aspects of the Sephardic influx from Portugal in the early eighteenth century', *Transactions of the Jewish Historical Society of England*, 25 (1973–5), 210–21 · *GM*, 1st ser., 34 (1764), 250

Mendes da Costa, Emanuel (1717–1791), naturalist, was born on 5 June 1717, the ninth and youngest child of John Abraham Mendes da Costa (1683–1763), a Jewish merchant of Portuguese descent who came to London from Rouen; his wife (and first cousin) was Esther (Ester), otherwise Johanna (1692–1749), of Budge Row, London, daughter of

Alvaro da *Costa, also of Portuguese origin. Philip Jacob *Mendes da Costa was his brother. His father, who lived in the City parish of St Christopher-le-Stocks, claimed to have provided Mendes da Costa with a good education; he was intended for the lower branch of the legal profession, and for a time served his articles in the office of a notary.

From his early years Mendes da Costa applied himself to the study of natural history, particularly conchology and mineralogy. In 1740 he was noted as a member of the Aurelian Society, and six years later he was elected an extra regular member of the Spalding Society, at which time he was described as a merchant. In November 1747 he was elected FRS; his knowledge of minerals and fossils was highly praised. From the time of his election he began enriching the society's *Philosophical Transactions* with many papers on his favourite subjects. On 20 April 1750 he married his cousin Leah (*d.* 1763), the third daughter of Samuel del Prado (also of Portuguese Jewish origin); the couple had no children. On 16 January 1752 he was admitted a fellow of the Society of Antiquaries; he was also a member of several other scientific associations.

By the middle of the eighteenth century Mendes da Costa had gathered an extensive collection of shells, minerals, and fossils. He had also generated an impressive network of correspondents, who assisted him in obtaining further specimens. He gained an early reputation as one of the key fossil experts of his time, in contact with many celebrated European naturalists; yet his life appeared to be a continual struggle with adversity. He was having financial problems by 1754, in which year he was imprisoned for debt and his cabinets held in bond; about this time he also ceased receiving financial support from his father. Upon his release in the following year he continued preparing his long-promised *Natural History of Fossils*. This work, first proposed in 1751, was intended to be issued in two volumes; however, only the first part of the first volume appeared in 1757. Nevertheless, his first work met with praise from eminent naturalists such as Carl Linnaeus, and by 1763 he had become a respected member of the scientific and antiquarian communities.

Through the efforts of supporters, who included the antiquary William Stukeley and the naturalist Peter Collinson, Mendes da Costa was elected clerk of the Royal Society on 3 April 1763, following the death of Francis Hauksbee; he was also elected the society's librarian, keeper of the repository, and housekeeper. About 1766 he married his second wife, Elizabeth Skillman (or Stillman), with whom he had one daughter. In addition to an annual payment of £50 for his duties, he and his family were housed rent-free on the society's premises at Crane Court in Fleet Street. He had been appointed for only five years when he was found to have obtained, for his own purposes, about £1500 of the society's funds. Responsible for the collection of subscriptions as part of his duties, he had misappropriated more than a hundred members' fees. He was summarily dismissed in December 1767, the family moved from Crane Court, and their possessions sold at auction. In May 1768 he was taken to court by the society,

and in November that year he was committed to the king's bench prison at St George's Fields. Furthermore, he was expelled from the Society of Antiquaries, and his books and specimens—the purchase of which had led him to debt, fraud, and imprisonment—were sold at auction.

Mendes da Costa remained in prison until 8 October 1772. While incarcerated he attempted to support himself by writing and lecturing on natural history, and in particular he gave a number of lecture series on fossils. He also revised and contributed additional notes to Gustav Engeström's translation of Axel Cronstedt's famous essay of 1758 on the new mineralogy (the English edition was published in 1770 as *Essay towards a System of Mineralogy*), and he carried out some translation work for the French edition of Dru Drury's *Illustrations of Natural History* (1770–82). He was eventually discharged from prison under the Insolvent Act, and from then until his death he struggled to make a living.

In 1774 Mendes da Costa petitioned to be allowed to read a course of lectures on fossils to the University of Oxford in the ensuing Trinity term; but his reputation preceded him, and permission was peremptorily refused. In addition to giving some lectures in London, he also resumed authorship—with some success. He published *Elements of Conchology, or, An Introduction to the Knowledge of Shells* in 1776, which was followed by *Historia naturalis testaceorum Britanniae, or, The British conchology, containing the … natural history of the shells of Great Britain and Ireland … in English and French* in 1778. Of the subscribers for this latter work, no fewer than twenty-two were fellows of the Royal Society.

Mendes da Costa died at his lodgings in the Strand in May 1791. He was buried on 22 May 1791 in the old cemetery of the Spanish and Portuguese congregation at 243 Mile End Road, London. Many of his manuscripts were preserved in the British Museum; the more important included letters to and from scientific friends, and covered a period of fifty years (1737–87). Mendes da Costa also mentioned his *Athenae Regiae Societatis Londinensis* (in three folio volumes), which he presented to the Royal Society's library in 1766, but all traces of this have disappeared.

YOLANDA FOOTE

Sources *The historical register*, 11 (1726), 26 • *GM*, 1st ser., 82/1 (1812), 21–4 • *GM*, 1st ser., 83/1 (1813), 429 • *GM*, 2nd ser., 26 (1846), 493 • Nichols, *Lit. anecdotes*, 2.292; 3.233, 757; 5.712; 6.80–81; 8.200; 9.607, 799, 812–13, 816 • review, *QR*, 139 (1875), 367–95, esp. 391 • Munk, *Roll* • will, June 1791, PRO, PROB 11/1205, sig. 279 • D. Lysons, *The environs of London*, 3 (1795), 478 • D. E. Allen, *The naturalist in Britain: a social history*, 2nd edn (1994) • *A selection of the correspondence of Linnaeus, and other naturalists, from the original manuscripts*, ed. J. E. Smith, 2 vols. (1821), vol. 2, pp. 482–3 • P. J. P. Whitehead, 'Emanuel Mendes da Costa (1717–91) and the *Conchology, or, Natural history of shells*', *Bulletin of the British Museum (Natural History)* [Historical Series], 6 (1977–80), 1–24 • *DNB*

Archives BL, corresp., commonplace book and papers, Add. MSS 9389, 28534, 28544, 29867, 29868, Egerton MS 2381 • Derby Local Studies Library, corresp. and papers • FM Cam., corresp. and papers • NHM, notebook relating to fossils in England • RCS Eng., catalogue of fossils and notary business • RS, papers | S. Antiquaries, Lond., corresp. with Michael Lost and Samuel Pegge • Warks. CRO, corresp. with Thomas Pennant

Mendes da Costa, Philip Jacob (1708–1780), merchant, was born in London on 24 February 1708, the elder surviving son of John Abraham Mendes da Costa (1683–1763), a rich Anglo-Jewish merchant of St Christopher-le-Stocks in the City of London, whose father had fled from Portugal to France to escape the attentions of the Inquisition. The family moved to London from Rouen about 1696 and joined other members of the family in the Anglo-Indian diamond trade and the import of gold and other commodities. In 1702 John Mendes da Costa married Johanna Ester (1692–1749), a daughter of the important merchant Alvaro da *Costa (1646–1716); they had nine children, the youngest of whom was the naturalist Emanuel *Mendes da Costa (1717–1791). As a youth, Philip Mendes da Costa spent some time in the Netherlands, presumably gaining mercantile experience with the Amsterdam branch of his family. Back in London in the mid-1720s, he led the life of a rich young blade and reputedly traded on his own account, presumably in the Anglo-Indian trade.

It seems that a marriage was intended between Philip Mendes da Costa and his first cousin, Catherine Rachel (Kitty) da Costa (1710–1747), but he acquired a dubious reputation as a rake and fortune-hunter and Kitty was married off in 1727 to the rich Joseph Isaac Villareal (1673–1730). When Villareal died, on 27 December 1730, Kitty speedily agreed to marry her former suitor, but under family pressure later rejected him. On 11 January 1732 Mendes da Costa, now using his Hebrew forename of Jacob, involved his family in a scandalous lawsuit by bringing an action against his cousin in the ecclesiastical court of arches, at Doctors' Commons, for breach of promise, the first Jew ever to do such a thing. His application for fulfilment of a marriage contract or damages of £100,000, and a subsequent suit for similar damages at the king's bench, were dismissed on the grounds that Kitty's promise of marriage had been conditional on her father's consent, which was refused. The vindictive Mendes da Costa promptly published a partial and embittered account of the trial, probably printed by the notorious Edmund Curll. M. J. Landa suggests that Mendes da Costa was the inspiration for the caricatural Jew in the second scene of Hogarth's *Harlot's Progress* of 1732.

Presumably as a consequence of the public scandal, Mendes da Costa, still only in his mid-twenties, was dispatched to Hamburg, which had one of the oldest Sephardic communities in Europe. He settled there permanently and formed a connection with the mercantile family of Bravo (which also had a branch in London) by marrying two daughters of the family in succession. During the course of the century, Hamburg, gradually dispensing with the intermediary services of Amsterdam, developed direct connections with London for the purchase of colonial goods of divers sorts, including coffee, hides, and tobacco, as well as diamonds. The Englishman may well have been a useful link between the cities. He was not, however, a successful businessman. In 1746 Frederick I invited rich Portuguese Jews to settle in Sweden as traders; 'Jacob Mendes da Costa of Hamburg Altona' acted as spokesman and negotiator for a group of twenty-two Jews. But the merchants were unenthusiastic and, worse, Mendes da Costa turned out to be bankrupt. The project was dropped. His subsequent career is unrecorded; he died at Altona in April or May 1780, leaving one daughter, Esther.   NORMA PERRY

Sources E. Mendes da Costa, 'Genealogical notes', *GM*, 1st ser., 82/1 (1812), 21–4 [BL, Add. MS 29867] · 'Proceedings … between Mr Jacob Mendes da Costa and Mrs Catherine da Costa Villareal … relating to a marriage contract', LPL, Process books of the court of arches, MSS EE9 187/1 and EEE 13 · J. Mendes da Costa, *The proceedings at large … between Mr Jacob Mendes da Costa and Mrs Catherine da Costa Villa Real … relating to a marriage contract* (1734) · M. J. Landa, 'Kitty Villareal, the Da Costas and Samson Gideon', *Transactions of the Jewish Historical Society of England*, 13 (1932–5), 271–91 · C. Roth, ed., *Anglo-Jewish letters (1158–1917)* (1938) · A. M. Hyamson, *The Sephardim of England: a history of the Spanish and Portuguese Jewish community, 1492–1951* (1951) · C. Roth, *A history of the Jews in England*, 3rd edn (1964)

Mendez [Mendes], **Moses** (1690?–1758), playwright and poet, was probably born in the City of London. He was a grandson of the Sephardi physician Fernando Mendes and the only son of James Mendez, of Mitcham, Surrey, a stockjobber, and Anne, of the Sephardi da Costa family. He married outside of his faith to Ann (Anne) Gabrielle (d. 1771), daughter and coheir of Sir Francis Head, baronet, of Hermitage, Higham, Kent. It is not known when Mendez was baptized.

Mendez may have received part of his education at St Mary Hall, Oxford, under Dr William King. At first he intended to become an advocate in Doctors' Commons, but instead took up stockjobbing, by which he made a fortune. He had a home at Mitcham, and bought St Andrews, a large estate at Old Buckenham, Norfolk. In 1737 he became steward, and the following year grand steward, in a masonic lodge, probably the British lodge that met at Braund's Head, New Bond Street.

Moses and his relative Solomon Mendez (d. 1762?) had friends in London literary circles, including Richard Savage, James Thomson, David Garrick, and Robert Dodsley, but there is some confusion between the two because of frequent lack of forenames in contemporary correspondence. It now seems that it was Solomon who in 1739 contributed to Alexander Pope's project of an allowance for the poet Savage, which Solomon withdrew in 1742; Thomson addressed a mock epitaph to Solomon and a birthday poem to his wife. Moses gave an account of a trip to Ireland in 1744 in a poem addressed to John Ellis, but Simpson's statement that he was friends with Swift (Simpson, 105) remains undocumented. David Garrick in 1745 called Moses 'very much my friend' (*Letters of David Garrick*, 70). Dodsley published several of his poems in his *Collection*, vol. 4 (1755). Mendez's *The Seasons* (1751), a set of Spenserian verses (a favourite form of his), opens with an elegy on Thomson's death.

Secure in his fortune, Mendez began a literary career. His first dramatic piece, *The Double Disappointment*, was the earliest published Jewish contribution to English literature. A farce with several songs (called a 'ballad opera'), it had its première at Drury Lane on 18 March 1746, and was revived the following season. The audience delighted in the exposing of national characters in the form of two Irish and French fortune hunters.

For Drury Lane, Mendez also provided three afterpieces. Most popular was *The Chaplet*, advertised as 'a New Pastoral Masque' or 'a New Musical Entertainment in Two Interludes' (*General Advertiser*), with music by William Boyce, which opened on 2 December 1749 and had revivals until April 1755. *Robin Hood*, set by Charles Burney, opened on 13 December 1750 for four performances, with only the music to recommend it. *The Shepherd's Lottery*, also set by Boyce, had its première on 19 November 1751, and was revived in two following seasons; it was also performed at the meeting of the Three Choirs at Hereford on 14 September 1754, under Boyce's direction. Songs from Mendez's plays, especially *The Chaplet*, were popular at the pleasure gardens and were widely disseminated in song sheets, songbooks, and magazines.

Mendez's poems appeared in numerous poetic miscellanies and collections; several were first printed in 1792 in the *European Magazine* (February, November, and December issues, along with a biographical sketch and portrait in the October issue). In the *Battiad*, in two cantos (1750), Mendez, assisted by Paul Whitehead and Dr Ralph Schomberg, satirized the part taken by William Battie against Schomberg in the latter's dispute with the College of Physicians.

The nearest contemporary source describes Mendez as a 'Person of considerable Genius, of an agreeable Behaviour and entertaining in Conversation [with] a very pretty Turn for Poetry' (Baker, vol. 2). Mendez was created an MA at Oxford University on 19 June 1750. He died at Old Buckenham, Norfolk, on 4 February 1758, and was buried there on 8 February.

Mendez's wife married Captain the Hon. John Roper (1734–1780) on 21 March 1760, and died on 11 December 1771. Mendez's sons Francis and James Roper were authorized to take their mother's maiden name (Head) by royal licence dated 11 May 1771. His cousin, Emanuel Mendes da Costa, was the noted English naturalist. His grandsons had military careers and served under Wellington. Sir George Head (1782–1855) was assistant commissary-general and deputy knight-marshal at the coronations of William IV and Queen Victoria; and Sir Francis Bond Head (1793–1875) became lieutenant-governor of Upper Canada and suppressed the rising of 1837–8.

THOMAS N. MCGEARY

Sources R. J. Bruce, introduction, in W. Boyce and M. Mendez, *The shepherd's lottery: a musical entertainment* (1751); facs. edn (1990) · [D. E. Baker], *The companion to the play-house*, 2 vols. (1764) · J. P. Simpson, 'Brother Moses Mendez, grand steward, 1738 (1690–1758)', *Ars Quartuor Coronatorum*, 18/2 (1905), 104–9 · A. Sherbo, 'Solomon Mendes, a friend of the poets', *Philological Quarterly*, 36 (1957), 508–11 · *European Magazine and London Review*, 22 (1792), 251–2 · J. M. Shaftesley, 'Jews in regular English freemasonry, 1717–1860', *Transactions of the Jewish Historical Society of England*, 25 (1973–5), 150–209 · *The correspondence of Robert Dodsley, 1733–1764*, ed. J. E. Tierney (1988) [incl. letter to Mendez] · *The letters of David Garrick*, ed. D. M. Little and G. M. Kahrl, 3 vols. (1963) · C. Roth, ed., *Anglo-Jewish letters (1158–1917)* (1938) · J. Sambrook, *James Thomson, 1700–1748: a life* (1991) · Foster, *Alum. Oxon.* · *The correspondence of Alexander Pope*, ed. G. Sherburn, 5 vols. (1956) · *DNB* · W. Van Lennep and others, eds., *The London stage, 1660–1800*, 5 pts in 11 vols. (1960–68) · *ESTC* · *BL cat.*

Likenesses W. Bromley, stipple and line engraving (after painting, now untraced), BM; repro. in *European Magazine and London Review*, facing p. 251

Wealth at death see probate, PRO, PROB 11/835, fols. 375v – 378r

Mendham, Joseph (1769–1856), Church of England clergyman and religious controversialist, was born in London on 14 February 1769 and baptized on 10 March of that year in the parish of St Stephen Walbrook. He was the sixth of the nine children of Robert Mendham (1737–1810), a successful merchant in the City of London, and his wife, Margaret Scott (*d.* 1812). He was educated at St Edmund Hall, Oxford, matriculating on 27 January 1789, and graduating BA in 1792 and MA in 1795. Here he imbibed a strongly evangelical atmosphere; St Edmund Hall has been described as 'the headquarters of evangelicalism at Oxford' (Reynolds, 58), and its vice-principal, Isaac Crouch, impressed evangelical values upon several generations of undergraduates. Mendham was ordained deacon in 1793 and priest in the following year, in each case by George Tomline, bishop of Lincoln. In 1795 the pattern for the rest of his life was set by his marriage on 15 December to Maria Riland (*d.* 1841), daughter of the Revd John Riland, rector of Sutton Coldfield. He and his wife had two children, a son, Robert Riland Mendham (*d.* 1857), and a daughter, Anna Maria Mendham (*d.* 1872). Equally significantly, Mendham immediately became curate to his father-in-law at Sutton Coldfield, and resided there until his death.

John Riland had been assistant to Henry Venn (1725–1797), vicar of Huddersfield and a leading evangelical; he was himself an admired figure in the evangelical revival and Mendham came to share his father-in-law's moderate Calvinism, his emphasis on the importance of personal salvation, and his devotion to pastoral duty. He served the parish of Sutton Coldfield conscientiously until he relinquished his curacy in 1826; he also served as warden of the corporation in 1807 and 1808. Having received substantial legacies from his parents, Mendham possessed sufficient financial independence to disdain the quest for clerical preferment and to concentrate upon his two principal interests, book collection and anti-Catholic controversial writing.

From his youth Mendham had amassed a library of religious literature, mainly from the sixteenth and seventeenth centuries. He was particularly interested in Reformation and post-Reformation controversies and had read widely among both protestant and Catholic authors. He strongly adhered to the protestant side in controversies of this nature, which he viewed in the context of contemporary Catholic campaigns for political emancipation. He devoted much attention to the alleged tyrannies and superstitions of the Church of Rome, which he attempted to expose by detailed quotation from Catholic sources. In the 1820s Mendham published three works of this kind, of which the most influential was *An Account of the Indexes, Prohibitory and Expurgatory, of the Church of Rome* (1826). However, the most important event of his career as a writer was the Catholic Emancipation Act of 1829, which led to allegations in some tory circles of betrayal of the protestant constitution. Mendham shared this opinion, supporting the British Society for Promoting the Religious Principles of the Reformation (or Reformation Society) and redoubling his literary efforts. His fear of growing Catholic numbers was made plain in his *Address to the Inhabitants of Sutton Coldfield* (1834), and his claim that the Catholic church was irremediably repressive was repeated in his *Index of prohibited books … being the latest specimen of the literary policy of the Church of Rome* (1840). His most scholarly work was *Memoirs of the Council of Trent* (1834, with a supplement in 1836), in which he reprinted a series of contemporary manuscript sources and displayed an impressive command of Spanish and Italian. His work was favourably reviewed in such strongly protestant periodicals as the *Church of England Quarterly Review* and the *Protestant Journal*, while his scholarly antiquarianism led him to make several contributions to the early issues of *Notes and Queries*.

In 1836 Mendham became perpetual curate of Hill, near Sutton Coldfield, where a chapel had been constructed to meet the needs of an increasing local population. But he was soon obliged by ill health to relinquish this living, and after the death of his wife in 1841 lived quietly with his son at Sutton Coldfield. He died there on 1 November 1856 at the age of eighty-seven, and was buried at Holy Trinity Church, Sutton Coldfield, on 6 November. His library of some 5000 volumes passed to his son and subsequently to his nephew, John Mendham, whose widow bequeathed it to the Law Society in 1869. Since the 1980s the collection has been on loan to Canterbury Cathedral Library.

By nature reserved and, latterly, almost reclusive, Mendham had little in common with the more raucous types of English anti-Catholicism of the mid-nineteenth century, although his work was used by popular protestant writers as a valuable source of information. But he represented a branch of conservative evangelical opinion in a period of increasing religious pluralism, and his genuine, if highly partial, scholarship amounted to a serious contribution to ecclesiastical history. G. M. DITCHFIELD

Sources G. M. Ditchfield, 'Joseph Mendham: collector and controversialist', *Catalogue of the Law Society's Mendham Collection … housed in Canterbury Cathedral Library*, ed. S. Hingley and D. Shaw (1994), 15–74 • J. Eales, 'The Mendham Collection: the contents and their historical context', *Catalogue of the Law Society's Mendham Collection … housed in Canterbury Cathedral Library*, ed. S. Hingley and D. Shaw (1994), 75–128 • J. Nicholson, *Catalogue of the Mendham Collection: being a selection of books and pamphlets from the library of the late Rev. Joseph Mendham, MA* (1871) [with suppl. (1874)] • Boase, *Mod. Eng. biog.* • W. K. R. Bedford, *Three hundred years of a family living: being a history of the Rilands of Sutton Coldfield* (1889) • W. K. R. Bedford, *History of Sutton Coldfield* (1891) • C. Haydon, *Anti-Catholicism in eighteenth-century England, c. 1714–80: a political and social study* (1993) • J. Wolffe, *The protestant crusade in Great Britain, 1829–1860* (1991) • J. S. Reynolds, *The evangelicals at Oxford, 1735–1871: a record of an unchronicled movement*, [2nd edn] (1975) • D. M. Lewis, ed., *The Blackwell dictionary of evangelical biography, 1730–1860*, 2 vols. (1995) • parish records of St Stephen Walbrook, GL, MS 8319/2 • parish records, Sutton Coldfield, Warks. CRO, DRB 2/10; DRB 2/15, fol. 129 • Warks. CRO, ZI/158, 6 • Crockford (1858)

Archives Law Society, London, collections relating to ecclesiastical history and law | Bodl. Oxf., collection relating to Council of Trent, corresp. and papers • Chetham's Library, Manchester, letters to Thomas Jones • LPL, Golightly MSS and Incorporated Church Building Society • Warks. CRO, Sutton Coldfield parish records

Wealth at death approx. £50,000—incl. Mendham's library: will, Ditchfield, 'Joseph Mendham: collector and controversialist', appx 1

Mendip. For this title name *see* Ellis, Welbore, first Baron Mendip (1713–1802).

Mendl, Sir Charles Ferdinand (1871–1958), information officer, was born in London on 14 December 1871, the second son of Ferdinand Mendl, businessman, and his wife, Jeannette Rachel, *née* Hyam. His elder brother was Sir Sigismund Ferdinand Mendl, financier and Liberal MP for Plymouth, 1898–1900. His father had been born at Tarbor in Bohemia and was sent to London as a youth to work on the Baltic exchange; he subsequently formed a small family grain firm and became a British subject. After Harrow School, Mendl entered the family firm and later started a branch in Buenos Aires. In 1912 he went to Paris as financial agent for several South American railways. On the outbreak of the First World War he volunteered as a private soldier but was seriously injured in an accident while an interpreter with the 25th infantry brigade and was invalided out in 1915. After working in Paris on intelligence for the Admiralty in 1918, he was attached to the British embassy during the peace conference and in 1920 was appointed Paris representative of the Foreign Office news department. He was knighted in 1924.

On 10 March 1926 Mendl married Ella Anderson (Elsie) de Wolfe (1865–1950), daughter of Stephen de Wolfe, doctor, of New York. She was a fashionable interior decorator, who had made a fortune in New York before moving to Paris. She rented the Villa Trianon at Versailles, where she entertained lavishly. From his own apartment in the avenue Montaigne, Mendl, who was appointed press attaché in 1926, hosted smaller and more intimate gatherings. Quickly he established good connections across a broad spectrum of the French establishment. When socialist leader Léon Blum led the popular front to power in 1936, ambassador Sir George Clerk was at a disadvantage since he had not met the new premier. Mendl, however, knew him well enough to telephone immediately and invite him to dine at the embassy. Contrary to legend Mendl was not a kind of grey eminence, but he was certainly an influential figure. At a time when Paris was still the United Kingdom's most important and most prestigious mission, Mendl, as well as being the embassy's antennae, played a proactive and significant role in shaping both élite and mass opinion. His talent and drive in exploiting to the full the potential of the newly created post of press attaché contributed to his success. His wife's social position helped, as did his own close relations with two of the inter-war ambassadors, Lord Tyrrell and Sir Eric Phipps.

Pierre Laval, the French premier from 1931 to 1932 and again from 1935 to 1936, believed Mendl to be working for British intelligence, alleging that the attaché had boasted that the British government had spent more money to bring down his government than on a colonial war. Laval blamed him for the press leak that torpedoed the Hoare–Laval plan on Abyssinia in December 1935. These allegations cannot be proved or disproved. Mendl did not write memoirs and left no papers. By its nature his activity left few traces. Yet some of Mendl's interventions can be documented, and there may well have been a secret service link. The Foreign Office was the paymaster of the Secret Intelligence Service and in 1922 part of Mendl's salary came from the secret service funds.

Mendl's career peaked in the run-up to the Second World War. British and French leaders endeavoured to sustain public support for appeasement. For Mendl and ambassador Sir Eric Phipps, critical voices were unwelcome. In March 1938, following the *Anschluss* (the German annexation of Austria), Winston Churchill visited Blum. 'Churchill is a nobody, he does not count in England', Mendl warned Blum's chef de cabinet (Renouvin and Rémond, 358). The *Anschluss* signalled the start of a vicious press campaign against the Blum cabinet and the Franco-Czech alliance. Mendl was widely believed to have instigated and funded the campaign. His mistake was to identify himself too closely with one section of the political world. As a result, his advice was overly biased and unrepresentative. On 24 September 1938 Phipps, acting almost certainly on Mendl's evaluation, reported: 'all that is best in France is against war, almost at any price' (Adamthwaite, 177–8). This was a gross misrepresentation of opinion. The suppression of alternative opinions included those of Anthony Eden. In June 1939 Phipps and Mendl tried to prevent him speaking in Paris.

On the collapse of France the Mendls left for Lisbon and then the United States, where they settled in Beverly Hills; while there Mendl appeared in Alfred Hitchcock's *Notorious* (1946), as the Commodore. The Mendls returned to France after the war. Following his wife's death in 1950, in 1951 Mendl married Yvonne Marie Marguerite Isabelle, daughter of Jules Hector Henri Victor Steinbach of Brussels, and divorced wife of Baron de Heckeren. She died in 1956. Mendl himself died in Paris on 14 February 1958. There were no children from either marriage.

ANTHONY ADAMTHWAITE

Sources *The Times* (15 Feb 1958) · *DNB* · A. Adamthwaite, *France and the coming of the Second World War* (1977) · *The diplomatic diaries of Oliver Harvey, 1937–40*, ed. J. Harvey (1970) · G. Warner, *Pierre Laval and the eclipse of France* (1968) · P. Renouvin and R. Rémond, *Leon Blum: chef de gouvernement* (Paris, 1967) · C. Gladwyn, *The Paris embassy* (1976) · *WWW*, 1951–60 · Burke, *Peerage*
Archives CAC Cam., corresp. | Lpool RO, corresp. with seventeenth earl of Derby · PRO, reports to Lord Crewe and corresp. with Sir William Tyrell, FO 800
Likenesses W. Stoneman, photograph, 1930, NPG

Mendl, (**Gladys**) **Henrietta**. *See* Schütze, (Gladys) Henrietta (1884–1946).

Mendoza, Daniel (1765?–1836), pugilist, the son of Jewish parents, Abraham Mendoza and his wife, Esther, *née* Lopes, was born, according to the fighter's memoirs, on 5 July 1764 in the parish of Aldgate, London. However, the Spanish and Portuguese Synagogue records show he was circumcised on 12 July of the following year, making a birth date of 5 July 1765 much more probable.

Educated for some years at a Jewish school, Mendoza afterwards entered into employment with various tradesmen including a glass-cutter, fruiterer, tea merchant, and tobacconist. During this time he served his pugilistic apprenticeship, impressing the noted Richard Humphries, who later became his bitter rival. Mendoza's first fight of significance was when he beat Sam Martin, the Bath Butcher. The contest took place at Barnet on 17 April 1787 at the instigation of the prince of Wales. On the 22nd of the next month he married his cousin Esther Mendoza (*d.* 1855) and in the same year he opened an academy at Capel Court, Bartholomew Lane, where he taught the art of self-defence. His popularity encouraged young Jews to gain fistic proficiency, with the result, as Francis Place noted, that abusive treatment of the Jewish community began to lessen (George, 138).

An impromptu set-to with Humphries at Epping in September 1787 led to the first of their three encounters. The men fought at Odiham, Hampshire, on 9 January 1788 and initially Mendoza had the advantage. However, after about twenty-nine minutes, injury compelled him to concede. The result being considered unsatisfactory, they again met on 6 May 1789. An octagonal amphitheatre was specially erected for the occasion in a park, near Stilton, belonging to a Henry Thornton. During the contest Humphries fell without a blow but, following a prolonged dispute, Mendoza agreed to continue and, at length, prevailed. In 1789 he published a small book entitled *The Art of Boxing* and on 29 September 1790 he opposed Humphries for a final time. The battle, at an innyard in Doncaster, was well sustained and Humphries, despite fighting resolutely, was again beaten.

Thereafter Mendoza was in great demand for theatrical appearances but his return to the fistic arena was delayed until he met Bristolian Bill Ward (later erroneously called Warr) at Smitham Bottom, near Croydon, on 14 May 1792. Although Ward was favourite, Mendoza proved superior in every round except one and, in approximately thirty minutes, was hailed the victor. When the two met again at Bexley, Kent, on 12 November 1794, Ward took an early lead but was defeated in only fifteen minutes. In a brief, albeit severe, contest Mendoza lost to the much heavier and more powerful John Jackson at Hornchurch, Essex, on 15 April 1795. The latter increased his advantage by unfairly holding his antagonist's hair with one hand while hitting him with the other. A bystander, writing to *The Times* (20 April 1795), proffered the opinion that had it not been for this 'I have no doubt but he [Mendoza] would have won'.

Daniel Mendoza (1765?–1836), by Henry Kingsbury, pubd 1789 (after J. Robineau)

Subsequently Mendoza became landlord of the Admiral Nelson public house in Whitechapel. To a challenge from Jem Belcher in November 1801 he replied that he supported a family of six children by his exertions as a publican and would only consider returning to the ring to avenge his defeat by Jackson (*Star Daily Evening Advertiser*, 26 Nov 1801). This did not come to pass and his next encounter, as a result of a quarrel, was when he outclassed Harry Lee in fifty-three rounds at Grinstead Green, near Bromley. Mendoza declined Lee's request for a return match in a letter to *The Times* (6 January 1807) wherein he stated his time was devoted to 'teaching Gentlemen the art of self-defence; from whence I derive the means of supporting my family'. Pierce Egan thought him unrivalled as a teacher and believed that no man united the theory of sparring with the practice of boxing to greater advantage. Mendoza's last prize-ring appearance was a twelve-round defeat on 4 July 1820 in a grudge encounter with fellow veteran Tom Owen on Banstead Downs. The following month he gave a farewell address at the Fives Court, St Martin's Street, in which he voiced his opinion that he had the right to call himself the 'Father of the Science' (*Weekly Dispatch*, 3 Sept 1820).

About 5 feet 7 inches tall, Mendoza was well formed, had considerable courage and excellent endurance. His blows were quick, but deficient in force, and he struck more often and stopped more dexterously than any fighter before him. Despite his pugilistic success he periodically experienced financial difficulties, suffering the indignity of an occasional stay in a debtors' prison, and his last years

were spent in poverty and distress. He died at his home in Horseshoe Alley, Petticoat Lane, London, on 3 September 1836 and was buried the following day in the new cemetery of the Spanish and Portuguese Jews at Mile End.

TONY GEE

Sources fight reports, etc., *The Times*; *London Chronicle*; *Morning Post, and Daily Advertiser*; *Morning Chronicle*; *Star Daily Evening Advertiser*; *The World*; *Gazetteer, and New Daily Advertiser*; *General Evening Post*; *Public Advertiser*; *Diary, or, Woodfall's Register*; *The Oracle*; *Lloyd's Evening Post*; *Morning Herald*; *Reading Mercury and Oxford Gazette*; *English Chronicle, or, Universal Evening Post*; *Weekly Dispatch*; *British Luminary, or, Weekly Intelligencer*; *Morning Star*; *The Sun* • *The memoirs of the life of Daniel Mendoza*, ed. P. Magriel (1951) • L. Edwards, 'Daniel Mendoza', paper read before the Jewish Historical Society of England, 15 March 1938 • P. Egan, *Boxiana, or, Sketches of ancient and modern pugilism*, 1 (1812), 253–80 • P. Egan, *Boxiana, or, Sketches of ancient and modern pugilism*, 2 (1818), 11 • P. Egan, *Boxiana, or, Sketches of ancient and modern pugilism*, 3 (1821), 60–71, 488–90 • T. Fewtrell, *Boxing reviewed, or, The science of manual defence, etc.* (1790), 77–8 • R. D. Barnett and others, eds. and trans., *The circumcision register of Isaac and Abraham de Paiba, 1715–1775* (1991), 92 • M. D. George, *London life in the eighteenth century* (1925), 137–8 • *The Times* (20 April 1795) [letter to editor about Mendoza–Jackson match] • *The Times* (6 Jan 1807) [letter to editor from Mendoza] • *Weekly Dispatch* (3 Sept 1820) [Mendoza's farewell address] • *Star Daily Evening Advertiser* (26 Nov 1801) [challenge from Belcher] • H. D. Miles, *Pugilistica*, 1 (1880), 71–83, 86–8, 94–5, 112–13 • *Bell's Life in London* (4 Sept 1836) • *Bell's Life in London* (11 Sept 1836)

Archives Jewish Museum, London

Likenesses J. Grozer, engraving, 1788 (after painting by S. Einsle), Jewish Museum, London • J. Lumsden, engraving, 1788?, Jewish Museum, London • J. Gillray, two etchings, 1788–90, Jewish Museum, London, NPG • W. N. Gardiner, engraving, pubd 1789 (after J. Robineau), Jewish Museum, London • J. Grozer, engraving, 1789 (after drawing by T. Rowlandson), Jewish Museum, London • H. Kingsbury, mezzotint, pubd 1789 (after J. Robineau), BM, Jewish Museum, London [*see illus.*] • J. Grozer, engraving, 1790? (after drawing by C. R. Ryley), Jewish Museum, London • I. Cruikshank, engraving, 1792 (after caricature), Jewish Museum, London

Wealth at death died in poverty: *Bell's Life in London* (4 Sept 1836)

Mendoza y Ríos, Joseph de (1761–1816), astronomer, born in Seville, Spain, on 29 January 1761, was the son of Joseph-Ygancio de Mendoza and his wife, María-Romana Morillo y Ríos. He later added the prestigious name Ríos of his maternal grandmother to that of his father—a common practice at the time. He was educated at the Royal College of San Isidro, Madrid, where he showed a remarkable aptitude for mathematics, and then joined the army as a cadet in the Royal regiment of dragoons. However, he soon requested to be transferred to the navy, which was a much more attractive place from the point of view of astronomy and mathematics. The transfer became effective on 16 March 1776. In August 1779, while returning from Manila, his ship, the *Santa Inés*, engaged in combat with two English cruisers; Mendoza Ríos was taken prisoner to Cork, where he arrived in early September. He was released one year later, and returned to Cadiz in September 1780.

Other naval postings and promotions followed. During this period Mendoza Ríos wrote a treatise on navigation, which in early 1787 he submitted to the navy minister, *teniente general de la armada* Baylio Fray Antonio Valdés, a man dedicated to the modernization of the Spanish navy; he recommended its publication. Mendoza Ríos, released from duties at sea because of ill health, was sent to Madrid to oversee its printing. After his two-volume treatise was published, in late 1787, he was promoted to *capitan de fragata*. Thus he began a second career, as a scientist, in areas of naval interest.

Back in Cadiz, Mendoza Ríos submitted a proposal for an institute for the sciences of navigation, including a cartographic depot, to be located at the naval headquarters near Cadiz. His ideas were accepted and the king set aside a large sum of money for it. The intention was to collect, or copy, maps and documents held by former officers and members of the nobility in Spain, for which task Mendoza Ríos suggested a young naval officer, Martin Fernández de Navarrete. Another purpose was to acquire, from other European locations, maps and charts and books and instruments relevant to navigation, and to report on recent scientific and industrial advances. Mendoza Ríos undertook this aspect. He left Spain in October 1789, accompanied by another young naval officer, José María de Lanz.

Through the publication of his treatise on navigation, Mendoza Ríos's name became known in scientific circles in Europe; Sir Joseph Banks was his correspondent in London, and in Paris he became acquainted with some of the leading scientists of the time. He took a serious interest in the use of new materials (precious stones and newly available metals, such as platinum) in the design and improvement of a variety of scientific instruments. Some of the instruments he designed or improved were sent to Malaspina to be used by the scientists attached to his expedition. At the time of his stay in Paris, French scientists were considering the construction of a large telescope to emulate Herschel's achievements in England. Mendoza Ríos advocated testing platinum for the mirror of the projected French telescope; the matter was discussed by a committee which included Lavoisier. He was elected foreign correspondent to the French Academy of Sciences on 4 August 1792.

As the political situation became more unstable in Paris and the telescope project collapsed, Mendoza Ríos moved to the safety of London. In 1792 he visited a number of industrial establishments in England and wrote detailed confidential reports on them. On account of his contributions to nautical astronomy he was elected a fellow of the Royal Society on 11 April 1793.

In 1796 Mendoza Ríos sent to Spain, from London, a large and valuable collection of maps, charts, and scientific and geographic books. In the same year he opened negotiations for one of Herschel's large telescopes. However, once installed in Madrid, this instrument, then the second largest in Europe, was not used to its full potential. Mendoza Ríos made his home in England, where he married Anna Maria Parker on 8 November 1798. They had two daughters, Francisca and Anna Fermina (*b.* 1799); the latter married in 1829 Sir Patrick Bellew (1798–1866), afterwards Lord Bellew of Barmeath Castle, Dunleer, co. Louth, Ireland.

From the 1790s Mendoza Ríos was in the forefront of those who sought to modernize a wide range of activities in the Spanish Navy, such as chronometry, precision mechanics, optics, and numerical calculation. Through his acquaintance with the best instrument makers he was able to place young Spanish apprentices in their workshops, even having one of them instructed in precious stone cutting, a very secretive craft. He also played an important role in the introduction into Spain of modern lighthouse techniques.

Mendoza Ríos was interested in the use of mathematical tables as aids to nautical astronomy. Soon after his arrival in London he proposed the publication of such a collection of tables. In 1797 he contributed to the *Philosophical Transactions* of the Royal Society an important paper on the central problems of nautical astronomy. He succeeded in simplifying mathematical calculations considerably, reducing them to the reading of a few entries in a set of pre-calculated, compact, and easy-to-use auxiliary tables. In the design of these tables he displayed a great deal of mathematical ingenuity. For their construction he used several 'computers' working in parallel, each person doing a simple and repetitive task. In 1801 he published, again in *Philosophical Transactions*, a full description of his reflecting circle, an improvement of Borda's circle. After lengthy discussions Mendoza Ríos obtained funds to publish his tables, enabling him to reduce their price and make them widely available. He also persuaded Portugal, Russia, and other foreign powers to buy copies. From the early 1800s his various tables were reprinted a large number of times and published in several languages; the last editions were made in the first decades of the twentieth century.

In September 1796 Mendoza Ríos requested permission to retire from the Spanish Navy. No action was taken then, but in May 1800 the king of Spain decided to remove his name from the navy list, probably, although not explicitly stated, because he had not returned to Spain when his country was at war with England. However, the navy and the Spanish court continued to consult him on naval matters until the end of his life.

Mendoza Ríos had always suffered from ill health; there were frequent references to his health in his correspondence (even in his scientific works) throughout his life, and these became more insistent and obsessive towards the end of it, when he commuted between his London and Brighton homes. He died on 4 March 1816 as a result of hanging himself in his country home, in New Steine, Brighton. The coroner's report stated that 'being a lunatic he hanged himself'. On 11 March Mendoza Ríos was buried in the church of St Nicholas, Brighton. He left, when he died, a considerable amount of money in trust for his wife and daughters. He is probably the mathematician and astronomer of Spanish origin who has received the widest international recognition for his scientific work. However, secondary literature on him is rare and, while respecting his achievements, often hostile to his personality.   EDUARDO L. ORTIZ

Sources Barmeath Castle, Ireland, Lord Bellew's family MSS · Museo Naval, Madrid · Observatorio de la Armada, San Fernando · Archivo de Simancas, Simancas · RS · Archivo General de la

Nación, Madrid · Archivo-Museo 'Don Alvaro de Bazán', Ciudad Real · PRO · CUL, Royal Greenwich Observatory papers · Bureau des Longitudes, Paris · bank archives, London · bank archives, Madrid · bank archives, Paris · bank archives, Mexico · bank archives, USA · personal corresp., priv. coll. [mainly in Spain] · E. L. Ortiz, ed., *The works of José de Mendoza y Ríos* (2003) · E. L. Ortiz, 'Joseph Mendoza y Ríos: teoría, observación y tablas', *Gaceta de la Real Sociedad Matemática Española*, 4/1 (2001), 155–83

Archives Archivo General, Simancas · Archivo General de la Nación, Madrid · Archivo-Museo 'Don Alvaro de Bazán', Ciudad Real · CUL, Greenwich Observatory MSS · Museo Naval, Madrid · Observatorio de la Armada, San Fernando · RS · priv. coll., personal corresp. | Barmeath Castle, Ireland, Lord Bellew's family MSS

Likenesses T. Phillips, portrait, Barmeath Castle, Ireland

Wealth at death approx. 60,000 reales in Spain: will

Mends, Sir Robert (1767?–1823), naval officer, from a Pembrokeshire family, was probably born in 1767. He entered the navy in 1779 on board the *Culloden* with Captain George Balfour, and in her was present at the action off Cape St Vincent and the relief of Gibraltar in January 1780. Afterwards, in the frigate *Guadeloupe*, with Captain Hugh Robinson, he was present at the action off the mouth of the Chesapeake on 16 March 1781, and at the defence of Yorktown, where the *Guadeloupe* was destroyed and Mends, then not fourteen, lost his right arm, besides being wounded in the left knee. On his recovery he was again with Captain Balfour in the *Conqueror*, one of the van of the fleet in the battle of Dominica, where he was severely wounded in the head by a splinter. In 1786 he was in the *Grampus* with Commodore Edward Thompson on the coast of Africa. On 26 August 1789 he was promoted lieutenant. He was then for some time in the sloop *Childers* in the channel. In 1793 he was in the *Colossus* in the Mediterranean and was at the occupation of Toulon, and in 1795, still in the *Colossus*, was in the action off Lorient on 23 June, when he was severely burnt by a powder explosion. On 15 December 1796 he was promoted commander, and for the next three years commanded the sloop *Diligence* (16 guns) on the Jamaica station. He was advanced to post rank on 2 May 1800, and, continuing on the same station, successively commanded the *Abergavenny* (54 guns), the *Thunderer* (74 guns), and the frigate *Quebec* (32 guns). In September 1802 he returned to England in the *Néréide* (36 guns).

In 1805 Mends was appointed to command the sea fencibles of the Dublin district and in 1808 to the frigate *Arethusa* (46 guns) in the Bay of Biscay and on the north coast of Spain. On the morning of 6 April 1809 she assisted in the closing stage of the action between the *Amethyst* and *Niemen*. The *Arethusa*'s share in it was small, but Mends was severely wounded in the head by a splinter. In the summer of 1810, in command of a squadron on the coast of Spain, Mends destroyed several French batteries, for which service, in addition to a formal letter of thanks from the junta of Galicia, he received the order of the Cross of Victory of the Asturias and the nominal rank of major-general of the Spanish army. From 1811 to 1814 he was superintendent of the prison hulks in Portsmouth harbour. On 25 May 1815 he was knighted, on receiving permission to wear the cross of the order of Charles III of Spain; and in April 1816,

the pension of £7, which had been granted him for the loss of his arm, was increased to £300. In June 1821 he was appointed commodore and commander-in-chief on the west coast of Africa, with his broad pennant first in the *Iphigénie* (42 guns) and afterwards in the frigate *Owen Glendower*. He died on board the *Owen Glendower* at Cape Coast, on the Gold Coast, on 4 September 1823.

Mends married in 1802 a daughter of James Butler of Bagshot; they had three sons, of whom one, a midshipman of the *Owen Glendower*, died at Sierra Leone three months after his father; another, James Augustus Mends, died a captain on the retired list in 1875; the third, George Clarke Mends, was a retired vice-admiral at his death in 1885. Admiral Sir William Robert Mends (1812–1897) was the son of Sir Robert's brother Admiral William Bowen Mends (1781–1864).

J. K. LAUGHTON, *rev.* ROGER MORRISS

Sources J. Marshall, *Royal naval biography*, 2/1 (1824), 270 · O'Byrne, *Naval biog. dict.* · Boase, *Mod. Eng. biog.* · A. B. Rodger, *The war of the second coalition: 1798–1801, a strategic commentary* (1964)

Mends, Sir William Robert (1812–1897), naval officer, the eldest son of Admiral William Bowen Mends (1781–1864) and his wife, *née* Dawe, and the nephew of Sir Robert Mends, was born at Plymouth on 27 February 1812. After attending Haverfordwest grammar school and Plymouth School, in May 1825 he entered the Royal Naval College at Portsmouth, and shortly after passing out in December 1826 was appointed to the frigate *Thetis* (46 guns), going to the South American station. He was in the *Thetis* when she was wrecked on Cape Frio on 5 December 1830. It was Mends's watch when the ship struck, but as the night was dark with heavy rain he was held guiltless. He was considered to have behaved well in a difficult situation, and several of the members of the court offered to take him with them. After passing his examination he joined the *Actaeon* in the Mediterranean, which in 1832 was at Constantinople when a Russian army of upwards of 20,000 men arrived there after the defeat of the Turks by Ibrahim Pasha at Konya. The intervention of the western powers secured the withdrawal of this force, and Mends observed its embarkation, making careful notes of their methods of embarking the cavalry and guns. In the summer of 1834 the *Actaeon* returned to England and was paid off, and in January 1835 Mends was appointed to the *Pique* with Captain Henry John Rous. In July the ship was sent out to Canada, and on the homeward voyage, on 22 September, struck heavily on a reef off the coast of Labrador. After a perilous and for a time rudderless voyage, Mends reached St Helen's on 13 October, and learned that he had been promoted lieutenant on 11 August.

In December, Mends joined the *Vernon* at Malta. A year later he was moved into the *Caledonia* and then to the *Rodney*, from which, in July 1838, he went to be flag lieutenant of Sir John Louis, the second in command on the station and superintendent of Malta Dockyard. At Malta, in December 1837, he married Melita (d. 1894), the daughter of Dr Stilon, a Neapolitan by birth who had served as a medical officer in the French army at Maida and been sent as a prisoner to England, where he married and entered the navy; some years later he settled in private practice at Malta. Mends and his wife had a son and a daughter. Mends continued with Louis, sometimes afloat, but mostly at Malta, until July 1843. From November 1843 he was in the frigate *Fox* with Sir Henry Blackwood on the coast of Ireland and in the East Indies. On 2 January 1847 he received the news of his promotion, on 9 November 1846, to commander. In January 1848 he was appointed to the *Vanguard*, in which, a couple of months later, he lost some of the fingers of his left hand, which was carried into a block and badly crushed. It was this, more than the loss of the fingers, which caused trouble, and for years afterwards he suffered from severe attacks of neuralgia. The *Vanguard* went home and was paid off in March 1849, and in July 1850 Mends was appointed to the *Vengeance*, again with Blackwood, who, however, died after a short illness at Portsmouth on 7 January 1851, and was succeeded by Lord Edward Russell. Towards the end of the summer the *Vengeance* went to the Mediterranean, but came home in December 1852; on the 10th Mends was promoted captain in acknowledgement of the excellent order of the ship.

In October 1853 Mends was selected by Sir Edmund Lyons to be his flag captain in the Mediterranean, if Captain Symonds, then in the *Arethusa*, should prefer to remain in the frigate. If not, Mends would take the *Arethusa* [see Symonds, Sir Thomas Matthew Charles]. Mends took the *Agamemnon* out and joined the fleet in the Sea of Marmora on Christmas eve, and then took command of the *Arethusa*. In her he took a particularly brilliant part in the bombardment of Odessa on 22 April 1854, attacking the Mole fortifications. He was promptly recalled by the commander-in-chief, who seems to have considered that he was needlessly risking the ship.

> I expected a reprimand when I went on board the admiral to report, but the enthusiasm of the fleet and the cheers given to us as we passed along the lines mollified the chief, and I was simply told not to go in again. (Mends, 102)

In June, Lyons and Symonds had found that they did not get on well together, and Mends agreed to re-exchange into the *Agamemnon*. From that time his individuality is lost in that of the admiral. Lyons refused the services of a captain of the fleet because Mends was so successful in his dual role of flag captain and chief of Lyons's staff; he had the direction of those points of detail on which much depended. By far the most important of these were the admirably implemented embarkation of the troops at Varna and the landing of them in the Crimea on 14 September. Lyons and the navy fully recognized that the credit belonged to Mends.

In February 1855 Lyons moved his flag to the *Royal Albert*, and Mends accompanied him. In all the operations of the year he had his full share, and he was made a CB on 5 July. He continued in command of the *Royal Albert* until March 1857, when he was appointed to the *Hastings* and later the *Majestic*, guardships in the Mersey, from which, four years later, he was appointed deputy controller-general of the coastguard at the Admiralty. He held this office for about a

year, and in May 1862 was appointed director of transports, responsible for the transport department of the Admiralty. Here he remained more than twenty years, during which there were several exceptional calls on his department which were successfully met. Among these the most important were the initial organization of the Indian troopship service in the mid-1860s, the expedition to Abyssinia, moving Indian troops to Malta in 1879, the Anglo-Asante and Anglo-Zulu wars, and the occupation of Egypt in 1882. On 1 January 1869 Mends became a retired rear-admiral, although he remained in service. The decision to end his sea-going career was not taken lightly. He earned further appointments and promotions: KCB (20 May 1871), vice-admiral (1 January 1874), admiral (15 June 1879), and GCB (24 November 1882), the last with special reference to his work on the expedition to Egypt. In 1871 he went to India to report on the Indian marine.

In February 1883 Mends retired and settled down at Alverstoke, within easy distance of his many old friends at Portsmouth. Here he lived peacefully for the next twelve years. In July 1894 his wife died after a short illness, a blow that seriously affected him, though he survived for three years. He died at his home, 3A Anglesey Crescent, Alverstoke, Hampshire, on 26 June 1897, the day of the great jubilee naval review. Mends's career demonstrated the limits placed on even the most brilliant officers by a lack of connection and patronage in the mid-nineteenth-century navy. Only through his close connection with Henry Blackwood and Lord Lyons, both of whom appreciated his outstanding abilities as a seaman and organizer, did Mends rise as far as he did, and both men died before they could render him much service.

J. K. LAUGHTON, *rev.* ANDREW LAMBERT

Sources B. S. Mends, *Admiral Sir W. R. Mends* (1899) · S. M. Eardley-Wilmot, *Life of Vice-Admiral Edmund, Lord Lyons* (1898) · A. D. Lambert, *The Crimean War: British grand strategy, 1853–56* (1990) · D. Ellison, *Quarterdeck Cambridge* (1991) · J. W. D. Dundas and C. Napier, *Russian war, 1854, Baltic and Black Sea: official correspondence*, ed. D. Bonner-Smith and A. C. Dewar, Navy RS, 83 (1943) · A. C. Dewar, ed., *Russian war, 1855, Black Sea: official correspondence*, Navy RS, 85 (1945)

Archives W. Sussex RO, Lyons MSS

Likenesses F. Green, portrait, 1840, repro. in Mends, *Admiral Sir W. R. Mends*, 80 · West & Son, photograph, repro. in Mends, *Admiral Sir W. R. Mends*, 346

Wealth at death £1199 4s. 9d.: probate, 1 Nov 1897, *CGPLA Eng. & Wales*

Menefie, George (1596/7–1645/6), merchant and lawyer, was probably born in south-western England. His literacy suggests some early education, perhaps in law, as he is occasionally referred to as a lawyer or attorney. Much of the information about his life is the result of fortuitous survivals, at least one relevant document having been rescued from a mass of legal papers which the civil war troops of McClellan's army were burning to heat their coffee.

Menefie may have first visited Virginia in the early 1620s, as he stated in 1637 that he had resided in the colony for sixteen or seventeen years. In July of 1622 or 1623 he travelled to the colony in the *Samuell*, where he conducted at least some business with John and Richard Stephens and is noted (unmarried) in the 'Lists of the Livinge & the Dead in Virginia' dated 16 February 1624. During this period Menefie handled estate matters for several prominent settlers, including Thomas Hamer, Lieutenant George Harrison, Richard Cornish, John Pountis, and Ralph Hamer. By January 1625 Menefie had erected a house in New Town, on Jamestown Island. In August 1626 he became merchant for the corporation of James City, dealing and buying commodities for them at a flat fee of 12 per cent, and about the same time he set up a forge. He served as a member of the house of burgesses for James City in 1629.

On 5 March 1633 the Dutch sea captain David Piertersz de Vries records landing at Littleton:

> where there resided a great merchant, named Mr. Menifit, who kept us to dinner, and treated us very well. … Here was a garden of one morgen, full of Provence roses, apple, pear, and cherry trees, the various fruits of Holland, with different kinds of sweet-smelling herbs, such as rosemary, sage, marjoram, and thyme. Around the house were plenty of peach-trees, which were hardly in blossom. I was astonished to see this kind of tree, which I had never seen before on this coast. (de Vries, 50)

Menefie, along with Dr John Pott, was responsible for bringing a minister, Anthony Panton, over from England, perhaps suggesting a streak of religious independence.

By 1635 Menefie had married Elizabeth (whose surname may have been Booker or possibly Clements). In this year he was appointed to the governor's council. This group was drawn into a power struggle with Sir John Harvey, fuelled by the governor's own prickly personality, his perceived favouritism toward Maryland's Roman Catholic settlers, and his restriction of land grants based on 'headrights'. The flashpoint came when the governor had three dissidents arrested and wished to try them under martial law. At a council meeting in May 1635 Menefie was asked by Harvey 'What … they deserve, that have gone about, to persuade the people from their obedience to his Majesty's substitute?'. Menefie replied that he was 'but a young lawyer and dare not upon the sudden deliver his opinion' (Neill, 116). A moderate in the power struggle, Menefie initially 'did absolutely refuse his aide' in plans to arrest the governor:

> alleadging reasons that it was not fitt to deale soe wth his Maties substitute; hee went not home as he said, but to the back river where hee debated wth himselfe, desiringe of God to confirm his resolucon or abolish it, but the losse of the Country sticking in his stomacke at last hee came, resolved as the rest. (Neill, 119)

> The next day the Governor demanded of the Counsell if they had knowledge of … the peoples grievances. Mr. Minifie .. answered that their chiefest grievance was the not sending the answer of the late Assembly by theire agents chosen, to which the Governor rising from his place replied, do you say soe? I arrest you upon suspicion of treason to his Majesty, whereupon Captain Uty and Captain Mathewes both of the Counsell layd hands on the Governor using these words, 'and we you upon suspicion of treason to his Majesty.' (Sainsbury, 304)

Governor Harvey returned to England to lodge a complaint, while Menefie profited by his absence by claiming 60 headrights (half for black people brought from England) and securing the 1200 acre Rich Neck tract based on 24 other headrights (including one East Indian and one Turk). Harvey, however, succeeded in having Menefie removed from the council of state by February 1637 and summoned to England to appear before the Star Chamber. The passage to London, with five friends, Menefie's daughter Elizabeth, and 222 hogsheads of tobacco, was undertaken in a leaky vessel called the *Flower de Luce*. In testimony to the high court of admiralty taken in August 1637 Menefie recalls that the passengers and company had to pump the vessel day and night, while John Castle, the gunner's mate, swore that he had heard the merchant 'say he would give his whole estate that was in the ship so that he and his child were ashore' (PRO, ADM 13/53, fols. 312–14).

Menefie, who resided in the parish of St Helen during this stay, petitioned the king in July 1637, requesting leave to return to:

> his plantation and the managing of his factories [or] not only he but all his principalls whose estates to a great value depend upon him shall be sustained of wellnigh irretrievable losses, and so all the fruits of his long, hard and ingenuous labours will be lost.

He describes himself as 'agent for many men's estates residing in England' and notes that he 'ever did and still doth aim at nothing but the support of himself and family' and has 'paid to your Matie. great sums of money for Tobacco imported into England' (PRO, SP Col. 16/323). Leave to return was granted on 29 September upon payment of £1000 security, and by February 1638 Menefie had arrived back in the colony with a number of servants.

Two months later Menefie was selected to travel to England aboard the *Dove*, with tobacco to obtain workmen to erect a state house—a move, one suspects, not entirely unrelated to Governor Harvey's desire to have him out of the colony. By January 1639 Menefie had returned to Virginia (again aboard the *Dove*). His second wife was Izabella, *née* Smith, the widow of William Perry (and, previously, of Richard Pace). After Sir Francis Wyatt replaced Harvey as governor in November 1639, Menefie was restored to his position on the council of state. He bought and sold a great deal of property during the period 1638–42, disposing of some 2000 acres around Rich Neck to Secretary Kemp, but obtaining 6000 acres in the York River area through the exercise of headrights, acquiring Yorke plantation through a mortgage from Harvey, and augmenting the Buckland property of his stepson Henry Perry with other headrights. In August 1640 Menefie was recalled to London along with others to answer the Star Chamber suit, but he escaped punishment owing to the ill health of Harvey and the abolition of that court in August 1641. Menefie returned to Virginia and participated in the work of the governor's council in 1642 and 1644. In 1645, after the massacre by Native Americans of the previous April, Acting-Governor Kemp selected Menefie as one of two commissioners to purchase powder and shot to protect Virginia against them. Menefie's will, dated 31 December 1645, was probated in Charles City county on 20 January 1646 and in London on 25 February 1647, suggesting that he died in Virginia. He left a third wife, Mary, as executor, and was buried in the parish church of Weston, possibly in England, the county being uncertain.

SAMUEL PYEATT MENEFEE

Sources V. F. Meyer and J. F. Dorman, revs., *Adventurers of purse and person: Virginia, 1607–1624/5*, 3rd edn (1987), 199, 447–9 · E. D. Neill, *Virginia Carolorum: the colony under the rule of Charles I and II* (1886) · D. P. de Vries, *Voyages from Holland to America, AD 1632 to 1644*, trans. H. C. Murphy (1853); repr. (1971), 50 [repr. 1971] · W. N. Sainsbury, ed., 'Virginia in 1635: the deposing of Governor Harvey', *Virginia Magazine of History and Biography*, 8 (1900–01), 299–306 · H. R. McIlwain, ed., *Minutes of the council and general court of colonial Virginia* (1924) · N. M. Nugent and D. R. Hudgins, eds., *Cavaliers and pioneers: abstracts of Virginia land patents and grants, 1623–1800*, 1–3 (1934–79) · PRO, SP 16/323, fols. 136–9 · PRO, ADM 13/53, fols. 295–8, 312–14 · PRO, PROB 10/672 · will, PRO, PROB 11/199, sig. 31 · PRO, CO 1/3, fols. 63, 210 · D. O. Shilton and R. Holworthy, *High court of admiralty examinations (MS vol. 53): 1637–1638* (1932), 142, 150, 235–6 · P. W. Coldham, *English adventurers and emigrants, 1609–1660: abstracts of examinations in the high court of admiralty, with reference to colonial America* (1984), 50, 78, 80, 99–101 · W. W. Hening, ed., *The statutes at large: being a collection of all the laws of Virginia, from the first session of the legislature in the year 1619*, 2nd edn, 1 (1823); repr. (1969)
Archives PRO, high court of admiralty records, ADM 13/53 · PRO, state papers, SP 14, SP 16
Wealth at death see will, PRO, PROB 11/199, sig. 31; inventory, PRO, PROB 10/672

Menelaus, William (1818–1882), engineer and iron and steel manufacturer, was born in East Lothian on 10 March 1818. Little is known about his family background except that his father was a writer to the signet at Edinburgh, and his mother's maiden name was Darling. He was probably educated locally, and apprenticed to a millwright or to a firm of engineers at Haddington. On 26 August 1852, in Aberdâr, he married Margaret Janet, the second daughter of Jenkin Rhys of the Llwydcoed ironworks, but she died just ten weeks later in November 1852, possibly of cholera. Menelaus did not remarry but, childless himself, he brought up and educated two nephews: William Darling, who became a law lord, and Charles Darling, who became an MP and later a baron.

Menelaus came to south Wales in 1844 to remodel a corn mill for Rowland Fothergill of Hensol Park, who persuaded him to stay and eventually manage Fothergill's ironworks at Llwydcoed and Aber-nant. Around 1850 he was induced by Sir John Guest—offering, it was said, to double his salary to £600 a year—to join the Dowlais Iron Company, where, in early 1851, he became the engineer-manager of the mills and forges department. It was a risky time to join the company: the enterprise had been paralysed through most of the 1840s by the long failure to agree terms for the renewal of its lease; and when this was settled in 1848, stagnation continued because of the long illness of Guest, virtually the sole owner. There was some revival under the management by his widow, Lady Charlotte Guest, but a decade's neglect had taken a heavy toll. The real climb came after Lady Charlotte's remarriage in 1855 when overall control fell to the chief trustee, G. T. Clark, who then appointed Menelaus as general manager.

It was a remarkably successful combination: Clark as, in effect, managing director looking after overall strategy, and Menelaus in operational control. Menelaus astutely insisted on weekly reports on physical and financial performance from all departments. As well as this managerial data, he also ensured firsthand knowledge of production by daily walks through the extensive and exposed works. He and Clark explicitly based their main decisions on long-run considerations: the spurning of short-run profit maximization in favour of investment for long-run growth infused his magisterial 1857 report on the state of the Dowlais works. He was also responsible for another landmark report in 1861 pressing the case for Dowlais to enter the coal trade. And it was Menelaus who went to Spain in October 1871 to negotiate a long-run source of cheaper ores, culminating in the launching of the Orcenario Iron Ore Company in 1873, jointly owned by Dowlais, Consett, and Krupps. It paid off: from being close to closure in the mid-1850s and in a period when most of the other works—even the Crawshays of Cyfarthfa—failed, or slid into decline, Dowlais profits between 1863 and 1882 averaged nearly £120,000.

The success derived from innovation as well as organization. Menelaus invented several mechanical handling devices and designed the massive new two-directional Goat mill for iron rolling. He fostered the famous 1860s Bessemer experiments in steel making at Dowlais and quickly adopted the Siemens furnace: in the early 1870s Dowlais was already becoming a significant steel maker, with six Bessemer converters and four Siemens open-hearth furnaces. By the time of Menelaus's death Dowlais had substantially effected the difficult transition from iron to steel. He used small coal, a waste product, in the furnaces, releasing the large coal for the lucrative steam coal trade; he exploded the entrenched belief in long blast furnace campaigns by demonstrating that old worn-out furnaces were merely vehicles for destroying fuel; and in 1870 he was first to use the waste gas from the coking ovens to fuel the furnaces.

Menelaus took little part in local public life, although he was a lieutenant in the Dowlais works volunteer force and supported Sir W. T. Lewis in his unsuccessful attempt in 1880 to become Conservative MP for Merthyr. His public activities were mostly related to his professional enthusiasms. He was the driving force of the 1857 meeting at the Castle Hotel, Merthyr, which led to the foundation of the South Wales Institute of Civil Engineers, of which he was the first president. Similarly, he took the chair at the 1886 meeting at the Queen's Hotel, Birmingham, which led to the founding of the Iron and Steel Institute of Great Britain, and was its president from 1875 to 1877. In 1881 Menelaus was awarded the Bessemer medal. He also appeared before numerous parliamentary committees dealing with iron, coal, and the railways, and his evidence usually related to ways of reducing costs. With Dowlais 1000 feet above sea level and with raw materials increasingly coming in as well as products going out, he saw transport as particularly crucial: 'we shall not make large profits in coal, until we have a more direct road to Cardiff', he reported to Clark (Owen, 79). At his death he was said to have been responsible for all the existing rail connections to Dowlais, and he also fought for cheaper freights, being, as he told a select committee in 1881, 'strong enough to fight the railway companies ourselves' ('Select committee … conveyance of goods'). Although active in the South Wales Coalowners' Association—formed primarily to present a united front in dealing with the workmen—Menelaus's opposition to any 'artificial' price-fixing bordered on the mystical: supply and demand constituted 'a law of God's providence' (*Western Mail*, 31 March 1882).

By the 1880s Menelaus's salary was reputed to be £3500 p.a., while he had personally invested in several large coal and iron enterprises. All this was not to support an ostentatious lifestyle; indeed, his only extravagance seems to have been collecting works of art, which were said to fill his home in Merthyr. He was severe and autocratic at the works to which he came as 'a tall, strong handsome man' (*South Wales Daily News*, 31 March 1882) and was later characterized by his long, black hair and 'thoughtful face and piercing eye' (ibid.).

Menelaus died, after a lengthy illness, on 30 March 1882 at Charlton House, High Street, Tenby, Pembrokeshire. He had previously given part of his valuable art collection, which consisted of thirty-six items valued at £10,000, to Cardiff Free Library. He was buried on 4 April 1882 in a secluded spot in the mountain churchyard of Penderyn, near Merthyr, in the same brick grave that had already held his wife for thirty years.　　　JOHN WILLIAMS

Sources *South Wales Daily News* (31 March 1882) · *South Wales Daily News* (5 April 1882) · *Western Mail* [Cardiff] (31 March 1882) · L. J. Williams, 'Menelaus, William', *DBB* · M. J. Lewis, 'G. T. Clark and the Dowlais Iron Company: an entrepreneurial study', MSc Econ diss., U. Wales, 1983 · C. Wilkins, *The history of Merthyr Tydfil*, [new edn] (1908) · J. A. Owen, *The history of the Dowlais iron works, 1759–1970* (1977) · J. P. Addis, *The Crawshay dynasty: a study in industrial organisation and development, 1765–1867* (1957) · C. Wilkins, *The history of the iron, steel, tinplate, and other trades of Wales* (1903) · J. H. Morris and L. J. Williams, *The south Wales coal industry, 1841–1875* (1958) · 'Royal commission to inquire into … coal in the United Kingdom: general minutes and proceedings of committees', *Parl. papers* (1871), 18.219–20, C. 435-I · L. Ince, *The south Wales iron industry, 1750–1885* (1993) · *Cardiff and Merthyr Guardian* (3 Sept 1852) · 'Select committee to inquire into charges … for conveyance of goods', *Parl. papers* (1881), 13.622–7, no. 374

Archives Glamorgan RO, Cardiff, Dowlais MSS · NL Wales, Clark MSS

Wealth at death £193,290 1s. 8d.: resworn probate, Dec 1882, *CGPLA Eng. & Wales*

Menken, Adah Isaacs (1835?–1868), actress and poet, is thought to have been born on 15 June 1835 in New Orleans. At various times in her life she produced different versions of her parentage, giving her father's name as James McCord, Richard Spencer, Ricardo La Fiertes (or Fuertes), and James Campbell. Her mother was stated to be either Creole or Jewish of Franco-Spanish descent. W. Mankowitz, in his 'biographic quest' entitled *Mazeppa* (1982), has shown that her most likely maiden name was Ada Berthe Théodore and that her father was probably a wheelwright, probably called Auguste Théodore, a 'free man of colour', living in New Orleans, and that her mother was a

Adah Isaacs Menken (1835?–1868), by Sarony & Co.

native of Pensacola, possibly called Magdaleine Jean Louis Janneaux. She and her half-sister later appeared in a dancing act as 'The Sisters Theodore', which gives some credence to this conjecture. Further mystery surrounds her early life and, if the attribution of the name is correct, it is probable that she married a composer, W. H. Kneass, in Galveston, Texas, on 6 February 1855, during which year she was already giving readings from Shakespeare, advertised in the *Liberty Gazette*. 'Ada Theodore' also published three poems and some liberationist pieces on the situation of women in that journal. On 23 November 1855 another poem, 'New Advertisement', written from Austin, proclaimed her wish to find a 'beau idéal'. It is possible that this poem could have been seen by Alexander Isaac Menken, then a pit musician and conductor, from a wealthy Jewish Cincinnati dry goods family, who eventually married Ada on 3 April 1856 at Livingston, Polk, Texas. She then became Adah Isaacs (adding an 'h' to her own and an 's' to her husband's name) Menken, under which name she performed on the stage for the rest of her life. Mr Kneass was apparently conveniently forgotten.

Adah Menken's first recorded stage appearance was with the amateur Crescent Dramatic Association of New Orleans in 1856. She was then taken on for leading parts by James S. Charles for his stock company, touring Texan towns. Poems and articles were also written for the *New Orleans Sunday Delta* and the *Cincinnati Israelite*, some dated in Hebrew, and Adah was accepted into the Cincinnati Jewish community. Meanwhile her husband had become her agent, and he booked her for Dayton, Ohio, in her own version of the Jack Sheppard story, *Sixteen-String Jack*, which was an immediate success, especially with the local militia. Adah had ambitions to try her luck in New York and, leaving Menken behind for ever, went there in 1859 to play Widow Cheerly in Andrew Cherry's *The Soldier's Daughter*. Here she met and married, thinking herself divorced by rabbinical diploma, on 3 September 1859, John Carmel Heenan, 'the Benicia Boy', a prizefighter also looking for public recognition. Scandal followed her when Alexander Menken announced that, although he was currently seeking a divorce, at the time of the Heenan marriage Adah was still his wife. Heenan left for an important contest in England and returned with another woman on his arm, Adah meanwhile having suffered a miscarriage. A further divorce took place in November 1861.

Menken consorted with the literati and toured Milwaukee, Detroit, Albany, and Chicago in *The Soldier's Daughter*, Douglas Jerrold's *Black-Eyed Susan*, and J. T. Haines's *The French Spy*, plays which she repeated throughout her life. Her greatest success everywhere, however, was as the hero of H. M. Milner's *Mazeppa*, based on Byron's poem, at the climax of which she appeared strapped to a running horse and clad to give the appearance of nakedness. Captain John B. Smith launched this play on 7 June 1861 at the Green Street Theatre, Albany, where it was enthusiastically received; the exposure of the actress's shapely body and the scandalized pleasure it evoked only enhanced the popularity of the piece. Her press manager at this time and for the rest of her life was Edwin James of the *New York Clipper*, whom she addressed as 'brother' and to whom she wrote regularly. The play transferred to the Broadway Theatre, opening on 13 June. On 24 September 1862 she married again; her new husband was Robert Henry Newell, the literary editor of the New York *Sunday Mercury*, but she found that his expectations of her retirement to domestic bliss in Jersey City did not conform with her own, and she left for New York after a week. She then resumed her stage career in Baltimore, giving some anxiety to her manager through her Confederate leanings. But she had set her heart on appearances in California, which she hoped would lead to an engagement in London. *Mazeppa* was again sold out at the Opera House in San Francisco and in Sacramento; Newell was present and seeking reconciliation, and she was again surrounded by writers such as Mark Twain and Bret Harte. Adah then bought a brownstone house in New York, at 458 Seventh Avenue. James managed to arrange an engagement at Astley's Amphitheatre in London, though at a much lower salary than that to which Adah was by now accustomed, and she set

sail for England on 3 April 1864, having in the meantime organized a divorce from Newell.

Adah Menken first settled in London at Bunyard's Private Hotel in Norfolk Street, but soon moved to a suite at the Westminster Palace Hotel, where she prepared for the opening night of *Mazeppa* on 3 October. Her appearance garnered mixed notices, but during the run (which lasted until December) she became accepted by bohemian society and held court at her 'literary salon' at the hotel. Paris beckoned, and Menken departed, armed with introductions from Charles Fechter to Gautier and Alexandre Dumas *père* but no theatrical engagement eventuated. On her return to London a provincial tour was arranged, to Glasgow, Liverpool, and Leeds, of *The Children of the Sun*, a poor play written for her by the American actor John Brougham. By October 1865 she had another lover, 'Captain' James Paul Barkley, a handsome, wealthy American addicted to gambling, whom she had probably met on the boat coming to England and whom she entertained in her house, 255 Brompton Road. When he fell ill in New York she returned there, and appeared again in *Mazeppa* at the Broadway Theatre with a guaranteed $12,000 for twenty-four performances. When she found herself pregnant, she married Barkley, on 19 August 1866. The marriage lasted for three days. Menken then departed again for Paris without her husband. There is no record of the birth, probably in November 1866, of their son, Louis Dudevant Victor Emmanuel, whose godmother was George Sand, and reports vary as to whether he died in that same year or was adopted by an English family and his name changed. Menken's stay in Paris was notorious both for her affair with Alexandre Dumas *père* and for her mute role in *The Pirates of the Savannah*. A disastrous visit to Vienna later in 1867 followed, where she was the victim of antisemitism, an account of which, since admitted to be fabricated, is contained in Samuel Edwards's (Gerson) *Queen of the Plaza* (1964). By the autumn Menken was in London pursuing the publication of a collection of her poems entitled *Infelicia*, dedicated to Dickens. A strange affair with Algernon Charles Swinburne soon began, and Menken is said to be the 'Dolorida' in his poem of that name. *Mazeppa* was again put on at Sadler's Wells, the last performance being on 30 May 1868. Menken then accepted an offer to appear in Paris, preceded by a holiday at Le Havre, since she was depressed and exhausted by the London engagement, in the course of which she had been involved in a stage accident, and was probably already suffering from cancer. She became ill during rehearsals for *The Pirates* and died on 10 August 1868, attended by a rabbi and a devoted servant in a hotel in the rue Caumartin. She had insisted that the Orthodox embargo on a post-mortem be observed, and various rumours circulated as to the cause of her death—tuberculosis, peritonitis, or cancer. She was buried in the Jewish section of the Père Lachaise cemetery but later transferred by Edwin James, with a donation from Barkley, to the cemetery at Montparnasse, where a stone was erected bearing her desired enigmatical inscription, 'Thou knowest'.   J. GILLILAND

Sources W. Mankowitz, *Mazeppa* (1982) · B. Falk, *The naked lady* (1934) · S. D'Amico, ed., *Enciclopedia dello spettacolo*, 11 vols. (Rome, 1954–68) · W. S. Meadmore, *Adah Isaacs Menken* (1938) · H. Wyndham, *Victorian sensations* (1933) · P. Larousse, ed., *Grand dictionnaire universel du XIXe siècle*, 17 vols. (Paris, 1866–90) · M. Banham, ed., *The Cambridge guide to world theatre* (1988) · *The life and reminiscences of E. L. Blanchard, with notes from the diary of Wm. Blanchard*, ed. C. W. Scott and C. Howard, 2 vols. (1891) · *ILN* (22 Oct 1864) · S. Edwards [N. B. Gerson], *The queen of the plaza* (1964) · R. Dillon, *Great expectations—the story of Benicia, Calif.* (1976?) · A. I. Menken, preface, *Infelicia* (1888) · *Era Almanack and Annual* (1868) · personal knowledge (1894) [*DNB*]

Likenesses lithograph, *c*.1864, V&A · C. Reutlinger, carte-de-visite (as Mazeppa), NPG · Sarony & Co., photograph, NPG [*see illus.*] · photographs (with Dumas and Swinburne) · portrait, repro. in *Infelicia* · reproductions, repro. in Mankowitz, *Mazeppa* · sixteen lithographs and watercolours, Harvard TC

Menmuir. For this title name *see* Lindsay, John, of Balcarres, Lord Menmuir (1552–1598).

Mennes, Sir John (1599–1671), naval officer, was born at Sandwich, Kent, on 1 March 1599, the second son of Andrew Mennes and Jane, daughter of John Blechenden. The Mennes family was armigerous and had long been prominent in Sandwich, where both his grandfather Matthew and Matthew's elder brother Thomas had been several times mayor. Mennes was educated at the local grammar school, but while his intellectual accomplishments seem to imply a university education the supposition (derived from Wood) that he went on to Corpus Christi College, Oxford, cannot be reconciled with the college records, since the John Mynne admitted gentleman commoner there in 1615 was the son of a knight. Whatever the case he had gone to sea by his early twenties, for in 1620 he took part in a six-hour battle off Dominica in which the *Margaret and John*, taking passengers to Virginia, fought off two Spanish warships. The captain, James Chester, is said to have been Mennes's father-in-law, a term then used for a stepfather; alternatively it could indicate an early marriage. Mennes had already served in the English Channel under Sir William Monson and subsequently commanded the king's ship *Seahorse*. These details were given by Sir Alexander Brett in recommending Mennes for further service in April 1626.

In home waters As a young man Mennes was seemingly quarrelsome, but soon established himself as a reliable officer. On 23 November 1628 he was appointed to captain the *Adventure* and convoyed a fleet to Glückstadt. On his return with a prize he was instructed to cruise the channel looking for further ships to capture, and was praised for 'discreet and stout carriage' in taking a Hamburger sailing under Dutch colours (*CSP dom.*, *1628–9*, 524). He was frequently employed in taking ambassadors and other distinguished travellers across the channel. On 24 May 1629 he brought 'a gentleman' from the Netherlands at the king's invitation (ibid., 557); this was Rubens. It is fanciful to suppose that Mennes's interest in painting dated from this mission, though he was doubtless chosen for this and similar duties because of his social as well as professional competence. His elder brother, Matthew, had been made knight of the Bath at Charles I's coronation. When

Sir John Mennes (1599–1671), attrib. Sir Anthony Van Dyck, *c*.1640

Mennes was suggested for another command by Sir Henry Mervyn in 1630, it was in the hope of having a captain who had passed his 'a,b,c' (*CSP dom.*, *1629–31*, 343). The bailiffs of Yarmouth specifically requested Mennes for fishery protection duty, which he undertook in autumn 1630. On 11 December following he was appointed as captain of the *Garland* to patrol the channel; his lieutenant was his younger brother Andrew. In 1631 he sent Secretary Nicholas a manuscript by Monson which he thought of relevance to current naval concerns, and in 1633 it was rumoured he would be sent to the East Indies. On 30 March 1635 he was given command of the *Red Lion* and applied to have his brother again as lieutenant. On 7 October he was moved to the *Vanguard*, and by the 14th was named vice-admiral in the channel. On 13 March 1636 he was made captain of the *Convertine*; there was some question of his entitlement to this command over the claims of another officer, but he was in post by 18 May. In March 1637 he returned to the *Vanguard*, and in November he took up the captaincy of Walmer Castle. On 15 April 1638 he became captain of the *Nonsuch* and in May was deputed to carry an ambassador to Spain. On 5 March 1639 he was appointed to the *Victory*, in which he continued for the summer.

In 1640 Mennes temporarily left the sea, being appointed on 22 February to command a troop of Carabiniers in the war against the Scots. On 28 April he arrived at Newcastle, and continued in the north throughout the year. On 16 December he was promoted to command two troops of Wilmot's regiment, leaving York the following day to fetch a consignment of the money being paid to the Scottish army of occupation. In January 1641 he was back at York where by 9 February he had married and set up house with Jane (d. 1662), daughter of Thomas Liddell of Ravensworth, co. Durham, and widow of Robert Anderson.

In August 1641 Mennes was ordered to receive the king at Doncaster and on the 18th his regiment was disbanded as part of the general demilitarization of the north-east. In 1642 he was back in the navy and on 23 February, as captain of the *Lion*, was entrusted with taking the queen over to the Netherlands. Having landed Henrietta Maria at Helvoetsluys he returned at once; the king had waited at Dover for news of the queen's safe landfall, and when Mennes was able to report this on 25 February he was knighted. On 26 April he had orders to press men for the summer guard and on 1 May was named rear-admiral. He had originally been posted to the *St George*, but it was as captain of the *Victory* that he refused to acquiesce in the parliamentary takeover of the fleet on 2 July. He had, according to Clarendon, been ashore with Warwick, who refused to let him return to his own ship but took him aboard the flagship and tried to induce him to join the rebels. On his refusal, he was put ashore (Clarendon, *Hist. rebellion*, 2.218). However, the exchange of letters between Warwick and Mennes indicates that the latter, having on 2 July received the king's command to refuse Warwick's orders, had not attended aboard the *James* and was consequently told of his 'discharge' on 4 July (Powell and Timings, 15–17).

Army service Since the king no longer had a navy Mennes transferred to the army. In 1643 he was general of artillery in Lord Capel's forces in the north-west, based at Shrewsbury. In February 1644 he complained he could do no useful service because of the 'insulting people' and for lack of money; his own revenues were detained by the rebels or such of his tenants 'as have forgot to pay' (Warburton, 2.371–2). By June 1644 he had been appointed by Rupert as governor of north Wales, with headquarters at Beaumaris. Again he did his best with limited resources of men and money, and in the face of rivalry from the archbishop of York, Williams, who had taken upon himself the role of saviour of the king's cause in those parts. Williams inveighed against Mennes and Dudley Wyatt as 'sharks and children of fortune' (*CSP dom.*, *1644–5*, 405).

In May 1645 Mennes replaced Pennington as the king's nominal vice-admiral. With the revolt of 1648 the king had a fighting fleet once more and Mennes resumed service afloat, though losing his flag. He also lost his estates—chiefly property in Bedfordshire inherited from his recently dead elder brother—sequestered by parliament. When Rupert's squadron left Helvoetsluys in January 1649 Mennes was captain of the *Swallow*, in which he led a successful detachment in search of prizes. He then sailed with the rest of the royalist fleet to Lisbon. In 1650, while the ships were still in the Tagus, Mennes left to attach himself to the exiled court, with which he remained until the Restoration. He served principally as a secret agent (and since little is known of his activities he would seem to

have been effective); in March 1655 he was sent from Cologne, where the king was, to Flushing to monitor the posts. Mennes also acted as medical adviser to the exiled cavaliers, being an amateur venerealogist. He doubtless played a part in the negotiations for the king's return, since he was friendly with Arnold Braems, a Dover merchant with contacts with Lawson and Montagu and who was one of the king's intermediaries in 1659.

Comptroller of the navy At the Restoration Mennes was appointed a gentleman of the privy chamber. He petitioned for and received the return of the captaincy of Walmer, though he resigned by April 1663 after complaining of the costs involved. In March 1661 he and Robert Phillips, a groom of the bedchamber, sued for a reversion of the site of Cannington Priory in Somerset which was granted to them in August. Mennes had meanwhile been down to Chatham on 10 April 1661 to inspect the *Henry*, already designated his flagship. On 18 May he was formally commissioned vice-admiral in the narrow seas for the summer. While serving in this capacity he was named to succeed Slingsby as comptroller of the navy and he left the fleet on 30 October. He took his seat at the Navy Board on 2 November and his patent passed the great seal on the 28th. His junior colleague Pepys welcomed him as 'a good fair-conditioned man' (Pepys, *Diary*, 2.206), but he and others soon came to recognize the appointment as disastrous. Mennes wholly lacked the qualities of mind and application which the comprehensive duties of the comptroller demanded. Initially he retained his command, and on 16 November he delegated his office work to Penn. On 15 January 1662 he sailed for Tangier, delivering Lord Peterborough there as governor on the 29th. He then joined up with Sandwich in Lisbon and together they brought Catherine of Braganza to England as queen. Mennes had custody of the jewel chest; presumably the 'great Portugal jewel' of 180 diamonds set in gold, which he would bequeath, was a legitimate acquisition on this service. He returned to the Downs in May, having completed his last voyage.

Mennes had been suspicious of Sandwich as a former Cromwellian, and had warned the king that the fleet was not safe in his hands. But these fears proved groundless and Sandwich at least was disposed to be friendly. Mennes's true friends, however, were those like Clarendon and Carteret who shared his unwavering affection to the crown. Mennes became a member of the council for foreign plantations in 1661, master of Trinity House in 1661–2, a member of the Tangier committee from 1662, and a founder assistant of the Royal Fishery Company in 1664.

Declining years Criticisms of Mennes as incompetent, incoherent, and vacillating abound in Pepys's diary and white book. His frustration with the 'old dotard' (who was in poor health from 1663) was coloured by some hope of succeeding him. But dissatisfaction with the comptroller was general, and repeated attempts were made to remove him to a sinecure, or at least delegate his key duties. When in November 1663 Pepys proposed taking on some of these himself, Sir William Coventry warned that Mennes would react 'as a dog in a manger' (Pepys, *Diary*, 4.398). When the matter was generally aired at the board in January 1664 Mennes would have none of it. During the Second Anglo-Dutch War, although Mennes was as busy as his health allowed, he became 'every day less and less capable' (ibid., 7.76). In August 1666 he was reported to be dying, and Pepys prematurely composed his epitaph: 'a very good, harmless, honest gentleman, though not fit for the business' (ibid., 7.255). Mennes, however, recovered. It was then proposed that he be made a commissioner-at-large, with Penn and Lord Brouncker as joint comptrollers. This was achieved only in part. By an order in council of 16 January 1667 Brouncker was to assist Mennes in the treasurer's accounts, and Penn with those of victuallers and pursers. Mennes pretended that this was his own idea, but his discontent was plain.

This was still unsatisfactory for Pepys and Coventry, who continued to call for Mennes's complete removal from the board, which they felt could not function properly while he sat there. Indeed Coventry ruefully suggested that the king would have been better served in the war by giving Mennes £1000 per annum 'to have sat still' (Pepys, *Diary*, 8.571). In March 1668 there were rumours that Mennes might actually survive a general purge of the Navy Board, prompting Pepys to observe that his dotage and folly did the king more hurt 'than all the rest can do by their knavery if they had a mind to it' (ibid., 9.100). Ranks were closed when Pepys, Mennes, and others from the Navy Office stood before the bar of the Commons on 5 March, when Pepys's oratory saved the day. But a month later Pepys was resolved to do something about Mennes 'before it be long' (ibid., 9.151). In January 1669 Pepys and Brouncker raised the issue with the duke of York, who promised to speak to the king. Pepys reminded the duke of this during an audience on 2 April, and was assured 'that he had so often spoke of it to the King ... that he cannot doubt his Majesty's remembering it whenever there shall be occasion' (*Samuel Pepys and the Second Dutch War*, 192). Pepys then recommended that Brouncker should be given a further share of the comptroller's work. But Matthew Wren, the duke's secretary, contrived to restrict the matter to the accounts of Sir William Warren, for fear of discouragement to one who had served the king so long. The truth was that Mennes was well befriended at court (though after 1667 he was without the sympathetic support of Carteret and Clarendon). There was reluctance to dismiss him when this might seem to acknowledge opposition criticism of the Navy Office's management of the war. These criticisms came to a head when the Brooke House commission's charges were debated before the privy council in January and February 1670. Pepys, who single-handedly defended the board at these proceedings, managed to attribute the greater part of the collective failure to Mennes, while extolling him as 'a gentleman of strictest integrity', worn out in mind and body through service to the king (ibid., 342).

Pepys never let his despair at 'the old fool' diminish his affection for Mennes as a friend, a wit, and a raconteur; he particularly admired his talents as a 'mimique' (Pepys, *Diary*, 7.2) and an improviser in verse. He recalls one memorable evening when Mennes and Evelyn vied with one another in this literary parlour game. Mennes conceded defeat with characteristic generosity: his 'mirth ... to see himself out-done, was the crown of all our mirth' (ibid., 6.220). Mennes was himself a poet, writing in collaboration with Dr James Smith and possibly Sir John Suckling (to whom Mennes had also been an army colleague). These works enjoyed popularity in spite or because of their tending to vulgarity; but the particular quality of Mennes's own contribution cannot be identified. Mennes was a true virtuoso, with medical and scientific interests, and a competent eye for pictures. He was also something of a sexual connoisseur, candid about buggery, teasing about bestiality, though with a personal preference for the simple charms of the women of Bury St Edmunds.

Mennes died, still comptroller of the navy, on 18 February 1671 in London and was buried in St Olave, Hart Street, where a memorial was erected. He was also commemorated in Nonington church, Kent, where his kinsfolk were buried. His second wife had died in 1662 and he had no children. His principal estate—land at Loughton, Essex, and part of the rectory of Goodnesborough, Kent—went to Francis Hammond, son of his dead sister Mary. He made other bequests to his nieces Lady Heath, wife of Sir John Heath of Brasted, Kent, and Jane, wife of Anthony Moyle, and to their children.

The poems Mennes wrote in collaboration with Smith were republished by Thomas Park in 1817 and J. C. Hotten in 1874. Mennes is not to be judged by these trifles, nor by the insufficiency with which he exercised the comptrollership in his last years. He was then most aptly characterized by Coventry as 'like a lapwing; that all he did was to keep a flutter, to keep others from the nest that they would find' (Pepys, *Diary*, 5.313–14). His forty years of active service, involving high command on land and sea, deserve to be remembered more than the frailties of his old age.

C. S. KNIGHTON

Sources G. Callender, 'Sir John Mennes', *Mariner's Mirror*, 26 (1940), 276–85 • PRO, SP 16/24, no. 87 • *CSP dom.*, 1628–71 • T. Raylor, *Cavaliers, clubs and literary culture: Sir John Mennes, James Smith, and the Order of the Fancy* (1994) • Clarendon, *Hist. rebellion*, 2.218, 222, 223; 4.424–5; 5.372 • J. R. Powell and E. K. Timings, eds., *Documents relating to the civil war, 1642–1648*, Navy RS, 105 (1963), ix, 3, 4, 8, 15–18, 137–8 • *Memoirs of Prince Rupert and the cavaliers including their private correspondence*, ed. E. Warburton, 3 vols. (1849), vol. 2, pp. 371–4; vol. 3, pp. 55–6 • *A collection of original letters and papers, concerning the affairs of England from the year 1641 to 1660. Found among the duke of Ormonde's papers*, ed. T. Carte, 1 (1739), 49, 54, 67, 89 • Pepys, *Diary* • *Samuel Pepys and the Second Dutch War: Pepys's navy white book and Brooke House papers*, ed. R. Latham, Navy RS, 133 (1995) [transcribed by W. Matthews and C. Knighton] • J. D. Davies, *Gentlemen and tarpaulins: the officers and men of the Restoration navy* (1991), 123 • PRO, PROB 11/335, fols. 297r–297v • R. Hovenden, ed., *The visitation of Kent, taken in the years 1619–1621*, Harleian Society, 42 (1898), 107
Archives BL, letters, verses, etc.
Likenesses attrib. A. Van Dyck, oils, *c*.1640, priv. coll. [*see illus.*] • attrib. A. Van Dyck, oils, second version, NMM, NPG
Wealth at death modest landholding; £50 p. a. as comptroller: will, PRO, PROB 11/355, fols. 297r–297v

Mennons, John (1747–1818), printer and journal editor, was born on 22 February 1747 in the Canongate parish of Edinburgh, son of John Mennons (1718–1793), baker, and Rebecca Galloway. John junior was apprenticed as a printer, probably with the *Edinburgh Courant*. He set up on his own in 1778 when he published the *Scots and County Magazine*, with the imprint 'J. Mennons & Co., Brodie's Close, Lawnmarket'. Over the next four years he produced a variety of periodicals offering information and entertainment, such as the *Gentleman and Lady's Pocket Register* and the *Weekly Mirror* (assisted in the latter by the balloonist James Tytler). About 1772 he married Janet Moir. A daughter, Janet, was born on 19 January 1773 but died in infancy; she was followed by a son, Thomas (1774–1804), who became his father's business partner.

In 1782 Mennons moved to Glasgow and bought a secondhand press; on 27 January 1783 he published the first issue of a newspaper, the *Glasgow Advertiser*, from Duncan's Land, Gibson's Wynd, in the Saltmarket, claiming, as editors do, to 'preserve his mind as free as possible from any prejudice, which … might lead him to partial representation of the facts'. In fact, Mennons's statement was more than the standard declaration of impartiality, for the *Advertiser* was noteworthy for its independence from political faction.

After the death of his first wife, Mennons married in 1785 Jean Steedman (*d.* 1814), daughter of James Steedman, cutler in Glasgow, and Jean McNair. They had three sons and five daughters; the first son, James, and a daughter, Jean, died young. The surviving daughters—Jane, Mary, Marion, and Agnes—never married. The second son, John (*c.*1786–1843), worked with his father for a while and later was editor of the *Greenock Advertiser*. The third son, another James, died in 1817. By virtue of his second marriage Mennons was admitted burgess and guild brother of Glasgow in 1786. He joined the Stationers' Company in 1786. By 1789 he was established in the Tontine Close, near the Cross, the hub of the busy merchant city. There he accepted 'advertisements, commissions and articles of intelligence'.

In appearance Mennons was stolid and genial. There is no clear evidence of his religion or politics. The *Advertiser* soon proved itself of special service to commerce, while politically generally steering a middle course. However, in 1793 Mennons was indicted for treason, for publishing, on 23 November 1792, a report of a meeting of the Partick Sons of Liberty which declared that if nations adopted Thomas Paine's principles, 'tyrants and their satellites would vanish' (*Glasgow Advertiser*, 23 Nov 1792). The author of the article failed to appear for trial and the matter was dropped, ending this 'disagreeable situation' (*Glasgow Advertiser*, 1 Feb 1793).

Mennons continued to print the kinds of useful publication he had in Edinburgh, including *Jones's Directory* (1787 and 1789), the *Glasgow Almanack* (1784–1802), and the *Glasgow Magazine* (1783–4), as well as selling lottery tickets and patent medicines. In 1797 he bought Jeanfield House, near Camlachie, from his wife's cousin Robert McNair, for

£2435, but sold it a year later to John Finlayson, McNair's brother-in-law.

In 1802 Mennons sold the *Advertiser* and leased Eastmuir coalfield, near Shettleston, owned by Finlayson. This venture failed, and in 1809 he was declared bankrupt. Attempts to return to publishing—the *Western Star* (1807) and *The Scotchman* (1812–13)—also failed. After his wife's death in 1814 he moved to Irvine on the Ayrshire coast and in a small house at 15 High Street, with the help of his children, doggedly started afresh. The *Irvine and County of Ayr Miscellany* (1814–15) proved his swansong. He died at home of old age on 2 February 1818, and was buried in Irvine parish churchyard two days later.

Mennons was no innovator, just one of many entrepreneurs of fluctuating fortune in a city recovering from the American War of Independence. His legacy is the *Glasgow Advertiser*, which became Glasgow's longest-running newspaper under the successive titles the *Herald and Advertiser*, then the *Glasgow Herald*, and then *The Herald*.

HAMISH WHYTE

Sources J. Gourlay, 'Notes on the life of John Mennons', *A history of the Glasgow Herald, 1783–1948*, ed. A. Ewing (1949), 86–100 · J. Gourlay, 'John Mennons: an early Glasgow journalist', *Records of the Glasgow Bibliographic Society*, 8 (1930), 58–72 · *Glasgow Advertiser* (27 Jan 1783) · A. Phillips, *Glasgow's Herald, 1783–1983* (1982) · *The Glasgow Herald: the story of a great newspaper, 1783–1911* (1911)
Likenesses oils, *c.*1940, priv. coll.; repro. in Gourlay, 'John Mennons: an early Glasgow journalist' · oils, priv. coll.; repro. in Gourlay, 'John Mennons: an early Glasgow journalist'

Menon, (Vengalil Krishnan) Krishna (1896–1974), diplomatist and politician, was born on 3 May 1896 at his mother's ancestral house, Vengalil, Calicut, Malabar, south India, the third of the eight children of Komathu Krishnan Kurup (*d.* 1935), only son of the raja of Kartanad and leader of the Tellicherry bar, and his wife, Vengalil Lakshmi Kutty Amma (*d.* 1911), Sanskrit scholar and musician, and daughter of Koothali Nayar, one of Malabar's largest landlords. He was educated at the Native High School, Calicut, and graduated BA from Presidency College, Madras, in 1917. At his father's behest he joined the Madras Law College, but his real interest was in the educational and nationalist political work of Annie Besant's Theosophical Society, and it was with her encouragement that he travelled to Britain in 1924 and took up a job at the theosophists' school at Letchworth. Chiefly to ease his father's disappointment, he studied law in Britain and was finally called to the bar at the Middle Temple in 1934. In the meantime, however, he attended evening classes at the London School of Economics, obtaining a university teaching diploma in 1926, a first-class BSc in politics in 1927, and an MSc in politics in 1934. In 1930 he graduated as an MA in psychology from University College, London.

Menon planned initially to return to India to build a network of vernacular schools, but his years in London drew him into radical politics and journalism, especially propaganda for Indian independence. By late 1931 he had turned the timid Commonwealth of India League into the militant India League, and he gradually rallied a host of prominent personalities and Labour politicians to the call for immediate independence, among them Harold Laski, Bertrand Russell, Marie Seton, Barbara Castle, Stafford Cripps, Michael Foot, and the opera singer Emily (Anna) Polak, who was a particularly close and supportive friend. The league was run on a shoestring budget, dependent almost entirely on Menon's own scanty finances, but had some noteworthy successes, including its exposé of police brutality in India during Gandhi's civil disobedience movements in 1930–32. Menon travelled to India in 1932 as secretary to the league's fact-finding mission and oversaw the publication of its report, *The Condition of India* (1933), for which Eric Gill provided the cover and Bertrand Russell the preface.

In 1934 Menon, who lived in a St Pancras garret, was elected as a Labour member of the St Pancras borough council, a seat he held for fourteen years. As the dynamic, tireless chairman of the education and library committee he hugely improved the borough's library and arts services, especially their provision for children. In 1955 he was made a freeman of the borough. At the time of his election he was editing the Twentieth Century Library for Bodley Head, but in 1935 he left this job to help Allen Lane found Penguin Books. He was the brains behind the Pelican series of educational texts, but he fell out with Lane shortly after its launch in 1937 and thereafter credit for its success was claimed by the adult educationist W. E. (Bill) Williams. Menon's difficulties with Lane were partly the result of personal crisis. In 1935 his father had died and his long engagement to Barbara Macnamara, an India League volunteer twelve years his junior, had collapsed, apparently at her instigation. After years of overwork and semi-starvation on a diet of tea and unbuttered toast, Menon had a nervous breakdown and was hospitalized throughout the summer of 1935. He emerged from hospital heavily dependent on medication, unable to walk without a stick, and having lost much of the wit and spontaneity which had previously leavened his acerbic, austere character. Tall and perilously thin, with aristocratic, hawk-like features, he remained devastatingly attractive to women, but he was rarely to form trusting friendships after his illness. One exception to this was Jawaharlal Nehru, for whom, even in this year of crisis, Menon managed to co-ordinate a highly successful visit to London. Both atheists and sharing a background of Fabian socialism, the two men became intimate friends and allies, unswervingly loyal to each other and to the goal of a modern, secular Indian state.

The Second World War pulled Menon two ways: as a councillor and St Pancras air warden he was actively involved in the war effort, but as a spokesman for Indian aspirations he had to explain to the British public why the Indian National Congress was refusing to co-operate. In 1940 his long service to the Labour Party was rewarded with pre-selection for the safe seat of Dundee, but he was forced to surrender it on the grounds of his primary loyalty to India. This was a personal tragedy for Menon, as he was better suited to the British political arena than the Indian one. Bitterly disappointed, he resigned from the

Labour Party, but rejoined it in 1944 when, partly through his influence, it adopted a resolution demanding freedom for India.

In 1947 Nehru appointed Menon the first high commissioner for independent India in London. In spite of mutterings in Whitehall Menon proved to be a good choice; he was determined that India should stay in the Commonwealth, and the formula reconciling a republican constitution to Commonwealth membership owed much to his influence. He brought style and a confidence-bolstering grandeur to the high commission, but his volatile temper and sharp tongue often ruffled egos, and in 1952 his tenure was terminated in a furore over army jeep purchases. Soon after, however, he was appointed deputy leader and then leader of the Indian delegation to the United Nations, where he championed the cause of non-alignment and asserted the importance of African and Asian nations. He helped solve the deadlock over the issue of US prisoners of war in Korea and won respect as a mediator in the crises in Indo-China and Cyprus. The US characterized him as a communist stooge, especially after his refusal to condemn outright the Soviet intervention in Hungary, but Menon refused to be drawn into either of the cold war blocs. He attacked the Western powers on the issue of colonialism, but not out of any slavish adherence to dogma; indeed, had the British government accepted his plan to resolve the Suez crisis in 1956, it would probably have salvaged more of its interests than it gained by force.

Nehru aside, many of India's politicians disliked and were afraid of Menon, who refused to make any concessions to the emergence of regional, sectarian, and caste interests in Indian politics. Hostile to the imposition of Hindi as a national language and fluent only in English, he would have been an unlikely candidate for election had not his stirring defence in the UN of India's stand on Kashmir and Goa turned him into a national hero. In 1953 he was elected to the upper house of the Indian parliament, and in 1957 he won a seat in the lower house representing Bombay, whereupon Nehru appointed him defence minister. Menon was more alert than Nehru to the threat China posed to India's security, and tried, with a brusqueness that alienated army chiefs, to build up India's defences in the north-east. Nevertheless, in 1962, when poorly equipped troops were routed in a clash with the Chinese in the North-East Frontier Agency, India's embarrassed fury focused on Menon rather than Nehru, and he was forced to resign from the cabinet. He quit the Congress altogether in 1967 when party bosses said they must have a Marathi-speaking candidate for his Bombay seat and, although he was returned to parliament in 1969 as a left-sponsored independent, he devoted most of his final years to a successful law practice in the supreme court. He died in New Delhi on 6 October 1974 and was cremated in a simple ceremony, his ashes being immersed in the Arabian Sea off the Keralan coast. He had never married, although because he was a member of the matriarchal Nayar caste he had had the satisfaction of seeing his mother's ancestral house in Calicut descend to the children of his late sister, Janaki Amma, who had supported him financially and emotionally throughout his life.

KATHERINE PRIOR

Sources J. Ram, *V. K. Krishna Menon: a personal memoir* (1997) • *The Times* (7 Oct 1974), 14 • *The Times* (12 Oct 1974), 14 • *The Times* (14 Oct 1974), 16 • J. E. Morpurgo, *Allen Lane, King Penguin: a biography* (1979) • W. E. Williams, *Allen Lane: a personal portrait* (1973) • T. J. S. George, *Krishna Menon: a biography* (1964) • DNB
Archives Nehru Museum, New Delhi, MSS • priv. coll., collection of personal letters | priv. coll., Marie Seton MSS | FILM BFI NFTVA, current affairs footage • BFI NFTVA, news footage | SOUND BBC WAC • BL NSA, documentary recording • BL NSA, performance recording
Likenesses Jerome, photograph, 1941, repro. in Ram, *V. K. Krishna Menon*, pl. 14 • photographs, 1949–60, Hult. Arch. • L. Larsen, photograph, c.1960, repro. in George, *Krishna Menon*, frontispiece • sculpture, repro. in Ram, *V. K. Krishna Menon*, cover

Menon, Vapal Pangunni (1894–1966), public servant and author, son of C. Sankunni Menon and his wife, Vapal Kunhikutty Amma, was born on 30 September 1894 in Ottapalam, a town in the Malabar district of the Madras presidency. The circumstances of his family were modest, but this was no handicap to his intellectual development or his enterprise. He decided, after matriculating from Ottapalam high school, that he had completed his formal education, and ran away from home in order to avoid being sent to college.

Menon's first employment was with the Imperial Tobacco Company in Bangalore; then, independently, as a contractor in the Kolar goldfields. His first venture in this unfamiliar business succeeded, but his second was disastrous. Penniless, but too proud to return to his family, he travelled northwards, far from the scene of his failure. After a short experience as schoolmaster in Bhopal he decided to seek employment with the government of India. On his journey he was helped by an old Sikh, who gave him 20 rupees with his blessing, saying that he would consider himself repaid if Menon would one day, in turn, help another in need. In Simla, Menon found another benefactor in a fellow Malayali, Anantan, then a superintendent in the home department of the government of India. Anantan took him into his home and also found him a clerk's post in his department. In 1925 Menon married Anantan's niece, and they had two sons. This marriage was dissolved, and in 1941 he married Anantan's widow, Srimati Kanakamma, who brought up his sons with her own daughter as one family.

The year 1914 was a political and constitutional watershed. The First World War and India's share in it strengthened her claim for an advance towards self-government. The recommendations of the Montagu–Chelmsford report took shape in the Government of India Act of 1919, which gave place, after much discussion and not a little nationalist protest, to the Government of India Act of 1935. The subject of constitutional reform was handled in the home department, and Menon made good use of his opportunity to become expert in this field. His ability was noticed, and rewarded with the title of *rao bahadur*.

He joined the new reforms office in 1930, and went to London in 1931 as a member of the secretarial staff of the second Indian round-table conference on constitutional reform. In 1933 he was assistant secretary in the reforms office, in 1934 under-secretary, and in 1936 deputy secretary under Hawthorne Lewis, the reforms commissioner.

The outbreak of war in 1939 frustrated the hope of achieving the federal scheme of the act of 1935, and the political parties in India seized the opportunity to press their respective, irreconcilable claims as conditions for co-operation with the war effort. The reforms office was brought directly into the sphere of the governor-general's responsibilities, becoming part of his secretariat. Menon was appointed CIE in 1941, and in the next year succeeded H. V. Hodson as reforms commissioner, in which capacity he occupied a key position of trust and influence as constitutional adviser to the last three viceroys of India.

Moves towards independence occurred against a background of varying fortunes of war and increasing communal bitterness, in a series of three-cornered entanglements between the ruling power, the Congress Party, and the Muslim League. In the Simla conference of 1945, in discussion of the cabinet mission's proposals, the formation of the so-called interim government, and the final evolution and acceptance of the plan for the transfer of power, and in all the manoeuvring between these stages, Menon played an indispensable role. In May 1947 Menon saved from shipwreck Lord Mountbatten's negotiations with the party leaders, by successfully advocating his own plan for an early transfer of power to two central governments with dominion status, in substitution at the last moment for the unacceptable formula favoured by the British cabinet. Mountbatten had the highest regard for Menon's judgement and character.

Menon was equally influential over the question of the future of the Indian princely states. In July 1947, barely a month before the transfer of power, Mountbatten confessed that he had given very little thought to the problem of the princes. Having been appointed by Sardar Vallabhbhai Patel, the deputy prime minister of India, as secretary of a new states department, Menon proposed that the princes should be asked to accede to one of the two new dominions on the three central subjects of defence, external affairs, and communications. In the weeks leading up to the transfer of power he played an active role in persuading the princes to sign instruments of accession. On one notable occasion a reluctant maharaja pulled a gun on him before agreeing to sign. In less than two-and-a-half years after August 1947 Menon completed the task of integrating the Indian states more fully with the new dominion. More than 550 states, great and small, half a million square miles, and 87 million people were added to India. The solution was summary, but realistic; and except in disputed Kashmir and in Hyderabad it was accomplished peacefully.

Menon had been appointed CSI in 1946. On 3 January 1948 he received at the governor-general's hands the unique distinction of a certificate conferring on him the dignity of a knight commander in that order, without the title and insignia which, as a servant of the independent government of India, he could not accept.

When Patel died in December 1950 Menon had lost, in the space of three years, two powerful patrons. The British-Indian government had recognized and rewarded his exceptional talents; and, had Patel lived, these would have been employed for longer in his country's service. But Menon's spectacular record, and his close association with Patel, had attracted envy and ill will in high places. After a short appointment as governor of Orissa in 1951, then as member of the finance commission, he was retired from service prematurely in March 1952.

But Menon's retirement in Bangalore was productive. He fulfilled a promise to Patel by writing two books, *The Story of the Integration of the Indian States* (1956) and *The Transfer of Power in India* (1957), two masterly first-hand historical documents. A much shorter work, *An Outline of Indian Constitutional History*, was published in 1965.

Modest, for all his success, frank, and tenacious of purpose, Menon had many friends and few enemies. He was a staunch Indian patriot, and at the same time a friend and admirer of the British and their institutions. In this there was no conflict of loyalties. Menon contributed much to the reconciliation of differences between Britain and India, and he was one of the main architects of the bridge which ultimately spanned them. He died in Jubbulpore, Madhya Pradesh, on 1 January 1966, and was survived by his wife.   W. H. J. CHRISTIE, *rev.* S. R. ASHTON

Sources *The Times* (4 Jan 1966) · A. Campbell-Johnson, *Mission with Mountbatten* (1951) · H. V. Hodson, *The great divide* (1969) · private information (1981) · personal knowledge (1981) · N. Mansergh and others, eds., *The transfer of power, 1942–7*, 12 vols. (1970–83)
Archives Bodl. Oxf., corresp. with Lord Monckton · SOAS, corresp. with H. V. Hodson

Menpes, Mortimer Luddington (1855–1938), painter, was born 'inartisticly', as he put it himself, on 22 February 1855 in Port Adelaide in South Australia. There he was educated at the grammar school and for a time attended classes at the school of design under John Hood. He was nineteen in 1875 when he arrived in England to continue his studies at the National Art Training School, South Kensington, under Sir Edward Poynter. He took up etching and in 1880 exhibited two drypoints at the Royal Academy exhibition where, over the next twenty years, he exhibited over thirty-five etchings and paintings.

Like Walter Sickert who had enrolled at the same time at the Slade School of Fine Art, London, Menpes was bowled over by his first meeting with James McNeill Whistler: 'If you want to see some fun Menpes, come with me.' Completely falling under his spell, Sickert and Menpes by 1881 had become Whistler's studio assistants, and were permitted under his strict guidance to print up a number of etchings. Menpes's own work at this time closely imitated Whistler and together with Sickert they would record a now vanished Chelsea. Whistler was a judge of the Crystal Palace exhibition, so not unnaturally he said, 'You have the Gold Medal, Menpes and Du Maurier the Silver' (Menpes, 29). In 1883–4 Menpes and Sickert travelled with Whistler to St Ives in Cornwall, and Menpes

later recorded that invariably Sickert would paint alone whereas Menpes stuck to the master (ibid., 140). He found himself part of an inner circle whose sole duty was to fight for and protect the master. However, by 1888 Menpes was becoming increasingly critical of Whistler and the relationship began to disintegrate. Menpes, who hated quarrels, recorded, 'For Whistler when he forgave at all, forgave completely. All was happiness and sunshine' (ibid., 153). On 27 April 1875 Menpes had married, at All Souls, Marylebone, Rosa Mary Grosse (d. 1936), and when their youngest child was born in 1887, Whistler, as a gesture of friendship, agreed to be godfather; she was christened Dorothy Whistler Menpes. However, a year later Menpes committed an unpardonable act when he announced he was going to Japan—'Japan was reserved for the "master"' (ibid., 39). When he returned in 1888 with an exhibition of his drypoints from his Japanese tour at Dowdswell's Gallery, London, Menpes refused to sign himself 'Pupil of Whistler'. Whistler, in turn, ignored Menpes completely and resigned from the Royal Society of British Artists after the exhibition.

Outside the Whistler circle, Menpes would have been forgotten but for an article in the *Pall Mall Gazette* (1 December 1888) entitled 'The home of taste' focusing on Menpes's decoration of his new house at 25 Cadogan Gardens in Kensington which had been built for him by the architect Arthur Heygate Mackmurdo (1851–1942). (Photographs of the interior of the house were included in an article in volume 17 of *The Studio*, 1894.) Whistler immediately hammered the final nail into Menpes's professional coffin by referring to him as an 'Australian immigrant of Fulham who like the kangaroo of his country is born with a pocket and puts everything in it' (Menpes, xxiii). The International Society of Sculptors, Painters and Gravers was formed in February 1898 with Whistler elected president. Sickert's and Menpes's names were put forward and answered by a firm 'no' from Whistler. Whistler died on 17 July 1903; the funeral took place on 23 July at Chelsea Old Church and Menpes, who had long since been cast in the role of 'enemy', was gracious enough to attend and pay his respects. After all his rejections Menpes repeated plaintively, 'Whistler did not mean to hurt me—he was really very fond of me' (Pocock, 130) and produced as a memorial to their friendship *Whistler as I Knew Him* (1904), a long and affectionate memoir, and a series of etched portraits of the stinging butterfly. The Leicester Gallery also gave an exhibition, by way of memorial, of Menpes's personal collection of Whistler drypoints.

Three years before Whistler's death Menpes went out as a war artist to South Africa for the British periodical *Black and White*. In 1901 he published *War Impressions*, the first of a series of books illustrated in colour from his sketches, with, in most cases, a text written by his daughter Dorothy. The series included *Japan, a Record in Colour* (1888, 1901), *France, Spain and Morocco* (1893), *World's Children* (1903), *The Durbar* (1903), *Venice* (1904), *India* (text by F. A. Steel, 1905), *The Thames* (text by G. E. Mitton, 1906), *Paris* (1907), *China* (text by Sir H. A. Blake, 1909), *The People of India* (text by G. E. Mitton, 1910), *Lord Kitchener* (1915), and

Lord Roberts (1915). Of his five children, Claude, Walter, Toby, Maudie Rose, and Dorothy, the last married into the Flowers Brewery family and had a son, Richard, born in 1910. A pastel portrait of Richard was drawn by Menpes in 1916.

During 1907 Menpes founded the Menpes Fruit Farm Co. at Pangbourne in Berkshire where he lived in his house, Iris Court, until his death there on 1 April 1938.

Menpes's obituary refers to him as a 'painter, etcher, raconteur and rifle shot' (*The Times*, 5 April 1938). He described his early life as that of a 'rolling stone, travelling all over the world in record time, being unsurpassed even by Jules Verne and that as a result of meeting Whistler he had cultivated some of his mannerisms'.

MICHAEL PARKIN

Sources M. Menpes, *Whistler as I knew him* (1904) · E. R. Pennell and J. Pennell, *The Whistler journal* (1921) · *The Australian encyclopaedia*, 6 (1958) · E. Robins Pennell and J. Pennell, *The life of James McNeill Whistler*, 2 vols. (1908) · d. cert. · T. Pocock, *Chelsea reach: the brutal friendship of Whistler and Walter Greaves* (1970)
Archives JRL, letters to C. A. Howell and M. H. Spielmann · U. Glas. L., letters to J. A. M. Whistler
Wealth at death £3260 13s. 7d.: probate, 11 Aug 1938, *CGPLA Eng. & Wales*

Mensforth, Sir Holberry (1871–1951), engineer and engineering company executive, was born at Snow Hill, Bradford, Yorkshire, on 1 May 1871, the second son of Edward Mensforth and his wife, Dorcas, *née* Harrison. His father was a painter and decorator; his mother's family were machine makers, of Crabtree Harrison of Bradford. (Some socialist influence through his grandfather Thomas Mensforth probably led to his being named after a well-known Chartist leader, Samuel Holberry.)

Mensforth was educated until aged about twelve at Christ Church Day School in Bradford, worked briefly in a law office, and then became a millwright's apprentice at S. Clayton & Co., a Bradford gas engine maker. Before completing his time he acted as foreman. Further technical instruction followed at evening classes at the mechanics' institute in Bradford in 1893–4, after which he became an instructor in metalwork at the Hull Municipal Technical School in 1896–7. He emerged as a versatile mechanic and toolmaker (a full member of the Amalgamated Society of Engineers) and head of Clayton's engineering shop. In 1900 he married, at Shipley, Yorkshire, Alice Maud (d. 1948), third daughter of William Jennings of Rossington Grange Farm, near Doncaster, and Emmie Temperley. They had one daughter, Muriel (b. 1911), and two sons, Thomas (b. 1901) and Eric (b. 1906). Both sons had distinguished engineering careers.

After briefly running his own gear-cutting business, Mensforth joined B. H. Thwaite's heavy engineering firm in Westminster, London, which brought him experience in the installation of gas engines and blowers in iron- and steelworks. In 1903 he joined the Trafford Park works of the American firm Westinghouse in Manchester, as a technical engineer in the engine department. (The firm produced gas engines, steam turbines, and a complete range of electrical equipment.) He made rapid progress with the firm, becoming superintendent of the engineering department in 1909, then in 1917 general manager. Mensforth was particularly successful in handling wartime labour difficulties and in increasing the output of munitions. To combat the disruptive effect on factory labour caused by the war, he set up in 1917, nine months before the Whitley councils, a works committee and staff committee. He appreciated the value of a university training and the need to attract graduates to his works. He was also a founder member and chairman of the Manchester and District Armaments Committee, which through its constituent firms—Westinghouse, Crossley's, Armstrong Whitworth, and Mather and Platt—aimed at ensuring a continuous supply of shells. These efforts were rewarded by a CBE and by an honorary MSc from the Manchester College of Technology in 1919.

After the war Sir Eric Geddes, the minister of transport, recruited Mensforth to smooth the transition of the munitions factories from war work to peacetime operations. As director-general of factories from 1920 to 1926, Mensforth successfully reduced the workforce and number of factories, won the co-operation of the unions, and introduced more commercial businesses and practices. In 1923 he was created a KCB. He was also a member in 1925 of the Biles subcommittee, which aimed to investigate the royal dockyards and their administration—though the attempt to introduce more businesslike methods in this case was less successful.

Mensforth then took up a post as managing director of Bolckow, Vaughan & Co. Ltd, an ailing coal, iron, steel, and chemical producer in the north-east. Alongside Henry D. McLaren, second Baron Aberconway, he helped reorganize and modernize the works, characteristically introducing joint consultation with labour, and then in 1931 negotiated its merger with another troubled iron and steel producer, Dorman Long.

In 1930 Mensforth accepted the chairmanship of the English Electric Company, which had been reorganized under an American syndicate. He took two important decisions: he negotiated a comprehensive technical and commercial agreement with Westinghouse and, to run the business, he made the inspired choice of one of his old Westinghouse apprentices, George H. Nelson (later first Lord Nelson). He handed over the chairmanship of English Electric in 1933 to Nelson, who continued as managing director.

In 1933 McLaren invited Mensforth to join the board of John Brown & Co. Ltd of Sheffield, on which he served as non-executive director. Mensforth concerned himself with the engineering aspects of the collieries, steelworks, and shipyards of Browns and chaired a number of subsidiaries, such as Nasmyth Wilson of Manchester and Cravens of Sheffield. He made three influential contributions: the development of the Firth Brown Engineers' tool department in Sheffield for the manufacture of high-quality cutting tools; the purchase in 1936 of Markham & Co. Ltd of Chesterfield, which strengthened Browns' engineering interests; and the recruiting of the German refugee Ludwig M. Loewy, whose designs for aluminium extrusion presses enabled Browns to close a crucial gap in British aircraft production facilities. Mensforth remained on the board of Browns until his retirement in 1945.

A vice-president of the British Electrical and Allied Manufacturers' Association, Mensforth was also a member of the Institution of Civil Engineers and the Institution of Mechanical Engineers and contributed occasionally to debates. He was a member of the executive council of the National Union of Manufacturers, and in 1928 was part of a deputation received by Stanley Baldwin, calling for the safeguarding of British industries.

In all his posts Mensforth combined both practical skill and 'firmness but fairness and integrity in dealing with men and unions' (Mensforth, 55). He was not committed to any political party and served willingly either Labour or Conservative governments. He died of a cerebral thrombosis on 5 September 1951 at his home, the Red House, 347 St Johns Road, Hazlemere, Buckinghamshire.

GEOFFREY TWEEDALE

Sources G. Tweedale, 'Mensforth, Sir Holberry', *DBB* • E. Mensforth, *Family engineers* (1981) • J. Bissett, *History of the board of management of the Manchester & District Armaments Output Committee: 1915–1919* (1919) • J. Dummelow, *1899–1949: Metropolitan-Vickers Electrical Co.* (1949) • *The Engineer* (14 Sept 1951), 337–8 • *Engineering* (14 Sept 1951), 340 • A. J. Grant, *Steel and ships: the history of John Brown's* (1950) • *The Times* (6 Sept 1951) • d. cert.

Archives Institution of Mechanical Engineers, London, corresp. with Sir Henry Lewis relating to donation to Institution of Mechanical Engineers

Likenesses photograph, repro. in Tweedale, 'Mensforth, Sir Holberry'

Wealth at death £6206 13s. 10d.: probate, 17 Jan 1952, CGPLA Eng. & Wales

Menteith. For this title name *see* Comyn, Walter, earl of Menteith (*d.* 1258); Stewart, Walter Bulloch, earl of Menteith (1225x30–*c*.1293) [*see under* Stewart family (*per. c.*1110–*c*.1350)]; Graham, Malise, third earl of Strathearn and first earl of Menteith (1406x13–1490); Graham, William, first earl of Airth and seventh earl of Menteith (1591–1661).

Menteith, Sir John (*d.* 1323?), soldier and administrator, was the second son of Walter Menteith, fifth earl of Menteith (*d.* in or before 1296), and brother of Alexander, who succeeded to the title. Both John and Alexander were captured after the Scottish defeat at Dunbar in 1296, and John was sent to Nottingham Castle in May, along with, among others, Sir Edmund Comyn of Kilbride. As the price of liberation he agreed to serve Edward I on his campaign against the French in 1297 and his lands were consequently restored to him. Menteith, by now a knight, returned to Scotland in 1298, but later rejoined the patriotic side. There is no record of his activities between then and September 1303, when he and Sir Alexander Menzies approached the English lieutenant Sir Aymer de Valence (*d.* 1324) at Linlithgow to treat for peace, presumably on behalf of the Scottish guardian, Sir John Comyn of Badenoch. At this point Edward I and his army were advancing deep into the north-east of Scotland, and the Scots sensed that submission was the only truly viable option. Although the starving state of the Irish foot soldiers with Valence persuaded Menteith and Menzies that further

resistance was worthwhile, the majority of the Scots, led by the guardian, and presumably including Menteith, submitted in February 1304.

Menteith must have somehow impressed King Edward, since in March 1304 he was granted the keeping of the castle, town, and sheriffdom of Dumbarton. The area was not yet firmly under Edward's control even in 1305, however, and Menteith was permitted to postpone the hearing of his account 'until the land of Scotland is secure' (*CDS*, vol. 5, no. 400(2)). Some headway in that direction was undoubtedly made in August of the same year, when Sir William Wallace, still resolutely refusing to submit to the English king, was captured, perhaps by treachery, within Menteith's sheriffdom of Dumbarton (supposedly at Robroyston near Glasgow). The sheriff had no choice but to hand Wallace over to Edward and was duly rewarded with lands worth £100. His action brought Menteith lasting ignominy, however ill deserved: Walter Bower, writing in the 1420s, describes the reputations of the main players in this melodrama thus:

> Some ostentatiously make their name great for show, like the tyrant Edward; some scandalously make it cheap so that they are abhorred, like the said John Menteith; others virtuously make it worthy so that they are an inspiration to others, like William Wallace.   (Bower, 6.315)

Yet Menteith's career was far from over. With the murder of Sir John Comyn of Badenoch and the seizure of the throne by Robert Bruce early in 1306, Menteith remained loyal to Edward I. Although he was probably essentially a realist, willing as such to support a *de facto* government, it is also possible that he identified himself with the Comyn faction, which would explain his failure to support Bruce. There may even be some truth in Bower's story that Menteith made overtures to the new king of Scots at this time in an attempt to trap him in Dumbarton Castle; the plot was revealed to Robert by a servant, Roland Carpentar, who was certainly granted the lands of Eddlewood by the grateful king.

Given his family's interests in the western highlands, including Kintyre, where they had recently built a castle at Skipness, Menteith was well placed to help the English maintain control of the western seaboard. His activities were clearly appreciated by the English king, who granted him the earldom of Lennox, forfeited by Earl Malcolm in June 1306, as well as the temporalities of the bishopric of Glasgow 'towards Dumbarton'. This grant thereby united that earldom with control of its ancient caput of Dumbarton (separated by King William of Scotland in 1211). It should be noted, however, that Sir John's brother's earldom had been granted to Sir John Hastings (*d.* 1313) only a month earlier, and it might be supposed that even the Lennox was no compensation. But Menteith was still in control of his family's lands in Kintyre, since in September 1306 Edward ordered him to force the inhabitants of the area to provide those besieging Dunaverty Castle (where King Robert was erroneously supposed to be hiding) with provisions and other supplies. In the following year Menteith was commanded to join forces with Hugh Bisset, an Irish entrepreneur who also claimed lands in Scotland, most notably the strategically important island of Arran. These two, and the English mariner Sir Simon Montague, were responsible for policing the western seaboard with their galleys, at a time when Robert was most likely to be hiding on Rathlin, off the coast of Ulster.

The problematic nature of west highland politics, not to mention the expansionism of families such as the Menteiths, led to feuds. Menteith's greatest enemy was John MacSween, who challenged the Menteith claim to Knapdale. Early in the reign of Edward II MacSween wrote to the English king, claiming that he had gone to Knapdale, which lands had been granted to him by Edward. He then asserted: 'Here it was that John [MacDougall] of Argyll had invaded the said lands with armed strength and great power on the part of John Menteith, and prohibited me from having the said lands; whereby the said John of Menteith is your enemy' (Stevenson, 2.437). Menteith, MacSween, and MacDougall were all ostensibly followers of the English, but the loss of Knapdale might have prompted Menteith to join King Robert, whose parliament he attended in 1309. Having returned to the patriotic side, Menteith proved a loyal supporter of the Scottish king, who clearly valued his administrative abilities. He was almost immediately employed as envoy to Robert's father-in-law, Richard de Burgh, earl of Ulster (d. 1326), in August 1309, and his prominence in the king's entourage is attested by his appearance as the second most important secular witness on royal charters (after Walter Stewart) until 1318, when he changes places with Sir James Douglas (d. 1330). Menteith witnessed an impressive total of forty-six charters, and may also have been butler in the royal household until 1318, when Sir William Soulis reclaimed this heritable office. The earldom of Menteith was placed under his care during the minority of his nephew Alan, and on 1 August 1323 he received from King Robert the grant of Glen Breackerie, Argyll, and Ailsa, Ayrshire.

Menteith was employed by Robert I on diplomatic missions, going to England with Thomas Randolph, first earl of Moray, in November 1316, in the hope of persuading Edward II to be more generous with the conditions of the recent truce. In 1323 Moray and Menteith were again involved in diplomatic affairs, but this concerned a far weightier truce, designed to last for thirteen years. Menteith probably died in the same year. He left his heir, another John, and a second son, Alexander. His wife's identity is unknown. FIONA WATSON

Sources C. Moor, ed., *Knights of Edward I*, 3, Harleian Society, 82 (1930), 145–6 • W. Bower, *Scotichronicon*, ed. D. E. R. Watt and others, new edn, 9 vols. (1987–98), vol. 6 • *RotS*, vol. 1 • J. Stevenson, ed., *Documents illustrative of the history of Scotland*, 2 vols. (1870) • *CDS*, vols. 2, 4–5 • F. Palgrave, ed., *Documents and records illustrating the history of Scotland* (1837) • G. W. S. Barrow and others, eds., *Regesta regum Scottorum*, 5, ed. A. A. M. Duncan (1988) • *APS*, 1124–1423, 474

Menteith, Robert (*bap.* 1603, *d.* in or before 1660), author, was baptized in Edinburgh on 25 January 1603, the third son of Alexander Menteith, merchant and burgess of Edinburgh, and his wife, Rachel Sandilands. He was educated at the University of Edinburgh where he graduated MA on 14 July 1621; he subsequently spent four years as

Robert Menteith (*bap.* 1603, *d.* in or before 1660), by René Lochon, 1661 (after Pierre Mignard, 1656)

professor of philosophy at the protestant academy of Saumur in France, returning home some time before 1629.

Although French protestantism, including that of Saumur, was largely Calvinist, Menteith seems to have been early inclined to the Arminian doctrine, and therefore to episcopacy. Some of the Edinburgh clergy wished to promote the teaching of Arminianism, in line with the policy of Charles I, and this led them to put Menteith forward as candidate for the chair of divinity at Edinburgh University in 1629. This appointment was successfully opposed by Edinburgh's Calvinist ministers and Menteith reacted by writing a pasquinade on the leading Calvinists of the day, including Robert Bruce of Kinnaird, who later called him a 'debauched sycophant' (Wodrow, 139). Menteith's Arminianism plainly attracted favourable attention from government, as he was presented by Charles I as minister to the parish of Duddingston, being ordained at St Andrews by Archbishop Spottiswood and admitted on 28 December 1630. In his parish he apparently had contact with the often-persecuted Catholic Abercorn family, who lived in the neighbourhood, and this may have inclined him to the Catholicism which he later embraced in France. In the early 1630s Menteith was discovered to be having an affair with Anna Hepburn, wife of Sir James Hamilton of Priestfield, as a result of which she was pregnant. Menteith fled the country, and was denounced a rebel on 7 October 1632. Some time before 1632 he had married a Marion Broun, whose name occurs as his spouse on a document dated 3

May 1632 at Haddington. She does not seem to have left the country with him, and was dead before 1639.

Menteith went to Paris, joined the Catholic church, and obtained the favour of Cardinal Richelieu. It is said (Chambers, 2.70) that Richelieu asked about Menteith's family when they first met. Knowing that a pedigree was essential to success in France, Menteith said that he was a Menteith of Salmonet. He is supposed to have had this idea because his father was a fisherman who used a salmonnet, but the description of his father as a merchant (Watson, 356) argues a higher station, and there was once a place called Salmonet in Stirlingshire, with which Menteith's family may have been connected.

Menteith became secretary to De la Porte, grand prior of France, and later to the Cardinal de Retz, coadjutor of Paris, who made him a canon of Notre Dame. When Retz was imprisoned in 1652 for his part in the Fronde upheavals, Menteith was among those of his household who fled the city, spending fifteen months in the safety of Michel de Marolles's abbey of Baugerais. That year he wrote a 'Remonstrance' to Charles II, published in Paris. His movements after this are uncertain, although he may have visited Rome, as his portrait was painted by Mignard in that city in 1656. He died, probably in Paris, before 13 September 1660. His *Histoire des troubles de la Grand Bretagne* was published in Paris in 1661, and an English translation was made by James Ogilvy in 1785. The work covers the turbulent period of British history from 1633 to 1646, with emphasis on events in Scotland.

ALEXANDER DU TOIT

Sources *Fasti Scot.*, new edn, 1.18 · R. Chambers, *Domestic annals of Scotland from the Reformation to the revolution*, 2 vols. (1858), vol. 2, pp. 70, 501 · A. Bower, *The history of the University of Edinburgh*, 1 (1817), 172–3 · J. Scot, *The staggering state of Scottish statesmen from 1550 to 1650*, ed. C. Rogers (1872), 75 · *Memoires de Michel de Marolles*, 3 vols. (1755), vol. 1, pp. 243–4, 367; vol. 3, p. 360 · R. Wodrow, 'Collections as to the life of Mr Robert Bruce, minister at Edinburgh', *Sermons by the Rev. Robert Bruce* (1843), 137–9 · H. Paton, ed., *The register of marriages for the parish of Edinburgh, 1595–1700*, Scottish RS, old ser., 27 (1905), 486 · C. B. B. Watson, ed., *Roll of Edinburgh burgesses and guild-brethren, 1406–1700*, Scottish RS, 59 (1929), 356 · F. J. Grant, ed., *Comissariat record of Edinburgh: register of testaments* (1887), 286 · F. Michel, *Les écossais en France, les français en Écosse*, 2 vols. (1862), vol. 2, pp. 299–302 · G. Tallemant des Raux, *Les historiettes de Tallemant des Raux*, 2 vols. (1960–61), vol. 2, pp. 325, 329, 330, 1184 · *Index to particular register of sasines for sheriffdoms of Edinburgh, Haddington, Linlithgow and Bathgate*, 4 vols. (1953–7), vol. 3, pp. 49, 332 · *The letters and journals of Robert Baillie*, ed. D. Laing, 1 (1841), 164
Archives NL Scot., Nisbet MSS
Likenesses R. Lochon, engraving, 1661 (after painting by P. Mignard, 1656), BM, NPG, V&A; repro. in R. Menteith, *Histoire des troubles de la Grand Bretagne* (1661), frontispiece [*see illus.*]

Menuhin, Yehudi, Baron Menuhin (1916–1999), violinist and conductor, was born on 22 April 1916 at the Mount Lebanon Hospital in the Bronx district of New York city, the only son and first among the three children of Moshe Menuhin (1893–1982), teacher, and his wife, Marutha (1896–1998), daughter of Nachum Sher and his wife, Sara Liba. His parents were Russian Jews. His father was born into an Orthodox Jewish family in Gomel, then in White Russia, and his mother near the Black Sea resort of Yalta.

Both emigrated to Palestine, where they met. Moshe Mnuchin, as he then called himself, went to New York in 1913 and taught Hebrew. Through an accidental meeting he learned that Marutha and her family were living in Chicago. He wrote to her, she joined him, and they married on 7 August 1914. They moved to Elizabeth, New Jersey, in 1917 and to San Francisco in 1918. When Moshe became an American citizen in 1919, he changed the family name to Menuhin. Their second child, a daughter, Hephzibah, was born on 20 May 1920, and their third, Yaltah, on 7 October 1921. Neither parent toed the Orthodox Jewish line, which they despised. Although 'Yehudi' means 'Jew', Yehudi had hardly any Jewish upbringing. The family ate ham, for example. For years Yehudi never entered a synagogue. Neither of his wives was Jewish (his first marriage was on a Saturday, the Jewish sabbath), and he once agreed to give a recital on Yom Kippur, the day of Atonement, not realizing what date it was.

Child prodigy Taken to concerts at the age of three, Yehudi was enchanted by the sound of the violin. He had lessons for two years from 1921 with Sigmund Anker. In July 1923 he left Anker to study with Louis Persinger (1887–1966), leader of the San Francisco Symphony Orchestra. His first full-length solo recital, before his ninth birthday, was on 30 March 1925 at the Scottish Rite Auditorium in San Francisco. The programme included Mendelssohn's concerto, accompanied by Persinger on the piano. When Persinger moved to New York for the winter, Marutha took the three children there, enrolling Yehudi at the Institute of Musical Art (later the Juilliard School). This was his first taste of school, as up to then the three children had been taught at home. It was a serious kind of childhood. Although there were escapades and fun, mostly it was non-stop music, highbrow reading, learning several languages, no sport in case hands were injured, and never a visit to a baseball game.

On 17 January 1926, in the Manhattan Opera House, Menuhin gave his first New York concert. He made his début with orchestra in San Francisco at the Curran Theatre on 12 March 1926, when he played three movements of Lalo's *Symphonie espagnole* with Persinger conducting. Eight months later he played Tchaikovsky's concerto. Persinger now urged that Menuhin should study in Europe. He became a pupil of the Romanian George Enesco, with whose playing he had been enthralled in San Francisco in 1925. But before lessons began, Menuhin was engaged by Paul Paray to play the Lalo and Tchaikovsky works with the Lamoureux orchestra (6 and 12 February 1927). For this occasion he was bought a 1690 Grancino violin. Moshe Menuhin now gave up the Hebrew schools he ran in San Francisco to manage and publicize his son's career, a role he fulfilled with gusto, bravado, and a runaway imagination (for twenty years he subtracted nine months from Yehudi's age).

On 25 November 1927 Menuhin played Beethoven's concerto with the New York Symphony Orchestra conducted by Fritz Busch in Carnegie Hall. Olin Downes of the *New*

York Times wrote that 'a boy of eleven proved conclusively his right to be ranked with the outstanding interpreters of this music' (26 Nov 1927). Busch wrote to the Berlin Philharmonic urging the orchestra to engage the boy to play concertos by Bach (E major), Beethoven, and Brahms in one programme. This was to come to fruition, but before that Menuhin had his first taste of failure when he played the Tchaikovsky concerto on 28 and 29 December 1928 at two concerts by the newly merged Philharmonic-Symphony Orchestra of New York, conducted by Willem Mengelberg. He played on a borrowed violin and had little rehearsal. Downes's review was unfavourable. This concert was attended by Henry Goldman, of the banking firm Goldman Sachs. After hearing about the borrowed instrument, he invited Yehudi to 'choose any violin, no matter what the price' (Y. Menuhin, 95). Menuhin chose the 'Prince Khevenhüller' which Antonio Stradivarius had made in 1733 in his ninetieth year. The price was $60,000.

The Berlin three-concerto concert took place on 12 April 1929. A family bereavement prevented Busch from conducting and he was replaced by Bruno Walter, with whom Menuhin achieved a close rapport. The scientist Albert Einstein was reported to have greeted the young soloist with the words: 'I see that the day of miracles is not over. Our dear old Jehovah is still on the job.' Menuhin in his memoirs varied this to 'Now I know there is a God in heaven' (Y. Menuhin, 98). In June he began lessons, on Enesco's recommendation, with Fritz Busch's brother Adolf. This involved living in Basel, where Busch's home was, for the next two years. But tours continued, and on 4 November 1929 Menuhin made his London début playing the Brahms concerto with the London Symphony Orchestra under Fritz Busch. This was followed on 10 November by an Albert Hall recital attended by 6000 people. A few

days later Menuhin made his first recordings (Bach, Beethoven, and Mozart sonatas) for His Master's Voice (HMV).

The Elgar concerto and international touring While in Paris in the summer of 1932, Menuhin received a letter from Fred Gaisberg, recording manager of HMV (by then EMI), asking him to study and record Sir Edward Elgar's concerto with the composer conducting. Gaisberg had for many years been trying to persuade the work's dedicatee, Fritz Kreisler, to record it with Elgar, but in vain. Menuhin had never heard a note of Elgar, but loved the work when he read the score. In London on 9 July Menuhin played the concerto, accompanied by Ivor Newton, to the 75-year-old composer. At the break for lunch Elgar declared himself entirely satisfied and departed to Newmarket for the races. The recording was made in Abbey Road studio no. 1 on 14 and 15 July, with the London Symphony Orchestra; by 2002 it had remained in the catalogue uninterruptedly for seventy years, being regarded as one of the greatest classic recordings ever made. On the following 20 November Menuhin and Elgar collaborated again in the concerto in the Albert Hall. Elgar made his first flight in order to go to Paris to conduct the concerto for Menuhin at a gala concert in the Salle Pleyel on 31 May 1933.

In September 1933 in the EMI recording studio Hephzibah, aged thirteen, partnered her brother in Mozart's A major sonata K526. The recording won a French prize as best chamber music disc of the year. The brother and sister gave their first joint public recitals that autumn in Paris, London, and New York. They had a remarkably close rapport and described themselves as 'the incestuous sonata players' (Burton, 177). The year 1933, in which Menuhin became the highest-paid artist of the time, was also the year in which the Nazis came to power in Germany. The conductor Wilhelm Furtwängler, in a naïve attempt

Yehudi Menuhin, Baron Menuhin (1916–1999), by Myfanwy Pavelic, 1982

to show that Germany was still hospitable to Jews, invited several celebrated Jewish soloists, including Menuhin, to appear with the Berlin Philharmonic in the 1933–4 season. They refused. Menuhin's Jewish manager in Berlin had already been forced out of his job.

On 18 and 19 January 1934 Menuhin played the Beethoven concerto with the New York Philharmonic conducted by Arturo Toscanini (their sole collaboration). After strenuous tours he took a sabbatical in 1936 and then returned to the international circuit with a newsworthy discovery. This was Schumann's concerto, written in 1853 for Joseph Joachim; Joachim, however, never played it, and at his death in 1907 left it to the Prussian State Library in Berlin with a bar on performance for 100 years. In 1933 the Hungarian violinist Jelly d'Arányi, Joachim's great-niece, said she had received a spirit message from Schumann urging her to play the work. Menuhin wanted to give the first performance in November 1937, but the Nazis refused to let the material leave Germany, thereby allowing Georg Kulenkampff to give the first performance in Berlin on 26 November. Menuhin played the concerto with piano accompaniment in Carnegie Hall, New York, on 5 December and with orchestra in St Louis on 23 December. He recorded it with the New York Philharmonic conducted by John Barbirolli.

Marriages and the war On a seventy-concert autumn and winter tour, Menuhin was joined in some concerts and recitals by Hephzibah. He returned to Europe in February 1938. In London he was introduced to two Australians, Lindsay Nicholas and his nineteen-year-old sister Nola Ruby (1918/19–1978). Menuhin fell in love with Nola, and they announced their engagement on 10 May 1938. Days later Lindsay became engaged to Hephzibah. Yehudi and Nola were married at Caxton Hall register office on 26 May. Hephzibah gave up her career to live in Australia. Yehudi and Nola, although deeply in love, had little in common. They found married life problematical from the start. She was humiliated by her mother-in-law and also found it difficult being the wife of a travelling virtuoso. Their first child, Zamira, was born in California on 29 September 1939. Their second, a son named Krov, was born in Melbourne.

Following America's entry into the war in December 1941, Menuhin gave recitals at as many military camps and naval bases as he could fit into his schedule. He flew to England in the spring of 1943, and gave a memorable performance of Brahms's concerto with Sir Adrian Boult and the BBC Symphony Orchestra. At this time he decided he was not playing enough contemporary music, and was introduced to Bartók's second violin concerto, which he performed with Dimitri Mitropoulos conducting in New York in November 1943. Later he commissioned a sonata from Bartók; he gave the first performance of this very demanding work in Carnegie Hall on 26 November 1944. In the same year he gave the British première of the second concerto on 20 September. After a tour of Alaska, the Aleutians, and Hawaii, he played for the Royal Navy in Scapa Flow and in towns throughout Britain, following this tour with concerts on the western front, some of them under German shellfire. He gave recitals in Brussels and Antwerp and the first concert in the Paris Opéra after the liberation.

At a dinner party during his London visit Menuhin met the 31-year-old actress and ballet dancer Diana Rosamond Constance Grace Irene Gould (1912–2003), and within a few days told her he intended to marry her. On his return to America, he told Nola about Diana. Nola, too, had formed another relationship. They were divorced in 1947. At the end of July 1945 Menuhin went with Benjamin Britten as pianist to play to the survivors of the concentration camp at Belsen. On Hamburg radio he gave the first performance of Mendelssohn's concerto since the Nazis had banned music by Jews.

Ambassador for music After the war Menuhin saw his role as that of an international ambassador for music. This frequently led him into controversy, as when he defended the conductor Wilhelm Furtwängler, whose association with the Nazis, itself still controversial, made him *persona non grata* particularly with some Jews. Menuhin recorded the Beethoven concerto with him in 1947 and 1953. Already he was acquainted with most of the world's leading statesmen, and many of them over the next forty years could have been forgiven for believing that a visit from Menuhin went with the job. After concerts in Berlin in September 1947, Menuhin asked to give a recital for displaced persons. Few of them attended: they had been urged to boycott the recital because he had played for Germans. Next day Menuhin drove to the refugees' camp, where he encountered a hostile reception but told them: 'To behave towards the Germans the way the Nazis behaved towards us is to admit that we have grown to be like the Nazis' (Y. Menuhin, 235). He left the camp to cheers. On return to England, Menuhin and Diana were married at Chelsea register office on 19 October. Their first son, Gerard, was born on 23 July 1948.

Menuhin's playing still divided the critics. His technique was often suspect mainly because of a weakness of his bowing arm, causing the bow to 'stutter' on the strings. He traced the fault to his studies with Adolf Busch:

> If you look at the old photographs, the position of the bow arm is absolutely atrocious—the high elbow with a pressure exerted through the first finger and hence the lack of a proper balance in the bow. The trouble is I played too well. I never studied with a pedagogue like Carl Flesch. (Stack)

Nevertheless he was in demand everywhere and never learned to say 'No' when asked to help a cause. He continued to champion new works, giving the first performance of Walton's violin sonata in London on 5 February 1949 in partnership with Louis Kentner, the husband of Diana's sister. He took Shostakovich's first concerto into his repertory a few years later, and also works by Bloch and Berg. On a visit to South Africa in 1950 he spoke out against apartheid. His first visit to Israel in April 1950 brought him a death threat, but the tour was a success. On 6 May 1951 he and Hephzibah gave the first recital in London's new Royal Festival Hall, a hall Menuhin always intensely disliked. Visits to Australia, New Zealand, and

Japan preceded the birth of Jeremy Menuhin on 2 November 1951 in San Francisco. In New Zealand Menuhin read a book about yoga, which he practised for the rest of his life. He learned more about it when he toured India in March 1952. After discussing it with the Indian prime minister, Jawaharlal Nehru, he was challenged to stand on his head in full evening dress at a state reception. He did so, whereupon Nehru followed suit. He also formed a firm friendship with the great sitar player Ravi Shankar. Thereafter he was an enthusiast for Indian music and played in partnership with Shankar, just as some years later he played violin duos with the jazz virtuoso Stéphane Grappelli.

London and the Menuhin School The Menuhins left California in 1956 and built a house in Gstaad, Switzerland, where in 1957 Menuhin established a festival. In the following year he became artistic director of the Bath festival, a post he held until 1968. Menuhin felt increasingly drawn to London and in 1957 bought a seventeenth-century house: 2 The Grove, Highgate, London. He appeared on the BBC programme *The Brains Trust*, lectured to the Royal Society, helped found a health-food shop in Baker Street, and participated in almost every good (and sometimes bad) cause which knocked on the door of no. 2. He had occasionally conducted before 1958, but with the formation of the Bath festival chamber orchestra he took up conducting enthusiastically. He attracted many distinguished musicians to the festival as soloists, but gave opportunities also to young performers, including the sixteen-year-old Jacqueline du Pré.

Menuhin had begun giving violin lessons in 1954 at Nadia Boulanger's academy in Fontainebleau, France. After serving on various competition juries he became worried about falling standards. Impressed by what he saw in the Soviet Union but unimpressed by the methods there, he decided to begin his own all-year-round school with an intake from the age of seven. The school opened in London in September 1963 and moved after a year to larger premises at Stoke d'Abernon, Surrey. Menuhin engaged distinguished musicians and teachers for the staff, and visiting teachers such as Boulanger herself and Hans Keller. Menuhin himself was on the governing body and was a visiting teacher, but was never merely a figurehead. He involved himself deeply with every aspect of the school. It is his noblest memorial.

From 1969 to 1975 Menuhin was president of UNESCO's international music council. He used the office in 1971 to attack the Soviet Union for lack of cultural freedom in a speech in Moscow. He cited the achievements of Shostakovich, Yevtushenko, Solzhenitsyn, and others, all of them dissidents in the Soviet view, and deplored the enforced absence from the hall of Rostropovich.

In 1980 Menuhin toured America with Hephzibah, who had lived in London since the late 1950s with her second husband. She died on 1 January 1981. From 1982 he reduced his violin-playing engagements and increased his conducting, making a series of recordings with the Royal Philharmonic Orchestra and also conducting opera. In 1994 he recorded the nine Beethoven symphonies with the Sinfonia Varsovia. His name filled halls, and the fee

that he earned as a conductor became as high as that which he had taken as a violinist. In 1985 he became a British citizen (while not renouncing American citizenship) and became able to style himself Sir Yehudi Menuhin, having been appointed honorary KBE in 1965. He and Diana had left Highgate in 1983 and now lived in Chester Square, Belgravia. In 1987 he was appointed to the Order of Merit. On the occasion of his seventy-fifth birthday in 1991, Channel 4 screened a two-hour 'family portrait' by Tony Palmer. This drew heavily on interviews with Menuhin's children exposing his shortcomings as a father (he knew these, once saying that his mother had taught him that to show emotion to children was to be 'too Jewish'), and expounding the theory, not easily dismissed as fallacious, that he had allowed Marutha and Diana to dominate him. More pleasant were the award of the Wolf prize at the Knesset in Israel and the conferment of a life peerage, as Baron Menuhin, in 1993.

Last years and assessment Despite the onset of deafness Menuhin worked on towards his eightieth birthday, visiting South Africa again to conduct black singers in Handel's *Messiah*. His last public appearance as a violinist was at the fortieth Gstaad festival in 1996. Urged by his daughter Zamira to slow down he replied: 'Darling, I'd miss the airports. I couldn't imagine life without the whirlwind.' In March 1999 he embarked on an eighteen-day tour of Germany conducting thirteen concerts with the Sinfonia Varsovia. He was worried about Diana's frail health after a stroke and concealed from her the fact that he himself had a heart problem (instead of consulting a doctor, he bought homeopathic medicines). In Berlin a doctor diagnosed pneumonia and pleurisy of both lungs. Menuhin entered the Martin Luther Hospital there, and on 12 March 1999 died after a massive heart attack; his wife survived him. He was buried in the grounds of his school at Stoke d'Abernon on 19 March. A memorial service was held in Westminster Abbey in June 2000.

Whatever imperfections there may have been in his technique on occasions, there is no question that Menuhin was among the greatest of all violinists. At its best his playing had a seraphic spiritual quality which seemed to come from some supernatural source. His recordings of Elgar with Elgar, Beethoven with Furtwängler, and Brahms with Boult are permanent testimony to artistry and interpretative insight of the very highest quality. And where technique is concerned, his performances of Bartók answer most criticisms. Yet it was in the music of Bach, which he had loved from the day when he first heard Persinger play it, that he achieved the apotheosis of his art. As a conductor he had many special qualities too. His humanity and warmth are evident particularly in his recordings of Elgar and Vaughan Williams. It is ample testimony to his strength of character that he emerged from his years as a prodigy, when his life was controlled and manipulated by his parents, into adult musicianship. He regarded music as a healing art and himself as a power for good. He was fearless in his criticisms of injustice and inhumanity wherever he found them; a friend intended it as a compliment when she said that 'all who love him would like to see him a little more critical of the people he is ready to help instead of pouring his love indiscriminately on the worthy and unworthy alike' (Burton, 295).

MICHAEL KENNEDY

Sources H. Burton, *Menuhin* (2000) • Y. Menuhin, *Unfinished journey* (1976); repr. (1996) • M. Menuhin, *The Menuhin saga* (1984) • T. Palmer, *A family portrait* (1991) • R. Magidoff, *Yehudi Menuhin* (1973) • D. Menuhin, *Fiddler's moll* (1984) • D. Menuhin, *A glimpse of Olympus* (1996) • J. Stack, 'A conversation with Yehudi Menuhin', *New England Today* (18 June 1980) • *The Independent* (13 March 1999) • *The Times* (13 March 1999) • *The Guardian* (13 March 1999) • m. certs.
Archives BBC WAC, archive | Rice University, Houston, Texas, Woodson Research Center, corresp. with Sir Julian Huxley • Tate collection, corresp. with Lord Clark • U. Reading L., corresp. with Edward Thompson of Heinemann • U. Warwick Mod. RC, corresp. with Victor Gollancz | FILM Channel 4, 1991
Likenesses J. Epstein, bust, 1945; formerly in possession of Menuhin • D. Wynne, bust, 1963 • M. Pavelic, oils, 1982, NPG [*see illus.*] • C. Baron, portrait (eightieth birthday), repro. in Menuhin, *Unfinished journey*

Menzies, Archibald (1754–1842), naval surgeon and botanical collector, was born at the house of Styx or Stix, near Aberfeldy, Perthshire, on 15 March 1754, the son of James and Ann Menzies. He had three brothers and four sisters, and was educated at the parish school at Weims. His elder brother, William, was employed in the Royal Botanic Garden, Edinburgh, and Archibald too became a gardener. John Hope, then professor of botany, enabled him to train as a surgeon at the University of Edinburgh and Menzies took his degree in 1781. After making a botanical tour through the highlands and Hebrides in 1778, he became assistant to a surgeon at Caernarfon. He subsequently entered the navy as assistant surgeon on board the *Nonsuch*, under Captain Truscott, and was present at Rodney's victory over the Comte de Grasse on 12 April 1782. On the declaration of peace he was sent to the Halifax station, where he corresponded with Sir Joseph Banks and sent him seeds, and in 1786 he was engaged as surgeon on board the *Prince of Wales*, under Lieutenant Colnett, on a fur-trading voyage of discovery to the north-west coast of America. They visited Staten Island, the Sandwich Islands, and China, returning direct from the latter in 1789.

In 1790 Menzies was elected fellow of the Linnean Society, in whose *Transactions* for 1791 and 1798 he published accounts of his natural historical findings. In the same year he was chosen as naturalist and surgeon on the *Discovery*, under Captain George Vancouver. The party was to explore and chart the coasts of north-west America. They visited the Cape, King George's Sound, New Zealand, Tahiti, and the Sandwich and Galápagos islands, as well as north-west America. Vancouver praised his services in the preface to his account of the voyage; only one man died from ill health on the expedition, which returned in October 1795.

Menzies made the first recorded ascent by a European of Wha-ra-rai and Mauna Loa, an active volcano over 13,000 feet in height, in Hawaii (Sandwich Islands); he determined their altitude by the barometer, and collected specimens in all the countries visited, especially at Valparaiso

and at Nootka Sound. He brought back a great variety of plants, including *Ribes speciosum*, *Araucaria imbricata*, and *Abies menziesii*, and numerous cryptogams, besides other natural history objects. The plants were transported in a glazed frame which foreshadowed the Wardian case, though many died after a disagreement between Menzies and Vancouver as to their handling. The new species of plants were described by Sir J. E. Smith, Robert Brown, and Sir W. J. Hooker, and Menzies himself gave an account of the voyage in the first and second volumes of John Loudon's *Magazine of Natural History*. Menzies' Olympic peninsula journal was published in 1992, and his Alaska journal was published in 1993. His Hawaii or Sandwich Island journals recording three separate visits to the islands were published in 1920. The long delays were due to his having given his five-volume journal to Banks rather than publish it himself.

Menzies was made honorary MD of Aberdeen University in 1799 and in the same year he joined the *Sanspareil* in the West Indies, under Lord Hugh Seymour. Soon after his return he retired from the navy, and he practised for some time in London, living in Chapel Place, Cavendish Square. He had married late in life and had no children. His wife died in 1836. From 1826 he lived at 2 Ladbroke Terrace, Notting Hill, where he died on 15 February 1842; he was buried at Kensal Green cemetery beside his wife. His herbarium of grasses, sedges, and cryptogams was bequeathed to the Royal Botanic Garden, Edinburgh; in 1886 other specimens were acquired by the British Museum.

Menzies is commemorated in the names of several of the plants he collected, though some have subsequently been renamed. Although skilled in botanical collection, description, and illustration, he never achieved eminence, because he relied on others to make his work public.

ELIZABETH BAIGENT

Sources *GM*, 2nd ser., 17 (1842), 668–9 • J. M. Naish, *The interwoven lives of George Vancouver, Archibald Menzies, Joseph Whidbey and Peter Puget* (1996) • J. J. Keevil, 'Archibald Menzies, 1754–1842', *Bulletin of the History of Medicine*, 22 (1948), 796–811 • J. Grinnell, 'Archibald Menzies, first collector of California birds', *The Condor*, 34 (1932), 243–52 • E. W. Groves, *Archibald Menzies* (1992) • W. K. Lamb, *Banks and Menzies* (1992) • F. R. S. Balfour, 'Archibald Menzies, 1754–1842: botanist, zoologist, medico and explorer', *Proceedings of the Linnean Society of London*, 156th session (1943–4), 170–83; pubd separately (1945)
Archives BL, journal of voyage in the *Discovery*, Add. MS 32641 • British Columbia Archives and Records Service, Victoria, corresp. and papers • Linn. Soc., journal [copy] • NL Aus., journal [copy] • U. Edin., New College, journal relating to Sandwich Islands • University of Washington, papers | Linn. Soc., letters to Sir James Smith • NHM, zoological notes made during Captain Vancouver's voyage to the Pacific Ocean • RBG Kew, corresp. with Sir Joseph Banks
Likenesses lithograph, 1835 (after E. U. Eddis), Wellcome L. • E. U. Eddis, oils, 1836, Linn. Soc. • Miss Turner, lithograph (after E. U. Eddis), BM, NPG

Menzies, Sir Frederick Norton Kay (1875–1949), medical officer of health, was born at Caernarfon on 2 November 1875, the second son of John Menzies, a civil engineer, and his wife, Edith Madeline, the daughter of Robert Kay, of

Burnley, Lancashire. He was educated at Llandovery College and at the University of Edinburgh, where he graduated MB in 1899 and in 1903 gained his MD degree and became member of the Royal College of Physicians of Edinburgh. He spent some time in postgraduate study in Vienna and Berlin and held resident posts at the Edinburgh Royal Infirmary, and in London at the Hospital for Sick Children, Great Ormond Street, the Brompton Hospital, and the Western Fever Hospital of the Metropolitan Asylums Board.

In 1905 Menzies obtained the diploma in public health, and in 1907 he was appointed demonstrator and lecturer in public health at University College, London, under Henry Richard Kenwood. In the same year he became deputy medical officer of health of the metropolitan borough of Stoke Newington in north London, and in 1909 he joined the staff of the London county council as a part-time officer. Two years later he was appointed a full-time assistant medical officer and began school medical work in the East End of London. His next important role was to prepare and implement schemes for the control of tuberculosis and venereal diseases in London. This task brought him into close contact with the managements and staffs of the then voluntary hospitals, a happy association which broadened with the years.

Menzies married in 1916 Harriet May, daughter of Edward Honoratus Lloyd KC, a leader of the parliamentary bar. They had two sons and one daughter; the elder son, a regular soldier, was killed in action in Normandy in 1944. In 1923 Menzies inherited Thorpe Abbotts Place, Diss, Norfolk, from his cousin, the daughter of Sir Edward Ebenezer Kay. For many years before her death he had managed the estate for her. He was so greatly attached to it that he gave up his London house and went to live there. In 1924 he resigned his post with London county council to become director of hospitals and medical services for the joint council of the British Red Cross Society and the order of St John of Jerusalem, and he also carried out a great deal of work for the Voluntary Hospital Commission. However, he was persuaded to remain on the county council's part-time staff as a consultant on the tuberculosis and venereal diseases schemes. During these years he visited large numbers of hospitals to inspect them, laying the basis for his work in the 1930s.

In 1926 Menzies returned to full-time work for the county council, succeeding his old chief, Sir William Hamer, as county medical officer of health. A few years later, torn between his own wish to settle down on his Norfolk estate and the increasing demands made upon him by his official duties, he took the decision to devote all his energies to London and sold the estate.

After 1926, although his responsibilities as county medical officer of health covered a very wide field, Menzies' main preoccupation was with hospital administration and preparing for moves to reform the poor law. In 1930 seventy-two general and special hospitals of the Metropolitan Asylums Board and of the twenty-five metropolitan boards of guardians were, on the abolition of those bodies, transferred to the control of the county council, with

Menzies as their chief medical adviser. The immense task of welding them into an integrated hospital service was possible only because of Menzies' unique knowledge of hospitals of all classes. Nevertheless, it was smoothly accomplished, and Menzies turned these hospitals into a co-ordinated group. He 'regarded the LCC as an ideal prototype hospital and health region'. In 1941 he described regionalization as 'the order of the day, the "New Order" or "New Deal", already adopted for wartime purposes and destined to be generally applied in peacetime' (Webster, 82–3). So successful was he that he received the most unusual distinction of mention in the published report of a government department. The annual report of the Ministry of Health for 1934–5 stated that 'the London County Council … were, indeed, fortunate in having a county medical officer whose personality and experience have been so largely responsible for the successful results which have been achieved'. On his retirement from office in 1939 the LCC recorded in its minutes the outstanding value of Menzies' services to London.

Menzies then returned to his native Caernarvonshire, where he acted as inspector of hospitals and convalescent homes in north Wales for the British Red Cross Society and the order of St John of Jerusalem. In 1945 he went back to London and was much in demand for committee work of which he had so much previous experience. He had been a member of government committees on venereal diseases, the training and employment of midwives, the scientific investigation of crime, and on nursing. He was for many years a ministry of health representative on the Central Midwives' Board and the General Nursing Council. He also played an active part in the establishment of the University of London's postgraduate medical school, at Hammersmith Hospital, while he was a medical officer of health. A great upholder of voluntary effort, he was a member of the council of King Edward's Hospital Fund for London, the Nuffield Provincial Hospitals Trust, and of the boards of St Thomas's Hospital, the London Hospital, and Queen Mary's Hospital, Roehampton. He was a member of the council of the National Association for the Prevention of Tuberculosis and of the appeals committee of the British Broadcasting Corporation.

Menzies, who was of commanding stature, possessed good judgement, the gift of exposition, and a persuasive tongue. He studied every problem thoroughly, and when he had found the solution he refused to compromise with expediency. In 1932 he was appointed KBE and in 1937 he was made honorary physician to the king. Already elected fellow of the Royal College of Physicians of Edinburgh in 1907, he was awarded its Cullen prize in 1934; in 1932 he became FRCP, London, and was presented with its Bisset-Hawkins gold medal in 1941. In 1927 he was elected a fellow of the Royal Society of Edinburgh and in 1933 he received the honorary degree of LLD from the University of Edinburgh. He was a knight of grace of the order of St John of Jerusalem.

During the later years of his life Menzies' health was not good. In February 1949, in his capacity as chairman of the

London committee, he went to Port Said to inspect the British hospital there. He was taken ill on the return voyage but was able to reach London, where he died, somewhat suddenly, at his home, 41 Melbury Court Gardens, on 14 May 1949. He was survived by his wife.

ALLEN DALEY, *rev.* PATRICK WALLIS

Sources *The Times* (16 May 1949) • *BMJ* (21 May 1949), 913–14 • *The Lancet* (21 May 1949) • J. Sheldrake, 'The L.C.C. hospital service', *Politics and the people of London: the London county council, 1889–1965*, ed. A. Saint (1989), 187–98 • *The annual address: delivered to the Royal College of Physicians of London on Monday 3 April 1950 by the president, Lord Moran* (1950) • personal knowledge (1959) • C. Webster, *The health services since the war*, 1 (1988) • *CGPLA Eng. & Wales* (1949)

Archives RCP Lond., memorandum on the London Council Hospital service | HLRO, letters to David Lloyd George

Likenesses W. Stoneman, photograph, 1947, NPG

Wealth at death £159,787 17s. 6d.: probate, 21 July 1949, *CGPLA Eng. & Wales*

Menzies, John (1624–1684), Church of Scotland minister and university professor, was born in Aberdeen. He was said to have been brought up a Roman Catholic, but must have converted to protestantism at an early age; his parents are unknown. He was admitted to Marischal College, Aberdeen, in 1638, and after graduating he was regent in logic until 1649, when he was first ordained and admitted to the second charge of St Nicholas, Aberdeen. He was then appointed professor of divinity in Marischal College and was translated to the Greyfriars Church, which was connected with it. He married Margaret Forbes, eldest daughter of Sir William Forbes of Craigievar, Aberdeenshire; they had one son, who died in Menzies' lifetime.

In the divisions which split the Scottish church in 1650 and 1651 Menzies became a protester leader, but in 1652 he supported Cromwell and became an Independent. As a result he faced prosecution by the synod of Aberdeen, but proceedings were stopped by order of the commandant of the English garrison. Menzies was called by Cromwell to London, with other protesters, to prepare an ordinance for the admission of ministers to parishes in Scotland, and was appointed a 'trier' for his own part of the country. In 1658, however, he returned to presbyterianism.

At the Restoration Menzies initially refused to conform to episcopacy, but when summoned before the privy council and threatened with deposition by the bishop and synod if he did not comply before January 1663 he accepted the change and retained his offices. He took an active part in the controversies with Roman Catholics and Quakers: his *Papismus Lucifugus, or … The Papers Exchanged betwixt Mr J. Menzies … and Mr F. Dempster, Jesuit* (1668) and *Roma mendax, or, The Falsehood of Rome's High Pretences to Infallibility and Antiquity Evicted* (1675) reveal a strident anti-Catholicism and anti-Quakerism and express a defence of predestinarianism indicative of Calvinist theology. His stance so recommended him to the authorities that there were rumours that he would be made a bishop. He held a post as rector in King's College, Aberdeen, from 1677 to 1682 and, after some hesitation, accepted the professorship of divinity in the college in 1678, but resigned shortly afterwards and was reinstated in his professorship in Marischal College and in the charge of Greyfriars Church. In

1681 he refused the test imposed by parliament and was deprived of his office, but the following year he changed his mind and was restored. That year he also published a funeral sermon for Sir Alexander Fraser of Doores.

Menzies died in Aberdeen on 1 February 1684, his conscience troubled both on account of his having conformed to episcopacy and of his having taken the test. He professed penitence for his vacillation and requested his brother-in-law to publish his declaration to that effect.

G. W. SPROTT, *rev.* R. P. WELLS

Sources *Fasti Scot.*, new edn, 6.2, 8 • R. Wodrow, *The history of the sufferings of the Church of Scotland from the Restoration to the revolution*, ed. R. Burns, 1 (1828), 315–16 • R. Wodrow, *The history of the sufferings of the Church of Scotland from the Restoration to the revolution*, ed. R. Burns, 2 (1829), 188 • R. Wodrow, *The history of the sufferings of the Church of Scotland from the Restoration to the revolution*, ed. R. Burns, 3 (1829), 310–11 • *Fasti academiae Mariscallanae Aberdonensis: selections from the records of the Marischal College and University, MDXCIII–MDCCLX*, 2, ed. P. J. Anderson, New Spalding Club, 18 (1898), 12, 34–5, 51, 588–9 • J. Stuart, ed., *Selections from the records of the kirk session, presbytery, and synod of Aberdeen*, Spalding Club, 15 (1846) • G. Grub, *An ecclesiastical history of Scotland*, 4 vols. (1861), vol. 3, pp. 155, 162–3, 265 • *DSCHT*, 559–66 • P. J. Anderson, ed., *Officers and graduates of University and King's College, Aberdeen, MVD–MDCCCLX*, New Spalding Club, 11 (1893), 11–12, 70 • *The letters and journals of Robert Baillie*, ed. D. Laing, 3 (1842), 273, 282, 364, 568 • J. Stuart, ed., *Extracts from the council register of the burgh of Aberdeen, 1625–1747*, 2, Scottish Burgh RS, 9 (1872), 131, 187, 224, 247, 263

Menzies, John (*fl.* 1710–1753), Jacobite agent, was born in Aberdeen, though details of his parents and upbringing are unknown. Menzies was a principal contact between the Stuart court and tory ministers and Jacobite MPs in Queen Anne's reign. Service in the rising of 1715 apparently earned Menzies Lord Mar's patronage. He resided in London during 1716–20, and was entrusted with crucial and sensitive correspondence during the Jacobite–Swedish plot of 1717–18, and in secret negotiations with whig minister Charles, third earl of Sunderland, in 1721. Later accused of embezzlement, Menzies fell foul of prominent Jacobites such as Francis Atterbury, bishop of Rochester. Mar vigorously defended Menzies' reputation, but the resulting rift between Mar, Atterbury, and the earl of Oxford consequently helped create fractious rival Jacobite groups. As with most Jacobite exiles, penury was a constant reality for Menzies. After his meagre pension expired, Menzies lived in France from 1720 to 1721 and sold chocolate to French nobles as a sideline. Mar's betrayal of the Jacobites seriously compromised Menzies' stature, yet James III (James Francis Edward Stuart) maintained confidence in him. Menzies was not directly involved in the Atterbury plot, but had been selected by the English Jacobite Charles, fourth earl of Orrery, to go to Russia in 1722 as an emissary. These plans collapsed when Orrery was imprisoned and Menzies again fled the authorities.

Menzies' poverty and his supposed slander of his own replacement, coupled with Atterbury's abhorrence of Mar and reports of that nobleman's underlings spying on leading Jacobites, effectively terminated Menzies' activities. After 1725 he resided in France permanently, continuing to correspond with Rome for decades, but his opinions were unsolicited. In 1736 he recounted his long service in a desperate appeal for money for him and his family, about which little is known, not even his wife's name. His last letter to Rome is dated May 1753, after which there exist no further details of his life or death.

Menzies' evident facility in French was recognized yet, like many minor Jacobite figures, he drew criticism for alleged incompetence and indiscretions, as well as for his protestantism. Desperate individuals who often were disrespected by nobles, Menzies and other agents inevitably were cast as scapegoats when conspiracies went sour. LAWRENCE B. SMITH

Sources Royal Arch., Stuart papers · *Calendar of the Stuart papers belonging to his majesty the king, preserved at Windsor Castle*, 7 vols., HMC, 56 (1902–23) · J. Macpherson, ed., *Original papers: containing the secret history of Great Britain*, 2nd edn, 2 vols. (1776) · Nairne MSS, Bodl. Oxf., MS Carte 212
Archives PRO, state papers domestic, SP 35 · PRO, state papers domestic, entry books, SP 44 · PRO, state papers foreign, France SP 78 | BL, Newcastle MSS, 1707–34, Add. MSS 32686, 32745–32749, 32752–32753, 32761, 32771–32774, 33198–33199 · BL, Stowe MSS 226–227 · Bodl. Oxf., Nairne MSS, MS Carte 212 · CUL, Cholmondeley (Houghton) MSS, MSS of Sir Robert Walpole, earl of Orford · NA Scot., Mar and Kellie MSS, GD 124 · Royal Arch., Stuart MSS

Menzies, John, of Pitfodels (1756–1843), benefactor, was born on 15 August 1756, the last member of a Roman Catholic family long resident at Pitfodels, Aberdeenshire. His father had died earlier in 1756, and Menzies was raised by his mother, a member of the house of Kirkconnel, who for a time moved the family to Belgium. He was educated at the Jesuit college at Dinant until its disbandment, probably in 1774. His mother then, unsuccessfully, petitioned Bishop George Hay for permission to employ Alexander Strachan, the former Jesuit missionary at Kirkconnel, as her son's tutor. In 1811 Menzies—who was known as Menzies of Pitfodels—benefited from the Relief Act when he was appointed deputy lieutenant of the counties of Aberdeen and Kincardine and convener of Aberdeenshire. By this time Menzies was, in Christine Johnson's opinion, 'perhaps the wealthiest and most influential Catholic in Scotland' (Johnson, 209) on account of his inheriting the estate and house at Blairs, near Aberdeen. In the next three decades he used his wealth to become an active promoter and benefactor of Catholic worship and education in Scotland. In 1812 he gave £2000 to purchase a site for the building of a new chapel on Leith Walk, Edinburgh. In 1827 he donated his estate to the Scottish Mission to found a new national seminary to replace the existing (and, in Menzies' view, inadequate) institutions at Lismore and Anquhorties. Places for sixty boys were provided at St Mary's College, Blairs, which opened on 2 June 1829 and, until 1874, remained the only Scottish seminary. In the year he gave up his estate, Menzies was described by Sir Walter Scott as 'a bauld crack that auld papist body, and well informed … He is very angry with the Irish demagogues, and a sound well-thinking man' (*Journal*, 1.349). In the following decade he participated in raising funds for the convent of St Margaret, Edinburgh, which opened in 1835. He was a member of the Abbotsford Club, to which, in 1842, he presented his *Extracta e variis cronicis*

Scocie. He died, unmarried, at Greenhill Cottage, near Edinburgh, on 11 October 1843. Blairs College, the legacy of this the only Catholic laird who 'backed the Scottish Mission financially to any significant extent' (Johnson, 146), was enlarged in 1897 and closed in 1986.

PHILIP CARTER

Sources C. Johnson, *Developments in the Roman Catholic church in Scotland, 1789–1829* (1983) · *DSCHT* · J. Ritchie, *Memorial of the centenary of St Mary's College, Blairs* (1929) · *The journal of Sir Walter Scott*, 2 vols. (1890–91) · *DNB*
Archives Scottish Catholic Archives, Edinburgh, the Presholme letters

Menzies, John (1808–1879), wholesale distributor and newsagent, was born in Edinburgh, the son of John Menzies, merchant, and his wife, Catherine Lindsay. He was educated at the Royal High School, Edinburgh. After a stiff and joyless apprenticeship (1823–30) to an Edinburgh bookseller named Sutherland, he moved to London, where he worked (December 1831 until February 1833) for Charles Tilt, a Fleet Street publisher of a famous Miniature Library. In consequence of his father's sudden death he returned to Edinburgh, and in 1833 opened a small shop at 61 Princes Street selling books, stationery, and prints. London life had given him a taste for innovation. He made a daring experiment in selling *The Scotsman* across his counter at a time when newspapers were customarily sold direct by their publishers to subscribers. In 1845 Menzies married Rossie Marr, daughter of a Leith merchant; they had two sons and three daughters.

At that time a retail bookseller acted as agent for a few publishers, whose books he exclusively displayed and sold; there were only loose connections between London publishers and Edinburgh retailers owing to the difficulties of travel. To remedy this situation Menzies inaugurated a wholesale book department, his chief business being on behalf of Tilt and (from 1837) Chapman and Hall. He secured the agency for *Punch* magazine (1841). He built up a prosperous business, although he never showed great ambitions and received some of his finest satisfactions from meeting or corresponding with literary figures like Charles Dickens. He was Edinburgh agent for the sale of *Mr Humphrey's Clock*, and for all of Dickens's works in east Scotland.

In 1835 Menzies issued his first trade stocklist, and from 1845 circulated a monthly catalogue to country buyers and other interested parties. He was irritable with customers who delayed settling their accounts, and implacable in pursuing small debts. He enjoyed publishing as a sideline of his business, and issued a series of Scottish guidebooks and books of Scottish views. His most lavish production was *The Costumes of the Clans* (1845) by the troublesome John Carter Allen, written in the name of John Sobieski Stolberg Stuart, soi-disant Count d'Albanie.

For a time Menzies ran an export department, but his most lucrative business was in railway bookstalls, of which he opened his first in 1857. These bookstalls proliferated, and he also recruited boys carrying baskets of

John Menzies (1808–1879), by unknown artist [detail]

reading matter to stand on platforms to service the passengers of through trains. Such were the rewards of railway station business that he abandoned his shop and moved to new warehouse premises on Hanover Street, Edinburgh, in 1859. John Menzies & Co. was formed as a partnership in 1867. A Glasgow wholesale branch was opened in 1868, and branches were set up in other Scottish towns during 1872–3. John Menzies died of heart failure on 6 December 1879 at his home, 3 Grosvenor Crescent, Edinburgh.

Menzies' elder son, **John Ross Menzies** (1852–1935), wholesale distributor and newsagent, was born on 17 September 1852 at 28 North Nelson Street, Edinburgh. He was a pawky, industrious Scot with foresight and ambition. Whereas his father had enjoyed the personal contacts of bookselling and wholesaling, he had a hard-headed interest in commercial matters. His driving force confirmed Menzies as the principal 'multiple' of newsagencies and booksellers in Scotland equivalent to the firms of W. H. Smith in England and of Eason in Ireland. He shared Smith's terror of handling salacious or lurid reading material. Local Scottish booksellers and newsagents resented the expansion of Menzies railway bookstalls, which were exempt from early-closing legislation, rates, and taxes. The large, prominent Menzies kiosks at the great urban termini were popular as rendezvous with generations of Scottish travellers and lovers. J. R. Menzies together with his brother, Charles Thompson Menzies (1858–1943), extended the company's wholesale warehouses to Dundee, Carlisle, and Aberdeen. The company opened its first English outlet, a railway bookstall at Carlisle, in 1888, although an informal understanding was later reached with W. H. Smith that neither company would invade the other's business territory. Menzies' annual profits averaged about £8000 in the 1880s. The firm continued in a small way as publishers until 1905, the last book appearing under their imprint being

Horsebreaking, a monograph on the schooling of ponies by the marchioness of Breadalbane. The business was constituted as a limited company in 1906, at which date it operated 357 railway bookstalls (second only in the United Kingdom to W. H. Smith). John Menzies became chairman and joint managing director of the company in 1906. The company began advertising at Edinburgh in 1913 (though not until 1926 in Glasgow), which stimulated the wholesaling business. But the 1920s were a period of stagnation: John Menzies retired as joint managing director in 1927 and as chairman in 1932.

The Menzies brothers worked long hours and preferred to eat sandwiches rather than leave their desks for lunch. They were patriarchal, sternly benevolent employers who devised incentives for their staff, including the payment of quarterly commissions. They started a rambling club in 1886, and were proud of their social and sports clubs. The most junior staff could rise through the management to the board of directors.

When young, John Ross Menzies yachted on the Clyde; later he was a devoted golfer. He had a craggy, forbidding appearance, shunned the limelight, and never married. He died of arteriosclerosis on 5 March 1935 at West Links House, North Berwick. The firm continued to be a family concern, under the direction of the children of his brother Charles.   RICHARD DAVENPORT-HINES

Sources *The Scotsman* (6 March 1935) · J. Menzies & Co., *The house of Menzies* (1958) · J. Menzies & Co., *The Menzies group* (1965) · L. Gardiner, *The making of John Menzies* (1983) · d. cert. · old parochial register (births and baptisms), 12 Nov 1852, Edinburgh, Scotland [John Ross Menzies] · d. cert. [John Ross Menzies] · *DSBB* · *CGPLA Eng. & Wales* (1935) [John Ross Menzies] · *The Times* (7 March 1935) · b. cert. [John Ross Menzies]

Likenesses double portrait, oils (with John Ross Menzies), repro. in Menzies & Co., *House of Menzies*, facing p. 22 · oils, repro. in Menzies & Co., *House of Menzies*, frontispiece · oils, John Menzies, Edinburgh [*see illus.*]

Wealth at death £137,949—John Ross Menzies: confirmation, 17 May 1935, *CGPLA Eng. & Wales*

Menzies, John Ross (1852–1935). *See under* Menzies, John (1808–1879).

Menzies [Menzey], **Michael** (d. 1766), advocate and inventor of agricultural and mining machinery, was probably one of the Menzies of Culter-Allers, Lanarkshire; little is known of his origins, but a younger brother was 'sheriff-depute' of Haddingtonshire. Menzies was admitted a member of the Faculty of Advocates on 31 January 1719. Menzies may have been the first to suggest threshing grain by a machine, and his idea was to imitate the action of the ordinary flail. A number of flails were attached to a horizontal axis, which was moved rapidly to and fro through half a revolution, the grain to be threshed being placed on either side. He took out a patent for his invention in 1734 (no. 544), and it was described in the *Transactions* of the Society of Improvers in Agriculture in 1743. It was not a practical success.

Menzies also took out a patent in 1750 (no. 653) for a machine to convey coal from the worked face to the bottom of the shaft, and in 1761 he obtained another patent (no. 762) for working and draining coal mines. Menzies' designs were very complicated, but at least several of the coal-conveying machines were built, and one was in use at Chatershaugh colliery, on the Wear, in 1753. J. C. Curr wrote in 1797 that 'The most ancient machine in my knowledge, now in use, is that invented by Menzey' (Curr, 33). His method of raising coals up the shaft, however, was only applicable where there was a stream of water with a fall of about half the depth of the pit. Menzies died at Edinburgh on 13 December 1766.

R. B. PROSSER, *rev.* ROBERT BROWN

Sources J. C. Curr, *The coal viewer and engine builder's practical companion* (1797) · R. Bald, *A general view of the coal trade of Scotland* (1812) · G. B. Hepburn, *A general view of the agriculture and rural economy of East Lothian* (1794) · R. L. Galloway, *Annals of coal mining and the coal trade*, 1st ser. (1898) · *Farmer's Magazine*, 17 (1816), 401 · *Scot's Magazine* (1766), 671

Menzies, Dame Pattie Maie (1899–1995). *See under* Menzies, Sir Robert Gordon (1894–1978).

Menzies, Sir Robert Gordon (1894–1978), prime minister of Australia, was born on 20 December 1894 at Jeparit, in the Wimmera district of Victoria, the fourth of the five children of James Menzies and his wife, Kate Sampson. The forebears were Scots on the paternal side and Cornish on the maternal. James was Jeparit's general storekeeper and local community leader, a lay preacher and prominent in activities ranging from sporting clubs to the district shire council.

Early life and career Though themselves not formally well educated, Menzies' parents were well read and anxious that their children should have the best instruction that could be arranged. They were accordingly sent to school in the nearby city of Ballarat. Bob did best, topping the state scholarship examination in 1907, studying subsequently at Wesley College, Melbourne, and on an exhibition at the University of Melbourne. In an outstanding undergraduate career he won a galaxy of prizes and the award in 1918 of the degree of master of laws.

Admitted to the bar, Menzies read with Owen Dixon, the leading Victorian junior and later chief justice of Australia. In 1920, as advocate for the Amalgamated Society of Engineers, Menzies won in the high court a case which proved a landmark in the augmentation of commonwealth powers over those of the states. The court's verdict brought Menzies 'sudden fame' professionally: more important personally, it gave him, as a young man of twenty-five, the means to marry. His bride was Pattie Maie (Pat) Leckie (1899–1995) [*see below*], daughter of J. W. Leckie, a manufacturer who had served in the Victorian parliament. They were married on 27 September 1920 at the Kew Presbyterian Church.

This was a period of political ferment in Melbourne, principally among young and respectable men. They wanted to bring a new sense of public responsibility to state politics, then notoriously moribund, even corrupt, and in organizations such as the Constitutional Club promoted speaking classes, a library, and a model parliament. Menzies imbibed the atmosphere of the time and, as a successful young professional, felt obliged to undertake 'a

Sir Robert Gordon Menzies (1894–1978), by Elliott & Fry, 1941

certain amount of public work'. He drifted into the service of the Nationalist Party, the conservative political formation spawned when Labor split over conscription during the late war. As a member of this party he entered the Victorian upper house, the legislative council, in 1928 at a by-election, and then, in the lower house, captured the Nunawading seat at the general election of the following year. He was soon a founder and leader of the 'Young Nationals', a ginger group dedicated to revitalizing the Nationalist Party, and as such had won by 1931 the presidency of the national federation, the governing body of the party apparatus. After the defeat of the ruling state Labor government in 1932 he was the first 'young nat.' to receive full cabinet rank when he became attorney-general and minister for railways in the Nationalist ministry headed by Sir Stanley Argyle.

Menzies was meanwhile being progressively drawn into federal politics by the crisis of the great depression. In the early 1930s the depression brought suffering to split James Scullin's ruling Labor government between those who thought salvation lay in balanced budgets and those for whom unusual troubles required unusual remedies, most particularly the expansion of credit. 'Honest Joe' Lyons, by late 1930 Scullin's acting treasurer, took the former attitude, as did Menzies and a 'Group of Six' prominent non-Labor men, who took the lead in virtually establishing a new political party to replace the existing Nationalists. The new organization, the United Australia Party (UAP), which altered the whole structure of Australian politics, was in fact largely the product of a powerful coalition of forces triggered by a mushrooming of citizens' leagues through which responsible elements from many levels of society gave expression to their fears of civil dislocation as depression conditions bit. Menzies and his compatriots persuaded Lyons to leave the Labor Party and become leader of the non-Labor federal opposition. The existing opposition leader, J. G. Latham, resigned and Lyons, at the head of the new party of redemption, became opposition leader. A federal election late in 1931 installed him as prime minister of Australia, after a sweeping victory in which eight Labor ministers lost their seats. In 1934 Menzies was persuaded to stand for the federal seat of Kooyong, which became vacant when its incumbent, Latham, left politics altogether. Elected with ease, Menzies took Latham's place, as attorney-general, in Lyons's cabinet. He was to hold the Kooyong seat until his voluntary retirement from parliament in 1966.

In 1935, at the age of forty-one, and accompanied by his wife, Menzies made his first trip to England, one of a small party of Australian ministers visiting London to take part in the silver jubilee celebration of George V's reign. As attorney-general he was also involved in official trade talks. He found these tedious but nothing could dim his joy in experiencing, as he put it in his diary, the reflections which 'can so strangely move the souls of those who go "home" to a land they have never seen' (Martin and Hardy, 1.148). For weeks he revelled in the actuality—in stones and architecture, countryside and ceremony—of the Britain that his education had taught him was also his. He met political notables, travelled widely, was entertained at Buckingham Palace, and won plaudits as a public speaker. Subsequent official visits, again largely for trade talks, enhanced his reputation and confirmed his affection for British culture, but evoked further aversion at what he saw as the ruthlessness of British businessmen.

Prime minister On Lyons's death in 1939 the UAP elected Menzies to party leadership. Page, leader of the Country Party, announced that his party would no longer work in coalition with the UAP, and launched on Menzies an attack described by the *Sydney Morning Herald* as 'a violation of the decencies of debate without parallel in the annals of the Federal Parliament' (Martin and Hardy, 1.274). Page asserted that, with war threatening, Menzies was incapable of leading the nation, because he had been disloyal to Lyons and because he had failed to enlist in the First World War. Though the full reasons for this animus are not altogether clear, Page—a simple if pompous soul—was well known as a butt for Menzies' often cutting wit and uncanny gifts as a mimic. Menzies perforce formed a new, all-UAP cabinet, which in September 1939 became a war cabinet when Menzies and his ministers assumed, without dissent, that since Britain had declared war on Germany after the latter's invasion of Poland, Australia would do so too.

The government took steps at once to put Australia on a war footing. War Precautions Acts gave new powers over industry and civil life, and recruitment of a second Australian Imperial Force began. Menzies resisted as long as he could 'minds ... heavily indoctrinated by the "old soldiers'

point of view"' (Martin and Hardy, 1.289) which pressed for rapid deployment of an expeditionary force to come to Britain's aid. Equally, he was worried about the Japanese threat. Late in 1940 he decided to visit London to remonstrate at Britain's failure to strengthen Singapore, which was then seen as the key bastion in Australia's Pacific defence. But even before he left, a general election had reduced his majority in the federal parliament to two (and independents at that), and already Labor was refusing to take part in a national government. When he arrived in England the first, 'phoney', stage of the European war was over: Britain was facing aerial blitz and daily fear of invasion from the continent. Assisting Australia, as Menzies asked, was out of the question. Invited by courtesy to sit while in London in the British cabinet, Menzies developed a curious love–hate relationship with Churchill whom he privately blamed for many of the disasters of this stage of the war, including the heavy losses Australian and New Zealand expeditionary troops suffered in the abortive Greek and Cretan campaigns.

It was an open secret that during Menzies' absence plotting took place against his leadership. He was not universally popular, not being good—as his political opponent but personal friend John Curtin once put it—'at handling his men' (Martin and Hardy, 1.385), and having alienated sections of the electorate through his social position, intelligence, and sometimes arrogant ways. Though welcomed on his return to Australia by great public meetings, to which he gave rousing patriotic addresses, Menzies soon came to feel that under his leadership the UAP could not prosper and the war effort might suffer. He offered Labor more proposals for a national government. When these were rejected, he called an emergency cabinet meeting at which a majority of his ministers agreed that a new leader was needed. Menzies forthwith resigned, to offer what he called 'real prospects of unity in the ranks of the Government parties' (ibid., 1.383). For him it was a deep personal blow; for the government parties it proved an ineffectual move. Before 1940 was out Labor, under John Curtin, was in office and Menzies on the opposition benches.

Menzies showed remarkable resilience after the first shock of resignation. The aged W. M. Hughes was elected party leader but proved ineffectual when Labor swept the polls in 1943, and Menzies was re-elected. With the passing of the crisis which had given it birth, the UAP was evidently in decline, and a series of 'post-mortems' on the 1943 defeat counselled a new start. Thus in 1944–5 was formed the Liberal Party, in whose gestation Menzies' influence was prominent.

Though elected leader of the new party, Menzies' position remained for some time uncertain. He was still not universally trusted and when defeated badly in the 1946 election toyed with the idea of leaving politics altogether. What saved him was the decision of Curtin's successor, Ben Chifley, to nationalize the Australian banks in 1947. Menzies took the lead in fighting this move, using it as symbolic of what he saw as the key issue of post-war politics: a struggle between socialism and planning for social justice on the one hand and the growth of freedom and prosperity through spontaneous, especially economic, development on the other.

In 1948 Menzies' party, after long argument, decided to dissolve the Communist Party of Australia if it came to office. The early cold war was taking shape. The Australian Liberal Party had been deeply moved by the communist coup in Prague and the death of Jan Masaryk. Menzies himself was in London in 1948, when the first Berlin blockade so stirred fears, only three years from the end of the Second World War, that another conflagration was about to break out.

The Menzies era The 1949 election fanned the flames of anti-communism and told against a Labor government which stood on a record of austerity whose virtues were not cherished on every side. The Liberals won and so began that period of ascendancy known as the 'Menzies era'. It lasted a record sixteen years and involved his winning seven general elections in a row. Not all were unequivocal victories: close calls were registered in 1954 and 1961 and, particularly after the formation of the Democratic Labor Party, the Liberals sometimes benefited fortuitously from their opponents' disarray. For all that, Menzies enjoyed formidable support in his own right. Occasional complaints about his leadership style notwithstanding, experience brought mellowness, and none could gainsay the extraordinary skill he developed over years of experience in handling the arts and mechanisms of politics. There was also the comfortable assumption he and some of his supporters cultivated that he was the 'natural' leader of the respectable, middle-of-the-road elements of the post-war community. His own early 'fireside talk' broadcasts, his concern, from the beginning, that women—most particularly the country's sound matrons—should be well represented in the new Liberal organization, and the relative permanence and autonomy of that organization itself were further factors in the development of this atmosphere.

The period of Menzies' ascendancy was marked by extraordinary economic growth. This 'long boom' was experienced in most advanced economies, but the Menzies governments' stability, their declared policies of 'development', and their continuance of the ambitious immigration programme initiated by Labor helped to transform Australian material life, as indicated by markers as various as growth in population and home ownership, the ubiquity of white goods, and a great jump in motor-vehicle ownership.

Predictably, communism and cold war fears dominated in the first years of Menzies' ascendancy. After one false start, the government carried legislation to dissolve the Communist Party, but this was declared invalid by the high court. Having successfully engineered a dissolution of both houses of parliament, the government won a second election and asked at referendum for constitutional powers to deal with communism in the same terms as had the nullified act. The opposition, under H. V. Evatt, narrowly defeated the referendum, depicted by its detractors

as an attack on civil liberties. Menzies travelled extensively in his first year or so of office, consulted many politicians and men of affairs, and decided as early as 1951 that Australia faced the danger of war in three years' time. Legislation established a National Security Resources Board to advise on the stockpiling of strategic materials, compulsory military training for eighteen-year-olds was instituted, and new equipment was planned for the army and navy. These measures were meant to accompany and strengthen the new anti-communist powers asked for at referendum. But, together with loans contracted abroad to give extensive stimulation to economic development (the other declared objective of the Liberals), they involved sometimes crippling expenditure which countered efforts to hold a lid on inflation.

Menzies benefited vicariously from the extraordinarily popular Australian tour of the young Queen Elizabeth in 1954, but sourness supervened when, on the eve of the election in that year, Vladimir Petrov and his wife defected from the Soviet embassy with alleged evidence of Russian spying activities. Some pundits, watching electoral trends, had thought Evatt a likely winner of the coming contest, but he behaved erratically before a royal commission appointed to inquire into the affair and soon gave evidence of a decaying mind, alleging that the Petrovs were not genuine witnesses and that the episode was a plot hatched by Menzies and the head of the secret service, Brigadier Spry, to keep him out of office. Though the allegation passed into Labor mythology, it has frequently been disproven.

In 1950 Menzies had believed that the chief communist threat was to Europe, and that in the event of world war Australia would provide forces to guard the Middle East. His first two ministers for external affairs, Percy Spender and Richard Casey, however, saw south-east Asia as the crucial area for Australian defence, and were chiefly responsible for the Australia–New Zealand–United States treaty (1951) and the formation of the South-East Asia Treaty Organization (1954). Menzies accepted the aim of such agreements: to sustain the commitment of the United States to the region and to look for security through 'great and powerful friends'. He also formally agreed in 1955 to Australian participation in the British-organized Far East Strategic Reserve; in consequence Australia was involved in conflicts arising from the Malayan emergency and Indonesia's policy of confrontation. Henceforth the Menzies administrations were committed to the concept of 'forward defence', a notion which, combined with increasing dependence on the United States, led almost inexorably to involvement, near the end of Menzies' prime ministership, in the Vietnam War.

In the years after 1958, when the minister for trade and industry, John McEwen, was leader of the Country Party, the fear of communism was a less important political imperative, and promotion of Australian exports through protection, tariff manipulation, and aggressive trade negotiations became characteristics of the Menzies era. McEwen's department was sometimes at odds with the treasury, occasionally to Menzies' displeasure. Nevertheless, though temperamentally different Menzies and McEwen saw eye to eye on most matters. On the eve of one federal election in the 1960s Menzies could write to McEwen: 'There never has been such a partnership as this in the political history of Australia.'

Achievements Preservation of the Liberal–Country Party coalition was in fact one of the three achievements on which, near the end of his parliamentary career, Menzies looked back with most pride. Given the natural tension that had always existed between the two parties, this accomplishment reflected the great political acumen and prestige of the mature Menzies. The other two feats he thought memorable were the extension of federal involvement in education and the physical development of Canberra as the national capital. The highlight of the first was the appointment in 1956 of Sir Keith Murray's committee to inquire into the then financial plight of Australia's universities, and Menzies' insistence that the committee's recommendations be fully implemented. The highlight of the second was his insistence in 1960 that funds be appropriated for the construction of the long-delayed lake that Walter Burley Griffin had originally made the centrepiece of his design for Canberra.

Menzies belonged to the generation for whom to be Australian was automatically to be British. It was an outlook that involved veneration for inherited institutions such as parliament and the courts because they were the creation of time and history, and respect for the crown as the focus of loyalty which held a family of disparate British societies together. In the 1950s and 1960s Menzies became something of the 'grand old man' at Commonwealth prime ministers' conferences, but he was privately unhappy at a scenario in which hitherto subject peoples increasingly became equals of the old 'white' self-governing dominions. His good friend Harold Macmillan tried gently to get him to accept 'the winds of change', but personally Menzies never quite did so. His almost sentimental old-fashioned Britishness led him into a few stances that had regrettable overtones, the prime example, perhaps, being his support of the Eden government's policies in the Suez crisis of 1956.

Menzies retired from politics at the peak of his power, in January 1966. He subsequently delivered by invitation at the University of Virginia a series of lectures later published as *Central Power in the Australian Commonwealth* (1967). In 1965 Harold Wilson had nominated him to succeed Winston Churchill as warden of the Cinque Ports, and on his annual trips to fulfil consequent honorific duties he was able to keep up with old friends in England. Among Menzies' many honorary degrees were those from Melbourne, Oxford, and Cambridge universities. His other honours included CH (1951) and FRS (1965). He was sworn of the privy council in 1937, and became a knight of the Thistle (1963) and a knight of the Order of Australia (1976).

Menzies wrote two volumes of reminiscences, *Afternoon Light* (1967) and *The Measure of the Years* (1970). In 1971 he suffered a severe stroke which incapacitated him physically and put limits on his public appearances. He died on 15 May 1978 at his home, 2 Hayerbrack Avenue, Malvern, Victoria, and was accorded a state funeral. He was privately cremated, and in June 1996 his ashes were interred, with those of his wife, in a newly established prime ministers' memorial garden in Melbourne general cemetery.

Large-framed and handsome, Menzies had a ready wit and superb command of language. His outward mien suggested a tendency towards imperiousness but it also covered a certain shyness. Intimates knew a man of great good humour and kindness. Life for him was a gift to be enjoyed with gusto; he took pleasure in food and drink, revelled in letting his hair down at his favourite Savage and West Brighton clubs in Melbourne, and enjoyed watching sports, being a connoisseur of the art of cricket. After Alfred Deakin and before Gough Whitlam, Menzies was probably the most well-read prime minister Australia has had, though he was not given to parading his erudition. He enjoyed nineteenth-century classical novels, could quote hundreds of lines of Shakespeare and of the Bible, and on boring train and aeroplane trips was given to probing 'who-dunnits'. An intensely private man, he strictly separated personal matters, such as his family life, from public affairs. Paul Hasluck, who knew Menzies well, wrote of him: 'I think the sort of tribute he would have appreciated most would not have been praise of his great talents or a recital of what he had accomplished but rather a statement that he was a man of character, honourable in conduct and decent in behaviour. He was that and I offer the tribute' (Martin, 'Menzies, Sir Robert Gordon', 15.361).

Dame Pattie Maie [Pat] **Menzies** (1899–1995) was born on 2 March 1899 at Alexandria in Victoria. Her father, John William Leckie, of Scottish descent, was Australian-born. Her mother, May Beatrix, died when Pattie was eleven, and as a growing girl she was close to and shared politics with her father, for a time a member of the Victorian parliament. She married Robert Menzies in 1920, and after he entered federal politics took part in most of his electioneering campaigns. In 1954 she was appointed by Queen Elizabeth II dame grand cross in the Order of the British Empire for her public work in hospitals and her representation of Australia on a number of occasions overseas. She died at Canberra on 30 August 1995.   A. W. MARTIN

Sources A. W. Martin and P. Hardy, *Robert Menzies: a life*, 2 vols. (1993–9) • A. W. Martin, 'Menzies, Sir Robert Gordon (1894–1978)', *AusDB*, 15.354–61 • A. W. Martin, 'The politics of the depression', *The Australian century*, ed. R. Manne (1999), 80–118 • I. Hancock, *National and permanent?* (2000) • S. Prasser, J. R. Nethercote, and J. Warhurst, *The Menzies era* (1995) • D. Lowe, *Menzies and the 'great world struggle': Australia's cold war, 1948–1954* (1999)

Archives NL Aus., MS 4936 • priv. coll., family MSS | FILM BFI NFTVA, current affairs footage • BFI NFTVA, documentary footage • BFI NFTVA, news footage

Likenesses Elliott & Fry, photograph, 1941, NPG [*see illus.*] • photographs, *c.*1941–1964, Hult. Arch. • W. Dargie, oils, Clothworkers' Headquarters, London • W. Dargie, oils, University of Melbourne, Australia • W. Dargie, portrait, Menzies Foundation, East Melbourne • W. Dargie, portrait, priv. coll. • W. Dobell, oils, New South Wales Art Gallery • I. Hele, oils, priv. coll. • I. Hele, oils, Parliament House, Canberra • I. Hele, oils, Gray's Inn, London • I. Hele, oils,

Victorian Bar Council · J. Longstaff, oils, Savage Club, Melbourne, Australia · C. Wheeler, oils, Western Australian Art Gallery
Wealth at death £201,306: probate

Menzies, Sir Stewart Graham (1890–1968), intelligence officer, was born at 46 Upper Grosvenor Street, London, on 30 January 1890, the second son of John Graham Menzies (1861–1911) and his wife, Susannah West Wilson (1865–1943), daughter of Arthur Wilson, of Tranby Croft. Following the death of John Menzies, in 1911, his widow in the following year married Lieutenant-Colonel Sir George Holford (1860–1926), an officer in the Life Guards who was equerry-in-waiting to Queen Alexandra and extra equerry to George V.

Stewart Menzies entered Eton College in 1903, and there won prizes for languages that included the king's prize for German in 1907. He was a popular boy and a fine athlete, master of the beagles, and president of the Eton Society ('Pop') in 1908 and 1909. Immediately on leaving school, in 1909, he was commissioned in the Grenadier Guards, but transferred to the Life Guards in the following year. While in the army he acquired a love of horses and of hunting that remained with him for the rest of his life and to which he returned with special zest in his retirement. His country home was at Luckington in Wiltshire and he hunted mainly with the duke of Beaufort's hounds. He was well into his seventies when a fall in the hunting field started a decline in his health. While resident in London he enjoyed an active social life. He was a great frequenter of White's Club and also belonged to St James's and the Turf.

Menzies first came into contact with the intelligence world during the First World War. He was sent to France in 1914 with the British expeditionary force, and by the end of the year had been awarded a DSO, as a subaltern. In 1915 he was awarded the MC, and after recovering from a gas attack was posted to a security intelligence appointment at general headquarters. The work appealed to him, and he showed a flair for it, aided by his knowledge of European languages. He ended the war with the rank of brevet major, and in 1919 was again selected for an intelligence appointment, this time with MI1(c), later the Secret Intelligence Service (SIS), also known as MI6. He thus began a career in professional intelligence, mainly as head of SIS's military section and deputy to the chief, which was to continue for thirty-two years. He was promoted colonel in 1932 and, though he had resigned from the Life Guards in 1929, he was promoted major-general during the Second World War.

Menzies became 'C', in full command of the SIS, only two months after the outbreak of war in 1939. It was a crucial moment in the history of his service. Between the wars it had been starved of funds by successive governments and consequently entered the war ill prepared for the tasks demanded by total warfare. Expansion and reconstruction had to take place simultaneously, and these tasks were further complicated by set-backs such as that at Venlo in November 1939, when SS men infringed Dutch neutrality by crossing the German–Dutch border to

Sir Stewart Graham Menzies (1890–1968), by Vandyk, 1953

kidnap two SIS officers who had gone there to meet contacts who were actually SS officers masquerading as members of an underground opposition in Germany.

The whole character of the SIS gradually changed. Hitherto staff had been recruited mainly from retired service officers; now that it could attract men and women of talent from all walks of life the management problems were new and intricate. Added to these Menzies had to steer his service through a complicated maze of inter-service relations created by the existence of a new British secret service—Special Operations Executive (SOE)—and, later, a new American service—the office of strategic services—operating in parallel (and often in competition) with his own in neutral and enemy territories. These and other circumstances—such as the lack of agents already in place in 1940—meant that it was to take some time before SIS could develop a momentum of its own and forge those links with allied intelligence and resistance organizations that were to prove valuable in the later stages of the war.

Besides commanding SIS Menzies was responsible for the overall supervision of the Government Code and Cypher School (GCCS), whose greatest achievement in the war was the breaking, with considerable initial Polish and French help, of the German 'Enigma'. This was an electromechanical enciphering and deciphering machine that was widely used by units of the German army, navy, and air force. German experts had rendered their machine so sophisticated that by the outbreak of the war they believed it safe even if captured. It was therefore used to communicate vital German war secrets. These began to be made available by GCCS by the end of 1940, and by the end of 1943 the school was decrypting as many as 40,000 naval and 50,000 army and air force messages a month. It is therefore not difficult to imagine the crucial importance of this source of intelligence to the allied war effort. But it was also a highly vulnerable source, for the security of which Menzies was finally responsible. This could mean refusing some forceful operational commander the right to act on its intelligence if by so doing he might endanger the source. In retrospect this responsibility was admirably discharged and the secret of the GCCS's remarkable cryptographic successes was preserved until the end of the war (and indeed for two decades afterwards). Not surprisingly, with such excellent information at his disposal Menzies' influence with the prime minister, the war cabinet, and the chiefs of staff was considerable.

The stamina and toughness that Menzies displayed during the war years came as something of a surprise to those acquainted with his easy and affluent way of life between the wars. Running his service and supervising GCCS meant exceptionally long hours of office work, besides which he became in time a member of Churchill's intimate circle of war advisers. This meant being on call to brief the prime minister at any hour of the day or night. On such occasions he had to answer for more than his own responsibilities, for he was the only intelligence director to enjoy this privileged position. As an intelligence man his strength lay in a quick grasp and understanding of operational issues and in his shrewd management of a network of powerful contacts. Organization and long-term planning were not his strong points. He preferred the getting of intelligence to the mosaic work of the assessors, and in this respect he resembled one of his American opposite numbers, Allen Dulles, another man to enter intelligence from a patrician background.

Menzies was married three times. His first wife, whom he married on 29 November 1918, was Lady Avice Ela Muriel Sackville (d. 1985), daughter of the eighth Earl De La Warr. They divorced in 1931, and on 12 December 1932 Menzies married Pamela Thetis (1903–1951), daughter of Rupert Evelyn Beckett (nephew of the first Baron Grimthorpe), and the divorced wife of James Roy Notter Garton. He married third, in 1952, as her fourth husband, Audrey Clara Lilian Chaplin, daughter of Sir Thomas Paul Latham, first baronet. He had one daughter, with his second wife.

To many foreigners Menzies came to seem the personal embodiment of an intelligence mystique that they believed characteristically and historically British. Whatever the truth of this might be it contributed to his international influence and was a potent factor in establishing the Anglo-American and other allied intelligence alliances. During the war years his service had a greater role to play than ever before. By the time that he retired, in 1951, the pressures of the cold war had caused the intelligence world to develop in major ways and to acquire potent technological resources; it was a very different world from the one that Menzies had entered in 1919 but

one in which, for SIS, the human source was still paramount.

Menzies was appointed CB in 1942, KCMG in 1943, KCB in 1951, and received a number of foreign decorations. He died in the King Edward VII Hospital for Officers, Beauchamp Place, London, on 29 May 1968.

[ANON.], rev. A. O. BLISHEN

Sources A. Cave Brown, *The secret servant: the life of Sir Stewart Menzies, Churchill's spymaster* (1989) · *WW* (1962) · personal knowledge (1981) · private information (2004) · *The Times* (31 May 1968) · *The Times* (6 June 1968) · *CGPLA Eng. & Wales* (1968)
Likenesses two photographs, *c.*1915–1932, Hult. Arch. · W. Stoneman, photograph, 1953, NPG · Vandyk, photograph, 1953, NPG [*see illus.*] · photograph, repro. in Brown, *Secret servant* · photograph, repro. in D. Stafford, *Churchill and secret service* (1997) · photographs, priv. coll.; repro. in Brown, *Secret servant*
Wealth at death £352,287: probate, 22 July 1968, *CGPLA Eng. & Wales*

Menzies, Sir William John (1834–1905), lawyer and financier, was born in Edinburgh on 14 October 1834. His father, Allan Menzies (1804–1856), was a writer to the signet and professor of conveyancing (1847–56) in the university. His mother, Helen Cowan, was the daughter of Alexander Cowan, paper maker. Menzies was educated at Edinburgh Academy, the University of Edinburgh, and in Germany. He trained as a lawyer, was admitted writer to the signet in 1858, and subsequently established his own practice. In 1859 he married Helen Marshall, a widow, the daughter of Alexander Adie, an optician. Three years after her death in 1867 he married Ellen, the youngest daughter of William Young and the widow of William Tweedie. In 1878 his second wife, Ellen, died and in 1879 he married a third widow, Annie Percival, the eldest daughter of J. A. Drought of Whigsborough, King's county, Ireland, whose late husband had been T. S. Jones of the National Bank of India.

In 1864, 1867, and 1872 Menzies travelled to the United States on behalf of clients. Greatly impressed by the economic potential and higher rates of return on capital there he formed the idea of founding a foreign investment company. Existing investment trusts were fixed trusts or legal trusts which terminated at a defined date and held a portfolio of securities that normally were not changed. Menzies instead proposed an investment company which would manage a flexible portfolio. The Scottish American Investment Company Ltd, formed on 29 March 1873, was the first investment company established in Scotland and the first to invest exclusively in the United States.

Menzies devised a capital structure which showed a shrewd understanding of the savings market. Investors could participate in either or both the equity and the loan capital. The nominal capital was £1 million, but to start with only 50,000 shares of £10 each were for sale, and only £2 of each £10 was to be paid up. For the loan capital, the company proposed to issue debenture stock bearing interest at 5.5 per cent and secured on the amount of unpaid capital and on the investments themselves. Investors who wished to participate in the risk or equity capital thus had access to a large quantity of low-priced loan capital. By issuing 50,000 shares of £10 each—a total capital of

£500,000—but collecting only £100,000 (50,000 shares at £2) the company could borrow up to £400,000 in debentures at 5.5 per cent. This could then be invested in the United States where interest rates were 7 per cent and above. The income to pay the ordinary shareholders would come from the difference between home and overseas interest rates. Substantial capitalists who had sufficient cash to take a risk with only the security of the underlying investment could buy the ordinary shares, while people who wanted a safe and steady return, yet a higher yield than was available in Britain, could purchase debentures with double security. In just over a month the equity shares were fully subscribed. Debentures were also popular, and by March 1874 the company had reached the limits of its borrowing powers.

Scottish American proved extremely successful. The ordinary dividend from 1874 to 1903, when Menzies retired, never fell below 10 per cent. Investments rose from £436,000 to £3.4 million in 1903. This record contrasted with the single-purpose ventures that Menzies and his coterie operated in mining, ranching, and forestry, where fraud, legal complications over foreign ownership of American land, managerial weakness arising from absentee ownership, and speculation without regard for the underlying value of assets lost money for investors.

Scottish American usually avoided single-purpose ventures, but in 1883 part of the reserve funds were invested in town sites in the Northwest Territories of Canada. Site values fell and Menzies was severely criticized by shareholders who demanded that he should drop his promotional activities and concentrate on Scottish American's business. When another of his ventures, the California Redwood Company, failed two years later the press blamed the directors of Scottish American. Public enthusiasm for overseas investment nevertheless remained high and by 1890 Menzies had achieved international recognition as an expert on American investment. In 1895 he published *America as a Field for Investment*.

Menzies served both God and Mammon. He was active in the Church of Scotland as an elder, as representative of the presbytery of Skye at the general assembly, and as agent for the church (1868–1905). He was prominent in the campaign against the disestablishment and disendowment of the Church of Scotland in the 1885 general election. He jointly wrote the petition *Appeal to the People of Scotland*, which was circulated among the electors of W. E. Gladstone's Midlothian constituency and delivered to Gladstone, who was staying with Lord Rosebery at Dalmeny. In May 1903, at Holyrood, Menzies was knighted for his services to the church.

Ill health forced Menzies to retire as managing director of Scottish American in 1903. He died on 14 October 1905 at his home in Canaan Lane, Morningside, Edinburgh, leaving his widow, Annie, who died in 1923, and a family of six sons and two daughters.   RONALD B. WEIR

Sources W. T. Jackson, *The enterprising Scot: investors in the American west after 1873* (1968) · R. B. Weir, *A history of the Scottish American Investment Company Limited, 1873–1973* (1973) · J. Clay, *My life on the range* (1962) · I. Machin, 'Voluntaryism and reunion, 1874–1929', *Church, politics and society: Scotland, 1408–1929*, ed. N. Macdougall (1983)
Likenesses Tiffany & Co., cast copper, Scot. NPG
Wealth at death £31,447 17s. 1d.: confirmation, 8 Dec 1905, CCI

Mepham [Meopham]**, Simon** (*c.*1275–1333), archbishop of Canterbury, took his name from Meopham in Kent, some miles south of Gravesend. He had at least two brothers, Edmund and Thomas (who became a friar), while Joan, wife of John Dene, seems to have been his sister. In 1327 Simon and Edmund joined with John Dene in securing a licence for the alienation of property and rents in Kent (including Meopham) for the establishment of a chantry in the chapel of St James de la Dene within Meopham church for the souls of the founders, of Joan, their parents, relatives, and benefactors. Two years later Simon was to issue an indulgence for those visiting the church and praying for the souls of his parents.

An Oxford MA by 1295, Mepham continued his studies in the theological faculty, receiving a licence to study for a year in February 1314. By the following year he was DTh and member of a commission of doctors who condemned certain theological errors. He was ordained acolyte in his native diocese on 28 May 1295 and priest two years later on 21 September. By the latter date he had been instituted to Tunstall, Kent, a rectory earlier held by his brother Edmund (who appears to have been slightly his senior), and one retained until his promotion as archbishop. The prebend of Hova Villa in Chichester Cathedral he likewise resigned in 1328 and Edmund on that occasion succeeded him by papal provision. Although he was also canon and prebendary of Llandaff from 1295—Edmund followed him there in 1327—and from 1299 archdeacon of Shropshire, he was only a moderate pluralist.

Election to Canterbury Archbishop Walter Reynolds died on 16 November 1327, and following his burial eleven days later the election process was set in motion. However, it was not until 7 December that the two monks sent to the king returned with the *congé d'élire*, which was recited in chapter the following day. The election followed on the 11th when the convent, adopting the method of 'compromise', chose Mepham. On 15 December a deputation of two monks sought out the elect at Chichester and after the conventional interval, this time of six days, he gave his assent and accompanied the monks to the king, whom they reached at Lichfield on 2 January 1328. It was, of course, Queen Isabella and Roger Mortimer who decided the issue. Mepham was graciously admitted and letters were dispatched to the pope and cardinals describing the elect as bereft of worldly goods but replete with virtue. Mepham then went to Avignon, where all went smoothly. On 27 May, in full consistory, Pope John XXII (r. 1316–34) confirmed the election and a special mandate authorized Pierre des Prés, cardinal-bishop of Palestrina, to consecrate Mepham in the house of the Friars Preacher. Four days later Mepham received the pallium. He dispatched apostolic letters to apprise the Canterbury chapter of the outcome and appointed his brother Edmund vicar-general. On 5 September he disembarked at Dover armed with bulls that would, if the need arose, enable him to

Simon Mepham
(c.1275–1333), seal

resume visitation of dioceses interrupted by royal or papal service. On the 19th he performed fealty to Edward at Bishop's Lynn, mandates for livery of the temporalities being issued the same day.

What lay behind the election is harder to determine. The political situation was tense: Edward II's body lay unburied until December, a rift was opening up between the supporters of Isabella and Mortimer and those of Henry of Lancaster, and the Scottish situation necessitated a parliament at York in February 1328. The negotiations at Edinburgh were ratified at Northampton in April amid popular outcry. It was clearly important to have a pliant figure at Canterbury. Despite his initial political stance, there is no certainty that the bishop of Lincoln, Henry Burghersh (d. 1340), was the candidate of Isabella and Mortimer and Mepham the Lancastrian nominee. It is true that Burghersh was *persona grata* at court, and that his name was suggested to the pope in letters of April and May 1328, but only if some impediment prevented Mepham's confirmation. Burghersh was a formidable and well-known figure—in May 1328 he was made chancellor. Mepham may have been appointed because he was a political nonentity, ostensibly harmless.

Involvement in politics Initially events proved otherwise. The other-worldly archbishop, whom the Rochester chronicler William Dene describes as remote from the affairs of ordinary men—'modum et mores hominum totaliter ignorans' (Dene, fol. 51v)—attended the Salisbury parliament of October 1328. There he adhered to the faction of Henry of Lancaster and Edmund, earl of Kent, who under colour of the utility of the realm opposed the 'rulers'—the queen and Mortimer. Letters from Lancaster and the earl of Norfolk, sent to the Rochester diocesan, Hamo Hethe (d. 1352), complained that the king's forces were devastating the countryside and taking the goods of the church, contrary to Magna Carta and the king's coronation oath. He was invited to discuss the situation in London, a suggestion reinforced by Mepham. When Hethe refused, Mepham denounced his lack of co-operation. The bishop is said to have retorted privately that it was beyond belief that in the depth of winter the archbishop should travel to London at the festive season of Christmas to bandy words with feckless upstarts unskilled in affairs— 'cum iuvenibus et inprovidis ac imperitis' (Dene, fol. 52r).

Proceedings opened at St Paul's on the Sunday before Christmas (18 December 1328) when Mepham preached. How many bishops responded is unknown—possibly only John Stratford of Winchester and Stephen Gravesend of London. The confederates decided to send the archbishop and the bishop of London, with the earls of Kent and Norfolk, to threaten the young king with armed resistance to his scheduled *chevauchée* and to his prises on the church and people. Mepham promised to precede the earls with cross and banner raised and, alleged Dene, was bound to them by oath.

Meanwhile the royalist forces advanced from the west to the neighbourhood of Bedford. According to Dene, the impetuous archbishop outdistanced his companions and then consulted Thomas Aledon, a Kentish knight, as to whether he should pay his respects to the king. The reply was in the affirmative, but with the caution that he should not divulge his mission until the morning, by which time his companions would have arrived. But, reports Dene, having greeted the king and Queen Isabella, Mepham, as soon as he had imbibed—tired by his journey and by the work he had done—waxed loquacious and revealed all. The government's view of the situation was then expounded to him. Accepting it totally, he bound himself by oath. Thereupon he was instructed to return to his companions and to urge them (with four exceptions) to submit to the king's grace. Initially greeted with enthusiasm in the Lancastrian camp, Mepham, once the truth became known, was ridiculed there. The abject submission of Lancaster and his supporters subsequently averted civil war but demonstrated the archbishop's ineptitude. However, Dene, though he had access to excellent sources of information, is undoubtedly an opinionated critic, and the chroniclers Knighton and Murimuth, by contrast, are not condemnatory, the latter regarding Mepham as a peacemaker.

Visiting his diocese Mepham's enthronement was delayed until 22 January 1329. Neither king nor great lords attended, and of the bishops only Rochester and London put in an appearance. Gravesend introduced a discordant note by claiming London's right to enthrone the archbishop, but the veteran Henry Eastry (d. 1331), the prior of Christ Church, Canterbury, was able to make the point that he had enthroned the last three—Pecham, Winchelsey, and Reynolds. Over a year later, on 18 February 1330, Mepham himself crowned Edward III's consort, Philippa of Hainault (d. 1369). In the meantime the archbishop had turned his attention to his diocese, although because of the loss of his register information is scarce about its administration. Lacking episcopal experience, he had no pool of clerks from which to draw, and the attempts of his brothers to find suitable men attracted the contempt of Dene (fol. 51v): they were seeking angels rather than men ('angelos et non homines quesierunt')! He began a visitation of his diocese the thoroughness of which is unknown, but it did involve a disastrous dispute with St Augustine's Abbey, Canterbury. As was normal practice, he required evidence of the house's appropriations, but the monks claimed complete exemption. Eastry counselled caution, but in vain. For failure to respond in the archbishop's court the abbot was declared contumacious, but appeal was made to the papal curia and Itier de Concoreto, the nuncio in England, was appointed judge-delegate. The notary serving the court summons arrived at Slindon, where the archbishop had fallen ill while visiting Chichester diocese. He and his party were set upon by Mepham's servants. The archbishop denied instigation, but despite a testimonial dispatched by his fellow bishops he was pronounced guilty of the outrage when the case was heard at Avignon. In due course Itier also found against Mepham, and under threat first of suspension, then of excommunication, condemned him to pay £700 to St Augustine's, a demand he ignored. Itier's ruling was to be replaced by a composition arranged by Mepham's diplomatic successor, John Stratford.

Provincial council and visitation Meanwhile on 27 January 1329 Mepham opened his provincial council at St Paul's with a sermon. At the end of proceedings, on 10 February, he declared the excommunication of the murderers of Bishop Walter Stapeldon (*d.* 1326), and of the plunderers of the abbeys of Bury St Edmunds and Abingdon. The constitutions that Mepham issued in 1329, though short, were sufficiently significant for William Lyndwood (*d.* 1446) to gloss eight of the nine. A resounding preamble, *Zelari oportet*, reminded prelates of the gravity of their obligations. There followed two canons requiring respectively the observation of Good Friday without servile work that would interrupt the obligations of piety, though not precluding such operations as were essential for the poor, and the solemn celebration of the feast of the Conception of the Blessed Virgin Mary. The third canon reiterated legislation against those who violated the immunity of the church or injured clerics. There followed two concerning testaments: the first under penalty of excommunication upheld the right of servants and villeins to make wills, while the second laid down that for those who had goods worth less than 100s., probate and the commission of administration to executors was to be free. The next canon released advocates and proctors from their oath to observe a regulation of the Exeter consistory (once believed to have been a statute of an Oxford council) prohibiting frivolous appeal from judicial *gravamen* before definitive sentence, on the grounds that this deprived the oppressed of remedy. A lengthy canon upheld the integrity of offerings and tithes, another condemned clandestine marriages, while the final one required a proper calculation of defects in benefices.

To follow up his provincial council Mepham had determined on a visitation of his province, beginning with Rochester, where he arrived on 2 October 1329. The *parti pris* Dene alleged that he brought eighty horsemen to the cathedral monastery, gave none of the customary *douceurs*, and incurred expenses of £24. Then it was Hethe's turn, against whom twenty-five charges were brought, many of them inspired by his own chapter. These were put to Hethe by Mepham's clerks, led by Master Laurence Fastolf. Eventually, despite the seriousness of some of the allegations, they were dropped, at a price ('mediante tamen pecunia') if Dene (fol. 55*r*) is to be believed. The diocese, the chronicler claims, was then visited roughly and inhumanely ('inhumaniter et dure'; ibid., fol. 53*v*), above all at the expense of Hethe, who considered himself victimized for failing to adopt the advice of the archbishop's relatives.

Prior Eastry supplied Mepham with a standard set of interrogatories for the visitations that took place between the spring of 1331 and the summer of 1332 in the dioceses of Chichester, Salisbury, Bath and Wells, and Exeter. He arrived at Exeter on 1 June 1332, in defiance of Bishop John Grandison's appeal to the apostolic see and his recently acquired papal privileges, only to find the cathedral fortified against him. Some of his followers were injured in the ensuing scuffles. The king, who had been kept informed, now intervened, but the bishop claimed that despite royal mandates the mayor had allowed copies of his privileges and of the parties' appeals to be torn down. Mepham withdrew, forced to rest content with his appeal against the *gravamina* he had suffered. Bishop Hethe urged perseverance, so Mepham summoned a council to St Paul's for 4 September 1332. There the bishops, closing ranks, presented three *gravamina* that impugned the summons on technical grounds. When Mepham refused to compromise, Bishop Adam Orleton (*d.* 1345) of Worcester launched an appeal, allegedly supported by all the bishops save Hethe, whereupon the assembly was dissolved with nothing accomplished.

Dispute with York, depression, and death Another conflict—the long-standing dispute over the bearing of one metropolitan's cross in the province of the other—was scarcely of Mepham's making. A tenable view is that he was responding to provocation. The problem was exacerbated by Archbishop William Melton's appointment as treasurer in December 1330, since this entailed his being regularly in the southern province. Mepham issued several mandates on the topic to his suffragans and, according to Dene, absented himself (though perhaps only initially) from the Westminster parliament of November 1330 because the northern primate was bent on arriving with his cross elevated. Lobbying his fellow bishops against York's pretensions produced a sole supporter—Hethe. Rochester's advice was that Mepham, having obtained royal licence, should withdraw from parliament, but the clerks of the archbishop's council warned that this might entail deprivation of his temporalities. That, Hethe rejoined ironically, could prove fortuitous: it would rid him of superfluous goods and *familia*, enable him to recover his reputation (*fama*), and permit him to raise a subsidy from his clergy. Allegedly Mepham liked the advice, but faced with a royal mandate sensibly did not take it. In 1332 the king again intervened with a warning not to impede Melton in the September parliament at Westminster. It is uncertain whether Mepham attended, but he was certainly not present with Melton for the parliament in York in December 1332. Nothing further is heard of the business.

While the archbishop remained at Mayfield in Sussex in a state of deep depression—'in magna tristicia sedentem' (Dene, fol. 66r)—he was visited by Hethe, who tried to console him and suggested how he might secure absolution from excommunication. Mepham expressed no interest, and on 12 October 1333 he died. On the 26th, after absolution, his body was buried in St Peter's Chapel south of the high altar at Canterbury. His shrine-like tomb of black marble now lies within a double screen across the entrance to St Anselm's Chapel. His principal executor, Laurence Fastolf, released £50 to augment the annual rent of 40s. for the celebration of Mepham's anniversary.

His archiepiscopate is a sorry tale of a tactless man who at one time or another alienated the pope (who suspended him more than once), the government, his suffragans, and his cathedral prior, the infuriatingly, patronizingly avuncular Henry Eastry. He began with little knowledge of how to conduct the affairs of the English church and, with minor exceptions such as the Norwich *sede vacante* composition of August 1330, he persistently demonstrated an inability to compromise. Zealous in the defence of his province, he was the first archbishop known to have formally adopted (on occasion) the title 'apostolice sedis legatus', but he lacked either the stature of Pecham or Winchelsey, themselves stubborn defenders of church and province, or the legal competence and political sagacity of Stratford. The *Speculum regis Edwardi* formerly attributed to him is now ascribed to William Pagula (*d.* 1332?). ROY MARTIN HAINES

Sources Vatican Archives, Reg. Aven. 31, fols. 122v, 130v · transcript of Andrea Sapiti's notebook, PRO, PRO 31/9/17A, fols. 84v–85r · Canterbury Cathedral archives · LPL, registers I and Q · A. C. Ducarel, 'Fragmenta sequentia registrorum Simonis de Mepeham et Johannis de Stratford Cantuar' archiepiscoporum', BL, Add. MS 6066 · W. Dene, 'Historia Roffensis', BL, Cotton MS Faustina B.v · 'Chronica Guillielmi Thorne', *Historiae Anglicanae scriptores X*, ed. R. Twysden (1652) · *Adae Murimuth continuatio chronicarum. Robertus de Avesbury de gestis mirabilibus regis Edwardi tertii*, ed. E. M. Thompson, Rolls Series, 93 (1889) · J. B. Sheppard, ed., *Literae Cantuarienses: the letter books of the monastery of Christ Church, Canterbury*, 1, Rolls Series, 85 (1887) · [H. Wharton], ed., *Anglia sacra*, 1 (1691) · W. Lyndwood, *Provinciale* (1679) · Chancery records · I. J. Churchill, *Canterbury administration: the administrative machinery of the archbishopric of Canterbury*, 2 vols. (1933) · R. M. Haines, *Ecclesia Anglicana: studies in the English church of the later middle ages* (1989) · R. M. Haines, *The church and politics in fourteenth-century England: the career of Adam Orleton, c. 1275–1345*, Cambridge Studies in Medieval Life and Thought, 3rd ser., 10 (1978) · R. M. Haines, *Archbishop John Stratford: political revolutionary and champion of the liberties of the English church*, Pontifical Institute of Medieval Studies: Texts and Studies, 76 (1986) · R. M. Haines, 'Bishops and politics in the reign of Edward II: Hamo de Hethe, Henry Wharton, and the "Historia Roffensis"', *Journal of Ecclesiastical History*, 44 (1993), 586–609 · R. M. Haines, 'Some criticisms of bishops in the xivth and xvth centuries', *Miscellanea historiae eccclesiasticae VIII*, ed. B. Vogler (1987) · R. M. Haines, 'The innocent abroad: the career of Simon Mepham, archbishop of Canterbury, 1328–33', *Bibliothèque d'Humanisme et Renaissance*, 92 (1997), 555–96 · J. R. Wright, *The church and the English crown, 1305–*

1334: a study based on the register of Archbishop Walter Reynolds (1980) · F. M. Powicke and C. R. Cheney, eds., *Councils and synods with other documents relating to the English church, 1205–1313*, 2 vols. (1964) · L. E. Boyle, 'William of Pagula and the *Speculum regis Edwardi III*', *Mediaeval Studies*, 32 (1970), 329–36 · Emden, *Oxf.*
Archives Canterbury Cathedral archives · LPL, registers I and Q
Likenesses effigy, Canterbury Cathedral; repro. in G. H. Cook, *Portrait of Canterbury Cathedral* (1949), illus. 31 · seal, BL; Birch, *Seals*, 1220 [*see illus.*]

Merbury, Charles (*d.* 1597), author, was the son of John and Alice Merbury of Ulceby, Lincolnshire. John served Charles Brandon, duke of Suffolk, as his comptroller. The second son (with an elder brother, Thomas, and two sisters) and a minor when his father made his will on 26 January 1553 (proved on 20 October), Charles was left some rents at Burwell, Lincolnshire, and £133 6s. 4d. An Oxford BA of 1570, he studied under 'Master Humfrey', presumably Laurence Humphrey, the president of Magdalen College. He entered Gray's Inn in 1571, but spent much time in Italy. A letter of 1577 announced his recent arrival in Florence. Henry Unton, who later encouraged him to write the work for which he is known, *A Briefe Discourse of Royall Monarchie*, recommended him to serve Thomas Radcliffe, earl of Sussex. Merbury apparently did not settle, although he mentioned much 'vacant' time spent 'attending in courte upon her majestie's service' before publishing his *Discourse* in 1581 (Merbury, *Discourse*, sig. *iiir).

The *Discourse* appeared novel, necessitating special vetting by the parliamentarian Thomas Norton, but its praise for monarchy as the best form of government owed much to Aristotle and Roman lawyers. The principal discussion of its place in political theory seems overemphatic in calling it 'a new departure' as 'the first English writing to show the influence of Bodin' (Allen, 250–51). Merbury disclaimed theoretical pretensions:

> I proceede not therin by way of rules and preceptes, as Cicero, Aristotle, and Plato did in their commonweales … not presuming to teache any … but meaning onely to put the learned reader in minde of that which he already knoweth, and if by chaunce there shall be anything new therin, and not in this our native language before time written, humbly to recommend the same unto his courteous correction. (Merbury, *Discourse*, 6)

On questions of the sovereign's legislative powers, as they 'doe require good advisement and better authority, I think good to suspende them until a more convenient time, or else to commende them unto those that are of more approved judgement and better warranted to deale with them' (ibid., 51). The attached Italian proverbs owe much to Stefano Guazzo, but testify to protracted travel in Italy—besides mentions of Tuscany, Merbury claimed to have encountered Spanish aspirations to 'preheminence' at 'Milan, Naples, Messina, Syracusa, Malta'. Supplemented by flattery of the linguistic abilities of Elizabeth I, its dedicatee, the *Discourse* depicted the 'prosperous estate', 'honour', and 'estimation' of the nation as deriving from 'the excellencie of royall monarchie'—republicans such as Italians and 'Flemings', however, lived 'abroade with less reputation, and for the most parte upon some bare and handycrafte occupation' (ibid., 2–5). Merbury was far from uncritical of Italians, who he complained thought 'none knew what civilitie mente but they' (ibid., 33).

In 1581, just after writing his Italianate book, Merbury lamented (in Italian) 'the extreme disgrace of my last, most unhappy journey' (BL, Lansdowne MS 33, fol. 205); this was perhaps the same occasion on which he was robbed 'passing the seas … to serve the duke of Anjou betweene Rye and Deepe' (*APC, 1581–2*, 366). Merbury took letters between Walsingham and Sir Henry Cobham, ambassador in France, in 1582. There he pursued a quest for reparation for his losses to pirates and also for similarly afflicted merchants of Chester. Letters to Anthony Bacon from France in 1583–4 complained increasingly of shortage of money while relaying (distinctly hearsay) intelligence; he planned to leave Paris in early 1584 for Angers 'to staye some tyme and to study yf I can the civil lawe' (LPL, MS 647, fol. 175). He acted again as a courier in 1585, for Sir Edward Stafford who noted him as 'verie good and honest and redie allwaies to doe what service he coulde', readiness which helped Merbury to get Walsingham's approval 'to continew my cours of travaile' (PRO, SP 78/13/48; 78/14/21). In April 1586 he was planning to go to Germany, but by 9 September 1589 he was back, and married Frances, probably *née* Angevine, at Healing near Grimsby.

Merbury described himself in his will as 'a royal servant', but was not the man granted the clerkship of the faculties in February 1594—according to Lord Burghley, this was a Thomas Marbery, of whom several were then active. Charles did acquire part of the crown lease of Markby, near his family's Lincolnshire lands. This seemed to be his main property when, 'beinge sicke and weake in body', he made his will on 26 July 1597 (PRO, PROB 11/90, fol. 345), leaving the Markby lease and over £130 in specified legacies to various relatives; he mentioned no surviving wife or children. The will was proved on 12 November 1597. JULIAN LOCK

Sources PRO, SP 78/7 · PRO, SP 78/13–15 · A. R. Maddison, ed., *Lincolnshire pedigrees*, 2, Harleian Society, 51 (1903), 637 · C. Merbury, *A briefe discourse of royall monarchie* (1581) · will, Charles Merbury, 1597, PRO, PROB 11/90, fol. 345 · will, John Merbury, 1553, PRO, PROB 11/36, fols. 135v–136r · C. Merbury, letters, BL, Lansdowne MSS 25, 33, 36, 108 · T. Birch, *Memoirs of the reign of Queen Elizabeth*, 1 (1754), 42–4 · *APC, 1581–2*, 366 · S. J. Gunn, *Charles Brandon, duke of Suffolk, c.1484–1545* (1988), 162 · J. Strype, *Annals of the Reformation and establishment of religion … during Queen Elizabeth's happy reign*, new edn, 3/1 (1824), 104–6 · H. R. Woudhuysen, 'Leicester's literary patronage: a study of the English court, 1578–1582', DPhil diss., U. Oxf., 1981, 84–6 · C. Merbury, 'Proverbi vulgari', ed. C. Speroni, *University of California Publications in Modern Philology*, 28 (1944–52), 63–157 · J. L. Lievsay, *Stefano Guazzo and the English Renaissance, 1575–1675* (1961), 123–7 · J. W. Allen, *A history of political thought in the sixteenth century* (1928); repr. (1960), 250–51 · R. Eccleshall, *Order and reason in politics: theories of absolute and limited monarchy in early modern England* (1978) · *N&Q*, 171 (1936), 256–8 · J. Foster, *The register of admissions to Gray's Inn, 1521–1889, together with the register of marriages in Gray's Inn chapel, 1695–1754* (privately printed, London, 1889), 41 · *A collection of state papers … left by William Cecill, Lord Burghley*, ed. W. Murdin, 2 (1759), 802 · Merbury to Anthony Bacon, LPL, MS 647

Wealth at death over £130—in specified legacies: will, PRO, PROB 11/90, fol. 345

Mercadier (*d.* 1200), adventurer and mercenary, rose from obscure Provençal origins to become a general and intimate of Richard I. He receives his first mention in October 1183 fighting for Richard against rebellious lords in Aquitaine following the death of Henry, the Young King. Knowledge of Mercadier's campaigns in Aquitaine ends abruptly with the termination of Geoffroi de Vigeois's chronicle in 1184, and nothing certain is known of his activities until 1194. He may well, however, have been among the Brabançon *routiers* who aided Richard in his conquest of the Quercy from Raymond (V), count of Toulouse, in 1188. Certainly in or after 1189 Mercadier was rewarded with the lands of Ademar de Beynac in Périgord. It seems unlikely that he accompanied Richard on the third crusade. Although Mercadier's name appears in a charter dated at Acre on 3 August 1191, listed among those sent back to France by Richard on business who were to draw credit from the Pisan merchant Giacomo de Jhota, this charter has been shown to be one of the notorious nineteenth-century *collection courtoise* forgeries.

Mercadier is next found at Richard's side at the rout of the retreating French at Fréteval on 5 June 1194, when he handed the king a fresh horse during his relentless pursuit of Philip Augustus. In March 1195 he was visiting his lands in Périgord, but in July he took the key castle of Issoudun, occupied part of Berry, and captured Gui, count of the Auvergne. The following year he headed a powerful army during Richard's invasion of Brittany, while in 1197, on 19 May, he and Count John captured Richard's hated enemy Philippe, bishop of Beauvais, in battle outside his castle of Milli. Later that year, in support of Baudouin (IX), count of Flanders, Mercadier plundered the fairs around Abbeville, seizing rich booty from French merchants.

In September 1198 Mercadier played a significant role in cutting off a French incursion into the Norman Vexin, forcing Philip to flee to Vernon. Subsequently, having been sent out to reconnoitre, it was he who advised Richard to attack Philip's numerically superior army at Gisors on 28 September, and Richard afforded Mercadier special mention in his letter describing the ensuing triumph. While heading south from Normandy into Aquitaine in early 1199 he and his band were badly mauled by some of Philip's vassals despite the prevailing truce. It was when reconnoitring the walls of Châlus-Chabrol with Mercadier on 26 March 1199 that Richard was struck by a crossbow bolt, and it was Mercadier's surgeon who first attended the king's fatal wound. Though Richard had spared the life of his assailant, one Peter Basil, and ordered his release, Mercadier vented his grief at the king's death by having the man flayed alive and hanged.

Mercadier now transferred his loyalties to John, and by the end of April 1199 was aiding Eleanor of Aquitaine to subdue Anjou by ravaging the lands of the supporters of Arthur of Brittany. Mercadier was then dispatched by John to Gascony, where the excesses of his *routiers* in the service of Helias, archbishop of Bordeaux, later prompted Innocent III to order an inquiry.

Of Mercadier the man little is known, save for that gleaned from his charter of March 1195 to the monks of Cadouin: a thank-offering and act of spiritual insurance which expresses his pride at being the king's loyal servant and heir to Ademar de Beynac. The witness list reveals that he married into the local aristocracy, his wife being the sister of Pons Amanieu de Madaillan, *seigneur* of Lesparre. Mercadier was murdered in Bordeaux on 10 April 1200, by a follower of Brandin, a rival captain, now seneschal of Gascony. To F. M. Powicke, Mercadier was 'a fit companion for the king with whose history his life is bound up', a nobler type than John's *routier* cut-throats and turncoats (Powicke, 232). How far contemporaries would have shared this view is uncertain, but Richard, at least, recognized his loyalty, daring, and, doubtless, ruthlessness. MATTHEW STRICKLAND

Sources *Chronica magistri Rogeri de Hovedene*, ed. W. Stubbs, 4 vols., Rolls Series, 51 (1868–71) · Geoffrey of Vigeois, 'Ex chronica Gaufredi coenobitae monasterii sancti Martialis Lemovicensis ac prioris Vosiensis coenobii', *Recueil des historiens des Gaules et de la France / Rerum Gallicarum et Francicarum scriptores*, ed. M. Bouquet and others, new edn, 12 (Paris, 1877), 421–51 · H. Géraud, 'Le Comte-Évêque', *Bibliothèque de l'École des Chartes*, 5 (1844–5) · F. M. Powicke, *The loss of Normandy, 1189–1204: studies in the history of the Angevin empire*, 2nd edn (1961) · H. Géraud, 'Mercadier: les routiers au XIIIe siècle', *Bibliothèque de l'École des Chartes*, 3 (1841–2), 417–45 · L. Landon, *The itinerary of King Richard I*, PRSoc., new ser., 13 (1935) · Paris, *Chron.*, 2.421

Mercator, Nicolaus [*formerly* Niklaus Kauffman] (1620?–1687), mathematician and astronomer, was born near Cismar or in Eutin (both in Holstein, Germany, then united with Denmark), the son of Martin Kauffman (*c.*1587–1637/8), who had been a Lutheran preacher (*diakon*) from 1619 in Eutin, and from 1623 in Oldenburg (Holstein), and his wife, Heilwig (*d.* 1677).

Mercator matriculated in 1632 at the University of Rostock and graduated *magister philosophiae* on 15 May 1641, with Jacob Fabricius (1576?–1652), a former student of Tycho Brahe, presiding. In 1642 he registered at the University of Leiden in the Netherlands, where he became acquainted with the English mathematician John Pell. Towards the end of the Thirty Years' War he took up a post at the University of Copenhagen. There he was in contact with the professor of mathematics Georg Fromme (1605–1651), another student of Brahe, and his circle.

When Copenhagen University was closed late in 1654 on account of an outbreak of the plague, Mercator travelled to London for a brief stay, and then moved to Paris. Regular correspondence with Samuel Hartlib testifies to their close relations. He returned to England in June 1657 and for about a year acted as tutor at Petworth House to Joceline Percy, son of the tenth earl of Northumberland; then until 1682 he lived in London, teaching mathematics.

In 1666 Mercator made and presented to Charles II a special marine timekeeper. Shortly afterwards he was elected fellow of the Royal Society. In the spring of 1669 he seems to have proposed to the French statesman J. B. Colbert not only his method of sailing into the wind, but also of improving the pendulum clock for use at sea. Years later Colbert commissioned him to construct the fountains at Versailles; in December 1682 he set out for France, but he did not receive the payment that had been agreed upon.

Mercator was married; nothing seems to be known of his wife, but they had a son David. Aubrey described Mercator as:

> of little stature, perfect black haire, of a delicate moyst curle; darke grey eie, but of great vivacity of spirit. He is of a soft temper, of great temperance, and of a prodigious invention. He will be acquainted (familialy) with nobody. (*Brief Lives*, 58)

His frequent moves may have been caused by his constant preoccupation with earning a livelihood.

While in Copenhagen, Mercator published a series of elementary university textbooks. In his *Cosmographia* (1651) he described the physical geography of the earth, while his *Astronomia* (1651) presented the elements of spherical astronomy. Also issued in 1651 was *Trigonometria sphaericorum logarithmica*. In *Rationes mathematicae* (1653) Mercator made a principal distinction between rational and irrational numbers and discussed the consequences for science. For music, Mercator maintained, this implied the distinction between harmony and dissonance, for astronomy that between a Keplerian world harmonics and the observable celestial motions. He also proposed a calendrical reform in *De emendatione annua* (1653?). His first book printed in England was a small study on the motion of planets, *Hypothesis astronomica nova* (1664). In it Mercator accepted Kepler's first law describing orbits as ellipses but rejected Kepler's second law, the area law, which determines the speed of the planets, in favour of his own hypothesis. In 1669 Mercator demolished Jean-Dominique (Giandomenico) Cassini's method of determining the line of apsides of a planetary orbit from three solar sightings.

Mercator's *Institutiones astronomicae* (in two books, 1676), intended for use at the University of Cambridge, emphasized the role of observation and presented an excellent summary of contemporary theory, including that Kepler's third law substantiated the Copernican instead of Brahe's intermediate planetary system. Among others, Newton (with whom Mercator exchanged letters on lunar theory) studied the work carefully, and it was used as a textbook at other universities. Noteworthy in Mercator's *Institutio brevis in geometriam* (1678) are original definitions of geometrical objects based on his concept of motion or inspired by physical phenomena.

Mercator was also a practical scientist: the 1666 gift to Charles II, of a marine watch from which the equation of time could be obtained, was his own invention; his proposal to Colbert of a pendulum clock for use at sea provoked criticism from Christiaan Huygens who had his own vested interest. Mercator also sought to clarify the theory of map projection of Gerardus Mercator, to whom he was not related, by an article in the *Philosophical Transactions* (13, 4 June 1666, 215–18).

Among all Mercator's achievements, the publication of his small book *Logarithmotechnia* (1667; enlarged edn, 1668) is the most outstanding. In it he constructed logarithms from first principles based on rational operations only, and expressed the area under the segment of a hyperbola by a logarithm. Most important, this book was the first to publish a function in the form of an infinite series—obviously independent of similar revolutionary results obtained by Jan Hudde and Newton. Mercator accepted such series as a new type of function in mathematical analysis. His complementary but unpublished *Cyclomathia* series contained expansions of circle integrals. Also of historical relevance is his Latin translation of the Dutch *Algebra ofte Stel-Konst* by Gerard Kinckhuysen. It was sent by John Collins to Newton who, from 1673 onwards, introduced revised versions of substantial passages from Mercator into his Lucasian lectures on arithmetic and algebra. Mercator died in Paris in January or February 1687 (according to J. Moller, writing in 1744, from grief at not receiving payment for his Versailles work); he left unpublished works including Latin translations of an astrological text by Benjamin Worsley (*c.*1657), his own 'Astrologia rationalis', versions of a treatise on music theory which applied logarithms to the division of the musical scale (*c.*1672), and theorems on the solution of equations, the method of differences, and the construction of tables.

CHRISTOPH J. SCRIBA

Sources J. E. Hofmann, *Nicolaus Mercator (Kauffman): sein Leben und Wirken, vorzugsweise als Mathematiker* (Wiesbaden, 1950), 43–103 · M. Folkerts, 'Mercator, Nicolaus', *Neue deutsche Biographie*, ed. Otto, Graf zu Stolberg-Wernigerode, 17 (Berlin, 1994) · D. T. Whiteside, 'Mercator, Nicolaus', *DSB* · W. Applebaum, 'A descriptive catalogue of the manuscripts of Nicolaus Mercator, FRS, 1620–1687, in Sheffield University Library', *Notes and Records of the Royal Society*, 41 (1986–7), 21–37 · *Brief lives, chiefly of contemporaries, set down by John Aubrey, between the years 1669 and 1696*, ed. A. Clark, 2 (1898), 58–9, 109, 263 · *DNB*
Archives BL, copy of *Logarithmotechnia*, with MS notes by Pell, MS 4403, no. 1 · University of Sheffield, Hartlib collection
Wealth at death in debt: Hofmann, *Nicolaus Mercator*; H. W. Turnbull, ed., *James Gregory tercentenary memorial volume* (1939), 153

Mercer, Andrew (1775–1842), poet and topographer, was born in Selkirk. He was destined for the ministry, and in 1790 entered the University of Edinburgh. Ultimately he gave up theology, studied the fine arts, and tried unsuccessfully to make a living in Edinburgh as a miniature-painter, teacher of drawing, and man of letters. He wrote both in prose and verse for Edinburgh periodicals and edited the *North British Magazine* during its short existence. He subsequently settled in Dunfermline, where he lived by teaching and by drawing patterns for the damask manufacturers. His best-known work was a *History of Dunfermline from the Earliest Records* (1828). Also published under his name was a *Historical and Chronological Table of the Ancient Town of Dunfermline from 1064 to 1834*, which was really an abridgement, with the consent of the original author, E. Henderson, of a manuscript volume entitled *Annals of Dunfermline from the Earliest Records to 1833*. He was the author of a poem, *Dunfermline Abbey* (1819), and a volume of verse, *Summer Months among the Mountains* (1838). A man of considerable ingenuity and scholarship, Mercer lacked self-discipline, however, and his last years were spent in poverty. He died at Dunfermline on 11 June 1842.

J. C. HADDEN, *rev.* H. C. G. MATTHEW

Sources P. Chalmers, *Historical and statistical account of Dunfermline*, 2 vols. (1844–59) · J. G. Wilson, ed., *The poets and poetry of Scotland*, 2 (1877) · D. Foskett, *British portrait miniatures* (1963) · Bénézit, *Dict.*
Archives NL Scot., letters to Robert Anderson

Mercer, Cecil William [*pseud.* Dornford Yates] (1885–1960), novelist and short story writer, was born on 7 August 1885 at Wellesley House, Upper Walmer, Kent, the only child of Cecil John Mercer (1850–1921), solicitor, and his wife, Helen Wall (1858–1918). He was a first cousin of the writer H. H. *Munro (Saki). He was educated at St Clare School, Walmer (1894–9), Harrow School (1899–1904), where he was taught by N. K. Stephen, and University College, Oxford, where he was president of the Oxford University Dramatic Society (1906–7) and took a third in jurisprudence. He was called to the bar by the Inner Temple in 1909. As pupil to Travers Humphreys he attended the Crippen trial, and began to obtain a knowledge of the criminal underworld that he was to incorporate into his fiction. Before the First World War Mercer combined legal work with writing; he contributed a piece to *Punch* in 1910, published stories in the *Windsor Magazine*—collected as *The Brother of Daphne* (1914)—and ghosted C. M. Stamper's *What I Know* (1913), a memoir of Edward VII and his motor cars. All these appeared under the pseudonym Dornford Yates, derived from family surnames on his father's and mother's sides respectively.

In 1914 Mercer was commissioned into the 3rd County of London yeomanry. He was posted to Egypt, and then served in Salonika with the 8th mounted brigade, before being invalided home in 1917 with severe rheumatism, and seconded to the Ministry of Labour. He ended the war with the acting rank of captain: he retained his commission until 1924. He was awarded the 1914–15 Star.

After the war Mercer abandoned the law for literature. With Oscar Asche he wrote the lyrics for the musical *Eastward Ho!*, which ran for 124 performances at the Alhambra, London, in 1919, but thereafter he concentrated on fiction. On 22 October 1919 Mercer married Bettine Stokes Edwards (1890–1973), an American actress, and in July 1920 his only child, Richard, was born. Mercer divorced Bettine in 1933, and on 10 February 1934 he married (Doreen) Elizabeth Lucie Bowie (1905–1964), whom he referred to as Jill after one of his characters. For reasons of health and economy Mercer settled in Pau, south-western France, in the early 1920s; later he moved south from the Villa Maryland there to a house of his own design, named Cockade, at Eaux Bonnes, completed in 1939. A fictionalized account of its construction can be found in *The House that Berry Built* (1945). In 1940 the German advance caused the Mercers to evacuate, and to flee by car across Spain to Portugal, from where they sailed to South Africa. Mercer was commissioned into the Royal Rhodesian regiment, rising to the rank of major. After the war changed conditions in France led the Mercers to return to Southern Rhodesia to settle. He built himself a house in Umtali, called Sacradown: completed in 1948, it incorporated pieces from Waterloo Bridge, London, originally installed at Cockade.

Between 1914 and 1958 Mercer published thirty-five books, selling over 2 million copies for estimated earnings of over £400,000 in royalties. Many of his novels and short stories appeared first in magazines, especially the *Windsor Magazine*, whose star he was. The ten Berry books are light-hearted romantic comedies, recounting the witty conversations and often farcical misadventures of Berry Pleydell and his wealthy and well-born relatives, possessors of an ancestral estate, White Ladies, in Hampshire. These stories are narrated by Boy Pleydell, and often contain auto-biographical elements, along with wish fulfilment and some occasional occult whimsy. The last two Berry books, *As Berry and I were Saying* (1952) and *B-Berry and I Look Back* (1958), are essentially Mercer's memoirs in fictional garb. The nine Chandos books, narrated in a mannered, archaic style by Richard Chandos, are fast-paced adventure thrillers, mostly set in Austria, the south of France, or Riechtenburg, Mercer's Ruritania. Jonah Mansel, Berry's cousin and Chandos's mentor, appears in both series. There are four other thrillers, which follow the Chandos formula of updated Gothic, featuring courtly but ruthless gentlemen-heroes, car chases (usually involving Rolls-Royces), ancient castles, hidden treasure, and private revenge. Other notable works include a fantasy, *The Stolen March* (1926); *Lower than Vermin* (1950), a defence of conservative values; and *Ne'er do Well* (1954), his only who-dunnit.

Mercer died at the Isolation Hospital, Umtali, Southern Rhodesia, on 5 March 1960, of pneumonia and lung cancer; he was cremated and his ashes immured in the north porch of St John's Church, Umtali.   STEPHEN DERRY

Sources A. J. Smithers, *Dornford Yates: a biography* (1982) · R. Usborne, 'Introduction', in D. Yates, *Perishable goods* (1984), vii–xiii · *DNB*
Archives BL, corresp. with Society of Authors, Add. MS 63351 · Bodl. Oxf., corresp., with a memoir concerning H. H. Munro
Likenesses photograph, repro. in D. Yates, *Fire below*, dust wrapper · photographs, repro. in Smithers, *Dornford Yates*
Wealth at death £141 19s. 3d. in England: Rhodesian probate sealed in England, 21 March 1961, *CGPLA Eng. & Wales*

Mercer, David Stuart (1928–1980), playwright and script-writer, was born on 27 June 1928 at the Maternity Hospital, Blenheim Road, Wakefield, amid the coalfields of west Yorkshire, the younger son of Edward Mercer, a railway engine driver, and his wife, Helen Elizabeth, *née* Steadman, who had been 'in service' before the marriage. Both of David Mercer's grandfathers were miners. Raised in a time of considerable hardship, he came from a strict and respectable upper-working-class family. His parents, who, when he was young, had left Methodism for low-church Anglicanism, were ambitious for him and his brother, Reuben; the family dictum, David recalled later, was 'do owt as long as tha doesn't get th'hands mucky' (*Theatre Quarterly*). A childhood illness incarcerated him in plaster for a time, giving him opportunity to read, yet he failed to follow his brother to grammar school.

After leaving elementary school at fourteen, Mercer found work as a pathology laboratory assistant at the local hospital. Three years later, in what he subsequently described as an act of misguided patriotism, he joined the Royal Navy, and was employed there in a pathology lab. He was shore based for eighteen months, then posted to HMS *Vanguard*. Apart from treating his marine colleagues for venereal disease, Mercer spent most of his time reading escapist fiction, and he discovered then that he longed for the education he had missed. He won his release in 1948 and used his former serviceman's grant to attend Wake-field Technical College. He matriculated in a year and went on to study chemistry at University College, Durham, but he soon switched to King's College, Newcastle upon Tyne (then affiliated with the University of Durham), to study fine art; he gained a 2:2 BA honours degree in 1953. During his time at college, Mercer devoured books on poetry, politics, philosophy, history, and psychiatry.

On 5 June 1953, just after graduation, Mercer married his first wife, Jitka Sigmund (*b.* 1926/7), a refugee from Olomouc, Czechoslovakia, who had been studying economics at King's. He travelled to Paris to become a painter, and lived there with his wife among other émigrés from communist regimes. On realizing that he was not cut out to be a painter, he burnt all his canvasses and turned to writing novels, all of which remained unpublished. Back in England after two years, he settled in London, earning a subsistence living as a supply teacher. In 1957 he started a relationship with Dilys Johnson, a graduate civil servant in the Ministry of Housing; his marriage collapsed, he had a nervous breakdown, and he was accepted at the pioneering Tavistock Clinic as 'a suitable case for treatment'.

It was while undergoing analysis in 1959 that Mercer started writing his first play. He had begun to visualize ideas in the form of images and speeches, and when he went to see Shelagh Delaney's *A Taste of Honey* he thought he could do better. The result was *A Death in the Family*, a script that drew heavily on his own background. By the good luck of an accidentally circuitous route, the script landed on the desk of the formidable play agent Margaret (Peggy) Ramsay. Within twelve months Mercer had received commissions to write plays for radio and television, and in the following year, 1961, he gave up teaching and became a full-time playwright instead. The breakthrough, however, did not come in the theatre, as Mercer and Ramsay had intended, but in television, the dramatic output of which was barely taken seriously at the time. Mercer changed that. He became the pathfinder and opened the way for writers like Dennis Potter, creating new benchmarks for the medium through his unconventional and compelling narrative technique, his urgent treatment of ideas, and the sharpness of the interplay between the political and the personal.

Mercer's first television play was a revised version of *A Death in the Family*, retitled *Where the Difference Begins*. It formed the opening part of the innovative trilogy entitled *The Generations* (1961–3), a typically astringent portrait of waning ideals, set in the world of the anti-nuclear movement and the cold war. In some of his television plays, however, Mercer focused more upon the individual, as in *A Suitable Case for Treatment* (1962) or *In Two Minds* (1967), works in which he explored madness, as either the only strategy for, or the personal cost of, survival.

Mercer's career as a playwright took off in 1965 with *The Governor's Lady*, performed by the Royal Shakespeare Company (RSC), which was to stage six of his plays, and, in the West End, with *Ride a Cock Horse*, in which Peter O'Toole played a successful working-class writer whose sense of self is undermined by his anxiety at the way he treats the three important women in his life. Friends maintain that the first of these women was modelled on Dilys Johnson, whom Mercer had married on 3 December 1960. She had seen him through the breakdown, but found it hard to share him as his circle widened and he became a striking figure on the literary scene. His desire for abundance—in money, drink, and women—did not help, and the second marriage disintegrated too. A long string of relationships, including one with novelist Penelope Mortimer (1918–1999) and another with a German actress, Maria Machado, with whom he had a daughter, ended only with his third and last marriage, on 5 November 1974, to Israeli speech therapist Dafna Hemdi (*b.* 1950). Their daughter, Rebecca, was born the following year. Mercer spent much of his later life in Israel. He was the inspiration behind the character of Malcolm Sloman in Trevor Griffith's play *The Party* (1973), in which the drunken working-class writer punctures the political pretensions of the assembled revolutionary sloganizers.

In all Mercer had two plays broadcast on radio, twenty-six plays broadcast on television, sixteen stage plays produced, and five screenplays made into films. He won three Writers' Guild awards for television scripts (*A Suitable Case for Treatment*, 1962; *In Two Minds*, 1967; *Let's Murder Vivaldi*, 1968), the 1965 *Evening Standard* award for most promising dramatist (*Ride a Cock Horse*), the 1966 BAFTA award for best screenplay (*Morgan*), the French Film Academy César award for *Providence* (1977), and an Emmy award in 1980 for the television play *A Rod of Iron*. The BBC wiped much of his television work (as was its custom then), but texts were published. As for his stage writing, Mercer was always frustrated by lack of recognition, despite the success of *After Haggerty* (1970), the first new play from the RSC to transfer to the West End.

An internationalist and anti-Stalinist Marxist who became disillusioned with the shortcomings of all his favourite causes, Mercer never stinted in asking the awkward questions. A huge bear of a man, topped by a full mop of hair and fronted by a cropped moustache and beard, he was, like his work, full of volatile contradictions: vulnerable and violent, loving and loathing. He excoriated his masculinity but could not escape it; he raged at injustice worldwide but felt powerless before the enormity of it—and so he wrote his plays, which bear the stamp of his passion and his pain. David Stuart Mercer died of a heart attack on 8 August 1980 in Haifa, Israel, where he was buried, many miles from Wakefield.

COLIN CHAMBERS

Sources 'Birth of a playwriting man [Interview with the editors and Francis Jarman]', *Theatre Quarterly*, 3 (Jan–March 1973), 43–57 · C. Chambers, *Peggy: the life of Margaret Ramsay, play agent* (1997) · personal knowledge (2004) · private information (2004) [C. Chambers] · T. Dunn, 'Mercer, David Stuart', *Playwrights*, ed. D. Pickering (1994), vol. 2 of *International dictionary of theatre* · C. Barker, 'Mercer, David Stuart', *Contemporary dramatists*, ed. D. L. Kirkpatrick, 4th edn (1988) · R. Cook, 'Garlic and keystone burgundy: student life in Newcastle during the 1950s', *Northern Review*, 4 (1996), 20–28 · D. Taylor, *Days of vision: working with David Mercer* (1990) · C. Chambers and M. Prior, *Playwrights' progress: patterns of postwar British drama* (1987) · J. R. Taylor, *The second wave* (1978) · P. Mortimer, *About time too* (1993) · P. Madden, ed., *David Mercer: where the difference begins* (1981) · F. Jarman, J. Noyce, and M. Page, eds., *The quality of Mercer: a bibliography of writings by and about David Mercer* (1974) · S. Lang, 'Introduction', in D. Mercer, *Plays one* (1990) · m. cert., 1953 · b. cert. · CGPLA Eng. & Wales (1981)

Archives BBC WAC, corresp. with staff of BBC · BFI, corresp. with Joseph Losey · BL, Margaret Ramsay collection

Likenesses photographs, probably priv. coll.

Wealth at death £164,389: probate, 8 April 1981, CGPLA Eng. & Wales

Mercer, Hugh (1725–1777), physician and revolutionary army officer in America, was born in Aberdeen, the son of William Mercer, possibly a minister, and his wife, Anna Munro. He studied medicine at Marischal College, Aberdeen, from 1740 to 1744. He joined the Jacobite army of Prince Charles Edward in 1745 as a surgeon's mate, and was present at the battle of Culloden.

Mercer fled to America in 1746 or 1747, and settled as a doctor at the Conococheague frontier settlement, near what became Mercersburg, Pennsylvania. He served in the failed expedition against Fort Du Quesne, under General Edward Braddock, and was wounded at the Monongahela on 9 July 1756, for which he received a medal from the corporation of Philadelphia. Mercer became a lieutenant-colonel of provincials in 1758, and accompanied the expedition under Brigadier-General John Forbes against the new Fort Du Quesne. He was for several months commander of the fort (renamed Fort Pitt), and he conducted negotiations with the Six Nations Amerindians in 1759. At the conclusion of the war Mercer returned to medical practice, and established himself, apparently at the suggestion of George Washington, at Fredericksburg, Virginia. There he was a member of the same masonic lodge as Washington, and was a regular visitor to the latter's home. He married Isabella Gordon of the town; they had four sons and one daughter.

At the outbreak of the American War of Independence Mercer was commander of the minute men. He was appointed colonel of the 3rd Virginia regiment, and in June 1776, at Washington's request, was promoted to brigadier-general by congress. He accompanied Washington in his retreat through New Jersey. He executed the successful attack on the Hessians at Trenton on 26 December 1776, and advised the night march on Princeton, in which he led the advance. During the battle his horse was disabled, and Mercer was knocked to the ground and severely bayoneted. He died of his wounds several days later, at a nearby farm, on 12 January 1777. He was buried at Christ Church yard, Philadelphia, but his remains were moved in 1840 to the Laurel Hill cemetery in Philadelphia.

In 1790 congress made provision for the education of his youngest son and the erection of a monument in his honour. Mercer county, Kentucky, is named after him.

H. M. CHICHESTER, *rev.* TROY O. BICKHAM

Sources J. T. Golrick, *The life of Gen. Hugh Mercer* (1906) · *Pennsylvania Evening Post* (18 Jan 1777) · E. E. Curtis, 'Mercer, Hugh', *DAB* **Archives** BL, letters to Colonel Bouquet, Add. MSS 21643–21655 **Likenesses** J. Trumbull, drawing, 1791, Fordham University, New York · J. Trumbull, drawing, Metropolitan Museum of Art, New York · J. Trumbull, five drawings (studies for *Death of General Mercer*), Princeton University Library

Mercer, James (*bap.* 1734, *d.* 1804), poet and soldier, was baptized in Aberdeen on 16 February 1734, the elder of two sons of Thomas Mercer (*d.* 1760x69), merchant, and his wife, Margaret Rickart (*d.* 1780x89). His father belonged to a cadet branch of the prominent Jacobite family Mercer of Aldie, and was himself a Jacobite who had fought at Culloden in 1746, and subsequently fled to France. Mercer was educated at Aberdeen grammar school and in 1748 he entered the four-year arts course at Marischal College, Aberdeen, graduating MA in 1752. There Thomas Blackwell, the principal of the college, instilled in Mercer a lifelong love of classical literature. Mercer joined his father in France, but wanting a military career, and contrary to the wishes of his Jacobite parents, he returned to England at the outbreak of the Seven Years' War in 1756. He took part in an unsuccessful expedition to Cherbourg, then served as an officer in a highland battalion in the army in Germany, under Prince Ferdinand of Brunswick. Among other engagements he was involved in the battle of Minden in 1761. He was once taken prisoner and his French captors were astonished by his knowledge of French language and customs.

Mercer returned briefly to Aberdeen, first about 1761–2 and then again at the peace of 1763, when he was married on 13 September 1763 to Katherine Douglas (*bap.* 1743, *d.* 1802), daughter of John Douglas of Fechil, and sister of Sylvester *Douglas (later Lord Glenbervie). They had two daughters. Mercer probably became a friend of the poet and philosopher James Beattie about this time, though they had been contemporaries at Marischal College. Mercer purchased a company and served for about nine years in the army in Ireland. During this time he was pressed by the archbishop of Cashel to take holy orders and to receive a lucrative living, but he declined. He became a major in 1770, but was becoming disillusioned with army life. He left the army in 1772, disappointed that an agreement that he should be promoted lieutenant-colonel was not honoured. He returned to Aberdeen, but in 1775 made an extended trip to the south of France for his wife's health. In 1778 Mercer took a commission in the duke of Gordon's fencibles, a company of militia, and was in Glasgow and Edinburgh. When the American War of Independence ended he finally retired to Aberdeenshire. At first the Mercers lived in a small cottage near Aberdeen. His mother, who had disapproved of Mercer's serving in the Hanoverian army, had left the family estate to Mercer's younger brother, David. However, Mercer inherited

it on David's death in 1787, and was then able to build the house Sunny Bank in Aberdeen.

Mercer is chiefly remembered as a friend of James Beattie. Beattie once wrote:

> He was the only person in this place whose taste and studies are similar to mine … I know not six persons in Scotland who understand Greek so well as he. If his health would permit, he would soon be the greatest scholar in Europe (letter to Robert Arbuthnot, 27 April 1769, NL Scot., acc. 4796, Fettercairn box 91)

He and Beattie shared a taste for comic banter and they exchanged light-hearted poems about their mutual friends, including the banker Sir William Forbes. Mercer was one of the very few friends Beattie saw regularly in his final years. Lord Glenbervie published an elegant quarto edition of Mercer's *Lyric Poems* anonymously in 1795, and with Mercer's name in 1804. A posthumous edition by Glenbervie in 1806 has some notes on the poems and a 'Life'. Gentle pieces such as 'Novelty' and 'Home' have contrasting images of stormy voyages and of domestic tranquillity and rural retirement, with echoes of Horace and also of James Beattie's poems. William Walker commented 'Mercer will be carried down to posterity more by his connection with Dr Beattie … than by any of his poetical efforts' (Walker, 336).

The last years of Mercer's life were saddened by the divorce of his elder daughter, Katherine, in 1796 and by the death of his wife on 3 January 1802. He gave Sir William Forbes some early assistance in preparing the biography of Beattie, who died on 18 August 1803. However, Mercer became mentally confused in May 1804 and he died at Sunny Bank on 27 November 1804. He was buried in St Nicholas's churchyard, Aberdeen.

ROGER J. ROBINSON

Sources S. Douglas, Baron Glenbervie, 'An account of the life of James Mercer, Esquire', in *Lyric poems by the late James Mercer, with an account of the life of the author, by Sylvester Lord Glenbovie*, 3rd edn (1806), xi–lxiv · W. Forbes, *An account of the life and writings of James Beattie*, 2 vols. (1806), esp. vol. 2, p. 377 · J. F. George, 'The "Auld Hoose" of Sunnybank', *The book of Powis*, ed. J. A. C. Coutts (*c.*1906), 50–53 · W. Walker, *The bards of Bon-Accord, 1375–1860* (1887), 333 · *Fasti academiae Mariscallanae Aberdonensis: selections from the records of the Marischal College and University, MDXCIII–MDCCCLX*, 2, ed. P. J. Anderson, New Spalding Club, 18 (1898), 320 · M. Forbes, *Beattie and his friends*, ed. M. Knight and M. Forbes (1904); repr. (1990) · R. J. Robinson, 'The poetry of James Beattie: a critical edition', PhD diss., U. Aberdeen, 1997 · parish register, Aberdeen, 16 Feb 1734 [baptism] **Archives** NL Scot., MS Acc. 4796, Fettercairn boxes 91–3 · NL Scot., corresp. with Lord Glenbervie · U. Aberdeen, corresp. with James Beattie, MSS 30/1 and 30/2 **Likenesses** C. Picart, engraving (after Irvine), repro. in J. Mercer, *Lyric poems*, 3rd edn, frontispiece

Mercer, James (1883–1932), mathematician, was born at Bootle, Liverpool, on 15 January 1883, the son of Thomas Mercer, an accountant, and his wife, Sarah Alice Mercer. He was educated at University College, Liverpool, and at Trinity College, Cambridge, where he obtained a scholarship in 1902. He was bracketed senior wrangler with John Edensor Littlewood in 1905, was a Smith's prizeman in 1908, and was elected a fellow of Trinity in 1909. He married, in 1911, Annie, fourth daughter of William Barnes, of

Walton, near Liverpool; a son survived him. After a short period of service as an assistant lecturer in Liverpool University, Mercer was recalled to Cambridge as a fellow and mathematical lecturer of Christ's College in 1912, and, up to the outbreak of war in 1914, was active in both teaching and research. During the First World War he was a naval instructor, and saw action at the battle of Jutland.

Mercer, although he wrote comparatively little, and almost all of it before he was thirty, was a mathematician of high originality and great skill, who made important advances in more than one branch of analysis. He was one of the first English mathematicians to occupy himself with the then novel theory of integral equations, to which, and to the closely related theory of orthogonal series, he contributed a number of striking theorems. One theorem in particular, concerning 'kernels' with positive eigenvalues, has become famous, and appears under his name in every treatise on the subject. A second Mercer's theorem, published in 1909, plays an important part in the modern theory of divergent series.

After the war the high hopes raised by Mercer's early mathematical work were never fully realized. He resumed his activity on his return to Cambridge, and was elected FRS in 1922, but his health, which had always been uncertain, began to fail, and led to resignation of his lecturership in 1926. He never recovered his powers, and died in St Paul's Hospital, Endell Street, London WC2, on 21 February 1932.   G. H. HARDY, rev. JOHN BOSNELL

Sources E. W. Hobson, *Obits. FRS*, 1 (1932–5), 164–5 · E. W. Hobson, *Journal of the London Mathematical Society*, 8 (1933), 79–80 · private information (1949) · personal knowledge (1949) · d. cert. · *CGPLA Eng. & Wales* (1932)
Likenesses W. Stoneman?, photograph, RS · photograph, repro. in Hobson, *Obits. FRS*, facing p. 164
Wealth at death £8181 18s. 9d.: resworn probate, 5 April 1932, *CGPLA Eng. & Wales*

Mercer, John (c.1300–1380), merchant, was the son of Thomas Mercer of Perth, and became the most prominent Scottish merchant of his day. The Mercers were closely associated with Perth, and John held several properties there and served as alderman. Nevertheless, little is known of his early career, and he must have been well advanced in years when he rose to national prominence in David II's service, perhaps coming to royal attention as a burgh representative negotiating the king's ransom in 1357. He represented Perth at a general council in 1365 and in parliament in 1370, and from 1359 to 1380 he was custumar of the town. In 1359–62 and 1374–7 he was in charge of arrangements for paying the ransom of David II, raised through the wool customs and collected in Flanders. He was later special deputy of the chamberlain (1364), receiver of the king's money (1376–7), and auditor of the sheriffs' accounts (1374). Mercer undertook diplomatic missions to Flanders in 1367 and to England in 1379. He was said to be in great favour with the king of France; this may have been true, but the John Mercer who was the French king's councillor in 1384 was probably a relative, perhaps his son.

Throughout his life John Mercer continued his mercantile activities, trading in England, Flanders, and France, often in partnership with his son Andrew. In a celebrated incident which brought him to the attention of English chroniclers he was shipwrecked during a voyage off the English coast in 1376 and was imprisoned by the earl of Northumberland. The earl of Douglas, Mercer's patron, protested to Edward III, and Mercer was freed, much to the regret of Thomas Walsingham, who believed that if he had been ransomed 'he would have enriched both the king and the kingdom by his vast wealth' (*Historia Anglicana*, 1.369). Mercer deducted 2000 merks from the royal ransom payments to compensate for his losses. His son Andrew took more drastic action and in 1378 raised a fleet of Spanish, French, and Scottish ships that attacked and plundered ships at Scarborough. In response the London merchant John Philipot (d. 1384) assembled his own fleet and captured Andrew and his booty. Andrew was released later that year. According to family tradition, an engraved cup commemorates this event, although the cup itself is probably later in date. Thomas Mercer, archdeacon of Glasgow and perhaps another son of John's, was imprisoned in England when returning from an embassy to France; the date is uncertain, but he was released under safe conduct in October 1379.

John Mercer died in 1380, and was buried in St John's Church, Perth. A probably inaccurate tradition maintains that the family traded their mills on the north and south inches of Perth for the right of burial in the church:

> Folk say the Mercers tried the town to cheat,
> When for two Inches they did win two feet.
> (*Our Seven Centuries*, 6)

During his career Mercer amassed substantial holdings in Perth and Perthshire, including Lyndoch, Tullybeagle, Meikle Kinnaird, Pettland, and Meikleour, and his marriage to Ada Murray of Tullibardine, Perthshire, c.1327, brought Aldie in Kinross-shire to the family. Their son Sir Andrew Mercer (d. c.1389) married Jonet, kinswoman of Margaret Berclay, the wife of Robert II's son Walter, thereby establishing ties of kinship to the royal family; his standing is shown by his acting as arbitrator in a lawsuit between John Logie, David II's stepson, and Robert Stewart, earl of Fife, Robert II's second son, in 1385. Among John's other sons may have been the Robert Mercer whose family became lairds of Innerpeffray in Strathearn, and John Mercer, canon of Dunkeld, whose petition for a papal dispensation in 1372 was supported by the kings of both Scotland and France. Thomas Walsingham described Mercer as 'skilful in matters relating to commerce, and fertile in expedient and prudent in counsel' (*Historia Anglicana*, 1.369). He represents the growing prominence of medieval merchants, who, through their financial importance to the crown, were able to exert increasing influence on national affairs, and to ensure the upward social mobility of their families.   ELIZABETH EWAN

Sources G. Burnett and others, eds., *The exchequer rolls of Scotland*, 1–3 (1878–80) · J. M. Thomson and others, eds., *Registrum magni sigilli regum Scotorum / The register of the great seal of Scotland*, 11 vols. (1882–1914) · *RotS* · *Thomae Walsingham, quondam monachi S. Albani,* *historia Anglicana*, ed. H. T. Riley, 2 vols., pt 1 of *Chronica monasterii S. Albani*, Rolls Series, 28 (1863–4), vol. 1, pp. 369–70 · *The Mercer chronicle, by an Irish Sennachy* (private circulation, London, 1866) · *Our seven centuries: an account of the Mercers of Aldie and Meikleour and their branches, from AD 1200 to the present time* (1868) · Bannatyne and Maitland Clubs, *Liber ecclesie de Scon* (1843) · *CDS*, vol. 4 · D. E. R. Watt, *A biographical dictionary of Scottish graduates to AD 1410* (1977) · R. S. Fittis, *The mercers of Innerpeffray and Inchbreakie from 1400 to 1513* (1877) · *APS*, 1124–1423 · W. Fraser, ed., *The Red Book of Menteith*, 2 (1880), 260

Archives NA Scot., corresp., photograph of cup, GD172/1263/1–22 | Meikleour House, Perthshire, Lansdowne MSS
Likenesses effigy, St John's Church, Perth
Wealth at death 'inestimably wealthy': *Historia Anglicana*, vol. 1, p. 369

Mercer, John (1791–1866), calico printer and chemist, was born on 21 February 1791 at Dean, in the parish of Great Harwood, near Blackburn, Lancashire, the eldest of three children of Robert Mercer (*d.* 1800), a hand-loom weaver and farmer, and his wife, Elizabeth Clayton. He received no formal education and began work as a bobbin winder in 1800, at the age of nine. A workman in the Oakenshaw calico-printworks taught him reading, writing, and arithmetic. Mercer also gave much time to music, to which he remained sensitive through life. In 1807, following his mother's marriage to a Thomas Mercer, the sight of his baby stepbrother in an orange coloured dress set him 'all on fire to learn dyeing' (Parnell, 10). In September 1809 Mercer was apprenticed in the colour shop of the Oakenshaw printworks, but within a year he had to surrender his indentures when the Fort brothers were forced to reduce their staff because of Napoleon's confiscation of British merchandise on the continent. Mercer then became a hand-loom weaver, and invented many ingenious designs in weaving. He also gave much attention to the study of mathematics, in which he was helped by an excise surveyor, John Lightfoot, whose sons were calico printers. In 1813 he experienced an evangelical conversion and joined the Wesleyans. In the same year he became engaged to Mary Wolstenholme (1785–1859), whom he married on 17 April 1814. They had two sons and two daughters.

In 1813 Mercer had resumed work as a dyer, while still continuing to weave, but it was not until 1814 that his attention was directed towards chemistry by the *Chemical Pocket-Book* (3rd edn, 1803) of James Parkinson, which 'introduced him into a new world' (Parnell, 22). This inspired his first major discovery, a method for fixing antimony sulphide on cloth to produce orange prints (no good orange dye suitable for calico printing had been previously known). In 1818 the Fort brothers re-engaged Mercer, this time as a chemist in their colour shop, at a salary of 30s. a week. He soon developed novel printing effects by applying his knowledge of inorganic chemistry. In 1823 Mercer rediscovered and introduced into England a method of applying to cotton cloth lead chromate, a yellow dye of great importance. He also discovered the use of manganese salts as bronze dyes, greatly improved the methods of printing indigo by using potassium

John Mercer (1791–1866), by unknown photographer

ferricyanide and potash, and made many other minor inventions with inorganic colours. Mercer was a partner in the firm of Fort Brothers between 1825 and 1848, when the firm dissolved in the face of foreign competition. The profits of the undertaking had been considerable, and the now wealthy Mercer was free to pursue researches sketched out during his busy years with Forts.

Mercer took a keen interest in theoretical chemistry, and this interest was greatly stimulated and strengthened by the influence of Lyon Playfair, who advanced his reputation both academically and socially. The two men had become friends in 1841, Playfair being then one of the chemists at James Thomson's printworks at Clitheroe. Playfair and a few scientific friends met once a week at Whalley to discuss scientific matters, and it was at one of these meetings that Mercer propounded a theory of catalysis. He posited the formation of unstable chemical intermediates by the catalyst which weakened chemical unions that were otherwise immune from attack. He read a paper on the subject at the Manchester meeting of the British Association for the Advancement of Science in 1842, and the theory was more fully developed and illustrated by Playfair (*Memoirs of the Chemical Society*, 3.348). Certain observations of Mercer's made in 1843 and discussed at the Whalley meetings also led Playfair to the discovery of a new class of compounds, the nitroprussides. In 1847 Mercer joined the Chemical Society.

Mercer's major discovery came in 1844 when he investigated the action of caustic soda, sulphuric acid, and zinc chloride on cotton cloth, paper, and other materials made from vegetable fibres. These experiments (which were carried out in commercial partnership with Robert Hargreaves of Broad Oak, near Accrington, and at his works) led to the discovery of the textile process known as mercerizing, and to the preparation of parchment paper, patented by Mercer in 1850. By treating cotton cloth with any one of the reagents mentioned, in a solution of a certain concentration, the individual cotton fibres became thicker and shorter, and the strength of the cloth was greatly increased. It also became semitransparent, and better able to absorb dyes than ordinary cloth, this being due to the swelling up of the cell walls in the fibre. However, the expense of the treatment meant that it was not widely adopted until the 1890s. Other fruits of this work were the demonstration that cotton (or cellulose) would dissolve in copper-ammonium solutions, a process that later became important for the production of artificial silk; and the demonstration that the chlorination of wool fabrics (delaines) made them printable. In 1851 Mercer was one of the jurors of the Great Exhibition. Excluded from the ordinary distinctions, he was awarded a council medal for the discovery of mercerization. In June 1852, on Playfair's action, he reluctantly assented to becoming a fellow of the Royal Society.

At the Leeds meeting of the British Association in 1858 Mercer noted simple mathematical relations between the atomic weights of the elements, but the observation was without influence. Chemistry, the effects of light on textiles, and their printing with natural colours inevitably combined to make him a keen experimental photographer. At the same meeting he contributed a paper on the reducing action of light on complex salts of iron, which yields a blue colour, varying in depth according to the intensity of light to which they have been exposed. The discovery of this photochemical action (blue-printing), which Mercer had made originally in 1828, proved a boon to drawing offices. Mercer himself proposed to utilize blueprints for recording the intensity of sunlight, and the process was adopted in some meteorological stations.

An unselfish, self-made man, Mercer was given to stimulating flights of scientific speculation among his friends, and in his experimental discoveries he displayed fertility of invention and a remarkable insight into chemistry. There can be little doubt that had he devoted himself entirely to research he would have been among the most distinguished chemists of the day. Endowed with the perseverance and business capacity necessary to raise himself from poverty to affluence, he was never grasping, and although he patented some of his inventions, he freely gave away many others which brought large sums of money to those who profited by them. Through life he took an evangelical interest in religion and religious affairs, giving popular lectures at Clayton-le-Moors on a variety of scientific topics from a natural theological perspective. In 1849 he returned to Anglican worship, but, with characteristic liberality of mind, continued to give material help to local Methodist institutions. Politically he was a reformer, and as a member of the Anti-Corn Law League his views on free trade and industrial values were greatly influenced by the calico printer Richard Cobden,

who acted as the London agent for Forts from 1828 until 1831.

Following his wife's death in 1859, Mercer's inventiveness plummeted. In 1861 he was made a justice of the peace for Lancashire, but was judged by those who knew him to be too merciful for a magistrate (Parnell, 266). In 1862 he served as a juror for the second International Exhibition. A severe cold, brought on by falling into a water reservoir in 1864, was the putative cause of a painful kidney disease, of which Mercer died at his home, Oakenshaw House, Oakenshaw, Clayton-le-Moors, on 30 November 1866. He was buried in the family vault in St Bartholomew's Church, Great Harwood. A clock tower memorial was unveiled in Great Harwood in June 1903.

P. J. HARTOG, rev. W. H. BROCK

Sources E. A. Parnell, *The life and labours of John Mercer* (1886) · R. S. Crossley, *Accrington: captains of industry* (1930) · A. Nieto-Galan, 'Calico printing and chemical knowledge in Lancashire in the early 19th century: the life and "colours" of John Mercer', *Annals of Science*, 54 (1997), 1–28 · A. W. Baldwin, 'Mercer and mercerization', *Endeavour*, 3 (1944), 138–43 · d. cert. · parish records (baptism), Great Harwood

Archives Clayton-le-Moors Public Library, autobiography and MSS · Lancs. RO, autobiography and papers · Man. CL, Manchester Archives and Local Studies, pattern book · MHS Oxf., recipe and trial books | Manchester Literary and Philosophical Society, letters to Lord Playfair · Rothamsted Agricultural Station, Warington MSS

Likenesses photographs, MHS Oxf. [*see illus.*]

Wealth at death under £16,000: probate, 7 March 1867, *CGPLA Eng. & Wales*

Mercer, Joseph (1914–1990), footballer and football manager, was born on 9 August 1914 at 32 Queen Street, Ellesmere Port, Wirral, Cheshire, the eldest in the family of three boys and one girl of Joseph Powell Mercer, professional footballer, of Ellesmere Port, and his wife, Ethel Breeze. He was educated at Cambridge Road School and John Street Senior Mixed School, Ellesmere Port, playing football for the Cheshire schools' team. His father, a former Nottingham Forest player, was wounded in the First World War, and became a bricklayer. He died when Mercer was twelve. After leaving school, Mercer worked for Shell in a variety of unskilled jobs, and played football first for the village of Elton Green and for the Shell Mex team, and later for Ellesmere Port. Spotted at Elton Green by an Everton scout, he played for Everton as an amateur for two years before signing on as a professional in 1931. He became a regular first-team player during the 1935–6 season as a wing-half, and got his first England cap in 1938. He appeared five times for England during the 1938–9 season, in which Everton won the League championship. In September 1939 Mercer joined the army after Stanley Rous, secretary of the Football Association, had circularized footballers urging them to join the Army Physical Training Corps, so that they would keep fit. He became a sergeant-instructor, and ended the Second World War as a sergeant-major. He played in twenty-seven wartime internationals, captaining England on several occasions, and also played for Aldershot. On 3 September 1941 he married

Joseph Mercer (1914–1990), by Sefton Samuels

Norah Fanny (*b.* 1919/20), daughter of Albert Edward Dyson, provision merchant. They had one son.

After the war Mercer was unhappy at Everton, and suffered from knee trouble. He was contemplating retirement in order to devote himself to running a grocery business in Wallasey when Arsenal offered £7000 for him in November 1946. He agreed to go on condition that he could live and train in Liverpool, and he continued to do so throughout his eight years with Arsenal. He became a half-back, and went on to captain Arsenal to two League championships, in 1948 and 1953, and to success in the FA cup final against Liverpool in 1950, a few days after being voted Footballer of the Year. In April 1954 he broke his leg, playing against Liverpool, and retired.

For the next twenty years Mercer pursued a successful career as a football manager. He became manager of Sheffield United, who were relegated to the second division at the end of his first season there, in 1955—an inauspicious start. In December 1958 he replaced Eric Houghton as manager of Aston Villa, who were also relegated at the end of the season. But, under his management, Aston Villa came top of the second division in the 1959–60 season, and won the League cup in 1961. Mercer had a nervous breakdown in 1964, after a disappointing season when the club came nineteenth in the League championship, and he resigned.

Mercer was out of football for fourteen months before becoming manager of Manchester City in 1965. He brought in Malcolm Allison as assistant manager and coach, and for five seasons this was a highly successful partnership. Manchester City came top of the second division in Mercer's first season there, won the League championship in 1968 and the FA cup in 1969, and in 1970 won both the League cup and the European Cupwinners' cup, beating the Polish team Gornik Zabrze 2–1 in the final. It was the first English club to win a domestic and a European trophy in the same season. Mercer's relationship with Allison soured after Allison, ambitious for promotion, became involved in boardroom intrigues, and Mercer left in 1972 to become manager of Coventry City. In May 1974, after the resignation of Sir Alf Ramsey, the England manager, Mercer agreed to be caretaker manager for the rest of the season. He was in charge for seven matches, with a record of three wins, three draws, and one loss. He was appointed OBE in 1976.

Mercer was regarded as the greatest wing-half of his generation, and had the Second World War not interrupted his career he would have won many more England caps. As a manager, his greatest successes were with Manchester City, previously overshadowed by their neighbours and rivals, Manchester United. He was a popular manager, much loved for his amiable manner and his big smile. He was famous for his bandy legs and was often mistaken for the jockey Joe Mercer. Mercer died of Alzheimer's disease on 9 August 1990 at his home in St Margaret's Road, Hoylake, Wirral, Cheshire. He was cremated at Landican five days later after a funeral service at Hoylake parish church.   ANNE PIMLOTT BAKER, *rev.*

Sources *The Times* (11 Aug 1990) · *The Independent* (11 Aug 1990) · J. Mercer, *The great ones* (1964) · E. Thornton, *Manchester City: Meridith to Mercer—and the Cup* (1969) · A. Ward, *The Manchester City story* (1984) · b. cert. · m. cert. · *CGPLA Eng. & Wales* (1990) · G. James, *Joe Mercer: football with a smile* (1993) · G. James, *Manchester: the greatest city* (1997), 227–87
Likenesses photographs, 1946–74, Hult. Arch. · S. Samuels, photograph, NPG [*see illus.*] · photograph, repro. in James, *Joe Mercer* · photograph, repro. in *The Times*
Wealth at death under £115,000: probate, 16 Nov 1990, *CGPLA Eng. & Wales*

Mercer, Mabel [*real name* Mabel Wadham] (1900–1984), cabaret singer, was born on 3 February 1900 at 30 James Street, Burton upon Trent, the daughter of Emily Mabel Wadham (*b.* 1879), variety artiste, who was the daughter of the painter Benjamin Braffet Wadham. Her father was an African-American musician whose identity is not established; his name may have been Mercer, but this is not verifiable. She was raised by her grandmother and educated (1907–14) at a convent school at Blackley, Manchester.

Mabel Wadham began her stage career dancing with the Romany Five, the family act of her aunt Rhoda King. When the act broke up about 1916, she joined a dance troupe and came to the notice of Nannette Horton Boucher, daughter of the pioneer African nationalist Africanus Horton, who took her into her household; there she associated for the first time with others of African descent. Consequently some contemporaries from this era recalled her as Mabel Boucher. In 1917–19 she toured with

Mabel Mercer (1900–1984), by unknown photographer

the show *Coloured Society* as a dancer and pianist. In mid-1920, when she appeared in London with the Southern Syncopated Orchestra, she was still billed as Mabel Wadham, but in the early 1920s she worked intermittently in an act called Kay and Mercer, travelling to Belgium and Luxembourg. She had a relationship at this time with Robert Williams, part of an African-American act known as Williams and Taylor, who worked in revue with Kay and Mercer.

Mercer appeared in Paris in 1924–5 at Le Grand Duc and Chez Florence; and then as a chorus girl in *Blackbirds of 1926* in Paris and London and with the African-American band leader Sam Wooding. She had a small part in *Show Boat* at the Drury Lane Theatre, London, in 1928. In 1931 she was working at Chez Florence with the band of her then-partner, the African-American drummer Harvey White (*b*. 1896), when she joined Ada Smith (known as Bricktop) in the management of her new club. Mabel Mercer began singing at the tables, soon becoming a Parisian institution and a favourite with British and American visitors, including royalty. In 1936 she appeared in the British film *Everything is Rhythm*. In February–March 1938 she appeared in Amsterdam with the band of the African-American jazz violinist Eddie South. Although in this period she frequently worked with jazz artistes, she was never herself a jazz singer.

Mabel Mercer moved to the United States in October 1938 for a six-month engagement at the Ruban Bleu Club in New York and was reunited with her mother, recently married to an American. In 1940 she went to the Bahamas for a holiday, but stayed on professionally after finding she would not be readmitted to the USA. Mabel Mercer reportedly performed frequently at private functions for the duke and duchess of Windsor. During 1941 she married Kelsey Pharr, a member of the Delta Rhythm Boys, a vocal group, in order to secure readmission to the USA. Although she never lived with her husband, who was openly homosexual, they remained married until he died in 1964. In New York Mercer worked again at the Ruban Bleu, then briefly at a new club called Bricktop's with Ada Smith. Through a relationship with the pianist Cyril F. (Cy) Walter, she secured a residency at the club Tony's at 59 West 52nd Street, which continued for seven years. She moved in 1949 to the Byline Room at 137 East 52nd Street, and with the club in 1955 to a new location on West 56th Street. When this engagement ended in summer 1958, she moved to the RSVP Room.

During the 1950s Mabel Mercer's singing gained wider currency through a series of LP albums for the Atlantic label, including *Sings Cole Porter* (Atlantic 1213) and *Once in a Blue Moon* (Atlantic 1301), on which she performs songs from the standard repertory of American popular song of the pre-rock era. She became a US citizen in 1952. For much of the 1960s she worked only intermittently, making some of her appearances outside New York. An engagement at the St Regis Hotel in 1972 fuelled a return to prominence. In 1977 Mercer revisited Europe, where she appeared at the Playboy Club, London, and made a BBC television series, *Miss Mercer in Mayfair*. Despite failing health, she continued working until hospitalized with angina in January 1984. She died in Pittsfield, Massachusetts, on 20 April 1984, survived by Harry Beard, a manager, her companion from the late forties. Whitney Balliett said that her singing 'lay somewhere between the concert hall and jazz. She had a rich, low mezzo-soprano and considerable range' (Balliett, 'Profiles', 55).

HOWARD RYE

Sources J. Haskins, *Mabel Mercer, a life* (1987) · H. Rye, 'Visiting firemen 15: the Southern Syncopated Orchestra (Part 2)', *Storyville*, 143 (1990), 165–78 · W. Balliett, 'Profiles, a queenly aura', *The New Yorker* (18 Nov 1972), 55–64 · L. McGlohan, 'Miss Mercer, you done good', *C.R.C. Newsletter* [Decatur, GA], 10/4 (1984), 2 · W. Balliett, 'Our footloose correspondents: in the country', *The New Yorker* (6 Sept 1982), 40–49 · Bricktop [A. Smith] and A. Haskins, *Bricktop* (1983) · J. Gill, 'Mercer, Mabel Alice Wadham', *Encyclopedia of African-American culture and history*, ed. J. Salzman, D. L. Smith, and C. West (1996)
Archives NYPL, Schomburg Center for Research in Black Culture, papers | NYPL, Schomburg Center for Research in Black Culture, Bricktop papers
Likenesses J. Kudler, photograph, *c*.1978, Hult. Arch. · photograph, Redferns Music Picture Library, London [*see illus.*] · photographs, repro. in Haskins, *Mabel Mercer*

Mercer, Thomas (1822–1900), maker of marine chronometers, watches, and clocks, was born in November 1822 at St Helens, the second of three children of Richard Mercer (*d*. 1830), sail maker and barge builder, and his wife, Sarah. In 1836 Sarah married Samuel Fletcher, manager of the Bridgewater Canal. Fletcher did not accept young Thomas, who was therefore apprenticed to his grandfather William Walker (1783–1860), a watch-movement maker at Duke Street, St Helens. His apprenticeship duties included on occasion walking from St Helens to Liverpool to deliver a basket of uncased watch movements to his uncle at 108 Homer Street, though his grandmother insisted that he should also attend the local school. In 1843 he went to work for Thomas Russell at 30–32 Slater Street, Liverpool, in order to learn from the top of the trade. In his free time he made watches, which he signed and sold under his own name. While in Liverpool, he absorbed the radical views then current, his support for these ideas earning him the nickname of 'Radical Tom', though he did not join any political group.

In 1854, having decided that the English watch and clock industry held no future for him, Mercer took a coach to London and purchased a one-way ticket to America, a land where, he said, everyone was equal and where he would be able to make progress. Fate decided his future, however, for while awaiting passage he saw a marine chronometer in the shop window of John Fletcher, one of the most important chronometer makers of the day. He entered the shop to ask for work, and was accepted as a watch springer and finisher. During this period, the Greenwich premium trials were being held, to enable the Royal Navy to find makers capable of supplying and servicing chronometers that could be relied on to perform accurately and consistently under the extremes of temperature and motion encountered at sea. High prices were paid for chronometers that passed these trials. Mercer left Fletcher's service in 1858 to set up on his own as a chronometer maker at New North Road, London, moving to 45 Spencer Street, Clerkenwell, in 1860 and later to other addresses in Clerkenwell. He had to face considerable competition in his chosen craft. Thomas Earnshaw and John Arnold, the two great modernizers of the marine chronometer, were long dead, but Dent, Frodsham, Blackie, the Poole brothers, Reid, and the Scandinavians Kullberg and Johannsen were all established and active in this lucrative field.

Mercer became involved in the British Horological Institute, which had been established in 1858 and was reputed to be the oldest professional institute in the world for that discipline. He served as its honorary treasurer from 1875 to 1895, and lectured there on the need to modernize the industry and to train young people. In 1874 he moved to St Albans, setting up a factory behind his house at 14–15 Prospect Road. Each Friday he travelled the 20 miles to collect finished parts from his specialist outworkers in Clerkenwell and call into the Horological Institute. In 1890, feeling the need to have a London address on his dials and letterheads, he took an office at 81 Westmoreland Place, City Road.

Mercer's marriage to Mary Thompson, daughter of a St Albans newspaper reporter, on 15 May 1875, was held at the church of St John in Holloway, so that many of his old friends and competitors could attend. The couple had seven children in six years: three boys and two sets of girl twins. Success in the Greenwich trials was the key to Mercer's profitable business: he entered at least one chronometer each year and he was placed second in 1881, his son Frank being placed first in 1911. Thomas Mercer was appointed as judge for the horological class at the Universal Exhibition held in Paris in 1900. Unfortunately he caught a cold on the ferry crossing to France and died at the Hôtel Internationale, Paris, on 29 September 1900. He was buried in St Stephen's Church, St Albans. At the time of his death he had been responsible for the manufacture of over 5000 chronometers, sold to the Royal Navy and to the navies of the world. The obituary of Mercer, published in the *British Horological Journal* for November 1900, attested:

> The annexed portrait affords a very fair idea of the man. Straightforward and self-reliant, he was, nevertheless, of retiring and unpretentious disposition, rarely mixing in public gatherings, yet taking an absorbing interest in all that pertained to horology, and especially in any proposal or device connected with improved methods of manufacture. Unswerving honesty was his prominent characteristic; this, coupled with the large amount of sound common sense with which he was endowed, enabled him by plodding industry to attain a position second to none in the trade.

F. A. MERCER

Sources private information (2004) · T. Mercer [F. A. Mercer], *Mercer chronometers: Radical Tom Mercer and the house he founded* (1978) · R. T. Gould, *The marine chronometer: its history and development* (1923); repr. (1989) · Prescot Watch and Clock Museum, archives · *Horological Journal*, 43 (1900–01), 31–2 · IGI
Archives NMM, Greenwich, Royal Observatory, archives · Prescot Watch and Clock Museum · priv. coll.
Likenesses photograph, repro. in *British Horological Journal*, 31 · photograph, repro. in Mercer, *Mercer chronometers*
Wealth at death £25,754 3s. 5d.: probate, 16 Feb 1901, CGPLA Eng. & Wales

Mercer, Sir Walter (1890–1971), surgeon, was born on 19 March 1890 at Cockholmbank, Stow, Midlothian, the second son of Ebenezer Beattie Mercer, a woollen manufacturer, and his wife, Jessie Mary Graham (née Greenfield). He was educated at George Watson's College, Edinburgh, and matriculated at Edinburgh University in 1907. From there he graduated MB, ChB in 1912, and then held a number of posts as house officer in hospitals at Carlisle and Berwick upon Tweed. In 1915 he joined the King's Own Scottish Borderers as the regimental medical officer, and later the Royal Scots Fusiliers. He served on the western front at the battle of the Somme, on the Messines Ridge at the third battle of Ypres, and at base hospitals in France and Italy. During the war Mercer received a permanent injury to the index finger of his left hand, but this was never allowed to interfere with his dexterity as a surgeon.

In 1918 Mercer joined the Edinburgh War Hospital at Bangour, West Lothian. There he met several distinguished American orthopaedic surgeons, who aroused his interest in orthopaedics. After demobilization in 1920 he was appointed as surgeon in charge of the Tynecastle Orthopaedic Clinic, Edinburgh, which was set up to care for disabled ex-servicemen. In 1921 he became a fellow of the Royal College of Surgeons of Edinburgh. In the same year he became assistant surgeon to Professor John Fraser at the Royal Infirmary, Edinburgh, where he was responsible for both the emergency and the elective work in orthopaedic surgery as well as being a clinical tutor. On 14 March 1923 Mercer married Helen May Margaret (Maisie) Lunan (b. 1899/1900), daughter of George Lunan, a pharmaceutical chemist, and his wife, Sarah Jane (*née* Milne). They adopted a son, David. In 1925 Mercer was appointed consultant surgeon to the South Eastern Counties of Scotland Sanatorium, East Fortune, East Lothian, which specialized in caring for patients with tuberculosis and where he was especially interested in the effects of tuberculosis on the bones and joints. He later became a consultant in tuberculosis at the City Hospital, Edinburgh, and at Bangour, where he established the thoracic unit for the east of Scotland during the Second World War.

Mercer published *Orthopaedic Surgery* in 1932 and this became a standard textbook, running to eight editions. It was his most important publication. He also wrote many articles on orthopaedics. In recognition of his work he was elected a fellow of the Royal Society of Edinburgh in 1935. During the war Mercer was appointed consultant in orthopaedic surgery to the Department of Health, Scotland, and chaired the Ministry of Health advisory committee on artificial limbs. Despite all this Mercer was essentially still a general surgeon, skilfully performing operations in abdominal, thoracic, and vascular surgery. To extend his range, immediately after the war he went to the USA to train in cardiac surgery under Alfred Blalock at Baltimore, where he also undertook research on babies born with congenital heart defects. Mercer then returned to Edinburgh, to concentrate on heart surgery at the Royal Infirmary. In 1948 he became the first occupant of the Law chair in orthopaedic surgery at Edinburgh University, and he devoted himself exclusively to orthopaedics. His teaching ward rounds were attended by large numbers of postgraduates from all over the world. He set high standards for his surgical trainees, by whom he was greatly respected, and was universally recognized as a most skilled and dexterous surgeon in all aspects of surgery. His reputation was enhanced by his becoming chairman of the editorial board of the *Journal of Bone and Joint Surgery* from 1954 to 1961 and vice-president of the British Orthopaedic Association.

In 1951 Mercer became president of the Royal College of Surgeons of Edinburgh; hitherto the college had acted merely as a surgical examining body, but under Mercer it adopted a more active role. Mercer started short courses in surgery to help postgraduates, especially those from overseas, to prepare for their fellowship and other examinations. For the fellows he founded the *Journal of the Royal College of Surgeons of Edinburgh* in 1955 and organized regular clinical meetings, to enable them to keep abreast with the latest surgical developments and with college news. He then laid plans to redevelop the college buildings, and the work began in 1960. Mercer was knighted in 1956 and made an honorary fellow of the Royal College of Surgeons of England. In the next year he retired as professor of orthopaedic surgery and as president of the college. From 1959 to 1971 he was honorary librarian of the Royal College of Surgeons of Edinburgh. In 1960 he was appointed a deputy lord lieutenant of the county of the city of Edinburgh.

A contemporary noted that Mercer

moved and spoke with a briskness characteristic of his operating. He never wasted time but always had an ear for any approach worthy of consideration. He was impatient of irrelevance and vague discussion and preferred the direct approach to any problem surgical or personal. To his intimate circle he showed a sense of humour and a warm understanding of problems which superficially might have seemed contrary to his outward, almost mechanical, efficiency. (*Lancet*, 501)

Mercer, whose hobbies had included tennis and golf, died in Edinburgh on 23 February 1971 of heart disease. He was survived by his wife and son. ALISON M. STEVENSON

Sources *The Scotsman* (24 Feb 1971) · *Journal of the Royal College of Surgeons of Edinburgh*, 16 (1971), 239–41 · J. P. Ross and W. R. Le Fanu, *Lives of the fellows of the Royal College of Surgeons of England, 1965–1973* (1981) · *WW* (1965) · *Journal of Bone and Joint Surgery*, 52B (1970), 1–7 · b. cert. · m. cert. · *BMJ* (6 March 1971), 559–60; (20 March 1971), 676 · *The Lancet* (6 March 1971), 500–01 · *Evening News* (23 Feb 1971)
Archives Royal College of Surgeons of Edinburgh, lecture notes and articles
Likenesses photograph, repro. in *BMJ* (6 March 1971), 559
Wealth at death £50,925.08: confirmation, 30 June 1971, *CCI*

Mercer, William (*b. c.*1605, *d.* in or after 1675), poet and army officer, was a son of John Mercer (*d.* 1637/8), who was minister of Methlick in Aberdeenshire at the time of William's birth, and later minister of Slains. For much of William's life the only evidence is that found in his own publications. Thus he wrote, in his characteristic doggerel verse, that after running away from school at the age of fifteen to become a soldier,

I serv'd an Emperor, and in much ado
I serv'd in Denmark, and Gustavus too.
(Laing, 342)

By the time he was twenty-four he had served six monarchs, but then, disillusioned by lack of pay, he returned home and got an appointment in 1630 as a chorister of the Chapel Royal at Stirling from Charles I, with the parsonage and vicarage of Glenlyon to provide an income. This musical side to his interests makes it likely that he was the 'William Merser, musician' who was admitted a burgess of Edinburgh in 1631 (Wood, 3.95). His first poetic work, *A Description of the Creation* (1632), a miscellany, included fulsome praise for Edinburgh's magistrates.

Some time thereafter Mercer moved to Ulster, where his brother was a Presbyterian minister. After the Irish rising of October 1641 he fought against the rebels, who had killed his brother, but by October 1642 he was serving as a captain in the English parliamentary army of the earl of Essex, and he witnessed the battle of Edgehill. However, obtaining pay again proved a problem. He was petitioning parliament for arrears by March 1643, and his campaign culminated in the verse *Angliae speculum, or, England's Looking-Glasse* (1646), addressing Essex as his patron and pleading for payment of £900 sterling from parliament. Essex's death soon afterwards prompted an elegy. Earlier in the year Mercer had also produced an elegy for his own father-in-law, Sir Henry Mervyn. In later verses he was to record that he had 'maried four fyne wives'—two maids between two widows—'A Murray, Mervyn, Conway and a Duff', the surnames suggesting that he acquired widows in Scotland, maids in England (Laing, 350).

Mercer next surfaces in Scotland. In 1648 he supported the engagers who were unsuccessful in their attempt to free Charles I from imprisonment in England, and it was probably in the engager army that he became a lieutenant-colonel, for that was his rank in February 1650 when he petitioned the commission of the general assembly of the Church of Scotland. Declaring his repentance for having supported the engagement, he indicated that he was ready to give public satisfaction for his sin. He was referred to the presbytery of Perth, indicating that he was resident in that area. But when in May the commission, considering his 'necessitous condition', recommended him for 'charitable supplie', it did so to the presbytery of Edinburgh (Mitchell and Christie, 363, 416). Mercer then disappears from view again until 1669, when he was in Ireland, publishing *A Welcom in a Poem* on the entry to Dublin of Lord Robartes of Truro, the new lord lieutenant.

When his eldest son was offered in marriage to the daughter and heir of Sir James Mercer of Aldie, Mercer returned to Scotland in 1672 to negotiate, but the proposed bride's family backed out of the arrangement. He sued them for damages, seeking to help his case by producing verses praising the court of session judges and begging for their favour, calling himself 'a Servant to Mars, and a Lover of the Muse' (NL Scot., Adv. MS 99.3.45). He lost his case, but in 1675 he was awarded the expenses he had incurred in coming from Ireland. *The Moderate Cavalier, or, The Soldier's Description of Ireland* (1675) has been wrongly attributed to him (the William Mercer who wrote that work having served in the English civil war as a royalist) but he was responsible for *News from Parnassus, in the Abstracts and Contents of Three Crown'd Chronicles*, which served to announce the forthcoming publication of a vast verse chronicle of events since 1638, a 'big book' on which he had been working for twenty years (Laing, 356). That this never appeared need be little lamented, for 'Mercer's writings are mainly valuable for their autobiographical details. The majority of his verses are mere doggerel, and display an inordinate self-conceit' (*DNB*). But his conceit did at least ensure that enough information survived to reconstruct the outline of his life.

DAVID STEVENSON

Sources D. Laing, 'Some account of Lieut.-Colonel William Mercer', *Proceedings of the Society of Antiquaries of Scotland*, 3 (1857–60), 341–57 · *DNB* · M. Wood, ed., *Extracts from the records of the burgh of Edinburgh, 1626–1641*, [8] (1936) · A. F. Mitchell and J. Christie, eds., *The records of the commissions of the general assemblies of the Church of Scotland*, 3, Scottish History Society, 58 (1909), 363, 416

Merceron, Joseph (*c.*1764–1839), parochial politician, was reputedly born, and certainly grew up, in Brick Lane, Bethnal Green, London. His parents have not been identified, but members of his family were office-holders in the parish. Bethnal Green was run by an 'open' (elected) vestry, which offered opportunities for political manipulation. Merceron's political career began in 1787, and within a few years he had become a vestryman, a tax commissioner, and a justice of the peace. Supporters could be rewarded with favourable tax assessments or the renewal

of public-house licences. Bethnal Green fell under Merceron's domination and became notorious for corruption. Merceron, according to Sidney and Beatrice Webb, 'amassed a considerable fortune, which he invested in public houses and cottage property within the parish, thus adding the power of the landlord to that of the parish officer and licensing justice'.

Merceron's position was briefly threatened in 1804, when the vestry instigated an audit of the parish accounts. Merceron promptly resigned as treasurer, but no one could be found to take his place, and he was re-elected in 1805. A more serious challenge began in 1809, led by a new rector, Joshua King. A prosecution for altering the parish assessments failed, and the vestry not only passed a vote of confidence in Merceron but paid his expenses out of parish funds. The turning point came when King was supported by the long-serving vestry clerk, who gave evidence against Merceron before a House of Commons committee in 1816, and then instigated a prosecution for the appropriation of £925 of parish funds and partiality in the renewal of liquor licences. At the Easter vestry in 1818 Merceron was voted out, and shortly afterwards he was convicted of the charges against him and imprisoned for eighteen months.

However, the succeeding regime of the rector and the new vestrymen was less than efficient, and Merceron was able to make a comeback through the manoeuvres of his son-in-law and those of his former supporters who were still in office. Merceron was not reappointed as a justice of the peace, but in other respects he was as much in control (either directly or through his brother-in-law, who became vestry clerk) as he had been before 1809. The abolition of the open vestry in 1823 did not, apparently, affect his position; he survived a parliamentary inquiry in 1830 without obvious difficulty. He died in Bethnal Green on 14 July 1839; he was reputed to be worth about £300,000, 'though he always appeared to be in poor circumstances'. His funeral was as well orchestrated as his political meetings had been.

IAN DOOLITTLE, *rev.*

Sources S. Webb and B. Webb, *English local government*, 1: *The parish and the county* (1906), 79–90
Wealth at death £300,000: *DNB*

Mercia. For this title name *see* Leofric, earl of Mercia (*d.* 1057); Ælfgar, earl of Mercia (*d.* 1062?); Eadwine, earl of Mercia (*d.* 1071) [*see under* Ælfgar, earl of Mercia (*d.* 1062?)].

Mercier, Honoré (1840–1894), lawyer and politician in Canada, was born on 15 October 1840 in the parish of St Athanase, Iberville county, Lower Canada, the fourth child of Jean-Baptiste Mercier, a farmer, and his wife, Catherine Kemeneur (or Timineur). His family had farmed in Canada since 1647. He grew up in a radical and nationalist household, but his studies (1854–62) at Montreal's Jesuit college, the Collège Ste Marie, immersed him in a conservative atmosphere of ultramontane Catholicism.

Having left college because of nervous tension before the end of his final year, Mercier entered a law office at St

Hyacinthe, some 30 miles east of Montreal, and then accepted the editorship of the local Conservative Party newspaper, the *Courrier de St-Hyacinthe*. He resigned in July 1864 in protest against the project of British North American confederation which the Conservatives had undertaken, and which he feared would destroy the French-Canadian nationality.

Mercier returned to legal studies at the Collège Ste Marie and was admitted to the bar in April 1865. He set up practice at St Hyacinthe, and rapidly became known as a talented criminal lawyer. On 29 May 1866 he married Léopoldine Boivin, the daughter of a local merchant. A child, Élisa, was born in 1867, but Léopoldine died two years later. On 9 May 1871 Mercier married Virginie Saint-Denis (*b.* 1852), with whom he had five children.

Mercier remained enamoured of politics. He broke definitively from the Conservatives in 1866, but the alternative was the Liberal Party, which was frowned on by the Catholic church. In 1871 he and others tried to re-form the Liberals as a *parti national*. They proclaimed themselves loyally Catholic and for the nation above all else. Under their banner Mercier was elected to the House of Commons in 1872. A passionate speech appealing to French Quebec MPs on behalf of Catholic schools displeased Liberal Party leaders, and in the 1874 elections they refused Mercier a nomination. But in May 1879, after winning a provincial by-election, he became solicitor-general of Quebec under the Liberal premier Henri-Gustave Joly. Two months later Joly's government fell.

The Liberals were still embarrassed by their radical elements, who provoked the church's antipathy. In 1880–81, therefore, Mercier secretly attempted, with the Conservative leader, J.-A. Chapleau, to form a union of moderate men from both parties. They failed, and in 1883 Mercier became leader of the still intact Quebec Liberals.

In 1885 a rebellion broke out in the Canadian northwest, led by the métis Louis Riel. Quebec volunteers helped put it down, but after Riel's arrest the French-language press argued that extenuating circumstances ought to dictate clemency towards him. When Riel was hanged for treason in November 1885, Quebeckers believed him the victim of racial and religious prejudice, killed for his nationality and religion. On 22 November Mercier told an enormous Montreal protest rally that Riel's death had been 'a blow struck at the heart of our race', which had left 'two million Frenchmen in tears' (Rumilly, 1.281–2). French Canadians must therefore unite in defence of their nationality and strengthen themselves in their province of Quebec. This appealed to ultramontane nationalists in the Conservative Party, and after the 1886 elections several of them threw their weight behind Mercier, enabling him to form a 'National' government of Quebec in January 1887.

To keep their support, Mercier organized a conference of premiers, demanding more autonomy and financial resources for the provinces; he named a popular priest deputy minister of colonization; he encouraged the building of colonization railways; he attended a eucharistic congress in Baltimore as political representative of Canadian Catholicism; and he successfully resolved an ancient dispute concerning properties held by the Jesuit order before its dissolution in 1773, taken over by the crown in 1800, and now claimed by various religious and educational institutions. His Jesuits' Estates Act of 1888 settled the matter in a way that was fair to protestants yet favourable to the Jesuits and officially approved by the pope.

This act earned Mercier the Vatican's grand cross of the order of St Gregory, but it provoked hostile reaction in English Canada, where many thought it authorized foreign (papal) interference in Canadian affairs. Mercier also provoked anger by his dramatic affirmations of Quebec's distinctiveness and autonomy. On a tour of Europe in 1891 he was received almost as the head of an independent state, becoming a commander of the Légion d'honneur in France, commander of the order of Leopold in Belgium, and count palatine in the Vatican. All this made English Canadians fear for confederation's survival. Many argued that it could endure only if its citizens spoke a common language and shared a common identity. Soon official use of French and public funding of Catholic schools were abandoned by the prairie provinces, and French was banned from Ontario and western public schools. The result was decades of bitter resentment.

In 1890 voters returned Mercier to office with a larger majority than before. But his government had run up a considerable debt, and his hope of raising money in Europe was disappointed. In these circumstances, his personal extravagance came under attack. In 1891 his ministry was accused of paying a $175,000 subsidy to a railway contractor in return for a $100,000 contribution to the National Party. Although Mercier himself was not implicated, the lieutenant-governor dismissed him. In the elections that followed, on 8 March 1892, he was overwhelmingly defeated.

Humiliated and weakened by diabetes, Mercier resigned the Liberal leadership and withdrew to the country. A charge of misappropriating government funds followed him, and though his trial that October ended in acquittal, it left him in complete financial ruin. He died of diabetes at the Notre Dame Hospital, Montreal, on 30 October 1894; a crowd of 70,000 followed his funeral. He was buried in Montreal's Côte-des-Neiges cemetery on 2 November.

Mercier's scandals were buried with him; his nationalist glories lived on. Although Quebeckers later rejected the Catholicism which defined his conception of French Canada, most still share his view of Quebec as the homeland of a French-speaking people needing autonomy and national recognition.

A. I. SILVER

Sources P. Dufour and J. Hamelin, 'Mercier, Honoré', *DCB*, vol. 12 • R. Rumilly, *Honoré Mercier et son temps*, 2 vols. (1975) • G. Gallichan, *Honoré Mercier: la politique et la culture* (1994) • H. B. Neatby, *Laurier and a liberal Quebec* (1973), chap. 3 • J. R. Miller, *Equal rights: the Jesuits' Estates Act controversy* (1979) • P. Charbonneau, *Le projet québécois d'Honoré Mercier* (1980) • P. Roy, ed., *Devant la statue de Mercier* (1912) • parish records of St-Athanase and St-Hyacinthe,

Archives Nationales de Québec, Montreal · *The Globe* [Toronto] (31 Oct–3 Nov 1894) · *The Gazette* [Montreal] (2 Nov 1894) · *The Gazette* [Montreal] (3 Nov 1894) · *La Patrie* (2 Nov 1894) · *La Presse* (2 Nov 1894)
Archives Archives Nationales de Québec, Montreal · NA Canada
Likenesses P. Chevré, statue, 1912, Parliament Building lawn, Quebec · W. Notman, photographs, McCord Museum, Montreal
Wealth at death bankrupt: Dufour and Hamelin, 'Mercier, Honoré'; Rumilly, *Honoré Mercier*

Mercier, Philip [*formerly* Philippe] (**1691–1760**), painter and etcher, was born in Berlin, the son of Philippe Mercier, a Huguenot tapestry weaver at the royal factory in that city. 'Reicrem' (his surname in reverse) was sometimes used as a signature on his paintings. He studied in Berlin at the Akademie der Künste and under Antoine Pesne, from 1711 court painter to Frederick I of Prussia, whose brother-in-law, George, elector of Hanover, became king of England (as George I) in 1714. It was probably in 1716 that, 'recommended from the Court at Hanover' (Vertue, *Note books*, 3.37), Mercier went to London, bringing a portrait of Frederick, the little grandson of George I (probably of the type represented at the Welsh Girls' School, Ashford, Middlesex). On 17 July 1719 he married Margaret Plante at St Martin-in-the-Fields and between 1720 and 1727 lived in Leicester Fields. Between 1726 and 1735 he attended the annual dinners of the St Luke's Club, acting as steward in 1728.

In the early 1720s Mercier's work was dominated by the influence of Watteau, with whose work he was clearly intimately acquainted. He etched a number of Watteau's works and painted variations on the theme of the *fête-champêtre* with either *commedia dell'arte* figures or English family groups of loyal Hanoverian courtiers. Such groups, of which there are fine examples at Belton House, Lincolnshire, and in the Tate collection, launched the conversation piece in British painting. Mercier was also active at this time as a picture dealer, selling a number of paintings 'collected abroad' (Cock's, 21 April 1724).

In December 1728 Frederick, having attained his majority, went to London and the following January was made prince of Wales. Mercier painted a series of whole-length portraits of the prince and his three sisters, the princesses Anne, Amelia, and Caroline (Shire Hall, Hertford), all four being engraved by John Simon, who described them as painted in 1728. They presumably brought about Mercier's appointments in 1729 as the prince's principal painter (on 17 February) and page of the bedchamber (on 6 March). On 26 January 1730 he was also made library keeper. In addition he shared with the prince an interest in the theatre; in 1729 they collaborated in a production of Thomas Doggett's *Hob* at Richmond, and in 1733 Mercier was a shareholder in Rich's Theatre at Covent Garden, London. His informal portrait of Handel (*c*.1730, priv. coll.) further suggests his interest in the performing arts. He painted more portraits of the prince in 1730 (priv. coll.) and about 1736 (National Portrait Gallery, London), and in 1733 he contrived an informal musical group of the prince with his three sisters (versions in the Royal Collection;

Philip Mercier (1691–1760), by John Faber junior, 1735 (after self-portrait)

National Portrait Gallery, London; and Cliveden, Buckinghamshire). Frederick's patronage, however, proved capricious. By 1736 he had sat to at least five other artists in London and there were rumours of a quarrel between Mercier and his royal patron. In October 1736 Mercier left his service, though he continued to receive payment as librarian until 1738.

On 25 June 1735 Mercier, described as a widower of St Giles-in-the-Fields, married Dorothy Clapham of St James's, Westminster. In 1736 he withdrew to an estate in the country, probably in Northamptonshire. Between October 1737 and May 1739 he was living in the Great Piazza, Covent Garden, but by October 1739 he had settled in York, where he stayed some thirteen years. While he found plentiful employment as a portrait painter, he also produced an increasing number of fancy pieces, often reminiscent of Chardin, for engraving in London. These addressed a popular market and included literary illustrations, domestic scenes, groups of children, and sets of, for example, the Seasons, the Times of Day, and the Senses.

Mercier visited Ireland in 1747 and Edinburgh in 1750, but in 1751 he let his house in York and returned to London. In 1752 he went to Portugal, where he was joined by his family. It is not known how long he stayed, but one of his last portraits, of the Burton family of London (Musée du Louvre, Paris), may be dated to about 1755. From this last decade there are some fancy pictures, painted with increasing economy, two of which, a *Girl Sewing* and a *Girl Washing* (both untraced), he exhibited with the Society of Artists in 1760.

Philip Mercier died in London on 18 July 1760, and was survived by his second wife. Although his best portraits have a fine French elegance, his work was inconsistent, and in his later years it apparently failed to sell. His influence on British painting was, however, considerable. His second wife, Dorothy, painted on a small scale in her husband's manner. She became a printseller in Little Windmill Street, Soho, London, in 1762 and retired from business in June 1768. Their daughter Charlotte Mercier (1738–1762) also practised in pastel, but she died in reduced circumstances in the workhouse of St James's, Westminster, London, in February 1762.　　　　　JOHN INGAMELLS

Sources J. Ingamells and R. Raines, *Philip Mercier* (1969) [exhibition catalogue, York City Art Gallery and Kenwood House, London] · J. Ingamells and R. Raines, 'A catalogue of the paintings, drawings and etchings of Philip Mercier', *Walpole Society*, 46 (1976–8), 1–70 · parish register, London, St Martin-in-the-Fields [marriage], 17/7/1719 · parish register, London, Whitechapel, St Mary [marriage], 25/6/1735 · *GM*, 1st ser., 30 (1760), 347 · Vertue, *Note books*, 3.37

Likenesses P. Mercier, etching, c.1723–1725 (after his portrait), BM · J. Faber junior, mezzotint, 1735 (after P. Mercier), BM, NPG [*see illus.*]

Mercier, Winifred Louise (1878–1934), educationist and college head, was born on 20 May 1878 at Ilford, Essex, second daughter of Lewis Mercier (*d.* 1928), a stockbroker of Huguenot ancestry, and his wife, Agnes Stedman (*d.* 1934). Her father's failure on the stock exchange meant that he was never again able to support his family, and her mother took them to live at the vicarage of her own father, Revd Paul Metheun Stedman, at Thurston, Suffolk. Winifred was educated at home and then at a private school, Wynaud House in Bowes Park, kept by Miss Pater, a cousin of Walter Pater. After her grandfather's death this school, where she was a student teacher, became for a time the only home she had. In 1897 she went to Maria Grey College at Brondesbury and in 1899 obtained the Cambridge teachers' certificate. Already her scholarly interest and ability as a teacher were apparent.

Winifred Mercier's first post (1899) was at St George's School, Edinburgh, and in 1904 the unexpected generosity of a relative enabled her to go to Somerville College, Oxford, where she gained the Margaret Evans historical prize (1904) and a first class in modern history (1907). Her academic brilliance had found its right expression. She returned to teaching at the Manchester High School for Girls (1907–9), under Sara Burstall, where she displayed both her 'intense pastoral instinct' (Grier, 63) and a progressive approach to history teaching. She used the assignment system, enabling girls to achieve some 'specialisation, slight or childish though it be' which would 'create mountain peaks in the flat sea of knowledge' (ibid., 68). Her membership of the new Historical Association brought her into contact with Tout and other historians at the university. She took an interest at this period in the cause of women's suffrage, but did not divert her energy from her profession: 'women Educationalists' were, she believed, 'much more open-minded, more liberal, and more enterprising than men' (ibid., 72).

Miss Mercier's reputation in education was growing, and in 1909 she was offered the post of director of studies and lecturer in history at Girton College. As a supervisor she combined stringency with accessibility, stimulating intellectual enthusiasm among her pupils. She launched Eileen Power on her career as a historian, and formed her 'subsequent notions about what a don ought to be like' (Dyhouse, 147). Yet Miss Mercier was not the complete academic: she was not interested in research—the life of pure scholarship did not appeal to her, she did not like writing, and she found a Cambridge women's college, at a time when women were not university teachers, too sequestered. She was primarily a teacher. Moreover she had in 1910 settled her parents in a home at King's Somborne, Hampshire, and she needed a better income.

In 1913 Miss Mercier accepted the post of vice-principal of the Leeds Municipal Training College and began the work to which she devoted the rest of her life, preparing elementary school teachers. Eileen Power recalled that 'she believed passionately that education was the root of all social progress' (Power, 21), and regarded this as the most important work she could do. Her entry into this work was not easy. She came to a mixed college, the pride of the civic authority, with many more women students than men, with an established and popular male principal (Walter Parsons). The appointment of a woman vice-principal had been insisted upon by the Board of Education, but her duties were ill-defined. For two terms Miss Mercier was able to pursue modestly reforming policies, to organize separate training for infant teachers, and to begin to improve Scripture teaching. But although on appointment she had insisted on an independent sphere of operation, and particularly did not want her authority to be limited to the social and domestic lives of the women students, arrangements for this were not made. She had no direct access to the governing body or to James Graham, the secretary for education in the local authority, who wished to turn the college into a branch of local government. All the problems were aggravated by the war, when the imbalance between men and women students was made worse.

Miss Mercier realized that educational progress was impossible, and resigned in May 1916. When Graham gave an abrasive talk to the resident women staff in the following month, nine of them also resigned. Miss Mercier and her colleagues received much support from fellow educationists, such as Michael Sadler, and from the British Federation of University Women, of whose local branch she was president (Dyhouse, 174). A lively press campaign, a petition, and a question in the House of Commons forced the Board of Education to set up a commission of inquiry, held in private in August 1916. The commissioners were impressed by Miss Mercier's evidence, and their report (November 1916) decided in her favour, stating she had performed her duties with distinction and was not responsible for the difficulties which had led to her resignation (Grier, 144). The first 'Battle of Leeds' had been won, and although she lost the second, to get the report published, this victory for the autonomy of the training colleges was of national importance.

The Leeds case had made Miss Mercier, according to John Dover Wilson, one of the 'leaders of English education' (Grier, xxvi). From 1916 to 1918 there was an interlude in her career. She was lecturer in education and tutor to secondary training students at the University of Manchester and also worked in the Leeds education department, though even the support of Sadler did not secure a permanent appointment. In 1915 she had been elected as fellow of the Royal Historical Society and was later, from 1929 to 1931, on its council. In 1917 she was made a member of the archbishops' first commission of enquiry into the teaching office of the church.

In 1918 Miss Mercier was approached to take the principalship of Whitelands College, the oldest and most prestigious of Anglican training colleges. She hesitated at first, because although Whitelands was already admitting nonconformist students she did not altogether approve of denominational colleges. However, after trying other services, she had found in the Church of England 'her true spiritual home' and in 1918 she began her work at Whitelands, then still in the King's Road, Chelsea. The Education Act of 1918 was already making an impact, and from the beginning of her principalship Miss Mercier kept Whitelands in the van of response to change. With the help of the London School of Economics she set up a course for training teachers for the new continuation schools and in 1920 twelve of its students were examined, though this initiative was soon frustrated by cuts in government expenditure.

Under Miss Mercier, Whitelands grew rapidly in numbers—from 190 students to 241. The Chelsea premises were unsatisfactory and noisy and the leases were due to run out. She persuaded the Church of England to acquire a large and leafy site in Putney, and to employ Giles Gilbert Scott to design a building worthy of her students. She supervised every detail of its planning and construction. She herself chose in Holland the fireplace tiles for the new study bedrooms. The building was occupied in October 1930 and opened by Queen Mary in June 1931—a royal acknowledgement of the rising status of teacher training. In 1933 Miss Mercier was appointed OBE.

In 1919 Winifred Mercier became president of the Training Colleges' Association. She gave evidence in 1923 before the Board of Education departmental committee on the training of teachers for public elementary schools. She did not accept that all teachers should be graduates, defending variety and more appropriate training for teachers of young children. It was said that she saved the lives of the training colleges that ran two-year courses. But she campaigned for closer connection between the universities and the training colleges, and in 1921 she became the colleges' representative on the Board of Education Conference on the Training Colleges and Universities. The University of London took over from the board, on a five-year trial, the examining for the teachers' certificate, and Miss Mercier, 'as an acknowledged scholar, was able to influence the syllabuses and examinations so that the professional education of teachers remained sound'

(Cole, 36). This arrangement was then adopted nationwide. In January 1928 Miss Mercier presided over the Conference of the Training Colleges' Association and the Association of Directors and Secretaries for Education, and her address on the curriculum of the colleges was a notable success.

Miss Mercier believed in an organic relationship between religion and education. She was widely read in theology and biblical studies, and was a supporter of the Life and Liberty Movement. She was also a hard-working member of the committee which prepared the influential *Cambridgeshire Syllabus of Religious Teaching for Schools* (1924), and it incorporated many of her ideas about the school as a religious community and the experiential approach to the Bible. She was also a member of the commission on religious education set up by the archbishops of Canterbury and York in 1926, and was responsible for the chapter entitled 'The church and the teaching profession' in its final report (1929). In 1931 the Association of Teachers of Religious Knowledge was launched, with Sir William Hadow as its president and Miss Mercier chair of the standing committee, which guided its policy. She was also chair of its publication committee and wrote the section on the Psalms in *The Teachers' Commentary* (1932). In all this she was a pioneer at a period when parents were more and more leaving the religious education of their children to the teacher.

Miss Mercier was never strong and all these labours taxed her to the limit. In 1931 cancer was diagnosed, and in spite of surgery and constant treatment she died at the house she had bought for her mother, 30 Rose Hill Park, West Sutton, Surrey, on 2 September 1934. Her ashes were buried in King's Somborne churchyard in her parents' grave.

MARGARET BRYANT

Sources L. Grier, *The life of Winifred Mercier* (1937) [incl. introduction by J. D. Wilson] • M. Cole, *Whitelands College, the history* (1982) • *WWW* • K. T. Butler and H. I. McMorran, eds., *Girton College register, 1869–1946* (1948) • E. Power, appreciation, *Girton Review*, Michaelmas term (1934) • H. M. Wodehouse, review of L. Grier, *The life of Winifred Mercier*, *Girton Review*, Easter term (1938) • *The Times* (4 Sept 1934) • *The Times* (5 Sept 1934) • J. D. Wilson, appreciation, *The Times* (7 Sept 1934) • *Manchester Guardian* (4 May 1936) • University of Surrey, Roehampton, London, Whitelands College • C. Dyhouse, *No distinction of sex? Women in British universities, 1870–1939* (1995) • probate • *CGPLA Eng. & Wales* (1934)

Archives University of Surrey, Roehampton, London, Whitelands College MSS

Likenesses photograph, 1906, repro. in Grier, *Life of Winifred Mercier*, facing p. 45 • Elliott & Fry, photograph, 1929, University of Surrey, Roehampton, London, Whitelands College, archives, H8733A • O. Birley, oils, 1938 (posthumous), University of Surrey, Roehampton, London, Whitelands College • photographs, University of Surrey, Roehampton, London, Whitelands College, archives

Wealth at death £3201 16s. 10d.: probate, 5 Dec 1934, *CGPLA Eng. & Wales*

Mercury, Freddie [*formerly* Faroukh Bulsara] (**1946–1991**), singer and song-writer, was born at the Government Hospital in Zanzibar on 5 September 1946, the eldest son of Bomi Bulsara, civil servant, and his wife, Jer. His parents were both from Bombay and were Zoroastrians. At five he

Freddie Mercury (1946–1991), by Peter Still, 1985 [performing at the Live Aid concert]

was enrolled at the local missionary school, and his sister, Kashmira, was born in 1952. Two years later the family moved back to Bombay, and he was enrolled at St Peter's, a prestigious English boarding-school some 50 miles from the city. Here he took piano lessons, joined the school choir, and formed his first band, the Hectics. After O levels, he returned briefly to Zanzibar before his family moved to England, settling at Feltham, Middlesex. Here he enrolled at Isleworth Polytechnic School, supporting himself in the holidays with a variety of jobs. Having gained an A level in art, he took a course in graphic design at Ealing College of Art (1966–9). There he met an astrophysics student and guitarist, Brian May, and a dentistry student and drummer, Roger Taylor, both of whom were playing in a group called Smile. Mercury (he changed his name to Freddie Mercury by deed poll in 1970) briefly joined a Liverpudlian group, Ibex, and then Sour Milk Sea, before forming Queen in 1970 with May and Taylor. They were joined in 1971 by bass player John Deacon, and the line-up of the band remained unchanged for the rest of its history. Mercury also met Mary Austin, manager of the London boutique Biba, and lived with her for seven years. She was to be a lifelong friend.

Signed to EMI as a glam rock band, Queen scored its first success with 'Seven Seas of Rhye' (1973), which peaked at number ten in the British charts. The albums *Queen* (1973) and *Queen II* (1974) followed with limited commercial success, due perhaps to the somewhat peculiar mix of styles

and references. Both were essentially hard rock, but are notable for early examples of Mercury's wit and innuendo. Titles such as 'My Fairy King' and 'The Fairy Feller's Masterstroke' (both composed by Mercury), combined with his use of falsetto, implied an underlying sexual ambiguity; this ambiguity, a characteristic of many glam rock musicians, stood in sharp contrast to the vigorous heterosexuality of traditional rock and popular music. The band also had its first American tour, supporting Mott the Hoople, but the audience initially regarded them as a joke, responding to the musicians' glam rock Zandra Rhodes silks, nail varnish, and make-up.

The band's first major success came in 1974 with the release of the *Sheer Heart Attack* album, which contained the number two British chart single, 'Killer Queen'. Written by Mercury and notable for its studio mix and feel for narrative, it gave Queen its first American top twenty hit and became the gay anthem for the winter of 1974, as well as gaining an Ivor Novello award for Mercury. The album cover was particularly striking, with a photograph of the members of the band collapsed in a heap, Mercury's trousers undone and black nail varnish on his left hand, against a black background with gaudy red lettering, which reinforced the ambiguities already surrounding Mercury's image as a macho rock hero, blending showmanship with high camp. Queen, however, was never perceived as a gay band, and Mercury's campery was regarded by its growing number of fans as evidence of a flair for theatricality, treading the line between the outrageous and bad taste. Mercury's adoption of the union flag, which was often emblazoned on his jackets or draped around his shoulders, and his wearing of a crown and ermine-trimmed robes, led to mass singing of 'God Save the Queen' even before the band recorded a version of it in 1975.

Queen's final breakthrough was made in 1975 with the release of *A Night at the Opera*, which took its title from the classic Marx Brothers film. The pre-release publicity for the album emphasized its production costs (£35,000), the three months it took to record, and the use of six different recording studios for its completion. Its most important track was 'Bohemian Rhapsody', which heralded what was to become Mercury's performance hallmark, an operatic vocal style. It lasted just short of six minutes (twice the length of an average single), had three tempo changes, and featured a pseudo-operatic passage of contrived pathos, so the record company was initially reluctant to issue it as a single; it was taken up by the disc jockey Kenny Everett, and reached number one in the British and number nine in the American charts. It won Queen its first platinum disc, gained a second Ivor Novello award for Mercury, and, at the 1977 Brit awards, was named joint best single of the preceding twenty-five years, with Procul Harum's 'A Whiter Shade of Pale'. 'Bohemian Rhapsody' was accompanied by one of the first promotional videos, with Mercury camping it up in a parody of Paderewski, hunched over a grand piano which he played with excessive gestures.

As Queen's popularity broadened, they became prime

movers in 'stadium rock', spectacularly lit and costumed performances for huge audiences in increasingly large venues, such as football stadiums, giving full scope to Mercury's commanding stage presence and idiosyncratic use of his detachable microphone stand. He was able to project both music and image to vast audiences, many of whom could see the stage only by virtue of live-relay video screens, 'prancing down multi-layered catwalks in a sequinned, skin-tight jump suit and ballet slippers, preening his way through a myriad of costume changes and singing in his majestic, slightly frayed tenor voice' (*The Times*). The appeal of the band was international: a concert in February 1981 at São Paulo, Brazil, was attended by a record audience for a rock concert, of 231,000 people.

In addition to his work with Queen, Mercury had a solo career which began in 1973 when he released a version of the Beach Boys' song 'I Can Hear Music' under the name Larry Lurex. His first solo hit was in 1984 with 'Love Kills' from the Giorgio Moroder soundtrack to the film *Metropolis*. His next single, 'I was Born to Love You', reached the British top twenty in 1985, and in 1987 a kitsch revival of the Platters' 'Great Pretender' reached the British top five. Later that year he teamed up with the opera singer Monserrat Caballé, whom he had long admired, for the top ten success 'Barcelona'. An album of the same title appeared in 1988, and Mercury and Caballé performed live at the Avinguda de Maria Cristina Stadium in Barcelona on 8 October 1988; it was to be Mercury's last performance on stage.

Meanwhile, Queen's hits continued unabated into the 1980s, including 'We Will Rock You', 'Radio Ga-Ga', and 'I Want to Break Free', which was reputed to have been adopted by the then incarcerated Nelson Mandela as the anthem of the African National Congress. *The Game* (1980) was Queen's first album to reach number one in the American charts, and one of its tracks, 'Another One Bites the Dust', by John Deacon, stayed at the top of the American singles charts for five weeks and sold 3 million copies. Like several other Queen songs, notably 'We are the Champions', it became a frequently sung anthem at sporting events. In November 1980 the single from Queen's *Flash Gordon* soundtrack album also broke new ground in incorporating snatches of dialogue from the film of the same name. A month later, when the band performed at the National Exhibition Centre in Birmingham, Mercury was carried onto the stage on the shoulders of his minder, who was dressed as Darth Vader from *Star Wars*. By 1982 the band members were recorded as Britain's highest-paid executives. They were famous for their extravagant end-of-tour and album launch parties, where guests were flown in from around the world. In 1984 Queen was placed on the United Nations' blacklist, for having played for eight nights at Sun City, South Africa, during the anti-apartheid cultural boycott. Its members were ostracized and heavily fined by the Musicians' Union, and were not forgiven until their appearance at the Live Aid concert organized by Bob Geldof in 1985 for famine relief in Ethiopia. Their twenty-minute set was one of the highlights of the show, and successfully re-presented the band to a younger audience. They then contributed to the soundtrack for Russell Mulcahy's fantasy film *Highlander*, and the songs were released on *A Kind of Magic*, which topped the British charts in the summer of 1986 and reached the top ten in forty other countries.

In 1990 Queen was presented with a British Phonographic Industry award for its contribution to British music, and in 1991 released *Innuendo*, a celebration of the band's twentieth anniversary. Queen's last single, 'The Show Must Go On', and the accompanying video which showed excerpts from the previous twenty years, had a decidedly nostalgic feeling. Mercury had been ill for some time, and seldom left Garden Lodge in Logan Mews, the Kensington home which he shared with Jim Hutton and numerous cats during his last year. The day before he died, he issued a statement 'for my friends and fans around the world', confirming that he had AIDS and that he had 'felt it correct to keep this information private to date in order to protect the privacy of those around me' (*The Independent*, 26 Nov 1991). He succumbed to bronchial pneumonia at his home on 24 November 1991. Hundreds of fans queued up outside Garden Lodge to pay their respects. His funeral took place three days later at the Kensal Green crematorium, attended only by close friends and family, and was conducted according to the Zoroastrian faith of his family. 'Bohemian Rhapsody' was re-released as a double A-side with 'These are the Days of our Lives' on 9 December and returned to the top of the charts; the royalties were donated to the HIV and AIDS charity the Terence Higgins Trust. Other tributes followed, including a concert at Wembley stadium on 20 April 1992, at which many major stars, including David Bowie, Elton John, and Liza Minnelli, performed. In 1995 Mercury's last seven songs were released from the archives, and the remaining members of Queen added their music and backing vocals. *Made in Heaven* went to the top of the charts. The sleeve for the album showed Brian May, John Deacon, and Roger Taylor in silhouette with their backs to the camera in the grounds of Mercury's Swiss home, Duck House, gazing across Lake Geneva past a statue of Mercury.

SHEILA WHITELEY

Sources D. Bret, *The Freddie Mercury story: living on the edge* (1996) · *The Independent* (26 Nov 1991) · *The Guardian* (26 Nov 1991) · *Melody Maker* (30 Nov 1991) · C. Larkin, ed., *The Guinness encyclopedia of popular music*, concise edn (1993), 1672 · *The Times* (26 Nov 1991) · S. Rider, *Queen: these are the days of our lives* (1992) · J. Hutton, *Mercury and me* (1994) · queen-fip.com [official Queen website], 20 May 1999
Archives FILM BFI NFTVA, 'Freddie Mercury: the untold story', BBC1, 8 Dec 2000 · BFI NFTVA, documentary footage · BFI NFTVA, performance footage | SOUND BL NSA, documentary recordings · BL NSA, performance recordings
Likenesses P. Still, photograph, 1985, Redferns Music Picture Library, London [*see illus.*] · twenty-one photographs, Hult. Arch.
Wealth at death £8,649,940: probate, 1992, *CGPLA Eng. & Wales*

Meredith, Edward (1648–1715), Jesuit, was born in Cornwall in 1648, the son of Edward Ameredith (*d.* 1661), Anglican rector of Landulph, and his wife, Alice Kekewitch (*bap.* 1625). He was sent to Westminster School about 1661 and in 1665 proceeded to Christ Church, Oxford, leaving three years later, apparently without taking a degree. In the following year he went to Spain as secretary to his kinsman Sir William Godolphin, who was sent there as ambassador. In Spain in 1671 both Meredith and Godolphin converted to Catholicism. Meredith was back in England by August 1671 when he took part in religious debates with the Anglican clergyman Edward Stillingfleet, an account of which Meredith published in 1687 as *The Sum of the Conference between Two Divines*. He was also present in 1676 at a rather similar religious disputation. Until 1684 Meredith received a pension of £100 a year from Godolphin, 'he having told me he looked upon me as his son' (MS will, English College, Rome).

Meredith probably left England at the time of the Popish Plot. In 1682, in a brief pamphlet, entitled *Some Remarques upon a Late Popular Piece of Nonsence called Julian the Apostate*, he defended the duke of York and the principles of passive resistance against the attacks of the whig apologist, Samuel Johnson. In 1684 Meredith joined the Society of Jesus under the alias of Edward Langsford, and enrolled at the noviciate at Watten in the Southern Netherlands. In this he was following in the footsteps of his brother, Amos. Edward remained a Jesuit for the rest of his life, although he was never ordained and did not proceed beyond the position of scholastic in the order. He returned to London in 1686 and published several pamphlets over the next two years, enjoying the freer atmosphere which the accession of James II had brought. His favourite device was to engage in controversial exchanges with protestant pamphleteers, using as a starting point a number of oral debates which took place between Catholic and protestant theologians. He also published a translation from a selection of Catholic meditative passages. When, late in 1687, James II attempted to impose a number of fellows sympathetic to his views on Magdalen College, Oxford, Meredith was among their number.

The revolution of 1688 resulted in Meredith's flight from England, and he joined the Jacobite settlement at St Germain-en-Laye. He moved to the Jesuit establishment in Rome in 1696, and then was in Naples for several years after 1702. He can be traced to Paris in 1711. He spent some time also at the English College, Rome. He was in poor health and his eyesight was failing. His last years were passed helping secure a benefaction for the English school at St Omer from the estate of Godolphin, who had made him a trustee for a fund of 4000 Spanish doubloons in his much disputed will. In one of Meredith's last letters, dated early in 1715, he emphasized his Jacobitism, claiming that 'the King's example is now the strongest motive for conversion' (Holt, *Letter Book*, 230). He died at Rome shortly afterwards. His will contains elaborate instructions for spending Godolphin's trust funds in repaying various debts and in helping the indigent English Catholics.

PETER HOLMES

Sources Gillow, *Lit. biog. hist.* · H. Foley, ed., *Records of the English province of the Society of Jesus*, 7 (1882–3), civ, 502 · G. Holt, *The English Jesuits, 1650–1829: a biographical dictionary*, Catholic RS, 70 (1984) · *DNB* · *The letter book of Lewis Sabran*, ed. G. Holt, Catholic RS, 62 (1971) · Wood, *Ath. Oxon.*, new edn, 1.xcv; 4.393, 653 · Foster, *Alum. Oxon.* · *Old Westminsters*, vol. 2 · T. H. Clancy, *English Catholic books, 1641–1700: a bibliography*, rev. edn (1996) · C. Dodd [H. Tootell], *The church history of England, from the year 1500, to the year 1688*, 3 vols. (1737–42), vol. 2, p. 465 · G. Holt, 'Two seventeenth-century Hebrew scholars: Thomas Fairfax and Edward Slaughter', *Recusant History*, 22 (1994–5), 482–90 · *CSP dom.*, 1687–9, 124, 139–40 · J. Polsue, *A complete parochial history of the county of Cornwall*, 2 (1868), 404, 407 · J. L. Vivian, ed., *The visitations of Cornwall, comprising the herald's visitations of 1530, 1573, and 1620* (1887)

Wealth at death considerable funds: will, English College, Rome, archives, MS will

Meredith, George (1828–1909), novelist and poet, was born at 73 High Street, Portsmouth, Hampshire, on 12 February 1828, the only child of Augustus Urmston Meredith (1797–1876) and Jane Eliza (1802–1833), daughter of Michael Macnamara, an innkeeper. Settled in the Portsmouth area at least from the middle of the eighteenth century, the Meredith family became prominent during the time of George's grandfather Melchizedec (*c.*1763–1814), a flamboyant naval outfitter, who as the larger-than-life tailor, the Great Mel, dominates his grandson's second novel, *Evan Harrington* (1861).

Youth, early career, and marriage Little is known of Meredith's childhood. His mother died when he was five; Augustus, unable to maintain the family business, was declared bankrupt in 1838 and moved to London. George went to St Paul's School in Southsea, then to boarding-school in Suffolk, and finally in August 1842 set off to Germany to the School of the Moravian Fathers in Neuwied near Koblenz on the Rhine. This school, chosen presumably for reasons of economy, had many advantages and was formative in important ways. Meredith's experience in its supportive environment gave him facility in languages—he had good French and German—and a perspective on England in relation to Europe. His later strong views on the need for women to be educated may in part have derived from the fact that girls as well as boys attended the school, though their accommodation was separate as were most classes and other activities. It is unclear why Meredith returned to England in January 1844, or how he spent the next couple of years. His annual income of £60, derived from a legacy from his mother together with her share of the estate of a sister who died in 1840, enabled him to be articled to Richard Stephen Charnock, a London solicitor and a man of literary tastes, in February 1846, though he seems never to have applied himself seriously to the law. He had little contact with his father, especially after Augustus migrated to South Africa in 1849 with his second wife, Matilda Buckett, said to have been his cook. They returned to England in the early 1860s, settling in Southsea, where Augustus died in 1876, and Matilda in 1885.

Meredith soon made his way into literary circles. Among the would-be authors he met was Edward Gryffydh Peacock, a son of the novelist Thomas Love Peacock, who shared rooms near the British Museum with his sister, a widow, Mary Ellen Nicolls (1821–1861). Described by Holman Hunt as 'a dashing type of horsewoman who attracted much notice from the "bloods" of the day' (Stevenson, 46), Mary had a five-year-old daughter from her first

George Meredith (1828–1909), by Frederick Hollyer, 1890?

marriage in January 1844 to Lieutenant Edward Nicolls RN. Nicolls had drowned within months of the wedding in an attempt to rescue one of his men. Mary was a contributor to a manuscript journal, the 'Monthly Observer', begun in 1848, in which Meredith and others also participated. Meredith's acquaintance with Mary, seven years older than him, was soon more than casual: they were married on 9 August 1849, at St George's, Hanover Square, London. Following their honeymoon in the Rhineland, they were back in London by November 1849, and for some years lived somewhat impecuniously, usually in the country near London, occasionally by the sea at Seaford, Sussex. Meredith later maintained, 'No sun warmed my roof-tree; the marriage was a blunder' (Clodd, 21), yet the relationship, always volatile, was sometimes ecstatic. Though Mary became pregnant more than once, only one child survived infancy, Arthur Gryffydh, born on 13 June 1853.

Early in their marriage both George and Mary worked on literary projects, and published articles in *Fraser's Magazine*. George had some poems accepted, the first in 1849, and soon assembled a volume, *Poems* (1851). Critical reaction can be summarized in R. H. Hutton's condescending verdict that *Poems* displayed 'more of promise than performance' (Williams, 28). Meredith's first volume of fiction was a prose allegory, *The Shaving of Shagpat: an Arabian Entertainment* (1856), which he claimed to have 'written … at Weybridge with duns at the door' (Clodd, 21). It attracted some highly favourable though not extensive critical comment, George Eliot in *The Leader* greeting it as

'a work of genius, and of poetical genius' (Williams, 41). A similar stylistic virtuosity and fascination with pastiche and generic experiment was exercised in *Farina: a Legend of Cologne* (1857), a slighter comic grotesque tale set in medieval Germany. Meredith meanwhile continued to seek work wherever he could, maintaining his output of verse, and succeeding George Eliot as the author of the 'Belles lettres' section of the *Westminster Review* from April 1857 to January 1858. In this capacity he took the opportunity to review his own work, asserting that '*Farina* is both an original and an entertaining book' (ibid., 58).

By 1856 George's relationship with Mary had frayed to breaking point. The painter Henry Wallis was known to them both, George having been the model for the dead poet in Wallis's most famous painting, *The Death of Chatterton*, exhibited at the Royal Academy in 1856. A strong attraction developed between Mary and Wallis: in spring 1857 Mary, pregnant by her lover, went to join him in Wales, leaving Arthur and her daughter Edith Nicolls with her former mother-in-law Lady Nicolls. Meredith claimed Arthur from Lady Nicolls in the autumn and assumed sole charge of the boy, taking rooms in Chelsea, London, until 1859 when he moved to Esher after the publication in June of his first full-length novel, *The Ordeal of Richard Feverel: a History of Father and Son*. Both this work and the poem sequence *Modern Love* (1862) were fuelled by the trauma of sexual betrayal.

Mary's affair with Wallis did not last long after the birth of their child, registered as Harold Meredith (later known as Felix Wallis). Mary and the baby joined Wallis in Capri in summer 1858, returning to England without him early in 1859, shifting from one set of lodgings to another, and moving to Oatlands Park near Weybridge in spring 1861, where she died from kidney disease on 22 October. Meredith allowed Arthur to see his mother during her last illness, but kept himself at a distance. Having been away in the week Mary died, he wrote euphemistically to his new friend William Hardman, 'When I entered the world again, I found that one had quitted it who bore my name: and this filled me with melancholy reflections which I rarely give way to' (*Letters*, 1.108).

While Meredith creatively transformed some aspects of his shame as a deserted husband in the situation of Sir Austin Feverel in *The Ordeal of Richard Feverel*, the novel is diminished if read simply as personal displacement. It is a startlingly original work, particularly in its stylistic diversity and sexual frankness, with a rich literary genealogy that includes 'new comedy' as well as the novel of education and chivalric romance. Elements of his philosophy, which became influential, were already distinctively demonstrated. The commitment to trust in natural energy and instinct over the constraints of system and reason, reiterated through all Meredith's writing, encouraged belief in the persistence of mystery and wonder in the natural world without requiring adherence to Christian myth (Darwin's *On the Origin of Species* was published in the same year). *Feverel*'s originality was recognized, but at the cost of some notoriety. 'I am tabooed from all decent drawing-room tables' (*Letters*, 1.39), Meredith lamented when

Mudie's circulating library, which had taken 300 copies, withdrew the novel. Though he revised *Feverel* several times, he never modified the treatment of Richard's adultery or the glimpses of the *demi-monde* which were presumably the source of offence. A different kind of recognition of Meredith's calibre came from an influential quarter. Jane Carlyle was initially exasperated by *Feverel*, but persevered, reading some of it to Thomas, who offered the opinion that 'The man's no fool' (Clodd, 24).

Experiment, 1860–1864 Meredith's next novel, *Evan Harrington, or, He would be a Gentleman* (1861), was serialized in *Once a Week* from February to October 1860. He was hard put to meet the demands of weekly serial publication, documenting the pains of composition in correspondence with the editor Samuel Lucas: 'Your advice is good. This cursed desire I have haunting me to show the reason for things is a perpetual obstruction to movement. I *do* want the dash of Smollett and know it' (*Letters*, 1.57). Stylistically *Evan Harrington* is plainer than its predecessors, working a topical vein of novels about class and gentlemanliness to similar effect but in a more comic, picaresque mode than its near-contemporary, Dickens's *Great Expectations*. Like *Richard Feverel*, it was in many ways a confessional novel, depending heavily on family history but also introducing characters drawn from other friends and acquaintances, notably Rose Jocelyn, avowedly based on Janet, the daughter of Sir Alexander and Lady Duff Gordon. Meredith met the Duff Gordons first at Weybridge in 1849–50, and the friendship resumed soon after Meredith's move to Esher when Janet rescued Arthur from being trampled by a runaway horse. By some accounts Meredith's attachment to the young woman who called him 'my Poet' went deeper than the courtly badinage recorded in his letters. Certainly he was devoted to her even after her marriage in December 1860 to H. J. Ross, a banker twenty years older than her, and they corresponded to the end of his life.

Always conscious of the priorities represented by 'baker's bills and Boy' (*Letters*, 1.250), Meredith took on a variety of jobs. He became a publisher's reader for Chapman and Hall, who had published *Feverel*, in succession to John Forster in 1860, a role he famously filled for over thirty years. He also read manuscripts for Saunders and Otley in the early 1860s. In his capacity at Chapman and Hall he encouraged several younger writers who went on to become figures of consequence. Thomas Hardy was one who appreciated his 'trenchant, turning kind' comments, recalling that 'he gave me no end of good advice, most of which, I am bound to say, he did not follow himself' (Stevenson, 174). George Gissing and Olive Schreiner were among others to profit from his counsel. He also made some spectacular miscalculations, in 1861 roundly stating of *East Lynne* that he was 'emphatically against it', thus opening the way for Bentley to make immense profits from Ellen Wood's novel. His pithy reports on the large quantity of reading he got through—averaging about ten manuscripts a week—were relished in the Chapman and Hall office.

In addition Meredith became an editorial writer for the tory *Ipswich Journal* at the invitation of a Weybridge acquaintance, Thomas Eyre Foakes. For some years his weekly columns earned a welcome £200 annually, despite the horrors of the 'Foakesday' deadlines. He none the less undertook other journalism, not all of it identified, including articles for the *Morning Post*, as well as publishing poems and short stories. For a time in 1862–3, in order to facilitate his London commitments, he spent Thursday nights in Dante Gabriel Rossetti's household in Chelsea, of which the poet Algernon Swinburne was also part. Perhaps because of the concentration of artistic energies under the same roof, the arrangement did not last long for all that in some respects it was productive. Another resident, the painter Frederick Sandys, told of an outing with Meredith, Rossetti, and Swinburne, when each of his companions wrote a poem between Waterloo station and their destination, Hampton Court.

From the years at Esher date many of Meredith's most enduring friendships. Chief among these friends was Captain Frederick Augustus Maxse RN, a Crimean War hero, whose mother was a daughter of the fifth earl of Berkeley. Maxse was an idealistic enthusiast whose personal idiosyncrasies and family history contributed substantially to *Beauchamp's Career*. He was not the only one of Meredith's friends to be used as a source for his fiction: William Hardman, a barrister and later editor of the *Morning Post*, whom Meredith got to know in autumn 1861, appears as Blackburn Tuckham in *Beauchamp's Career*; and the character of Adrian Harley in *Richard Feverel* was based on the eccentric Maurice Fitzgerald, a nephew of the poet Edward Fitzgerald. A little later Meredith met such up-and-coming men of letters as John Morley and Leslie Stephen (who became Vernon Whitford in *The Egoist*). Augustus Jessopp, clergyman and headmaster of the King Edward VI School in Norwich, introduced himself in a flattering letter in November 1861. Their correspondence became acquaintance, and in September 1862 Arthur Meredith was enrolled at Jessopp's school.

Most of these men shared Meredith's pleasure in long walks in the Surrey countryside, and some of them the passion for the Alps which infuses his writing, especially *The Egoist*. His first alpine holiday was in July and August 1861 in company with Arthur and the sometimes tiresome William Charles Bonaparte Wyse, described by Meredith as 'half Prince, half Paddy' (*Letters*, 1.125) because of his descent from a brother of Napoleon Bonaparte on his mother's side, and Irish landowners on his father's. Wyse later figured as Richmond Roy in *The Adventures of Harry Richmond*. Meredith's exhilarated letters, especially to Maxse, trace their itinerary from Germany into Switzerland and on to Italy. While his resistance to orthodox Christian belief was shaken momentarily, his belief in the transcendent if inscrutable power of the natural world was affirmed:

> My first sight of the Alps has raised odd feelings. Here at last seems something more than earth, and visible, if not tangible. They have the whiteness, the silence, the beauty and mystery of thoughts seldom unveiled within us, but which conquer Earth when once they are. In fact they have

made my creed tremble.—Only for a time. Our great error has been (the error of all religion, as I fancy) to raise a spiritual system in antagonism to Nature. (ibid., 1.93)

The Liberal statesman and editor John Morley later commented pertinently on this passage, that 'This hardly comes to much for purposes of controversial logic', proceeding, however, to a qualification which speaks of the attraction that Meredith's vigorous communion with the natural world held not only for Morley himself but for others of the next generation: 'the train of latent thought and feeling, thus suddenly started in his soul, carried him far into new regions of art, faith, and life' (Morley, 1.45).

Many accounts of Meredith in person derive from his years at Esher. Frank Burnand, later editor of *Punch*, described their first meeting in terms coloured by subsequent friendship:

> George Meredith never merely walked, never lounged; he strode, he took giant strides. He had ... crisp, curly, brownish hair, ignorant of parting; a fine brow, quick, observant eyes, greyish—if I remember rightly—beard and moustache, a trifle lighter than the hair. A splendid head; a memorable personality. Then his sense of humour, his cynicism, and his absolutely boyish enjoyment of mere fun, of any pure and simple absurdity. His laugh was something to hear; it was of short duration, but it was a roar; it set you off—nay, he himself, when much tickled, would laugh till he cried (it didn't take long to get to the crying), and then he would struggle with himself, hand to open mouth, to prevent another outburst. (Burnand, 1.361–2)

Such accounts of Meredith's boisterous physical presence are numerous: this one aligns with the author himself the philosophy of the tonic properties of laughter which appears in a rudimentary form in *Shagpat*, and later in a more mandarin presentation in *The Egoist*. '[A] born tease' (Clodd, 28), Meredith was renowned to the end of his days as 'a brilliant and indefatigable leader of talk' (Sully, 324). His oral delivery had none of the dense obliquity of his written prose:

> 'By God,' said one of the Victorian wits to him one day, 'George, why don't you write like you talk?' It is true that his conversation, particularly as he grew deafer, tended to become a monologue, but it was sprinkled with gems and never bored. He was a great improvisatore and nothing could be more exhilarating than to watch him, with his splendid head and his eyes aflame, stamping up and down the room, while he extemporized at the top of his resonant voice a sonnet in perfect form on the governess's walking costume, or a dozen lines, in the blankest of Wordsworthian verse, in elucidation of Haldane's philosophy. (Asquith, 1.37)

In many respects his talking and writing were of a piece. A critic commented that it was difficult in his novels to distinguish 'where record of sober fact had ended and where the innocent mendacity of the novelist had begun' (Hammerton, 110). This tendency was apparent also in Meredith in person. His propensity for improvisation, sometimes in verse as Asquith describes, and sometimes in prose narratives, maybe triggered by advertisements in the daily papers, has considerable relevance to his fictional practice, where 'facts' are frequently discernible, as in the use of friends and acquaintances as prototypes for characters.

Even in his letters Meredith fictionalized his correspondents, characterizing them often through extravagant jokes based on nicknames.

Meredith repeatedly worked through personal trauma in his writing, at a greater or lesser remove. Those 'melancholy reflections' occasioned by the death of Mary before long assumed powerful shape in the poem sequence *Modern Love* (1862). The fifty sixteen-line 'sonnets' play out the end of a love affair in a narrative which dwells on representing states of mind and shifts of perception rather than on an objective account of what actually took place. Even Maxse, the dedicatee, complained of obscurity in a review in the *Morning Post*, while others went on the attack. 'Mr George Meredith is a clever man, without literary genius, taste or judgement' whose work 'has no kind of right to the title "Modern Love": "Modern Lust" would certainly be ... more accurate', ranted R. H. Hutton in *The Spectator*, his earlier dismissiveness transformed to overt hostility (Williams, 95). In reply Swinburne provided dignified and detailed advocacy for Meredith as a poet 'whose work, perfect or imperfect, is always as noble in design as it is often faultless in result' (ibid., 98).

Literary merit aside, *Modern Love* is a curiously evenhanded working through of the dynamics of Meredith's first marriage from which there was no evident trauma carried over into his second marriage. Marie Vulliamy (1840–1885) was the youngest daughter of an English mother and a French father. Meredith met the family, which had settled in Mickleham following Justin Vulliamy's retirement from his wool business in Normandy, in autumn 1863. The handsome young widower was subjected to intense interrogation about his previous marriage and his financial situation by his prospective father-in-law before permission for the wedding was forthcoming. The marriage was celebrated by Augustus Jessopp in Mickleham parish church on 20 September 1864.

Meredith waxed rhapsodic about his bride: 'I knew when I spoke to her that hers was the heart I had long been seeking, and that my own in its urgency was carried on a pure though a strong tide' (*Selected Letters*, 41). Once adjusted to conjugal life, he described her as 'a mud fort. You fire broadsides into her, and nothing happens' (Stevenson, 185). Marie was a handsome woman, capable of effective domestic diplomacy, an accomplished pianist whose favourite composer was Chopin, and a capable scholar whose translation of Charles de Mazade's *Life of Cavour* was published by Chapman and Hall in 1877. There were two children: William Maxse (*b.* 1865) and Marie Eveleen (Mariette; *b.* 1871). Though the new Mrs Meredith was fond of her stepson, Arthur was away at school and did not become part of the family circle. Early in 1867 Meredith transferred him from Jessopp's school in Norwich to Hofwyl School near Bern, where G. H. Lewes's three sons had been pupils. Neither his visits to Hofwyl nor Arthur's visits home were frequent.

When he met Marie, Meredith was finishing *Emilia in England* (1864; re-titled *Sandra Belloni* when it was reissued in 1886). The novel was from the first conceived as part of a diptych, in which Meredith made yet another generic departure, interlacing comedy of manners with political adventure. The struggle for Italian unification provides a strong undertow, with Meredith drawing on the Rossettis and others with Italian connections, as well as depicting Swinburne in a minor character, Tracy Runningbrook. Always a good self-critic, though unable to act on his criticisms, he observed accurately that 'the novel has good points, and some of my worst ones. It has no plot, albeit a current series of events: but being based on character and development it is not unlikely to miss a striking success' (*Letters*, 1.247). Yet despite generally lukewarm if sympathetic reviews, Meredith's reputation was consolidating. A milestone was the appraisal of his work to date by Justin McCarthy, later a politician and journalist, in 'Novels with a purpose' (*Westminster Review*, July 1864), which praised its distinctiveness but cautioned that the author is 'too often … induced to sink the story-teller in the critic, the poet in the social philosopher' (Williams, 135).

Consolidation, 1864–1875 Brimming with ideas, desperate for popularity and profit, Meredith tried 'an English novel, of the real story-telling order' (*Letters*, 1.250), a version of the traditional squire-and-milkmaid seduction plot used to good effect as recently as 1859 by George Eliot in *Adam Bede*. As always he encountered problems in his efforts 'to "finish off" *Rhoda Fleming* in one volume, now swollen to two—and Oh, will it be three?—But this is my Dd. Dd. Dd. uncertain workmanship' (ibid., 1.302). The work did run to three volumes: *Rhoda Fleming: a Story* was published by Tinsley in 1865.

Meredith attempted redress for the flat reception of *Emilia* in its sequel, which had the working title 'Emilia in Italy'. *Vittoria* came out in 1866 (serialized in *The Fortnightly*, and published in three volumes by Chapman and Hall): 'all story … no Philosopher present: action: excitement: holding of your breath, chilling horror: classic sensation' (*Letters*, 1.255). To no avail. Geraldine Jewsbury, who had found *Emilia in England* 'a charming story' though the style 'becomes fatiguing after a while', described *Vittoria* as an 'unmerciful novel' (Williams, 111, 113, 153). Meredith's partisan enthusiasm for Italian nationalist movements had another outcome, however, when he was commissioned to cover the Austro-Prussian War for the *Morning Post*. He was in Italy from June to November 1866 (though the war was over in July), producing lively coverage. He undertook other journalistic roles, deputizing as editor of *The Fortnightly* in 1867 when Morley went to America, and in the following year contributing a number of essays to the *Pall Mall Gazette*. About this time he began to read aloud for a couple of hours a week to Mrs Benjamin Wood, an eccentric widow with failing sight who lived at Eltham, for which he earned a substantial £300 a year well into the 1880s.

Late in 1867 the Merediths made a move of great significance. Having lived since their marriage in rented houses in Esher and Norbiton, they bought Flint Cottage, Box Hill, Dorking, which was to be Meredith's home for the remaining forty-two years of his life. The relatively small house was imaginatively extended in 1876 by the construction of a chalet as Meredith's study. The building was

at Marie's expense, her annual income of £200 at marriage having increased following her father's death in 1870. Meredith was delighted by the arrangement, boasting to Morley:

> You should know, I work and sleep up in my cottage at present, and anything grander than the days and nights at my porch you will not find away from the Alps: for the dark line of my hill runs up to the stars, the valley below is a soundless gulf. There I pace like a shipman before turning in. (*Letters*, 1.539)

Settled in Flint Cottage, Meredith finished a long-nurtured project, *The Adventures of Harry Richmond*, which ran in the *Cornhill Magazine* from September 1870 to November 1871, illustrated by the rising George Du Maurier, then appeared in three volumes from Smith Elder dated 1871. Elements of earlier novels were reworked in this 'History of father and son': like *Evan Harrington*, *Harry Richmond* has picaresque elements; and like the *Emilia* novels, it has a distinct political inflection. The distancing in time and place often associated with its romance adventure genre is qualified as the hero's adventures take him through a recognizably mid-nineteenth-century Europe where the divine right of kings is everywhere in question and exposure of patriarchal egoism goes along with demonstration of female strength and suffering. Meredith had claimed for *Modern Love*, the most painfully personal of his works, wider relevance as 'a dissection of the sentimental passion of these days' (*Letters*, 1.160). His concern to analyse contemporary life became even more explicit from the 1870s, not only in his fiction but also in the topical commentary that provides the substance of five Peacockian 'Up to midnight' dialogues which appeared in *The Graphic* in December 1872 and January 1873.

Popular acclaim, 1875–1885 Though Meredith had published *Harry Richmond* with Smith Elder, he returned amicably to Chapman and Hall for the publication of *Beauchamp's Career* (1876). Always engaged in generic experiment, in *Beauchamp's Career* he produced a political novel. Serialization in *The Fortnightly* (August 1874–December 1875) marked the end of some years' estrangement from its touchy editor, John Morley, who in 1871 had complained to Meredith about his abrasive comments on Morley's 'opinions, ideas, and likings' (*Letters*, 1.443); later Morley expressly recognized Meredith's dignified and generous behaviour during the rift. Of all Meredith's friends from the 1850s and 1860s, Morley achieved the greatest worldly success, first in literature (as editor and author) and then in politics (he took office first under Gladstone in 1886, as chief secretary for Ireland, and was secretary of state for India from 1905 to 1910). Morley was only one of the key figures in the Liberal Party to whom Meredith was close, especially from the 1880s on: others included Herbert Asquith, a future prime minister, and Richard Haldane, a future lord chancellor. Not only did Meredith engage in his fiction with political issues, but increasingly he also consorted with public figures, and intervened in current debates through journal essays and letters to the newspapers.

Beauchamp's Career can be read as Meredith's contention

with Morley. Meredith's awareness of the power of impulse and chance in human affairs pervades the novel, implicitly undermining the basic conviction of Morley and his positivist colleagues of the inexorable power of reason to effect personal, social, and political change. In this sense Morley is a presence in the novel, though he is represented in no single character. The titular hero, however, was avowedly based on Meredith's closest friend, Frederick Maxse. While the focus is on the revolt of the radical hero against his aristocratic establishment formation, sexual politics become more insistent than in earlier work. The career of Nevil Beauchamp is marked out through his relationships with women, which successively define the damaging contradictions and limitations of his radical idealism. In particular the complex characterization of the tory heiress, Cecilia Halkett, brings out the extent to which male authority painfully circumscribes women.

Meredith later suggested of this novel that 'There is a breezy, human interest about it; and the plot has a consistency and logical evolution which *Feverel* lacks' (Clodd, 24)—a comment that downplays the extent to which *Beauchamp's Career*, like its almost exact contemporaries, George Eliot's *Daniel Deronda* and Anthony Trollope's *The Way we Live now*, is concerned to anatomize the England of the day. It also downplays the extent to which his characteristic narrative tactics are fully matured in this work: major confrontations are reported, not shown, because their significance resides not in the action itself, but in its implications and effects. The reception of *Beauchamp's Career* established Meredith as a major literary presence, who because of the density of his style was often compared to Browning.

In the middle 1870s Meredith was again working on a number of projects, including a never-completed play, 'The sentimentalists', as well as poetry and short fiction. *The House on the Beach: a Realistic Tale*, *The Case of General Ople and Lady Camper*, and *The Tale of Chloe* were published in the *New Quarterly Magazine* in the late 1870s, but not in book form until the 1890s. He also made a start on two novels: *The Amazing Marriage*, which he rewrote and published in 1895, and *Celt and Saxon*, to which he did not return (it was posthumously published in 1910). In these novels emerged a personal mythology cast in terms of racial characteristics—the dialectic of fiery Celt and stoic Saxon—that became more central in *Diana of the Crossways*, though the superiority of the Welsh in spirit and imagination to the phlegmatic, materialistic English was a subject of his fiction as early as *Emilia in England*. Meredith, calling himself half-Welsh and half-Irish, laid comprehensive claim to Celtic attributes at a time when ideologies of race and political issues such as home rule were topical.

The momentum of Meredith's work in this phase was generated by exploration of comedy—always a genre that engaged him. He delivered his lecture on comedy at the London Institution on 1 February 1877 (published in the *New Quarterly Magazine* in April, and in book form in 1898).

The essay was part of his preparation for *The Egoist: a Comedy in Narrative* (serialized in the *Glasgow Weekly Herald*, June 1879–Jan 1880; then issued in 3 volumes by Kegan Paul, 1879). Now acknowledged as his masterpiece, this highly structured novel both articulates Meredith's particular idea of comedy as 'the ultimate civilizer' (*Egoist*, 'Prelude') and draws on the traditions of stage comedy of Molière and Congreve. While celebrating these various literary traditions, *The Egoist* also engages with such significant Victorian discourses as evolution and imperialism. Sir Willoughby Patterne, like Sir Austin Feverel, invokes science to control his domain, but even more comprehensively than Sir Austin he is thwarted by the elemental energies of nature associated particularly with women and the lower orders. In his presentation of the female characters, especially the beautiful heroine Clara Middleton and the witty widow Mrs Mountstuart Jenkinson, Meredith's advocacy for women becomes more explicit. As always, some reviewers objected to Meredith's preciosity, but others responded with enthusiasm to the novel's verbal brilliance. By now he had another generation of devotees among younger writers, including Robert Louis Stevenson (to whom Meredith confided that Sir Willoughby Patterne 'is all of us' (Williams, 521)), and W. E. Henley (who reviewed the novel four times).

Throughout his career certain of Meredith's works set up dialogues with their predecessors. *The Tragic Comedians: a Study in a Well-Known Story* (serialized in *The Fortnightly*, Oct 1880–Feb 1881, and published in 2 volumes by Chapman and Hall, 1880) provides an excellent case in point. Again he homed in on the egoism and self-deception of the central characters, in a grim negative demonstration of the corrective capacities of the comic spirit. Meredith reinterpreted the love affair of the German socialist Ferdinand Lassalle, a Jew, with a much younger woman from an aristocratic Roman Catholic family, which ended in Lassalle's death in a duel. Here the novel foreshadows its successor by drawing on the history of a public figure for significant aspects of the plot.

It was *Diana of the Crossways* (1885) that finally gained Meredith significant popular acclaim. Readers could see resemblances in the account of Diana Merion's tribulations to the close relationships of Caroline Norton with Lord Melbourne (Lord Dannisburgh in the novel) and Sidney Herbert (Percy Dacier), and the allegation that she betrayed a political secret (concerning the corn law repeal). Possibly because of threats of legal action the serialization in the *Fortnightly Review*, which ran from June to December 1884, was abruptly terminated after twenty-six chapters. There were seventeen more in the three-volume version brought out by Chapman and Hall in February 1885—and the novel went into two further editions before the end of the year. Diana's double disadvantage as an Irish woman tapped into two highly topical issues, home rule and women's rights, on both of which Meredith was increasingly drawn to make public pronouncement. In addition, like many of Meredith's novels, *Diana* contains commentary on the aims and techniques of fiction, made particularly potent by Diana's being herself a novelist dedicated to 'reading the inner as well as exhibiting the outer' (*Diana*, chap. 1).

Meredith was now prospering as never before. In 1882, by the death of a distant cousin he secured a reversion from the estate of a great-uncle, which, he observed inimitably, 'relieves me of the constant harassment of the sense of neediness' (*Letters*, 2.659). Despite his complaints about financial problems early in his career, Meredith had been able to support himself by his writing and related activities with assistance from his inheritance and the income of his second wife. This additional legacy, together with effective management of his business affairs from the mid-1890s at the hands of his son Will, contributed to his substantial estate, declared at £33,701 15s. 10d. (ibid., 2.1067n.).

Meredith's health was no longer robust, however. Always subject to gastric ailments, he adopted a vegetarian diet for a time in the late 1870s. Digestive problems paled beside the onset of motor ataxia from the end of 1881, a cruel affliction given his commitment to vigorous physical exercise. The contemporary diagnosis of locomotor ataxia, a possible symptom of tertiary-stage syphilis, was questioned by twentieth-century medical opinion, which suggested that Meredith suffered—painfully but less dramatically—from osteoarthritis. Whatever the cause, his physical mobility was severely restricted from the late 1880s, when increasing deafness further limited his social interactions. Travel abroad was now difficult, so he holidayed in the British Isles: in August 1887 he went to St Ives to be with Leslie Stephen and his family; in 1888 he made his first visit to Wales to visit Will, who was with an engineering firm there; and in August 1890 he journeyed to Scotland.

The death of Marie on 17 September 1885, from cancer of the throat, was a grievous blow. Meredith's poem 'A Faith on Trial' movingly sets her mortal illness in the larger context of decay and death as necessary for renewal, and he mourned her as 'the most unpretending, brave and steadfast friend ever given for a mate' (*Letters*, 2.789). Of necessity, some lifestyle change followed, notably the employment of a governess for the fourteen-year-old Mariette, his strong-willed but devoted daughter. His concern for instance that Mariette should not go about unchaperoned can be seen as intelligibly inconsistent with his advocacy of equality for women. Less intelligible was his gradual estrangement from his elder son, whose schooling in Germany had been followed by employment in Le Havre and Lille. In the early 1880s there was some rapprochement when Meredith, remorseful on learning that Arthur had tuberculosis, spent time with him both in England and in Italy. But Arthur's affinities were rather with his half-sister Edith (Mrs Charles Clarke) than with his Meredith kin, and he was being cared for by her at home in Woking when he died on 3 September 1890. Meredith did not attend the funeral.

Late phase, 1885–1909 The success of *Diana* encouraged Chapman and Hall to put out a collected ('new') edition of Meredith's work, of which the first titles were issued in 1885. With his fiction (some of it lightly revised) now in circulation, it became the subject of significant critical surveys—some, inevitably, hostile, like William Watson's censure of his artificiality (Williams, 317–30); but an increasing proportion were admiring, notably the book-length studies by Richard Le Gallienne in 1890 and Hannah Lynch in 1891. His reputation was not only English: Roberts Brothers' uniform edition, issued simultaneously with the New Edition, did well in the United States; and his continental reputation, especially in France, consolidated through the 1890s.

Meredith turned again to poetry: *Poems and Lyrics of the Joy of Earth* (1883) was followed by four more volumes—*Ballads and Poems of Tragic Life* (1887), *A Reading of Earth* (1888), *Modern love: a reprint, to which is added 'The sage enamoured and the honest lady'* (1892), and *Poems: the Empty Purse* (1892)—over the next decade. All were published by Macmillan, Meredith having made a strategic decision to bring out his verse from a publisher other than Chapman and Hall, though he assembled his work under one imprint when he moved to Constable in the mid-1890s. That house published *Odes in Contribution to the Song of French History* (1898) and *A Reading of Life* (1901), and also issued a number of selections: *Selected Poems* (1897), *The Nature Poems* (1898), and two posthumous volumes, *Last Poems* and *Poems Written in Early Youth* (both 1909). Meredith was of the view that his poems would outlive his novels, for all that 'Only a few read my verse, and yet it is that for which I care most … I began with poetry and I shall finish with it' (Clodd, 23). While his technical virtuosity is still acknowledged, readers turn to his poetry now for its emphatic articulation of his philosophy of life. That philosophy, which is likely to appear anachronistic and arcane to readers in the twenty-first century, however sympathetic they may be to Meredith's environmentalism, was potent for his contemporaries. The most thoroughgoing testimony to the influence and impact of Meredith's ideas is G. M. Trevelyan's *The Poetry and Philosophy of George Meredith* (1906), the historian's only book on a living person and, additionally, an index to the admiration for Meredith among the intelligentsia and the Liberal establishment. John Morley pungently summarized Meredith's vitalist ethic:

> Live with the world. No cloister. No languour. Play your part. Fill the day. Ponder well and loiter not. Let laughter brace you. Exist in everyday communion with Nature. Nature bids you take all, only be sure you learn how to do without. (Morley, 1.38)

Morley delineates the tonic power of Meredith's 'deep companionship of the large refreshing natural world [which] brought unspeakable fullness of being to him, as it was one of his most priceless lessons to men of disposition more prosaic than his own' (ibid., 39). Others were similarly exhilarated. '[T]he glory of George Meredith is that he combined subtlety with primal energy: he criticized life without losing his appetite for it', declared G. K. Chesterton in his obituary in the *Illustrated London News* (22 May 1909), succinctly identifying Meredith's appeal for a post-Darwinian world.

Meredith's creative energies were not all directed to

poetry, for there were three more novels: *One of our Conquerors* (serialized in *The Fortnightly*, Oct 1890–May 1891, simultaneously in *The Sun* (New York) and *Australasian*, and published in 3 volumes by Chapman and Hall, 1891), *Lord Ormont and his Aminta* (serialized in the *Pall Mall Magazine*, Dec 1893–July 1894, and issued in 3 volumes by Chapman and Hall, 1894), *The Amazing Marriage* (serialized in *Scribner's Magazine*, Jan–Dec 1895, and published in two volumes by Constable and Scribner, 1895). Claimed to be 'a broad and a close observation of the modern world' (*Letters*, 2.999), *One of our Conquerors* is the most challenging of all Meredith's works in the extravagance of its address to such familiar themes as the social injustices experienced by women, and the connections among egoism, capitalism, orthodox Christianity, and militarism. Both *Lord Ormont and his Aminta* and *The Amazing Marriage* continue an exploration of sexual relationships apparently or actually illicit, and of the range of comedy. Although these are mellower works than the relentlessly tragic *One of our Conquerors*, each is challenging in subject matter and narrative method.

Meredith's world was gradually closing in. The household at Flint Cottage following Mariette's marriage in 1894 to Henry Parkman Sturgis, a businessman, was made up of a nurse, Bessie Nicholls, and gardener, Frank Cole, together with dogs, and later a donkey to pull the trap in which Meredith took outings once he could no longer walk. He now left Box Hill only rarely, though in some years he had seaside holidays in Norfolk. His health became increasingly frail: he underwent surgery for urinary problems and gallstones in the 1890s; then, after a serious illness in winter 1903–4, he broke his right ankle in 1905. None the less, he maintained a wide circle of acquaintances, receiving guests, and developing new friendships, a number of them with young women. The letters and poems he wrote from the mid-1880s to Hilda de Longueil, Jean Palmer, Alice Meynell, and especially Ulrica Duncombe, a Girton graduate and daughter of the earl of Faversham, are sympathetic, playful, and seemingly flirtatious, oddly complementary to the bonhomie of earlier letters to his male peers.

Although Meredith accepted few public responsibilities, he succeeded Tennyson as president of the Society of Authors in 1892. At times reluctantly, he assented to recognition of various kinds including an honorary doctorate from the University of St Andrews in 1892. Because he was unable to attend the appropriate ceremonies he later declined similar degrees from the universities of Oxford and Wales. Edward Clodd organized a dinner in his honour at the Burford Bridge Inn close to Flint Cottage in 1895, at which Hardy and Gissing spoke of their admiration and indebtedness. For his seventieth birthday in 1898 Leslie Stephen instigated a testimonial, signed by thirty 'comrades in letters'. The highest public honour came in 1905 with his installation as the twelfth of twenty-four members of Edward VII's new Order of Merit, which Meredith whimsically described as the 'Order of Old Men'.

A process of setting his affairs on a more business-like basis began when Meredith employed W. Morris Colles as

his literary agent in 1892, and accelerated when his son Will took over in 1895, having joined the publisher Constable—a move which ended Meredith's long relationship with Chapman and Hall. Constable promptly capitalized on their acquisition, bringing out *The Amazing Marriage*, and then the De Luxe Edition of his works, including fiction, poetry, and non-fiction prose (36 vols., 1896–8, 1910–11). Other complete editions followed: the Library Edition from 1897, the Pocket Edition from 1906, and the Memorial Edition from 1909. Though he continued to speak of 'new' fictional works, especially one called 'The journalists', none eventuated: he wrote only poetry and the occasional short prose piece.

By the turn of the century Meredith was well ensconced as the Sage of Box Hill. He volunteered public pronouncements in letters to the press, and was sought out for interviews, commenting wryly that 'the British public (who never cared to read my books)' now 'wanted to know what I eat for breakfast, and what coloured tie I generally wear' (Butcher, 130). For all this self-deprecation, his status was not simply that of celebrity, but of public intellectual. His political position, usually implicit in his fiction, was now explicit, and consistently if idiosyncratically Liberal and anti-imperialist. He supported home rule, and opposed the Second South African War; generally interested in military matters, he followed closely the Russian Revolution of 1905. He could be relied on for pungent anti-clerical statements: 'Parsondom has always been against progress; they treat Christianity, not as a religion but as an institution' (Clodd, 26); for all this he bore with Anglican rites of marriage, baptism, and burial. He was much in demand for comment in the brief campaign leading to the 1906 general election, won by the Liberal Party following the resignation of Balfour and his Conservative government in December 1905. With his Liberal connections now holding high office, Meredith's influence was probably at its height: but the Fabian George Bernard Shaw's description of him at this time as 'a Cosmopolitan Republican Gentleman of the previous generation' (Stone, 96) was ominous.

The political issue with which he came particularly to be identified was women's rights and the suffrage. Throughout his fiction, women's disadvantage in a patriarchal society is tellingly presented, and also argued out in his poetry, notably in 'A Ballad of Fair Ladies in Revolt' (*Fortnightly Review*, 1 Aug 1876). He developed his ideas in interviews, typically pointing out to W. T. Stead in 1903 'a certain contempt on the part of man for the creature he has subdued and made a minister to his own gratification' (Stead, 230), and sensationally proposing to a *Daily Mail* interviewer in 1904 that marriage should be for a probationary term of ten years.

He was, however, emphatically opposed to militancy; in a letter to *The Times* he deplored the flawed tactics of a suffragist demonstration in the outer lobby of the House of Commons ('The mistake of the women has been to suppose that John Bull will move sensibly for a solitary kick'), while maintaining the line he had consistently advanced, that men must come to see 'that women have brains, and can be helpful to the hitherto entirely dominant muscular creature who has allowed them some degree of influence in return for servile flatteries and the graceful undulations of the snake—admired yet dreaded' (*Letters*, 3.1576–7).

Much publicity attended Meredith's eightieth birthday in 1908. In high spirits, he instructed an interviewer to 'Say that I am very well, and that you found me sitting in my chair, delivering myself freely of very Radical sentiments' (Hammerton, 49). But he was failing. He took a chill after his donkey-cart outing on 14 May 1909, and died at home in Flint Cottage on 18 May. Following cremation at Woking, on 22 May his ashes were buried beside Marie in Dorking cemetery in a grave lined with whitebeam and wild briar. Inscribed on the gravestone is a quotation from *Vittoria*:

Life is but a little holding, lent
To do a mighty labour.

Though a petition that he be buried in Westminster Abbey was denied, a memorial service was held there at noon on the day of the funeral, attended by his friend the prime minister H. H. Asquith and Miss Asquith, the American ambassador, and prominent literary figures. Newspaper reports noted that there were many wreaths from women's suffrage societies, and that mourners included a notable representation of young women. The organ of the non-militant suffragists, the *Common Cause*, carried an extended obituary editorial which delivered a telling personal testimony to Meredith's influence, expanded into an evaluation of how he had 'changed the world':

Beyond everything, what he brought to the younger generation of women was hope and self-revelation … Now woman feels that she belongs to herself, that she possesses herself, and that unless or until she does so the gift of herself is impossible. You cannot give what you have not got. Women … would force men to look at things as they are; at women's lives as they are; at the purely masculine world in which they are compelling women to live and to which the women cannot and ought not to adapt themselves.   (27 May 1909, 91–2)

Such tributes might have gratified Meredith, who in his later years had frequently proclaimed, 'I think that all right use of life, and the one secret of life, is to pave ways for the firmer footing of those who succeed us' (*Letters*, 2.876). Other obituaries dwelt on different accomplishments. *The Times* was suitably representative: its full authority was invested in its eulogy, which pronounced that 'in the end he achieved the position of the greatest man of letters of his age', delineating with conviction:

the once great walker, great talker, great writer, the poet with the noble head, the keen-eyed, keen-tongued foe of pretence and folly, [who] watched with almost unabated interest the life of which so many different features appealed to him, from cricket to tragic love, from old wine to contemporary politics.   (19 May 1909)

Afterlife Certain obituaries celebrating Meredith as the last of the Victorians, anticipated the inevitable eclipse of his late-blooming fame, which did not long survive him.

Neither Meredith's intellectual attraction, nor the currency of his writing, lasted much beyond 1920. His declining reputation coincided with the downturn in the political fortunes of the Liberal Party, by the late 1920s—with the rise of Labour—no longer a potential party of government. The novelist E. M. Forster, whose early work shows some Meredithian influence, denounced his predecessor in 1927:

Meredith is not the great name he was twenty or thirty years ago, when much of the universe and all Cambridge trembled … His philosophy has not worn well. His heavy attacks on sentimentality—they bore the present generation, which pursues the same quarry with neater instruments … And his visions of Nature—they do not endure like Hardy's, there is too much Surrey about them, they are fluffy and lush … What with the faking, what with the preaching, which was never agreeable and is now said to be hollow, and what with the home counties posing as the universe, it is no wonder Meredith now lies in the trough.   (Forster, 62–3)

Similar sentiments were expressed by Harold Nicolson thirty years later, in an Oxford rather than a Cambridge milieu, reminiscing with David Cecil and Maurice Bowra:

We discuss how the books which we admired in our youth survive into old age. The one who comes out worst of this discussion is Meredith, who must have meant to us the subtleties that Freud provided for our successors but which seem to us just crinkum-crankum.   (Nicolson, 313)

The Cambridge critic F. R. Leavis, himself a redoubtable maker and breaker of literary reputations, acknowledged the efficacy of Forster's attack in his post-war stocktake of the history of the English novel:

As for Meredith, I needn't add anything to what is said about him by Mr E. M. Forster, who, having belonged to the original *milieu* in which Meredith was erected into a great master, enjoys peculiar advantages for the necessary demolition-work.   (Leavis, 23)

In the second half of the twentieth century, there were none the less occasional attempts to revive Meredith and restore at least his literary reputation, notably about 1970 with the publication of C. L. Cline's edition of the letters and several critical studies. But his work was only partially and erratically in print, and by 1997 John Sutherland could pronounce that 'he is to all intents and purposes a literary corpse—a well-remembered and abstractly revered corpse but apparently beyond critical exhumation' (Sutherland, 5).

It is arguable, however, that the nature and extent of Meredith's achievement is best demonstrated by his formative influence on the next generation of novelists, including James Joyce. Even E. M. Forster allowed that 'he is the finest contriver that English fiction has ever produced'. This judgment was shared by Virginia Woolf, daughter of Meredith's friend Leslie Stephen, who accurately saw in him 'a great innovator'. He was always a writer's writer. The exasperated and ambivalent comments of his contemporary Oscar Wilde, declaring that he is 'an incomparable novelist', defined the paradoxes constituted by his work: 'His style is chaos illumined by flashes of lightning. As a writer he has mastered everything except language: as a novelist he can do everything, except tell a story: as an artist he is everything, except articulate' (Williams, 315–16). A similar irritation was more than once expressed by Henry James, another contemporary, who exercised particular authority about the art of the novel. Discussing 'the unspeakable *Lord Ormont*', James expostulated: 'not a difficulty met, not a figure presented, not a scene constituted' (ibid., 406–7); and yet at Meredith's death he generously declared, 'He did the best things best' (ibid., 406). Thomas Hardy, a fellow practitioner both in poetry and prose, and no believer in the afterlife, published an eighteen-line poem, 'G. M. 1828–1909', in *The Times* on the day of Meredith's funeral. Its concluding line, 'His words wing on—as strong words will' (later amended to 'as live words must'), points to the capacity of Meredith to speak to later generations. Hardy's tribute also provides important evidence in support of the verdict that Meredith holds a central place in the literary history of the Victorian era, as poet, journalist, and publisher's reader, and primarily as novelist.

MARGARET HARRIS

Sources L. Stevenson, *The ordeal of George Meredith* (1953) · *The letters of George Meredith*, ed. C. L. Cline, 3 vols. (1970) · E. Clodd, 'George Meredith: some recollections', *Fortnightly Review*, 86 (1909), 19–31 · S. M. Ellis, *George Meredith: his life and friends in relation to his work* (1919) · J. A. Hammerton, *George Meredith: his life and art in anecdote and criticism*, 2nd edn (1911) · I. Williams, ed., *George Meredith: the critical heritage* (1971) · M. Collie, *George Meredith: a bibliography* (1974) · *Selected letters of George Meredith*, ed. M. Shaheen (1997) · *The notebooks of George Meredith*, ed. G. Beer and M. Harris, Salzburg Studies in English literature: Romantic Reassessment, 73/2 (1983) · A. Butcher, *Memories of George Meredith, O. M.* (1919) · J. Ross, *The fourth generation: reminiscences* (1912) · W. T. Stead, 'Character sketch: George Meredith', *Review of Reviews* (10 March 1904), 224–30 · E. M. Forster, *Aspects of the novel* (1927); repr. (1974) · F. R. Leavis, *The great tradition* (1948) · J. Lucas, 'Meredith's reputation', *Meredith now: some critical essays*, ed. I. Fletcher (1971) · J. Sutherland, 'A revered corpse: the peculiar unreadability of George Meredith', *TLS* (15 Sept 1997) · M. B. Forman, *Meredithiana: being a supplement to the bibliography of Meredith* (1924) · John, Viscount Morley, *Recollections*, 2 vols. (1918) · H. Nicolson, *Diaries and letters, 1945–1962*, ed. N. Nicolson (1968) · Earl of Oxford and Asquith, *Memories and reflections, 1852–1927*, 1 (1928) · J. S. Stone, *George Meredith's politics as seen in his life, friendships, and works* (1986) · G. M. Trevelyan, *The poetry and philosophy of George Meredith* (1906) · R. A. Gettmann, 'Meredith as publisher's reader', *Journal of English and Germanic Philology*, 48 (1949), 45–56 · B. W. Matz, 'George Meredith as publisher's reader', *Fortnightly Review*, 86 (1909), 282–98 · F. C. Burnand, *Records and reminiscences personal and general*, 2 vols. (1904) · J. Sully, *My life and friends: a psychologist's memories* [1918] · D. Johnson, *The true history of the first Mrs. Meredith and other lesser lives* (1973) · J. Lindsay, *George Meredith: his life and work* (1956) · V. Woolf, 'The novels of George Meredith', *Collected essays*, ed. L. Woolf (1966)
Archives Dartmouth College Library, literary papers · Hunt. L., corresp. and literary MSS · L. Cong., literary papers · Morgan L., literary papers · NYPL, literary papers · Princeton University Library, New Jersey, papers · Ransom HRC, papers · Yale U., Beinecke L., letters and papers | BL, letters to Sir William Hardman · BL, corresp. incl. family corresp. with Macmillans · Bodl. Oxf., letters to various members of the Lewis family · Bodl. Oxf., letters to James Thomson · LUL, letters to M. Lewin and T. H. Lewin · LUL, corresp. with Henry Salt · NL Scot., letters to Lord Haldane · UCL, letters to James Sully · W. Sussex RO, letters mainly to F. A. Maxse
Likenesses H. Wallis, oils, 1856 (*The death of Chatterton*; Meredith as model), Tate collection · D. G. Rossetti, sketch, *c.*1860 (*Mary Magdalene at the gate of Simon the Pharisee*; Meredith as model) · Hillyer,

photograph, 1887 · H. Roller, photograph, 1888 · F. Hollyer, cabinet photograph, 1890?, NPG [*see illus.*] · G. F. Watts, oils, 1893, NPG · J. S. Sergent, charcoal drawing, 1896, FM Cam. · M. Menpes, drypoint etching, 1900 · J. S. Sergent, drawings, 1901 · A. L. Coburn, photograph, Oct 1904, NPG; repro. in T. Cooper and others, *Men of mark: a gallery of contemporary portraits* (1913) · W. Strang, oils, 1906, NPG · W. Strang, chalk drawing, 1908, Royal Collection · T. Spencer-Simson, bronze medallion, before 1910, NPG · M. Beerbohm, caricature, AM Oxf.; repro. in *VF* (24 Sept 1896) · M. Beerbohm, double portrait, caricature, sketch (with Kipling), NYPL, Hall Caine and Swinburne collection · C. Holroyd, bronze medals, NPG, Tate collection · E. T. Reid, caricature, repro. in *Punch* (28 July 1894) · Violet, duchess of Rutland, pencil drawing, Scot. NPG · Mrs S. Trower, photograph (aged sixty-eight) · E. J. Wheeler, caricature, repro. in *Punch* (19 Dec 1891) · photograph (aged thirty-five) · photograph (aged eighty) · photograph, University College Medical School, London · photographs, repro. in *The memorial edition*, 27 vols. (1909–11) · photographs, repro. in Ellis, *George Meredith* · photographs, repro. in Hammerton, *George Meredith* · photographs, repro. in W. M. Meredith, *Letters of George Meredith*, 2 vols. (1912)
Wealth at death £32,359 3*s.* 10*d.*: probate, 1909, *CGPLA Eng. & Wales* · £33,701 15*s.* 10*d.*: *Letters of George Meredith*, ed. Cline, 2, 1067n

Meredith [*née* Twamley], **Louisa Anne** (1812–1895), writer and naturalist, was born on 20 July 1812 at 47 Newhall Street, Birmingham, the daughter of Thomas Twamley (1757–1834), miller and corn inspector, and his wife, Louisa Anne Meredith (1769–1840). Educated at home, as a young adult she became a centre of lively interest in Birmingham literary, artistic, and Chartist groups. By 1836 she was a published poet and artist. Leigh Hunt was impressed by her early volume *Poems* (1835), and in his poem 'Blue Stocking Revels' teasingly wrote:

> Then came young Twamley, nice sensitive thing,
> Whose pen and whose pencil give promise like Spring
> (Miller, 89)

On 18 April 1839 at Edgbaston old church, near Birmingham, Louisa Twamley married her cousin Charles Meredith (1811–1880), from Van Diemen's Land, and embarked with him to Sydney on the *Letitia* in June 1839, arriving on 27 September. One economically unsuccessful year in New South Wales produced Meredith's first child and her sharply observed *Notes and Sketches of New South Wales* (1844), and occasioned the couple's retreat to the Meredith family estates in Van Diemen's Land, where they arrived in Hobart Town on 21 October 1840 on the *Sir George Arthur*.

Here began a permanent colonial exile for Louisa Meredith, except for one visit to England at the age of seventy-nine. Following Charles's lacklustre career they moved from one Meredith property to another: Cambria, Riversdale, and Spring Vale, near Swansea; Lath Hall and Poyston at Port Sorell, where Charles was police magistrate; Plas Newydd, where Meredith wrote her second book of social history, *Over the Straits: a Visit to Victoria* (1861); Twamley, on Prosser's Plains, and Malunnah, Orford. One break from settler life spent at Government House in Hobart in late 1845 allowed Meredith to mix with Hobart's impressive group of artists, including John Skinner Prout, and

Louisa Anne Meredith (1812–1895), by unknown photographer

reawaken her talent for social engagement and commentary. It was a visit to Victoria in 1856 that produced *Over the Straits*.

In the 1860s and 1870s, while Louisa Meredith was sharing and orchestrating her husband's successes as a founding member of the parliament of Tasmania, her career as writer, botanist, and artist brought her at last to individual prominence in England and Australia. Following on her early naturalist English books and poems, and mostly publishing in both London and Hobart, she combined her narrative, naturalist, and artistic talents to produce gorgeous folio celebrations of the natural life of Tasmania. Her valuable record of life and landscape, vivid, accurate, and readable, is also punctuated with elegiac passages on the rapid destruction of that world by the settler invasion.

Louisa Meredith's best writing uses an engaging personal narrative to convey accurate descriptive information. Her major works, *Notes and Sketches*, *Over the Straits*, and *My Home in Tasmania* (1852), reveal a shrewd observer, appreciative and accurate. *My Home in Tasmania* is invaluable as the first detailed account of this colony by a woman settler. By contrast to the sharp-sighted realism of this writing, Meredith's verse, though confidently fluid, is conventional in sentiment, and became increasingly moralistic. Even so, the late *Grandmama's Verse-Book for Young Australia* (1878) is significant as the first book of lively poems written for Tasmanian children about their own bushland creatures.

Though she always regretted her Tasmanian exile, Louisa Meredith's rich appreciation of the island produced not only a valuable historical record of colonial Tasmania, but a first evolving aesthetic and scientific view of the island inscribed and illustrated in fine books for its own people and the English-speaking world. She won literary distinctions, awards, and medals at exhibitions around the world and was a notable scientific collector and correspondent.

Between 1840 and 1847 Louisa and Charles Meredith had four sons, the second dying in infancy. Class-conscious and racially prejudiced, but always energetically creative, independently minded, and resourceful, Louisa Meredith died in Fitzroy, a small inner suburb of Melbourne at the home of friends, 171 Victoria Parade, on 21 October 1895, and was buried in Swansea, Tasmania.

ELIZABETH LAWSON

Sources V. Rae-Ellis, *Louisa Anne Meredith: a tigress in exile* (1979) · J. M. Buchanan, 'Mrs Charles Meredith: a biography, 1812–1895', MA thesis, University of Melbourne, 1950 · L. Meredith, *My home in Tasmania* (1852) · Mrs C. Meredith, *Notes and sketches in New South Wales* (1844) · L. A. Meredith, *Over the straits* (1861) · M. Swann, 'Mrs Meredith and Miss Atkinson, writers and naturalists', *Royal Australian Historical Society Journal and Proceedings*, 15 (1929–30), 1–29 · D. C. Miller, 'Mrs Louisa Anne Meredith and her colour printed books', *Antiquarian Book Monthly Review*, 14 (1987), 88–95
Archives Royal Society of Tasmania, Hobart family corresp. · State Library of Tasmania, Hobart family MSS · University of Tasmania, Hobart family letters | Mitchell L., NSW, letters to Sir Henry Parkes
Likenesses C. A. Woolley, photograph, 1866, Allport Library and Museum of Fine Arts, Hobart, Tasmania · J. W. Beattie, photograph, 1895, Allport Library and Museum of Fine Arts, Hobart, Tasmania · photograph, Allport Library and Museum of Fine Arts, Hobart, Tasmania [*see illus.*]
Wealth at death relative poverty: Rae-Ellis, *Louisa Anne Meredith*, 257

Meredith, Richard (d. 1597), Church of Ireland bishop of Leighlin, was a native of Denbighshire and a son of Robert Meredith ap Gronw and his wife, Margaret, daughter of William John ap Gronw. Meredith matriculated at Oxford in 1568, taking the degree of BA at Jesus College on 4 March 1573 and that of MA on 1 June 1575. In 1578 he became prebendary at Brecon collegiate church and rector of Barton in Pembrokeshire. In 1579 he became vicar of Llanafan Fawr, Brecknockshire, and in 1580 rector of Nangle in Pembrokeshire and cursal prebendary of St David's. He married Sarah Batho, with whom he had at least three sons and three surviving daughters. Her brother became his steward.

In 1584 Meredith was appointed chaplain to the new lord deputy of Ireland, Sir John Perrot, whom he accompanied to Dublin. In June 1584 he became dean of St Patrick's Cathedral, Dublin. In this office he seems to have acquitted himself well, and in July 1588 he was noted for 'diligent preaching' and keeping 'a good house to the relief of many people which likeness was not done this 30 years by his predecessors' (PRO, SP 63/135/79). He was a loyal supporter of Perrot, and, when the lord deputy was opposed by Archbishop Loftus in his proposals for diverting revenues of St Patrick's to the establishment of a university, Meredith took his part.

On 13 April 1589 Meredith was appointed by letters patent to the see of Leighlin and was consecrated by Archbishop Adam Loftus of Dublin. Meredith was not also bishop of Ferns, as noted in the *Dictionary of National Biography*. A later carving on his monument at St Patrick's Cathedral described him as being of Leighlin and Ferns, but this was an error. The state papers make this clear, as do the several episcopal lists and biographies that deal with the period: Hugh Allen (*d.* 1599) was bishop of Ferns during this time. Leighlin and Ferns were not merged until 1600, on the accession of Robert Grave. Because of the poverty of his new diocese, worth some £50 a year, Meredith was allowed to hold the deanery of St Patrick's *in commendam*, it yielding, according to the bishop's own calculations, 'in tithe corn, one year with another, 2500 pecks of castle measure, besides rent beeves' (PRO, SP 63/164/34). On Perrot's return to England in 1588, attempts were made by his enemies to implicate him in treasonous correspondence with the king of Spain. Bishop Meredith produced evidence suggesting that papers which substantiated the charges were forgeries composed by a priest, Denis O'Rowghan, and an accomplice, Henry Bird. As a result of his support for Perrot, Meredith was imprisoned in the Fleet. Although a servant who had 'wrongly charged' the bishop recanted his statement (PRO, SP 63/164/33), Meredith appeared before the Star Chamber in May 1592 and was fined £2000. This was remitted in March 1593, on condition that Meredith pay the queen an annuity of 300 marks for ten years.

By 1593 Meredith was in poor health and 'not like to live', but this did not preclude his being summoned before the Dublin court of castle chamber in January 1594. Arising from a dispute within Leighlin concerning the stipend of a schoolmaster named Brock, the subsheriff, under warrant of the lord deputy, had 'taken up' certain moneys from the bishop's steward. In response, Meredith was declared to have said publicly that within the diocese of Leighlin the lord deputy would 'do what I will him to do with his sword and I will command him and his sword' (PRO, SP 63/173/13). For these 'undutiful speeches', he was fined £20 with a sentence of eight days in prison. But Meredith's tribulations seem to have left him unbroken in spirit, and he was noted for his wit and humour. In prison he was reported to be 'as merry as ever he was'. He had a rueful view of Irish political life, remarking to a newly appointed bishop who had charged him with a broken promise that 'when you have been in Ireland a twelvemonth, no man will believe a word that you speak' (PRO, SP 63/157/37iii, 63/202/57).

Bishop Meredith died at Dublin on 3 August 1597 and was buried in St Patrick's Cathedral. He was survived by his wife. Although he had re-edified the episcopal buildings of his see, he appears to have retained significant financial resources. Bishop Lyon of Cork had once rather sourly noted that Meredith could 'as well skill to buy and sell matters belonging to the church as some meaner can'

(PRO, SP 63/141/21vii). His will dated 28 July 1587 bequeathed money to his daughters, provided they remained chaste until marriage, and £100 to Dublin corporation. His youngest son inherited an estate in Pembrokeshire. The eldest son, Robert, knighted on 6 September 1635 by the earl of Strafford, was an Irish privy councillor and chancellor of the Irish exchequer. Meredith's second son, Thomas, also knighted, held lands at Dollardstown, co. Meath.   HELEN COBURN WALSHE

Sources PRO, State papers, Ireland, Elizabeth I, SP 63 · *CSP Ire., 1509–1625* · W. M. Mason, *History … of the cathedral church of St Patrick's* (1819) · H. Cotton, *Fasti ecclesiae Hibernicae*, 2 (1848) · W. M. Brady, *The Irish Reformation* (1867) · J. Morrin, ed., *Calendar of the patent and close rolls of chancery in Ireland*, 3 vols. (1861–3) · *Wood, Ath. Oxon.*, new edn · *DNB* · J. Lodge, *The peerage of Ireland*, rev. M. Archdall, rev. edn, 7 vols. (1789)

Wealth at death some property left to offspring; £100 to Dublin corporation; allowance to poor; £800 due to estate from Archbishop Loftus and sons: will, 28 July 1597, noted Mason, *History*

Meredith, Richard (1558/9–1621), dean of Wells, was born in Bath and admitted scholar of Winchester College, aged fourteen, in 1573. He was admitted scholar of New College, Oxford, in 1576, and elected fellow in 1578; he proceeded BCL in 1584. On 20 November 1584 he was presented to the living of the former abbey church of Sts Peter and Paul, Bath; he also held the rectory of Portishead from May 1597, at the presentation of Sir Thomas Cecil, Lord Burghley's eldest son. From 1598 he appears as chaplain to Sir Robert Cecil, Burghley's second son, and from 1599 was appointed to preach at court on the special Lent rota. He was made chaplain to James I, and in February 1606 preached two sermons before him that contained scathing indictments of sermon centred piety and urged a renewed commitment to liturgical worship. These, Meredith's only surviving works, were licensed for printing by another Cecil chaplain, Richard Neile, and are some of the earliest published expressions of the avant-garde conformity later more widely promulgated by Neile and William Laud.

On 9 November 1607 Meredith was presented by the king to the deanery of Wells, and was admitted a canon residentiary shortly afterwards; thereupon he resigned the rectory of Bath but retained Portishead. He appears to have remained thereafter in Somerset, only appearing as a court Lent preacher again in 1608 and 1611. In 1609 he also became ordinary of St Cuthbert's, Wells. His wife (whose identity is unknown) and daughter were buried in the cathedral in 1613, and he seems neither to have remarried nor to have left an heir. Meredith's churchmanship was marked by a nostalgia for pre-Reformation forms that could be judged extreme even by later Laudian standards. In 1620 and in his will of July 1621 he left a total of £200 for the installation of new organs in the cathedral. He also instructed the vicars choral of the cathedral to 'singe my Requiem', and expressed the hope 'that my soule shalbe carried forthwith by Angels into Abrahams bosome'— both striking allusions to proscribed Roman rites for the dead. The beneficiaries named in his will include no relations, but many associates from the clerical and civic élites of Bath and Wells, several of whom were later key supporters of William Laud during his brief tenure of the see from 1626 to 1628. These include Sir Arthur Duck, then chancellor of Bath and Wells and later Laud's chief legal aide, and Duck's relations by marriage, Sir Henry Southworth and Thomas Southworth, the latter recorder of Wells. Meredith instructed that his library be divided between 'our towne church' (presumably St Cuthbert's) and Dr Timothy Revett, canon of Wells and archdeacon of Bath. A wealthy man, Meredith also left £200 for a marble monument, and requested burial in Wells Cathedral choir 'as neare as possible may be to my Stalle' (will). He died in Wells on 15 August 1621.　　　　P. E. McCULLOUGH

Sources will, PRO, PROB 11/139, fols. 136–7 · R. Meredith, *Two sermons* (1606) · *Calendar of the manuscripts of the dean and chapter of Wells*, 2, HMC, 12 (1914) · *Fasti Angl., 1541–1857*, [Bath and Wells] · F. W. Weaver, ed., *Somerset incumbents* (privately printed, Bristol, 1889) · *Calendar of the manuscripts of the most hon. the marquis of Salisbury*, 24 vols., HMC, 9 (1883–1976) · Westminster Abbey muniment book 15, Westminster Abbey library, London · T. F. Kirby, *Winchester scholars: a list of the wardens, fellows, and scholars of … Winchester College* (1888) · BL, Lansdowne MS 984 · Foster, *Alum. Oxon.*
Wealth at death cash bequests of approx £1000; plus books, diamond rings, and gold: will, PRO, PROB 11/139, fols. 136–7

Meredith [*née* Lloyd], **Susanna** (1823–1901), philanthropist, was born in southern Ireland, the eldest of four daughters of the governor of Cork county gaol. Her early life is obscure. Her physician husband died of cholera a few years after they married, leaving her a childless widow; she never remarried. At about this time she was teaching local poor women to earn a living by crocheting lace. In 1860 her father died and she went with her mother and sister, Mary Anne Lloyd, to live in London.

Susanna Meredith joined the governing body of the London Free Hospital and became familiar with philanthropic women in London. One of these described the suffering of the women prisoners of London: Meredith interpreted this as a call from God for her to redeem female prisoners, and in 1865 she set up the London Prison Mission. She and her fellow missioners visited the female convicts in Brixton Convict Prison and Fulham Women's Refuge in London. She was given free and unsupervised access to every woman in Brixton. However, with the rise of Sir Edmund Du Cane as chairman of directors of convict prisons and, after 1877, chairman of the Prison Commission which governed the newly nationalized local prisons, missionary schemes of prisoner redemption were sidelined. Her access to prisoners was increasingly blocked except under strict conditions, which she refused to accept. Thenceforth she attended only women who specifically asked her to visit.

In protest Susanna Meredith led several hundred volunteer women to establish prison gate missions outside the London women's prisons, such as Tothill Fields. Rooms were rented opposite these prisons and a breakfast was available to all being released. Employment was offered at a laundry owned by the mission, known as the Marble Laundry. By the late nineteenth century about 100 women were employed there at any one time: indeed, in 1893 about 800 women worked a total of nearly 17,000 days' work. The laundry served sick and destitute people in the Clapham area; the women former prisoners arrived at 8 o'clock for prayers and, taking their lunch on the premises, worked through the day until 7 o'clock in the evening. Alcohol was prohibited and the women were placed in nearby lodgings selected by the staff of the prison mission: their rent was paid direct out of their earnings at the laundry.

Susanna Meredith's second long-term project was the rescue of the daughters of criminals. Convinced that they were at risk of moral corruption she established the Princess Mary Village Homes at Addlestone in Surrey in 1871. Here her mission built twenty semi-detached cottages, in each of which were placed ten girls and a housemother assisted by an elder girl monitor. By 1901 over 1000 had passed through Addlestone. The aim was to create an intimate, tender, and highly moral family ethos to replace the presumed criminal and immoral model of the earlier family. Dr Barnardo drew from Meredith's model of cottage homes as an alternative to great barrack-like establishments when he planned his own homes for children in the early 1870s.

Separation from a contaminating social environment and exposure to a new pure moral ethos was an abiding theme of Susanna Meredith's general theory of the origins of crime. Thus her prison gate missions were designed to combat the influence of gang leaders who assembled outside the prisons to lure newly released women back to crime. She and her missionaries visited women former prisoners in the most notorious areas of London to induce them to break from criminal associates. A familiar figure, she was tolerated even by the gangs themselves in these areas. At her laundry, close supervision aimed to prevent any contamination, and evening behaviour was reported upon by the landlady.

But Susanna Meredith and her volunteer helpers, most of them deaconesses of the Church of England, saw themselves primarily as savers of souls. She started from the premise that all people are sinners, being prone to the 'natural enmity of the human heart' and separated by sin from their redeemer: redemption, she argued, is only possible through acceptance of Christ's atonement on the cross. She offered a counter-thesis to the hereditarian neo-Darwinian positivist criminology which was widely urged in the 1880s and 1890s: Meredith was convinced that, although heredity did establish character predisposition, it did not eliminate responsibility or capacity for remorse, nor did heredity alter the essence of the human being as child of God gone astray.

Susanna Meredith identified particular criminal patterns, arguing that individuals were characteristically subject to mercurial mood swings, and engaged in unstable and transient relationships and projects. Believing them volatile, false, and evasive, she saw them as slaves to instant self-gratification, very often addicted to the stupefying effects of alcohol. They met challenge with hardness of heart or self-exculpatory special pleading, and, despite attractive quirks, they were lost souls stumbling through their broken and destructive lives separated by the malicious wiles of Satan from the superabundant love of God. It was that superabundance upon which Meredith called as she pounded out her urgent message of repentance and salvation. She warned of the horror of 'the lake that burneth with everlasting fire', seeing a clear parallel between Satan's kingdom and the complexity of the criminal underworld with its power, temptation, malice, and terror. She grounded her mission on the teachings of scripture and resolutely met prevarication or falsehood with an appropriate biblical text, believing that criminals always won arguments based on logic chopping. Mrs Meredith believed that her relationships with women prisoners must be compassionate as well as firm, and that condescension, contempt, and hard-hearted piety merely alienated. She was, however, most passionate in her appeal to women offenders, and extremely direct and candid. It was those qualities of honesty and concern for the women which they claimed to remember most about her.

Susanna Meredith was a significant figure among Victorian middle-class women philanthropists of the period: like many others she saw it as her duty to reclaim souls, advancing what was, in part, a conservative vision of the role of women in society—as courageous nurturers, dutiful rescuers, benevolent representatives of middle-class charity, and, by implication, guarantors of wholesome social ties between the classes and the family base of Victorian society. Consequently, Susanna Meredith was strongly supported by the royal family and by Victorian aristocrats, including Lord and Lady Rookwood and the earl and countess of Meath, as well as by well-known figures in the Victorian legal and penal worlds.

Yet such philanthropic women were innovators, entering the field of social policy in a way which was new for women: Susanna Meredith was, for example, called in evidence before the Gladstone committee on prisons in 1895. Like many other women philanthropists she asserted her right to an independent life of public service, and challenged the attempt of the exclusively male prison commissioners to silence her, advancing her practice with considerable success.

Susanna Meredith was also interested in medical missions and in the 1870s ran the Battersea medical mission in London. She set up the Christian Women's Union and the Women's Missionary Association, the latter providing nursing and dispensary care in Palestine and Lebanon from 1894 onwards. She herself visited philanthropic projects and penal establishments in North America in 1879 and 1889, and imitative prison missions were set up in North America, Scotland, Sweden, and Ireland. Mrs Meredith wrote many pamphlets and reports about her work, but her beliefs are most plainly set out in *A Book about Criminals* and *Saved Rahab*, both published in 1881.

Susanna Meredith spent the last few years of her life living at Fairview, Woburn Hill, near the children's village at Addlestone, and in June 1895 she had a stroke from which she never fully recovered. She died there on 18 December 1901, and was buried in Brookwood cemetery near Woking in Surrey. Throughout her life she was greatly helped by her sister Mary Anne Lloyd. She was remembered for her intense sympathy for suffering people and her great love of young people. A most natural personality, uninhibited in humour and self-expression, her most noted trait was her entirely genuine kindness of heart.

BILL FORSYTHE

Sources S. Meredith, *Saved Rahab* (1881) · M. A. Lloyd, *Susanna Meredith: record of a vigorous life* (1903) · 'Departmental committee on prisons', *Parl. papers* (1895), 56.1, C. 7702; 56.55, C. 7702-I · 'Directors of convict prisons', *Parl. papers* (1867–8), 34.519, no. 4083; (1868–9), vol. 30, no. 4212; (1870), vol. 38, C. 204 [annual reports] · L. Zedner, *Women, crime, and custody in Victorian England* (1991) · Baroness Burdett-Coutts [A. G. Burdett-Coutts], ed., *Woman's mission: a series of congress papers on the philanthropic work of women* (1893) · J. Parker, *Women and welfare: ten Victorian women in public service* (1988) · F. K. Prochaska, *Women and philanthropy in nineteenth-century England* (1980) · *The Times* (19 April 1901) · *The Times* (12 July 1901) · *The Times* (25 March 1901) · S. Meredith, *A book about criminals* (1881) · E. M. Tomkinson, *The world's workers: Sarah Robinson, Agnes Weston, Mrs Meredith* (1887) · CGPLA Eng. & Wales (1902)
Archives Surrey HC, papers of the Princess Mary Village Homes
Likenesses photograph (after portrait?), repro. in Tomkinson, *World's workers*
Wealth at death £1200 12s. 8d.: probate, 5 April 1902, CGPLA Eng. & Wales

Meredith, Sir William, third baronet (*bap.* 1724, *d.* 1790), politician, was baptized at St John the Baptist, Chester, on 10 March 1724, the first son of Amos Meredith (1688–1744) and his wife, Joanna (*bap.* 1692), daughter of Thomas Cholmondeley MP, of Vale Royal, Cheshire. He was admitted to Westminster School in October 1738 and matriculated from Christ Church, Oxford, on 24 March 1743. On his father's death at Bath on 6 May 1744 he became heir to the family title and estates, which descended to him on the demise of his grandfather, Sir William Meredith, second baronet (1655–1752), in January 1752. He remained a bachelor, although his marriage on 17 November 1747 to Miss Cheetham of Mellor, Derbyshire, was mistakenly announced in the *Gentleman's Magazine* (17, 1747, 544).

Meredith considered himself a tory at this stage and the University of Oxford showed its approval of his politics by conferring the degree of DCL upon him on 14 April 1749. Both his father and his maternal uncle Charles Cholmondeley (1685–1756) were close friends of the prominent Jacobite James Barry, fourth earl of Barrymore. At the general election of 1754 Meredith was returned at Wigan, Lancashire, with Barrymore's second son, the Hon. Richard Barry (1720?–1787). Unsurprisingly these political connections prompted Richard Rigby to condemn Meredith for being 'as determined a Jacobite' 'as any in the House of Commons' (*Correspondence of … Bedford*, 2.159). Horace Walpole similarly portrayed him later as 'a convert from Jacobitism' (Walpole, *Memoirs*, 1.279), an accusation that Meredith strenuously denied.

Meredith's position at Wigan became untenable when the whigs secured the mayoralty in their favour in 1760 following two years of heated litigation. At the general election of 1761 he therefore turned his attention to Liverpool instead, where his success in the contest owed much to the support of the independently minded lower trades-men and dissenters against the Anglican dominated cor-poration interest. He was now considered a follower of Lord Bute and he initially supported George Grenville. However, when his supporters secured the mayoralty in their favour in late October 1763 Meredith's position was sufficiently well consolidated for him to reveal his true feelings. On 5 November 1763 he expressed his 'irrepar-able' (Jucker, 214) disappointment over Grenville's refusal to allow him to dispose of local patronage:

> Having acted with Administration without a thought for myself against the sense of my constituents … I own I did hope to have been allowed the same degree of credit as my predecessors did … especially after Lord Bute had told me '*I might command* (I repeat his words) as much regard from him as was ever shewn to a Member for Liverpool'.   (ibid., 215)

Ten days later Meredith voted against Grenville on the Wilkes case. On 14 February 1764 Meredith marked him-self out as a leading opponent by moving that a general warrant was 'not warranted by law' (*JHC*, 29.843). His brother-in-law Frederick Vane (1732–1801), who had mar-ried Henrietta Meredith in 1758, seconded the motion. Meredith now joined the opposition Wildman's Club and entered into a connection with the duke of Portland, one of the most enthusiastic of the Rockingham whigs. Late in 1764, after submitting his text to the duke of Newcastle for comment, Meredith published an anonymous *Reply to the 'Defence of the Majority in the House of Commons on General Warrants'* by Charles Lloyd. On 29 January 1765 he again unsuccessfully moved the illegality of general warrants. Walpole now described him as 'inflexibly serious, and of no clear head', but whose words were 'worth attending to by those who had patience for it', 'an honest man, though not without personal views, which a little sharpened his scorn of those who had unlike views, and were not equally honest' (Walpole, *Memoirs*, 1.279).

As MP for a great trading centre Meredith naturally developed colonial contacts. During the passage of the American Currency Bill in April 1764 he acted as a medi-ator between the Board of Trade and the colonial agents watching the Commons debate from the gallery. On 6 Feb-ruary 1765 he spoke against Grenville's Stamp Act, warn-ing that

> We ought … to be extremely delicate in imposing a burden upon others which we not only do not share ourselves but which is to take it far from us. If we tax America we shall supersede the necessity of their assembling.
> ('Parliamentary diaries of Nathaniel Ryder', 259)

He opposed the bill again on 15 February and presented a petition from Virginia against it.

On the formation of the Rockingham ministry in July 1765 Meredith became a lord of the Admiralty. As the Stamp Act crisis raged he overrode attempts by the Liver-pool corporation to suppress a circular in favour of repeal from the London North American merchants committee. He also co-operated with local mercantile interests who were preparing evidence on the detrimental effects of the act for presentation to a Commons committee. On 22 April 1766 he worked with Sir George Savile to obtain the

long cherished, but purely symbolic resolution declaring general warrants illegal.

When the Chatham administration was formed in July 1766 Meredith was among those who initially remained in office, but he joined the Rockinghams when they entered into opposition in late November 1766. Meredith was soon urging the union of the opposition parties, particularly in a series of enthusiastic letters to Portland. In February 1767 he sent Newcastle his analysis of the voting in the land tax division. Despite his eagerness, Rockingham's immediate circle maintained a lingering distrust of Mere-dith's earlier allegiances. On 17 February 1768 Meredith's impassioned speech on the Nullum Tempus Bill, which affected Portland's interests, thoroughly alarmed Rock-ingham: 'He was weak and strained his voice to a degree that I feared his lungs would suffer. He fairly exhausted himself of bodily strength but not before the strength of his arguments had made real impression' (BL, Add. MS 32988, fols. 369–70). Walpole later recorded that he spoke on this occasion 'with more applause than he had ever done' (Walpole, *Memoirs*, 3.115).

At the general election of 1768 mobs armed with bludgeons caused violent pro-corporation unrest against Meredith and Richard Pennant at Liverpool, but the pair were returned unopposed. Meredith's carefully cultivated interest, based on strong support from the lower freemen and tradesmen, ensured that he was now a considerable figure in his own right in parliament even without his party connection with Rockingham. An assiduous elec-tioneer, he was also active on Portland's behalf at Wigan, where he had been building up a party in the duke's inter-est since 1763. He also assisted in securing the return of Portland's brother-in-law Booth Grey at Leicester and of Lord John Cavendish at Lancaster.

In 1769 and 1770 Meredith opposed the government in the Commons over Wilkes and the Middlesex election. He also composed a pamphlet, *The question stated, whether the freeholders of Middlesex lost their right by voting for Mr. Wilkes*, a draft of which was discussed by the Rockinghams at a meeting on 17 May 1769. Meredith argued that the legal right to elect was a property right, which could not be taken from freeholders by an arbitrary resolution of the Commons. Nathaniel Forster produced an antagonistic answer and the constitutional expert Sir William Black-stone published his *Letter to Sir William Meredith*. Meredith himself replied with *A Letter to Dr. Blackstone* (1770), the draft of which was read by Rockingham, who approved of it 'most exceedingly' (Rockingham to Portland, 17 Dec 1769, Portland MSS). Despite his strong feelings on the issue, Meredith was wary of inflaming controversy in Liv-erpool and gave only grudging assistance to his local sup-porters when they decided to join the petitioning move-ment. As he informed Rockingham on 18 October 1769, he urged them to exercise restraint because 'they were con-tinually asking the assistance of ministers and should therefore be cautious of offending them' (Rockingham MSS).

Other issues also attracted Meredith's attention. In

March 1770 he joined his future brother-in-law Barlow Trecothick in urging a repeal of the American tea duty. On 11 February 1771 he introduced an ultimately unsuccessful bill to repeal a clause in the Nullum Tempus Act, an amendment which would have worked in Portland's favour. When the printers' case arose in 1771 Meredith warned the government that it risked involving the kingdom in unnecessary distress and on 27 March 1771 he spoke against committing Brass Crosby to the Tower. Earlier that day he had fearlessly intervened to rescue Lord North, who was hurt when a large and excited mob smashed the windows of his coach and proceeded to wreck the vehicle. In gratitude North bestowed on Sir William's younger brother, Theophilus Meredith (1731?–1775), then rector of Linton, Herefordshire, the more lucrative benefice of nearby Ross-on-Wye.

As the opposition to North collapsed Meredith began to drift away from the Rockinghams. On 14 November 1770, the day after Grenville's death, John Calcraft reported optimistically to Chatham that Meredith was 'impatient to see your Lordship, and adopt your plans' (*Correspondence of William Pitt*, 3.448). The Rockinghams had their suspicions confirmed on 7 March 1771 when Meredith spoke against Dowdeswell's Jury Bill and adopted Chatham's argument that the bill should be declaratory not enacting. By 1772 he was 'supposed by the Rockingham party to lean to the court' (*Last Journals of Horace Walpole*, 1.43) over the Royal Marriage Bill, but he voted against the measure. Subsequently, he continued to cause North's administration some discomfiture. As a member of Burgoyne's committee on East India affairs, he was 'hot on the pursuit of Clive' (ibid., 1.230) and on 10 May 1773 he seconded Burgoyne's resolutions of censure. As one of the 'particular friends' (ibid., 1.371) of George III's brother, the duke of Gloucester, who had been secretly married since 1766, Meredith was present at the birth of the duchess's child on 29 May 1773. None the less, Meredith kissed hands in March 1774 as 'comptroller of the household and privy councillor' and he was soon forced to acquiesce in a royal command not to visit the duke. He also curried favour with North by publishing *A Letter to the Earl of Chatham on the Quebec Bill* (1774), which prompted an anonymous *Letter to Sir William Meredith* (1774) in reply. Meredith's transfer of loyalty utterly destroyed his reputation. Horace Walpole now described him disparagingly as 'that fluctuating patriot who has broken with all parties and at last has dropped anchor at his own interest' (ibid., 1.311).

Meredith was more favourably remembered for his unsuccessful championing of religious dissent and reform of the criminal law. John Jebb addressed his *Letter on Subscription* (1772) to Meredith personally and Sir William contributed a piece on religious toleration to the *Gentleman's Magazine* (43, 1773, 216–17). On 6 February 1772 he presented to the Commons a petition signed by almost 250 'clergy men of the Church of England, and certain members of the professions of civil law and physic, and some others, who prayed for relief from subscription to the 39 Articles' (*Annual Register*, 1772, 171–3). It was rejected and his motions against subscription on 23 February 1773

and 5 May 1774 were also unsuccessful. Walpole described Meredith as 'remarkably averse to punishments that reached the lives of criminals' (Walpole, *Memoirs*, 3.208) and he moved for an inquiry into the state of the criminal law on 27 November 1770. He raised the issue again on 13 May 1777 with a reasoned plea against capital punishment for minor offences. His speech was published shortly afterwards as *Punishment of Death* (1777), but Meredith was far in advance of prevailing opinion. However, in the changing climate of the early 1830s the third edition of his text ran to 60,000 copies and further reprints followed.

At the general election of 1774 Meredith was once again returned unopposed for Liverpool. On 20 December 1774, as the American crisis escalated, he 'imputed all the present troubles to the Declaratory Act asserting the supremacy of Great Britain' (Almon, 1.29). This view was reiterated on 10 February 1775, when he claimed to have opposed the act and asserted that he 'would never have taken the part he did, could he have supposed the ministers who gave up the advantages would have maintained the principle of taxing America' (ibid., 1.177). However, former Rockinghamite ministerial colleagues argued that he had never previously objected to the act. Meredith's resignation in early December 1777 was even more controversial. He was 'treated by both sides with equal contempt' (*Last Journals of Horace Walpole*, 2.81) because it coincided almost exactly with the public announcement of Burgoyne's surrender at Saratoga. On 10 December he was accused in the Commons of 'deserting his principles, and his friends the ministers, in the hour of their dismay' (Almon, 8.156), and his insistence 'that he had never voted for any one measure that tended to create or to support this war' (ibid.) carried little weight. The Rockinghams were not prepared to forgive his inconsistency and never accepted him back. Subsequently, Meredith moved unsuccessfully for the repeal of the Declaratory Act on 6 April 1778 and for peace with America on 11 June 1779. Thirty copies of his learned *Historical Remarks on the Taxation of Free States* (1778) were also printed anonymously at this time.

In 1779 Meredith's extravagance finally obliged him to sell the family property at Henbury for £24,000. By the time of the parliamentary dissolution in 1780, his chief Liverpool antagonist, Bamber Gascoyne, and the corporation had won control of the constituency and Meredith announced his decision not to stand, pleading illness. He attempted to regain the seat in 1784, but withdrew before the end of the poll. In late 1785 there were rumours that he would be appointed to assist William Eden in the commercial negotiations at Paris, but he was becoming an increasingly obscure figure. Following his death at Lyons, France, on 2 January 1790, the baronetcy became extinct.

PATRICK WOODLAND

Sources J. Brooke, 'Meredith, Sir William', HoP, *Commons, 1754–90* · H. Walpole, *Memoirs of the reign of King George the Third*, ed. G. F. R. Barker, 4 vols. (1894) · *The last journals of Horace Walpole*, ed. Dr Doran, rev. A. F. Steuart, 2 vols. (1910) · Rockingham MSS, Sheff. Arch., Wentworth Woodhouse muniments · Sheff. Arch., Wentworth Woodhouse muniments · U. Nott. L., Portland MSS · 'Parliamentary diaries of Nathaniel Ryder, 1764–7', ed. P. D. G. Thomas, *Camden miscellany, XXIII*, CS, 4th ser., 7 (1969) · *The Jenkinson papers,*

1760–1766, ed. N. S. Jucker (1949) • *GM*, 1st ser., 17 (1747), 544 • *GM*, 1st ser., 36 (1766), 166–9, 209–12 • *GM*, 1st ser., 43 (1773), 171–3 • *GM*, 1st ser., 60 (1790), 85–6, 272 • *IGI* • G. Ormerod, *The history of the county palatine and city of Chester*, 2nd edn, ed. T. Helsby, 3 (1882), 650, 708 • Foster, *Alum. Oxon.* • *Annual Register* (1772), 171–3 • *Correspondence of John, fourth duke of Bedford*, ed. J. Russell, 3 vols. (1842–6) • *Correspondence of William Pitt, earl of Chatham*, ed. W. S. Taylor and J. H. Pringle, 4 vols. (1838–40) • J. Almon, ed., *The parliamentary register, or, History of the proceedings and debates of the House of Commons*, 17 vols. (1775–80), vol. 1, p. 177 • R. J. S. Hoffman, *The marquis: a study of Lord Rockingham, 1730–1782* (1973) • F. O'Gorman, *The rise of party in England: the Rockingham whigs, 1760–1782* (1975) • P. Langford, *The first Rockingham administration, 1765–1766* (1973) • P. D. G. Thomas, *John Wilkes: a friend to liberty* (1996) • G. Rudé, *Wilkes and liberty: a social study of 1763 to 1774* (1962) • J. Brooke, *The Chatham administration, 1766–1768* (1956) • P. D. G. Thomas, *British politics and the Stamp Act crisis: the first phase of the American revolution, 1763–1767* (1975) • P. D. G. Thomas, *The Townshend duties crisis* (1987) • J. Brewer, *Party ideology and popular politics at the accession of George III* (1976) • L. B. Namier, *England in the age of the American revolution*, 2nd edn (1963) • *DNB*

Archives Sheff. Arch., letters to Charles, second marquess of Rockingham • U. Nott. L., letters to duke of Portland
Likenesses T. Watson, mezzotint, pubd 1773 (after D. Gardner), BM, NPG
Wealth at death Henbury, Cheshire, sold for £24,000, 1779 because of mounting debts; most presumably dissipated before death: Ormerod, *History of the county palatine and city of Chester*, 3.708

Meredith, William Henry [Billy] (**1874–1958**), footballer, was born on 30 July 1874 at Blackpark, Chirk, Denbighshire, the ninth of ten children of Henry Meredith (*d.* 1904), mining engine winder, and his wife, Jane, *née* Hughes (*d.* 1904). Both parents were Welsh, originally of farming stock, having travelled in 1873 from Trevonin to Chirk in search of work. Meredith attended the local Chirk School until the age of twelve, when he obtained work at the nearby Black Park colliery, initially as a pony driver and 'hutcher' before later becoming a boiler-firer. His ambition was then to become a mining engineer, but he was already a precocious footballer.

By the age of fifteen Meredith was playing for Chirk reserves; by eighteen was a first team member, and in 1894 he won a Welsh cup medal. Uncertainty in the mining industry in 1893 led him to follow the example of his brother Sam, then a professional with Stoke City, to play semi-professionally for Northwich Victoria of the second division of the Football League. In September 1894 he signed professional forms for Manchester City, also in the second division, and in January 1895 he finally gave up his job at Black Park.

Meredith was a forward, a right-winger, noted for his 'Scottish-style' close ball control and trickery. He was also a prolific goalscorer, and set many records for both club and country. In his first ten years with Manchester City he captained the club to promotion to the first division and, in 1904, to the club's first significant trophy, the FA cup. Meredith scored the only goal in a 1–0 victory over Bristol City at Crystal Palace.

The following season Meredith was accused by the Football Association of accepting illegal wage payments and of attempting to fix the result of a crucial league match, an

William Henry [Billy] **Meredith** (**1874–1958**), by Francis Fielding, *c.*1904

accusation he always denied. He was suspended from September 1905 to January 1907 and was banned from playing for Manchester City for life. He was subsequently bought by Manchester United, and made his début for them in January 1907. He played for Manchester United for the next eight seasons, before professional football closed down in 1915 for the duration of the First World War. With Manchester United he won two league championships in 1908 and 1911 and helped the club to its first FA cup win in 1909.

Meredith also had a prolific international career for Wales. For many years he held the record for the highest number of appearances in a Welsh jersey (forty-eight) and he was, along with brother Sam, a member of the first Welsh team to win the home international championship, in the 1906–7 season.

Angered by the financial restrictions placed upon professional footballers and wanting to create more secure working conditions for professionals, Meredith was instrumental in forming the Players' Union in December 1907, and chaired its inaugural meeting at the Imperial

Hotel, Manchester. The abolition of the maximum wage, the ending of restrictions on the freedom of movement of players between clubs, and the recognition by the FA that professional footballers were bona fide workers with the same rights of access to employment law as other workers—these were key aims of the union. Insurance against injury and the establishment of a pension fund were also important items on the new union's agenda.

The organization struggled for two years to establish itself before, in March 1909, the Football Association—annoyed at the union's insistence on taking clubs to court in pursuit of unpaid wages rather than addressing their complaints to the association as supreme governing body—decided to abolish it. Meredith and his Manchester United colleagues refused to resign from the union and were 'locked out' by their club. In September 1909, faced with a possible strike by professional players in support of Meredith and his 'outcasts' (as the locked-out men had become known), the FA relented and allowed the union to continue in existence. Meredith, though he never served in an official capacity in the organization, continued for the rest of his career to promote and publicize the union, principally via newspaper articles.

Meredith returned to Manchester City as a 'guest' player during the First World War and played in the war leagues for three years. In 1921 his registration with Manchester United was cancelled and he finished his playing career with Manchester City. His last competitive match was an FA cup semi-final in 1923 against Newcastle, when he was a couple of months short of his fiftieth birthday, an exceptional age for a full-time professional player.

Meredith was a popular subject for newspaper caricaturists during an era when sports photography was rudimentary. His toothpick, which he chewed incessantly while playing, was a readily identifiable trademark. He claimed he chewed toothpicks and matches instead of the traditional miner's tobacco twist, the latter being considered inappropriate for a footballer, since there were no convenient spittoons available at pitch-side. Fans would send him packets of toothpicks. His fitness was legendary: in a career of almost twenty years of top-class football, he hardly missed more than a dozen matches through injury. He was a strict teetotaller, a non-smoker, and a keen dietician, his spare, almost spindly frame leading to nicknames such as Old Skin, which he disliked. He was also ahead of his time where training was concerned: in an era when jogging and physical jerks were considered sufficient preparation for a game, he wrote many articles placing great emphasis on developing ball control. Until his fiftieth year he continued to polish his skills, insisting that no professional player could ever cease learning his trade.

Meredith married Ellen Negus (1879–1933), a local Chirk girl, in April 1900 at St Mark's Church, Clowes Street, Manchester, and lived for some years in Nut Street, Belle Vue, Manchester. They had two children: Lily, born in 1903, and Winifred, born in 1906. In 1904 he opened a sports goods shop in St Peter's Square, Manchester. The shop closed following a fire in 1909, however, and Meredith was declared bankrupt. In 1914 he took a public house, the Church Hotel in Longsight, Manchester, and in the 1920s and 1930s he and his wife managed a second public house, the Stretford Hotel, Stretford Road, Manchester.

In 1926 Meredith starred in a feature film, *The Ball of Fortune*, as well as a number of short coaching films. He would appear on stage in cinemas showing his films and answer questions from the audience. He was good friends with many music-hall stars of the pre-Second World War period, including George Robey (who designed Manchester United's cup final shirts in 1909) and Harry Weldon (who played Stiffy the Goalkeeper in a Fred Karno sketch that also featured Charlie Chaplin). The catch-phrase 'Meredith, we're in!' from another pre-First World War Karno sketch was said to have been inspired by Meredith.

In retirement Meredith lived in Manchester with his daughter Winifred, a champion dancer and later principal of her own dancing school. He died at his home, in Burton Road, Withington, Manchester, on 19 April 1958 from heart failure and was buried four days later in the southern cemetery, Manchester.   JOHN HARDING

Sources J. Harding, *Football wizard: the story of Billy Meredith* (1998) • personal knowledge (2004) • private information (2004) • b. cert. **Archives** Man. CL, Misc/897/1–76 | FILM Northwest Film Archive, Portland, Oregon, *Ball of Fortune*, 1926 | SOUND priv. coll., tape recording of interview, *c.*1947 [BBC Radio Wales, 'Sporting call']

Likenesses F. Fielding, photograph, *c.*1904, PRO [*see illus.*] • photographs, Greater Manchester County RO, Documentary Photography Archive

Meredith, Sir William Ralph (1840–1923), politician and judge in Canada, was born in the township of Westminster, Middlesex, Upper Canada (later Ontario), on 31 March 1840, the eldest son of John Walsingham Cooke Meredith (1809–1881), of London, Ontario, and his wife, Sarah, the daughter of Anthony Pegler, of the same town. His father was a farmer and businessman of Irish birth, and a graduate of Trinity College, Dublin. Meredith was educated at the London district grammar school; in 1859 he won a two-year scholarship to the Toronto law school, and in 1861 was called to the bar of Upper Canada. He took the degree of LLB at the University of Toronto in 1867. He practised law in London, Ontario, and became QC in 1875 and a bencher of the Law Society of Upper Canada in 1876. In 1888 he moved to Toronto, where from February to October 1894 he held the office of corporation counsel and head of the legal department of the city. He was knighted in 1896.

Meanwhile, in 1872, Meredith had been elected to represent London as a Conservative in the legislative assembly of Ontario, and in 1878 he became leader of the opposition. Although a forceful speaker and a man of great energy, Meredith was a failure in politics. He had not the political subtlety of Oliver Mowat, the Liberal leader in the provincial house, and his opinions were really much more radical than conservative. As early as 1875 he advocated manhood suffrage, and soon after made the compensation of workers for accidents a plank in his platform. He was too independent to see eye to eye with Sir John A. Macdonald, the Conservative leader in the federal house. At the same time his own views on federal–provincial relations led him to support Macdonald in his fight with Mowat on questions of provincial rights, such as Ontario's north-west boundary, and the ownership of crown lands.

Meredith opposed the Liberal policy of placing the department of education under a political minister, and urged that control be given to a non-political superintendent. An Anglican, he came into conflict with two outspoken bishops of the Roman Catholic church over educational policy, since he wished to curtail the power of the clergy over the separate (Catholic) schools. His political disputes with prominent Roman Catholic clerics over these issues embarrassed his federal leader, who depended largely upon the support of Francophone, Roman Catholic Quebec.

In 1894 Meredith retired from political life, and was appointed by the federal (Conservative) government chief justice of the common pleas division of the high court of justice of Ontario. During the breakup of the federal (Conservative) government in 1895–6, repeated but unsuccessful efforts were made, especially by Sir Charles Tupper, to induce him to leave the bench and to take a portfolio in the ministry. In 1912 he became chief justice of Ontario and thereby president *ex officio* of the appellate division. As a judge, Meredith took an important part in codifying the laws of the province. In 1896 he had been appointed a member of the commission for the revision of the provincial statutes, and did most of the work upon it. In 1910 he was the chairman of a provincial commission on whose report was based a substantial revision of the provincial statute awarding compensation to workers for injuries.

In 1895 Meredith was appointed to the senate of the University of Toronto, and served as its chancellor from 1900 to his death. In 1905 the Conservative provincial administration appointed a commission under Meredith's chairmanship to look into the affairs of the university, which had long been hampered by political interference. Following its recommendations, an act of 1906 placed the university under an independent board of governors, and greatly increased its financial support. Meredith was the first chair of the board of governors created by the 1906 act, and until his death advised the government in all matters relating to the university.

Meredith was a man of firm principles, great industry, and forceful personality. He died in Montreal on 21 August 1923, of a chill brought on by swimming. He was survived by his wife, Mary (d. 1930), the daughter of Marcus Holmes, of London, Ontario, whom he had married in June 1862. Their only son died on active service during the First World War; their three daughters survived him.

W. L. GRANT, rev. J. R. MILLER

Sources H. J. Morgan, ed., *The Canadian men and women of the time* (1898) • H. J. Morgan, ed., *The Canadian men and women of the time*, 2nd edn (1912) • P. E. P. Dembski, 'William Ralph Meredith: leader of the conservative opposition in Ontario, 1878–1894', PhD diss., University of Guelph, Canada, 1977 • P. E. P. Dembski, 'A matter of conscience: the origins of William Ralph Meredith's conflict with Archbishop John Joseph Lynch', *Ontario History*, 73 (1981), 131–44 • J. R. Miller, *Equal rights: the Jesuits' Estates Act controversy* (1979) • *The Globe* [Toronto] (22 Aug 1923) • *Daily Mail and Empire* [Toronto] (22 Aug 1923) • A. M. Evans, *Sir Oliver Mowat* (1992) • R. White, *Ontario, 1610–1985* (1985) • S. J. R. Noel, *Patrons, clients, brokers: Ontario society and politics, 1791–1896* (1990) • C. Armstrong, *The politics of federalism: Ontario's relations with the federal government, 1867–1942* (1981) • J. S. Willison, *Sir Wilfrid Laurier and the Liberal Party*, 2 vols. (1903)

Archives NA Canada | NA Canada, Sir John A. Macdonald MSS • Public Archives of Ontario, Toronto, Sir Oliver Mowat MSS • Public Archives of Ontario, Toronto, Sir James P. Whitney MSS

Meredyth. For this title name *see* Somerville, William Meredyth, first Baron Athlumney and first Baron Meredyth (1802–1873).

Meres, Francis (1565/6–1647), writer and translator, was the son of Thomas Meres of Kirton in Holland, Lincolnshire. He may be the Francis Meres baptized on 19 August 1565 in Grantham, Lincolnshire, or the one baptized on 10 March 1565 in Colsterworth, Lincolnshire, but neither identification is certain. The family had long been prominent in the county's affairs, supplying many members of parliament and high sheriffs during the fifteenth century. In Easter term 1584 Francis matriculated as a sizar at Pembroke College, Cambridge, graduating BA in 1587 and MA in 1591. On 10 July 1593 he was incorporated MA at Oxford, making him 'Maister of Arts in both Universities', as he called himself on the title-pages of several of his books.

For a time Meres returned to Lincolnshire and lived in Auborne at the house of his kinsman John Meres, high sheriff of the county, whose help he had earlier received in his unsuccessful quest for a postgraduate position at Cambridge. With his kinsman's further help, Meres sought a position with his powerful relative Lawrence Meres, member of the queen's council of the north. When that suit was also unsuccessful, Meres moved to London, where he began the brief but intense period of writing and translation upon which his fame rests.

He may be the F. M. who wrote a poem for *The Paradise of Dainty Devices* (1595), but his first definite publication is a 36-page sermon on the virtues of marriage entitled *Gods Arithmeticke*, published by Richard Jones in 1597. In a lengthy dedication to John Meres, one-third as long as the sermon itself, Meres contrasts godly addition and multiplication with the devil's operations of subtraction and division, using this metaphor as a springboard for his discussion of holy matrimony (which proves that 'two are better than one'). At the end of the dedication Meres expresses thanks for his kinsman's generosity, signing it 'From my Chamber in Saint Marie Buttolph-lane, neere London-Stone this 10 of October 1597' (sig. A7v).

After this original work Meres turned his attention to translating the religious works of Luis de Granada out of Spanish. The first of these, *The sinners guyde*, was entered on the Stationers' register on 2 August 1597 but not published until the following year, when it was issued by Paul Linley and John Flasket as a 525-page quarto. In his dedication to privy councillor Sir Thomas Egerton, thick with classical allusions and dated 10 May 1598, Meres calls the translation 'the fruites of a poor schollers study' (sig. A3v). One day later Meres wrote the dedication for his second translation, *Granados Devotion*, published by Cuthbert Burby as a 576-page octavo. Meres dedicated this volume to William Sammes of the Middle Temple, whom he called 'the kinde entertainer of vertue, the mirrour of a goode minde', promising to dedicate a future work 'to the immortalizing of your Religion, Learning, Bounty, and Courtesy' (sig. A6v).

Meres's next book is the one for which he is known to posterity: *Palladis tamia, Wits Treasury*. It was entered on the Stationers' register on 7 September 1598, and Meres's dedication to Thomas Eliot of the Middle Temple is dated 19 October. In this dedication Meres describes Sentence, Similitude, and Example as the 'three channels' through which all wit flows, and which form the basis of the present work. He also says that this book is a sequel to Nicholas Ling's popular *Politeuphuia, Wits Commonwealth* (1597), though the compilers of the later *England's Helicon* (1600) apparently did not consider Meres's book an official part of the series. In addition to the dedication, Meres wrote a Latin address to the reader in which he apologizes for the book's limitations and blames publisher Cuthbert Burby's stinginess with paper. This address was torn out of most copies of the first edition, no doubt by Burby, but one full copy survives.

Most of the 666-page book consists of similes comparing the natural world with the spiritual world, for example: 'As dogges feede themselves in butchers shambles: so devils feed themselves in unchast and incontinent mens soules' (fol. 109v). Meres also uses examples from the Bible and classical literature, and he groups all his similes into chapters with such headings as 'Chastity', 'Women', and 'Schollers'. Despite the superficial appearance of classical learning, Meres translated most of *Palladis tamia* directly from Erasmus's *Parabolae sive similiae* and from J. Ravisius Textor's *Officina*, a Latin quotation book commonly used as a text in grammar schools. He also drew on such pedagogical texts as Roger Ascham's *The Scholemaster* (1570) and William Kempe's *The Education of Children in Learning* (1588), and his prose style is influenced by John Lyly's *Euphues* (1578).

Modern interest in *Palladis tamia* centres primarily on the chapter entitled 'A comparative discourse of our English poets, with the Greeke, Latine, and Italian poets'. This chapter uses the simile format to compare classical authors to their contemporary English counterparts, and it constitutes a unique and extremely valuable survey of English literature at the end of the sixteenth century. The most famous passages are those in which Meres mentions Shakespeare's 'sugred Sonnets among his private friends' and names twelve of Shakespeare's plays (fols. 281v–282), but he also praises many other poets, playwrights, translators, and satirists, some eighty English writers in all. He praises Michael Drayton even more fulsomely than Shakespeare, addresses Thomas Nashe as 'gallant young Juvenall' and 'sweete Tom' (fol. 286), and records gossip about

the deaths of Robert Greene, George Peele, and Christopher Marlowe. In two shorter but no less important chapters Meres also names twenty-one contemporary artists and sixteen musicians.

Meres cribbed much of his poetry chapter from William Webbe's *Discourse of English Poetrie* (1586), George Puttenham's *Arte of English Poesie* (1589), and Sir Philip Sidney's *Apologie for Poetrie* (1595), but it is evident that he also had contacts in the contemporary literary scene. His dedications for *Granados Devotion* and *Palladis tamia* show that he had friends at the Middle Temple, and Shakespeare and Drayton, the subjects of his most detailed and personal comments, both had close ties to that institution. Wright suggests Anthony Munday as another likely source of Meres's theatrical information: not only was Munday closely involved in editing and publishing the series of which *Palladis tamia* formed a part, but Meres singles him out for praise as 'our best plotter' (fol. 283v) and otherwise emphasizes Munday's fellow writers for the Admiral's Men.

Although his greatest fame has come in modern times, Meres enjoyed a certain amount of renown from *Palladis tamia* in his own day. Charles Fitzgeoffries, whom Meres had praised as 'that high touring Falcon' (fol. 285v), returned the favour by addressing a Latin poem to Meres in his *Affaniae* (1601), calling him 'theologus et poeta' (*Affaniae*, 62). Ben Jonson alludes to Meres's praise when he notes that Anthony Munday is 'in print as our best plotter' while satirizing him as Antonio Balladino in *The Case is Altered* (printed 1609, but written earlier; (*Works of Ben Jonson*, 108)). Thomas Heywood praises Meres's scholarship in *An Apology for Actors* (1612) and says that his account of poetry is learnedly done, while Edmund Howes includes him in a list of Elizabethan poets in the 1615 continuation of Stow's *Annales*.

Following *Palladis tamia*, Meres capped off his *annus mirabilis* of 1598 with one final publication, a third translation from Luis de Granada entitled *Granados Spirituall and Heavenlie Exercises*. His dedication 'to the valorous and nobleminded Gentleman, Captaine John Sammes, Esquire' (sig. A3), in which he compares Sammes to a long list of famous warriors, is dated 24 November 1598. A second edition of this work, with the dedication omitted, was published in Edinburgh in 1600, but by that time Meres had forsaken literary endeavours for a spiritual life. He was ordained deacon at Colchester, Essex, on 29 September 1599, and made a priest the following day. He became canon of Teigh, Rutland, in 1602, and rector of Wing, Rutland, on 14 July of the same year.

For the remaining forty-five years of his life Meres lived in Wing, serving as master of the grammar school in addition to carrying out his ecclesiastical duties. During his early years at Wing he married a woman named Mary (1576/7–1631), and in late 1607 they had a son named Francis, who matriculated at Trinity College, Cambridge, in 1625, graduated BA in 1628–9 and MA in 1632, and followed his father into the priesthood, dying in 1683. The younger Francis wrote a commendatory poem for fellow Cambridge student Thomas Randolph's *The Jealous Lovers*

(1640). A second edition of *The Sinner's Guide* was published by Edward Blount in 1614, and reissues of *Palladis tamia* were published in 1634 (under the title *Wits Common-wealth*) and 1636 (as *Witts Academy*), but there is no indication that Meres was involved with these editions.

However, in 1631 Meres commemorated the death of his wife on 2 May with a touching four-page lament in the Wing parish register which shows that, even at that late date, he remained interested in literature. Near the top of the first page he wrote:

> That poet Sr Philip Sidney sayde of Argalus and Parthenia,
> I may justly say of Mye-Selfe and my deare Wyfe:
> Her beinge was in him alone,
> And she not beinge he was none.
> (Leics. RO, DE 1846/1)

He minutely describes her final illness and recites her virtues at length in both English and Latin, quoting Suetonius, Horace, and St Augustine in passages which strongly recall the *imitatio* style of *Palladis tamia*. After his wife's death, Meres lived another sixteen years as rector of Wing before dying there on 29 January 1647 at the age of eighty-one.   DAVID KATHMAN

Sources D. C. Allen, 'Francis Meres's treatise "Poetrie": a critical edition', *University of Illinois Studies in Language and Literature*, 16 (1933), 345–500 · D. C. Allen, introduction, in F. Meres, *Palladis tamia*, facs. edn (1938) · F. Meres, *Palladis tamia: wits treasury, being the second part of wits common-wealth* (1598) · F. Meres, *Gods arithmeticke* (1597) · L. de Granada, *The sinners guyde*, trans. F. Meres (1598) · L. de Granada, *Granados devotion*, trans. F. Meres (1598) · L. de Granada, *Granados spirituall and heavenlie exercises*, trans. F. Meres (1598) · C. T. Wright, 'Anthony Mundy and the Bodenham miscellanies', *Philological Quarterly*, 40 (1961), 449–61 · Venn, *Alum. Cant.*, 1/3.171 · parish register, Wing, Rutland, Leics. RO, DE 1846/1 · IGI [parish register, Colsterworth, Lincolnshire] · *The works of Ben Jonson*, ed. C. H. Herford and P. Simpson, 3 (1927)
Archives Leics. RO, Wing parish register, DE 1846/1

Meres [Meeres], **John** (1698–1761?), printer, was born in London, the son of Thomas Meres, the disinherited son of Sir Thomas *Meres (*bap.* 1634, *d.* 1715). On 9 February 1713 John Meres was apprenticed to William Stephens, a London printer, for seven years and while it remains uncertain when Meres formally entered the book trade, it was most likely his relative Hugh Meres who gave him a formal introduction to the profession. Hugh Meres was a director of Sun Fire Insurance and the printer of the *British Mercury* and, from 1721 onwards, the *Historical Register*. In October 1719 he commenced a new daily newspaper, the *Daily Post*, and three years later was printer of the *British Journal*, before he died on 19 April 1723. His widow, Cassandra, the daughter of Thomas Grover the typefounder, continued the printing business until her own death in February 1726, at which time her son-in-law, Richard *Nutt, assumed control. In December 1727 Nutt started the *London Evening-Post*, which by 1737 was under the printing management of John Meres.

By this time, Meres was established in the Old Bailey. He had married Sarah Robinson on 2 June 1732 at St Botolph without Bishopsgate; they had one son, John. The *Daily Post*, alongside the *London Evening-Post* and the weekly *Universal Spectator*, became the focus of Meres's energies, and he dropped the *Historical Register* to concentrate on the

management of these three papers. With three newspapers printed from the same office, there were clear indications of reproducing news from each other, which was typical of the London papers of the time. While the *Universal Spectator* claimed that 'this Journal … contains about six Times more Domestick News than the Common Journals; with several material Paragraphs of fresh News, not in any other Paper', Meres was not loath to admit that in every issue of the *London Evening-Post* 'we copy the principal Paragraphs from the Morning Papers (without which our Evening Paper would be of no service to the Country)' (Harris, 161). Despite this process of news sharing, Meres's papers still offered enough space for competing commentaries. Indeed, in 1738 he was tried for inserting disparaging remarks in the *Daily Post* concerning the king of Sweden. Initially, he refused to find sureties for his good behaviour and was confined to Newgate prison, but he eventually changed his mind and Robert Gosling and George Strahan, both booksellers, offered sureties in his favour. However, within two years remarks in the *Daily Post* reflecting upon an act of parliament dealing with the embargo of provisions saw Meres called to the bar of the House of Commons on 2 December 1740, and he was subsequently held in gaol until 10 February 1741. Upon his release, Meres was cautioned for selling the *London Evening-Post*. Meres was also implicated in the legal action taken against Nutt in 1754 over the publishing of an allegedly seditious letter in the *London Evening-Post*, which led to Nutt's conviction and imprisonment the following year. Meres reputedly died in 1761, but no record of his death or burial has been located. The records of the Stationers' Company detail apprentices bound to and freed by Meres after 1761 though this may be the result of confusing Meres with his son, who was freed by patrimony in 1758. The son inherited the business and discontinued publication of the *Daily Post* in 1772.

Further confusion is caused by John Nichols identifying **William Mears** (*bap.* 1686, *d.* 1739) as John Meres, although there is no clear relationship between the two men. William Mears, bookseller, was baptized on 24 October 1686 at Faversham, Kent, the son of Leonard Meeres, mariner, and his wife, Elizabeth. He was bound to the bookseller Israel Harrison on 9 September 1700 and on 6 October 1707, he was made free of the Stationers' Company. On 2 May 1709 he married Mary, daughter of the prominent bookseller and member of the Stationers' Company Daniel Browne, in St Dunstan-in-the-West parish. Between 1713 and 1727, he traded from an office at the Lamb without Temple Bar before moving to Ludgate Hill. He was master to several apprentices, including his son, William, who was bound on 6 June 1727. In 1713 he issued a catalogue of English plays and the following year he co-published, with his father-in-law, *The Persian and Turkish Tales* translated from Pétis de la Croix. He published no fewer than eight more works during the course of his career, including Defoe's *New Voyage Round the World* (1725) and *Tour through Great Britain* (1724–7), before his death in 1739 from an unknown cause.   MICHAEL T. DAVIS

Sources D. F. McKenzie, ed., *Stationers' Company apprentices*, 3 vols. (1961–78), vols. 2–3 · H. R. Plomer and others, *A dictionary of the printers and booksellers who were at work in England, Scotland, and Ireland from 1726 to 1775* (1932) · H. R. Plomer and others, *A dictionary of the printers and booksellers who were at work in England, Scotland, and Ireland from 1668 to 1725* (1922); repr. (1968) · M. Harris, *London newspapers in the age of Walpole* (1987) · *DNB* · *IGI* · private information (2004) [M. Treadwell, Trent University, Canada]

Meres, Sir Thomas (*bap.* 1634, *d.* 1715), politician, was baptized on 17 September 1634 at St Margaret's, Lincoln, the eldest son of Robert Meres DD (1595/6–1652), chancellor of Lincoln Cathedral, and Elizabeth (*d.* 1639), daughter of Hugh Williams of Y Wig, Caernarvonshire, and widow of William *Dolben DD, prebendary of Lincoln. He was educated at Sleaford grammar school before being admitted to Sidney Sussex College, Cambridge, on 23 January 1651; he entered the Inner Temple in 1653. In January 1658 he married Anne (*d.* 1698), daughter and coheir of Sir Erasmus de la Fountaine of Kirby Bellars, Leicestershire. They had three sons and three daughters; only one son and one daughter definitely survived their father.

Meres entered parliament in 1659 for Lincoln, and was re-elected to the Convention in April 1660. On 30 May 1660 he was called to the bar, but there is no evidence that he practised, politics, both local and national, engrossing his attention. He was knighted on 11 June 1660. He was an active justice of the peace in Lindsey and Kesteven, and captain of a company of Lincoln's trained band. He also sat in every parliament for Lincoln before 1688. Nor was he content to play a minor role at Westminster. In the Cavalier Parliament, 1661–79, he delivered more than 500 recorded speeches in addition to his work on committees and tellerships. Not surprisingly, given his ecclesiastical connections, Meres proved a staunch supporter of the established church, although one keen to promote a moderate settlement. In 1661 the presbyterian Baron Wharton considered him a friend. Meres seems to have advocated the comprehension of moderate nonconformists within the church and opposed the toleration of sectaries outside it. On other matters he adopted the stance of a country supporter, conscious of the privileges of the Commons, and evincing a concern for low taxation and honest administration.

Meres was 'very knowing in the order[s] of the House' (*Diary of Sir Edward Dering*, 90), and as such was seen by many as a potential speaker. He was thought to be the king's preferred choice for speaker in February 1673, but was elected only to chair the committee of elections. In this session he opposed the declaration of indulgence, and fear of popery seems to have softened his attitude towards toleration for protestant nonconformists. During the summer of 1673 he hoped to gain the speaker's chair if Sir Edward Seymour received office, or office himself as he coveted the post of secretary to the new lord treasurer, Thomas Osborne, earl of Danby. Neither came his way and Meres became a more trenchant critic of the court. Danby believed him to be an adherent of the earl of Arlington, and it was Meres who thirded the impeachment of Danby in April 1675.

Although perceived as a potential court adherent as early as 1676, Meres was still an opponent of the court at the time of the Popish Plot, and he again backed the impeachment of Danby. Following the dissolution of the Cavalier Parliament, Meres retained his seat at Lincoln and was the court candidate for speaker. However, the Commons responded to Meres with shouts of 'away with him, no upstarts' (Crossette). Nevertheless, he retained the chairmanship of the committee of elections, albeit by a narrow margin. The earl of Shaftesbury still considered him 'worthy', and at last on 14 May 1679 he attained office as an Admiralty commissioner at a salary of £1000 p.a. He voted for the committal of the Exclusion Bill and was re-elected for Lincoln in August 1679. In the Oxford Parliament of 1681 he spoke in favour of proposals for a regency, which received scant support. Meres lost his office on 19 May 1684 when the duke of York took over the Admiralty.

Meres was re-elected to the 1685 parliament and was again put forward as speaker; this time he was defeated by the candidate of George Jeffreys, lord chief justice (later first Baron Jeffreys). He remained an active speaker in debate. He lost his local offices in March 1688 'for refusing to be one of the repealers' (*Portland MSS*, 3.406) of the Test Act and penal laws. He received royal backing in the form of a letter from the earl of Sunderland in the run up to James II's abortive parliament in 1688, but he may not have even stood for election to the convention of 1689. He remained out of parliament for over a decade.

Meres was returned to the Commons for Lincoln in February 1701. He was quickly into his stride as a debater, generally voicing the opinions of a country tory in support of the impeachment of William III's whig ministers and for measures such as reviving the commission of accounts. He did not stand in the election of November 1701, but was returned in the election following the accession in 1702 of Queen Anne. On the major issue of the 1704–5 session he 'sneaked' off rather than vote on the tack of the Occasional Conformity Bill to the Land Tax Bill. He was also somewhat equivocal on the constitutional question raised by the Ashby *v.* White case, wherein the whigs wished to allow the electors who had been disfranchised to appeal to the law courts, which would have had the effect of challenging the right of the Commons to determine their own membership. He was a frequent speaker on the Regency Bill of 1706, again espousing a country viewpoint. Almost his last parliamentary act was to vote against the impeachment of Dr Henry Sacheverell in 1710.

Meres retired from parliament at the 1710 election. He died at his house in Bloomsbury Square, London, on 9 July 1715. He was buried on the 23rd at Kirby Bellars in Leicestershire, which he had inherited from his wife, much to the chagrin of her brother, John (*d.* 1708), who denounced Meres in his will for persuading his father to divide the estate to his own advantage. He was succeeded by his son, Sir John Meres.   STUART HANDLEY

Sources J. S. Crossette, 'Meres, Sir Thomas', HoP, *Commons, 1660–90* · P. Watson and P. Gauci, 'Meres, Sir Thomas', HoP, *Commons, 1690–1715* [draft] · E. Deacon, *Deacon of Elstowe and London and allied families* (1898), 297–300 · A. R. Maddison, ed., *Lincolnshire pedigrees*, 2,

Harleian Society, 51 (1903), 666 · A. Grey, ed., *Debates of the House of Commons, from the year 1667 to the year 1694*, new edn, 10 vols. (1769) · J. W. F. Hill, *Tudor and Stuart Lincoln* (1956), 168, 184–5 · C. Holmes, *Seventeenth-century Lincolnshire*, History of Lincolnshire, 7 (1980), 229, 237–8 · *The diary of John Milward*, ed. C. Robbins (1938), 196, 201, 216, 225, 249 · *The parliamentary diary of Sir Edward Dering, 1670–1673*, ed. B. D. Henning (1940), 90 · M. Knights, *Politics and opinion in crisis, 1678–1681* (1994), 44, 46, 50, 98, 125–6, 359 · P. Seaward, *The Cavalier Parliament and the reconstruction of the old regime, 1661–1667* (1988), 96–7 · *Lincolnshire Notes and Queries*, 2 (1891), 116, 151, 187 · *The manuscripts of his grace the duke of Portland*, 10 vols., HMC, 29 (1891–1931), vol. 3
Archives Lincs. Arch., corresp. and papers
Wealth at death substantial; several estates; London house

Merewether, Edward Rowland Alworth (1892–1970), factory inspector, was born on 2 March 1892 at 33 Arbour Square, Stepney, London, the only son and eldest of the three children of Alworth Edward Merewether (*b. c.*1870) later a Royal Navy surgeon, and his wife, Jane Victoria, *née* McKay (*c.*1870–1919). His father died from malaria in 1906. Merewether was educated at Tavistock House School in Sheerness, at Christ's Hospital in London, and, from 1909, at Durham University. As an undergraduate he won the Tulloch scholarship (1911), the Durham University Medical Society essay prize (1913), and the Charlton scholarship (1914). He graduated MB, BS, with second-class honours, in 1914.

Merewether was briefly a house physician at the Royal Victoria Infirmary, Newcastle upon Tyne, but at the outbreak of the First World War he enlisted as a temporary surgeon-lieutenant in the Royal Navy. He saw service in France, the Balkans, and with the Grand Fleet. One of his postings, in 1915, was as medical officer in charge of the British naval mission in Serbia, for which he was mentioned in dispatches. Merewether's work in controlling the typhus epidemics then rife in the region earned him the order of St Sava of Serbia (4th class). It also provided him with material for his Durham MD thesis: 'Some medical aspects of the war in Serbia with special reference to the British naval mission', in 1916, and in the same year for his article 'Report on the late medical conditions in Serbia with special reference to the typhus fever epidemic' in the *Journal of the Royal Naval Medical Service*. On 3 April 1918 Merewether married Ruth Annie Hayton (1890/91–1971), a nurse with the Red Cross and daughter of Robert Waddell, a market gardener, of Corbridge-on-Tyne. The marriage produced three daughters.

After the war Merewether lived for a time in Hanwell, Middlesex, where he combined general practice with chairmanship of the medical board of the Ministry of Pensions and, subsequently, with the post of medical member of the Pensions Appeal Tribunal. In the early 1920s an inheritance enabled him largely to dispense with medical practice. He moved to Ascot in Berkshire, while he studied for the bar at Gray's Inn in London, with a view to becoming a coroner. His only medical appointments during this time were as assistant tuberculosis officer for Sheffield, from 1922, and as assistant school medical officer for Salford (1926–7). Merewether was called to the bar in 1926,

but in the following year he joined HM medical inspectorate of factories, in which organization he spent the rest of his career. Initially based at the inspectorate's Glasgow office, Merewether relocated to Birmingham in the early 1930s before moving to London in 1939. In 1943 he was promoted senior medical inspector of factories, a post he held until his retirement in 1957.

Merewether had been in the inspectorate for only a short time when he was instructed, in March 1928, to investigate the occurrence of pulmonary disease among asbestos workers. By October 1929 he had completed a report which was later amalgamated with a study on preventive measures conducted by Charles Price, from HM engineering inspectorate of factories. In 1930 their findings were jointly published as *Report on Effects of Asbestos Dust in the Lungs and Dust Suppression in the Asbestos Industry*, for the first part of which Merewether was responsible. The report, which quickly came to be regarded as a classic, conclusively established that prolonged inhalation of asbestos dust at heavy concentrations could lead to potentially fatal fibrosis of the lungs. Its findings were directly responsible for the establishment of a compensation scheme and of the asbestos industry regulations (1931) which sought to control dust emission in asbestos factories. Throughout the rest of his career Merewether took a special interest in occupational chest ailments, including asbestos-related disease. Although not the first person to suspect that exposure to asbestos dust could cause lung cancer, in the 1940s and 1950s it was Merewether who produced official data suggestive of an association, if not a causal link.

Merewether was not a prolific author, but he published, in addition to his contributions to the annual reports of HM chief inspector of factories, several important papers on dust diseases in scientific and medical journals. He also edited, though did not otherwise contribute to, a three-volume work entitled *Industrial Medicine and Hygiene* (1954–6). Merewether's eminence in the fields of pulmonary disease and occupational health was recognized by the conferment of a number of honours and appointments: he was made honorary physician to George VI (1944–7), FRSE (1940), FRCP (1946), CBE (1948), and CB (1956); in 1946 the Society of Apothecaries awarded him an honorary diploma in public health; and later he became an officer of the order of St John of Jerusalem. He was also a member of the industrial health research board, honorary fellow of the American Public Health Association, scientific adviser to the Empire Rheumatism Council, corresponding committee member on industrial hygiene to the International Labour Office, and, briefly, medical adviser to the Ministry of Agriculture and Fisheries.

Merewether travelled widely on official business, including to the USA during the Second World War; and he continued to do so after retirement, when he spent some time as a consultant, especially on legal aspects of industrial medicine. In 1964 he undertook a tour of the Far East on behalf of the International Labour Organization advising on the establishment of occupational health services.

In appearance Merewether was bespectacled and somewhat spare of frame; he went bald at a comparatively early age. He had an engaging personality and a strong sympathy for the 'underdog'. In later life he had a weakness for alcohol which he regularly indulged during long lunch breaks away from his office, often at the Savage Club. In retirement he lived at Pyrford in Surrey. He died, of cerebral thrombosis and cerebral arteriosclerosis, in hospital at Weybridge, Surrey, on 13 February 1970. He was cremated at Woking. His wife survived him by some eighteen months.   P. W. J. BARTRIP

Sources *BMJ* (28 Feb 1970), 571–2 · *The Lancet* (28 Feb 1970), 477–8 · *The Times* (23 Feb 1970) · private information (1998) · *WWW, 1961–70* · registration and presentation MSS, GL, Christ's Hospital MSS · Munk, *Roll* · U. Durham · b. cert. · m. cert. · d. cert.
Likenesses photograph, repro. in *BMJ*
Wealth at death £1356: administration, 2 July 1970, *CGPLA Eng. & Wales*

Merewether, Henry Alworth (1780/81–1864), serjeant-at-law, was the eldest son of Henry Merewether of Calne, Wiltshire. He was educated at Reading School under Dr Richard Valpy, was called to the bar at the Inner Temple on 5 May 1809, was created serjeant-at-law on 25 June 1827, and received a patent of precedence in 1832. He practised on the western circuit with much success, became recorder of Great Yarmouth in 1832, and afterwards recorder of Reading. In 1845 he was appointed attorney-general to Adelaide, the queen-dowager, in succession to Serjeant Taddy. He received the degree of DCL from the University of Oxford on 12 June 1839.

Merewether was elected town clerk of the corporation of London on 23 June 1842, by a majority of twenty-six votes, in competition with William Pritchard, then high bailiff of Southwark. Almost certainly he owed this appointment to an able pamphlet he had written in support of the alleged right of the corporation to the foreshore of the Thames, which was the subject of litigation at that time. By accepting the clerkship he relinquished an annual income of over £5000 at the bar. It was said by those among the corporation who knew him that the office of town clerk had never been filled with such dignity as in his time. He appeared on behalf of the corporation in the court of chancery and elsewhere on several occasions, and defended their interests with great learning and ability. He was also the author of several legal works, the principal being *The History of the Boroughs and Municipal Corporations of the United Kingdom*, written with Archibald John Stephens (3 vols., 1835) and *A New System of Police* (1816).

Merewether resigned the office of town clerk on 10 February 1859 and was granted a pension of £1000 p.a. He died at his family seat, Castlefield House, near Calne, Wiltshire, on 22 July 1864, in his eighty-fourth year. Twice married, he was survived by his second wife, Cecilia Maria Merewether, and by several children. His eldest son, Henry Alworth (1812–1877), was recorder of Devizes and a bencher of the Inner Temple, and was appointed QC in 1853. A younger son, Sir William Lockyer *Merewether, by

his first marriage (to Eliza Maria, daughter of Thomas Lockyer of Wembury House, Devon) served in the Indian army and administration.

CHARLES WELCH, *rev.* ALEC BRIAN SCHOFIELD

Sources Boase, *Mod. Eng. biog.* · J. E. Martin, ed., *Masters of the bench of the Hon. Society of the Inner Temple, 1450–1883, and masters of the Temple, 1540–1883* (1883) · *Law Times* (30 July 1864), 442 · *Law List* · H. Le Strange, *Norfolk official lists* (1890) · GL, Corporation of London MSS · d. cert.
Archives BL, corresp. with Sir Robert Peel and others, index to MSS, VII, 1985
Likenesses Miss Turner, lithograph (after J. Lucas), BM, NPG
Wealth at death under £4000: probate, 22 Nov 1864, *CGPLA Eng. & Wales*

Merewether, John (1797–1850), dean of Hereford, son of John Merewether of Blackland, Wiltshire, was born at Marshfield, Gloucestershire. His father was a great-grandson of the John Merewether of Devizes (1655–1724) who attended Bishop Ken in his last illness, and whose daughter married William Hawkins, a grandson of Izaac Walton, and author of the *Short Account of Ken's Life* (1713). He was a distant cousin of Serjeant Henry Alworth Merewether, attorney-general to Queen Adelaide, and nephew of Henry Alworth. Merewether matriculated from Queen's College, Oxford, in 1814, obtained third-class honours in classics and graduated BA in 1818, MA in 1822, and BD and DD in 1832. He was ordained deacon in 1819 and priest in 1820 by the bishop of Salisbury, and served curacies at Gillingham, Dorset, and Hampton, Middlesex. While at Hampton he was instrumental in building a chapel of ease at Hampton Wick, and attracted the favourable notice of the duke of Clarence, later William IV, then residing at Bushey. He was chaplain to the duchess of Clarence, later Queen Adelaide, in 1824, and spent a number of Christmases and Easters at court.

In 1828 Merewether was presented by the lord chancellor to the living of New Radnor, and in 1832, on the promotion of the Hon. Edward Grey to the bishopric, he succeeded him as dean of Hereford. On 13 January 1833 William IV appointed him one of the deputy clerks of the closet, and is said to have asked Lord Melbourne to appoint Merewether to the first available bishopric. In 1836 he was instituted to the vicarage of Madeley, Shropshire, in the gift of the dean and chapter of Hereford. A staunch tory, he was passed over for episcopal preferment in favour of Melbourne's political appointments. He later suffered from Peel's refusal to consider political applicants to the bench, Merewether having organized the tory party in Hereford elections. As dean, Merewether attempted to reform the cathedral, initiating weekly rather than monthly chapters, and attempting to make the vicars-choral more regular in attendance of cathedral services. He was also responsible for the appointment of Samuel Wesley as organist. The effect of his reforms was limited by his failure to carry the chapter with him. In 1837 he started a long feud with the chapter about custody and use of the chapter seal. Merewether objected to its use in his absence, while the chapter objected to his absences. An appeal to the bishop resulted in Merewether backing down.

In 1847 Merewether was a strenuous opponent of the election of Renn Dickson Hampden to the see of Hereford, regarding certain of Hampden's opinions as dangerous, even heretical. After a fruitless memorial to the queen, he announced to Lord John Russell, prime minister, in a lengthy letter, his intention of voting against Hampden's election in the chapter meeting, and he received in reply the laconic note: 'Sir, I had the honour to receive your letter of the 22nd inst. in which you intimate to me your intention of violating the law' (S. Walpole, *The Life of Lord John Russell*, 1, 1891, 498n.). Merewether questioned the legality of the eventual election and finally refused to affix the seal of the dean and chapter to the document recording the bishop's formal election. He also refused to attend the enthronement.

Merewether, who was an enthusiastic local antiquary, was elected FSA in 1836, and communicated to the *Archaeologia* accounts of discoveries made during the restoration of Hereford Cathedral. He took a general interest in sacred architecture, and visited several cathedrals to determine which type of repair would be appropriate at Hereford. In 1843 he wrote *Statement on the Condition and Circumstances of the Cathedral Church of Hereford*, describing the condition of the structure, and contributed £500 to the restoration fund. He was also an enthusiastic rather than scientific member of the Archaeological Institute. In 1849, for example, he opened up thirty-five barrows on Marlborough downs. His notes were posthumously published in 1851 as *Diary of a dean: being an account of the examination of Silbury Hill and of various barrows and other earthworks on the downs of north Wilts.*

Merewether married Mary Ann Baker (1807/8–1879) of Wiley, Wiltshire. They had six sons and three daughters. Merewether died at Madeley vicarage on 4 April 1850, and was buried in the lady chapel of Hereford Cathedral. The five lancet windows at the east end of the minster were fitted with stained glass to his memory with the inscription 'In Memoriam Johannis Merewether, S.T.P. ecclesiae Heref. decani, quo strenuo fautore huius sacræ ædis restitutio feliciter est inchoata'.

THOMAS SECCOMBE, rev. ELLIE CLEWLOW

Sources GM, 2nd ser., 33 (1850), 536–7, 562 · *Manchester Guardian* (10 April 1850), 257 · *ILN* (13 April 1850), 247 · *Annual Register* (1850), 217 · Foster, *Alum. Oxon.* · P. Barrett, *Barchester: English cathedral life in the nineteenth century* (1993) · O. Chadwick, *The Victorian church*, 3rd edn, 2 vols. (1971–2) · B. M. Marsden, *The early barrow diggers* (1974) · G. V. Cox, *Recollections of Oxford* (1868), 342 · J. Jones, *Hereford cathedral and city: a handbook*, 2nd edn (1858), 74 · F. T. Havergal, *Fasti Herefordenses* (1869), 41
Archives BL, corresp. with Robert Peel, Add. MSS 490–562 · NA Scot., letters to Fox Maule, 1848, GD45
Likenesses C. Baugniet, lithograph, 1848, BM · portrait, repro. in *ILN*, 247

Merewether, Sir William Lockyer (1825–1880), army and political officer in India, son of Serjeant Henry Alworth *Merewether (1780/81–1864) and his first wife, Eliza Maria Lockyer, was born at 51 Chancery Lane, London, on 6 February 1825. Educated at Westminster School, he entered the Bombay army as a second-lieutenant in March 1841. He served with the 21st Bombay native infantry during the Sind War of 1843 and was at the battle of Hyderabad. Appointed afterwards to the irregular horse, stationed on the north-west border of Sind, he was recalled to his former regiment for service in the southern Maratha country, but rejoined the frontier force in 1847, eventually (1859) to become its commandant, in succession to General John Jacob. In 1847, with 133 Sind horsemen, he defeated 700 Baluch outlaws, which helped to secure the peace of the frontier. In 1848–9 he was second in command of Sir George Malcolm's detachment of Sind horse, serving with the army of the Punjab, and was present at the siege and surrender of Multan, the battle of Gujrat, and the occupation of Peshawar. In 1856, during General Jacob's absence in Persia, he received the brevet of captain and was left in charge of the Sind frontier; he succeeded in suppressing not only the rebellion of local peoples but the insubordination of troops under his control.

In 1854 Merewether married Harriett, youngest daughter of J. Dale of Coleshill, Warwickshire. Made a CB in 1860, he was nominated military secretary, as major, to the government of Bombay in 1861, and political agent at Aden in 1865. In the last post he undertook operations against the Fadhli Arabs, who attempted to intercept the supplies of grain and food provided for the garrison by the inhabitants of the interior. These operations, though subsequently approved by government, were carried out by Merewether on his own personal responsibility. He subsequently negotiated with King Theodore of Abyssinia, and on the outbreak of war with him took command as lieutenant-colonel of the pioneer force dispatched from Bombay in September 1867 and rendered other valuable assistance to General Lord Napier. He was made KCSI, and received the thanks of parliament (1868) and brevet of colonel. Appointed chief commissioner in Sind in June 1867, it was not until July in the following year that he could be spared to take up the appointment. In 1876 he returned home to take his seat in the Council of India. A generous and popular companion, Merewether was generally considered a true soldier, a shrewd politician, and an enlightened administrator. He died at his home, 31 Linden Gardens, Bayswater, London, on 4 October 1880, survived by his wife and three sons.

F. J. GOLDSMID, rev. JAMES FALKNER

Sources *Indian Army List* · *Army List* · *Hart's Army List* · P. Cadell, *History of the Bombay army* (1938) · Boase, *Mod. Eng. biog.* · CGPLA Eng. & Wales (1880)
Archives BL OIOC, corresp. and papers, MS Eur. D 625 | BL, corresp. with Sir A. H. Layard, Add. MSS 38991–38994, 39113–39120 · BL, letters to Sir Stafford Northcote, Add. MS 50030 · BL OIOC, corresp. with Sir Frederic Goldsmid, MS Eur. F 134 no. 33 · BL OIOC, letters to Sir Lewis Pelly, MS Eur. F 126
Likenesses group portrait, photograph, c.1867, repro. in J. Falconer, *Photography and the Royal Engineers* (1982) · wood-engraving, NPG; repro. in *ILN* (5 Sept 1868)
Wealth at death under £4000: administration with will, 7 Dec 1880, CGPLA Eng. & Wales

Merfyn Frych (d. 844), king of Gwynedd, was the son of Gwriad ab Elidir and Esyllt ferch Gynan. Merfyn ruled the kingdom of Gwynedd in north-west Wales from 825 until his death in 844. He was the first member of the so-called 'second dynasty of Gwynedd', which through the descendants of his son Rhodri Mawr came to rule most of Wales in the tenth and later centuries. Merfyn's connection with the earlier kings of Gwynedd was not through his father, Gwriad, but through his mother, Esyllt (though some genealogies represent her as his wife). Esyllt's father, Cynan Dindaethwy, had died in 816 when fighting his dynastic rival Hywel Fychan. On Hywel's death in 825 Merfyn assumed the kingship though, as far as can be established, he was not a direct agnatic relative of the earlier rulers. His father's origins and therefore the precise nature of Merfyn's claim to the kingship are difficult to determine, and attempts to do so have been coloured by later medieval dynastic legend and early modern speculation. A connection with 'Manaw' has been interpreted as being either the Isle of Man or the (by then extinct) kingdom of Manaw of Gododdin in north Britain (Lothian, Scotland); other locations such as Ireland, Galloway in Scotland, and Powys in north-east Wales have also been posited. Merfyn's only known genealogical connection with Powys is his union with Nest, the sister of Cyngen ap Cadell, king of Powys (r. 808–54/5).

Little is known of Merfyn's nineteen-year reign. He was probably one of the Welsh kings who were defeated by Ecgberht of Wessex in 830, but the implications of this defeat for his rule are unknown. Merfyn's court, perhaps on Anglesey, appears to have fostered Latin and (to a lesser extent) Greek learning, judging from the few hints that survive. The anonymous *Historia Brittonum* was composed in Merfyn's fourth year and probably in Gwynedd. It drew on a variety of sources, including Welsh, Irish, Anglo-Saxon, continental and classical history and pseudo-history. The so-called 'Bamberg Cryptogram' of Dubthach reveals a similar variety of contacts. It seems that Dubthach, an Irishman at Merfyn's court, posed the cryptogram to visiting Irish scholars *en route* for the continent. It took the form of a brief greeting from Merfyn to his brother-in-law Cyngen ap Cadell, and had been translated into Greek by one Suadbarr. Merfyn Frych (the epithet means 'the Freckled') died in 844: that year also witnessed the battle of 'Cedyll', but attempts to link this battle with Merfyn's death are unwarranted. The kingship of Gwynedd then passed to his famous son *Rhodri Mawr.

DAVID E. THORNTON

Sources J. Williams ab Ithel, ed., *Annales Cambriae*, Rolls Series, 20 (1860) · T. Jones, ed. and trans., *Brenhinedd y Saesson, or, The kings of the Saxons* (1971) [another version of *Brut y tywysogyon*] · T. Jones, ed. and trans., *Brut y tywysogyon, or, The chronicle of the princes: Peniarth MS 20* (1952) · T. Jones, ed. and trans., *Brut y tywysogyon, or, The chronicle of the princes: Red Book of Hergest* (1955) · P. C. Bartrum, ed., *Early Welsh genealogical tracts* (1966) · T. Mommsen, ed., *Chronica minora saec. IV. V. VI. VII.*, 3, MGH Auctores Antiquissimi, 13 (Berlin, 1898) · R. Derolez, 'Dubthach's cryptogram', *L'Antiquité Classique*, 21 (1952), 359–75 · *ASC*, s.a.828 [texts A, E] · J. E. Lloyd, *A history of Wales from the earliest times to the Edwardian conquest*, 3rd edn, 2 vols. (1939); repr. (1988) · N. K. Chadwick, 'Early culture and learning in north Wales', in N. K. Chadwick and others, *Studies in the early British church* (1958), 29–120 · D. E. Thornton, *Kings, chronologies and genealogies: studies in the political history of early medieval Ireland and Wales* [forthcoming]

Meriton, George (d. 1624), dean of York, was born in Hertfordshire, probably at Braughing. His father was a tenant of Thomas Howard, first earl of Suffolk (1561–1626), who was born under the earl's roof. He matriculated from St John's College, Cambridge, in 1581, graduated BA in 1585, and MA in 1588, and was on 4 July 1589 elected a fellow of Queens' College, Cambridge. There he was junior bursar in 1595/6 and senior bursar the following year, and proceeded BD in 1596 and DD in 1601. Fuller reports that Meriton defended the ceremonies of the Church of England in frequent, contentious discussion with Thomas Brighton when both were at Queens' College. Later, in Scotland, Meriton continued this defence of conformity and the royal supremacy in *A Sermon Preached before the General Assembly at Glasgow* (1611). His Calvinist sympathies are well documented in his other published sermons: *A Sermon of Nobility* (1607), preached before the king; *The Christian Man's Assuring House and a Sinner's Conversion* (1614), preached before the young Prince Charles; and *A Sermon of Repentance* (1607).

Meriton was presented to the rectory of Hadleigh in Suffolk by Archbishop Whitgift in 1599, and thus to the deanery of Bocking (usually held in conjunction with the rectory) on 24 May 1599. Hadleigh registers record the baptism of several children of Meriton and his wife, Mary Rands, granddaughter of Henry Rands, bishop of Lincoln. Meriton was chaplain to James I and to James's wife Anne of Denmark, and was made dean of Peterborough on 12 June 1612, dean of York on 27 March 1617, and prebendary of Tockerington in the cathedral church of York on 5 March 1617; he resigned Hadleigh in 1618. Meriton died on 23 December 1624 and was buried in York Minster.

BERTHA PORTER, rev. LORI ANNE FERRELL

Sources W. Dugdale, *The visitation of the county of Yorke*, ed. R. Davies and G. J. Armytage, SurtS, 36 (1859), 107 · T. Fuller, *The church-history of Britain*, 11 pts in 1 (1655), pt 10, p. 49 · F. Drake, *Eboracum, or, The history and antiquities of the city of York* (1736), 510, 559, 565 · R. Newcourt, *Repertorium ecclesiasticum parochiale Londinense*, 2 (1710), 66–8 · T. Baker, *History of the college of St John the Evangelist, Cambridge*, ed. J. E. B. Mayor, 1 (1869), 198 · Venn, *Alum. Cant.* · G. Meriton, *A sermon of nobility* (1607)
Archives BL · Hunt. L.

Meriton, George (b. 1634, d. in or before 1711), legal writer, was born in July 1634 (aged thirty and eleven months at the visitation of 28 August 1665), the eldest son of Thomas Meriton (1606–1654?) and Grace, daughter of Francis Wright of Bolton upon Swale, Yorkshire. His grandfather was George *Meriton, dean of York in 1617–24, and his younger brother was Thomas *Meriton. Meriton inherited the paternal estate at Castle Leavington, in the North Riding of Yorkshire, in 1653 or 1654, studied law, and became an attorney at nearby Northallerton. About this time he married Mary, daughter of John Palliser of Kirby Wiske, near Thirsk and Northallerton. They had five sons and a daughter—the eldest, Thomas, born in October 1657. Meriton's two sisters Grace and Ann also married into the Palliser family, to his wife's brothers, Thomas and Francis. Of perhaps greater importance was their cousin,

William Palliser, who was educated at Northallerton but who found preferment as an Irish bishop.

In the mid-1660s Meriton began to publish legal works, beginning with *Land-Lords Law* (1665), which went through several editions, and was followed by *A Touchstone of Wills* (1668) and *A Guide for Constables, Churchwardens etc.* (1669). A different kind of work followed in 1675 with the publication of *Anglorum gesta, or, A Brief History of England*. Other works followed—*The Parson's Monitor* (1681) and *Nomenclatura clericalis* (1685). In 1683 he published in both London and York *The Praise of Yorkshire Ale*, which contained the following advice to the reader:

> That man is too morose, and much to blame
> That doth condemn all mirth to be profane.

This work contained dialogue in a Yorkshire dialect. Meriton returned to legal themes with *A Guide to Surveyors of the Highways* (1694), and then moved on to the reformation of manners with *Immorality, Debauchery, and Profaneness Exposed* (1698).

Meriton's next work was published in Dublin in 1700, *An abridgement of the Irish statutes, from the third year of the reign of King Edward II … with an abridgement of English statutes enacted since Sir Edward Poynings's law relating to the kingdom of Ireland*. On the title-page he was described as 'barrister at law'. In that same year he was granted an LLB from the University of Dublin. When exactly Meriton moved to Dublin is unclear: it may well have coincided with William Palliser's achievement of episcopal office in 1693. Ralph Thoresby noted in his diary on 18 May 1703 that he had enquired after Meriton, but been told 'that he had removed into Ireland, where he was said to be a judge, but whether alive or dead, unknown' (*Diary*, 1.426). In Dublin in 1701 there appeared *An abridgement of the act of parliament for the better execution of His Majesty's declaration for the settlement of … Ireland*.

Meriton made his will on 26 September 1701, and it was proved on 15 March 1711. He was survived by his wife and all his children except for George (1660–1680), who died while studying at Cambridge.   STUART HANDLEY

Sources *Dugdale's visitation of Yorkshire, with additions*, ed. J. W. Clay, 2 (1907), 486–7 · Burtchaell & Sadleir, *Alum. Dubl.*, 575 · J. W. Clay, ed., *Abstracts of Yorkshire wills in the time of the Commonwealth*, Yorkshire Archaeological Society, 9 (1890), 64 · *The diary of Ralph Thoresby*, 2 vols. (1830), 1.426 · H. W. F. Harwood, ed., *The Genealogist*, new ser., 23 (1906–7), 164–5 · W. O. Cavenagh, 'Castletown and its owners', *Journal of the Royal Society of Antiquaries of Ireland*, 6th ser., 2 (1912), 44–5 · Allibone, *Dict.*, 2.1268 · Watt, *Bibl. Brit.*, 2.665 · J. G. Marvin, *Legal bibliography, or, A thesaurus of American, English, Irish and Scotch law books* (1847), 510 · R. Davies, *A memoir of the York press: with notices of authors, printers, and stationers, in the sixteenth, seventeenth, and eighteenth centuries* (1868), 114–16

Meriton, John (1630/31?–1704), Church of England clergyman, whose life has been the subject of some confusion, is often difficult to distinguish and reconcile with those of contemporary namesakes. Contrary to previous accounts, and with some reservations, he was probably born in 1630 or 1631, the son of Henry Meriton (*d.* 1656?), sometime rector of King's Ripton and Stilton, Huntingdonshire, and Susan, his wife. This John Meriton was admitted as a sizar to Magdalene College, Cambridge, on 2 June 1645, aged fourteen, proceeding BA in 1649 and MA in 1652, and is probably the same John Meriton who was incorporated MA at Oxford on 14 July 1657. Meriton proceeded DD at Cambridge in 1669.

Meriton can first be identified with some certainty from 22 January 1653 when he was elected Sunday afternoon lecturer for the church of St Martin-in-the-Fields, Westminster, a post which he appears to have held without interruption until his death. He is probably synonymous with the Meriton who was a delegate for the third classis of the presbyterian London provincial assembly from 29 April 1652 until 23 January 1660. He assumed ministerial duties for the parish of St Nicholas Acons, London (in the third classis), some time prior to 2 November 1653, and was confirmed in that capacity with the assent of Oliver Cromwell on 19 January 1656. He is probably the same Meriton who was named as a commissioner in An Act for Approbation and Admission of Ministers of the Gospel to Benefices and Public Lectures just prior to the Restoration, and seems likely to have been one of the presbyterian ministers signatory to *The Humble and Grateful Acknowledgement* (1660) thanking Charles II for his declaration on ecclesiastical affairs. On 5 June 1661 Nathaniel Hardy and Matthew Smalwood jointly testified to the bishop of London that Meriton was 'of unblameable Conversation of Loyale affection to the Kings Majesty orthodox in Judgement & Conformable to the Church of England' (Guildhall Library, MS 10116/1). Meriton was reinstituted to the rectory of St Nicholas Acons on 18 July 1661. On 5 April 1664 he resigned the benefice and was installed to the rectory of the parish of St Michael Cornhill, London, which he held until his death. From 1661 to 1701 Meriton was a lecturer at St Mary-at-Hill, London. He was a second assistant at Sion College, 1656, 1657, and 1658, and president in 1676–7. As well as contributing a sermon to *The Morning Exercise Methodized* (ed. Thomas Case, 1660) Meriton published three sermons and a book of daily prayers.

By his own account Meriton was one of the few ministers who stayed at his post during the plague of 1665, and he is known to have been highly active in efforts to rebuild and reunite the city churches after the fire of 1666. After three or four years of incapacity brought on by 'the Drs Age and infirmity' Meriton died on 5 December 1704 and was interred in his vault in the chancel of St Michael Cornhill on 11 December 1704 (Guildhall Library, MS 4072/2, p. 26). Meriton was predeceased by his wife, Elizabeth (*d.* 1680), who was buried in his vault on 29 December 1680. They had baptized some twelve children: eight boys and four girls.

Of the various misrepresentations that have attended accounts of Meriton's life the suggestion that Meriton is synonymous with that 'old dunce Meriton' and 'my old acquaintance, that dull fellow Meriton' that Samuel Pepys refers to in his diaries, and furthermore that he was deprived of the lectureship of St Olave's, Southwark, for fanaticism (in October 1683)—as Bliss in his edition of *Athenae Oxonienses* maintains—can both be corrected: these assertions have more correctly been shown to have referred to a Thomas Meriton, probably Thomas Meriton

(d. 1705), minister and rector of St Nicholas Cole Abbey, London (1658–1705), and hence brother of John—as Pepys himself implies.

Meriton is most easily confounded with John Meriton (1635/6–1696?) sometime vicar of St Ives, Huntingdonshire, and chaplain to Henry Bennet, earl of Arlington. This Meriton—in contrast to other accounts—was probably born in 1635 or 1636, the son of Richard Meriton of Northallerton, Yorkshire, was schooled privately at Danby Wiske, Yorkshire, and admitted a sizar at St John's College, Cambridge, on 18 October 1652, aged sixteen. He did not matriculate or graduate, but was created MA at Cambridge by the king's letters mandatory on 26 September 1660. It was probably he who was ordained a deacon at Lincoln in July 1661, and who—contrary to the account of Venn—was rector of Walsoken, Norfolk, in 1661 and of Little Fakenham, Suffolk, in 1662. Similarly, it was probably he and not the former who was rector of St Mary Bothaw, London, from 25 June 1666 to 1669. His one publication was an assize sermon preached at Huntingdon at the summer assizes of 1670. He probably died in 1696.

Meriton can clearly be distinguished from two other namesake Church of England clergymen. John Meriton (1604/5–1669), of unknown parentage, matriculated sizar at Trinity Hall, Cambridge, in Michaelmas term 1620, graduating BA in 1622 and proceeding MA in 1626. He took out a licence to marry Susan Ederidge (c.1612–1641) on 24 April 1633. He was rector of Sacomb, Hertfordshire, from 1633 until his death on 20 December 1669. He was buried at Sacomb two days later. And John Meriton (1662–1717) was the son of Henry Meriton, rector of Oxburgh in Norfolk (1667–1707) and other parishes. He was admitted a pensioner at Gonville and Caius College, Cambridge, in 1679, matriculated in 1680, graduated BA in 1683, and proceeded MA in 1686. He was ordained deacon by the bishop of London in 1683, and was rector of Boughton, Norfolk (1687–1717), Caldecote, Cambridgeshire (1688–1717), and Oxburgh (1708–17). He joined his father in controversy with Quakers, taking part in a conference with some at West Dereham, Norfolk, in 1698. The following year he wrote a letter to Humphrey Prideaux about an anti-Quaker petition and published a tract denouncing their beliefs. He was buried at Oxburgh on 2 August 1717.

IAN L. O'NEILL

Sources DNB · Venn, *Alum. Cant.* · Wood, *Ath. Oxon.*, new edn · C. H. Firth and R. S. Rait, eds., *Acts and ordinances of the interregnum, 1642–1660*, 3 vols. (1911) · E. Calamy, *An historical account of my own life, with some reflections on the times I have lived in, 1671–1731*, ed. J. T. Rutt, 2 vols. (1829) · G. Hennessy, *Novum repertorium ecclesiasticum parochiale Londinense, or, London diocesan clergy succession from the earliest time to the year 1898* (1898) · *Reliquiae Baxterianae, or, Mr Richard Baxter's narrative of the most memorable passages of his life and times*, ed. M. Sylvester, 1 vol. in 3 pts (1696) · J. L. Chester and G. J. Armytage, eds., *Allegations for marriage licences issued from the faculty office of the archbishop of Canterbury at London, 1543 to 1869*, Harleian Society, 24 (1886) · W. Brigg, ed., *The register book of the parish of St. Nicholas Acons, London, 1539–1812* (1890) · J. L. Chester, ed., *The parish registers of St Michael, Cornhill, London*, Harleian Society, register section, 7 (1882) · W. A. Littledale, ed., *The registers of St Vedast, Foster Lane, and of St Michael le Quern, London*, 2, Harleian Society, register section, 30 (1903) · E. H. Pearce, *Sion College and Library* (1913) · C. E. Surman,

ed., 'The records of the provincial assembly of London, 1647–1660', DWL [2 vols.] · S. Dunn, *Memoirs of the seventy-five emminent divines whose discourses form the morning exercises at Cripplegate, St. Giles in the Fields, and in Southwark* (1844) · R. Newcourt, *Repertorium ecclesiasticum parochiale Londinense*, 2 vols. (1708–10) · W. Kennett, *A register and chronicle ecclesiastical and civil* (1728) · J. Meriton, *Curse not the king* (1661) · *VCH Hertfordshire* · admon, PRO, PROB 6/32, fol. 273r [Henry Meriton of Stilton, Huntingdonshire, 12 Nov 1656] · vestry minute book, St Martin-in-the-Fields, 1651–66, City Westm. AC, F2003, p. 13 · vestry minute book, St Martin-in-the-Fields, 1683–1716, City Westm. AC, F2005, p. 339 · records of the provincial assembly of London, 1647–60, LPL, ARC.L40.2, E17, fols. 123r, 253v · St Nicholas Acons vestry minute book, GL, MS 4060/1, p. 93 · correspondence with Archbishop Sancroft, Bodl. Oxf., MS Tanner 44, fols. 239, 242 · Commonwealth records: register of approvals of ministers, LPL, MS COMM. III/4, fol. 456r · presentation and admission to St Nicholas Acons, LPL, MS COMM. II/460; MS COMM. III/4 · admission to rectory of St Nicholas Acons, GL, MS 9050/8, fol. 49 · admission to rectory of St Michael Cornhill, GL, MS 9050/8, fol. 84 · petition of Nathaniel Hardy and Matthew Smalwood, 1661, GL, MS 10116/1 · speech of John Meriton at vestry meeting, St Michael's, London, 1673, Bodl. Oxf., MS Rawl. C. 24, 3, fol. 71 · declaration on admission to St Nicholas Acons, Drapers' Company Archive, Q21/3 · certificate of resignation from St Nicholas Acons, Drapers' Company Archive, Q21/2 · Rowland Meriton's petition for the profits of the livery of St Michael Cornhill, Drapers' Company Archive, Q21/4 · parish register, St Michael Cornhill, GL, MS 4063/1, fols. 165r, 187r · St Michael Cornhill vestry minute book, GL, MS 4072/2, p. 26 [order appointing curate for John Meriton] · Pepys, *Diary*, 7.365, 8.222 · letter from representatives of St Olave's, Southwark, re Thomas Meriton, July 1683?, PRO, SP29/429, no. 236 · J. Meriton, letter to Humphrey Prideaux, 1699, Bodl. Oxf., MS Tanner 22, fol. 5

Archives Bodl. Oxf., transcript of a speech, MS Rawl. C24, 3. p. 71 | Bodl. Oxf., corresp. with W. Sancroft, Tanner MS 44, fols. 239, 242

Meriton, Thomas (b. 1637/8), playwright, was the second son of Thomas Meriton (1606–1654?) of Castle Leavington, Yorkshire, and Grace, daughter of Francis Wright of Bolton upon Swale, North Riding of Yorkshire. His paternal grandfather was George *Meriton (d. 1624), dean of York; his elder brother was the legal writer George *Meriton (b. 1634, d. in or before 1711).

Thomas was educated at a private school at Danby Wiske, North Riding of Yorkshire. When he was admitted to St John's College, Cambridge, on 9 May 1662, he was twenty-four—an unusually old student, seven or eight years older than many of his peers. By the time he embarked on his first degree Thomas had already written at least four plays, two of which were published in 1658: *The Wandering Lover, a Tragy-Comedie*, dedicated to Francis Wright, and *Love and War, a Tragedy*, which he dedicated to his brother, George. Neither seems to have been staged in public, but *The Wandering Lover*, was as its author proudly informs his readers in the subtitle, 'acted severall times privately at sundry places by the Author and his friends with great applause'. The other two plays he had written, 'The Severall Affairs, a Comedy', and 'The Chast Virgin, a Romance', never went into print, which Langbaine considers a mercy: he disparages Meriton as 'the meanest writer that ever England produced' whose 'stupidity' makes him 'the dullest of poets' (Langbaine, 367). Though Langbaine's remarks are exaggerated the style Meriton employed, especially in *Love and War*, is indeed full of the 'bombast' of which Langbaine accuses him (ibid.).

Meriton, who graduated BA (1665) and MA (1669), was ordained priest on 23 August 1669 and became rector of Normanton, Lincolnshire. The date of his death is not known. ARTEMIS GAUSE-STAMBOULOPOULOU

Sources Venn, *Alum. Cant.*, 1/3.177 · G. Langbaine, *An account of the English dramatick poets*, 2 (1691); facs. edn with introduction by J. Loftis, 2 vols. (1971), vol. 2, pp. 367–70 · [G. Jacob], *The poetical register, or, The lives and characters of the English dramatick poets*, [1] (1719), 181 · *The English verse drama full-text database*, Chadwyck-Healey Ltd (1994–6) [CD-ROM] · *DNB*

Meritt [Maetzker], **Paul John** (1843/4–1895), playwright and theatre manager, was born in Kiev, Russia. His father, originally from Prague, was a naturalized Briton and sometime private secretary to Sir Edward Earle Gascoyne Bulwer. Although formally his surname remained Maetzker, Paul Meritt always used the Anglicized version. On his father's death in 1854, his Yorkshire-born mother, whose maiden name was Elissens, sent him to school in Leeds, where he was known as Russian Jack. There his juvenile melodrama ('Roderick the Ruthless'), written in 1859–60, earned him a flogging for misuse of school paper. In 1861 he made his acting début at the Theatre Royal in Hull, initially as Wilford in *The Iron Chest* by George Colman the younger, but his main employment was as an office clerk in Leeds and, from 1868, in London. Meritt began writing professionally about 1870 and between 1871 and 1874 was a mainstay author at the Grecian Theatre, where his early sensational melodramas ('works strung together almost at haphazard to please an east-end audience'; Archer, 227) included *Sid, or, The Family Legend* (first performed in Doncaster in 1870), *Glin Gath*, and the farce *Chopsticks and Spikins*.

Meritt could write forceful melodramatic dialogue; but none of his pieces had pretensions to literary quality, an aspiration which he tended to disparage. Probably his greatest success was *The New Babylon* (Manchester, 1878; Duke's, 1879), which became the talk of London and ran for 361 performances. It astounded audiences by the verisimilitude, diversity, and brilliance of its settings and effects: a ship collision in mid-Atlantic; representations of Cremorne Gardens, Goodwood racecourse, and the Thames Embankment; and a night scene at the notorious slum of Seven Dials. Equally ingenious and almost as exhilarating was *The World* (1880; with Augustus Harris), which drew on familiar plot-lines such as insurance fraud and thwarted family inheritance, set against an especially thrilling shipboard explosion, a nerve-tingling rescue from a raft (which *The Theatre* suggested was worthy to 'be recorded in the famous annals of melodrama'; p. 176), and the fatal precipitation of the villain down a hotel lift-shaft. Another collaboration with Harris, *Youth* (1881), was notable for the authenticity of its rendering of the convict-yard at Portsmouth gaol, which Meritt had previously visited to absorb the atmosphere.

During the early 1880s Meritt partnered George Conquest at the Surrey Theatre, which led to several jointly written plays and equal sharing of the profits. Indeed, most of Meritt's forty-odd pieces were collaborations, if not with Conquest or Harris, then with Tom Taylor, Henry Spry, or Henry Pettitt. As there was also money to be made from novels based on popular plays, Meritt recruited a Surrey colleague, the actor W. Howell Poole, who dabbled a little in fiction, to produce a novelistic version of *The New Babylon*. It was published jointly in 1882, but Meritt, having contributed little beyond the basic framework, received only a one-third royalty. He later quarrelled with Poole over 'Hidden Millions', a prose version of his earlier play *Glin Gath*, published under Meritt's sole name in *Pictorial World* (Christmas 1882). As principal author, Poole claimed a £200 royalty rather than the £45 Meritt actually paid; but after a two-day court hearing in 1885, irreconcilable conflicts in evidence emerged, preventing the jury from agreeing on a verdict. Meritt's last exposure on the London stage was the revival of *The World* (1894), which ran for fifty performances. According to *The Times*, it had aged well for a fourteen-year-old play and, as a spectacular, episodic melodrama, was still 'a striking work of its class' (26 Feb 1894).

A large-framed man, well-built, and bespectacled, with a rather chubby appearance, Meritt possessed, in William Archer's opinion, powers of invention which could have fitted him 'for better things' (Archer, 231). But within his range he enjoyed real success and made enough money to indulge his passion of collecting theatrical portraiture. A member of the Savage Club and the Dramatic Authors' Society, he knew the theatre intimately and was a friend of leading figures such as Arthur Pinero and Henry Irving. Actively involved in the production of his plays, he attended the majority of first nights personally. About a quarter of his dramatic output was published, all in Lacy's *Acting Edition*. Meritt died on 7 July 1895 at his home, The Hollies, Pembroke Square, Kensington, London, and was buried on the 11th in Brompton cemetery in London. He was survived by his wife, Annie.

JOHN RUSSELL STEPHENS

Sources *The Era* (13 July 1895), 9 [incl. play bibliography] · *The Graphic* (13 July 1895), 38 · P. Meritt, 'My first drama, and what became of it', *Era Almanack and Annual* (1888), 85–6 · W. Archer, *English dramatists of to-day* (1882), 226–32 · C. Pascoe, *Dramatic notes: a chronicle of the London stage, 1879–1882* (1883) · C. Scott, review, *The Theatre*, 3rd ser., 2 (1880), 174–7 · *The Times* (1 May 1885), 3 · *The Times* (2 May 1885), 6 · *The Times* (26 Feb 1894), 12 · Boase, *Mod. Eng. biog.* · A. Nicoll, *Late nineteenth century drama, 1850–1900*, 2nd edn (1959), vol. 5 of *A history of English drama, 1660–1900* (1952–9), 485–7, 806 · J. P. Wearing, *The London stage, 1890–1899: a calendar of plays and players*, 2 vols. (1976) [performance data for the 1890s] · *CGPLA Eng. & Wales* (1895) · d. cert.
Likenesses London Stereoscopic Co., photograph, repro. in *The Graphic*
Wealth at death £4863 18s. 4d.: probate, 23 Aug 1895, *CGPLA Eng. & Wales*

Merivale, Charles (1808–1893), historian and dean of Ely, second son in the large family of John Herman *Merivale (1779–1844), commissioner in bankruptcy, and Louisa Heath (1787–1873), daughter of Joseph *Drury, was born at 14 East Street, Red Lion Square, London, on 8 March 1808.

Charles Merivale (1808–1893), by unknown photographer

His father being a Unitarian and his mother an Anglican, he was brought up in a climate of undogmatic and practical piety. At the age of fifteen he joined the Church of England with other members of the family. Initially taught by his mother, he showed an early enthusiasm for education, especially for Roman history, which, with his brother Herman *Merivale, he converted into a game which they played with their hoops in Queen Square. He also briefly attended a private day school kept by Dr Lloyd in Keppel Street, Bloomsbury, and was afterwards grounded in Greek by his father. In January 1818 he was entered at Harrow School, of which his grandfather had been headmaster. Here his contemporaries included Charles Wordsworth, Richard Chenevix Trench, and Henry Edward Manning. While at Harrow he wrote much Latin verse and committed to memory the *Eclogues* and *Georgics* of Virgil, all of Catullus and of Juvenal, and the greater part of Lucan. He also passed muster in the cricket field, and in 1824 played in the match against Eton. On the offer of an Indian writership in 1824 he transferred to Haileybury College, where he took prizes in classics and Persian, and was first in the class list. But a casual perusal of Edward Gibbon's *Autobiography* awakened conflicting interests. As his enthusiasm for the life of a scholar grew, the prospect of a career in the Indian Civil Service lost its appeal. His father agreed to send him to Cambridge, and the writership was instead given to John Laird Muir Lawrence.

Merivale was admitted to St John's College, and matriculated in 1826. He graduated BA (senior optime and fourth classic) in 1830, having in the preceding year gained the Browne medals for Latin verse, and proceeded MA in 1833, BD in 1840, and DD in 1871. He also rowed for the university in the first boat race with Oxford at Henley in 1829, and in the following summer accomplished the feat of walking from Cambridge to London in one day. In his early graduate days he belonged to the élite society, the Apostles, many of whose members were destined for high office in church and state, and to a smaller society called the Hermathenae. Among his friends were Henry Alford (afterwards dean of Canterbury), William Hepworth Thompson (afterwards master of Trinity), Joseph Williams Blakesley (afterwards dean of Lincoln), James Spedding, and John Mitchell Kemble, the philologist. Merivale was at this time a liberal, and interest in the Belgian revolution drew him to the Netherlands in the summer of 1831. On his return he briefly pursued interests in Anglo-Saxon, Saint-Simonianism, and freemasonry, but on his election to a fellowship in 1833, he took holy orders and settled down to historical research. In the reaction against the parliamentary Reform Act of 1832, his political opinions became conservative, as they were to remain for the rest of his life. Nevertheless, the high toryism of St John's College proved uncongenial, and he was only reconciled to continued residence there by his failure in 1835 to win the chair of classics at King's College, London, and several subsequent disappointments. Meanwhile he studied German, travelled to Bavaria and Austria (1836), and cultivated a growing interest in Roman history. He was a conscientious, though unenthusiastic, tutor, and in 1836 and 1837 was one of the examiners for the classical tripos. His religious views were moderate, and the four sermons which he delivered as select preacher to the university in November 1838 were warmly commended by William Whewell, and led to his appointment in the following year as select preacher at Whitehall. As a scholar he was more of a Latinist than a Grecian, and a devotee to Latin verse composition. Although he had studied political economy under Malthus at Haileybury, he retained no interest in the subject or sympathy with his master's opinions—he was a lifelong protectionist. Nevertheless, in academic matters he was a moderate reformer, and helped to establish the law, moral sciences, and natural sciences triposes, which, however, he subsequently described as 'sickly growths' (*Autobiography*, 105). He was naturally inclined to a retired life, and, even when absorbed in the study of Roman history, was satisfied with a single brief visit to Rome in the autumn of 1845.

To secure leisure for his studies, Merivale accepted the rectory of Lawford, Essex, a college living, in 1848, and relinquished his fellowship. Now able to wed, he married on 2 July 1850, Judith Mary Sophia (1817–1906), youngest daughter of George Frere of Lincoln's Inn. They had three sons and two daughters.

Merivale had contributed a version of 'Der Kampf mit dem Drachen' to his father's translation of the minor poems of Schiller (1844); but subsequently his German studies were subordinate to his historical work. He was collaborating on a *History of Rome*, for the Society for the Diffusion of Useful Knowledge, when its failure set him free to recast and continue the work independently on a large scale as the *History of the Romans under the Empire* (7 vols., 1850–64; new edn, 8 vols., 1865). The value of this work, which formed a prelude to Gibbon's *Decline and Fall of the Roman Empire*, was largely uncontested by contemporaries. Despite Merivale's neglect of epigraphical and numismatic sources, it made his reputation and was translated into German, French, and Italian. The popularity of the first three volumes induced him to publish a popular epitome in one volume, *The Fall of the Roman Republic* (1853), which reached a fifth edition in 1863. He also edited as parerga *C. Sallustii Crispi Catilina et Jugurtha* (1852) and *An account of the life and letters of Cicero, translated from the German of Bernhard Rudolf Abeken* (1854), and contributed the article on Niebuhr to the *Encyclopaedia Britannica* in 1857. He wrote for the conservative journal, the *Saturday Review*, for some years, and produced an apologetic lecture for the Christian Evidence Society, entitled *The Contrast between Pagan and Christian Society* (1872). His *General History of Rome from the Foundation of the City to the Fall of Augustulus* (1875) was a convenient epitome of a vast subject: an abridgement by C. Puller appeared in 1877. Other historical writings included *The Roman Triumvirates* (1876), *St Paul at Rome* (1877), and *Four Lectures on some Epochs of Early Church History* (1879). He also published several works of Latin verse, but *Homer's Iliad in English Rhymed Verse* (1869), which appeared when there was keen competition among translators, did not add to his reputation. Other publications included sermons and discourses, as well as a pamphlet entitled *Open Fellowships: a Plea for Submitting College Fellowships to University Competition* (1858), and a memoir of his brother Herman (1884). He was Hulsean lecturer in 1862, was reappointed select preacher at Whitehall in 1864, and delivered the Boyle lectures in 1864 and 1865. In 1862 and 1871 he examined for the Indian Civil Service. He acted as chaplain of the House of Commons from 1863 until 1869, and in November of that year, having declined the regius chair of modern history at Cambridge, accepted the deanery of Ely from Gladstone. Further honours included the honorary degree of DCL from the University of Oxford in 1866, and in 1884 that of LLD from Edinburgh. St John's made him an honorary fellow in 1874.

Merivale made no figure in convocation, and after only a few months withdrew from the committee for the revision of the Authorized Version of the New Testament, observing that he had come to translate, not to construe. His dry humour was reserved for private circles. He identified himself with no ecclesiastical party, abhorred polemics, and as a preacher was judicious rather than eloquent. Although he favoured the toleration of diversity as the only means of avoiding the disruption of the church, he approved the controversial Public Worship Regulation Act of 1874 which was intended to check ritualism. His later years were spent in almost entire seclusion at Ely, where he enlarged the school. His most memorable act as

dean was to organize an elaborate commemoration in 1873 of the foundation of Ely Minster, of which he published an account. His nephew, Christopher Wordsworth, described him as 'the most imperturbable and sedentary of men in later years' (Wordsworth, 162). On 17 February 1892 he had a slight attack of paralysis; a second, towards the close of November 1893, was followed by his death on 27 December at the deanery at Ely. He was buried in Ely cemetery on 2 January 1894; his monument was placed in Ely Cathedral. His *Autobiography*, a fragment reaching no further than his ordination, was edited with his correspondence by his daughter, Judith Anne Merivale, for private circulation and published in 1899.

J. M. RIGG, *rev.* JOHN D. PICKLES

Sources *Autobiography and letters of Charles Merivale*, ed. J. A. Merivale (1899) • A. W. Merivale, *Family memorials* (privately printed, Exeter, 1884) • C. Wordsworth, *Cambridge Review* (18 Jan 1894) • C. Wordsworth, *Cambridge Review* (25 Jan 1894) • J. E. Sandys, *The Eagle*, 18 (1895), 183–96 • H. C. Merivale, *Bar, stage and platform: autobiographic memoirs* (1902), 82–96 • *The Times* (28 Dec 1893) • *The new Cambridge bibliography of English literature*, [2nd edn], 3, ed. G. Watson (1969), 1493–4 • P. Allen, *The Cambridge Apostles: the early years* (1978) • Burke, *Gen. GB* [Frere pedigree] • probate • *CGPLA Eng. & Wales* (1894) • *Cambridge Chronicle* (29 Dec 1893)

Archives CUL, letters • Emory University, Atlanta, Georgia, Pitts Theology Library, corresp. with H. E. Manning • NL Wales, letters to George Stovin Venables • UCL, letters to Society for the Diffusion of Useful Knowledge

Likenesses C. W. Walton, lithograph, *c*.1893, St John Cam. • marble medallion, *c*.1900, Ely Cathedral • engraving (in old age; after photograph), repro. in *ILN* (6 Jan 1894), 5 • photograph (in old age), NPG [*see illus.*]

Wealth at death £11,216 1s. 4d.: probate, 26 Jan 1894, *CGPLA Eng. & Wales*

Merivale, Herman (1806–1874), civil servant and economist, was born on 8 November 1806 at Cockwood House, Dawlish, Devon, the eldest of twelve children of John Herman *Merivale (1779–1844), commissioner in bankruptcy, and his wife, Louisa Heath (1787–1873), daughter of the Revd Dr Joseph *Drury. Charles *Merivale, dean of Ely, was a younger brother. Merivale was a boy of extraordinary precocity. He read Latin when four years old with his grandfather Drury. In January 1817 he was sent to Harrow School, to the house of his uncle, Henry Joseph Thomas *Drury. He was captain of the school before he was sixteen, read much in his uncle's library and became, like his father, a good Italian scholar. He wrote long letters to his father on Tasso's *Jerusalem Delivered* (1819) and Gibbon's account of the Arian controversy (1820). He won all the school prizes, and was taken by his father to see Coleridge at Highgate. He went into residence at Oriel College, Oxford, in January 1824. In 1825 he won an open scholarship at Trinity College and was elected as first holder of the Ireland scholarship. After a first class in classical honours in 1827, he was elected to a fellowship at Balliol in December 1828, and was Eldon scholar in 1831. Called to the bar at the Inner Temple in 1832, he practised on the western circuit. He was highly respected in his profession, and was, when he had a favourable opportunity, a very

Herman Merivale (1806–1874), by unknown engraver, pubd 1874 (after Dickinson)

effective speaker, but his practice was not in proportion to his reputation, perhaps because he was not disposed to the oratorical efforts which were admired at quarter sessions. He was appointed recorder of Falmouth, Helston, and Penzance in 1841. He married at Dawlish, on 29 October 1834, Caroline Penelope (d. 1881), eldest daughter of the Revd William Villiers Robinson and sister of Sir George Stamp Robinson.

On 2 March 1837 Merivale was elected to the professorship of political economy at Oxford, founded by Henry Drummond in 1825. He held it for the usual term of five years and delivered a course of lectures on the colonies. The lectures made a great impression, containing a very able criticism of the Wakefield scheme of colonization, and were published in 1841 (reprinted in 1861) as *Lectures on Colonization and Colonies*. The book led to his appointment in November 1847 as assistant under-secretary of state for the colonies, and in 1848 he succeeded Sir James Stephen as permanent under-secretary. Here, as always, he was a person of great promptitude of judgement, and vigorous, if not combative, in defending it. His tight, perceptive minutes reflected both colonial history and knowledge of America. He believed in colonial self-government, the utility of colonies, and the durability of empire, united by loyalty to the crown in some form of federation. As in the India Office later, he tended to let sleeping dogs lie, and did not leave his imprint on the colonies as much as did Stephen and Sir Frederic Rogers. Edward Bulwer-Lytton, when resigning the secretaryship for the colonies in June 1859, expressed his gratitude for Merivale's services in the warmest terms, and later described him as one of the

most remarkable men he had ever met. His intellectual characteristic was 'massiveness', and he could be compared 'to no other of less calibre than Macaulay'. He was held in the highest esteem by his official colleagues.

In 1860 Merivale became permanent under-secretary in the new India Office, by invitation of Sir Charles Wood, with the distinction of CB. For someone who believed that a changed dispatch was a bad dispatch, the elaborate consultative process, involving the Council of India, smacked of too many cooks. Notwithstanding, his Colonial Office experience provided valuable guidance in Indian affairs, which included complex legal problems. He lent stature to the permanent under-secretaryship, his opinion being sought by council members and the secretary of state alike.

Strong of features and thickset, Merivale was unassuming and unambitious, with a formidable capacity for work (which even Sir Louis Mallet admired). He was a lover of heraldry, geology, and trees enjoyed on a visit to America. He talked little, but always well and with humour; he refused a KCB, seeing no use of it, and sought relaxation by playing indifferent whist, dabbling in poetry, and writing. His literary works, except the *Lectures on Colonization*, were written in intervals between more absorbing business and scarcely give a full impression of his powers. These include a variety of articles in the *Edinburgh Review*, *Foreign Quarterly*, *Quarterly Review*, and *Pall Mall Gazette*. His other works include his *Introductory Lecture upon Political Economy* (1837); a collection of reports of legal cases in the queen's bench (with A. Davison, 1844); *Historical Studies* (1865); *Memoirs of Sir Philip Francis* (1867); and the second volume of the *Life of Sir Henry Lawrence* (1872).

Merivale received an honorary DCL from Oxford in 1870. In politics he was a staunch Liberal, believing in the rights of subject peoples. In private life he showed a singularly affectionate nature, both in early life to his parents, brothers, and sisters, and afterwards among his own family and friends. He suffered intense grief at the death in 1872 of his daughter Agnes. He had another daughter, Isabella, and a son, Herman Charles *Merivale, the playwright. By his mother's death in 1873 he inherited the family estate of Barton Place. He died on 8 February 1874 at his house, 13 Cornwall Gardens, South Kensington, London, and was buried in Fulham cemetery. In his funeral encomium, C. J. Vaughan, master of the Temple, described him as one of 'that order of true and real men who are not for show, but for use, who scramble not for place or title, but do an unobtrusive work well [and] cultivate intellect not for its emoluments, but for its blessings'. LESLIE STEPHEN, rev. DONOVAN WILLIAMS

Sources A. W. Merivale, *Family memorials* (privately printed, Exeter, 1884) · C. Merivale, 'Herman Merivale, C.B.', *Report and Transactions of the Devonshire Association*, 16 (1884), 570–80 · W. P. Morrell, *British colonial policy in the mid-Victorian age* (1969) · J. W. Cell, *British colonial administration in the mid-nineteenth century: the policy-making process* (1970) · S. R. Stenbridge, *Parliament, the press, and the colonies, 1846–1880* (1982) · K. N. Bell and W. P. Morrell, eds., *Select documents on British colonial policy, 1830–1860* (1928); repr. (1986) · H. C. Merivale, *Bar, stage and platform: autobiographic memoirs* (1902) · A. West,

Contemporary portraits: men of my day in public life (1920) • D. Williams, *The India Office, 1858–1869* (1983) • *Wellesley index* • *Pall Mall Gazette* (9 Feb 1874), 5
Archives BL, letters to Macvey Napier, Add. MSS 34617–34626 • BL OIOC, letters to Sir Henry Sumner-Maine • Herts. ALS, corresp. with Lord Lytton • U. Nott., letters to duke of Newcastle
Likenesses drawing (after Dickinson), repro. in *The Graphic* (21 Feb 1874), 178 • wood-engraving (after Dickinson), NPG; repro. in *ILN* (21 Feb 1874), 168 [*see illus.*]
Wealth at death under £14,000: probate, 25 Feb 1874, *CGPLA Eng. & Wales*

Merivale, Herman Charles (1839–1906), playwright and novelist, born in London on 27 January 1839, was the only son of Herman *Merivale (1806–1874), a barrister, writer, and civil servant who was permanent under-secretary of the India Office, and his wife, Caroline Penelope Robinson (*d.* 1881), daughter of the Revd William Villiers Robinson. Merivale had two sisters. He was educated first at a preparatory school, and then at Harrow School, where he was a favourite of C. J. Vaughan, the headmaster. A detailed account of his often unhappy schooldays is found in his reminiscences, *Bar, Stage and Platform: Autobiographic Memoirs* (1902). On leaving school in 1857 he entered Balliol College, Oxford, where A. C. Swinburne and Charles Bowen were his contemporaries. He graduated BA in 1861, with a first class in classical moderations and a second in the final classical school. From early youth he had been devoted to drama, and was a good amateur actor who unsuccessfully attempted to start a drama club at Oxford.

Called to the bar of the Inner Temple, London, on 26 January 1864, Merivale went on the western circuit, and also the Norfolk circuit, where Matthew Arnold was his companion. Later, through his father's influence, he was junior counsel for the government on Indian appeals, and in 1867 boundary commissioner for north Wales under the Reform Act. From 1870 to 1880 he edited the *Annual Register*. At his father's home he met many distinguished men, including Lord Robert Cecil (afterwards Lord Salisbury), who became a lifelong friend. His friends in literary and dramatic circles included William Makepeace Thackeray, Edward Bulwer-Lytton, Matthew Arnold, Anthony Trollope, W. S. Gilbert, Edmund Yates, and others.

After his father's death in 1874 Merivale gave up law and, following his real tastes, devoted himself to literature and drama. As early as 1867 he had written, under the pseudonym of Felix Dale, a farce, *He's a Lunatic*, in which John Clayton played the main role, and in 1872 Hermann Vezin produced at London's Court Theatre *A Son of the Soil*, which had been adopted by Merivale from François Ponsard's *Le lion amoureux*.

Merivale's first dramatic success was *All for Her*, based on Charles Dickens's *A Tale of Two Cities*, written in collaboration with J. Palgrave Simpson, and produced by John Clayton at the Mirror Theatre on 18 October 1875. In the autumn of 1879 Genevieve Ward produced *Forget-Me-Not*, by Merivale and F. C. Grove, taking the part of the heroine, Stéphanie de Mohrivart—a role that she would continue to play more than 2000 times over a period of ten years in many different countries. In 1882, at the invitation of the

Herman Charles Merivale (1839–1906), by Elliott & Fry

actor and manager Sir Squire Bancroft, Merivale adapted Victorien Sardou's *Fédora*. His poetic drama, *The White Pilgrim* was produced by Vezin in 1883, and in the same year he published the piece in a volume with other poems.

Merivale wrote many farces and burlesques. At John Hollingshead's invitation he produced *The Lady of Lyons Married and Settled* (Gaiety Theatre, 5 October 1878), and *Called There and Back* (Gaiety, 15 October 1884). *The Butler* (1886) and *The Don* (1888) were both written for the actor J. L. Toole. In writing *The Don*, and other works, Merivale was assisted by his wife, Elizabeth, daughter of John Pittman. They were married in London on 13 May 1878, and she was to be his constant companion and support until the end of his life. His mental state was 'always precarious' (Sutherland, 430), leading to occasional mental and physical breakdowns throughout his life. In 1879 he published *My Experiences in a Lunatic Asylum*, written 'By a Sane Patient', in which he stated that nervous illness was 'aggravated tenfold by this unutterable cruelty' of committal (*My Experiences in a Lunatic Asylum*, 166).

In 1882 Merivale sold the acting rights of *Edgar and Lucy*, a play adapted from Sir Walter Scott's *Bride of Lammermoor*, to Henry Irving, who produced it on 20 September 1890 under the title of *Ravenswood*. Merivale's well-received novel *Faucit and Balliol* was published also in 1882, the earlier chapters of which provide a lively evocation of Oxford life. He also demonstrated his literary facility with a fairytale for children, *Binko's Blues* (1884), and *Florien*, a five-act tragedy in verse (1884), and in frequent contributions to periodicals. His legal training was put to the use of the Dramatic Authors' Society, and with J. Palgrave Simpson, W. S. Gilbert, and others he led the fight for the reform of dramatic copyright.

Merivale's unstable health required him to live at Eastbourne on the Sussex coast. There he interested himself in politics as an ardent Liberal, working hard for the party between 1880 and 1890. A brilliant speaker, he refused many invitations to stand for parliament, including the offer of an Irish seat from Charles Stewart Parnell. He had a fair complexion, a full fair beard, and was slightly rotund, and although he had a cheerful presence he probably suffered from depression; in 1891 he was unable to complete a memoir of his friend Thackeray for the Great Writers series of Messrs Walter Scott. (Sir Frank Marzials finished the work in 1891.) Ordered to take a long sea voyage to Australia, Merivale and his wife were shipwrecked, and they returned to England after having been rescued. On leaving for Australia he had been induced to give his solicitor and trustee Cartmell Harrison a 'power of attorney', and in 1900, through Harrison's default, he lost the whole of his fortune of £2000 a year. A civil-list pension of £125 was awarded him on 25 May 1900. In June a matinée was given for his benefit at Her Majesty's Theatre in London.

A few years before his death Merivale had become a Roman Catholic. He died suddenly of heart failure on 14 January 1906 at 69 Woodstock Road, Acton, Middlesex, and was buried in his father's grave in Brompton cemetery. He had no children and his widow was granted a civil-list pension of £50 in 1906.

ELIZABETH LEE, rev. WILLIAM BAKER

Sources H. C. Merivale, *Bar, stage and platform: autobiographic memoirs* (1902) · *The Times* (17 Jan 1906), 6 · J. R. Stephens, *The profession of the playwright: British theatre, 1800–1900* (1992), 101–3, 181 · J. A. Sutherland, 'Merivale, Herman Charles', *The Stanford companion to Victorian fiction* (1989), 430 · L. W. Conolly and J. P. Wearing, *English drama and theatre, 1800–1900* (1978), 143–4 · R. Foulkes, ed., *British theatre in the 1890s* (1992), 19, 44–5, 60–61 · B. Stoker, *Personal reminiscences of Henry Irving*, 2 vols. (1906) · H. C. Black, *Pen, pencil, baton, and mask: biographical sketches* (1896), 180 · *Reminiscences of J. L. Toole*, ed. J. Hatton (1892), 264–5 · J. Hollingshead, *Gaiety chronicles* (1898) · M. E. Bancroft and S. Bancroft, *The Bancrofts: recollections of sixty years* (1909) · A. Nicoll, *A history of late nineteenth century drama, 1850–1900*, 2 (1946); repr. (1949), 487 [repr. (1949)] · *The letters and private papers of William Makepeace Thackeray*, ed. G. N. Ray, 2 (1945), 662, 59n. · m. cert. · d. cert.

Likenesses C. Calthrop, portrait; formerly in possession of Mrs Merivale, 1912 · Elliott & Fry, photograph, repro. in Merivale, *Bar, stage, and platform*, frontispiece [*see illus.*] · portrait; formerly in possession of Mrs Merivale, 1912

Wealth at death £2832 9s. 6d.: probate, 24 Feb 1906, *CGPLA Eng. & Wales*

Merivale, John Herman (1779–1844), lawyer and literary scholar, was born in Exeter, Devon, on 5 August 1779, the only son of John Merivale (1752–1831), of Barton Place, Exeter, and Bedford Square, London, and Ann Katenkamp (1754–1829), daughter of a German merchant settled in Exeter. The earliest records of the Merivale (originally spelt Mervayle) family are to be found in the parish registers of Middleton Cheney, Northamptonshire, dating back to 1558.

Samuel Merivale (1715–1771), John Herman's grandfather, was born on 21 November 1715 in Northampton, the son of John Merivale (1668–1733), a stocking weaver and milliner, and Hannah Moore (*b.* 1693). Samuel Merivale was brought up as a Baptist, attending the Independent Baptist Academy about 1731. He then came under the influence of Dr Philip Doddridge, attending his academy in Northampton in 1733, and became a Presbyterian. He began to officiate as 'stated' minister at Sleaford, Lincolnshire, in 1737. In 1743 he received a 'call' to Tavistock, where he underwent the ceremony of ordination. In 1748 he married Elizabeth Schellaber. She died in 1761; in that same year Samuel Merivale accepted the post of tutor to the Presbyterian Theological Seminary, founded in that year at Exeter. He married in 1766 Betsy Manning, *née* Bottrell (*d.* 1805). Samuel Merivale died in Exeter in December 1771 and was buried in the Unitarian burial-ground there. He had published *Daily Devotions for the Closet: to which are Added Prayers on Particular Occasions* (3rd edn 1796).

Samuel Merivale's grandson, John Herman Merivale, was himself brought up a Unitarian, so that although he attended St John's College, Cambridge, he left in 1796 without taking a degree. After 1819 he conformed to the Church of England. On 17 December 1798 he entered Lincoln's Inn, London, and was called to the bar in 1804. On 10 July 1805 Merivale married Louisa Heath (1787–1873), daughter of the Revd Joseph *Drury, headmaster of Harrow School. They had six sons and six daughters. Their eldest son was Herman *Merivale (1806–1874); their second son was Charles *Merivale (1808–1893), dean of Ely and historian of the Roman empire.

In 1811, at the request of the Society for the Diffusion of Knowledge, Merivale published a work concerning the death penalty and the improvement of prison discipline, entitled *A brief statement of the proceedings in both houses of parliament in the last and present sessions upon the several bills introduced with a view to the amendment of the criminal law*. He practised in chancery and bankruptcy, and published *Reports of Cases Argued and Determined in the High Court of Chancery* (3 vols., 1817–19). He sat on the chancery commission of 1824, concurring with its report, but expounded a wider scheme of reform in *A Letter to William Courtenay, Esq., on the Subject of the Chancery Commission* (1827). On 2 December 1831 he was appointed to a commissionership in bankruptcy, which he held until his death.

Merivale was an accurate and elegant scholar, accomplished alike in classical and romantic literature. He was a friend of Byron's. With Robert Bland he published *Translations Chiefly from the Greek Anthology: with Tales and Miscellaneous Poems* (1806), including translations by Henry Drury and Thomas Denman, though usually called simply 'Bland and Merivale'. It was greatly admired by Byron, who praised the compilers in *English Bards and Scotch*

Reviewers (line 881), and bitterly regretted not having the book in Greece. A revised and enlarged edition, retitled *Collections from the Greek Anthology and from the Pastoral, Elegiac, and Dramatic Poets of Greece* (1813) did not sell so well as had been hoped. In 1814 Merivale published *Orlando in Roncesvalles*, a poem in *ottava rima*, based on the *Morgante maggiore* of Luigi Pulci. This too was liked by Byron, who wrote: 'your measure is uncommonly well chosen and wielded' (*Byron's Letters and Journals*, 4.12), and by Ugo Foscolo in his article, 'Narrative and Romantic poems of the Italians' (*QR*, 21, 1819, 486–556). When making his own translation of the first canto of *Morgante maggiore* Byron recommended Merivale as an Italian linguist to John Murray (*Byron's Letters and Journals*, 7.54). In 1815 Merivale tried unsuccessfully to establish himself as a playwright, submitting co-written dramatic works to Drury Lane through Byron, who said, 'I have some doubts of it—but none of your part therein' (*Byron's Letters and Journals*, 4.301). In 1820 he brought out a free translation, again in *ottava rima*, of the first and third cantos of Fortiguerra's *Ricciardetto*. A collective edition of Merivale's *Poems, Original and Translated*, appeared in two volumes in 1838; it included a continuation of Beattie's *Minstrel*, previously published anonymously in 1808. At the age of sixty Merivale learned German, and shortly before his death published accurate translations of some of Schiller's poems as *The Minor Poems of Schiller of the Second and Third Periods* (1844).

Merivale was a frequent contributor to the *Quarterly Review*, other reviews, and periodicals. He made some collections for a history of Devon. Nicknamed 'Merry', he was universally popular in the literary circle which formed around Henry Drury (Hodgson, 1.45, 47). Byron recalled him as 'a very good-natured fellow' (*Byron's Letters and Journals*, 3.247). Merivale died suddenly at his London residence in Bedford Square on 25 April 1844; his wife survived him. His memorial in Hampstead church, where he was buried, omits his literary attainments, merely stating he was 'one of the commissioners in Her Majesty's court of bankruptcy'. J. M. RIGG, *rev.* RALPH LLOYD-JONES

Sources A. W. Merivale, *Family memorials* (privately printed, Exeter, 1884) · E. H. A. Koch, *Leaves from the diary of a literary amateur: John Herman Merivale, 1819–1844* (1911) · *Byron's letters and journals*, ed. L. A. Marchand, 3 (1974), 247; 4 (1975), 12, 301; 7 (1977), 54 · [J. T. Hodgson], *Memoir of the Rev. Francis Hodgson BD scholar, poet and divine*, 2 vols. (1878) · [U. Foscolo], 'Narrative and Romantic poems of the Italians', *QR*, 21 (1819), 486–556 [review] · *GM*, 2nd ser., 22 (1844), 96 · W. P. Baildon, ed., *The records of the Honorable Society of Lincoln's Inn: admissions*, 1 (1896) · review of *The minor poems of Schiller*, *The Athenaeum* (30 March 1844), 285–7 · *The Athenaeum* (4 May 1844), 407 · review of *Poems, original and translated*, *QR*, 64 (1839), 396–411 · *LondG* (6 Dec 1831) · 'Merivale's poems', *Dublin University Magazine*, 16 (1840), 403–9 · 'The Greek anthology', *Blackwood*, 33 (1833), 865–88 · 'The Greek anthology', *Blackwood*, 34 (1833), 115–40, 258–84, 373–406, 961–98 · C. Merivale, 'Herman Merivale, C.B.', *Report and Transactions of the Devonshire Association*, 16 (1884), 570–80 · *Memoirs, journal and correspondence of Thomas Moore*, ed. J. Russell, 6 (1854), 320 · will, PRO, PROB 11/2000/479, 1844

Archives BL, Add. MSS 40362, 40501, 44058 · Devon and Exeter Institution Library, Exeter, sketches of church monuments, etc. | BL, letters to Joseph Hunter, Add. MS 24871 · Bodl. Oxf., letters to Isaac Disraeli · John Munnby Ltd, London · LUL, letters to Lord Brougham · NL Scot., corresp. with Blackwoods · UCL, letters to Society for the Diffusion of Useful Knowledge

Likenesses J. Posselwhite, stipple, pubd *c.*1844 (after E. U. Eddis), NPG · E. U. Eddis, drawing, 1848, Hampstead church; repro. in Koch, *Leaves from the diary of a literary amateur* · group portrait, oils, priv. coll.

Wealth at death over £20,000—incl. property in Exeter and in Bedford Square: will, 1844, PRO, PROB 11/2000/479

Merivale, Samuel (1715–1771). *See under* Merivale, John Herman (1779–1844).

Merk [Merke], **Thomas** (*d.* 1409/10), bishop of Carlisle, was of unknown origin, but there was a Merk family holding land in Drayton, Middlesex, whose members had frequent dealings with the Benedictines of Westminster Abbey between 1365 and 1429. Merk entered that house as a novice *c.*1376. Abbot William Colchester, probably his mentor and possibly a kinsman, included just him alongside his parents and himself in an anniversary mass established in 1411.

Merk was BTh of Oxford in 1392–3 and DTh by 1395, when he was prominent enough to be one of a university delegation to submit to the king for alleged misdeeds during a recent controversy with Archbishop Arundel. At some point he composed *De moderno dictamine*, a guide to letter-writing for apprentice estate managers which won immediate popularity and provided sharp evidence that here was no ordinary monk–scholar. In 1393 he was appointed as a visitor for the Benedictine order by the provincial chapter, apparently as deputy for Abbot Colchester. The abbey enjoyed Richard II's personal patronage, and evidently Merk had especially caught the king's eye. He accompanied him to Ireland in 1395 and may even have hoped to become bishop of Worcester in that year. This was premature, but certainly he was now *persona grata* with the king, and henceforward used heavily by him. He was included in an embassy to Paris from 19 June to 18 August 1396 to seal the king's second marriage; perhaps Merk was to contribute theological expertise.

On 4 January 1397 Merk was papally provided to the see of Carlisle, entirely to gain status and a modestly comfortable income, not at all to run it. He received its temporalities on 18 March and had been consecrated by 23 April. Richard was at this time promoting to bishoprics several religious from a circle of such men that he was gathering at court. They were able men, but their constant intimacy, presence, and advancement were unusual, and attracted critical comment, Merk by name as a carouser with the king. On the other hand, he was away on embassies to Cologne (18 May–26 August 1397), to France and the empire (5 November 1397–5 February 1398), and to Paris to collect Queen Isabella's dowry (19 October–28 November 1398). In between he was always with the king, and undertook the controversial errand on 20 September 1397 of warning off Archbishop Arundel from coming into parliament to fight his banishment.

Merk accompanied the king on his fateful expedition to Ireland (having been named as both an executor and legatee in his will), returned with him to Milford Haven, and was among the handful chosen to speed with him up the

Welsh coast to Conwy in the vain bid to out-race Henry Bolingbroke and muster the Ricardian powerhouse of Cheshire. Whatever the varying reliability of the many accounts, he was clearly regarded as a major influence on the king, one whose safety Richard sought to protect in the negotiations that ensued, and said to be sceptical of Bolingbroke's avowed guarantees to the king. The chronicler Jean Creton, who was a bystander at the usurpation, says that Merk was one of just five men whom Bolingbroke demanded be tried for treason. On the other hand, once the king had been taken near Flint, it is also reported that Bolingbroke sought to content the bishop and, for whatever reasons on each side, it seems that Merk did take his place in the deposition assembly on 30 September. A very unreliable French chronicle (the *Chronique de la traïson et mort de Richart Deux, roy Dengleterre*) almost at once, English chroniclers predictably much later, and Shakespeare latest of all and most famously asserted that the bishop alone, or as one of very few, dared speak out and refuse to believe that Richard had abdicated freely unless he were brought into public to confirm it:

> My lord of Hereford here, whom you call king,
> Is a foul traitor to proud Hereford's king;
> And if you crown him, let me prophesy,
> The blood of English shall manure the ground
> And future ages groan for this foul act.
> (*Richard II*, IV.i)

Whatever the exact truth, and recent scholars doubt the dramatic incident, Merk was removed immediately to St Albans Abbey 'for his safety' (*Johannis de Trokelowe … chronica*, 314), and became one of only two bishops to lose their sees; indeed, the other, Roger Walden, had to suffer because he was occupying Archbishop Arundel's place but was not held in custody. Merk was translated by a pliant pope to the *in partibus* see of Salmas by 19 October 1399, when he took an oath of obedience to the archbishop of York, but he could not gain confirmation of even this titular see. On 29 October he was charged in parliament with complicity in the murder of the duke of Gloucester in 1397, and possibly he had indeed been in or near Calais at the crucial time. Despite 'a fine speech' of which Walsingham heard, and which perhaps underlies the legend of his brave loyalty to Richard II, he suffered forfeiture and exclusion from the general amnesty on 19 November. In practice, though, he was simply left under the nominal surveillance of the abbot of St Albans, and was able to become involved in preparations for the 'Epiphany plot' by Richard II's closest supporters, allegedly (but this is again the ever confident *Traïson et mort*) even meeting with them on 17 December in Westminster Abbey. Partly because the plot was so confused in execution, he took no part in its actual misfire, but he was imprisoned in the Tower of London on 10 January and found guilty of treason (by a jury of laymen) on 4 February. He was sentenced to death, and the king set about seeking his degradation from orders and surrender to secular authority.

For whatever reason, Merk suddenly found mercy. On 23 June 1400 he was simply committed to the very friendly custody of Abbot Colchester at Westminster and pardoned formally on 28 November. Merk had no wish to resume a cloistered life and surprising efforts were made to help him. He was licensed by the king in view of his 'notable poverty' (*CPR, 1399–1401*) to obtain benefices from the pope worth 100 marks a year in March 1401, and indeed 300 marks by November. His quest was further supported by Oxford University, to which he had returned by June 1401, and where he resumed scholarship and preaching until at least 1405. In a series of surviving letters, assuming they were all sent and not Merk's own wishful thinking, the university wrote extravagantly to the pope, king, and a cardinal to repent its support for his deprivation and press for his rehabilitation as one defamed and as an effective defender of orthodoxy. He failed to secure the 'golden prebend' of Masham in York Minster, but armed with a papal dispensation to hold a cure he obtained the vicarage of Sturminster Marshall, Dorset, on the presentation of the king himself in December 1403. In May 1404 he obtained a licence from the pope to farm this out for ten years while he was studying, serving a prelate, or living in the curia. Abbot Colchester then presented him to the rectory of Todenham, Gloucestershire, in August 1404. He served as suffragan bishop to the aged Bishop William Wykeham in the Winchester diocese from January 1403, and during the vacancy following Wykeham's death was asked by Archbishop Arundel to perform ordinations in October 1405. On 14 May 1405 John Porter, rector of Barrowby, Lincolnshire, was granted three years' leave for non-residence while in Merk's service. His rehabilitation was furthered when he was chosen to preach in the southern convocation on 10 May 1406, and even to prorogue the session whenever the bishops were engaged in parliament.

Hereafter Merk's life becomes obscure. He was said to have been in Lucca in May 1408 and, more reliably, at the Council of Pisa in May 1409. Perhaps he died abroad. He was certainly dead by 13 January 1410 and perhaps even by October 1409.   R. G. DAVIES

Sources R. G. Davies, 'The episcopate in England and Wales, 1375–1443', PhD diss., University of Manchester, 1974, 3.cxcvi–cxcviii [incl. ref. for death] • E. H. Pearce, *The monks of Westminster* (1916) • Emden, *Oxf.*, 2.1263–4 • B. Williams, ed., *Chronicque de la traïson et mort de Richart Deux, roy Dengleterre*, EHS, 9 (1846) • *The chronicle of Adam Usk, 1377–1421*, ed. and trans. C. Given-Wilson, OMT (1997) • C. Given-Wilson, ed. and trans., *Chronicles of the revolution, 1397–1400: the reign of Richard II* (1993) • [J. Creton], 'Translation of a French metrical history of the deposition of King Richard the Second … with a copy of the original', ed. and trans. J. Webb, *Archaeologia*, 20 (1824), 1–423 • *Johannis de Trokelowe et Henrici de Blaneforde … chronica et annales*, ed. H. T. Riley, pt 3 of *Chronica monasterii S. Albani*, Rolls Series, 28 (1866) • *CPR, 1399–1401*, 450
Likenesses portrait, 15th cent. (meeting of Richard II and Henry IV at Flint Castle, *Histoire du roy d'Angleterre Richard II*), BL, Harley MS 1319, fol. 50

Merle, William (*d.* in or before **1347**), meteorologist, has been said to have been a fellow of Merton College, Oxford, but his name does not appear in fourteenth-century college records. The established facts of his life are these: he became rector of Driby, Lincolnshire, in May 1331, a position which he held until his death, which had occurred by

March 1347; in 1335 he obtained licence to study at Oxford for two years and his licence for university study was renewed four times between 1338 and 1346; he had become MA by 1339. Although Merle's Oxford college or hall affiliation remains unknown, his association with contemporary Merton fellows John Ashenden, Simon Bredon, and William Rede is well documented. He borrowed books from Bredon; one medical volume he never returned. The extant copy of Merle's weather diary, *Consideraciones temperiei pro septem annis Christi* (Bodl. Oxf., MS Digby 176, fols. 4–8), belonged to William Rede, and John Ashenden freely borrowed from Merle's writings for the meteorological portions of his astrological compendium, the *Summa judicialis de accidentibus mundi*.

Each of Merle's three known writings has to do with meteorology. The *De pronosticatione aeris* of 1340 (Bodl. Oxf., MS Digby 147) concerns the identification of natural signs thought to precede changes of weather. In this remarkable work Merle draws upon medieval folk wisdom of the 'red sky at night, sailor's delight' variety, as well as upon the usual ancient authorities, Aristotle, Pliny, Ptolemy, and Virgil. Merle's *Consideraciones temperiei* represents a unique achievement in the fourteenth century—a systematic record of the weather over an extended period of time. From January 1337 to January 1344 Merle recorded temperatures (in a relative, qualitative sense), winds (often their force and direction), the incidence of rain, snow, frost, fog, hail, thunder, and lightning. For much of these seven years he was based at Oxford, but he also made observations from Driby and, on 28 March 1343, experienced an earthquake strong enough to topple chimneys in Lindsey, Lincolnshire. Merle firmly believed in the coincidental, if not causal, relationship between astronomical and terrestrial phenomena. His brief tract, *De futura temperie aeris pronosticanda* (Bodl. Oxf., MS Digby 97), enumerates the considerations one should make in drafting an astrological weather prediction. He stresses the correct application of astrological *regulae*, checked against the observation of natural signs, as vital to an accurate forecast. Unfortunately, Merle's empirical approach to meteorology did not make a great impact on scholastic Oxford; and, ironically, despite his considerable study and experience, not a single weather prediction by him is now extant. KEITH SNEDEGAR

Sources Emden, *Oxf.* · H. M. Carey, *Courting disaster: astrology at the English court and university in the later middle ages* (1992) · Merle's MS *Consideraciones temperiei pro 7 annis*, trans. G. J. Symons (1891)

Archives Bodl. Oxf., MSS Digby 97, 147, 176

Merle [*later* de Merle], **William Henry** [*pseuds.* A. B., A. Bird, the White Blackbird] (**1791–1878**), author, was born on 18 September 1791, and was baptized at St Bartholomew-the-Great, London, on 16 November 1791. He was the only son of William Merle (*d.* 1822), a London banker and JP of Collier's Wood, Mitcham, Surrey, and Elizabeth, daughter of John Halcrow. Merle entered Eton College on 15 September 1805, lodging in the same remove as the diarist Charles Fulke Greville.

A rich Regency bachelor, Merle visited the studio of George Cruikshank (1792–1878) in May 1814, in order to suggest a caricature lampooning Lord Cochrane, then accused of manipulating the stock exchange by spreading news that Napoleon had been killed. From that point on Merle bombarded the artist with ideas for prints and publishing projects—including an extraordinary send-up of the Horticultural Society (British Museum, *Catalogue of Political and Personal Satires*, 15155, 1 January 1826) and an unpublished variant of Mulready's 1840 design for a post-office envelope. Excessively fond of verbal/visual and multilingual puns (he also translated simple verses from Greek and Latin), Merle often signed with the initials A. B., or as A. Bird or the White Blackbird (*merle*, 'blackbird'), alluding to his French ancestors who had escaped to England after the revocation of the edict of Nantes.

Apparently Merle's father suffered severe financial reverses, for when he died in 1822, Merle became involved in protracted suits trying to recover property. During the next two decades, in straitened circumstances, Merle contributed verse and prose to numerous periodicals, including *The Times*, the *New Monthly Magazine*, the *Literary Gazette*, the *Morning Chronicle*, *Bentley's Miscellany*, and *George Cruikshank's Omnibus*.

In May 1829 Merle sketched the 'almost … mediaeval festivity' celebrating the coming-of-age of his friend John George Pole of Shute House, Axminster, Devon, and arranged for Pole to commission Cruikshank to etch his sketch, anticipating wrongly that Pole's family and friends would buy many copies. (Only one print is known to exist.) However, a wood-engraving from that design was published to illustrate an account of the 'eventful birthday' in George P. R. Pulman's *Book of the Axe* (1875). Also in 1829 Merle married Mary, daughter of John Norman of Iwood, Congresbury, Somerset. Two years later Cruikshank took Merle's designs and redrew them for wood-engravings, supplying one original etching as well, all illustrating a collection of Merle's journalistic pieces, *Odds and Ends in Verse and Prose* (April 1831; 2nd edn, 1836). Merle also published *Costanca, a Poem*, in 1828, and two novels, *Glenlonely* (1837), and the quasi-autobiographical *Melton de Mowbray, or, The Banker's Son* (1838).

Some time in the 1840s Merle's finances stabilized. From that time forward he resided at a succession of West End addresses, in the west country, or in Europe, mixing with old Etonians and others of the upper middle classes, and frequented the Athenaeum, to which he was elected in February 1838. After the death of his first wife, who left him her estate in Somerset, on 16 June 1853, in Clifton, Merle married Ann, only daughter of Henry Norman, a surgeon, of Portbury, Kenn Court, and Bleadon, Somerset. Though this was a second very happy union for Merle, there were burdens: his 'wee wife' suffered much from ill health and her brother's family became dependent on Merle when an agent defalcated while her brother was fighting in the Crimea. Moreover, Merle's own sister became another dependent when her husband ran through his fortune and hers.

Merle cultivated Cruikshank, but also badgered him; he often braced the artist when a project failed, or lent him money, but he exacted repayment by repeatedly submitting manuscripts through Cruikshank for publication. One novel, *Bathurst* (1850), was finally placed with T. C. Newby after Merle and Cruikshank had tried for nearly a decade to interest other publishers. Cruikshank was willing to illustrate it but Newby rushed out the book without undertaking the dubious additional expense.

Cruikshank's perpetual indebtedness alternately mystified and infuriated Merle. 'You have no children crying out for—"bread!"' (Merle to G. Cruikshank, 21 April 1861, quoted in Patten, 2.391), he protested, uninformed about Cruickshank's mistress and ten children. None the less he assiduously collected his friend's books, prints, and drawings and contributed modestly to various testimonials and other fund-raisers. Their amity lasted more than sixty years, although ill health and family troubles kept Merle close to home in his last decades, when he served as lord of the manor of Kenn and one of the deputy lieutenants for Somerset.

Merle died of pneumonia at his home, Ward Hill, Rowledge, Frensham, Surrey, on 29 September 1878, only eight months after Cruikshank, and was buried in Congresbury church, where there is a memorial stained-glass window. His wife survived him by more than a decade.

ROBERT L. PATTEN

Sources Princeton University, George Cruikshank MSS, corresp. of W. H. Merle and George Cruikshank, c.1816–1878 · R. L. Patten, *George Cruikshank's life, times, and art*, 2 vols. (1992–6) · Walford, *County families* (1875–88) · Boase, *Mod. Eng. biog.* · *The Times* (2 Oct 1878) · d. cert. · IGI
Archives Princeton University, New Jersey, George Cruikshank collection
Wealth at death over £50,000—estate, presumed value: Cruikshank MSS, Princeton University

Merlin [Myrddin] (*supp. fl.* **6th cent.**), poet and seer, is a figure whose historicity is not proven. He is known in Welsh sources as Myrddin and from the twelfth century also as Merlinus or Merlin. No definite conclusion can be drawn from Myrddin's absence from tenth-century Welsh genealogies and from the list included in the *Historia Brittonum*, written in 829 or 830, of five Brittonic poets renowned in the sixth century. On the other hand, approving references to him by twelfth- and thirteenth-century Welsh court poets do not necessarily signify that he was a flesh-and-blood early medieval poet. The possibly sixth- or seventh-century poem *Y Gododdin, gwenwawt Mirdyn* ('The fair [or "blessed"] song [possibly "inspiration"] of Myrddin') is said to have been 'defended' by a hero, Morien, but it is uncertain whether this line was part of the original composition or a later addition. Similar uncertainty surrounds an interpretation, based on the evidence of a single line, that Myrddin was regarded as a vaticinatory authority by the tenth-century south-west Walian author of the political prophecy, *Armes Prydein*.

The biographical strands of what is regarded as the native Welsh, pre-Geoffrey of Monmouth, tradition about Myrddin can be pieced together from six poems which also contain prophetic material: the eleventh-century *Ymddiddan Myrddin a Thaliesin* ('The dialogue of Myrddin and Taliesin'), and the twelfth- and thirteenth-century poems, *Yr afallennau* ('The apple trees'), *Yr hoianau* ('Greetings [to a pig]'), *Cyfoesi Myrddin a Gwenddydd ei chwaer* ('The prophecy of Myrddin and his sister, Gwenddydd'), *Gwasgargerdd Myrddin yn y bedd* ('Myrddin's diffuse poem from the grave'), and *Peirian faban* ('Commanding youth'). The first of these connects Myrddin with Dyfed, as well as with the north-British battle at Arthuret (Arfderydd), dated 573 in the *Annales Cambriae*. From the other poems it can be gathered that Myrddin was the son of Morfryn, that his lord, Gwenddoleu, fell in the battle at Arthuret (near Carlisle) fought against King Rhydderch of Strathclyde, that Myrddin was responsible for the deaths of two of the children of his sister Gwenddydd, and that four of his own brothers were also killed. Guilt and confusion caused him to lose his reason and flee to Coed Celyddon (the Caledonian forest), where he lived in fear of Rhydderch, communed with trees and wild animals, and gained the prophetic powers that are displayed particularly in the last three poems mentioned. The colloquy with Gwenddydd suggests that brother and sister were eventually reconciled.

The words *llallogan* and *llallawg* used here in addressing Myrddin may simply represent a term of affection ('friend' or similar), or a pet name, but there is undoubtedly a close connection with the name and the story of the Strathclyde seer Lailoken (orthographical variants Lalochen, Laloecen, Laloicen) who lost his reason after inciting battle, according to two fragments, one or both of which may have formed part of the anonymous life of Kentigern composed for Bishop Herbert of Glasgow in the mid-twelfth century (Lailoken plays a much smaller part in the later twelfth-century life by Jocelin of Furness). It has been suggested that Llallogan was the Myrddin original, and that relocalization of the tradition to Welsh soil involved taking on a new name, perhaps derived from a false interpretation of the place name Caerfyrddin (Carmarthen) as *caer* ('fortress') and *myrddin* (which, in the place name, really derives from the British *moridunon*, 'sea-fortress'). There are other possibilities, however: Myrddin may have been the real name of Llallogan, or there may have been two or more poets or seers, northern or Welsh, or both, whose traditions contaminated one another or were conflated—witness the similarity to the Irish Suibhne Geilt who supposedly went mad and took to the woods after the battle of Mag Roth in 637.

The influential *Historia regum Britanniae*, written in the 1130s by Geoffrey of Monmouth, makes no mention of the northern figure: it draws on the account in the *Historia Brittonum* of a fatherless wonder-child, Ambrosius (in Welsh, Emrys), who interpreted an omen of warring white and red reptiles as representing the struggle between the Saxons and the people of Vortigern. Geoffrey renamed the youth as Merlinus, an acceptable Latinization of Myrddin, fashioned him into a wizard associated with Dyfed and Carmarthen in particular, and included a selection of his prophecies, which appear to be mostly the author's own invention. By 1148–51, when he wrote his life of Merlin (*Vita Merlini*), Geoffrey had access to more Merlin material. This may have included some of the Welsh poems already mentioned, and perhaps poems no longer extant in which the Lailoken element used by Geoffrey (such as the motif of the triple death, by falling, hanging, and drowning in his version) may have been more evident. In the life, Merlin is depicted as a king of Dyfed, drawn into northerly events through his sister, Ganieda (Gwenddydd), wife of Rodarchus (Rhydderch), here friend rather than foe. But Merlin's grief and madness after battle accord with the Welsh poems, as does his conversation with his sister, and to a lesser degree, his extended debate with the poet Taliesin.

Geoffrey of Monmouth's identification of Myrddin–Merlin with *Ambrosius, who apparently flourished some one hundred years earlier than the Myrddin connected with the battle of Arthuret, created a problem of chronology that appears to have been resolved first by Gerald of Wales. He differentiated between two Merlins: one, Merlinus Ambrosius, from Carmarthen, who prophesied in the time of Vortigern, while a northern Merlinus Celidonius (or Silvester), contemporary with Arthur, was, like Lailoken, driven mad by a monstrous apparition seen in battle. According to Gerald's account in his *Itinerarium Cambriae*, both foretold the destruction of the kingdom of Britain and the advent of the Saxons and the Normans; Gerald records his discovery at Nefyn in 1188 of a manuscript of the prophecies of the latter, more prolific Merlin. Welsh poets from the fifteenth century onwards occasionally make a similar distinction between Myrddin Emrys and Myrddin Wyllt (Merlin the Wild), but most references are simply to Myrddin, above all to his prophetic and bardic powers (often coupled with those of Taliesin), to an obscure tradition about him being 'on a pole' (which has been connected with the death of Lailoken who was skewered on a pole in a fish pond), and to his reputation as a lover who went into a house of glass for the sake of his mistress.

Merlin is first brought into contact with *Arthur in the late twelfth-century French verse romance *Merlin* by Robert de Boron. This was adapted in the early thirteenth-century prose *Merlin*, and continued in *Le livre d'Artus* and *Suite du Merlin*. Merlin arranges for the round table to be made, and is responsible for the test of the sword in the anvil which establishes Arthur's right to kingship. The thirteenth-century vulgate *Merlin* continuation develops Merlin's role as Arthur's mentor and describes how the maiden Viviane consigns him to an enchanted prison in the Forest of Broceliande. *Le Morte d'Arthur* by Sir Thomas Malory drew on these French texts, and was to be an important source for the mid-nineteenth-century Arthurian revival, in particular Tennyson's treatments of Merlin in *Enid and Nimuë* (1857), *Vivien* (1859), and *Idylls of the King* (1869), which inspired Pre-Raphaelite portraits such as the Oxford Union mural *Merlin being Imprisoned beneath a Stone by the Damsel of the Lake* (1857) by Edward Burne-Jones and the same artist's *The Beguiling of Merlin* (1873–7).

The prominence of Merlin is a striking feature of modern Arthurian fiction in Britain and America. Particularly influential works include *A Connecticut Yankee at the Court of King Arthur* (1898) by Mark Twain (who portrayed Merlin as a fraud who is unmasked when he is confronted with modern technology), and T. H. White's series of novels, *The Once and Future King* (1958), and *The Book of Merlyn* (1977). A resuscitated Merlin acts as *deus ex machina* on behalf of Christian morality in *That Hideous Strength: a Modern Fairy-Tale for Grown-Ups* by C. S. Lewis (1945). He is a central character in Mary Stewart's Merlin trilogy (1970–79), the first novel of which was the basis for the BBC1 television series *Merlin and the Crystal Cave* (1991). He appears as the benign Professor Merriman Lyon in *The Dark is Rising* series (1965–77) by Susan Cooper. From the early nineteenth century onwards Merlin has had a powerful appeal to German writers including Dorothea Schlegel, Christoph Martin Wieland, Ludwig Uhland, Heinrich Heine, and Gerhart Hauptmann. German translations of T. H. White and Mary Stewart led to a number of works in the 1970s and 1980s (notably Tankred Dorst's play *Merlin, oder, Das wüste Land* (1981)) which coincided with a spate of French Merlin adaptations and novels such as *L'enchanteur* by René Barjavel (1984).

Merlin appears in musical works from the mid-eighteenth century onwards, in masques, operas, choral works, and musicals. The best-known is *Camelot* (1960), the stage musical based on White's *The Once and Future King*, which was made into a film in 1967. Several of the numerous Arthurian films made in the twentieth century give prominence to the figure of Merlin: Walt Disney's animation *The Sword in the Stone* (1963), also based on White's work, had a wide popular appeal. More ambitious was John Boorman's *Excalibur* (1981) in which Merlin, curiously, talks in Old Irish.   M. E. HAYCOCK

Sources *Llyfr Du Caerfyrddin*, ed. A. O. H. Jarman (1982) • J. G. Evans, ed., *The poetry in the Red Book of Hergest* (1911) • *Ymddiddan Myrddin a Thaliesin*, ed. A. O. H. Jarman (1951) • A. O. H. Jarman, ed., 'Peiryan Vaban', *BBCS*, 14 (1950–52), 104–8 • Geoffrey of Monmouth, *Vita Merlini / Life of Merlin*, ed. and trans. B. Clarke (1973) • *The Historia regum Britannie of Geoffrey of Monmouth*, ed. N. Wright, 1: *Bern, Bürgerbibliothek, MS 568* (1985) • I. Williams, ed., *Canu Aneirin* (1938) • Taliesin, *Armes Prydein / The prophecy of Britain*, ed. I. Williams, trans. R. Bromwich (1972) • I. Williams, ed., 'Y cyfoesi a'r afallennau yn Peniarth 3', *BBCS*, 4 (1927–9), 112–29 • Nennius, 'British history' and 'The Welsh annals', ed. and trans. J. Morris (1980) • *Gir. Camb. opera* • R. Jarman, *Trioedd ynys Prydein*, 2nd edn (1978) • A. O. H. Jarman, 'The Merlin legend and the Welsh tradition of prophecy', *The Arthur of the Welsh*, ed. R. Bromwich, A. O. H. Jarman, and B. F. Roberts (1991), 117–45 • P. Goodrich, ed., *The romance of Merlin: an anthology* (1990) • N. J. Lacy, G. Ashe, and D. N. Mancoff, *The Arthurian handbook* (1997)

Merlin, John Joseph (1735–1803), inventor, was born or baptized, or possibly both born and baptized, on 17 September 1735 at Huy, Southern Netherlands, into a family who were probably inventors. He was the third child of Maximilien Joseph Merlin (born at Cambrai, 8 January 1710) and Marie-Anne Levasseur.

By about 1754 he was working in Paris, gaining for himself a reputation for mechanical ability. In 1760 he came to England in the suite of the Spanish ambassador, the conde de Fuentes, and lived in Soho Square, London.

By 1763 Merlin had left the service of Fuentes and was living, and most probably working (for a goldsmith named Sutton), in New Street, Covent Garden. Shortly afterwards he moved to work at Cox's Museum in Spring Gardens, becoming 'the first or principal mechanic' (*Kirby's … Museum*, 274). The museum housed a collection of large automata which had a profound influence on Merlin, but realizing that the museum was financially unstable, Merlin decided in 1773 to set up on his own as a maker of mathematical instruments. In the same year Merlin designed and patented a dutch oven (not unlike a present-day rotisserie) and in the following year he patented a down-striking piano action which could be fitted to a harpsichord, enabling the player, by the operation of a foot pedal, to use the instrument as either a piano or a harpsichord. A second pedal allowed the player to produce a crescendo or decrescendo when using the harpsichord alone by slowly bringing on the unison and octave registers, or on release of the pedal, removing first the octave register and then the two unisons. In 1780 Merlin built a single-manual harpsichord to which his down-striking piano action was fitted, thereby making it a compound instrument. It has the unusual specification of one 16 ft register, two 8 ft registers, and one 4 ft register. It also incorporates an ingenious recording device: as the performance proceeds, pencils attached to trackers make marks on a roll of paper attached to a clockwork rotating drum. Though innovative, the system was never likely to succeed because the marks on the paper had subsequently to be deciphered and converted to standard musical notation.

Merlin's other inventions included extending the compass of the piano (at the suggestion of his friend Dr Charles Burney) and combining the square piano with an organ (making the square claviorganum). He popularized roller skates (most probably invented in Holland about 1700), and is immortalized in a passage in Busby's *Concert Room and Orchestra Anecdotes*:

> One of his ingenious novelties was a pair of skaites … Supplied with a pair of these and a violin he mixed in the motley group of one of the celebrated Mrs. Corneily's masquerades at Carlisle House, Soho Square; when, not having provided the means of retarding his velocity, or commanding its direction, he impelled himself against a mirror of more than five hundred pounds value, dashed it to atoms, broke his instrument to pieces and wounded himself most severely. (Busby, 2.137)

He also invented the forerunner of the present-day wheelchair, a form of scales for weighing human beings, a number of specialized watches and clocks, and a small portable scale for weighing gold coinage. Among his more bizarre inventions were a rotating table which enabled a hostess to fill up to twelve cups of tea without leaving her place, and a device to enable blind persons to play cards. All of these were to be seen at Merlin's Mechanical Museum, near Hanover Square, a popular place of entertainment for London society, with whom, despite his incomplete Anglicization, Merlin was much in demand. He never married, but was highly thought of, as witnesses his obituary in the *Gentleman's Magazine*, which reported that 'he hardly ever let a moment slip by unemployed'

(*GM*, 1st ser., 73/1, 1803, 485). He died in London on 4 May 1803, and left his property to his two brothers and a sister, all of whom lived abroad.   CHARLES MOULD

Sources *John Joseph Merlin: the ingenious mechanick* (1985) [exhibition catalogue, Iveagh Bequest, Kenwood, London, 19 July – 26 Aug 1985] · *Kirby's wonderful … museum*, 6 vols. (1803–20), vol. 1, pp. 274–9 · T. Busby, *Concert room and orchestra anecdotes of music and musicians, ancient and modern*, 2 (1825), 137 · P. A. Scholes, *The great Dr Burney: his life, his travels, his works, his family and his friends*, 2 vols. (1948) · D. H. Boalch, *Makers of the harpsichord and clavichord, 1440–1840*, 3rd edn, ed. C. Mould (1995), 128–30, 505
Likenesses T. Gainsborough, oils, Iveagh Bequest, Kenwood House, Hampstead, London; repro. in *John Joseph Merlin* · G. P. Harding, stipple and etching?, NPG; repro. in *Kirby's wonderful … museum*, vol. 1

Merret [Merrett], **Christopher** (1614–1695), physician and writer on natural philosophy, was born at Winchcombe, Gloucestershire, on 16 February 1614, the son of a non-gentry father of the same name, who was at some time involved in a tobacco growing project in the west midlands. On entering Oxford University in 1631 he was initially at Gloucester Hall but moved to Oriel College, graduating BA in January 1635; reverting to Gloucester Hall, he then studied medicine, proceeding BM in June 1636 and DM in January 1643. Around that time he married Ann Jenour (or Jenner, the name of a kinsman mentioned in his *Pinax*), of Kempsford, near Fairford, Gloucestershire, with whom he had at least two sons.

Having settled in practice in London about 1640, Merret was admitted to fellowship of the College of Physicians in 1651 and speedily rose to distinction in it. In 1654, besides being Goulstonian lecturer, he was nominated by his friend from Oxford days, William Harvey, to the keepership of the new library and museum which Harvey had given the college; Merret later compiled the first catalogue, which was printed in 1660. This post not only carried a stipend of £20 a year, but also brought Merret rent-free accommodation in the college house in Amen Corner. Subsequently he was also to serve seven terms as its censor.

At the meeting at Gresham College in November 1660 preparatory to the founding of the Royal Society, Merret was one of the forty people, and one of the fourteen medical men, it was agreed to invite to become fellows at the very outset. He quickly became a very active member, serving on the council, contributing several papers to the *Philosophical Transactions*, and impressing with his knowledge of applied natural philosophy. In December 1662 Merret gave a paper to the society describing the addition of sugar to a finished wine to induce a second fermentation for the specific purpose of making it sparkle. The earliest French document to mention sparkling champagne was written in 1718 and referred to its emergence twenty years before, making Merret's discovery a generation ahead of French claims. Undertaking at Robert Boyle's suggestion a translation of Antonio Neri's *L'arte vetraria*, he went to the trouble of repeating the experiments described and added so many original observations from his own deep study of the subject as to almost double the length of what appeared in 1662 as *The Art of Glass*. This work is said to have given a considerable impetus to glass-making in various parts of Europe. In June 1664 he was consequently the Royal Society's choice as chairman of a committee for the history of trades. The report of that, if it was ever produced, has not survived. Earlier in 1664 the society also charged Merret and Walter Charleton with the task of drawing up a list of animals appropriate for its projected museum and with providing instruction on how to preserve these when dead.

About the same time Merret was invited, together with a fellow London physician, John Dale, to produce a new catalogue of the British fauna, flora, and fossils in lieu of an intended revised edition of William How's *Phytologia Britannica* (1650) which had been aborted by How's premature death. Merret's interest and knowledge was mainly in geology and enabled him to produce a remarkably detailed account of the fossils and mineral wealth of England and Wales. Dale was to have covered the botany, but died almost at once. John Ray (who was to be scathing about what ultimately emerged) ought to have been asked to take that over, but Merret unwisely determined to cope with it as well. To that end he augmented the many pre-existing records by drawing on John Goodyer's manuscripts loaned by his executor and employing the ex-soldier Thomas Willisel for five seasons to search for north of England rarities; Merret's own two sons also assisted with plant-hunting forays. For illustrations he was able to purchase 800 plant engravings made for Thomas Johnson but never used. Inevitably, though, the lengthy botanical part of the resulting small octavo, *Pinax rerum naturalium Britannicarum*, betrayed by its many inaccuracies Merret's insufficient command of that subject. The work was further ill-starred by appearing just before the great fire, which apparently consumed most of the first impression. Surviving copies tend to bear the next year's date, 1667. Disowning that edition, Merret announced that he was preparing a revised one on a new method for publication later that year, but nothing materialized.

London's twin disasters of those years were to prove Merret's undoing far more direly. During the plague he took refuge in the country and in his absence the college was broken into and its treasure chest emptied. The great fire then destroyed the college house and most of its library and records. The loss of records was especially critical, for in a court case during the Commonwealth in 1656 there had been a ruling which undermined the statutory powers long enjoyed by the college to exercise control over medical practice in London. Reversing that ruling, and making good the loss of prestige that resulted, was one of the college's most pressing priorities following the Restoration, and it fell to Merret as librarian to try to produce the necessary documentary evidence. In this he proved sufficiently successful to be able to publish a collection which, at least in his view, sustained the college's position. Despite that coup, when he sought to further his aim of converting the college to the new empiricism by proposing that it share a meeting room with the Royal Society instead of building a replacement for its own one

lost to the fire, the opposition proved too great. Returning to the attack by subtler means, in 1669 he published *A Short View of the Frauds and Abuses Committed by Apothecaries*, in which he urged the physicians to outflank those increasingly influential professional rivals by drawing on the discoveries of the new experimentalism to dispense remedies that were thereby superior. That was hardly an argument likely to prevail, however, for it appeared to require the physicians to concede their enemies' case by concentrating on therapy.

Merret's chances of winning over his colleagues to a greater empiricism had meanwhile been rendered the more vain by the college's decision to abolish his post—on the reasonable view that the near-destruction of the library and museum had made it superfluous. The lease of the building was accordingly resigned and he was paid off with £50 by way of compensation. Merret nevertheless insisted that his appointment had been for life and embarked on a protracted campaign to secure his reinstatement, twice appealing unsuccessfully to the king's bench. Eventually, in September 1681, the college was driven to deprive him of his fellowship, nominally on the ground that he had failed to attend a meeting to which he had been summoned. Four years later the Royal Society expelled him, too, for having been in arrears with his subscriptions since about 1668.

Merret spent his last, no doubt embittered, years in a house in Hatton Garden, dying there on 19 August 1695. He was buried 'twelve feet deep' (according to Wood, *Ath. Oxon.*) in St Andrew's Church, Holborn. A genus of unicellular algae was named *Merrettia* by S. F. Gray many years later in his honour.   D. E. ALLEN

Sources C. E. Raven, *English naturalists from Neckam to Ray: a study of the making of the modern world* (1947) · H. J. Cook, *The decline of the old medical regime in Stuart London* (1986) · H. J. Cook, 'Physicians and the new philosophy: Henry Stubbe and the virtuosi-physicians', *The medical revolution of the seventeenth century*, ed. R. K. French and A. Wear (1989), 246–71 · Munk, *Roll* · R. T. Gunther, *Early British botanists and their gardens* (1922) · M. Hunter, *Establishing the new science: the experience of the early Royal Society* (1989) · M. Hunter, 'The social basis and changing fortunes of an early scientific institution: an analysis of the membership of the Royal Society', *Notes and Records of the Royal Society*, 31 (1976–7), 9–114 · M. Hunter, *The Royal Society and its fellows, 1660–1700: the morphology of an early scientific institution* (1982) · J. Britten and J. E. Dandy, eds., *The Sloane herbarium* (1958) · B. Henrey, *British botanical and horticultural literature before 1800*, 1 (1975) · H. Lyons, *The Royal Society, 1660–1940: a history of its administration under its charters* (1944) · W. E. S. Turner, 'A notable British seventeenth-century contribution to the literature of glass-making', *Glass Technology*, 6 (1962), 201–13 · C. Webster, *The great instauration: science, medicine and reform, 1626–1660* (1975) · Wood, *Ath. Oxon.* · T. Stevenson, *A world encyclopedia of champagne and sparkling wine* (1998) · C. Merret, *Short view of frauds by apothecaries* (1670) · *DSB*

Archives NHM, specimens | BL, papers, Sloane MS 3914, fols. 2–16, 57

Likenesses G. P. Harding, watercolour engraving, RCP Lond.

Merrey, Walter (*bap.* **1723**, *d.* **1799**), hosier and numismatist, was baptized on 15 December 1723 at the church of St Martin's-le-Grand, Coney Street, York, the son of Samuel

Merrey and his wife, Mary Knapton. According to the Nottingham historian John Blackner (1815), Merrey was originally apprenticed to a Nottingham surgeon, but following the latter's death was assigned to a hosier and woolcomber in the same town . At Sneinton, Nottinghamshire, on 17 April 1746 he married by licence Mary Hardy (b. 1718/19) of Brewhouse Yard, Nottingham, five years his senior; they subsequently had at least five children. By 1774 he had become a master hosier, in other words a merchant dealing in stockings knitted on hand-operated stocking frames in domestic houses, which was then the staple industry of Nottingham. By 1783 he was in partnership with his son Joseph as 'manufacturers of hose in general'; they later became dyers as well. In 1776 he was appointed one of the two trustees of Walker's charity in St Nicholas's parish, Nottingham, and in 1794 treasurer to the corporation; by 1799 he was also a land tax commissioner for the borough.

Merrey acquired a wide knowledge of coinage and currency and owned 'an immense collection' of ancient coins, many discovered in the Nottingham area. In 1789 he published a treatise entitled Remarks on the Coinage of England from the Earliest to the Present Times (8 vols.; 2nd edn, 1794), dedicated to Dr William White of York. In this he used his knowledge of the history of coinage in Britain to explain the current scarcity of silver in circulation, which he attributed to the overvaluation of gold. His proposed solution was to reduce the value of the guinea from 21s. to 20s. 6d. He was especially concerned at the effects on the poor of the circulation of base copper coinage in the place of silver. He had signed an association with a number of other employers not to offer their employees more than 6d. worth of copper in their wages, but was forced to admit that this caused problems for them in obtaining change for small purchases.

Merrey died at his home in Castle Gate, Nottingham, on 9 August 1799. In his will he remarked that his partnership was owed 'several large sums of money', no doubt owing to wartime conditions. Most of his property was left to his son Joseph, but no mention was made of his coin collection, the subsequent fate of which is unknown.

ADRIAN HENSTOCK

Sources J. Blackner, The history of Nottingham (1815) · D. Gray and V. W. Walker, Records of the borough of Nottingham, 1760–1800 (1947), vol. 7 of Records of the borough of Nottingham · will, 6 March 1800, Notts. Arch., PRNW · Reports of charity commissioners for Nottinghamshire (1820–37) · Registers of St Mary, Castlegate, York, Yorkshire Parish Record Society, 136 (1972) · Registers of St Martin, York, Yorkshire Parish Record Society, 36 (1909) · parish registers, Sneinton, Notts. Arch. · Nottingham Poll Book (1774) · W. Bailey, Directory of Nottingham (1783) · title deed, 1799, Notts. Arch., M24, 620 · DNB · GM, 1st ser., 59 (1789), 728 · GM, 1st ser., 69 (1799), 815

Wealth at death over £300—total estate: will, Notts. Arch.

Merrick, James (1720–1769), biblical and classical scholar and translator, was born at Reading on 8 January 1720, the son of John Merrick MD (1669/70–1757) and Elizabeth (d. 1764), daughter of Richard Lybbe of Hardwick, Oxfordshire. The Latin inscription on his parents' graves in Caversham church, Reading, was written by Merrick. He was educated at Reading School, where he was senior

scholar. The school had a scholarship on Sir Thomas White's foundation at St John's College, Oxford, but Merrick was not elected: he is said to have received the votes of the aldermen but not those of the burgesses, and he may have been the innocent victim of some dispute between them. Merrick matriculated at Trinity College, Oxford, on 14 April 1736. He became a scholar of the college in 1737, and graduated BA in 1739 and MA in 1742.

Merrick was a child prodigy: he published Messiah: a Divine Essay in 1734, one of many eighteenth-century poems of that title, and an undistinguished example of the type. As a scholar of Trinity College he published The destruction of Troy; being the sequel of the Iliad. Translated from the Greek of Tryphiodorus (1739). The first edition was preceded by a long and impressive list of subscribers, which suggests that he was a young man of some renown, even as an undergraduate, and the preface indicates that he had already been in correspondence with Reimarus. He published the Greek and Latin texts of Tryphiodorus in 1741. Merrick became a fellow of the college in 1744 (probationer-fellow, 21 May 1744, fellow, 21 May 1745). Among his pupils were Lord North and Lord Dartmouth.

Merrick took holy orders, and preached an ordination sermon at Christ Church in 1747, and in Trinity College chapel in 1749, but he never engaged in any parochial duties, probably owing to ill health. Merrick was subject to acute pains in his head, frequent lassitude, and feverish complaints. He retired to Reading, where he interested himself in the welfare of those in the debtors' prison. He wrote the poem over the 'debtors' grate' in Castle Street:

> Oh ye, whose hours exempt from sorrow show,
> Behold the seat of pain, and want, and woe:
> Think, while your hands th'intreated alms extend,
> That what to us ye give, to God ye lend.

Merrick also took much notice of the soldiers in the garrison at Reading. He distributed 10,000 copies of a pamphlet, The Christian Monitor by John Rawlet of Newcastle upon Tyne, and also produced An encouragement to a good life: particularly addressed to some soldiers quartered in Reading, Berks (1759).

Merrick's most celebrated publication, other than The Destruction of Troy, was The Psalms, Translated or Paraphrased in English Verse (1765; a second edition was called for within a year), which was also preceded by a splendid list of subscribers. Merrick described it as 'a mixture of Translation and Paraphrase' (preface), and acknowledged the assistance of the great Hebrew scholar Robert Lowth. The psalms were widely admired: Merrick was a scholar and a poet, and he had the leisure to pursue the matter properly. He also provided notes to elucidate the difficult or obscure passages. According to Charles Coates, the historian of Reading, Merrick was to be congratulated on his clarity and accuracy. Coates noted

> the successful manner in which the probable meaning of the Psalmist is, for the most part, ascertained. It is a lively Commentary and Exposition of abstruse passages. Many of those hasty transitions, by which we had been hitherto startled and perplexed, are rendered easy and intelligible. (Coates, 441)

Originally the psalms were not intended to be sung, if

only because Merrick found that he 'could not confine himself in general to stanzas, nor, consequently, adopt the measures to which the tunes used in our Churches correspond'. Additionally, he 'knew not how, without neglecting the Poetry, to write in such language as the common sort of people would be likely to understand' (preface). But it was a tribute to his work that a number of them were set to music and found their way into hymnbooks.

Merrick was evidently aiming to capture a different audience from the nonconformists who were singing Isaac Watts's *The Psalms of David* of 1719: he seems to have been attempting a version which would be an alternative to Watts for the Church of England, and which would also 'answer the purposes of private devotion' (preface). He used a number of metres; the majority were couplets in octosyllabics or of seven syllables. The popularity of the book is shown by its frequent reprinting, and by an edition 'divided into stanzas and adapted for devotion' by W. D. Tattersall (1794). Before that, twenty-one of Merrick's psalms had appeared in J. Ash and C. Evans's *A Collection of Hymns Adapted to Public Worship* (1781), over the signature 'M'; they were set to music by William Hayes (1775) for use in Magdalen College chapel, Oxford. Further editions with musical settings followed, including settings by Haydn. According to Julian's *Dictionary of Hymnology*, Merrick's psalm versions were popular in the early nineteenth century, but had by 1892 'fallen very much into disuse' (p. 725, col. 2). It is not difficult to see why: although they were commended by Robert Lowth (who of course had a hand in them, and who described Merrick as 'one of the best of men, and most eminent of scholars'), they were described by a contemporary critic as tame and diffuse, and James Montgomery has some sharp comments on their verbosity. They are now forgotten. They were greatly admired, however, in Merrick's own time: Thomas Warton said that they evidenced 'a flow of poetical language, and a richness of imagery, which give dignity to the subject, without departing from the sense of the inspired writer' (Coates, 439).

Merrick followed up his version of the psalms with *Annotations on the Psalms* (1768), which provoked a small controversy between Robert Lowth, bishop of Oxford, Thomas Secker, archbishop of Canterbury, and Gregory Sharpe, master of the Temple. The *Letter to the right reverend the lord bishop of Oxford, from the master of the Temple. Containing remarks upon some strictures made by his grace the late archbishop of Canterbury, in the Revd. Mr. Merrick's annotations on the psalms* (1769) is concerned principally with the interpretation of Psalm 110. The dispute was about the possibility, or not, of the psalm containing a prophecy concerning Christ (the 'priest for ever after the order of Melchizedek'), and is of little value except as evidence of the contemporary interest in Merrick's work. Merrick died at Reading on 5 January 1769 after a long illness and was buried at Caversham church with his family.

J. R. WATSON

Sources C. Coates, *The history and antiquities of Reading* (1802) • Foster, *Alum. Oxon.* • J. Ash and C. Evans, *A collection of hymns adapted to public worship* (1781) • N. Temperley, *The music of the English parish church*, 2 vols. (1979) • J. Julian, ed., *A dictionary of hymnology* (1892) • 'Oxoniensis', *N&Q*, 2nd ser., 4 (1857), 291 • *DNB* • Caversham church records

Archives Bodl. Oxf., corresp. and papers | Bodl. Oxf., corresp. with Robert Lowth

Merrick, Joseph Carey [*called* the Elephant Man] (1862–1890), freak show novelty and medical curiosity, was born at 50 Lee Street, Leicester, on 5 August 1862, the elder son (there was also a daughter) of Joseph Rockley Merrick (*b.* 1835/6), a warehouseman and machine operator in a cotton factory, and Mary Jane Potterton (1834/5–1873), who taught in a Baptist Sunday school. His younger brother died at an early age from scarlet fever and his sister was born disabled, but it seems likely that Merrick was a normal, healthy baby. However, between the age of two and five years old he began to show signs of the condition (possibly Proteus syndrome) which would subsequently earn him the epithet Elephant Man. At about the same time hip disease (possibly following a fall) began to make him increasingly lame. Nevertheless, he attended day school in Leicester until the age of eleven or twelve.

Following the death of Merrick's mother in 1873, his father married Emma Wood Antill (*née* Warner), a widow with several children of her own. Subsequently, Merrick 'never … had one moment's comfort' and was so taunted by his step-mother that he would 'stay in the streets with a hungry belly rather than return [home] for anything to eat' (Merrick). He was now also looking for work, but his worsening appearance made it difficult for him to find and keep a job.

Finally, in December 1879, after living with an uncle for two years (and spending periods working as a cigar-roller and a haberdashery peddler) Merrick was reduced to entering the Leicester union workhouse. His time there must have been almost unbearable—two years after he finally signed himself out he still shrank 'with the greatest of horror' (F. Carr Gomm, *The Times*, 4 Dec 1886) from any possible return to such a place. Nevertheless, he had to endure the grim routine for four long years. His only respite was in 1882, when he spent a short period in the Leicester Infirmary, so that surgeons could remove a projection from his upper lip which was making eating difficult and his speech almost unintelligible.

Early in 1884 Merrick began to realize that the only alternative to a life in the workhouse was to turn his appearance to profit as a 'novelty'. He contacted the owner of a Leicester music-hall, Sam Torr, who formed a syndicate to exhibit 'the Elephant Man, Half-a-Man and Half-an-Elephant'. To accompany the act, Torr also printed *The Autobiography of Joseph Carey Merrick* (n.d. [1884]), a seven-paragraph pamphlet (of uncertain authorship) from which Merrick received half the profits. In November 1884, after several months in the midlands, the act set up (under the management of Tom Norman) in a vacant shop in Whitechapel Road, opposite the London Hospital. As a result, Merrick came to the attention of a number of surgeons including Frederick Treves who, on 2 December 1884, exhibited him to the Pathological Society of London. Engravings of Merrick from this date show a grotesquely

Joseph Carey Merrick [the Elephant Man] (1862–1890), by unknown photographer, c.1889

disfigured young man. His head was already quite deformed by numerous bony protuberances and soft-tissue swellings, and brown 'cauliflower' skin covered much of his twisted body. Indeed, from about this time, his appearance was such that he could venture outside only under cover of a black theatrical cape and a huge yachting cap, from which was hung a curtain-like cloth with a wide slit through which he could see.

It was the Victorian appetite for 'novelties' that had brought Merrick freedom from the workhouse. However, by the mid-1880s the tide of public opinion was beginning to turn against such 'degrading' spectacles and, a few days after his appearance before the Pathological Society, the authorities moved him on from Whitechapel. Following a period under the management of Sam Roper, he travelled to Europe with a fourth manager (possibly named Ferrari). In June 1886 this manager stole Merrick's savings (said to be some £50) and abandoned him in Brussels. Refused passage from Ostend to Dover, Merrick probably caught the Antwerp–Harwich mail packet and the boat-train to Liverpool Street Station, where he arrived in a distressed state on 24 June 1886. He produced Treves's calling card and the

surgeon was duly called to the station. Treves took Merrick back to the London Hospital, but this was probably intended only as a temporary measure—at that time the hospital was forbidden to house 'incurables'. However, Merrick's condition moved the hospital's director, Frederick Carr Gomm, to make an appeal to the public in The Times (4 December 1886), and within a week sufficient funds were obtained to convert several hospital rooms into an apartment in which Merrick could live out his days.

Accounts of Merrick's life at the hospital are nearly all derived from Treves's The Elephant Man and Other Reminiscences (1923), written in the last year of Treves's life. Although the work contains a number of factual errors, it remains clear that Merrick had found a sanctuary of sorts. He talked with Treves most days, and the surgeon became impressed with the young man's intelligence and sensitivity. He soon acquired a library and spent much time reading and model making. Something of a cause célèbre following Carr Gomm's letter to The Times, he received numerous visitors, including several celebrities and the princess of Wales. On at least one occasion arrangements were made for him to attend a pantomime, where he sat in a private box—screened from public gaze by three nurses. He also made several trips to the country (staying on the estate of Lady Kneightley, near Daventry), the last shortly before his death.

Although Merrick's condition had made a long life unlikely, his sudden death at the London Hospital, on the afternoon of 11 April 1890, was unexpected. It is thought he suffocated as a result of attempting to sleep in a normal position—he usually slept sitting up. Recognizing that it might one day be possible to diagnose conclusively Merrick's condition, Treves arranged for casts to be made of Merrick's body, took skin samples, and probably oversaw the bleaching and mounting of his skeleton. Despite this, by the late 1990s the exact nature of Merrick's condition remained uncertain—his symptoms still did not seem to be entirely consistent with either Proteus syndrome or neurofibromatosis (the popular diagnosis from the 1880s to the 1980s). Merrick's DNA probably holds the answer, but the skin samples were lost during the Second World War and early attempts (1997) to extract genetic material from his tooth pulp proved unsuccessful.

Interest in Merrick has continued to resurface at periods throughout the twentieth century, and his life has been the subject of a number of works, both factual and dramatic. The latter include The Elephant Man (1979), a play by Bernard Pomerance; a 1980 film (of the same title) directed by David Lynch and starring John Hurt; and a radio play, Emma Hamilton and the Elephant Man (1997), by David Constantine. PETER OSBORNE

Sources P. Graham and F. Oehlschlager, Articulating the Elephant Man (1992) · M. Howell and P. Ford, The true history of the Elephant Man, 3rd edn (1992) · QED, 'The true story of the Elephant Man', BBC documentary, 1997 · J. C. Merrick, The autobiography of Joseph Carey Merrick [n.d., 1884?] · G. R. Seward, The Elephant Man (1992) · J. A. R. Tibbles and M. M. Cohen, 'The Proteus syndrome: the Elephant Man diagnosed', BMJ (13 Sept 1986), 683–5 · 'The Elephant Man', BMJ (11 Dec 1886), 1188–9 · 'Death of the "Elephant Man"',

BMJ (19 April 1890), 916–17 · m. cert. [Joseph Rockley Merrick and Emma Wood Antill] · d. cert. [Mary Jane Merrick] · F. Treves, *The Elephant Man and other reminiscences* (1923) · b. cert.

Archives Royal London Hospital, Archives and Museum, cardboard model of building assembled by subject · Royal London Hospital, Archives and Museum, numerous X-rays, C-T scans, etc. of subject's skeleton · Royal London Hospital, Archives and Museum, photograph of handbill advertising the 'Elephant Man' act · St Bartholomew's School of Medicine and Dentistry, London, Pathology School Museum, subject's skeleton, hat, and plaster casts of body | Royal London Hospital, Archives and Museum, minutes of the house committee of the London Hospital · Royal London Hospital, Archives and Museum, minutes of the board of governors for the London Hospital medical college

Likenesses photograph, *c*.1889, Royal London Hospital Archives and Museum [*see illus.*] · photographs, Royal London Hospital Archives and Museum · portraits, repro. in Graham and Oehlschlager, *Articulating the Elephant Man* · portraits, repro. in Howell and Ford, *True history* · two lithographs, repro. in *Transactions of the Pathology Society of London*, 36 (1885), pl. xx

Merrick [*formerly* Miller], **Leonard William** (1864–1939), writer, was born on 21 February 1864 at 51 Belsize Park, London. His early years are clouded in obscurity, but he seems to have been the only son of William Miller and Esther Davis. His father, a businessman, and his family—of Jewish origin—planned his education in private schools, at Heidelberg University, and in law, but Merrick's father lost money in a business venture, and Merrick left his school, Brighton College, early. At the age of eighteen he was sent to South Africa and to the Kimberley goldfield area, where initially he superintended black labourers; later he worked as a magistrate's clerk, finally entering a Kimberley solicitor's office. A serious attack of camp fever nearly killed him. These experiences form the setting for Merrick's *The Worldlings* (1900).

After his return to London in the 1880s, he changed his name by deed poll to Merrick, and for two years toured England as an actor, playing largely in melodramas. Disillusioned with acting, he then turned to writing short stories for a London paper, *Wit and Wisdom*. His first novel, *Mr Bazalgette's Agent* (1888), although critically and commercially unsuccessful, is remarkable for its use of the selective confessional diary form in the voice of what must be the first female detective. A depressed Merrick went to New York to seek his fortune on the stage with a borrowed £50, but while unemployed there he wrote his second novel, *Violet Moses* (1891), which satirically draws upon the Anglo-Jewish background of the St John's Wood and Maida Vale areas of late Victorian London. He returned to London in 1891 to discover that the novel had achieved limited critical recognition. On 1 February 1894, at St Pancras parish church, London, Merrick married Hope Sarah Augusta Butler-Wilkins (d. 1917), of Northampton, the daughter of a dentist and the author of at least two novels, *When a Girl's Engaged* (1905) and the posthumously published *Mary-Girl* (*c*.1920). Between 1891 and 1911, when his last novel, *The Position of Peggy Harper*, was published, Merrick wrote nine other novels, and many short stories, and he collaborated in the writing of at least ten plays. After 1911 he concentrated his creative energies on writing short stories for high-paying magazines.

Merrick's work is characterized by an obsession with style. Michael Sadleir observes in his *XIX Century Fiction: a Bibliographical Record* (1951) that the uniform edition of Merrick's writing published in 1918–19 by Hodder and Stoughton in London

> represented an attempt by a group of fellow-writers to force on public notice and appreciation a delicate and conscientious artist in fiction, whose merits had never been recognized as they deserved. It is sad to record that the generous undertaking failed of its purpose. Merrick was, remained, and still is an 'author's author'. (Sadleir, 1.262–3)

Among the writers contributing introductions to the works in this edition were Sir James Barrie (for *Conrad in Search of his Youth*, 1903), Sir Arthur Pinero (for *The Position of Peggy Harper*), Neil Munro (for *The Worldlings*), Maurice Hewlitt (for *Cynthia, a Daughter of the Philistines*, 1896), Granville Barker (for *One Man's View*, 1897), and G. K. Chesterton (for *The House of Lynch*, 1907). Each introduction stressed Merrick's craftsmanship, his use of theatrical setting, his realism, and his concern to expose fraud. A late collection of short stories, *Four Stories* (1925), draws skilfully upon the bohemian latin quarter of Paris where Merrick spent some of his last years. He had moved there with his only daughter, Lesley, after the death of his wife in 1917, as he found it cheaper and more comfortable than London. During the late 1920s and 1930s he made several round-the-world cruises with his daughter, who left a vivid photographically illustrated account of them, in her *A Good Time* (1936).

H. G. Wells noted in his introduction to Merrick's *The Quaint Companions* (1903) that the book

> is about the tragedy of racial miscegenation. It is, perhaps, the most sympathetic and understanding novel, in its intimate everyday way, about the clash of colour and race prejudice and racial quality that has ever been written in England, and its merits make its limitation of length and scope more regrettable. (Wells, ix)

Indeed it is George Orwell in his introduction to a projected 1945 reprint of *The Position of Peggy Harper* who summed up the reason why Merrick's work failed to achieve either best-seller status or critical acclaim: his gloomy works primarily focus on artists. Yet Merrick's realism, his concern for the outsider, and his originality of plotting ensure him a permanent place in British literary history.

From all accounts Merrick was shy and diffident, rarely seen at the Savage, his London club. His opposition to hunting seems to have been one of his few firm public stances. His hobbies were, according to his obituary in the *New York Times*, 'music, reading other persons' novels, and seeing other persons' plays'. In his *Contemporary Portraits* Frank Harris described him as 'a small, handsome man, slight but wiry and healthy, with melancholy, dark brooding eyes, long and straight nose, and large black moustache' (Harris, 94). Merrick died in a London nursing home at 3 Courtfield Gardens on 7 August 1939 and was cremated at Golders Green, Middlesex. His daughter edited a posthumous collection of his short stories, *The Leonard Merrick Omnibus* (1950).

WILLIAM BAKER

Sources W. Baker, D. Lass, and S. E. Tabachnick, 'Leonard Merrick: an annotated bibliography of writings about him', *English Literature in Transition, 1880–1920*, 21 (1978), 79–109 • W. Baker, 'Leonard Merrick: a forgotten master?', *Antiquarian Book Monthly Review*, 15 (1988), 140–44 • E. W. McDiarmid, *Leonard Merrick, 1864–1939* (1980) • *New York Times* (8 Aug 1939) • F. Harris, 'Leonard Merrick', *Contemporary portraits: fourth series* (1924), 94–111 • L. Merrick, *A good time* (1936) • L. Merrick, 'Introduction', *The Leonard Merrick omnibus*, ed. L. Merrick (1950), vii • G. Orwell [E. A. Blair], 'Introduction to "The position of Peggy Harper"', in *The collected essays, journalism, and letters of George Orwell*, ed. S. Orwell and I. Angus, 4: *In front of your nose, 1945–1950* (1968), 52–6 • M. Sadleir, 'Leonard Merrick', *XIX century fiction: a bibliographical record based on his own collection*, 1 (1951), 262–3 • H. G. Wells, 'Introduction', in L. Merrick, *The quaint companions* (1924), v–ix • b. cert. • m. cert. • d. cert. • *CGPLA Eng. & Wales* (1940)

Archives Harvard U., Houghton L., literary MSS and papers • University of Minnesota, Minneapolis | Bodl. Oxf., letters to A. St John Adcock

Likenesses portrait, repro. in Baker, 'Leonard Merrick', 140 • portrait, repro. in Merrick, *Good time*

Wealth at death £17,016 19s. 11d.: probate, 7 Aug 1940, *CGPLA Eng. & Wales*

Merrick, Rice [Rhys Meurug] (c.1520–1587), landowner and antiquary, was descended from one of the native Welsh families of Miskin, according to bardic tradition and the genealogical tracts. His contemporary the Glamorgan bard Dafydd Benwyn maintained that he was the son of Meurug ap Hywel ap Philip, of the line of Caradog Freichfras. Merrick's father came originally from Llantrisant, but moved to Bonvilston in south Glamorgan about 1520 on the occasion of his marriage to the daughter of William ap John. It was probably in Bonvilston that Rice, who seems to have been their only son, was born shortly afterwards. By 1554 Merrick had moved to Pen-coed in the parish of St Fagans, possibly at the time of his marriage to Mary (c.1525–1589), the daughter of Christopher Fleming of Flemingston and his wife, Elizabeth Mansel of Oxwich; Mary was thus related to one of the most influential contemporary Glamorgan families.

Rice Merrick probably began to practise as an attorney when he was fairly young. He was appointed clerk of the peace by William Herbert (d. 1570) and Henry Herbert (d. 1601), the first and second earls of Pembroke of the second creation, who were successively *custodes rotulorum* of Glamorgan. Furthermore, some of the estreat rolls for the manor of Glynrhondda show that in 1583 Merrick was deputy steward to William Mathew, and in 1585 to George Herbert. It is likely that he acted also as deputy steward for Miskin. In 1546 the manor of Tre-hyl, which had formerly belonged to a family called Cotrel, had been sold to Meurug ap Hywel ap Philip by Walter Herbert of Dunraven. By 1554 this had passed to Merrick, who, some time between 1554 and 1563, moved to a new residence situated near to the remains of Cotrel Court, once the seat of the by then extinct Cotrel family. In 1574/5 he purchased the adjoining manor of Bonvilston from William Bassett of Beaupré. Rice Merrick and his father managed to acquire freeholds in both the manors, and before his death Rice possessed the nucleus of an estate that, at a later date, comprised the western part of the parish of St Nicholas, the greater part of Bonvilston, and small portions of Llancarfan and Pendeulwyn.

Merrick may well have begun his researches into the history and chorography of Glamorgan when he was still a young man, and his appointment as clerk of the peace obviously gave him an excellent opportunity to visit every part of Glamorgan in his search for materials, the fruit of which was his celebrated *Morganiae archaiographia*, or *A Book of Glamorganshire's Antiquities*. Begun probably in 1578 but never finally completed, and based on a rich and interesting variety of sources both written and oral, this work is the first historical and topographical study of any Welsh county and is, therefore, an important landmark in Welsh historiography. It was first published by Thomas Phillipps at his private press in Middle Hill, Worcestershire, in 1825, but for many years it was best known by the 1887 second edition by James Andrew Corbett. Both of these editors used a corrupt and incomplete copy, transcribed some time between 1660 and 1680 and now deposited in the library of the Queen's College, Oxford. Another copy, transcribed possibly c.1674–1675, is in Cardiff Central Library and corresponds fairly closely with the Oxford version, and with another copy preserved in the National Library of Wales, although some small differences suggest that it is an independent copy of an exemplar that is now lost. It contains a variant version of the dissension that allegedly arose between Iestyn ap Gwrgant (*fl. c.*1081–1093), the last independent ruler of Glamorgan, and Rhys ap Tewdwr (d. 1093), king of Deheubarth, based, it is stated therein, on 'the Records of the auncient Abbey of Neth', a source that is no longer extant.

It seems that the original holograph of Merrick's *magnum opus* has been lost, although it may have been one of the manuscripts that Thomas Wilkins (d. 1699), the rector of St Mary Church, had in his possession. Furthermore, this may well have been one of the Glamorgan manuscripts to which Edward Lhuyd (d. 1709) had access, probably during his visit to south Wales in 1697, for Edward Williams (Iolo Morganwg; d. 1826) claimed that he had seen the manuscript in 1799 at Hafoduchtryd, a mansion in the Ystwyth valley, Cardiganshire, 'with the arms of ancient families finely blazoned in rich colours'. A new, fuller, and more accurate edition of Merrick's work was published in 1983.

Morganiae archaiographia, which deservedly won for its author the distinction of being the most important of the older historians of Glamorgan, was not the only product of Merrick's scholarly researches. In it he refers to other works he had written or compiled, such as the 'Treatice of Wales' or 'that booke which treateth of Cambria', a work that may have discussed the political divisions of the country, and a 'Short Treatice of the Bishoprick of Landaph', a work that was probably based mainly on his study of *Liber Landavensis*, a twelfth-century manuscript which, in his day, was still in the possession of the chapter of Llandaff Cathedral. Frequent mention of another work which he calls 'Peramb.' is probably a reference to William Lambarde's book, *A Perambulation of Kent* (1576), which chiefly inspired Merrick to undertake the task of writing a book on Glamorgan.

In his day Merrick was renowned throughout the whole of Wales both as a historian and a genealogist, and Lewys Dwnn, the distinguished genealogist, sang to his great learning and scholastic accomplishments. According to Dwnn, he had compiled 'one of the finest books in Wales about the whole island of Britain'. This is probably a reference to his substantial collection of genealogies, often referred to as the Cottrell book. The professional poets Dafydd Benwyn and Sils ap Siôn both sang elegies to him. Following his death at Cotrel on 1 March 1587 Rice Merrick was buried in the parish church at St Nicholas, of which he was one of the patrons. He and his wife, Mary, had three sons, Morgan, their heir, William, and John, as well as several daughters, one of whom married Roger Williams, the scholarly rector of St Nicholas from 1582 to 1626, who probably acquired most of Merrick's manuscripts after the latter's death; it may have been from one of his descendants that the manuscripts eventually passed into the possession of Thomas Wilkins. This collection may well have included the final holograph of Merrick's pioneering work on Glamorgan, which in time found its way to Hafoduchtryd, where it was completely destroyed in the fire that badly damaged the mansion in 1807.

C. W. Lewis

Sources C. W. Lewis, 'The literary history of Glamorgan from 1550 to 1770', *Glamorgan county history*, ed. G. Williams, 4: *Early modern Glamorgan* (1974), 535–639 · G. J. Williams, *Traddodiad llenyddol Morgannwg* (1948), 203–14 · T. J. Hopkins, 'Rice Merrick (Rhys Meurug) of Cottrell', *Morgannwg*, 8 (1964), 5–13 · R. Merrick, *Morganiae archaiographia: a book of the antiquities of Glamorganshire*, ed. B. Ll. James (1983), xi–xxxvii · G. T. Clark, *Limbus patrum Morganiae et Glamorganiae* (1886) · C. F. Shepherd, *St Nicholas* (1934) · E. Lhuyd, *Parochialia*, ed. R. H. Morris, 3 (1911), 116–47 [suppl. to *Archaeologia Cambrensis*] · J. M. Traherne, ed., *Stradling correspondence: a series of letters written in the reign of Queen Elizabeth* (1840), 167–8, 169 · *The account of the official progress of His Grace Henry first duke of Beaufort … through Wales in 1684*, ed. R. W. Banks (1888), 271, 346 · M. Robbins, 'The agricultural, domestic, social and cultural interests of the gentry of south-east Glamorgan, 1540–1640', PhD diss., U. Wales, 1974 · NL Wales, Aberdâr MS 1 · NL Wales, MS 11700E · NL Wales, Peniarth MS 120 E · NL Wales, MS 5262 · NL Wales, Llanover MS C 16, fol. 270 · NL Wales, Llanover MS C 34, fol. 19 · NL Wales, Llanover MS C 45, fol. 28 · NL Wales, Peniarth MS 96, fols. 245 ff. · estreat rolls for the manor of Glynrhondda, NL Wales, Bute Collection, Box 88, B.I. · Queen's College, Oxford, MS 288 · Cardiff Central Library, MS 4.33 · Cardiff Central Library, MS 5.8 · Cardiff Central Library, MS 3.464 · Cardiff Central Library, MS 10, fol. 113 · Cardiff Central Library, MS 2.277, fols. 344–6 · Coll. Arms, MS 36/5g · Coll. Arms, MS 36/25 · F. Jones, *Report … on the Welsh manuscripts contained in the muniments of the College of Arms* (1957) · P. Morgan, *Oxford libraries outside the Bodleian* (1973) · *Archaeologia Cambrensis*, 5th ser., 7 (1890), 321–2 · *Llên Cymru*, 1 (1950–51), 48 · J. Simmons, ed., *English county historians* (1978)
Archives Glamorgan RO, Cardiff, MSS, CL/BRA 247, nos. 18, 19, 21, 22, 24, 26, 28, 42, 318 · NL Wales, Talbot of Hensol collection, MSS nos. 543, 544, 548

Merrifield, Charles Watkins (1827–1884), mathematician, was born on 20 October 1827 at Nelson Square, Southwark, London, the son of John Merrifield (1788/9–

1877), barrister, formerly of Tavistock, Devon, and his wife, Mary Philadelphia, *née* Watkins (1804–1889) [*see* Merrifield, Mary Philadelphia], a writer on art and literature. After receiving a good general education he entered the education department in 1847 at Whitehall, and was subsequently appointed an examiner, a post he held to within a few months of his death. Although called to the bar in January 1851, he did not practise. He devoted his leisure time to mathematics, and especially to naval architecture, amassing an extensive knowledge of applied mechanics and hydraulics. On 12 October 1858 he married Elizabeth Ellen, daughter of John Nicholls of Trekenning, St Colomb; she died on 23 March 1869 at their home, 23 Scarsdale Villas, South Kensington.

In 1858 Merrifield published a paper 'The geometry of the elliptic equation' in the *Philosophical Magazine*, which revealed remarkable mathematical ability. Important papers on the calculation of elliptic functions followed, resulting in his election on 4 June 1863 as a fellow of the Royal Society. On 19 March 1866 he was elected a member of the London Mathematical Society, becoming a member of its council on 10 November 1870, vice-president (1876–8), president (1878–80), and treasurer from November 1880 until his resignation, due to ill health, on 14 December 1882.

On the establishment in 1867 of the Royal School of Naval Architecture and Marine Engineering at South Kensington, Merrifield accepted the office of vice-principal at the request of the authorities, succeeding shortly afterwards to the post of principal. He held this office until 1873, when, on the transference of the school to Greenwich, he returned to the education office. From 1864 to 1875 Merrifield was member and secretary of the Institution of Naval Architects, from which he received a handsome testimonial on his retirement.

He was also a member of the Association for the Improvement of Geometrical Teaching, and he sat on many committees of the British Association for the Advancement of Science, being president of section G (on mechanical science) at the Brighton meeting of 1875 and at the Glasgow meeting of 1876. In his presidential address of 1876 he stressed the importance of practical education, urging more language and less grammar, more drawing and less geometry, or, as he himself put it, 'more marching and less drill' (*PRS*). He served on various commissions, including the royal commission on the unseaworthiness of ships in 1869, and the royal commission which reported on Charles Babbage's famous analytical engine. He frequently acted as assessor in the wreck commissioner's court, and was superintendent of the naval museum at South Kensington.

Merrifield was a frequent contributor to mathematical journals, although few of his papers were of any great length. More than a hundred were published in the *Transactions of the Institution of Naval Architects*, with other papers appearing in the Royal Society's *Philosophical Transactions*, the *Assurance Magazine*, *British Association Reports*, and the *Proceedings of the London Mathematical Society*. For many years he also edited Longman's Text-books of Science series, contributing his own *Technical Arithmetic and Mensuration* in 1870.

Merrifield's particular skill lay in mathematical arithmetic, methods of interpolation and tabular work in general, talents which he fully exploited by producing extended mathematical tables to reduce the amount of manual calculation required for particular mathematical applications. Thus it was largely to Merrifield that the revolution from 'rule of thumb' to exact science in naval architecture was attributed by his mathematical peers.

In addition to his scientific attainments, Merrifield was well versed in Latin and Greek, and was also able to write and speak French and Italian fluently. Some of his papers on the difficult and scientifically interesting subject of sea-waves were translated into Italian for the *Revista Marittima*, in which they appeared with a footnote from the editor bearing testimony to the author's extensive knowledge and excellence of style. Merrifield recovered from an attack of apoplexy in April 1882, but on 18 October 1883 suffered another attack; he died at his home, 45 Church Road, Hove, Sussex, on 1 January 1884, aged fifty-six.   ADRIAN RICE

Sources *PRS*, 36 (1883–4), i–iii · *Proceedings of the London Mathematical Society*, 1st ser., 15 (1883–4), 281–4 · *Nature*, 29 (1883–4), 270 · Boase & Courtney, *Bibl. Corn.*, 1.350 · G. C. Boase, *Collectanea Cornubiensia: a collection of biographical and topographical notes relating to the county of Cornwall* (1890) · *The Times* (4 Jan 1884), 6c · *The Athenaeum* (5 Jan 1884), 25
Archives CUL, letters to Sir George Stokes
Likenesses photograph, Sci. Mus.
Wealth at death £2302 17s. 10d.: probate, 4 Feb 1884, *CGPLA Eng. & Wales*

Merrifield [*née* Watkins], **Mary Philadelphia** (1804–1889), writer on art and algology, was born on 15 April 1804 in Brompton, London, the daughter of a conveyancing barrister, Sir Charles Watkins. In 1827 she married John Merrifield of Tavistock (1788/9–1877), who was called to the bar in Middle Temple in 1828 and practised for many years in Brighton, where the family lived. Her earliest work appears to be her translation, entitled *Treatise of Painting* (1844), of Cennino Cennici's early fifteenth-century work, which had been recently discovered and published in 1821 by the Italian antiquary Giuseppe Tambroni. This led to her employment by the royal commission on the fine arts, investigating the history of painters' materials and techniques, which resulted in the publication of her *The Art of Fresco Painting* (1846). Reflecting the royal commission's deep concern about the absence of a British school of history painting, it was at once a collection of historical texts on the techniques of twelfth- to eighteenth-century fresco painters and a manual for the practising artist; it long remained a useful work and was reprinted in 1952. Her two sons, Charles Watkins *Merrifield (1827–1884), later a marine engineer and mathematician, and Frederick Merrifield, assisted her researches. Mrs Merrifield followed this important work with *Original Treatises on the Arts of Painting* (1849), a collection of early technical information which remained of value for many years and was reprinted in 1967.

In 1851 Mary Merrifield published *Practical Directions for Portrait-Painting in Watercolours*, which was followed in 1854 by *Dress as a Fine Art*, a reprint of essays which had first appeared in the *Art Journal* and the *London Magazine*; both works seem to be intended for a readership of young middle-class women. In *Dress* Mrs Merrifield declared herself in favour of practical, modest, and elegant fashions, and displayed a considerable sympathy for the dress reforms of Amelia Bloomer. Her *Handbook of Light and Shade with Reference to Model Drawing* (1855) was possibly written at the request of her son Charles, who was then an examiner in the education office.

On 2 May 1857 Mary Merrifield was granted a civil-list pension of £100 in recognition of her services to literature and art. Ironically her literary career now took a new direction: in the same year she published *Brighton Past and Present*, a lively guidebook featuring a good many Regency anecdotes, which was followed by *A Sketch of the Natural History of Brighton* (1864). This reflected her new interest in botany: over the next twenty years, taking advantage of her seaside residency, she became an accepted authority on seaweeds, publishing articles on marine algae in the *Journal of the Linnean Society*, the *Journal of Botany*, and the *Annals of Botany*. From 1875 until her death she also contributed frequently to the important scientific journal *Nature*, exhibiting a keen sensitivity to both the beauty and the antiquity of her subject matter. She assisted in the arrangement and display of natural history exhibits at the Brighton Museum, and in her later years learned Danish and Swedish to read scientific literature in these languages. A species of marine algae was named after her, and her herbarium is held at the natural history department of the British Museum.

After the death of her husband in 1877 Mary Merrifield went to live with her daughter, who had married a clergyman, at Stapleford vicarage, near Cambridge; she died there on 4 January 1889. Her contributions to both art history and science show how a linguistically accomplished middle-class woman could establish herself in Victorian cultural and scholarly circles: C. R. Sherman has emphasized how translations—rather than original writings—could serve as 'passports for women's publications in the arts' (Sherman, 13), while the essentially taxonomic and descriptive project of late Victorian botany offered Merrifield an opportunity to establish a niche in one of the few sciences considered suitable for her sex.

ROSEMARY MITCHELL

Sources A. C. Sewter, 'Introduction', in M. P. Merrifield, *The art of fresco painting*, new edn (1952), vii–x · Desmond, *Botanists*, rev. edn, 483 · Boase, *Mod. Eng. biog.* · d. cert. · d. cert. [John Merrifield] · *Nature*, 39 (1888–9), 255 · C. R. Sherman and A. M. Holcomb, eds., *Women as interpreters of the visual arts, 1820–1979* (1981), 13 · D. Robertson, *Sir Charles Eastlake and the Victorian art world* (1978), 70–71, 438
Archives RBG Kew · U. Cam., department of plant sciences

Merriman, (Frank) Boyd, Baron Merriman (1880–1962), judge, was born at Knutsford on 28 April 1880, the eldest son of Frank Merriman JP (1852–1920) of Knutsford, and his wife, Mariquita (d. 1930), fourth daughter of John Pringle Boyd. N. J. Merriman was his great-uncle. Boyd, as he was called by most who knew him well, was educated at Winchester College where he won the English speech prize and played an active part in the debating society. Circumstances did not permit him to enter a university and he became articled to a firm of Manchester solicitors. Later he decided to go to the bar and he was called by the Inner Temple in 1904. He became a pupil in the chambers of the future lord chief justice Gordon Hewart.

In the First World War Merriman served with distinction in the Manchester regiment and on the staff. He was thrice mentioned in dispatches and in 1918 appointed OBE. On his return to civilian life he made such rapid progress that in 1919 he was able to take silk. In 1920 he was appointed recorder of Wigan. In the meantime he took a keen interest in politics and was adopted as Conservative candidate for the Rusholme division of Manchester. In 1924 he won this seat after a contest with the Liberal candidate C. F. G. Masterman and retained it until his elevation to the bench in 1933, when he joined other Wykehamists of his generation who also became High Court judges. He gave up the recordership of Wigan when in March 1928 he succeeded Sir Thomas Inskip as solicitor-general. This period of office ended in June 1929; in January 1932 he was reappointed. Then in September 1933 he became president of the Probate, Divorce, and Admiralty Division and was subsequently sworn of the privy council.

The Admiralty work of the division was much shrunken by a worldwide decline in shipping. Probate work continued much as it had been before Merriman's appointment, but the flood of divorce cases increased and continued to do so during the whole of his presidency. His work in that office was carried out with great energy and efficiency, all the more because he had little experience in the class of work he had to perform. He had previously had a substantial practice as a junior and as a silk at the common-law bar on the northern circuit and in London. One memorable case in which he appeared was an action brought by Captain Peter Wright against Lord Gladstone arising out of defamatory statements made by Wright concerning W. E. Gladstone. The thankless task of appearing for Wright he performed with ability, tact, and good taste which won general admiration.

In September 1929 Merriman appeared before the commission appointed to report on the Palestine disturbances of August 1929. He led the team of barristers who appeared for the Palestine Zionist Executive and the Zionist Organization. The complaints made by his clients against the *mufti* of Jerusalem and the Palestine Arab Executive were that they were influenced by the general political motive of determined opposition to the policy of the Jewish national home based on the Balfour declaration.

At the bar Merriman was vigorous and fair in controversy, and the same qualities were recognized by his fellow members of the House of Commons. On the bench he was above all conscientious and anxious to give of his best, never sparing himself in the attempt to arrive at a just conclusion in every case. The amount of work required from him and the other judges of the division rose with the number of divorce petitions presented, from less than 5000 in 1933, when he was appointed, to over 50,000 in 1947. The judicial strength of the division increased from three to eleven before the end of his presidency.

The act of 1937 which enlarged the grounds for divorce was no doubt in part responsible for this vast increase in the work, but Merriman never questioned the propriety of the act. As a judge he did all he could to surmount the difficulties in his way. His occasional explosions of anger were always directed at what appeared to him to be unjust or otherwise objectionable, and he earned the respect and affection of those who practised before him. He was a just and upright judge who remained in office until he died at the age of eighty-one without losing the capacity to deal judicially and thoroughly with each case which he had to try. At the last he was engaged in a matrimonial appeal in the House of Lords on which he was due to deliver his opinion on the day of his death. The greater part of it was included in the opinion of one of the colleagues who had been sitting with him.

During a happy childhood at Knutsford as a member of a large family with many relations in the neighbourhood, Merriman developed a love of music, the theatre, and sport, particularly fishing and golf. These interests were with him to the end. He did not abandon his attachment to Knutsford, which he visited regularly when opportunity offered in order to take part in various church and civil occasions; he retained many friendships there. In London he was a popular member of the Savile Club; at the Inner Temple he was appointed a bencher in 1927, and in 1949 deputized for King George VI as treasurer. From 1941 to 1946 he was chairman of the bishop of London's commission on City churches. He was an honorary member of the American and Canadian bar associations and an honorary LLD of McGill University. He was knighted in 1928, created a baron in 1941, and appointed GCVO in 1950.

On 11 September 1907 Merriman married Eva Mary (*d.* 1919), second daughter of the late Revd Henry Leftwich Freer, with whom he had two daughters. On 18 December 1920 he married his second wife, Olive McLaren (*d.* 1952), third daughter of Frederick William Carver, of Knutsford. On 1 January 1953 he married his third wife, Jane Lamb, younger daughter of James Stormonth, of Belfast. Merriman died in London on 18 January 1962. He was survived by his third wife. HODSON, *rev.*

Sources personal knowledge (1981) · private information (1981) · *The Times* (19 Jan 1962) · Burke, *Peerage* (1959) · *CGPLA Eng. & Wales* (1962)
Archives NRA, papers
Likenesses W. Stoneman, photograph, 1955, NPG · J. Merton, portrait, priv. coll.
Wealth at death £20,254 6s. 4d.: probate, 16 May 1962, *CGPLA Eng. & Wales*

Merriman, Brian (*c.*1750–1805), Irish-language poet, was probably born in the neighbourhood of Ennistimon, co. Clare, the son of a stonemason. His mother was a woman of the Mac Uilcín (Quilkin) family, a surname usually associated with counties Mayo and Galway. He had two or perhaps more sisters. A tradition persisted throughout the nineteenth century that Merriman had been born out of wedlock, and that the surname by which he was known was simply 'a fancy patronymic' (O'Grady, 493, 495). Moreover, it has also been suggested that his family may have been 'an offshoot of the MacNamaras' (MacLysaght, 215), possibly linking him with the seventeenth-century Gaelic poet Murchadh Riabhach Mac Con Mara. Those sections of his poetry that deal with the question of illegitimacy, while borrowing many well-wrought themes, treat the illegitimate child and erring mother in such a positive and sympathetic manner that many readers have suspected a less than purely dispassionate interest. In the absence of any hard proof, however, the question of his birth must remain conjectural.

The Merriman family soon moved east to the parish of Feakle and settled near Lough Graney, which features prominently in the opening lines of his best-known poem, *Cúirt an mheonoíche* ('The Midnight Court', 1780). While Merriman's first language was undoubtedly Irish, his education, received locally, probably comprised a good grounding in English grammar and in the various branches of mathematics, although an 1836 manuscript categorically states that he knew no Greek or Latin (see Ó Foghludha, 1949, 7).

A vibrant literary culture was maintained in counties Clare and Limerick in the second half of the eighteenth century by a network of scribes and poets. Merriman would have been exposed to some of the poetry of this group from youth and doubtlessly absorbed their compositional techniques. However, he was not animated to partake actively until 1780 when he composed his *Cúirt an mheonoíche*. It is highly probable that his contribution was connected with the formation of the 'Ennis group', composed of a number of contemporary literati who had decided to establish a court of poetry, a type of literary guild, and set down rules to regulate the work of the court. One such rule directs members who may have access to old books or manuscripts to have them 'renewed' or copied, a stipulation which provides a valuable insight into Merriman's literary formation and background.

The three lengthy monologues that make up Merriman's *Cúirt* are informed by a tension between the desire on the part of lovers for freedom to act independently and the imperatives of the arranged marriage. The role of the dowry within an arranged marriage is key to his forthright discussion of the lack of marital equilibrium and its social and psychological consequences: young women unable to attract marriage partners and so resorting to prostitution; young men marrying well-dowried but infecund women, or holding out for 'a better deal'; young women frustrated in marriage to old men and their consequent inclination to adultery; old men being deceived into marriage with promiscuous, and sometimes pregnant women; and children conceived outside wedlock. This catalogue of marital danger is approached by Merriman in a comical mode, making highly effective use of irony, satire, ambiguities, and the well-understood hint. It is as if he feels that his readership or audience—for the poem must have been transmitted orally on a wide scale—knows full well about these matters, but has never had them discussed so fully and openly. His language is bold and fluent as he juxtaposes colloquial and literary registers. The entire effort is harnessed in an innovative verse form and while the import of the whole is for the most part humorous, at certain junctures the anxieties of Merriman's women crystallize, and these lines can be seen to betray a serious side to the poet's interest and may well reflect some personal anxieties surrounding the circumstances of his own conception and birth, and his failure, as yet, to marry.

Five scholarly editions of *Cúirt an mheonoíche* (or sometimes entitled *Cúirt an mheán oíche*) have appeared in the twentieth century, the latest (1982) based on what is now accepted as the poet's autograph copy. This manuscript, preserved in Cambridge University Library (Cambridge Add. MS 6562), not only contains Merriman's version of the *Cúirt* and two other minor pieces of his, but also an anthology of Munster verse in the poet's own hand. This latter is most illuminating in determining allusions, resonances, and influences in Merriman's own work. Of telling significance is the devotional verse ascribed in the manuscript to Murchadh Riabhach Mac Con Mara. These verses, dated between 1687 and 1688, contemplate the transience of life, the inevitability of death, and the formidable test of the last judgment. In content and general outlook this poetry forms an antithesis to the high-spirited worldliness found in the *Cúirt*. But the replication in Merriman of the diction, the phraseology, and so many rhetorical devices of Mac Con Mara suggests a deep familiarity with his work. More crucially, however, it can be seen to reflect a determination on the part of Merriman to exorcise the sombre influences of the elder (and perhaps ancestral) poet by incorporating them into a poem that challenged the very basis of Mac Con Mara's philosophy.

Merriman established and kept a good school of mathematics in the environs of Lough Graney. Having married a certain Cáit Ní Choileáin (Kate Collins) about 1783, he moved south to within a half a mile of the village of Feakle and rented a 7 or 8 acre farm at Aill from a minor noble of the MacNamaras. He seems to have been progressive and innovative in his approach to farming, and was awarded two spinning-wheels as prizes for his flax crop in 1796. He farmed and taught a successful school at Aill for some twenty years. He and his wife had two daughters, and he later moved his family to Limerick city, where he again maintained a successful mathematics school at Old Clare Street for two years. As he was walking in Old Clare Street on the morning of 27 July 1805, he was taken ill and carried back to his home, Corner and Archway House where he died, survived by his wife. He was buried in the cemetery at Feakle. Subsequent reports of his death in Irish newspapers mentioned his position as teacher of mathematics, but ignored his major contribution to Irish literature. A less prurient and less easily shocked generation of readers and scholars, however, have been captivated by Merriman's innovativeness and originality, even as enigmas concerning the man and his poem persist and continue to engage.   L. P. Ó MURCHÚ

Sources L. P. Ó Murchú, ed., *Cúirt an mheon-oíche le Brian Merriman* (1982) · B. Merriman, *Cúirt an mheadhon oidhche*, ed. R. Ó Foghludha (1912) · B. Merriman, *Cúirt an mheadhon oidhche*, ed. R. Ó Foghludha (1949) · P. De Brún and M. Herbert, eds., *Catalogue of Irish manuscripts in Cambridge libraries* (1986) · NL Ire., MS G844 · S. H. O'Grady, ed., *Catalogue of Irish manuscripts in the British Museum*, 1 (1926) · E. MacLysaght, *The surnames of Ireland*, 2nd edn (1969) · B. Ó Cuív, 'Rialacha do chúirt Éigse i gContae an Chláir', *Éigse*, 11 (1964–6), 216–18 · *Report of the linen board of Ireland* (1796) · *General Advertiser, or, Limerick Gazette* (29 July 1805)
Archives CUL, Add. MS 6562
Wealth at death mathematical schools were financially successful: NL Ire., MS G844

Merriman, Henry Seton. *See* Scott, Hugh Stowell (1862–1903).

Merriman, John (1774–1839). *See under* Merriman, Samuel (1771–1852).

Merriman, John Xavier (1841–1926), politician in South Africa, was born on 15 March 1841 at Street, Somerset, the eldest of the nine children of Nathaniel James *Merriman (1809–1882), later bishop of Grahamstown, and his wife, Julia, *née* Potter (1820–1910). Merriman was educated at the Diocesan College, Cape Town (1851–6), and at Radley College, near Oxford (1856–8). He then worked in London for three years as a clerk in a tea and silk importing firm, and in 1862 returned to the Cape.

Earning a living Merriman qualified as a surveyor, and from 1863 worked in the Cape border districts, enjoying the outdoor life and reading prodigiously. From 1870 to 1874 he was a diamond buyer at early Kimberley: he had no knack for this tricky trade, but made lasting friendships, notably with Cecil Rhodes, whom he persuaded to enter politics as 'the only intellectual pursuit open to a colonist'. On 16 September 1874 he married Agnes (1854–1923), the younger daughter of Joseph Vintcent, a Netherlands-born merchant and member of the legislative council; their exceptionally happy marriage was childless. Still in search of a livelihood, Merriman in 1874 joined a wine firm in Cape Town and opened a crayfish canning factory, but abandoned these trades with relief when he became a cabinet minister in 1875. Between spells in office he was a newspaper correspondent (1879–81), and, in 1885, tried to amalgamate the diamond mines, but failed when Rhodes withdrew his support. While at Kimberley he was horrified at the working conditions of the Africans there: 'a scandal and a disgrace for everyone whose moral sense is not blunted by the habit of looking at them as mere working animals'. In 1887 he joined the Transvaal gold rush, but preferred the beautiful Barberton goldfields to the squalid Johannesburg mining camp. Like many others he was duped into buying a 'salted' mine. In 1889 he became manager of the Langlaagte mine near Johannesburg, but was unfairly extruded. In 1892 he at last found the secondary occupation he loved: he bought

John Xavier Merriman (1841–1926), by Edward Roworth

and transformed a beautiful, derelict farm, Schoongezicht, in Stellenbosch, and became an innovative wine producer and fruit grower and exporter.

Opposing confederation The 'chief object' in Merriman's life was parliament: 'the government and ordering of society under the reign of freedom and of law … the highest and best side of politics'. He believed that a 'good Opposition is essential to good government' and his own example confirmed this. Of his fifty-four years in parliament he spent forty-one as a towering figure in opposition. He was first elected in 1869 for Aliwal North, and in 1875 John Molteno, the first prime minister under responsible government, invited him to join the cabinet as commissioner for crown lands and public works, with responsibility for railway development. He at once proved his capability. With his tall stature and handsome appearance, his quick wit, debating skill, and sparkling eloquence—enhanced by his beautiful speaking voice—he was the most conspicuous figure in parliament.

Politically Merriman collided with the current imperialism. In May 1875 Lord Carnarvon, the British secretary of state for the colonies, launched a premature South African confederation scheme which Molteno repudiated and Merriman derided. Merriman vehemently denounced the arbitrary annexation of Transvaal, and the appointment of Sir Bartle Frere as Cape governor and South African high commissioner, with the special duty—unknown to Merriman—to accomplish confederation. However, Frere's brilliance and distinction at first overawed Merriman. In November 1877 they worked amicably together to subdue a frontier uprising with the use of Cape troops, and Frere commended Merriman's 'energy and efficiency'. But with a renewed outbreak Frere changed his line: in February 1878 he abruptly dismissed the ministry for unconstitutionally deploying the Cape forces, and made Merriman the scapegoat. Frere's 'vindictive duplicity' distressed Merriman deeply and considerably damaged his reputation. The new prime minister, the pliable Gordon Sprigg, adopted Frere's policy of advancing confederation by destroying an alleged 'native conspiracy'— which Merriman dismissed as 'balderdash'—by forcibly disarming suspected nations. The results were disastrous. In 1881 the Sprigg ministry fell and to Merriman's relief Frere was recalled for provoking the unauthorized Anglo-Zulu War.

A new force, the Afrikaner Bond, now dominated Cape politics. With the outbreak of the First South African War (1880), Merriman collaborated with the shrewd Cape Afrikaner leader J. H. Hofmeyr to help restore Transvaal peace and autonomy. In other ways the two men were antipathetic. Hofmeyr, in Merriman's view, undermined parliamentary government by refusing the responsibility of power and rejecting the premiership. The result was the safe choice of the mild Thomas Scanlen, in whose cabinet Hofmeyr reluctantly served. Hofmeyr resigned after quarrelling with his fellow cabinet minister Merriman over the return of (now chronically rebellious) Basutoland and Transkei to British control, and over Merriman's attack on Afrikaner nationalism as 'the detestable doctrine that a man's political views should follow his race and language'. Perhaps most potent of all, however, was Hofmeyr's resentment at Merriman's nickname for him—'the Mole'. Against expectations, Merriman succeeded in the transfer of Basutoland, which became a British protectorate and eventually independent, but the Bond defeated him on Transkei and the ministry fell in 1884.

Rhodes and the Jameson raid Merriman's next term of office (1890–93) was as treasurer and minister of agriculture in the Rhodes ministry. His excellent banking law, Gladstonian budgets, and promising reforms in agriculture were the fruits of his admirable administration. But politically he was frustrated. Rhodes was engrossed with developing the north by means of his chartered British South Africa Company, and left cabinet control to the unscrupulous James Sivewright, who thwarted the 'liberal trio' of Merriman and his close friends J. W. Sauer and James Rose-Innes. The breaking-point came when Sivewright granted his friend J. D. Logan a railway catering monopoly for eighteen years: once exposed it had to be cancelled. The trio informed Rhodes that if Sivewright did not resign, they would do so; but Rhodes tricked them into delaying, and in July 1894 successfully reformed his cabinet, dropping all four ministers, though he was at pains to whitewash Sivewright. To Merriman, Rhodes's immoral conduct was the prelude to his complicity in the Jameson raid (December 1895), the cataclysm which cost Rhodes the Cape premiership, polarized South African loyalties, and left Merriman isolated. Because chartered troops had violated Transvaal independence, Merriman was convinced that the British South Africa Company's charter should be cancelled. 'I have a duty to perform … and if I stand alone I must do it', he wrote to Rose-Innes (whose priority was redress of Uitlander grievances) on 20 April 1896 (*Selections from the Correspondence*, 2.221). In addition, Rhodes had compromised Hofmeyr, who had earlier accepted a gift of the company's shares. Both Merriman's motion and Rose-Innes's amendment were defeated. Instead, the moderate W. P. Schreiner—Hofmeyr's choice as next prime minister—proposed a parliamentary committee of inquiry into Cape involvement in the raid; Merriman served on the committee and wrote its report, which confirmed Rhodes's guilt, but with no means of exacting retribution.

The peace party In the war crises that followed Merriman supported the Bond as the party working for peace, and was reviled as a renegade and a traitor. In 1897 he moved a vote of no confidence in the inert Sprigg government, but was defeated by the speaker's casting vote. In 1898 Schreiner was successful as the mover of the same motion. In the embittered elections that ensued Merriman was a prime target; after twenty years' service he had to withdraw from his Namaqualand constituency, but the Wodehouse Bond branch came to his rescue (to his lasting gratitude), and he won this difficult seat. The Bond–South African Party came in with a majority of one, and the Schreiner 'Peace Ministry' took office under shadow of impending war, with Merriman in the cabinet.

The instigators of war, as Merriman stressed in his exhortations to British Liberal Party supporters, were Rhodes, the British colonial secretary, Joseph Chamberlain, and the Cape governor and high commissioner, Sir Alfred Milner, whose militancy was particularly alarming. Merriman tried his hardest, by deed, word, and letter, to promote Transvaal reform, considering the war that began in October 1899 to be 'unjust and unjustifiable'. He was personally affected when invasion by the Orange Free State triggered an uprising in adjoining Cape districts, including Wodehouse, despite all his calming efforts. Once subdued, the problem of punishing the rank-and-file rebels split the Schreiner ministry irremediably. Milner and Chamberlain demanded the statutory life disfranchisement, while Merriman argued passionately for amnesty, following the precedent set by Lord Durham after the 1837–9 Canadian uprising. Even Schreiner and Richard Solomon, the attorney-general, both under Milner's influence, were converted by Merriman's powerful amnesty minute, but they reverted when Chamberlain rejected it. (He eventually reduced the penalty to five years, to help Schreiner.) At the party meeting, Schreiner was defeated and resigned (June 1900), and the opposition leadership passed to Merriman.

Leader of the opposition In mid-1900, after apparent Boer defeat and British annexation, a new phase of mobile warfare brought heartrending reprisals. Fearing a second Cape rising, in January 1901 Merriman went to London to petition for peace on the basis of immediate self-government. As he expected, he failed; and when he translated his peace mission into tense and dangerous public meetings, he feared it would become inflammatory. Before leaving England he had a long talk with Sir Henry Campbell-Bannerman which might well have influenced the Liberal Party leader's speech the next day denouncing the British 'methods of barbarism'.

When Merriman returned to Schoongezicht he suffered the indignity of farm arrest under martial law regulations, although Rose-Innes and Solomon soon obtained his release on parole; he spent much of the rest of the war in seclusion on the farm. When peace came in May 1902 his hopes for a better, united South Africa burgeoned after meeting the Transvaal leaders, General Louis Botha and General Jan Christiaan Smuts, whose ability he had long admired. Lord Milner's campaign to suspend the Cape constitution as the pivot of an imperially-dominated federation infuriated Merriman. Chamberlain, while refusing, did not disown the project, and when the Cape parliament met, Merriman denounced Milner's conspiracy in a rousing, mocking speech in which he described Milner's coterie of Oxford helpers as the 'Milner Kindergarten' (an epithet which became a label of honour).

As Merriman had foreseen, rebel disfranchisement caused a 'pro-British' triumph in the 1904 elections. The Progressive Party, headed by Dr Jameson, defeated the South African Party, and Merriman himself lost his seat, though the Bond member for Victoria West resigned in his favour. While Jameson's party split into rival pressure groups, Merriman's interests ranged over the wider South African scene. They encompassed his attack on Chinese labour (on humane not racial grounds), his evidence to the South African native affairs commission decrying segregation and expounding Cape liberalism, and his seminal correspondence on closer union with Smuts and former 'President' H. T. Steyn of the Orange Free State. Merriman rejoiced when the British Liberal Party victory in 1906, which hinged on 'Chinese slavery', caused Milner's downfall, thus hastening self-government for the new colonies. He cogently argued with Smuts in favour of the Cape qualified, non-racial franchise instead of white manhood suffrage, but could not succeed beyond (as he hoped) ensuring the entrenchment of the Cape franchise in the future constitution of South Africa. He also vainly raised the need to protect civil liberties by a bill of rights, and to send experts abroad to study existent unions and federations, with special attention to the Swiss example.

Prime minister and South African union In February 1908, after a sweeping South African Party victory, Merriman became prime minister on the dual programme of restoring Cape solvency and achieving closer union. By stringent taxation and retrenchment he balanced his budgets, but at great cost to his popularity. He also took charge of 'native' affairs; in his twenty-seven months of office he paid particular attention to migrants' hardships, to higher education, and in general to the grievances and rights as citizens of the black population. But he was too busy to continue his detailed preparations for the

national convention and it was Smuts who drew up the constitutional blueprint.

The national convention of October 1908 to May 1909, despite the extolling of 'the Convention spirit', proved very disillusioning to Merriman. Smuts was often shifty and Botha sullen when crossed. The worst feature was the prevailing illiberalism. But Merriman missed one signpost: the special protection of the Cape franchise was linked with the abolition of the right—never exercised—of black voters to stand for parliament in the Cape, a grave injustice and ambivalence. On the other hand, when the devout F. S. Malan (the leading Bondsman at the convention) moved to insert a religious reference in the preamble of the constitution, Merriman leapt up and declared that the name of the Almighty could not be used in a document that violated the doctrine that all men are equal. The last phase—the passage of the Act of Union through the British parliament—went smoothly, despite Schreiner's courageous attempt to have the franchise amended. Merriman, ahead of the other prime ministers, was sworn of the privy council. For the rest, he was ignored, while Botha was fêted as the coming premier of the union. It was no surprise: Rose-Innes had already forewarned him. But what Merriman did not know was that Hofmeyr had already opted for Botha, not for any reason of statesmanship but because the choice of Merriman would split Afrikaner unity. Jameson also favoured a 'Best Man Government' led by Botha. This 'miasma of intrigue' was completely alien to Merriman: the choice of first union premier, he believed, was the governor-general's prerogative and not the business of politicians. His forebodings about union increased. 'The Convention Spirit!! … [It] was damnable', he wrote to Rose-Innes. 'Sauer and I had … to listen to things [against the black population] that made our blood boil.' And he admitted to the historian Basil Williams: 'I wondered whether I had done the right thing'. Because he condemned the nostrum of a 'Best Man Government' he was attacked on public platforms and in the press, which berated him as a 'reactionary and a crank', hostile to the mines, and a renegade towards empire. (Two editors who pressed his claims were dismissed.)

The first union governor-general, Lord Gladstone, who was primed in favour of Botha in London, slanted his interviews accordingly. The three Bondsmen in Merriman's cabinet opted for Botha, who had promised them the positions that they craved; but the considerable pro-Merriman Bond, South African Party, and Orange Free State support was not plumbed. Nor was the fair-minded and highly reputed Judge Rose-Innes consulted. His continued view was that Merriman's 'brilliant intellect' and great services 'marked him as leader of a new dominion … Botha did not keep so firm a grip … or exercise so wholesome a restraint as Merriman would have done'.

Elder statesman Botha, as prime minister from May 1910, offered Merriman a seat in the cabinet, which he refused, for he knew that their cultural and political differences were insuperable. Merriman retired to the back benches as 'a humble musketeer' and the government's 'candid friend', to its frequent discomfiture. In this last phase of his parliamentary career he won singular honour and regard for his defence of liberal principles, his compassionate insights, and his attacks on financial laxity and unauthorized executive action. (When Smuts in 1914 ended a mining strike by deporting the labour leaders, Merriman shamed this 'ruthless philosopher' when they met ceremonially by standing aside and pronouncing, 'dictators first!'.) But in the difficult and divisive war and post-war years he gave Botha and Smuts powerful support. In the 1915 elections he courageously stood in nationalist Stellenbosch. After his victory he gave a party 'for supporters, white and coloured, all classes. Went off I think well, about 500 turned up. Tea, strawberries, and wine-cup'. His diary exudes a Pepysian contentment.

Merriman's influence extended far beyond politics. His love of literature and learning flowed into innumerable public speeches and lectures. For many years he was chairman of the South African Library and the museum, and on the councils of Cape Town and Stellenbosch universities. He presided over literary, scientific, and philosophical societies, encouraged young writers and scholars, and wrote prefaces for their books. His most enduring influence came through his collected letters, which have informed and enlightened generations of scholars.

Merriman's wife, Agnes, died on 10 September 1923. That night Merriman had a stroke, but survived, though mentally disabled, for three more years. He died on 2 August 1926 at his farm, Schoongezicht, Stellenbosch, at the age of eighty-five, and was buried at Schoongezicht. His obituaries rang with praises: he had outlived his feuds, his ambitions, his lost causes. Now the headlines chorused, 'The great John X. is dead'.   PHYLLIS LEWSEN

Sources P. Lewsen, *John X. Merriman: paradoxical South African statesman* (1982) · *Selections from the correspondence of J. X. Merriman*, ed. P. Lewsen, 4 vols. (1960–69) · *Sir James Rose-Innes: selected correspondence, 1884–1902*, ed. H. M. Wright (1972) · *James Rose-Innes … an autobiography*, ed. B. A. Tindall (1949) · E. A. Walker, *W. P. Schreiner: a South African* (1937) · J. H. Hofmeyr and F. W. Reitz, *The life of Jan Hendrik Hofmeyr (Onze Jan)* (1913) · R. I. Rotberg, *The founder: Cecil Rhodes and the pursuit of power* (1988) · J. L. Garvin, *The life of Joseph Chamberlain*, 1–3 (1932–4) · L. M. Thompson, *The unification of South Africa, 1902–1910* (1960) · T. R. H. Davenport, *The Afrikaner Bond* (1966) · W. K. Hancock, *Smuts*, 1: *The sanguine years, 1870–1919* (1962) · G. H. L. Le May, *British supremacy in South Africa, 1899–1907* (1965) · P. Lawrence, *The life of John Xavier Merriman* (1930) · private information (2004)
Archives BL, memoranda and letters to Sir J. C. Molteno, Add. MS 39299 · National Library of South Africa, Cape Town · Rhodes University, Grahamstown, South Africa, Cory Library for Historical Research, papers and letter-book · University of Cape Town Library, corresp. | Bodl. Oxf., Bryce MSS · Cumbria AS, Carlisle, letters to Lord Howard of Penrith · National Library of South Africa, Cape Town, Rose-Innes, Currey, Schreiner MSS · NL Aus., corresp. with Alfred Deakin · Rhodes University, Grahamstown, South Africa, Cory Library for Historical Research, telegrams mainly to John Hemming · Rhodes University, Grahamstown, South Africa, Cory Library for Historical Research, corresp. with Sir John Gordon Sprigg
Likenesses P. T. Cole, portrait, Houses of Parliament, Cape Town, South Africa · E. Roworth, drawing, Transvaal Archives Department, Pretoria, South Africa [*see illus.*] · E. Roworth, pen-and-ink drawing, University of Cape Town, South Africa, Jagger Library · E. Roworth, portrait, St Barnabas rectory, Cape Town, South Africa · W. H. Schröder, caricatures, repro. in *Excalibur Supplement* (1882)
Wealth at death £858 17s. 4d.: administration with will, 6 Jan 1927, CGPLA Eng. & Wales

Merriman, Nathaniel James (1809–1882), bishop of Grahamstown, Cape Colony, was born in Marlborough, Wiltshire, on 4 April 1809, the third son of Thomas Merriman of Marlborough. Educated at Winchester College and at Brasenose College, Oxford, where he was Hulme exhibitioner, he graduated BA with second-class honours in *literae humaniores* in 1831 (MA, 1834). He was ordained deacon in 1832 and priest in 1833, and became perpetual curate of Over Darwen in Lancashire. In 1841 he moved to the vicarage of Street in Somerset. He had married on 19 February 1840 Julia (1820–1910), daughter of John Potter of Darwen, Lancashire. They had six daughters and three sons. The eldest of his sons, John X. *Merriman, was premier of the Cape Colony from 1908 to 1910.

In 1848 Merriman accepted an offer of the projected archdeaconry of Grahamstown made to him by Robert Gray, bishop of Cape Town. By the end of the year he was in Africa, and at the beginning of 1849 he started on his first visitation of the archdeaconry, which comprised the eastern half of the Cape Colony. He soon came to do most of his travelling on foot, often covering 40 miles in a day, and taught himself, as a necessary concomitant, to do his own shoe repairs. 'He is a very remarkable man', wrote the bishop that year; 'his self-denial and energy both of body and mind are greater than in any other man I have ever met with … the record of his life for the past year would astonish any one'. In 1850 Merriman offered to undertake a mission to the Xhosa people of British Kaffraria, and although Gray refused to release him for this work the successful establishment of a mission there was largely due to Merriman's exertions.

In 1863, at the trial of Bishop Colenso, Merriman, representing the clergy of his archdeaconry, was one of the accusers. When the archdeaconry in 1853 had been constituted as the see of Grahamstown, Merriman had declined the bishopric, as indeed—at his wife's insistence—he declined the offer of several other South African dioceses. Gray's determination to use Merriman, and Mrs Merriman's determination to protect her husband from overwork, were a perpetual source of tension. Eventually, after a short period as dean of Cape Town in 1870, Merriman was consecrated third bishop of Grahamstown, on 5 December 1871. In the late 1870s he became embroiled in a bitter and often unseemly dispute with his dean, Frederick Williams, who, after being a vigorous opponent of Bishop Colenso, became his equally ardent champion. Williams claimed that Merriman possessed no jurisdiction over the cathedral and was tried in an ecclesiastical court for contumacy. For refusing to recognize the authority of the court, Williams was automatically excommunicated in 1880. The dispute eventually came before the judicial committee of the privy council, as the court of appeal in colonial causes, whose judgment contrived to justify the position of both parties. Merriman's essential fairmindedness was demonstrated by the fact that at about

Nathaniel James Merriman (1809–1882), by Samuel Alexander Walker

this time he sided publicly with Colenso in his championship of the Zulu.

Merriman was the author of some lectures on Shakespeare (1857–8), and of *The Kafir, the Hottentot, and the Frontier Farmer* (1854) and *The Bishop's Ride through Independent Kaffraria to Natal and back* (1872). Merriman died in Grahamstown on 16 August 1882 from a carriage accident.

C. A. HARRIS, *rev.* PETER HINCHLIFF

Sources *DSAB* · P. M. Whibley, *Merriman of Grahamstown* (1982) · D. H. Varley and H. M. Matthew, eds., *The Cape journals of Archdeacon Merriman* (1957) · P. B. Hinchliff, *The Anglican church in South Africa* (1963), 115–29 · C. Lewis and G. E. Edwards, *Historical records of the church of the province of South Africa* (1934), 175–9, 236–73 · *Cape Argus* (18 Aug 1882) · *The Times* (18 Aug 1882) · complete record of *Merriman v. Williams*, Bishopscourt, Cape Town · R. Gray, *Life of Bishop Gray* (1876)
Archives diocesan archives, Grahamstown · National Library of South Africa, Cape Town | LPL, corresp. with A. C. Tait and related papers · Rhodes University, Grahamstown, South Africa, diocese of Grahamstown MSS
Likenesses S. A. Walker, photograph, NPG [*see illus.*]

Merriman, Samuel (1731–1818), physician, born on 29 December 1731 at Marlborough, Wiltshire, was the third son of Nathaniel Merriman, grocer, and his wife, Elizabeth Hawkes. He entered Edinburgh University in 1748, and graduated there as MD in 1753; his thesis 'De conceptu', published in 1753, was well regarded and was reprinted by William Smellie in the second volume of his *Thesaurus medicus* (1779). In 1753 he married one of the daughters and coheirs of William Dance, surgeon, of Marlborough; they had fourteen children, of whom one alone, Ann, wife of his nephew Samuel Merriman, survived him. His wife died in 1780.

Merriman first settled as a physician in Bristol, and afterwards moved to Andover, Hampshire. However, when he moved to London in April 1757, he commenced practice in Queen Street, Mayfair, as an apothecary, in partnership with Oakley Halford, who was about to retire. He remained an apothecary for about twenty years, before practising as a physician, finally retiring in 1812. His speciality was midwifery. He is said to have attended more than ten thousand labours; in one year alone he attended 362. His leisure was devoted to literature and biblical studies.

Merriman died at his son-in-law's house, 26 Half Moon Street, London, on 17 August 1818.

GORDON GOODWIN, *rev.* SUSAN SNOXALL

Sources private information (1894) · *GM*, 1st ser., 88/2 (1818), 189 · *The Lancet* (30 Nov 1850), 610
Likenesses J. Corner, engraving (after Richmond) · T. Richmond, miniature

Merriman, Samuel (1771–1852), physician and accoucheur, was born on 25 October 1771 at Marlborough, Wiltshire, the only son of Benjamin Merriman, brewer, and Mary, eldest daughter of William Hawkes. Merriman received his early education at the free grammar school, Marlborough. In 1784 the family moved to London and he continued his education at a school in Old Burlington Street before embarking on a protracted medical education. Merriman trained mainly with his paternal uncle, also Samuel Merriman, a distinguished obstetrician, moving into his home in Queen Street, Mayfair. He studied anatomy under Matthew Baillie and George Cruikshank at the famous Windmill Street School and in 1795 attended the midwifery lectures of Dr Thynne at the Westminster Lying-in Hospital. He also gained clinical experience by visiting the patients of his cousin William Merriman. Merriman qualified in 1800, becoming a member of the Society of Apothecaries. The previous year the close relationship between the two branches of the Merriman family was cemented when Samuel married Ann, his uncle's only surviving daughter. The couple continued to live in the family Mayfair home. They had two daughters and a son.

Although Merriman initially practised as an apothecary, he acquired a reputation by following his uncle's example and specializing in midwifery. He built his skills through a number of institutional posts. From 1808 he was, in turn, physician accoucheur, consulting physician accoucheur, and vice-president at the Westminster Dispensary, obtaining the necessary MD degree from Marischal College, Aberdeen, through a personal examination by Dr Henry Vaughan (later Sir Henry Halford, bt). In 1808 Merriman was also employed by the board of St George's, Hanover

Square, to attend all difficult births in the parish. The following year he was appointed physician accoucheur to the Middlesex and Westminster lying-in hospitals.

These institutional appointments provided the clinical material which formed the basis of Merriman's many publications on obstetrical practice. In 1810 he produced a pamphlet on retroversion of the uterus. His *Synopsis of the Various Kinds of Difficult Parturition* (1814), a collection of case histories of complicated births and their clinical management, was widely praised. It went through several editions and was translated into a number of languages. Merriman also published a large number of papers in medical journals, some under pseudonyms, describing difficult forms of delivery. From 1810 he lectured on obstetrics at the Middlesex Hospital and in 1820–21 he also taught at St Bartholomew's Hospital. In addition to his publications on midwifery Merriman revised Underwood's *Treatise on the Diseases of Children* (1827) and defended the new practice of smallpox vaccination against the extravagant objections of Benjamin Moseley in *Observations on some Late Attempts to Depreciate the Value and Efficiency of Vaccination* (1805). Merriman briefly ventured into medical politics in 1833 with *The Validity of the Thoughts on Medical Reform*, defending the licensing procedures of the Society of Apothecaries, for whom he served as examiner in midwifery. He also contributed a large number of articles on midwifery, history, and archaeology to the *Gentleman's Magazine*.

By the late 1820s Merriman's professional reputation was secure and he gradually gave up his institutional posts and teaching to concentrate on his private practice. This brought in sufficient income for Merriman to buy a house in Grosvenor Square and an estate at Rodbourne Cheney in his native Wiltshire. Merriman's standing among his contemporaries was such that he received the unusual accolade of a long and glowing biography in *The Lancet*, which praised him as the beau ideal of man-midwives. He was active in a range of societies, including the Medical Society of London, the Linnean Society, the Royal Medical and Chirurgical Society, and the Society for the Relief of Widows and Orphans of Medical Men, serving as treasurer to the two latter institutions. He was also treasurer of the Middlesex Hospital from 1840 to 1845.

Merriman died at his home at 34 Brook Street, Grosvenor Square, on 22 November 1852. He was survived by only two children, his son, Samuel William (who had followed his father into the field of obstetrics), and his younger daughter, his wife, Ann, having died on 10 March 1831 and his elder daughter in 1844.

John Merriman (1774–1839), first cousin to Samuel Merriman, was born on 26 October 1774 at Marlborough, Wiltshire, the son of Nathaniel Merriman and Elizabeth, daughter of Thomas Baverstock of Alton, Hampshire. In 1794 he moved to London to complete his medical training, and became a member of the Royal College of Surgeons and the Society of Apothecaries. He practised medicine in partnership with Thomas Hardwick of Kensington, and their professional relationship was strengthened

when Merriman married Hardwick's niece Jane. Merriman enjoyed an extensive practice and rose to become one of the medical attendants to the royal household. He attended the duchess of Kent, the Princess Victoria, and the Princess Sophia at Kensington Palace. With Victoria's accession to the throne in 1837 Merriman and his two sons, John and James Nathaniel, with whom he worked in partnership, jointly held the post of apothecary-extraordinary to her majesty. Merriman died on 17 June 1839 at Kensington Square after a long illness.

DEBORAH BRUNTON

Sources *The Lancet* (30 Nov 1850), 610–15 · *GM*, 2nd ser., 39 (1853), 207–9 · *Medical Times and Gazette* (27 Nov 1852), 557 · *DNB*
Likenesses Maynall, portrait · drawing (after daguerreotype), repro. in *The Lancet* · stipple, BM

Merrington, Martha Crauford (*b.* 1830/31, *d.* in or after 1901), poor-law guardian, emerged from an obscure background. Nothing is known of her personal life but she was well connected. For instance, her close associates included Caroline Biggs (editor of the *Englishwomen's Review* and member of the Committee for Promoting the Return of Women as Poor Law Guardians), Helen Taylor and Augusta Webster (members of the London school board in the 1870s and 1880s), the educationist Emily Anne Shirreff, and the philanthropist Mary Anne Donkin. The earliest reference to any public activity on the part of Martha Merrington is a minute of the London school board (10 January 1872), where it is recorded that she had joined Chelsea divisional committee in January 1872. This was a local body formed to assist the London school board in the struggle over school attendance, and Martha Merrington served alongside Emily Shirreff, the co-founder of the National Union for the Improvement of the Education of Women of all Classes. Later that same year Mary Anne Donkin joined the committee. A worker for the Charity Organization Society, she lived just the other side of Kensington High Street from Martha Merrington (London school board minutes, 18 Dec 1872). By June 1874 Miss Merrington was manager of three elementary schools in Notting Hill (ibid., 7 May and 22 Oct 1873, 17 June 1874). In these years she also established crèches for the babies of working women in Kensington.

In the spring of 1875 Martha Merrington put herself forward as a candidate for the Kensington board of guardians. She polled 3893 votes and was elected eighteenth of eighteen successful candidates (Kensington board of guardians minute book, 16 April 1875). The first woman to be elected to a poor-law guardianship, she was appointed to a local relief committee, as well as becoming a visitor to the workhouse and the workhouse infirmary. Six months later, when one of her male colleagues from the visiting committee, Frederick Edgcombe, pressed the appointment of a committee to visit the asylums and schools, she joined him on it.

For the next three years Martha Merrington took an active interest in poor-law administration. Authorized to reorganize the staffing of the workhouse infirmary, she earned the gratitude of her male colleagues when she managed to produce a weekly saving on the wages bill of

£4 17s. 6d. (Kensington board of guardians minute book, 16 March 1876). She had previously visited a school at Herne Bay, Kent, where some Kensington pauper children were boarded. Her concern led the guardians to appoint a lady volunteer visitor and in December 1875 Mary Anne Donkin was deputed to produce a further report. The experiment was a success. Miss Donkin submitted a list of recommendations and the guardians thanked her 'for the careful and efficient manner in which she had conducted the enquiry' (ibid., 30 Dec 1875). In April 1877 the efforts of Martha Merrington were acknowledged when she was elected twelfth of eighteen guardians. For two years she prioritized her duty visits to the infirmary and pauper schools and became an infrequent attender at board meetings (ibid., April 1877 to May 1879). She was disqualified from serving in 1879 when a ratepayer took legal action against her candidacy on the grounds that she was moving house when the election took place.

In November 1879 Martha Merrington joined the controversy over the administration of Upton House, the London school board's new truant school. Replying to a letter from Helen Taylor informing her of the conditions at the school, she proposed a radically different approach. In particular, she pressed the case for altering the management of the day schools in order to promote school attendance. First, she suggested that there should be a good fire in the entrance room or hall; second, that a 'kind old woman *not a teacher*' should greet the children, reward the early arrivals with a 'bun or sugarplum', take their outer clothing, and 'send them into the schoolroom warm and happy—whereas they now go in cold and crying to undergo school discipline' (Merrington to H. Taylor, 18 Nov 1879, Mill–Taylor MSS). Writing as the school board faced the triennial elections, she also offered her services as a public speaker and informed Helen Taylor of a campaign meeting to be held at her home in Harrington Gardens on behalf of Augusta Webster. Martha Merrington set a precedent for female involvement in local government. It seems fitting that in 1881 Mary Anne Donkin inherited her seat on the Kensington board of guardians.

In 1881 Martha Merrington was living with her schoolmistress sister, Emily, at 10 Harrington Gardens, Kensington, on income derived from property; twenty years later she was living with two young nieces in Croydon, as a self-employed teacher of languages.   JANE MARTIN

Sources minute books, 1875–80, LMA, Kensington board of guardians archives · London school board minutes, 1870–80, LMA · P. Hollis, *Ladies elect: women in English local government, 1865–1914* (1987); pbk edn (1989) · London School of Economics, Mill–Taylor collection · census returns, 1881, 1901
Archives LMA, Kensington board of guardians · London School of Economics, Mill–Taylor collection

Merriot, Thomas (1589–1662), grammarian, was born at Steeple Langford, near Salisbury, Wiltshire, of unknown parents. He entered Winchester College in 1601, and on 14 October 1608 matriculated at New College, Oxford. A fellow from 1610 to 1624, he was admitted scholar of civil law on 21 October 1611 and received the degree of bachelor of civil law on 22 November 1615. Merriot taught in the grammar school adjoining the cloister. On 15 January 1624 the warden and fellows of New College appointed him vicar of the church of St Peter and Paul, Swalcliffe, near Banbury, Oxfordshire, home to a branch of the Wickham family claiming kinship with William of Wykeham, founder of Winchester College and New College, and an area positioned strategically (between Edgehill and Oxford) to witness early events of the civil war. As vicar of Swalcliffe he held the tithes of Epwell, his chief means, on condition he officiate there.

A forthright man of strong principles, and vicar of Swalcliffe for thirty-five years, Merriot had disagreements with parishioners. On 10 May 1637 the council of state responded favourably to his petition 'complaining of very hard measure offered him in the rate assessed on him for ship-money by his parishioners'. The council found the vicarage to be 'of very small value, and the vicar poor, though very well affected to any public work for church or commonwealth' and held it 'very unjust that his parishioners should make the service of the shipping a stale to wreak their spleen upon him for another occasion wherein his forwardness merited encouragement and their disaffection was deservedly overruled' (*CSP dom.*, 1637, 90). The circumstances of this tantalizing 'another occasion' (ibid.) are not recorded. That Merriot signed a declaration, based on personal and parish evidences, denying claims by the Swalcliffe Wickhams to kinship with William of Wykeham may have antagonized that locally influential family. In February 1642 Merriot, a staunch royalist, and 163 male parishioners signed the protestation oath required by the House of Commons.

Parish disputes were soon eclipsed by broader political concerns. On 26 July 1642 Merriot was summoned to appear before the House of Commons 'to answer his Contempt, for using some reproachful Terms upon the Parliament, and publishing the last Declaration of his Majesty's' (*JHC*, 2.692). Though his living was sequestered by the Westminster assembly, Merriot successfully petitioned the committee for plundered ministers and was granted a hearing by the committee of his county (31 August 1646). He resigned the vicarage on 10 March 1659 and was succeeded by Humphrey Smart.

Wood described Merriot as 'a good Latinist and orator' and in his youth Merriot penned 'several Latin copies of verses, dispersed in books', including at least four occasional poems about members of the royal family, published at Oxford in anthologies between 1612 and 1623 (Wood, *Ath. Oxon.: Fasti*, 1.362; Wood, *Ath. Oxon.*, 3.590). Decades later, in advancing age, as 'T. M.' he published *Vulgaria, sive, Miscellanea prosaica* (1652), a commonplace book, with maxims and aphorisms drawn largely from classical authors. Curiously the work contains only the first five of the nine sections ('classes') announced in the table of contents, probably because 'the cost of printing … induced him to "scrap" the last four' (Madan, 3.18). His *Grammaticall miscellanies, wherein, the truth of many rules, both in the English rudiments, and Latine grammar is examined* (1660), written in a style combining English and Latin in the same sentence, is an extensive commentary on William Lily's grammar, which Merriot had studied at Winchester, in answer to certain 'litigious' Oxford academics who apparently insisted on Lily's infallibility (sig. A2r). It is also a defence of rhetoric—no 'pettie verbal Art' (sig. A3v)—which he claims is equal in importance to mathematics or metaphysics. He believes that grammar is the 'foundation on which the superstructure of all Arts and Sciences is grounded, and the Porter as it were opening the door to give a free ingress into them' (sig. A3v). The work is divided into 136 sections ('members'), each discussing an aspect of Latin grammar. In his preface Merriot pays tribute to the 'famous D. Reynolds', presumably John Rainolds, dean of Christ Church, Oxford (sig. A5r).

The 'progress notes' of Warden Michael Woodward offer glimpses into Merriot's last years at Swalcliffe. He had, for example, turned 'an Hovell' (Woodward, 89) at the end of his house into a school, but by 1659 his school, house, and barns were greatly in need of rafting and thatching. On 19 July 1662, 'very poore & worth nothing (his debts being paid)' (Woodward, 88), Merriot died; he was buried two days later in the churchyard, the brass plate on his gravestone later being removed to the chancel floor. Parish disputes continued, for on 7 October 1663 'Mistriss Merriott' (presumably his widow) had to be persuaded to 'returne unto Mr. Smart the vicar, the Barnes doore, that shee carryed from the vicaridge' (Woodward, 89).   PAGE LIFE

Sources Wood, *Ath. Oxon.*, new edn, 3.589–90 · Wood, *Ath. Oxon.: Fasti* (1815), 362 · M. Woodward, 'Swalcliffe', *The progress notes of Warden Woodward round the Oxfordshire estates of New College, Oxford, 1659–1675*, ed. R. L. Rickard, Oxfordshire RS, 27 (1949), 87–93 · *JHC*, 2 (1640–42), 692 · *Parochial collections made by Anthony à Wood and Richard Rawlinson*, ed. and trans. F. N. Davis, 3, Oxfordshire RS, 11 (1929), 291–2 · C. S. A. Dobson, ed., *Oxfordshire protestation returns, 1641–2*, Oxfordshire RS, 36 (1955), 30–31 · *Reg. Oxf.*, 2/1.272; 2/2.302; 2/3.342 · T. F. Kirby, *Winchester scholars: a list of the wardens, fellows, and scholars of … Winchester College* (1888) · C. E. Keyser, 'An architectural account of Swalcliffe church, Oxfordshire', *Archaeological Journal*, 61 (1904), 85–101 · 'Descent of the family of Wickham of Swalcliffe, co. Oxon and their kindred to the founder of New College', *Collectanea Topographica et Genealogica*, 3 (1836), 178–239, 345–76 · *CSP dom.*, 1637, 90; *addenda, 1625–49*, 570 · Foster, *Alum. Oxon.*, 1500–1714, 3.1002 · *IGI* · *DNB* · F. Madan, *Oxford literature, 1450–1640*, and *1641–1650* (1912), vol. 2 of *Oxford books: a bibliography of printed works* (1895–1931); repr. (1964) · F. Madan, *Oxford literature, 1651–1680* (1931), vol. 3 of *Oxford books: a bibliography of printed works* (1895–1931); repr. (1964)

Archives BL, Register-book of the Proceedings of the Committee of the House of Commons, Add. MS 15670, fol. 198

Wealth at death 'Mr. Merriot dieing very poore & worth nothing (his debts being paid)': Woodward, 'Swalcliffe'

Merrison, Sir Alexander Walter (1924–1989), nuclear physicist, was born on 20 March 1924 in Wood Green, London, the only child of Henry Walter Merrison, fitter's mate, who rose to be service manager in the local gas board and a respected chairman of the Tottenham group of hospitals, and his wife, Violet Henrietta Mortimer, from Ipswich. Alec (as he was known) attended Tottenham grammar school and Enfield grammar school. He went to King's College, London, where he graduated in physics in 1944, after which he was 'placed' on wartime radar at the

Signals Research and Development Establishment at Christchurch. After two years he requested transfer to the Atomic Energy Research Establishment at Harwell (1946). There he helped to equip an electron accelerator to produce short pulses of neutrons, a new technique for probing the structure of matter, the subject on which he was to publish his first papers. In 1948 he married Beryl Glencora (d. 1968), daughter of Frank Bruce Le Marquand, a brewer in Jersey. They had two sons.

In 1951 Merrison accepted a lectureship at the University of Liverpool, where the physicists were constructing a proton cyclotron large enough to produce the newly discovered 'pi-mesons', the particles then thought to be responsible for binding together the atomic nucleus. Having assisted in the completion of the machine, he was awarded a PhD in 1957 for his first experiments on the interaction of pi-mesons with nuclear matter. From that time on he was a dedicated particle physicist. He had a gift for designing clean experiments, creating new equipment and making it work properly, and inspiring physicists and engineers to work together hard but amicably. He also became an inspiring teacher, able to communicate his bubbling enthusiasm to his students. From 1957 to 1960 he was at the Conseil Européen de Recherches Nucléaires (CERN), the newly established European accelerator laboratory near Geneva. Together with G. Fidecaro he confirmed that the weak nuclear force responsible for radioactivity was a universal interaction. In 1960 he returned to Liverpool as professor of experimental physics, but remained closely connected with CERN for the rest of his life.

In 1962 Merrison was engaged by the Science Research Council (SRC) to build an electron synchrotron at Daresbury in Cheshire, but was allowed to retain his chair. The machine was finished on time and on budget, and worked straightaway. The Daresbury laboratory quickly became an important centre of research in particle and radiation physics, and as its director he began to take an active part in policy matters at the SRC and elsewhere. He was a member of the government's Council for Scientific Policy (1967–72). Needing a change of home and work when his first wife died in 1968, he gladly accepted the vice-chancellorship of the University of Bristol (where the pi-mesons had originally been discovered). He was elected FRS in 1969.

Merrison arrived in Bristol in 1969 to find the university in confrontational turmoil and its academic quality depleted. He quickly gained the confidence of staff and students alike, made new academic appointments, and introduced far-reaching reforms of the senate, administration, and personnel management. In 1970 he married Maureen Michèle Barry, a lecturer in the history department at Bristol and daughter of John Michael Barry, entertainer. They had a daughter and a son.

Merrison personally prepared a tough and detailed plan of action for Bristol University when faced with the financial cuts of 1981. It was unavoidably controversial, and difficult negotiations in the senate followed. Nevertheless, he eventually succeeded in his objective. Soon after becoming vice-chancellor, Merrison accepted a series of chairmanships of important government committees. The first was the committee of inquiry into the design and erection of box girder bridges (1970–73), which set new worldwide standards (the Merrison rules) for the design of such bridges. He was knighted in 1976 and became an honorary fellow of the Institution of Structural Engineers in 1981. Bristol gave him an honorary LLD in 1971, and he had six other honorary degrees. He also chaired the committee of inquiry into the regulation of the medical profession (1972–5). He was vice-chairman of the South West Regional Health Authority and was a popular choice to chair the royal commission on the National Health Service when it was appointed in 1976. This reviewed the entire service and in 1979 issued a report with suggestions about how it could be improved. Many of the proposals were gradually implemented by administrative action in the ensuing years.

Merrison played a full part in the Committee of Vice-Chancellors and Principals, being its chairman in 1979–81. During this time he had to deal with the government's new policy of high fees for overseas students. He became chairman of the Advisory Board for the Research Councils (1979–83), where he supervised the planning of the nation's basic research in the universities and research council laboratories and criticized the government's cuts. He was a devoted European, but never forgot the abiding value of the Commonwealth. He was president of the council of CERN in 1982–5, and simultaneously (1982–3) chairman of the council of the Association of Commonwealth Universities. At home he was elected president of the Institute of Physics (1984–6). He retired from the Bristol vice-chancellorship in 1984.

He was sought after by business for technological prowess as much as administrative flair. He became chairman of the Bristol Regional Board, and director of Lloyds Bank (1986–9) and of the Western Provident Association (1985–9), thereby extending his interests in medicine. He was a director of the Bristol Waterworks Company from 1984. Business was perhaps not his most natural habitat, but he threw himself into these new pursuits with characteristic zeal and open-minded curiosity. He became a governor in 1969, then chairman (1971–87), of the Bristol Old Vic, not only satisfying his love for the theatre but skilfully guiding it through its redevelopment programme. He was a director of the Bristol *Evening Post* (1979–89), was appointed deputy lieutenant of the county of Avon (1974), and served as high sheriff (1986–7).

Merrison was stockily built, 5 feet 10 inches in height, with clear blue eyes and high cheek-bones. His voice became boisterous when he was excited. The greatest pleasure of Merrison and his second wife was to entertain friends and colleagues at Maes-y-ffin, their farmhouse in the Llanthony valley, and, after Merrison's retirement, at The Manor, Hinton Blewett, near Bristol. He died in Bristol on 19 February 1989.   BRIAN FLOWERS, *rev.*

Sources *The Times* (21 Feb 1989) • *WWW* • private information (1996) • personal knowledge (1996) • *CGPLA Eng. & Wales* (1989)

Wealth at death £154,837: probate, 8 Dec 1989, *CGPLA Eng. & Wales*

Merritt, Anna Massey Lea (1844–1930), figure painter and etcher, was born on 13 September 1844 in Philadelphia, Pennsylvania, the daughter of Joseph Lea jun., a textile manufacturer, and Susanna Massey. They were a prominent and affluent Quaker family, and Anna was the eldest of six sisters. She was educated at the progressive Eagleswood School in Bryn Mawr, Pennsylvania, 1858–60, followed by the Agassiz School in Cambridge, Massachusetts, 1861, and then studied anatomy at the Women's Medical College, Philadelphia. In 1865 she moved to Europe with her family, and took private lessons with Heinrich Hoffman, professor at the Dresden Academy, and Stefano Ussi in Florence. She studied briefly with Léon Cogniet in Paris and Alphonse Legros in Basel before moving to Britain owing to the outbreak of the Franco-Prussian war in 1870. In 1871 Lea took a studio in Devonshire Street and took lessons from Henry *Merritt (1822–1877), a picture conservator and art critic, who became her mentor. Merritt stringently supervised the production and direction of her work, recommending, for example, that she focus on portraiture rather than genre pictures, despite the latter's greater likelihood of success during the period. Lea married Merritt on 17 April 1877 and, tragically, he died only three months later on 10 July, leaving her to pursue a prolific career. *Art Criticism and Romance*, a selection of Henry Merritt's writings, which included Anna Marritt's hagiographic biography of her husband and was illustrated with twenty-three of her etchings, was published in 1879. Merritt was made a member of the Royal Society of Painters and Etchers and lived in Britain for the remainder of her life, but made frequent extended trips to the USA, and continued to exhibit in both countries. Her sitters and patrons included American as well as British citizens; her portrait *Horace Howard Furness* (1895) is now in the Furness Library, University of Pennsylvania, and *The Shipley Sisters* (1902) is in Shipley School, Bryn Mawr, Pennsylvania. Her work was occasionally exhibited at the Pennsylvania Academy of Fine Arts from 1867 until 1924, and in 1888 she exhibited thirty-three etchings in the 'Work of the Women Etchers of America' at New York's Union League Club. Her work received awards at the Centennial Exposition in Philadelphia (1876) and in the Columbian Exposition in Chicago (1893). In the latter exhibition *Eve Overcome by Remorse* won a medal in the British section; she also completed three decorative mural panels for the Woman's Building on the theme of traditional women's occupations: needlework, education, and charity. In Britain she exhibited at the Royal Academy from 1871 until 1917, as well as at the Grosvenor Gallery and New Gallery in London. *War* (1883; Bury Art Gallery and Museum) was apparently inspired by news of Gordon's death at Khartoum; the picture actually focuses on the suffering of women through the depiction of a widow and her female friends watching a neo-classical victory parade. Female patrons of Merritt's work included Mrs Warren de la Rue, who commissioned *Romeo and Juliet* in 1883. During the 1880s the propriety of women artists painting from the nude model was doubtful and Merritt's *Eve* (exh. RA, 1885) received unfavourable reviews. Her memorial to her husband, *Love Locked Out* (exh. RA, 1890; Tate collection) which shows a naked youth, was, however, the first painting by a woman artist acquired for the nation through the Chantrey Bequest. During this period her celebrity status meant that she moved in London art circles with artists such as William Holman Hunt, Edward Burne-Jones, Lawrence Alma-Tadema, G. F. Watts, James McNeill Whistler, and Frederic Leighton. In 1900 her article 'A letter to artists: especially women artists' offered advice on the challenges facing women in the profession. She lamented that 'The chief obstacle to a woman's success is that she can never have a wife', and she opposed the segregation of women's work, 'separate exhibitions of women's work were in opposition to the views of the artists concerned who knew that it would lower their standard and risk the place they already occupied' (Merritt, 463–9). In 1890 she settled in Hurstbourne Tarrant, Hampshire, for health reasons, where she wrote and illustrated two garden books in *A Hamlet in Old Hampshire* (1902) and *An Artist's Garden* (1908). After several years of failing eyesight Merritt died in Hurstbourne Tarrant, on 5 April 1930.

MEAGHAN E. CLARKE

Sources P. G. Nunn, ed., *Canvassing women: recollections by six Victorian women artists* (1986) • P. G. Nunn, *Victorian women artists* (1987) • *Love locked out: the memoirs of Anna Lea Merritt*, ed. G. Gorokhoff [n.d., 1982?] [incl. a checklist of her paintings] • W. S. Sparrow, *Women painters of the world* (1905) • Graves, *Artists* • Graves, *RA exhibitors*, vol. 3 • D. Gaze, ed., *Dictionary of women artists*, 2 vols. (1997) • D. Cherry, *Painting women: Victorian women artists* (1993) • A. L. Merritt, 'A letter to artists: especially women artists', *Lippincott's Magazine*, 65 (1900), 463–9 • P. Peet, 'Merritt, Anna Massey Lea', *ANB* • Wood, *Vic. painters*, 3rd edn • CGPLA Eng. & Wales (1930) • d. cert.

Wealth at death £830 10s. 11d.: probate, 12 June 1930, CGPLA Eng. & Wales

Merritt, Henry (1822–1877), picture conservator and art critic, was born in Oxford on 8 June 1822, the son of Joseph Merritt, a tailor. The fifth of nine children, his early years were passed in considerable poverty. His mother encouraged his education at an infant school, and, from the age of eleven, at the Blue Coat School for Boys in Church Street, Oxford. He also sang in the choir of Carfax church, and it was the choirmaster there who introduced him to the Bodleian picture gallery in the Upper Library. Having worked as an errand boy, at fifteen he was apprenticed to a framemaker, but he also found time to copy pictures in the Bodleian. He met the painter Alfred William Delamotte, who gave him free drawing lessons. In 1846 he walked to London, where he found casual work as a gilder and picture copyist. He gradually established himself as a picture conservator, and in 1851 was asked to restore a collection of paintings for a wealthy gentleman, Joseph Parrinton. He began to write art criticism for *The Reasoner*, under the pseudonym Christopher, and from 1852 contributed to *The Leader*. These articles were republished in 1854 in the *Cabinet of Reason*, with a preface by his landlord, G. J. Holyoake, under the title *Dirt and Pictures Separated in the Works of the Old Masters*. In 1866 he became art critic for *The Standard*.

An Oxford acquaintance introduced Merritt to Sir Charles Eastlake, who commissioned him to conserve some works in the National Gallery. Through the recommendation of the painter George Richmond, in 1865 he was entrusted by Dean Stanley with the task of cleaning the portrait of Richard II in Westminster Abbey. He removed the overpainting and afterwards worked on the portrait of Henry VII in the National Portrait Gallery, on various pictures at Hampton Court Palace, and on the scenes from the first duke of Marlborough's campaigns, by Louis Laguerre, on the staircases of Marlborough House, London. Merritt was sensitive and discreet in his restorations. He was also proud of his ability to overcome the hardships of his youth and to make the acquaintance of distinguished men such as Gladstone and John Ruskin. (His 'Story of a Feather' was published by Ruskin in *Fors Clavigera*.) In 1865 he published anonymously *Robert Dalby and his World of Troubles*, an account, in the form of a romance, of his own early life. This was described by the editor of his writings as possessing 'a certain roughness of expression' but 'a true and refined pathos'. He also began to write a story called *The Oxford Professor*, which was published posthumously.

Merritt suffered from a weak chest and heart for many years, possibly exacerbated by his pipe-smoking, and he travelled abroad only briefly, visiting Paris in 1856. In 1870 he had met the young American painter Anna Massey Lea (1844–1930) [*see* Merritt, Anna Massey Lea], who became his pupil and friend. Despite their mutual affection he felt unable to marry her, as he had to support three other families of friends and relatives. However, after her prolonged visit to America in 1876–7 they were married quietly, in St Pancras parish church on 17 April 1877. Merritt died just three months later, on 10 July 1877, at his home, 54 Devonshire Street, Pollard Place, London. He was buried initially in the family vault of Frederick Willis Farrer in Brompton cemetery; his remains were later removed to Brookwood, Surrey, to fulfil his request that an elm should be planted over his grave. His wife painted *Love Locked Out* (Tate collection) as a memorial to him. There were no children of the marriage. A selection of Merritt's writings were edited by Basil Champneys and published in London in 1879, by his widow, as *Art Criticism and Romance*.

A. F. POLLARD, *rev.* SUZANNE FAGENCE COOPER

Sources H. Merritt, *Art criticism and romance, with recollections and 23 etchings by Anna Lea Merritt*, ed. B. Champneys, 2 vols. (1879) • *Love locked out: the memoirs of Anna Lea Merritt*, ed. G. Gorokhoff [n.d., 1982?] • IGI • CGPLA Eng. & Wales (1877) • VCH Oxfordshire, 4.445 • J. J. L. Whiteley, 'The university galleries', *Hist. U. Oxf.* 6: 19th-cent. Oxf., 611–30, esp. 611 • N&Q, 6th ser., 1 (1880), 471 • *The Times* (14 July 1877) • E. Croft-Murray, *Decorative painting in England, 1537–1837*, 1 (1962), 253

Likenesses A. L. Merritt, etching, repro. in Merritt, *Art criticism and romance*, frontispiece • photograph, repro. in Gorokhoff, ed., *Love locked out*, pl. 30

Wealth at death under £5000: probate, 2 Aug 1877, CGPLA Eng. & Wales

Merrivale. For this title name *see* Duke, Henry Edward, first Baron Merrivale (1855–1939).

Merry, Anthony (1756–1835), diplomatist, was born on 2 August 1756 at 17 Laurence Pountney Lane, London, the only son and younger child of Anthony Merry, a City wine merchant and shipowner, and his wife, Susanna Chitty. After a counting-house education and employment in Malaga, he became British consul in Majorca in 1783. Appointed consul-general in Madrid in 1787, he served as chargé d'affaires before leaving Spain in 1796. In 1799 he went as consul-general to Denmark, Prussia, and Sweden and was chargé d'affaires in Copenhagen. Secretary to the embassy that negotiated the treaty of Amiens with France, he served in 1802 as minister *ad interim* in Paris. On 21 January 1803 he married at St Mary's, High Street, Marylebone, Elizabeth Leathes (*née* Death) (*d.* 1824), the widow of John Leathes of Herringfleet Hall, Suffolk. Their marriage was childless.

Named minister to the United States in 1803, Merry was the first British minister to reside in the new American capital of Washington. Ever sticklers for protocol, he and his wife took umbrage at the democratic etiquette of President Thomas Jefferson's administration. The Napoleonic war severely strained Anglo-American affairs, owing to the problems arising from a belligerent–neutral relationship, and Merry clashed with the Americans in defending both the British impressment of seamen and the restrictions on neutral trade to colonial and blockaded ports. Approached by American conspirators such as Aaron Burr, who sought British aid in their plots of disunion, Merry listened to the plotters but never abetted them. Despite his long and honourable career, he is mainly remembered for his American ministry, the unfavourable accounts of which reflected Jefferson's animosity towards Britain and Merry.

Recalled from America in 1806 by the Grenville–Fox government, Merry, a Pittite, did not expect reassignment, but a new administration in 1807 sent him on a futile mission to conciliate Denmark following the British bombardment of Copenhagen. In 1808 he received his last assignment, which sent him to Sweden as minister. He retired in 1809 after twenty-six years in the diplomatic service. According to an associate, he performed his duties 'strictly *en règle* … like clockwork' and without imagination. Esteemed, nevertheless, by foreign secretaries such as Robert Banks Jenkinson and George Canning, he was used by them to train budding diplomats, including Augustus John Foster and Stratford Canning. Dour and meticulous, Merry was respected, however, especially by younger colleagues, who nicknamed him Toujours Gai.

In retirement Merry lived first at Herringfleet Hall in Suffolk, where he was a justice of the peace, and then at Dedham House in Dedham, Essex. He died at home on 14 June 1835 and was buried at St Mary the Virgin, Dedham, where there is a mural tablet to his memory.

MALCOLM LESTER

Sources M. Lester, *Anthony Merry redivivus: a reappraisal of the British minister to the United States, 1803–1806* (1978) • B. Mayo, ed., *Instructions to the British ministers to the United States, 1791–1812* (1941) • *IGI* • parish register, London, St Laurence Pountney [birth], 2 Aug 1756

Archives CKS, corresp. and papers | BL, letters to Lord Auckland, Add. MSS 34428–34434 • L. Cong., Augustus John Foster MSS • L. Cong., John Franklin Jameson MSS • L. Cong., Thomas Jefferson MSS • L. Cong., James Madison MSS • National Archives and Records Administration, Washington, DC, state department records • NL Scot., corresp. with Sir Robert Liston • PRO, Foreign Office papers • PRO, corresp. F. J. Jackson, FO 353 • Sandon Hall, Staffordshire, Harrowby Manuscript Trust, letters to Lord Harrowby
Likenesses G. Stuart, oils, 1805 (after glass negative), L. Cong., J. F. Jameson MSS; repro. in Lester, *Anthony Merry redivivus*
Wealth at death £35,000: probate registry

Merry, James (1805–1877), ironmaster and coalmaster, was born at Nettleholes Farm in the parish of New Monkland, Lanarkshire, the son of James Merry, coalmaster, and Janet Creelman. His father was already in business in a small way as a colliery proprietor, supplying the Glasgow market along the recently opened Monkland Canal. Merry's early education was at the local parish schools in Langloan and Airdrie, followed from 1815 by attendance at Glasgow high school after his parents moved to Glasgow to control their mining concerns from an office opened at the canal basin at Port Dundas. He afterwards attended classes at Glasgow University, where he probably first met his future partner, Alexander Cunninghame, whose family already operated mines on the family lands of Craigends in Renfrewshire.

Merry began his business training as assistant to his father, learning from him in the 1820s all the practical aspects of mining, and details of accounts and leases. He was taken into partnership in 1831, and when his father retired in 1835 Merry was sole proprietor of the firm of James Merry Junior, coalmaster. During the next twenty years he built a large business empire, in partnership with Cunninghame. The opportunity came with the spectacular growth of the Scottish pig-iron trade following J. B. Neilson's innovation, in 1828, of the hot blast in the manufacture of iron. The Monklands area, where Merry held his mineral leases at the eastern end of the Monkland Canal, was rich in coal and iron seams and was also being opened up by Scotland's first railways. Seven new ironworks had opened in the area between 1828 and 1838, and Merry joined in partnership with Cunninghame and a Leith merchant, Alexander Allison, to raise the capital to open the Carnbroe Iron Works, operated by the new partnership of Allison & Co. The opening of the Glasgow, Paisley, Kilmarnock, and Ayr Railway in 1840 carried the new iron industry into Ayrshire, where in 1842 Allison & Co. bought out the leases from an insolvent partnership that had partly erected blast furnaces at Glengarnock. Merry, Allison, and Cunninghame operated this venture as the Glengarnock Iron Company, and when Allison retired in 1845, the controlling firm became that of Merry and Cunninghame, which soon added a third ironworks at Ardeer in 1854. By then the firm operated three ironworks, twelve collieries, and numerous iron mines and was the second-largest producer of pig iron, and third in rank as colliery operators, in Scotland.

During this rapid expansion Merry was the dominant partner, daily in the offices of the works, and controlling every aspect of operations. He combined technical expertise with a detailed knowledge of local mineral leases, systematically negotiating a mineral bank of leasehold agreements with landowners in Ayrshire and Lanarkshire. He was forceful, even ruthless in business, and had a reputation for aggressiveness in management, regularly breaking strikes at his works by importing highland and Irish labour. His companies were the most notorious operators of truck shops in the mining districts, controlling one-third of those operating in Scotland.

By the early 1860s daily management was in the hands of Cunninghame and his cousin, John, for from 1855 Merry had used his industrial wealth to develop other interests; indeed from 1866, when Alexander Cunninghame died, John Cunninghame was in partnership with Merry and ran the business. In 1847, aged forty-two, Merry had married Anne McHardie, whose father, James McHardie, was sheriff-clerk of Glasgow and owner of the Cleddens estate near Glenboig, Lanarkshire, another rich coal and iron area; they had two sons. The marriage was his entrée into Glasgow society, as his wife was a noted beauty and socialite. The following year Alexander Cunninghame married Anne's sister, binding the families in ties that were more than commercial.

Merry's ambitions, however, were wider still and developed in parallel with his consuming passion for horse-racing. He had been a figure on the Scottish racing circuits from the 1830s, but in 1855, the year he opened Ardeer, he also purchased the famous yellow and black racing colours left free on the death of the marquess of Westminster. That year he won the Two Thousand Guineas for the first time with Lord of the Isles, his first son was born, and he and his family moved from their house in Athole Place, Glasgow, to their new residence, Culdees Castle, at Auchterarder in Perthshire. About 1857 they moved again, to their estate of Belladrum at Beauly, Inverness-shire.

From this platform Merry contested Glasgow as a Liberal in 1857 and lost. Later that year he fought and won the Falkirk burghs, defeating George Baird of Gartsherrie in a contest that was the subject of a petition to the House of Commons on grounds of corrupt practices during the election. Merry was unseated, but in 1859 he regained the house and served continuously as MP for the Falkirk burghs until his retiral at the general election of 1874, when he was already in ill health. London society was opened up to him through his Westminster seat, and during the period from 1859 to 1875 he developed a highly successful stable, winning virtually every major race, including twice taking the St Leger and Two Thousand Guineas, and the Derby; he also won the Oaks. In London he based himself at his residence in Eaton Square, and enjoyed membership of Brooks's and the Reform Club.

In ill health in 1874, Merry attempted to take advantage of the new joint stock legislation to convert the partnership to a public company with £1.5 million capital to purchase the partners' shares. The flotation collapsed with the ending of the mid-Victorian boom in 1873–4, and Merry was obliged to repurchase the issued shares at par, the company reverting to co-partnery. This coincided with

his sale of his stables, which realized 21,650 guineas. With this reverse he retired from the partnership, which had received less and less of his attention in the twenty years since he had taken to country living and enjoying his life as an MP and a horse-racing patron. In Inverness-shire he was a deputy lieutenant of the county and also a justice of the peace.

The dominant partner in Merry and Cunninghame, Merry created a business empire which ranked second only to the Bairds of Gartsherrie among the coal and iron dynasties of mid-nineteenth-century Scotland. Nevertheless, when he died on 3 February 1877, it was at his London home, 68 Eaton Square, far from the grime of the coal and iron districts of the west of Scotland. He was survived by his wife.
ANTHONY SLAVEN

Sources *The Bailie* (26 May 1875) · J. Foster, *Members of parliament, Scotland … 1357–1882*, 2nd edn (privately printed, London, 1882) · *The Post Office directory of Glasgow* [annuals] · J. McArthur, *New Monkland parish: its history, industries and people* (1890) · A. Miller, *The rise and progress of Coatbridge* (1962) · C. A. Oakley, *Our illustrious forebears* (1980) · *Glasgow Herald* (5 Feb 1877) · *DSBB* · *CGPLA Eng. & Wales* (1877) · NA Scot., SC 29/44/25
Archives NA Scot., letters to William Cuninghame
Likenesses sketch, Mitchell L., Glas.
Wealth at death £680,402 9s. 7d.: confirmation, 22 March 1877, *CCI*

Merry, Robert (1755–1798), poet, was born in London in April 1755, the eldest son of Robert Merry, governor of the Hudson's Bay Company. His grandfather Captain Merry, sailing in search of the north-west passage, discovered and gave its name to Merry Island. He was directly descended from Sir Henry Merry, who was knighted by James I in 1621. His mother was the eldest daughter of Sir John Willes, lord chief justice, friend of Addison and Gay and occasional contributor to *The Spectator*. Merry's education was entrusted to his father's sister, who sent him to Harrow School, where his tutor was the celebrated Latin scholar Samuel Parr, and then to Christ's College, Cambridge, where he was admitted on 2 April 1771. He 'lived irregularly' (Venn, *Alum. Cant.*), and so left without taking a degree, going on to study at Lincoln's Inn, where he had been entered, by his father's wish, on 5 November 1770. He was never called to the bar, but seized the opportunity, on the death of his father, to purchase a commission in the Horse Guards. As an adjutant of the first troop he developed the propensities for fashionable living and heavy play which would embarrass him throughout his life, and his dwindling fortune obliged him to sell out his commission at the age of twenty-five. Several years of travel on the continent led him, by 1784, to the English colony settled at Florence.

It was here that Merry first made the acquaintance of the literary coterie, consisting of expatriate English writers and a few dissident Italian poets, with whom he collaborated to produce, first the *Arno* (1784) and then the more famous *Florence Miscellany* (1785). These collections of verse by Hester Lynch Piozzi, Bertie Greatheed, William Parsons, and Merry were written, according to Mrs Piozzi's preface, 'to divert ourselves and to say kind things of each

Robert Merry (1755–1798), by unknown artist, in or before 1793

which Bell brought out in 1789. It ran to four editions, but did not survive the effect of Gifford's satirical attack in *The Baviad* (1791) on the style which had come to be known as Della Cruscan, here characterized as 'Truth sacrificed to letters, sense to sound' (Gifford, 12). An abrupt end to the exchange of effusions in *The World* had already been effected by a first and last meeting between the literary lovers, in the spring of 1789. A final poem by Della Crusca, 'The Interview', indicated his heartbroken deference to 'stern DUTY', since Anna Matilda was already married, but less impassioned readers attributed the cooling of his ardour to stern reality, since she was also aged forty-six and rather fat.

The newspapers continued to promote the mystery surrounding the identity of Della Crusca, a diversion Merry may have continued to promote in order to evade his creditors, although his poem of 1788, *Diversity*, is the last he published under his assumed name. Mrs Piozzi reports at this period that 'Merry is a dissipated man become truly wicked' (K. C. Balderston, ed., *Thraliana*, 1951, 2.714). A focus for his energies was provided in 1789 by political events on the continent, and his revolutionary sympathies became increasingly apparent in his work. He managed to introduce into his *Ode on the Restoration of his Majesty* the proviso 'Long may he rule a *willing* land'. The ode was read at a celebration at the Opera House on 21 April 1789 by Mrs Siddons dressed as Britannia (Boaden, 277–8). Merry visited Paris after the storming of the Bastille and was inspired to write *The Laurel of Liberty* (1790), the radical fire of which Walpole disparaged as proceeding from the old sexual jealousy he had suffered in Florence (*Extracts*, 252–3). His freely canvassed political opinions may have cost him the laureateship, despite a campaign on his behalf in *The World*. On 14 July 1791 his ode celebrating the fall of the Bastille, in part a reply to Burke's *Reflections*, was read at a meeting at the Crown and Anchor in the Strand of '1,500 English gentlemen' sympathizers with the French Revolution (*GM*, 61, 673). Merry was at this time back in Paris, presenting a treatise on the nature of a free government to the convention and renewing an acquaintance with the painter David, to whom he was apparently indebted for a passport home.

Merry was also enjoying a degree of success as a dramatist. His tragedy *Lorenzo*, a verse drama featuring piratical Moors and Turks, and a hero rescued from captivity by a besotted handmaiden, opened at the Theatre Royal, Covent Garden, on 5 April 1791. It was well received, though severely handled by newspapers unreceptive to its political tendencies (Oulton, 81). Furthermore, the part of Zoriana was taken by the well-known actress Ann Brunton (1769–1808), who, as Fanny Burney notes, 'performed his heroine so highly to his satisfaction, that he made his addresses to her' (*Diary and Letters of Madame D'Arblay*, 1842, 5.264). They were married on 26 August 1791. His wife was the daughter of John Brunton, a grocer turned actor and manager of provincial theatre, and the sister of Louisa, countess of Craven. She had been introduced to the public at Bristol aged fifteen, then transplanted to the London

other'. The mixture of Italian and English verses, the use of Italian metres and rhyme schemes, the allusions to Dante and Petrarch, and the frequent references to Italian liberty suggest, however, that the later volume at least was conceived with more serious aims than the mutual flattery of the collaborators. Merry's subsequent adoption of the pseudonym Della Crusca indicates his commitment to the ideals of the Accademia Della Crusca, founded to further Italian culture as it is celebrated in the *Miscellany*, and abolished in 1783 by the Grand Duke Leopold. The intellectual defiance of Austrian hegemony implied by Merry's poetic stance was given a certain edge by the open knowledge among the colony of his liaison with the Countess Cowper, at that time the mistress of the grand duke. This rivalry caused a scandal which Merry suspected was fomented by his co-writers. When he left Florence in the spring of 1787, he left behind him some satirical verses which effectively dissolved the literary circle he had helped to create.

Merry arrived in England, where he found a former fellow officer in the horseguards, Captain Topham, eager to capitalize on the amorous notoriety he had achieved in Florence. *The World*, a journal edited by Topham with ambitions to middle-brow literary gentility, first published Merry's 'Adieu and Recall to Love' on 29 June 1787, under the pen name Della Crusca, and then played enthusiastic host to the escalating poetic exchanges occasioned by Hannah Cowley's reply of 12 July, 'The Pen', signed Anna Matilda. Ensuing issues saw the development of a sentimental dialogue which attracted countless readers and imitators and was reprinted in the *British Album*, stage by the manager Harris. She made her début as Horatia at Covent Garden in 1785, after which the novelty of her youth, with her sweet voice and expressive eye, created a great following which waned after her first season (Genest, *Eng. stage*, 76). It was generally agreed that she lacked the energy and commanding presence of Sarah Siddons (Dunlap, 335), but this did not prevent her from taking major tragic roles at Covent Garden (Genest, *Eng. stage*, 75). She continued to act for a season following her marriage, under the name of Mrs Merry, but, her spotless reputation notwithstanding, her husband's family considered this a great indelicacy, and she left the stage in the spring of 1792.

After the failure of his comic opera, *The Magician No Conjuror*, which ran for just four nights, the Merrys travelled to France, and in August and September 1792 Merry was once again in Paris. He turned down the offer of a seat at the king's trial, and, if Walpole is to be believed, narrowly escaped the guillotine at the hands of a mob who had mistaken him for the Abbé Maury (Walpole, 492). Back in London in 1793, they were deterred from further excursions to the continent by reports of the dangers to travellers, and settled instead in cheap lodgings in Scarborough. From here Merry wrote in October to the poet Samuel Rogers, requesting financial assistance and insisting that his whereabouts remain a secret. Several of his letters were opened before delivery at this period, possibly owing to the activities of Pitt's Post Office spies (Clayden, 283). Merry occupied the following years in writing epigrams against the government in *The Telegraph* under the name of Tom Thorne, and published a play, *Fénelon*, in 1795. Neither these nor even the relatively warm reception which greeted his poem *The Pains of Memory* (1796) served to alleviate the increasingly straitened financial circumstances in which he found himself. When his wife was offered an engagement by Wignell, of the New Theatre, Philadelphia, pressing debts and an eagerness to taste life in a republic prompted Merry to consent to her return to the stage, and they landed at New York on 10 October 1796. From her first appearance in Philadelphia, on 5 December, Mrs Merry won a reputation across the principal theatres of the union which entitled her, according to Dunlap, 'to the character of the most perfect actress America has seen' (p. 334).

Robert Merry was an affectionate husband (*Journals and Correspondence of Thomas Sedgwick Whalley*, 415), and, already inclined to corpulence, he grew increasingly indolent with his wife's growing success. The *Monthly Magazine* for August 1798 announced a work in preparation by Merry 'on the State of Society and Manners in America'. On the morning of 24 December of this year, however, Merry was walking in his garden in Baltimore when he fell in an apoplectic fit and died three hours later. He was forty-three years old, and his death was attributed to a lack of exercise. His wife survived him, married Thomas Wignell in 1803, with whom she had her only child, and after his death married William Warren, a manager of the Philadelphia and Baltimore theatres, in 1806. She died in childbirth at Alexandria, Virginia, in 1808.

Robert Merry's reputation has not improved with posterity. The conclusions of Gifford's satire continue to dominate the critical climate, in which the criticisms levelled by Wordsworth's 'Preface' to the *Lyrical Ballads* (1800) at the Della Cruscan school are seen to have effected an irreversible literary revolution away from such stylistic excesses. Macaulay, however, in an essay of 1830, recognized Merry as a forerunner, howbeit inferior, of the reformers of English poetry from 'the monotony of the correct school' (repr. in T. B. Macaulay, *Literary and Historical Essays*, 1932, 176), and such late twentieth-century critical attention as has been directed at the poetry of Della Crusca has begun to adopt this approach. James Clifford, in his study of Merry (1943) identifies him as a 'Pre-Byronic Hero'. Jerome McGann has in a recent work (1996) sought to rehabilitate the Della Cruscan school as a *fin de siècle* movement with a far-reaching influence on subsequent literary history.

Corinna Russell

Sources GM, 1st ser., 61 (1791), 673 · GM, 1st ser., 69 (1799), 252–4 · GM, 1st ser., 78 (1808), 749 · W. Gifford, *The Baviad, and Maeviad*, new edn (1797), *passim* · *Autobiography, letters, and literary remains of Mrs Piozzi*, ed. A. Hayward, 2 (1861), 36 · P. W. Clayden, *The early life of Samuel Rogers* (1887) · H. Walpole, *Letters addressed to the countess of Ossory, from the year 1769 to 1797*, ed. R. V. Smith, 2 (1848), 492 · *Extracts of the journals and correspondence of Miss Berry*, ed. M. T. Lewis, 2nd edn, 3 vols. (1865–6), vol. 1, pp. 252–3 · J. Boaden, *Memoirs of Mrs Siddons*, 2 (1827), 277–8 · *European Magazine and London Review*, 24 (1793), 411–12 · *Monthly Review*, enlarged ser., 4.56–62; 5.201–5, 344; 19.274–7; 21.149–55 · *Monthly Magazine*, 1.46; 4.129; 7.255–8 · D. E. Baker, *Biographia dramatica, or, A companion to the playhouse*, rev. I. Reed, new edn, rev. S. Jones, 1 (1812), 507 · W. C. Oulton, *The history of the theatres of London*, 2 (1796), 80–81, 107 · Genest, *Eng. stage*, 7.25, 29–30, 75 · W. Dunlap, *History of the American theatre*, 1 (1833), 334–40 · *Journals and correspondence of Thomas Sedgwick Whalley*, ed. H. Wickham, 2 (1863), 415 · R. Marshall, *Italy in English literature, 1755–1815* (1934), *passim* · J. L. Clifford, *Robert Merry: a pre-Byronic hero* (1943) · J. J. McGann, *The poetics of sensibility* (1996), 74–93 · ANB · IGI

Archives Harvard U., MSS · L. Cong., literary MSS and family MSS | JRL, poem and letters to H. L. Piozzi

Likenesses J. Collyer, line engraving, 1790 (after engraving by H. D. Hamilton, 1789), BM, NPG; repro. in *The British album*, 3rd edn (1790) · oils, in or before 1793, priv. coll. [*see illus.*] · stipple, BM; repro. in *European Magazine*; and *London Review*

Merry, William Walter (1835–1918), classical scholar, was born at Evesham on 6 September 1835, the only son of Walter Merry, of that town, and his wife, Elizabeth Mary Byrch. He entered Cheltenham College as a day boy in 1846 and was elected to an open scholarship at Balliol College, Oxford, in 1852. He obtained a first class in classical moderations (1854) and a second class in *literae humaniores* (1856). In 1858 he gained the chancellor's Latin essay prize and in the following year he was elected a fellow of Lincoln College, where he filled the office of classical lecturer until his election to the rectorship twenty-five years later. Merry was ordained deacon in 1860, priest in the next year, and in 1862 was presented by his college to the perpetual curacy of All Saints, Oxford. As this living was also a college chaplaincy his tenure of it enabled him to retain his fellowship on his marriage later in the same year to

William Walter Merry (1835–1918), by unknown photographer

Alice Elizabeth (d. 1914), only daughter of Joseph Collings, jurat of the royal court of Guernsey, with whom he had two sons and two daughters.

While holding this living Merry acquired considerable popularity as a preacher. He was select preacher before the university in 1878–9 and 1889–90, and Whitehall preacher in 1883–4. He also found time to pursue his studies in the Greek classics. His friendship with James Riddell, who had been his tutor at Balliol, at first fixed him as a student of Homer. After Riddell's early death (1866) he completed for the Clarendon Press and published in 1876 the large edition of the *Odyssey*, books i–xii, which Riddell had begun. He was also entirely responsible for the minor edition of the whole of the *Odyssey* which was issued by the Clarendon Press in two volumes in 1870 and 1878. Later he edited for the same press the plays of Aristophanes: the *Clouds* (1879), the *Acharnians* (1880), the *Frogs* (1884), the *Knights* (1887), the *Birds* (1889), the *Wasps* (1893), and the *Peace* (1900). Erudite, full of sound learning, and spiced with congenial humour, these editions were familiar to several generations of students.

Merry's Latinity was at least on a par with his Greek. He had remarkable verbal knowledge of the Latin poets and of Cicero, and great facility as a writer of Latin verse. The distinctive mark of his scholarship, however, was his power of interpretation. His colleague, William Warde Fowler, observed that he never found anyone quite so helpful in divining the meaning of a difficult passage: 'He took the bearings of it with wonderful rapidity, and then

looked straight into it without the least hesitation or confusion' (*Oxford Magazine*, 15 March 1918). In 1875 he published a volume entitled *Greek Dialects* and another in 1891 entitled *Selected Fragments of Roman Poetry*.

In 1880 Merry was appointed public orator of the university, an office which he held until 1910; and in 1884 he succeeded Mark Pattison as rector of Lincoln College, not long after the election of his colleague, Thomas Fowler, as president of Corpus Christi College. His fine presence, his lively wit, and the extraordinary lucidity of his Latin, which was aided by his delivery, made him an ideal public orator. He was described as being able to turn the diction of Cicero to the topics of the day in such a way as to make it somehow quite intelligible to undergraduates who had little Latin, and ladies who had none. His *Orationes tum Creweianae tum gratulatoriae* were published by the Clarendon Press in 1909.

Merry's rectorship was long and provided much needed peace after the frictions caused by the rule of Mark Pattison. His affability and genial humour, together with his care for the interests of all members of the college, made him popular with the fellows and with many generations of undergraduates. However, he lacked the qualities of leadership which could have improved the college's academic reputation: it remained small and comparatively undistinguished. By contrast he had great qualities as a host, as he showed when he filled the office of vice-chancellor from 1904 to 1906 and maintained the tradition of hospitality associated with that office.

Merry died in Lincoln College on 5 March 1918 and was buried beside his wife in Holywell cemetery, Oxford.

E. I. Carlyle, rev. Richard Smail

Sources *The Times* (7 March 1918) · *Oxford Magazine* (15 March 1918) · *Classical Review*, 32 (1918), 85–6 · E. Hilliard, ed., *The Balliol College register, 1832–1914* (privately printed, Oxford, 1914) · V. Green, *The commonwealth of Lincoln College, 1427–1977* (1979), 511–13 · CGPLA Eng. & Wales (1918)
Likenesses C. Johnson, oils, exh. RA 1898, Lincoln College, Oxford · photograph, NPG [see illus.]
Wealth at death £14,188 5s. 10d.: probate, 26 April 1918, CGPLA Eng. & Wales

Merry del Val, Rafael María José Pedro Francisco Borja Domingo Gerardo de la Santísma Trinidad (1865–1930), papal administrator, was born on 10 October 1865 at 33 Portman Square, Gloucester Place, London, the second of the four sons of Rafael Merry del Val (1831–1917), secretary to the Spanish legation in London, a monarchist supporter of Alfonso XII, and Sofia Josefa de Zulueta (d. 1925), elder daughter of Pedro José de Zulueta, count of Torre Díaz, of the London bank of Zulueta & Co., and his wife, Sophia Ann Wilcox, who was of Scottish and Dutch ancestry. The del Vals were an Aragonese family originally from Saragossa claiming descent from a twelfth-century Breton crusader; the name of Merry came from a line of Irish merchants from co. Waterford, Ireland, who settled in the late eighteenth century in Seville. The Zuluetas were an old Basque family ennobled as counts de Torre Díaz in the nineteenth century. Merry del Val's elder brother,

Rafael María José Pedro Francisco Borja Domingo Gerardo de la Santísma Trinidad Merry del Val (1865-1930), by unknown photographer

Alfonso, marquess of Merry del Val (b. 1864), was Spanish ambassador to Great Britain between 1913 and 1931.

Early life Merry del Val was baptized on 11 October 1865 in the Spanish embassy chapel, St James's, Spanish Place, and was educated from the age of nine at Bayliss House, a private school in Slough. From the age of twelve, when his father became the Spanish minister to Belgium, he attended the Jesuit colleges of Notre Dame de Namur and of St Michel in Brussels. As a boy, he 'loved dancing, swimming, and shooting', and was 'an excellent shot and a fearless rider' (Forbes, 19–20). His international upbringing gave him fluency in English, French, Spanish, and Italian; he later learned German. As a seminarian at Ushaw in 1883 he popularized tennis, played in the college theatricals, notably the devil in *Les mémoires du diable*, and once for a dare broke the ice to swim across the college bathing place. His college nickname was Merry Devil (Forbes, 17, 21). He was ordained to minor orders in 1885, when he accompanied his father, then Spanish ambassador to Vienna, to Rome to complete his training for the priesthood.

Merry del Val was entered at the Scots College in Rome, but at a papal audience Leo XIII insisted that he be trained at the Accademia dei Nobili Ecclesiastici. On a visit to his family in September 1886 he acted as secretary to Francis Schönborn, archbishop of Prague, who ordained him sub-deacon in Prague Cathedral in 1887. In 1887, though not yet ordained, he wore the uniform of private chamberlain supernumary to the pope, with the title of monsignor, as secretary and interpreter for the papal delegation led by Monsignor Ruffo Scilla to London for Queen Victoria's golden jubilee. In 1888 he accompanied papal delegations to Berlin for the funeral of Wilhelm I and the coronation of his successor, Friedrich III, and to the court of Franz Joseph. Lucido Maria Cardinal Parocchi, vicar of Rome, ordained him to the diaconate on 27 May 1888 and on 30 December to the priesthood. He said his first mass in the oratory of St Ignatius adjoining the Gesù. He completed his studies at the Accademia and the Gregorian in 1891, including a course in ecclesiastical diplomacy, a doctorate in theology, and a degree in canon law. He also began in 1890 his work as spiritual director of the Christian Brothers' school in the Roman slum quarter of the Trastevere, and founded an Association of the Sacred Heart for boys and young men. He taught them football and tried to teach them cricket, found them jobs, blessed their weddings, and counselled their marriages. He always claimed to have wanted a pastoral ministry in England, and his Roman pastorate was his only outlet for this.

Papal adviser Authority, however, decreed otherwise. In 1891 Merry del Val was appointed *cameriere segreto partecipante* and in 1893 master of the robes and privy chamberlain to the pope, with a duty of attendance upon him. When on holiday in San Sebastian in 1891 and 1892 he gave religious instruction to the Spanish royal children and prepared the young Alfonso XIII for his first communion. He kept a confessional for the English in San Silvestro in Capite, where he also preached in English, and he was spiritual director of the Spanish College.

He was also called upon to advise on English affairs. He wrote the conclusion of Leo XIII's letter of 1895, *Ad Anglos*, and in 1896 was secretary to the pontifical commission to investigate the validity of Anglican orders, arising from the ecumenical conversations between Charles Lindley Wood, second Viscount Halifax and the Abbé Fernand Portal. The secretary of state, Cardinal Rampolla, was sympathetic to their cause. Merry del Val helped shape the pope's view of the issue, and he was in close contact with Cardinal Vaughan of Westminster and those members of the commission (Canon James Moyes, Francis Gasquet, the Franciscan David Fleming, and the Spanish Capuchin, Calasanzio de Llevaneras) who advised that Anglican orders were defective in form and intention, against those who thought that they were valid or doubtful (the historian the Abbé Louis Duchesne, the Jesuit Emilio de Augustinis, the English Thomas B. Scannell, and Pietro Gasparri, later secretary of state). Merry del Val drafted the pope's encyclical letter of 13 September 1896, *Apostolicae curae*, which declared Anglican orders 'absolutely null and utterly void' (Hughes, 198) and greatly influenced Anglican–Roman Catholic relations in the twentieth century.

Merry del Val's ancestry is one key to his convictions. His maternal grandfather, the second count de Torre Díaz, conformed to the Church of England, and returned to the Roman Catholic church under the influence of the Oxford

Movement; his wife, Sophia, was a convert from evangelicalism. Merry del Val inherited their convert zeal. He had been taught by an ex-parson and took delight in converting Anglicans. There was also a Spanish dimension to his mind. The first count de Torre Díaz was a noted liberal who had to leave Spain, and the family's reversion to Catholicism was a self-conscious return to the conservatism which Merry del Val showed throughout his life.

As apostolic delegate to Canada in 1897 Merry del Val adjudicated with tact in the controversy over the Manitoba laws on state support for Catholic schools. Ottawa University made him an LLD. In 1898 he helped establish the Beda College in Rome for older ordinands. In 1899 he was appointed president of the Accademia, of which he was a recent graduate, and met there Nicola Canali, who served him for the rest of his life. In 1900 he was consecrated titular archbishop of Nicaea. He celebrated the occasion not with a banquet, but with a dinner for two hundred of the Roman poor. In 1902 he published *The Truth of Papal Claims*, a reply to *The Validity of Papal Claims* by F. N. Oxenham, chaplain of All Saints' Church on the via del Babuino in Rome. In 1902 Merry del Val travelled to London to represent the pope at Edward VII's coronation. Cardinal Vaughan wanted him as his successor at Westminster, and his name was on the chapter's original *terna* for the see, with the Benedictines J. C. Hedley and F. N. Gasquet. The duke of Norfolk regarded this 'Cockney Spaniard' (Leslie, 80) as a foreigner, and successfully opposed his candidature.

Secretary of state In 1903, on the death of Leo XIII, Merry del Val was appointed secretary to the conclave to elect his successor, and took up residence in the Sala Borgia. He refused to transmit to the conclave the emperor Franz Josef's veto of Cardinal Rampolla as Leo's successor. As secretary to the conclave he acted as pro-secretary of state to the new pope, Pius X, who on 18 October 1903 appointed him secretary of state, and on 9 November made him cardinal priest and titular of the Basilica of Santa Prassede, rendered famous in English as St Praxed's in Browning's poem *The Tomb of St Praxed*. He was just thirty-eight.

The new pope was a peasant, a pastor, and an administrator of genius, with a natural manner which delighted ordinary Italians. He had, however, no experience of the church outside his native northern Italy, and Merry del Val had the diplomatic and linguistic skills which the pope himself was wholly lacking. Merry del Val's pastoral work in Rome and his rigorous piety were additional recommendations. The pope was, moreover, intent on a complete restructuring of the Vatican bureaucracy and a codification of canon law, and sensed in Merry del Val an efficiency and an adamantine spirit like his own. Merry del Val was one of the triad of dominant figures in the papal entourage, with the Capuchin J. C. Vives y Tutó and Gaetano Cardinal De Lai. Merry del Val's attitudes have been called 'an untroubled but rigid intransigence' (Aubert, 391). He continued for four years, however, to take advice from his *sostituto* (under-secretary) Giacomo della Chiesa, who had held the same post under his allegedly more flexible predecessor Rampolla, and who later became Benedict XV.

A full understanding of Merry del Val's work as secretary of state must await the opening of the Vatican archives for these years. Like his pope, he was not a native Roman, and felt his isolation. His authority was increased by Pius X's sweeping reorganization of the curia. The secretariat of state was assigned the congregation for extraordinary ecclesiastical affairs and the secretariat of briefs, while the consistorial congregation became responsible for some of the major missionary countries, Great Britain and Ireland, the United States, Canada, and the Netherlands, formerly under the jurisdiction of the sacred propaganda.

Two matters injured Merry del Val's reputation, his handling of the church–state crisis in France and his part in the papal condemnation of modernism. The conflict in France, gathering force for two decades, brought about the expulsion of the religious orders in 1901. The final breakdown in church–state relations was precipitated in 1904 by the visit of President Loubet to the king of Italy, formally acknowledging the Italian state partly created from the states of the church. A compromise proposal for a meeting between Merry del Val and the French foreign minister at the French embassy in Rome was torpedoed by publicity in the French newspaper *Le Figaro*. The cardinal then drafted a confidential protest to France dated 28 April 1904, which was hardly stronger than those of Rampolla, but he rashly sent copies of the document, with an additional sentence offensive to the anticlerical French administration, to other heads of state, one of whom, the prince of Monaco, leaked the document to the socialist newspaper *l'Humanité*. France recalled its ambassador to Rome, and after a row over episcopal appointments unilaterally abolished the Napoleonic concordat of 1801 by the law of separation of 1905. Merry del Val encouraged the pope to override the wish of the majority of French bishops to compromise with the state's decision to lease church's properties to *associations culturelles*, predominantly lay committees not controlled by the clergy, arguing that this would subject the bishops to the laity and abolish papal authority. The impoverished French church, deserted by the state, was henceforth wholly in papal hands.

Condemnation of modernism Merry del Val's role in the modernist crisis was also a complicated one, but it is unlikely that future research will greatly change the present picture, to distinguish the servant from his master. The pope was responsible for the acts of his pontificate, and Merry del Val was his willing instrument. The cardinal's anti-modernism predated his elevation to the office of secretary of state. He was hostile to the heresy of 'Americanism', condemned by Leo XIII's apostolic letter *Testem benevolentiae*, in 1899. In a letter to his cousin Denis Sheil in 1899 Merry del Val complained of the future modernist George Tyrrell's *External Religion*, and in the same year protested to Cardinal Vaughan about the heresies of the scientist St George Jackson Mivart. He promised papal approbation of Vaughan's plan for the hierarchy's joint pastoral letter condemning liberal Catholicism in 1900. In

1903 he wrote the covering letter to Cardinal Richard of Paris for the decree of the Holy Office placing five of the Abbé Alfred Firmin Loisy's books on the index, and repudiated Loisy's subsequent qualified submission. In 1905 he was drawn into Tyrrell's attempts to leave the Society of Jesus, Tyrrell observing that the Jesuit general and the cardinal were 'as identical as any two persons of the Trinity' (Barmann, 172). Merry del Val commissioned Joseph Lemius to draft the encyclical *Pascendi* of 1907, denouncing modernism as 'the synthesis of all the heresies' (*Pascendi*, edition of 1937, 39). He conveyed to Bishop Peter Amigo of Southwark Tyrrell's deprivation of the sacraments in 1907. Merry del Val's other acts show the same temper. In 1912 he applauded the archbishop of Rouen's reaffirmation of the legend that Lazarus, Martha, and Mary had first brought Christianity to Gaul. From 1911, however, he can be distinguished from the extreme anti-modernists, and tried to curb the activities of Umberto Benigni and his Sodalitium Pianum, who roundly abused him for his diplomatic behaviour (Poulat, 77). Benigni had a mania for codenames and aliases, and referred to Merry del Val as 'Miss Romey' and 'George' (Holmes, *Triumph*, 277).

Merry del Val's other actions confirm his sympathies for a conservative Catholic integralism. He wrote the letter of 1904 dissolving the Italian Opera dei Congressi, to bring the Italian lay bodies directly under the church's authority through Catholic Action. He favoured a similar dependence for the centre party in Germany. He was party to the papal condemnation of the left leaning French movement of the Sillon in 1910, and encouraged critics of the social modernism of the Catholic trade unions in northern France, for 'emphasizing justice at the cost of charity' (Misner, 311). His other responsibilities included the Swiss guards, the presidency of the commission of cardinals for the administration of the resources of the Holy See, and the prefecture of the Sacred Congregation of Loreto. In 1914 he was appointed archpriest of St Peter's and superior of its chapter. He secured the cardinalate conferred on Francis Gasquet in 1914, when he also signed the concordat with Serbia.

Final years Pius X died shortly after the outbreak of the First World War. The new pontiff, Benedict XV, made Merry del Val secretary of the Holy Office. Benedict had been accused of modernism himself, and brought the anti-modernist campaign to a close. Merry del Val's period of great influence on papal policy was now over. He remained a rallying point for conservatism in the church, and received twelve and seventeen votes in two of the ballots in the papal conclave of 1922. He lived simply in the upper rooms of the Palazzina, built for Cardinal Henry of York. His remaining career centred round his positions at the Holy Office, camerlengo and archpriest, in which his tall and handsome presence and knowledge of languages made him a gracious host to distinguished visitors and at conferences and receptions. He presided at the congresses of the International Women's League in 1922 and Rome in 1925, and was appointed its protector. As protector of the

Friars Minor he was the papal legate in 1926, when the Italian church and state came together for the celebrations for the seventh centenary of the death of St Francis. The legate's papal train, the first since 1870, was greeted with gun salutes at every station, and at Assisi he publicly praised Mussolini on the day that the Duce ordered the negotiations which resolved the Roman question by the Lateran treaties between Italy and the papacy in 1929.

The cardinal guarded the memory of Pius X. He said mass every month at his tomb on the anniversary of his death, and helped the pope's family when they came as war refugees to Rome. From 1924 he went mountain climbing around Arabba in the Dolomites, calling in on Pius X's home village of Riese. His ties with England remained strong. In 1925, the year of the silver jubilee of his consecration as bishop, he celebrated mass in St Peter's in the presence of Cardinal Bourne and 1200 English pilgrims. In 1926 he consecrated as bishop his old school friend from Ushaw, the future Cardinal Hinsley. In 1927 he revisited England and Ushaw. He became cardinal protector of the English College in succession to Gasquet in 1929.

Merry del Val loved simple practical jokes and liked to travel incognito. His bouts of withdrawal, exhaustion, and depression were the dark side of his profound piety as a Servite tertiary, with a favourite devotion to Our Lady of Sorrows. A discipline and hairshirts, one of them of wire, with evidence of their use, were found in his rooms after his death. He was protector of the Society of the Sacred Heart, and devoted much of his time to counselling young religious. He donated all he could to Roman charities, regularly giving away his bedlinen and slipping money in envelopes to a large and humble clientele. In his work among the youth of the Trastevere he built them a club in corrugated iron with theatre, billiard, and reading rooms, wrote the music for their religious ceremonies, and followed their fortunes through the First World War. He died in Rome during an operation for appendicitis on 26 February 1930. His body was carried by boys from the Trastevere to the crypt of St Peter's and buried near the tomb of Pius X. The inscription on his marble cenotaph reads 'Da mihi animas—Coetera tolle' ('give me souls—take the rest'), a mystical application of Genesis 14: 21. At the request of the Spanish hierarchy the cause for his canonization was introduced in 1953. The informative process was completed in 1956 and published in 1957 as *Romana beatificationis et canonizationis servi dei Raphaelis card. Merry del Val informatio*. In 1965 Mrs Joan de Trafford founded the international Legion of Merry del Val to press for his canonization, and it held a conference in Rome in 1971. His cause seems to have made little progress since.

SHERIDAN GILLEY

Sources F. A. M. Forbes, *Rafael, Cardinal Merry del Val: a character sketch* (1932) · P. Cenci, *Il Cardinale Raffaele Merry del Val* (1933) · M. C. Buehrle, *Rafael Cardinal Merry del Val* (1957) · P. Fairlie, OSB, ed., *Let God act: selections from the writings of Cardinal Rafael Merry del Val* (1974) · 'Cardinal Merry del Val', *Ushaw Magazine*, 40 (1930), 44–9 · 'Some records and recollections of Cardinal Merry del Val', *Ushaw Magazine*, 41 (1931), 82–91 · J. D. Holmes, 'Cardinal Raphael Merry del Val, an uncompromising ultramontane: gleanings from his correspondence with England', *Catholic Historical Review*, 60 (1974), 55–64 • J. J. Hughes, *Absolutely null and utterly void: the papal condemnation of Anglican orders, 1896* (1968) • R. Aubert, 'Pius X: a conservative reform pope', *History of the church: the church in the industrial age*, ed. H. Jedin (1981), vol. 9 of *History of the church*, 381–93 • J. McManners, *Church and state in France, 1870–1914* (1972) • R. Merry del Val, *Memories of Pope Pius X* (1939) • *CGPLA Eng. & Wales* (1931) • S. Leslie, *Cardinal Gasquet: a memoir* (1953) • L. F. Barmann, *Baron Friedrich von Hügel and the modernist crisis in England* (1972) • E. Poulat, *Intégrisme et Catholicisme intégral* (1969) • J. D. Holmes, *The triumph of the Holy See* (1978) • P. Misner, *Social Catholicism in Europe from the onset of industrialisation to the First World War* (1991)

Archives Archivio Vaticano, Vatican City • Westm. DA | Downside Abbey, near Bath, Gasquet MSS • Ushaw College, Durham, corresp. relating to Ushaw College

Likenesses F. D'Ignazio, portrait, Holy Office, Rome • B. Georgieu, portrait, St Peter's, Rome, treasury • Italian school, portrait, Ushaw College, co. Durham • G. H. Wrede de Elima, bust, Ushaw College, co. Durham • photograph, repro. in Cenci, *Cardinale Raffaele Merry del Val*, frontispiece [*see illus.*]

Wealth at death £15,589 16s. 4d.: administration with will, 27 May 1931, *CGPLA Eng. & Wales*

Merryweather, Henry (1839–1932). *See under* Brailsford, Mary Ann (*bap.* 1791, *d.* 1852).

Mersey. For this title name *see* Bigham, John Charles, first Viscount Mersey (1840–1929).

Mersington. For this title name *see* Swinton, Sir Alexander, Lord Mersington (1621x30?–1700).

Merthyr. For this title name *see* Lewis, William Thomas, first Baron Merthyr (1837–1914).

Merton, Sir Thomas Ralph (1888–1969), physicist, was born in Wimbledon, Surrey, on 12 January 1888, the only son (there were also two daughters) of Emile Ralph Merton (1850–1921) and his wife, Helen (*b.* 1860, *d.* after 1921), daughter of Thomas Meates. Emile Merton, of German origin but of British nationality when his children were born, was for a time partner in the family business of Henry R. Merton & Co., metal traders, founded by his elder brother in London in 1860; another brother, William, had founded the Metallgesellschaft in Frankfurt am Main in 1881. Merton was educated at Farnborough School and at Eton College, where Dr T. C. Porter, the physics master, encouraged him to begin research. Between leaving Eton in 1905 and going up to Balliol College, Oxford, in 1906, he worked at King's College, London, where he made a lifelong friend of Herbert Jackson and met J. W. Nicholson. He went to Balliol with distinguished fellow Etonians Julian Grenfell, Ronald Knox, and Julian Huxley.

In view of his delicate health and his promise as a scientist, the university allowed Merton to go straight to a research thesis without taking his final exams, a unique privilege well justified by subsequent events. His investigation of the properties of solutions of caesium nitrate earned him a BSc in 1910. Meanwhile he had been reading widely and conceived many ideas for improving the techniques of spectroscopy. While still a schoolboy he had set up a room in his father's house as a primitive laboratory.

Sir Thomas Ralph Merton (1888–1969), by John Merton, 1951

After his marriage in 1912 to Violet Marjory (*d.* 1976), daughter of Lieutenant-Colonel William Harcourt Sawyer, his spectroscopic laboratory was moved to his London house in Gilbert Street.

After 1913 a steady stream of papers came from Merton's private laboratory, in which he assembled the latest spectroscopic equipment. His early work was on the absorbtion spectra of solutions, but he soon changed to the spectra of gases and to astrophysics, which were to be the main fields of his investigations. His early papers were distinguished by the beauty and accuracy of his experimental techniques. In 1916 he obtained his DSc from Oxford and was appointed lecturer in spectroscopy at King's College, London. In the same year his first joint paper with J. W. Nicholson appeared. It was a fortunate chance which brought together Nicholson's brilliant mathematical analysis and Merton's experimental skill. The paper dealt with the broadening of spectral lines in a condensed discharge. By an ingenious technique Merton measured the discontinuities in the lines due to their partial breaking up into components under the influence of the magnetic field between adjacent atoms. The two men applied the same technique to the measurement of the spectra of hydrogen and helium, reproducing the distribution of intensity of some stellar lines in the laboratory for the first time.

The First World War scarcely interrupted these

researches. Merton, having been rejected for active service on grounds of health, was commissioned in 1916 as a lieutenant in the Royal Naval Volunteer Reserve in the secret service, the first scientist to be so appointed. His success in identifying the secret ink carried by German spies in their clothing, and inventing a new means of secret writing, won a mention in dispatches.

In 1919 Balliol elected Merton to a research fellowship and Oxford made him reader (from 1923 professor) in spectroscopy. He worked on a series of problems, usually with a young student as his assistant. He was elected to the Royal Society in 1920 and in 1922, with Sydney Baratt, gave the society's Bakerian lecture, on the spectrum of hydrogen. They cleared up a number of discrepancies in the secondary spectrum of hydrogen which were shown to be due to the hydrogen molecule, and they also showed the profound influence that traces of impurities can exert on gas spectra. In 1923 Merton, who had inherited about £80,000 under his father's will, left Oxford to live at Winforton House in Herefordshire, the estate he had acquired with 3 miles of salmon fishing on the Wye. He was a good shot and a most skilful fisherman. He transferred his laboratory to Winforton, so that he was able to combine a sporting life with his scientific research.

There is a gap of nearly twenty years between Merton's scientific papers of 1928 and 1947. In this interval he was busy in the laboratory and was taking out patents for his inventions. Diffraction gratings were one of his lifelong interests and here his inventive genius best showed itself. The rarity and expense of good diffraction gratings led him to devise, in 1935, a method of copying them without loss of optical quality by applying a thin layer of a cellulose ester solution to an original plane grating. When the solvent had evaporated he detached this pellicle and applied its grooved surface to a moist gelatine film on a glass plate. When dry, the gelatine bore a faithful record of the original rulings.

In 1948 Merton made an important basic advance in the art of ruling diffraction gratings. Since 1880 these had been ruled groove by groove by the method used by Rowlands. In place of this, Merton ruled a very fine helix continuously on a steel cylinder which he then opened out upon a plane gelatine-coated surface by his copying method. No lathe could, however, rule a helix free from errors of pitch and these Merton eliminated by an ingenious device. It consisted of a 'chasing lathe' by which he cut a secondary helix on the same cylinder with a tool mounted on a 'nut' lined with strips of cork pressed upon the primary lathe-cut helix. Periodic errors were thus averaged and eliminated by the elasticity of the cork.

Merton handed these processes over to the National Physical Laboratory (NPL) for further development and they formed the basis of a considerable research programme. The 'blazed' gratings made by the Merton–NPL method were of great value in making available cheap infra-red spectrometers of high resolving power for research and industry, while long gratings ruled by this method came into use for engineering measurement and machine tool control.

In the laboratory at his father's house Merton had bombarded various newly discovered phosphorescent powders with cathode rays. He was surprised to find that while all lit brilliantly, the afterglow was brief and feeble. By experiment, he discovered that this was because the excitation and emission lines of the spectra barely overlapped, and that by mixing suitable powders he could increase the afterglow. He realized that persistent afterglow could be got by a double layer of powders, in which the light emitted by the back layer excited the front layer, but as this technique seemed to have no practical use he forgot about it for thirty-three years, until 1938 when Sir Henry Tizard asked if he could achieve such a long afterglow. Merton was able to reply by return of post, and soon after was asked to join the air defence committee where he learned that his discovery had made possible the two-layer long-persistence radar screens which helped to bring victory in the battle of Britain. His other wartime inventions included a black paint which reduced the proportion of light reflected from bombers in a searchlight to less than one per cent; the use of nitrous oxide in the fuel to accelerate fighter aircraft; and a diffraction rangefinder for fighters, which was used against doodlebugs.

From 1939 to 1956 Merton was treasurer of the Royal Society, where his knowledge and experience of business were of considerable benefit. He formed a committee of experts to control its finances, and it was on his initiative that charitable bodies were given power to invest in equities, where they had previously been limited to gilt-edged stock. The income of all the society's funds showed a large increase during his treasurership.

In 1930 John, the eldest of the Mertons' five sons, brought home the drawing prize from Eton and this proved a turning point in both his and his father's lives. It awoke in Merton some latent interest and he spent months in Italy with his son seeing all the great collections of Renaissance paintings. His study of the techniques of the Florentine paintings was reflected in his son's pictures. He began to make a remarkable collection of pictures of the period 1450–1520. From 1944 until his death he was a member of the scientific advisory board of the National Gallery, and its chairman from 1957 to 1965. He was also a trustee of the gallery, and of the National Portrait Gallery from 1955 to 1962. Merton was knighted in 1944 for his services during the war and in 1956 was appointed KBE. He was awarded the Holweck prize in 1951 and the Rumford medal of the Royal Society in 1958.

In 1947 Merton bought Stubbings House, at Maidenhead Thicket, Berkshire. Its spacious rooms made an admirable setting for his collection of pictures. As a man of considerable wealth, he maintained what was probably the last private physics laboratory in Britain. Papers and patents continued to appear, based on his researches there. In 1957 he had several serious operations and thereafter he rarely left his home, where he died on 10 October 1969.

HAROLD HARTLEY, *rev.* ISOBEL FALCONER

Sources H. Hartley and D. Gabor, *Memoirs FRS*, 16 (1970), 421–40 · *The Times* (13 Oct 1969) · personal knowledge (1981)

Archives CAC Cam., corresp. with A. V. Hill · IWM, corresp. with Tizard and others · Nuffield Oxf., corresp. with Lord Cherwell
Likenesses J. Merton, drawing, 1951, priv. coll. [*see illus.*] · photograph (after drawing by J. Merton), RS; repro. in Hartley and Gabor, *Memoirs FRS*, facing p. 421
Wealth at death £1,920,337: probate, 2 March 1970, *CGPLA Eng. & Wales*

Merton, Walter of (*c.*1205–1277), administrator, bishop of Rochester, and founder of Merton College, Oxford, was the son of William Cook (le Kuk, le Keu) of Basingstoke, Hampshire, and in his early years was known as Walter of Basingstoke. His father, who died *c.*1245, was connected with Richard Herriard, a royal minister and justice in the reigns of Richard I and John: the kinship was most probably through William's mother, whose name is unknown. William Cook's own wife, Walter's mother, was Christina Fitzace, a member of a family of free tenants of the royal manor of Basingstoke. She died in 1238, and left a small estate to her son, who received other lands from her kin.

Walter of Merton was the only son of his parents' marriage, but he had seven sisters, and through their marriages at least thirteen nephews and three nieces. The pious commemoration of his parents, and an appropriate provision for his sisters and their children, were two of his principal concerns throughout his career. He appears to have owed his education to the Augustinian canons of Merton, Surrey, though whether in the priory itself or elsewhere is uncertain. He evinced no scholarly tastes, and his principal professional skill seems to have been in conveyancing and the routines of the common law. He was, however, deeply grateful to the priory for its patronage, and not only took its name himself but also explicitly conferred it upon his college. He was certainly not professed at Merton, but he witnessed deeds for the priory from the early 1230s, and in 1233 was presented to one of its livings: Cuddington, in Surrey. At that time he was a clerk, but apparently not in priestly orders, for a letter written by the Franciscan Adam Marsh (*d.* 1259), recommending him for the subdiaconate, dates from *c.*1236. The letter is addressed to another Franciscan, Adam Bechesoveres, and speaks of Merton's being about to be ordained by Robert Grosseteste, bishop of Lincoln (*d.* 1253). The implication is that he was in Grosseteste's diocese, and with it a possibility that he was then at Oxford.

Within two years, however, Walter of Merton had entered the king's service. In 1236 there was a parliament at Merton Priory, and Henry III frequently visited the house. It seems that on some such occasion the chancellor's household gathered in a promising recruit. By 1238 Merton was evidently familiar with the workings of the writs office, and he was able to secure a charter from the king, in support of his title to his mother's lands, in circumstances that suggest some degree of privilege. The first explicit record of his employment by the crown comes in 1240, when he was appointed to conduct a survey of the royal demesne in Essex, Kent, Hertfordshire, and Middlesex. Shortly afterwards Merton bought up the Surrey lands of William Wateville, one of his fellow commissioners in 1240. He had already acquired land to

Walter of Merton (*c.*1205–1277), seal

provide a marriage settlement for his sister Agnes, and he displayed an assured skill in the complicated transactions which were then involved. To secure the Wateville fee he had not only to discharge Wateville's debt of £100 to Aaron, son of Abraham of London, to whom the land was mortgaged, but also to negotiate his way through two titles in dower, and buy out another claimant. The transaction was not completed until 1249, when he obtained a grant of free warren in his lands, presumably to enhance his title and status. He was, however, probably already contemplating something beyond the ordinary ambitions of the lesser country gentry.

By that time Merton had served for four years in the chancery of the bishop of Durham, Nicholas Farnham (*d.* 1257), whose colleague in the king's service he had been when Farnham was the royal physician. His employment at Durham could be regarded rather as an extension than as an interruption of his work for the king. It certainly broadened his administrative experience, and gave him some connections in the north, including the benefices of Sedgefield and Staindrop in co. Durham, and Haltwhistle in Northumberland. He also held Benningbrough in Yorkshire, Branston in Lincolnshire, and Potton in Bedfordshire. He returned to the royal administration in 1247, and probably served again as a member of the chancellor's household. He became protonotary of the chancery, and from 1255 he emerged as a regular recipient of royal favours. He had custody of the great seal in 1258, when the chancellor, Henry Wingham (*d.* 1262), was ill, and he acted regularly as Wingham's deputy in the following year. In 1259 he received the prebend of Kentish Town at St Paul's, which at that time was in the king's gift, and a prebend at Exeter. He later exchanged Kentish Town for another London prebend, Finsbury, and also held two prebends at Salisbury, one at Lincoln, and the archdeaconry of Bath.

He did not, however, succeed Wingham as chancellor in 1260, but was passed over in favour of Nicholas of Ely (*d.* 1280), a baronial nominee. In the course of the previous decade the king's expenditure and the extravagances of his policies had excited a movement among the baronage for administrative reform, which issued in the parliaments held at Westminster and Oxford in 1258. As a royal clerk without other affiliations Merton was naturally the king's man. The confidence the king now placed in him as a competent and reliable administrator made him unacceptable to the reformers, but a further change in Henry's fortunes brought him into office as chancellor in July 1261.

Merton's private actions over the next three years are closely related to his role in the public affairs of the kingdom. In the time of his success he no doubt felt the precariousness of his position. As early as 1240 he had founded a hospital at Basingstoke dedicated to St John, in honour of his parents, and he had since carefully built up his lands in Surrey. In 1262 he persuaded the king to take over the hospital as a royal foundation, and he assigned his manors of Malden, Chessington, and Farleigh to Merton Priory to hold in trust to support university students. To that end he obtained a confirmation from the superior lord of the fee, Richard de Clare, earl of Gloucester and Hertford, but Richard's sudden death in July 1262 left his heir Gilbert (d. 1295) a minor, and the transaction incomplete. In June 1263 Simon de Montfort (d. 1265) seized power; Merton again gave place to Nicholas of Ely, and his manors and prebendal lands were sacked by Montfort's followers. In the course of the next year the Surrey manors were formally occupied by Gilbert de Clare, who at that time was one of Montfort's supporters.

Merton continued to act for the king, accompanying Henry to Amiens in January 1264, and arguing his cause there before Louis IX (r. 1226–70). He was nevertheless able to make his peace with Montfort, who was intent upon stable government, and to recover control of his lands. At the end of August 1264 Merton realized the plans that he had been maturing, in an innovative and powerfully influential way. Instead of continuing with Merton Priory as his trustee, he founded an independent college of priests at Malden, Surrey, under a warden, endowed it with the manors of Malden and Farleigh, and charged it with the maintenance of twenty scholars at Oxford or elsewhere. The beneficiaries were to be apt for advanced studies, and they were to be recruited first from suitably qualified members of Merton's own kin, and then principally from the diocese of Winchester. What was novel was that although the college was to be subject to a visitor, the bishop of Winchester, the scholars themselves had the right and duty to scrutinize its management.

Merton did not become chancellor again when Henry recovered his authority after the battle of Evesham (4 August 1265), but he was secure in royal favour and able to give close attention to his foundation. He acquired a substantial plot of land in Oxford, including the church and churchyard of St John the Baptist, and several houses, between St John's Lane, now Merton Street, and the south wall of the city, and established his scholars there. They had previously been lodged in Bull Hall, in Pennyfarthing (later Pembroke) Street. Besides the advowson of St John's

Church he gave them the rectory of St Peter's-in-the-East, with two chapels of ease, and the manor of Holywell, which made the college an extensive landholder to the north-east and north of the city.

In 1270 Merton published new statutes for the college, elaborating the provisions of 1264, and incidentally appointing St John's Hospital, Basingstoke, as an asylum for fellows superannuated through sickness. One of the houses in St John's Street had been adapted to provide a residence for the warden, and by 1274, when Merton issued his final statutes, the whole collegiate body was assembled in Oxford. A large common hall was raised, and the church, rededicated to St John and St Mary, sumptuously rebuilt to house both the college chapel and the displaced parishioners of St John's. Over the same years Merton greatly enlarged the endowment with six further churches, one of them in Northumberland, at Ponteland, and seven manors, including a valuable property in Cambridge. He later persuaded Edmund, earl of Lancaster (d. 1296), to add the rectory of Embleton, Northumberland, to the tale.

On Henry III's death in 1272 Merton became chancellor again, and held the great seal until Edward I returned to England in 1274. In July 1274 he was elected bishop of Rochester, and in the following month he published his last statutes for the college, which refine the provisions of 1270 in a manner that reflects the successful unification of the house. He paid final visits to Oxford and to Durham in the spring and summer of 1277, and died on 27 October 1277, probably at Saleby in Lincolnshire, after an accident while fording a river. He was buried in the north transept of Rochester Cathedral in accordance with the instructions in his will, which reveal that it had been his intention, if he had died in Hampshire, to be buried beside his parents in St Michael's, Basingstoke. His Limoges enamel memorial and a commemorative window at Rochester were destroyed at the Reformation. His monument there was replaced in 1598 on the initiative of Sir Henry Savile (d. 1622), and then again, in its medieval form, in 1852. A chalice was removed from the grave and taken to Oxford in 1598.

Merton owed his career and his wealth to his administrative ability, and his experience moved him to a remarkable act of familial and public piety. His own connection with the university schools is problematic, but he worked with graduates, and evidently thought well of them. He resolved to add to their numbers, and he did so in a distinctive way. He established his college to serve both church and state by nurturing talent, and he hoped that its members would mark their success in the wider world by augmenting his benefactions, and so furthering the community that he had created. His great accomplishment was to make the house of the scholars of Merton an autonomous and self-regulating body, which became a widely accepted and long-enduring model.

G. H. MARTIN

Sources J. R. L. Highfield, ed., *The early rolls of Merton College, Oxford*, OHS, new ser., 18 (1964) · G. H. Martin and J. R. L. Highfield,

A history of Merton College, Oxford (1997) • *Chancery records* • P. S. Allen and H. W. Garrod, eds., *Merton muniments*, OHS, 86 (1928) • J. Blair, 'The Limoges enamel tomb of Walter de Merton', *Postmaster* [published by Merton College] (Sept 1994), 35–41 • *Ann. mon.*, vol. 4

Archives Merton Oxf., Merton College muniments, executors' accounts

Likenesses figure, *c.*1790, Merton Oxf.; similar painting, BL • corbel head, Merton Oxf., chapel; plaster copy, Queen's Room, Merton Oxf. • seal (as bishop of Rochester, 1274–7), Merton Oxf., Merton College records, 2871 • seal (as bishop of Rochester, 1274–7), BL; Birch, *Seals*, 2154 [*see illus.*]

Wealth at death approx. £5000: Highfield, ed., *Early rolls of Merton College*, 56–8

Mervyn [Mervin], **Sir Audley** (1603?–1675), lawyer and politician, was the second son of Sir Henry *Mervyn (*bap.* 1583, *d.* 1646), naval officer, and his wife, Christian Touchet, daughter of George Audley, first earl of Castlehaven. He matriculated from Christ Church, Oxford, on 10 June 1618. His grandfather Castlehaven had secured extensive properties under the Ulster plantation, an interest maintained by various members of the Audley and Mervyn families. By 1641 Mervyn was in possession of extensive Ulster properties, particularly in co. Tyrone, where he resided at Trillick (or Castle Touchett). On 19 June 1638 he married Mary, widow of lieutenant Francis Windsor of Ballydermot, co. Londonderry, and daughter of John Dillon of Castle Dillon, co. Armagh; they had at least one son and one daughter. He later married Martha (*d.* 1685), daughter of Sir Hugh Clotworthy of co. Antrim and his wife, Mary (*née* Langford), and sister of politician Sir John Clotworthy; they had at least two sons and one daughter. If his successive marriages linked him to other protestant New English families in Ireland, his family connections, by blood and marriage, also included Catholic families, among them the Touchetts and the Maguires. In 1640 he held the rank of captain in the new army intended by the lord lieutenant, the earl of Strafford, for service against the covenanters in Scotland.

Mervyn was elected to the Irish parliament of 1640 for co. Tyrone, and by the following year had emerged as one of the most active MPs and a leader of the parliamentary attack on Strafford's regime. On 27 February 1641 he presented the articles of impeachment against four of Strafford's associates, a move designed not merely to undermine the position of the beleagured lord lieutenant, but also to establish the illegality of recent government practices, and to assert the rights of the Irish parliament, including that of impeachment. It was a case grounded on the common powers of parliaments in England and Ireland, regardless of the lack of precedent in the latter case, a position put forward by Mervyn in speeches to parliament, subsequently published.

Following the outbreak of the 1641 rising Mervyn secured a military command among the protestant forces raised in western Ulster, rising to the rank of colonel. His brother-in-law Rory Maguire became a leading insurgent, and attempted unsuccessfully to persuade him to deliver terms from the Irish in arms; his cousin James Touchet, third earl of Castlehaven, became a general among the

Sir Audley Mervyn (1603?–1675), by unknown artist, 1660s

confederate Catholics. In 1642 he was one of a group of protestant officers who travelled to England to request supplies from Charles I and the English parliament. His report to the latter on events in Ulster in 1641–2 was published by order of the Commons as *An exact relation of all such occurrences as have happened in the several counties of … the north of Ireland* (1642). By 1643 protestant opinion in Ireland was faced with the choice between the alternative policies of the warring camps in England, with Charles I sponsoring peace negotiations with the confederate Catholics, and renewed war in Ireland being advocated by the English parliamentarians and their Scottish allies. Mervyn was named governor of Londonderry in 1644, and the royalist lord lieutenant, Ormond, looked to him to uphold Charles I's position in the north-west, including resistance to attempts to draw Ulster protestants into the solemn league and covenant. He indeed supported moves to oppose the covenant in the Irish parliament and his correspondence with Ormond shows his continued commitment to that institution, by now reduced to a protestant membership and meeting only occasionally. Back in Ulster, however, the pressure of local opinion was too strong for him as his opposition to the covenant, which he depicted as a source of division among protestants, in fact left him increasingly isolated amid an often enthusiastic reception of the covenant. He reluctantly subscribed, though he continued to profess loyalty to Ormond, attempted to gloss his acceptance of the covenant with his own interpretation, and protested the necessity of his action if he was to retain any influence in Derry.

Mervyn served in the renewed fighting in Ulster, under the banner of the English parliament. By 1648 new lines of division in the three kingdoms had opened in the aftermath of the New Model Army's intervention into politics in England, and the engagement between a faction of the Scottish covenanters (including some in Ulster) and the king. Mervyn came under suspicion at Westminster and orders were transmitted for his arrest and dispatch to England, which was duly accomplished. He was allowed to return to Ulster in May 1649, but was soon to be found active in an emerging royalist coalition directed against parliament's commander in Londonderry, Sir Charles Coote. By the summer of 1649 he was involved in negotiations on Ormond's behalf with the Ulster Catholic leader Owen Roe O'Neill. However, the arrival of Cromwellian forces in Ulster soon spelt the collapse of resistance to the newly proclaimed English Commonwealth, and Mervyn appears to have prudently moved to make terms with Coote. His activities in the 1650s are unclear. He may have been detained in 1655. In Trinity term 1658 he was admitted to King's Inns, Dublin. He was reported to have been associated in the Dublin coup of December 1659 directed against the military regime in London which had recently displaced the restored Rump Parliament.

In 1660 Mervyn was elected to the Irish convention for co. Tyrone, and in May was appointed one of twelve commissioners sent from the convention to Charles II. He was knighted and on 20 September 1660 was appointed prime serjeant-at-law in Ireland, the most senior law office but a post which perhaps held more prestige than influence by this time. Early in 1661 he was named as one of thirty-six commissioners to implement the king's declaration for the settlement of Ireland, embracing the preliminary stage in the controversial and convoluted question of a land settlement. Over the next few years he would emerge as a defender of the protestant interest, particularly on the land question. He had himself gained property as a reward for past service and acted as a trustee for the protestant '49 officers' (who sought recompense for military service before the regicide).

Elected to the 1661–6 parliament, again for co. Tyrone, Mervyn was the Commons' choice for speaker in May 1661. He spent nine months in England engaged in negotiations about the shape of the forthcoming Act of Settlement, returning to Ireland and his role as speaker in May 1662. His position as speaker was recognized as an influential one, and he resumed an old habit by publishing some of his parliamentary speeches. At the same time his legal office saw him participate in the activities of the court of claims set up to assess conflicting land claims, and a

source of concern to many protestants who feared the loss of recent acquisitions. Not surprisingly in view of his multiple roles and the possibility of personal losses, accusations of both corruption and self-interest were levelled against him. In February 1663, as speaker, he presented a series of demands from the Commons restricting the powers of commissioners charged with adjudicating land claims and articulating protestant grievances at the manner of implementing the Act of Settlement, which he dubbed 'the law of laws … the Magna Carta Hiberniae' (Prendergast, 440). His speech, duly published, caused considerable resentment, both to the lord lieutenant, Ormond, and to Charles II—Clarendon reported that he had 'never seen the King more offended' (Routledge, 301). Its notoriety saw it cited by a group of protestant malcontents as expressive of their grievances. Their unsuccessful conspiracy included an attempt to seize Dublin Castle in 1663, and Mervyn was among those subsequently suspected of involvement, though no action was taken against him. With the dissolution of parliament in 1666 his influence appears to have declined. He continued to play a role in the land courts, and is noticed practising law in a chancery case in 1671, but his later years are obscure. He died at Dublin on 24 October 1675 and was buried there in St Werburgh's Church.

Opinions concerning Mervyn, both in his own day and since, have been various, but rarely complimentary, with frequent accusations of corruption, lack of scruple, or the pursuit of self-interest above principle. There is no denying his propensity to safeguard his own position, yet there remain elements of consistency in his opinions, not least concerning the powers and rights of the parliament of Ireland. Perhaps the twists and turns of his career indicate not only an individual of some ability and resilience but also the complex dilemmas facing any individual seeking to pilot a political career through the turbulence of mid-17th century Ireland and Britain.

R. M. ARMSTRONG

Sources A. R. Hart, 'Audley Mervyn: lawyer or politician?', *Explorations in law and history*, ed. W. N. Osborough (1995), 83–105 · J. P. Prendergast, 'Some account of Sir Audley Mervyn', *TRHS*, 4 (1874), 421–54 · B. McGrath, 'A biographical dictionary of the membership of the Irish House of Commons, 1640–1641', PhD diss., University of Dublin, 1997 · *DNB* · L. J. Arnold, *The Restoration land settlement in county Dublin, 1660–1688* (1993) · M. Perceval-Maxwell, *The outbreak of the Irish rebellion of 1641* (1994) · A. Clarke, *Prelude to the Restoration in Ireland* (1999) · *CSP Ire.* · *Calendar of the Clarendon state papers preserved in the Bodleian Library*, 5: 1660–1726, ed. F. J. Routledge (1970) · *Miscellanea Genealogica et Heraldica*, new ser., 1 (1874), 423, 426 · 'Some funeral entries of Ireland', *Journal of the Association for the Preservation of the Memorials of the Dead, Ireland*, 7 (1907–9)
Likenesses portrait, 1660–69, priv. coll. [see illus.]

Mervyn, Sir Henry (*bap.* 1583, *d.* 1646), naval officer, was baptized at Rogate, Sussex, on 26 December 1583, eldest of the twelve children born to Edmund Mervyn (*d.* 1604), of Durford and Petersfield, Hampshire, and his wife, Anna (*d.* 1625x8), daughter of William Jephson of Froyle, Hampshire. He married Christian Touchet, daughter of George,

Lord Audley of Heleigh, who was created Lord Castlehaven in 1617, the year of his death, and Lucy Mervyn. On the death of his wife's grandfather Sir James Mervyn he succeeded to the Fountel Giffard estates. Two sons and five daughters reached adulthood.

Mervyn entered the navy and in 1617 was appointed admiral and captain-general of the narrow seas. His son James (d. 1641) commanded the king's ship *St Claude* under him in 1626. In 1623, as admiral in the narrow seas, he was arrested and briefly imprisoned on a charge of piracy for his seizure of a Spanish ship carrying treasure to Dunkirk, much to the displeasure of the French and Spanish ambassadors. Coinciding as it did with the infanta incident the seizure caused quite a diplomatic dispute. It was treated as piracy and only Mervyn's confession and repentance followed by his replacement as admiral calmed the situation. Earlier he had seized a Dutch East Indiaman worth £100,000 for not striking her sails to him in the narrow seas. This also was returned, on request of the ambassador of the states general of the United Provinces.

Mervyn's disgrace was temporary and by 1627 he was back in command. He was highly dissatisfied with the condition of the fleet caused by lack of finance, materials, and victuals. In December 1627 he wrote to Nicholas (Buckingham's secretary) that soon he would have more ships than men, 'all the ships are so infectious that I fear if we hold the sea a month we shall not bring men enough home to moor the ships' (Oppenheim, 231). Mervyn commanded the *St George* in the Ré fleet but was weather-bound at Yarmouth and therefore escaped the indignities of that particular expedition. In 1629, again in command in the narrow seas, Mervyn listed the seamen's complaints: 'These neglects be the cause that mariners fly to the service of foreign nations to avoid His Majesty's'. In the same year he also wrote to the lords of the admiralty that 'Foul weather, naked bodies & empty bellies make the men voice the King's service worse than a galley slave' (ibid., 235). This concern with the welfare of the seamen was a constant thread in his writings and one that failed to endear him to naval administration.

By 1630 Mervyn was considering his future and entered negotiations with Sir Kenholm Digby for the sale of his command of the narrow seas. For this he wanted £5,000 arrears plus £3,000 to compensate for his original purchase. The negotiations were fruitless and by August 1630 he was again in command in the narrow seas. He asked for the appointment of Sir John Mennes to the fleet so that he would have at least one captain who had 'passed his A B C' (Oppenheim, 287).

As rear-admiral in the 1636 fleet Mervyn commanded the *James* and managed to force some fishing licences on Dutch busses. This was one of the fleet's few successes. Mervyn served as rear-admiral again in 1637 (on the *Bonaventure*) and in 1638 (on the *Victory*) but refused reappointment in 1639. In the same year he decided to sue the king for unpaid wages. Northumberland's secretary, Thomas Smith, was determined that this suit would not succeed. Shortly after his decision to sue the king, and possibly as a

result of Smith's hostility, Mervyn decided to retire to Trillick Castle together with his son Audley *Mervyn. He took no further part in naval affairs.

Mervyn's son James died on 12 July 1641 and was buried at Dublin; Audley then became heir to his father. He settled in Ireland, where he attained eminence in the law, and in 1661 was elected speaker of the Irish House of Commons. Sir Henry Mervyn died at Trillick, in late May or early June 1646. He was an active and capable admiral who at all times showed concern for the health and material comfort of his seamen and the professionalism of his officers. Unlike many of his colleagues in the navy he was never tainted by the endemic corruption of a navy that served him poorly.   ROY McCAUGHEY

Sources CSP dom. · *The naval tracts of Sir William Monson*, ed. M. Oppenheim, 5 vols., Navy RS, 22–3, 43, 45, 47 (1902–14) · M. Oppenheim, *A history of the administration of the Royal Navy* (1896) · DNB · IGI · A. P. McGowan, 'The Royal Navy under the first duke of Buckingham', PhD diss., U. Lond., 1971 · *The autobiography of Phineas Pett*, ed. W. G. Perrin, Navy RS, 51 (1918) · G. E. Manwaring and W. G. Perrin, eds., *The life and works of Sir Henry Mainwaring*, 2 vols., Navy RS, 54, 56 (1920–22) · G. E. Aylmer, *The king's servants: the civil service of Charles I, 1625–1642*, rev. edn (1974) · C. E. Fayle, 'The ship-money fleets', *EdinR*, 234 (1921), 375–89 · F. E. Dyer, 'The ship money fleet', *Mariner's Mirror*, 23 (1937), 198–209 · *Miscellanea Genealogica et Heraldica*, new ser., 1 (1874), 422–3

Meryon, Charles Lewis (1783–1877), physician, son of Lewis Meryon of Rye in Sussex, of an old Huguenot family, was born on 27 June 1783. He was the uncle of Edward *Meryon (bap. 1807, d. 1880). Meryon was educated at Merchant Taylors' School, London, from 1796 to 1802, and obtained a Stuart's exhibition to St John's College, Oxford; he matriculated on 29 March 1803, and graduated BA in 1806, MA in 1809, and BM and DM in 1817. He studied medicine at St Thomas's Hospital, London, under Henry Cline, on whose recommendation he was in 1810 engaged to accompany Lady Hester Stanhope, as her medical attendant, on a voyage to Sicily and the Middle East. He travelled with her for seven years, saw her finally settled at Mount Lebanon, and then returned to England in 1817 to take his medical degrees.

Meryon married shortly after his return and pursued his medical career. He was admitted as a candidate of the Royal College of Physicians on 26 June 1820, and as a fellow on 25 June 1821. Shortly afterwards he became domestic physician to Sir Gilbert Heathcote, but in 1827, at the earnest request of Lady Hester, he set out once more for Syria and Lebanon in company with his wife. They were attacked and plundered *en route* by pirates off Crete, and returned to Leghorn in Italy, where Mrs Meryon was unwilling to continue with their journey. The couple returned to England in 1828 but soon set out again; they arrived at Mount Lebanon in 1830. Lady Hester was then at the zenith of her power, and Meryon subsequently described with the utmost minuteness her complicated living arrangements, her tyranny, and her interminable conversations and cross-questionings, of which he himself was often a victim. Owing to disagreements, chiefly resulting from Lady Hester's intolerance of his wife,

Charles Lewis Meryon (1783–1877), by Arminius Meyer, c.1846

Meryon left Mount Lebanon in April 1831 and spent several years living in Nice. But along with his wife and daughter Eugenia he paid Lady Hester a final visit between 1837 and August 1838. After finally settling in London he published his *Memoirs of the Lady Hester Stanhope* (3 vols.), in 1845. Although published earlier the *Memoirs* are in reality a sequel to the scarcely less entertaining *Travels of Lady Hester Stanhope* (2 vols., 1846). His relationship with Narcisse Chaspoux, a French ballet dancer, produced a son, also named Charles Meryon (1821–1867). Meryon died in London on 11 September 1877, at his home, 88 The Grove, Hammersmith, aged ninety-four.

THOMAS SECCOMBE, *rev.* MICHAEL BEVAN

Sources V. Childs, *Lady Hester Stanhope* (1990) · Foster, *Alum. Oxon.* · C. J. Robinson, ed., *A register of the scholars admitted into Merchant Taylors' School, from AD 1562 to 1874*, 2 (1883), 166 · Munk, *Roll* · Allibone, *Dict.* · *CGPLA Eng. & Wales* (1878)

Archives Bodl. Oxf., corresp. | Wellcome L., corresp., incl. letters to Lady Hester Stanhope · Wellcome L., papers interleaved in volume of travels of Lady Hester Stanhope

Likenesses A. Meyer, oils, c.1846, RCP Lond. [*see illus.*] · photograph (as an old man), BM · portrait, repro. in [C. L. Meryon], *Travels of Lady Hester Stanhope* (1846), 3

Wealth at death under £5000: resworn probate, 29 Sept 1878, *CGPLA Eng. & Wales*

Meryon, Edward (*bap.* 1807, *d.* 1880), physician, was baptized in Rye, Sussex, on 10 December 1807, the son of John Meryon (*bap.* 1776, *d.* 1857), harbour commissioner, merchant, and innkeeper, who was descended from a Huguenot family who emigrated to England from France about 1682, and Jane Gatland or Gateland (*bap.* 1787, *d.* 1858), of Rye, spinster and dressmaker. He was the nephew of Charles Lewis Meryon (1783–1877). Edward's parents never married and little is known of his early life. However, in 1829 he entered the newly established London University to study medicine, where he was an outstanding student, gaining many distinctions and prizes. Between 1830 and 1831 he was apprenticed to Frederick Bellingham, an apothecary. In 1831 Meryon became a member of the Royal College of Surgeons and a licentiate of the Society of Apothecaries, London. Meryon married Catherine Baily (*bap.* 1811, *d.* 1897) of Falkingham, Lincolnshire, on 5 February 1833 and the couple had four daughters—Lucy Elizabeth (*b.* 1834), Anne (*b.* 1835), Julia (*b.* 1841), Evelyn Jane (*b.* 1846)—followed by a son, John Edward (1851–1896).

In 1836 Meryon published *The Physical and Intellectual Constitution of Man Considered* and in 1838 he went into partnership with Thomas Wood, surgeon, at 4 Bolton Street. In 1840 Meryon became one of the founder members of the Microscopical Society of London. Two years later he was appointed lecturer in comparative anatomy at St Thomas's Hospital, London, and in 1844 was awarded an MD degree from the University of London. Meryon gradually established himself as a respected physician with a special interest in nervous and muscle diseases. In 1846 he was elected a fellow of the Royal Medical and Chirurgical Society of London (later to become the Royal Society of Medicine). In 1850 he became a member of the Athenaeum and had his portrait painted by John Linnell. It was exhibited that year at the Royal Academy.

In December 1851 Meryon presented a paper, 'On granular and fatty degeneration of the voluntary muscles', at a meeting of the Royal Medical and Chirurgical Society. This was published in the *Transactions* of the society the following year (*Medico-Chirurgical Transactions*, 35, 1852, 73–84). Some years later he expanded his observations in a chapter of his book, *Practical and Pathological Researches on the Various Forms of Paralysis* (1864). In these two publications he reported his studies on several extensive families with a disease subsequently to be referred to as Duchenne muscular dystrophy after Duchenne de Boulogne (1806–1875), who described the disease some years later. In fact Edward Meryon was the first to make a systematic and detailed study of the disease. He showed that the disorder affected only males, was familial, essentially a disease of muscle and *not* the nervous system because he demonstrated that the spinal cord was normal, and finally, based on his microscopic observations, he concluded that the basic defect was a breakdown of the muscle fibre membrane (sarcolemma). These observations were made many years before Duchenne and others. In fact it was some 135 years later that the basic defect was proved to be the absence of the muscle fibre membrane protein dystrophin.

Several factors might account for the fact that Meryon's contributions went unrecognized at the time of their publication. His paper presented to the Royal Medical and Chirurgical Society, and later published in the *Transactions* of the society in 1852, was a relatively brief article running to just twelve pages. This was enlarged into a short chapter (fifteen pages) in his *Practical and Pathological Researches*. By comparison, Duchenne's main contributions on muscular dystrophy were published in several very extensive papers (totalling 124 pages) in a single year, 1868. In addition, Duchenne incorrectly dismissed Meryon's publication of 1852 as describing cases of 'progressive muscular atrophy', a neurogenic disorder, rather than muscular dystrophy, a disease of muscle. This misinterpretation by Duchenne was perpetuated by later researchers, and though corrected in a publication in 1879 by Sir William Gowers, Meryon's contribution never gained the recognition given to Duchenne for having first described childhood muscular dystrophy. Duchenne was perhaps also a better publicist of his findings than Meryon.

Meryon was elected a fellow of the Geological Society in 1857, and a fellow of the Royal College of Physicians in 1859. In 1861 he published a first volume of *The History of Medicine*, but planned further volumes were never completed. He was a council member of the Geological Society (1862–4) and vice-president 1865 and the following year published some further observations, in his 'On granular degeneration of the voluntary muscles' (*The Lancet*, 1, 1866, 258–60).

In 1869 Meryon was elected vice-president of the Royal Medical and Chirurgical Society. From this time his main hospital appointment was as physician to the newly established London Infirmary for Epilepsy and Paralysis, which eventually moved to Portland Terrace, Regent's Park, as the Hospital for Diseases of the Nervous System.

Meryon's *On the functions of the sympathetic system of nerves, as a physiological basis for a rational system of therapeutics* (1872) drew heavily in the first part on the work of the celebrated French physiologist Claude Bernard (1813–1878). In the second part, however, Meryon emphasized the possible future role of the system in therapy, prescient by some fifty years of subsequent work on neurotransmission. In 1875 he was elected to the council of the Royal College of Physicians. About this time he also wrote a play, partly in verse, entitled *The Huguenot* (1876), a historical romance between a young Catholic girl and her childhood love who was a Huguenot, set in France in 1572 at the time of the St Bartholomew's day massacre.

Meryon resigned his hospital appointment owing to ill health in 1879 and died on 8 November 1880 at his home, 14 Clarges Street, Piccadilly, London, from heart disease and gout. He was buried at Brompton cemetery, London, on 12 November. His obituaries demonstrate that he was a much-liked and respected physician. Meryon bequeathed everything to his wife, Catherine, the estate being valued at less than £4000.

ALAN E. H. EMERY and MARCIA L. H. EMERY

Sources A. E. H. Emery, 'Duchenne muscular dystrophy—Meryon's disease', *Neuromuscular Disorders*, 3 (1993), 263–6 · A. E. H. Emery and M. L. H. Emery, 'Edward Meryon and muscular dystrophy', *Journal of Medical Genetics*, 30 (1993), 506–11 · A. E. H. Emery and M. L. H. Emery, 'Edward Meryon's contribution to muscular dystrophy', *The history of a genetic disease* (1995), 25–48 · A. E. H. Emery and M. L. H. Emery, 'The life of Edward Meryon', *The history of a genetic disease* (1995), 49–66 · A. E. H. Emery and M. L. H. Emery, 'Edward Meryon (1807–1880): his life and Huguenot background', *Journal of Medical Biography*, 6 (1998), 1–10
Likenesses J. Linnell, oils, 1850, priv. coll.
Wealth at death under £4000: probate, 1880

Merz, Charles Hesterman (1874–1940), electrical engineer, was born at Gateshead on 5 October 1874, the eldest child of John Theodore Merz, a naturalized British subject of German descent, who was an industrial chemist and author of *A History of European Thought in the Nineteenth Century* (1896–1914). His mother was Alice Mary, daughter of Edward Richardson, a well-known Quaker of Newcastle upon Tyne. Charles Merz, his two brothers, and his sister, were brought up in a highly intellectual atmosphere at The Quarries, Benwell, Newcastle upon Tyne, the home of the Merz family.

Owing to his mother's Quaker connection, Merz was educated at Bootham School, York, after which he studied at the Armstrong College (later King's College), Newcastle upon Tyne. In 1892 he went as a pupil to the Pandon Dene generating station of the Newcastle upon Tyne Electric Supply Company (NESCo), which had been founded in 1889 by his father and Robert Spence Watson, who had married his mother's sister. In 1894 he became a pupil at the Robey engineering works in Lincoln. He then went to the Bankside station of the City of London Electric Lighting Company, superintending contracts for the British Thomson-Houston Company (BTH), manufacturers of electrical plant, of which company his father was at that time a director. At the age of twenty-three he was appointed manager and engineer to operate the plant which BTH had provided for electricity supply in Croydon. So successful was he in this that he was given charge of a similar and larger contract at Cork, which also included tramways. Here he came into contact with William McLellan, who in 1902 became his partner in the well-known firm of Merz and McLellan, consultative electrical engineers (established first at Newcastle upon Tyne and later also in London), until McLellan's death in 1934.

Charles Merz's principal claim to fame as an electrical engineer rests on his innovations for electricity supply in Britain. He designed Neptune Bank, a Tyneside power station, the first in Britain to supply three-phase current for public supply. It was opened by Lord Kelvin in 1901. Merz next designed the Carville power station, commissioned in 1904, also on the Tyne. This was widely recognized as the first large generating station of the modern type and it established his engineering reputation. His paper 'Power station design', written with W. McLellan and presented at the Institution of Electrical Engineers (IEE), was published in the institution's *Journal* (74, 1904, 697). It explained his principles of design to achieve economy of production and reliability of supply. In the same paper he identified the need for further development:

> Since the early days of the distribution of electrical energy an amount of attention has been directed to the Power Station as compared with the Distribution System which is hardly warranted by its importance from either an engineering or a commercial standpoint.

He recognized before anyone else that in Britain, with

industries concentrated in certain areas, such as the north-east, public electricity supply needed to be cheaper and more reliable than private electricity. To capture this market Merz conceived the idea of interconnecting several power stations by high voltage. This would greatly reduce the number of power stations compared to independent operation, improve reliability, and allow the most economical stations to supply most electricity. However, Merz saw that such an interconnection would, under fault conditions, cause major damage unless the faulty transmission or component could be isolated automatically and quickly. His novel solution, with Bernard Price, was the invention of balanced protection, which led to many later developments in system protection technology. With system protection Merz was free to develop a new transmission system for NESCo to supply electricity cheaper than any other British undertaking. In 1916, in an IEE discussion on the electricity supply of Great Britain, Merz described the principle of an interconnected system with its many advantages.

Merz married on 18 June 1913 Stella Alice Pauline Byrne de Satur (*b*. 1883/4), daughter of Edmond Charles R. Byrne de Satur, artist of Dublin; they had a son and a daughter. In the First World War Merz served the government diligently, and chaired the subcommittee on electricity power supply. From this time he believed that Britain needed a new electricity supply system to replace the many small uneconomic undertakings still in use. In 1926, in a technical report to the Weir committee, he outlined the concept, economic feasibility, and practicality of an efficient national transmission system, later known as the national grid. Merz made many visits to the United States, India, South Africa, South America, and Australia, promoting power supply and railway electrification. These visits helped to retain for Britain a large share of overseas electrical developments.

A photograph of Merz in 1903 shows him standing with Lord Kelvin and George Westinghouse. He was then twenty-nine, of middle height, clean-shaven, and of average build. His later formal portrait, painted in 1944, after his death, shows him little changed, but with the same modest and self-confident air.

Before technical committees Merz was a superb expert witness, calm, collected, lucid, accurate, and penetrating. These characteristics were conspicuously in evidence during the protracted proceedings of the Administrative County of London Electric Power Bill in 1904–5, when he was only thirty years of age. After passing all committee stages the bill failed through lack of parliamentary time, and a great opportunity for consolidating the chaotic London position was lost.

Although Merz was a vice-president of the IEE (1912–15), his dislike of public speaking restrained him from accepting nomination for the presidency. He greatly valued the bestowal (1931) of the Faraday medal by the institution, the honorary degree of DSc (1932) from Durham University, and the vice-presidency of the Royal Institution. He characteristically declined all pecuniary recompense or titular honours in respect of his work for the government.

Merz, his two children, and two servants, were killed by an enemy bomb at his home, 14 Melbury Road, Kensington, London, on the night of 14–15 October 1940. The house was completely demolished, only Mrs Merz escaping, though injured. In the field of electricity supply Merz ranks as the premier electrical engineer in the first half of the twentieth century.

R. A. S. Redmayne, *rev.* Albert Snow

Sources J. R. B., *Journal of the Institution of Electrical Engineers*, 87 (1940), 708–10 · J. Rowland, *Progress in power* (1960) · A. Snow, 'The role of electrical power transmission systems in Britain, 1875–1948', PhD diss., Open University, 1995 · C. H. Merz, discussion on 'The electricity supply of Great Britain', *Journal of the Institution of Electrical Engineers*, 54 (1916), 588 · C. H. Merz and W. McLellan, *National electricity supply technical scheme* (1926) · C. H. Merz and W. McLellan, 'Power station design', *Journal of the Institution of Electrical Engineers*, 33 (1903–4), 696–746, esp. 691 · A. Snow, 'The first national grid', *Journal of the Institution of Electrical Engineers*, 2/5 (1993), 215–24 · J. N. Waite, 'NESCo, forerunner of the grid', *Electrical Industries* (April 1951), 98 · R. M. Black, *The history of electrical wires and cables* (1983), 198 · 'Electric power supply at Newcastle-upon-Tyne', *The Electrician* (21 June 1901), 319 · L. Hannah, *Electricity before nationalisation: a study in the development of the electricity supply industry in Britain to 1948* (1979) · personal knowledge (1949)
Archives Inst. EE, corresp. and papers · Institution of Mechanical Engineers, London, volume of autobiographical notes · U. Newcastle, Robinson L., notes for a memoir
Likenesses A. Mason, oils, 1944 (posthumous), Inst. EE · photographs, repro. in Rowland, *Progress in power*
Wealth at death £200,480 13s. 11d.: probate, 29 Jan 1941, CGPLA Eng. & Wales

Meschin, William le (*d.* 1129x35). *See under* Ranulf (I), third earl of Chester (*d.* 1129).

Mesmes, Jean-Antoine de, count of Avaux in the French nobility (1640–1709), diplomat, was the fourth son of Jean-Antoine de Mesmes, count of Avaux (*d.* 1673), president of the French parliament, and his wife, Anne Courtin. He was the nephew of Claude de Mesmes, count of Avaux (1595–1650), the most distinguished diplomat of his day. Avaux joined Louis XIV's service young, and was ambassador at Venice from 1672 to 1674. In 1675 he was the French plenipotentiary at the congress of Nijmegen and on his return in 1678 he was appointed ambassador to the Netherlands, a post he held for ten years. Saint-Simon wrote of Avaux: 'He was a very good looking and elegant man, and gallant. He was honourable, very aristocratic, charming, noble and very courteous' (Saint-Simon, 3.43). The count was recalled to Paris in November 1688 after William III invaded England. Louis appointed him an extraordinary ambassador to King James, whom he accompanied to Ireland in March 1689.

Avaux was entrusted with half a million livres, 300,000 of which were to be put at James's disposal, and the remainder of which were to form a secret fund to be spent at his own discretion. His instructions were to look after French interests in Ireland, to ensure that James acted prudently, and to send frequent reports back to France. The archive of his candid correspondence provides the most detailed account of the first year of the civil war in

Ireland. From the outset he noted that 'our chief difficulty will be the irresolution of King James, who often changes his mind and then decides not always for the best' (Hogan, 1.23), and that in Ireland it 'takes three days to get done what in France would take one' (ibid., 1.27).

James placed Avaux with Richard Talbot, duke of Tyrconnell, and John Drummond, earl of Melfort, on a three-man council, from where Avaux exerted great influence in the running of the country. Whereas James aimed to re-establish himself in England, Avaux saw French interests would be better served by establishing Ireland as a French satellite. To this end he cultivated Tyrconnell, who he felt was sympathetic, and assisted in the dismissal of Melfort, who he felt was not. When an English army was expected in the north, James rejected Avaux's advice to disarm and arrest the protestants in the chief towns as a precaution, and to disperse the prisoners in small parties throughout the country. Avaux argued that the 'pity shown to the protestants would be an act of cruelty on the catholics' (Hogan, 1.379). He was unjustly accused by Macaulay, in his *History of England* (chap. 14), of advocating a general massacre. This difference of objectives strained his relationship with James: 'The king was dissatisfied with his haughty and disrespectful manner of conducting himself' (Berwick, 59).

Avaux was recalled following a court intrigue at Versailles mounted by his replacement, Count Lauzun, who was held in high esteem by Mary of Modena, and who was able to use Avaux's criticism of James against him. In order to get veteran French troops sent to Ireland, Avaux proposed that a French brigade be exchanged for a larger brigade of Irish recruits who could be trained in France. He devoted his last three months in Ireland to recruiting the regiments which he was to take with him.

On 12 March 1690 Lauzun arrived in Ireland with the promised French brigade, and on 8 April 1690 Avaux sailed from Cork. With him went Justin MacCarthy and the six thousand men who proved to be the first regiments of the Irish brigade which endured as a distinct formation in the French army for the next hundred years. Avaux served from 1692 until 1699 as ambassador to Sweden. His last posting was in 1701 when he was again appointed Louis's ambassador to Holland. He never married. He died in Paris on 10 February (new style) 1709.

PIERS WAUCHOPE

Sources *Négociations de M. le Comte d'Avaux en Irlande, 1689–90*, ed. J. Hogan, 2 vols., IMC (1934–58) · Marquis MacSwiney of Mashanaglass, 'Some unpublished letters of the Count d'Avaux in the National Library of Ireland', *Proceedings of the Royal Irish Academy*, 40C (1931–2), 296–307 · D. C. de Kavanagh Boulger, *The battle of the Boyne* (1911) · D. C. Boulger, 'The charge against Count d'Avaux', *The Athenaeum* (9 Dec 1911), 732–3 · J. J. Jusserand, ed., *Recueil des instructions données aux ambassadeurs et ministres de France*, 25 (1929), 421–50 · F.-A. de La Chenaye-Desbois, *Dictionnaire de la noblesse: contenant les généalogies, l'histoire et la chronologie des familles nobles de la France*, 3rd edn, 19 vols. (Paris, 1863–76); repr. (1969) · L. de Rouvray, duc de Saint-Simon Vermandois, *Mémoires*, ed. G. Truc (1964) · J. Fitzjames [Duke of Berwick], *Mémoires du maréchal de Berwick*, 2 vols. (Paris, 1778) · J. Balteau and others, eds., *Dictionnaire de biographie française*, 1 (Paris, 1933), pt 1, pp. 838–42

Archives BL, letters and papers, index of MSS, VII, 1985 · PRO, official corresp. and papers, FO 95/543–578 | Archives du Ministère des Affaires Étrangères, Paris, papers · Archives Nationales, Paris, ministère de la guerre papers

Mess, Henry Adolphus (1884–1944), social worker and sociologist, was born on 9 June 1884 at 10 Grayling Terrace, Stoke Newington, London, the son of Henry Adolphus Mess, a commercial clerk, and his wife, Mary Ann Thornton. He was educated at Bancroft's School, Woodford, and at Birkbeck College, where he obtained an external BA degree (1901–5). He then studied for an MA degree in English (1906–9) at King's College, London. Mess spent seven years, from 1912 to 1919, in the East End of London as secretary of the Mansfield House University Settlement, in the dockland area of Canning Town. While there he wrote *Casual Labour at the Docks* (1916), an account of the casual labour system and its effects on the dockers in Canning Town, and *The Facts of Poverty* (1920), in which he tries to define poverty, drawing on his experiences at Mansfield House.

Mess left Mansfield House in 1919 to become social study secretary of the Student Christian Movement. In 1920 he married Sofie, daughter of Captain H. N. Hansen; they had two sons and one daughter. He was much concerned with the social message of Christianity, and published a pamphlet, *Outline Studies in the Christian Gospel for Society* (1923), to help students to discover how the gospels threw light on the social problems of the age. In *The Message of C.O.P.E.C.* (1924) he summarized the reports submitted to the conference on Christian politics, economics, and citizenship, held in Birmingham in April 1924. While with the Student Christian Movement he worked on a study of factory legislation, published as *Factory Legislation and its Administration, 1891–1924* (1926), in a series by writers connected with the London School of Economics, in which he acknowledges his debt to R. H. Tawney. He stressed that industry was more dangerous in 1924 than in 1891, and urged the government to reduce the high accident rate by bringing in safety legislation. From 1924 to 1925 Mess was lecturer in social science to the Lancashire and Yorkshire Congregational unions. In 1926 he was awarded an external PhD degree from King's College, London, in economics. He then became a research scholar at the London School of Economics.

Mess was appointed director of the new bureau of social research for Tyneside in 1925. It was set up by a group of Christians who believed that accurate information about social conditions was needed in order to tackle the social problems of Tyneside. Mess spent three years collecting information before publishing *Industrial Tyneside* (1928), a study of the eleven municipal districts along both sides of the Tyne as they had changed over the previous century, with recommendations for the future. He paints a grim picture of poor housing, poor health, poor education, and high unemployment. At the same time he organized courses of lectures and discussion groups for clergy and social workers, and the publication of a series of 'Tyneside papers' on such topics as the pollution of the Tyne estuary, infant welfare in Tyneside, tuberculosis in Tyneside, and unemployment at the shipyards. In 1929 the Tyneside Council of Social Service, with Mess as director, took over from the bureau.

In 1935 Mess was appointed reader in sociology at the University of London, attached to Bedford College, a position he held until his death. He published *Social Groups in Modern England* (1940), and *Social Structure* (1942). His most important work, *Voluntary Social Services since 1918* (1947), was planned in the early years of the war, when he realized that the statutory social services would grow rapidly after the war. Addressing the question of whether the voluntary social services had outlived their usefulness, he wanted to show what they had achieved between the wars, to make sure that there would still be a role for them in the post-war world. Mess died after writing three chapters and starting on three more, and the book was expanded and completed by his colleague at Bedford College, Gertrude Williams, who invited other sociologists to contribute chapters.

Mess became part-time director of studies to the National Council of Social Service in 1942. He wrote *Dispersal* (1944), which grew out of a study for the Bank of England of the experience of the wartime evacuation of bank staff, and he began to collect data for a study of the social problems of small towns. The material he had collected by his death was later published as *The Size and Social Structure of a Town* (1953), and was an important influence on post-war planning. Henry Mess died from pneumonia on 23 January 1944 in a London nursing home, Granard House, 98 Dovehouse Street, Fulham Road, London, and was survived by his wife.   ANNE PIMLOTT BAKER

Sources M. Brasnett, *Voluntary social action: a history of the National Council of Social Service, 1919–1969* (1969), 121–3 · G. Williams, foreword, in H. Mess, *Voluntary social services since 1918* (1947) · *Newcastle Journal* (24 Jan 1944) · *The Times* (25 Jan 1944) · WWW · CGPLA Eng. & Wales (1944) · b. cert. · d. cert.
Likenesses photograph, repro. in *Newcastle Journal*
Wealth at death £821 17s. 10d.: probate, 18 May 1944, CGPLA Eng. & Wales

Messel, Oliver Hilary Sambourne (1904–1978), artist and stage designer, was born on 13 January 1904 at 27 Gloucester Terrace, Hyde Park, London, the youngest of the three children of Lieutenant-Colonel Leonard Charles Rudolph Messel (1872–1953), of Nymans, Cuckfield, Sussex, a soldier and stockbroker of German extraction, and his wife, Maud Frances (1875–1960), daughter of the artist Edward Linley *Sambourne (1844–1910). Theirs was an artistic, fashionable, and moneyed milieu, with no material wants, in which Oliver as a young child came to meet collectors, actors, artists, and museum curators. Influences from such people of culture and vivacity helped to direct his life, as did the effect on him of his family's varied domestic surroundings, principal among which were their two Sussex country houses, Balcombe House and Nymans (now in the hands of the National Trust). The painter Glyn Philpot was a particularly influential figure to Messel from an early age, teaching him to observe and

to draw, and encouraging him in his early attempts at stage design. In the 1920s Philpot and Messel travelled regularly on the continent together.

Between 1917 and 1921 Messel was at Eton College but, having determined from childhood to be an artist, he left early to enter the Slade School of Fine Art, under Henry Tonks. There he impressed his teachers and friends by the masks worn at student parties that he modelled from wax and papier mâché. This light-hearted affair soon burgeoned into the revival of the ancient art of theatrical mask-making. In 1925 Messel held an exhibition of his masks at the Claridge Galleries in London, which awakened considerable interest and led to his first professional commission—to decorate with masks a scene from the ballet *Zephyr and Flora*, directed by Georges Braque at the London Coliseum. C. B. Cochran, alert as ever to young talent, engaged Messel to design masks for his *Cochran's Revue* at the London Pavilion in 1926. They revealed early proof of their creator's flair for suggesting diverse periods and nationalities, which he later developed in designs for opera, ballet, and the cinema.

For the rest of the 1920s Messel contributed designs for costume and scenery to a succession of Cochran revues, of which perhaps the most notable is his setting for Noël Coward's song 'Dance, Dance, Little Lady', from *This Year of Grace* (1928). In Messel's *mise en scène* each performer was masked to exhibit a vapid and fundamentally unhappy visage, reflecting facets of society at that period.

In 1932 Messel embarked on two highly ambitious theatrical ventures with Cochran, making designs that were among the most distinguished of his career. For the revival of *Helen!* (Adelphi Theatre, 1932), directed by Max Reinhardt, he contrived a beautiful and imaginative decor, draping the bedroom and bathroom scenes almost wholly in white and clothing Helen herself (played by Evelyn Laye) entirely in white for the final scene. The set received an ovation every night. For Reinhardt's *The Miracle* (Lyceum Theatre, 1932) he was responsible for the costume. Though inevitably restricted in what was a version of a medieval mystery play he managed to insert doses of fantasy, for example in the forest scene, with its macabre 'personalized' trees, and in the costumes for the banquet scene—diverse but always kept within their medieval patterns.

By the end of 1932 Messel was established as one of the foremost stage designers in Britain and his name became as great a draw for a production as that of any star actor. During the Second World War, while a captain in the camouflage corps in Norwich 'designing frightfully pretty baroque pill boxes' (Lord Snowdon, in Castle, 114), he saved and restored the city's assembly rooms when the building was requisitioned as a camouflage school.

Messel's talents in later years were stimulated by the development of a new strain in contemporary poetical drama exemplified by his designs for Christopher Fry's *Ring around the Moon* (Globe Theatre, 1950). In opera his designs for *The Magic Flute* (Covent Garden, 1947), *Queen of Spades* (Covent Garden, 1950), and *Der Rosenkavalier*

(Glyndebourne, 1959) gave his imaginative fantasy full scope. For ballet his designs had the rare quality of furthering as well as decorating the dramatic action, a technique particularly noticeable in the scenery for *Francesca da Rimini* (Covent Garden and New York, 1937), which was adapted from early Renaissance paintings. His scenery for the revival in 1946 of *Sleeping Beauty*, in London and New York, was a major contribution to its success also.

Between 1934 and 1959 Messel designed costume and sets for films, notably *Romeo and Juliet* (for which he was nominated for two Oscars in 1936), *Caesar and Cleopatra* (directed by George Cukor, 1946), and *Suddenly Last Summer* (directed by J. L. Mankiewitz, 1959). In 1956 he was made a fellow of University College, London, and in 1958 he was appointed CBE.

At the beginning of their careers in the early 1920s both Messel and Rex Whistler were confronted in the theatre, and to a lesser extent in opera and ballet, with a general standard of decor that was competent but unimaginative. Naturalism was then at a premium with theatrical management, and theatre design in London and the regions tended to reproduce upper-class late-Victorian and Edwardian domestic backgrounds. Working independently and in different styles, Messel and Whistler changed all that and raised the standard of stage decor into an eclectic and well-appreciated art. Essentially Messel's decoration suggested baroque, Whistler's rococo. In 1982 the earl of Snowdon, Messel's nephew, lent for an indefinite period to the Theatre Museum, London, the Oliver Messel collection, comprising masks, head-dresses and costumes, models and maquettes, and designs and drawings for virtually every production that Messel had undertaken.

Messel was charming, hospitable, the host of spectacular parties. He was short and immaculately dressed, with dark hair, sparkling eyes, and an elf-like smile that was a lifelong characteristic. He giggled a great deal and could cry at will—an extrovert, emotional quality that had its dark side, when he could be angry, moody, temperamental, and the author of sudden, vehement letters. He gradually withdrew from theatre design in London in the late 1950s as the fashion for 'kitchen-sink drama', in the wake of John Osborne's *Look Back in Anger* (Royal Court Theatre, 1956), began to change theatrical perspective as fundamentally as Messel himself had done in the 1930s. He designed productions for the Metropolitan Opera House in New York, including *The Marriage of Figaro* (1959) and *Ariadne auf Naxos* (1962); he designed a shoe shop, Raynes, in Old Bond Street, London (1959); and he oversaw the redecoration of Flaxley Abbey, Gloucestershire (1962–3).

More significantly, however, Messel fell in love with Barbados, where he moved in 1966 and spent the last twelve years of his life with his long-term companion and manager, Vagn Riis-Hansen. In Barbados he reinvented himself as an architect, designing and decorating houses for private clients, and on nearby Mustique as the architect to the island's owner, the Hon. Colin Tennant. He became beset by ill health and severe financial problems, and died at the home that he had designed for himself—Maddox, St James, Barbados—on 13 July 1978. His ashes are buried in the magnolia garden at Nymans.

D. Pepys-Whiteley, rev. James Hamilton

Sources *DNB* · C. Castle, *Oliver Messel: a biography* (1986) · C. W. H. Beaton and R. Pinkham, *Oliver Messel* (1983) [exh. cat., Theatre Museum, London] · *The Times* (15 July 1978) · *The Times* (21 July 1978) · O. Messel, *Stage designs and costumes* (1933) · J. Laver, *Between the wars* (1961) · J. Laver, *Costume in the theatre* (1964) · private information (2004) · b. cert.
Archives Theatre Museum, London | priv. coll., Thomas Messel collection
Likenesses C. Beaton, photographs, NPG · Snowdon, photographs, NPG
Wealth at death died in debt

Messel, Rudolph (1848–1920), industrial chemist, was born on 14 January 1848 in Darmstadt, the second of five children of Simon Messel, banker and his wife, Amelia. After his father died in 1859 he was sent to a Huguenot school in Friedrichsdorf. He attended the federal polytechnic in Zürich, then studied under Emil Erlenmeyer in Heidelberg, and finally received a DSc studying chemistry under Adolf Strecker in Tübingen. In 1870 he went to Manchester and became assistant first to Frederick Grace Calvert (1819–1873) and then to Henry Roscoe (1833–1915).

At the outbreak of the Franco-Prussian War in July 1870 Messel was recalled to Germany; he served as a stretcher-bearer in the army of the Loire and was wounded. After his recovery he returned to England, where he remained for the rest of his life. He applied for naturalization in 1907 at the age of fifty-nine and took the oath of allegiance on 6 May that year.

Messel became assistant to William Stevens Squire (1834–1906) of Dunn, Squire & Co., initially at Stratford in Essex, then at Silvertown, also in Essex. Shortly afterwards, Squire formed the company Squire, Chapman & Co., and took Messel with him. Messel developed a form of the contact or catalytic process for the manufacture of fuming sulphuric acid, in great demand as a raw material in the dyestuffs industry. The key to the process was the combination of pure sulphur dioxide and oxygen gases using a platinized pumice catalyst. One of Messel's important contributions was his study of the catalytic reaction and the poisoning of the platinum catalyst. The process was patented by Squire in 1875, and Squire and Messel described and demonstrated it before the Chemical Society the following April. Clemens Winkler in Germany simultaneously developed a similar process, but acknowledged the independence of Messel's work. In 1878 Messel succeeded Squire as managing director of the firm which became Spencer, Chapman, and Messel Ltd. He resigned in 1915 owing to ill health.

Messel was a founder member of the Society of Chemical Industry (1881), was its foreign secretary for a number of years from 1910, and served as its president in 1911–12 and 1914. His presidential address in New York dwelt on the importance of communication between science and industry. He was elected FRS in 1912. He was a vice-president of the Chemical Society (1906–9), vice-chairman of West Ham chamber of commerce, and a member of the board of studies in chemistry at the University of London and the governing body of the Imperial College of Science and Technology, London.

Messel remained a bachelor and lived in the works at Silvertown until he retired, when he went to live at his London address, 147 Victoria Street. Despite many years in England he never lost his German accent. A modest and sincere man, his indefatigable hard work and innate sense of justice made him popular with his workforce. He was in great demand socially and became an admired figure at the Savage Club. He died at his London home on 18 April 1920 leaving an estate of more than £174,000. In his will he stated that he considered his immediate relatives to be well provided for and that he wished to leave the bulk of his fortune for the furtherance of scientific objectives in his adopted country. After a number of small bequests he left four-fifths of his residuary estate to the Royal Society and the remainder to the Society of Chemical Industry, stipulating that the capital should be kept intact and the income used to encourage scientific research. In 1921 the Society of Chemical Industry instituted the Messel medal, its senior award, given every second year.

ANN K. NEWMARK

Sources E. F. A., *PRS*, 110A (1926), i–iv · *Nature*, 105 (1920) · *The Times* (20 April 1920) · naturalisation, PRO, HO144/851/150, 575 · d. cert.

Wealth at death £174,537 16s. 9d.: probate, 22 June 1920, *CGPLA Eng. & Wales*

Messervy, Sir Frank Walter (1893–1974), army officer, was born on 9 December 1893 in Trinidad, the elder son and eldest of three children of Walter John Messervy, a bank manager of Trinidad, and later England, and his wife, Myra Naida de Boissiere. Messervy was educated at Eton College and the Royal Military College, Sandhurst. He was commissioned into the Indian army in 1913, serving in the First World War in Hodson's Horse in France, Palestine, Syria, and Kurdistan. He became a distinctive and high-spirited cavalry officer, with a high handicap at polo.

In 1925–6 Messervy attended the Staff College, Camberley; he then served on regimental duties in India and as brigade-major at Risalpur on the north-west frontier of India. He next went as instructor at the Staff College in Quetta (where a fellow instructor was Colonel Bernard Montgomery (later Viscount Montgomery of Alamein). From Quetta he went to command the 13th Duke of Connaught's Own lancers (1938–9) and saw them through mechanization. In 1927 Messervy married Patricia, daughter of Lieutenant-Colonel Edward Arthur Waldegrave Courtney. They had a daughter and two sons, the younger of whom died in a car accident in 1965.

From 1939 to 1940 Messervy was GSO1 in the 5th Indian infantry division, with which he went to the Sudan after the outbreak of the Second World War. He was given command of a small raiding force, the gazelle force, which hunted Italians. When the British advanced into Ethiopia he commanded the 9th infantry brigade which captured the fort at the battle of Keren (1941). He was then given command of the 4th Indian division in the western desert,

Sir Frank Walter Messervy (1893–1974), by Walter Stoneman, 1946

distinguishing himself in the battle of Sidi ʿUmar (November 1941).

Messervy was an extraordinary figure: tall and athletic looking, with a facial expression that clearly showed his strong sense of purpose. In battle, sometimes in somewhat irregular headgear, his spare figure moving among his troops in his own fearless fashion was well known to them and a source of constant inspiration. His religious faith was resolute. He said repeatedly of the way to pronounce his name: 'The accent is not on the Mess, but on the Serve' (personal knowledge). He took part in Sir Claude Auchinleck's advance to Benghazi in the winter of 1941 and the subsequent retreat. When Major-General J. C. Campbell, the commander of the 7th armoured division, was killed, Messervy succeeded him in the command of the Desert Rats. One of Rommel's battle groups overran his headquarters and he was captured. He removed his badges of rank, pretended to be a batman, and escaped back to the British lines within twenty-four hours.

Messervy was posted to India in 1943 with the rank of major-general. In command of the 7th Indian division he took part in the battle of Arakan (1944), causing the Japanese force to disintegrate. He then fought in the battles at

Kohima and Imphal, leaving in October 1944 to command 4th corps. General W. J. Slim, who promoted him to this post, wrote that he 'had the temperament, sanguine, inspiring, and not too calculating of odds' (Maule, 333). He was also heard to say: 'I want a man who will throw his hat over the Chindwin and lead his troops after it—and Messervy's that man' (ibid.). Messervy did precisely that. The daring thrust of 4th corps on Rangoon played a decisive part in the defeat of the Japanese army in Burma.

After the Japanese surrender Messervy was appointed general officer commanding-in-chief, Malaya, where he took the surrender of 100,000 Japanese. In 1946 he returned to India as general officer commanding-in-chief, northern command, and on the creation of Pakistan in 1947 he became that government's first commander-in-chief. He retired in 1948 with the honorary rank of general. He was colonel of the 16th light cavalry (1946–9) and of the Jat regiment (1947–55).

Messervy was appointed to the DSO (1941), to which a bar was added in 1944. He was created CB in 1942, KBE (1945), and KCSI (1947). He was also a commander of the US legion of merit. Messervy died on 2 February 1974 at his home, North End House, Heyshott, near Midhurst, Sussex. R. G. SATTERTHWAITE, *rev.*

Sources H. Maule, *Spearhead general, the epic story of General Sir Frank Messervy and his men in Eritrea, north Africa and Burma* (1961) · personal knowledge (1986) · *The Times* (4 Feb 1974) · *WWW* · *CGPLA Eng. & Wales* (1974)

Archives King's Lond., Liddell Hart C., corresp. and MSS | FILM IWM FVA, 'Surrender of swords by Gen. Itagaki and staff', South-East Asia Command Film Unit, 22 Feb 1946, J/FUB/528 · IWM FVA, actuality footage · IWM FVA, news footage | SOUND IWM SA, 'British officer's account of winning of VC near Buthidaung, Burma', BBC Sound Archives, 30 May 1944, 2563 · IWM SA, oral history interview

Likenesses B. Hailstone, oils, 1945, IWM · T. Hennell, watercolour drawing, 1945, IWM · W. Stoneman, photograph, 1946, NPG [*see illus.*] · G. Argent, photograph, 1968, NPG

Wealth at death £14,331: probate, 5 Nov 1974, *CGPLA Eng. & Wales*

Meston, James Scorgie, first Baron Meston (1865–1943), administrator in India, was born at Aberdeen on 12 June 1865, the eldest son of James Meston, registrar for the parish of Old Machar, Aberdeen, and his wife, Jane Greig, daughter of James Scorgie, of Aberdeen. At the Aberdeen grammar school he was dux and gold medallist. From the University of Aberdeen he passed the Indian Civil Service examination of 1883, and then went to Balliol College, Oxford, for his probation. At the close of 1885 he was posted to the North-Western Provinces and Oudh United Provinces (later renamed the United Provinces of Agra and Oudh). He married on 10 December 1891 Jeanie (*d.* 1946), only daughter of James McDonald, banker, of Mossat, Aberdeenshire; they had two sons, of whom the elder died in boyhood. In 1897 he was made director of land records and agriculture. He was financial secretary to government from 1899 to 1903—an anxious period on account of failed monsoons and consequent famine conditions. From 1905 to 1906 his services were loaned to the

James Scorgie Meston, first Baron Meston (1865–1943), by Elliott & Fry

Cape Colony and Transvaal governments to advise on civil service reform.

In the middle of 1906 Meston officiated as secretary to the government of India in the finance department and was confirmed in the post in the following year. He quickly mastered the intricacies of Indian finance and made them more intelligible to his colleagues by minutes and drafts invariably well couched and in beautiful calligraphy. In the viceroy's legislature he was able to disarm critics by his lucid and persuasive speeches.

In the autumn of 1912 Meston returned to Lucknow to be lieutenant-governor of the United Provinces. The heavy labours of the office were enhanced in 1914 by the outbreak of war, with its demands on manpower and supplies from India. His reluctance to refuse any reasonable request, irrespective of the work it might entail, added to his burdens, but did not lessen his zeal in promoting local self-government, industrial expansion, and education.

In these years also Meston did much to prepare the way for Indian political advance. On his invitation Lionel Curtis, whom he had met in South Africa, went to India in the autumn of 1916 for discussions on the subject. Although Meston could take no public part in the unofficial moves which followed, he gave much help behind the scenes in preparing the way for the substantial constitutional reforms of 1919. In 1917, with Sir Satyendra Prasanno (later Lord) Sinha and the Maharaja Ganga Singh of Bikaner, he assisted the secretary of state in representing India in the imperial war cabinet and conference.

In 1918 Meston was called to the executive council as finance member. His effective tenure was very short. He was in London again in the summer of 1919, giving evidence for his government before the joint select committee of parliament on Indian reform which had before it the report on the issue by the viceroy, Lord Chelmsford, and the secretary of state for India, E. S. Montagu. Later in the year the state of Meston's eyesight compelled him to relinquish his finance membership and to decline the invitation of Montagu to be permanent under-secretary at the India Office. In recognition of his services and with the idea of his assisting Lord Sinha, the parliamentary under-secretary for India, he was created in November 1919 Baron Meston of Agra and of Dunnottar, Kincardineshire.

The Government of India Act of 1919 was now on the statute book, and the devolution of considerable power to the provinces, and within the provinces to elected ministers on specified topics, was clearly going to necessitate new financial relations between the provinces and the centre. Meston was made chairman of a small expert committee to recommend adjustments and to work out an equitable plan of provincial contributions to the central exchequer varying according to circumstances. His gift for conciliation amounted to genius, but the resulting 'Meston settlement' gave rise to much inter-provincial tension, particularly as these years were times of extreme financial stringency because of wider economic conditions. The Indian statutory (Simon) commission, reporting in 1930, regarded these long-drawn-out controversies as inherent in the terms of reference rather than as due to any error of judgement by the Meston committee. Later the idea of utilizing Meston's experience for presiding over parliamentary inquiries was chilled by some years of delay in reporting the conclusions of a committee set up under his chairmanship in 1922 by the chancellor of the exchequer to investigate the system of percentage grants in aid of local administration, especially for educational purposes. The issue was, however, not wholly free from party differences.

Another reason for delay was the variety of activities engaged in by Meston. Meston and Lionel Curtis in combination were the main designers of the Institute of International Affairs, at Chatham House, St James's Square, London, which in turn provided the model for other institutions of the kind, especially in Commonwealth countries. Meston was chairman of the first governing body (1920–26). He was also for many years chairman of the publications committee and of the editorial board of *International Affairs*, and he served on the council to the end. Here as elsewhere he won the affectionate loyalty of the staff. The library at Chatham House bears his name. As vice-chairman of the supervisory commission of the League of Nations, he achieved remarkable success in bringing about adjustments of the finances of the league.

At home Meston was best known for his steadfast fidelity to the Liberal Party in the years of its decline. As president of the Liberal Party organization from 1936 he made frequent speeches in various parts of the country and they often attracted attention in the press. He was for many years to his death chairman of the National Liberal Club. He was also prominent in freemasonry, being installed at the end of 1926 grand superintendent of the provincial grand chapter of Royal Arch masons of Berkshire. With these many voluntary activities he combined much work in the City. He was chairman of the Galloway Hydro-Electric Power Company, of the Calcutta Electric Supply Corporation, and of three other limited companies, and was on the boards of nine others. He also wrote short but eminently readable contributions to the literature of Indian reform: the Rede lecture at Cambridge in 1920, published as *India at the Crossways*, and *Nationhood for India*, (1931).

Meston was appointed CSI in 1908 and KCSI in 1911 and received the volunteer decoration in 1914. He was a knight of grace of the order of St John of Jerusalem, and received honorary degrees from the universities of Aberdeen, Edinburgh, and Zürich, and he was an honorary fellow of University College, London. He received the freedom of the cities of London and Manchester in 1917 and of his native city in 1935. His chancellorship of Aberdeen University, from 1928 to his death, gave him particular pleasure. Meston died at Wayside, Cookham Road, Maidenhead, Berkshire, on 7 October 1943, and was succeeded by his only surviving son, Dougall. His wife survived him. He was interred at Allenvale cemetery, Aberdeen.

F. H. BROWN, rev. FRANCIS ROBINSON

Sources *India Office List* · *The Times* (8 Oct 1943) · *Annual Report of the Council of the Royal Institute of International Affairs* · Meston MSS · *CGPLA Eng. & Wales* (1944)

Archives BL OIOC, corresp. and papers, MSS Eur. F 136 · JRL, letters to the *Manchester Guardian* · U. Cam., Centre of South Asian Studies, corresp. and papers | BL OIOC, letters to Walter Lupton, MSS Eur. E 391 · Bodl. Oxf., corresp. with L. G. Curtis · Bodl. Oxf., corresp. with Gilbert Murray · CUL, corresp. with Lord Hardinge · U. Birm. L., corresp. with Austen Chamberlain

Likenesses W. Stoneman, photograph, 1917, NPG · Elliott & Fry, photograph, NPG [*see illus.*] · M. F. de Montmorency, oils, National Liberal Club, London

Wealth at death £66,244 4s. 11d.: probate, 6 March 1944, CGPLA Eng. & Wales

Meston, William (c.1680–1745), poet and teacher, was born in Midmar in Aberdeenshire, the eldest son of William Meston (1645–1723), a blacksmith, and his wife, Katherine Leonard. He studied at Marischal College, Aberdeen, graduating AM in 1698. He taught at the grammar school of New Aberdeen from 1701 to 1713, then became tutor to James Keith, brother of George, tenth and last Earl Marischal. In the rising of 1715 he accompanied the Earl Marischal with drawn sword to proclaim the Old Chevalier at the Cross of Aberdeen. Shortly afterwards he was appointed professor of philosophy in Marischal College and governor of Dunnottar Castle. While skulking in the hills after the rising with the highland poet Alexander Robertson of Strowan, he composed satirical verses and songs to amuse his companions.

After the Indemnity, Meston lived in the household of the dowager Countess Marischal at Inverugie near Peterhead until her death in 1729. Thereafter, he set up a series of private schools with his brother Samuel at Elgin, Turriff, Montrose, and Perth, before becoming tutor to the children of a prominent Jacobite, Laurence Oliphant of Gask, in 1736.

Jacobite politics formed Meston's principal theme, and in poems like *The Tale of a Man and his Mare* (1721), *The Knight of the Kirk, or, The Ecclesiastical Adventures of Sir John Presbyter* (1723), *Old Mother Grim's Tales* (1737–8), and *Mob contra Mob* (1738), he directed a stream of witty and energetic Hudibrastic satire against the whigs and Presbyterians. The knight, for example,

> would make out this paradox
> By logick, that his friend *John Knox*
> And *Andrew Melvil*, could invent
> A better scheme of Government
> Ecclesiastic, and far meeter
> For us, than either *Paul* or *Peter* …
> As when St. *Paul* writes to the *Romans*,
> That all their peers as well as commons
> Should subject be to supreme powers,
> That was for their times, nor for ours
> (*Poetical Works*, 18–19)

His squire is a conventicling west country whig:

> An *ignis fatuus* kind of preacher,
> Who led his kirk, where few could reach her,
> Thro' dub and mire, and bogs and mosses,
> And edify'd her with his glosses,
> In her affliction and distresses,
> On mountain sides and wildernesses.
> (*Poetical Works*, 53)

Meston's portrait of the sister draws on an equally well-established tradition equating canting puritanism with unbridled sensual appetite:

> For her religion, it appears,
> To go no further than her ears
> And tongue; which I can tell you truly,
> Is still a member most unruly:
> Tho' not the only one about her …
> She fainted, if she chanc'd to look
> Upon the *common-prayer book*:
> And rav'd out *Popery* and the *mass*,
> When she was roused with a glass
> Of citron-water, which is better
> Than *usquebaugh*: then reads a *letter*
> In *Rutherford*; and never misses
> To pitch on those which mention kisses.
> (*Poetical Works*, 53–6)

Meston's reputation suffered severely during the nineteenth century at the hands of whiggish and unionist critics. He was branded (unjustly) as a mere plagiarist of Samuel Butler, and dismissed as 'a gay, thoughtless, clever, extravagant, restless, indolent, careless, unsteady, witty, dissipated dog' (Robertson). As standards of morality changed, his 'coarseness' became an unsurmountable barrier to recognition, and in the twentieth century he was virtually forgotten.

In character, Meston seems indeed to have been a man of high conviviality, a bon viveur and wit, and as such was memorably recreated in Alexander Allardyce's *Balmoral: a Romance of the Queen's Country* (1893), which, although fictional, probably gives a pretty fair idea of what he was actually like.

Towards the end of his life Meston moved to Peterhead,

then a noted spa, as a pensioner of the countess of Erroll, niece of his old protectoress, Lady Keith. He died in Aberdeen in the spring of 1745 and was buried in an unmarked grave in the Spital kirkyard.   WILLIAM DONALDSON

Sources J. T. Findlay, 'The ingenious and learned William Meston, A.M.', *Transactions of the Buchan Field Club*, 7 (1902), 91–122 [incl. bibliography of Meston's works] · *The poetical works of the ingenious and learned William Meston, A.M.* (1767) · Chambers, *Scots.* (1855) · W. Donaldson, *The Jacobite song: political myth and national identity* (1988) · R. L. Emerson, *Professors, patronage, and politics: the Aberdeen universities in the eighteenth century* (1992) · J. Robertson, 'Aberdonian worthies: chapter the second—William Meston', *Aberdeen Magazine*, 1 (1831), 666–72 · W. Walker, *The bards of Bon-Accord, 1375–1860* (1887) · J. Hogg, *Jacobite relics of Scotland* (1819–21) · A. Jervise, *Epitaphs and inscriptions from burial grounds and old buildings in the north-east of Scotland*, 2 vols. (1875–9) · J. B. Pratt, *Buchan*, rev. R. Anderson, 4th edn (1901) · G. Meston, *Meston genealogy* (1977)
Archives NL Scot., P. J. Anderson letters, MS 6536 · NL Scot., Blaikie collection · NL Scot., Edward Lumsden letters, MS 296

Metacom [Philip; *called* King Philip] (*c.***1630–1676**), leader of the Algonquian Indians, was born in or near Mount Hope in what is now Rhode Island, the second son of *Massasoit (also known as Osamequin) (*c.*1600–1661), Wampanoag sachem, who, in 1620, greeted the first pilgrims in the land they named Plymouth. Although Massasoit initially welcomed the newcomers, over the course of his lifetime he and his people became increasingly aggrieved at the incursion of more and more English settlers onto their homelands. None the less, after Massasoit's death in 1661 his sons Metacom and Wamsutta appeared before the Plymouth court to pledge their fidelity to the English authorities. Soon afterwards Wamsutta, who had succeeded his father to the sachemship, died under mysterious circumstances; rumours emerged that he had been poisoned.

At Wamsutta's death in 1662 Metacom, who had taken the name Philip, became sachem, and retained the sachemship until his death. During this period he attempted to lead his people in resisting Christianity, and he himself scoffed at the attempts of English missionary John Eliot and Indian missionary John Sassamon to convert him. He wrangled with the Plymouth authorities time and again over questions of political, military, and cultural autonomy. In 1671 he was brought before the court and ordered to surrender his arms and renew his pledge of faith to the colonists. He grudgingly complied, but throughout the late 1660s and early 1670s appeared to be preparing for war.

The execution of John Sassamon's alleged murderers in June 1675 sparked the war that to many seemed inevitable, and within days Wampanoag warriors began attacking English towns in Plymouth Colony. Soon they were joined by Narragansett, Pocumtuck, and Nipmuck Indians, as well as former Christian Indians and, eventually, Abenakis in the north. In fourteen months of fighting, this loose coalition of Algonquians, led by Philip, threatened to expel the English from New England. In the course of the war Philip and many of his people travelled north and west, into western Massachusetts and New York, to camp for the winter and attempt to forge an alliance with neighbouring Mohawks.

When the tide of the war turned in the spring of 1676 Philip headed home, towards his birthplace, Mount Hope. It was there that he was killed, on 12 August 1676, by an Indian soldier named Alderman, in the employ of the English captain Benjamin Church. Church ordered Metacom quartered and decapitated, his limbs and trunk scattered, declaring that since Metacom 'had caused many an Englishman's body to be unburied, and to rot above ground, not one of his bones should be buried' (Church, 125–6). English soldiers then staked his head on a pole and carried it back to Plymouth, where it stood for decades, a grisly monument to a grisly war.

Weeks before Metacom's death English soldiers captured his wife, Wootonekanuske, and his son (whose name has not survived). Both were imprisoned and later apparently sold into slavery and sent out of the colonies to the West Indies. It is not likely that either survived for long. Metacom's death effectively marked the end of the war, but his story captured the imagination of subsequent generations of Americans, especially in the first half of the nineteenth century, when white American poets, playwrights, and novelists romanticized his plight.

JILL LEPORE

Sources T. Church, *Entertaining passages relating to Philip's War which began in the month of June, 1675* (Boston, 1716); 2nd edn as *The history of Philip's War* (1829); repr. (1989) • W. Hubbard, *A narrative of the troubles with the Indians in New-England* (1677); repr. in *The history of the Indian wars in New England*, ed. S. G. Drake, 2 vols. (1865) • D. E. Leach, *Flintlock and tomahawk: New England in King Philip's War* (1958) • J. Lepore, *The name of war: King Philip's War and the origins of American identity* (1998) • I. Mather, *A brief history of the war with the Indians in New-England* (1676); repr. as *The history of King Philip's war*, ed. S. G. Drake (1862)

Metcalf, John [called Blind Jack of Knaresborough] (1717–1810), road builder and surveyor, was born on 15 August 1717 at Knaresborough, of parents of modest means. He was sent to school at the age of four but two years later became blind after an attack of smallpox. Despite his blindness he became an accomplished rider, swimmer, and card player. He enjoyed a wager and was involved in cockfighting, horse-racing, and philandering. Metcalf played the violin and oboe and from the age of fifteen earned a living entertaining wealthy visitors to the rapidly developing spa of Harrogate. He was also a successful horse dealer.

According to the *Memoirs* that Metcalf published in 1795, at the age of twenty he became enamoured of a local innkeeper's daughter, Dorothy Benson (1716/17–1778), but, owing to an indiscretion with another woman, had to leave the area. He travelled to the coast and at Whitby boarded a ship for London. While in the capital he renewed some of his earlier contacts. One of these acquaintances, Colonel Liddell, was about to travel to Harrogate and offered to take Blind Jack with him. However, Jack, aware of the poor condition of the roads, struck a wager that he would get to Harrogate more quickly on foot than by coach. Jack took five and a half days to walk about 210 miles and won the wager.

Shortly after his return in 1739 Metcalf discovered that Dorothy was to be married. He ascertained her continuing affection for him and on the eve of her wedding they eloped. They subsequently married and settled in Knaresborough. The couple had four surviving children. In addition to continuing his career as a musician Metcalf established the first public chaise enterprise in Harrogate and a business carrying fresh fish from the coast to Leeds and Manchester. He soon gave up this latter venture, finding the profits small for the effort expended.

In 1745 Metcalf became involved in suppression of the Jacobite rising, raising troops locally for William Thornton of York. Metcalf accompanied the troops north, and was present at the battle of Falkirk, and later at Culloden. While with the army Metcalf established a number of contacts and on his return home traded in textiles from Scotland. He also conveyed army baggage and, despite some near disasters, carried contraband such as tea, brandy, and rum. In 1751, when he was thirty-four years old, Metcalf established a stage-wagon service between York and Knaresborough. His extensive travelling meant that he was fully conversant with the poor state of roads in the area and when the opportunity arose to embark on a new career of road building, he took it.

In 1752 the first Turnpike Act in the locality authorized a route between Boroughbridge and Harrogate. Metcalf approached Thomas Ostler, the surveyor, and contracted to build a 3 mile section, which he successfully completed ahead of schedule. As a consequence of the high quality of his work and of his novel ideas of construction, he was awarded the contract to build a bridge at Boroughbridge. Despite obstruction from his competitors he completed the bridge successfully and by August 1754 had received over £500 for his work. Metcalf sold his stage-wagon business in order to concentrate on this new and more profitable career. His next major contract was a 6 mile stretch between Harrogate and Harewood, near Leeds, for which he received £1200. As Metcalf's reputation grew he was awarded contracts in other parts of Yorkshire and, subsequently, in Lancashire, Derbyshire, and Cheshire. A contemporary noted that Metcalf was 'a projector and surveyor of highways in difficult and mountainous parts' using only his staff as a guide (Bew, 173).

Metcalf frequently undertook projects that other people refused and managed to complete all his contracts, though on occasions he lost financially. In order to deal with marshy areas he devised a method of laying heather and gorse as the foundation and building the road on top. This proved very successful and in many places enabled a more direct route to be taken. He built several stretches of moorland road linking Yorkshire and Lancashire and altered many routes in the Peak District. Metcalf was meticulous in his surveys and was so convinced as to the correctness of his routes and methods that for a new Pennine road over Pule and Standish common he offered to bear the cost if his scheme was not successful. He used his heather and gorse remedy and employed 400 men for the 9 mile stretch. Metcalf proudly notes that this section of road required no repairs for twelve years. For the whole contract of 21 miles he received £4500. His next projects were in Cheshire and for a total of 26 miles he received

£6500. In addition to road building, Metcalf occasionally constructed houses.

In 1778 Metcalf's wife died in Stockport, where she had been seeking a cure for her rheumatism. Metcalf subsequently established a cotton-spinning business with his son-in-law in Cheshire. It was not successful and after a brief foray into cotton weaving he returned to road building which he continued until 1792 when he was seventy-five years old.

In the course of his career Metcalf had constructed over 120 miles of high-quality road, for which he received in excess of £40,000. Metcalf attributed his success to his excellent memory for detail, which had developed as a result of his blindness. He made a valuable contribution to communications in the late eighteenth century by improving routes and thus enabling wheeled vehicles to move more easily in the critical period of rapid industrial expansion.

Metcalf retired to a smallholding in Spofforth near Wetherby, but remained active, dealing in hay and timber. Having dictated memoirs of his remarkable life, Metcalf published these in 1795, selling them to visitors in Harrogate. He died, aged ninety-two, in Spofforth, on 27 April 1810 and was buried on 30 April in All Saints' churchyard, Spofforth. An epitaph on his gravestone praises his great achievements, despite being 'one whose infant sight/Felt the dark pressure of an endless night'.

CHRISTINE S. HALLAS

Sources *The life of John Metcalf, commonly called Blind Jack of Knaresborough* (1795); facs. edn (1989) • S. Smiles, *Lives of the engineers*, 1 (1861), 208–34 • parish register, Spofforth, All Saints, 30 April 1810, N. Yorks. CRO, MIC1645, vol. 9 [burial] • turnpike trust accounts, Harrowgate–Boroughbridge, 1752–1876, N. Yorks. CRO, TD16/1-2, MIC669 • E. Hargrove, *The history of the castle, town, and forest of Knaresborough*, 7th edn (1832) • G. Bew, 'Observations on blindness and on the employment of the other senses to supply the loss of sight', *Memoirs of the Literary and Philosophical Society of Manchester*, 1 (1785), 159–84, esp. 172–4, 176 • *The life of John Metcalf, commonly called Blind Jack of Knaresborough*, 3rd edn (1804) • Harrogate Library, Harrogate, boxfile on John Metcalf, chapbooks • T. Treddlehoyle, *Bairnsla foaks annual* (1847), 2–30 • S. Smiles, *Life of Telford* (1867), 74–98 • parish registers, Knaresborough, 1710–30, N. Yorks. CRO, MIC2397, vol. 1/4 [baptisms; no mention of the baptism of a Metcalf] • *Three celebrities of Knaresborough* [n.d.], 23–48 • M. Hartley and J. Ingilby, *Yorkshire portraits* (1961), 71–4

Likenesses J. R. Smith, line drawing, 1795, BM, NPG; repro. in Metcalf, *Life of John Metcalf* (1795)

Metcalfe, Sir Charles Herbert Theophilus, sixth baronet (1853–1928), civil engineer, born at Simla, India, on 8 September 1853, was the only child of Sir Theophilus John *Metcalfe, fifth baronet (1828–1883), of the Bengal civil service, and his first wife, Charlotte, daughter of Lieutenant-General Sir John *Low. His mother died shortly after his birth (26 September 1853). He was educated at Harrow School (from 1867) and at University College, Oxford (1874–7), where he played rugby and ran the quarter-mile for the university, and graduated with second class honours in law and history. He succeeded his father as baronet in 1883.

Metcalfe was articled to the engineering firm Fox & Sons from 1878 to 1881, serving as assistant engineer in the construction of the Southern Railway of Ireland and on the West Lancashire Railway. In 1882 and 1883 he was resident engineer for the Southport and Cheshire Lines Railway, for the reclamation of the Hesketh Marsh, and in 1884 for the Liverpool, Southport, and Preston Junction Railway. In 1886 he and Douglas Fox were jointly appointed consulting engineers for the Liverpool and St Helens and South Lancashire Railway.

From 1882 Metcalfe lived and worked increasingly in southern Africa, initially for Fox, ultimately as a partner in the firm of Sir Douglas Fox & Partners, becoming involved in the construction of many of the region's major railway lines. His athletic enjoyment found expression in walking huge distances—often more by choice than by necessity—in the course of surveying and construction. With Douglas Fox he was engineer for the extension of the rail line northwards from Kimberley, and was in charge of the survey from 1888 to 1891. In 1892 Metcalfe returned to South Africa to supervise construction to Vryburg, coming once again into contact with Cecil Rhodes, a friend from his Oxford days. He supported Rhodes's dreams for Rhodesia's development—for which railways were essential—and spent a lot of time travelling with his friend, particularly during the 1896 Matabele (Ndebele) uprising. In 1902 Metcalfe was one of the few friends present at Rhodes's funeral in the Matopos.

Metcalfe went on to act as consulting engineer for all the lines which became the Rhodesia railway system, linking South Africa northward to the Belgian Congo (Zaïre), westward to Angola, and eastward to northern Mozambique. Construction of the link began at Vryburg in 1893, the line reaching Mafeking in October 1894 and Bulawayo in October 1897. Sufficient traffic to cover the cost of building and operating the railways failed to materialize. The line was originally intended to go via Gwelo to Lake Tanganyika, but when work was resumed after the Second South African War (1899–1902) what was initially referred to as a branch line was built towards the rich Wankie coalfields near Victoria Falls. The line was completed to the falls and across the Zambezi River in 1904. In January 1906 the line reached the Broken Hill zinc and lead mines which, despite assurances by Edmund Davies that all financial difficulties would be resolved, for technical reasons did not generate the large volume of traffic originally anticipated. Financial salvation came in the form of the Rhodesia–Katanga Junction railway, completed in 1909, to the Katanga border and rapidly linked to the rich Katanga copper mines. The Rhodesia–Katanga line was built at the instigation of another of Rhodes's colleagues, Robert Williams. In October 1902 the railway via Gwelo reached Salisbury (Harare), where it met the line from Beira completed three years earlier.

Metcalfe and the Fox partnership were also consulting engineers for the Benguela railway across Angola from Lobito Bay, an enterprise also spearheaded by Williams. The Portuguese granted a concession for the line in November 1902, construction beginning the next year. The most difficult terrain had been crossed when the First

World War broke out in 1914, but financial and political factors delayed the line's completion; it reached the Congo frontier on 28 August 1928. Conflicting economic pressures among the colonial powers ensured that this line never fully realized its potential as a western outlet for Northern Rhodesia and Katanga, or as a significant part of an east-west transcontinental network of which Metcalfe and others had expected the Rhodesian lines to form the centre.

Metcalfe also contributed to establishing rail communication between Nyasaland and Beira, Mozambique. He was joint consulting engineer for the Shire Highlands Railway from Blantyre to Port Herald, on which, after some nine years' delay, construction began in 1904 and was completed in 1908. This line, together with the Central Africa Railway from Port Herald to Chindio on the Zambezi, became the Nyasaland Railways Company in 1931. Metcalfe also supervised the survey of the Trans-Zambesia Railway from Beira to Muracca on the Zambezi, completed only in 1922, eight years after he had left Africa.

Metcalfe became an associate of the Institution of Civil Engineers in 1885, a member in 1897, and was a member of the council from 1904 to 1906. He was a director of the Victoria Falls Power Company (later the Victoria Falls and Transvaal Company) from its registration in 1906 to his retirement in 1914. In 1901 he took the chair at a meeting arranging an annual engineers conference which led to the formation of the South African Association for the Advancement of Science.

In 1914 Metcalfe retired to Winkworth Hill, Hascombe, near Godalming, Surrey, devoting himself to gardening and experimentation in colour photography. In 1919 he visited Palestine to report to a Zionist organization on the future development of the country. He died, unmarried, at Winkworth Hill on 29 December 1928, and was buried at Busbridge, Godalming. He was a noted raconteur, widely considered an excellent companion, loved good company, and shone in it, although most of his working life was arduous and solitary. In an emergency he was cool and resourceful. He was succeeded as seventh baronet by his cousin, Theophilus John Massie Metcalfe (b. 1866).

E. I. CARLYLE, rev. SIMON KATZENELLENBOGEN

Sources *The Times* (1 Jan 1929) · *PICE*, 228 (1928–9), 352–3 · S. E. Katzenellenbogen, *Railways and the copper mines of Katanga* (1973) · *The South and East African Year Book and Guide*, Union-Castle Steamship Company · Burke, *Peerage* · *CGPLA Eng. & Wales* (1929)

Wealth at death £119,201 19s. 4d.: resworn probate, 23 Feb 1929, *CGPLA Eng. & Wales*

Metcalfe, Charles Theophilus, Baron Metcalfe (1785–1846), colonial governor, was born on 30 January 1785 at the Lecture House, Calcutta, the second son of Sir Thomas Theophilus Metcalfe, first baronet (1745–1813), a major in the East India Company's Bengal army. The family originated in Yorkshire, but Metcalfe's immediate ancestors were Anglo-Irish gentry, like many of the East India Company's servants. Metcalfe's grandfather was a king's army officer; his father reached India as a cadet in 1767. There, in 1782, he married Susannah Sophia (d. 1815), widow of

Charles Theophilus Metcalfe, Baron Metcalfe (1785–1846), by Frederick Richard Say

Major John Smith. Her father, John Debonnaire, was a merchant at Madras and later at the Cape of Good Hope. Young Metcalfe was sent to Mr Tait's school at Bromley in Kent, and then to Eton College (1796), where he became a competent classical scholar. Meanwhile his father became successively a director of the East India Company and MP for Abingdon; he was created a baronet in 1802. Metcalfe's brother Theophilus was sent to the company's factory in Canton (Guangzhou) as writer, while he himself arrived in India on 2 January 1801, a few weeks before his sixteenth birthday.

Early career Metcalfe's rapid promotion in the company's service was due to his sharpness and linguistic ability, but a powerful influence in his favour was the friendship between his father and Richard Wellesley, Lord Mornington, governor-general of Bengal, and also an Etonian. Wellesley was in the midst of a determined campaign to entrench British paramountcy in India. Having defeated Tipu Sultan, he was about to move against the Marathas. He also sought to establish the independent authority of the governor-general against that of the directors, founding his own academy, Fort William College, and creating a private office through which he could channel able young civilians devoted to himself. Metcalfe was the first pupil to sign on at Fort William College, but his real education in

Indian politics and language did not begin until he reached the court of Daulat Rao (Sindhia), the leading Maratha chieftain, where his first public office was assistant to the resident, Colonel J. Collins. This relationship was not a success; Metcalfe wrote of his superior: 'To say the best of him, he is a man one ought immediately to quit' (Thompson, 35). Returning to Calcutta, Metcalfe was temporarily drafted in April 1803 into the governor-general's private office, which was running at high alert following the outbreak of war with the Marathas. Metcalfe now joined the staff of the commander-in-chief, Lord Lake, participating in the storming of the fortress of Dig (24 December 1804). This earned him valuable credit among the military, with whom he preserved easier relations than did many civilian officers.

The decisive point in Metcalfe's early career came late in 1805 when John Malcolm, the company's leading diplomatist, sought him out and persuaded him that the political (that is, diplomatic) service offered a more interesting future than did ordinary administration. Metcalfe's initial appointment in this line, which foreshadowed a career in the Muslim successor states to the Mughal empire, was as first assistant to the resident in Delhi (appointed 15 August 1806). The city, which had been captured from the Marathas only three years earlier, was then poised on the western extremities of the company's territory. It was a 'listening post' and a diplomatic base for all British attempts to head off dangerous combinations against them in the north and west, whether these were believed to emanate from Ranjit Singh's newly united Punjab, Afghanistan, the Jat state of Bharatpur or, more distantly, from the feints of France or the Russians. British policy was to neutralize the Mughal emperor, whose power was reduced to the confines of his palace but whose charisma remained formidable, especially among the Muslims of the subcontinent. It was also deemed necessary to prevent combinations between the powerful Sikhs and any other Indian power and to maintain a loose suzereinty over the princes of nearby Rajputana.

Mission to the Punjab, 1808–1809 Working with Archibald Seton, the knowledgeable but eccentric resident at Delhi, Metcalfe had only begun to grasp the politics of the imperial court and turn his mind to suppressing the gang robbery in the dispirited capital when he was abruptly dispatched on a diplomatic mission to the north-west. He was to lead an embassy to the court of Ranjit Singh in an attempt to draw him into a defensive alliance. The periodic chimera of French interference in the Persian world had been raised again by Napoleon Bonaparte's invasion of Russia and unfavourable changes in Persian politics. Metcalfe's mission was part of an effort which also included Elphinstone's delegation to Kabul and Malcolm's to Persia. The mission (August 1808 to June 1809) was formally a failure. Ranjit Singh persistently evaded Metcalfe's attempt to bind him into alliance with the company. The Punjab ruler evidently feared that any type of treaty relationship would begin to erode his independence in the same way in which the system of subsidiary alliances had undermined princes east and south of the

Jumna. Yet the fuller knowledge of British aims, and the fighting abilities of the small military force which accompanied Metcalfe, dissuaded this cautious sovereign from allying with the company's enemies among the Marathas, as some of his advisers and the more zealous Sikhs advised. The French 'threat' evaporated while the mission was in progress. Metcalfe also managed to take the heat out of the cross-border conflicts between British and Sikh protégés in the Delhi region. Henceforth, until the Sikh state disintegrated in the 1840s, the British tempered their interference beyond the Sutlej River, and the Sikhs abandoned their political ambitions in the Delhi region for a more expansive policy in the Muslim north-west. Besides this, Metcalfe returned from the mission with a much deeper knowledge of the politics of the north-west.

According to Kaye's *Life* and his entry in the *Dictionary of National Biography*, the portly, equable Metcalfe 'never married', reserving his warmest affections for his sister Georgina. Edward Thompson believed, however, that it was from this embassy that Metcalfe returned with a Sikh wife. They had three boys, one of whom, James *Metcalfe, survived him and was recognized though not named as a son in his will (Thompson, 412). James became a senior army officer and aide-de-camp to Lord Dalhousie. This information was omitted from the official record to spare the blushes of Victorian England. Metcalfe's signal generosity to Eurasian charities is presumably explained by the marriage.

Resident at Delhi, 1811–1819 On his return from the Punjab, Metcalfe spent the next eighteen months as deputy secretary to the governor-general and acting resident at Sindhia's court at Gwalior. On 25 February 1811, however, he was appointed resident at Delhi, a position for which he was superbly qualified. Here he continued the spirit of Seton's policies, gradually eroding the remaining authority of the royal house, and trying to set the administration of the Delhi territories on a firmer basis. In this project, Metcalfe revealed the moderate radicalism which was his most conspicuous political trait. He sought to refound the social order of the territories, which had been subject to continuous military incursions in the previous century, on the bedrock of the local peasant landowner (here also called *zamindar*, but a self-cultivator rather than one of the great rentier *zamindars* of Bengal). Metcalfe considered Cornwallis's 1793 permanent settlement of Bengal with great landowners to be an unmitigated disaster. It resulted in excessive land taxes and the creation of 'sham proprietors' who oppressed the people. Every field, he thought, had its 'natural owner'. The British had consistently confused the political office of revenue collector with underlying proprietary right. As he later instructed Bentinck, castigating a generation of revenue policy:

> The Government is not proprietor of the land, and cannot make proprietors of the land. The real proprietors of the land are generally individuals of the village communities, who are also, for the most part, the natural cultivators and occupiers of the land. (*Correspondence of … Bentinck*, 1.604)

His belief that a 'natural' body of honest small proprietors had been overturned by the eighteenth century 'anarchy' and the effects of British government, led Metcalfe to lay similar stress on the role of property owners in the framing of his police regulations in the Delhi territory. Metcalfe's general view of the political impact of Britain on India was a gloomy one, which dwelt on over-assessment and the destruction of traditional institutions. But this Indian whiggism which was later to recommend itself to Lord William Bentinck did not translate into English radicalism. He thought the English people were 'disaffected and rebellious' and did not seriously consider returning to England until much later.

Resident at Hyderabad, 1820–1825 In 1819 Metcalfe was brought to Calcutta as political and private secretary to the governor-general, but the desire to 'set his flag' in central India, as well as machinations of his enemies in London and Calcutta, soon ensured that he was sent to Hyderabad as resident (appointed 26 December 1820). Here he succeeded his relative by marriage Henry Russell. Hyderabad was both tool and victim of British expansion in southern India. A Mughal élite, supported by north Indian commercial communities, exercised a troubled hegemony over a large range of Maratha and Telugu chieftains and landowners. Through the operations of a subsidiary alliance and moneylending by financiers based in Bombay, the British creamed off much of the surplus of the state which had not already been consumed by its indigenous suzereins. The resident exercised influence through Lala Chandu Lal, the *diwan* (chief financial officer) of the state, but he in turn was hamstrung by European financiers in the form of the business house of Palmer & Co., which held virtually the whole state in hock. William Palmer, a Eurasian merchant, and Thomas Rumbold, a hanger-on of the governor-general, Lord Hastings, had set up their commercial house at Hyderabad in 1816, dealing in cotton, timber, and forest produce. By the time Metcalfe arrived there, in late 1820, Palmer & Co. were virtual rulers of the state, financing the nobility and even the *nizam* himself. The exactions that this fiscal apparatus had visited on the peasantry resulted in 1819 in an uprising which had to be suppressed by British troops. Metcalfe quickly came to realize that the condition of Hyderabad could not be improved unless the 'pillage' of the house of Palmer was stopped and its interested alliance with Chandu Lal was broken. In proceeding against Palmers, and suggesting that the debt to them be paid off by a 6 per cent loan guaranteed by the British government, Metcalfe ran into stiff opposition from the governor-general, Rumbold's patron. By the time he left the state in 1825, Metcalfe (who had succeeded his brother as third baronet in 1822) had had some success in reviving cultivation under the agency of British collectors who had been drafted in. Hyderabad's treasury had begun to improve. Yet the 'plunderers' were still largely in place, though their activities had now become more discreet. Soon after Hastings's return to England the directors did in fact pay off the debt, and Palmer & Co. rapidly became bankrupt.

In Delhi again, 1825–1827 Metcalfe's final period 'in the field' was spent back in Delhi from 1825 to 1827, as resident and civil commissioner and as agent to the governor-general in Rajputana. Once again his main duties were to tame the volatile politics of the Indian princely states and to contain their rulers through treaty or, if possible, by subjecting them to British educational and cultural influences. The major event of this period of Metcalfe's career was the defeat, in January 1826, of the Jat state of Bharatpur which had halted the British advance in 1805 and was regarded as 'the very Palladium of native authority and independence'. It is striking that a pro-consul so important in the extension of British paramountcy throughout India should have been so sceptical of its consequences, though this pessimism he held in common with Malcolm and Munro. Metcalfe was convinced that India was at all times looking out for the downfall of the British: 'Our hold is so precarious that a very little mismanagement might accomplish our expulsion' (*Correspondence of ... Bentinck*, 1.309). It was perhaps this sombre view that led him to welcome with particular alacrity the appointment in 1827 of the whig Lord William Bentinck as governor-general. Bentinck's coming would, he hoped, loosen the grip of the 'secretaries in Calcutta' and open the way for a general reformation of Indian government on more rational principles. In particular, he hoped that the relentless expansion of the borders of British India (which he had so signally aided) could now be brought to a halt.

Administering India On 29 June 1827 Metcalfe was summoned to take his place in the supreme council in Calcutta during the last few months of Lord Amherst's administration. With his extensive knowledge of the Indian states, he was ideally suited to take a key position in Bentinck's new administration. At first, Metcalfe's relations with Bentinck were not as open as the former had hoped. Thereafter, however, they became allies on a number of critical and controversial issues: the reduction of the perquisites of British officers (the half-*batta* issue), general matters of economy, and the abolition of suttee (widow-burning). These measures earned Bentinck, and with him Metcalfe, great hostility among European and more orthodox Indian residents of Calcutta. Metcalfe was subjected to innuendo concerning the large sums his Indian subordinates were alleged to have made during his earlier career. Nevertheless, during Bentinck's long absences from the capital on tour, Metcalfe was effectively 'King of Calcutta'. He generally exercised a moderating influence over the governor-general and his agents in their relations with princely states, who, though hostile in principle to annexation, often meddled in their affairs. Despite continued calls for intervention against 'misgovernment', the semi-independence of the state of Oudh survived for another twenty years. By contrast, Mysore was annexed on the grounds of 'ungovernability', even though the royal authorities had already succeeded in putting down rebellion. In this case the resident and officers in Madras misled Metcalfe and Bentinck as to the real situation in the state.

Towards the end of Bentinck's administration Metcalfe,

who had been passed over for the governorships of Madras and Bombay because of opposition from the directors, was appointed governor of the new province of Agra. But further dissension in London held up the appointment of a successor to the ailing Bentinck and, on 20 March 1835, Metcalfe was appointed acting governor-general of India. The appointment was anomalous and was never to be made substantive. Both whigs and tories now held that the governor-general should not be a company servant but a British politician. This alone would secure the link between British and Indian government and the subordination of the company to parliament. Metcalfe's tenure was to last only one year. But in that year, against the wishes of the directors and many retired officials, he passed an act which conceded greater freedom to the British press in India, which had been subject to censorship and restrictions, particularly since Secretary John Adam had clamped down on it during the First Anglo-Burmese War (1824–6). Metcalfe had acted partly in the spirit of Bentinck's administration, but true to his moderate whig beliefs he also believed a free press would help 'pour the enlightened knowledge and civilisation, the arts and sciences of Europe, over the land' (Thompson, 321).

Metcalfe's final post in India was as lieutenant-governor of the province of Agra, recently reduced in status, which he held from April 1836 to February 1838. Auckland had succeeded as governor-general, and Metcalfe, the man who had urged British power forward into north-western India, now spent his last few months in India warning the newcomer against the headstrong interventions in the politics of the Punjab, the Indus valley, and Afghanistan which were to be Auckland's downfall. Metcalfe wrote that the Russian 'threat' to the Indian empire would prove as chimerical as Napoleon's supposed 'threat' which had galvanized his own embassy to Ranjit Singh thirty years earlier (Metcalfe to Auckland, 15 Oct 1836, BL, Auckland MSS, Add. MS 37690).

Governing Jamaica and Canada, 1839–1845 Metcalfe's final two public offices were as governor of Jamaica (from July 1839 to July 1842) and as governor-in-chief of British North America (from March 1843 to December 1845). In both of these posts his policies were designed to uphold the authority of the crown in parliament and to pursue conciliation and 'enlightenment'. In Jamaica he attempted to deal with the consequences of the abolition of slavery and to steady the relationship between the new class of emancipated black small-holders and the still dominant planters. Metcalfe felt he had to secure the disciplined labour of the black former slaves, whom he regarded as both prosperous and insubordinate by comparison with the Indian peasant. Yet at the same time he was determined to stop the planters securing their labour by force and oppression. He also contracted a dislike of the Baptist missionaries, whose 'baneful effect', he thought, had been to stir up the former slaves to demand an unjustifiable price for their labour. Though Metcalfe was able to re-establish a degree of political harmony in the island, he was unable to solve the labour problem, or, given his limited view of the role of the state, to avert its longer term racial and economic problems. He often found himself caught between the local assembly (which had powerful supporters in the British parliament) and Lord John Russell's whig ministry, which was, in some respects, more radical than Metcalfe.

A comparable stalemate faced Metcalfe in Canada. During 1837–8 the colonies had been convulsed by a French-Canadian and Irish-American revolt. Lord Durham had expounded the principle of 'responsible government' but the meaning of this was as unclear as the means of putting it into practice. Loyalist, republican, British, French, landowning, and commercial interests were pitted against each other. Metcalfe was faced with inconclusive elections in 1843, a recalcitrant representative assembly, and a nominated council which often ignored him and resigned *en masse* in November 1843. Fitted by training in India and by temperament for government as an enlightened executive, and to maintaining as much as possible of the executive's power, especially in the matter of appointments, he was unable to cope with politics which were both democratic and archaic, in that Canadians wanted him to be not a governor supported by a representative assembly, but a substitute monarch.

Death and burial The rapid deterioration of his health as a result of an advancing cancer of the face forced the British ministry and Metcalfe himself to contemplate his retirement. He returned to England in 1845 and was created Baron Metcalfe, but died at Malshanger, near Basingstoke, on 5 September 1846; he was buried at Winkfield, near Fern Hill, where the family vault contains a stirring epitaph by Macaulay. His barony became extinct, and his brother, Thomas Theophilus *Metcalfe, succeeded as fourth baronet. His will included a bequest of £50,000 to his illegitimate son James *Metcalfe.   C. A. BAYLY

Sources J. W. Kaye, *Life and correspondence of Charles, Lord Metcalfe*, 2 vols. (1854) · E. Thompson, *The life of Charles, Lord Metcalfe* (1937) · *The correspondence of Lord William Cavendish Bentinck, governor-general of India, 1828–1835*, ed. C. H. Philips, 2 vols. (1977) · *Records of the Delhi residency and agency* (Lahore, 1911) · *The speech of the Rt. Hon. Sir C. T. Metcalfe, bart. governor of Jamaica, on the proroguing of the Jamaica legislature on 11 April, 1840* (1840) · T. G. P. Spear, 'The twilight of the Mughals: studies in late Mughal Delhi', in M. Francis, *Governors and settlers: images of authority in the British colonies, 1820–60* (1992), chap. 9 · J. Rosselli, *Lord William Bentinck: the making of a liberal imperialist, 1774–1839* (1974) · T. B. Higginson, 'Lord Metcalfe: a Canadian appreciation', *Canadiana Review*, 1 (1963) · Z. Yazdani, *Hyderabad during the residency of Henry Russell, 1811–20* (1976) · E. Stokes, *The English utilitarians and India* (1959) · D. N. Panigrahi, *Charles Metcalfe in India, ideas and administration, 1806–35* (1968) · P. A. Buckner, *The transition to responsible government: British policy in British North America, 1815–1850* (1985) · DNB · BL, Auckland MSS

Archives BL OIOC, corresp. and papers relating to India · BL OIOC, family papers relating to India, reel 576 [microfilm] · NA Canada, corresp. and papers | BL, Auckland MSS · BL OIOC, letters to Lord Amherst, MS Eur. F 140 · BL OIOC, Bayley MSS · BL OIOC, government of India, foreign and political proceedings · Lincs. Arch., letters to his sister Viscountess Ashbrook · Lincs. Arch., corresp. with the Monson family · Lpool RO, letters to Lord Stanley · NRA, priv. coll., corresp. with William Fraser · NRA, priv. coll., dispatches to Lord Stanley · PRO, Colonial Office records,

Jamaica and Canada • U. Nott. L., corresp. with Lord William Bentinck

Likenesses J. Hopper, portrait, *c.*1799, priv. coll. • J. J. Masquerier, oils, *c.*1800, Eton • G. Chinnery, oils, *c.*1830, NPG • A. Haycock, portrait, 1845, Canada • E. A. Baily, plaster bust, Metcalfe Hall, Calcutta; copy, BL OIOC • attrib. C. Krieghoff, oils, Château de Ramezay, Montreal, Canada • T. B. Macaulay, epitaph, Metcalfe family vault, Winkfield, near Fern Hill, Berkshire • A. Maurin, lithograph (after A. Duperly), BM • F. R. Say, oils, Oriental Club, London [*see illus.*] • oils, Royal Commonwealth Society, London

Wealth at death £100,000—personal estate: Thompson, *Metcalfe*, 411

Metcalfe, Edward Dudley [Fruity] (1887–1957), soldier and courtier, was born on 16 January 1887 in Dublin, the only son of Edward Metcalfe of the Irish General Prisons' Board, and his wife, Edith Maud Mary Howard-Hamilton. He was educated privately and at Trinity College, Dublin, from which he graduated in 1907. Intellectually unambitious and devoted to horses, he naturally looked to the cavalry for a career; as he was also impecunious, he chose the Indian army. He was commissioned in Skinner's horse in 1909.

Metcalfe's conviviality and charm, combined with his horsemanship, ensured his popularity in the Indian cavalry, if not necessarily commensurate promotion. In 1914 he was appointed adjutant to the governor of Bengal's bodyguard and would no doubt have continued in such sociable and decorative roles if the First World War had not thrust him into a rougher form of soldiering. He served with distinction in France and Mesopotamia, was mentioned in dispatches, and in 1916 was awarded the Military Cross. After the war he took part in the Waziristan campaign of 1919–21.

Metcalfe's life changed dramatically in November 1921, when the prince of Wales visited India and Metcalfe was appointed aide-de-camp with special responsibility for the prince's polo and other equine diversions. He treated the prince with an irreverent affection that impressed and delighted his new employer, and quickly became part of the royal entourage. The prince's regular staff were less enchanted. 'Metcalfe is not *at all* a good thing for HRH,' wrote Admiral Halsey. 'He is an excellent fellow, always cheery and full of fun, but far, far too weak and hopelessly irresponsible. He is a *wild, wild* Irishman' (Ziegler, 143). When the prince returned to Britain with his new friend still in attendance King George V took alarm and insisted that Metcalfe return to India. After a prolonged battle the king had his way, but not before Metcalfe had further enhanced his prospects by marrying in 1925 Lady Alexandra Naldera Curzon (1904–1995), younger daughter of the former foreign secretary Lord Curzon of Kedleston.

'Fruity' Metcalfe, as he was invariably known, retired from the army in 1927 with the rank of major. Though not offered a position at court when the prince of Wales acceded as King Edward VIII in 1936, he remained a close friend, and he and his wife were among the little band who attended his marriage, as duke of Windsor, to Mrs Simpson. After the outbreak of war he returned to Britain with the duke, and became equerry when the duke was

appointed to the British military mission in France. In May 1940, in the face of the German advance, the duke left Paris for the south of France to rejoin his wife. Metcalfe felt that he had been callously abandoned, but the duke may well have found it impossible to get in touch with him. At all events, though he left the duke's service, their friendship was resumed after the war without any evident recrimination.

Back in Britain, Metcalfe enlisted in the Royal Air Force and served on the ground staff in the Middle East. After the war he joined the film industry, where his charm and wide contacts made him a valuable recruit. His marriage foundered and Lady Alexandra divorced him in 1955 after three years of separation, but the relationship remained amicable. They had had a son and two daughters.

Metcalfe had always been a heavy smoker: he contracted lung cancer and died at his London home, 182 St James's Court, Buckingham Gate, on 18 November 1957. He was, wrote Lord Brownlow in a posthumous tribute, 'a man who prized friendship and loyalty above all qualities in mankind' (*The Times*). His importance rests on his relationship with the prince of Wales; it can be argued that he encouraged the prince in irresponsible self-indulgence, but his friendship and loyalty were never in question.

Metcalfe was tall and lanky, strikingly good-looking and attractive to women. He seems never to have been painted except as part of a group-portrait of members of White's club, by Simon Elwes.   PHILIP ZIEGLER

Sources private information (2004) [David Metcalfe] • F. Donaldson, *Edward VIII* (1974) • P. Ziegler, *King Edward VIII: the official biography* (1990) • *The Times* (21 Nov 1957) • CGPLA Eng. & Wales (1958) • b. cert. • entry in Register Book of Non Royal Marriages, 21 July 1925, Chapel Royal

Archives priv. coll., MSS

Likenesses C. Beaton, group portrait, photograph, 1937 (*Wallis at the window*), NPG • S. Elwes, group portrait, 1957 (with members of White's Club), White's Club, London

Wealth at death £17,175 3s. 9d.: probate, 14 March 1958, CGPLA Eng. & Wales

Metcalfe, Fanny (1829–1897), headmistress, was born on 1 February 1829, the younger daughter (there was also at least one son) of Charles James Metcalfe, gentleman, of Roxton House, Roxton, Bedfordshire, and his wife, Elizabeth (1791–1885). She was educated at home and in Berlin, where she and her sister, Anna Sophia Metcalfe (1826–1910), went about 1850 to acquire the linguistic and other competences which would enable them to earn their living by schoolkeeping, 'the family money having somehow melted away' (Capper). In 1858 they joined their mother in opening a select boarding-school for girls in a rented villa in the equally select hamlet of Brent Street, Hendon, transferring it in 1863 to purpose-built premises on an extensive site at Golders Green. Under the joint vigorous direction thereafter of the two sisters, who remained unmarried, Highfield achieved such outstanding success that it soon became pre-eminent among private girls' boarding-schools.

Wishing to see the benefits of education extended to

girls beyond their schooldays, Fanny Metcalfe, with her sister's backing, supported from the outset the college, afterwards Girton College, founded at Hitchin in 1869 on the initiative of Emily Davies. Known to Emily Davies through their joint membership since 1866 of the London Association of Schoolmistresses, Fanny Metcalfe was invited to advise on curricular and disciplinary matters (her particular spheres of responsibility at Highfield) while the college was still at the planning stage. She also played a personal part in efforts to recruit students for the new venture, sending out the college prospectus from her Highfield address to heads of other proprietary schools with a letter 'To the pupils' inviting them, as the persons who should be most anxious for its success, to share in a project 'which I believe will one day add materially to the long list of England's glories'. In 1869 an already close association with the college was formalized by her appointment to the executive committee, in effect the governing body, of which she remained a member until shortly before her death.

Used to managing a large residential establishment, Fanny Metcalfe was well able to advise the committee on practical matters: she contributed, with others, to the planning of Girton's first permanent buildings, kept an eye on the housekeeping, and, perceiving a wasted asset, financed with contributions from herself and Highfield well-wishers some overdue and imaginatively conceived improvements to the grounds and gardens. In regard to the students, Fanny Metcalfe's experience and good sense made her sceptical of bland assurances that young women facing the rigours of Cambridge degree courses, and much less well-prepared than their brothers, could take care of themselves. With Barbara Bodichon she pressed in 1874 for a more clearly defined tutorial system, for some elementary health care, and, in a more radical vein (though without success), for the appointment to the executive committee of some person—they had in mind Louisa Lumsden, pioneer Girton student promoted to resident lecturer—able to speak to the committee, which was based in London, from the students' viewpoint.

After Girton was firmly established, Fanny Metcalfe assisted in the founding (1882) and development of Westfield College, where a former Girtonian, Constance Maynard, was installed as mistress. A proposal made by Fanny and her sister to locate the college on a site adjacent to Highfield, possibly with a view to its incorporation with the school, did not materialize, but in its eventual home on the Finchley Road in Hampstead, Westfield was only a short carriage drive away. Both sisters served on the Westfield council—Anna from the start, Fanny from 1890. Of the two, Fanny was undoubtedly Constance Maynard's preferred confidante: 'delightful, thorough and kind' (Constance Maynard diaries, 11 Feb 1888, Westfield College Archives).

Although dogged in later years by illness, apparently asthma, Fanny Metcalfe remained active until her death, on 30 May 1897, at 33 Devonshire Place, Marylebone, London. She was buried in the churchyard of St Mary's, Hendon, on 3 June. A prize for medieval and modern languages was founded at Girton by 'Old Highfielders' in her memory. JANET SONDHEIMER

Sources *The Times* (11 June 1897) • *Girton Review* (Aug 1897) • *Englishwoman's Review*, 28 (1897), 203–4 • E. E. Capper, 'Recollections of Hendon in the '50s', 1927, Hendon Public Library, Archives and Local Studies Centre • Girton Cam., Davies MSS • Girton Cam., Bodichon MSS • B. Stephen, *Emily Davies and Girton College* (1927) • Queen Mary College, London, Westfield College Archives • Boase, *Mod. Eng. biog.* • d. cert.
Archives Girton Cam., letters to Barbara Bodichon
Likenesses Burgess, oils, Girton Cam.
Wealth at death £7747 14s. 6d.: probate, 20 Dec 1897, CGPLA Eng. & Wales

Metcalfe, Frederick (1815–1885), Church of England clergyman and Scandinavian scholar, was born in Gainsborough, Lincolnshire, the fifth son of Morehouse or Moorhouse Metcalfe, a merchant. After attending Shrewsbury School, he was elected scholar of St John's College, Cambridge, in 1834 from which he graduated BA in 1838 as junior optime with a second class in classics. He taught at the Wesleyan Proprietary School, Sheffield, in 1842–4, the City of London School in 1844–6, and Brighton College in 1847–9. He graduated MA in 1845, and received deacon's orders in 1845 and priest's in 1846. He was fellow of Lincoln College, Oxford, from 1844 to 1885 and lived in Oxford from 1849 where he was also incumbent of St Michael's, a living in the gift of the college. In 1851 he became sub-rector and in 1853 Greek lecturer at the college. He graduated BD in 1855.

Metcalfe was irascible (it was rumoured that he had once killed a man in a fight) and tiresome. Throughout his career as a fellow he was a 'consistent opponent of reform, an ardent and litigious upholder of his rights, and often at loggerheads with his colleagues, even those who were of similar political views' (Green, 432). During the forty years in which he was chaplain of St Michael's he created nearly as much dissension in the parish as he did in the college. He once boasted that when he first went to the parish there were only ten dissenters, but that the number had since increased to eighty. In 1850, as college bursar, he made a consummate mess of the accounts, but when due to present them to the fellows, he simply hid himself and refused to answer questions about them. Mark Pattison described Metcalfe as 'a vulgar and conceited fellow' (Green, 432). Metcalfe unsuccessfully opposed Pattison's election to the rectorship in 1861 and was particularly embittered in his last years in college. On 17 January 1859 he had married Rosamund, daughter of Henry Robinson, describing himself as a 'sad and unwilling' husband (Green, note to 475). Although his wife died within two years, he found that, under the terms of a college by-law, his having married prevented his preferment to college livings in addition to his chaplaincy of St Michael's. His appeal to the college visitor in 1861 to intercede on his behalf was refused. There was relief in college when he died on holiday in Christiania, Norway, on 24 August 1885. His fellowship carried the substantial stipend of £424 a year and by the end of his incumbency the living of St Michael's gave him £230 a year, allowing him to leave more than £17,000 in his will.

Despite his shortcomings Metcalfe was a respected Scandinavian scholar, and twice an unsuccessful candidate for the Rawlinson chair of Anglo-Saxon at Oxford. He frequently spent his summer holidays in Scandinavia and wrote accounts of his travels as *The Oxonian in Norway* (1856), in *Thelemark* (2 vols., 1858), and in *Iceland* (1861). Among his more serious literary work is an edition of *Passio et miracula beati Olavi* from a manuscript in Corpus Christi College, Oxford. The more recent coverage of his unattractive personality has obscured earlier accounts of his contribution to scholarship.   ELIZABETH BAIGENT

Sources V. Green, *The commonwealth of Lincoln College, 1427–1977* (1979) · Boase, *Mod. Eng. biog.* · Venn, *Alum. Cant.* · *CGPLA Eng. & Wales* (1886) · *The Times* (29 Aug 1885) · m. cert.
Wealth at death £17,606 1s. od.: probate, 16 March 1886, *CGPLA Eng. & Wales*

Metcalfe, James (1817–1888), army officer in the East India Company, illegitimate son of Charles Theophilus *Metcalfe, Baron Metcalfe (1785–1846), was educated at Addiscombe College (1834–5), and in 1836 was appointed an ensign to the 3rd Bengal native infantry, of which regiment he was adjutant from 1839 to 1846, when, on the death of his father, he inherited £50,000. He was aide-de-camp to the marquess of Dalhousie from 1848 to 1853, receiving his captaincy in 1850. In 1852 he married José Eliza, daughter of Evelyn Meadows Gordon, Bengal civil service. On the outbreak of the Indian mutiny Metcalfe was appointed interpreter to the commander-in-chief. In that capacity, as well as in that of aide-de-camp and commandant at headquarters, he went through much of the mutiny with Sir Colin Campbell. Promoted to major in 1858, he commanded a wing of the 4th Bengal European infantry at Lucknow. Metcalfe was made CB and brevet lieutenant-colonel. He retired in 1861, and died at 44 Harcourt Terrace, West Brompton, London, on 8 March 1888, survived by his wife.

H. M. CHICHESTER, *rev.* JAMES FALKNER

Sources *Indian Army List* · *GM*, 2nd ser., 26 (1846), 534–6 · H. M. Vibart, *Addiscombe: its heroes and men of note* (1894)
Likenesses T. J. Barker, oils, 1859, NPG
Wealth at death £63,532 17s. 6d.: probate, 2 June 1888, *CGPLA Eng. & Wales*

Metcalfe [*married name* Michelmore], **Jean** (1923–2000), broadcaster, was born on 2 March 1923 at 34 Howard Road, Reigate, Surrey, the eldest child of Guy Vivian Metcalfe, a clerk at the Southern Railway's Waterloo terminus, and his wife, Gwendoline Annie, *née* Reed. She described her family as 'Ovaltiney people', after the popular malted milk bedtime drink. They were lower middle-class, without a bathroom, and used Southern Railway privilege tickets to get them to their most ambitious holiday destination, Cornwall.

At the local county school Metcalfe gave the first indications of her future career by excelling at elocution and art. At home she formed a passionate love of the radio as the passport to a wider world, and eagerly followed Christopher Stone talking about the gramophone, the gardener

Jean Metcalfe (1923–2000), by unknown photographer, 1943

C. H. Middleton talking about his cabbages, the avuncular Uncle Mac talking about life—and *Children's Hour*, with Larry the Lamb and Mr Grouser. She joined the *Children's Hour* radio circle and entered for competitions which entitled the winners to visit Broadcasting House, headquarters of the BBC, to speak into the microphone. Though the competitions were stopped when she had entered only two, her enthusiasm for radio remained. She also excelled at school dramatics, and once played Queen Victoria.

After leaving school at sixteen in 1939, Metcalfe went to secretarial college, then one of the few routes to a career open to a woman. Her father, who wanted her to follow him in working for the Southern Railway, mistrusted her desire to join the BBC. It was true that the corporation then recruited even its secretaries from the daughters of the professional classes. Nevertheless in 1940 she applied for a job at the BBC. By describing her father as a 'welfare officer'—because he had done a certain amount of voluntary work for injured railwaymen—and also invoking grandparents living in Norfolk to give a 'county' impression, she succeeded in getting a job with the variety department at £2 5s. 6d. a week. A chance to feature on air came when a producer, unsatisfied with Gerald Bullitt's interpretation of Thomas Ashe's poem 'Spring, the sweet spring', for the *Books and People* programme, produced for the Empire Service from offices at 200 Oxford Street, asked her to read it instead. Her first broadcast was on 21 May 1941.

Metcalfe was auditioned as an announcer for the new

General Forces programme, a joint BBC–War Office venture which was the BBC's first worldwide service and the first to use women announcers. Shortly afterwards she began her period of service with the programme that made her famous: *Forces Favourites*, a request programme in which members of the armed forces abroad could ask the 'compère', as presenters were called, to play their favourite music, and families at home (though no girlfriends or boyfriends) could ask for music for members of the forces serving abroad. She began the job after five hours of studying the programme under its editor, Margaret Hubble. It was while doing the programme from London that she 'met' her male colleague at the Hamburg end of the operation, Squadron Leader Arthur Clifford (Cliff) Michelmore (*b.* 1919). They married on 4 March 1950 (after the programme had been converted to the peacetime *Two-Way Family Favourites*) and had a son, Guy, who became a television presenter, and a daughter, Jenny, who studied to be an actress.

Also in 1950, replacing Olive Shapley, Metcalfe started to present *Woman's Hour* on BBC radio, a programme which at that time had a long list of forbidden topics. She caused consternation when she stated on air that Henry James could be considered an 'erotic' (instead of 'esoteric') novelist. Self-effacing and gently spoken, she none the less pioneered the art of interviewing stars in their own homes and getting them to talk frankly about themselves when a more pushy personality might have clammed them up. The wartime 'forces' sweetheart' singer Vera Lynn, the irascible television personality Gilbert Harding, the song and dance man Frankie Vaughan, and the stiff-upper-lipped film actor Kenneth More all succumbed to her gently probing manner. In 1955 the *Daily Mail* made her broadcasting personality of the year and in 1963 she won a Variety Club of Great Britain radio personality award.

In 1964 Metcalfe gave up broadcasting to raise her family (it was in that year that Karsh of Ottawa took her photograph, a sure sign that she was a celebrity) and did not return full-time until 1971, when she presented *If You Think You've Got Problems*, a programme in which a broad range of human problems were discussed, including sexual subjects, discussion of which would not have been allowed when she began her association with *Woman's Hour*. Though the BBC objected to one of her programmes, on lesbianism, because it would be going out on a Sunday, she was now the lay chairman of groups of experts who could and did discuss almost anything, including transvestism and orgasms.

Metcalfe's career in television was less successful than her career on radio. She made her début with Robert Beatty in *Saturday Night Out* and did guest spots for *Juke Box Jury* and *Wednesday Magazine*, but it was for her calm, caring, and intelligent voice rather than her appearance that she was most remembered. When *If you Think you've Got Problems* was dropped in 1979, she went back to the talent she had shown at school by painting and drawing for Christmas cards and books. In 1986 she published a joint autobiography with her husband, *Two-Way Story*. She died

at Petersfield Hospital, Petersfield, Hampshire, on 28 January 2000. She was survived by her husband and their two children.   DENNIS BARKER

Sources C. Michelmore and J. Metcalfe, *Two-way story* (1986) • *The Guardian* (29 Jan 2000) • *The Times* (29 Jan 2000) • *The Independent* (31 Jan 2000) • *The Scotsman* (31 Jan 2000) • private information (2004) • personal knowledge (2004) • b. cert. • m. cert. • d. cert.
Likenesses photograph, 1943, Hult. Arch. [*see illus.*] • double portrait, photograph, 1949 (with Cliff Michelmore), repro. in *The Scotsman* • photograph, 1951, repro. in *The Independent* • Karsh of Ottawa, photograph, 1964, repro. in *The Guardian* • photograph, repro. in *The Times* • photographs, Hult. Arch.
Wealth at death £74,776—gross; £73,546—net: probate, 16 Aug 2000, *CGPLA Eng. & Wales*

Metcalfe, Nicholas (*d.* **1539**), college head, was a native of the North Riding of Yorkshire, being the son of Richard and Agnes Metcalfe of the parish of Askrigg, near Aysgarth. He graduated BA at Cambridge in 1495 and MA in 1498, proceeding BTh in 1504, and DTh in 1507. He was rector of Stourmouth (1509–10), vicar of Kemsing (1509–17), St Werburgh's, Hoo (1517–34), and Southfleet (1531–7), all in Kent, as well as being rector of Henley, Oxfordshire (1510–21), Woodham Ferrers, Essex (1517–39), and canon and prebendary of Lincoln (1526–39).

Metcalfe's promotions all derived from his proximity to John Fisher, bishop of Rochester. In 1498 the master of Michaelhouse, John Fothede, and other clerks who included Fisher and Metcalfe, were associated in grants of property in Cambridge; it is highly probable that the clerks mentioned were the fellows, and therefore that Fisher and Metcalfe were contemporaries at Michaelhouse. In 1507 Metcalfe was dispensed by Cambridge University from lecturing duties in order to undertake business with the chancellor, an office held by Fisher since 1504. In 1512 Metcalfe became archdeacon of Rochester, where Fisher was bishop.

Between 1 November and 3 December 1518 Metcalfe assumed the mastership of St John's College, Cambridge, an office he held until 4 July 1537. He inherited the government of a society which stood in need of endowments if it was properly to sustain its intended complement of fellows and scholars. Metcalfe acted as Fisher's agent both in securing the properties of two nunneries granted by the king—Higham Priory in Kent and Broomhall Priory in Berkshire—and in managing the acquisition of further benefactions, many of them given by northerners. Roger Ascham in *The Scholemaster* excused Metcalfe's alleged partiality to men of the north on the grounds of their contribution to the early endowment of the college. He also praised Metcalfe for his advancement of learning and virtue.

As master of St John's, Metcalfe was also involved in Fisher's polemical work in defence of Catholic doctrine against Luther. Metcalfe himself preached against Luther in 1526, at a time when under his leadership a number of fellows of the college also supported Fisher's defence. He was not, however, in the forefront of scholars, but rather continued to act as an agent and intermediary. John Watson, fellow of St John's, wrote to him in 1519 at Rochester asking for copies of Fisher's *De unica Magdalena* to send to William Melton and others of Fisher's friends in Yorkshire. Later Metcalfe was asked by Fisher to borrow from the university library Chrysostom's sermons *Contra Judeos*, needed for his polemical work.

During his mastership, Metcalfe contributed to the physical development of St John's. An additional court at the south-west corner of the first court of the college, visible on Hammond's Cambridge plan of 1592 before the erection of the present second court, was financed at least partly by his gift. His gift of £40 towards the new chambers was recorded in an early college register, but subsequently deleted. The master's accounts record payments for stone and timber in 1529–30. He is also recorded as having given £80 which was used to buy land worth £4 a year. This cannot be certainly identified, but may have been land at Babraham, Fen Drayton, Conington, and Swavesey, Cambridgeshire, bought by the college during 1528 and 1529.

After Fisher's execution in 1535, Metcalfe, who had supported the bishop's opposition to Henry VIII's divorce and supremacy over the church in convocation, himself fell under suspicion of disloyalty to the king. Summoned to London, he was interviewed by Thomas Cromwell and ordered to resign his mastership: an eyewitness later recorded how on 4 July 1537, in the college chapel, Metcalfe 'dyd in the presence of all the fellows resygne the Mastershippe, saying that he was commaunded to do so, whych he dyd with weepyng tears' (Scott, 332). The event is commemorated by a brass plate in the college antechapel, on which a petition for the prayers of the faithful was subsequently defaced.

Metcalfe requested burial in his church of Woodham Ferrers, to which in his will of 1539, proved on 16 October, he left ornaments and altar cloths. He bequeathed 40s. to St John's for his exequies, 10s. to Michaelhouse, and, after personal bequests, the residue of his goods to be distributed among poor scholars towards their maintenance at Cambridge.   MALCOLM G. UNDERWOOD

Sources Emden, *Cam.*, 403 · R. Rex, *The theology of John Fisher* (1991) · T. Baker, *History of the college of St John the Evangelist, Cambridge*, ed. J. E. B. Mayor, 1 (1869), 85–109 · will, 1539, PRO, PROB 11/27, sig. 31 · *Fasti Angl., 1300–1541*, [Monastic cathedrals], 42 · R. Ascham, *English works: … The scholemaster*, ed. W. A. Wright (1904), 278–9 · J. Watson, letters to Nicholas Metcalfe, 25 March 1519, 1 April 1519, St John Cam., Archives, D56.45; D56.40 · R. Sharpe, letter to Nicholas Metcalfe, 20 Oct 1523?, St John Cam., Archives, D56.41 · master's accounts, 1523–37, St John Cam., Archives, D106.11, fols. 115v, 119 · *An inventory of the historical monuments in the city of Cambridge*, Royal Commission on Historical Monuments (England), 2 (1959), 191a · inventories of arms in windows, 1868, St John Cam., Archives, D33.3.9, memos. 40–41 · A. C. Crook, *From the foundation to Gilbert Scott: a history of the buildings of St John's College, Cambridge, 1511 to 1885* (1980), 108, 167 · Cooper, *Ath. Cantab.*, 1.62 · Trinity Cam., Michaelhouse muniments, no. 121 · St John Cam., Archives, D20.60 · letters from his mother and aunt, 1521, St John Cam., D105.38, D105.39 · R. F. S. [R. F. Scott], 'Notes from the college records', *The Eagle*, 31 (1909–10), 32 · C. Whaley, *The parish of Askrigg* (1890)
Likenesses Clayton and Bell, ceiling figure, 1867–8, St John Cam.

Wealth at death £12 in money; also provision for two lifetime annuities of 26s. 8d. and one of the same amount for duration of a nephew's residence at King's College (actually seven years): will, PRO, PROB 11/27, sig. 31

Metcalfe, Robert (1579–1652/3), Hebraist and benefactor, was the son of Alexander Metcalfe of St John's parish in Beverley, Yorkshire. He was educated at Beverley grammar school and at St John's College, Cambridge, where he was admitted as a scholar in 1594, graduated BA about 1605, and proceeded MA in 1606. The Beverley corporation accounts for this period record small payments to Alexander Metcalfe 'to the use of his son at Cambridge' (Poulson, 1.453).

On 10 April 1606 Metcalfe was admitted a fellow of St John's College; he was incorporated at Oxford University in 1610, and took the degree of BD in 1613. On the festival of St Mark 1616 he was elected a preacher of St John's College and became vicar of Burwell in Cambridgeshire in 1618. About 1622 he followed Andrew Byng of St John's College as regius professor of Hebrew. He subsequently migrated to Trinity College, from which he proceeded doctor of divinity in 1630. Citing his age and infirmities he resigned his chair in October 1645, and was succeeded by Ralph Cudworth. On 14 August 1646 he was appointed college lecturer in Hebrew and in October of the same year vice-master of Trinity, an office he held until his death.

James Duport in *Musae subsecivae* refers to Metcalfe as a man of singularly retired habits, leading a solitary life among his books in his college chamber. Nicholas Hookes of Trinity College, who composed two elegies, one Latin and one English, to his memory, praises both his wisdom and charity, and especially his generosity to poor deserving students.

Metcalfe's will, dated 9 October 1652, further attests his concern for education and the poor. Having provided for his sister, Prudence Metcalfe, with an annuity of £20 in addition to a legacy of £100, and set aside £200 for the poorest of his Wensleydale kin, he left almost all the rest of his estate, worth in excess of £2000, to charity. The libraries of Trinity and St John's colleges each received £100 to buy divinity books. He remembered the poor of his Burwell parish with an annual rent charge of 30s., and the poor of All Saints and St Michael's, Cambridge, with a gift of £5, though his birthplace featured by far the most prominently among his bequests. To the corporation of Beverley he left in perpetuity two recently purchased farms in Guilden Morden and Over, in Cambridgeshire, to pay annually £10 each to the lecturer and schoolmaster; £6 13s. 4d. each to three native-born poor scholars at Cambridge; and £20 to the town poor. The exact date of Metcalfe's death is unknown, but probate was granted on 15 April 1653. His arms, with a few lines relating to him, are in the 'Liber memorialis' of Trinity College, where he was buried in the chapel.   CLAIRE CROSS

Sources will, CUL, department of manuscripts and university archives, vice-chancellor's court wills, Packet 14 [attested copy in East Riding of Yorkshire Archives Service, Beverley DD BC 9/22, 'Beverley charity wills', 1–13] · R. Metcalfe, letter resigning the regius chair, CUL, department of manuscripts and university archives, CUR 39.3, art. 4 · G. Poulson, *Beverlac, or, The antiquities and history of the town of Beverley*, 1 (1829) · *VCH Yorkshire East Riding*, vol. 6 · J. D. [J. Duport], *Musae subsecivae, seu, Poetica stromata* (1676) · N. Hookes, *Amanda: a sacrifice to an unknown goddesse* (1653) · Venn, *Alum. Cant.*, 1/3 · Foster, *Alum. Oxon.* · T. Baker, *History of the college of St John the Evangelist, Cambridge*, ed. J. E. B. Mayor, 1 (1869) · W. W. Rouse Ball and J. A. Venn, eds., *Admissions to Trinity College, Cambridge*, 1 (1916) · East Riding of Yorkshire Archives Service, Beverley, PE/129/1

Archives CUL, department of manuscripts and university archives, letter, CUR 39.3 [art. 4]

Wealth at death over £2100: will, CUL, department of manuscripts and university archives, vice-chancellor's court wills, Packet 14

Metcalfe, Theophilus (*bap.* 1610, *d.* 1645/6), stenographer, was baptized at St Mary's, Richmond, Yorkshire, on 3 June 1610, the tenth child of Matthew Metcalfe and his wife, Maria (*née* Taylor). Through his father he was descended from the Metcalfes of Askrigge, Yorkshire. His mother's brothers were Thomas *Taylor (1576–1632), the puritan preacher, and Theophilus Taylor, rector of St Lawrence's Church, Reading, from 1610 to 1640.

By 1633 Theophilus Metcalfe was living and teaching shorthand in London. By 1635 he was apparently living in the parish of St Katharine by the Tower and had married Ann, with whom he had five sons and two daughters. His shorthand system, which was heavily dependent upon Thomas Shelton's work, *Short-Writing*, known in later editions as *Tachygraphy*, adopting many of Shelton's symbols and rules, first appeared as *The Art of Stenography*, entered in the Stationers' Company register on 18 April 1633. No copy is known to be extant. The earliest surviving example of Metcalfe's primer appeared as the first issue of the sixth edition, published by himself in 1645 from St Katharine's Court, by which time the title had changed to *Short Writing the Most Easie Exact Lineall and Speedy Method*. By the spring of 1646 Metcalfe was dead. The sixth edition of that year was reissued by John Hancock, to whom Metcalfe's widow had assigned her rights in her husband's works on 10 April.

Subsequently Metcalfe's shorthand system was republished many times in several editions, the last of which, the so-called fifty-fifth edition, appeared in 1721. *A Schoolmaster to Radio-Stenography*, a learning aid to 'short writing', appeared in 1649 and in 1668. Metcalfe's system was used, and recommended to others, by the hymn writer Isaac Watts (1674–1748). There is a copy of the Bible written by William Holder in 'short writing' in the British Library (Add. MS 30385), and a manuscript copy of the 1674 edition of *Short Writing* in the National Library of Scotland (Warden MS Acc. 5706/9) written, with additions and improvements, by James Douglas in 1681. Metcalfe's system was popular in seventeenth century New England, where it was used to record the Salem witch trials of 1692. 'Short writing' was later adopted by James Weston for his *Stenography Compleated* (1727). There is nothing to support the claim, often made by nineteenth-century writers, that the charge of a hand and pen in the Metcalfe family crest

was granted to the stenographer. It was issued to his great-grandson, Sir Thomas Theophilus Metcalfe, baronet (1745–1813), of Chilton, Berkshire, in 1802.

FRANCES HENDERSON

Sources W. J. Carlton, *Shorthand books* (1940), 48–55 · R. C. Alston, *A bibliography of the English language from the invention of printing to the year 1800*, 8: *Treatises on shorthand* (1966), 14–18 · T. Metcalfe, *Short writing: the most easie, exact, lineall and speedy method that hath ever yet been obtained*, 6th edn (1646) · T. Metcalfe, *A schoolmaster to radio-stenography, or, Short writing* (1649) · *Yorkshire Post* (17 Nov 1906) · BL, Add. MS 30385 · NL Scot., Warden MS Acc. 5706/9 · I. Watts, *The improvement of the mind* (1868) · personal information (2004) [Michael Mendle]

Likenesses T. Cross, engraving, repro. in Metcalfe, *Short writing*

Metcalfe, Sir Theophilus John, fifth baronet (1828–1883), administrator in India, was born at Metcalfe House, Delhi, on 28 November 1828, the eldest son of Sir Thomas Theophilus *Metcalfe, fourth baronet (1795–1853), of the Bengal civil service, and his second wife, Felicity Annie (*d.* 1842), daughter of J. Browne of the Bengal medical board. His father's eldest brother, Sir Theophilus John Metcalfe, second baronet, was president of the select committee at Canton (Guangzhou), and died in 1822. Theophilus John was sent to England as a child and placed in Mrs Bragge's school at Clifton. In 1845, while enrolled at the East India Company's military college at Addiscombe, he was struck down by an illness which left him blind in the right eye. His hopes of a military career thus destroyed, in 1847 he transferred to Haileybury College and two years later sailed for India to take up a civilian appointment in the Delhi territories. On 14 October 1851 he married Charlotte, daughter of General Sir John Low. She died at Simla on 26 September 1853, shortly after giving birth to a son, the year also that Metcalfe succeeded to the baronetcy.

In 1857 Metcalfe was appointed joint magistrate and deputy collector at Meerut and Fatehpur. On the morning of 11 May 1857 he brought information to Delhi that the Meerut mutineers were crossing the Jumna River to the city. Having sounded the alarm, Metcalfe aided the escape of some of the European inhabitants and then made good his own escape with the assistance of the nawab of Jhajjar, whom he later accused of treachery and declined to save from execution. The uprising enabled Metcalfe to fulfil the military ambitions thwarted by his teenage illness and in battles around Delhi he acquired a reputation as a fearless fighter. His familiarity with Delhi was of great advantage to the besieging troops and on 14 September 1857, in the third of four columns of assault on the city, he successfully guided the 52nd regiment of light infantry through back streets and gardens into Chandni Chauk and up to the heavily fortified Jama Masjid.

After the city's recapture Metcalfe hurled himself into a frenzy of retributive slaughter. His father's magnificent house, crammed with treasures and housing a library of 25,000 volumes, had been gutted by the mutineers and no amount of revenge seemed to compensate Metcalfe for the loss. For decades the Metcalfe men and their palatial residence had symbolized British power in the region and, although Metcalfe was not the senior civil officer in Delhi at this time, it was his vengeance that the terrified Indians feared most. Even the Europeans in Delhi seem to have accepted that Metcalfe was in charge, although the commissioner was actually C. B. Saunders. One Englishwoman, Mrs Coopland, praising Metcalfe's 'lynx eye for detecting culprits', observed how he was a law unto himself: 'One day, when passing General Penney's house, amongst a guard of sowars, he detected a murderer, and instantly singled him out, tried, and condemned him' (Coopland, 272–3).

As news of the indiscriminate killing reached Benares and Calcutta, many senior officers urged restraint and John Lawrence in particular thought that Metcalfe should be punished for his excesses. Metcalfe was not disciplined but, regardless, his Indian career was virtually at an end. In 1859, after a stint as assistant to the agent at Delhi and deputy collector of Fatehpur, he went to Britain on sick furlough, never to return. He was made CB in 1864 and retired on an invalid pension in 1866. On 26 August 1876 he married Katharine Hawkins (d. 1911), daughter of James Whitehead Dempster of Dunnichen. He died in Paris on 8 November 1883, aged fifty-four, and was succeeded as baronet by his only child, Charles Herbert Theophilus *Metcalfe (1853–1928), the railway engineer.

KATHERINE PRIOR

Sources E. Bayley, *The golden calm*, ed. M. M. Kaye (1980) · N. Gupta, *Delhi between two empires, 1803–1931* (1981) · R. M. Coopland, *A lady's escape from Gwalior* (1859) · W. W. Ireland, *History of the siege of Delhi by an officer who served there* (1861) · *DNB* · T. R. E. Holmes, *A history of the Indian mutiny* (1883) · Burke, *Peerage* (1954)
Archives BL OIOC, family papers relating to India [microfilm] · BL OIOC, papers relating to Indian mutiny, MS Eur. D 610 | priv. coll., Metcalfe, Bayley, and Ricketts family MSS
Wealth at death £8613 1s. 7d.: confirmation, 16 Jan 1884, *CCI*

Metcalfe, Sir Thomas Theophilus, fourth baronet (1795–1853), East India Company servant, was born on 2 January 1795, the fourth child of Sir Thomas Theophilus Metcalfe, first baronet (1745–1813), a major in the Bengal army, and his wife, Susannah Sophia, *née* Debonnaire (d. 1815), who was formerly married to Major John Smith. He was younger brother of Charles Theophilus *Metcalfe, third baronet and Baron Metcalfe, successively governor in India, Jamaica, and Canada. Thomas's father, who had made a fortune in India, on his return to England was elected a director of the East India Company, a position which he held from 1789 until his death in 1813. In 1796 Thomas senior was elected a member of parliament, and he was created a baronet in 1802. Thomas junior attended elementary school at Bromley in Kent and may have followed his two older brothers to Eton College. In 1812, when he was seventeen, the family sent him to India. After several months' study at Fort William College, Calcutta, he proceeded to Delhi in October 1813 to work for his brother Charles, recently appointed resident at Delhi. He remained uninterruptedly in Delhi for the next forty years. From 1819 to 1822 he was assistant resident under Sir David Ochterlony; subsequently he served again under his brother Charles during the latter's second term as resident (1825–7). In 1835, after the murder of William Fraser, he became himself civil commissioner and agent to the governor-general, as the post of resident was then called. In this position, which he retained until his death in 1853, he not only conducted the company's diplomatic relations with the Mughal court, but was responsible for the civil administration of the Delhi territory.

Metcalfe's early years were troubled by a series of personal crises. A spendthrift as a youth, he squandered an inheritance of £10,000, and left his father and then his brother Charles to pay his bills. His first wife, Grace Clarke, whom he married on 7 June 1815, died in Delhi in 1824, and their two sons died in infancy. He then married, on 13 July 1826, Felicity Anne Browne, with whom he had two sons, including Theophilus John *Metcalfe, and four daughters, before her death at Simla on 26 September 1842. About 1830 Thomas built as his residence the famed Metcalfe House on the banks of the Jumna, adjacent to the old city of Delhi. The house was a spacious flat-roofed bungalow with a columned veranda and curved portico surrounded by lakes and gardens. Lavishly furnished, the house contained Metcalfe's extensive library and art collection, including an entire room devoted to memorabilia of Napoleon Bonaparte. At the extreme opposite end of Delhi, near the Qutb Minar, Metcalfe converted a small domed octagonal Muslim tomb into a country garden house. Beside it he erected a small guest house known as Dilkusha ('heart's delight'). Within these residences Metcalfe lived the life at once of nabob and of squire. His daughter Emily Bayley [see below] remembered him as a man meticulous in personal habits, who every morning, punctually at ten o'clock, on his way to his carriage, 'passed through a row of servants, one holding his hat, another his gloves, another his handkerchief, another his gold-headed cane, and another his despatch-box'. A patron of Indian arts, and a student of Mughal architecture, Metcalfe in 1844 commissioned a Delhi artist to produce a set of illustrations entitled *Reminiscences of Imperial Dehlie* [sic]. When his brother Charles died in 1846, Metcalfe inherited the baronetcy and the family estate, but chose to remain at his post in Delhi. On 3 November 1853, aged fifty-eight, he died under mysterious circumstances. His family believed that he had been poisoned by the Mughal queen Zinat Mahal Begam in revenge for his part in the exclusion of her son Jivan Bahkt from the imperial title.

Emily Anne Theophila Bayley [née Metcalfe], Lady Bayley (1830–1911), Metcalfe's eldest daughter, was born in Meerut. She was sent at the age of five to be brought up by relatives in England, where, with her sister Georgiana, she lived with various members of the family and at a boarding house in Suffolk under the care of a governess. In 1848 Emily returned to India, where she lived with her widowed father in Delhi for two years. On 6 March 1850 she married Sir Edward Clive *Bayley (1821–1884), then under-secretary of the foreign department of the government of India. During their twenty-eight years together in India she bore her husband thirteen children, two of whom died in infancy. One of the family's periodic home leaves coincided with the outbreak of the Indian mutiny in May 1857, when Metcalfe House was sacked by rebel sepoys. After Sir Edward's retirement in 1878, Emily returned to England, where her husband died in 1884. She died at her home, The Wilderness, Ascot, Berkshire, on 6 March 1911. Her book of reminiscences, written in retirement and published in 1980 as *The Golden Calm*, provides a nostalgic account of her family life and personal experiences both in England and in India.

THOMAS R. METCALF

Sources E. Bayley, *The golden calm*, ed. M. M. Kaye (1980) · P. Spear, *Twilight of the Mughuls* (1951) · M. Archer, 'Artist and patrons in "residency" Delhi', *Delhi through the ages*, ed. R. E. Frykenberg (1986) · E. Thompson, *Life of Charles, Lord Metcalfe* (1937) · Burke, *Peerage* (1939) · *CGPLA Eng. & Wales* (1911) [Emily Anne Theophila Bayley]
Archives BL OIOC, reminiscences of Delhi · NRA, priv. coll., letters to his children
Wealth at death £4275 6s. 10d.—Emily Anne Theophila Bayley: probate, 6 April 1911, *CGPLA Eng. & Wales*

Metcalfe, William (*fl.* 1778–1799). *See under* London Corresponding Society (*act.* 1792–1799).

Meteyard, Eliza (1816–1879), writer and advocate of women's rights, was born in Lime Street, Liverpool, on 21 June 1816, the third child and only daughter of the six children of William Meteyard (*d.* 1842), a surgeon, and his wife, Margaret, the youngest daughter of Zebedee Beckham, merchant, of Great Yarmouth. Eliza worshipped her father, who, in 1818, was appointed surgeon to the Shropshire militia and moved the family to Shrewsbury, where they were acquainted with the parents of Charles Darwin. In 1829, following a severe case of scarlet fever—which may have contributed to her subsequent deafness—Eliza was sent to live with a recently widowed, childless aunt near Norwich. A few years later, in 1833, Eliza's literary career began when she assisted her eldest brother in preparing his reports as a tithe commissioner for East Anglia.

In 1840 Mrs Christian Isabel Johnstone, the editor of *Tait's Edinburgh Magazine*, published the first of Eliza Meteyard's eight novels in serial form in the periodical. Encouraged by its reception, and thrown onto her own resources by the death of her father in 1842, Eliza determined to try her luck in London. She joined in the radical community around Douglas Jerrold, who gave her the pseudonym Silverpen when she wrote an editorial in 1845 for the first issue of his *Weekly Newspaper*. That year her *Tait's* serial was published as a book with the title *Struggles for Fame*, an ironic title, considering that it dealt with the problems faced by an aspiring writer forced to choose between marriage and a career. But, as she wrote of her heroine, 'her masculine mind and energy were worthy of her descent' (Gleadle, 184–5). In 1846 the Quaker writers William and Mary Howitt became firm friends and, with their assistance, Eliza became a prolific contributor to such radical weeklies as *Howitt's Journal* (1847–8), *Eliza Cook's Journal* (1848–9), *People's Journal* and *Chambers's Journal* (both 1846), *Cassell's Journal* (1849–52), *Ladies' Journal* (1855–7), the *Home Companion* (1846), and *Everybody's Journal* (1860), as well as to monthly magazines like *Tait's*. In the preface to her second novel, *The Doctor's Little Daughter* (1850), Meteyard stated that it was written 'in such

moments as are occasionally spared time from my occupation on the weekly press'; Mary Howitt believed this novel portrayed Eliza's childhood. She spent the £50 she received for it to buy her penniless younger brother a passage to Australia.

As a writer of serious popular journalism advocating social reform in the areas of public sanitation, art education, and provision of cemeteries, Eliza Meteyard eagerly joined the Whittington Club when Douglas Jerrold proposed it in 1846. With women as equal members with men, Eliza became an active member of the club's council and of the committee of women who vetted prospective female members—there were 400 of them in 1850, out of a total membership of 1900. This vibrant club, described as women's 'own feminist adult recreation institution' (Gleadle, 53), was seen by Eliza as 'meeting the great sexual question of society' where 'glorious minds might thus be brought to bear upon the spirit of the age in all their high example of womanly grace combined with intellectual strength' (*Jerrold's Weekly Newspaper*, 24 Oct 1846; Gleadle, 152). It is most likely that Eliza met George Dawson (1821–1876), the eclectic Birmingham preacher, a favourite lecturer at the club, and she wrote several articles (later reprinted as *The Nine Hours Movement: Industrial and Household Tales*, in 1872) supporting Dawson's early closing movement during the late 1840s. Eliza believed in 'social and industrial communities, and was even solicited to join and head a community in the western states of North America' (Meteyard, xiii; Kent, 43). Echoing her lifelong friend Samuel Smiles (1812–1904), Eliza related how an artisan was led, after reading her articles, to 'self-culture and social elevation', becoming the editor of an important provincial daily newspaper.

Eliza Meteyard's life was not easy, having to adjust her style of writing to each particular periodical, sinking to the '*chatty* resume', as she described it, in 1857 (Smith, 2.108) for *Chambers's Journal* and rising to a higher stream of knowledge for the quality quarterly journals. Editors frequently rejected her articles, complaining that they were excessively radical, and she often acquiesced by writing conventional stories in order to make a living. But by June 1851 her straitened circumstances constrained her to apply to the Royal Literary Fund for financial support, and she was granted a total of £240 between 1851 and 1868. Gladstone also awarded her an annual civil-list pension of £60 in 1869, which was increased to £100 in 1874.

Eliza Meteyard's interest in archaeology, passed on by her father, resulted in the publication, in 1862, of *Hallowed Spots of Ancient London*. Its dedicatee, Charles Roach Smith (1807–1890), described her as 'good-looking, very conversational and cheerful, although so deaf she used an ear-trumpet' (Smith, 2.111). She had been familiar with the Wedgwood family from her association with the Darwins in childhood (the two families were related), and in 1865 she published her two-volume biography of Josiah Wedgwood, which remains a 'standard work' (Meteyard, i). Although the Howitts had secured £1000 for her from the publisher, she had to pay £215 of that stipend towards securing better-quality engravings for the book and complained to her friends that 'every possible means had been taken to strip her of every shilling of profit' for her work (ibid., 110). She had earlier published *Lilian's Golden Hours* (1857), a domestic novel set in the family of a china manufacturer, and she published later works on the Wedgwoods, including *A Group of Englishmen, 1795–1815: Records of the Younger Wedgwoods and their Friends* (1871), *Memorials of Wedgwood: a Selection from his Fine Art Works* (1874), and *The Wedgwood Handbook: a Manual for Collectors* (1875).

Throughout her life Eliza Meteyard moved house within London repeatedly, finding it difficult to maintain a home in her favourite Hampstead, and, in 1876, Dean Stanley and his wife gave her a comfortable cottage at 2 Stanley Place, Fentiman Road, South Lambeth, where she died of bronchitis on 4 April 1879. According to Caroline A. White (White, 181), Eliza Meteyard died in her arms, but her friends were told neither of her death, nor of her funeral in Woking, Surrey, where she was buried, at her request, in the grave of her aunt Mary Ann Beckham. Long before her death her 'visionary ideas sank into oblivion [while] feminists concentrated on short-term strategies which might make headway among the general public' (Gleadle, 170), and twentieth-century feminists have generally ignored her pioneering role.   FRED HUNTER

Sources E. Meteyard, *The life of Josiah Wedgwood, from his private correspondence and family papers*, 2 vols. (1865–6); facs. edn with introduction by R. W. Lightbown (1970) · K. Gleadle, *The early feminists: radical Unitarians and the emergence of the women's rights movement, 1831–51* (1995) · C. Kent, 'The Whittington Club: a bohemian experiment in middle-class social reform', *Victorian Studies*, 17 (1973–4), 31–55 · C. A. White, *Sweet Hampstead and its associations* (1900), 76, 180–81 · C. R. Smith, *Retrospections, social and archaeological*, 2 (1886), 106–12 · Blain, Clements & Grundy, *Feminist comp.*, 734 · S. Mitchell, *The fallen angel* (1981) · M. Howitt, letters to E. Meteyard, Harvard U., Houghton L., MS Eng 883–883.1
Archives BL, Gladstone, Add. MSS 44405–44406 · BL, letters to Royal Literary Fund, loan 96 · Holborn Library, Camden, London, Camden Local Studies and Archives Centre, letters to Joseph Mayer and letters to Charles Roach Smith, corresp., 091.5, A163–173 · RBG Kew, letters to Joseph Dalton Hooker · Royal Literary Fund, London, archives, case no. 1269, reel 46 · U. Reading L., letters to George Bell & Sons
Likenesses G. Fontana, marble medallion
Wealth at death under £200: resworn administration with will, Jan 1881, *CGPLA Eng. & Wales* (1879)

Metford, William Ellis (1824–1899), engineer, was born on 4 October 1824, the elder son of William Metford, physician, of Flook House, Taunton, and his wife, M. E. Anderdon. He was educated at Sherborne School between 1838 and 1841; his contemporaries remembered him as an agreeable and intelligent boy, showing little aptitude for study, but even then enthusiastic about rifle shooting, for his father was a keen sportsman and had set up a rifle range near his house. Metford also developed a taste for mechanics, pursued in his father's workshop, where he made his own tools and built a model steam engine. This presumably encouraged him to adopt engineering as a profession.

Metford was apprenticed to W. M. Peniston on the Bristol and Exeter Railway, then from 1846 to 1850 employed on the Wilts, Somerset, and Weymouth Railway. At this time his chief hobby was the making of rockets and fireworks. In 1850 he applied for the post of surveyor of Bristol, but although recommended by Isambard Kingdom Brunel, he failed to secure the appointment, working instead under T. E. Blackwell in connection with Bristol traffic schemes. This experience led him, in collaboration with the instrument maker Thomas King of Bristol, to adapt the surveyor's theodolite and level, with the intention of making them easier to set up on rough ground. In 1856 he described these instruments to the Institution of Civil Engineers and was elected to that body. He then worked briefly on the Penistone and Wycombe Railway.

On 12 February 1857 Metford married Caroline, daughter of George Wallis MD, at Bedminster. He was appointed engineer to the East Indian Railway, and in March 1857 the couple sailed to Calcutta and proceeded to Monghyr, where they found themselves immediately caught up in the mutiny. For six weeks, until English troops reached the town, Metford organized a small defence force, and himself manufactured the bullets for its rifles. The strain of this episode undermined his health and in 1858 he returned to England, to live on private means, and to pursue his other interests, particularly his passion for ballistics.

In 1852 Metford had begun experiments with alloys, the shape of bullets, and their rifling. In 1856 he had devised an explosive bullet which passed government tests, only to be dropped while he was in India. The design was finally adopted in 1863 but these bullets were declared illegal by the St Petersburg Convention in 1868. After a struggle with the authorities, Metford was awarded £1000 on top of his expenses for this work.

Metford's chief contribution to the development of the rifle was to be the first to substitute very shallow grooving and a hardened cylindrical bullet expanding into it, for deep grooving and bullets of soft lead. In 1865 his first match rifle appeared, having five shallow grooves and shooting a hardened bullet of special design. In 1870 he embarked seriously on the production of a breech-loading rifle, paying the closest attention to every detail of the barrel and cartridge, and at Wimbledon in 1871 Sir Henry St John Halford, since 1862 his friend and assistant, carried off the principal prize for military breech-loading rifles. From 1877 the Metford rifle scored an unbroken succession of triumphs. Between that date and 1894 it failed only four times to win the duke of Cambridge's prize, while it took most of the other prizes.

The advance in military small arms abroad, and especially the increased rapidity of loading, caused the appointment of a committee in February 1883 to examine British capability in this field. Metford designed for it the detail of the .42 bore for the rifle provisionally issued for trial early in 1887, and when the .303 magazine rifle, known as the Lee-Enfield, was adopted, assisted in designing the barrel, chamber, and cartridge. In 1888 the War Office committee on small arms selected as the pattern for British use a rifle which combined the Metford bore with the bolt action and detachable magazine invented by the

American, James P. Lee. This arm, known as the Lee-Metford rifle, was long in use.

Though devoted to scientific pursuits, Metford read widely and was interested in politics, history, and religion, for he was above all a God-fearing man. He abhorred cant and hypocrisy. He returned from India with a chronic headache which seldom left him but he bore this affliction with patience. Brunel commented in his *Memoir* of Metford that his handiwork was of a high order; that his achievements in India and in Britain merited wider appreciation than they received at the time; and that he had no obvious successor in the world of rifles. In the summer of 1892 a sharp attack of his old illness caused Metford to cease all experiments and after a few years of failing strength he died peacefully at his home, Redland Villa, Upper Redland, near Bristol, on 14 October 1899.

E. I. CARLYLE, rev. ANITA McCONNELL

Sources [H. M. Brunel and T. F. Fremantle], *Memoir of William Ellis Metford* (1900) · *PICE*, 15 (1855–6), 246–50 · *The Engineer* (20 Oct 1899), 392; (27 Oct 1899), 432 · 'Correspondence between the war office and Mr. Metford', *Parl. papers* (1864), 35.539–50, no. 543 [explosive percussion bullet] · *CGPLA Eng. & Wales* (1899) · marriage announcements, *The Times* (Feb 1857) · d. cert.

Likenesses photograph, repro. in Fremantle, *Memoir of William Ellis Metford*

Wealth at death £13,141 15s. 7d.: resworn probate, March 1900, *CGPLA Eng. & Wales* (1899)

Methley [Furth], **Richard** (1450/51–1527/8), Carthusian monk and mystical writer, is recorded in a manuscript annotation with the surname Furth; presumably he took the name of his birthplace, a village near Leeds, on his entry into religion, as was customary. According to his own account he entered the Mount Grace Charterhouse *c.*1476, following the death of an invalid anchoress to whom he had privately given a large sum in alms, while openly giving only as little as the others who were with him at the time. When the anchoress's servant disclosed the extent of his alms-giving, some of his companions praised him, while others criticized his altruism. The anchoress died a few days later, and Methley followed her into the solitary life as a Carthusian. He served at one point as vicar of Mount Grace, as also did his confrère Thurstan Watson, to whom he dedicated his Latin translation of the anonymous fourteenth-century mystical treatise *The Cloud of Unknowing*. An autograph letter addressed to Henry, tenth Baron Clifford (BL, Add. MS 48965, no. 10), dealing with monastic business affairs, would date from his time as vicar.

Methley's surviving works comprise a set of short treatises dealing with various aspects of the contemplative life, and Latin translations of the *Cloud* and of the Middle English version of Marguerite Porete's *Mirror of Simple Souls*. The unique copies of all of these works survive in three manuscripts. The latter half of the *Experimentum veritatis* and the English 'Letter to Hugh Hermit, of solitary life nowadays' occur among a collection of letters and papers dated 1533–6 in PRO, SP I/239. Three autobiographical spiritual treatises, the *Scola amoris languidi* (dated by internal references to August 1481), the *Dormitorium dilecti dilecti* (written in 1485, when the author gives his age as

thirty-four) and the *Refectorium salutis*, which records graces and experiences from 6 October to the Saturday before the third Sunday of Advent (15 December), 1487, survive in Cambridge, Trinity College, MS O.2.56. In these works Methley defends the hermitic life, discusses the discernment of the truth or falsehood of such experiences as visions, voices, and prophecies, and relates his own emotional, sensory mystical graces, including ecstatic visions of Christ and the saints, and gifts of loving languor and heavenly song similar to those described in the works of Richard Rolle. Methley also refers in these works to at least four other treatises that are not known to survive.

Methley's translations of *The Cloud of Unknowing* and *The Mirror of Simple Souls* survive in Cambridge, Pembroke College, MS 221. The colophon of the *Cloud* dates its completion to the second day after the feast of St Lawrence (12 August) 1491. Both of these works appear to have been translated because Methley misidentified their authors as Carthusians: he comments in one annotation to the *Cloud* that its author's reference to hermitic vocation proves that he was a member of the order; and a later annotation to the *Mirror* identifies it as the work of Jan van Ruusbroec (or Ruysbroeck), who is further mistakenly identified as prior of the Charterhouse of Paris. Both these translations, along with Methley's own *Scola amoris languidi*, are provided with full sets of explanatory annotations. Methley is also known from a series of marginal annotations in the sole surviving manuscript of the Book of Margery Kempe (a manuscript that belonged to Mount Grace) comparing Margery's spiritual gifts with those of Methley and his confrère John Norton, whose unedited mystical writings survive in Lincoln Cathedral Chapter Library, MS A.6.8.

Methley died, no doubt still at Mount Grace, during the year preceding 3 May 1528, when his name was entered among the obits recorded at the Carthusian general chapter.

MICHAEL SARGENT

Sources 'The self-verification of visionary phenomena: Richard Methley's *Experimentum veritatis*', ed. M. G. Sargent, *Kartäusermystik und -mystiker* [Tückelhausen 1981], ed. J. Hogg, 2 (Salzburg, 1982), 121–37 · J. Hogg, ed., *Richard Methley: "To Hew Heremyte a pystyl of solytary lyfe nowadayes"* (1977), 91–119 · W. E. Campbell, ed., 'Richard Methley: "To Hew Heremyte a pystyl of solytary lyfe nowadayes"', *The thought and culture of the English Renaissance: an anthology of Tudor prose, 1481–1555*, ed. E. M. Nugent (1956), 387–93 · 'The *Scola amoris languidi* of Richard Methley of Mount Grace Charterhouse, transcribed from the Trinity College Cambridge MS O.2.56', ed. J. Hogg, *Kartäusermystik und -mystiker* [Tückelhausen 1981], 2 (Salzburg, 1982), 138–65 · 'A mystical diary: the *Refectorium salutis* of Richard Methley of Mount Grace Charterhouse', ed. J. Hogg, *Kartäusermystik und -mystiker* [Tückelhausen 1981], 1 (Salzburg, 1982), 208–38 · 'The *Dormitorium dilecti dilecti* of Richard Methley of Mount Grace Charterhouse transcribed from the Trinity College Cambridge MS O.2.56', ed. J. Hogg, *Kartäusermystik und -mystiker* [Tückelhausen 1981] (Salzburg, 1982), 79–103 · A. G. Dickens, ed., *Clifford letters of the sixteenth century*, SurtS, 172 (1962) · J. Hogg, ed., *Mount Grace Charterhouse and late medieval English spirituality*, 2 (1978) · E. Colledge and R. Guarnieri, 'The glosses by "M.N." and Richard Methley to "The mirror of simple souls"', *Archivio italiano per la storia della pietà*, 5 (1968), 357–82 · J. Hogg, *Carthusian materials in the London Public Record Office collection SP1/239* (Salzburg, 1977), 134–44 · D. Knowles [M. C. Knowles], *The religious orders in England*, 2

(1955) • K. Lochrie, *Margery Kempe and translations of the flesh* (1991) • M. G. Sargent, 'The transmission by the English Carthusians of some late medieval spiritual writings', *Journal of Ecclesiastical History*, 27 (1976), 225–40 • *The book of Margery Kempe*, ed. S. B. Meech and H. E. Allen, EETS, 212 (1940)

Archives BL, Add. MS 48965, no. 10 • Pembroke Cam., MS 221 • Trinity Cam., MS O.2.56 | PRO, SP I/239

Methold, Sir William (*c.*1560–1620?), judge, was the eldest son of William Methold of Rushworth and South Pickenham, Norfolk, and Susanna, daughter of George Alington of Swinhope, Lincolnshire, and Rushworth, Norfolk. He attended Lyon's Inn, was admitted a member of Lincoln's Inn on 20 February 1581, and called to the bar in 1589. In 1607 he was deputy treasurer at Lincoln's Inn, was Lent reader there and a bencher in 1608, and in 1612 was made a serjeant. On 16 March 1612 he was appointed chief baron of the exchequer in Ireland, a member of the Irish council, and was knighted by James I. Lord Deputy Chichester defended Methold, 'a Judge of clean Hands and a good integrity', when, in September 1614, it was rumoured that he would be removed or demoted for lack of ability ('Letter-book', 134–5). He sat in the Irish House of Lords in the 1613–15 parliament and served as an assize justice. At some point he is reported to have delivered a 'diatribe on recusancy' when the Dublin aldermen sought to present a junior alderman for mayor, his seniors refusing to take the oath of supremacy (Ball, 1.243). He was appointed a joint keeper of the great seal on 10 April 1619, holding that post for the few weeks until the appointment of the next lord chancellor. He married Margaret (*d.* 1640), daughter of John Southwell of Barham, Suffolk. They had an only daughter, Elizabeth, who on 18 July 1608 married at Dagenham, Essex, Thomas Potts, master of the harehounds to James I and Charles I, and after her husband's death suffered so much poverty that the council of state, on 25 May 1655, granted her a pension of 10*s.* a week. Methold died in Dublin, probably on 7 March 1620. He was buried in Christ Church, Dublin. Lady Methold survived her husband, and married Sir Thomas Rotherham, one of the privy council of Ireland. She died on 23 December 1640, in the lifetime of her second husband, and was buried at Christ Church, Dublin, on the 26th.

GORDON GOODWIN, *rev.* JUDITH HUDSON BARRY

Sources *CSP Ire., 1611–25* • R. Lascelles, ed., *Liber munerum publicorum Hiberniae … or, The establishments of Ireland*, later edn, 2 vols. in 7 pts (1852), vol. 1 • F. E. Ball, *The judges in Ireland, 1221–1921*, 2 vols. (1926), vol. 1, p. 324 • 'Letter-book of Sir Arthur Chichester, 1612–1614', ed. R. D. Edwards, *Analecta Hibernica*, 8 (1938), 3–177 • W. R. Prest, *The rise of the barristers: a social history of the English bar, 1590–1640* (1986) • W. A. Shaw, *The knights of England*, 2 (1906), 151

Methuen [*formerly* Stedman], **Sir Algernon Methuen Marshall**, baronet (1856–1924), publisher, was born Algernon Methuen Marshall Stedman at 171 Union Street, Southwark, London, on 23 February 1856, the third son of John Buck Stedman, surgeon, of Godalming, at one time mayor of that town, and his wife, Jane Elizabeth Marshall, daughter of Richard Marshall, of King's Lynn. He was educated at Berkhamsted School from 1869 and at Wadham College, Oxford, where he took his BA degree in classics in 1878 and proceeded MA in 1881. While at Oxford he wrote

Sir Algernon Methuen Marshall Methuen, baronet (1856–1924), by unknown artist

a book about the university, entitled *Oxford Life* (1878), which was not very favourably received by the authorities. On leaving Oxford he acted for a while as tutor in a coaching establishment at Friar Park in Henley-on-Thames, and in 1880 opened Highcroft, a private school of his own at Milford, Surrey. On 5 January 1884 he married Emily Caroline (*b.* 1856/7), daughter of Edwin Bedford, solicitor, of Ladbroke Terrace, London. They had no children. During his period as a schoolmaster he wrote a number of textbooks of elementary Latin, Greek, and French. It was primarily with the idea that he might handle these little books more profitably himself that, in June 1889, under the style Methuen & Co., he opened a small publishing office at 19 Bury Street, Bloomsbury, London, with a manager in charge. From the beginning educational works were an important part of his production, but the business of the firm was gradually extended to every department of letters. Prominent on the list from the start, and establishing a fruitful relationship with women writers, was Edna Lyall, a polemical novelist and supporter of women's emancipation. The early list was strong on liberal humanist texts such as A. F. Robbins's *Early Public Life of William Ewart Gladstone*, and the Social Questions of Today series, which included works on trade unionism and the co-operative movement.

The first important success was the publication in 1892 of Rudyard Kipling's *Barrack-Room Ballads*. By 1894 the firm had enjoyed five years of solid growth and took larger premises at 36 Essex Street and a new manager, G. E. Webster.

In 1895 Stedman gave up his school and concentrated on publishing. Kipling's poetry continued to be published by him, but novels built up the company. The popularity of the novels of Marie Corelli, most of which bore the Methuen imprint, was another source of profit. As Maureen Duffy has documented, Methuen needed the best-sellers in order to finance publication of Ibsen's *Brand* (1894), which began Methuen's long tradition of a prestigious drama list, and Henry James, whose *The Golden Bowl* (1905) was a popular success.

In the 1890s Methuen diversified into children's fiction (*The Wind in the Willows* and A. A. Milne headed the list in the early 1900s). By the late 1890s Stedman, who changed his name to Algernon Methuen in 1899, was able to rebuild his house, New Place, near Haslemere, on the profits, although the sixpenny paperbacks (reprints of the classics known as the Universal Library and later the Standard Library, which competed with Dent's Everyman series) had disappointing sales. In the early 1900s the Arden Shakespeare and a complete Dickens with notes and illustrations by George Gissing were launched. The firm also issued a *History of England* in seven volumes (1904–13) by leading historians, which met with marked success. Algernon Methuen's range was catholic: he boldly published Wilde's *De Profundis* in 1905 and succeeded in his desire to 'rehabilitate' Wilde's name, with three editions in two months. Less fortunate, however, was the choice of D. H. Lawrence's *The Rainbow* (1915), described by another Methuen author, Robert Lynd, as 'a monstrous wilderness of phallicism' (Duffy, 57). Copies of *The Rainbow*, judged as an obscene publication, were seized by Scotland Yard from Essex Street. Algernon Methuen, much to Lawrence's bitterness, was quietly regretful at the trial. The book was seen as an insult to the memory of the war dead and Methuen's uncharacteristically muted response was perhaps due to his public support of Asquith's government.

In politics, of which he was a constant observer, Methuen was at one time a tariff reformer and follower of Joseph Chamberlain; he changed his mind, however, and in 1905 wrote *England's Ruin*, a pamphlet in favour of free trade. In 1910 he contested the Guildford division of Surrey as a Liberal, but was unsuccessful. In 1901 he wrote a pamphlet opposing the Second South African War, called *Peace or War in South Africa*, afterwards expanded into *The Tragedy of South Africa* (1905), and, in 1911, *A Simple Plan for a New House of Lords*.

In 1905 Algernon Methuen suffered serious illness and afterwards increasingly conducted business from his home in Surrey. The firm was turned into a limited liability company in 1910; E. V. Lucas was made a director with Methuen as chairman. Algernon Methuen still governed editorial policy and sought new titles such as T. S. Eliot's *The Sacred Wood* (1920). After the Lawrence débâcle, which caused considerable damage to the business, Methuen drastically reduced the fiction titles and played safe. They shied away from modernism and the serious fiction list was dominated by Arnold Bennett. By 1920 the company was reliant on westerns, the Tarzan books, and the Fu Manchu thrillers. Science also proved lucrative and Methuen secured the most significant title of all: Einstein's *Relativity: the Special and the General Theory* (1920).

In 1921 Algernon Methuen compiled *An Anthology of English Verse*, following it in 1922 with a sequel, *Shakespeare to Hardy*, both of which met with a warm welcome. He also produced a little book on rock plants, entitled *An Alpine A.B.C.* (1922), gardening being the constant delight of his spare hours. In 1909 he was appointed a justice of the peace and he was created a baronet in 1916. He died on 20 September 1924 at his home, New Place, Thursley, near Haslemere, where he was buried on 24 September. He was survived by his wife.

In business Methuen was vigilant, imaginative, and constructive, concealing under a diffident and even detached manner great shrewdness. In private life he was urbane and philanthropic, much concerned in schemes for social welfare. By his will he left large sums to Berkhamsted School and to Wadham College.

E. V. LUCAS, rev. CLARE L. TAYLOR

Sources *Sir Algernon Methuen, baronet, a memoir* (1925) · M. Duffy, *A thousand capricious chances: a history of the Methuen list, 1889–1989* (1989) · m. cert. · d. cert. · J. Rose and P. J. Anderson, eds., *British literary publishing houses, 1881–1965*, DLitB, 112 (1991)
Likenesses A. G. Wyon, bronze portrait tablet, 36 Essex Street, London · A. G. Wyon, marble portrait tablet, priv. coll. · drawing, Methuen Publishing Ltd, London [*see illus.*]
Wealth at death £279,654 2s. 6d.: probate, 14 Nov 1924, CGPLA Eng. & Wales

Methuen, John (1650–1706), diplomat, was born at Pipper Street, Bradford-on-Avon, Wiltshire, the eldest son of Paul *Methuen (d. 1667), reckoned by Aubrey the 'greatest cloathier of his time', and his wife, Grace (d. 1700), daughter of John Ashe of Freshford, Somerset. He matriculated from St Edmund Hall, Oxford, on 21 April 1665 but does not appear to have taken a degree, entered the Inner Temple, and was called to the bar in 1674. In February 1672 he married Mary Chevers, daughter of Seacole Chevers, a wealthy Wiltshire clothier. They had three sons and two daughters, four of their children being baptized at Bradford. Some time after the birth of their youngest child, but before Methuen was sent overseas, he appears to have separated from his wife.

On 20 June 1685 Methuen was appointed a master in chancery, a post which he held for the rest of his life. He contested the 1690 general election for Devizes, and eventually obtained a seat there upon petition in December 1690. He continued to represent the borough until his death, save for one short interruption in 1701. On 13 May 1691 he was appointed minister to Portugal, arriving in Lisbon in the spring of 1692 to what he anticipated to be 'a pleasant and not too onerous post in an agreeable climate' (Francis, 5). His first stint of service there allowed him to develop good relations with Pedro II and he returned to England from December 1694 to June 1695 to attend the Commons, leaving his eldest son, Paul *Methuen (c.1672–1757), to deputize. On 15 May 1696 Methuen was appointed to the council of trade, despite his reluctance, and ordered back to England, but not replaced as minister to Portugal,

Paul again deputizing. His performance in parliament attracted the attention of James Vernon, influential under-secretary to the secretary of state, the duke of Shrewsbury, and led to his appointment as lord chancellor of Ireland on 24 January 1697 (patent dated 11 March), Paul Methuen now formally taking over as minister in Lisbon.

Methuen took his seat as speaker of the Irish House of Lords on 15 June 1697 and became the main figure in a faction-driven Irish administration, divided over the division of political and property spoils resulting from the defeat of the Jacobites, and over policies towards Jacobites and dissenters. Both factions had been effectively decapitated during 1696 by the deaths of Lord Deputy Henry Capel and Lord Chancellor Sir Charles Porter, respectively an English whig and an English tory. Thomas Brodrick, one of the leaders of the Capel faction, who was in close correspondence with the whig Shrewsbury, had recommended the appointment of an Englishman 'and anything but a tory' (CSP dom., 1696, 457–8). Vernon recommended Methuen to Shrewsbury for his 'prudence and principles' and his appointment was welcomed by Capel's supporters in the Irish administration and parliament, a compliment returned by Methuen shortly after his arrival, making clear his preference for 'my Lord Capel's friends' (Buccleuch MSS, 2.490–91).

Almost immediately upon his arrival in Ireland the inexperienced Methuen was embroiled in the preparations for a new session of the Irish parliament, in which a number of controversial matters were raised. A strong church party in the Lords, among them William King, bishop of Derry, led opposition to bills for reversing outlawries, for ratifying (in part) the articles of Limerick and a security bill which had its origins in a 1696 plot to assassinate William III. The first of these bills had to be substantially amended, the second passed only narrowly in the Lords, and the third was rejected there. As effectively speaker of the Lords, Methuen was heavily involved, and claimed that he visited the house twenty-two times during the debate on the articles. The reporting of these events in England damaged him, giving the impression that a pro-Jacobite party was active in the Irish parliament, whereas in fact the objections to the bills related mainly to their impact on individual protestants. The administration's new penal measures against Catholics were passed without difficulty. In addition the administration managed to weaken the potential opposition from the old Porter faction by means of apparently promising, but never delivering, a lucrative revenue post to one of its leaders, Philip Savage, who generally remained 'on side' throughout the session. Vernon complimented Methuen's 'dexterity' during the session and he vigorously defended his conduct in letters to Vernon and Robert Harley, to whom he compared his efforts in Ireland to 'soliciting my disputable election for the Devizes' (Portland MSS, 3.588–9).

When parliament met again during the winter of 1698–9 Methuen found himself further undermined by English parliamentary resolutions on Irish matters. William Molyneux's Case of Ireland Stated, disputing the English parliament's right to legislate for Ireland, had been denounced in the English Commons where Methuen himself had had little choice but to lead and, it would appear, blunt the attack. Irish anger was exacerbated by the English parliament's suppression of Irish woollen exports, and by King William's decision to get around opposition (from Methuen himself among others) to a standing army in England by placing five Huguenot regiments on the Irish establishment. The Dublin administration managed to survive opposition attacks in relation to the supply, the woollen industry, and the regiments though it suffered what were seen as serious defeats in the Commons on a bill to develop an Irish linen industry (as an alternative to wool) and on an amended security bill. A further challenge to Irish protestant interests, and to Methuen's authority, emerged in 1700 in the form of the trustees appointed by the English parliament to examine the disposal of lands and goods forfeited by Jacobites after the war of 1689–91. Methuen had opposed ('skilfully' according to Vernon) the Resumption Act which set up the trust, in its passage through the English Commons. He engaged in prolonged legalistic fencing with the trustees on their arrival in Dublin in June 1700 on matters where he considered they were encroaching on his and the administration's powers and also alleged to the whig ministry in London that the tory appointed trustees were favouring Catholics in their determinations. He also appears to have used this episode to attempt to rebuild his shattered prestige among Irish protestants and with the king and the ministry. Shortly before this he appears to have considered resignation because of his perception that the king had lost confidence in him.

For most of his six years of active service as lord chancellor Methuen was the leading figure in an Irish administration headed by a succession of weak or inexperienced lords justices—or by the mostly absentee lord lieutenant, the earl of Rochester, who, though a leading high-church tory, retained him in office and seems to have worked tolerably well with him. His own lengthy absences, a trait shared with more celebrated lord chancellors, prompted criticism, but some at least were involuntary as when recalled to account for events in Ireland, or when defending Irish interests in the English Commons. Towards the end of his period in Ireland he claimed that in his management of parliament he faced the rival courting of MPs by the powerful duke of Ormond. Assessments of his role have reflected the opinion of hostile commentators, Swift or Archbishop King, though the English lord chancellor and Junto magnate, Lord Somers, also appears to have had an extremely low opinion of his abilities and performance. Even so he was allowed to retain his Irish post after being reassigned to Portugal.

Methuen was dispatched to Portugal as a special envoy in April 1702 and, though Paul Methuen remained minister, 'in practice he became subordinate to his father' (Francis, 111). In 1701, with the disputes which would result in the War of the Spanish Succession looming, Portugal had attached itself to France. Methuen was unable to detach Portugal ahead of the outbreak of war (15 May 1702) and returned to England in June. He was mandated to return as ambassador, even while his patent as lord chancellor of Ireland was renewed (26 July) but chose not to take ambassadorial rank. He was back in Portugal by 8 August 1702 and helped ensure that the Portuguese broke the French alliance a few weeks later. Formal negotiations to attach Portugal to the allies opened in December and, though Methuen's orders were to return within weeks if no treaty could be obtained, he persisted with negotiations until April. He then departed to report to London, leaving full powers to treat with his son, who refused any concessions not made by his father and concluded offensive and defensive treaties with Portugal on 16 May 1703.

John Methuen returned to Portugal in September 1703, with ambassadorial rank as of 18 June, but was no longer lord chancellor, to his disappointment. He concluded a commercial treaty on 27 December 1703, opening Portugal to English cloth in return for preferential customs duties on Portuguese as against French wines, both being commodities in which, incidentally, he had interests. Despite criticisms of his conduct and probity, he continued as ambassador in Portugal until his death, at Lisbon on 2 July 1706, following several weeks' illness described as a mixture of rheumatism and gout, the latter being a chronic complaint. His body was embalmed and buried in Westminster Abbey on 17 September 1708, his son Paul succeeding as ambassador.

Opinions of Methuen, contemporary and later, were widely polarized. To the tory Swift he was 'a profligate rogue without religion or morals; but cunning enough; yet without abilities of any kind'. Certainly he does not appear to have been a devout man, while rumours of his liaison with Sarah Earle, wife of the consul in Lisbon, may have been confirmed by his subsequent bequest. With the return to power of the whigs, tory criticism was eclipsed by a Methuen legend, encompassing John and Paul Methuen, the commercial treaty being sometimes mistakenly ascribed to the latter. Though the Portuguese alliance of 1703 contributed to English maritime power in the Mediterranean, the trade treaty, John Methuen's 'distinctive achievement' (Francis, 334), arguably had more pronounced effects. Mutual trade increased significantly in the coming decades, and to the treaty has been ascribed the traffic in port wine. 'The name of Methuen was indissolubly linked with port-wine' (Francis, 353), though in its later form this was not a product of John Methuen's own day. The commercial treaty has been considered 'a coup of considerable importance for Portugal', ensuring 'regular exports to balance its imports', while 'England gained unhindered sales of textiles and clothing in a small but significant market where there was no longer a significant local industry', and outlets in the Atlantic colonies (D. Birmingham, *A Concise History of Portugal*, 1993, 64). In 1721 it was even remarked that Methuen

> deserved to have his Statue erected in every Trading Town in Great Britain ... his great Abilities did not only enrich his Country, whilst he lived, but left us a most valuable inheritance behind him, and we reap the Fruits of his Wisdom and Love to his Country at this Hour. (Francis, 355)

G. F. R. BARKER, rev. THOMAS DOYLE

Sources A. D. Francis, *The Methuens and Portugal* (1966) · *CSP dom.*, 1696–1702 · *Report on the manuscripts of his grace the duke of Buccleuch and Queensberry ... preserved at Montagu House*, 3 vols. in 4, HMC, 45 (1899–1926), vol. 2 · PRO, SP 63/360, 361 · *Private and original correspondence of Charles Talbot, duke of Shrewsbury*, ed. W. Coxe (1821) · T. Doyle, 'Politics and parliament in Ireland in the reign of William III', MA diss., University College Dublin, 1992 · T. Doyle, 'The politics of protestant ascendancy: politics, religion and society in protestant Ireland, 1700–1710', PhD diss., National University of Ireland, 1996 · *The manuscripts of his grace the duke of Portland*, 10 vols., HMC, 29 (1891–1931), vol. 3 · W. King, correspondence, TCD, MSS 750/1, 750/2/1, 1995–2008 · *Letters illustrative of the reign of William III from 1696 to 1708 addressed to the duke of Shrewsbury by James Vernon*, ed. G. P. R. James, 3 vols. (1841) · N. Luttrell, *A brief historical relation of state affairs from September 1678 to April 1714*, 6 vols. (1857) · *The correspondence of Henry Hyde, earl of Clarendon, and of his brother Lawrence Hyde, earl of Rochester*, ed. S. W. Singer, 2 (1828) · J. R. O'Flanagan, *The lives of the lord chancellors and keepers of the great seal of Ireland*, 1 (1870), 489–96 · *DNB*

Archives Wilts. & Swindon RO, corresp., accounts, and papers | BL, letters to John Ellis, Add. MSS 28872–28916 · BL, letters to Lord Godolphin, Add. MSS 28056–28057 · BL, letters to first marquess of Halifax, C5 · CKS, corresp. with Alexander Stanhope

Likenesses W. Humphrey, mezzotint, pubd 1774, BM, NPG · A. Carpentiers, oils, Corsham Court, Wiltshire · oils, Corsham Court, Wiltshire

Methuen, Paul. *See* Methven, Paul (*d*. in or before 1607).

Methuen, Paul (1613–1667), clothier, was born on 13 October 1613 at Frome, Somerset, eldest son of Anthony Methuen (*c*.1574–1640), vicar of Frome (of Scottish extraction), and his wife, Jane (1579–1641), daughter and heir of Thomas Taylor of Bristol. He is not known for certain to have been in trade in Bradford-on-Avon, Wiltshire, until 1646, but had probably moved there some years earlier.

Paul Methuen was married twice; his first wife, Sarah, was living in 1641, and must have been the subject of an inscription mentioned in his will as being already on his tombstone. No children are known to have survived. His second marriage, probably in the late 1640s, was to Grace (*d*. 1700), daughter of John Ashe of Freshford, clothier, and granddaughter of James Ashe of Westcombe in Batcombe; their eldest son was born about 1650. James was prominent among a group of clothiers from the Shepton Mallet area who had made their fortunes in the manufacture of medley cloths from the newly introduced Spanish wool. His son John (*d*. 1658) moved to Freshford, and began to make Spanish cloths there in the late 1620s. In the two years covering 1641–3 he is known to have sent over 1400 cloths worth almost £26,000 for sale in London. In 1656 he was said to be worth £60,000. By 1646 he took a lease of his largely medieval house (later called The Priory), and bought it in 1657 (it was demolished in 1938).

Paul Methuen's name first appears in surviving Ashe family account books in 1642. John Aubrey's statement that Methuen succeeded his father-in-law in trade can only apply to the later years of his business. Aubrey also stated that Methuen was the greatest clothier of his time (Aubrey, *Natural History of Wiltshire*). The Ashe account books show that he sent cloths to London for sale from time to time, but most of his output must have gone to other agents. In 1659 he bought 159 bags of Spanish wool, certainly indicative of a very large trade. Shortly before this Methuen had brought from Amsterdam 'for his own use and benefit' a Dutch spinner and his family. This is the first known attempt to take advantage of the advanced Dutch techniques in using Spanish wool.

Methuen's exact date of death is unknown; he was buried in Bradford church on 18 July 1667. His monument does not survive. His will suggests that he shared the political views of his parliamentarian father-in-law, John Ashe; in it, he spoke of himself as one of the elect, but he had not separated himself from the Church of England; he bequeathed to Bradford church a pulpit cloth, which was to bear both his coat of arms, and his clothmark. He left property in Bradford worth £70 a year, an annuity of £20, and £1200 to his wife. He owned other property in Bradford at his death, and left monetary legacies of £7000. His wife was married twice more, first to Edward Pearce of London (d. c.1673), then to a man named Andrews. She died in 1700, a widow, at Leyton, Essex.

Methuen's heir was his son John *Methuen. He made provision for his second son Anthony to succeed to the trade, leaving him workshops, dyehouses, and fulling mills. A younger son, Turner, who was to be bred a scholar and divine, went to St Edmund Hall, Oxford, in 1677, but must have died a young man. Two other sons and an unmarried daughter were living in 1700.

K. H. ROGERS

Sources will, Wilts. & Swindon RO, 1742/6400 · will, Wilts. & Swindon RO, 1742/6401 [Grace Methuen] · deeds of Bradford property, Wilts. & Swindon RO, 1742/3248–9, 3268 · Ashe family account books, PRO, C107/17–20 · J. de L. Mann, *The cloth industry in the west of England from 1660 to 1880* (1971) · W. H. Jones, *Bradford-on-Avon: a history and description* (1907) · F. Brown, ed., *Abstracts of Somersetshire wills*, 3 (privately printed, London, 1889), 44 · T. Borenius, *Catalogue of the pictures at Corsham Court* (1939) · J. Aubrey, *The natural history of Wiltshire*, ed. J. Britton (1847); facs. edn (1969)
Archives Wilts. & Swindon RO, MSS
Likenesses oils, Corsham Court, Wiltshire
Wealth at death legacies of £12,000

Methuen, Sir Paul (c.1672–1757), diplomat, was the eldest son of John *Methuen (1650–1706), diplomat, and his wife, Mary Chevers. Educated privately and from 1681 to 1684 at a Jesuit school in Paris, Methuen accompanied his father upon the latter's appointment as minister to Lisbon on 13 May 1691. In this capacity he gained valuable diplomatic experience, won the esteem of King Pedro, and made useful contacts among influential elements of the Portuguese nobility. These qualifications led to his appointment in March 1697 as chargé d'affaires standing in for his father who had become lord chancellor of Ireland. As minister at Lisbon (1697–1702) Methuen skilfully promoted British trading interests but, lacking adequate funds, could not prevent Portugal from allying with France in 1701, preparatory to hostilities over the Spanish succession.

Following the return of John Methuen in May 1702, father and son worked tirelessly to break up the Franco-Portuguese agreement, their efforts succeeding when Portugal changed sides and acceded to the grand alliance in 1703. This treaty, widely regarded as a great diplomatic victory over France, provided the English and Dutch with useful naval facilities in the Mediterranean. It also paved the way for the famous Methuen commercial treaty, signed on 27 December 1703, which formed the basis of Britain's monopoly of Portugal's trade in the eighteenth century.

In July 1705 Methuen was present during the successful expedition against Gibraltar, followed by a mission to Morocco to purchase corn and horses for the allied army and to counteract French diplomatic manoeuvres in this area. Later that year he accompanied Charles III of Spain at the siege of Barcelona and then returned to England for the purpose of raising further military supplies. While there, Queen Anne appointed him minister to Savoy. In July 1706 he succeeded his deceased father as ambassador to Portugal, remaining in this capacity until 1708, when he obtained a leave of absence upon his election to parliament for the borough of Devizes, Wiltshire. He represented this constituency from 1708 to 1711, when he was wrongly accused of corruption and disqualified. Disillusioned he stayed away from parliament until 1714 when he was elected the member for Brackley, Northamptonshire, a seat he held continuously until 1747.

From November 1709 to December 1710 Methuen held the post of lord of the Admiralty, and from October 1714 to April 1717 he served in the same capacity at the Treasury, but refused a diplomatic mission to Holland to arrange the yearly Dutch naval quota. In 1715 Methuen was appointed ambassador to Spain and was sent on a special mission to conclude a new commercial treaty with Spain. Illness forced his return to England after four months, leaving as chargé d'affairs his assistant George Bubb Dodington, who ultimately secured the treaty building upon Methuen's groundwork. On 29 October 1715 he was sworn of the privy council. During James Stanhope's absence from England in 1716 he acted in his place as secretary of state for the south, becoming full secretary when upon his return Stanhope took over the northern department. Despite poor health, Methuen remained in this position until 1717 when, after Viscount Townshend's dismissal from office, he resigned with Robert Walpole and William Pulteney. He returned to office with Walpole, and became comptroller of the royal household (1720), a dignity he exchanged in 1725 for that of treasurer of the household, which he occupied until 1730. In recognition of his services he was made a knight of the Bath on the revival of that order by George I in May 1725. Townshend endeavoured in 1730 to obtain his reappointment as secretary of state, but failed in the effort, and from that year Methuen remained out of office. He led the opposition to Viscount Bolingbroke's partial pardon, spoke vehemently against Walpole's excise measure, and in December 1741 carried George Lee by three votes as chairman of committees in opposition to Walpole's nominee. Methuen was highly esteemed by many of his contemporaries as a man of ability and charm. He was one of several prominent politicians to whom Joseph Addison and Richard Steele dedicated the first collected edition of *The Spectator* (1714); the third volume of Charles King's *British Merchant* (1721) was also dedicated to him. As a diplomat, Methuen was shrewd, industrious, and highly competent, qualities which enabled him to secure major economic and diplomatic gains that greatly facilitated Britain's rising imperial success.

Methuen died, unmarried, on 11 April 1757, and was buried near his father in the south aisle of Westminster Abbey. His heir was his cousin Paul Methuen for whom he bought Corsham Court, in which to place his furniture and valuable collection of pictures. Through his liberality all his servants were left with board wages for the rest of their lives, and he left other generous legacies to numerous relatives and friends.

KARL WOLFGANG SCHWEIZER

Sources A. D. Francis, *The Methuens and Portugal, 1691–1708* (1966) · H. E. Fisher, 'Anglo-Portuguese trade, 1700–1770', *Economic History Review*, 2nd ser., 16 (1963–4), 219–33 · W. Coxe, *Memoirs of the life and administration of Sir Robert Walpole, earl of Orford*, 3 vols. (1798) · J. Aubrey, *The natural history of Wiltshire*, ed. J. Britton (1847) · J. McLachlan, *Trade and peace with old Spain* (1940) · *The letters and dispatches of John Churchill, first duke of Marlborough, from 1702 to 1712*, ed. G. Murray, 5 vols. (1845) · D. B. Horn, ed., *British diplomatic representatives, 1689–1789*, CS, 3rd ser., 46 (1932) · E. Prestage, *Portugal and the War of the Spanish Succession* (1938) · B. Williams, *Stanhope: a study in eighteenth-century war and diplomacy* (1932) · P. Smithers, *Life of Joseph Addison* (1954) · L. Frey and M. Frey, *A question of empire: Leopold I and the War of the Spanish Succession* (1983) · R. R. Sedgwick, 'Methuen, Paul', HoP, *Commons, 1715–54*

Archives BL, corresp. and papers, Add. MSS 29590, 34335 · BL, naval papers, Add. MSS 5437–5441 · BL, political papers relative to Portugal, Add. MS 9744 · PRO, state papers foreign, Lisbon letters, 89/88 · PRO, state papers foreign, 89/16–20 (Portugal) · Wilts. & Swindon RO, papers | BL, Southwell MSS, Blathwayt corresp., Add. MS 34335 · BL, letters to George B. Dodington, Egmont MSS 2172–2174 · BL, Hatton Finch MSS, letters and Lisbon corresp., Add. MS 29590 · BL, letters to James Vernon and William Blathwayt, Add. MS 21491 · BL, corresp. with Charles Whitworth, Add. MS 37363 · BL, letters to H. Worsley, Add. MS 15936 · CKS, corresp. with Alexander Stanhope · CKS, corresp. with James Stanhope · NA Scot., corresp. with Lord Polwarth

Likenesses B. Lens, miniature, 1723, Corsham Court, Wiltshire · A. Carpentiers, oils, after 1725, Corsham Court, Wiltshire · J. Highmore, oils, 1725, NPG · attrib. J. Riley, oils (as a boy), Corsham Court, Wiltshire · P. Scheemakers, marble bust, Corsham Court, Wiltshire · miniature, Corsham Court, Wiltshire · oils, Corsham Court, Wiltshire

Wealth at death £70,000 on deposit in Bank of England; plus house in Grosvenor Square, estate in Wiltshire (Corsham Court); valuable pictures and much furniture: Francis, *The Methuens*, 352–3

Methuen, Paul Ayshford, fourth Baron Methuen (1886–1974), painter and landowner, was born on 29 September 1886 at Corsham, near Chippenham, Wiltshire, the eldest child in the family of three sons and two daughters of Field Marshal Paul Sanford *Methuen, third Baron Methuen of Corsham (1845–1932), and his second wife, Mary Ethel (d. 1941), daughter of William Ayshford Sanford of Nynehead Court, Somerset. From Eton College he went to New College, Oxford, to read natural sciences (zoology) and engineering, receiving a second class in 1910. His father had links with South Africa, and from 1910 to 1914 he worked as assistant at the Transvaal Museum in Pretoria. His interest in zoology was lifelong: he later refused the chair of zoology in a South African university only because he felt committed to the preservation of Corsham Court. In works of reference he described himself as

'painter and zoologist'. In 1915 he married Eleanor (Norah; d. 1958), daughter of William James Hennessy, landscape painter, of Rudgwick, Sussex. They had one son, who died at birth. In the First World War he served first with the Royal Wiltshire yeomanry and then with his father's regiment, the Scots Guards. From 1924 until 1932, when he succeeded to the peerage, he made use of his scientific training as livestock officer, and later marketing officer, in the Ministry of Agriculture. The inspection of slaughterhouses, which was one of his duties, converted him permanently to vegetarianism.

Methuen had been taught drawing at Eton by 'Sammy' and Sidney Evans, of the long-established dynasty of drawing masters, and in Oxford at the Ruskin School and by the Slade professor Charles Holmes, but he was over forty before his individual style was formed. In 1927 he responded to an advertisement from Walter Sickert soliciting pupils. The master's conduct of his small class was so casual that it soon drifted away, but his influence on this pupil was decisive. The sombre, restrained tonality of Methuen's paintings, the rough, broken touch, and the emphasis on contour in the rendering of architecture obviously come from Sickert, but the artistic personality that he developed was quite distinctive. He had a strong feeling for architecture, as for natural history, and his preferred subjects were urban views and outdoor scenes with buildings, animals, and plants, notably the magnolias and orchids that he cultivated at Corsham. In these the sensitivity of the artist is combined with the exact observation of the scientist.

In 1939 Methuen rejoined his regiment and served on the staff as a captain until 1944, when he was transferred to the procurement and fine arts branch formed to protect historic buildings and works of art at risk during the invasion of the continent. He was posted to northern France, and in 1952 published an account of his activities (which extended to French Flanders, Belgium, and Holland) in *Normandy Diary*, a book of permanent value to the antiquarian and architectural historian, and one that can be read with pleasure by the non-specialist as an engaging but unconscious self-portrait.

The chief preoccupation of Methuen's later years, apart from his painting, and one for which he denied himself many luxuries, was the restoration, maintenance, and improvement of Corsham Court, the family seat, and of the collection of pictures that hung in the magnificent gallery built and furnished for them in the 1760s. He bought back as many as possible of those that his father had sold, and added a few more; in 1971 he published a useful short account of the history of the collection, together with a handlist based on the latest critical opinion; and he designed, and had woven in Spain, a carpet for the gallery, a room 72 feet long, with a pattern repeating the intricate stucco-work of the ceiling.

Methuen was a good-looking man, tall and fair, with a ruddy complexion. His distinguished presence was enhanced by a certain absent-mindedness about the way he wore his clothes. A peer who practises one of the arts inevitably risks being labelled a dilettante, but Methuen overcame the handicap of his rank and was accepted as a serious professional artist. In 1951 he was elected an associate of the Royal Academy and in 1959 Royal Academician. For more than thirty years he was president of the Royal West of England Academy in Bristol. Following the destruction of its premises in 1942, Methuen offered the Bath School of Art a site at Corsham Court until the school's closure in 1972. The school was notable for its distinguished teaching staff who included Peter Lanyon, Gillian Ayres, and Howard Hodgkin. He was a trustee of the National Gallery (1938–45) and of the Tate Gallery (1940–45), a fellow of the Society of Antiquaries and an honorary fellow of the Royal Institute of British Architects. Methuen died in Bath on 7 January 1974 and his brother Anthony Paul (b. 1891) succeeded to the peerage.

J. A. GERE, rev.

Sources The Times (8 Jan 1974) · E. Croft-Murray (1973) [exhibition catalogue, Fieldborne Gallery, London] · J. Pope-Hennessy and E. Croft-Murray, Memorial exhibition catalogue (1975) [Fieldborne Gallery, London] · personal knowledge (1993) · private information (1993) · Methuen: paintings and drawings (1989) [exhibition catalogue, Victoria Art Gallery, Bath]
Likenesses W. Stoneman, three photographs, 1919–51, NPG · Tunbridge, photograph, 1941, Hult. Arch. · D. McFall, bronze bust, c.1956, Corsham Court, Wiltshire · P. de Laszlo, oils, Corsham Court, Wiltshire · P. A. Methuen, self-portrait, pencil drawing, BM · photograph, repro. in The Times (18 Nov 1989)
Wealth at death £191,680: probate, 31 Dec 1974, CGPLA Eng. & Wales

Methuen, Paul Sanford, third Baron Methuen (1845–1932), army officer, was born at Corsham Court, Corsham, near Chippenham, Wiltshire, on 1 September 1845, the eldest of the three sons of Frederick Henry Paul Methuen, second Baron Methuen (1818–1891), and his wife, Anna Horatia Caroline (d. 1899), only child of John Sanford, rector of Nynehead, Somerset. He was descended from a brother of John *Methuen, who negotiated the Methuen treaty with Portugal. His grandfather Paul Methuen, first Baron Methuen (1779–1849), was an independent and sometimes radical MP for Wiltshire in several parliaments.

After Eton College (1858–60) and two years in the Royal Wiltshire yeomanry, Methuen joined the Scots Fusilier Guards as ensign and lieutenant (by purchase) in November 1864. He was promoted lieutenant and captain (by purchase) in December 1867; captain and lieutenant-colonel in July 1876; and regimental major in October 1882, after serving as adjutant of the 1st battalion from August 1868 to November 1871. He was brigade major, home district (1871–6), and assistant military secretary in Ireland (1877). He witnessed the Prussian army in France in 1871, and from 1878 to 1881 was military attaché in Berlin. In February 1881 he tried to rescue a man from the icy Spree River, for which he was awarded the gold medal for saving life. Apparently a military 'Prussophile', he attempted to introduce some German practices into the British army. Nevertheless, he did not favour conscription or compulsory training in Britain, but supported the volunteers and later the Territorial Force. He also favoured Cardwellian short service. He saw active service at Amoaful in the Second

Anglo-Asante War of 1873–4 on the staff of Sir Garnet Wolseley. On 18 June 1878 he married Evelyn (d. of tuberculosis 2 June 1879), eldest daughter (by his second marriage) of Sir Frederick Hutchinson Hervey-Bathurst, third baronet, of Clarendon Park, Wiltshire; they had no children.

Methuen received his brevet-colonelcy in 1881. He served as assistant adjutant and quartermaster-general, home district (1881–4). He was commandant at headquarters in Egypt for three months in 1882, being present at the battle of Tell al-Kebir, and was awarded the Osmanie (third class). Favoured by the queen and prince of Wales, he was a member of neither the Wolseley nor the Roberts ring and worked with both, but 'preferred the company of other aristocratic officers' (Miller, 19). On 9 January 1884 he married his cousin Mary Ethel (d. 11 May 1941), second daughter of William Ayshford Sanford, of Nynehead Court and formerly in the colonial service; they had three sons and two daughters, the elder of whom predeceased her father. The eldest child was the painter Paul Ayshford *Methuen. Methuen served in Sir Charles Warren's Bechuanaland expedition (1884–5), where he commanded Methuen's Horse, a corps of mounted rifles raised for the expedition, and obtained his first experience of South Africa and the Boers. Warren found him 'over-zealous and pushy' (Miller, 48). He was bitterly disappointed when Wolseley did not select him for the Gordon relief expedition. He obtained a land concession north of Mafeking, but his speculation failed.

In 1875 Methuen had been accepted at the Staff College and decided against attending, but in 1887 he attended some courses there. He was promoted major-general in May 1888 and substantive colonel in November 1888. He served as deputy adjutant-general in South Africa (1888–90), and wanted conciliation with the Boers. He agreed with their view of Africans and considered the English view 'philanthropic and rotten' (Miller, 52). In June 1890 he inspected Rhodes's pioneer column and, on behalf of the high commissioner, authorized its departure. In 1891 he succeeded his father in the title. He commanded the home district from 1892 to 1897, and organized the armed forces in the 1897 jubilee procession. In 1897 he went privately as an observer to the Tirah campaign, and he served as press censor at its headquarters; the campaign was his first experience of hill warfare. He was promoted lieutenant-general in April 1898, and on the outbreak of the Second South African War he was given command of the 1st division, though Milner wanted him made commander-in-chief in South Africa.

By the time Methuen reached South Africa, early in November 1899, the original plans had had to be abandoned. Methuen was ordered to relieve Kimberley, though neither Wolseley nor Lansdowne thought him capable of 'an almost independent command' (Gooch, 62–3). He had under 10,000 men, including few mounted troops. For lack of them, although he dislodged the Boers from positions at Belmont (23 November) and Graspan (25 November), these successes could not be exploited by an effective pursuit. At Graspan, although soldiers were available, he used the naval brigade as assault infantry, and they suffered heavy losses; he blamed them for not extending. However, contemporaries, including William Laird Clowes in his classic *The Royal Navy: a History*, condemned Methuen's misuse of the naval brigade. Attacking again on 28 November, he found the Boers' skilfully chosen position at the Modder River difficult to capture, but his left eventually crossed the river, and in the night the Boers retired. He was slightly wounded. Possibly he should have pressed on: the suspension of the advance allowed the Boers to draw reinforcements from Kimberley and Natal and to make their next position, at Magersfontein (north of the Modder River), formidable.

Methuen planned to attack the Boers at Magersfontein by means of the Highland brigade making a night march and a dawn attack. He failed to secure adequate reconnaissance or use his observation balloon, and so did not know where the Boer defences were: his artillery bombarded the wrong place. In the early morning of 11 December the highlanders met intense rifle fire from the concealed Boer trenches, and suffered heavy casualties; their commander, Major-General A. G. Wauchope, was killed. The attack failed, although for a time the issue apparently hung in the balance. Methuen blamed Wauchope and bad luck. The Highland brigade survivors, bitterly hostile, blamed Methuen. This 'disaster', one of the three defeats in 'black week', shocked the British. Methuen was much criticized in Britain, but General Sir Redvers Buller, though advised by Lansdowne in a cable to sack him, refused to make him a scapegoat by superseding him, and Lord Roberts, Methuen's friend, retained him in his command and declared that the task set Methuen had been impossible with that force. However, he quickly removed the Highland brigade from Methuen as 'it would not be safe to trust him in action with it' (Gooch, 154).

After French had relieved Kimberley (15 February), Methuen's force occupied the area. Relatively favourable to the Boers, Methuen disliked Rhodes and what he considered Rhodes's interference in military matters. During the operations which ended in initial failure at Paardeberg (18 February 1900), Methuen at the Modder River helped to detain General Piet Cronje in his position. Subsequently he conducted operations in the Kimberley–Boshof area during the advance on Pretoria with considerable success and continued actively engaged, mainly in western Transvaal, until the end of the war. Most officers of his seniority had gone home, but he remained, effectively demoted, chasing the elusive C. R. de Wet with skill and persistence. He had many minor successes, notably against General Jacobus Hendrik De la Rey near Klerksdorp on 19 February 1901; he gave his opponents no rest, made many captures, thwarted them again and again, and gained their respect as well as the trust and affection of his own men.

Towards the end of the war, at Tweebosch on 7 March 1902, Methuen's column—largely inexperienced yeomanry and colonial units—was attacked by De la Rey's commando. Many of the inexperienced troops panicked and fled. The regulars, especially the gunners, fought well, but the column was forced to surrender; this was the worst British defeat in the guerrilla war. Methuen, severely wounded in the thigh, was the only British general captured by the Boers. De la Rey sent him to the nearest British hospital; because of his wound, he had to use a stick for the rest of his life. In 1903 Methuen gave evidence to the Elgin royal commission on the war in South Africa, advocating the use of mounted infantry rather than traditional cavalry, and reforms including improved training and an improved status and role for the Staff College. Appointed colonel of the Scots Guards in May 1904, an appointment which gave him great pleasure, Methuen was promoted general the same month and in June received command of the Fourth Army corps. This was transformed into the eastern command in 1905, and there he put into practice the lessons he had learned in South Africa, particularly on accurate rifle fire. As a trainer and administrator he contributed to the high standard of the British expeditionary force in 1914.

In April 1908 Methuen was appointed general officer commanding-in-chief in South Africa, a post which he held until 1912. He was popular, particularly with his former opponents, and helped to improve relations between the Boers and the British. He was governor and commander-in-chief of Natal in 1910, and was promoted field marshal in June 1911.

Despite his age, Methuen was governor and commander-in-chief of Malta from February 1915 to May 1919, and it was due largely to his foresight that Malta was well equipped with hospitals and staff for the Dardanelles expedition. At the end of 1919 he was appointed constable of the Tower. He lived chiefly at Corsham Court, doing much to help the British Legion, the Church Lads' Brigade, the Boy Scouts, the VAD organization, and local movements and causes, winning affection and respect. He was appointed CB in 1882, CMG in 1886, KCVO in 1897, KCB in 1900, GCB in 1902, GCVO in 1910, and GCMG in 1919. He was a Liberal Unionist. Methuen died at Corsham Court on 30 October 1932.

C. T. ATKINSON, rev. ROGER T. STEARN

Sources *The Times* (31 Oct 1932) • J. F. Maurice and M. H. Grant, eds., *History of the war in South Africa, 1899–1902*, 4 vols. (1906–10) • private information (1949) • S. M. Miller, *Lord Methuen and the British army: failure and redemption in South Africa* (1999) • L. S. Amery, ed., *The Times history of the war in South Africa*, 7 vols. (1900–09) • T. Pakenham, *The Boer War* (1979) • Marquess of Anglesey [G. C. H. V. Paget], *A history of the British cavalry, 1816 to 1919*, 4 (1986) • P. Warwick and S. B. Spies, eds., *The South African War: the Anglo-Boer War, 1899–1902* (1980) • Burke, *Peerage* (1959) • GEC, *Peerage* • *Hart's Army List* (1891) • W. L. Clowes, *The Royal Navy: a history from the earliest times to the present*, 7 vols. (1897–1903), vol. 7 • A. Keppel-Jones, *Rhodes and Rhodesia: the white conquest of Zimbabwe, 1884–1902* (1983) • H. H. R. Bailes, 'The influence of continental examples and colonial warfare upon the reforms of the late Victorian army', PhD diss., U. Lond., 1980 • K. Surridge, '"All you soldiers are what we call pro-Boer": the military critique of the South African War, 1899–1902', *History*, new ser., 82 (1997), 582–600 • J. Gooch, ed., *The Boer War: direction, experience and image* (2000) • D. Lowry, ed., *The South African War reappraised* (2000)

Archives Wilts. & Swindon RO, corresp. and papers, WRO 1742 | BL, corresp. with Lord Gladstone, Add. MS 46009 • BL, corresp. with Lord Selborne, Add. MS 46003 • NAM, letters to Earl Roberts,

7101/23, 8310/155–62 · NAM, letters to Professor Spenser Wilkinson, relating to military training, 9011–42 · NRA, priv. coll., corresp. with Sir John Ewart · PRO, letters to Odo Russell, FO 918/54 · Wilts. & Swindon RO, corresp. with Viscount Long, WRO 947/132/619–21 | FILM BFI NFTVA, news footage

Likenesses Window & Grove, photograph, c.1899, repro. in H. W. Wilson, *With the flag to Pretoria*, 1 (1900), 124 · W. Carter, oils, 1904, Corsham Court, Wiltshire · J. S. Shirley-Fox, portrait, 1905, Corsham Court, Wiltshire · P. A. Methuen, oils, 1920, NPG · R. T., wood-engraving, NPG; repro. in *ILN* (6 Dec 1884) · Spy [L. Ward], caricature, chromolithograph, NPG; repro. in *VF* (17 Dec 1892)

Wealth at death £165,911 17s. 7d.: probate, 22 Feb 1933, CGPLA Eng. & Wales

Methven. For this title name *see* Stewart, Henry, first Lord Methven (c.1495–1553/4); Smythe, David, Lord Methven (1746–1806).

Methven, Sir (Malcolm) John (1926–1980), industrialist, was born on 14 February 1926 at Southampton, the younger of two sons of Lieutenant-Colonel Malcolm David Methven OBE, of Ledbury, and his wife, Helen Marion Watson. He was educated at Mill Hill School and at Gonville and Caius College, Cambridge, where he was a Tapp exhibitioner in law and a Tapp postgraduate law scholar. He gained a first class in part two of the law tripos in 1949 and was admitted solicitor in 1952. On 19 April the same year he married Margaret Field (b. 1922/3), daughter of Air Commodore Charles Henry Nicholas; they had three daughters.

In 1952 Methven joined Birmingham corporation as a solicitor but left local government service in 1957 to move to the metals division of ICI where he worked in the legal department in Birmingham, later moving to Millbank. He became head of the central purchasing department in 1968 and in 1970 was made deputy chairman of the Mond division.

In 1973 Methven left ICI to become the first director-general of the newly created office of fair trading (OFT). As the first consumer watchdog he strove to maintain a balance of interest between consumers on the one hand and trade and industry on the other—a feat which he performed with considerable skill, aided by his knowledge of the law, his experience as a former member of the Monopolies Commission, and a genuine interest in the needs of consumers.

Although previously unaccustomed to working in the public eye, Methven took in his stride the speaking engagements and media interviews necessary to ensure that the aims and activities of the OFT were known to a wide and diverse audience, and came to regard publicity as a major tool in attaining his objectives. He developed a close working relationship with journalists, who appreciated his accessibility and his straightforward and disarming manner. An early interviewer described him as '… a mild man; mild steel'. As the consumer's champion he brought about changes in standards, safety, and consumer information, and encouraged trade associations to adopt voluntary codes of practice as an alternative to legislation. In particular, he stimulated the advertising industry to improve its self-regulatory procedures.

In 1976 Methven became director-general of the Confederation of British Industry. He wanted it to be an organization with teeth which would provide an alternative voice to the TUC. He determined to broaden its base by attracting trade and commerce into membership in addition to the large manufacturing industries, to develop sound well-argued policies, and to publicize them widely in order to ensure that the case for private enterprise did not go unheard by default.

Methven was quickly recognized by the government, trade union leaders, and Whitehall officials as a tough opponent and a lucid and persistent advocate for industry. CBI members saw in him the ability, tenacity, and vigour to weld together a diverse organization and to provide leadership at a time of political and economic difficulty. Led by him they reacted vigorously against the Bullock report on industrial democracy and, in answer to his rallying call, 1300 delegates turned up at the first national CBI conference, held in Brighton in 1977 to argue the case for British business. One CBI member was heard to say as he waited nervously to speak on this first national occasion: 'I worked my way to the top, I didn't talk my way there'; but, under Methven's leadership, talk they did. In order to ensure the conference's success in media terms Methven walked Fleet Street, confronting editors in their offices, chivvying them to ensure that their papers were well represented in Brighton. As one editor commented, 'Whatever Methven does, he means it'. Methven's marriage was dissolved in 1977, and in that year he married Karen Jane, daughter of Walter Anderson Caldwell, research chemist.

Methven was knighted in 1978. A hard taskmaster, he drove no one harder than himself, and even at times of great personal achievement was driven to self-examination and to moments of self-doubt. He was always quick to seek, and listen to, the advice of others. Tall, lean, and somewhat lugubrious in appearance he was a lively and challenging colleague whose warm, whimsical, and engaging manner won him friends in every walk of life. Music, particularly opera, was one of his greatest pleasures. With his second wife he developed a love of sailing and found time to be one of the chief fund-raisers for the British entry *Lionheart* in the America's Cup. Methven died in London at the King Edward VII Hospital, Beaumont Street, Westminster, on 23 April 1980 at the age of fifty-four.
DOROTHY DRAKE, *rev.*

Sources *The Times* (24 April 1980) · *The Times* (26 April 1980) · *The Times* (20 May 1980) · personal knowledge (1986) · m. cert. · d. cert.

Archives U. Warwick Mod. RC, papers relating to CBI

Likenesses F. Belsky, sculptured head, Confederation of British Industry, London

Wealth at death £104,624: administration, 22 July 1980, CGPLA Eng. & Wales

Methven [Methuen], Paul (d. in or before 1607), Scottish minister and Church of England clergyman, was born at Falkland in Fife. Originally a baker in Dundee, he became an early convert to protestantism. He had certainly opportunity to profit from reforming and English influences then circulating in Dundee and went south 'to leirne letteris and to preach godis word' (*Historie and Cronicles*, 2.136) in England, where he received instruction from Miles Coverdale and married an Englishwoman. When forced to flee from England under Mary Tudor, he returned home by 1558 to preach in Dundee and elsewhere in Forfarshire and in Fife at the homes of lairds. He administered the sacraments at Lundie, and in April 1558 was active in destroying images. He is also known to have administered communion at Cupar 'in the Lady Brackmonthis hous, at the begynnyn of the religion' (Fleming, 1.286). When he was summoned, with others from Dundee, to appear in Edinburgh before the queen regent and privy council on 20 July 1558 to answer for his actions, the case was deferred on account of the presence of nobles sympathetic to his cause.

Methven's services as a protestant preacher were sought by the bailies of Aberdeen anxious to recruit him in 1559 but his first public ministry was in Dundee, the earliest burgh to exhibit the face of a reformed church from 1558. In November 1558 he was summoned by the bishops and, in his absence, was 'condemned to be banished' (Calderwood, 1.347), though his supporters in Dundee continued to protect him. When the queen regent ordered his arrest the provost of Dundee, the latter alerted Methven to avoid the town. On 10 May 1559 he and other prominent reformers were sent for trial before the justiciary court in Stirling for usurping the ministerial office, for administering without the consent of ordinaries the sacrament of the altar in a manner different from that of the Catholic church at Easter in Dundee, Montrose, and elsewhere in Forfarshire and Kincardineshire by convening the lieges, and for preaching erroneous doctrines and inciting disturbances. Denounced as a rebel and outlawed for usurping the authority of the church, Methven found succour as the lords of the congregation began to mobilize their forces to defend the preachers.

With the success of the Reformation, Methven was translated in 1560 from Dundee to Jedburgh in the borders and was present at early general assemblies of the church, but was deposed from the ministry and excommunicated in 1563 for adultery with his servant. Knox, who played a principal part in these proceedings, admitted that 'the trial and examination of that crime was difficult' (*Knox's History*, 1.66). To the indignation of the Scottish church, Methven fled to England and entered the ministry there, where he seems to have been commended by Coverdale and Edmund Grindal, bishop of London, to John Parkhurst, bishop of Norwich, who welcomed him as a learned and excellent preacher. Between 1564 and 1566 the general assembly was ready to hear his contrition and admit him to repentance, but it refused his request to have his case expunged from the register, insisting he appear in church in Edinburgh as a penitent in sackcloth, bareheaded and barefooted, to profess his sorrow and request the congregation's forgiveness and then to repeat the procedure at Dundee and Jedburgh. On returning to Scotland in 1566, Methven began the process of submission but left for England before completing his task. In

1570 he obtained English naturalization and was instituted to four benefices in south-west England. He also remarried: his second wife was Anne Rogers of Cannington (*d.* 1610). On 12 August 1577 he was collated to the prebend of Combe XI in Wells Cathedral, resigning it in favour of his son Anthony in 1590, when he was installed in Combe X instead. In 1584 he was in contact with the earl of Leicester and the exiled Scottish ministers. Paul Methven had died by 23 April 1607. His descendants prospered as clothiers, diplomats, and landowners, and were raised to the peerage as barons Methuen in 1838.　　JAMES KIRK

Sources *The historie and cronicles of Scotland … by Robert Lindesay of Pitscottie*, ed. A. J. G. Mackay, 3 vols., STS, 42–3, 60 (1899–1911) • G. Buchanan, *Opera omnia* (1725) • D. Laing, ed., *The miscellany of the Wodrow Society*, Wodrow Society, [9] (1844) • D. Calderwood, *The history of the Kirk of Scotland*, ed. T. Thomson and D. Laing, 8 vols., Wodrow Society, 7 (1842–9) • *CSP Scot., 1547–85* • T. Thomson, ed., *Acts and proceedings of the general assemblies of the Kirk of Scotland*, 3 pts, Bannatyne Club, 81 (1839–45) • J. Row, *The history of the Kirk of Scotland, from the year 1558 to August 1637*, ed. D. Laing, Wodrow Society, 4 (1842) • J. Spottiswood, *The history of the Church of Scotland*, ed. M. Napier and M. Russell, 3 vols., Bannatyne Club, 93 (1850) • *John Knox's History of the Reformation in Scotland*, ed. W. C. Dickinson, 2 vols. (1949) • *The works of John Knox*, ed. D. Laing, 6 vols., Wodrow Society, 12 (1846–64) • T. McCrie, *The life of John Knox* (1812) • R. Pitcairn, ed., *Ancient criminal trials in Scotland*, 7 pts in 3, Bannatyne Club, 42 (1833) • W. Page, ed., *Letters of denization and acts of naturalization for aliens in England, 1509–1603*, Huguenot Society of London, 8 (1893) • *Registrum Matthei Parker, diocesis Cantuariensis, AD 1559–1575*, ed. W. H. Frere and E. M. Thompson, 1, CYS, 35 (1928) • H. Robinson, ed. and trans., *The Zurich letters, comprising the correspondence of several English bishops and others with some of the Helvetian reformers, during the early part of the reign of Queen Elizabeth*, 1, Parker Society, 7 (1842) • *Calendar of the manuscripts of the most hon. the marquis of Salisbury*, 2, HMC, 9 (1888) • F. W. Weaver, ed., *Somerset incumbents* (privately printed, Bristol, 1889) • D. H. Fleming, ed., *Register of the ministers, elders, and deacons of the Christian congregation of St Andrews*, 2 vols., Scottish History Society, 4, 7 (1889–90) • *Fasti Angl., 1541–1857*, [Bath and Wells] • Burke, *Peerage* (1999)

Methwold [Methold], **William** (*bap.* 1590, *d.* 1653), administrator in India, was baptized in September 1590, the son of Thomas Methwold of South Pickenham, near Swaffham, Norfolk, and his wife, Susan, daughter of Anthony Hogan (or Hoogan) of Castle Acre, also near Swaffham. The judge Sir William Methold was his uncle. Aged sixteen he was apprenticed to an English merchant, serving four years in London, five in Middelburg in the Netherlands. He knew Latin, became fluent in Dutch and French, and later could converse in Persian, the language of the Mughal court and high officials.

In September 1615 Methwold was accepted for service in the East India Company and sailed in the *Unicorn* in its 1616 fleet, arriving in Surat, Gujarat, in September of that year. During the voyage he was transferred, as a linguist, to the flagship, which engaged an aggressive Portuguese carrack, which was disabled, ran ashore, and was burned by her crew. While based at Surat he toured some of the inland markets. In March 1617 he sailed in command of the *Unicorn* as chief merchant, to obtain pepper and deliver it to Bantam, Java. Spending over four of the hottest months in Tiku, Sumatra, buying pepper, he was attacked by the bloody flux (dysentery), and many of his crew died of infections for which there were no known preventions or cures. He survived, as few contemporaries did, nearly fifteen years in company service abroad, including prolonged voyages. The company's council at Bantam, then controlling its interests on the east coast of India, appointed him chief merchant on the Coromandel coast, based in Masulipatam, where he arrived in May 1618 and remained until October 1622. To his indignation he was recalled to London to answer allegations of dishonesty. He freely admitted to private trading, then totally forbidden though widely practised, and was held responsible for the loss of an investment in diamonds, stolen from his servant by brigands. Other charges proved groundless. From April 1624 Methwold ceased to be officially connected to the company, but appears to have maintained close relations with it, and to have traded on his own account. He married Mary Wright (d. 1652), daughter of William Wright of Sevenoaks, Kent, in April 1624. They had two sons and three daughters. Their elder son, William, was apprenticed to the company, sailing to the Coromandel coast in 1643, aged thirteen, and Methwold willed that their younger son, Thomas, be apprenticed to a Levant company merchant.

In June 1628 Methwold accepted the freedom of the East India Company, entitling him to become a shareholder. Invited to become chief factor in Persia in 1629, he demanded a higher salary than the company would pay. From 1630 to 1633 he held the ceremonial appointment of deputy swordbearer of the city of London. In the latter year he was appointed president at Surat, which now also controlled the Coromandel coast. He arrived at Surat in November 1633 and found the hinterland to have been depopulated by successive droughts, followed by famine and disease. Business remained precarious until 1636. In that year the company was held responsible for attacks on Surat shipping by English pirates, and he suffered imprisonment until an indemnity was provided from company funds. Meanwhile, in 1635, he had concluded a very valuable pact with the Portuguese viceroy at Goa, which henceforth ended hostilities and allowed the English the use of Portuguese ports, the protection of their fortresses, and access to their stores. He persistently advocated the potentialities of Portuguese-owned Bombay as harbour, base, and gateway to the riches of India; the company would acquire it in 1667 from Charles II, to whom Bombay had been ceded in his wife's dowry.

Invited to serve the company at home, Methwold sailed in command of the Mary in January 1639. An attack by Malabar pirates was repulsed, but prolonged delays by contrary winds resulted in the voyage taking almost twelve months. On arrival in England one of his first duties was to appear before Charles I in support of a remonstrance against the Courteen Company, which was infringing the East India Company's charter. As contriver of the Goa pact, he held successful discussions with the Portuguese ambassador to ensure its terms remained effective now that Portugal had regained its independence from Spain. Appointed a committee (director) of the company in 1640, he was elected deputy governor in 1643

and was re-elected annually until his death. About 1640 he acquired Hale House and adjoining land in Kensington, which became his home.

Methwold negotiated the amalgamation of the East India Company's interests with those of the rival Assada Company in 1649. His negotiating skills were noticed in government, but in 1649 he declined an invitation to become ambassador in Madrid. His wife died in October 1652 and in the following February he married Sarah (d. 1678?), daughter of Sir Richard Deane and widow of William Rolfe of Ealing, Middlesex. He made her executrix of his will on 20 February and died only days later on 5 March 1653, at Hale House. He was buried, under the name Meathall, in St Mary Abbots Church, Kensington, on 10 March. The company's records show that he had bought its shares to a considerable value and had purchased large quantities of Eastern commodities for resale, and he died a wealthy man.

Apart from forthright letters and reports to the company, partly published, he composed a 'Relation of Golconda', a brilliant description of that part of India, which appeared in the 1626 edition of Samuel Purchas's *Purchas his Pilgrimage*. It included brief descriptions of the kingdoms of Arakan, Pegu, and Tenasserim, based on trade information, not personal observation. An extensively annotated edition of the text was published by W. H. Moreland in 1931. MICHAEL STRACHAN

Sources W. H. Moreland, ed., *Relations of Golconda*, Hakluyt Society, 2nd ser., 66 (1931) · A. R. Ingram, *The gateway of India: the story of Methwold and Bombay* (1938) · *CSP col.*, vols. 2–4, 6, 8 · E. B. Sainsbury, ed., *A calendar of the court minutes … of the East India Company*, 11 vols. (1907–38) · F. C. Danvers and W. Foster, eds., *Letters received by the East India Company from its servants in the east*, 6 vols. (1896–1902) · *DNB* · R. C. Prasad, *Early English travellers in India* (1965); 2nd rev. edn (1980) · S. Purchas, *Purchas his pilgrimage*, 4th edn (1626) · L. E. Pennington, ed., *The Purchas handbook: studies of the life, time and writings of Samuel Purchas*, 2 vols., Hakluyt Society, 2nd ser., 185–6 (1997) · *The embassy of Sir Thomas Roe to the court of the great mogul, 1615–1619*, ed. W. Foster, Hakluyt Society, 2nd ser., 1–2 (1899); rev. edn (1926) · E. Terry, *A voyage to East India* (1655) · J. B. Tavernier, *Travels in India*, ed. V. Ball, 2 vols. (1889) · PRO, PROB 11/231, fols. 20v–22r · parish register, London, Kensington, St Mary Abbots, 10 March 1653 [burial]

Archives BL OIOC

Wealth at death wealthy; property in Norfolk, Somerset, London, and Yorkshire: will, PRO, PROB 11/231, fols. 20v–22r

Métivier, Georges (1790–1881), Guernsey patois poet and philologist, was born on 29 January 1790 in Fountain Street, St Peter Port, Guernsey, the second of the five children of Jean-Carey Métivier (1757–1796), advocate, and his wife, Esther (1762–1839), daughter of Jean Guille. He came of a French Huguenot family. His grandfather had fled from France, finding refuge first in the Netherlands, later in Guernsey. Jean-Carey Métivier was an able advocate but died while comparatively young.

Very little can be ascertained about the early years of Métivier. After the death of his father, in 1796 the family went to live at St George, the home of his mother's family, in the Castel parish. According to tradition, Métivier spent many years of his early manhood away from the island.

One source suggests that he pursued medical studies at Edinburgh University. The university has no record of his matriculating or taking a degree; it should be remembered, however, that at that time it was not unusual for students to attach themselves privately to a tutor. Métivier may indeed have studied at Edinburgh. It was perhaps while there that he became interested in ancient languages. During the course of his life he learned Hebrew, Chaldaic, Arabic, Latin, Greek, and several modern languages and dialects. There is also a tradition that he spent some time in commerce. This may be a plausible inference, since two of his brothers (Charles and Carey Henry) became established as merchants in Bristol, and a third (Jean) at Cartagena. These brothers were part of a large network of Guernsey merchants involved in international trade based on St Peter Port (Guernsey) and Rio de Janeiro (Brazil).

Métivier returned to Guernsey about 1830. An obituary, generally well informed, states that he resided in the island of his birth 'from the year 1830 till his death' (*Guernsey Magazine*). Soon after his return he published his first collection of poems in the Guernsey patois, *Rimes Guernesiaises par un Câtelain* (1831); a Câtelain is an inhabitant of the Castel parish. This was followed by a stream of poems published in local newspapers and magazines, some of them republished as *Fantaisies Guernesiaises* (1866). Another collection, *Poésies Guernesiaises et Françaises*, was published posthumously in 1883. Métivier's patois poems belong to the nineteenth-century tradition of regional lyricism. In a letter to him, Victor Hugo summarized the Guernseyman's verses as 'si savants dans leur naïveté, si gracieux dans leur rudesse' ('so perceptive in their innocence, so polished in their ruggedness'; Hugo to Métivier, 18 June 1866). Paul Stapfer, French master at Elizabeth College and friend of Hugo, observed that some of Métivier's poems were in fact translations of works by Burns, Béranger, and others (Stapfer, 228). Métivier's 'supporters' defended him on the ground that many of his productions, 'unlike most translations, turned out superior to the originals, notably that of his French version of "Tupper's Proverbial Philosophy"' (*Guernsey Magazine*).

Métivier's interest in philology led him to correspond with William Barnes on matters linguistic and to join the London Philological Society. In 1862 Prince Lucien Buonaparte visited him, and this led to Métivier's rendering of the gospel of Matthew into patois (1863) and a translation of the sermon on the mount and the parable of the sower. His philological research culminated in his great opus, *Dictionnaire franco-normand, ou, Recueil des mots particuliers au dialecte de Guernesey, faisant voir leurs relations romanes, celtiques et tudesques* (1870). This was a magnificent gallimaufry of scholarship, antiquarianism, eccentricity, and poetry. Despite some curious etymologies the book was many years later still regarded as an important resource, 'being the only full bilingual dictionary with Guernesiais lemmata' (Coates, 80).

Métivier lived as something of a recluse.

He never moves away from his retired little hermitage, where he lives with one old Welshwoman as servant. I suspect that his worldly means are very small, and chiefly confined to very old books, of which he has a curious collection scattered about his little dark den,

recorded Charles Tennant in a letter to William Barnes (Baxter, 219). Métivier's contemporaries recognized both his greatness and his shortcomings. 'Had he but possessed system and method in the arrangement and dissemination of his knowledge, he would have been one of the lights not only of Guernsey but of the world', observed an obituarist (*Guernsey Magazine*). He was remembered as a charming companion 'when in conversation he could be pinned to a given subject. His remarks were … often intermingled with a spice of wit and humour' (ibid.). He died, unmarried, in Guernsey on 23 March 1881 and was buried there six days later in St Martin's churchyard.

GREGORY COX

Sources 'Insular biography', *Guernsey Magazine*, 9/4 (1881), [8] · R. Lebarbenchon, *La grève de Lecq: Guernesey et Jersey* (Cherbourg, 1988) · R. Lebarbenchon, ed., *Des filles, une sorcière, Dame Toumasse et quelques autres* (Cherbourg, 1980) · P. J. Girard, 'George Metivier, Guernsey's "national" poet', *Report and Transactions* [Société Guernesiaise], 20 (1976–80), 617–33 · V. Hugo, letter to G. Métivier, 18 June 1866, priv. coll. [Gregory Stevens Cox] · R. Coates, *A bibliography of Channel Islands French and the general linguistic situation in the islands to 1997* (1998) · P. Stapfer, *Causeries Guernesiaises* (1869) · L. Baxter, *The life of William Barnes, poet and philologist* (1887) · Greffe, Royal Court, Guernsey, Métivier family files · Métivier family file, Priaulx Library, Guernsey

Likenesses engraving (after photograph), repro. in G. Métivier, *Dictionnaire franco-normand* (1870) · portrait; formerly Guille-Allès Library, Guernsey

Mettingham, John of (d. 1301), justice, makes his first appearance in surviving records in 1270, when he brought an action of trespass in the common bench as rector of Shotley in Suffolk. He was probably already a clerk of Gilbert of Preston (d. 1274), the chief justice of that court, and his service to Preston may date back to at least 1265. After Preston's death he received appointment as one of the regular justices of the newly established assize circuits in 1274. When arrangements were made in the summer of 1278 to create two permanent circuits of the general eyre he was one of the justices appointed to the 'northern' circuit. He sat as a junior justice on every eyre of that circuit until 1288. He became chief justice of the circuit for the Dorset eyre of 1288. Mettingham seems to have been assigned special responsibility for hearing *quo warranto* and related pleas on his eyre circuit, but this was certainly not the only business that he heard. Extant reports and other evidence show that he also sat in on the hearing of ordinary civil litigation in at least five counties.

From 1285 onwards Mettingham was also (like most of his colleagues) assigned to take assizes during vacations in one of the newly reorganized assize circuits. Mettingham was fortunate to escape conviction during the so-called 'state trials' of 1289–93. When one complainant alleged that Mettingham had been sitting in the common bench while the complainant had had his proper challenges to jurors refused, the auditors of complaints simply accepted his statement that he had been sitting on the bench not as a justice but as a well-wisher of the complainant's opponent (the prior of Sempringham). In a series of other cases from eyres where Mettingham had been one of the justices, the auditors accepted his 'record' that he had not been sitting in the court when the case concerned was decided. By the time these cases were heard Mettingham had replaced the disgraced Thomas of Weyland (*d.* 1298) as chief justice of the common bench, a post he held from the beginning of 1290 until the time of his death. During this period, as the surviving reports show, Mettingham was clearly the major figure in his court, though this dominance came increasingly to be shared from the mid-1290s with his colleague William Bereford (*d.* 1326).

John of Mettingham was a beneficed clergyman and seems to have left no children. He died between the end of Trinity term and 19 September 1301, when Ralph Hengham (*d.* 1311) replaced him as chief justice of the common bench. PAUL BRAND

Sources Common Pleas rolls, PRO, CP40 · Eyre Rolls, PRO, JUST 1 · *Chancery records* · unpubd law reports, BL; CUL · D. Crook, *Records of the general eyre*, Public Record Office Handbooks, 20 (1982)

Metzler, Johann Georg. *See* Giesecke, Charles Lewis (1761–1833).

Meudwy Môn. *See* Jones, Owen (1806–1889).

Meulan. For this title name *see* Beaumont, Robert de, count of Meulan and first earl of Leicester (*d.* 1118); Waleran, count of Meulan and earl of Worcester (1104–1166).

Meuland [Meuleng, Meulent, Molend], **Roger de** [Master Longespée] (*c.*1215–1295), bishop of Coventry and Lichfield, was a kinsman of Henry III. He is once referred to by the chronicler Matthew Paris as Master Longespée (Paris, *Chron.*, 5.644), and it is thus possible that he was a son of William *Longespée, earl of Salisbury (*d.* 1226), who was Henry III's uncle. The reason why Roger was styled de Meuland (Meuleng, Meulent, and Molend are among the variant forms of his name) is unclear, although it probably indicates some connection with Meulon in Normandy. Perhaps it was there that he was born or brought up.

Nothing seems known of Meuland's early career. By 1257 he was a canon of Lichfield and a papal chaplain. He owed his election to the bishopric of Coventry and Lichfield, in the January of that year (his consecration followed on 10 March 1258), to the influence of the king's brother, Richard, earl of Cornwall. Later in 1257 Meuland went out to Germany with Richard, where the latter had been elected king. He repeated the journey in 1258. Meuland was no mere creature of Henry III and his brother, however. In 1259 he incurred Henry's wrath by attempting to subject the royal free chapels in his diocese to episcopal control, a dispute that rumbled on until Meuland's final capitulation in 1281.

On the other hand, Meuland cannot be ranked as one of the episcopal supporters of Simon de Montfort. In July 1263 the king empowered him, with Richard of Gravesend, bishop of Lincoln, and Henry of Sandwich, bishop of London, to reach a settlement with Montfort, but the reimposition of the provisions of Oxford that resulted reflected the realities of the political situation rather than Meuland's own political stance. The latter is seen more clearly in March 1264 when Meuland represented Henry III in the abortive negotiations before the final outbreak of hostilities. He was prepared to co-operate with the subsequent regime of Simon de Montfort—in December 1264 he helped to arrange a temporary settlement with the marcher barons—but he was not one of the bishops suspended from office after the battle of Evesham. Between 1258 and 1272 Meuland, like previous bishops of Coventry and Lichfield, was frequently appointed to be the king's representative in negotiations with the Welsh. After 1272 this and any other political activity ceased. Despite being, as Henry III expressed it, 'bound to the king by right of blood [*iure sanguinis*] before all other prelates of the realm' (*Close Rolls*, 10.486), Meuland appears to have played but a modest part in affairs of state.

As bishop of Coventry and Lichfield, Meuland's record was mixed. In 1282 Archbishop John Peckham, after a visitation of the bishopric, wrote him a blistering letter of criticism. Peckham had discovered the prevalence of incest, an infinite multitude of children lacking confirmation, the appropriation of churches to the great damage of the cure of souls and Meuland himself, 'as though not caring about these things and others', living outside the diocese. Meuland was ordered to appoint a suffragan bishop 'knowing the language' (Martin, 2.479–80), a hint perhaps that Meuland himself (who may have been brought up in France) did not. While there is evidence to support some of Peckham's accusations, especially over appropriations, they were made when Meuland was already a sick man in decline: when he died, on 16 December 1295, he was described as of great age. On the more positive side, Meuland and his officials ordained or enlarged at least five vicarages. He was also the first bishop of Coventry and Lichfield to keep an episcopal register (later lost).

If Meuland did neglect his diocese, he certainly spoke of his 'devotion to his spouse, the church of Lichfield' (Savage, 164) and did much to display it. 'For the increase of divine worship' (though also to provide patronage for his protégés), he created three new prebends, one endowed with land he himself had acquired. One of his last acts was to issue new statutes governing the conduct of the chapter, which increased the daily provision for each prebendary. Earlier, in 1278, when Meuland permitted the appropriation by Stafford Priory of the church of Stowe by Chartley, he made no stipulation about the creation of a vicarage, but he did obtain an annual pension of 10 marks for the dean and chapter of Lichfield's common fund. Likewise, when he secured an annual pension of 30 marks from the church of Wigan, he assigned 10 marks to the fabric fund of the cathedral and 20 marks to the sacrist, of which half was to be assigned to six boys appointed by the bishop.

The reference to the fabric fund is significant. It was during Meuland's episcopate that the whole of the present nave of Lichfield Cathedral was built, together with the lower part of the great west front. Meuland may have played a significant part in raising funds for the enterprise. He may also have inspired certain elements of the design. In particular, the unique clerestory windows, consisting of three trefoiled circles, were modelled on the external triforium windows of Henry III's Westminster Abbey, perhaps a graceful tribute by Bishop Roger to his royal kinsman. Roger de Meuland's record, both as a political and as a diocesan bishop, was mediocre. As a builder he has at least a claim, albeit an unprovable one, to fame.

D. A. CARPENTER, rev.

Sources H. E. Savage, ed., *The great register of Lichfield Cathedral known as Magnum registrum album*, William Salt Archaeological Society, 3rd ser. (1924, [1926]) · *Registrum epistolarum fratris Johannis Peckham, archiepiscopi Cantuariensis*, ed. C. T. Martin, 3 vols., Rolls Series, 77 (1882–5) · *VCH Staffordshire*, vol. 3 · P. Brieger, *English art, 1216–1307* (1957) · *Close rolls of the reign of Henry III*, 10, PRO (1931)

Meulen, Steven van der (*d.* **1563/4**), painter, was the son of Rinnold (or Rumold) van der Meulen. In 1543 he was a pupil of the Antwerp artist Willem van Cleve (*fl.* 1530–1564). In 1552 he registered with the Guild of St Luke in Antwerp and by September 1560 he had arrived in London. In early 1561 van der Meulen travelled to Stockholm to paint Erik XIV of Sweden, who was vying for the hand of Elizabeth I of England. The portrait that resulted, painted in March of that year, so pleased Erik that he gave the artist 100 daler and in June 1561 it was presented to Elizabeth (Nationalmuseum, Gripsholm Castle, Stockholm). Van der Meulen appears to have made more than one copy of the portrait as a note on the rear of a smaller version (Nationalmuseum, Gripsholm Castle, Stockholm) states that the canvas was intended for a proposed match with a princess of Hesse-Cassel, Prussia. On 22 June 1561 van der Meulen is mentioned in a list of members of the Dutch church; he became a naturalized citizen of England on 4 February 1562. An inventory of Lord Lumley's collection taken in 1590 refers to portraits by the 'famous paynter Steven' of Lord and Lady Lumley dated 1563 (priv. coll.), 'the last Earl of Arundell drawn twise' (priv. coll.) and of the count of Egmont. Reference to the artist's will, dated 5 October 1563 and proved on 20 January 1564, has dramatically narrowed the artist's *œuvre* by excluding portraits attributed to van der Meulen made after January 1564, before which date he had died in London, probably of the plague. In his will, van der Meulen's wife is named as Gertrude Stubbeleeren (or Stubbeleren); his two children, Rumold (or Rinnold) and Eric, are also mentioned in addition to his father, to whom he left his property overseas with the proviso that this would pass, on his father's death, to his brothers and sisters. Van der Meulen also left specific bequests to his mother's sister, his brother, Hadrian, and an unmarried sister. His children are referred to in his will in terms that imply a previous marriage. Van der Meulen's work reflects the dissemination in Elizabethan England of the style developed by his more famous contemporary Anthonis Mor.

P. G. MATTHEWS and ELIZABETH DREY-BROWN

Sources K. Hearn, ed., *Dynasties: painting in Tudor and Jacobean England, 1530–1630* (1995), 60–61, 71, 93–4, 96, 158, no. 47 [exhibition catalogue, Tate Gallery, London, 12 Oct 1995 – 7 Jan 1996] ·

R. Strong, *Tudor and Jacobean portraits*, 2 vols. (1969), 119–34 · E. Auerbach, *Tudor artists* (1954), 177 · S. Strömbom, 'Erik XIV's porträtt', *Nationalmuseui Årsbok* (1933), 12–48 · W. G. Constable, 'A new work by "the famous paynter Steven"', *Burlington Magazine*, 67 (1935), 135–6 · K. E. Steneberg, *Vasarenässansens porträttkonst* (1935), 25–9 · S. Strömbom, 'A Flemish painter at the Swedish court, 1561', *Actes du XVIIme congrès international d'histoire de l'art* (1955), 361–4 · G. F. Hill, 'Two Netherlandish artists in England: Steven van Herwijk and Steven van der Meulen', *Walpole Society*, 11 (1922), 29–32 · PRO, PROB 11/47, fol. 14r

Meulles, Nicholas de. *See* Moels, Sir Nicholas de (*d.* 1268/9).

Meurig [Mauricius Morganensis, Maurice] (*fl.* **1210**), Welsh-language poet, was probably also the treasurer of the diocese of Llandaff. The date of his activity is apparently determined by a passage in Gerald of Wales's 'De principis instructione' (§3, chap. 28). This work states that a long-deceased soldier–poet appeared in a vision to Meurig (Mauricius) and invited him to complete a poem prophesying the interdict imposed on England in the reign of King John. Gerald asserts in the same work that Meurig, whom he describes as 'vir bonus et copiose litteratus', was a Glamorgan man and a brother of Clement, abbot of Neath. John Bale confirms his origins in calling him Mauricius Morganensis and, like Gerald, refers to his literary talents, attributing to him a book of Latin epigrams and several volumes in Welsh. It has therefore been concluded that this Mauricius may reasonably be identified with the Meurig who was treasurer of Llandaff in Gerald's time.

In the Iolo manuscripts Meurig is said to have been the author of 'Y cwta cyfarwydd', a history of the whole island of Britain, a book of proverbs, works on Welsh poetry and theology, and a translation of the gospel of St John from Latin into Welsh, with commentaries. No trace of these works has been found, probably because they did not exist. The extant manuscript called 'Y cwta cyfarwydd' was written in the first half of the fifteenth century, somewhere in west Glamorgan or the Gower, possibly by a certain 'Dauyd', whose name is recorded on one of its pages and who may have been a monk at Neath Abbey.

C. W. LEWIS

Sources *Gir. Camb. opera*, 8.162, 310 · G. Owen, *The description of Penbrokshire*, ed. H. Owen, 4 vols., Honourable Society of Cymmrodorion, Cymmrodorion Record Series, 1 (1892–1936), pts 1–2 · NL Wales, MS 9266 · T. Williams, ed., *Iolo manuscripts* (1848) · *Report on manuscripts in the Welsh language*, 2 vols. in 7, HMC, 48 (1898–1910), vol. 1, p. 389 · G. Williams, ed., *Glamorgan county history, 3. The middle ages*, ed. T. B. Pugh (1971) · Bale, *Index*

Meurug, Rhys. *See* Merrick, Rice (*c.*1520–1587).

Meux [*formerly* Lambton], **Sir Hedworth** (1856–1929), naval officer, was born in London on 5 July 1856, the third son of George Frederick D'Arcy Lambton, second earl of Durham (1828–1879), and his wife, Lady Beatrix Frances (*d.* 21 Jan 1871), the second daughter of James *Hamilton, first duke of Abercorn. He was educated at Cheam School and entered the *Britannia* as a cadet in 1870. He went to sea in December 1871 in the frigate *Endymion*, of the channel squadron, and in August 1874 was transferred to the flagship *Agincourt*, under Sir Beauchamp Seymour. From the beginning of 1875, until promoted sub-lieutenant at the end of that year, he was with the flagship *Undaunted* in the East Indies. From the end of 1876 to March 1879 he served in the flagship *Alexandra*, in the Mediterranean under Sir Geoffrey Hornby. After being promoted lieutenant in February 1879, in 1880 he returned to the *Alexandra* as flag lieutenant to his old chief Sir Beauchamp Seymour, under whom he was present at the bombardment of Alexandria (11 July 1882) and took part in the ensuing operations on the coast of Egypt. Admiral Seymour (created Lord Alcester for his services), on leaving his command to join the Board of Admiralty in March 1883, secured a 'haul-down' promotion for his flag lieutenant. Following his return home, Lambton went to Dublin as aide-de-camp to the lord lieutenant, the fifth Earl Spencer. In July 1886 he returned to the Mediterranean in command of the sloop *Dolphin*, and in February 1888 he was appointed to command the royal yacht *Osborne*, a post he held until he was promoted captain in 1889. He was a friend of the prince of Wales (later Edward VII). From 1890 to 1892 he was flag captain to Charles Hotham in the *Warspite* on the Pacific station.

In July 1894 Earl Spencer, then first lord of the Admiralty, appointed Lambton his naval private secretary, a post he retained under Spencer's successor, Viscount Goschen, until 1897. In this important office both ministers placed great reliance on Lambton's judgement on senior officers' appointments; more than once Lambton advised his chief to make appointments to which the naval lords objected. He was not popular with the officers with whom he dealt through the lack of consideration which he showed them, although he was far junior to most of them in rank and to all of them in age.

In 1897 Lambton went to the China station in command of the large protected cruiser *Powerful*—with her sister ship, the *Terrible*, the largest warship of her day—and on his voyage home in her in October 1899 he was sent to Durban, at a critical time early in the Second South African War. On his way he called at Mauritius, and on his own initiative embarked the 2nd battalion, South Yorkshire regiment. Sir George White, commanding at Ladysmith, had been sending urgent messages for more powerful guns. Captain Percy Scott, in the *Terrible*, which had arrived at the Cape on its way to replace the *Powerful* on the China station, improvised field-carriages for naval guns, and with four long 12-pounders and two 4.7 inch guns Lambton landed with a naval brigade and arrived at Ladysmith on 30 October, just in time to prevent its surrender to the besieging Boers. The naval guns, though short of ammunition, countered the Boer artillery throughout the siege. The naval brigade gained much press coverage and praise: G. W. Steevens of the *Daily Mail* wrote that 'this handful of sailors have been the saving of Ladysmith' (Steevens, 141). Lambton was, in White's words, 'the life of the garrison' until its relief (28 February). Lambton was created CB, and on the arrival of the *Powerful* in England was welcomed with great popular enthusiasm.

At the end of 1900 Lambton was persuaded by Lord Rosebery and by his brother, Lord Durham, to stand at the general election as a Liberal candidate for Newcastle upon Tyne, but he was unsuccessful. In April 1901 he was appointed to command the royal yacht *Victoria and Albert*, and three months later was made commodore in charge of the king's yachts; he retained this command until April 1903, having been promoted rear-admiral in October 1902. From June 1903 he had a year's service afloat as second in command to Lord Charles Beresford in the Channel Fleet, and from November 1904 to December 1906 he commanded the cruiser division of the Mediterranean Fleet. In 1902–3 he criticized Fisher's Selborne scheme of officer training. In the subsequent polarization of naval officers into rival groups, Fisher's 'fishpond' and Beresford's 'syndicate of discontent', Lambton (formerly friendly with Fisher) was from 1906 a leader of the latter group. In January 1908 he was appointed vice-admiral and commander-in-chief in China.

Lambton returned home in April 1910, and on 18 April married Mildred Cecilia Harriet (27 Feb 1869 – 17 Sept 1942), the third daughter of Henry Gerard *Sturt, first Baron Alington (1825–1904), and the widow of Viscount Chelsea (d. 1908), the second son of the fifth Earl Cadogan. In the following December he came into a large fortune under the will of Valerie Susie, the widow of Sir Henry Brent Meux, third baronet, a brewer, of Theobald's Park, Waltham Cross. During the Second South African War Lady Meux, hearing of the landing of the naval guns for the defence of Ladysmith, had ordered six naval 12-pounders on travelling carriages to be made at Elswick and sent to Lord Roberts in South Africa. They were known as the Elswick battery. On his return to England later that year, Lambton had called on Lady Meux, described the work of his guns at Ladysmith, and praised her patriotic action in sending similar guns to the front. Touched by this tribute, Lady Meux, after making many wills, decided to make Lambton her heir on the sole condition that he changed his name to Meux. This he did by royal licence in September 1911.

Meux was promoted admiral in March 1911, and later that year was considered as the next first sea lord (to replace Sir Arthur Wilson). His friend George V initially favoured his appointment. However, the Fisherite Sir Francis Bridgeman was selected, and Meux remained on half pay until July 1912, when he was appointed (as George V wanted, but to Fisher's anger) commander-in-chief at Portsmouth. He retained this office until February 1916, having been selected for the rank of admiral of the fleet in March 1915.

On the outbreak of war in 1914 Meux's principal duty was to defend the transports taking the British expeditionary force to France and the army's main line of communication from Southampton to Le Havre. This was achieved with complete success; moreover, on his own initiative, Meux organized a life-saving patrol service of yachts and other small craft, sailing under the blue ensign with a red cross at the main. On giving up his command he was persuaded to enter parliament as Unionist MP for

Portsmouth, being unopposed at the by-election consequent on Lord Charles Beresford's elevation to the peerage. He was popular in the House of Commons and several times spoke vigorously on naval subjects; but he was not really interested in parliamentary work, and retired at the 1918 general election.

Meux was now free to devote himself to the turf, since boyhood his greatest interest outside the navy. He had started breeding bloodstock in 1882, and had had some good horses trained by Tom Green at Stapleton Park, Pontefract. He won the Grand Military gold cup with Ruy Lopez in 1895, and was elected to the Jockey Club in 1906. On inheriting Theobald's Park, where Lady Meux had a racing stable, he bred his own horses there, and with them won the Hardwicke stakes at Ascot three times, the Manchester November handicap (top weight), the Liverpool cup, the Chester Cup, and many other races. He was a shrewd judge of racing, breeding, and all turf matters, and would have been an even more successful owner had he not been too fond of his horses to sell them.

For Meux, an aristocrat and court favourite and so an atypical naval officer, the service was apparently an interest rather than a profession. According to Arthur J. Marder, he was 'a very able sea-officer with no great administrative talent … but lazy and rather spoiled' (Marder, 1.257, 407). He was made CVO (1901), KCVO (1906), KCB (1908), and GCB (1913). He died on 20 September 1929 at Danebury, an estate which he had bought near Stockbridge, Hampshire. His will was proved at £910,465 gross, with net personalty £734,265. He had no children, and he left his fortune, subject to his widow's interest, to her grandson Sir Ian Hedworth John Little Gilmour, third baronet (b. 1926), later a Conservative MP and cabinet minister. V. W. BADDELEY, rev. ROGER T. STEARN

Sources official naval records, PRO • private information (1937) • R. Gardiner and A. Lambert, eds., *Steam, steel and shellfire: the steam warship, 1815–1905* (1992) • T. Pakenham, *The Boer War* (1979) • R. F. MacKay, *Fisher of Kilverstone* (1973) • P. Scott, *Fifty years in the Royal Navy* (1919) • *Fear God and dread nought: the correspondence of Admiral of the Fleet Lord Fisher of Kilverstone*, ed. A. J. Marder, 2 (1956) • A. J. Marder, *From the Dreadnought to Scapa Flow: the Royal Navy in the Fisher era, 1904–1919*, 5 vols. (1961–70), vol. 1 • R. Hough, *First sea lord: an authorized biography of Admiral Lord Fisher* (1977) • G. W. Steevens, *From Capetown to Ladysmith* (1900) • *WWW*, 1929–40 • *WWBMP* • Burke, *Peerage* • M. Wilson and L. Thompson, eds., *The Oxford history of South Africa*, 2 vols. (1971), vol. 2
Archives Lambton Park, Chester-le-Street, Durham, corresp. and papers
Likenesses P. de Laszlo, portrait; formerly in possession of his widow, 1937 • A. McEvoy, portrait; formerly in possession of his widow, 1937 • Spy [L. Ward], cartoon, chromolithograph caricature, NPG; repro. in *VF* (28 June 1900)
Wealth at death £910,465 16s. 0d.: probate, 19 Nov 1929, *CGPLA Eng. & Wales*

Meverell, Othowell (1586x8–1648), physician, was born in Derbyshire, the second son of George Meverell of Throwley, Staffordshire, and Constance Allen, daughter of Ottewell Allen of Whetsone, Derbyshire. After education at home he matriculated as a pensioner at Christ's College, Cambridge, which he entered in July 1604, graduating BA in 1608. While living in college, Meverell had an illness, probably smallpox. The method of treatment during the seventeenth century included the closing of all openings to the sick-room, and this often resulted in the partial asphyxiation of the patient when almost convalescent. Meverell became unconscious and was thought dead. Fortunately, the preparations for his burial exposed him to fresh air and he was revived, thereby narrowly escaping being buried alive.

Meverell went to Leiden, entered on the medical line on 14 February 1613, and graduated MD there on 1 October 1613. On his first appearance before the College of Physicians, London, in 1614, Meverell claimed that he had been created a master at Christ's by a grace in 1611. His Leiden degree was incorporated at Cambridge on 15 March 1616. He settled in practice in the City of London, and was elected a fellow of the College of Physicians on 21 April 1618. Meverell was censor for eight years between 1624 and 1640, registrar from 1639 to 1640, and president from 1641 to 1644. He was physician to the Bethlem Hospital from at least 1638, if not earlier. Possessing a modest house in the parish of St Lawrence Jewry, Meverell was none the less grouped among London's wealthiest inhabitants by the City's aldermen in 1640. Meverell and his wife, Katherine, daughter of Richard Ironside of London, had at least five children, Ottwell, Samuel, Margaret, Katherine, and Sarah, who in 1646 married George Ent, a fellow of the College of Physicians. Meverell's most significant achievement was his strong leadership of the college into the parliamentary camp at the opening of the civil war, a policy continued by his treasurer, Dr John Clarke, who succeeded him as president in 1645, Meverell becoming treasurer. Meverell and Clarke also acted in concert in reforming college statutes to allow licentiates to present foreign medical degrees without having to incorporate on them in English universities. Meverell's and Clarke's friendship and co-operation may have had their origin in their student days together in the intensely puritan atmosphere of Christ's College, Cambridge. Meverell's graduation thesis at Leiden is extant in manuscript (probably BL, Sloane MS 2606). Also in manuscript are the notes of the anatomy lectures which he read at the College of Physicians in November 1628 (BL, Sloane MS 2614).

On 28 December 1637 it was resolved by the court of assistants of the Barber–Surgeons' Company that 'Dr Meverell shall be Reader of our anatomical lectures at the next publique discection to be held in the new erected Theater'; and on 8 November 1638, that:

> there shalbe presented as the guift of this Compaine to Mr. Doctor Meverell a peece of plate with the Compaines scutchion ingraven thereon for his paynes in readeing at our last publique anatomye in the new Theater before the Lords of his Majesties most honourable privye Councell and others, spectators in the time of those 3 dayes readings.

The lectures began with a prayer, followed by an introduction in Latin; then the dissection was carried out under the lecturer's direction with his explanations, and at the end he again gave a short address. Its last words were: 'vos autem gratias agite chirurgiae proceribus et anatomiae magistris his quia dextri et artificiose putridum hoc cadaver dissecaverunt' ('Give thanks, moreover, to these most expert masters of surgery and anatomy, who have dextrously and skilfully dissected this gory cadaver'). In his pocket notebook he wrote below, 'Sic perorabam in theatro anatomico chirurgorum, Londin: 13 April 1638' ('This [lecture] was concluded at the anatomy theatre of the surgeons [at Barber-surgeons Hall]'; BL, Sloane MS 2614). He resigned the office of reader at the end of that year. Meverell's notebooks show that he was well read in Cicero, and—what might not have been expected of a Ciceronian and Grecian—he quotes al-Razi as well as Hippocrates and Galen. The notebooks also contain a few notes of cases, general notes on diseases, and numerous prescriptions, as well as a rhythmical declamation in Latin on 'The fear of the Lord is the beginning of wisdom'.

Meverell died on 13 July 1648 in the parish of St Lawrence Jewry, London, and was buried in the church there. He left £40 to the College of Physicians, and to several of the fellows a gold ring with the inscription 'Medici morimur, medicina perennis' ('doctors die, but medicine is eternal'; Hamey). He is to be distinguished from Dr Andrew Meverell of Trinity College, Cambridge, elected a fellow of the College of Physicians in December 1664.

Other manuscripts of Othowell Meverell's found in the British Library are: 'De causis signis & Curatione morborum, & symptomatum particularium' (BL, Sloane MS 2606); 'Observationes medico-practica, excerpta ex variis authoribus' (BL, Sloane MS 2622); and 'Praxis medica' (BL, Sloane MS 2636). The physician's will, written in 1646, indicates that he owned a country house in Chertsey, Surrey, which ultimately devolved on his eldest son, Ottwell (PRO, PROB 11/205, sig. 127).

NORMAN MOORE, rev. WILLIAM BIRKEN

Sources R. W. Innes Smith, *English-speaking students of medicine at the University of Leyden* (1932) · *The visitation of London, anno Domini 1633, 1634, and 1635, made by Sir Henry St George*, 2, ed. J. J. Howard, Harleian Society, 17 (1883) · G. J. Armytage, ed., *A visitation of the county of Surrey, begun … 1662, finished … 1668*, Harleian Society, 60 (1910) · Munk, *Roll* · B. Hamey, 'Bustorum aliquot reliquiae …', RCP Lond. · annals, RCP Lond. · S. Young, *The annals of the Barber–Surgeons of London: compiled from their records and other sources* (1890), 367 · W. Birken, 'The Royal College of Physicians of London and its support of the parliamentary cause in the English civil war', *Journal of British Studies*, 23/1 (1983–4), 47–62 · H. J. Cook, *The decline of the old medical regime in Stuart London* (1986) · G. Clark and A. M. Cooke, *A history of the Royal College of Physicians of London*, 3 vols. (1964–72) · *CSP dom.*, 1637–8 · Venn, *Alum. Cant.*

Wealth at death property in London and in Chertsey, Surrey; also £40 and several gold rings: will, PRO, PROB 11/205, sig. 127

Mew, Charlotte Mary (1869–1928), poet, was born on 15 November 1869 at 30 Doughty Street, London, the eldest daughter and third child of the seven children of Frederick Mew (1833–1898), and his wife, Anna Maria Marden (1837–1923), daughter of H. E. Kendall, an architect. Frederick Mew, an innkeeper's son from the Isle of Wight, was an architect who worked as Kendall's assistant. Charlotte recalled her childhood as intensely happy, although three of her brothers died in infancy and both the eldest brother and the youngest sister were confined to asylums. After her father's death she was left, with her much-loved sister

Anne, to look after their demanding mother. It is said that they made a vow never to marry, for fear of passing on what they thought of as the family 'taint'.

Charlotte Mew attended the Gower Street School, where she became passionately attached to the headmistress, Lucy Harrison. All her life she was sexually attracted to clever, strong-minded women. Her own personality, it soon became clear, was divided between a correct, late Victorian 'Miss Lotti' and a wild, talented, 'priceless' Charlotte. Very small (she took size two in boots), a brilliant pianist and mimic, with a hoarse voice like an urchin's, she could be riotously funny and then fall, without warning, into a black depression.

In 1888 the Mews moved to 9 Gordon Street, where they lived in genteel near-poverty. Anne painted and decorated furniture, and Charlotte began to write. She fitted in well with the new women of the period, rolling her own cigarettes and going where she pleased. Her story 'Passed' appeared in the second volume of the *Yellow Book*, and she contributed to various journals until 1914. It was through the *Yellow Book* that she met and was deeply attracted to its dashing assistant editor, Ella D'Arcy. In 1902 she went to meet Ella in Paris, but the visit was a bitter disappointment. Ten years later she fell in love with the novelist May Sinclair, and apparently chased her into the bedroom, where she was humiliatingly rejected. Her divided nature made these emotional disasters particularly painful because her ladylike side, the 'Miss Lotti', totally disapproved of them.

Charlotte Mew wrote very little verse until in 1909 her 'Requiescat' appeared in *The Nation*. 'The Farmer's Bride', also in *The Nation* (February 1913), attracted much more attention. This was the first to be published of her characteristic monologues, which speak for the frustrated, the guilty, the bereaved, and the outcast. The speakers are of both sexes, but the men, like the tormented clerk of 'In Nunhead Cemetery', who watches the burial of the woman he loves, are hesitating and pitiable, whereas the women are physically passionate and strong in the face of loss. Some of the most interesting pieces have autobiographical elements. Charlotte Mew wrote movingly about the deaths of children, and about mentally handicapped people. In 'Fame' and 'The Quiet House' she struggles with the ordeal of self-identification: 'Some day I *shall* not think; I shall not *be*!' ('The Quiet House'). The metre in these monologues follows the pressure of what is being felt or said, resulting in broken phrases, striking outbursts, and ambiguous closes.

Charlotte Mew also wrote short lyrics of great intensity ('Jour de fête', 'A quoi bon dire', 'Sea Love'). She was quite clear as to what she wanted from poetry. It was the *cri de coeur*, giving 'not only the cry but the gesture and the accent—and so one goes on—calling up witnesses to the real thing!' (C. Mew to Mrs Hill, 4 Jan 1917, State University of New York, Buffalo). Although she possessed two large trunks said to be full of manuscripts, Charlotte was fiercely self-critical and published very little. Sometimes she agreed to read her poems aloud, and is said to have read like one possessed. In November 1915 she was invited by Alida Monro, who managed the Poetry Bookshop in Devonshire Street, to come to one of their evening meetings. Asked on arrival whether she was Charlotte Mew, she replied, 'I am sorry to say I am.' But Alida persevered, and in May 1916 the Poetry Bookshop published Charlotte's first collection, *The Farmer's Bride*. A new edition, with eleven additional poems, was published in 1921, appearing in America as *Saturday Market*.

Through Alida Monro, Charlotte met a great admirer of her work, Sydney Cockerell, director of the Fitzwilliam Museum, who became a fussy but loyal friend. He in turn recommended *The Farmer's Bride* to Thomas Hardy, and in 1918 and 1926 Charlotte was invited to stay with the Hardys at Max Gate. In spite of this modest success—and Hardy believed that Charlotte Mew would still be read long after other women poets were forgotten—these were hard times for the Mew sisters. They moved from Gordon Street to 86 Delancey Street in north London, where their mother died in 1923, and although Cockerell managed to obtain a civil-list pension of £75 a year for Charlotte, they were reduced to living in Anne's studio, which had only one cold-water tap. Then in 1925 Anne developed inoperable cancer, and Charlotte, who nursed her tirelessly, was overcome with self-imposed guilt. She had begun to look, according to a contemporary, like a reluctant visitor from another world, frightened at what she had undergone in this one. After Anne's funeral she retreated to a nursing home at 37 Beaumont Street, London, and on 24 March 1928 committed suicide by swallowing disinfectant.

Charlotte Mew was buried, as she requested, in the same grave as her sister in Hampstead cemetery. A second collection of her poetry, *The Rambling Sailor*, was published by the Poetry Bookshop in 1929.   PENELOPE FITZGERALD

Sources A. Monro, 'Charlotte Mew: a memoir', in *Collected poems of Charlotte Mew* (1953) • M. C. Davidow, 'Charlotte Mew: biography and criticism', PhD diss., Brown University, Rhode Island, 1960 • *Charlotte Mew: collected poems and prose*, ed. V. Warner (1982) • P. M. Fitzgerald, *Charlotte Mew and her friends* (1984) • M. Watts, *Mrs Sappho: the life of C. A. Dawson Scott, mother of International PEN* (1987) • S. Cockerell, diaries, BL, Add. MSS 45926–45927, 52623–52773 • J. Grant, *Harold Monro and the Poetry Bookshop* (1967) • T. Boll, 'The mystery of Charlotte Mew and May Sinclair: an enquiry', *Bulletin of the New York Public Library*, 74 (1971), 445–53 • J. Freeman, 'Charlotte Mew', *The Bookman*, 76 (1929), 145–6 • V. Meynell, ed., *Friends of a lifetime: letters to Sydney Carlyle Cockerell* (1940) • personal information (2004) • b. cert. • *The Times* (25 March 1928)
Archives BL, literary MSS and corresp. of and relating to her, Add. MSS 57754–57755 • State University of New York, Buffalo, MSS and letters | NYPL, Berg collection • priv. coll., F. B. Adams collection
Likenesses group photograph, *c*.1890 (with Elizabeth Goodman), NPG • photograph, *c*.1923, NPG • D. Hawksley, pen and wash, 1926, NPG
Wealth at death £8729 10*s*. 0*d*.: probate, 24 May 1928, *CGPLA Eng. & Wales*

Mews, Peter (1619–1706), bishop of Winchester, son of Elisha Mews and his wife, Elizabeth Winniffe, was born at Purse Caundle in Dorset on 25 March 1619. His uncle Dr Thomas *Winniffe, who was dean of St Paul's, supported him through Merchant Taylors' School in London. He went from there to St John's College, Oxford, where he

was elected a scholar on 11 June 1637. He graduated BA on 13 May 1641 and MA on 21 April 1645. By the latter date, however, his mind was certainly not on academic matters because three years before he had joined the king's army, rising to the rank of captain. He was wounded several times and was taken prisoner at the battle of Naseby. He was ejected from the fellowship which he had obtained at St John's by the parliamentary visitors after the war. Apparently undeterred by these setbacks, he went to the United Provinces on the king's service in 1648.

Royalist conspirator Mews briefly toyed with returning to academic life under the Commonwealth, though not in England. In August 1653 he applied through his friend Sir Edward Nicholas for the princess of Orange's support to obtain the post of professor of philosophy at Breda. This encountered a sceptical response from Sir Edward Hyde on the grounds of Mews's long absence from his books. Even Nicholas seems to have regarded the post merely as a good cover for royalist conspiracy and Mews's application did not proceed. It was to royalist plotting rather than academic study that Mews devoted the next seven years.

Between December 1653 and March 1655 Mews acted as a sort of liaison officer with John Middleton and others involved in the rebellion in Scotland against the protectorate government, risking his life on several occasions. Unfortunately neither the good opinion of Nicholas nor the good standing he apparently enjoyed with the royalist community in England could save Mews from the backbiting and intrigue which dogged the exiled court. As a result, a furious row erupted between Mews and Hyde in the spring of 1655, leaving Nicholas caught in the middle. Mews remonstrated: '[a]ll my designes have bin, and ever shall be, built upon Religion and honour' (*Nicholas Papers*, 2.311). However, Mews did not abandon the royal cause but enlisted under the duke of York in Flanders and was still being used as a messenger by the exiled court as late as April–May 1660.

It is unclear at what stage Mews was ordained. He is known almost invariably in royalist sources as Captain Mews, right down to the Restoration, which seems odd if he was already ordained. Needless to say his role throughout most of the 1650s was hardly a usual one for a clergyman, and at the end of May 1655 he was writing openly to Nicholas about the possibility of challenging a person who had slandered him to a duel, which would have been even more unclerical.

Post-Restoration preferment and bishop of Bath and Wells At the Restoration Mews did at last return to his books, petitioning the king for money to pay off debts contracted in his service and to buy books to further his studies. On 12 September 1660 he was installed as archdeacon of Huntingdon and he was created DCL at Oxford on 6 December. Preferments followed in quick succession. He was made vicar of St Mary's, Reading, rector of South Warnborough in Hampshire, and rector of Worplesdon in Surrey (in September 1661). He was also restored to his fellowship at St John's College; the king wrote to the president and fellows, ordering that he be maintained in it despite the absences necessitated by his other posts. In 1662 these were further augmented by canonries at Windsor and St David's. He also became a royal chaplain. Finally in 1665 his portfolio of posts was given some element of geographical coherence, when he exchanged the archdeaconry of Huntingdon for that of Berkshire.

Mews remained well connected at court, as well as being part of the Anglican-royalist establishment at Oxford. A regular correspondent of Sir Joseph Williamson, he was one of the delegates who negotiated peace with the Dutch in 1667. He married Mary, daughter of Dr Richard *Baylie (1585–1667), president of St John's; when Baylie died Henry Bennet, earl of Arlington, wrote on the king's behalf to the college, recommending that Mews succeed him, which he duly did on 5 August 1667. From there he went on to become vice-chancellor of the university between 1669 and 1673. He continued to acquire church preferments, receiving the 'golden prebend' at St David's and being made dean of Rochester, under another former royalist officer, Bishop John Dolben, in 1670.

Despite his ordination and change of role since the 1640s and 1650s Mews simply continued in a sense to fight the civil war by other means. He was involved in persecuting dissenters in Reading as early as January 1663, accusing one of wanting to repeat the 'old rebellion' (CSP dom., 1663–4, 11). He was even involved in taking action against dissenters in the town of Oxford while he was vice-chancellor, in particular targeting a conventicle at the house of a former Cromwellian officer. He always fiercely opposed indulgence towards dissent; even as late as 1674, when reporting on dissenters in Somerset, he did so in quasi-military terms: 'they [the ringleaders] shall have no Quarter from mee' (Bodl. Oxf., MS Tanner 42, fol. 119).

By this time Mews had become bishop of Bath and Wells, where he was elected on 19 December 1672 and consecrated on 9 February 1673. Burnet, who later resented Mews's longevity in the highly sought after see of Winchester, attributed his rise to 'obsequiousness and fury' and derided his alleged lack of learning as childish (Burnet's History, 2.432). Mews certainly lacked neither court connections nor zeal and his approach to Archbishop Sheldon smacks somewhat of obsequiousness. Yet it is not clear that he was altogether lacking in learning. True, he did not produce scholarly works, but he seemed capable of delivering the Latin orations that were called for by his various academic, diplomatic, and episcopal roles and on at least one occasion was praised for the appropriateness of what he said. He could observe and lament clerical ignorance in his diocese from an apparent position of strength. The Ex-ale-tation of Ale, which he published in 1671, was an eccentric piece which associated alehouses with political loyalty in contrast to the burgeoning coffee houses. Given his political stance it is hardly surprising that Mews should become caught up in the partisan politics of the exclusion crisis. He joined other bishops in opposing exclusion and was dubbed a 'Yorkist' for his pains by the local citizens of Bath, an epithet which he typically resolved to wear with pride (CSP dom., 1679–80, 429). He was particularly active in the tory cause in the

general election of 1681, exhorting his clergy to turn out at the polls against whig candidates, which they did in unprecedented numbers.

Bishop of Winchester In the political climate which prevailed after 1681 Mews as an active tory was clearly destined for promotion; this duly came in November 1684, when he was appointed to succeed George Morley as bishop of Winchester. As a self-confessed Yorkist, he was doubtless relieved at the peaceful succession of James II just three months later. However, the peace was short-lived and the outbreak of Monmouth's rebellion afforded Mews a rare chance to relive his adventurous youth in an area where he had until recently been the diocesan. Hurrying down to join the royal army in the west country, he found himself in the camp on the night of 5–6 July, in the battle of Sedgemoor. Mews's role on this occasion has lost nothing in the telling, partly no doubt because of the sheer incongruity of a 66-year-old bishop's having any part in a major battle. In reality, Mews's role was modest but practical; perceiving that the potentially decisive Royal Artillery were at some distance, he had two of the cannon brought up using the horses from his own carriage, which contributed to the ultimate victory. He was wounded in the fighting and after the battle was rewarded with a medal from the king. Despite his earlier belligerent stance towards west country dissenters, Mews did urge clemency for the rebels, sadly to no avail.

The sense of common purpose between James II and tories like Mews which marked the summer of 1685 was soon a thing of the past, though Mews remained in touch with the king and had several one-to-one conversations with him between 1686 and 1688. In February 1686 Mews wrote to Sancroft warning that directions to preachers would be a preferable solution to the problem of contentious preaching than the suppression of all afternoon lectures regardless, which was then being contemplated. Unfortunately the directions to preachers did not settle the matter to the king's satisfaction and there followed the establishment of the ecclesiastical commission and action against Bishop Compton. Mews actively encouraged the fellows of Magdalen College, Oxford (where he was visitor), in defying James II. In April 1687 he wasted no time in writing to them urging them to hold an election according to the statutes and he hastily admitted John Hough as president, when it was already known that the king favoured another candidate and might take action to block such a move. He told the fellows that he admired their courage. Mews was totally sidelined as visitor in the deepening confrontation between king and college and he had no effective role in the matter until the royal policy went into reverse in the autumn of 1688. Before that, though, he continued to be involved in the episcopal opposition to royal policies: only a particularly draining course of medical treatment seems to have prevented him from joining the seven bishops in petitioning James II. He wrote to Sancroft on 24 June, expressing his fellow feeling with them.

However, opposition to a Stuart king did not come easily to Mews and he spent much of the rest of the year seeking to save James's crown. A lack of imagination at times meant that he did more harm than good to his royal master. His unnecessary delays in restoring the fellows of Magdalen in October 1688 infuriated his fellow tories and enabled the king's enemies to present this concession as insincere. He was very active among the Guildhall peers, who acted as a sort of provisional government after James's first flight in December, but he failed to prevent the disastrous second flight.

In parliament Mews voted against the transfer of the crown to William and Mary, but he did not become a nonjuror: he conformed to the revolution. He lived on for another seventeen years after it but his effectiveness as a bishop was much reduced in this period. This is apparent from several sources, including the manoeuvring already afoot in 1701 for his successor and the petition framed at the time of his death by local gentry for a more effective new bishop to take his place. It was an accidental administration of the wrong medicine that finally caused Mews's death on 9 November 1706 at the bishop's palace of Farnham Castle, Surrey. He was buried in Winchester Cathedral. The significant surviving portraits of Mews are from later in his life, where he appears as a white-haired but alert old man, a civil-war wound on his cheek covered by a patch, from which he came to be known as Old Patch.

ANDREW M. COLEBY

Sources Wood, *Ath. Oxon.*, new edn · *The life and times of Anthony Wood*, ed. A. Clark, 5 vols., OHS, 19, 21, 26, 30, 40 (1891–1900) · *The Nicholas papers*, ed. G. F. Warner, 2, CS, new ser., 50 (1892) · J. R. Bloxam, ed., *Magdalen College and James II, 1686–1688: a series of documents*, OHS, 6 (1886) · *Calendar of the Clarendon state papers preserved in the Bodleian Library*, 2: 1649–1654, ed. W. D. Macray (1869); 3: 1655–1657, ed. W. D. Macray (1876); 4: 1657–1660, ed. F. J. Routledge (1932); 5: 1660–1726, ed. F. J. Routledge (1970) · Sancroft papers, Bodl. Oxf., MSS Tanner · *Burnet's History of my own time*, ed. O. Airy, new edn, 2 vols. (1897–1900) · R. Beddard, ed., *A kingdom without a king: the journal of the provisional government in the revolution of 1688* (1988) · *Hist. U. Oxf. 4: 17th-cent. Oxf.* · Bodl. Oxf., MS Rawl. D. 666 · *CSP dom., 1660–1706* · L. von Ranke, *A history of England: principally in the seventeenth century*, 4 (1875) · L. Brockliss, G. Harriss, and A. Macintyre, *Magdalen College and the crown: essays for the tercentenary of the restoration of the college, 1688* (1988) · *Fasti Angl., 1541–1857*, [Bath and Wells] · *Fasti Angl., 1541–1857*, [Canterbury] · H. Hyde, earl of Clarendon and S. Gale, *The history and antiquities of the cathedral church of Winchester* (1715) · will, PRO, PROB 6/82, fol. 239v

Archives Hants. RO, household account book | BL, letters to Sir Edward Nicholas and others · Bodl. Oxf., Tanner MSS, Sancroft papers · Magd. Oxf., archives · Oxf. UA · St John's College, Oxford, archives

Likenesses D. Loggan, miniature, *c*.1680, NPG · D. Loggan, miniature, *c*.1680, BM · oils, after 1684, Magd. Oxf. · oils, after 1684, St John's College, Oxford · attrib. M. Dahl, oils (seated with robes of Garter Prelate), St John's College, Oxford · line engraving (after Loggan), BM, NPG · monument, Winchester Cathedral · portrait (with Garter robes), Bishop's palace, Wells · portrait, Farnham Castle · portrait, Dunster Castle, Somerset

Wealth at death see administration, PRO, PROB 6/82, fol. 239v

Mewtas [Mewtis], **Sir Peter** (*d.* 1562), soldier and courtier, was the son of Philip Mewtas and Elisabeth Foxley, and grandson of Frenchman John Mewtas, French secretary to Henry VII and Henry VIII between 1491 and 1522. He was a man of action: tall, thickset, with a long fair beard, and expert in small arms, first coming to notice in Thomas Cromwell's circle. He was active in the suppression of the Pilgrimage of Grace in 1536 and was said in 1538 to have been to France in order to shoot Cardinal Pole, though this may have misinterpreted missions of 1537–8, when Henry sent him to explore the king's marrying Marie de Guise.

Mewtas was appointed gentleman of the privy chamber (1536), master of Bethlem Hospital (1536), comptroller of the mint (1537), overseer of artillery (1537), keeper of Wanstead Park (1540), governor of Guernsey (1545), and chancellor of the tenths of the household (by 1546). He married Jane Astley, a lady of the queen's privy chamber, in 1537; and, by 1552, another Jane, perhaps surnamed Angersley, about whom little is known. In 1539 he and the first Jane were granted lands at West Ham, Essex, to which was added the adjacent manor of Bretts in 1540. A child was baptized in February 1539, probably Henry, or perhaps Frances, later gentlewoman of the chamber to Elizabeth I and wife of Henry, Viscount Howard of Bindon. There were other sons, Thomas and Hercules, the youngest. Mewtas's widow and Frances were given a new lease of Bretts in 1565 and, in 1567, enjoyment of it for Jane's life; she died in 1577.

Mewtas was one of the English dignitaries greeting Anne of Cleves at Calais in 1540. It was probably about this time that he received from Duke Philip of Bavaria, who was of the same party and a suitor to the Princess Mary, that 'best diamonte' bequeathed in his will to Frances. Mewtas resigned the comptrollership of the mint in 1542. The following year he furnished 200 men for service at Guînes. He was knighted on 18 May 1544 on campaign at Butterden, leading 500 hackbutters. In Guernsey he oversaw works at Castle Cornet, including the construction of the Mewtas Bulwark, employing the engineer John Rogers. In 1546 he appears to have gone undercover in France: an English agent matching his appearance was sighted in Normandy that October.

Henry VIII willed 200 marks to Mewtas, as one deserving a token of special affection. In February 1547 he conveyed to France notice of Edward VI's accession. At Rye on 6 July 1551 he was deputed to greet Jean d'Albon, Maréchal de St André, on the latter's embassy to invest Edward with the order of St Michel, apparently receiving from the *maréchal* a brooch and chain which Frances also came to inherit. Under Edward, Mewtas continued to supervise the defences of Guernsey and represent royal interests in the island, where he was ordered to see that reformed church services were observed and ecclesiastical goods protected from misappropriation.

At the king's death Mewtas joined Northumberland's attempt to subvert the Tudor succession, reputedly contributing a significant contingent of followers. This led to his imprisonment and loss of office by September 1553. He was also implicated in an attack with a knife upon a resident of a village near London who favoured the mass. He was committed to close prison in the Fleet in March 1555, but the following month was permitted to enter a £500 recognizance.

Elizabeth's accession saw Mewtas's return to favour. In August 1559 he visited François II with the queen's condolences on the death of Henri II. Throckmorton, impressed

by Mewtas's protestantism, repeatedly recommended he should succeed him as ambassador in France. In 1561 Mewtas was in Scotland, pursuing ratification of the treaty of Edinburgh. Back in France in July 1562, on a somewhat ill-defined mission to the prince de Condé, he fell sick at Dieppe, dying there in August or September 1562, and was buried there in September, in the course of activities representative of his career and ancestry: on French business, employing diplomatic and martial experience in the interests of protestantism and the English crown.
D. M. OGIER

Sources LP Henry VIII · PRO, SP 1 · W. C. Metcalfe, ed., *The visitations of Essex*, 2 vols., Harleian Society, 13–14 (1878–9) · M. St C. Byrne, ed., *The Lisle letters*, 6 vols. (1981) · CSP Spain, 1553 · D. M. Ogier, *Reformation and society in Guernsey* (1996) · will, PRO, PROB 11, 23 Streat
Archives Island Archive Service, Guernsey, signed and sealed appointment of Helier Gosselin as Bailiff of Guernsey, 1549

Mey, John (*d.* 1456), archbishop of Armagh, was a native of the diocese of Meath and a bachelor of civil and canon laws. He first appears on the records as an expert in laws at the Armagh provincial council held in Drogheda in October 1433. When, in July 1434, he received by papal provision the rectory of St Mary's, Painestown, diocese of Meath (valued at 34 marks), he was required to resign the perpetual vicarage of Stamullen (valued at 20 marks). Mey was one of the five diocesan tellers whose election of William Silk as bishop of Meath was declared null when Pope Eugenius IV provided Silk to that see.

In December 1438, when Mey was perpetual vicar of Delvin, he received a papal dispensation to hold another benefice, and obtained the vicarage of Kilmessan also. He was judge or official of the Meath diocesan court. With the death of Archbishop John Prene in June 1443 vigorous efforts were made again to persuade Archbishop Richard Talbot of Dublin to accept a translation to Armagh, to which he had first been elected in 1416 but not consecrated. Talbot at first consented to this latest attempt, which in the end came to nothing. On 26 August 1443 Pope Eugenius IV provided Mey to the archiepiscopal see of Armagh. He was consecrated on 20 June 1444, and enthroned in Armagh Cathedral by the dean, Cathal Ó Mealléin, on 9 July.

While Mey was of Anglo-Irish background, his new diocese was divided along political and racial lines. That part roughly coterminous with the modern county of Louth was called Armagh *inter Anglicos*, and lay within the area of English control and language, ruled from Dublin. The archbishop lived in this area in his manors at Termonfeckin near Drogheda, and Dromiskin.

The northern part of the diocese, Armagh *inter Hibernicos*, roughly coterminous with the modern county of Armagh, was Gaelic-speaking, and was ruled by Irish chiefs. At this time junior branches of the powerful Ó Néill clan of Tír Eoghain sought to expand into this area and establish sub-lordships by dispossessing the minor clans and hereditary ecclesiastical families who had occupied these lands for generations. This was a source of frequent conflict between Archbishop Mey and the Ó Néill clan, as the archbishop sought to remedy the injustices to his tenants, and to prevent further loss of income to himself resulting from the loss of church lands. The forlorn hope of saving church lands and protecting the tenants is a constant theme in Mey's register. The newcomers and their followers resented the archbishop and his authority, and sought to prevent him and his messengers from travelling to Armagh. Episcopal visitations were hampered, and exactions of food and lodgings for soldiers were made from the church tenants. Priests who kept concubines were attacked and had property confiscated. The archbishop as justice of the peace even had to spend £100 in defending Louth from the attacks of the clans of Ó Néill, Ó hAnluain, and Mac Mathghamhna.

In 1449 the archbishop vainly sought protection by giving Ó Néill a pension of money and later this was changed to cloth. Such pensions only proved to be a key to further exactions. In 1451 Mey listed these and other injuries before placing Eóghan Ó Néill and his entire lordship under interdict. By 1455 relations between the archbishop and Ó Néill had improved. Eóghan Ó Néill yielded to his son, Éinrí, whom Archbishop Mey instituted as chief at Tullaghoge. Three months later, in a concordat between the new chief and the archbishop, Éinrí swore to be a protector and patron of the church. This gave the archbishop peace for the remainder of his term of office.

Mey's influence in Armagh *inter Anglicos* was considerable, and he regularly attended parliaments held within his province, at Trim and Drogheda. However, because of the primatial cross-bearing controversy with the archbishop of Dublin, Mey refused to attend in person those parliaments held at Dublin or Naas, which were outside his province. He insisted on this right when he held the office of deputy lieutenant to the earl of Ormond in 1453–4. Two years later Ormond still owed him over £200 for expenses incurred in this office.

Mey was not politically ambitious, nor was he keen to engage in administration and military hostings. From these latter he repeatedly sought to be excused, saying that although he was prepared to work for peace, the duties of his pastoral office obliged him to use spiritual rather than secular means. As metropolitan Mey was zealous in the performance of his pastoral duties. He held at least four provincial councils, and he personally carried out canonical visitations in all except two of the most distant dioceses. He demanded high standards from the bishops, and he sought to promote reform and extirpate corruption and abuses from the clergy and from the monasteries. The monasteries had grown disorderly, and in some cases, such as that of the Augustinian house of Sts Peter and Paul, Armagh, quite notorious, and Mey's efforts at reform met with little success. Moreover, he was frequently hindered by Rome's intervention in favour of unworthy appointees. Only among the mendicant friars did he find any sense of religious duty or observance of the rule.

Late in 1455 Mey made provision for his peace of soul by providing financial aid to increase the maintenance of priests at the chantry of St Anne in the church of St Peter, Drogheda, to pray for his eternal rest and that of his predecessors and successors. His death occurred in 1456, after 16 September.

ANTHONY LYNCH

Sources W. G. H. Quigley and E. F. D. Roberts, eds., *Registrum Iohannis Mey: the register of John Mey, archbishop of Armagh, 1443–1456* (1972) · K. Simms, 'The archbishops of Armagh and the O'Neills, 1347–1471', *Irish Historical Studies*, 19 (1974–5), 38–55 · K. Simms, 'The concordat between primate John Mey and Henry O'Neill (1455)', *Archivium Hibernicum*, 34 (1976–7), 71–82 · J. Watt, '*Ecclesia inter Anglicos et inter Hibernicos*: confrontation and coexistence in the medieval diocese and province of Armagh', *The English in medieval Ireland*, ed. J. Lydon (1984), 46–64 · *CEPR letters*, vol. 9 · H. F. Berry and J. F. Morrissey, eds., *Statute rolls of the parliament of Ireland*, 4 vols. (1907–39), vol. 2 · A. Lynch, 'The province and diocese of Armagh, 1417–71', MA diss., University College Dublin, 1979 · F. J. Byrne, 'Bishops, 1111–1534', *A new history of Ireland*, ed. T. W. Moody and others, 9: *Maps, genealogies, lists* (1984), 264–332 · *The whole works of Sir James Ware concerning Ireland*, ed. and trans. W. Harris, 1 (1739), 86
Archives PRO NIre., register

Meyer [*née* Levis], **Adele**, **Lady Meyer** (1862/3–1930), campaigner for social reform, was the eldest daughter of Julius Levis of 35 Belsize Park Gardens, London. Her family was Jewish and her father was a merchant, but nothing is known about her early life. On 14 March 1883 she married Carl Ferdinand *Meyer (1851–1922), a financier whose connection with the merchant banking house of Rothschilds brought them both into touch with the prominent financial and political personalities of the time. The couple had a son and a daughter. Her husband was created a baronet in 1910.

Adele Meyer played a prominent role in the social life of the *fin de siècle*; and it was later noted that she 'always recalled with pleasure the admiration her delicate colouring and prematurely grey hair and her quick intelligence provoked' (*The Times*, 21 Jan 1930). However, the life of a socialite was not sufficient for her, and she became associated with a number of campaigns to improve the position of women in society, the first of which was the St Pancras School for Mothers. In order to improve the physical state of the poor, she organized cooking lessons for women in their own homes. This development was so successful that it was adopted elsewhere in the United Kingdom and overseas. She acted as chair of this organization until 1928, when she was forced to resign through ill health.

Adele Meyer's concern for health and diet motivated her to establish, in 1910, the first rural health centre in Britain, which was based near Shortgrove, her country home at Newport, Essex. The centre included a school for mothers, a welfare club, a girls' club, and a dental clinic, and penny dinners were organized for schoolchildren. As with the St Pancras School for Mothers, this was a model that was followed in other parts of the country. It remained open until the outbreak of the First World War. In addition, Meyer was among the founders of Queen Mary's Hostel for Women, a branch of King's College, London, known for the study of social and domestic science. According to one of her obituaries, this 'claimed much of her thought during the latter period of her life' (*Manchester Guardian*, 20 Jan 1930). Unlike many of her social circle, she was a supporter of the movement to extend voting rights to women.

Adele Meyer's concern for women also extended to the abuses many of them suffered in their jobs. From 1906 she became involved, with Clementina Black, in a detailed investigation into the work of women in London in the unregulated tailoring, dressmaking, and underclothing trades. The resulting publication, *Makers of our clothes, being the results of a year's investigation into the work of women in London in the tailoring, dressmaking and underclothing trades*, written by Meyer and Black, appeared in 1909. The conclusion of the investigation was that: 'If there is any immediate means by which legislation might diminish the evil of underpayment, it is the highest time that legislation should intervene in aid of a law-abiding, industrious, and greatly oppressed, class of citizens' (p. 18).

Adele Meyer continued to act as a hostess, both in London and in the splendid Queen Anne home in Essex beside the River Cam. The banker Charles Addis recorded a visit to the country home in 1909. He was impressed, but rather patronizingly described her as agreeable but 'not deep or learned with good impulses in her fashionable way'. He added that 'She ripples along about higher education and vocation schools and health culture and music' (Kynaston, 2.331–2). In appearance she was 'A short plump blonde, [with] wavy grey hair, very dark eyebrows and eyelashes, beautiful white teeth' (ibid., 331). Both she and her husband were enthusiastic patrons of the opera and discriminating buyers of paintings. After her husband's death in 1922 she served on the committee of the Shakespeare Memorial Theatre in Stratford.

A memorable portrait of Adele Meyer, depicting her and her two children, was painted in 1897 by John Singer Sargent and hung in the dining-room at Shortgrove during her lifetime. It was exhibited at the Royal Academy and has been described as a consummation of *fin de siècle* opulence. Henry James praised its 'wonderful rendering of life, of manners, of aspects, of types, of textures, of everything' (Kynaston, 2.332). After his visit Addis agreed that it was a superb portrait.

Despite all Adele Meyer's involvements with social reform, the writer of her obituary in *The Times* felt that 'her chief interests … lay with those near to her', namely her children and grandchildren, 'concerning whose welfare she was vigilant and active' (*The Times*, 21 Jan 1930). Lady Meyer died of heart failure on 17 January 1930 at her home in Kent, Chipstead Place, Chevening.

SERENA KELLY

Sources *The Times* (21 Jan 1930) · *Manchester Guardian* (20 Jan 1930) · Mrs C. Meyer [A. Meyer] and C. Black, *Makers of our clothes, being the results of a year's investigation into the work of women in London in the tailoring, dressmaking and underclothing trades* (1909) · m. cert. · d. cert. · Burke, *Peerage* · D. Kynaston, *The City of London*, 4 vols. (1994–2001) · J. Lomax and R. Ormond, *John Singer Sargent and the Edwardian age* (1979)
Likenesses J. S. Sargent, oils, 1897
Wealth at death £86,109 13s. 6d.: probate, 12 March 1930, *CGPLA Eng. & Wales*

Meyer, Sir Carl Ferdinand, first baronet (1851–1922), financier, was born at Hamburg, Germany, on 23 December 1851, the second son of Siegmund Meyer (1815–1882) and his wife, Elise Rosa (d. 1855), daughter of Reuben Hahn. He was educated abroad and went to London in 1872 to work as a clerk at Rothschilds' merchant bank. On 14 March 1883 he married Adele *Meyer (1862/3–1930), daughter of Julius Levis, merchant, of London; they had a son and daughter.

At Rothschilds, Meyer's promotion to senior clerk was rapid and he carried a partner's workload. Particular concerns were Rothschilds' extensive yet unlikely finance of southern African diamond and gold mining and the 1886 formation of the pioneering and immensely successful Exploration Company. He handled Rothschilds' relationship from 1887 with Cecil Rhodes, which began his lifelong association with De Beers Consolidated Mines Ltd. As a De Beers director from shortly after its formation, he experienced headlong conflict with Rhodes and his South African cronies in seeking to impose good business practice. Meyer became a major figure in mining finance, acting as director of several southern African companies. He served as deputy chairman of De Beers from 1888 to 1921.

At Rothschilds Meyer grew close to another of their allies, Sir Ernest Cassel, and the two worked on bond issues for foreign governments. But in the mid-1890s, when Cassel failed to persuade Rothschilds to back his Egyptian projects, such as the Aswan Dam, he drifted away from them, and in 1896 took Meyer with him. They remained lifelong friends and collaborators. Meyer, whom Rothschilds kept out of their partnership and were happy to see sit in their general office until at least 1890, was pleased to go, but he did so on good terms and continued as their representative on several boards. However, in allowing his departure, Rothschilds deprived themselves of vital leadership for a generation. He worked with Cassel on the successful Egyptian projects and in 1898 was appointed a director to watch over Cassel's substantial interest in his newly promoted National Bank of Egypt. Henceforth Meyer operated from the bank's London head office and remained a director until his death.

Meyer's interests also extended to China, then a battlefield on which the imperial powers fought for economic influence. He was chairman of the Pekin Syndicate Ltd, formed in 1897 to operate concessions for railways and mines, and regarded as a major instrument of British influence. This led to Meyer's 1899 appointment to the London committee of the Hongkong and Shanghai Bank and, in 1904, to his directorship of Central China Railways Ltd. However, the Pekin Syndicate made slow progress, and in 1910 Meyer fell victim to the machinations of French shareholders who forced his resignation, although he held on to his railway company directorship until 1914.

Away from business, Meyer's interests included music, shooting, and racehorse-owning, while in London his connections included the National Hospital and the Shakespeare Memorial Theatre. His promotion of the latter in 1909 with the first contribution, of £70,000, to a £500,000 building fund was rewarded with a baronetcy a year later. About 1905 he acquired a country estate, Shortgrove, at Newport, Essex, and he became a county figure, sitting on the bench, and supporting Newport grammar school and Saffron Walden Hospital. His wife—'a society beauty fashionably interested in movements and causes' (Kynaston, 2.331)—was active in local affairs and, further afield, was a well-informed chair of the St Pancras School for Mothers. With his wife he was an enthusiastic patron of opera and a discriminating collector of pictures. He had a neat, dapper appearance.

Despite being a naturalized British subject since 1877 and having his son on active service, Meyer suffered great prejudice during the First World War. Following the torpedoing of the *Lusitania* in 1915, he led hundreds of former German citizens in declaring in *The Times* loyalty to the crown and detestation of German methods of warfare, but to little effect. Depressed by ostracism, his health broke down in 1916, when the Hongkong Bank was quick to encourage his resignation. In 1918 his fellow magistrates gave him the benefit of the doubt over the hoarding of 56 lbs of tea.

Meyer died at his London home, 12 Park Crescent, Portland Place, on 18 December 1922. He was survived by his wife. Although born into a Jewish family, he received a Christian burial at St Marylebone cemetery, East Finchley, on 22 December, and his death went uncommented upon by the Jewish press. His son, Frank, succeeded him in the baronetcy.

JOHN ORBELL

Sources D. Kynaston, *The City of London*, 4 vols. (1994–2001) · F. H. H. King, *The history of the Hongkong and Shanghai Banking Corporation*, 2 (1988) · S. D. Chapman, 'Rhodes and the City of London: another view of imperialism', *HJ*, 28 (1985), 647–66 · R. V. Turrell and J.-J. Van Helten, 'The Rothschilds, the Exploration Company and mining finance', *Business History*, 28 (1986), 181–205 · P. Thane, 'Financiers and the British state: the case of Sir Ernest Cassel', *Business History*, 28 (1986), 80–99 · Burke, *Peerage* · *The Times* (19 Dec 1922) · *The Times* (23 Dec 1922) · Y. Cassis, *City bankers, 1890–1914*, trans. M. Rocque (1994) [Fr. orig., *Banquiers de la City à l'époque édouardienne, 1890–1914* (1984)] · CGPLA Eng. & Wales (1923) · WWW
Archives priv. coll., letter-books
Likenesses H. von Herkomer, oils, 1908, priv. coll.; repro. in H. A. Chilvers, *The story of De Beers* (1939), facing p. 195 · Spy [L. Ward], lithograph, repro. in *VF*, 1163 (March 1909)
Wealth at death £478,000: resworn probate, 15 Feb 1923, CGPLA Eng. & Wales

Meyer, (Frederic-)Charles (1780–1840). *See under* Meyer, Philip James (1737–1820).

Meyer, Frederick Brotherton (1847–1929), Baptist minister, was born on 8 April 1847 in Lavender Terrace, Clapham, Surrey, the son of Frederick Meyer, a London businessman, and great-grandson of John Sebastian Meyer, a sugar refiner from Worms who settled in London in the eighteenth century. His mother was Ann, daughter of Henry Sturt, chief executive of the firm Ward, Sturt, and Sharp. He had three sisters. The social background from which he came was to make F. B. Meyer (as he was known) unusual among nonconformist ministers. He was educated at Brighton College and spent two years in clerical work, employed by Allen, Murray & Co., Billiter

Square, London. Meyer's family attended Bloomsbury Chapel, a fashionable Baptist church. Meyer was baptized at New Park Road Chapel, Brixton, in 1864. Partly through the influence of William Brock, Bloomsbury's minister, Meyer felt drawn towards Baptist ministry. In 1866 he began training at Regent's Park College and in 1869 graduated with a BA from London University.

Meyer married Jane Eliza Jones (1845–1929) from Birkenhead on 20 February 1871. They had one daughter, Hilda, who became Mrs Tatam, and who had three children. Meyer's wife was something of an invalid, taking little active part in his church affairs. His friend and main biographer, W. Y. Fullerton, refers to Meyer's 'feminine virtues' and it is conceivable that there was a homosexual orientation in Meyer's nature. Yet his gentleness of character and appearance were combined with an autocratic style of management. He had a determination to succeed in many diverse areas. Financially, he was able to be independent for much of his life, mainly owing to the sales of his devotional and topical books. He wrote over seventy books and booklets and their circulation by the time of his death had reached 5 million copies.

From 1870 to 1872 Meyer was assistant and then associate minister at Pembroke Chapel, Liverpool, as a colleague of C. M. Birrell, father of the MP Augustine Birrell. The biblical preaching and cultured style which characterized Birrell made a deep impression on Meyer. He later came to feel, however, that he should share his true self more fully. Personal revelations became a distinctive feature of his preaching. During his first full pastorate (1872–4), at Priory Street Baptist Church, York, Meyer encountered America's foremost evangelist, Dwight L. Moody. Through Moody's impact Meyer came to believe that he had been freed from a conventional ministry, and he became convinced that an evangelism that attracted those outside the churches should be his priority. He moved to the respectable Victoria Road Nonconformist Church in Leicester in 1874, but found that his commitment to reaching the unchurched sectors of society, especially industrial workers, was not shared by the church leadership. He resigned in 1878.

Meyer remained in Leicester as minister of a new church which was formed largely by former members of Victoria Road, including several from prominent nonconformist families. Melbourne Hall was built to Meyer's specifications as a centre for evangelistic activity, educational and social agencies, and Christian nurture. It drew congregations of 1500, and growth in membership throughout the 1880s made it one of the most significant Baptist churches outside London. Meyer was known particularly because of his work with former prisoners in Leicester. By the time he left the city in 1888 he had met more than 4500 discharged prisoners and had provided employment and accommodation for many. Two businesses were set up by Meyer, one selling firewood and the other offering window-cleaning services. He also emerged during the 1880s as a leading supporter of 'gospel temperance' and as a crusader against mass gambling. His most spectacular gesture while at Leicester was a public protest at the races

against drinking and gambling. Meyer was able to point out that the races were later discontinued.

Meyer moved to London in 1888, to a ministry at the Regent's Park Chapel, which was unusual among Baptist churches for having an upper-class congregation. The church grew rapidly under his care. The remainder of his life was spent in London, at Regent's Park (1888–92 and 1909–15), and at Christ Church, Westminster Bridge Road, Lambeth (1892–1907 and 1915–20). Christ Church was affiliated to the London Congregational Union. Although it was not a Baptist church, Meyer insisted that a baptistery be installed. He built up an evening congregation at Christ Church numbering 2500, his weekly Sunday afternoon 'brotherhood' meeting attracted 800 working-class men, and he created a huge network of societies serving the needs of the area. He became the most prominent free-church campaigner in south London on behalf of the 'social purity' movement, and through his efforts more than 700 brothels were closed between 1895 and 1907. Meyer hired a disused factory which was converted into a youth centre for gymnastics and carpentry. The term 'hooligan' was derived from a family of that name encountered by Meyer's staff.

Opposition to the Conservative government's Education Bill of 1902, which nonconformists saw as discriminating against them, drew Meyer into political controversy. In May 1903, with John Clifford and Sylvester Horne, he led a demonstration against the legislation that drew 140,000 people to Hyde Park. He also denounced the government's Licensing Bill as 'pro-beer'. The run-up to the 1906 general election saw Meyer campaigning for the Liberal Party. From 1907 to 1909 he was a travelling representative of the free churches, and in 1910 he became honorary secretary of the National Free Church Council, a body which co-ordinated the activities of the free churches at national level. Although his priority was the council's spiritual work, he pressed for free churches to deal with causes of injustice and attacked the vested interests of the House of Lords. Meyer came to personify the nonconformist conscience. In 1911 he mounted opposition to a fight at Earls Court for a world boxing title. His belief, which gained him many enemies, was that because Jack Johnson, the title holder, was a black person and his challenger, Bombardier Wells, was white, the contest would be seen as a test of racial superiority. Winston Churchill, then home secretary, eventually cancelled the event.

Peace and justice were important to Meyer. Nonconformist opinion had been divided over the Second South African War, and he had produced in 1901 a manifesto which attempted to express a consensus opinion. As a representative of the free churches and the British peace groups, he presented congratulations in 1911 to President Taft for his work on behalf of international arbitration. During the First World War, although not a pacifist, Meyer assisted No-Conscription Fellowship members in their work on behalf of conscientious objectors. He visited prisoners in France and relayed to Asquith, the prime minister, and Lord Kitchener the concerns felt about the ill treatment of conscientious objectors. Bertrand Russell supplied him with material for a book about conscientious objectors entitled *The Majesty of Conscience*, and after the war Meyer argued that those who had been imprisoned should use their experience to agitate for a reformatory approach to imprisonment.

Meyer was the leading nonconformist in the Keswick Holiness, or higher Christian life, movement, which took its name from an annual convention held in the Lake District. The Keswick Convention, which attracted up to 6000 people, was predominantly Anglican and tended to be supported by the better off. Meyer's urbane manner enabled him to mix easily with this constituency and he became a highly popular and effective Keswick speaker. He spoke first at Keswick in 1887, and from then until his death spoke at twenty-six Keswick Conventions, as well as at important regional conventions in, for example, Llandrindod Wells in Wales and Bridge of Allan in Scotland. He introduced the Keswick Movement's teaching into the Baptist denomination by the formation, in 1887, of a prayer union which attracted wide support among Baptist ministers.

From the 1890s Meyer became Keswick's leading international representative. In 1891 he spoke for the first time at Dwight L. Moody's annual conference in Northfield, Massachusetts. Subsequently Meyer made nearly twenty visits to the United States and Canada. He was, in 1897, the first English speaker at the German Blankenburg Convention. In 1902 he spoke in Jamaica. By 1903 he was able to report on the effects of Keswick teaching in Europe, having spoken several times in Europe, notably in Germany and Scandinavia. In 1908 he spent six months addressing meetings in South Africa, where he had spiritual and political discussions with Gandhi, and in 1909 he undertook a 25,000 mile preaching tour to the Middle and Far East, including China. An ambition to speak in Australia was fulfilled in 1923. In Los Angeles in 1905 Meyer reported on the Welsh revival of 1904–5, and his message influenced the early Pentecostal movement.

With the support of several Keswick leaders Meyer launched, in 1917, the Advent Testimony and Preparation Movement, which taught that Jesus Christ would soon return and inaugurate a millennial reign. Meyer led the movement and saw it become the most influential body promoting premillennial views in Britain. Large meetings were held, most notably in 1927 in the Royal Albert Hall, when Christabel Pankhurst was the speaker. Pankhurst, who had been converted to belief in the second advent and had abandoned her previous commitment to the women's movement, had been nurtured by Meyer.

Several significant offices were held by Meyer. In 1904–5 and again in 1920–21 he was president of the National Free Church Council. He was elected to the presidency of the Baptist Union, serving with distinction in 1906–7. He was president of the World's Sunday School Association in 1907–10, and in the 1920s was director and general secretary of the Regions Beyond Missionary Union and for a short time principal of All Nations College. McMaster University in Canada awarded him an honorary DD in 1911.

Within Baptist life Meyer's influence was mainly felt through the Prayer Union, in his sponsorship of the deaconess movement, which he began in 1890, and through fund raising. J. H. Shakespeare, the secretary of the Baptist Union, used Meyer's talents to appeal for money in the period 1912–14. Through the efforts of Shakespeare and Meyer £250,000 was collected for a sustentation fund to give support to poorer ministers. Meyer also raised $66,000 at a Baptist World Alliance congress in Philadelphia in 1911 for a Baptist seminary in Russia.

But Meyer's personality and experience were such that he was essentially transdenominational. He co-operated not only with nonconformists but with Anglican and Catholic leaders, including Archbishop Davidson and Cardinal Bourne. His doctrinal convictions were evangelical but he drew from varied spiritual sources, especially from within the mystical tradition. He related to both the more liberal and the more conservative wings of evangelicalism. In this, as in his unique ability to combine social action and Keswick devotion, he was the most important bridge builder in the evangelical world of his day. Meyer died at 3 Owls Road, Bournemouth, on 28 March 1929 and was buried in Bournemouth. At his death he left more than £7000, with substantial legacies going to the Regions Beyond Missionary Union and to Meyer's Homeless Children's Aid and Adoption Society.   IAN M. RANDALL

Sources W. Y. Fullerton, *F. B. Meyer: a biography* (1929) · M. J. Street, *F. B. Meyer, his life and work* (1902) · F. B. Meyer, *Reveries and realities, or, Life and work in London* (1896) · I. M. Randall, 'Mere denominationalism: F. B. Meyer and Baptist life', *Baptist Quarterly*, 35 (1993–4), 19–34 · I. M. Randall, 'Spiritual renewal and social reform: attempts to develop social awareness in the early Keswick movement', *Vox Evangelica*, 23 (1993), 67–86 · I. M. Randall, 'A Christian cosmopolitan: F. B. Meyer in Britain and America', *Amazing grace: evangelicalism in Australia, Britain, Canada and the United States*, ed. G. A. Rawlyk and M. A. Noll (1994)
Archives BLPES, corresp. with E. D. Morel · Bodl. Oxf., Asquith MSS · Richmond Local Studies Library, London, Sladen MSS
Likenesses J. Collier, oils, 1907?, Baptist Union, London · portrait, Baptist Church House, Didcot
Wealth at death £7367 9s. 2d.: probate, 1929, *CGPLA Eng. & Wales*

Meyer, Henry Hoppner (1782/3–1847), portrait painter and engraver, was born in London and baptized on 10 February 1784 at St Paul's, Covent Garden, Westminster, London, the son of John Henry Meyer, engraver, and his wife, Elizabeth. He was the nephew of John *Hoppner (1758–1810), painter; listing the mourners at Hoppner's funeral, the painter Joseph Farington recorded 'Mier [Meyer], miniature painter, Hoppner's nephew' (Farington, *Diary*, 10, 3594, 8 Feb 1810). He was a pupil of Francesco Bartolozzi, in whose stippled manner he learned to engrave; he also worked in mezzotint. He painted portraits in oil and watercolours and exhibited twelve of these at the Royal Academy between 1821 and 1826, including one of the author George Dyer (1819, exh. RA, 1821; FM Cam.). He also painted portraits of Dr George Pinckard, physician to the dispensary; William Blair, surgeon to the dispensary; and Stephen Hough, vestryman, which he presented in 1823/4 to the Bloomsbury Dispensary (the Bloomsbury Sick Infirm Poor Fund), by whom the portraits were later loaned to the church of St Giles-in-the-Fields, London.

Meyer was a foundation member of the Society of British Artists, of which he was president in 1828. He retired from that office in the following year, however, and ceased to exhibit with the society in 1833. To its first exhibition in 1824 he sent eight portraits, two sketches in chalk, and forty-three engravings. In 1826 he exhibited a drawing of Thomas Telford and a half-length portrait of Charles Lamb (1826; BL, India Office Collections, F107; reduced-size copy, NPG). Crabb Robinson recorded, on 26 May 1826, calling

> on Meyer of Red Lion Square, where Lamb was sitting for his portrait. A strong likeness but it gives him the air of a thinking man and is more like the framer of a system of Philosophy than the genial and gay author of *The Essays of Elia*. (Walker, 1.304)

Meyer's own engraving after the portrait was published by Henry Colburn in Leigh Hunt's *Lord Byron and some of his Contemporaries* (1828). He exhibited a portrait of the actor Benjamin Webster in 1831; his portrait of Edmund Kean as Alanienouidet, chief and prince of the Huron tribe of Indians (exh. 1833), is in the Garrick Club, London, together with further actors' portraits by Meyer.

Meyer's refined stipple engravings, for which he is now chiefly remembered, form elegant portraits of leading figures of literary and artistic, as well as court, society. Several of these (he produced over 200) were published between 1810 and 1820 in *Contemporary Portraits* and the *New Monthly Magazine*. They included Byron, after James Holmes and G. H. Harlow; Scott, after Raeburn; Samuel Rogers; Francis Jeffrey; Wordsworth; and Coleridge, after C. R. Leslie. His small engraving (proof impression, BM) after a portrait of Keats by Joseph Severn, which was reproduced in Hunt's *Lord Byron* (1828), is particularly fine. Among the artists whose portraits he engraved were Benjamin West, Sir David Wilkie, James Northcote, Gainsborough, and John Hoppner (the last two after self-portraits). In his diary Farington records the progress of Meyer's engraving of his own portrait by Sir Thomas Lawrence. His other engraved subjects included the actresses Mrs Mardyn (1836, from a portrait painted in 1816) and Eliza O'Neill (as 'Belvedera', after A. W. Devis); the publisher John Boydell, after Gilbert Stuart; and Erasmus Darwin.

Of Meyer's engravings after three separate portraits of Byron—by George Sanders (*c*.1812), George Henry Harlow (1815), and James Holmes (1815/16)—the latter, engraved by 1818, when Byron requested his publisher, John Murray, to send 'half a dozen of the coloured prints from Holmes's miniature' (*Byron's Letters and Journals*, 6.27), is Meyer's most successful engraving of the poet, who took a keen interest in the reproduction of his portraits. A few of Meyer's prints were hand-coloured by Holmes, who worked closely with the engraver to provide copies for the publisher and wrote to Murray that 'the colour'd copy will be similar to the portrait of Lord Byron & the plain impression will be highly finished' (Peach, 74). Byron later wrote to a young admirer that 'A painter by the name of Holmes made (*I think the very best*) one of me in 1815—or 1816—and from this there were some good engravings taken' (*Byron's Letters and Journals*, 10.75).

Meyer's engravings of portraits of royalty include those of George IV; Prince Leopold, afterwards king of the Belgians; Princess Charlotte, after whole-lengths by A. E. Chalon; and Frederick William, duke of Brunswick, after J. P. Zahn. He contributed illustrations to Sir George Nayler's sumptuously produced *The Coronation of His Majesty George IV* (1837). His engraved portraits of the aristocracy included those of Admiral Viscount Nelson; Marquess Wellesley; Lady Leicester, afterwards Lady de Tabley, as 'Hope', after Sir Thomas Lawrence; and Sarah Sophia, countess of Jersey, after a miniature by George Sanders. He also engraved historical and subject pictures, of which a list is given in the *Dictionary of National Biography*. He died in London on 28 May 1847, aged sixty-four.

ANNETTE PEACH

Sources DNB · *Engraved Brit. ports.* · H. Meyer, prints, BM, department of prints and drawings · NPG, Heinz Archive and Library · R. Walker, *National Portrait Gallery: Regency portraits*, 2 vols. (1985) · *GM*, 2nd ser., 27 (1847), 665 · *IGI* · S. C. Hutchison, 'The Royal Academy Schools, 1768–1830', *Walpole Society*, 38 (1960–62), 123–91, esp. 157 · Farington, *Diary* · Graves, *RA exhibitors* · G. Ashton, *Pictures in the Garrick Club*, ed. K. A. Burnim and A. Wilton (1997) · catalogue. wellcome.ac.uk/search~S5/a [Wellcome Institute iconographic catalogue, on Meyer, Henry], 29 Jan 2003 · *Byron's letters and journals*, ed. L. A. Marchand, 12 vols. (1973–82); suppl. (1994) · A. Peach, 'Portraits of Byron', *Walpole Society*, 62 (2000), 1–144 · prodigi.bl. uk/iosm/PDform.asp (shelfmark F107) [detailed record on portrait of Charles Lamb], 29 Jan 2003

Meyer, Jeremiah (1735–1789), miniature painter, was born at Tübingen, Württemberg, on 18 January 1735. He was brought to England at the age of twelve by his father, who was described by William Hayley, Meyer's great friend, as portrait painter to the duke of Württemberg and by Edward Edwards as 'a painter of small subjects, of no great talent' (Edwards, 158). His father was possibly Wolfgang Dietrich Majer (1698–1762), who, according to Bénézit, worked in Tübingen and London. For two years, in 1757 and 1758, Meyer studied enamel painting under C. F. Zincke. Zincke had retired in 1746 with failing eyesight but for over thirty years he had been the foremost enamellist in England. Enamel painting was an expensive practice and Hayley records that Meyer paid Zincke £200 for tuition and £200 for materials (Hayley, 68). Edwards noted that 'Meyer surpassed his master, in the elegance and gusto of his portraits, a superiority, which he acquired by his attention to the works of Sir Joshua Reynolds' (Edwards, 159). Richard Redgrave also attributes Meyer's 'great power and elegance' and 'life-like truth and expression' to his study of Reynolds (Redgrave, *Artists*, 292). In 1761 Meyer was awarded a gold medal by the Society of Arts for a 'profile likeness of George III from memory, intended to be, but not actually, used as a die for the coinage' (Woods, 191).

Hayley records confusingly that Meyer 'had belonged to the society in St Martin's Lane, supported by a subscription of artists' (Hayley, 69). This seems to indicate that Meyer attended the informal academy run by Hogarth in St Martin's Lane (confirmed in 1823; Hardcastle, 176–80n.). Meyer also exhibited at the first public exhibition of artists' works held in 1760 in the Strand in the property of the

Jeremiah Meyer (1735–1789), self-portrait

Society of Arts. The following year, when planning another exhibition, the original group split into the Free Society of Artists and the Society of Artists (based at Spring Gardens, Charing Cross). Meyer joined the latter group and, when it became the Incorporated Society of Artists in 1765, he became one of its directors; he exhibited in 1761–3, 1765, and 1767. When this society in turn split in 1768 he joined the group who the same year founded the Royal Academy. Hayley described Meyer as 'one of the most active, and most respected, of its earliest members' and it was due to his initiative that the Royal Academy pension fund was established in 1775 (Hayley, 69). Meyer exhibited as an academician at the academy from 1769 to 1778 and in 1783, his work including portraits of the royal family. Horace Walpole noted in his RA catalogue for 1771, '131. A Portrait in Enamel—Lord Granby, fine. The King bought it' (no longer in the Royal Collection).

Meyer had first trained as an enamel painter. In contrast British-born miniaturists such as Spencer and Finney began their careers working in watercolour on ivory. The success of dedicated enamellists such as Zincke had encouraged these miniaturists to learn and additionally to offer their customers enamel miniatures. As Meyer began his career the increasing popularity of watercolour conversely meant that he was encouraged to offer his customers the choice of both watercolour and enamel. In Thomas Mortimer's trade directory of 1763, *The Universal Director*, Meyer was described as 'Enamel and Miniature Painter'. In 1764 he was appointed miniature painter to Queen Charlotte, and painter in enamel to George III. While visiting Buckingham House in 1783 Horace Walpole recorded seeing 'some modern enamels by Meyer' (Walpole, 79).

Samuel Finney had also been appointed miniature painter to the queen in 1763 and felt a keen sense of competition towards Meyer. In his autobiographical account

Finney recalled his dislike of Meyer—'that rascal Miers'—whom he accused of personal slights, such as the 'rascally acquisition of the late Mr Spencers enamel colours which they had agreed to divide equally' (Finney, 'Historical Survey', 385–411, 373–85). Others had a higher estimation of Meyer. In 1783 Joshua Reynolds commended to his nephew in India Meyer's son George, describing him as 'the son of a particular friend of mine' (F. W. Hilles, ed., *Letters of Sir Joshua Reynolds*, 1929, 97–8). Meyer was also a friend of George Romney, who painted the Meyer family after his return from Italy in 1776. It was Meyer who introduced Romney to William Hayley, a gentleman of leisure and a poet, who was to exercise a strong influence on Romney's life and was his future biographer. Hayley, in his biography of Romney, recalled Meyer as their mutual friend and his account of Meyer is the major source for Meyer's life.

Meyer was naturalized in 1762. In 1763 he married Barbara Marsden, who as a child had herself won premiums from the Society of Arts—in 1755 and 1756 for drawings, and in 1757 and 1758 for ornamental designs. The 1758 award was in a class limited to candidates under fourteen, so she must have been under twelve years of age when she won her first award in 1755, the society's first competition; this drawing has survived in the society's archive. There is some confusion about the number of children in the Meyer family. Farington records the death of one son, George, who joined the East India Company and shot himself in 1793 in Calcutta. Two years later, on 12 January 1795, he reports: 'Captn. Meyer, 2nd son of Meyer … died yesterday' and adds, 'Mrs Meyer has now one son and four daughters living', which implies that Meyer had three sons (Farington, *Diary*, 2.291). Joshua Reynolds painted one daughter, Mary, as a girl in 1771, in the character of Hebe (Rothschild collection, Ascott). Reynolds was close to the Meyer family and there is no payment recorded in his ledger for this portrait, which he exhibited in 1772.

Meyer lived for many years in Tavistock Row, Covent Garden; he retired to Kew, where he died on 20 January 1789 after catching a chill. He was buried in Kew churchyard, and in Kew church there is a mural tablet to his memory with a medallion relief portrait and eulogistic verses by his friend Hayley, of which the following is an extract:

Age after age may not one Artist yield
Equal to thee in painting's nicer field
And ne'er shall sorrowing earth to heaven command
A fonder parent, or a truer friend.

Meyer is one of the artists depicted in Zoffany's group portrait *The Royal Academicians* (1772; Royal Collection). There is also a portrait drawing of him (RA) by George Dance RA, etched by William Daniell (NPG), and there are prints of him after N. Dance by W. Pether, and after P. Falconet by D. Pariset.

The Royal Collection reflects Meyer's role as miniature painter to the royal family with nineteen portraits. Other examples of his work are in the Victoria and Albert Museum, London, the Fitzwilliam Museum, Cambridge, and the Ashmolean Museum, Oxford, where there is also an interesting album of drawings by Meyer and his family. Although Meyer trained as an enamel painter modern assessments of his career recognize the significant part he played in the development of watercolour on ivory. V. J. Murrell concluded: 'The first artist to realise fully the great potential of miniature painting on ivory was Jeremiah Meyer … and to him must go the main credit for the renaissance of the art in the late 18th century' (Murrell, 18). A contemporary, writing in 1774, noted the key reason for Meyer's revolutionary originality:

> The Miniatures excell all others in pleasing Expression, Variety of Tints, and Freedom of Execution, being performed by hatching and not stipling as most Miniatures are. Indeed in this Branch of the Art Mr Meyer seems to stand unrivalled, and I believe he may justly be reckoned the first Miniature Painter in Europe.   (Murrell, 19)

KATHERINE COOMBS

Sources W. Hayley, *The life of Romney* (1809) · Bénézit, *Dict.*, new edn · I. Bignamini, 'George Vertue, art historian, and art institutions in London, 1689–1768', *Walpole Society*, 54 (1988), 1–148, esp. 19–148 · E. Hardcastle [W. H. Pyne], *Wine and walnuts, or, After dinner chit-chat*, 1 (1823), 176–80 · Redgrave, *Artists*, 2nd edn · E. Edwards, *Anecdotes of painters* (1808); facs. edn (1970), 158–60 · H. T. Woods, *A history of the Royal Society* (1913), 190–91 · Graves, *RA exhibitors* · H. Walpole, 'Horace Walpole's journals of visits to country seats', *Walpole Society*, 16 (1927–8), 9–80, esp. 79 · J. Murrell, 'The craft of the miniaturist', in J. Murdoch and others, *The English miniature* (1981), 18–19 · S. Finney, 'An historical survey of the parish of Wilmslow', MS, Ches. & Chester ALSS [incl. 'Autobiographical account'] · S. Finney, correspondence, Ches. & Chester ALSS, Finney of Fulshaw MSS, DFF 28–39 · R. Walker, *The eighteenth and early nineteenth century miniatures in the collection of her majesty the queen* (1992), nos. 249–69 · D. B. Brown, *Catalogue of the collection of drawings in the Ashmolean Museum*, 4 (1982), no. 1361

Archives Ches. & Chester ALSS, Finney of Fulshaw MSS, corresp. · Ches. & Chester ALSS, S. Finney, 'Autobiographical account', in 'An historical survey of the parish of Wilmslow'

Likenesses J. Zoffany, group portrait, oils, 1772 (*The Royal Academicians*), Royal Collection · G. Dance, drawing, RA · W. Daniell, etching (after drawing by G. Dance), NPG · D. P. Pariset, stipple (after P. Falconet), BM · W. Pether, mezzotint (after N. Dance), BM · relief, Kew parish church; B. Reading, altered version, BM, NPG · self-portrait, drawing, AM Oxf. [*see illus.*]

Meyer, Margaret Theodora (1862–1924), university teacher, was born in September 1862 in Ulster, the second child and eldest daughter of Thedore Jonah Meyer, a Presbyterian minister and a naturalized British subject from 1855, and his wife, Jane Ann, the daughter of William Stevenson. Her elder brother, Sir William Stevenson *Meyer (1860–1922), served as first high commissioner for India (1920–22). She spent much of her childhood in Italy, but attended the North London Collegiate School for Girls, going from there to Girton College, Cambridge, in 1879. The holder of a college scholarship, she was in the second class in the mathematical tripos in 1882—for her a disappointing result. Later she gained the MA at Trinity College, Dublin.

After three years (1885–8) as assistant mistress at Notting Hill high school, London, Meyer returned to Girton as resident lecturer in mathematics, and for thirty years took a prominent part in almost every aspect of the life of the college. An outstanding teacher, well liked by her colleagues, she was an influential figure during a period of marked change in the college's administration. As part of her work as one of the first directors of studies in mathematics (1903–18) she served on the education board, set up in 1904 to bring the concerns of the teaching staff to the attention of the governing executive committee; in 1910 she was nominated staff representative on this committee (renamed council). Although not active in research, Meyer strongly supported women students aiming in that direction; she herself was one of the earliest women members of the London Mathematical Society (admitted 1889). Valuing close college–school connections, she was for a time Girton representative to the Cambridge and County School for Girls. One of Meyer's most remarkable contributions to the college, and perhaps the one for which she is best remembered, is the carving of the oak panelling around the chancel of the college chapel. The work was done mostly by herself and former students working under her direction. It was completed in 1926 in her memory.

During much of the First World War, along with many mathematics lecturers, Meyer undertook calculational work for the War Office in her spare time. In 1918, after a period of poor health and at a time when mathematics enrolments were low, she resigned her college positions and took a post with the Air Ministry, which was related to aircraft design and construction. She then returned for a time to teaching, both privately and as a coach at University College, London, and in addition served on London county council schools committees. Social work among Indian students, to which she was perhaps drawn through her brother's connection with India, also occupied her.

Outside of mathematics and Girton College, Meyer's special interest was astronomy. Although she did not publish original work in this field she had considerable formal background, the mathematical tripos curriculum of her time having included mathematical astronomy. When the Royal Astronomical Society opened its fellowship to women, she was one of the first to be elected, in 1916.

An ardent climber, fearless, quick, and possessing great stamina, Meyer loved the mountains. From 1890, except during the war, she went to the Alps almost every summer. She was an early member of the Ladies' Alpine Club, having joined in 1909, and served as its deputy president (1913–15) and president (1916–19). Two of her especially notable climbs were described in the club's journal. Her friends and colleagues valued her kindliness and ready sympathy; she was a person to be relied on, especially in times of difficulty. She died in Bishop's Road, Paddington, London, on 27 January 1924 after colliding with a bus while bicycling; she was buried in Boscombe cemetery on 31 January. Her bequests to Girton included £2000 for the benefit of women mathematics students.

MARY R. S. CREESE

Sources A. S. D. M., *The Observatory*, 47 (1924), 99 · *Monthly Notices of the Royal Astronomical Society*, 85 (1924–5), 314 · *Girton Review*, Easter term (1924), 6–7 · K. T. Butler and H. I. McMorran, eds., *Girton College register, 1869–1946* (1948), 646 · 'Meyer, Sir William Stevenson', *DNB* · B. Stephen, *Girton College, 1869–1932* (1933) · *The Times* (30 Jan 1924) · *Proceedings of the London Mathematical Society*, 1st ser., 20

(1888–9), 88, 109 • *The Times* (22 March 1924) • private information (2004) • d. cert.

Archives Girton Cam., mathematics books • Ladies' Alpine Club, London, Alpine books

Wealth at death £13,450 13s. 1d.: probate, 15 March 1924, *CGPLA Eng. & Wales*

Meyer, Michael Leverson (1921–2000), translator and writer, was born at 59 Hamilton Terrace, North Marylebone, London, on 11 June 1921, the third and youngest son of Percy Barrington Meyer, manager of the timber-importing company of Montague Meyer, and Eleanor Rachel (Nora), *née* Benjamin (d. 1928/9), who died when he was seven. He was educated at Wellington College and Christ Church, Oxford, where he switched from classics to English literature and was taught by the poet and critic Edmund Blunden. At Oxford Meyer edited *Eight Oxford Poets* (1941) with his friend Sidney Keyes, and after Keyes's death two years later in the Second World War he edited *Collected Poems of Sidney Keyes* (1945, revised 1989). Although he had been a conscientious objector, Meyer served from 1942 to 1945 in Bomber Command headquarters near High Wycombe, where he translated technical military jargon into readable English. After the war he became a lecturer in English literature from 1947 to 1950 at Uppsala University in Sweden, where he wrote a noteworthy novel of adolescence, *The End of the Corridor* (1951), based on his days at Wellington College. He also wrote a play set in Sweden, *The Ortolan*, staged in 1953 (two years after it was completed) with Maggie Smith in the lead, and revived in 1965 with Helen Mirren.

During his Swedish tenure Meyer learned Swedish and Norwegian, translating Frans G. Bengtsson's poem *The Long Ships* (1951), an endeavour that brought him to the attention of the BBC, which commissioned translations of Ibsen during that decade: *Little Eyolf* for radio, and *The Lady from the Sea* and *John Gabriel Borkman* for television, with Laurence Olivier starring in the latter. In 1959 the young director Michael Elliott produced Meyer's new version of *Brand* for Casper Wrede's 59 Theatre Company at the Lyric, Hammersmith, with Patrick McGoohan in the lead.

Meyer's abilities were now recognized worldwide, and the American publisher Doubleday commissioned him to translate sixteen Ibsen plays. In 1960 the first four of these were published: *Brand, The Lady from the Sea, John Gabriel Borkman,* and *When we Dead Awaken*; the last, *Rosmersholm,* appeared in 1966. Meyer became the first Briton to receive the gold medal from the Swedish Academy, in 1964, the year of his first eight Strindberg translations, comprising *The Father, Miss Julie, Creditors, The Stronger, Playing with Fire, Erik the Fourteenth, Storm,* and *The Ghost Sonata.* He also had time that year to write a television play, *The Summer in Gossensass,* about Ibsen's love for a teenaged girl. Meyer's skill as a translator lay in his sensitivity to the original text and his ability to convert its nuances of meaning and atmosphere into a richly evocative English. With *Brand* in 1959 Meyer converted Ibsen into a modern master, profoundly influenced directors about how the playwright's material should be approached, and raised the standards for translators. Ibsen previously had been performed mostly in the Victorian English of William Archer, whose fatiguing six-hour version of *Brand,* for example, was laid out in rhyming couplets. Meyer retained the poetry in blank verse and, among other improvements, revitalized Ibsen's humour.

Meyer next turned his energies to a three-volume biography of Ibsen: *Henrik Ibsen: the Making of a Dramatist* (1967), *Henrik Ibsen: the Farewell to Poetry* (1971), and *Henrik Ibsen: the Top of a Cold Mountain* (1971), the latter winning the Whitbread biography prize for 1971. His other renowned biography, that of Strindberg (1985), assured his place as a literary writer of note. In 1977 he added a radio play about Strindberg's love life, *Lunatic and Lover,* later performed at the Edinburgh Festival. In the following year he was a visiting professor of drama at Dartmouth College in Hanover, Massachusetts, the first of five such American positions. The others were at the University of Colorado, Boulder (1986), Colorado College at Colorado Springs (1988), Hofstra University at Hempstead, New York (1989), and the University of California, Los Angeles (1991).

Meyer's autobiography, *Not Prince Hamlet* (1989)—published in the USA as *Words through a Window Pane*—displayed both his wit and his sensitive understanding of the theatre and the famous actors and writers with whom he was associated, including Ralph Richardson, George Orwell, and Graham Greene. Meyer never married but he was attractive to women, and with Maria Rossman had a daughter, Nora, who was born when he was past fifty. He was a witty, gregarious, and generous man, stocky and rubicund, an enthusiastic public speaker and one who embraced the active life, from real tennis to hockey. He was a member of the Marylebone Cricket Club and an enthusiastic spectator of virtually any sport. He was also competitive in board games, once playing Scrabble with Graham Greene during a round-the-world trip in 1959–60 (and bemoaning Greene's cheating). Meyer mischievously added eating and sleeping as recreations under his *Who's Who* entry; he had a passion for food, and served on the committee of *The Good Food Guide.* He was also a member of the Garrick and Savile clubs.

Meyer remained active through his seventies, translating *Road to Auschwitz: Fragments of a Life* (1990) by Hedi Fried, Ibsen's *Master Olof* (1991), and *Three Danish Comedies* (1999) by Ludvig Holberg and J. L. Heiberg. He also wrote a fantasy, *A Meeting in Rome* (1991) about Ibsen and Strindberg coming together, as they never did. In 1995 Meyer became the first Briton to receive Norway's order of merit. He died at St Mary's Hospital, Praed Street, Westminster, on 3 August 2000 of heart disease. His translations of Strindberg and Ibsen continue to be performed in the twenty-first century, particularly in the United Kingdom and the United States. JOHN D. WRIGHT

Sources *The Times* (7 Aug 2000) • *The Guardian* (7 Aug 2000) • *WWW, 1996–2000* • *WW* (1989)

Wealth at death £3,844,948 gross; £2,962,580 net: probate, 5 March 2001, *CGPLA Eng. & Wales*

Meyer, Philip James (1737–1820), musician, was born in Strasbourg, Alsace, France, and studied for the ministry at the protestant college there, singing in the church choir and playing the organ. After he discovered an old German harp and learned to play it, he left the college about 1757 and went to Paris, where he had lessons from Christian Hochbrucker, nephew of Jacob Hochbrucker, usually regarded as the inventor of the single-action pedal harp: Christian Hochbrucker, later *maître de harpe* to Queen Marie-Antoinette, was the first composer to publish music for the pedal harp. The pedal harp gradually replaced the old 'hook harp', on which semitones were produced by hooks turned with the left hand during performance. The addition of pedals to turn the hooks left both hands free. Meyer's first solo performance was for the Concert Spirituel in Paris in 1761, and he performed there until 1764, often playing his own works. He later studied German music with Johann Gottfried Müthel, a composer and organist, who had had lessons from Johann Sebastian Bach shortly before Bach's death. In 1763 he published one of the earliest tutors for the harp, *Essai sur la vraie manière de jouer de la harpe*, for beginners and amateurs, and this was followed by *Nouvelle méthode pour apprendre à jouer de la harpe* (1774). In these he gave instructions for playing both the hook harp and the pedal harp. Meyer was married in Strasbourg in 1768, and had two sons, both harpists.

Meyer first visited London in 1772, and is thought to have been the first person to play the pedal harp in England. For the next few years he divided his time between London, Strasbourg, and Paris, which had become the centre of the harp industry, especially after the arrival of Marie-Antoinette, already an accomplished player, in 1770. He turned his hand to opera with *Damète et Zulmis* (1780) and, probably, *Apollon et Daphné* (1782) (although this was possibly written by the Bohemian composer Anton Mayer), both failures when performed at the Paris Opéra, and his *Vénus et Adonis* (1782) was withdrawn without being performed. The playwright Pierre-Augustin Caron de Beaumarchais asked him to compose a score for his new edition of Voltaire's libretto of *Samson*, originally written for Jean-Philippe Rameau in 1734, but Meyer's version was rejected by the Académie Royale de Musique in 1783.

Meyer settled permanently in London in 1784 and devoted the rest of his life to teaching the harp, which had become very fashionable (especially among young ladies), and composing. His earliest compositions, including six divertimenti for harp and violin (1767) and two sets of six sonatas for solo harp (1768 and 1770), were published in Paris. In London, his published works included sonatas for harp and strings, duets for harp and keyboard and for two harps, and a *Collection of Hymns and Psalms* (1815) for harp and piano, dedicated to Princess Charlotte. He also arranged many songs for the harp. Meyer died in London on 17 January 1820.

Philip James Meyer (1770–1849), musician, the elder son of Philip James Meyer, was born in Paris and moved to London with his family in 1784. Regarded as an excellent performer, with a sensitivity compared to that of Anne-Marie Krumpholz, he accompanied the leading singers of the day, including Gertrude Elizabeth Mara (1749–1833). A popular work was the arrangement for harp and piano by Thomas Greatorex (1758–1831) of the glee 'O strike the

harp', first performed by Meyer and Greatorex on 27 April 1798 at the King's Theatre Room. Meyer also accompanied ballets, including *Les follies d'Espagne* at the King's Theatre on 15 June 1789, played in concerts at Covent Garden and Drury Lane and at private parties, and played for the Covent Garden oratorios in 1791 and for the Drury Lane oratorios in 1791–2. He also composed for the harp. He was appointed harpist to Queen Charlotte. Meyer wrote an unpublished biography of his father, which he sent to John Sainsbury in 1823 when he was compiling his *Dictionary of Musicians* (1824). He died at Pentonville, London, on 18 October 1849.

(Frederic-)Charles Meyer (1780–1840), musician, the younger son of Philip James Meyer, was born in Strasbourg. Although he is recorded as having performed on the harp at Covent Garden and the Pantheon in 1791–2, and for the ballet *La foire de Smyrne* at the Haymarket Theatre on 14 April 1792, and he played in the Drury Lane oratorios in 1794, he was primarily a teacher and composer. He composed sonatas for the harp, and also published *Divertimento Delia*, *Il pensieroso*, *Introduction and Solo*, and *Fantasia and Solo*, and his harp tutor, *A New Treatise on the Art of Playing upon the Double Movement Harp*, appeared about 1825. Meyer was one of the performers of 'A New Bardic Overture' for six harps at the King's Theatre on 25 April 1816. He died in 1840.   ANNE PIMLOTT BAKER

Sources R. Rensch, *Harps and harpists* (1989), 153–79 • Highfill, Burnim & Langhans, *BDA* • M. E. Bartlett, 'Beaumarchais and Voltaire's "Samson"', *Studies in Eighteenth-Century Culture*, 11 (1982), 33–49 • S. McVeigh, *Concert life in London from Mozart to Haydn* (1993) • H. J. Zingel, 'Meyer, Philippe-Jacques', *New Grove*, 2nd edn • *GM*, 1st ser., 90/1 (1820), 187 • *GM*, 2nd ser., 32 (1849), 663 • *DNB* • [J. S. Sainsbury], ed., *A dictionary of musicians*, 2 vols. (1824)
Likenesses W. Beechey, portrait ((Frederic-)Charles Meyer); Sothebys, 1975

Meyer, Philip James (1770–1849). *See under* Meyer, Philip James (1737–1820).

Meyer, Rollo John Oliver [Jack] (1905–1991), educationist and cricketer, was born on 15 March 1905 at the rectory, Clophill, Bedfordshire, the son of Canon (Horace) Rollo Meyer, Church of England clergyman, and his wife, Arabella Crosbie Ward. His education commenced at what he called a dame-school in Middlesex, followed by a preparatory school in Blackheath, where he was accepted on favourable terms—a sign of things to come. In 1918 he moved to Haileybury College, to which he won an unexpected scholarship. He didn't enjoy himself much there, but did well at sports. From Haileybury he went on to Pembroke College, Cambridge, where as well as a good deal of very successful cricket (he was for three years a Cambridge cricket blue, as well as a rackets blue and very nearly a golf blue) he inclined towards schoolmastering. He spent a short period teaching, and then went to India, using his sporting fame and perhaps his less than glamorous academic results in search of a fortune. He worked as a cotton broker for Gill & Co., Bombay, from 1926 to 1929. He then worked as a private tutor in Limboli and Porbandar, and became headmaster of Dhrangadhra Palace School in 1930. In 1931 he married Joyce Evelyn Symons, with whom he had two daughters, one of whom died young. The marriage worked, but India did not. However, he started to find his feet as a schoolmaster there, and he began to coach sons of the Indian aristocracy for entry into Oxford and Cambridge.

In 1935 Meyer took five of his Indian pupils to England, and Millfield School was thus established. It grew rapidly. Meyer—universally known as the Boss—built on three successful pillars. First, he recognized the value of what came to be called 'comprehensive' schooling; it may have been based on money rather than on more social attitudes, but it worked and Millfield prided itself on being the first public comprehensive and co-educational school. Secondly, and following from this, he recognized the issue of what was later called 'diversity'; he would, to put it crudely, educate not-so-bright children of rich parents at high fees, while taking on bright pupils—whether academic, artistic, or sporting—for little or nothing in payment. The third and most important strand in Meyer's approach was that as a born pedagogue, in the best sense of the word, he recognized that there was no child who had not got some good in him or her, and aimed to bring this out. Millfield thrived on this formula and became a large organization—a senior school, preparatory school, and pre-preparatory school, with very substantial academic, artistic, and sporting achievements to the credit of its pupils. Meyer was appointed OBE in 1967. In later years Millfield's headmaster was a member of the headmaster's conference, a sign of respectability denied, many said unfairly, to Meyer in his day.

Of course there was a downside. Meyer's autocratic, even roguish, approach went out in the more straight-laced post-war years, and a board of governors was established. His stern if whimsical discipline—he was a great one for corporal punishment—went out of fashion too. Some of Millfield's advantages in the immediate post-war years—for instance keeping class sizes small by employing, on the cheap, retired teachers from other schools—lost their effect. In 1970 Meyer resigned and exiled himself to Greece, in what appeared, in public anyway, to be slightly unseemly circumstances. His work in Greece was by no means a failure, with the true schoolmastering skills still coming through, as founder and first headmaster of St Lawrence College, Athens, from 1979 to 1986 and co-founder and first rector of Byron College, Athens, from 1986 to 1987. He retired through ill health in the latter year.

Meyer was a great sportsman. As with his schoolmastering his success was based not on book knowledge or learning, but on instinct and natural flair. He played cricket for Somerset (and was captain in 1947) and his career included taking 412 first-class wickets, including those of some of the very best batsmen of the day, including Woolley, Edrich, and Bradman. He took these interests with him to Millfield but contrary to popular belief did not overdo the sporting side—this mistake, if mistake it was, was left to his successors.

Meyer died at Bristol General Hospital on 9 March 1991 and was survived by his wife and one daughter, the other daughter having predeceased him in a car accident. He was a difficult, talented man in very many fields. But in the field of teaching he was a genius. Millfield and indeed educational thinking more widely stand as monuments to his ideas, enthusiasm, and skill. The recognition that every child has a winning streak in him or her, and that it is the job of the school to bring this forward, may not have been entirely new, but Meyer certainly made it real.

PETER KEMP

Sources M. Goater, *Jack Meyer of Millfield* (1993) · *The Times* (1 March 1991); (14 March 1991); (16 March 1991) · *The Independent* (12 March 1991) · *WWW, 1991–5* · personal knowledge (2004) · private information (2004) · b. cert. · d. cert. · *CGPLA Eng. & Wales* (1991)
Likenesses photograph, repro. in *The Times* (11 March 1991) · photograph, repro. in *The Independent*
Wealth at death under £115,000: probate, 11 April 1991, *CGPLA Eng. & Wales*

Meyer, Sir William Stevenson (1860–1922), administrator in India, was born at Galatz, Moldavia, during a temporary visit of his parents, on 13 February 1860. He was the elder son of the Revd Theodore Jonah Meyer, a minister of the Presbyterian Church of England who was naturalized as a British subject in 1855, and his wife, Jane Ann, daughter of William Stevenson. He was educated at a mission school at Blackheath, at University College School, and at University College, London. He obtained third place in the open competition for the Indian Civil Service in 1879. Meyer joined the service in Madras in 1881, and remained in that presidency until becoming deputy secretary in the government of India finance department in 1898. On 1 June 1895 he married Mabel Henrietta (d. 1914), daughter of Major William W. Jackson of the Indian army; they had a son and daughter, both of whom predeceased their father.

Meyer was heavily involved in the financial administration of the British empire in India for the next twenty years, becoming financial secretary in the government of India, in 1905, secretary of military finance in 1906, and finance member of the viceroy's council in 1913, a post he held throughout the First World War. He also acted as Indian editor of the *Imperial Gazetteer of India* (3rd edn, 1902–5), was a member of the royal commission on decentralization in India (1907–9), the representative of the British and Indian governments at the International Opium Conference at The Hague (1911–12), and became the first president of the central recruiting board in India, which he converted from a regimental to a civil agency. In recognition of his public services he was made KCIE (1909), KCSI (1915), and GCIE (1918). In 1918 he retired from the Indian Civil Service, and was appointed in October 1920 first high commissioner of India, taking over from the India Office certain agency functions in London, under the new political reforms embodied in the Government of India Act of 1919. In this capacity Meyer headed the Indian delegations at the first and second assemblies of the League of Nations (1920–21). He was also chairman of the finance subcommittee of the Earl Haig's Officers' Association and a member of the imperial shipping committee.

Sir William Stevenson Meyer (1860–1922), by Walter Stoneman, 1919

Meyer's career in the financial administration of India was heavily bound up with the issue of the cost of imperial defence. India's large army, paid for by the Indian taxpayer, formed an important part of the defence force of the British empire, and in addition Indian revenues contributed to the costs of British army troops garrisoned in the subcontinent. By the first decade of the twentieth century it had been established that the Indian exchequer should not be liable for expenditure by India-based troops fighting overseas in areas in which India had no defence interest, but even this level of military outlay left the government of India vulnerable to attack by nationalist critics of the cost of imperial rule. The cost of fighting the First World War, especially the campaign that the Indian army undertook on Britain's behalf in Iraq (Mesopotamia), strained the Indian financial and monetary systems to the limit, and led to considerable friction with London, especially when the Mesopotamia campaign foundered through lack of resources. By 1917 the government of India could only survive by printing money, resulting in inflation, severe remittance difficulties, and a serious run on the paper currency.

Meyer coped with these unprecedented problems with some skill, and secured a number of important concessions—notably the de-linking of the rupee from its fixed exchange rate with sterling in 1916 and the imposition of revenue tariffs on British cotton goods in 1917—that helped to establish the relative autonomy of Indian financial administration from London in the post-war years. In

1919–20 the government of India succeeded in removing the defence of the Middle East from the list of its strategic obligations in future imperial defence planning.

Meyer's attitude to Indian political reform after the war was liberal, although he was cautious about allowing devolution of power over finance into untried hands. He was one of the proponents of the term 'diarchy' to describe the executive system introduced by the 1919 Government of India Act, in which the duties of provincial government were shared between officials appointed by the crown and ministers elected by new legislative councils. As high commissioner for India from 1920 to 1922 he helped to establish India's fiscal autonomy from Britain over tariff policy, and made the system for purchasing government stores more competitive, removing established preferences in favour of British manufacturers. His campaign to secure Indian membership of the International Labour Organization bore fruit after his death, which occurred suddenly on the way to the Westminster Hospital in London on 19 October 1922.

B. R. TOMLINSON

Sources *DNB* · B. R. Tomlinson, *The political economy of the raj, 1914–1947* (1979) · Burke, *Peerage* (1907) · *Dod's Peerage* (1918) · *CGPLA Eng. & Wales* (1922)
Archives CUL, Hardinge MSS
Likenesses W. Stoneman, photograph, 1919, NPG [*see illus.*]
Wealth at death £22,702 16s. 9d.: probate, 21 Nov 1922, *CGPLA Eng. & Wales*

Meynell [*née* Thompson], **Alice Christiana Gertrude** (1847–1922), poet and journalist, was born at Barnes, Surrey, on 11 October 1847, the younger daughter of Thomas James Thompson (1809×11–1881) and his wife, Christiana Jane Weller (1825–1910), daughter of Thomas Edmund Weller (1799–1884) and his wife, Elizabeth Dixon Southerden.

Thomas James Thompson was born in Jamaica, the son of an Englishman, James Thompson, and his Creole mistress. His grandfather Dr Thomas Pepper Thompson had emigrated from Liverpool and had grown rich on the ownership of sugar plantations, and when his son James predeceased him Dr Thompson brought his grandson to England. At his death he left him a substantial legacy. After leaving Cambridge without taking a degree, Thomas James dabbled in politics and the arts. He was a widower in his mid-thirties when he married Christiana Weller at Barnes parish church on 21 October 1845. Their two daughters, Alice, and the elder Elizabeth (1846–1933) [*see* Butler, Elizabeth Southerden, Lady Butler], were educated entirely by himself; his teaching was to be a great influence on them.

Christiana Weller, to whom Thompson was introduced by his friend Charles Dickens, was a concert pianist and an amateur painter. It was perhaps from her that Elizabeth inherited a talent which was to make her famous as a painter of battle scenes under her married name, Lady Butler.

Thompson's prosperity did not last, and it was partly for reasons of economy that he and his family travelled constantly, living in rented houses which were sometimes in

Alice Christiana Gertrude Meynell (1847-1922), by Sherril Schell, 1913

England but more often in Italy. From 1851, when Alice was four, they seldom stayed long in the same place, but it was the Ligurian coast of Italy that they chiefly frequented—Albaro, Nervi, Sori, Portofino (then a fishing village)—and the two young girls learned to speak Italian fluently, but with a Genoese accent. Alice's legacy from these years was a lifelong love of Italy.

In 1868 the Thompsons stayed for a time at Malvern, Worcestershire, and it was there that Alice took instruction and was received into the Roman Catholic church, on 20 July at St George's, Worcester. As an Anglican she had been religious from childhood. Her mother had joined the Catholic church some time before without telling her family. It seems that there was no later discussion on the matter between her and Alice, as the parents apparently were unaware of their daughter's intention. Thomas James was to convert to Catholicism shortly before his death in 1881. Alice's faith became the most important thing in her life. 'I saw when I was very young', she wrote many years later, 'that a guide in morals was even more necessary than a guide in faith. It was for this that I joined the Church. Other Christian societies may legislate, but the Church administers legislation' (A. Meynell to her daughter Olivia, n.d., Meynell MSS). And, again in later years, she said that the antithesis of slavery was not so much liberty as voluntary obedience which gives the truest freedom (Meynell MSS).

In the course of Alice's instruction at Worcester by Father Dignam, a young Jesuit priest, the two became friends, but this later developed into a hopeless love. Dignam asked to be sent abroad and communication between them ceased. Alice had been writing poetry for the two or three years prior to her conversion, and now her deep sorrow, though unnamed, was the subject of several fine poems which would later become well known, among them 'Renouncement', a piece often found in anthologies. Her first published poems appeared as *Preludes* in 1875 and met with praise from Tennyson, Coventry Patmore, Aubrey de Vere, and John Ruskin. Wilfrid John Meynell (1852-1948), a young Roman Catholic journalist in London, read a review of her work in the *Pall Mall Gazette*, and his admiration for the poems led to a meeting. The couple fell in love and, after overcoming parental opposition over Meynell's lack of money, they were married in London at the church of the Servite Fathers on 16 April 1877.

The Meynells settled in Kensington, at 47 Palace Court and worked hard at journalism, which was their only income. Their first child—a son—was born in 1878, and thereafter they had seven more children, of whom one died in infancy, but Alice Meynell managed to be a very loving mother while continuing the essential journalistic work. Wilfrid Meynell, with Alice's help, edited the *Weekly Register* (known to the family as *The Reggie*) for seventeen years, and both made considerable contributions to it. During one of Wilfrid's rare absences, Alice edited it by herself and wrote to him: 'My own Love ... Never again shall I fear taking *The Reggie* for you; I am going in at a canter with both hands down' (A. Meynell to W. Meynell, 1893, Meynell MSS).

From 1883 to 1895 the Meynells also edited *Merry England*, a monthly. On a fairly regular basis Alice contributed articles, mainly of literary criticism, to *The Spectator*, *The Tablet*, the *Saturday Review*, *The World*, and the *Scots Observer*. Her first volume of essays, *The Rhythm of Life*, published in 1893, consisted mainly of work reprinted from periodicals. Of the essay that gave the book its title, W. E. Henley, editor of the *Scots Observer*, wrote that it was 'one of the best things it has so far been my privilege to print' (W. E. Henley to A. Meynell, 1889, Meynell MSS). In 1893 Alice Meynell began to write a weekly column in the *Pall Mall Gazette* which was widely read and much admired, and she became sought after by lionizing hostesses.

In this busy household the children, as they grew older, sat under the dining-room table editing their own 'magazine', while their parents used the table-top as their working area. Two of the children, Viola Mary Gertrude *Meynell (1885-1956) and Francis Meredith Wilfrid *Meynell (1891-1975), both became well-known writers, Viola publishing a memoir of her mother in 1929 and one of her father in 1952.

Alice Meynell became acquainted with Coventry Patmore through her review of his poems, and an increasingly close friendship developed between them. For her it was an *amitié amoureuse* but Patmore (widowed twice and married to his third wife) fell in love with her. She felt that their relationship was a threat to her happy marriage, and thus severed all communication with him.

Francis Thompson (not a relative) had become a part of the Meynells' lives through their editorship of *Merry England*, and from then until his death in 1907 they cared for this brilliant but most impractical poet as if he were one of their own children. He loved Alice Meynell with hopeless adoration, and George Meredith, too, had fallen in love with her. She had an intense admiration for the poetry of Patmore, Thompson, and Meredith and was very proud of their public acclaim of her own work, but their love for her was not always easy to deal with, and it created jealousy among them. Her capacity to inspire deep affection in people of all ages was intensely strong throughout her life.

Five more volumes of Alice Meynell's essays appeared, as well as a book on Ruskin, and an anthology of Patmore's poetry and one of English lyric poetry. During a period of almost twenty years, when motherhood and journalism claimed her time, she wrote no poetry, but after 1895 (the year in which she was mentioned as a possible Poet Laureate) she returned to poetry, and this second part of her literary life produced some of her finest work, including some poems on the First World War. She had always been a staunch supporter of women's suffrage and more general principles of women's rights—at the age of eighteen she had written in her diary: 'Of all the crying evils in the depraved earth … the greatest, judged by all the laws of God and humanity, is the miserable selfishness of men that keeps women from work' (Schlueter and Schlueter, 323). This questioning of women's social status is seen in her later work, especially in the meditative *Mary, the Mother of Jesus* (1923).

In the year before she died Alice Meynell experienced a final creative period of productivity, her outburst of song, like the swan's, preceding her silence. In her poems written then, as in her prose, there is tightly packed thought, with every line and paragraph having been subjected to a stern discipline. The rules of her art echoed those of her life. She died at her London home, 2A Granville Place, on 27 November 1922 and was buried in Kensal Green cemetery. Her husband survived her.   JUNE BADENI

Sources V. Meynell, *Alice Meynell: a memoir* (1929) · J. Badeni, *The slender tree: a life of Alice Meynell* (1981) · P. Schlueter and J. Schlueter, eds., *An encyclopedia of British women writers* (1988) · Meynell MSS, Greatham, near Pulborough, Sussex · private information (2004) · *DNB* · *CGPLA Eng. & Wales* (1923) · m. cert. [Thomas James Thompson and Christiana Jane Weller] · d. cert. [Thomas James Thompson] · d. cert. [Christiana Jane Thompson]
Archives Boston College, literary papers · CUL · Hunt. L., letters · L. Cong. · NRA, corresp. and literary papers · priv. coll. | Bodl. Oxf., letters to Elizabeth, Lady Lewis · Ransom HRC, corresp. with John Lane · Somerville College, Oxford, letters with poems to Percy Withers · U. Leeds, Brotherton L., letters to Edmund Gosse · U. Nott. L., letters to Fred Page · UCL, letters to Arnold Bennett
Likenesses A. Stokes, watercolour sketch, 1877, priv. coll. · J. S. Sargent, pencil drawing, 1895, NPG · W. Rothenstein, lithograph, 1897, NPG · W. Rothenstein, two lithographs, 1897, BM, NPG · S. Schell, platinum print photograph, 1913, NPG [*see illus.*] · O. Sowerby, drawing, 1921, priv. coll. · J. Russell & Sons, photograph, NPG · photograph, NPG
Wealth at death £538 17s. 10d.: administration, 18 Oct 1923, *CGPLA Eng. & Wales*

Meynell [*née* Kilroy]**, Dame Alix Hester Marie**, Lady Mey-nell (1903–1999), civil servant, was born at Felixstowe, The Park, Nottingham, on 2 February 1903, the second

Dame Alix Hester Marie Meynell, Lady Meynell (1903–1999), by Walter Bird, 1958

daughter and second child in the family of four daughters and one son of Lancelot Kilroy (*d.* 1941), surgeon in the Royal Navy, and his wife, Hester Mary Agnes, *née* Dowson (1867–1941). Her parents were not very compatible. Lancelot Kilroy, of Irish protestant origins, had strong opinions and limited means, but was devoted to his wife. Hester Kilroy, child of prosperous midlands Unitarians, active in progressive causes, was not so devoted to her husband. Another complication was that she had become a Roman Catholic, which the Dowson family characteristically tolerated, but which caused Lancelot Kilroy's father, also a doctor in the armed services, to disown his son before the marriage.

Education and early life Alix Kilroy grew up as part of the extended Dowson family, and financially supported by it. Her father was mostly away at sea, and her parents rarely lived long together. After early private education (at home, at Miss Churley's Academy for Young Ladies, Nottingham, and at St Michael's, Tavistock) she went to Malvern Girls' College (1916–1920), which she remembered without affection. In the end, after her mother took her away to Switzerland mid-term, she—or perhaps her mother—was, in effect, expelled. Absorbed back into the Dowson family at Nottingham, she now worked for entrance to Oxford and went on energetic Swiss walking tours with her uncles. She was awarded a minor scholarship to Somerville College, and after a winter of naval socializing in Malta, went up to Oxford in 1922.

At Oxford Kilroy read philosophy, politics, and economics ('modern Greats'), had John Macmurray as her philosophy tutor, and always remembered how after she had written a balanced academic essay on Descartes he simply said 'Yes, but what do *you* think?' (Meynell, *Public Servant, Private Woman*, 67). This was the Oxford tutorial system working as it should, but Mrs Macmurray once set an alarm clock to go off during their lengthy discussions: very naturally perhaps, for Kilroy and her friend Jane Martin were already university stars, and Kenneth Clark, who later married Jane Martin, claimed that he hardly ever attended a lecture except in the hope of sitting next to a pretty undergraduate named Alix Kilroy. But although Kilroy had had enough of wholly female society at Malvern, and spent as little leisure time in Somerville as she could, it was there that she met her close lifelong friend Evelyn *Sharp. In 1925 she took a second-class degree.

Civil servant It had been intended that Kilroy would join the family law firm in Nottingham, but she was now attracted to practising at the bar in London. However, the examination for the administrative grade of the civil service was for the first time opened to women in 1925. She entered, came twelfth out of the 200 candidates, and with two other women (Enid Russell Smith and Mary Smeiton) obtained an appointment. Her grandmother Alice Maud Dowson found the announcement in *The Times* and said 'None of my children has set the Thames on fire, but now one of my granddaughters has' (Meynell, *Public Servant, Private Woman*, 79). Appointed to the Board of Trade, and treated objectively from the start, she was soon secretary to inquiries that were vetting claims by two minor industries for tariff protection, and later investigated the problems caused to the Lancashire cotton industry by the emerging cotton industries of the East. After 1929 she served as a private secretary, the usual stepping-stone to promotion, and then in 1932, after only the slightest official hesitation, became the first of the woman examination entrants to become a principal. Import tariffs had been introduced in November 1931 on goods from foreign countries. This led to much negotiation about reciprocal reductions. As a principal Kilroy had responsibility for negotiations with Sweden, and she typically made a lifelong friend (on her side wholly platonic) of Björn Prytz, head of the Swedish delegation and of SKF, the largest ball-bearing manufacturer. There followed a series of other trade assignments, including the negotiation of import quotas for agricultural products, and then the vetting of applications by German refugees to settle in Britain.

Throughout this period Kilroy was involved with the Council of Women Civil Servants, and particularly in arguing for open access for women to the diplomatic service. It helped the argument that the trade negotiations she had conducted might have been conducted elsewhere by male diplomatic staff. The chairman of the committee charged with investigating the admission of women, Sir Claud Schuster, was swayed, but the ban on women was not lifted completely until 1946. Kilroy never argued in favour of positive discrimination for women, which she viewed as dangerously close to denigration. The principle she supported was that success should be by merit in equal competition between colleagues, male and female. Her own progress showed what became possible for women on this basis.

The Second World War gave maximum scope for creative civil servants and introduced a civilian nation to total war. Kilroy, working under Laurence Watkinson, and very soon an assistant secretary, was successively concerned with food-import control, limiting the production of inessential goods, and identifying, indeed inventing, storage and factory space for war purposes. In 1941, by which time she was a principal assistant secretary, her department had responsibility for introducing Hugh Dalton's policy for furniture rationing and 'utility' furniture. From 1943 to 1945 she served, again with Watkinson, in a new reconstruction department. This prepared for the dismantling of wartime controls. She also had considerable responsibility for the creation of the Institute of Management and the Council of Industrial Design; and she made a large contribution to the combination of industrial development certificates and building licences, by which post-war government was expected to help old and declining industrial areas. During the war she was also privately involved with several groups aiming to influence future public policy. Long afterwards she considered that the Second World War really was the nation's 'finest hour', and that for a few years London had been the true capital of Europe. In her official career it was certainly her finest hour also.

Kilroy became an under-secretary in 1946 (shortly before her marriage to Sir Francis Meredith Wilfrid *Meynell (1891–1975), poet, publisher, and typographer) and had official responsibility for price control and food rationing. There was outcry from the press and the fashion industry when she publicly resisted the introduction from Paris of the 'new look' longer skirt. There were good economic arguments for her opposition, but she recognized later than she had been slow to realize that civil servants in peacetime could not be as prominent as was acceptable in war. In 1949 she was made a DBE, the conventional award of the lower CB not yet being open to women. Shortly afterwards she was seconded to be the first secretary of the Monopolies and Restrictive Practices Commission, which took her away from the centre of affairs. She developed a system for identifying and carrying out inquiries and by 1952 three substantial reports had been completed. By then she had been an under-secretary for six years. She returned to the Board of Trade's headquarters in 1952, but it became clear to her that personalities had changed and that promotion would not happen. She retired in 1955, eight years before reaching pensionable age.

'Private woman' Alix Meynell's autobiography later gave a vivid account of the private life which accompanied her official successes, very much unobserved by her colleagues at the Board of Trade. She was a good skier and ballroom dancer, and came gradually to adapt to Bloomsbury sexual values. Between 1924 and December 1931 she had a complicated relationship with (George) Garrow Tomlin (1898–1931), barrister, and second son of Thomas James Chesshyre Tomlin, Baron Tomlin. Garrow Tomlin—described as 'sophisticated [but] hopelessly unstable' (MacCarthy)—insisted that love and sex were quite separate, and that he could never commit himself to love or marriage. Kilroy resisted this point of view, but she suffered the deepest grief when Tomlin died as a result of a flying accident. In a Bloomsburian (even Murdochian) conclusion she went to the funeral with Francis Meynell, together with Vera Meynell (his wife), and another woman friend. Her diary reported:

> Thought how futile popular morals are, according to which G behaved abominably. There were us three, Vera, Barbara and me, with all of whom G had slept and all felt we had lost perhaps the most worthwhile person we'd known.
> (Meynell, *Public Servant, Private Woman*, 125)

From 1933 Kilroy and Francis Meynell were 'one another's best' (MacCarthy). This did not exclude other relationships, and they could not marry, because Vera Meynell did not want a divorce, and she and Francis had a young son. The Meynell code allowed Francis and Alix many weekends and holidays together, but Alix could not have the children she wished for. During the war they started to live together permanently, and after Francis and Vera were finally divorced, they married on 29 August 1946. By then she felt she had stepped unknowingly from youth to middle age. She and Francis Meynell bought Cobbold's Mill in Suffolk, between Monks Eleigh and Chelsworth. Here they gardened, kept ducks, hens, and swans, and later some cows and 100 pigs, all treated with particular consideration. There was also a river bathing pool, and in the years after the war there was rarely a weekend when they went there alone. The guests were often from their various families but were wonderfully varied. One was Stephen Potter, a friend from before the war, who asked Francis Meynell one weekend to read over the first draft of what became *Gamesmanship*, which was later dedicated to him.

Retirement Retirement released Alix Meynell to independent public life. She campaigned against British involvement in Suez and in favour of British nuclear disarmament. She was called to the bar in 1956, simply to fulfil an old ambition. She was a member of the South Eastern Gas Board (1956–69) and chair for seven years of its consumer council, a member of Harlow New Town corporation (1956–65) and of the Monopolies Commission (1965–8). She was on Cosford rural district council from 1970 to 1974. Later still—in 1986—she stood unsuccessfully as a candidate for the Social Democratic Party in the Suffolk county council elections.

Throughout the 1950s, and until 1967, the Meynells farmed and entertained at Cobbold's Mill, and holidayed many times at Gordon Waterfield's converted castle in Italy. In 1967 they moved to Lavenham, where Francis Meynell died in 1975. This loss, Alix Meynell wrote, permanently deprived her of joy. She continued, however, to be constructive and lively into extreme old age. In 1988,

when she was eighty-five, Gollancz published her autobiography, *Public Servant, Private Woman*. This was lively, funny, and exact, and a very candid self-portrait. The Virago Press was said to have rejected it because 'You make it all too easy' and they wanted 'Blood on the floor' (*Somerville College Report*), but it was true to Meynell's own experience. It was even more remarkable that she published, on her ninety-fifth birthday, *What Grandmother Said*, a serious biographical study of her Dowson grandmother which stylishly recreated affluent, late Victorian life in the midlands and north-west, and the adult characters of her own childhood. Her grandmother (who had had ten children) was active in the movement for women's suffrage. Alix Meynell herself retained the Dowson family temperament, though in a Bloomsbury mutation. Her autobiography quoted a definition of unitarianism—'Protestantism without its black insistence on guilt … breathing the spirit of prudent optimism in which [Unitarians] were inclined to view this world and the next'. She commented that this accorded well with the Dowson ethos and that 'I find it attractive myself' (Meynell, *Public Servant, Private Woman*, 36).

What Grandmother Said was Meynell's last published work, though she planned another, to be called 'Before the package tour', about holidays in France and Italy. Until the very end of her life she was still active, this time pressing the Labour government of 1997 to restore railway porters for the benefit of elderly travellers. She died at Laxfield House, Cundy's Lane, Brent Eleigh, Suffolk, on 31 August 1999, of heart failure and mitral valve disease. She was survived by numerous nephews and nieces.

ARTHUR GREEN

Sources A. Meynell, *Public servant, private woman: an autobiography* (1988) · A. Meynell, *What grandmother said* (1998) · F. MacCarthy, *The Guardian* (2 Sept 1999) · *The Times* (3 Sept 1999) · *Daily Telegraph* (3 Sept 1999) · J. Commander, *The Independent* (2 Sept 1999) · S. Hicklin, *Somerville College Report* (1999) · WWW · private information (2004) [Benedict Meynell; Hilary Law; Fiona MacCarthy; John Commander] · b. cert. · m. cert. · d. cert.
Likenesses attrib. M. Potter, portrait, *c*.1940, priv. coll. · W. Bird, photograph, 1958, NPG [*see illus.*] · R. Kilroy, double portrait, *c*.1960 (with Sir Francis Meynell), repro. in Meynell, *Public servant* · double portrait, photograph (with Sir Francis Meynell), repro. in *The Guardian* · photograph, repro. in Commander, *The Independent*

Meynell, Charles (1828–1882), Roman Catholic priest, was probably born at Wolverhampton. He was educated at Sedgley Park School, near Wolverhampton (1843–5), and at St Mary's College, Oscott (1845–9). In 1849 he entered the English College at Rome, where he was ordained in 1856 and awarded a DD. He returned to Oscott as professor of philosophy. In 1863 he published *The 'Colenso' Controversy Considered from the Catholic Standpoint*, which was written jointly with the Revd J. S. Northcote, then president of Oscott. This was followed in 1866 by *Short Sermons on Doctrinal Subjects*. H. I. D. Ryder, who recalled that his sermons were often above the heads of the Oscott pupils, nevertheless emphasized his gift for encouraging boys to think for themselves.

Among the pupils was the future poet and traveller Wilfrid Scawen Blunt, who subsequently claimed that Meynell's emphasis on the importance of reason as the basis of religious faith had sowed the seeds of his later agnosticism. In the late 1870s Blunt wrote to Meynell for assistance with his increasing doubts: their correspondence, which discussed the existence of God and the possibility of an afterlife, was edited by Aubrey de Vere and published in 1878 under the title *Proteus and Amadeus: a Correspondence*. Meynell's influence on Blunt was not just a theological one: Blunt testified to Meynell's instinctive love of poetry, commenting that the professor taught him to rate Keats and Shelley above Scott, Byron, and Wordsworth.

Meynell's friendship with another great nineteenth-century figure, J. H. Newman, had less problematic results. While contributing articles to *The Rambler* (he also supervised the philosophy section for some time), Meynell cemented an acquaintance with Newman, who in 1869 asked him to read and criticize his *Grammar of Assent*. The correspondence of the two scholars reveals Meynell's modesty and tact, as well as his keen philosophic mind. Newman subsequently presented him with an inscribed silver chalice as an expression of his gratitude.

In 1870 Meynell was moved to Birmingham, where he was attached to the cathedral, St Chad's, for three years. In 1873 he took charge of the small mission of Caverswall, in north Staffordshire. He died in Caverswall, after an operation, on 3 May 1882, and was buried there on 8 May. His last work, *Sermons for the Spring Quarter*, was published posthumously in 1883, and was reviewed favourably by a critic in *The Tablet*, who commented that it was 'not easy to lay down once we have taken it up, and there are not many sermons which can pretend to this praise' (*Tablet*, 17 March 1883, 410).

Although Meynell was an accomplished scholar, he left few publications; after his death his contemporaries dwelt more on his appealing personality than his erudition. Fond of children and animals (he once domesticated a wild grey rabbit), Meynell was popular with both Catholics and protestants in his mission at the Potteries. Ryder recalled that, despite 'a certain shy gentleness', he was 'quite endlessly amusing' and 'attracted everyone who came near him without effort' (Ryder, ix).

ROSEMARY MITCHELL

Sources *The Tablet* (6 May 1882), 692 · *The Tablet* (13 May 1882), 753 · *The Tablet* (17 March 1883), 409–10 · Gillow, *Lit. biog. hist.* · H. I. D. Ryder, 'Introductory memoir', in C. Meynell, *Sermons for the spring quarter* (1883) · E. Finch, *Wilfrid Scawen Blunt, 1840–1922* (1938), 27–28, 374–5 · *The letters and diaries of John Henry Newman*, ed. C. S. Dessain and others, [31 vols.] (1961–), vols. 18–30 · J. L. Altholz, *The liberal Catholic movement in England: the 'Rambler' and its contributors, 1848–1864* [1962], 64 · *Wellesley index* · *N&Q*, 5th ser., 8 (1895), 451
Archives CUL, letters to Lord Acton
Likenesses Moloney, portrait; Newbuildings Place, Sussex, in 1938

Meynell, Sir Francis Meredith Wilfrid (1891–1975), typographer and publisher, was born on 12 May 1891 at 47 Palace Court, Bayswater, London, the youngest of seven children (three sons and four daughters) of Wilfrid John

Meynell (1852–1948), manager of the publishing firm Burns and Oates, and his wife, Alice Christiana Gertrude *Meynell (1847–1922), poet and the daughter of Thomas James Thompson. His sister was the writer Viola Mary *Meynell (1885–1956). Francis Meynell was educated at St Anthony's School, Eastbourne, and from fourteen at Downside School. In 1909 he entered Trinity College, Dublin, but he left early in his third year without taking a degree.

Meynell began work in his father's firm, and shortly afterwards took charge of design and production. Much of the firm's printing was then done by Bernard Newdigate of the Arden Press, Letchworth, but besides Newdigate Meynell also got to know Stanley Morison, who joined Burns and Oates in 1913 with no previous experience of book production. Meynell and Morison found that they shared a sympathy for left-wing politics and interests in the seventeenth-century Fell types at Oxford University Press, in arabesque ornament in typography, and in good book design generally.

On 29 August 1914 Meynell married Hilda Peppercorn (1886–1962), better known as the concert pianist Hilda Saxe; they had a daughter, Cynthia, in 1915. In 1913 Meynell had also been appointed manager of *The Herald*. A socialist in politics, he supported the women's suffrage movement, while in the First World War he was a conscientious objector, helping in 1916 to found the Guild of the Pope's Peace with Morison. He also helped to found the Anglo-Russian Democratic Alliance in March 1917 (he openly admired the Russian Revolution). At *The Herald* (from 31 March 1919 the *Daily Herald*), where he became assistant editor to George Lansbury and the associate editor Gerald Gould, he waged a campaign of support for the communist cause. The Russian government offered to help subsidize the paper and Meynell even became involved in smuggling diamonds out of Russia. The full story of his early political career is recorded in his autobiography *My Lives* (1971). He resigned from the *Daily Herald* in September 1920, and from January to June 1921 was editor of *The Communist*.

In 1916 Meynell had founded the Pelican Press, which initially was closely connected with *The Herald*, and set himself 'to do good printing for the daily, not the exceptional, purpose', as he phrased it. Much of Meynell's design was influenced by the American typographer Bruce Rogers, but he also began to install some of the typefaces issued by the Lanston Monotype Corporation, sometimes adding modifications of his own. With the publication of *The Herald* as a daily paper in 1919, Meynell relinquished the management of the Pelican Press to Stanley Morison, but in 1921 he returned to it after the end of his association with *The Communist*. The press quickly gained a reputation not only for the quality of its book printing, but also for the imagination of its advertisement setting. Some of its most characteristic work is in the publicity book *Typography*, compiled by Meynell and first issued in 1923.

In 1923 Meynell founded the Nonesuch Press with the help of David Garnett and Vera Rosalind Wynn Gordon (née Mendel; 1895–1947), whom he married on 11 June 1925, after his divorce in 1923; they had a son, Benedict, in 1930. Stanley Morison was not part of the Nonesuch enterprise: Meynell's gradual disillusionment with the Roman Catholic faith in the early 1920s, and both men's different marital difficulties, helped to make the friendship less close in later years than it had been, although they remained friends until Morison's death in 1967. The Nonesuch Press began business in the cellar of the Birrell and Garnett bookshop in Gerrard Street, Soho, London. It was unlike the great private presses with which it has sometimes been confused. It possessed only a modicum of type, used chiefly for setting specimen pages. Instead it relied on the best modern types available commercially, chiefly from among the revivals of classic faces being issued under Morison's auspices by Monotype in the 1920s, and on the best of the new continental designs from Germany, the Netherlands, and France. The press issued both limited and unlimited editions. Its first production, John Donne's *Love Poems* (issued on 3 May 1923), appeared in an edition of 1250 copies; and although one of its earliest publications, *The Book of Ruth*, was published in an edition of only 250 copies, many of the volumes in the Compendious Series, beginning with Geoffrey Keynes's edition of William Blake's *Poetry and Prose* (1927), were reprinted many times over. *The Week-End Book*, an anthology edited by Meynell and his wife, Vera, and first published in 1924, caught the mood of the times; by December 1932 sales had reached over 120,000 copies according to the press's advertisements. In a different way, besides the Compendious Edition of Blake, the press also played a major part in the development of modern literary taste. Keynes had already edited Blake for the press in 1925, and among the more notable Nonesuch books were two selections of Blake's drawings (1927 and 1956) and the first facsimile of Blake's so-called Rossetti notebook (1935). Montague Summers's edition of William Congreve was published in 1923, followed by editions of Wycherley (1924), Rochester (1926), Otway (1927), Vanbrugh (1928), Farquhar (1930), and Dryden (1931). The press published two of John Evelyn's works for the first time, while the edition by John Hayward of John Donne's *Complete Poetry and Selected Prose* (1929) scored an immediate and lasting success. Nor did Meynell neglect illustrated books. Among those published by the press the *Anacreon* (1923) of Stephen Gooden, the *Genesis* (1924) of Paul Nash, and E. McKnight Kauffer's pictures for Burton's *Anatomy of Melancholy* (1925) may be accounted some of the best books of their kind in the period.

Meynell published a full account of the press to date in *The Nonesuch Century*, written with A. J. A. Symons and Desmond Flower, in 1936; but although the Nonesuch Press survived the depression it did so finally only with the help of George Macy, who had founded the Limited Editions Club in America in 1929. After lengthy negotiations Macy took over the press in 1936, with Meynell remaining as designer. Several of the books issued by Macy in the following years, however, bore little resemblance to the old Nonesuch style, although the great Nonesuch Dickens appeared during this period, designed largely by Harry Carter and supervised by Meynell.

Although the Nonesuch Press took up much of Meynell's time, the depression in the book trade in the 1930s forced him to turn also for a living elsewhere. In 1929 he had written *The Typography of Newspaper Advertisements*, which immediately became required reading in publicity circles, and in 1930 he joined Charles W. Hobson's advertising agency for four years. In 1935 Meynell returned briefly to journalism at the *News Chronicle*, before being employed successively by United Artists and the Gaumont-British Picture Corporation and the advertising agency Mather and Crowther. In 1940 he became an adviser on consumer needs to the Board of Trade, and in 1946 he was appointed to the Cement and Concrete Association, where he became director and remained until 1958. He was married for a third time, on 29 August 1946, to Alix Hester Marie Kilroy (1903–1999) [*see* Meynell, Dame Alix Hester Marie], under-secretary at the Board of Trade from 1946 to 1955, who was appointed DBE in 1949. Meynell was knighted in 1946, and appointed royal designer for industry in 1945.

Much to Meynell's pleasure George Macy returned the Nonesuch Press to him in 1951. Meynell thereupon resumed publication in association with Max Reinhardt and thus later with the Bodley Head. In 1953 he published a coronation Shakespeare, and he continued to wage his campaign for better book production by turning in 1963 to a new series of children's classics, the Nonesuch Cygnets. In 1961 he published his own *Poems & Pieces, 1911 to 1961*, where he brought together his poems in a more satisfactory format than he had been able to in the wartime *Fifteen Poems* (1944). The last book to be published by the press in Meynell's lifetime was a collection of poems by Tennyson, illustrated by Aubrey Beardsley, in 1968.

Meynell was a member of the Royal Mint advisory committee from 1954 to 1970, and as honorary typographic adviser to HM Stationery Office from 1945 to 1966 was responsible for much of the official printing for the Festival of Britain in 1951 and the coronation in 1953. He was vice-president of the Poetry Society from 1960 to 1965, and the University of Reading gave him the honorary degree of DLitt in 1964. He was known for his grace in his appearance and manners. Meynell died at his home, the Grey House, Barn Street, Lavenham, Suffolk, on 10 July 1975. He was cremated and his ashes were scattered in Sussex.

DAVID MCKITTERICK

Sources F. Meynell, *My lives* (1971) · J. Dreyfus, D. McKitterick, and S. Rendall, *The Nonesuch Press* (1981) · private information (2004) [family]
Archives Boston PL, corresp. · CUL, papers · NRA, corresp. and literary papers | Bodl. Oxf., letters to George Rostrevor Hamilton · Col. U., Random House papers · King's AC Cam., letters to John Hayward · U. Reading L., letters to Bodley Head Ltd · U. Texas,

Limited Editions Club papers · Welwyn Garden City Central Library, Hertfordshire, corresp. with Sir Frederic Osborn
Likenesses E. Gill, drawing, 1933; in possession of family, in 1986 · W. Orpen, double portrait, oils (with the artist's wife), AM Oxf. · engraving (after E. Gill), repro. in F. Meynell and others, *The Nonesuch century* (1936) · photographs, CUL, Meynell papers
Wealth at death £22,879: administration with will, 28 Oct 1975, *CGPLA Eng. & Wales*

Meynell, Hugo (1735–1808), huntsman and politician, was born in June 1735 at Bradley Park, Derbyshire, his family being 'of long standing' in the region (*Sporting Magazine* 33.182). He was the second son of Littleton Pointz Meynell and his first wife, Judith, daughter of Thomas Alleyne of Barbados. Meynell's father acquired a large fortune from gambling, some of which, according to Samuel Johnson, he lent to Frederick, prince of Wales, in return for the promise of a peerage. Hugo Meynell inherited both wealth and status and throughout his life occupied a number of important social positions in the Leicestershire and Derbyshire area. In 1758 he became high sheriff for Derbyshire, and in 1761 and 1768 he was elected MP for Lichfield. In February 1769 he became MP for Lymington, Hampshire, and in 1774 for Stafford, which he represented until 1780. He also held the position of master of the royal staghounds in 1770 and 1772.

In June 1754 Meynell married Anne (d. 1757), daughter of John Gell of Hopton, Derbyshire; they had one son, Godfrey (b. 1755). Anne died at Hopton in June 1757 and in June the next year Meynell married Anne Boothby Skrymsher (c.1737–1814), daughter of Thomas Boothby Skrymsher of Tooley Park, Leicestershire. Their union produced two sons, Hugo (1759–1800) and Charles (b. 1768); the latter went on to become the master of the royal tennis court.

In 1754 Meynell purchased Quorndon Hall in Leicestershire and set about improving the estate. His occupancy lasted until 1800, when he sold it to the earl of Sefton. Throughout the latter half of the eighteenth century Quorndon Hall was a magnet attracting numerous aristocrats, drawn by the 'very splendid entertainment's' (*Sporting Magazine*, 33.182) on offer. Meynell showed himself to be a good landlord, behaved generously towards the poor, and was esteemed by every rank of society. While such behaviour attracted much local admiration, Meynell's principal fame was based on his achievements in the field of fox-hunting, a sport that he effectively transformed. Between 1753 and 1800 he hunted the Quorn country around Melton Mowbray in Leicestershire. The Quorn pack had been established in 1698 but it was not until Meynell took charge that the hunt attained its reputation. Until the 1750s the favourite quarry of the chase had been the hare, a much slower animal than the fox, which could be caught by the scenting skills of harrier packs. Given the fox's comparative speed in relation to hounds, the only way that a hunter could hope to catch one was to begin the meeting at daybreak, before the fox had digested its food, and use the hounds to sniff the animal out. Far from being a chase, this pursuit was carried out at a very slow pace 'walking him to death', and culminated in the fox's being

Hugo Meynell (1735–1808), by Sir Joshua Reynolds, 1756?–1758

literally dug out, with spade and shovel, from its lair. Meynell transformed all this by 'breeding a fast pack of hounds with first rate noses and tremendous drive which showed sport such as no fox-hunter had before enjoyed' (Bovill, 198–9). Also, whereas previously it had been almost unknown for thoroughbred horses to be used in the chase, every member of Meynell's pack enjoyed such mounts. Fox-hunts under Meynell started at about midday and were based upon speed and hard riding, dependent upon high-quality hounds and horses.

Inevitably the provision and maintenance of such packs was an extremely expensive undertaking and by 1780 Meynell was forced to relinquish his exclusive control of the pack. Whereas previously, like most significant fox-hunting landowners, he had financed the pack entirely out of his own pocket, the onerous costs forced him to transform the Quorn hunt into a subscription pack whose members shared in the expenses. Although it might be expected that such a concession would undermine Meynell's authority in the hunt, particularly as many 'dashing young men' became members, this was not the case. When two of the foremost well born and spirited men of their day, Harvey Aston and Charles Windham, started racing one another before the hounds, 'by force of his laughter and the pleasantry of his observation upon them, they were called back to order, and acknowledged their error'. Evidently, said Meynell, 'the hounds were following the gentlemen, who were very kindly gone forward to see what the fox was about' (*Sporting Magazine*, 33.182). Such a mixture of humour and tact enabled him to retain his authority, instilling some discipline into the pack.

Meynell's contemporaries conceded that he was unequalled in running a subscription pack and he was unanimously hailed as the foremost fox-hunter in the kingdom. He understood that it was important to retain the active support of local farmers in order to ensure that they would preserve foxes rather than destroy them. To this end, he would often delay the hunt on market days in order to enable the farmers to participate. This, and a number of other displays of tact and consideration, meant that the Quorn, while under his direction, blossomed into the foremost hunt of the day. Meynell's departure from the Quorn area in 1800 was a devastating blow to the fox-hunting there, and in 1803 the Leicestershire country was described as being 'in the last stages of decline' (*Sporting Magazine*, 21.348).

Meynell died at his London home in Chapel Street, Mayfair, on either 13 or 14 December 1808. Having passed through Quorndon Hall his body was interred at his family's ancestral burial place at Bradley Park on either 21 or 22 December. He was survived by his second wife, Anne, but because of the earlier death of his eldest son Meynell left much of his money, £11,000 a year, to his grandson Hugo Meynell of Hore-Cross-hall, Staffordshire. Meynell's death was widely mourned, his tact and generosity having ensured that he enjoyed substantial popular affection.

The modern method of fox-hunting is often referred to as the 'Meynellian system'. In historiographical terms, while scholars correctly observe that some of Meynell's contemporaries were influential in helping to create the Quorn pack, and promote hunts based upon the hot pursuit of foxes by carefully bred horses and hounds, Meynell's reputation remains largely intact. It is significant that even Raymond Carr, while maintaining that Meynell's influence is 'somewhat exaggerated', acknowledges that he 'revolutionised the hunt' (Carr, 38–40). It was under Meynell that fox-hunting became an exciting, fashionable sport. Indeed, at the time of his retirement, meetings occurred on a regular basis throughout England, with almost all of them endeavouring to imitate the sport established by the Quorn under his leadership. Of course, the continuance, and indeed expansion, of the Meynellian system long after its creator's death owed much to others. While it was Meynell who had originally glamorized fox-hunting, with an emphasis on speed and daring, the dissemination of such an image was heavily dependent on the skills of others. The most notable of these were sporting journalists such as Nimrod (Charles James Apperley) and Robert Smith Surtees, whose invigorating prose captivated large numbers of readers, and artists and engravers, notably the German-born Rudolph Ackermann, whose pictures magnified the seductive drama of the chase, highlighting its most thrilling aspects. Cumulatively the product of so much prose and picture was an arresting image of the English countryside that still exerts power today.   ADRIAN N. HARVEY

Sources *Sporting Magazine*, 33 (1809), 182 · *Sporting Magazine*, 21 (1803), 348 · E. W. Bovill, *English country life 1780–1830* (1962) · R. Longrigg, *The English squire and his sport* (1977) · R. Carr, *English fox-hunting* (1977) · *GM*, 1st ser., 78 (1808), 1134, 1186 · J. Brooke, 'Meynell, Hugo', HoP, *Commons, 1754–90* · D. C. Itzkowitz, *Peculiar privilege: a social history of English foxhunting, 1753–1885* (1977)
Likenesses J. Reynolds, portrait, 1756?–1758, priv. coll. [*see illus.*]
Wealth at death £11,000 p.a. and other bequests: *Sporting Magazine* (1809); *GM*, 1186

Meynell, Laurence Walter (1899–1989), author, was born at Grasmere, Oaks Crescent, Wolverhampton, Staffordshire, on 9 August 1899, the youngest son of Herbert Meynell, chairman of a brass-founding company, and his wife, Agnes Mary Sollom. The family was Roman Catholic, and Meynell was educated at St Edmund's College, Old Hall, Ware, Hertfordshire. During the First World War he served in the Honourable Artillery Company. Upon discharge he declined to enter the family business and was for a time an articled pupil in a land agency, an estate agent, and a schoolmaster, before settling on a career as a professional writer. He travelled a great deal throughout the 1920s, in Europe and on foot through Britain. While living in a garret in Paris he wrote his first novel, *Mockbeggar* (1924). A satire on the 'bright young things' of the 1920s, it won the Harrap fiction prize. On 22 September 1932 he married a fellow writer, Shirley Ruth Darbyshire (1903–1955), daughter of Taylor Darbyshire, a journalist. They had one daughter. He served in the Royal Air Force during the Second World War and was mentioned in dispatches.

Laurence Meynell was a prolific writer in a variety of genres. He wrote stories for girls, using the pseudonym Valerie Baxter, historical biographies which reflected his interest in engineering and craftsmanship, including one on Brunel, books on cricket, novels, career stories for children, and, most notably, mystery novels and books for boys. As A. Stephen Tring, he earned himself a modest place in literary history with his first children's book, *The Old Gang* (1947), which broke free of the stilted language and archaic boarding-school setting typical of school stories of the time. With its brisk, colloquial dialogue and theme of rivalry between pupils at grammar and secondary modern schools, it set a new standard for school stories. Although not a great book (Meynell's social attitudes and contemporary schoolboy slang have dated it), it was both readable and firmly within the experience of the ordinary boy. The book was recognized by contemporary critics as a welcome innovation. One critic said of it, 'if the moribund boy's story is to recover its vitality a transfusion of Stephen Tring is our best hope' (Trease, 112). Meynell also wrote a series of books about a young boy named Barry Briggs, who at the beginning of the first story is about to sit the eleven-plus exam, which too was distinguished for its realistic characters and dialogue.

Meynell had written a number of 'Ruritanian adventure stories' in his early days, but he developed as a serious mystery writer late in his career (*The Times*). His most memorable creation in this genre was the private eye Hooky Hefferman, the genial, clubbable 'man of the bars' (Pederson, 748). Meynell's characteristic style was good-natured and civilized, reflecting traits that friends recognized in the man himself. His writing, even in his hard-boiled detective novels, reflected his affection for civility and good manners.

After the death of his first wife in 1955, Meynell married on 26 September 1956 the actress Joan Belfrage (1903/4–1986), whose previous marriage had been dissolved; she was the daughter of Francis Joseph Henley, a major in the Oxfordshire and Buckinghamshire light infantry. Between 1955 and 1957 Meynell edited the series Men of the Counties for the Bodley Head and from 1958 to 1960 was literary editor of Time and Tide in the difficult period following the death of Lady Rhondda. He was a devotee of the works of Samuel Johnson and served for a time as president of the Johnson Society. In his Who's Who entry he listed his recreations as 'walking [and] trying to write a play'. His publications included one play among over 150 other books. Meynell died at 14 New Church Road, Hove, Sussex, on 14 April 1989.

The traits that made Meynell's books for children accessible in the 1940s and 1950s—their colloquial language and topical situations—have caused them to date. But he will be remembered as one of the first, if not the greatest, exponents of the lively, realistic, and topical children's story that came to dominate the literature of the late twentieth century.   ELIZABETH J. MORSE

Sources The Times (18 April 1989), 18 · T. Chevalier, ed., Twentieth-century children's writers, 3rd edn (1989) · WWW · J. P. Pederson, ed., St James guide to crime and mystery writers, 4th edn (1996) · G. Trease, Tales out of school: a survey of children's fiction (1964) · H. Carpenter and M. Prichard, The Oxford companion to children's literature (1984) · B. Doyle, The who's who of children's literature (1968) · b. cert. · m. certs. · d. cert.
Archives Boston University, Mugar Memorial Library
Likenesses photograph, repro. in The Times, 18
Wealth at death £288,314: probate, 31 Oct 1989, CGPLA Eng. & Wales

Meynell [married name Dallyn], **Viola Mary Gertrude** (1885–1956), novelist and short-story writer, was born on 15 October 1885 at 21 Upper Phillimore Place, London, the fifth of the seven children of Wilfrid Meynell (1852–1948), journalist and author, and his wife, Alice Christiana Gertrude *Meynell, née Thompson (1847–1922), poet and essayist. Her parents built a house at 47 Palace Court in Kensington in 1889, and she attended the convent school of the Sisters of Sion as a day student from about 1893 until 1901. She grew up in a strongly Roman Catholic literary atmosphere, helping her parents with their many journalistic tasks from an early age; many of her later novels and short stories reflect her Catholic upbringing, exploring themes of moral transgression and the possibility of redemption and the interaction of divine providence in the individual's life. She was especially close to her mother, adopting a great deal of her philosophy and values. Her first novels, Martha Vine (1910) and Cross-in-Hand Farm (1911), are relatively simple tales of love and morality, although already marked by the acute psychological analyses that are her fiction's great strength; her mother was supportive of her early fiction, but was concerned that it was too self-revelatory. With Lot Barrow

(1913), she turned to an ironic rural tragedy, in the manner of Thomas Hardy, and began to find a wider and respectful audience; her reputation was solidified with the much lighter comic romance, Modern Lovers (1914).

In 1911 Meynell's father bought property in Greatham, Sussex, and she and the family thereafter divided their time between the country home and London. An early engagement to the Irish-born painter Charles Stabb was broken off by 1912. Many literary friends from London came to stay with the Meynells at Greatham: D. H. Lawrence lived there for six months in 1915, and a story he wrote during that time, 'England, My England', was perceived by the Meynells as a cruel attack on their family. Among Meynell's good friends in this period were Maitland Radford (whose marriage proposal she turned down in 1915), the novelists Ivy Low and Gladys Huntington, and the poet and children's author Eleanor Farjeon.

Although her brother Francis was a vocal pacifist, Meynell produced two books supporting the war effort: Julian Grenfell (1917) a short, impassioned biography of the soldier hero; and a translation of Eugène Lemercier's Lettres d'un soldat (1917). The novels she wrote during the war—Columbine (1915) and Narcissus (1916)—dealt directly with questions of sin and moral responsibility, and reflect the sombre mood of the times. She was engaged to her publisher, Martin Secker, but broke off with him just before their planned 1919 wedding. Her short volume of Verses (1919) was respectfully reviewed.

Meynell's next two novels, Second Marriage (1918) and Antonia (1921), were experiments in wedding psychological realism to mythic and allusive plot structures; Antonia was roundly damned by critics, who found it incoherent. Meynell surprised family and friends when she finally went through with a marriage proposal, marrying a local Sussex farmer and merchant who was neither literary nor Catholic, John William Dallyn (1879–1947), on 28 February 1922; she gave birth to a son, Jacob, in January 1923. Her mother's death in November 1922 was a turning point in her life. On the one hand, it liberated her artistically, as she turned to the short story (with the 1924 collection, Young Mrs Cruse and four later collections) and used it as a vehicle to portray her personal experiences more directly than she had done with her novels; on the other hand, her mother's memory continued to haunt her, and she spent some years researching and writing Alice Meynell: a Memoir (1929) and rededicating her time and efforts to the Meynell family. She and her husband separated finally in 1929 (as a Catholic, she never considered divorce, and continued to use her married name everywhere but on her published work), and she moved back to London while her son attended the Froebel school there. She lived at 14 St Mary Abbot's Terrace until 1930, when she moved back into the family home at Palace Court. By 1935 she had returned to Greatham, and lived there with only brief exceptions until her death. Much of her time at Greatham was occupied with caring for her aged and increasingly infirm father.

Meynell wrote fewer novels, producing instead reviews and articles for magazines and newspapers, and turning to editing projects such as an edition of the letters of J. M. Barrie (1942), which she took on at the request of her good friend Lady Cynthia Asquith, and two volumes of letters addressed to Sir Sydney Carlyle Cockerell (1940 and 1956), to whom she was very close in the last few decades of her life. But during this period she also produced what may be her masterpiece, the ambitious novel *Follow thy Fair Sun* (1935), the fullest development of her psychological insights and her Catholic themes. She radically revised it—shortening it and eliminating its allegorical elements—and republished it under the title *Lovers* in 1944. She also produced more short stories, many of which, set on farms or in small villages, give insight into her life and experiences; her later stories are increasingly dark in tone and outlook.

Meynell's health deteriorated in the late 1940s, and she was eventually diagnosed as having muscular dystrophy. Despite a growing weakness and paralysis, she wrote one more novel (*Ophelia*, 1951), a memoir of her father's friendship with the poet Francis Thompson (1952), and more short stories. Four of her stories appeared in the *New Yorker*

in 1955–6; one of these, 'The Veranda', is directly autobiographical in its depiction of her illness. She died at her home, Humphrey's Homestead, Greatham, on 27 October 1956, and was buried the same month in the Catholic cemetery in nearby Houghton. At her death, she was working on a volume of *Collected Stories*, published in 1957. Her body of work includes a dozen novels and some forty short stories in addition to her memoirs and miscellaneous poetry and prose. Her fame was at its height during the decade following the First World War, but her later work also found many readers and much critical acclaim for the beauty of its style and the depth of its probings into human motivation.   RAYMOND N. MACKENZIE

Sources Meynell's letters, priv. coll. [at family home, Greatham, Sussex] · private information (2004) [family] · V. Meynell, *Alice Meynell: a memoir* (1929) · V. Meynell, *Francis Thompson and Wilfrid Meynell* (1952) · b. cert. · d. cert.
Archives NRA, priv. coll., corresp. and literary papers | BL, letters to Sydney Carlyle Cockerell · Bodl. Oxf., letters to George Rostrevor Hamilton · Indiana University, Bloomington, letters to Martin Secker · Tate collection, letters to Anita Bartle
Wealth at death £1644 13s. 5d.: administration, 1 May 1957, *CGPLA Eng. & Wales*

PICTURE CREDITS

Martindale, Louisa (1872–1966)—
© Estate of Frank O Salisbury 2004.
All rights reserved, DACS; New
Sussex Hospital, Brighton;
photograph National Portrait
Gallery, London

Martineau, Harriet (1802–1876)—
© National Portrait Gallery, London

Martineau, James (1805–1900)—
© National Portrait Gallery, London

Martineau, Jane (1812–1882)—Royal
Holloway College; photograph
National Portrait Gallery, London

Martins, Emmanuel Alhandu (1899–
1985)—Collection Stephen Bourne

Martyn, Henry (1781–1812)—© National
Portrait Gallery, London

Martyn, John (1699–1768)—© National
Portrait Gallery, London

Martyn, Thomas (1735–1825)—
© National Portrait Gallery, London

Marvell, Andrew (1621–1678)—
© National Portrait Gallery, London

Marx, (Jenny Julia) Eleanor (1855–
1898)—© National Portrait Gallery,
London

Marx, Karl Heinrich (1818–1883)—Marx
Memorial Library, London

Mary [of Guise] (1515–1560)—Scottish
National Portrait Gallery

Mary (1542–1587)—The Royal
Collection © 2004 HM Queen
Elizabeth II

Mary, princess royal (1631–1660)—
private collection

Mary [of Modena] (1658–1718)—
© National Portrait Gallery, London

Mary, Princess (1723–1772)—© National
Portrait Gallery, London

Mary (1867–1953)—© Estate of Bertram
Park / Camera Press; collection
National Portrait Gallery, London

Mary I (1516–1558)—Museo del Prado,
Madrid / Bridgeman Art Library

Mary II (1662–1694)—The Royal
Collection © 2004 HM Queen
Elizabeth II

Mary Adelaide, Princess, duchess of
Teck (1833–1897)—© National
Portrait Gallery, London

Masefield, John Edward (1878–1967)—
© National Portrait Gallery, London

Maskell, Daniel (1908–1992)—Getty
Images - Hulton Archive

Maskelyne, Nevil (1732–1811)—© The
Royal Society

Mason, Charlotte Maria Shaw (1842–
1923)—© reserved

Mason, James Neville (1909–1984)—
© Dennis Reed; British Film Institute

Mason, John Monck (1726?–1809)—
© National Portrait Gallery, London

Mason, William (1725–1797)—
Pembroke College, Cambridge

Massey, Daniel Raymond (1933–1998)—
© Tom Hustler / National Portrait
Gallery, London

Massey, Raymond (1896–1983)—
© National Portrait Gallery, London

Massey, William Ferguson (1856–
1925)—© National Portrait Gallery,
London

Massingberd, Sir Archibald Armar
Montgomery- (1871–1947)—
© National Portrait Gallery, London

Massinger, Philip (1583–1640)—
© National Portrait Gallery, London

Massingham, Henry William (1860–
1924)—© National Portrait Gallery,
London

Masson, David Mather (1822–1907)—
Scottish National Portrait Gallery

Massue de Ruvigny, Henri de, earl of
Galway, and marquess of Ruvigny in
the French nobility (1648–1720)—
© National Portrait Gallery, London

Masterman, Sir John Cecil (1891–
1977)—© National Portrait Gallery,
London

Masters, John (1914–1983)—© reserved

Mather, Alexander (1733–1800)—
© National Portrait Gallery, London

Mather, Cotton (1663–1728)—
© American Antiquarian Society

Mather, Increase (1639–1723)—
© National Portrait Gallery, London

Mather, Robert Cotton (1808–1877)—
© National Portrait Gallery, London

Matheson, Sir (Nicholas) James
Sutherland, first baronet (1796–
1878)—© National Portrait Gallery,
London

Mathew, Theobald (1790–1856)—
© National Portrait Gallery, London

Mathew, Sir Theobald (1898–1964)—
© National Portrait Gallery, London

Mathews, Charles (1776–1835)—
© National Portrait Gallery, London

Mathews, Charles Edward (1834–
1905)—Alpine Club Photo Library,
London

Mathews, Dame Elvira Sibyl Maria
Laughton (1888–1959)—© National
Portrait Gallery, London

Mathews, Thomas (1676–1751)—
© National Maritime Museum,
London, Greenwich Hospital
Collection

Mathias, William James (1934–1992)—
© reserved; photograph National
Portrait Gallery, London

Mathieson, (James) Muir (1911–1975)—
Getty Images - Baron

Matilda [of England] (1102–1167)—
Master and Fellows of Corpus Christi
College, Cambridge

Matthew, (Henry) Colin Gray (1941–
1999)—© Judith Aronson

Matthew, Sir Robert Hogg (1906–
1975)—© National Portrait Gallery,
London

Matthew, Tobie (1544?–1628)—Christ
Church, Oxford

Matthew, Sir Toby (1577–1655)—
© National Portrait Gallery, London

Matthews, Drummond Hoyle (1931–
1997)—Godfrey Argent Studios

Matthews, Henry, Viscount Llandaff
(1826–1913)—© National Portrait
Gallery, London

Matthews, Jessie Margaret (1907–
1981)—© Tom Hustler / National
Portrait Gallery, London

Matthews, Sir Stanley (1915–2000)—
Getty Images - Hulton Archive

Matthews, Victor Collin, Baron
Matthews (1919–1995)—courtesy Sue
Adler / The Observer; collection
National Portrait Gallery, London

Matthews, Walter Robert (1881–1973)—
© reserved; collection National
Portrait Gallery, London

Mattocks, Isabella (1746–1826)—
Garrick Club / the art archive

Maturin, Charles Robert (1780–1824)—
© National Portrait Gallery, London

Maty, Paul Henry (1744–1787)—Scottish
National Portrait Gallery

Maud, Princess (1869–1938)—
© National Portrait Gallery, London

Maud, John Primatt Redcliffe, Baron
Redcliffe-Maud (1906–1982)—
© National Portrait Gallery, London

Maude, Aylmer (1858–1938)—
© National Portrait Gallery, London

Maude, Clementina, Viscountess
Hawarden (1822–1865)—© reserved

Maudling, Reginald (1917–1979)—
© National Portrait Gallery, London

Maudslay, Henry (1771–1831)—
© National Portrait Gallery, London

Maudsley, Henry (1835–1918)—
Wellcome Library, London

Mauduit, Israel (1708–1787)—
© reserved

Maugham, Frederic Herbert, first
Viscount Maugham (1866–1958)—
© reserved; collection Trinity Hall,
Cambridge; © reserved in the
photograph

Maugham, (William) Somerset (1874–
1965)—© reserved / Tate, London,
2004

Maugham, (Gwendoline Maud) Syrie
(1879–1955)—Wellcome Library,
London

Maule, Fox, second Baron Panmure
and eleventh earl of Dalhousie
(1801–1874)—© National Portrait
Gallery, London

Maule, Harry, styled fifth earl of
Panmure (1659–1734)—Scottish
National Portrait Gallery

Maule, Henry (1676–1758)—National
Gallery of Ireland

Maule, James, fourth earl of Panmure
(1658/9–1723)—in the collection of
Brechin Castle; photograph courtesy
the Scottish National Portrait Gallery

Maule, William, earl of Panmure of
Forth (1699/1700–1782)—in a private
Scottish collection; photograph
courtesy the Scottish National
Portrait Gallery

Maurice, prince palatine of the Rhine
(1621–1652)—© reserved

Maurice, Sir Frederick Barton (1871–
1951)—© National Portrait Gallery,
London

Maurice, (John) Frederick Denison
(1805–1872)—© National Portrait
Gallery, London

Maurice, Sir John Frederick (1841–
1912)—© National Portrait Gallery,
London

Mavor, Osborne Henry [James Bridie]
(1888–1951)—courtesy Vincent
Cianni Photographs / Lida Moser

Maxfield, Thomas (d. 1784)—
© National Portrait Gallery, London

Maxse, Sir (Frederick) Ivor (1862–
1958)—© National Portrait Gallery,
London

Maxton, James (1885–1946)—by
courtesy of Felix Rosensteil's Widow
& Son Ltd., London, on behalf of the
Estate of Sir John Lavery; collection
National Portrait Gallery

Maxwell, Sir Herbert Eustace, seventh
baronet (1845–1937)—Scottish
National Portrait Gallery

Maxwell, James Clerk (1831–1879)—
© National Portrait Gallery, London

Maxwell, (Ian) Robert (1923–1991)—
© National Portrait Gallery, London

Maxwell, Sir William Stirling, ninth
baronet (1818–1878)—private
collection; photograph © National
Portrait Gallery, London

Maxwell, Winifred, countess of
Nithsdale (1672–1749)—Traquair
House Charitable Trust

May, George Ernest, first Baron May
(1871–1946)—© National Portrait
Gallery, London

May, Peter Barker Howard (1929–
1994)—© Brian Griffin; collection
National Portrait Gallery, London

May, Philip William (1864–1903)—
© National Portrait Gallery, London

May, Robert (b. 1588?, d. in or after
1664)—© National Portrait Gallery,
London

May, Thomas (b. in or after 1596,
d. 1650)—© National Portrait Gallery,
London

May, Thomas Erskine, Baron
Farnborough (1815–1886)—
© National Portrait Gallery, London

Maybrick, Florence Elizabeth (1862–
1941)—Getty Images - Hulton
Archive

Mayer, Joseph (1803–1886)—Board of
Trustees of the National Museums
and Galleries on Merseyside (Walker
Art Gallery, Liverpool)

Mayerl, William Joseph [Billy] (1902–
1959)—© reserved; collection
National Portrait Gallery, London

Mayerne, Sir Theodore Turquet de
(1573–1655)—North Carolina
Museum of Art, Raleigh, purchased
with funds from the State of
Carolina

Mayhew, Christopher Paget, Baron
Mayhew (1915–1997)—© National
Portrait Gallery, London

Mayhew, Henry (1812–1887)—
© National Portrait Gallery, London

Maynard, Sir Henry (b. 1547, d. 1610)—
© National Portrait Gallery, London

Maynard, Sir John (1604–1690)—
© National Portrait Gallery, London

Mayow, John (bap. 1641, d. 1679)—
© National Portrait Gallery, London

Mazzini, Giuseppe (1805–1872)—in a
private collection; photograph

courtesy the Scottish National Portrait Gallery

Mboya, Thomas Joseph (1930–1969)— © reserved; East African Newspapers (Nation) Ltd; photograph National Portrait Gallery, London

Meacham, Gwendoline Emily [Wendy Wood] (1892–1981)—© Scottish National Portrait Gallery

Mead, Richard (1673–1754)—Coram Foundation, Foundling Museum, London; photograph National Portrait Gallery, London

Meade, James Edward (1907–1995)— © National Portrait Gallery, London

Meade, Matthew (1628/9–1699)— © National Portrait Gallery, London

Meagher, Thomas Francis (1823– 1867)—National Gallery of Ireland

Mee, Anne (c.1770–1851)—V&A Images, The Victoria and Albert Museum

Mee, Arthur Henry (1875–1943)— © Estate of Frank O Salisbury 2004. All rights reserved, DACS; photograph National Portrait Gallery, London

Mehmet Ali (c.1769–1849)—photograph by courtesy Sotheby's Picture Library, London

Mehta, Sir Pherozeshah Merwanjee (1845–1915)—© National Portrait Gallery, London

Meiggs, Russell (1902–1989)—Balliol College, Oxford / Michael Noakes

Meighen, Arthur (1874–1960)— © National Portrait Gallery, London

Meikle, Andrew (1719–1811)— © National Portrait Gallery, London

Meinertzhagen, Richard (1878–1967)— Trustees of the Col. R. Meinertzhagen Trusts / Rhodes House Library

Meitner, Lise (1878–1968)—© reserved; Bildarchiv Österreichische Nationalbibliothek

Melba, Dame Nellie (1861–1931)— © reserved; Royal Opera House Archive

Meldola, Raphael (1849–1915)— © National Portrait Gallery, London

Mellish, Robert Joseph, Baron Mellish (1913–1998)—© National Portrait Gallery, London

Mellon, Paul (1907–1999)—© National Portrait Gallery, London

Mellon, Sarah Jane (1824–1909)— © National Portrait Gallery, London

Melville, David, third earl of Leven and second earl of Melville (1660–1728)— Scottish National Portrait Gallery

Melville, George, fourth Lord Melville and first earl of Melville (1636– 1707)—private collection; photograph National Portrait Gallery, London

Mendelssohn Bartholdy, (Jacob Ludwig) Felix (1809–1847)— © National Portrait Gallery, London

Mendoza, Daniel (1765?–1836)— © Copyright The British Museum

Menken, Adah Isaacs (1835?–1868)— © National Portrait Gallery, London

Mennes, Sir John (1599–1671)—private collection, on loan to Plymouth Art Gallery; © reserved in the photograph

Menteith, Robert (bap. 1603, d. in or before 1660)—© National Portrait Gallery, London

Menuhin, Yehudi, Baron Menuhin (1916–1999)—© National Portrait Gallery, London

Menzies, John (1808–1879)—by kind permission of John Menzies plc

Menzies, Sir Robert Gordon (1894– 1978)—© National Portrait Gallery, London

Menzies, Sir Stewart Graham (1890– 1968)—© National Portrait Gallery, London

Mepham, Simon (c.1275–1333)—The British Library

Mercer, John (1791–1866)—© Museum of the History of Science, University of Oxford

Mercer, Joseph (1914–1990)—© Sefton Samuels / National Portrait Gallery, London

Mercer, Mabel (1900–1984)— photograph Michael Ochs Archives / Redferns

Mercier, Philip (1691–1760)— © National Portrait Gallery, London

Mercury, Freddie (1946–1991)— photograph Peter Still / Redferns

Meredith, George (1828–1909)— © National Portrait Gallery, London

Meredith, Louisa Anne (1812–1895)— Allport Library and Museum of Fine Arts, State Library of Tasmania

Meredith, William Henry [Billy] (1874– 1958)—Public Record Office

Merivale, Charles (1808–1893)— © National Portrait Gallery, London

Merivale, Herman (1806–1874)— © National Portrait Gallery, London

Merivale, Herman Charles (1839– 1906)—© National Portrait Gallery, London

Merrick, Joseph Carey [the Elephant Man] (1862–1890)—Royal London Hospital Archives and Museum

Merriman, John Xavier (1841–1926)— © reserved

Merriman, Nathaniel James (1809– 1882)—© National Portrait Gallery, London

Merry, Robert (1755–1798)—© reserved

Merry, William Walter (1835–1918)— © National Portrait Gallery, London

Merry del Val, Rafael María José Pedro Francisco Borja Domingo Gerardo de la Santísma Trinidad (1865–1930)— © National Portrait Gallery, London

Merton, Sir Thomas Ralph (1888– 1969)—private collection

Merton, Walter of (c.1205–1277)—The British Library

Mervyn, Sir Audley (1603?–1675)— private collection

Meryon, Charles Lewis (1783–1877)—by permission of the Royal College of Physicians, London

Messervy, Sir Frank Walter (1893– 1974)—© National Portrait Gallery, London

Meston, James Scorgie, first Baron Meston (1865–1943)—© National Portrait Gallery, London

Metcalfe, Charles Theophilus, Baron Metcalfe (1785–1846)—Oriental Club; photograph National Portrait Gallery, London

Metcalfe, Jean (1923–2000)—Getty Images – Hulton Archive

Methuen, Sir Algernon Methuen Marshall, baronet (1856–1924)— Methuen Publishing Limited; photograph National Portrait Gallery, London

Meyer, Jeremiah (1735–1789)— Ashmolean Museum, Oxford

Meyer, Sir William Stevenson (1860– 1922)—© National Portrait Gallery, London

Meynell, Alice Christiana Gertrude (1847–1922)—© National Portrait Gallery, London

Meynell, Dame Alix Hester Marie, Lady Meynell (1903–1999)—© National Portrait Gallery, London

Meynell, Hugo (1735–1808)—Christie's Images Ltd. (2004)